WHO'S WHO IN SCOTLAND
4th EDITION 1992-93

Who's Who
in
Scotland

4th EDITION 1992-93

Carrick Media

Published by Carrick Media
2/7 Galt House, 31 Bank Street, Irvine KA12 0LL
0294 311322

Set by The Format Factory, Mansfield
Printed in Great Britain by Bookcraft, Midsomer Norton, Avon

British Library Cataloguing-in-Publication Data
A catalogue record for this book is available from the British Library

ISBN 0 946724 30 X

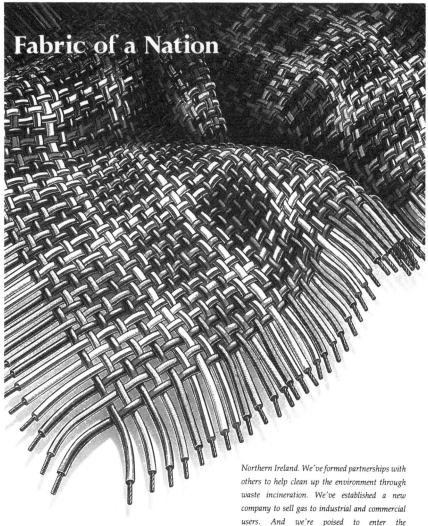

Fabric of a Nation

O VER 75 % of Scots depend on us for their electricity. Power for industry, for homes, for offices, for retail outlets. Power for hospitals, schools, farms, leisure centres and theatres.

But nowadays there's very much more to ScottishPower than power in Scotland.

We're active and successful energy traders south of the border. We have proposals to combine with Northern Ireland Electricity to supply power to Northern Ireland. We've formed partnerships with others to help clean up the environment through waste incineration. We've established a new company to sell gas to industrial and commercial users. And we're poised to enter the telecommunications market.

In fact you could say that we're providing the fabric that helps make the nation successful.

ScottishPower

THE CHARTERED INSTITUTE OF PUBLIC FINANCE AND ACCOUNTANCY

CIPFA Scottish Secretary: Ian P Doig, IPFA
Technical Manager: Derek S Yule, BCom, IPFA
Conferences and Courses Organiser: Carolyn Wildy
CIPFA Careers Adviser: Anne Ray

The Chartered Institute of Public Finance and Accountancy (CIPFA) is a professional accountancy body founded in 1885 with the following objectives and purposes:

✳   to advance the science of public finance and accountancy

✳   to promote education in public finance and accountancy

✳   to promote and publish the results of studies and research into public finance and accountancy

The CIPFA Scottish Office is involved in a wide range of Institute activities affecting financial management in the public services including the education and training of accountants, policy issues, accounting, auditing and research. Also conferences and courses, publications, research, statistics and liaising with the press.

CIPFA Scottish Office
8 North West Circus Place
Edinburgh EH3 6ST
Tel: 031 220 4316   Fax: 031 220 4305

With its impressive riverside location, moments from the city centre and adjacent to the award winning Scottish Exhibition and Conference Centre, the Moat House International Glasgow professionals stand ready to make your conference an outstanding success.

Meeting Your Needs

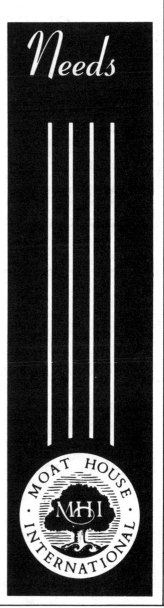

From small meetings to major events, friendly and expert service, coupled with purpose designed facilities and extensive support services, will meet your every need.

The spectacular design of the hotel affords inspiring panoramic views from each of the 300 luxury rooms, including 15 suites. Work up your appetite in our Waterside Club leisure centre, take a favourite pre-dinner cocktail in the Quarter Deck and then enjoy gourmet Scottish and international haute cuisine in the Mariner or informal dining in the Pointhouse cafe, overlooking the River Clyde.

And after your conference don't be surprised if you're tempted back for a holiday.

Preface

It is two years since the publication of the third edition of Who's Who in Scotland. This new, completely revised, edition contains around 5,000 entries, many appearing for the first time.

All walks of Scottish life are represented: politics and public service, law, religion and education, business and finance, science and medicine, the arts and sport. Prominent Scots living outwith Scotland are not included.

Entries are arranged in alphabetical order, according to surname. A typical entry contains full name, present occupation, date and place of birth, followed by details of family, education and career, publications, recreations and address. The following abbreviations are commonly used: b. (born); m. (married); s. (son); d. (daughter).

Great care has been taken to ensure that information given is accurate and up to date, but during the period in which the book has been in preparation, it is inevitable that some circumstances will have changed. The publishers cannot accept liability for any errors.

A

Abbott, Mollie Pearson, CBE (1984), DPE, MEd; b. 4.2.28, Peebles. Educ. Edinburgh Ladies' College; Dunfermline College of Physical Education. Assistant Teacher of Physical Education in Edinburgh schools; Temporary Lecturer, Moray House College of Education, Edinburgh, 1952-56; Senior Lecturer, Ripon Training College, 1956-62; Principal Lecturer, Aberdeen College of Education, 1962-63; HM Inspector of Schools, 1964-70; Principal, Dunfermline College of Physical Education, 1970-83. Past Chairman: Association of Higher Academic Staff in Colleges of Education in Scotland, Scottish Central Committee on Physical Education, Scottish Joint Consultative Committee on Physical Education; former Member: General Teaching Council for Scotland, Court of Heriot Watt University, National Committee for the In-Service Training of Teachers, Scottish Arts Council, Scottish Council of Physical Education, Scottish Sports Council. Recreations: golf; reading; skiing; swimming; walking; wind-surfing; listening to music. Address: (h.) Janefield House, Kirkcudbright, DG6 4UR; T.-0557 30119.

Aberdeen and Temair, Marchioness of (Beatrice Mary June Gordon), CBE, DL. Musical Director and Conductor, Haddo House Choral and Operatic Society, since 1945.

Adair, Robert, OBE, JP, LAE, INC.E, MIMI, TQ. Honorary Sheriff, Shetland, since 1982; Chairman, Shetland Committee for Employment of Disabled, since 1986; b. 8.7.22, Yorkshire; m., Thomasina Jane Yates; 3 d. Educ. Darlington College of Further Education; Jordanhill College of Education. Territorial Army, 1939-46 - RASC, UK and Europe, war service; Member, Executive Committee, NHS General Practitioners, 1955-74; Town and County Councillor, 1963-66; Town Councillor, 1969-74; Chairman, Working Party on NHS Reorganisation, Shetland, 1971-74; Shetland Health Board: Chairman Designate, 1973, Chairman, 1974-85; Member, Scottish Planning Council, NHS, 1974-85; first Chairman, Children's Panel Advisory Committee; Shetland College of Further Education: Lecturer in Engineering, 1966, Senior Lecturer, 1978-87; Chairman, Shetland Scouts County Association; Chairman, County Valuation Court. Recreations: swimming; golf; computers; reading; horses; fishing; radio. Address: (h.) 41 Gilbertson Road, Lerwick, Shetland, ZE1 OHN; T.-0595 3576.

Adam, Edmund Ian, MBChB, DRCOG. Medical Adviser, Lothian Regional Council, since 1985; Clinical Assistant, Department of Medicine, Western General Hospital, Edinburgh, since 1969; Medical Officer, Company of Merchants of City of Edinburgh, since 1973; b. 26.5.31, Edinburgh; m., Norma Barbara; 2 s. Educ. Daniel Stewart's College, Edinburgh; University of Edinburgh. House Officer (Surgery), General Hospital, Kirkcaldy, 1956-57; House Officer (Medicine), Bangour General Hospital, 1957; Medical Officer (Captain, RAMC), Intelligence Corps Depot, Sussex, 1957-59; House Officer (Obstetrics), Craigtoun Maternity Hospital, St. Andrews, 1959-60; Trainee Assistant, general practice, Dunkeld, 1960-61; Partner, general practice, Edinburgh, 1961-85; School Medical Officer, Daniel Stewart's and Melville College, Edinburgh, 1972-85. Moderator, Society of High Constables of Edinburgh, 1987-89; Honorary Physician: Scottish Schools Rugby Union, since 1977, Scottish Badminton Union, 1977-90. Recreation: golf. Address: (h.) Norian, 60 Hillview Terrace, Edinburgh EH12 8RG; T.-031-334 3498.

Adam, Ian Clark, CA. Partner in charge, Price Waterhouse Scotland, since 1986; Partner, Price Waterhouse, since 1976; b. 2.9.43, Dundee; m., Betty Anne; 1 s.; 1 d. Educ. Harris Academy, Dundee. Trained as CA, Henderson & Logie, Dundee, 1962-67; Price Waterhouse Peat & Co., Rio de Janeiro, 1967-70; Price Waterhouse, Bristol, 1970-76; opened Edinburgh office, 1976. Treasurer, Royal Burgess Golfing Society of Edinburgh; Treasurer, Royal Scottish Society for the Prevention of Cruelty to Children. Recreations: golf; reading; walking. Address: (b.) Albany House, 58 Albany Street, Edinburgh EH1 3QR; T.-031-557 9900.

Adam, Ian Simpson Thomson, QFSM, GIFireE. Firemaster, Central Region Fire Brigade, since 1984; b. 4.5.40, Dunfermline; m., Norma; 1 s. Educ. Beath Secondary, Cowdenbeath. Retained Firefighter, Fife, 1960; wholetime Firefighter, Fife, 1964; Leading Firefighter, Fife, 1968; Sub Officer, Fife, 1969; Station Officer, Fife, 1972; Assistant Divisional Officer, Fife, 1974; Divisional Officer, Fife, 1978; Third Officer, SDO, Fife, 1979; Depute Firemaster, Central, 1982. Recreations: gardening; photography. Address: (h.) Norwood, Smithy Loan, Dunblane.

Adams, David Austey, MA. Principal, Northern College of Education, formerly Aberdeen College of Education, since 1983; b. 2.3.42, Wakefield, Yorkshire; m., Margaret Ishbel; 1 s.; 1 d. Educ. Harris Academy, Dundee; St. Andrews University. Teacher of English and History, High School of Dundee; Principal Teacher of English, Arbroath Academy; Assistant Director of Education: Angus County Council, Tayside Regional Council. Member, Scottish Examination Board; Chairman, Committee of Principals of Scottish Centrally Funded Colleges. Recreations: fishing; shooting. Address: (b.) Northern College of Education, (Aberdeen Campus), Hilton Place, Aberdeen, AB9 1FA; T.-0224 283500.

Adams, Gordon Cassie, MBE. Member, Aberdeen District Council, since 1974; b. 4.2.24, Aberdeen; m., Jean Murray; 2 d. Commissioned Officer, Reconnaisance Corps, 1942-47. Technical Advisor: Government of Pakistan, 1962-68; University of Minas Gerais, Brazil, 1968-70. JP, 1974-84; Parliamentary candidate, Aberdeen North, 1979; former Secretary, Scotland in Europe Movement, 1979; Leader, Conservative Group, Aberdeen City Council, 1976-84; Member, Aberdeen Local Health Council, 1975-79. Recreations: Indian/African history; music; writing; reading. Address: (h.) 11c Kings Gate, Aberdeen; T.-Aberdeen 645834.

Adams, Irene, JP. MP (Labour), Paisley North, since 1990; b. 1948.

Adams, James Gordon Leitch, MA, PhD. Director of Investment and Planning, Scottish Tourist Board, since 1988 (formerly Director of Development); b. 17.10.40, Glasgow; m., Rowan Hopwood; 1 s.; 1 d. Educ. Dundee High School; St Andrews University; Queen's University, Canada; McGill University. Economist: Canadian Federal Government, 1966-70, Highlands and Islands Development Board, 1970-75; Lecturer, Glasgow University, 1975-82; Visiting Lecturer in Poland, 1978, and India, 1981; United Nations Adviser in Saudi Arabia, 1989. Recreations: mountaineering; golf. Address: (h.) 5 Corrennie Drive, Edinburgh; T.-031-447 8073.

Adams, Professor James Hume, MD, PhD, FRSE, FRCPath, FRCP(Glas), DSc. Professor of Neuropathology, Glasgow University, since 1971; b. 31.12.29, Glasgow; m., Eileen Rachel Lawson; 3 s. Educ. Paisley Grammar School; Glasgow University. Specialist Pathologist, RAMC, 1955-57; MRC Research Fellow, Institute of Psychiatry, London, 1957-59; Lecturer/Senior Lecturer/Reader in Neuropathology, Glasgow University, 1959-71. President, British Neuropathological Society, 1968-76; Secretary-General, International Society of Neuropathology, 1978-86,

President, since 1990. Publications: three books and more than 100 papers in scientific journals. Recreations: golf; bridge. Address: (h.) 31 Burnhead Road, Newlands, Glasgow, G43 2SU; T.-041-637 1481.

Adams, Robert William, OBE, FCMA, FCCA, JDipMA. Scottish Chairman, Writers' Guild; Director, John Cairney & Co. Ltd., since 1983; Chairman, Burns Musical Co. Ltd., since 1987; Member, Committee of Management, Hanover Housing Association, since 1982; b. 27.9.22, Glasgow; m., Mary Ann Ritchie; 2 s.; 1 d. Educ. Shawlands Academy, Glasgow. H.C. Stewart & Co., CA, Glasgow; Lieutenant, Parachute Regiment; South of Scotland Electricity Board; James Colledge (Cocoa) Ltd., West Africa; Highland Home Industries Ltd.; Managing Director, A.H. McIntosh & Co. Ltd., until 1982. Member, Glenrothes Development Corporation, 1976-84; former Member: Scottish Sports Council; Council, Institute of Cost and Management Accountants; Scottish Sports Council; former Convenor, Scottish Athletic Coaching Committee. Recreations: tennis; golf. Address: (h.) Achray, Shore Road, Aberdour, Fife; T.-0383 860269.

Adams, William Ralph McClymont, Esq., OStJ, FSA (Scot), FHSS. Vice President Heraldry Society of Scotland, since 1988 (Secretary, 1983-87) and Fellow of Society; b. 6.3.15, Banton, by Kilsyth; m., Joan Graham Barry; 1 s.; 2 d. Educ. Dollar Academy; Hillhead High School, Glasgow; Perth Academy; Heriot Watt College, Edinburgh; Edinburgh College of Art. Architectural training, Perth and Edinburgh; Civil Servant, 1939-80; specialised in conservation of carved stone, decorated plaster, painted ornament and heraldic blazons; Senior Conservation Officer for Scotland, from 1953; Officer, Most Venerable Order of St John of Jerusalem, since 1982; Honorary Guildsman, Ancient Royal Archers Guild of St Sebastian of Knokke, Belgium, 1984. Recreations: horticulture; photography; research and lecturing on heraldry, history, historic buildings and gardens. Address: (h.) Limegrove, High Street, Gifford, Haddington, East Lothian EH41 4QU; T.- 062 081 617.

Adamson, Iain Thomas Arthur Carpenter, BSc, MSc, AM, PhD. Senior Lecturer in Mathematics and Computer Science, Dundee University, since 1965; b. 17.6.28, Dundee; m., Robin Andison; 1 d. Educ. Morgan Academy, Dundee; St. Andrews University; Princeton University. Assistant in Instruction, Princeton University, 1950-52; Lecturer: Queen's University of Belfast, 1952-59, Queen's College, Dundee (St. Andrews University), 1960-65; visiting appointments, University of Western Australia, 1965-66, 1972-73, 1978. President, Edinburgh Mathematical Society, 1983-84; Session Clerk: Dundee Meadowside Church, 1975-81, Meadowside St. Paul's Church, 1982-84; ordained as Auxiliary Minister, Church of Scotland, 1986. Books: Introduction to Field Theory; Rings, Modules and Algebras; Elementary Rings and Modules; Elementary Mathematical Analysis. Recreation: reading. Address: (h.) 3 Chalmers Street, Dundee; T.-0382 453980.

Adamson, Norman Joseph, CB, QC. Assistant Counsel to Lord Chairman of Committees in House of Lords, since 1989; Legal Secretary to the Lord Advocate and First Parliamentary Draftsman for Scotland, 1979-89; b. 29.9.30; m., Patricia Mary Guthrie; 4 d. Educ. Hillhead High School, Glasgow; Glasgow University. Faculty of Advocates, Scotland, 1957; called to English Bar, Gray's Inn, 1959; Army Legal Aid (Civil) (UK), 1956-57; practice at Scottish Bar, 1957-65; Standing Junior Counsel, Bible Board, 1962; Standing Junior Counsel, MoD (Army), 1963-65; Honorary Sheriff Substitute, 1963-65; Parliamentary Draftsman and Legal Secretary, Lord Advocate's Department, London, since 1965. Elder, Church of Scotland. Recreations: music; theatre.

Adamson, Rev. Sidney, MA, BD. Minister, Church of Scotland; b. 3.8.11, Arbroath; m., Margaret T. Sharpe, JP; 1 s. Educ. Dumbarton Academy; Glasgow University and Trinity College; Royal Scottish Academy of Music and Drama. Ministries: St Ninian's, Sanquhar, 1937-47 (including war service), Trinity Church, Renfrew, 1947-54, High Kirk of Rothesay, 1954-59, St Michael's Inveresk, Musselburgh, 1959-85. Moderator of Presbytery: Dumfries, 1939, Dunoon, 1958, Dalkeith, 1964 and 1965; former Moderator, Synod of Lothian and Tweeddale; Army Chaplain, India, 1944-47; Territorial Army Chaplain, 1952-66; Chaplain, Royal British Legion (Scotland), Paisley, Renfrew, Rothesay, Musselburgh, and Honorary Vice President, Edinburgh & Lothian Area Council, 1973; Industrial Chaplain, Babcock & Wilcox Ltd., Renfrew, 1948-54; Chaplain, British Sailors' Society, 1955-85; Editor, Homeward Bound (Forces magazine, India), 1946-47. Publications: Two Centuries of Service (history of Sanquhar congregation), 1939; St Michael's Kirk at Inveresk (four editions between 1963 and 1984). Recreations: (at suitable periods) ballroom dancing; shooting; swimming; (always) reading; theatre; freelance journalism; ex-service welfare. Address: 48 Hailes Gardens, Colinton, Edinburgh, EH13 0JH; T.-031-441 2471.

Addison, Alexander, MB, ChB, FRCGP, DObstRCOG. Senior Partner, Addison, Scott, Kane & Ferguson, since 1978; Chairman, Lanarkshire LMC, since 1988; Member, Scottish Committee, BMA, since 1984; b. 23.8.30, Kerala; m., Joan Wood; 3 s. Educ. Keith Grammar School; Aberdeen Grammar School; Aberdeen University. House Surgeon and Physician, Woodend General Hospital, Aberdeen, 1954-55; Captain, RAMC; Junior Medical Specialist, Cowglen MH, 1955-58; SHO, Bellshill MH, 1958-59; GP in Douglas and Physician to Lady Home Hospital, since 1959; Member, West of Scotland Faculty of GP College, 1967-79 and of Scottish Council, 1976-78; Member, Lanarkshire LMC, since 1972, and of AMAC, since 1975; Chairman, Lanarkshire AMAC, 1982-86; Chairman, Scottish Association of General Practitioner Hospitals, 1985-87; Member, Scottish Committee of Medical Commission on Accident Prevention, since 1976; Member, National Medical Consultative Committee, 1977-83; Honorary Surgeon, St. Andrews Ambulance Association, 1959-89. Recreations: curling; golf; reading. Address: (h.) 7 Addison Drive, Douglas, Lanarkshire ML11 0PZ; T.-0555 851302.

Adler-Bell, Marianne. Dress Designer, since 1939; Member, Board of Directors, Citizens' Theatre, Glasgow, since 1973; b. 17.1.15, Berlin, Germany; m., John Bell (deceased); 1 s. Educ. Staatliche Augusta Schule, Berlin; Art School, Berlin. Former Vice-Chairman, Citizens' Theatre Society. Awarded Bundesverdienstkreuz (similar in Germany to OBE) for work in furthering Scottish-German relations. Recreations: opera; gardening. Address (h.) 348 Knightswood Road, Glasgow, G13 2BT; T.-041-959 1696.

Affolter, Michael Theodore, BA (Hons), PhD, DipTP, MRTPI. Assistant Secretary, Scottish Office, since 1989; b. 11.5.40, Bangor, Northern Ireland; m., Margaret Elizabeth; 2 s. Educ. Bangor Grammar School; Queen's University of Belfast. Planning Officer, Ministry of Development, Northern Ireland, 1963-66; joined Scottish Development Department, 1967; lateral transfer from professional to administration (Principal level), 1978. Recreations: skiing; badminton; cricket; golf; hill walking. Address: (h.) 1 Mortonhall Road, Edinburgh EH9 2HS. T.-031-667 4716.

Affrossman, Stanley, BSc, PhD. Senior Lecturer in Chemistry, Strathclyde University, since 1974; b. 22.9.36, Glasgow; m., Patricia Maclean; 2 d. Educ. Whitehill Senior Secondary School; Glasgow University. Fellow, National Research Council of Canada, Ottawa, 1961-63; Assistant

Lecturer, Royal College of Science and Technology, Glasgow, 1963-65; Lecturer, Strathclyde University, 1965-74. Recreations: caravanning; hill-walking. Address: (h.) 46 Stirling Drive, Bearsden, Glasgow; T.-041-942 0287.

Agnew of Lochnaw, Sir Crispin Hamlyn. 11th Baronet (created 1629); Chief of the Agnews; Advocate, since 1982; Unicorn Pursuivant of Arms, 1981-86, Rothesay Herald of Arms, since 1986; b. 13.5.44, Edinburgh; m., Susan Rachel Strang Steel; 1 s.; 3 d. Educ. Uppingham School; Royal Military Academy, Sandhurst. Commissioned Royal Highland Fusiliers, 1964, as 2nd Lieutenant; Major, 1977; Retired, 1981. Member: Royal Navy Expedition to East Greenland, 1966; Joint Services Expedition to Elephant Island, Antarctica, 1970-71; Army Nuptse Himal Expedition, 1975; Army Everest Expedition, 1976; Leader: Army East Greenland Expedition, 1968; Joint Services Expedition to Chilean Patagonia, 1972-73; Army Api Himal Expedition, 1980. Publications: articles in various newspapers and journals. Recreations: mountaineering; offshore sailing. Address: 6 Palmerston Road, Edinburgh, EH9 1TN; T.-031 667 4970.

Agnew, Ian, MA (Hons) (Cantab). Rector, Perth High School, since 1975; b. 10.5.32, Newcastle-upon-Tyne; m., Gladys Agnes Heatherill; 1 d. Educ. King's College School, London; Pembroke College, Cambridge. Assistant Teacher of Modern Languages, Melville College, Edinburgh, 1958-63; Assistant Teacher of Modern Languages, then Principal Teacher of Russian, George Heriot's School, Edinburgh, 1964-70; Housemaster, Craigmount Secondary School, Edinburgh, 1970-73; Deputy, Liberton High School, Edinburgh, 1973-75. Chairman, Tayside Regional Working Party on Religious Education, since 1977; Minute Secretary, Headteachers Association of Scotland, 1979-81; Committee Member, SCCORE; President: Perthshire Musical Festival, 1978-88, Perth Chamber Music Society, 1982-89; Past President, Rotary Club of Perth St. John's; Past Chairman: Barnton and Cramond Conservative Association and West Edinburgh Conservative and Unionist Association; Elder, St. Andrew's Parish Church, Perth; Serving Officer (OStJ), Priory of Scotland of the Most Venenerable Order of St. John. Recreations: music (opera); reading; tennis; gardening. Address: (h.) Northwood, Heughfield Road, Bridge of Earn, Perthshire, PH2 9BH; T.-0738 81 2273

Aiken, Peter David, LLB. Senior Partner, Menzies Dougal WS, since 1988 (Partner, since 1973); b. 16.8.46, Manchester; m., Sally; 2 s. Educ. Dundee High School; St. Andrews University. Apprentice to Strathern & Blair, WS; joined Menzies Dougal & Milligan, WS, 1972; Stockholm University, 1975-77 (Diploma of International Law). Recreations: golf; tennis. Address: (b.) 12 Bruntsfield Crescent, Edinburgh; T.-031-447 1035.

Ailsa, The Marquess of (Archibald David Kennedy), OBE; b. 3.12.25, Witham, Essex; m., Mary Burn; 2 s.; 1 d. Educ. Nautical College, Pangbourne. Commissioned Scots Guards, 1944; served with Royal Northumberland Fusiliers in Korea; commissioned 4/5th Bn., Royal Scots Fusiliers TA (commanded, 1966-68); commanded 3rd Bn., Royal Highland Fusiliers T&AVR; Honorary Colonel, Ayr and Renfrew Bn., Army Cadet Force. Recreation: sailing. Address: (h.) Cassillis, Maybole, Ayrshire, KA19 7JN.

Airlie, 13th Earl of (David George Coke Patrick Ogilvy), KT, GCVO, PC, JP. Lord Chamberlain of Her Majesty's Household; Ensign, Queen's Body-Guard for Scotland (Royal Company of Archers), since 1975; Chairman, General Accident Fire & Life Assurance Corporation plc, since 1987 (Deputy Chairman, 1975-87); Director, Royal Bank of Scotland Group, since 1983; Director, Royal Bank of Scotland plc, since 1991; Director, Stratton Investment Trust plc, since 1986; Lord Lieutenant, Angus; Chancellor of the

Royal Victorian Order; President, Scout Association Scotland; b. 17.5.26, London; m., Virginia Fortune Ryan; 3 s.; 3 d. Educ. Eton College. Lieutenant, Scots Guards, 1944; serving 2nd Bn., Germany, 1945; Captain, ADC to High Commissioner and C-in-C Austria, 1947-48; Malaya, 1948-49; resigned commission, 1950; Chairman, Ashdown Investment Trust Ltd., 1968-82; Director, J. Henry Schroder Wagg & Co. Ltd., 1961-84 (Chairman, 1973-77); Chairman, Schroders plc, 1977-84; Scottish and Newcastle Breweries plc, until 1983. Address: (h.) Cortachy Castle, Kirriemuir, Angus; T.-Cortachy 231.

Aitchison, James Douglas, MA (Hons), MEd (Hons). Head Teacher, Boclair Academy, Bearsden, since 1991 (Head Teacher, Gleniffer High School, Paisley, 1984-91); b. 2.7.47, Glasgow. Educ. High School of Glasgow; Glasgow University; University of Marburg. Teacher, Lycee Faidherbe, Lille; Principal Teacher, Bearsden Academy; Assistant Head Teacher, Gryffe High School, Houston. Recreations: curling; walking; travel. Address: (h.) 44 Keystone Road, Milngavie; Glasgow G62 6QG; T.-041-956 6693.

Aitken, Professor Adam Jack, MA, DLitt. Editor, A Dictionary of the Older Scottish Tongue, 1956-86; Editorial Consultant and Pronunciation Editor, Concise Scots Dictionary, 1975-85; b. 19.6.21, Edinburgh; m., Norma Ward Manson; 3 s.; 1 d. Educ. Lasswade Secondary School; Edinburgh University. Assistant Lecturer in English Language, Edinburgh University, 1947-48; Research Fellow, Universities of Glasgow, Aberdeen and Edinburgh, 1948-54; Lecturer, Universities of Glasgow and Edinburgh, 1954-64 (Assistant Editor and Editor, Dictionary of the Older Scottish Tongue); Edinburgh University: Honorary Senior Lecturer, 1965-71, Senior Lecturer (part-time) in English Language, 1971-75, Reader (part-time) in English Language, 1975-79; Chairman, Language Committee, Association for Scottish Literary Studies, 1971-76; Chairman, Universities' Forum for Research on the Languages of Scotland, 1978-81; Vice-President, Scottish Text Society, since 1985; Biennial Sir Israel Gollancz Prize of British Academy, 1981; Honorary Professor, Edinburgh University, since 1984. Publications: Edinburgh Studies in English and Scots, 1971; The Computer and Literary Studies, 1973; Lowland Scots, 1973; Bards and Makars, 1977; Languages of Scotland, 1979. Address: (h.) 5 Bellevue Crescent, Edinburgh, EH3 6ND; T.-031-558 1534.

Aitken, Colin Graeme Girdwood, BSc, PhD. Senior Lecturer, Department of Mathematics and Statistics, Edinburgh University, since 1991; b. 20.6.51, Glasgow; m., Elizabeth McRoberts; 1 s.; 1 d. Educ. Glasgow Academy; Edinburgh University; Cambridge University; Glasgow University. Fellow, Royal Statistical Society; Fellow, Institute of Statisticians, Member, Forensic Science Society. Publication: The Use of Statistics in Forensic Science (Co-Editor). Recreations: golf; bridge; country dancing; hill walking. Address: (b.) Department of Mathematics and Statistics, Edinburgh University, Mayfield Road, Edinburgh EH9 3JZ; T.-031-650 4877.

Aitken, Rev. Fraser Robert, MA, BD. Minister, Ayr: St. Columba Church, since 1991 (Minister, Girvan North Parish Church, 1984-91); b. 8.1.53, Paisley. Educ. John Neilson Institution, Paisley; Glasgow University. Assistant D'Anglais, CEG Anduze, France, 1972-73; Probationer Assistant, Fairmilehead Parish Church, Edinburgh, 1977-78; Minister, Neilston Parish Church, 1978-84. Chaplain, Ayr Bn., Boys' Brigade, 1985-91; Editor, Ayr Way (Presbytery Supplement), since 1985. Recreations: reading; music. Address: (h.) The Manse, 2 Hazelwood Road, Ayr; T.-0292 283125.

Aitken, George Pattullo Hogg, TD, BL. Assistant Secretary, Scottish Home and Health Department, 1975-90; b. 19.2.30, Dundee; m., Agnes Gray; 5 d. Educ. Morgan Academy;

Edinburgh University. Senior Examiner, Estate Duty Office, Edinburgh, 1958-69; Principal: Scottish Home and Health Department, 1969-72, Scottish Courts Administration, 1972-75. Kirk organist. Address: (h.) The Coach House, 13 High Street, Musselburgh, East Lothian.

Aitken, Joan Nicol, MA (Hons), SSC. Solicitor, since 1978; Partner, Messrs Rollo Davidson and McFarlane, Cupar, since 1985; Editor, Journal of the Law Society of Scotland; b. 26.2.53, Glasgow; m., Alistair Bruce Dodds; 1 d. Educ. James Gillespie's High School for Girls; Dundee University. Member: Scottish Consumer Council; Council, Law Society of Scotland. Was first lady member of Society of Solicitors in the Supreme Courts of Scotland. Address: (h.) Shepherd's Lodge, Glaickbea, Kiltarlity, Beauly IV4 7HR; T.-0463 74369.

Aitken, Professor Robert Cairns Brown, MB, ChB, DPM, MD, FRCPEdin, FRCPsych. Professor of Rehabilitation Studies, Edinburgh University, since 1974 (Dean, Faculty of Medicine, 1990-91, Vice-Principal, since 1991); Honorary Consultant in Rehabilitation Medicine, Lothian Health Board, since 1974; b. 20.12.33, Dunoon; m., Audrey May Lunn; 1 s.; 1 d. Educ. Dunoon Grammar School; Cargilfield School, Edinburgh; Sedbergh School, Yorkshire; Glasgow University. Institute of Aviation Medicine, RAF, 1959-62; Orpington and Maudsley Hospitals, 1962-66; Senior Lecturer/Consultant Psychiatrist, Royal Infirmary and Royal Edinburgh Hospital, 1967-74. President, International College of Psychosomatic Medicine, 1985-87; Chairman, Napier Polytechnic of Edinburgh Governors, 1983-90; Member, Council for Professions Supplementary to Medicine, 1983-90; Member, General Medical Council, since 1991; Director, Lothian Health Board, since 1991; Editor, Journal of Psychosomatic Research, 1979-85; occasional WHO consultant; Foundation Secretary, then President, Society for Research in Rehabilitation, 1981-83. Publications: papers on measurement of mood; flying phobia; management of disability. Recreations: people, places and pleasures of Edinburgh, Scotland and beyond. Address: (h.) 11 Succoth Place, Edinburgh, EH12 6BJ; T.-031-337 1550.

Aitken, Robin Elliot Guild, TD, MB, ChB, MSc, MFCM, MFPHM. Senior Medical Officer, Scottish Home and Health Department; b. 7.11.39, Edinburgh; m., 1, Gillian Ann Odell (deceased); 1 s.; 2, Helen Grace Broughton. Educ. Robert Gordon's College, Aberdeen; Aberdeen University. Medical Officer, 23 Parachute Field Ambulance, 1965-68; Regimental Medical Officer, 1st Bn., Black Watch, 1968-69; Army Health Specialist, 1969-72; retired as Major, 1972; Community Medicine Specialist, Grampian Health Board, 1972-79. Commanding Officer, 252 Field Ambulance (TA) as Lieutenant Colonel, 1977-79; Regimental Medical Officer (Lieutenant Colonel), 2nd 52nd Lowland Volunteers (TA), 1980-83; Elder, Colinton Parish Church. Recreations: running; mountaineering; skiing; cycling; fishing; shooting. Address: (h.) Carnferg, 31 Dreghorn Loan, Colinton, Edinburgh, EH13 ODF; T.-031-441 6116.

Aitken, William Duff, MM (FG). Director, William Aitken Highland Exports Ltd., since 1973; Member, Board of Directors, Eden Court Theatre, 1984-88; Member, Inverness District Council, 1984-88; b. 12.3.27, Newton Mearns; m., Eva Alexandra Kjellsson; 2 d. Educ. Terra Nova, Birkdale; Merchant Taylors'; Liverpool Nautical College. Seafaring, 1943-53; tanning industry, 1953-72. Member, SSAT. Recreations: philately; swimming; RNXS; TNAUK. Address: (h) The Thistles, 24 MacLeod Road, Balloch, by Inverness, IV1 2JW; T.-0463 791234.

Aitken, William Russell, MA, PhD, FLA. Bibliographer; b. 7.2.13, Calderbank, Lanarkshire; m., Betsy Mary Murison; 1 d. Educ. Dunfermline High School; Edinburgh University.

Assistant Librarian, Scottish Central Library, 1936-40; war service, RAF, 1941-46; County Librarian: Clackmannanshire, 1946-49, Perth and Kinross, 1949-58, Ayr, 1958-62; Lecturer, then Senior Lecturer, latterly Reader, Department of Librarianship, University of Strathclyde, 1962-78. President, Scottish Library Association, 1965; Friends Historical Society, 1989. Editor, Library Review, 1964-76. Books: A History of the Public Library Movement in Scotland, 1971; William Soutar's Poems in Scots and English (Editor), 1961, 1975; The Complete Poems of Hugh MacDiarmid (Editor, with Michael Grieve), 1978, 1985; Scottish Literature in English and Scots (a bibliographical guide), 1982; Poems of William Soutar: a new selection (Editor), 1988. Address: (h.) 6 Tannahill Terrace, Dunblane, FK15 OAX; T.-Dunblane 823650.

Aitkenhead, John M., MA (Hons), MEd, JP. Headmaster and Founder, Kilquhanity House International School for Boys and Girls, since 1940; b. 21.5.10, Glasgow; m., Morag MacKinnon; 2 s.; 2 d. Educ. Ardrossan Academy; Glasgow University. Worked in Scottish education system until 1940; conscientious objector during World War II; established school inspired by work and writing of A.S. Neill; ardent Scottish nationalist. Recreations: singing; poetry; Scottish country dancing; Gaelic; gardening. Address: Kilquhanity, Castle Douglas DG7 3DB; T.-055 665 242.

Alcock, Professor Leslie, OBE, MA, FSA, FRHistS. Professor of Archaeology, Glasgow University, 1973-90; b. 24.4.25, Manchester; m., Elizabeth A. Blair; 1 s.; 1 d. Educ. Manchester Grammar School; Brasenose College, Oxford. 7th Gurkha Rifles, 1943-47; Archaeological Survey of Pakistan, 1950-52; Lecturer, Reader, Professor of Archaeology, University College, Cardiff, 1953-73; Member, Board of Trustees, National Museum of Antiquities of Scotland, 1973-85; Member, Ancient Monuments Board, Scotland, 1974-90; Commissioner: Royal Commission on Ancient Monuments of Scotland, since 1977, RCAM Wales, 1986-90; President, Cambrian Archaeological Association, 1982-83; President, Society of Antiquaries of Scotland, 1984-87. Publications: Arthur's Britain, 1971; Economy, Society and Warfare, 1987. Recreations: mountain and coastal scenery; music. Address: (h.) 29 Hamilton Drive, Glasgow G12 8DN.

Alcock, Stephen Robert, MB, ChB, PhD. Senior Lecturer in Bacteriology, Glasgow University, since 1981; Honorary Consultant in Bacteriology, Greater Glasgow Health Board, since 1981; b. 24.6.45, Sutton Coldfield; m., Jean Margaret Diack; 1 s.; 1 d. Educ. Aberdeen Academy; Bearsden Academy; Aberdeen University. House Officer appointments, Aberdeen Royal Infirmary, 1970; Lecturer, Aberdeen University, 1970-81; consultancy work with diving industry, 1974-81, and Sultanate of Oman, 1984-88. Recreations: angling; books. Address (h.) 2 Midlothian Drive, Shawlands, Glasgow; T.-041-649 1521.

Alexander, Professor Alan, MA. Professor of Local Government, Strathclyde University, since 1987; Director, Scottish Local Authorities Management Centre, since 1987; b. 13.12.43, Glasgow; m., Morag MacInnes; 1 s.; 1 d. Educ. Possil Secondary School, Glasgow; Albert Secondary School, Glasgow; Glasgow University. Lecturer/Assistant Professor, Political Science, Lakehead University, Ontario, 1966-71; Lecturer in Politics, Reading University, 1971-87. Member of Board, Housing Corporation, 1977-80; Member, Standing Research Committee on Local and Central Government Relations, Joseph Rowntree Memorial Trust, since 1988; conducted inquiry into relations between Western Isles Islands Council and BCCI, 1991. Publications: Local Government in Britain since Reorganisation, 1982; The Politics of Local Government in the UK, 1982; L'amministrazione locale in Gran Bretagna, 1984; Borough Government and Politics:

Reading, 1835-1985, 1985. Recreations: theatre; cinema; hill-walking; avoiding gardening. Address: (b.) SLAMC, Strathclyde Graduate Business School, 130 Rottenrow, Glasgow, G4 0GE; T.-041-553 4143.

Alexander, David Alan, MA (Hons), PhD, Fel.BPS. Senior Lecturer, Medical School, Aberdeen University, since 1980 (Director of Course for the Diploma in Psychotherapy, since 1983) and Deputy Head of Department; b. 28.8.43, Ellon, Aberdeenshire. Educ. George Watson's College, Edinburgh; Morgan Academy, Dundee; St. Andrews University; Dundee University. Holder of MRC scholarship; Lecturer in Mental Health, Aberdeen University; Senior Lecturer in Mental Health, Aberdeen University and External Examiner, University of West Indies and University of London. Consultant to Police Foundation and Consultant to Grampian Police. Publications: co-author of three books and regular contributor to professional journals. Recreations: badminton; squash; climbing. Address: (b.) Department of Mental Health, Medical School, Foresterhill, Aberdeen; T.-Aberdeen 681818.

Alexander, Major-General David Crichton, CB. Commandant, Scottish Police College, 1979-87; b. 28.11.26, Aberdour; m., Diana Joyce (Jane) Fisher; 1 s.; 1 step-s.; 2 d. Educ. Edinburgh Academy; Staff College, Camberley; Royal College of Defence Studies. Royal Marines, 1944-77 (2nd Lieutenant to Major-General, including Equerry and Acting Treasurer to Duke of Edinburgh); Director-General, English Speaking Union, 1977-79. Governor, Corps of Commissionaires; Member, Civil Service Final Selection Board, 1978-88; Chairman, Edinburgh Academy, 1985-90; Freeman, City of London; Liveryman, Painter Stainers' Company; Member, Transport Users Consultative Committee for Scotland. Recreations: fishing; golf; gardening. Address: (h.) Baldinnie, Park Place, Elie KY9 1DH; T.-0333 330882.

Alexander, David Richard Watson, CBE (1972), MA; b. 12.8.18, Montrose; m., Mrs M.A.E. James; 1 s., 1 d. by pr. m.; 3 step-s. Educ. Montrose Academy; Edinburgh University. Served World War II in Hong Kong, India, Ceylon and Malaya (2nd Royal Scots, 12th Frontier Force Regt. and Force 136 (S.O.E.)); final rank, Lieutenant Colonel; awarded MBE (Mil.) for gallant and distinguished service with S.O.E. behind Japanese lines in Malaya. Colonial Administrative Service: appointed Assistant District Officer, Nigeria, 1946; resigned, 1947; re-appointed, 1948, Administrative Officer, Somaliland - on secondment to Cyrenaica (Libya) for service with War Office, then Foreign Office Administration of African Territories, finally Government of Cyrenaica; appointments: PA to Chief Administrator, BMA Benghazi, Political Secretary, District Commissioner Derna, District Adviser, Benghazi, Chief Secretary, Ministry of Interior; transferred to Hong Kong, 1953; appointments: Commissioner Essential Services Corps and Chief Staff Officer Civil Aid Services, Director of Social Welfare, Commissioner of Labour, Director of Urban Services and Chairman, Urban Council, Chairman, Housing Authority; Honourable Member, Legislative Council; retired, 1975. Elected Member, Lothian Regional Council, 1982-86 (Chairman, Planning and Development Committee). Address: (h.) 2 Crarae Avenue, Edinburgh, EH4 3JD.

Alexander, Rev. Douglas Niven, MA, BD. Minister, Erskine Parish Church, Bishopton, since 1970; Convener, Church of Scotland Board of Communication, 1987-91; b. 8.4.35, Eaglesham; m., Dr. Joyce O. Garven; 1 s.; 2 d. Educ. Hutchesons' Boys' Grammar School, Glasgow; Glasgow University (President, SRC, 1958); Union Theological Seminary, New York. Assistant Minister, St. Ninian's Church, Greenock, 1961-62; Warden, Iona Community House, Glasgow, 1963-70. Secretary, Scottish Union of Students, 1958; Assessor to Lord Rector, Glasgow University,

1969-71; Chaplain to Erskine Hospital, since 1970; Moderator, Paisley Presbytery, 1984; Mair Memorial Lecturer, Glasgow University, 1987; Chairman, British Churches Committee for Channel 4 TV, 1986-88; Member: Scottish Committee, IBA, 1988-90; Scottish Viewers Consultative Committee, ITC, since 1991; National Religious Advisory Committee, IBA, 1988-90; National Religious Advisory Committee, ITC, since 1991; Central Religious Advisory Committee, since 1988. Recreation: researching ways of salmon poachers! Address: The Manse, Newton Road, Bishopton, Renfrewshire, PA7 5JP; T.-0505 862161.

Alexander, Rev. Eric J., MA, BD. Minister, St. George's-Tron Parish Church, Glasgow, since 1977; b. 9.5.32, Glasgow; m., Margaret D. Connell; 1 s.; 1 d. Educ. Allan Glen's School, Glasgow; Glasgow University. Publications: The Search for God, 1962; Plainly Teaching the Word, 1989. Address: (h.) 12 Dargarvel Avenue, Glasgow, G41.

Alexander, James, BSc, PhD. Reader, Department of Immunology, Strathclyde University, since 1990; b. 14.11.49, Glasgow; m., Margaret Jean Wendon; 1 s. Educ. St. Mungo's Academy, Glasgow University. Scientific Staff, Division of Leprosy and Mycobacterial Research, National Institute for Medical Research, London, 1975-79; Research Fellow, Department of Biology, Imperial College of Science and Technology, London, 1979-85; Strathclyde University: Wellcome Trust Lecturer, Immunology, 1985, Senior Lecturer, 1989. Recreations: gardening; reading. Address: (b.) Todd Centre, Taylor Street, Strathclyde University, Glasgow G4 0NR; T.-041-552 4400.

Alexander, John Huston, BLitt, MA, DPhil Oxon. Senior Lecturer in English, Aberdeen University, since 1984; Editor, Scottish Literary Journal; Field Editor, Abstracts of English Studies, since 1988; b. 5.4.41, Coleraine, Northern Ireland; m., Flora Ross; 2 s.; 2 d. Educ. Campbell College, Belfast; St. Edmund Hall, Oxford. Sessional Lecturer in English, University of Saskatchewan, Canada, 1966-67; Lecturer in English, Aberdeen University, 1968-84. Editor, The Scott Newsletter, since 1982. Publications: Two Studies in Romantic Reviewing, 1976; The Lay of the Last Minstrel: Three Essays, 1978; The Reception of Scott's Poetry By His Correspondents: 1796-1817, 1979; Marmion: Studies in Interpretation and Composition, 1981; Scott and his Influence (Editor, with David Hewitt), 1983; Reading Wordsworth, 1987; Executive Editor, Edinburgh Edition of the Waverley Novels. Recreation: music. Address: (h.) 45A Queen's Road, Aberdeen, AB1 6YN; T.-0224 317424.

Alexander, Keith, BSc (Hons), BArch, RIBA, ARIAS, MBIM. Director, Centre for Facilities Management, Strathclyde University, since 1990; b. 20.9.49, Nottingham; m., Marie-Yvonne; 2 s.; 1 d. Educ. Wellingborough Grammar School; Welsh School of Architecture; University of Wales Institute of Science and Technology. Architect, new town development authorities, 1971-75; Principal, private practice, Northern Ireland and Scotland, 1975-78; Senior Lecturer, Ulster College, Northern Ireland Polytechnic, 1975-78; Consultant, Building Performance Design and Appraisal, 1978-90; Strathclyde University: Lecturer, Department of Architecture and Building Science, 1978-90, Director, Building Performance and Research Unit, 1984-90; Visiting Lecturer, School of Architecture, National University of Singapore, 1982-84; Architect, private practice, Singapore, 1982-84. Chairman, European Facilities Management Network. Recreations: rugby; golf. Address: (b.) Centre for Facilities Management, Strathclyde University, 50 George Street, Glasgow, G1 1QE. T.-041-553 4165.

Alexander, Sir Kenneth John Wilson, BSc (Econ), LLD, DUniv, FRSE, CBIM, Hon. Fellow, RIAS. Principal and Vice-Chancellor, Stirling University, 1981-86; b. 14.3.22,

Edinburgh; m., Angela-May; 1 s.; 4 d. Educ. George Heriot's School, Edinburgh; School of Economics, Dundee. Taught at Universities of Leeds, Sheffield and Aberdeen; Professor of Economics, Strathclyde University, 1963-80; Chancellor, Aberdeen University, since 1986; Member, Advisory Committee on University of the Air, 1965; Chairman: Committee on Adult Education in Scotland, 1970-73, Social Science Research Council, 1975-76; President, Section F, British Association, 1974; Chairman, Highlands and Islands Development Board, 1976-80; Economic Consultant to the Secretary of State for Scotland, since 1968; Member, Scottish Development Agency, 1975-85; Chairman, Council for Applied Science in Scotland, 1980-85; Governor, Technical Change Centre, 1981-87; Director, Scottish Television Ltd., since 1981; Member, Council for Tertiary Education in Scotland, 1981-82; Deputy Chairman, Scottish Council (Development and Industry), since 1982; Honorary President: The Highland Fund, since 1983; Scottish National Dictionary Association Ltd., since 1983; President, Town and Country Planning (Scottish Section), since 1982; Chairman, Michael Kelly Associates, since 1986; Director, Stakis plc, since 1987; Chairman, Edinburgh Book Festival, since 1987; Chairman, Scottish Industrial Trade Exhibitions, since 1990. Publications. The Economist in Business, 1967; Fairfields, a study of industrial change (with C.L. Jenkins), 1971; The Political Economy of Change (Editor), 1976. Recreation: Scottish antiquarianism. Address: (h.) 9 West Shore, Pittenweem, Fife, KY10 2NV; T.-0333 310593.

Alexander, Professor Michael Joseph, BA, MA (Oxon). Berry Professor of English Literature, St. Andrews University, since 1985; b. 21.5.41, Wigan; m., 1, Eileen Mary McCall (deceased); 2, Mary Cecilia Sheahan; 1 s.; 2 d. Educ. Downside School; Trinity College, Oxford; Perugia University; Princeton University. Editor, William Collins, London, 1963-65; Lecturer, University of California, 1966-67; Editor, Andre Deutsch, London, 1967-68; Lecturer: East Anglia University, 1968-69, Stirling University, 1969; Senior Lecturer, 1977; Reader, 1985. Publications: Earliest Anglish Poems (Translator), 1966; Beowulf (Translator), 1973; Twelve Poems, 1978; The Poetic Achievement of Ezra Pound, 1979; Macmillan Anthology of English Literature, 1989. Address: (b.) Department of English, St. Andrews University, St. Andrews KY16 9AL; T.-0334 76161.

Alexander, Samuel, BL. Honorary Sheriff, Dumbarton, since 1983; b. Glasgow; m., Isabella Kerr Ligertwood; 2 s. Educ. Govan High School; Glasgow University. Consultant (formerly Senior Partner), Keyden Strang & Co., Solicitors, Glasgow. Recreations: golf; reading. Address: (h.) 1 Hillneuk Avenue, Bearsden, Glasgow, G61; T.-041-942 4674.

Alexander, William Nelson, OBE, JP, CEng, MICE, MIHT. Depute Chief Executive, Dumfries and Galloway Regional Council, since 1989; b. 13.5.36, Glasgow; m., Eleanor Smith McNaught; 2 d. Educ. Allan Glen's School, Glasgow; Royal College of Science and Technology, Glasgow (part-time); Paisley Technical College (part-time). Trained as Civil Engineer, Dumbarton County Council, 1953-58; National Service, 1959-61; various appointments with local roads authorities in Scotland, 1961-79; Personal Assistant to Chief Executive, Dumfries and Galloway Regional Council, 1979-84; Depute Director of Roads and Transportation, 1984-87; Assistant Chief Executive, 1987-89. Municipal Engineer of the Year, 1989. Recreations: golf; walking; photography. Address: (h.) Nethercairn, 10 Georgetown Drive, Dumfries, DG1 4EH; T.-0387 61103.

Ali, Nasir, MB, BS, DPM, MRCPsych. Consultant Psychiatrist, since 1973; Honorary Senior Lecturer, Aberdeen University, since 1982; b. 21.8.39, Lucknow, India; m., D. Rosemary; 1 s.; 1 d. Address: (h.) Balmachree House, Dalcross, Inverness, IV1 2JQ; T.-Inverness 790602.

Ali, Yaqub, OBE. Chairman, Castle/AA Brothers Ltd.; Director, Hunza Foods Ltd.; Director, Strathclyde Vintners Ltd.; b. 12.12.31; m., Nancy; 1 s. Non-Executive Director, Landmark Cash & Carry Group; Member: Scottish Police Advisory Board, Scottish Industry Development Advisory Board, Queens College Council, Glasgow. Recreation: gardening. Address: (b.) 525 Crown Street, Glasgow, G5 9XR; T.-041-429 6188.

Alison, Graham, BSc, MEd. General Secretary, Scottish Further and Higher Education Association, since 1982; b. 15.6.31, Clydebank; m., Norma McA. Perry; 2 d. Educ. Dumbarton Academy; Glasgow University. Education Officer, RAF; Educational Psychologist, Lecturer in Psychology and (until it closed) Vice-Principal, Hamilton College of Education. Recreations: theatre; golf; bowling. Address: (b.) 90 Mitchell Street, Glasgow, G1 3NQ; T.-041-221 0118.

Allan, Andrew D.C., MA (Hons). Head Teacher, Mainholm Academy, Ayr, since 1974; b. 16.4.31, Irvine; m., Margaret M.N. Lamont; 2 d. Educ. Irvine Royal Academy; Glasgow University; Jordanhill College of Education. National Service, RAEC, 1954-56; Mathematics Teacher, Kilmarnock Academy, 1956-58; Principal Teacher of Mathematics: Dalry High School, 1958-62, John Neilson Institution, 1962-65, Kilmarnock Academy 1965-71; Assistant Head Teacher, Kilmarnock Academy, 1970-72; Depute Head Teacher, Ardrossan Academy, 1972-74. Elder, Church of Scotland, since 1956; President, Alloway Rotary Club, 1986-87; Governor, Craigie College of Education, 1979-87, and Jordanhill College, since 1991; Member, Education Committee, Church of Scotland. Recreations: golf; walking; travelling. Address: (h.) 46 Taybank Drive, Ayr; T.-Alloway 41067.

Allan, David Smith, BSc (Hons). DipEd. Headmaster, Preston Lodge High School, Prestonpans, since 1970; b. 17.1.35, Prestonpans; m., Alexandra; 2 s.; 1 d. Educ. Preston Lodge School, Prestonpans; Edinburgh University. Teacher, George Heriot's School, Edinburgh, 1958-63; Principal Teacher of Science, Preston Lodge High School, Prestonpans, 1963-70. Hon. President, Preston Lodge FP Club; Past President, Lothian Headteachers Association. Recreations: rugby committee work; golf. Address: (b.) Preston Lodge High School, Prestonpans, East Lothian; T.-Prestonpans 811170.

Allan, D. Stuart, LLB, NP. Solicitor and Notary Public; Director of Corporate Services, Fife Regional Council; b. 11.11.49, Dundee. Educ. Morgan Academy; Dundee University. Chairman, Society of Directors of Administration in Scotland, 1991-92. Address: (b.) Fife House, Glenrothes, KY7 FLT; T.-0592 754411.

Allan, Gary James Graham, LLB. Partner, Hughes Dowdall, Solicitors, Glasgow, since 1986; b. 21.1.58, Aberdeen; m., Margaret Muriel Glass. Educ. Aberdeen Grammar School; Aberdeen University. Apprenticeship, McGrigor Donald and Company, Solicitors, Glasgow and Edinburgh; joined Hughes Dowdall, 1982. Executive Member, Glasgow Bar Association, since 1983; Parliamentary Liaison Officer, Law Society of Scotland, until 1988. Recreations: sport; reading; music; fishing; the company of good friends. Address: (b.) 216 Bath Street, Glasgow, G2 4HS; T.-041-332 5321.

Allan, George Alexander, MA (Hons). Headmaster, Robert Gordon's College, Aberdeen, since 1978; b. 3.2.36, Edinburgh; m., Anne Violet Veevers; 2 s. Educ. Daniel Stewart's College, Edinburgh; Edinburgh University. Teacher of Classics, Glasgow Academy, 1958-60; Daniel Stewart's College: Teacher of Classics, 1960-63, Head of Classics,

1963-73 (appointed Housemaster, 1967); Schoolmaster Fellow Commoner, Corpus Christi College, Cambridge, 1972; Deputy Headmaster, Robert Gordon's College, 1973-77. Former Chairman and former Secretary, Headmasters' Conference (Scottish Division) (Member, National Committee, 1982 and 1983); Governor, Welbeck College, 1980-89; Council Member, Scottish Council of Independent Schools, since 1988. Recreations: gardening; golf; music. Address: 24 Woodend Road, Aberdeen, AB2 6YH; T.-0224 321733.

Allan, James Morrison, FRICS, ACIArb. Chartered Surveyor; b. 1.10.43, Edinburgh; m., Elizabeth Howie Sneddon Jack; 2 s. Educ. George Watson's College; Heriot Watt College. Joined Phillips Knox & Arthur as Apprentice Quantity Surveyor, 1960; qualified ARICS, 1965; FRICS, 1975; RICS: Chairman, National Junior Organisation, 1975-76; Chairman, Quantity Surveyors Committee in Scotland, 1988-89; Chairman, RICS in Scotland, 1991-92; Scottish nominee, RICS General Council. Recreations: family; caravanning and motoring; golf. Address: (b.) 9 Park Crescent, Liberton, Edinburgh, EH16 6JD; T.-031-658 1113.

Allan, John Balfour, MA, LLB. Divisional Solicitor, Office of Solicitor to Secretary of State for Scotland, since 1982; b. 11.10.33, Linlithgow Bridge. Educ. George Watson's College, Edinburgh; Edinburgh University. Legal Assistant, Auld & Macdonald, WS, 1958-60; Office of Solicitor to Secretary of State for Scotland: Legal Assistant, 1961-66, Senior Legal Assistant, 1967-71; Divisional Solicitor, 1971-72; Secretary, Scottish Law Commission, 1972-79; Deputy Solicitor to Secretary of State for Scotland, 1979-82. Recreation: men's hockey. Address: (h.) 10 Craigleith Hill Gardens, Edinburgh, EH4 2JJ; T.-031-332 6420.

Allan, Sheriff John Douglas, BL, DMS, FBIM. Sheriff of Lanark, since 1988; b. 2.10.41, Edinburgh; m., Helen E.J. Aiton; 1 s.; 1 d. Educ. George Watson's College, Edinburgh; Edinburgh University. Solicitor in private practice, Edinburgh, 1963-67; Procurator Fiscal Depute, Edinburgh, 1967-71; Solicitor, Crown Office, Edinburgh, 1971-76; Assistant Procurator Fiscal, then Senior Assistant Procurator Fiscal, Glasgow, 1976-79; Solicitor, Crown Office, Edinburgh, 1979-83; Procurator Fiscal for Edinburgh and Regional Procurator Fiscal for Lothians and Borders, 1983-88. Part-time Lecturer in Law, Napier College, Edinburgh, 1963-66; Holder, Scout "Medal of Merit"; Session Clerk, Greenbank Parish Church of Scotland. Recreations: Scouts; youth leadership; walking; Church. Address: (b.) Sheriff Court House, Lanark ML11 7NQ; T.-0555 61531.

Allan, Norman James Wilson, MA, FSA Scot, FRCS(C), FRCOG. Member, Grampian Regional Council, since 1986; b. 23.4.22, Dufftown; 1 s.; 1 d. Educ. Hutchesons' Grammar School, Glasgow; Aberdeen University; Glasgow University. Merchant Navy; SHO, Hammersmith Hospital, London; Registrar, Edinburgh; Senior Registrar, Northampton; Associate Professor, University of Ottawa; Consultant Obstetrician and Gynaecologist, Ottawa General Hospital; Consultant in Maternal Welfare, Government of Ontario. Publication: Scotland, The Broken Image, 1983. Address: (h.) Glenbrae, 2 Campbell Street, Banff, AB45 1JR; T.-0261 815291.

Allan, Norman Colvin, MB, ChB, FRCP, FRCPath. Consultant Haematologist, Western General Hospital, Edinburgh, since 1967, and part-time Senior Lecturer in Medicine, Edinburgh University; b. 30.6.29, N. Nigeria; m., Margaret Eurwen; 2 s.; 3 d. Educ. Daniel Stewart's College, Edinburgh; Edinburgh University. RAMC, 1953-55; Registrar, 1956-60; Senior Registrar, Haematology, Ibadan, 1960-62; Senior Lecturer, Haematology, Ibadan, 1962-67.

Recreation: photography. Address: (h.) 11 Crarae Avenue, Edinburgh, EH4 3JD; T.-031-332 4748.

Allan, Robert, MBE. Chief Executive, Scottish Fishermen's Federation, since 1982; b. 14.11.33, Peterhead; m., Moira W. Morrison; 2 d. Educ. Aberdeen Grammar School. Audit Assistant, R.C. Kelman & Shirreffs, CA, Aberdeen, 1949-62; Assistant Secretary, latterly Secretary, Aberdeen Fishing Vessel Owners' Association Ltd. and Scottish Trawlers' Federation, 1962-71; Chief Executive, Aberdeen Fishing Vessel Owners' Association Ltd. and Aberdeen Fish Producers' Organisation Ltd., 1971-82. Recreation: keen follower of the fortunes of Aberdeen FC. Address: (h.) 40 Parkhill Circle, Dyce, Aberdeen, AB2 OFN; T.-0224 724366.

Allan, Scott Birnie, MA, DipEd. Vice-Principal, Queen Margaret College, since 1989; b. 16.3.37, Paisley; m., Margaret Coulthard; 2 s. Educ. Greenock Academy; King's School, Rochester; St. Andrews University; University of Surrey. Education Officer, Royal Army Education Corps, 1961-65; Lecturer, National Police Staff College, Bramshill, 1965-74; Senior Lecturer, latterly Head, Department of Communication and Information Studies, Queen Margaret College, 1974-89. Recreations: theatre; music; travel. Address: (b.) Queen Margaret College, Clerwood Terrace, Edinburgh, EH12 8TS; T.-031-317 3203.

Allanbridge, Hon. Lord (William Ian Stewart), QC. Senator of the College of Justice in Scotland, since 1977; b. 8.11.25. Called to the Bar, 1951; Advocate-Depute, 1959-64; Home Advocate-Depute, 1970-72; Solicitor-General for Scotland, 1972-74; Temporary Sheriff Principal, Dumfries and Galloway, 1974.

Allcock, Ronald, FIWEM, LRSC. Director, Tay River Purification Board, since 1987; b. 9.1.40, Mancot; 1 s.; 1 d. Educ. Holywell Grammar School; Doncaster College of Technology. Research Chemist, Coalite Chemicals, 1962; District Inspector, Trent River Authority, 1966; Divisional Pollution Officer: Yorkshire Water, 1972, Clyde River Purification Board, 1978. Recreations: golf; reading; amateur football. Address: (b.) 1 South Street, Perth, PH2 8NJ; T.-Perth 27989.

Allen, Professor John Anthony, PhD, DSc, FIBiol, FRSE. Director, University Marine Biological Station, Millport, 1976-91; Professor of Marine Biology, London University, 1976-91; b. West Bridgford; m., Margaret Porteous Aitken; 1 s.; 1 d.; 1 step s. (adopted). Assistant Lecturer, Glasgow University; Reader in Marine Biology, Newcastle upon Tyne University. Member, Natural Environmental Research Council, 1977-83 (Chairman, University Affairs Committee, 1978-83); Member, Nature Conservancy Council, 1982-90 (Chairman, Advisory Committee on Science, 1984-90); Council, Marine Biological Association, 1981-83, since 1989. Recreations: appreciating gardens; pub lunching; wildlife. Address: (h.) Drialstone, Isle of Cumbrae; T.-0475 530479.

Allen, Professor John Walter, MA, FSAS, FRSE. Professor of Solid State Physics, St. Andrews University, since 1980; b. 7.3.28, Birmingham. Educ. King Edward's High School, Birmingham; Sidney Sussex College, Cambridge. RAF, 1949-51; Staff Scientist, Ericsson Telephones Ltd., 1951-56; Services Electronics Research Laboratory, 1956-68; Visiting Associate Professor, Stanford University, 1964-66; joined Department of Physics, St. Andrews University, 1968. Recreations: archaeology; country dancing. Address: (b.) Department of Physics and Astronomy, St. Andrews University, North Haugh, St. Andrews, Fife, KY16 9SS; T.-0334 76161.

Allen, Professor Kevin John, BA. Professor and Director, European Policies Research Centre, Strathclyde University;

b. 25.11.41, Warrington; m., Kirsten Margaret Paton; 1 s.; 1 d. Educ. Boteler Grammar School, Warrington; Nottingham University; Newcastle University. Lecturer in Applied Economics, Glasgow University, 1964-75; Research Fellow, International Institute of Management, Berlin, 1975-77; Co-Director, then Director, Centre for the Study of Public Policy, Strathclyde, 1977-87. Recreations: fly fishing; photography. Address: 141 St. James Road, Glasgow, G4 0LT; T.-041-552 4400.

Allison, Professor Arthur Compton, BSc, DipNumMath, PhD, MBCS. Vice Principal for Science and Engineering and Professor of Computing Science, Glasgow University, since 1986 (Director, Board of Studies in Information Technology); b. 24.3.41, Belfast; m., Dr. Joyce Allison; 3 d. Educ. Queen's University, Belfast; Glasgow University. Glasgow University, 1962-67; Smithsonian Institution, Boston, 1967-73; Glasgow University, 1973-83; Northeastern University, Boston, 1983-84; Glasgow University, since 1984. Elder, Church of Scotland. Recreations: running; squash; curling. Address: (b.) Department of Computing Science, Glasgow University, Glasgow, G12 8QQ; T.-041-339 8855, Ext. 4453.

Allison, Charles William, MBChB, FFARCS. Consultant Anesthetist, Stracathro Hospital, Brechin, since 1982; Consultant, Dundee teaching hospitals; Honorary Senior Lecturer, Dundee University; b. 1.7.52, Newport on Tay; m., Elspeth Stratton; 2 d. Educ. Madras College, St. Andrews; Dundee University. Training grades in anaesthesia, Dundee, 1976-81; Clinical Research Fellow, Hospital for Sick Children, Toronto, 1982. Publication: Preoperative Starvation in Children (paper). Recreations: golf; photography. Address: Summerbank House, Brechin, Angus DD9 6HL; T.-0356 623624.

Allison, John Andrew, MA, LLB. Solicitor, since 1963; Honorary Sheriff, Cupar, since 1986; b. 10.5.36, Glasgow; m., Elizabeth; 2 s.; 1 d. Educ. Paisley Grammar School; Glasgow University. Legal apprenticeship, McGrigor Donald & Co., Glasgow; Legal Assistant, Glenrothes Development Corporation; Partner, Pagan, Osborne, Grace and Calders, WS, Fife; Dean, Society of Solicitors for Eastern District of Fife; Member, Council, Law Society of Scotland. Recreations: hill-walking; sailing. Address: (h.) Craigrothie House, by Cupar, Fife; (b.) 12 St. Catherine Street, Cupar, Fife; T.-0334 53777.

Allison, Joseph Philip Sloan, MA (Cantab), CertEd. Headmaster, St. Mary's Music School, Edinburgh, since 1979; b. 6.2.44, Leeds; m., Caroline Margaret Paton; 3 s.; 1 d. Educ. Rugby; Churchill College, Cambridge; Moray House College of Education. Jardine Matheson & Co. Ltd., Hong Kong, 1967-70; Assistant Master, then Assistant Head, Belhaven Hill, Dunbar, 1970-77; Deputy Head, St. Mary's Music School, 1977-79. Recreations: sailing; bird-watching; hill-walking. Address: (h.) 4 Raeburn Street, Edinburgh, EH4 1HY; T.-031-332 9768.

Allison, Marjorie Elisabeth Marion, BSc, MD, FRCP. Senior Lecturer in Medicine, Glasgow University, since 1977; Honorary Consultant Nephrologist, Glasgow Royal Infirmary, since 1977; b. 7.9.40, Glasgow. Educ. Hamilton Academy; Glasgow University. Clinical training in nephrology, Glasgow Royal Infirmary, 1966-69; Research Fellow in Kidney Pathophysiology, University of North Carolina, 1969-72, 1979-81. Publications: contributed chapters on acute kidney failure to textbooks. Recreations: gardening; cooking; medical antiquities. Address: (b.) Renal Unit, Glasgow Royal Infirmary, Glasgow; T.-041-552 3535, Ext. 5292.

Allsop, Douglas Thomson, MBE. Executive Director, Scottish Council on Alcohol, since 1979; b. 5.11.32, Arbroath; m., Elizabeth Blair Marshall; 1 s. Educ. Arbroath

High School. Clydesdale Bank Ltd., 1949-72 (latterly as Investment Manager); Regional Director, Slater, Walker Ltd., Merchant Bankers, 1973-77. Recreations: gardening; walking. Address: (b.) 137/145 Sauchiehall Street, Glasgow, G2 3EW; T.-041-333 9677.

Allsop, Rev. Thomas Douglas, MA, BD. Minister, Beechgrove Church, Aberdeen, since 1977; b. 2.3.34, Kilmaurs; m., Marion Morrison Urie; 2 s.; 1 d. Educ. Kilmarnock Academy; Glasgow University and Trinity College. Assistant Minister, St. Marnock's, Kilmarnock; Minister: Kirriemuir South (after a union called Kirriemuir St. Andrew's), 1959-65; Minister, Knightswood St. Margaret's, Glasgow, 1965-77. Founder Chairman, Kirriemuir Round Table; Moderator, Dumbarton Presbytery, 1975; Burgess, City of Aberdeen. Recreations: photography; golf; musical appreciation. Address: 156 Hamilton Place, Aberdeen, AB2 4BB; T.-0224 642615.

Alstead, Brigadier (Francis) Allan (Littlejohns), CBE, MPhil, FCIT, FBIM, FIPM, FInstAM. Chief Executive, Scottish Sports Council, since 1990; b. 19.6.35, Glasgow; m., Joy Veronica Edwards; 2 s. Educ. Glasgow Academy; Royal Military Academy, Sandhurst; Royal Naval Staff College; Joint Services Staff College; University of Wales, Aberystwyth. Commissioned into King's Own Scottish Borderers, 1955; commanded 1st Bn., KOSB, 1974-76; Military Assistant to Quarter-Master-General, 1976-79; Instructor, Army Staff College, Camberley, 1979-81; Assistant Chief of Staff, BAOR, 1981-84 (Colonel); Commander, 51st Highland Brigade, 1984-87 (Brigadier); NATO Research Fellow, 1987-88; NATO Reinforcement Co-ordinator, 1988-90. Member, Royal Company of Archers (Queen's Bodyguard in Scotland); Regimental Trustee, KOSB; Deputy Hon. Colonel, Edinburgh and Heriot Watt Universities OTC; Governor, Moray House College. Recreations: running; swimming; tennis; sailing. Address: (b.) South Gyle, Edinburgh, EH12 9DQ; T.-031-317 7200.

Ambler, Professor Richard Penry, MA, PhD, FSAS. Professor of Protein Chemistry and Head, Institute of Cell & Molecular Biology, Edinburgh University; b. 26.5.33, Bexley Heath; m.; 2 d. Educ. Haileybury and ISC; Pembroke College, Cambridge. Research Fellow, Pembroke College, Cambridge, 1959-62; scientific staff, MRC Laboratory of Molecular Biology, Cambridge, 1960-65; joined Department of Molecular Biology, Edinburgh University, 1965. Address: (b.) Institute of Cell & Molecular Biology, Darwin Building, University of Edinburgh EH9 3JR; T.-031-650 5366.

Ambrose, Timothy Michael, BA (Hons), CertEd, FMA. Director, Scottish Museums Council, since 1986; b. 8.12.49, Devizes; m., Hon. Angela Ambrose; 2 d. Educ. Dauntsey School; Southampton University. Archivist, Ashmolean Museum Library, Oxford University, 1972; Research Assistant, Danebury Trust, 1973; Publications Assistant, Department of Environment, 1973; Research Assistant in European Archaeology, Oxford University, 1975; Assistant Keeper of Archaeology, Lincolnshire Museums, 1977; Scottish Museums Council: Depute Director, 1982, Acting Director, 1986. External Examiner, Department of Museum Studies, Leicester University, since 1990; Board Member, Business in the Arts Scotland, since 1991. Publications: New Museums – A Start-up Guide, 1987; Education in Museums, Museums in Education, 1987, Working with Museums, 1988; Presenting Scotland's Story, 1989; Money, Money, Money and Museums, 1991; Forward Planning: A Handbook (Co-editor), 1991; Museum Basics (Co-author), 1992. Recreation: gardening. Address: (h.) 7 Plewlands Avenue, Morningside, Edinburgh; T.-031-447 1218.

Amin, Professor Sayed-Hassan, LLB, LLM, PhD. International Lawyer; Vice-President, Scottish Institute of

International and Comparative Law; Visiting Professor, Tehran University, since 1988; Member, Chartered Institute of Arbitrators, since 1984; b. Persia. Educ. University of Tehran; Glasgow University. Senior Lecturer, then Reader in Law, Glasgow Polytechnic, 1981-91; Middle East Editor, Oil and Gas Law and Taxation Review, since 1985; Director and Representative for Scotland and N.I., World Development Movement, since 1989; Member, Council for National Academic Awards, since 1989. Publications: 27 books on international, Middle Eastern and Islamic law. Recreations: walking; book collecting. Address: (h.) Royston, Crown Road North, Glasgow, G12 9DH; T.-041-339 1867.

Ancram, Michael Andrew Foster Jude, MA, LLB. MP (Conservative), Devizes, since 1992; b. London; m., Lady Jane Fitzalan-Howard; 2 d. Educ. Ampleforth; Christ Church, Oxford; Edinburgh University. Advocate, Scottish Bar, 1970; MP, Berwickshire and East Lothian, February to September, 1974; Chairman, Conservative Party in Scotland, 1980-83; MP, Edinburgh South, 1979-87; Minister for Home Affairs and Environment, Scottish Office, 1983-87; Chairman, Northern Corporate Communications Ltd. 1989-91. Recreations: skiing; folk singing; photography. Address: (h.) Monteviot, Jedburgh, Roxburghshire TD8 6UQ.

Anderson, Rev. Andrew Fraser, MA, BD. Minister, Greenside Parish Church, since 1981; b. 2.9.44, Aberdeen; m., Hazel Neary; 2 s. Educ. Harrow School; Magdalen College, Oxford; Edinburgh University. Industrial management, Dickinson Robinson Group Ltd., 1967-77. Recreations: music; gardening. Address: (h.) 80 Pilrig Street, Edinburgh, EH6 5AS; T.-031-554 3277.

Anderson, Andrew John. Director, National Outdoor Centre, Glenmore Lodge, since 1986; Member, Management Team, Scottish Sports Council, since 1987; b. 30.10.44, Altrincham; m., Catriona Mary; 1 d. Army, 1964-73; Instructor in Outdoor Activities; Instructor in Mountaineering, Glenmore Lodge, 1973-79; Deputy Director, Inverclyde National Sports Training Centre, Largs, 1979-86. Training Officer, Mountain Rescue Committee of Scotland. Recreations: mountaineering; golf. Address: (h.) Director's House, Glenmore Lodge, Aviemore, PH22 1QU; T.-047-986 256.

Anderson, Charles Mitchell, MA, DPA. Chief Executive, Ettrick and Lauderdale District Council, since 1985; b. 3.9.45, Kirkcaldy; m., Margaret; 2 s. Educ. Kirkcaldy High School; Edinburgh University; Strathclyde University (part-time). Divisional Assistant Secretary, Freight Transport Association; Administrative Officer, Irvine Development Corporation; Principal Administrative Officer, Highland Regional Council; Assistant Director of Administration and Legal Services, Central Regional Council; Assistant Secretary, Convention of Scottish Local Authorities. Address: (b.) PO Box 4, Council Chambers, Paton Street, Galashiels, TD1 3AS; T.-0896 4751.

Anderson, David, MBE, JP. Member, Grampian Regional Council, 1974-90 (Depute Convener, 1986-90, Liberal Democrat Group Leader, 1982-90); b. 17.1.16, St. Andrews; m., Jessie Watt Taylor; 2 s.; 1 d. Educ. Madras College, St. Andrews. Employed in forestry, various estates in Fife, until 1939; Sergeant, Royal Corps of Signals, 1939-46; various posts in Forestry Commission, 1946-81, latterly as Chief Forester in charge, Huntly Forest; Member, Aberdeen County Council, 1961-74; Chairman, Education Committee, 1973-74. Chairman, Rhynie Branch, Royal British Legion. Recreation: bowling. Address: (h.) Burmah, 6 Watson Avenue, Huntly, Aberdeenshire, AB5 5BF; T.-Huntly 2878.

Anderson, David Colville, VRD, QC, BA Oxon, LLB; b. 8.9.16, Cupar; m., Juliet Hill Watson; 2 s.; 1 d. Educ.

Glenalmond College; Pembroke College, Oxford; Edinburgh University. RNVR, 1935-61; served World War II in destroyers; mentioned in Despatches, 1942; special operation, Norway, 1945; King Haakon VII Freedom Medal; Admiralty's Egerton Prize, 1943; Lieutenant Commander, 1947. Advocate, 1946; Lecturer in Scots Law, Edinburgh University, 1947-60; Standing Junior Counsel, Ministry of Works, 1954-55, and War Office, 1955-57; QC, 1957; Solicitor-General for Scotland, 1960-64; MP (Conservative) for Dumfries, 1963-64; Honorary Sheriff, 1965-72; Chairman, Industrial Appeal Tribunals, 1970-72; Chief Reporter for Public Inquiries and Under-Secretary, Scottish Office, 1972-74; Commissioner, Northern Lighthouses, 1960-64. Subject of play, The Case of David Anderson QC, by John Hale (Lyric, Hammersmith, 1981, etc.). Recreations: travel; hill-walking; golf. Address: (h.) 8 Arboretum Road, Edinburgh, EH3 5PD; T.-031-552 3003.

Anderson, David Rae, MA (Hons), LLB, LLM, WS, NP. Solicitor, since 1961 (Senior Partner in private practice); part-time Legal Chairman, Industrial Tribunals, since 1971; Honorary Sheriff, since 1981; b. 27.1.36, Stonehaven; m., Jean Strachan. Educ. Mackie Academy, Stonehaven; Aberdeen University; Edinburgh University; Australian National University, Canberra. Barrister and Solicitor of Supreme Court of Victoria, Australia, 1962; Legal Officer, Attorney-General's Department, Canberra, 1962-65; part-time research student, Law Faculty, Australian National University, Canberra, and part-time Lecturer in Legal History, 1962-65; returned to Scotland, 1965, in private legal practice, Edinburgh, 1965-67, Alloa and Central Scotland, since 1967; Interim Town Clerk, Burgh of Alva, 1973; former part-time Reporter to Secretary of State for Scotland for public enquiries; former Dean, Society of Solicitors of Clackmannanshire; Member, Council, Law Society of Scotland; former Convener, International Relations Committee, currently Convener 1992 Committee and Convener, Committee on the Constitution; former Member, UK Delegation, Council of the Bars and Law Societies of the European Community; Member, Stirling University Conference; Elder, Church of Scotland; Parliamentary candidate, 1970 and 1971; formerly served, RNVR; Past President, Alloa Rotary Club. Recreations: climbing and hill-walking; reading, especially historical biography and English literature; music; interested in current affairs, architecture, stately homes and travel. Address: (h.) 3 Smithfield Loan, Alloa, FK10 1NJ; T.-0259 213096; (b.) 8 Shillinghill, Alloa, FK10 1JT; T.-0259 723201.

Anderson, Don S.H., IPFA, FRVA. Director of Finance, Clydesdale District Council, since 1983; b. 9.1.43, Forfar; m., Irene R.; 3 d. Educ. Mackie Academy, Stonehaven. Trainee Accountant, Clackmannan County Council, 1961-66; Accountancy Assistant, Airdrie Town Council, 1966-69; Accountant, Kilmarnock Town Council, 1969-75; Finance Manager, Clydesdale District Council, 1975-83. Recreations: golf; swimming. Address: (b.) District Offices, South Vennel, Lanark, ML11 7JT; T.-0555 61331, Ext. 134.

Anderson, Dorothy Elizabeth, BSc (Hons), MB, ChB, MRCP(UK), DMRD, FRCR, FRCP(Glas). Consultant Radiologist, Glasgow Royal Infirmary, since 1981; Honorary Clinical Lecturer, Glasgow University, since 1982; b. 26.9.50, Glasgow; m., David Anderson; 1 s.; 1 d. Educ. Glasgow High School for Girls; Glasgow University. Pre-registration posts, Stobhill Hospital and Glasgow Royal Infirmary; post-registration year, Respiratory Unit, Knightswood Hospital; trained in radiology, Western Infirmary, Glasgow (Registrar, then Senior Registrar). Recreation: choral singing. Address: (h.) 18 Milverton Avenue, Bearsden, Glasgow G61 4BE; T.-041-942 7510.

Anderson, Douglas Kinloch, OBE, MA. Chairman, Kinloch Anderson Ltd., Edinburgh, since 1975; Board Member, Scottish Tourist Board, since 1986; Deputy Chairman, Edinburgh Marketing Ltd.; Director: Lothian and Edinburgh Enterprise Ltd., Edinburgh's Capital Ltd., Scottish Eastern Investment Trust PLC; b. 19.2.39, Edinburgh; m., Deirdre Anne; 2 s.; 1 d. Educ. George Watson's Boys College; St. Andrews University. Joined Kinloch Anderson Ltd., 1962 (fifth generation in family business); Assistant on Master's Court, Edinburgh Merchant Company, 1976-79; elected Honorary Member, St. Andrew's Society of Washington DC, 1985; Member, Edinburgh Festival Council, 1988-90; President, Edinburgh Royal Warrant Holders Association, 1987-88; Member, Scottish Committee, Institute of Directors; President, Edinburgh Chamber of Commerce, 1988-90; Master, Edinburgh Merchant Company, since 1990. Recreations: golf; fishing; watching schoolboy rugby; travel (non-business). Address: (b.) Commercial Street/Dock Street, Leith, Edinburgh EH6 6EY; T.-031-555 1355.

Anderson, Douglas M.W., DSc, PhD, CChem, FRSC, FRSE. Reader in Chemistry, Edinburgh University, since 1954; b. 10.11.25, Edinburgh; m., Margaret Joan Laing; 1 s.; 3 d. Educ. Montrose Academy; Edinburgh University. War Service, RAF, 1943-46 (Radar duties). Secretary and General Scientific Adviser, International Natural Gums Association for Research Ltd.; adviser and consultant to industry; Editor, two series of monographs on aspects of analytical chemistry. Recreations: music; angling; philately; all kinds of DIY. Address: (b.) Chemistry Department, The University, Edinburgh, EH9 3JJ; T.-031-667 1081, Ext. 3446.

Anderson, Gordon Alexander, CA, FCMA. Chartered Accountant; b. 9.8.31, Glasgow; m., Eirene Cochrane Howie Douglas; 2 s.; 1 d. Educ. High School of Glasgow. Apprentice CA, Moores Carson & Watson, Glasgow, 1949-54; qualified CA, 1955; National Service, Royal Navy, 1955-57 (Sub Lieutenant); Partner, Moores Carson & Watson, 1958 (firm name changed to McClelland Moores, 1958, Arthur Young McClelland Moores, 1968, Arthur Young, 1985, Ernst & Young, 1989); Chairman, Arthur Young, 1987-89; Deputy Senior Partner, Ernst & Young, 1989-90; Member, Council on Tribunals and of its Scottish Committee, since 1990; Chairman, Bitmac Ltd., since 1990; Director: TSB Bank Scotland plc, since 1991, High School of Glasgow Ltd., 1975-81, Douglas Firebrick Co. Ltd., 1960-70; Member, Scottish Milk Marketing Board, 1979-85; Institute of Chartered Accountants of Scotland: Member, Council, 1980-84, Vice President, 1984-86, President, 1986-87. Recreations: golf; gardening; rugby football (as spectator). Address: (h.) Ardwell, 41 Manse Road, Bearsden, Glasgow, G61 3PN; T.-041-942 2803.

Anderson, Rev. Professor Hugh, MA, BD, PhD, DD, FRSE. Professor of New Testament Language, Literature and Theology, Edinburgh University, 1966-85; b. 18.5.20, Galston, Ayrshire; m., Jean Goldie Torbit; 1 s.; 1 s. (deceased); 1 d. Educ. Kilmarnock Academy; Glasgow University. Chaplaincy work, Egypt and Palestine, 1945-46; Lecturer in Old Testament, Glasgow University, 1946-51; Minister, Trinity Church, Pollokshields, Glasgow, 1951-57; Professor of Biblical Criticism, Duke University, North Carolina, 1957-66; special appointments including A.B. Bruce Lecturer in New Testament, Glasgow University, 1954-57; Katharine McBride Visiting Professor, Bryn Mawr College, Pennsylvania, 1972-73; Kenan Distinguished Visiting Professor, Meredith College, North Carolina, 1982-83; Pendergrass Visiting Professor, Florida Southern College, 1985-86, 1987-88. Awarded Schweitzer Medal from North Carolina History and Science Foundation. Publications: Psalms 1-45; Historians of Israel; The New Testament in Historical and Contemporary Perspective (Editor with W. Barclay); Jesus and Christian Origins; Jesus; The Gospel of Mark: Commentary; 3 and 4 Maccabees (Commentary). Recreations: golf; gardening; music. Address: (h.) 5 Comiston Springs Avenue, Edinburgh, EH10 6NT.

Anderson, Iain Buchanan, MA, DipEd, LGSM. Music Presenter/Sports Commentator, BBC, since 1985; b. 21.6.38, Stirling; m., Marion Elizabeth; 3 s.; 1 d. Educ. Bellahouston Academy, Glasgow; Glasgow University; Guildhall School. Lecturer in Speech and Drama, Jordanhill College, 1967; Arts Editor/Presenter, Radio Clyde, 1974. Rugby Correspondent, Scotland on Sunday. Address: (h.) Elmhurst, Station Road, Langbank, PA14 6YA; T.-047 554 733.

Anderson, Iain Howe, BSc, PhD, CChem, FRSC. Director of Planning and Research, Scottish Vocational Education Council, since 1991; b. 8.2.37, Glasgow; m., Anne I. Morrison; 1 s.; 1 d. Educ. Gordon Schools, Huntly; Aberdeen University. Lecturer in Chemistry: Heriot-Watt College, 1961-66, Heriot-Watt University, 1966-71; Assistant Secretary, Scottish Association for National Certificates and Diplomas, 1971-73; Education Officer, then Senior Education Officer, Scottish Technical Education Council, 1973-86. Publications: Chemistry for the Applied Sciences (Co-author); research papers. Recreations: sailing; angling. Address: (h.) 5 Duchess Park, Helensburgh, G84 9PY, T.-0436 73263.

Anderson, Ian, MA, PhD. Senior Lecturer in Mathematics, Glasgow University, since 1985; Member, Editorial Board, Glasgow Mathematical Journal; Treasurer, British Combinatorial Committee; b. 27.11.42, Haddington; m., Margaret Greig; 2 s.; 1 d. Educ. St. Andrews University; Nottingham University. Assistant Lecturer, then Lecturer, Glasgow University, 1967-85. Publications: A First Course in Combinatorial Mathematics, 1974; Combinatorics of Finite Sets, 1987; Combinatorial Designs, 1990; more than 20 research papers. Recreations: music; hill-walking; Church activities. Address: (b.) Department of Mathematics, Glasgow University, Glasgow, G12 8QW; T.-041-339 8855, Ext. 4751.

Anderson, James Alexander, BL, NP. Solicitor, since 1948; Member, Glasgow and North Argyll Legal Aid Committee, 1960-86; Honorary Sheriff at Oban, since 1980; b. 17.5.21, Glasgow; m., Jean Jeffrey Brown; 2 s.; 1 d. Educ. Elgin Academy; Edinburgh University. Army, 1942-46 (Staff Captain, RA); joined Anderson Banks & Co., Solicitors, Oban, 1950 (Senior Partner, until 1986); Local Representative, Legal Aid Committee, 1960-79; Dean of Faculty, Oban Procurators, 1975-78. Treasurer, Lorn & Mull Presbytery; Treasurer, Oban and District Christian Aid Committee. Recreations: writing; gardening; golf; pool. Address: (b.) 4/6 Stevenson Street, Oban, Argyll; T.-0631 63158.

Anderson, James Andrew, MA (Hons), DipEd, MRTPI. Director of Planning, Shetland Islands Council, since 1987; b. 19.11.45, Whalsay, Shetland. Educ. Anderson Educational Institute, Lerwick; Aberdeen University. Teachers For East Africa Scheme (Ministry of Overseas Development): recruited, 1967, Diploma in Education, Makerere University, Uganda, 1968, Education Officer, Kenya; Teacher, New Zealand, 1971; Hamilton City Council, New Zealand: Senior Town Planning Assistant, 1971, Assistant Town Planning Officer, Statutory Planning Department, 1974; Senior Planning Assistant, Shropshire County Council, 1976; Depute Director of Planning, Shetland Islands Council, 1978. Trustee, Shetland Amenity Trust. Recreations: hill walking; learning languages; foreign travel. Address: (h.) 12 Fogralea, Lerwick, Shetland Islands; T.-0595 3535.

Anderson, James Frazer Gillan, CBE, JP, DL. Member, Scottish Development Agency, 1986-89; Convener, Central

Regional Council, 1974-86; b. 25.3.29, Maddiston, by Falkirk; m., May Harley; 1 s.; 1 d. Educ. Maddiston School; Graeme High School, Falkirk. Convener, Stirling County Council, 1971-75; Member: Health and Safety Commission, 1974-80; Montgomery Committee, 1982-84; Scottish Economic Council, 1983-87; Treasurer, Maddiston Old Folks Association; awarded Honorary Degree, Doctor of University (Stirling). Recreations: gardening; walking; reading. Address: (b.) Viewforth, Stirling; T.-Stirling 442000.

Anderson, James Killoch, OBE, MB, ChB, FFCM, FCR, JP. Former Unit Medical Officer, Glasgow Royal Infirmary and Royal Maternity Hospital, Glasgow (retired, 1988); b. 3.2.23, Johnstone; m., Irene Webster Wilson; 1 s.; 2 d. Educ. High School of Glasgow; Glasgow University. Deputy Medical Superintendent, Glasgow Royal Infirmary and Associated Hospitals, 1954; appointed Medical Superintendent, 1957; District Medical Officer, Eastern District, Greater Glasgow Health Board, 1974; Unit Medical Officer, Unit East 1, Greater Glasgow Health Board, 1984. Corps Commandant and Council Member, St Andrew's Ambulance Association, 1957-82; Member of Committee, Scottish Ambulance Service, 1957-74; Director, North Parish, Washing Green Society, Glasgow, since 1957; Member, Scottish Technical Education Council, since 1974; Member, Science Development Team, 16-18s Action Plan, Scottish Education Department. Recreations: gardening; golf. Address: (h.) 15 Kenilworth Avenue, Helensburgh, G84 7JR; T.-0436 3739.

Anderson, John, MA (Hons). Rector, High School of Stirling, since 1982; Chairman, General Teaching Council of Scotland, 1985-87; b. 20.11.37, Oyne, Aberdeenshire; m., Christina M. Murray; 2 d. Educ. Banchory Academy; Aberdeen University. Assistant Teacher, Robert Gordon's College, Aberdeen, 1961-65; Principal Teacher of Geography, Buckie High School, 1965-70; Rector, Speyside High School, 1970-82. Council Member, SCOTVEC; Governor, Scottish Council for Education Technology. Recreations: golf; fishing. Address: (b.) High School of Stirling, Ogilvie Road, Torbrex, Stirling; T.-Stirling 72451.

Anderson of Pittormie, Captain John Charles Lindsay, VRD (and clasp), OStJ, MA (Oxon), LLB, RNR. Solicitor; Consultant to Messrs J.L. Anderson; Honorary Sheriff, Tayside, Central and Fife, since 1986; Arable and Fruit Farmer; Quarrymaster, Fife Redstone and Brackmont Quarries; b. 8.9.08, Cupar; m., Elsie Margaret Begg; 1 s.; 2 d. Educ. St. Salvators, St. Andrews; Glenalmond College; Pembroke College, Oxford; Edinburgh University. Solicitor, since 1931; Member, St. Andrews Town Council, 1938-51 (Honorary Treasurer, 1945-51); Parliamentary candidate (Conservative), West Stirling, 1945; joined RNVR as Sub Lt., 1930; served World War II, Northern Patrol, Convoys, Gunnery Specialist; Captain, RNR, 1954; commanded HMS Unicorn, Tay Division RNVR/RNR, 1954-59; RNR ADC to The Queen, 1959-60; Founder Governor, Unicorn Preservation Society, since 1968; Member, Business Committee, Edinburgh University General Council, since 1982; Member, Council, Law Society of Scotland, 1983-86; former Dean of Faculty, Cupar; President, Royal Caledonian Curling Club, 1978-79; Chairman: Kirkcaldy Ice Rink, 1978-88, Scottish Ice Rinks Association, 1986-88, Fife Housing Co. Ltd., Cupar Corn Exchange Co. Ltd., Fife Redstone Quarry Co. Ltd., Brackmont Quarry Ltd.; Honorary President, St. Andrews Branch, Royal British Legion. Recreations: curling; shooting; golf; tennis. Address: (h.) Inverbeg, 22 Hepburn Gardens, St Andrews, KY16 9DE; T.-0334 72348.

Anderson, John MacKenzie, MB, ChB, DPath, FRCPath. Consultant Histopathologist, Dundee Hospitals, since 1975; Honorary Senior Lecturer in Pathology, Dundee University, since 1975; b. 13.8.35, Dundee; m., Mary Ursula Nolan; 2 s.; 2 d. Educ. Dollar Academy; St. Andrews University. Medical Officer, RAMC, 1960-63; Assistant Pathologist, Glasgow Royal Infirmary, 1959-60 and 1963-65; Maudsley Hospital, London, 1965-67; Consultant Pathologist, Greenock Hospitals, 1967-69; Stobhill Hospital, Glasgow, 1969-70; Royal Hospital for Sick Children, Edinburgh, 1970-75. Recreations: golf; gardening; music. Address: (b.) Department of Pathology, Ninewells Hospital, Dundee; T.-Dundee 60111, Ext. 2667.

Anderson, Joseph Aitken, BA (Hons), CSD, MBIM. Managing Director, North of Scotland Milk Marketing Board, since 1982; Director, Company of Scottish Cheesemakers, since 1983; Director, Norlink Ltd., since 1985; Chairman, ITC Viewers Consultative Committee for Scotland, since 1990; b. 1.7.36, Prestonpans; m., Sheila Armstrong; 2 s. Educ. Preston Lodge; Open University. Managing Secretary: Carluke Co-operative Society, 1962-65, East Fife Co-operative Society, 1965-71; Depute Chief Executive, Central and East Fife Co-operative Society, 1971-79; Executive Officer and Secretary, Fife Regional Co-operative Society, 1979-82. Member, United Kingdom Dairy Association Council; Past Chairman, NE Branch, Society of Dairy Technology; President, Inverness and District Chamber of Commerce. Recreations: golf; fly fishing; photography. Address: (b.) Balmakeith Industrial Estate, Forres Road, Nairn IV12 5QW; T-0667 53344.

Anderson, Kathleen Janette, OBE, BSc, PhD, CBiol, FIBiol, CChem, FRSC. Depute Principal, Napier Polytechnic of Edinburgh, since 1983; b. 22.5.27, Glasgow; m., Mark Elliot Muir Anderson; 1 s.; 1 d. Educ. Queens Park School, Glasgow; Glasgow University. Lecturer, West of Scotland Agricultural College, Glasgow, 1948-54; Johnson and Florence Stoney Research Fellow, University of Sydney, Australia, 1952-53; Commonwealth Travelling Research Fellow, Australia and New Zealand, 1953; Sir James Knott Research Fellow, Durham University, 1955-57; King's College, Durham University: Lecturer in Biochemistry, 1958-59, Lecturer in Microbiology, 1962-63, Lecturer (part-time) in Landscape Horticulture, 1963-65, Lecturer (part-time), Extra-Mural Department, 1959-65; Lecturer (part-time), Department of Extra-Mural Studies, Edinburgh University, 1965-68; Napier College, Edinburgh: Senior Lecturer, Department of Biological Sciences, 1968-69, Head of Department, Biological Sciences, 1969-83. Crown Trustee, National Library for Scotland, since 1981; Deacon, Church of Scotland, 1974-78, Elder, since 1978; CNAA Environmental Sciences Board, 1978-84; Chairman, Joint Committee for Biology, SCOTEC, 1979-85; Institute of Biology: Chairman, Scottish Branch, 1977-79, Member of Council, 1977-80, Fellowship Committee, 1980-83, Environment Division, 1982-86; Founder Chairman, Heads of Biology in Tertiary Education, 1975-77; Heads of Biology in Polytechnics, 1974-83; Nurse Education Committee, Royal Edinburgh Hospital, 1974-77; SCOTVEC: Council Member and Chairman, Education Policy Committee, since 1984, Vice Chairman, since 1989; Chairman, Edinburgh Branch, Glasgow Graduates Association, 1985-86; Member, Scottish National Committee, English Speaking Union, since 1987; Trustee, Royal Observatory (Edinburgh) Trust, since 1987; Member: Radioactive Waste Management Advisory Committee, since 1988; Agriculture Industries Training Board, since 1989; Scottish Committee, University Funding Council, since 1989; Governor, St George's School, since 1989; Governor, George Watson's School, since 1990. Publications: Discover Lothian Beaches; Holyrood Park Teachers Handbook; Safety in Biological Laboratories. Recreations: grand-children; charity work; gardening; foreign travel. Address: (b.) Napier Polytechnic of Edinburgh, 219 Colinton Road, Edinburgh, EH14 1DJ; T.-031-444 2266.

Anderson, Kenneth D., MA. Rector, Grove Academy, Broughty Ferry, since 1981; b. 13.11.31, Glasgow; m., Heather; 1 s. Educ. Glasgow Academy; University College, Oxford. Teacher of Classics, Dunfermline High School, 1955-62; Principal Teacher of Classics: Beath High School, 1962-64, Robert Gordon's College, Aberdeen, 1964-72; Assistant Head Teacher, Portobello High School, Edinburgh, 1972-75; Deputy Rector, Perth Grammar School, 1975-81. Recreations: choral singing; Church work. Address: (b.) Grove Academy, Camperdown Street, Broughty Ferry, Dundee; T.-0382 730284.

Anderson, Leslie William. Home Affairs Correspondent, BBC Scotland, since 1990 (Parliamentary Correspondent, 1984-89); b. 3.8.40, Edinburgh; m., Alexandra; 2 d. Educ. Daniel Stewarts College, Edinburgh. Reporter, Lennox Herald, Dumbarton, 1960-63; News Reporter, Scottish Daily Mail, Glasgow, 1963-66; Scottish Daily Express: News Reporter, 1966-67, Deputy Industrial Correspondent, 1967-70, Industrial Correspondent, 1970-78; Industrial Correspondent, BBC Scotland, 1979-84. Recreation: rugby (spectating). Address: (h.) 10 Seggielea Road, Jordanhill, Glasgow; T.-041-954 3369.

Anderson, Professor Malcolm, MA, DPhil (Oxon). Professor of Politics, Edinburgh University, since 1979, and Dean, Faculty of Social Sciences; b. 13.5.34, Knutsford; m., Jacqueline Larrieu; 2 s.; 1 d. Educ. University College, Oxford. Lecturer in Government, Manchester University, 1960-63; Research Fellow, Institut National des Sciences Politiques, 1964-65 and 1986-87; Senior Lecturer, then Professor, Warwick University, 1965-79; Visiting Fellow, Institute of Higher Studies, Vienna, 1977-78; Associate Professor, Sorbonne-Pantheon, 1987-88. Chairman, European Community Studies Association. Publications: Government in France, 1970; Conservative Politics in France, 1974; Frontier Regions in Western Europe, 1983; Women, Equality and Europe (Co-editor), 1988; Policing the World, 1989. Recreations: walking; reading; photography. Address: (h.) 13 Northumberland Street, Edinburgh, EH3 6LL; T.-031-556 2113.

Anderson, Moira, OBE. Singer; b. Kirkintilloch; m., Dr. Stuart Macdonald. Educ. Ayr Academy; Royal Scottish Academy of Music, Glasgow. Began with Kirkintilloch Junior Choir, aged six; made first radio broadcast for BBC in Scotland, aged eight; was Teacher of Music in Ayr before becoming professional singer; made first professional broadcast, White Heather Club, 1960; has toured overseas, had her own radio and TV series; has introduced Stars on Sunday, ITV; appeared in summer shows, cabaret, pantomime and numerous other stage shows; several Royal Variety performances.

Anderson, Robert David, MA, DPhil. Reader in History, Edinburgh University, since 1985; b. 11.7.42, Cardiff. Educ. Taunton School, Somerset; Queen's and St. Antony's Colleges, Oxford. Assistant Lecturer, Glasgow University, 1967-69; Lecturer, then Senior Lecturer, Edinburgh University, 1969-85. Publications: Education in France 1848-1870, 1975; France 1870-1914: Politics and Society, 1977; Education and Opportunity in Victorian Scotland, 1983 (winner, Scottish Arts Council Literary Award, 1984); The Student Community at Aberdeen, 1860-1939 (1988). Address: (b.) Department of History, Edinburgh University, Edinburgh; T.-031-650 3786.

Anderson, Robert Geoffrey William, MA, DPhil, FSA, FSA Scot, FRSE. Director, The British Museum (Director, National Museums of Scotland, 1985-92); b. 2.5.44, London; m., Margaret Elizabeth Callis Anderson; 2 s. Educ. St. John's College, Oxford. Assistant Keeper, Royal Scottish Museum, 1970-75; Assistant Keeper, Deputy Keeper, Keeper, Science Museum, 1975-84; Director, Royal Scottish Museum, 1984-85. Dexter Award, American Chemical Society, 1986; President, International Commission on Scientific Instruments, since 1982; President, British Society for History of Science, 1988-90. Publications: books on history of science and museology. Address: (h.) 11 Dryden Place, Edinburgh EH9 1RP; T.-031-667 8211.

Anderson, Thomas Alfred, CEng, FICE, FIWEM, FIHT, FIOSH, FBIM. Director of Sewerage, Strathclyde Regional Council, since 1991; b. 9.11.34, Glasgow; m., Margaret; 3 d. Educ. Strathbungo Senior Secondary School; Royal Technical College, Glasgow; Paisley College of Technology. City Engineer's Department, Corporation of the City of Glasgow: Senior Civil Engineer, 1964-68, Assistant Chief Civil Engineer, 1968-75; Strathclyde Regional Council: Assistant Director of Sewerage, 1975-81, Depute Director of Sewerage, 1981-91. Institution of Municipal Engineers National Medal and Prize Winner, 1980; Examiner, Institution of Civil Engineers, since 1977. Address: (b.) Strathclyde House, 20 India Street, Glasgow G2 4PF; T.-041-227 3721.

Anderson, William, CBE. Managing Editor, The Sunday Post (Editor, 1967-90); b. 10.2.34, Motherwell; m., Margaret Cross McClelland; 3 s. Educ. Dalziel High School; Glasgow University. Journalist since first producing school newspapers, with interruptions as cook steward, male nurse, medical student and Army officer. Recreations: fishing; sailing; cooking. Address: (b.) Courier Building, Meadowside, Dundee; T.-0382 23131.

Anderson, William, FRICS, IRRV. Regional Assessor, Tayside Region, since 1986; b. 17.9.37, Leven; m., Margaret Johnstone Forgan; 1 s.; 1 d. Educ. Buckhaven High School; College of Estate Management, Reading. Apprentice Surveyor, then Valuation Assistant, Fife County Council Assessor's Department, 1956-63; Valuer, then Depute County Assessor, Perth & Kinross Joint Valuation Authority, 1963-75; Depute Regional Assessor (Angus), then Senior Depute Assessor, Tayside Regional Council, 1975-86. Secretary, Scottish Assessors' Association. Recreations: music; theatre; fishing. Address: (b.) Tayside House, 28 Crichton Street, Dundee, DD1 3RH; T.-0382 23281.

Anderson, William Archibald, MC, TD, JP, MA. Member, Shetland Islands Council, since 1982 (Vice-Convener, since 1990); b. 22.12.19, Edinburgh; m., Patricia Smith (daughter of late Ex-Provost James A. Smith); 2 s. Educ. Daniel Stewart's College; Aberdeen University. Served with Black Watch (RHR), 1939-46. Woollen manufacturer, 1946-52; schoolmaster, 1952-82. Recreations: gardening; golf. Address: (h.) The Sea Chest, East Voe, Scalloway, Shetland; T.-Scalloway 326.

Anderson, Professor Sir (William) Ferguson, Kt (1974), OBE, KStJ, MD, FRCP(Lond), (Glas), (Edin), (C), (I), FACP. Professor Emeritus, Geriatric Medicine, Glasgow University; Vice-President, Scottish Retirement Council; Honorary President, Crossroads (Scotland) Care Attendant Scheme; Honorary Vice-President, Age Concern (Scotland); Patron, Abbeyfield Society, Scotland; b. 8.4.14, Glasgow; m., Margaret Gebbie; 1 s.; 2 d. Educ. Glasgow Academy; Glasgow University. Assistant Lecturer, Materia Medica, Glasgow University, 1939-41; Major, RAMC, 1941-46; Senior Lecturer, Materia Medica, Glasgow University, 1946-48; Senior Lecturer, Materia Medica, Glasgow University, 1946-48; Senior Lecturer, Welsh National School of Medicine, 1948-52; Honorary Consultant Physician, Cardiff Royal Infirmary, 1948-52; Consultant Physician in Geriatric Medicine and Advisor in diseases of old age and chronic sickness, Western Regional Board, 1952-65; Professor of Geriatric Medicine, Glasgow University, 1965-79. St. Mungo Prize, City of Glasgow; Ed Henderson Award, American

Geriatrics Society; Brookdale Award, Gerontological Society of America. Recreation: golf. Address: (h.) Rodel, Moor Road, Strathblane, Glasgow, G63 9EX; T.-Blanefield 70862.

Andrawes, Professor Kamal Zaki, BSc (Eng), MSc, PhD. Professor of Geotechnical and Highway Engineering, Strathclyde University, since 1989; b. 12.11.39, Cairo, Egypt; m., Linda; 1 s.; 1 d. Educ. Manchester University; Cairo University; Southampton University. Address: (b.) Department of Civil Engineering, Strathclyde University, Glasgow; T.-041-552 4400.

Andrew, William, MA. Writer; b. 31.8.31, Glasgow. Educ. Shawlands Academy, Glasgow; Glasgow University. Taught English in London and Glasgow; turned to full-time writing, 1979; plays for stage, radio and television, including Project Flora, The Best Baby, Behind the Circle; short stories. Recreations: local history; music.

Andrews, Anthony Peter Hamilton, MA. Director, The British Council, Scotland, since 1990; b. 23.12.46. Royal Marines Officer, 1964-71; studied, Andrews University and University College of North Wales, Bangor; British Council: Assistant Director, Kano, Nigeria, 1976-78, Assistant Representative, Yugoslavia, Belgrade, 1979-81, Assistant Representative, Oman, Muscat, 1981-85, Director, North East Brazil, Recife, 1985-89; Director, Glasgow, 1989-90; founded Scottish International Resource Project, 1990. Recreations: literature; art; music; natural history, especially trees and shrubs and entomology; angling; sailing. Address: (b.) The British Council, 3/4 Bruntsfield Crescent, Edinburgh EH10 4HD; T.-031-447 4716.

Angus, David George, MA (Hons), DipEd. Freelance Writer and Lecturer; b. 20.4.25, Brora; m., Florence Jean Manson. Educ. Inverness Royal Academy; Lanark Grammar School; Edinburgh University. Assistant Teacher of English, Beath High School, 1951-59; freelance Writer, Edinburgh, 1959-61; Special Assistant Teacher of English, Alloa Academy, 1961-71; Extramural Lecturer in Scottish Literature, Stirling University, ten years; has published verse in Scots, English and French; contributed prose in Scots to Lallans magazine and The Scotsman and in English to Scots Magazine and The Scotsman; former Historian, Edinburgh Wax Museum; former Council Member and Vice-Chairman, Saltire Society; founder Member and former Secretary, Scots Language Society. Publication: Roses and Thorns - Scottish Teenage Verse (Editor). Recreations: historical, literary and genealogical research. Address: (h.) 122 Henderson Street, Bridge of Allan, Stirling, FK9 4HF; T.-832306.

Angus, Rev. James Alexander Keith, LVO, TD, MA. Minister, Braemar and Crathie Parish Churches, since 1979; Domestic Chaplain to The Queen; b. 16.4.29, Aberdeen; m., Alison Jane Daly; 1 s.; 1 d. Educ. High School of Dundee; St. Andrews University. Assistant Minister, Glasgow Cathedral, 1955-56; Minister: Hoddam Parish Church, 1956-67; Gourock Old Parish Church, 1967-79. TA: Captain, Royal Artillery, 1950-56, Chaplain, 1957-77; Convener, Committee of Chaplains to HM Forces, General Assembly, 1981-85; LVO, 1990. Recreations: hill-walking; fishing; golf. Address: (h.) The Manse of Crathie, Crathie, near Ballater, Aberdeenshire; T.-Crathie 208.

Angus, Rae, MA (Hons), MLitt, MBIM. Depute Principal, Aberdeen College of Further Education, since 1991; b. 1.4.47, Ellon; m., Winifred Stewart; 2 d. Educ. Peterhead Academy; Aberdeen University. Further Education Lecturer, 1975; Research Fellow, Aberdeen Universiy, 1978-80; Aberdeen College of Commerce, 1981-91, latterly as Depute Principal. Recreations: reading; walking; computing. Address: (h.) 4 Curlew Avenue, Newburgh, Aberdeen.

Angus, William Jestyn, FIPM, MIMC. Director-Scotland, Knight Wendling Executive Search Ltd., since 1982; Director, Glasgow Chamber of Commerce; Director, Merchants House of Glasgow; Vice-President, Glasgow and West of Scotland Outward Bound Association; b. 12.12.30, Northumberland; m., Eleanor Gillian Attwood; 1 s.; 1 d. Educ. Gordonstoun School; Harvard Business School. Eighteen years with George Angus & Co. Ltd., latterly part of Dunlop Holdings Ltd.; from 1953 in marketing, export sales, general management and group personnel management; joined Matthew Hall Group, 1971; Senior Consultant, MSL, 1973-82. Recreations: hill-walking; skiing; tennis; wine. Address: (h.) Braeriach, Helensburgh, G84 9AH; T.-0436 72393.

Angus, Col. William Turnbull Calderhead, CEng, MRAeS, FBIM, FIQA. Honorary Sheriff, North Strathclyde, since 1986; b. 20.7.23, Glasgow; m., Nola Leonie Campbell-Gillies; 2 s.; 2 d. Educ. Govan High School; Glasgow University; Royal Military College of Science. Commissioned Royal Regiment of Artillery, 1944; King's African Rifles and GSO2, DAAG (Major), HQ East Africa Command, 1945-47; Technical Staff Course, Royal Military College of Science, 1949-51; TSO2 (Major), Inspectorate of Armaments, 1951-54; BAOR and Cyprus, 1954-57; GSO2 (Major), G(Tech) HQ BAOR, 1957-60; TSO2 (Major), Ordnance Board, 1960-63; TSO2 (Major), Trials Establishment Guided Weapons, RA, 1963-65; postgraduate Guided Weapons Course, Royal Military College of Science, 1965-66; TSO1 (Lt. Col.), Royal Armament Research and Development Establishment, 1966-69; Assistant Director, Guided Weapons Trials (Col.), MOD Procurement Executive, 1970-73; Member (Col.), Ordnance Board, 1973-74; retired, 1974; self-employed holiday cottages proprietor and Scottish Manager for Blakes Holidays; Past President, Campbeltown Rotary Club. Recreations: wood-turning and manufacture of spinning wheels; creationism studies. Address: Kilchrist Castle, Campbeltown, Argyll, PA28 6PH; T.-0586 53210.

Annan, Hugh Ross, BL. Procurator Fiscal, Linlithgow, since 1976; b. 27.12.34, Perth; m., Sheila McNicol; 2 s. Educ. Bell-Baxter School, Cupar; St. Andrews University. Solicitor 1959; Procurator Fiscal, Cupar, February-October, 1976. Recreations: reading; astronomy. Address: (h.) 14 Deacons Court, Linlithgow, West Lothian; T.-Linlithgow 844684.

Annand, David Andrew, DA, ARBS. Sculptor; b. 30.1.48, Insch, Aberdeenshire; m., Jean; 1 s.; 1 d. Educ. Perth Academy; Duncan of Jordanstone College of Art, Dundee. Lecturer, Sculpture Department, Duncan of Jordanstone College of Art, Dundee, 1972-74; Art Department, St. Saviours High School, Dundee, 1975-88; full-time sculptor, since 1988; public commissions include: Deer Leap, Dundee Technology Park, Man Feeding Seagulls, Glasgow Garden Festival, Grey Heron, Edinburgh Botanic Gardens, Beatrix Potter Garden, Perth and Kinross Heritage Trust; Royal Scottish Academy: Latimer Award, 1976, Benno Schotz Award, 1978, Ireland Alloys Award, 1982; one man exhibition, Open Eye Gallery, Edinburgh, 1990; winner, High Street commission, Perth Partnership Sculpture Competition, 1990; winner, Irvine Development Corporation Almswall Road Sculpture Competition, 1990. Recreations: music; bird watching; children watching; cooking; eating; drinking wine. Address: Pigscrave Cottage, The Wynd, Kilmany, Cupar, Fife KY15 4PU. T.-082 624 714.

Annand, James King, MA. Writer; b. 2.2.08, Edinburgh; m., Beatrice Violet Lindsay (deceased); 4 d. Educ. Broughton Secondary School, Edinburgh; Edinburgh University. Assistant Teacher, James Clark School, Edinburgh, 1932-49 (War Service, Royal Navy, 1941-46); Lecturer in Current Affairs, Regent Road Day Release Centre, 1949-53; Principal Teacher of History, James Clark School, 1953-58; Headmaster, Whithorn Junior Secondary School, 1959-62;

Principal Teacher of History, Firrhill Secondary School, Edinburgh, 1962-71. Founder Member and holder of various offices, Scottish Youth Hostels Association, since 1931; Council Member: Saltire Society, 1951-54, Historical Association of Scotland, 1954-58; founder Member, Scots Language Society, 1972 (Vice-Preses, 1983, Hon. Preses, 1990); Councillor, Royal Burgh of Whithorn, 1960-62; Editor: The Rebel Student, 1929, Lines Review, 1958-59, Lallans, 1973-83. Awarded Burns Chronicle Poetry Prize, 1955; Scottish Arts Council Special Award for contribution to Scottish poetry, 1979. Publications: Sing it Aince for Pleisure, 1965; Two Voices, 1968; Twice for Joy, 1973; Poems and Translations, 1975; Songs from Carmina Burana, 1978; Thrice to Show Ye, 1979; Dod and Davie, 1986; Early Lyrics by Hugh MacDiarmid (Editor), 1968; A Scots Handsel (Editor), 1980; A Wale o Rhymes, 1989. Recreations: mountaineering; natural history; photography; book-binding. Address: (h.) 173/314 Comely Bank Road, Edinburgh, EH4 1DJ; T.-031-332 6905.

Annand, Louise Gibson, MBE, MA (Hons), AMA. Artist; Member, Royal Fine Art Commission for Scotland, 1979-86; b. 27.5.15, Uddingston; m., 1, Alistair Matheson (deceased); 2, Roderick MacFarquhar (deceased). Educ. Hamilton Academy; Glasgow University. Teacher, primary and secondary schools, Glasgow, 1939-49; Assistant, Schools Museum Service, 1949-70; Museums Education Officer, 1970-80. Past Chairman: Scottish Educational Film Association (Glasgow Production Group); Glasgow Lady Artists Club Trust; National Vice-Chairman, Scottish Educational Media Association, 1979-84; President: Society of Scottish Women Artists, 1963-66 and 1980-85; Glasgow Society of Women Artists, 1977-79, 1988-91; Visiting Lecturer in Scottish Art, Regina University, 1982; Chairman, J.D. Fergusson Foundation, since 1982 (Trustee, since 1983); Member, Business Committee, General Council, University of Glasgow, 1981-85, 1988-91; exhibited widely since 1945; produced numerous 16mm films, including the first on Charles Rennie Mackintosh, 1966. Recreations: mountaineering (Ladies Scottish Climbing Club). Address: (h.) 22 Kingsborough Gardens, Glasgow, G12 9NJ; T.-041-339 8956.

Annandale and Hartfell, 11th Earl of (Patrick Andrew Wentworth Hope Johnstone of Annandale and of That Ilk). Farmer; Chief, Clan Johnstone; Baron of the Barony of the Lands of the Earldom of Annandale and Hartfell, and of the Lordship of Johnstone; Hereditary Steward, Stewartry of Annandale; Hereditary Keeper, Keys of Lochmaben Castle; Deputy Lieutenant, Dumfriesshire, since 1987; b. 19.4.41, Auldgirth, Dumfriesshire; m., Susan Josephine; 1 s.; 1 d. Educ. Stowe School; Royal Agricultural College, Cirencester. Member: Dumfriesshire County Council, 1970-75, Dumfries and Galloway Regional Council, 1975-85, Scottish Valuation Advisory Council, 1982, Solway River Purification Board, 1973-85; Underwriter, Lloyds, London, 1976. Address: (b.) House of Lords, London SW1.

Anstruther, Sir Ralph (Hugo), of that Ilk, 8thBt. of Balcaskie and 12th of Anstruther, KCVO, MC, DL, BA. Equerry to the Queen Mother, since 1959, and Treasurer since 1961; b. 13.6.21. Educ. Eton; Magdalene College, Cambridge. Major (ret.), Coldstream Guards. Member, Queen's Bodyguard for Scotland (Royal Company of Archers); DL, Fife, 1960; DL, Caithness-shire, 1965. Address: Balcaskie, Pittenweem, Fife; Watten, Caithness.

Anthony, William Burns, FRICS. Building Manager, National Museums of Scotland, since 1988; b. 29.10.47, Edinburgh; m., Pamela Pickering; 1 s.; 1 d. Educ. Daniel Stewart's College, Edinburgh; Napier College, Edinburgh. J. and J. Hall, Chartered Architects and Surveyors, Galashiels: Apprentice Quantity Surveyor, 1964-70, Assistant Quantity

Surveyor, 1970-71; Senior Quantity Surveyor: John D. Hutchison Chartered Surveyors, Edinburgh, 1971-77, Kirkcaldy District Council, 1977-78; Principal Quantity Surveyor, Scottish Health Service Common Services Agency, Building Division, 1978-88. Member, Scottish Council, RICS; Chairman, Quantity Surveyors Divisional Committee, RICS in Scotland, 1990-91. Recreations: curling; scouting. Address: Royal Museum of Scotland, Chambers Street, Edinburgh EH1 1JF; T.-031-225 7534.

Anton, Alexander Elder, CBE, MA, LLB, FBA; b. 1922; m., Doris May Lawrence; 1 s. Educ. Aberdeen University. Solicitor, 1949; Lecturer, Aberdeen, 1953-59; Professor of Jurisprudence, Glasgow University, 1959-73; Honorary Professor, 1984, Aberdeen University; Member, Scottish Law Commission, 1966-82; UK Delegate to Hague Conference on Private International Law, 1964-82; Chairman, Scottish Rights of Way Society, 1988-92. Publications: Private International Law, 1967; Civil Jurisdiction in Scotland, 1984. Recreation: hill-walking. Address: (h.) 9 Baillieswells Terrace, Bieldside, Aberdeen, AB1 9AR.

Arbuthnot, Peter Geoffrey. Managing Director, Christie's Scotland Limited, since 1989; b. 18.9.50, London; m., Belinda Terry-Engell; 1 s.; 1 d. Educ. Stowe School; Trinity College, Cambridge. Research in Indian Archaeology, 1974-76; Specialist, Ethnographic Art, Christie's Auctioneers, London, 1976-80; Commodity Trader, E.D. and F. Man, 1980-83; Christie's in the City, 1983-88. Recreations: squash; skiing; hockey; travel; public speaking. Address (b.) 164-166 Bath Street, Glasgow G2 4TG; T.-041-332 8134.

Arbuthnott, 16th Viscount of (John Campbell Arbuthnott), CBE, DSC, FRSE, FRSA, KStJ, MA. Lord Lieutenant, Grampian Region (Kincardineshire), since 1977; Director: Clydesdale Bank PLC, Britoil, Scottish Widows'; Member, BP Scottish Advisory Board; b. 26.10.24; m.; 1 s.; 1 d. Educ. Fettes College; Gonville and Caius College, Cambridge. Member, Countryside Commission for Scotland, 1967-71; Chairman, Red Deer Commission, 1969-75; Member, Aberdeen University Court, 1978-84; President, Scottish Landowners Federation, 1974-79; President, Royal Scottish Geographical Society, 1984-87; Chairman, Scottish Widows' Fund and Life Assurance Society, 1984-87; Lord High Commissioner to the General Assembly of the Church of Scotland, 1986-87; President, Royal Zoological Society of Scotland, since 1976; President, Scottish Agricultural Organisation Society, 1980-83; President, Federation of Agricultural Cooperatives (UK), 1983-87; Deputy Chairman, Nature Conservancy Council, 1980-85, and Chairman, Scottish Committee, NCC; Chairman, Aberdeen and Northern Marts Ltd., 1986-91, Director, 1973-91; Prior of Scotland, The Order of St. John, since 1983; Member, Royal Commission on Historical Manuscripts, since 1988. Address: (h.) Arbuthnott House, by Laurencekirk, Kincardineshire.

Arbuthnott, Professor John Peebles, PhD, ScD, FIBiol, HonFTCD. Principal and Vice Chancellor, Strathclyde University, since 1991; b. 8.4.39; m., Elinor Rutherford Smillie; 1 s.; 2 d. Educ. Glasgow University; TrinityCollege, Dublin. Assistant Lecturer, then Lecturer, Department of Bacteriology, Glasgow University, 1960-67; Fellow of the Royal Society, 1968-72; Senior Lecturer, Department of Microbiology, then Senior Lecturer, Department of Bacteriology, Glasgow University, 1972-75; Professor of Micriobiology, Trinity College, Dublin, 1976-88. Member: Veterinary Products Committee for MAFF, AFRC Food Research Committee, Lister Institute, Department of Health/Department of Agriculture Steering Group on Microbiological Safety of Food, Board of Public Health Laboratory Service; Chairman, MRC Polysaccharide Vaccine Subcommittee. Recreations: attending soccer matches; golf.

Address: (b.) Strathclyde University, Glasgow, G1 1XQ; T.-041-552 4400.

Arbuthnott, The Hon. William David, MBE. Regimental Secretary, The Black Watch, since 1978; b. 5.11.27, Colchester; m., Sonja Mary Thomson; 1 s.; 2 d. Educ. Fettes. Army Officer, The Black Watch, 1948-78. Recreations: gardening; reading; civil engineering. Address: (h.) The Old Manse, Trochry, by Dunkeld, PH8 ODY; T.-Trochry 205; (b.) RHQ The Black Watch, Balhousie Castle, Hay Street, Perth, PH1 5HS; T.-Perth 21281, Ext. 8530.

Archer, Gilbert Baird, Chairman, Tod Holdings Ltd, since 1970; Chairman, John Dickson & Sons Ltd, since 1985; b. 24.8.42, Edinburgh; m., Irene Conn; 2 d. Educ. Melville College. Vice Convenor, George Watson's College, 1978-80; Governor, Fettes College, 1986-90; Director, Scottish Council of Independent Schools, 1988-91; Council Member, Governing Bodies Association of Independent Schools, 1988-91; Governor, Napier Polytechnic of Edinburgh; Governor, St. Columba's Hospice; President, Edinburgh Chamber of Commerce & Manufactures; Vice Chairman, Cancer Support Therapy Fund; Chairman, Edinburgh Common Purpose; Moderator, High Constabulary of the Port of Leith; Liveryman, Worshipful Company of Gunmakers, London. Recreations: fishing; shooting. Address: (b.) 12 Broughton Place, Edinburgh EH1 3RX; T.-031-556 4518.

Argent, Edward, DipRADA, FGSM. Director, School of Drama, Royal Scottish Academy of Music and Drama, since 1974; b. 21.8.31, London; m., Christine Tuck; 1 s.; 2 d. Educ. Mercers' School, London; RADA. Actor, Director, Stage Manager, 1954-70; Teacher, 1962-70; Principal Lecturer and Head, School of Theatre, Manchester Polytechnic, 1970-74. Director: Citizens' Theatre, Scottish Mask and Puppet Centre, Prime Productions, National Council for Drama Training, Conference of Drama Schools (Executive Committee). Recreations: theatre-going; reading; grandparenting. Address: (b.) 100 Renfrew Street, Glasgow, G2 3DB; T.-041-332 4101.

Argyll, 12th Duke of, (Ian Campbell). Chief of Clan Campbell; Hereditary Master of the Royal Household, Scotland; Hereditary High Sheriff of the County of Argyll; Admiral of the Western Coast and Isles; Keeper of the Great Seal of Scotland and of the Castles of Dunstaffnage, Dunoon, and Carrick and Tarbert; b. 28.8.37.

Armour, Archibald, MA (Hons), FEIS. Head Teacher, Camphill High School, Paisley, 1975-85; b. 3.6.20, Paisley; m., Margaret B.L. Hebditch; 1 s.; 1 d. Educ. Camphill Senior Secondary School, Paisley; Glasgow University. Teacher, Camphill Senior Secondary School, 1950-54; Principal Teacher of English: Abercorn Junior Secondary School, Paisley, 1954-61, Renfrew High School, 1961-68 (Depute Head, 1965-68); Head Teacher, Mount School (later Cowdenknowes High School), Greenock, 1968-75. President, Educational Institute of Scotland, 1976-77 (Vice-President, 1971-72). Recreations: golf; gardening; bridge; Burns Suppers. Address: (h.) Marvin, 9 Douglas Avenue, Elderslie, Johnstone, PA5 9ND; T.-Johnstone 20884.

Armour, Professor James, CBE, PhD, Dr hc Utrecht, MRCVS, FRSE. Vice-Principal (Planning - External Relations), Glasgow University, since 1991; Dean, Faculty of Veterinary Medicine, 1986-91, and Professor of Veterinary Parasitology (Personal Chair), Glasgow University, since 1976; b. 17.9.29, Basra, Iraq; m., Irene Morris (deceased); 2 s.; 2 d. Educ. Marr College, Troon; Glasgow University. Colonial veterinary service, Nigeria, 1953-60; Research Scientist, Wellcome Ltd., 1960-63; Glasgow University: Research Fellow, 1963-67, Lecturer/Senior Lecturer, 1967-73, Reader, 1973-76. Chairman, Government Committee on Animal Medicines, since 1987; Chairman, Editorial Board,

In Practice (veterinary journal); Chairman, Governing Body, Institute of Animal Health. Publications: joint author of textbook on veterinary parasitology; editor, two books; 150 scientific articles. Recreation: golf. Address: (h.) 10 Willockston Road, Troon, Ayrshire; T.-0292 314068.

Armour, Mary Nicol Neill, DA, RSA, RSW, RGI, LLD Glasgow (1980). Artist; b. 27.3.02, Blantyre; m., William Armour. Educ. Hamilton Academy; Glasgow School of Art. Elected ARSA, 1941; RSW, 1956; RSA, 1958; RGI, 1977; Honorary President: Glasgow School of Art, 1982; Royal Glasgow Institute of the Fine Arts, 1983; Vice President, Paisley Art Institute, 1983. Guthrie Award, RSA, 1937; Cargill Prize, RGI, 1972; Fellow, Paisley College of Technology, since 1989. Recreations: gardening; dress-making. Address: 2 Gateside Place, Kilbarchan, PA10 2LY; T.-Kilbarchan 2873.

Armour, Robert Malcolm, MBA, LLB (Hons), DipLP, WS, NP. Company Secretary, Scottish Nuclear Limited, since 1990; Director, IMS Trust, since 1990; b. 25.9.59, Edinburgh; m., Anne Ogilvie White. Educ. Daniel Stewart's and Melville College, Edinburgh; Edinburgh University. Solicitor: Haldaner McLaren and Scott, WS, Edinburgh, 1983-86; Partner, Wright, Johnston and MacKenzie, Edinburgh, 1987-90. Recreations: golf; curling. Address: Scottish Nuclear, Peel Park, East Kilbride G74 5PR; T.-03552 62000.

Arnold, James Edward, MBE, MA (Hons), BA, CertEd. Manager, New Lanark Conservation Trust, since 1974; b. 16.3.45, Glasgow; m., Rose. Educ. Caludon Castle Comprehensive School; York University; London University. Recreations: New Lanark and life. Address: (b.) Mill Number Three, New Lanark, Lanark; T.-0555 61345.

Arnott, James Mackay, TD, BL, WS, SSC. Solicitor; Partner, MacRoberts, Glasgow and Edinburgh, since 1963; b. 22.3.35, Blackford, Perthshire; m., Jean Barbara Allan; 3 s. Educ. Merchiston Castle School, Edinburgh; Edinburgh University. National Service, RAF, 1957-60; TA, 1961-77. Council Member, Law Society of Scotland, 1983-85 (Convenor, Law Reform Committee); Secretary, Scottish Building Contract Committee. Recreation: cricket. Address: (b.) 152 Bath Street, Glasgow, G2 4TB; T.-041-332 9988; 27 Melville Street, Edinburgh, EH3 7JF; T.-031-226 2552.

Arnott, John Michael Stewart, BA. Member, South East Regional Board, Scottish Natural Heritage, since 1992; b. 12.6.33; m., Lynne Gladstone-Millar; 1 s.; 1 d. Educ. Peterhouse, Cambridge. Pilot, RAF, 1952-54; Announcer, Producer, Editor Talks and Features, Edinburgh Manager, BBC Scotland, 1960-90; Member, 1982-92, Vice-Chairman, 1986-92, Countryside Commission for Scotland; Member, Committee for Scotland, Nature Conservancy Council, 1986-91; Member, NCC Advisory Committee on Birds, 1990; Chairman, CCS Advisory Panel on Management of Mountain Areas, 1989-90; Member, National Parks of England and Wales Review Panel, 1990. Sony Award for Radio Feature, 1985. Recreations: ornithology; hill-walking. Address: (h.) East Redford House, 133 Redford Road, Edinburgh, EH13 0AS; T.-031-441 3567.

Arnott, Professor Struther, BSc, PhD, FIBiol, FRSE, FRS. Principal and Vice-Chancellor, St. Andrews University, since 1986; b. 25.9.34, Larkhall; m., Greta Edwards; 2 s. Educ. Hamilton Academy; Glasgow University. King's College, London: Scientist, MRS Biophysics Research Unit, 1960-70, Demonstrator, Physics, 1960-67, Director of Postgraduate Studies in Biophysics, 1967-70; Purdue University, Indiana, USA: Professor of Molecular Biology, 1970, Head, Department of Biological Sciences, 1975-80, Vice-President for Research and Dean, Graduate School, 1980-86; Oxford University: Senior Visiting Research Fellow, Jesus College,

1980-81, Nuffield Research Fellow, Green College, 1985-86, Guggenheim Memorial Foundation Fellow, 1985. Recreations: birdwatching; botanizing. Address: (b.) College Gate, North Street, St. Andrews KY16 9AJ; T.-0334 76161.

Aronson, Sheriff Hazel Josephine, QC, LLB. Sheriff of Lothian and Borders at Edinburgh, since 1983; Chairman, Mental Welfare Commission for Scotland; b. 12.1.46, Glasgow; m., John A. Cosgrove; 1 s.; 1 d. Educ. Glasgow High School for Girls; Glasgow University. Advocate at Scottish Bar, 1968-79; Sheriff of Glasgow and Strathkelvin at Glasgow, 1979-83. Recreations: walking; Langlauf; opera; foreign travel. Address: (h.) 14 Gordon Terrace, Edinburgh, EH16 5QR; T.-031-667 8955.

Arthur, Alexander David. Member, Shetland Islands Council, since 1986 (Vice-Chairman, General Services Committee); b. 16.12.24, Lerwick; m., 1, Elizabeth Sandison (deceased); 1 s.; 2 d.; 2, Georgina Herculson. War Service, REME. Member, Shetland Council of Social Service; Vice Chairman, Shetland Citizens Advice Bureau Advisory Committee; Vice Chairman, Shetland Local Health Council. Recreations: collector of antiques and coins; licensed radio amateur. Address: (h.) Roadside, Girlsta, Shetland, ZE2 9SQ.

Arthur, David S.C., MA (Hons), DipEd. Scottish Regional Director, Cystic Fibrosis Trust; Director of Training, DDTA (Dumbarton), 1987-88; b. 23.2.30, Kenya; m., Mary Frost; 3 d. Educ. Loretto School, Musselburgh; Edinburgh University; Moray House College of Education. Assistant Teacher: Larchfield, 1954-56, Melville College, 1957-62; Senior History Master, Robert Gordon's College, 1962-68; Depute Rector, High School of Stirling, 1968-70; Rector, Greenfaulds High School, 1970-76; Principal, Lomond School, Helensburgh, 1977-86. Chairman: Samaritans Inc., 1972-76; Secretary, Dumbarton District Business Club; Board, Young Enterprise Dunbartonshire. Publication: Someone To Turn To. Recreations: gardening; hill-walking; photography; tennis. Address: (h.) Inverallan, 26 Argyle Street, Helensburgh G84 8DB; T.-0436 76494.

Arthur, Lt. General Sir Norman, KCB (1985); DL (Stewartry of Kirkcudbright); b. 6.3.31, London (but brought up in Ayrshire, of Scottish parents); m., Theresa Mary Hopkinson; 1 s.; 1 d.; 1 s. (deceased). Educ. Eton College; Royal Military Academy, Sandhurst. Commissioned Royal Scots Greys, 1951; commanded Royal Scots Dragoon Guards, 1972-74, 7th Armoured Brigade, 1976-77, 3rd Armoured Division, 1980-82; Director, Personal Services (Army), 1983-85; commanded Army in Scotland, and Governor of Edinburgh Castle, 1985-88; retired, 1988; Honorary Colonel, Royal Scots Dragoon Guards, since 1984; Col. Comdt. Military Provost Staff Corps, 1983-88; Honorary Colonel, 205 (Scottish) General Hospital, Territorial Army, since 1988; mentioned in Despatches, 1974. Officer, Royal Company of Archers; President, Scottish Conservation Projects Trust, since 1989; Vice President, Riding for the Disabled Association, Edinburgh and the Borders, since 1988; Chairman, Army Benevolent Fund, Scotland; Member, British Olympic equestrian team (three-day event), 1960. Recreations: riding; country sports; country life; reading. Address: (h.) Newbarns, Dalbeattie, Kirkcudbrightshire; T.-055 663 227.

Ashcroft, Brian Kemp, BA (Hons), MA. Director, Fraser of Allander Institute, Strathclyde University, since 1989; Member, Secretary of State's Panel of Economic Consultants, since 1991; b. 5.3.47, Stockton-on-Tees; m., Janet; 1 s.; 2 d. Educ. Stockton Grammar School; Lancaster University. Rock musician, 1962-65; Construction Industry: labourer, clerk, office manager, 1965-70; Lecturer, Glasgow Polytechnic, 1974-76; Strathclyde University: Lecturer/Senior Lecturer, 1976-89, Research Director, Fraser of Allander Institute,

1989. Publications: over 30 academic papers/books. Recreations: photography; jogging; trying to hide his English origins. Address: (b.) 100 Cathedral Street, Glasgow, G4 0LN; T.-041-552 4400.

Ashcroft, William Alexander, BSc, MSc, PhD, FGS. Senior Lecturer, Department of Geology, Aberdeen University, since 1980; b. 16.6.36, Morayshire; m., Margaret Jean Cotching; 2 s. Educ. Aberlour High School; Aberdeen University; Birmingham University. Seismologist, Seismograph Services Ltd., 1959-62; postgraduate student, 1962-65; Assistant Lecturer, then Lecturer, then Senior Lecturer, Aberdeen University, since 1966. Recreation: skiing. Address: (b.) Department of Geology and Petroleum Geology, King's College, Aberdeen AB9 2UE; T.-0224 273458.

Asher, Catherine Archibald, OBE, BA, RGN, SCM, RNT. Director of Nurse Education, Glasgow Eastern College of Nursing and Midwifery, since 1974; Chairman and Elected Member, National Board for Nursing, Midwifery and Health Visiting for Scotland, since 1983; b. 6.7.33, Edinburgh. Educ. Sir Percy Jackson's Grammar School, Doncaster; Woodside Senior Secondary School, Glasgow; Open University; Edinburgh University. Staff Nurse, then Ward Sister, Glasgow Royal Infirmary, 1956-61; Edinburgh University Certificate in Nursing Studies (Education), 1961-63. Elected Member, General Nursing Council (Scotland), 1976-83; Member, UK Central Council for Nursing Midwifery and Health Visiting. Publication: An Outline of Basic Nursing Care (Co-author). Recreations: golf; swimming; gardening. Address: (h.) 68 Fifth Avenue, Glasgow, G12 0AT; T.-041-339 5072.

Asher, Professor R.E., BA, PhD, FRSE, FRAS. Professor of Linguistics, Edinburgh University, since 1977; Dean, Faculty of Arts, 1986-89; Vice-Principal, since 1991; b. 1926, Nottinghamshire. Educ. Edward VI Grammar School, Retford; University College, London. Assistant, Department of French, University College London, 1951-53; Lecturer in Linguistics/Tamil, School of Oriental & African Studies, London, 1953-65; joined Department of Linguistics, Edinburgh University, 1965. Elected Fellow, Kerala Sahitya Akademi, India, 1983; awarded Gold Medal of the Akademi for distinguished services to Malayalam language and literature. Publications: A Tamil prose reader, 1971; Some landmarks in the history of Tamil prose, 1973; Towards a history of phonetics (Co-editor), 1981; Tamil, 1982; Studies on Malayalam language and literature, 1989. Address: (b.) Department of Linguistics, Edinburgh University, Adam Ferguson Building, Edinburgh EH8 9LL.

Ashmall, Harry Alfred, MA, MLitt, FBIM. Rector, Morrison's Academy, since 1979; presenter of religious programmes on radio and television, since 1976; b. 22.2.39, Stirling; m., Edna Reid; 2 d. Educ. Kilsyth Academy; Glasgow University. Teacher and Careers Master, High School of Glasgow, 1961-66; Principal Teacher of History and Modern Studies, Lochend Secondary School; Principal Teacher of History, High School of Glasgow; Rector, Forfar Academy, 1971-79. Vice Chairman, UNICEF UK; Member, Scottish Council for Research in Education; Chairman, Educational Broadcasting Council for Scotland; Member, Executive Committee, British Council ECS. Publications: The High School of Glasgow: a history, 1976; Belief yet Betrayal, 1971; Preparing a Staff Manual, 1977; Pupils and their courses, 1981. Recreations: reading; skiing; golf. Address: (b.) Morrison's Academy, Crieff, PH7 3AN; T.-0764 3885.

Ashton, Pauline Mary, BEd. General Secretary, Girl Guides Association (Scotland), since 1988; b. 1.1.59, Wincanton. Educ. Alcester Grammar School; St. Mary's College, Fenham. Teacher, Newcastle-upon-Tyne; Training Manager,

Girl Guides Association. Recreations: good food and wine; travel; historic houses. Address: (b.) 16 Coates Crescent, Edinburgh, EH3 7AH; T.-031-226 4511.

Ashworth, Bryan, MD, FRCP(Lond), FRCP(Edin). Honorary Librarian, Royal College of Physicians of Edinburgh, 1982-91; Consultant Neurologist, Royal Infirmary and Western General Hospital, Edinburgh, and Senior Lecturer in Medical Neurology, Edinburgh University, since 1971; b. 5.5.29, Oundle, Northants. Educ. Laxton School; Oundle School; St. Andrews University. National Service, Captain RAMC, Northern Nigeria, 1953-55; junior hospital posts, Manchester and Bristol; Wellcome-Swedish Travelling Research Fellow, Karolinska Hospital, Stockholm, 1965-66; Lecturer in Clinical Neurology, Manchester University, and Honorary Consultant Physician, Manchester Royal Infirmary, 1967-71; Director (non-executive), Robert Bailey and Son, PLC, Stockport, since 1978. Publications: Clinical Neuro-ophthalmology, 2nd edition, 1981; Management of Neurological Disorders, 2nd edition, 1985; The Bramwells of Edinburgh, 1986. Recreations: writing; walking. Address: (h.) 13/5 Eildon Terrace, Edinburgh, EH3 5NL; T.-031-556 0547.

Ashworth, John Brian, FCA, CBIM. Managing Director, Chivas Brothers Ltd., since 1974, and Seagram Distillers PLC, since 1984; b. 2.9.36, Wakefield; m., Valerie; 2 s.; 1 d. Educ. Ackworth School; British College of Accountancy. Articled chartered accountancy, Leeds; Accountant, John Smiths Tadcaster Brewery Co. Ltd.; Commercial Director, Shaw Carpet Co. Ltd.; Founder/Managing Director, Crimpfil Ltd. Member, Council, CBI Scotland; Chairman, Renfrewshire Enterprise Ltd.; Governor, Paisley University; Member, Council, Scotch Whisky Association; Master, Keepers of the Quaich. Recreations: golf; travel. Address: (b.) 111 Renfrew Road, Paisley; T.-041-842 2211.

Athanas, Christopher Nicholas, MA, LLB. Partner, Dundas & Wilson, Solicitors, Edinburgh, since 1969; b. 26.8.41, Aden; m., Sheena Anne Stewart; 1 s.; 2 d. Educ. Blairmore Preparatory School, Aberdeenshire; Fettes College, Edinburgh; Aberdeen University. Law Apprentice, then Legal Assistant, Paull & Williamsons, Advocates, Aberdeen, 1964-68; Legal Assistant, Dundas & Wilson, Solicitors, Edinburgh, 1968-69. Member, Society of Writers to the Signet; Member, Law Society of Scotland Investor Protection Committee; Invited Member, Edinburgh Registrars Group; former Director, Edinburgh Junior Chamber of Commerce. Recreations: art; angling; golf; walking. Address: (b.) Dundas & Wilson, 25 Charlotte Square, Edinburgh; T.-031-225 1234.

Atholl, The Duke of ((George) Iain Murray), DL (Perthshire), MA. Chairman, Westminster Press Ltd.; Chairman, RNLI, 1979-89; Vice-President, National Trust for Scotland, since 1975; Honorary President, Scottish Wildlife Trust, since 1974; President, Scottish Landowners Federation, 1986-91; b. 19.6.31, London. Educ. Eton; Christ Church, Oxford. Past Convener, Scottish Landowners Federation; Member, Committee on the Preparation of Legislation; Member, Red Deer Commission, 1969-83. Recreations: golf; bridge; shooting; stalking. Address: (h.) Blair Castle, Blair Atholl, Perthshire; T.-Blair Atholl 212.

Atkinson, Professor David, BSc, PhD, MIBiol, CBiol, MIEEM, FRSA. Professor of Agriculture (Land Resources), Aberdeen University, since 1988; Head, Land Resources Department and Vice-Dean Research, Scottish Agricultural College, Aberdeen; b. 12.9.44, Blyth; m., Elisabeth Ann Cocks; 1 s.; 2 d. Educ. Newlands County Secondary Modern School; Hull University; Newcastle-upon-Tyne University. East Malling Research Station, Maidstone, 1969-85; Macaulay Institute for Soil Research, 1985-87; Macaulay Land Use Research Institute, 1987-88. Chairman, Programme Committee, 1991 BCPC Conference. Recreations: music; reading thrillers; quotations. Address: (b.) 581 King Street, Aberdeen, AB9 1UD; T.-0224 480291.

Atkinson, Jacqueline Mary, BA, PhD, CPsychol. Senior Lecturer, Glasgow University, since 1991; b. 24.6.50, Hampton, Middx. Educ. Thames Valley Grammar School; Hull University. Research Psychologist, Guy's and St. Olave's Hospital, 1974-77; Lecturer, Glasgow University, 1977-91. Member, Management Committee, National Schizophrenia Fellowship (Scotland). Publications: Coping with Schizophrenia; Schizophrenia at Home; Coping with Stress at Work. Recreations: quilt art; writing romantic fiction (as Fiona Sinclair and Mhairi McBeth). Address: (b.) Department of Public Health, Glasgow University, 2 Lilybank Gardens, Glasgow, G12 8RZ; T.-041-339 8855, Ext. 5009.

Atkinson, Valerie, MA (Hons). Deputy Editor, News and Current Affairs, BBC Scotland, since 1988; Editor, Focal Point, BBC Scotland, since 1988; b. 28.12.44, Glasgow; m., Ian Atkinson; 1 s.; 1 d. Educ. Hillhead High School, Glasgow; University of Glasgow. BBC Scotland, News and Current Affairs: Researcher, Radio, Reporter, TV, Director, TV, Producer, TV. TRICS Award, Best News, Current Affairs or Topical Events Programme, 1986. Recreations: tennis; theatre; skiing. Address: (h.) 43 Cleveden Road, Glasgow G12 0PH; T.-041-339 6738.

Auchinachie, Henry Williamson, ACIS, AIB (Scot). Former Member, Grampian Regional Council (Finance Chairman, 1978-86); Farmer; retired Bank Manager; b. Keith, Banffshire; m., 1, Edith Russell Taylor (deceased); 1 s.; 4 d.; 2, Anne Barclay Thomson Walker. Educ. Keith Grammar School; Metropolitan College (Correspondence). Cadet Officer, Mercantile Marine; Bank Official (branches, Inspection and Legal Departments, finally Branch Manager). Former JP; former Member: Banchory Town Council; Kincardine County Council; Aberdeen County Council; Deer District Council; former Treasurer, Lonmay Parish Church (35 years); Secretary/Treasurer, Lonmay Public Hall, 37 years; Life Member: British Show Jumping Association; Fraserburgh Burns Club; Co-Founder, Banchory Festival of Scottish Music. Recreations: music; horses. Address: (h.) Mill of Crimond, Fraserburgh, Aberdeenshire, AB4 4XQ; T.-0346 32216.

Avonside, Rt. Hon. Lord (Ian Hamilton Shearer), PC, QC. Senator of the College of Justice in Scotland, 1964-84; b. 6.11.14.

B

Bade, Rev. Raymond John, DipTh. Minister, United Reformed Churches in Coaltown of Balgonie, Dundee and Falkirk, since 1991; Vice Chairman, Scottish Churches Council, 1986-90; Vice Chairman, Mid Scotland District, United Reformed Church, since 1990; b. 20.4.31, Ilford; m., Cathreen Birrell Kenny. Educ. Ilford County High School; Overdale Theological College, Birmingham. Entered ministry of Churches of Christ, 1957; first charge, Leeds, until 1961; Falkirk Church of Christ, 1961-65; Dalkeith Road,

Edinburgh, 1965-91; became United Reformed Church minister after union, 1981. Chairman, Ark Southside House Management Committee, 1984-91. Recreations: caravanning; exercising the dog; listening to records. Address: (h.) 3 Parbroath Road, Glenrothes, Fife KY7 4TH; T.-0592 772948.

Bagnall, John Michael, MA (Cantab), DipLib, MIInfSci. University Librarian, Dundee University, since 1987; b. 22.4.45, South Yorkshire; m., Carol. Educ. Mexborough Grammar School; Sidney Sussex College, Cambridge. Diploma in Librarianship, University College, London; Assistant Librarian and Sub-Librarian, Newcastle upon Tyne University. Recreations: music; bird-watching; languages. Address: University Library, Dundee, DD1 4HN; T.-0382 23181.

Bailey, Michael, BA (Hons). Curator, Maclaurin Art Gallery, Ayr, since 1976; Visual Arts Development Officer, Kyle & Carrick District Leisure Service; b. 11.11.37, Stockport; m., Bernadette Donnelly; 4 s. Educ. Moseley Hall; Open University; Meteorological Office College. Meteorologist, 1956-61; marine biology research, UKAEA, 1961-64; meteorologist, 1964-76. Recreations: music and drama; visual arts; travel. Address: (b.) Rozelle House, Rozelle Park, Ayr, KA7 4NQ; T.-0292 45447.

Bailey, Raymond James, CEng, MIEE. Principal, Cardonald College, Glasgow, since 1986; b. 31.8.34, Glasgow; m., Maria Anne Mallon; 3 s. Educ. St. Mungo's Academy. Address: (b.) Cardonald College, Mosspark Drive, Glasgow, G52 3AY; T.-041-883 6151.

Baillie, Professor John, MA, CA. Visiting Professor of Accountancy, Heriot-Watt University, Edinburgh, since 1989; Johnstone-Smith Professor of Accountancy, Glasgow University, 1983-88; Partner, KPMG Peat Marwick (formerly KMG Thomson McLintock), since 1978; b. 7.10.44; m., Annette Alexander; 1 s.; 1 d. Educ. Whitehill School. Member, various technical and professional affairs committees, Institute of Chartered Accountants of Scotland. Recreations: keeping fit; reading; music; golf. Address: (h.) The Glen, Glencairn Road, Kilmacolm, Renfrewshire; T.-Kilmacolm 3254.

Baillie, Ian David Hunter, CQSW. Director of Social Work, Church of Scotland Board of Social Responsibility, since 1990; Director, Social Care Association (Education), since 1987; Auxiliary Minister, United Reformed Church; b. 18.12.40, Dundee; m., Margaret MacCallum McFarlane; 3 d. Educ. Hutchesons Boys Grammar School. Eight years in life assurance; 25 years, to date, in social work; former Depute Director of Social Work, Strathclyde Regional Council. Manager, Kirk Care Housing Association; Member, Executive, International Christian Federation for Prevention of Alcoholism and Drug Addiction. Recreations: sport (watching); reading. Address: (b.) Church of Scotland Board of Social Responsibility, 121 George Street, Edinburgh, EH2 4YN; T.-031-225 5722.

Baillie, Marion, MA (Hons). Chairman, Carers National Association (Strathclyde); Member, Committee of Management, Carers National Association; Governor, Morrison's Academy; Member, Board of Managers, Jordanhill School. Educ. Glasgow University. Teacher of English, until 1963; Lecturer in English, until 1965; Headmistress, Morrison's Academy Girls' School, until 1972; Assistant Principal, Jordanhill College of Education, until 1987. Address: (h.) 12 Napier Road, Killearn, Glasgow; T.-Killearn 50580.

Bain, Professor Andrew David, MA, PhD, FRSE. Visiting Professor, Glasgow University, since 1991; Board Member, Scottish Enterprise, since 1991; Economic Consultant, since 1991; b. 21.3.36, Glasgow; m., Eleanor Riches; 3 s. Educ. Glasgow Academy; Cambridge University. Various posts, Cambridge University, 1959-67; Professor of Economics: Stirling University, 1967-77, Strathclyde University, 1977-84; Group Economic Advisor, Midland Bank, 1984-90. Member: Committee to Review the Functioning of Financial Institutions, 1977-80, Monopolies and Mergers Commission, 1980-81. Publications: The Control of the Money Supply, 1970; The Economics of the Financial System (2nd Edition), 1992. Address: (b.) Department of Political Economy, Glasgow University, Glasgow, G12 8RT; T.-041-339 8855.

Bain, Professor William Herbert, MD, FRCS. Titular Professor in Cardiac Surgery, Glasgow University, since 1981; Consultant Cardio-Thoracic Surgeon, since 1962; b. 20.11.27, Kilmacolm; m., Helen Craigie; 2 s.; 1 d. Educ. Glasgow High School; Glasgow University. Graduated MB, ChB; House Officer posts, Glasgow, 1950-51; McIntyre Research Scholar, 1952-53; Registrar in General Surgery, Glasgow Royal Infirmary, 1954-58; Lecturer in Experimental Surgery, Honorary Senior Registrar, 1958-62; Andrews Fellow, University of Chicago, 1961; Senior Lecturer/Reader in Surgery, Glasgow, 1962-81; Consultant Surgeon, Royal Infirmary, Western Infirmary, Stobhill Hospital. Examiner for Glasgow and Edinburgh Royal Colleges; Member, British Standards Institute; Past President, Scottish Thoracic Society; President, Society of Cardiothoracic Surgeons of Gt. Britain and Ireland, 1989. Publications: Blood Flow Through Tissues and Organs, 1968; Essentials of Cardiovascular Surgery, 1974; Intensive Care, 1980. Recreations: sailing; fishing. Address: (h.) 37 Dunellan Road, Milngavie, Glasgow G62 7RE; T.-041-956 3218.

Bainton, Ian, MA, MBIM. Headteacher, Uddingston Grammar School, since 1987; b. 30.8.38, Edinburgh; m., Agnes Anne; 2 s.; 1 d. Educ. Linlithgow Academy; Edinburgh University. Education Officer, Government of Kenya, seven years; Central Region, seven years; Assistant Principal, Inveralmond Community High School, four years; Depute Rector, Grangemouth High School, three years. Recreations: reading; gardening; DIY. Address: (b.) Station Road, Uddingston, Glasgow, G71 7BS.

Baird, Alister. Chief Executive, Hamilton District Council; b. 11.12.38, Glasgow; m., Lynne; 2 s. Educ. Eastbank Academy, Glasgow. Student Sanitary Inspector, then Assistant Sanitary Inspector, Airdrie Town Council, 1957-63; Senior Assistant Sanitary Inspector, Fife County Council, 1963-65; Depute Director of Environmental Health, East Kilbride Town Council, 1965-75; Director of Environmental Health, Hamilton District Council, 1975-86. Recreations: golf; music; art. Address: (b.) Municipal Buildings, 102 Cadzow Street, Hamilton ML3 6HH; T.-0698 282323.

Baird, Professor David Tennent, BA (Cantab), MB, ChB, DSc, FRCP Edin, FRCOG, FRS(Ed). Medical Research Council Professor of Reproductive Endocrinology, Edinburgh University, since 1985; Consultant Obstetrician and Gynaecologist, Simpson Memorial Maternity Pavilion, Edinburgh Royal Infirmary, since 1970; b. 13.3.35, Glasgow; m., Frances Lightveld; 2 s. Educ. Aberdeen Grammar School; Aberdeen University; Trinity College, Cambridge; Edinburgh University. After clinical training in endocrinology as well as obstetrics, spent three years (1965-68) as an MRC travelling Research Fellow at Worcester Foundation for Experimental Biology, Shrewsbury, Mass., USA, conducting research on reproductive endocrinology; Deputy Director, MRC Unit of Reproductive Biology, Edinburgh, 1972-77; Professor of Obstetrics and Gynaecology, Edinburgh University, 1977-85; served on a number of national and international committees. Publications: four books on reproduction. Recreations: ski mountaineering; music; sport. Address: (b.) Department of Obstetrics and Gynaecology, Edinburgh

University, Centre for Reproductive Biology, 37 Chalmers Street, Edinburgh, EH3 9EW; T.-031-229 2575.

Baird, Isabel Duncan. General Secretary, United Free Church of Scotland, since 1981; b. 15.9.34, Aberdeen; m., Ronald C.F. Baird; 1 s. Educ. Rosemount Secondary School; Central School (commercial course). Shorthand typist, 1950; private secretary, 1953; private secretary to General Secretary, United Free Church of Scotland, 1971-81. Boys' Brigade officer, 1968-77. Recreations: reading; knitting; Boys' Brigade; local/national Church. Address: (b.) 11 Newton Place, Glasgow, G3 7PR; T.-041-332 3435.

Baird, John Alexander, MD, MRCPsych, DCH. Physician Superintendent, State Hospital, Carstairs, since 1985; b. 28.8.47, Edinburgh; m., Ann Easson; 3 s. Educ. Daniel Stewart's College, Edinburgh; Edinburgh University. Consultant Psychiatrist, State Hospital, Carstairs, 1981-85. Standing Committee on Difficult Prisoners: Member, 1985-88, Chairman, 1988-91; Member, Parole Board for Scotland, since 1992. Recreations: hill walking; wine; watching rugby. Address: (b.) State Hospital, Carstairs Junction, Lanark, ML11 8RP; T.-0555 840 293.

Baird, Joyce Deans, MA, MB, ChB, FRCPEdin. Reader in Medicine, Edinburgh University, and Honorary Consultant Physician, Western General Hospital, Edinburgh; b. 24.6.29, Glasgow; m., John Alexander Penman Splitt; 1 d. Educ. St. Leonards School, St. Andrews; Aberdeen University. Medical staff appointments, Royal Infirmary, Edinburgh, 1954-64; Research Fellow, Department for Endocrine and Metabolic Diseases, Western General Hospital, Edinburgh, 1965-68; Medical Officer, Scottish Home and Health Department, 1968-70; Lecturer in Medicine, Western General Hospital, Edinburgh, 1971-76; Vice-President, European Association for the Study of Diabetes. Recreations: music; painting; hillwalking; skiing; travel; reading. Address: (h.) Manor House, Boswall Road, Edinburgh, EH5 3RR; T.-031-552 2030.

Baird, Susan, CBE, OStJ, JP, DUniv. Lord Provost of Glasgow, 1988-92; b. 26.5.40, Glasgow; m., George; 3 s.; 1 d. Educ. St. Mark's Secondary School, Glasgow. Worked in a city centre office; joined Labour Party, 1969; became Councillor for Parkhead, 1974; elected Bailie of the city, 1980; former Convener, Manpower Committee, latterly Vice-Convener, Parks and Recreation Committee. Address: (b.) City Chambers, George Square, Glasgow, G2 1DU; T.-041-221 9600.

Baird, William Bramwell, LLB (Hons), LLM, ACII. Commander, The Salvation Army, Scotland, since 1990; b. 20.11.27, Glasgow; m., Rita Gravett. Educ. Kilmarnock Academy; London University. Salvation Army: served in corps, business and social work, 1949-66, Finance Officer, Pakistan, 1966-69, Secretary, The Mothers' Hospital, 1970-73, Personnel Officer, Social Services, 1973-74, Legal Officer, International Headquarters, 1974-82, Chief Secretary, Social Services, 1982-84, Chief Secretary, Scotland, 1984-90. Recreation: music. Address: 19 Viewfield Avenue, Bishopbriggs, Glasgow G64 2AG.

Baird, Rev. William Gordon Glen, DPA, ACII. Minister, Inverkeithing St. John's and North Queensferry Churches, since 1977; b. 7.1.28, Glasgow; m., Morag Thorburn Crichton; 1 s.; 1 d. Educ. William Hulme's Grammar School, Manchester; Glasgow University; Glasgow and West of Scotland Commercial College; Edinburgh University. Inland Revenue, 1944-46; Royal Navy, 1946-48; Ministry of National Insurance, 1948-66; Senior Executive Officer, HM Treasury (O & M Division), Scottish Branch, 1967-68; Training Officer for Scotland, Department of Health and Social Security, 1969-72; student, University of Edinburgh, 1972-74; Assistant Minister, St. Ninian's Church,

Corstorphine, Edinburgh, 1974-75. Recreations: gardening; railways; the solitude of the Western Isles. Address: St. Johns Manse, 34 Hill Street, Inverkeithing, Fife; T.-0383 412422.

Baker, Frances J.T., MSc, BA, RGN, OHNC, Cert Ed. Senior Regional Nursing Officer, British Gas Scotland, since 1982; Member, National Board for Nursing, Midwifery and Health Visiting for Scotland, since 1988; b. 29.4.34, Ayr; m., Alan; 1 s.; 1 d. Educ. Ayr Academy; London University (External); Manchester University. Casualty Staff Nurse, Ayr County Hospital; Sister, NCB, North Staffs; Lecturer, Senior Lecturer, Head of Health and Nursing Studies, Stoke on Trent Cauldon College, 1975-82. Publication: Role of Occupational Health Nurse in the Care of the Pregnant Woman at Work. Recreations: opera and classical music; theatre; swimming; gardening; tapestry; reading. Address: (b.) Granton House, Marine Drive, Edinburgh, EH5 1YB.

Baker, James Robert, RGN, RNT. Principal, Argyll and Clyde College of Nursing and Midwifery, since 1983; b. 8.5.34, Liverpool; Edna M.; 2 s. Educ. Longview Secondary Modern School, Liverpool; London University. Nurse Teacher, Whiston, Lancashire, 1963-66; Principal Tutor: Inverclyde and Bute College of Nursing and Midwifery, 1966-69, Law Hospital, Carluke, 1969-74; Inverclyde and Bute College of Nursing and Midwifery: Principal Nursing Officer (Teaching), 1974-76, Director of Nurse Education, 1976-85. Chairman, Scottish Directors of Nurse Education Group, since 1985. Recreations: walking; swimming. Address: (h.) 1 Anderson Road, Bishopton, PA7 5EN; T.-0505 863063.

Baker, Professor Michael John, TD, BA, BSc (Econ), DipM, CertITP (Harvard), DBA (Harvard), FCIM, F.SCOTVEC, FCAM, FRSA. Professor of Marketing, Strathclyde University, since 1971 (Deputy Principal, since 1984); Chairman, Institute of Marketing, 1987; b. 5.11.35, Debden; m., Sheila; 1 s.; 2 d. Educ. Worksop College; Bede, Gosforth and Harvey Grammar Schools; Durham University; London University; Harvard University. Royal Artillery, 1956 (2nd Lt.); Richard Thomas & Baldwins (Sales) Ltd., 1958-64; Lecturer: Medway College of Technology, 1964-66, Hull College of Technology, 1966-68; FME Fellow, Harvard Business School, 1968-71; Member, Vice-Chairman and Chairman, SCOTBEC, 1973-85; Member, SSRC Management Committee, 1976-80; Dean, Strathclyde Business School, 1978-84; Chairman, Marketing Education Group, 1974-87; Member, SHERT, since 1983; Member, UGC Business and Management Sub-Committee, 1986-89; Member, Chief Scientist's Committee, since 1985; Governor, CAM; Director: Stoddard Sekers International PLC, ARIS PLC; Governor, Lomond School. Publications: Marketing New Industrial Products, 1975; Market Development, 1983; Marketing Strategy and Management, 1985; Marketing, 5th edition, 1991; The Marketing Book (Editor), 1991; The Role of Design in International Competitiveness, 1989; Marketing and Competitive Success, 1989; Dictionary of Marketing & Advertising (2nd edition), 1990; Research for Marketing, 1991; Perspectives on Marketing Management (Editor), 1991. Recreations: sailing; gardening; travel; DIY. Address: (b.) Strathclyde University, 173 Cathedral Street, Glasgow, G4 ORQ; T.-041-552 4400.

Baker, Professor Thomas Neville, BMet, PhD, DMet, FIM, FInstP, CEng, CPhys. Professor, Department of Metallurgy and Engineering Materials, Strathclyde University; b. 11.1.34, Southport; m., Eileen May Allison. Educ. King George V School, Southport; Sheffield University. Research Metallurgist, Nelson Research Laboratories, English Electric Co., Stafford, 1958-60; Scientist, Project Leader, Tube Investments Research Laboratories, Hinxton Hall, Cambridge, 1961-64; Department of Metallurgy, Strathclyde University: SRC Research Fellow, 1965, Lecturer, 1966,

Senior Lecturer, 1976; Head, Division of Metallurgy and Engineering Materials, 1988-90. Recreations: music; literature; creating a garden. Address: (b.) Department of Metallurgy and Engineering Materials, Strathclyde University, Colville Building, 48 N. Portland Street, Glasgow; T.-041-552 4400.

Baldwick, Allan Thomas, JP. Chairman, Annandale and Eskdale Licensing Board, since 1988; Chairman, Physical Planning, Dumfries and Galloway Regional Council, since 1990; b. 14.11.48, Dumfries; m., Isabella; 1 d. Educ. Lockberbie Academy. Dumfries and Galloway Regional Councillor, since 1986; Annandale and Eskdale District Councillor, since 1988; Hoddom and Ecclefechan Community Councillor, since 1982. Address: (h.) Hunters Lea, Hoddom Road, Ecclefechan, DG11 3BY; T.-05763 456.

Balekjian, Wahe Hagop, Dr (Law), Dr (pol sc), PhD. Honorary Senior Research Fellow, School of Law, Glasgow University, since 1990 (Reader in European Law, 1976-90, Head of Department, 1976-88); Visiting Titular Professor, University of Salzburg, Austria, since 1981; Titular Professor, European Faculty, Land Use Planning, Strasbourg, since 1982; Honorary Senior Research Fellow, School of Law, Glasgow University, since 1990; b. 2.10.24, Cairo; m., Eva Birgitta. Educ. College of Arts and Sciences, Cairo; Vienna University; Manchester University. Diploma, Hague Academy of International Law. Lecturer, Vienna University, 1957-73; Simon Research Fellow, Manchester University, 1963-65; Head of Department, European Studies, National Institute of Higher Education, Limerick, 1973-76. Publications: Legal Aspects of Foreign Investment in the EEC, 1967 (awarded Prize of European Communities, 1967); The Status of Unrecognised States in International Law (published in German, 1971). Recreations: hill-walking; piano playing; languages. Address: (b.) School of Law, The University, Glasgow, G12 8QQ; T.-041-339 8855, Ext. 5539.

Balfour of Burleigh, Lord. Chairman: Turing Institute, Edinburgh Cablevision plc, Capella Nova, Canongate Press plc; Deputy Governor, Bank of Scotland, 1977-91; b. 6.1.27, London. Educ. Westminster School, London. Graduate Apprentice, English Electric Company, 1951; various positions in manufacturing mangement; started English Electric's manufacturing operations in India as General Manager of new company in Madras, 1957-64; returned to Liverpool as General Manager; appointed General Manager, D. Napier & Son, before leaving the company in 1968; joined Bank of Scotland as a Director, 1968; also Director: Scottish Investment Trust plc; William Lawson Distillers Ltd.; Infolink UAPT plc; Bo'ness Heritage Trust. Forestry Commissioner, 1971-74; Chairman, Scottish Arts Council, 1971-80; Chairman, Edinburgh Book Festival, 1982-87; Member, British Railways (Scottish) Board; Treasurer, Royal Society of Edinburgh; Treasurer, Royal Scottish Corporation; President, Friends of Vellore; President, Franco Scottish Society; Chancellor, Stirling University, since 1988. Recreations: woodwork; hill-climbing; music. Address: c/o Royal Society of Edinburgh, 22 George Street, Edinburgh.

Balfour, 4th Earl of (Gerald Arthur James Balfour), JP, b. 23.12.25; m. Educ. Eton; HMS Conway. Member, East Lothian County Council, 1960-75. Address: (h.) The Tower, Whittingehame, Haddington.

Balfour, Ian Leslie Shaw, MA, LLB, BD, PhD, SSC, NP. Solicitor (Senior Partner, Balfour & Manson), since 1955; b. 16.6.32, Edinburgh; m., Joyce Margaret Ross Pryde; 3 s.; 1 d. Educ. Edinburgh Academy; Edinburgh University. Qualified as Solicitor, 1955; commissioned, RASC, 1955-57; Partner, Balfour & Manson, since 1959; Secretary, Oliver & Son Ltd., 1959-89; Fiscal to Law Society of Scotland, since 1981. Baptist Union of Scotland: President, 1976-77, Law

Agent, since 1964, Secretary, Charlotte Baptist Chapel, Edinburgh, since 1980, Secretary, Scottish Bapist College, since 1983; Secretary, Elba Housing Society Ltd., since 1969; Council, Society for Computers and Law, since 1988; Director, Edinburgh Medical Missionary Society. Recreations: hill-walking; home computing; lay preaching. Address: (b.) 58 Frederick Street, Edinburgh; T.-031-225 8291.

Balfour, Peter Edward Gerald, CBE. President, Scottish Council (Development and Industry), since 1985 (Chairman, 1978-85); Director, Royal Bank of Scotland, 1972-90; Chairman, Charterhouse plc, 1985-91; Chairman, Selective Assets Trust and First Charlotte Assets Trust; b. 9.7.21, Woking; m., 1, Grizelda Ogilvy, 2, Diana Wainman; 3 s.; 2 d. Educ. Eton College. Served Scots Guards, 1940-54; joined William McEwan & Co., brewers, 1954; appointed Director, 1958; Director, Scottish Brewers, 1959; Scottish and Newcastle Breweries, 1961 (Chairman and Managing Director, 1970-83); Director and Vice Chairman, RBS Group, 1978; Director, British Assets Trust. Recreations: farming; forestry. Address: (h.) Scadlaw House, Humbie, East Lothian; T.-087 533 252.

Balfour, William Harold St. Clair. Solicitor; b. 29.8.34, Edinburgh; m., 1, Patricia Waite (m. dissolved); 1 s.; 2 d.; 2, Alice Ingsay McFarlane; 2 step. d. Educ. Hillfield, Ontario; Edinburgh Academy; Edinburgh University. Partner, Balfour & Manson, Nightingale & Bell, since 1962; Clerk to Admission of Notaries Public, since 1971; Prison Visiting Committee, 1965-70; Chairman, Basic Space Dance Theatre, 1980-86; Friends of Talbot Rice Art Centre, since 1982, Garvald Trustees, since 1980, Wellspring Management, since 1990, Scottish Arts Council, since 1988; Secretary: Scottish Photography Gallery, Fruit Market Gallery, Edinburgh; Trustee, Edinburgh Rudolf Steiner School. Recreations: sailing; walking; wine. Address: (b.) 58 Frederick Street, Edinburgh, EH2 1LS; T.-031-225 8291.

Balharrie, Brigadier John Charles, MBE, MC, KStJ, TD. Deputy Lieutenant, Dunbartonshire, 1983-90; b. 21.12.19, Glasgow; m., Sara Jean Ferguson. Educ. Glasgow Academy. Commissioned, 1938; active service, Middle East and NW Europe, 1939-45 (twice wounded), Palestine, Cyprus and Aden, 1945-59; commanded Royal Scots Greys, 1962-64; Chief Staff Officer, 52nd Lowland Division, 1964-67; Assistant Director, Armoured Warfare Studies, Ministry of Defence, 1967-69; Commander, Lowland Area, Edinburgh Castle, 1969-73; retired as Brigadier, 1974, and served as Secretary, Lowland TAVR Association, 1974-84. Honorary Colonel, Glasgow and Lanarkshire Bn., Army Cadet Force, 1985-90; President: Glasgow Area HQ Branch, Royal British Legion Scotland, since 1975, Joint Council, City of Glasgow Naval, Army and Air Force Associations, since 1974; Member of Chapter, Order of St. John in Scotland, 1981-90; Chairman: Glasgow Branch, Forces Help Society and Lord Roberts Workshops, 1976-85, Glasgow and West of Scotland Branch, Royal Scots Dragoon Guards Association, 1980-92; Glasgow Branch, St. John Association in Scotland, 1977-87; Vice-Convenor, Chaplains Committee, Church of Scotland, 1985-88; Vice-Chairman, Skeabost Community Council, Isle of Skye, since 1989. Recreations: country pursuits. Address: (h.) Crepigill Lodge, Skeabost Bridge, Isle of Skye, IV51 9PB; T.-047032 244.

Ball, Derek William, MB, MRCPsych. Composer; Consultant Psychiatrist; b. 30.12.49, Letterkenny, Ireland; m., Marie Knox; 1 d. Educ. Kings Hospital, Dublin; Royal Irish Academy of Music; Trinity College, Dublin. Studied composition with Dr. Archie Potter; writes chamber and orchestral music; numerous performances in Dublin; pieces performed at festivals in Paris and Bordeaux. Founder Member, Association of Young Irish Composers; Secretary/Treasurer,

Scottish Society of Composers. Address: (h.) Mazagon, 4 Glen Road, Lennoxtown, G65 7JX.

Ball, Geoffrey A., FCA. Chairman, CALA plc (Group Managing Director, since 1974); b. 4.8.43, Bristol; m., Mary Elizabeth; 3 s.; 1 d. Educ. Cotham Grammar School, Bristol. Former Managing Director, Greencoat Properties Ltd.; non-executive Director: Standard Life Assurance Company; Scottish Mortgage & Trust p.l.c.; Stenhouse Western Ltd. Chairman, School Governing Council, George Watson's College, Edinburgh. Recreations: golf; music. Address: (b.) 42 Colinton Road, Edinburgh, EH10 5BT; T.-031-346 0194.

Ball, Graham Edmund, BDS, FDS, RCS (Eng). Chief Administrative Dental Officer, Orkney Health Board, since 1991; b. 14.12.53; m., Carolyn Bowyer; 1 s.; 2 d. Educ. King Edward VI School, Southampton; Welsh National School of Medicine. Registrar, Oral and Maxillofacial Surgery, Portsmouth hospitals, 1979-81; Associate Specialist (part-time), Oral Surgery, Wessex Cardiothoracic Unit, 1982 84; general dental practice, 1984-88; Clinical Community Dental Officer, Orkney Health Board, 1988-91. Recreations: sailing; walking. Address: (h.) North Coubister, Firth, Orkney; T.-0865 76515.

Ball, Professor John Macleod, BA (Cantab), DPhil. Professor of Applied Analysis, Department of Mathematics, Heriot-Watt University, Edinburgh, since 1982; Senior Fellow, Science and Engineering Research Council, 1980-85; b. 19.5.48, Farnham, Surrey. Educ. Mill Hill School; St. John's College, Cambridge. SERC postdoctoral research fellowship, 1972-74, at Department of Mathematics, Heriot-Watt University, and Lefschetz Center for Dynamical Systems, Brown University, Providence, Rhode Island, USA; Heriot-Watt University: Lecturer in Mathematics, 1974-78, Reader in Mathematics, 1978-82. Elected Fellow, Royal Society of Edinburgh, 1980; Whittaker Prize, Edinburgh Mathematical Society, 1981; Junior Whitehead Prize, London Mathematical Society, 1982; Keith Prize, Royal Society of Edinburgh, 1991; elected Fellow, Royal Society, 1989; President, Edinburgh Mathematical Society, 1989-90; Executive Editor, Proceedings of Royal Society of Edinburgh (A). Recreations: music; travel. Address: (h.) 11 Gloucester Place, Edinburgh, EH3 6EE.

Ballantyne, Rev. Duncan Alexander, BD, FSA(Scot), CertMin. Minister, Ascog with Craigmore St. Brendan's, Bute, since 1986; b. 30.7.55, Houston, Renfrewshire. Educ. Linwood High School; Trinity College, Glasgow. Former Sales Manager in the jewellery trade; Probationer, Trinity Church, Rothesay, 1985. Voluntary Adult Literacy Teacher. Recreations: hill-walking; badminton. Address: (h.) The Manse, 1 Albany Terrace, Craigmore, Rothesay, Isle of Bute; T.-Rothesay 502506.

Ballinger, Brian Richard, MA, BM, BCh, FRCPEd, FRCPsych, DPM. Consultant Psychiatrist, Dundee Psychiatric Service, since 1971; Honorary Senior Lecturer, Dundee University; Medical Director, Mental Health Unit and Chairman, Dundee Division of Psychiatry; b. 1.6.37, Newport, Gwent; m., Dr. C. Barbara Ballinger; 2 s. Educ. Manchester Grammar School; University College, Oxford; St. Mary's Hospital Medical School, London. Postgraduate training in London, Oxford, Sheffield and Dundee; special interest in psychiatry of old age. Recreations: painting; music; travel. Address: (b.) Royal Dundee Liff Hospital, Dundee; T.-0382 580441.

Balls, Rev. Ernest George, MA, BD, STM, DD. Clerk to Ardrossan Presbytery, 1980-89; b. 25.6.14, London; m., Elspeth Russell Alexander; 2 s.; 1 d. Educ. Perth Academy; St. Andrews University; Union Seminary, New York. Former Convener, Church and Nation Committee, General Assembly; former Representative, Church of Scotland: Central Committee of World Council of Churches, Scottish Religious Advisory Committee (BBC), Central Religious Advisory Committee (BBC and ITA); Past Chairman, Multilateral Church Conversation. Recreations: gardening; angling. Address: (h.) 67 High Road, Stevenston, KA20 3DZ; T.-Stevenston 63512.

Bancroft, John Henry Jefferies, MA, MD, FRCP, FRCPE, FRCPsych. Clinical Consultant, MRC Reproductive Biology Unit, since 1976; Honorary Senior Lecturer, Department of Psychiatry, Edinburgh University, since 1976; b. 18.6.36, Peterborough; 2 s.; 1 d. Educ. Bedford School; Caius College, Cambridge. Clinical Reader, Department of Psychiatry, Oxford, 1969-76. President, International Academy of Sex Research, 1976-77; Chairman, British Association for Behavioural Psychotherapy, 1983-84; Member, Scientific Advisory Board, Kinsey Institute for Research in Sex and Gender Reproduction; President, Lothian Marriage Guidance Council, since 1988. Publications: Deviant Sexual Behaviour, 1974; Human Sexuality and its Problems, 1983 (2nd edition, 1989); Annual Review of Sex Research (Editor). Recreation: music. Address: (h.) 28 Elbe Street, Leith, Edinburgh, EH6 7HW; T.-031-553 7221.

Band, Thomas Mollison. Chief Executive, Scottish Tourist Board, since 1987; Director, Taste of Scotland Ltd., since 1987; Deputy Chairman, Forth Bridge Centenary Trust, since 1989; Director, Edinburgh Chamber of Commerce Ltd., since 1989; b. 28.3.34, Aberdeen; m., Jean McKenzie Brien; 1 s.; 2 d. Educ. Perth Academy. Principal, Tariff Division, Board of Trade, London, 1969-73; Director (Location of Industry), Department of Industry, Glasgow, 1973-76; Assistant Secretary (Industrial Policy), Scottish Economic Planning Department, 1976-78; Assistant Secretary (Housing), Scottish Development Department, 1978-82; Assistant Secretary (Finance), Scottish Office, 1982-84; Director, Historic Buildings and Monuments, Scottish Development Department, 1984-87. Recreations: gardening; skiing; beating. Address: (h.) Heathfield, Pitcairngreen, Perthshire; T.-073 883 403.

Banks, Philip, MA, MEd. HM Inspector of Schools, since 1983; b. 17.1.46, Stockton-on-Tees; m., Inger Haagensen-Banks; 1 s.; 1 d. Educ. St. Chad's College, Wolverhampton; Trinity Hall, Cambridge; Edinburgh University. Teacher, Ipswich School and Edinburgh Academy, 1969-73; Principal Teacher of English, Queen Anne High School, Dunfermline, 1973-81; Development Officer, Scottish Education Department, 1981-83. Recreations: reading; squash; walking. Address: (b.) Corunna House, 29 Cadogan Street, Glasgow; T.-042-204 1220.

Banks, Robert Lewis McIntyre, BL, NP. Senior Partner, Anderson, Banks and Co., Solicitors, Oban, since 1986 (Partner, since 1954); b. 24.3.32, Oban; m., Ishbel Gordon. Educ. Oban High School; Edinburgh University. Dean, Oban Faculty of Solicitors, 1986-89; appointed Honorary Sheriff at Oban, 1989; Honorary Secretary, RSSPCC, Oban and District Branch, 1961-92; President, Comunn Gaidhealach an Obain, since 1982; Vice Chairman, Gaelic Language Promotion Trust. Recreations: hill walking; amateur drama; association football. Address: (h.) Gowanbrae, Ardconnel Road, Oban, Argyll; T.-0631 62850.

Bannister, John Roy, Clerk to the Scottish Traffic Commissioner, since 1987; b. 3.11.46, London; m., Jan; 1 s.; 1 d. Educ. Edmonton County Grammar School. Department of Transport: London, 1965-72, 1984-87, Newcastle upon Tyne, 1972-83; Manager, International Road Freight Office, Newcastle upon Tyne, 1983-84. Recreations: home brewing/wine; foreign travel; railways. Address: (h.) 13 Warrender Court, North Berwick, East Lothian; T.-0620 4683.

Barbenel, Professor Joseph Cyril, BDS, BSc, MSc, PhD, LDS RCS(Eng), CBiol, FIBiol, CPhys, FInstP, FRSE. Professor, Bioengineering Unit, Strathclyde University, since 1982 (Head, Tissue Mechanics Division, since 1970); b. 2.1.37, London; m., Lesley Mary Hyde Jowett; 2 s.; 1 d. Educ. Hackney Downs Grammar School, London; London Hospital Medical College; Queen's College, Dundee (St. Andrews University); Strathclyde University. Dental House Surgeon, London Hospital, 1960; National Service, RADC, 1960-61 (Lieutenant, 1960, Captain, 1961); general dental practice, London, 1963; student, 1963-67; Lecturer, Department of Dental Prosthetics, Dental School, Dundee, 1967-69; Senior Lecturer, Strathclyde University, 1970-82. Member of Committee, and Secretary for Standardisation, International Society for Bioengineering and the Skin; Member, Steering Committee, Forum on Clinical Haemorheology; Member, Administrative Council, International Federation of Medical and Biological Engineering, and Chairman, European Working Group. Recreations: music; theatre. Address: (b.) University of Strathclyde, Bioengineering Unit, 106 Rottenrow, Glasgow, G4 ONW; T.-041-552 4400.

Barber, Professor James Hill, MB, ChB, MD, FRCGP, FRCPSG, DRCOG. None Miller Professor of General Practice, Glasgow University, since 1974; Principal, Greater Glasgow Health Board, since 1972; Honorary Consultant, Medicine, Royal and Western Infirmaries, Glasgow, since 1972; b. 28.5.33, Dunfermline; m., Patricia M. Burton (deceased); 1 s.; 3 d. Educ. Edinburgh Academy; University of Edinburgh. Medical Branch, RAF, 1958-63; General Practitioner: Callander, 1964-66, Livingston, 1966-72; Senior Lecturer, General Practice, Glasgow University, 1972-74. Publications: General Practice Medicine, 1975 and 1985; Towards Team Care, 1980. Recreations: sailing; model fishing-boat construction; photography. Address: (b.) Woodside Health Centre, Barr Street, Glasgow; T.-041-332 9977.

Barber, Rev. Peter Horne, MA, BD. General Secretary, Baptist Union of Scotland, since 1980; b. 25.8.30, Edinburgh; m., Isobel; 1 s.; 2 d. Educ. Boroughmuir Secondary School, Edinburgh; Edinburgh University and New College. Minister: East Kilbride Baptist Church, 1955-73; Upton Vale Baptist Church, Torquay, 1973-80. Centenary President, Baptist Union of Scotland, 1969-70. Recreations: golf; swimming; music. Address: (b.) 14 Aytoun Road, Glasgow, G41 5RT; T.-041-423 6169.

Barbour, Very Rev. Robert Alexander Stewart, KCVO, MC, MA, BD, STM, DD, DipEd. Minister, Church of Scotland, since 1954; Dean, Chapel Royal in Scotland, 1981-91; Prelate, Priory of Scotland, Order of St. John, since 1977; b. 11.5.21, Edinburgh; m., Margaret Pigot; 3 s.; 1 d. Educ. Rugby School; Balliol College, Oxford; St. Mary's College, St. Andrews. Army (Scottish Horse), 1940-45; Territorial Army, 1947-54; Editorial Assistant, Thomas Nelson & Sons, 1948-49; Secretary, Edinburgh Christian Council for Overseas Students, 1953-55; Lecturer and Senior Lecturer in New Testament Language, Literature and Theology, New College, Edinburgh University, 1955-71; Professor of New Testament Exegesis, Aberdeen University, 1971-86; Master, Christ's College, Aberdeen, 1977-82; Moderator, General Assembly of the Church of Scotland, 1979-80; Chaplain to the Queen in Scotland, 1976-91, Extra Chaplain, since 1991; Honorary Secretary, Novi Testamenti Societas, 1970-77. Recreations: music; forestry; walking. Address: (h.) Fincastle, Pitlochry, PH16 5RJ; T.-0796 473209.

Barclay, Kenneth Forsyth, BL, NP. Secretary, Scottish Law Commission; b. 1.2.38, Glasgow; m., Jean Broom Curwen; 1 s.; 1 d. Educ. Woodside Senior Secondary School, Glasgow; Glasgow University. Solicitor in private practice, 1960-71; Principal Solicitor, Cumbernauld Development Corporation, 1971-73; joined Office of Solicitor to Secretary of State for Scotland, 1973; Legal Secretary, Royal Commission on Legal Services in Scotland, 1976-80, then Divisional Solicitor, Scottish Office. Recreations: golf; walking; tennis; badminton; reading. Address: (b.) 140 Causewayside, Edinburgh, EH19 1PR; T.-031-668 2131.

Barge, Lt. Commander Ronald Mansfield, DSC, VRD, DL. Chairman, Otter Ferry Salmon Ltd., since 1977; Chairman, Onshore Aquaculture Ltd., since 1981; Past Chairman, Bitmac Ltd.; b. 10.11.20, Rawal Pindi; m., Elizabeth Ann Lamberton; 3 s.; 3 d. Educ. Cargilfield; Glenalmond; Glasgow School of Art; Durham University; Royal College of Art, London. RNVR, 1937; Navy, 1939-46; Lt. Commander, Clyde Division, RNVR; Director, William Robertson Shipowners Ltd., Glasgow; farming, Argyll, from 1971; pioneer of salmon farming in Scotland; Director, Scottish Society for Prevention of Cruelty to Animals; Past Chairman, Glasgow and West of Scotland SPCA. Recreations: gardening; sailing; art. Address: (h.) Whistlers' Hill, Rhu, Dunbartonshire; T.-0436 820 285.

Barker, Professor John Reginald, BSc, MSc, PhD, FRSE. Titular Professor, Department of Electronics and Electrical Engineering, Glasgow University, since 1985; b. 11.11.42, Stockport; m., Elizabeth Carol; 2 s.; 1 d. Educ. New Mills Grammar School; Edinburgh University; Durham University; Warwick University. Warwick University: SERC Personal Research Fellowship, 1969-70, Lecturer (Physics), 1970-84, Senior Lecturer, 1985-85; Affiliate Professor, Colorado State University, 1979-83. Member, SERC/DTI Devices Committee, since 1988; Chairman, SERC Molecular Electronics Committee, since 1990; Member, SERC Electronic Materials Committee, and Materials Commission, since 1991. Publications: Physics of Non-Linear Transport in Semiconductors (Co-author), 1979; Granular Nanoelectronics, 1991; over 140 scientific papers. Recreations: hill-walking; reading; cooking. Address: (b.) Nanoelectronics Research Centre, Department of Electronics and Electrical Engineering, Glasgow University, Glasgow, G12 8QQ; T.-041-339 8855.

Barker, Pamela Margaret Wentworth, BSc, MB, ChB, DPM, MRCPsych. Consultant Psychiatrist, Highland Health Board, since 1978; Clinical Senior Lecturer in Mental Health, Aberdeen University, since 1981; b. 5.11.29, London. Educ. Ipswich High School; Leeds University. House Physician and House Surgeon, General Infirmary, Leeds; Senior House Officer, Pinderfields General Hospital, Wakefield; Registrar, Stanley Royd Hospial, Wakefield; Assistant Psychiatrist, Yorkshire Regional Health Authority. Recreation: motor vehicle maintenance. Address: (h.) Burnside, Leachkin Road, Inverness, IV3 6NW; T.-0463 234101.

Barker, Thomas Christopher, MA, FSA Scot. Secretary to Trustees, Scottish National War Memorial, Edinburgh Castle, since 1987; b. 28.6.28, Brighton; m., Griselda Helen Cormack; 2 s.; 1 d. Educ. Uppingham; New College, Oxford. 2nd Lt., 1st Bn., The Worcestershire Regiment, 1946-48; HM Diplomatic Service: 3rd Secretary, Paris, 1953-55; 2nd Secretary, Baghdad, 1955-58; Foreign Office, 1958-62; 1st Secretary, Head of Chancery and Consul, Mexico City, 1962-67; Counsellor and Head of Chancery, Caracas, 1969-71; Foreign and Commonwealth Office, 1971-75; Under Secretary, Northern Ireland Office, Belfast, 1976. Curator, Scottish National War Memorial, 1978-87; Treasurer, St. Ninian's Cathedral, Perth, 1983-86. Address: (h.) Carmurie, South Street, Elie, KY9 1DN.

Barlow, Professor (Arthur) John, PhD, DIC, BSc, ACGI, MIEE, CEng. Titular Professor, Electronics and Electrical Engineering Department, Glasgow University; b. 17.3.34, Nottinghamshire; m., Alma Marshall; 1 s.; 1 d. Educ. Nottingham High School; Imperial College. Turner and

Newall Research Fellow, Imperial College, 1958-61; Glasgow University: Lecturer, 1961-66, Senior Lecturer, 1966-68, Reader, 1968-75. Address: (h.) 5 Auchencruive, Milngavie, Glasgow, G62 6EE.

Barnes, Robin Adam Boyd, MA (Hons), MEd. Director of Education, Shetland Islands Council, since 1975; b. 3.4.27, Glasgow; m., Cecilia; 3 d. Educ. Glasgow Academy; Glasgow University. Royal Navy, 1945-48; Teacher of English, Larkhall Academy, Lanarkshire, 1953-54; Special Assistant Teacher of English, Kelvinside Academy, Glasgow, 1954-64; Assistant Director of Education, Edinburgh, 1964-72; Director of Education, Zetland County Council, 1972-75. Education Officer, RNR Glasgow, 1958-64; Member, East of Scotland Schools/Industry Liaison Working Party with SED, 1966-68; Secretary, Edinburgh Primary Schools Working Party, 1968-72. Recreations: performing music (piano); walking; gardening. Address: (b.) Education Office, 1 Harbour Street, Lerwick, Shetland, ZE1 0LS; T.-0595 3535, Ext. 254.

Barnet, James Paul, MA, LLB. Partner, Macbeth Currie & Co., Solicitors, since 1965; Honorary Sheriff, Tayside Central and Fife, at Dunfermline; Dean, Dunfermline District Society of Solicitors; b. 20.7.37, Darlington; m., Margaret Smart; 4 s. Educ. Dunfermline High School; Edinburgh University. Admitted as Solicitor, 1961. Council Member, Law Society of Scotland, 1985-88; Local Secretary, Scottish Garden City Housing Society Ltd.; Captain, Scottish Universities Golfing Society, 1980-81; President, Dunfermline Rotary Club, 1985-86. Recreations: golf; reading; quoting Dr. Johnson. Address: (h.) Bonnyton House, Dunfermline, Fife, KY12 9HT; T.-Dunfermline 731011.

Barnett, Robert Hall, FIMI. Managing Director, Barnetts Motor Group Ltd, since 1965; b. 22.1.36, Dundee; m., Alison; 1 s.; 1 d. Educ. Morgan Academy. Dundee and Tayside Chamber of Commerce: Deputy President, 1991-92, President, since 1992. Recreations: golf; sailing; motorcycling. Address: (b.) Riverside Drive, Dundee; T.-0382 68622.

Barnett, Robert James Charles, LLB (Hons). Director of Administration and Legal Services and Depute Chief Executive, Western Isles Islands Council, since 1986; Returning Officer, Western Isles Islands Area, since 1986; b. 10.5.53, Birmingham; m., Christine Mary; 1 s.; 1 d. Educ. Homelands Technical High School, Torquay; Bristol Polytechnic; Guildford College of Law. Served articles with Torbay Borough Council, 1975-77; qualified as Solicitor, 1978; Assistant Solicitor, then Senior Assistant, then Principal Assistant Solicitor, Plymouth City Council, 1978-86. Recreations: music; reading; walking; family. Address: (b.) Western Isles Islands Council, Council Offices, Sandwick Road, Stornoway, Isle of Lewis, PA87 2BW; T.-0851 703773, Ext. 200.

Barr, Rev. Alexander Craib, MA, BD. Minister, St. Nicholas' Cardonald Parish Church, Glasgow, since 1947; Moderator, Presbytery of Glasgow, 1987-88; b. 10.2.27, Glasgow; m., Agnes Morrison Robertson; 3 d. Educ. Daniel Stewart's College, Edinburgh; Edinburgh University. Ordained Probationer Assistant, Bathgate High Church, 1950-52; Minister: Hawick Burnfoot Parish Church, 1952-58, Methil Parish Church, 1958-67. Moderator, Presbytery of Kirkcaldy, 1964-65. Recreations: gardening; photography. Address: (h.) 25 Fisher Drive, Phoenix Park, Paisley, PA1 2TP.

Barr, Professor Allan David Stephen, BSc, PhD, CEng, FIMechE, FRSE. Jackson Professor of Engineering, Aberdeen University, since 1985; Dean, Faculty of Engineering and Mathematical and Physical Sciences; b. 11.9.30, Glasgow; m., Eileen Patricia Redmond. Educ. Daniel

Stewart's College, Edinburgh; Edinburgh University. Student apprentice, Bristol Aeroplane Company; Lecturer, Department of Engineering, Edinburgh University; Fulbright Scholar, Visiting Associate Professor, Department of Theoretical and Applied Mechanics, Cornell University, USA; Senior Lecturer, then Reader, Department of Mechanical Engineering, Edinburgh University; Professor and Head, Department of Mechanical Engineering, Dundee University. Recreations: fly fishing; oil painting. Address: (b.) Department of Engineering, Kings College, University of Aberdeen, AB9 2UE.

Barr, David, DPE. Director of Physical Education, Dundee University, since 1968; b. 7.3.34, Motherwell; m.; 1 s.; 1 d.; 1 step d. Educ. Dalziel High School, Motherwell; Scottish School of Physical Education, Jordanhill College of Education, Glasgow. Physical Fitness Officer, RAF, 1957-60; Games Master, Glyn Grammar School, Ewell, Surrey, 1960-63; Assistant Director of Physical Education, Aberdeen University, 1963-66; Director of Physical Recreation, Bradford University, 1966-68. Played water polo for Scotland, 1955-61, for Great Britain, 1958-61; national water polo coach, Great Britain, 1961-65; director of water polo, Scotland, 1972-75; team manager/coach, water polo, GB at World Student Games, Budapest, 1965, Turin, 1970, Moscow, 1973. Publications: A Guide to Water Polo, 1964; Play Better Water Polo, 1970; Water Polo, 1980. Recreations: golf; gardening. Address: (b.) Department of Physical Education, The University, Dundee, DD1 4HN; T.-Dundee 23181, Ext. 4117.

Barr, Rev. David, MA, BD. Hospital Chaplain, Glasgow Royal Infirmary and Canniesburn Hospital, 1962-84; b. 14.6.14, Airdrie. Educ. Airdrie Academy; Glasgow University and Trinity College. Student Assistant, New Monkland Parish Church, 1935-37; Minister, Kirkintilloch South Church, 1938-42; part-time Hospital Chaplain, Broomhill and Lanfine Hospitals; Minister, St. Mary's, Partick, 1942-62; part-time Hospital Chaplain, Glasgow Western Infirmary, 1960-62. Moderator, Glasgow Presbytery, 1969-70; Chairman, National Association of Whole-Time Hospital Chaplains for England, Scotland and Wales, 1978-82. Recreations: motoring; reading; topography; ecclesiology; medicine. Address: (h.) 17 Victoria Park Gardens South, Broomhill, Glasgow, G11 7BX; T.-041-339 5364.

Barr, David George Dryburgh, MB, ChB, FRCPEd, DCH. Consultant Paediatrician, Lothian Health Board, since 1971; part-time Senior Lecturer, Department of Child Life and Health, Edinburgh University, since 1977; b. 14.2.36, Edinburgh; m., Anna Blair; 2 s.; 1 d. Educ. Daniel Stewart's College, Edinburgh; Edinburgh University. Senior Registrar, Royal Hospital for Sick Children, Edinburgh, 1965-69; Research Fellow, Children's hospital, Zurich, Switzerland, 1969-70; Consultant Paediatrician, Edinburgh Northern and West Fife Hospitals, 1971-77; Consultant Paediatrician, Royal Hospital for Sick Children and Simpson Memorial Maternity Pavilion, since 1977; seconded to Ministry of Health and University of Riyadh, Saudi Arabia, 1980-83. Address: (b.) Royal Hospital for Sick Children, Sciennes Road, Edinburgh; T.-031-667 1991.

Barr, Rev. George Russell, BA, BD. Minister, St. Luke's Parish Church, Greenock, since 1988; Vice-President, Scottish Churches Theology Society, since 1990; b. 15.10.53, Kilmarnock; m., Margaret Wyllie; 1 s.; 1 d. Educ. Kilmarnock Academy; Langside College; Edinburgh University. Assistant Minister, Jedburgh Old linked with Ancrum linked with Edgerston, 1978-79; Minister, Garthamlock and Craigend East, Glasgow, 1979-88. Recreations: sport; Scotch Malt Whisky Society. Address: (h.) 50 Ardgowan Street, Greenock, PA16 8EP; T.-0475 21048.

Barr, Ian. Chairman, Post Office Scotland (formerly Chairman, Scottish Postal Board), 1984-88; Board Member, Girobank Scotland, 1984-88; Chairman, Association for Business Sponsorship of the Arts, Scotland, 1986-88; b. 6.4.27, Edinburgh; m., 1, Gertrud Karla Odefey; 2 d; 2, Margaret Annie McAlpine Barr. Educ. Boroughmuir High School. Post Office: Assistant Postal Controller (North Western Region, England), 1955; Inspector of Postal Services, 1957; Assistant Controller (Planning), 1962 (both in Post Office HQ, London); Staff College, Henley on Thames, 1965-66; Principal, 1966, and Member, Civil Service Selection Board, 1966-71; Assistant Secretary, 1971; Regional Director (Eastern Postal Region, England), 1976; Post Office Headquarters Director of Buildings, Mechanisation and Transport, 1978; Director, Post Office Estates Executive, 1981-84; Chairman, Post Office National Arts Committee, 1976-87; Chairman, Saltire Society, 1986-87; Director, Scottish National Orchestra, since 1988; President, Conference Europeenne des Postes et des Telecommunications (Batiments), 1982-86; Member, British Materials Handling Board, 1978-81; Member, Scottish Council, CBI, 1984-88; Fellow, Institute of Directors, 1984; Director, St Mary's Music School, since 1986, and Chairman, Management Committee, 1988-90; Trustee, Endocrine Research Trust, since 1987; Director, Friedman Camerata of St Andrew, 1988-89; Trustee, Lamp of Lothian Collegiate Trust, Haddington, since 1988; Member, Edinburgh Festival Council, 1988-89; Member, Scottish Constitutional Steering Committee, 1988. Recreations: composing serial music; constructing a metaphysical system. Address: Scott House, Newcastleton, Roxburghshire, TD9 0QU.

Barr, James, ACMA, MBIM, MIPM. Chief Executive, Inverclyde Enterprise Trust, since 1991; b. 21.5.34, Greenock; m., Mary Halliday Barr; 1 s.; 2 d. Educ. Greenock High School. Clerical Officer, Civil Service, 1951-53; National Service, RAF, 1953-55; clerical, Thos. Black and Sons (camp outfitters), 1955-57; Cost Accountant, John Walker and Sons (sugar refiners), 1957-70; various management to senior management posts, IBM (UK) Ltd, Greenock, 1970-91. President, Renfrewshire Section, Scottish Football Referees Association. Recreations: football refereeing; road running. Address: 64/66 West Blackhall Street, Greenock, PA15 1XG.

Barr, Rev. John Gourlay Crichton. Deputy Secretary, Law Society of Scotland, 1978-88; non-stipendiary Priest, Scottish Episcopal Church, since 1985; b. 10.5.23, Berwick-upon-Tweed; m., Mary Wanklyn Branford; 2 s. Educ. Struan School, Berwick; George Watson's College, Edinburgh; Edinburgh University. Royal Navy, 1942-46; mentioned in Despatches, Normandy, 1944; admitted Solicitor, 1947; Partner: Robertson Dempster & Co., Perth, 1956-74, Condie, Mackenzie & Co., Perth, 1974-78. Former Member of Board, Royal Lyceum Theatre and Perth Repertory Theatre (Chairman, 1972-78); Scottish Episcopal Church: Lay Reader, Diocese of St Andrews, 1958-78, Diocesan Registrar, 1974-78; involved in team ministry, St. Mark's Episcopal Church, Portobello, since 1981; Past Chairman: Laity Committee, Scottish Churches Council; Perth Council of Churches; Council Member, Law Society of Scotland, 1968-77; Member, EAST (Ecumenical AIDS Support Team), since 1987 (Secretary, since 1988); Unionist candidate, West Stirlingshire, 1964; Lieutenant, RNVR, 1946. Recreations: theatre; bird-watching; creative writing. Address: (h.) 3 Hamilton Terrace, Edinburgh, EH15 1NB; T.-031-669 3300.

Barr, Sheriff Kenneth Glen, MA, LLB. Sheriff, South Strathclyde, Dumfries and Galloway, at Dumfries, since 1976; b. 20.1.41.

Barr, William James, OBE, CEng, MICE, FIIM. Chairman and Managing Director, Barr Limited (which includes W. and J. Barr and Sons (Scotland) Limited, Ayrshire Crane, Barmix Concrete, Barr Construction, Solway Engineers, Solway Precast, Solway Crane), since 1969; b. 12.3.39, Ayr; m., Marlean Ramage; 2 s.; 1 d. Educ. Girvan High School; Glasgow University; Paisley College. Chairman, Freeport (Scotland) Ltd; Chairman, Thomas Telford Services Ltd; Director: Thomas Telford Ltd, Construction T.A. Services (Swindon) Ltd, C.T.A. Projects Limited; Member, Council and Executive, Institution of Civil Engineers; Former Chairman, Glasgow and West of Scotland Association, Institution of Civil Engineers; Visiting Professor, Strathclyde University; Chairman, Craigie College of Education; Vice-Chairman, Ayr College Board; Member, Board of Governors, Paisley College; Chairman, Ayr Locality Enterprise and Resource Trust; Member, Governing Council, ScotBIC; Chairman, Ayrshire Pick Up Training Project; Vice Chairman and Fund Raising Director, Ayrshire Hospice; Vice Chairman, Enterprise Ayrshire; Board Member and Past President, Ayr Chamber of Commerce; Board Member, Ayrshire Chamber of Industry and Commerce. Recreations: the works of Robert Burns and Thomas Telford; walking; reading. Address: (h.) Harkieston, Maybole, Ayrshire KA19 7LP; T.-0655 83123; (b.) Heathfield, Ayr, KA8 9SL; T.-0292 281311.

Barratt, Michael, MA (Hons). Headmaster, Rannoch School, since 1982; b. 31.12.40, Edinburgh; m., Valerie Anne Dixon; 1 s.; 1 d. Educ. George Watson's College, Edinburgh; Merchiston Castle School; St. Andrews University; St. Edmund Hall, Oxford. Assistant Master, Epsom College, Surrey, 1964-73; Housemaster, Strathallan School, Perth, 1973-82. Recreations: golf; gardening; mountaineering; theatre. Address: Headmaster's House, Rannoch School, Rannoch, Perth, PH17 2QQ; T.-088 22 332.

Barratt, Oliver William. Secretary, Cockburn Association (Edinburgh Civic Trust), since 1971; Secretary, Cockburn Conservation Trust, since 1978; b. 7.7.41, Belfast. Educ. Radley College; East of Scotland College of Agriculture. Vice Chairman, Scottish Association for Public Transport; Trustee, Scottish Historic Buildings Trust and Lothian Building Preservation Trust. Recreations: the hills; travel; most of the arts. Address: (h.) 1 London Street, Edinburgh, EH3 6LZ; T.-031-556 5107.

Barratt, Robin, DLC, BEd (Hons). Director, National Sports Training Centre; b. 8.2.33, Scarborough; m., Ann; 2 s. Educ. Scarborough Boys High School; Lancaster University; Loughborough University. Recreations: sailing; squash. Address: (b.) Inverclyde National Sports Training Centre, Largs; T.-0475 674666.

Barrett, Professor Ann, MB, BS, FRCR, FRCP, MD. Professor of Radiation Oncology, Glasgow University, since 1986; Consultant, Royal Hospital for Sick Children, since 1986; b. 27.2.43, London; m., Adrian Bell; 1 s.; 2 d. Educ. Queen Elizabeth's Grammar School; St. Bartholomew's Hospital. Formerly Consultant in Radiotherapy and Oncology, Royal Marsden Hospital; Director, Beatson Oncology Centre, Glasgow, 1986-91; Member, COMARE; Member, Council, Royal College of Radiologists. Publications: Cancer in Childhood (Co-editor); Practical Radiotherapy Planning (Co-author). Recreations: walking; music; 19th-century novels. Address: (b.) Beatson Oncology Centre, Western Infirmary, Glasgow; T.-041-339 8822.

Barrie, Alistair T., BSc (Hons), DipTP, MRTPI. Chief Planning Officer, City of Dundee District Council, since 1974; b. 19.2.38, Dundee; m., Elizabeth; 2 s.; 1 d. Educ. Harris Academy, Dundee; St. Andrews University; Heriot-Watt University. Past Chairman and former Hon. Secretary and Treasurer, Scottish Society of Directors of Planning. Recreation: athletics. Address: (b.) City of Dundee District

Council, 21 City Square, Dundee, DD1 3BS; T.-0382 23141, Ext. 4400.

Barrie, Lesley, DPA, MHSM, DipHSM, MBIM. General Manager, Forth Valley Health Board, since 1991; b. 20.9.44, Glasgow. Educ. Glasgow High School for Girls; Glasgow University. NHS administrative trainee, 1963-66; hospital management, 1966-77; District General Manager: Inverclyde District, 1977-81, Glasgow South East, 1981-83; Director Administrative Services, Glasgow Royal Infirmary, Glasgow Royal Maternity Hospital, Glasgow Dental Hospital, 1983-87; Unit General Manager, Stirling Royal Infirmary, 1987-91. Member, Forth Valley Health Board, since 1991; Children's Panellist, 1975-79; Chairman, Social Security Appeal Tribunals, 1978-90; Table Tennis Internationalist for Scotland, 1963-70; formerly National and International Secretary, Scottish Table Tennis Association. Recreations: table tennis; badminton; reading. Address: (b.) Forth Valley Health Board, 33 Spittal Street, Stirling; T.-0786 51454.

Barron, James Walter. Keeper of the Registers of Scotland, since 1990; b. 22.8.34, Edinburgh; m., Elizabeth Coutts; 2 d. Educ. Broughton Secondary School. Entered Civil Service, 1951, as Clerical Officer, Admiralty (Rosyth); transferred Department of Registers as Assistant Examiner, 1956; Examiner, 1965; Senior Examiner, 1973; seconded Lands Tribunal for Scotland as Clerk, 1970-73; transferred Scottish Office, 1976, as Principal, SDD; transferred Superannuation Division, 1980; promoted Assistant Secretary, 1985. Assistant Secretary, Edinburgh University Open Studies Association; Session Clerk, Portobello St. James Parish Church; Secretary, Portobello Recorded Music Society. Recreations: music; reading; rugby; informal further education. Address: (b.) Meadowbank House, London Road, Edinburgh; T.-031-659 6111.

Barron, Professor Laurence David, DPhil, BSc, MInstP. Professor of Chemistry, Glasgow University, since 1984; b. 12.2.44, Southampton; m., Sharon Aviva Wolf; 1 s.; 1 d. Educ. King Edward VI Grammar School, Southampton; Northern Polytechnic, London; Lincoln College, Oxford. Post-doctoral research, Cambridge University, 1969-75; Ramsay Memorial Fellow, 1974-75; Glasgow University: Lecturer in Chemistry, 1975-80, Reader, 1980-84. Corday-Morgan Medal, Chemical Society, 1977; G.M.J. Schmidt Memorial Lecturer, Weizmann Institute of Science, 1984; F.L. Conover Memorial Lecturer, Vanderbilt University, 1987. Publication: Molecular Light Scattering and Optical Activity, 1982. Recreations: walking; music; radio-controlled model aircraft. Address: (b.) Chemistry Department, The University, Glasgow, G12 8QQ; T.-041-339 8855.

Barrow, Professor Geoffrey Wallis Steuart, MA (Hons), BLitt, DLitt, FBA, FRSE, FSA, FSA Scot, FRHistS, Hon. DLitt (Glasgow). Sir William Fraser Professor of Scottish History and Palaeography, Edinburgh University, since 1979; b. 28.11.24, Headingley, Leeds; m., Heather Elizabeth Agnes Lownie; 1 s.; 1 d. Educ. St. Edward's School, Oxford; Inverness Royal Academy; St. Andrews University; Pembroke College, Oxford. Royal Navy and RNVR (Sub-Lieutenant), 1943-46; Lecturer in History, University College, London, 1950-61; Professor of Medieval History, Newcastle-upon-Tyne University, 1961-74; Professor of Scottish History, St. Andrews University, 1974-79. Member, Royal Commission on Historical Manuscripts, 1984-90; Royal Historical Society: Council Member, 1963-74, Joint Literary Director, 1964-74, Vice President, 1982-86; Past Chairman of Council, Scottish History Society (President, 1973-77); President, Saltire Society, 1987-90. Publications: Feudal Britain, 1956; Acts of Malcolm IV, 1960; Robert Bruce, 1965 and 1988; Acts of William I, 1971; The Kingdom of the Scots, 1973; The Scottish Tradition (Editor), 1974; The Anglo-Norman Era in Scottish History, 1980; Kingship and Unity:

Scotland 1000-1306, 1981. Recreations: hill-walking; visiting graveyards; travel. Address: (h.) 12A Lauder Road, Edinburgh, EH9 2EL; T.-031-668 2173.

Barry, Rt. Rev. Mgr. John Charles McDonald, MA (Cantab), DCL. Parish Priest, Church of Our Lady, Star of the Sea, North Berwick, since 1989; b. 26.9.17, Edinburgh. Educ. Abbey School, Fort Augustus; Trinity College, Cambridge; University of Fribourg, Switzerland; Oscott College, Birmingham; Gregorian University, Rome. Ordained priest, 1944; appointed Curate, St. Patrick's, Kilsyth; sent to Rome to study canon law, 1946; appointed to St. Cuthbert's, Edinburgh, 1949; transferred to St. Anthony's, Polmont, 1950; St. Andrew's College, Drygrange: Lecturer, 1953, Rector, 1960; St. Mark's, Edinburgh, 1977-89; Editor, Canon Law Abstracts, Canon Law Society of Great Britain, 1959-84; Consultor to the Pontifical Commission for the Revision of Canon Law, 1966-78. Recreations: golf; walking. Address: 9 Law Road, North Berwick, EH39 4PN; T.-0620 2195.

Bartholomew, John Christopher, MA, FRSE, FRGS. President, Royal Scottish Geographical Society, since 1987; b. 15.1.23, Edinburgh; m., Genevieve Achard-James; 5 s. Educ. Edinburgh Academy; Gordonstoun; Edinburgh University. Military Service, Royal Engineers (Survey), Middle East and East Africa, 1943-47; rejoined family firm on graduation, 1950, to share editorial responsibility for The Times Atlas of the World, Mid-century Edition and all subsequent editions, 1967-82, and other atlases; Editorial Director, John Bartholomew & Son Ltd., 1960-84. President, British Cartographic Society, 1970-71; Vice-President, International Cartographic Association, 1972-80; President, Edinburgh University Graduates' Association, 1980-82; Director, Scottish Rights of Way Society, since 1984. Recreations: hill-walking; photography; weather observation. Address: (h.) 26 Braid Farm Road, Edinburgh, EH10 6LF; T.-031-447 2655.

Bartlett, Professor Christopher John, BA, PhD, FRHistS, FRSE. Professor of International History, Dundee University, since 1978 (Head of Modern History Department, 1983-88); Member, Scottish Examination Board; b. 12.10.31, Bournemouth; m., Shirley Maureen Briggs; 3 s. Educ. Queen Elizabeth's Grammar School, Wimborne; University College, Exeter; London School of Economics. Assistant Lecturer, Edinburgh University, 1957-59; Lecturer, University of the West Indies, Jamaica, 1959-62; Lecturer, Queen's College, Dundee, 1962-68; Reader, Dundee University, 1968-78. Publications: Great Britain and Sea Power 1815-53; Castlereagh; The Long Retreat; The Rise and Fall of the Pax Americana; A History of Postwar Britain 1945-74; The Global Conflict 1880-1970; British Foreign Policy in the Twentieth Century; The Annual Register 1987 (United Kingdom and Scotland chapters). Address: (b.) Department of History, The University, Dundee.

Barty, James Webster, OBE (1981), MA, LLB. Retired Solicitor; Honorary President, Scottish Law Agents Society, since 1984; b. 9.3.12, Dunblane; m., Elisabeth Beryl Roebuck; 1 s.; 2 d. Educ. Hurst Grange School, Stirling; Fettes College, Edinburgh; St. Andrews University; Edinburgh University. Qualified as Solicitor, 1935; Partner, Tho. & J.W. Barty, Dunblane, 1937-84; Scottish Law Agents Society: Secretary, 1940-82, President, 1982-84; Honorary Sheriff, since 1970. Clerk, Dunblane Cathedral Kirk Session, 1949-69; Council Member, Friends of Dunblane Cathedral, 1940-84 (Vice-Chairman, 1974-84). Recreations: life-long interest in sport (rugby, tennis, cricket, badminton) and in all arts, including theatre, opera, ballet, literature and painting. Address: (h.) Easterton, Argaty, Doune, Perthshire; T.-0786 841 372.

Basson, John Vincent, MB, ChB, BSc (Hons), MPhil, FRCPsych. Principal Medical Officer, Scottish Home and Health Department; b. 23.11.45, Manchester. Educ. De La Salle College, Salford; Edinburgh University. Fellowship in Community Psychiatry, 1976-78; Consultant Psychiatrist, Royal Edinburgh Hospital and HM Prison, Saughton, 1978-88. Member, Secretary of State's Committee on Difficult Prisoners, 1979-82; Past Chairman, Edinburgh Cyrenian Trust; Member, McClelland Committee on AIDS and Drug Abuse. Recreations: gardening; keep fit; golf; travel. Address: (b.) St. Andrew's House, Edinburgh; T.-031-244 2805.

Bastable, Arthur Cyprian, OBE, BSc, CEng, FIEE, FBIM. General Manager, Ferranti plc, Dundee, 1958-86; Director, Ferranti Astron Ltd., 1983-86; Director, Ferranti Industrial Electronics Ltd., 1984-86; Deputy Chairman, Dundee Port Authority, since 1981 (Member, since 1967, Convener, Corporate Planning Committee, since 1975); b. 9.5.23, Kobe, Japan; m., Joan Cardwell; 1 s.; 1 d. Educ. St Georges School, Harpenden; Manchester University. Joined Ferranti, 1950; President, Dundee & Tayside Chamber of Commerce, 1970-71 (Convener, Overseas Trade and Development, 1973-91); Member, Tayside Development Authority, 1972-75; Vice-Chairman, Board of Governors, Dundee College of Technology, 1975-77; Member, Scottish Council, CBI, 1980; Member, Dundee Project Steering Committee, 1983-91; Director: Edinburgh Instruments Ltd., 1983-85; Taytec Ltd., 1985-88; Dundee Unitech Ltd., since 1985; Dundee and Tayside ITEC Ltd., 1985-88; Chairman, Tayside 1992 Committee, since 1988. Recreations: sailing; skiing; ornithology. Address: (h.) Hunters Moon, 14 Lorne Street, Monifieth, Dundee, DD5 4DU.

Baster, Jeremy, BA, MPhil. Director of Economic Development, Orkney Islands Council, since 1985; b. 5.2.47, New York; m., Miriam Landor; 2 s.; 1 d. Educ. Leighton Park School, Reading; St. John's College, Oxford; University College, London. Early career in consultancy; Economist, Scottish Council (Development and Industry), 1975-80; Economist, Orkney Islands Council, 1980-85. Fellow, The Smallpeice Trust; Director, Soulisquoy Printmakers Ltd.; Director, Orkney Enterprise. Address: (b.) Council Offices, School Place, Kirkwall, KW15 1NY; T.-0856 3535.

Bates, Peter James, CertSocAdmin, DipSocWk. Director of Social Work, Tayside Regional Council, since 1987; b. 6.5.45, Birmingham; m., Ann Gordon; 1 s.; 3 d. Educ. Birmingham University. Left school at 15 and completed five year apprenticeship; became active in youth work and community action in Handsworth; attended Birmingham University from the age of 23; moved to Scotland, 1969, as a social worker in Greenock; senior social worker, Edinburgh, later Director of a Community Development Project in the Grassmarket; a Social Work Manager with Lothian Regional Council; Principal Child Care Officer, later Deputy Director of Social Work, Strathclyde Regional Council. Recreations: running; climbing; photography. Address: (b.) Social Work Department, Tayside House, 28 Crichton Street, Dundee, DD1 3RN; T.-Dundee 23281.

Batey, Thomas, BSc, PhD, FIBiol, CIAgrE, MISoilSci. Senior Lecturer in Soil Science, Aberdeen University, since 1974; Director, Soil and Land Use Consultants Ltd, since 1988; b. 20.3.33, West Woodburn; m., Elizabeth L.; 2 s. Educ. Gosforth County Grammar; Durham University. Advisory Soil Scientist, MAFF: Cambridge, 1959-64, Reading, 1964-71; Lecturer, Aberdeen University, 1971-74. British Society of Soil Science: Honorary Treasurer, 1979-90, Vice-President, 1991-92; Member, Royal Society Study Group on the Nitrogen Cycle in the UK, 1979-83; Convenor, Working Group F, International Soil Tillage Research Organisation, since 1990; Member, Editorial Advisory Board, Soil Technology, since 1990; Visiting Lecturer, Lincoln College,

Canterbury University, New Zealand, 1980; Visiting Research Fellow, New England University, Australia, 1990. Publication: Soil Husbandry – a Practical Guide to the Use and Management of Soils, 1988. Recreations: music; hill walking; skiing; bridge. Address: (b.) Department of Plant and Soil Science, Aberdeen University, Aberdeen, AB9 2UE; T.-0224 272262.

Baxby, Keith, BSc, MB, BS, FRCS. Consultant Urological Surgeon, Tayside Health Board, since 1977; Honorary Senior Lecturer, Dundee University, since 1977; Clinical Director, Special Surgical Services, Dundee Royal Infirmary, since 1991; b. 17.4.44, Sheffield. Educ. King Edward VII School, Sheffield; Durham University. House Officer, Royal Victoria Infirmary, Newcastle-upon-Tyne, 1968-69; Surgical Registrar, Newcastle University Hospitals, 1969-73; Northern Counties Kidney Fund Research Fellow, 1973-74; Senior Urological Registrar, Newcastle General Hospital, 1974-77; Visiting Professor of Urology, Louisiana State University, 1981; WHO Fellow in Clinical Urodynamics, 1984. Recreation: deer stalking. Address: (b.) Department of Urology, Royal Infirmary, Dundee; T.-0382 23125.

Baxter, Audrey Caroline, BA, DipACC. Commercial Director, W.A. Baxter and Sons Ltd, Fochabers, since 1990; b. 25.5.61; m., Colin McNiven. Educ. St. Leonard's School; Heriot-Watt University. International banking, Kleinwort Benson Ltd, London, 1983-87; Director, Corporate Planning, Baxters of Speyside, 1988-90. Director, Moray, Badenoch and Strathspey LEC, since 1991; Member, Council, Moray College, since 1991; Member, Council, CBI Scotland, since 1990; Director, Quality Scotland Foundation, since 1991. Recreations: fishing; tennis; water sports; reading; all music. Address: (b.) W.A. Baxter and Sons Ltd, Fochabers, Moray.

Baxter, Brian Newland, BSc, MSc, PhD, CEng, FRINA, MIES. Marine Consultant; Visiting Professor, Department of Ship and Marine Technology, Strathclyde University, since 1980; Nautical Assessor (Naval Architect), Home Office, since 1974; Moderator for Engineering Council Examinations, since 1977; b. London; m., Nadina McLeod; 2 d. Educ. King's College, Newcastle, Durham University. Scientific Officer, Royal Naval Scientific Service, 1948-50; Lecturer in Naval Architecture, King's College, Newcastle, 1950-57; Chief Representative, Bureau Veritas in the UK, 1957-62; Director, Yarrow & Co., Glasgow, 1962-79; Deputy Managing Director, Yarrow Shipbuilders, Glasgow, 1967-81; Director, British Shipbuilders Training and Education Co., 1981-84. President, Institution of Engineers and Shipbuilders in Scotland, 1979-81; Hon. Secretary, Seagull Trust, since 1984. Recreations: reading; writing; walking; golf. Address: (h.) Dunelm, Kilmacolm, Renfrewshire, PA13 4DQ; T.-050 587 2092.

Baxter, Carole Mary, BSc. Co-Presenter, The Beechgrove Garden, BBC Scotland, since 1986 (Head Gardener, The Beechgrove Garden, since 1984); b. 30.6.57, Maidstone. Educ. Maidstone School for Girls; Sussex University. Undergardener, Kildrummy Castle Gardens Trust, Aberdeenshire, 1979-80; Gardener/Caretaker, Aberdeen University Air Squadron, 1980-83; Assistant Gardener, The Beechgrove Garden, Aberdeen, 1983-84. Publication: The Beechgrove Garden (Co-author). Recreations: skiing; walking; swimming; gardening. Address: (b.) BBC, Beechgrove Terrace, Aberdeen, AB9 2ZT; T.-0224 625233.

Baxter, Mary Ross, MBE, MA, LRAM. Immediate Past President, International PEN Scottish Centre; b. 23.9.27, Glasgow. Educ. Park School, Glasgow; Glasgow University. John Smith & Son, Booksellers, Glasgow, 1952-56; British European Airways, Glasgow Office, 1956-60; National Book League (now known as Book Trust), 1960-89; started the Scottish Office in 1961. Honorary Member, Scottish Library

Association. Recreations: music; books; home-decorating; cooking; gardening. Address: (h.) 18 Crown Terrace, Glasgow, G12 9ES; T.-041-357 0327.

Baxter, (William) Gordon, OBE, DL, LLD. Chairman, W.A. Baxter & Sons Ltd., since 1971; b. 8.2.18, Fochabers, Moray; m., Ena E. Robertson; 2 s.; 1 d. Educ. Ashville College, Harrogate; Aberdeen University. ICI Explosives Ltd., 1940-45 (Research and Development Manager, various military projects); joined family business, 1946; Managing Director, 1947-71; Member, British Export Council Committee for Exports to USA, 1964-69; Member, North American Advisory Group, DTI, 1982-88; former Director, Grampian Regional Board, Bank of Scotland; Member of Council, Royal Warrant Holders Association, London; former Member, Scottish Conservative Party's Business Group. Recreations: fishing; tennis. Address: (h.) Speybank House, Fochabers, Moray; T.-0343 821 234.

Bayliss, Anthony Paul, MB, ChB, FRCR, DMRD. Consultant Radiologist, Aberdeen Royal Infirmary, since 1975; b. 7.2.44, Oldham; m., Margaret Anne; 3 s. Educ. Oldham Hulme Grammar School; St. Andrews University. Medical Intern., Mount Sinai Hospital, Minneapolis, 1969-70; House Officer, Ballochmyle Hospital, Ayrshire, 1970-71; Trainee Radiologist, Western Infirmary, Glasgow, 1971-75. Recreation: golf. Address: (h.) School House, Drumoak, Aberdeen; T.-Drumoak 650.

Baynham, John William, BSc, PhD, DIC. Chairman, Lothian Health Board, since 1990; Chairman, Board of Governors, Moray House College, since 1991; Non-Executive Director, Lawrie & Symington Ltd., since 1987; b. 20.1.29, Blantyre; m., Marie B. Friel; 1 d. Educ. Bathgate Academy; Aberdeen University; Imperial College, London. Scottish Agricultural Industries PLC, 1955-87, latterly as Agribusiness Director. Member, Lothian Health Board, 1987-90. Recreations: golf; grandchildren. Address: (h.) 2/18 Succoth Court, Succoth Park, Edinburgh, EH12 6BZ; T.-031-337 2813.

Bealey, Professor Frank William, BSc (Econ), DSc (Econ). Professor of Politics, Aberdeen University, 1964-90; b. 31.8.22, Bilston, Staffordshire; m., Sheila Hurst; 1 s.; 2 d. Educ. King Edward VI Grammar School, Stourbridge; London School of Economics. Extra-Mural Lecturer, Manchester University, 1951-52; Lecturer, Keele University, 1952-64; Temporary Lecturer, Birmingham University, 1958-59. Treasurer and founder Member, Society for the Study of Labour History, 1960-63; Convener, Committee for Social Science, Aberdeen University, 1970-74 and 1986-89; Fellow, Royal Historical Society, 1971; Editorial Board, Political Studies, 1975-83; Visiting Fellow, Yale University, 1980; Organiser, Parliamentary All-Party Group, Social Science and Policy, 1984-89. Publications: Labour and Politics 1900-1906 (Co-author); Constituency Politics (Co-author); The Social and Political Thought of the British Labour Party; The Post Office Engineering Union; The Politics of Independence (Co-author); Democracy in the Contemporary State. Recreations: reading poetry; darts; eating and drinking; watching football and cricket. Address: (h.) Morag House, Oyne AB52 6QT; T.-Old Rayne 457.

Beastall, Graham Hedley, BSc, PhD, MRCPath. Top Grade Biochemist (Endocrinology), Glasgow Royal Infirmary, since 1981; Honorary Lecturer, Glasgow University, since 1983; b. 11.12.47, Liverpool; m., Judith; 2 s. Educ. Liverpool Institute High School for Boys; Liverpool University. Lecturer in Biochemistry, Liverpool University, 1971-72; Lecturer in Steroid Biochemistry, Glasgow University, 1972-76; Senior Biochemist (Endocrinology), then Principal Biochemist (Endocrinology), Glasgow Royal Infirmary, 1976-81. National Meetings Secretary, Association of

Clinical Biochemists, since 1988; Area Commissioner, Greater Glasgow Scout Council, 1980-88. Recreations: Scouting; gardening; sport. Address: (b.) Department of Clinical Biochemistry, Royal Infirmary, Glasgow, G4 OSF; T.-041-552 3535, Ext. 4632.

Beat, Janet Eveline, BMus, MA. Composer; Lecturer, Royal Scottish Academy of Music and Drama, since 1972; Artistic Director and Founder, Soundstrata (electro-acoustic ensemble); b. 17.12.37, Streetly. Educ. High School for Girls, Sutton Coldfield; Birmingham University. Freelance Orchestral Player, 1960s; Lecturer: Madeley College of Education, 1965-67, Worcester College of Education, 1967-71; founder Member, and former Council Member, Scottish Society of Composers; writes musical criticism for The Scotsman; G.D. Cunningham Award, 1962; her compositions include The Gossamer Web, 1975; Dancing on Moonbeams, 1980 (released on gramophone record); Journey of a Letter, 1986; Fireworks in Steel, 1987; Aztec Myth, 1987; A Vision of the Unseen, 1988; Kist O'Ayres, 1989; her works have been performed throughout Scotland as well as in Switzerland, Poland, North America, South America, Greece and Japan. Recreations: travel; reading; photography. Address: (h.) 5 Letham Drive, Glasgow, G43 2SL; T.-041-637 1952.

Beattie, Alastair, MA, LLB. Chief Executive, Caithness District Council, since 1974; b. 11.10.37, Aberdeen; m., Rosaline; 2 s.; 1 d. Educ. Robert Gordon's College, Aberdeen; Aberdeen University. Legal/Principal Legal Assistant, Dumfries County Council, 1961-67; Caithness County Council: Depute County Clerk, 1967-74, Chief Executive, 1974. Recreations: bowls; gardening; bridge. Address: (b.) Council Offices, Market Square, Wick, Caithness; T.-0955 3761.

Beattie, Alistair Duncan, MD (Hons), FRCPGlas, FRCPLond. Consultant Physician, Southern General Hospital, Glasgow, since 1976; Honorary Clinical Lecturer, Glasgow University, since 1977; b. 4.4.42, Laurencekirk; m., Gillian Margaret McCutcheon; 3 s.; 2 d. Educ. Paisley Grammar School; Glasgow University. Junior hospital appointments, Royal Infirmary and Western Infirmary, Glasgow, 1965-69; Department of Materia Medica, Glasgow University: Research Fellow, 1969-73, Lecturer, 1973-74; MRC Research Fellow, Royal Free Hospital, London, 1974-75. Honorary Treasurer, Medical and Dental Defence Union of Scotland. Recreations: golf; music. Address: (h.) 228 Queen Victoria Drive, Glasgow, G13 1TN; T.-041-959 7182.

Beattie, Henry Thomson, OBE (1974). Member, Perth and Kinross District Council, since 1980 (Convenor of Architectural Services, 1982-85, Leader, Conservative Group, 1985-86); b. 14.6.20, Glasgow; m., Harriet Hall Hughes; 2 s. Educ. Hutchesons' Grammar School, Glasgow. Pilot, RAF, 1944-45; joined Rivers Steam Navigation Co., 1946; Controlling Agent, Assam, 1954-64 (Director, Assam Sillimamite Co. Ltd., 1956-64); General Manager, Assam Railways & Trading Co. Ltd., 1965-73; Chairman, Nocte Timber Co. Ltd., 1965-73; Housemaster, Morrison's Academy, Crieff (retired, 1985). Appointed MBE, 1964, for services to British people during Chinese incursion into India; Chairman, Assam branch, UK Citizens Association, 1968-72; Chairman, Crieff Community Council, 1975-78. Recreations: fencing; golf. Address: The Cottage, Rectory Road, Crieff, PH7 3DZ; T.-Crieff 2295.

Beattie, Rev. Walter Gordon, MA, BD. Minister, Arbroath Abbey Church, since 1977, Arbroath Old and Abbey Church, since 1990; b. 25.4.32, Aberdeen; m., Catherine Fiona Matheson; 1 s.; 2 d. Educ. Robert Gordon's College, Aberdeen; Aberdeen University. Assistant Minister, St. Machar's Cathedral, Aberdeen, 1956-57; Minister: Sorbie Parish, Wigtownshire, 1957-62; Fraserburgh West Church,

1962-77. Hospital and school Chaplain. Recreations: reading; gardening; walking. Address: 51 Cliffburn Road, Arbroath, Angus, DD11 5BA; T.-Arbroath 72196.

Beaumont, Professor Phillip Barrington, BEcon (Hons), MEcon, PhD. Professor, Department of Social and Economic Research, Glasgow University, since 1990 (Senior Lecturer, 1984-86, Reader, 1986-90); b. 13.10.49, Melbourne, Australia; m., Patricia Mary Ann McKinlay; 1 s. Educ. Camberwell High School, Melbourne; Monash University, Melbourne; Glasgow University. Research Fellow, then Lecturer, Glasgow University, 1976-84; Visiting Professor: Massachusetts Institute of Technology, Boston, 1982, McMaster University, 1986, Case Western Reserve University, 1988, Cornell University, 1990. Publications: Bargaining in the Public Sector, 1978; Safety at Work and the Trade Unions, 1981; Job Satisfaction in Public Administration, 1983; The Decline of Trade Union Organization, 1987; Change in Industrial Relations, 1990; Public Sector Industrial Relations, 1991. Recreations: tennis; badminton; shooting; fishing. Address: (b.) The University, Glasgow, G12 8QQ; T.-041-339 8855.

Bechhofer, Professor Frank, MA. Professor of Social Research, Edinburgh University, since 1987 (Director, Research Centre for Social Sciences, since 1984); b. 10.10.35, Nurnberg, Germany; m., Jean Barbara Conochie; 1 s.; 1 d. Educ. Nottingham High School; Queens' College, Cambridge. Junior Research Officer, Department of Applied Economics, Cambridge University, 1962-65; Edinburgh University: Lecturer in Sociology, 1965-71, Reader in Sociology, 1971-87. Address: (b.) Research Centre for Social Sciences, 56 George Square, Edinburgh, EH8 9JU; T.-031-650 4068.

Beck, Professor John Swanson, BSc, MD, FRCPGlas, FRCPEdin, FRCPath, FIBiol, FRSE. Professor of Pathology, Dundee University, since 1971; Honorary Consultant Pathologist, Tayside Health Board, since 1971; b. 22.8.28, Glasgow; m., Marion Tudhope Paterson; 1 s.; 1 d. Educ. Glasgow Academy; Glasgow University. House Officer, Western Infirmary and Royal Hospital for Sick Children, Glasgow, 1953-54; Trainee Pathologist, Western Infirmary and Glasgow University, 1954-63; Clinical Research Fellow, National Institute for Medical Research, London, 1960-61; Senior Lecturer in Pathology, Aberdeen University, 1963-71. Chairman, Clinical and Biomedical Research Committee, Chief Scientist Organisation, Scottish Home and Health Department, since 1983 (Member, Chief Scientist Committee, since 1983); Chairman, Breast Tumour Panel, Medical Research Council, 1979-89; Member, Tayside Health Board, 1983-91; Member, Medical Advisory Group, LEPRA, since 1988; Member, National Biological Standards Board, since 1988; Chairman, Scientific Policy Advisory Committee, since 1991; former Member, Cell Biology and Disorders Board, Medical Research Council; former Assistant Editor, Journal of Pathology. Recreation: DIY. Address: (b.) Department of Pathology, Ninewells Hospital and Medical School, PO Box 120, Dundee, DD1 9SY; T.-0382 60111, Ext. 2169.

Beckett, Rev. David Mackay, BA, BD. Minister, Greyfriars Tolbooth and Highland Kirk, Edinburgh, since 1983; Secretary, General Assembly Panel on Doctrine; b. 22.3.37, Glasgow; m., Rosalie Frances Neal; 2 s. Educ. Glenalmond; Trinity Hall, Cambridge; St. Andrews University. Assistant Minister, Dundee Parish Church (St. Mary's), 1963-66; Minister, Clark Memorial Church, Largs, 1966-83. Convener, Committee on Public Worship and Aids to Devotion, General Assembly, 1978-82; President, Church Service Society, 1986-88. Publication: The Lord's Supper, 1984. Address: (h.) 12 Tantallon Place, Edinburgh, EH9 1NZ; T.-031-667 8671.

Bedborough, William F., MA (Hons), DipEdTech. Rector, Jordanhill School, since 1989 (Rector, Forfar Academy, 1979-89); b. 6.11.42, Glasgow; m., Sheena J. McLullich; 1 s.; 1 d. Educ. Hutchesons' Boys' Grammar School, Glasgow; Glasgow University. Assistant Teacher (History), Hutchesons' Boys Grammar School, 1965-68; Special Assistant Teacher (History), Hamilton Academy, 1968-69; Principal Teacher (History), Bellshill Academy, 1969-72; Assistant Rector, Arbroath Academy, 1972-75; Depute Rector, Galashiels Academy, 1975-79. Recreations: sailing; golf; squash. Address: (b.) Jordanhill School, Chamberlain Road, Glasgow; T.-041-959 1897.

Bedi, Tarlochan Singh, JP, MB, BS, MRCPsych, DPM. Consultant Psychiatrist, Southern General Hospital, Glasgow, since 1980; b. India; m., Dr. T.H. Ratani; 1 s. Educ. Poona University, India. Junior House Officer, Aga Khan Hospital, Nairobi; Senior House Officer, Glenside and Barrow Hospital, Bristol; Registrar, Coneyhill Hospital, Gloucester; Senior Registrar, Gartnavel and Southern General Hospital, Glasgow; Consultant Psychiatrist, Woodilee Hospital, Lenzie. Past President: Scottish Asian Action Committee, Glasgow; Indian Social and Cultural Association, Glasgow; Indian Graduates Society, Glasgow. Recreations: music; photography; culinary arts. Address: 156 Prestonfield, Milngavie, G62 7QA; T.-041-445 2466.

Begg, David, BA (Hons). Chairman of Finance, Lothian Regional Council, since 1990 (Councillor, since 1986); Lecturer in Economics, Napier Polytechnic, since 1981; b. 12.6.56, Edinburgh; m., Karen. Educ. Portobello High School; Heriot-Watt University. Economic Researcher, PEIDA, 1979; management employee, BR, 1979-81. Publications: articles on transport economics and local government finance. Recreations: golf; watching Hibernian F.C. Address: (b.) Parliament Square, Edinburgh; T.-031-469 3347.

Begg, Professor Hugh MacKemmie, MA, PhD, DipTP, FRTPI, FRSA. Director, School of Town and Regional Planning, Duncan of Jordanstone College of Art, Dundee, since 1981; b. 25.10.41, Glasgow; m., Jane Elizabeth Harrison; 2 d. Educ. High School of Glasgow; St. Andrews University; University of British Columbia. Lecturer in Political Economy, St. Andrews University; Research Fellow, Tayside Study; Lecturer in Economics, Dundee University; Assistant Director of Planning, Tayside Regional Council; Visiting Professor, Technical University of Nova Scotia; Consultant, UN Regional Development Project, Saudi Arabia; Consultant, Industry Department Scotland. Recreations: local history; reading; rugby. Address: (h.) 4 Esplanade, Broughty Ferry, Dundee; T.-0382 79642.

Begg, Ian McKerron, DA, FRIAS, FSA Scot. Architect (own practice), since 1983; Vice President, Architectural Heritage Society of Scotland; Member, Council, Saltire Society; b. 23.6.25, Kirkcaldy; 3 d. Educ. Kirkcaldy High School; Edinburgh College of Art. Partner, Robert Hurd & Partners, 1951-83; Interim Director, Edinburgh New Town Conservation Committee; Architectural Advisor, National Trust for Scotland; Interim Director, Edinburgh Old Town Committee for Conservation and Renewal. Recreations: travel, particularly to Paris; supporting Scotland's identity. Address: Ravens'Craig Tower, Plockton, Ross-shire, IV52 8UB; T.-059 984 265.

Begg, Norman Roderick Darroch, MA, LLB. Secretary, Aberdeen University; b. 23.12.41, London; m., Fiona Schofield; 3 d. Educ. Aberdeen Grammar School; Aberdeen University. Administrative Assistant, East Anglia University, 1964-66; Aberdeen University, since 1966: Administrative Assistant; Assistant Secretary; Registry Officer; Clerk to Senatus; Deputy Secretary. Member, Children's Panel,

Grampian Region, 1984-87; Past Chairman, Aberdeen Studio Theatre Group; Director, Edinburgh Festival Fringe Society, 1980-83; Hon. Vice-President, Aberdeen Opera Company, since 1988. Recreation: amateur drama. Address: (h.) Rae's Cottage, Udny Green, by Ellon, Aberdeenshire; T.-06513 2065.

Begg, Robert William, CBE (1977), MA, CA, FRSA, DUniv (Glas). Member, Museums and Galleries Commission, 1988-91; b. 19.2.22; m., Sheena Margaret Boyd; 2 s. Educ. Greenock Academy; Glasgow University. Royal Navy, 1942-46 (Lt., RNVR) (Despatches). Consultant, Moores & Rowland, since 1987 (Partner, Mann Judd Gordon, Glasgow, 1951-86). Honorary Treasurer, Royal Philosophical Society of Glasgow, 1952-62; Honorary Treasurer, Royal Glasgow Institute of Fine Arts, 1975-87, President, 1987-90; Member, Board of Governors, Glasgow School of Art, 1955-77 (Chairman, 1970-76); Trustee, National Galleries of Scotland, 1974-91 (Chairman, 1980-87); Council Member, National Trust for Scotland, 1984-90 (Executive, 1985-90); Member of Court, Glasgow University, 1986-90. Address: (h.) 3 Colquhoun Drive, Bearsden, Glasgow, G61 4NQ; T.-041-942 2436.

Begg, Thomas N.A., OBE, JP, BA, PhD. Economic Historian and Lecturer; Board Member, Scottish Homes, since 1988; Member, Council of Management, Scottish Special Housing Association, 1980-89; b. 8.1.42, Stirling; m., Mary E.; 1 d. Educ. Balfron High School; Strathclyde University. Publications: The CWD File, 1980; Fifty Special Years, 1987. Recreations: hill-walking; music; reading. Address: Department of Applied Consumer Studies, Queen Margaret College, Edinburgh; T.-031-317 3000.

Behan, Professor Peter Oliver, MD, ChB, FRCP(Lond), FRCP(I), FRCP(Glas), FACP. Consultant Neurologist, Greater Glasgow Health Board, since 1976; Professor of Neurology, Glasgow University; b. 8.7.35, Co. Kildare; m., Dr. Wilhelmina Behan; 2 s.; 1 d. Educ. Sir John Cass College, London; Leeds University Medical School. Demonstrator in Pathology, Cambridge University, 1965-66; Research Fellow in Psychiatry, Harvard University, 1966-67; Special Research Fellow, Oxford University, 1968-70; Lecturer in Neurology, then Senior Lecturer, then Reader, Glasgow University, from 1971. Patron, Motor Neurone Disease Association of Scotland; awarded Pattison Medal for contributions to neurology; Chief Editor, Journal of Neuroimmunology. Recreations: salmon fishing; Samuel Johnson. Address: (h.) 17 South Erskine Park, Bearsden, Glasgow; T.-041-942 5713.

Behrens, Reinhard. Artist; President, Society of Scottish Artists, since 1989; Board Member, Crawford Arts Centre, St. Andrews, since 1990; b. 14.11.51, Scheessel, Germany; m., Margaret L. Smyth; 1 d. Educ. Kirchenpauer Gymnasium, Hamburg; Hamburg College of Art; Academy of Arts, Vienna; Edinburgh College of Art. Draughtsman, German Archaeological Institute, Pergamon, Turkey, 1976; Writer and Illustrator, German publishers, 1980-82; Lecturer in Drawing and Painting, Edinburgh College of Art, 1981-83; Visiting Lecturer, Glasgow School of Art, Duncan of Jordanstone College of Art, Dundee, 1984-86; Lecturer, Grays School of Art, Aberdeen, 1986-87; exhibitions of drawings, prints, paintings throughout Scotland, Europe, Canada and USA. German Academic Exchange Award, 1979; Andrew Grant Major Award, 1980; EIS Award, 1981, 1986; Benno Schotz Award, 1983; IBM Award, 1985; Scottish Arts Council Major Bursary, 1987. Publications: From the Land; SSA – The First 100 years. Address: 9 Calman's Wynd, Pittenweem, Fife, KY10 2NS; T.-0333 312083.

Belch, Alexander Ross, CBE (1972), LLD Strathclyde (1978), BSc, FRSE, FRINA, CBIM, CEng. Company Director; b. 13.12.20, London; m., Janette Finnie Murdoch

(deceased); 4 d. Educ. Morrison's Academy, Crieff; Glasgow University. Lithgows Ltd.: Director and General Manager, 1954, Managing Director, 1964; Managing Director, Scott Lithgow Group, 1969-80; Member, Board, British Shipbuilders, 1977-79; President, Shipbuilders and Repairers National Association, 1974-76; Chairman: Jebsens Travel Ltd., Capelrig Ltd., Murray Hotels (Crieff) Ltd., Kelvin Travel Ltd., Altnacraig Shipping plc, Orico Systems Ltd., Amprotech Ltd., Ferguson Marine plc, Ferguson Shipbuilders Ltd.; a Director, Jebsens (UK) Ltd. Chairman, Trustees of the Scottish Maritime Museum. Address: (h.) Altnacraig House, Lyle Road, Greenock, PA16 7XT; T.-0475 21124.

Belch, Jill J.F., MBChB, FRCP, MD (Hons). Senior Lecturer and Honorary Consultant Physician, University Department of Medicine, Ninewells Hospital, Dundee, since 1987; b. 22.10.51, Glasgow; m., Tom Van Der Ham; 1 s.; 2 d. Educ. Morrison's Academy; Glasgow University. Secretary/Treasurer, Royal Society of Medicine Forum on Angiology, since 1986; Treasurer, Scottish Heart and Arterial Risk Prevention Group, since 1989; Board Member, Scottish Medical Journal, since 1989; Member, Editorial Board, Platelet, since 1989; Editor, Vascular Medicine Review, since 1989. Publications: 150 papers. Recreations: skiing; family. Address: (b.) University Department of Medicine, Ninewells Hospital, Dundee, DD1 9SY; T.-0385 60111.

Bell, Albert Elliot, MA, MB, ChB, MFCM. Honorary Senior Lecturer, Department of Community Medicine, Edinburgh University, 1987-89; b. 26.11.24, Edinburgh; m., Dr. Fiona McCully; 3 s. Educ. Glasgow University. Industry, 1939-51 (RAF, 1944-47, Sgt. Pilot); Deputy Medical Superintendent, Glasgow Royal Infirmary Group, 1962-63; Assistant Dean, Faculty of Medicine, Glasgow, 1963-70; Scottish Home and Health Department, 1970-85; Community Medicine Specialist, Fife Health Board, 1985-87. Recreations: golf; art. Address: (h.) 6B Juniper Park Road, Edinburgh; T.-031-453 3692.

Bell, Alexander Gilmour, BL. Chief Reporter for Public Inquiries, Scottish Office, since 1979; b. 11.3.33.

Bell, Alexander Scott, FFA, FPMI. Managing Director, Standard Life Assurance Company, since 1988; b. 4.12.41, Falkirk; m., Veronica Jane Simpson; 2 s.; 1 d. Educ. Daniel Stewart's College, Edinburgh. Joined Standard Life, 1958; General Manager (Finance), 1985-88. Director: Bank of Scotland, Hammerson Property Investment and Development Corporation plc, Scottish Financial Enterprise. Recreations: golf; travel. Address: (b.) 3 George Street, Edinburgh, EH2 2XZ; T.-031-245 6011.

Bell, Sheriff Andrew Montgomery, BL. Sheriff of Lothian and Borders, at Edinburgh, since 1990 (Sheriff of Glasgow and Strathkelvin, at Glasgow, 1984-90); b. 21.2.40, Edinburgh; m., Ann Margaret Robinson; 1 s.; 1 d. Educ. Royal High School, Edinburgh; Edinburgh University. Solicitor, 1961-74; called to Bar, 1975; Sheriff of South Strathclyde, Dumfries and Galloway, at Hamilton, 1979-84. Address: (h.) 5 York Road, Edinburgh, EH5 3EJ; T.-031-552 3859.

Bell, Sheriff Archibald Angus, QC (Scot), MA, LLB. Sheriff of Glasgow and Strathkelvin, at Glasgow, since 1973; b. 13.4.23.

Bell, Colin John, MA (Hons). Broadcaster; Journalist; Author; Rector, Aberdeen University, 1991-93; b. 1.4.38, London; m., Caroline Rose Bell; 1 s.; 3 d. Educ. St. Paul's School; King's College, Cambridge. Journalist, The Scotsman, 1960-62 and 1975-78; Columnist/Contributor, London Life, Sunday Times, Sunday Telegraph, Daily Mirror, Sunday Mail, etc.; Lecturer, Morley College, 1965-

68; College Supervisor, King's College, Cambridge, 1968-75; Parliamentary candidate (SNP), West Edinburgh, 1979; European Parliamentary candidate (SNP), North East Scotland, 1979; Vice-Chairman, SNP, 1978-84; Campaign Director, Euro Election, 1984; a Senior Fellow, the 21st Century Trust, 1990. Publications: City Fathers, 1969; Boswell's Johnson, 1971; Scotch Whisky, 1985; Radical Alternative (Contributor), 1978; The Times Reports (Series) (Editor). Recreations: jazz; Scottish history. Address: (h.) Cockburnhill, Balerno, Midlothian.

Bell, Professor Colin Roy, BA, MScEcon, FRSE. Professor of Sociology, Edinburgh University, since 1988; b. 1.3.42, Enfield; m., Dr. Janette Webb; 1 s.; 3 d. Educ. The Judd School, Tonbridge; Keele University; University of Wales. University teaching posts at Essex; Professor of Sociology, Universities of New South Wales and Aston; research posts, Universities of Leicester and Edinburgh. Publications: Middle Class Families; Community Studies; Doing Sociological Research; Property, Paternalism and Power; numerous other academic papers and books. Recreations: jazz and blues; Munros; Penguins; gardening. Address: (b.) Sociology Department, Edinburgh University, 18 Buccleuch Place, Edinburgh, EH8; T.-031-667 1011.

Bell, Professor David Nevin Fraser, MA, MSc, PhD. Professor of Economics, Stirling University, since 1990; b. 16.12.51, Inverness; m., Gill; 1 s.; 1 d. Educ. Dornoch Academy; Aberdeen University; London School of Economics; Strathclyde University. Lecturer, St. Andrews University, 1974-75; Research Fellow: Fraser of Allander Institute, Strathclyde University, 1975-83, Macroeconomic Modelling Bureau, Warwick University, 1983-85; Lecturer, Glasgow University, 1985-90. Economic Consultant to Secretary of State for Scotland. Recreations: golf; five-a-side football; hill walking; photography; more golf. Address: (b.) Department of Economics, Stirling University, Stirling, FK9 4LA; T.-0786 67486.

Bell, Donald Atkinson, BSc, PhD, FIMechE, CEng, MIEE, FBCS. Director, Marchland Consulting Ltd., since 1990 (Director, National Engineering Laboratory, 1983-90); b. 28.5.41, Belfast; m., Joyce Louisa Godber; 2 s. Educ. Royal Belfast Academical Institution; Queen's University, Belfast; Southampton University. National Physical Laboratory, Teddington, 1966-77; Electronics Applications Division, Department of Industry, 1978-82. Address: (b.) Marchland Consulting Ltd., 108 East Kilbride Road, Glasgow G76 8JF; T.-041-644 2000.

Bell, George Armour, JP, BSc, MB, ChB. Member, Lanarkshire Health Board, 1981-91 (Chairman, Finance Committee); b. 8.7.20, Bellshill; m., Elizabeth Davidson Porteous; 2 s. Educ. Bellshill Academy; Glasgow University. War Service, 609 Squadron, SMO Prestwick, SMO Brize Norton, RAF. Retired General Practitioner, Bellshill; Founder Chairman, Crime Prevention Panel, Bellshill and District; former Red Cross Detachment Medical Officer, Bellshill; former Chairman, Lanarkshire Branch, Tenovus Scotland; Member, National Committee, Tenovus Scotland; Founder Chairman, Community Council for Mossend; Honorary Medical Officer, Bellshill Bn., Boys Brigade; President, Bellshill Branch, Arthritis Care; Honorary Member, Rotary. Address: (h.) Chudleigh, 449 Main Street, Bellshill, Lanarkshire, ML4 1DB; T.-749084.

Bell, George Scott, AIB, AIB (Scot). Honorary Sheriff, Tayside, Central and Fife, at Dunfermline, since 1976; b. 27.6.14, Johnstone; m., 1, Agnes Ewing Stark (deceased); 2, Violet Woolcock; 1 d. Educ. Madras College, St. Andrews. Began career with British Linen Bank, St. Andrews, 1931; as Member, RAFVR, called up for active service, 1939; mentioned in Despatches, 1946; British Linen Bank: Assistant

Trustee Manager, 1952, Manager, Linlithgow, 1957, Manager, Dunfermline, 1963 (merged with Bank of Scotland, 1971); part-time Lecturer in banking subjects, Heriot-Watt College, Edinburgh, three years; Examiner, Institute of Bankers in Scotland, 10 years; retired from Bank, 1974. Elder, Church of Scotland, since 1957; at various times Treasurer, St. Michael's Church, Linlithgow, and St. Margaret's Church, Dunfermline. Recreations: golf; bowls. Address: (h.) Kilrymont, 16 Over Haven, Limekilns, Dunfermline, Fife, KY11 3JH; T.-0383 872484.

Bell, G. Susan, ACIS, FSA (Scot). Founder Director, Scotland Direct (Holdings) Limited; Gourmet Scotland Limited; Bell Lawrie of Biggar (Developments) Ltd.; Board Member, SCOTVEC; b. 31.8.46; m., Arthur J.A. Bell; 2 s.; 2 d. Educ. College of Commerce, Glasgow. Investment Analyst, Edinburgh, 1970-74; Conservative Parliamentary candidate: Motherwell, 1970, Caithness & Sutherland, February 1974; Chairman, Conservative Candidates Association, 1971-74; Member, Council, CBI Scotland; Founder Chairwoman, Phoenix Group, 1987; Board Member, Scottish Tourist Board, 1983-88; Member, Council, National Trust for Scotland, 1983-88. Recreations: garden; riding; reading. Address: (h.) Culter House, Coulter, Biggar; T.-0899 20064.

Bell, Emeritus Professor Henry B., BSc, PhD, FIM, CEng. Professor of Metallurgy, Strathclyde University; b. 3.7.22, Greenock; m., Barbara M. Smith; 1 d. Educ. Greenock High School; Royal College of Science and Technology. Assistant Metallurgist, Scotts Shipbuilding and Engineering Company; Research Assistant, Lecturer, Reader, Metallurgy Department, Strathclyde University; Visiting Professor, Concepcion University, Witwatersrand University, Toronto University; Distinguished Visiting Scientist, National Research Council, Halifax. Kroll Medallist, Institute of Metals; Member, Editorial Panel, Ironmaking and Steelmaking. Recreation: gardening. Address: (h.) 89 Finlay Rise, Milngavie, Glasgow G62 6QL; T.-041-956 1473.

Bell, Jeanne Elisabeth, BSc, MD, MRCPath. Senior Lecturer in Pathology, Edinburgh University, since 1984; Honorary Consultant in Neuropathology, Western General Hospital, Edinburgh, since 1984; b. 10.8.42, England; m., Dr. Denis Rutovitz; 1 s. Educ. Newcastle-upon-Tyne University. Lecturer, Department of Anatomy, Newcastle-upon-Tyne, 1967-70; part-time Scientific Officer, MRC Clinical and Population Cytogenetics Unit, Edinburgh, 1975-79; Senior Registrar in Paediatric Pathology, Royal Hospital for Sick Children, Edinburgh, 1979-84. Address: (b.) Neuropathology Laboratory, Western General Hospital, Crewe Road, Edinburgh, EH4 2XU; T.-031-332 2525.

Bell, Neil, MusB, GRSM, ARMCM, ARCO, CertEd. Director of Music, Broughton High School, Edinburgh, and Director, Lothian Specialist Music Scheme, since 1980; b. 17.10.43, York. Educ. Nunthorpe Grammar School, York; Manchester University; Royal Manchester College of Music. Assistant Music Master, Cheadle Hulme School, 1967; Head of Music, West Bridgford School, Nottingham, 1971; joined teaching staff, South Nottinghamshire School of Music, becoming Vice Principal, then Principal; professional Singer, formerly with BBC Northern Singers, John Currie Singers; Musical Director: Dundee Choral Union, Lothian Region Schools Choir. Recreations: the arts; gardening; hill-walking. Address: (b.) Broughton High School, Carrington Road, Edinburgh, EH4 1EG; T.-031-332 7805.

Bell, Robin, MA, MSc. Poet and Broadcaster; b. 4.1.45, Dundee; m., Suzette; 2 d. Educ. Morrison's Academy, Crieff; St. Andrews University; Perugia University, Italy; Union College, New York; Columbia University, New York. Formerly: Director of Information, City University of New

York, Regional Opportunity Program; Assistant Professor, John Jay College of Criminal Justice, City University of New York; Member, US Office of Education Task Force in Educational Technology; Audio-Visual Editor, Oxford University Press; Editor, Guidebook series to Ancient Monuments of Scotland; Secretary, Poetry Association of Scotland. Scottish Radio and Television Industries Award for Best Radio Feature, 1984; Sony Award, Best British Radio Documentary, 1985. Publications: The Invisible Mirror; Culdee, Culdee; Sawing Logs; Strathinver: A Portrait Album 1945-53; Collected Poems of James Graham, Marquis of Montrose (Editor); Radio Poems; The Best of Scottish Poetry; An Anthology of Living Scottish Poets (Editor). Address: (h.) 38 Dovecot Road, Edinburgh, EH12 7LE; T.-031-334 5241.

Bell, Sheriff Principal Stewart Edward, MA (Cantab), LLB (Glas), QC. Sheriff Principal of Grampian, Highland and Islands, 1983-88; b. 4.8.19, Glasgow; m., 1, Isla Spencer (deceased); 2, Mavis Kydd; 3 d.; 2 step d. Educ. Kelvinside Academy; Trinity Hall, Cambridge; Glasgow University. Commissioned Loyal Regiment, 1939; served with 2nd Bn. in Singapore and Malaya, 1940-42; PoW in Singapore and Korea, 1942-45; admitted Advocate, 1948; practised in Malacca, Malaya as Advocate and Solicitor, 1949-51; at Scottish Bar, 1951-61; Sheriff of Lanarkshire (later of Glasgow and Strathkelvin) at Glasgow, 1961-82. Honorary Pipe-Major, Royal Scottish Pipers Society, 1975-77; Past President and former Honorary Pipe Major, Glasgow Highland Club; Chairman, Scottish Far East PoW Association. Recreation: Highland bagpipe. Address: (h.) 14 Napier Road, Edinburgh, EH10 5AY.

Bell, Thomas Grant Law, LDS, RFPS(Glas). Regional Dental Officer, Scottish Home and Health Department, 1979-88; b. 17.2.26, Motherwell; m., Edith Barnett Porter; 1 s.; 1 d. Educ. Bellshill Academy; Anderson College of Medicine; Glasgow Dental Hospital and School. Captain, Royal Army Dental Corps, 1949-51; Assistant in general practice, 1951-54; Senior Dental Officer, Burgh of Motherwell and Wishaw, 1955-65; Principal in general practice, 1965-79; former Secretary and Treasurer and Past Chairman, Lanarkshire Section, BDA; Past Chairman, Local Dental Committee, Lanarkshire, and Lanarkshire Steering Committee, NHS Reorganisation; Lanarkshire Health Board: former Dental Secretary, Area Dental Committee, and former Member, GP Sub-Committee and Dental Service Committee; former Honorary Visiting Dental Surgeon, Edinburgh Dental Hospital. Recreations: fishing; shooting; boating; photography; philately. Address: (h.) Cabrach, 10 Laburnum Crescent, Wishaw, ML2 7EH; T.-0698 384930.

Bellany, John, RA. Artist; b. 18.6.42. One-man exhibition, National Portrait Gallery, 1986; retrospective exhibition, Scottish National Gallery of Modern Art, 1986; works in major galleries and private collections throughout the world.

Bell-Scott, Euan Toddy Morrison, LLB, NP, WS. Partner, Russel & Aitken, Falkirk, since 1981; Member, Forth Valley Health Board; b. 12.2.54, Edinburgh; m., Elizabeth Anne Hartley; 1 s.; 1 d. Educ. Edinburgh Academy; Aberdeen University. Secretary, Falkirk Victims Support. Recreations: family; road and cross-country running; tennis; golf; watching rugby internationals. Address: (h.) The Tower, 37 High Street, Dollar FK14 7AZ.

Beloff, Halla, BSc, PhD, FBPS. Senior Lecturer, Department of Psychology, Edinburgh University, since 1963; b. 11.5.30; m., John Beloff; 1 s.; 1 d. Educ. South Hampstead High School; London University; Illinois University; Queen's University, Belfast. Former Editor, British Journal of Social and Clinical Psychology; former Member, Psychology Committee, Social Science Research Council; President, British Psychological Society, 1983-84. Occasional broad-

caster, BBC Radio Scotland; Convener, Committee on Arts, Scottish Council on Disability, since 1986. Publications: Psychology Survey 5 (Co-Editor), 1984; Camera Culture, 1985, Getting into Life, 1986; Psychology Survey 6, 1987. Recreations: following the arts and not being shocked by the new; needlework. Address: (h.) 6 Blacket Place, Edinburgh, EH9 1RL; T.-031-667 3200.

Belton, Neville Richard, BSc, PhD, CChem, MRSC. Senior Lecturer, Department of Child Life and Health, Edinburgh University, since 1975; Honorary Biochemist, Lothian Health Board; b. 5.10.37, Nottingham; m., Elisabeth Foster Inglis; 1 s.; 1 d. Educ. Nottingham High School; Birmingham University. Research Associate, Children's Memorial Hospital, Chicago, 1963-67; Lecturer in Pharmacology and Associate in Paediatrics, Northwestern University, Chicago, 1964-67; Lecturer, Department of Child Life and Health, Edinburgh University, 1967-75. Member: DHSS Working Party on the Composition of Infant Foods, 1974-80; Committee, Nutrition Society (Scottish Group and Reproduction and Growth Group); Elder, Cramond Kirk. Publication: Textbook of Paediatric Nutrition (Joint Editor), 1991. Recreations: travel; sport (squash, tennis, hockey); music. Address: (h.) 6 St. Bernards Crescent, Edinburgh, EH4 1NP; T.-031-332 0392.

Beltrami, Joseph, BL, NP. Solicitor (Beltrami & Co.); b. 15.5.32, Rutherglen; m., Brigid D.; 3 s. Educ. St. Aloysius College, Glasgow; Glasgow University. Intelligence Corps, 1954-56 (Sgt.); qualified as Solicitor, 1956; specialised in criminal law; has instructed in more than 500 murder cases; closely associated with two cases of Royal Pardon. Chairman, soccer testimonials: Jim Johnstone and Bobby Lennox, 1976; Danny McGrain, 1980. Publications: The Defender, 1980; Glasgow - A Celebration (Contributor), 1984; Tales of the Suspected, 1988; A Deadly Innocence, 1989. Recreations: bowls; soccer; snooker; writing; boxing. Address: (h.) 5 St. Andrew's Avenue, Bothwell, Lanarkshire; T.-Bothwell 852374.

Benedetti, Giovanni. Chairman, Benedetti Holdings; Chairman, Pendigo Ltd.; Director, Silcock Express; Director, Prince's Scottish Youth Business Trust; Director, ASSET; b. 6.3.43, Italy; m., Francesca; 2 d. Arrived in Britain aged 11; worked in uncle's cafe until age of 19; started his own business with two dry-cleaning shops; opened his first factory in Ardrossan, 1970; company bought by BET, 1989. Recreations: skiing; sailing.

Benington, (Charles) Kenneth, BSc, PhD, CEng, FIMechE. Industrial Adviser to Secretary of State for Scotland, since 1988; b. 1.4.31, Belfast; m., Margaret Malcolm; 1 s.; 1 d. Educ. Dalriada Grammar School, Ballymoney; Queen's University, Belfast; Heriot-Watt University. Graduate apprentice and design engineer, Associated Electrical Industries Ltd., 1953-60; Assistant Chief Engineer, Trials, British Ship Research Association, 1960-63; Lecturer, Heriot-Watt University, 1963-72; Senior Engineer, Marine Industries Centre, Newcastle University, 1972-74; Brown Brothers & Co. Ltd.: Systems Manager, 1974-75; Technical Manager, 1975-77; Technical Director, 1977-80; Assistant Managing Director and Technical Director, 1980-81; Managing Director, 1981-86; Technical Director, Vickers Marine Engineering Division, 1986-88;Member, Executive Committee, Scottish Employers' Association, 1984-86; Member, Board of Unilink, Heriot Watt University, 1987-90. Address: (b.) Industry Department for Scotland, Alhambra House, 45 Waterloo Street, Glasgow, G2 6AT.

Bennett, Bruce, MB, ChB (Hons), MD (Hons), FRCP, FRCPath, FRCPEd. Reader in Medicine, Aberdeen University; b. 5.7.38, Gorakhpur, India; m., Dr. G. Adey Bennett. Educ. Brechin High School; Aberdeen University.

Aberdeen University: Ashley Mackintosh Research Fellow, 1964; MRC Junior Research Fellow, 1965; Lecturer in Medicine, 1967; Eli Lilly Travelling Research Fellow, then Visiting Research Fellow, Case Western Reserve University, Cleveland, Ohio, 1970-72; Wellcome Senior Research Fellow, Aberdeen University, 1973; appointed Senior Lecturer, 1978. Address: (b.) Department of Medicine and Therapeutics, Polwarth Building, Foresterhill, Aberdeen; T.-0224 681818, Ext. 53025.

Bennett, David Andrew, MA, LLB, WS, NP. Partner, Bennett & Robertson, Solicitors, Edinburgh and Glasgow, since 1964; Chairman, Oswalds of Edinburgh Ltd., since 1964; b. 27.3.38, Edinburgh; m., Marion Miller Park; 2 d. Educ. Melville College, Edinburgh; Fettes College, Edinburgh; Edinburgh University. Director, Jordan Group Ltd.; Member, Council, Law Society of Scotland, 1984-90. Session Clerk, Liberton Kirk, since 1975; Honorary Secretary, Scottish Hockey Association, 1973-82; Scottish Editor, Palmer's Company Law, since 1970, and Gore-Browne on Companies, since 1975. Recreations: most sports and arts. Address: (b.) 16 Walker Street, Edinburgh, EH3 7NN; T.-031-225 4001.

Bennett, Howard Grimwade. Publisher and Managing Director, The Oban Times Ltd., since 1983; b. 17.6.40, London; m., Joan Peake Hughes; 1 s.; 1 d. Educ. Lady Manners Grammar School, Derbyshire. Reed International, 1959-65; The McCorquodale Group, 1966-75; Holmes McDougall Ltd., 1975-81; Petersburg Press, USA, 1981-83. Recreations: classical music; modern art. Address: (h.) Church Lodge, Dalmally, Argyll PA33 1AX.

Bennett, James Douglas Scott, MA, CA. Group Financial Director, John Menzies plc, since 1981; Director, East of Scotland Industrial Investments PLC, since 1984; Director, Scottish Provident Institution, since 1989; b. 1.3.42, Forfar; m., Lorna Elizabeth Margaret Peat; 2 s. Educ. Fettes College; Edinburgh University. Binder Hamlyn, 1968-71; Financial Director, Chloride Group, 1972-75. Member, Commission for Local Authority Accounts in Scotland, since 1983; Member, Group of Scottish Financial Directors; Member, Edinburgh University Business Studies Advisory Committee; Fellow, Royal Society of Arts. Recreations: golf; reading. Address: (b.) John Menzies plc, 108 Princes Street, Edinburgh, EH2 3AA; T.-031-225 8555.

Bennett, Ronald Alistair, CBE (1986), QC (Scot), MA, LLB. Vice-President for Scotland, Value Added Tax Tribunals, since 1977; Member, Scottish Medical Practices Committee, 1976-88; b. 11.12.22; m., Margret Magnusson; 3 s.; 3 d. Educ. Edinburgh Academy; Edinburgh University; Balliol College, Oxford. Lt., 79th (Scottish Horse) Medium Regiment, RA, 1943-45; Captain, attached RAOC, India and Japan, 1945-46; called to Scottish Bar, 1947; Standing Counsel to Ministry of Labour and National Service, 1957-59; Sheriff-Principal: Roxburgh, Berwick and Selkirk, 1971-74, South Strathclyde, Dumfries and Galloway, 1981-82, North Strathclyde, 1982-83, Highlands and Islands, 1990-91; Chairman, Medical Appeal Tribunals (Scotland), since 1971; Chairman, Agricultural Wages Board for Scotland, since 1973; Chairman, Local Government Boundary Commission for Scotland, 1974-89; Chairman, Industrial Tribunals (Scotland), since 1977; Chairman, Pension Appeal Tribunals (Scotland) since 1984. Address: (h.) Laxamyri, 46 Cammo Road, Barnton, Edinburgh, EH4 8AP.

Bennie, Alexander McArthur, BDS. Chief Administrative Dental Officer, Highland Health Board, since 1989; b. 7.12.32, Cambuslang; m., Annabelle Davidson Armstrong; 1 s.; 3 d. Educ. Rutherglen Academy; Glasgow University. National Service Aircrew Officer, 1951-53; General Dental Practitioner, 1959-66; Chief Dental Officer, County of

Sutherland, 1966-75; District Dental Officer/Assistant Chief Dental Officer, 1975-89. Member, National Dental Consultative Committee, 1975-84 (Vice Chairman, 1981-84); Honorary Clinical Senior Lecturer, Department of Oral Medicine and Pathology, Glasgow University. Recreations: golf; reading; gardening; cycling; walking. Address: (h.) Filmhor, Dornoch, Sutherland; T.-0862 810474.

Bennie, Thomas, FIB (Scot). General Manager, Bank of Scotland, since 1984; b. 7.11.32, Falkirk; m., Jean M. Bennie; 2 s.; 2 d. Educ. Falkirk High School. British Linen Bank (later merged with Bank of Scotland): entered, 1949; appointed Assistant Superintendent of Branches, 1969; Assistant General Manager, Bank of Scotland Finance Co. Ltd., 1973; Deputy Chief Executive and Assistant Director, British Linen Bank Ltd. (subsidiary of Bank of Scotland), 1977; appointed Director, British Linen Bank Ltd., 1978; Divisional General Manager, Bank of Scotland International Division, 1980-84. Recreations: fishing; golf; bowls; gardening. Address: (b.) Bank of Scotland, 110 St. Vincent Street, Glasgow, G2 5EJ.

Bentham, Professor Richard Walker, BA, LLB, Barrister. Professor of Petroleum and Mineral Law and Director of the Centre for Petroleum and Mineral Law Studies, Dundee University, 1983-90; b. 26.6.30, Holywood, Co. Down; m., Stella Winifred Matthews; 1 d. Educ. Campbell College, Belfast; Trinity College, Dublin. Lecturer in Law: Tasmania University, Hobart, 1955-57; Sydney University, New South Wales, 1957-61; Legal Department, British Petroleum Co., 1961-83 (Deputy Legal Adviser to the Company, 1979-83). Council Member: British Branch, International Law Association; International Bar Association (Section on energy and natural resources law); elected FRSA, 1986; Board Member, Scottish Council for Arbitration; Council Member, ICC Institute of International Business Law and Practice; British nominated Member, IEA Dispute Settlement Centre's Panel of Arbitrators. Recreations: cricket; military history and military modelling. Address: (h.) West Bryans, 87 Dundee Road, West Ferry, Dundee; T.-0382 77100.

Berry, Professor David Richard, MA, MSc, PhD, DSc, CBiol, FIBiol. Professor, Department of Bioscience and Biotechnology, Strathclyde University; b. 1.3.41, Huddersfield; m., Elisabeth Ann; 1 s.; 1 d. Educ. Holme Valley Grammar School; St. Peter's College, Oxford. Scientific Officer, Glaxo Ltd., Ulverston, 1962-64; graduate student, 1964-70; Lecturer, then Senior Lecturer, then Reader, Strathclyde University; Member, Scottish Examination Board Biology Panel. Address: (b.) Department of Bioscience and Biotechnology, Strathclyde University, George Street, Glasgow; T.-041-552 4400.

Berry, Graham, CA. Director of Finance and Administration, Scottish Arts Council, since 1989; b. 12.1.45, Edinburgh; 1 s.; 1 d. Educ. Royal High School, Edinburgh; CA Apprentice, Edinburgh, 1963-68; CA, Price Waterhouse, London, 1968-70; Divisional Chief Accountant, Trust House Forte, London, 1970-74; Company Secretary, 1974-86: Scottish Film Council, Scottish Council for Educational Technology, Glasgow Film Theatre, Filmhouse Ltd., Scetlander Ltd.; Finance Officer, Stirling University, 1986-89. Recreations: mountaineering; photography. Address: (b.) Scottish Arts Council, 12 Manor Place, Edinburgh, EH3 7DD; T.-031-226 6051.

Berry, John, CBE (1968), DL (Fife) (1969), BA (Cantab), MA (Cantab), PhD (St. Andrews) Hon. LLD Dundee (1970), HonDSc St. Andrews (1991), FRSE (1936). Adviser and Consultant on environmental and wildlife conservation (retired); b. 5.8.07, Edinburgh; m., Hon. Bride Fremantle; 2 s.; 1 d. Educ. Ardvreck School, Crieff; Eton College; Trinity College, Cambridge. Salmon Research Officer, Fishery Board for Scotland, 1930-31; Biological Research Station,

University College, Southampton: Research Officer, 1932-36; Director, 1936-39; Chief Press Censor for Scotland, 1940-44; Biologist and Information Officer, North of Scotland Hydro-Electric Board, 1944-49; Environment Conservation Adviser, 1944-89 (to South of Scotland Electricity Board, 1969-89, to Scottish Landowners Federation, 1984-87); Director of Nature Conservation in Scotland, 1949-67; consultancy work 1968-90. Honorary Life Member, Swiss League for Protection of Nature, 1946; founder Member (1948), International Union for Conservation of Natural Resources and first President, International Union Commission on Ecology; Member, Executive Board, International Waterfowl Research Bureau, 1963-72; Honorary Corresponding Member, Danish Natural History Society, since 1957; Vice-President and Honorary Life Fellow, Royal Zoological Society of Scotland, since 1959; Honorary Life Fellow: Wildfowl Trust, 1983; Glasgow Natural History Society, 1951; Member, Dundee University Court, 1970-78; Director, British Pavilion, Expo 71, Budapest; Member, Scottish Marine Biological Association, 1947-71 (Council, 1947-54 and 1957-66). Recreations: natural history (especially insects, water birds and fish); music. Address: (h.) The Garden House, Tayfield, Newport-on-Tay, Fife, DD6 8HA; T.-0382 543118.

Berry, William, MA, LLB, WS, NP. Senior Partner, Murray Beith & Murray, WS, Edinburgh, since 1967; Deputy Chairman, Scottish Life Assurance Co.; Director: Scottish American Investment Co. Plc, Fleming Universal Investment Trust Plc, Dawnfresh Seafoods Ltd., Inchape Family Investments Ltd., and other companies; b. 26.9.39, Newport-on-Tay; m., Elizabeth Margery Warner; 2 s. Educ. Ardvreck, Crieff; Eton College; St. Andrews University; Edinburgh University. Interests in farming, forestry, etc. Depute Chairman, Edinburgh Festival Society, 1985-89; Member Council/Board: New Town Concerts Society Ltd., Thistle Foundation. Performer in three records of Scottish country dance music. Recreations: music; shooting; forestry. Address: (b.) 39 Castle Street, Edinburgh, EH2 3BH; T.-031-225 1200.

Besson, John Alexander Owen, BSc, MB, ChB, DPM, MRCPsych. Senior Lecturer in Mental Health, Aberdeen University, since 1985 (Wellcome Senior Lecturer, 1981-85); Honorary Consultant Psychiatrist, since 1981; b. 29.6.44, New Amsterdam, Guyana; m., Margaret Jean Adair. Educ. Edinburgh University. Consultant Psychiatrist, Lothian Health Board, 1977-80. Address: (b.) Department of Mental Health, University Medical Buildings, Foresterhill, Aberdeen; T.-Aberdeen 681818.

Bethel, Archibald A, BSc, MBA, CEng, MIMechE. Chief Executive, Lanarkshire Development Agency, since 1991; b. 9.2.53, Uddingston; m., Doreen; 1 s.; 1 d. Educ. Hamilton Academy; Strathclyde University. Vetco Gray Inc.; Managing Director, Engineering Division, Morrison Construction Group. Recreations: golf; computers; football. Address: (b.) 166 Park Street, Motherwell; T.-0698 51411.

Bethell, John, BSc (Hons). Chief Executive, Scottish Seed Potato Development Council, since 1982; Company Secretary, VT Growers Ltd., since 1984; Company Secretary, SE Growers Ltd., since 1989; b. 30.4.39, Nuneaton; m., Gillian; 1 s.; 3 d. Educ. Hutchesons' Boys' Grammar School; Glasgow University. Geologist, Government of Sierra Leone; District Manager, Texaco Africa Ltd., Sierra Leone; Managing Director, Argus of Ayr Ltd.; Chairman, Argoventure Ltd.; Chairman, River Tyne Trust; Recreations: climbing; underwater fishing; fish-farming. Address: Gillisland, The Sands, Haddington, EH41 3EY; T.-062 082 4133.

Bevan, John Stuart, BSc (Hons), MBChB (Hons), MD, MRCP (UK), FRSM, MRCPEdin. Consultant Physician and Endocrinologist, Aberdeen Royal Infirmary, since 1991; Honorary Senior Clinical Lecturer, Aberdeen University, since 1991; b. 18.9.53, Portsmouth; m., Sheena Mary; 2 s.; 2 d. Educ. Portsmouth Northern Grammar School; Dunfermline High School; Edinburgh University. Registrar in Endocrinology, Radcliffe Infirmary, Oxford, 1981-83; Medical Research Council Training Fellow in Endocrinology, Oxford, 1984-86; Senior Registrar in Medicine and Endocrinology, University Hospital of Wales, Cardiff, 1987-90. Publications: papers on clinical neuroendocrinology, particularly the treatment of human pituitary tumors. Recreations: cricket; guitar; ornithology. Address: (b.) Department of Endocrinology, Aberdeen Royal Infirmary, Foresterhill, Aberdeen, AB9 2ZB; T.-0224 681818.

Bevan, Jonquil, MA, DPhil (Oxon). Reader in English Literature, Edinburgh University, since 1991; b. 15.3.41, Brecon, Wales. Educ. Godolphin and Latymer School; Lady Margaret Hall, Oxford. Assistant Lecturer, Edinburgh University, 1967. Publications: edition of Izaak Walton's The Compleat Angler, 1983; Izaak Walton's The Compleat Angler: The Art of Recreation, 1988; various articles. Recreations: music; hill walking; book collecting. Address: (h.) 1 London Street, Edinburgh, EH3 6LZ; T.-031-556 8285.

Bevan-Baker, John Stewart, FRCO. Composer and freelance Musician; b. 3.5.26, Staines, Middlesex; m., June Mary Findlay; 1 s.; 4 d. Educ. Blundells School, Tiverton; Royal College of Music, London. Bevin boy, 1944-46; City Carillonneur, Aberdeen, 1958-63; Music Teacher in London, Aberdeen, Highlands of Scotland, and Glasgow. Recreations: gardening; reading; conservation. Address: (h.) 12 Academy Street, Fortrose, Ross-shire, IV10 8TW; T.-0381 20936.

Beveridge, Crawford William, BSc, MSc. Chief Executive, Scottish Enterprise, since 1991; b. 3.11.45, Edinburgh; m., Marguerite Devoe; 1 s.; 1 d. Educ. Daniel Stewart's College; Edinburgh University; Bradford University Management Centre. Training Officer, Hewlett Packard, 1968; European Personnel Director, Digital, 1977; Vice President Human Resources, Analog Devices, 1982; Vice President Corporate Resources, Sun Microsystems, 1985. Recreations: cooking; music; paperweights. Address: (b.) Scottish Enterprise, 120 Bothwell Street, Glasgow, G2 7JP; T.-041-248 2700.

Beveridge, George William, MB, ChB, FRCPE. Consultant Dermatologist, Edinburgh Royal Infirmary, since 1965; Honorary Senior Lecturer, Edinburgh University, since 1965; b. 23.2.32, Edinburgh; m., Janette Millar; 2 s.; 2 d. Educ. Dollar Academy; Edinburgh University. President, Scottish Dermatological Society, 1982-85; Elder, Church of Scotland. Recreations: golf; gardening. Address: (h.) 8 Barnton Park View, Edinburgh, EH4 6HJ.

Beveridge, John Lawrence, BSc, DipAgric(Cantab), MS (Iowa), MA. Deputy Principal, The Scottish Agricultural College, Edinburgh, since 1986; b. 23.7.33, Glasgow; m., Margaret Ann; 1 s.; 2 d. Educ. Hillhead High School; Glasgow University; Cambridge University; Iowa State University. Research Assistant, University College of North Wales, 1958-59; University Demonstrator, Cambridge University, 1959-65; Lecturer: West of Scotland Agricultural College, 1965-69, Edinburgh University, 1969-81; Assistant to Principal, East of Scotland College of Agriculture, 1981-86. Recreations: music; gardening; golf. Address: (h.) St Andrews, Duns Road, Gifford, Haddington, East Lothian, EH41 4QW; T.-062-081 694.

Bewsher, Peter Dixon, MB, ChB, MD, FRCPE. Reader in Therapeutics, Aberdeen University, since 1977; Honorary Consultant Physician, Grampian Health Board, since 1969; b. 6.4.34, Cockermouth; m., Marlyn Crichton; 2 s.; 1 d. Educ. Cockermouth Grammar School; St. Andrews University.

34   WHO'S WHO IN SCOTLAND

Medical Registrar, Aberdeen Hospitals; Research Associate, Indiana University; Lecturer, then Senior Lecturer in Therapeutics, Aberdeen University. Recreations: music; golf; hill-walking. Address: (h.) 83 Abbotshall Drive, Cults, Aberdeen, AB1 9JJ; T.-Aberdeen 868078.

Biddulph, 5th Lord (Anthony Nicholas Colin). Interior Designer and Sporting Manager; b. 8.4.59. Educ. Cheltenham; RAC, Cirencester. Recreations: shooting; design; fishing. Address: Address: (h.) Makerstoun, Kelso, TD5 7PA; T.-05736 234.

Biggart, Thomas Norman, CBE (1984), WS, MA, LLB. Partner, Biggart Baillie & Gifford, WS, Solicitors, Glasgow and Edinburgh, since 1959; b. 24.1.30; m., Eileen Jean Anne Gemmell; 1 s.; 1 d. Educ. Morrison's Academy, Crieff; Glasgow University. Royal Navy, 1954-56 (Sub-Lt., RNVR). Law Society of Scotland: Council Member, 1977-86; Vice-President, 1981-82; President, 1982-83; President, Business Archives Council, Scotland, 1977-86; Member, Executive, Scottish Council (Development and Industry), since 1984; Member, Scottish Tertiary Education Advisory Council, 1984-87; Member, Scottish Records Advisory Council, since 1985; Director: Clydesdale Bank, since 1985; New Scotland Insurance Group, since 1986 (Chairman, since 1989); Chairman, Beechwood, Glasgow, since 1989; Trustee, Scottish Civic Trust, since 1989; Member, Council on Tribunals (Chairman, Scottish Committee), since 1990; Honorary Member, American Bar Association, 1982; OStJ, 1968. Recreations: golf; hill-walking. Address: (h.) Gailes, Kilmacolm, Renfrewshire, PA13 4LZ; T.-Kilmacolm 2645.

Binnie, Frank Hugh. Director, The Design Council Scotland, since 1990; Director, UK Clothing and Textile Initiative, since 1990; b. 1.3.50, Edinburgh; m., Kaye; 3 s. Educ. Loughborough Grammar; Leicester Polytechnic. Design Management Trainee, Corahs Textiles, Leicester, 1970-73; Manufacturing Manager, Floreal Knitwear, Mauritius, 1973-76; Sales Manager, Kemptons Knitwear, Leicester, 1976-79; General Manager Design, Texport Unilever, 1979-82; Manufacturing Manager, Kilspindie Knitwear, 1982-85; Director and Company Secretary, Midlothian Enterprise, 1985-88; Managing Director, Perkins, Hodgkinson and Gillibrand (Coxmore plc) North and Scotland, 1988-90. Recreations: yachting; running. Address: (b.) Ca' d'Oro Building, 45 Gordon Street, Glasgow, G1 3LX; T.-041-221 6121.

Binns, John Kenneth, MB, ChB, FRCPEdin, FRCPsych. Physician Superintendent, Leverndale Hospital, Glasgow, since 1969 (Consultant Psychiatrist, since 1964); Honorary Clinical Lecturer, Glasgow University, since 1964; b. 25.6.28, Halifax; m., Sylvia Sharp; 1 s.; 1 d. Educ. Rishworth School, West Yorkshire; Edinburgh University. Fulbright Scholar and Rotating Intern., Erie, Pa., 1951-52; Medical Officer, RAMC, 11th Hussars, 1952-54; psychiatric training, Royal Edinburgh Hospital, 1956-64. Member of numerous professional committees at various times. Publication: Psychiatry in Medical Practice (Contributor). Recreations: gardening; photography. Address: (h.) 1 Balvie Avenue, Giffnock, Glasgow, G46 6NE.

Bird, Professor Colin C., MBChB, PhD, FRCPath, FRCPE. Professor of Pathology and Head, Department of Pathology, Edinburgh University, since 1986; b. 5.3.38, Kirkintilloch; m., Ailsa M. Ross; 2 s.; 1 d. Educ. Lenzie Academy; Glasgow University. McGhie Cancer Research Scholar, Glasgow Royal Infirmary, 1962-64; Lecturer in Pathology: Glasgow University, 1964-67, Aberdeen University, 1967-72; MRC Goldsmiths Travelling Fellow, Chicago, 1970-71; Senior Lecturer in Pathology, Edinburgh University, 1972-75; Professor and Head, Department of Pathology, Leeds University, 1975-86. Recreations: golf; skiing; hill walking; music. Address: (h.) 45 Ann Street, Edinburgh, EH4 1PL.

Birnie, Rev. Charles John, MA. Minister of Aberdour linked with Tyrie, since 1982; b. 19.7.25, Kininmonth, Lonmay; m., Isabel Moir; 2 s.; 1 d. Educ. Peterhead Academy; Kings College, Aberdeen; Christs College, Aberdeen. Higher Diploma in Religious Education. Teacher of English, Bowmore, Islay, 1950-53; Head Teacher: Watten Primary School, Caithness, 1953-59; Melness Junior Secondary School, Sutherland, 1959-61; English-teaching posts in Banffshire, 1961-67; Minister, Annbank, Ayrshire, 1969-82. Publication: Makar's Quair anthology (Editor), 1968. Recreations: composition of original bothy ballads; collecting Scottish anecdotes; writing scripts featuring vocabulary and rural life of Buchan; country concerts. Address: The Manse, Tyrie, Fraserburgh, AB4 4DN; T.-Memsie 325.

Birnie, George David, BSc, PhD. Senior Scientist, Beatson Institute for Cancer Research, since 1969; Honorary Lecturer in Biochemistry, Glasgow University, since 1982; b. 8.8.34, Gourock; m., Jean Gray McCaig; 2 s.; 1 d. Educ. Gourock High School; Greenock High School; Glasgow University. Assistant Lecturer in Biochemistry, Glasgow University, 1959-60; Postdoctoral Fellow, McArdle Memorial Laboratory, University of Wisconsin, 1960-62; Scientist, Imperial Cancer Research Fund Laboratories, London, 1962-69. Kitchener Scholarship, 1952-56; Fulbright Travel Scholarship, 1960-62; US Public Health Service Fellowship, 1960-62; Member, Editorial Advisory Panel, Biochemical Journal; editor of five books, author of more than 120 papers. Deacon, Giffnock Congregational Church. Recreation: gardening. Address: (b.) Beatson Institute for Cancer Research, Garscube Estate, Switchback Road, Bearsden, Glasgow, G61 1BD; T.-041-942 9361.

Birse, Graham Robertson. Director, Public Relations, Scottish Tourist Board, since 1987; b. 21.9.57, Newport on Tay; m., Elaine; 2 s. Educ. Glenrothes High School; Napier Polytechnic. Public Relations Manager, Royal Automobile Club, 1984. PR Advisor: Forth Bridge Centennial Committee, 1990, Mental Health Foundation (Scotland) Jubilee Appeal Committee, 1989. Recreations: Scotland; hill walking; ornithology; reading; football; environment. Address: (b.) 23 Ravelston Terrace, Edinburgh, EH4 3EU; T.-031 332 2433.

Birss, Rev. Alan David, MA (Hons), BD (Hons). Minister, Paisley Abbey, since 1988; b. 5.6.53, Ellon; m., Carol Margaret Pearson. Educ. Glenrothes High School; St. Andrews University; Edinburgh University. Assistant Minister, Dundee Parish Church (St. Mary's), 1978-80; Minister, Inverkeithing Parish Church of St. Peter, 1982-88. Secretary, Scottish Church Society; Member, Council, Church Service Society; Chairman, Scottish Committee, Royal School of Church Music. Address: The Manse of Paisley Abbey, 15 Main Road, Castlehead, Paisley, PA2 6AJ; T.-041-889 3587.

Birt, Christopher Alan, MA, MSc, MB, BChir, FRCP, FFPHM, DRCOG. Consultant in Public Health Medicine, Highland Health Board, since 1987; Honorary Clinical Senior Lecturer in Public Health, Aberdeen University, since 1990; Honorary Clinical Senior Lecturer in Public Health, Glasgow University, since 1989; b. 10.1.42, Woking; m., Lesley Gillian Jones; 1 s.; 3 d. Educ. Wellington College, Crowthorne; King's College, Cambridge; St. Thomas's Hospital Medical School, London; University of Manchester Medical School. Postgraduate training in general medicine; training in community medicine/public health medicine, Manchester; Consultant, North Derbyshire, 1976-78; Area Medical Officer, District Medical Officer, Chief Medical Officer, Stockport, 1979-86; Chief Administrative Medical Officer, Western Isles, 1986-88. Recreations: foreign travel; skiing; walking; vegetarian food; wine. Address: (h.) Fodderty Lodge, Dingwall, Ross-shire, IV15 9UE; T.-0997 421207.

Bishop, Alan Henry, CB (1989), MA (Hons). HM Chief Inspector of Prisons for Scotland, since 1989; b. 12.9.29, Edinburgh; m., Marjorie Anne Conlan; 1 s.; 1 d. Educ. George Heriot's School, Edinburgh; Edinburgh University. Private Secretary to Parliamentary Under Secretaries of State for Scotland, 1958-59; Principal, Department of Agriculture and Fisheries for Scotland, 1959; First Secretary, Food and Agriculture, Copenhagen and The Hague, 1963-66; Assistant Secretary: Commission on the Constitution, 1969-73, Devolution Division, Scottish Office, 1973-76, Health Building and Liaison Divisions, SHHD, 1976-80; Assistant Under-Secretary of State, Scottish Office, London, 1980-84; Principal Establishment Officer, Scottish Office, 1984-89. President, Scottish Bridge Union, 1979-80. Recreations: contract bridge; theatre. Address: (b.) St. Andrew's House, Edinburgh, EH1 3DE; T.-031-244 2335.

Bishop, Christopher Sayles, MA. Chief Executive, Royal Scottish Orchestra, since 1988; b. 1.4.32, Woodford Green; 1 s.; 1 d. Educ. Forest School; Caius College, Cambridge. Commissioned, Intelligence Corps, Director of Music, Magdalen College School, Oxford, 1956-59; Director of Music, Bishop's Stortford College, 1959-64; General Manager, International Classical Division, EMI Ltd., 1964-79; Managing Director, Philharmonia Orchestra, 1979-88. Recreation: sailing. Address: (b.) RSO Centre, 73 Claremont Street, Glasgow, G3 7HA; T.-041-226 3868.

Bishop, Gordon, MA (Hons), DipEd. Head Teacher, Tarbert Academy, since 1984; Vice-Convener, EIS Central Advisory Committee for English, 1976-88; b. 17.12.35, Glasgow; m., Jean Bonner; 2 s. Educ. Possil Senior Secondary School, Glasgow; Glasgow University. Taught in further education and schools, since 1966; Principal Teacher of English: Woodside Secondary School, Glasgow, 1972-75, Elgin Academy, 1975-77; Head Teacher, Tobermory High School, 1977-84. Recreations: golf; badminton; music; theatre. Address: (b.) Tarbert Academy, School Road, Tarbert, Argyll, PA29 6TE; T.-08802 269.

Bisset, Lt. Col. Alexander Galletly, FCIT. Secretary, Multiple Sclerosis Society in Scotland, since 1981; b. 5.10.30, Edinburgh; m., Elizabeth Margaret Bertram; 2 d. Educ. George Watson's College; Royal Military Academy, Sandhurst. Commissioned Royal Army Service Corps, 1951; transferred to Royal Corps of Transport, 1965; Elder, Cramond Kirk. Address: (b.) 2A North Charlotte Street, Edinburgh EH2 4HR; T.-031-225 3600.

Bisset, Rev. Peter Thomas, MA, BD. Evangelist, Church of Scotland, since 1974; Warden, St. Ninian's Training Centre, Crieff, since 1974; b. 16.6.27, Motherwell; m., Margaret Russell; 1 s.; 2 d. Educ. Rutherglen Academy; Glasgow University. Minister: Livingstone Church, Stevenston, 1953-60, Rutherford Church, Glasgow, 1960-68, High Church, Bathgate, 1968-74. Publications: Ten Growing Churches (Contributor); Prospects for Scotland (Contributor); The Kirk and Her Scotland; Religion, State and Society in Modern Britain (Contributor). Address: St. Ninian's, Comrie Road, Crieff, Perthshire, PH7 4BG; T.-0764 3766/7.

Black, Antony, MA (Cantab), PhD (Cantab). Reader in Political Science, Dundee University, since 1990; Author; b. 23.6.36, Leeds; m., Aileen Pow; 4 s.; 1 d. Educ. Shrewsbury School; King's College, Cambridge. Assistant Lecturer, Department of Political Science, Queen's College, Dundee, 1963-66; Lecturer, Department of Political Science, Dundee University, 1967-80; Visiting Associate Professor, School of Government and Public Administration, The American University, Washington, DC, 1975-76. Publications: Monarchy and Community: political ideas in the later conciliar movement (1430-50); Council and Commune: the Council of Basle and the 15th-century heritage; Guilds and

civil society in European political thought from the 12th century to the present; State, Community and Human Desire; Community in Historical Perspective (Editor). Recreation: hill-walking. Address: (b.) Department of Political Science, Dundee University, Dundee; T.-Dundee 23181, Ext. 4592.

Black, Bruce, MA. Senior Depute Secretary, Convention of Scottish Local Authorities, since 1986; Secretary, Scottish Constitutional Convention, since 1989; b. Kirkcaldy; m., Isabel; 1 s.; 2 d. Educ. Buckhaven High School; Edinburgh University. Employed in steel industry, 1964-68; administrative post, Glasgow Corporation, 1968-73; Project Co-ordination Officer, Ross & Cromarty County Council, 1973-75; Assistant Chief Executive, Highland Regional Council, 1975-86. Recreations: current affairs; travel; sport. Address: (b.) COSLA, Rosebery House, 9 Haymarket Terrace, Edinburgh, EH12 5XZ; T.-031-346 1222.

Black, Hugh Blair, MA (Hons). Head Teacher, Greenock High School, 1968-85; Minister, Struthers Memorial Church, Greenock, since 1956; b. 22.7.22, Kilmacolm; m., Isobel B.M. Wright; 3 d. Educ. Greenock High School; Glasgow University; Jordanhill College of Education. History Teacher, latterly Principal Teacher of History, Port Glasgow High School, 1951-64; Head Teacher, Mount School, Greenock, 1964-68. Chairman, Central Committee on Social Subjects, seven years; Chairman, Social Subjects Centre, Jordanhill, seven years. Address: (h.) 27 Denholm Street, Greenock; T.-Greenock 87432.

Black, Hugh Finlayson, BSc (Hons), MBA. Depute Director Development, Highland Regional Council, since 1984; Company Manager, Highland Opportunity Limited, since 1986; Regional Manager, Prince's Scottish Youth Business Trust, since 1988; b. 16.6.46, Johnstone; m., Lydia Mary McRae; 1 s.; 3 d. Educ. Paisley Grammar School; Aberdeen University; Strathclyde University; Glasgow University. Development Officer, West Cumberland Farmers, 1973-75; Regional Manager, Pan Britannica Industries, 1976-79; Principal Officer, Grampian Regional Council, 1980-84. Recreations: walking; swimming; gardening; reading. Address: (b.) Development Department, Highland Regional Council, Glenurquhart Road, Inverness, IV3 5NX; T.-0463 234121, Ext. 402.

Black, Rev. James G., BD, DPS. Minister, Westwood Parish Church, East Kilbride, since 1986; b. 10.2.52, Motherwell; m., Isobel-Ann T. Hamilton; 1 d. Educ. Dalziel High School, Motherwell; Glasgow University. Minister: Hamilton North, 1978-82, Burnbank/Hamilton North, 1982-86. Editor, Church of Scotland Year Book; Secretary, Scottish Christian Conservative Forum. Recreations: reading; music. Address: 16 Inglewood Crescent, East Kilbride; T.-03552 23992.

Black, Professor Robert, QC, LLB (Hons), LLM, FRSA. Professor of Scots Law, Edinburgh University, since 1981; General Editor, The Laws of Scotland: Stair Memorial Encyclopaedia, since 1988 (formerly Deputy and Joint General Editor); Temporary Sheriff, since 1981; b. 12.6.47, Lockerbie. Educ. Lockerbie Academy; Dumfries Academy; Edinburgh University; McGill University, Montreal. Advocate, 1972; Lecturer in Scots Law, Edinburgh University, 1972-75; Senior Legal Officer, Scottish Law Commission, 1975-78; practised at Scottish bar, 1978-81; QC, 1987. Publications: An Introduction to Written Pleading, 1982; Civil Jurisdiction: The New Rules, 1983. Recreations: beer and books, not necessarily in that order. Address: (h.) 6/4 Glenogle Road, Edinburgh, EH3 5HW; T.-031-557 3571.

Black, Robert Reid, MBE, ARSA, DA, ARIBA, FRIAS. Partner, Baxter Clark & Paul, Architects, Dundee, since 1965; b. 1.11.35, Arbroath; m., Moyra Christine Deuchar; 1 s.; 3 d. Educ. Arbroath High School; Dundee College of Art; Duncan of Jordanstone School of Architecture. Apprenticeship, Arbroath Town Council, 1951-55; Architectural Assistant, Arbroath Town Council, 1958; Northern Ireland Housing Trust, 1958-59; private practice, 1960; Baxter Clark & Paul, since 1961. Member, Housing Awards Panel, Saltire Society, since 1970 (currently Convener). Address: (b.) 20 South Tay Street, Dundee; T.-0382 27511.

Black, Robert William, MA (Hons, Econ), MSc (Town Planning), MSc (Public Policy). Chief Executive, Tayside Regional Council, since 1990 (Chief Executive, Stirling District Council, 1985-90); b. 6.11.46, Banff; m., Doreen Mary Riach; 3 s.; 1 d. Educ. Robert Gordon's College, Aberdeen; Aberdeen University; Heriot-Watt University; Strathclyde University. Nottinghamshire County Council, 1971-73; City of Glasgow Corporation, 1973-75; Strathclyde Regional Council, 1975-85. Fellow, Royal Statistical Society. Recreations: hill-walking; cycling; golf; swimming; music and art. Address: (b.) Tayside House, Crichton Street, Dundee DD1 3RA; T.-Dundee 23281.

Black, W.J. Murray, BSc, PhD, ARICS, JP. Farms Director, Edinburgh School of Agriculture, since 1970; Honorary Senior Lecturer, Edinburgh University, since 1970; b. 26.7.35, Reading; m., Ann Warren; 3 d. Educ. Leighton Park School, Reading; Reading University; Durham University; College of Estate Management, Reading. Lecturer in Agriculture, Newcastle University, 1959-64; Principal Scientific Officer, Agricultural Institute, Dublin, 1964-70. Member: Farm Animal Welfare Council, London, since 1988, NCCS (SNH) S.E. Scotland Regional Board, since 1991, UK Register of Organic Food Suppliers R. & D. Committee, London, since 1989; Honorary Secretary/Treasurer, British Society of Animal Production, since 1980. Publications: 45 scientific papers. Recreations: DIY houses and restoration of old cars; holidays in France. Address: The Pines, Bush, Penicuik, EH26 0PH; T.-031-445 3136.

Blackburn, Richard A.M, BSC (Hons), MEd (Hons), MBA. Chief Executive, Banff and Buchan District Council, since 1990; b. 27.10.49, Rutherglen; m., Andrina; 2 d. Educ. Hamilton Academy; Glasgow University. Recreation: golf. Address (b.) St. Leonards, Sandyhill Road, Banff; T.-0261 812521.

Blackie, Professor John Walter Graham, BA (Cantab), LLB. Professor of Law, Strathclyde University, since 1991 (Senior Lecturer in Scots Law, Edinburgh University, 1988-91, Lecturer, 1975-88); Director, Blackie & Son Ltd., publishers, since 1970; Advocate, since 1974; b. 2.10.46, Glasgow; m., Jane Ashman. Educ. Uppingham School; Peterhouse, Cambridge; Harvard; Merton College, Oxford; Edinburgh University. Open Exhibitioner, Peterhouse, Cambridge, 1965-68; St. Andrews Society of New York Scholar, Harvard, 1968-69; practised at Scottish bar, 1974-75. Recreations: music; sailing. Address: (h.) 17 Parsonage Square, Glasgow G1 1PX.

Blacklaws, Allan Farquharson, OBE, CBIM, CIPM. Human Resource Consultant, since 1983; Director, Edinburgh International Folk Festival; b. 24.7.24, Glasgow; m., Sylvia Noble; 3 d. Educ. Whitehill School, Glasgow; University College, Swansea. Personnel Director, Scottish & Newcastle Breweries p.l.c., 1962-83; original Member, National Industrial Relations Court; Member: Employment Appeal Tribunal; ACAS Panel of Arbitrators. Recreations: bowls; hill-walking; folk music. Address: (h.) Craigmore House, 25 Craigmillar Park, Edinburgh, EH16 5PE; T.-031-667 3765.

Blair, Alastair William, MB, ChB, FRCPE, DCH. Consultant Paediatrician, Fife Area Health Board, since 1970; Honorary Senior Lecturer: Department of Biochemistry and Microbiology, St. Andrews University, since 1975;

Department of Child Life and Health, Edinburgh University, since 1979; Secretary, Scottish Paediatric Society, since 1987; b. 11.8.36, Preston; m., Irene Elizabeth McFee; 2 s. Educ. Harris Academy, Dundee; St. Andrews University. House Officer/Senior House Officer: Arbroath Infirmary; Maryfield Hospital, Dundee; Kings Cross Hospital, Dundee; Hospital for Sick Children, Great Ormond Street, London; Lecturer in Child Health, St. Andrews University; Registrar in Medical Paediatrics, Hospital for Sick Children, Great Ormond Street, London; Lecturer in Child Health, Aberdeen University; Wellcome-Swedish Research Fellow, Karolinska Children's Hospital, Stockholm; Senior Registrar in Paediatrics, Southmead Hospital, Bristol. Publication: Prenatal Paediatrics: a handbook for obstetricians and paediatricians (Co-author and Editor), 1971. Recreations: private aviation; camping; restoring old property; sailing; jazz. Address: (h.) Bellcraig Farm, by Leslie, Fife, KY6 3JE; T.-0592 741754.

Blair, David Alexander Busbridge, MA, LLB. Chief Executive, Lochaber District Council, since 1981; b. 24.4.48, Perth. Educ. Perth Junior and Senior Academies; Edinburgh University. A Trustee, Abbeyfield Ballachulish Society, since 1983; Chairman, Outward Bound Loch Eil, since 1988; a Trustee, Outward Bound Trust (UK), since 1988. Recreations: botany; skiing; hill-walking. Address: (h.) Loyhurst, Muirshearlich, Banavie, Fort William, PH33 7PB; T.-0397 81 777.

Blair, James Ballantyne, BL, InstAM (Dip). Honorary Sheriff, Grampian, Highland and Islands at Stonehaven, since 1989; b. 16.8.24, Dailly, Ayrshire; m., Margaret M.J. McCafferty (deceased); 2 s.; 2 d. Educ. Peebles High School; Edinburgh University. Post Office, Peebles, 1941-44; Royal Signals, 1944-48 (GHQ (I) Signals, New Delhi, 1945-47); Sheriff Clerk's Offices, Edinburgh, Inverness, Peebles, Dingwall, Glasgow, 1948-73; Sheriff Clerk of Aberdeenshire at Aberdeen, 1973-82. Recreations: opera/operetta; reading (current affairs and law reports). Address: 41 Woodcot Park, Stonehaven, AB3 2HG; T.-0569 62067.

Blair, James Eric, BL. Solicitor, since 1948; Honorary Sheriff, since 1980; b. 18.3.23, Airdrie. Educ. Glasgow Academy; Glasgow University. Past Captain, Airdrie Golf Club. Recreation: golf. Address: (h.) Dunedin, Forrest Street, Airdrie.

Blair, John Samuel Greene, OBE (Mil), TD, CStJ, BA, Hon. DLitt (St. Andrews), ChM, FRCSEdin, FICS, D(Obst)RCOG. Lecturer, History of Medicine, Dundee University, since 1990; Consultant Surgeon, Perth Royal Infirmary, 1966-90; Vice-President, British Society for the History of Medicine, since 1991; President, Scottish Society of the History of Medicine; b. 31.12.28, Wormit, Fife; m., Ailsa Jean Bowes; 2 s.; 1 d. Educ. Dundee High School; St. Andrews University (Harkness Scholar, 1946-50). National Service, RAMC, 1952-55; Tutor, Department of Anatomy, St. Salvator's College, St. Andrews, 1955; surgical and research training, Manchester, Dundee, Cambridge, London, 1957-65; Member, Court of Examiners, Royal College of Surgeons of Edinburgh, 1965; postgraduate Clinical Tutor, Perth, 1966-74; first North American Travelling Fellow, St. Andrews/Dundee Universities, 1971; Secretary, Tayside Area Medical Advisory Committee, 1974-83; Member, Education Advisory Committee, Association of Surgeons, 1984-88; Secretary, Perth and Kinross Division, British Medical Association, 1982-90; Member, Scottish Council and Chairman's Sub-Committee, BMA, 1985-89; Fellow of the BMA, 1990; Honorary Colonel (TA), RAMC; Member, Principal's Council, St Andrews University, since 1989; Elder, Church of Scotland; Hospitaller, Priory of Scotland, Order of St. John of Jerusalem. Publications: books on medical history and anatomy. Recreations: golf; history; travel;

bridge. Address: (h.) 143 Glasgow Road, Perth; T.-Perth 23739.

Blair, Robin Leitch, MB, ChB, FRCSEdin, FRCS(C), FACS. Head, Department of Otolaryngology, Ninewells Hospital and Medical School, Dundee, since 1984; Consultant Otolaryngologist, Tayside Health Board, since 1984; b. 28.11.45, Gourock; m., Elizabeth Anne White; 2 d. Educ. Greenock Academy; Edinburgh University; University of Toronto. House Surgeon, Royal Infirmary, Edinburgh; Lecturer, Department of Anatomy, Glasgow University; Assistant Professor, Department of Otolaryngology, University of Toronto. Address: (b.) Department of Otolaryngology, Ninewells Hospital and Medical School, Dundee, DD1 9SY; T.-0382 60111, Ext. 2726.

Blair, Robin Orr, MA, LLB, WS. Managing Partner, Dundas & Wilson, CS, since 1988. Educ. Rugby School; St. Andrews University; Edinburgh University. Partner, Dundas & Wilson, since 1967; Purse Bearer to Lord High Commissioner to General Assembly of Church of Scotland; Honorary Secretary, Association of Edinburgh Royal Tradesmen. Address: (b.) 25 Charlotte Square, Edinburgh, EH2 4EZ; T.-031-225 1234.

Blair, Rev. Thomas James Loudon, MA, BD. Minister, Galston Parish Church, since 1980; Clerk, Irvine and Kilmarnock Presbytery, 1985-91; b. 24.7.40, Glasgow; m., Patricia Anne Bell; 1 s.; 2 d. Educ. Hutchesons' Grammar School, Glasgow; Glasgow University. Minister: Campsie Trinity and Milton of Campsie, 1965-71; Wallacetown Parish Church, Dundee, 1971-80; Mid Craigie Parish Church, Dundee (temporarily linked with Wallacetown), 1975-80. Recreations: golf; reading. Address: The Manse, Galston, Ayrshire; T.-Galston 820246.

Blair-Kerr, Sir Alastair, KB (1973), MA, LLB. President of the Court of Appeal for Bermuda, 1979-89; President of the Court of Appeal for the Bahamas, 1978-81; Member, Gilbraltar Court of Appeal, 1981-86; b. 1.12.11, Killin, Perthshire; m., Esther Margaret Fowler Wright (deceased); 1 s.; 1 d. Educ. McLaren High School, Callander; Edinburgh University. Solicitor, 1939; Advocate, Scots bar, 1951; Advocate and Solicitor, Singapore, 1939-41; Straits Settlements Volunteer Force, 1941-42; escaped from Singapore, 1942; Indian Army: Staff Capt., "A" Bombay District HQ, 1942-43; DAAG 107 Line of Communication area HQ, Poona, 1943-44; British Army: GS02, War Office, 1944-45; SO1 Judicial, BMA Malaya, 1945-46; Colonial Legal Service (HM Overseas Service), Hong Kong: Magistrate, 1946-48; Crown Counsel, 1949; President, Tenancy Tribunal, 1950; Crown Counsel, 1951-53; Senior Crown Counsel, 1953-59; District Judge, 1959-61; Puisne Judge, Supreme Court, 1961-71; Senior Puisne Judge, Supreme Court, 1971-73; Acting Chief Justice of Hong Kong; President, various commissions of inquiry. Recreations: music; walking. Address: Gairn, Kinbuck, Dunblane, Perthshire, FK15 ONQ; T.-0786 823377.

Blake, Professor Christopher, CBE, FRSE, MA, PhD. Bonar Professor of Applied Economics, Dundee University, 1974-88; Chairman, Glenrothes Development Corporation, since 1987; b. 28.4.26; m.; 2 s.; 2 d. Educ. Dollar Academy; St. Andrews University. Royal Navy, 1944-47; teaching posts, 1951-53; Assistant, Edinburgh University, 1953-55; Stewarts & Lloyds Ltd., 1955-60; Lecturer, then Senior Lecturer, St. Andrews University, 1960-67; Senior Lecturer, then Professor of Economics, Dundee University, 1967-74; Director, Alliance Trust plc, since 1974; Director, William Low & Co. plc, 1980-90 (Chairman, 1985-90). Recreation: golf. Address: (h.) Westlea, Wardlaw Gardens, St. Andrews, Fife, KY16 9DW.

Blakey, Rev. Ronald Stanton, MA, BD, MTh. Deputy Secretary, Department of Education, Church of Scotland, since 1981; Secretary, Assembly Council, from 1 Aug., 1988; b. 3.7.38, Glasgow; m., Kathleen Dunbar; 1 s. Educ. Hutchesons' Boys' Grammar School, Glasgow; Glasgow University. Minister: St. Mark's, Kirkconnel, 1963-67; Bellshill West, 1967-72; Jedburgh Old Parish with Edgerston and Ancrum, 1972-81. Member, Roxburgh District Council, 1974-80 (Chairman of Council, 1977-80); Religious Adviser, Border Television, 1973-81; Member, Borders Region Children's Panel, 1974-80; JP, 1974-80. Publication: The Man in the Manse, 1978. Recreation: collecting antiquarian books on Scotland. Address: (h.) 61 Orchard Brae Avenue, Edinburgh EH4.

Blanche, John Jamieson, CA. Chairman, West of Scotland Assured Homes PLC; Director, Scottish Veto Investment Company; Director, Apex Trust Scotland Ltd.; Director, Chorus Trust Ltd.; Governor, Strathallan School; Member, Common Services Agency (Scottish NHS) Management Committee; Member, Food From Britain Council; b. 10.7.29, Paisley; m., Fiona; 1 s.; 1 d. Educ. Glasgow Academy; Strathallan School. Director, Allied-Lyons PLC, 1986-89; Chairman, Allied Distillers Ltd., 1984-89; William Teacher & Sons Ltd.: Managing Director, 1979-84, Chairman, 1984-89; Chairman and Managing Director, Stewart & Son of Dundee Ltd., 1969-79; Allied-Lyons Eastern Ltd.: Chief Executive, 1988-89, non-executive Director, 1989-91; Director, Clyde Port Authority, 1980-86; Member, East European Trade Council, 1988-91; President, Junior Chamber Scotland, 1967. Recreations: golf; hill-walking; fishing; gardening; travel; music. Address: (b.) Daldrishaig, Aberfoyle, Stirling, FK8 3TQ; T.-087 72 223.

Bland, Keith Preston, BSc (Hons), PhD, FRES. Senior Lecturer in Preclinical Veterinary Sciences, Royal (Dick) School of Veterinary Studies, Edinburgh, since 1990; b. 20.11.41, Beetham; m., Valerie Ann Dunningham; 2 s. Educ. Heversham Grammar School; Nottingham University; London University. Research Assistant, Institute of Psychiatry, London University, 1963-68; Research Associate, Iowa State University, 1968-69; Lecturer in Veterinary Physiology, Edinburgh University, 1969-90. Secretary, Edinburgh Entomological Club. Recreation: entomology. Address: (h.) 35 Charterhall Road, Edinburgh EH9 3HS; T.-031-667 7013.

Blaxter, Professor John Harry Savage, MA (Oxon), DSc (Oxon), FIBiol, FRSE. Deputy Chief Scientific Officer, Scottish Marine Biological Association, 1985-91; Reader, then Hon. Professor, Stirling University, since 1969; Hon. Professor, St. Andrews University, since 1990; b. 6.1.29, London; m., Valerie Ann McElligott; 1 s.; 1 d. Educ. Berkhamsted School; Brasenose College, Oxford. SO, then SSO, Marine Laboratory, Aberdeen, 1952-64; Lecturer, Zoology Department, Aberdeen University, 1964-69; PSO, 1969, SPSO, 1974, Scottish Marine Biological Association, Oban. Recreations: sailing; gardening. Address: (h.) Dems Lodge, Barcaldine, Oban PA37 1SF; T.-0631 72228.

Bleasdale, Cyril, OBE, FCIT, MBIM, FRSA. Director, ScotRail, since 1990; b. 8.7.34, Liverpool; 2 d. Educ. Evered High School. Managing Director, Freightliner, 1975-82; Director, InterCity, British Rail, 1982-86; General Manager, BR London Midland Region, 1986-90. Recreations: music; fitness. Address: (b.) ScotRail House, 58 Port Dundas Road, Glasgow, G4 0HG; T.-041-335 3355.

Bluck, Professor Brian John, BSc, PhD, DSc, FGS, FRSE. Titular Professor of Geology, Glasgow University, since 1989; b. 29.8.35, Bridgend, Wales; m., Mary; 1 s.; 1 d. Educ. Bridgend County Grammar School; University College, Swansea. Assistant Lecturer, 1963; Lecturer, 1965; Senior

Lecturer 1976; Reader, 1981. Keith Medal, Royal Society of Edinburgh, 1981; Lyell Award, Geological Society of London, 1981. Recreations: hill-walking; theatre; music. Address: (b.) Glasgow University, Glasgow, G12 8QQ.

Blyth, Professor Thomas Scott, BSc, DSc (St. Andrews), D-es-Sc (Paris), CMath, FRSE, FIMA. Professor of Pure Mathematics, St. Andrews University, since 1977; b. 3.7.38, Newburgh, Fife; m., Jane Ellen Christine Pairman; 1 d. Educ. Bell-Baxter High School, Cupar; St. Andrews University. NATO Research Scholar, Sorbonne, 1960-63; St. Andrews University: Lecturer in Mathematics, 1963-72, Senior Lecturer, 1972-73, Reader, 1973-76; Visiting Lecturer, University of Western Australia, 1966; Visiting Professor, University of Western Ontario, 1968-69, New University of Lisbon, 1988-91, University of Minho, 1989-91. Past President, Edinburgh Mathematical Society; former Executive Editor, Proceedings A, Royal Society of Edinburgh; Corresponding Member, Royal Society of Sciences of Liege. Publications: Residuation Theory (Co-author), 1972; Set Theory and Abstract Algebra, 1975; Module Theory, 1977; Algebra Through Practice, Books 1 to 6 (Co-author), 1984-85; Categories, 1986; Essential Student Algebra, Volumes 1 to 5 (Co-author), 1986. Address: (h.) Wheaton Cottage, 4 Main Street, Strathkinness, Fife, KY16 9RU; T.-0334 85661.

Blyth, William, MA, LLB, BCom, SSC, NP. Director of Administration, City of Edinburgh District Council, since 1980; b. 3.8.37, Kirkcaldy; m., Anna Cecilia; 2 s.; 1 d. Educ. George Heriot's School, Edinburgh; Edinburgh University. Edinburgh Corporation: Head of Conveyancing and Contracts, 1971; Senior Depute Director of Administration, 1974. Recreation: gardening. Address: City Chambers, High Street, Edinburgh; T.-031-225 2424.

Boag, Archibald, BSc. Examination Secretary, CSE (Grampian) Examination Board, since 1988 (Rector, Lossiemouth High School, 1973-88); b. 1.7.31, Ardnadam, Dunoon; m., Fiona Wilson Mackenzie; 2 s. Educ. Dunoon Grammar School; Glasgow University; Jordanhill College of Education. National Service, 2nd Lt., Royal Artillery, 1955-57; Teacher of Mathematics and Science, Dunoon Grammar School, 1957-61; Principal Teacher of Mathematics, Bankhead Academy, Bucksburn, 1961-73. Publication: Mathematics for General Education (Chairman of Joint Authors). Recreations: bridge; bowling; sailing. Address: (h.) Torfness, James Street, Lossiemouth, Moray, IV31 6QZ; T.-0343 812544.

Boddy, Francis Andrew, MB, ChB, FRCPEdin, FFPHM, DPH. Director, Public Health Research Unit (formerly Social Paediatric and Obstetric Research Unit), Glasgow University, since 1978; b. 1.3.35, York; m., Adele Wirszubska; 2 d. Educ. Prince Henry's Grammar School, Otley; Edinburgh University. Research Associate, New York City Department of Health; Senior Lecturer, Department of Community Medicine, Glasgow University. Honorary Secretary, Society for Social Medicine, 1982-87; Convener, Scottish Affairs Committee, Faculty of Public Health Medicine, since 1991. Publications on socio-medical and public health topics. Recreations: fishing; photography. Address: (b.) 1 Lilybank Gardens, Glasgow, G12; T.-041-339 3118.

Boe, Norman W., LLB (Hons). Deputy Solicitor to Secretary of State for Scotland, since 1987; b. 30.8.43, Glasgow; m., Margaret; 1 s.; 1 d. Educ. George Heriot's School, Edinburgh; Edinburgh University. Legal apprenticeship, Lindsays WS, 1965-67; Legal Assistant, Menzies & White, WS, 1967-70; Office of Solicitor, Scottish Office: Legal Assistant, 1970, Senior Legal Assistant, Divisional Solicitor. Recreations: golf; dog-walking; holidaying. Address: (b.) New St. Andrew's House, Edinburgh; T.-031-244 4884.

Bogie, David Wilson, MA, LLB, FSAScot. Sheriff of Grampian, Highland and Islands at Aberdeen and Stonehaven, since 1985; b. 17.7.46, Dundee. Educ. George Watson's College; Grenoble University; Edinburgh University; Balliol College, Oxford. Admitted Member, Faculty of Advocates, 1972; Temporary Sheriff, 1981. Recreations: architectural history; heraldry. Address: (b.) Sheriff's Chambers, Aberdeen; T.-0224 572780.

Bold, Alan. Writer; b. 20.4.43, Edinburgh; m., Alice Howell; 1 d. Educ. Broughton Secondary School; Edinburgh University. Full-time writer and visual artist since 1966; has published numerous books of poetry including: To Find the New; The State of the Nation; a selection in Penguin Modern Poets 15; In This Corner: Selected Poems 1963-83; collaborated on A Celtic Quintet, Haven and Homage to MacDiarmid; Editor, numerous anthologies, including: The Penguin Book of Socialist Verse; The Martial Muse; Cambridge Book of English Verse 1939-75; Making Love; The Bawdy Beautiful; Mounts of Venus; Drink To Me Only; The Poetry of Motion; books of criticism including: Thom Gunn & Ted Hughes; George Mackay Brown; The Ballad; Modern Scottish Literature; MacDiarmid: The Terrible Crystal; Muriel Spark; MacDiarmid: A Critical Biography (McVitie's Prize for Scottish Writer of the Year, 1989); Scotland: A Literary Guide; A Burns Companion; Editor: The Thistle Rises: a MacDiarmid Miscellany; The Letters of Hugh MacDiarmid; author of novel, East Is West; has exhibited Illuminated Poems in a variety of venues; regular reviewer with Glasgow Herald and contributor to Sunday Times. Recreations: walking; playing alto saxophone; watching films; gardening. Address: (h.) Balbirnie Burns East Cottage, near Markinch, Glenrothes, Fife, KY7 6NE; T.-0592 757216.

Bolton, Lyndon, Managing Director: Alliance Trust PLC, Dundee, Second Alliance Trust PLC; b. 24.1.37, London; m., Rosemary Jane Toler Mordaunt; 2 s. Educ. Wellington College; Royal Military Academy, Sandhurst. National Service, Royal Artillery, 1955-57; Deloitte Plender Griffiths & Co., London, 1957-63; Alliance Trust, Dundee, since 1964; Trustee, Trustee Savings Bank, 1963-83; Board Member, TSB Group, 1979-83; Director, TSB Group, since 1983; Director, General Accident Fire and Life Assurance Corporation PLC, since 1982. Governor, Dundee College of Education, 1980-85; Member of Court, Dundee University, since 1985. Recreations: sailing; golf; fishing; painting. Address: (h.) Arrat's Mill, Brechin, Angus, DD9 7PR; T.-Bridge of Dun 220.

Bomont, Robert George, BSc (Econ), IPFA, JP. University Secretary, Stirling University, since 1973; b. 6.5.35, Preston; m., Marian; 1 s.; 2 d. Educ. Preston Grammar School; London University. Trainee and qualified accountant, Lancashire County Council, 1951-64; Assistant Finance Officer, Lancaster University, 1964-66; Accountant, then Accountant and Deputy Secretary, Stirling University, 1966-73. General Commissioner of Income Tax, since 1977; Chairman, Executive Committee, Strathcarron Hospice. Recreations: golf; gardening; DIY. Address: (h.) Wester Ardoch, Feddal Road, Braco, by Dunblane, Perthshire.

Bonallack, Michael Francis, OBE. Secretary, Royal and Ancient Golf Club of St. Andrews, since 1983; b. 31.12.34.

Bond, Professor Michael R., MD, PhD, FRCSEdin, FRCPsych, FRCPSGlas, DPM. Professor of Psychological Medicine, Glasgow University, since 1973; b. 15.4.36, Balderton, Nottinghamshire; m., Jane; 1 s.; 1 d. Educ. Magnus Grammar School, Newark; Sheffield University. Vice-Principal, Glasgow University; Chairman, Medical Sub-Committee, Universities Funding Council; Member, SHHD Chief Scientist Committee; Councillor, International Association for the Study of Pain. Recreations: reading;

music; painting. Address: (b.) 6 Whittinghame Gardens, Great Western Road, Glasgow; T.-041-334 9826.

Bone, (James) Drummond, MA. Dean, Faculty of Arts, Glasgow University, since 1992; b. 11.7.47, Ayr; m., Vivian. Educ. Ayr Academy; Glasgow University; Balliol College, Oxford. Lecturer in English and Comparative Literary Studies, Warwick University; Lecturer and Senior Lecturer, English Literature, Glasgow University. Academic Editor and Advisory Editor, The Byron Journal. Recreations: music; skiing. Address: (h.) The Old Manse, Bow of Fife, Cupar.

Bone, Thomas R., CBE, MA, MEd, PhD, FCCEA. Principal, Jordanhill College, since 1971; Chairman, General Teaching Council for Scotland, since 1991; b. 2.1.35, Port Glasgow; m., Elizabeth Stewart; 1 s.; 1 d. Educ. Port Glasgow High School; Greenock High School; Glasgow University; Jordanhill College. Teacher of English, Paisley Grammar School, 1957-62; Lecturer in Education, Jordanhill College, 1962-63; Lecturer in Education, Glasgow University, 1963-67; Head of Education Department, Jordanhill College, 1967-71. Member, Dunning Committee, 1975-77; Chairman, Educational Advisory Council, IBA, 1985-88; Vice-Chairman: Scottish Examination Board, 1977-84; Scottish Tertiary Education Advisory Council, 1984-87; Chairman: Scottish Council for Educational Technology, 1981-87; Standing Conference on Studies in Education, 1982-84; Council for National Academic Awards Board for Organisation and Management, 1983-87; Chairman, Council for National Academic Awards Committee for Teacher Education, 1987-89; Chairman, General Teaching Council for Scotland, 1990-91. Publication: School Inspection in Scotland, 1968. Recreation: golf. Address: (b.) Jordanhill College of Education, Southbrae Drive, Glasgow, G13 1PP; T.-041-950 3200.

Bonnar, Anne Elizabeth, MA. Director, Bonnar Keenlyside; Arts Management Consultant; Chair, Federation of Scottish Theatres, since 1991; b. 9.10.55, St. Andrews; m., Fernley Thompson; 1 s.; 2 d. Educ. Dumbarton Academy; Glasgow University; City University, London; Jordanhill College of Education. Theatre Manager, Young Vic Theatre, London, 1980; Director, Circuit, 1982, 1983; Press and Publicity, Mayfest, 1984, 1985; Publicity Officer, Citizens' Theatre, Glasgow, 1981-85; Arts Public Relations Consultant, 1985-86; General Manager, Traverse Theatre, 1986-91. Address: (h.) The Grange, Burntisland, Fife KY3 0AA; T.-0592 874478.

Bonnar, Desmond Michael, PhD, MBA, DipTP. Chief Executive, Lothian and Edinburgh Enterprise Ltd, since 1991; b. 26.7.47, Wishaw; m., Maureen; 1 s.; 1 d. Educ. Reading University; Glasgow University; Glasgow School of Art. Scottish Development Agency: Regional Director, Edinburgh/Lothians, Head, Service Industry Group, Head, Special Projects Division, Project Executive, Glasgow Eastern Area Renewal Project. Recreations: skiing; windsurfing. Address: (b.) Apex House, 99 Haymarket Terrace, Edinburgh, EH12 5HD; T.-031-313 4000.

Bonner, Geoff, BSc, MRTPI, MBIM. Chief Executive, Stirling District Council, since 1990; b. 13.1.54, Luton. Educ. Luton Grammar School; Luton VI Form College; University of Aston in Birmingham; City of Birmingham Polytechnic. Planning Assistant, Luton Borough Council, 1975-79; Principal Planning Assistant, West Midlands County Council, 1979-85; Assistant Executive, West Midlands County Council, 1985-86; Assistant Chief Executive, Highland Regional Council, 1986-90. Recreation: dabbling. Address: (b.) Municipal Buildings, Corn Exchange Road, Stirling; T.-0786 79000.

Bonomy, John, MA, LLB. Chief Executive and Director of Administration, Motherwell District Council, since 1983; b. 25.4.38, Motherwell; m., Isabella Margaret; 3 s. Educ. Dalziel High School, Motherwell; Glasgow University. Depute Town Clerk: Arbroath, 1966; Motherwell and Wishaw, 1966-74; Director of Administration, Motherwell, 1974-83. Recreations: golf; reading. Address: (b.) Civic Centre, Motherwell; T.-Motherwell 66166.

Borland, Marjorie Kirsteen, DA, RIBA, ARIAS, SpDip, FRTPI. Planning Consultant; Commissioner, Royal Fine Art Commission for Scotland, since 1986; b. 13.1.25, Glasgow; m., John Charles Holmes, MC; 1 s.; 1 d. Educ. Westbourne School for Girls; Glasgow School of Architecture; School of Planning, London. Planner, London CC; Partner, Jack Holmes & Partners, Architects; Principal, The Jack Holmes Planning Group; Planning Consultant. Past Convener: RIAS Environment Committee, GIA Environment Committee. Recreations: rough gardening; listening to music. Address: (h.) Drumhead, Cardross, Dunbartonshire; T.-038 984 1217.

Borley, Lester. Director, National Trust for Scotland, since 1983; b. 7.4.31.

Borthwick, Professor Edward Kerr, MA (Aberdeen), MA, PhD (Cantab). Professor of Greek, Edinburgh University, 1980-89; b. 9.6.25, Aberdeen; m., Betty Jean Orton; 2 s.; 1 d. Educ. Aberdeen Grammar School; Aberdeen University; Christ's College, Cambridge. Croom Robertson Fellow, Aberdeen University, 1948-51; Lecturer in Classics, Leeds University, 1951-55; Edinburgh University: Lecturer in Greek, 1955-67, Senior Lecturer, 1967-70, Reader, 1970-80. Recreations: music; tennis; golf. Address: (h.) 9 Corrennie Drive, Edinburgh, EH10 6EQ; T.-031-447 2369.

Borthwick of that Ilk, Lord (John Henry Stuart Borthwick), TD (1943), DL, JP, NN, OL, GCLJ. 23rd Lord Borthwick; Baron of Heriotmuir, Borthwick and Locherwart; Chairman: Heriotmuir Properties Ltd., since 1965; Heriotmuir Exporters Ltd., since 1972; Director, Ronald Morrison & Co. Ltd., since 1972; b. 13.9.05, Borthwick; m., Margaret Frances Cormack (deceased); 2 s. Educ. Fettes College, Edinburgh; King's College, Newcastle-upon-Tyne. Diploma in Agriculture. Formerly RATA, re-employed 1939; served NW Europe, Allied Military Government Staff (Junior Staff College, SO 2), 1944; CCG (CO 1, Lt.-Col.), 1946; Department of Agriculture for Scotland, 1948-50; farming own farms, 1950-71; National Farmers Union of Scotland: Midlothian Branch Committee, 1963; Mid and West Lothian Area Committee, 1967-73 (President, 1970-72); Council Member, 1968-72; Member: Lothians Area Committee, NFU Mutual Insurance Society, 1969-85; Chairman, Monitoring Committee, Scottish Tartans, 1976; Scottish Southern Regional Committee, Wool Marketing Board, 1966-85; Chairman, Area Committee, South of Scotland Electricity Board Consultative Council, 1972-76; Member, Midlothian County Council, 1937-50; Member: Local Appeal Tribunal (Edinburgh and the Lothians), 1963-75; Midlothian Valuation Appeal Committee, 1966; Member: Standing Council of Scottish Chiefs; The Committee of the Baronage of Scotland; Member Corresponding, Istituto Italiano di Genealogie e Araldica, Rome and Madrid, 1964; Honorary Member: Council of Scottish Clans Association, USA, 1975; Royal Military Institute of Canada, 1976; Kt of Justice and Honour, GCLJ (Grand Croix, 1975); CL (Commander of the Rose of Lippe), 1971; NN, 1982. Recreations: shooting; travel; history. Address: Crookston, Heriot, Midlothian, EH38 5YS; T.-Heriot 232.

Borthwick, Kenneth White, CBE, DL, JP; b. 4.11.15, Edinburgh; m., Irene Margaret; 2 s.; 1 d. Educ. George Heriot's School, Edinburgh. War Service, RAF; Lord Provost and Lord Lieutenant, City of Edinburgh, 1977-80; Chairman,

1986 Commonwealth Games Organizing Committee; Dean of Consular Corps of Edinburgh and Leith, since 1991; Hon. Consul, Republic of Malawi. Recreations: golf; gardening; painting. Address: (h.) 17 York Road, Edinburgh, EH5 3EJ; T.-031-552 2519.

Boscawen, James Townshend. Land Management Consultant; b. 8.5.32, London; m., Deirdre E.E. Curtis-Bennett; 2 d. Educ. Sunningdale; Downhouse. Grenadier Guards, 1950-54; forestry management, Bowater Paper Corporation, 1954-64; Member Queen's Bodyguard for Scotland (Royal Company of Archers); Council, Timber Growers Ltd.; Chairman, Mid Scotland Committee, Timber Growers Ltd.; Member, Executive Council, Erskine Hospital. Recreations: shooting; fishing. Address: Boltachan House, Aberfeldy, Perthshire; T.-0887 20496.

Bossy, Rev. Michael J.F., SJ, MA. Jesuit Priest, since 1962; Rector and Parish Priest, St. Aloysius, Glasgow, since 1988; b. 22.11.29, London. Educ. St. Ignatius College, London; Heythrop College; Campion Hall, Oxford. Assistant Teacher, St. Ignatius College, London, 1956-59; St. Francis Xavier's College, Liverpool, 1963-64; Stonyhurst College, Lancashire, 1965-71; Head Teacher, Stonyhurst, 1971-85; Curate, St. Aloysius Church, Glasgow, 1986-88. Recreation: watching games. Address: (b.) 56 Hill Street, Glasgow, G3 6RH; T.-041-332 3039.

Bouchier, Professor Ian Arthur Dennis, CBE, MB, ChB, MD, FRCP, FRCPEdin, FIBiol, FRSE, FRSA. Professor of Medicine, Edinburgh University, since 1986; b. 7.9.32, Cape Town, South Africa; m., Patricia Norma Henshilwood; 2 s. Educ. Rondebosch Boys High School; Cape Town University. Instructor in Medicine, School of Medicine, Boston University, 1964; London University: Senior Lecturer in Medicine, 1965; Reader in Medicine, 1970; Professor of Medicine, Dundee University, 1973-86. Member: Court, Dundee University; Chief Scientist, Scotland; Council, Royal Society, Edinburgh; Medical Research Council; President, World Organization of Gastroenterology; former Dean, Faculty of Medicine and Dentistry, Dundee University; Chairman, Education Committee, British Society of Gastroenterology. Publications: Clinical Skills (2nd edition), 1982; Gastroenterology (3rd edition), 1982; Textbook of Gastroenterology, 1984; Inflammatory Bowel Disease, 1986. Recreations: music; history of whaling; cooking. Address: (b.) Department of Medicine, Royal Infirmary, Edinburgh, EH3 9YW; T.-031-229 2477, Ext. 3176.

Boulton, Professor Geoffrey Stewart, FRS, BSc, PhD, DSc, FRSE, FGS. Regius Professor of Geology and Mineralogy, Edinburgh University, since 1986; b. 28.11.40, Stoke-on-Trent; m., Denise Bryers; 2 d. Educ. Longton High School; Birmingham University. Geological Survey of GB, 1962-64; University of Keele, 1964-65; Birmingham University, 1965-67; Water Supply Department, Kenya, 1968; University of East Anglia, 1968-81; Extraordinary Professor, University of Amsterdam, 1981-86. President, Quaternay Research Association, since 1991; President, British Glaciological Society, 1989-91; President, Geological Society of Edinburgh, since 1991; Member, Nature Conservancy Council for Scotland Science Board, 1991-92; Governor, Strathallan School, since 1990; Kirk Bryan Award of the Geological Society of America, 1976. Recreations: violin; mountaineering. Address: (h.) 19 Lygon Road, Edinburgh, EH16 5QD; T.-031-667 2531.

Bovey, Keith S., BL. Solicitor, since 1951; President, Scottish CND; b. 31.7.27, Renfrew; m., Helen Cameron; 1 s.; 1 d. Educ. Paisley Grammar School; Glasgow University. Army, 1944-48. Publication: Misuse of Drugs, A Handbook for Lawyers. Address: (b.) 126 Morningside Road, Edinburgh EH10 4DT; T.-031-452 8822.

Bowen, Edward Farquharson, TD, LLB. Advocate; b. 1.5.45, Edinburgh; m., Patricia Margaret Brown; 2 s.; 2 d. Educ. Melville College, Edinburgh; Edinburgh University. Admitted Solicitor, 1968; Advocate, 1970; Standing Junior Counsel, Scottish Education Department, 1976; Advocate Depute, 1979-83; Sheriff of Tayside, Central and Fife, at Dundee, 1983-90; Partner, Thorntons WS, 1990-91; Governor, Dundee Institute of Technology, 1987-90. Served RAOC TA/TAVR, 1964-80. Recreation: golf. Address: (h.) Westgate, 12 Glamis Drive, Dundee.

Bowen, Stanley, CBE (1972). Honorary Sheriff, Lothian and Borders, since 1975; b. 4.8.10, Carnoustie; m., Mary Shepherd Greig; 2 s.; 1 d. Educ. Barry School, Angus; Grove Academy, Dundee; University College, Dundee. Qualified as Solicitor in Scotland, 1932; entered Procurator Fiscal service, 1933; Depute Procurator Fiscal, Hamilton, 1937; Interim Procurator Fiscal, Airdrie, 1938; Crown Office: Legal Assistant, 1941, Principal Assistant, 1945, Crown Agent for Scotland, 1967-74; since 1974, has served on a number of bodies connected with criminal procedure, police administration, forensic pathology services, the law of human transplants and the care and resettlement of offenders; Chairman, Corstorphine Trust. Recreations: golf; gardening. Address: (h.) Achray, 20 Dovecot Road, Corstorphine, Edinburgh, EH12 7LE; T.-031-334 4096.

Bowes, Professor Donald Ralph, MSc, PhD, DSc, DIC, FRSE, FGS. Professor, Department of Geology, Glasgow University, since 1974; b. 9.9.26, Australia; m., Mary Morris; 2 s.; 1 d. Educ. Unley High School; Adelaide University; Imperial College, London. Lecturer in Geology, University of Adelaide, University College of Swansea; Senior Lecturer, Reader, Professor in Geology, Glasgow University. 1851 Exhibitioner, Tate Medallist; former Vice President, Royal Society of Edinburgh. Publications: 200 scientific papers; two books. Recreations: gardening; music; opera. Address: (b.) Department of Geology and Applied Geology, Glasgow University, Glasgow, G12 8QQ; T.-041-339 8855.

Bowie, Graham Maitland, MA, LLB. Chief Executive, Lothian Regional Council, since 1986 (Director of Planning, 1975-86); b. 11.11.31, Alloa; m., Jennifer; 1 s.; 2 d. Educ. Alloa Academy; St. Andrews University; Glasgow University. Glasgow Chamber of Commerce, 1957-59; Ford Motor Co., 1959-64; Edinburgh Corporation Education Department, 1964-69; Inner London Education Authority, 1969-75. Recreations: music; golf; walking. Address: (b.) Lothian Regional Council, Regional Headquarters, George IV Bridge, Edinburgh, EH1 1UQ; T.-031-469 3001.

Bowling, Dudley James Francis, DSc, BSc, PhD, CBiol, MIBiol. Reader in Plant Science, Aberdeen University, since 1981; b. 20.5.37, Kingston upon Hull; m., Sheila Mary Daun. Educ. Hull Grammar School; Nottingham University; Aberdeen University. Aberdeen University: Assistant in Botany, 1961; Lecturer in Botany, 1963; Senior Lecturer in Botany, 1974; Visiting Scientist, DSIR, Palmerston North, New Zealand, 1976-77. Publication: Uptake of Ions by Plant Roots, 1976. Recreations: gardening; model railways. Address: (b.) Department of Plant and Soil Science, St. Machar Drive, Old Aberdeen, AB9 2UD; T.-Aberdeen 272693.

Bowlt, Kenneth Stuart, BSc, ARICS. Chartered Surveyor; Member, Royal Institution of Chartered Surveyors Scottish Council, since 1990; b. 7.7.52, Nairn; m., Edith Bowman. Educ. Queen Victoria School, Dunblane; Edinburgh University. Voluntary Service Overseas, Zambia, 1975-80; set up Bowlts (chartered surveyors practice), 1991. Member, Royal Institution of Chartered Surveyors in Scotland Rural Practice Divisional Committee, since 1988; Secretary/Treasurer, West Ross Deer Management Group, since 1991. Recreations: fishing; stalking; five-a-side football; keep fit. Address: (h.) Muirfield, 27 Forteath Avenue, Elgin; T.-0343 549278.

Bowman, Allan John, MA, CQSW, DMS. Director of Social Work, Fife, since 1986; b. 3.1.50, Perth; m., Marilyn Norah Cosgrove; 1 s.; 3 d. Educ. Perth Academy; Edinburgh University; Robert Gordon's Institute of Technology; Anglian Regional Management Centre. Social Worker and Senior Social Worker, Dundee Corporation, then Tayside Region, 1972-78; Senior Social Worker, Depute Area Social Work Organiser and Area Social Work Organiser, Essex County Council, 1978-84; Depute Director and Director of Social Work, Fife Regional Council, 1985. Member, Tayside Education/ Industry Liaison Committee, 1977-78; Chair, Essex BASW, 1982-84; Chair, Tayforth Training Consortium. Recreations: horse racing; guitar; theatre; swimming; cricket; golf. Address: (b.) Social Work Department, Fife House, North Street, Glenrothes, KY7 5LT; T.-0592 754411, Ext. 3883.

Bowman, Bernard Neil, LLB, NP. Senior Partner, Bowman Gray Robertson & Wilkie, Solicitors, Dundee, Forfar and Blairgowrie, since 1984; first Lord President, Court of Deans of Guild of Scotland, 1989; Lord Dean of Guild of Guildry Incorporation of Dundee, 1987-90; President, Scottish Cricket Union, 1989; Secretary, Dundee Institute of Architects, since 1970; Director, High School of Dundee, 1980-90; Chairman, High School of Dundee Scholarship Fund, 1987-90; Clerk, Three United Trades of Dundee and to Mason Trade, Wright Trade and Slater Trade of Dundee, since 1970; Co-opted Member, Law Society of Scotland Committees – Public Relations and Conference, 1982-90, Complaints, 1987-90; Member, Working Party on "Corporate Conveyancing", 1989; Member, School Age Team Sports Enquiry, 1989; b. 11.11.43, Dundee; m., Pamela Margaret Munro Wright; 2 d. Educ. High School of Dundee; Edinburgh University; St. Andrews University. Apprenticeship, Sturrock Morrison & Gilruth, Solicitors, Dundee, 1967-69; admitted Solicitor, 1969; Notary Public, 1970; assumed Partner, Gray Robertson & Wilkie, 1971. Secretary: Dundee Building Trades (Employers) Association, 1970-89; Dundee Construction Industry Group Training Association, since 1970; Tayside Construction Safety Association, 1975-89; Joint Secretary, Local Joint Council for Building Industry, 1970-89, and Local Joint Apprenticeship Committee for the Building Industry, 1970-89; President, Scottish Counties Cricket Board, 1981; Committee Member and National Selector, Scottish Cricket Union, 1974-83; Selector, 1990. Recreations: cricketophile; breeding Highland cattle. Address: (b.) 27 Bank Street, Dundee; T.-0382 222667.

Bowman, Professor William Cameron, BPharm, PhD, DSc, FIBiol, FRSE, FRSA, FRPharmS, HonFFARCS. Head, Department of Physiology and Pharmacology, Strathclyde University, since 1990 and 1966-87; b. 26.4.30, Carlisle; m., Anne Wyllie Stafford; 1 s.; 1 d. Educ. Carlisle Grammar School; London University. RAF (commissioned officer), 1955-57; Lecturer, then Reader in Pharmacology, London University, 1952-66. Dean, School of Pharmaceutical Sciences, Strathclyde University, 1974-77; Vice Principal, Strathclyde University, 1986-90. Member: Nomenclature Committee, BP Commission, 1964-67; Biology Committee, MOD, 1966-75; TCT and SEAR Sub-Committees, CSM, 1972-83; Biomedical Research Committee, SHHD, 1980-85; Chairman, Committee, British Pharmacological Society, 1981-84, Foreign Secretary since 1992; Chairman of Committee, Heads of UK Pharmacology Departments, since 1990. Publications: Textbook of Pharmacology, 1968, 1980; Pharmacology of Neuromuscular Function, 1980, 1990; Dictionary of Pharmacology, 1986; many research articles in scientific journals. Address: Department of Physiology and

Pharmacology, Strathclyde University, Glasgow, G1 1XW; T.-041-552 4400.

Bown, Professor Lalage Jean, OBE, MA (Oxon), DrUniv (Open University), FRSA, FEIS, FRSE. Professor and Director, Department of Adult and Continuing Education, Glasgow University, 1981-92; Hon. Professor, Warwick University, since 1992; b. 1.4.27, Croydon. Educ. Wycombe Abbey School, Buckinghamshire; Cheltenham Ladies' College; Somerville College, Oxford. Resident Tutor: University College of the Gold Coast, 1949-55; Makerere University College, Uganda, 1955-59; successively Tutorial Advisor, Assistant Director, Deputy Director, Extra-Mural Department, Ibadan University, 1960-66 (Associate Professor, 1962-66); Director of Extra-Mural Studies and Professor Ad Personam, University of Zambia, 1966-70; Professor of Adult Education, Ahmadu Bello University, Nigeria, 1971-76; Commonwealth Visiting Professor, Edinburgh University, 1974; successively Professor of Adult Education and Dean of Education, Lagos University, 1977-80. Former Member, Scottish Community Education Council; Member: Board of Trustees, National Museums of Scotland; Board of Governors, Newbattle Abbey College; Council, INSITE Trust; former Board Member, The British Council; former Member, Governing Body, Institute of Development Studies; Member, Commonwealth Standing Committee on Student Mobility and Higher Education Co-operation; Past President, British Comparative and International Education Society; Past President, Development Studies Association; Vice-President, National Union of Townswomen's Guilds; Vice-President, WEA. Publications: 10 academic books. Recreation: travel. Address: (h.) 37 Partickhill Road, Glasgow G11 5BP; T.-041-339 1714.

Bowser of Argaty and the King's Lundies, David Stewart, JP, BA (Agric). Trustee, Scottish Forestry Trust, 1983-89 (Chairman, 1987); Member, Queen's Bodyguard for Scotland (Royal Company of Archers); Chairman, Scottish Council, British Deer Society, since 1988; b. 11.3.26; m.; 1 s.; 4 d. Educ. Harrow; Trinity College, Cambridge. Captain, Scots Guards, 1944-47; Forestry Commissioner, 1974-82; President, Highland Cattle Society, 1970-72; Member, Perth County Council, 1954-61. Address: Auchlyne, Killin, Perthshire.

Boyd, Alan Robb, LLB, BA, NP. Legal Adviser, Irvine Development Corporation, since 1984; b. 30.7.53, Glasgow; m., Frances Helen Donaldson; 2 d. Educ. Irvine Royal Academy; Dundee University. Admitted Solicitor, 1976; Principal Legal Assistant, Shetland Islands Council, 1979-81; Principal Solicitor, Glenrothes Development Corporation, 1981-84. Council Member, Law Society of Scotland, since 1985 (Chairman, Public Service and Commerce Group, 1986-88, Convenor, Law Reform Committee, since 1989). Recreations: golf; music; gardening. Address: (b.) Perceton House, Irvine, Ayrshire, KA11 2AL; T.-0294 214100.

Boyd, Gavin, CBE (1977), MA (Hons), LLB. Consultant, Boyds, Solicitors, since 1978; Director, Scottish Opera Theatre Royal (Chairman, 1973-88); b. 4.8.28; m., Kathleen Elizabeth Skinner; 1 s. Educ. Glasgow Academy; Glasgow University. Partner, Boyds, Solicitors, 1955-77; Director, Stenhouse Holdings p.l.c., 1970-79 (Chairman, 1971-78); Director, Scottish Opera, 1970-88; Director, North Sea Assets plc, 1972- 88 (Deputy Chairman, 1980-88); Director, Paterson Jenks plc, 1972-81; Director, Scottish Television plc, since 1973; Director, Ferranti plc, 1975-88; Director, British Carpets plc, 1977-81; Director, Merchant House of Glasgow, since 1982. Chairman, Court, Strathclyde University, 1983-88; Trustee, Scottish Hospital Endowments Research Trust; Hon. LLD, Strathclyde, 1982, and Fellow, 1991. Recreations: music and the performing arts; yacht cruising; hill-walking. Address: (h.) Tigh Geal, 6 Milton Hill, Dumbarton, G82 2TS.

Boyd, Ian Mair, MSc, CA. Group Finance Director, The Weir Group PLC, since 1981; Director, Glasgow Income Trust plc, since 1990; b. 4.9.44, Ayr; m., Theodora; 2 s.; 1 d. Educ. Ayr Academy; London Business School. The Weir Group PLC: Financial Controller International Division, 1975-78, Group Chief Accountant, 1978-81. Council Member, Institute of Chartered Accountants of Scotland; Chairman, Group of Scottish Finance Directors, since 1990. Recreations: golf; hill-walking; fishing. Address: (b.) Weir Group PLC, Cathcart, Glasgow, G44 4EX; T.-041-637 7111.

Boyd, James Edward, CA. Director and Financial Adviser, Denholm group of companies, since 1968; b. 14.9.28; m., Judy Ann Christey Scott; 2 s.; 2 d. Educ. Kelvinside Academy; The Leys School, Cambridge. Chairman, Ayrshire Metal Products plc, since 1991 (Director, since 1965); Deputy Chairman, Scottish Widows' Fund & Life Assurance Society, since 1988 (Director, since 1981); Director, Shanks & McEwan Group Ltd., since 1983; Governor, British Linen Bank Ltd., since 1986; Director, Bank of Scotland, since 1984; Deputy Chairman, BAA plc, since 1985. President, Institute of Chartered Accountants of Scotland, 1982-83. Recreations: tennis; golf; gardening. Address: (h.) Dunard, Station Rpad, Rhu, G84 8LW; T.-0436 820441.

Boyd, James Ferguson, MD, FRCPEdin, FRCPath, FRCPGlas. Senior Lecturer in Pathology of Infectious Diseases, Glasgow University, since 1961; Honorary Consultant Pathologist, Greater Glasgow Health Board, since 1961; b. 6.5.25, Kilbirnie, Ayrshire; m., Christina M. MacLeod; 2 s.; 2 d. Educ. Hillhead High School, Glasgow; Carrick Academy, Maybole; Glasgow University. Resident, Hairmyres Hospital, East Kilbride, and Royal Alexandra Infirmary, Paisley, 1948-49; Royal Army Medical Corps, 1949-51; Resident, Western Infirmary, Glasgow, 1951-52; trainee posts in pathology, Western Infirmary, Glasgow, and Area Laboratory, Stirling Royal Infirmary, 1952-57; Lecturer in Pathology, Glasgow University, 1957-61, with secondment to Royal Maternity Hospital and Royal Hospital for Sick Children, Glasgow; Senior Lecturer, Ruchill Hospital, Western Infirmary, Gartnavel General Hospital and Knightswood Hospital, Glasgow, since 1961. Recreations: golf; walking. Address: (h.) 44 Woodend Drive, Jordanhill, Glasgow, G13 1TQ; T.-041-959 2708.

Boyd, John Morton, CBE, BSc, PhD, DSc, FIBiol, CBiol, FRSE, FRSA, HonFRSGS, HonFRZSS. Consultant to Scottish Hydro-Electric plc, since 1990; Consultant to National Trust for Scotland, since 1985; b. 31.1.25, Darvel; m., Winifred Isobel Rome; 4 s. Educ. Darvel School; Kilmarnock Academy; Glasgow University. War service, 1943-47 (Flt. Lt., RAF). Nature Conservancy Council: Regional Officer, 1957-68, Assistant Director, 1969-70, Director (Scotland), 1971-85; Nuffield Travel Fellow, Mid-East and East Africa, 1964-65; Leader, British Jordan Expedition, 1966; Member, Royal Society Aldabra Expedition, 1967; Member, Council, Royal Zoological Society of Scotland, 1963-69, 1980-89, since 1990; Member, BBC Scotland Agricultural Advisory Committee, 1973-76; Member, Council, National Trust for Scotland, 1971-85; Member, Council, Royal Society of Edinburgh, 1978-81; Member, Seals Advisory Committee, NERC, 1973-79; Member, Consultative Panel on Conservation of Phoenix and Line Islands (Central Pacific), 1981-90; Co-Chairman, Area VI Anglo-Soviet Environmental Protection Agreement, 1977-85; Member, Council, Scottish Wildlife Trust, 1985-91; Vice-President, Scottish Conservation Projects Trust, since 1985; Member, Commission on Ecology, IUCN, since 1976; Member, CCS Panel on Popular Mountain Areas, 1989;

General Editor (Island Biology), Edinburgh University Press, since 1985; Consultant Editor, Discover Scotland, 1989-90; Lecturer, Swan (Hellenic) Ltd. and Serenissima Travel Ltd.; Neill Prize, Royal Society of Edinburgh, 1985. Publications: St. Kilda Summer (Co-author), 1960; Mosaic of Islands, 1963; Highlands and Islands (Co-author), 1964; Travels in the Middle-East and East Africa, 1966; Island Survivors (Co-author), 1974; The Natural Environment of the Hebrides (Co-editor), 1979 and 1983; Fraser Darling's Islands, 1986; The Hebrides – a natural history (Co-author), 1990. Recreations: hill-walking; travel; painting; photography. Address: (h.) 57 Hailes Gardens, Edinburgh, EH13 OJH; T.-031-441 3220; Balephuil, Tiree, Argyll; T.-Scarinish 521.

Boyd, Michael, MA (Hons). Artistic Director, Tron Theatre, Glasgow, since 1984; b. 6.7.55, Belfast; m., Marcella Evaristi; 1 s.; 1 d. Educ. Latymer Upper School, London; Daniel Stewart's College, Edinburgh; Edinburgh University. Director, Malaya Bronnaya Theatre, Moscow; Belgrade Theatre, Coventry; Crucible Theatre, Sheffield; freelance work, Lyric Hammersmith, Haymarket Leicester, Royal Court, Traverse Edinburgh, Cambridge Theatre Co., Harbourfront, Toronto. Recreations: reading; music; travel. Address. (b.) Tron Theatre, Trongate, Glasgow; T.-041-552 3748.

Boyd, William Dalziel, MB, ChB, FRCPEdin, FRCPsych, DPM. Chairman, Age Concern Scotland; Honorary Treasurer, Royal College of Psychiatrists; b. 9.11.30, Cupar, Fife; m., Betty Ledingham Gordon; 3 s.; 1 d. Educ. Trinity College, Glenalmond; Edinburgh University. National Service, Royal Army Medical Corps; training posts at Rosslynlee Hospital, Midlothian; Edinburgh Royal Infirmary; Royal Edinburgh Hospital; Consultant Psychiatrist: Herdmanflat Hospital, Haddington; Royal Edinburgh Hospital; Physician Superintendent, Royal Edinburgh Hospital; Consultant Psychiatrist, Lothian Health Board (retired); former Vice-Chairman and Medical Commissioner, Mental Welfare Commission for Scotland. Recreation: improving old houses and old gardens. Address: (h.) Kirkbrae House, 10 Randolph Cliff, Edinburgh, EH3 7UA; T.-031-225 3289.

Boyes, John, MA (Hons). HM Inspector of Schools, since 1974; b. 20.5.43, Greenock; m., Margaret Anne Peat; 1 s.; 1 d. Educ. Greenock High School; Glasgow University. Taught French and German, Alloa Academy and Denny High School, 1967-74. Recreation: puns and spoonerisms. Address: (b.) Scottish Education Department, Corunna House, 29 Cadogan Street, Glasgow; T.-041-204 1220.

Boyle, Rt. Rev. Mgr. Hugh Noonan, PhL, STL. Administrator, Metropolitan Cathedral Church of St. Andrew, Glasgow, since 1983 (Canon, Chapter of Metropolitan Cathedral Church, since 1984); Prelate of Honour, since 1987; Archivist, Archdiocese of Glasgow, since 1973; b. 14.1.35, Glasgow. Educ. St. Aloysius' College, Glasgow; Glasgow University; Pontifical Scots College and Pontifical Gregorian University, Rome, 1956-63. National Service, RAF, 1954-56; ordained priest, Rome, 1962; Assistant Priest: St. Philomena's, Glasgow, 1963-66, St. Eunan's, Clydebank, 1966-76; Archdiocese of Glasgow: Assistant Archivist, 1967-73; Chancellor, 1976-83. Editor, Catholic Directory for Scotland and Western Catholic Calendar, since issues of 1975; Member: Scottish Catholic Communications Commission, 1979-87; Scottish Catholic Heritage Commission, since 1981; Patron, Hutchesons' Hospital, since 1983. Recreations: music (listening); walking. Address: St. Andrew's Cathedral House, 90 Dunlop Street, Glasgow, G1 4ER; T.-041-221 3096.

Boyle, Iain Thomson, BSc (Hons), MB, ChB, FRCP, FRCP (London and Glasgow), FSA (Scot). Reader in Medicine, Glasgow University and Glasgow Royal Infirmary, since

1984; Medical Advisor, Strathclyde University, since 1991; Chairman, Board of Management, Scottish Medical Journal, since 1987; Hon. Treasurer, Bone and Tooth Society, since 1989; b. 7.10.35, Glasgow; m., Elizabeth Johnston Carmichael; 1 s.; 2 d. Educ. Paisley Grammar School; Glasgow University. Lecturer in Medicine, Glasgow University and Glasgow Royal Infirmary, 1964-70; Hartenstein Research Fellow, Wisconsin University, 1970-72; Senior Lecturer in Medicine, Glasgow University and Glasgow Royal Infirmary, 1973-84. Editor, Scottish Medical Journal, 1978-83; Co-Editor, Bone, since 1983; Council Member, Royal College of Physicians and Surgeons, 1984-88; Secretary: Scottish Society for Experimental Medicine, 1984-88; Scottish Society of Physicians, 1984-88; President, Caledonian Philatelic Society, 1983-84. Fletcher Prize, Royal College of Physicians and Surgeons of Glasgow, 1973. Recreations: philately; Scottish social history; angling; gardening; golf. Address: (h.) 7 Lochbrae Drive, High Burnside, Rutherglen, Glasgow, G73 5QL.

Boyle, John Stirling, MA, DPA. Director, Corporate Affairs (Scotland), British Railways Board, since 1992; b. 17.9.39, Paisley; m., Helen Dickson; 2 s.; 1 d. Educ. Camphill School, Paisley; Glasgow University. School Teacher, 1960-61; Reporter, Sunday Post, 1961-62; Technical Writer, Harland Engineering Company, 1962-64; Health Education Officer, Stirling County, 1964-66; Public Relations Officer, Heriot-Watt University, 1966-73; Director, External Relations, Scottish Council (Development and Industry), 1973-83; Director of Public Affairs (Scotland), British Rail, 1983-92. Recreations: motor cycling; music; Munros. Address (b.) 23 Chester Street, Edinburgh.

Bradley, Rev. Dr. Ian Campbell, MA, BD, DPhil. Writer and Broadcaster; Head of Religious Broadcasting, BBC Scotland, 1990-91; b. 28.5.50, Berkhamsted; m., Lucy Patricia; 1 s.; 1 d. Educ. Tonbridge School, Kent; New College, Oxford; St. Andrews University. Research Fellow, New College, Oxford, 1971-75; Staff Journalist, The Times, 1976-82; ordained into Church of Scotland, 1990. Publications: The Call to Seriousness, 1974; William Morris and his World, 1975; The Optimists, 1976; The Penguin Annotated Gilbert & Sullivan, 1980; The Strange Rebirth of Liberal Britain, 1982; Enlightened Entrepreneurs, 1986; The Penguin Book of Hymns, 1989; God is Green, 1990; O Love That Wilt Not Let Me Go, 1990; Marching to the Promised Land, 1992. Recreations: music; walking; family; spas. Address: (h.) 7 Strathkinness High Road, St. Andrews KY16 9UA; T.-0334 75389.

Brady, Paul A., BSc (Hons), PhD. Head, Higher Education Division, Scottish Education Department; b. 28.7.49, Glasgow; 2 s.; 1 d. Educ. St. Mungo's Academy, Glasgow. Joined Scottish Office, 1974; posts in Industry, Police, Education and Energy areas, 1974-88; headed team advising on electricity privatisation, 1988-90; Private Secretary to Parliamentary Under Secretary of State, Scottish Office, 1977-79. Recreations: walking; music; family. Address: (b.) Scottish Education Department, 43 Jeffrey Street, Edinburgh; T.-031-244 5402.

Brain, Rev. Isobel Jarvie, MA. Minister, Ballantrae Parish Church, since 1987; Member, Probationers and Transference of Ministers Committee, since 1990; b. 4.7.30, Glasgow; m., Rev. E.J. Brain; 1 d. Educ. Hillhead High School; Glasgow University; Jordanhill College. Teacher in Glasgow, 1952-62; Head, English Department, then Deputy and Head Teacher in Liverpool secondary schools, 1963-85; Attached Assistant Minister, Jordanhill Parish Church, 1985-86. First prizewinner (Mezzo Soprano Class), International Eisteddfod, Llangollen, 1949; Governor, Liverpool Central College of Further Education, 1976-85. Recreations: music; theatre;

reading biographies. Address: (h.) The Manse, Ballantrae, Girvan, KA26 0NH; T.-046583 252.

Braithwaite, Robert Barclay, BSc, CEng, FICE, MASCE. General Manager, Aberdeen Harbour Board, since 1990 (Assistant, then Deputy General Manager and Harbour Engineer, 1986-89); b. 17.2.48, Glasgow; m., Christine Isobel Ross; 2 s. Educ. Hutchesons' Boys' Grammar School; Strathclyde University. Graduate/Assistant Engineer, Rendel Palmer & Tritton, Consulting Civil Engineers, London, 1969-74; Deputy Harbour Engineer, 1974-75, Harbour Engineer, 1976-86, Aberdeen Harbour Board. Chairman, Aberdeen Maritime Museum Appeal; Council Member, Aberdeen Chamber of Commerce; Director, British Ports Federation. Recreations: hill-walking; badminton; other sports; reading. Address: (b.) Harbour Office, 16 Regent Quay, Aberdeen, AB9 1SS; T.-0224 592571.

Brand, Professor Charles Peter, MA, PhD. Professor of Italian, Edinburgh University, 1966-88 (Vice-Principal, 1984-88); b. 7.2.23, Cambridge; m., Gunvor Hellgren; 1 s.; 3 d. Educ. Cambridgeshire High School; Trinity Hall, Cambridge. Lecturer in Italian, Cambridge University, 1952-66; Fellow and Tutor, Trinity Hall, Cambridge, 1958-66. Editor, Modern Language Review, 1970-76. Holder, Commendatore della Repubblica Italiana. Publications: Italy and the English Romantics, 1957; T. Tasso, 1965; L. Ariosto, 1974; Writers of Italy (Editor). Recreations: sport; gardening. Address: (h.) 21 Succoth Park, Edinburgh, EH12 6BX; T.-031-337 1980.

Brand, David Allan, LLB (Hons), NP. Solicitor; Partner, Thorntons WS, Dundee; b. 4.3.50, Dundee; 1 d. Educ. Grove Academy, Broughty Ferry; Dundee University. Member, Council, Law Society of Scotland; Member, Council, Faculty of Procurators and Solicitors in Dundee; Reporter to Scottish Legal Aid Board; Member, Council, NHBC Scotland; Past Chairman: Solicitors Property Centres Group Scotland, Tayside Solicitors Property Centre, Social Security Tribunals. Recreations: all types of music; amateur operatics. Address: (b.) Whitehall Chambers, 11 Whitehall Street, Dundee, DD1 4AE; T.-0382 29111.

Brand, Hon. Lord (David William Robert Brand), QC (Scot). Senator of the College of Justice in Scotland, 1972-89; b. 21.10.23.

Brand, Janet Mary Valentine, BA (Hons), DipTP, MRTPI. Senior Lecturer, Strathclyde University, since 1973 (Member of Senate, 1984-91; Member of Court, 1989-91; Convener, Programme of Opportunities for Women Committee, since 1990); b. 19.4.44, Bath; 2 d. Educ. County High School for Girls, Brentwood; Exeter University; Mid Essex Technical College. Local authority appointments in Departments of Planning, Essex County Council, London Borough of Barking and City of London, 1965-70; Senior Lecturer, Department of Planning, South Bank Polytechnic, 1970-73. Convener, Education Committee, Scottish Branch, RTPI, 1983-88); Moderator and Reviser, SCOTVEC, 1978-88. Recreations: the environment; gardening; family pursuits; travelling. Address: (b.) Centre for Planning, Strathclyde University, 50 Richmond Street, Glasgow; T.-041-552 4400, Ext. 3905/6.

Brand, John Arthur. Senior Lecturer in Government, formerly Politics, Strathclyde University; b. 4.8.34, Aberdeen; 1 d. Educ. Aberdeen Grammar School; Aberdeen University; London School of Economics. Assistant in Politics, Glasgow University, 1959-61; Lecturer in Politics, Reading University, 1961-63; Lecturer in the Politics of Education, London University, 1963-64; joined Strathclyde University as Lecturer in Politics, 1964. Chairman: Campaign for a Scottish Assembly, 1979-83; Glasgow Community Relations Committee, 1968-71. Recreations: skiing; tennis; music.

Address: (h.) 17 Kew Terrace, Glasgow, G12 OTE; T.-041-339 1675.

Brannan, Micheline H., MA. Head of Parole and Life Sentence Prisoner Review Division, Scottish Office Home and Health Department, since 1991; b. 23.10.54, Glasgow; m., Michael N. Brannan; 2 s. Educ. Hutchesons' Grammar School; St. Hilda's College, Oxford. Scottish Office: joined as administrative trainee, 1976, promoted to Principal, 1982, Industry Department for Scotland, 1982-84, Scottish Education Department, 1985-88, Home and Health Department Criminal Justice Division, 1989-91. Secretary, Edinburgh Jewish Literary Society. Recreations: Scottish country dancing; folk dancing; Jewish cultural activities. Address: (b.) Calton House, Redheughs Rigg, Edinburgh, EH12 9HW; T.-031-244 8526.

Branscombe, Professor Peter John, MA (Oxon), PhD. Professor of Austrian Studies, St. Andrews University, since 1979; b. 7.12.29, Sittingbourne, Kent; m., Marina Riley; 2 s.; 1 d. Educ. Dulwich College; Worcester College, Oxford; Bedford College, London. Joined St. Andrews University, 1959, as Lecturer, then Senior Lecturer, in German. Governor, Royal Scottish Academy of Music and Drama, 1967-73; served on Awarding Panel for Schlegel-Tieck Prize, 1971-79 (Convener, 1974-77); Member: Music Committee, Scottish Arts Council, 1973-80; Scottish Arts Council, 1976-79; Chairman, SAC Working Party investigating the record industry in Scotland, 1976-77; Chairman, Conference of University Teachers of German in Scotland, 1983-85. Publications: Heine: Selected Verse, 1967 (2nd edition, 1986); Austrian Life and Literature 1780-1938: eight essays (Editor), 1978; Schubert Studies (Editor), 1982; Mozart: Die Zauberflote, 1991. Recreations: natural history; walking; music; theatre. Address: (b.) Department of German, The University, St. Andrews, Fife, KY16 9PH; T.-St. Andrews 76161, Ext. 331.

Brant, Douglas, CIPFA, FRVA, MBIM. Director of Finance, Strathkelvin District Council, since 1974; b. 27.6.42, Motherwell; m., Valerie Margaret; 1 s.; 1 d. Educ. Dalziel High School, Motherwell; Scottish College of Commerce. Trainee and Accountancy Assistant, Burgh of Motherwell and Wishaw, 1959-64; Burgh of Bishopbriggs: Assistant and Depute Town Chamberlain, 1964-68, Town Chamberlain, 1968-75. Past Chairman, Scottish Branch, CIPFA. Recreations: golf; curling. Address: (b.) PO Box 4, Tom Johnston House, Civic Way, Kirkintilloch, G66 4TJ.

Bray, Jeremy William, PhD. MP (Labour), Motherwell South, since 1983; Opposition Spokesman on Science and Technology, since 1983; b. 29.6.30, Hong Kong; m., Elizabeth Trowell; 4 d. Educ. Aberystwyth Grammar School; Kingswood School, Bath; Jesus College, Cambridge; Harvard University. Technical Officer, Wilton works, ICI, 1956-62; MP, Middlesbrough West, 1962-70; Member, Select Committee on Nationalised Industries, 1962-64; Chairman, Labour Science and Technology Group, 1964-66; Member, Economic Affairs Estimates Sub-Committee, 1964-66; Parliamentary Secretary, Ministry of Power, 1966-67; Joint Parliamentary Secretary, Ministry of Technology, 1967-69; Director, Mullard Ltd., 1970-73; Chairman, Fabian Society, 1971-72; Co-Director, Programme of Research into Econometric Methods, Imperial College, 1971-74; Consultant, Battelle Research Centre, Geneva, 1973; Senior Research Fellow, Strathclyde University, 1974, and Visiting Professor, 1974-79; Deputy Chairman, Christian Aid, 1972-83; MP, Motherwell and Wishaw, 1979-83; Member, Treasury and Civil Service Select Committee, 1979-83; Chairman, Sub-Committee, Treasury and Civil Service Select Committee, 1981-82; Visiting Research Fellow, Imperial College, London, since 1989. Publications: Decision in Government, 1970; Production Purpose and Structure, 1982.

Recreation: sailing. Address: (b.) House of Commons, London, SW1A 0AA.

Breaks, Michael Lenox, BA, DipLib. University Librarian, Heriot-Watt University, since 1985; b. 12.1.45, Plymouth; m., Barbara Lawson; 1 s.; 1 d. Educ. St. George's College, Weybridge; Leeds University. Assistant Librarian: University College, Swansea, York University; Social Sciences Librarian, University College, Cardiff, 1977-81; Deputy Librarian, University College, Dublin, 1981-85. Recreations: gardening; horse-riding; walking. Address: (h.) 15 Corrennie Gardens, Edinburgh, EH10 6DG; T.-031-447 7193.

Breen, James William, DPE. Deputy Chief Executive, Scottish Sports Council, since 1989; b. 1.7.53, Glasgow; m., Fiona; 2 d. Educ. Victoria Drive Secondary School, Glasgow; Jordanhill College of Education. Physical Education Teacher, 1974-78; Assistant Recreation Officer, Strathkelvin District Council, 1978-82; Chief Assistant Recreation Management, Moray District Council, 1982-86; Assistant Director of Leisure Services, Motherwell District Council, 1986-89. Leader, Scottish Kayak Expedition to NW Norway, 1980. Recreations: sport; geography/geology of West Scotland; gardening; DIY; car mechanics. Address: (h.) 1 Castle Grove, Kilsyth, Glasgow G65 9NB; T.-0236 825482.

Breeze, David John, BA, PhD, FSA, PPSA Scot, FRSE, MIFA. Chief Inspector of Ancient Monuments, Scotland, since 1989; President, Society of Antiquaries of Scotland, 1987-90; b. 25.7.44, Blackpool; m., Pamela Diane Silvester; 2 s. Educ. Blackpool Grammar School; Durham University. Inspector of Ancient Monuments, Scotland, 1969-88; Principal Inspector of Ancient Monuments, Scotland, 1988-89. Member, International Committee of the Congress of Roman Frontier Studies, since 1969; Member, Hadrian's Wall Advisory Committee, since 1977; Trustee, Senhouse Roman Museum, since 1985; Council Member, Society of Antiquaries of London, 1984-86. Publications: The Building of Hadrian's Wall, The Army of Hadrian's Wall and Hadrian's Wall (all Co-author); Roman Scotland: a guide to the visible remains; Roman Scotland: some recent excavations (Editor); The Romans in Scotland (Co-author); The Northern Frontiers of Roman Britain; Roman Forts in Britain; Studies in Scottish Antiquity (Editor); Hadrian's Wall, a souvenir guide; A Queen's Progress, an introduction to the buildings associated with Mary Queen of Scots in Scotland; The Second Augustan Legion in North Britain; Service in the Roman Army (Co-editor); Invaders of Scotland (Co-author). Recreations: reading; walking; swimming; travel. Address: (h.) 36 Granby Road, Edinburgh, EH16 5NL; T.-031-667 8876.

Bremner, David Neill, MB, ChB, FRCSEdin. Consultant General Surgeon, Borders Health Board, at Borders General Hospital, Melrose, since 1976; b. 4.2.42, Forfar; m., Janette Marlyn; 3 s.; 1 d. Educ. Forfar Academy; Queen's College, St. Andrews University. House Surgeon, Inverness Hospitals, 1966-68; Registrar Surgeon: Ayr hospitals, 1969-71, Edinburgh hospitals, 1971-74; Senior Registrar, Professorial Department of Surgery, Edinburgh, 1974-76. South Medical Advisor, Scottish Rugby Union; Honorary Vice President, Gala Rugby Club; Regional Advisor, Royal College of Surgeons of Edinburgh. Recreations: gardening; rugby. Address: (h.) 26 Abbotsford Road, Galashiels, TD1 3DS; T.-0896 2558.

Bremner, James W., FCCA, IRRV, MBIM. Director of Finance, Highland Regional Council, since 1975; b. 29.5.33, Forfar; m., Ethel; 1 s.; 1 d. Educ. Forfar Academy. RAF, 1951-54; Accountant, Angus County Council, 1955-65; Ross and Cromarty County Council: Depute County Treasurer, 1965-70; County Treasurer, 1970-75. Recreation: golf.

Address: (b.) Highland Regional Council, Glenurquhart Road, Inverness; T.-0463 234121.

Brew, David Allan, BA, MSc. Assistant Secretary, Scottish Office Industry Department, since 1991; b. 19.2.53, Kettering. Educ. Kettering Grammar School; Heriot-Watt University; Strathclyde University; European University Institute, Florence. Administration Trainee and HEO(D), Scottish Office, 1979-81; Administrator, DGV, Commission of the EC, 1981-84; Principal, Scottish Office Industry Department, Glasgow, 1984-88, Edinburgh, 1988-90; Assistant Secretary, since 1990; Head, Electricity Privatisation Division, 1990-91; Head, European Funds and Co-ordination Division, since 1991. Member, Court, Heriot-Watt University, 1985-91. Recreations: languages; music; film; gastronomy. Address (h.) Flat 4, 1 Dundas Street, Edinburgh, EH3 6QG; T.-031-556 4692.

Brewster, Ernest Ralph, BSc, PhD, MBCS, MBIM, CChem. Director of Computer and Management Services, Borders Regional Council, since 1987; b. 29.12.47, Romford; 2 d. Educ. Royal Liberty Grammar School, Romford; Exeter University. Research Assistant, Exeter University, 1972-73; Research Fellow, Oxford University, 1973-75; Senior Scientific Officer, MAFF, 1975-80; Professional Technological Officer, later Principal, Central Computer and Telecommunications Agency, HM Treasury, 1980-85; Information Systems Manager, Norfolk County Council, 1985-87; Secretary, Borders Branch, British Institute of Management, 1990-91. Recreations: chess; running; horse riding. Address: (h.) Midraw, 11 North Street, Duns, Berwickshire, TD11 3AP; T.-0361 83597.

Brian, Paul Vaughan, BSc. Rector, Biggar High School, since 1985 (Rector, Hutchesons' Grammar School, Glasgow, 1984-85); b. 14.6.42, Wokingham; m., Helen Margaret Balneaves; 1 s.; 1 d. Educ. Perth Academy; Edinburgh University; Heriot-Watt College. Assistant Headmaster, Garnock Academy, Kilbirnie, 1974; Depute Rector, Marr College, Troon, 1977; Headteacher, Gryffe High School, Bridge of Weir, 1979. Scientific Officer, Scottish Hindu Kush Expedition, 1968. Recreations: mountaineering; golf; gardening. Address: (b.) Biggar High School, Biggar, Lanarkshire.

Bridges, Professor Roy Charles, BA, PhD, FRGS, FRHistS. Professor of History, Aberdeen University, since 1988 (Chairman, African Studies Group, since 1983); b. 26.9.32, Aylesbury; m., Jill Margaret Bridges; 2 s.; 2 d. Educ. Harrow Weald County Grammar School; Keele University; London University. Lecturer in History, Makerere University, Uganda, 1960-64; joined Aberdeen University as Lecturer, 1964; Senior Lecturer, 1971-88; Head, History Department, 1977-82, 1985-88, since 1990; Secretary, African Studies Group, 1966-83. Member, History Panel, Scottish Examination Board, 1983- 89; Chairman, Joint Working Party on Higher and Post-Higher History, 1988-90; Visiting Professor, Indiana University; President, Aberdeen Branch, Historical Association; Treasurer, Scottish Institute of Missionary Studies. Publications: Nations and Empires (Co-author), 1969; J.A. Grant in Africa, 1982. Recreations: cricket; geology; walking. Address: (b.) Department of History, King's College, Aberdeen, AB9 2UB; T.-Aberdeen 272452.

Britton, Professor Celia Margaret, MA (Cantab), PhD. Carnegie Professor of French, Aberdeen University, since 1991; b. 20.3.46, Stanmore, Middx. Educ. North London Collegiate School; New Hall, Cambridge. Temporary Lecturer in French, Kings College, London, 1972-74; Lecturer in French Studies, Reading University, 1974-91. Publications: Claude Simon: Writing The Visible, 1987; articles on French literature and cinema. Address: (b.)

Department of French, Aberdeen University, Old Aberdeen, AB9 2UB; T.-0224 272163.

Broadie, Professor Alexander, MA, BLitt, PhD, FRSE. Professor in Philosophy, Glasgow University. Educ. Edinburgh University; Balliol College, Oxford. Publications: A Samaritan Philosophy, 1981; George Lokert: Late-Scholastic Logician, 1983; The Circle of John Mair, 1985; Introduction to Medieval Logic, 1987; Notion and Object, 1989; The Tradition of Scottish Philosophy, 1990; Paul of Venice: Logica Magna, 1990. Address: (b.) Philosophy Department, The University, Glasgow, G12 8QQ; T.-041-339 8855.

Brock, Professor David John Henry, BA (Oxon), PhD, MRCPath, FRSE, FRCPE, FIBiol. Professor of Human Genetics, Edinburgh University, since 1985; Director, Human Genetics Unit, Edinburgh University, since 1983; b. 5.6.36, London; m., Sheila Abercromby; 4 s. Educ. Diocesan College, Cape Town; Cape Town University; Oxford University. Postdoctoral Fellow: Massachussets Institute of Technology, 1962-63; Harvard University, 1963-66; Oxford University, 1966-67; Senior Scientific Officer, ARC Animal Breeding Research Organisation, 1967-68; joined Edinburgh University as Lecturer in Human Genetics, 1968; appointed Reader, 1978. Address: (b.) Human Genetics Unit, Western General Hospital, Edinburgh; T.-031-332 7917.

Brockie, Rev. Colin Glynn Frederick, BSc(Eng), BD. Minister, Grange Church, Kilmarnock, since 1978; b. 17.7.42, Westcliff-on-Sea, Essex; m., Barbara Katherine Gordon; 2 s.; 1 d. Educ. Musselburgh Grammar School; Aberdeen Grammar School; Aberdeen University. Probationer Assistant, Mastrick Church, Aberdeen, 1967-68; Minister, St. Martin's Church, Edinburgh, 1968-78. Chaplain, Ayrshire Mission to the Deaf, since 1982; Honorary Secretary and Treasurer, Scottish Church History Society. Recreations: billiards; photography; computing. Address: Grange Manse, 14 Portland Road, Kilmarnock; T.-Kilmarnock 25311.

Brockington, John Leonard, MA, DPhil. Reader in Sanskrit, Edinburgh University, since 1989 (Senior Lecturer, 1982-89); b. 5.12.40, Oxford; m., Mary Fairweather; 1 s.; 1 d. Educ. Mill Hill School; Corpus Christi College, Oxford. Lecturer in Sanskrit, Edinburgh University, 1965-82. Publications: The Sacred Thread, 1981; Righteous Rama, 1984. Address: (h.) 3 Eskvale Court, Penicuik, Midlothian EH26 8HT; T.-0968 78709.

Brocklebank, Ted. Head of Documentaries and Features, Grampian Television, since 1985 (Head of News and Current Affairs, 1977-85); b. 24.9.42, St. Andrews; 2 s. Educ. Madras College, St. Andrews. D.C. Thomson, Dundee, 1960-63; Freelance Journalist, 1963-65; Scottish TV, 1965-70; Reporter, Grampian TV, 1970-76. Won BAFTA Award for What Price Oil?; Radio Industries Club of Scotland Special Award (Documentary) for Tale of Two Cities; Norwegian Amanda award for eight-part series on world oil business, networked on Channel Four and throughout USA on PBS. Recreations: rugby; music; reading; living in Scotland. Address: (b.) Grampian TV, Queen's Cross, Aberdeen, AB9 2XJ.

Brocklesby, Professor David William, Dr.Vet.Med. (Zurich), FRCPath, FRCVS, CMG. Professor of Tropical Animal Health and Director, Centre for Tropical Veterinary Medicine, Edinburgh University, since 1978-90; b. 12.2.29, Grimsby; m., Jennifer Mary Hubble; 1 s.; 3 d. Educ. Sedbergh School, Yorkshire; Royal Veterinary College, London; London School of Hygiene and Tropical Medicine. Veterinary Research Officer, East African Veterinary Research Organisation, Muguga, Kenya (Head, Division of Protozoal Diseases), 1955-66; Head, Department of Animal

46 WHO'S WHO IN SCOTLAND

Health, Fisons Pest Control Ltd., Saffron Walden, 1966-67; Head, Department of Parasitology, AFRC Institute for Research on Animal Diseases, Compton, Berkshire, 1967-78. Recreations: walking dogs; reading The Times; watching TV. Address: (h.) 3 Broomieknowe, Lasswade, Midlothian, EH18 1LN; T.-031-663 7743.

Brodie, Martin Jeffrey, MD, FRCP(G), FRCP(E). Consultant Physician and Clinical Pharmacologist; Senior Lecturer in Medicine and Therapeutics, Glasgow University; b. 14.1.46, Glasgow; m.; 1 s.; 1 d. Educ. Hutchesons' Boys Grammar School; Glasgow University. Lecturer in Materia Medica, Glasgow University, 1974-77; Lecturer in Clinical Pharmacology, Royal Postgraduate Medical School, London, 1977-81. Chairman, Committee of Management, Prescribers' Journal, DHSS, London; Chairman, West of Scotland Epilepsy Research Group. Publications: Practical Prescribing; 200 medical reviews and papers. Recreations: chess; reading; dog walking. Address: (b.) Epilepsy Research Unit, University Department of Medicine and Therapeutics, Western Infirmary, Glasgow; T.-041-339 8822, Ext. 4572.

Brodie, Robert, CB, MA, LLB. Solicitor to Secretary of State for Scotland, since 1987 (Deputy Solicitor, 1984 87); b. 9.4.38, Dundee; m.; Jean Margaret McDonald; 2 s.; 2 d. Educ. Morgan Academy, Dundee; St. Andrews University; Queen's College, Dundee. Scottish Office: Legal Assistant, 1965; Senior Legal Assistant, 1970; Deputy Director, Scottish Courts Administration, 1975; Assistant Solicitor, Scottish Office, 1982. Recreations: music; hill-walking. Address: (h.) 45 Stirling Road, Edinburgh; T.-031-552 2028.

Brodie, William, BSc, CBiol, MBiol. Rector, Wallace High School, Stirling, since 1984; b. 16.9.37, Hamilton; m., Helen Bland; 1 s.; 1 d. Educ. Hamilton Academy; Glasgow University; Paisley College of Technology. Teacher, Wishaw High School, 1965-67; Principal Teacher of Biology, Hutchesons' Grammar School, Glasgow, 1967-74; Assistant Rector, Graeme High School, Falkirk, 1974-79; Depute Rector, Kirkintilloch High School, 1979-81; Rector, Balfron High School, 1981-84. Treasurer, Headteachers' Association of Scotland. Recreations: golf; tennis; gardening. Address: (b.) Wallace High School, Dumyat Road, Stirling; T.-0786 62166.

Brodie of Brodie, (Montagu) Ninian Alexander, DL, JP; b. 12.6.12, Forres; m., Helena Penelope Budgen (deceased); 1 s.; 1 d. Educ. Eton. Trained Webber-Douglas School of Dramatic Art, 1933-35; professional Actor and Director, occasional broadcasts, 1935-40; served with Royal Artillery, including North Africa and Italy, 1940-45; returned to stage, with occasional films and broadcasts, 1945-50; managed estate, market garden, etc., Brodie Castle, from 1950; gave Brodie Castle and part of estate to National Trust for Scotland, 1979; voluntary work as guide etc., since 1980. Life Member, National Trust for Scotland. Recreations: shooting; hill-walking; collecting paintings. Address: (h.) Brodie Castle, Forres, Moray, IV36 0TE.

Broni, David Alexander Thomas. Head of Secretariat, Scottish Enterprise, since 1991; b. 25.10.57, Glasgow; m., Ann Frances; 1 s.; 1 d. Educ. St. Mungo's Academy. Joined civil service, 1975; Manpower Services Commission, 12 years, Training Agency, 2 years, Scottish Office Industry Department, 2 years. Recreations: running; cycling; swimming; rugby; opera. Address: (b.) 120 Bothwell Street, Glasgow, G2 7JP; T.-041-228 2854.

Brooke, (Alexander) Keith, ARAgS. Honorary President, Blackface Sheep Breeders' Association, since 1989; Director: Animal Diseases Research Association, since 1981, Royal Highland and Agricultural Society of Scotland, since 1986, Scottish, English and Welsh Wool Growers Ltd., since 1988,

Wallets Marts PLC, British Rouge De L'Ouest Sheep Society Ltd., Wigtownshire Quality Lamb Ltd.; Member, Panel of Arbiters; Farmer; b. 11.2.46, Minnigaff; m., Dilys K. Littlejohn; 1 s.; 3 d. Educ. George Watson's College, Edinburgh. Address: (h.) Carscreugh, Glenluce, Newton Stewart, DG8 0NU; T.-058 13 334.

Brooker, William Dixon, BSc. Chairman, North East Mountain Trust, since 1990; Director, Department of Adult Education and Extra-Mural Studies, Aberdeen University, 1981-89; b. 13.12.31, Calcutta; m., Margaret Laura Parkinson; 1 s.; 1 d. Educ. Aberdeen Grammar School; Aberdeen University. Principal Teacher of Geography: Aberlour High School; Keith Grammar School; King Richard School, Dhekelia, Cyprus; Keith Grammar School; Tutor Organiser in Extra-Mural Studies, Aberdeen University, 1966. President, Scottish Mountaineering Club, 1972-74 (Honorary Editor, SMC Journal, 1975-86); Vice-Chairman: Mountaineering Council of Scotland, 1979-81; Scottish Mountain Leader Training Board, 1978-80. Recreations: mountaineering; skiing; travel; photography. Address: (h.) 25 Deeview Road South, Cults, Aberdeen; T.-0224 861055.

Brookes, Brian Sydney, MBE, BSc, MSc, MIBiol. Freelance Naturalist and Ecologist, and Consultant in environmental education and conservation, since 1985; b. 4.5.36, Beckenham, Kent; m., Margaret Mary; 3 s.; 1 d. Educ. Beckenham and Penge Grammar School; King's College, London; Dundee University. Teaching in London schools, seven years; Assistant Warden, field centre in Devon, two years; Warden, Kindrogan Field Centre, Perthshire, 18 years. Sometime Council Member, Botanical Society of the British Isles; various committees, Scottish Wildlife Trust. Recreations: bee-keeping; photography. Address: (h.) Borelick, Trochry, Dunkeld, Perthshire, PH8 0BX; T.-035 03 222.

Brookes, Douglas Whittaker, TD. Secretary, Inverness and District Chamber of Commerce, since 1980; b. 3.1.19, Sheffield; m., May; 1 s.; 1 d. War Service, 1939-46 (Captain, RE); AI Welders Ltd., Inverness, 1946-80: Sales Manager; Sales Director; Managing Director and Chief Executive. Served with local regiment, TA, Lovat Scouts, 1950-66 (latterly Major, Second-in-Command). Recreations: golf; hill-walking; reading. Address: (h.) 13A Island Bank Road, Inverness, IV2 4QN; T.-0463 233570.

Brooks, Professor Charles Joseph William, PhD, DSc, DIC, ARCS, CChem, FRSC, FRSE. Professor Emeritus of Chemistry, Glasgow University; b. 28.9.27, London; m., Gillian M.W. Staniforth; 1 s.; 1 d. Educ. Surbiton County Grammar School; Royal College of Science, London University. Assistant Lecturer, Department of Chemistry and Biochemistry, St. Thomas's Hospital, London, 1954-56; Member, MRC scientific staff, research units, Glasgow, 1956-63; Chemistry Department, Glasgow University: Lecturer, 1963; Senior Lecturer, 1966; Reader, 1973; Titular Professor, 1976-90; Visiting Professor: Baylor College of Medicine, Houston, Texas, 1963 and 1965; Japan Society for Promotion of Science, 1977; Walker-Ames Professor, University of Washington, Seattle, May 1987. Editor, Gas Chromatography - Mass Spectrometry Abstracts, 1974-85; Member, Editorial Advisory Board: Biological Mass Spectrometry, Rapid Communications in Mass Spectrometry; Editorial Advisor, Biochemical Journal. Recreations: travel; music. Address: (b.) Chemistry Department, Glasgow University, Glasgow, G12 8QQ; T.-041-339 8855.

Brooks, Professor David Neil, BA, MSc, PhD. Titular Professor, Department of Psychological Medicine, Glasgow University (Head of Clinical Psychology Training); Director, Case Management Services Ltd.; Consultant Neuropsychologist, ScotCare Brain Injury Unit; Chartered

Clinical Psychologist; b. 6.3.44, Huddersfield; m., Christine; 2 s.; 1 d. Educ. William Hulme's School, Manchester; University of Wales; Leeds University; Glasgow University. Past President, International Neuropsychological Society; Vice President, European Brain Injury Society; Project Director, EEC Concerted Action on Brain Injury. Recreations: shooting; working. Address: (h.) 16 Dougalston Gardens North, Milngavie, Glasgow, G62 6HN.

Brooks, James, BTech (Hons), MPhil, PhD, FRSC, CChem, FGS, FInstPet, AssocBIT. Senior Partner, Brooks Associates Glasgow, since 1986; Visiting Lecturer, Glasgow University, since 1978; Chairman/Director, Petroleum Geology '86 Limited, since 1985; b. 11.10.38, Co. Durham; m., Jan Slack; 1 s.; 1 d. Educ. University of Bradford. Research Scientist, British Petroleum, 1969-75; Senior Research Fellow, Bradford University, 1975-77; Research Associate/Section Head/Senior Scientist, British National Oil Corporation/Britoil PLC, 1977-86. Geological Society: Vice President, 1984-87, Secretary, 1987-90; Founder and Chairman, The Petroleum Group; AAPG Distinguished Lecturer to North America, 1989-90. Publications: 18 books; 80 research papers. Recreations: travel; reading; writing; sport (English soccer!); Christian work. Address: (h.) 10 Langside Drive, Newlands, Glasgow, G43 2EE; T.-041-632 3068.

Brooks, Patrick William, BSc, MB, ChB, DPM, MRCPsych. Senior Medical Officer, Scottish Home and Health Department, since 1981; b. 17.5.38, Hereford. Educ. Hereford High School; Bishop Vesey's Grammar School, Sutton Coldfield; Edinburgh University. Royal Medical and associated hospitals, including State Hospital, Carstairs, and Western General Hospital, Edinburgh: Senior House Officer, 1964-66; Registrar, 1966-69; Senior Registrar, 1969-74; Medical Officer, Scottish Home and Health Department, 1974-81. A founder Member, Edinburgh Festival Fringe Society, 1959 (Vice-Chairman, 1964-71); Chairman, Edinburgh Playhouse Society, 1975-81; Secretary, Lothian Playhouse Trust, 1981-83; Chairman, Scottish Arts Lobby (SALVO); Joint Vice-Chairman, Royal Lyceum Theatre Club; Secretary and Treasurer, Edinburgh Friends of Scottish Ballet. Recreations: opera; ballet; music; theatre; cinema; modern Scottish art; travel. Address: (h.) 11 Thirlestane Road, Edinburgh, EH9 1AL.

Broom, Andrew Munro, MA, LLB. Deputy Keeper, Scottish Record Office, since 1985; b. 18.3.33, Glasgow; m., Katherine Mary Scott; 1 s.; 1 d. Educ. Hutchesons' Boys' Grammar School, Glasgow; Glasgow University; Edinburgh University. National Service, RASC, 1955-57; PA to Deputy Director, Army Legal Services, War Office, 1956-57; joined Scottish Record Office as Assistant Keeper, Grade II, 1957; Grade I, 1963; Secretary, National Register of Archives (Scotland), 1963-71; seconded to Registrar-General for Scotland as Departmental Record Officer, 1974-77; Secretary, Committee on Conservation and Restoration, International Council on Archives, 1981-88. Chairman, Society of Archivists (Scottish Region), 1987-90. Recreations: swimming; photography; assisting Edinburgh Hospitals Broadcasting Service. Address: (b.) Scottish Record Office, HM General Register House, Edinburgh, EH1 3YY; T.-031-556 6585.

Broster, Rev. David, BA. Minister, Kilbirnie: St. Columba's, since 1983; Clerk, Ardrossan Presbytery, since 1989; Moderator, Synod of Ayr, 1991-92; b. 14.3.44, Liverpool; m., Margaret Ann; 2 d. Educ. Liverpool Institute High School; United Theological College, University of Wales; Open University. Dip., Theology; Cert., Pastoral Studies. Ordained by Presbyterian Church of Wales, 1969; Minister: Park Place, Tredegar, Gwent, 1969-78, Clubmoor Presbyterian Church of Wales, Liverpool, 1978-83; Clerk, Association in East, Presbyterian Church of Wales, 1981-83. Recreations: com-

puters; gardening; advanced driving. Address: St. Columba's Manse, Kilbirnie, Ayrshire, KA25 7JU; T.-0505 683342.

Broun, Rev. Canon Claud Michael, BA (Oxon). Rector, Greyfriars, Kirkcudbright, and St. Mary's, Gatehouse of Fleet, since 1988; b. 9.2.30, Edinburgh; m., Janice Ann Broun (qv); 2 s.; 1 d. Educ. Edinburgh Academy; Brasenose College, Oxford. Rector: St. Cuthbert's, Cambuslang, 1962-75, St. Mary's, Hamilton, 1975-88; Canon, St. Mary's Cathedral, Glasgow, since 1983. Recreations: cricket; hill-walking; crosswords. Address: Greyfriars Rectory, 54 High Street, Kirkcudbright, DG6 4JX; T.-0557 30580.

Broun, Janice Anne, BA. Freelance journalist; East European Correspondent, News Network International, since 1989; Author; b. 24.3.34, Tipton; m., Canon Claud Broun (qv); 2 s.; 1 d. Educ. Dudley Girls High School; St. Anne's College, Oxford. Publications: Conscience and Captivity: Religion in Eastern Europe, 1988; Prague Winter, 1988; Albania: Religion in a Fortress State, 1989; Bulgaria: Religion Denied, 1989; Romania: Religion in a Hardline State, 1989. Recreations: swimming; cycling; table tennis; music; art history; travel. Address: Greyfriars Rectory, 54 High Street, Kirkcudbright, DG6 4JX; T.-0557 30580.

Brown, Alan Cameron, BSc (Hons), PhD, CBiol, MIBiol. Principal, Lauder College, Dunfermline, since 1987; b. 18.1.43, Rothesay; m., Noel Robertson Lyle. Educ. Rothesay Academy; Glasgow University. Assistant Teacher of Science, Ayr Academy, 1969-70; Principal Teacher of Biology, Loudon Academy, 1970-71; Principal Teacher of Biology, Ravenspark Academy, 1971-72; Depute Director of Education, Berwick County Council, 1972-75; Assistant Director of Education, Borders Regional Council, 1975-80; Depute Principal, Galashiels College of FE, 1980-84; Depute Principal, Borders College of FE, 1984-87. Recreations: cycling; swimming. Address: (b.) Lauder College, Halbeath, Dunfermline, Fife; T.-Dunfermline 726201.

Brown, Professor Alan Geoffrey, BSc, MB, ChB, PhD, FRSE, FIBiol. Professor of Veterinary Physiology, Edinburgh University, since 1984; b. 20.4.40, Nottingham; m., Judith Allen; 1 s.; 1 d. Educ. Mundella School, Nottingham; Edinburgh University. Assistant Lecturer, then Lecturer in Veterinary Physiology, Edinburgh University, 1964-68; Beit Memorial Fellow for Medical Research, 1968-71; Research Fellow supported by MRC, 1971-74; Lecturer, then Reader in Veterinary Physiology, Edinburgh University, 1974-84; holder, MRC Research Fellowship for academic staff, 1980-85. Member, Editorial Boards, several scientific journals. Recreations: music; gardening; walking; reading. Address: (b.) Department of Preclinical Veterinary Sciences, Edinburgh University, Edinburgh, EH9 1QH; T.-031-667 1011.

Brown, Catherine, FSA Scot. Freelance Food Writer, since 1973; b. Glasgow; m., Iain Brown; 2 d. Educ. Hutchesons Grammar School; Queens College, Glasgow. Lecturer, catering subjects; professional cook in hotels and restaurants; senior researcher, Scottish Hotel School, for book, British Cookery, published 1976; freelance food writer. Publications: Scottish Regional Recipes, 1981; Scottish Cookery, 1985; A Flavour of Edinburgh, 1986; Broths to Bannocks, 1990. Recreations: mountain climbing; fishing. Address: (h.) 4 Belhaven Terrace, Glasgow G12 0TF; T.-041-357 4920.

Brown, Charles, JP. Member, Glasgow District Council, since 1980 (Bailie, since 1988); full-time official, National Union of Tailor and Garment Workers, since 1956; Chairman, Glasgow Sports Promotion Council; b. 4.11.21, Stirling; m., Margaret; 2 d. Educ. Pirn Street Advanced School, Glasgow. Governor, Baillies Institution; former Member, Glasgow Northern Hospital Board; Past Chairman, Glasgow Trades

Council. Recreations: bowling; swimming; golf. Address: (h.) 340 Golfhill Drive, Glasgow, G31 2NY.

Brown, Professor Charles Malcolm, BSc, PhD, DSc, FRSA, FIBiol, FRSE. Professor of Microbiology, Heriot-Watt University, since 1979 (Head, Department of Biological Sciences); Director, International Centre for Brewing and Distilling, since 1989; b. 21.9.41, Gilsland; m., Diane Mary Bryant; 3 d. Educ. Houghton-le-Spring Grammar School; Birmingham University. Lecturer in Microbiology, Newcastle-upon-Tyne University, 1966-73; Senior Lecturer, Dundee University, 1973-79. Editor-in-Chief, Microbiological Sciences; Council Member: Scottish Marine Biological Association; Society for General Microbiology; Director, Bioscot Ltd; Editor, Process Biochemistry. Recreations: music; walking. Address: (b.) Heriot-Watt University, Riccarton, Edinburgh, EH14 4AS; T.-031-449 5111.

Brown, Daniel Martin, MA (Hons). Principal, Barmulloch College, 1977-89; b. 4.12.28, Clydebank; m., Isabella Montgomery; 1 s.; 1 d. Educ. Clydebank High School; Dumbarton Academy; Glasgow University; Jordanhill College. Education Officer, RAF, 1952-54 (final rank, flying officer); Teacher of English and History: Vale of Leven Academy, 1954-56; Gordon Schools, Huntly, 1956-62; Teacher of English, Dunfermline High School, 1962-64; Senior Lecturer in English, Langside College of Further Education, Glasgow, 1964-70; Cardonald College, Glasgow: Head, Department of Communication Arts, 1970-75; Depute Principal, 1975-77. Chairman, Moderating Committee, SCOTBEC, 1975-78; Further Education Representative, Strathclyde Regional Council, 1980-83; Member, Officer Group on Post-Compulsory Education; Further Education Representative, Strathclyde Regional Council Joint Planning Group for Training in Community Work; College Organiser, College Public Speaking Annual Competition, Glasgow Junior Chamber of Commerce, 1978-86. Recreations: reading (especially 20th-century novelists); theatre; films; angling; bowling. Address: (h.) 45 Lanton Road, Newlands, Glasgow, G43 2SR; T.-041-637 8169.

Brown, David Blair, MA, LLB. Rector, Dunfermline High School, since 1983; b. 6.5.38, Glasgow; m., Marjory Kathleen Muir; 2 s.; 1 d. Educ. Hutchesons' Boys Grammar School, Glasgow; Glasgow University; Jordanhill College of Education. Teacher, Hutchesons' Boys Grammar School; Principal Teacher of History, Renfrew High School, 1970-74; Assistant Rector, Stonelaw High School, 1974-78; Depute Rector and Acting Head, Dalbeattie High School, 1978-81; Assistant Rector, Musselburgh Grammar School, 1981-83. Member, Children's Panel, since 1976. Recreations: walking; cycling; swimming; gardening; theatre; music. Address: (h.) 3 Craigluscar Court, Dunfermline.

Brown, Dennis Henry, FBCS. Director, Midlothian Campaign Ltd, since 1986; b. 19.8.22, London; m., Betty Joan; 2 s. Educ. Highbury County School. Finance Officer, London County Council, 1939-64; RAF, 1942-47; Chairman/Managing Director, family computer bureau, 1964-79; Business Consultant, 1979-86. District Councillor, Midlothian District Council, 1977-80 (Convenor, Finance Committee, 1977-80); College Councillor, Jewel and Esk Valley College, since 1988; Chairman, IBM Computer Users Association, 1970-72 (Honorary Life President); Chairman, Glenesk Scout District, 1977-83. Recreations: music; travel. Address: (h.) 5 Greenlaw Grove, Glencorse, Penicuik, Midlothian, EH26 0RF; T.-0968 672671.

Brown, Professor Ewan, MA, LLB, CA. Merchant Banker; Director: Noble Grossart Ltd., since 1971; Scottish Development Finance; John Wood Group Plc; Pict Petroleum Plc; Stagecoach Holdings Plc; James Walker (Leith) Ltd.; b.

23.3.42, Perth; m., Christine; 1 s.; 1 d. Educ. Perth Academy; St. Andrews University. CA apprentice with Peat Marwick Mitchell, 1964-67. Honorary Professor in Finance, Heriot Watt University; Trustee, Carnegie Trust for the Universities of Scotland; Governor, George Watsons College; Council Member, Institute of Chartered Accountants of Scotland; Assistant, Merchant Company of Edinburgh; Council Member, Scottish Business School, 1974-80; Director, Scottish Transport Group, 1983-88; Governor, Edinburgh College of Art, 1986-89. Recreations: family; golf; skiing; Scottish watercolours; Mah Jongg. Address: (b.) 48 Queen Street, Edinburgh; T.-031-226 7011.

Brown, George, BL. Chief Executive Officer, Dunfermline District Council, since 1974; b. 2.1.33, Falkirk; m., Sarah; 2 s.; 1 d. Educ. Falkirk High School; Edinburgh University. Solicitor. Assistant Solicitor: Allan Dawson Simpson & Hampton, WS, 1954-55; Falkirk Burgh, 1955-59; Dunfermline Burgh, 1959-62; Town Clerk and Chamberlain, Linlithgow Burgh, 1962-70; Town Clerk and Chief Executive, Bathgate Burgh, 1970-74. Past Chairman, Scottish Branch, SOLACE. Recreations: gardening; philosophy. Address: (b.) City Chambers, Dunfermline, Fife; T.-Dunfermline 722711.

Brown, George Mackay, OBE, MA, Hon. MA (Open University), Hon. LLD (Dundee), Hon DLitt (Glasgow), FRSL. Poet and story-teller; b. 17.10.21, Stromness, Orkney. Educ. Stromness Academy; Newbattle Abbey College; Edinburgh University. Author of: (short stories) A Calendar of Love, A Time to Keep, Hawkfall, The Sun's Net, Andrina, The Masked Fisherman; (poetry) Selected Poems, Winterfold, Voyages, The Wreck of the Archangel; (novels) Greenvoe, Magnus, Time in a Red Coat, The Golden Bird; various plays for stage and television; three books for children; Editor, Selected Prose of Edwin Muir; two books on Orkney. Winner, 1988 James Tait Black prize for The Golden Bird. Address: (h.) 3 Mayburn Court, Stromness, Orkney, KW16 3DH.

Brown, (James) Gordon. MA, PhD. MP (Labour), Dunfermline East, since 1983; Shadow Chancellor of the Exchequer, since 1992; b. 20.2.51. Educ. Kirkcaldy High School; Edinburgh University. Rector, Edinburgh University, 1972-75; Temporary Lecturer, Edinburgh University, 1976; Lecturer, Glasgow College of Technology, 1976-80; Journalist and Current Affairs Editor, Scottish Television, 1980-83. Contested (Labour) South Edinburgh, 1979; Chairman, Labour Party Scottish Council, 1983-84; Opposition Chief Secretary to the Treasury, 1987; Shadow Minister for Trade and Industry, 1989. Publications: The Red Paper on Scotland (Editor), 1975; The Politics of Nationalism and Devolution (Co-Editor), 1980; Scotland: The Real Divide, 1983; Maxton, 1986; Where There is Greed, 1989. Recreations: reading and writing; football; golf; tennis. Address: 21 Ferryhills Road, North Queensferry, Fife.

Brown, Gordon Lamont. Scottish Rugby International and British Lion; Author and After-Dinner Speaker; b. 1.11.47, Troon; m., Linda; 1 s.; 1 d. Educ. Marr College, Troon. Bank Clerk, British Linen Bank, 1965-71; Building Society Manager: Leicester Building Society, 1971-76, Bristol & West Building Society, since 1976. Played for Scotland, 30 times; toured with British Isles Rugby Team ("Lions), New Zealand 1971, South Africa 1974, New Zealand 1977; holds world record for number of tries scored by a forward on a tour (eight); Vice-Chairman, Stars Organisation for Spastics (Scotland); Finance Committee Member, National Playing Fields Association. Publications: Broon from Troon (autobiography); Rugby is a Funny Game (rugby anecdotes). Recreation: golf. Address: (h.) 65 Bentinck Drive, Troon, Ayrshire; T.-0292 314070.

Brown, Hamish Macmillan. Author, Lecturer, Photographer and Mountaineer; b. 13.8.34, Colombo, Sri Lanka. Educ. several schools abroad; Dollar Academy. National Service, RAF, Middle East/East Africa; Assistant, Martyrs' Memorial Church, Paisley; first-ever full-time appointment in outdoor education (Braehead School, Fife); served many years on Scottish Mountain Leadership Board; has led expeditions world-wide for mountaineering, skiing, trekking, canoeing, etc. Publications: Hamish's Mountain Walk, 1979 (SAC award); Hamish's Groats End Walk, 1981 (Smith's Travel Prize shortlist); Time Gentlemen, Some Collected Poems, 1983; Eye to the Hills, 1982; Five Bird Stories, 1984; Poems of the Scottish Hills (Editor), 1982; Speak to the Hills (Co-Editor), 1985; Travels, 1986; The Great Walking Adventure, 1986; Hamish Brown's Scotland, 1988; Climbing the Corbetts, 1988; Great Walks Scotland (Co-author), 1989; Scotland Coast to Coast, 1990; Walking the Summits of Somerset and Avon, 1991. Recreations: gardening; "bird" philately; books; music. Address: 21 Carlin Craig, Kinghorn, Fife, KY3 9RX; T.-0592 890422.

Brown, Ian, CSSD, LUDipDA. Artistic Director, Traverse Theatre Company, since 1988; b. 8.3.51, Sawbridgeworth. Educ. The King's School, Ely; Central School of Speech and Drama, London. Drama Teacher; Community Arts Worker, Cockpit Theatre, London; English Language Teacher, Berlitz School, Paris; Director, Cockpit Youth Theatre, London; Associate Director, Theatre Royal, Stratford East; Artistic Director, TAG Theatre Company, Glasgow. Board, Sue McLennon Dance Company; Spirit of Mayfest Award for Great Expectations, 1988; Scotland on Sunday Paper Boat award for Bondagers, Mayfest, 1991. Address: (b.) Traverse Theatre, 112 West Bow, Edinburgh, EH2 2HH; T.-031-226 2633.

Brown, Ian. Chief Executive, Edinburgh Chamber of Commerce; b. 14.7.45, Hawick; m., Moira Blyth; 1 s.; 1 d. Educ. Hawick High School. Chief Executive, Chamber Developments Ltd., Who's Who in Business in Scotland Ltd., Edinburgh's Capital Ltd. Recreations: golf; curling; walking; music. Address: (b.) 3 Randolph Crescent, Edinburgh, EH3 7UD; T.-031-225 5851.

Brown, Ian Forbes, FIB (Scot). Director: Wilson Distributors (Scotland) Ltd.; G.A. Holdings Ltd.; Credential Holdings Ltd.; Thorburn PLC; Norman Cordiner Ltd.; Chairman: Anglo Scottish Properties Plc; Bondsure Ltd.; b. 5.3.29; m., Margaret Catherine; 1 s.; 1 d. Educ. Glasgow High School. Address: (h.) 8 Ardchoille Park, Strathmore Street, Perth PH2 7TL.

Brown, Ian Johnston Hilton, MA (Hons). Rector, Lanark Grammar School, since 1986 (Rector, Strathaven Academy, 1976-86); b. 5.10.37, Aberdeen. Educ. Royal High School, Edinburgh; Edinburgh University; Moray House College of Education. Teacher, Kirkcaldy High School, 1961-66; Principal Teacher, Bishopbriggs High School, 1966-71; Assistant Head Teacher, Cathkin High School, 1971-74; Depute Rector, Hunter High School, 1974-76. Recreations: hill-walking; badminton; theatre. Address: (b.) Lanark Grammar School, Lanark, ML11 9AQ; T.-Lanark 2471.

Brown, James Armour, RD, BL, FSA (Scot). Partner, Kerr, Barrie & Duncan (formerly Kerr, Barrie & Goss), Solicitors, Glasgow, 1957-91 (Consultant since 1991); b. 20.7.30, Rutherglen; m., Alexina Mary Robertson McArthur; 1 s. Educ. Rutherglen Academy; Glasgow University. National Service, Royal Navy, 1951-53; commissioned RNVR, 1952; served with Clyde Division, RNVR/RNR, 1953-72; Captain, 1972; Senior Reserve Supply Officer on staff of Admiral Commanding Reserves, 1973-76; Naval ADC to The Queen, 1975-76; Member, Suite of Lord High Commissioner to General Assembly of Church of Scotland, 1961-63; Session Clerk, Stonelaw Parish Church, Rutherglen, 1964-81; Member, Church of Scotland Committee on Chaplains to HM Forces, 1975-82 (Vice-Convener, 1979-82); Clerk, Incorporation of Bakers of Glasgow, 1964-89; Deacon, Society of Deacons and Free Preseses of Glasgow, 1978-80; Member, Glasgow Committee, Order of St. John of Jerusalem, since 1961 (Chairman, since 1982); Member, Chapter of the Priory of Scotland of the Order of St. John, since 1970; KStJ, 1975; Preceptor of Torphichen, Priory of Scotland, since 1984; Hon. Chairman, Orders and Medals Research Society (Scottish Branch), 1987- 91. Recreations: music; historical research. Address: (h.) 25 Calderwood Road, Rutherglen, Glasgow, G73 3HD; T.-041-647 2051.

Brown, Jenny, MA (Hons). Freelance journalist and presenter of Scottish Television's book programmes; b. 13.5.58, Manchester; 2 s. Educ. George Watson's College; Aberdeen University. Assistant Administrator, Edinburgh Festival Fringe Society, 1980-82; Director, Edinburgh Book Festival, 1983-91. Address: (b.) Scottish Television, Cowcaddens, Glasgow G2 3PR.

Brown, Professor John Campbell, BSc, PhD, DSc, FRAS, FRSE. Professor of Astrophysics, Glasgow University, since 1984; b. 4.2.47, Dumbarton; m., Dr. Margaret I. Brown; 1 d. Educ. Dumbarton Academy; Glasgow University. Glasgow University Astronomy Department: Research Assistant, 1968-70, Lecturer, 1970-78, Senior Lecturer, 1978-80, Reader, 1980-84; Nuffield Fellow, 1983-84; Kelvin Medallist, 1983-86; DAAD Fellow, Tubingen University, 1971-72; ESRO/GROC Fellow, Space Research Laboratory, Utrecht, 1973-74; Visitor: Australian National University, 1975, High Altitude Observatory, Colorado, 1977; NASA Associate Professor, Maryland University, 1980; NSF Fellow, University of California at San Diego, 1984; Brittingham Professor, University of Wisconsin, 1987. SERC Solar System Committee, 1980-83; Council, Royal Astronomical Society, 1984-87, since 1990 (Vice-President, 1986-87); Member, International Astronomical Union, since 1976. Recreations: cycling; walking; painting; lapidary; conjuring; photography; woodwork. Address: (b.) Department of Physics and Astronomy, Glasgow University, Glasgow, G12 8QW; T.-041-330 5182.

Brown, John Clouston, AIB (Scot). Member, Orkney Islands Council, since 1978; b. 4.10.14, Stromness, Orkney; m., Maria Sinclair Flett; 2 s.; 1 d. Educ. Stromness Academy. Joined Union Bank of Scotland Ltd., Stromness, Orkney, 1931; RAF, Burma and India, 1941 45; Manager, Stromness Branch, Union Bank of Scotland (subsequently Bank of Scotland), 1954-74. Past Chairman, Stromness Golf Club; former Secretary: Stromness Chamber of Commerce, Kirkwall Arts Club; former Treasurer, Orkney Agricultural Society. Recreations: golf; fishing; drama. Address: (h.) Breck, Birsay, Orkney, KW17 2LY; T.-Birsay 349.

Brown, Professor Kenneth Alexander, BSc, MSc, PhD. Professor of Mathematics, Glasgow University, since 1990; b. 19.4.51, Ayr; m., Irene M.; 2 s. Educ. Ayr Academy; Glasgow University; Warwick University. Recreations: reading; running; drinking beer; talking. Address: (b.) Mathematics Department, Glasgow University, Glasgow, G12 8QW; T.-041-339 8855, Ext. 6535.

Brown, Kenneth Clarke, CIPFA. Director of Finance, Nithsdale District Council, since 1984; Clerk and Treasurer, Solway River Purification Board, since 1989; b. 28.5.44, Dumfries; m., Olivia; 1 s.; 1 d. Educ. Dumfries Academy. Commenced career as Audit Examiner with District Audit in Chelmsford, 1966; moved to Carlisle; appointed Chief Internal Auditor, Skelmersdale and Holland UDC, 1971; moved to similar post, Chorley Borough Council, 1974; Depute Director of Finance, Nithsdale District Council, 1976-

84. Honorary Treasurer, Ellisland Trust. Recreations: golf; football; keep-fit; DIY. Address: (h.) Kilmory, 51 Rotchell Park, Dumfries, DG2 7RL; T.-0387 54889.

Brown, Madeline, MB, ChB, MRCPsy, DPsy. Consultant Child Psychiatrist, Royal Aberdeen Children's Hospital, since 1982; b. 30.10.37, Aberdeen; m., Ian R. Brown; 2 s. Educ. Aberdeen Academy; Aberdeen University. Recreations: hill-walking; badminton; drama. Address: (h.) 37 Argyll Place, Aberdeen; T.-0224 633996.

Brown, Neil Dallas, DA. Painter; Lecturer, Department of Fine Art Studies (Painting Studios), Glasgow School of Art, since 1979; b. 10.8.38, Elgin; m., Georgina Ballantyne; 2 d. Educ. Bell Baxter High School, Cupar; Duncan of Jordanstone College of Art, Dundee; Royal Academy Schools, London. Visiting Lecturer, School of Design, Duncan of Jordanstone College of Art, since 1968; Visiting Lecturer in Painting, Glasgow School of Art, since 1976; since completing training, 36 one-man exhibitions, in Dundee, Manchester, Edinburgh, London (nine), Glasgow, York, Basle, Paris, Stirling, Belfast, Aberdeen and Kirkcaldy; won 10 awards for painting; has been Guest Artist, Dollar Summer School for the Arts, Croydon College of Art, Strathclyde University, Ulster Polytechnic, Grays School of Art (Aberdeen), Maryland Institute College of Art (Baltimore), Newport College of Art (Wales). Recreations: fishing; running. Address: (h.) Aerie, 55 Abbeywall Road, Pittenweem, Fife, KY10 2NE; T.-311852.

Brown, Professor Peter Evans, PhD, FRSE. Professor of Geology, St. Andrews University, since 1990; b. 5.4.30, Kendal; m., Thelma Smith; 2 s. Educ. Kendal School; Manchester University. Mineralogist/Geologist, Geological Survey of Tanganyika; Lecturer/Senior Lecturer in Geology, Sheffield University; Professor of Geology, Aberdeen University. Fellow, Geological Society. Recreations: mountaineering; exploration. Address: (b.) Department of Geography and Geology, Purdie Building, St. Andrews, KY16 9ST.

Brown, Professor Peter Melville, MA (Oxon), DPhil. Professor Emeritus, Glasgow University, since 1986 (Stevenson Professor of Italian, 1975-86); b. 7.7.26, Todmorden; m., Aileen Taylor Tough; 2 s.; 1 d. Educ. Todmorden Grammar School; Magdalen College, Oxford; Scuola Normale Superiore, Pisa. Aberdeen University: Assistant Lecturer in Italian, 1955-57, Lecturer in Italian, 1957-66, Senior Lecturer in Italian, 1966-72; Professor of Italian, Hull University, 1972-75. Publication: Lionardo Salviati: A Critical Biography, 1975. Recreation: travel. Address: (h.) 23 Osborne Place, Aberdeen, AB2 4BX; T.-0224 640473.

Brown, Robert Edward, LLB (Hons), NP. Solicitor; Member, Glasgow District Council, and Leader, Liberal Group (now Liberal Democrat Group), since 1977; b. 25.12.47, Newcastle-upon-Tyne; m., Gwen Morris; 1 s.; 1 d. Educ. Gordon Schools, Huntly; Aberdeen University. Legal apprenticeship, Aberdeen, 1969-71; Procurator Fiscal Depute, Dumbarton, 1972-74; Assistant, then Partner, Ross Harper & Murphy, Rutherglen and Glasgow, since 1974. Parliamentary candidate (Liberal), Rutherglen, October 1974, 1979, 1983, 1987; first Liberal, Glasgow District Council; former Secretary, North Aberdeen Liberals; former Member, Scottish Liberal Party Executive and Local Government Organiser; Debates Convenor, Strathclyde Junior Chamber, 1973; Chairman, Rutherglen Citizens' Advice Bureau, 1980-83; Honorary President, Rutherglen Bowling Club, since 1977. Recreations: politics; reading; history; science fiction. Address: (h.) 3 Douglas Avenue, Rutherglen, Glasgow; T.-041-634 2353.

Brown, Robert Iain Froude, MA, MEd, ABPsS, CPsychol. Senior Lecturer, Department of Psychology, Glasgow University, since 1968; b. 16.1.35, Dundee; m., Catherine G.; 2 d. Educ. Daniel Stewart's College, Edinburgh; St. Andrews University; Edinburgh University; Glasgow University. Education Department, Corporation of Glasgow; Department of Psychological Medicine, Glasgow University. National Training Adviser, Scottish Council on Alcohol; Member, Executive, Scottish Council on Alcohol; Chairman, Society for the Study of Gambling, London; Chairman, Glasgow Council on Alcohol; Chairman, Confederation of Scottish Counselling Agencies. Recreations: travel; music. Address: (h.) 13 Kirklee Terrace, Glasgow, G12 0TH; T.-041-339 7095.

Brown, Rev. Robin Graeme, BA, BD. Principal, St. Colm's Education Centre and College, since 1984; b. 27.11.32, Alverstoke, Hampshire; m., Sibyl Enid Clarke; 1 s.; 2 d. Educ. Fettes College, Edinburgh; Cambridge University; Edinburgh University; Heidelberg University. Principal, St. Columba's College, Alice, South Africa, 1971-73; Leader, Iona Community, 1974-81. Address: (h.) 24 Inverleith Terrace, Edinburgh, EH3 5NU; T.-031-332 1156.

Brown, Professor Sally, BSc, MA, PhD. Professor of Education, Stirling University, since 1990; b. 15.12.35, London; m., Professor Charles Brown (deceased); 2 s. Educ. Bromley High School GPDST; University College, London; Smith College, Massachusetts; Stirling University. Lecturer in College of Education, London, and College of Technology, Nigeria; University Lecturer, Nigeria; School Science Teacher, Helensburgh; University Researcher, Stirling; Research Adviser to Scottish Education Department; Director, Scottish Council for Research in Education, 1986-90. Publications: 60 (articles, monographs, books) on educational research and education generally. Recreations: squash; reading. Address: (b.) Department of Education, Stirling University, Stirling, FK9 4LA.

Brown, Professor Stewart J., BA, MA, PhD. Professor of Ecclesiastical History, Edinburgh University, since 1988; b. 8.7.51, Illinois; m., Teri B. Hopkins-Brown; 1 s.; 1 d. Educ. University of Illinois; University of Chicago. Fulbright Scholar, Edinburgh University, 1976-78; Whiting Fellow in the Humanities, University of Chicago, 1979-80; Assistant to the Dean, College of Arts & Sciences, and Lecturer in History, Northwestern University, 1980-82; Associate Professor and Assistant Head, Department of History, University of Georgia, 1982-88; Visiting Lecturer, Department of Irish History, University College, Cork, 1986. Publication: Thomas Chalmers and the Godly Commonwealth in Scotland, 1982 (awarded Agnes Mure Mackenzie Prize from Saltire Society). Recreations: swimming; hill-walking. Address: (h.) 160 Craigleith Hill Avenue, Edinburgh, EH4 2NB; T.-031-343 1712.

Brown, William, CBE (1971), Dr hc (Edin). Chairman, Scottish Arts Council; Deputy Chairman, Scottish Television, since 1990 (Managing Director, 1966-90); b. 24.6.29, Ayr; m., Nancy Jennifer Hunter; 1 s.; 3 d. Educ. Ayr Academy; Edinburgh University. STV: London Sales Manager, 1958-61, Sales Director, 1961-63, Deputy Managing Director, 1963-66. Lord Willis Award for services to TV, 1982; Royal Television Society Gold Medal for outstanding services to TV, 1984; Chairman, Council, ITCA, 1968-69, 1978-80; Director, ITN, 1972-77 and 1988-90; Director, ITP, 1968-89; Director, Channel 4, 1980-84; Director, Scottish Amicable Life Assurance Society, since 1981, Chairman, since 1989. Recreation: golf. Address: (b.) STV, Cowcaddens, Glasgow, G2 3PR.

Brown, William, BL, SSC, NP. Solicitor; Partner, Tods Murray WS; b. 18.3.32, Dunfermline; m., Anne Sword; 2 d.

Educ. Dunfermline High School; Edinburgh University. National Service commission, RAOC, 1952; Partner, Ranken & Reid, 1960-90. Member, Society of High Constables of Edinburgh. Recreations: golf; music; shooting. Address: (h.) Greenlawns, 45 Barnton Avenue, Edinburgh, EH4 6JJ; T.-031-336 4227.

Browne, Ronald Grant, DA. Folk Entertainer ("The Corries"), since 1961; Portrait Painter, since 1979; b. 20.8.37, Edinburgh; m., Patricia Isabella Elliot; 2 s.; 1 d. Educ. Boroughmuir School, Edinburgh; Edinburgh College of Art. Teacher of Art and Painting, 1959-63; folk entertaining, 1963-79; folk entertaining and portrait painting, since 1979.

Browning, Rev. Derek, MA, BD. Parish Minister, Cupar Old and St. Michael of Tarvit Parish Church, since 1987; b. 24.5.62, Edinburgh. Educ. North Berwick High School; Corpus Christi College, Oxford; St. Mary's College, St. Andrews. Assistant Minister, Troon St. Meddan's, 1986. Member, Cupar Community Council, since 1989; Convener, Presbytery of St. Andrews Christian Education Committee. Recreations: reading; music; cooking; dog-walking; travel. Address: Eden Manse, Cupar, KY15 4HQ; T.-0334 53196.

Browning, J. Robin, BA (Hons), FIB (Scot). General Manager, Bank of Scotland, since 1986 (Divisional General Manager, 1983-86); b. 29.7.39, Kirkcaldy; m., Christine Campbell; 1 s.; 1 d. Educ. Morgan Academy, Dundee; Strathclyde University; Harvard Business School. Bank of Scotland: Assistant Management Accountant, 1971-74, Assistant Manager (Corporate Planning), 1974-77; British Linen Bank Ltd.: Manager, 1977-79, Assistant Director, 1979-81, Director, 1981-82; Assistant General Manager, Bank of Scotland, 1982-83. Recreations: curling; gardening; DIY enthusiast. Address: (b.) Bank of Scotland, Head Office, The Mound, Edinburgh, EH1 1YZ; T.-031-243 5541.

Brownlie, William Steel, MC, TD, MA; b. 12.10.23, Cambusnethan; m., 1, Margaret Mitchell (deceased); 2, Netta Russell (deceased); 1 s.; 1 d. Educ. Greenock Academy; Glasgow University. Royal Armoured Corps, 1942-47; 2nd Fife and Forfar Yeomanry, 1944-47; Captain, NW Europe; Ayrshire (ECO) Yeomanry, 1950-68; Lt.-Col. Commanding, 1966-68; Teacher, John Neilson High School, Paisley, 1951-84 (Principal Teacher, Modern Languages); Contributor, Lingo Column, Times Educational Supplement; Editor, The Scottish Schoolmaster; Editor, The Yeoman (Ayrshire Yeomanry). Publications: The Proud Trooper (History of the Ayrshire Yeomanry), 1964; Thirteen Letters from a Scottish Solider (Editor), 1988. Recreations: military history; philately; photography; philology. Address: (h.) Orchard Cottage, Law Brae, West Kilbride, KA23 9DD; T.-0294 822216.

Bruce, David, MA. Director, Scottish Film Council, since 1986; b. 10.6.39, Dundee; m., Barbara; 1 s.; 1 d. Educ. Dundee High School; Aberdeen Grammar School; Edinburgh University. Freelance (film), 1963; Assistant Director, Films of Scotland, 1964-66; Director, Edinburgh International Film Festival, 1965-66; Promotions Manager, Mermaid Theatre, London, 1966-67; Executive Officer, British Universities Film Council, 1967-69; joined Scottish Film Council as Assistant Director, 1969; Depute Director, SFC and Scottish Council for Educational Technology, 1977-86. Chairman, Mental Health Film Council, 1982-84; Chairman, Scottish Society for History of Photography, 1983-86; Chairman, Association of European Film Institutes. Recreations: movies; music; photo-history. Address: (b.) Downahill, 74 Victoria Crescent Road, Glasgow, G12 9JN; T.-041-334 4445.

Bruce, Fraser Finlayson, RD, MA (Hons), LLB, FSA(Scot). Permanent Chairman, Industrial Tribunals for Scotland, since 1982; Temporary Sheriff, since 1984; Solicitor, since 1956; b. 10.10.31, Kirkcaldy; m., Joan Gwendolen Hunter; 2 step-

s. Educ. St. Andrews University. National Service, Royal Navy, 1956-58, commissioned Sub-Lieutenant, RNVR; Legal Assistant: Lanark County Council, 1958-60, Inverness County Council, 1960-66; Depute County Clerk: Argyll County Council, 1966-70, Inverness County Council, 1970-72; County Clerk, Inverness County Council, 1972-75; Joint Director of Law and Administration, Highland Regional Council, 1975-82. Served RNVR, 1956-76, retiring as Lieutenant-Commander RNR. Recreations: hill walking; golf; reading (in philosophy and naval/military history). Address: (h.) 1 Hazel Drive, Dundee DD2 1QQ; T.-0382 68501.

Bruce, George, OBE (1984), MA, LittD. Writer/Lecturer; b. 10.3.09, Fraserburgh; m., Elizabeth Duncan; 1 s.; 1 d. Educ. Fraserburgh Academy; Aberdeen University. Teacher, English Department, Dundee High School, 1928-46; BBC Producer, Aberdeen, 1946-56; BBC Talks (Documentary) Producer, Edinburgh, with special responsibility for arts programmes, 1956-70; first Fellow in Creative Writing, Glasgow University, 1971-73; Visiting Professor, Union Theological Seminary, Richmond, Virginia, and Writer in Residence, Prescott College, Arizona, 1974; Visiting Professor of English, College of Wooster, Ohio, 1976-77; Scottish-Australian Writing Fellow, 1982; E. Hervey Evans Distinguished Fellow, St. Andrews Presbyterian College, North Carolina, 1985; Vice-Chairman, Council, Saltire Society; Council Member, Advisory Council of the Arts in Scotland; Extra-Mural Lecturer, Glasgow, St. Andrews and Edinburgh Universities; Executive Editor, The Scottish Review, 1975-76. Publications: verse: Sea Talk, 1944; Selected Poems, 1947; Landscapes and Figures, 1967; Collected Poems, 1970; The Red Sky, 1985; Perspectives: poems 1970-86, 1987; prose: Scottish Sculpture Today (Co-author), 1947; Anne Redpath, 1974; The City of Edinburgh, 1974; Festival in the North, 1975; Some Practical Good, 1975; A Scottish Postbag (Co-author), 1986; as Editor: The Scottish Literary Revival, 1962; Scottish Poetry Anthologies 1-6 (Co-Editor), 1966-72. Recreation: visiting friends. Address: 25 Warriston Crescent, Edinburgh, EH3 5LB; T.-031-556 3848.

Bruce, John Wilkinson, AHWC, CChem, MRSC, BSc, BA. Member: Dumfries and Galloway Regional Council, 1986-90; Annandale and Eskdale District Council, 1984-88; b. 10.2.25, Leith; 2 d. Educ. Broughton Secondary School, Edinburgh; Heriot-Watt College, Edinburgh. Industrial Chemist: Stewart and Lloyds, Corby, 1945-47, SCWS Junction Mills, Leith, 1947-52; Teacher: Earlston, Berwickshire, 1954-58, Duns, 1958-63; Principal Teacher of Science, Langholm, 1963-83 (also Deputy Rector, 1965-83). Educational Institute of Scotland: President, Berwickshire Branch, 1962-63, President, Dumfriesshire Branch, 1968-69; President, Langholm Congregational Church, 1966-70; Member, Langholm Town Council, 1966-72, and 1973-75; President, Honours Graduate Teachers' Association, 1980-84. Recreations: bridge; bowls; amateur operatics; philosophy. Address: (h.) 14 John Street, Langholm, Dumfriesshire, DG13 OAD.

Bruce, Malcolm Gray, MA, MSc. MP (Liberal), Gordon, since 1983; Rector, Dundee University, 1986-89; b. 17.11.44, Birkenhead; m., Jane Wilson; 1 s.; 1 d. Educ. Wrekin College; St. Andrews University; Strathclyde University. Trainee Journalist, Liverpool Daily Post & Echo, 1966-67; Section Buyer, Boots the Chemist, 1968-69; Fashion Retailing Executive, A. Goldberg & Sons, 1969-70; Research and Information Officer, NESDA, 1971-75; Marketing Director, Noroil Publishing, 1975-81; Director, Aberdeen Petroleum Publishing; Editor/Publisher, Aberdeen Petroleum Report, 1981-83; Co-Editor, Scottish Petroleum Annual, 1st and 2nd editions. Vice Chairman, Political, Scottish Liberal Party, 1975-84. Recreations: reading; music; theatre; hill-walking;

cycling; travel. Address: (h.) Grove Cottage, Grove Lane, Torphins, Banchory AB31 4HJ.

Bruford, Alan James, BA, PhD. Archivist, School of Scottish Studies, Edinburgh University, since 1965; Editor, Tocher, since 1971; b. 10.5.37, Edinburgh; m., Morag B. Wood; 1 d. Educ. Edinburgh Academy; Winchester College; St. John's College, Cambridge; Edinburgh University. Junior Research Fellow, 1965; Assistant Lecturer, 1965; Lecturer, 1968; Senior Lecturer, 1984; fieldwork throughout Scotland, especially Orkney and Shetland, collecting folktales and other traditions, songs, fiddle music and oral history; Treasurer, Scottish Association of Magazine Publishers, 1974-79; Convener, Scottish Oral History Group, since 1987; Organising Secretary, 7th Congress, International Society for Folk-Narrative Research, 1979. Publications: Gaelic Folk-Tales and Mediaeval Romances, 1969; The Green Man of Knowledge and Other Scots Traditional Tales, 1982. Recreations: music (traditional, baroque, composition); travel in Scotland; quizzes. Address: (h.) South Mains, West Linton, Peeblesshire, EH46 7AY.

Brumfitt, Professor John Henry, MA, DPhil (Oxon). Emeritus Professor, St. Andrews University, since 1986 (Professor of French, 1969-86); b. 5.4.21, Shipley; m., 1, Patricia Renee Grand; 2, Margaret Anne Ford; 1 s.; 2 d. Educ. Bradford Grammar School; Queen's College, Oxford. Laming Travelling Fellow, Queen's College, Oxford, 1947-48; Lecturer in French, University College, Oxford, 1948-51; St. Andrews University: Lecturer in French, 1951-59, Senior Lecturer, 1959-69; Member, Editorial Boards, French Studies and Forum for Modern Language Studies. Publications: The French Enlightenment; Voltaire Historian. Address: (h.) 22 Buchanan Gardens, St. Andrews, Fife; T.-0334 73079.

Brunt, Peter William, MD, FRCP(Lond), FRCP(Edin). Consultant Physician, Aberdeen Royal Infirmary, since 1970; Clinical Senior Lecturer in Medicine, Aberdeen University, since 1970; Physician to The Queen in Scotland, since 1984; b. 18.1.36, Prestatyn; m., Marina Evelyn Anne Lewis; 3 d. Educ. Manchester Grammar School; King George V School; Liverpool University. Recreations: mountaineering; music. Address:(h.) 17 Kingshill Road, Aberdeen, AB2 4JY; T.-Aberdeen 232034.

Bruton, Professor Kevin John, BA, MA, PhD. Chair of Spanish, Head of Department and Head, School of Modern Languages, Stirling University, since 1990; b. 9.5.47, Cardiff; m., Ann Elisabeth; 1 s.; 1 d. Educ. St. Illtyd's College, Cardiff; King's College and Birkbeck College, London University. Marketing Management, Reckitt-Colman (Overseas) Ltd., 1970-72; Marketing Consultant, S. P. & M., 1972-76; Middlesex Polytechnic, 1977-78; Heriot-Watt University, 1978-81; Lecturer in Spanish, Salford University, 1981-89. National Council, IHESC; Councillor, Salford City Council, 1984-90. Recreations: rugby; cricket; golf (playing); cycling; astronomy; walking. Address: Department of Spanish; Stirling University, Stirling FK9 4LA; T.-0786 73171.

Bryant, Anthony B., FRICS. Regional Director, Highlands, National Trust for Scotland, since 1986; b. 25.1.38; m., Jane E.A.; 1 s.; 1 d. Educ. Bryanston School. Trained as land agent, Chatsworth Estate, 1956-60, returning there 1964-69 after working for the Duchy of Cornwall; joined National Trust for Scotland as Depute Factor, 1969; Factor, 1976; Head Factor, 1984. Recreations: music; painting. Address: (b.) Abertarff House, Church Street, Inverness 1V1 1EU; T.-Inverness 232034.

Bryant, Professor David Murray, BSc, PhD, ARCS, DIC. Professor, Department of Biological and Molecular Sciences, Stirling University, since 1989; b. 24.9.45, Norwich; m., Victoria Margaret Turton; 1 s.; 1 d. Educ. Greshams School,

Holt; Imperial College, London. Lecturer/Senior Lecturer/Reader, Stirling University, since 1970. Recreations: skiing; birds; theatre. Address: (h.) Kenilworth Road, Bridge of Allan, FK9 4EH.

Bryce, Professor Charles F.A., BSc, PhD, DipEdTech, CBiol, FIBiol, CChem, FRSC. Professor and Head of Department, Biological Sciences, Napier Polytechnic, since 1983; b. 5.9.47, Lennoxtown; m., Maureen; 2 s. Educ. Lenzie Academy; Shawlands Academy; Glasgow University; Max Planck Institute, Berlin. Executive Editor, Computer Applications in the Biosciences; Chairman, UK Interest Group on Education in Biotechnology; Chairman, European Federation of Biotechnology Working Party on Education. Recreations: distance running; competitive bridge; collecting wine. Address: (b.) Napier Polytechnic, 10 Colinton Road, Edinburgh, EH10 5DT; T.-031-455 2525.

Bryden, Bill. Director/Writer; Associate Director, National Theatre, since 1974; Head of Drama, BBC Scotland, since 1985; b. 12.4.42, Greenock; m., Hon. Deborah Morris; 1 s.; 1 d. Educ. Greenock High School. Researcher, STV, 1964; Assistant Director, Royal Court Theatre, 1966; Associate Director, Royal Lyceum Theatre, Edinburgh, 1969, Member, Board of Directors, Scottish Television, 1982-85; Director (National Theatre): The Mysteries, Glengarry Glen Ross; author of plays: Willie Rough, Benny Lynch; film scripts: Long Riders, Ill Fares The Land, The Holy City; opera: Parsifal; Cunning Little Vixen. Recreation: music. Address: (b.) BBC, Queen Margaret Drive, Glasgow; T.-041-339 8844.

Bryson, Adam., MBChB, MRCGP, MPH, MFPHM. Medical Executive, Western Infirmary Unit, Greater Glasgow Health Board, since 1987; Consultant in Public Health Medicine, since 1987; b. 4.8.45, Motherwell; m., Wendy; 3 s. Educ. Dalziel High School; Glasgow University. General Medical Practitioner, Kirkintilloch, 1972-78; Consultant in Primary Care, Military Hospital, Saudi Arabia, 1978-82; Trainee in Public Health Medicine, Greater Glasgow Health Board, 1982-85; Acting Unit Medical Officer, Unit West-2, Greater Glasgow Health Board, 1985-87. Littlejohn-Gairdner Memorial Prize, 1988. Recreations: golf; DIY; furniture restoration. Address: Minerva Lodge, Seven Sisters, Lenzie G66 3AW; T.-041-776 7875.

Bryson, William McNicol, FIMI. Director, Scottish Motor Trade Association, 1985-89; b. 6.3.28, Lanark; m., 1, Marion Rankin Cowper (deceased); 1 s.; 1 d.; 2, Mary K. Hamilton. Educ. Lanark Grammar School. Trained as aircraft mechanic, RAF Technical School, Cosford; Rossleigh Ltd.: joined as salesman/buyer, 1949; General Manager, Glasgow, 1961-71; Marketing Director, Edinburgh, 1971-73; Managing Director and General Manager, 1973-77; Regional Director and Managing Director, Heron Rossleigh, 1977-82; Deputy Chairman and Managing Director, Taggart Motor Group, 1982-85. Lord Cornet, Royal Burgh of Lanark, 1959. Recreations: shooting; horse-riding; classic cars. Address: (h.) Marclann, 3 Friarsfield Road, Lanark; T.-0555 2817.

Buccleuch, 9th Duke of, and Queensberry, 11th Duke of (Walter Francis John Montagu Douglas Scott), KT (1978), VRD, JP. Hon. Captain, RNR; Captain, Queen's Bodyguard for Scotland (Royal Company of Archers); Lord Lieutenant of Roxburgh, since 1974, and of Ettrick and Lauderdale, since 1975; b. 23.9.23, London; m., Jane McNeill, daughter of John McNeill, QC, Appin, Argyll; 3 s.; 1 d. Educ. Eton; Christ Church, Oxford. Served World War II, RNVR; MP (Conservative), Edinburgh North, 1960-73; PPS to the Scottish Office, 1961-64; Chairman, Conservative Party Forestry Committee, 1967-73; Chairman, Royal Association for Disability and Rehabilitation, since 1978; President: Royal Highland and Agricultural Society of Scotland, 1969, St. Andrew's Ambulance Association, Royal Scottish

Agricultural Benevolent Institution, Scottish National Institution for War Blinded, Royal Blind Asylum and School, Galloway Cattle Society, East of England Agricultural Society, 1976, Commonwealth Forestry Association; President (Scotland), Malcolm Sargent Cancer Fund for Children; President, Golden Globe Charitable Trust, since 1990; Chairman, Living Landscape Trust, since 1985; Chairman, Buccleuch Heritage Trust, since 1986; Vice-President: Royal Scottish Society for Prevention of Cruelty to Children, Disablement Income Group Scotland, Disabled Drivers Motor Club, Spinal Injuries Association; Honorary President: Animal Diseases Research Association, Scottish Agricultural Organisation Society; DL: Selkirk, 1955, Midlothian, 1960, Roxburgh, 1962, Dumfries, 1974. Recreations: travel; country sports; painting; photography; classical music. Address: Bowhill, Selkirk; T.-Selkirk 20732; and Drumlanrig Castle, Thornhill; T.-Thornhill 30248.

Buchan, Alexander. Honorary Sheriff, since 1974; Chairman, Angus JPs, since 1963; Member, Angus District Council, since 1974; 4.4.24, Brechin; m., May Milne Melvin. Educ. Brechin High School. Brechin Town Council, 1962-75; Angus County Council, 1964-75; Tayside Regional Council, 1974-82; Provost of Brechin, 1966-75. Member: General Medical Council, Scottish Health Service Advisory Committee, Tayside Health Council. Recreation: golf. Address: (h.) Fairways, 3 North Latch Road, Brechin, DD9 6LF; T.-03562 2564.

Buchan, Alexander Stewart, MB, ChB, FFARCS. Consultant in charge of Obstetric Anaesthesia, Simpson Memorial Maternity Pavilion, Edinburgh, since 1988; b. 7.9.42, Aberdeen; m., Henrietta Young Dalrymple; 1 s. Educ. Loretto School; Edinburgh University. Anaesthetic training in Edinburgh, apart from work in Holland, 1972; appointed Consultant in NHS, 1975; Royal Infirmary, Edinburgh, Royal Hospital for Sick Children, and Princess Margaret Rose Orthopaedic Hospital. Publication: Handbook of Obstetric Anaesthesia, 1991. Recreations: sailing; fishing; golf. Address: (h.) 21 Chalmers Crescent, Edinburgh, EH9 1TS; T.-031-667 1127.

Buchan, Janey. Member, European Parliament, for Glasgow, since 1979; b. 30.4.26.

Buchan of Auchmacoy, Captain David William Sinclair, JP, KStJ. Chief of the Name of Buchan; b. 18.9.29; m., The Hon. Susan Blanche Fionodbhar Scott-Ellis, 4 s., 1 d. Educ. Eton; Royal Military Academy, Sandhurst. Commissioned Gordon Highlanders, 1949; served Berlin, BAOR and Malaya; ADC to GOC-in-C, Singapore, 1951-53; retired 1955. Member, London Stock Exchange; Senior Partner, Messrs Gow and Parsons, 1963-72. Changed name from Trevor through Court of Lord Lyon King of Arms, 1949, succeeding 18th Earl of Caithness as Chief of Buchan Clan. Member: Queen's Body Guard for Scotland (Royal Company of Archers); The Pilgrims; Friends of Malta GC; Alexandra Rose Day Council; Council, St. John's Ambulance, London; Council, Royal School of Needlework, 1987; Conservative Industrial Fund Committee, 1988; Governor, London Clinic, 1988; Vice-President, Bucks CCC, since 1984; Member, Council for London, Order of St. John. Recreations: cricket; tennis; squash. Address: Auchmacoy House, Ellon, Aberdeenshire.

Buchanan, Rev. Fergus Cameron, MA (Hons), BD (Hons). Minister, St. Paul's Parish Church, Milngavie, since 1988; Member, Executive, Board of Social Responsibility, Church of Scotland, since 1991; b. 26.9.54, Glasgow; m., Gabrielle; 3 s. Educ. Crookston Castle Secondary School; Glasgow University. Assistant Minister, Glasgow Cathedral, 1981-83; Minister, Ardeer Parish Church, 1983-88. Recreations: run-

ning; reading; Rangers. Address: 8 Buchanan Street, Milngavie, G62 8DD; T.-041-956 1043.

Buchanan, Hugh Ross, BA. Artist; b. 29.5.58, Edinburgh; m., Ann de Rohan; 2 d. Educ. Belhaven; Wellington; Edinburgh College of Art. Architectural watercolourist, with special interest in baroque and classicism; exhibitions: Henderson Gallery, Edinburgh, 1981; Scottish Gallery, 1984, 1987, 1991; Francis Kyle Gallery, London, 1986, 1988, 1990, 1992; several mixed shows; collections: Prince of Wales, House of Commons, City of Edinburgh, Bank of Scotland. Member, Council, National Trust for Scotland; Member, Conservative Arts and Heritage Committee. Recreation: motorcycle maintenance. Address: (h.) Thirdpart, by Crail, Fife, KY10 3XD; T.-0333 50441.

Buchanan, James Glen Stewart, MB, ChB, FRCGP, DCH, DRCOG. Chairman, Scottish Council on Alcohol, since 1987; b. 11.6.24, Annan; m., Elizabeth Urquhart Macgregor; 2 s. Educ. Dumfries Academy; Edinburgh University. General Practitioner, Vale of Leven, 1958-87; Past President, Glasgow Psychosomatic Society. Recreations: hill-walking; fishing; reading. Address: (h.) Landalla Cottage, Glenisla, Blairgowrie, PH11 8PH; T.-057582 318.

Buchanan, Professor John (Iain) Thomson, BSc, MSc, PhD. Professor of Computer Science, Strathclyde University, since 1988; b. 25.7.46, Glasgow; m., Margaret Moffat. Educ. Allan Glen's School, Glasgow; Glasgow University; Strathclyde University. Lecturer, Manchester University, 1971-75; Lecturer, Strathclyde University, 1976-88. Recreations: yachting; mountains; music; food and wine. Address: (b.) Department of Computer Science, Strathclyde University, Glasgow, G1 1XH; T.-041-552 4400.

Buchanan, Nigel Walter, BA, LLB. Solicitor; b. 22.7.33, Stirling; m., Caroline Grotrian. Educ. Rugby School; Oxford University; Glasgow University. National Trust for Scotland: Member, Executive and Finance Committee; Convenor, Countryside Advisory Panel; Council Member, Society for Computers and Law. Recreations: shooting; curling; needlework. Address: (b.) 48 Castle Street, Edinburgh, EH2 3LX; T.-031-225 3912.

Buchanan, William Menzies, DA. Deputy Director, Glasgow School of Art, since 1990 (Head of Fine Art Studies, since 1977); b. 7.10.32, Caroni Estate, Trinidad, West Indies. Educ. Glasgow School of Art. Art Teacher, Glasgow, 1956-61; Exhibitions Officer, then Art Director, Scottish Arts Council, 1961-77. Chairman, Stills Gallery, Edinburgh, 1987. Publications: Scottish Art Review, 1965, 1967, 1973; Seven Scottish Painters catalogue, IBM New York, 1965; The Glasgow Boys catalogue, 1968; Joan Eardley, 1976; Mr Henry and Mr Hornel Visit Japan catalogue, 1978; Japonisme in Art (Contributor), 1980; A Companion to Scottish Culture (Contributor), 1981; The Stormy Blast catalogue, Stirling University, 1981; The Golden Age of British Photography (Contributor), 1984; The Photographic Collector (Contributor), 1985; Willie Rodger: A Retrospective (Contributor to catalogue), 1986; Scottish Photography Bulletin (Contributor), 1988; History of Photography (Contributor), 1989; Mackintosh's Masterwork (Editor), 1989; British Photography in the 19th Century (Contributor), 1989. Recreations: gardening; cooking. Address: (b.) Glasgow School of Art, 167 Renfrew Street, Glasgow, G3 6RQ; T.-041-332 9797.

Buchanan-Jardine, Sir Andrew Rupert John, MC. Landowner; Deputy Lieutenant; b. 2.2.23, London; 1 s.; 1 d. Educ. Harrow; Royal Agricultural College. Joined Royal Horse Guards, 1941; served NW Europe; retired as Major, 1949. Joint Master, Dumfriesshire Foxhounds, 1950; JP.

Recreation: country pursuits. Address: (h.) Dixons, Lockerbie, Dumfriesshire; T.-Lockerbie 2508.

Buchanan-Smith, Robin D., BA, ThM. Member, Board of Directors, Scottish Television, since 1982; Chancellor's Assessor, St. Andrews University, 1981-85; Chairman, Scotland's Heritage Hotels, 1988-91; b. 1.2.36, Currie, Midlothian; m., Sheena Mary Edwards; 2 s. Educ. Edinburgh Academy; Glenalmond; Cambridge University; Edinburgh University; Princeton Theological Seminary. Minister, Christ's Church, Dunollie, Oban, 1962-66; Chaplain, St. Andrews University, 1966-73. Chaplain: 8th Argylls, 1962-66, Highland Volunteer, 1967-69; British Council of Churches Preacher to USA, 1968; Commodore, Royal Highland Yacht Club, 1977-81. Recreations: sailing; Scotland. Address: Isle of Eriska, Ledaig, Argyll, PA37 1SD; T.-0631 72 371.

Buck, Andrew Robin, BCom, CA. Managing Director, Dinwiddie Grieve Ltd., Dumfries, since 1979; Partner, DG Format, Dumfries, since 1985; Chairman, Corporate Presentation Systems Ltd., since 1989; b. 6.2.44, Carlisle; m., Rowena Rosemary Morewood; 2 d. Educ. Bradfield College, Berkshire; Edinburgh University. Qualified CA with Wallace & Somerville, CA, Edinburgh, 1967; Shell International Group, Philippines and Nigeria, 1967-73; Edward Bates Ltd., Edinburgh, 1974; Peat Marwick Mitchell & Co., Hong Kong, 1975-78. Member, Council, Institute of Chartered Accountants of Scotland, since 1989; Chairman, South West area, since 1991. Recreations: skiing; sailing; bringing up two small children. Address: 109 Irish Street, Dumfries, DG1 2QN.

Buehler, Joachim. Director, Goethe-Institut Glasgow, the German Cultural Institute in Scotland, since 1987; b. 27.7.30, Berlin; 1 s.; 2 d. Educ. North West German Music Academy, Detmold. Director of Music, Salem Schools, Germany, 1952-68; Representativ for Music in Africa and Asia, Goethe-Institute, Munich, 1968-73; Director, German Cultural Institute, Bombay, 1973-82; Director, Goethe-Institut, Seoul, 1983-87. Principal Conductor, Bombay Philharmonia, Cantata Choir, Bombay, 1973-82; Guest Conductor, Korean National Symphony Orchestra, Seoul Philharmonic, 1983-87. Address: (b.) 3 Park Circus, Glasgow, G3 6AX; T.-041-332 2555.

Bullough, Professor Donald Auberon, MA, FSA, FRHistS. Professor of Mediaeval History, St. Andrews University, 1973-91 (Dean, Faculty of Arts, 1984-88); Emeritus Professor, since 1991; Visiting Professor, Rutgers University, NJ, since 1991; b. 13.6.28, Stoke; m., Belinda Jane Turland; 2 d. Educ. Newcastle-under-Lyme High School; St. John's College, Oxford. National Service, RA, 1946-48; studied abroad, 1950-52; Fereday Fellow, St. John's College, Oxford, 1952-55; Lecturer, Edinburgh University, 1955-66 (Reader Elect, 1966); Warden, Holland House, Edinburgh University, 1960-63; Visiting Professor, Southern Methodist University, 1965-66; Professor of Mediaeval History, Nottingham University, 1966-73; Director, Paul Elek Ltd., 1968-79; Acting Director, British School at Rome, 1984 (Chairman, Faculty of History, Archaeology and Letters, 1975-79); Ford's Lecturer in English History, Oxford University, 1979-80; Andrew Mellon Lecturer, Catholic University, Washington, 1980; Raleigh Lecturer, British Academy, 1985; Hector Munro Chadwick Lecturer, Cambridge University, 1990. Recreations: talk; looking at buildings; postal history. Address: (b.) c/o Murray and Donald, Kinburn Castle, St. Andrews KY16 9DS.

Bunch, Antonia Janette, MA, FLA, FIInfSc, FSA Scot. Director, Scottish Science Library, since 1987; b. 13.2.37, Croydon. Educ. Notting Hill and Ealing High School; Strathclyde University. Assistant Librarian, Scottish Office, 1962-65; Librarian, Scottish Health Service Centre, 1965-81; Lecturer, Strathclyde University, 1981-86. Founding Chairman, Association of Scottish Health Sciences Librarians; Member, Standing Committee on Science and Technology Libraries, IFLA, 1987-91; Member, Advisory Committee, British Library Science Reference and Information Service, since 1987. Publications: Libraries in Hospitals (Co-author), 1969; Hospital and Medical Libraries in Scotland: an Historical and Sociological Study, 1975; Health Care Administration: an Information Sourcebook, 1979. Recreations: breeding and showing Welsh mountain ponies; gardening; music; travelling in Italy. Address: (b.) National Library of Scotland, 33 Salisbury Place, Edinburgh, EH9 1SL; T.-031-226 4531.

Bundy, Professor Alan Richard, BSc, PhD, FRSA. Professor, Department of Artificial Intelligence, Edinburgh University, since 1990; b. 18.5.47, Isleworth; m., D. Josephine A. Maule; 1 d. Educ. Heston Secondary Modern School; Springrove Grammar School; Leicester University. Tutorial Assistant, Department of Mathematics, Leicester University, 1970-71; Edinburgh University: Research Fellow, Metamathematics Unit, 1971-74, Lecturer, Department of Artificial Intelligence, 1974-84, Reader, 1984-87, Professorial Fellow, 1987-90. Editorial Board: Artificial Intelligence Journal, Journal of Automated Reasoning, AJ & Society Journal, Journal of Logic and Computation. Publications: Artificial Intelligence: An Introductory Course, 1978; The Computer Modelling of Mathematical Reasoning, 1983; The Catalogue of Artificial Intelligence Tools, 1984; Symbolic Computation (Series Editor). Recreations: wine and beer making; walking. Address: (b.) Department of Artificial Intelligence, Edinburgh University, 80 South Bridge, Edinburgh, EH1 1HN; T.-031-650 2716.

Bunn, Professor Philip Robertson, BSc, MSc, PhD, MInstMC, MIEE, CEng. Dean of Engineering, Paisley University, since 1990; Professor and Head, Department of Electrical and Electronic Engineering, Paisley University, since 1988; b. 19.2.43, Hertford; m., Katrina McKenzie; 1 s.; 1 d. Educ. St. Albans School; Leicester University; Bradford University. Elliott Automation Ltd (later GEC Elliott Process Automation Ltd), 1964-72; International Combustion Ltd, 1972-73; Principal Lecturer, Computer Engineering, Teesside Polytechnic, 1973-88. Recreation: golf. Address: Department of Electrical and Electronic Engineering, Paisley University, High Street, Paisley, PA1 2BE; T.-041-848 3400.

Bunney, Herrick, LVO, BMus, FRCO, FRSAMD, ARCM. Honorary Fellow, Edinburgh University; Organist and Master of the Music, St. Giles' Cathedral, Edinburgh, since 1946; b. London; m., Mary Howarth Cutting; 1 s.; 1 d. Educ. University College School; Royal College of Music. Organist to Edinburgh University, until 1981; former Conductor: Edinburgh Royal Choral Union, Edinburgh University Singers, The Elizabethan Singers (London), St. Cecilia Singers. Recreations: hill-walking; bird-watching. Address: (h.) 3 Upper Coltbridge Terrace, Edinburgh, EH12 6AD; T.-031-337 6494.

Burchell, Professor Brian, BSc (Hons), PhD, MRCPath. Professor of Medical Biochemistry and Clinical Director, University Department of Biochemical Medicine, Dundee; Honorary Top Grade Biochemist; b. 1.10.46, Bosworth; m., Ann; 1 s.; 1 d. Educ. King Edward VII Grammar School, Coalville; St. Andrews University. Lecturer in Biochemistry: Loughborough University of Technology, 1974-75, Dundee University, 1976-78; Wellcome Trust Special Research Leave Fellow, 1978-80; Wellcome Trust Senior Lecturer in Biochemistry, Dundee University, 1980-88. Editor and Deputy Chairman, Editorial Board, Biochemical Journal. Publications: over 100 scientific papers and reviews. Recreation: golf. Address: (b.) University Department of

Biochemical Medicine, Ninewells Hospital and Medical School, Dundee, DD1 9SY; T.-0382 60111, Ext. 2164.

Burdon, Professor Roy Hunter, BSc, PhD, CBiol, FIBiol, FRSA, FRSE. Professor of Molecular Biology, Strathclyde University; m., Margery Grace Kellock; b. 27.4.38, Glasgow; 2 s. Educ. Glasgow Academy; St. Andrews University. Assistant Lecturer, Glasgow University, 1959; Research Fellow, New York University, 1963; Glasgow University: Lecturer in Biochemistry, 1964, Senior Lecturer, 1967, Reader, 1974, Professor of Biochemistry (Titular), 1977; Guest Professor of Microbiology, Polytechnical University of Denmark, 1977-78; Governor, West of Scotland College of Agriculture; Biochemical Society (UK): Honorary Meeting Secretary, 1981-85, Honorary General Secretary, 1985-89, Chairman, 1989-92; Chairman, British Co-ordinating Committee for Biotechnology; Chairman, Scientific Advisory Committee, European Federation of Biotechnology, 1991; Auditor, International Union of Biochemistry and Molecular Biology, 1991-94. Recreations: music; painting; golf. Address: (h.) 144 Mugdock Road, Milngavie, Glasgow, G62 8NP; T.-041-956 1689.

Bureau, James Roger, BA. Senior Lecturer, Marketing Department, Strathclyde University, since 1987; Director, Cappella Nova, since 1988; b. 14.5.32, Antwerp, Belgium; m., April M.M. Connacher; 2 s.; 2 d. Educ. Kirkham Grammar School; University College, Durham University. Trainee Graduate, Market Research Department, Benton and Bowles, 1956-61; Gillette UK: Market Research Section Head, later Manager, 1961-67; Brand Manager, later Group Brand Manager, Marketing Department, 1968-73; Marketing Director, Jeyes UK, 1973-76; Marketing Department, Strathclyde University, since 1976. Founder Organiser, Balquhidder Summer Music Concerts. Publication: Brand Management, 1981. Recreations: classical music; history; astronomy; poetry; not gardening; political structures. Address: (h.) The Bank House, Buchlyvie, Stirling; T.-036 085 435.

Burgess, Charles Douglas, FRICS, IRRV. Partner, David Watson, Property Agents, Surveyors and Valuers, Glasgow, since 1973; Chairman, Royal Institution of Chartered Surveyors in Scotland, 1990-91; b. 20.12.33, Glasgow; m., Margaret (Rita) Helen Blackwood; 2 d. Educ. High School of Glasgow; Royal Technical College, Glasgow. National Service, 1956-58; Assistant Surveyor, Hendry & Steel, 1958-65; Partner, 1965-73. President, Property Owners and Factors Association, Glasgow, Ltd., 1977-79; President, Property Owners and Factors Association, Scotland, Ltd., 1986-88; Past Preses, Weavers Society of Anderston; Past President, Sandyford Burns Club, Glasgow; Past President, Glasgow and District Burns Association. Recreations: sailing; music; the works of Robert Burns. Address: (b.) 926 Govan Road, Glasgow, G51 3AE; T.-041-445 3741.

Burgess, John Moncrieff, BSc, MIEDO. Director of Research and Development, Shetland Islands Council, since 1975; b. 8.9.36, Scousburgh; m., Patricia Margaret; 2 s. Educ. Anderson Educational Institute; Aberdeen University. Lecturer, North of Scotland College of Agriculture, 1961-64; Assistant Lands Officer, then Lands Officer, Department of Agriculture and Fisheries for Scotland, 1964-75. Recreations: boating; fishing. Address: (b.) 93 St. Olaf Street, Lerwick, Shetland; T.-0595 3535.

Burgess, Moira, MA, FLA. Novelist and Short Story Writer; b. 19.3.36, Campbeltown; m., Archie Stirling (deceased); 1 s.; 1 d. Educ. Campbeltown Grammar School; Strathclyde University. Librarian, 1953-73; author of: The Day Before Tomorrow (novel), 1971; A Rumour of Strangers (novel), 1987; Editor, short story anthologies: Streets of Stone (with Hamish Whyte), 1985, Streets of Gold (with Hamish Whyte),

1989, The Other Voice, 1987; compiler, The Glasgow Novel, 2nd edition, 1986 (bibliography). Creative Writing Fellow, Renfrew District Libraries, 1990 92. Recreations: reading; embroidery; theatre.

Burgess, Professor Robert Arthur, LLB, PhD. Professor of Business Law, Strathclyde University, since 1989; b. 24.2.46, Northwich; m., Frances I.L. Burns; 1 s.; 1 d. Educ. Sir John Deane's Grammar School, Northwich; University College, London; Edinburgh University. National Provincial Bank, 1967-69; Lecturer in Law, Southampton University, 1969-72; Lecturer in Taxation and Investment Law, Edinburgh University, 1972-78; Reader in Law, University of East Anglia, 1978-89. Publications: Perpetuities in Scots Law; Corporate Finance Law; Law of Borrowing. Recreations: food and drink; travel. Address: (b.) Law School, Strathclyde University, 173 Cathedral Street, Glasgow, G4 0RQ; T.-041-552 4400.

Burgon, Robert Douglas, BA, MLitt, APMI. Director and Secretary, Scottish & Northern Ireland Plumbing Employers' Federation, since 1988; Secretary and Pensions Manager, Plumbing Pensions (UK) Ltd., since 1988; b. 3.8.55, Haddington; m., Sheila Georgina Bryson. Educ. North Berwick High School; Heriot Watt University. SNIPEF: Assistant Industrial Relations Officer, 1978, Assistant to the Director, 1979, Secretary, 1983. Recreation: music (church organist). Address: (b.) 2 Walker Street, Edinburgh, EH3 7LB; T.-031-225 2255.

Burley, Elayne Mary, BA (Hons). Director, Napier Enterprise Centre, Napier University, since 1991; b. 17.10.44, Cheshire; 2 s.; 1 d. Educ. Astley Grammar School for Girls; Leeds University. Leeds Polytechnic, 1966-68; Lecturer, Gordon Institute of Technology, Victoria, Australia, 1970-72; Lecturer, Open University in Scotland, 1972-84; Head of Training, Scottish Council for Voluntary Organisations, 1984-91. Founder Member, Confederation of Scottish Counselling Agencies; Member, Management Committee, Wellspring. Recreations: golf; bridge; performing arts; walking on the beach; collecting blue and white china. Address: (b.) 10 Colinton Road, Edinburgh; T.-031-455 2311.

Burley, Lindsay Elizabeth, MB, ChB, FRCPE, MRCGP, LHSM. Director of Planning and Development, Lothian Health Board; b. 2.10.50, Blackpool; m., Robin Burley. Educ. Queen Mary School, Lytham; Edinburgh University. Address: (b.) Lothian Health Board, 148 The Pleasance, Edinburgh EH8 9RR; T.-031-229 5888.

Burnet, George Wardlaw, LVO, BA, LLB, WS, KStJ, DL. Senior Partner, Murray Beith & Murray, WS, 1983-91; Chairman: Life Association of Scotland Ltd., since 1985; Caledonian Research Foundation, since 1988; b. 26.12.27, Edinburgh; m., Jane Elena Moncrieff; 2 s.; 1 d. Educ. Edinburgh Academy; Lincoln College, Oxford; Edinburgh University. Brigadier, Queen's Bodyguard for Scotland (Royal Company of Archers); former Midlothian County Councillor; Convenor, Church of Scotland Finance Committee, 1980-83; Hon. Fellow, Royal Incorporation of Architects in Scotland; Deputy Lieutenant, Midlothian. Address: (h.) Rose Court, Inveresk, Midlothian, EH21 7TD.

Burnett, Charles John, KStJ, DA, AMA, FSAScot, FHSS. Ross Herald of Arms; Curator of Fine Art, Scottish United Services Museum, Edinburgh Castle, since 1985; Vice-President, Heraldry Society of Scotland, since 1986; Vice-Patron, Genealogical Society of Queensland, since 1986; b. 6.11.40, Sandhaven, by Fraserburgh; m., Aileen E. McIntyre; 2 s.; 1 d. Educ. Fraserburgh Academy; Gray's School of Art, Aberdeen; Aberdeen College of Education. Advertising Department, House of Fraser, Aberdeen, 1963-64; Exhibitions Division, Central Office of Information, 1964-68 (on team which planned British pavilion for World Fair, Montreal, 1967); Assistant Curator, Letchworth Museum and Art Gallery, 1968-71; Head, Design Department, National Museum of Antiquities of Scotland, 1971-85. Heraldic Adviser, Girl Guide Association in Scotland, since 1978; Librarian, Priory of the Order of St. John in Scotland, since 1987; Council Member, Society of Antiquaries of Scotland, 1986-88; Honorary Citizen of Oklahoma, 1989. Recreations: reading; visiting places of historic interest. Address: (h.) 3 Hermitage Terrace, Morningside, Edinburgh; T.-031-447 5472.

Burnett, James Murray, FRICS, DipTP. Partner, Donaldsons, Chartered Surveyors, since 1987; Board Member, Cumbernauld Development Corporation, since 1990; Director, Broadwood Developments plc, since 1992; b. 7.2.44, Edinburgh; m., Elizabeth Anne; 1 s.; 2 d. Educ. Boroughmuir School; Heriot-Watt University; Edinburgh College of Art. Joined Donaldsons in 1970, giving development consultancy advice for large shopping centres. Chairman, General Practice Division, Royal Institution of Chartered Surveyors in Scotland, 1992-93. Recreations: golf; gardening. Address: (h.) 438 Lanark Road, Colinton, Edinburgh; T.-031-441 2200.

Burnett, Robert Gemmill, LLB, SSC, NP. Solicitor, since 1972; b. 18.1.49, Kilmarnock; m., Patricia Margaret Masson; 1 s.; 2 d. Educ. George Heriot's School, Edinburgh; Edinburgh University. Apprentice, then Assistant, then Partner, Drummond Miller WS. President, Edinburgh Bar Association; Secretary, Lothian Allelon Society; Solicitor to General Teaching Council. Recreations: golf; gardening. Address: (b.) 31/32 Moray Place, Edinburgh; T.-031-226 5151.

Burnett, Rodney Alister, MB, ChB, FRCPath. Consultant Pathologist responsible for diagnostic services, University Department of Pathology, Western Infirmary, Glasgow, since 1985; b. 6.6.47, Congleton; m., Maureen Elizabeth Dunn; 2 d. Educ. Sandbach School; St. Andrews University. Lecturer in Pathology, Glasgow University, 1974-79; Consultant in administrative charge, Department of Pathology, Stobhill Hospital, Glasgow, 1979-85. Secretary, Association of Clinical Pathologists, Caledonian Branch. Address: (h.) 134 Brownside Road, Cambuslang, Glasgow, G72; T.-041-641 3036.

Burnett, Rupert Gavin, BCom, CA, FCMA. Director, Student Loans Company Limited, since 1991; Director, Scottish Conveyancing and Executry Services Board, since 1991; b. 6.11.39, India; m., Elspeth MacLean; 2 s.; 1 d. Educ. George Watson's College; Edinburgh University; Harvard Business School. CA apprenticeship, Geoghegan and Co., Edinburgh, 1957-62; Management Accountant, Procter and Gamble Ltd., 1963-65; Management Consultant, McLintock, Moores and Murray, 1965-68; Chartered Accountant, Arthur Young McClelland Moores and Co., 1968-91 (subsequently Arthur Young, then Ernst and Young, Partner, latterly Senior Partner, 1970-91). Honorary Professor, Stirling University, since 1991; Member, Council, Institute of Chartered Accountants of Scotland, since 1990; Chairman, North Strathclyde Area Committee, Audit Practices Committee, CCAB, 1986-91; Trustee, Church of Scotland Trust, 1992. Recreations: watching rugby; fishing; theatre; country cottage; hill walking; church treasurer. Address: (h.) 7 Ralston Road, Bearsden, Glasgow, G61 3SS; T.-041-942 5513.

Burnett-Stuart of Crichie, George Slessor. Farmer and Landowner, since 1969; b. 3.1.48, Cobham; m., Patricia De Lavenne; 2 d. Educ. Winchester College; Bordeaux University. Member, Council, Scottish Conservation Projects; Member, Council, National Trust for Scotland; Member, Council, Stewart Society; Chairman, Grampian Farming

Forestry Wildlife Group; Director, Association of Agriculture Scotland; Treasurer, Friends of Grampian Stones. Recreations: kite-flying; travelling; tree-planting. Address: Crichie House, Stuartfield, Peterhead, AB4 8DY; T.-0771 24202.

Burns, Jessica Martha, BA (Hons), LLB, SSC. Senior Lecturer, Faculty of Law, Aberdeen University, since 1986; part-time Chairman, Social Security Appeal Tribunals, since 1987; b. 4.10.52, Dumfries; m., Bill Findlay; 2 d. Educ. Carlisle and County High School for Girls; Stirling University; Edinburgh University. Lecturer in Law, Glasgow University, 1983-85. Member, Parole Board for Scotland, since 1990; Member, Police Advisory Board for Scotland, since 1988; Governor, Scottish Police College, since 1988; Visiting Professor, School of Law, Maryland University, since 1988; part-time Chairman, Disability Appeal Tribunals, since 1992; Chairman, Nursery Trust, Aberdeen University. Recreations: relaxing with family; theatre; music; good company. Address: Faculty of Law, Aberdeen University, Aberdeen, AB9 2UB; T.-0224 272416.

Burns, Michael John, MA, LLB; b. 11.3.32, Dingwall; m., Janet Susan; 3 d. Educ. Dingwall Academy; Fettes College; St. Andrews University; Edinburgh University. National Service commission, Seaforth Highlanders; Partner, T.S.H. Burns and Son, Dingwall; Honorary Sheriff Substitute; Area Chairman, Rent Tribunal. Recreations: golf; cultivation of garden and friends. Adress: The Shieling, Ferry Road, Dingwall; T.-0349 62255.

Burstall, Professor Rodney M., MA, MSc, PhD. Professor of Computer Science, Edinburgh University, since 1979; b. 11.11.34, Liverpool; m., Seija-Leena (deceased); 3 d. Educ. George V Grammar School, Southport; King's College, Cambridge; Birmingham University. Operational Research Consultant, Brussels, 1959; Operational Research and Programming, Reed Paper Group, Kent, 1960; Research Fellow, Birmingham University, 1962; Research Fellow, Lecturer, Reader, Professor, Department of Artificial Intelligence, Edinburgh University, 1964-79. Emissary to UK for Venerable Chogyam Trungpa Rinpoche, Buddhist Meditation Master, 1982; Member, Academia Europaea, 1989. Address: (b.) Department of Computer Science, Edinburgh University, King's Buildings, Mayfield Road, Edinburgh, EH9 3JZ; T.-031-667 1081.

Burt, Gillian Robertson, MA (Hons). Headmistress, Craigholme School, Glasgow, since 1991; b. 7.2.44, Edinburgh; m., Andrew Wallace Burt; 1 s.; 1 d. Educ. Mary Erskine School; Edinburgh University; Moray House College of Education. Teacher of Geography, Tabeetha Church of Scotland School, Jaffa, Israel, 1966-67; Teacher of Geography, Boroughmuir Secondary School, 1967-70; Head of Geography, St. Hilary's School, Edinburgh, 1970-71, 1976-86, Head of Careers, 1986-91 (merged with St. Margaret's School, 1983). Recreations: music; theatre; walking; cooking; foreign travel. Address: (h.) 277 Nithsdale Road, Glasgow, G41 5LX; T.-041-427 2034.

Burton, Anthony Winston, OBE, BA (Hons). Director, The Planning Exchange, since 1975; b. 14.10.40, Leicester; 2 s.; 1 d. Educ. Wyggeston; Keele University. Deputy Chairman, Consumers' Association; Member, National Consumer Council; Member, European Commission's Consumers' Consultative Council. Recreation: sailing. Address: (h.) 9 Marchmont Terrace, Glasgow, G12; T.-041-334 7697.

Burton, Derek Arthur, BSc, MA, ABPsS. Honorary Senior Lecturer in Clinical Psychology, St. Andrews University, since 1977; b. 27.8.32, Staffordshire. Educ. North Staffordshire College; Leicester University; Hull University. Research Assistant, Institute of Neurology, London; Senior

Psychologist, Leicester; Principal Psychologist, Leicester Area Psychology Service; Consultant Psychologist, Fife Adult Psychology Service. Collingwood Philosophy Prizewinner; Honorary Fellow, Edinburgh University. Recreations: hill walking; music; theatre. Address: (b.) Department of Psychology, St. Andrews University, St. Andrews; T.-St. Andrews 76161.

Burton, Gillian Robertson, MA (Hons). Headmistress, Craigholme School, Glasgow, since 1991; b. 7.2.44, Edinburgh; m., Andrew Wallace Burt; 1 s.; 1 d. Educ. Mary Erskine School; Edinburgh University; Moray House College of Education. Teacher of Geography: Tabeetha Church of Scotland, Jaffa, Israel, 1966-67, Boroughmuir Secondary School, Edinburgh, 1967-70; Head of Geography, St. Hilary's School, Edinburgh, 1970-71; rejoined St. Hilary's School, 1976, as Head of Geography; Head of Careers, St. Margaret's School, Edinburgh, 1986-91. Recreations: music; theatre; walking; cooking; foreign travel. Address: (h.) 277 Nithsdale Road, Glasgow, G41 5LX; T.-041-427 2034.

Burton, Lord (Michael Evan Victor Baillie). Landowner and Farmer; Member, Inverness District Council, since 1984; Executive Member, Scottish Landowners Federation, since 1963; b. 27.6.24, Burton-on-Trent; m., 1, Elizabeth Ursula Foster Wise (m. diss.); 2, Coralie Denise Cliffe; 2 s.; 4 d. Educ. Eton; Army. Scots Guards, 1942 (Lt., 1944); Lovat Scouts, 1948; Member, Inverness County Council, 1948-75; JP, 1961-75; Deputy Lieutenant, Inverness, 1963-65; has served on numerous committees. Recreations: shooting, fishing and hunting (not much time); looking after the estate. Address: Dochfour, Inverness; T.-046 386 252.

Bushe, Frederick, RSA (1987), DA, DAE. Sculptor, since 1956; Director, Scottish Sculpture Workshop, since 1979; b. 1.3.31, Coatbridge; m., Fiona M.S. Marr; 1 d.; 3 s., 1 d. by pr. m. Educ. Our Lady's High School, Motherwell; Glasgow School of Art. Lecturer in Sculpture: Liverpool College of Education, 1962-69, Aberdeen College of Education, 1969-79; full-time Artist since 1979; established Scottish Sculpture Workshop and Scottish Sculpture Open Exhibition; exhibited in numerous one man and group exhibitions, since 1962. Recreation: listening to music. Address: (h.) Rose Cottage, Lumsden, Huntly, Aberdeenshire.

Busuttil, Professor Anthony, MD, FRCPath, FRCP, FRCPE, DMJ(Path), MRCP (UK). Regius Professor of Forensic Medicine, Edinburgh University, since 1987; Honorary Consultant Pathologist, Lothian Health Board, since 1976; Police Surgeon, Lothian and Borders Police, since 1980; b. 30.12.45, Rabat, Malta; m., Angela; 3 s. Educ. St. Aloysius' College, Malta; Royal University of Malta. Junior posts, Western Infirmary, Glasgow; Lecturer in Pathology, Glasgow University. Address: (h.) 78 Hillpark Avenue, Edinburgh, EH4 7AL; T.-031-336 3241.

Bute, 6th Marquess of (John Crichton-Stuart), JP. Hereditary Sheriff of Bute; Hereditary Keeper of Rothesay Castle; Lord Lieutenant, Argyll and Bute, since 1990; b. 27.2.33; m., 1, Nicola Weld-Forester (m. diss.); 2 s.; 1 d.; 1 d. (deceased); 2, Jennifer Percy. Educ. Ampleforth College; Trinity College, Cambridge. Chairman, Scottish Standing Committee for Voluntary International Aid, 1964-68; Chairman, Council and Executive Committee, National Trust for Scotland, 1969-84 (President, since 1991); Chairman: National Museums of Scotland, since 1985; Scottish Committee, National Fund for Research into Crippling Diseases, since 1966; Historic Buildings Council for Scotland, 1983-88; Scottish Advisory Committee of the British Council, since 1987; Chairman, Museums Advisory Board (Scotland), 1984-85; Trustee, National Galleries of Scotland, 1980-86; Member, Countryside Commission for Scotland, 1970-78; Honorary Sheriff-Substitute, Bute, 1976; Convener, Buteshire

County Council, 1967-70; DL Bute, 1961; Lord Lieutenant, 1967-75; Hon. LLD, Glasgow, 1970; Hon. FRIAS, 1985. Address: (h.) Mount Stuart, Rothesay, Isle of Bute PA20 9LR.

Butler, Anthony Robert, BSc, PhD, DSc, AKC. Reader in Chemistry, St. Andrews University, since 1965; b. 28.11.36, Croydon, Surrey; m., Janet Anderson. Educ. Selhurst; King's College, London; Cornell University. Consulting Editor, Longman-Cartermill Publishing, 1980; Lecturer, Fleming Centenary Celebration, Darvel, 1981. Recreations: hill-walking; road-running; music; writing Chinese characters. Address: (h.) Red Gable, Denhead, St. Andrews; T.-033485 521.

Butler, Rev. John Michael Francis, DipTh, DipMS, MBIM, MIPM. Minister of Religion (Congregational), since 1953; b. 12.3.28, Petersfield; m., Charlotte Matilda; 2 s.; 1 d. Educ. Churchers College, Petersfield; New College, London. Minister: Laira and Plympton Congregational Churches, 1953-59; Helensburgh Congregational Church, 1959-64; General Secretary, Scripture Union – Scotland, 1965-88; Minister, Partick Congregational Church, since 1988. Recreations: Christian activity; reading and book reviewing; sailing; bad photography. Address: (h.) 2 Southview, Dalmuir, Clydebank, G81 3LA; T.-041-952 1338.

Butler, Vincent Frederick, RSA, RGI. Sculptor. Address: (h.) 17 Deanpark Crescent, Edinburgh, EH4 1PH; T.-031-332 5884.

Butlin, Ron, MA, DipAECD. Poet and Novelist; b. 17.11.49, Edinburgh. Educ. Dumfries Academy; Edinburgh University. Writer in Residence, Lothian Region Education Authority, 1979, Edinburgh University, 1981, 1984-85; Scottish/Canadian Writing Exchange Fellow, University of New Brunswick, 1983-84; Writer in Residence for Midlothian, 1989-90. Publications: poetry: Stretto, 1976; Creatures Tamed by Cruelty, 1979; The Exquisite Instrument, 1982 (Scottish Arts Council Book Award); Ragtime in Unfamiliar Bars, 1985 (SAC Book Award, Poetry Book Society recommendation); prose: The Tilting Room (short stories), 1983 (SAC Book Award); The Sound of My Voice (novel), 1987; Blending In (play), 1989. Recreations: music; travel. Address: (h.) 9 Moncrieff Terrace, Edinburgh, EH9 1NB; T.-031-667 0394.

Butter, Sir David Henry, KCVO, MC. Lord Lieutenant, Perth and Kinross, since 1975; Landowner and Company Director; b. 18.3.20, London; m., Myra Alice Wernher; 1 s.; 4 d. Educ. Eton College; Oxford University. Served in World War II, 2nd Lt., Scots Guards, 1940; served in Western Desert, North Africa, Sicily and Italy (ADC to GOC 8th Army, 1944); Temporary Major, 1946; retired, 1948; Brigadier, Queen's Bodyguard for Scotland (Royal Company of Archers); President, Highland TAVR, 1979-84; Member, Perth County Council, 1955-74; Deputy Lieutenant, Perthshire, 1956; Vice Lieutenant, Perthshire, 1960-71; Lord Lieutenant of County of Perth, 1971-75, of Kinross, 1974-75; Governor, Gordonstoun School, 1954-86; Governor, Butterstone House School; Honorary President, Perthshire Battalion, Boys Brigade. Recreations: golf; skiing; travel; shooting. Address: Cluniemore, Pitlochry, Perthshire; T.-0796 2006.

Butter, Professor Peter Herbert. Regius Professor of English Language and Literature, Glasgow University, 1965-86; b. 7.4.21, Coldstream; m., Bridget Younger; 1 s.; 2 d. Educ. Charterhouse; Balliol College, Oxford. Royal Artillery, 1941-46; Lecturer in English, Edinburgh University, 1948-58; Professor of English, Queen's University, Belfast, 1958-65. Secretary/Treasurer, International Association of University Professors of English, 1965-71. Publications: Shelley's Idols of the Cave, 1954; Francis Thompson, 1961;

Edwin Muir, 1962; Edwin Muir: Man and Poet, 1966; Shelley's Alastor, Prometheus Unbound and Other Poems (Editor), 1971; Selected Letters of Edwin Muir (Editor), 1974; William Blake: Selected Poems (Editor), 1982; The Truth of Imagination: Uncollected Prose of Edwin Muir (Editor), 1988; Complete Poems of Edwin Muir (Editor), 1991. Recreations: gardening; hill-walking. Address: (h.) Ashfield, Prieston Road, Bridge of Weir, Renfrewshire, PA11 3AW; T.-Bridge of Weir 613139.

Butterfield, Alan W., MA, DipEd, JP. Rector, Hamilton Grammar School, since 1971; b. 1.5.33, Dundee; m., Rosemary; 1 s.; 1 d. Educ. Dundee High School; St. Andrews University. Teacher of English and History, Harris Academy, Dundee; Special Assistant of English and History, Dunfermline High School; Principal Teacher of English: Broxburn Academy, Trinity Academy, Edinburgh; Depute Rector, Falkirk High School. President, Headteachers' Association of Scotland, 1984-85. Recreation: Rotary. Address: (h.) 23 Langside Road, Bothwell, Lanarkshire; T.-853505.

Butters, Benjamin. Chairman and Managing Director, Butters Engineering Services Ltd., since 1980; Member, Lands Valuation Appeal Tribunal; Chairman, Glasgow College of Nautical Studies; Director, Merchants House of Glasgow; b. 28.3.27, Glasgow; m., Norah Lindsay Hill; 1 s.; 2 d. Educ. Loretto; Glasgow Technical College. Sales Director, Butters Bros & Co. Ltd., 1954-63; Managing Director, Butters Cranes Ltd., 1963-78; Director, Abbot Engineering Ltd., 1960-78; Past President, Scottish Engineering Employers Association. Recreation: golf (Royal Troon). Address: (h.) Flat 8, 4 Barcapel Avenue, Newton Mearns, Glasgow, G77 6QJ; T.-041-639 3128.

Butterworth, Neil, MA, HonFLCM. Chairman, Scottish Society of Composers, since 1991; Music Critic, Times Educational Supplement, since 1983, and The Sunday Times Scotland, since 1988; Broadcaster; b. 4.9.34, Streatham, London; m., Anna Mary Barnes; 3 d. Educ. Rutlish School, Surrey; Nottingham University; London University; Guildhall School of Music, London. Lecturer, Kingston College of Technology, 1960-68; Head, Music Department, Napier College, Edinburgh, 1986-87. Conductor: Sutton Symphony Orchestra, 1960-64, Glasgow Orchestral Society, 1975-83 and since 1989; Chairman, Incorporated Society of Musicians, Edinburgh Centre, since 1981; Chairman, Inveresk Preservation Society, since 1988; Churchill Fellowship, 1975. Publications: Haydn, 1976; Dvorak, 1980; Dictionary of American Composers, 1983; Aaron Copland, 1984; Samuel Barber, 1988; Vaughan Williams, 1989; Neglected Music, 1991; over 300 compositions. Recreations: autographs; collecting books and records; giant jigsaw puzzles. Address: (h.) The White House, Inveresk, Musselburgh, Midlothian; T.-031-665 3497.

Buxton, Paul Kenneth, MA (Cantab), MB, BChir, FRCP(C), FRCPEdin. Consultant Physician in Dermatology, Fife Health Board and Royal Infirmary, Edinburgh, since 1981; Member, Clinical Teaching Staff, Edinburgh University, since 1981; b. 28.2.36, Harrar, Ethiopia; m., Heather; 1 s.; 1 d. Educ. Trinity College, Cambridge; St. Thomas's Hospital, London. Dermatologist, Royal Jubilee Hospital, Victoria, BC, Canada, 1971-81. President, Fife Branch, BMA, 1986-87; Fellow, Royal Society of Medicine; Member, Ethical Committee, Fife Health Board; Member, Editorial Board, Ethics and Medicine. Publication: ABC of Dermatology. Recreations: seafaring; books; art; country pursuits. Address: (h.) Old Inzievar House, Dunfermline, KY12 8HA; T.-0383 880297.

Byers, Rev. Alan James. Minister, Gamrie linked with King Edward, since 1988; b. 7.4.26, Girvan; m., Mairi Catriona Laing; 3 s.; 1 d. Educ. Girvan Secondary School; Edinburgh University; New College. RAF, 1944-48; Chaplain to hydro-electric workers' camps, 1955-56; Assistant Minister, Ardchattan, 1959; Minister: Presbyterian Church of Ghana (Northern Ghana), 1960-71; Boddam Parish Church, Peterhead, 1971-88. Recreations: photography; DIY. Address: The Manse, King Edward, Banff, AB45 3NQ; T.-02616 258.

Byrne, John. Playwright. Works include The Slab Boys (stage play) and Tutti Frutti (television serial).

C

Caddie, James Murdoch, MBIM. Adviser to voluntary organisations; former Chief Executive Officer, Epilepsy Association of Scotland; Association of Scotland, since 1977; b. 2.11.27, Glasgow; m., Grace Betty (deceased); 2 d. Educ. Whitehill Senior Secondary School, Glasgow. Administrator: South of Scotland Electricity Board, 1948-71, National Health Service, 1971-77. Member: local Health Council, 1978-83; Glasgow Council for Welfare of the Disabled; Chairman, Joint Epilepsy Associations Committee, 1980-88. Recreations: gardening; travel. Address: (h.) 35 Baldric Road, Glasgow, G13 3QT; T.-041-959 7250.

Caddy, Brian, BSc, PhD, CChem, MRIC. Senior Lecturer in Forensic Science and Director, Forensic Science Unit, Strathclyde University, since 1978; Editor, Journal of the Forensic Science Society; b. 26.3.37, Burslem, Stoke-on-Trent; m., Beryl Ashworth; 1 s.; 1 d. Educ. Middleport Secondary Modern School; Longton High School; Sheffield University. Strathclyde University: MRC Research Fellow, 1963, Director, Forensic Science Unit, 1966. Council Member, Forensic Science Society; Visiting Professor, University of Birmingham, Alabama; Adviser, UN Narcotics Division. Recreations: music; reading; gardening; walking the dog; relaxing. Address: (b.) Forensic Science Unit, Strathclyde University, Glasgow; T.-041-552 4400.

Cadell, Colin Simson, CBE, DL, MA, AMIEE; b. 7.8.05, Colinton; m., Rosemary Elizabeth Pooley; 2 s.; 1 d. Educ. Merchiston; Edinburgh University; Ecole Superieure d'Electricite. Commissioned RAF, 1926; Director of Signals, RAF, 1944; AOC, 66 Group, 1946; Managing Director, International Aeradio, 1947; Vice-Lieutenant for West Lothian, 1972-86; Chairman, Edinburgh Airport Consultative Committee, 1972-83. Member, Royal Company of Archers (Queen's Bodyguard for Scotland); Legion of Merit (US). Address: (h.) 2 Upper Coltbridge Terrace, Edinburgh, EH12.

Cadell, Patrick Moubray, BA, FSA (Scot). Keeper of the Records of Scotland, since 1991; b. 17.3.41, Linlithgow; m., Sarah King; 2 s.; 1 d. Educ. Merchiston Castle School, Edinburgh; Cambridge University; Toulouse University. Information Officer, British Museum; Assistant Keeper, Department of MSS, British Museum; Keeper of Manuscripts, National Library of Scotland, 1983-90. Clerk, Abbey Court of Holyrood; Recorder of the Council of Lord High Commissioners; Past President, West Lothian History and Amenity Society. Recreations: walking; music. Address:

(b.) Scottish Record Office, HM General Register House, Edinburgh EH1 3YY; T.-031-556 6585.

Cadell of Grange, William Archibald, DL, MA (Cantab), RIBA, FRIAS. Architect, since 1960; b. 9.3.33, Aldershot; m., Mary-Jean Carmichael; 3 s. Educ. Merchiston Castle; Cambridge University; Regent Street Polytechnic. Robert Matthew, Johnson Marshall and Partners; Associate, Ian G. Lindsay and Partners; started William A. Cadell Architects, 1968. DL, West Lothian, 1982; Member, Executive and Curatorial Committees, National Trust for Scotland; former Chairman, RIAS Conservation Working Group; former Chairman, West Lothian History and Amenity Society. Recreations: gardening; local history; exhibition design; theatre. Address: Grange, Linlithgow, West Lothian; T.-0506 842946.

Caie, Professor Graham Douglas, MA, PhD. Professor of English Language, Glasgow University, since 1990; b. 3.2.45, Aberdeen; m., Ann Pringle Abbott; 1 s., 1 d. Educ. Aberdeen Grammar School; Aberdeen University; McMaster University, Canada. Teaching Assistant, McMaster University, 1968-72; Amanuensis and Lektor, Copenhagen University, 1972-90. Chairman, Medieval Centre, Copenhagen University, 1985-90; Visiting Professor: McMaster University, 1985-86, Guelph University, 1989; Associate Fellow, Clare Hall, Cambridge, 1977-78; International Secretary, New Chaucer Society; Member, Board, McMaster Old English Texts series; Editorial Committee, Scottish Texts Society; Erasmus Academic Advisory Group (EC Commission). Publications: The Theme of Doomsday in Old English Poetry; Beowulf; Bibliography of Junius XI MS; numerous articles. Address: (h.) 12B Upper Glenburn Road, Bearsden, Glasgow, G61 4BW; T.-041-943 1192.

Caird, Professor Francis Irvine, MA, DM, FRCP, FRCPSGlas. David Cargill Professor of Geriatric Medicine, Glasgow University, since 1979; b. 24.8.28, Glastonbury; m., Angela Margaret Alsop (deceased); 1 s.; 2 d. Educ. Winchester College; New College, Oxford. Medical Registrar, General Hospital, Birmingham, and RPGMS, Hammersmith; Senior Registrar and Medical Tutor, Radcliffe Infirmary, Oxford; Senior Lecturer and Reader in Geriatric Medicine, Glasgow University. Recreation: travel. Address: (h.) 4 Colquhoun Drive, Bearsden, Glasgow, G61 4NQ; T.-041-942 7785.

Cairncross, Robert George, MB, ChB, FRCP (Ed), MRCGP. Deputy Secretary, Scottish Council for Postgraduate Medical Education, since 1984; Honorary Lecturer, Centre for Medical Education, Dundee University, since 1984; b. 6.7.44, Dundee. Educ. Robert Gordon's College, Aberdeen; Aberdeen University. Registrar, Lothian Health Board, 1972-75; trainee General Practitioner, Edinburgh University, 1975-76; Lecturer in Medical Education, Dundee University, 1976-81; Educational Adviser, College of Medicine, Abha, Saudi Arabia, 1981-83; Project Director, Dundee University, 1983-84. Address: (b.) Scottish Council for Postgraduate Medical Education, 12 Queen Street, Edinburgh, EH2 1JE; T.-031-225 4365.

Cairns, Gordon McLean, MA, LLB, NP. Solicitor; Honorary Sheriff, Stranraer, since 1981; b. 31.7.38, Calcutta; m., Elizabeth; 1 s.; 1 d. Educ. Edinburgh Academy; Edinburgh University. Solicitor in private practice, since 1961. Address: (h.) Birchgrove, Whitehouse Road, Stranraer; T.-0776 2984.

Cairns, Rev. John Ballantyne, LTh, LLB. Parish Minister, Riverside Church, Dumbarton, since 1985; b. 15.3.42, London; m., Dr. Elizabeth Emma Bradley; 3 s. Educ. Sutton Valence School, Kent; Bristol University; Edinburgh

University. Messrs Richards, Butler & Co., Solicitors, City of London, 1964-68; Administrative Assistant, East Lothian County Council, 1968-69; Assistant Minister, St. Giles, Elgin, 1973-75; Minister, Langholm, Ewes and Westerkirk Parish Churches, 1975-85, also linked with Canonbie, 1981-85; Clerk, Presbytery of Annandale and Eskdale, 1980-82; Convener, Maintenance of the Ministry Committee and Joint Convener, Board of Ministry and Mission, Church of Scotland, 1984-88; Divisional Chaplain, Strathclyde Police. Publications: Keeping Fit for Ministry, 1988; Democracy and Unwritten Constitutions, 1989. Recreations: golf; curling. Address: (b.) High Street, Dumbarton, G82 1NB; (h.) 5 Kirkton Road, Dumbarton, G82 4AS.

Cairns, Michael Francis, BSc, CQSW, DMS. Director, Age Concern Scotland, since 1989; b. 30.10.48, Dumbarton; m., Krystyna Anna Makar; 2 s.; 1 d. Educ. St. John's College, Southsea; Bedford and Goldsmiths Colleges, London University. Inner London Probation Service, 1973-76; Senior Social Worker, LB of Wandsworth, 1976-80; Assistant Divisional Director of Social Work, Berkshire CC, 1980-85; Divisional Director of Social Work, Lothian Region, 1985-89. Recreations: golf; gardening; music. Address: (b.) 54A Fountainbridge, Edinburgh, EH3 9PT; T.-031-228 5656.

Cairns, Robert, MA, DipEd. Member, City of Edinburgh District Council, since 1974 (Convener, Planning and Development Committee, since 1986); b. 16.7.47, Dundee; m., Pauline Reidy; 2 s. Educ. Morgan Academy; Edinburgh University; Moray House College of Education. Assistant Editor, Scottish National Dictionary, 1969-74; Parliamentary candidate (Labour), North Edinburgh, 1973, February 1974; Teacher, James Gillespie's High School, since 1975; Vice Chairman, Edinburgh Old Town Committee; Board Member: Edinvar Housing Association, Old Town Renewal Trust, Old Town Community Development Project, Edinburgh Military Tattoo. Recreations: gardening; theatre. Address: (h.) 34 Fountainhall Road, Edinburgh; T.-031-667 2974.

Cairns, Professor Robert Alan, BSc, PhD, FInstP. Professor, Department of Mathematical and Computational Sciences, St. Andrews University, since 1991 (Reader, 1985-91); b. 12.3.45, Glasgow; m., Ann E. Mackay. Educ. Allan Glen's School, Glasgow; Glasgow University. Lecturer in Applied Mathematics, St. Andrews University, 1970-83; Senior Lecturer, 1983-85; Consultant, UKAEA Culham Laboratory, since 1984. Committee Member, Plasma Physics Group, Institute of Physics, 1981-84; Member, SERC Laser Committee, since 1990; Member, SERC Atomic and Molecular Physics Sub-Committee, since 1990; Member, Editorial Board, Plasma Physics, 1983-85. Publications: Plasma Physics, 1985; Radiofrequency heating of plasmas, 1991. Recreations: music (listening to and playing recorder and baroque flute); golf; hill-walking. Address: (b.) Department of Mathematical and Computational Sciences, St. Andrews University, North Haugh, St. Andrews, Fife, KY16 9SS; T.-0334 76161, Ext. 8135.

Calder, Professor Andrew Alexander, MD, FRCP(Glas), FRCOG. Professor of Obstetrics and Gynaecology, Edinburgh University, since 1987; Consultant Gynaecologist, Edinburgh Royal Infirmary and Consultant Obstetrician, Simpson Memorial Maternity Pavilion, Edinburgh, since 1987; b. 17.1.45, Aberdeen; m., Valerie Anne Dugard; 1 s.; 2 d. Educ. Glasgow Academy; Glasgow University. Clinical training posts in obstetrics and gynaecology, 1969-72: Queen Mother's Hospital, Western Infirmary, Royal Maternity Hospital and Royal Infirmary, (all Glasgow); Research Fellow, Nuffield Department of Obstetrics and Gynaecology, Oxford University, 1972-75; Lecturer in Obstetrics and Gynaecology, Glasgow University, 1975-78, Senior Lecturer, 1978-86. Secretary, Munro Kerr Society for the Study of Reproductive Biology, 1980-86, Chairman, since 1989; Blair

Bell Memorial Lecturer, RCOG, 1977; WHO Travelling Fellow, 1985. Recreations: music; golf; curling. Address: (h.) 21 Braid Avenue, Edinburgh, EH10 4SR; T.-031-447 0490.

Calder, Angus Lindsay, MA, DPhil. Reader and Staff Tutor in Arts, Open University in Scotland, since 1979; Co-Editor, Journal of Commonwealth Literature, 1980-87; Convener, Scottish Poetry Library, 1983-88; b. 5.2.42, Sutton, Surrey; m., 1, Jennifer Daiches; 1 s.; 2 d.; 2, Catherine Kyle; 1 s. Educ. Wallington County Grammar School; Kings College, Cambridge. Lecturer in Literature, Nairobi University, 1968-71; Visiting Lecturer, Chancellor College, Malawi University, 1978. Member, Board of Directors: Fruitmarket Gallery, Royal Lyceum Theatre Company, 7-84 Theatre Company; Editorial Committee, Cencrastus; Member, Panel of Judges, Saltire Society Scottish Book of the Year Award, since 1983; Eric Gregory Award for Poetry, 1967. Publications: The People's War: Britain 1939-1945, 1969 (John Llewellyn Rhys Memorial Prize); Revolutionary Empire, 1981 (Scottish Arts Council Book Award); The Myth of the Blitz, 1991. Recreations: curling; cricket. Address: (b.) 60 Melville Street, Edinburgh, EH3 7HF; T.-031-226 3851.

Calder, Finlay, OBE. Grain Exporter; b. 20.8.57, Haddington; m., Elizabeth; 1 s.; 1 d. Educ. Daniel Stewart's and Melville College. Played rugby for Scotland, 1986-90; captained Scotland, 1989; captained British Isles, 1989. Recreation: work! Address: (b.) 3 John's Place, Leith, EH6 7EL; T.-031-554 6263.

Calder, George D., BA (Hons), LLB. Assistant Secretary, Scottish Office, since 1987; b. 20.12.47, Edinburgh; m., Kathleen Bonar; 2 d. Educ. George Watson's College; Pembroke College, Cambridge; Edinburgh University. Department of Employment, 1971-73; European Commission, 1973-76; HM Treasury, 1976-79; Manpower Services Commission Scotland, 1979-83; MSC Director for Northern England, 1983-85; MSC Director for Scotland, 1985-87. Recreations: hill-walking; football; reading; writing; book collecting. Address: (b.) 16 Waterloo Place, Edinburgh; T.-031-244 3848.

Calder, Jenni, BA, MPhil. Freelance Writer; Publications Editor, National Museums of Scotland, Edinburgh, since 1987; b. 3.12.41, Chicago, Illinois; 1 s.; 2 d. Educ. Perse School for Girls, Cambridge; Cambridge University; London University. Freelance writer, 1966-78; taught and lectured in Scotland, England, Kenya and USA; Lecturer in English, Nairobi University, 1968-69; Education Officer, Royal Scottish Museum, 1978-87. Member, Scottish Arts Council Book Awards Panel; Member, Scottish Writers Against the Bomb. Publications: Chronicles of Conscience: a study of George Orwell and Arthur Koestler, 1968; Scott (with Angus Calder), 1969; There Must be a Lone Ranger: the Myth and Reality of the American West, 1974; Women and Marriage in Victorian Fiction, 1976; Brave New World and Nineteen Eighty Four, 1976; Heroes: from Byron to Guevara, 1977; The Victorian Home, 1977; The Victorian Home from Old Photographs, 1979; RLS, A Life Study, 1980; The Robert Louis Stevenson Companion (Editor), 1980; Robert Louis Stevenson and Victorian Scotland (Editor), 1981; The Strange Case of Dr Jekyll and Mr Hyde (Editor), 1979; Kidnapped (Editor), 1981; Catriona (Editor), 1981; The Enterprising Scot (Editor), 1986; Island Landfalls (Editor), 1987; Bonny Fighters: The Story of the Scottish Soldier, 1987; Open Guide to Animal Farm and Nineteen Eighty Four, 1987; The Wealth of a Nation (Editor), 1989; St. Ives, a new ending, 1990; Scotland in Trust, 1990. Recreations: music; films; walking the dog. Address: (h.) 18 Springfield Road, South Queensferry, West Lothian; T.-031-331 2765.

Calder, John, Honorary Sheriff, Lothians; Vice Lieutenant, West Lothian; b. 11.7.14, Dundee; m., Vida Carmichael; 1 s.;

1 d. Educ. Morgan Academy, Dundee; University College, Dundee; Edinburgh University. Solicitor; Depute Town Clerk, Kirkcaldy; County Clerk, West Lothian; retired. District Governor, Rotary International District 102, 1962; Verdienstkreuz Am Bande (FDR) awarded by Bundesprasident, 1983. Address: (h.) Woodlands, 8 Dundas Street, Bo'ness, West Lothian; T.-0506 822311.

Calder, Robert Russell, MA. Critic, Philosophical Writer, Historian of Ideas, Poet, Freelance Journalist, Book Reviewer; b. 22.4.50, Burnbank. Educ. Hamilton Academy; Glasgow University; Edinburgh University. Co-Editor, Chapman, 1974-76 and since 1988; Editor, Lines Review, 1976-77; Theatre Critic and Feature Writer, Scot, 1983-86; books: A School of Thinking, 1992; Narcissism, Nihilism, Simplicity (Editor), 1992; poetry: Il Re Giovane, 1976, Ettrick & Annan, 1981; Serapion, 1992. Recreations: music - opera singing; jazz piano. Address: (h.) 23 Glenlee Street, Burnbank, Hamilton, ML3 9JB; T.-0698 824244.

Calderwood, Sir Robert, Kt. Chief Executive, Strathclyde Regional Council, since 1980; b. 1.3.32; m., Meryl Anne; 3 s.; 1 d. Educ. William Hulme's School, Manchester; Manchester University (LLB Hons). Town Clerk: Salford, 1966-69, Bolton, 1969-73, Manchester, 1973-79. Director, Glasgow Garden Festival 1988 Ltd., 1985-88; Chairman, Strathclyde Buses Ltd., since 1989; Member: Parole Board for England and Wales, 1971-73; Society of Local Authority Chief Executives, since 1974 (President, 1989-90); Scottish Consultative Committee, Commission for Racial Equality, 1981-88; Director, European Summer Special Olympic Games 1990 (Strathclyde) Ltd., 1989-90; Member, Council, Industrial Society, since 1983; Director, GEC (Scotland) Ltd., since 1991; Director, Scottish Opera, since 1991; CBIM; Companion, IWEM, 1983-89. Recreations: theatre; watching rugby; interested in United Nations activities. Address: Strathclyde Regional Council, 20 India Street, Glasgow, G2 4PF.

Caldwell, David Cleland, SHNC, MA, BPhil. Secretary, The Robert Gordon Institute of Technology, since 1984; seconded as Secretary, Conference of Scottish Centrally-Funded Colleges, 1988-90; b. 25.2.44, Glasgow; m., Ann Scott Macrae; 1 s.; 1 d. Educ. George Watson's College, Edinburgh; St. Andrews University; Glasgow University. Warwick University: Lecturer in Politics, 1969-76, Administrative Assistant, 1976-77, Assistant Registrar, 1977-80; Registry Officer, Aberdeen University, 1980-84. Member: Warwick District Council, 1979-80, Grampian Regional Council, 1983-84; Parliamentary candidate (Labour), North East Fife, 1983; Member, Aberdeen Grammar School Council, 1983-88 (Chairman, 1985-88); Member, St. Andrews University Court, since 1986. Address: (b.) The Robert Gordon Institute of Technology, Schoolhill, Aberdeen, AB9 1FR; T.-0224 633611.

Caldwell, David Hepburn, MA, PhD, FSAScot. Curator in Charge of the Scottish Medieval Collections, Royal Museum of Scotland; b. 15.12.51, Kilwinning, Ayrshire; m., Margaret Anne McGovern; 2 d. Educ. Ardrossan Academy; Edinburgh University. Joined staff, National Museum of Antiquities, 1973. Publications: The Scottish Armoury, 1979; Scottish Weapons and Fortifications, 1981. Recreation: travelling. Address: (h.) 3 James Park, Burntisland, Fife, KY3 9EW; T.-872175.

Caldwell, Rev. James, MA. Minister of Religion (retired); former Member, Tayside Health Board; b. 12.5.16, Larkhall, Lanarkshire; m., Marjory Bruce Harvie; 2 s.; 1 d. Educ. Hamilton Academy; St. Andrews University; St. Mary's College, St. Andrews. Ordained by Glasgow Presbytery; Assistant Minister, Govan Old Parish Church, 1943; inducted Rossland Church, Bishopton, 1945; inducted Kirriemuir,

1952; Moderator, Forfar Presbytery, 1955-56; translated to Shawlands Old Parish Church, 1958; became Minister, united charge with Langside Avenue Church, 1963; Chaplain, Victoria Infirmary, Glasgow, 1962-78; translated to Abernethy and Dron Parish Church, Perthshire, 1978; linked with Arngask, Glenfarg, 1979; Member, Advisory Board of Church of Scotland, 1980-81; Moderator, Perth Presbytery, 1983-84; first Chairman, Glasgow (SE) Health Council, 1975-78; Tayside Health Board: Convener, General Medical Practitioners' Committee and Special Leave Committee, 1984-85; Chairman, Arbroath Probus Club, 1989-90. Recreations: walking; gardening; travel; choral singing; writing and journalism. Address: (h.) 26 Dalhousie Place, Arbroath, DD11 2BT; T.-Arbroath 70670.

Caldwell, Sheila Marion, BA (Hons). General Secretary, Glasgow Association of University Women; Member, Committee, Royal Scottish Geographical Society; b. England; m., Major Robert Caldwell, TD. Educ. Tunbridge Wells Grammar School; University College, London. Founder/Principal, Yejide Girls' Grammar School, Ibadan, Nigeria; first Principal, Girls' Secondary (Government) School, Lilongwe, Malawi; Depute Head, Mills Grammar School, Framlingham, Suffolk; Head, St. Columba's School, Kilmacolm, 1976-87; Treasurer, Secondary Heads' Association, Scotland, 1984-87. Recreations: exploring new places and new ideas; reading; walking; music/opera; interior design (theory and practice). Address: (h.) 27 Oxford Road, Renfrew, PA4 0SJ; T.-041-886 2296.

Callen, Rev. John Robertson, MA, BD. Minister, Lochgilphead Parish Church, since 1962; Member, Board of Social Responsibility, General Assembly; b. 12.12.35, Glengarnock; m., Isobel Annie Morrison; 2 s. Educ. Spier's School; Glasgow University and Trinity College. Moderator: Inveraray Presbytery, 1966, 1973, South Argyll Presbytery, 1983; Chaplain, Lochgilphead Hospitals; Local Office-Bearer, National Bible Society of Scotland, since 1963; first Chairperson, Lochgilphead Community Council, 1977-79; Leader, Holy Land tour, 1983; Lyon Court grant of arms, 1968; Member, Council of Christians and Jews. Publication: Social Directory of Lochgilphead, 1972. Recreations: hill-walking; cycling. Address: Parish Manse, Manse Brae, Lochgilphead, Argyll, PA31 8QZ; T.-0546 602238.

Calman, Professor Kenneth Charles, MD, PhD, FRCP, FRCS, FRSE. Chief Medical Officer, Department of Health, since 1991; Chief Medical Officer, Scottish Home and Health Department, 1989-91; b. 25.12.41, Glasgow; m., Ann; 1 s.; 2 d. Educ. Allan Glen's School, Glasgow; Glasgow University. Lecturer in Surgery, Western Infirmary, Glasgow, 1968-72; MRC Clinical Research Fellow, London, 1972-73; Professor of Oncology, Glasgow University, 1974-84; Dean of Postgraduate Medicine, 1984-89. Recreations: golf; jogging; gardening. Address: (h.) 585 Anniesland Road, Glasgow; T.-041-954 9423.

Cameron, Alasdair. Farmer and Crofter; Commissioner, Crofters Commission; b. 12.6.44, Dingwall; m., Jeannette Benzie; 2 d. Educ. Dingwall Academy. Member, Scottish Agricultural Arbiters Association; Member, Northern Counties Valuators Association; Member, Committee, Highland Farming and Forestry Advisory Group; Hon. President, Black Isle Farmers Society; Member, Scottish Vernacular Buildings Working Group; Member, Historic Farm Buildings UK; Past Chairman, Dingwall Round Table. Recreations: photography; industrial archaeology; local history; the countryside. Address: Wellhouse Farm, Black Isle, Muir of Ord, Ross-shire, IV6 7SF; T.-0463 870416.

Cameron, Alexander, BA, CertASS, CQSW. Director of Social Work, Borders Regional Council, since 1987; b. 29.4.50, Glasgow; m., Linda Dobbie; 2 s. Educ. Duncanrig

Senior Secondary, East Kilbride; Strathclyde University; Aberdeen University. Social Worker, Clackmannan County Council, 1973-75; Central Regional Council: Research/Planning Officer, 1975-79, Principal Officer (Fieldwork), 1979-81, Assistant Director of Social Work, 1981-87. Assistant Secretary, Association of Directors of Social Work; Council Member, Central Council for Education and Training in Social Work; Member, Scottish Health Service Advisory Council. Recreations: rugby; trying to spend time with family. Address: (h.) Glencairn, Gattonside, Melrose, Roxburghshire; T.-0896 82 2831.

Cameron, Allan John, MBE, VL, JP. Convener, Ross and Cromarty District Council; Farmer and Landowner, since 1947; b. 25.3.17, Edinburgh; m., Elizabeth Vaughan-Lee; 2 s.; 2 d. Educ. Harrow; Royal Military College. Regular officer, Queen's Own Cameron Highlanders, 1936-47 (ret. Major); Member, Ross and Cromarty County Council, 1955-75 (Chairman, Education Committee, 1962-75); former Commissioner: Red Deer Commission, Countryside Commission for Scotland; former Member, BBC Council for Scotland; President, Royal Caledonian Curling Club, 1963; President, International Curling Federation, 1965-69. Recreations: curling; golf; shooting; fishing; gardening. Address: (h.) Allangrange, Munlochy, Ross and Cromarty; T.-046381 249.

Cameron, Rev. Andrew Bruce. Priest, Scottish Episcopal Church; Convener, Mission Board, Scottish Episcopal Church, since 1988; Rector, St. John's Episcopal Church, Perth, since 1988; b. 2.5.41, Glasgow; m., Elaine Cameron; 2 s. Educ. Eastwood Secondary School; Edinburgh Theological College. Curate, Helensburgh and Edinburgh, 1964-70; Chaplain, St. Mary's Cathedral, Edinburgh, 1970-75; Diocesan and Provincial Youth Chaplain, 1969-75; Rector, St. Mary's Church, Dalmahoy, and Anglican Chaplain, Heriot Watt University, 1975-82; Churches Development Officer, Livingston Ecumenical Parish, 1982-88. Former Chair, Livingston Voluntary Organisations Council. Recreations: music; theatre; various sports; gardening. Address: 23 Comely Bank, Perth, PH2 7HU; T.-0738 25394.

Cameron, Younger of Lochiel, Donald Angus, MA, FCA, DL. Director, J. Henry Schroder Wagg & Co. Limited, since 1984; b. 2.8.46, London; m., Lady Cecil Kerr; 1 s. 3 d. Educ. Harrow; Christ Church, Oxford. 2nd Lieutenant, Queen's Own Cameron Highlanders (TA), 1966-68; Chartered Accountant, 1971. DL, Lochaber, Inverness, Badenoch and Strathspey. Address: (h.) Achnacarry, Spean Bridge, Inverness-shire.

Cameron of Lochiel, Colonel Sir Donald (Hamish), KT (1973), CVO, TD, JP. 26th Chief of the Clan Cameron; Lord Lieutenant, County of Inverness, 1971-86; Chartered Accountant; b. 12.9.10; m.; 2 s.; 2 d. Educ. Harrow; Balliol College, Oxford. Lt.-Col. commanding: Lovat Scouts, 1944-45; 4/5th Bn. (TA), Queen's Own Cameron Highlanders, 1955-57; Colonel, 1957 (TARO); Vice-Chairman, Royal Bank of Scotland, 1969-80; Chairman, Culter Guard Bridge Holdings Ltd., 1970-76; Chairman, Scottish Widows Life Assurance Society, 1964-67; President, Scottish Landowners Federation, 1979-84; President, Royal Highland and Agricultural Society of Scotland, 1971, 1979, 1987; Member, Scottish Railways Board (Chairman, 1959-64). Address: (h.) Achnacarry, Spean Bridge, Inverness-shire.

Cameron, Dugald, DA, FCSD. Director, Glasgow School of Art, since 1991; Director, Squadron Prints, since 1977; Industrial Design Consultant, since 1965; b. 4.10.39, Glasgow; m., Nancy Inglis. Educ. Glasgow High School; Glasgow School of Art. Industrial Designer, Hard Aluminium Surfaces Ltd., 1962-65; Visiting Lecturer, Glasgow School of Art, 1963-70; Head of Product Design, Glasgow School of Art, 1970-82; Head of Design, 1982-91; Member: Engineering Advisory Committee, Scottish Committee, Council of Industrial Design, since 1966, Industrial Design (Engineering) Panel and 3D Design Board, CNAA, since 1978, Scottish Committee of Higher Education, Design Council. Publications: Glasgow's Own (a history of 602 City of Glasgow Squadron, Royal Auxiliary Air Force), 1987; Glasgow's Airport, 1990. Recreations: railways; flying (lapsed private pilot). Address: (h.) Achnacraig, Skelmorlie, Ayrshire.

Cameron, Duncan Inglis, OBE, JP, BL, DUniv, CA, FRSGS. Director of Administration and Secretary, Heriot-Watt University, 1965-90; b. 26.8.27, Glasgow; m., Elizabeth Pearl Heron; 2 s.; 1 d. Educ. Glasgow High School; Glasgow University. RAF, 1945-48; CA apprentice, Alfred Tongue & Co., 1948-51; Qualified Assistant, Cooper Brothers & Co., 1951-52; Assistant Accountant, Edinburgh University, 1952-65; Commonwealth Universities Administrative Fellow, 1972. President, Edinburgh Junior Chamber of Commerce, 1962-63; Governor, Keil School, Dumbarton, 1967-85; Chairman of Council, Royal Scottish Geographical Society, 1983-88 (Trustee, since 1973); Governor, Scottish College of Textiles, since 1991; Chairman, Bioscot Ltd., 1983-84; Chairman, Edinburgh Conference Centre Ltd., 1987-90; Director, Heriot-Watt Computer Application Services Ltd., 1987-90; Chairman, Scottish Textile and Technical Centre Ltd., since 1991; Member, Universities Central Council on Admissions, 1967-90; Member, Directing Group, Programme on Institutional Management in Higher Education, OECD, Paris, 1986-90; Member, Executive Committee, Federation Superannuation System for Universities, since 1988; Member, Board of Management, Petroleum Science and Technology Institute, since 1989; Chairman, Edinburgh Society of Glasgow University Graduates, 1984-85; Session Clerk, St. Ninian's Church, Corstorphine, since 1969; Honorary Fellow, Royal Scottish Geographical Society, 1989; Honorary Doctor, Heriot-Watt University, 1991; Officer of the Royal Norwegian Order of St. Olav, 1979. Recreations: travel; photography. Address: (h.) 30 Belgrave Road, Edinburgh EH12 6NF; T.-031-334 3444.

Cameron, Ewen, OBE, JP. Highland Cattle Breeder; Managing Director: Lochearnhead Hotel, since 1947, Lochearnhead Development Company, since 1955; Member, Perth and Kinross District Council, since 1980 (Convenor, Leisure and Recreation Committee); Member, Tayside Health Board; Member, Scottish Sports Council; Member, Electricity Consultative Council for the North of Scotland; b. 23.12.26, Lochearnhead; m., Davina Anne Frew; 1 s.; 1 d. Educ. Glenalmond College (Victor Ludorum). Royal Navy (South East Asia Command), 1944-47; played rugby for Perthshire Acas, 1946-50; Member: Perth County Council, 1964-75, Stirling District Council, 1974-77 (Environmental Health Convener); Vice-Chairman, Cumbernauld Development Corporation, 1973-77 (Member, 1963-73); former Member, Consultative Council, Scottish Tourist Board; Chairman, British Water Ski Federation, 1965-70; President, Balquhidder, Lochearnhead and Strathyre Highland Games; Chairman, Visiting Committee, Perth Prison, 1980-84; Vice-President, Royal Highland Agricultural Society, 1981. Highland Games Champion of Scotland (Heavy Events), 1953. Recreations: curling; shooting; golf; dominos. Address: (h.) Ben Ouhr, Lochearnhead, Perthshire; T.-05673 231.

Cameron, Brigadier Ewen Duncan, OBE. Director of Administrative Services, National Trust for Scotland, since 1986; b. 10.2.35, Bournemouth; m., Joanna Margaret Hay; 2 d. Educ. Wellington College; Royal Military Academy, Sandhurst. Commissioned The Black Watch, 1955; DS, The Staff College, 1972-75; Commanding Officer, 1st Bn., The Black Watch, 1975-78; Commander, Royal Brunei Armed Forces, 1980-82; Indian College of Defence Studies, Delhi, 1983; Divisional Brigadier, Scottish Division, 1984-86. Member, Queen's Bodyguard for Scotland (Royal Company of Archers). Recreations: music; bird-watching; squash; ski-ing; gardening. Address: (h.) The Old Manse, Arngask, Glenfarg, Perthshire, PH2 9QG; T.-05773 394.

Cameron, Professor George Gordon, BSc, PhD, DSc, FRSE. Professor of Physical Chemistry, Aberdeen University, since 1984; b. 1.12.32, Stirling; m., Aileen Elizabeth Sinclair; 1 s.; 2 d. Educ. Stirling High School; Glasgow University. Lecturer in Chemistry, St. Andrews University, 1961; Lecturer in Physical Chemistry, then Senior Lecturer, then Reader, Aberdeen University, 1966-84. Recreations: outdoor activities (walking, skiing); music. Address: (b.) Department of Chemistry, Aberdeen University, Aberdeen, AB9 2UE; T.-0224 272903.

Cameron, Gordon Stewart, RSA, DA. Artist; b. 27.4.16, Aberdeen; m., Ellen Malcolm, RSA. Educ. Robert Gordon's College, Aberdeen; Gray's School of Art, Aberdeen. Part-time Lecturer, Gray's School of Art, 1946-51; Lecturer, Dundee College of Art, 1952; Senior Lecturer, Duncan of Jordanstone College of Art, 1967-81; elected, ARSA, 1958, Academician, 1971; work in public galleries in Scotland and in private collections in various parts of the world. Address: (h.) 7 Auburn Terrace, Invergowrie, Dundee; T.-Dundee 562318.

Cameron, Sheriff Ian Alexander, MA, LLB. Sheriff of Lothian and Borders at Edinburgh, since 1987; b. 5.11.38, Elgin; m., Dr. Margaret Anne Cameron; 1 s. Educ. Elgin Academy; Edinburgh University; Aberdeen University. Partner, Stewart and McIsaac, Solicitors, Elgin, 1962-86. part-time Reporter to Children's Panel, 1971-84. Recreations: travel; railway history, hill walking. Address: Achnacarry, Elgin, IV30 1NU; T.-0343 542731; 19/4 Damside, Dean Village, Edinburgh, EH4 3BB; T.-031-220 1548.

Cameron, Rev. Professor James Kerr, MA, BD, PhD, FRHistS. Professor of Ecclesiastical History, St. Andrews University, 1970-89; b. 5.3.24, Methven; m., Emma Leslie Birse; 1 s. Educ. Oban High School; St. Andrews University; Hartford Theological Seminary, Hartford, Connecticut. Ordained as Assistant Minister, Church of the Holy Rude, Stirling, 1952; appointed Lecturer in Church History, Aberdeen University, 1955; Lecturer, then Senior Lecturer in Ecclesiastical History, St. Andrews University; Dean, Faculty of Divinity, 1978-83. President: Ecclesiastical History Society, 1976-77, British Sub-Commission, Commission Internationale d'Histoire Ecclesiastique Comparee, since 1979; Vice-President, International Association for Neo-Latin Studies, 1979-81. Publications: Letters of John Johnstone and Robert Howie, 1963; First Book of Discipline, 1972; contributions to: Acta Conventus Neo-Latini Amstelodamensis, 1973; Advocates of Reform, 1953; The Scottish Tradition, 1974; Renaissance and Renewal in Christian History, 1977; Reform and Reformation: England and the Continent, 1979; Origins and Nature of the Scottish Enlightenment, 1982; A Companion to Scottish Culture. Recreation: gardening. Address: (h.) Priorscroft, 71 Hepburn Gardens, St. Andrews, KY16 9LS; T.-0334 73996.

Cameron, John Bell, CBE, FRAgricS, AIAgricE. Chairman, British Railways (Scottish) Board, since 1988; Member, British Railways Board, since 1988; Farmer, since 1961; b. 14.6.39, Edinburgh; m., Margaret Clapperton. Educ. Dollar Academy. Vice President, National Farmers' Union of Scotland, 1976-79, President, 1979-84; Member, Agricultural Praesidium of EEC, 1979-84; Chairman, EEC Advisory Committee for Sheepmeat, 1982-90; Chairman, World Meats Group, (IFAP), since 1983; Chairman, Board of Governors, Dollar Academy, since 1985; Chairman, United Auctions

Ltd., since 1985; Member, Board of Governors, Macaulay Land Use Research Institute, since 1987. Long Service Award, Royal Observer Corps. Recreations: flying; shooting; travelling. Address: (h.) Balbuthie Farm, by Leven, Fife; T.-0333 730210.

Cameron, Hon. Lord (John Cameron), KT (1978), Kt (1954). Senator of the College of Justice in Scotland and Lord of Session, 1955-85; b. 1900. Sheriff of Inverness, Elgin and Nairn, 1945; Sheriff of Inverness, Moray, Nairn and Ross and Cromarty, 1946-48; Dean, Faculty of Advocates, 1948-55.

Cameron, John Alastair, QC, MA (Oxon). Vice-Dean, Faculty of Advocates, since 1983; President, Pensions Appeal Tribunal for Scotland, since 1985; b. 1.2.38, Newcastle-upon-Tyne; m., Elspeth Mary Dunlop Miller; 3 s. Educ. Trinity College, Glenalmond; Pembroke College, Oxford. Called to the Bar, Inner Temple, 1963; admitted Member, Faculty of Advocates, 1966; Advocate-Depute, 1972-75; Standing Junior Counsel to Department of Energy, 1976-79, Scottish Development Department, 1978-79; Legal Chairman, Pensions Appeal Tribunals for Scotland, since 1979. Publications: Medical Negligence: an Introduction, 1983; Reproductive Medicine and the Law (Contributor). Recreations: travel; sport; Africana. Address: (h.) 4 Garscube Terrace, Edinburgh, EH12 6BQ; T.-031-337 3460.

Cameron, Professor John Robinson, MA, BPhil. Regius Professor of Logic, Aberdeen University, since 1979; b. 24.6.36, Glasgow; m., 1, Mary Elizabeth Ranson (deceased); 2, Barbara Elizabeth Blair; 1 s.; 2 d. Educ. Dundee High School; St. Andrews University. Harkness Fellow, USA, 1959-61; Lecturer in Philosophy, Queen's College, Dundee, 1962 (Dundee University from 1967); appointed Senior Lecturer in Philosophy, 1973. Recreation: bricolage. Address: (b.) Department of Philosophy, Aberdeen University, King's College, Aberdeen, AB9 2UB; T.-Aberdeen 272365.

Cameron, (John Roderick) Hector, LLB, NP. Partner, Dorman Jeffrey & Co., Solicitors, since 1990; b. 11.6.47, Glasgow; m., Rosemary Brownlee; 1 s.; 1 d. Educ. High School of Glasgow; Friends School, Wigton; St. Andrews University. Admitted Solicitor, 1971; Partner, Bishop, Milne Boyd & Co., 1973; Chairman, Glasgow Junior Chamber of Commerce, 1981; Managing Partner, Bishop & Co., 1985; Director, Merchants House of Glasgow, 1986; Director, Glasgow Chamber of Commerce, 1987. Chairman, Strathclyde Appeal Committee, Help the Aged, 1987. Recreations: reading; gardening; sailing; golf. Address: (b.) Madeleine Smith House, 6/7 Blythswood Square, Glasgow G2 4AD.

Cameron, Rev. Dr. John Urquhart, BA, BSc, PhD, BD, ThD. Minister, Parish of Broughty Ferry, since 1974; b. 10.6.43, Dundee; m., Jill Sjoberg; 1 s.; 1 d. Educ. Falkirk High School; St. Andrews University; Edinburgh University; University of Southern California. Marketing Executive, Beechams, London, 1969-73; Assistant Minister, Wellington Church, Glasgow, 1973-74; Chaplain, Royal Naval Reserve, 1976-81; Marketing Consultant, Pergamon Press, Oxford, 1977-81; Religious Education Department, Dundee High School, 1980-87; Sports Journalist and Travel Writer, Hill Publications, Surrey, since 1981; Physics Department, Dundee College of Further Education, since 1987; Chaplain, Royal Caledonian Curling Club. National and international honours in both summer and winter sports, 1960-85; sports scholarship, University of Southern California, 1962-64. Recreations: golf; skiing; curling. Address: St. Stephen's Manse, 33 Camperdown Street, Broughty Ferry; T.-0382 77403.

Cameron of Lochbroom, Lord (Kenneth John Cameron), Life Baron (1984), PC (1984), MA (Oxon), LLB, QC, FRSE.

Senator of the College of Justice, since 1989; Chairman, Scottish Civic Trust; b. 11.6.31, Edinburgh; m., Jean Pamela Murray; 2 d. Educ. Edinburgh Academy; Corpus Christi College, Oxford; Edinburgh University. Advocate, 1958; Queen's Counsel, 1972; President, Pensions Appeal Tribunal for Scotland, 1976; Chairman, Committee of Investigation Under Agricultural Marketing Act 1958, 1980; Advocate Depute, 1981; Lord Advocate, 1984; Hon. Bencher, Lincoln's Inn; Hon. Fellow, Corpus Christi College, Oxford. Recreations: fishing; sailing. Address: (h.) 10 Belford Terrace, Edinburgh.

Cameron, Sheriff Lewis, MA, LLB. Solicitor, since 1962; Sheriff of South Strathclyde Dumfries and Galloway at Dumfries, since 1988; b. 12.8.35, Glasgow; m., Sheila Colette Gallacher; 2 s.; 2 d. Educ. St. Aloysius College; Blairs College; St. Sulpice, Paris; Glasgow University. RAF, 1954-56; admitted Solicitor, 1962. Member, Legal Aid Central Committee, 1970-80; Legal Aid Secretary, Airdrie, 1978-87; Chairman, Social Security Appeal Tribunals, 1983-88; Dean, Airdrie Society of Solicitors, 1984-85; Tutor, Strathclyde University, 1981-88; Treasurer, Monklands Victim Support Scheme, 1983-88; Chairman, Dumfries and Galloway Family Conciliation Service, 1988-92; Chairman, Dumfries and Galloway, Scottish Association for the Study of Delinquency, since 1988; Member, Scotland Committee, National Children's Homes, since 1991; Trustee, Oscar Marzaroli Trust, since 1990. Recreations: cinema; theatre; music; travel; tennis. Address: (h.) Rose Cottage, Johnstone Bridge, Dumfries and Galloway; (b.) Sheriff Court House, Dumfries, DG1 2AN; T.-0387 62334.

Cameron, Monica Joan, BA (Oxon), MA, PGCE. Headmistress, St. Margaret's School, Edinburgh, since 1984; b. 27.2.31, Alloa; m., Rev. D.E.N. Cameron; 2 s.; 2 d. Educ. Cheltenham Ladies' College; St. Hugh's College, Oxford; Durham University. Deputy Head, Northallerton Grammar School, 1974-82; Assistant Head, Firrhill High School, Edinburgh, 1983-84. Recreations: Christian activities; walking; reading. Address: (h.) 6 Redford Terrace, Colinton, Edinburgh; T.-031-441 3022.

Cameron-Head of Inverailort, Lucretia Pauline Rebecca Ann, OBE, JP, DL. Convenor, Glenfinnan Gathering, since 1957; Chairman, Lochaber Handicapped Association, since 1981; Vice-President, Sunart & District Agricultural Society; b. 21.8.17, Glasgow; m., Francis Cameron-Head of Inverailort (deceased). County Councillor, Inverness-shire, 1945-75; Vice Chairman, Lochaber Hospital Board; Member, Northern Regional Hospital Board; Chairman, Children's Committee, Health Committee, Social Work Committee, Inverness-shire; Chairman, Drug Accounts Committee for Scotland; Chairman, Nurse Training North of Scotland; Vice Chairman, Red Cross, Inverness; Vice-Chairman, Inverness Girl Guides; Chairman, Agricultural Executive (Land Girls) Scotland. Recreations: gardening; current affairs. Address: (h.) Inverailort Castle, Lochailort, Inverness-shire; T.-Lochailort 234.

Campbell, Alan Grant, LLB. Chief Executive, Grampian Regional Council, since 1991; b. 4.12.46, Aberdeen; m., Susan Black; 1 s.; 2 d. Educ. Aberdeen Grammar School; Aberdeen University. Aberdeen County Council: Law apprentice/Solicitor, 1968-72, Senior Legal Assistant, 1972-75; Grampian Regional Council: Assistant Director of Law and Administration, 1975-79, Depute Director, 1979-84, Director of Law and Administration, 1984-91; Seminar Leader, Diploma in Legal Practice, Aberdeen University. Recreation: cycling. Address: Woodhill House, Westburn Road, Aberdeen, AB9 2LU; T.-0224 682222, Ext. 4400.

Campbell, Professor Alexander George Macpherson, MB, ChB, FRCPEdin, DCH. Professor of Child Health, Aberdeen

University, since 1973; Honorary Consultant Paediatrician, Grampian Health Board, since 1973; b. 3.2.31, Glasgow; m., Sheila Mary Macdonald; 1 s.; 2 d. Educ. Dollar Academy; Glasgow University. Paediatric Registrar, Royal Hospital for Sick Children, Edinburgh, 1959-61; Senior House Officer, Hospital for Sick Children, London, 1961-62; Assistant Chief Resident, Children's Hospital of Philadelphia, 1962-63; Fellow in Paediatric Cardiology, Hospital for Sick Children, Toronto, 1963-64; Fellow in Fetal and Neonatal Physiology, Nuffield Institute for Medical Research, Oxford, 1964-66; Lecturer in Child Health, St. Andrews University, 1966-67; Assistant, then Associate Professor of Paediatrics, Yale University School of Medicine, 1967-73. Chairman, Joint Committee for Vaccination and Immunisation, Department of Health. Recreation: golf. Address: (b.) Department of Child Health, Aberdeen University, Aberdeen; T.-0224 681818, Ext. 52471.

Campbell, Alistair Bromley, OBE. Chairman of Council, Scottish Conservation Projects Trust, since 1984; Director Training, Craft Ltd., Pathcraft Ltd. and SCP Services Ltd. b. 23.6.27, Charing, Kent; m., Rosemary Pullar; 1 s.; 2 d. Educ. Tonbridge School. Training in agriculture, 1944-47; self-employed Farmer, 1948-81; Agricultural Consultant, Arbiter, Valuer, 1968-81; Agricultural Adviser and Valuer, South of Scotland Electricity Board, 1972-81; Vice-Chairman, Countryside Commission for Scotland, 1972-81; Member, Secretary of State's Panel of Agricultural Arbiters, 1968-81; Member, Scottish Land Court, 1981-92; Member, Council of Management, Strathcarron Hospice, Denny; former Council Member, British Trust for Conservation Volunteers (Chairman, Scottish Regional Committee, 1975-84); Church Warden, St. Mary's Episcopal Church, Dunblane, since 1960; Honorary Vice-President and a Director, Doune and Dunblane Agricultural Society; former Convener, Legal Committee, NFU of Scotland; General Commissioner of Income Tax, since 1971; Chairman, Scottish Executive Committee, Association of Agriculture, 1980-86. Recreations: work; shooting; enjoying countryside; farming. Address: (h.) Grainston Farm, Kilbryde, Dunblane, Perthshire, FK15 9NF; T.-0786 823304.

Campbell, Arthur McLure, CBE. Principal Clerk of Session and Justiciary, Scotland, 1982-89; Clerk of Committees (Temporary), House of Lords, 1991; b. 15.8.32, Glasgow. Educ. Queen's Park School, Glasgow. Admiralty Supplies Directorate, 1953-54; entered Scottish Court Service (Sheriff Clerk Branch), 1954; Departmental Legal Qualification, 1956; Sheriff Clerk Depute, Kilmarnock, 1957-60; Sheriff Clerk of Orkney, 1961-65; seconded HM Treasury (O. & M.), 1965-69 (Secretary, Lord Chancellor's Committee on Re-sealing of Probates and Confirmations, 1967-68, and Secretary, Scottish Office Committee on Money Transfer Services, 1968-69); Sheriff Clerk, Airdrie, 1969-72; Principal, Scottish Court Service Staff Training Centre, 1973-74; Assistant Sheriff Clerk of Glasgow, 1974-81. Chairman, Sheriff Clerks' Association, 1971-72; Member, Secretary of State for Scotland's Review Body on Use of Judicial Time in the Superior Courts, 1985-86. Address: c/o Bank of Scotland, Kirkwall, Orkney, KW15 1HJ.

Campbell, Catherine, JP, BSc, BA (Hons), MSc. Educational Psychologist; Member, Scottish Milk Marketing Board, since 1981; Chairman, Cumbernauld "I" Tech, since 1984; b. 10.1.40, Glasgow; m., John Campbell; 2 s.; 1 d. Educ. Notre Dame High School; Glasgow University; Open University; Strathclyde University. Teacher of Mathematics, 1962-68; Member, Cumbernauld and Kilsyth District Council, 1969-78; Member, Cumbernauld Development Corporation, 1975-84. Jubilee Medal, 1977. Recreations: horse riding; homecrafts. Address: (h.) 10 Westray Road, Cumbernauld, G67 1NN; T.-023 67 24834.

Campbell, Sir Colin Moffat, Bt, MC. Chairman, James Finlay plc, 1975-90; Director, James Finlay plc; b. 4.8.25; m., Mary Anne Chichester Bain; 2 s.; 1 d. (deceased). Educ. Stowe. Scots Guards, 1943-47 (Captain); joined James Finlay & Co. Ltd., 1947. President, Federation of Kenya Employers, 1962-70; Chairman, Tea Board of Kenya, 1961-71; Chairman, East African Tea Trade Association, 1960-61, 1962-63, 1966-67; Member, Scottish Council, CBI, 1979-85; Member, Council, CBI, since 1981; Deputy Chairman, Commonwealth Development Corporation, 1983-89, Board, 1981-89. Recreations: gardening; racing; cards. Address: (h.) Kilbryde Castle, Dunblane, Perthshire.

Campbell, David A., MA. Assistant Secretary, Scottish Office, since 1978; b. 5.11.34, Concepcion, Chile; m., Philippa Louise Bunting; 1 s.; 3 d. Foundation Scholar, King's College, Cambridge. King's Own Scottish Borderers (Malayan emergency), 1956-58; travel in the Antipodes and Africa, 1958-60, as tram conductor, docker, schoolmaster and Private Secretary to the Commissioner of the Cameroons; HM Diplomatic Service, 1960-78. Trustee, Rudolf Steiner School of Edinburgh. Recreations: books; the arts; horses. Address: (h.) Old Costerton, Midlothian; T.-Humbie 682.

Campbell, David Ross, FISD, MCIM. Chairman and Chief Executive, West Independent Newspapers Ltd.; Chairman: Guthrie Newspaper Group; Glasgow Guardian Group; Alloa Printing and Publishing Co.; Director, Clyde Cablevision Holdings Ltd.; Director, Strathclyde News Holdings Ltd.; Chairman, Clansman Travel & Leisure Ltd.; b. 27.9.43, Glasgow; m., Moira. Educ. Whitehill School, Glasgow; James Watt Memorial College, Greenock. Previously worked for: international marine radio company; Union Castle SS Company; Sperry Rand; Scottish and Universal Group of companies. Immediate Past President, Glasgow Chamber of Commerce (Director, since 1981); Vice Chairman, Enterprise Ayrshire; Member, Commonwealth Press Union; Liveryman of the City of London. Recreations: golf; walking; swimming. Address: (b.) Herald Street, Ardrossan, KA22 8BX; T.-0294 64321.

Campbell, Professor Donald, CBE, MB, ChB, FCAnaesth, FRCP(Glas), FRCS(Eng). Professor of Anaesthesia and Dean of Medicine, Glasgow University; Past Chairman, Scottish Council for Postgraduate Medical Education; b. 8.3.30, Rutherglen; m., Catherine Conway Bradburn; 1 s.; 3 d. Educ. Pitlochry High School; Hutchesons Grammar School, Glasgow; Glasgow University. Honorary Consultant Anaesthetist, Greater Glasgow Health Board; former Dean, Faculty of Anaesthetists, Royal College of Surgeons of England; former Vice-President, Royal College of Surgeons of England; Past President, Scottish Society of Anaesthetists; former Vice-President and Member of Council, Association of Anaesthetists of Great Britain and Ireland; Member, Medical Advisory Committee, British Council; Visitor, RCPS (Glas), since 1990. Recreations: curling; angling. Address: (b.) 27 Tannoch Drive, Milngavie, Glasgow, G62 8AR; T.-041-956 1736.

Campbell, Doris Margaret, MD, FRCOG. Senior Lecturer in Obstetrics and Gynaecology and Reproductive Physiology, Aberdeen University, since 1984; b. 24.1.42, Aberdeen; m., Alasdair James Campbell; 1 s.; 1 d. Educ. Aberdeen High School for Girls; Aberdeen University. Resident house officer posts, Aberdeen, 1967-69; Research Fellow, Aberdeen University, 1969-73; Registrar in Obstetrics and Gynaecology, Aberdeen Hospitals, 1973-74; Lecturer in Obstetrics and Gynaecology and Physiology, Aberdeen University, 1974-84. Former Member, Scottish Women's Hockey Council. Recreations: bridge; badminton; guiding. Address: (h.) 77 Blenheim Place, Aberdeen; T.-Aberdeen 639984.

Campbell, Rev. Effie Crawford, BD. Minister, Crichton West Church, Cumnock, 1981-91; Moderator, Synod of Ayr, 1987; b. 7.3.22, Glasgow; m., George Campbell; 1 d. Educ. Battlefield Secondary School, Glasgow; Glasgow University. Before marriage, office worker, SCWS; housewife for 25 years, before full-time study; first ordained woman minister in Ayr Presbytery; first woman to be Moderator, Synod of Ayr. Recreations: reading; knitting; motoring; speaking. Address: (h.) 7 Lansdowne Road, Ayr KA8 8LS; T.-0292 264282.

Campbell, Elizabeth (Libby), RGN, RM, MSc. Director of Nursing Services, St. John's Hospital, West Lothian, since 1989; b. 9.8.50, Dundee. Educ. Mary Erskine School for Girls, Edinburgh; Edinburgh University. Assistant, then Deputy, Director of Nursing Services, Bangour General Hospital, West Lothian, 1985-89. Vice Chairman, National Association of Theatre Nurses, 1989-92 (Chairman, 1992-95); Member, National Board for Nursing, Midwifery and Health Visiting, 1989-94. Recreations: singing; travelling; Munro bagging; music. Address: 3 Saxe Coburg Terrace, Edinburgh, EH3 5BU; T.-031-332 7984.

Campbell, Wing Commander George, MBE, EsqStJ, DL, MBIM. County Director, British Red Cross Society (Dunbartonshire), since 1983; b. 24.11.22, Renton; m., Marion T.H. Halliday; 1 s.; 1 d. Educ. Vale of Leven Academy. Joined RAF, 1941; served in UK, India, Burma, Malaya, Singapore; demobilised, 1946, and continued in Royal Air Force Voluntary Reserve (Training Branch), serving with Air Training Corps; formed 2319 (Vale of Leven) Squadron, 1956; appointed to Wing Staff, Glasgow, and Western Wing, 1973; promoted to Wing Commander, 1978; retired, 1983; attended Bisley Shooting as competitor, coach, and team captain for 42 years; Chairman, County Scout Committee; Vice Chairman, Duke of Edinburgh Award (County Co-ordinating Committee); Elder, Church of Scotland; County Representative, Royal Air Forces Benevolent Fund; Past President, Dumbarton Rotary Club; Past Chairman, RNLI, Dumbarton Branch. Address: (h.) Valeview, Comley Bank, Oxhill, Dumbarton; T.-Dumbarton 63700.

Campbell, Rev. George Houstoun. Minister, John Knox Church, Stewarton, since 1971; Moderator, Synod of Ayr, 1988-89; b. 29.4.27, Glasgow; m., Elspeth Gibb Campbell Adams; 1 s.; 3 d. Educ. Whitehill Senior Secondary School, Glasgow; Glasgow University; Trinity College. Post Office and Civil Service, 1941-52; Missionary of Church of Scotland to Church of Central Africa Presbyterian, Malawi, 1957-71. Moderator, Presbytery of Irvine and Kilmarnock, 1980-81; President, Scottish Feed the Minds. Publications: Lonely Warrior; Tikuwababitiziraci Wana? Recreations: reading; gardening; visiting new places. Address: John Knox Manse, 27 Avenue Street, Stewarton, Kilmarnock, KA3 5AP; T.-0560 82418.

Campbell, George William, HND Agric, DipFBOM, MIAM. Director, Scottish Crofters Union, since 1990; b. 27.12.64, Inverness. Educ. Ullapool Junior Secondary School; Dingwall Academy; School of Agriculture, Aberdeen. Project Officer, North West Development Programme, 1988-90. Assessor for Crofters Commission. Recreations: motorcycling; racquet sports. Address: (b.) Old Mill, Broadford, Isle of Skye; T.-0471 822 529.

Campbell of Croy, Baron (Gordon Thomas Calthrop Campbell), PC (1970), MC (and Bar). Consultant, oil industry, since 1975; Director, Alliance and Leicester Building Society and Chairman of its Scottish Board; Chairman, Stoic Insurance Services, since 1979; b. 8.6.21; m.; 2 s.; 1 d. Educ. Wellington. Commissioned, Regular Army, 1939; RA, 1942 (Major); wounded and disabled, 1945; entered HM Foreign Service, 1946 and served in the Foreign Office, at the UN, in the Cabinet Office (Private Secretary to the Secretary of the Cabinet) and in the Embassy in Vienna; MP (Conservative), Moray and Nairn, 1959-74; Government Whip, 1961-62; Lord Commissioner of the Treasury and Scottish Whip, 1962-63; Parliamentary Under-Secretary of State, Scottish Office, 1963-64; Secretary of State for Scotland, 1970-74; Chairman, Scottish Committee, International Year of Disabled, 1981; Partner, Holme Rose Estate and Farms; Trustee, Thomson Foundation, since 1980; Chairman, Advisory Committee on Pollution of the Sea, 1987-89. Address: (h.) Holme Rose, Cawdor, Nairnshire.

Campbell, Hugh Hall, QC, BA (Hons), MA (Oxon), LLB (Hons), FCIArb. Queen's Counsel, since 1983; b. 18.2.44, Glasgow; m., Eleanor Jane Hare; 3 s. Educ. Glasgow Academy; Trinity College, Glenalmond; Exeter College, Oxford; Edinburgh University. Called to Scottish Bar, 1969; Standing Junior Counsel to Admiralty, 1976. Recreations: music; hill-walking; golf. Address: (h.) 12 Ainslie Place, Edinburgh, EH3 6AS; T.-031-225 2067.

Campbell, Ian, MA, PhD. Reader in English Literature, Edinburgh University; b. 25.8.42, Lausanne, Switzerland. Educ. schools in Lausanne, Rothiemay, Findochty, Buckie and Stonehaven; Aberdeen University; Edinburgh University. Joined Edinburgh University as Assistant Lecturer, then Lecturer in English Literature; visiting appointments in France, Switzerland, Germany, Japan, Canada and USA; Visiting Professor of English, UCLA. President, Carlyle Society; Associate Editor, Carlyle Letters; Past President, Scottish Association for the Speaking of Verse. Recreations: music; sport; travel; history. Address: (b.) Department of English, Edinburgh University, George Square, Edinburgh, EH8 9JX; T.-031-650 1000.

Campbell, Sir Ian, CBE, OStJ, VRD, JP. Deputy Chairman, Collins Halden (Scotland), since 1987; Chairman, Select Assured Properties PLC, since 1989; Director, Travel System Ltd., since 1987; Director, Hermiston Securities, since 1990; b. 3.2.23, Edinburgh; m., Marion Kirkhope Shiel; 1 d. Educ. Daniel Stewart's College, Edinburgh. Royal Navy, 1942-46; Royal Naval Reserve, 1946-64 (retired with rank of Commander); John Line & Sons, 1948-61 (Area Manager, West of England); Managing Director, MacGregor Wallcoverings Ltd., 1965-77; Finance Director, Scottish Conservative Party, 1977-89. Councillor, City of Edinburgh, 1984-88; Member, Transport Users Consultative Committee for Scotland, 1981-87. Recreations: golf; vintage cars; water colour painting. Address: (h.) Merleton, 10 Boswall Road, Edinburgh, EH5 2PR; T.-031-552 4825.

Campbell, Sir Ilay Mark, MA (Oxon). Chairman, Christie's Scotland, since 1978; Director, High Craigton Farming Co.; b. 29.5.27, Edinburgh; m., Margaret Minette Rohais Anderson; 2 d. Educ. Eton; Christ Church, Oxford. Christie's: Scottish Agent, 1968, Joint Scottish Agent, 1973-92; Honorary Vice-President, Scotland's Garden Scheme; Trustee, Crarae Gardens Charitable Trust, since 1978; Past President, Association for the Protection of Rural Scotland; former Convener, Church of Scotland Committee on Artistic Matters; Member, Historic Buildings Council for Scotland; former Member, Council, Executive Committee and Gardens Committee, National Trust for Scotland; former Scottish Representative, National Arts Collection Fund. Recreations: heraldry; genealogy; collecting heraldic bookplates. Address: (h.) Crarae Lodge, Inveraray, Argyll, PA32 8YA; (b.) Cumlodden Estate Office, Inveraray, Argyll, PA32 8YA; T.-0546 86633.

Campbell, James Hugh, BL. Senior Partner, Bird Semple Fyfe Ireland, WS, since 1987; b. 13.11.26, Old Kilpatrick; m., Iris Burnside Hercus; 2 s.; 1 d. Educ. Bearsden Academy;

Glasgow University. Senior Partner, Bird Son & Semple, 1965-73, and Bird Semple Crawford Herron, 1973-87. Member, Council, Law Society of Scotland, since 1986 (President, 1991-92). Recreations: music; reading; golf. Address: (b.) 249 West George Street, Glasgow, G2 4RB; T.-041-221 7090.

Campbell, John Craig. Member, Grampian Regional Council Appeals Committee; Grampian Regional Representative, War Pensions Association; Director, Langstane Press Ltd., Aberdeen, since 1946; b. 28.3.15, Aberdeen; m., Anna Wilson Harrison; 1 s. Educ. Morgan Academy, Dundee. Past President, Aberdeen Master Printers; Past Chairman, South Aberdeen Conservative Association; former Member: Manpower Services Commission (Scotland), Scottish Master Printers Education Committee, Paper Publishing Industry Training Board, Grampian Regional Council, Grampian/Tayside Area Manpower Board, Convention of Scottish Local Authorities, Scottish Joint Negotiating Committee (Education); former Governor: Robert Gordon's Institute of Technology, Robert Gordon's College; Past Chairman, Oakbank School Managers; Past Chairman, Grampian Regional Council Education Committee. Recreation: golf. Address: (h.) 110 Mastrick Drive, Aberdeen; T.-0224 691122.

Campbell, Joseph. Managing Director, West Sound Radio, since 1983; b. 16.8.39, Glasgow; m., Sheila Margaret Craig; 1 s.; 2 d. Educ. Kirkcudbright Academy. Managing Director, United Scottish Farmers, 1969-77; Managing Director, Kintyre Farmers, 1977-83. Chairman, Scottish Agricultural Managers' Association, 1975-77; Scottish Council Member, Animedica International, 1977-79; Council Member, Scottish Agricultural Organisation Society, 1979-83; Chairman, Ayrshire Nursing Homes Federation, 1985-90; Director, Ayr Chamber of Commerce, since 1985; Director, Ayrshire Local Enterprise Company, since 1990; Managing Director, South West Sound, since 1990; Vice Chairman, Opera West, since 1986. Royal Humane Society Award, 1963. Recreations: music; painting; reading; golf. Address: (h.) 30 Racecourse Road, Ayr, KA7 2UX; T.-0292 266033.

Campbell, Rev. Keith, BSc, BD. Minister, Broughty Ferry: St. Aidan's, Dundee, since 1968; Moderator, Dundee Presbytery, 1990-91; Vice-Chairman, Tayside Health Board; Chairman, St Aidan's Project; b. 19.12.32, Gourock; m., Christine Mary Beaton MacFarlane; 1 s. (deceased); 2 d. Educ. Strathallan School; Glasgow University. Minister, Edinkillie, Morayshire, 1963-68; Convener, Business Committee, Presbytery of Dundee, 1984-88; Past Chairman, Dundee Local Health Council; former Depute Chairman, Dundee College of Education. Recreations: swimming; sailing; gardening; photography. Address: St. Aidan's Manse, 63 Collingwood Street, Barnhill, Dundee; T.-0382 79253.

Campbell, Malcolm, MA (Hons), PhD. Reader in Greek, St. Andrews University, since 1984 (Chairman, 1987-91); b. 10.11.43, Shrewsbury; m., Dorothy Helen Fear; 2 s. Educ. Boroughmuir School, Edinburgh; Edinburgh University; Balliol College, Oxford. Lecturer, St. Andrews University, since 1968. Publications: A Commentary on Quintus Smyrnaeus, Posthomerica XII, 1981; Echoes and Imitations of Early Epic in Apollonius Rhodius, 1981; Index verborum in Apollonium Rhodium, 1983; Studies in the Third Book of Apollonius Rhodius' Argonautica, 1983; A Lexicon to Triphiodorus, 1985; Index verborum in Moschum et Bionem, 1987; Index in Arati Phaenomena, 1988; Moschus Europa (Editor), 1991. Recreations: music; philately. Address: (b.) Department of Greek, The University, St. Andrews, Fife.

Campbell, Malcolm, MBChB, FRCGP. General Medical Practitioner, Kirkintilloch, since 1975; Assistant Regional Adviser in General Practice, West of Scotland, since 1991;

Honorary Clinical Senior Lecturer, Department of Postgraduate Medical Education, Glasgow University, since 1991; b. 12.4.47, Rawcliffe; m., Patricia; 1 s.; 2 d. Educ. Greenock High School; Glasgow University. House Officer posts in medicine and surgery, Hairmyres Hospital, 1971; Obstetric Senior House Officer, Glasgow Royal Maternity Hospital, 1972; Paediatric Senior House Officer, Royal Hospital for Sick Children, 1972; Registrar in Medicine, Falkirk Royal Infirmary, 1973; Trainee in general pratice, Dunblane, 1974. Member, West of Scotland Faculty Board, RCGP; Examiner, RCGP. Recreations: sailing; supporting St. Johnstone F.C. Address: (h.) 47 Victoria Road, Lenzie, Glasgow, G66 5AP; T.-041-776 5694.

Campbell, Rev. Neil Gregor, BA, BD. Minister, Penninghame St. John's Parish Church, Newton Stewart, since 1989; b. 5.5.61, Brighton; m., Elizabeth Campbell; 2 s. Educ. George Watson's College, Edinburgh; Edinburgh University. Assistant Minister, Palmerston Place Church, Edinburgh, 1987-89. Recreations: reading (mainly modern literature); hill-walking. Address: The Manse, York Road, Newton Stewart, DG8 6HH; T.-0671 2259.

Campbell, Niall Gordon, BA. Under Secretary, Social Work Services Group, Scottish Office Home and Health Department, since 1989; b. 9.11.41, Peebles; m., Alison M. Rigg; 3 s. Educ. Edinburgh Academy; Merton College, Oxford. Entered Scottish Office 1964; Assistant Secretary, 1978; various posts in Scottish Education Department and Scottish Development Department. Address (h.) 15 Warriston Crescent, Edinburgh.

Campbell, Robert Craig, BSc, MCIM. Chief Economist, Scottish Council (Development and Industry), since 1988; b. 29.4.47, Glasgow; m., Elizabeth Helen C.; 2 d. Educ. Glasgow Academy; St. Andrews University. Scottish Council: Research Executive, 1970-77, Research Director, 1977-84, Director, Overseas Projects Unit, 1984-86, Policy Research Director, 1986-88. Recreation: angling. Address: (b.) Scottish Council (Development and Industry), 23 Chester Street, Edinburgh; T.-031-225 7911.

Campbell, Rev. Roderick D.M., BD, FSA Scot. Minister, Mearns Parish Church, since 1979; b. 1.8.43, Glasgow; m., Susan Norman; 2 d. Educ. Daniel Stewart's College, Edinburgh; Arbroath High School; Jordanhill College of Education; New College, Edinburgh University. Teacher, Technical Subjects, Glasgow, Tanzania and London, 1967-70; Associate Minister, St. Andrew's, Nairobi, 1975-78; Chieftain, Caledonian Society of Kenya, 1978; founder Member, Undugu Society of Kenya, 1975; Chairman, Institute of Advanced Motorists (Kenya), 1977-78. Convener, Lodging House Mission, Glasgow Presbytery, 1981-86; Convener, National Church Extension Committee, Church of Scotland, 1987-89; Chaplain, 1/52 Lowland Volunteers, TA; Vice-Convener, Maintenance of the Ministry Committee, General Assembly; Member, Greater Glasgow Health Board; Chairman, The 1988 Forum, 1988-91; Chairman, Glasgow Churches Council for Overseas Students, since 1987; Vice Chairman, Eastwood Conservative Association, since 1988. Recreations: swimming; horse-riding; hill-walking. Address: The Manse of Mearns, Newton Mearns, Glasgow, G77 5BU; T.-041-639 1410.

Campbell, Walter Menzies, CBE, QC, MA, LLB. MP (Liberal Democrat), North East Fife, since 1987; Advocate, since 1968; Queen's Counsel, since 1982; part-time Chairman, VAT Tribunal, 1984-87; Member: Legal Aid Central Committee, 1983-86, Scottish Legal Aid Board, 1986-87; Chairman: Medical Appeal Tribunals, 1985-87, Royal Lyceum Theatre, Edinburgh, 1984-87; Member, Broadcasting Council for Scotland, 1984-87; Member, Select Committee on Members Interests, 1987-90; Member, Select

Committee on Trade and Industry, since 1990; Member, North Atlantic Assembly, since 1989; Party Spokesman on Defence and Sport, since 1988; b. 22.5.41, Glasgow; m., Elspeth Mary Urquhart. Educ. Hillhead High School, Glasgow; Glasgow University; Stanford University, California. President, Glasgow University Union, 1964-65; took part in Olympic Games, Tokyo, 1964; AAA 220-yards champion, 1964, 1967; Captain, UK athletics team, 1965-66; 1966 Commonwealth Games, Jamaica; UK 100-metres record holder, 1967-74. Advocate Depute, 1977-80; Standing Junior Counsel to the Army in Scotland, 1980-82. Parliamentary candidate (Liberal): Greenock and Port Glasgow, February, 1974, and October, 1974, East Fife, 1979, North East Fife, 1983; Chairman, Scottish Liberal Party, 1975-77; Member: UK Sports Council, 1965-68; Scottish Sports Council, 1971-81. Recreations: all sports; music; theatre. Address: (b.) House of Commons, London, SW1A 0AA; T.-071-219 4446.

Campbell, William Kilpatrick, MA (Hons). Director, Mainstream Publishing, since 1978; b. 1.3.51, Glasgow; m., Marie-France Callie; 2 d. Educ. Kilmarnock Academy; Edinburgh University. Postgraduate research, Universities of Edinburgh and California; world travel, 1975; Publications Manager, Edinburgh University Student Publications, 1976-78. Publications: Alternative Edinburgh (Co-Editor), 1972; Another Edinburgh, 1976. Recreations: soccer; tennis; swimming; wine; books; people. Address: (b.) 7 Albany Street, Edinburgh, EH1 3UG; T.-031-557 2959.

Campbell, William Wallace Meek, RMN, RGN, MSc. Research and Development Manager, Grampian Health Board, since 1992; b. 27.11.42, Greenock; 2 s. Educ. Greenock High School; Edinburgh University. Director of Nursing Service (North District), Grampian Health Board, 1984-87; Director of Nursing Services, Community Health Unit, Aberdeen, 1987-90; General Manager, Community Health Sector, and Acting Divisional General Manager, Priority Services Unit, 1991-92. Recreations: music; poetry; bowling (indoor and outdoor); film buff. Address: (h.) 4 Pinkie Gardens, Newmachar, Aberdeenshire; T.-Newmachar 2743.

Campbell-Gibson, Lt.Comdr. R.N. (Ret.) Hugh Desmond. Member, Council, Association for Protection of Rural Scotland; Member, Executive Committee, and County Organiser, Argyll, Scotland's Gardens Scheme; b. 18.8.24; m., Deirdre Wilson; 2 s.; 1 d. Educ. Royal Naval College, Dartmouth. Naval cadet, 1937-41; served Royal Navy, 1941-60; war service convoy duties, Atlantic and Mediterranean; farmed Glenlussa, by Campbeltown, 1960-68; farmed and ran hotel, Dunmor, Seil, Argyll, 1969-83; now manages family woodlands at Melfort. Recreations: gardening; skiing. Address: (h.) Tighnamara, Melfort, Kilmelford, Argyll; T.-Kilmelford 224.

Campbell-Preston, Robert Modan Thorne, OBE, MC, TD. Deputy Lieutenant of Argyll and Bute; b. 7.1.09; m., the Hon. Angela Murray (deceased); 1 d. Educ. Eton; Christ Church, Oxford. Lt., Scottish Horse, 1930; Lt.-Col., 1945; Hon. Col., Fife & Forfar Yeomanry/Scottish Horse, 1962-67; retired Member, Royal Company of Archers (Queen's Bodyguard for Scotland); Joint Managing Director, Alginate Industries Ltd., 1949-74; DL, 1951; JP, 1950; Silver Star, USA, 1945; Chairman, Argyll and Bute Trust. Recreations: shooting; fishing; gardening. Address: Ardchattan Priory, by Oban, Argyll; T.-Bonawe 274.

Campsie, Alistair Keith, SDA. Author, Journalist and Piper; b. 27.1.29, Inverness; m., Robbie Anderson; 2 s.; 1 d. Educ. West Sussex High School; Lanark Grammar School; West of Scotland College of Agriculture. Inspector of Agriculture, Sudan Government Service, 1949; Cocoa Survey Officer,

Nigeria, 1951; experimental staff, National Institute of Agricultural Engineering (Scotland), 1953; Country Editor, Weekly Scotsman, 1954; Sub-Editor, Verse Writer, Scottish Daily Mail, 1955; Founder Editor, East African Farmer and Planter, 1956; Chief Sub-Editor, Weekly Scotsman, 1957; designed and appointed first Editor, Geneva Weekly Tribune, 1958; Chief Feature Writer, Scottish Daily Mail, 1959; Columnist, Science Correspondent and Senior Writer, Scottish Daily Express, 1962-73; founded The Piper's Press, 1988; two Scottish Arts Council writer's bursaries; two SAC publisher's awards. Publications: Poems and a Pibroch (with Hugh MacDiarmid), 1972; By Law Protected, 1976; The MacCrimmon Legend or The Madness of Angus Mackay, 1980; We Bought a Country Pub (under pen-name Alan Mackinnon), 1984; Perfect Poison, 1985; Pibroch: the Tangled Web (radio series), 1985; Dundas or How They Murdered Robert Burns (play), 1987; The Clarinda Conspiracy, 1989; The True Story of The Ball of Kirriemuir, 1989; Cary Grant Stopped Me Smoking, 1991. Recreations: bagpipes (playing and composing); good whisky; self-important people. Address: Piper's Restaurant and Private Hotel, Union Place, Montrose; T.-0674 72298.

Canavan, Dennis, BSc (Hons), DipEd. MP (Labour), Falkirk West, since 1983; b. 8.8.42, Cowdenbeath. Educ. St. Bride's and St. Columba's Schools, Cowdenbeath; Edinburgh University. Principal Teacher of Mathematics, St. Modan's High School, Stirling, 1970-74; Assistant Head, Holyrood High School, Edinburgh, 1974; Leader, Labour Group, Stirling District Council, 1974; MP, West Stirlingshire, 1974-83; Chairman, Scottish Parliamentary Labour Group, 1980-81; Vice-Chair, PLP Northern Ireland Committee, since 1983; Member, Foreign Affairs Select Committee, since 1982; Founder and Convener, All Party Parliamentary Scottish Sports Group, since 1987. Recreations: marathon running; hill-climbing; fishing; swimming; football (former Scottish Universities football internationalist). Address: (h.) 15 Margaret Road, Bannockburn, Stirling, FK7 OJG; T.-0786 812581.

Candlish, Kenneth Henry, BL, JP, DL. Retired Solicitor; Deputy Lieutenant, Berwickshire; b. 22.8.24, Edinburgh; m., Isobel Robertson-Brown; 2 d. Educ. George Watson's; Edinburgh University. Depute County Clerk, West Lothian, 1951-64; County Clerk, Berwickshire, 1964-75. Recreations: photography; wine-making; music. Address: (h.) The Elms, Duns, Berwickshire; T.-Duns 83298.

Cant, Harry Wallace, MA, LLB, WS, NP. Solicitor, since 1954; Clerk and Treasurer, Iona Cathedral Trust, 1965-85; b. 5.7.18, Edinburgh; m., Mary Fleming Hamilton; 3 s.; 1 d. Educ. George Watson's College, Edinburgh; Edinburgh University. War Service, 1939-46 (Capt., Royal Artillery, 51st Highland Division, Western Desert, Sicily, France and Germany); wounded France, 1944; Partner: Menzies & Thomson, WS, 1954, J. & F. Anderson, WS, 1966; Consultant, J. & F. Anderson, WS, 1984-87; Secretary, Edinburgh Musical Festival Association, 1958-67; Secretary, Scottish Society of Women Artists, 1960-68; Treasurer, Scottish Action on Dementia, 1987-89. Recreations: golf; reading. Address: (h.) 77 Craiglockhart Road, Edinburgh, EH14 1EL; T.-031-441 3512.

Cant, Rev. Harry William Macphail, MA, BD, STM. Extra Chaplain to the Queen in Scotland, since 1991; Minister, St. Magnus Cathedral, Orkney, 1968-90; b. 3.4.21, Edinburgh; m., Margaret Elizabeth Loudon; 1 s.; 2 d. Educ. Edinburgh Academy; Edinburgh University; Union Theological College, New York. Lt., KOSB, 1941-43; Captain, King's African Rifles, 1944-46; TA Chaplain, 7th Argyll and Sutherland Highlanders, 1962-70; Assistant Minister, St. Nicholas Parish Church, Aberdeen, 1950-51; Minister, Fallin Parish Church, Stirling, 1951-56; Scottish Secretary, Student Christian

Movement, 1956-59; Minister, St. Thomas' Parish Church, Leith, 1960-68. Publications: Preaching in a Scottish Parish Church; Springs of Renewal in Congregational Life; Light in the North (Co-editor). Address: Cathedral Manse, Kirkwall, Orkney, KW15 1NA; T.-0856 3312.

Cantley, Maurice, BSc, PhD. Director, Industry and Export Services, Highlands and Islands Enterprise, since 1991; b. 6.6.37, Cambuslang; m., Rosalind Diana Jones; 2 d. Educ. Bedford Modern and Bristol Grammar; Bristol University. Unilever Ltd., 1961-67; McCann Erickson Advertising, London, 1967-76; Director of Recreation and Tourism, Tayside Regional Council, 1976-82; Head of Tourism, HIDB, 1982-85; Marketing Director, Highlands and Islands Development Board, 1985-91. Chairman, Association of Directors of Recreation, Leisure and Tourism, 1980-82; Hon. Education Officer, Society of Cosmetic Chemists of GB, 1963-66. Recreations: driving north of Ullapool; natural history; hill-walking. Address: (h.) Oldshorebeg, Kinlochbervie, Sutherland, IV27 4RS; T.-097182 257.

Caplan, Hon. Lord (Philip Isaac Caplan), MA, LLB, QC. Senator of the College of Justice, since 1989; b. 24.2.29, Glasgow, iii., Joyce Stone (2nd m.); 2 s.; 2 d. Educ. Eastwood School; Glasgow University. Solicitor, 1952-56; called to Bar, 1957; Standing Junior Counsel to Accountant of Court, 1964-70; Chairman, Plant Varieties and Seeds Tribunal, Scotland, 1977-79; Sheriff of Lothian and Borders, at Edinburgh, 1979-83; Sheriff Principal of North Strathclyde, 1983-88; Member, Sheriff Courts Rules Council, 1984-88; Commissioner, Northern Lighthouse Board, 1983-88; Chairman, Scottish Association for the Study of Delinquency, 1985-89, Hon. Vice President, 1990; Member, Advisory Council on Messengers at Arms and Sheriff Officers, 1987-88; Chairman, Scottish Association of Family Conciliation Services. FRPS (1988), AFIAP (1985). Recreations: photography; bridge; music; reading. Address: (b.) Court of Session, Parliament House, Edinburgh.

Capperauld, Ian, MB, ChB, DObst, RCOG, FRCSEdin, FRCSGlas, FRCSEng. Executive Director, Research and Development, Ethicon Ltd., since 1969; Consultant Surgeon, since 1962; Medical Director, Huntly Nursing Home, since 1981; Member, Lothian Health Board, since 1981; b. 23.10.33, New Cumnock; m., Wilma Hyslop Young; 2 s. Educ. Cumnock Academy; Glasgow University; Edinburgh University. Served as Major, RAMC, 1959-69 (Consultant Surgeon). Recreations: fishing; shooting. Address: (b.) Ethicon Ltd., PO Box 408, Bankhead Avenue, Edinburgh; T.-031-453 5555.

Carbery, Emeritus Professor Thomas Francis, OBE, MSc, PhD, DPA. Former Professor, Strathclyde Business School, Strathclyde University; Chairman, South of Scotland Consumers Committee/Office of Electricity Regulation, since 1990; Member: Scottish Legal Aid Board, since 1986, Data Protection Tribunal, since 1985; b. 18.1.25, Glasgow; m., Ellen Donnelly; 1 s.; 2 d. Educ. St. Aloysius' College, Glasgow; Glasgow University; Scottish College of Commerce. Cadet navigator/meteorologist, RAF, 1943-47; civil servant, 1947-61; Lecturer, then Senior Lecturer, Scottish College of Commerce, 1961-64; Strathclyde University: Senior Lecturer in Government-Business Relations, 1964-75, Head, Department of Office Organisation, 1975-79, Professor of Office Organisation, 1979-85, Professor of Business Information, 1985-88; part-time Professor of Marketing, 1988-90. Member: Independent Broadcasting Authority, 1970-79, Broadcasting Complaints Commission, 1981-86, Royal Commission on Gambling, 1975-77, Transport Users Consultative Committee (Chairman, Scottish TUCC), 1975-81, Press Council, 1987-90, Scottish Consumer Council (latterly Vice-Chairman), 1976-84; Chairman, Scottish Transport Research Group, 1983-87; Member,

Church of Scotland Committee on Higher Education, 1986-87; Chairman, Strathclyde University Inter-denominational Chaplaincy Committee, 1981-87; Joint Editor, Bulletin of Society for Co-operative Studies; Chairman, Scottish Catholic Communications Commission; Member, Scottish Catholic Education Commission. Recreations: conversation; watching television; spectating at association football; very bad golf. Address: (h.) 24 Fairfax Avenue, Glasgow, G44 5AL; T.-041-637 0514.

Cargill, Kenneth George, MA, LLB. Head of News, Current Affairs and Sport, Television, BBC Scotland, since 1988; b. 17.2.47, Arbroath; m., Una Gallacher. Educ. Arbroath High School; Edinburgh University. BBC TV Scotland: Researcher, Current Affairs, 1972; Reporter, Current Account, 1973; Film Director, Public Account, 1978; Producer, Current Account, 1979, Agenda, 1981, People and Power (London), 1983; Editor of the day, Reporting Scotland, 1983; Editor, Scotland 2000, 1986-87; Deputy Editor, News and Current Affairs, Television, 1984-88. Publication: Scotland 2000 (Editor), 1987. Address: (b.) Broadcasting House, Queen Margaret Drive, Glasgow, G12 8DG; T.-041-330 2250.

Carlyle, Walter, BSc, ARIC. General Manager, BP Oil Grangemouth Refinery Limited, since 1987; b. 5.4.37, Bo'ness; m., Beatrice S. Henderson; 2 s.; 1 d. Educ. Bo'ness Academy; Heriot-Watt University. BP: Development Chemist, Aden Refinery, 1961-67; Branch Manager, Design, Refineries Department, 1967-75, Manager, Investment Branch, London, 1980-82, Manager, Development Division, Manufacturing, London, 1982, Assistant Works Manager, BP Oil Grangemouth Refinery Ltd., 1982, Works Manager, Grangemouth, 1983-87. Council Member, CBI Scotland. Recreations: golf; walking; the performing arts. Address: (b.) BP Oil Grangemouth Refinery Limited, Bo'ness Road, Grangemouth, FK3 9XQ; T.-Grangemouth 483422.

Carmichael, Hugh Alisdair, MB, ChB, FRCP(Glas). Consultant Physician, Vale of Leven Hospital, Alexandria, since 1979; b. 21.11.45, Dingwall; m., Rosamund Mary Brannan; 1 s.; 3 d. Educ. Ardrossan Academy; Glasgow University. Glasgow Royal Infirmary: Resident House Surgeon, 1970-71, Resident House Physician, 1971, Senior House Officer in Haematology, 1971-72, Senior House Officer in Medicine, 1972-74, Registrar in Medicine and Gastroenterology, 1974-77; Senior Registrar in Medicine, Western Infirmary, Glasgow, and Gartnavel Hospital, 1977-79. Address: (b.) Vale of Leven Hospital, Alexandria, Dunbartonshire; T.-Alexandria 54121.

Carmichael, Margaret Mary, BMus, ARCM. Principal, Oxenfoord Castle School, Pathhead, since 1979; b. 1.2.40, Alyth, Perthshire. Educ. Bedford High School; Guildhall School of Music and Drama, London. Head of Music, City of London School for Girls, 1970-74; Lecturer in Music, Goldsmiths' College, London University, 1975-78. Chairman: Music at Oxenfoord, 1980-90, Scottish Independent Schools' Orchestra, 1986-89. Recreations: theatre; travel. Address: (b.) Oxenfoord Castle School, Pathhead, Midlothian, EH37 5UD; T.-0875 320241.

Carmichael of Kelvingrove, Baron (Neil George Carmichael). Life Peer; b. 1921. MP (Labour), Woodside, 1962-74, Kelvingrove, 1974-83.

Carmichael, Peter, CBE, DSc; b. 26.3.33, Dunblane; m., June; 2 s.; 4 d. by pr. m. Educ. McLaren High School, Callander; Glasgow University. Design engineer, Ferranti Ltd., Edinburgh, 1958-65; Hewlett-Packard, South Queensferry: Project Leader, 1965-67, Production Engineering Manager, 1968-73, Engineering Manager, 1973-75, Manufacturing Manager, 1975-76, Division General

Manager, 1976-82, Joint Managing Director, 1980-82; Scottish Development Agency: Director, Small Business and Electronics, 1982-88, Group Director East, 1988-89. Chairman: Wolfson Microelectronics Co., Esmee Fairbairn Economic Institute, Strathclyde Fabricators; Partner, Craiglea Clocks. Recreations: fishing; antique clock restoration. Address: (h.) 86 Craiglea Drive, Edinburgh; T.-031-447 6334.

Carmichael of Carmichael (Richard John). 26th Baron of Carmichael, since 1980; 30th Chief of Name and Arms of Carmichael, since 1981; Chartered Accountant; Farmer; b. 1.12.48, Stamford; m., Patricia Margaret Branson; 1 s.; 2 d. Educ. Hyton Hill Preparatory School; Kimbolton School; Coventry College of Technology. Audit Senior, Coopers and Lybrand, Tanzania, 1972; Audit Manager, Granger Craig Tunnicliffe, Tauranga, New Zealand, 1974; ACA, 1971; FCA, 1976; Factor/Owner, Carmichael Estate, 1980; Director: Carmichael Heritage Leisure Ltd., Clydesdale Development Co. Ltd., Scottish Orienteering 6-Day Event Co. Ltd.; claims family titles: Earldom of Hyndford, Viscountcies of Inglisberry and Nemphlar, and Lordship Carmichael of Carmichael. Member, Supreme Council of Scottish Chiefs; Secretary Carmichael Anstruther District Charitable Association; New Zealand Orienteering Champion, 1977; Grade One Controller, British Orienteering Federation. Recreations: orienteering; skiing; Clan Carmichael Association. Address: Carmichael House, Carmichael, by Biggar, Lanarkshire, ML12 6PG; T.-08993 336.

Carnall, Geoffrey Douglas, MA, BLitt. Reader in English Literature, Edinburgh University, since 1969; b. 1.2.27, Croydon, Surrey; m., Elisabeth Seale Murray; 1 s.; 2 d. Educ. Perse School, Cambridge; Magdalen College, Oxford. Lecturer in English, Queen's University, Belfast, 1952-60; Lecturer, then Senior Lecturer in English Literature, Edinburgh University, 1960-69. Chairman, Edinburgh Council for Nuclear Disarmament, 1963-70; Elder, South-East Scotland Monthly Meeting, Society of Friends (Quakers), 1970-87; Chairman, Edinburgh Christian Campaign for Nuclear Disarmament, 1982-85; Vice-Chair, Scottish Christian CND, 1987. Publications: Robert Southey and His Age, 1960; Robert Southey, 1964; The Mid-Eighteenth Century (Volume 8, Oxford History of English Literature) (Co-author), 1979; The Impeachment of Warren Hastings (Co-editor), 1989. Recreation: demonstrating against nuclear weapons. Address: (b.) Department of English Literature, David Hume Tower, George Square, Edinburgh, EH8 9JX; T.-031-667 1011.

Carnegy-Arbuthnott, David, TD, DL, LLD, CA. Landowner; b. 17.7.25, London; m., Helen Adamson Lyell; 2 s.; 2 d. Educ. Stowe. Emergency commission, The Black Watch, 1944-47; Chartered Accountant, 1953; in practice, Dundee, 1956-86; TA, 1955-69; Brevet Colonel, 1969; Hon. Colonel, 1st Bn., 51st Highland Volunteers (TA), 1980-89; Deputy Lieutenant, County of City of Dundee, 1973-89, Angus, since 1989; Member, Queen's Bodyguard for Scotland (Royal Company of Archers), since 1959; Governor, Dundee College of Education, 1985-87; Governor, Northern College of Education, 1987-91; President, Dundee Chamber of Commerce, 1971-72; Member of Court, Dundee University, 1977-85; Convener, Standing Committee, Scottish Episcopal Church, since 1987. Recreations: shooting; country pursuits. Address: (h.) Balnamoon, Brechin, Angus, DD9 7RH; T.-035 66 208.

Carnegie, Leslie Thompson, CBE (1980), BL, JP, Solicitor. Chief Executive, Dumfries and Galloway Regional Council, 1974-85; Honorary Sheriff, since 1960; b. 16.8.20, Aberdeen; m., Isobel Jane McCombie, JP. Educ. Aberdeen Grammar School; Aberdeen University. Legal Department, Aberdeen Corporation, 1939-48; Depute County Clerk, East Lothian,

1948-54; County Clerk, Dumfries County Council, 1954-75. Past President, Society of County Clerks in Scotland; Clerk, Dumfries Lieutenancy, 1954-85. Recreations: gardening; music appreciation; sporting activities. Address: (h.) Marchhill Park, Dumfries.

Carnegy of Lour, Baroness (Elizabeth Patricia), DL. Life Peer, since 1982; Member, House of Lords Select Committee on European Communities, Sub-Committee D; President for Scotland, Girl Guides Association, 1979- 89; Member of Council and of Finance Committee, Open University, since 1984; Member, Scottish Economic Council, since 1980; Hon. President, Scottish Library Association, since 1989; Member of Court, St. Andrews University, since 1991; Farmer, 1956-89; b. 28.4.25. Educ. Downham School. Cavendish Laboratory, Cambridge, 1943-46; Girl Guides Association: Training Adviser for Scotland, 1958-62 and for Commonwealth HQ, 1963-65; co-opted Angus County Council Education Committee, 1967-75; Councillor, Tayside Regional Council, 1974-82; Chairman, Education Committee, 1976-82; Chairman, Working Party on Professional Training in Community Education Scotland, 1975-77; Commissioner, Manpower Services Commission, 1979-82, and Chairman, Committee for Scotland, 1980-83; Member, Scottish Council for Tertiary Education, 1979-84; Chairman, Scottish Council for Community Education, 1980-88; Honorary Sheriff, 1969-84; Deputy Lieutenant, District of Angus, 1988; Fellow, Royal Society of Arts, 1987; Honorary LLD, Dundee University, 1991. Address: (h.) Lour, Forfar, Angus, DD8 2LR; T.-0307 82 237.

Carnie, Colin Greig, DIC, CEng, MICE. Partner, Crouch Hogg Waterman since 1966; Director, Glasgow Development Agency, since 1991; b. 12.11.34, Glasgow; m., Elizabeth Haddo Neill; 3 s.; 2 d. Educ. Loretto; Imperial College, London. Engineer, Crouch and Hogg, 1962-66. Director, Scottish Industrial Estates Corporation, 1972-78; Member, Glasgow Action, 1986-91; Member, Broadcasting Council for Scotland, 1973-78; Director, Glasgow Chamber of Commerce; Vice Chairman, The Salmon Conservancy; Honorary Consul in Scotland for Costa Rica. Recreations: fishing; sailing; shooting. Address: (b.) The Octagon, 35 Baird Street, Glasgow G4 0EE; T.-041-552 2000.

Carr, John Roger, CBE, JP, FRICS, FRSA. Chairman, Countryside Commission for Scotland, since 1985 (Member, since 1979); Member, Macaulay Land Use Research Institute, since 1987; Director, UK 2000 Scotland, since 1990; President, Ramblers Association Scotland, since 1992; Manager, FWAG, since 1984; b. 18.1.27, Ackworth, Yorkshire; m., Cathrine Elise Dickson-Smith; 2 s. Educ. Ackworth & Ayton (Quaker) School. Royal Marines, 1945-47; Gordon Highlanders TA, 1950-55; Factor, Walker Scottish Estates Co., Ballater; Factor, subsequently Director and General Manager, Moray Estates Development Co., Forres; former Convenor, Scottish Recreational Land Association; former Council Member, Scottish Landowners Association; former District Councillor, Moray. Recreations: most country pursuits. Address: (b.) Bradbush, Darnaway, Moray, IV36 0SH; T.-03094 249.

Carrol, Charles Gordon, MA, DipEd. Director, Commonwealth Institute, Scotland, since 1971; b. 21.3.35, Edinburgh; m., Frances Anne Sinclair; 3 s. Educ. Melville College, Edinburgh; Edinburgh University; Moray House College of Education. Education Officer: Government of Nigeria, 1959-65, Commonwealth Institute, Scotland, 1965-71. Lay Member, Press Council, 1978-83. Recreations: walking; angling; reading; cooking. Address: (h.) 11 Dukehaugh, Peebles; T.-0721 21296.

Carroll, Professor Robert Peter, MA, PhD. Professor, Department of Biblical Studies, Glasgow University, since

1991 (Dean, Faculty of Divinity, 1991-93); b. 18.1.41, Dublin; m., Mary Anne Alice Stevens; 2 s.; 1 d. Educ. High School, Dublin; Trinity College, Dublin University; Edinburgh University. After postgraduate degree, worked as swimming pool attendant, barman, brickie's mate, secondary school teacher; Glasgow University: Assistant Lecturer in Semitic Languages, 1968, Lecturer in Old Testament Language and Literature, 1969, Senior Lecturer in Biblical Studies, 1981; Reader, 1986. Publications: When Prophecy Failed, 1979; From Chaos to Covenant, 1981; Jeremiah: A Commentary, 1986; Jeremiah (JSOT Guide), 1989; Wolf in Sheepfold, 1991. Recreations: cinema; day-dreaming; writing imaginary books in my head. Address: (h.) 5 Marchmont Terrace, Glasgow, G12 9LT; T.-041-339 0440.

Carse, George, MA, BL; b. 30.10.19, Edinburgh; m., Ann Elisabeth C. Rankine; 1 d. Educ. Edinburgh Academy; Edinburgh University. Assistant, St. Cuthbert's Parish Church, Edinbugh, 1943-44; Chaplain, Royal Navy, 1944-47; Minister: Lethendy and Kinloch Parish Church, 1947-49, Liberton Northfield Parish Church, 1949-59; admitted Faculty of Advocates, 1965. President, Edinburgh Natural History Society, 1967-70; President, Lothians Branch, Scottish Wildlife Trust, since 1978; Chairman, Liberton Association, 1967-73. Recreations: walking; ornithology; natural history. Address: (h.) 121 Liberton Brae, Edinburgh, EH16 6LD; T.-031-664 2070.

Carson, Jack. Convener, Cunninghame District Council, since 1988; Member, Board, Irvine Development Corporation, since 1989; b. 30.4.33, Irvine; m., Mary Carson Hill; 2 s.; 2 d. Educ. Irvine Royal Academy. Member, Irvine Burgh Council, 1972-75; Cunninghame District Council: Vice-Convener, 1980-88, Chairman, Miscellaneous Services Committee, 1980-88, Chairman, Economic Development Committee, 1984-88; Vice-Chairman, Cunninghame Justices of the Peace Advisory Committee; Member, Scottish Prisons Visiting Committee; Vice-Chairman, Scottish Maritime Museum, Irvine; Chairman, Cunninghame District Council Municipal Bank. Recreations: golf; football. Address: (b.) Cunninghame House, Friars Croft, Irvine, KA12 8EE; T.-0294 74166, Ext. 2327.

Carswell, Joyce Mary, BA. Deputy Director (Age Care), Board of Social Responsibility, Church of Scotland, since 1987; b. 9.4.49, Ayr. Educ. Larkhall Academy; Strathclyde University; Edinburgh University. Social Worker, 1971-74; Training Officer, Board of Social Responsibility, 1974-87; External Assessor to Certificate on Social Service, 1981-86. Secretary of State Appointee, Saughton Prison Visting Committee. Recreations: handcrafts; reading; involvement with local churches in setting up care groups for elderly people. Address: (b.) Church of Scotland, 121 George Street, Edinburgh, EH2 4YN; T.-031-225 5722.

Carter, Christopher John, BA (Hons), PhD, MRTPI, FBIM, FRSA. Vice Principal, Duncan of Jordanstone College of Art, since 1981; b. 5.2.41, Capel, Surrey; m., Ann Fisher Prince; 1 s.; 1 d. Educ. Ottershaw School, Chertsey, Surrey; Birmingham University; Glasgow University. Town Planning Assistant, Cumbernauld Development Corporation, 1963-64 and 1967-68; Visiting Lecturer in Geography, Brock University, St. Catharines, Ontario, 1968-69; Lecturer/Senior Lecturer in Planning, Glasgow School of Art, 1969-76; Principal Lecturer in Planning, Coventry (Lanchester) Polytechnic, 1976-78; Senior Lecturer/Head, Department of Town and Regional Planning, Duncan of Jordanstone College of Art, 1978-81. Winner, RTPI Prize, 1970.Member: Board of Governors, Dundee Institute of Technology, since 1989; Scottish Committee, Universities Funding Council, since 1989. Publications: Innovations in Planning Thought and Practice at Cumbernauld New Town 1956-62; The Designation of Cumbernauld New Town (case study) (Co-

author). Recreations: skiing; running; photography; music. Address: (h.) 39 Haston Crescent, Kinnoull, Perth; T.-0738 36802.

Carter, Professor David Craig, MB, ChB, MD, FRCSEdin, FRCSGlas. Regius Professor of Surgery, Edinburgh University, since 1988; Honorary Consultant, Edinburgh Royal Infirmary, since 1988; Member, Broadcasting Council for Scotland, since 1989; Chairman, Scottish Council for Postgraduate Medical Education; b. 1.9.40, Penrith; m., Ilske; 2 s. Educ. St. Andrews University. Lecturer in Clinical Surgery, Edinburgh University, 1969-74; 12-month secondment as Lecturer in Surgery, Makerere University, Kampala, Uganda, 1972; Senior Lecturer in Surgery, Edinburgh University, 1974-79; St. Mungo Professor of Surgery, Glasgow University, 1979-88; Honorary Consultant, Glasgow Royal Infirmary, 1979-88; 12-month secondment as Associate Professor of Surgery, University of California, 1976. Council Member, Royal College of Surgeons of Edinburgh, 1980-89. Moynihan Prize, 1973; James IV Association of Surgeons Travelling Fellow, 1975. Recreations: golf; music. Address: (b.) University Department of Surgery, Royal Infirmary, Edinburgh, EH3 9YW; T.-031-229 2477.

Carter, George Robert, MIPM, MBIM. Personnel Services Controller, Christian Salvesen PLC, 1974-90; Director, Christian Salvesen (Food Services) Ltd., since 1977; Member, CBI Employment Policy Committee, since 1987; Member, EAT, since 1985; b. 26.2.31, Youghal, Ireland; m., Margaret Elizabeth Andrew; 2 s.; 1 d. Educ. Christian Brothers Primary and Secondary School. Merchant Navy, 1949-54; trade union official, 1954-63; various personnel management roles, Chrysler (UK) Ltd., 1963-68; Consultant, Department of Employment, 1968-70; Personnel Director, Beaverbrook Newspaper Group, 1970-74. Member: Administration Committee, Scottish Business Education Council, 1977-79, CBI Industrial Relations Committee (Scotland), 1977-80, CBI (Scotland) Council, 1980-88; Chairman, CBI (Scotland) Employment Committee, 1980-88; Member, Manpower Services Committee (Scotland), 1980-87. Recreations: music; reading; photography. Address: (h.) 12A Ravelston Park, Edinburgh, EH4 3DX; T.-031-332 7914.

Carter, Tom, OBE, ACIS, ACMA, CIPFA. Chairman, Castlehill Housing Association; Chairman, Partnership Housing Ltd.; Governor, Robert Gordon's Institute of Technology; Temporary Acting Director of Finance, Western Isles Island Council; b. 27.12.23, Carlisle; m., Gill (m. diss.); 2 s. Educ. Birkenhead Park High School. 7th Bn., Royal Tank Rgt., 1942-44; various clerical posts, mainly with former LMS Railway, 1939-47; Birkenhead: Clerk, Parks and Cemeteries Department, 1947-48, Accountancy Assistant, 1948-55; Technical Assistant, rising to Assistant Secretary, former IMTA, 1955-61; Deputy County Treasurer, Holland (Lincolnshire), 1961-68; County Treasurer, Moray and Nairn, 1968-75; Director of Finance, Grampian Regional Council, 1975-87. Past Chairman, Directors of Finance (Scotland) Section, CPFA; Member, Local Government Finance Working Party; former Commissioner, Public Works Loan Board. Recreations: walking; bridge; gardening; wine-making; reading. Address: (h.) 24 Gordon Road, Mannofield, Aberdeen, AB1 7RL.

Carty, Anthony John, LLB, LLM, PhD. Senior Lecturer, Public International Law, Glasgow University, since 1990; guest Professor in Law and Politics, Free University, Berlin, since 1991; b. 26.5.47, Belfast. Educ. Queen's University, Belfast; Jesus College, Cambridge. Lecturer, English Law, University of Paris II; Alexander Von Humboldt Fellow, Max Planck Institute for Public Law, Heidelberg; guest Professor, University of Laval (Quebec), Michigan Law School. Publications: Power and Manoeuvrability (Editor), 1978; editor of several books on international law and economic developments. Recreation: foreign languages. Address: Department of Public Law, Glasgow University, Glasgow; T.-041-339 8855.

Carty, Matthew John, MB, ChB, FRCSEdin, FRCPSGlas, FRCOG. Consultant Obstetrician and Gynaecologist, Southern General Hospital, Glasgow, since 1977; b. 8.3.42, Hamilton; m., Caroline Martin; 2 s.; 2 d. Educ. St. Aloysius College, Glasgow; Glasgow University. Lecturer in Midwifery, Nairobi University, Kenya, 1970-71; Lecturer in Midwifery, Glasgow University, 1972-77. Recreations: squash; golf; tennis; jogging. Address: (h.) 31 Monreith Road, Newlands, Glasgow; T.-041-632 1033.

Cash, John David, BSc, MB, ChB, PhD, FRCPath, FRCPE. National Medical and Scientific Director, Scottish National Blood Transfusion Service, since 1979; Honorary Professor, Department of Medicine, Edinburgh University, since 1987; b. 3.4.36, Reading; m., Angela Mary Thomson; 1 s.; 1 d. Educ. Ashville College, Harrogate; Edinburgh University. Edinburgh and South East Scotland Blood Transfusion Service: Deputy Director, 1969, Regional Director, 1974. Adviser in Blood Transfusion, WHO. Recreations: fishing; gardening. Address: (b.) Scottish National Blood Transfusion Service, Headquarters, Ellen's Glen Road, Liberton, Edinburgh EH17 7QT; T.-031-664 2317.

Cash, Phillip, BSc, PhD. Senior Lecturer in Medical Microbiology, Aberdeen University, since 1989; b. 27.1.53, Stockport; m., Beatriz. Educ. Stockport School; University of Wales, Swansea; Glasgow University. Research Fellow, Alabama University, 1978-80; Lecturer, Medical Microbiology, Aberdeen University, 1980-89. Publications: research papers on molecular virology. Recreations: photography; reading; gardening. Address: Department of Medical Microbiology, Aberdeen University, Aberdeen AB9 2ZD.

Caskie, Rev. Donald Murdoch, MA, HCF; b. 27.2.08, Glasgow; m., Jane (Sheana) Mathieson; 3 s.; 1 d. Educ. Buchanan Institute and John Street Secondary; Glasgow University and Trinity College. Minister: Cumbrae, 1932-37, Coatbridge: Coats, 1937-47; Army Chaplain, 1941-45; Minister, Monkton and Prestwick, 1947-81; Moderator, Presbytery of Ayr, 1960-61. Past President, Prestwick Rotary Club; Life Member and Past President, Prestwick Burns Club. Address: (h.) 5 Tramore Crescent, Prestwick KA9 1LT; T.-Prestwick 78534.

Caskie, Rev. J. Colin, BA, BD. Parish Minister, Carnoustie, since 1983; Member, Board of Stewardship and Finance, General Assembly; b. 17.8.47, Glasgow; m., Alison McDougall; 2 s.; 1 d. Educ. Knightswood Secondary School; Strathclyde University; Glasgow University. Parish Minister, Penilee, Glasgow, 1977-83. Recreations: stamp collecting; gardening. Address: 44 Terrace Road, Carnoustie, Angus, DD7 7AR; T.-0241 52289.

Cassels, James Rendall Thomson, BSc, MSc, PhD, CChem, FRSC. Head Teacher, Bellahouston Academy, Glasgow, since 1986; b. 23.4.45, Irvine; m., Angela; 3 d. Educ. Irvine Royal Academy; Strathclyde University; Glasgow University. Assistant Head Teacher, Camphill High School, Paisley, 1977-84; Depute Head Teacher, Mearns Castle High School, Glasgow, 1984-86. Formerly: Member, Chemistry Panel, Scottish Examination Board; Chairman, Joint Working Party on Standard Grade Chemistry; Member, advisory committee, Scottish Council for Research in Education; awarded medal, Education Division, Royal Society of Chemistry, 1980. Recreation: bird-watching. Address: (b.) 30 Gower Terrace, Glasgow, G42 5QE; T.-041-427 2251.

Cassidy, Anthony (Tony) F., BSc (Hons). Chief Executive, Renfrewshire Enterprise, since 1991; Non-Executive Director, EFM Dragon Investment Trust, since 1987; Non-Executive Director, Castle Cairn Investment Trust, since 1990; b. 17.11.44, Kilbarchan; m., Laura Jane; 2 s. Educ. Glasgow University. Lecturer, Mechanical Engineering, Glasgow University, 1969-72; British Council official: India, 1972-76, Japan, 1976-81, France, 1983-84; Director, Japan/Asia, Locate in Scotland, 1984-91. Recreations: opera; orchestral music; rowing; sailing; skiing. Address: (b.) Merlin House, Mossland Road, Hillington, Glasgow, G52 4XZ; T.-041-882 6288.

Catley, Brian John, MA, PhD. Senior Lecturer in Biochemistry, Department of Biological Sciences, Heriot-Watt University, since 1978; b. 15.11.36, Salisbury, Wiltshire; m., Elizabeth Ferguson Eyres; 1 s.; 1 d. Educ. Bradford Grammar School; St. Catherine's College, Oxford. Research Chemist, Ilford Ltd., 1961-64; Assistant Lecturer, London University, 1965-67; Guest Investigator, Rockefeller University, New York, 1967-68, Assistant Professor, Miami University, 1968-72; Lecturer, Heriot-Watt University, 1972-78. Convenor, Reserve Management Committee, Balerno, Scottish Wildlife Trust. Recreations: photography; travel. Address: (b.) Department of Biological Sciences, Heriot-Watt University, Riccarton, Edinburgh, EH14 4AS; T.-031-449 5111, Ext. 4685.

Cattanach, John Harkness, VM, JP. Member, Highland Regional Council, 1982-86; Member, Nairn District Council, since 1974; b. 19.1.19, Torbermory; m., Williamina Fraser; 1 s. Educ. Kingussie Secondary School; Skerry's College, Glasgow. Army Officer, 1938-46 (Captain); ran own business, 1946-50; accountant, 1950-55; own business, 1956-74. Awarded Order of the Silver Cross of Virtuti Militari by the Polish Government in exile; Hon. Lt. Col., Polish Armed Forces (Govt. in exile). Address: (h.) Lorne House, Geddes, by Nairn, IV12 5SB; T.-06677 279.

Catto, Professor Graeme R.D., MB, ChB (Hons), MD (Hons), DSc, FRCP, FRCPE, FRCPGlas. Dean, Faculty of Clinical Medicine, since 1992, and Professor in Medicine and Therapeutics, Aberdeen University, since 1988; Honorary Consultant Physician/Nephrologist, since 1977; b. 24.4.45, Aberdeen; m., Joan Sievewright; 1 s.; 1 d. Educ. Robert Gordon's College; Aberdeen University. Research Fellow/Lecturer/Senior Lecturer/Reader in Medicine, Aberdeen University, 1970-88; Harkness Fellow of Commonwealth Fund of New York, 1975-77 (Fellow in Medicine, Harvard Medical School and Peter Bent Brigham Hospital, Boston). Recreations: curling; fresh air; France. Address: (b.) Department of Medicine, Aberdeen University, Foresterhill, Aberdeen, AB9 2ZB; T.-0224 681818.

Cawdor, 6th Earl (Hugh John Vaughan Campbell), FSA, FRICS, FRSA; b. 6.9.32; m., 1, Cathryn Hinde (m. diss.); 2 s.; 3 d.; 2, Countess Angelika Ilona Lazansky von Bukowa. Educ. Eton; Magdalen College, Oxford; Royal Agricultural College, Cirencester. Address: (h.) Cawdor Castle, Nairn.

Cawthra, David Wilkinson, BSc, FEng, FICE, FIHT, CBIM. Chief Executive, The Miller Group Limited, since 1992; b. 5.3.43, Halifax; m., Maureen Mabel Williamson; 1 s.; 1 d. Educ. Heath Grammar School, Halifax; Birmingham University. Mitchell Construction Company Ltd., 1964-73; Tarmac Construction Ltd., 1973-79; Balfour Beatty Ltd., 1979-91. Member, NEDO Construction Industry Sector Group, 1990-92. Recreations: hill-walking; American history. Address: (b.) Miller House, 18 South Groathill Avenue, Edinburgh, EH4 2LW; T.-031-332 2585.

Cay, Elizabeth Lorna, MD, FRCP, FRCPsych, DPM. Consultant in Rehabilitation Medicine, since 1975; Honorary

Senior Lecturer, Edinburgh University, since 1976; b. 11.1.31, Cawdor, Nairn; m., David Robert Bellamy Cay (deceased); 1 s.; 1 d. Educ. Elgin Academy; Peebles Burgh and County High School; Edinburgh University. Temporary Advisor, WHO; Member, Scientific Council on Rehabilitation, International Society and Federation of Cardiology. Recreations: convertibles; breeding dogs; travel. Address: (h.) 12 India Street, Edinburgh, EH3 6EZ; T.-031-225 3640.

Chalmers, Rev. John Pearson, BD. Minister, Palmerston Place Church, Edinburgh, since 1986; b. 5.6.59, Bothwell; m., Elizabeth Barbara Boning; 2 s.; 1 d. Educ. Marr College; Strathclyde University; Glasgow University. Minister, Renton Trinity, 1979-86; Clerk, Dumbarton Presbytery, 1982-86. Governor, Donaldson College, since 1987 (Vice Chairman, since 1992). Recreations: bee-keeping; golf. Address: 37 Caiyside, Edinburgh, EH10 7HW; T.-031-445 5197.

Chalmers, Rev. William Riddell, MA, BD, STM. Minister, Dunbar Parish Church, since 1966; b. 24.10.27, Uddingston. Educ. Uddingston Grammar School; Glasgow University and Trinity College; Union Theological Seminary, New York. Minister, Fort Washington Presbyterian Church, Broadway, NY, 1953-57; Minister, St. Nicholas', Cardonald Parish Church, Glasgow, 1958-66. Recreations: football (played with Ayr United FC, US All-Star Team); cricket (played with Uddingston CC); golf. Address: The Manse, Dunbar, East Lothian, EH42 1AB; T.-Dunbar 63749.

Chambers, Ernest George Wilkie, MBA, BSc (Hons). Director of Water, Strathclyde Regional Council, since 1988; b. 10.5.47, Dundee; m., Jeanette; 1 s.; 1 d. Educ. Harris Academy, Dundee. Assistant Engineer, East of Scotland Water Board and Lower Clyde Water Board, 1969-75; SRC Water Department: Area Engineer (Renfrew), 1975-79, Divisional Operations Engineer, Lower Clyde Division, 1979-84, Assistant Divisional Manager, 1984-86, Assistant Director (Operations & Maintenance), 1986-88. President, Scottish Branch, Association of Water Officers, 1991-92; UK Representative, International Water Supply Association Management and Training Committee, 1992. Recreations: Boys Brigade; sailing; DIY. Address: (b.) 419 Balmore Road, Glasgow, G22 6NU; T.-041-355 5101.

Chapman, Charles Duncan, OBE, MA, LLB. Honorary Sheriff, since 1960; b. 11.2.13, Denny, Stirlingshire; m., Margaret Martin Henry (deceased); 1 s.; 1 d. Educ. Morrison's Academy, Crieff; Edinburgh University. Legal apprentice; Royal Artillery, 1939-45 (Major, 1943); Kirkcaldy Town Council, 1945-75: Legal Assistant, Depute Town Clerk, Town Clerk; Chief Executive, Kirkcaldy District Council, 1975-78. Past Chairman, Law Committee, Convention of Burghs; former Member, Central Probation Council; served on a number of Government committees and working parties; former Council Member, Law Society of Scotland; Director, Link Housing Association. Publication: The Licensing Scotland Act 1976. Address: (h.) 15 Stanley Park, Kirkcaldy; T.-0592 201270.

Chapman, Francis Ian, CBE, FRSA, CBIM. Chairman, Radio Clyde Ltd., since 1972; Director, United Distillers PLC, since 1988; Chairman and Managing Director, Chapmans Publishers Ltd., since 1989; Chairman, Guinness Publishing, since 1991; b. 26.10.25, St. Fergus, Aberdeenshire; m., Marjory Stewart Swinton; 1 s.; 1 d. Educ. Shawlands Academy, Glasgow; Ommer School of Music. War Service: RAF air crew cadet, 1943-44; National Service coal mines, 1945-47. William Collins: trainee, 1947, Sales Representative, New York Branch, 1951, General Sales Manager, London, 1955, appointed to main operating Board as Group Sales Director, 1960; appointed to Board, William Collins (Holdings) Ltd. as Joint Managing Director, 1967; Deputy Chairman, William Collins (Holdings) Ltd., 1976;

Chairman, William Collins Publishers Ltd., 1979; Chairman and Chief Executive, William Collins PLC, 1981-89; Chairman, Hatchards Ltd., 1976-89; Board Member, Pan Books Ltd., 1962-84; Chairman, Harvill Press Ltd., 1976-89; Board Member, Book Tokens Ltd., since 1981; Member, Governing Council, SCOTBIC, since 1983; Board Member, IRN Ltd., 1983-85; President, Publishers Association, 1979-81; Trustee, Book Trade Benevolent Society, since 1982; Board Member, Scottish Opera Theatre Royal Ltd., 1974-79; Director, Stanley Botes Ltd., 1985-89; Non-Executive Director, Guinness PLC, since December 1986; Joint Chairman and Chief Executive, Harper and Row, New York, 1987-89. Scottish Free Enterprise Award, 1985; Hon. DLitt, Strathclyde, 1990. Recreations: golf; swimming; skiing; music. Address: (b.) Radio Clyde, Clydebank Business Park, Clydebank.

Chapman, Professor John N., MA, PhD, FInstP, FRSE. Titular Professor, Physics and Astronomy, Glasgow University, since 1988; b. 21.11.47, Sheffield; m., Judith M.; 1 s.; 1 d. Educ. King Edward VII School, Sheffield; St. John's College and Fitzwilliam College, Cambridge. Research Fellow, Fitzwilliam College, Cambridge; Lecturer, Glasgow University. Publication: Quantitative Electron Microscopy (Co-Editor). Recreations: photography; walking; squash. Address: (b.) Department of Physics and Astronomy, Glasgow University, Glasgow, G12 8QQ; T.-041-339 8855, Ext. 4462.

Chapman, Robert Sutherland, MB, ChB (Hons), FRCP(Glas), FRCP(Edin), FRCP(Lond). Consultant Dermatologist, Greater Glasgow Health Board and Forth Valley Health Board, since 1971; Clinical Lecturer, Glasgow University, since 1973; b. 4.6.38, Cults, Aberdeenshire; m., Dr. Rosalind S. Slater; 2 s.; 1 d. Educ. Turriff Academy; Aberdeen University. House Officer, Aberdeen Royal Infirmary; Research Fellow, Department of Materia Medica and Therapeutics, Aberdeen University; Registrar and Senior Registrar in Dermatology, Aberdeen Hospitals; Senior Registrar in Dermatology, Middlesex Hospital and St. John's Hospital for Diseases of the Skin, London. Recreations: gardening; hill-walking. Address: (h.) 4 Seafield Avenue, Bearsden, Glasgow, G61 3LB; T.-041-942 8993.

Charlton, Professor Graham, BDS, MDS, FDSRCS. Professor of Conservative Dentistry and Head of Department, Edinburgh University, 1978-91; b. 15.10.28, Newbiggin-By-Sea, Northumberland; m., Stella Dobson; 2 s.; 1 d. Educ. Bedlington Grammar School; St. John's, York; Durham University. CertEd. Teacher in Northumberland, 1948-52 (including period of National Service); Dental School, 1952-58; general dental practice, 1958-64; Lecturer, then Senior Lecturer/Honorary Consultant, Bristol University, 1964-78 (Clinical Dean, Dental School, Bristol, 1975-78). Dean of Dental Studies, Edinburgh University, 1978-83. Address: (h.) Carnethy, Bog Road, Penicuik, Edinburgh EH26 9ET; T.-0968 73639.

Chatfield, William Robertson, MD, ChB, FRCS Glas, FRCS Edin, FRCOG, DFM. Consultant Obstetrician, Queen Mother's Hospital, Glasgow; Consultant Gynaecologist, Western Infirmary, Glasgow; Honorary Senior Lecturer, Glasgow University; b. 19.9.39, Glasgow; m., Mary McIndeor McArthur; 2 s.; 1 d. Educ. Glasgow Academy; Glasgow University. Hall Tutorial Fellow, Glasgow University; Lecturer, Nairobi University, Kenya; Senior Lecturer, Otago University, New Zealand. Recreation: golf. Address: (h.) 49 Carlaverock Road, Glasgow, G43 2QL; T.-041-632 2966.

Chatterji, Professor Monojit, BA, MA, PhD. Bonar Professor of Applied Economics, Dundee University, since 1989; Lecturer, Essex University, since 1975; b. 15.1.51,

Bombay; m., Anjum Rahmatulla; 1 s.; 1 d. Educ. Cathedral School, Bombay; St. Columba's, Delhi; Elphinstone College, Bombay; Christ's College, Cambridge. Recreations: tennis; cinema; history; theology. Address: (b.) Department of Economics, Dundee University, Dundee; T.-0382 23181.

Cheetham, Professor Juliet, MA. Professor and Director, Social Work Research Centre, Stirling University, since 1986; b. 12.10.39, Jerusalem; m., Christopher Paul Cheetham; 1 s.; 2 d. Educ. St. Andrews University; Oxford University. Probation Officer, Inner London, 1959-65; Lecturer in Applied Social Studies and Fellow of Green College, Oxford, 1965-86. Member: Committee of Enquiry into Working of the Abortion Act; Northern Ireland Human Rights Commission; Commission of Racial Equality; Social Security Advisory Committee; Council for National Academic Awards. Recreation: canal boats. Address: (b.) Social Work Research Centre, Stirling University, Stirling, FK9 4LA; T.-0786 67724.

Cherry, Rev. Alastair Jack, BD. Minister, Stamperland Parish Church, Glasgow, since 1987 (Scoonie Kirk, Leven, 1982-87); Convener, Church of Scotland Working Group on Special Educational Needs, and Advisor, Church Advisorate in Special Education Needs; b. 13.3.44, Glasgow; m., Fiona Mairi Murchison; 2 s. Educ. Bellahouston Academy, Glasgow; Glasgow University. Staff, Clydesdale Bank Ltd., 1964-76; studied for ministry, 1976-82. Recreations: music; dramatic art; walking; swimming. Address: Manse of Stamperland, 109 Ormonde Avenue, Glasgow, G44 3SN; T.-041-637 4976.

Chester, Richard Waugh, ARAM, GRSM, ARCM. Administrator, National Youth Orchestra of Scotland, since 1987; b. 19.4.43, Hutton Rudby; m., Sarah Chapman-Mortimer; 1 s.; 2 d. Educ. The Friends' School, Great Ayton; Royal Academy of Music. Flautist: BBC Northern Ireland, 1965, Scottish National Orchestra, 1967; Conductor; Teacher; Examiner. Director, Glasgow Festival Strings; Member, Music Committee, Scottish Arts Council; Governor, St. Mary's Music School, Edinburgh. Recreations: squash; swimming; cricket; good food. Address: (h.) Milton of Cardross, Port of Menteith, Stirling, FK8 3JY; T.-08775 634.

Cheyne, Rev. Professor Alexander Campbell, MA (Hons), BLitt, BD, HonDLitt (Memorial University, Newfoundland). Professor of Ecclesiastical History, Edinburgh University, 1964-86; Principal, New College, Edinburgh, 1984-86; Moderator, Edinburgh Presbytery, Church of Scotland, 1987-88; b. 1.6.24, Errol, Perthshire. Educ. Kirkcaldy High School; Edinburgh University; Oriel College, Oxford; Basel University, Switzerland. National Service, Black Watch and RAEC (Instructor, Army School of Education), 1946-48; Glasgow University: Assistant Lecturer, 1950-51, Lecturer in History, 1951-53; New College and Basel University, 1953-57; Lecturer in Ecclesiastical History, Edinburgh University, 1958-64. Carnegie Scholar, 1948-50; Aitken Fellow, 1956-57; Visiting Professor, Wooster College, Ohio, 1973; Chalmers Lecturer (Trinity College, Glasgow, and Christ's College, Aberdeen), 1976-80; Visiting Fellow, Wolfson College, Cambridge, 1979; Burns Lecturer, Knox College, Dunedin, New Zealand, 1980; President, Scottish Church History Society, 1986-89. Publications: The Transforming of the Kirk: Victorian Scotland's Religious Revolution, 1983; The Practical and the Pious: Essays on Thomas Chalmers 1780-1847 (Editor), 1985; contributions to: Reformation and Revolution: Essays presented to Hugh Watt, 1967, The Westminster Confession in the Church Today, 1982; introduction to Movements of Religious Thought in Britain during the Nineteenth Century, 1971. Recreations: classical music; walking; foreign travel. Address: (h.) 12 Crossland Crescent, Peebles, EH45 8LF; T.-0721 22288.

Cheyne, Alexander Ian, MB, ChB, DPM, FRCPsych, FRCP(Glas). Consultant Psychiatrist, Nuffield Hospital, Glasgow, formerly at Gartnavel Royal Hospital, Glasgow; b. 29.9.30, Rangoon, Burma; m., Jean MacDonald Edmonds; 3 d. Educ. Aberdeen Grammar School; Aberdeen University. House Officer: Aberdeen Royal Infirmary, 1954-55, Glasgow Royal Infirmary, 1955; Medical Officer, RAMC, 1955-57; Trainee, general practice, Banchory, 1957-58; Principal, general practice, Cambridgeshire, 1958-64; Registrar, Crichton Royal, Dumfries, 1965-67; Psychiatrist, Hillcrest Hospital, Adelaide, 1967-68; Senior Registrar, Gartnavel Royal Hospital, Glasgow, 1968-70. Recreations: farming; golf; walking. Address: (h.) Bridge of Frew, Kippen, Stirlingshire FK8 3JA; T.-Kippen 678.

Chick, Jonathan Dale, MA (Cantab), MB, ChB, MPhil, FRCPE, FRCPsych. Consultant Psychiatrist, Royal Edinburgh Hospital, since 1979; part-time Senior Lecturer, Edinburgh University, since 1979; b. 23.4.45, Wallasey; m., Josephine Anna; 2 s. Educ. Queen Elizabeth Grammar School, Darlington; Corpus Christi College, Cambridge; Edinburgh University. Posts in Edinburgh teaching hospitals, 1971-76; scientific staff, MRC Unit for Epidemiological Studies in Psychiatry, 1976-79. Adviser, WHO; awarded Royal College of Psychiatrists Research Medal and Prize. Publication: Drinking Problems (Co-author), 1984. Recreations: music; literature; visual arts. Address: (h.) 8 Abbotsford Park, Edinburgh; T.-031-447 6027.

Chisholm, Rev. Archibald Freeland, MA. Minister, Braes of Rannoch with Foss and Rannoch, since 1984; b. 27.10.32, Glasgow; m., Margaret Downer Rice; 4 d. Educ. Perth Academy; St. Andrews University; New College, Edinburgh. Minister, Bantu Presbyterian Church of South Africa, Gordon Memorial, Natal, 1958-67; Tutor, Federal Theological Seminary of Southern Africa, 1964-65; Minister: Stamperland Parish Church, Glasgow, 1968-76, St. Andrew's Parish Church, Leven, 1976-84. Address: The Manse, Kinloch Rannoch, Pitlochry, PH16 5QA; T.-08822 381.

Chisholm, Duncan Douglas, MB, ChB, MRCPsych, DPM, DPsychother. Consultant Child and Adolescent Psychiatrist, Department of Child and Family Psychiatry, Royal Aberdeen Children's Hospital, since 1975; Clinical Senior Lecturer, Department of Mental Health, Aberdeen University, since 1975; b. 8.10.41, Grantown-on-Spey; m., Rosemary Galloway Doyle; 2 d. Educ. Grantown Grammar School; Aberdeen University. Pre-registration House Officer, Aberdeen, 1965-66; post-registration Senior House Officer/Registrar, Royal Cornhill Hospital and Ross Clinic, Aberdeen, 1966-70; Senior Registrar in Child and Adolescent Psychiatry, 1970-75 (including one-year sabbatical, Clarke Institute of Psychiatry, Toronto, 1973-74). Vice-President, Grampian Family Conciliation Service; Chairman, Association for Family Therapy, Grampian Branch. Recreations: reading; chess; crosswords; literature, history and culture of Scotland and Scottish Highlands; bowls. Address: (h.) Figurettes, 51 Fountainhall Road, Aberdeen, AB2 4EU; T.-0224 640074.

Chisholm, Duncan Fraser, JP. Managing Director, Duncan Chisholm & Sons Ltd., Inverness, since 1979; Member, Inverness District Council, since 1984; Vice-Chairman, Inverness, Loch Ness and Nairn Tourist Board, since 1988; Member, Board of Governors, Eden Court Theatre, Inverness, 1984-88; President, Clan Chisholm Society, 1978-89; b. 14.4.41, Inverness; m., Mary Rebecca MacRae; 1 s.; 1 d. Educ. Inverness High School. Council Member, Inverness, Loch Ness and Nairn Tourist Board, since 1979; President, Inverness and Highland Chamber of Commerce, 1983-84 (Vice-President, 1982-83); Elder, Church of Scotland; Past President, Inverness Wine Appreciation Society; Assistant Area Scout Commissioner, 1975-78. Recreations: swimming;

badminton. Address: (b.) 47-53 Castle Street, Inverness; T.-0463 234599.

Chisholm, Duncan John, FRICS. Regional Assessor, Fife Regional Council, since 1990; Electoral Registration Officer, Fife Regional Council, since 1990; Community Charges Registration Officer, Fife Regional Council, since 1990; b. 22.1.53, Musselburgh; m., Ann Thomson; 1 s.; 1 d. Educ. Trinity Academy, Edinburgh. Apprentice Surveyor, Midlothian County Assessor, 1970-74; Valuer, Midlothian County Assessor, 1974-75; Valuer, Senior Valuer, Divisional Assessor, Lothian Regional Assessor, 1975-89. Recreations: golf; music; eating; real ale. Address (b.) Fife House (03), North Street, Glenrothes, Fife; T.-Glenrothes 757371.

Chisholm, Professor Geoffrey Duncan, ChM, FRCS, FRCSEdin, FRCPEdin, HonFRACS, FRCPS Glas, Hon. FCS (SA). Professor of Surgery, Edinburgh University, since 1977; Director, Nuffield Transplant Unit, Edinburgh, since 1977; Honorary Senior Lecturer, Institute of Urology, London University, since 1972; b. 30.9.31, Hawera, New Zealand; m., Angela Jane; 2 s. Educ. Malvern College; St. Andrews University. Research Fellow, John Hopkins Hospital, Baltimore, 1961-62; Consultant Urological Surgeon, Hammersmith Hospital, London, 1967-77; Honorary Senior Lecturer, Royal Postgraduate Medical School, 1967-77. Chairman, British Prostate Group, 1975-80; Vice President, British Association of Surgical Oncologists, 1980-81; President, British Association of Urological Surgeons, 1985-87; Chairman, European Society of Urological Oncology and Endocrinology, 1985-86; Council Member, Royal College of Surgeons of Edinburgh, since 1984; President, Royal College of Surgeons of Edinburgh, 1988-91; Managing Editor, Urological Research, 1977-81; Editor, British Journal of Urology, since 1977; Chairman, Conference of Medical Royal Colleges and Faculties (Scotland), 1989-91; Chairman, Joint Committee on Higher Surgical Training, since 1991; Chairman, Edinburgh Postgraduate Medical Board, since 1991. Publications: Scientific Foundation of Urology (Joint Editor); Clinical Practice in Urology (Series Editor). Recreations: gardening; wine tasting; squash racquets. Address: (h.) 8 Ettrick Road, Edinburgh, EH10 5BJ; T.-031-229 7173.

Chisholm, Malcolm. MP (Labour), Edinburgh Leith, since 1992.

Chiswick, Derek, MB, ChB, MPhil, FRCPsych. Honorary Senior Lecturer in Forensic Psychiatry, Edinburgh University; Consultant Forensic Psychiatrist, Lothian Health Board; b. 7.1.45, Hampton, Middlesex; m., Ann Williams; 3 d. Educ. Preston Manor County School, Wembley; Liverpool University. Parole Board for Scotland: Member, 1983-88, Vice-Chairman, 1984-88; Chairman, Working Group on Suicide Precautions, Glenochil Young Offenders' Institution and Detention Centre, 1984-85. Recreation: relaxing with family. Address: (h.) 6 St. Catherine's Place, Edinburgh, EH9 1NU; T.-031-667 2444.

Christian, Professor Reginald Frank, MA (Hons) (Oxon). Professor of Russian and Head of Department, St. Andrews University, since 1966; b. 9.8.24, Liverpool; m., Rosalind Iris Napier; 1 s.; 1 d. Educ. Liverpool Institute High School; Queen's College, Oxford. RAF, 1943-46 (aircrew), flying on 231 Sqdn. and 6 Atlantic Ferry Unit (Pilot Officer, 1944); Foreign Office (British Embassy, Moscow), 1949-50; Lecturer and Head of Russian Department, Liverpool University, 1950-55; Senior Lecturer, then Professor of Russian and Head of Department, Birmingham University, 1955-66; Visiting Professor: McGill University, Montreal, 1961-62, Institute of Foreign Languages, Moscow, 1964-65; Dean, Faculty of Arts, St. Andrews University, 1975-78; Member, University Court, 1971-73, 1981-85. President,

British Universities Association of Slavists, 1967-70; Member, International Committee of Slavists, 1970-75; Honorary Vice-President, Association of Teachers of Russian; Member, UGC Arts Sub-Committee on Russian Studies. Publications: Russian Syntax (with F.M. Borras), 1959 and 1971; Korolenko's Siberia, 1954; Tolstoy's War and Peace: A Study, 1962; Russian Prose Composition (with F.M. Borras), 1964 and 1974; Tolstoy: A Critical Introduction, 1969; Tolstoy's Letters, edited, translated and annotated, 1978; Tolstoy's Diaries, edited, translated and annotated, 1985. Recreations: violin; fell-walking; Russian philately; formerly association football. Address: (h.) 20 Shoregate, Crail, Fife; T.-0333 50101.

Christie, Alexander Duncan, PhD, BSc, CEng, MIEE, AFRAeS. Head, Department of Diagnostic Ultrasound, Ninewells Medical School, Dundee, since 1971; b. 14.6.30, Detroit; m., Beatrice R. Phemister; 2 d. Educ. Robert Gordon's College, Aberdeen; Aberdeen University. Pilot, RAF, 1953-63; Lecturer, Bristol College of Technology, 1963-67; Lecturer, Aberdeen University, 1967-70; Principal Physicist, Tayside Health Board, and Honorary Senior Lecturer, Dundee University, from 1971; Professor, WHO Collaborating Centre, University of Zagreb, 1986; Visiting Professor, University of Hong Kong, 1988-89. Publication: Ultrasound and Infertility, 1981. Address: (b.) Department of Obstetrics and Gynaecology, Dundee University, Dundee; T.-0382 60111.

Christie, Andrew John McPhedran, BAcc, CA, ATII. Partner, Arthur Andersen (Chartered Accountants), since 1983; b. 17.7.50, Glasgow; m., Barbara Isabel Tait; 2 s. Educ. Hillhead High School, Glasgow; Glasgow University. Joined Arthur Andersen, 1971; appointed Honorary Professor, Heriot-Watt University, 1990. Convener, Taxation Committee, ICAS. Recreations: golf; skiing. Address: (b.) 18 Charlotte Square, Edinburgh, EH2 4DF; T.-031-225 4554.

Christie, Campbell. General Secretary, Scottish Trades Union Congress, since 1986; b. 23.8.37, Carsluith, Kirkcudbrightshire; m., Elizabeth Brown Cameron; 2 s. Educ. Albert Senior Secondary School, Glasgow; Woolwich Polytechnic, London. Civil Servant, Department of Health and Social Security, 1954-72; National Officer, then Deputy General Secretary, Society of Civil and Public Servants, 1972-86. Member, EEC Economic and Social Committee; Member, Scottish Economic Council; Director, Wildcat Theatre Company, Scottish National Orchestra, Theatre Royal Opera Company. Address: (h.) 31 Dumyat Drive, Falkirk; T.-0324 24555; (b.) 16 Woodlands Terrace, Glasgow, G5; T.-041-332 4946.

Christie, Rev. James, SJ, MA, MSc, CQSW, MInstGA. Director, The Garnethill Centre, Glasgow, since 1980; b. 3.7.40, Bellshill, Lanarkshire. Educ. Our Lady's High School, Motherwell; St. Aloysius College, Glasgow; Campion Hall, Oxford; Columbia University; Southampton University; London School of Economics. Ordained Priest, Society of Jesus, 1970; parish work and training in Paris, 1970-71; on staff of Fons Vitae Institute, Johannesburg, 1971-72; School Counsellor, Wimbledon College, 1973-75; Depute Director, The Dympna Centre, London, 1977-80. Recreation: hill-walking. Address: 56 Hill Street, Glasgow, G3 6RE; T.-041-332 3039.

Christie, John Belford Wilson, CBE, BA (Cantab), LLB, HonLLD (Dundee, 1977). Advocate; b. 4.5.14, Allanton, Lanarkshire; m., Christine Isobel Syme Arnott; 4 d. Educ. Merchiston Castle School; Cambridge University; Edinburgh University. Admitted to Faculty of Advocates, 1939; on active service, RNVR, 1939-46; Sheriff-Substitute, Western Division, Dumfries and Galloway, 1948-55; Sheriff of Tayside, Central and Fife, at Dundee, 1955-83. Member,

Parole Board for Scotland, 1967-73; Member: Queen's College Council, St. Andrews University, 1960-67, University Court, Dundee University, 1967-75; Honorary Lecturer, Department of Private Law, Dundee University; Knight of the Holy Sepulchre of Jerusalem, 1988. Recreation: golf. Address: (h.) Annsmuir Farm, Ladybank, Fife; T.-0337 30480.

Christie, Robert Alexander, LLB. Chief Executive and Director of Administration, Berwickshire District Council, since 1977; b. 24.1.45, Preston. Educ. Balshaw's Grammar School, Leyland, Lancashire; St. Andrews University. Dumfries County Council: Principal Legal Assistant, 1969-71, Depute County Clerk, 1971-73; Depute County Clerk, Argyll County Council, 1973-75; Depute Director of Administration, Argyll and Bute District Council, 1975-76; Chief Executive, Lochaber District Council, 1976-77. Recreations: cooking; reading; listening to music. Address: (b.) District Council Offices, 8 Newtown Street, Duns, Berwickshire, TD11 3DT; T.-0361 82600.

Christie, Robert Johnstone Stevenson, BSc (Hons). Scottish Secretary, Professional Association of Teachers, since 1989; b. 7.8.46, Edinburgh; m., Anne Elisabeth Fraser Macleod; 3 d. Educ. Grangemouth High School; Paisley College of Technology; Jordanhill College of Education; Glasgow University. Chemist, British Petroleum Chemicals Ltd., 1964-68; Principal Teacher of Physics, Tain Royal Academy, 1976-88. Recreations: family; music; history; sailing; Rotary. Address: (b.) 22 Rutland Street, Edinburgh, EH1 2AN; T.-031-228 4231.

Christie, Terry, BSc (Hons). Head Teacher, Musselburgh Grammar School, since 1987; b. 16.12.42, Edinburgh; 2 s.; 1 d. Educ. Holy Cross Academy, Edinburgh; Edinburgh University. Depute Rector, Trinity Academy, 1978-82; Head Teacher, Ainslie Park High School, 1982-87. Played football for Dundee, Raith Rovers and Stirling Albion, 1960-74; former Manager, Meadowbank Thistle FC. Recreations: golf; bridge; snooker; reading. Address: (h.) 76 Meadowfield Terrace, Edinburgh, EH8 7NU; T.-031-661 1486.

Christie, Sheriff William James, LLB. Sheriff of Tayside, Central and Fife, at Kirkcaldy, since 1979; b. 1.11.32.

Clapham, David Charles, LLB, SSC. Solicitor (Principal, private practice, since 1984); Vice President, Glasgow Bar Association, since 1991; Secretary, Strathclyde Region Local Valuation Panel, since 1988; b. 16.10.58, Giffnock; m., Debra Harriet Samuels. Educ. Hutchesons' Boys' Grammar School, Glasgow; Strathclyde University. Legal apprenticeship, 1979-81; admitted Solicitor, 1981; admitted Notary Public, 1982; founded own legal practice, 1984; Tutor, Strathclyde University, since 1984; part-time Lecturer, Glasgow University, since 1991. Secretary, Glasgow Bar Association, 1987-91; Director, Legal Defence Union. Recreations: reading and collecting books; research into war crimes trials. Address: (b.) 79 West Regent Street, Glasgow, G2 2AW; T.-041-332 5537.

Clark, Alastair Trevor, CBE (1976), LVO (1974), MA (Oxon), FSA Scot. Barrister; Member, Scottish Museums Council, 1980-90 (Chairman, 1981-84 and 1987-90); Member, Lothian Health Board, 1981-89; Member, City of Edinburgh District Council, 1980-88; Member, Race Relations Assessors Panel, Scottish Sheriff Courts, since 1983; Member, Edinburgh Academical Club Council, 1978-84 and 1986-90; a Governor, Edinburgh Filmhouse, 1980-84 and since 1987; Member, National Museums of Scotland Charitable Trust, since 1987; b. 10.6.23, Glasgow; m., Hilary Agnes Mackenzie Anderson. Educ. Giffnock Academy; Glasgow Academy; Edinburgh Academy; Magdalen College, Oxford; Inns of Court (Middle Temple); Ashridge

Management College. War service, Queen's Own Cameron Highlanders and Royal West African Frontier Force, Nigeria, India and Burma, 1942-46; Administrative Branch, HM Colonial Service (later HMOCS): Nigeria, 1949-59 (Secretary to Cabinet, Northern Region; Senior District Officer), Hong Kong, 1960-72 (Director of Social Welfare; Deputy and Acting Director of Urban Services; Acting Chairman Urban Council; Clerk of Councils; Principal Assistant Colonial Secretary, etc.), Western Pacific, 1972-77 (Chief Secretary Western Pacific High Commission; Deputy and Acting Governor, Solomon Islands); retired, 1977; Vice-President, Hong Kong Scout Association, 1965-72; Joint Founder, HK Outward Bound School; Honorary Secretary, St. John's Cathedral Council, 1963-72; Country Leader Fellowship to USA, 1972; Selector, Voluntary Service Overseas, 1978-80; Leverhulme Trust Grant, 1979-81; Vice-Chairman, Committee of Area Museum Councils, 1983-84; Member: Secretary of State's Museums Advisory Board, 1983-85, Museums Association Council, 1983-86 and since 1990; Trustee, National Museums of Scotland, 1985-87; Member, Edinburgh International Festival Council, 1980-86 and since 1990; a Director, Royal Lyceum Theatre Company, 1982-84; Member, Court of Directors, Edinburgh Academy, 1979-84. Publication: A Right Honourable Gentleman – Abubakar from the Black Rock, 1991. Recreations: music; books; theatre; netsuke; cartophily. Address: (h.) 11 Ramsay Garden, Edinburgh, EH1 2NA; T.-031-225 8070.

Clark, Alex. Member, Board of Directors: Mayfest (Founder and Hon. President), Scottish Opera, Scottish Ballet, Glasgow Jazz Festival, Glasgow Film Theatre; Trustee, James Milne Memorial Trust; Trustee, Hugh MacDiarmid Memorial Trust; b. 2.1.22, Larkhall; m., Jessie Beveridge McCulloch; 1 s.; 1 d. Educ. Larkhall Academy. Grain miller, 1936-39; coal miner, 1939-53; political organiser, 1953-69; Scottish and Northern Ireland Secretary, British Actors Equity Association, 1969-84; created the post of STUC Arts Officer, 1985-87; founder Member, Boards, Scottish Youth Theatre, Scottish Theatre Company, Royal Lyceum Theatre Company; also served on Boards of Pitlochry Festival Theatre and Cumbernauld Theatre Company; Member, Scottish Arts Council's Review Committee on Scottish Theatre Company, 1987; Member, Working Party on a National Theatre for Scotland, 1987; Lord Provost's Award for services to the city of Glasgow, 1987; Member, STUC Entertainment and Arts Committee, since foundation. Recreations: reading; music; theatre; walking; gardening. Address: (h.) Ponfeigh, 8 Strathwhillan, Brodick, Isle of Arran.

Clark, Alistair Campbell, MA, LLB, WS. Partner, Blackadder, Reid, Johnston (formerly Reid, Johnston, Bell & Henderson), Solicitors, Dundee, since 1961; President, Law Society of Scotland, 1989-90 (Council Member, since 1982); Honorary Sheriff, Tayside Central & Fife, since 1986; b. 4.3.33, Dundee; m., Evelyn M. Clark; 3 s. Educ. Grove Academy, Broughty Ferry; St. Andrews University. Dean, Faculty of Procurators and Solicitors in Dundee, 1979-81; Secretary, Royal Dundee Blind Craft Products; Founder Chairman, Broughty Ferry Round Table; Founder President, Claverhouse Rotary Club, Dundee. Recreations: family; travel; erratic golf. Address: (b.) 34 Reform Street, Dundee; T.-0382 29222.

Clark, David Findlay, OBE, MA, PhD, CPsychol, FBPsS, ARPS. Consulting Clinical Psychologist; former Director, Area Clinical Psychology Services, Grampian Health Board and Clinical Senior Lecturer, Department of Mental Health, Aberdeen University; b. 30.5.30, Aberdeen; m., Janet Ann Stephen; 2 d. Educ. Banff Academy; Aberdeen University. Flying Officer, RAF, 1951-53; Psychologist, Leicester Industrial Rehabilitation Unit, 1953-56; Senior, then Principal Clinical Psychologist, Leicester Area Clinical Psychology Service, and part-time Lecturer, Leicester University and

Technical College, 1956-66; WHO short-term Consultant, Sri Lanka, 1977; various lecturing commitments in Canada and USA, since 1968. Honorary Sheriff, Grampian and Highlands; former Governor, Aberdeen College of Education; Member, Grampian Children's Panel, 1970-85; Safeguarder (in terms of Social Work Scotland Act), since 1985; Past Chairman, Clinical Division, British Psychological Society. Publication: Help, Hospitals and the Handicapped, 1984. Recreations: photography; squash; sailing; chess; guitar playing; painting and drawing. Address: (h.) Glendeveron, 8 Deveron Terrace, Banff, AB45 1BB; T.-0261 812624.

Clark, Frank, CBE, MHSM, DipHSM. General Manager, Lanarkshire Health Board, since 1985; Vice Chairman of Governors, Queen's College, Glasgow, since 1990; b. 17.10.46, Aberdeen; m., Linda Margaret; 2 d. Educ. Aberdeen Academy. Greater Glasgow Health Board: Assistant District Administrator, 1977-81, District General Administrator, 1981-83; Lanarkshire Health Board: Director of Administrative Services, 1983-84, Secretary, 1984-85. Member: Scottish Health Services Advisory Council, since 1990, Advisory Group on Acute Services, since 1990, Chief Scientists Health Service Research Committee, since 1989, National Nursing Strategy Group, since 1990, Scottish Overseas Health Support Policy Board, since 1990; West of Scotland Dental Education Trust Distance Learning Unit Appeal Committee, since 1992; Chairman: Joint Management Executive/General Managers Manpower Group, since 1990, West of Scotland Health Service Research Network, since 1990; Vice Chairman, Scottish Health Board General Managers' Group, since 1990. Recreations: reading; music; gardening; driving; swimming; DIY; poetry. Address: (b.) Lanarkshire Health Board, 14 Beckford Street, Hamilton, ML3 0TA; T.-0698 281313.

Clark, Graham M. BSc, PhD, CChem, FRSC, MBIM. Principal, Angus College of Further Education, since 1990; b. 2.8.41, Dumfries; m., Linda A.; 3 d. Educ. George Watson's College, Edinburgh; Edinburgh University. Research Fellow, Hull University, 1966-67; Lecturer, Huddersfield Polytechnic, 1967-79; Head of Applied Science, North East Surrey College of Technology, 1980-85; Deputy Director, Nene College, Northampton, 1986-89. Editor, Thermal Analysis Reviews and Abstracts, 1986-92. Recreations: golf; hill walking; UK philately. Address: (b.) Angus College of Further Education, Arbroath, DD11 3EA; T.-0241 72056.

Clark, Guy Wyndham Nial Hamilton, JP, DL. Deputy Lieutenant, Renfrewshire, since 1987; Director, Greig, Middleton & Co. Ltd., since 1986; b. 28.3.44; m., Brighid Lovell; 2 s.; 1 d. Educ. Eton. Commd. Coldstream Guards, 1962-67; Investment Manager, Murray Johnstone Ltd., Glasgow, 1973-77; Partner, R.C. Greig & Co. (Stockbrokers), Glasgow, 1977-86; Member, Executive Committee, Erskine Hospital; Chairman, JP Advisory Committee, since 1991. Recreations: hunting; shooting; fishing; racing. Addrss: (h.) Braeton, Inverkip, PA16 0DU; T.-0475 520 619.

Clark, Hector Goodfellow, QPM. Deputy Chief Constable, Lothian and Borders Police, since 1984; b. 4.4.34, Felton; m., Anne; 1 s. Educ. Skerry's College, Newcastle upon Tyne. Joined Northumberland Constabulary (later Northumbria police), 1955: Head of CID, 1976-81, Assistant Chief Constable (Operations) and (Crime), 1981-84. Recreations: travel; walking; golf. Address: (b.) Police Headquarters, Fettes Avenue, Edinburgh, EH4 1RB; T.-031-311 3131.

Clark, Rev. John, FPhS. Minister, St. Blane's, Dunblane, 1980-88; b. 28.6.23, Kilmarnock; m., Mary Cameron Graham; 2 d. Educ. Kilmarnock Academy; Glasgow University; Trinity College, Glasgow. RAC, 1942-46; Assistant Minister, Riccarton Parish Church, Kilmarnock,

1948-49; Minister, St. Serf's Church, Dysart, 1949-55; first Minister, Drumry: St. Mary's Parish Church, Drumchapel, Glasgow, 1955-60; Minister, Kennoway Parish Church, 1960-80; Moderator, Kirkcaldy Presbytery, 1966-67; Moderator, Stirling Presbytery, 1984-85. Publication: New Ways to Worship (Contributor), 1980. Recreations: driving; swimming; painting; crosswords; listening to music. Address: (h.) 25 Buchan Drive, Dunblane, FK15 9HW.

Clark, John Kenneth, BA (Hons), MA. Glasspainter; b. 1.12.57, Dumbarton. Educ. Dumbarton Academy; Glasgow School of Art. Commissions include: Cafe Gandolfi, Glasgow (Saltire Award); Paisley Abbey (Saltire Award); Heaton Memorial Window, Ledbury; Lockerbie Memorial Window; Queens Park Synagogue, Glasgow. Address: (h.) 11A Maxwell Drive, Glasgow, G41 5DR.

Clark, Kenneth James, CBE, MA, LLB, JP. Chief Executive, Borders Regional Council, since 1974; b. 30.4.33, Perth; m., Marion; 3 s. Educ. Dundee High School; St. Andrews University. National Service, Queen's Own Cameron Highlanders, 1955-57; Legal and Administrative Assistant, Roxburgh County Council, 1962 63; Banff County Council: Legal and Administrative Assistant, 1963-64, Assistant County Clerk, 1964-65, Depute County Clerk, 1965-66; Depute County Clerk, Berwick County Council, 1966-71; County Clerk, Ross and Cromarty County Council, 1971-74. Member, Working Group for Scotland on Handling of Complaints against the Police, 1974; Member, Committee of Inquiry into Local Government in Scotland (The Stodart Committee), 1981. Address: (b.) Regional Headquarters, Newtown St. Boswells, Melrose, TD6 OSA; T.-0835 23301.

Clark, Robert Andrew, BA, AMA. Depute Director, Scottish Museums Council, since 1989; b. 3.7.55, London; m., Pamela Ruth Diamond. Educ. Highgate School, London; Magdalen College, Oxford; Leicester University. Junior Curator, Beamish Musuem, Co. Durham, 1979-84; Museum Director, Chatterley Whitfield Mining Museum, Stoke on Trent, 1984-86; organised museum services for small local authorities and trusts, Northamptonshire, 1986-89. Scottish representative, Vintage Motor Cycle Club Management Comittee; Museum Professional Advisor, National Association of Mining History Organisations. Recreations: vintage motor cycling; gardening. Address: (h.) 10 Miller Place, Airth, FK2 8JY; T.-Airth 846.

Clark, Robert John Whitten. Head, Fisheries Regimes Fishstock Management, Marketing and Trade Division, Department of Agriculture and Fisheries for Scotland, 1985-87; b. 29.9.32, Edinburgh; m., Christine Margaret Reid; 1 s.; 1 d. Educ. George Heriot's School, Edinburgh. Scottish Education Department: various appointments, 1949-69, including Private Secretary to Secretary of Department, 1960-61, Head, Teacher Training Branch, 1967-69, Head, Schools Branch, 1969-73, Head, Children's Hearings Branch, Social Work Services Group, 1973-75, Head, Children's Division, Social Work Services Group, 1975-76, Head, List D (Approved) Schools Division, Social Work Services Group, 1976-79; Head, Home Defence and Emergency Services Co-ordination Division, Scottish Home and Health Department, 1979-85. Former Captain and Past President, Edinburgh and District Civil Service Golfing Society; Captain, Scottish Education Department Golf Club, 1984-85; former Vice-Captain, Scottish Civil Service Golfing Society. Recreations: travel; golf; reading; gardening. Address: (h.) 39 Gordon Road, Edinburgh, EH12 6LZ; T.-031-334 4312.

Clark, Robert Phillip, SSC, NP. Solicitor (retired); b. 20.4.20, Dundee; m., Helen Joan Forman; 3 s. Educ. Logie Secondary School, Dundee; University College, Dundee. Commenced legal training, 1937; War service, 1940-45: Royal Armoured Corps; Royal Military College, Sandhurst;

commissioned 2nd Fife & Forfar Yeomanry; Regimental Signals Officer; wounded 1944; resumed legal training, 1947-50; qualified Solicitor, 1950; Court procurator, 1952-56; Honorary Sheriff of Tayside Central and Fife at Dundee, since 1977; former Dean, Faculty of Procurators and Solicitors in Dundee; former Vice-President, Scottish Law Agents Society; Clerk, Hammerman Incorporation of Dundee. Recreations: tennis and golf; hill-walking; photography. Address: (h.) Kilry Lodge, Alyth, Perthshire.

Clark, Robert William, MA (Cantab). Chairman, Nobel's Explosives Co. Ltd., since 1989; Chief Executive Officer, ICI International Explosives, since 1991 (Principal Executive Officer, 1989-91); b. 27.6.37, Middlesbrough; m., Moira Elizabeth; 1 s.; 1 d. Educ. Acklam Hall Secondary Grammar School, Middlesbrough; Trinity College, Cambridge University. Heavy Organic Chemicals Division (engineering and production management), ICI Ltd., 1960-71; London Business School, 1971-72; ICI Ltd.: senior management positions, Petrochemicals Division, 1972-78, appointed Director, Petrochemicals Division, 1978, Director, Petrochemicals and Plastics Division, 1981, Director, Nobel's Explosives Company Ltd., 1984. Board Member, Tees and Hartlepool Port Authority, 1981-84; Member, Advisory Committee on Major Hazards, 1981-84; Sloan Fellow, London Business School. Recreations: gardening; walking; travel. Address: (b.) Nobel House, Stevenston, KA20 3LN; T.-0294 87600.

Clark, Roland Arthur, MB, ChB, BSc (Hons), MRCP(UK), FRCP. Consultant Physician, Kings Cross/Ninewells Hospitals, Dundee, since 1977; Honorary Senior Lecturer in Medicine, Dundee University, since 1977 (Head, Department of Respiratory Diseases, since 1985); b. 8.9.40, Bexleyheath; m., Ann Havard; 2 s.; 4 d. Educ. Dartford Grammar School; Edinburgh University; Zagreb University; Ibadan University. House Officer, Senior House Officer, Research Fellow and Registrar, Departments of Respiratory Diseases, Cardiology, Neurology, Gastroenterology and General Medicine, Edinburgh University; Senior Registrar, Departments of Medicine/Respiratory Diseases, Sheffield University; Consultant Physician and Honorary Lecturer, Lodge Moor/Northern General Hospitals, Sheffield, and Department of Medicine, Sheffield University. Recreations: golf; fishing; gardening; photography; archaeology. Address: (h.) 4 Lawhead Road East, St. Andrews, Fife; T.-0334 77025.

Clark, Terence Gilbert, CEng, MIEE, MMS, MHSM. Chief Administrator and Secretary, Tayside Health Board, since 1986; b. 19.3.39, Bristol; m., Jennifer Mary; 1 s.; 1 d. Educ. Katharine Lady Berkeley's Grammar School; Bristol College of Science and Technology. Design engineer, 1955-64; work study officer, East Anglian Regional Health Board, 1964-70; Chief Work Study Officer, then General Administrator, Tayside Health Board, 1970-86. Recreations: squash; vintage cars and motorcycles. Address: (b.) Vernonholme, Riverside Drive, Dundee; T.-Dundee 645151.

Clark, William. Scottish Political Correspondent, Glasgow Herald, since 1981; b. 18.8.39, Motherwell; m., Anne F. Henry, AIMLT; 1 s.; 2 d. Educ. Dalziel High School. Indentured Motherwell Times, 1956-61; Deputy Night News Editor, Scottish Daily Mail, Glasgow, 1961-68; Scottish Industrial Correspondent, Glasgow Herald, 1976-81. Address: (b.) 195 Albion Street, Glasgow.

Clarke, Eric Lionel. MP (Labour), Midlothian, since 1992; b. 9.4.33, Edinburgh; m., June; 2 s.; 1 d. Educ. Holy Cross Academy; W.M. Ramsey Technical College; Esk Valley Technical College. Coal miner, 1949-77; General Secretary, NUM Scottish Area, 1977-89; County Councillor, Midlothian, 1962-74; Regional Councillor, Lothian, 1974-78. Recreations: fly fishing; gardening; carpentry. Address:

(h.) 32 Mortonhall Park Crescent, Edinburgh; T.-031-664 8214.

Clarke, Professor Joseph Andrew, BSc, PhD. Director, Energy Simulation Research Unit, Strathclyde University, since 1987; Director, Engineering Faculty MSc in Energy Systems, since 1990; Director, International Building Performance Simulation Association, since 1990; b. 6.3.52, Glasgow; m., Kathryn Ann; 1 s.; 2 d. Educ. Whitehill Senior Secondary School; Strathclyde University. SERC Research Fellow, 1977-79; SERC Senior Research Fellow, 1979-83; SERC Advanced Research Fellow, 1983-87. Recipient, Royal Society Esso Energy Award, 1989. Publication: Energy Simulation in Building Design, 1985. Recreations: running; family activities. Address: (b.) ESRU, Department of Architecture, Strathclyde University, Glasgow, G1 1XQ; T.-041-552 4400, Ext. 3986.

Clarke, Owen James. Controller, Inland Revenue, Scotland, since 1990; b. 15.3.37, Edinburgh; m., Betty; 2 s.; 1 d. Educ. Portobello High. Entered Civil Service, 1955; served in London, Merseyside, North of England; in Scotland: Greenock, Falkirk, Wick, Edinburgh; three years in Revenue fraud squad; six years, special anti-avoidance office. Secretary, Scottish Judo Federation; Secretary, Commonwealth Judo Federation. Recreations: jogging; squash; golf. Address: (b.) 80 Lauriston Place, Edinburgh, EH3 9SL; T.-031-229 9344.

Clarke, Peter, CBE, BSc, PhD, LLD, CChem, FRSC. Chairman, Scottish Vocational Education Council, 1985-91; Chairman, Aberdeen Enterprise Trust, since 1984; Chairman, Council for National Academic Awards Committee for Scotland, 1982-87; Member, Council for Professions Supplementary to Medicine, 1977-85; Chairman, Industrial Training Centre, Aberdeen, since 1989; Director, Creative Capital Nominees Ltd., since 1982; b. 18.3.22, Mansfield; m., Ethel; 2 s. Educ. Queen Elizabeth's Grammar School, Mansfield; University College, Nottingham. Principal, Robert Gordon's Institute of Technology, Aberdeen, 1970-85. President, Association of Principals of Colleges, 1980-81; Member, Science and Engineering Research Council, 1978-82; Trustee, Gordon Cook Foundation, since 1988. Recreations: walking; gardening. Address: (h.) Dunaber, 12 Woodburn Place, Aberdeen, AB1 8JR; T.-0224 311132.

Clarke, Peter James, MA (Cantab). Secretary to the Forestry Commissioners, since 1976; b. 16.1.34, London; m., Roberta Anne Browne; 1 s.; 1 d. Educ. Enfield Grammar School; St. John's College, Cambridge. Executive Officer, War Office, 1952-62; Higher Executive Officer, 1962; Senior Executive Officer, Forestry Commission, 1967; Principal, 1972; Principal, Department of Energy, 1975. Recreations: gardening; hill-walking; sailing. Address: (h.) 5 Murrayfield Gardens, Edinburgh, EH12 6DG; T.-031-337 3145.

Clarke, Professor Roger John, ALCM, BA, BTech, MSc, PhD, CEng, MIEE, MIEEE. NCR Professor of Electronic Engineering, Heriot Watt University, since 1989; b. 1.10.40, Ewell, Surrey; m., Yvonne Clarke; 1 s. Educ. Gravesend Grammar School; Loughborough University. Development Engineer, STC Ltd., Woolwich, 1962-64; Research Associate, then Lecturer in Electrical Engineering, Loughborough University, 1964-86; Reader in Electrical Engineering, Heriot Watt University, 1986-89. Recreations: gardening; playing the cello; Shakespeare. Address: (b.) Department of Electrical and Electronic Engineering, Heriot Watt University, 31-5 Grassmarket, Edinburgh, EH1 2HT; T.-031-225 6465.

Clarke, Thomas, CBE, JP. MP (Labour), Monklands West, since 1983; Shadow Secretary of State for Scotland, since 1992; b. 10.1.41, Coatbridge. Educ. Columba High School,

Coatbridge. Former Assistant Director, Scottish Council for Educational Technology; Provost of Monklands, 1975-82; Past President, Convention of Scottish Local Authorities; MP, Coatbridge and Airdrie, 1982-83; author, Disabled Persons (Services Consultation and Representation) Act, 1986. Recreations: films; walking; reading. Address: (h.) 37 Blairhill Street, Coatbridge, ML5 1PG; T.-0236 22550.

Clayson, Christopher William, CBE (1974), OBE (1966), MB, ChB, DPH, MD, FRCPEdin, FRCPLond, Hon.FACP, Hon.FRACP, Hon.FRCP(Glas), Hon.FRCGP, Hon. FRCP Edin. Physician (retired); b. 11.9.03, Ilford. Educ. George Heriot's School, Edinburgh; Edinburgh University. Assistant Physician: Southfield Sanatorium, Edinburgh, 1931-44, City Hospital, Edinburgh, 1939-44; Lecturer, Edinburgh University, 1939-44; Medical Superintendent, Lochmaben Sanatorium, 1944-48; Consultant Physician, Dumfries and Galloway Hospitals, 1948-68; President, RCPEdin, 1966-70; Chairman, Departmental Committee on Scottish Licensing Law, 1971-73; Chairman, Scottish Council on Postgraduate Medical Education, 1970-74; William Cullen Prizeman, RCPEdin, 1978. Address: (h.) Cockiesknowe, Lochmaben, Lockerbie, DG11 1RL; T.-0387 810231.

Cleall, Charles, MA(Wales), BMus(Lond), ADCM, FRCO(CHM), GTCL, LRAM, HonTSC. Author and Writer; b. 1.6.27, Heston, Middlesex; m., Mary Turner; 2 d. Educ. Hampton School, Middlesex; Trinity College of Music; London University; Jordanhill College of Education, Glasgow; University College of North Wales. Organist and Choirmaster, St. Luke's, Chelsea, 1945-46; Command Music Adviser to Royal Navy, Plymouth Command (Instr. Lieut., RN) 1946-48; Professor of Solo Singing and Voice Production, and of ear-training and of choral repertoire, Trinity College of Music, London, 1949-52; Choral Scholar, Westminster Abbey, 1949-52; Organist and Choirmaster, Wesley's Chapel, City Road, London, 1950-52; Conductor, Morley College Orchestra, 1950-52; Conductor, Glasgow Choral Union, 1952-54; BBC Music Assistant, Midland Region, 1954-55; Music Master, Glyn County School, Ewell, 1955-66; Conductor, Aldeburgh Festival Choir, 1957-60; Organist and Choirmaster, St. Paul's, Portman Square, W1, 1957-61; Organist and Choirmaster, Holy Trinity, Guildford, 1961-65; Lecturer in Music, The Froebel Institute, Roehampton, 1967-68; Adviser in Music, London Borough of Harrow, 1968-72; Northern Divisional music specialist, HM Inspectorate of Schools in Scotland, 1972-87; Editor, Journal, Ernest George White Society, 1983-88; has given many lectures on singing and choir training; has written scores of articles and book reviews. Limpus Fellowship Prizeman, Royal College of Organists; International Composition Prizeman, Cathedral of St. John the Divine, New York. Publications: Voice Production in Choral Technique, 1955-1970; The Selection and Training of Mixed Choirs in Churches, 1960; Sixty Songs from Sankey, 1960; John Merbecke's Music for the Congregation at Holy Communion, 1963; Music and Holiness, 1964; Plainsong for Pleasure, 1969; Authentic Chanting, 1969; A Guide to Vanity Fair, 1982. Recreations: writing; reading; natural history; walking. Address: (h.) 10 Carronhall, Stonehaven, Aberdeen, AB3 2HF.

Cleary, Michael, BA (Hons), AHSM; Secretary and Director of Administration, Greater Glasgow Health Board, since 1987; b. 1.3.43, Swansea; m., Dorothy May; 1 s.; 1 d. Educ. Bishop Gore School, Swansea; King's College, London University. Bristol Royal Infirmary, 1968-70; Bristol Dental Hospital, 1970-71; Gartnavel General Hospital, 1971-74; Glasgow South West District, 1974-81; Glasgow North District, 1981-84; Glasgow Health Board, 1984-87. Recreations: music; choral singing (Member, Glasgow Phoenix Choir); eating; good conversation. Address: (h.) Wellwood Cottage, Cleghorn, Lanark.

Cleland, John, BSc (Hons). Depute Principal, Kilmarnock College, since 1984; b. 3.11.35, Darvel; m., Janet G. Ross; 1 s.; 1 d. Educ. Darvel Junior Secondary School; Kilmarnock Academy; Glasgow University. Assistant Teacher of Mathematics, then Assistant Teacher of Science, Kilmarnock Academy; Assistant Teacher of Chemistry, then Senior Assistant Teacher, then Head of Department, Kilmarnock Technical College; Head, Department of Mathematics and Science, Kilmarnock College. FE Representative, SCEEB Chemistry Syllabus Panel, 1974-77; Joint Setter, SCE "H" Grade Chemistry, 1984; Member, Ayr Friends of the Hospice Committee. Recreations: bridge; golf. Address: (b.) Holehouse Road, Kilmarnock, KA3 7AT; T.-0563 23501.

Clements, Professor John Barklie, BSc, PhD, FRSA, FRSE. Titular Professor in Virology, Glasgow University, since 1987 (Reader, 1984-87); b. 14.3.46, Belfast. Educ. Belfast Royal Academy; Queen's University, Belfast. Research Fellow, California Institute of Technology, 1971-73; joined Institute of Virology, Glasgow University, 1973; Cancer Research Campaign Travelling Fellow, Department of Biochemistry and Molecular Biology, Harvard University, 1983; Council Member, Society for General Microbiology, 1984-88; Member, MRC Physiological Systems and Disorders Board, 1990-94. Recreations: walking; golf; music. Address: (b.) Department of Virology, Institute of Virology, Glasgow University, Glasgow; T.-041-330 4027.

Clemson, Gareth, BMus (Auckland), BMus (Edinburgh). Teacher of violin and viola, since 1975; Composer; b. 1.10.33, Thames, New Zealand; m., Thora Clyne; 2 s.; 1 d. Educ. St. Peter's School, New Zealand; King's College, New Zealand; Auckland University; Edinburgh University. Music teaching, New Zealand, Edinburgh and West Lothian, 1960-65; String Teacher, West Lothian, 1975-85, Fife Region, since 1985; lessons in composition from Thomas Wilson, 1963-65; chamber works including Nexus I and II, Waters of Separation, The Singing Cat, Invocation; broadcasts, New Zealand and Scotland; recent compositions, Imago for violin and viola, Cronos for strings, Stray Birds for voice and ensemble, Shrew in the Kitchen for piano trio, Anything You Can Do for trumpet and cello, Overtones for school orchestra. Recreations: drawing and painting; photography; philately; cats. Address: (h.) Tillywhally Cottage, Milnathort, Kinross-shire, KY13 7RN; T.-Kinross 64297.

Clerk of Penicuik, Sir John Dutton, 10th Bt, CBE (1966), VRD, FRSE, JP. Lord Lieutenant of Midlothian, 1972-92; b. 30.1.17; m.; 2 s.; 2 d. Educ. Stowe. Ensign,, Queen's Bodyguard for Scotland (Royal Company of Archers). Address: (h.) Penicuik House, Penicuik, Midlothian, EH26 9LA.

Clifford, Timothy Peter Plint, BA, AMA. Director, National Galleries of Scotland, since 1984; b. 26.1.46; m., Jane Olivia Paterson; 1 d. Educ. Sherborne; Perugia University; Courtauld Institute, London University. Manchester City Art Galleries: Assistant Keeper, Department of Paintings, 1968-72, Acting Keeper, 1972; Assistant Keeper: Department of Ceramics, Victoria and Albert Museum, London, 1972-76, Department of Prints and Drawings, British Museum, London, 1976-78; Director, Manchester City Art Galleries, 1978-84. Chairman, International Committee for Museums of Fine Art, 1980-83; Member, Museums and Galleries Commission, 1983-88; Member, Executive Committee, Scottish Museums Council; Vice President, Turner Society, 1984; Hon. Vice-President, Frigate Unicorn Preservation Society, since 1987; Member, Academic Committee, Accademia Italiana, since 1987; Cavaliere all'Ordine del Merito della Repubblica Italiana, 1988; Member, Advisory Council, Friends of Courtauld Institute, since 1990; Vice-President, NADFAS, since 1990. FRSA; FSA (Scot). Recreations: shooting; bird-watching;

collecting butterflies and moths. Address: (b.) National Galleries of Scotland, The Mound, Edinburgh, EH2 2EL.

Clinkenbeard, Rev. William Ward, BSc, BD, STM. Minister, Carrick Knowe Parish Church, since 1971; Moderator, Edinburgh Presbytery, since 1992; b. 25.8.37, Lincoln, Nebraska; m., Dr. Janette McKay Hunter; 2 s.; 1 d. Educ. Lincoln High School; University of Nebraska; McCormick Theological Seminary; Glasgow University; Yale. Minister, Wood River Presbyterian Church, Nebraska. Publication: The Contemporary Lesson. Recreations: golf; walking; photography. Address: (h.) 40A Harlaw Road, Balerno, Edinburgh, EH14 7AX; T.-031-449 6984.

Clive, Eric McCredie, MA, LLB, LLM, SJD. Full-time Member, Scottish Law Commission, since 1981; b. 24.7.38, Stranraer; m., Kay McLeman; 1 s.; 3 d. Educ. Stranraer Academy; Stranraer High School; Edinburgh University; University of Michigan; University of Virginia. Department of Scots Law, Edinburgh University: Lecturer, 1962-69, Senior Lecturer, 1969-75, Reader, 1975-77, Professor, 1977-81. Publications: The Law of Husband and Wife in Scotland, 2nd edition, 1982; Scots Law for Journalists (Co-author), 5th edition, 1988. Recreations: hill-walking; chess. Address: (h.) 14 York Road, Edinburgh, EH5 3EH; T.-031-552 2875.

Clouting, David Wallis, BDS, MSc, LDSRCS (Eng), DDPH. Chief Administrative Dental Officer, Borders Health Board, since 1990; b. 29.3.53, London; m., Dr. Margaret M.C. Bacon; 3 s.; 1 d. Educ. Leyton County High School for Boys; University College Hospital Dental School, London; Institute of Dental Surgery, London; Joint Department of Dental Public Health, London Hospital Medical College and University College, London. Senior Dental Officer for Special Needs, East and North Hertfordshire Health Authorities, 1983-90. Representative, Scottish Chief Administrative Dental Officers Group, Health Education Authority District Dental Officers Liaison Group. Recreations: amateur radio; DIY; swimming; hill walking; sailing. Address: (b.) Borders Health Board Headquarters, Huntlyburn, Melrose, TD6 9BP; T.-089682 2662.

Clow, Robert George Menzies. Chairman (since 1979) and Managing Director (since 1969), John Smith & Son (Glasgow) Ltd.; b. 27.1.34, Sian, Shensi, North China; m., Katrina M. Watson. Educ. Eltham College, London. Interned by Japanese as a child; National Service, RAF; trained as a bookseller, Bumpus London; worked in Geneva; joined John Smith & Son (Glasgow), 1960. Founded, with others, The New Glasgow Society, 1965 (Chairman 1967, 1968); worked for 12 years in rehabilitating St. Vincent Crescent, Glasgow, as founder member, St. Vincent Crescent Area Association; Secretary, First Glasgow Housing Association, since 1978; restored Aiket Castle (winner of an Europa Nostra Merit Award, 1989), 1976-79; National Trust for Scotland: elected to Council 1978 and 1991; elected Member, Committee, Strathclyde Building Preservation Trust, 1986; appointed to Architectural Heritage Fund Executive, 1989. Recreations: farming; bee keeping; opera; restoring old houses; swimming; skiing; reading on holiday. Address: Aiket Castle, Dunlop, Ayrshire; T.-(b.) 041-221 7472.

Clunie, Henry, DipTech, JP. Honorary Sheriff, since 1967; b. 30.6.07, Leith; m., Harriot Shearer Wilson; 1 s.; 1 d. Educ. Trinity Academy, Leith; Moray House College of Education. Deputy Rector, Dornoch Academy, 1968-72; Town Councillor, Royal Burgh of Dornoch, 1958-74 (Provost, 1965-74); created Freeman of the Burgh, 1973; appointed Commissioner of Income Tax; Member, Sutherland District Council, 1974-78. Recreations: music; amateur drama. Address: (h.) 29 Macdonald Road, Dornoch, Sutherland; T.-0862 810201.

Clunies-Ross, Professor Anthony Ian, BA (Melbourne), MA (Cantab). Professor in Economics, Strathclyde University, since 1978; b. 9.3.32, Sydney, New South Wales; m., Morag McVey; 2 s.; 2 d. Educ. Knox Grammar School, Sydney; Scotch College, Melbourne; Melbourne University; Pembroke College, Cambridge. Tutor in History, Melbourne University, 1958-59; Lecturer, then Senior Lecturer in Economics, Monash University, 1961-67; Senior Lecturer, then Professor in Economics, University of Papua New Guinea, 1967-74; Temporary Lecturer, then Senior Lecturer in Economics, Strathclyde University, 1975-78. Chairman, Australian Student Christian Movement, 1963-66; Member, St. Andrews Diocesan Synod, Scottish Episcopal Church, 1984-86. Publications: One Per Cent: The Case for Greater Australian Foreign Aid, 1963 (Co-author); Australia and Nuclear Weapons (Co-author), 1966; Alternative Strategies for Papua New Guinea, (Co-author), 1973; The Taxation of Mineral Rent (Co-author), 1983; Migrants from Fifty Villages, 1984; Economic Stabilisation for Developing Countries, 1991. Recreations: swimming; gardening. Address: (h.) Railway Cottage, Kinbuck, Dunblane, Perthshire, FK15 ONL; T.-Dunblane 822684.

Clyde, Hon. Lord (James John Clyde), QC (Scot), BA (Oxon), LLB. Senator of the College of Justice, since 1985; b. 29.1.32, Edinburgh; m., Ann Clunie Hoblyn; 2 s. Educ. Edinburgh Academy; Corpus Christi College, Oxford; Edinburgh University. Called to Scottish Bar, 1959; QC, 1971; Advocate Depute, 1973-74; Chancellor to Bishop of Argyll and the Isles, 1972-85; a Judge of the Courts of Appeal of Jersey and Guernsey, 1979-85; Chairman, Medical Appeal Tribunal, 1974-85; Chairman, Committee of Investigation for Scotland on Agricultural Marketing, 1984-85; Chairman, Scottish Valuation Advisory Council, since 1987 (Member, since 1972); Member, UK Delegation to CCBE, 1978-84 (Leader, 1981-84). Director, Edinburgh Academy, 1979-88; Chairman, St. George's School for Girls, since 1989; Governor, Napier Polytechnic of Edinburgh, since 1989; Assessor to Chancellor of Edinburgh University, since 1989; Trustee and Manager, St. Mary's Music Society, since 1976; Trustee, National Library of Scotland, since 1978. Recreations: music; gardening. Address: (h.) 9 Heriot Row, Edinburgh, EH3 6HU; T.-031-556 7114.

Clydesmuir, Baron (Ronald John Bilsland Colville), KT (1972), CB (1965), MBE (1944), TD. Lord Lieutenant, Lanarkshire, since 1963; Captain General, Queen's Bodyguard for Scotland (Royal Company of Archers); b. 21.5.17; m.; 2 s.; 2 d. Educ. Charterhouse; Trinity College, Cambridge. Served in The Cameronians (Scottish Rifles), 1939-45; commanded 6/7th Bn., The Cameronians, TA, 1953-56; Director, Colvilles Ltd., 1958-70; Governor, British Linen Bank, 1966-71; Governor, Bank of Scotland, 1972-81; Director, Scottish Provident Institution, 1954-88; Director, Barclays Bank, 1972-82; Chairman, North Sea Assets Ltd., 1972-88; Scottish Council (Development and Industry): Chairman, Executive Committee, 1966-78, President, 1978-87; President, Scottish Council of Physical Recreation, 1964-72; Hon. LLD, Strathclyde, 1968; Hon. DSc, Heriot-Watt, 1971. Address: (h.) Langlees House, Biggar, Lanarkshire ML12 6NP.

Clyne, Rev. Douglas Roy, BD. Minister, Old Parish Church, Fraserburgh, since 1973; b. 9.11.41, Inverness; m., Annette Taylor; 1 s. Educ. Inverness High School; Aberdeen University. Accountancy (Inverness County Council and Highland Printers Ltd.), 1956-68; studied for the ministry, 1968-72; Assistant Minister, Mastrick Parish Church, Aberdeen, 1972-73. Address: Old Parish Church Manse, 97 Saltoun Place, Fraserburgh, AB4 5RY; T.-0346 28536.

Coates, Leon, MA (Cantab), LRAM, ARCO. Lecturer in Music, Edinburgh University, since 1965; b. 15.6.37,

Wolverhampton; m., Heather Patricia Johnston. Educ. Derby School; St. John's College, Cambridge. Composer, pianist, organist, St. Andrew's and St. George's Church, Edinburgh, since 1981; Conductor: Edinburgh Chamber Orchestra, 1965-75, Edinburgh Symphony Orchestra, 1973-85; Conductor, Edinburgh Studio Orchestra, since 1986; Harpsichordist, Scottish Baroque Ensemble, 1970-77; broadcasts as pianist and harpsichordist; compositions broadcast on Radio 3, Radio 4 Scotland and Radio Eireann. Recreation: hill-walking. Address: (h.) 35 Comely Bank Place, Edinburgh EH4 1ER; T.-031-332 4553.

Coats, Sir William David, Kt, DL, HonLLD (Strathclyde), 1977. Chairman, Coats Patons PLC, 1981-86; Deputy Chairman, Clydesdale Bank PLC, since 1985; b. 25.7.24, Glasgow; m., The Hon. Elizabeth L.G. MacAndrew; 2 s.; 1 d. Educ. Eton College. Joined J. & P. Coats Ltd., 1948, as management trainee; held various appointments and became a Director, 1957; appointed Director, Coats Patons PLC, on its formation, 1960; Deputy Chairman, 1979. Chairman, Glasgow Coordinating Committee, Cancer Research Campaign. Recreations: golf; shooting. Address: (h.) The Cottage, Symington, Ayrshire, KA1 5QG.

Cobbe, Professor Stuart Malcolm, MA, MD, FRCP. Professor of Medical Cardiology, Glasgow University, since 1985; b. 2.5.48, Watford; m., Patricia Frances; 3 d. Educ. Royal Grammar School, Guildford; Cambridge University. Training in medicine, Cambridge and St. Thomas Hospital, London; qualified, 1972; specialist training in cardiology, National Heart Hospital, London, and John Radcliffe Hospital, Oxford; research work, University of Heidelberg, 1981; Consultant Cardiologist and Senior Lecturer, Oxford, 1982-85. Recreation: walking. Address: (b.) Department of Medical Cardiology, Queen Elizabeth Building, Royal Infirmary, Glasgow, G3; T.-041-552 3535, Ext. 4722.

Cochran, Hugh Douglas, BA (Oxon), LLB. Advocate in Aberdeen, since 1958; b. 26.4.32, Aberdeen; m., Sarah Beverly Sissons; 4 s.; 2 d. Educ. Loretto; Trinity College, Oxford; Edinburgh University. Partner: Cochran & Macpherson, 1958-80, Adam, Cochran, since 1980. Secretary, Aberdeen Association for the Prevention of Cruelty to Animals, since 1972; Registrar, Diocese of Aberdeen and Orkney, since 1984. Recreations: cycling; collecting stamps. Address: 6 Bon Accord Square, Aberdeen, AB9 1XU; T.-Aberdeen 588913.

Cochran, William, MB, ChB, FRCSEdin, FRCSGlas. Consultant Paediatric and Neonatal Surgeon, Royal Hospital for Sick Children, Glasgow, since 1977; Honorary Clinical Senior Lecturer, Glasgow University, since 1978; b. 4.5.27, Sandhead, Wigtownshire; m., Pamela White; 2 s.; 1 d. Educ. Allan Glen's School, Glasgow; Fraserburgh Academy; Aberdeen University. Demonstrator, Department of Anatomy, Aberdeen University; Paediatric Surgical Registrar, Edinburgh Northern Group Hospitals; Senior Paediatric Surgical Registrar, Royal Hospital for Sick Children, Belfast; Consultant Paediatric Surgeon, Belfast Hospitals and Honorary Clinical Lecturer, Queen's University, Belfast. Former Member, Special Advisory Committee (A/E) to Committee for Higher Surgical Training. Address: (h.) 4 Greenwood Drive, Bearsden, Dunbartonshire, G61 2HA; T.-041-943 0579.

Cochran, Professor William, BSc, PhD, MA, FRS, FRSE. Professor of Natural Philosophy, Edinburgh University, 1975-87; b. 30.7.22, Newton Mearns; m., Ingegerd Wall; 1 s.; 2 d. Educ. Boroughmuir School, Edinburgh; Edinburgh University; Cambridge University. Demonstrator/ Lecturer/Reader, Cambridge University, 1948-64; Fellow, Trinity Hall, Cambridge, 1951-64; Professor of Physics, Edinburgh University, 1964-75; Dean, Faculty of Science,

1978-81; University Vice Principal, 1984-87; Honorary Fellow, Trinity Hall, Cambridge, since 1983; awards from Institute of Physics, 1966, Royal Society, 1978, Franklin Institute, 1985. Recreations: family history; Scots verse. Address: (h.) 71 Clermiston Road, Edinburgh; T.-031-334 6612.

Cochrane, Alexander Kitchener, DL. Retired Company Chairman; b. 6.6.16, Edinburgh; m., Ethel Scott Seatter; 3 s. Educ. Morrison's Academy. Commissioned TA RE, 1937; served 1939-45; attached Indian Army, 1940-45, and on deputation to Government of India; joined family business and retired as Chairman of group, Cochrane Vehicle Holdings Ltd. Recreations: fishing; shooting; gardening. Address: Mount Chasse, Broomieknowe, Lasswade, EH18 1LN; T.-031 663 7906.

Cochrane, James Aikman (Peter), MA, DSO, MC. Member, Scottish Arts Council; b. 12.5.19, Glasgow; m., Louise Morley; 2 d. Educ. Loretto; Wadham College, Oxford. 2nd QO Cameron Highlanders, 1940-45; Staff College, Quetta, HQ ALFSEA, 1945-46; Publisher, Chatto & Windus (Partner), 1946-51; Director, Butler & Tanner, 1952-79. Publications: Dr. Johnson's Printer; Charlie Company; Scottish Military Dress. Recreations: fishing; looking at Romanesque churches. Address: (h.) 12 Warrender Park Terrace, Edinburgh, EH9 1EG; T.-031-229 4615.

Cockburn, Professor Forrester, MD, FRCPGlas, FRCPEdin, DCH. Samson Gemmell Professor of Child Health, Glasgow University, since 1977; b. 13.10.34, Edinburgh; m., Alison Fisher Grieve; 2 s. Educ. Leith Academy; Edinburgh University. Early medical training, Edinburgh Royal Infirmary, Royal Hospital for Sick Children, Edinburgh, and Simpson Memorial Maternity Pavilion, Edinburgh; Research Fellow in Paediatric Metabolic Disease, Boston University; Visiting Professor, San Juan University, Puerto Rico; Nuffield Fellow, Institute for Medical Research, Oxford University; Wellcome Senior Research Fellow, then Senior Lecturer, Department of Child Life and Health, Edinburgh University. Publications: a number of textbooks on paediatric medicine, neonatal medicine, nutrition and metabolic diseases. Recreation: sailing. Address: (b.) University Department of Child Health, Royal Hospital for Sick Children, Yorkhill, Glasgow, G3 8SJ; T.-041-339 8888.

Cockburn, James Masson Thomson, BSc (Hons), CEng, FICE, FIWEM, FBIM. Director of Water Services, Grampian Regional Council, since 1988; b. 22.1.47, Aberdeen; m., Avril; 2 s. Educ. Robert Gordon's College; Dundee University. Assistant Engineer, East of Scotland Water Board, 1969-75; Assistant Divisional Manager (Dundee), Department of Water Services, Tayside Regional Council, 1975-76; Assistant Director, Department of Water and Sewerage, Dumfries and Galloway Regional Council, 1976-79; Depute Director, Department of Water Services, Grampian Regional Council, 1979-88. Past President, Scottish Section, Institution of Water Engineers and Scientists; Member of Council, Institution of Water and Environmental Management, 1987-91; Secretary, Scottish Association of Directors of Water and Sewerage, since 1989. Recreations: hill-walking; sailing; skiing; curling; Rotary. Address: (b.) Grampian Regional Council, Woodhill House, Westburn Road, Aberdeen, AB9 2LU; T.-0224 664900.

Cocker, Douglas, DA, ARSA. Sculptor, since 1968; Lecturer in Sculpture, Grays School of Art, Aberdeen, 1982-90; b. 23.3.45, Alyth, Perthshire; m., Elizabeth Filshie; 2 s.; 1 d. Educ. Blairgowrie High School; Duncan of Jordanstone College of Art, Dundee. SED Travelling Scholar, Italy and Greece, 1966; RSA Andrew Carnegie Travelling Scholar, 1967; RSA Benno Schotz Award, 1967; Greenshields Foundation (Montreal) Fellowship, 1968-69 (studies in New

York and Greece); RSA Latimer Award, 1970; Arts Council of GB Award, 1977; East Midlands Arts Award, 1979; Scottish Arts Council Major Bursary, 1989; Essex Fine Art Fellowship, 1991-92; Visiting Artist: Newcastle Polytechnic, Duncan of Jordanstone College of Art, Edinburgh College of Art and Tyler University, Philadelphia. Fourteen one-man exhibitions, 1969-84; numerous group and mixed exhibitions, 1970-85; various commissions. Recreations: reading; travel; sport. Address: (h.) Craigveigh, Gordon Crescent, Aboyne, Aberdeenshire; T.-Aboyne 86011.

Coggins, Professor John Richard, MA, PhD, FRSE. Professor of Biochemistry, Glasgow University, since 1986; Managing Director, Biomac Ltd., since 1988; b. 15.1.44, Bristol; m., Dr. Lesley F. Watson; 1 s.; 1 d. Educ. Bristol Grammar School; Queen's College, Oxford; Ottawa University. Post-doctoral Fellow: Biology Department, Brookhaven National Laboratory, New York, 1970-72, Biochemistry Department, Cambridge University, 1972-74; Lecturer, Biochemistry Department, Glasgow University, 1974-78, Senior Lecturer, 1978-86. Chairman, Molecular Enzymology Group, Biochemical Society, 1982-85; Chairman, Biophysics and Biochemistry Committee, SERC, 1985-88; Member, DTI-SERC Joint Advisory Board for Biotechnology, 1989-91; Member of Council, AFRC, 1991-94; Biochemistry Adviser to UFC, 1989-91. Recreations: sailing; travelling. Address: (b.) Department of Biochemistry, Glasgow University, Glasgow, G12 8QQ; T.-041-339 8855, Ext. 5267.

Coghill, William Francis, BA, DipCrim. Collector of Customs and Excise, Edinburgh, since 1988; b. 4.4.34, Glasgow; m., Dr. Vera Maybelle Rockwell; 2 s.; 1 d. Educ. Allan Glen's School, Glasgow; Open University; London University. Joined HM Customs and Excise, 1951; after service in London, Manchester and Glasgow, joined Investigation Branch, London, 1960, and remained there until 1985, reaching rank of Deputy Chief Investigation Officer and Head of Anti-Drugs Smuggling Group; Deputy Collector, London Port, three years. Recreations: playing golf; sports spectating. Address: (b.) 44 York Place, Edinburgh, EH1 3JW; T.-031-556 2433.

Cohen, Professor Anthony Paul, BA, MSc (SocSc), PhD. Professor and Head, Department of Social Anthropology, Edinburgh University, since 1989; b. 3.8.46, London; m., Dr. Bronwen J. Cohen; 3 s. Educ. Whittinghame Collge, Brighton; Southampton University. Assistant Professor, Queen's University, Kingston, Ontario, 1970-71; Lecturer/Senior Lecturer in Social Anthropology, Manchester University, 1971-89. Publications: The Management of Myths; The Symbolic Construction of Community; Whalsay: Symbol, Segment and Boundary in a Shetland Island Community; Belonging (Editor); Symbolising Boundaries (Editor). Recreations: day-dreaming; music; novels; political spectating. Address: (b.) Adam Ferguson Building, Edinburgh University, George Square, Edinburgh, EH8 9LL; T.-031-650 3934, Ext. 6373.

Cohen, Cyril, OBE, JP, FRCPEdin, FRCPGlas. Honorary Fellow, Dundee University; retired Consultant Physician, Geriatric Medicine, and Hon. Senior Lecturer, Geriatric Medicine, Dundee University; Member, Chief Scientist's Health Services Research Committee; Chairman, Advisory Group on Health Education for Elderly People, Health Education Board, Scotland; b. 2.11.25, Manchester; m., Dr. Sarah E. Nixon; 2 s. Educ. Manchester Central High School; Victoria University, Manchester. Embarked on career in geriatric medicine, 1952. Past Member/Chairman, Angus District and Tayside Area Medical Committees; Secretary/Chairman, Tayside Area Hospital Medical Services Committee; Member, Scottish and UK Central Committee, Hospital Medical Services, and Chairman, Geriatric Medicine Sub-

committee; Past Chairman, Scottish Branch, British Geriatric Society (former Council Member); Member, Panel on Nutrition of the Elderly, COMA; Honorary Vice-President, Dundee and District Branch, British Diabetic Association; Life Member, Manchester Medical Society; Past Member, Chief Scientist's Committee for Research on Equipment for the Disabled; Member, Angus Access Panel and REMAP; Honorary Vice-President, Dundee and District Branch, British Diabetic Society; Chairman, Radio North Angus (Hospital Radio); former Member, Brechin and Forfar School Councils, Forfar Academy School Board and Central Committee on Primary Education; Secretary, Aberlemno Community Council; Vice-Chairman, Angus Association of Voluntary Organisations and Member, Brechin Day Care Centre Committee; former Director, Scottish Hospital Advisory Service; Past President, Montrose Burns Club and Brechin Arts Guild; Member, Executive, Age Concern Scotland; Member, Advisory Board, Bird Semple Ireland and Fyffe; Member, League of Friends, Forfar Hospitals; Chairman, Angus Care of the Elderly Group. Publications: many on geriatric medicine and care of the elderly. Recreations: photography; short walks; being at home. Address: (h.) Mansefield, Aberlemno, Forfar, DD8 3PD; T.-030-783 259.

Cohen, George Cormack, MA, LLB. Advocate; b. 16.12.09, Glasgow; m., Elizabeth Wallace; 1 s.; 1 d. Educ. Kelvinside Academy, Glasgow; Glasgow University. Admitted to Faculty of Advocates, 1935; Sheriff of Caithness at Wick, 1944-51; Sheriff of Ayrshire at Kilmarnock, 1951-55; Sheriff of Lothians and Peebles at Edinburgh, 1955-66. Recreations: gardening; travel. Address: (h.) 37B Lauder Road, Edinburgh, EH9 1UE; T.-031-668 1689.

Cohen, Patricia Townsend Wade, BSc, PhD. Head of Molecular Biology and Senior Scientist, Medical Research Council Protein Phosphorylation Unit, Department of Biochemistry, Dundee University, since 1991; b. 3.5.44, Worsley, Lancashire; m., Professor Philip Cohen (qv); 1 s.; 1 d. Educ. Bolton School; University College, London. Postdoctoral Research Fellow, Department of Medical Genetics, Washington University, Seattle, USA, 1969-71; Department of Biochemistry, Dundee University: Science Research Council Fellowship, 1971-72, Research Fellow (part-time), 1972-83, Lecturer (part-time), 1983-90, Senior Lecturer, 1990-91. Publications: 70 papers and reviews in scientific journals. Recreations: reading; skiing; golf. Address: (h.) Inverbay II, Invergowrie, Dundee, DD2 5DQ; T.-0382 562328.

Cohen, Professor Philip, BSc, PhD, FRS, FRSE. Royal Society Research Professor, Dundee University, since 1984; Honorary Director, Medical Research Council Protein Phosphorglation Unit, since 1990; b. 22.7.45, London; m., Patricia Townsend Wade (qv); 1 s.; 1 d. Educ. Hendon County Grammar School; University College, London. Science Research Council/NATO postdoctoral Fellow, Department of Biochemistry, University of Washington, 1969-71; Dundee University: Lecturer in Biochemistry, 1971-78, Reader in Biochemistry, 1978-81, Professor of Enzymology, 1981-84. Federation of European Biochemical Societies Anniversary Prize, 1977; Colworth Medal, British Biochemical Society, 1978; CIBA Medal and Prize, British Biochemical Society, 1992. Publications: 250 papers and reviews, one book. Recreations: chess; golf; natural history. Address: (h.) Inverbay II, Invergowrie, Dundee; T.-0382 562328.

Coke, Professor Simon, MA (Oxon). Professor of International Business, Edinburgh University, since 1972; b. 27.6.32, Bicester, Oxfordshire; m., Diana Margaret Evison; 1 s.; 2 d. Educ. Ridley College, Ontario; Pembroke College, Oxford. Marketing Executive, Beecham Overseas, 1958-64; General Manager, Japan, etc., Johnson & Johnson, 1964-68;

Head, Department of Business Studies, Edinburgh University, 1984; Dean, Scottish Business School, 1981-83; Director, Edinburgh University Management School; Director: Nippon Asset Trust, IeS Optimum Income Trust PLC, Jiig-Cal Ltd., Lastolite Ltd.   Address: (b.) Edinburgh University Management School, 7 Bristo Square, Edinburgh EH8.

Cole, Professor Alfred John, BSc, MSc, PhD, FBCS. Professor of Computational Science, St. Andrews University, 1969-88; b. 11.4.25, London; m., Christina Brotherson Carnie; 1 s. Educ. Preston Manor County School; University College, London. Lecturer: Heriot-Watt College, Edinburgh, 1952-55, Queen's College, Dundee, 1955-61; Senior Lecturer and Director, Computing Laboratory, Leicester University, 1961-65; Reader and Director, Computing Laboratory, St. Andrews University, 1965-69 (Head, Department of Computational Science). Publication: Macroprocessors, 1976. Recreations: beer and wine-making; concertina playing; East Fife FC supporter. Address: (h.) Inisheer, Barnyards, Kilconquhar, Fife; T.-033 334 378.

Cole-Hamilton, Arthur Richard, BA, CA, FIB(Scot). Chief Executive, Clydesdale Bank PLC, since 1987; b. 8.5.35, Kilwinning; m., Prudence Ann; 1 s.; 2 d. Educ. Ardrossan Academy; Loretto School; Cambridge University. Partner, Brechin Cole-Hamilton & Co., CA, 1962-67; various appointments, Clydesdale Bank, 1967-82; appointed Chief Executive, 1982, Director, 1984. Former Council Member, Institute of Chartered Accountants of Scotland (Chairman, Finance and General Purposes Committee, 1981-85); Chairman, Committee of Scottish Clearing Bankers, since 1991; President, Institute of Bankers in Scotland, 1988-90; Deputy Chairman, Scottish Council (Development and Industry); Director, Glasgow Chamber of Commerce, 1985-91; Trustee, National Galleries of Scotland, since 1986. Recreation: golf. Address: (b.) 30 St. Vincent Place, Glasgow; T.-041-248 7070.

Cole-Hamilton, Professor David John, BSc, PhD, FRSC, FRSE. Irvine Professor of Chemistry, St. Andrews University, since 1985; b. 22.5.48, Bovey Tracey; m., Elizabeth Ann Brown; 2 s.; 2 d. Educ. Haileybury and ISC; Hertford; Edinburgh University. Research Assistant, Temporary Lecturer, Imperial College, 1974-78; Lecturer, Senior Lecturer, Liverpool University, 1978-85. Sir Edward Frankland Fellow, Royal Society of Chemistry, 1984-85; Corday Morgan Medallist, 1983. Address: (b.) Department of Chemistry, The Purdie Building, St. Andrews, Fife, KY16 9ST; T.-0334 76161.

Collee, Professor John Gerald, CBE, MD, FRCPath, FRCPEdin. Professor and Head, Department of Bacteriology, Edinburgh University, 1979-91; Chief Bacteriologist, Edinburgh Royal Infirmary, 1979-91; b. 10.5.29, Bo'ness; m., Isobel McNay Galbraith; 2 s.; 1 d. Educ. Bo'ness Academy; Edinburgh Academy; Edinburgh University. House Physician, 1951-52; Army medical service, 1952-54 (Captain, RAMC); General Practitioner, 1954-55; Lecturer in Bacteriology, Edinburgh, 1955-63; WHO Visiting Professor of Bacteriology, Baroda, India, 1963-64; Edinburgh University: Senior Lecturer and Honorary Consultant Bacteriologist, 1964-70, Reader in Bacteriology, 1970-74, Personal Professor of Bacteriology, 1974-79; Editor and Past Chairman, Journal of Medical Microbiology. Recreations: woodwork; mechanics; fishing; music; painting. Address: (h.) 204 Newhaven Road, Edinburgh EH6 4QE; T.-031-552 8810.

Collie, George Francis, CBE (Civil), MBE (Military), JP, BL. Honorary Sheriff, Grampian Region, at Aberdeen, since 1974; retired Advocate in Aberdeen and Notary Public; b. 1.4.09, Aberdeen; m., Margery Constance Fullarton Wishart; 2 s. Educ. Aberdeen Grammar School; Aberdeen University. Partner, then Senior Partner, James & George Collie,

Advocates in Aberdeen; Deputy Chairman, then Chairman, Board of Management for Aberdeen Special Hospitals, 1952-68. Honorary Colonel, 51st Highland Division, RASC (TA) and later Honorary Colonel, 153 Highland Regiment, RCT (V), 1964-72. Address: (h.) Morkeu, Cults, Aberdeen, AB1 9PT; T.-0224 867636.

Collie, Ian, MA, MEd, MBIM, FSA Scot. Director of Education, Central Regional Council, since 1975; b. 20.7.33, Grantown-on-Spey; m., Helen; 1 s.; 1 d. Educ. Kingussie Secondary School; Aberdeen University; Glasgow University. Army, 1956-58; teacher, Renfrewshire, 1958-64; lecturer, Glasgow, 1964-66; Junior Assistant Director of Education, then Senior Assistant Director, Stirlingshire, 1966-69; Depute Director, Dunbartonshire, 1969-73; Sole Depute, Stirlingshire, 1973-75. Chairman, Scottish Mountain Leader Training Board; Chairman, Saltire Society Education Committee. Publication: Selections from Modern Writings (Editor). Recreations: hill-walking; squash. Address: (b.) Viewforth, Stirling; T.-Stirling 442679.

Collier, H. Bruce, DCA, MITSA. Director of Consumer and Trading Standards, Strathclyde Regional Council, since 1991; b. 24.5.46, Dumbarton; m., Margaret; 3 d. Educ. Clydebank High School. Senior Trading Standards Officer, Clydebank, 1975; Assistant Divisional Trading Standards Officer, Ayr, 1979; Assistant Director, Department of Consumer and Trading Standards, Strathclyde Regional Council, 1985. Chairman, Association of Petroleum and Explosives Acts Administration, 1973; Chairman, Institute of Trading Standards Scotland, 1986; Vice President, European Inter-Regional Institute of Consumer Affairs, since 1991; Chairman, Irvine CAB, since 1982. Recreations: reading; walking. Address: (b.) Strathclyde House, 20 India Street, Glasgow, G2 4PF; T.-041-227 3105.

Collier, Michael H., IPFA. Director of Finance, NHS in Scotland, since 1990; President, Chartered Institute of Public Finance and Accountancy, since 1991; b. 30.3.43, Stoke-on-Trent; m., Cynthia Jean; 1 s.; 1 d. Educ. King's Grammar School, Macclesfield. Macclesfield Borough Council, 1960-67; Group Accountant, Salop County Council, 1968-71; Chief Accountant, Birkenhead County Borough Council, 1971-73; Senior Assistant Director of Finance, Stockport Metropolitan District Council, 1973-77; Regional Treasurer, Mersey Regional Health Authority, 1978-85; District General Manager, Liverpool District Health Authority, 1985-90. Member, Council, Chartered Institute of Public Finance and Accountancy, since 1981. Recreations: fell walking; bridge; badminton; theatre. Address: (b.) Room 178, St. Andrew's House, Regent Road, Edinburgh; T.-031-244 3464.

Collin, William Robert, BSc. Headteacher, Dunbar Grammar School, since 1983; b. 3.7.43, Edinburgh; m., Valerie; 2 s.; 1 d. Educ. Eyemouth High School; Berwickshire High School; Edinburgh University; Moray House College of Education. Teacher, then Principal Teacher: Eyemouth High School, Arbroath High School; Assistant Head Teacher, Dunbar Grammar School; Depute Head Teacher, Selkirk High School. Elder, Church of Scotland. Recreations: history of east coast fishing industry; gardening; walking. Address: (h.) Rosebery Place, Dunbar, EH42 1AQ; T.-0368 63162.

Collins, Dennis Ferguson, MA, LLB, WS. Senior Partner, Carlton Gilruth, Solicitors, Dundee; Honorary Sheriff; b. 26.3.30, Dundee; m., Elspeth Margaret Nicoll; 1 s.; 1 d. Educ. High School of Dundee; St. Andrews University. Part-time Lecturer in Scots Law, St. Andrews University, then Dundee University, 1960-79; Agent Consulaire for France in Dundee, since 1976; Hon. Secretary, Dundee Society for Prevention of Cruelty to Children, 1962-90; Treasurer, Dundee Congregational Church, since 1966; Past President, Dundee and District Philatelic Society; Past President, Association of

Scottish Philatelic Societies; Dean, Faculty of Procurators and Solicitors in Dundee, 1987-89. Recreations: Chinese postal history; gardening; Sherlock Holmes pursuits. Address: (h.) Stirling House, Craigiebarn Road, Dundee, DD4 7PL; T.-0382 458070.

Collins, Kenneth Darlingston, BSc (Hons), MSc. Member (Labour), European Parliament, since 1979; b. 12.8.39, Hamilton; m., Georgina Frances Pollard; 1 s.; 1 d. Educ. St. John's Grammar School; Hamilton Academy; Glasgow University; Strathclyde University. Steelworks apprentice, 1956-59; University, 1960-65; Planning Officer, 1965-66; WEA Tutor, 1966-67; Lecturer: Glasgow College of Building, 1967-69; Paisley College of Technology, 1969-79; Member: East Kilbride Town and District Council, 1973-79, Lanark County Council, 1973-75, East Kilbride Development Corporation, 1976-79; Chairman, NE Glasgow Children's Panel, 1974-76; European Parliament: Deputy Leader, Labour Group, 1979-84, Chairman, Environment Committee, 1979-84 and since 1989 (Vice-Chairman, 1984-87), Socialist Spokesman on Environment, Public Health and Consumer Protection, 1984-89. Honorary Vice-President: International Federation on Environmental Health, Institute of Trading Standards Administration, European Food Law Association, Royal Environmental Health Institute of Scotland; European Advisor to BECTU, EETPU and NALGO. Recreations: music; boxer dogs; cycling. Address: (b.) 11 Stuarton Park, East Kilbride, G74 4LA; T.-03552 37282.

Collins, Kenneth E., PhD, MRCGP. Chairman, Glasgow Jewish Board of Education, since 1989; Honorary Treasurer, Glasgow Jewish Representative Council, since 1989; b. 23.12.47, Glasgow; m., Irene Taylor; 1 s.; 3 d. Educ. High School of Glasgow; Glasgow University. General medical practitioner in Glasgow, since 1976; Medical Officer, Newark Lodge, Glasgow, since 1978; Research Associate, Wellcome Unit for the History of Medicine, Glasgow University. Publications: Aspects of Scottish Jewry, 1987; Go and Learn: International Story of the Jews and Medicine in Scotland, 1988; Second City Jewry, 1990. Address: (b.) c/o Glasgow Jewish Board of Education, Calderwood Road, Glasgow, G43.

Colquhoun of Luss, Captain Sir Ivar (Iain), 8th Bt, JP, DL. Honorary Sheriff; Chief of the Clan; b. 4.1.16.

Coltart, George John Letham, TD, MA, MSc, CEng, MICE. Priory Secretary, Order of St. John of Jerusalem, since 1991; b. 2.2.29, Edinburgh; m., Inger Christina Larsson; 1 s.; 1 d. Educ. George Watson's College, Edinburgh; Royal Military Aademy, Sandhurst; King's College, Cambridge; Cornell University, USA. Commissioned, Royal Engineers, 1949; Captain, Adjutant, 23 Engineer Regiment, 1957-58; Staff College, Camberley, 1962; DAA & QMG 5 Bde, 1963-65; OC 51 Field Squadron, 1965-66; trasferred to Reserve, 1966; Senior Lecturer in Civil Engineering, Heriot-Watt University, 1966-91 (Deputy Head of Department, 1987-90). Convener, Edinburgh and Heriot-Watt Universities Joint Military Education Committee, 1988-91; Commanding Officer, Edinburgh and Heriot-Watt UOTC, 1971-74; TA Colonel, Lowlands, 1975-80; Chairman, Lowland TAVRA, 1987-90. Recreations: reserve forces; forestry; DIY. Address: Napier House, 8 Colinton Road, Edinburgh EH10 5DS; T.-031-447 6314; Polskeoch, Thornhill, DG3 4NN.

Coltrane, Robbie, DA. Actor/Director; b. 31.3.50, Glasgow. Educ. Trinity College, Glenalmond; Glasgow School of Art. Film credits: Subway Riders, 1979, Balham Gateway to the South, 1980, Britannia Hospital, 1981, Scrubbers, 1982, Krull, 1982, Ghost Dance, 1983, Chinese Boxes, 1984, The Supergrass, 1984, Defense of the Realm, 1985, Revolution, 1985, Caravaggio, 1985, Absolute Beginners, 1985, Mona Lisa, 1985, Eat the Rich, 1987, The Fruit Machine, 1987,

Slipstream, 1988, Bert Rigby, You're a Fool, 1988, Danny Champion of the World, 1988, Let It Ride, 1988, Henry V, 1988, Nuns on the Run, 1989, Perfectly Normal, 1989; theatre credits: The Bug, 1976, Mr Joyce is Leaving, 1978, The Slab Boys, 1978, The Transfiguration of Benno Blimpie, 1978, The Loveliest Night of the Year, 1979-80, Dick Whittington, 1979, Snobs and Yobs, 1980, Yr Obedient Servant (one-man show), 1987, Mistero Buffo (one-man show), 1990; television credits include: roles in several The Comic Strip Presents productions, lead role in Tutti Frutti (BBC Scotland), Mistero Buffo; films: Pope Must Die, 1990, Alive and Kicking, 1991, Comfort Creek, 1991. Honorary President, Heriot-Watt University. Recreations: vintage cars; sailing; painting; reading; movies. Address: c/o CDA, 47 Courtfield Road, London, SW7; T.-071-370 0708.

Comley, David John, BSc, PhD, FIH. Director of Housing, Glasgow City Council, since 1988; b. 25.4.50, Carshalton. Educ. Ashlyns School, Berkhamsted; Birmingham University. Housing Management Trainee, then District Housing Manager, Dudley Metropolitan Borough, 1976-80; District Housing Manager, then Assistant Director, then Depute Director, Glasgow City Council, from 1980. Adviser to COSLA, since 1988; Member, Hamish Allan Trust; Board Member, Scottish Jazz Network. Recreations: jazz; classical music; saxophone; hill-walking; literature; cinema; theatre. Address: (b.) Lomond House, 9 George Square, Glasgow, G2 1TG; T.-041-227 4613.

Compton, John Cole, MBE, BSc (Agric) (Hons). Council Member, Scottish Landowners Federation, since 1976 (Past Chairman, Land Use Committee); Member, Executive Committee, National Trust for Scotland, since 1987; Member, Scottish Agricultural Research and Development Advisory Council, since 1987; Member, Tay River Purification Board, since 1964 (Vice Chairman for many years); b. 1.1.23, Chippenham; m., Elizabeth Beatrice Cox; 2 d. Educ. Blundell's; Edinburgh University. Commissioned Royal Engineers, War service, 1941-45; mixed farming in Angus since 1949; former NFU Branch Chairman; non-party Angus County Councillor, 1968-75; Past Chairman, Scottish Polo Association; Member, Committee for Scotland, Nature Conservancy Council, 1981-90; Council Member, Scottish Wildlife Trust, 1982-91; founder Member, Angus and Tayside Children's Panel Advisory Committee; former Member, Noranside Borstal Institution Visiting Committee. Recreations: riding; sailing; wildlife and countryside matters at home and overseas; foreign travel. Address: (h.) Ward of Turin House, Forfar, DD8 2TF; T.-030 783 253.

Condliffe, John, BA (Oxon), MPhil. Managing Director, Strategy and LEC Operations, Scottish Enterprise (Director, Finance and Information, Scottish Development Agency, 1987-90; Director, North East, 1984-87); b. 17.9.46, Portsmouth. Educ. Portsmouth Grammar School; Magdalen College, Oxford; University College, London. Corporate planning, Greater London Council; Industrial Development Executive, London Docklands Development Team; Senior Lecturer in Economics, Polytechnic of Central London; Head of Area Programmes, Scottish Development Agency. Recreations: music; visual arts. Address: (b.) Scottish Enterprise, 120 Bothwell Street, Glasgow; T.-041-248 2700.

Conn, Stewart. Head, Radio Drama Department, BBC Scotland; b. 1936. Author of numerous stage plays; poetry includes An Ear to the Ground and Under the Ice.

Connarty, Michael, BA, DipEd, DCE, JP. MP (Labour), Falkirk East, since 1992; b. 3.9.47, Coatbridge; m., Margaret Doran; 1 s.; 1 d. Educ. Stirling University; Jordanhill College of Education; Glasgow University. Member, Scottish Executive, Labour Party, 1981-92; Chair, Labour Party Scottish Local Government Committee, 1987-90; Member,

Convention of Scottish Local Authorities, 1980-90 (Depute Labour Leader, 1988-90); Member, Stirling District Council, 1977-90 (Council Leader, 1980-90); Vice-Chair, Socialist Educational Association, 1983-85; Council Member, Educational Institute of Scotland, 1984-85; Founding Secretary, Labour Coordinating Committee (Scotland). Address: (h.) 47 Bo'ness Road, Grangemouth FK3 8AP.

Connelly, David, MA (Oxon), FSAScot. Secretary, Buildings of Scotland Trust, since 1990; Chairman, Cockburn Conservation Trust, Edinburgh, since 1990; b. 23.2.30, Halifax; m., Audrey Grace Salter; 1 s.; 1 d. Educ. Heath Grammar School, Halifax; Queen's College, Oxford. Colonial Administrative Service, Tanganyika, 1954-62; Assistant Secretary, St. Andrews University, 1962-63; Principal, Commonwealth Relations Office, 1963-64; First Secretary, British High Commission, New Delhi, 1964-66; Principal, Scottish Office, 1966-73; Assistant Secretary, 1973-87; Director, Historic Buildings and Monuments, Scotland, 1987-90. Recreations: opera; literature; history; architecture; walking the hills; country life. Address: c/o Royal Bank of Scotland plc, 36 St. Andrew Square, Edinburgh, EH2 2YB.

Connon, Iain Urquhart, MRTPI. Director of Environment Division, Dunfermline District Council, since 1991; b. 14.8.39, Perth; m., Eileen Margaret; 2 d. Educ. Perth Academy; Dundee College of Art. Rowand, Anderson, Kinninmouth & Paul, Architects, Edinburgh, 1962-67; Robert Matthew, Johnson Marshall & Partners, Architects, Edinburgh, 1967-70; Planning Department, Burgh of Dunfermline, 1970-75; Dunfermline District Council, since 1975. Recreations: Italian language and literature; ski mountaineering; cycling. Address:(b.) 3 New Row, Dunfermline, KY12 7NN; T.-0383 736321.

Connor, Professor James Michael, MD, BSc (Hons), MB, ChB (Hons), FRCP. Professor of Medical Genetics and Director, West of Scotland Regional Genetics Service, since 1987 (Wellcome Trust Senior Lecturer and Honorary Consultant in Medical Genetics, Glasgow University, 1984-87); b. 18.6.51, Grappenhall, England; m., Dr. Rachel A.C. Educ. Lymm Grammar School, Cheshire; Liverpool University. House Officer, Liverpool Royal Infirmary; Resident in Internal Medicine, Johns Hopkins Hospital, USA; University Research Fellow, Liverpool University; Instructor in Internal Medicine, Johns Hopkins Hospital, USA; Consultant in Medical Genetics, Duncan Guthrie Institute of Medical Genetics, Yorkhill, Glasgow. Publications: Essential Medical Genetics (Co-author), 1984 (3nd edition, 1990); various articles on aspects of medical genetics. Recreations: fly fishing; windsurfing; skiing. Address: (h.) East Collarie Farm, by Fenwick, Ayrshire; T.-Fenwick 790.

Conroy, Stephen, Painter; b. 1964, Helensburgh. Educ. Glasgow School of Art. Group exhibitions, Royal Glasgow Institute of Fine Arts, Scottish National Gallery of Modern Art, Cincinnati and tour; one-man exhibitions, London.

Conti, Rt. Rev. Mario Joseph, STL, PhL, DD. Bishop of Aberdeen, since 1977; Member, Pontifical Council for the Promotion of Christian Unity, Rome, since 1984; Member, International Commission for English in the Liturgy, 1978-87; b. 20.3.34, Elgin. Educ. St. Marie's Convent; Springfield School, Elgin; Blairs College, Aberdeen; Scots College, Pontifical Gregorian University, Rome. Ordained priest, Rome, 1958; Curate, St. Mary's Cathedral, Aberdeen, 1959-62; Parish Priest, St. Joachim's, Wick and St. Anne's, Thurso, 1962. Commendatore, Order of Merit, Italian Republic; President-Treasurer, SCIAF, 1977-85; President, National Liturgy Commission, 1978-86; Chairman, Scottish Catholic Heritage Commission; President, Commission for Christian Doctrine and Unity, since 1986; first Convener, Central Council, ACTS, 1990; Knight Commander of the Holy Sepulchre, 1989; Conventual Chaplain Ad Honorem, Knights of Malta, 1991. Recreations: music; art. Address: Bishop's House, 156 King's Gate, Aberdeen; T.-0224 319154.

Conway, Rt. Rev. Mgr. Michael Joseph, BA, MSc (Econ). Catholic Chaplain, Glasgow University, since 1977; Prelate of Honour, since 1988; b. 5.3.40, Newry. Educ. St. Colman's College, Newry; St. Kieran's College, Kilkenny; University College, Dublin; London School of Economics. St. James's, Coatbridge, 1963-65; St. David's, Plains, Airdrie, 1965-66; St. Theresa's, Newarthill, 1966-69; St. Monica's, Coatbridge, 1975-77. Recreations: golf; hill-walking; reading; listening to music. Address: (b.) Turnbull Hall, 13-15 Southpark Terrace, Glasgow, G12 8LG; T.-041-339 4315.

Cook, Alexander Bethune, BSc (Hons). Chief Planning Officer, Dunfermline District Council, since 1991; b. 3.10.46, Kirkcaldy; m., Jennifer; 2 s. Educ. Kirkcaldy High School; Heriot Watt University. Planning Assistant, Cumbernauld Development Corporation; Senior Planning Assistant, Dumfries and Galloway Regional Council; joined Dunfermline D.C. as Principal Planning Officer. Recreations: guitar music; hill-walking; golf. Address: (b.) 3 New Row, Dunfermline, KY12 7NN; T.-0383 736321.

Cook, Colin. General Manager, BT Scotland, since 1990; b. 21.7.41, Dumfries; m., Marion; 1 s.; 1 d. Sales/marketing background; General Manager UK (Sales), BT commercial sector. Address: (b.) 11 Hope Street, Glasgow; T.-041-220 2244.

Cook, Fraser Murray, OBE, BSc, MIMechE, CEng, FInstPet. Chairman, Highlands and Islands Development Consultative Council, 1986-88; Vice Chairman, Forth Ports Authority, 1985-88; Member, Court, Stirling University, since 1986; b. 29.12.17, Conon Bridge, Ross-shire; m., Eve Smith Reid (deceased). Educ. Inverness Royal Academy; Morgan Academy, Dundee; St. Andrews University. Engineering graduate apprentice, Pumpherston Oil Co. Ltd., 1939-41; REME, South East Asia Command, 1941-46; Assistant to Manager, Pumpherston Oil Co. Ltd., 1946-48; Production Engineer, latterly Oil Construction Engineer, Southern Africa, 1948-53; Engineer, BP Oil Grangemouth Refinery Ltd., 1953-56; Manager, Pumpherston Oil Co. Ltd., 1956-62; Works Manager: BP Oil Grangemouth Refinery Ltd., 1962-66, BP Oil Llandarcy Refinery Ltd., 1966-69; General Manager, then Managing Director and General Manager, BP Oil Grangemouth Refinery Ltd., 1969-77. Chairman, Cumbernauld Development Corporation, 1983-86; Chairman, East Strathearn Community Council, since 1989. Recreations: some golf; photography. Address: Littleton Cottage, Cultoquhey, by Crieff, Perthshire, PH7 3NF; T.-Crieff 3537.

Cook, Rev. James Stanley Stephen Ronald Tweedie, BD, DipPSS. Minister, Hamilton West Parish Church, since 1974; b. 18.8.35, Tullibody; m., Jean Douglas McLachlan; 2 s.; 1 d. Educ. Whitehill Senior Secondary School, Glasgow; St. Andrews University. Apprentice quantity surveyor, Glasgow, 1953-54; regular soldier, REME, 1954-57; Assistant Preventive Officer, Waterguard Department, HM Customs and Excise, 1957-61; Officer, HM Customs and Excise, 1961-69; studied for the ministry, 1969-74. Chairman, Cruse (Lanarkshire); Member, National Training Group, Cruse, since 1987; Chairman, Hamilton Crime Prevention Panel, 1986-87; Member, Action Research for Crippled Child Committee, since 1977;Substitute Provincial Grand Master, Lanarkshire (Middle Ward), 1983-88; Honorary Provincial Grand Chaplain, since 1989; founder Member, Wishaw Victims Support Scheme, 1985; Chaplain, Hartwood Hospital for Mental Health, since 1988. Recreations: music; photography; DIY. Address: West Manse, 43 Bothwell Road, Hamilton, ML3 OBB; T.-Hamilton 458770.

Cook, John, FIB (Scot), FCIS, FBIM. General Manager, Corporate and International Banking, Clydesdale Bank PLC, since 1988; b. 6.6.38, Hamilton; m., Maureen Muir; 2 s. Educ. Rutherglen Academy. Joined Clydesdale Bank in Glasgow, 1955; held appointments in Glasgow and London; Assistant General Manager, 1982; Operations Director, Corporate Banking, 1987. Recreations: Church work; reading; walking; travel. Address: (b.) 30 St. Vincent Place, Glasgow, G1 2HL; T.-041-248 7070.

Cook, Rev. John Weir, MA, BD. Minister, St. Philip's, Joppa, since 1988 (Henderson Church, Kilmarnock, 1970-88); b. 10.2.37, Greenock; m., Elizabeth Anne Gifford; 1 s.; 2 d. Educ. Greenock Academy; High School of Glasgow; Glasgow University. Peter Marshall Scholar, Princeton, 1962; Minister, St. Andrews Church, Calcutta, 1963-70; accredited by British Association for Counselling, 1984 and 1989. Recreations: reading; sport; after-dinner speaking. Address: 6 St. Mary's Place, Edinburgh, EH15 2QF; T.-031-669 2410.

Cook, Michael Blyth, BSc, AHWU. Rector, Queen Anne High School, Dunfermline, since 1988; b. 8.6.39, Dunfermline; m., Sheena Rodger; 4 d. Educ. Beath High School, Cowdenbeath; Edinburgh University; Heriot Watt University. Teacher, Special Assistant, Beath High School, 1963-68; Principal Teacher of Maths, St. Columba's, Dunfermline, 1968-71, and Buckhaven High School, 1971-74; Assistant Rector, then Depute Rector, Woodmill High School, 1974-87. Recreations: golf; bridge; hill-walking. Address: (b.) Queen Anne High School, Broomhead, Dunfermline; T.-Dunfermline 728188.

Cook, Michael David, CA, IPFA, MHSM, JP. General Manager, Dumfries and Galloway Health Board, since 1985; b. 30.1.45, Glasgow; m., Deirdre; 1 s.; 1 d. Educ. Wishaw High School; Glasgow University. Treasurer, Orkney Health Board, 1973-74; Area Management Accountant, then District Finance Officer, Ayrshire and Arran Health Board, 1974-82; Treasurer, Dumfries and Galloway Health Board, 1982-85. Recreations: sailing; reading; hill-walking. Address: (b.) Nithbank, Dumfries; T.-0387 46246.

Cook, Robin. MP (Labour), Livingston, since 1983 (Edinburgh Central, 1974-83); b. 28.2.46.   Opposition Spokesman on Health and Social Security, since 1987.

Cooke, David John, BSc, MSc, PhD, CPsych, FBPsS. Head of Forensic Clinical Psychology, Greater Glasgow Health Board, since 1984; Honorary Lecturer, since 1984, and Honorary Senior Research Fellow, Glasgow University, since 1989; Visiting Professor, Glasgow Polytechnic, since 1990; b. 13.7.52, Glasgow; m., Janet Ruth Salter; 2 d. Educ. Larbert High School; St. Andrews University; Newcastle-upon-Tyne University; Glasgow University. Clinical Psychologist, Gartnavel Royal Hospital, 1976-83; Cropwood Fellow, Institute of Criminology, Cambridge University, 1986. Recreations: sailing; opera; cooking. Address: (b.) Douglas Inch Centre, 2 Woodside Terrace, Glasgow, G3 7UY; T.-041-332 3844.

Cooke, Joseph Henry, BSc (Hons), MA, DipEd. Head Teacher, Kyle Academy, Ayr, since 1985; b. 30.12.32, Kingston, St. Vincent, West Indies; m., Mary A. Marshall; 3 s. Educ. Methodist College, Belfast; Queen's University, Belfast. Teacher, Down High School, Downpatrick, 1956-67; Head, Geography Department: Strathearn School, Belfast, 1967-74, Ravenspark Academy, Irvine, 1975-79; Assistant Head Teacher, then Depute Head Teacher, Garnock Academy, Kilbirnie, 1979-85. Session Clerk, Alloway Parish Church. Recreations: travel; bowls; photography; gardening; DIY. Address: (h.) 3 Corsehill Park, Ayr, KA7 2UG; T.-0292 284745.

Cooke, Nicholas Huxley, MA (Oxon). Director, The Scottish Conservation Projects Trust, since 1984; b. 6.5.44, Godalming, Surrey; m., Anne Landon; 2 s.; 3 d. Educ. Charterhouse School; Worcester College, Oxford. Retail management, London, 1967; chartered accountancy training, London, 1968-71; British International Paper, London, 1972-78; Director (Scotland), British Trust for Conservation Volunteers, 1978-84. Member: Policy Committee, Scottish Council for Voluntary Organisations; Age Resource Scotland Steering Group; Executive Group, UK 2000 Scotland; Chairman, Scottish Advisory Panel, Shell Better Britain Campaign; Member, Scottish Committee, European Year of the Environment, 1987-88. Recreations: fishing; walking; photography; outdoor conservation work. Address: (b.) Balallan House, 24 Allan Park, Stirling, FK8 2QG; T.-0786 79697.

Cooke, Professor Timothy, MD, FRCS, MB, ChB. St. Mungo Professor of Surgery, Glasgow University, since 1989; Honorary Consultant Surgeon, Royal Infirmary, Glasgow; b. 16.9.47, Liverpool; m., Lynn; 1 s.; 1 d. Educ. Birkenhead Institute; Liverpool University. Surgical training, Liverpool University, 1973-79; Lecturer in Surgery, Southampton University, 1980-83; Senior Lecturer and Honorary Consultant Surgeon, Charing Cross & Westminster Medical School, 1983-86; Senior Lecturer and Honorary Consultant Surgeon, Liverpool University and Royal Liverpool and Broadgreen Hospitals, 1986-89. Hunterian Professor, Royal College of Surgeons of England. Publications: numerous scientific articles about cancer research. Recreations: playing wide range of indoor and outdoor sports; lifetime supporter, Liverpool FC. Address: (b.) University Department of Surgery, Royal Infirmary, Glasgow, G31 2ER; T.-041-552 3535, Ext. 5429.

Coombs, Professor Graham H., BSc, PhD. Professor of Zoology, Glasgow University, since 1990 (Head of Department, since 1991); b. 22.9.47, Coventry; m., Isabel; 1 d. Educ. King Henry VIII School, Coventry; University College, London. Research Fellow, University of Kent, 1972-74; Lecturer, Department of Zoology, Glasgow University, 1974-86, Senior Lecturer, 1986-88, Reader, 1988-90. Recreation: golf. Address: (b.) Department of Zoology, Glasgow University, Glasgow, G12 8QQ; T.-041-339 8855, Ext. 4777.

Cooper, Professor Neil Louis, BA, MA, BPhil, FRSE. Professor of Moral Philosophy, Dundee University, since 1981 (Head, Department of Philosophy, since 1984); b. 25.4.30, Ilford; m., Beryl Barwell Turner; 1 s.; 1 d. Educ. Westminster City School; City of London School; Balliol College, Oxford (Domus Exhibitioner); Senior Scholar, New College, Oxford, 1953-55; John Locke Scholar, 1954. RAF, 1948-49; Lecturer in Philosophy, Queen's College, St. Andrews University, 1956-67; Dundee University: Senior Lecturer in Philosophy, 1967-69, Reader in Philosophy, 1969-81, Dean of Students, Faculty of Social Sciences and Letters, 1972-74, Member of Senate, since 1978, and of Court, since 1986; Editorial Chairman, The Philosophical Quarterly, since 1985; FRSE, 1987. Publications: The Definition of Morality (Contributor), 1970; Weakness of Will (Contributor), 1971; The Diversity of Moral Thinking, 1981; Philosophers on Education (Contributor), 1986; The Analytic Tradition (Co-Editor), 1990; New Inquiries into Meaning and Truth (Co-Editor), 1991. Recreations: conversation; reading; listening to music; playing with ideas. Address: (h.) 2 Minto Place, Dundee, DD2 1BR; T.-Dundee 66518.

Cooper, Patricia, BA, DMS, CertEd. Lecturer in Consumer Studies, Robert Gordon's Institute of Technology, Aberdeen, since 1983; Council Member, Scottish Consumer Council, since 1987; Member, Food Policy Committee, National Consumer Council, since 1988; Director, Scottish

Agricultural College (Aberdeen) since 1991; b. 24.11.42, South Elmsall; m., John M. Cooper; 2 s. Teacher/Lecturer in Home Economics, since 1963. Member, British Telecom Consumer Liaison Panel, 1986; Secretary, Aberdeen Consumer Group, 1985. Recreations: entertaining; reading diverting novels. Address: (b.) R.G.I.T., Kepplestone Premises, Queens Road, Aberdeen, AB9 2PG; T.-0224 633611.

Cooper, Sheena M.M., MA. Rector, Aboyne Academy and Deeside Community Centre; b. 7.3.39, Bellshill. Educ. Dalziel High School, Motherwell; Glasgow University. Teacher of History, Dalziel High School, Motherwell, 1962-68; Lecturer in History, Elizabeth Gaskell College of Education, Manchester, 1968-70; Woman Adviser, then Assistant Rector, Montrose Academy, 1970-76; Rector, John Neilson High School, Paisley, 1976-83. Member: Council for Tertiary Education in Scotland, 1979-83, Scottish Examination Board, since 1984, Scottish Vocational Education Council, 1985-88, Religious Advisory Council, BBC, 1980-91, Broadcasting Council for Scotland, since 1991; President, Education Section, British Association for Advancement of Science, 1978-79. Recreation: walking. Address: (b.) Aboyne Academy and Deeside Community Centre, Aboyne; T.-0339 86222, Ext. 24.

Copeland, Professor Laurence Sidney, BA (Hons), MA (Econ), PhD. Ivory Professor of Finance, Stirling University, since 1991; b. 8.9.46, Manchester; m., Rebecca; 2 s. Educ. Manchester Grammar School; Brasenose College, Oxford. Lecturer, Manchester University, 1976-91. Visiting Professor, New York University, 1982, 1983; Visiting Research Fellow, Lancaster University, 1990. Publication: Exchange Rates and International Finance, 1989. Recreation: running. Address: Department of Accounting and Finance, Stirling University, Stirling, FK9 4LA; T.-0786 67283.

Coppock, Professor John Terence, CBE, MA, PhD, FBA, FRSE. Emeritus Professor of Geography, Edinburgh University; Secretary and Treasurer, Carnegie Trust for the Universities of Scotland, since 1987; Member, Scottish Sports Council, 1976-88; b. 2.6.21, Cardiff; m., Sheila Mary Burnett; 1 s.; 1 d. Educ. Penarth County School; Queens' College, Cambridge. Civil Servant, 1938-47 (Lord Chancellor's Department, Ministry of Works, Customs and Excise); War Service, Army, 1939-46 (Commissioned, 1941); Departmental Demonstrator, Department of Geography, Cambridge University, 1949-50; University College, London: Assistant Lecturer, 1950-52, Lecturer, 1952-64, Reader, 1964-65; Ogilvie Professor of Geography, Edinburgh University, 1965-86. Institute of British Geographers: Vice-President, 1971-73, President, 1973-74; Vice-President, Royal Scottish Geographical Society, since 1975; Vice-President, British Academy, 1985-87. Recreations: walking; natural history; listening to music. Address: (b.) Carnegie Trust for the Universities of Scotland, 22 Hanover Street, Edinburgh, EH2 2EN; T.-031-220 1217.

Corbet, Professor Philip Steven, BSc, PhD, DSc, ScD, FIBiol, FESC, FRSE, FRSA. Biologist and Author; Professor of Zoology, Dundee University, 1980-90 (Head, Department of Biological Sciences, 1983-86); Professor Emeritus, since 1990; b. 21.5.29, Kuala Lumpur, Malaysia; m., Mary Elizabeth Canvin; 1 d. by pr. m. Educ. Dauntsey's School, Wiltshire; Reading University; Gonville and Caius College, Cambridge. Zoologist, East African Fisheries Research Organisation, Jinja, Uganda, 1954-57; Entomologist: East African Virus Research Organisation, Entebbe, Uganda, 1957-62; Entomology Research Institute, Canada Department of Agriculture, Ottawa, 1962-67; Director, Research Institute, Canada Department of Agriculture, Belleville, Ontario, 1967-71; Professor and Chairman, Department of Biology, Waterloo University, Ontario, 1971-74; Professor and

Director, Joint Centre for Environmental Sciences, Canterbury University and Lincoln College, New Zealand, 1974-78; Professor, Department of Zoology, Canterbury University, New Zealand, 1978-80. Entomological Society of Canada: President, 1971, Gold Medal, 1974, Fellow, 1976; Commonwealth Visiting Professor, Cambridge University, 1979-80; Member, New Zealand Government Independent Fact-Finding Group on Nuclear Energy, 1975-77; Member, New Zealand Environmental Council, 1976-79; Member, Committee for Scotland, Nature Conservancy Council, 1986-90; Societas Internationalis Odonatologica, Member of Honour, 1985; President, British Dragonfly Society, since 1983. Publications: A Biology of Dragonflies, 1962; research papers on medical entomology and pest management. Recreations: natural history; music. Address: (h.) 29 Mentone Terrace, Edinburgh EH9 2DF; T.-031-662 4696.

Corke, Donald Stevenson, BA, LLB. Advocate; b. 5.8.59, Salisbury (now Harare); m., Helen Louise White. Educ. Mount Pleasant School, Salisbury; Cape Town University; Witwatersrand University. National Service, Rhodesia, 1978-79; admitted as Advocate, Supreme Court of South Africa, 1985; Member, Faculty of Advocates (Scotland), since 1988 Address: (h.) 43 Marchmont Crescent, Edinburgh, EH9 1HF; T.-031-228 6263.

Cormack, Professor Richard Melville, MA, BSc, DipMathStat, PhD, FRSE. Professor of Statistics, St. Andrews University, since 1972; b. 12.3.35, Glasgow; m., Edith Whittaker. Educ. Glasgow Academy; Cambridge University; London University (External); Aberdeen University. Lecturer in Statistics, Aberdeen University, 1956-66; Assistant Professor, University of Washington, 1964-65; Senior Lecturer, Edinburgh University, 1966-72. Honorary Secretary, Biometric Society (British Region), 1970-77, President, 1990-92; President (International), Biometric Society, 1980-81; Member, Natural Environment Research Council, 1983-89; Member, Scottish Universities Council on Entrance, 1982-89; Member, Science Board, Nature Conservancy Council, Scotland, 1991-92. Publications: The Statistical Argument; Sampling Biological Populations (Editor), Spatial and Temporal Analysis in Ecology (Editor). Recreations: photography; music; hill-walking. Address: (h.) 58 Buchanan Gardens, St. Andrews, Fife; T.-0334 76970.

Cormie, James E.D., BL. Chief Executive and Director of Administration and Legal Services, Perth and Kinross District Council, since 1981; b. 30.7.30, Edinburgh; m., Stella Anne Moir; 1 s.; 1 d. Educ. Robert Gordon's College, Aberdeen; Aberdeen University. Solicitor, private practice, 1953-55; Solicitor, Aberdeen Town Council, 1955-66; Depute Town Clerk, Perth, 1966-75; Director of Administration and Legal Services, Perth and Kinross District, 1975-81. Clerk to Lieutenancy, Perth and Kinross; Company Secretary: Perth and Kinross Recreational Facilities Ltd., Perth Festival of the Arts Ltd., Bowerswell Memorial Homes (Perth) Ltd.; Member, Society of High Constables of the City of Perth; Member, Secretary of State's Advisory Committee on Scotland's Travelling People. Recreations: photography and film-making; golf; hill-walking. Address: (b.) Council Building, 2 High Street, Perth, PH1 5PH; T.-0738 39911.

Corner, David John, BA (Oxon), FRHS. Secretary, St. Andrews University, since 1991; Honorary Lecturer, Department of Mediaeval History, St. Andrews University, since 1991; b. 24.10.47, Birmingham; m., Carol Ann; 2 s. Educ. King Edward VI Grammar School, Aston, Birmingham; Worcester College, Oxford. Prize Fellow, Magdalen College, Oxford, 1972-75; Lecturer, Department of Mediaeval History, St. Andrews University, 1975-91. Governor, Newbattle Abbey College, since 1991; President, St. Andrews Association of University Teachers, 1985-88. Recreations: cinema; sport. Address: St. Andrews University,

College Gate, North Street, St. Andrews, KY16 9AJ; T.-0334 76161.

Corner, Douglas Robertson, FIB (Scot). General Manager, Retail Banking West, Clydesdale Bank PLC, since 1990; b. 19.5.44, Glasgow; m., Alice Cairns; 1 s.; 1 d. Educ. Duncanrig Secondary School, East Kilbride. Royal Bank of Scotland, 1962-68; Rolls-Royce Ltd., 1968-69; Clydesdale Bank, since 1969. Director, Quarriers Homes; Member, Council, Institute of Bankers in Scotland; Treasurer, The Prince's Trust (Strathclyde); Director, Glasgow Chamber of Commerce. Recreations: golf; bowls; walking. Address: (b.) 30 St. Vincent Place, Glasgow, G1 2HZ; T.-041-248 7070.

Cornish, Melvyn David, BSc, PGCE. Deputy Secretary, Edinburgh University, since 1991; b. 29.6.48, Leighton Buzzard; m., Eileen Joyce Easterbrook; 1 s.; 1 d. Educ. Cedars Grammar School, Leighton Buzzard; Leicester University. Chemistry Teacher, Jamaica and Cumbria, 1970-73; Administrator, Leicester Polytechnic, 1973-78, Senior Administrative Officer, Assistant Secretary, Director of Planning, Edinburgh University, 1978-91. Recreations: walking; cinema; travel; family. Address: (b.) Old College, South Bridge, Edinburgh; T.-031-650 2136.

Cornwell, Professor John Francis, PhD, BSc, DIC, ARCS, FRSE. Professor of Theoretical Physics, St. Andrews University, since 1979 (Chairman, Physics Department, 1984-85); b. 28.1.37, London; m., Elizabeth Margaret Burfitt; 2 d. Educ. Ealing Grammar School; Imperial College, London. Lecturer in Applied Mathematics, Leeds University, 1961-67; St. Andrews University: Lecturer in Theoretical Physics, 1967-73, Reader, 1973-79. Publications: Group Theory in Physics, three volumes, 1984, 1989; Group Theory and Electronic Energy Bands in Solids, 1969. Recreations: sailing; hill-walking; tennis; badminton; golf. Address: (b.) Department of Physics and Astronomy, St. Andrews University, North Haugh, St. Andrews, Fife, KY16 9SS; T.-0334 76161.

Cornwell, Professor Keith, BSc, PhD, CEng, FIMechE. Professor and Head, Department of Mechanical Engineering, Heriot-Watt University, since 1989; b. 4.4.42, Abingdon; m., Sheila Joan Mott; 1 s.; 1 d. Educ. City University, London. Research Fellow, then Lecturer, Middlesex Polytechnic; Lecturer, Heriot-Watt University. Publications: The Flow of Heat; numerous journal papers. Recreations: walking; old cars. Address: (h.) 33 Park Avenue, Duddingston, Edinburgh, EH15 1JS.

Corrie, John Alexander. Farmer; Chairman, Scottish Transport Users Consultative Committee, since 1989; Member, Central Transport Consultative Committee, since 1989; Director, Ayrshire Agricultural Society, since 1990; Council Member, Royal Agricultural Society of England, since 1991; b. 1935; m.; 1 s.; 2 d. Educ. Kirkcudbright Academy; George Watson's College, Edinburgh; Lincoln Agricultural College, New Zealand. Commissioned from the ranks, New Zealand Army, 1957; National Chairman, Scottish Young Conservatives, 1964; Council Member, National Farmers Union of Scotland, 1965; Chairman, Kirkcudbright Conservative Association, 1966; Lecturer, British Wool Marketing Board, 1967-74, and Agricultural Training Board, 1969-74; MP (Conservative), Bute and North Ayrshire, 1974-83, North Cunninghame, 1983-87; appointed Scottish Conservative spokesman on education, 1974; Member, European Parliament, 1975 and 1977-79; Vice President, EEC/Turkey Committee; appointed Opposition Whip, 1975 (resigned, 1976); elected to Council, Belted Galloway Cattle Society, 1978; PPS to Secretary of State for Scotland, 1979-81; elected to Council, National Cattle Breeders Association, 1979; introduced private member's Bill on abortion law reform, 1979; Chairman, Scottish

Conservative Backbench Committee, 1981; elected Leader, Conservative Group on Scottish Affairs, 1982; Member, Council of Europe, 1983-87; Member, Western European Union (Defence Committee), 1983-87; Industry Fellowship with Conoco Oil, 1987; Vice Chairman, FAO Committee in Rome for Council of Europe; awarded Wilberforce Plaque for humane work, 1981; farms family farm in Kirkcudbright. Address: (h.) Park of Tongland, Kirkcudbright, DG6 4NE.

Corsar, Charles Herbert Kenneth, LVO, OBE, TD, JP, DL, MA. Farmer, since 1953; Secretary for Scotland, Duke of Edinburgh's Award, 1966-87; b. 13.5.26, Edinburgh; m., Mary Drummond Buchanan-Smith (see Mary Drummond Corsar); 2 s.; 2 d. Educ. Merchiston Castle; King's College, Cambridge. Commissioned, The Royal Scots TA, 1948; commanded 8/9 Bn.,The Royal Scots TA, 1964-67; Edinburgh and Heriot-Watt Universities OTC, 1967-72; TA Colonel, 1972-75; Hon. ADC to The Queen, 1977-81; Honorary Colonel, 1/52 Lowland Volunteers, 1975-87; Chairman, Lowland TA and VR Association, 1984-87; Zone Commissioner, Home Defence, East of Scotland; County Councillor, Midlothian, 1958-67; Deputy Lieutenant, Midlothian; Vice President, The Boys Brigade, 1970-91 and President, Edinburgh Bn., Boys Brigade, 1969-87 (Hon. President, Edinburgh Bn., since 1987); Chairman, Scottish Standing Conference of Voluntary Youth Organisations, 1973-78; Governor: Merchiston Castle School, Clifton Hall School; Chairman, Wellington List D School, 1978-84; Chairman, Earl Haig Fund Scotland, 1984-90; Secretary, Royal Jubilee and Princes' Trusts (Lothian and Borders); Member, Scottish Sports Council, 1972-75; Elder, Church of Scotland, since 1956. Recreations: gardening; bee-keeping; shooting. Address: (h.) Burg, Torloisk, Ulva Ferry, Isle of Mull PA74 6NH; T.-Ulva Ferry 289; 11 Ainslie Place, Edinburgh, EH3 6AS; T.-031-225 6318.

Corsar, The Hon. Mrs Mary Drummond, MA. Chairman, Women's Royal Voluntary Service, since 1988 (Vice Chairman, 1984-88); Chairman Scotland, WRVS, 1981-88; b. 8.7.27, Edinburgh; m., Colonel Charles H.K. Corsar (qv); 2 s.; 2 d. Educ. Westbourne, Glasgow; St. Denis, Edinburgh; Edinburgh University. Midlothian Girl Guides: Secretary, 1951-66, County Commissioner, 1966-72; Deputy Chief Commissioner, Girl Guides Scotland, 1972-77; Member: Parole Board for Scotland, 1982-89; Executive Committee, Trefoil Centre, since 1975; Visiting Committee, Glenochil Detention Centre, since 1976; Management Committee, Church of Scotland Youth Centre, Carberry, 1976-82; Governor, Fettes College; Member of Convocation, Heriot Watt University. Recreation: hill-walking. Address: Burg, Torloisk, Ulva Ferry, Isle of Mull, PA74 6NH; T.-068 85 289.

Coull, Professor Alexander, BSc, PhD, CEng, FRSE, FICE, FIStructE, DSc. Regius Professor of Civil Engineering, Glasgow University, since 1977; b. 20.6.31, Peterhead; m., Frances Bruce Moir; 1 s.; 2 d. Educ. Peterhead Academy; Aberdeen University. Research Assistant, MIT, USA, 1955; Structural Engineer, English Electric Co. Ltd., 1955-57; Lecturer in Engineering, Aberdeen University, 1957-62; Lecturer in Civil Engineering, Southampton University, 1962-66; Professor of Structural Engineering, Strathclyde University, 1967-76. Chairman, Clyde Estuary Amenity Council, 1981-86; awarded Telford Premium, 1973, and Trevithick Premium, 1974, Institution of Civil Engineers. Publications: Tall Buildings, 1967; Fundamentals of Structural Theory, 1972; Tall Building Structures, 1991. Recreations: golf; hill-walking; skiing. Address: (h.) 11 Blackwood Road, Milngavie, Glasgow, G62 7LB; T.-041-956 1655.

Coull, James West. Honorary Sheriff, Dundee, since 1971; b. 30.5.14, Dundee; m., Jean Fairley; 1 s.; 1 d. Educ. Morgan Academy, Dundee; St. Andrews University. Solicitor (retired)

and Notary Public; Burgh Prosecutor, Carnoustie, 1963-75; Dean, Faculty of Procurators and Solicitors in Dundee, 1971-73. Recreations: gardening; watercolour painting. Address: (h.) 2A Guthrie Street, Carnoustie, Angus.

Coull, Rev. Morris Cowper, BD. Minister, Hillington Park Parish Church, Glasgow, since 1983; b. 12.4.41, Largs; m., Ann Duthie; 1 s.; 1 d. Educ. Allan Glen's School; Newbattle Abbey College; Glasgow University; Trinity College. Assistant Minister, Bearsden South Parish Church, 1972-74; Minister, New Cumnock (Old) Parish Church, 1974-83. Address: 61 Ralston Avenue, Glasgow, G52; T.-041-882 7000.

Coulsfield, Hon. Lord (John Taylor Cameron), QC, BA, LLB. Senator of the College of Justice, since 1987; b. 24.4.34, Dundee; m., Bridget Deirdre Sloan. Educ. Fettes College; Corpus Christi College, Oxford; Edinburgh University. Admitted to Faculty of Advocates, 1960; Queen's Counsel, 1973; Lecturer in Public Law, Edinburgh University, 1960-64; Advocate Depute, 1977-80; Keeper of the Advocates Library, 1977-87; Chairman, Medical Appeal Tribunals, 1985-87; Judge of the Appeal Courts of Jersey and Guernsey, 1986-87

Coulthard, William George, LLB. Solicitor, since 1971; Honorary Sheriff, since 1988; b. 13.3.48, Whitehaven; m., Fiona Jane McQueen; 1 s.; 2 d. Educ. Glasgow Academy; Glasgow University. Partner in legal firm, since 1974; Dean, Faculty of Procurators, Stewartry of Kirkcudbright, 1986-88; Chairman, Castle Douglas High School Board, since 1990. Recreations: golf; squash; hill-running. Address: (h.) Netherby, Castle Douglas, DG7 1BA; T.-0556 2965.

Courtney, Professor James McNiven, BSc, PhD, Dr sc nat, ARCST, CChem, FRSC, FPRI. Professor, Bioengineering Unit, Strathclyde University, since 1989 (Reader, 1986-89, Senior Lecturer, 1981-86); Visiting Professor, University of Rostock, Germany, since 1978; b. 25.3.40, Glasgow; m., Ellen Miller Courtney; 2 s.; 1 d. Educ. Whitehill Senior Secondary School; Royal College of Science and Technology; Strathclyde University. Rubber technologist: MacLellan Rubber Ltd., Glasgow, 1962-65, Uniroyal Ltd., Dumfries, 1965-66; Lecturer, Bioengineering Unit, Strathclyde University, 1969-81. Recreation: football supporter (Glasgow Rangers). Address: (b.) Strathclyde University, Bioengineering Unit, 106 Rottenrow, Glasgow; T.-041-552 4400.

Cousin, (David) Alastair (Henry), BVMS, MRCVS, DBR, JP. Partner, veterinary practice, Kintyre, since 1972; Honorary Sheriff, Campbeltown Sheriff Court, since 1990; b. 19.4.44, Kincardine on Forth; m., Anne Macleod; 1 s.; 1 d. Educ. Balfron High School; Glasgow University; Liverpool University. Veterinary practice, Campbeltown: Veterinary Assistant, 1966, Junior Partner, 1972, Senior Partner, 1982. Recreations: sailing; shooting; gardening; music. Address: (h.) Southpark, Kilkerran Road, Campbeltown; T.-0586 553108.

Coutts, Findlay Macrury, MA, LLB. Director of Central Services, Dunfermline District Council, since 1991 (Director of Administration, 1975-91); b. 16.3.43, Aberdeen; m., Christine; 1 s.; 1 d. Educ. Aberdeen Grammar School; Aberdeen University. Law apprentice/Legal Assistant, Hamilton Town Council, 1966-69; Town Clerk, Cupar, 1969-75. Recreations: good food; golf; town twinning. Address: (b.) City Chambers, Dunfermline; T.-Dunfermline 722711.

Coutts, Brigadier Francis Henderson, CBE, DL. Trustee, The Seagull Trust; b. 8.7.18, Glasgow; m., Morag Russell Fullerton; 2 d. Educ. Glasgow Academy; Army Staff College, Camberley. Metropolitan Police, 1937-40; in the ranks,

London Scottish, 1940-41; commissioned King's Own Scottish Borderers, 1941-73; Colonel, 1970-80. General Secretary, Royal British Legion Scotland and Earl Haig Fund Scotland, 1973-83; President, Scottish Rugby Union, 1977-78; Elder, Colinton Parish Church; Hon. Secretary, Friends of St. Andrew's, Jerusalem; Hon. President, Legion Housing Scotland. Recreations: gardening; golf; Grouse; piping. Address: (h.) 5 Gillsland Road, Edinburgh, EH10 5BW; T.-031-337 4920.

Coutts, Rev. Fred, MA, BD. Hospital Chaplain, Foresterhill Hospitals Unit, Aberdeen, since 1989; b. 13.1.47, Forfar; m., Mary Lawson Fraser Gill; 2 s.; 1 d. Educ. Brechin High School; Dollar Academy; St. Andrews University; Edinburgh University. Assistant Minister, Linwood Parish Church, 1972-74; Minister: Buckie North, 1974-84, Mastrick, Aberdeen, 1984-89. Chairman: Buckie Community Council, 1981-83, Moray Firth Community Radio Association, 1982-83. Recreations: music; photography; home computing. Address: 9A Millburn Street, Aberdeen, AB1 2SS; T.-Aberdeen 583805.

Coutts, Herbert, SBStJ, AMA, FMA, FSAScot. City Curator, Edinburgh City Museums and Art Galleries, since 1973; b. 9.3.44, Dundee; m., Angela E.M. Smith; 1 s.; 3 d. Educ. Morgan Academy, Dundee. Assistant Keeper of Antiquities and Bygones, Dundee City Museums, 1965-68; Keeper, 1968-71; Superintendent, Edinburgh City Museums, 1971-73; Vice-President, Museum Assistants Group, 1969-70; Member: Government Committee on future of Scotland's National Museums and Galleries, 1979-80; Council, Museums Association, 1977-78, 1987-88; Council, Society of Antiquaries of Scotland, 1981-82; Board, Scottish Museums Council, 1985-88; Museums Adviser, COSLA, 1985-90; Member, Paxton House Trust, since 1988; Member, East Lothian Community Development Trust, since 1989. Contested Angus South (Lab), 1970. Publications: Ancient Monuments of Tayside; Tayside Before History; Edinburgh: An Illustrated History; Gold of the Pharaohs (Editor); Dinosaurs Alive! (Editor); Sweat of the Sun – Gold of Peru (Editor). Recreations: family; gardening; opera; writing; reading; walking. Address: (h.) Kirkhill House, Queen's road, Dunbar, EH42 1LN; T.-0368 63113.

Coutts, John R.T., BSc, PhD. Reader in Obstetrics and Gynaecology/Reproductive Medicine, Glasgow University, since 1987; b. 10.7.41, Dundee; m., Marjory R.B.; 1 s.; 2 d. Educ. Morgan Academy, Dundee; St. Andrews University. Dundee University: Research Fellow in Obstetrics and Gynaecology, 1966-69, Honorary Lecturer in Obstetrics and Gynaecology, 1969-70; Lecturer, then Senior Lecturer, Glasgow University, 1970-87. Publications: The Functional Morphology of the Human Ovary (Editor); many journal articles. Recreations: squash; bowling. Address: (b.) Department of Obstetrics and Gynaecology, Glasgow Royal Infirmary, 10 Alexandra Parade, Glasgow; T.-041-552 3535.

Coutts, Norman Alexander, BSc, MB, ChB, FRCP(Glas), FRCP(Edin), FRCP(Lond). Consultant Paediatrician, Argyll and Clyde Health Board, since 1969; Honorary Senior Clinical Lecturer, Paediatrics, Glasgow University, since 1980; b. 20.1.33, Glasgow; m., Margaret Sargeant; 2 s.; 1 d. Educ. Woodside School, Glasgow; Glasgow University. House Officer posts, Glasgow, 1958-59; Captain, RAMC, 1959-61; Registrar posts, Lincoln, Leeds, York and Glasgow, 1961-69. Member of Council, British Paediatric Association, 1985-88. Recreations: walking; philately. Address: (h.) 1 Elm Gardens, Bearsden, Glasgow, G61 3BH; T.-041-942 7194.

Coutts, T(homas) Gordon, MA, LLB, QC. Queen's Counsel, since 1973; Chairman, VAT Tribunals, since 1990; Temporary Judge, Court of Session, since 1991; b. 5.7.33, Aberdeen; m., Winifred K. Scott; 1 s.; 1 d. Educ. Aberdeen

Grammar School; Aberdeen University. Advocate, 1959; Chairman, Industrial Tribunals, 1972; Chairman, Medical Appeal Tribunals, 1984. Recreations: golf; stamp collecting. Address: (h.) 6 Heriot Row, Edinburgh.

Coventry, Molly Jean, RGN, SCM, RNT, BA. Director of Nurse Education, Glasgow South College of Nursing, since 1985; b. 16.5.35, Glasgow. Educ. Largs Higher Grade School; Ardrossan Academy; Open University. General nurse training, Victoria Infirmary, 1953-56; qualified as midwife, 1957; Director of Nurse Education, Glasgow South East College of Nursing and Midwifery, 1977-85. Scottish Representative, Royal College of Nursing Association of Nurse Education, 1976-80; Member, National Nursing and Midwifery Advisory Committee; elected Member, National Board for Nursing, Midwifery and Health Visiting for Scotland. Recreations: singing; bird-watching; woodwork; swimming; photography; travel. Address: (b.) South College of Nursing, 2001 Govan Road, Glasgow, G51; T.-041-445 2466, Ext. 4276.

Cowan, Brigadier Colin Hunter, CBE, MA, FRSA, CEng, MICE. Chief Executive, Cumbernauld Development Corporation, 1970-85; b. 16.10.20, Edinburgh; m., 1, Elizabeth Williamson (deceased); 2 s.; 1 d.; 2, Mrs Janet Burnett. Educ. Wellington College; Trinity College, Cambridge. Commissioned, Royal Engineers, 1940; service in India and Burma, Royal Bombay Sappers and Miners, 1942-46; staff and regimental appointments, UK and Malta, 1951-60; commanded Field Engineer Regiment, Germany, 1960-63; Defence Adviser, UK Mission to UNO, New York, 1964-66; Chief Staff Officer to Engineer-in-Chief (Army), Ministry of Defence, 1966-68; Brigadier, Engineer Plans (Army), Ministry of Defence, 1968-70. Recreations: hill-walking; photography; music. Address: (h.) 12B Greenhill Gardens, Edinburgh, EH10 4BW; T.-031-447 9768.

Cowan, David Lockhart, MB, ChB, FRCSEdin. Consultant Otolaryngologist, City Hospital, Royal Hospital for Sick Children and Western General Hospital, Edinburgh, since 1974; Honorary Senior Lecturer, Edinburgh University; b. 30.6.41, Edinburgh; m., Eileen M. Masterton; 3 s.; 1 d. Educ. George Watson's College, Edinburgh; Trinity College, Glenalmond; Edinburgh University. Scottish Representative, Council, British Association of Otolaryngologists. Publications: Logan Turner's Diseases of the Ear, Nose and Throat (Co-author); Paediatric Otolaryngology (Co-author). Recreations: golf; all sport. Address: (h.) 28 Braid Hills Road, Edinburgh, EH10 6HY; T.-031-447 3424.

Cowan, John, MBE, BSc (Hons), MSc, PhD, DEng, FIStructE, FEIS. Director, Open University in Scotland, since 1987 (Professor of Engineering Education, Heriot Watt University, 1982-87); b. 19.3.32, Glasgow; m., Audrey Walker Cowan; 3 s.; 1 d. Educ. High School of Glasgow; Edinburgh University; Heriot-Watt University. Design engineer, Blyth & Blyth, Edinburgh, 1952-64; joined Heriot-Watt College as Lecturer, 1964; awards, Institution of Structural Engineers and Czech Ministry of Higher Education, for work in engineering education research. Recreations: reading; music; photography. Address: (b.) 60 Melville Street, Edinburgh, EH3 7HF; T.-031-226 3851.

Cowan, Margaret Morton (Lady Cowan), MA, JP. National Trust for Scotland: Member, Council, since 1989; Member, Executive Committee, since 1991; Member, Scottish Advisory Committee, British Council, since 1991; b. 4.11.33, Newmilns; m., Sir Robert Cowan (qv); 2 d. Educ. St. George's School for Girls, Edinburgh; Edinburgh University. British Petroleum Company, 1955-59; Teacher, West Midlands Education Authority, 1965-76; Consultant and Lecturer in Use of Language, Hong Kong, 1976-81. Member, Justice of the Peace Committee, Inverness, since

1985. Address: (h.) The Old Manse, Farr, Inverness-shire, IV1 2XA; T.-080 83 209.

Cowan, Sir Robert, KB, LLD, MA. Chairman, Highlands and Islands Enterprise, since 1991 (Chairman, Highlands and Islands Development Board, 1982-91); Board Member, Scottish Development Agency, 1982-91; Member, General Advisory Council, BBC; Member, Court, Aberdeen University; Member, Scottish Post Office Board; Governor, Napier College, Edinburgh; b. 27.7.32, Edinburgh; m., Margaret Morton Dewar (see Margaret Morton Cowan); 2 d. Educ. Edinburgh Academy; Edinburgh University. Fisons Ltd., 1958-62; Wolsey Ltd., 1962-65; PA Management Consultants Ltd., 1965-82. Hon. LLD, Aberdeen University, 1987; Hon. DUniv, Stirling University. Recreations: gardening; sailing. Address: (h.) The Old Manse, Farr, Inverness-shire; T.-08083 209.

Cowe, Alan Wilson, MA, LLB. Secretary and Clerk, Church of Scotland General Trustees, since 1964; b. 9.8.38, Kelso; m., Agnes Cunningham Dick. Educ. Dunfermline High School; Edinburgh University. Law apprentice, Simpson Kinmont & Maxwell, WS, Edinburgh; Assistant to Secretary, Church of Scotland General Trustees, 1963-64. Recreations: long-distance running; hill-walking. Address: (b.) 121 George Street, Edinburgh; T.-031-225 5722.

Cowie, Professor John McKenzie Grant, BSc, PhD, DSc, CChem, FRSC, FRSE. Professor of Chemistry of Materials, Heriot-Watt University, since 1988 (Professor of Chemistry, Stirling University, 1973-88); b. 31.5.33, Edinburgh; m., Agnes Neilson Campbell; 1 s.; 1 d. Educ. Royal High School, Edinburgh; Edinburgh University. Assistant Lecturer, Edinburgh University, 1956-58; Research Officer, National Research Council of Canada, Ottawa, 1958-67; Lecturer, Essex University, 1967-69; Senior Lecturer, Stirling University, 1969-73. Staff Assessor, Bangladesh Agricultural College; Vice Chairman, Scottish Spinal Cord Injury Association; Hon. President, Scottish Council on Disability (Stirling District); Vice Chairman, Scottish Council on Disability, 1989-90; Hon. President, Council of Social Services (Stirling District). Recreations: reading; painting; listening to music. Address: (h.) Traquair, 50 Back Road, Dollar, Clackmannanshire; T.-Dollar 42031.

Cowie, Hon. Lord (William Lorn Kerr Cowie), MA (Cantab), LLB (Glas). Senator of the College of Justice in Scotland, since 1977; b. 1.6.26, Glasgow; m., Camilla Henrietta Grizel Hoyle; 2 s.; 2 d. Educ. Fettes College, Edinburgh; Clare College, Cambridge; Glasgow University. RNVR, 1944-47 (Sub. Lt.); Member, Faculty of Advocates, 1952; QC, 1967. Scottish rugby internationalist, 1953. Recreation: fishing. Address: (h.) 20 Blacket Place, Edinburgh; T.-031-667 8238.

Cowley of Innerwick, Col. Victor Charles Vereker, TD, JP, DL. Land Owner and Farmer; b. 4.4.18, Glasgow; m., Moyra McClure; 1 s.; 2 d. Educ. St. Mary's, Melrose; Merchiston Castle School. Young master printer, 1937; commissioned, RATA, 1939; served France, North Africa, Sicily, Italy, Burma, Indo China; Col. Depute CRA 51st Highland Division; Chairman, Brownlie Scandrett and Graham Ltd. (retired 1960); Vice Convener, East Lothian County Council, 1973; Regional Councillor, Lothian, 1975; Commissioner of Income Tax, East Lothian, 1965-87. Recreations: shooting; golf. Address: Crowhill, Innerwick, Dunbar, EH42 1QT; T.-036 84 279.

Cowpe, Jonathan George, BDS (Hons), FDSRCS Ed, PhD. Senior Lecturer in Dental Surgery, Dundee University, since 1985; Honorary Consultant in Oral Surgery, since 1985; Head, Department of Dental Surgery, since 1990; b. 23.4.52, Manchester; m., Marianne; 1 s.; 1 d. Educ. Cheltenham

College; Manchester University. Resident House Officer in Oral Surgery, Manchester Dental Hospital, 1975-76; Resident Senior House Officer in Oral Surgery, Bolton General Hospital, 1976-78; Dundee Dental Hospital: Registrar in Oral Surgery, 1978-80, Lecturer and Honorary Senior Registrar in Oral Surgery, 1980-84. Toller Research Prize, 1981; Howard Elder Research Prize, 1983; President, Dundee Dental Club, 1985-86. Recreations: golf; squash; hill-walking. Address: (h.) 13 Westacres Drive, Wormit, Fife.

Cox, Gilbert Kirkwood, DL. General Manager Scotland, Associated Perforators & Weavers Ltd., since 1971; Director/Trustee, Airdrie Savings Bank, since 1987 (Vice President, 1992); b. 24.8.35, Chapelhall, Airdrie; m., Marjory Moir Ross Taylor; 2 s.; 1 d. Educ. Airdrie Academy. National Coal Board, 1953-63; David A. McPhail & Sons Ltd., 1963-68; D.A. Monteith Holdings, 1968-71. Deputy Lieutenant, Lanarkshire; founder Member and Past President, Monklands Rotary Club; Member, Scottish Kidney Research Fund. Recreations: golf; gardening; walking. Address: (h.) Bedford House, Commonhead Street, Airdrie, ML6 6NS; T.-0236 63331.

Coyle, Very Rev. Mgr. Francis Coyle, JCL. Parish Priest, St. Philomena's, Glasgow; b. 2.8.24, Glasgow. Educ. St. Aloysius College, Glasgow; St. Peter's College, Bearsden; Gregorian University, Rome. Assistant Priest, St. Andrew's Cathedral, 1949-52; Secretary, Archdiocese of Glasgow, 1952-68; Personal Secretary, Archbishop Scanlan, 1968-72; Assistant Priest, St. Charles, 1952-71; Chancellor, Archdiocese of Glasgow, 1971-74; Catholic Representative, Strathclyde Region Education Committee, 1974-83; Vice President, Catholic Education Commission, 1974-83. Chaplain of Honour to the Pope, 1972; JP, Glasgow, 1980. Recreations: golf; photography. Address: St. Philomena's, 1255 Royston Road, Glasgow, G33; T.-041-770 4237.

Coyne, Peter, MBA, ARICS. Regional Manager, British Waterways in Scotland, since 1988; b. 1955, Milngavie; m., Janice Paterson; 2 s.; 1 d. Educ. St. Aloysius College, Glasgow; Paisley College; Glasgow University. Valuation Surveyor: William O'Neil & Partners, Glasgow, 1972, Glasgow Corporation Estates, 1974; Estate Surveyor, British Waterways (Scotland), 1976. Director, The Nolly Company, since 1990. Recreations: golf; hill-walking. Address: (h.) 96 Beechwood Drive, Glasgow, G11; T.-041-334 3153.

Cracknell, Professor Arthur Philip, MA, MSc, DPhil, CPhys, FInstP, FRSE. Professor of Theoretical Physics, Dundee University, since 1978; b. 18.5.40, Ilford; m., Margaret Florence Grant; 1 s.; 2 d. Educ. Chigwell School; Pembroke College, Cambridge; Queen's College, Oxford. Lecturer in Physics: University of Singapore, 1964-67, University of Essex, 1967-70; Senior Lecturer in Physics, then Reader, Dundee University, 1970-78. Editor, International Journal of Remote Sensing. Publications: 20 books; 200 scientific papers. Address: (b.) Dundee University, Dundee, DD1 4HN; T.-0382 23181.

Cracknell, (William) Martin. Chief Executive, Glenrothes Development Corporation, since 1976; b. 24.6.29, Leicester; m., Gillian Goatcher; 2 s.; 2 d. Educ. St. Edwards School, Oxford; Royal Military Academy, Sandhurst. Army, Royal Green Jackets, 1947-69; British Printing Industries Federation, 1969-76. Board Member, Glenrothes Enterprise Trust, 1983-89; Member, Executive, Scottish Council (Development and Industry), 1984-89; Chairman, Glenrothes University Industry Dining Club; Chairman, Committee for Scotland, German Chamber of Industry and Commerce in the UK. Address: (b.) Carleton House, Markinch, Glenrothes, Fife KY7 6AH; T.-0592 754343.

Craig, Alex. R., BSc. Headmaster, Hillhead High School, Glasgow, since 1976; b. 27.10.28, Cleland; m., Nessie; 2 s.; 1 d. Educ. Wishaw High School; Glasgow University. Secretary, Wishaw Bowling Club. Recreations: bowling; photography; DIY. Address: (b.) Hillhead High School, Oakfield Avenue, Glasgow; T.-041-339 8200.

Craig, Emeritus Professor Gordon Younger, BSc, PhD, CGeol, FRSE. Emeritus Professor of Geology, Edinburgh University, since 1984; President, International Commission on the History of the Geological Sciences, 1984-89; b. 17.1.25, Milngavie; m., Mary Thornton; 2 s. Educ. Hillhead High School; Bearsden Academy; Glasgow University; Edinburgh University. Joined Edinburgh University as Lecturer, 1947; James Hutton Professor of Geology, 1967-84. President, Edinburgh Geological Society, 1967-69; Clough Medal, Edinburgh Geological Society, 1987; History of Geology Division Award, Geological Society of America, 1990. Publications: Geology of Scotland (Editor), 1991 (3rd ed.); James Hutton: The Lost Drawings (Co-author), 1977; A Geological Miscellany (Co-author), 1982. Recreations: golf; gardening. Address: (h.) 14 Kevock Road, Lasswade, Edinburgh, EH18 1HT; T. 031-663 8275.

Craig, James, OBE, MA, LLB, WS, NP. Retired Solicitor; b. 15.9.14, Ardrossan; m., Alice Norris Leith; 1 s.; 1 d. Educ. Aberdeen Grammar School; Aberdeen University. Qualified as Solicitor, 1938; Royal Navy and Fleet Air Arm (Lt. Cmdr., RNVR); Partner, R. Addison Smith & Co., WS, Edinburgh, 1952-82; former Assistant Registrar of Friendly Societies for Scotland; former Assistant Certification Officer for Trade Unions and Employers Associations for Scotland; former Treasurer, HM Commissioners Trust Funds for Queen Victoria School, Dunblane; former Secretary and Treasurer, Scottish Naval, Military and Air Force Veterans Residences; Consultant, Balfour & Manson, Solicitors, Edinburgh, 1982-84. Recreations: now only golf and travel. Address: (h.) 12 Royal Circus, Edinburgh; T.-031-226 6432.

Craig, James Leith Johnstone, MA, LLB, WS. Solicitor; Assistant Registrar of Friendly Societies for Scotland, since 1981; Assistant Certification Officer for Trade Unions and Employers Associations for Scotland, since 1980; b. 23.5.44, Aberdeen; m., Susan Mary McDowell; 1 s.; 1 d. Educ. George Watson's College; Edinburgh University. Apprentice, W. & J. Burness, WS, Edinburgh, 1966-68; Assistant, A. & J.L. Innes, Solicitors, Kirkcaldy, 1968-71; Partner, R. Addison Smith & Co., WS, Edinburgh, 1972-82; Partner, Balfour & Manson, Solicitors, Edinburgh, since 1982. Recreations: golf; skiing. Address: (b.) 58 Frederick Street, Edinburgh; T.-031-225 8291.

Craig, John Alexander, BSc, DipTP, MICE. Head, Department of Town and Country Planning, Edinburgh College of Art/Heriot-Watt University, 1978-90; Dean, Faculty of Environmental Studies, Heriot-Watt University, 1983-86; b. 18.5.32, Warrington, Lancashire; m., Jessie Crawford Inglis; 1 s.; 2 d. Educ. Invergordon Academy; Glasgow University; Edinburgh College of Art. National Service, RAF, 1955-57; Structural Engineer, P. & W. McLellan Ltd., Glasgow, 1957-59; Assistant Civil Engineer: Cumbernauld Development Corporation, 1959-63; Livingston Development Corporation, 1963-66; Lecturer, Department of Town and Country Planning, Edinburgh College of Art, 1966-78; private practice as Consultant Civil Engineer, 1968-77; part-time Lecturer, Coatbridge Technical College, 1957-63; Examiner, Glasgow and West of Scotland Committee for Technical Education, 1961-63; Member, Executive Committee, Scottish Branch, RTPI, 1979-83. Recreations: gardening; DIY house and car maintenance; photography. Address: (h.) 1 Newland Avenue, Bathgate, West Lothian, EH48 1EE; T.-0506 53824.

Craig, John Garrioch, TD. Director, Craig Caledonian Company Limited, since 1975; Chairman, Epilepsy Association of Scotland, since 1987; b. 26.5.34, Glasgow; m., Caroline Bourke Maclean; 2 s.; 1 d. Educ. Loretto; Royal College of Science and Technology. Commissioned, The Cameronians (Scottish Rifles), 1952-54; TA, 1954-67; Director, Colvilles Ltd., 1967-68; Group Manager, then Divisional Manager, British Steel Corporation, 1968-78. Director, Merchants House of Glasgow, since 1978; Director, Scottish United Investors plc, since 1981; Chairman, Paisley Abbey Octo and General Funds, since 1983; Council Member, Quarrier's Homes, since 1990. Recreations: farming; shooting; golf. Address: (h.) South Branchal Farm, Bridge of Weir, PA11 3SJ; T.-Kilmacolm 2985.

Craig, John Warrender, LDS, FDS, RCSE, DPD. Chief Administrative Dental Officer, Lothian Health Board, since 1974; Consultant in Community Dental Health; Honorary Senior Lecturer, Department of Preventive Dentistry, Edinburgh University, since 1974; b. 21.3.28, South Africa; m., Hazel Campbell Henry; 2 s. Educ. George Heriot's School, Edinburgh; Edinburgh University; St. Andrews University. Chief Dental Officer, Inverness County Council, 1958; Senior Hospital Dental Officer, Eastern Regional Hospital Board, and Clinical Lecturer in Operative Dental Surgery, Department of Orthodontics and Children's Dentistry, St. Andrews University, 1961; Chief Dental Officer, City of Edinburgh, 1965. British Dental Association: former Secretary, Highland and Dundee Sections, President, East of Scotland Branch, 1976-77; British Paedodontic Society: Chairman, East of Scotland Branch, 1970-73, National President, 1972-73; National President, British Association for the Study of Community Dentistry, 1978-79. Publications: The Management of Traumatized Incisor Teeth of Children (Co-author), 1970. Recreations: music; gardening. Address: (h.) 1 Liberton Gardens, Edinburgh, EH16 6JX; T.-031-664 3195.

Craig, Rev. Maxwell Davidson, MA, BD, ThM. General Secretary, Action of Churches Together in Scotland, since 1990 (Minister, St. Columba's Parish Church, Bridge of Don, Aberdeen, 1989-91); Chaplain to the Queen in Scotland, since 1986; Convener, Church and Nation Committee, Church of Scotland, 1984-88; b. 25.12.31; m., Janet Margaret Macgregor; 1 s.; 3 d. Educ. Bradford Grammar School; Harrow School; Oriel College, Oxford; Edinburgh University. National Service, 1st Bn., Argyll and Sutherland Highlanders (2nd Lt.), 1954-56. Assistant Principal, Ministry of Labour, 1957-61; Private Secretary to Parliamentary Secretary, 1959-61; left London and civil service to train for ministry of Church of Scotland, 1961; ThM, Princeton, 1965; Minister, Grahamston Parish Church, Falkirk, 1966-73; Minister, Wellington Church, Glasgow, 1973-89; Chairman: Falkirk Children's Panel, 1970-72, Hillhead Housing Association Ltd., 1975-89; Member, Strathclyde Children's Panel, 1973-86. Recreations: hill-walking; dinghy sailing; squash. Address: (h.) 9 Kilbryde Crescent, Dunblane, Perthshire FK15 9BA; T.-0786 823147.

Craig, Rev. Neil Douglas, MA, BD. Minister, Craignair linked with Urr, 1980-87; b. 7.8.22, Waterbeck; m., Florence Grimmond Sproul; 1 s.; 1 d. Educ. Royal High School, Edinburgh; Edinburgh University. Minister: St. Andrews Church, Hawick, 1947-53, Carstairs and Carstairs Junction, 1953-61, Craignair Church, Dalbeattie, 1961-80; former Convener, Youth Committee, Lanark Presbytery; Convener, Maintenance of the Ministry Committee, Dumfries Presbytery; Convener, General Assembly Committee on Probationers and Transference of Ministers. Recreations: cricket; golf; gardening. Address: (h.) Rossett, 33 Albert Road, Dumfries, DG2 9DN; T.-0387 52187.

Craig, Very Rev. Professor Robert, CBE (1981), MA, BD, STM, PhD, DLitt, LLD, DD, Hon. FZweIE, Hon. CF. Moderator, General Assembly of the Church of Scotland, 1986-87; b. 22.3.17, Markinch, Fife; m., Olga Wanda Strzelec; 1 s.; 1 d. Educ. Coaltown of Balgonie and Falkland Public Schools; Bell-Baxter, Cupar; St. Andrews University; Union Theological Seminary, New York. Assistant Minister, St. John's Kirk, Perth, 1941-42; ordained, 1942; served as Army Chaplain, 1942-47, in Europe and Middle East; mentioned in despatches, Normandy, 1944; Deputy Leader, Iona Community, 1948-50; Professor of Divinity, Natal University, 1950-57; Professor of Religion, Smith College, University of Zimbabwe (formerly Rhodesia); Minister, St. Andrew's Scots Memorial Church, Jerusalem, 1980-85; Hon. CF 1947; Hon. Chaplain, Scottish Branch, Palestine Police Old Comrades' Association, since 1986, and Fife and Angus Branch, Normandy Veterans' Association, since 1987; Hon. DD, St. Andrews, 1967; Hon. LLD, Witwatersrand, 1979, Birmingham, 1980, Natal, 1981; Hon. DLitt, Zimbabwe, 1981; Hon. Fellow, Zimbabwe Institution of Engineers, 1976; Golden Jubilee Medal, Witwatersrand University, 1977; City of Jerusalem Medal, 1985; Member, The Jerusalem Foundation, since 1989. Address: (h.) West Port, Falkland, Fife, KY7 7BL; T.-033757 238.

Craig, Robert, BA, MA, ALA. Executive Secretary, Scottish Library Association, since 1984; b. 2.7.43, Hamilton; m., Ann Beaton; 1 s.; 1 d. Educ. Dalziel High School; Strathclyde University. Depute County Librarian, Lanark County Council, 1974-75; Principal Education Librarian, Glasgow Division, Strathclyde Regional Council, 1975-79; Lecturer, Strathclyde University, 1979-84. Publications: Scottish Libraries (Editor); Lights in the Darkness (Co-editor); Scotland 1939 (Co-author). Recreations: reading; gardening; football. Address: (b.) Motherwell Business Centre, Coursington Road, Motherwell, ML1 1PW; T.-0698 52526.

Craig, Robert Harvey, RD, CA. Chartered Accountant in professional practice, since 1955; Honorary Sheriff, North Strathclyde at Campbeltown, since 1986; b. 18.12.29, Campbeltown; m., Marion Caldwell; 1 s.; 1 d. Educ. Campbeltown Grammar School; Glasgow University. Admitted to Institute of Chartered Accountants of Scotland, 1953; Fleet Air Arm, 1953-55; later commanded a Naval Reserve minesweeper; Director of various companies. Recreations: sailing; skiing. Address: (h.) Ferndean, Campbeltown, Argyll, PA28 6EN; T.-0586 52495.

Craig, Robert James, MB, ChB, MRCPsych, MPhil. Consultant Psychiatrist; Consultant, Rosslynlee Hospital; b. 13.5.47, Newcastle; m., Elaine Catherine May; 1 s. Educ. Daniel Stewart's College; Edinburgh University. House Officer: Head Injuries and Neurosurgery, Edinburgh Royal Infirmary and Western General Hospital, Edinburgh, General Medicine, Eastern General Hospital, Edinburgh; Senior House Officer, General Medicine, Edenhall Hospital, Musselburgh; Registrar, Psychiatry, Rosslynlee Hospital, Roslin; Senior Registrar, Psychiatry, Royal Edinburgh Hospital. Address: (b.) Rosslynlee Hospital, Roslin, Midlothian, EH25 9QE; T.-031-440 2313.

Craik, Professor Alexander Duncan Davidson, BSc, PhD, FRSE. Professor of Applied Mathematics, St. Andrews University, since 1988 (Reader, 1974-87); b. 25.8.38, Brechin; m., Elizabeth Mary Farmer; 1 s.; 1 d. Educ. Brechin High School; St. Andrews University; Cambridge University. St. Andrews University: Lecturer in Applied Mathematics, 1963-70, Senior Lecturer, 1970-74. Publication: Wave Interactions and Fluid Flows, 1985. Address: (h.) 92 Hepburn Gardens, St. Andrews, KY16 9LN; T.-0334 72992.

Craik, Sheriff Roger George, QC (Scot). Sheriff of Lothian and Borders, at Edinburgh, since 1984; b. 22.11.40.

Craik, Professor Wendy Ann, BA, PhD. Professor of English, Middle East Technical University, Ankara, since 1989; b. 7.2.34, London; 1 s. Educ. Tiffin School, Kingston-on-Thames; Leicester University. Part-time Tutor, WEA and University Extension Courses, Vaughan College, Leicester, 1959-63; Principal English Teacher, Oadby Beauchamp Grammar School, Leicester, 1963-65; Lecturer in English, Aberdeen University, 1965-72, Senior Lecturer, 1972-87, Reader, 1987-89. Publications: Jane Austen: the Six Novels; Jane Austen in her Time; Elizabeth Gaskell and the 19th Century Novel; The Bronte Novels. Address: (b.) Department of English, Kings College, Aberdeen; T.-0224 272632.

Cramb, Rev. Erik McLeish, LTh. Organiser for Tayside, Scottish Churches Industrial Mission, since 1989; b. 26.12.39, Glasgow; m., Elizabeth McLean; 2 s.; 3 d. Educ. Woodside Secondary School, Glasgow; Glasgow University and Trinity College. Minister: St. Thomas' Gallowgate, Glasgow, 1973-81, St. Paul's United Church, Kingston, Jamaica, 1981-84, Yoker, Glasgow, 1984-89. Socialist; Member, Iona Community; Member, Disablement Income Group; Chair, Dundee Money Advice Project. Recreation: supports Partick Thistle. Address: (h.) 65 Clepington Road, Dundee, DD4 7BQ; T.-0382 458764.

Cramond, Kenneth William, JP, BL, NP. Chief Executive, Roxburgh District Council, since 1986; b. Arbroath; m., Georgina B. Silver; 3 s. Educ. St. Andrews University. Legal Assistant, Clydebank Town Council; Senior Legal Assistant, Inverness County Council; Town Clerk Depute, Hawick Town Council; Director of Administrative and Legal Services, Roxburgh District Council. Address: (b.) District Council Offices, High Street, Hawick, TD9 9EF; T.-0450 75991.

Cramond, Ronald Duncan, CBE (1987), MA, FBIM, FSA Scot. Chairman, Scottish Museums Council, since 1990; Commissioner, Countryside Commission for Scotland, since 1988; Trustee: National Museums of Scotland, since 1985, Scottish Civic Trust, since 1988, Cromarty Arts Trust, 1988-91, Bo'ness Heritage Trust, since 1989; Vice President, Architectural Heritage Society of Scotland, since 1989; b. 22.3.27, Leith; m., Constance MacGregor (deceased); 1 s.; 1 d. Educ. George Heriot's School; Edinburgh University. Commissioned Royal Scots, 1950; entered War Office, 1951; Private Secretary to Parliamentary Under Secretary of State, Scottish Office, 1956; Principal, Department of Health for Scotland, 1957; Mactaggart Fellow, Glasgow University, 1962; Haldane Medallist in Public Administration, 1964; Assistant Secretary, Scottish Development Department, 1966; Under Secretary, 1973; Under Secretary, Department of Agriculture and Fisheries for Scotland, 1977. Deputy Chairman, Highlands and Islands Development Board, 1983-88; Member, Scottish Tourist Board, 1985-88. Recreations: golf; hill-walking; testing a plastic hip. Address: (b.) c/o Scottish Museums Council, 20 Torphichen Street, Edinburgh EH3 8JB.

Crampin, Stuart, BSc, PhD, ScD, FRSE, FRAS. Deputy Chief Scientific Officer (Individual Merit), British Geological Survey, since 1987; Principal Scientist, Edinburgh Anisotropy Project, since 1988; Honorary Professor, Geophysics Department, Edinburgh University, since 1988; Chairman, IASPEI Commission on Wave Propagation in Real Media, 1983- 89; b. 22.10.35, Tiptree, Essex; m., Roma Eluned Williams; 2 d. Educ. Maldon Grammar School; King's College, London; Pembroke College, Cambridge. Research Fellow, Uppsala University, 1963-65; Gassiot Fellow in Seismology, NERC, 1966-69; Principal Scientific Officer, Institute of Geological Sciences, 1969-76; Senior Principal Scientific Officer (Individual Merit), British Geological Survey, 1976-87; Conrad Schlumberger Award, EAEG, 1986; Virgil Kauffman Gold Medal, SEG, 1988. Recreations: hill-walking; travelling. Address: (b.) British Geological Survey, Murchison House, West Mains Road, Edinburgh, EH9 3LA; T.-031-667 1000.

Crampsey, Robert A. McN., MA (Hons), ARCM. Freelance Broadcaster and Writer; b. 8.7.30, Glasgow; m., Dr. Veronica R. Carson; 4 d. Educ. Holyrood School, Glasgow; Glasgow University; London University (External). RAF, 1952-55 (demobilised in rank of Flt. Lt.); Head of History Department, St. Aloysius College, Glasgow, 1967-71; Assistant Head Teacher, Holyrood Secondary School, 1971-74; Rector, St. Ambrose High School, Coatbridge, 1974-86. Winner, Brain of Britain, BBC, 1965; Churchill Fellow, 1970; semi-finalist, Mastermind, 1972-73; BBC Sports Commentator. Publications: History of Queen's Park FC; Puerto Rico; The Manager; The Scottish Footballer; The Edinburgh Pirate (Arts Council Award); The Run Out; Mr Stein (a biography); The Young Civilian; The Glasgow Golf Club 1787-1987; The Empire Exhibition; The Somerset Cricket Quiz Book; The Surrey Cricket Quiz Book; Ranfurly Castle Golf Club – a centenary history; The Official Centenary History of the Scottish Football League. Recreations: travel; things Hispanic; listening to and playing music; cricket. Address: (h.) 15 Myrtle Park, Glasgow, G42; T.-041-423 2735.

Cranston, Professor William Ballantyne, PhD, CEng, FICE, FIStructE, FACI, MIABSE, MIOD. Professor and Head, Department of Civil Engineering, Paisley College, since 1988; b. 7.12.33, Edinburgh; m., Agnes Muir Anderson; 4 s.; 1 d. Educ. Dollar Academy; Glasgow University. Assistant to Professor of Civil Engineering, Glasgow University, 1957-61; Cement and Concrete Association: Research Engineer, 1961-77, Head, Design Department, 1977-83, Director (Technical Applications), 1984-87. Former Slough Borough and Berkshire County Councillor. Recreations: sailing; fly-fishing. Address: (h.) Flat 8, 8 Riverview Place, Glasgow, G5 8EB; T.-041-429 8169.

Crawford, Alexander A., BSc (Hons). Rector, Irvine Royal Academy, since 1984; b. 12.1.39, Glasgow; m., Anne; 2 d. Educ. Stranraer High School; Glasgow University; Jordanhill College of Education. Teacher of Mathematics, then Principal Teacher, King's Park Secondary, Glasgow, 1962-74; Assistant Head Teacher, Park Mains High School, Erskine, 1974-78; Depute Head Teacher, Kilmarnock Academy, 1978-84. Recreations: golf; cycling; jazz. Address: (b.) Academy Road, Irvine, KA12 8RN; T.-0294 76221.

Crawford, Henry Paton Fowler, MBE. Member, Scottish Agricultural Development Council; Member, Scottish Agricultural Consultative Panel; b. 14.1.21, Harthill; m., Robina Cessford; 2 s.; 1 d. Educ. Harthill School. Left school aged 14 and worked on farm for 17 years; took up post as District Organiser, Scottish Farm Servants Union (subsequently known as the Scottish Agriculture, Horticulture and Forestry Section, TGWU); appoined Sectional Secretary for Scotland; now retired. Address: (h.) 9 Woodside Park, Kelso, Roxburghshire; T.-Kelso 24328.

Crawford, James, MA, LLB, NP. Consultant, Neill Clerk, Solicitors, since 1988; Honorary Sheriff, Greenock, since 1987; b. 10.10.23, Greenock; m., Ruth Gibson; 1 s.; 1 d. Educ. Greenock Academy; Glasgow University. Army, 1942-46, commissioned Reconnaissance Corps, 1944, and served in West Africa and Burma; private practice, Gourock, 1949-88; 277th Field Regiment, RA, TA, 1949-53, retiring as Captain. Appointed General Commissioner for Income Tax, Renfrewshire, 1989; Hon. Secretary, Inverkip Society, 1962-83 (now Trustee); Chairman, Greenock Provident Bank,

1965-66. Recreations: gardening; fishing; travel. Address: (h.) 4 Edinburgh Drive, Gourock, PA19 1AG; T.-0475 31413.

Crawford, Robert, MA, DPhil. Lecturer in Modern Scottish Literature, Department of English, St. Andrews University, since 1989; Co-Editor, Verse Magazine, since 1984; Poetry Editor, Polygon, since 1991; Poet and Critic; b. 23.2.59, Bellshill; m., Alice Wales. Educ. Hutchesons' Grammar School, Glasgow; Glasgow University; Balliol College, Oxford. Snell Exhibitioner & Carnegie Scholar, Balliol College, Oxford, 1981-84; Elizabeth Wordsworth Junior Research Fellow, St. Hugh's College, Oxford, 1984-87; British Academy Postdoctoral Fellow, Department of English Literature, Glasgow University, 1987-89. Publications: The Savage and the City in the Work of T.S. Eliot, 1987; A Scottish Assembly, 1990; Sharawaggi (Co-author), 1990; About Edwin Morgan (Co-Editor), 1990; Other Tongues: young Scottish poets in English, Scots and Gaelic (Editor), 1990; The Arts of Alasdair Gray (Co-Editor), 1991; Devolving English Literature, 1992; Talkies, 1992. Recreation: being private. Address: (b.) Department of English, St. Andrews University, St. Andrews, KY16 9AL; T.-0334 76161, Ext. 471.

Crawford, 29th Earl of, and Balcarres, 12th Earl of (Robert Alexander Lindsay), PC, DL. Premier Earl of Scotland; Head of House of Lindsay; b. 5.3.27; m., Ruth Beatrice Meyer; 2 s.; 2 d. Educ. Eton; Trinity College, Cambridge. Grenadier Guards, 1945-49; MP (Conservative), Hertford, 1955-74; Welwyn and Hatfield, February to September, 1974; Opposition Front Bench Spokesman on Health and Social Security, 1967-70; Minister of State for Defence, 1970-72; Minister of State for Foreign and Commonwealth Affairs, 1972-74; Chairman, Lombard North Central Bank, 1976-80; Director, National Westminster Bank, 1975-88; Director, Scottish American Investment Co., 1978-88; Vice-Chairman, Sun Alliance & London Insurance Group, 1975- 91; President, Rural District Councils Association, 1959-65; Chairman, National Association of Mental Health, 1969-70; Chairman, Historic Buildings Council for Scotland, 1976-83; Chairman, Royal Commission on Ancient and Historical Monuments of Scotland, since 1985; First Crown Estate Commissioner, 1980-85; Deputy Lieutenant, Fife; Chairman, National Library of Scotland, since 1990. Address: (h.) Balcarres, Colinsburgh, Fife, KY9 1HL.

Crawford, Robert Caldwell. Composer; b. 18.4.25, Edinburgh; m., Alison Braedine Orr; 1 s.; 1 d. Educ. Melville College, Edinburgh; Keswick Grammar School; Guildhall School of Music, London. Freelance Composer and Critic until 1970; BBC Music Producer, 1970-85; Chairman, Music Advisory Committee for Sir James Caird's Travelling Scholarships Trust, since 1978. Recreations: carpentry; hill-walking; gardening; beekeeping. Address: (h.) 12 Inverleith Terrace, Edinburgh, EH3 5NS; T.-031-556 3600.

Crawford, Professor Robert MacGregor Martyn, BSc, DocSciNat (Liege), FRSE, FInstBiol. Professor of Plant Ecology, St. Andrews University, since 1977; b. 30.5.34, Glasgow; m., Barbara Elizabeth Hall; 1 s. Educ. Glasgow Academy; Glasgow University; Liege University; Munich University; Moscow University. Lecturer, then Reader in Botany, St. Andrews University; Past President, Edinburgh Botanical Society; Editor, Flora. Recreations: European languages; music; photography. Address: (b.) The University, St. Andrews, KY16 9AJ; T.-0334 76161.

Crawford, Robert MacKay, BA, PhD. Director, Locate in Scotland, since 1991; b. 14.6.51, Largs; m., Linda; 1 s.; 1 d. Educ. St. Michael's Adademy, Kilwinning; Strathclyde University; Harvard University; Glasgow University. Assembler, IBM, 1969-71; Research Officer, SNP, 1977-79;

Citibank, London, 1982-83; Research Fellow, Fraser of Allander Institute, 1983-86; Locate in Scotland, since 1986. Recreations: running; hill walking; reading (literature, history of ideas). Address: (b.) 120 Bothwell Street, Glasgow, G2 7JP; T.-041-248 2700.

Crawford, Rudy, BSc (Hons), MBChB, FRCS (Glas). Consultant in Accident and Emergency Care, Royal Infirmary, Glasgow, since 1990; Honorary Clinical Senior Lecturer, Glasgow University, since 1991; b. 5.5.49, Glasgow; m., Jane Crawford; 1 s.; 1 d. Educ. Glasgow University. Temporary Lecturer in Anatomy, Glasgow University; general surgery training; specialist training in accident and emergency medicine and surgery, Glasgow and Aberdeen; formerly member of offshore specialist team providing medical support for North Sea oil emergencies including Piper Alpha Disaster; founder Member and Local Project Director, Scottish Trauma Audit Group and Scottish Child Accident Research and Audit Group; Member, Council, St. Andrew's Ambulance Association; Member, Scottish Management Efficiency Group Working Party on Accident and Emergency Services. Recreations: running; photography; travel; Rotary International. Address: (b.) Accident and Emergency Department, Royal Infirmary, Glasgow, G4 0SF; Ext. 041-552 3535, Ext. 5116.

Crawford, Thomas, MA. Hon. Reader in English, Aberdeen University, since 1985; Convener, Publications Board, Association for Scottish Literary Studies, since 1988; b. 6.7.20, Dundee; m., Jean Rennie McBride; 1 s.; 1 d. Educ. Dunfermline High School; Edinburgh University; University of Auckland. University of Auckland: Lecturer in English, 1953-60, Senior Lecturer, 1960-62, Associate Professor, 1963-65; Lecturer in English, Edinburgh University, 1965; Commonwealth Research Fellow, Hamilton, Ontario, 1966; Senior Lecturer in English, then Reader, Aberdeen University, 1967-85; Warnock Fellow, Yale University, various times, since 1978. Past President, Association for Scottish Literary Studies; former Editor, Scottish Literary Journal; Council Member, Scottish Text Society. Publications: Burns: a study of the poems and songs, 1960; Scott, 1965; Scott, selected poems (Editor), 1972; Love, Labour, and Liberty, 1976; Society and the Lyric, 1980. Recreations: walking and rambling; music. Address: (h.) 61 Argyll Place, Aberdeen, AB2 4HU; T.-0224 635862.

Crean, Gerard Patrick, PhD, FRCPE, FRCPG, FRCPI. Consultant Physician and Physician-in-charge, Gastro-Intestinal Centre, Southern General Hospital, Glasgow, since 1967; Director, Diagnostic Methodology Research Unit, Southern General Hospital, Glasgow, since 1970; Honorary Lecturer, Glasgow University, since 1970; b. 1.5.27, Courtown Harbour, County Wexford; m., Janice Dodds Mathieson; 1 s.; 2 d. Educ. Rockwell College, Cashel, County Tipperary; University College, Dublin. House appointments, Mater Misericordiae Hospital, Dublin, Western General Hospital, Edinburgh and Edinburgh Royal Infirmary; Registrar, then Senior Registrar, Western General Hospital, Edinburgh; Member, scientific staff, Medical Research Council Clinical Endocrinology Unit, Edinburgh; Honorary Lecturer, Department of Therapeutics, Edinburgh University; Visiting Professor in Physiology, Pennsylvania University. Clarke Prize, Edinburgh Pathological Club; contributed to several textbooks. Past President, British Society of Gastroenterology; President, Scottish Fiddle Orchestra. Recreations: fiddle playing; traditional music; history of Antarctic exploration; golf. Address: (h.) St. Ronan's, Duchal Road, Kilmacolm, PA13 4AY; T.-Kilmacolm 2504.

Creanor, Stephen Leonard, BDS, PhD. Clinical Senior Lecturer in Oral Biology, Glasgow University Dental School, since 1990; b. 17.2.57, Broxburn; m., Elaine Ann; 1 s.; 1 d. Educ. St. Conval's High School, Cumnock; Glasgow

University. House Surgeon, Glasgow Dental Hospital, 1980-81; Resident Senior House Surgeon, Department of Oral Surgery, Victoria Infirmary, Glasgow, 1981-83; Glasgow University Dental School: Research Fellow, Department of Oral Medicine and Pathology, 1983-87, Clinical Lecturer, Oral Biology Group, 1987-90. Recreations: music; reading; cooking. Address: Oral Biology Group, Glasgow University Dental School, 378 Sauchiehall Street, Glasgow, G2 3JZ; T.-041-332 7020, Ext. 376.

Cresser, Professor Malcolm Stewart, PhD, DIC, BSc, ARCS, FRSC, CChem. Professor of Plant & Soil Science, Aberdeen University, since 1989; b. 17.4.46, London; m., Louise Elizabeth Blackburn; 1 s.; 2 d. Educ. St. Ignatius College, Tottenham; Imperial College, London. Lecturer, Senior Lecturer, Reader, Department of Soil Science, Aberdeen University, 1970-89; awarded 11th SAC Silver Medal, 1984. Publications: Solvent Extraction in Flame Spectroscopic Analysis; Environmental Chemical Analysis (Co-author); Acidification of Freshwaters (Co-author). Recreations: painting; drawing; gardening. Address: (b.) Department of Plant and Soil Science, Meston Building, Old Aberdeen, AB9 2UE; T.-0224 272259.

Cresswell, Lyell Richard, BMus (Hons), MusM, PhD. Composer; b. 13.10.44, Wellington, New Zealand; m., Catherine Mawson. Educ. Victoria University of Wellington; Toronto University; Aberdeen University. Music Organiser, Chapter Arts Centre, Cardiff; Forman Fellow in Composition, Edinburgh University; Canadian Commonwealth scholarship, 1969-70; Dutch Government bursary, 1974-75; Ian Whyte Award, 1978; APRA Silver Scroll, 1979; Cramb Fellow, Glasgow University, 1982-85. Address: (h.) 4 Leslie Place, Edinburgh, EH4 1NQ; T.-031-332 9181.

Crichton, Charles Maitland Makgill, of That Ilk. Chief of the Crichtons; Owner, Monzie and Largo Estates, since 1968; Chairman, Monzie Joinery Ltd., since 1979; Chairman, Butinox Timber Finishes Ltd., since 1986; b. 25.7.42, Crieff; m., Isla Susan Gloag; 1 s. Educ. Winchester. Economics Intelligence Department, Bank of England, 1963-68. President, Crieff Branch, NFU; Chairman, Kinross and West Perthshire Conservative Association; Conservative candidate, Greenock and Port Glasgow, 1983, Northumbria (European Election), 1984; Chairman, Scottish Branch, Association of Independent Electricity Producers, since 1990. Recreation: cross-country skiing. Address: Monzie Castle, Crieff, Perthshire; T.-0764 3110.

Crichton, Rev. James, MA, BD, MTh. Minister, Crosshill linked with Dalrymple, since 1981; Clerk, Ayr Presbytery, since 1991; b. 1.10.44, Glasgow; m.; 2 s.; 1 d. Educ. Eastbank Academy; Glasgow University. Minister, Crosshill, 1969-81; Chaplain, Ayr County Hospital, 1982-84 and since 1988; Member, South Ayrshire Health Council, since 1984; Moderator, Ayr Presbytery, 1984-85; Chairman, Scottish Reformation Society, since 1982; Vice-President, Scottish Covenanters Memorials Association, since 1989. Publications: The Story of the Crosshill Churches; The Carrick Covenanters; Ayr Presbytery 1581-1981 (Co-author); Mixed Company. Recreation: worrying about Rangers. Address: 30 Garden Street, Dalrymple, Ayrshire; T.-Dalrymple 263.

Crichton, John. Member, Western Isles Islands Council, since 1974 (Chairman, Manpower Committee, since 1978; Vice-Chairman, Policy and Resources Committee, since 1984); Chairman, Stornoway Trust, 1983-89; Chairman, Crofters Union, 1985-91; Liaison Officer and Assessor, Crofters Commission, since 1979; b. 27.3.23, Stornoway; m., Joan Finlayson; 2 s.; 1 d. Educ. Knock Public School. Address: (h.) 21 Swordale, Point, Isle of Lewis, PA86 0BP.

Crichton, Maurice, CA. Director, Woolwich Building Society and Chairman, Scottish and Northern Ireland Local Board, since 1977; Chairman, Irvine Development Corporation, since 1991; Director, Macphie of Glenbervie Ltd., since 1986; b. 4.6.28, Glasgow; m., Diana Russell Lang; 3 s.; 1 d. Educ. Kelvinside Academy; Cargilfield School; Sedbergh School. Partner, Touche Ross & Co., Chartered Accountants, 1955-86. Deacon Convener, Trades House of Glasgow, 1988-89; Member, Board, Bield Housing Association; Elder, Paisley Abbey. Recreations: golf; music; trout fishing; shooting. Address: (h.) Hall of Caldwell, Uplawmoor, Glasgow; T.-050 585 248.

Crichton, Robert, MC, DL, JP, SDA. Farmer; b. 17.11.22, Linlithgow; m., Joan Patricia Watts, BSc; 3 s.; 2 d. Educ. Edinburgh Academy; Edinburgh and East of Scotland College of Agriculture. Army, 1942-46, 2nd Lothians and Border Horse; agricultural student, 1947-49; farming, since 1949. Commandant, Edinburgh, Lothians and Peebles Army Cadet Force, until 1963; JP, since 1958; Deputy Lieutenant, County of West Lothian, since 1961. Recreation: gardening. Address: Niddry Mains, Winchburgh, Broxburn, West Lothian, EH52 6QR; T.-0506 890213.

Crichton, Thomas Kennedy, MBIM. Director of Industrial Liaison, Heriot-Watt University, Edinburgh, 1982-90; b. 4.8.25, Edinburgh; m., Davida Anne Whiteford; 1 s.; 3 d. Educ. Daniel Stewart's College, Edinburgh; Heriot-Watt College, Edinburgh. Entered Royal Navy, 1943; commissioned, 1944; active service in light coastal forces in Channel, North Sea and Atlantic; Parts and Service Manager, James Ross & Sons (Motors) Ltd., Edinburgh, 1947-62; Divisional Manager, SAAB (Gt. Britain) Ltd., 1962-78; joined Heriot-Watt University, 1979. Elder, Cramond Kirk. Recreations: family; golf; walking and gardening. Address: (h.) 1 Braehead Crescent, Barnton, Edinburgh, EH4 6BP; T.-031-339 4917.

Critchley, Frank. Honorary Sheriff, Grampian, Highland and Islands, since 1984; b. 7.10.14, Inverness; m., Joyce; 1 s.; 1 d. Educ. Inverness Royal Academy; George Watson's College, Edinburgh; Edinburgh University. Solicitor, 1938-84, retiring as Senior Partner of MacNeill & Critchley, Inverness; Royal Corps of Signals, 1939-46 (Major); President, Inverness Rotary Club, 1954-55; Member, Craig Dunain Hospitals Board of Management, 1952-58 (Chairman of Finance); Registrar, Diocese of Moray Ross and Caithness, 1971-86; Member, Council, Law Society of Scotland, 1971-77; Dean, Faculty of Solicitors of Inverness-shire, 1979-82; Chairman, Regional Advisory Committee, North of Scotland Conservancy, Forestry Commission. Recreations: reading; walking; gardening; golf; theatre. Address: (h.) Malwa, 9 Mayfield Road, Inverness; T.-Inverness 233516.

Critchlow, Howard Arthur, BDS, FDSRCS(Eng), FDSR-CPS(Glas). Consultant Oral Surgeon (Honorary Senior Lecturer), Glasgow Dental Hospital, Stobhill General Hospital and Royal Hospital for Sick Children, Glasgow, since 1976; b. 22.4.43, Littleborough; m., Avril; 1 s.; 1 d. Educ. Nottingham High School for Boys; Sheffield University. General dental practice, Sheffield; oral surgery training posts. Chairman, Greater Glasgow Health Board Area Dental Committee and Dental Ethical Committee; Chairman, Glasgow Northern Hospitals Ethical Committee. Recreations: gardening; hill-walking; riding; running. Address: (b.) Glasgow Dental Hospital and School, 378 Sauchiehall Street, Glasgow, G2 3JZ; T.-041-332 7020.

Croan, Sheriff Thomas Malcolm, MA, LLB. Sheriff of North Strathclyde at Kilmarnock, since 1983; b. 7.8.32, Edinburgh; m., Joan Kilpatrick Law; 1 s.; 3 d. Educ. St. Joseph's College, Dumfries; Edinburgh University. Admitted to Faculty of Advocates, 1956; Standing Junior Counsel, Scottish Development Department, 1964-65 and (for highways work), 1967-69; Advocate Depute, 1965-66; Sheriff of Grampian, Highland and Islands at Banff and Peterhead, 1969-83. Recreation: sailing. Address: (h.) Overdale, 113 Bentinck Drive, Troon.

Crofton, Sir John Wenman, KB, MD, FRCP, FRCPE. Vice-Chairman, Scottish Committee, Chest, Heart and Stroke Association, 1976-90; Chairman, Tobacco and Health Committee, International Union Against Tuberculosis and Lung Disease, 1984-88; b. 27.3.12, Dublin; m., Eileen Chris Mercer, MBE; 2 s.; 3 d. Educ. Tonbridge; Sidney Sussex College, Cambridge. Professor of Respiratory Diseases, Edinburgh University, 1952-77; Dean, Faculty of Medicine, 1963-66; Vice-Principal, 1969-70; President, Royal College of Physicians of Edinburgh, 1973-76; Chairman, Scottish Health Education Co-ordinating Committee, SHHD, 1981-86. Recreations: history; music; mountains. Address: (h.) 13 Spylaw Bank Road, Edinburgh, EH13 0JW; T.-031-441 3730.

Crofts, Roger Stanley, BA, MLitt, CertEd. Chief Executive, Scottish Natural Heritage, since 1991 (Assistant Secretary, Rural Affairs Division, Scottish Development Department, 1988-91); b. 17.1.44, Leicester. Educ. Hinckley Grammar School; Liverpool University; Leicester University. Research Assistant in Geography: Aberdeen University, 1966-72; University College, London, 1972-74; entered Scottish Office, 1974; Senior Research Officer, 1974-78; Principal Research Officer, 1978-84; Assistant Secretary, Highlands and Tourism Division, Industry Department, 1984-88. Recreations: gardening; choral singing; hill-walking. Address: (h.) 19 Manor Place, Edinburgh, EH3 7DX; T.-031-225 1177.

Cromarty, James, QHP, MB, ChB, MFPHM, DPH,MRE-HIS,MIHSM. General Manager, Orkney Health Board, since 1985; b. 28.12.28, Stromness; m., Joyce Bilton; 2 s. Educ. Stromness Academy; Edinburgh University. RAF, 1952-76; Commanding Officer: 3 RAAF Hospital NSW, 1968-70, RAF Aviation Medicine Training Centre, 1970-73, Joint Services Medical Rehabilitation Unit, 1974-76; Chief Administrative Medical Officer, Orkney Health Board, since 1976. Recreations: reading; fishing. Address: (h.) Waterfiold, Orphir, Orkney; T.-Orphir 327.

Crompton, Professor David William Thomasson, MA, PhD, ScD, FIBiol, FRSE. John Graham Kerr Professor of Zoology, Glasgow University, since 1985; b. 5.12.37, Bolton; m., Effie Mary Marshall; 1 s.; 2 d. Educ. Bolton School; Sidney Sussex College, Cambridge. National Service, commission, King's Own Royal Regiment, 1957; Assistant in Research, Cambridge University, 1963-68; Fellow, Sidney Sussex College, 1964-85; Vice-Master, 1981-83; Lecturer in Parasitology, Cambridge University, 1968-85; Joint Editor, Parasitology, 1972-82; Adjunct Professor, Division of Nutritional Sciences, Cornell University, New York, since 1981; Aquatic Life Sciences Committee, Natural Environment Research Council, 1981-84; Director, Company of Biologists Ltd., since 1985; Member, WHO Expert Committee on Parasitic Diseases, since 1985; Scientific Medal, Zoological Society of London, 1977; Head, WHO Collaborating Centre for Ascariasis, Glasgow University. Recreations: mountain walking; fishing; books; bull terriers. Address: (b.) Department of Zoology, Glasgow University, Glasgow, G12 8QQ; T.-041-330 5395; (h.) 7 Kirklee Terrace, Glasgow, G12 0TQ; T.-041-357 2631.

Crompton, Graham Kenneth, MB, ChB, FRCPE, FCCP. Consultant Physician, Lothian Health Board, since 1969; Senior Lecturer (part-time) in Medicine and Respiratory Medicine, Edinburgh University, since 1969; b. 14.2.35, Salford; 2 s. Educ. Salford Grammar School; Edinburgh University. Appointed Consultant Physician, 1969; Director of Studies, Faculty of Medicine, 1977-88; Member, Medical

Advisory Committee, Asthma Society, 1981-88. Publications: Diagnosis and Management of Respiratory Diseases; chapters in seven medical text books; numerous papers. Recreation: watching sport. Address: (h.) 1B/3 Fairacre Court, Abbotsford Crescent, Edinburgh, EH10 5DY; T.-031-447 1022.

Crosbie, Ian Martin, FCII. Former Moderator, Society of High Constables of Edinburgh; Editor, Scottish Life Staff Journal, since 1987; b. 26.5.22, Edinburgh; m., Lily; 1 s. Educ. Daniel Stewart's College, Edinburgh. Joined Scottish Life Assurance Company, 1939; RAF, 1941-46; management, Scottish Life Assurance Company, 1970-84; Council Member, Insurance Society of Edinburgh, 1973-83 (Honorary Treasurer, 1978-83); Member, Lothian Regional Council, 1982-88. Recreations: golf; tennis; travel; music; gardening; photography; oil and water-colour painting. Address: (h.) 4 Braehead Avenue, Edinburgh, EH4 6BA; T.-031-339 6233.

Crosby, William Scott, CBE (1982), BL. Lawyer; b. 31.7.18, Hawick; m., Margaret Elizabeth Bell; 3 s. Educ. Hawick High School; Edinburgh University. Army Service, 1939-46; Croix de Guerre, 1945; acted as Brigade Major 152 Brigade, 1945; Former Senior Partner, Storie, Cruden & Simpson, Advocates, Aberdeen; Chairman, Grampian Health Board, 1973-82; President, Society of Advocates in Aberdeen, 1984-85. Recreations: golf; swimming; walking; music; language study; gardening. Address: (h.) 82 Beaconsfield Place, Aberdeen; T.-Aberdeen 643067.

Crosfield, Rev. Canon George Philip Chorley, OBE, MA (Cantab). Provost, St. Mary's Cathedral, Edinburgh, 1970-90; Hon. Canon, St. Mary's Cathedral, since 1991; b. 9.9.24, London; m., Susan Mary Jullion; 1 s.; 2 d. Educ. George Watson's College, Edinburgh; Selwyn College, Cambridge. Royal Artillery, 1942-46 (Captain); Priest, 1952; Assistant Curate: St. David's, Pilton, Edinburgh, 1951-53, St. Andrew's, St. Andrews, 1953-55; Rector, St. Cuthbert's, Hawick, 1955-60; Chaplain, Gordonstoun School, 1960-68; Canon and Vice-Provost, St. Mary's Cathedral, Edinburgh, 1968-70. Recreations: gardening; walking; carpentry. Address: (h.) 21 Biggar Road, Silverburn, near Penicuik EH26 9LQ; Tel.-0968 676607.

Cross, John Nelson, MA, PGCE, MLC. Headmaster, Westbourne School, since 1988; b. 29.3.43, Kendal; m., Julia Mackessack-Leitch; 1 s.; 1 d. Educ. Sedbergh; St. Peter's College, Oxford. Head, Outdoor Education, Gordonstoun School, 1968-72; Director of Expeditions, Aiglon College, Switzerland, 1972-84; Deputy Head, Abbots Hill School, Hemel Hempstead, 1984-88. Recreations: skiing; walking; climbing; linguistics. Address: (h.) Easter Drumquhassle Farm, Drymen, Glasgow; T.-0360 60893.

Crossling, Frank Turner, MB, ChB, FRCSG, FRCSEng. Consultant General Surgeon, Stobhill General Hospital, Glasgow, since 1962; b. 16.8.27, Aberdeen; m., Margaret Elizabeth Abdy; 1 s. Educ. Robert Gordon's College, Aberdeen; Aberdeen University. Series of surgical posts in Aberdeen, London and Glasgow; seconded to University of East Africa, Nairobi, 1967, to help set up a medical school. Recreations: photography; classical music; gardening; dry fly fishing. Address: (h.) 28 North Grange Road, Bearsden, Glasgow, G61 3AF; T.-041-943 0409.

Crowden, Kenneth Harry, FITB, MBIM. General Manager Scotland, Astra Training Services Limited, since 1990; b. 22.6.47, Edinburgh; m., Isobel Mary. Educ. Boroughmuir School, Edinburgh. Ministry of Labour, Employment Benefits Service; Manpower Services Commission, Job Centre Manager, Regional Marketing and Sales Manager; exchange with French Civil Service; Marketing and Product Development Manager/Regional Operations Manager/

Director for Scotland, Skills Training Agency, Department of Employment. Past President, Rutherglen Junior Chamber; Senator, Junior Chamber International. Recreations: sailing; skiing. Address: (h.) 686 Clarkston Road, Netherlee, Glasgow G44 3YS; T.-041-637 3615.

Cruickshank, Alistair Booth, MA. Secretary, Royal Scottish Geographical Society, since 1986; b. 3.8.31, Dumfries; m., Sheena Carlin Brown; 2 s.; 1 d. Educ. High School of Stirling; Glasgow University; Georgia University. Flying Officer, Education Branch, RAF, 1956-58; Glasgow University, 1958-61; Nottingham University, 1961-65; Glasgow University, 1965-86. Member, Clackmannan District Council, 1974-77; Member, Forth Valley Health Board, 1977-89; Chairman, Scout Association, Clackmannanshire, 1986-91; ordained Auxiliary Minister, Church of Scotland, 1991; Deputy Lieutenant, County of Clackmannan, since 1991. Recreations: fly fishing; peoples and places. Address: (b.) 10 Randolph Crescent, Edinburgh, EH3 7TU; T.-031-225 3330.

Cruickshank, Donald Gordon, MA, CA, MBA. Chief Executive, NHS in Scotland, since 1989; Member of Council, Manchester Business School, since 1986; b. 17.9.42, Elgin; m., Elizabeth Taylor; 1 s.; 1 d. Educ. Fordyce Academy; Robert Gordon's College; Aberdeen University; Manchester University. Consultant, McKinsey & Co. Inc., 1972-77; General Manager, the Sunday Times, Times Newspapers Ltd., 1977-80; Managing Director, Finance and Administration, Pearson plc, 1980-84; Managing Director, Virgin Group plc, 1984-89. Chairman, Wandsworth Health Authority, 1986-89. Address: (b.) St. Andrew's House, Edinburgh, EH1 3DE; T.-031-244 2410.

Cruickshank, Harvey. Consultant, Condies, Solicitors, Perth, since 1984; Honorary Sheriff at Perth, since 1966; b. 25.5.15, Perth; m., Muriel Helen Marshall; 1 s.; 1 d. Educ. Perth Academy. Apprenticeship, 1932-37, qualifying as Solicitor, 1937; Assistant, Condie, Mackenzie & Co., WS, Perth, 1937-39; enlisted, RAOC, 1940; commissioned, RAOC, 1941; Staff Captain, War Office, 1942; Major, 1944; demobbed 1945; Condie, Mackenzie & Co., WS: Partner, 1945, Senior Partner, 1962, retired, 1984. Recreations: golf; photography. Address: (h.) 13 Viewlands Road, Perth, PH1 1BL; T.-0738 21882.

Crummy, Helen Murray, MBE, DL, JP; b. 10.5.20, Edinburgh; m., Larry Crummy; 3 s. Educ. James Clark's School. Founder Member and Organising Secretary, 23 years, Craigmillar Festival Society; served on Morris Committee (Housing and Social Work); former Member: Scottish Council for Community Education, Scottish Arts Council Development Committee, various Gulbenkian committees, DHSS Appeals Tribunal, Lothian Regional Council Education Advisory Committee. Recreations: writing; historical research; reading; gardening. Address: (h.) 4 Whitehill Street, Newcraighall, Musselburgh, EH21 8RA; T.-031-669 7344.

Cruttenden, Timothy Peter, BEd, DipPE, FILAM. Director of Leisure Services, East Kilbride District Council, since 1980; b. 6.9.45, Portsmouth; m., Hazel; 2 s. Educ. Warblington School, Havant; Bristol University; St. Paul's, Cheltenham. Taught in Hampshire and Gloucestershire, 1967-72; sports centre management, 1973-77; recreation administration, since 1977. Winner, Sports Council Management Award, Scotland, 1977; served on various national bodies and working parties, including Countryside Commission for Scotland and Scottish Sports Council. Recreations: squash; hockey; golf; sailing. Address: (b.) Civic Centre, East Kilbride, G74 1AB; T.-03552 71277.

Cubie, Andrew, LLB (Hons), NP, WS. Chairman, Bird Semple Fyfe Ireland, WS, since 1991; b. 24.8.46,

Northallerton; m., Dr. Heather Ann Cubie; 1 s.; 2 d. Educ. Dollar Academy; Edinburgh University. Partner, Fyfe Ireland & Co., WS, 1971; Senior Partner, Corporate Department, Bird Semple Fyfe Ireland, WS, 1987; formerly: Tutor, Faculty of Law, Edinburgh University, Examiner, Law Society of Scotland; External Examiner, Diploma in Law, Edinburgh University; Member, Scottish Council, CBI; Assistant of Merchant Company of Edinburgh; Governor, George Watson's College; Vice Chairman, RNLI Scotland; Member, Committee of Management, RNLI. Recreation: sailing. Address: (b.) Orchard Brae House, 30 Queensferry Road, Edinburgh, EH4 2HG; T.-031-343 2500.

Cull, Roger Ewart, BSc (Hons), PhD, MB, ChB, FRCPE. Consultant Neurologist, Royal Infirmary, Edinburgh, since 1981; Senior Lecturer in Medical Neurology, Department of Clinical Neurosciences, Edinburgh University, since 1981; b. 24.10.47, Leigh, Lancs; m., Dr. Ann M. Cull; 2 d. Educ. Rydal School, Colwyn Bay; Edinburgh University. House Physician, Western General Hospital, Edinburgh, 1971-72; House Surgeon, Longmore Hospital, Edinburgh, 1972; MRC Research Fellow, Department of Physiology, Edinburgh University, 1972-75; Lecturer in Medical Neurology, Edinburgh University, 1976 79; Clinical Lecturer in Neurology, National Hospital for Nervous Diseases, London, 1979-81. Recreations: jazz guitar and piano. Address: (b.) Department of Medical Neurology, Royal Infirmary, Lauriston Place, Edinburgh; T.-031-229 2477.

Cullen, Professor Christopher, BA, PhD, FBPsS, CPsychol. SSMH Chair of Learning Difficulties, St. Andrews University, since 1986; Honorary Clinical Psychologist, Fife Health Board, since 1986; b. 25.12.49, Manchester. Educ. North Manchester Grammar School; University College of North Wales, Bangor. Project Director, Hester Adrian Research Centre, Manchester University, 1981-83; Director of Clinical Psychology Services to Mentally Handicapped People, Salford Health Authority, 1983-86. Chair, Professional Affairs Board, British Psychological Society, 1987-90. Recreations: climbing; fell-running. Address: (b.) Psychological Laboratory, St. Andrews University, St. Andrews, KY16 9JU; T.-0334 76161, Ext. 7168.

Cullen, Hon. Lord (William Douglas Cullen), QC. Senator of the College of Justice, since 1986; b. 18.11.35. Advocate-Depute, 1978-81; Chairman, Court of Inquiry into the Piper Alpha Disaster, 1988-90.

Culshaw, Professor Brian, BSc, PhD, CEng, MIEE. Professor of Electronics, Strathclyde University, since 1983; b. 24.9.45, Ormskirk; m., Patricia Brigid Cargan; 2 d. Educ. Ormskirk Grammar School; University College, London. Research Fellow, Cornell University, 1970; Technical Staff Member, Bell Northern Research, Ottawa, 1970-73; University College, London: Research Fellow, 1974-75, Lecturer, 1975-82; Senior Research Fellow, Stanford University, 1982; Reader, University College, London, 1983. Recreations: walking; photography; music and opera; theatre. Address: (h.) Cromdale, Gryffe Road, Kilmacolm, Renfrewshire, PA13 4BD; T.-050587 2460.

Cuming, Henry George, CBE, MA, PhD, DIC, CEng, FIMA, MRAeS. Principal, Dundee Institute of Technology, since 1969; b. 11.12.27, London; m., Valerie Margaret Bennett; 1 s.; 1 d. Educ. Owen's School, London; St. Catharine's College, Cambridge; London University. Scientific Officer, Royal Aircraft Establishment, Farnborough, 1951-55; Lecturer in Mathematics, Birmingham College of Advanced Technology, 1955-58; Senior Lecturer in Mathematics, 1958-60; Head, Department of Aeronautical Engineering, Lanchester College of Technology, Coventry, 1960-66; Depute Principal, Napier College of Science and Technology, Edinburgh, 1966-69.

Address: (b.) Bell Street, Dundee, DD1 1HG; T.-0382 308000.

Cumming, Alexander James, MA (Hons), CIMA, IPFA. Director of Finance and Treasurer, Grampian Health Board, since 1986; b. 7.3.47, Aberdeen; m., Margaret Callan; 1 s.; 2 d. Educ. Fordyce Academy; Robert Gordon's College; Aberdeen University. VSO, 1968-70; Accountant, Company Secretary, Chief Accountant, 1970-75; joined Grampian Health Board, 1975. Treasurer, Langstane Housing Association. Address: (b.) 7 Albyn Place, Aberdeen; T.-0224 589901.

Cumming, Robert Currie, BL, FIBS, ACIB, FRCSEdin (Hon.). Chairman, English Speaking Union – Scotland, 1984-90; Non-Executive Director, Adam & Co. Group PLC, since 1983; b. 21.5.21, Strathaven; m., Mary Jean McDonald Crombie. Educ. Hutchesons' Grammar School, Glasgow; Glasgow University. Former Executive Director, Royal Bank of Scotland Group PLC and Royal Bank of Scotland PLC. Trustee and Finance Convener, Royal Scottish Geographical Society; Member, Investment Committee and Finance Committee, Royal College of Surgeons, Edinburgh; Representative to University Conference, Stirling University. Recreations: fishing; golf; walking. Address: (h.) 3 Succoth Park, Edinburgh, EH12 6BX; T.-031-337 1910.

Cumming, Ronald Patrick, MB, ChB, FRCSEdin. Consultant Surgeon, Shetland Hospitals, 1957-85; Honorary Senior Lecturer in Surgery, Aberdeen University, 1980-85; b. 15.8.23, Golspie; m., Norma Gladys Kitson; 2 s. Educ. Golspie Secondary School; Aberdeen University. General practice assistant, Huntly and Rhynie, Aberdeenshire; Assistant Lecturer in Anatomy, Aberdeen University; junior surgical posts in Worcester, Burnley, and Aberdeen; Fellow, British Medical Association; Senior Fellow, Association of Surgeons of Great Britain and Ireland. JP; Honorary Sheriff; Chairman, Shetland Committee for Employment of Disabled People, until 1985; former Member, Lerwick Town Council and Shetland County Council; Junior Bailie, Lerwick Town Council, 1972-75; President, Shetland Fiddlers, 1973-85. Publication: Aspects of Health and Safety in Oil Development (Co-Editor). Recreations: golf; badminton; gardening; reading; music. Address: (h.) 62 Hammerfield Avenue, Aberdeen; T.-0224 313192.

Cummins, John George, MA, PhD. Reader in Spanish, Aberdeen University, since 1980 (Head, Department of Spanish, 1979-90); b. 26.9.37, Hull; m., Elaine S. Rockett; 2 s.; 1 d. Educ. Malet Lambert School, Hull; Manchester University. Assistant in Spanish, St. Andrews University, 1961-63; Lecturer in Spanish, Birmingham University, 1963-64; Aberdeen University: Lecturer in Spanish, 1964-72, Senior Lecturer in Spanish, 1972-80. Recreations: shooting; fishing. Address: (b.) Department of Spanish, King's College, Aberdeen University, Old Aberdeen; T.-Aberdeen 272540.

Cunningham, Professor Ian M.M., CBE, FRSE, FIBiol, FRAgS, Hon. Assoc. RCVS, Bsc, PhD. Member of Council: Agriculture and Food Research Council, National Trust for Scotland; Chairman, Board, Macaulay Land Use Research Institute; Member, Board, Institute of Grassland and Environmental Research; General Council Assessor, Court, Edinburgh University; Professor of Agriculture, Glasgow University, and Principal, West of Scotland Agricultural College, 1980-87; b. 30.9.25, Kirknewton; m., Agnes Whitelaw Frew. Educ. Lanark Grammar School; Edinburgh University. Assistant Economist, West of Scotland Agricultural College, 1946-47; Lecturer in Agriculture, Durham School of Agriculture, 1947-50; Lecturer, then Senior Lecturer, Edinburgh University, 1950-68; Director, Hill Farming Research Organisation, 1968-80. Member: Farm Animal Welfare Council, Hill Farming Advisory Committee,

Scotland; George Hedley Memorial Award for services to the sheep industry; Massey Ferguson Award for services to British agriculture; Sir William Young Award for services to livestock production in Scotland; Hon. Assoc., RCVS. Address: (h.) Bruaich, Hazlieburn, West Linton, Peeblesshire.

Cunningham, Rev. John, JCD. Roman Catholic Priest; President, Roman Catholic Scottish National Tribunal, since 1986; b. 22.2.38, Paisley. Educ. St. Mary's College, Blairs, Aberdeen; St. Peter's College, Cardross; Scots College and Gregorian University, Rome. Assistant Priest, Our Lady of Lourdes, Bishopton, 1964-69; Professor of Canon Law, St. Peter's College, Cardross and Newlands (Glasgow), 1967-81; Advocate of the Roman Catholic Scottish National Tribunal, 1970-82; Assistant Priest, St. Columba's, Renfrew, 1974-86; Vice-President, RC Scottish National Tribunal, 1982-86. Address: 22 Woodrow Road, Glasgow, G41 5PN; T.-041-427 3036.

Cunningham-Jardine, Ronald Charles, Lord Lieutenant, Dumfries, since 1991; Farmer; b. 19.9.31, Edinburgh; m., Constance Mary Teresa Inglis; 1 s.; 1 d. Educ. Ludgrove; Eton; Royal Military Academy, Sandhurst. Royal Scots Greys (retired as Captain), 1950-58. Recreations: fishing; coursing; shooting. Address: (h.) Fourmerkland, Lockerbie, Dumfriesshire, DG11 1EH; T.-0387 810226.

Curnow, John, BMedSci (Hon), BM, BS. Consultant Communicable Disease and Environmental Medicine, Grampian Health Board, since 1990; Senior Clinical Lecturer in Public Health Medicine, Aberdeen University, since 1990; Medical Officer, No. 2 Maritime Headquarters Unit, since 1991; b. 25.8.42, Bodmin, Cornwall; m., Mary Elizabeth; 1 s.; 2 d. Educ. Churston Ferras Grammar School; Nottingham University. Commissioned Officer, RAF (Pilot), 1962-80; Nottingham University, 1980-85; NHS, 1985-86; Registrar, Senior Registrar, Trent Training Scheme and Community Medicine, 1986-89; Consultant, Public Health Medicine, Central Nottingham Health Authority, 1989-90. Fellow, Society of Public Health; Expedition Trainer, Duke of Edinburgh Award Scheme. Recreations: mountain walking; field sports. Address: (h.) 2 Shorehead, Stonehaven, Kincardineshire.

Curran, Professor Sir Samuel Crowe, Kt, DL, MA, BSc, PhD, DSc, FInstP, FInstE, FRSE, FRS, CEng, DEng, FEng. Visiting Professor of Energy Studies, Glasgow University; Scientific Adviser to various organisations; b. 23.5.12, Ballymena, Northern Ireland; m.; 3 s.; 1 d. Educ. Wishaw High School; Glasgow University; Cambridge University; California University. Research, Glasgow University, Cambridge University; war research, MAP and Ministry of Supply in radar and atom bomb (Manhattan project); staff, Physics Department, Glasgow University; Chief Scientist, UKAEA at AWRE (also on board, UKAEA, Harwell); Principal, Royal College of Science and Technology, Glasgow; Principal and Vice-Chancellor, Strathclyde University. Publications: books on nuclear radiation, energy, and issues in science and higher education. Recreations: golf; horology. Address: (h.) 93 Kelvin Court, Glasgow, G12 OAH; T.-041-334 8329.

Currie, Professor Sir Alastair Robert, Kt, MB, ChB, Dr hc, Hon DSc, Hon LLD, FRCP, FRCPEdin, FRCPGlas, FRCSE, FRCPath, FRSE. Emeritus Professor of Pathology, Edinburgh University; Chairman, Board of Governors, Beatson Institute for Cancer Research; Chairman of Council, Paterson Institute for Cancer Research; Vice-President, Cancer Research Campaign; President, Royal Society of Edinburgh; Deputy Chairman, Caledonian Research Foundation; b. 8.10.21, Isle of Islay; m., Jeanne Marion Clarke, MB, ChB; 3 s.; 2 d. Educ. Port Ellen Public School; High School of Glasgow; Glasgow University. Lecturer and

Senior Lecturer in Pathology, Glasgow University and Glasgow Royal Infirmary, 1945-59; Head, Division of Pathology, Imperial Cancer Research Fund, London, 1959-62; Regius Professor of Pathology, Aberdeen University, 1962-72; Professor of Pathology, Edinburgh University, 1972-86. Recreation: reading. Address: (h.) 42 Murrayfield Avenue, Edinburgh, EH12 6AY; T.-031-337 3100.

Currie, Alexander Monteith, OBE, BA, BLitt, Dr hc (Edin), HonLLD (Sheffield). Secretary, Edinburgh University, 1978-89; b. 2.5.26, Stevenston; m., Pamela Mary Breeze; 2 s. Educ. Stevenston Higher Grade School; Portmadoc Grammar School; Bangor University; St. Catherine's College, Oxford. Administrative Officer, Manchester University, 1952-61; Academic Secretary, Liverpool University, 1962-65; Registrar and Secretary, Sheffield University, 1965-78. Officer (First Class), Royal Order of the Polar Star (Sweden). Address: (h.) 13 Moray Place, Edinburgh, EH3 6DT; T.-031-225 7775.

Currie, Rev. David Edward Paxton, BSc, BD. Minister, West Kirk, East Kilbride, since 1983; b. 27.6.50, Glasgow; m., Gwen; 2 s.; 2 d. Educ. Hunter High School, East Kilbride; Duncanrig Senior Secondary School, East Kilbride; Strathclyde University; Glasgow University. Apprentice metallurgist, Rolls Royce, Hillington, 1967-70; studied, Strathclyde University, 1970-74; Rolls Royce: Production Engineer, Hillington, 1974-77, Development Engineer, East Kilbride, 1977-79; studied for the ministry, 1979-82; probationery year, Rutherglen Stonelaw, 1982-83. Recreations: reading; music; hill-walking; skiing; golf. Address: 1 Barr Terrace, West Mains, East Kilbride, G74 1AP; T.-East Kilbride 20753.

Currie, John (Ian) C., CChem, MRSC, FIWEM. Director and River Inspector, Tweed River Purification Board, since 1964; b. 19.10.33, Glasgow; m., Margaret A.; 3 s.; 1 d. Educ. Shawlands Academy, Glasgow; Paisley Technical College. Assistant Inspector and Chemist, Tweed River Purification Board, 1955-61; Assistant Inspector, Clyde River Purification Board, 1961-64; Pollution Prevention Officer, Usk River Authority, 1964. Recreation: golf. Address: (b.) Burnbrae, Mossilee Road, Galashiels; T.-0896 2425.

Currie, Rev. Robert, MA. Honorary Associate Minister, Paisley Abbey; b. 9.12.24, Aberdeen; m., Sheila Thomson; 1 s.; 2 d. Educ. Robert Gordon's College; Central School, Aberdeen; Aberdeen University and Christ's College, Aberdeen. Minister: Boquhanran, Clydebank, 1955-69, Dowanhill, Glasgow, 1969-84, Community Minister, Partick, Glasgow, 1984-89. Chaplain, Queen Mother's Hospital; Chaplain, West of Scotland War Training Corps, 1959-69; Honorary Secretary, Scottish Pastoral Association, 1963-67; Member, Iona Community, 1953-90 (Convener, Reviewing Committee, 1972-87, Convener, Mainland Committee, 1986-88). Recreation: choral and organ music. Address: 61 Dowanside Road, Glasgow, G12 9DL; T.-041-334 5111.

Currie, Professor Ronald Ian, CBE (1977), CBiol, FIBiol, FRSE, BSc (Hons). Professorial Fellow, Grant Institute of Geology, Edinburgh University, 1988-90; Director and Secretary, Scottish Marine Biological Association, 1966-87; b. 10.10.28; m., Cecilia de Garis; 1 s.; 1 d. Educ. Glasgow University; Copenhagen University. Joined Royal Naval Scientific Service, 1949; seconded to National Institute of Oceanography; William Scoresby Expedition, South Africa, 1950; Discovery Expedition, Antarctica, 1951; Chairman, Biological Planning Committee, International Indian Ocean Expedition, 1960; Indian Ocean Expedition, 1963 and 1964; Secretary: International Association for Biological Oceanography, 1964-66 (President, 1966-70), Scientific Committee on Oceanic Research, International Council of

Scientific Unions, 1972-78; Honorary Secretary, Challenger Society, 1956-88; Honorary Professor, Heriot-Watt University, 1979. Recreations: cooking; hill-walking; shooting; local history. Address: (h.) Kilmore House, Kilmore, by Oban, Argyll; T.-Kilmore 248.

Curtis, Professor Adam Sebastian Genevieve, MA, PhD. Professor of Cell Biology, Glasgow University, since 1967; b. 3.1.34, London; m., Ann Park; 2 d. Educ. Aldenham School; Kings College, Cambridge. University College, London: Honorary Research Assistant, 1957-62, Lecturer in Zoology, 1962-67. Director, Company of Biologists Ltd., since 1961; Governor, Westbourne School, 1985-90; Council Member, Royal Society of Edinburgh, 1983-86; President, Society of Experimental Biology; Editor, Scottish Diver magazine, 1978-91; President, Scottish Sub-Aqua Club, 1972-76. Recreations: sports diving; gardening. Address: (h.) 2 Kirklee Circus, Glasgow, G12 OTW; T.-041-339 2152.

Curtis, G. Ronald, BSc, CEng, FICE, FSA Scot. Consulting Civil Engineer, Supervising Engineer (Reservoir Safety); Chairman, Historic Roads and Bridges Committee, Association for the Protection of Rural Scotland, 1983-90; b. 24.4.25, Edinburgh; m.; 4 s. Educ. George Watson's College, Edinburgh; Edinburgh University. Design of sewage works, J.D. & D.M. Watson, Consulting Civil Engineers, London, 1947-49; design and construction of sewerage and water supply schemes, Babtie Shaw and Morton, Consulting Civil Engineers, Glasgow, 1949-58; North of Scotland Hydro-Electric Board, 1958-87. Elder, Church of Scotland, 1962-87; Leader, Scout Movement, 1943-75. Recreations: Scotland; archaeology; historic Highland roads and bridges; megalithic astronomy. Address: (h.) 4 Braid Mount Rise, Edinburgh, EH10 6JW; Olcote, New Park, Callanish, Isle of Lewis, PA86 9DZ.

Curtis, Michael, MBChB, MRCPath. Forensic Pathologist, since 1988; b. 4.12.54, Wallsend. Educ. Dame Allan's School, Newcastle upon Tyne; Dundee University. Lecturer in Pathology, Newcastle upon Tyne University, 1979-86; Consultant Pathologist, North Manchester General Hospital, 1986-88; Senior Lecturer in Forensic Medicine/Consultant, Glasgow University, since 1988. Recreations: flying; clay pigeon shooting. Address: (h.) Ardfern, 20 Glen Road, Lennoxtown, Glasgow, G65 7JX; T.-0360 310632.

Cuschieri, Professor Alfred, MD, ChM, FRCSEd, FRCSEng, FIBiol. Professor and Head, Department of Surgery, Dundee University, since 1976; b. 30.9.38, Malta; m., Dr. M.P. Holley; 3 d. Educ. St. Aloysius College; Royal University of Malta; Liverpool University. Lecturer/Senior Lecturer/Reader in Surgery, then Professor of Surgery, Liverpool University. Recreations: fishing; music. Address: (h.) 6 Balnacarron Avenue, St. Andrews, KY16 9LT; T.-0382 60111.

Cusine, Professor Douglas James, LLB. Professor, Department of Conveyancing and Professional Practice of Law, Aberdeen University, since 1990; Member, Council, Law Society of Scotland, since 1988; Member, Lord President's Advisory Council on Messengers-at-Arms and Sheriff Officers, since 1989; b. 2.9.46, Glasgow; m., Marilyn Calvert Ramsay; 1 s.; 1 d. Educ. Hutchesons' Boys' Grammar School; Glasgow University. Solicitor, 1971; Lecturer in Private Law: Glasgow University, 1974-76, Aberdeen University, 1977-82; Senior Lecturer, 1982-90. Publications: Marine Pollution: Law and Practice (Co-Editor), 1980; Cases and Materials in Commercial Law (Co-Editor), 1987; A Scots Conveyancing Miscellany (Editor), 1987; New Reproductive Techniques: a legal perspective, 1988; Law and Practice of Diligence (Co-author), 1989; Reproductive Medicine and the Law (Co-Editor), 1990; Standard Securities, 1990; various articles on medico-legal issues and conveyancing.

Recreations: swimming; walking; bird-watching. Address: (h.) New Mearns, Downies, Portlethen, Aberdeen; T.-0224 780334.

D

Cuthbert, James R., MA, MSc, DPhil. Chief Statistician, Scottish Office, since 1988; b. 20.7.46, Irvine. Educ. Glasgow University; Sussex University. Lecturer in Statistics, Glasgow University, 1970-74; civil servant (Scottish Office and HM Treasury), since 1974. Address: (b.) Scottish Office, New St. Andrew's House, Edinburgh, EH1 3SX.

Cuthbertson, Iain. Actor; b. 4.1.30. Acted, Citizens', Glasgow, 1958-60; made London debut with the Citizens' in Gay Landscape, 1958; played title role in The Wallace, Edinburgh Festival, Edinburgh Festival, 1960; Member, Pitlochry Festival company, 1961; General Manager and Director of Productions, Citizens', 1962-65; there created the role of Armstrong in Armstrong's Last Goodnight; Associate Director, Royal Court Theatre, London, 1965; there played Musgrave in Sergeant Musgrave's Dance; Director, Perth Theatre, 1967-68; played the leading role in Sutherland's Law (TV series).

Cuthbertson, Ian Jardine, LLB, NP, MIPA, MSPI, FInstD. Licensed Insolvency Practitioner; Partner, Dorman, Jeffrey & Co., Solicitors, Glasgow and Edinburgh, since 1979; b. 8.5.51, Glasgow; m., Sally Jane; 1 s.; 2 d. Educ. Jordanhill College School, Glasgow; Glasgow University. Apprenticeship, Messrs Boyds; admitted as Solicitor, 1974; Partner, Messrs Boyds, 1978; jointly founded firm of Dorman Jeffrey & Co., 1979. Honorary Legal Adviser, Glasgow Group, Riding for the Disabled Association. Recreations: rugby; swimming; reading; computers. Address: (b.) Madeleine Smith House, 6/7 Blythswood Square, Glasgow; T.-041-221 9880; 20 Ainslie Place, Edinburgh; T.-031-225 9999.

Cuthell, Rev. Thomas Cuthbertson, MA, BD. Senior Minister, St. Cuthbert's Parish Church, Edinburgh, since 1976; b. 18.2.41, Falkirk. Educ. Bo'ness Academy; Edinburgh University. Assistant Minister, St. Giles Cathedral, Edinburgh, 1964-66; Minister, North Kirk, Uphall, 1966-76. Recreations: yacht racing; music; squash. Address: (h.) 22 Learmonth Terrace, Edinburgh, EH4 1PG; T.-031-332 6138.

Czerkawska, Catherine Lucy, MA (Hons); MA (postgraduate). Novelist and Dramatist; b. 3.12.50, Leeds; m., Alan Lees; 1 s. Educ. Queen Margaret's Academy, Ayr; St. Michael's Academy, Kilwinning; Edinburgh University; Leeds University. Wrote and published two books of poetry (White Boats and a Book of Men); taught EFL in Finland and Poland for three years; returned to Scotland to work as Community Writer in Fife; thereafter, full-time freelance writer working on radio and television drama, original plays and adaptations, short stories, features, etc.; author, Shadow of the Stone and The Golden Apple; Pye Radio Award for Best Play of 1980, O Flower of Scotland; Scottish Radio Industries Club Award, 1983, for Bonnie Blue Hen. Recreations: travel; films; local history; swimming; genealogy. Address: c/o Peters Fraser and Dunlop, 5th Floor, The Chambers, Chelsea Harbour, Lots Road, London, SW10 0XF; T.-01-376 7676.

Dagg, John Hunter, MD (Hons), FRCPGlas, FRCPEdin. Consultant Physician, Western Infirmary, Glasgow, since 1972; Honorary Lecturer in Medicine, Glasgow University, since 1962; b. 23.3.33, Rutherglen. Educ. High School of Glasgow; Glasgow University. Junior hospital posts, Glasgow and Paisley, 1958-65; Senior US Public Health Service Fellow, University of Washington Medical School, 1965-67; Senior Wellcome Fellow in Clinical Science, University Department of Medicine, Western Infirmary, Glasgow, 1968-72. Member, Board of Examiners, Royal Colleges of Physicians, UK. Recreations: classical music, especially as pianist; hill-walking; gardening. Address: (h.) Ardvulan, Gartmore, By Stirling, FK8 3RJ.

Daiches, Professor David, CBE, MA (Edin), DPhil (Oxon), Hon DLitt (Edinburgh, Glasgow, Sussex, Brown, Guelph), Docteur de l'Universite (Sorbonne), DUniv (Stirling), Dottore in Lettere (Bologna). Writer; b. 2.9.12, Sunderland; m., Isobel J. Mackay (deceased); 1 s.; 2 d. Educ. George Watson's College, Edinburgh; Edinburgh University; Balliol College, Oxford. Professor of English, Cornell University, 1946-51; University Lecturer in English and Fellow of Jesus College, Cambridge, 1951-61; Professor of English, Sussex University, 1961-77; Director, Institute for Advanced Studies in the Humanities, Edinburgh University, 1980-86. President, Saltire Society, 1981-87, now Vice-President; Past President, Association for Scottish Literary Studies. Publications: numerous works of criticism and biography, including A Critical History of English Literature; Robert Burns; Sir Walter Scott and His World; The Paradox of Scottish Culture; God and the Poets (Gifford Lectures, 1983). Recreations: music; talking. Address: (h.) 12 Rothesay Place, Edinburgh, EH3 7SQ.

Daiches, Lionel Henry, MA, LLB. Queen's Counsel, since 1956; Fellow, International Academy of Trial Lawyers, since 1976; b. 8.3.11, Sunderland; 2 s. Educ. George Watson's College, Edinburgh; Edinburgh University. Solicitor, Scotland, 1936-39; Army service, 1940-46, including Judge Advocate-General's Branch, Central Mediterranean Forces, North Africa and Italy (including Anzio Beachhead); Advocate, Scots Bar, 1946; QC Scotland, 1956; broadcaster on television and radio. Publication: Russians at Law, 1960. Recreations: walking and talking. Address: (h.) 10 Heriot Row, Edinburgh, EH3 6HU; T.-031-556 4144.

Dair, Thomas Morrison, JP. Education Chairman, Fife Regional Council, since 1978; b. 13.3.35, Cowdenbeath; m., Helen; 1 s.; 1 d. Educ. Beath High School; Lauder College. Former mining engineer; Town Councillor, 1972-75; Regional Councillor, since 1974; Member: Scottish Examinations Board, Health and Safety Executive Education Advisory Committee, Teachers and College Lecturers Negotiating Body, Scottish Television Education Advisory Committee; Chairman, Board of Governors, Fife College of Technology. Recreations: golf; gardening; reading. Address: (h.) 5 Barclay Street, Cowdenbeath, Fife; T.-0383 510434.

Dake, Laurence Patrick, OBE, BSc (Hons). Consultant, Reservoir Engineering (Hydrocarbon), since 1982; Honorary Professor, Petroleum Engineering, Heriot Watt University, since 1982; b. 11.3.41, Warrington; m., Grace Anderson. Educ. Douglas High School, Isle of Man; Glasgow University. Reservoir Engineer, Shell International, 1964-74; Head of Reservoir Engineering Training, The Hague, Holland, 1974-78; Chief Reservoir Engineer, BNOC, Glasgow, 1978-82. Adviser to governments and oil companies; worked on more than 100 projects worldwide; awarded OBE for services to reservoir engineering. Publication:

Fundamentals of Reservoir Engineering. Recreations: golf; cooking. Address: The Chapel, 10 Dublin Meuse, Edinburgh, EH3 6NW; T.-031-558 3147.

Dalby, Martin, BMus, ARCM. Executive Music Producer, BBC Scotland, since 1990 (Head of Music, 1972-90); b. 25.4.42, Aberdeen; m., Hilary. Educ. Aberdeen Grammar School; Royal College of Music. Music Producer, BBC Radio 3, 1965-71; Cramb Research Fellow in Composition, Glasgow University, 1971-72; freelance Composer. Recreations: flying; railways; bird-watching; hill-walking. Address: (h.) 23 Muirpark Way, Drymen, near Glasgow, G63 ODX; T.-0360 60427.

Dale, Brian Graeme, LLB, WS, NP. Partner, Brooke & Brown, WS, Dunbar, since 1974; Convener, Board of Administration, General Synod, Scottish Episcopal Church, 1980-90; b. 20.11.46, London; m., Judith Gail de Beaufort Franklin; 4 s.; 2 d. Educ. Bristol Grammar School; Aberdeen University. Legal apprentice, Shepherd & Wedderburn, WS, Edinburgh, 1968-70; Assistant, then Partner, Stuart & Stuart WS, Edinburgh, 1970-85; Treasurer, 1971, Secretary, 1974-90, Registrar, 1974, Diocese of Edinburgh, Scottish Episcopal Church; Honorary Secretary, Abbeyfield Society (Dunbar) Ltd. Recreations: music; armchair sport; singing; family life. Address: (h.) 5 The Doon, Spott, Dunbar, East Lothian; T.-Dunbar 62059.

Dale, Colin, BSc, MBIM. Manager, Scotland and Northern Ireland, British Technology Group, since 1979; b. 2.3.39, Edinburgh; m., Norma Mary Reilly; 1 s.; 2 d. Educ. Royal High School, Edinburgh; Heriot-Watt University. Research Chemist in industry, 1962-69; Executive, Scottish Council (Development and Industry), 1969-77; Manager, Scottish Development Agency, 1977-79. Chairman, Telford College Council, Edinburgh; Secretary, Harmeny Athletic Club, Edinburgh. Recreations: outdoors; gardening; athletics; reading history. Address: (b.) 23 Chester Street, Edinburgh, EH3 7ET; T.-031-220 2860.

Dale, Jack, MA, BD, STM. Further and Higher Education Secretary, Educational Institute of Scotland, since 1985; b. 15.5.38, Glasgow; m., Dr. Maureen G. Dale; 1 s.; 2 d. Educ. North Kelvinside Secondary School, Glasgow; Glasgow University; Union Theological Seminary, New York. Minister, Glengarry Parish, Church of Scotland, 1964-67; Senior Lecturer in Philosophy, Paisley College of Technology, 1967-85. Trustee, National Library of Scotland, since 1988. Address: (h.) Kincarse, Kinnaird, Inchture, Perthshire PH14 9QY.

Dale, Professor John Egerton, BSc, PhD, FRSE, FIBiol. Professor of Plant Physiology, Edinburgh University, since 1985 (Head, Department of Botany, since 1987, Head, Division of Biological Sciences, since 1990); b. 13.2.32, London; m., Jacqueline Joyce Benstock; 1 s.; 2 d. Educ. City of London School; Kings College, London. Plant Physiologist, Empire Cotton Growing Corporation, Uganda, 1956-61; Lecturer in Botany, then Reader, Edinburgh University, 1961-85. Secretary, Society for Experimental Biology, 1974-79; Secretary General, Federation of European Societies of Plant Physiology, 1978-84. Publications: 90 papers on growth of leaves and related topics. Recreations: travel; gardening. Address: (h.) The Old Bothy, Drem, North Berwick, EH39 5AP; T.-062 085 394.

Dalgety, The Hon. Mr Justice, (Ramsay Robertson Dalgety), QC, LLB (Hons). Supreme Court Judge, Kingdom of Tonga, since 1991; b. 2.7.45, Edinburgh; m., Mary Margaret Bernard; 1 s.; 1 d. Educ. High School of Dundee; St. Andrews University. Advocate, 1972; QC, 1986; Temporary Sheriff, 1987-91. Member, City of Edinburgh District Council, 1974-80; Director, Scottish Opera Ltd.,

1980-90; Director, Scottish Opera Theatre Trust Ltd., 1987-90; Deputy Chairman, Hibernian FC Shareholders Association, since 1990. Address: Apartment N, 116 Queensferry Road, Edinburgh EH4 2BT.

Dalhousie, Earl of (Simon Ramsay), KT, GCVO, GBE, MC, LLD. Lord Lieutenant, County of Angus, 1967-89; Lord Chamberlain to Queen Elizabeth, the Queen Mother, since 1965; Chancellor, Dundee University, 1977-92; b. 17.10.14, London; m., Margaret Elizabeth Mary Stirling; 3 s.; 2 d. Educ. Eton; Christ Church, Oxford. Major, 4/5 Black Watch TA; served overseas, 1939-45 (prisoner); MP, Forfar, 1945-50; Conservative Whip, 1946-48; Governor-General, Federation of Rhodesia and Nyasaland, 1957-63. Address: (h.) Brechin Castle, Brechin, Angus; T.-035-62 2176.

Dalrymple, Major The Hon. Colin James, DL, JP, BA. Farmer and Landowner, since 1956; b. 19.2.20, Ford, Midlothian; m., Fiona Jane Edwards; 1 s.; 3 d. Educ. Eton College; Trinity College, Cambridge. Served with Scots Guards, 1939-56; Member, Midlothian County Council, 1967-75; active supporter, Scottish Landowners Federation and National Farmers Union of Scotland. Recreations: shooting, fishing. Address. Oxenfoord Mains, Dalkeith.

Dalrymple, Fiona Jane, OBE. Hon. President, National Farmers Union of Scotland, since 1991 (Vice President, Lothian Area); Chairman, Home Grown Cereals Authority Advisory Committee, Food From Britain, since 1992; b. 15.1.34, London; m., Hon. Colin Dalrymple (qv); 1 s.; 2 d. Educ. Downham. Former Convener, Pigs Committee and Animal Health and Welfare Group, National Farmers Union of Scotland; former Chairman, Large White Breed Council. Organiser, Midlothian, Scotland's Gardens Scheme. Recreations: gardening; needlework; bridge. Address: (h.) Oxenfoord Mains, Dalkeith, Midlothian; T.-0875 320208.

Dalrymple, Sir Hew (Fleetwood) Hamilton-, 10th Bt (created 1697), KCVO, 1985 (CVO, 1974). Lord Lieutenant, East Lothian, since 1987; Vice-Chairman, Scottish & Newcastle Breweries, 1983-86 (Director, 1967-86); Chairman, Scottish American Investment Co., 1985-91 (Director, since 1967); b. 9.4.26; m., Lady Anne-Louise Mary Keppel; 4 s. Educ. Ampleforth; Staff College, Camberley, 1957. Commissioned Grenadier Guards, 1944; DAAG HQ 3rd Division, 1958-60; Regimental Adjt., Grenadier Guards, 1960-62; retired, 1962; Captain, Queen's Bodyguard for Scotland (Royal Company of Archers). DL, East Lothian, 1964; JP, 1987. Address: Leuchie, North Berwick, East Lothian; T.-North Berwick 2903.

Dalrymple, John Francis, BA, PhD, MInstP, CPhys, FSS. Head, Department of Management Science, Stirling University, since 1990 (Senior Lecturer in Management Science, 1989-90, Lecturer, 1979-89); Governor, BMT Quality Assurance Ltd., since 1990; Chairman, Scottish Association of Children's Panels, 1983-88; b. 18.9.49, Rosyth; 1 d. Educ. St. Andrew's High School, Kirkcaldy; Stirling University; Strathclyde University. Research Fellow, then Lecturer, Department of Applied Physics, Strathclyde University, 1974-79. Member, Strathclyde Region Children's Panel, since 1977. Recreations: skiing; walking; reading; swimming. Address: (b.) Management Science Department, School of Management, Stirling University, Stirling, FK9 4LA; T.-0786 73171, Ext. 2606.

Dalrymple-Hamilton, Christian Margaret, MBE, DL; b. 20.9.19, Devon. President, Wigtownshire Girl Guides. Address: (h.) Cladyhouse, Cairnryan, Stranraer, Wigtownshire.

Dalrymple-Hamilton of Bargany, Captain North Edward Frederick, CVO, MBE, DSC, JP, DL (Ayrshire). Ensign,

Queen's Bodyguard for Scotland (Royal Company of Archers); b. 17.2.22; m., 1, Hon. Mary Colville (deceased); 2 s.; 2, Antoinette Beech. Educ. Eton. Director of Naval Signals, 1965, Director, Weapons Directorate Surface, 1967, retired, 1970. Address: (h.) Lovestone House, Bargany, Girvan, Ayrshire, KA26 9RF; T.-0465 87227.

Dalyell, Tam. MP (Labour), Linlithgow (formerly West Lothian), since 1962; Weekly Columnist, New Scientist, since 1967; Member, Ancient Monuments Board for Scotland; Chairman, Bo'ness Heritage Trust; b. 9.8.32, Edinburgh; m., Kathleen Wheatley; 1 s.; 1 d. Educ. Edinburgh Academy; Harecroft; Eton; King's College, Cambridge; Moray House, Edinburgh. National Service, Scots Greys; Teacher, Bo'ness Academy, 1957-61; Deputy Director of Studies, Ship-School Dunera, 1961-62; Member, Public Accounts Committee, 1962-66; PPS to R.H.S. Crossman, 1964-70; Vice-Chairman, Parliamentary Labour Party, 1974-76; Member, European Parliament, 1975-78; Member, National Executive Committee, Labour Party, 1986-87; Member, Historic Buildings Council for Scotland, 1975-87. Publications: Case for Ship Schools, 1959; Ship-School Dunera, 1961; Devolution: the end of Britain?, 1978; A Science Policy for Britain, 1983; One Man's Falklands, 1983; Misrule, 1987; Dick Crossman: a portrait, 1989. Address: (h.) The Binns, Linlithgow, EH4 7NA; T.-0506 83 4255.

Dalzel-Job, Lt. Cdr. Patrick. Deputy Lieutenant, Lochalsh, since 1979; b. 1.6.13, London; m., Bjorg Bangsund (deceased); 1 s. Educ. Berkhamsted; in Switzerland. Owner/Master, topsail schooner Mary Fortune, mainly Norwegian and Arctic waters, until start of Second World War; as a junior Sub Lt., organised landing of Allied Expeditionary Force, North Norway, 1940, and evacuation of civilians from Narvik before German bombing; thanked by King of Norway; awarded Knight's Cross (1st Class) of St. Olav with swords; Special Service Operations, Norway, France, Germany; Canadian Navy, post-war; retired to West Highlands, 1960. Publications: The Settlers, 1957; From Arctic Snow to Dust of Normandy, 1991. Recreations: skiing; sailing; woodland garden. Address: (h.) Nead-An-Eoin, by Plockton, Ross-shire; T.-059 984 244.

Dalziel, Colonel William Alexander, CBE (1980), OStJ, TD, JP, DL, KLJ. Chairman, Transport Users Consultative Committee for Scotland; Chairman, Gas Consumers Council for Scotland; Chairman, Magistrates Committee, Edinburgh; Deputy Lord Lieutenant, Edinburgh, since 1977; b. 6.5.21, Dumbarton; m., Elizabeth Alexander Melville; 1 d. Army Service (Colonel); Deputy Chief Signals Officer, Scottish Command; worked in retail clothing trade, transport industry, fishing industry. Recreations: golf; gardening. Address: (h.) Gowanfield, 6 Orchard Road South, Edinburgh, EH4 3HF.

Daniels, Peter William, MA (Hons). Chief Executive, Clydesdale District Council, since 1983; b. 8.6.49, Wishaw; m., Anne; 3 s.; 1 d. Educ. Brandon High School, Motherwell; Dalziel High School, Motherwell; Glasgow University; Jordanhill College of Education. Lecturer (A) in Public Administration, Bell College of Technology, Hamilton, 1972-75; Personal Assistant to Chief Executive, Renfrew District Council, 1975-81; Assistant Chief Executive, Leicester City Council, 1981-83. Member, Scottish Symphony Orchestra Trust; former elected Member, East Kilbride District Council; former Vice-Chairman, Manpower Committee, COSLA. Recreations: running; football; classical music; playing piano and clarinet; Cub Scout leader. Address: (b.) Clydesdale District Council, District Offices, South Vennel, Lanark, ML11 7JT; T.-Lanark 61331.

Darling, Alistair Maclean. MP (Labour), Edinburgh Central, since 1987; Advocate; b. 28.11.53.

Dareau, Margaret Grace, MA. Editor, Dictionary of the Older Scottish Tongue, since 1984; b. 11.3.44, Dumfries; m., Michel Dareau; 1 s.; 2 d. Educ. Annan Academy; Edinburgh University. Research Assistant on Middle English Dialects Atlas, 1967; Kennedy Scholarship to study linguistics, MIT, 1967; began work at Dictionary of Older Scottish Tongue, 1968; Editor, Concise Scots Dictionary, 1976-77, 1980-84. Recreations: horse riding and schooling. Address: (h.) The Old Manse, Howgate, Penicuik, EH26 8QB; T.-0968 73028.

Darwent, Rt. Rev. Frederick Charles, LTh (Hon), JP. Bishop of Aberdeen and Orkney, since 1978; b. 20.4.27, Liverpool; m., 1, Edna Lilian Waugh (deceased); 2 d.; 2, Roma Evelyn Fraser. Educ. Warbreck School, Liverpool; Ormskirk Grammar School; Wells Theological College, Somerset. Followed a banking career, 1943-61; War Service, Far East, 1945-48; ordained Deacon, 1963, Priest, 1964, Diocese of Liverpool; Curate, Pemberton, Wigan, 1963-65; Rector: Strichen, 1965-71, New Pitsligo, 1965-78, Fraserburgh, 1971-78; Canon, St Andrew's Cathedral, Aberdeen, 1971; Dean of Aberdeen and Orkney, 1973-78. Recreations: amateur stage (acting and production); calligraphy; music. Address: (b.) Diocesan Centre, 39 King's Crescent, Aberdeen, AB2 3HP; T.-0224 636653.

Das, Sachinandan, MB, BS, FRCR, DMRT. Consultant in administrative charge, Ninewells Hospital, Dundee, and Head, University Department, Dundee University, since 1987, Clinical Director, since 1991; Chairman, Area Oncology Committee, since 1987; Council Member, Scottish Radiological Society, since 1987; Regional Postgraduate Education Advisor in Radiotherapy and Oncology, since 1987; b. 1.8.44, Cuttack, India; m., Dr. Subhalaxmi; 1 s.; 1 d. Educ. Ravenshaw Collegiate School; SCB Medical College, Cuttack, India; Utkal University. Senior House Officer in Radiotherapy, Plymouth General Hospital, 1969-70; Registrar in Radiotherapy and Oncology, then Senior Registrar, Mersey Regional Centre for Radiotherapy, Liverpool, 1970-77; Member: Standing Scottish Committee, National Medical Consultative Committee, Scottish Paediatric Oncology Group, Joint Radiological Safety Committee, Radiation Hazards Sub-Committee, Unit Medical and Dental Advisory Committee. Recreations: hill-walking; table tennis; reading. Address: (h.) Grapevine, 42 Menzieshill Road, Dundee, DD2 1PU; T.-Dundee 642915.

Datta, Dipankar, MB, BS, FRCPGlas. Consultant Physician (with special interest in gastroenterology), since 1975; Chairman, Scottish India Forum; Project Director, Scottish Overseas Aid; b. 30.1.33, Chittagong, India; m., Dr. J.B. Datta (qv); 1 s.; 1 d. Educ. Calcutta University. Former Member, Central Executive Committee, Scottish Council, United Nations Association; former Vice Chairman, UN Association, Glasgow; Chairman, Overseas Doctors' Association, Scottish Division; former Member, Lanarkshire Health Board; Member, Executive Committee, Scottish Council, Royal Commonwealth Society for the Blind. Recreations: reading - history, economics and international politics. Address: (h.) 9 Kirkvale Crescent, Newton Mearns, Glasgow, G77 5HB; T.-041-639 1515.

Datta, Jean Bronwen, MB, ChB, MRCP(Glas), DObstRCOG, DCH. Associate Specialist in Infectious Diseases, Belvidere Hospital and Ruchill Hospital, Glasgow, since 1970; Honorary Senior Clinical Lecturer, Glasgow University, since 1985; b. 2.2.32, Glasgow; m., Dr. Dipankar Datta (qv); 1 s.; 1 d. Educ. Rutherglen Academy; Glasgow University. Various hospital appointments, including Registrar in Paediatrics, Sheffield Children's Hospital and Royal Maternity Hospital, Glasgow. Publication: Infections in Current Medical Practice (Contributor), 1986. Recreations: walking; skiing; gardening; music. Address: (h.) 9 Kirkvale

Crescent, Newton Mearns, Glasgow, G77 5HB; T.-041-639 1515.

Davenport, Professor John, BSc, MSc, PhD, DSc, FIBiol, FZS. Director, University Marine Biological Station, Millport, since 1991; Professor of Marine Biology, London University; b. 12.2.46; m., Julia Ladner; 2 d. Educ. Bablake School, Coventry; London University; Southampton University; University of Wales. Demonstrator in Marine Biology, University of Wales at Bangor, 1970-72; Researcher, NERC Unit of Marine Invertebrate Biology, 1972-83 (promoted Principal Scientific Officer, 1980); Lecturer, then Senior Lecturer, School of Animal Biology, University of Wales at Bangor, 1983-88; Reader in Marine Biology, School of Ocean Sciences, Marine Sciences Laboratories, Menai Bridge, 1988-91. Publications: Animal Osmoregulation (Co-Author), 1981; Environmental Stress and Behavioural Adaptation, 1985; Animal Life at Low Temperature, 1992. Recreations: skiing; sailboarding; swimming; birding; badminton. Address: (b.) University Marine Biological Station, Isle of Cumbrae, KA28 0EG.

Davidson, Alan Ingram, ChM, FRCSEdin, DObstRCOG. Consultant Surgeon, Aberdeen Royal Infirmary, since 1974; Honorary Senior Lecturer in Surgery, Aberdeen University, since 1974; b. 25.3.35, Aberdeen; m., Margaret Elizabeth Mackay; 1 s.; 1 d. Educ. Robert Gordon's College, Aberdeen; Aberdeen University. House Officer, Aberdeen Royal Infirmary, 1959-60; National Service, Royal Army Medical Corps, 1960-62; Lecturer, Department of Pathology, Aberdeen, 1963-64; Registrar and Senior Registrar, Aberdeen Royal Infirmary, 1964-74. Recreations: gardening; watching TV; music. Address: (h.) 20 Hillview Road, Cults, Aberdeen; T.-Aberdeen 867347.

Davidson, Hon. Lord (Charles Kemp Davidson), MA, LLB, FRSE. Chairman, Scottish Law Commission, since 1988; Senator of the College of Justice, since 1983; Deputy Chairman, Boundaries Commission for Scotland, since 1985; b. 13.4.29, Edinburgh; m., Mary Mactaggart; 1 s.; 2 d. Educ. Fettes College, Edinburgh; Oxford University; Edinburgh University. Advocate, 1956; QC (Scot), 1969; Keeper, The Advocates Library, 1972-77; Vice Dean, Faculty of Advocates, 1977-79; Dean, 1979-83; Procurator to the General Assembly of the Church of Scotland, 1972-83; Chairman, National Health Service Tribunal for Scotland, 1970-83. Address: (h.) 22 Dublin Street, Edinburgh, EH1 3PP; T.-031-556 2168.

Davidson, Professor Colin William, BSc, DipER, PhD, CEng, FIEE, FRSA. Consulting Engineer; Emeritus Professor, Heriot-Watt University; b. 18.9.34, Edinburgh; m., Ranee M.N. Cleland; 2 d. Educ. George Heriot's School; Edinburgh University. Lecturer, Edinburgh University, 1956-61; Electronics Engineer, Nuclear Enterprises (GB) Ltd., 1961-64; Lecturer, Heriot-Watt College/University, 1964-67; Associate Professor, Chulalongkorn University, Bangkok, 1967-68; Heriot-Watt University: Senior Lecturer, 1968-85, Professor of Electrical Engineering, 1985-88, Dean of Engineering, 1976-79 and 1984-87, Head of Department, 1979-87. Vice-President, Institution of Electrical Engineers; Member, Lothian Regional Council, since 1990. Recreation: sailing (Royal Highland Yacht Club). Address: (h.) 20 East Barnton Avenue, Edinburgh, EH4 6AQ; T.-031-336 5806.

Davidson, Douglas, FCR, DCR, SRR. Area Adviser in Radiography, Aberdeen Royal Infirmary, since 1982; Member, Grampian Health Board, 1978-91; Council Member, College and Society of Radiographers, 1991-92; b. 8.2.32, Aberdeen; m., Margaret Farquhar; 1 s.; 1 d. Educ. Robert Gordon's College, Aberdeen; Grampian School of Radiography. National Service, RAMC, 1950-52; Radiographer: Chalmers Hospital, Banff, 1954-55, Aberdeen

Royal Infirmary, since 1955. Harry West Memorial Award, 1986. Recreations: golf; swimming; watching sport of all kinds. Address: (h.) 23 Ronaldsay Road, Aberdeen, AB2 6ND; T.-0224 310486.

Davidson, Duncan Lewis Watt, BSc (Hons), MB, ChB, FRCPEdin. Consultant Neurologist, Tayside Health Board, since 1976; Honorary Senior Lecturer in Medicine, Dundee University, since 1976; b. 16.5.40, Kingston, Jamaica; m., Dr. Anne V.M. Maiden; 4 s.; 1 d. Educ. Knox College, Jamaica; Edinburgh University. House Officer, Senior House Officer, Registrar and Senior Registrar posts in medicine and neurology, Edinburgh, 1966-75; Peel Travelling Fellowship, Montreal, 1973-74; MRC clinical scientific staff, MRC Brain Metabolism Unit, Edinburgh, 1975-76. Recreations: gardening; golf. Address: (h.) Brooksby, Queens Terrace, St. Andrews, Fife; T.-0334 76108.

Davidson, Eric Dalgleish, DA (Edin), RIBA, FRIAS. Director, Scottish Health Service, Common Services Agency, Building Division, 1985-89; b. 7.9.28, Musselburgh; m., June Mary Ryman; 2 s.; 2 d. Educ. Musselburgh Grammar School; Heriot-Watt University; Edinburgh College of Art. Assistant Regional Architect, South Eastern Regional Hospital Board, 1961-74; Lecturer in Advanced Practice and Management, Department of Architecture, Edinburgh University, 1966-74; Assistant Director and Chief Architect, Scottish Health Service, Common Services Agency, Building Division, 1974-85. Council Member, RIAS, 1984-88; Member, Scottish Building Contracts Committee, 1987-91; Member, Scottish Building Standards Committee (Research Sub-Committee), 1986-91; Committee Member, Disability Scotland. Address: (h.) 27 Belgrave Road, Edinburgh, EH12 6NG; T.-031-334 5231.

Davidson, Ewan Irvine, BCom, CQSW. Director, Alzheimer's Scotland, since 1987; b. 12.11.48, Peebles; m., Carol Brown; 1 s.; 1 d. Educ. Peebles High School; Edinburgh University; Glasgow University. Co-operative Officer, Swaziland, 1969; Co-ordinator, Drug Abuse Unit (Western Australia), 1974; Volunteer Director, CSV (London), 1978; Development Officer, Lothian Regional Council, 1980; Projects Manager, Key Housing Association, Glasgow, 1985. Recreations: marathon running; digging the allotment. Address: (b.) 33 Castle Street, Edinburgh; T.-031-225 1453.

Davidson, Fraser Paul, LLB, PhD. Senior Lecturer in Law, Dundee University, since 1990; b. 10.7.54, Dundee; m., Fiona Joyce Tullis. Educ. Lawside Academy, Dundee; Dundee University; Edinburgh University. Tutor: Department of Jurisprudence, Dundee University, 1976-77, Department of Public Law, Edinburgh University, 1977-78; Lecturer in Law, Dundee University, 1978-90. Publications: The Judiciary and the Development of Employment Law, 1984; A Guide to the Wages Act 1986, 1986; International Commercial Arbitration: Scotland and the Uncitral Model Law, 1991. Recreations: reading; music; theatre; cinema; spectator sports. Address: (h.) Invergowrie House, Ninewells, Dundee, DD2 1UA; T.-0382 645639.

Davidson, Ian Graham, MA (Hons). MP (Labour), Glasgow Govan, since 1992; Chairman, Strathclyde Education Committee, since 1990; Chairman, COSLA Education Committee, since 1990; b. 8.9.50, Jedburgh; m., Morag Mackinnon; 1 s.; 1 d. Educ. Jedburgh Grammar School; Galashiels Academy; Edinburgh University; Jordanhill College of Education. Address: (h.) 71 Queen Margaret Drive, Glasgow, G20 8PA; T.-041-946 3887.

Davidson, Rev. Ian Murray Pollock, MA, BD. Minister, Allan Park South Church and Church of the Holy Rude, Stirling, since 1985; Vice Chairman, General Trustees, Church of Scotland, since 1990; b. 14.3.28, Kirriemuir; m.,

Isla; 2 s. Educ. Montrose Academy; St. Andrews University. National Service, 1949-51; Minister: Crieff North and West Church (St. Andrew's), 1955-61, Grange Church, Kilmarnock, 1961-67, Cambuslang Old Church, 1967-85; Convener, Maintenance of the Ministry Committee and Board, Church and Ministry Department, 1981-84; General Trustee, since 1975. Publication: At the Sign of the Fish (history of Cambuslang Old Parish Church), 1975. Recreations: travel; photography; reading; writing. Address: (h.) 21 Drummond Place, Stirling, FK8 2JE; T.-0786 74154.

Davidson, John F., MB, ChB, FRCPEdin, FRCPath. Consultant Haematologist, Glasgow Royal Infirmary, since 1969; b. 11.1.34, Lumphanan; m., Laura G. Middleton; 1 s.; 1 d. Educ. Robert Gordon's College, Aberdeen; Aberdeen University. Surgeon Lt., RN; Registrar in Medicine, Aberdeen Royal Infirmary; Research Registrar in Medicine, then Senior Registrar in Haematology, Glasgow Royal Infirmary. Secretary, British Society for Haematalogy, 1983-86; President, British Society for Haematology, 1990-91; Chairman, BCSH Haemostasis and Thrombosis Task Force, 1986-81; Chairman, Steering Committee NEQAS in blood coagulation, 1986-91; Editor, Progress in Fibrinolysis, Volumes I to VII; Chairman, International Committee on Fibrinolysis, 1976-84; Co-Editor in Chief, Fibrinolysis. Recreation: gardening. Address: (b.) Department of Haematology, Glasgow Royal Infirmary, Glasgow; T.-041-304 4669.

Davidson, John Knight, OBE, MD, FRCPEdin, FRCPGlas, FRCR, FACR (Hon), FRACR (Hon). Consultant Radiologist; b. 17.8.25, Edinburgh; m., Edith E. McKelvie; 2 s.; 1 d. Educ. George Watson's Boys College, Edinburgh; Edinburgh University. Consultant Radiologist in Admin. Charge, Western Infirmary and Gartnavel General, Glasgow, 1967-90; Royal College of Radiologists: Member, Council, 1984-87, Chairman, Examining Board, 1976-79, Scottish Committee, 1985-89; Member, Council, Royal Glasgow Institute of Fine Arts, 1978-88; Member, Medical and Dental Defence Union Council; Adviser in Hyperbaric Research, MRC and Aberdeen; Member, Executive, and Chairman Health Policy, Scottish Conservative and Unionist Association; Deputy President, Glasgow and Renfrewshire, British Red Cross Society. International Skeletal Society Silver Medal, 1992; Rohan Williams Professor, Australasia, 1977; Aggarwal Memorial Oration, India, 1988; Editor, Aseptic Necrosis of Bone and numerous publications. Recreations: golf; painting; bridge; meeting people; skiing. Address: (h.) 31 Newlands Road, Glasgow, G43 2JG; T.-041-632 3113; (b.) Lifewatch, 5/6 Park Terrace, Glasgow, G3 6BY; T.-041-332 8010.

Davidson, John Marr, MA, LLB, WS. Partner, W. & J. Burness, WS, 1954-86; b. 22.6.23, Lanark; m., Sylvia Russell; 1 s.; 1 d. Educ. Edinburgh Academy; Edinbrgh University. Service in Italy, Middle East, Europe, with Cameronians (Scottish Rifles), attaining rank of Captain, 1942-46; Law Apprentice, then Partner, Auld and Macdonald, WS, 1946-54. High Constable, Holyrood; Director, various limited companies. Recreations: shooting; fishing; travel. Address: (h.) 66 Barnton Park Crescent, Edinburgh, EH4 6EN; T.-031-339 5387.

Davidson, Julie Wilson. Writer and Broadcaster; Television Critic, Glasgow Herald, since 1981; Freelance Contributor, BBC, Granada TV, The Times, The Observer, etc., since 1981; b. Motherwell; m., Harry Reid (qv); 1 d. Educ. Aberdeen High School for Girls. Trainee Journalist, D.C. Thomson Ltd., Dundee, 1961-64; Feature Writer and Sub-Editor, Aberdeen Press & Journal, 1964-67; The Scotsman: Feature Writer, 1967-77, Columnist, 1977-81. Columnist/Critic of the Year, Scottish Press Awards, 1985; Critic of the Year, Scottish Press Awards, 1988-89-92.

Recreations: reading; walking; travelling; lunching. Address: (h.) 15 Albion Buildings, Ingram Street, Glasgow; T.-041-552 8403.

Davidson, Neil McDonald, MA, DM, FRCP, FRCPE. Consultant Physician, Eastern General Hospital, Edinburgh, since 1978; Senior Lecturer in Medicine, Edinburgh University, since 1978; Assistant Director of Studies (Medicine), Edinburgh Postgraduate Board for Medicine, since 1985; Member, General Medical Council, since 1989; b. 15.5.40, Leamington Spa; m., Jill Ann; 3 s.; 1 d. Educ. Epsom College; Merton College, Oxford; St. Thomas's Hospital, London. House Officer, St. Thomas's Hospital and Hammersmith Hospital, London; Medical Registrar, St. Thomas's Hospital, London; Senior Medical Registrar, Lecturer and Senior Lecturer in Medicine, Ahmadu Bello University, Zaria, Nigeria; Lecturer in Medicine, Edinburgh University. Recreation: collecting antique maps. Address: (h.) 43 Blackford Road, Grange, Edinburgh, EH9 2DT; T.-031-667 3960.

Davidson, Professor Robert, MA, BD, DD, FRSE. Moderator, General Assembly of the Church of Scotland, 1990-91; Professor of Old Testament Language and Literature, Glasgow University, 1981-91; b. 30.3.27, Markinch, Fife; m., Elizabeth May Robertson; 5 s.; 4 d. Educ. Bell-Baxter School, Cupar; St. Andrews University. Lecturer in Biblical Studies, Aberdeen University, 1953-60; Lecturer in Hebrew and Old Testament Studies, St. Andrews University, 1960-66; Lecturer/Senior Lecturer in Old Testament, Edinburgh University, 1966-72. Publications: The Bible Speaks, 1959; The Old Testament, 1964; Geneses 1 - 11, 1973; Genesis 12 - 50, 1979; The Bible in Religious Education, 1979; The Courage to Doubt, 1983; Jeremiah Volume 1, 1983; Jeremiah Volume 2, Lamentations, 1985; Ecclesiastes, Song of Songs, 1986; Wisdom and Worship, 1990. Recreations: music; gardening. Address: (h.) 30 Dumgoyne Drive, Bearsden, Glasgow, G61 3AP; T.-041-942 1810.

Davidson, William Keith, CBE, JP, FRCGP, DPA; b. 20.11.26, Glasgow; m., Dr. Mary W.A. Davidson; 1 s.; 1 d. Educ. Coatbridge Secondary School; Glasgow University. Medical Officer, 1st Bn., RSF, 1950; Maj. 2 i/c 14 Field Ambulance, 1950-51; Medical Officer, i/c Holland and Belgium, 1952; General Medical Practitioner, 1953-90; Chairman, Glasgow Local Medical Committee, 1971-75; Chairman, Scottish General Medical Services Committee, 1972-75; Member, Scottish Council on Crime, 1972-75; Fellow, BMA, 1975; Deputy Chairman, General Medical Services Committee (UK), 1975-79; Member, Scottish Medical Practices Committee, 1968-80; Chairman, Scottish Council, BMA, 1978-81; Chairman, Scottish Health Services Planning Council, 1984-89; Member, Scottish Health Services Policy Board, 1985-89; Vice President, BMA, since 1983; Hon. President, Glasgow Eastern Medical Society, 1984-85; Member, General Medical Council, since 1984; Member, Greater Glasgow Health Board, 1989-91; Chairman, Strathclyde Aids Forum, since 1990; Chairman, Greater Glasgow Health Board Aids Forum, since 1990; Chairman, Greater Glasgow Health Board Drugs & Alcohol Forum, since 1990; Vice Chairman, Chryston High School Board, since 1990; Elder, Church of Scotland, since 1956. Recreation: gardening. Address: (h.) Dunvegan, Hornshill Farm Road, Stepps, Glasgow, G33 6DE; T.-041-779 2103.

Davidson, William Powell, MREHIS, MInstWM, MILAM. Director of Environmental Health & Leisure Services, Stewartry District Council, since 1982; Secretary, Scottish Food and Drugs Co-ordinating Committee, since 1983; b. 28.8.48, Paisley; m., Elizabeth Ann Davidson; 1 s. Educ. Camphill Senior Secondary School, Paisley; Langside College, Glasgow; Bell College, Hamilton. Trainee, then

Assistant Sanitary Inspector, Renfrew County Council, 1966-71; Sanitary Inspector, Paisley Burgh Council, 1971-72; Assistant District Sanitary Inspector, Perth and Kinross Joint County Council, 1972-75; Area Environmental Health Officer, Argyll and Bute District Council, 1975-76; Regional Manager, Ciba Geigy Public Hygiene Project, Saudi Arabia, 1976-77; Senior Environmental Health Officer, Perth and Kinross District Council, 1977-79; Depute Director of Environmental Health, Stewartry District Council, 1979-82. Recreations: golf; gardening; travel; jogging; football. Address: (b.) Environmental Health & Leisure Services Department, Cannonwalls, High Street, Kirkcudbright.

Davie, Elspeth, DA. Writer; b. Kilmarnock; m., George Elder Davie; 1 d. Educ. George Watson's College; Edinburgh University; Edinburgh Art College. Taught Art for several years in the Borders, Aberdeen and Northern Ireland; author of four novels: Providings, Creating A Scene, Climbers on a Stair, Coming to Light; four collections of short stories: The Spark, The High Tide Talker, The Night of the Funny Hats, A Traveller's Room, Death of a Doctor; two Arts Council Awards; received Katherine Mansfield Prize, 1978. Recreations: reading; walking; films. Address: (h.) 155/17 Orchard Brae Gardens, Edinburgh, EH4; T.-031-332 8297.

Davie, Ivor Turnbull, MB, ChB, FFARCS. Consultant Anaesthetist, Western General Hospital, Edinburgh, since 1971; Honorary Senior Lecturer, Edinburgh University, since 1979; Lecturer, Central Midwives Board (Scotland), since 1974; b. 23.2.35, Edinburgh; m., Jane Elizabeth Fleischmann; 1 s.; 1 d. Educ. Royal High School, Edinburgh; Edinburgh University. Member, Board of Examiners, Faculty of Anaesthetists, Royal College of Surgeons of England (Primary FFARCS, 1978-84, Part II FFARCS, 1985-86, Part III FFARCS, 1987-88, Part III FCAnaes, 1988-90); President, Edinburgh and East of Scotland Society of Anaesthetists, 1990-91; Tutor, Faculty of Anaesthetists, 1979-87; Regional Educational Adviser, College of Anaesthetists, since 1988; Member, Editorial Board, British Journal of Obstetrics and Gynaecology, 1980-84; Visiting Medical Officer, Westmead Centre, Sydney, NSW, 1983. Address: (b.) Department of Anaesthesia, Western General Hospital, Edinburgh, EH4 2XU; T.-031-332 2525.

Davie, Robert Alastair, MA, BCom. Secretary/Director, Sea Fish Industry Authority, since 1981; b. 28.10.38, Edinburgh; m., Carol Haig; 2 s. Educ. George Watson's College; Edinburgh University. Recreation: golf. Address: (h.) 4 Riselaw Place, Edinburgh, EH10 6HP; T.-031-447 5168.

Davies, Professor Alan, MA, PhD, DipEd, DipGenLing. Professor of Applied Linguistics, Edinburgh University, since 1992; b. 17.2.31, Neath; 1 s.; 3 d. Educ. Alderman Newton's School, Leicester; Corpus Christi College, Oxford. School Teacher, England and Kenya, 1955-62; Senior Research Associate, Birmingham University, 1962-65; Lecturer, Senior Lecturer, Reader, Edinburgh University, 1965-92; seconded: Professor of English and Head of Department, Tribhuvan University, Kathmandu, 1969-71, Visiting Professor and Director, National Languages Institute of Australia Language Testing Centre, Melbourne University, 1990-91. Past Chairman, British Association of Applied Linguistics; Secretary-General, International Association of Applied Linguistics; President, TESOL (Scotland); Editor, Language Testing, since 1992. Publications: Principles of Language Testing, 1990; The Native Speaker in Applied Linguistics, 1991. Address: (b.) Department of Applied Linguistics, Edinburgh University, 14 Buccleuch Place, Edinburgh, EH8 9LN; T.-031-650 3497.

Davies, Christopher Henry, BA (Hons), DipEd, FBIM. Chief Executive, Sea Fish Industry Authority, since 1989; b. 6.11.39, Wolverhampton; m., Elisabeth; 2 s. Educ. Wolverhampton Grammar School; University College, Durham; Queens' College, Cambridge. General Manager: Commercial Plastics GMBH, Austria, Nairn Australia; International Operations Director, Nairn International Ltd., Newcastle; Sales/Marketing Director, Nairn Floors Ltd., Kirkcaldy; Managing Director, Forbo Nairn Ltd., Kirkcaldy. Recreations: music; walking; board-sailing; golf. Address: (h.) 7 West Carnethy Avenue, Colinton, Edinburgh; T.-031-441 2152.

Davies, David Lloyd, MD, FRCP. Senior Lecturer in Medicine, Glasgow University, since 1973; Honorary Consultant Physician; b. 1.3.38, Swansea; m., Catherine G. Drummond; 1 d. Educ. Llandovery College; St. Mary's Hospital, London. Various hospital appointments: St. Mary's Hospital, London, Colonial Hospital, Gibraltar, Postgraduate Medical School, Hammersmith, Chelmsford and Essex Hospital, Western Infirmary, Glasgow. Recreations: marquetry; music; gardening; sport. Address: (h.) Rosebud Cottage, 23 Main Street, Killearn G63 9RJ; T.-0360 50990.

Davies, David Somerville, FTCL, ARCM, Conductor, Artistic Director, Paragon Ensemble of Scotland, since 1980; b. 13.6.54, Dunfermline. Educ. Dunfermline High School; Royal Scottish Academy of Music; Edinburgh University; Marseille Conservatoire. Assistant Principal Flute, Scottish National Orchestra; Principal Flute, Scottish Opera; Freelance Conductor; Assistant Conductor, Marseille Opera; Lecturer and Head of Woodwind, Royal Scottish Academy of Music; Tovey Memorial Prize; Clutterbuck Scholarship; Sir James Caird Scholarship; Scottish Arts Council Music Award; Scottish International Education Trust Award; Performing Rights Society/Scottish Society of Composers Award for services to contemporary Scottish music. Recreations: reading; photography; computing. Address: (b.) c/o Paragon Ensemble, 2 Port Dundas Place, Glasgow G2 3LB; T.-041-332 9903.

Davies, Ivor, MA, DipEd, PhD, MILAM. Director of Planning, Scottish Sports Council, since 1975; b. Scotland. Educ. Edinburgh University. Founded and developed Department of Geography, Lakehead University, Thunder Bay, Ontario, and became first Chairman of Department. Recreations: sport; music. Address: (b.) Caledonia House, South Gyle, Edinburgh, EH12 9DQ; T.-031-317 7200.

Davies, John Geraint, MA. Secretary General, General Synod, Scottish Episcopal Church, since 1986; Administrator, SEC Pension Fund, since 1988; b. 5.7.38, Wrexham; m., Frances Gillian Peacock; 2 s.; 1 d. Educ. Oxford. Rolls Royce, 1959-63; Ferranti, 1963-71; Scottish Office, 1971-85. Address: (b.) 21 Grosvenor Crescent, Edinburgh, EH12 5EE.

Davies, Patrick P., LLB. Solicitor; Partner, Peterkins, since 1971; Member, Council, Law Society of Scotland, since 1985; b. 5.10.44, Cheltenham; m., Caroline Jane Gray; 1 d. Educ. Bristol Grammar School; Aberdeen University. Recreations: hill-walking; driving pre-war motor cars. Address: (b.) 7/9 King Street, Aberdeen, AB2 3AA; T.-Aberdeen 626300.

Davies (a.k.a. Glasse-Davies), Professor R. Wayne, MA, PhD, ScD. Robertson Professor of Biotechnology, Glasgow University, since 1989; b. 10.6.44, Cardiff; m., Victoria Glasse; 3 s.; 1 d. Educ. Queen Elizabeth's Hospital, Bristol; St. John's College, Cambridge. Research Fellow, University of Wisconsin, 1968-71; H3 Professor, Universitat Zu Koln, FRG, 1971-77; Lecturer, University of Essex, 1977-81; Senior Lecturer, UMIST, 1981-83; Vice-President, Scientific and Research Director, Allelix Biopharmaceuticals, Toronto, 1983-89. Recreations: poetry and literature; politics; skiing. Address: (b.) Robertson Institute of Biotechnology,

Department of Genetics, Glasgow University, Church Street, Glasgow, G11 5JS; T.-041-339 8855, Ext. 5102.

Davies, Terry, BSc (Hons), MSc, MInstP, FIPC. Principal, James Watt College, since 1990; b. 14.12.40, Llanelli. Educ. Llanelli Boys' Grammar School; University College of Swansea; Nottingham University. Lecturer (Physics), Middlesex Polytechnic, then Preston Polytechnic, 1964-73; Depute Head, Department of Engineering, Science and Construction, Lewes Technical College, 1973-79; Head, Department of Science, Mathematics and Computing, Telford College of Further Education, Edinburgh, 1979-85; Depute Principal, Telford College of FE, 1985-90. Recreations: rugby; cricket; squash; tennis. Address: (b.) James Watt College, Finnart Street, Greenock, PA16 8HF; T.-0475 24433.

Davis, Christine A.M., MA, DipEd. Chairman, Scottish Legal Aid Board, since 1991; Member, Scottish Agricultural Wages Board, since 1990; Member, Scottish Economic Council, since 1987; Member, Scottish Committee of the Council on Tribunals, since 1989; b. 5.3.44, Salisbury; m., Robin John Davis; 2 d. Educ. Perth Academy; Ayr Academy; St. Andrews University; Aberdeen University; Aberdeen College of Education. Teacher of History and Modern Studies, Cumbernauld High School and High School of Stirling, 1967-69; joined Dunblane Town Council and Perth and Kinross Joint County Council, 1972; undertook research in Canada on Ontario Hydro and small claims in Ontario courts, 1977-78; Chairman, Electricity Consultative Council for North of Scotland, 1980-90; Member, North of Scotland Hydro Electric Board, 1980-90; Clerk, London Yearly Meeting, Society of Friends (Quakers); a President, Council of Churches for Britain and Ireland. Recreations: embroidery; bird-watching; walking. Address: (h.) 24 Newton Crescent, Dunblane, Perthshire, FK15 ODZ; T.-Dunblane 823226.

Davis, Margaret Thomson. Novelist; b. Bathgate; 2 s. Educ. Albert Secondary School. Worked as children's nurse; Red Cross nurse; short story writer; novelist; author of autobiography, The Making of a Novelist; novels include The Breadmakers, A Baby Might Be Crying, A Sort of Peace, The Prisoner, The Prince and the Tobacco Lords, Roots of Bondage, Scorpion in the Fire, The Dark Side of Pleasure, A Very Civilised Man, Light and Dark, Rag Woman Rich Woman, Daughters and Mothers, Wounds of War, A Woman of Property; Committee Member: International PEN (Scottish Branch); Society of Authors; Lecturer in Creative Writing; Honorary President, Strathkelvin Writers Club; Committee Member, Swanwick Writers' School. Recreations: reading; travelling; being with friends. Address: c/o Heather Jeeves Literary Agency, 15 Campden Hill Square, London, W8.

Davis, Robert Clive, CEng, MIMarE. Marine Engineer Superintendent, Scottish Fisheries Protection Agency, since 1991; b. 29.8.38, Brighton; m., Elizabeth Mary Warren; 2 s. Educ. Marist Brothers, Durban, South Africa; Glasgow College of Nautical Studies. Apprenticeship, James Brown, Durban, South Africa; joined Merchant Navy, 1959; served with Safmarine, Bank Line, Jardine Matheson; Boiler Inspector, 1970-72; joined Scottish Office, 1972; promoted Chief Engineer, 1979. Recreations: golf; gardening; DIY. Address: (h.) 19 Duddingston Park South, Edinburgh, EH15 3NY; T.-031-669 5320.

Davis, Robert Gunn. Member, Mental Welfare Commission for Scotland, since 1984; Social Work Adviser (Mental Health), Strathclyde Region, since 1977; b. 11.5.38, Edinburgh; m., Mildred Bennett; 1 s.; 1 d. Educ. Daniel Stewart's College, Edinburgh. Certificate of Qualification in Probation Work, Jordanhill College, 1968. Probation Officer, City of Glasgow, before 1969; Senior Social Worker, then Social Work Training Officer, Lanark County Council, 1970-

75; Recruitment and Training Officer, Strathclyde Region Social Work Department, 1975-77. Founder Member, British Association of Social Workers. Recreations: vintage/classic motorcycle and vehicle rallies. Address: (h.) 5 Braid Green, Livingston, West Lothian, EH54 8PN; T.-Livingston 39148.

Davison, Edward Cowper. Assistant Secretary, Scottish Office, since 1984; b. 31.10.40, Darlington; m., Anna Fay Henderson; 2 d. Educ. Dame Allan's School, Newcastle-upon-Tyne; Glasgow University; London University Institute of Education. Assistant Master, Tottenham County School, 1964-68; administrative staff, Glasgow University, 1969-75; Principal, Scottish Office, 1975-84. Address: (h.) 14 Plewlands Terrace, Edinburgh, EH10 5JZ; T.-031-447 3289.

Davison, Timothy Paul, BA (Hons), AHSM, MBA. Unit General Manager, Glasgow Mental Health Services, since 1991; b. 4.6.61, Newcastle upon Tyne; m., Hilary; 1 s. Educ. Kenton Comprehensive School, Newcastle upon Tyne; Stirling University; Glasgow University. Joined NHS as management trainee, 1983; Hospital Administrator, Glasgow Royal Infirmary, 1988-90; Sector Manager, Gartnavel Royal Hospital, 1990-91; Visiting Lecturer on Health Services Management, Queen Margaret College; Member, Management Committee, Glasgow Association for Mental Health. Recreations: sport; military and political history; writing unfinished novels. Address: (b.) Mental Health Unit, Gartnavel Royal Hospital, 1055 Great Western Road, Glasgow, G12 0XH; T.-041-334 4416.

Dawson, James Ronald, FRICS. Chairman, Royal Institution of Chartered Surveyors in Scotland, since 1992; b. 28.5.41, Glasgow; m., Marion; 1 s.; 1 d. Educ. High School of Glasgow; Stow College of Building, Glasgow. Apprentice Quantity Surveyor, Baxter Dunn & Gray, Chartered Surveyors, Glasgow, 1958-63; Assistant Surveyor Associate and Partner, Robert H. Soper & Company, Chatered Surveyors, Cumbernauld and Edinburgh, 1965-72; Joint Founding Partner, Robertson and Dawson Chartered Surveyors, since 1972. Captain, Ward XXIII, Society of High Constables of Edinburgh. Recreations: golf; walking. Address: (b.) Robertson and Dawson, Chartered Surveyors, 6 Manor Place, Edinburgh, EH3 7DD; T.-031-225 2219.

Dawson, Professor John Alan, BSc, MPhil, PhD, MIPDM. Professor of Marketing, Edinburgh University, since 1990; b. 19.8.44, Hyde; m., Jocelyn Barker; 1 s.; 1 d. Educ. Lady Manners School, Bakewell; University College, London; Nottingham University. Lecturer, Nottingham University; Lecturer, Senior Lecturer, Reader, St. David's University College, Wales; Fraser of Allander Professor of Distributive Studies, Stirling University; Visiting Lecturer, University of Western Australia; Visiting Research Fellow, Australian National University; Visiting Professor: Florida State University, Chuo University. Former Member, Distributive Trades Committee, NEDC; former Honorary Secretary, Institute of British Geographers; Board Member, Cumbernauld Development Corporation. Publications: Evaluating the Human Environment, 1973; Man and His World, 1975; Computing for Geographers, 1976; Small-Scale Retailing in the UK, 1979; Marketing Environment, 1979; Retail Geography, 1980; Commercial Distribution in Europe, 1982; Teach Yourself Geography, 1983; Shopping Centre Development, 1983; Computer Methods for Geographers, 1985; Retailing in Sconland 2005, 1988; Evolution of European Retailing, 1988; Retailing Environments in Developing Countries, 1990. Recreations: sport; writing. Address: (b.) Edinburgh University, 50 George Square, Edinburgh; T.-031-650 1000.

Dawson, J.A.L., BSc, CEng, FIHT, MICE. Director of Roads, Scottish Office, since 1989; Chief Road Engineer, Scottish Development Department, since 1988; b. 6.2.50,

Hillingdon; m., Frances Anne Elizabeth; 2 d. Educ. Mill Hill School; Southampton University. British Rail Engineering Scholar, 1968-72; Department of Environment, 1972-76; Department of Transport, 1976-81; Overseas Transport Consultant, 1981-85; Director (Transport), London Regional Office, Department of Transport, 1985-88. Recreation: touring. Address: (b.) New St. Andrews House, Edinburgh, EH1; T.-031-244 4283.

Dawson, Thomas Cordner, QC (Scot). Solicitor-General for Scotland, since 1992; b. 14.11.48. Advocate, 1973; QC, 1986.

Day, Alan Frederick, BA, MA, PhD, FRHistS. Senior Lecturer in History, Edinburgh University, since 1987; Associate Director, International Office, Edinburgh University, since 1989; b. 23.5.44, Bristol; m., Dr. Katherine J. Day; 1 s.; 2 d. Educ. Queen Elizabeth's Hospital, Bristol; Southampton University; McMaster University, Canada; Johns Hopkins University, USA. Fulbright Scholar, 1968-71; Ford Foundation Fellow, 1970-71; History Department, Edinburgh University: Temporary Lecturer, 1971-74, Lecturer, 1974-87; Visiting Professor of History, Northern Virginia Community College, 1983-84. Publications: A Social Study of Lawyers in Maryland, 1660-1775; A Biographical Dictionary of the Maryland Legislature, 1634-1789 (Joint Editor). Recreations: American and British sport; US politics; travel; vacuuming. Address: (b.) Department of History, Edinburgh University, William Robertson Building, George Square, Edinburgh, EH8 9JY; T.-031-650 3771.

Deane, Robert Fletcher, MB, ChB, MSc, FRCSEdin, FRCSGlas. Consultant Urological Surgeon, since 1971; b. 25.3.38, Glasgow; m., Sylvia Allison Yuill; 3 s. Educ. Hillhead High School, Glasgow; Glasgow University. Consultant Urologist, Western Infirmary, Glasgow, since 1971; Senior Consultant Surgeon to Family Planning Association, Glasgow; Member, Specialist Advisory Committee (Urology); Founder, Board of Intercollegiate Specialty Board in Urology. Publication: Urology Illustrated. Recreations: golf; music. Address: (h.) 27 Bellshaugh Lane, Glasgow, G12 0PE; T.-041-334 8102.

Deans, Rev. Graham Douglas Sutherland, MA, BD (Hons). Minister, St. Mary's Parish Church, Dumfries, since 1987; b. 15.8.53, Aberdeen; m., Marina Punler. Educ. Mackie Academy, Stonehaven; Aberdeen University. Assistant Minister, Craigsbank Parish Church, Corstorphine, 1977-78; Minister, Denbeath and Methilhill Parish Churches, 1978-87; Depute Clerk and Treasurer, Kirkcaldy Presbytery, 1981-87; Vice-Convener, Committee on Maintenance of the Ministry, Convener, Committee on Glebes, Dumfries and Kirkcudbright Presbytery, since 1991; Member, General Assembly Committees: Maintenance of the Ministry, Probationers and Transference of Ministers, since 1991. Publication: A History of Denbeath Church, 1980. Recreation: music. Address: 47 Moffat Road, Dumfries, DG1 1NN; T.-0387 54873.

Deans, Joyce Blair, MBE, BArch, PRIAS, RIBA, ACIArb, FRSA. Architect; President, Royal Incorporation of Architects in Scotland, since 1991; b. 29.1.27, Glasgow; m., John Albert Gibson Deans; 2 s.; 2 d. Educ. Laurel Bank School for Girls; Strathclyde University. Re-entered profession as Assistant, private practice, 1968; appointed Associate, 1972; established own practice, 1981. First female President, Glasgow Institute of Architects, 1986-88; first female Vice President, Royal Incorporation of Architects in Scotland, 1986-88; Member, Building Standards Advisory Committee, 1990-93; Governor, Glasgow School of Art. Recreations: gardening; golf; walking; reading; theatre. Address: 11 South Erskine Park, Bearsden, Glasgow, G61 4NA; T.-041-942 6795.

Deans, Rodger William, CB. Regional Chairman, Social Security Appeal Tribunal and Medical Appeal Tribunals for Scotland, 1984-90 (retired); b. 21.12.17, Perth; m., Joan Radley; 1 s.; 1 d. Educ. Perth Academy; Edinburgh University. Served World War II, RA and REME, Major; Military Prosecutor, Palestine, 1945-46; Solicitor to Secretary of State for Scotland and to HM Treasury, 1971-80 (Assistant Solicitor, 1962-71, Senior Legal Assistant, Scottish Office, 1951-62, Legal Assistant, 1947-50); Consultant Editor, Green & Son, Edinburgh, 1981-82; Senior Chairman, Supplementary Benefit Appeal Tribunals, 1982-84. Recreations: hill-walking; gardening. Address: (h.) 25 Grange Road, Edinburgh, EH9 1UQ; T.-031-667 1893.

Deb, Saumitra, MBBS, MRCPsych. Clinical Senior Lecturer, Department of Mental Health, Aberdeen University, since 1989; Consultant Psychiatrist; b. 16.12.53, Calcutta, India; m., Arundhati; 1 d. Educ. Calcutta University. Registrar in Psychiatry: University Hospital of Wales, 1983-85, Charing Cross and Westminster Hospital, London, 1985-86; Senior Registrar in Psychiatry and Clinical Teacher, Faculty of Medicine, Leicester University, 1986-88. Recreations: art; music; drama. Address: (b.) Woodlands Hospital, Cults, Aberdeen, AB1 9PR; T.-0224 681818, Ext. 51575.

Demarco, Richard, OBE, RSW, SSA, Hon. FRIAS. Artist and Writer; Director, Richard Demarco Gallery, since 1966; External Assessor, Stourbridge College of Art, since 1988; b. 9.7.30, Edinburgh; m., Anne Muckle. Educ. Holy Cross Academy, Edinburgh; Edinburgh College of Art. National Service, KOSB, 1954-56; Art Master, Duns Scotus Academy, Edinburgh, 1957-67; Vice-Chairman, Board, Traverse Theatre Club, 1963-67; Director, Sean Connery's Scottish International Education Trust, 1972-73; Member, Board of Governors, Carlisle School of Art, 1970-74; Member, Edinburgh Festival Society, since 1991; Contributing Editor, Studio International, 1982-84. Gold Order of Merit, Polish People's Republic; awarded insignia of Chevalier de L'Ordre Des Arts Et Des Lettres; Order of Cavaliere Della Republica d'Italia; Scottish Arts Council Award for services to Scotland's visual arts, 1975; Honorary Member, Scottish Arts Club and Chelsea Arts Club. Publications: The Road to Meikle Seggie; The Artist as Explorer. Recreation: walking "The Road to Meikle Seggie". Address: (h.) 23(a) Lennox Street, Edinburgh; T.-031-343 2124.

Denholm, James Allan, CA. Director, William Grant & Sons Ltd., since 1975; Chairman, East Kilbride Development Corporation, since 1983 (Member, since 1979); Director, Scottish Mutual Assurance Society, since 1987; Director, Scottish Cremation Society Limited, since 1980; Vice President, Institute of Chartered Accountants of Scotland, since 1989; b. 27.9.36, Glasgow; m., Elizabeth Avril McLachlan, CA; 1 s.; 1 d. Educ. Hutchesons Boys Grammar School, Glasgow; Institute of Chartered Accountants of Scotland. Apprenticed, McFarlane Hutton & Patrick, CA, Glasgow (Sir William McLintock prizeman); Chief Accountant, A. & W. Smith & Co. Ltd., Glasgow, 1960-66; Secretary, William Grant & Sons Ltd., since 1968; Council Member, Institute of Chartered Accountants of Scotland, 1978-83. Director and Treasurer, Glasgow YMCA, 1966-79; Chairman, Glasgow Junior Chamber of Commerce, 1972-73; Member, CBI Scottish Legal Panel, since 1987; Elder, New Kilpatrick Parish Church, since 1971; Visitor of the Incorporation of Maltmen in Glasgow, 1980-81; President, 49 Wine and Spirit Club of Scotland, 1983-84; Trustee: Scottish Chartered Accountants Trust for Education, The Queen's College, Glasgow Educational Trust, Scottish Cot Death Trust; Fellow, Society of Antiquaries of Scotland, since 1987. Recreations: shooting; golf. Address: (h.) Greencroft, 19 Colquhoun Drive, Bearsden, Glasgow; T.-041-942 1773.

Denholm, John Clark, MA (Hons), MIPA. Managing Director, Leith Advertising Agency Ltd., since 1984; Chairman, One to One Direct Communications Ltd., since 1990; b. 10.9.50, Chesterfield; m., Julia; 1 s.; 1 d. Educ. Buckhaven High School; St. Andrews University. Product Manager, The Boots Company, Nottingham, 1972-76; Brand Manager, Scottish & Newcastle Breweries, 1976-80; Account Director, Hall Advertising, Edinburgh, 1980-84. Recreation: golf. Address: (b.) 1 Canon Street, Edinburgh; T.-031-557 5840.

Dennis, Richard Benson, PhD, BSc. Managing Director, Edinburgh Instruments Ltd.; Director, Edinburgh Sensors Ltd.; Senior Lecturer, Heriot-Watt University; Founder, Mintek GmbH, West Germany; b. 15.7.45, Weymouth; m., Beate Stamm; 2 d. Educ. Weymouth Grammar School; Reading University. SRC Postdoctoral Fellow, Reading; Guest Fellow, Freiburg University, 1968-70; Lecturer/Senior Lecturer, Heriot-Watt University, 1970-91; Alexander von Humboldt Fellow, Munich University, 1976-78; Treasurer, UK Laser and Electro-Optic Trade Association;Council Member, Scottish Consultative Committee on the Curriculum, since 1991; Chairman, Balerno High School Board; Joint Winner, Department of Industry EPIC Award (Education in Partnership with Industry and Commerce), 1982. Recreations: bridge; sport. Address: (b.) Edinburgh Instruments Ltd., Riccarton, Currie, Edinburgh; T.-031-449 5844.

Dennison, Brigadier Malcolm Gray. Lord Lieutenant of Orkney, since 1990; b. 19.3.24, Nyasaland. Educ. Lincoln School; Edinburgh University. RAF, 1942-52: Bomber Command, 1944-45, Senior Intelligence Officer, 219 and 205 Groups, Egypt, 1946-47, MECAS, 1947-48, HQ Middle East Air Force Intelligence, 1948-51; Bahrain Petroleum Co., 1953-55; Intelligence, Sultan Armed Forces, Oman, 1955-75, Adviser to Sultan, 1975-83. Order of Oman (Military); DSM (Oman). President, SSAFA, Orkney. Recreation: book collecting. Address: (h.) Roeberry House, St. Margaret's Hope, Orkney, KW17 2TW; T.-0856 83 228.

Denny, Margaret Bertha Alice, OBE, DL, BA (Hons), PhD. Member, Council and Executive Committee, National Trust for Scotland, since 1974 (Vice President, since 1981); b. 30.9.07, Chatham; m., Edward Leslie Denny. Educ. Dover County School; Bedford College for Women, London University. Entered Civil Service as Principal, Ministry of Shipping, 1940; Assistant Secretary, 1946; Under Secretary, 1957; Governor, Bedford College; Member, Scottish Advisory Council for Civil Aviation, 1958-67; Member, Western Regional Hospital Board, 1960-74; Member, Scottish Committee, Council of Industrial Design, 1961-71; Member, General Advisory Council, BBC, 1962-66; Member, General Nursing Council, Scotland, 1963-78; Member, Board of Management, State Hospital, Carstairs, 1966-76; Vice-Chairman, Argyll and Clyde Health Board, 1974-77; County Commissioner, Girl Guides, Dunbartonshire, 1958-68; DL, Dunbartonshire, since 1973; Officer, Order of Orange Nassau, 1947. Recreations: gardening; needlework; music. Address: (h.) Gartochraggan Cottage, Gartocharn, by Alexandra, Dunbartonshire; T.-038 983 272.

Dent, John Anthony, MD, FRCS (Edin), DipMEd. Senior Lecturer in Orthopaedic and Trauma Surgery, Dundee University, since 1990; Honorary Consultant, Tayside Health Board, since 1990; b. 4.3.53, Kendal; m., Frances Jane Wyllie; 1 s. Educ. Heversham Grammar School; Dundee University. House Officer, Professorial Therapeutics Unit and Professorial Surgical Unit, Ninewells Hospital, Dundee; Registrar, Orthopaedics and Trauma Training Scheme, Tayside Health Board; Hand Research Fellow, Princess Margaret Rose Hospital, Edinburgh; Kleinert Hand Fellow, Louisville Hand Surgery Associates, Kentucky; Lecturer and Honorary Senior Registrar, Dundee University and Tayside Health Board. Fellow, British Orthopaedic Association. Recreations: history; church involvement. Address: (b.) University Department of Orthopaedic Surgery, Caird Block, Royal Infirmary, Dundee; T.-0382 23125.

Denyer, Professor Peter Brian, BSc, PhD. Advent Professor of Integrated Electronics, Edinburgh University, since 1986; b. 27.4.53, Littlehampton; m., Fiona Margaret Lindsay; 2 d. Educ. Worthing Technical High School; Loughborough University. Wolfson Microelectronics Institute, 1976-80; Lecturer, then Reader, Edinburgh University, 1981-86. Chairman, SERC/DTI Microelectronics Design Sub-Committee, 1989-91; Director, VLSI Vision Ltd., since 1990. Publications: Introduction to MOSLSI Design, 1983; VLSI Signal Processing: A Bit-Serial Approach, 1985. Recreations: family; walking; renovation. Address: (h.) 91 Colinton Road, Edinburgh, EH10 5DF; T.-031-337 3432.

Deregowski, Professor Jan Bronislaw, BSc, BA, PhD, DSc, FBPsS. Professor of Psychology, Aberdeen University, since 1986 (Reader, 1981-86); b. 1.3.33, Pinsk, Poland; m., Eva Loft Nielsen; 2 s.; 1 d. Educ. London University. Lecturer, then Senior Lecturer, Aberdeen University, 1969-81. Publications: Illusions, Patterns and Pictures: a cross-cultural perspective; Distortion in Art; Perception and Artistic Style (Co-author). Address: (b.) Department of Psychology, King's College, Old Aberdeen, AB9 2UB; T.-Aberdeen 272247.

Dervaird, Hon. Lord (John Murray), MA (Oxon), LLB (Edin). Dickson Minto Professor of Company and Commercial Law, Edinburgh University, since 1990; Chairman, Scottish Council for Arbitration, since 1989; Council Member, London Court of International Arbitration, since 1990; Vice-President, Comite Europeen de Droit Rural, Paris, since 1990; Chairman, Scottish Ensemble, since 1988; Hon. President, Advocates' Business Law Group, since 1988; b. 8.7.35, Stranraer; m., Bridget Jane Godfrey; 3 s. Educ. Stranraer schools; Edinburgh Academy; Corpus Christi College, Oxford; Edinburgh University. Advocate, 1962; QC, 1974; Law Commissioner (part-time), 1979-88; Senator of the College of Justice, 1988-89. Publications: Stair Encyclopaedia of Scots Law (Contributor); articles on legal and ornithological subjects. Recreations: farming; gardening; bird-watching; music; curling. Address: (b.) Faculty of Law, Old College, South Bridge, Edinburgh.

Devereux, Alan Robert, CBE, DL, CEng, MIEE, CBIM. Chairman, Quality Scotland Foundation; International Director, Gleneagles PLC, since 1990; Chairman, Scottish Tourist Board, 1980-90; Director, Scottish Mutual Assurance Society, since 1976; Director, Walter Alexander PLC, 1980-90; Scottish Adviser, Hambros Bank Ltd., 1984-90; Director, Hambros Scotland Ltd., 1984-90; Member, British Tourist Authority, 1980-90; Director, Solsgirth Investment Trust Ltd., 1981-90; b. 18.4.33, Frinton-on-Sea; m., 1, Gloria Alma Hair (deceased); 1 s.; 2, Elizabeth Tormey Docherty. Educ. Colchester School; Clacton County High School; Mid Essex Technical College. Marconi's Wireless Telegraph Company: apprentice, 1950-55, Standards Engineer, 1955-56; Technical Production Manager, Halex Division, British Xylonite Company, 1956-58; Technical Sales Manager, SPA Division, Sanitas Trust, 1958-65; General Manager, Dobar Engineering, 1965-67; various managerial posts, Norcros Ltd., 1967-69; Group Managing Director, Scotcros Ltd., 1969-78; Deputy Chairman, Scotcros Ltd., 1978-80. CBI: Chairman, Scotland, 1977-79 (Deputy Chairman, 1975-77), Council Member, 1972-84, Member, President's Advisory Committee, 1979; UK Regional Chairman, 1979; Chairman, Small Industries Council for Rural Areas of Scotland, 1975-77; Member, Scottish Development Agency, 1977-83; Chairman, Scottish Appeals Committee, Police Dependants'

Trust; Member: David Livingstone Memorial Trust; Malcolm Sargent Cancer Fund for Children; Scottish Free Enterprise Award, 1978; Deputy Lieutenant, Renfrewshire, since 1985; Chairman, Special Appeals Committee, Mental Health Foundation, since 1990. Recreations: work; amateur radio; reading. Address: (h.) 293 Fenwick Road, Giffnock, Glasgow, G46 6UH; T.-041-638 2586.

Devine, Rt. Rev. Joseph. Bishop of Motherwell, since 1983; b. 7.8.37.

Devine, Professor Thomas Martin, BA, PhD, DLitt, FRHistS. Professor of Scottish History, Strathclyde University, since 1988 (Chairman, Department of History, since 1990); Chairman, Economic and Social History Society of Scotland, 1984-88; b. 30.10.46, Motherwell; m., Catherine Mary Lynas; 2 s.; 3 d. Educ. Our Lady's RC High School, Motherwell; Strathclyde University. Lecturer, then Senior Lecturer and Reader, Department of History, Strathclyde University, 1969-88; Visiting Professor, University of Guelph, Canada, 1983 and 1988 (Adjunct Professor in History, since 1988); Joint Founding Editor, Scottish Economic and Social History, 1980-84. Publications: The Tobacco Lords, 1975; Lairds and Improvement in Enlightenment Scotland, 1979; Ireland and Scotland 1600-1850 (Co-Editor), 1983; Farm Servants and Labour in Lowland Scotland 1770-1914, 1984; A Scottish Firm in Virginia 1767-77, 1984; People and Society in Scotland 1760-1830 (Co-Editor), 1988; The Great Highland Famine, 1988; Improvement and Enlightenment (Editor), 1989; Conflict and Stability in Scottish Sociey (Editor), 1990; Irish Immigrants and Scottish Society in the Eighteenth and Nineteenth Centuries (Editor), 1991. Recreations: walking and travelling in the Hebrides; watching Celtic FC. Address: (b.) Department of History, McCance Building, 16 Richmond Street, Glasgow, G1 1XQ; T.-041-552 4400, Ext. 2931.

de Vink, Peter Henry John, BComm. Managing Director, Edinburgh Financial and General Holdings Ltd., since 1978; b. 9.10.40, Amsterdam; 1 s.; 1 d. Educ. Edinburgh University. National Service, Dutch Army, 1961-63; Edinburgh University, 1963-66; Ivory and Sime Investment Managers, 1966-78, latterly as Director. Address: (b.) 7 Howe Street, Edinburgh, EH3 6TE; T.-031-225 6661; (h.) Huntly Cot, Temple, Midlothian.

Dewar, Donald Campbell, MA, LLB. MP (Labour), Glasgow Garscadden, since 1978; Opposition Spokesman on Scottish Affairs, 1983-92, Social Services, since 1992; b. 21.8.37, Glasgow; 1 s.; 1 d. Educ. Glasgow Academy; Glasgow University. Practised as Solicitor in Glasgow; MP, Aberdeen South, 1966-70; PPS to Tony Crosland, 1967; Chairman, Select Committee on Scottish Affairs, 1980-81; Member, Scottish front bench team, since 1981; elected to Shadow Cabinet, 1984. Address: (h.) 23 Cleveden Road, Glasgow, G12; T.-041-334 2374.

Dewar, Lawrence, MIGD. Chief Executive, Scottish Grocers' Federation, since 1980; b. 12.1.36, Blackford; m., Nancy Kelly; 2 s.; 2 d. Educ. Dunfermline High School. Grocer of the Year, 1967; President, Scottish Grocers' Federation, 1975; Member, Board, SCOTBEC, 1981-85; Member, Sector Sector Board 5, SCOTVEC, since 1986; Secretary, Institute of Grocery Distribution (Scottish Branch), 1984. Recreations: golf; reading; TV. Address: (b.) 3 Loaning Road, Edinburgh, EH7 6JE; T.-031-652 2482.

Dhir, Professor Ravindra Kumar, BSc, PhD, CEng, MIMM, FGS. Professor of Concrete Technology, Dundee University, since 1991; Director of Concrete Technology Unit, since 1989; b. 3.11.35, Nakodar, India; m., Bharti; 3 d. Educ. Nakodar Ayar High School, India; Durham University; Sheffield University. Management Trainee, National Coal Board, 1965-67; Dundee University: Lecturer in Civil Engineering, Senior Lecturer, 1977, Reader, 1988. Publications: Civil Engineering Materials (Co-Author); Protection of Concrete (Co-Author); Advances in Concrete Slab Technology (Co-Author). Address: (b.) Department of Civil Engineering, Dundee University, Dundee; T.-0382 23187.

Diamond, Harry, FIPR. Head of Public Relations, City of Glasgow, 1974- 91; b. 15.12.26, Glasgow; 2 s. Educ. Strathbungo Senior Secondary School. Daily newspaperman, 1942-62; PR in gas industry, 1962-69; PR consultant, 1969-74. Winner, Tallents Medal for exceptional achievement, Institute of Public Relations; Member: Executive Committee, Erskine Hospital; Board of Directors, Architectonic Research Institute; Prince and Princess of Wales Hospice Company; Executive Committee, Jewish Representative Council; Council, Garnethill Hebrew Congregation. Recreations: writing; music; talking. Address: (h.) 20 Thorncliffe Gardens, Glasgow, G41 2DE; T.-041-632 8839.

Dick, David, OBE, DIC, CEng, FIEE. Principal, Stevenson College of Further Education, Edinburgh, 1969-87; Chairman, Fire Services Examination Board (Scotland), 1968-86; Member, Construction Industry Training Board, 1976-85; Member, Electrical Engineering Services Committee, CITB, 1976-88; b. 20.3.29, Edinburgh; m., Muriel Elsie Margaret Buchanan; 5 d. Educ. Boroughmuir School, Edinburgh; Heriot-Watt College, Edinburgh; Imperial College, London. Electrical Engineer, North of Scotland Hydro-Electric Board, 1951-54; Lecturer, Dundee College of Technology, 1954-60; Head, Department of Electrical Engineering, Coatbridge Technical College, 1960-64; Depute Principal, Napier College of Science and Technology, Edinburgh, 1964-69. Manpower Services Commission: Chairman, Lothian District Manpower Committee, 1981-82, Member, Lothian and Borders Area Manpower Board, 1982-85; Member and Chairman, various committees: Scottish Technical Education Council, Scottish Business Education Council, 1969-87; Past Chairman, Scottish Committee, Institution of Electronic and Radio Engineers; former Honorary President, Edinburgh and District Spastics Association. Recreations: music (flute); gardening; writing historical biographies. Address: (h.) West Lodge, Clerkinglon, near Haddington, East Lothian.

Dick, Professor Heather M., MD, FRCPGlas, FRCPath, FIBiol, FRSE. Professor of Medical Microbiology, Dundee University, since 1984; Visiting Professor (Immunology), Strathclyde University, since 1981; b. 14.11.32, London; m., Alex. L. Dick; 1 d. Educ. Harris Academy, Dundee; Queen's College, Dundee (St. Andrews University). Resident House Officer, Dundee Royal Infirmary and Ruchill Hospital, Glasgow, 1957-59; Assistant, Department of Bacteriology, St. Andrews University, 1959-61; Lecturer, Department of Bacteriology, Glasgow University, 1964-71; Consultant in Clinical Immunology, Glasgow Royal Infirmary, 1971-84. Publication: Topley and Wilson's Principles of Bacteriology and Immunity, 8th edition (Joint Editor, Volume 1). Recreation: music. Address: (b.) Department of Medical Microbiology, Ninewells Hospital, Dundee, DD1 9SY; T.-0382 60111, Ext. 2166.

Dick, James, BA, DMS. Director of Social Work, Highland Regional Council, since 1986; b. 19.5.39, Kirkcaldy; m., Isabella Hazell Grieve; 1 d. Educ. Open University; Robert Gordon's Institute of Technology; Jordanhill College of Education. Probation Officer, Edinburgh Combined Probation Area, 1967-69; Child Care Officer/Social Worker, Moray and Nairn County Councils, 1969-71; Senior Social Worker, Perth and Kinross County Councils, 1971-73; Principal Social Worker/Divisional Officer, Borders Region, 1973-78; Divisional Officer, Banff/Buchan, Grampian Region, 1978-

85; Senior Depute Director, Highland Region, 1985-86. Recreations: golf; gardening; bowls. Address: (h.) Heatherlie, 31 Sunnyside, Culloden Moor, by Inverness; T.-Inverness 790727.

Dick, Rev. John Hunter Addison, MA (Hons), MSc, BD (Hons). Minister, Ferryhill Parish Church, Aberdeen, since 1982; b. 27.12.45, Dunfermline; m., Gillian Averil Ogle-Skan; 3 s. Educ. Dunfermline High School; Edinburgh University. Research Assistant, Air Pollution Survey, Edinburgh University, 1967-70; Senior Tutor in Geography, Queensland University, Australia, 1970-78; student of divinity, 1978-81; Assistant Minister, Fairmilehead Parish Church, Edinburgh, 1981-82. Recreations: music; philately; golf. Address: The Manse, 54 Polmuir Road, Aberdeen, AB1 2RT; T.-0224 586933.

Dick, Maria M., MA. Head Teacher, Auchenharvie Academy, since 1989; b. 3.3.49, Irvine; m., James Dick. Educ. Irvine Royal Academy, Glasgow University. Teacher of English, then Principal Teacher, Irvine Royal Academy, 1972-77; Principal Teacher of English: James Hamilton Academy, 1977-80, Ravenspark Academy, 1980-83; Divisional Curriculum Development Officer, 1983-84; Assistant Head Teacher, then Temporary Depute Head Teacher, Auchenharvie Academy, 1984-89. Recreations: two large Belgian shepherds! Address: (b.) Auchenharvie Academy, Saltcoats Road, Stevenston, Ayrshire, KA20 3JW.

Dickie, Rev. Michael Mure, BSc (Agric). Minister, Ayr: Castlehill, since 1967; b. 7.7.28, Glasgow; m., Marjory Jack Smith; 1 s.; 2 d. Educ. Dundee High School; Melville College, Edinburgh; Edinburgh University. 2nd Bn., Royal Scots; Minister: Rothiemay Parish, 1955-61, St. David's Church, Bathgate, 1961-67; Member, West Lothian Education Committee, 1963-67; first Chairman, Ayr Burgh Children's Panel; Secretary, Steering Committee for Community Councils in Ayr; Member, Forehill and Holmston Community Council, three years; Chaplain, "R" Division, Strathclyde Police. Recreations: hill-walking; drawing. Address: Castlehill Manse, 3 Hillfoot Road, Ayr, KA7 3LF; T.-Ayr 267332.

Dickie, Thomas, JP. Chairman, Garnock Valley Development Executive, 1984-88; Member, Cunninghame District Council, since 1975 (Convener, 1980-84); Chairman, Cunninghame District Licensing Board, since 1980; b. 5.12.30, Beith; m., Janette Coulter Brown. Educ. Beith Academy; Speirs' Secondary School; Glasgow and West of Scotland Commercial College. Office boy to Personnel Manager, Redpath Engineering Ltd., 1946-80; Member, Board, Irvine Development Corporation, 1981-84; Secretary, Cunninghame North Constituency Labour Party, since 1990. Recreations: caravanning; walking; music. Address: (h.) 45 Loadingbank Court, Kilbirnie, Ayrshire, KA25 6JX; T.-0505 682205.

Dickinson, Professor Harry Thomas, BA, DipEd, MA, PhD, DLitt, FRHistS. Professor of British History, Edinburgh University, since 1980; Professor of British History, Nanjing University, since 1987; b. 9.3.39, Gateshead; m., Jennifer Elizabeth Galtry; 1 s.; 1 d. Educ. Gateshead Grammar School; Durham University; Newcastle University. Teacher of History, Washington Grammar School, 1961-64; Earl Grey Fellow, Newcastle University, 1964-66; History Department, Edinburgh University: Assistant Lecturer, 1966-68, Lecturer, 1968-73, Reader, 1973-80; Visiting Professor, Nanjing University, China, 1980 and 1983. Fulbright Scholar, 1973; Huntington Library Fellowship, 1973; Folger Shakespeare Library Fellowship, 1973; Winston Churchill Fellow, 1980; Leverhulme Award, 1986-87; Ahmanson Fellowship, UCLA, 1987; Anstey Lecturer, University of Kent, 1989; Chairman, Publications Committee, Historical Association, 1991-93;

Vice-President, Royal Historical Society, 1991-95; Member, Humanities Committee, CNAA, 1991-93. Publications: Bolingbroke; Walpole and the Whig Supremacy; Liberty and Property; British Radicals and the French Revolution; The Correspondence of Sir James Clavering; Politics and Literature in the 18th Century; The Political Works of Thomas Spence; Caricatures and the Constitution 1760-1832; Britain and the French Revolution; many essays and reviews. Recreations: reading; films. Address: (h.) 44 Viewforth Terrace, Edinburgh, EH10 4LJ; T.-031-229 1379.

Dickinson, Professor John Philip, MA, MSc, PhD, FASA CPA, ACIS, FRSA, FBIM. Professor of Accountancy, Glasgow University, since 1985; Director, Glasgow Business School, since 1987; Dean, Faculty of Law and Financial Studies, Glasgow University, since 1989; b. 29.4.45, Morecambe; m., Christine Houghton; 1 s.; 2 d. Educ. Morecambe Grammar School; Cambridge University; Leeds University. Lecturer, Department of Management Studies and Associate Lecturer in Operational Research, Leeds University, 1968-71; Lecturer, Department of Accounting and Finance, Lancaster University, 1971-75; Senior Lecturer, Department of Accounting and Finance, University of Western Australia, 1975-80; Senior Lecturer, Department of Accountancy, Dundee University, 1980-81; Professor of Accountancy, Stirling University, 1981-85. Publications: Portfolio Theory, 1974; Risk and Uncertainty in Accounting and Finance, 1974; Statistics for Business Finance and Accounting, 1976; Portfolio Analysis and Capital Markets, 1977; Statistical Analysis in Accounting and Finance, 1990. Recreations: photography; wine and beer-making; travel. Address: (b.) Department of Accounting and Finance, Glasgow Business School, 65-69 Southpark Avenue, Glasgow, G12 8LE; T.-041-330 5428.

Dickson, Captain Alexander Forrest, OBE, RD, FRIN. Commissioner of Northern Lighthouses, since 1979; b. 23.6.20, Edinburgh; m., Norma Houston; 3 s.; 2 d. Educ. George Watson's; Leith Nautical College. Apprentice, P. Henderson and Co., 1936-39; Royal Navy service in destroyers, 1939-45; Lecturer, Leith Nautical College, 1945-49; Shell International Marine Co. Ltd., 1949-79 (Director Operations, 1968-79). Honorary Sheriff, Perth. Recreations: fishing; gardening; golf. Address: (h.) Birchburn, Kenmore, Perthshire; T.-08873 283.

Dickson, Campbell S., MA, DipEd. Rector, Nairn Academy, since 1987; b. 25.11.44, Edinburgh; 2 s. Educ. Boroughmuir High School, Edinburgh; Edinburgh University. Teacher of Modern Languages, Dunfermline High School, 1968-71; Principal Teacher of Modern Languages, Golspie High School, 1971-79; Assistant Rector, Banff Academy, 1979-82; Depute Rector, Lochaber High School, 1982-87. Member, Scottish Central Committee on Modern Languages, 1977-80. Recreations: sport (squash, curling, skiing); walking; bridge; reading. Address: (b.) Nairn Academy, Duncan Drive, Nairn, IV12 4RD; T.-0667 53700.

Dickson, Ian Archibald. Secretary to Northern Lighthouse Board, since 1987; b. 3.5.42, Edinburgh; m., Moira Evelyn McLean; 1 s. Educ. George Heriot's, Edinburgh. Northern Lighthouse Board: Executive Officer, 1960-73, Personnel Officer, 1973-77, Deputy Secretary, 1977-86. Elder, Church of Scotland. Address: (b.) 84 George Street, Edinburgh; T.-031-226 7051.

Dickson, James Holms, BSc, MA, PhD, FLS. Senior Lecturer in Botany, Glasgow University, since 1979; b. 29.4.37, Glasgow; m., Camilla Ada Lambert; 1 s.; 1 d. Educ. Bellahouston Academy; Glasgow University; Cambridge University. Assistant, then Senior Assistant in Research, Botany School, Cambridge University, 1961-70; Member, Royal Society Expedition to Tristan da Cunha, 1962;

Research Fellow and Official Fellow, Clare College, Cambridge, 1963-70; Lecturer in Botany, Glasgow University, 1970-79. President, Glasgow Natural History Society, 1976-79 and 1987-90; Leader, Trades House of Glasgow Expedition to Papua New Guinea, 1987; Scientific Adviser to Britoil's exhibition, Glasgow Garden Festival, 1988; President, Botanical Society of Scotland, 1990-92. Publication: Wild Plants of Glasgow, 1991. Recreation: gardening. Address: (h.) 113 Clober Road, Milngavie, Glasgow, G62 7LS; T.-041-956 4103.

Dickson, Leonard Elliot, CBE, MC, TD, DL, BA (Cantab), LLB. Retired Solicitor; b. 17.3.15, Edinburgh; m., Mary Elisabeth Cuthbertson; 1 s.; 1 d. Educ. Uppingham; Magdalene College, Cambridge; Glasgow University. 1st Bn., Glasgow Highlanders HLI, 1939-46; former Senior Partner, Dickson, Haddow & Co., Solicitors, Glasgow (retired, 1985); Clerk, Clyde Lighthouses Trust, 1953-65; Secretary, Glasgow Society of Sons of Clergy, 1953-83; serving Officer, TA, 1939-55 (Lt. Col. commanding 1st Bn., Glasgow Highlanders, 1952-55); Chairman, Lowland TAVR, 1968-70; Member, Glasgow Executive Council, NHS, 1956-74 (Vice Chairman, 1970-74). Recreations: travel; gardening. Address: (h.) Bridge End, Gartmore, Stirling, FK8 3RR; T.-087 72 220.

Dickson, Sheriff Robert Hamish, LLB, WS. Sheriff of South Strathclyde, Dumfries & Galloway at Airdrie, since 1988; b. 19.10.45, Glasgow; m., Janet Laird Campbell; 1 s. Educ. Glasgow Academy; Drumtochty Castle; Glenalmond; Glasgow University. Solicitor, Edinburgh, 1969-71, and Glasgow, 1971-86; Partner, Brown Mair Gemmill & Hislop, Solicitors, Glasgow, 1973-86; apppointed floating Sheriff of South Strathclyde, Dumfries & Galloway at Hamilton, 1986. Recreations: golf; music; reading. Address: (b.) Airdrie Sheriff Court, Airdrie; T.-Airdrie 751121.

Dickson, William Thomas. Convener, Social Work Committee, Central Regional Council, since 1991; b. 5.6.53, Dumfries; m., Elizabeth; 1 s.; 1 d. HM Forces (KOSB), 1970-76; elected, Central Regional Councillor, 1990. Member, Executive, Age Concern (Scotland). Recreation: sport (spectator). Address: (b.) Central Regional Council, Viewforth, Stirling, FK8 2ET; T.-0786 443379.

Dillon, J. Shaun H., DRSAM (Comp), FSA Scot. Professional Musician; Composer, Oboist and Teacher of Woodwind; b. 30.12.44, Sutton Coldfield. Educ. Berwickshire High School; Fettes College; Royal Scottish Academy of Music; Guildhall School of Music. Studied composition with Frank Spedding and Edmund Rubbra; awarded prize for composition for Leicestershire Schools Orchestra, 1965; commissions from various bodies, including Scottish Amateur Music Association; Instructor of Woodwind: Edinburgh Corporation, 1967-72, Aberdeen Corporation (latterly Grampian Region), 1972-81; Freelance Musician, since 1981; sometime Director of Music, St. Mary's Cathedral, Aberdeen; Suite of Airs and Graces for strings published; Secretary, Association of Instrumental and Vocal Specialists, 1975-78. Recreations: reading, especially history, literature; crosswords; playing flute (badly) in ceilidh bands. Address: (b.) 34 Richmond Street, Aberdeen, AB2 4TR; T.-Aberdeen 630954.

Dilworth, Rt. Rev. Gerard Mark, OSB, MA, PhD, FRHistS, FSA Scot. Abbot, Fort Augustus Abbey, since 1991; b. 18.4.24. Educ. St. Andrew's School, Edinburgh; Fort Augustus Abbey School, Invernessshire; Oxford University; Edinburgh University. Fort Augustus Abbey School: Senior Modern Languages Master, 1956-59, Headmaster, 1959-72; Parish Priest, Fort Augustus, 1974-79; Editor, The Innes Review, 1979-84; Keeper, Scottish Catholic Archives, Edinburgh, 1979-91. Publications: The Scots in Franconia;

George Douglas: priest and martyr. Address: (b.) Columba House, 16 Drummond Place, Edinburgh, EH3 6PL; T.-031-556 3661.

Dinsdale, Professor Jack, MA, MSc, CEng, MIMechE, MIEE, FIQA. NCR Industrial Professor of Mechatronics, Dundee University, since 1989; Director, Advanced Mechatronics Research Centre, since 1990; b. 25.12.37, London; 4 s.; 1 d. Educ. Mill Hill School, London; Trinity College, Cambridge; Cranfield Insitute of Technology. Project Manager, Elliott Automation (now GEC), 1960; Principal Research Engineer, Cranfield Unit for Precision Engineering (CUPE), 1968; Professor of Machine Systems, Cranfield Institute of Technology, 1984. Recreations: music-making; photography. Address: (b.) Dundee University, Dundee, DD1 4HN; T.-0382 23181.

Dixon, Brian Ringrose, ACIB. Scotland Director, Barclays Bank PLC, since 1983; Director, Strathclyde Innovation, since 1989; b. 4.1.38, Market Weighton; m., Annette Robertson; 2 s. Educ. Pocklington School, York. Council Member, Scottish Enterprise Foundation; Member, Governing Council, Scottish Business in the Community. Recreations: rugby; gardening; golf; walking. Address: (b.) 90 St. Vincent Street, Glasgow, G2 5UQ; T.-041-221 9585.

Dixon, Charles, BSc, PhD, FIMA, FRMetS, MBCS, CMaths. Senior Lecturer in Mathematics, Dundee University, since 1976 (Adviser of Studies, Faculty of Science and Engineering, since 1975); b. 27.2.35, Dundee. Educ. Morgan Academy, Dundee; St. Andrews University. Assistant Lecturer in Mathematics, Queen's College, Dundee, and St. Andrews University, 1957-60; Research Assistant, Department of Meteorology, Imperial College, London, 1960-62; Lecturer in Mathematics, Queen's College, Dundee, then Dundee University, 1962-76; Visiting Senior Lecturer, University of Western Australia, 1969 and 1974; Visiting Professor, New Mexico State University, 1980. Vice-President, Dundee Bn., Boys Brigade. Publications: Applied Mathematics of Science and Engineering, 1971; Numerical Analysis, 1974; Advanced Calculus, 1981. Recreations: curling; playing bagpipes. Address: (b.) Department of Mathematics and Computer Science, Dundee University, Dundee, DD1 4HN; T.-0382 23181, Ext. 4495.

Dixon, Professor Geoffrey Richard, BSc, PhD, FIHort. Professor of Horticulture, Strathclyde University, since 1987; Head, Department of Horticulture, Scottish Agricultural College, Auchincruive, Ayr, since 1987; b. 13.6.42, London; m., Kathleen Hilda Edwards; 1 s.; 1 d. Educ. Pewley County School, Guildford; Wye College, London University. Plant Pathologist, National Institute of Agricultural Botany, Cambridge, 1968-78; Head, Horticulture Division and Chairman, Crop Production and Protection Group, and Senior University Lecturer, Aberdeen School of Agriculture, 1978-87; Chairman, International Clubroot Working Group; Visiting Professor, Mansourah University, Egypt; Vice-Chairman, Education and Training Committee, Council Member and Chairman, Scottish Branch, Institute of Horticulture; created Freeman Citizen of Glasgow and Member, Incorporation of Gardeners of Glasgow; Member of the Master Court. Wain Fellowship, AFRC. Publications: Vegetable Crop Diseases; Plant Pathogens and their control in horticulture; 100 scientific papers. Recreations: gardening; photography; travel; hill-walking. Address: (h.) Helenton Mote, Symington, by Ayr, KA1 5PP; T.-0563 830251.

Dixon-Carter, Clare. Chairman, Scottish Central Council Branch, British Red Cross Society; b. 18.9.38, London. Educ. Moira House School, Eastbourne. Technical staff, EMI; hotel management, 1959-65; Assistant Regional Organiser for Scotland, World Wildlife Fund, 1969-77; joined Inverness-shire Branch, British Red Cross Society, 1965; Branch

Director, 1979-86; awarded British Red Cross Society Voluntary Medical Service Medal, 1983; BRCS Badge of Honour for Distinguished Service and Life Membership of Society, 1986; Vice Chairman, Scottish Central Council Branch, 1986-90. Recreations: photography; travel; music. Address: (h.) Easter Balnabaan, Drumnadrochit, Inverness-shire, IV3 6UX; T.-04562 310.

Dobie, Margaret G.C., OBE, MA, DipSocStud. Member, Broadcasting Council for Scotland, 1987-91; Vice Chair, Scottish Association for the Study of Delinquency, since 1989; Chair, Children's Panel Advisory Group, 1985-88; Chair, Dumfries and Galloway Children's Panel Advisory Committee, 1982-89; b. Galloway; m., James T.J. Dobie; 3 s. Educ. Benedictine Convent, Dumfries; Dumfries Academy; Edinburgh University. Medical Social Worker; Chair, Dumfries and Galloway Regional Children's Panel, 1971-77; Social Worker, Child Guidance Service, Dumfries; National Secretary, Scottish Association for the Study of Delinquency, 1982-87; Chair, Dumfries & Galloway Valuation Panel, since 1987; Member, Dumfries & Galloway Family Conciliation Service Executive Committee. Recreations: travel; tennis; reading. Address: (h.) Mansepark, Kirkgunzeon, Dumfries, DG2 8LA; T.-038 776 661.

Dobson, Roger, FITD, MIPM. Personnel Director, Operations, United Distillers, since 1988; b. 15.11.46, Manchester; m., Jane Philippa Wardley; 3 s.; 1 d. Educ. Bolton School; Strathclyde University. Hoover, 1972-74; Philips, 1974-76; Scottish & Newcastle Breweries, 1976-85; B & Q PLC, 1985-88. Chairman, Scotvec Business, Administration and Management Sector Board; Chairman, Stirling University Human Resource Management Centre Advisory Committee; Chairman, Scottish Interactive Technology Centre; Member, Scottish Examination Board. Recreations: long-distance walking and sailing. Address: (b.) Distillers House, 33 Ellersly Road, Edinburgh, EH12 6JW; T.-031-337 7373.

Dobson, Ronald Matthew, MA, PhD. Honorary Lecturer in Zoology, Glasgow University (Lecturer in Agricultural Zoology, 1959-74, Senior Leader, 1974-90); b. 18.12.25, Blackburn, Lancashire; m., Ruth Hilda Nash; 2 s.; 3 d. Educ. Queen Elizabeth's Grammar School, Blackburn; Cambridge University; London University. Insect Infestation Inspector, Ministry of Food, then Department of Agriculture for Scotland, 1945-49; Research Assistant, Wye College, London University, 1950-53; Scientific Officer, then Senior Scientific Officer, Rothamsted Experimental Station, 1953-59. Fellow, Royal Entomological Society of London; Honorary Editor, Glasgow Naturalist. Publications: Insects and Other Invertebrates in Colour (adaptation); numerous scientific and natural history articles. Recreations: music; house renovation; boating. Address: (h.) 7 Netherburn Avenue, Glasgow, G44 3UF; T.-041-637 3659.

Dodd, Raymond Henry, MA, BMus, ARAM. Cellist and Composer; b. 31.3.29; m., Doreen Joyce; 1 s.; 1 d. Educ. Bryanston School; Royal Academy of Music; Worcester College, Oxford. Music Master, Sedbergh School, 1951-55; Aberdeen University: Lecturer in Music, 1956, Senior Lecturer in Music, 1971-91; Visiting Professor of Music, Wilson College, USA, 1972-73. Various orchestral and chamber music compositions; a Director: North East of Scotland Music School, Scottish Music Information Centre; awarded Szymanowski Medal, Polish Ministry of Art and Culture, 1982. Address: (h.) 14 Giffordgate, Haddington, East Lothian, EH41 4AS; T.-062 082 4618.

Doig, Andrew, MB, ChB, FRCPEdin, FRCP. Consultant Physician, Edinburgh Royal Infirmary, 1963-89; Senior Lecturer in Medicine, Edinburgh University, 1963-89; b. 18.12.24, Edinburgh; m., Anne Bisset Duthie; 1 s.; 1 d. Educ.

Boroughmuir School, Edinburgh; Edinburgh University; Illinois University. Junior medical posts, Edinburgh Royal Infirmary, Victoria Hospital (Burnley), Edinburgh University; postdoctoral Research Fellow, United States Public Health Service; President, Scottish Society of Physicians, 1985-86; President, Harveian Society of Edinburgh, 1989-90. Recreations: hill-walking; photography; 18th-century history. Address: (h.) 13 Nile Grove, Edinburgh, EH10 4RE; T.-031-447 4160.

Doig, Very Rev. Andrew Beveridge, MA, BD, DD. Moderator, General Assembly of the Church of Scotland, 1981-82; b. 18.9.14, Carluke; m., 1, Nan Carruthers (deceased); 1 d.; 2, Barbara Young; 1 s.; 1 d. Educ. Hyndland Secondary School, Glasgow; Glasgow University; Trinity College, Glasgow; Union Theological Seminary, New York. Missionary, Church of Scotland, to Nyasaland, 1939; Senior Chaplain to the Forces, East Africa Command, 1940-45; Secretary, Blantyre Mission Council, 1946-53; Member: Government Advisory Committee on African Education, 1948-53, Nyasaland Legislative Council, 1946-53; seconded from missionary service to be Nominated Member for African Interests, Central Africa Federal Assembly, 1953-58; General Secretary, Blantyre Synod, Church of Central Africa, Presbyterian, 1958-62; Minister, St. John's and King's Park, Dalkeith, 1962-72; Clerk, Dalkeith Presbytery, 1965-72; Member, Overseas Council, Church of Scotland, and Convener, Christian Aid, 1967-70; General Secretary, National Bible Society of Scotland, 1972-82; Member, Executive Committee for Europe in worldwide United Bible Societies, 1974-82. Recreation: golf. Address: (h.) The Eildons, Moulin Square, Pitlochry, PH16 5EW; T.-0796 2892.

Doig, John Scott. Regional Sheriff Clerk, Grampian Highland and Islands; b. 24.11.38, Dundee; m., Margaret; 1 s.; 1 d. Educ. Harris Academy, Dundee. Sheriff Clerk Service since 1956 in Glasgow, Perth, Campbeltown, Linlithgow, Glasgow, Dumbarton; Secretary, Sheriff Court Rules Council, 1973-79. Recreations: bowls; snooker. Address: (b.) The Castle, Inverness; T.-0463 230782.

Donachy, John Archibald, OBE, MA, FBIM. Governor, British Film Institute, since 1974; Chairman, Scottish Film Council, since 1984; b. Edinburgh; m., Jilly Pollard; 1 s.; 1 d. Educ. George Heriot's School; High School of Glasgow; Glasgow University. Recreations: gardening; cooking; films; music. Address: (h.) Clerkington Mill, Haddington, East Lothian, EH41 4NJ; T.-062 082 2429.

Donald, George Malcolm, ARSA, RSW, DA, ATC, MEd. Lecturer, Edinburgh College of Art; Printmaker; b. 12.9.43, Ootacamund, South India; 1 s.; 1 d. Educ. Robert Gordon's College; Aberdeen Academy; Edinburgh College of Art; Hornsey College of Art; Edinburgh University. Joined Edinburgh College of Art as Lecturer, 1969; Visiting Lecturer, five Faculties of Art in India, 1979; Visiting Professor of Art, 1981, and Visiting Professor, Drawing and Anatomy, 1985, University of Central Florida; Visiting Professor, Strasbourg, 1986, Belgrade, 1987, Sechuan Fine Art Institute, China, 1989; Latimer Award, RSA, 1970; Guthrie Award, RSA, 1973; Scottish Arts Council Bursary, 1973; RSA Gillies Bequest Travel Award to India, 1978; SAC Travel and Study Award, Indiana, 1981; RSA Gillies Prize, 1982; RSW Mary Marshall Brown Award, 1983; RGI Cargill Award, 1987; former Council Member, Printmakers Workshop (Edinburgh); former Member, Scottish Arts Council Awards Committee; one man shows, Florida, 1985, Helsinki, 1985, Edinburgh Festival, 1985, Belgrade, 1987, Florida, 1987, Edinburgh, 1988, 1990. Address: (h.) Bankhead, by Duns, Berwickshire, TD11 3QJ; T.-0361 83014.

Donald, James Forrest. Director, His Majesty's Theatre, Aberdeen, since 1971; b. 14.3.34, Aberdeen; m., Anne Gerrie; 1 s.; 1 d. Educ. Gordonstoun School. Recreation: golf. Address: (b.) His Majesty's Theatre, Aberdeen; T.-Aberdeen 637788.

Donald, James Turner, BSc (Eng). General Manager, Common Services Agency, Scottish Health Service, since 1986; Member, Management Committee, Common Services Agency, since 1986; b. 12.9.36, Paisley; m., Muriel Elizabeth Ramsay; 1 s.; 1 d. Educ. Gordonstoun; Glasgow University. Inveresk Group Ltd.: joined, 1962; General Manager, Woodhall, 1970-72, Caldwells, 1972-74, Carrongrove, 1974-76, Westfield, 1981-85, Divisional Chairman, 1974-80, Director, Inveresk Group Ltd., 1976-81. Chairman, Scottish Division, British Paper and Board Federation, 1976-79; Regional Councillor, CBI Scotland, 1976-82; Member, Post Qualification Education Board for Pharmacists, since 1989; Liveryman, Worshipful Company of Stationers and Newspaper Makers. Recreations: restoring 18th-century listed building (second time); horses; photography; music. Address: (b.) Trinity Park House, South Trinity Road, Edinburgh, EH5 3SE; T.-031-552 6255.

Donald, William J., BSc. Principal, Thurso College, since 1989; Director, Caithness and Sutherland Enterprise Co., since 1991; b. 6.9.31, Cullen; m., Elizabeth M. Young; 1 s.; 1 d. Educ. Fordyce Academy; Aberdeen University; Aberdeen College of Education. Teacher of Agriculture, Perth and Kinross Education Committee, 1956-67; Thurso College: Lecturer in Agriculture, 1967-72, Head, Department of Mathematics and Science, 1972-74, Depute Principal, 1974-89. Recreations: golf; Rotary; horticulture; travel; reading. Address: (h.) Kinnoull, 30 Ormlie Hill, Thurso, KW14 7DY; T.-0847 63230.

Donaldson, Professor (Charles) Ian (Edward), BA (Hons), MA, FAHA. Regius Professor of Rhetoric and English Literature, Edinburgh University, since 1991; b. 6.5.35, Melbourne, Australia; m., Grazia Gunn; 1 s., 1 d. by pr. m. Educ. Melbourne Grammar School; Melbourne University; Oxford University. Senior Tutor in English, Melbourne University, 1958; Oxford University: Fellow and Lecturer in English, Wadham College, 1962-69; CUF Lecturer in English, 1963-69; Australian National University: Professor of English, 1969-91, Director, Humanities Research Centre, 1974-90. Publications: The World Upside-Down: Comedy from Jonson to Fielding, 1970; Ben Jonson Poems (Editor), 1975; The Rapes of Lucretia, 1982; Jonson and Shakespeare, 1983; Transformations in Modern European Drama, 1983; Seeing the First Australians (Co-Editor), 1985; Ben Jonson, 1985. Address: (h.) 25 Northumberland Street, Edinburgh, EH3 6LR; T.-031-557 6050.

Donaldson, David Abercrombie, RSA, RP, RGI, LLD, DLitt, HonDLitt (Glasgow). Painter; Painter and Limner to The Queen in Scotland, since 1977; b. 29.6.16, Chryston; m., 1, Kathleen Boyd Maxwell; 1 s.; 2, Maria (Marysia) Mora-Szorc; 2 d. Educ. Coatbridge Secondary School; Glasgow School of Art. Head of Painting School, Glasgow School of Art, 1967-81; Hon. LLD, Strathclyde, 1971. Recreations: music; cooking. Address: (h.) 5 Cleveden Drive, Glasgow, G12 0SB; T.-041-334 1029.

Donaldson, Professor Gordon, CBE, DLitt, FBA, FRSE. HM Historiographer in Scotland, since 1979; Professor Emeritus, since 1979; b. 13.4.13, Edinburgh. Educ. Royal High School, Edinburgh; Edinburgh University; London University. Assistant, Scottish Record Office, 1938-47; Lecturer in Scottish History, Edinburgh University, 1947; Reader, 1955; Professor of Scottish History and Palaeography, 1963; Member, Royal Commission on the Ancient and Historical Monuments of Scotland, 1964-82;

Member, Scottish Records Advisory Council, 1964-87; President: Scottish Ecclesiological Society, 1963-65, Scottish Church History Society, 1964-67, Scottish History Society, 1968-72, Scottish Record Society, since 1981, Stair Society, since 1987. Publications: The Making of the Scottish Prayer Book, 1954; Register of the Privy Seal of Scotland, V-VIII, 1957-82; Life in Shetland under Earl Patrick, 1958; Scotland: Church and Nation, 1960, 1972; Scottish Reformation, 1960, 1972; Scotland: James V to James VII, 1965, 1971; The Scots Overseas, 1966; Northwards by Sea, 1966, 1978; Scottish Kings, 1967, 1977; First Trial of Mary Queen of Scots, 1969; Mary Queen of Scots, 1974; Scotland: The Shaping of a Nation, 1974, 1980; The Queen's Men, 1983; Isles of Home, 1983; Scottish Church History, 1985; Sir William Fraser, 1985; Reformed by Bishops, 1988; The Faith of the Scots, 1990; A Northern Commonwealth: Scotland and Norway, 1990. Address: (h.) 6 Pan Ha', Dysart, Fife, KY1 2TL; T.-0592 52685.

Donaldson, Professor Gordon Bryce, MA, PhD, FInstP, FRSE. Professor, Department of Physics and Applied Physics, Strathclyde University, since 1985; b. 10.8.41, Edinburgh; m., Christina Martin; 1 s.; 1 d. Educ. Glasgow Academy; Christ's College, Cambridge. Cavendish Laboratory, Cambridge, 1962-65; Lecturer in Physics, Lancaster University, 1966-75; Strathclyde University: Lecturer, 1976, Senior Lecturer, 1978; Visiting Scientist and Fulbright Scholar, University of California, 1975; Visiting Professor, University of Virginia, 1981; Chairman, Institute of Physics Low Temperature Group, since 1990; DTI/SERC Coordinator for National Superconductivity Programme, since 1990. Governor, Glasgow Academicals Memorial Trust. Address: (b.) Department of Physics and Applied Physics, Strathclyde University, Glasgow, G4 ONG; T.-041-552 4400.

Donaldson, Graham H. C., MA (Hons), MEd. Her Majesty's Chief Inspector of Schools, Northern Division, since 1991; b. 11.12.46, Glasgow; 2 s.; 1 d. Educ. High School of Glasgow; Glasgow University. Teacher of History and Modern Studies, Craigbank Secondary School; Principal Teacher, Curriculum Development, Dunbartonshire County Council; Evaluation Officer, Consultative Committee on the Curriculum; HMI, Western Division; HMI, Education 14-18. Publication: James IV – a Renaissance King. Recreations: reading; walking; golf; watching football. Address: Lasswade, Bridgeview Road, Aboyne, AB34 5HB; T.-03398 86784.

Donaldson, Professor Iain Malcolm Lane, BSc, MB, ChB, MA, FRCPE, MRCP. Professor of Neurophysiology, Edinburgh University, since 1987; b. 22.10.37; m.; 1 s. Educ. Edinburgh University. House Physician and Surgeon, Research Fellow, Honorary Lecturer, Honorary Senior Registrar, Departments of Medicine and Surgical Neurology, Edinburgh University, 1962-69; Anglo-French Research Scholarship, University of Paris, 1969-70; Research Officer, University Laboratory of Physiology, Oxford, 1970-79; Fellow and Tutor in Medicine, St. Edmund Hall, Oxford, 1973-79; Professor of Zoology, Hull University, 1979-87; Emeritus Fellow, St. Edmund Hall, Oxford, since 1979. Recreation: studying the past. Address: (b.) Department of Pharmacology, Edinburgh University, 1 George Square, Edinburgh.

Donaldson, James Andrew, BDS, BA, DFM. Principal, general dental practice; b. 28.2.57, Glasgow; m., Patricia H. Winter; 2 d. Educ. Coatbridge High School; Dundee University; Open University; Glasgow University. Dental Adviser, British Antarctic Survey, since 1986; Member: National Council, General Dental Practitioners Association, since 1989, Scottish General Dental Services Committee, since 1991, Aberdeen District Council, 1984-86, Grampian Regional Council, 1986-88; Director, "Open Wide" Dental

Courses. Recreations: skiing; squash; scuba diving. Address: (h.) Ellon Castle, Ellon, AB41 9QN; T.-0358 21865.

Donaldson, James T., BA (Hons), MEd. HM Chief Inspector of Schools, since 1988 (HM Inspector of Schools, 1982-88); b. 4.3.45, Ecclefechan; m., Maureen; 1 s.; 2 d. Educ. Wallace Hall Academy; Strathclyde University; Edinburgh University. Lecturer, Edinburgh College of Commerce, 1968-73; Lecturer/Senior Lecturer, Queen Margaret College, Edinburgh, 1973-79; Head, Department of Business Studies, Telford College of Further Education, Edinburgh, 1979-82. Recreations: golf; running. Address: (b.) Scottish Education Department, Room 4/103 New St. Andrews House, Edinburgh; T.-031-244 5324.

Donaldson, William, MA, PhD. Writer, Researcher, Traditional Musician; b. 19.7.44, Fraserburgh. Educ. Fraserburgh Academy; Aberdeen University. Publications: Popular Literature in Victorian Scotland, 1986; The Jacobite Song, 1988; The Language of the People, 1989. Recreation: piobaireachd player. Address: (b.) 13 Mile End Avenue, Aberdeen.

Donaldson, (William) Blair (MacGregor), MB, ChB, FRCS, FCOphth, DO. Consultant Ophthalmic Surgeon, since 1979; Senior Lecturer in Ophthalmology, Aberdeen University, since 1979; Designer of surgical instruments; b. 24.12.40, Edinburgh; m., Marjorie Stuart; 1 d. Educ. Edinburgh Academy; Edinburgh University. Junior hospital appointments in Tasmania and Scotland. Recreations: skiing; tennis; golf; shooting; oil painting; silversmithing. Address: (h.) 45 Carlton Place, Aberdeen, AB2 4BR; T.-0224 641166.

Donnachie, Ian, MA MLitt, PhD, FSA (Scot). Staff Tutor in History, Open University in Scotland, since 1970; Senior Lecturer, Open University in Scotland since 1985; b. 18.6.44, Lanark. Educ. Lanark Grammar School; Glasgow University; Strathclyde University. Research Assistant, Galloway Project, Strathclyde University, 1967-68; Lecturer in Social Studies: Napier Polytechnic, 1968-70, Deakin University, Victoria, 1982; Visiting Fellow: Deakin University, Victoria and Sydney University, NSW, 1985; Adult and Continuing Education Lecturer for Aberdeen University, Edinburgh University and Glasgow University, since 1966. Trustee, Scottish Brewing Archive; Consultant: National Library of Scotland, Scottish Tourist Board, Scottish Office Education Department; Member: Universities Council for Adult and Continuing Education (Scotland), International Council for Distance Education. Publications include: A History of the Brewing Industry in Scotland; Industrial Archaeology in the British Isles (jointly); Scottish History 1560-1980 (jointly); That Land of Exiles: Scots in Australia (jointly); Forward! Labour Politics in Scotland 1888-1988 (Co-Editor); A Companion to Scottish History from the Reformation to the Present (jointly); The Manufacture of Scottish History (Co-editor). Recreations: walking; curling; eating; drinking. Address: (b.) 60 Melville Street, Edinburgh, EH3 7HF; T.-031-226 3851.

Donnelly, Dougie. Radio and Television Broadcaster, since 1976; b. 7.6.53, Glasgow; m., Linda; 3 d. Educ. Hamilton Academy; Strathclyde University. Studied law at University; joined Radio Clyde to present music programmes, 1976, and BBC TV Scotland as Sports Presenter and Commentator, 1978; Presenter, Friday Night With Dougie Donnelly, BBC TV Scotland (two series); Presenter, Dougie Donnelly Mid Morning Show, Radio Clyde (ninth year). Scottish Radio Personality of Year, 1979, 1982 and 1985; Scottish TV Personality of Year, 1982; Member: Stars Organisation for Spastics, Lords Taverners. Recreations: golf; reading; socialising; work. Address: (b.) c/o David John Associates,10 Queen's Gate Lane, Glasgow, G12 9DF; T.-041-357 0532.

Donnison, Professor David. Professor of Town and Regional Planning, Glasgow University, since 1980; b. 19.1.26. Lecturer: Manchester University, 1950-53, Toronto University, 1953-55; London School of Economics and Political Science: Reader, 1956-61, Professor, 1961-69; Director, Centre for Environmental Studies, London, 1969-75; Chairman, Supplementary Benefits Commission, 1975-80. Address: (b.) Glasgow University, Glasgow, G12 8RT.

Donohoe, Brian H. MP (Labour), Cunninghame South, since 1992; b. 10.9.48, Kilmarnock; m., Christine; 2 s. Educ. Irvine Royal Academy; Kilmarnock Technical College. Secretary, Irvine and District Trades Council, 1973-81; Chair, North Ayrshire and Arran LUC, 1977-79; Chair, Cunninghame Industrial Development Committee, 1975-79; former full-time trade union official (NALGO). Recreation: gardening. Address: (h.) 5 Greenfield Drive, Irvine, Ayrshire; T.-0294 74419.

Donovan, Professor Robert John, BSc, PhD, CChem, FRSC, FRSE. Professor of Chemistry, Edinburgh University, since 1979; b. 13.7.41, Nantwich; m., Marion Colclough; 1 d. Educ. Sandbach School; University College of Wales, Aberystwyth; Cambridge University. Research Fellow, Gonville and Caius College, 1966-70; Edinburgh University: Lecturer in Physical Chemistry, 1970-74, Reader in Chemistry, 1974-79. Member, Physical Chemistry Panel, Science & Engineering Research Council, 1977-80; Member, Management Committee, SERC Synchrotron Radiation Source, Daresbury, 1977-80; Member, SERC Synchrotron Radiation Facility Committee, 1979-84; Chairman, SERC Laser Facility Committee, 1989-92; Member, SERC Science Board, 1989-92; awarded Corday-Morgan Medal and Prize, Royal Society of Chemistry, 1975; Member, Faraday Council, Royal Society of Chemistry, 1981-83, 1991-93. Recreations: hill-walking; skiing; sail-boarding; cross-country riding. Address: (b.) Department of Chemistry, Edinburgh University, West Mains Road, Edinburgh, EH9 3JJ; T.-031-650 4722.

Doran, Frank, LLB. MP (Labour), Aberdeen South, 1987-92; b. 13.4.49, Edinburgh; m., Pat; 2 s. Educ. Dundee University. Solicitor with own business in Dundee; Member, General Management Committee, Dundee City Labour Party; Party Solicitor in Dundee; Lecturer and Writer on child care and mental health law; Founder Member, Scottish Legal Action Group and "Scottish Child"; Past Chairman, Dundee Association for Mental Health; Front Bench Spokesman, Oil and Gas Industry, since 1988. Recreations: football; cinema.

Dorman, Arthur Brian, LLB, FBIM. Solicitor; Founding and Senior Partner, Dorman, Jeffrey & Co., Glasgow and Edinburgh; b. 21.6.45, Glasgow; 1 s.; 1 d. Educ. Hillhead High School; Glasgow University. Recreation: occasional golf. Address: (b.) Madeleine Smith House, 6/7 Blythswood Square, Glasgow, G2 4AD; T.-041-221 9880.

Dorrian, Alexander Moore, BSc, FIMechE, FIMarE, FRINA, MIESS. Managing Director, BAeSEMA Ltd.; b. 19.9.46, Glasgow; m., Frances Graham; 1 s.; 1 d. Educ. Strathclyde University. Apprenticeship with G. & J. Weir, Cathcart, Glasgow; worked through ranks, YARD Ltd. Recreation: golf. Address: (b.) 1 Atlantic Quay, Broomielaw, Glasgow, G2 8JE.

Dorward, Adam Paterson, FCFI. Member, Borders Health Board (Convener, Finance Committee), 1978-89; b. 11.6.22, Galashiels; m., Jean MacPherson Ovens; 2 s. Educ. Sedbergh School; St. John's College, Cambridge; Dundee School of Economics; Tailor & Cutter Academy; Stevenson College. RAF, 1942-46 (Flt. Lt. Pilot, Flying Instructor); J. & J. Dorward Ltd., Gala Forest: joined, 1946, appointed Designer/Production Manager, 1948, appointed Director,

1952, Managing Director, 1972, Chairman, 1978; negotiated amalgamation with Dawson International, remaining Managing Director for 18 months; administration, Youth Opportunities Programme and Youth Training Scheme, Borders Regional Council, 1982-84; Business Consultant, 1984; Production Co-ordinator, clothing manufacturer, 1985-87. Former Governor, Scottish College of Textiles; Town and County Councillor, 1955-60; Member, Board, Galashiels Further Education College, 1955-60; Deacon, Galashiels Manufacturers' Corporation, 1960; a Governor, St. Mary's Preparatory School, Melrose, 1960; Council Member, Clothing Manufacturers' Federation of GB, 1973-81; Chairman, Scottish Clothing Manufacturers' Association, 1975-79; Past Chairman, Border Counties TSB; former Trustee, TSB of South of Scotland; Member, Eildon Housing Association, since 1978; Trustee, R.S. Hayward Trust. Recreations: sports; gardening. Address: (h.) Caddon Lynns, Clovenfords, Galashiels, TD1 3LF; T.-0896 85 259.

Dorward, David Campbell, MA, GRSM, LRAM. Composer, since 1944; Music Producer, BBC, 1962-91; b. 7.8.33, Dundee; m., Janet Offord; 1 s.; 2 d. Educ. Morgan Academy, Dundee; St. Andrews University; Royal Academy of Music. Teaching, 1960-61; Freelance, 1961-62. Arts Adviser, Lamp of Lothian Collegiate Trust, since 1967; Member, Scottish Arts Council, 1972-78; Consultant Director, Performing Right Society, 1985-90; Patron's Fund Award, 1958; Royal Philharmonic Prizewinner, 1958; compositions include four string quartets, symphony, four concertos, Tonight Mrs Morrison (one-act opera), A Christmas Carol (musical), and incidental music for TV, radio, film and stage. Recreations: photography; computers; walking in the country. Address: (h.) 10 Dean Park Crescent, Edinburgh, EH4 1PH; T.-031-332 3002.

Dorward, David Philip, MA, LLB. Secretary, St. Andrews University, 1989-91; b. 10.4.31, Dundee; m., Joy Stewart; 2 s.; 1 d. Educ. Dundee High School; St. Andrews University. Appointed Administrative Assistant, St. Andrews University, 1959; successively Assistant Secretary and Deputy Secretary. Publications: Scottish Surnames, 1978; The Place Names of Scotland, 1979. Recreations: music; golf; gardening; travelling. Address: (h.) 7 Drumcarrow Crescent, Strathkinness, Fife, KY16 9XT; T.-0334 85 630.

Douglas, Rev. Andrew Morrison, MA. Minister, High Church, Hilton, Aberdeen; Clerk, Aberdeen Presbytery; Moderator, Aberdeen Presbytery, 1987-88; b. 23.2.30, Orange, Australia; m., Margaret Rennie; 2 s.; 2 d. Educ. Robert Gordon's College; Aberdeen University. Minister: Lochcraig Church, Fife, 1957-63, Bonaccord St. Paul's, Aberdeen, 1963-72, Southesk, Brechin, 1972-77. Chaplain, Aberdeen Maternity and Sick Children's Hospitals, 1968-71. Recreations: gardening; games. Address: 24 Rosehill Drive, Aberdeen, AB2 2JJ; T.-Aberdeen 484155.

Douglas, Rev. Iain Mackechnie, MA, BD, MPhil, DipEd. Minister, St. Andrew's Parish Church, Montrose, since 1980, linked with Farnell Parish Church, 1990; b. 25.6.35, Eccles, Berwickshire; m., E.W. Shirley Harris; 2 s. Educ. Eccles Public School; George Watson's Boys' College, Edinburgh; Edinburgh University. Missionary, Church of Scotland, 1960-68; ordained, Madras Diocese, Church of South India, 1960; Lecturer, Tamilnad Theological College, 1963-68; Teacher of Religious Education, Hawick High School, 1969-74; Principal Teacher of Religious Education, Morgan Academy, Dundee, 1974-80; Governor, Northern College of Education, since 1986. Publications: Famulus Christi (Contributor), 1976; Sacris Erudiri (Contributor), 1974-75. Address: 49 Northesk Road, Montrose, DD10 8TQ; T.-Montrose 72060.

Douglas, Rev. Ian Percy, LTh. Minister, Craigiebuckler Parish Church, Aberdeen, since 1982; b. 2.5.38, Inverurie;

m., Celia Gerrard; 2 s. Educ. Inverurie Academy; Aberdeen University. Junior Salesman, Isaac Benzie Ltd., Aberdeen, 1954-56; 1st Bn., Seaforth Highlanders, 1956-59; Departmental Manager, Isaac Benzie Ltd., 1960-65; Training and Personnel Officer, House of Fraser, 1965-67; studied for the ministry, 1967-73; Minister, Viewforth Parish Church, Edinburgh, 1974-82. TA Chaplain, 205 General Hospital Unit, 1979-81; Burgess of Guild of Burgh of Aberdeen; Patron, Seven Incorporated Trades of Aberdeen. Recreations: music; bowls. Address: Craigiebuckler Manse, Springfield Road, Aberdeen, AB1 8AA.

Douglas, James Hall, MA, LLB. Honorary Sheriff, since 1983; b. 16.9.21, Glasgow; m., Louisa Hemsworth. Educ. Whitehill Senior Secondary School, Glasgow; Glasgow University. RAF, 1940-46; Procurator Fiscal service, 1951-82, at Ayr, Glasgow, Stranraer and Dunfermline; Procurator Fiscal, Dunfermline, 1967-82. Recreations: reading; gardening; music; philately. Address: (h.) 1 Canmore Grove, Dunfermline, KY12 OJT; T.-Dunfermline 725486.

Douglas, John Aitken, DPE, DMS, MBIM, FILAM. Director of Recreation Services, Inverclyde District Council, since 1974; b. 8.4.41, Duns; m., Anne; 1 s.; 1 d. Educ. Berwickshire High School, Duns; Scottish School of Physical Education, Jordanhill College of Education; Glasgow College of Technology. Teacher of Physical Education, Dollar Academy, 1963-65; Assistant Lecturer in Physical Education, Glasgow University, 1965-66; Lecturer in Physical Education, Strathclyde University, 1966-67; Manager, Bellahouston Sports Centre, Glasgow, 1967-71; Recreation Officer, Bishopbriggs Burgh Council, 1971-74. Churchill Fellow, 1970; Past Chairman: British and Irish Basketball Federation, 1972-73, Association of Recreation Managers, 1973-74 and 1979-80; former Member, National Executive, Institute of Leisure and Amenity Management, and Past Chairman, Scottish Region; former Member, Executive, Association of Directors of Recreation, Leisure and Tourism; former Officer Adviser, COSLA. Recreations: hockey; squash; caravanning; skiing; sailboarding. Address: (b.) Municipal Buildings, Greenock; T.-0475 24400.

Douglas, Neil James, MD, FRCP. Reader in Respiratory Medicine, Edinburgh University, since 1983; Consultant Physician, since 1983; Chairman, Editorial Board, Clinical Science, 1990-92; b. 28.5.49, Edinburgh; m., Dr. Sue Galloway; 1 s.; 1 d. Educ. Dundee High School; Trinity College, Glenalmond; St. Andrews University; Edinburgh University. Lecturer in Medicine, Edinburgh University, 1974-83; MRC Travelling Fellow, University of Colorado, 1980-81. Recreations: fishing; gardening; eating. Address: (b.) Department of Respiratory Medicine Unit, City Hospital, Greenbank Drive, Edinburgh; T.-031-447 1001.

Douglas, Patricia, MBE. Director, Charles Rennie Mackintosh Society; m., Thomas H. Douglas; 2 s. Recreations: tennis; bridge. Address: (b.) Queen's Cross, 870 Garscube Road, Glasgow, G20 7EL; T.-041-946 6600.

Douglas, Sadie Naomi, MBE. Administrative Director, Scottish Civic Trust, since 1983; b. Huddersfield; m., Alexander Douglas (deceased); 1 s. Educ. Longley Hall, Huddersfield; Huddersfield Technical College. Worked with Oxfam, 1966-70; Organising Secretary, Facelift Glasgow, 1970-73; Trust Secretary, Scottish Civic Trust, 1973-83. Member, Countrywide Holiday Association (President, Glasgow CHA Club); Member, Scottish Countryside Activities Council. Recreation: hill-walking. Address: (h.) Hillhouse, Ardneil Avenue, West Kilbride, Ayrshire, KA23; T.-0294 822465; (b.) 24 George Square, Glasgow, G2 1EF; T.-041-221 1466.

Douglas-Hamilton, Lord James Alexander, MA, LLB. MP (Conservative), Edinburgh West, since 1974; Parliamentary Under Secretary of State, Scottish Office, for Home Affairs and the Environment, since 1987; b. 31.7.42, Strathaven; m., Susan Buchan; 4 s. Educ. Eton; Balliol College, Oxford; Edinburgh University. Advocate at Scots Bar, 1968; Member, Edinburgh Town Council, 1972; Scottish Conservative Whip, 1977; a Lord Comr, HM Treasury, and Government Whip for Scottish Conservative Members, 1979-81; PPS to Malcolm Rifkind MP, at Foreign Office, later Scottish Office; Captain, Cameronian Coy., 2nd Bn., Lowland Volunteers (RARO), 1972; Honorary President, Scottish Amateur Boxing Association, since 1975; President, Royal Commonwealth Society in Scotland, 1979-87; President, Scottish Council, United Nations Association, 1981-87. Oxford Boxing Blue, 1961; President, Oxford Union Society, 1964. Publications: Motive For A Mission: The Story Behind Hess's Flight to Britain, 1971; The Air Battle for Malta: The Diaries of a Fighter Pilot, 1981; Roof of the World, 1983. Recreations: golf; forestry. Address: (h.) 12 Quality Street Lane, Davidsons Mains, Edinburgh; T.-031-336 4213.

Douglas-Home, Hon. (Lavinia) Caroline, FSA Scot. Estate Factor, Douglas and Angus Estates, since 1959; Trustee, National Museum of Antiquities of Scotland, 1982-85; Deputy Lieutenant, Berwickshire, since 1983; b. 11.10.37 (daughter of Baron Home of the Hirsel, KT, PC). Educ. privately. Woman of the Bedchamber (Temporary) to Queen Elizabeth the Queen Mother, 1963-65; Lady-In-Waiting (Temporary) to HRH Duchess of Kent, 1966-67. Recreations: fishing; reading; antiquities. Address: (h.) Dove Cottage, The Hirsel, Coldstream, Berwickshire; T.-0890 2834.

Dourish, James Anthony, MA (Hons). Rector, Trinity High School, Renfrew, since 1979; b. 7.2.37, Glasgow; m., Honor Burns; 3 s.; 1 d. Educ. St. Aloysius' College, Glasgow; Glasgow University. Teacher of Classics, St. Aloysius' College, Glasgow, 1960-67; Principal Teacher of Classics: St. Gregory's, Glasgow, 1967-71, Holyrood, Glasgow, 1972-73; Assistant Head Teacher, St. Margaret Mary's, Glasgow, 1974-77; Depute Head Teacher, Cardinal Newman High School, Bellshill, 1977-79. Choirmaster/Organist, St. Andrew's Cathedral, Glasgow, 1975-82; Past President, Rutherglen Lawn Tennis Club. Recreations: tennis; hill-walking; music. Address: (h.) 46 Viewpark Drive, Burnside, near Glasgow; T.-041-647 1021.

Dover, Sir Kenneth James, BA, MA, DLitt, Hon.LLD (St. Andrews, Birmingham), Hon.LittD (St. Andrews, Bristol, London, Liverpool, Durham), Hon.DHL (Oglethorpe), FRSE, FBA. Chancellor, St. Andrews University, since 1981; b. 11.3.20, Croydon; m., Audrey Ruth Latimer; 1 s.; 1 d. Educ. St. Paul's School, London; Balliol College, Oxford; Merton College, Oxford. Fellow and Tutor, Balliol College, Oxford, 1948-55; Professor of Greek, St. Andrews, 1955-76; President, Corpus Christi College, Oxford, 1976-86. Served in Royal Artillery, 1940-45; President, Hellenic Society, 1971-74; President, Classical Association, 1975; President, British Academy, 1978-81; Foreign Honorary Member, American Academy of Arts and Sciences, since 1979; Foreign Member, Royal Netherlands Academy, since 1979; Honorary Fellow, Balliol, Corpus Christi and Merton Colleges, Oxford. Recreations: lonely country; historical linguistics. Address: (h.) 49 Hepburn Gardens, St. Andrews, Fife, KY16 9LS; T.-0334 73589.

Dow, Professor Alexander Carmichael, MA, PhD. Professor and Head, Department of Economics, Glasgow Polytechnic, since 1989; b. 28.8.46; m., Sheila Christine; 2 d. Educ. Perth Academy; St. Andrews University; Simon Fraser University; University of Manitoba. Research Officer, Commonwealth Secretariat; Lecturer and Assistant Professor, University of Toronto; Lecturer, Stirling University.

Recreations: curling; travel. Address: (b.) Department of Economics, Glasgow Polytechnic, Cowcaddens Road, Glasgow, G4 0BA; T.-041-331 3310.

Dow, Lt. Col. Leslie Phillips Graham, OBE. Producer, Edinburgh Military Tattoo, since 1975; b. 13.1.26, Glasgow; m., Joan Robinson; 2 d. Educ. Belhaven Hill, Dunbar; Marlborough College. Commissioned, The Cameronians (Scottish Rifles), 1946; 1st Bn., Gibraltar, Trieste, Hong Kong and Malaya, 1947-51; C-in-C's Staff, Singapore, 1952-54; Adjt., 1st Bn., 1955; Staff College, 1956; Staff (Brigade Major), 1957-59; Company Commander, 1st Bn., Kenya and BAOR, 1959-61; Company Commander, RMA, Sandhurst, 1962-64; MA to GOC Kenya, 1965; with 1st Bn., 1966-68; commanded in Aden until standdown, Douglas, Lanarkshire, May, 1968; voluntary retirement, 1969. Member, The Monks of St. Giles. Recreations: shooting; gardening; French wine; classical music; composing indifferent light verse. Address: (h.) 22A Northumberland Street, Edinburgh, EH3 6LS; T.-031-557 0467.

Dow, Sheila Christine, MA (Hons), PhD. Reader in Economics, Stirling University, since 1988; b. 16.4.49, Dumfries; m., Professor Alexander Dow; 2 d. Educ. Hawick High School; St. Andrews University; University of Manitoba; McMaster University; Glasgow University. Overseas Office, Bank of England, 1970-72; Economist, then Senior Economist, Department of Finance, Government of Manitoba, 1973-77; Lecturer, Department of Economics, Stirling University, 1979-88. Treasurer, Scottish Economic Society. Publications: Macroeconomic Thought, 1985; Financial Markets and Regional Economic Development, 1990; Money Matters (Co-author), 1982. Recreations: travel; various sports. Address: (b.) Department of Economics, Stirling University, Stirling, FK9 4LA; T.-0786 73171, Ext. 7474.

Downie, Rev. Alexander George. Minister, Saline linked with Blairingone, since 1958; b. 15.6.23, Tarland; m., Jean; 1 s.; 2 d. Educ. Morpeth Grammar School; St. Andrews University. Army, 1942-47; commissioned, 1945, attached to 1st Mahratta Light Infantry; with British Occupation Forces, Japan, 1947; promoted Captain, 1947. Assistant Minister, St. Ninian's Parish Church, Stirling, 1951-53; Minister, Saline Parish Church, 1953-58. Moderator, Dunfermline and Kinross Presbytery, 1964-65. Address: The Manse, Saline, Fife; T.-New Oakley 852240.

Downie, James Hubert. FRSA. Deputy Lieutenant; Member, Western Isles Health Board; Barrister; b. 13.5.23, Northwood, Middlesex; m., Joyce Wyllie Milne; 3 d. Educ. Merchant Taylor's School, Northwood. Royal Navy, 1941-58 (retired as Lt.-Comdr); Shell-Mex & BP Ltd.: joined, 1959, Manager, Industrial Relations and Manpower Division, 1966-67, Manager, Trade Relations Division, 1967-75. Recreations: angling; gardening; bird-watching. Address: (h.) Dunarin Strond, Isle of Harris, Western Isles; T.-0859 82 247.

Downie, Professor Robert S., MA, BPhil, FRSE. Professor of Moral Philosophy, Glasgow University, since 1969 (Stevenson Lecturer in Medical Ethics, 1984-88); b. 19.4.33, Glasgow; m., Eileen Dorothea Flynn; 3 d. Educ. High School of Glasgow; Glasgow University; Queen's College, Oxford. Tutor, Worcester College, Oxford, 1958-59; Glasgow University: Lecturer in Moral Philosophy, 1959-68, Senior Lecturer, 1968-69; Visiting Professor: Syracuse University, New York, 1963-64, Dalhousie University, Nova Scotia, 1976. Publications: Government Action and Morality, 1964; Respect for Persons, 1969; Roles and Values, 1971; Education and Personal Relationships, 1974; Caring and Curing, 1980; Healthy Respect, 1987; Health Promotion: models and values, 1990. Recreation: music. Address: (b.)

Department of Philosophy, Glasgow University, G12 8QQ; T.-041-339 8855.

Downs, Ian, DipArch, DipTP, RIBA, MRTPI, FRIAS. Chief Architect/Planner and Director of Technical Services, Irvine Development Corporation; b. 21.2.37, Withernsea, East Yorkshire; 1 s.; 1 d. Educ. Withensea High School; Hull School of Architecture; Manchester University. Architect, Cumbernauld Development Corporation, 1960-63; Architect/Planner: United States (private practice, working on New Towns), 1964-65, Wilson & Womersely, 1965-66; Group Architect, Livingston Development Corporation, 1966-69; Assistant Chief Architect: Redditch Development Corporation, 1969-76, West Midlands Metropolitan County Council, 1976-79. Recreation: sailing. Address: (b.) Irvine Development Corporation, Perceton House, Irvine; T.-Irvine 214100.

Dowson, Henry Richard, BSc, PhD, FRSE. Reader in Mathematics, Glasgow University, since 1975; Editor-in-Chief, Glasgow Mathematical Journal, since 1975; b. 2.3.39, Newcastle-upon-Tyne. Educ. Royal Grammar School, Newcastle-upon-Tyne; King's College, Newcastle-upon-Tyne; St. John's College, Cambridge. Assistant Lecturer, Department of Pure Mathematics, University College of Swansea, 1963-65; Lecturer, Department of Mathematics, Newcastle-upon-Tyne University, 1965-66; Assistant Professor, Illinois University, 1966-68; Department of Mathematics, Glasgow University: Lecturer, 1968-73, Senior Lecturer, 1973-75. Publication: Spectral Theory of Linear Operators, 1978. Recreation: bridge; numismatics. Address: (b.) Department of Mathematics, University Gardens, Glasgow, G12 8QW; T.-041-339 8855, Ext. 5179.

Doyle, Professor Christopher John, BA, MSc. Head of Economics, Marketing and Management Department, Scottish Agricultural College, Auchincruive, since 1989; Adjunct Professor of Agricultural Economics, Glasgow University, since 1989; Vice Dean (Education), Scottish Agricultural College, Auchincruive, since 1991; b. 21.8.48, Sale, Cheshire; m., Alice. Educ. St. Ambrose College, Cheshire; Keele University; Newcastle upon Tyne University. Departmental Demonstrator in Agricultural Economics, Oxford University, 1972-76; Research Officer, Centre for Agricultural Strategy, Reading University, 1976-79; Principal Scientific Officer, Institute for Grassland and Animal Production, 1979-86; Senior Economist, Ruakura Research Centre, MAF, New Zealand, 1987; Principal Scientific Officer, Institute for Grassland and Animal Production, 1988-89. Publications: 80 scientific papers and publications. Recreations: languages; foreign travel; modern history; theatre. Address: (b.) Scottish Agricultural College, Auchincruive, Ayr, KA6 5HW; T.-0292 520331.

Doyle, Rev. Ian Bruce, MA, BD, PhD. General Secretary, Department of National Mission, 1984-89; b. 11.9.21, Methil, Fife; m., Anne Watt Wallace; 2 s. Educ. Buckhaven High School; St. Andrews University; New College, Edinburgh. Served with Church of Scotland Huts, Germany, 1945-46; Assistant to Rev. D.P. Thomson, Evangelist, 1946; Minister: St. Mary's, Motherwell, 1946-60, Eastwood, Glasgow, 1960-77; Convener: Home Mission Committee, 1970-74, Home Board, 1974-77; Secretary, Department of Home Mission, 1977-84; Joint Secretary, Department of Ministry and Mission, 1984-89; Secretary, Prison Chaplaincies Board, since 1977. Publications: This Jesus; Reformation and Revolution (Contributor); The Word for All Seasons (Contributor); Local Church Evangelism (Contributor); D.P.: a memoir of Dr. D.P. Thomson. Recreation: reading. Address: (h.) 21 Lygon Road, Edinburgh; T.-031-667 2697.

Draper, Ivan Thomas, MB, ChB, FRCPEdin, FRCPGlas. Consultant Neurologist, Institute of Neurological Sciences,

Glasgow, since 1965; b. 11.9.32, Derby; m., Muriel May Munro. Educ. Bemrose School; Aberdeen University. Fellow, Department of Medicine, Johns Hopkins Hospital, Baltimore, 1962-63. Past President, Scottish Ornithologists Club; Curate, St. Bride's Episcopal Church, Glasgow. Publication: Lecture Notes on Neurology, 6th Edition. Recreations: birds; books; fish. Address: (b.) Institute of Neurological Sciences, Southern General Hospital, Govan Road, Glasgow.

Draper, Professor Paul Richard, BA, MA, PhD. Professor of Finance, Strathclyde University, since 1986 (Head, Department of Accounting and Finance, since 1990); b. 28.12.46, Hayes; m., Janet Margaret; 1 s.; 1 d. Educ. Exeter, Reading and Stirling Universities. Lecturer: St. Andrews and Edinburgh Universities. Publication: Scottish Financial Sector (Co-author), 1988; Investment Trust Industry in the UK, 1989. Recreations: renovating country cottages; home computing. Address: (h.) 19 Upper Gray Street, Newington, Edinburgh; T.-031-667 4087.

Draper, Professor Ronald Philip, BA, PhD. Regius Chalmers Professor of English, Aberdeen University (Professor, since 1973, Head of Department, since 1984); b. 3.10.28, Nottingham; m., Irene Margaret Aldridge; 3 d. Educ. Nottingham High School; Nottingham University. Tutorial Assistant, Nottingham University, 1951-53; Education Officer, RAF, 1953-55; Lecturer in English, Adelaide University, 1955-56; Leicester University: Assistant Lecturer in English, 1957-58, Lecturer, 1958-68, Senior Lecturer, 1968-73. Publications: D.H. Lawrence, 1964; D.H. Lawrence (Profiles in Literature), 1969; D.H. Lawrence, The Critical Heritage (Editor), 1970; Hardy, The Tragic Novels (Editor), 1975, 1991; George Eliot, The Mill on the Floss and Silas Marner (Editor), 1978; Tragedy, Developments in Criticism (Editor), 1980; Shakespeare, A Midsummer Night's Dream, 1980; Shakespeare, Cymbeline, 1980; Lyric Tragedy, 1985; Shakespeare, The Winter's Tale, 1985; D.H. Lawrence, Sons and Lovers, 1986; Hardy, Three Pastoral Novels (Editor), 1987; Shakespeare, Twelfth Night, 1988; The Literature of Region and Nation (Editor), 1989; An Annotated Critical Bibliography of Thomas Hardy (Co-author), 1989; The Epic: Developments in Criticism (Editor), 1990. Recreations: reading; listening to music; walking. Address: (b.) English Department, Taylor Building, King's College, Old Aberdeen, AB9 2UB; T.-0224 272623.

Drever, Harry Sinclair, MBE, JP, AIB (Scot). Consultant, Gerald Eve Chartered Surveyors, London, since 1974; Honorary Sheriff, Grampian, Highlands and Islands at Shetland, since 1961; b. 28.10.05, St. Margaret's, Hope, Orkney. Educ. St. Margaret's Hope Secondary School. Union Bank of Scotland Ltd. and Bank of Scotland, 1921-70 (Manager, Lerwick and Scalloway Branches, 1950-70); Shetland County Councillor, 1958-70 (sometime Chairman, Finance Committee); Member, Board of Management, Shetland Hospitals, 1959-70 (latterly Chairman, Finance Committee); Chairman, Zetland Territorial and Air Forces Association, until 1968; former Honorary Secretary, Shetland Branch, National Savings Committee; former Honorary Treasurer: Shetland Branch, British Red Cross Society, Shetland Tourist Association, Shetland Dog Trials Association, Shetland Swimming Pool Association. Recreations: golf; billiards; restoring antique furniture. Address: (h.) Vogalee, 78 St. Olaf Street, Lerwick; T.-0595 3783.

Drewry, James Michael, FITSA, DCA. Director of Trading Standards, Lothian Regional Council, since 1989; b. Hexham. Trained, Northumberland County Council; Inspector of Weights and Measures, Cheshire County Council; Senior Assistant Chief Trading Standards Officer, Humberside County Council, 1976-79; County Consumer Protection Officer, Durham County Council, 1980-89. Vice Chairman,

Institute of Trading Standards Administration; President, European Consumer Product Safety Association. Recreations: squash; golf; travel. Address: (b.) Chesser House, 500 Gorgie Road, Edinburgh EH11 3YJ; T.-031-469 5454.

Drummond, Alastair Wilson, MB, ChB, MRCPsych. Director, Scottish Hospital Advisory Service, since 1988; b. 7.5.32, Cumbria; m., Jean; 2 s. Educ. Ulverston Grammar School; Manchester University. Consultant Psychiatrist, West Cumberland Hospital, Whitehaven, 1963-82, Rosslynlee Hospital, Roslin, 1982-87. Recreations: fishing; skiing; music. Address: (h.) 10 Crichton Cottages, Pathhead, Midlothian, EH37 5UY; T.-Ford 320445.

Drummond, Humphrey, MC. Writer and Farmer; Proprietor and Managing Director, The Historical Press; b. 18.9.22, Old Buckenham, Norfolk; m., Cherry Drummond, 16th Baroness Strange; 3 s.; 3 d. Educ. Eton; Trinity College, Cambridge. Captain, 1st Mountain Regiment; former General Secretary, Council for Preservation of Rural Wales; Welsh Representative, National Trust; Chairman, Society of Authors (Scotland), 1976-82. Publications: Our Man in Scotland; The Queen's Man; The King's Enemy; Falconry For You; Falconry. Recreations: mechanical musical instruments; pre-Raphaelitism. Address: Megginch Castle, Errol, Perthshire; T.-Errol 222.

Drummond, Rev. John Whiteford, MA, BD. Minister, Rutherglen West Parish Church, since 1986; b. 27.6.46, Glasgow; m., Barbara S. Grant; 1 s.; 3 d. Educ. Bearsden Academy; Glasgow University. Probationer Assistant, St. Francis-in-the-East Church, Bridgeton, Glasgow, 1970-71; ordained Assistant, King's Park Parish Church, Glasgow, 1971-73; Minister, Linwood Parish Church, 1973-86. Recreations: family; reading. Address: (h.) 12 Albert Drive, Rutherglen, Glasgow, G73 3RT; T.-041-643 0234.

Drummond, Rev. Norman Walker, MA, BD. Headmaster, Loretto School, since 1984; b. 1.4.52, Greenock; m., Lady Elizabeth Kennedy; 2 s.; 2 d. Educ. Crawfordton House, Dumfriesshire; Merchiston Castle School; Fitzwilliam College, Cambridge; New College, Edinburgh. Chaplain to the Forces, 1976-82; Depot, The Parachute Regiment and Airborne Forces, 1977-78; 1st Bn., The Black Watch (Royal Highland Regiment), 1978-82; Chaplain, Fettes College, 1982-84. Member, Queen's Bodyguard for Scotland (Royal Company of Archers); Member of Court, Heriot-Watt University; Member, Scottish Committee, Duke of Edinburgh's Award Scheme; Chairman, Musselburgh and District Council of Social Services. Publication: The First Twenty Five Years (the official history of the Black Watch Kirk Session). Recreations: rugby football; cricket; golf; curling; traditional jazz; Isle of Skye. Address: Headmaster's House, Loretto School, Musselburgh, East Lothian; T.-031-665 2567.

Drummond, Thomas Anthony Kevin, LLB, QC. Advocate Depute, Crown Office, 1985-90; Member, Criminal Injuries Compensation Board, since 1990; Member, Firearms Consultative Committee, since 1989; b. 3.11.43, Howwood, Renfrewshire; m., Margaret Broadley; 1 d. Educ. Blairs College, Aberdeen; St. Mirin's Academy, Paisley; Edinburgh University. Civil Service, 1962-66; Solicitor, 1970-74; Bar, since 1974; QC, 1987. Cartoonist (Tak), Scots Law Times, since 1981. Recreations: shooting; hill-walking. Address: (h.) Pomathorn House, Howgate, Midlothian; T.-Penicuik 74046.

Dryden, Professor Myles Muir, BSc (Econ), MBA, PhD. Professor of Management Studies, Glasgow University, since 1972; b. 21.9.31, Dundee; m., Margaret Mary Cargill; 1 s.; 1 d. Educ. Kirkcaldy High School; London School of Economics; Cornell University. National Service, 1st Bn., Black Watch, BAOR, 1950-52; Assistant Professor of Finance, Sloan School of Industrial Management, Massachusetts Institute of Technology, 1960; Lecturer, then Reader in Economics, Edinburgh University, 1963-72; appointed to first Chair of Management Studies, Glasgow University, 1972 (Head of Department, until 1980); Member, Scottish Business School Council, 1975-79; has published in a number of professional journals; research on capital budgeting, share price behaviour and portfolio management. Recreations: pottering about in the garden or with microcomputers. Address: (b.) Department of Management Studies, 55 Southpark Avenue, Glasgow, G12 8LF; T.-041-330 4664.

Drysdale, Thomas Henry, LLB, WS. Solicitor; Deputy Keeper of Her Majesty's Signet, since 1991; Partner, Shepherd & Wedderburn, WS, Edinburgh, since 1967 (Managing Partner, since 1988); b. 23.11.42, Buchlyvie; m., Caroline Shaw; 1 s.; 2 d. Educ. Cargilfield; Glenalmond; Edinburgh University. Recreations: skiing; walking; reading. Address: (b.) 16 Charlotte Square, Edinburgh, EH2 4YS; T.-031-225 8585.

Dudgeon, Alexander (Sandy) Stewart, MA, CA. Deputy Managing Director, Adam & Company PLC, since 1991; b. 16.10.57, Edinburgh; m., Jennifer J.K. Waddell; 2 s. Educ. Trinity College, Glenalmond; Aberdeen University. Adam & Company PLC: Company Secretary, 1983-86, Director, since 1989; Director, Adam & Company International Ltd., since 1989; Director, Adam & Company Investment Management Ltd., since 1990; Member, Horseracing Advisory Council, 1985-90; Director, John Letters of Scotland Ltd., since 1991. Recreations: racing; farming; squash; golf; bridge. Address: (h.) 8 Cluny Drive, Edinburgh, EH10 6DW; T.-031-447 1979.

Dudley Edwards, Owen, BA, FRHistS. Reader in Commonwealth and American History, Edinburgh University, since 1979; b. 27.3.38, Dublin; m., Barbara Lee; 1 s.; 2 d. Educ. Belvedere College, Dublin; University College, Dublin; Johns Hopkins University, Baltimore. Visiting Lecturer in History, University of Oragon, 1963-65; Assistant Lecturer in History, Aberdeen University, 1966-68; Lecturer in History, Edinburgh University, 1968-79; Visiting Lecturer, California State University of San Francisco, 1972-73; Visiting Associate Professor, University of South Carolina, 1973; Sir David Owen Evans Lecturer, University College of Wales, Aberystwyth, 1987; Journalist and Broadcaster, notably for Irish Times, since 1959, and BBC, since 1969; contributor to various journals, especially The Scotsman. Life Member: American Historical Association, Organisation of American Historians; External Examiner: Queen's University, Belfast, Bradford University, Manchester University, Sorbonne, University College Cardiff. Publications: Celtic Nationalism (with Gwynfor Evans, Ioan Rhys and Hugh MacDiarmid), 1968; The Sins of Our Fathers - Roots of Conflict in Northern Ireland, 1970; The Mind of an Activist - James Connolly, 1971; P.G. Wodehouse - a Critical and Historical Essay, 1977; Burke and Hare, 1980; The Quest for Sherlock Holmes: a Biographical Study of Arthur Conan Doyle, 1982; Eamon de Valera, 1987; Macaulay (Historians on Historians), 1988; The Edinburgh Festival, 1990; City of 1000 Worlds – Edinburgh in Festival, 1991; as Editor/Contributor: 1916 - The Easter Rising (with Fergus Pyle), 1968; Conor Cruise O'Brien Introduces Ireland, 1969; James Connolly: Selected Political Writings (with Bernard C. Ransom), 1973; Scotland, Europe and the American Revolution (with George Shepperson), 1976; Christmas Observed (with Graham Richardson), 1981; Edinburgh (with Graham Richardson), 1983; A Claim of Right for Scotland, 1989; The Fireworks of Oscar Wilde, 1989; A. Conan Doyle: The Exploits of Brigadier Gerard, 1991. Recreations: Scottish Nationalism; playing chess badly. Address: (b.) Department of History, Edinburgh University, George Square, Edinburgh; T.-031-664 3526.

Duff, John Hume, MA (Cantab), MA (Edin), DipEd (Oxon). Rector, Kelvinside Academy, since 1980; b. 24.4.40, Edinburgh. Educ. St. Mary's School, Melrose; Edinburgh Academy; Corpus Christi College, Cambridge; Edinburgh University; Brasenose College, Oxford. Housemaster and Head of History Department, Kelly College, Tavistock, Devon, 1967-80. Major, TA. Recreations: squash rackets; skiing; hill-walking; foreign travel. Address: (b.) Kelvinside Academy, 33 Kirklee Road, Glasgow, G12 OSW; T.-041-357 3376.

Duffty, Paul, MB, ChB, MRCP, LMCC. Consultant Paediatrician, since 1982; Senior Lecturer in Child Health, Aberdeen University, since 1982; b. 1.9.46, Leeds; m., Lesley Marjory Macdonald; 2 d. Educ. Leeds Central High School; Aberdeen University. Lecturer in Child Health, Aberdeen University, 1972-75; Trainee in General Practice, Aberdeen, 1975-76; Lecturer in Child Health, Aberdeen University, 1976-78; Fellow in Neonatology, Toronto University, 1978-80; Staff Paediatrician, Hospital for Sick Children, Toronto, and Assistant Professor, Toronto University, 1980-82. Recreations: hill-walking; cross-country skiing; philately. Address: (h.) 13 Louisville Avenue, Aberdeen; T.-0224 317072.

Duffus, John Henderson, BSc, PhD, DSc, CBiol, MIBiol, CChem, FRSC. Director, Edinburgh Centre for Toxicology (EdinTox); Senior Lecturer in Environmental Toxicology, Heriot-Watt University, since 1980. Educ. Arbroath High School; Edinburgh University; Heriot-Watt University. Research Fellow: Warwick University, 1965-67, Edinburgh University, 1967-70; Lecturer, Heriot-Watt University, 1970-80; WHO Consultant, Toxicology and Chemical Safety, since 1981; Member, UK Department of the Environment Advisory Committee on Hazardous Substances, since 1991; Titular Member, IUPAC Commission on Toxicology, since 1991. Publications: Environmental Toxicology, 1980; Carbohydrate Metabolism in Plants (Co-author), 1984; Environmental Toxicology and Ecotoxicology, 1986; Magnesium in Mitosis and the Cell Cycle (Co-author), 1987; Yeast: A Practical Approach (Co-Editor), 1988; The Toxicology of Chemicals, Series 1, Carcinogenicity, Vol III (Co-Editor), 1991; Toxic Substances in Crop Plants (Co-Editor), 1991. 1988. Address: (b.) Heriot-Watt University, Riccarton, Edinburgh, EH14 4AS; T.-031-449 5111.

Duffy, Mgr. Francis Provost, VG. Vicar General to RC Bishop of Galloway, since 1975; Parish Priest, Troon, since 1982; b. 15.10.14, Edinburgh. Educ. Holy Cross Academy, Edinburgh; Blairs College, Aberdeen; Pontifical Scots College, Rome; Gregorian University, Rome. Ordained Priest (Rome), 1938; Curate, Ayr, 1939-41; Professor, Blairs College, Aberdeen, 1941-55; parish work in various towns, since 1955; Monsignor, since 1972. RC Religious Adviser, Scottish Television, 1958-78; Member, Dumfries Education Committee, 1963-72; Composer of congregational Church music and hymns. Address: 4 Cessnock Road, Troon, KA8 6NJ; T.-Troon 313541.

Duffy, John Alastair, BSc, PhD, DSc, CChem, FRSC. Reader in Chemistry, Aberdeen University, since 1991; Consultant to British Steel Corporation, 1987-91; Chairman, Molten Salts Discussion Group, Royal Society of Chemistry, 1986-88; b. 24.9.32, Birmingham; m., Muriel F.L. Ramsay; 1 s.; 1 d. Educ. Solihull School, Warwickshire; Sheffield University. Research Chemist, Albright & Wilson, Oldbury, 1958-59; Lecturer in Inorganic Chemistry, Wolverhampton Polytechnic, 1959-61; Senior Lecturer in Inorganic Chemistry, NE Wales Institute, 1961-65; Lecturer in Chemistry, Aberdeen University, 1966-77; Assessor in Inorganic Chemistry for Ordinary and Higher National Certificates and Diplomas in Scotland, 1971-82; Consultant to Schott Glaswerke, Mainz, West Germany, 1984-86; Past

Chairman, NE Scotland Section, Royal Society of Chemistry. Publications: General Inorganic Chemistry, 1966; Bonding Energy Levels and Bands in Inorganic Solids, 1990. Recreations: 20th-century opera; music. Address: (h.) 35 Beechgrove Terrace, Aberdeen, AB2 4DR; T.-0224 641752.

Duffy, Sheila Sinclair, MA. Women's Editor, Radio Clyde, since 1973; Freelance Journalist, since 1967; b. 6.8.46, Silloth, Cumberland; m., Paul Young; 2 d. Educ. St. Joseph's, Nicosia; Boroughmuir School, Edinburgh; Edinburgh University. Auxiliary nurse, Edinburgh Royal Infirmary, 1965-66; croupier, Edinburgh night club, 1966-67; graduate trainee, Scottish Television, 1967-68; Reporter, Scottish Television, 1968-73; Presenter, Dateline Early/Edinburgh Film Festival programmes/Moneywise. Glenfiddich Food Writer Award, 1986. Recreations: children; husband; genealogy; cooking; reading; cake decorating; walking; sampler embroidery. Address: (b.) Young Casting Agency, 7 Beaumont Gate, Glasgow; T.-041-339 5180.

Duggan, Professor Arthur William, BSc, MB, BS, MD, PhD. Professor of Veterinary Pharmacology, Edinburgh University, since 1987; b. 14.6.36, Brisbane; m., Gwyndolyn Helen Randall; 2 s.; 1 d. Educ. Brisbane Grammar School; Queensland University. Medical practice, 1961-67; medical research, Institute of Advanced Studies, Australian National University, Canberra, 1968-87. Publications: over 100 scientific papers. Address: (h.) 5c Strathalmond Road, Edinburgh, EH4 8AB.

Dukes, Professor Paul, BA (Cantab), MA, PhD. Professor of History, Aberdeen University, since 1988; b. 5.4.34, Wallington; m., Rosemary Mackay; 1 s.; 1 d. Educ. Wallington County Grammar School; Cambridge University. Advisory Editor, History Today. Publications: several books on aspects of Russian, American and European history. Recreations: hill-walking; travel. Address: (b.) History Department, Aberdeen University, Aberdeen; T.-0224 272465.

Dulverton, 2nd Baron (Frederick Anthony Hamilton Wills), CBE, TD, MA, DL; b. 19.12.15, London; m., Ruth Violet Mary; 2 s.; 1 d. Educ. Eton; Magdalen College, Oxford. Commissioned Lovat Scouts, 1935 (Major, 1943); President: Bath and West Agricultural Society, 1973, Three Counties Agricultural Society, 1975, Timber Growers United Kingdom, 1983; Chairman, Dulverton Trust; Council Member, WWF (UK) and Wildfowl Trust; awarded Gold Medal, Royal Forestry Society; appointed Commander of Order of Golden Ark by Prince Bernhard of Netherlands for services to wildlife, 1985. Recreations: field sports; nature photography. Address: (h.) Fassfern, Kinlocheil, Fort William, Inverness-shire; T.-039783 232.

Dunbar, Sir Archibald Ranulph, MA, DipAgric (Cantab), DTA (Trin). Retired; b. 8.8.27, London; m., Amelia M.S. Davidson; 1 s.; 2 d. Educ. Wellington College; Pembroke College, Cambridge. Military Service, Cameron Highlanders (attached Gordon Highlanders), 1945-48; Imperial College of Tropical Agriculture, Trinidad, 1952-53; Agricultural Officer, Colonial Service, Uganda (later Overseas Civil Service, Uganda) 1953-70; Landowner, Duffus Estate, Elgin, since 1970. Honorary Sheriff, Sheriff Court District of Moray, since 1989; Knight of Honour and Devotion, Sovereign Military Order of Malta, 1989. Recreations: swimming; railways; model railways; military models. Address: (h.) The Old Manse, Duffus, Elgin, Moray; T.-0343 830270.

Dunbar, John Greenwell, MA, FSA, FSA Scot, HonFRIAS. Secretary, Royal Commission on the Ancient and Historical Monuments of Scotland, 1978-90; b. 1.3.30, London; m., Elizabeth Mill Blyth. Educ. University College School, London; Balliol College, Oxford. joined staff, Royal

Commission on the Ancient and Historical Monuments of Scotland, 1953; Member, Ancient Monuments Board for Scotland, 1978-90. Publications: The Historic Architecture of Scotland, 1966; Accounts of the Masters of Works, Volume 2 (1616-1649), (Joint Editor), 1982. Address: (h.) Paties Mill, Carlops, by Penicuik, Midlothian, EH26 9NF; T.- West Linton 60250.

Dunbar, Morrison Alexander Rankin, FCIOB, FFB, FBIM, FRSAMD, FRSA. Lord Dean, Guild of Merchants House of Glasgow, since 1991; Chairman, Epilepsy Association of Scotland, since 1990; Director, Kensington Contracts Ltd. and Property Cos., since 1962; b. 27.4.29, Glasgow; m., Sally Joan Sutherland; 2 s.; 1 d. Educ. Belmont House; Gresham House. Managing Director, Morrison Dunbar Ltd. Builders, 1957-81. President: Scottish Building Contractors Association, 1968, Scottish Building Employers Federation, 1975, Building Employers Confederation, 1980, Builders Benevolent Institution, 1987; Chairman, Royal Scottish Academy of Music and Drama, 1987 91; Trustee and Director, St. Mary's Music School, Edinburgh; Trustee, University of Strathclyde Foundation; Member, Lloyds of London; Member, Trades House of Glasgow. Recreations: music; art galleries; golf. Address: (h.) 18 Devonshire Terrace Lane, Glasgow, G12 9XT; T.-041-357 1289.

Dunbar-Nasmith, Rear Admiral David Arthur, CB, DSC, DL. Chairman, Moray and Nairn Newspaper Company, 1982-91; Director, Cairngorm Chairlift Company, 1973-91; b. 21.2.21, Glen of Rothes, Rothes; m., Elizabeth Bowlby; 2 s.; 2 d. Educ. Lockers Park; Royal Naval College, Dartmouth. To sea, 1939; War service, Atlantic and Mediterranean; Commanding Officer, HM Ships Haydon, 1943-44, Peacock, 1945-46, Moon, 1946, Rowena, 1946-48, Enard Bay, 1951, Alert, 1954-56, Berwick and 5th Frigate Squadron, 1961-63, Commodore Amphibious Forces, 1966-67; Naval Secretary, 1967-70; Flag Officer Scotland and Northern Ireland, 1970-72; Member, Highlands and Islands Development Board, 1972-83 (Chairman, 1981-82, Deputy Chairman, 1972-81); Member: Countryside Commission for Scotland, 1972-76, British Waterways Board, 1980-87, North of Scotland Hydro Electric Board, 1982-85; Gentleman Usher of the Green Rod to the Order of the Thistle; Vice Lieutenant, County of Moray; Member, Queen's Bodyguard for Scotland (Royal Company of Archers). Recreations: sailing; shooting; skiing. Address: (h.) Glen of Rothes, Rothes, Moray; T.-03403 216.

Dunbar-Nasmith, Professor Emeritus James Duncan, CBE, BA, DA, RIBA, PPRIAS, FRSA, FRSE. Professor and Head, Department of Architecture, Heriot-Watt University and Edinburgh College of Art, 1978-88; Partner, The Law and Dunbar-Nasmith Partnership, Architects, Edinburgh and Forres, since 1957; b. 15.3.27, Dartmouth. Educ. Lockers Park; Winchester College; Trinity College, Cambridge; Edinburgh College of Art. Lt., Scots Guards, 1945-48; ARIBA, 1954; President: Edinburgh Architectural Association, 1967-69, Royal Incorporation of Architects in Scotland, 1971-73; Member, RIBA Council, 1967-73 (Vice-President and Chairman, Board of Architectural Education, 1972-73); Council, ARCUK, 1976-84, Board of Education, 1976-88 (Vice Chairman, 1977); Member: Royal Commission on Ancient and Historical Monuments of Scotland, since 1972, Ancient Monuments Board for Scotland, 1969-82 (interim Chairman, 1972-73), Historic Buildings Council for Scotland, since 1966; Trustee: Scottish Civic Trust, Architectural Heritage Fund, Theatres Trust, Holyrood Brewery Foundation, Thirlestane Castle Trust; Member: Edinburgh New Town Conservation Committee, Council of Europa Nostra; Deputy Chairman, Edinburgh Festival Society, 1981-85. Recreations: music; theatre; skiing; sailing. Address: (b.) 16 Dublin Street, Edinburgh, EH1 3RE; T.-031-556 8631.

Duncan, Alan James, BSc (Hons), MS, PhD, CPhys, FInstP. Reader in Physics, Stirling University, since 1989; b. 4.11.38, North Berwick; m., Helen Irene Thompson; 1 s.; 1 d. Educ. North Berwick High School; St. Andrews University; Stanford University. Research Officer: Tube Investments Ltd., 1961-63, International Research and Development Company Ltd., 1963-65; Research Assistant, Stanford University, 1965-70; Lecturer in Physics, Stirling University, 1970-89. Chairman, Scottish Branch, Institute of Physics, 1983-85; Member, Atomic Molecular and Optical Physics Committee, Institute of Physics. Recreations: reading; swimming. Address: (h.) 13 Newton Crescent, Dunblane, FK15 0DZ; T.- 0786 822806.

Duncan, Angus, OBE, FRICS. Former Deputy Chief Quantity Surveyor and Assistant Director in Scottish Office Building Directorate (retired); b. 4.12.28, Sorbie. Educ. Bell-Baxter School, Cupar; Newbattle Abbey College; Heriot-Watt College. Joined Department of Health for Scotland, 1957, dealing with prison buildings, later advising various Scottish Office Departments on housing, education, and health building matters. Chairman, Quantity Surveyors Committee, Scottish Branch, RICS, 1982-83. Member, Committee of Management, Kirk Care Housing Association, since 1988; Board Member, Queensberry House Hospital, since 1990. Recreations: travel; walking; photography; reading; bird-watching. Address: (h.) 4/9 Dun-Ard Garden, Oswald Road, Edinburgh, EH9 2HZ; T.-031-667 1596.

Duncan, Professor Archibald Alexander McBeth, MA, FBA, FRSE, FRHistS. Professor of Scottish History, Glasgow University, since 1962; b. 17.10.26, Pitlochry; m., Ann Hayes Sawyer; 2 s.; 1 d. Educ. George Heriot's School, Edinburgh; Edinburgh University; Balliol College, Oxford. Lecturer: Balliol College, 1950-51, Queen's University, Belfast, 1951-53, Edinburgh University, 1953-61; Leverhulme Fellow, 1961-62; Clerk of Senate, Glasgow University, 1978-83. Publications: Scotland, The Making of the Kingdom; revised 3rd edition of W.C. Dickinson's Scotland from Earliest Times to 1603; Regesta Regum Scottorum, v., The Acts of Robert I 1306-29, 1988. Recreation: swimming. Address: (h.) 17 Campbell Drive, Bearsden, Glasgow, G61 4NF: T.-041-942 5023.

Duncan, David Graham Bruce, DipArch, DipTP, RIBA, MRTPI, RIAS. Director of Planning, City of Edinburgh District Council, since 1988; b. 23.8.36, Derby; m., Helen Teresa; 2 s. Educ. George Heriot's School, Edinburgh; Edinburgh College of Art. Architect/Planner, R.E. & B.L.C. Moira, Architects and Planning Consultants, Edinburgh, 1960-63; Architect/Planner, Government of State of Singapore, 1963-67; Assistant Planner, then Depute County Planning Officer, East Lothian County Council, 1967-75; Director of Planning, East Lothian District Council, 1975-88. Address: 1 Cockburn Street, Edinburgh; T.-031-225 2424.

Duncan, Geoffrey Cheyne Calderhead, BL, NP. Partner, Kerr, Barrie & Duncan, since 1970-91; b. 6.10.29, Whitecraigs, Glasgow; m., Lorna Dowling; 1 s.; 1 d. Educ. Belmont House School; Glasgow Academy; Glasgow University. Partner, Aitken, Hamilton & Duncan, 1951-70; Chairman, Glasgow Junior Chamber of Commerce, 1963-64; Director, The Girls' School Company Ltd., 1964-90 (Chairman, 1977-90); Chairman, St. Columba's School, 1972-83; Director, The West of Scotland School Company Ltd., since 1972 (Chairman, since 1989); Member, Board of Management, Glasgow South Western Hospitals, 1964-69; Member, Clyde River Purification Board, 1969-75; Director, Glasgow Chamber of Commerce, 1972-92; Chairman, Glasgow Post Office Advisory Committee, 1974-84; Member, Post Office Users' National Council, 1974-87; Chairman, Post Office Users' Council for Scotland, 1984-87; Chairman, Advisory Committee on Telecommunications for

Scotland, 1984-87; Secretary, Clyde Cruising Club, 1964-69; Council Member, Clyde Yacht Clubs' Association, 1967-73; Member, Scottish Council, Royal Yachting Association, 1967-73; Director, The Merchants' House of Glasgow, since 1982; Member, Glasgow Committee, Royal National Lifeboat Institution, since 1980; Council Member, Royal Faculty of Procurators in Glasgow, 1981-84; Trustee, George Craig Trust Fund, since 1980 (Chairman, since 1989); Trustee, Ferguson Bequest Fund, since 1987; Member, Executive Committee, Abbeyfield Quarrier's Society, since 1981 (Chairman, since 1988); Member, Council of Management, Quarrier's Homes, since 1985; Director, The Scottish Cremation Society Ltd., since 1982; Member, Iona Cathedral Management Board, since 1990. Recreations: golf; curling; gardening; photography. Address: (h.) Mid Clevans, Bridge of Weir, Renfrewshire; T.-Bridge of Weir 612566.

Duncan, Rev. Graham Alexander, BEd, BD (Hons). Minister, Cumbernauld Old Parish Church, since 1988; b. 15.6.49, Aberdeen; m., Sandra Todd. Educ. Hilton Secondary School; Aberdeen Academy; Aberdeen University. Teacher, Aberdeen, 1971-74; Missionary-in-Charge, Lovedale Institution, RSA, 1978-81; Tutor and Vice Principal, Albert Luthuli College, Federal Theological Seminary of Southern Africa, 1982-87. Address: The Manse, Baronhill, Cumbernauld, G67 2SD; T.-0236 721912.

Duncan, Ian Douglas, MB, ChB, FRCOG. Reader in Obstetrics and Gynaecology, Dundee University, since 1978; Honorary Consultant in Obstetrics and Gynaecology, Tayside Health Board, since 1978; President-Elect, International Federation for Cervical Pathology and Colposcopy; b. 7.11.43, Edinburgh; m., Jennifer Ross Conacher; 2 s.; 1 d. Educ. Harris Academy, Dundee; St. Andrews University. House Officer, Surgery and Medicine, Maryfield Hospital, Dundee, 1967-68; Senior House Officer, Urology, Ballochmyle Hospital, Mauchline, 1968-69; Registrar in Obstetrics and Gynaecology, Dundee Royal Infirmary, 1969-72; Faculty Fellow in Gynaecologic Oncology, Duke University Medical Center, 1972-74; Senior Registrar/Lecturer in Obstetrics and Gynaecology, Ninewells Hospital, Dundee, 1974-78. John Kynoch Scholarship, 1967; Senior Fulbright Scholarship, 1972; British Society for Colposcopy and Cervical Pathology: Treasurer, 1979-82, Secretary, 1982-85, President, 1985-88; Treasurer, British Gynaecological Cancer Society, 1985-88, President, 1988-91; Deacon, Bonnetmaker Craft of Dundee, 1987-89. Recreations: golf; gardening. Address: (h.) Invertay, 299 Strathmartine Road, Dundee, DD3 8NS; T.-Dundee 826628.

Duncan, Rev. James, BTh, DipTh, MPhS, FSA Scot. Minister, Blair Atholl and Struan, since 1980; b. 28.1.26, Glasgow; m., Christine Margaret Fisher; 2 s. Educ. Eastbank Academy, Glasgow; Glasgow University. War Service, 1943-46; seconded to Colonial Office, London, 1944; seconded to Australian Army in British North Borneo; ADC Chief Civil Affairs Staff Officer, British Borneo; Harrisons and Crosfield, British Borneo, 1946-47; various Sales Representative jobs, until 1956; joined Unilever (Batchelors Catering Supplies) as Special Accounts Manager. Recreations: music; watching TV; wine-making; good food and wine. Address: The Manse, Blair Atholl, Pitlochry, PH18 5SX; T.-079681 213.

Duncan, Professor James Lindsay, BVMS, PhD, MRCVS. Professor in Veterinary Parasitology, Glasgow University, since 1987; b. 26.2.41, Law, Carluke; m., Helen M.; 1 s.; 1 d. Educ. Wishaw High School; Glasgow University. Veterinary Practice, UK, and clinical teaching posts, Kenya, 1964-70; Glasgow University: Research Fellow, Department of Veterinary Parasitology, 1970-76, Lecturer, 1976-79, Senior Lecturer, 1979-82, Reader, 1982-87; Consultant, joint FAO/IAEA Animal Health Division, International Atomic Energy Agency, Vienna; Co-author of several textbooks.

Recreations: tennis; squash; golf; music. Address: (h.) Eastfield of Wiston, Biggar, Lanarkshire; T.-Lamington 270.

Duncan, James Wann, MBE, JP, MIMFT. Former Vice-Chairman, Tayside Health Board (Convener, General Purposes Committee); Convener, Personnel and Accommodation Sub-Committee, Management Committee, Common Services Agency; retired Senior Chief Maxillofacial Technician, Dundee Royal Infirmary; b. 14.7.25, Dundee; m., Hilda Mackenzie Gray; 3 d. Educ. Stobswell Secondary School; Dundee College of Technology. Former Convener, Property Equipment Supplies Committee, General Board of Management, Dundee General Hospitals; former Vice-Convener, General Purposes Committee, General Board of Management, Dundee Northern Hospitals; former Member, Dundee Town Council (Senior Magistrate); former Convener: Dundee Art Galleries and Museums Committee, Further Education Committee, Dundee Police Committee; former Member, Board of Governors, Scottish Police College; Member, Dundee District Council, 1974-77 (Convener, Planning and Development Committee); Chairman, Dundee City Labour Party, 1960-62; former Member, Scottish Council, SDP; Scottish Representative, National Committee for Dental Technicians, USDAW; former Member: STUC Health and Social Services Committee, Dundee University Court. Recreations: golf; gardening; DIY. Address: (h.) 13 Clive Road, Downfield, Dundee, DD3 8LP; T.-0382 825488.

Duncan, John Lindsay, BSc, PhD, DSc, FRSE, FRSA. Reader in Chemistry, Aberdeen University, since 1982; Convener, Science Panel, Scottish Universities Council on Entrance, 1983-89; b. 3.2.37, Edinburgh; m., Anne Shearer; 2 d. Educ. Melville College, Edinburgh; Edinburgh University. ICI Research Fellow, Reading University, 1961-64; Aberdeen University: Lecturer, 1964-74, Senior Lecturer, 1974-82. Publication: The Determination of Vibrational Anharmonieity in Molecules from Spectroscopic Observations, 1991. Recreations: music; art; gardening. Address: (b.) Department of Chemistry, Aberdeen University, Meston Walk, Old Aberdeen, AB9 2UE; T.-0224 272911.

Duncan, Leslie James, CA. Managing Partner, Scottish Region, Grant Thornton, since 1989; b. 17.11.44, Glasgow; m., Liz; 2 s. Educ. George Heriot's, Edinburgh; Robert Gordon's, Aberdeen; Aberdeen University. Grant Thornton: Partner, Glasgow Office, 1975, Managing Partner, Glasgow Office, 1988. Recreation: Treasurer, Riley RM Club. Address: (b.) 112 West George Street, Glasgow, G2 1QF; T.-041-332 7484.

Duncan, Malcolm, MA, LLB. Chief Executive, East Lothian District Council, since 1987; b. 14.7.45, Cupar; m., Stephanie; 1 s.; 1 d. Educ. Royal High School, Edinburgh; Edinburgh University. Legal apprentice, Midlothian County Clerk, 1969-72; East Lothian District Council: Legal Assistant, 1972-75, Director of Administration, 1974-87. Address: (b.) Council Buildings, Haddington, East Lothian, EH41 3HA; T.-062 082 4161.

Duncan, Professor William. MBChB, FRCPE, FRCSE, FRCPC, FRCR, FACR (Hon). Professor of Radiation Oncology, Edinburgh University, since 1971; Head, Department of Clinical Oncology, Edinburgh University, since 1990; b. 29.4.30, Aberdeen; m., Joyce Mary Gellatly; 3 s. Educ. Robert Gordon's College, Aberdeen; Aberdeen University. Consultant, Christie Hospital and Holt Radium Institute, Manchester; Lecturer, Manchester University; Director, South East Scotland Regional Radiotherapy Services; Honorary Consultant, Lothian Health Board; Chief, Department of Radiation Oncology, Ontario Cancer Institute, Princess Margaret Hospital, Toronto. Publication: Clinical Radiobiology (Co-author). Recreations: painting; gardening;

music. Address: 30A Inverleith Place, Edinburgh, EH3 5QB; T.-031-552 2898.

Duncan Millar, Ian Alastair, CBE, MC, MA, MICE, CEng, FIFM, DL. Chairman, Consultative Committee on Freshwater Fisheries, 1981-86; Vice President, Scottish Landowners Federation, 1986-90; Member, Queen's Bodyguard for Scotland (Royal Company of Archers); b. 22.11.14, Alloa; m., Louise Reid McCosh; 2 s.; 2 d. Educ. Greshams School, Holt; Trinity College, Cambridge. Civil Engineer, Sir Alexander Gibb & Partners, 1937-51 (except War years); War Service, Corps of Royal Engineers, Western Desert, Europe (with Highland Division); wounded; twice mentioned in Despatches; retired as Major; Resident Engineer i/c Pitlochry Dam and Power Station, 1946-51; Member: Perth and Kinross County Council, 1946-74 (Convener, 1970-74), Tayside Regional Council, 1974-78 (Convener, 1974-78), North of Scotland Hydro Electric Board, 1956-70 (Depute Chairman, 1970-72); Director: Macdonald Fraser & Co., Perth, 1961-84, United Auctions (Scotland) Ltd., 1963-74 (Chairman, 1967-74); fought Parliamentary elections as Liberal, Banff, 1945, Kinross and West Perth, 1949 and 1963. Director, Hill Farming Research Organisation, 1966-78; Chairman, Scottish Branch, Institute of Fisheries Management, 1980-83; Vice President, Royal Highland and Agricultural Society of Scotland, 1972. Recreations: fishing; shooting; knowing about salmon. Address: (h.) Reynock, Remony, Aberfeldy, Perthshire; T.-Kenmore 400.

Dundas-Bekker, Althea Enid Philippa, DL. Deputy Lieutenant, Midlothian, since 1991; Vice Chairman, Midlothian Tourist Association, since 1988; b. 4.11.39, Gorebridge; m., Aedrian Ruprecht Bekker (deceased); 2 d. Educ. Business College, Auckland. Secretarial work abroad, in London, and with the National Trust for Scotland; inherited Arniston House, 1970, and restoring ever since. Committee Member, Scottish Historic Houses Association; Trustee, SBAAT; Member, Curatorial Committee, National Trust for Scotland; Member, Council, Scottish Records Advisory Council; Trustee, Arniston Village Improvement Trust; Chairman, Gorebridge Local History Society. Recreation: walking dogs. Address: (h.) Arniston House, Gorebridge, Midlothian, EH23 4RY; T.-087530 238.

Dundee, Earl of (Alexander Henry Scrymgeour). Hereditary Royal Standard-Bearer for Scotland; b. 5.6.49.

Dundonald, 15th Earl of (Iain Alexander Douglas Blair); b. 17.2.61; m., Marie Beatrice Louise Russo; 1 s. Educ. Wellington College; Royal Agricultural College, Cirencester. Company Director. Address: Lochnell Castle, Ledaig, Argyll.

Dunion, Kevin Harry, MA (Hons), MSc. Director, Friends of the Earth Scotland, since 1991; b. 20.12.55, Bridge of Allan; 2 d. Educ. St. Andrew's High School, Kirkcaldy; St. Andrews University; Edinburgh University. HM Inspector of Taxes, 1978-80; Administrator, Edinburgh University Students Association, 1980-84; Scottish Campaigns Manager, Oxfam, 1984-91. Editor, Radical Scotland, 1982-85; Chair, Scottish Education and Action for Development, since 1990. Address: (b.) Bonnington Mill, 72 Newhaven Road, Edinburgh, EH6 5QG; T.-031-554 9977.

Dunlop, Alastair Barr, OBE, FRICS. Member, Lothian Health Board, 1983-91 (Vice Chairman, 1989-91); Chairman, Central and South, Scottish Conservative and Unionist Association, 1985-88; b. 27.12.33, Calcutta; m., Catriona C.L.H. MacLaurin; 1 s.; 1 d. Educ. Radley. National Service, 1952-54 (active service, Malaya: 2nd Lt., 1st Bn., RWK); commerce, City of London, 1954-58; agricultural student, 1959-61; Land Agent, Inverness, 1962-71 (Partner, Bingham Hughes & Macpherson); Joint Founding Director, Martin Paterson Associates Ltd., 1971. Chairman, Edinburgh and

Borders Branch, RICS, 1977; General Commissioner for Income Tax, since 1991; Trustee, Paintings in Hospitals Scotland; Member, Lothian Ethics of Medical Research Committee; Life Member, Institute of Directors; Chairman, Edinburgh Branch, World Wildlife Fund; President, Edinburgh South Conservative Association. Recreations: golf; skiing; fine arts. Address: 46 Dick Place, Edinburgh, EH9 2JB; T.-031-667 5343.

Dunlop, Alexander Scott, MA (Hons). Rector, Blairgowrie High School, since 1978; b. 24.2.34, Stevenston; m., Elspeth Jean Mitchell; 4 s. Educ. Stevenston Higher Grade School; Ardrossan Academy; Glasgow University; Jordanhill College. Teacher: Irvine Royal Academy, 1957, Ardrossan Academy, 1959; Special Assistant, Ardrossan Academy, 1965; Principal Teacher of English, Stevenston High School, 1968; Assistant Rector, Auchenharvie Academy, 1971; Depute Rector, Garnock Academy, Kilbirnie, 1974. Organist and Choirmaster: St. John's Church of Scotland, Ardrossan, 1958-68, St. Cuthbert South Beach Church, Saltcoats, 1968-78, St. Andrew's, Blairgowrie, since 1984; Member, Royal College of Organists; Member, National Rose Society. Recreations: music; growing and exhibiting sweet peas, roses; golf. Address: (b.) The High School, Blairgowrie, Perthshire, PH10 6PW; T.-Blairgowrie 3445/6.

Dunlop, Rev. Alistair John, MA, FSA Scot. Minister, Saddell and Carradale, since 1979; Presbytery Clerk, South Argyll, 1986-91; b. 18.3.39, Glasgow; m., Elaine Marion Seton Smith; 4 s. Educ. Hutchesons' Boys' Grammar School; Glasgow University; Trinity College, Glasgow. Assistant Minister, Dunblane Cathedral, 1964-65; Minister: Kirriemuir St. Ninian's, 1965-70, Beith: High, 1970-79; Moderator: Ardrossan Presbytery, 1974-75, South Argyll Presbytery, 1982. Scout Leader, 28th Argyll Scout Troop. Recreations: gardening; TV watching; thinking about working. Address: The Manse, Carradale, Campbeltown, Argyll, PA28 6QG; T.-058 33 253.

Dunlop, Eileen. Children's Writer; b. 13.10.38, Alloa; m., Antony Kamm (qv). Educ. Alloa Academy; Moray House College. Publications: Robinsheugh, 1975; A Flute in Mayferry Street, 1976; Fox Farm, 1978; The Maze Stone, 1982 (SAC Book Award); Clementina, 1985 (SAC Book Award); The House on the Hill, 1987 (commended, Carnegie Medal); The Valley of Deer, 1989; (with Antony Kamm) Scottish Verse to 1800, 1985; A Book of Old Edinburgh, 1983; Finn's Island, 1991. Recreations: reading; gardening; theatre. Address: (h.) 46 Tarmangie Drive, Dollar, FK14 7BP; T.-0259 42007.

Dunlop, Professor John, BSc, MSc, PhD, CEng, MIEE, MIEEE. Professor of Electronic Systems Engineering, Strathclyde University, since 1989; b. 18.4.44, Cardiff; m., Irene Margaret Reynish; 1 d. Educ. Canton High School for Boys, Cardiff; University College of Swansea. Lecturer in Telecommunications, Strathclyde University, 1969-85; Senior Lecturer, 1985-87; Reader, 1988-89. Publications: Telecommunications Engineering (textbook); numerous papers. Recreations: Great Western Railway; cycling. Address: (b.) Department of Electronic and Electrical Engineering, Strathclyde University, Glasgow, G1 1XW; T.-041-552 4400.

Dunn, Bill, BA. Chief Executive, Ayr Locality Enterprise Resource Trust (ALERT), since 1988 (Managing Director, Garnock Valley Development Executive, 1984-88); b. 26.2.48, Ayr; m., Sheila; 2 s.; 2 d. Educ. Ayr Academy; Strathclyde University. Transport Manager, National Freight Corporation/British (later Scottish) Road Services, 1970-73; Administrator, Ayrshire Joint Police Committee, 1973; Internal Audit Department, British Steel Corporation, Glasgow, 1973-81; Garnock Valley Task Force: Project Co-ordinator, 1981-83, Business Development Consultant, 1983-84. Recreations: family; golf; football; music; DIY; model railways. Address: (b.) 16 Smith Street, Ayr, KA7 1TD; T.-0292 264181.

Dunn, Professor Douglas Eaglesham, BA, FRSL, Hon.LLD (Dundee, 1987). Professor, Department of English, St. Andrews University, since 1991; b. 23.10.42, Inchinnan. Educ. Renfrew High School; Camphill Senior Secondary School, Paisley; Hull University. Books of poems: Terry Street, 1969, The Happier Life, 1972, Love or Nothing, 1974, Barbarians, 1979, St. Kilda's Parliament, 1981, Elegies, 1985, Selected Poems, 1986, Northlight, 1988; Secret Villages (short stories), 1985; Andromache (translation), 1990; Poll Tax: The Fiscal Fake, 1990; books edited: Choice of Lord Byron's Verse, 1974, The Poetry of Scotland, 1979, A Rumoured City: New Poets from Hull, 1982; Two Decades of Irish Writing: a Critical Survey, 1975; The Essential Browning, 1990; Scotland: an anthology, 1991; Faber Book of Twentieth Century Scottish Poetry, 1992; author of plays, and TV films using commentaries in verse. Gregory Award, 1968; Somerset Maugham Award, 1972; Geoffrey Faber Memorial Prize, 1975; Hawthornden Prize, 1982; Whitbread Award for Poetry and Whitbread Book of the Year Award, 1985; Cholmondeley Award, 1989. Honorary Visiting Professor, Dundee University, 1987; Fellow in Creative Writing, St. Andrews University, 1989-91; Honorary Fellow, Humberside College, 1987. Address (b.) Department of English, St. Andrews University, St. Andrews, KY16 9AL.

Dunn, Col. George Willoughby, CBE, DSO (and Bar), MC, TD, DL. Retired Solicitor; Member, Queen's Bodyguard for Scotland (Royal Company of Archers); b. 27.3.14, Carmyle, Lanarkshire; m., Louise Wilson; 2 d. Educ. Trinity College, Glenalmond; Glasgow University (BL). Solicitor, 1937; served Second World War with 51st Highland Division, Middle East, N. Africa, Sicily and NW Europe; Col. late TA The Black Watch; Chairman, Royal British Legion Scotland, 1971-74; DL, Angus, 1971. Recreations: golf; fishing. Address: David's Hill, St. Vigeans, Arbroath, Angus; T.-Arbroath 72538.

Dunnachie, James Francis, JP. MP (Labour), Glasgow Pollok, since 1987; b. 17.11.30.

Dunne, John Joseph, MA (Hons), MPhil, PhL, AFBPsS, CPsychol. Consultant Clinical Psychologist and Head, Community Clinical Psychology Service, Forth Valley Health Board, since 1985; Honorary Lecturer in Psychology, Stirling University, since 1986 (Director, Macmillan Nursing Research Project, since 1987); Member, Advisory Group to "Partnership in Cancer Care"; b. 31.8.42, Kirkcaldy; m., Marie Anne Cecile. Educ. Blairs College, Aberdeen; Gregorian University, Rome; St. Andrews University; Edinburgh University. Clinical Psychologist, Royal Edinburgh Hospital, 1977-81; Senior Clinical Psychologist (Primary Care), Dedridge and Craigshill Health Centres, Livingston, 1981-85; Honorary Fellow, Edinburgh University, since 1984. Address: (b.) Community Clinical Psychology Service, Department of Psychology, Stirling University, Stirling; T.-0786 67680.

Dunnet, Professor George Mackenzie, OBE, BSc, PhD, DSc, FRSE, FIBiol, FRSA. Regius Professor of Natural History, Aberdeen University, 1974-92 (Dean, Faculty of Science, 1984-87); Chairman, Salmon Advisory Committee, since 1986; Chairman, Fish Farming Advisory Committee, since 1990; Member of Council, NCC, and Chairman, its Advisory Committee on Science, 1990-91; Member, Council, NCCS, and Chairman, its Science, Research and Development Board, 1991-92; Member of Council, Scottish Natural Heritage, since 1992; Chairman, Shetland Oil Terminal Environmental Advisory Group, since 1977; b.

19.4.28, Dunnet, Caithness; m., Margaret Henderson Thomson; 1 s.; 2 d. Educ. Peterhead Academy; Aberdeen University. Research Fellow, Oxford University, 1952; Research Officer, CSIRO, Australia, 1953-58; Lecturer/Senior Lecturer in Zoology, Aberdeen University, 1958-71; Professor of Zoology, Aberdeen University, 1971-74; Senior Research Fellow, DSIR, New Zealand, 1968-69. Member, Committees: The Nature Conservancy, Nature Conservancy Council, Natural Environment Research Council, British Council; Chairman, Advisory Committees for Protection of Birds (Scotland, and England and Wales), 1979-81; Council Member, Scottish Marine Biological Association; President, British Ecological Society, 1979-81; Member, Red Deer Commission, 1975-80. Recreations: walking; croquet. Address: (h.) Whinhill, Inverebrie, Ellon, Aberdeen, AB4 9PT; T.-03587 215.

Dunnett, Alastair MacTavish, HonLLD (Strathclyde). Director, Thomson Scottish Petroleum Ltd., 1979-87; b. 26.12.08, Kilmacolm; m., Dorothy Halliday (see Dorothy Dunnett); 2 s. Educ. Overnewton School; Hillhead High School, Glasgow. Entered Commercial Bank of Scotland Ltd., 1925; Co-Founder, The Claymore Press, 1933-34; Glasgow Weekly Herald, 1935-36; The Bulletin, 1936-37; Daily Record, 1937-40; Chief Press Officer, Secretary of State for Scotland, 1940-46; Editor: Daily Record, 1946-55, The Scotsman, 1956-72; Managing Director, Scotsman Publications Ltd., 1962-70 (Chairman, 1970-74); Chairman, Thomson Scottish Petroleum Ltd., Edinburgh, 1971-79; Member, Executive Board, Thomson Organisation Ltd., 1973-78; Director, Scottish Television, 1975-79; a Governor, Pitlochry Festival Theatre, 1958-84; Member: Press Council, 1959-62, Scottish Tourist Board, 1962-70, Council, National Trust for Scotland, 1962-70, Scottish International Education Trust, Scottish Theatre Ballet Committee, Scottish Opera Committee. Publications: Treasure at Sonnach, 1935; Heard Tell, 1946; Quest by Canoe, 1950; Highlands and Islands of Scotland, 1951; The Donaldson Line, 1952; The Land of Scotch, 1953; The Duke's Day, No Thanks to the Duke, 1978; Among Friends (autobiography), 1984; The Scottish Highlands (Co-author), 1988; End of Term, 1989; author of plays: The Original John Mackay, 1956; Fit to Print, 1962. Recreations: sailing; riding; walking. Address: (h.) 87 Colinton Road, Edinburgh, EH10 5DF; T.-031-337 2107.

Dunnett, Dorothy. Writer, since 1960; Portrait Painter, since 1950; b. 25.8.23, Dunfermline; m., Alastair M. Dunnett (qv); 2 s. Civil Service: Assistant Press Officer, Scottish Government Departments, Edinburgh, 1940-46, Executive Officer, Board of Trade, Glasgow, 1946-55; Trustee for the Secretary of State for Scotland, Scottish National War Memorial, since 1962; Director, Scottish Television p.l.c., since 1979; Fellow, Royal Society of Arts, since 1986; Trustee, National Library of Scotland, since 1986; Director, Edinburgh Book Festival, since 1990. Publications (novels): Game of Kings, 1961; Queens' Play, 1964; The Disorderly Knights, 1966; Dolly and the Singing Bird, 1968; Pawn in Frankincense, 1969; Dolly and the Cookie Bird, 1970; The Ringed Castle, 1971; Dolly and the Doctor Bird, 1971; Dolly and the Starry Bird, 1973; Checkmate, 1975; Dolly and the Nanny Bird, 1976; King Hereafter, 1982; Dolly and the Bird of Paradise, 1983; Niccolo Rising, 1986; The Spring of the Ram, 1987; The Scottish Highlands (Co-author), 1988; Race of Scorpions, 1989; Moroccan Traffic, 1991; Scales of Gold, 1991; Contributor to Scottish Short Stories, anthology, 1973. Recreations: travel; medieval history; opera; orchestral music; ballet. Address (h.) 87 Colinton Road, Edinburgh, EH10 5DF; T.-031-337 2107.

Dunnett, Major Graham Thomas, TD, DL. Vice Lord Lieutenant, Caithness, since 1986; b. 8.3.29, Wick; 3 s. Educ. Wick High School; Archbishop Holgate's Grammar School,

York. Commissioned into Seaforth Highlanders, 1950. Address: Cathel Shieling, Loch Calder, Thurso, Caithness.

Dunning, Norman Moore, BA (Oxon), CQSW. Director, Scottish Society for the Mentally Handicapped, since 1991; Divisional Manager (East and North Scotland), RSSPCC, 1987-91; Chairman, British Association for the Study and Prevention of Child Abuse and Neglect, 1986-89; Honorary Lecturer, Department of Child and Adolescent Psychiatry, Glasgow University, since 1984; Vice-Chairman, Scottish Child Law Centre; b. 15.4.50, Crewe; m., Diana Mary; 2 s. Educ. Sandbach School; Jesus College, Oxford; Manchester University. Probation Officer, City of Manchester and Salford, 1973-75; Social Worker, NSPCC, 1975-77; Leader, RSSPCC Overnewton Centre, Glasgow, 1978-87. Former Joint Director, Family Research Project and Child Abuse Interventions Research Project, Glasgow University; Director: SSMH (Homes) Ltd., Care Cards Ltd., Scotcap Ltd., SSMH Trustee Service Ltd. Recreations: running; cycling; swimming. Address: (h.) / The Ness, Dollar, Clackmannanshire; T.- 0259 43354.

Dunsire, Thomas, MA, LLB, WS. Partner, then Consultant, J. & J. Milligan, WS, Edinburgh (now Morton, Fraser & Milligan, WS), 1951-90; b. 16.11.26, Rangoon, Burma; m., Jean Mary. Educ. Morrison's Academy, Crieff; Edinburgh University. Royal Navy; Solicitor and WS, 1950. Chairman, Governors, Morrison's Academy, since 1984. Recreations: formerly rugby, football, golf and cricket. Address: (h.) 40 Liberton Brae, Edinburgh.

Durham, Jane Mary Stow. Commissioner, Royal Commission for Ancient and Historical Monuments of Scotland, since 1983; Vice President, Architectural Heritage Society of Scotland, since 1985; President, Tain and Easter Ross Civic Trust, since 1990; b. 26.5.24, Invergordon; m., P.E. Durham, RN (retd.); 3 s. Chairman, Tain Pilgrimage Centre Committee; FSA Scot; former Chairman, Scottish Vernacular Buildings Group. Recreations: trying to save buildings of merit; identifying settlement patterns from the past; driving a gig. Address: (h.) Scotsburn, Kildary, Ross-shire, IV18 0PE; T.-086 284 2241.

Durie, Alastair, MA, PhD, FRHistS. Senior Lecturer, Economic History, Glasgow University, since 1989; former Director, Overseas Office, Aberdeen University; b. 4.8.46, Edinburgh; m., Catherine Elizabeth; 1 s.; 1 d. Educ. Edinburgh Academy; Edinburgh University. Lecturer and Writer on Scottish economic and social history; Member, Scottish History Council, 1976-80; Visiting Professor of History, University of Guelph, Canada, 1983; Council Member, British Universities Transatlantic Committee, since 1984; Publications: The Scottish Linen Industry in the Eighteenth Century, 1978; George Washington Wilson and Edinburgh, 1987; Sport and Leisure in Victorian Scotland, 1989. Recreations: squash; shooting; snooker. Address: (b.) Department of Economic History, Glasgow University, Glasgow; T.-041-339 8855.

Durnin, Professor John V.G.A., MA, MB, ChB, DSc, FRCP, FRSE, FIBiol. Professor of Physiology, Glasgow University, since 1977; b. 23.4.23, Stirling; m., Joan Grimshaw; 4 s.; 2 d. Educ. Robert Gordon's College, Aberdeen; Aberdeen University; Glasgow University. Resident Hospital Officer in Medicine, Surgery and Clinical Pathology, four years; Lecturer/Reader, Institute of Physiology, Glasgow University; WHO and FAO Consultant in Nurtrition in several developing countries, including Burma, Ghana, Ethiopia, Mexico, Peru and Chile; Honorary Civilian Consultant to the Army in Physiology and Nutrition. Recreations: golf; skiing; hill-walking; ballet. Address: (h.) Buchanan Castle, Drymen, Glasgow; T.-Drymen 60677.

Durrani, Professor Tariq Salim, BSc (Hons), MSc, PhD, FIEE, CEng, FIEEE. Professor, Department of Electronic and Electrical Engineering, Strathclyde University, since 1986; b. 27.10.43, Amraoti, India; m., Clare Elizabeth; 1 s.; 2 d. Educ. Marie Colaco High School, Karachi; Engineering University, Dacca; Southampton University. Research Fellow, Southampton University, 1970-76; joined academic staff, Strathclyde University, 1976; Director, SERC/DTI Scottish Regional Transputer Centre, since 1987; Director, DTI Centre for Parallel Signal Processing, since 1988; Director/Chairman, Scottish Electronics Technology Group; Member, AdCom, Signal Processing Society; Chairman, Management Committee, IT Associate Companies Scheme (ITACS). Publications: six books; over 130 technical research papers. Recreation: playing occasional golf badly. Address: (b.) Department of Electronic and Electrical Engineering, Strathclyde University, Glasgow; T.-041-552 4400, Ext. 2883.

Durward, William Farquharson, MB, ChB, FRCP(Edin), FRCP(Glas). Consultant Neurologist, Greater Glasgow and Lanarkshire Health Boards, since 1977; Honorary Clinical Senior Lecturer in Neurology, Glasgow University, since 1978; Director, Cloburn Quarry Co. Ltd.; b. 16.9.44, Kilmarnock; m., Ann Roy Paterson; 1 s.; 1 d. Educ. Kilmarnock Academy; Glasgow University; Boston University. Employed by NHS, since 1968; specialist training grades, 1969-77. Recreations: walking; reading; railway conservation. Address: (h.) Overdale, 20 South Erskine Park, Bearsden, Glasgow, G61 4NA; T.-041-942 3143.

Dutch, Rev. Henry D.M., FIPR, FSA (Scot). Head of Public Relations, Strathclyde Regional Council, since 1975; b. 9.6.28, Montrose; m., Nan Martin; 2 d. Educ. Montrose Academy. Journalist, Glasgow Herald, 1954-67; Public Relations Officer, Scottish Special Housing Association, 1967-72; Head of Public Relations, Corporation of City of Glasgow, 1972-75. Chairman, Local Government Group, Institute of Public Relations, 1991; Auxiliary Minister (ordained 1986), Church of Scotland. Recreations: golf; hill-walking. Address: (b.) Strathclyde House, 20 India Street, Glasgow, G2 4PF; T.-041-227 3425.

Duthie, Sir Robert Grieve, CBE (1978), CA, LLD, CBIM, FRSA, FRIAS, DTech (Napier). Chairman: Scottish Development Agency, 1979-88, Britoil PLC, 1988-90, Insight International Tours Ltd., Capital House Investment Management PLC, since 1988; Director: Carclo Engineering Group PLC, since 1986, Investors Capital PLC, since 1986, Sea Catch PLC, since 1987, Royal Bank of Scotland plc, since 1978, British Assets Trust plc, since 1977; Member, Board, British Polythene Industries plc, since 1989; Member, Court, Strathclyde University, since 1988; Member, Board of Governors, Beatson Institute for Cancer Research, since 1989; b. 2.10.28, Greenock; m., Violetta Noel Maclean; 2 s.; 1 d. Educ. Greenock Academy. Apprentice Chartered Accountant, Thomson Jackson Gourlay and Taylor, CA, 1946-51; joined Blacks of Greenock, 1952; appointed Managing Director, 1962; Chairman, Black & Edgington, 1972-83. Chairman, Inverkip Society, 1966; Director, Greenock Chamber of Commerce, 1966; Member, Clyde Port Authority, 1971-83 (Chairman, 1977-80); Director, Greenock Provident Bank, 1969-75 (Chairman, 1975); Member, Scottish Telecommunications Board, 1972-77; Council Member, Institute of Chartered Accountants of Scotland, 1973-78; Member: East Kilbride Development Corporation, 1976-78, Strathclyde Region Local Valuation Appeal Panel, 1976-83; CBI Tax Liaison Officer for Scotland, 1976-79; Chairman, Made Up Textile Association of Great Britain, 1972; Member: British Institute of Management Scottish Committee, 1976, Glasgow and West of Scotland Committee, Scottish Council (Development and Industry), 1975-79; Chairman, Greenock Club, 1972; Captain, Greenock Cricket

Club, 1960-61; Commissioner, Queen Victoria School, Dunblane, 1972-89; Commissioner, Scottish Congregational Ministers Pension Fund, since 1973; Member, Scottish Economic Council, since 1980; Member of Council, Royal Caledonian Curling Club, 1984-88; Treasurer, Nelson Street EU Congregational Church, Greenock, since 1970. Awarded Honorary Degree of Doctor of Laws, Strathclyde University, 1984. Recreations: curling; golf. Address: (h.) Fairhaven, 181 Finnart Street, Greenock, PA16 8JA; T.-Greenock 22642.

Dutton, Ian Murray, BSc, MSc, DipEd. Director of Education, Borders Regional Council, since 1990; b. 26.4.41, West Bridgeford; m., Margaret; 2 d. Educ. Jarrow Grammar School; Durham University; Bristol University. Chemistry Teacher, 1963-74; Northumberland County Council: Assistant Director of Education, 1975-87, Deputy Director of Education, 1988-90. Recreations: fishing; golf; gardening. Address: (b.) Regional Headquarters, Newtown St. Boswells, Melrose, TD6 0SA; T.-0835 23301.

Duxbury, Professor Geoffrey, BSc, PhD, CPhy, FInstP. Professor, Chemical Physics, Strathclyde University; b. 6.11.42, Blackburn; m., Mary R.; 1 s.; 1 d. Educ. Cheadle Hulme School, Sheffield University. Junior Research Fellow, National Physical Laboratory, 1967-69; Research Assistant, Research Associate, Lecturer in Chemical Physics, Bristol University, 1970-80; Senior Lecturer/Reader, Strathclyde University, 1981-86. Marlow Medal, Faraday Division, Royal Society of Chemistry, 1975. Address: (b.) Department of Physics and Applied Physics, Strathclyde University, Glasgow, G4 0NG; T.-041-552 4400.

Dyer, Iain James Anthony, MBE, JP, MA, LLB, DL. Lecturer in Private Law, Glasgow University, since 1980; b. 21.4.38, Tanzania; m., Elizabeth Anne Barry; 2 s. Educ. Dumfries Academy; Glasgow University. Parliamentary candidate (Conservative), Hamilton, 1964, 1967; Member, City of Glasgow Council, 1974-88; Lord Provost's Assessor, Court of Glasgow University, 1977-80; Leader of the Opposition and Bailie, 1984-88; Deputy Lieutenant, City of Glasgow, since 1987; Vice Chairman, Scottish Housing Training Board, 1985-88; Member, Board, The Housing Corporation, 1983-89; Member, Scottish Advisory Council, Shelter, since 1989; Member, Board, East Kilbride Development Corporation, since 1990. Recreation: music. Address: (h.) Orleans, 2 Dalziel Drive, Glasgow, G41 4PT; T.-041-423 5949.

Dyer, James A.T., MB, ChB (Hons), MRCPsych. Medical Commissioner, Mental Welfare Commission for Scotland, since 1991; Honorary Senior Lecturer in Psychiatry, Edinburgh University, since 1981; b. 31.12.46, Arbroath; m., Lorna M.S.; 2 s.; 1 d. Educ. Bo'ness Academy; Robert Gordon's College, Aberdeen; Aberdeen University. Trainee General Practitioner, Skene, Aberdeenshire, 1971-72; junior clinical appointments, then Senior Registrar in Psychiatry, Royal Edinburgh Hospital, 1972-77; Scientific Officer, MRC Unit for Epidemiological Studies in Psychiatry, Edinburgh, 1977-80; Consultant Psychiatrist, Royal Edinburgh Hospital, 1981-91. Member, Medical Action for Global Security. Recreations: walking; reading; photography. Address: (h.) 86 Morningside Drive, Edinburgh, EH10 5NT; T.-031-447 8148.

Dyke, Michael Christopher, CIPFA. Director of Management Services, Glenrothes Development Corporation, since 1990 (Director of Finance, 1988-89); b. 25.12.46, Blackpool. Educ. St. Joseph's College, Blackpool; Manchester College of Commerce. Deputy Director of Finance, Alnwick DC, 1973-78; North East Derbyshire DC, 1978-80; Assistant Director of Finance, then Director of Finance/Depute Chief Executive, North East Fife District Council, 1980-87. Member, Scottish Branch Executive Committee, CIPFA. Recreations: swimming; reading; walk-

ing; music; travel in Scotland. Address: (b.) Balgonie Road, Markinch, Glenrothes, Fife.

Dyker, George Simpson, MBChB, FRCP (Glas), FRCGP. Principal, general practice, since 1967; Deputy Regional Adviser in General Practice, since 1989; b. 6.7.41, Aberdeen; m., Dr. Elspeth J.C. Dyker; 1 s.; 2 d. Educ. Hutchesons' Grammar School; Glasgow University. Pre-registration jobs, Stobhill Hospital, Glasgow and Royal Infirmary, Glasgow, 1964-65; Faulds Research Fellowship, (Department of Materia Medica, Glasgow University, Stobhill Hospital, Glasgow), 1965-66; Examiner, Royal College of General Practitioners, since 1985; Examiner, Diploma in Geriatric Practice, Glasgow University, since 1991. Chairman, Faculty Board (West of Scotland), Royal College of General Practitioners, 1991-94. Recreations: occasional golf; walking. Address: (h.) 4 Old Coach Road, East Kilbride, Glasgow, G74 4DP; T.-03552 20045.

E

Eadie, Alexander. MP (Labour), Midlothian, 1966-92; b. 23.6.20, Glasgow; m., Janice C. Murdoch; 1 s. Educ. Buckhaven Senior Secondary School. Coal miner, 1934-65; trade union official, 1965-66; served in local government in Fife, 20 years; Parliamentary Labour Candidate, Ayr, 1959, 1964; PPS to Rt. Hon. Margaret Herbison, Minister of Social Security, 1967; Under Secretary of State for Energy, 1974-79; Secretary, PLP Miners' Group, since 1983; former Chairman, Parliamentary Power and Steel Group; JP; awarded BEM, 1960. Recreations: reading; writing; bowling.

Eadie, John, BSc (Hons), FRAgS. Director, Scottish Forestry Trust (Director, Hill Farming Research Organisation, 1980-87); b. 6.11.30, Polton, Midlothian; m., Jean Young Dunlevie; 1 s.; 2 d. Educ. Linlithgow Academy; Edinburgh University. National Agricultural Advisory Service, MAFF, 1954-61; Hill Farming Research Organisation: joined, 1961, Head of Animal Production and Nutrition, 1974-80. Research Medal, Royal Agricultural Society of England, 1978. Address: (b.) Scottish Forestry Trust, c/o TG (UK), 5 Dublin Street Lane, Edinburgh, EH1; T.-031-557 0944.

Eagles, John Mortimer, MBChB, MPhil, MRCPsych. Consultant Psychiatrist, Royal Cornhill Hospital, Aberdeen, since 1985; Honorary Senior Lecturer in Mental Health, Aberdeen University, since 1985; b. 21.10.52, Newport-on-Tay; m., Janette Isobel Rorke; 2 d. Educ. Bell-Baxter High School, Cupar; Aberdeen University; Edinburgh University. Resident House Officer posts, Aberdeen, 1977-78; Senior House Officer/Registrar in Psychiatry, Royal Edinburgh Hospital, 1978-82; Lecturer, Department of Mental Health, Aberdeen University, 1982-85; Psychiatric Tutor for trainee psychiatrists, Aberdeen, 1987-92. Chairman, North-East Regional Postgraduate Medical Education Committee, since 1990. Recreations: cricket; golf; travel; reading. Address: (h.) 41 Binghill Park, Milltimber, Aberdeen, AB1 0EE; T.-0224 732434.

Earnshaw, Rev. Phillip, BA, BSc, BD. Minister, Parish of Pollockshields, Glasgow, since 1991 (Minister, Parish of

Stromness and Graemsay, Orkney, 1986-91); Member, Board of Communication, Church of Scotland, since 1988; Convener, Life and Work Committee, since 1991; b. 27.12.38, Holmfirth, near Huddersfield; m., Anne R.P. MacAndrew; 2 s.; 1 d. Educ. Penistone Grammar School; Open University; Stirling University; Glasgow University. Recreations: music; gardening; walking; astronomy. Address: (h.) The Manse, 36 Glencairn Drive, Pollockshields, Glasgow G41 4PW; T.-041-423 4000.

Eason, Professor George, MSc, PhD, FIMA, FRSE. Honorary Professor, Strathclyde University, since 1986 (Professor of Mathematics for Applied Scientists, 1970-86); b. 19.3.30, Chesterfield; m., 1, Olive Holdstock (deceased); 2, Esme Beryl Burgess; 2 d. Educ. Clay Cross Tupton Hall Grammar School; Birmingham University; Keele University. Scientific Officer, RARDE, Ministry of Defence, 1954-56; Lecturer in Applied Mathematics, Newcastle-upon-Tyne University, 1957-61; Senior Lecturer, then Reader, Strathclyde University, 1961-70; Visiting Professor, Wisconsin University, 1968-69. IMA: Chairman, Scottish Branch, 1974-76, Council Member, 1976-79. Publication: Mathematics and Statistics for the Biosciences (Co-author). Recreations: hill-walking; gardening; music. Address: (h.) 4 Kinord Drive, Aboyne AB34 5JZ; T.-03398 86873.

Eastmond, Clifford John, BSc, MD, FRCP, FRCPE. Consultant Rheumatologist, Grampian Health Board, since 1979; Clinical Senior Lecturer, Aberdeen University, since 1979; b. 19.1.45, Ashton-under-Lyne; m., Margaret Wadsworth; 2 s.; 1 d. Educ. Audenshaw Grammar School; Edinburgh University. House Officer posts, Edinburgh, one year; moved to Liverpool for further training, subsequently to Rheumatism Unit, Leeds. Elder, Church of Scotland. Recreations: skiing; hill-walking; music. Address: (h.) Whinmoor, 34 Leslie Crescent, Westhill, Skene, Aberdeenshire; T.-0224 741009.

Easton, Rev. David John Courtney, MA, BD. Minister, Burnside Parish Church, Glasgow, since 1977; Moderator, Glasgow Presbytery, 1989-90; 7.10.40, Bogota, Colombia; m., Edith Stevenson; 2 s.; 1 d. Educ. Arbroath High School; Aberdeen University. Minister, Hamilton-Bardrainney Parish Church, Port Glasgow, 1967-77. Past Chairman, Scottish Tear Fund Advisory Committee; Member, Rutherford House Council. Recreation: music. Address: 59 Blairbeth Road, Burnside, Rutherglen, Glasgow, G73 4JD; T.-041-634 1233.

Easton, Sir Robert William Simpson, CBE (1980), DUniv, CEng, FIMechE, FIMarE, FRINA. Chairman, Yarrow Shipbuilders Ltd., since 1979; Chairman, GEC Scotland, since 1990; Chairman and Chief Executive, GEC Naval Systems, since 1991; Director, Glasgow Enterprise, since 1990; Chairman, Clyde Port Authority, since 1983; Director, Supermarine Consortium Ltd., since 1986; b. 30.10.22, Glasgow; m., Jean Fraser; 1 s.; 1 d. Educ. Govan High School, Glasgow; Royal Technical College, Glasgow. Apprentice, Marine Engineer, 1939-51; Manager, Yarrow & Co. Ltd., 1951-65; Yarrow Shipbuilders Ltd.: Director, 1965-70, Deputy Managing Director, 1970-77, Managing Director, 1977-91; Main Board Director, Yarrow & Co. Ltd., 1971-77. Vice-President, Clyde Shipbuilders Association, 1972-79; Member, Worshipful Company of Shipwrights, 1982; Freeman, City of London, 1982; Council Member, RINA, 1983; Trustee, Seagull Trust, 1984; Member, Merchant House of Glasgow, 1988; Member, Incorporation of Hammermen, 1989; President, Institute of Welding, since 1991. Recreations: sailing; golf; walking; family. Address: (h.) Springfield, Stuckenduff Road, Shandon, Dunbartonshire, G84 8NW; T.-0436 820 677.

Easton, Robin Gardner, MA, DipEd. Rector, High School of Glasgow, since 1983; b. 6.10.43, Glasgow; m., Eleanor

Mary McIlroy; 1 s.; 1 d. Educ. Kelvinside Academy; Sedbergh School; Christ's College, Cambridge; Wadham College, Oxford. Teacher of French and German, Melville College, Edinburgh, 1966-72; Housemaster and Deputy Head, French Department, Daniel Stewart's and Melville College, 1972-78; Head, Modern Languages, George Watson's College, 1979-83. Elder, Church of Scotland. Recreations: watching rugby; tennis; hill-walking; visiting ancient monuments. Address: (h.) 21 Stirling Drive, Bearsden, Glasgow, G61 4NU; T.-041-943 0368.

Eastwood, Martin Anthony, MB, MSc, FRCPE. Consultant Gastroenterologist, Western General Hospital, since 1968; Reader in Medicine, Edinburgh University, since 1987; b. 7.8.35, Hull; m., Jenny; 3 s.; 1 d. Educ. Minster Grammar School, Southwell; Edinburgh University. Lecturer in Therapeutics, Royal Infirmary, Edinburgh, 1964-68. Publications: papers on physiology of the colon and nutrition; Human Nutrition and Dietetics (Co-Editor), 1986. Address: (b.) Wolfson Laboratory, Gastrointestinal Unit, Western General Hospital, Edinburgh, EH4 2XU; T.-031-332 2525.

Eccles, Alexander Charles William Anderson, RD–, BA, LLB, WS. Temporary Sheriff, since 1984; part-time Chairman, Social Security Appeals Tribunals, since 1985, and Rent Assessment Committee, since 1975; part-time Chairman, Industrial Tribunals, since 1991; b. 8.1.33, Newcastle upon Tyne; m., Judith Margaret Hardy; 2 s.; 2 d. Educ. Loretto; Gonville and Caius College, Cambridge; Edinburgh University. National Service, 1951-53 (commissioned HLI); TA, Royal Scots, 1953-59; qualified Solicitor and WS, 1960; Assistant with various firms and local authorities, 1960-68; Partner, J.L. Anderson & Co., Solicitors, Cupar, Kinross, Glenrothes and Cowdenbeath, 1968-84. Lt. Cdr., RNR, 1966-85; Rugby Blue, Edinburgh University (played for Scottish Universities and Durham County). Recreations: rugby; squash; reading military history. Address: (h.) 152 Hyndland Road, Glasgow, G12 9PN; T.-041-334 5801.

Eccleshall, David Ernest, ACIB. General Manager, Clydesdale Bank PLC, since 1987; b. 3.3.42, Welshpool; m., Thelma Margaret; 1 s.; 1 d. Educ. Welshpool Grammar School. Midland Bank plc, 1958-87. Recreations: gardening; walking; golf. Address: (h.) Cartref, 1 Katrine Drive, Newton Mearns, Glasgow, G77 5NJ; T.-041-639 5293.

Eccleston, Gillian Margaret, BSc, PhD, MRPS. Senior Lecturer in Pharmaceutics, Strathclyde University; b. Morpeth, Northumberland; m., Peter James; 1 d. Educ. Erdington Grammar School for Girls, Birmingham; Leeds University. Development Pharmacist, Boots Pure Drug Co., Nottingham, 1968; Research Assistant, Lecturer, Senior Lecturer in Pharmacy, Portsmouth Polytechnic, 1969-78; Lecturer in Pharmaceutics, Strathclyde University. Visiting Professor, Cincinnatti University; Lecturer, European Continuing Education College. American Society of Cosmetic Chemists Best Paper Award. Recreation: gardening. Address: (b.) Department of Pharmaceutical Sciences, Strathclyde University, Glasgow.

Eckford, James Millar, OBE, FCIS, FHSM, FBIM. Chief Executive, Ayrshire and Arran Health Board, since 1985; b. 8.7.36, Edinburgh; m., Joan Miller. Educ. George Heriot's School, Edinburgh. General Administrator, Aberdeen General Hospitals; Senior Administrator, Dundee General Hospitals; Hospital Secretary, Western General Hospital, Edinburgh; Assistant Secretary, South-Eastern Regional Hospital Board; Edinburgh Northern Hospitals: Deputy Secretary and Treasurer, Acting Secretary and Treasurer; District Administrator, East Fife District, Fife Health Board, 1974-79; Secretary, Forth Valley Health Board, 1979-85. Member: Scottish Health Service Advisory Council; Scottish

Management and Efficiency Group; Board, Ayrshire Enterprise; Council, Ayr College; Chairman, Dalmellington and District Conservation Trust. Recreations: bowling; fishing; curling; Ayr United FC. Address: (h.) 22 Abbot's Way, Doonfoot, Ayr; T.-0292 42323.

Eddy, Forrest Brian, BSc, PhD. Reader in Zoology, Dundee University, since 1991; b. 5.11.41, Kitale, Kenya; m., Rosemary; 1 s.; 1 d. Educ. Prince of Wales School, Nairobi; London University; Bristol University. Dundee University: Lecturer in Zoology, 1974, Senior Lecturer, 1986. Recreation: antiques. Address: (b.) Department of Biological Sciences, Dundee University, Dundee, DD1 4HN; T.-0382 23181.

Eden, Professor Colin, BSc, PhD. Professor and Head, Department of Management Science, Strathclyde Business School, since 1988; b. 24.12.43, Birmingham; m., Christine Eden. Educ. Moseley Grammar, Birmingham; Leicester University; Southampton University. Operational Researcher, engineering industry; Management Consultant; Bath University: Lecturer in Decision Analysis, Senior Lecturer, Reader; Director, Strategic Decision Support Research Unit. Publications: four books; over 60 papers. Recreations: sailing; skiing; hill walking. Address. (h.) 7 Albion Gate, Glasgow; T.-041-553 4142.

Eden, Hon. Ronald John. Author; b. 5.3.31, London; m., Rosemary Crowder; 2 s. Educ. Trinity College, Glenalmond; Christ Church, Oxford. Stockbroker, 1954-72; General Commissioner of Income Tax, 1970-72. Publications: Going to the Moors, 1979; The Sporting Epicure, 1991. Recreations: reading; writing; the countryside. Address: (h.) Cromlix, Dunblane, Perthshire, FK15 9JT; T.-0786 822125.

Eden, Tim Osborn Bryan, MB, BS, D(Obst)RCOG, MRCP, FRCPEdin. Consultant Paediatric Haematologist/Oncologist, Royal Hospital for Sick Children, Edinburgh, since 1982; part-time Senior Lecturer, Edinburgh University, since 1982; b. 2.4.47, Birmingham; m., Randi Forsgren; 1 s.; 1 d. Educ. Grimsby Wintringham Grammar School; University College and Hospital, London. House Physician, University College Hospital, London; Senior House Physician (Obstetrics), Isle of Wight; Registrar, Paediatrics, Royal Hospital for Sick Children, Edinburgh; Registrar, Haematology, Edinburgh Hospitals; Postdoctoral Fellow, Stanford University, California; Lecturer in Child Life and Health, Edinburgh University; Consultant Clinical Haematologist, Bristol Children's Hospital. Chairman, United Kingdom Children's Cancer Study Group; Coordinator, MRC Eighth Childhood Leukaemia Trial; Trustee and Member, Scottish Committee, Malcolm Sargent Fund. Recreations: family; politics. Address: (b.) Royal Hospital for Sick Children, Edinburgh; T.-031-667 1991.

Edge, David Owen, BA, MA, PhD, FRAS, FRSA. Director, Science Studies Unit, Edinburgh University, 1966-89 (Reader in Science Studies, since 1979); b. 4.9.32, High Wycombe; m., Barbara Corsie; 2 s.; 1 d. Educ. Aberdeen Grammar School; Leys School, Cambridge; Gonville and Caius College, Cambridge. Assistant Physics Master, Perse School, Cambridge; Producer, Science Unit, Talks Department, BBC Radio, London, 1959-66; Senior Fellow, Society for the Humanities, and Senior Research Associate, Science, Technology and Society Program, Cornell University, 1973; Member, Edinburgh University Court, 1983-86; Scottish HQ Adviser for Students, Scout Association, 1966-85; President (Past Chairman), Scout & Guide Graduate Association; Circuit Steward, Methodist Church, Edinburgh and Forth Circuit, 1983-86; Editor, Social Studies of Science, since 1971; Member, various CNAA panels and committees, since 1972; President, Society for Social Studies of Science (4S), 1985-87; Fellow, American Association for the Advancement of Science. Publications: Astronomy Transformed (Co-

author), 1976; Science in Context (Co-Editor), 1982. Recreations: hill-walking; music; watching sport - especially soccer and baseball. Address: (h.) 25 Gilmour Road, Edinburgh, EH16 5NS; T.-031-667 3497.

Edward, Judge David Alexander Ogilvy, CMG, QC, MA, LLB, FRSE. Judge of the Court of First Instance of the European Communities, since 1989; Advocate, since 1962; Trustee, National Library of Scotland, since 1966; b. 14.11.34, Perth; m., Elizabeth Young McSherry; 2 s.; 2 d. Educ. Sedbergh School; University College, Oxford; Edinburgh University. National Service, RNVR, 1956-57 (Sub-Lt.); Clerk, Faculty of Advocates, 1967-70, Treasurer, 1970-77; President, Consultative Committee, Bars and Law Societies of the European Community, 1978-80; Salvesen Professor of European Institutions, Edinburgh University, 1985-89; Member, Law Advisory Committee, British Council, 1974-88; Chairman, Continental Assets Trust plc, 1986-89; Director, Adam & Company plc, 1984-89; Director, Harris Tweed Association Ltd., 1985-89; Member, Panel of Arbitrators, International Centre for Settlement of Investment Disputes, 1981-89; Specialist Adviser to House of Lords Select Committee on the European Communities, 1985-88; Chairman, Hopetoun House Preservation Trust. Chairman, Scottish Council for Arbitration, 1988-89 (Honorary President, since 1989). Address: (h.) 32 Heriot Row, Edinburgh EH3 6ES; (b.) European Court of First Instance, L-2925 Luxembourg; T.-010-352-4303-3494.

Edwards, Professor Christopher Richard Watkin, MA, MB, BChir, MD, FRCP, FRCPEdin, FRSE. Professor of Clinical Medicine, Edinburgh University, since 1980 (Dean, Faculty of Medicine, since 1991); Honorary Consultant Physician, Lothian Health Board, since 1980; Chairman, Department of Medicine, Western General Hospital, since 1981; b. 12.2.42, Irvinestown, Northern Ireland; m., Dr. Sally Edwards; 2 s.; 1 d. Educ. Marlborough; Cambridge University. Junior House Officer posts, St. Bartholomew's Hospital; Senior House Officer posts, Brompton and Hammersmith Hospitals; Lecturer, St. Bartholomew's Hospital Medical College, 1968-72; Visiting Fellow, Bethesda, USA, 1972-73; Senior Lecturer and Honorary Consultant Physician, St. Bartholomew's Hospital, 1975-80. Recreations: drawing; painting; golf. Address: (b.) Department of Medicine, Western General Hospital, Edinburgh; T.-031-332 2525.

Edwards, Elizabeth Alice, BSc, SRN, SCM. Chief Area Nursing Officer, Tayside Health Board, since 1988 (Dumfries and Galloway Health Board, 1980-88); b. Coleraine. Educ. Coleraine High School; Edinburgh University. Ward Sister, Royal Victoria Hospital, Belfast, 1960-65; nursing in North America, 1966-67; Department Sister and Assistant Matron, Royal Victoria Hospital, Belfast, 1967-69; full-time student at University, 1969-72; Principal Nursing Officer, Edinburgh Northern Hospitals Group, 1972-74; District Nursing Officer, North Lothian District, Lothian Health Board, 1974-80. Member, National Board for Nursing, Midwifery and Health Visiting for Scotland, since 1983, Deputy Chairman, since 1985; Member, United Kingdom Central Council for Nursing, Midwifery and Health Visiting, 1984-88. Address: (b.) Tayside Health Board, Vernonholme, Riverside Drive, Dundee.

Edwards, Frederick Edward, RD, MUniv, BA, DipASS, FBIM. Director of Social Work, Strathclyde Regional Council, since 1976; b. 9.4.31, Liverpool; 2 s.; 1 d. Educ. St. Edward's College, Liverpool; Glasgow University. Midshipman to Second Officer, Alfred Holt & Co., 1948-57; awarded Perm. Commn. RNR, 1953; Lt.-Cmdr., 1963; Reserve Decoration, 1972; Clasp, 1982; Management Trainee, Morgan Crucible Group, 1957-60; Probation Service, Liverpool, 1960-69; Director of Social Work, Joint

County Council of Moray and Nairn, 1969-75; Director of Social Work, Grampian Region, 1975-76; Visiting Professor of Social Administration and Social Work, Glasgow University, since 1988. Recreations: hill-walking; natural history; Scottish country dancing. Address: (b.) 20 India Street, Glasgow, G2 4PF; T.-041-227 2343.

Edwards, George Lowden, CEng, MIMechE, MIEE, FBIM, FInstPet. Head of Public Affairs, Clydesdale Bank PLC; Trustee, Scottish Civic Trust; Deputy Chairman, Scottish National Committee, English-Speaking Union; b. 6.2.39, Kirriemuir; m., Sylvia Izatt; 1 d. Educ. Webster's Seminary, Kirriemuir; Dundee Institute of Technology. Production Engineer, Burroughs Machines Ltd., Cumbernauld, 1961-64; Development Division, Scottish Council (Development and Industry), Edinburgh, 1964-67; General Manager, GR Designs Ltd., Perth, 1967-68; London Director, Scottish Council (Development and Industry), 1968-78; Manager, Public Affairs Scotland, Conoco (UK) Ltd., Aberdeen, 1978-83; Manager, Public Affairs, Conoco (UK) Ltd., London, 1983-85. Recreations: music; travel; food and wine. Address: (h.) 1 Back Dean, Ravelston Terrace, Edinburgh, EH4 3UA.

Edwards, Neil, DMS, DCA, MITSA. Director of Trading Standards and Consumer Protection, Fife, since 1988; b. 6.10.45, Wrexham, N. Wales; m., Stefania; 1 s.; 1 d. Educ. Yale High School, Wrexham; Liverpool Polytechnic. Inspector of Weights and Measures, Denbighshire CC, 1967-74; Area Officer, Department of Trading Standards, Clwyd CC, 1974-78; retail management, Italy, 1978-81; Trading Standards Officer, Durham CC, 1981-83; Principal Trading Standards Officer, West Midlands CC, 1983-86; Depute Director of Trading Standards, Dumfries and Galloway RC, 1986-88. Recreation: sport. Address: (b.) Fife House (03), North Street, Glenrothes, Fife KY7 5LT; T.-0597 766353.

Edwards, Professor Paul Geoffrey, MA (Cantab), BA. Professor Emeritus of English and African Literature, Edinburgh University; b. 31.7.26, Birmingham; m., Maj Ingbritt Nilsson; 2 d. Educ. St. Philip's School, Birmingham; Hatfield College, Durham; Emmanuel College, Cambridge. Taught English, St. Augustine's College, Cape Coast, Ghana, 1954-57; Lecturer in English, Sierra Leone University, 1957-63; joined Edinburgh University, 1963; Visiting Professor, at various times: University of California, New York State University, Bangkok University, Singapore University. Publications: West African Narrative, 1963; Through African Eyes, 1966; Equiano's Travels, 1967; Legendary Fiction in Medieval Iceland (Co-author), 1970; Black Personalities in the Era of the Slave Trade (Co-author), 1983; Icelandic Sagas (Co-translator); The Life of Equiano, 1988; Vikings in Russia (Co-author), 1989; Black Writers in Britain (Co-editor), 1991. Recreations: teaching; translating sagas. Address: (h.) 82 Kirk Brae, Edinburgh, EH16 6JA.

Egginton, Gay, BSc (Hons), PGCE. Headmistress, Laurel Bank School, Glasgow, since 1984; b. 28.2.44, Woking. Educ. St. George's School, Edinburgh; Harrogate College, Yorkshire; London University. Teacher of Chemistry, Priory Comprehensive School, Lewes, 1965-70; Head of Chemistry, Priory County Grammar School, Shrewsbury, 1970-75; Head of Chemistry and Upper School, St. Margaret's School, Edinburgh, 1975-84. Scottish Chairman, Girls' School Association, 1987-90. Recreations: travel; theatre. Address: (b.) Laurel Bank School, 4 Lilybank Terrace, Glasgow, G12.

Eilbeck, Professor John Christopher, BA, PhD, FIMA, FRSE. Professor, Department of Mathematics, Heriot-Watt University, since 1986 (Head of Department, 1984-89); b. 8.4.45, Whitehaven; m., Lesley; 3 s. Educ. Whitehaven Grammar School; Queen's College, Oxford; Lancaster University. Royal Society European Fellow, ICTP, Trieste, 1969-70; Research Assistant, Department of Mathematics,

UMIST, Manchester, 1970-73; Heriot-Watt University: Lecturer, Department of Mathematics, 1973-80, Senior Lecturer, 1980-85, Reader, 1985-86; Long-term Visiting Fellow, Center for Nonlinear Studies, Los Alamos National Laboratory, New Mexico, 1983-84. Publications: Rock Climbing in the Lake District (Co-author), 1975; Solitons and Nonlinear Wave Equations (Co-author), 1982. Recreation: mountaineering. Address: (b.) Department of Mathematics, Heriot-Watt University, Riccarton, Edinburgh, EH14 4AS; T.-031-451 3220.

Elders, Rev. (Iain) Alasdair, MA, BD. Minister, Broughton McDonald Parish Church, Edinburgh, since 1973; b. 17.4.39, Sunderland; m., Hazel Stewart Steven; 1 s.; 1 d. Educ. Daniel Stewart's College, Edinburgh; Edinburgh University. Assistant Minister: Edinburgh: St. Andrew's, 1961-63, Edinburgh: High (St. Giles Cathedral), 1963-65; Minister, Cumbernauld: Abronhill (church extension charge), 1965-73. Secretary, Cumbernauld Council of Churches, 1967-72; Chairman, Council of East End Churches of Edinburgh, 1978-82; Chairman, New Town Community Council, 1986-89; Scout Commissioner, 1966-90; Secretary, East End Churches Together, since 1989; Vice-Chairman, Edinburgh and East of Scotland Society for the Deaf. Address: Broughton McDonald Manse, 103 East Claremont Street, Edinburgh, EH7 4JA; T.-031-556 7313.

Elgin, 11th Earl of, and Kincardine, 15th Earl of, (Andrew Douglas Alexander Thomas Bruce), KT (1981), DL, JP; 37th Chief of the Name of Bruce; Lord Lieutenant, Fife Region, since 1987; Ensign, Queen's Bodyguard for Scotland (Royal Company of Archers); Chairman, Scottish Money Management Association; President, Royal Scottish Automobile Club; b. 17.2.24; m., Victoria Usher; 3 s.; 2 d. Educ. Eton; Balliol College, Oxford. President, Scottish Amicable Life Assurance Society, since 1975; Chairman, National Savings Committee for Scotland, 1972-78; Member, Scottish Postal Board, since 1980; Lord High Commissioner, General Assembly, Church of Scotland, 1980-81; Grand Master Mason of Scotland, 1961-65; President, Royal Caledonian Curling Club, 1968-69; Hon. LLD, Dundee, 1977, Glasgow, 1983. Address: (h.) Broomhall, Dunfermline, KY11 3DU.

Eliott of Redheugh, Margaret Frances Boswell. Chief of Clan Elliot; Chairman, Elliot Clan Society and Sir Arthur Eliott Memorial Trust; b. 13.11.48; m., 1, Anthony Vaughan-Arbuckle (deceased); 1 s.; 1 d.; 2, Christopher Powell Wilkins. Educ. Hatherop Castle School. Recreations: reading; hunting; sailing; gardening. Address: Redheugh, Newcastleton, Roxburghshire.

Ellington, Professor Henry Irvine, BSc, PhD, CEng, FIEE, CPhys, FInstP, FCollP. Director, Educational Development Unit, Robert Gordon's Institute of Technology, since 1988; Professor, since 1990; b. 17.6.41, Aberdeen; m., Lindsay Moir Sheldon; 1 s.; 1 d. Educ. Robert Gordon's College, Aberdeen; Aberdeen University. Scientific Officer, AERE, Harwell, 1963-65; Robert Gordon's Institute of Technology: Lecturer, School of Physics, 1966-73, Senior Lecturer in charge, Educational Technology Unit, 1973-88; consultancy work in educational technology for numerous organisations. Publications: eight books; over 150 papers. Recreations: reading; music; golf. Address: (h.) 164 Craigton Road, Aberdeen; T.-0224 316274.

Ellington, Marc Floyd, DL. Baron of Towie Barclay (Feudal Barony); Laird of Gardenstown and Crovie; Deputy Lieutenant, Aberdeenshire, since 1984; b. 16.12.45; m., Karen Leigh; 2 d. Member, National Committee, Architectural Heritage Society of Scotland; Member, British Heritage Commission (representing Scottish Tourist Board); Vice-President, Buchan Heritage Society; Trustee, Scottish Historic

Building Trust; Chairman, Heritage Press (Scotland); Director: Aberdeen University Research Ltd., Gardenstown Estates Ltd.; Soundcraft Audio; Partner, Heritage Sound Recordings; awarded Saltire Award, 1973, Civic Trust Award, 1975, European Architectural Heritage Award, 1975; Producer, documentary films and television programmes; Member, Historic Buildings Council for Scotland, since 1980; SBStJ; FSA. Recreations: sailing; historic architecture; art collecting; music. Address: Towie Barclay Castle, Auchterless, Turriff, Aberdeenshire, AB5 8EP; T.-08884 347.

Elliot, Sir Gerald Henry. Chairman, Scottish Opera, since 1987; Chairman, Biotal Limited, 1987-90; Chairman, Martin Currie Unit Trusts, 1988-90; b. 24.12.23, Edinburgh; m., Margaret Ruth Whale; 2 s.; 1 d. Educ. Marlborough College; New College, Oxford. Chairman, Christian Salvesen PLC, 1981-88; Chairman, Scottish Provident Institution, 1983-89; Chairman, Scottish Arts Council, 1980-86; Vice Chairman, Scottish Business in the Community, 1987-89; Chairman, Prince's Scottish Youth Business Trust, since 1987; Trustee, National Museums of Scotland, 1987-91; Member of Court, Edinburgh University, since 1984; Chairman, Scottish Unit Managers Ltd., 1984-88; Chairman of Trustees, David Hume Institute, since 1985; Chairman, Institute of Directors, Scottish Division, since 1989; Fellow, Royal Society of Edinburgh, since 1977; Honorary Consul for Finland in Edinburgh and Leith, 1957-89. Address: (b.) 8 Howe Street, Edinburgh, EH3 6TD; T.-031-220 3739.

Elliot, John. Farmer; Vice Chairman, British Wool Marketing Board, for Southern Scotland; b. 29.5.47, Duns, Berwickshire; m., Joan Kathleen Wight; 1 s.; 1 d. Educ. St. Mary School, Melrose; Edinburgh Academy. Nuffield Scholar, US and Canada, 1982. Recreations: spectator sports; reading; writing; agriculture. Address: Rawburn, Duns, Berwickshire, TD11 3PG; T.-036 17 221.

Elliot, Thomas, MBE, JP. Farmer; a Director, Royal Highland and Agricultural Society of Scotland; a Director, Animal Diseases Research Association; Member, Hill Farming Advisory Committee for Scotland; b. 6.4.26, Galashiels; m., Patrena Jennifer Mundell; 1 s.; 2 d. Educ. St. Mary's School; Loretto. President, Border Area, NFU of Scotland, 1974-76; Chairman, Selkirk Branch, 1968; President, South Country Cheviot Society, 1971-73; Member, Southern Regional Committee, British Wool Board. Played rugby, Gala RFC, 1945-58; 14 caps for Scotland, 1955-58; Barbarians, 1956; British Lions, South African tour, 1955. "Border Man of the Year", Tweeddale Press, 1979; Elder and Session Clerk, Caddonfoot Church. Recreations: watching rugby; reading books; farming. Address: Newhall, Clovenfords, Galashiels; T.-Clovenfords 260.

Elliot of Harwood, Baroness (Katharine Elliot), DBE (1958), JP. Life Peer; President, Royal Highland Agricultural Society, 1986; b. 15.1.03; m., Rt. Hon. Walter Elliot, PC, CH, MP (deceased). Educ. Abbot's Hill, Hemel Hempstead; Paris. Chairman: National Union of Conservative and Unionist Associations, 1956-67, Carnegie UK Trust, 1940-86, Consumer Council, 1963-68; UK Delegate to General Assembly, United Nations, 1954-56-57; Member, Roxburgh County Council, 1946-75 (Vice-Convener, 1974); Member, King George's Jubilee Trust, 1936-68; Hon. LLD, Glasgow, 1959. Address: (h.) Harwood, Bonchester Bridge, Hawick, Roxburghshire.

Elliott, Professor Robert F., BA (Oxon), MA. Professor of Economics, Aberdeen University, since 1990; b. 15.6.47, Thurlow, Suffolk; m., Susan Elliott Gutteridge; 1 s. Educ. Haverhill Secondary Modern School, Suffolk; Ruskin College and Balliol College, Oxford. Joined Aberdeen University, 1973, as Research Fellow, then Lecturer; acted as Consultant to numerous public and private sector organisa-

tions, including Megaw Committee of Inquiry into Civil Service Pay, the EEC Commission and Highlands and Islands Development Board, on issues of pay and employment. Publications: books on Pay in the Public Sector, 1981; Incomes Policies, Inflation and Relative Pay, 1981; Incomes Policy, 1981; Unemployment and Labour Market Efficiency, 1989; Labour Market Analysis, 1990. Recreations: music; reading; golf. Address: (h.) 11 Richmondhill Place, Aberdeen, AB2 4EN; T.-0224 314901.

Elliott, Hon. Lord (Walter Archibald Elliott), QC, MC, BL. President, Lands Tribunal for Scotland, since 1971; Chairman, Scottish Land Court, since 1978; Brigadier, Queen's Bodyguard for Scotland (Royal Company of Archers), since 1983; b. 6.9.22, London; m., Susan Isobel MacKenzie Ross; 2 s. Educ. Eton College; Edinburgh University. 2nd Bn., Scots Guards, 1943-45 (Staff Captain, 1947); Advocate and at the Inner Temple, Barrister-at-Law, 1950; QC (Scotland), 1963; conducted Edinburgh ring road inquiry, 1967. Publication: Us and Them: a study of group consciousness, 1986. Recreations: gardening; skiing; shooting. Address: (h.) Morton House, 19 Winton Loan, Edinburgh, EH10 7AW; T.-031-445 2548.

Ellis, Charles William, OBE, BA (Hons), LLD. Chairman, Grampian Health Board, 1982-89; Member, Whitley Council for Professions Allied to Medicine, 1987-89; b. 15.11.21, Horsham, Sussex; m., Maureen Patricia Radley; 1 s.; 3 d. Educ. Oxted County School; University College London. Indian Army and Royal Artillery, 1941-64; completed degree in modern history, 1964-66 (begun in 1940-41); Junior Lecturer to Head, School of Social Studies, Robert Gordon's Institute of Technology, Aberdeen, 1966-85. Councillor, City of Aberdeen, 1971-75 (Convener, Education Committee, 1974-75); Councillor, Grampian Regional Council, 1974-78 (Leader, Labour Group). Recreations: International affairs; family; genealogy. Address: (h.) 50 Hammerfield Avenue, Aberdeen, AB1 6LJ; T.-Aberdeen 310098.

Ellis, Frank, MA, BA (Hons), MEd. Rector, Denny High School, since 1987; b. 30.1.44, Shotts; m., Moreen Russell McLean; 1 s. Educ. Our Lady's High School, Motherwell; Glasgow University; London University; Stirling University. Teacher of Classics, Cumbernauld High School, 1966-71; Principal Teacher of Classics: Cumbernauld High School, 1971-73, Lornshill Academy, Alloa, 1973-78; Assistant Rector, Falkirk High School, 1978-84; Depute Rector, McLaren High School, Callander, 1984-87. Member, CCC, 1980-83. Recreations: squash; hill-walking; reading; music (listening); skiing. Address: (h.) 43 Westerlea Drive, Bridge of Allan, Stirling, FK9 4DQ; T.-Bridge of Allan 833177.

Ellis, Jean B.M., OBE, BSc, MB, ChB, JP. Member, Mental Welfare Commission for Scotland, 1984-88; Member, Scottish Hospital Endowment Research Trust, since 1978; President, Aberdeen and NE Association for Mental Health; b. 13.9.20, Poona, India; m., Richard T. Ellis (qv); 2 s.; 2 d. Educ. Malvern Girls College; Aberdeen University. Past Chairman: Aberdeen Marriage Guidance Council, Royal Cornhill and Associated Hospitals Board of Management; former Member: NE Regional Hospital Board, Nurses and Midwives Whitley Council (Management Side), Grampian Health Board. Address: (h.) 18 Rubislaw Den North, Aberdeen, AB2 4AN; T.-0224 316680.

Ellis, Laurence Edward, MA, AFIMA. Rector, The Edinburgh Academy, 1977-92; b. 21.4.32, Great Yarmouth; m., Elizabeth Ogilvie; 2 s.; 1 d. Educ. Winchester College; Trinity College, Cambridge. National Service, Rifle Brigade, 1950-52 (2nd Lt.); Assistant Master and Housemaster, Marlborough College, 1955-77. Reader, Church of England; Co-author, SMP Mathematics texts; article in Dictionary of National Biography on A.L.F. Smith. Recreations: music;

reading; crosswords; woodwork. Address: (h.) 50 Inverleith Place, Edinburgh, 3.

Ellis, Richard Tunstall, OBE, DL, MA, LLB; b. 6.9.18, Liverpool; m., Jean Bruce Maitland Porter (see Jean B.M. Ellis); 2 s.; 2 d. Educ. Merchant Taylors School, Crosby; Silcoates School, Wakefield; Aberdeen University. Captain, Royal Signals, 1939-45 (POW, Germany); Partner, Paull & Williamsons, Advocates, Aberdeen, 1949-83, Senior Partner, 1970-83; Chairman, Trustee Savings Bank Scotland, 1983-86; Chairman, TSB Scotland p.l.c., 1986-89; Director, TSB Group p.l.c., 1986-89; Chairman, Board of Governors, Dunfermline College of Physical Education, 1964-67; Governor, Aberdeen College of Education, 1969-75; Member: Scottish Board, Norwich Union Insurance Society, 1973-80, Aberdeen Board, Bank of Scotland, 1972-82, Aberdeen University Court, since 1984, Council, National Trust for Scotland, 1984-89; Chairman, Scottish Division, Institute of Directors, 1988-89. Recreations: golf; hill-walking; skiing. Address: (h.) 18 Rubislaw Den North, Aberdeen, AB2 4AN; T.-0224 316680.

Elvidge, John William, BA (Oxon). Assistant Secretary, Scottish Office, Head of Scottish Enterprise and Employment Division; b. 9.2.51, Edmonton, Middlesex. Educ. Sir George Monoux School, Walthamstow; St. Catherine's College, Oxford. Recreations: appreciating other people's creativity; observing other people's politics. Address: (b.) Room 5/111, New St. Andrews House, Edinburgh, EH1; T.-031-244 4684.

Emmanuel, Professor Clive Robert, BSc (Econ), MA, PhD, ACIS. Professor of Accounting and Head of Department, Glasgow University; b. 23.5.47; m.; 1 s.; 2 d. Educ. UWIST; Lancaster University; UCW, Aberystwyth. Steel Company of Wales, Port Talbot, 1964-68; Lecturer, Lancaster University, 1974-78; Senior Lecturer, then Reader, UCW, Aberystwyth, 1978-87; Associate Professor, University of Kansas, 1980-82. Address: (b.) Department of Accounting and Finance, Glasgow University, Glasgow.

Emmanuel, Francis Xavier Soosaipillai, MB, BS, MSc, PhD, MRCPath. Consultant Medical Mircobiologist, Lothian Health Board, since 1986; Honorary Senior Lecturer in Medical Microbiology, Edinburgh University, since 1988; b. 24.8.48, Jaffna, Sri Lanka; m., Jacintha; 2 d. Educ. Ceylon University; Birmingham University. Lecturer, Ceylon University, 1973-77; Research Fellow, Birmingham University, 1977-80; Registrar in Microbiology, Western General Hospital, Edinburgh, 1980-83; Senior Registrar in Microbiology, Oxfordshire Health Authority, 1983-86. Recreations: cooking; reading. Address: (h.) 14 Polwarth Terrace, Merchiston, Edinburgh, EH11 1ND; T.-031-228 4476.

Emond, Professor William John, BSc, FIMA, FSS. Vice Principal, Dundee Institute of Technology, since 1985; b. 23.8.42, Bellshill; m., Helen Catherine Elliott; 1 s.; 2 d. Educ. Allan Glen's School; Strathclyde University. Lecturer, then Senior Lecturer, polytechnics in England; former Head, Department of Mathematics and Computer Studies, Dundee Institute of Technology; Member, General Teaching Council; Member, SCOTVEC; Member, SCRE. Past Chairman: Alyth Musical Society, Perthshire Youth Brass Association. Recreations: golf; sailing; choral singing. Address: (h.) Kinbrae, Alyth, Perth, PH11 8ES; T.-08283 2446.

Emslie, Rt. Hon. Lord (George Carlyle), MBE, PC, LLD, FRSE. Lord Justice General of Scotland, 1972-89; Lord President of the Court of Session, 1972-89; b. 6.12.19, Glasgow; m., Lilias Ann Mailer Hannington; 3 s. Educ. High School of Glasgow; Glasgow University. Commissioned A. & S.H., 1940; served War of 1939-45 (Despatches), North Africa, Italy, Greece, Austria, 1942-46; p.s.c. Haifa, 1944;

Brigade Major (Infantry), 1944-46; Advocate, 1948; Advocate-Depute (Sheriff Courts), 1955; QC (Scotland), 1957; Sheriff of Perth and Angus, 1963-66; Dean, Faculty of Advocates, 1965-70; Senator of the College of Justice, 1970-72; Chairman, Scottish Agricultural Wages Board, 1969-73; Member, Council on Tribunals (Scottish Committee), 1962-70; Hon. Bencher, Inner Temple, 1974, and Inn of Court of N. Ireland, 1981; PC, 1972; Baron (Life Peer), created 1980. Recreation: golf. Address: (h.) 47 Heriot Row, Edinburgh, EH3 6EX; T.-031-225 3657.

Emslie, John Andrew Noble, MD, DipBact. Consultant in the Epidemiology of Communicable Diseases, since 1975; Honorary Clinical Senior Lecturer, Glasgow University, since 1990; b. 24.1.36, Glasgow; m., Patricia Margaret Lawn; 1 s.; 1 d. Educ. Hutchesons' Boys' Grammar School; Glasgow University. House Officer, Medicine/Surgery, Victoria Infirmary, Glasgow; Senior House Officer/Registrar, Western Infirmary, Glasgow, 1961-64; Trainee Bacteriologist, Public Health Laboratory Service, London, 1964-65; Bacteriologist (later Acting Director), Public Health Laboratory Service, Middlesbrough, 1965-68; Consultant-in-Charge, Microbiology Department, Ayrshire Laboratory Service, 1968-75. National Secretary, British Society for the Study of Infection. Recreations: railways; photography; model-making; travel. Address: (b.) Communicable Diseases (Scotland) Unit, Ruchill Hospital, Glasgow, G20 9NB; T.-041-946 7120, Ext. 1488.

Emslie-Smith, Donald, SBStJ, MD (Hons), ChB, FRCP, FRCPEdin, FSA Scot. Honorary Fellow, Dundee University (Reader in Medicine, 1971-87, Head, Department of Medicine, 1986-87); Honorary Consultant Physician (Cardiologist), Tayside Health Board, 1961-87; b. 12.4.22, Aberdeen; m., Ann Elizabeth Milne; 1 s.; 1 d. Educ. Trinity College, Glenalmond; Aberdeen University. House Physician, Aberdeen Royal Infirmary; RAFVR (Medical Branch), UK and Middle East; Registrar in Cardiology, Dundee Royal Infirmary; Edward Wilson Memorial Research Fellow, Baker Institute, Melbourne; Tutor and Senior Registrar in Medicine, Royal Postgraduate Medical School and Hammersmith Hospital, London; Senior Lecturer in Medicine, St. Andrews University. Council Member, Association of Physicians of Great Britain and Ireland, 1977-80; Chairman, British Cardiac Society, 1987; President, Harveian Society of Edinburgh, 1986-87, Harveian Orator, 1987. Publications: Textbook of Physiology (Co-author and Editor) (8th to 11th editions); Accidental Hypothermia, 1977. Recreations: fly-fishing; dinghy-sailing; music. Address: (b.) University Department of Medicine, Ninewells Hospital and Medical School, Dundee, DD1 9SY; T.-0382 60111.

English, Peter Roderick, BSc (Hons), NDA (Hons), PhD. Reader in Animal Husbandry, Aberdeen University; b. 9.3.37, Glen Urquhart, Inverness-shire; m., Anne Dunlop Mackay; 2 s.; 1 d. Educ. Balnain Public School; Arnisdale School; Glen Urquhart Senior Secondary School; Inverness Royal Academy; Aberdeen University. Farm Manager, Aberdeen University: Assistant Lecturer, Research Fellow, Lecturer, Reader. Won David Black Award, 1984, for major contribution to British pig industry. Publications: The Sow - Improving Her Efficiency; Glen Urquhart; The Growing and Finishing Pig. Recreations: athletics; shinty (first Editor, Shinty Yearbook); writing; travel; hard labour. Address: (h.) Arnisdale, 13 Fintray Road, Aberdeen, AB1 8HL; T.-Aberdeen 319306.

Entwistle, Professor Noel James, BSc, PGCE, PhD, FilDr (h.c.), FBPsS. Bell Professor of Education, Edinburgh University, since 1978; Director, Godfrey Thomson Unit for Educational Research, since 1978; b. 26.12.36, Bolton; m., Dorothy Bocking; 1 d. Educ. King's School, Ely; Sheffield University; Aberdeen University. Teacher, Rossall School,

Fleetwood, 1961-64; Research Fellow, Aberdeen University, 1964-68; Department of Educational Research, Lancaster University: Lecturer, 1968, Senior Lecturer, 1971, Professor, 1972. Editor, British Journal of Educational Psychology, 1975-79; Governor, St. Margaret's School, Edinburgh. Recreations: reading; walking; golf. Address: (b.) 10 Buccleuch Place, Edinburgh, EH8 9JT; T.-031-667 1011.

Entwistle, Raymond Marvin, ACIB. Managing Director, Adam & Company Plc, since 1991; b. 12.6.44, Croydon; m., Barbara Joan Hennessy; 2 s.; 1 d. Educ. John Ruskin Grammar School. Several managerial appointments with Lloyds Bank. Governor, Edinburgh College of Art; Chairman, Fruit Market Gallery, Edinburgh. Recreations: golf; shooting; fishing; antiques. Address: (b.) 22 Charlotte Square, Edinburgh, EH2 4DF; T.-031-225 8484.

Erdal, David Edward, MA, MBA. Chairman, Tullis Russell & Co. Ltd., since 1985; b. 29.3.48, Umtali, Zimbabwe; 1 s.; 1 d. Educ. Glenalmond; Brasenose College, Oxford; Harvard Business School. English Language Teacher, London, 1972-74; Foreign Language Institute, People's Republic of China, 1974-76; joined Tullis Russell, 1977. Trustee, Baxi Partnership; Fellow, Royal Society of Arts. Recreations: sailing; skiing; reading. Address: (b.) Tullis Russell & Co. Ltd., Markinch, Glenrothes, KY7 6PB; T.-0592 753311.

Erickson, Professor John, MA, FRSE, FBA, FRSA. Director, Centre for Defence Studies, Edinburgh University, since 1967; b. 17.4.29, South Shields; m., Ljubica; 1 s.; 1 d. Educ. South Shields High School; St. John's College, Cambridge. Research Fellow, St. Antony's College, Oxford; Lecturer, Department of History, St. Andrews University; Lecturer/Reader, Department of Government, Manchester University; Reader/Professor, Defence Studies, Edinburgh University. President, Association of Civil Defence and Emergency Planning Officers, until 1984; Visiting Professor, Yale University, 1987. Publications: The Soviet High Command, 1962; The Road to Stalingrad, 1975; The Road to Berlin, 1984; Soviet Ground Forces, An Operational Assessment, 1986. Recreation: model-making. Address: (b.) 31 Buccleuch Place, Edinburgh; T.-031-650 4263.

Erskine, Donald Seymour, DL, FRICS. Factor and Director of Estates, National Trust for Scotland, 1961-89; b. 28.5.25, London; m., Catharine Annandale McLelland; 1 s.; 4 d. Educ. Wellington College. RA (Airborne), 1943-47 (Captain); Pupil, Drumlanrig Estate, 1947-49; Factor, Country Gentlemen's Association, Edinburgh, 1950-55; Factor to Mr A.L.P.F. Wallace, 1955-61. Member, Queen's Bodyguard for Scotland (Royal Company of Archers); Deputy Lieutenant, Perth and Kinross; Elder and General Trustee, Church of Scotland. Recreations: shooting; singing. Address: (h.) Cleish House, Cleish, Kinross-shire, KY13 7LR; T.-057 75 232.

Espley, Arthur James, MB, ChB, DObstRCOG, FRCSEdin. Consultant Orthopaedic Surgeon, Bridge of Earn Hospital, since 1981; Honorary Senior Lecturer, Department of Orthopaedic and Traumatic Surgery, Dundee University, since 1981; b. 19.2.44, Southend; m., Erica Strang; 1 s.; 2 d. Educ. Belfast Royal Academy; Edinburgh University (Rugby Blue, 1968). Member, Scottish and British Universities Rugby XV, 1968. Recreations: golf; gardening; curling. Address: (h.) Couttie Bridge Cottage, Coupar Angus, PH13 9HF; T.-0828 27301.

Essery, David James. Under Secretary, Scottish Office Home and Health Department, since 1991; b. 10.5.38, Greenock; m., Nora Loughlin Sim; 2 s.; 1 d. Educ. Royal High School, Edinburgh. Entered Department of Health for Scotland, 1956; Private Secretary to Minister of State, Scottish Office, 1968-69; Principal, Scottish Development Department, 1969-76; Assistant Secretary, Scottish Economic Planning Department, 1976-81; Scottish Development Department, 1981-85; Under Secretary, Department of Agriculture and Fisheries for Scotland, 1985-91. Recreations: reading; music; cricket; squash. Address: (b.) St. Andrew's House, Edinburgh EH1 3DE; T.-031-244 2127.

Esson, George Albert, QPM, LLB. Chief Constable, Dumfries & Galloway Constabulary, since 1989; b. 30.3.42, Alford, Aberdeenshire; m., Margurita; 1 d. Educ. Alford Academy; Aberdeen University. Constable, Stirling and Clackmannan, 1961; transferred to Aberdeen City; Sergeant, 1967; attended Aberdeen University as police-sponsored student; Grampian Police: Inspector, 1974; Chief Inspector, 1979; Superintendent, 1982; Chief Superintendent, 1984; Assistant Chief Constable, 1986; Deputy Chief Constable, 1987. Recreations: sport in general, golf and curling in particular. Address: (b.) Police Headquarters, Loreburn Street, Dumfries, DG1 1HP; T.-0387 52112.

Eunson, Edwin Russell, OBE (1986), KFO, JP. Convener, Orkney Islands Council, 1978-90 (Chairman, Policy and Resources Committee, 1978-90); Director, Orkney Islands Property Development PLC; Director, Orkney Homes Trust PLC; b. 25.12.17, Kirkwall; m., Margaret Ross Nicolson. Educ. Kirkwall Grammar School. Member, Kirkwall Town Council, 1947-68 (Dean of Guild, 1955, Treasurer, 1955-57, Bailie, 1957-68); Member, Orkney County Council, 1947-55; Member, Orkney Islands Council, 1974-90 (Chairman: Development, Planning and Control Committee, 1974-77, Social Work and Environmental Health Committee, 1977-78); Member: Highlands and Islands Development Consultative Council, 1974-90; Scottish Council (Development and Industry) Executive Committee, 1974-90; Chairman, Orkney Committee for Employment of Disabled Persons, 1981-91; Member, Executive Committee, COSLA, 1982-90; Session Clerk, Kirkwall East Church, 1955-87; Chairman: Orkney Liberal Association, 1962-78, Orkney Council of Social Service, 1968-74, Kirkwall Chamber of Commerce, 1970-72; Commander, Royal Norwegian Order of Merit; Freeman of Orkney; President, Orkney Age Concern. Recreations: reading; walking dogs. Address: (h.) Newhallea, Glaitness Road, Kirkwall, Orkney; T.-0856 3367.

Evans, Charles, CEng, MIMechE, MIRTE. Chief Executive and Managing Director, Lothian Region Transport plc, since 1986 (Director of Public Transport, Lothian Regional Council, 1978-86); Chairman, Bus and Coach Council - Scotland, 1987-88; b. 30.8.37, Chadderton, Lancashire; m., Cherie; 3 s.; 1 d. Educ. North Chadderton Secondary Modern School; Oldham Technical College. Apprentice Engineer/Engineer, Oldham Corporation Passenger Transport, 1952-63; Assistant Engineer, Manchester Corporation, 1963-65; Edinburgh Corporation: Assistant Chief Engineer, 1965-71, Chief Engineer, 1971-75; Depute Director, Lothian Regional Council, 1975-78. President, Bus and Coach Council, 1986-87; Director, Edinburgh Chamber of Commerce, since 1990. Recreations: golf; caravanning. Address: (b.) 14 Queen Street, Edinburgh, EH2 1JL; T.-031-554 4494.

Evans, Sheriff George James, MA, LLB. Sheriff of Glasgow and Strathkelvin, at Glasgow, since 1983; b. 16.7.44.

Evans, James, RD, JP, DL, BSc, CEng, FRINA, MIMechE. Managing Director, Thomas Evans (Berwick) Ltd.; Chairman, Berwickshire District Council, since 1980; Chairman, Fishing Boat Builders Association, 1979- 90; b. 9.5.33, South Shields; m., Patricia Alexena Kerr; 1 s.; 2 d. Educ. Merchiston Castle School; Kings College, Durham. Apprenticeship, 1950-56; Royal Navy, 1956-58; YARD, 1958-63; UKAEA, 1963-68; RNR, 1956-80 (retired as Captain (E) RNR); Member, Eyemouth Burgh Council, 1972-75; Berwickshire County Council; Vice-Chairman and

Finance Chairman, Berwickshire District Council, 1974-80; awarded Silver Medal, Nuclear Engineering Society, 1962; Hon ADC, The Queen, 1979-80; Deputy Lieutenant, Berwickshire, since 1978; Chairman, Berwick Freemen's Guild, since 1975. Address: (h.) Makore, Northburn View, Eyemouth, Berwickshire; T.-Eyemouth 50231.

Evans, Martyn Robert Rowlinson, BA (Hons), MA (Econ). Director, Shelter (Scottish Campaign for the Homeless), since 1987; b. 11.7.52, Hamilton; m., Angela May Morton; 2 s. Educ. Warwick School; City of Birmingham Polytechnic; Manchester University. Department of Health and Social Security, 1974-75; Directorate for Voluntary Services, 1975-76; Tameside MBC, 1976-78; Centre for Housing Research, Glasgow University, 1979-80; Housing Aid Worker, Shelter, 1980-83; Depute Director, Shelter Scotland,1983-87. Chair, Glasgow Council for Single Homeless, 1984-87; Convener, Board of Trustees, Glasgow Stopover, 1986-87; Non-Executive Director, Scottish Council for Voluntary Organisations. Recreations: golf; music. Address: (h.) 30 Teviotdale Place, Edinburgh; T.-031-332 1463.

Eveling, Stanley, BA, BPhil. Fellow, Edinburgh University; Playwright; Television Critic, The Scotsman; b. 4.8.25, Newcastle upon Tyne; m., Kate Howell; 2 s.; 2 d. Educ. King's College, Durham University; Lincoln College, Oxford. Recreations: golf; tennis; going abroad. Address: (b.) Fettes College, Edinburgh, EH4 1QX.

Everett, Peter, BSc (Hons), SPMB. Director, Scottish Hydro-Electric, since 1989; Director, Forth Ports Authority, since 1989; b. 24.9.31, London; m., Annette Patricia Hyde; 3 s.; 1 d. Educ. George Watson's College; Edinburgh University. Royal Engineers, 1953-55 (2nd Lt.); joined Shell International Petroleum Company, 1955; Managing Director, Brunei Shell Petroleum Co. Ltd., 1979-84; Managing Director, Shell UK Exploration and Production, 1985-89; retired, 1989. Honorary Professor, Heriot Watt University, 1989. Recreation: golf. Address: (h.) Cluain, Castleton Road, Auchterarder, Perthshire PH3 1JW.

Everett, Robert Anthony, BA, BSc, CPhys, MInstP, AFIMA, ASTA. Headteacher, Kilchuimen Academy, since 1971; b. 5.6.31, Battle, Sussex; m., Christina Laird Hastings Brown; 3 s.; 2 d. Educ. St. Mary's Academy, Bathgate; Edinburgh University; Moray House College of Education; Open University. National Service, Royal Signals; Teacher of Science, Bathgate Academy; Principal Teacher of Science, Dornoch Academy; Principal Teacher of Physics: Camphill Senior Secondary School, Paisley, Galashiels Academy; Headteacher, Leverhulme Memorial Secondary School, Leverburgh, Isle of Harris. Sometime Secretary, Fort Augustus Village Council; former Secretary, Fort Augustus/Glenmoriston Community Council; Past Chairman, Fort Augustus Royal British Legion (Scotland); Elder, Fort Augustus Church of Scotland. Recreation: swimming. Address: (h.) The Schoolhouse, Fort Augustus, Inverness-shire, PH32 4DR; T.-0320 6235.

Ewan, Edmund Alan, MA, DipEd, DPhil. Vice-Principal, Moray House College of Education, Edinburgh, since 1984 (re-named Moray House Institute of Education, Heriot-Watt University, 1991); b. 30.10.31, Bridge of Earn; m., Elizabeth Miller Calder; 2 s. Educ. Perth Academy; St. Andrews University; Oxford University. Assistant Director of Education, Fife County Council, 1961-66; Head, Department of Educational Management and Administration, Moray House College of Education, 1967-84. Recreation: hill-walking. Address: (b.) Moray House College Institute of Education, Heriot-Watt University, Holyrood Road, Edinburgh, EH8 8AQ; T.-031-558 6164.

Ewen, Robert, OBE, TD, MA. Secretary of the University Court, Glasgow University, since 1985; b. 3.3.39, Clydebank; m., Eleanor Irene Grayson; 1 s.; 1 d. Educ. Inverness Royal Academy; Aberdeen University. Aberdeen University: Clerk, Faculty of Arts, 1964-73, Clerk, Senatus Academicus, 1973-79, Deputy Secretary, 1976-85. Lt. Col., Royal Engineers (TA). Recreations: golf; squash; shooting; hill-walking. Address: (b.) University of Glasgow, Glasgow, G12 8QQ; T.-041-339 8855.

Ewing, Lord (Harry Ewing), MP (Labour), Falkirk East, 1983-92 (Stirling and Falkirk, 1971-74, Stirling, Falkirk and Grangemouth, 1974-83); b. 20.1.31.

Ewing, Margaret Anne, MA, BA (Hons). MP (Moray), since 1987; Parliamentary Leader, SNP, since 1987; b. 1.9.45, Lanark; m., Fergus Stewart Ewing. Educ. Biggar High School; Glasgow University; Strathclyde University; Jordanhill College. Schoolteacher, 1968-74 (Principal Teacher of Remedial Education, St. Modan's, Stirling, 1972-74); SNP MP (East Dunbartonshire), 1974-79; Freelance Journalist, 1979-81; Co-ordinator, West of Scotland CSS Scheme, 1981-87. Recreations: grdening; reading; arts in general. Address: (h.) Burns Cottage, Tulloch's Lane, Tulloch's Brae, Lossiemouth, Moray, IV31 6QY; T.-034381 3218/2222.

Ewing, Winifred Margaret, MA, LLB, NP. Member (SNP), European Parliament, since 1975; President, Scottish National Party; President, European Free Alliance, since 1991; b. 10.7.29, Glasgow; m., Stewart Martin Ewing; 2 s.; 1 d. Educ. Queen's Park School; Glasgow University. Solicitor, since 1952; former Secretary and President, Glasgow Bar Association; President, Soroptimist Club (Glasgow), 1966; MP (SNP), Hamilton, 1967-70, Moray and Nairn, 1974-79; Vice President of Group (Rainbow Alliance) in European Parliament. Recreations: walking; reading; painting; swimming. Address: (h.) Goodwill, Miltonduff, Elgin, IV30 3TL

F

Fair, James Stuart, MA, LLB, WS, NP. Solicitor; Senior Partner, now Consultant, Thorntons, WS, Dundee; Honorary Sheriff and Temporary Sheriff; former Lecturer in Taxation and Professional Ethics, Dundee University; Clerk, Commissioners of Inland Revenue (Dundee District); Director of private investment trust companies; b. 30.9.30, Perth; m., Anne Lesley Cameron; 2 s.; 1 d. Educ. Perth Academy; St. Andrews University; Edinburgh University. Chairman, University Court, Dundee; Member, Dundee Port Authority; Past President, Dundee and Tayside Chamber of Commerce & Industry; Past Chairman, Review Committee, Perth Prison; Member, Scottish Solicitors' Discipline Tribunal, 1978-88; President, Dundee Choral Union; Trustee, Sir James Caird's Travelling Scholarship Trust; Member, Committee on Medical Ethics, Ninewells Hospital and Medical School, Dundee. Address: (h.) Beechgrove House, 474 Perth Road, Dundee, DD2 1LL.

Fairbairn, The Hon. Mrs Elizabeth Mary, BA (Hons). Member, Planning and Resources Committee, Scottish Arts

Council, since 1991 (Chairman, Combined Arts Committee, 1988-91); Council Member, The Cockburn Association, since 1988; Chairman, Live Music Now! (Scotland), since 1990; Secretary/Administrator, The Gulliver Award for the Performing Arts in Scotland, since 1990; Chairman, Castle Rock Housing Association, since 1987; b. 21.6.38, Galashiels; 3 d. Executive, Edinburgh Financial and General Holdings Ltd., 1979-86 (Director, 1981-86); part-time Consultant, CASCO Ltd., 1987; Financial Controller, Nicholas Groves-Raines Architects, 1988-89; Administrator, Edinburgh Festival Forum, 1989; Administrator, Edinburgh International Festival Endowment Fund, since 1989; Member, Edinburgh Festival Council, 1983-86; Chairman, Lothian Housing Association; Chairman, Friends of the Edinburgh International Festival; Director, Lothian Homes Ltd.; Director, DBF Television Ltd.; Patron, Artlink; Trustee, The Glasite Meeting House Trust; Trustee, Action Against Addiction. Recreation: music. Address: (h.) 38 Moray Place, Edinburgh, EH3 6BT; T.-031-225 2724.

Fairbairn of Fordell, Sir Nicholas Hardwick, QC, KLJ, KOSJ, KPR, FSA(Scot), MA, LLB. MP (Conservative), Perth and Kinross, since 1983; Queen's Counsel, since 1972; Chairman, Historic Buildings Council for Scotland; b. 24.12.33, Edinburgh; m., Suzanne Mary Wheeler; 3 d. Educ. Loretto; Edinburgh University. Called to the Scots Bar, 1957; MP, Kinross and West Perthshire, 1974-83; Solicitor General, 1979-82; Commissioner of Northern Lighthouses, 1979-82. Honorary President and Founder: Society for Preservation of Duddingston, Edinburgh Brook Advisory Centre; Honorary President, Dysart and Dundonald Pipe Band; Trustee, Royal Museums of Scotland; Vice President, Society of Scottish Women Artists. Publications: Alastair MacLean's Scotland (Contributor); A Life is Too Short. Recreations: painting; broadcasting. Address: (h.) Fordell Castle, by Dunfermline, Fife.

Fairgrieve, Brian David, OBE, DL, MB, ChB, FRCSEd. General Surgeon, Falkirk Royal Infirmary, 1960-87; Deputy Lieutenant, Falkirk and Stirling Districts; b. 21.2.27, Glasgow. Educ. Glasgow Academy; Glasgow University. RMO, 2/6th Gurkha Rifles, 1952-54; initial medical training, Western Infirmary, Glasgow, Stobhill General Hospital, Killearn Hospital; Area Scout Commissioner, 21 years; President, Forth Valley Area Scout Council; Past President, Rotary Club of Falkirk; Lecturer and Examiner, Scotish Police College; Member, Council, St. Andrew's Ambulance Association; former Director, Incorporated Glasgow Stirlingshire & Sons of the Rock Society; Hon. Vice President, Grangemouth Rugby Club; awarded Silver Wolf, 1983, and OBE, 1986, for services to International Scouting. Recreations: photography; travel. Address: (h.) 19 Lyall Crescent, Polmont, Falkirk, FK2 0PL; T.-0324 715449.

Fairgrieve, James Hanratty, DA, ARSA, RSW. Painter; Lecturer in Drawing and Painting, Edinburgh College of Art, since 1968; b. 17.6.44, Prestonpans; m., Margaret D. Ross; 2 s.; 1 d. Educ. Preston Lodge Senior Secondary School; Edinburgh College of Art. Postgraduate study, 1966-67; Travelling Scholarship, Italy, 1968; President, SSA, 1978-82; exhibited in Britain and Europe, since 1966. Recreation: angling. Address: (h.) Burnbrae, Gordon, Berwickshire; T.-Gordon 357.

Fairgrieve, Sir (Thomas) Russell, CBE, TD, JP. Chairman, Belwood Nurseries Ltd., Quality Guaranteed PLC, Vincent Taylor & Company; Director, Central Scottish Woodlands Ltd., William Baird PLC, Bain Clarkson Ltd. (Inchcape); b. 3.5.24, Galashiels; m., Millie Mitchell; 1 s.; 3 d. Educ. St. Mary's School, Melrose; Sedbergh School, Yorkshire. Commissioned, 8th Gurkha Rifles (Indian Army), 1943; Company Commander, 1/8th Gurkha Rifles, 1944-46 (Burma, Malaya and Java); TA, 4th KOSB, 1947-63 (Major).

Director, Laidlaw & Fairgrieve Ltd., 1953-68 (Managing Director, 1958-68); Director, Dawson International PLC, 1961-73 (Group Yarn Sales Director, 1965-68); Chairman, Scottish Young Conservatives, 1950-51; President, Scottish Conservative Association, 1965-66; MP, Aberdeenshire West, 1974-83; Chairman, Scottish Conservative Group for Europe, 1974-78; Scottish Conservative Whip, 1975; Chairman, Scottish Conservative Party, 1975-80; Under-Secretary of State for Scotland, 1979-81; Member, Consultative Assembly, Council of Europe and WEU, 1982-83. Address: (h.) Pankalan, Bolside, Galashiels; T.-0896 2278.

Fairley, Charles John, BSc, PhD. Chief Executive, Scottish Enterprise Tayside, since 1991; Chairman, Cogent Diagnostics Ltd., since 1989; b. 15.8.41, Burntisland; m., Judith Anne Brown; 1 s.; 3 d. Educ. Daniel Stewart's College; Edinburgh University. Lecturer, Edinburgh University, 1964-67; Brooke Bond Liebig: Scientist/Corporate Planner, 1967-72, Commercial Manager, 1972-74; General Manager, Gulf Oil (Scotland), 1974-77; Scottish Development Agency: Investment Manager, 1977-81, Divisional Head, 1987-88; Director, Strategic Management, Ernst & Young, 1988-89; Owner, CM Consultants, since 1989. Director, Dundee Repertory Theatre; former President, Licensing Executive Society (UK & Ireland). Recreations: golf; canal cruising; real ale. Address: (h.) Burlington House, Perth Road, Dunblane, FK15 0HA; T.-0786 825543; (b.) 0382 23100.

Fairlie of Myres, David Ogilvy, MBE. Landowner; Chairman, East Fife Branch, Arthritis and Rheumatism Council; b. 1.10.23, Edinburgh. Educ. Ampleforth College, York; Oriel College, Oxford. Officer, Royal Signals, Europe, Ceylon, Singapore, Java, Malaya, Korea, SHAPE Paris; retired, 1959; former Cupar District Commissioner and Fife Area Commissioner for Scouts; awarded Silver Acorn and Silver Wolf; DL, Fife; JP; Member, Queen's Bodyguard for Scotland; Knight of the Holy Sepulchre of Jerusalem (Chancellor of the Lieutenancy of Scotland). Publication: Fairlie of that Ilk. Recreations: genealogy; photography; walking; shooting; gardening; bee-keeping. Address: Myres Castle, Auchtermuchty, Cupar, Fife, KY14 7EW.

Fairlie, Peter James Morrison. Managing Director, Glenturret Distillery Ltd., since 1989; Member, Scottish Sports Council, since 1990; b. 18.12.57, Bridge of Allan; m., Anne (Louise) Moon; 1 s.; 1 d. Educ. Strathallan School. Glenturret Distillery Ltd., since 1977. Vice Chairman, Association of Scottish Visitor Attractions, since 1988. Recreations: squash (Internationalist, 1980-87); golf; skiing; angling. Address: (h.) Woodend, Craigmill, by Stirling, FK9 5PP; T.-0786 71252.

Fairrie, Lt. Col. Adam Angus. Regimental Secretary, Queen's Own Highlanders, since 1978; b. 9.12.34, Bromborough; m., Elizabeth Rachel Pryor; 1 s.; 1 d. Educ. Stowe; Royal Military Academy, Sandhurst. Commissioned, Queen's Own Cameron Highlanders, 1955; to Queen's Own Highlanders, 1961; Staff College, Camberley, 1966; National Defence College, Latimer, 1973-74; Commanding Officer 1st Bn. Queen's Own Highlanders, 1974-77. Publications: Cuidich 'n Righ (a history of the Queen's Own Highlanders); The Northern Meeting 1788-1988. Address: (b.) RHQ, Queen's Own Highlanders, Cameron Barracks, Inverness; T.-Inverness 224380.

Fairweather, Andrew Burton, OBE, TD, BA, MBIM. General Secretary, Abbeyfield Society for Scotland, since 1991; b. 26.2.31, Edinburgh; m., Elizabeth Brown; 3 s. Educ. Royal High School, Edinburgh; Edinburgh University; Open University. Clerical Officer, HM Customs and Excise, 1949; Executive Officer: Accountant of Court for Scotland, 1949, Department of Health for Scotland, 1951 (Secretary, Scottish

Medical Practices Committee, 1954-58); Higher Executive Officer, Department of Health for Scotland and Scottish Development Department, 1958; Senior Executive Officer, Scottish Development Department, 1965 (Secretary, Rent Assessment Panel for Scotland, 1965-67); Principal: Chief Administrative Officer, Civil Service College, Edinburgh, 1970, Scottish Economic Planning Department, 1972, Scottish Development Department, 1974 (Secretary, Local Government Staff and Property Commissions, 1974-77), Scottish Office Central Services, 1981; Senior Principal, Scottish Office Central Services, 1982. Rifle Brigade, RAEC; Royal Scots (TA) and Royal Corps of Transport (TA); Commanding Officer, 495 Liaison Unit (BAOR), Royal Corps of Transport (TA), 1977-81; Colonel, Regular Army Reserve of Officers, 1982. Address: (h.) 127 Silverknowes Gardens, Edinburgh.

Fairweather, Rev. Ian C.M., MA (Hons), BD. Associate Minister, Glasgow Cathedral, 1985-90; b. 7.3.20, Glasgow; m., Joan Margaret Dickinson. Educ. Hutchesons' Boys' Grammar School, Glasgow; Glasgow University. Professor of Philosophy, Scottish Church College, Calcutta, and Murray College, Sialkot, 1945-47; Minister, Perceton & Dreghorn Parish Church, 1948-63; Lecturer in Religious Studies and Religious Education, Jordanhill College of Education, 1964-82. Church of Scotland Representative, General Teaching Council for Scotland, 1983-91; Hon. Fellow, New College, Edinburgh, 1984-85. Publications: The Quest for Christian Ethics: an inquiry into ethics and Christian ethics (Co-author); Religious Education (Co-author). Recreation: gardening. Address: (h.) Seaforth, 10 Hillside Road, Cardross, G82 5LX; T.-0389 841551.

Falchikov, Michael George, BA, DipPSA. Senior Lecturer in Russian, Edinburgh University, since 1989; b. 26.5.37, London; 1 s.; 1 d. Educ. Welwyn Garden City Grammar School; Oriel College, Oxford. National Service, RAF, 1956-58; Careers Advisor, Newcastle-upon-Tyne, 1962-64; Edinburgh University: Assistant Lecturer, 1965, Lecturer, 1968, Head, Department of Russian, 1990-91, Convener, Board of Asian and Modern European Languages, since 1991. Parliamentary candidate (Liberal Democrats), Linlithgow, 1992. Recreations: watching football (especially Hibs); traditional jazz; cinema; travel. Address: (h.) 51 Thirlestane Road, Edinburgh, EH9; T.-031-650 3671.

Falconer, Alex. Member (Labour), Mid Scotland and Fife, European Parliament, since 1984; b. 1.4.40.

Falconer, Ian McLeod, BSc, CEng, MICE. Buildings Officer, Dundee University, since 1979; b. 21.7.31, Aberdeen; m., Brenda; 2 s.; 1 d. Educ. Aberdeen Academy; Aberdeen University. Worked in hydro-electric, building and civil engineering contracting throughout Scotland until 1979; commissioned in Royal Engineers during National Service, 1956; appointed Specialist Adviser, House of Commons Committee on Scottish Affairs, 1982, for inquiry into dampness in housing. Recreations: swimming; golf; Rotary; reading. Address: (b.) The University, Dundee; T.-0382 23181.

Falconer, Lake. Solicitor (retired); b. 21.10.27, Oban; m., Winifred Margaret Payne; 2 s. Educ. Oban High School; Glasgow University. RAF, 1946-48; qualified Solicitor, 1951; Partner, then Senior Partner, D.M. MacKinnon & Co., WS, Oban, 1953-89; Council Member, Law Society of Scotland, 1980-90; Vice President, 1985-86; Dean, Oban Faculty of Solicitors, 1983-86; Honorary Sheriff of North Strathclyde at Oban, since 1988; Chairman, Oban Social Security Appeal Tribunal; Commodore, Royal Highland Yacht Club, 1974-77; Chairman and Depute Launching Authority, Oban Lifeboat, since 1972; Chairman, North Argyll District Scout Council, since 1982; Session Clerk, Kilmore and Oban Church of Scotland; Member, Judicial Commission, General

Assembly of Church of Scotland. Recreation: sailing. Address: (h.) Birkhill, Glenmore, Oban, PA34 4PG; T.-0631 62940.

Fallon, Edward Brian. Deputy Leader, Lothian Regional Council, since 1990 (Chair, General Purposes Committee, since 1986); Convener, COSLA Protective Services Committee, since 1990; b. 10.11.47, Edinburgh; m., Jennifer Mary; 1 s.; 1 d. Educ. St. Anthony's School, Edinburgh; Napier College; Edinburgh School of Building. Elected, Lothian Regional Council, 1982. Member: Torness Local Liaison Committee, Edinburgh Prison Visiting Committee. Recreations: golf; football; reading; swimming. Address: (b.) Regional Chambers, Parliament Square, Edinburgh, EH1 1TT; T.-031-469 3325.

Fallon, Ronald John, BSc, MD, FRCPath, FRCPGlas. Consultant in Laboratory Medicine, Ruchill Hospital, Glasgow, since 1961; Honorary Senior Clinical Lecturer in Bacteriology, Immunology and Infectious Diseases, Glasgow University, since 1961; b. 1.2.28, Wallasey; m., Valerie Frances Kirkham; 4 d. Educ. Wallasey Grammar School; Liverpool University. Temporary Assistant Lecturer in Bacteriology, Liverpool University, 1953-55; Junior Bacteriologist, Royal Naval Hospital, Plymouth, 1955-57; Lecturer in Bacteriology, Glasgow University, 1957-61. Member: Advisory Committee on Dangerous Pathogens, Microbiological Advisory Committee DOH; Member, SHHD Sterile Supplies Policy Advisory Group; Past Chairman, Scottish Branch, British Society for the Study of Infection; Past Chairman, Central Sterilising Club. Recreations: singing; country dancing; gardening. Address: (b.) Department of Laboratory Medicine, Ruchill Hospital, Glasgow; T.-041-946 7120.

Fannin, A. Lorraine, BA (Hons), DipEd. Director, Scottish Publishers Association, since 1987; b. Belfast; m., Nigel Fannin; 2 s.; 1 d. Educ. Victoria College, Belfast; Queen's University, Belfast; Reading University. Teacher of Modern Languages, Henley-on-Thames and Edinburgh; opened children's bookshop, 1979; Partner, Whigmaleerie Story Cassettes, since 1985. Recreations: theatre; gardening; antique-hunting; reading. Address: (b.) 137 Dundee Street, Edinburgh, EH11 1BG; T.-031-228 6866.

Fargus, Col. Brian Alfred, OBE, DL. Deputy Lieutenant, Midlothian, since 1986; b. 3.1.18, Ollerton; m., Shiona Margaret Lay MacKichan; 1 s.; 1 d. Educ. Cargilfield; Rugby; Royal Military College, Sandhurst; Staff College, Camberley. Commissioned The Royal Scots, 1938; served Hong Kong, 1938-41, and North West Europe - Adjutant, 8th Bn., The Royal Scots, 1944-45; C.O. Depot The Royal Scots, 1957-59; Senior Intelligence Officer, Middle East Command, 1966-67; Colonel General Staff, HQ Scotland, 1968-70; Military Attache, British Embassy, Pretoria, 1971-72; Assistant Regimental Secretary, then Regimental Secretary, The Royal Scots, 1973-83. Recreations: golf; gardening; fishing. Address: St. Arvans, Nisbet Road, Gullane, East Lothian, EH31 2BQ; T.-0620 84 2440.

Farley-Sutton, Captain Colin David, CEng, EurIng, FIMechE, DL. Independent Consulting Engineer; Deputy Lieutenant, Caithness, since 1986; b. 20.12.31, Rugby; m., Sheila Wilson Baldwin; 2 s.; 2 d. Educ. Rugby College of Technology and Arts; RN Engineering College, Plymouth; RN College, Greenwich. Royal Navy, 1950-82 (Captain Superintendent, HMS Vulcan, Dounreay, 1980-82); Bookseller, Thurso, 1983-87; Lecturer, Thurso Technical College, 1984-87; President, Caithness Branch, Red Cross, since 1991. Address: (h.) Shepherd's Cottage, Lynegar, Watten, Caithness, KW1 5YJ; T.-Watten 697.

Farmer, John Gregory, BSc, PhD, CChem, FRSC. Senior Lecturer in Environmental Chemistry, Edinburgh University, since 1990; b. 18.2.47, Market Bosworth; m., Margaret Ann McClimont, 2 s.; 1 d. Educ. Kilmarnock Academy; Glasgow University. Post-Doctoral Investigator, Woods Hole Oceanographic Institution, Mass., USA, 1972-74; Research Assistant and Fellow, Department of Forensic Medicine and Science, Glasgow University, 1974-86; Lecturer in Environmental Chemistry, Edinburgh University, 1987-90. Chairman, 8th International Conference on Heavy Metals in the Environment, Edinburgh, 1991. Recreations: football; cricket; hill walking. Address: Department of Chemistry, Edinburgh University, West Mains Road, Edinburgh; T.-031-650 4757.

Farmer, Tom, CBE. Chairman and Chief Executive, Kwik-Fit Holdings PLC, since 1984; b. 10.7.40, Edinburgh; m., Anne Drury Scott; 1 s.; 1 d. Educ. Holy Cross Academy. Address: (b.) 17 Corstorphine Road, Edinburgh; T.-031-337 9200.

Farquhar, Agnes B.F., MA, LLB. Senior Partner, R.D. Hunter & Co.; Member, Council, Law Society of Scotland, 1985-91, Member, Scottish Solicitors Discipline Tribunal; Member, Scottish Records Advisory Council; Kilmarnock; m., James W. McGirk (deceased); 1 s. Educ. Kilmarnock Academy; Glasgow University. Elder, Church of Scotland. Address: (h.) Moorfield, Cumnock, Ayrshire; T.-0290 21185.

Farquhar, Charles Don Petrie, JP, DL. Member, Dundee District Council, since 1974; b. 4.8.37, Dundee; m., Mary Martin Gardiner; 2 d. Educ. Stobswell Secondary School; Dundee Trades College; NCLC. Time-served engineer; elected Dundee Corporation, 1965; former Magistrate and Chairman of various Committees; served Royal Engineers (TRG NCO); Supervisory Staff, Plant Engineering Division, NCR; elected Dundee District Council, 1974; Lord Provost and Lord Lieutenant, City of Dundee District, 1975-77; Chairman, District Licensing Board and District Licensing Committee; Chairman, Tayside Committee for Employment of Disabled People. Recreations: fresh-water angling; numismatics; DIY; pool; golf. Address: (h.) 15 Sutherland Crescent, Dundee, DD2 2HP.

Farquhar, William John, MA, DSA, FHSM. Secretary, Scottish Health Service Advisory Council, since 1989; Secretary, Clinical Resource and Audit Group, NHS in Scotland, since 1989; b. 29.5.35, Maud, Aberdeenshire; m., Isabel Henderson Rusk; 4 s. Educ. Peterhead Academy; Aberdeen University; Manchester University. National Administrative Trainee, Scottish Health Service; Hospital Secretary, Whitehaven Hospital, Cumberland; Deputy Secretary and Treasurer, West Cumberland Hospital Management Committee; Regional Staff Officer, South-Eastern Regional Hospital Board; Deputy Secretary, Eastern Regional Hospital Board; Lothian Health Board: District Administrator, South Lothian District, then Administrator, Operational Services. Secretary, Scottish Health Service Planning Council, 1985-89; Director, Planning Unit, Scottish Home and Health Department, 1987-90; Council of Europe Medical Fellowship, 1988; Elder, Colinton Parish Church; Vice-Convener, Church of Scotland National Board for Mission, since 1991. Recreations: gardening; walking. Address: (h.) Craigengar, 7 Harelaw Road, Colinton, Edinburgh, EH13 0DR; T.-031-441 2169.

Farquhar, Angus Durie Miller, DL, MA, FRICS. Vice Lord Lieutenant, Aberdeenshire, since 1988 (DL, 1984); b. 27.3.35, Haydon Bridge; m., Alison Mary Farquharson of Finzean; 2 s.; 1 d. Educ. Trinity College, Glenalmond; Downing College, Cambridge. Chartered Surveyor, Estate Factor, Farmer and Forester; Council Member, Scottish Landowners Federation, 1980-88; Member: Regional Advisory Committee, Forestry Commission, since 1980; Nature Conservancy Committee for Scotland, 1986-91; Nature Conservancy Council for Scotland NE Committee, since 1991; President, Deeside Field Club; Hon. President, Kincardine/Deeside Scouts; Director, Lathallan School; Member, Church of Scotland Judicial Committee. Recreations: shooting; fishing; gardening; nature conservation. Address: (h.) Finzean House, Finzean, Banchory, Aberdeenshire, AB3 5ED; T.-033045 229.

Farquharson, Sister Barbara Frances, RSCJ, BD (Hons), DipPriEd, PGCE. Religious of the Society of the Sacred Heart, since 1962; Headmistress, Kilgraston School, Bridge of Earn, since 1987; b. 22.8.38, Glasgow. Educ. Elmwood School, Bothwell; Heythrop College, London University; Craiglockhart College of Education, Edinburgh. Teacher, 1960-67; Lecturer, Nkozi Teacher Training College, Uganda, 1967-71; Head of RE Department/Resident Mistress and Housemistress, Kilgraston School, 1974-87. Recreations: yoga; walking; reading; theatre; music; travel. Address: Kilgraston School, Convent of the Sacred Heart, Bridge of Earn, Perthshire, PH2 9BQ; T.-0738 812257.

Farquharson, Captain Colin Andrew, JP, DL, FRICS. Lord Lieutenant of Aberdeenshire, since 1987; Chartered Surveyor and Land Agent, since 1953; Member, Grampian Health Board, 1981-89; Director, MacRobert Farms (Douneside), 1971-87; b. 9.8.23; m., 1, Jean Sybil Mary Hamilton (deceased); 2 d.; 1 d. deceased; 2, Clodagh, JP, DL, widow of Major Ian Houldsworth of Dallas, Morayshire; 3 step s.; 2 step d. Educ. Rugby. Grenadier Guards, 1942-48; ADC to Field Marshal Sir Harald Alexander (Earl Alexander of Tunis), 1942-48; Member, Board of Management, Royal Cornhill Hospitals, 1962-74; Chairman, Gordon Local Health Council, 1975-81; DL, Aberdeenshire, 1966; Vice Lord Lieutenant, Aberdeenshire, 1983-87; Member, Queen's Bodyguard for Scotland (Royal Company of Archers), since 1964. Recreations: shooting; fishing; farming. Address: Whitehouse, Alford, Aberdeenshire, AB33 8DP.

Farquharson, Gordon Alexander, MA, DipEd. Head Teacher, Tobermory High School, since 1984; b. 7.2.42, Dumfries; m., Elizabeth M. Naismith; 1 s. Educ. Dumfries Academy; Edinburgh University; Moray House College of Education. Teacher of English, Dumfries Academy, 1966-70; Assistant Principal Teacher of English, Queen Anne High School, Dunfermline, 1970-72; Principal Teacher of English, Dunoon Grammar School, 1972-84. Elder, Church of Scotland; Director, Mull Little Theatre. Recreations: drama; choral singing. Address: (h.) Avoch, Western Road, Tobermory, Isle of Mull; T.-0688 2405.

Farquharson, Sir James Robbie, KBE, BSc, CEng, FICE. Upland farmer, since 1965; b. 1.11.03, Kirriemuir; m., Agnes Binny Graham; 2 s. Educ. Websters High School, Kirriemuir; Royal Technical College, Glasgow; Glasgow University. Trainee Civil Engineer, LMS Railway, 1923-25; Civil Engineer, Kenya and Uganda Railway, 1925-37; Tanganyika Railway: Assistant to General Manager, 1937-41, Chief Engineer, 1941-45; General Manager, 1945-48; Deputy General Manager and Chief Engineer, East African Railways andHarbours, 1948-52; General Manager, Sudan Railways, 1952-57; General Manager, East African Railways and Harbours, 1957-61; Assistant Crown Agent and Engineer-in-Chief, Crown Agents, 1961-65. Fellow, Scottish Council Development and Industry; Former Member, Executive Committee, Scottish Council Development and Industry; undertook missions to Nigeria, Malawi, Jordan and Philippines for Overseas Development Administration; advised African Development Board on transport matters. Publication: Tanganyika Transport, 1945. Recreation: farming in retirement. Address: (h.) Kinclune, Kirriemuir, Angus, DD8 5HX; T.-0575 74710.

Farrell, Sheriff James Aloysius, MA, LLB. Sheriff of Lothian and Borders, since 1986; b. 14.5.43, Glasgow; m., Jacqueline Allen; 2 d. Educ. St. Aloysius College; Glasgow University; Dundee University. Admitted to Faculty of Advocates, 1974; Advocate-Depute, 1979-83; Sheriff of Glasgow and Strathkelvin, 1984-85; Sheriff of South Strathclyde, Dumfries and Galloway, 1985-86. Recreations: sailing; cycling; hill-walking. Address: (b.) Sheriff's Chambers, Edinburgh; T.-031-226 7181.

Farrington, Dennis Joseph, BSc, DPhil, LLM, CChem, MRSC, FBIM. Deputy Secretary and Registrar, Stirling University, since 1986; b. 13.8.47, Ellesmere Port; m., Julia Baverstock; 1 s.; 1 d. Educ. Ellesmere Port County Grammar School; University of Kent; University of Ulster. Civil Service, 1972-81: Customs and Excise, 1972-73, Northern Ireland Office, 1973-78, HM Stationery Office, 1978-81; Personnel Officer, Hull University, 1981, Administrative Secretary, 1986. Secretary, Conference of University Administrators, 1982-88; Chairman, Cancer Research Campaign, Stirling, 1987-91. Publication: Universities and the Law (Co-author), 1990. Recreations: DIY; home computing. Address: (b.) Stirling University, Stirling, FK9 4LA; T.-0786 67020.

Farry, James. Chief Executive, The Scottish Football Association Ltd., since 1990 (Secretary, The Scottish Football League, 1979-89); 1.7.54, Glasgow; m., Elaine Margaret; 1 s.; 1 d. Educ. Queens Park Secondary School; Hunter High School; Claremont High School. Recreations: occasional fishing; regular spectating football matches. Address: (b.) 6 Park Gardens, Glasgow, G3 7YF; T.-041-332 6372.

Fasken, Robert Alexander, CBE. Governor, Eden Court Theatre, Inverness; Honorary President, Scottish Youth Hostels Association; b. 5.11.22, Edinburgh; m., Nancy Blanch; 1 s. Educ. George Watson's College. Department of Agriculture and Fisheries for Scotland, 1939-65; Secretary, Advisory Panel on Highlands and Islands, 1961-65; Secretary, Highlands and Islands Development Board, 1965-75; Member, HIDB, 1975-84; Chairman, Highlands and Islands Tourism Council, 1976-84; Member, Scottish Tourist Board, 1975-84. Recreations: reading; chess; gardening. Address: (h.) 79 Stratherrick Road, Inverness, IV2 4LL; T.-0463 233378.

Fass, Michael J., MA. Director, West Lothian Enterprise Ltd., since 1983; b. 22.6.44, Sonning, Berks; m., Iola Mary Ashton; 1 s.; 2 d. Educ. Eton College; Trinity College, Cambridge; IMD, Lausanne. Served C Squadron (Berkshire Yeomanry) Berkshire and Westminster Dragoons (TA), 1963-68; worked in industry at Hays Wharf, Miles Druce-GKN, and DTI's Small Firms Service; Director, Prince's Scottish Youth Business Trust; Honorary Fellow, Edinburgh University; Lay Minister, St. John's Church, Princes Street, Edinburgh; Corporate Member's Representative, Scottish Council Development and Industry. Publication: The Vital Economy, Integrating Training and Enterprise (Co-Author). Address: 20 Fountainhall Road, Edinburgh, EH9 2NN.

Faulkner, Professor Douglas, WhSch, PhD, RCNC, FEng, FRINA, FIStructE, FRSA, MSNAME. Professor and Head, Department of Naval Architecture and Ocean Engineering, Glasgow University; b. 29.12.29, Gibraltar; m., Isobel Parker Campbell; 3 d. Educ. Sutton High School, Plymouth; HM Dockyard Technical College, Devonport; Royal Naval College, Greenwich. Aircraft carrier design, 1955-57; production engineering, 1957-59; structural research, NCRE Dunfermline, 1959-63; Assistant Professor of Naval Construction, RNC, Greenwich, 1963-66; Structural Adviser to Ship Department, Bath, 1966-68; Naval Construction Officer attached to British Embassy, Washington DC, 1968-70; Member, Ship Research Committee, National Academy of Sciences, 1968-71; Research Associate and Defence Fellow, MIT, 1970-71; Structural Adviser, Ship Department, Bath, and Merrison Box Girder Bridge Committee, 1971-73; UK Representative, Standing Committee, International Ship Structures Congress, 1973-85; Member, Marine Technology Board, Defence Scientific Advisory Council; Head, Department of Naval Architecture and Ocean Engineering, Glasgow University, since 1973; Board of Governors, BMT Quality Assurance Ltd., since 1990; David W. Taylor Medal, Society of Naval Architects and Marine Engineeers. Recreations: hill-walking; music; chess; GO. Address: (h.) 57 Bellshaugh Place, Glasgow, G12 OPF; T.-041-357 1748.

Fawkes, Rev. George Miller Allan, BA, BSc, JP. Minister, Lonmay linked with Rathen West, since 1979; b. 20.3.35, Glasgow; m., Beatrice B.A. Forbes; 1 s.; 1 d. Educ. Irvine Royal Academy; Glasgow University; Open University; Aberdeen University. FSS, 1961-71; MInstP, 1976-80. Statistician, Pilkington Bros., St. Helens, 1957-58; Education Officer, RAF, 1958-61; Statistician, Stewarts and Lloyds, Clydesdale Works, 1961-64; Lecturer, Inverness Technical College, 1964-77. Buchan Presbytery: Moderator, 1986-87, Convener, Maintenance of the Ministry Committee, 1984-88; Chaplain, HM Prison, Peterhead, since 1988. Recreations: reading; family history; relationship between religion and science; photography. Address: The Manse, Lonmay, Fraserburgh, AB4 4UJ; T.-0346 32227.

Fee, Kenneth, MA, FRCS. Editor, Scots Independent, since 1985; b. 14.7.31, Glasgow; m., Margery Anne Dougan; 3 s.; 1 d. Educ. Gourock High School; Hamilton Academy; Glasgow University. President, Glasgow University SRC and Scottish Union of Students; Editor, Gum, Ygorra and GU Guardian; sometime in military intelligence; Sub-Editor, Glasgow Herald; Strathclyde Publishing Group; itinerant teaching; Member, Scottish Executive, NASUWT, since 1983; various SNP branch, constituency and national offices, since 1973. Publication: How to Grow Fat and Free. Recreations: chess; gastronomy; campaigning. Address: (h.) 157 Urrdale Road, Dumbreck, G41 5DG; T.-041-427 0117.

Fenton, Professor Alexander, CBE, MA, BA, DLitt, HonDLitt (Aberdeen), FRSE, FSA, FRSGS, FSA Scot. Director, National Museum of Antiquities of Scotland, 1978-85; Research Director, National Museums of Scotland, 1985-89; Director, European Ethnological Research Centre, since 1989; Chair of Scottish Studies and Director, School of Scottish Studies, Edinburgh University, since 1990; b. 26.6.29, Shotts; m., Evelyn Elizabeth Hunter; 2 d. Educ. Turriff Academy; Aberdeen University; Cambridge University. Senior Assistant Editor, Scottish National Dictionary, 1955-59; part-time Lecturer, English as a Foreign Language, Edinburgh University, 1958-60; National Museum of Antiquities of Scotland: Assistant Keeper, 1959-75, Deputy Keeper, 1975-78; part-time Lecturer, Department of Scottish History, Edinburgh University, 1974-80; Honorary Fellow, School of Scottish Studies, since 1969; Foreign Member: Royal Gustav Adolf Academy, Sweden, since 1978, Royal Danish Academy of Sciences and Letters, since 1979; Honorary Member: Volkskundliche Kommission fur Westfalen, since 1980, Hungarian Ethnographical Society, since 1983; Jury Member, Europa Prize for Folk Art, since 1975; President, Permanent International Committee, International Secretariat for Research on the History of Agricultural Implements; Secretary, Permanently Standing Organising Board, European Ethnological Atlas; President, Scottish Vernacular Buildings Working Group; President, Scottish Country Life Museums Trust; Secretary and Trustee, Friends of the Dictionary of the Older Scottish Tongue; Secretary and Trustee, Scottish Land Inheritance Fund; Co-Editor: Tools and Tillage, since 1968, The Review of Scottish Culture, since 1984. Publications: The Various Names of Shetland, 1973, 1977; Scottish Country Life, 1976 (Scottish

Arts Council Book Award); The Diary of a Parish Clerk (translation from Danish), 1976; The Island Blackhouse, A Guide to the Blackhouse at 42 Arnol, Lewis, 1978 (re-issued, 1989); A Farming Township, A Guide to Auchindrain, Museum of Argyll Farming Life, 1978; The Northern Isles, Orkney and Shetland, 1978 (Dag Stromback Award); The Rural Architecture of Scotland (Co-author), 1981; The Shape of the Past 1, 1985; If All The World Were a Blackbird (translation from Hungarian), 1985; The Shape of the Past II, 1986; 'Wirds an' Wark 'e Seasons Roon on an Aberdeenshire Farm, 1987; Country Life in Scotland, Our Rural Past, 1987; Scottish Country Life, 1989; The Turra Coo, 1989. Recreation: languages. Address: (b.) European Ethnological Research Centre, National Museums of Scotland, Queen Street, Edinburgh, EH2 1JD; T.-031-225 7534.

Fenton, Professor George Wallace, MB, FRCPEdin, FRCPsych, MRCP, DPM. Professor of Psychiatry, Dundee University, since 1983; Honorary Consultant Psychiatrist, Tayside Health Board, since 1983; Chairman, Scottish Division, Royal College of Psychiatrists; b. 30.7.31, Londonderry; m.; 1 s. Educ. Ballymena Academy; Queen's University, Belfast. Lecturer, Academic Department of Psychiatry, Middlesex Hospital, 1964-66; Maudsley Hospital, London: Consultant Psychiatrist, 1967-75, Consultant in Charge, Epilepsy Unit, 1969-75, Consultant Neurophysiologist, 1968-75; Senior Lecturer, Institute of Psychiatry, London University, 1967-75; Professor of Mental Health, Queen's University, Belfast, 1976-83. Publications: Event Related Potentials in Personality and Psychopathology (Co-author), 1982; numerous papers on clinical neurophysiology and neuropsychiatry. Recreations: sailing; history; literature. Address: (b.) University Department of Psychiatry, Ninewells Hospital and Medical School, Dundee, DD1 9SY; T.-Dundee 60111, Ext. 3111.

Fenwick, Hubert Walter Wandesford. Architectural Historian and Lecturer; Chairman, Royal Martyr Church Union; b. 17.7.16, Glasgow. Educ. Huntley School, New Zealand; Royal Grammar School, Newcastle-upon-Tyne. Architectural student; qualified, 1950; office of Ian G. Lindsay, then Lorimer & Matthew, Edinburgh; gave up architectural career, 1958; RIBA Examiner for Scotland in History of Architecture, until post abolished; Assistant Secretary and PRO, Scottish Georgian Society, 1960-65; Council Member, Cockburn Association, 1966; Scottish Editor, Church Illustrated, 1959-64; Editor and Manager, Edinburgh Tatler and Glasgow Illustrated, 1966-67; regular contributor to Scots Magazine, 25 years, and other journals. Publications: Architect Royal; Auld Alliance; Scotland's Historic Buildings; Scotland's Castles; Chateaux of France; Scotland's Abbeys and Cathedrals; View of the Lowlands; Scottish Baronial Houses. Recreations: foreign travel; architectural history; sketching and photography (for own books and articles); gardening. Address: 15 Randolph Crescent, Edinburgh, 3; T.-031-225 7982.

Fenwick, Kenneth George, FIH. Director of Housing, Angus District Council, since 1987; b. 28.7.38, Forfar; m., Marion Elizabeth Anderson; 3 s.; 1 step d. Educ. Forfar Academy; Dundee Technical College. Town Planning Assistant, Angus County Council, 1956-57 and 1960-62 (National Service, RAF, 1958-60); Housing Assistant, Glenrothes Development Corporation, 1962-65; Housing Manager, Selkirk Town Council, 1965-66; District Housing Officer, Glenrothes Development Corporation, 1966-67; Assistant Town Factor, then Town Factor, Forfar Town Council, 1967-75; Depute Director/Area Housing Manager, Angus District Council, 1975-76; Director of Housing, Glenrothes Development Corporation, 1976-82; Director of Housing, Kirkcaldy District Council, 1982-87. Recreations: football; swimming; hill-walking; reading. Address: (b.) County Buildings, Forfar, Angus; T.-Forfar 65101.

Ferguson, Professor Allister Ian, BSc, MA, PhD, FInstP, CPhys. Professor of Photonics, Strathclyde University, since 1988; b. 10.12.51, Aberdeen; m., Kathleen Ann Challenger. Educ. Aberdeen Academy; St. Andrews University. Lindemann Fellow, Stanford University, 1977-79; SERC Research Fellow, St. Andrews, 1979-81; SERC Advanced Fellow, Oxford, 1981-86; Junior Research Fellow, Merton College, Oxford, 1981-83; Lecturer, then Senior Lecturer, Southampton University, 1983-88. Address: (b.) Department of Physics and Applied Physics, Strathclyde University, Glasgow, G4 0NG; T.-041-552 4400.

Ferguson, Professor Anne, PhD, FRCP, FRCPath, FRSE. Professor of Gastroenterology, Edinburgh University, since 1987; b. 26.7.41, Glasgow; 1 s.; 1 d. Educ. Notre Dame High School; Glasgow University. Appointments in medicine and immunology, Glasgow and Edinburgh Universities. Address: (b.) Western General Hospital, Crewe Road, Edinburgh EH4 2XU.

Ferguson, Professor James, ARCST, BSc, PhD, DSc, FRSC, CChem. Professor, Department of Chemistry and Head, Fibre and Textile Research Unit, Strathclyde University, since 1991 (Reader, 1981-91); b. 30.3.35, Paisley; m., Jean Leslie; 2 s.; 2 d. Educ. Camphill Secondary School, Paisley; Glasgow University; Royal College of Science and Technology. Research Chemist, Shell Research, 1960-63; Lecturer in Textile Chemistry, Strathclyde University, 1963-76; Senior Lecturer, 1976-81; Consultant to UNIDO, 1985 and 1987. Deacon, Incorporation of Weavers of Glasgow, 1984-88; President, British Society of Rheology, 1988-90; Visiting Professor, Ohio University, 1988. Recreations: golf; travel. Address: 29 Limetree Crescent, Newton Mearns, Glasgow, G77 5BJ; T.-041-639 3405.

Ferguson, James Brown Provan, MB, ChB, DipSocMed, FFPHM. Chief Administrative Medical Officer, Director of Public Health, Lanarkshire Health Board, since 1988; b. 23.10.35, Armadale; m., Sheila Capstick; 3 d. Educ. Bathgate Academy; Edinburgh University. Group Medical Superintendent, Edinburgh Northern Hospitals; District Medical Officer, North Lothian District, Lothian Health Board; Senior Medical Officer, Scottish Home and Health Department. Elder, Old Parish Church, Uddingston. Recreations: art; reading; walking. Address: (b.) Lanarkshire Health Board, 14 Beckford Street, Hamilton, ML3 0TA.

Ferguson, James Gordon Dickson, BA. Chairman, Stewart Ivory and Company Limited, since 1989; b. 12.11.47, Belfast; m., Nicola Hilland Stewart; 2 s.; 1 d. Educ. Winchester College; Trinity College, Dublin. Stewart Ivory (formerly Stewart Fund Managers): joined 1970, Director, 1974; Former Deputy Chairman, Association of Investment Trust Companies; Non-Executive Director: Value and Income Trust PLC, OLIM Convertible Trust PLC. Address: (b.) 45 Charlotte Square, Edinburgh EH2 4HW; T.-031-226 3271.

Ferguson, James Murray, BSc (Econ), MPhil, DipEd, FCIS, FIPM, FBIM, FRSA, FSA Scot. Principal and Chief Executive, Aberdeen College of Further Education, since 1990; b. 21.4.28, Almondbank, Perthshire; m., Moira McDougall, BA; 2 d. Educ. Perth Academy; London University; Edinburgh University; Dundee University; Moray House College of Education. Military Service, 1946-79: full-time, Army Emergency Reserve, Territorials, T&AVR; Regular Army Reserve of Officers (final rank of Major); variety of business appointments, mainly in insurance, investment and finance, 1952-64; lectureships in range of management subjects, various higher educational establishments, 1965-76; Principal, Elmwood College, Fife, 1976-82; Principal, Aberdeen College of Commerce, 1982-90. Governor: Further Education Staff College, Coombe Lodge, Bristol, 1982-87, Aberdeen College of Education, 1983-87. Recreations: sporting: badminton, tennis, hill-walking; non-sporting: reading, writing, public speaking, local history studies. Address: (h.) 45 Desswood Place, Aberdeen, AB2 4EE; T.-Aberdeen 631480.

Ferguson, Rev. John, Lth, BD. Minister of Portree, since 1980; b. 30.3.37, North Uist; m., Effie MacPhail; 2 s.; 1 d. Educ. Bayhead Junior Secondary School; Glasgow University and Trinity College. Labourer, 1952-59; Faith Mission Bible College, 1959-61; evangelism, 1961-66; Assistant, Strath, Skye, 1966-68; student, 1968-73; Minister, Cross, Ness, 1973-80. Recreations: art; fishing; gardening. Address: The Manse, Viewfield Road, Portree, IV51 9ES; T.-0478 2019.

Ferguson, Kenneth Gordon, OBE, FRICS, ACIOB, JP. Senior Partner, Ferguson and Partners, Chartered Quantity Surveyors, since 1979; Member, City of Edinburgh District Council, since 1977; b. 17.2.44, Edinburgh; m., Jennifer Day Love; 2 d. Educ. Leith Academy; Heriot-Watt University; Napier College. Vice-President, Scottish Conservative and Unionist Association, 1985-87; Chairman, Planning Committee, Edinburgh District Council, 1983-84. Recreations: numismatics; writing; travel. Address: (h.) Glebeside, 2 Pentland Avenue, Edinburgh, EH13 0HZ; T.-031-441 3046.

Ferguson, Moira. Executive Officer/Company Secretary, Scottish Pre-school Play Association, since 1988; b. 28.5.35, Glasgow; m., Douglas Ferguson; 3 d. Educ. Glasgow High School for Girls. J. & P. Coats; Glasgow Education Department; Greater Glasgow Health Board. Chairman, SPPA, 1982-84; Chairman, Scope in Scotland, 1984-85; Membr, Board, Scottish Child and Family Alliance. Recreations: reading; theatre; Open University. Address: (b.) 14 Elliot Place, Glasgow, G3 8EP; T.-041-221 4148.

Ferguson, Patricia Ann, BSc, JP. Chairman, Fife Health Board, since 1987; Director, Hatrick-Bruce Group, since 1977; b. Dundee; m., Euan Ferguson. Educ. St. Margaret's, Aberdeen; St. Andrews University; Royal Military College of Science. Member, Fife Health Board, since 1983. Recreation: dressage. Address: Lydiard House, Milton of Balgomie, Fife.

Ferguson, Robert Greig, MREHIS, MIWM. Director of Environmental Health, Caithness District Council, since 1974; b. 30.7.42, Saltcoats, Ayrshire; m., Ruth; 1 s.; 2 d. Educ. Ardrossan Academy; School of Building, Cambuslang; David Dale College, Glasgow; Coatbridge Technical College; Dundee University. Student Sanitary Inspector, Ayr County Council, 1961-65; Assistant Sanitary Inspector: Ayr County Council, 1965-66, Clackmannan County Council, 1966-67; District Sanitary Inspector, Angus County Council, 1967-70; Caithness County Council: Depute County Sanitary Inspector, 1970-71, County Sanitary Inspector, 1971-74. Recreations: golf; snooker; cartophily; bowls. Address: (b.) Council Offices, 77 High Street, Wick; T.-Wick 3761, Ext. 236.

Ferguson, Rev. Ronald, MA, BD, ThM. Minister, St. Magnus Cathedral, Orkney, since 1990 (Leader, Iona Community, 1981-88); b. 27.10.39, Dunfermline; m., Cristine Jane Walker; 2 s.; 1 d. Educ. Beath High School, Cowdenbeath; St. Andrews University; Edinburgh University; Duke University. Journalist, Fife and Edinburgh, 1956-63; University, 1963-71; ordained Minister, Church of Scotland, 1972; Minister, Easterhouse, Glasgow, 1971-79; exchange year with United Church of Canada, 1979-80; Deputy Warden, Iona Abbey, 1980-81. Publications: Geoff: A Life of Geoffrey M. Shaw, 1979; Grace and Dysentery, 1986; Chasing the Wild Goose, 1988; The Whole Earth Shall Cry Glory (Co-Editor), 1985; George MacLeod, 1990. Recreation: supporting Cowdenbeath Football Club. Address:

(h.) Cathedral Manse, Berstane Road, Kirkwall, Orkney, KW15 1NA; T.-0856 3312.

Ferguson, William James. Farmer, since 1954; Vice Chairman, Aberdeen and District Milk Marketing Board; Vice Chairman, Scottish Agricultural College; Deputy Lieutenant, Grampian Region; b. 3.4.33, Aberdeen; m., Carroll Isobella Milne; 1 s.; 3 d. Educ. Turriff Academy; North of Scotland College of Agriculture. National Service, 1st Bn., Gordon Highlanders, 1952-54, serving in Malaya during the emergency. Member, Scottish Country Life Museums Trust Ltd. Recreations: golf; field sports. Address: Rothiebrisbane, Fyvie, Turriff, Aberdeenshire, AB53 8LE; T.-0651 891 213.

Fergusson of Kilkerran, Sir Charles, 9th Bt; b. 10.5.31.

Fergusson, Professor David Alexander Syme. MA, BD, DPhil. Professor of Systematic Theology, Aberdeen University, since 1990; b. 3.8.56, Glasgow; m., Margot McIndoe; 1 s. Educ. Kelvinside Academy; Glasgow University; Edinburgh University; Oxford University. Assistant Minister, St. Nicholas Church, Lanark, 1983-84; Associate Minister, St. Mungo's Church, Cumbernauld, 1984-86; Lecturer, Edinburgh University, 1986-90. Chaplain to Moderator of the General Assembly, 1989-90. Publication: Bultmann, 1992. Recreations: football; golf; jogging. Address: 44 Ashley Road, Aberdeen, AB1 6RT; T.-0224 583817.

Fergusson, James A., MB, ChB, MRCGP. Regional Medical Officer, Scottish Home and Health Department, 1973-89; b. 17.7.24, Glasgow; m., Christine Irvine; 2 s.; 1 d. Educ. Hillhead High School; Glasgow University. Medical Assistant: Gynaecology Department, Western Infirmary, Glasgow, 1948, Obstetric Department, Stobhill Hospital, Glasgow, 1948-49, Medical Department, Victoria Infirmary, Glasgow, 1949; General Medical Practitioner, Glasgow, 1949-73; Physician, Cowglen Hospital, 1964-73. Session Clerk, Giffnock South Parish Church. Publication: Potassium Studies in Elderly, 1971. Recreations: golf; fishing; bowls. Address: (h.) 10 Dorian Drive, Glasgow, G76 7NP; T.-041-638 9847.

Fernie, Professor Eric Campbell, BA, FSA, FSA Scot. Watson Gordon Professor of Fine Art, Edinburgh University, since 1984 (Dean, Faculty of Arts, since 1989); Chairman, Ancient Monuments Board for Scotland, since 1989; b. 9.6.39, Edinburgh; m., Margaret Lorraine; 1 s.; 2 d. Educ. Marist Brothers College, Johannesburg; Witwatersrand University; London University. Lecturer, Witwatersrand University, 1964-67; East Anglia University: Lecturer, 1967-74, Senior Lecturer, 1974-84, Dean, School of Fine Art and Music, 1977-81. Publications: The Architecture of the Anglo-Saxons; The Communar and Pitancer Rolls of Norwich Cathedral Priory (Co-author). Address: (b.) 19 George Square, Edinburgh, EH8 9LD; T.-031-667 1011.

Ferrell, William Russell MBChB, PhD. Reader in Physiology, Glasgow University, since 1991; b. 5.3.49, St. Louis, USA; m., Anne Mary Scobie; 3 s.; 1 d. Educ. St. Aloysius College, Glasgow; Glasgow University. House Officer, NHS, 1973-74; Lecturer in Physiology, 1977; Senior Lecturer in Physiology, 1989. Recreations: DIY; computing; classical music. Address: (b.) Institute of Physiology, Glasgow University, Glasgow, G12 8QQ; T.-041-339 8855, Ext. 4762.

Ferrier, Alan Gray, TD, DL. Manager, Norwich Union Insurance Group, Wick, since 1973; b. 23.5.39, Glasgow; m., Jean; 1 s.; 1 d. Educ. Hillhead High School; Strathclyde University. Joined Norwich Union, 1962; commissioned TA, 1964; appointed Company Commander, Infantry, 1976;

Deputy Lieutenant, Caithness, since 1984; Squadron Commander,236 Field Squadron (ADR) (V), Royal Engineers, 1986-90; Chairman, Royal British Legion and Earl Haig Fund Wick; Secretary and Past President, Rotary Club of Wick; Vice Chairman, Northern Area, Committee of Highland TAVRA; Company Commander, 3/51 Highland Volunteers Wick, 1976-81. Recreation: fishing. Address: (h.) 81 Willow Bank, Wick, Caithness, KW1 4PE; T.-0955 3178.

Ferrier, Professor Robert Patton, MA (Cantab), BSc, PhD, FInstP, FRSE. Professor of Natural Philosophy, Glasgow University, since 1973; Head, Department of Physics and Astronomy, since 1989; b. 4.1.34, Dundee; m., Valerie Jane Duncan; 2 s.; 1 d. Educ. Morgan Academy, Dundee; Queen's College, Dundee, St. Andrews University. Scientific Officer, AERE Harwell, 1959-61; Research Associate, Massachusetts Institute of Technology, 1961-62; Senior Research Assistant, Cavendish Laboratory, Cambridge, 1962-65; Fellow, Fitzwilliam College, Cambridge, 1964-73; Assistant Director of Research, Cavendish Laboratory, Cambridge, 1965-71; Lecturer in Physics, Cambridge University, 1971-73; Guest Scientist, IBM Research Division, California, 1972-73. Member, Physics Committee, SERC, 1979-82 (Chairman, Semiconductor and Surface Physics Sub-Committee, 1979-82). Recreations: tennis; reading crime novels; garden and house maintenance. Address: Department of Physics and Astronomy, The University, Glasgow, G12 8QQ; T.-041-330 5388.

Fewson, Professor Charles Arthur, BSc, PhD, FRSE, FIBiol. Titular Professor, Department of Biochemistry, Glasgow University, since 1982; b. 8.9.37, Selby, Yorkshire; m., Margaret C.R. Moir; 2 d. Educ. Hymers College, Hull; Nottingham University; Bristol University. Research Fellow, Cornell University, New York, 1961-63; Department of Biochemistry, Glasgow University: Assistant Lecturer, 1963-64, Lecturer, 1964-68, Senior Lecturer, 1968-79, Reader, 1979-82. Recreation: watching cricket. Address: (h.) 39 Falkland Street, Glasgow, G12 9QZ; T.-041-339 1304.

Fiddes, Sheriff James Raffan, QC (Scot), MA, BA. Sheriff of South Strathclyde, Dumfries and Galloway, at Hamilton, 1977-88; b. 1.2.19. Educ. Aberdeen Grammar School; Glasgow University and Balliol College, Oxford. Advocate, 1948. Recreations: reading the classics; walking. Address: (h.) 23 South Learmonth Gardens, Edinburgh, EH4 1EZ; T.-031-332 1431.

Fife, 3rd Duke of (James George Alexander Bannerman Carnegie). Master of Southesk; b. 23.9.29; m., Hon. Caroline Cicely-Dewar (m. diss.); 1 s.; 1 d. Educ. Gordonstoun. National Service, Scots Guards, Malaya, 1948-50; Royal Agricultural College; Clothworkers' Company and Freeman, City of London; President, ABA, 1959-73, Vice-Patron, 1973; Ships President, HMS Fife, 1964-87; a Vice-Patron, Braemar Royal Highland Society; a Vice-President, British Olympic Association. Address: Elsick House, Stonehaven, Kincardineshire, AB3 2NT.

Findlay, Donald Russell, QC, LLB (Hons). Advocate, since 1975; Member, Lothian Health Board, 1987-91; Director, Glasgow Rangers FC; b. 17.3.51, Cowdenbeath; m., Jennifer E. Borrowman. Educ. Harris Academy, Dundee; Dundee University. Sometime Lecturer in Commercial Law, Heriot-Watt University. Recreations: Glasgow Rangers FC; Egyptology; archaeology; wine; ethics. Address: (b.) Advocates Library, Parliament House, Parliament Square, Edinburgh, EH1 1RF; T.-031-226 2881.

Findlay, James A.M., MBChB, FRCS. Consultant Surgeon, Royal Alexandra Hospital, Paisley, since 1972; part-time Unit Medical Officer, since 1990; b. 1.1.35, Fraserburgh; m., Dr. Mary Findlay; 1 s.; 2 d. Educ. Fraserburgh Academy;

Aberdeen University. House Officer, 1959-60; Anatomy Departments, Aberdeen University, Glasgow University, 1960-62; Chief Resident, Orthopaedics, Ottawa University, 1969-70; Senior Registrar, Orthopaedics, Leeds, 1970-72. Recreations: economics; Scottish home rule. Address: (h.) 27 Berryhill Drive, Giffnock, G46 7AA; T.-041-638 5901.

Findlay, Richard, DDA, FInstD. Managing Director, Radio Forth, since 1977; m., Elspeth; 2 s.; 1 d. Educ. Royal Scottish Academy of Music and Drama. Chairman, Association of Independent Radio Contractors, 1984-86 and 1988-90; former Hon. President, Heriot Watt University Students Association and Member, University Court; Director: Scottish and Irish Radio Sales Ltd., Radio Clyde Holdings PLC, Lothian Health Board, Moray Firth Radio Ltd., Central FM (Holdings) Ltd; Chairman, Radio Tay Ltd.; Chairman, Radio Borders Ltd. Address (b.) Radio Forth Ltd., Forth House, Forth Street, Edinburgh.

Findlay, Richard Martin, LLB, NP. Partner, Tods Murray WS, Edinburgh, since 1990 (Partner, Ranken & Reid SSC, Edinburgh, 1979-90); b. 18.12.51, Aberdeen. Educ. Gordon Schools, Huntly; Aberdeen University. Trained, Wilsone & Duffus, Advocates, Aberdeen; Legal Assistant, Commercial Department, Maclay Murray & Spens, Glasgow and Edinburgh, 1975-78. Company Secretary: Edinburgh Capital Group Limited, Edinburgh Arts and Entertainment Limited; Director, West Lothian Youth Theatre and Edinburgh International Jazz Festival. Recreations: music; theatre; opera; cinema. Address: (b.) 66 Queen Street, Edinburgh, EH2 4NE; T.-031-226 4771.

Fine, Anne, BA (Hons). Writer; b. 7.12.47, Leicester; m., Kit; 2 d. Educ. Northampton High School for Girls; Warwick University. Published books: for children: The Summer-house Loon, 1978, The Other, Darker Ned, 1979, The Stone Menagerie, 1980, Round Behind the Ice-house, 1981, The Granny Project, 1983, Scaredy Cat, 1985, Anneli the Art Hater, 1986, Madame Doubtfire, 1987, Crummy Mummy & Me, 1988, A Pack of Liars, 1988, Bill's New Frock, 1989, Goggle-Eyes, 1989; for adults: The Killjoy, 1987, Taking the Devil's Advice, 1990. Winner. Carnegie Medal, 1989; Guardian Children's Fiction Award, 1989. Recreations: reading; walking. Address: (b.) c/o Murray Pollinger, 4 Garrick Street, London, WC2E 9BH.

Fink, Professor George, MB, BS, MD, MA, DPhil, FRSE. Director, MRC Brain Metabolism Unit, since 1980; Honorary Professor, Edinburgh University, since 1984; b. 13.11.36, Vienna; m., Ann Elizabeth; 1 s.; 1 d. Educ. Melbourne High School; Melbourne University; Hertford College, Oxford. House Officer appointments, Royal Melbourne and Alfred Hospitals, 1961-62; Demonstrator and Lecturer, Department of Anatomy, Monash University, 1963-64; Nuffield Dominions Demonstrator, Oxford, 1965-67; Senior Lecturer, Monash University, 1968-71; University Lecturer, Oxford, 1971-80; Official Fellow and Tutor in Physiology and Medicine, Brasenose College, Oxford, 1974-80. Member of Council, European Neuroscience Association, 1980-82; President, European Neuroendocrine Association, since 1991. Publications: Neuropeptides: Basic and Clinical Aspects (Co-Editor), 1982; Neuroendocrine Molecular Biology (Co-Editor), 1986; 250 papers on neuroendocrinology and psychoneuroendocrinology. Recreations: skiing and squash. Address: (b.) MRC Brain Metabolism Unit, Department of Pharmacology, Edinburgh University, 1 George Square, Edinburgh, EH8 9JZ; T.-031-650 3548.

Finlay, Ian, CBE, MA, HRSA, FRSA. Professor of Antiquities, Royal Scottish Academy; Writer and Art Historian; b. 2.12.06, Auckland, New Zealand; m., Mary Scott Pringle; 2 s.; 1 d. Educ. Edinburgh Academy; Edinburgh University. Joined Royal Scottish Museum, 1932; Deputy

Regional Information Officer Scotland (Ministry of Information), 1942-45; Secretary, Royal Fine Art Commission for Scotland, 1953-61; Royal Scottish Museum: Keeper, Department of Art and Ethnography, 1955-61, Director, 1961-71. Former Member: International Council of Museums, Counseil de Direction Gazette des Beaux Arts; former Vice-Chairman, Scottish Arts Council; Freeman, City of London; Member, Livery Worshipful Company of Goldsmiths; Guest, State Department, US, 1960. Publications: Scotland, 1945; Scottish Art, 1945; Art in Scotland, 1948; Scottish Crafts, 1948; A History of Scottish Gold and Silver Work, 1956; Scotland (enlarged edition), 1957; The Lothians, 1960; The Highlands, 1963; The Lowlands, 1967; Celtic Art: An Introduction, 1973; Priceless Heritage: The Future of Museums, 1977; Columba, 1979 (Scottish Arts Council Award); A History of Scottish Gold and Silver Work (new edition, 1991). Address: (h.) Currie Riggs, Balerno, Midlothian, EH14 5AG; T.-031-449 4249.

Finlayson, David Munro, BSc, PhD. Senior Lecturer in Physics, St. Andrews University, since 1964; b. 2.5.19, Dunnet, Caithness; m., Angela; 2 d. Educ. Wick High School; St. Andrews University. Army Service, 1940-46 (Sgt., Royal Artillery, Captain, REME); Visiting Lecturer, Purdue University, Indiana, 1951-52; Lecturer in Physics, Aberdeen University, 1952-64. St. Andrews University: Member of Court, 1973-77, Member of Senate, 1973-82, Dean of Science, 1979-82; Fellow, Society of Antiquaries of Scotland; Editor, Proceedings, 11th Low Temperature Conference, 1968; Editor, Localisation and Interaction, 1986. Recreations: hill climbing; gardening; country dancing; woodworking. Address: Greenloaning, Kingsbarns, St. Andrews, KY16 8ST; T.-0334 88214.

Finlayson, Niall Diarmid Campbell, MB, ChB, PhD, FRCP, FRCPEdin. Consultant Physician, Edinburgh Royal Infirmary, since 1973; Honorary Senior Lecturer, Department of Medicine, Edinburgh University, since 1973; b. 21.4.39, Georgetown, Guyana; m., Dale Kristin Anderson; 1 s.; 1 d. Educ. Loretto School, Musselburgh; Edinburgh University. Lecturer in Therapeutics, Edinburgh University, 1965-69; Assistant Professor of Medicine, New York Hospital-Cornell Medical College, New York, 1970-72. Address: (h.) 10 Queens Crescent, Edinburgh, EH9 2AZ; T.-031-667 9369.

Finn, Anthony, MA (Hons). Rector, St. Andrew's High School, Kirkcaldy, since 1988; Member, General Teaching Council and Vice-Convener of its Education Committee; Teachers' Representative, National Committee for the Staff Development of Teachers; Member, EIS National Council; Governor, Moray House College of Education; Chair, Organisation Committee, Fife Secondary Teachers Association; b. 4.6.51, Irvine; m., Margaret Caldwell. Educ. St. Joseph's Academy, Kilmarnock; Glasgow University. Teacher, Principal Teacher, Assistant Head Teacher, Depute Head Teacher, Acting Head Teacher, St. Andrew's Academy, Saltcoats, 1975-88. Recreations: sport; travel; literature; current affairs. Address: (h.) 1 Blair Place, Kirkcaldy, KY2 5SQ; T.-0294 640109.

Finn, Kathleen, DCE. Schoolteacher; Past President, Educational Institute of Scotland (now Parliamentary Convener); Chair, STUC Women's Committee and Member, STUC General Council; Member, Scottish Arts Council Drama Committee; b. 22.2.43, Glasgow. Educ. Possil Secondary School; Jordanhill College. Union activist since start of teaching career. Member, Board of Directors, Wildcat; Member, Trade Union Committee, Mayfest. Recreations: swimming; reading; political theatre; cat lover. Address: (h.) 18 Marywood Square, Glasgow, G41 2BJ; T.-041-423 1796.

Finnie, James Ross, CA. Member, Inverclyde District Council, since 1977; Financial Consultant; Director, J.B.

Butchart & Sons Ltd.; b. 11.2.47, Greenock; m., Phyllis Sinclair; 1 s.; 1 d. Educ. Greenock Academy. Member, Executive Committee, Scottish Council (Development and Industry), 1976-87; Convener, Planning and Development Committee, Inverclyde District Council, 1977-80; Chairman, Scottish Liberal Party, 1982-86. Address: (h.) 91 Octavia Terrace, Greenock, PA16 7PY; T.-0475 31495.

Firth, Professor William James, BSc, PhD, CPhys, FRSE. Professor of Physics and Head, Department of Physics and Applied Physics, Strathclyde University, 1990-93; b. 23.2.45, Holm, Orkney; m., Mary MacDonald Anderson; 2 s. Educ. Perth Academy; Edinburgh University; Heriot-Watt University. Lecturer to Reader, Physics, Heriot-Watt University, 1967-85. Recreation: sports (Edinburgh University Hockey Blue, 1967-68). Address: (b.) John Anderson Building, 107 Rottenrow, Glasgow, G4 0NG.

Fischer, Conan James, BA, MA, DPhil. Senior Lecturer in History, Strathclyde University, since 1989; b. 14.6.51, Wellington, New Zealand; m., Mary Christie Dudgeon; 2 d. Educ. Bristol Grammar School; East Anglia University; Sussex University. Lecturer in German Studies, University of Aston in Birmingham; Lecturer in History: Heriot-Watt University, 1979-89, Strathclyde University, 1989-90. Publications: Stormtroopers: a Social, Economic and Ideological Analysis, 1929-35, 1983; The German Communists and the Rise of Nazism, 1991. Recreations: hill walking; politics; the arts. Address: (b.) Department of History, Strathclyde University, 16 Richmond Street, Glasgow, G1 1XQ; T.-041-552 4400, Ext. 2231/2236.

Fisher, Gregor. Actor (television, theatre, film). Credits include: Rab C. Nesbitt series (leading role), BBC TV; Naked Video series, BBC TV; Rab. C. Nesbitt's Christmas Show (leading role), BBC TV; Scotch and Wry Hogmanay Show, BBC TV. Address: (b.) c/o Julian Belfrage Associates, 68 St. James's Street, London, SW1.

Fisher, Howard Andrew Powell, BSc, PhD, MRSC, CChem. Director of Development and Planning, Grampian Regional Council, since 1989; b. 15.7.40, London; m., Fiona Elizabeth Munro; 1 s.; 1 d. Educ. Cranleigh; Glasgow University. Civil Service, 1967-84. Recreations: painting; interest in design. Address: (b.) Woodhill House, Westburn Road, Aberdeen, AB9 2LU.

Fisher, Rev. Ian Riddock, MA. Secretary, Board of Stewardship and Finance, Church of Scotland, since 1989; Convener, St. Andrew Press Executive Committee, 1985-89; Vice-Chairman, National Bible Society of Scotland, 1987-90; b. 12.2.33, Glasgow; m., Mairi Matheson; 2 d. Educ. Kelvinside Academy, Glasgow; Glasgow University; Edinburgh University. Scottish Travelling Secretary, Inter-Varsity Fellowship, 1960-64; Minister, Maybole West Parish Church, 1964-72; Minister, Fernhill and Cathkin Parish Church, Rutherglen, 1972-89. Address: (h.) 157 Nithsdale Road, Glasgow, G41 5RD; T.-041-423 1773.

Fisher, Kenneth Holmes, BA, ACIS, AInstM, DipABCC. Depute Principal, North Glasgow College, since 1987; b. 19.3.41, Glasgow. Educ. Hillhead High School, Glasgow. Administrative appointments, Colvilles Ltd., 1957-67; Lecturer and Senior Lecturer, Anniesland College, Glasgow, 1967-75; Head, Department of Business Studies, Cumbernauld College, 1975-80; Head, Department of Commerce, Anniesland College, Glasgow, 1980-86. Address: (b.) North Glasgow College, 186 Rye Road, Glasgow, G21 3JY; T.-041-558 9071.

Fisher, Robert Walker, DipM, MCIM. Managing Director, Bartholomew, since 1989; b. 14.8.48, Glasgow; m., Myra; 2 d. Educ. Bearsden Academy; Metropolitan College, London;

Strathclyde University Business School. William Collins Sons & Co., Glasgow, 1966-71; William Collins (Africa) (Pty) Ltd., South Africa, as Sales Representative, then Product Manager, 1972-78; Managing Director: Vaal Book Distributors (Pty) Ltd., South Africa, 1978-80, Collins Vaal (Pty) Ltd., South Africa, 1980-85; Chairman and Managing Director, Collins Publishers (SA) (Pty) Ltd., South Africa, 1985-86; Managing Director, William Collins Publishers Ltd., New Zealand, 1987-89. Recreations: reading; music; photography; hill-walking. Address: (b.) 12 Duncan Street, Newington, Edinburgh, EH9 1TA; T.-031-667 9341.

Fitzgerald, Brian John, BSc, CEng, FICE. Chairman and Managing Director, Laing Scotland, since 1989; Director, John Laing Construction Ltd., since 1989; Director, John Laing Developments Ltd., since 1990; b. 17.9.46, Glasgow; m., Maren Lina Hunter; 2 s. Educ. Salesian College, Farnborough; Glasgow University. Whatlings plc: Engineer, Manager, Director, Managing Director, 1969-88; Director: Alfred McAlpine Construction Ltd., 1985-88, Health Care International (Scotland) Ltd., since 1991, Norcity Homes plc, since 1988, Norcity II plc, since 1989, Norhomes plc, since 1989, Manchester Village Homes plc, since 1989. Recreation: squash. Address: (b.) John Laing Construction Ltd., 175 Elderslie Street, Glasgow; T.-041-332 7055.

Fladmark, Jan Magnus, DA (Edin), DipTP, FRTPI, FSA Scot. Assistant Director, Countryside Commission for Scotland, since 1976; Convener, Patrick Geddes Planning Award, since 1989; Visiting Lecturer, Duncan of Jordanstone College of Art, since 1990; b. 12.2.37, Romsdal, Norway; m., Caroline Ashton Miller; 1 s.; 3 d. Educ. Hamar Cathedral School; Gjermundnes Agricultural College; Military College; Edinburgh College of Art. Press Photographer, Sunnmørsposten, 1953-55; National Service, Norwegian Army, 1957-58; Architect, Moira and Moira, 1964-66; Research Fellow, Edinburgh College of Art, 1966-67; Planning Officer, Scottish Office, 1967-70; Lecturer and ODA Programme Director, Edinburgh University, 1970-76; lecture tour, Latin America, 1973; Adviser: Metropolitan Government of Lima, 1975, Mezzogiorno Development Agency (FORMEZ), 1980, Vesuvian Research Institute, 1985; Chairman, RTPI Scotland, 1981-82; Governor, Edinburgh College of Art, 1982-88; Scottish Committee, RIBA Festival of Architecture, 1983-84; Founding Secretary, Patrick Geddes Planning Award, 1983-89; Council Member, Saltire Society, 1984-88; Assessor, Architectural Competition for Iona Community, 1985; Chairman, Scottish Inter-Agency Liaison Group, 1987-90; Founding Chairman, Countryside Around Towns Forum, 1989-91; MOD Liaison Committee on Environmental Matters, 1989-92; Recreation Committee, Scottish Landowners' Federation, since 1990; Assessor, Loch Lomond Park Authority, Scottish Wildlife Trust and Central Scotland Countryside Trust, 1990-91; Andrew Grant Bequest Travel Scholar, 1964, and Research Fellowship, 1966; Honorary Fellow, Edinburgh University, 1971; Fellow, Salzburg Seminar in American Studies, 1973; Founding Honorary President, Edinburgh University Parachute Club, 1975; Fladmark of Fladmark, since 1981; Fellow, RTPI, 1984; Glenfiddich Living Scotland Award, 1986; Fellow, Society of Antiquaries of Scotland, 1988. Publications: The Countryside Around Towns, 1988; Tomorrow's Architectural Heritage, 1991. Recreations: Viking history; marathons; riding. Address: Macduff House, Auchtermuchty, Fife KY14 7AP; T.-0337 28281.

Flatman, Peter William, MA, PhD. Senior Lecturer in Physiology, Edinburgh University, since 1991; b. 1.8.53, Woodford; m., Jane Morris; 1 s.; 1 d. Educ. East Ham Grammar School; King's College, Cambridge. MRC Research Assistant, Physiological Laboratory, Cambridge, 1977-80; Lecturer in Physiology, Edinburgh University, 1980-91. Member: Editorial Board, Magnesium Research,

since 1988, Scientific Committee, 3rd European Congress on Magnesium, 1989, Editorial Board, Journal of Trace Elements and Electrolytes in Health and Disease, since 1990; Fellow, Cambridge Philosophical Society, since 1975; Honorary Member, Gesellschaft Fur Mineralstoffe und Spurenelemente, since 1991; Heinz Zunkley Prize; 1991. Recreations: walking; reading; sailing. Address: Department of Physiology, University Medical School, Teviot Place, Edinburgh, EH8 9AG; T.-031-650 3254.

Fleming, Archibald Macdonald, MA, BCom, PhD, FRSA. Director of Continuing Education, Strathclyde University, since 1987 (Director, Management Development Programmes, Strathclyde Business School, 1984-87); Lecturer, Department of Information Science, Strathclyde University, since 1968; Consultant on Management Training and Development, since 1970; b. 19.6.36, Glasgow; m., Joan Moore; 1 s.; 1 d. Educ. Langholm Academy; Dumfries Academy; Edinburgh University. W. & T. Avery, 1961-63; IBM (UK) Ltd., 1963-64; Sumlock Comptometer Ltd., 1964-68; Consultancies: Scottish Co-operative Wholesale Society, 1969, Hotel and Catering Industry Training Board, 1971, Scottish Engineering Employers Association, 1973. Member, Strathclyde Children's Panel; Member, Committee on Food Processing Opportunities in Scotland, Scottish Council (Development and Industry); Vice-Chairman, Universities Council for Adult and Continuing Education (Scotland), since 1990; Member, American Association for Adult and Continuing Education. Publication: Scottish Business Dictionary (with B. McKenna). Recreation: reading, observing and talking on Scotland and the Scots. Address: (b.) 16 Richmond Street, Glasgow, G1 1XQ.

Fleming, Professor George, BSc, PhD, FEng, FICE, FRSA, MIWEM. Professor of Civil Engineering, Strathclyde University, since 1985; Member of Council, Institution of Civil Engineers, since 1986; Member, Environment Committee, SERC, since 1986; b. 16.8.44, Glasgow; m., Irene Fleming; 2 s.; 1 d. Educ. Knightswood Secondary School, Glasgow; Strathclyde University; Stanford University, California. Research Assistant, Strathclyde University, 1966-69, Stanford University, 1967; Senior Research Hydrologist, Hydrocomp International, California, 1969-70; Research Associate, Stanford University, 1969-70; Director and Vice President, Hydrocomp International, Palo Alto and Glasgow, 1970-79; Lecturer, then Senior Lecturer, then Reader in Civil Engineering, Strathclyde University, 1971-85; Visiting Professor, University of Padova, Italy, since 1980; Vice Dean, Engineering Faculty, Strathclyde University, 1984-87; Member, Overseas Projects Board, DTI, 1991. Publications: Computer Simulation in Hydrology, 1975; The Sediment Problem, 1977; Deterministic Models in Hydrology, 1979. Recreations: farming; fishing; food; film-making. Address: (b.) John Anderson Building, 107 Rottenrow, Glasgow, G4 0NG; T.-041-552 4400, Ext. 3168.

Fleming, Maurice. Editor, The Scots Magazine, 1974-91; b. Blairgowrie; m., Nanette Dalgleish; 2 s.; 1 d. Educ. Blairgowrie High School. Trained in hotel management before entering journalism; worked on various magazines; has had five full-length plays performed professionally, as well as one-act plays by amateurs; founder Member: Traditional Music and Song Association of Scotland, Scottish Poetry Library; Past Chairman, Blairgowrie, Rattray and District Civic Trust; Past Chairman, Blair in Bloom. Publication: The Scots Magazine – A Celebration of 250 Years (Co-Editor). Recreations: theatre; reading; bird-watching; enjoying the countryside; folksong and folklore. Address: (h.) Craigard, Perth Road, Blairgowrie; T.-Blairgowrie 3633.

Fleming, Tom. Actor and Director; b. 29.6.27, Edinburgh. Co-Founder, Edinburgh Gateway Company, 1953; directed and acted in numerous productions there; joined Royal

Shakespeare Company at Stratford upon Avon, 1962, and played several classical roles, including Brutus in Julius Caesar, the Earl of Kent in King Lear, and the title role in Cymberline; toured with RSC in USSR, USA and Europe, 1964; appointed Director, new Royal Lyceum Theatre Company, 1965; there played title role in Galileo; appeared on television in title role of Jesus of Nazareth; Television Commentator on ceremonial occasions; played Divine Correction, The Thrie Estates, Edinburgh Festival, 1959 and 1973; author of play, Miracle at Midnight; former Artistic Director, Scottish Theatre Company.

Fletcher, Colonel Archibald Ian, OBE. Justice of the Peace for Argyll and Bute, since 1971; Deputy Lieutenant, since 1975; Vice Lord Lieutenant, since 1990; b. 9.4.24, London; m., Helen Clare de Salis; 1 s.; 2 d. Educ. Ampleforth College. Recruit, Guards Depot, 1942; Troop Leader, 3rd Tank Bn., Scots Guards, NW Europe, 1944-45; served Palestine, N. Africa, Malaya, Kenya; commanded 1st Bn., Scots Guards, 1963-66, Malaya and Borneo, and Regiment, 1967-70; retired to farm in Argyll; County Councillor, 1972-74; Member, NFU of Scotland Council, 1972-85, Honorary President, 1985-86, President, Cowal Area, 1987-89; Council Member, Timber Growers UK, 1986-91; Director (Deputy Chairman), Argyll and the Islands Enterprise, since 1991; Chairman, Colintraive and Glendaruel Community Council, since 1977. Recreation: country pursuits. Address: (h.) Dunans, Glendaruel, Colintraive, Argyll; T.-Glendaruel 235.

Fletcher, Professor Roger, MA, PhD, FIMA, FRSE. Professor of Optimization, Department of Mathematics and Computer Science, Dundee University, since 1984; b. 29.1.39, Huddersfield; m., Mary Marjorie Taylor; 2 d. Educ. Huddersfield College; Cambridge University; Leeds University. Lecturer, Leeds University, 1963-69; Principal Research Fellow, then Principal Scientific Officer, AERE Harwell, 1969-73; Senior Research Fellow, then Senior Lecturer, then Reader, Dundee University, 1973-84. Publications: Practical Methods of Optimization, 2nd edition, 1987. numerous others. Recreations: hill-walking; music; bridge. Address: (h.) 43 Errol Road, Invergowrie, Dundee, DD2 5BX; T.-0382 562452.

Flett, Ian Stark, CBE (1984), MA, MEd, ABPS. Chairman, Scottish Centre for Tuition of the Disabled, 1980-89; Chairman, National Association for Gifted Children Scotland, since 1985; b. 26.1.20, Aberdeen; m., Moyra. Educ. Aberdeen Grammar School; Aberdeen University; Aberdeen College of Education. RAF, Signals and Intelligence Branch, 1940-46; Teacher, Aberdeen, 1947-49; Adviser, Durham, 1949-54; Assistant Education Officer, Lancashire, 1954-59; Deputy, 1959-63; Deputy Education Officer, City of Hull, 1963-66; Member, Dalegacy Institute of Education, Hull University, 1963-66; Director of Education, Fife, 1966-85; General Secretary, Association of Directors of Education in Scotland, 1975-85; President, 1979-80; Adviser to Association of County Councils, 1970-74; Principal Adviser, Convention of Scottish Local Authorities, 1975-84; Member, Consultative Committee on the Curriculum, 1977-87; Member, General Teaching Council, 1976-84; Governor, Craiglockhart College of Education, 1977-83; Chairman, Scottish Association of Educational Management and Administration, 1981-84. Publication: The Years of Growth 1945-75, 1989. Recreations: music; gardening. Address: (h.) 5 Townsend Place, Kirkcaldy, Fife, KY1 1HB; T.-0592 260279.

Flett, James. JP. Honorary Sheriff, Lothians and Borders; Past Chairman, City of Edinburgh Valuation Appeal Committee; b. 26.1.17, Findochty; m., Jean Walker Ross; 1 s. Educ. Findochty Public School; Heriot-Watt University; Royal Military College, Sandhurst. Commissioned Seaforth Highlanders; Chief Official, Royal Burgh of Linlithgow (retired). Governor, West Lothian Educational Trust; former

Member, JP Advisory Committee; former Member, Scottish Home Department Interviewing Committee at Edinburgh Prisons; former Member, West Lothian Licensing Board. Recreations: gardening; travel; walking. Address: (h.) Craigenroan, Linlithgow, West Lothian; T.-Linlithgow 842344.

Flint, Professor David, TD, MA, BL, CA, FRSA. Professor of Accountancy, Glasgow University, 1964-85 (Vice-Principal, 1981-85); b. 24.2.19, Glasgow; m., Dorothy Mary Maclachlan Jardine; 2 s.; 1 d. Educ. High School of Glasgow; Glasgow University. Royal Signals, 1939-46 (Major; mentioned in Despatches); Partner, Mann Judd Gordon & Company, Chartered Accountants, Glasgow, 1951-71; Lecturer (part-time), Glasgow University, 1950-60; Dean, Faculty of Law, 1971-73; Council Member, Scottish Business School, 1971-77; Institute of Chartered Accountants of Scotland: President, 1975-76, Vice-President, 1973-75, Convener, Research Advisory Committee, 1974-75 and 1977-84, Convener, Working Party on Future Policy, 1976-79, Convener, Public Sector Committee, 1987-89, Convener, Taxation Review and Research Sub-Committee, 1960-64; Trustee, Scottish Chartered Accountants Trust for Education, 1981-87; Member, Management Training and Development Committee, Central Training Council, 1966-70; Member, Management and Industrial Relations Committee, Social Science Research Council, 1970-72 and 1978-80; Member, Social Sciences Panel, Scottish Universities Council on Entrance, 1968-72; Chairman, Association of University Teachers of Accounting, 1969; Member, Company Law Committee, Law Society of Scotland, 1976-85; Scottish Economic Society: Treasurer, 1954-62, Vice-President, 1977-88, Hon. Vice-President, since 1988; Member, Commission for Local Authority Accounts in Scotland, 1978-80; President, European Accounting Association, 1983-84. Publication: Philosophy and Principles of Auditing, 1988. Recreation: golf. Address: (h.) 16 Grampian Avenue, Auchterarder, Perthshire, PH3 1NY; T.-0764 63978.

Flockhart, (David) Ross, BA, BD. Director, Scottish Council for Voluntary Organisations, 1972-91; Member, Court, Stirling University, since 1989; b. 20.3.27, Newcastle, NSW, Australia; m., Pamela Ellison Macartney; 3 s.; 1 d.; 1 d. (deceased). Educ. Knox Grammar School, Sydney; Sydney University; Edinburgh University. Royal Australian Engineers, 1945-46; Chaplain to Overseas Students, Edinburgh, 1955-58; Parish Minister (Church of Scotland), Northfield, Aberdeen, 1958-63; Warden, Carberry Tower, Musselburgh, 1963-66; Lecturer and Senior Lecturer, School of Community Studies, Moray House College of Education, 1966-72; Member, Scottish Arts Council, 1976-82; Trustee, Community Projects Foundation. Recreations: bee-keeping; sailing; bread-baking. Address: (h.) Longwood, Humbie, East Lothian; T.-Humbie 208.

Florey, Professor Charles du Ve, MD, MPH, FFCM, FRCPE. Professor of Epidemiology and Public Health, Dundee University, since 1983. Instructor, Assistant Professor, Yale University, 1963-69; Member, Scientific Staff, MRC, 1969-71; Senior Lecturer, then Reader, then Professor, St. Thomas's Hospital Medical School, 1971-83; Member, Committee on Data Protection, 1976-78. Publications: Introduction to Community Medicine; Methods for Cohort Studies of Chronic Airflow Limitation. Address: (b.) Department of Epidemiology and Public Health, Ninewells Hospital and Medical School, Dundee, DD1 9SY; T.-0382 632124.

Fluendy, Malcolm A.D., MA, DPhil, DSc, CChem, FRSC, MInstP, CPhys, FRSE. Reader in Chemistry, Edinburgh University; b. 28.3.35, London; m., Annette Pidgeon; 2 s. Educ. Westminster City School; Balliol College, Oxford. National Service, 1953-55 (Lt., Royal Signals); Royal Naval

Scientific Service, 1955-56; Balliol College, Oxford, 1956-62; Research Fellow: University of California, Berkeley, 1962-63, Harvard University, 1963-64; joined Edinburgh University as Lecturer, 1964. Chairman, Molecular Beam Group, Chemical Society, 1974-79; Physical Secretary, RSE, since 1989. Publication: Molecular Beams. Recreations: sailing; cruising (yachtmaster). Address: (b.) Department of Chemistry, West Mains Road, Edinburgh, EH9 3JJ; T.-031-667 1081.

Foley, Hugh Smith. Principal Clerk of Session and Justiciary, since 1989; b. 9.4.39, Falkirk; m., Isobel King Halliday. Educ. Dalkeith High School. Entered Scottish Court Service (Court of Session Branch), 1962; Assistant Clerk of Session, 1962-71; Depute Clerk of Session, 1972-80; seconded to Sheriff Court, Edinburgh, 1980-81; Principal Sheriff Clerk Depute, Glasgow, 1981-82; Sheriff Clerk, Linlithgow, 1982; Deputy Principal Clerk of Session, 1982-86; Senior Deputy Principal Clerk, 1986-89. Member, Lord President's Committee on Procedure in Personal Injuries Litigation in Court of Session, 1978-79. Address: (b.) Parliament House, Edinburgh, EH1 1RQ; T.-031-225 2595.

Foot, Professor Hugh Corrie, BA, PhD, FBPsS. Professor of Psychology, Strathclyde University, since 1992; b. 7.6.41, Northwood, Middx; m., Daryl M.; 1 s.; 1 d. Educ. Durham University; Queen's College, Dundee. Research Fellow, Dundee University, 1965-68; University of Wales Institute of Science and Technology: Lecturer, 1968-77, Senior Lecturer, 1977-88; Reader, University of Wales College of Cardiff, 1989-91. Recreations: tennis; hill walking. Address: Department of Psychology, Strathclyde University, Turnbull Building, 155 George Street, Glasgow, G1 1RD; T.-041-552 4400, Ext. 2580.

Forbes, Professor Charles Douglas, DSc, MD, MB, ChB, FRCP, FRCPGlas, FRCPEdin, FRSA. Professor of Medicine, Dundee University, and Honorary Consultant Physician, Tayside Health Board, since 1987; b. 9.10.38, Glasgow; m., Janette MacDonald Robertson; 2 s. Educ. High School of Glasgow; Glasgow University. Assistant Lecturer in Materia Medica, Glasgow University; Lecturer in Medicine, Makerere, Uganda; Registrar in Medicine, Glasgow Royal Infirmary; Reader in Medicine, Glasgow University; Fellow, American Heart Association; Fullbright Fellow; Director, Regional Haemophilia Centre, Glasgow. Recreation: gardening. Address: (h.) East Chattan, 108 Hepburn Gardens, St. Andrews, KY16 9LT; T.-0334 72428.

Forbes, Very Rev. Graham J.T., MA, BD. Provost, St. Mary's Cathedral, Edinburgh, since 1990 (Provost, St. Ninian's Cathedral, Perth, 1982-90); b. 10.6.51, Edinburgh; m., Jane Miller; 3 s. Educ. George Heriot's School, Edinburgh; Aberdeen University; Edinburgh University. Curate, Old St. Paul's, Edinburgh, 1976-82; Chairman, Canongate Youth Project, 1977-83; Chairman, Lothian Association of Youth Clubs, 1981-88; Member, Scottish Community Education Council, 1982-88; Chairman, Scottish Intermediate Treatment Resource Centre, 1982-89; Member, Edinburgh Area Board, Manpower Services Commission, 1980-83; Chairman, Youth Affairs Group, Scottish Community Education Council, 1982- 88; Non-Executive Director, Radio Tay, 1987-90; Member, Parole Board for Scotland, since 1991. Address: 8 Lansdowne Crescent, Edinburgh, EH12 5EQ.

Forbes, Professor Jill Elizabeth, BA, DPhil, FRSA. Professor of French, Strathclyde University, since 1991; b. 21.6.47, London; 1 s. Educ. North London Collegiate School; Manchester University; Somerville College, Oxford; University of Paris III. Lectrice d'anglais, Ecole Normale Superieure, 1971-74; Lecturer in French: Leicester Polytechnic, 1975-77, Loughborough University, 1977-84;

Head, Department of Modern Languages, South Bank Polytechnic, 1984-91; Visiting Professor: University of Paris III, 1987-88, University of Paris IV, 1990-91. Governor, British Film Institute, 1976-80. Publications: The Cinema in Contemporary France; Contemporary France: Politics, Economics, Society. Recreations: cinema; opera; the French provinces; detective fiction. Address: (b.) Department of Modern Languages, Strathclyde University, Glasgow; T.-041-552 4400.

Forbes, Sheriff John Stuart, MA, LLB. Sheriff of Tayside, Central and Fife, at Dunfermline, since 1980; b. 31.1.36.

Forbes, 22nd Lord (Nigel Ivan Forbes), KBE (1960), JP, DL. Premier Lord of Scotland; Chairman, Rolawn Ltd., since 1975; President, Scottish Scout Association, 1970-88; b. 19.2.18; m., Hon. Rosemary Katharine Hamilton-Russell; 2 s.; 1 d. Educ. Harrow; Sandhurst. Retired Major, Grenadier Guards; Representative Peer of Scotland, 1955-63; Minister of State, Scottish Office, 1958-59; Member, Scottish Committee, Nature Conservancy, 1961-67; Member, Aberdeen and District Milk Marketing Board, 1962-72; Chairman, River Don District Board, 1962-73; President, Royal Highland and Agricultural Society of Scotland, 1958-59; Member, Sports Council for Scotland, 1966-71; Chairman, Scottish Branch, National Playing Fields Association, 1965-80; Deputy Chairman, Tennant Caledonian Breweries Ltd., 1964-74. Address: (h.) Balforbes, Alford, Aberdeenshire,AB33 8DR; T.-09755 62516.

Forbes, Ronald, DA. Artist; Director, Master of Fine Art Degree Course, Duncan of Jordanstone College of Art, Dundee, since 1983; b. 22.3.47, Braco; m., Sheena Henderson Bell; 1 s.; 2 d. Educ. Morrison's Academy, Crieff; Edinburgh College of Art. Leverhulme Senior Art Fellow, Strathclyde University, 1973-74; Head of Painting, Crawford School of Art, Cork, Ireland, 1974-78; Artist-in-Residence, Livingston, 1978-80; Scottish Arts Council Studio Bursary, Amsterdam, 1980; Lecturer, Glasgow School of Art, 1979-83. Prizes include RSA Guthrie Award, Royal Scottish Academy, 1979. Recreations: cinema; theatre; gardening. Address: (h.) 13 Fort Street, Dundee, DD2 1BS; T.-0382 641498.

Forbes, Captain William Frederick Eustace. Vice Lord-Lieutenant of Stirling and Falkirk, since 1984; b. 6.7.32; m.; 2 d. Educ. Eton. Coldstream Guards, 1950-59; Chairman, Scottish Woodland Owners' Association, 1974-77; Chairman, Scottish Branch, National Playing Fields Association, 1980-90. Address: (h.) Dinning House, Gargunnock, Stirling, FK8 3BQ.

Ford, Harold Frank, BA, LLB; b. 17.5.15, Dirleton, East Lothian; m., Lucy Mary Burnet; 1 s.; 3 d. Educ. Winchester College; University College, Oxford; Edinburgh University. War Service, 1940-45, Lothians and Borders Yeomanry; PoW, Germany; Scottish Bar, 1945; Legal Adviser to UNRRA and IRO in British Zone of Germany, 1947; Sheriff Substitute of Forfar and Perth, 1951-71; Sheriff at Perth, 1971-80. Governor, Patrick Allan Fraser of Hospitalfield Trust, Arbroath; Past Chairman, Perth Prison Visitors' Centre. Recreations: gardening; golf. Address: Millhill, Meikleour, Perth, PH2 6EF; T.-Caputh 311.

Ford, James Allan, CB, MC. Author; Trustee, National Library of Scotland, 1981-91; b. 10.6.20, Auchtermuchty; m., Isobel Dunnett; 1 s.; 1 d. Educ. Royal High School, Edinburgh; Edinburgh University. Employment Clerk, Ministry of Labour, 1938-39; Executive Officer, Inland Revenue, 1939-40; Captain, The Royal Scots, 1940-46 (POW, Far East, 1941-45); Executive Officer, Inland Revenue, 1946-47; Department of Agriculture for Scotland, 1947-66 (Assistant Secretary, 1958); Registrar General for Scotland, 1966-69; Under Secretary, Scottish Office, 1969-

79. Publications (novels): The Brave White Flag, 1961; Season of Escape, 1963; A Statue for a Public Place, 1965; A Judge of Men, 1968; The Mouth of Truth, 1972. Recreations: trout fishing; gardening. Address: (h.) 29 Lady Road, Edinburgh, EH16 5PA; T.-031-667 4489.

Ford, James Angus, MB, ChB, FRCPEdin, FRCPGlas, DCH. Consultant Paediatrician, since 1975; Chairman, Scottish Council, British Medical Association; Chairman, Scottish Committee of Hospital Medical Services, 1983-86; b. 5.11.43, Arbroath; m., Dr. Veronica T. Reid. Educ. Kelvinside Academy; Glasgow University. House appointments: Glasgow Royal, Southern General, Stobhill, Belvidere; Registrar/Senior Registrar, Stobhill; Consultant appointments: Rutherglen Maternity Hospital, Royal Hospital for Sick Children, Glasgow; Territorial Army: six years, 6/7th Bn., Cameronians (Scottish Rifles), Captain; BMA: Chairman, Hospital Junior Staff Committee (Scotland), Deputy Chairman, HJSC (UK), Member of Council (Scottish and UK), Member, Joint Consultants Committee (Scottish and UK). Recreation: gardening. Address: (h.) 20 Ralston Road, Bearsden, Glasgow; T.-041-942 4273.

Forde, Professor Michael Christopher, BEng, MSc, PhD, CEng, MICE, MIHT, FINDT. Tarmac Professor of Civil Engineering Construction, Edinburgh University, since 1990; b. 15.2.44, Sale; m., Edna Johnson Williams; 1 s.; 1 d. Educ. De La Salle College; Birmingham University; Liverpool University. Site Engineer, Christani-Shand, 1966-67; County Surveyors Department, Cheshire County Council, 1967-69; Research Student, Birmingham University, 1969-73; Edinburgh University: Lecturer, 1973-84, Senior Lecturer, 1984-89. Medal of City of Grenoble, 1979. Publications: over 70 papers published. Recreations: travel; armchair cricketer. Address: (h.) Tintern House, 46 Cluny Gardens, Edinburgh, EH10 6BN; T.-031-447 4960.

Forrest, Professor Sir (Andrew) Patrick (McEwen), Kt (1986), BSc, MD, ChM, FRCS, FRCSEdin, FRCSGlas, DSc (Hon), LLD (Hon), FACS (Hon), FRACS (Hon), FRCSCan (Hon), FRCR (Hon), FIBiol, FRSE. Professor Emeritus, Honorary Fellow, Visiting Worker, ICRF Clinical Oncology Unit, Edinburgh University; b. 25.3.23, Mount Vernon, Lanarkshire; m., Margaret Anne Steward; 1 s.; 2 d. Educ. Dundee High School; St. Andrews University. House Surgeon, Dundee Royal Infirmary; Surgeon Lieutenant, RNVR; Mayo Foundation Fellow; Lecturer and Senior Lecturer, Glasgow University; Professor of Surgery, Welsh National School of Medicine; Regius Professor of Clinical Surgery, Edinburgh University; Visiting Scientist, National Cancer Institute, USA; Chief Scientist (part-time), Scottish Home and Health Department, 1981-87; Chairman, Working Group, Breast Cancer Screening, 1985-86; President, Surgical Research Society, 1974-76; President, Association of Surgeons of Great Britain and Ireland, 1988-89; Lister Medal, Royal College of Surgeons of England, 1987; Member, Kirk Session, St. Giles Cathedral. Publications: Prognostic Factors in Breast Cancer (Co-author), 1968; Principles and Practice of Surgery (Co-author), 1985; Breast Cancer: the decision to screen, 1990. Recreations: sailing; golf. Address: (h.) 19 St. Thomas Road, Edinburgh, EH9 2LR; T.-031-667 3203.

Forrest, Robert Jack. Director, Royal Highland & Agricultural Society of Scotland, since 1989, Hon. Treasurer, 1985-88, Chairman, 1989-90, Hon. Secretary since 1991; b. 4.1.39, Duns; m., Jennifer McCreath; 2 s.; 1 d. Educ. Loretto School; East of Scotland College of Agriculture. Director, Robert Forrest Ltd. (Farmers), since 1960, Chairman since 1986; President, British Simmental Cattle Society, 1983-84; judged pedigree cattle and sheep at home and abroad; Member, Panel of Scottish Agricultural Arbiters; Vice Chairman, Scottish Agricultural Benevolent Institution, 1991; Council Member, Royal Agricultural Society of the

Commonwealth; Elder, Bonkyl Church. Address: (h.) Preston, Duns, Berwickshire, TD11 3TQ; T.-0361 82826.

Forrester, Professor Alexander Robert, BSc, PhD, DSc, FRSC, FRSE. Professor of Chemistry, Aberdeen University, since 1985 (Head of Department, 1987-90, Dean, Faculty of Engineering and Mathematical and Physical Sciences, 1990-91); Vice-Principal (Sciences), since 1991; b. 14.11.35, Kelty, Fife; m., Myrna Ross; 1 s.; 3 d. Educ. Alloa Academy; Stirling High School; Heriot-Watt University; Aberdeen University (PhD). Chairman, North of Scotland Section, Royal Society of Chemistry, 1987-90; Council Member: Royal Society of Chemistry, 1987-90, Perkin Division, Royal Society of Chemistry, since 1991; Member, Committee, Scottish National Library, since 1988; Member, Grants Committee, 1988-91, and BP Fellowship Committee, 1988-91, Royal Society Edinburgh; Director, Aberdeen University Research and Industrial Services, since 1990. Recreations: golf; cricket; football (free transfers from Third Lanark and Partick Thistle). Address: (b.) Chemistry Department, Aberdeen University, Aberdeen; T.-Aberdeen 272944.

Forrester, Rev. Professor Duncan Baillie, MA (Hons), BD, DPhil. Principal, New College, Edinburgh, since 1986, and Professor of Christian Ethics and Practical Theology, since 1978; Member, WCC Faith and Order Commission, since 1983; President, Society for Study of Theology, 1991-94; President, Society for Study of Christian Ethics, 1991-94; Church of Scotland Minister; b. 10.11.33, Edinburgh; m., Rev. Margaret McDonald; 1 s.; 1 d. Educ. Madras College, St. Andrews; St. Andrews University; Chicago University; Edinburgh University. Part-time Assistant in Politics, Edinburgh University, 1957-58; Assistant Minister, Hillside Church, Edinburgh, and Leader of St. James Mission, 1960-61; as Church of Scotland Missionary, Lecturer and then Professor of Politics, Madras Christian College, Tambaram, South India, 1962-70; ordained Presbyter, Church of South India, 1962; part-time Lecturer in Politics, Edinburgh University, 1966-67; Chaplain and Lecturer in Politics, Sussex University. Publications: Caste & Christianity, 1980; Encounter with God (Co-author), 1983; Studies in the History of Worship in Scotland (Co-Editor), 1984; Christianity and the Future of Welfare, 1985; Theology and Politics, 1988; Just Sharing (Co-author), 1988; Beliefs, Values and Policies 1989; Worship Now Book II (Co-editor), 1989; Theology and Practice (Editor), 1990. Recreations: hill-walking; reading; listening to music. Address: (h.) 25 Kingsburgh Road, Edinburgh, EH12 6DZ; T.-031-337 5646.

Forrester, Frederick Lindsay, MA (Hons), DipEd, MBIM, FEIS. Organising Secretary, Educational Institute of Scotland, since 1975; b. 10.2.35, Glasgow; m., Ann V. Garrity; 1 s.; 1 d. Educ. Victoria Drive Senior Secondary School, Glasgow; Glasgow University; Jordanhill College of Education. Teacher of English, Glasgow secondary schools, 1962-64; Teacher of English and General Studies, Coatbridge Technical College, 1964-67; Assistant Secretary, Educational Institute of Scotland, 1967-75. Contributor to Times Educational Supplement Scotland and Education Herald. Recreations: walking; cycling; swimming; foreign travel. Address: (h.) 145 South Gyle Gardens, Edinburgh EH12 7XH; T.-031-334 4242.

Forrester, Ian Stewart, QC, MA, LLB, MLC. Honorary Visiting Professor in European Law, Glasgow University, since 1991; Member, European Advisory Board, Tulane University Law School, since 1992; b. 13.1.45, Glasgow; m., Sandra Anne Therese Keegan; 2 s. Educ. Kelvinside Academy, Glasgow; Glasgow University; Tulane University of Louisiana. Admitted to Faculty of Advocates, 1972; admitted to Bar of State of NY, 1977; Maclay, Murray & Spens, 1968-69; Davis Polk & Wardwell, 1969-72; Cleary Gottlieb Steen & Hamilton, 1972-81; established independent chambers, Brussels, 1981; Co-Founder, Forrester & Norall, 1981 (Forrester Norrall & Sutton, 1989), practising before European Commission and Court. Chairman, British Conservative Association, Belgium, 1982-86. Recreations: politics; wine; cooking; restoring old houses. Address: Advocates' Library, Parliament House, Edinburgh, EH1 1RF.

Forrester, Professor John Vincent, MD, FRCSEdin. Cockburn Professor of Ophthalmology, Aberdeen University, since 1984; Honorary Consultant Ophthalmologist; b. 11.9.46, Glasgow; m., Anne Gray; 2 s. 2 d. Educ. St. Aloysius College, Glasgow; Glasgow University. Ophthalmologist in training, Glasgow hospitals, 1972-79; MRC Travelling Fellow, Columbia University, New York, 1976-77; Consultant Ophthalmologist, Southern General Hospital, Glasgow, and Honorary Clinical Lecturer, Glasgow University, 1979-84. Recreation: family life. Address: 12 Urie Crescent, Stonehaven; T.-0569 62303.

Forrester, Rev. Margaret Rae, MA, BD. Minister, St. Michael's, Edinburgh, since 1980; Convener, Board of World Mission and Unity, Church of Scotland, since 1992; b. 23.11.37, Edinburgh; m., Duncan B. Forrester; 1 s.; 1 d. Educ. George Watson's Ladies' College; Edinburgh University and New College. Assistant Pastor, Madras; Minister, Telscombe Cliffs URC, Sussex; Assistant Minister, St. George's West, Edinburgh; Chaplain, Napier College, Edinburgh. Recreation: gardening. Address: 25 Kingsburgh Road, Edinburgh, EH12 6DZ; T.-031-337 5646.

Forster, Ada Mary Maude, RGN. Staff Nurse, Cottage Hospital, Hawick, since 1986; Member, Scottish National Board for Nursing, Midwifery and Health Visiting, since 1988; Member, United Kingdom Central Council for Nursing, Midwifery and Health Visiting, since 1989; b. 29.9.42, Hawick; m., Maurice Oliver Forster; 2 d. Educ. Craigmount School, Minto, Hawick; Edinburgh Royal Infirmary. Staff Nurse, Edinburgh Royal Infirmary, 1964; Ward Sister, Borders Health Board, 1966. Member, Borders Health Board, 1987-91. Recreations: gardening; shotting. Address: Newbigging House, Jedburgh TD8 6NA.

Forsyth of That Ilk, Alistair Charles William, JP, KHS, FSCA, FSA Scot, FInstPet, CStJ. Baron of Ethie; Chief of the Name and Clan of Forsyth; b. 7.12.29; m., Ann Hughes; 4 s. Educ. St. Paul's School; Queen Mary College, London. Company Director; Priory Chapter, Most Venerable Order of St. John of Jerusalem, since 1978; Member, Angus District Council, since 1988 (Chairman, Industrial Committee). Recreations: Scottish antiquities; hill-walking. Address: (h.) Ethie Castle, by Arbroath, Angus, DD11 5SP.

Forsyth, Bill. Film Director and Script Writer; b. 1947, Glasgow. Films include: Gregory's Girl, 1981, Local Hero, 1983, Comfort and Joy, 1984.

Forsyth, Constance Catherine, MB, ChB, MD, FRCPLond, FRCPEdin. Reader, Department of Child Health, Dundee University, 1975-88; b. 25.7.23, Edinburgh. Educ. George Watson's Ladies' College, Edinburgh; Edinburgh University. Carnegie Research Scholar, Edinburgh University; Research Fellow, Toronto University; Registrar, then Research Fellow, Hospital for Sick Children, Great Ormond Street, London; Dundee University: Lecturer, Department of Child Health, 1955-62, Senior Lecturer, 1962-75. Recreations: hill-walking; golf; swimming; music; travelling; caravanning. Address: (h.) 5A Glamis Drive, Dundee, DD2 1QG; T.-Dundee 66412.

Forsyth, James, MA. Head, Department of Russian, Aberdeen University, since 1964; b. 8.12.28, Edinburgh; m., 1, Mary A. Brown; 2, Tanya Maseeva; 3, Josephine Newcombe; 1 d. Educ. George Heriot's School; Edinburgh University. Edinburgh Public Library, 1946-58; Russian

Department, Keele University, 1958-61; Russian Department, Glasgow University, 1961-64. Publications: Russian through Reading (Co-author), 1962; Practical Guide to Russian Stress, 1963; A Grammar of Aspect, 1970; Chuckle with Chekhov (Co-author), 1975; Listening to the Wind, 1977. Recreations: walking; swimming; art; listening to music. Address: (h.) 9 Kirkbrae Avenue, Cults, Aberdeen; T.-Aberdeen 861727.

Forsyth, Michael Bruce, MA. MP (Conservative), Stirling, since 1983; Minister of State, Department of Employment, since 1992; b. 16.10.54, Montrose; m., Susan Jane; 1 s.; 2 d. Educ. Arbroath High School; St. Andrews University. National Chairman, Federation of Conservative Students, 1976; Member, Westminster City Council, 1978-83; Member, Select Committee on Scottish Affairs; Parliamentary Private Secretary to the Foreign Secretary, 1986-87; Past Chairman, Scottish Conservative Party; former Parliamentary Under Secretary of State, Scottish Office. Publications: Reservicing Britain; Reservicing Health; The Myths of Privatisation; Down with the Rates; Politics on the Rates; The Case for a Poll Tax. Recreations: mountaineering; astronomy. Address: House of Commons, London, SW1.

Forteviot, 3rd Baron (Henry Evelyn Alexander Dewar), MBE (1943), DL; b. 23.2.06; 2 s.; 2 d. Educ. Eton; St. John's College, Oxford. Black Watch (RHR), 1939-45; Deputy Lieutenant, Perth, 1961; Chairman, John Dewar & Sons Ltd., 1954-76. Address: (h.) Dupplin Castle, Perth.

Fortune, David Ramsay, CA. Vice President, Citibank NA, Edinburgh, since 1988; b. 14.5.47, Edinburgh; 3 d. Educ. Fettes College; Institute of Chartered Accountants of Scotland. Senior Accountant, Whinney Murray, London, 1973-76; appointed Assistant Manager, Chemical Bank, London and Edinburgh, 1977-80; joined Citibank, 1980, and appointed Resident Vice President, Edinburgh Branch, 1982; Director, Stanecastle Assets Ltd., 1986-87. Recreations: shooting; yachting; gardening. Address: (h.) 35 Great King Street, Edinburgh, EH3 6QR; T.-031-557 8829.

Forty, Professor Arthur John, CBE, BSc, PhD, DSc, LLD, FRSE. Principal and Vice-Chancellor, Stirling University, since 1986; b. 4.11.28, Shrivenham; m., Alicia Blanche Hart; 1 s. Educ. Headlands School, Swindon; Bristol University. RAF, 1953-56; Senior Scientist, Tube Investments Ltd., 1956-58; Lecturer, Bristol University, 1958-64; founding Professor of Physics, Warwick University, 1964-86; Pro-Vice-Chancellor, Warwick Univ., 1970-86; Member, Physics and Materials Science Committees, SERC, 1970-74; Member, UGC, 1982-86 (Vice-Chairman, 1985-86); Member, Computer Board, Universities and Research Councils, 1982-85 (Chairman, 1988-91); Member, British Library Board, since 1987; Chairman, Information Systems Committee, UFC, since 1991; author of "Forty Report" on future facilities for advanced research computing. Recreations: dinghy sailing; gardening. Address: (h.) Principal's House, Stirling University, Stirling, FK9 4LA.

Forwell, Harold Christie. Member, Fife Health Board, 1981-89; Member, Industrial Tribunals (Scotland); Director, Fife Chamber of Commerce; b. 16.8.25, Kirkcaldy; m., Isobel Russell Stuart; 1 s.; 1 d. Educ. George Watson's College, Edinburgh; Queen's University, Belfast. Past Chairman, National Joint Committee for Scottish Baking Industry; former Member, Retail Wages Council (BFCS Scotland); Past President; Scottish Association of Master Bakers, Kirkcaldy Rotary Club. Queen's Jubilee Medal, 1977. Recreations: sailing; travel. Address: (h.) 4 West Fergus Place, Kirkcaldy, Fife; T.-0592 260474.

Foster, Ann, MA. Director, Scottish Consumer Council, since 1991; b. 28.9.49, St. Andrews. Educ. Hutchesons' Girls' Grammar School, Glasgow; St. Andrews University; Reading

University. Lecturer, ILEA, 1972-78; Consultant, National Consumer Council, 1978-91; Visiting Fellow, Institute of Food Research; Council Member, Coronary Prevention Group; Member, Committee, Medical Aspects of Food Policy. Recreations: skiing; theatre; opera. Address: (b.) 314 St. Vincent Street, Glasgow, G3 8XW; T.-041-226 5261.

Foster, John, CBE, FRICS, FRTPI, RIBA, ARIAS, FRSA. Vice President, Ramblers Association (Scotland); Director, Countryside Commission for Scotland, 1968-85; b. 13.8.20, Glasgow; m., Daphne Househam. Educ. Whitehill School, Glasgow; Royal Technical College, Glasgow. Surveyor with private firm in Glasgow, 1937; Air Ministry during War; Assistant Planning Officer: Kirkcudbright County Council, 1945-47, Holland Joint Planning Committee, Lincolnshire, 1947-48; Deputy County Planning Officer, Holland County Council, 1948-52; Deputy Planning Officer, Peak Park Planning Board, 1952-54; Director, Peak District National Park Board, 1954-68. Honorary Vice-President, Countrywide Holidays Association; Honorary Fellow, Royal Scottish Geographical Society; Member, Scottish Council, RICS (Penfold Silver Medallist); Life Member, National Trust for Scotland; George Waterston Memorial Award, 1991. Recreations: walking; swimming; photography; philately; reading; travel. Address: (h.) Birchover, Ferntower Road, Crieff, PH7 3DH; T.-0764 2336.

Foster, Professor John Odell, MA, PhD. Professor of Applied Social Studies, Paisley College, since 1981; b. 21.10.40, Hertford; m., Renee Prendergast. Educ. Guildford Grammar School; St. Catherine's College, Cambridge. Postdoctoral Research Fellow, St. Catherine's College, Cambridge, 1965-68; Lecturer in Politics, Strathclyde University, 1966-81. Publications: Class Struggle and the Industrial Revolution, 1974; Politics of the UCS Work-In, 1986; Track Record: the Caterpillar Occupation, 1988. Recreation: hill-walking. Address: (h.) 845 Govan Road, Glasgow, G51.

Foster, Professor Roy, MA, DPhil, DSc, FRSC, FRSE. Emeritus Professor; Professor of Physical-Organic Chemistry, Dundee University, 1969-86; b. 29.7.28, Leicester; m., Delwen Eluned Rodd; 1 s.; 2 d. Educ. Wyggeston School, Leicester; Wadham College, Oxford. Research Fellow, Department of Pharmacology, Oxford University, 1953-56; Queen's College, Dundee (St. Andrews University): Senior Edward A. Deeds Fellow, 1956-59, Lecturer in Organic Chemistry, 1959-63, Senior Lecturer, 1963-66, Reader, 1966-67 (thence Dundee University, 1967-69). British Association for the Advancement of Science: Member of Council, Member, General Committee, Chairman, Tayside and Fife Branch, 1977-84; Dundee University: sometime Member of Court, Dean, Faculty of Science, Head, Department of Chemistry. Recreation: gardening. Address: (b.) Chemistry Department, Dundee University, Dundee, DD1 4HN; T.-0382 23181.

Fothergill-Gilmore, Linda Adams, BS, PhD, FSA Scot. Reader in Biochemistry, Edinburgh University, since 1989; b. 16.4.43, Boston, Massachusetts; 1 s.; 1 d. Educ. Provincetown High School; Michigan State University; Aberdeen University. Research Fellow in Biochemistry, then Research Officer in Biochemistry, Aberdeen University, 1969-83; Lecturer in Biochemistry, Aberdeen University, 1983-86; Senior Lecturer in Biochemistry, Edinburgh University, 1986-89. Recipient, Wellcome Trust University Award, 1986-91. Recreations: choral singing; travel; house renovations. Address: (b.) Department of Biochemistry, Edinburgh University, George Square, Edinburgh, EH8 9XD; T.-031-667 1011, Ext. 2492.

Foulds, Emeritus Professor Wallace Stewart, CBE, MD, ChM, FRCS, FRCSGlas, DO, FCOphth, Hon. DSc (Strathclyde), Hon. FRACO. Emeritus Professor of Ophthalmology, Glasgow University; b. 26.4.24, London; m., Margaret Holmes Walls; 1 s.; 2 d. Educ. George Watson's Boys College, Edinburgh; Paisley Grammar School; Glasgow University. RAF Medical Branch, 1946-49; training posts, Moorfields Eye Hospital, London, 1952-54; Research Fellow, Institute of Ophthalmology, London University, and Senior Registrar, University College Hospital, London, 1954-58; Consultant Ophthalmologist, Addenbrookes Hospital, Cambridge, 1958-64; Honorary Lecturer, Cambridge University and Research Fellow, London University,1958-64; Past President: Ophthalmological Society of UK, Faculty of Ophthalmologists; Past Chairman, Association for Eye Research; Past President, College of Ophthalmologists. Recreations: sailing; diving. Address: (b.) Ross Hall Hospital, 221 Crookston Road, Glasgow, G63 3NQ; T.-041-810 3151.

Foulis, Alan Keith, BSc, MD, MRCPath. Consultant Pathologist, Royal Infirmary, Glasgow, since 1983; b. 25.5.50, Glasgow; m., Anne Don Foulis; 1 s.; 1 d. Educ. Glasgow Academy; Glasgow University. Trained in pathology, Western Infirmary, Glasgow, following brief flirtation with surgery at Aberdeen Royal Infirmary; C.L. Oakley Lecturer, Pathological Society, Oxford, 1987; Bellahouston Medal, Glasgow University, 1987; R.D. Lawrence Lecturer, British Diabetic Association, Manchester, 1989. Publications: research papers on diseases of the pancreas. Recreations: choral and Leider singing; walking; cycling; arctophilia; natural history. Address: (h.) 32 Tannoch Drive, Milngavie, Glasgow; T.-041-956 3092.

Foulkes, George, JP, BSc. MP (Labour and Co-operative), Carrick, Cumnock and Doon Valley, since 1979; Opposition Spokesman on Foreign Affairs, since 1984; b. 21.1.42, Oswestry; m., Elizabeth Anna; 2 s.; 1 d. Educ. Keith Grammar School; Haberdashers' Aske's School; Edinburgh University. President, Scottish Union of Students, 1964-66; Director: European League for Economic Co-operation, 1967-68, Enterprise Youth, 1968-73, Age Concern Scotland, 1973-79; Chairman: Lothian Region Education Committee, 1974-79, Education Committee, COSLA, 1975-79; Rector's Assessor, Edinburgh University, 1968-71; Chairman, John Wheatley Centre. Recreation: boating; watching football (Heart of Midlothian and Ayr United). Address: (h.) 8 Southpark Road, Ayr, KA7 2TL; T.-Ayr 265776.

Fourman, Professor Michael Paul, BSc, MSc, DPhil. Professor of Computer Systems, Edinburgh University, since 1988; Director, Abstract Hardware Ltd., since 1986; b. 12.9.50, Oxford; m., Jennifer Robin Head; 1 s.; 1 d. Educ. Allerton Grange, Leeds; Bristol University; Oxford University. Junior Research Fellow, Wolfson College, Oxford, 1974-78; J.F. Ritt Assistant Professor of Mathematics, Columbia University NY, 1976-82; Department of Electrical & Electronic Engineering, Brunel University: Research Fellow, 1983-86, HIrst Reader in Integrated Circuit Design, 1986, Professor of Formal Systems, 1986-88. Recreations: cooking; sailing. Address: (b.) Computer Science Department, JCMB, King's Buildings, Edinburgh, EH9 3JZ; T.-031-650 5197.

Fowler, Agnes Isobel, BSc. Secretary/Treasurer, Royal Scottish Academy of Music and Drama; b. 13.2.42, Glasgow; m., William M. Fowler; 2 s.; 1 d. Educ. Jordanhill College School; Glasgow University. Governor, Associated Board, Royal Schools of Music. Recreations: hill-walking; swimming; gardening; Church. Address: (h.) Hillside, 7 Main Street, Drymen, Glasgow; T.-0370 60009.

Fowlie, Hector Chalmers, OBE, MB, ChB, FRCPEdin, FRCPsych, DPM. Retired Consultant Psychiatrist; Vice-Chairman, Mental Welfare Commission for Scotland, 1984-89; b. 21.6.29, Dundee; m., Christina N.M. Walker; 2 s.; 1 d.

Educ. Harris Academy, Dundee; St. Andrews University. House Officer, Maryfield Hospital, Dundee, and Perth Royal Infirmary; Registrar, Dundee Royal Mental Hospital; Lecturer, Department of Psychiatry, Medical School, Dundee University; Consultant Psychiatrist and Deputy Physician Superintendent, Gartnavel Royal Hospital, Glasgow; Physician Superintendent, Royal Dundee Liff and Strathmartine Hospitals; Consultant Psychiatrist, Tayside Health Board. Sometime Vice-Chairman, Parole Board for Scotland; Member, Tayside Health Board; Council of Europe Scholar; Consultant, WHO; Governor, Dundee Institute of Technology; Chairman, Dundee Association for Mental Health; Member, Dundee Retirement Council. Recreations: reading; walking. Address: (h.) 21 Clepington Road, Dundee; T.-0382 456926.

Fox, Christopher Howard Christian, MRAC, ARICS. Regional Director, South West Region, Scottish Natural Heritage, since 1992; b. 13.1.41, Whitehaven; m., Caroline Jane Porter; 1 s.; 1 d. Educ. Fettes College; Edinburgh; Royal Agricultural College, Cirencester. Assistant Land Agent; W.H. Cooke & Arkwright, Chartered Surveyors, Hereford, 1963-69, Nature Conservancy Council, Edinburgh, 1969-73; Area Land Agent, North Scotland, Nature Conservancy Council, 1973-83; Senior Land Agent (Scotland), Nature Conservancy Council, 1983-91; Regional Director, South West Scotland, Nature Conservancy Council for Scotland, 1991-92. Director, Scottish Agricultural College, Auchincruive; Member, West Advisory Committee, Scottish Agricultural College. Recreations: country sports; contemporary Scottish painters; music. Address: (h.) 6 Afton Terrace, Edinburgh, EH5 3NG; T.-031-552 5894.

Fox, George Frew, CA. Past Chairman, Dundee United Football Club; b. 18.11.13, Carnoustie; m., Violet J. Low; 2 d. Educ. Grove Academy, Dundee. Commenced practice as CA, 1938; War Service, 1940-46; resumed practice, 1946; retired, 1978; former Treasurer, Scottish Football Association (Life Member); Life Member: Carnoustie Golf Club, Broughty Golf Club, Forfarshire Football Association, Tayside Athletic Club; Honorary President, Carnoustie Panmure PC; Honorary Vice President, Broughty Operatic Society. Recreation: golf. Address: (h.) 17 Lochty Street, Carnoustie, Angus.

Fox, Professor Keith Alexander Arthur, BSc (Hons), MB, ChB, FRCP. Duke of Edinburgh Professor of Cardiology, Edinburgh University, since 1989; b. 27.8.49, Salisbury, Rhodesia; m., Aileen E.M.; 1 s.; 1 d. Educ. Falcon College; Edinburgh University. Assistant Professor of Medicine, Washington University School of Medicine, 1980-85; Senior Lecturer in Cardiology and Consultant Cardiologist, University Hospital of Wales College of Medicine, 1985-89. Address: (b.) Cardiovascular Research Unit, Edinburgh University, Hugh Robson Building, George Square, Edinburgh, EH8 9XF; T.-031-650 3696.

Fraile, Professor Medardo, PhD. Writer; Emeritus Professor in Spanish, Strathclyde University, since 1985; b. 21.3.25, Madrid; m., Janet H. Gallagher; 1 d. Educ. Madrid University. Teacher of Spanish language and literature, Ramiro de Maeztu Secondary School, Madrid, 1956-64; Assistant in Spanish, Southampton University, 1964-67; Strathclyde University: Assistant Lecturer in Spanish, 1967-68, Lecturer, 1968-79, Reader, 1979-83, Personal Professor, 1983-85. Travelling Scholarship for authors, 1954; Premio Sesamo for short story writing, 1956; literary grant, Juan March Foundation, 1960; Book of the Year award, 1965; La Estafeta Literaria Prize for short stories, 1970; Hucha de Oro Prize for short stories, 1971; research grant, Carnegie Trust, 1975; Ibanez Fantoni Prize for journalism, 1988. Publications: several collections of short stories (Complete Short Stories, Madrid, 1991), a novel and books of literary criticism.

Recreations: swimming; walking. Address: (h.) 24 Etive Crescent, Bishopbriggs, Glasgow, G64 1ES; T.-041-772 4421.

Frame, John Neil Munro, LLB. Director, Bell Lawrie White & Co.; Member, Scottish Sports Council; b. 8.10.46, Edinburgh; m., Susan Macmillan; 2 s.; 2 d. Educ. Edinburgh University. Recreations: jogging slowly; golfing erratically; reading profusely. Address: 30 Murrayfield Road, Edinburgh, EH12 6ER; T.-031-346 0077.

Frame, Roger Campbell Crosbie, CA. Secretary, Royal Scottish Society of Painters in Water Colours, since 1986; Secretary, Glasgow Eastern Merchants and Tradesmen's Society, since 1983; Treasurer, Glasgow Group of Artists, 1983-88; b. 7.6.49, Glasgow; m., Angela M. Evaristi; 2 s.; 1 d. Educ. Glasgow Academy. Qualified CA, 1973; formed Frame & Co., CA, 1976. Deacon, Incorporation of Coopers of Glasgow, 1985-86. Recreations: clay pigeon shooting; art. Address: (b.) 29 Waterloo Street, Glasgow, G2 6BZ; T.-041-226 3838.

France, Anthony James, MA, MB, BChir, MRCP. Consultant Physician, Tayside Health Board, since 1989; Honorary Senior Lecturer, Dundee University, since 1989; b. 5.4.54, London; m., Rosemary; 1 s.; 2 d. Educ. Perse School, Cambridge; Magdalene College, Cambridge; St. Thomas' Hospital, London. Qualified 1978; specialises in management of HIV infection and other communicable diseases. Recreations: photography; gardening; decorating an old house. Address: (b.) King's Cross Hospital, Clepington Road, Dundee, DD3 8EA; T.-0382 816116.

France, Professor Peter, MA, PhD, FBA. Professor of French, Edinburgh University, 1980-90, Endowment Fellow, since 1990; b. 19.10.35, Londonderry; m., Sian Reynolds; 3 d. Educ. Bradford Grammar School; Magdalen College, Oxford. Fellow, Magdalen College, Oxford, 1960-63; Lecturer, then Reader in French, Sussex University, 1963-80; French Editor, Modern Language Review, 1979-85. Publications: Racine's Rhetoric, 1965; Rhetoric and Truth in France, 1972; Poets of Modern Russia, 1982; Diderot, 1982; Rousseau: Confessions, 1987; Politeness and its Discontents, 1991. Address: (b.) 60 George Square, Edinburgh, EH8 9JU; T.-031-667 1011.

Francis, John Michael, BSc, ARCS, PhD, DIC, FRSGS, FRSE. Chief Executive, Nature Conservancy Council for Scotland (Director Scotland, Nature Conservancy Council, 1984-91); b. 1.5.39, London; m., Eileen; 2 d. Educ. Gowerton Grammar School, near Swansea; Imperial College of Science and Technology, London University. CEGB Berkeley Nuclear Laboratories, 1963-70; Director, Society, Religion and Technology Project, Church of Scotland, 1970-74; Senior Research Fellow, Heriot-Watt University, 1974-76; Principal, Scottish Development Department, 1976-81; Assistant Secretary, Scottish Office, 1981-84. Consultant, World Council of Churches, 1971-83; Chairman, SRT Project, Church of Scotland; Member, Oil Development Council for Scotland, 1973-76; Member, Advisory Committee for Scotland, Nature Conservancy Council, 1973-76; Council Member, National Trust for Scotland, since 1984; Chairman, Edinburgh Forum, since 1986. Publications: Scotland in Turmoil, 1972; Changing Directions, 1973; Facing Up to Nuclear Power, 1976; The Future as an Academic Discipline, 1975; The Future of Scotland, 1977; contributions to scientific journals. Recreations: theatre; hill-walking; ecumenical travels. Address: (h.) 49 Gilmour Road, Newington, Edinburgh, EH16 5NU; T.-031-667 3996; (b.) Headquarters, Nature Conservancy Council for Scotland, 12 Hope Terrace, Edinburgh, EH9 2AS; T.-031-447 4784.

Franks, Graham, RGN, RMN, RNMH, DipN, MHSM, Dip. HSM. Chief Area Nursing Officer, Fife Health Board, since 1987; b. 30.10.43, Leicester; m., V.J. Franks. Educ. Guthlaxton Grammar School, Leicester. Manager, Patient Care Services, East Cumbria Health Authority; Director of Nursing Services, Carlisle Acute Hospitals; Area Nurse Planning/Personnel, Cumbria Area Health Authority; Regional Nursing Officer, Newcastle Regional Hospital Board. Address: (b.) Glenrothes House, Fife; T.-Glenrothes 754355.

Fraser, Alan Alexander, BSc (Hons), MBChB, MRCPsych. Consultant Psychiatrist, Southern General Hospital, Glasgow, since 1987; Honorary Senior Lecturer in Psychiatry, Glasgow University, since 1988; b. 17.10.55, Kilbirnie. Educ. Spier's School, Beith; Glasgow University. Address: (h.) 50 Westbourne Gardens, Glasgow, G12 9XF; T.-041-357 2283.

Fraser, Brian Mitchell, BA (Hons), PhD, DGA, MIPM. Assistant Principal, Glasgow Polytechnic; b. 31.7.43, Paisley; m., Hannah Orr Weir Burt; 3 s. Educ. Camphill High School, Paisley; London University; Strathclyde University. Civil Servant, 1962-70; Senior Administrator, Paisley College of Technology, 1970-78; Director of Personnel, Glasgow University, 1978-91; Boys' Brigade historian and leader. Publications: Sure and Stedfast - A History of the Boys' Brigade (Co-author), 1983; A Legacy of Scots (Co-author), 1988; Kirk and Community, 1990. Recreations: youth work; historical research. Address: (h.) Dunedin, Holehouse Road, Eaglesham; T.-Eaglesham 2416.

Fraser, Callum George, BSc, PhD, FAACB. Top Grade Biochemist, Ninewells Hospital and Medical School, since 1983; Honorary Senior Lecturer, Dundee University, since 1983; Honorary Senior Lecturer, St. Andrews University, since 1988; b. 3.1.45, Dundee; m., Stella Sim; 2 d. Educ. Dunfermline High School; Perth Academy; Aberdeen University. Postdoctoral Fellow, National Research Council of Canada, 1969-70; Lecturer in Chemical Pathology, Aberdeen University, and Honorary Biochemist, Grampian Health Board, 1970-75; Chief Clinical Biochemist, Flinders Medical Centre, South Australia, 1975-83; Honorary Senior Lecturer, then Honorary Associate Professor, Flinders University of South Australia, 1975-83. Chairman, Education Division, International Federation of Clinical Chemistry; former Member, Commission on Teaching of Clinical Chemistry, International Union of Pure and Applied Chemistry; Member, Editorial Board, Advances in Clinical Chemistry. Recreations: sailing; gardening; reading; travel. Address: (b.) Department of Biochemical Medicine, Ninewells Hospital, Dundee, DD1 9SY; T.-0382 60111.

Fraser, Sir Charles Annand, KCVO, WS, DL. Partner, W. & J. Burness, WS, since 1956; Chairman: Adam and Company PLC; Director: British Assets Trust PLC, Grosvenor Developments, Scottish Widows' Fund and Life Assurance Society, Scottish Television PLC, Scottish Business in the Community; Vice Chairman, United Biscuits (Holdings) PLC; b. 16.10.28, Humbie, East Lothian; m., Ann Scott-Kerr; 4 s. Educ. Hamilton Academy; Edinburgh University. Purse Bearer to Lord High Commissioner to General Assembly of Church of Scotland, 1969-88; served on Court, Heriot-Watt University, 1972-78; Council Member, Law Society of Scotland, 1966-72; Trustee, Scottish Civic Trust. Recreations: gardening; skiing; squash; piping. Address: (h.) Shepherd House, Inveresk, Midlothian; T.-031-665 2570.

Fraser, Donald Chisholm, MCCEd, DipTechEduc, DipEducTech. Secretary to the Council and Director, Policy and Administration, Scottish Consultative Council on the Curriculum, since 1988; b. 27.7.32, Inverness; m., Patricia A. Ross; 1 s.; 2 d. Educ. Inverness High School; Jordanhill

College of Education; Dundee Institute of Technology. Teacher, Inverness-shire, 1955-62; Principal Teacher, Millburn Academy, Inverness, 1962-63; Head of Technical/Engineering, High School of Dundee, 1963-71; Lecturer in Technical Education, Dundee College of Education, 1971-74; Assistant Director, Scottish Centre for Mathematics, Science and Technical Education, 1974-82; Director, Scottish Curriculum Development Service (Dundee Centre), 1982-88. Member, Scottish Advisory Committee, The British Council. Recreations: gardening; angling; dabbling in oils; travel. Address: (h.) 7 Ralston Road, Broughty Ferry, Dundee; T.-Dundee 76587.

Fraser, Douglas Jamieson. Poet; b. 12.1.10, Edinburgh; m., Eva Nisbet Greenshields; 2 s.; 1 d. Educ. George Heriot's School. Spent 44 years with Standard Life Assurance Company, Edinburgh; awarded Queen's Silver Jubilee Medal. Publications: Landscape of Delight; Rhymes o' Auld Reekie; Where the Dark Branches Part; Treasure for Eyes to Hold. Recreation: painting. Address: (h.) 2 Keith Terrace, Edinburgh, EH4 3NJ; T.-031-332 5176.

Fraser, Elwena D.A. Honorary Sheriff, Tayside, Central and Fife, since 1982; Member, Rateable Valuation Appeal Committee, 1975-85; Governor, Dundee Institute of Technology, 1969-89, Fellow of Dundee Institute, since 1990; b. 5.9.31, Lowestoft; m., Dr. Ian Tuke Fraser; 2 s.; 1 d. Educ. Craigholm School, Glasgow; Calder Girls' School, Seascale. Journalist, Scottish Daily Express, 1950-54; Member, Perth Town Council, 1969-72; Member, Education Committee, Perth County Council, 1969-72; Member, Dundee University Adult Education Committee, 1969-72; Member, Executive Committee, Perth Tourist Association, 1969-72; Member, Executive Committee, Perth Festival of the Arts, 1971-81; Board Member, Perth College of Further Education, 1972-78 (Chairman, 1975-78); Honorary Manager, Trustee Savings Bank (Perthshire), 1973-75; Member, Gas Consumers Council for Scotland, since 1973; Member, BBC Broadcasting Council for Scotland, 1977-80. Recreation: gardening. Address: (h.) 15 Spoutwells Avenue, Scone, Perthshire, PH2 6RP; T.-0738 51310.

Fraser, Eugenie. Writer, since 1980; b. 10.12.05, Archangel, Russia; m., Ronald Fraser; 2 s. Educ. Archangel; Bruce's Business College, Dundee. Housewife since marriage in 1935; spent 26 years travelling to and from India; four years to and from Thailand. Scottish Arts Council Award-winner. Recreations: swimming; sewing; embroidery; travel. Address: (h.) 5 Braid Crescent, Edinburgh, EH10 6AX; T.-031-447 3855.

Fraser, Hugh Donald George, MBE, QPM, DipSM, OStJ, FBIM, MIPM, MIIRSM. Former Senior Assistant Secretary, Heriot-Watt University; Member, Lothian Regional Council, since 1982; Honorary Secretary, Scottish Chamber of Safety, since 1979; b. Edinburgh; m., Margaret Jane Stothard; 1 s.; 2 d. War Service, RAF Aircrew, 1939-45 (Pilot); Edinburgh City Police, 1941-71; Chief Superintendent, Research and Planning Branch, Home Office, London, 1966-68; Deputy Commandant, Scottish Police College, 1968-71. Honorary Secretary, Edinburgh and District Spastic Association, 14 years; Member: Edinburgh Accident Prevention Council, Lothian Retirement Committee. Recreations: Burns' enthusiast; work with senior citizens; jogging; the theatre. Address: (h.) 181 Braid Road, Edinburgh, EH10 6JA; T.-031-447 1270.

Fraser, Ian Ross, OBE, MA (Hons), MEd. Rector, Inverness Royal Academy, since 1971; b. 16.4.30, Carmyle, Lanarkshire; m., Trudy C. Marshall; 3 s.; 1 d. Educ. Aberdeen Grammar School; Aberdeen University; Aberdeen College of Education. Principal Teacher of Geography, Elgin Academy, 1960-66; Rector, Waid Academy, Anstruther,

1966-71; Member, Ruthven Committee on Ancillary Staff in Secondary Schools, 1973-76; Honorary Secretary, 1975-77, and President, 1978-79, Headteachers' Association of Scotland; Chairman, Highland Region Curriculum Coordinating Group, 1980-84; Chairman, Scottish Central Committee on Social Subjects, 1981-83; Chairman, Steering Committee, S1/2 Social Subjects Development Programme, 1983-87; Vice Chairman, Scottish Consultative Council on the Curriculum, SCCC Board of Management, SCCC Secondary Committee (Convener, 1987-91). Recreations: tennis; fishing; hill-walking. Address: (h.) Yendor, Dores Road, Inverness, IV2 4XE; T.-0463 232862.

Fraser, Ian Scott, BSc (Econ), LLB, DEc, DPA, FBIM. Barrister-at-Law; Advocate; b. 21.7.18, Dundee; m., Kathleen Mary Fraser; 1 s.; 1 d. Educ. Fort William High School; London University. Civil Service: Admiralty, 1936-46, Ministry of Pensions and National Insurance, 1946-55 and 1961-63, Treasury, 1955-57 (seconded to NATO (Shape) Paris 1956-57); United Nations official, 1957-61 and 1963-76, serving in Ethiopia and other African countries, New York, Middle East, and South America; travel and further education, 1976-81; practising Advocate, 1981-86; Chairman, Board of Directors, Scottish Rights of Way Society Ltd., 1983-86; Life Member, National Trust for Scotland and Royal Scottish Geographical Society. Recreations: travel; photography; motor caravanning; walking. Address: (h.) 1 Mayfield Gardens, Edinburgh, EH9 2AX; T.-031-667 3681.

Fraser, Professor Sir James David, 2nd Bt, FRCSEdin, FRCS, ChM, BA, MBChB. Postgraduate Dean, Faculty of Medicine, Edinburgh University, 1981-89; b. 19.7.24.

Fraser, James Edward, CB, MA (Aberdeen), BA (Cantab), FSA (Scot). Secretary of Commissions for Scotland, since 1992; b. 16.12.31, Aberdeen; m., Patricia Louise Stewart; 2 s. Educ. Aberdeen Grammar School; Aberdeen University; Christ's College, Cambridge. Royal Artillery, 1953-55 (Staff Captain, "Q", Tel-El-Kebir, 1954-55); Assistant Principal, Scottish Home Department, 1957-60; Private Secretary to Permanent Under-Secretary of State, Scottish Office, 1960-62; Private Secretary to Parliamentary Under-Secretary of State, Scottish Office, 1962; Principal, 1962-69: SHHD, 1962-64, Cabinet Office, 1964-66, HM Treasury, 1966-68, SHHD, 1968-69; Assistant Secretary: SHHD, 1970-76, Scottish Office Finance Division, 1976; Under Secretary, Local Government Finance Group, Scottish Office, 1976-81, Scottish Home and Health Department, 1981-91. President, Scottish Hellenic Society, Edinburgh and Eastern Scotland. Recreations: reading; music; walking; Greece, ancient and modern. Address: (b.) St. Andrew's House, Edinburgh, EH1 3DG.

Fraser, John, MA (Hons). Rector, Mackie Academy, Stonehaven, since 1975; b. 8.8.36, Inverness; m., Judith Helen Procter; 2 d. Educ. Inverness Royal Academy; Aberdeen University; Aberdeen College of Education. Teacher, Harris Academy, 1960-66; Principal Teacher of History, Buckie High School, 1966-72; Assistant Head Teacher and Depute Rector, Peterhead Academy, 1972-75; Governor, Aberdeen College of Education, since 1984; Member: GTC, 1979-83 and 1990-91, Grampian Region Education Committee, 1975-78; Regional Convener, SSTA, 1976-86. Conductor: Buckie Choral Union, 1968-72; Peterhead Choral Society, 1972-75; Organist in various churches; President, Stonehaven Rotary Club, 1988-89. Recreations: music; DIY. Address: (b.) Slug Road, Stonehaven; T.-Stonehaven 62071/2.

Fraser, John A.W., MA, FEIS, JP, DL. Headmaster, Scalloway Junior High School, 1966-88; Deputy Lieutenant for Shetland, since 1985; b. 9.11.28, Lerwick; m., Jane Ann Jamieson; 2 s. Educ. Anderson Educational Institute; Edinburgh University; Moray House College of Education.

Education Officer, RAF, 1950-52; Teacher, Baltasound Junior Secondary School, 1952-54; Head Teacher: Haroldswick Primary School, 1954-59, Aith Junior High School, 1959-66. Former Member, National Council, EIS; Chairman, Scalloway Development Association; Member, Shetland Valuation Appeals Committee; General Commissioner of Income Tax. Recreations: genealogy; travel; gardening. Address: (h.) Broadwinds, Castle Street, Scalloway, Shetland; T.-Scalloway 644.

Fraser, Rev. John Gillies. Chairman, Lord's Day Observance Society, Scottish Council, 1985-89; Chairman, Church of Scotland Total Abstainers Society, since 1980; Vice-Chairman, National Church Association, since 1986; Minister, Macgregor Memorial Church, Glasgow, 1960-70, Elderpark Macgregor Memorial Church, 1970-86; 5.7.14, Glasgow; m., Jessie MacKenzie Mayer; 1 s.; 3 d. Educ. Shawlands Academy; Glasgow University and Trinity College. Public Assistance Department (later Social Service Department), Glasgow Corporation, 1931-48; Ministry of National Insurance, 1948; divinity student, 1948-50; Minister/Missionary, Church of Scotland, Northern Rhodesia, 1950-60; Minister, Macgregor Memorial Church, 1960-70. Scottish Assistant Secretary, Crusaders' Union, 1935-47; Secretary, South West Glasgow Sunday School Union, 1942-47. Recreation: gardening. Address: (h.) 17 Beaufort Gardens, Bishopbriggs, Glasgow, G64 2DJ; T.-041-772 2987.

Fraser, Rev. John Hamilton, LTh. Minister, Castle Douglas Parish Church, since 1990; b. 2.12.40, Irvine; m., Mary Clark Kirkland; 2 s.; 1 d. Educ. Irvine Royal Academy; Glasgow University and Trinity College. Eleven years in engineering before going to university; Minister, Paisley: St. Columba Foxbar, 1973-79; Rutherglen: Wardlawhill, 1979-83; United Reformed Church minister, York and Bradford, 1983-90. Recreations: reading; painting; drawing. Address: (h.) 1 Castle View, Castle Douglas; T.-Castle Douglas 2171.

Fraser of Carmyllie, Lord (Peter Fraser), QC. Minister of State, Scottish Office, since 1992; b. 29.5.45. MP (Conservative), Angus South, 1979-83, Angus East, 1983-87; Solicitor-General for Scotland, 1982-89; Lord Advocate, 1989-92.

Fraser, Raymond Morris, LLB (Hons). Advocate, since 1971; b. 16.2.47, Edinburgh. Educ. George Heriot's School, Edinburgh; Edinburgh University. Conservative Parliamentary candidate, Orkney and Shetland, October 1974; instigator of visit to Angola, 1976, to defend British mercenaries at war crimes trial; Hon. President, Auchinleck Boswell Society, 1989-90. Address: (h.) Bonaly Tower, Edinburgh; T.-031-441 6522.

Fraser, Robert W., BSc (Hons), CEng, FICE, FIWEM. Director, Water and Drainage Services, Borders Regional Council, since 1981; b. 13.5.39, Kirkcaldy; m., Elizabeth; 1 s.; 1 d. Educ. Kirkcaldy High School; Edinburgh University. Address: (b.) West Grove, Waverley Road, Melrose, TD6 9SJ; T.-Melrose 2056.

Fraser, Simon Cumming. Director, Scottish Landowners' Federation, since 1989; b. 18.9.35, Sevenoaks; m., Elspeth Dickson; 1 s.; 1 d. Educ. RN College, Dartmouth. Royal Navy, 1949-88, as a Commander, Staff Planning Officer to Flag Officer Scotland, 1984-88. Recreations: hill-walking; gardening. Address: (b.) 25 Maritime Street, Edinburgh; T.-031-555 1031.

Fraser, Sheriff Simon William Hetherington, LLB, NP. Sheriff of North Strathclyde at Dumbarton, since 1989; b. 2.4.51, Carlisle; m., Sheena Janet; 1 d. Educ. Glasgow Academy; Glasgow University. Solicitor, 1973; Partner, Flowers & Co., Solicitors, Glasgow, 1976-89; Temporary

Sheriff, 1987-89. Glasgow Bar Association: Secretary, 1977-79, President, 1981-82. Recreations: cricket; snooker. Address: (b.) Sheriff Court, Church Street, Dumbarton; T.-0389 63266.

Fraser, Professor William Douglas, BSc, MSc, PhD, FRICS. Professor and Head, Department of Land Economics, Paisley College, since 1986; b. 3.1.40, Edinburgh. Educ. Edinburgh Academy; London University; Strathclyde University. Partner, Bingham, Hughes and Macpherson, Chartered Surveyors, Inverness, 1970-72; Lecturer, Department of Land Economics, Paisley College, 1972-83; Lecturer, Centre for Property Valuation and Management, City University, London, 1983-86. Publication: Principles of Property Investment and Pricing, 1984. Recreations: climbing; gardening. Address: (b.) Department of Land Economics, Paisley College, High Street, Paisley, PA1 2BE; T.-041-848 3450.

Fraser, William Hamish, MA, DPhil. Reader in History, Strathclyde University (Dean, Faculty of Arts and Social Studies, since 1987); b. 30.6.41, Keith; m., Helen Tuach; 1 d. Educ. Keith Grammar School; Aberdeen University; Sussex University. Lecturer in History, Strathclyde University, 1966-77. Publications: Trade Unions and Society 1850-1880, 1973; Workers and Employers, 1981; The Coming of the Mass Market, 1982; Conflict and Class: Scottish Workers 1700-1838, 1988; People and Society in Scotland 1830-1914, 1990. Recreations: hill-walking; skiing; cleaning canals. Address: (h.) 112 High Station Road, Falkirk, FK1 5LN; T.-0324 22868.

Fraser, Sir William Kerr, GCB (1984), LLD, FRSE. Principal and Vice Chancellor, Glasgow University, from October 1988; Permanent Under Secretary of State, Scottish Office, 1978-88; b. 18.3.29; m., Marion Anne Forbes; 3 s.; 1 d. Educ. Eastwood Secondary School; Glasgow University. RAF, 1952-55; various posts in Scottish Office, 1955-78, including Principal Private Secretary to Secretary of State for Scotland, 1966-67. Director, Scottish Mutual Assurance Society; Governor, Caledonian Research Foundation. Address: (b.) Glasgow University, Glasgow, G12 8QQ; T.-041-339 8855.

Freeman, Christopher Paul, BSc, MB, ChB, MPhil, FRCPsych. Consultant Psychiatrist, Royal Edinburgh Hospital, Edinburgh, since 1980; Senior Lecturer, Department of Psychiatry, Edinburgh University, since 1980; Psychiatric Tutor, Royal Edinburgh Hospital, since 1983; b. 21.4.47, York; m., Katherine; 2 s. Educ. Nunthorpe School, York; Edinburgh University. Royal College of Psychiatrists Gaskell Gold Medal. Publication: Research Methods in Psychiatry (Co-author), 1989. Recreations: tennis; squash; growing bonsaii trees. Address: (h.) The Old Farmhouse, Wester Pencaitland, East Lothian, EH34 5DE; T.-0875 340 612.

Freeman, James Martin, BSc, MSc, DipEd. Rector, Lawside RC Academy, Dundee, since 1986; b. 7.11.34, Edinburgh; m., Mary Agnes; 2 s.; 1 d. Educ. St. Anthony's RC School, Edinburgh; Edinburgh University; University of East Anglia. Assistant Headteacher, Liberton High School, Edinburgh, 1976-82; Depute Headteacher, Holy Rood High School, Edinburgh, 1982-86; Lecturer in Education, Makerere University, Kampala, 1969-73. Recreations: sailing; walking; reading; family. Address: (b.) School House, Dundee; T.-0382 825 801.

Freeman, Peter A., MA (Cantab), MB, BChir, FRCS, FRCS(Glas). Consultant Orthopaedic Surgeon; b. 24.1.25, Birmingham; m., Daphne Nicholson Crockett; 1 s.; 2 d. Educ. Christ's College, Cambridge; St. Bartholomew's Hospital, London. House Surgeon appointments, London, 1949-54; SHO and Registrar, Robert Jones and Agnes Hunt

Orthopaedic Hospital, Oswestry, 1954-57; Senior Registrar, Western Infirmary, Glasgow, 1957-61; Orthopaedic Assistant, Massachusetts General Hospital, Boston, 1959-61; Consultant Orthopaedic Surgeon, Victoria Infirmary and Associated Hospitals, Glasgow, 1961-89; Surgeon in Charge, West of Scotland Spinal Injuries Unit, Philipshill Hospital, Busby, 1980-88. Address: (h.) The Barracks, Auchenmalg, Newton Stewart, DG8 0LA; T.-058 15 274.

Freemantle, Andrew, MBE, FBIM. General Manager, Scottish Ambulance Service, since 1991; b. 26.9.44, Bournemouth; m., Patricia Mary; 4 d. Educ. Framlingham College; Royal Military College of Science. Commissioned, Royal Hampshire Regiment (Germany, Malaya, Borneo), 1965-69; Australian SAS Regiment (Australia, South Vietnam), 1969-72; Royal Hampshire Regiment, (Hong Kong, UK, Northern Ireland), 1972-76; Staff College, Camberley, 1978; Directing Staff, Staff College, 1983-84; Commanding Officer, Royal Hampshire Regiment (mention in Dispatches, 1987), 1985-87; Commander, 19 Infantry Brigade (Brigadier), 1987-89; Member, Royal College of Defence Studies, 1990. Recreations: running; cooking; field sports. Address: (b.) National Headquarters, Scottish Ambulance Service, Tipperlinn Road, Edinburgh, EH10 5UU; T.-031-447 7711.

Freer, Professor John Henry, BSc, MSc, PhD. Titular Professor in Microbiology, Glasgow University, since 1986, and Head of Botany/ Microbiology/Zoology Planning Unit, since 1991 (Reader, 1982-86; Head, Department of Microbiology, 1984-91); b. 17.11.36, Kasauli, India; m., Jocelyn Avril Williams; 4 d. Educ. Durham University; Nottingham University; Birmingham University. Lecturer in Microbiology, New South Wales University, Australia, 1962-65; New York University Medical Centre: Associate Research Scientist, then Assistant Professor, Microbiology, 1965-68; Senior Lecturer, Microbiology Department, Glasgow University, 1968-82; Editor-in-Chief, Journal of General Microbiology. Publication: Bacterial Protein Toxins (Joint Editor), 1988, 1990, 1992; Sourcebook of Bacterial Protein Toxius, 1991; 100 scientific articles. Recreations: sailing; painting. Address: (b.) Department of Microbiology, Glasgow University, Glasgow, G12 8QQ; T.-041-330 4642.

Friedman, Leonard Matthew. Artistic Director, Friedman Ensemble (and Players), since 1973; Artistic Director, Camerata of St. Andrew, since 1988; Recitalist with Allan Schiller; b. 11.12.30, London; 2 s.; 3 d. Educ. Coopers Company School; Guildhall School of Music and Drama. Artistic Director, Scottish Ensemble, 1969-86; Founder/Co-Founder/Leader/or Director of: Hadyn Orchestra, Kalmar Chamber Orchestra, Tilford Bach, London Bach, Bremen Bach, Northern Sinfonia, Cremona Quartet, International Mozart Ensemble, Friedman Ensemble, Scottish Baroque, Aleph Ensemble, Scottish Ensemble; Guest Leader/Deputy Leader of: Royal Philharmonic, Bremen Philharmonic, Westphalia Symphony, English Opera Group, Glyndebourne, Scottish Opera, Scottish Ballet, Italian Opera Company, Festival Ballet, English Chamber, Scottish Chamber, Royal Ballet, etc.; numerous broadcasts, summer schools, festivals, lectures, records; Gold Medal, Guildhall School of Music and Drama; Citizen of the Year, Edinburgh, 1980, for aiding the development of SBE, SCO and Queen's Hall; Leader, Scottish Philharmonic, five Edinburgh Festivals; Artistic Director, Mendelssohn on Mull Festival, 1988; Ensemble Coach, St. Mary's Music School. Recreations: relative religion; philosophy; cricket; politics (global). Address: (h.) 17 William Street, Edinburgh EH2 4PY.

Friend, James, MA, MB, ChB, FRCPEdin. Consultant in Thoracic Medicine, Grampian Health Board, since 1973; Clinical Senior Lecturer in Medicine, Aberdeen University, since 1973; b. 2.6.38, Edinburgh; m., Elizabeth; 1 s.; 2 d.

Educ. Edinburgh Academy; Gonville and Caius College, Cambridge; Edinburgh University. Hospital posts in Edinburgh and Oxford; Dorothy Temple Cross Fellowship, Seattle, 1971-72; British Thoracic Society: Council Member, 1983-91, Treasurer, 1984-91; Chairman, Grampian Action on Smoking and Health, since 1989. Recreation: the Scottish hills. Address: (b.) City Hospital, Aberdeen, AB2 1NJ; T.-0224 681818, Ext. 58303.

Frier, Brian Murray, BSc (Hons), MD, FRCP (Edin), FRCP (Glas). Consultant Physician, Royal Infirmary, Edinburgh, since 1987; Honorary Senior Lecturer in Medicine, Edinburgh University, since 1987; b. 28.7.47, Edinburgh; m., Dr. Isobel M. Wilson; 1 d. Educ. George Heriot's School, Edinburgh; Edinburgh University. Medical Registrar, Ninewells Hospital, Dundee, 1974-76; Research Fellow in Diabetes and Metabolism, Cornell University Medical Centre, The New York Hospital, 1976-77; Senior Medical Registrar, Royal Infirmary, Edinburgh, 1978-82; Consultant Physician, Western Infirmary and Grartnavel General Hospital, Glasgow, 1982-87. R.D. Lawrence Lecturer, British Diabetic Association, 1986; Governor, George Heriot's Trust, Edinburgh. Recreations: appreciation of the arts; ancient and modern history. Address: (h.) 100 Morningside Drive, Edinburgh, EH10 5NT; T.-031-447 1653.

Frizzell, Edward W. MA (Hons). Chief Executive, Scottish Prison Service, since 1991; Board Member, Quality Scotland Foundation, since 1991; b. 4.5.46, Paisley; m., Moira Calderwood; 2 s.; 1 d. Educ. Paisley Grammar School; Glasgow University. Scottish Milk Marketing Board, 1968-73; Scottish Council (Development and Industry), 1973-76; DAFS, Scottish Office, 1976-78; First Secretary, Fisheries, Office of the UK Permanent Representative to European Communities, Brussels (Foreign and Commonwealth Office), 1978-82; Assistant Secretary (Grade 5), Scottish Education Department, Higher Education Division, 1982-86; Scottish Office Finance Division, 1986-89; Director, Locate in Scotland, Scottish Office Industry Department (Grade 4), 1989-91. Recreations: fewer and fewer. Address: (b.) Calton House, 5 Redheughs Rigg, Edinburgh, EH12 9HW; T.-031-244 8522.

Froude, Rev. J. Kenneth, MA, BD (Hons). Minister, St. Brycedale Church, Kirkcaldy, since 1979; b. 8.12.50, Glasgow. Educ. Hillhead High School; Aberdeen University. Trained in personnel management; Assistant Minister, Northfield, Aberdeen, 1978-79; Business Committee Convener, Kirkcaldy Presbytery; Member, local Careers Service Committee; Presenter, BBC Schools radio programme. Recreations: running; singing; squash; mountaineering. Address: 6 East Fergus Place, Kirkcaldy; T.-0592 264480.

Frutin, Bernard Derek, MBE. Entrepreneur and Inventor; Chairman and Managing Director: Rocep Lusol Holdings Ltd., since 1973, Rocep Pressure Packs Ltd., since 1987; b. 7.2.44, Glasgow; m., Victoria Ellen; 3 d. Educ. Kelvinside Academy, Glasgow. Winner of nine international innovator awards since 1989, including John Logie Baird and British Institute of Packaging Environmental Awards; Finalist, 1992 Prince of Wales Award. Recreations: sailing; skiing; fine food; listening to music. Address: (b.) Rocep Lusol Holdings Ltd., Glasgow Road, Deanpark, Renfrew, PA4 8XY; T.-041-885 2222.

Fry, Stephen C., BSc, PhD. Reader in Botany, Edinburgh University, since 1989; b. 26.11.53, Sheffield; m., Verena Ryffel; 3 d. Educ. Thornbridge School, Sheffield; Leicester University. Postdoctoral Research Fellow, Cambridge University, 1978-79; Royal Society Rosenheim Research Fellow, Cambridge University, 1979-82; Senior Research Associate, University of Colorado, 1982-83; Lecturer in Botany, Edinburgh University, 1983-89. Margaret Wallace

Henry Prize, Leicester University, 1975; President's Medal, Society for Experimental Biology, 1988. Publication: The Growing Plant Cell Wall: Chemical and Metabolic Analysis, 1988. Recreations: hill-walking; paper chromatography. Address: (b.) Division of Biological Sciences, Edinburgh University, King's Buildings, Mayfield Road, Edinburgh, EH9 3JH; T.-031-650 5320.

Fullarton, John Hamilton, ARIAS, DipTP. Consultant Architect and Town Planner; Director of Technical Services, Scottish Special Housing Association, 1979-89; b. 21.2.31, Dalry, Ayrshire; m., Elvera Peebles; 1 s. Educ. Dalry High School; Glasgow School of Art; Royal Technical College, Glasgow; Edinburgh College of Art. Architect with local authorities before joining Scottish Office, 1964; Superintending Architect, Scottish Development Department, 1970-78; Head of New Towns, Construction Industry Division, Scottish Economic Planning Department, 1978-79. Research Fellowship, Urban Planning, Edinburgh College of Art, 1966-67. Publications: Scottish Housing Handbooks: Space Standards, 1969; Housing for the Elderly, 1970; Waverley Park Conservation Study, 1977. Address: (h.) 7 Queens Crescent, Edinburgh, EH9 2AZ; T.-031-667 5809.

Fulton, Rikki, OBE. Actor; b. 15.4.24, Glasgow; m., Kate Matheson. Educ. Whitehill Secondary School. Invalided out of RNVR as Sub-Lt., 1945; began professional career broadcasting with BBC in Glasgow; Presenter, BBC Showband, London, 1951-55; appeared in numerous pantomimes and revues with Howard & Wyndham from 1955, including Five Past Eight shows; television work including Scotch & Wry (creator, Rev. I.M. Jolly) and starring roles in The Miser and A Winter's Tale; films including The Dollar Bottom, Gorky Park, Local Hero, Comfort and Joy and The Girl in the Picture. Scottish TV Personality of the Year, 1963 and 1979; Best Light Entertainment Performance of the Year, 1969 and 1983; President's Award, Television and Radio Industries Club, 1988. Recreations: bridge; chess; reading; music (listening and piano); writing; painting.

Fulton, William Francis Monteith, BSc, MD (Hons), MB, ChB, FRCP, FRCPGlas, FRCPEdin. Reader, Department of Materia Medica, Glasgow University, 1977-84; Consultant Physician, Stobhill General Hospital, Glasgow, 1958-84; b. 12.12.19, Aberdeen; m., Dr. Frances I. Melrose; 1 s.; 1 d. Educ. Bryanston School, Dorset; Glasgow University. Resident Physician and Surgeon, Western Infirmary, Glasgow, 1945-46; National Service, Merchant Navy, 1946-48 (Ship's Surgeon); joined National Health Service, 1950; Research Assistant, Cardiology, Edinburgh University, 1952-53; Senior Lecturer, Department of Materia Medica, Glasgow University, 1958-77; Senior Fellow, Cardiology, Johns Hopkins Hospital, Baltimore, 1963-64; Foundation Professor of Medicine, Nairobi University, 1967-72. Publications: The Coronary Arteries, 1965; Modern Trends in Pharmacology and Therapeutics, 1967. Address: (h.) Woodhill, Braemar, AB3 5XX; T.-033 97 41239.

Furnell, James R.G., MA (Hons), DCP, PhD, LLB, FBPsS, DipLP. Consultant Clinical Psychologist (Child Health), Forth Valley Health Board, since 1980; Honorary Fellow, Edinburgh University, since 1987; b. 20.2.46, London; m., Lesley Anne Ross; 1 s.; 1 d. Educ. Leighton Park Society of Friends School, Reading; Aberdeen University; Glasgow University; Stirling University; Dundee University. Clinical Psychologist, Royal Hospital for Sick Children, Glasgow, 1970-72; Senior Clinical Psychologist, Forth Valley Health Board, 1972-80. Member, National Consultative Committee of Scientists in Professions Allied to Medicine, 1984-87 (Secretary, Clinical Psychology Sub-Committee); Member, Forth Valley Health Board, 1984-87; Chairman, Division of Clinical Psychology, British Psychological Society, 1988-89. Recreations: flying; cross-country skiing. Address: (h.)

Glensherup House, Glendevon, by Dollar, Perthshire, FK14 7JY; T.-Muckhart 234.

Furness, Professor Raymond Stephen, BA, MA, PhD. Professor of German, St. Andrews University, since 1984; b. 25.10.33, Builth Wells; m., Janice Fairey; 1 s.; 2 d. Educ. Welwyn Garden City Grammar School; University College, Swansea. Modern Languages Department, University of Manchester Institute of Science and Technology; Department of German, Manchester University. Publications: Expressionism; Literary History of Germany 1890-1945; Wagner and Literature; A Companion to Twentieth Century German Literature. Recreation: old horror films. Address: (h.) The Dirdale, Boarhills, St. Andrews, KY16 8PP; T.-033 488 469.

Furness, Lt. Col. Simon John, DL. Landowner; Vice Lord Lieutenant, Berwickshire, since 1990; b. 18.3.36, Ayton. Educ. Charterhouse; RMA, Sandhurst. Commissioned Durham Light Infantry, 1956, 2nd Lt.; served Far East, UK, Germany; active service, Borneo, Northern Ireland; retired, 1978; appointed Deputy Colonel (Durham) The Light Infantry, 1989. Member, Executive, National Trust for Scotland (Chairman, Gardens Committee). Recreations: field sports; gardening. Address: The Garden House, Netherbyres, Eyemouth, Berwickshire, TD14 5SE; T.-08907 50337.

Fyfe, Maria, BA (Hons). MP, Glasgow Maryhill, since 1987; b. 25.11.38, Glasgow; 2 s. Educ. Notre Dame High School, Glasgow; Strathclyde University. Glasgow District Councillor, 1980-87; Senior Lecturer, Central College of Commerce, 1977-87; Member, Scottish Executive Committee, Labour Party, 1981-87. Address: (b.) House of Commons, London, SW1A 0AA; T.-071-219 4430/6819; 041-945 1495.

Fyfe, William Stevenson, OBE (1987). Chairman, Ayrshire and Arran Health Board, since 1981; Chairman, Scientific & Professional Staffs Whitley Council, 1989-91; Chairman, Coastal Crafts and Printing Ltd., since 1982; Fellow, Institution of Industrial Managers, since 1985; b. 10.6.35, Glasgow; m., Margaret H.H. Auld; 1 s.; 1 d. Educ. Dollar Academy; Scottish College of Commerce. Town Councillor, Prestwick, 1967-73 (Magistrate, 1970-73, Acting Treasurer, 1971-73); Ayr County Councillor, 1970-73; appointed to Ayrshire and Arran Health Board, 1973 (Financial Convener, 1973-81); Chairman, Scottish Health Service Advisory Council, 1989-93; Member, General Whitley Council, 1989-91. Recreation: golf. Address: (h.) Ford House, Pennyglen, Culzean, KA19 8JW.

Fyfe, William Stuart Fraser, BSc (Agric). Depute Principal, Elmwood College, Cupar; b. 26.5.29, Dundee; 2 s.; 1 d. Educ. Morgan Academy, Dundee; Aberdeen University. Teacher of Science Subjects, Webster Seminary, Kirriemuir, 1955; Lecturer of Agricultural Subjects, Elmwood Agricultural Centre, Cupar, 1956. Head of Centre (Non-Vocational Evening Classes), Elmwood, 1980. Recreations: hill-walking; skiing; international holidays; family. Address: (h.) Royston, Carslogie Road, Cupar, Fife; T.-0334 55090.

G

Galbraith, Rev. David Douglas, MA, BD, BMus, MPhil. Chaplain to St. Andrews University, since 1987; b. 22.6.40,

Kirkintilloch; m., Dr. Jillian Galbraith; 2 d. Educ. Ardrossan Academy; High School of Dundee; St. Andrews University; Glasgow University. Associate Minister, Craigmillar, Edinburgh, 1970-77; Minister, Strathkinness Parish Church, 1977-80; Lecturer in Practical Theology, St. Andrews University, 1980-81; Professor of Ministry and Mission, Trinity Theological College, Brisbane, 1981-86. Music Director, Craigmillar Festival Society, 1972-77; Secretary, Queensland Branch, Royal School of Church Music, 1982-86; founder Editor, One Voice, Australian church music magazine; Co-Editor, Trinity Occasional Papers; 1992 Morrison Lecturer, Western Australia. Publications: Square Dance in Heaven; New Ways to Worship (Co-author); Worship in the Wide Red Land (Editor). Recreations: musical composition; dinghy sailing. Address: (b.) Chaplaincy Centre, 3A St. Mary's Place, St. Andrews, KY16 9UY; T.-0334 76161, Ext. 569.

Galbraith, Philip Andrew, BSc (Hons), DipEd. Rector, Greenwood Academy, Irvine, since 1987; b. 8.7.46, Edinburgh; m., Dorothy; 1 s.; 2 d. Educ. Mackie Academy, Stonehaven; Aberdeen University. Principal Teacher, Geography, Marr College, Troon; Assistant Rector, Auchinleck Academy; Depute Rector, Auchenharvie Academy. Immediate Past President, Scottish Association of Geography Teachers. Recreations: golf; walking; aviation. Address: (b.) Greenwood Academy, Dreghorn, Irvine; T.-0294 213124.

Galbraith, Roderick Allister McDonald, BSc, PhD (Cantab), CEng, MRAeS. Head of Aerospace Engineering, Glasgow University, since 1989; b. 4.8.47, Lowmoor, England; m., Lynn Margaret Fraser. Educ. Greenock High School; James Watt Memorial College; Paisley College of Technology; Cambridge University. Apprentice Draughtsman/Engineer, Scott's Shipbuilding & Engineering Co. Ltd., 1964-72; Department of Aerospace Engineering, Glasgow University: joined 1975; Reader, 1989. Publications: over 100 reports and publications on aerodynamics. Recreations: sailing; walking. Address: (b.) Department of Aerospace Engineering, Glasgow University, Glasgow, G12 8QQ; T.-041-330 5295.

Galbraith, Samuel Laird, BSc, MBChB, MD, FRCSGlas. MP (Labour), Strathkelvin and Bearsden, since 1987; Neurosurgeon; b. 18.10.45.

Gall, James, LDS, RFPS. Deputy Chief Dental Officer, Scottish Home and Health Department, 1976-87; Honorary Visiting Dental Surgeon, Glasgow Dental School and Hospital, since 1964; Senior Dental Adviser, Prisons Division, Scottish Office, and Senior Dental Adviser, Supplies Division and Building Division, Common Services Agency, NHS, 1977-87; b. 21.4.24, Wishaw; m., Margaret Law Cram; 1 s.; 2 d. Educ. Bellshill Academy; Glasgow University. General Dental Practitioner, 1948-74; joined SHHD as Dental Officer, 1974; elected to local Dental Committee, Lanarkshire, 1958-74 (Member, Executive Council); Member, Area Dental Committee, Lanarkshire Health Board, 1974-85; Dental Member, Scottish Dental Estimates Board, 1971-74; Chairman, Scottish Branch, British Society of Medical and Dental Hypnosis Society, 1970 (National Chairman, 1977-80, President, 1980-82); International Fellow, American Society of Clinical Hypnosis; Life Founder Fellow, Federation Dentaire International; Provincial Fellow, Royal Society of Medicine; Life Fellow, Royal Zoological Society of Scotland. President, Clyde Toastmasters Club, 1962; served in Boys Brigade as Officer, 1st Bellshill. Publication: Modern Trends in Hypnosis (Contributor), 1983. Recreations: gardening; golf; boating; music; reading; bridge;

152   WHO'S WHO IN SCOTLAND

football. Address: (h.) The Bungalow, Douglas Gardens, Uddingston, Glasgow; T.-Uddingston 812878.

Gallacher, Tom. Writer; b. 16.2.34, Alexandria. Stage plays: Our Kindness to 5 Persons, 1969; Mr Joyce is Leaving Paris, 1971; Revival, 1972; Three to Play, 1972; Schellenbrack, 1973; Bright Scene Fading, 1973; The Only Street, 1973; Personal Effects, 1974; A Laughing Matter, 1975; Hallowe'en, 1975; The Sea Change, 1976; A Presbyterian Wooing (adapted from Pitcairne's The Assembly), 1976; The Evidence of Tiny Tim, 1977; Wha's Like Us - Fortunately!, 1978; Stage Door Canteen, 1978; Deacon Brodie (adapted from Stevenson and Henley), 1978; Jenny, 1979; Natural Causes, 1980; The Parole of Don Juan, 1981; The Treasure Ship (adapted from Brandane), 1982. Publications: (fiction): Hunting Shadows, 1981; Apprentice, 1983; Journeyman, 1984; Survivor, 1985; The Jewel Maker, 1986; The Wind on the Heath, 1987; The Stalking Horse, 1989; Gainful Perjury, 1990. Address: (b.) Alan Brodie Representation, 91 Regent Street, London, W1R 7TB.

Gallagher, Rt. Rev. Monsignor Hugh Provost. Parish Priest, St. Mary's, Greenock, since 1972; Diocesan Treasurer, since 1964; Canon of Cathedral Chapter, since 1975; b. 30.4.20, Clydebank. Educ. St. Patrick's High School, Dumbarton; St. Peter's College, Bearsden. Assistant Priest, Gourock, 1945-56; Vice Rector, Royal Scots College, Valladolid, Spain, 1956-63; Chaplain, Little Sisters of the Poor, Greenock, 1964-69; Parish Priest, St. Columba's, Renfrew, 1969-72; Prelate of Honour by Pope John Paul II, 1987. President, Inverclyde Voluntary Association for Mental Health. Recreations: golf; music. Address: St. Mary's Rectory, 14 Patrick Street, Greenock, PA16 8NA; T.-Greenock 21084.

Gallagher, Sister Maire T., OBE, MA (Hons), DCE. Superior, Convent of Notre Dame, Dumbarton; Sister of Notre Dame Religious Congregation, since 1959; Chairman, Scottish Consultative Council on the Curriculum, 1987-91 (Chairman, Committee on Secondary Education, 1983-87); Member, Main Committee, 1986; b. 27.5.33, Glasgow. Educ. Notre Dame High School, Glasgow; Glasgow University; Notre Dame College of Education. Principal Teacher of History, Notre Dame High School, Glasgow; Lecturer in Secondary Education, Notre Dame College of Education; Headteacher, Notre Dame High School, Dumbarton, 1974-87. Member, Consultative Committee on the Curriculum, since 1976; Member, Executive, Secondary Heads Association (Scottish Branch), 1976-83; Coordinator, Christian Life Movement Groups, West of Scotland. Recreations: reading; dress-making; bird-watching. Address: (h.) Convent of Notre Dame, Cardross Road, Dumbarton, G82 4JH; T.-Dumbarton 62361.

Gallie, Philip (Phil) Roy, TEng, MIPhE. MP (Conservative), Ayr, since 1992; b. 3.6.39, Portsmouth; m., Marion Wands; 1 s.; 1 d. Educ. Dunfermline High School; Kirkcaldy Technical College. Former electrical engineer, Ben Line Steamers; SSEB/CEGB/SSEB, laterly Manager Galloway and Lanark Hydros and Inverkip Power Station. Conservative constituency chairman (twice); District Councillor, 1980-84; Elder, Church of Scotland. Recreations: sports; politics. Address: (b.) 1 Wellington Square, Ayr; T.-0292 263991.

Galloway, George. MP (Glasgow Hillhead), since 1987; Vice-Chair, Parliamentary Foreign Affairs Committee; b. 16.8.54, Dundee; m., Elaine Fyffe; 1 d. Educ. Harris Academy, Dundee. Production Worker, Michelin Tyres, 1974; Dundee Labour Party Organiser, 1977; General Secretary, War on Want, 1983. Chairman, Scottish Labour Party, 1981-82; Member, Scottish Labour Party Executive Committee, 1974-84; Founder and first General Secretary, Trade Union Friends of Palestine, 1979. Recreations: foot-

ball; music; films. Address: (b.) House of Commons, Westminster, London; T.-071-219 4084.

Galloway, Janice. Writer/Music Critic; b. 2.12.56, Kilwinning. Educ. Ardrossan Academy; Glasgow University. Variety of paid and unpaid work, including 10 years' teaching English in Ayrshire; music criticism for Glasgow Herald and The Observer Scotland; fiction writing, including one collection of short stories and one novel. Publications: The Trick Is To Keep Breathing, 1990; The Trick, 1991; Blood, 1991; New Writing Scotland (Co-Editor), 1990-91. Address: (h.) 25 Herriet Street, Pollokshields, Glasgow, G41 2NN; T.-041-429 0300.

Galloway, Peter George, BA, DipComm. Rector, Trinity Academy, Edinburgh, since 1983; b. 21.3.44, St. Andrews; m., Elizabeth; 1 d. Educ. Buckhaven High School; Heriot Watt University; Moray House College of Education. Teacher, Broughton Secondary, Edinburgh, 1967-69; Principal Teacher, Liberton High School, 1969-76; Assistant Rector, Royal High School, Edinburgh, 1976-80; Depute Head, James Gillespie's High School, Edinburgh, 1980-83. Recreations: rugby football, as a spectator; golf; tennis; cinema; travel; cooking. Address: (b.) Trinity Academy, Craighall Avenue, Edinburgh, EH6 4RT; T.-031-552 8101.

Galt, Rose Ann, MA (Hons), FEIS. Depute Registrar (Education), General Teaching Council for Scotland; Vice-Chairman, Scottish Council for the Validation of Courses for Teachers, since 1987; b. 19.3.37, Glasgow; m., William Galt; 1 d. Educ. Possil Secondary School, Glasgow; Glasgow University; Jordanhill College. Started teaching, Albert Secondary, Glasgow, 1960; appointed Principal Teacher (Guidance), 1970; after career break, resumed teaching, Our Lady's High School, Cumbernauld, 1971, and became Principal Teacher of English, Greenfaulds High School, 1975; EIS: Chairman, Glasgow Local Association, 1970-71, President, Dumbarton Local Association, 1976-77, National Vice-President, 1978-79, National President, 1979-80, Convener, Parliamentary Committee, 1987-89, Member, National Executive, 1987-89; Convener, Education Committee, General Teaching Council, 1982-86, Vice-Chairperson, 1985-87, Chairperson, 1987-89; Member, Scottish Examination Board, 1982-90; Member, European Executive Committee, World Confederation of Organisations of the Teaching Profession (WCOTP), 1988-89; Member, Strathclyde Regional Council Equality Working Party, 1986-87. Recreations: reading; cooking; fiendishly difficult crosswords. Address: (h.) 38 Meadow View, Cumbernauld, Glasgow; T.-0236 722028.

Gammell, James Gilbert Sydney, MBE, CA; b. 4.3.20, Camberley; m., Susan Patricia Bowring; 5 s.; 1 d. Educ. Winchester College. Major, Grenadier Guards, Second World War; Partner, Ivory & Sime, 1949, Chairman, 1974-85; former Director, Bank of Scotland, Standard Life. Recreation: farming. Address: (h.) Foxhall, Kirkliston, West Lothian, EH29 9ER; T.-031-333 3275.

Gammerman, Alexander, BSc, PhD. Reader in Computer Science, Department of Computer Science, Heriot-Watt University, since 1990; b. 2.11.49, Alma-Ata, USSR; m., Susan Caroline; 1 s.; 1 d. Educ. 6th High School, Tallinn, Estonia; Leningrad University. Post-Doctoral Research Fellow, Agrophysical Research Institute, Leningrad, 1969-76; Deputy Director of Computer Centre, Academy Science, Leningrad, 1976-80; Senior Research Fellow, Computer Centre, Health Service Bureau, Leningrad, 1980-83; Computer Science Department, Heriot-Watt University: Lecturer, 1983-87, Senior Lecturer, 1987-90. Recreations: Russian poetry and literature; chess; athletics. Address: (h.) 3 Polwarth Grove, Edinburgh, EH11 1LZ; T.-031-337 6744.

Garden, Neville Abbot. Presenter, BBC Radio Scotland (Queen Street Garden, since 1990, Good Morning Scotland, 1978-90, The Musical Garden, since 1979); Writer and Lecturer on musical and media matters; b. 13.2.36, Edinburgh; m., Jane Fowler; 1 s., 1 d.; 3 d. by pr. m. Educ. George Watson's College, Edinburgh. Reporter, Sub-Editor, Feature Writer, Evening Dispatch, 1953-63; Daily Columnist and Music Critic, Edinburgh Evening News, 1963-64; Senior Feature Writer, Scottish Daily Express, 1964-78; Music Critic and Columnist, Sunday Standard, 1981-83; Music Writer, Scotland on Sunday, since 1988; Conductor: Edinburgh Grand Opera, seven years; Edinburgh Ballet Theatre, nine years; Artistic Director, The Salon Orchestra (members of BBC Scottish Symphony Orchestra), since 1989; Musical Director, Southern Light Opera Company, since 1979. Publication: Bloomsbury Good Music Guide. Address: (b.) BBC, Queen Margaret Drive, Glasgow.

Gardiner, Iain Derek, FRICS. Chartered Surveyor, since 1957; Senior Partner, Souter & Jaffrey, Chartered Surveyors, since 1986; Vice Chairman, Royal Institution of Chartered Surveyors in Scotland, since 1991; b. 22.12.33, Glasgow; m., Kathleen Elizabeth Johnson; 2 s.; 1 d. Educ. Hutcheson's Grammar School, Glasgow; Royal Technical College, Glasgow. Trainee and Assistant Quantity Surveyor, John H. Allan & Sons, Glasgow, 1950-57; National Service, Royal Engineers, 1957-59; Souter & Jaffrey, Inverness: Quantity Surveyor, 1959-63, Partner, 1963-86. Chairman, Inverness Area, RICS in Scotland, 1969-70; Chairman, Quantity Surveyors Committee, RICS in Scotland, 1989-90; Chairman, Friends of Eden Court Theatre, 1981-82; Treasurer, Inverness Area Scout Council, since 1979. Recreations: swimming; travel; cookery. Address: (b.) 33 Academy Street, Inverness, IV1 1JN; T.-0463 239494.

Gardner, Angela Joy, BSc (Hons). Educational Affairs Coordinator Scotland, British Petroleum, since 1990; Member, Scottish Examinations Board, since 1991; b. 16.9.62, Wolverhampton; m., Andrew Ronald Gardner. Educ. Codsall High School; UMIST. BP Chemicals Ltd., South Wales and Grangemouth, 1984-90; BP Schools Link Officer, 1985-90. Member, General Teaching Council for Scotland, since 1990. Address: (b.) P.O. Box 44, Bo'ness Road, Grangemouth, FK3 9TA; T.-0324 476054.

Gardner, David Alistair. Chairman: Moray Firth Radio Limited, 1980-90, Hi-Line, Dingwall, since 1985; b. 10.10.30, Glasgow; m., Sheila Maree Stewart; 1 d. Educ. Fettes College, Edinburgh; Ross Hall, Scottish Hotel School, Glasgow. National service, RAF, 1949-50; involved in hotel/licensed trade as Manager/Owner/Director, since 1950; Past President, Inverness and Highland Region Licensed Trade Association; freelance, BBC Radio, 1958-80; own programme, Moray Firth Radio, since 1982; former Senior Bailie, Dornoch Town Council; former Member, Sutherland County Council; Past Chairman, North of Scotland Water Board. Co-Founder, Inverness Hospitals Broadcasting Service. Recreations: broadcasting; travel; golf. Address: (h.) Altyre, 10 Abertarff Road, Inverness, IV2 3NW; T.-0463 230684.

Gardner, Dianne Alicia, BA (Hons). Headmistress, Wellington School, Ayr, since 1988; b. 15.9.47, Wolverhampton; m., John W. Gardner. Educ. Ounsdale School; Liverpool University. Museum Assistant, 1969-71; Teacher of History, 1971-72; Head of History, then Senior Mistress, Wellington School, 1972-88. Recreations: painting; gardening. Address: (b.) Carleton Turrets, Ayr, KA7 2XH; T.-0292 269321.

Gardner, James, BSc. Rector, Dunblane High School, since 1989; b. 3.2.41, Glasgow; m., Margaret Catherine; 1 s.; 1 d. Educ. Allan Glen's School, Glasgow; Glasgow University;

Strathclyde University. Teacher of Mathematics, Allan Glen's School, 1968-76; Principal Teacher of Mathematics, Cranhill Secondary, Glasgow, 1976-80; Assistant Head Teacher, Dunoon Grammar School, 1980-84; Depute Rector, Wallace High School, Stirling, 1984-89. Member, British Antarctic Survey, 1963-66. Recreations: climbing; skiing; orienteering; chess. Address: (b.) Dunblane High School, Highfields, Dunblane; T.-0786 823823.

Gardner, Raymond Alexander. Features Editor, Glasgow Herald, since 1978 (also "Trencherman", Restaurant and Hotel Critic, since 1982, and weekly wine column); b. 6.11.44, Glasgow. Educ. High School of Glasgow. Various editorial positions, Fleet Street and Scotland; Columnist, Travel Writer and Author; Contributor to Decanter Magazine, A la Carte, Harpers, Homes and Gardens, Quick Magazine (Munich), Options, The Scotland Book, Motor Boat and Yachting, Radio Clyde, Radio Scotland, RTE. Publications: Land of Time Enough - A Journey Through the Waterways of Ireland; Glasgow - A Celebration (Contributor); Glasgow Herald Book of Glasgow. Recreation: doing nothing on boats in Ireland. Address: (b.) Glasgow Herald, 195 Albion Street, Glasgow, G1; T.-041-552 6255.

Garland, Professor David William, LLB, MA, PhD. Professor of Penology, Faculty of Law, Edinburgh University, since 1992; b. 7.8.55, Dundee; m., Anne Jowett; 2 d. Educ. Harris Academy, Dundee; Edinburgh University; Sheffield University. Edinburgh University: Lecturer, Faculty of Law, 1979-90, Reader, 1990-92; Davis Fellow, History Department, Princeton University, 1984-85; Visiting Professor: Boalt Law School, University of California, Berkeley, 1988, Department of Sociology, New York University, 1992, School of Law, New York University, 1992-93. Publications: Punishment and Welfare, 1985 (winner of Denis Carroll Prize, International Society of Criminology); Punishment and Modern Society (awarded Distinguished Scholar Award, American Sociological Association and Outstanding Scholarship Award, American Society for the Study of Social Problems). Recreations: football; squash; sociology. Address: Old College, South Bridge, Edinburgh, EH8 9YL; T.-031-650 2032.

Garner, John Angus McVicar, MB, ChB, DRCOG, DCH, MRCGP. Principal in general practice, since 1980; Vice-Chairman, Scottish General Medical Services Committee, since 1989; Member, Scottish Council, British Medical Association, since 1989; Chairman, Lothian Local Medical Committee, since 1991; b. 4.9.50, London; m., Catherine Lizbeth; 1 s.; 1 d. Educ. Eltham College; Edinburgh University. Secretary, Lothian Local Medical Committee, 1986-89; Member, General Medical Services Committee, since 1989; Member, National Medical Advisory Committee, since 1989. Recreations: amphibians and photographing fungi. Address: (h.) 25 Murrayfield Avenue, Edinburgh, EH12 6AU; T.-031-337 6120.

Garner-Smith, Brigadier Kenneth James, OBE, DL, MA. Deputy Lieutenant, Inverness-shire, since 1964; Honorary Sheriff, Inverness-shire, since 1967; Member, Queen's Bodyguard for Scotland (Royal Company of Archers), since 1953; b. 30.3.04; m., Mary Macdonald of Aird and Vallay; 1 s.; 2 d. Educ. Charterhouse; Trinity College, Oxford. Commissioned Seaforth Highlanders, 1925; campaigns: Palestine (Despatches, 1936), North Africa, 1942-43; Staff College (various staff appointments); Military Attache: HM Embassy, Oslo, 1945-48, HM Embassy, Ankara, 1954-57; Member, Inverness County Council, 1961-75; Chairman, Inverness CC Education Committee, 1967-75. Address: (h.) Cottage of Aird, Aird House, Inverness, IV1 2AA; T.-0463 231212.

Garraway, Professor William Michael, MD, MSc, FRCPE, FRCGP, FFCM, FACE, DObstRCOG, DCH. Professor of Public Health, Edinburgh University, since 1983; b. 26.1.42, Dumfries; m., Alison Mary Haggart; 1 s.; 1 d. Educ. Carlisle Grammar School; Edinburgh University; London University; Mayo Graduate School of Medicine. Lecturer, Department of Community Medicine, Edinburgh University, 1972-77 (Senior Lecturer, 1978-81); Consultant Epidemiologist, Mayo Clinic, Rochester, USA, 1981-83. Recreations: hill-walking; cross-country skiing. Address: (b.) Medical School, Teviot Place, Edinburgh, EH8 9AG.

Garrett, James Allan, MB, ChB, FRCSEdin, FRCSGlas. Consultant Surgeon, Stobhill Hospital, Glasgow, since 1967; b. 8.3.28, Glasgow; m., Margaret Keddie; 1 s.; 1 d. Educ. Hutchesons' Grammar School, Glasgow; Glasgow University. Captain, RAMC, 1952-54; House Officer, Registrar and Senior Registrar, Glasgow Royal Infirmary, 1954-67. Address: (h.) 12 Richmond Drive, Cambuslang, Glasgow, G72 8BH; T.-041-641 3333.

Gartside, Peter, BEd (Hons). Freelance education and training consultant; Research Officer, Scottish Council for Research in Education, 1987-88; Advisor, Scottish Council for Educational Technology, 1980-86; Secretary, Scottish Committee on Open Learning, 1983-86; b. 31.10.32, Oldham; m., Kathleen; 1 s. Educ. East Oldham High School; Chester Diocesan Training College; Charlotte Mason College of Education. National Service, Royal Scots Greys, 1951-53; Teacher, Hollinwood County Secondary School, Oldham, 1955-57; Housemaster, The Blue Coat School, Oldham, 1957-68; Head of House, Hattersley County Comprehensive School, 1968-70; Warden, Workington Teachers' Centre, Cumbria, 1970-76; Education Department, Independent Broadcasting Authority, 1977-78; Warden, West Cumbria Teachers' Centre, 1978-79. Former Honorary Secretary, National Committee of Teachers' Audio/Visual Aids Groups; former Member, BBC Radio Carlisle Education Education Advisory Panel. Recreations: walking; travel; music. Address (h.) 73 Argyle Way, Dunblane, FK15 9DY.

Garvie, Alexander Femister, MA. Reader, Department of Classics, Glasgow University, since 1987 (Senior Lecturer, 1972-87); b. 29.1.34, Edinburgh; m., Jane Wallace Johnstone; 1 s.; 1 d. Educ. George Watson's College, Edinburgh; Edinburgh University; Cambridge University. Assistant, then Lecturer, Department of Greek, Glasgow University, 1960-72; Visiting Gillespie Professor, College of Wooster, Ohio, 1967-68; Visiting Assistant Professor, Ohio State University, 1968; Visiting Professor, University of Guelph, 1986. Publications: Aeschylus' Supplices: Play and Trilogy, 1969; Aeschylus Choephori: Introduction and Commentary, 1986. Recreations: music; hill-walking. Address: (h.) 93 Stirling Drive, Bishopbriggs, Glasgow; T.-041-772 4140.

Garvie, Ian Graham Donaldson, MA (Hons), BLitt, DipEd. Rector, Auchmuty High School, Glenrothes, 1976-90; b. 7.6.29, Perth; m., Margaret M.C. McIntosh. Educ. Perth Academy; Edinburgh University; Moray House College; Exeter College, Oxford. Vice-Chairman, Scottish Talking Newspaper Group. Recreation: hill-walking. Address: (h.) 23 Lakeside Road, Kirkcaldy, KY2 5QJ; T.-0592 266886.

Gaskin, Professor Maxwell, DFC (and bar), MA. Jaffrey Professor of Political Economy, Aberdeen University, 1965-85; b. 18.11.21, Liverpool; m., Brenda Stewart; 1 s.; 3 d. Educ. Quarry Bank School, Liverpool; Liverpool University. War Service, RAF, 1941-46; Lecturer and Senior Lecturer in Economics, Glasgow University, 1951-65; Head, Department of Political Economy, Aberdeen University, 1965-81; Economic Consultant to Secretary of State for Scotland, 1965-87; Member, Scottish Agricultural Wages Board, 1972-90; Chairman, Foresterhill and Associated Hospitals Board, 1972-

74; Chairman, Flax and Hemp and Retail Bespoke Tailoring Wages Councils, since 1978; Member, Civil Engineering EDC, 1978-84; Chairman, Section F, British Association, 1978-79; President, Scottish Economic Society, 1981-84; Fellow, Royal Economic Society. Publications: The Scottish Banks: A Modern Survey, 1965; North East Scotland: A Survey of its Development Potential (Co-author), 1969; Economic Impact of North Sea Oil on Scotland (Co-author), 1978; Employment in Insurance, Banking and Finance in Scotland, 1980; The Political Economy of Tolerable Survival (Editor), 1981. Recreations: music; gardening. Address: (h.) Westfield, Ancrum, Roxburghshire, TD8 6XA; T.-08353 237.

Gautam, Prasanna Chandra, MBBS (Hon), MRCP (UK). Consultant Physician, Grampian Health Board, since 1989; Clinical Senior Lecturer in Medicine, Medical School, Aberdeen, since 1989; b. 3.4.45, Nepal; m., Leela Mani; 1 s.; 1 d. Educ. Padmodaya High School, Wathmandu; Bangalore Medical College, India. HMG of Nepal: Medical Officer, 1970-76, Senior Medical Officer, 1977-78; Senior House Officer in General Medicine, UK, 1977-81; Registrar in Cardiology, Liverpool, 1981-84; Registrar in Geriatric Medicine, Liverpool, 1984-86; Senior Registrar in General Medicine and Geriatrics, 1986-89. Chairman, Nepalese Doctors Association (UK); Executive Member, Scottish Branch, BGS. Publications: several books in Nepali; publications on hypothermia and cardiac problems in the elderly. Recreations: chess; travelling; gardening; walking. Address: (b.) Department of Medicine for the Elderly, Woodend Hospital, Aberdeen; T.-0224 681818, Ext. 56319.

Gavin, Anthony John, BSc, DipEd. Rector, St. Saviour's High School, Dundee, since 1979; b. 11.10.41, Perth; m., Charlotte Duffy; 2 d. Educ. Perth Academy; St. Andrews University. TVEI Adviser for Scotland, 1986-90; Depute Head Teacher, St. Augustine's High School, Edinburgh; Assistant Head Teacher, St. David's High School, Dalkeith. President, Scottish Schools Hockey Association, 1978-82. Recreations: music; golf. Address: (b.) Drumgeith Road, Dundee; T.-0382 500727.

Gavin, Derek, FRICS, IRRV. Chartered Surveyor, since 1971; Executive Director, Stirling Enterprise Park, since 1984; Board Director, Stirling Business Links Ltd.; b. 12.12.46, Perth; m., Terry; 1 s. Educ. Perth Academy; College of Estate Management. Trainee Surveyor, Bell Ingram, Perth, 1964-69; Management Surveyor, Scottish Industrial Estates Corporation, Glasgow, 1969-72; Valuation Surveyor, Bell Ingram, Perth, 1972-77; Estates Property Manager, Central Regional Council, 1977-84. Recreations: veteran hockey player; golf. Address: (b.) John Player Building, Players Road, Stirling; T.-0786 63416.

Gavin, Kevin George, MA (Hons), DipEd. Chief Adviser, Strathclyde Regional Council Education Department, since 1990 (HM Inspector of Schools, 1985-90); b. 4.7.48, Aberdeen; m., Jessie M.C. Connell; 1 d. Educ. Aberdeen Academy; Aberdeen University; Aberdeen College of Education. Assistant Head Teacher, Silverwood Primary School, Kilmarnock, 1974-77; Head Teacher, Monkton Primary School, 1977-80; Adviser in Primary Education: Grampian, 1980-83, Strathclyde, 1983-85. Recreations: walking; gardening; food and drink; art; motor-cycling. Address: (b.) Strathclyde Regional Council, Education Department, Glasgow; T.-041-249 4233.

Gawthrop, Professor Peter John, MA, DPhil, MIEE, MInstMC, CEng. Wylie Professor of Mechanical Engineering, Glasgow University, since 1987; b. 10.3.52, Seascale; m., Angela; 2 d. Educ. Whitehaven Grammar School; Queen's College, Oxford. W.W. Spooner Research Fellow, New College, Oxford; Lecturer, then Reader, Sussex University. Recreation: hill-walking. Address: (b.)

Department of Mechanical Engineering, James Watt Building, Glasgow University, Glasgow, G12 8QQ; T.-041-339 8855.

Gayre of Gayre and Nigg, Lt. Col. Robert, MA, DPhil, DFSc, DSc; Grand Commander, Order of St. Lazarus; b. 6.8.07; m., Mary Nina Terry (deceased); 1 s. Educ. Edinburgh University; Exeter College, Oxford. Commissioned Officer, Supplementary Reserve Royal Artillery, 1931; War Service, 1939; transferred to Regular Army Reserve, 1941; Staff Officer for Education, HQ Airborne Forces, 1941; Major HQ, Oxford District, 1941; Lt. Col., Educational Adviser, Allied Military Government for Italy, 1943; Professor of Anthropology, University of Saugor, India, 1954. Member, Royal Society of Naples. Recreation: sailing. Address: Minard Castle, Argyll.

Gaze, Professor Raymond Michael, LRPE. LRCSE, LRFPSG, MA, DPhil, FSA Scot, FRSE, FRS. Head, MRC Neural Development and Regeneration Group, ICAPB (Department of Zoology), Edinburgh University, since 1984; b. 22.6.27, Blackpool; m., Robinetta Mary Armfelt; 1 s.; 2 d. Educ. Medical School of Royal Colleges of Edinburgh; Oxford University. Lecturer in Physiology, Edinburgh University, 1955-62; Alan Johnston, Lawrence and Mosely Research Fellow of the Royal Society, 1962-66; Reader in Physiology, Edinburgh University, 1966-70; Head, Division of Developmental Biology, National Institute for Medical Research, London, 1970-83; Deputy Director, National Institute for Medical Research, London, 1977-83; Honorary Professor of Zoology, Edinburgh University, since 1988. Recreations: hill walking; music; drawing. Address: (h.) 37 Sciennes Road, Edinburgh, EH9 1NS; T.-031-667 6915.

Geary, Martin Charles, RD, MA, LLB. Advocate, since 1980; b. 25.8.50, Taplow, Berkshire; m., Irene Maud Bailey; 2 d. Educ. Abingdon School; Edinburgh University. Qualified as Solicitor, 1979; commenced pupillage at Bar, 1979; called to Bar, 1980. Member, Royal Naval Reserve, since 1969 (Lt. Commander). Recreations: walking; skiing; sailing. Address: (b.) Advocates Library, Parliament House, Edinburgh, EH1 1RF; T.-031-226 5071.

Geddes, Rev. Alexander John, MA, BD. Minister, St. Columba's Parish Church, Stewarton, since 1989; b. 27.7.36, Aberdeen; m., Elizabeth Mary Scott Henderson; 1 s.; 2 d. Educ. Robert Gordon's College, Aberdeen; High School of Stirling; Glasgow University. Assistant Minister, St. Machar's Cathedral, Aberdeen, 1960-61; Minister: St. Andrew's Church, Peebles, 1961-66, St. John's Church, Paisley, 1966-79, The Langstane Kirk, Aberdeen, 1979-89. Convener, Church of Scotland In-Service Training Committee, 1983-86; Vice Convener, Church of Scotland Education for the Ministry Committee, 1983-86; Church of Scotland Selection School Assessor, since 1987; Member, Church of Scotland Board of Communication and St. Andrew Press Executive, since 1990. Recreations: travel; photography; golf. Address: (h.) 1 Kirk Glebe, Stewarton, Kilmarnock, KA3 5BJ; T.-0560 82453.

Geddes, Keith, BEd. Leader, Labour Group, Lothian Regional Council, since 1990; Vice-Chair, COSLA Finance Committee, since 1990; b. 8.8.52, Selkirk; m., Linda McCracken. Educ. Galashiels Academy; Edinburgh University; Moray House College. Regional Councillor, since 1982; Chair, LRC Education Committee, 1987-90; Chair, LRC Policy and Resources Committee, since 1990. Recreations: hill-walking; golf; cricket; film. Address: (h.) 9 Willowbrae Avenue, Edinburgh; T.-031-661 7935.

Gellatly, David Andrew Stewart, LLB, CA. Partner, Miller McIntyre & Gellatly, Chartered Accountants, since 1977; b. 25.10.50, Perth; m., Gael Douglas-Scott Mackintosh; 1 s.; 1

d. Educ. Perth Academy; Sharp's Institution; Edinburgh University. Member, Council, Institute of Chartered Accountants of Scotland. Recreations: curling; golf. Address: (h.) Latch Cottage, Blebocraigs, Cupar, Fife, KY15 5UG; T.-033 485 330.

Gellatly, Ian Robert George, CA. Past President, Scottish Football League; Past Chairman, International Committee, Scottish Football Association; Director, Dundee Football Club PLC, since 1969 (Chairman, 1972-86); b. 5.11.38, Dundee; m., Anne May Horsburgh; 1 s.; 1 d. Educ. Dundee High School; Lathallan Preparatory School; Merchiston Castle School. Partner, Miller McIntyre Gellatly, CA, Dundee, 1964-88. Recreations: golf; curling. Address: (h.) The Paddock, Mains of Fowlis, Invergowrie, by Dundee, DD2 5LQ.

Gemmell, Curtis Glen, BSc, PhD, MIBiol, FRCPath. Reader in Bacteriology, Glasgow University, since 1990 (Senior Lecturer, 1976-90); Honorary Bacteriologist, Greater Glasgow Health Board, since 1976; b. 26.8.41, Beith, Ayrshire; m., Anne Margaret; 2 d. Educ. Spier's School, Beith; Glasgow University. Glasgow University: Assistant Lecturer, 1966-68, Lecturer, 1968-69; Paisley College of Technology: Lecturer, 1969-71, Senior Lecturer, 1971-76; Visiting Assistant Professor, University of Minnesota, Minneapolis, 1979-80. Recreations: gardening; golf. Address: (h.) Sunninghill, 19 Lawmarnock Crescent, Bridge of Weir, PA11 3AS; T.-Bridge of Weir 613350.

Gemmell, Gavin John Norman, CA. Senior Partner, Baillie, Gifford & Co., since 1989 (Partner, since 1967); Chairman, Toyo Trust Baillie Gifford Ltd., since 1989; Director, Scottish Widows Fund & Life Assurance Society, since 1984, Guardian Baillie Gifford Ltd., since 1990, TSB Bank Scotland PLC, since 1991; b. 7.9.41, Edinburgh; m., Kathleen Fiona Drysdale; 1 s.; 2 d. Educ. George Watson's College. CA Apprentice, John M. Geoghegan & Co., 1959-64; joined Baillie, Gifford & Co., 1964; Chairman, AITC Tax Committee, 1980-89. Recreations: golf; squash; foreign travel. Address: (b.) 1 Rutland Court, Edinburgh, EH3 8EY; T.-031-222 4000.

Gemmill, Colin William Ramsay, BA (Cantab), LLB, NP. Partner, Montgomerie & Co., Solicitors, Glasgow, since 1966; b. 30.12.35, Glasgow; m., Patricia Margaret Wallace; 2 s. Educ. Glenalmond College, Perthshire; Cambridge University; Glasgow University. Trained with Maclay Murray & Spens, Solicitors, Glasgow. Member, Council, Law Society of Scotland, since 1986. Recreations: rugby union (officiating); tennis; squash; golf; theatre; music. Address: (h.) 31 Henderland Road, Bearsden, Glasgow, G61 1JQ; T.-041-942 2891.

Gennard, Professor John, BA (Econ), MA (Econ), FIPM. Professor of Industrial Relations, Strathclyde University, since 1981; Dean, Strathclyde Business School, since 1987; b. 26.4.44, Manchester; m., Florence Anne Russell; 1 s.; 1 d. Educ. Hulme Grammar School for Boys; Sheffield University; Manchester University. Research Officer, Industrial Relations Department, then Lecturer in Industrial Relations, London School of Economics, 1968-81. Publications: The Reluctant Militants (Co-author), 1972; Financing Strikers, 1978; Industrial Relations and Job Security, 1979; The Closed Shop in British Industry, 1984; A History of the National Graphical Association, 1990. Recreations: football; swimming; politics; trade unions; food and drink. Address: (h.) 4 South Avenue, Carluke, Lanarkshire; T.-0555 51361.

Gent, William, RNMH. Director of Nursing, Mental Handicap Services, Forth Valley Health Board, since 1985; b. 3.3.44, Crawcrook, Co. Durham; m., Audrey Charlton; 1

s.; 1 d. Educ. Hookergate Grammar School. Student/staff nurse, 1963-66; charge nurse, 1966-69; Deputy Principal Nursing Officer, Earls House, Durham, 1969-73; Senior Nurse, RSNH, Stirlingshire, 1973-85. Member, National Board for Scotland, 1983-88 and 1988-93; Member, UK Central Council, 1988-93. Recreation: hill-walking. Address: (b.) Royal Scottish National Hospital, Larbert; T.-0324 556131.

George, John Charles Grossmith, FSA(Scot), FHS. Kintyre Pursuivant of Arms, since 1986; b. 15.12.30, London; m., Margaret Mary Maria Mercedes Weld. Educ. Ampleforth. Lt., Hertfordshire Yeomanry, 1951-54; films and television advertising, 1952-62; College of Arms, 1962-72; Earl Marshal's Liaison Officer with the Churchill family, 1965; Green Staff Officer, Prince of Wales's Investiture, 1969; Garioch Pursuivant, 1976. Chairman, Philbeach Light Opera Society, 1961-63; Vice President, BBC "Mastermind" Club, 1979-81; Knight of Obedience, Sovereign Military Order of Malta, 1975; Commander, Order Pro Merito Melitensi, 1983; Colonel and Hon. ADC to Governor, State of Kentucky, 1991. Publications: The Puffin Book of Flags, 1975; The French Heralds (paper), 1985; numerous historical articles. Recreations: English light opera and musical comedies; hagiographies; sports. Address: (h.) 115 Henderson Row, Edinburgh, EH3 5BB; T.-031-557 1605.

George, Judith Wordsworth, MA (Oxon), PhD. Deputy Scottish Director, The Open University, since 1984; b. 26.8.40, Bradford; 2 d. Educ. Heath Grammar School, Halifax; Somerville College, Oxford. Tutor in Philosophy, St. Andrews University; Lecturer in History of Fine Art, Manchester University; Tutor in Classics, Open University; Senior Counsellor, Open University in Scotland. Recreations: gardening; classical music; hill-walking. Address: (b.) 60 Melville Street, Edinburgh, EH3 7HF; T.-031-226 3851.

George, Professor William David, MB, BS, FRCS, MS. Professor of Surgery, Glasgow University, since 1981; b. 22.3.43, Reading; 1 s.; 3 d. Educ. Henley Grammar School; London University. Lecturer in Surgery, Manchester University, 1973-77; Senior Lecturer in Surgery, Liverpool University, 1977-81. Member, National Committees, British Association of Surgical Oncology and Surgical Research Society. Recreations: veteran rowing; golf. Address: (b.) University Department of Surgery, Western Infirmary, Glasgow, G11 6NT; T.-041-339 8822.

Gerrard, John Henry Atkinson, ARIAS, DA (Edin), MA (Cantab), FRSA. Technical Director, Scottish Civic Trust, since 1984; b. 15.9.34, Leicester; m., Dr. Margaret Mackay. Educ. Abbotsholme; Corpus Christi College, Cambridge; Edinburgh College of Art. Assistant Architect: Sheffield Corporation, 1961-63, Planning Department, Oxford City Council, 1965-68; Assistant Director, Scottish Civic Trust, 1968-84. Recreation: travelling hopefully. Address: (b.) Scottish Civic Trust, 24 George Square, Glasgow; T.-041-221 1466.

Gerson, Jack Barton. Dramatist and Novelist; b. 31.7.28, Glasgow; 1 d. Educ. Hillhead High School, Glasgow. RAF, two years; worked in advertising and cinema distribution, 1949-59; writing full-time since 1959; won BBC Television Play Competition, 1959, for Three Ring Circus; has written more than 100 hours of television drama; created two series, The Regiment and The Omega Factor; 14 radio plays; novels include Whitehall Sanction, Assassination Run, Treachery Game, The Back of the Tiger, and Deaths Head Berlin. Recreations: cinema; reading; swimming; Caribbean Islands; sleeping in front of television set. Address: (b.) c/o Harvey Unna & Stephen Durbridge, 24 Pottery Lane, Holland Park, London, W11 4LZ; T.-01-727 1346.

Gerstenberg, Frank Eric, MA (Cantab), PGCE. Principal, George Watson's College, Edinburgh, since 1985; b. 23.2.41, Balfron; 1 s.; 2 d. Educ. Trinity College, Glenalmond; Clare College, Cambridge; London University. Assistant Master, Kelly College, Tavistock, 1963-67; Housemaster and Head of History, Millfield School, 1967-74; Headmaster, Oswestry School, 1974-85. Governor, Beaconhurst School, Bridge of Allan. Recreations: skiing; sailing; travelling; music. Address: (h.) 27 Merchiston Gardens, Edinburgh, EH10 5DD; T.-031-337 6880.

Gerver, Professor Elisabeth, BA (Hons), MA, PhD. Professor of Continuing Education and Director, Centre for Continuing Education, Dundee University, since 1990; b. 15.4.41, Winnipeg; m., Dr. David Gerver (deceased); 1 s.; 1 d. Educ. Wolfville High School, Nova Scotia; Dalhousie University, Canada; Toronto University; King's College, London. Lecturer in Communications, Newcastle upon Tyne Polytechnic, 1968-69; part-time staff, Open University, 1971-84; Lecturer in Communication, Queen Margaret College, Edinburgh, 1974-83; Director, Scottish Community Education Microelectronics Project, Glasgow, 1981-82; Director, Scottish Institute of Adult and Continuing Education, 1983-90. Council Member, Scottish Community Education Council, 1979-83; Member, BBC Continuing Education Advisory Council, 1983-86; Executive Member, Scottish Institute of Adult Education, 1979-83 (Chairman, 1980-83); Vice-President, European Bureau of Adult Education, 1986-90; Member, Board of Directors, Network Scotland Ltd., 1984-88; Governor, Queen Margaret College, 1985-88; Chair, Editorial Board, Computers in Adult Education and Training, since 1986; Member, IBA Educational Advisory Council, 1988-90. Publications: Computers and Adult Learning, 1984; Humanising Technology, 1985; Strategic Women: how do they manage in Scotland? (Co-author), 1991. Recreations: spare time spent with children, at the performing arts, in the garden and on the hills. Address: (h.) 29 Moray Place, Edinburgh, EH3 6BX; T.-031-225 1036.

Gibbons, John Ernest, PhD, DipArch, DipTP, ARIBA, ARIAS, FSA(Scot), FRSA. Director of Building and Chief Architect, Scottish Office, since 1984; b. 20.4.40, Halesowen; m., Patricia Mitchell; 1 s.; 2 d. Educ. Oldbury Grammar School; Birmingham School of Architecture, Aston University; Edinburgh University. Lecturer, Birmingham School of Architecture and Aston University, 1962-65; Research Fellow, Architecture Research Unit, then Lecturer in Architecture, Edinburgh University, 1966-72; Principal, Architect's Division, Scottish Development Department, 1972-78; Visiting Research Scientist, CSIRO, Melbourne, 1975; Assistant Director, Building Directorate, SDD, 1978; Deputy Director, Scottish Office Building Directorate, 1982-84. Member of Council, EAA and RIAS, 1977-80; Member, Council, ARCUK, since 1984; Assessor, Design Council, 1984-88. Address: (h.) Crichton House, Pathhead, Midlothian, EH37 5UX; T.-0875 320085.

Gibbs, Ronald Percy, OBE. Chairman, PHAB Scotland, since 1984; Concert Organiser, Edinburgh Bach Society, 1981-91; Convener, History Section, The Cramond Association, since 1983; b. 1.6.21, London; m., Margaret Eleanor Dean; 3 s.; 1 d. Educ. Owen's School, Islington. Ministry (later Department) of Transport, 1938-81; set up the Ports Office for Scotland in Edinburgh, 1973, and remained Head of that Office until retiral in 1981. Board Member, PHAB Ltd. and Vice-Chairman, Handicabs (Lothian) Ltd. Recreations: transport and communications; music; local and industrial history; photography. Address: (h.) 13 Inveralmond Drive, Edinburgh, EH4 6JX; T.-031-312 6034.

Gibbs, Stephen Cokayne, Director, Vaux Group PLC, since 1970; b. 18.7.29, Hertingfordbury, England; m., Lavinia

Bacon; 2 s.; 1 d. Educ. Eton College. Served with KRRC (60th Rifles), 1947-49; TA, service with QVR (TA), 1951-63: Lt., 1951, Captain, 1956, Major, 1958; Port Line Ltd., 1949-62: Assistant Manager, 1957, London Manager, 1959; Charles Barker PLC, 1962-87: Director, 1962, Deputy Chairman, 1982-87. Member, Executive, National Trust for Scotland, since 1987, and Council, since 1991; Governor, Belhaven Hill School, since 1987. Recreations: shooting; fishing. Address: The Estate Office, Dougarie, Isle of Arran, KA27 8EB; T.-0770 84259.

Gibson, Sir Alexander (Drummond), KB (1977), CBE (1967), Hon. RAM, Hon. FRCM, Hon. FRSAM, Hon. RSA, OStJ, FRSE, FRSA, Hon. LLD (Aberdeen), Hon. DMus (Glasgow), DUniv (Stirling), Hon. Doctor (Open University), Hon. DMus (Newcastle upon Tyne), LRAM, ARCM, ARCO. Conductor Laureate, Scottish Opera, since 1987 (Artistic Director, 1962-85, Music Director, 1985-87); Honorary President, Scottish National Orchestra, since 1985 (Principal Conductor and Musical Director, 1959-84); b. 11.2.26, Motherwell; m., Anne Veronica Waggett; 3 s.; 1 d. Educ. Dalziel High School, Motherwell; Glasgow University; Royal College of Music; Mozarteum, Salzburg, Austria; Accademia Chigiano, Siena, Italy. Royal Signals, 1944-48; Repetiteur and Assistant Conductor, Sadler's Wells Opera, 1951-52; Assistant Conductor, BBC Scottish Orchestra, Glasgow, 1952-54; Sadler's Wells Opera: Staff Conductor, 1954-57, Musical Director, 1957-59; Principal Guest Conductor, Houston Symphony Orchestra, 1981-82 and 1982-83. Freeman, Burgh of Motherwell and Wishaw, 1964; St. Mungo Prize, 1970; Arnold Bax Memorial Medal for Conducting, 1959; ISM Musician of the Year Award, 1976; Sibelius Medal, 1978; Musician of the Year, British Music Year Book, 1980.

Gibson, Archibald Turner, FIB (Scot). General Manager, Bank of Scotland, since 1988 (Joint General Manager, 1983-88); b. 6.6.32, Paisley; m., Ellen Campbell McNiven; 1 s.; 2 d. Educ. Paisley Grammar School; Harvard Business School. Bank of Scotland: Assistant General Manager, International Division, 1974-80, Divisional General Manager, Marketing and Development, 1980-83. Recreations: tennis; gardening; theatre; art. Address: (b.) Bank of Scotland, Head Office, The Mound, Edinburgh; T.-031-243 5554.

Gibson, Edgar Matheson, MBE, TD, DL, DA. Assistant Rector, Kirkwall Grammar School, 1988-90; Chairman, St. Magnus Cathedral Fair, since 1982; Chairman, Northern Area, Highland TA&VR Association, since 1987; Deputy Lieutenant, Orkney, since 1976; Chairman, Orkney Branch, SSAFA, since 1990; b. 1.11.34, Kirkwall; m., Jean McCarrick; 2 s.; 2 d. Educ. Kirkwall Grammar School; Gray's College of Art, Aberdeen. National Service, 1958-60; TA and TAVR service to 1985 with Lovat Scouts, reaching Lt. Col.; Battalion Second in Command, 2/51 Highland Volunteers, 1973-76; Joint Services Liaison Officer for Orkney, 1980-85; Cadet Commandant, Orkney Lovat Scouts ACF, 1979-86, Honorary Colonel, since 1986. Recreations: painting; sculpture; whisky tasting. Address: (h.) Transcona, New Scapa Road, Kirkwall, Orkney; T.-0856 2849.

Gibson, Ernest Douglas, DPE, DCE. Provost, Nithsdale District Council, since 1988; b. 30.11.28, Edinburgh; m., Isobel Doreen Gass; 2 s.; 1 d. Educ. Portobello High School; Jordanhill College. Teacher, 1950; National Service, RAF, 1950-52; Teacher, 1952-59; Head Teacher, 1959-84; elected to Nithsdale District Council, 1977. Recreations: golf; fishing; gardening. Address: (h.) 29 Ardwall Road, Dumfries, DG1 3AQ; T.-0387 54651.

Gibson, Rev. Henry Montgomerie, MA, BD, PhD. Minister, The High Kirk, Dundee, since 1979; b. 11.6.36, Wishaw; m., Dr. Anne Margaret Thomson; 1 s. Educ.

Wishaw Academy; Hamilton Academy; Glasgow University. Assistant Minister, Glasgow Cathedral, 1960; Minister: Carmunnock Parish Church, Glasgow, 1961-71, Aberfeldy, 1971-79; Convener, Church of Scotland Working Party on Alcohol and Drugs, 1975-81. Recreations: reading; table tennis (occasionally). Address: High Kirk Manse, 6 Adelaide Place, Dundee, DD3 6LF; T.-Dundee 22955.

Gibson, John Alan, MD, FLS, FSA. Director, Scottish Natural History Library, since 1974; Chairman, Clyde Area Branch, Scottish Wildlife Trust, since 1969; Honorary Secretary, British Medical Association, since 1957; b. 15.5.26, Kilbarchan; m., Dr. Mary M. Baxter; 1 d. Educ. Lindisfarne School; Paisley Grammar School; Glasgow University. Family Doctor, village of Kilbarchan; Editor, The Scottish Naturalist (founded 1871); Scottish Representative and former Vice-President, Society for the Bibliography of Natural History; Scientific Meetings Secretary, Society for the History of Natural History; Chairman, Scottish Natural History Trust; Honorary Secretary, Scottish Society for the Protection of Birds; Chairman, Friends of Glasgow University Library; Honorary Secretary, Clyde Bird Club; former Secretary, Royal Physical Society of Edinburgh; Gold Medal, Scottish Society for the Protection of Birds, 1967; Queen's Silver Jubilee Medal, 1977; Fellowship, BMA, 1982; Fellow, Royal Society of Medicine. Publications: over 300 scientific papers and books on Scottish natural history, 1943-90. Recreations: natural history; golf (Royal Troon). Address: (h.) Foremount House, Kilbarchan, PA10 2EZ; T.-Kilbarchan 2410.

Gibson, Rev. Professor John Clark Love, MA, BD, DPhil. Professor of Hebrew and Old Testament Studies, Edinburgh University, since 1987; b. 28.5.30, Coatbridge; m., Agnes Gilmour Russell, MA ; 4 s.; 1 d. Educ. Coatbridge High School; Glasgow University; Magdalen College, Oxford. Licensed as Probationer, Church of Scotland, 1956; Assistant Minister, Bellshill West, 1956; Minister, Newmachar, 1959-62; Edinburgh University: Lecturer in Hebrew and Semitic Languages, 1962-73, Reader, 1973-87. Publications: Textbook of Hebrew Inscriptions, 1971; Textbook of Aramaic Inscriptions, 1975; Canaanite Myths and Legends, 1978; Textbook of Phoenician Inscriptions, 1982; Daily Study Bible (Old Testament) (General Editor and author of volumes on Genesis and Job), 1981-86; Reader's Digest Family Guide to the Bible (Features Editor), 1984; The Bible in Scottish Life and Literature (Contributor), 1988. Recreations: the Bible in Scots; Burns; golf. Address: 10 South Morton Street, Edinburgh; T.-031-669 3635.

Gibson, Peter Robert, MA (Hons). Consumer Affairs Consultant, since 1991; Vice-Chair, Citizens Advice Scotland, since 1991; b. 11.9.47, Dunlop, Ayrshire; m., Amanda Kate Britain; 1 d. Educ. Glasgow Academy; Elk Grove Senior High School, California; St. Andrews University; University of California, Davis. Teaching Assistant, University of California, Davis, 1969-70; Marketing Trainee, Unilever, 1970-71; Regional Organiser, Shelter, Surrey and Hampshire, 1971-73; National Groups Organiser, War on Want, 1973-74; Director, Shelter Scotland, 1974-77; Director, Scottish Consumer Council, 1977-90; Deputy Director, The Planning Exchange, 1990-91. Member, Scottish Housing Advisory Committee, 1977-79. Recreations: home improvement (involuntary); Italy; eating out; trashy TV and cinema; cats. Address: (h.) Dunluce House, Prospect Road, Dullatur, G68 OAN; T.-0236 724247.

Gibson, William John Alexander, MB, ChB, DMRD (Lond). Consultant Diagnostic Radiologist with administrative responsibility, Stracathro Hospital, Brechin; Hon. Senior Lecturer, Dundee University; President, Scottish Radiological Society, 1991-93; b. 20.5.36, Ayr; m., Daphne; 2 s. Educ. Douglas-Ewart High School, Newton Stewart; Glasgow

University. Various posts, Victoria Infirmary and Glasgow Royal Infirmary; Senior Registrar, Dundee Royal Infirmary; appointed Consultant, Stracathro Hospital, 1968; Secretary, Scottish Radiological Society, 1977-80; Chairman, Group Medical Staff Committee, Angus Hospitals Group, 1991-93. Recreations: bowling; motor sport; TV sport; philately. Address: (h.) 12 Cedar Road, Broughty Ferry, Dundee, DD5 3BB; T.-0382 79446.

Gibson-Smith, Chris, BSc, MSc, PhD. Chief Executive, BP Exploration Europe, since 1992; b. 8.9.45, Newcastle; m., Marjorie; 2 d. Educ. Taunton School; Durham University; Newcastle University; Stanford University. Oil exploration and production geologist with BP in a variety of world-wide posts, 1970-84; Sloan Fellow, Stanford University, 1984; President, BP Alaska Exploration Inc., 1985-87; Assistant General Manager, BP Corporate Planning Department, 1987-89; General Manager, Developments, BPX Europe, 1989-91; Deputy Chief Executive, BP Exploration Europe, 1991-92. Council Member, CBI Scotland; Chairman, Business in the Arts, Scotland. Recreations: sport; music; modern art; history; literature. Address: (b.) 301 St. Vincent Street, Glasgow, G2 5DD; T.-041-225 8266.

Gilbert, Colin, BA (Hons). Head of Comedy, BBC Scotland, since 1986; b. 3.4.52, Glasgow; m., Joanna; 1 s.; 1 d. Educ. St. Paul's School; York University. Script Editor, Not The 9 O'Clock News, 1980-82; Producer: A Kick Up the Eighties, 1983, Naked Radio, 1984, Naked Video and City Lights, 1986-87-88-89, Rab C. Nesbitt, 1990, I, Lovett, 1990. Address: (b.) BBC Scotland, Queen Margaret Drive, Glasgow, G12 8DG.

Gilchrist, Sir Andrew Graham, KCMG (1964), BA (Oxon). Fruitgrower and Author, formerly Diplomat; b. 19.4.10, Lesmahagow; m., Freda Grace Slack (deceased); 2 s.; 1 d. Educ. Edinburgh Academy; Exeter College, Oxford. Foreign Service, 1933-70, including appointments as Ambassador at Reykjavik, Djakarta, Dublin, with time out for two years Army service (Major, Force 136) in South-East Asia; on retirement, made Chairman, Highlands and Islands Development Board, 1970-76. Publications: Bangkok Top Secret; Cod Wars and How to Lose Them; Malaya, 1941: the fall of a fighting empire; six novels (latest: Did Van Gogh Paint his Bed?, 1991). Recreations: music; fishing; curling (oldest playing member, Lesmahagow Curling Club). Address: (h.) Arthur's Crag, Hazelbank, by Lanark; T.-055586 263.

Gilchrist, Archibald, MA. Director, Lilley plc, since 1987; Board Member, Scottish Legal Aid Board, since 1986; b. 17.11.29, Glasgow; m., Elizabeth Jean; 2 s.; 1 d. Educ. Loretto School; Pembroke College, Cambridge. Barclay Curle & Co. Ltd., 1954-64; Brown Bros. & Co. Ltd., 1964-72; Govan Shipbuilders Ltd., 1972-79; Vosper Pte Ltd., Singapore, 1980-86. Governor, Glasgow Polytechnic; Chairman, Council, St. Leonards School; Vice Chairman, Royal Scottish Orchestra; Member, Scottish Committee, CNAA. Recreations: shooting; fishing; golf. Address: (h.) 35 Barnton Avenue, Edinburgh, EH4 6JJ; T.-031-336 4288.

Gilchrist, Bernard, MBE, MA (Hons) (Oxon). Chief Executive, Scottish Wildlife Trust, 1965-85; b. 20.5.19, Manchester; m., Jean W. Gregory; 2 s.; 1 d. Educ. Manchester Grammar School; Queen's College, Oxford. Tanganyika: Forest Officer, HM Colonial/Overseas Civil Service, 1942-62 (Conservator of Forests, 1960), Conservator of Forests, Tanganyika/Tanzania Government Service, 1962-65. Recreations: countryside; natural history; hill-walking; photography. Address: (h.) 9 Murrayfield Gardens, Edinburgh, EH12 6DG; T.-031-337 3869.

Gilchrist, Thomas, BSc, PhD, CChem, FRSC. Managing Director, Ross Fraser Ltd. and Giltech Ltd., since 1984; b. 18.6.36, Ayr; m., Fiona Christina Brown; 2 d. Educ. Ayr Academy; Glasgow University. Assistant Lecturer in Chemistry, Glasgow University, 1961-62; Research Chemist: Canadian Industries Ltd., Quebec, 1962-64, ICI Ltd., Stevenston, Ayrshire, 1964-69; Strathclyde University: Lecturer in Bioengineering, 1969, Head, Division of Artificial Organs, Bioengineering Unit, 1972, Senior Lecturer in Bioengineering, 1975-84. Section Editor, International Journal of Artificial Organs. Recreations: golf; curling. Address: (h.) The Lodge, 67 Midton Road, Ayr, KA7 2TW; T.-Ayr 266088.

Giles, Cecilia Elspeth, CBE, MA. Member, Transport Users Consultative Committee for Scotland, since 1989; Member, Church of Scotland Board of Stewardship and Finance, since 1986, Vice Convener since 1990; b. Dumfries. Educ. Queen Margaret's School, Yorkshire; Edinburgh University. Administrative staff, Khartoum University, 1956-57; joined Administrative staff, Edinburgh University, 1957; Assistant Secretary, Edinburgh University, 1972-87; Committee of Vice-Chancellors and Principals' Administrative Training Officer (seconded part-time), 1983-85. President, Edinburgh University Graduates' Association, 1889-91; Member, Business Committee, General Council, Edinburgh University, since 1988. Publication: Tourism in Scotland (Co-author). Recreations: entertaining friends, family and godchildren; theatre. Address: (b.) Graduates' Association, 5 Buccleuch Place, Edinburgh, EH8 9LW.

Gillespie, Adam, BSc (Hons), CPhys, MInstP. Head Teacher, Greenfaulds High School, Cumbernauld, since 1986; b. 22.3.44, Glasgow; m., Agnes C. Ferrie; 2 s. Educ. Glasgow University. Teacher of Physics, Dumbarton Academy, 1966-68; Principal Teacher of Physics, Jordanhill College School, 1968-78; Assistant Head Teacher, then Depute Head Teacher, Vale of Leven Academy, 1978-86. Former Member, Scottish Branch Committee, Institute of Physics. Recreations: music; gardening; walking. Address: (h.) 14 Carseview Drive, Bearsden, G61 3NJ; T.-041-942 9593.

Gillespie, Archibald, CA, ACMA, IPFA. Director of Finance, Strathclyde Regional Council, since 1986; b. 4.9.35, Greenock; m., Alice Finlayson; 2 s.; 2 d. Educ. Greenock High School. Chief Internal Auditor, Greenock Corporation, 1964-67; County Treasurer, Bute County Council, 1967-75; Senior Depute Director of Finance, Strathclyde Regional Council, 1975-86. Member, Executive Committee, CIPFA, Scottish Branch. Recreations: golf; badminton. Address: (h.) 64 South Street, Greenock; T.-0475 81904.

Gillespie, Professor John Spence, MB, ChB, PhD, FIBiol, FRCPGlas, FRSE. Professor and Head of Department of Pharmacology, Glasgow University, since 1968; b. 5.9.26, Dumbarton; m., Jemima Simpson Ross; 4 s.; 1 d. Educ. Dumbarton Academy; Glasgow University. National Service as RMO, 1950-52; McCunn Research Scholar in Physiology, Glasgow University, 1953-55; Faulds Fellow, then Sharpey Scholar, Physiology Department, University College, London, 1955-57; Lecturer in Physiology, Glasgow University, 1957-59; Sophie Fricke Research Fellow, Royal Society, Rockefeller Institute, 1959-60; Glasgow University: Senior Lecturer in Physiology, 1961-63, Henry Head Research Fellow, Royal Society, 1963-68; Vice-Principal, Glasgow University, since 1983; Honorary Secretary, Physiological Society, 1966-72; Council Member, Research Defence Society, 1974-77; Committee Member, British Pharmacological Society, 1973-76. Recreations: gardening; painting. Address: (b.) Department of Pharmacology, Glasgow University, Glasgow, G12 8QQ; T.-041-339 8855, Ext. 4565.

Gillies (nee McCall-Smith), Anne Bethea, MA, LLB. Advocate; Honorary Sheriff of South Strathclyde, Dumfries and Galloway, at Lanark, since 1960; Member, Valuation Appeal Panel, Strathclyde, 1974-88; b. 12.4.22, Lochgilphead, Argyll; m., Sheriff Principal M.G. Gillies, T.D., Q.C. (qv). Educ. Sherborne School for Girls, Dorset; Edinburgh University. Served in WAAF, until 1946; called to Scottish Bar, 1951; married, 1954. Recreations: gardening; cats. Address: (h.) 1 The Warren, Gullane, East Lothian, EH31 2BE; T.-Gullane 842857.

Gillies (Maurice) Gordon, TD (and Bar), QC (Scot). Sheriff Principal of South Strathclyde, Dumfries and Galloway, 1982-88; b. 17.10.16.

Gillies, Norman Neil Nicolson, BA, MBIM, FRSA. Director, Sabhar Mor Ostaig, since 1988; Vice Chairman, Skye & Lochalsh Local Enterprise Company, since 1990; b. 1.3.47, Flodigarry, Isle of Skye; m., Jean Brown Nixon; 1 s.; 2 d. Educ. Portree High School; Strathclyde University; Open University. Managerial experience in hotel and catering industry, 1968-75; managerial experience in the building industry; College Secretary, Sabhal Mor Ostaig, 1983-88. Chairman, Steering Committee, Gaelic Terminology Database Project; Director, Highland Training and Development Ltd.; Member, Gaelic Advisory Council, Scottish Television; Member, BARAIL (Centre for Highlands and Islands Policy Studies); Board Member, Comunn Na Gaidhlig, 1986-90. Recreations: reading; family. Address: (h.) Innis Ard, Ardvasar, Isle of Skye, IV45 8RT; T.-04714 281.

Gillies, Rev. Dr. Robert Arthur, BD, PhD. Rector, St. Andrew's Episcopal Church, St. Andrews, since 1991; b. 21.10.51, Cleethorpes; m., Elizabeth; 2 s. Educ. Barton-upon-Humber Grammar School; Edinburgh University; St. Andrews University. Medical Laboratory Technician, 1968-72; Curate, Christ Church, Falkirk, 1977-80; Curate, Christ Church Morningside, and Chaplain, Napier College, 1980-84; Chaplain, Dundee University, 1984-90. Hon. Lecturer, Department of Philosophy, Dundee University, since 1985. Recreations: family; garden; Scotland's mountains. Address: St. Andrew's Rectory, Queen's Terrace, St. Andrews, Fife, KY16 9QF; T.-0334 73344.

Gillies, Valerie, MA (Hons), MLitt, FSA Scot. Poet; b. 4.6.48, Edmonton, Canada; m., Professor William Gillies; 1 s.; 2 d. Educ. Trinity Academy, Edinburgh; Edinburgh University; University of Mysore, South India. Writer-in-School: Boroughmuir High School, The Edinburgh Academy; Scriptwriter, BBC Radio and Schools TV; Poet to the Borders Festival, 1989; Writer-in-Residence, Duncan of Jordanstone College of Art and Dundee District Libraries, 1988-90. Eric Gregory Award; SAC Book Award. Publications include: Each Bright Eye; Bed of Stone; Tweed Journey; The Chanter's Tune. Recreations: field-walking; map-reading. Address: (h.) 67 Braid Avenue, Edinburgh, EH10 6ED; T.-031-447 2876.

Gillies, Professor William, MA (Edin), MA (Oxon). Professor of Celtic, Edinburgh University, since 1979; b. 15.9.42, Stirling; m., Valerie; 1 s.; 2 d. Educ. Oban High School; Edinburgh University; Corpus Christi College, Oxford; Dublin University. Dublin Institute for Advanced Studies, 1969-70; Lecturer, Edinburgh University, 1970-79; Fellow, Royal Society of Edinburgh, 1990. Director, SNDA Ltd. Recreations: walking; gardening; music. Address: (h.) 67 Braid Avenue, Edinburgh, EH10 6ED.

Gillis, Charles Raphael, MD, FRCP(Glas), FFCM. Director, West of Scotland Cancer Surveillance Unit, since 1973; Director, WHO Collaborating Centre; Honorary Clinical Senior Lecturer, Glasgow University, since 1973; b. 23.10.37,

Glasgow; m., Judith Ann Naftalin; 1 s.; 1 d. Educ. High School of Glasgow; Glasgow University. Lecturer in Epidemiology and Preventive Medicine, then Senior Lecturer and Honorary Consultant Epidemiologist, Glasgow University, 1965-73. Past Chairman, Cancer Education Co-ordinating Group of the UK and Republic of Ireland; Past Chairman, West of Scotland Oncological Organisation. Address: (b.) West of Scotland Cancer Surveillance Unit, Ruchill Hospital, Bilsland Drive, Ruchill, Glasgow, G20 9NB; T.-041-946 7120.

Gillon, Rev. Charles Blair, BD. Parish Minister, Ibrox, Glasgow, since 1980; b. 19.8.38, Montrose; m., Linda Smith; 3 s.; 3 d. Educ. Morgan Academy, Dundee; George Heriot's, Edinburgh; Trinity College, Glasgow University. Library Assistant, Edinburgh Corporation Libraries, 1957-59; Senior Library Assistant, Edinburgh University Library, 1959-63; Librarian, Animal Breeding Library, Commonwealth Agricultural Bureau, Edinburgh, 1963-69; student, 1970-75; Parish Minister, Kilbarchan East, 1975-80. Member, Incorporation of Skinners, Trades House, Glasgow. Address: 3 Dargarvel Avenue, Glasgow, G41 5LD; T.-041-427 1282.

Gillon, Hamish William, FFA, FPMI. General Manager (Finance) and Actuary, Scottish Provident Institution, since 1988; b. 22.1.40, Edinburgh; m., Sandra; 1 s.; 1 d. Educ. Royal High School, Edinburgh. Various appointments, Scottish Provident Institution, since 1965. Hon. Treasurer, Faculty of Actuaries; Chairman, Finance and General Purposes Committee, The Scout Association. Address: (b.) 6 St. Andrew Square, Edinburgh, EH2 2YA; T.-031-556 9181.

Gilmour, Colonel Allan Macdonald, KCVO, OBE, MC (and Bar), DSC (USA). Lord Lieutenant of Sutherland, 1972-91; Member, Highland Regional Council, since 1976; Member, Sutherland District Council, 1974-88 (Chairman, 1974-78); President, Highland Territorial & Auxiliary Reserve Association, 1988-91; b. 23.11.16, Edinburgh; m., Jean Wood; 3 s.; 1 d. Educ. Cargilfield, Edinburgh; Winchester College; Trinity College, Oxford. Commissioned Seaforth Highlanders, 1939; served War in Middle East, Sicily and NW Europe; Regimental and Staff appointments, 1945-69, including Instructor, Staff College, Quetta, and Chief of Staff, Ghana Armed Forces; Member, Sutherland County Council, 1970; Member, Highland Health Board, 1974 (Chairman, 1982-84); DL, Sutherland, 1969; Member: Highland River Purification Board, since 1978, Highlands and Islands Development Consultative Council, 1980-88; Chairman, East Sutherland Council of Social Service, 1972-76; Board Member, Scottish National Orchestra Society, 1976-86. Recreation: fishing. Address: (h.) Invernauld, Rosehall, Lairg, Sutherland; T.-054 984 204.

Gilmour, Andrew Parr, BSc (Hons). Rector, Rothesay Academy, since 1983; b. 26.4.46, Glasgow; m., Elizabeth Morrison MacPherson; 1 s.; 2 d. Educ. Allan Glen's School, Glasgow; Glasgow University. Teacher of Chemistry, Allan Glen's School, 1969; Dunoon Grammar School: Principal Teacher of Chemistry, 1972, Assistant Rector, 1975; Depute Head Teacher, Mearns Castle High School, 1981. Recreations: sailing; badminton; rugby (spectating nowadays); swimming; cycling; windsurfing; gardening. Address: (h.) Millford, 34 Mount Stuart Road, Rothesay, Isle of Bute; T.-Rothesay 503336.

Gilmour, Douglas Graham, BSc (Hons), MB, ChB, MD, FRCS. Consultant Vascular Surgeon, Glasgow Royal Infirmary, since 1983; b. 15.4.47, Glasgow; m., Evelyn Jean; 2 s.; 2 d. Educ. Kelvinside Academy, Glasgow; Glasgow University. House Surgeon/Physician, then Senior House Officer/Registrar in Surgery, Western Infirmary, Glasgow, 1971-77; Glasgow Royal Infirmary: Senior Registrar in Surgery, 1977-80, Senior Lecturer (Honorary Consultant) in

Surgery, 1980-83. Recreations: family; golf; skiing. Address: (b.) Vascular Surgery Department, Royal Infirmary, Glasgow; T.-041-552 3535, Ext. 5503.

Gilmour, Hugh Montgomery, MB, ChB, FRCPath. Senior Lecturer in Pathology, Edinburgh University, since 1979; Honorary Consultant, Lothian Health Board, since 1979; b. 17.5.43, Edinburgh; m., Alison Mary Little; 2 s. Educ. George Heriot's School; Edinburgh University. House Officer appointments in medicine and surgery, Bangour General Hospital, 1967-68; Lecturer, Department of Pathology, Edinburgh University, 1968-79. Recreations: golf; gardening. Address: (b.) University Medical School, Teviot Place, Edinburgh, EH8 9AG; T.-031-650 3001.

Gilmour, John, DL, MFH. Farmer; b. 15.7.44, Edinburgh; m., Valerie Janine Russell; 2 s.; 2 d. Educ. Eton; Aberdeen College. Captain, FFY/SH (TA); Member, Queen's Bodyguard for Scotland (Royal Company of Archers). Trustee, ADRA (Moredun Institute). Recreations: fishing; reading. Address: Balcormo Mains, Leven, Fife; T.-033 336 229.

Gilmour, John Andrew George, MA, LLB, NP. Solicitor; Marketing Consultant; Honorary Sheriff at Dumbarton, since 1991; b. 17.11.37, Balloch; m., Roma Aileen; 3 d. Educ. Morrison's Academy, Crieff; Edinburgh University. Partner, McArthur Brown Robertson; Partner, McArthur Stanton; President, Strathclyde Junior Chamber of Commerce, 1973; Director, Dumbarton Enterprise Trust, since 1985; Dean, Faculty of Dunbartonshire Solicitors, 1988-90. Recreations: sport; music; gastronomy. Address: (h.) Cramond Cottage, 19 East Lennox Drive, Helensburgh; T.-0436 75057.

Gilmour, Sir John Edward, 3rd Bt, DSO, TD, JP, BA. Lord Lieutenant of Fife, 1980-87; b. 24.10.12, Edinburgh; m., Ursula Mabyn Wills; 2 s. Educ. Eton College; Trinity Hall, Cambridge; Dundee School of Economics. Served with Fife and Forfar Yeomanry, 1939-45; served on Fife County Council, 1951-61; MP (Conservative), East Fife, 1961-79; Chairman, Conservative Party in Scotland, 1965-67; Lord High Commissioner, General Assembly, Church of Scotland, 1982, 1983. Recreation: gardening. Address: (h.) Montrave, Leven, Fife, KY8 5NY; T.-Leven 26159.

Gilmour, William McIntosh, OStJ, BL. Honorary Sheriff, Dumbarton; Lawyer; b. 9.3.23, Newcastle-upon-Tyne; m., Elinor Adams. Educ. Hillhead High School; Cally House, Gatehouse of Fleet; Glasgow University. Early experience with legal firms in Glasgow; became Partner, latterly Senior Partner, in firm in Dunbartonshire; now in practice in Glasgow; former Dean, Faculty of Solicitors in Dunbartonshire; founder Member and Past President, Clydebank Rotary Club; Past Deacon, Society of Deacons and Free Presces; Chairman for Dunbartonshire, Order of St. John; Member, Incorporation of Gardeners (Glasgow Trades House). Recreations: dog-walking (formerly, motor sport). Address: (h.) 65 Killermont Road, Bearsden, Glasgow; T.-041-942 0498.

Gilmour, Rev. William Mayne, MA, BD. Minister, Lecropt Kirk, Bridge of Allan, since 1983; b. 18.10.42, Glasgow; m., Helen Grant Dewar; 1 s.; 1 d. Educ. Albert Secondary School, Glasgow; Aberdeen University. Minister: Townhead Church, Coatbridge, 1969-79, Chalmers linked with Lecropt Church, Bridge of Allan, 1979-83. Recreation: reading. Address: Lecropt Kirk Manse, 5 Henderson Street, Bridge of Allan, FK9 4NA; T.-0786 832382.

Gimingham, Professor Charles Henry, OBE, BA, PhD, ScD, FRSE, FIBiol. Regius Professor of Botany, Aberdeen University, 1981-88; b. 28.4.23, Leamington; m., Elizabeth Caroline Baird; 3 d. Educ. Gresham's School, Holt, Norfolk;

Emmanuel College, Cambridge. Research Assistant, Imperial College, London, 1944-45; Department of Botany, Aberdeen University: Assistant, 1946-48, Lecturer, 1948-61, Senior Lecturer, 1961-64, Reader, 1964-69, Professor, since 1969, Head of Department, 1981-88; Member: Scottish Committee of Nature Conservancy, 1966-69, Scottish Advisory Committee, Nature Conservancy Council, 1970-80, Countryside Commission for Scotland, since 1980; President, Botanical Society of Edinburgh, 1982-84; Vice-Chairman, NE Regional Board, Nature Conservancy Council for Scotland, 1991-92; Member, Board of Management, Hill Farming Research Organisation, 1981-87; Member, Governing Body, Aberdeen College of Education, 1981-87; Member, Council of Management, Macaulay Institute for Soil Research, 1983-87; Member, Board of Management, Macaulay Land Use Research Institute, 1987- 90; British Ecological Society: Joint Secretary, 1956-61, Vice-President, 1962-64, Joint Editor, Journal of Ecology, 1975-78, President, 1986-87. Publications: Ecology of Heathlands, 1972; Introduction to Heathland Ecology, 1975. Recreations: hill-walking; photography; history and culture of Japan. Address: (h.) 4 Gowanbrae Road, Bieldside, Aberdeen.

Gimson, George Stanley, QC (Scot). Chairman, Pensions Appeals Tribunals, Scotland, since 1975; Chairman, Medical Appeal Tribunals, 1985-91; b. 1915. Educ. High School of Glasgow; Glasgow University. Advocate, 1949; Sheriff Principal of Aberdeen, Kincardine and Banff, 1972-74; Sheriff Principal of Grampian, Highland and Islands, 1975-82; Member, Edinburgh Central Hospitals Board, 1960-70 (Chairman, 1964-70); Director, SNO Society Ltd., 1962-80; Trustee, National Library of Scotland, 1963-76; Chairman, RSSPCC, Edinburgh, 1972-76; Hon. LLD, Aberdeen, 1981. Address: (h.) 11 Royal Circus, Edinburgh, EH3 6TL.

Girdwood, Professor Ronald Haxton, CBE, MB, ChB (Hons), MD, PhD, FRCPEd, FRCP, FRCPI, FRCPath, Hon. FACP, Hon. FRACP, FRSE. President, Royal College of Physicians of Edinburgh, 1982-85; Chairman, Scottish National Blood Transfusion Association, since 1981; b. 19.3.17, Arbroath; m., Mary Elizabeth Williams; 1 s.; 1 d. Educ. Daniel Stewart's College, Edinburgh; Edinburgh University; Michigan University. Army service, RAMC, UK and India, 1942-46, successively as Lt., Captain, Major and Lt.-Col. (when posted to Burma); Lecturer, then Senior Lecturer, Reader in Medicine, Edinburgh University, 1946-62; Research Fellow, Michigan University, 1948-49; Consultant Physician, Edinburgh Royal Infirmary, 1950-82; Professor of Therapeutics and Clinical Pharmacology, Edinburgh University, 1962-82 (Dean, Faculty of Medicine, 1975-79); Chairman, Scottish Group, Nutrition Society, 1961-62; President, British Society for Haematology, 1963-64; Chairman, Executive Committee, Edinburgh and SE Scotland Blood Transfusion Association, since 1970; Member, UK Committee on Safety of Medicines, 1972-83; Chairman, Medico-Pharmaceutical Forum, 1985-87; President, University of Edinburgh Graduates' Association, 1991-92; Member, Board of Governors, St. Columba's Hospice, since 1985; Suniti Panja Gold Medal, Calcutta School of Tropical Medicine, 1980; given the Freedom of Sirajgunj, Bangladesh, 1984; Oliver Memorial Awards for services to blood transfusion, 1991. Publications: Travels with a Stethoscope, 1991; editor of four medical books and more than 300 medical papers. Recreations: writing; photography. Address: (h.) 2 Hermitage Drive, Edinburgh, EH10 6DD; T.-031-447 5137.

Glasby, Michael Arthur, BM, BCh, MA, MSc (Oxon), MA (Cantab), FRCS (Eng). Reader in Anatomy, Edinburgh University, since 1992; b. 29.10.48, Nottingham; m., Celia M.E. Robinson. Educ. High Pavement Grammar School, Nottingham; Christ Church, Oxford; Oxford Medical School. Senior Scholar and Assistant Tutor in Physiology, Christ Church, Oxford, 1971-76; Surgeon, Harefield Hospital

Transplant Trust, 1981-83; Fellow and Lecturer in Anatomy, New Hall, Cambridge, 1983-87; Lecturer in Anatomy, Royal College of Surgeons of England, 1984-87; joined Edinburgh University as Lecturer, 1987. Editor, anatomy textbook for surgeons and physiology textbook for surgeons; numerous articles. Recreations: golf; Latin and Greek literature; music; beekeeping; wine. Address: (b.) Department of Anatomy, Edinburgh University, Edinburgh, EH8 9AG; T.-031-650 3112.

Glasgow, 10th Earl of (Patrick Robin Archibald Boyle). Television Director/Producer; b. 30.7.39; m., Isabel Mary James; 1 s.; 1 d. Educ. Eton; Paris University. Sub.-Lt., RNR, 1959-60; Producer/Director, Yorkshire TV, 1968-70; free-lance Film Producer, since 1971; formed Kelburn Country Centre, 1977. Address (b.) Kelburn Castle, Fairlie, Ayrshire, KA29 0BE; T.-0475 568685.

Glasier, Anna, MB, ChB, BSc, MRCOG, MD. Director, Lothian Health Board Family Planning and Well Woman Services, since 1990; Senior Lecturer, Department of Obstetrics and Gynaecology, Edinburgh University, since 1990; Consultant Gynaecologist, Lothian Health Board, since 1989; b. 16.4.50, Salisbury. Educ. Lord Digby's School, Sherborne. Clinical Research Scientist, Medical Research Council Centre for Reproductive Biology, Edinburgh, 1989-90. Recreations: ski mountaineering; sailing. Address: (b.) 18 Dean Terrace, Edinburgh, EH4 1NL; T.-031-332 7941.

Glass, Alexander, MA, DipEd. Rector, Dingwall Academy, since 1977; b. 1.6.32, Dunbar; m., Edith Margaret Duncan Baxter; 3 d. Educ. Dunbar Grammar School; Edinburgh University; Heidelberg University; University of Aix-en-Provence. Teacher of Modern Languages, Montrose Academy, 1958-60; Special Assistant Teacher of Modern Languages, Oban High School, 1960-62; Principal Teacher of Modern Languages, Nairn Academy, 1962-65; Principal Teacher of French and Assistant Rector, Perth Academy, 1965-72; Rector, Milne's High School, Fochabers, 1972-77. Chairman, COSPEN; former President, Highland Secondary Headteachers' Association; former Chairman, Highland Region Working Party for Modern Languages; Regional Chairman, Highland Region Children's Panel; Reader, Church of Scotland; Chairman, Inverness District, Scottish Community Drama Association; Chairman and Secretary, Scottish Secondary Schools' Travel Trust; Churchill Fellow, 1991. Recreations: amateur drama; foreign travel; Rotary. Address: (h.) Craigton, Tulloch Avenue, Dingwall, IV15 9LH; T.-0349 63258.

Glasser, Professor Fredrik Paul, BA, PhD, DSc, FRSE. Professor of Chemistry, Aberdeen University, since 1981; b. 2.5.29, New Haven; m., Lesley Dent; 1 s.; 2 d. Research Fellow, Pennsylvania State University, 1957-59; joined Aberdeen University as Research Fellow, 1959; Lecturer, 1961-69; Senior Lecturer, 1969-76; Reader, 1976-81. Recreations: gardening; walking. Address: (h.) The Grange, 26 Gilbert Road, Bucksburn, Aberdeen; T.-0224 712605.

Glen, Alastair Campbell Agnew, MD, BSc, FRCP(Glas). Consultant Clinical Biochemist, Victoria Infirmary, Glasgow, since 1970; Honorary Senior Lecturer, Glasgow University, since 1991; b. 3.8.36, Glasgow; m., Lesley Gordon; 2 s.; 1 d. Educ. Glasgow Academy; Glasgow University. Research Associate, Massachusetts Institute of Technology, 1966. Recreations: almost anything from skiing and angling to Scottish politics. Address: (h.) 276A Nithsdale Road, Glasgow, G41 5LP; T.-041-427 2131.

Glen, Alexander Iain Munro, MB, ChB, FRCPsych, FRCP(Glas), DPM. Consultant Psychiatrist, Highland Health Board, since 1981; Hon. Senior Lecturer, Aberdeen University, since 1986; Research Director, Highland Psychiatric Research Group, since 1981; Member (SNP), Highland Regional Council, since 1990; b. 25.5.30, Glasgow; m., Dr. Evelyne Glen; 2 s.; 2 d. Educ. Albert Road Academy, Glasgow; Glasgow Academy; Glasgow University. National Service as Surgeon Lt., RNVR, 3rd Frigate Squadron, Far East, 1955-57; Research Fellow, Psychiatry, Glasgow University, 1964-68; Medical Research Council Clinical Psychiatry Unit, 1968-72; MRC Brain Metabolism Unit, Research Fellow, Pharmacology, Edinburgh University, 1972-81. Recreations: politics; poetry; Scotland. Address: (h.) Dalnavert Community Co-operative, Dalnavert, by Kincraig, PH21 1NG; T.-054 04 347.

Glen, Duncan Munro, FCSD. Writer and Lecturer; Partner, Galliard Publishers; b. 11.1.33, Cambuslang; m., Margaret Eadie; 1 s.; 1 d. Educ. West Coats, Cambuslang; Edinburgh College of Art. Book Designer, HM Stationery Office, London; Lecturer in Typography; Editor, Robert Gibson & Co. Ltd.; Sole Owner, Akros Publications; Lecturer, then Senior Lecturer, then Head of Graphic Design, Lancashire Polytechnic; Professor and Head, Department of Visual Communication, Nottingham Polytechnic (Emeritus Professor); Editor, Akros, poetry magazine, 1-51. Author and editor of many books including Hugh MacDiarmid and The Scottish Renaissance, Selected Essays of Hugh MacDiarmid, In Appearances: Poems, The Autobiography of a Poet, Makars' Walk, The Poetry of the Scots, Selected Poems 1965-1990, A Journey Into Scotland. Recreation: walking. Address: (h.) 18 Warrender Park Terrace, Edinburgh, EH9 1EF; T.-031-229 3680.

Glen, Eric Stanger, MB, ChB, FRCSGlas, FRCSEdin. Consultant Urological Surgeon, Walton Urological Teaching and Research Centre, Southern General Hospital, Glasgow; Honorary Clinical Senior Lecturer, Glasgow University; Member, Surgical Examination Panel, Royal College of Physicians and Surgeons of Glasgow; b. 20.10.34, Glasgow; m., Dr. Patricia. Educ. Glasgow University. Pre-Consultant posts, Western and Victoria Infirmaries, Glasgow; Ship Surgeon, Royal Fleet Auxiliary. Chairman, Greater Glasgow Health Board Incontinence Resource Group; Founder and former Secretary, International Continence Society; Founder, Urological Computing Society. Publications: chapters in books; papers on urodynamics, urology and computing. Recreations: travel; writing; computer applications. Address: (h.) 9 St. John's Road, Pollokshields, Glasgow, G41 5RJ; T.-041-423 0759.

Glen, James Robert, CA. Chairman, The Scottish Life Assurance Co., since 1987 (Director, since 1971); Director, Scottish Investment Trust PLC, since 1981; b. 27.5.30, Perth; m., Alison Helen Margaret Brown; 3 s. Educ. Merchiston Castle School. 2nd Lt., RA, 1954-56; Secretary, C.W. Carr, 1956-58; Baillie, Gifford & Co., 1958-62; joined Scottish Investment Trust, 1962. Address: (b.) 6 Albyn Place, Edinburgh; T.-031-225 7781.

Glen, Norman MacLeod, CBE, TD, MA, JP. Leader, Conservative Group, Dumbarton District Council, since 1974; b. 22.12.11, Glasgow; m., Dr. Janet M.S. Glen (deceased); 2 s.; 2 d. Educ. Glasgow Academy; Glasgow University. Retail trade as Buyer, Director and Managing Director, John Glen & Co. Ltd., Glasgow, 1932-74; War Service, six years; TA (mostly 474 HAA Regt RA), 1938-56 (Lt. Colonel, 1954-56); Parliamentary candidate (Liberal), 1945, (Conservative), 1951, 1955, 1959, 1964, 1966 and By-Election, Woodside, 1962; elected, Helensburgh Town Council, 1966 (last Provost of Helensburgh, 1970-75); Elder, West Kirk of Helensburgh. Recreation: walking. Address: (h.) Flat 11, Queen's Court, Helensburgh, G84 7AH; T.-0436 3497.

Glenarthur, 4th Baron (Simon Mark Arthur), Bt. Chairman, St. Mary's Hospital, Paddington, NHS Trust, since

1991; Consultant, British Aerospace PLC, since 1989; Hanson PLC, since 1989; Minister of State, Foreign and Commonwealth Office, 1987-89; DL, Aberdeenshire, since 1987; b. 7.10.44; m.; 1 s.; 1 d. Educ. Eton. Retired Major, 10th Royal Hussars (PWO); Helicopter Captain, British Airways, 1976-82; a Lord in Waiting, 1982-83; Parliamentary Under Secretary of State: Department of Health and Social Security, 1983-85, Home Office, 1985-86; Minister of State, Scottish Office, 1986-87; Member, Queen's Bodyguard for Scotland (Royal Company of Archers). Address: (b.) House of Lords, London, SW1A 0PW.

Glencross, Rev. William McCallum, LTh. Minister, Macdonald Memorial Church, Bellshill, since 1973; b. 29.7.34, Sanquhar; m., Agnes Jane Crate; 3 d. Educ. Sanquhar Academy; Dumfries Academy; Glasgow University. Mining Surveyor, NCB, 1950-63; Parish Minister, Whalsay and Skerries (Shetland Islands), 1968-73. Address: Macdonald Memorial Manse, 346 Main Street, Bellshill, Lanarkshire; T.-Bellshill 842177.

Gloag, Matthew Irving. Director, Matthew Gloag & Son Ltd., since 1971; b. 1.12.47, Perth; m., Dilly Moon; 2 d. Chairman, Scottish Licensed Trade Association, 1984-85. Address: (b.) 33 Kinnoull Street, Perth, PH1 5EU; T.-0738 21101.

Glover, Professor David Moore, BA, PhD, FRSE. Professor of Biochemistry, Dundee University, since 1989; Director, Cancer Research Campaign Cell Cycle Group, since 1989; b. 28.3.48, Chapeltown; m., Barbara A. Spruce. Educ. Broadway Grammar School, Barnsley; Fitzwilliam College, Cambridge. Postdoctoral Fellow, Stanford University, California, 1972-75; Imperial College, London, 1975-89, latterly as Head, Biochemistry Department. Publications: 80 scientific papers; two books; Editor, eight books. Address: (b.) CRC Laboratories, Medical Sciences Institute, Dundee, DD1 4HN; T.-0382 307793.

Glover, Rev. Robert Lindsay, BMus, BD, ARCO. Minister, St. George's West, Edinburgh, since 1985; b. 21.7.45, Watford; m., Elizabeth Mary Brown; 2 s.; 2 d. Educ. Langholm Academy; Dumfries Academy; Glasgow University. Minister, Newton Parish, near Dalkeith, 1971-76; Minister, St. Vigeans Parish, Arbroath, 1976-85. Recreations: music (organ and accordion); caravanning; reading. Address: 24 Queensferry Street Lane, Edinburgh, EH2 5PF; T.-031-225 7001.

Glover, Sue, MA. Writer; b. 1.3.43, Edinburgh; m., John Glover; 2 s. Educ. St. George's School, Edinburgh; Montpellier University; Edinburgh University. Original drama and other scriptwriting for radio, television and theatre; theatre productions include The Seal Wife, Edinburgh Festival, 1980, An Island in Largo, Byre Theatre, 1981, The Bubble Boy, Glasgow Tron, 1981, The Straw Chair, Traverse Theatre, 1988; Bondagers, Traverse Theatre, 1991 (winner, 1990 LWT Plays on Stage Award); television work includes The Spaven Connection and Mme Montand and Mrs Miller; televised version of The Bubble Boy won a silver medal, New York Film and Television Festival, and a merit, Chicago International Film Festival, 1983. Recreations: house and garden. Address: Castlefield Cottage, Castlebank Road, Cupar, Fife; T.-Cupar 53664.

Goddard, Kenneth George, BA, IPFA. Director of Finance, Skye and Lochalsh District Council, since 1981; b. 14.1.47, Pembroke Dock; m., Jennifer; 2 s. Educ. Pembroke Grammar School; St. Davids University, Lampeter. Inland Revenue, 1970-72; Pembroke Borough Council, 1972-74; South Pembrokeshire District Council, 1974-78; joined Skye and Lochalsh District Council, 1978. Address: (b.) Park Road, Portree, Isle of Skye, IV51 9EP; T.-0478 2341.

Godden, Anthony John, BSc (Hons), FRSH, AIHE. Principal, West Lothian College of Further Education, since 1987; b. 26.3.46, Swansea; m., Kelly; 1 s.; 1 d. Educ. Dynevor Grammar School; North East London Polytechnic; Open University. Lecturer, Bridgnorth College of Further Education, 1970-73; Social Tutor, Airedale and Wharfedale College of Further Education, 1973-75; Warden, Mildmay Hall, and Head, Section of General Studies and Information Sciences, Essex Institute of Higher Education, 1975-78; Assistant Inspector, Kent County Council Education Department, 1978-82; Principal, Gainsborough College of Further Education, 1982-86. Director, East of Scotland Training Consortium. Recreations: armchair sport; theatre; guitar; travel. Address: (b.) West Lothian College, Marjoribanks Street, Bathgate, EH48 1QJ; T.-0506 634300.

Godden, Tony Richard Hillier, CB, BSc (Econ). Member, The Council on Tribunals and its Scottish Committee, since 1988; Member, Advisory Board on Ancient Monuments, since 1990; Secretary, Scottish Development Department, 1980-87; b. 13.11.27, Barnstaple; m., Marjorie Florence Snell; 1 s.; 2 d. Educ. Barnstaple Grammar School; London School of Economics. Commissioned, RAF Education Branch, 1950; entered Civil Service, 1951; first appointed to Colonial Office; Private Secretary to Parliamentary Under Secretary of State, 1954-55; seconded to Cabinet Office, 1957-59; joined Scottish Home Department, 1961; Assistant Secretary, Scottish Development Department, 1964; Under Secretary, 1969; Secretary, Scottish Economic Planning Development, 1973-80. Address: c/o New Club, Edinburgh, EH2 2BB.

Godfray, Martin Francis, BSc, CChem, FRSC, MChemA. Public Analyst, Official Agricultural Analyst and Scientific Adviser, Lothian, Borders and Highland Regional Councils and Orkney and Shetland Islands Councils, since 1980; b. 10.5.45, Barry, Glamorgan; m., Heather Jean; 1 s.; 2 d. Educ. Barry Boys Grammar Technical School; Birmingham University. Deputy Public Analyst and Deputy Agricultural Analyst, London Boroughs of Southwark, Greenwich, Islington and Tower Hamlets, 1973-80. Address: (b.) Regional Laboratory, 4 Marine Esplanade, Edinburgh, EH6 7LU; T.-031-553 1171.

Godman, Norman. MP (Labour), Greenock and Port Glasgow, since 1983; b. 1937.

Gold, Lex. Managing Director, Scottish Enterprise, since 1990; b. 14.12.40, Rigside; m., Eleanor; 1 s.; 1 d. Educ. Lanark Grammar School. Sub-Editor, Daily Record; professional footballer; joined Civil Service, Glasgow, 1960; Inland Revenue, two years; Civil Service Department, four years; Home Office, 21 years; Training Agency, three years. Recreations: theatre; opera; reading; football; golf; running. Address: (b.) 9 St. Andrew Square, Edinburgh; T.-031-225 8500.

Goldberg, Professor Sir Abraham, KB, MD, DSc, FRCP, FRCPEdin, FRCPGlas, FRSE. Regius Professor of the Practice of Medicine, Glasgow University, 1978-89; Founder President, Faculty of Pharmaceutical Medicine of Royal Colleges of Physicians of UK, 1989; b. 7.12.23, Edinburgh; m., Clarice Cussin; 2 s.; 1 d. Educ. Sciennes School, Edinburgh; George Heriot's School, Edinburgh; Edinburgh University. House Physician, Royal Hospital for Sick Children, Edinburgh, 1946-47; RAMC, 1947-49 (granted rank of honorary Major on discharge); Nuffield Research Fellow, UCH Medical School, London, 1952-54; Eli Lilly Travelling Fellow in Medicine (MRC), Department of Medicine, Utah University, 1954-56; Glasgow University: Lecturer in Medicine, 1956-59, Titular Professor of Medicine, 1967-70, Regius Professor of Materia Medica, 1970-78. Chairman, Grants Committee 1, Clinical Research Board, MRC, 1973-77; Member, Chief Scientist's Committee,

SHHD, 1977-83; Chairman, Biomedical Research Committee, SHHD, 1977-83; Editor, Scottish Medical Journal, 1962-63; Chairman, Committee on Safety of Medicines, 1980-86; Fitzpatrick Lecturer, Royal College of Physicians, London, 1988; Goodall Memorial Lecturer, Royal College of Physicians and Surgeons of Glasgow, 1989; City of Glasgow Lord Provost's Award, 1988. Publications: Disorders of Porphyrin Metabolism (Co-author), 1987; Recent Advances in Haematology (Joint Editor), 1971; Clinics in Haematology "The Porphyrias" (Co-author), 1980. Recreations: medical history; literature; writing; walking; swimming. Address: (h.) 16 Birnam Crescent, Bearsden, Glasgow, G61 2AU.

Goldfinch, Paul, MA, MSc, MSc, CEng, MBCS, AFIMA, FSA Scot. Senior Lecturer and Depute Head, Undergraduate Teaching, Department of Computer Science, Strathclyde University, since 1988; b. 4.4.45, Bristol; m., Dr. Judith M. Goldfinch; 2 s. Educ. Wolverhampton Grammar School; King Edward VII School, Sheffield; St. Catherine's College, Oxford; Essex University; Edinburgh University. Department of Aeronautics and Fluid Mechanics, Glasgow University, 1968-72; Secretary's Office, Edinburgh University, 1972-78; Assistant Registrar, Strathclyde University, 1978-85. Member, Executive Committee, Scottish Youth Hostels Association, since 1972; Treasurer, Scottish Countryside Activities Council, since 1991. Recreations: hills; music; history; railways. Address: (b.) Department of Computer Science, Strathclyde University, Livingstone Tower, 26 Richmond Street, Glasgow, G1 1XH; T.-041-552 4400, Ext. 3230.

Goldie, David. Farmer; Member, Scottish Training Committee, Agricultural Training Board, 1982-86; Member, Scottish Agricultural Development Council, 1983-86; Director, Royal Highland and Agricultural Society, since 1976 (Chairman of Directors, 1987-88); b. 30.7.37, Dumfries; m., Ann Irving; 3 s. Educ. Wallace Hall Academy, Closeburn, Thornhill. Chairman, Annandale Young Farmers Club, 1958-59; Elder and Treasurer, Ruthwell Church, since 1968; founder Chairman, local Community Council, 1978-81; Chairman, Dumfries Agricultural Society, 1977-79. Address: (h.) Longbridgemuir, Clarencefield, Dumfries; T.-038 787 210.

Goodall, Alexander, MA (Hons). Principal, Wester Hailes Education Centre, since 1982; b. 25.8.38, Dolphinton, Peebles-shire; 1 s.; 1 d. Educ. Portobello High School; Edinburgh University; Moray House College of Education. Teacher of History, Niddrie Marischal Secondary School, 1961-64; Education Officer, Teso College, Uganda, 1964-69; Preston Lodge High School: Principal Teacher of History, 1969-74, Assistant Head Teacher, 1974-78; Depute Principal, Wester Hailes Education Centre, 1978-82. Editor, Scottish History Teaching Review. Publication: Economics and Development (Co-author). Recreations: trout angling; rubber bridge. Address: (b.) 5 Murrayburn Drive, Edinburgh; T.-031-442 2201.

Gollan, Rev. Alasdair, BA, BTh. Minister, Lochcarron Free Church, since 1985; Moderator, Free Church of Scotland, 1990; b. 23.2.23, Glasgow; m., Rachel Mary MacKinnon; 3 d. Educ. Woodside Secondary School, Glasgow; Edinburgh University; Free Church College, Edinburgh; Open University. Merchant Navy, 1941-46; Minister: Shiskine Free Church, 1950-59, Burghead Free Church, 1959-68, East Kilbride Free Church, 1968-70, Free Gaelic Church, Greenock, 1970-85. Provost of Burghead, 1966-68; JP; Member, Joint County Council of Moray and Nairn, 1966-68. Recreations: walking; cycling; bird-watching; reading. Address: Free Church Manse, Lochcarron, Ross-shire, IV54 8YQ; T.-052 02 208.

Gooday, Professor Graham W., BSc, PhD, FRSE. Professor of Microbiology, Aberdeen University, since 1984; b. 19.2.42, Colchester; m., Margaret A. Mealing; 1 s.; 2 d. Educ. Hove Grammar School for Boys; Bristol University. VSO, Sierra Leone, 1964; Research Fellowships: Leeds University, 1967, Glasgow and Oxford Universities, 1969; Lecturer, Senior Lecturer, Reader, Aberdeen University, 1972-84; Member, Aquatic Life Sciences Committee, NERC, 1984-87; Council Member, British Mycological Society, 1974-77, President, 1993; Council Member, Society for General Microbiology, 1976-80; awarded first Fleming Lectureship, Society for General Microbiology, 1976. Recreation: open countryside. Address: (b.) Department of Molecular and Cell Biology, Marischal College, University, Aberdeen, AB9 1AS; T.-0224 273147.

Goodman, Anthony Eric, MA (Oxon), BLitt (Oxon), FRHistS. Reader in History, Edinburgh University, since 1983; b. 21.7.36, London; m., Jacqueline; 1 d. Educ. Selhurst Grammar School, Croydon; Magdalen College, Oxford. Joined staff, Edinburgh University, 1961. Secretary, Edinburgh Branch, Historical Association, since 1975. Publications: The Loyal Conspiracy, 1971; A History of England from Edward II to James I, 1977; The Wars of the Roses, 1981; A Traveller's Guide to Medieval Britain (Co-author), 1986; The New Monarchy, 1471-1534, 1988. Recreation: getting to know the Borders. Address: (h.) 23 Kirkhill Gardens, Edinburgh, EH16 5DF; T.-031-667 5988.

Goodsman, James Melville. Director, The Conservative Party in Scotland, since 1990; b. 6.2.47, St. Andrews; m., Victoria Smitherman. Educ. Elgin Academy. Conservative Party Agent, 1968-80; Deputy Central Office Agent, North West Area, 1980-84; Assistant Director (Community Affairs), CCO, 1984-89; Head, Community and Legal Department, CCO, 1989-90. Recreations: golf; Church music; Scotland's heritage. Address: (b.) Suite 1/1, 14 Links Place, Leith, Edinburgh, EH6 7EZ; T.-031-555 2900.

Goodwin, Sir Matthew Dean, CBE, CA. Chairman, Hewden Stuart PLC; Director, Murray Ventures PLC; Chairman, Murray Enterprise PLC; Chairman, Scotcare Ltd.; Member, Irvine Development Corporation; Deputy Chairman, Scottish Conservative Party, since 1990 (Hon. Treasurer, 1983-90); b. 12.6.29, Dalserf; m., Margaret Eileen Colvil; 2 d. Educ. Glasgow Academy. Recreations: shooting; bridge; farming. Address: (b.) 135 Buchanan Street, Glasgow; T.-041-221 7331.

Gould, Lord (James Duncan), Life Peer (1987), Kt (1983), CA, FRSA, FCIOB, FFB, DL. Chairman, Scottish Conservative Party, 1983-89; Director: Mactaggart & Mickel Ltd., since 1965, American Trust PLC, since 1984, Gibson & Gould Ltd., since 1978, Edinburgh Oil & Gas PLC, since 1987, Biomac Ltd., since 1988, Strathclyde Graduate Business School Ltd., since 1990; b. 28.5.34, Glasgow; m., Sheena Paton; 2 s.; 1 d. Educ. Glasgow Academy. President: Scottish Building Contractors' Association, 1971, Scottish National Federation of Building Trades Employers, 1977-78; Honorary Treasurer, Scottish Building Employers' Federation, 1979-81; Chairman, Conservative Board of Finance Scotland, 1980-83; Honorary Treasurer, Scottish Conservative and Unionist Association, 1980-83; Honorary President, Eastwood Conservative Association, since 1978; Chairman, East Renfrewshire Conservative Association, 1974-77; Chairman, CBI Scotland, 1981-83; Chairman, Royal Scottish Orchestra, since 1991; Member, Scottish Hospital Endowments Research Trust; Member of Court, Strathclyde University, since 1988; President, Glasgow Bn., Boys Brigade, since 1987; Elder, Mearns Parish Church; Trustee, Ferguson Bequest; Vice President, Tenovus-Scotland. Recreations: golf; tennis; walking. Address: (b.)

107 West Regent Street, Glasgow, G2 2BH; T.-041-332 0001.

Gordon, (Alexander) Esme, RSA, FRIBA, FRIAS; b. 12.9.10, Edinburgh; m., Betsy McCurry (deceased); 2 s.; 1 d. Educ. Edinburgh Academy; School of Architecture, Edinburgh College of Art; RIBA. Owen Jones Scholar, 1934; worked for three years in London office of Sir John Burnet; Tait & Lorne, FFRIBA; set up own practice as Architect in Edinburgh, 1936; War Service, RE, Europe; President, Edinburgh Architectural Association, 1955-57; Member, Scottish Committee, Arts Council of GB, 1959-67; Honorary Secretary, RSA, 1972-77. Publications: A Short History of St. Giles Cathedral, 1954; The Principles of Church Building, Furnishing, Equipment and Decoration, 1963; The Royal Scottish Academy 1826-1976, 1976; The Making of the Royal Scottish Academy, 1988. Address: (h.) Flat 23, 2 Barnton Avenue West, Edinburgh, EH4 6EB; T.-031-339 8073.

Gordon, Boyd. Fisheries Consultant; Fisheries Secretary, Department of Agriculture and Fisheries for Scotland, 1982-86; b. 18.9.26, Musselburgh; m., Elizabeth Mabel Smith; 2 d. Educ. Musselburgh Grammar School. Military Service, Royal Scots; joined Civil Service, initially with Ministry of Labour, then Inland Revenue; joined Department of Agriculture and Fisheries for Scotland, 1953; Principal dealing with Salmon and Freshwater Fisheries Administration and Fisheries Research and Development, 1962-73; Assistant Secretary, Agriculture Economic Policy, EEC Co-ordination and Agriculture Marketing, 1973-82. Recreations: golf; gardening; local Church matters; violin playing. Address: (h.) 87 Duddingston Road, Edinburgh; T.-031-669 4380.

Gordon, Charles P., CA. Director of Finance, Edinburgh University, since 1990; b. 1.6.34, Glasgow. Educ. Allan Glen's School. Formerly Quaestor and Factor, St. Andrews University. Address: (b.) Old College, South Bridge, Edinburgh, EH8 9YL; T.-031-650 2182.

Gordon, Professor George, MA (Hons), PhD. Director of Academic Practice, Strathclyde University, since 1987; Governor, Jordanhill College of Education, since 1982 (Chairman, since 1987); b. 14.11.39, Edinburgh; m., Jane Taylor Collins; 2 d. Educ. George Heriot's School; Edinburgh University. Edinburgh University: Vans Dunlop Scholar, 1962-64, Demonstrator, 1964-65; Strathclyde University: Assistant Lecturer, 1965-66, Lecturer, 1966-80, Dean, Faculty of Arts and Social Studies, 1984-87; served on SUCE and SCE Geography Panels; Member, SCOVACT; served on General Teaching Council for Scotland and Council, Royal Scottish Geographical Society; Vice President, British Association for the Advancement of Science; former Member, General Assembly of Open University; Member, Senate, Strathclyde University. Publications: Regional Cities of the UK 1890-1980 (Editor), 1986; Perspectives of the Scottish City (Editor), 1985; Scottish Urban History, 1983; The Making of Scottish Geography (Co-author), 1984; Settlement Geography, 1983; Urban Geography, 1981. Recreations: theatre-going; watching sport. Address: (b.) Centre for Academic Practice, Strathclyde University, Richmond Street, Glasgow; T.-041-552 4400, Ext. 2637.

Gordon, George, MB, ChB, FRCSE, FRCOG. Consultant Obstetrician and Gynaecologist, Dumfries and Galloway, since 1969; b. 4.9.36, Markinch, Fife; m., Rosemary Gould Hutchison; 1 s.; 1 d. Educ. Bell Baxter School; Edinburgh University. Senior Registrar, Western General Hospital, Edinburgh, 1966-69; Chairman, Scottish Confidential Enquiry into Maternal Mortality; Member, Central Midwives Board for Scotland, 1978-84; External Examiner, Edinburgh University, 1978-82; Examiner, FRCS Edinburgh and DRCOG London; Secretary, RCOG Scottish Executive;

Administrative Consultant, Alexandra Hospice Unit; Honorary Secretary, Dumfries and Stewartry Division, BMA, 1975-87. Recreations: music; Scottish literature; golf; gardening. Address: (b.) Dumfries and Galloway Royal Infirmary, Bankend Road, Dumfries, DG1 4AP.

Gordon, George Park Douglas, BSc (Hons). HM Chief Inspector of Schools, Western Division and Special Educational Needs; b. 23.10.37, Peterhead; m., Karein L.M.; 1 s.; 1 d. Educ. Peterhead Academy; Aberdeen University; Aberdeen College of Education. Teacher of Science, Peterhead Academy, 1961-64; Principal Teacher of Science, Dornoch Academy, 1964-67; Assistant Adviser in Science, Glasgow, 1967-69; HM Inspector of Schools, 1969-75, Higher Grade, 1975-86; HM Chief Inspector of Schools, Education (Basic and Special), 1986-88; Education 5-14 and Special Educational Needs, 1988-89. Recreations: golf; squash; gardening; reading; walking; spending winter Saturdays watching football and supporting Aberdeen FC. Address: (h.) Suilven, 8 Ewing Walk, Fairways, Milngavie, G62 6EG; T.-041-956 5131.

Gordon, Sheriff Gerald Henry, QC, MA, LLB, PhD, LLD. Sheriff of Glasgow and Strathkelvin, since 1978; b. 17.6.29, Glasgow; m., Marjorie Joseph; 1 s.; 2 d. Educ. Queen's Park Senior Secondary School; Glasgow University. Advocate, 1953; Procurator Fiscal Depute, Edinburgh, 1960-65; Edinburgh University: Head, Department of Criminal Law and Criminology, 1965-72, Personal Professor of Criminal Law, 1969-72, Dean, Faculty of Law, 1970-73, Professor of Scots Law, 1972-76; Sheriff of South Strathclyde, Dumfries and Galloway, at Hamilton, 1976-77; Member, Interdepartmental Committee on Scottish Criminal Procedure, 1970-77. Publications: Criminal Law of Scotland, 1967, 1978; Renton & Brown's Criminal Procedure (Editor), 1972, 1983. Recreations: Jewish studies; coffee conversation; swimming. Address: (h.) 52 Eastwoodmains Road, Giffnock, Glasgow; T.-041-638 8614.

Gordon, Rev. Canon Hugh. Chaplain, St. Joseph's House, Edinburgh; b. 18.11.10, Inverness. Educ. Stonyhurst College, Lancashire; Heriot-Watt College, Edinburgh; Oscott College, Birmingham. Ordained, 1937; Curate, Inverness, 1937; Army Chaplain, 1940 (Egypt and El Alamain, 51st Highland Division); Osnabruck, 1946, developing civilian parish church and first Catholic school in Germany after the fall of Hitler; Priest: Stirling, Selkirk, St. Andrews, Edinburgh St. Margaret's and St. John the Evangelist, Linlithgow St. Michael's; founded Linlithgow Scripture Centre for Christian Unity; former Executive Member, Scottish Catholic Lay Apostolate Council; Member: Commission for Christian Doctrine and Unity; Order of Christian Unity; Fellowship of St. Andrew. Recreations: anything to help restoration of Christian unity; stopped tennis, golf, fishing. Address: 47 Gilmore Place, Edinburgh, EH3 9NG; T.-031-229 1929.

Gordon, James Stuart, CBE, MA (Hons). Managing Director, Radio Clyde, since 1973; Chairman, Scottish Exhibition Centre, 1983-89; Member, Scottish Development Agency, 1981-90; Member, Glasgow University Court, since 1984; b. 17.5.36, Glasgow; m., Anne Stevenson; 2 s.; 1 d. Educ. St. Aloysius College, Glasgow; Glasgow University. Political Editor, STV, 1965-73. Winner, Observer Mace Debating Tournament, 1957; Sony Special Award for Services to Radio, 1984; Member, Committee of Inquiry into Pay and Conditions of Teachers in Scotland, 1986. Recreations: his children; genealogy; golf. Address: (b.) Radio Clyde, Clydebank Business Park, Clydebank; T.-041-306 2202.

Gordon, Canon Kenneth Davidson, MA. Rector, St. Devenick's Episcopal Church, Bieldside, Aberdeen, since 1971; Examining Chaplain to Bishop of Aberdeen and

Orkney, 1978-86; Warden of Lay Readers, Diocese of Aberdeen and Orkney, since 1978; b. 27.12.35, Edinburgh; m., Edith Jessica Newing; 2 s. Educ. George Heriot's School, Edinburgh; Edinburgh University; Tyndale Hall, Bristol. Curate, St. Helens Parish Church, Lancashire, 1960-66 (with charge of St. Andrew's Mission Church, 1962-66); Vicar, St. George the Martyr's Parish Church, Bolton, 1966-71; Canon, St. Andrew's Cathedral, Aberdeen, since 1981. Member, Mission Board, General Synod, Scottish Episcopal Church. Recreations: bird-watching; golf; photography; model railways. Address: The Rectory, Bieldside, Aberdeen, AB1 9AP; T.-0224 861552.

Gordon, Rev. Peter Mitchell, MA, BD. Minister, Airdrie West Parish Church, since 1985; b. 1.7.30, Aberdeen; m., Fiona Selby McDonald; 2 s. Educ. Aberdeen Grammar School; Aberdeen University. Minister: Camperdown, Dundee, 1959-65, Brechin Cathedral, 1965-85. Recreations: gardening; local and family history. Address: West Parish Manse, Arthur Avenue, Airdrie; T.-0236 763022.

Gordon, Robert. Chartered Accountant; Senior Partner, Chiene & Tait, CA, Edinburgh; Director, Scottish Equitable Life Assurance Society, since 1975; b. 1930; m., Avril Wotherspoon; 3 s.; 2 d. Educ. Cargilfield; Loretto. Member, Commission for Local Authority Accounts in Scotland, 1976-85; Governor, Moray House College of Education, 1979-87; Member, Committee of Investigation for Scotland, since 1980; Governor, Loretto School (Chairman), since 1981; Member, Scottish Council of Independent Schools, 1987-89; Member, Society of High Constables and Guard of Honour of Holyroodhouse, since 1965. Recreation: yachting. Address: (b.) 3 Albyn Place, Edinburgh, EH2 4NQ; T.-031-225 7515.

Gordon, Professor William Morrison, MA, LLB, PhD. Douglas Professor of Civil Law, Glasgow University, since 1969; Solicitor (non-practising), since 1956; b. 3.3.33, Inverurie; m., Isabella Evelyn Melitta Robertson; 2 s.; 2 d. Educ. Inverurie Academy; Robert Gordon's College, Aberdeen; Aberdeen University. National Service, Royal Navy, 1955-57; Assistant in Jurisprudence, Aberdeen University, 1957-60; Glasgow University: Lecturer in Civil Law, 1960-65, Senior Lecturer in Law, 1965-69 (and Sub-Dean of Faculty); Dean of Faculty, 1974-76. Elder and Session Clerk, Jordanhill Parish Church; Literary Director, The Stair Society. Publications: Studies in Transfer of Property by Traditio, 1970; Scottish Land Law, 1989; articles. Recreation: golf. Address: (b.) Department of Legal History, Stair Building, University, Glasgow, G12 8QQ; T.-041-339 8855, Ext. 5387.

Goring, Rev. Iain McCormick, BSc, BD. Minister, Callander Kirk, since 1985; b. 22.7.50, Edinburgh; m., Janet Page; 2 s.; 1 d. Educ. Dunfermline High School; Edinburgh University. Civil Service (DHSS, London), 1971-72; after BD, Assistantship, St. Luke's, Milngavie, 1975-77; Minister, Lochwood Church, Glasgow, 1977-85. Address: The Manse, Aveland Park Road, Callander, Perthshire, FK17 8EN; T.-0877 30097.

Gorman, Brian, MA. Director, English-Speaking Union in Scotland, since 1984; b. 31.10.51, Wishaw. Educ. Our Lady's High School, Motherwell; Glasgow University; Jordanhill College of Education. Teacher of Modern Studies, Columba High School, Coatbridge, 1974-76; Principal Teacher of Modern Studies, St. John's High School, Dundee, 1976-78; Group Travel and Transport Manager, Cotters Travel and Leisure Group, 1978-84. Recreations: theatre; debating. Address: (b.) 23 Atholl Crescent, Edinburgh; T.-031-229 1528.

Gorrie, Donald Cameron Easterbrook, OBE, MA, JP. Leader, Liberal Democrat Group: Lothian Regional Council,

since 1974, City of Edinburgh District Council, since 1980; b. 2.4.33, India; m., Astrid Salvesen; 2 s. Educ. Hurst Grange, Stirling; Oundle School; Corpus Christi College, Oxford. Schoolmaster: Gordonstoun School, 1957-60, Marlborough College, 1960-66; Scottish Liberal Party: Director of Research, 1969-71, Director of Administration, 1971-75; Edinburgh Town Councillor, 1971-75. Director, 'Edinburgh Translations>; Member, Board: Royal Lyceum Theatre Company, Queens Hall, Lothian Association of Youth Clubs; former Scottish native record holder, 880 yards. Address: (h.) 54 Garscube Terrace, Edinburgh, EH12 6BN; T.-031-337 2077.

Gosden, Roger Gordon, BSc, PhD, DSc, FZS, FIBiol. Senior Lecturer in Physiology, Medical School, Edinburgh University, since 1976; b. 23.9.48, Ryde, Isle of Wight; m., Carole Ann Walsh; 2 s. Educ. Chislehurst and Sidcup Grammar School; Bristol University; Cambridge University. MRC Research Fellow, Cambridge University, 1973-74 and 1975-76; Population Council Research Fellow, Duke University, USA, 1974-75; Visiting Scientist, University of Southern California, 1979 and 1982. Publication: Biology of Menopause, 1985. Recreations: natural history; painting. Address: (b.) Department of Physiology, University Medical School, Edinburgh, EH8 9AG; T.-031-650 3267.

Goskirk, Rev. John Leslie, LTh. Minister, Lairg Parish Church, since 1968, and Rogart Parish Church, since 1970; b. 16.3.38, Glasgow; m., Myra Hendry Fisher; 2 s.; 2 d. Educ. High School of Glasgow; Glasgow University and Trinity College. Clerk, Sutherland Presbytery; Past Chairman, former Golspie, Rogart and Lairg District Council; Past Chairman, Lairg Community Council. Address: The Manse, Lairg, Sutherland.

Gossip, Michael A.J., OBE, JP, BL, FBIM. Chief Executive, Argyll and Bute District Council, since 1974; Honorary Sheriff, Dunoon, since 1989; b. 27.4.33, Edinburgh; m., Margaret; 1 s.; 2 d. Educ. George Watson's Boys' College, Edinburgh; Edinburgh University. Legal Assistant, Midlothian County Council, 1955-57; Dumfries County Council: Senior Legal Assistant, 1957-60, Depute County Clerk, 1960-71; Argyll County: Depute County Clerk, 1971-72, County Clerk, 1972-75. Recreations: bowls; gardening. Address: (b.) Kilmory Castle, Lochgilphead, Argyll; T.-0546 2127.

Gotts, Iain McEwan, DipLE, DipTP, FRICS, MRTPI. Director, PEIDA plc, Planning, Economic and Development Consultants, since 1976; b. 26.2.47, Glasgow; m., Pamela; 1 s.; 2 d. Educ. Jordanhill College School, Glasgow; Paisley College of Technology; Heriot-Watt University/Edinburgh College of Art. Trainee Surveyor, British Rail Property Department, Glasgow, 1965-68; further education, 1968-72; Surveyor/Land Economist, Wright & Partners, Edinburgh, 1972-76. Recreations: music; golf; rugby. Address: (b.) 10 Chester Street, Edinburgh, EH3 7RA; T.-031-225 5737.

Goudie, Andrew William, BA, MA, PhD. Senior Economic Adviser, Scottish Office, since 1990; b. 3.3.55, London; m., Christine Lynne Hurley; 2 s.; 1 d. Educ. Haberdashers' Aske's School; Queens' College, Cambridge University. Research Officer, Department of Applied Economics, Cambridge, 1978-85; Research Fellow, Queens' College, Cambridge, 1981-83; Fellow, Robinson College, Cambridge, 1983-85; Director, Cambridge Econometrics Ltd., 1983-85; Senior Economist, The World Bank, Washington DC, 1985-90. Address: (b.) Scottish Office Industry Department, Alhambra House, 45 Waterloo Street, Glasgow, G2 6AT; T.-041-242 5565.

Goudie, Professor Robert Barclay, MD, FRCPGlas, FRCPath, FRSE. St. Mungo (Notman) Professor of Pathology

(Emeritus), Glasgow University; General Secretary, Pathological Society of Great Britain and Ireland; b. 13.11.28, Glasgow; m., Lilian Duke Munro; 3 s.; 1 d. Educ. Hutchesons' Grammar School; Glasgow University. Squadron Leader, RAF Medical Branch, Institute of Pathology and Tropical Medicine, Halton, 1954-56; Lecturer, Senior Lecturer, Reader, University Department of Pathology, Western Infirmary, Glasgow, 1956-70; Nuffield Fellow in Medicine, Cambridge University, 1959-60. Recreation: golf. Address: (b.) University Department of Pathology, Royal Infirmary, Glasgow, G4 OSF; T.-041-552 3535, Ext. 4224.

Gough, Robert Kerr Livingstone, CBE, JP. Convener, Fife Regional Council, since 1978; b. 1.8.24, Buckhaven; m., Margaret; 2 s. Educ. Buckhaven High School. Member, Buckhaven and Methil Town Council, 1956; Vice-Convener, Fife Regional Council, 1975; Member and Vice Chairman, Glenrothes Development Corporation, 1986. Recreations: gardening; welfare of young, old and physically handicapped. Address: (h.) 46 Stark Street, Buckhaven, Fife; T.-0592 713308.

Gow, Professor Ian Thomas McVey, MA, PhD, DipJap. Deputy Principal and Director, Centre for Japanese Studies, Stirling University, since 1987; Chairman, Japan Society of Scotland, since 1988; Director, Ecosse Ltd., Glasgow, since 1989; b. 15.10.44, Liverpool; m., Kathrine; 4 s. Educ. Dunoon Grammar School; Edinburgh University; Sheffield University; Osaka University. Royal Navy, 1961-69; Librarian, Sheffield University, 1980-82; Research Director, Mitaka, 1983; Director, Japanese Programme, Aston University, 1984-85; Director, Japanese Business Unit, Warwick University, 1985-87. Member: Advisory Board, CNAA, since 1990, Council, British Association of Japanese Studies, UK-Japan 2000 Education Committee. Publications: Japan's Quest for Comprehensive Security, 1984 (Co-author); Okinawa, 1945 – Gateway to Japan, 1985; Making Managers, 1988. Recreations: golf; guitar. Address: 1 Victoria Place, Stirling; T.-0786 72080.

Gow, Sir (James) Michael, GCB. President, Royal British Legion Scotland, since 1986; President, Earl Haig Fund (Scotland), since 1986; b. 3.6.24, Sheffield; m. Jane Emily Scott; 1 s.; 4 d. Educ. Winchester College. Enlisted, Scots Guards, 1942; commissioned, 1943; served NW Europe 1944-45, Malayan Emergency, 1949; Equerry to the late HRH Duke of Gloucester, 1952-53; Brigade Major, 1955-57; Regimental Adjutant, Scots Guards, 1957-60; Instructor, Army Staff College, 1962-64; Command, 2nd Bn Scots Guards, Kenya and England, 1964-66; GSO1, HQ London District, 1966-67; Command, 4th Guards Brigade, 1968-69; Imperial Defence College, 1970; Brigadier General Staff (Int.) HQ, BAOR and Assistant Chief of Staff, G2 HQ, Northag, 1971-73; GOC 4th Div., BAOR, 1973-75; Director of Army Training, 1975-78; General Officer Commanding, Scotland, Governor of Edinburgh Castle, 1979-80; Commander-in-Chief, BAOR and Commander, Northern Army Group, 1980-83 (awarded die Plakette des deutschen Heeres); ADC Gen. to the Queen, 1981-84; Commandant, Royal College of Defence Studies, 1984-86. Colonel Commandant: Intelligence Corps, 1973-86, Scottish Division, 1979-80; Brigadier, Queen's Body Guard for Scotland, (Royal Company of Archers); UK Member, Eurogroup US Tour, 1983; UK Kermit Roosevelt Lecturer, USA, 1984; Vice President: Queen Victoria School, Dunblane, 1979-80, Royal Caledonian Schools, Bushey, since 1980; County Commissioner, British Scouts, W. Europe, 1980-83 (Silver Acorn); Freeman: City of London, 1980, State of Kansas, USA, 1984; Freeman and Liveryman, Painters' and Stainers' Company, 1980. Publications: Trooping the Colour: A History of the Sovereign's Birthday Parade by the Household Troops, 1989; Jottings in a General's Notebook, 1989; General Reflections, 1991. Recreations: sailing; music; travel;

reading. Address: (h.) 18 Ann Street, Edinburgh EH4 1PJ; T.-031-332 4752.

Gow, Sheriff Neil, QC (Scot). Sheriff of South Strathclyde, at Ayr, since 1976; b. 24.4.32.

Gowenlock, Professor Brian Glover, CBE, PhD, DSc, CChem, FRSC, FRSE. Professor of Chemistry, Heriot-Watt University, 1966-90 (Dean, Faculty of Science, 1969-72 and 1987-90); Member, University Grants Committee, 1976-85; Assessor Member, Scottish Tertiary Education Advisory Council, 1984-87; b. 9.2.26, Oldham; m., Margaret Davies; 1 s.; 2 d. Educ. Hulme Grammar School; Manchester University. Assistant Lecturer, then Lecturer in Chemistry, University College of Swansea, 1948-55; Lecturer, then Senior Lecturer in Chemistry, Birmingham University, 1955-66; Visiting Scientist, National Research Council of Canada, Ottawa, 1963; Erskine Memorial Fellow, Canterbury University, Christchurch, 1976; Leverhulme Emeritus Fellow, Heriot-Watt University, 1990-92. Recreations: genealogy; foreign travel. Address: (h.) 49 Lygon Road, Edinburgh, EH16 5QA; T.-031-667 8506.

Gowland, David Alexander, BA, PhD, PGCE. Senior Lecturer in Modern History, Dundee University, since 1982 (Director, School of Contemporary European Studies, since 1979); b. 1.4.42, Reading; m., Helen Janet Mackinlay; 3 d. Educ. Culford; Manchester University; London University. Dundee University: Assistant Lecturer in Modern History, 1967-69, Lecturer in Modern History, 1970-81, Dean of Students, Faculty of Arts and Social Sciences, 1979-83; Honorary Lecturer, Civil Service College, 1970-76; Open University Tutor, since 1971. Publications: Common Market or Community?, 1973; Methodist Secessions, 1979; Scottish Methodism in the Early Victorian Period, 1981; European Community, Past Present and Future, 1987; Never Call Retreat, 1989. Recreation: golf. Address: (b.) Department of Modern History, Dundee University, Dundee; T.-Dundee 23181.

Grace, Professor John, BSc, PhD. Professor of Environmental Biology, Edinburgh University, since 1992; b. 19.9.45, Northampton; m., Elizabeth Ashworth; 2 s.; 1 d. Educ. Bletchley Grammar School; Sheffield University. Lecturer, then Reader in Ecology, Edinburgh Univrsity, 1970-92. Co-Editor, Functional Ecology, since 1986; Technical Editor, International Society for Biometeorology, since 1983; Member, Terrestrial Life Sciences Committee, Natural Environment Research Council, 1986-89; Council Member, British Ecological Society, since 1983. Publications: Plant Response to Wind, 1977; Plants and their Atmospheric Environment (Co-Editor), 1981; Plant-atmosphere Relationships, 1983. Recreations: hill-walking; cycling; fishing; bridge. Address: (h.) 25 Craiglea Drive, Edinburgh, EH10 5PB; T.-031-447 3030.

Gracie, Alistair. Head of News and Current Affairs, Grampian Television, since 1986; b. 25.2.48, Aberdeen; m., Wendy; 1 s.; 2 d. Educ. Aberdeen Grammar School. Joined Aberdeen Journals as Trainee Journalist, 1966; worked on Press and Journal as Reporter and Evening Express as Sub-Editor; moved into television as Researcher/Reporter, 1972; Grampian Television: News Editor, 1974, Programme Editor, 1978. Recreations: mountaineering; squash; running; photography; reading; painting. Address: (b.) Grampian TV, Queen's Cross, Aberdeen, AB9 2XJ.

Graeme, Malcolm Laurie, SBStJ, VRD, MA, MB, BChir, MFPHM, DPH, MRCS, LRCP; b. 16.9.19, Guernsey; m., Dr. Patricia Doreen Shurly, MB, BS, MRCP; 1 d. Educ. Stowe; Jesus College, Cambridge; St. George's Hospital Medical School (Devitt-Pendlebury Scholarship). Surgeon, Lt.-Surgeon, Lt. Cdr., RNVR/RNR, 1944-64; Public Health

Service, London County Council, London Borough of Barnet and London Borough of Enfield, 1957-70; Medical Branch, Civil Service, Departments of Education and Science and Health and Social Security, 1970-79; Ordained Elder, Church of Scotland, 1970; Clerk to Congregational Board and Member, Kirk Session, Ceres Parish Church, since 1987; Life Governor, Royal Scottish Corporation of London; District Councillor (Conservative), NE Fife, 1980-84; Member, Fife Health Board, 1983-87; Hon. Vice-President, NE Fife Conservative Association, since 1987; Chairman, Fife and Kinross Committee, King George's Fund for Sailors and Member, Scottish Council, 1987-90; Life Member, St. John Association of Scotland and Vice-Chairman, Fife Committee. Recreation: gardening. Address: (h.) Little Baltilly, Ceres, by Cupar, Fife, KY15 5QG; T.-Ceres 238.

Graham, Rev. A. David M., BA, BD. Minister, Rosemount Parish Church, Aberdeen, since 1990; b. 17.7.40, Tralee; m., Mary A. Taylor; 2 s.; 1 d. Educ. Wesley College, Dublin; Methodist College, Belfast; Queen's University, Belfast; Glasgow University. Assistant, South Leith Parish; Secretary for Christian Education, Scottish National Council of YMCAs; Minister, Anderston Parish, Glasgow; Warden, Iona Abbey; Minister, Rutherford Parish, Aberdeen. Recreations: jogging; climbing. Address: 22 Osborne Place, Aberdeen, AB2 4DA; T.-0224 648041.

Graham, Lord Donald, BSc, MBA. Director of Information Technology, Adam & Company, since 1991; Director, Fruit Market Gallery, since 1992; Director, KDCL Ltd., Property Developers, since 1992; b. 28.10.56, Salisbury, Southern Rhodesia; m., Bridie; 2 d. Educ. St. Andrews College, South Africa; St. Andrews University; INSEAD. Recreations: piping; music. Address: (b.) Adam & Company plc, 22 Charlotte Square, Edinburgh, EH2 4DF; T.-031-225 8484.

Graham, Dennis C., DSc, PhD, CChem, FRSC, FInstBiol, FRSA, FRSE. Honorary Fellow, Edinburgh University, College of Agriculture; Former Director, Agricultural Scientific Services, Department of Agriculture and Fisheries for Scotland; b. 2.12.29, Carlisle. Educ. Carlisle Grammar School; Durham University; Edinburgh University. Recreation: cultivation of alpine plants. Address: 447 Lanark Road, Edinburgh, EH14 5BA; T.-031-453 3459.

Graham, James, MB, ChB, FRCSGlas, FRCSEdin. Consultant Orthopaedic Surgeon, Western Infirmary and Gartnavel General Hospital, Glasgow, since 1976; Honorary Clinical Lecturer, Glasgow University, since 1976; b. 2.3.36, Stonehouse; m., Wilma Edith Melville; 1 s.; 1 d. Educ. Hamilton Academy; Glasgow University. House Officer posts, Western Infirmary and Southern General Hospital, Glasgow; basic surgical training, Vale of Leven Hospital, Alexandria, and Western Infirmary, Glasgow; orthopaedic training in Western Infirmary, Royal Hospital for Sick Children and Southern General Hospital, Glasgow and Massachusetts General Hospital; appointed Senior Lecturer in Orthopaedics and Honorary Consultant Orthopaedic Surgeon, Western Infirmary and Gartnavel General Hospital, 1972; research, teaching and clinical fellowship to Harvard University and Massachusetts General Hospital, Boston, 1968-69; British Orthopaedic Association ABC Travelling Fellowship to North America, 1974. Recreations: rugby (watching); golf (participating); DIY. Address: (b.) Department of Orthopaedics, Western Infirmary, Glasgow, G11 6NT; T.-041-339 8822.

Graham, Marquis of (James Graham). Brigadier, Queen's Bodyguard for Scotland (Royal Company of Archers), since 1986 (Member, since 1965); b. 6.4.35; m., Catherine Elizabeth MacDonell; 2 s.; 1 d. Educ. Loretto. Order of St. John, 1978. Council Member, National Farmers' Union of

Scotland, 1982-84, 1987-90. Address: (h.) Auchmar, Drymen, Glasgow.

Graham, James Grierson, BSc, DipEd. Director of Education, Grampian Regional Council, since 1990; b. 27.3.37; m., Janette; 2 d. Educ. Dumfries Academy; Glasgow University; Jordanhill College of Education. Science Teacher, Dumfries County Council, 1960-63; Professional Assistant (Schools), Carlisle Corporation, 1963-65; Assistant Director of Education, Dundee Corporation, 1965-67; Junior Depute Director, Dundee Corporation, 1967-68; Senior Depute Director, Aberdeen County Council, 1968-75; Senior Depute Director, Grampian Regional Council, 1975-90. Chairman, Scottish Council for Educational Technology. Recreations: cycling; curling; badminton; skiing; golf. Address: (b.) Woodhill House, Westburn Road, Aberdeen, AB9 2LU; T.-0224 664600.

Graham, John James, OBE, MA, FEIS. Member, Shetland Islands Council (Chairman, Leisure & Recreation Committee), since 1982; Chairman, Shetland Movement, since 1982; Joint Editor, The New Shetlander, since 1956; b. 12.7.21, Lerwick; m., Beryl Smith; 3 s.; 2 d. Educ. Lerwick Central Secondary School; Edinburgh University. RAF Training Command, 1941-44, Bomber Command, 1944-46; Principal Teacher of English, Anderson Educational Institute, Lerwick, 1950-66; Headmaster: Lerwick Central Secondary School, 1966-70, Anderson High School, Lerwick, 1970-82; Member: Consultative Committee on the Curriculum, 1976-80, Broadcasting Council for Scotland, 1981-84; President, Shetland Folk Society. Publications: A Grammar and Usage of the Shetland Dialect (Co-author); Northern Lights (Joint Editor); The Shetland Dictionary; Shadowed Valley (novel). Recreations: local history; golf. Address: (h.) 10 Reform Lane, Lerwick, Shetland; T.-Lerwick 3425.

Graham, John Michael Denning, LLB (Hons), NP. Solicitor and Notary Public, since 1970; Chairman, Kilmacolm Developments Ltd.; Director: Select Assured Properties plc, John Smith & Son (Glasgow) Ltd.; ScotCare Group Ltd.; Chairman, Rent Assessment Committee, Glasgow, since 1983; Senior Tutor in Law, Glasgow University; Governor, Queens College, Glasgow; b. 7.9.44, Kirkintilloch; m., Christina Jeanne Sinclair; 2 s. Educ. Royal Belfast Academical Institution; Queen's University, Belfast. Senior Partner, Paterson Robertson & Graham, Solicitors, since 1971. Recreations: tennis; golf; hang-gliding. Address: (h.) St. Michael's, Garngaber Avenue, Lenzie, G66; T.-041-221 7691.

Graham, John Strathie, BA. Under Secretary, Local Government Group, Scottish Office Environment Department, since 1991; b. 27.5.50, Edinburgh; m., Anne Graham; 2 s.; 1 d. Educ. Edinburgh Academy; Corpus Christi College, Oxford. Joined Scottish Office, 1972; Principal, Scottish Economic Planning Department, 1976; Assistant Secretary, Industry Department for Scotland, 1982; Private Secretary to Secretary of State, 1983; Assistant Secretary: Planning Division, Scottish Development Department, 1985, Finance Division 1, 1990. Recreations: exploring Scotland; listening to music. Address: (b.) New St. Andrews House, Edinburgh, 1.

Graham, Professor Neil Bonnette, BSc, PhD, CChem, FRSC, FPRI, FRSE. Professor in Chemical Technology, Strathclyde University, since 1973; b. 23.5.33, Liverpool; 1 s.; 3 d. Educ. Alsop High School, Liverpool; Liverpool University. Research Chemist, Research Scientist, Canadian Industries Ltd., MacMasterville PQ, Canada, 1956-67; Assistant Group Head, then Group Head, Polymer Chemistry, ICI, Runcorn, Cheshire. Member: Advisory Committee on Dental and Surgical Materials, 1980-86, and sometime member of various committees, Society of Chemical Industry,

Royal Society of Chemistry and Plastics and Rubber Institute; Chairman, Glasgow Membrane Group, since 1986; Member, International Editorial Boards, Biomaterials, Biomedical Polymers and Journal of Controlled Release; Governor and Trustee, Keil School; Trustee, James Clerk Maxwell Trust. Recreations: music; walking. Address: (b.) Strathclyde University, Department of Pure and Applied Chemistry, Thomas Graham Building, 295 Cathedral Street, Glasgow, G1 1XL; T.-041-552 4400, Ext. 2133.

Graham, Nigel John O. Member, Highland Regional Council, since 1983; b. 28.7.27, Worcestershire; m., Margaret; 2 s.; 2 d. Educ. Marlborough College. Highland Light Infantry, 1945-53; TA, Queen's Own Cameron Highlanders, 1953-61; farmer, 1953-83; Member, Nairn County Council, 1966-72. Chairman, Inverness Nairn and Lochaber Conservative Association. Recreation: bird-watching. Address: (h.) Househill, Nairn; T.-Nairn 53241.

Graham, Sir Norman William, Kt (1971), CB (1961), MA, DLitt (Heriot-Watt), DUniv (Stirling), FRSE; b. 11.10.13, Dundee; m., Catherine Mary Strathie; 2 s.; 1 d. Educ. High School of Glasgow; Glasgow University. Assistant Principal, Department of Health for Scotland, 1936; Principal, Ministry of Aircraft Production, 1941; Principal Private Secretary to Minister, 1944; Assistant Secretary, Department of Health for Scotland, 1945; Under Secretary, 1956; Secretary, Scottish Education Department, 1964-73. Recreations: golf; gardening. Address: (h.) 6 Chesterhall Steading, Longniddry, East Lothian; T.-0875 52130.

Graham, Ronald Cairns, MB, ChB, DipSocMed, FRCP, FFCM. General Manager, Tayside Health Board, since 1985; Honorary Senior Lecturer, Dundee University, since 1969; b. 8.10.31, Airdrie; m., Christine Fraser Osborne; 2 s.; 1 d. Educ. Airdrie Academy; Glasgow University. Deputy Medical Superintendent, Edinburgh Royal Infirmary; Assistant Senior Administrative Medical Officer, South-Eastern Regional Hospital Board; Eastern Regional Hospital Board: Deputy Senior Administrative Medical Officer, Senior Administrative Medical Officer; Chief Administrative Medical Officer, Tayside Health Board, 1973-85. Recreation: fishing. Address: (h.) 34 Dalgleish Road, Dundee; T.-Dundee 455426.

Graham, Thomas. MP (Labour), Renfrew West and Inverclyde, since 1987; b. 1944.

Graham, William, MA. Freelance Writer; b. 27.2.13, Carluke; m., Jean C. Simpson; 1 s.; 1 d. Educ. Wishaw High School; Glasgow University; Jordanhill College of Education. Organist; Teacher; Nurseryman; Airman; Author. Former Secretary and President, Ayr Burns Club; Past Preses, Scots Language Society (now Hon. Vice-Preses). Publications: That Ye Inherit; Twa-Three Sangs and Stories; The Talking Scots Quiz Book; The Scots Word Book; October Sunset; The Handy Guide to Scots. Recreations: music; gardening. Address: (h.) 48 Mount Charles Crescent, Alloway, Ayrshire; T.-Ayr 43701.

Graham, William Peter, MA, BD. Minister, Chirnside Parish Church, since 1968, Bonkyl & Preston, Edrom-Allanton, since 1978; Clerk, Duns Presbytery, since 1982; b. 24.11.43, Edinburgh; m., Isabel Arnot Brown; 2 s. Educ. George Watson's College, Edinburgh; Edinburgh University. Assistant Minister, Dundee (St. Mary's) Parish Church, 1966-68. Convener, General Assembly's Nomination Committee, 1990; Hospital Chaplain, The Knoll, Duns, since 1985; Chairman, Cruse Bereavement Care, Berwickshire. Recreations: golf; cycling; gardening; reading. Address: (h.) The Manse, Chirnside, Duns, Berwickshire, TD11 3XL; T.-089081 269.

Grainger, John McGregor Leighton, FTS. Director of Tourism, Perthshire Tourist Board, since 1982; b. 3.9.43, Aberdeen; m., Kathleen; 1 s.; 2 d. Assistant Tourist Officer, Aberdeen Town Council, 1959-67; Tourism Manager, Dunbar Town Council, 1967-69; Tourism Manager, Perth Tourist Association, 1969-74; Senior Tourist Officer, Tayside Regional Council, 1974-82. Secretary, Scottish Tourism Awards Scheme; Secretary, Society of High Constables of the City of Perth. Recreations: fishing; hill-walking. Address: (b.) 45 High Street, Perth, PH1 5TJ; T.-0738 27958.

Grains, Florence Barbara, JP. Chairman, Shetland Health Board, since 1985; Member, Shetland Islands Council, since 1986; Member, OFFER, since 1991; b. 2.11.32, Shetland; m., Alistair M. Grains; 4 s. Educ. Whiteness School, Shetland; Lerwick FE Centre. Retired Sub-postmaster, Whiteness, Shetland. Vice Chairman, Shetland Council of Social Service; Chairman, Alting Debating Society; Trustee, Shetland Amenity Trust; Chairman, Shetland Branch, Post Office Users Council for Scotland; Supervisor, Whiteness and Weisdale Playgroup; Cub Scout Leader; Executive Member, SWRI; Chairman, Shetland Family History Society; Chairman, Foula Electricity Trust. Address: (h.) Hoove, Whiteness, Shetland; T.-0595 84 243.

Grant, Angus Watt. Member, Central Regional Council, 1982-86; b. 15.7.19, Ballater; m., Margaret Grant Park, MA. Educ. Aldenham School, Hertfordshire; Manchester Business School. Management Trainee, 1936-39; commissioned, Royal Marines, 1939-46; Personnel Officer/Manager, Dunlop Rubber Co., Birmingham and Durban (South Africa), 1946-52; Regional Director, National Development and Management Foundation, South Africa, 1953-54; Manager, Employment and Training, Stanvac Refining Co., Durban, 1954-56; Chairman, Executive Committee, Executive Director, Management Services and PA to Chairman, United Tobacco Co. Ltd., Johannesburg, 1956-74; Manager, Senior Management Studies, BAT Industries Ltd., 1974-80. Past Chairman: Programme Committee, Institute of Directors (South Africa Branch), Industrial Council for the Tobacco Industry, South Africa; former Member, Executive Committee, Computer Society of South Africa, and National Development and Management Foundation, South Africa. Recreations: nature conservation; photography. Address: (h.) 2 Bruce's Wynd, Pittenweem, KY10 2NR.

Grant, Professor Colin Drummond, BSc, PhD, CEng, FIChemE, FRSA. Roche Professor of Chemical Engineering, Strathclyde University, since 1989; b. 3.6.46, Glasgow; m., Maida Elizabeth; 2 s. Educ. Fettes College, Edinburgh; Strathclyde University. Student Apprentice, Babcock and Wilcox Ltd., 1963-67; Strathclyde University: Research Student, 1967-70, Lecturer, 1970-82, Senior Lecturer, 1982-83, Reader in Chemical Engineering, 1983-89. Secretary, Scottish Branch, Institution of Chemical Engineers, 1975-83; Member of Council, IChemE, since 1988. Recreations: mountaineering; tennis; squash. Address: (h.) 64 Eastcote Avenue, Jordanhill, Glasgow, G14 9ND; T.-041-959 7148.

Grant, Donald, QFSM, GIFireE. Firemaster, Highland and Islands Fire Brigade, since 1985; b. 11.1.41, West Linton; 1 s. Educ. Inverness High School. Fireman, 1961; Instructor, Scottish Fire Service Training School, 1965; Sub Officer, 1967; Station Officer, 1968; Assistant Divisional Officer, 1974; Divisional Officer, 1974; Deputy Firemaster, 1976. Past Chairman, British Fire Service Sports and Athletics Association; Chairman, Scottish Fire Service Sports and Athletics Association. Recreations: SFA referee; various sports. Address: The Limit, Lentran, Inverness; T.-0463 83616.

Grant, Donald Blane, CBE, TD, LLD, CA. Chairman, Scottish Legal Aid Board, 1986-91; Partner, Thomson,

McLintock & Co., 1950-86; Chairman, Tayside Health Board, 1984-91; Chairman, Dundee and London Investment Trust PLC; b. 8.10.21, Dundee; m., Lavinia Margaret Ruth Ritchie; 3 d. Educ. Dundee High School. Royal Artillery, 1939-46 (retired as Major). Chairman: Mathew Trust, Caird Travelling Scholarships Trust. Recreations: golf; fishing; shooting; gardening. Address: (h.) 24 Albany Road, Broughty Ferry, Dundee, DD5 1NT.

Grant, Donald Patrick James, FBIM, FRSA. Director, Cumbrae Properties (1963) Ltd., since 1977; Deputy Chairman, Bute Fabrics, Isle of Bute; Honorary Sheriff, Rothesay; b. 12.5.19, Fulwood, Yorkshire; m., Joan Winfield Grant; 1 s.; 1 d. Educ. Kings School, Macclesfield; Kings College, Durham University. Royal Navy, 1940-46, serving as Lieutenant RNVR in submarines, and as air engineering officer Flag Officer Air's staff, East Indies station; Vickers Ltd., Engineering Group, 1946-74, in various appointments as General Manager and Managing Director; Consultant, 1974-76. Address: (h.) Heathmount, 22 Crichton Road, Rothesay, PA20 9JR; T.-0700 503409.

Grant, Ian. Managing Director, Aberdeen Enterprise Trust, since 1991; b. 28.6.43, Saltcoats. Educ. Ardrossan Academy. Has worked for Shell UK, 30 years, latterly as Head of Management Information and Head of Commercial Services, Shell UK Exploration and Production; currently on three-year secondment. Address: (b.) First Floor, Seaforth Centre, 30 Waterloo Quay, Aberdeen; T.-0224 582599.

Grant, Ian David, CBE, FRAgS. Farmer; Chairman, Scottish Tourist Board, since 1990; President, National Farmers Union of Scotland, 1984-90; b. 28.7.43, Dundee; m., Eileen May Louisa Yule; 3 d. Educ. Strathallan School; East of Scotland College of Agriculture. Farms at Thorn, Alyth. Chairman, EEC Cereals Working Party, 1982-88 and International Federation of Agricultural Producers, Grains Committee, 1984-90; Vice Chairman, East of Scotland Farmers Ltd.; Member, Scottish Tourist Board, since 1988; Director, NFU Mutual Insurance Soc. Ltd., since 1990; Director, Clydesdale Bank PLC, since 1989; Member, Scottish Council, CBI, since 1984. Recreations: shooting; swimming; music. Address: (h.) Thorn, Alyth, Blairgowrie, PH11 8NP; T.-082-83 2253.

Grant, Ian Faulconer Heathcoat, JP, DL. Director: Glenmoriston Estates Limited, since 1964, McKinroy Limited, since 1981, Pacific Assets Trust PLC, since 1985, Royal Bank of Scotland PLC, since 1982, Royal Bank of Scotland Group plc, since 1985, Worldwide Value Fund Inc. (USA), since 1986; b. 3.6.39, Singapore; m., Sally; 1 s.; 3 d. Educ. Cargilfield; Sedbergh; Liverpool College of Commerce. ICI Ltd., 1957-62; various positions, Jardine Matheson & Co. Ltd., Hong Kong, 1962-73, culminating in directorship on Main Board. Address: (b.) Glenmoriston Estates Ltd., Glenmoriston, near Inverness; T.-0320 51202.

Grant, Rev. James Gordon, MA, BD. Minister, Dean Church, Edinburgh, since 1987 (Portland Church, Troon, 1965-87); b. 5.7.32, Glasgow; m., Susan Ann Hewitt; 2 s.; 1 d. Educ. High School of Stirling; St. Andrews University. Ordained, 1957; Probationer Assistant, St. Mungo's Parish Church, Alloa, 1957-59; Minister, Dyce Parish Church, Aberdeen, 1959-65; Convener, Inter-Church Relations Committee, 1983-84. Recreations: golf; climbing; ornithology. Address: (h.) 1 Ravelston Terrace, Edinburgh, EH4 3EF; T.-031-332 5736.

Grant, Major James MacAlpine Gregor, TD, NDA, MRAC. Landowner and Farmer, since 1961; b. 18.2.38, Nakuru, Kenya; m., Sara Marjory; 3 d. Educ. Eton; Royal Agricultural College, Cirencester. National Service, Queen's Own Cameron Highlanders, 1957-58; TA with 4/5th Queen's Own Cameron Highlanders; Volunteers with 51st Highland Volunteers. Address: Roskill House, Munlochy, Ross-shire, IV8 8PA; T.-Munlochy 207.

Grant, James Shaw, CBE, LLD, FRSE, FRAgS, MA. Author; b. 22.5.10, Stornoway; m., Catherine Mary Stewart. Educ. Nicolson Institute, Stornoway. Editor, Stornoway Gazette, 1932-63; Governor, Pitlochry Festival Theatre, 1954-84 (Chairman, 1971-83); Member, Crofters Commission, 1955-78 (Chairman, 1963-78); Director, Grampian TV, 1969-80; Member: Highlands and Islands Development Board, 1970-82, Scottish Advisory Committee, British Council, since 1972; Chairman, Harris Tweed Association Ltd., 1972-84; Member, Council, National Trust for Scotland, 1979-84; Governor, Eden Court Theatre, since 1980 (Vice Chairman, since 1987); author of plays: Tarravore, The Magic Rowan, Legend is Born, Comrade the King. Publications: Highland Villages, 1977; Their Children Will See, 1979; The Hub of My Universe, 1982; Surprise Island, 1983; The Gaelic Vikings, 1984; Stornoway and the Lews, 1985; Discovering Lewis and Harris, 1987; Enchanted Island, 1989. Address: (h.) Ardgrianach, Inshes, Inverness; T.-Inverness 231476.

Grant, Professor John Paxton, LLB, LLM. Professor, Department of Public Law, Glasgow University, since 1988 (Dean, Faculty of Law and Financial Studies, 1985-89; Convener, School of Law); b. 22.2.44, Edinburgh; m., Elaine E. Sutherland. Educ. George Heriot's School, Edinburgh; Edinburgh University; Pennsylvania University. Lecturer, Faculty of Law: Aberdeen University, 1967-71, Dundee University, 1971-74; Senior Lecturer, Department of Public International Law, Glasgow University, 1974-88; Visiting Professor: Saint Louis University School of Law, 1981, Northwestern School of Law, Lewis and Clark College, 1984 and 1986; Member, Children's Panel: Aberdeenshire and Kincardine, 1970-71, Dundee, 1971-74, Strathclyde, 1974-81. Publications: Independence and Devolution (Editor), 1976; The Impact of Marine Pollution: Law and Practice (Joint Editor), 1980; The Encyclopaedic Dictionary of International Law (Joint General Editor), 1985; Legal Education 2000 (Joint Editor), 1988. Recreations: walking; travelling. Address: (h.) 87 Warrender Park Road, Edinburgh, EH9 1EW; T.-031-229 7705.

Grant, John Peters, FCCA. Honorary Sheriff, Inverness since 1963; b. 24.12.98, Leith; m., Agnes M.R. Beaumont; 1 d. Educ. Broughton School, Edinburgh. Inland Revenue (Inspector of Taxes), 39 years; Councillor, Nairn Town Council and Moray and Nairn County Council, five years; Vice Chairman, Moray and Nairn Valuation Committee, and General Commissioner of Income Tax, until the age of 75. Freelance sports journalist. Recreations: golf; bowling. Address: (h.) 16 Seabank Road, Nairn, IV12 4EU; T.-Nairn 53376.

Grant, Lesley Dunbar, MBE, MA. Member, Scottish Sports Council; b. 10.1.33, Banchory. Former Chairman, North Angus and Mearns Conservative and Unionist Association; Former Chairman, Kincardine and Deeside Conservative and Unionist Association; Elder, Banchory-Ternan Church. Address: Ordeans, Banchory, AB31 3TN.

Grant, Very Rev. Malcolm Etheridge, BSc (Hons), BD (Hons). Provost and Rector, Cathedral Church of S. Andrew, Inverness, since 1991; b. 6.8.44, Maidstone; m., Katrina Russell Nuttall; 1 s.; 1 d. Educ. Dunfermline High School; Edinburgh University; Edinburgh Theological College. Assistant Curate: S. Mary's Cathedral, Glasgow, 1969-72, Grantham Parish Church, in charge of Church of the Epiphany, Earlesfield, 1972; Team Vicar, Earlesfield, Grantham Team Ministry, 1972-78; Priest-in-Charge, S. Ninian's, Invergordon, 1978-81; Provost and Rector,

Cathedral Church of S. Mary the Virgin, Glasgow, 1981-91; Examining Chaplain to Bishop of Moray, Ross and Caithness, 1979-81; Member, Highland Region Education Committee, 1979-81. Address: 15 Ardross Street, Inverness, IV3 5NS; T.-0463 233535.

Grant, Maurice Alexander, MA. Principal, Industry Department for Scotland, since 1983; b. 1.1.41, Portree; m., Isabel Alison MacDonald; 1 d. Educ. Dunoon Grammar School; Glasgow University. Executive Officer: Department of Health for Scotland, 1961-62, Scottish Development Department, 1962-66; Higher Executive Officer, then Senior Executive Officer, Scottish Development Department, 1966-81; Principal, Scottish Economic Planning Department, 1981-83. Publications: The Story of Donald Cargill, 1988; History of Free St. Columba's Church, 1991. Recreation: collecting antiquarian books. Address: (h.) 8 Nantwich Drive, Edinburgh, EH7 6QS; T.-031-669 7347.

Grant, Professor Nigel Duncan Cameron, MA, MEd, PhD, FRSE. Professor of Education, Glasgow University, since 1978; b. 8.6.32, Glasgow; m., Valerie Keeling Evans; 1 s.; 1 d. Educ. Inverness Royal Academy; Glasgow University. Teacher of English, Glasgow secondary schools, 1957-60; Lecturer in Education, Jordanhill College of Education, 1960-65; Lecturer in Educational Studies, then Reader, Edinburgh University, 1965-78. Past Chairman and President, British Comparative and International Education Society; former Executive Member, Comparative Education Society in Europe; Past Chairman, Scottish Educational Research Association; Chairman, Scottish Universities Council for Studies in Education; Educational Consultant, Comann Sgoiltean Da-Chananach Ghlaschu; Member, Executive Committee, Advisory Council for the Arts in Scotland; Member, Editorial Board, Comparative Education; Trustee, Urras Foghlam na Gaidhlig; Member, Scottish Constitutional Steering Committee; Hon. President, Glasgow Educational Colloquium. Publications: Soviet Education, 1964; Society, Schools and Progress in Eastern Europe, 1969; Education and Nation-Building in the Third World (Editor and Co-author), 1971; A Mythology of British Education (Co-author), 1974; Scottish Universities: The Case for Devolution (Co-author), 1976; Patterns of Education in the British Isles (Co-author), 1977; The Crisis of Scottish Education, 1982. Recreations: theatre; music; poetry; natural history; languages; art; travel; calligraphy. Address: (b.) Department of Education, Glasgow University, Glasgow, G12 8QQ; T.-041-339 8855.

Grant, Peter James. Chairman, Sun Life Corporation PLC, since 1983; Chairman, Sun Life Assurance Society PLC, since 1983 (Director, since 1973); b. 5.12.29, London; m., Paula Eugster; 2 s.; 3 d. Educ. Winchester; Magdalen College, Oxford. Lieutenant, Queen's Own Cameron Highlanders. Vice-Chairman, 1983-85, Deputy Chairman, 1985-88, Lazard Bros & Co.; Director, Scottish Hydro, since 1990; Deputy Chairman, then Chairman, LEP Group PLC, since 1989; Director, London Merchant Securities PLC, BNP UK Holdings Ltd.; Member, Industrial Development Advisory Board; Member, Council, Institute of Directors. Recreations: fishing; shooting; golf. Address: (h.) Mountgerald, near Dingwall, Ross-shire, IV15 9TT; T.-0349 62244.

Grant, Professor Peter Mitchell, BSc, PhD, CEng, FIEE. Professor of Electronic Signal Processing, Edinburgh University, since 1987; Director, EUMOS, Edinburgh, since 1985; b. 20.6.44, St. Andrews; m., Marjory Renz; 2 d. Educ. Strathallan School; Heriot-Watt University; Edinburgh University. Member, Communications and Distributed Systems Committee, Science and Engineering Council; Honorary Editor, Proceedings IEE (Part F). Publication: Adaptive Filters (Co-Editor), 1985; Signal Processing and Coding (Co-author), 1988. Address: (b.) Department of Electrical Engineering, Edinburgh University, Edinburgh, EH9 3JL; T.-031-650 5569.

Grant, Philippa. Member, Scottish Tourist Board, since 1991; Director, Moray, Badenoch and Strathspey Enterprise Company, since 1991; Proprietor, The Old School Shop, since 1984; b. 16.8.49, Windsor; m., John Peter Grant of Rothiemurchus (qv); 1 s.; 2 d. Educ. various educational establishments. Chairwoman, Highland Region, Scottish Pre-School Playgroups Association, 1979-83, Scottish Executive Committee, 1983-84; Board of Management, Scottish Council, YWCA Housing Society, 1985-91; Chairwoman, Voluntary Action in Badenoch and Strathspey, 1986-89; Chair, Highland Community Care Forum, since 1991. Recreations: reading; music; art; gardening; walking; skiing; show ponies; good food. Address: (h.) Doune of Rothiemurchus, by Aviemore, PH22 1QP; T.-0479 810123.

Grant, Richard Anthony, BSocSc, MSc. Head of Division, Land Use and Crofting, Scottish Office Agriculture and Fisheries Department, since 1991; b. 12.6.48, Leicester; m., Jacqueline Claire; 1 s.; 1 d. Educ. Loughborough College School; Birmingham University; Strathclyde University. Research Officer/Senior Research Officer, Scottish Education Department and Scottish Development Department, 1969-75; Principal Research Officer, Housing Research Unit, Scottish Development Department, 1975-77; Principal, Sports Policy Branch, Scottish Education Department, 1977-79; Principal Research Officer, Housing and Urban Renewal Research Unit, Scottish Development Department, 1979-85; Principal, Land Use and Conservation Branch, Department of Agriculture and Fisheries, 1986-89; Principal, NHS Management Executive, 1989-91. Recreations: cycling; hill-walking; cross-country skiing. Address: (b.) Room 350, Pentland House, Robbs Loan, Edinburgh; T.-031-224 6190.

Grant of Dalvey, Sir Patrick Alexander Benedict, 14th Bt, FSA Scot, LLB. Chieftain of Clan Donnachy; Company Director; b. 5.2.53.

Grant of Rothiemurchus, John Peter, DL. Landowner; Director: Scot Trout Limited, Cairngorm Recreation Trust; Member, Council, National Trust for Scotland; Vice President, Scottish Landowners Federation; b. 22.10.46, Rothiemurchus; m., Philippa (qv); 1 s.; 2 d. Educ. Gordonstoun. Past Chairman: Scottish Recreational Land Association; British Deer Producers Society; Highland Region Forestry, Farming and Wildlife Advisory Group; former Member, Forestry Commission Regional Advisory Committee; Patron, Highland Hospice. Recreations: skiing; shooting. Address: (b.) Doune of Rothiemurchus, by Aviemore; T.-0479 810647.

Grant-Wood, John, MA (Hons). Headmaster, Firrhill High School, Edinburgh, since 1975; b. 8.6.31, Ashton-under-Lyne; m., Pamela Irene; 1 s. Educ. Audenshaw Grammar School; Edinburgh University. Bank of Scotland; RAF; Headmaster, Livister Primary School, Shetland; Senior Housemaster, United World College of the Atlantic, South Wales; Depute Headmaster, Firrhill High School; twice elected to Court, Heriot-Watt University; Council Member, Headteachers Association of Scotland. Publication: Educating for Tomorrow (Contributor). Recreations: travel; railways; canals; music. Address: (h.) Rossarden, 20 Greenhill Gardens, Edinburgh; T.-031-447 3882.

Granville, 5th Earl (Granville James Leveson Gower), MC. Lord Lieutenant, Western Isles, since 1983 (Vice Lord-Lieutenant, 1976-83); b. 6.12.18.

Grassie, Professor Norman, BSc, PhD, DSc, CChem, FRSC, FRSE. Emeritus Professor of Chemistry, Glasgow University, since 1984; b. 28.5.24, Aberdeen; m., Catherine

Beaton; 1 s.; 2 d. Educ. Nicolson Institute, Stornoway; Aberdeen University. DSIR Senior Research Fellow, Birmingham University, 1948-50; ICI Research Fellow, Glasgow University, 1950-55; Glasgow University: Lecturer, 1955, Senior Lecturer, 1963, Reader, 1967, Titular Professor, 1971; Visiting Professor, Universities of: Mainz, 1967, Delaware, 1969, Malaysia, 1975-77, Merida (Venezuela), 1979. Publications: numerous books, mainly on topics related to polymer stability and degradation. Recreations: bridge; hill-walking; grandchildren; Church activities. Address: (h.) 15 Lovat Avenue, Bearsden, Glasgow, G61 3LQ; T.-041-942 8768.

Gratwick, Adrian Stuart, MA (Cantab), DPhil (Oxon). Reader in Humanity, St. Andrews University, since 1983; b. 31.3.43, Stanmore, Middlesex; m., Jennifer Rosemary Clark; 2 s.; 1 d. Educ. St. Aloysius' College, Glasgow; St. Brendan's College, Bristol; St. John's College, Cambridge; Balliol College, Oxford. St. Andrews University: Assistant Lecturer in Humanity, 1966, Lecturer, 1969. Recreations: walking; gardening; woodwork. Address: (b.) Department of Humanity, St. Salvator's College, St. Andrews, Fife; T.-0334 76161, Ext. 492.

Gravestock, Martin John. Crown Estate Receiver for Scotland, since 1985; b. 31.8.52, Carshalton, Surrey; m., Olwyn Claire; 3 s. Educ. Sutton County Grammar School. Crown Estate Office, since 1969: Legal, Foreshore and Seabed, General, and London Branches; Head, Personnel Branch, 1984; Head, Foreshore and Seabed Branch, 1984-85. Recreations: cars; gardening. Address: (b.) 10 Charlotte Square, Edinburgh; T.-031-226 7241.

Gray, Adam, NDA, NDD. Farmer; Director, Scottish Milk Marketing Board, since 1981; Director, Royal Highland & Agricultural Society; President, Scottish Agricultural Arbiters Association, since 1988; Chairman, UK Milk Publicity Council, since 1989; b. 6.8.29, Borgue, Kirkcudbright; m., Elaine West Russell; 3 s. Educ. George Watson's Boys College; West of Scotland Agricultural College. Nuffield Scholar, 1955; Past President, Stewartry NFU; Member, NFU Council; former Council Member, British Simmental Cattle Society; Past Chairman, SW Scotland Grassland Society; former Chairman, Kirkcudbright District Council; Honorary President, Stewartry Agricultural Society; Chairman, Scottish Agricultural Arbiters Association; Secretary, Kirkcudbright Burns Club; Past President, Kirkcudbright Rotary Club. Recreations: rugby; local history. Address: (h.) Ingleston, Borgue, Kirkcudbright; T.-05577 208.

Gray, Alasdair. Artist and Writer; b. 28.12.34, Glasgow; 1 s. Educ. Whitehill Senior Secondary School; Glasgow Art School. Part-time Art Teacher, 1958-62; Scene Painter, 1963-64; has since lived by drawing, painting, writing; Glasgow People's Palace has a collection of his portraits and cityscapes; has a mural in Palacerigg nature reserve, Cumbernauld. Publications: novels: Lanark; 1982 Janine; The Fall of Kelvin Walker; Something Leather; anthologies: Unlikely Stories, Mostly; Lean Tales (this last also containing work by Jim Kelman and Agnes Owens); Five Glasgow Artists (an exhibition catalogue); Saltire Self-Portrait No. 4. Scottish National Library has a collection of his unpublished plays and other material. Recreations: reading; talking to friends; drinking; walking.

Gray, Alexander, MA, LLB, DUniv, FSA Scot. Honorary Sheriff, Dumbarton; b. 6.5.12, Glasgow; m., Margaret; 2 s. Educ. Hillhead High School; Glasgow University; Edinburgh University. Town Clerk, Cove and Kilcreggan, 1948-67; Queen's Coronation Medal, 1953; Dean, Faculty of Procurators, Dumbarton, 1972; Clerk of Peace, Dunbartonshire,1974. Recreations: archaeology; Gaelic;

arthritis charity. Address: (h.) (h.) Borraichill, 116 Frederick Crescent, Port Ellen, Isle of Islay, PA42 7BQ.

Gray, Charles Ireland, JP. Leader, Strathclyde Regional Council, 1986-92 (Depute Leader, 1978-86); Member, Scottish Enterprise Board, since 1990; b. 25.1.29, Gartcosh; m., Catherine; 3 s.; 2 d. Educ. Coatbridge High School. Local government, since 1958; Director, Scottish Exhibition and Conference Centre; former Vice-Chairman, East Kilbride Development Corporation; former Member: Scottish Development Agency, Clyde Port Authority; former Vice-Chairman, Planning Exchange; Member, Single Market Committee, Scottish Economic Council, since 1989; Member, European Consultative Council for Local and Regional Authorities, since 1989. Recreations: music; reading; local government. Address: (b.) Strathclyde House, 20 India Street, Glasgow, G2 4PF.

Gray, David, DipArch (Aberdeen), RIBA, ARIAS, DipTP (Strath). Director of Architectural and Related Services, Strathclyde Regional Council, since 1991; b. 2.10.37, Aberdeen; m., Margaret Ross Allen Gordon; 1 s.; 2 d. Educ. Robert Gordon's College; Scott Sutherland School of Architecture; Strathclyde University. Apprentice architect/architect, Aberdeen, 1956-62; architect, Lanark County Council, 1962-66; architect/planner, East Kilbride Development Corporation, 1966-67; Group Leader/Assistant County Architect, then Depute County Architect, Renfrew County Council, 1967-75; Strathclyde Regional Council: Area Architect (Renfrew Division), 1975-76, Depute Director (Renfrew/Dumbarton/Argyll), 1976-78, Depute Director (Glasgow Division), 1978-87, Senior Depute Director, 1987-91. Vice-President/Hon. Secretary, Association of Chief Architects of Scottish Local Authorities; Council Member, Royal Institute of Architects in Scotland; Scottish Member, Public Sector Group, Royal Incorporation of British Architects. Recreations: sport; theatre; gardening. Address: (b.) Strathclyde Regional Council, Strathclyde House 2, 20 India Street, Glasgow, G2 4PF; T.-041-227 2100.

Gray, Ethel Marian, CBE, JP, MA, LLD, FEIS. Director, LEAD - Scotland, and Chairman, Advisory Committee; Convener, Adult Access to Education, Scottish Institute of Adult and Continuing Education, 1988-89 (President of Institute, 1984-87); Vice-Chairman, Board of Governors, The Queen's College, Glasgow, 1980-88; Chairman, Education Project for Older People, Age Concern Scotland, 1982-85; b. 19.4.23, Glasgow; m., George Deans Gray (qv). Educ. Hutchesons' Girls Grammar School; Paisley Grammar School; Glasgow University. Teacher of English, 1946-52; Lecturer in English and Drama, Jordanhill College, 1952-63; Founding Principal, Craigie College of Education, Ayr, 1963-75; Director, Scottish Adult Literacy Agency, 1976-79; Chairman, National Book League Scotland, 1977-81; Member of Court, Chairman of Staffing Committee and Joint Faculty Staff Review Board, Heriot-Watt University, 1979-84; Adviser in Adult Education, IBA, 1983-88; Member, Scottish Tertiary Education Advisory Council, 1984-87; Member, Scottish Advisory Committee, British Council, 1968-89; Member, STV Education Advisory Committee, since 1981; Member, Scottish Community Education Council, 1979-85 (Chairman, Communications and Technology Group and Chairman, Management Committee, Micro-Electronics Project); Member, Crawford Commission on Radio and Television Coverage, 1973-75; Member, Committee of Enquiry on the Police, 1977-79; Member, Consultative Committee on the Curriculum, 1965-71. Recreations: reading; travelling; theatre. Address: (h.) 7 Greenbank Crescent, Edinburgh, EH10 5TE; T.-031-447 5403.

Gray, George Bovill Rennie, OBE, DL, CDA, FBIM. Farmer; Chairman, G.B.R. Gray Ltd., since 1952; Member,

Board of Management, and Vice-Chairman, Hanover (Scotland) Housing Association Ltd.; Vice-President, Animal Diseases Research Association, Moredun, since 1974; Director, Moredun Animal Health Ltd.; b. 5.3.20, Edinburgh; m., Anne Constance Dale; 4 s.; 2 d. Educ. Clayesmore School, Dorset; Edinburgh and East of Scotland College of Agriculture. Past Chairman, East Lothian Area, National Farmers Union of Scotland; former Convenor, Cereals Committee, NFU of Scotland; former Member, Seed Production Committee, National Institute of Agricultural Botany, Cambridge; a Director, West Cumberland Farmers Ltd., 1955-85; Director, Scottish Society for Research in Plant Breeding, since 1957 (Trustee, since 1977); Member, Pig Industry Development Authority, 1958-68; Chairman, Oxford Farming Conference, 1972; Member, Agricultural and Veterinary Sub-Committee, UGC, 1972-82; Member, Lothian Regional Council, 1974-82; Member, Scottish Advisory Board, British Institute of Management, 1978-90; Member, Scientific Research Panel, Home Grown Cereals Authority, 1973-80; Hon. President, East Lothian Conservative and Unionist Association; Elder, Church of Scotland; former Assistant County Scout Commissioner; Director, Cruden Foundation. Recreations: gardening; arboriculture. Address: Smeaton Hepburn, East Linton, EH40 3DT; T.-0620 860275.

Gray, George Deans, CBE, MA. Member, Board of Education, Church of Scotland, 1980-87; b. 23.5.08, Edinburgh; m., Ethel Marian Rennie (see Ethel Marian Gray). Educ. Royal High School, Edinburgh; Edinburgh University. Teacher of Classics: Musselburgh Grammar School, 1931-37, George Watson's College, Edinburgh, 1937-45; Principal Teacher, Royal High School, Edinburgh, 1946-59; Secretary, Scottish Council for the Training of Teachers, 1959-66; Registrar (first), General Teaching Council for Scotland, 1966-72; Honorary General Secretary, Scottish Secondary Teachers Association, 1945-59; Chairman: Classical Association (Edinburgh and SE Centre), 1968-73, Scottish Dyslexia Association, 1980-82. Recreations: choral singing; classical music; piano; gardening. Address: (h.) 7 Greenbank Crescent, Edinburgh, EH10 5TE; T.-031-447 5403.

Gray, His Eminence Cardinal Gordon Joseph, MA, DD, FEIS, DUniv (Heriot-Watt). Archbishop of St. Andrews and Edinburgh, 1951-85 (retired, 1985); b. 10.8.10. Educ. Holy Cross Academy, Edinburgh; St. Joseph's, Sussex; St. John's, Surrey. Ordained Priest, 1935; Assistant Priest: St. Andrew's, Fife, 1935-41; Parish Priest, SS Mary and David, Hawick, 1941-47; Rector, St. Mary's College, Blairs, 1947-51; named Cardinal, 1969 (first resident Scottish Cardinal). Address: (h.) The Hermitage, Gillis College, Whitehouse Loan, Edinburgh, EH9 1BB.

Gray of Contin, Lord (Hamish Gray), PC, DL. Business and Parliamentary Consultant, since 1986; b. 28.6.27, Inverness; m., Judith W. Brydon; 2 s.; 1 d. Educ. Inverness Royal Academy. Queen's Own Cameron Highlanders, 1945-48; Director, family and other private companies, 1949-70; MP, Ross and Cromarty, 1970-83; Government Whip, 1971-74; Opposition Spokesman on Energy, 1975-79; Minister of State for Energy, 1979-83; Minister of State for Scotland, 1983-86; Spokesman for Government in Lords for Scotland, Employment and Energy, 1983-86. Vice President, Neighbourhood Energy Action; President, Energy Action Scotland; Vice President, Scottish Association of Youth Clubs. Recreations: golf; cricket; hill-walking; rugby. Address: (h.) Achneim House, Flichity, Inverness-shire, IV1 2XE.

Gray, Iain George Fowler. Scottish Office Industry Department, since 1990; b. 3.5.39, Glasgow. Educ. Albert Road Academy, Glasgow; Roseburn, Edinburgh; Royal High School, Edinburgh. Joined War Office as Executive Officer, 1960; PS/DUS (B), 1964-65; joined Scottish Office as Assistant Principal, 1965, Principal, 1969; SED to 1971; Private Secretary to Minister of State, 1971-72; SDD, 1973; SEPD, 1973-77; DAFS (Assistant Secretary), 1978-84; Finance Officer, DAFS/SED, 1985-89; Scottish Office Home and Health Department, 1989-90. Recreation: golf. Address: (b.) St. Andrews House, Edinburgh; T.-031-244 4680.

Gray, James Allan, MB, ChB, FRCPEdin. Consultant in Communicable Diseases, City Hospital, Edinburgh, since 1969; part-time Senior Lecturer, Department of Medicine, Edinburgh University, since 1969; Principal Medical Officer, Scottish Widows' Fund, Edinburgh, since 1990; President, British Society for the Study of Infection, 1989-91; b. 24.3.35, Bristol; m., Jennifer Margaret Newton Hunter; 1 s.; 2 d. Educ. St. Paul's School, London; Edinburgh University. House Surgeon and Physician posts, Edinburgh and Middlesbrough; Short Service Commission, RAF Medical Branch, 1960-63; Senior House Officer, Research Fellow and Registrar posts, Edinburgh, 1965-67; Registrar, Bristol Royal Infirmary, 1967-68; Senior Registrar, Royal Free Hospital (Department of Infectious Diseases), London, 1968-69; Assistant Director of Studies (Medicine), Edinburgh Post-Graduate Board, 1976-84; Fellow, Royal Medical Society (Senior President, 1958-59); Founder Editor, Res Medica, 1957-58; Assistant Editor, Journal of Infection, 1979-86. Publications: Antibacterial Drugs Today (Co-author), 1983; Infectious Diseases (Co-author), 1984, 1992. Recreations: hill-walking; pottery collecting; photography. Address: (h.) St. Andrews Cottage, 15 Lauder Road, Edinburgh, EH9 2EN; T.-031-667 4124.

Gray, Professor James Robertson, OBE, BSc, DipActMaths, FFA, FIMA, FSS. Professor and Head, Department of Actuarial Mathematics and Statistics, Heriot-Watt University, 1971-89 (now Emeritus); b. 21.2.26, Dundee; m., Catherine McAulay Towner. Educ. High School of Dundee; Edinburgh University. Actuarial Trainee, Scottish Life Assurance Company, 1947-49; St. Andrews University: Lecturer in Mathematics, 1949-50, Lecturer in Statistics, 1950-62, Senior Lecturer in Statistics (also Head of Department), 1962-71; Heriot-Watt University: established first Department of Actuarial Science in UK; Dean, Faculty of Science, 1978-81; Council Member, Faculty of Actuaries, 1969-87 (Vice President, 1983-87); Vice-Chairman, Scottish Examination Board, 1984-90 (Convener of Examinations Committee, 1982-90); former Vice-Chairman, Scottish Universities Council on Entrance; Past Chairman: Scottish Branch, Institute of Mathematics and Its Applications, Edinburgh Branch, Royal Statistical Society. Recreations: golf; hill-walking; bridge; music; Rotary. Address: (h.) Green Gables, 9 Cammo Gardens, Edinburgh, EH4 8EJ; T.-031-339 3330.

Gray, John Bullard, CA. Finance Director, Scottish Hydro-Electric PLC, since 1989; b. 4.7.41, Prestwick; m., Isobel Margaret Craig; 2 s. Educ. Strathallan School. Glenfield & Kennedy Ltd., 1966-68; McLintock Moores & Murray Ltd., 1968-72; Marathon Shipbuilding (UK) Ltd., 1972-76; David Brown-Vosper (Offshore) Ltd., 1976-80; Cammell Laird Shipbuilders Ltd., 1980-83; Vosper Thornycroft UK Ltd., 1983-85; VSEL Consortium PLC, 1985-89. Recreations: golf; hill-walking. Address: (b.) 16 Rothesay Terrace, Edinburgh, EH3 7SE; T.-031-225 1361.

Gray, John William Reid, MA, LLB, Advocate; b. 24.12.26, Aberdeen. Educ. Aberdeen Grammar School; Aberdeen University. Resident Magistrate, Uganda, 1954-62; Temporary Procurator-Fiscal Depute, Glasgow, 1962-63; Lecturer in Private Law, Queen's College, Dundee, then Dundee University, 1964-84; Warden, Airlie Hall, 1966-75; Member of Senate, 1971-75. Fellow, Saltzburg Seminar, 1964. Publications: articles in legal journals; The

Administration of Justice Act, 1982. Address: (h.) 24 Park Road, Dundee, DD3 8LA; T.-0382 815866.

Gray, Muriel, BA (Hons). Broadcaster; Director, Gallus Besom Productions; b. Glasgow. Educ. Glasgow School of Art. Worked as an illustrator; then as a designer with National Museum of Antiquities; was member of rock band, The Family Von Trapp; had own show with Radio Forth; was frequent presenter on Radio 1; co-presented The Tube, Channel 4; had own arts programme, The Works, Tyne Tees; own music programme, Studio 1, Border TV; presented Casebook Scotland, BBC Scotland; Frocks on the Box, Thames TV; Acropolis Now, ITV; presented The Media Show, Channel 4; Co-Producer and Presenter, Walkie Talkie, Channel 4; first woman Rector, Edinburgh University; Producer/Presenter/Director, The Munro Show, Scottish TV; Producer/Presenter, Art is Dead…Long Live TV!, Channel Four. Publication: The First Fifty. Recreation: being in the Scottish Highlands – gets grumpy and miserable if can't be up a mountain every few weeks. Address: (b.) Gallus Besom Productions, Greenside House, 25 Greenside Place, Edinburgh, H1 3AA.

Gray, Professor Peter Michael David, MA, DPhil, FBCS. Professor, Department of Computing Science, Aberdeen University, since 1989; b. 11.2.40, Abingdon; m., Doreen F. Ross; 1 s.; 1 d. Educ. Abingdon School; Queens' College, Cambridge; Jesus College, Oxford. Systems Analyst, Plessey Co., Poole, 1966-68; Research Fellow, Computer Research Group, Aberdeen University, 1968-72; Lecturer in Computing Science, Aberdeen University, 1972-84; Senior Lecturer, 1985-89. Reader, Church of Scotland. Publication: Logic, Algebra and Databases. Recreation: croquet. Address: (b.) Department of Computing Science, King's College, Aberdeen, AB9 2UB; T.-0224 272292.

Gray, Robert, CBE, OStJ, JP, LLD, DL, MICW. Lord Provost of Glasgow, 1984-88; Lord Lieutenant of Glasgow, 1984-88; Chairman, Greater Glasgow Tourist Board, 1984-88; Freelance Clerk of Works and Building Consultant; b. 3.3.28, Glasgow; m., Mary McCartney; 1 d. Educ. St. Mungo's Academy; Glasgow College of Building. Joiner; Clerk of Works; Lecturer and Senior Lecturer in Building Subjects; elected Member, Glasgow District Council, 1974; Chairman, Licensing Committee, 1975-77; Vice Chairman, JP Committee, 1976-77; City Treasurer, 1980-84; Governor, Glasgow College; Vice-Chairman, Mayfest; Member, Board, Glasgow Jazz Festival; Trustee, Child and Family Trust; Member, Incorporation of Wrights of the Trades House of Glasgow; formerly: Member, Scottish Confederation of Tourism, President, Prince and Princess of Wales Hospice, Honorary President, Save the Children Fund, Trustee, University of Glasgow Trust, Patron, Glasgow Branch, British Red Cross Society. Recreations: walking; spectator sports; reading; opera; music. Address: (b.) City Chambers, Glasgow, G2 1DU; T.-041-227 4002.

Gray, Professor Robert Hugh, BSc (Econ), MA (Econ), MBIM, FCA, CA. Mathew Professor of Accounting and Information Systems, Dundee University, since 1990; b. 1.4.52, Manchester; 2 s. Educ. De La Salle College, Salford; Hull University; Manchester University. Qualified as accountant with KPMG Peat Marwick, 1976; Lecturer, Lancashire Polytechnic, UCNW Bangor, University of East Anglia; Member, Research Board, Scottish National Heritage; Editor, British Accounting Review. Recreations: golf; sailing; rock music. Address: (b.) Department of Accountancy and Business Finance, Dundee University, Dundee, DD1 4HN; T.-0382 307789.

Gray, Professor Sidney John, BEc, PhD, FCCA, AASA CPA, ACIS, MBIM. Professor of Accounting and Finance, Glasgow University, since 1978 (Head, Department of Accountancy, 1980-87, and Director, Glasgow Business School, 1986-87); b. 3.10.42, Woodford; m., Hilary Fenella Jones; 1 s.; 1 d. Educ. Bedford Modern School; Sydney University; Lancaster University. Peirce Leslie and Co. Ltd., UK and India, 1961-67; Burns Philp Pty Ltd., Australia, 1967-68; Tutor in Accounting, Sydney University, 1972; Lecturer in Accounting and Finance, Lancaster University, 1974-78; Secretary General, European Accounting Association, 1982-83; Member, Accounting Standards Committee for UK and Ireland, 1984-87; Chairman, British Accounting Association, 1987. Publications: Mega-Merger Mayhem, 1989; International Financial Reporting, 1984; Information Disclosure and the Multinational Corporation, 1984; International Accounting and Transnational Decisions, 1983. Recreations: golf; tennis; travel. Address: (h.) 21 Lampson Road, Killearn, Stirlingshire, G63 9PD; T.-0360 50707.

Gray, Sir William (Stevenson), Kt (1974), JP, DL, HonLLD (Strathclyde), HonLLD (Glasgow). Solicitor and Notary Public, since 1958; Chairman, Norcity Homes PLC, since 1988; b. 3.5.28, Glasgow; m., Mary Rodger; 1 s.; 1 d. Educ. Hillhead High School, Glasgow; Glasgow University. Chairman: Scottish Special Housing Association, 1966-72, Clyde Tourist Association, 1972-75, Scotland West Industrial Promotion Group, 1972-75, WPHT Scotland Ltd. (formerly World of Property Housing Trust Scottish Housing Association Ltd.), since 1974, Irvine New Town Development Corporation, 1974-76, Scottish Development Agency, 1975-79, The Oil Club, since 1975, Research Trust for Institute of Neurological Sciences, since 1978, Glasgow Independent Hospital Ltd., 1982-89, Webtec Industrial Technology Ltd., since 1984, Barrell Selection Ltd., since 1987, Gap Housing Association Ltd., since 1988, Gap Housing Association (Ownership) Ltd., since 1988, Clan Homes plc, since 1988, Manchester Village Homes plc, since 1989, Norhomes plc, since 1989, Norcity II Plc, since 1989, Paragon Group, since 1990, Home Partners Plus Plc, since 1991. Member: Lower Clyde Water Board, 1971-72, National Trust for Scotland, 1971-72, Scottish Opera Board, 1971-72, Executive, Scottish Council (Development and Industry), 1971-75, Convention of Royal Burghs, 1971-75, Clyde Port Authority, 1972-75, Scottish National Orchestra Society, 1972-75, Advisory Council for Energy Conservation, 1974-84, Scottish Economic Council, 1975-83, Central Advisory Committee on JPs, since 1975, Glasgow Advisory Committee on JPs, since 1975, Third Eye Centre, since 1984 (Chairman, 1975-84), Hodgson Martin Ltd. Advisory Board, since 1988, Dermalase Ltd., since 1989. Vice President: Charles Rennie Mackintosh Society, since 1974, Glasgow Citizens' Theatre, since 1975 (Member, Board of Directors, 1970-75), Strathclyde Theatre Group, 1975-86, Scottish Association for Care and Resettlement of Offenders, 1982-86 (Chairman, 1975-82); Governor, Glasgow School of Art, 1961-75; Patron: Scottish Youth Theatre, 1978-86, Scottish Pakistani Society, since 1984; Member: Court, Glasgow University, 1972-75, Council, Strathclyde University Business School, since 1978, Glasgow Corporation, 1958-75 (Chairman, Property Management Committee, 1964-67); Treasurer, City of Glasgow, 1971-72; Lord Provost and Lord Lieutenant of the City of Glasgow, 1972-75. Recreations: sailing; theatre. Address: (b.) 13 Royal Terrace, Glasgow G3 7NY; T.-041-332 8877.

Green, Lawrence Love, MBE. Senior Secretary (Region 4), National Union of Seamen, Scotland and North East England; Joint Chairman, Scottish District Maritime Board; b. 17.9.23, Glasgow; m., Eileen Egan; 3 s. Educ. Lambhill Street Secondary School. Seafaring from 1940; entered trade union movement in 1955 as full-time officer, National Union of Seamen. Vice-Chairman, Port Welfare Committee; Member, Management Committee, Veteran Seafarers Association. Recreations: spectator sports (soccer, boxing, rugby).

Address: (h.) 1425 Paisley Road West, Glasgow; T.-041-882 6954.

Green, Malcolm Robert, MA, DPhil. Chairman, Environment Committee, Strathclyde Regional Council, since 1990 (Chairman, Education Committee, 1982-90); Chairman, Education Committee, Convention of Scottish Local Authorities, 1978-90; Lecturer in Roman History, Glasgow University, since 1967; b. 4.1.43, Leicester; m., Mary Margaret Pratley; 1 s.; 2 d. Educ. Wyggeston Grammar School, Leicester; Magdalen College, Oxford. Address: (b.) Strathclyde House, 20 India Street, Glasgow, G2 4PF; T.-041-227 3447.

Greenberg, Rabbi Philip T., BA, MPhil. Rabbi, Giffnock and Newlands Hebrew Congregation, Glasgow, since 1981; b. 28.6.37, Liverpool; m., Hannah Barber-Kestenberg; 1 s.; 1 d. Educ. Quarry Bank Grammar, Liverpool; Jews College, London University. Minister, Chingford Hebrew Congregation, 1959-68; Rabbi, Nottingham Hebrew Congregation, 1968-72; Head, Mishna Stream, Hasmonean Boys Grammar School, London, 1972-81. Member, Executive, Glasgow Council of Christians and Jews. Recreations: music, reading; photography. Address: (h.) 20 Ayr Road, Giffnock, Glasgow, G46 6RY; T.-041-638 0309.

Greene, John Gerald, MA, PhD, FBPsS. Head of Psychological Services, Western District, Greater Glasgow Health Board; Clinical Lecturer, Glasgow University; b. 10.3.38, Glasgow; m., Dr. Elisabeth Rose Hamil; 2 s.; 2 d. Educ. St. Aloysius College, Glasgow; Glasgow University. Clinical Tutor, Glasgow University Master of Applied Science degree in Clinical Psychology; Registrar, Board of Examiners for the Diploma in Clinical Psychology; Top Grade Psychologist, Greater Glasgow Health Board, since 1982; Chairman, National (Scotland) Scientific Consultative Committee on Clinical Psychological Services, 1985-87; Secretary (1975-77) and Chairman (1977-79), Consultative Committee on Psychological Services, Greater Glasgow Health Board; Secretary and Treasurer, Scottish Branch Committee, Division of Clinical Psychology, 1977-81. Publications: The Social and Psychological Origins of the Climacteric Syndrome, 1984; Clinical Psychology in the Scottish Health Service (Co-author), 1984. Recreations: music; tennis. Address: (b.) Psychology Department, Gartnavel Royal Hospital, Glasgow, G12 OXH.

Greene, John Henderson, MA, LLB. Partner, MacRoberts, Solicitors, Glasgow, Edinburgh and London; b. 2.6.32, Kilmarnock; m., Catriona McGillivray Scott; 1 s. Educ. Merchiston Castle School, Edinburgh; Edinburgh University. Assistant, Joseph Kirkland & Son, Solicitors, Saltcoats, 1958-60; Assistant, MacRoberts, Solicitors, 1960 (appointed Partner, 1961); Law Society of Scotland: Vice-Convener, Company Law Committee, former Member, Bankruptcy and Liquidation Committee; former Council Member, Royal Faculty of Procurators, Glasgow; founder Chairman, Troon Round Table, 1964; Captain, Royal Troon Golf Club, 1989; Elder, Portland Church, Troon; President, Glasgow Ayrshire Society, 1985-86. Publication: Law and Practice of Receivership in Scotland (Co-author). Recreations: golf; gardening. Address: (h.) Silvertrees, 7 Lady Margaret Drive, Troon, KA10 7AL; T.-Troon 312482.

Greenman, Professor Jonathan Vaughan, BA, MA, PhD. Professor of Mathematics and Its Applications, Stirling University, since 1990; b. 3.3.39, Cardiff; m., Barbara Phyllis; 2 s. Educ. Kingston Grammar School; Cambridge University. Harkness Scholar, University of California, Berkeley; Department of Physics, MIT; Stanford Research Institute, California; Department of Mathematics, Essex University; Tutor, Open University; Senior Analyst, Corporate Planning, British Petroleum plc; Industry Analyst, Centre for Global

Energy Studies. Recreations: cinema; walking; travel. Address: (b.) Department of Mathematics, Stirling University, Stirling, FK9 4LA; T.-0786 67460.

Greenock, William, MA. Principal, Clydebank College, since 1984; b. 3.2.37, Glasgow; 2 d. Educ. Allan Glen's School; Glasgow University. Teacher, secondary schools, 1959-65; David Dale College, 1965-68; Langside College, 1968-70; Reid Kerr College, 1970-75; Anniesland College, 1975-82; Ayr College, 1982-84. Session Clerk, Langside Parish Church, Glasgow. Recreation: golf. Address: (b.) Clydebank College, Kilbowie Road, Clydebank, G81 2AA; T.-041-952 7771.

Greenstead, Professor Christopher Stanford, BSc, MSc. Director, Strathclyde Graduate Business School, since 1986; b. 10.9.41, Leeds; m., Candace Helen; 1 s.; 1 d.; 1 s. by pr. m. Educ. Cranbrook School, Kent; Sir John Cass College, London; Strathclyde University. Chemist in pharmaceuticals, 1960-65; operational research/consultancy in food industry, 1966-68; appointed Lecturer in OR, Strathclyde, 1969, then in Accounting and Finance, 1974; was part-time Director of yacht chandlery company, eight years. RNR officer, eight years. President, European Network of Business Schools. Publications: three books; several articles on business statistics and management development. Recreations: sailing; golf (badly); theatre and concerts (infrequently). Address: (h.) 18 Carrick Drive, Glasgow, G32 0RW; T.-041-778 9120.

Greer, Rev. Arthur David Courtenay, MA, LLB, DMin. Minister, Dunscore with Glencairn and Moniaive, since 1985; b. 20.2.30, Glasgow; m., Kathleen Slessor; 1 s.; 3 d. Educ. Prestwick Public and High Schools; Ayr Academy; Glasgow University (Trinity College); NYTS. Assistant Minister, St. Quivox, Ayr, 1954-55; Minister: Presbyterian Church of Jamaica and Grand Cayman, 1956-63, Kelvingrove Church, Glasgow, 1964-78; Department of Education Staff Tutor, St. Colm's College, Edinburgh, 1978-81; Associate Minister, Whitfield, Dundee, 1981-85. Recreations: youth hostelling; philately. Address: The Manse, Wallaceton, Dumfries; T.-Dunscore 245.

Greer, Professor Ian Andrew, MB, ChB, MD (Glas), MRCP(UK), MRCOG. Muirhead Professor and Head, Department of Obstetrics and Gynaecology, Glasgow University, since 1991; Honorary Consultant Obstetrician and Gynaecologist, Glasgow Royal Infirmary and Glasgow Royal Maternity Hospital, since 1991; b. 16.4.58, Glasgow; m., Anne Smith; 2 s. Educ. Allan Glen's School, Glasgow; Glasgow University. Registrar in General Medicine, Glasgow Royal Infirmary; Registrar in Obstetrics and Gynaecology, Glasgow Royal Maternity Hospital and Glasgow Royal Infirmary; Lecturer in Obstetrics and Gynaecology, Edinburgh University; Clinical Research Scientist/Consultant Obstetrician and Gynaecologist, MRC Reproductive Biology Unit, Edinburgh. MRCOG Gold Medal; Blair-Bell Lectureship, Royal Collge of Obstetricians and Gynaecologists 1989; Travelling Fellowship, RCOG, 1989; Watson Prize Lecture, Royal College of Physicians and Surgeons of Glasgow, 1990. Address: (b.) Department of Obstetrics and Gynaecology, Glasgow University, Glasgow Royal Infirmary, Glasgow, G31 2ER; T.-041-552 8316.

Gregory, Paul, BA, DipTP, MRTPI. Director of Planning and Development, Borders Regional Council, since 1986. Educ. King Edward VII Grammar School, King's Lynn; Manchester University. Norfolk County Council; Scottish Development Department; Borders Regional Council. Address: (b.) Regional HQ, Newtown St. Boswells, Melrose, TD6 0SA; T.-0835 23301.

Gregson, William Derek Hadfield, CBE, DL, DFH, CEng, FIEE, CBIM, FRSA. Commissioner of Northern

Lighthouses; Director: Anderson Strathclyde, Brammer plc, East of Scotland Industrial Investments PLC; Consultant, ICI; b. 27.1.20; m., Rosalind Helen Reeves; 3 s.; 1 d. Educ. UK and Switzerland. Director, Ferranti Holdings, 1983-85; Deputy Chairman, British Airports Authority, 1975-85; Director, British Telecom (Scotland), 1977-85. Recreations: woodwork; books; automation in the home. Address: (h.) 5 Barnton Avenue, Edinburgh, EH4 6AJ; T.-031-336 3896.

Grier, Arnold Macfarlane, MB, ChB, FRCSEdin. Consultant Ear, Nose and Throat Surgeon, Highland Health Board, since 1962; National Vice-President, Scottish Association for the Deaf; b. 5.9.21, Musselburgh; m., Elisabeth J. Kluten; 2 s.; 1 d. Educ. Musselburgh Grammar School; Edinburgh University. Recreations: gardening; aviculture; painting. Address: (h.) Elmbank, 68 Culduthel Road, Inverness; T.-Inverness 234682.

Grier, Scott, OBE, MA, CA, MCIT. Managing Director, Loganair Limited, since 1983; b. 7.3.41, Kilmacolm; m., Frieda Gardiner; 2 s. Educ. Greenock High School; Glasgow University. Apprenticed, Grahams Rintoul & Co., 1962-66; Accountant, Ardrossan Harbour Company, 1967-76; Loganair: Financial/Commercial Manager and Secretary, 1976, Financial Director, 1977. Recreations: golf; philately. Address: (h.) Lagavulin, 15 Corsehill Drive, West Kilbride, KA23 9HU; T.-0294 823138.

Grieve, Professor Andrew Robert, DDS, BDS, FDS RCSEd. Professor of Conservative Dentistry, Dundee University, since 1980 (Senior Adviser of Studies in Dentistry, since 1982); Consultant in Restorative Dentistry, Tayside Health Board, since 1980; b. 23.5.39, Stirling; m., Frances M. Ritchie; 2 d. Educ. Perth Academy; St. Andrews University. Junior hospital appointments and general dental practice, 1961-65; Lecturer in Operative Dental Surgery and Dental Therapeutics, St. Andrews University, 1963-65; Lecturer in Conservative Dentistry, Birmingham University, 1965; appointed Senior Lecturer and Consultant in Restorative Dentistry, Birmingham Area Health Authority (Teaching), 1975. Member, Dental Council, Royal College of Surgeons of Edinburgh, 1983-88 and since 1989; President, British Society for Restorative Dentistry, 1986-87; Council Member, Royal Odonto-Chirurgical Society of Scotland, 1985-88; Chairman, Tayside Area Dental Advisory Committee, 1987-90; Member, General Dental Council, since 1989. Recreation: hill-walking. Address: (b.) Department of Conservative Dentistry, Dental School, The University, Dundee, DD1 4HN; T.-0382 26041.

Grieve, John. Actor; b. 14.6.24, Glasgow. Trained, Royal Scottish Academy of Music and Drama (James Bridie Gold Medallist), followed by five full seasons, Citizens' Theatre, Glasgow; also appeared in Guthrie's production of The Anatomist, Citizens', 1968; numerous other performances on the Scottish stage, including leading roles in The Bevellers, The Flouers o' Edinburgh, The Good Soldier Schweik, Twelfth Night; television work includes The Vital Spark, Oh Brother, Doctor at Sea, New Year shows; numerous appearances in pantomime; appeared with Scottish Theatre Company in Waiting for Godot and The Thrie Estaites. Address: (b.) c/o David White Associates, 2 Ormond Road, London, Surrey, TW10 6TH.

Grieve, Kathleen Zia, MBE, BSc. Organiser, Network Scotland Ltd., 1975-85; b. 25.9.20, Aberdeen; m., Rev. G.M. Denny Grieve; 2 s.; 1 d. Educ. St. Margaret's School for Girls, Aberdeen; Aberdeen University. Technical Assistant, BBC, 1941-44; service in Church of Scotland from 1944, including National Vice-Convener, Home Board, four years, National President, Woman's Guild, 1966-69; represented Church of Scotland, World Alliance of Reformed Churches meeting, Nairobi, 1970; Member, Church of Scotland Committee of

Forty (Honorary Secretary, 1972-78); appointed Organiser, Scottish Telephone Referral Service for Adult Literacy (which became Network Scotland Ltd.), 1975; founder Member, then Honorary Secretary, Dyslexia Scotwest; founder Member, Trustee and Administrator, Pet Fostering Service Scotland, 1985-87; Treasurer, Society for Companion Animal Studies, 1989. Recreations: walking dog; reading; helping in Hospice shop; chess; motoring; gardening. Address: (h.) 13 Montgomerie Terrace, Ayr, KA7 1JL; T.-0292 261768.

Grieve, Professor Sir Robert, Kt (1969). Honorary Professor, Heriot-Watt University; Professor Emeritus, Glasgow University; b. 11.12.10. Chief Planner, Scottish Office, 1960-64; Professor of Town and Regional Planning, Glasgow University, 1964-74; Chairman, Highlands and Islands Development Board, 1965-70.

Grieve, Professor Robert, MA, PhD, CPsych, FBPsS. Professor of Psychology, Edinburgh University, since 1987; b. 2.8.44, Bathgate; m., Anne; 1 s.; 2 d. Educ. Edinburgh University. Lecturer in Psychology, St. Andrews University; Senior Lecturer in Psychology, then Associate Professor of Psychology, University of Western Australia. Address: (b.) Department of Psychology, Edinburgh University, 7 George Square, Edinburgh, EH8 9JZ; T.-031-650 3441.

Grieve, Hon. Lord (William Robertson Grieve), VRD (1958), QC (Scot), MA, LLB. Senator of the College of Justice in Scotland, 1972-88; Chairman, Board of Governors, St. Columba's Hospice, since 1983; b. 21.10.17, Glasgow; m., Lorna St. John Benn (deceased); 1 s.; 1 d. Educ. Glasgow Academy; Sedbergh School; Glasgow University. Served with Royal Navy as an RNVR officer, 1939-45; Advocate, Scots Bar, 1947; QC, 1957; Sheriff Principal, Renfrew and Argyll, 1964-72; Judge of Appeal, Jersey and Guernsey, 1971-72; Procurator, Church of Scotland, 1968-72; Chairman, Governors, Fettes Trust, 1978-86. President, Glasgow University Union, 1938. Recreations: golf; painting. Address: (h.) 20 Belgrave Crescent, Edinburgh, EH4 3AJ; T.-031-332 7500.

Griffiths, Nigel, JP. MP (Labour), Edinburgh South, since 1987; Opposition Spokesman on Consumer Affairs, since 1989; b. 20.5.55; m., Sally McLaughlin. Educ. Hawick High School; Edinburgh University; Moray House College of Education. Secretary, Lothian Devolution Campaign, 1978; Rights Adviser, Mental Handicap Pressure Group, 1979-87; City of Edinburgh District Councillor, 1980-87 (Chairperson, Housing Committee); Member, Edinburgh Festival Council, 1984-87; Member, Edinburgh Health Council, 1982-87; Executive Member, Edinburgh Council of Social Service, 1984-87; Member, Wester Hailes School Council, 1981; Executive Member, Scottish Constitutional Convention (Chair, Finance Committee). Recreations: travel; live entertainment; badminton; hill-walking; rock-climbing; architecture; reading; politics. Address: (h.) 39 Thirlestane Road, Edinburgh, EH9 1AP; T.-031-447 1947.

Griffiths, Professor Peter Denham, CBE, BSc, MD, LRCP, MRCS, FRCPath, FBIM, FRSA. Emeritus Professor of Biochemical Medicine, Dundee University (Vice-Principal, 1979-85, Dean of Medicine and Dentistry, 1985-89); Consultant, Tayside Health Board, 1986-89; b. 16.6.27, Southampton; m., Joy Burgess; 3 s.; 1 d. Educ. King Edward VI School, Southampton; Guy's Hospital, London University. House appointments, Guy's Hospital, 1956-57; Junior Lecturer in Physiology, Guy's Hospital, 1957-58; Registrar and Senior Registrar, Guy's and Lewisham Hospitals, 1958-64; Consultant Pathologist, Harlow Hospitals Group, 1964-66; Senior Lecturer in Clinical Chemistry/Honorary Consultant, St. Andrews University, then Dundee University, 1966-68. Member, General Medical Council, since 1986;

President, 1987-89, and sometime Chairman of Council, Association of Clinical Biochemists; former Director, Dundee Repertory Theatre. Recreations: music; theatre; domestic activities. Address: (h.) 52 Albany Road, West Ferry, Dundee, DD5 1NW; T.-0382 76772.

Grimes, Alistair Bernard, MA (St. Andrews), MA (Durham), PhD (Edinburgh), MBA (Edinburgh). Group Funding Controller, The Wise Group, since 1988; b. 30.5.51, London. Educ. King Edward VI Grammar School, Nuneaton; St. Andrews University; Durham University; Edinburgh University. Age Concern Scotland, 1978-79; Scottish Council of Social Service, 1979-82; Lothian Regional Council, 1982-84; Assistant Director, Scottish Council for Voluntary Organisations, 1984-88. Founder Member, Past Chairman, Scottish Education and Action for Development. Publications: Cold as Charity, 1980; The Form of Ideology (Contributor), 1981; Scotland: The Real Divide, 1983. Recreations: good films; bad television; complaining about ScotRail; waiting with anticipation the fall of Michael Forsyth. Address: (h.) 108 Newhaven Road, Edinburgh, EH6 4BR; T.-031-553 1965.

Grimmond, Iain William, BAcc (Hons), CA. Treasurer, Erskine Hospital for Disabled Ex-Servicemen, since 1981; b. 8.8.55, Girvan; m., Marjory Anne Gordon Chisholm; 1 s.; 2 d. Educ. Hutchesons' Boys Grammar School; Glasgow University. Trainee CA, Ernst & Whinney, Glasgow, 1976-79; Assistant Treasurer, Erskine Hospital, 1979-81. Elder, Giffnock South Parish Church; Honorary Auditor, Paisley Art Institute. Recreations: golf; badminton; reading. Address: (h.) 9 Wemyss Avenue, Crookfur, Newton Mearns, Glasgow, G77 6AR; T.-041-639 4894.

Grimond, Baron (Joseph Grimond), TD, PC. Life Peer; b. 29.7.13. Director of Personnel, European Office, UNRRA, 1945-47; Secretary, National Trust for Scotland, 1947-49; MP (Liberal), Orkney and Shetland, 1950-83; Leader, Parliamentary Liberal Party, 1956-67.

Grimond, Lady Laura Miranda. President, Women's Liberal Federation, 1984-86; Honorary Sheriff, Kirkwall, 1977-89; Member, Board of Trustees, National Museum of Antiquities of Scotland, 1972-85; Member, Ancient Monuments Board of Scotland, 1979-90; b. 13.10.18, London; m., Rt. Hon Lord Grimond of Firth (qv); 2 s.; 1 s. (deceased); 1 d. Educ. privately. Magistrate, Richmond, Surrey, 1955-59; fought West Aberdeenshire as Liberal, 1970; Member, Orkney Islands Council, 1974-81; Trustee and Chairman, Management Committee, Hoy Trust, 1973-77; first Chairman, Orkney Heritage Society. Address: (h.) The Old Manse of Firth, Kirkwall, Orkney.

Grimson, Dermot, MRTPI. Director, Rural Forum, since 1987; b. 22.5.52, Glasgow; m., Fiona Moncrieff Gratton. Educ. Kelvinside Academy; Glasgow School of Art. Planner, Renfrew District Council; Planner, Banff and Buchan District Council. Former Member of Banff and Buchan Health Council; Past Chairman, Buchan Countryside Group; former Secretary, Banff and Buchan Constituency Labour Party; Chairman, Perth Civic Trust. Address: (h.) 10 St. John's Place, Perth; T.-0738 30014.

Grinyer, Professor John Raymond, MSc, FCA. Professor of Accountancy and Business Finance, Dundee University, since 1976 (Head, Department of Accountancy and Business Finance, 1976-90, Dean, Faculty of Law, 1984-85 and 1991); b. 3.3.35, London; m., Shirley Florence Marshall; 1 s.; 2 d. Educ. Central Park Secondary Modern School, London; London School of Economics. London Electricity Board, 1950-53; National Service, RAMC, 1953-55; Halifax Building Society, 1955-56; Martin Redhead & Co., Accountants, 1956-60; Hope Agar & Co., Chartered

Accountants, 1960-62; Kemp Chatteris & Co., Chartered Accountants, 1962-63; Lecturer, Harlow Technical College, 1963-66; City of London Polytechnic, 1966-71; Cranfield School of Management, 1971-76; Chairman, British Accounting Association, 1980-81 and 1990, and Scottish Representative, since 1984. Recreations: golf; dinghy sailing. Member, Royal Tay Yacht Club. Address: (b.) The University, Dundee, DD1 4HN; T.-Dundee 307192.

Grinyer, Professor Peter Hugh, MA (Oxon), PhD. Esmee Fairbairn Professor of Economics (Finance and Investment), St. Andrews University, since 1979; b. 3.3.35, London; m., Sylvia Joyce Boraston; 2 s. Educ. Balliol College, Oxford; London School of Economics. Senior Managerial Trainee, Unilever Ltd., 1957-59; Personal Assistant to Managing Director, E.R. Holloway Ltd., 1959-61; Lecturer and Senior Lecturer, Hendon College of Technology, 1961-64; Lecturer, The City University, London, 1965-69; The City University Business School: Senior Lecturer and Co-ordinator of Research, 1969-72, Reader, 1972-74, Professor of Business Strategy, 1974-79; Chairman, Department of Economics, St. Andrews University, 1979-85; Vice-Principal, 1985-87 (Acting Principal, 1986); Chairman, Department of Management, 1987-89; Chairman, St. Andrews Management Institute, since 1989; Chairman, St. Andrews Strategic Management Ltd., since 1989. Member, Sub-Committee on Management and Business Studies, University Grants Committee, 1979-85; Consultant to NEDO on Sharpbenders Project, 1984-86; Non-Executive Director: Glenrothes Enterprise Trust, 1983-86, John Brown plc, 1984-86, Don Bros. Buist plc (now Don and Low (Holdings) Ltd.) 1985-91, Ellis and Goldstein plc, 1987-88; Chairman (non-executive), McIlroy Coates, since 1991. Recreations: mountain walking; golf; listening to music. Address: (b.) Department of Management, St. Andrews University, Kinnessburn, Kennedy Gardens, St. Andrews, Fife, KY16 9DJ; T.-0334 76161, Ext. 8102.

Groat, John Malcolm Freswick, MBE, JP, DL. Company Director: J.M.F. Groat & Sons Ltd., Orkney Seaport Supplies Ltd.; Member, Orkney Health Board, since 1979; Member, Orkney Islands Council Pilotage Committee; Postmaster, Longhope, Orkney, since 1964; Secretary, Longhope Lifeboat, since 1962; b. 9.9.23, Longhope, Orkney; m., Edna Mary Yule. War service: joined RAFVR as Air Crew Cadet, 1943; operational service with No. 576 and No. 150 Lancaster Squadrons No. 5 Group, Bomber Command, RAF, until 1945, then in India and as Officer i/c transport, Air Command South East Asia, Changi, Singapore, until 1947; Clerk, Hoy and Walls District Council, 1953-74; Clerk, School Management Committee, Walls and Flotta, 1953-74; Registrar of Births etc., Hoy and Walls, 1953-74; Provincial Grand Master, Orkney and Zetland, 1979-84; Trustee, Longhope Lifeboat Disaster Fund, since 1969; Agent, Shipwrecked Mariners Society; Secretary, Longhope British Legion, 1948-53; Secretary, Longhope Sailing Club, 1950-60; Director, Orkney Islands Shipping Co., 1974-87; Member, Coastguard Lifesaving Company, Longhope, 1947-61; Founder Member, Orkney Flying Club, 1949; Secretary/Treasurer, Walls and Hoy Agricultural Society, 1950-60; R.W. Master, Lodge St. Colm No. 1022, 1964-69. Address: (h.) Moasound, Longhope, Orkney; T.-241.

Groom, Rev. Colin John, MA. Member, Fife Regional Council (Chairman, Protective & General Services Committee); Depute Administrator, Fife Local Health Council; b. 29.1.34, Harrow; m., Eileen; 1 s.; 1 d. Educ. Harrow County Grammar School; Wesley House, Cambridge University; New College, Edinburgh University. Methodist Minister, Telford, 1960-67; Methodist Minister and Industrial Chaplain, Leeds, 1967-70; Minister, Cardenden Parish Church, 1972-82. Member, Iona Community and Christian Socialist Movement. Recreations: hill-walking; cross country skiing. Address: (h.) 27 Scott Road, Glenrothes, Fife, KY6 1AB; T.-0592 756970.

Grossart, Angus McFarlane McLeod, CBE, LLD, MA, CA. Advocate; Merchant Banker; Chairman of the Trustees, National Galleries of Scotland, since 1988; Director: Hewden Stuart plc, since 1988, Alexander and Alexander, New York, since 1984, American Trust PLC, since 1973, Edinburgh Fund Managers PLC, since 1983 (Deputy Chairman), Noble Grossart Limited, since 1969, The Royal Bank of Scotland plc, since 1982, The Scottish Investment Trust PLC, since 1973 (Chairman), Scottish Television plc, since 1989; b. 6.4.37, Glasgow; m., Gay Kerr Dodd; 1 d. Educ. Glasgow Academy; Glasgow University. CA apprentice, Thomson McLintock, 1958-62; Advocate, Scottish Bar, 1962-69; Managing Director, Noble Grossart Ltd., since 1969. Former Scottish Editor, British Tax Encyclopaedia and British Tax Review. Recreations: golf; decorative arts. Address: (b.) 48 Queen Street, Edinburgh, EH2 3NR; T.-031-226 7011.

Grosset, Alan George, MA, LLB, WS, NP. Partner, Alex. Morison & Co., WS; b. 18.1.42, Edinburgh; 1 s.; 1 d. Educ. Royal High School, Edinburgh; Edinburgh University. Law Society of Scotland "Troubleshooter" from inception of scheme, until 1987; President, Scottish Lawn Tennis Association, 1983-84; Council Member, Lawn Tennis Association, 1980-89; first Chairman, Scottish Sports Association, 1984-90; Member, Scottish Sports Council, since 1984; Founder Member, Scottish Branch, Society for Computers and Law; Secretary, British Sports Forum, since 1991. Recreations: golf; tennis; squash. Address: (b.) 33 Queen Street, Edinburgh; T.-031-226 6541.

Grosz, David Peter, BA (Hons). Chairman, Ramblers' Association Scottish Council, since 1985; Founding Member and Committee Member, Scottish Council for National Parks, since 1991; b. 2.4.39, London. Educ. Wyggeston Boys' Grammar School, Leicester; Nottingham University; School of Education, Leicester University. School Teacher, Leicester, 1962-78, West Lothian, 1978-84. Member, RA National Executive Committee, since 1983; Member, Board of Directors, Scottish Rights of Way Society, since 1984; Chairman, Friends of New Lanark, 1985-89; Member, Council, National Trust for Scotland, since 1989. Recreations: walking; reading; campaigning with passion for public access and countryside conservation. Address: (h.) 10 Rosebery Place, Eliburn, Livingston, West Lothian, EH54 6RP; T.-0506 412902.

Groves, C. Arthur, JP. Member, Borders Regional Council, since 1986; Chairman, Justices Committee, Ettrick and Lauderdale, since 1984; Chairman, General Inland Revenue Commissioners, since 1983; b. 28.11.24, London. Educ. Raine's Foundation, London. Selkirk Town Council, 1961-75 (Hon. Treasurer); former Selkirk County Councillor (Chairman, Finance Committee). Recreation: equestrian activities. Address: (h.) 24 Hillview Crescent, Selkirk, TD7 4AZ; T.-0750 21126.

Guest, Charles Drysdale Graham, FRICS. Chartered Surveyor; Partner, Ryden Property Consultants and Chartered Surveyors, since 1981; b. 26.7.47, Edinburgh; m., Gail Meikle; 1 s.; 2 d. Educ. George Watson's College, Edinburgh; Merchiston Castle School, Edinburgh; Liverpool University. Richard Ellis, Chartered Surveyors, Johannesburg, 1970-72; Weatherall Green & Smith, London, 1972-77; joined Ryden, 1977. Recreations: shooting; fishing; skiing; tennis. Address: (b.) 46 Castle Street, Edinburgh, EH2 3BM; T.-031-225 6612.

Guild, Ivor Reginald, CBE, FRSE, MA, LLB, WS. Partner, Shepherd & Wedderburn, WS, since 1950; Procurator Fiscal to the Lyon Court; b. 2.4.24, Dundee. Educ. Cargilfield; Rugby; New College, Oxford; Edinburgh University.

Chairman: Dunedin Worldwide Investment Trust PLC, Dunedin Income Growth Investment Trust PLC, Edinburgh Investment Trust PLC; Director: Fleming Universal Trust PLC, Fulcrum Investment Trust. Editor, Scottish Genealogist; Bailie, Abbey Court of Holyroodhouse; Trustee, Edinburgh University; Secretary and Treasurer, Stair Society. Recreations: golf; genealogy. Address: (b.) 16 Charlotte Square, Edinburgh, EH2 4YS; T.-031-225 8585.

Guild, Stuart Alexander, TD, BL, WS, NP. Writer to the Signet, since 1950; Senior Partner, Guild and Guild WS, 1958-89; b. 25.1.24, Edinburgh; m., Fiona Catherine MacCulloch; 1 s.; 2 d. Educ. Edinburgh Academy; George Watson's College, Edinburgh; Queen's University, Belfast; Edinburgh University. Royal Artillery, 1942-47; Territorial Army (RA), 1947-65; County Cadet Commandant, Lothian Bn., ACF, 1967-69 (Hon. Lt-Col.); Honorary Treasurer, 1976-91, and Shooting Convener, Army Cadet Force Association (Scotland); Council Member, Army Cadet Force Association, 1976-91; Member, Lowland TA & VR Association; Deputy Chairman, Lothian & Borders, Royal Artillery Council of Scotland; President, Lothian & Peebles Home Guard Rifle Association, 1980-91; Vice-President, Lothian Smallbore Shooting Association; Governor, Melville College Trust, 1976-91; Chairman, Sandilands Memorial Trust; Assistant, The Company of Merchants of the City of Edinburgh, 1972-75; Vice-Convener, Mary Erskine School for Girls, 1973-75. Recreations: golf; target shooting; photography. Address: (h.) 7 Lockharton Gardens, Edinburgh, EH14 1AU.

Gulland, Anne. Member, Scottish Sports Council, 1979-90; b. 26.3.31, Dunblane; m., Neil W. Gulland; 1 s.; 2 d. Educ. McLaren High School, Callander. Treasurer, 11 years, Scottish Women's Hockey Association; one year as Vice-President; three years as President; Treasurer, Great Britain Olympic Committee (hockey). Elder, Church of Scotland. Address: (h.) 48 Dunmar Drive, Alloa, Clackmannanshire; T.-0259 212908.

Gulliver, Stuart, BSc (Econ). Chief Executive, Glasgow Development Agency, since 1991; b. 10.1.42, Sheffield; m., Barbara McKewan; 3 s.; 1 d. Educ. Firth Park Grammar School; London School of Economics. Research Fellow in Economics, Leeds University; Senior Lecturer, Leeds Polytechnic; commercial development, Warrington New Town Development Corporation; Regional Director, Scottish Development Agency. Visiting Professor in Economic and Social Research, Glasgow University. Recreations: cricket; tennis; watching football; music, especially modern jazz; theatre. Address: (b.) Atrium Court, 50 Waterloo Street, Glasgow, G2 6HQ; T.-041-204 1111.

Gunn, Alexander MacLean, MA, BD. Minister, Aberfeldy with Amulree and Strathbraan with Dull and Weem, since 1986; b. 26.2.43, Inverness; m., Ruth T.S.; 1 s.; 1 d. Educ. Edinburgh Academy; Beauly; Dingwall Academy; Edinburgh University and New College. Parish Minister: Wick St. Andrews and Thrumster, 1967-73; Member, Caithness Education Committee, 1968-73; Parish Minister, Glasgow St. David's Knightswood, 1973-86; Convener, Church of Scotland Rural Working Group, 1988-90; Convenor, General Assembly's Presbytery Development Committee, 1990-92; Convenor, General Assembly's Mission and Evangelism Resource Committee, since 1992. Chairman, Breadalbane Academy School Board, 1989-92. Address: The Manse, Taybridge Terrace, Aberfeldy, PH15 2BS; T.-0887 820656.

Gunn, James Forsyth Grimmond, BSc, CEng, FICE, FIStructE, ACIArb, MConsE. Chairman, Blyth & Blyth Group, since 1987; Director, Blyth & Blyth Associates, since 1976; b. 5.8.36, Edinburgh; m., Brenda; 1 s.; 1 d. Educ. George Watson's Boys' College; Edinburgh University.

Construction Engineer, Bovis, London and Manchester, 1960-61; joined Blyth & Blyth, 1962; Manager, Belfast Office, 1964-70; Associate, Edinburgh Office, 1970; Partner/Director, Edinburgh, 1976. Member, Scottish Council, CBI. Recreations: golf; fishing; hill-walking; music. Address: (h.) 8A Glencairn Crescent, Edinburgh, EH12 5BS; T.-031-226 6975.

Gunstone, Professor Frank Denby, BSc, PhD, DSc, FRSC, FRSE, CChem. Professor of Chemistry, St. Andrews University, 1971-89; Honorary Research Professor, since 1989; b. 27.10.23, Chadderton; m., Eleanor Eineen Hill; 2 s.; 1 d. Educ. Oldham Hulme Grammar School; Holt High School, Liverpool; Liverpool University. Lecturer, Glasgow University, 1946-54; St. Andrews University: Lecturer, 1954-59, Senior Lecturer, 1959-65, Reader, 1965-71. Lipid Award, American Oil Chemists' Society, 1973; Hildith Lecturer, 1975; Kaufmann Lecturer, 1976. Address: (h.) Rumgally House, Cupar, Fife, KY15 5SY; T.-0334 53613.

Gurdon, Col. Robert Temple, FBIM. Schools Liaison Officer for Army in Scotland, since 1983; b. 23.6.32, Colchester; m., Elizabeth Ann Terry; 1 s.; 1 d. (dec.). Educ. Rugby School. Commissioned The Black Watch, 1952; Staff College, 1963; National Defence College, 1973; commanded 1/51 Highland Volunteers, 1975-77; Chief of Staff Scotland, 1979-83; retired as Colonel, 1983. Chairman, Earl Haig Fund Scotland; Chairman, Highland Brigade Club. Recreations: shooting; golf. Address: (h.) 4 Middleby Street, Edinburgh, EH9 1TD; T.-031-667 3875.

Guthrie, James King, BSc, CEng, MICE. Director, Scotland Tarmac Construction Ltd.; b. 22.12.29, Glasgow; m., Katherine; 1 s.; 4 d. Educ. Jordanhill College School; Glasgow University. National Service, Royal Engineers, 1955-57 (2nd Lt.); Senior Engineer, G. Wimpey Ltd., 1957-64; Project Manager, A.M. Carmichael Ltd., 1964-70; Area Manager/Director, Tarmac Construction Ltd., 1970-80; Director, Aberdeen Construction Group PLC, 1981-86. Recreations: golf; sailing; music. Address (h.) Forest Lodge, Dollar, FK14 7LT; T.-02594 2600.

H

Haddow, Rev. Angus Halley, BSc. Minister, Methlick Parish Church, Aberdeenshire, since 1990 (Minister, Garthdee Parish Church, Aberdeen, 1981-90); Clerk, Aberdeen Presbytery, 1981-90; b. 27.11.32, Wishaw; m., Marjory Walsh; 1 s.; 2 d. Educ. Wishaw High School; Glasgow University and Trinity College. Science Teacher, Greenfield Secondary School, 1957-60; Assistant Minister, Newarthill, 1962-63; Minister: Largo St. David's Parish Church, 1963-71, Trinity Parish Church, Aberdeen, 1971-81; Minute Clerk, Aberdeen Presbytery, 1977-81. Publication: The Paranormal in Holy Scripture (Co-author). Recreations: reading; parapsychology; hill-walking; music. Address: The Manse, Methlick, Ellon, Aberdeenshire, AB41 0DS; T.-06514 215.

Hadley, Geoffrey, BSc (Hons), PhD. Convener, Grampian Regional Council, 1986-90; Honorary Senior Lecturer,

Aberdeen University, since 1985; Consultant Microbiologist, since 1985; b. 7.2.32, Stoke-on-Trent; m., Barbara Jean Ross; 3 d. by pr. m. Educ. Longton High School; Birmingham University. Research Fellow, Nottingham University, 1956-58; Lecturer, Glasgow University, 1958-60; Lecturer, then Senior Lecturer, Aberdeen University, 1960-85; seconded to University of Malaya, 1967-68; Member, Aberdeen County Council, 1973-75, Grampian Regional Council, since 1974; Vice-President, British Mycological Society, 1987; Chairman, Grampian Heart Campaign. Recreations: classical music; home brewing and wine-making; cricket; cycling; DIY. Address: (h.) 74 Don Street, Old Aberdeen, Aberdeen, AB2 1UU; T.-0224 494472.

Hagart-Alexander of Ballochmyle, Sir Claud, Bt, DL, JP, BA, CEng, MInstMC. Vice Lord-Lieutenant, Ayrshire and Arran, since 1983; b. 6.1.27, Peking; m., Hilda Etain Acheson; 2 s.; 2 d. Educ. Sherborne; Corpus Christi College, Cambridge. Address: (h.) Kingencleugh House, Mauchline, Ayrshire, KA5 5JL; T.-0290 50217.

Haggart, Rt. Rev. Alastair Iain Macdonald, MA, LLD. Retired Bishop, b. 10.10.15, Glasgow; m., 1, Margaret Agnes Trundle; 2 d.; 2, Mary Scholes. Educ. Edinburgh Theological College; Durham University. Curate, St. Mary's Cathedral, Glasgow; Curate, St. Mary's, Hendon, London; Precentor, St. Ninian's Cathedral, Perth; Rector, St. Oswald's, King's Park, Glasgow; Synod Clerk, Diocese of Glasgow; Provost, St. Paul's Cathedral, Dundee; Principal, Theological College, Edinburgh; Bishop of Edinburgh; Primus, Scottish Episcopal Church. Recreations: walking; reading; music; asking people questions. Address: (h.) 19 Eglinton Crescent, Edinburgh, EH12 5BY; T.-031-337 8948.

Haggart, David Ballantine, JP, MA. Writer and Broadcaster; Head of Careers Service, University, 1963-92; b. 15.3.34, Dundee; m., Gwendolen Hall; 3 s. Educ. Aberdeen Grammar School; Aberdeen University. National Service, Band of Royal Corps of Signals, 1956-58; Teacher, Perth and Kinross County Council, 1958-59; Youth Employment Officer, City of Aberdeen, 1959-63; Member, Justices' Committee, Aberdeen, since 1976; Member, Justice of the Peace Advisory Committee, since 1991; Chairman, Ferryhill Community Council, 1976-82; Chairman, Castlehill Housing Association, since 1991; Chairman, Aberdeen and NE Scotland Music Festival, 1982-84; Writer and Producer, educational television programmes, including The Interview (Royal Television Society award); Editor, Current Vacancies, since 1986; regular radio broadcasts, mainly on religious programmes; Presenter, Sunday Best, Northsound Radio, since 1981; Producer, since 1988. Recreations: songwriting; motoring; local history. Address: (h.) 24 Polmuir Road, Aberdeen, AB1 2SY; T.-0224 584176.

Haggart, Mary Elizabeth, OBE. Chairman, Scottish Board of Nursing Midwifery and Health Visiting, 1980-83; b. 8.4.24, Leicester; m., Rt. Rev. A.I.M. Haggart (qv). Educ. Wyggeston Grammar School for Girls, Leicester; Leicester Royal Infirmary and Children's Hospital. Leicester Royal Infirmary: Staff Nurse, 1947-48, Night Sister, 1948-50, Ward Sister, 1950-56, Night Superintendent, 1956-58, Assistant Matron, 1958-61; Assistant Matron, Brook General Hospital, London, 1962-64; Matron, Dundee Royal Infirmary and Matron Designate, Ninewells Hospital, Dundee, 1964-68; Chief Nursing Officer, Board of Managements, Dundee General Hospitals and Ninewells Hospital, 1968-73; Chief Area Nursing Officer, Tayside Health Board, 1974-82; President, Scottish Association of Nurse Administrators, 1972-77; Member, Scottish Board, Royal College of Nursing, 1965-70; Member, General Nursing Council for Scotland, 1965-70 and 1978-82; Member, Standing Nursing and Midwifery Committee, 1971-74 (Vice Chairman, 1973-74); Member, Action on Smoking and Health Scotland, 1978-82 (Chairman,

Working Party, Smoking and Nurses); Governor, Dundee College of Technology, 1978-82; Honorary Lecturer, Department of Community Medicine, Dundee University and Medical School, 1980-82; Member, Management Committee, Carstairs State Hospital, 1982; Member, United Kingdom Central Council for Nursing Midwifery and Health Visiting, 1980-82; Member, Scottish Hospital Endowments Research Trust, since 1986. Recreations: walking; music; travel. Address: (h.) 19 Eglinton Crescent, Edinburgh, EH12 5RY; T.-031-337 8948.

Haggarty, William McLaughlan, TD, BL. Solicitor, since 1950; Senior Partner, Mathie-Morton Black & Buchanan, Ayr; Honorary Sheriff, South Strathclyde, Dumfries and Galloway; b. 22.2.26, Glasgow; m., Olive Dorothy Mary Speirs; 1 s.; 1 d. Educ. High School of Glasgow; Glasgow University. War Service, Merchant Navy, 1943-47; Chairman, National Insurance Tribunal, North and South Ayrshire, 1963-88; Lt. Col. Commanding 264 (Scottish) Regiment, Royal Corps of Transport (TA), 1966; Dean, Ayr Faculty of Solicitors, 1982; Governor, Craigie College of Education, Ayr, 1983-91. Recreations: golf; travel; gardening. Address: (b.) 4 Alloway Place, Ayr; T.-0292 263549.

Hagman, Eric Martin, CA. Managing Partner, Arthur Andersen & Co., Scotland, since 1980; Past Chairman, Royal Scottish Automobile Club; Chairman, ICAS Audit Practice Committee; Member, ICAS Audit Accountancy Working Party; Member, Council, CBI Scotland; Treasurer, Council, Royal Glasgow Institute of the Fine Arts; Governor, Glasgow School of Art; Member, Board, Scottish Financial Enterprise; Trustee, National Galleries of Scotland; Treasurer, Strathclyde Police Dependants Trust; b. 9.7.46, Glasgow; m., Valerie; 4 s.; 1 d. Educ. Kelvinside Academy. Recreations: sailing; skiing; tennis; squash; wine. Address: (h.) Eriska, 49 Sutherland Avenue, Pollokshields, Glasgow; T.-041-427 0471.

Hague, Clifford Bertram, MA, DipTP, MRTPI. Head, Department of Planning and Housing, Heriot-Watt University/Edinburgh College of Art, since 1990; Course Tutor, Open University, 1974-88; b. 22.8.44, Manchester; m., Irene; 1 s.; 3 d. Educ. North Manchester Grammar School; Magdalene College, Cambridge; Manchester University. Planning Assistant, Glasgow Corporation Planning Department, 1968-69; Lecturer, Department of Town and Country Planning, Heriot-Watt University/Edinburgh College of Art, 1969-73, Senior Lecturer, 1973-90; Council Member, Royal Town Planning Institute, 1979-87 and since 1991 (Past Chairman, Scottish Branch). Publication: The Development of Planning Thought: A Critical Perspective, 1984. Recreation: cricket. Address: (b.) Department of Planning and Housing, Edinburgh College of Art, Edinburgh, EH3 9DF; T.-031-229 9311.

Haig, Andrew James Newton, BSc, PhD, CBiol, MIBiol, MIWEM. Assistant Director (Chief Scientist), Clyde River Purification Board, since 1989; b. 2.4.47, London; m., Barbara Mary Jackson; 1 s.; 1 d. Educ. King's School, Bruton; London University; Leeds University. Research Assistant, Leeds University Marine Laboratory, 1968-71; Clyde River Purification Board: Marine Biologist, 1971-74, Assistant Marine Survey Officer, 1974-75, Marine Survey Officer, 1975-89, Assistant Director, 1989. Member, Scottish Council, Institute of Biology, 1978-81. Recreations: natural history; gardening; angling. Address: (b.) Rivers House, Murray Road, East Kilbride, Glasgow, G75 0LA; T.-03552 38181.

Haig of Bemersyde, The Earl (George Alexander Eugene Douglas), OBE, DL, MA, ARSA, KStJ. Painter; b. 15.3.18, London; 1 s.; 2 d. Educ. Cargilfield; Stowe School; Christ Church, Oxford. 2nd Lt., Royal Scots Greys, 1938; retired on account of disability, 1951 (rank of Captain); attended

Camberwell School of Arts and Crafts; paintings in many public and private collections; served Second World War; taken prisoner, 1942; Member, Royal Fine Art Commission for Scotland, 1958-61; Chairman, SE South East Scotland Disablement Advisory Committee, 1960-73; Trustee, Scottish National War Memorial, since 1961 (present Chairman); Trustee, National Galleries of Scotland, 1962-72; Member, Scottish Arts Council, 1968-74; Past Chairman, Royal British Legion Scotland; President, Earl Haig Fund Scotland/Royal British Legion Scotland, 1980-86; President, Scottish Branch, Officers Association; President, Scottish Craft Centre, 1952-73; Vice President, Scottish National Institution for War Blinded and of Royal Blind Asylum, since 1960. Recreations: fishing; shooting. Address: (h.) Bemersyde, Melrose, TD6 9DP; T.-08352 2762.

Haines, Gerald, MA. Rector, Keith Grammar School, since 1989; b. 28.7.38, Glamorgan; m., Avril Esther Shearer; 1 s.; 1 d. Educ. Eastwood Senior Secondary, Glasgow; Glasgow University Teacher of English, Cumbernauld High School, 1964-69; Principal Teacher of English, then Assistant Head Teacher, Lossiemouth High School, 1969-78; Depute Rector, Keith Grammar School, 1978-89. Recreations: bridge; cricket; gardening; golf. Address: (b.) School Road, Keith, AB5 3ES; T.-05422 2461.

Haksar, Vinit, BA, MA, DPhil. Reader in Philosophy, Edinburgh University, since 1980; b. 4.9.37, Vienna; 2 s.; 1 d. Educ. Doon School; Oxford University. St. Andrews University: Assistant in Philosophy, 1962-64, Lecturer, 1964-69; Lecturer in Philosophy, Edinburgh University, 1969-80. Publications: Equality, Liberty and Perfectionism, 1979; Civil Disobedience, Threats and Offers, 1986; Indivisible Selves and Moral Practice, 1991. Recreation: tennis. Address: (h.) 63 Findhorn Place, Edinburgh; T.-031-667 3474.

Haldane, Johnston Douglas, MB, FRCPEdin, FRCPsych, DPM. Psychotherapist and Consultant; b. 13.3.26, Annan; m., Kathleen McKirdy; 3 s. Educ. Lockerbie Academy; Dumbarton Academy; Dumfries Academy; Edinburgh University. Consultant Psychiatrist, Department of Child and Family Psychiatry, Stratheden Hospital, Cupar; Senior Lecturer, Department of Mental Health, Aberdeen University. Recreations: gardening; the arts. Address: (h.) Tarlogie, 54 Hepburn Gardens, St. Andrews, Fife, KY16 9DG.

Haldane, John Joseph, BA, PGCE, BA, PhD. Reader in Moral Philosophy, St. Andrews University, since 1990; Director, Centre for Philosophy and Public Affairs, St. Andrews University, since 1988; b. 19.2.54, London; m., Hilda Marie Budas; 1 s.; 1 d. Educ. St. Aloysius College, Glasgow; Wimbledon School of Art; London University. Art Master, St. Joseph's Grammar School, Abbey Wood, 1976-79; Visiting Lecturer, School of Architecture, Polytechnic of Central London, since 1983; Lecturer in Moral Philosophy, St. Andrews University, 1983-90. Member, Editorial Board, The Philosophical Quarterly, since 1984 (Reviews Editor, since 1990); Member, Editorial Board, Journal of Medical Ethics, since 1991. Recreations: reading; photography; gardening; art. Address: (b.) Department of Moral Philosophy, St. Andrews University, St. Andrews, KY16 9AL; T.-0334 76161.

Halford-MacLeod, Lt.-Col. Aubrey Philip Lydiat, MA (Hons). Army Officer, The Black Watch (RHR), since 1962; Staff Officer, Grade 1, G1 Action and Support Team (Demob Cell), since 1992; b. 28.4.42, Bagdad; m., Alison Fiona Brown; 2 s.; 1 d. Educ. Winchester College; Magdalen College, Oxford. Entry into Sandhurst, 1961; commissioned into The Black Watch as 2nd Lt., 1962; Lt., 1964; Captain, 1968; Adjutant, then Training Major, 1/51 Highland, Perth, 1970-74; Major, 1975; Lt.-Col., 1985; Chief of Staff, Scottish Division, The Castle, Edinburgh, 1988-91; UK Liaison

Officer, US European Command, Stuttgart, 1991; appointed Commanding Officer, Glasgow and Strathclyde Universities OTC. Recreations: walking the dogs; shooting; fishing; opera; model soldiers; curling. Address: (b.) Army HQ, Craigiehall, Edinburgh, EH1; T.-031-310 2352.

Halford-MacLeod, Aubrey Seymour, CMG, CVO, MA (Oxon); b. 15.12.14, Birmingham; m., Giovanna M. Durst; 3 s.; 1 d. Educ. King Edward's School, Birmingham, and abroad; Magdalen College, Oxford. HM Diplomatic Service, Third Secretary, Foreign Office, 1937; Bagdad, 1939; Office of Minister of State, Algiers, 1943; reopened Embassy, Rome, 1944; Secretary, Advisory Council Italy, and Political Adviser to Allied Control Commission, 1943-46; PPS to Permanent Under Secretary, Foreign Office, 1946-49; Deputy Secretary-General, Council of Europe, 1949-52; Tokyo, 1953-55; Libya, 1955-57; Kuwait, 1957-59; Munich, 1959-65; Ambassador to Iceland, 1966-70. Director, Scottish Opera, 1972-77; President, Scottish Society for Northern Studies, 1972-75; Vice-President, Clan MacLeod Society of Scotland, 1973-77; Adviser, Scottish Council (Development and Industry), 1970-77. Recreations: fishing; ornithology. Address: (h.) Mulag House, North Harris, Western Isles, PA85 3AB; T.-Harris 2054.

Hall, Professor Denis R., BSc, MPhil, PhD, FInstP, FIEE, CEng. Professor of Optoelectronics, Heriot-Watt University, since 1986; b. 1.8.42; m.; 1 s.; 1 d. Educ. Manchester University; London University; Case Western Reserve University. NRC Postdoctoral Fellow, NASA Goddard Space Flight Center, 1971-72; Senior Research Scientist, AVCO Everett Research Laboratory, Boston, 1972-74; Principal Scientific Officer, Royal Signal and Radar Establishment, 1974-79; Senior Lecturer/Reader, Department of Applied Physics, Hull University, 1979-86. Address: (b.) Heriot-Watt University, Riccarton, Edinburgh, EH14 4AS.

Hall, Jacqueline, MA (Hons), DMS, DipM. Executive Director, Gordon Enterprise Trust, since 1990; b. 17.1.65, Aberdeen; m., Dennis J.W.G. Hall. Educ. Bankhead Academy, Aberdeen; Aberdeen University; Robert Gordon's Institute of Technology. Executive Officer, Civil Service, 1986-87; Assistant Director, Moray Enterprise Trust, 1987-90. Scottish Young Career Woman of the Year, 1991; Board Member, Grampian, Young Enterprise Scotland; Advisor, Young Enterprise Scotland; Advisor, Princes Scottish Youth Business Trust. Recreations: running; swimming; aerobics; reading; salmon fishing. Address: (b.) The Business Development Centre, Thainstone Agricultural Centre, Inverurie, AB51 9WU; T.-0467 21166.

Hall, Rev. Keith Ferrier, BD (Hons). Minister, Alloa Parish Church (St. Mungo's), since 1987; b. 20.10.55, Arbroath; m., Amilia Elaine Donaldson; 2 s.; 1 d. Educ. Arbroath High School; St. Andrews University. Assistant Minister, Dundee Parish Church (St. Mary's), 1980-81; Minister, Blairgowrie St. Mary's-South, 1981-87. Recreation: golf. Address: (h.) Manse of St. Mungo's, 37a Claremont, Alloa, FK10 2DG; T.-0259 213872.

Hall, Margaret McArthur, CBE, MA, LLB, NP. Director, Legal Services, Scottish Enterprise, since 1990; b. Johnstone; m., William Maurice Hall; 2 d. Educ. Camphill Secondary School, Paisley; Glasgow University. Private practice as Solicitor, 1957-63; East Kilbride Development Corporation, 1963-67; Scottish Enterprise and its predecessor organisations, since 1967; former Member, Council, Law Society of Scotland; Governor, Queen Margaret College, Edinburgh; Member, Secretary of State's Building Standards Advisory Committee. Recreations: walking; Scottish country dancing; orchid growing. Address: (b.) 120 Bothwell Street, Glasgow; T.-041-248 2700.

Hall, Martin R., BSc (Hons), MREHIS, MIEH. Director of Environmental Services, Shetland Islands Council, since 1992; b. 30.3.56, Irvine; m., Joyce; 1 s.; 2 d. Educ. St. Michael's Academy, Kilwinning; Strathclyde University. Student EHO, Saltcoats Town Council, 1974; EHO, Cunninghame DC, 1975-86; Depute Director, Environmental Health and Trading Standards, Shetland Islands Council, 1986-90; Director, EH&TS, 1990-92. Recreations: Scouting; golf. Address: (b.) 3 Commercial Road, Lerwick, ZE1 0LY; T.-0595 3535, Ext. 324.

Hall, Samuel James, BL, NP, WS. Solicitor, since 1951; Partner, Robson, McLean WS, since 1957; Legal Assessor, Professional Conduct Committee, United Kingdom Central Council for Nursing, Midwifery and Health Visiting; Solicitor to the Ministry of Defence (Navy Department) in Scotland; b. 29.5.30, Edinburgh; m., Olive Douglas Kerr; 2 s.; 1 d. Educ. Daniel Stewart's College, Edinburgh; Edinburgh University. Officer, Royal Army Service Corps, until 1953. Recreations: golf; good food. Address: (h.) Carron Vale, 2 Wardie Road, Edinburgh; T.-031-552 1836.

Hall, William, CBE, DFC, FRICS. Member, Lands Tribunal for Scotland, 1971-91; Member, Lands Tribunal for England and Wales, 1979-91; Honorary Sheriff, Paisley, since 1974; b. 25.7.19, Paisley; m., Margaret Semple Gibson; 1 s.; 3 d. Educ. Paisley Grammar School. Pilot, RAF, 1939-45 (Despatches); Senior Partner, R. & W. Hall, Chartered Surveyors, Paisley, 1949-79; Chairman, Royal Institution of Chartered Surveyors in Scotland, 1971; Member, Valuation Advisory Council, 1970-80; Executive Member, Erskine Hospital, since 1976. Recreation: golf. Address: (h.) Windyridge, Brediland Road, Paisley, PA2 9HF; T.-Brediland 3614.

Hall, William Andrew McDonald, MA (Hons). Head Teacher, Dalry Secondary School, Kirkcudbrightshire, since 1973; b. 12.2.37, Airdrie; m., Catherine R.; 1 s.; 2 d. Educ. Airdrie Academy; Glasgow University. Teacher of History, Hamilton Academy, 1962-66; Principal Teacher of History, Mackie Academy, Stonehaven, 1966-73. Recreations: reading; golf; Airdrieonians Football Club; cinema. Address: (b.) Dalry Secondary School, St. John's Town of Dalry, Kirkcudbrightshire, DG7 3UU; T.-064 43 259.

Hall, (William) Douglas, OBE (1985), BA, FMA. Keeper, Scottish National Gallery of Modern Art, 1961-86; b. 9.10.26, London; m., 1, Helen Elizabeth Ellis (m. diss.); 1 s.; 1 d.; 2, Matilda Mary Mitchell. Educ. University College School, Hampstead; University College and Courtauld Institute of Art, London University, 1948-52. Intelligence Corps, 1945-48 (Middle East); Manchester City Art Galleries: Keeper, Rutherston Collection, 1953-58, Keeper, City Art Gallery, 1958-59, Deputy Director, 1959-61. Recreations: music; travel; gardening; wall-building. Address: (h.) 4 Northumberland Place, Edinburgh, EH3 6LQ; T.-031-557 3393; Laidlaws, Spottiswood, Gordon, Berwickshire, TD3 6NQ; T.-05784 277.

Halliburton, Ian Scott. Director, James Finlay Investment Services Ltd., since 1978; b. 30.1.43, Huddersfield; m., Anne Whitaker; 1 s.; 1 d. Educ. Royal High School, Edinburgh; Royal Scottish Academy of Music and Drama. General banking training, Royal Bank of Scotland, 1961-63; RSAMD, 1963-66; professional actor, 1967-70; sales consultant, 1970-71; insurance broker, 1971-78. Director, New Beginnings (Strathclyde) Ltd. Recreations: hill-walking; listening to music; supporting the arts. Address: (h.) 259 Garrioch Road, Glasgow, G20 8QZ; T.-041-946 5426.

Halliday, James, MA, MLitt, JP. Chairman, Scots Independent Newspapers; b. 27.2.27, Wemyss Bay; m., Olive Campbell; 2 s. Educ. Greenock High School; Glasgow

University. Teacher: Ardeer FE Centre, 1953, Kildonan Secondary School, Coatbridge, 1954-56, Uddingston Grammar School, 1956-58, Dunfermline High School, 1958-67; Lecturer in History, Dundee College of Education, 1967-79; Principal Lecturer in History, 1979-87. Scottish National Party, 1956-60; Parliamentary candidate: Stirling and Falkirk Burghs, 1955 and 1959, West Fife, 1970. Publications: World in Transformation - America; Scotland The Separate; A Concise History of Scotland; Story of Scotland (Co-author). Recreations: reading; folk music; football spectating. Address: (h.) 15 Castleroy Crescent, Broughty Ferry, Dundee, DD5 2LU; T.-Dundee 77179.

Halliday, Rt. Rev. Robert Taylor, MA, BD. Bishop of Brechin, since 1990; b. 7.5.32, Glasgow; m., Dr. Gena M. Chadwin; 1 d. Educ. High School of Glasgow; Glasgow University; Trinity College, Glasgow; Episcopal Theological College, Edinburgh. Deacon, 1957; Priest, 1958; Assistant Curate, St. Andrew's, Edinburgh, 1957-60, St. Margaret's, Newlands, Glasgow, 1960-63; Rector, Holy Cross, Davidson's Mains, Edinburgh, 1963-83; External Lecturer in New Testament, Episcopal Theological College, Edinburgh, 1963-74; Canon, St. Mary's Cathedral, Edinburgh, 1973-83; Rector, St. Andrew's, St. Andrews, 1983-90; Tutor in Biblical Studies, St. Andrews University, 1984-90. Recreations: walking; reading; gardening. Address: 35 Carlogie Road, Carnoustie, DD7 6ER.

Halling, Professor Peter James, BA, PhD. Professor of Biocatalyst Science, Strathclyde University, since 1990; b. 30.3.51, London. Educ. Calday Grammar School; Churchill College, Cambridge; Bristol University. Postdoctoral Fellow, University College, London, 1975-78; Research Scientist, Unilever Research, Bedford, 1978-83. Recreation: orienteering. Address: (h.) 34 Montague Street, Glasgow, G4 9HX; T.-041-552 4400.

Halls, Michael, FREHIS, FRSH, MIWM. Director of Environmental Services, Ettrick and Lauderdale District Council, since 1975; b. 6.12.39, Galashiels; m., Sheila; 1 s.; 1 d. Educ. Galashiels Academy; Heriot-Watt. Trainee Burgh Surveyor, Galashiels Town Council, 1959-63; Additional Public Health Inspector, Thame Urban District Council, 1963-64; Galashiels Town Council: Assistant Burgh Surveyor and Sanitary Inspector, 1964-68, Depute Burgh Surveyor, 1968-71, Burgh Surveyor, 1971-75. Last Honorary Secretary, Scottish Institute of Environmental Health, 1978-83; first Senior Vice-President, Royal Environmental Health Institute of Scotland. Recreation: golf; philately; wine-making/drinking; music; eating; photography. Address: (b.) PO Box 4, Paton Street, Galashiels, TD1 3AS; T.-0896 4751.

Hamblen, Professor David Lawrence, MB, BS, PhD, FRCS, FRCSEdin, FRCSGlas. Professor of Orthopaedic Surgery, Glasgow University, since 1972; Honorary Consultant in Orthopaedic Surgery, Greater Glasgow Health Board, since 1972; Visiting Professor to National Centre for Training and Education in Prosthetics and Orthotics, Strathclyde University, since 1981; Hon. Consultant Orthopaedic Surgeon to Army in Scotland; b. 31.8.34, London; m., Gillian; 1 s.; 2 d. Educ. Roan School, Greenwich; London University. The London Hospital, 1963-66; Teaching Fellow in Orthopaedics, Harvard Medical School/Massachusetts General Hospital, 1966-67; Lecturer in Orthopaedics, Nuffield Orthopaedic Centre, Oxford, 1967-68; Senior Lecturer in Orthopaedics/Honorary Consultant, Edinburgh University/South East Regional Hospital Board, 1968-72; Member, Chief Scientist Committee and Chairman, Committee for Research on Equipment for Disabled, 1983-90; Member, Editorial Board, Journal of Bone and Joint Surgery, 1978-82 and 1985-89; Member, Physiological Systems Board, Medical Research Council, 1983-88; President, British Orthopaedic Association, 1990-91

(Chairman, Education Sub-Committee, 1986-89). Recreation: golf. Address: (b.) University Department of Orthopaedic Surgery, Western Infirmary, Glasgow, G11 6NT; T.-041-339 8822.

Hamer-Hodges, David William, MS, FRCS, FRCSE. Consultant Surgeon, Western General Hospital, Edinburgh, since 1979; Honorary Senior Lecturer, Edinburgh University, since 1979; b. 17.10.43, Portsmouth; m., Gillian Landale Kelman; 3 s.; 1 d. Educ. Portsmouth Grammar School; University College London. Senior Registrar, Aberdeen Teaching Hospitals; Research Fellow, Harvard Medical School; Resident Surgical Officer, St. Mark's Hospital, London. Address: (b.) 14 Moray Place, Edinburgh; T.-031-225 4843.

Hamill, Jim, BA (Hons), PhD. Senior Lecturer, International Business, Strathclyde University, since 1989; b. 23.6.55, Port Glasgow; m., Theresa Ann Thomson; 2 s. Educ. St. Columba's High School, Gourock; Paisley College. Lecturer in Economics, Napier College, Edinburgh, 1980-83; Postdoctoral Research Fellow, Strathclyde University, 1983-86; Lecturer (International Business), Strathclyde University, 1986-89; Co-Director, Strathclyde International Business Unit, 1989-91. Publications: five books; 30 journal articles. Recreations: Glasgow Celtic FC; five-a-side football. Address: (h.) 34 Ross Avenue, Renfrew; T.-041-886 4723.

Hamill, Sir Patrick, Kt (1984), QPM, OStJ, BA. Chief Constable of Strathclyde, 1977-85; b. 29.4.30, Clydebank; m., Nellie Gillespie; 4 s.; 1 d. Educ. St. Patrick's High School, Dumbarton. Joined Dunbartonshire Constabulary, 1950, and rose through the ranks until promoted Chief Superintendent, 1970; transferred to City of Glasgow Police, 1972; appointed Assistant Chief Constable, 1974; joined Strathclyde Police, 1975, and attended the Royal College of Defence Studies, 1976; President, Association of Chief Police Officers (Scotland), 1982-83, Honorary Secretary and Treasurer, 1983-85; Member, Board of Governors: St. Aloysius College, Glasgow, 1983-90, St. Andrew's College of Education, Bearsden, 1987-88; Chairman, Management and Development Board, St. Margaret's Hospice, Clydebank, since 1986. Recreations: walking; reading history; golf.

Hamilton, Alex. Writer; b. 14.4.49, Glasgow; 2 d. Educ. Glasgow. Publications: Three Glasgow Writers, 1976; Gallus, did you say? and other stories, 1982; many articles, poems, songs, stories. Recreations: language; literature; music; theatre. Address: (h.) 143 Peveril Avenue, Glasgow, G41 3SF; T.-041-632 2644.

Hamilton, Alexander Macdonald, CBE, JP, MA, LLB. Vice Chairman, Royal Bank of Scotland Group plc; Vice Chairman, Royal Bank of Scotland plc; Chairman, Scottish Committee, The Scout Association; b. 11.5.25, Motherwell; m., Catherine; 2 s.; 1 d. Educ. Hamilton Academy; Glasgow University. Former Senior Partner, now Consultant, McGrigor Donald & Company, Solicitors, Glasgow; former Member, Council, Law Society of Scotland, now Convener, Insolvency and Diligence Committees; President of the Society, 1977-78; former Member, Court House Committee, Royal Faculty of Procurators of Glasgow; Past President, Glasgow Juridical Society; Secretary, Cambuslang Old Parish Church; Vice-Chairman and Legal Adviser, Cambuslang Community Council. Recreations: sailing; golf. Address: (h.) 30 Wellshot Drive, Cambuslang; T.-041-641 1445.

Hamilton, 15th Duke of, and Brandon, 12th Duke of (Angus Alan Douglas Douglas-Hamilton). Premier Peer of Scotland; Hereditary Keeper of Palace of Holyroodhouse; b. 13.9.38; m., Sarah Scott; 2 s.; 2 d. Educ. Eton; Balliol College, Oxford. Flt.-Lt., RAF (retired, 1967); flying instructor, 1965; Instrument Rating Examiner, 1966; Test Pilot, Scottish

Aviation, 1971-72; Member, Queen's Bodyguard for Scotland (Royal Company of Archers), since 1975; KStJ, 1975, Prior for Scotland, 1975-82; Honorary Member, Royal Scottish Pipers, 1977; Council Member, Cancer Research Campaign, 1978; Honorary Air Commodore, Maritime Headquarters Unit 2, R.Aux.AF, 1982. Publication: Maria R, 1991. Address: (h.) Lennoxlove, Haddington, East Lothian.

Hamilton, Arthur Campbell, QC, BA, LLB. Queen's Counsel, since 1982; Judge of the Courts of Appeal of Jersey and of Guernsey, since 1988; President, Pensions Appeal Tribunals for Scotland, since 1992; b. 10.6.42, Glasgow; m., Christine Ann; 1 d. Educ. High School of Glasgow; Glasgow University; Worcester College, Oxford; Edinburgh University. Advocate, 1968; Standing Junior Counsel to Scottish Development Department, 1975-78, Inland Revenue (Scotland), 1978-82; Advocate Depute, 1982-85. Recreations: hill-walking; fishing; music; history. Address: (h.) 8 Heriot Row, Edinburgh, EH3 6HU; T.-031-556 4663.

Hamilton, Professor David Ian, MB, BS, FRCS(Eng), FRCS(Edin). Professor of Cardiac Surgery, Edinburgh University, since 1987; b. 22.6.31, Stockton-on-Tees; m., Myra McAra; 4 s. Educ. Leighton Park, Reading; Middlesex Hospital Medical School. Resident surgical appointments and Demonstrator, Department of Anatomy, Middlesex Hospital, 1957-63; Casualty Officer and Orthopaedics, Royal Surrey County Hospital; Comyns Berkeley Travelling Fellow, Presbyterian Medical Centre, San Francisco, 1967-68; Cardiac Surgeon, Liverpool Health Authority, 1969-86. Examiner, Postgraduate Fellowship in Cardio Thoracic Surgery, Royal College of Surgeons, Edinburgh, 1981-89. President, Society of Cardio Thoracic Surgeons of Gt. Britain & Ireland. Recreation: golf. Address: (h.) Colton, 44 Spylaw Bank Road, Colinton, Edinburgh, EH13 0JG; T.-031-441 1934.

Hamilton, Frank D., OBE. Director (Scotland), Royal Society for the Protection of Birds, since 1972; b. 13.11.32, Edinburgh; m., Kathleen; 1 s.; 1 d. Educ. George Watson's College, Edinburgh. Various posts in industry; joined RSPB, 1958, based first in London, then at HQ, Bedfordshire; developed UK film shows, education, sales and membership; established office in Northern Ireland; returned to Scotland, 1970. President, Scottish Ornithologists Club; Scottish Representative, International Council for the Protection of Birds (British Section). Recreations: bird-watching and bird surveys; walking; wine-making. Address: (h.) 23 Campbell Road, Longniddry, East Lothian, EH32 ONP.

Hamilton, Ian Robertson, QC (Scot), BL; b. 13.9.25, Paisley; m., Jeannette Patricia Mari Stewart; 1 s.; 1 d. by pr. m. Educ. John Neilson School, Paisley; Allan Glen's School, Glasgow; Glasgow University; Edinburgh University. RAFVR, 1944-48; called to Scottish Bar, 1954, and to Albertan Bar, 1982; Founder, Castle Wynd Printers, Edinburgh, 1955; Advocate Depute, 1962; Director of Civil Litigation, Republic of Zambia, 1964-66; Hon. Sheriff of Lanarkshire, 1967; retired from practice to work for National Trust for Scotland and later to farm in Argyll, 1969; returned to practice, 1974; Sheriff of Glasgow and Strathkelvin, May-December, 1984; returned to practice. Chief Pilot, Scottish Parachute Club, 1979-80. Publications: No Stone Unturned, 1952; The Tinkers of the World, 1957 (Foyle award-winning play); A Touch of Treason, 1990; To Steal a Stone, 1991. Recreation: hill-walking. Address: (b.) Advocates' Library, Parliament House, Edinburgh, EH1 1RF.

Hamilton, Rev. Ian William Finlay, BD, LTH, ALCM, AVCM. Minister, Nairn Old Parish Church, since 1986; b. 29.11.46, Glasgow; m., Margaret McLaren Moss; 1 s.; 2 d. Educ. Victoria Drive Senior Secondary School, Glasgow; Glasgow University and Trinity College. Initially employed

in banking, then in music publishing; ordained, Alloa North Parish Church, 1978. Moderator, Presbytery of Inverness, 1990-91. Publication: A Century of Christian Witness; several children's talks published in the Expository Times. Recreation: music (organ and piano). Address: Nairn Old Parish Church Manse, 3 Manse Road, Nairn, IV12 4RN; T.-0667 52203.

Hamilton, Loudon Pearson, CB (1987), MA (Hons). Chairman, Corstorphine Trust, since 1990; Chairman, Lothian Marriage Counselling Service, since 1984; b. 12.1.32, Glasgow; m., Anna Mackinnon Young; 2 s. Educ. Hutchesons Grammar School, Glasgow; Glasgow University. National Service, RA, 1953-55 (2nd Lt.); Inspector of Taxes, Inland Revenue, 1956-60; Assistant Principal, Department of Agriculture and Fisheries for Scotland, 1960; Private Secretary to Parliamentary Under Secetary of State for Scotland, 1963-64; First Secretary, Agriculture, British Embassy, Copenhagen and The Hague, 1966-70; Assistant Secretary, Department of Agriculture and Fisheries for Scotland, 1973-79; Principal Establishment Officer, Scottish Office, 1979-84; Secretary, Scottish Office Agriculture and Fisheries Department, 1984-92. Address: (h.) 5 Belgrave Road, Edinburgh, EH12 6NG; T.-031-334 5398.

Hamilton, Thomas Banks, BAcc, CA. Director, Stakis PLC, since 1991; Chief Executive, Ashbourne Homes PLC, since 1988; Managing Director, Elders PLC, since 1988; b. 22.11.55, Glasgow; 3 s. Educ. Glasgow Academy; Glasgow University. Member, Scottish Health Advisory Council; Director, Independent Healthcare Association. Recreations: hill-climbing; golf; painting; drawing. Address: (b.) 3 Atlantic Quay, Glasgow; T.-041-304 1000.

Hamilton, William, MB, ChB, MD, FRCPGlas, FRCPEdin, DPH, DCH. Paediatric Endocrinologist, in private practice; Paediatrician and Paediatric Endocrinologist, Department of Child Health, Royal Hospital for Sick Children, Glasgow, 1961-89; University Senior Lecturer, 1962-89; b. 22.12.22, Holytown, Lanarkshire; m., Elizabeth Janet Beveridge; 2 s. Educ. Holytown Public School; Dalziel High School, Motherwell; Glasgow University. House Physician/House Surgeon posts, Glasgow, 1952-54; general practice, 1954-56; Registrar medical post, Inverness, 1957-61; Senior Registrar in Paediatrics, 1961-62. Advisor on Postgraduate and Undergraduate Education and Training, Fatah Medical School, Tripoli, Libya. Publications: Clinical Paediatric Endocrinology, 1972; Surgical Treatment of Endocrine Disease; chapter in Diseases of the Fetus and Newborn. Recreations: gardening; vintage car enthusiast. Address: (h.) 81 Woodend Drive, Glasgow, G13 1QF; T.-041-954 9961.

Hamilton, Professor (William) Allan, BSc, PhD, FIBiol, FRSE. Professor of Microbiology, Aberdeen University (Vice Principal, 1988-90); Director, Aberdeen University Research and Industrial Services (AURIS) Ltd.; Chairman, National Collections of Industrial and Marine Bacteria Ltd.; b. 4.4.36, Glasgow. Educ. Hutchesons' Boys Grammar School; Glasgow University. Postdoctoral Research Fellow: Illinois University, 1961-62, Rio de Janeiro University, 1962-63; Scientist, Unilever Research, Bedford, 1963-67; Lecturer/Senior Lecturer, Department of Biochemistry, Aberdeen University, 1967-75; Senior Lecturer/Reader, Department of Microbiology, Aberdeen University, 1975-80. Council, Society of General Microbiology, 1972-76, 1985-89, Treasurer since 1992. Recreations: sailing; wine; skiing; fishing. Address: (h.) 175 Queen's Road, Aberdeen, AB1 8BS; T.-0224 313434.

Hamilton-Grierson, Philip John, MA. Board Member, Highlands and Islands Enterprise; Chairman, State Hospital, Carstairs; Chairman, Northern College; Chairman, Highland Hospice Ltd.; Director, Cromarty Firth Port Authority; b.

10.10.32, Inveresk; m., Pleasaunce Jill Cardew; 1 s.; 2 d. Educ. Rugby School; Corpus Christi College, Oxford. Contracts Manager, Bristol Aircraft Ltd.; Economic Adviser, Joseph Lucas Industries Ltd.; Secretary to Liberal Parliamentary Party; Director, Gallaher Ltd. Fellow, Royal Society of Arts. Recreations: hill-walking; tennis; music. Address: (b.) Bridge House, 20 Bridge Street, Inverness IV1 1QR; T.-Kessock 392.

Hamlin, Professor Michael John, BSc, FEng, FRSE, FICE, FIWEM, MASCE, Hon.LLD (St. Andrews), CBIM. Principal and Vice-Chancellor, Dundee University, since 1987; b. 11.5.30; m., Augusta; 3 s. Educ. St. John's College, Johannesburg; Bristol University; Imperial Coll., London. Consultant on water resources problems; Birmingham University: Professor, Water Engineering, 1971, Head of Department, 1980, Pro-Vice-Chancellor, 1985, Vice-Principal, 1986. Address: (b.) Dundee University, Dundee, DD1 4HN.

Hammerton, Desmond, BSc, CBiol, FIBiol, FIWEM, FBIM, FRSE. Director, Clyde River Purification Board, since 1975; Visiting Professor in Biology, Paisley University; Consultant, World Health Organisation, since 1977; b. 17.11.29, Wakefield, Yorkshire; m., Jean Taylor; 2 s.; 2 d. Educ. Harrow Weald County School; Birkbeck College, London University. Assistant Biologist, Metropolitan Water Board, 1953-55; Research Biologist, Bristol Waterworks, 1955-58; Principal Assistant, Lothians River Purification Board, 1958-62; Director, Hydrobiological Research Unit, Khartoum University, 1962-71; Deputy Director, Clyde River Purification Board, 1971-74. Member, Aquatic Life Sciences Grants Committee, Natural Environment Research Council, 1975-79; Member, Marine Pollution Monitoring Management Group and its Steering Committee, 1974- 91; Member, Steering Committee for the Development of Environmental Quality Objectives and Standards, Department of Environment, since 1981; Member, Scottish Council, Institute of Biology, 1973-76; elected to Committee of Environment Division, Institute of Biology, 1977 (Chairman, Environment Division, 1980-82); Member, Terrestrial and Freshwater Sciences Committee, Natural Environment Research Council, 1985-89; Member, Acid Rain Working Group, Watt Committee on Energy, since 1983; Member, Board of Governors, Paisley College, since 1989; Member of Council, Royal Philosophical Society of Glasgow, since 1990. Recreations: chess; tennis; hill-walking. Address: (h.) 7 Fairfield Place, Bothwell, Glasgow, G7 8RP; T.-Bothwell 852261.

Hammond, John Arthur, PhD, MRCVS, DVSM, DTVM, DAP&E. Senior Lecturer, Department of Tropical Animal Health, Royal (Dick) School of Veterinary Studies, Edinburgh University, since 1978; Editor, Tropical Animal Health and Production, since 1988; b. 21.5.25, Bale, Norfolk; m., Anne Marie Eggleton. Educ. Gresham's; Royal (Dick) School of Veterinary Studies, Edinburgh; London School of Hygiene and Tropical Medicine, London; Royal Veterinary College, London. Veterinary Officer, Tanganyika; Veterinary Research Officer, Tanganyika/Tanzania; Principal Scientific Officer, East African Veterinary Research Organisation, Kenya; Lecturer/Senior Lecturer, Department of Animal Health/Department of Tropical Animal Health, Edinburgh University. Recreations: sport (especially cricket); travel; reading; gardening. Address: (h.) 61 Fountainhall Road, Edinburgh, EH9 2LH; T.-031-667 6146.

Hampson, Stephen F., MA, BPhil. Assistant Secretary, Industry Department for Scotland, since 1984; b. 27.10.45, Grimsby; m., Gunilla Brunk; 1 s.; 1 d. Educ. The Leys School, Cambridge; University College, Oxford. Lecturer, Department of Political Economy, Aberdeen University, 1969-71; Economist, National Economic Development Office, 1971-75; Economic Adviser, Scottish Office, 1975-78 and 1982-84; First Secretary, British High Commission, New Delhi, 1978-81. Recreations: hill-walking; theatre. Address: (h.) Glenelg, Park Road, Kilmacolm, Renfrewshire; T.-Kilmacolm 2615.

Hanley, Clifford. Writer and Performer; Emeritus Professor, York University, Toronto; b. 28.10.22, Glasgow; m., Anna Clark (deceased); 1 s.; 2 d. Educ. Eastbank Academy, Glasgow. Journalist, since 1940; Novelist, since 1957; Songwriter; Broadcaster; Member, Scottish Arts Council, 1965-72; Member, Inland Waterways Advisory Council, 1970-73; Professor of Literature, York University, Toronto, 1979-80. Publications: Dancing in the Streets; Love from Everybody; The Taste of Too Much; Nothing but the Best; The System; The Redhaired Bitch; It's Different Abroad; The Italian Gadget; The Chosen Instrument; The Scots; Another Street, Another Dance. Recreations: music; talk; golf. Address: (h.) 35 Hamilton Drive, Glasgow, G12 8DW.

Hannay of Kirkdale and That Ilk, Ramsay William Rainsford. Landowner, Farmer, Caravan Park Operator, since 1964; Barrister-at-Law, Inner Temple; b. 15.6.11, India; m., Margaret Wiseman; 1 s.; 1 d. Educ. Winchester College; Trinity College, Cambridge (Hons. degree in Law). Called to the Bar and practised in the Bankruptcy Court; called up for service in the Forces, 1939; commissioned, HLI; served throughout the War in Europe, with a short spell in USA and Canada; demobilised with rank of Major; Legal Assistant, then Assistant Solicitor, Board of Trade, 1946-64; Honorary Sheriff, Stewartry of Kirkcudbright; Member, Queen's Bodyguard for Scotland (Royal Company of Archers); President, Dumfries and Galloway Boy Scouts Association; Chief of the Clan Hannay; President, Drystane Walling Association of Great Britain. Recreations: sailing; shooting; fishing. Address: (h.) Cardoness, Gatehouse-of-Fleet, Kirkcudbrightshire; T.-Mossyard 207.

Hansell, Michael Henry, BSc, DPhil. Senior Lecturer in Zoology, Glasgow University, since 1985; b. 5.3.40, Cromer; m., Norma Jean; 1 s.; 1 d. Educ. Malvern College, Worcs; Trinity College, Dublin; Oxford University. Lecturer in Zoology, University of Khartoum, 1966-68; Lecturer in Zoology, Glasgow University, 1968-85. Consulting Editor, Animal Behaviour Journal, 1976-91; Member, Executive Committee, Scottish Field Studies Association, 1989-91. Publications: two books; over 50 papers. Recreations: collecting unnecessary numbers of decorative artefacts from around the world and studio pottery in Britain; reading poetry. Address: (b.) Zoology Department, Glasgow University, Glasgow, G12 8QQ; T.-041-339 8855.

Hansom, James David, MA, PhD, FRGS. Senior Lecturer in Physical Geography, Glasgow University, since 1990; Editor, Applied Geography; b. 9.4.51, Dundee; m., Shelagh Margaret Mitchell; 3 s. Educ. Kirkton High School, Dundee; Aberdeen University. Lecturer in Geography, University College, Dublin, 1977-79; Sheffield University, 1979-90. Publications: (book) Coasts, 1988; 50 scientific papers. Recreations: hill-walking; expeditions; five-a-side football. Address: (b.) Department of Geography and Topographical Sciences, Glasgow University, Glasgow; T.-041-339 8855.

Hanson, William Stewart, BA, PhD, FSA, FSA Scot. President, Council for Scottish Archaeology, since 1989; Senior Lecturer in Archaeology, Glasgow University, since 1990; b. 22.1.50, Doncaster; m., Lesley MacInnes. Educ. Gravesend Grammar School; Manchester University. Lecturer in Archaeology, Glasgow University, 1975; Director, large-scale archaeological excavations at several sites in Scotland and northern England, including complete excavation of the Roman Fort at Elginhaugh, Dalkeith; recipient, Glenfiddich Living Scotland Award, 1987. Publications include: Agricola and the conquest of the north; Rome's north-west frontier: the Antonine Wall (Co-author); Scottish archaeology: new perceptions (Co-author); papers and articles. Recreations: tennis; film. Address: (h.) 4 Victoria Road, Stirling, FK8 2RH; T.-0786 65506.

Harbison, Rev. David John Hislop, MA, BD. Minister, Beith High Church, since 1979; b. 26.8.33, Greenock; m., Winifred Grace Harley Wright; 1 s.; 2 d. Educ. Greenock Academy; Glasgow University. Minister: Whalsay & Skerries (Shetland), 1958-67, Hillhouse, Hamilton, 1967-79. Recreations: fishing; golf. Address: 2 Glebe Court, Beith, KA15 1ET; T.-Beith 2686.

Hardie, Andrew Rutherford, QC (Scot). Treasurer, Faculty of Advocates, since 1989; b. 8.1.46, Alloa; m., Catherine Storrar Elgin; 2 s.; 1 d. Educ. St. Modan's High School, Stirling; Edinburgh University. Enrolled Solicitor, 1971; Member, Faculty of Advocates, 1973; Advocate Depute, 1979-83. Recreation: golf. Address: (h.) 27 Hermitage Gardens, Edinburgh, EH10 6AZ; T.-031-447 2917.

Hardie, Donald Graeme, TD, JP, FRPI. Director, Hardie Polymers Ltd., since 1976, Director, Ronaash Ltd., since 1988; Director, Hardie Polymers (England) Ltd., since 1989; b. 23.1.36, Glasgow; m., Rosalind Allan Ker; 2 s. Educ. Blairmore and Merchiston Castle. Commissioned 41st Field Regiment RA, 1955; Battery Commander 277 (Argyll & Sutherland Highlanders) Regiment RA (TA), 1966; Commanding Officer GSVOTC, 1973; TA Col. Lowlands, 1976; TA Col. DES, 1980; TA Col. Scotland, 1985; ACF Brigadier Scotland, 1987. UTR Management Trainee, 1956-59; F.W. Allan & Ker, Shipbrokers, 1960-61; J. & G. Hardie & Co. Ltd., 1961-81; Director, Gilbert Plastics Ltd., 1973-76. Lord Lieutenant, Strathclyde Region (Districts of Dumbarton, Clydebank, Bearsden & Milngavie, Strathkelvin, Cumbernauld & Kilsyth), since 1990; Hon. Col. 105 (Scottish & Ulster), Air Defence Regiment RA (V); Hon. Col. Glasgow & Lanarkshire ACF; Vice Chairman, Scottish Gunner Council; Member, Executive Committee, Erskine Hospital; Vice President, ACFA Scotland. Recreations: skiing; sailing; shooting; fishing. Address: (h.) Dun Ruadh, Gartocharn, Dunbartonshire, G83 8SB.

Hardie, Sir Douglas Fleming, CBE, JP, FRSA, CBIM. Chairman and Managing Director, Edward Parker & Co. Ltd., since 1960; Deputy Chairman, Scottish Development Agency, 1978-91; Chairman, Grampian Television PLC, since 1989; b. 26.5.23, Dundee; m., Dorothy Alice Warner; 2 s.; 1 d. Educ. Trinity College, Glenalmond. Trooper, 58 Training Regt., RAC, 1941; commissioned RMA Sandhurst, 1942, 1 Fife & Forfar Yeomanry Flamethrowing Tank Regt., NW Europe, 1942-46 (Despatches), Major. Director: Dayco Rubber (UK) Ltd., 1956-86, Clydesdale Bank plc, since 1981, The Alliance Trust plc, since 1982, The Second Alliance Trust plc, since 1982, Alliance Trust (Finance) Ltd., since 1982, SECDEE Leasing, since 1982, Alliance Trust (Nominees) Ltd., since 1982; Chairman, A.G. Scott Textiles, 1985-87; Member: CBI Grand Council, London, 1976-85, Scottish Economic Council, 1977-91; Councillor, Winston Churchill Memorial Trust, since 1985; Director, Prince's Scottish Youth Business Trust, 1987; Past President, Dundee Rotary Club; Vice-President, Fife & Forfar Yeomanry Regimental Association; Deacon Convener, Nine Incorporated Trades of Dundee, 1951-54; Elder, Dundee Parish Church (St. Mary's). Recreations: golf; fishing. Address: (h.) 6 Norwood Terrace, West Park, Dundee, DD2 1PB.

Hardie, Sally Patricia Connally, BA. Member, Executive, National Trust for Scotland, since 1985; Member of Court, St. Andrews University, since 1987; Lothians Chairman, National Art Collections Fund, since 1987; Trustee, Robert T. Jones Jr. Memorial Scholarship Fund; b. 6.2.26, Atlanta; m., John Donald M. Hardie; 2 s.; 1 d. Educ. The Spence School, New York; Vassar College. Recreations: conservation and study of our heritage; gardening; politics. Address: (h.) Chesterhill House, Humbie, East Lothian; T.-087 533 648.

Hardie, William Dunbar, MA, BA. Writer and Entertainer; b. 4.1.31, Aberdeen; m., Margaret Elizabeth Simpson; 1 s.; 1 d. Educ. Robert Gordon's College, Aberdeen; Aberdeen University; Sidney Sussex College, Cambridge. Administrative Assistant, then Assistant Secretary, NE Regional Hospital Board; District Administrator, North District, Grampian Health Board; Secretary, Grampian Health Board, 1976-83. Co-writer and performer, Scotland The What? (comedy revue); writer, Dod'N'Bunty column, Aberdeen Evening Express. Recreations: reading; TV-watching; film and theatre-going; sport; avid and totally biased follower of Aberdeen's football team, Scotland's rugby team, and England's cricket team. Address: (h.) 50 Gray Street, Aberdeen, AB1 6JE; T.-0224 310591.

Hare, Rev. Malcolm McNeill Walker, BA, BD. Minister, St. Kentigern's, Kilmarnock, since 1979; b. 21.11.28, Bangor, N. Ireland; m., Dr. Margaret Kathleen Buick Knox; 1 s.; 1 d. Educ. Sullivan Upper School, Holywood, Co. Down; Trinity College, Dublin; New College, Edinburgh. Minister: Charing Cross, Grangemouth, 1956-63, Langside Hill, Glasgow, 1963-79. Chairman, Scottish Council of the Leprosy Mission, 1982-85. Recreations: golf; music; gardening. Address: (h.) 21 Raith Road, Fenwick, Ayrshire; T.-Fenwick 388.

Hare, Professor Paul Gregory, BA, BPhil, DPhil. Professor of Economics and Head of Department, Heriot-Watt University, since 1985; b. 19.3.46, Hull; m., Susan Jennifer Robertson; 1 s.; 2 d. Educ. Malet Lambert High School, Hull; St. John's College, Cambridge; Nuffield College, Oxford. Technical Officer, ICI, 1967-68; Lecturer, Birmingham University, 1971-72; Lecturer, Senior Lecturer, Reader, Stirling University, 1972-85. Member, Lothian Region Children's Panel, 1981-89. Recreations: hill-walking; reading; listening to choral music. Address: (h.) 34 Saughtonhall Drive, Edinburgh, EH12 5TN; T.-031-337 7329.

Hare Duke, Rt. Rev. Michael Geoffrey, BA, MA. Bishop of St. Andrews, Dunkeld and Dunblane, since 1969; b. 28.11.25.

Hargreave, Timothy Bruce, MB, MS, FRCSEdin, FRCS. Consultant Urological and Transplant Surgeon, Western General Hospital, Edinburgh, since 1978; b. 23.3.44, Lytham; m., Molly; 2 d. Educ. Harrow; University College Hospital, London University. Senior Registrar: Western Infirmary, Glasgow, University College Hospital, London; Medical Officer, Paray Mission Hospital, Lesotho. President, British Andrology Society. Publications: Diagnosis and Management of Renal and Urinary Disease; Male Infertility (Editor); Practical Urological Endoscopy; The Management of Male Infertility. Recreation: skiing. Address: (h.) 20 Cumin Place, Edinburgh.

Harlen, Wynne, OBE, MA (Oxon), MA (Edin), PhD. Director, Scottish Council for Research in Education, since 1990; Visiting Professor, Liverpool University, since 1990; b. 12.1.37, Swindon; 1 s.; 1 d. Educ. Pate's Grammar School for Girls, Cheltenham; St. Hilda's College, Oxford; Bristol University. Teacher/Lecturer, 1958-66; Research Associate, Bristol University School of Education, 1966-73; Research Fellow, Project Director, Reading University, 1973-77; Research Fellow, Centre for Science Education, King's College, London, 1977-84; Sidney Jones Professor of Science Education, Liverpool University, 1985-90. Chair, SCAFA Early Years Forum; Member, Secretary of State's Working

Party on the Development of the National Curriculum in Science, 1987-88. Publications: 20 books; 100 papers. Recreations: concerts; opera; hill-walking. Address: (h.) 26 Torphin Road, Colinton, Edinburgh, EH13 0HW; T.-031-441 6130.

Harper, Professor Alexander Murray, MB, ChB, MD (Hons). Professor of Surgical Physiology, Glasgow University, since 1981; Honorary Consultant Clinical Physiologist, Greater Glasgow Health Board, since 1970; b. 31.5.33, Glasgow; m., Charlotte Maria Fossleitner; 2 s.; 1 d. Educ. Hutchesons' Grammar School; Glasgow University. House Physician and Surgeon, Southern General Hospital and Glasgow Royal Infirmary, 1957-58; McIntyre Research Scholar in Clinical Surgery, Glasgow Royal Infirmary, 1958-60; Scientific Assistant, Medical Research Council, 1960-63; Wellcome Senior Research Fellow in Clinical Science and Honorary Lecturer in Surgery, Glasgow University, 1963-68; Glasgow University: Senior Lecturer in Surgery and Surgical Physiology, 1968-69, Reader, 1969-81. Editor in Chief, Journal of Cerebral Blood Flow and Metabolism, 1981-89; Editor, Cerebrovascular and Brain Metabolism Reviews, since 1989; David Patey Prize, Surgical Research Society, 1966; H.G. Wolff Award, American Association for Study of Headache, 1968; Gold Medal, British Migraine Association, 1976; Honorary Fellow, American Heart Association (Stroke Council), 1980. Recreations: fishing; contract bridge; gardening. Address: (b.) Wellcome Surgical Institute, Glasgow University, Garscube Estate, Bearsden Road, Glasgow, G61 1QH; T.-041-942 2248.

Harper, Rev. Anne J. McInroy, BD, STM, MTh. Chaplain, Glasgow Royal Infirmary, since 1990; b. 31.10.49, Glasgow. Educ. Camphill Senior Secondary School, Paisley; Glasgow University; Union Theological Seminary, New York. Graduate Fellow, Union Theological Seminary, and Assistant Minister, 2nd Presbyterian Church, New York City, 1974-75; research, Church history and liturgics, Glasgow University, 1975-78; Assistant Minister, Abronhill Church, Cumbernauld, 1978-79; Christian Education Field Officer, Church of Scotland Department of Education, 1979-84; Minister, Linthouse St. Kenneth's Parish Church, 1984-90. Holder (first woman), The Scots Fellowship awarded by Union Theological Seminary, New York, 1974. Address: The Chaplain's Office, Glasgow Royal Infirmary, Glasgow, G4 0SF; T.-041-552 3535.

Harper, Professor Anthony John, BA, MA, PhD, CertEd. Professor of German Studies, Strathclyde University, since 1979; b. 26.5.38, Bristol; m., Sandra; 1 s.; 2 d. Educ. Clifton College, Bristol; Bristol University; Exeter University. Lecturer, Department of German, Edinburgh University, 1962-79. Publications: German Today (Co-author), 1967; David Schirmer - A Poet of the German Baroque, 1977; Time and Change, Essays on German and European Literature, 1982; Schriften zur Lyrik Leipzigs 1620-1670, 1985; The Song-Books of Gottfried Finckelthaus, 1988 Address: (b.) Department of Modern Languages, Strathclyde University, 26 Richmond Street, Glasgow, G1 1XQ; T.-041-552 4400.

Harper, Rev. David Little, BSc, BD (Hons). Minister, St. Meddan's Church, Troon, since 1979; Moderator, Presbytery of Ayr, 1991-92; b. 31.10.47, Moffat; m., Janis Mary Clark; 2 s. Educ. Morton Academy, Thornhill; Dumfries Academy; Edinburgh University. Assistant Minister, Cumbernauld St. Mungo's, 1971-72; first Minister, New Erskine Parish Church, 1972-79. Member, Scottish Advisory Committee, Independent Broadcasting Authority, 1974-79; Scottish Member, Religious Advisory Panel, IBA, 1978-79. Recreations: golf; hill-walking; swimming. Address: St. Meddan's Manse, 27 Bentinck Drive, Troon, Ayrshire; T.-0292 311784.

Harper, Douglas Ross, BSc, MD, FRCSEdin, FRCSEng, FRCSGlas. Consultant Surgeon, Forth Valley Health Board, since 1976; Examiner, Royal College of Surgeons of Edinburgh, since 1979; Examiner, Royal College of Surgeons of Glasgow, since 1987; Honorary Senior Lecturer, Department of Clinical Surgery, Edinburgh University, since 1976; b. 16.2.40, Aberdeen; m., Dorothy Constance Wisely; 1 s.; 3 d. Educ. Aberdeen Grammar School; Aberdeen University. House Officer, Registrar and Fellow in Vascular Surgery, Aberdeen Royal Infirmary, 1967-73; Senior Registrar, Edinburgh Royal Infirmary, 1973-76. Elder, Bridge of Allan Chalmers Church of Scotland. Recreations: hill-walking; geology; woodwork. Address: (h.) Glenallan, 16 Upper Glen Road, Bridge of Allan, Stirlingshire, FK9 4PX; T.-0786 832242.

Harper, Edward James, MA, BMus, ARCM, LRAM. Composer, since 1957; Reader in Music, Edinburgh University, since 1990; Director, New Music Group of Scotland, since 1973; b. 17.3.41, Taunton; m., Dorothy Caroline Shanks. Educ. King Edward VI School, Guildford; Royal College of Music, London; Christ Church, Oxford. Main works as a Composer: Piano Concerto, 1971, Bartok Games, 1972, Ricercari in Memoriam Luigi Dallapiccola, 1975, Fanny Robin (chamber opera), Chester Mass, 1979, Clarinet Concerto, 1981, Hedda Gabler (opera, commissioned for Scottish Opera), 1985; Fantasia V (for chamber orchestra), 1985; The Mellstock Quire (chamber opera), 1987; Homage to Thomas Hardy (baritone and orchestra), 1990. Address: (h.) 7 Morningside Park, Edinburgh, EH10 5HD; T.-031-447 5366.

Harper, John Ross, CBE, MA, LLB. Senior Partner, Ross Harper & Murphy and Harper McLeod, Solicitors, since 1962; b. 20.3.35, Glasgow; m., Ursula; 2 s.; 1 d. Educ. Hutchesons' Boys' Grammar School; Glasgow University. Parliamentary Commissioner; Professor of Law, Strathclyde University; Past President, Glasgow Bar Association; Past President, Law Society of Scotland; Chairman, Section on General Practice, International Bar Association; former President, Scottish Conservative & Unionist Association; former Chairman, Society of Scottish Conservative Lawyers; former Parliamentary candidate (Conservative), Hamilton and West Renfrewshire; Honorary Secretary, Scottish Conservative & Unionist Association. Publications: Glasgow Rape Case; My Client My Lord; A Practitioner's Guide to the Criminal Courts; Fingertip Criminal Law; Rates Revaluation; Devolution. Recreations: angling; bridge; shooting. Address: (b.) The Ca'd'oro, 45 Gordon Street, Glasgow, G1 3PE; T.-041-221 8888.

Harris, Rev. John William Forsyth, MA. Minister, Bearsden South Church, since 1987; b. 10.3.42, Hampshire; m., Ellen Lesley Kirkpatrick Lamont; 1 s.; 2 d. Educ. Merchant Taylors' School, London; St. Andrews University; New College, Edinburgh University. Ordained Assistant, St. Mary's Church, Haddington, 1967-70; Minister: St. Andrew's Parish Church, Irvine, 1970-77, St. Mary's Parish Church, Motherwell, 1977-87. Convener, Scottish Churches' Christian Aid Committee, 1986-90; Convener, Scottish Christian Aid Committee, since 1990; Member, Executive, General Assembly's Committee on Church and Nation, 1985-91, and Convener of its Economic and Industrial Interests Sub-Committee, 1987-91; Convener, Scottish Television Advisory Committee on Religious Broadcasting, since 1990; Member, Executive, Scottish Churches Council, 1986-90. Fencing Blue, St. Andrews and Edinburgh; Scottish Fencing Internationalist, 1963-66. Recreations: holiday home in Kintyre; walking. Address: 61 Drymen Road, Bearsden, Glasgow, G61 2SU; T.-041-942 0507.

Harris, Marshall James, DPA. Director, Scottish Educational Trust for United Nations and International

Affairs, since 1986; b. 14.3.28, Edinburgh; m., Matilda Currie Main; 2 s.; 1 d. Educ. Armadale Secondary; Glasgow University. Accountancy, pre-1958; Scottish National Officer, UN Association, 1958-86; Secretary, Scottish Standing Committee for Voluntary International Aid. Former Liberal and Alliance candidate. Recreations: reading; member of Rotary, Liberal International and Royal Institute of International Affairs. Address: (h.) Hopetoun, Charlotte Street, Brightons, Falkirk; T.-0324 715203.

Harris, Professor William Joseph, BSc, PhD. Professor of Genetics, Aberdeen University, since 1987; Managing Director, Scotgen Ltd., since 1987 (Chairman, since 1989); b. 17.11.44, Dundee; m., Linda McPherson; 2 s.; 1 d. Educ. Lawside Academy, Dundee; St. Andrews University. Lecturer, Aberdeen University, 1969-78; Head, Biotechnology, Inveresk Research International, 1978-86; Research and Development Director, Bioscot Ltd., 1986-88; Technical Manager, Biotechnology Investments Cogent Ltd, 1982-88. Awarded DTI Smart Awards, 1987-88-89; Regional Winner, Toshiba Year of Invention, 1989. Recreation: golf. Address: (h.) 3 Caesar Avenue, Carnoustie, Angus; T.-0241 53900.

Harrison, Anthony Frederick, CEng, FIEE, FBIM. Director of Telecommunications, Scottish Office, since 1974; b. 20.2.29, Northampton; m., Doreen Caughlin; 1 s. Educ. Tollington Grammar School, London; Hendon Technical College. Began career in GPO, London and Dollis Hill Research Station; helped introduce first error-correcting radiotelegraph system; joined MEL Equipment Ltd. as Project Manager, 1962; designed first GPO Data Test Set; joined Marconi Space and Defence as Project Group Manager, 1968; Leader, European Consortium, providing all electronics, communications and guidance for European Space Tug; Head of Telecommunications, Greater London Council, 1972-74. Address: (b.) St. Andrews House, Regent Road, Edinburgh, EH1 3DE; T.-031-244 2645.

Harrison, Professor Bryan Desmond, CBE, BSc, PhD, FRS, FRSE, Hon. DAgric. Professor of Plant Virology, Dundee University, since 1991; b. 16.6.31, Purley, Surrey; m., Elizabeth Ann Latham-Warde; 2 s.; 1 d. Educ. Whitgift School, Croydon; Reading University. Agricultural Research Council Postgraduate Research Student, 1952-54; Scientific Officer, Scottish Horticultural Research Institute, 1954-57; Senior and Principal Scientific Officer, Rothamsted Experimental Station, 1957-66; Scottish Horticultural Research Institute/Scottish Crop Research Institute: Principal Scientific Officer, 1966, Senior Principal Scientific Officer (Individual Merit), 1969, Deputy Chief Scientific Officer (Individual Merit), 1981; Head, Virology Department, 1966-91; Honorary Professor, Department of Biochemistry and Microbiology, St. Andrews University, 1987; Honorary Visiting Professor, Dundee University, 1988-91; Past President, Association of Applied Biologists. Recreation: gardening. Address: (b.) Department of Biological Sciences, Dundee University, Dundee, DD1 4HN; T.-0382 23181.

Harrison, Cameron, BSc (Hons), MEd. Chief Executive, Scottish Consultative Council on the Curriculum, since 1991; Rector, The Gordon Schools, Huntly, 1982-91; b. 27.8.45, Mauchline, Ayrshire; m., Pearl; 1 s.; 1 d. Educ. Cumnock Academy; Strathclyde University; Glasgow University; Stirling University. Teacher, Greenock Academy, 1968-71; Principal Teacher of Physics, Graeme High School, Falkirk, 1971-79; Depute Rector, Kirkcudbright Academy, 1979-82; Member, SEB; CCC Sub-Committees (Member, JWP on Higher Physics, 1976-79); Member, several research advisory committees; Chairman, Scottish Central Committee for Physical Recreation; General Secretary, CIDREE. Recreations: lay preacher; used to play rugby (still pretends

to!); music. Address: (h.) 9/3 Damside, Dean Village, Edinburgh.

Harrison, Lloyd, BA (Oxon). Rector, Dollar Academy, since 1984; b. 4.8.34, Bradford; m., Moira Middlemass; 2 s.; 1 d. Educ. Bradford Grammar School. Head of Classics, Glenalmond College, 1960-68; Head of Classics, Leeds Grammar School, 1968-70; Deputy Head, Colne Valley High School, 1970-75; Head, Steyning Grammar School, 1975-78; Head, Northallerton Grammar School, 1979-84. Recreations: cycling in Perthshire and France. Address: (h.) 2 Academy Place, Dollar, FK14 7DZ; T.-0259 42160.

Harrison, Professor Robert Graham, BSc (Hons), PhD, FRSE. Professor of Physics, Heriot-Watt University, since 1987; b. 26.2.44 Oxford; m., Rowena Indrania; 1 s.; 1 d. Educ. Wanstead High School; London University. Postgraduate and postdoctoral research, Royal Holloway College, London, and Culham Laboratories, UKAEA, 1966-72; Lecturer, Bath University; joined Physics Department, Heriot-Watt University. Publications: 160 scientific publications, including editorship of three books. Address: (b.) Physics Department, Heriot-Watt University, Riccarton, Currie, Edinburgh, EH14 4AS; T.-031-449 5111.

Harrison, Sydney, OBE. Proprietor, Paisley and Renfrewshire Gazette Group, 1963-87; Chairman, James Paton Ltd., Printers, 1970-87; Editor, Scot, 1981-87; b. 13.4.13, Glasgow; m., Joan Morris. Educ. Whitehill School, Glasgow. Journalist, various newspapers, 1927-37; Sub-Editor, Glasgow Herald, 1938-39; Army, 1939-46 (Lt.-Col., 1944); Editor, Scottish Field, 1946-63; Director, Scottish Counties Newspapers, 1950-63; Councillor, 4th District, Renfrewshire, 1956-67; Member, Council of Industrial Design, Board of Trade, 1955-65; Honorary Member, Scottish PEN; President, Paisley Burns Club, 1984-85; Past President, Rotary Club of Paisley. Recreations: curling; motoring; caravanning; travel. Address: (h.) Aviemore, Brookfield, Renfrewshire, PA5 8UG; T.-Johnstone 20634.

Hart, Maidie (Jenny Marianne), MA (Hons). Founder President, Scottish Convention of Women, since 1981; b. 15.12.16, Brookfield, Renfrewshire; m., William Douglas Hart; 2 d. Educ. St. Columba's School for Girls, Kilmacolm; St. Andrews University. Church of Scotland: Vice Convener, Home Board, 1967-70, National Vice-President, Woman's Guild, 1967-70, National President, Woman's Guild, 1972-75, Elder, since 1974; Executive Member, Women's National Commission, 1974-76; Member, Coordinating Committee, UK International Woman's Year, 1974-76 (Chairwoman, Scottish Steering Committee); first Chairwoman, Scottish Convention of Women, 1977; Vice President, British Council of Churches, 1978-81; Church of Scotland Delegate to World Council of Churches, 5th Assembly, 1975, WCC European Conference, 1978, WCC Human Rights and Mission Women's Conference, 1980, WCC Sheffield International Conference, 1981. Recreations: travel; walking; family; reading; garden; cooking. Address: (h.) Westerlea, Chapelhill, Dirleton, East Lothian, EH39 5HG; T.-062-085 278.

Hart, Morag Mary, RGN, RSCN, DL, JP. County Commissioner, Dunbartonshire Girl Guides, 1982-90; Deputy Lieutenant, Dunbartonshire, since 1989; Director, Scotsell Ltd., since 1982; b. 19.4.39, Glasgow; m., Tom Hart; 1 s.; 1 d. Educ. Westbourne School for Girls, Glasgow. Sick Children's Hospital, Glasgow, 1956-59; Western General Hospital, Edinburgh, 1960-62. Recreations: reading; gardening; sailing; walking. Address: (h.) 18 Campbell Drive, Bearsden, Glasgow, G61 4NE; T.-041-942 1216.

Hart, Professor Ralph Thomas, BCom, MA, FSS, FBIM, FInstD. Professor and Head, Business School, Robert Gordon's Institute of Technology, 1970- 91; Director: Wall

Colmonoy Ltd., Pontardawe, South Wales, since 1964, John Fleming & Co. (Holdings) Ltd., 1986-89, Aberdeen and District Milk Marketing Board, 1979-89; b. 20.4.30, Newcastle-upon-Tyne; m., Hazel Margaret Norton; 2 s.; 1 d. Educ. Dame Allan's Boys' School; King's College, Durham; Strathclyde University. Industrial appointments, 1950-59, with Electricity Authority, Metal Box Co. Ltd. and National Coal Board; Lecturer, Municipal College of Commerce and Rutherford College of Technology, Newcastle, 1959-62; Senior Lecturer, Scottish Woollen Technical College, 1962-65; Head, Management Studies, Scottish College of Textiles, 1965-70; Dean, Faculty of Arts, Robert Gordon's Institute of Technology, 1974-79; Member: Board for Diploma in Commerce, 1969-88; Scottish Business Education Council, 1973-85 (Chairman, Professional Studies Sector Committee); Member, various committees and boards, Council for National Academic Awards, 1973-83; Chairman, Appeals Committee, Aberdeen, Scottish Health Service, 1974; Member, MSC Training of Trainers Advisory Group, 1981-84; Member, Domestic Coal Users Consumers Council, since 1985. Recreations: fly fishing; tennis; Continental touring. Address: (h.) Grefsen House, Findon Village, Aberdeen; T.-Aberdeen 780330.

Hartnett, Frank Ernest Lawrence, OBE, BSc (Econ), CertEd, DipEdTech. General Manager, Grampian Health Board, since 1991; b. 3.9.40, Alton; m., Catherine Mary Adams; 1 s.; 1 d. Educ. Lord Wandsworth College; London University; Southampton University; Sussex University. Head, Economics Department, Cheshunt Grammar School; commissioned RAF, 1965; lead role in achieving organisational change in RAF training, 1972-75; involved in fast jet operations, RAF Germany, 1975-78; introduction of Tornado into RAF, 1978-81; OFFR and aircrew selection, 1982; OC Trg WG, RAF Hereford, 1982-85; OC Admin WG, RAF Cosford, 1985-87; General Manager, Maternity and Child Health, 1987-89, General Manager, Mental Health, 1989-91, Grampian Health Board. Recreations: hill-walking; shooting; badminton. Address: (b.) 1-5 Albyn Place, Aberdeen; T.-0224 589981.

Hartnoll, Mary C., BA (Hons). Director of Social Work, Grampian Regional Council, since 1978; b. 15.5.39, Bristol. Educ. Colston's Girls School, Bristol; Bedford College, London University; Liverpool University. Child Care Officer, Dorset County Council, 1961-63; various posts, Reading County Borough, 1963-74; Berkshire County Council: Assistant Director, 1974-75, Divisional Director, 1975-77. Member, Board of Directors: National Institute of Social Work, Northsound Radio; Secretary, Association of Directors of Social Work. Recreations: natural history; walking. Address: (b.) Woodhill House, Westburn Road, Aberdeen, AB9 2LU; T.-0224 664957.

Hartshorn, Christina, BA, MSc, DipCG. Enterprise Officer for Women in Scotland, since 1986; b. 18.12.46, Birmingham; 1 d. Educ. Bartley Green Girls' Grammar School, Birmingham; Essex University; Stirling University. Careers Officer, Senior Careers Officer, Fife Regional Council; Lecturer, Napier College, Edinburgh; Tutor, Extra Mural Department, Edinburgh University; Freelance Careers Advisor and Counsellor. Equal Opportunities Fellowship, German Marshall Fund of the United States, 1987. Recreations: friends; hill-walking; clarinet. Address: (b.) Scottish Enterprise Foundation, Stirling University, Stirling; T.-0786 73171.

Harvey, Professor Alan L., BSc, PhD. Director, Strathclyde Institute for Drug Research, since 1988; Professor in Physiology and Pharmacology, Strathclyde University, since 1986; b. 23.6.50, Glasgow. Educ. Hutchesons', Glasgow; Strathclyde University. Lecturer in Physiology and Pharmacology, Strathclyde University, 1974-83; Senior

Lecturer, 1983-86. British Pharmacological Society Sandoz Prize, 1983; British Pharmaceutical Conference Science Award, 1983. Publications: Toxicon (Editor); Snake Toxins, 1991. Address: (b.) Department of Physiology and Pharmacology, Strathclyde University, Glasgow, G1 1XW; T.-041-553 4155.

Harvey, Susan, MA, MIL. Vice-President, International Orienteering Federation, since 1988; Board Member, SE Regional Board, Scottish Natural Heritage, since 1992; Board Member, Training 2000: Scottish Alliance for Woemn's Training, since 1991; b. 3.7.43, Harpendon; m., Robin Harvey, MBE; 1 s. Educ. Claremont, Esher; Edinburgh University. General Secretary, World Orienteeering Championships, 1974-76; Director, Harvey Map Services Ltd., since 1977; President, Scottish Orienteering Association, 1979-80; Secretary General, International Orienteering Federation, 1983-86; Commissioner, Countryside Commission for Scotland, 1988-92. British Ladies Open Champion Orienteering, 1971. Recreations: orienteering; guitar; gardening; carpentry. Address: (h.) Mile End, Doune, FK16 6BJ; T.-0786 841202.

Harvey, Rev. William John, BA (Hons), BD (Hons). Minister, Church of Scotland, since 1964; Leader, The Iona Community, since 1988; b. 17.5.37, Glasgow; m., Isabel Mary Douglas; 2 s.; 2 d. Educ. Fettes College, Edinburgh; Oxford University; Glasgow University. National Service, Argyll & Sutherland Highlanders, 1956-58; Ordained Assistant, Govan Old Parish Church, 1964-66; Member, Gorbals Group Ministry, 1963-71; Minister, Laurieston-Renwick Parish Church, Glasgow, 1968-71; Warden, Iona Abbey, 1971-76; Minister, Raploch Parish Church, Stirling, 1976-81; Minister, Govan Old Parish Church, 1981-88. Member, Church of Scotland Committee on Church and Nation, 1978-86; Kerr Lecturer, Glasgow University, 1987. Recreations: reading; history; bread and wine-making. Address: (h.) Flat 2/1, 99 McCulloch Street, Glasgow, G41 1NT; T.-041-429 3774.

Harvey-Jamieson, Lt.-Col. Harvey Morro, OBE, TD, DL, WS; b. 9.12.08, Edinburgh; m., Frances Ridout; 3 s. Educ. Edinburgh Academy; RMC, Sandhurst; Edinburgh University (BL). 2nd Lt., King's Own Scottish Borderers, 1928; Captain, 1938; Major, RA TA, 1939; Lt. Col., 1943; CO 3rd Edinburgh Home Guard Bn. Royal Scots, 1954-57; Member, Royal Company of Archers (Queen's Bodyguard for Scotland), since 1934; Secretary and Legal Adviser, The Company of Merchants of City of Edinburgh, 1946-71; Member, Committee on Conveyancing Legislation, 1964-66; Chairman, Scottish Committee HMC Association of Governing Bodies of Boys and Girls Public Schools, 1956-70; Member, Council, Cockburn Association, 1957-78; Deputy Lieutenant, Edinburgh, since 1968. Recreation: travel. Address: (h.) 20 Dean Terrace, Edinburgh; T.-031-332 4589.

Harvie, John, MA (Hons). Headteacher, Claremont High School, since 1980; b. 17.8.33, Dalry, Ayrshire; m., Jean D.T. Wallace; 1 s.; 1 d. Educ. Dalry Senior Secondary School; Glasgow University. Teacher: Kilbirnie Junior Secondary School, 1959-61, Duncanrig Secondary School, East Kilbride, 1961-70; Claremont High School: Principal Teacher of Modern Languages, 1970-73, Head of Upper School, 1973-75; Headteacher, Rosehall High School, Coatbridge, 1975-80. President, East Kilbride Rotary Club. Recreations: golf; watching football. Address: (h.) Murrayfield, 3 Clamps Grove, East Kilbride, Glasgow, G74 2EZ; T.-East Kilbride 21352.

Haslett, Professor Christopher, BSc (Hons), MBChB (Hons), FRCP Edin, FRCP Lond. Professor of Respiratory Medicine, Edinburgh University, since 1990; Honorary Consultant Physician, Lothian Health Board, since 1990;

Visiting Professor, Department of Medicine, Royal Postgraduate Medical School, since 1990; b. 2.4.53, Chester; m., Jean Margaret; 1 s.; 1 d. Educ. Wirral Grammar School; Edinburgh University Medical School. House Physician, Department of Medicine, Royal Infirmary, Edinburgh, 1977-87; Rotating Medical Registrar, Ealing Hospital and Hammersmith Hospital, London, 1980-82; MRC Travelling Fellow, National Jewish Hospital, Denver, Colorado, 1982-85; MRC Senior Clinical Fellow and Senior Lecturer, Department of Medicine, Royal Postgraduate Medical School, Hammersmith Hospital, London, 1986-90. Vice-Chairman, National Asthma Campaign Research Committee; Member, British Lung Foundation Research Committee; Member, MRC Systems "A" Grants Committee; Secretary, Lung Injury Section, European Respiratory Society. Recreation: rugby union. Address: (h.) 12 Chalmers Crescent, Edinburgh, EH9 1TS; T.-031-667 6491.

Hastings, Gerard Bernard, BSc, PhD. Director, Advertising Research Unit, Department of Marketing, Strathclyde University, since 1987; Member, Forth Valley Health Board; b. 5.10.56, Ilkley; m., Shelley Anne; 3 s. Educ. St. Michael's College, Leeds; Newcastle upon Tyne Polytechnic; Strathclyde University. Recreations: hill-walking; travel; books. Address: (b.) Department of Marketing, Strathclyde University, 173 Cathedral Street, Glasgow, G4 0RQ; T.-041-552 4400.

Hatwell, Anthony, DFA(Lond). Sculptor; Head, School of Sculpture, Edinburgh College of Art, 1969-90; b. 21.6.31, London; m., Elizabeth; 2 d. Educ. Dartford Grammar School; Slade School of Fine Art; Borough Polytechnic; Bromley College of Art. Exhibited recently: Scottish Arts Council Edinburgh Festival Exhibition, 1978; British Sculpture in the 20th Century, Whitechapel Gallery, 1981; Built in Scotland exhibition in Edinburgh, Glasgow, and London, 1983; Slade Postgraduate Scholarship, 1956; Boise Travelling Scholarship, 1957; Assistant to Henry Moore, 1958; Member, London Group, 1959-69 (Vice-President, 1961-63); works in collections of Scottish National Gallery of Modern Art, Arts Council of GB, Scottish Arts Council and private collections. Address: (h.) 4 North Street, Belhaven, Dunbar, East Lothian.

Havergal, Giles. Director, Citizens' Theatre, Glasgow, since 1969; b. 9.6.38.

Hawkins, Anthony Donald, BSc, PhD, FSA Scot, FRSE. Director of Fisheries Research for Scotland, since 1987 (Deputy Director, 1983-87); Honorary Professor, Aberdeen University; b. 25.3.42, Dorset; m., Susan Mary; 1 s. Educ. Poole Grammar School; Bristol University. Entered Scottish Office as Scientific Officer, Marine Laboratory, Aberdeen, 1965; Senior Scientific Officer, 1969, Principal Scientific Officer, 1972, Senior Principal Scientific Officer, 1978, Deputy Chief Scientific Officer, 1983; conducts research into behaviour and physiology of fish; awarded A.B. Wood Medal, Institute of Acoustics, 1978; Honorary Lecturer in Marine Biology, St. Andrews University. Publications: books on fish physiology and aquarium systems. Recreations: reading; angling; soccer; breeding whippets. Address: (b.) Marine Laboratory, PO Box 101, Victoria Road, Torry, Aberdeen; T.-0224 876544.

Haworth, John Roger, BA (Hons),MRTPI, MCIT. Director of Economic Development, Ross and Cromarty District Council; b. 4.2.46, Worsley, Manchester; m., Margaret; 2 s.; 2 d. Educ. Bolton School; Manchester University. Planning Assistant, Stirling County Council, 1968-71; Ross and Cromarty County Council: Assistant Planning Officer, 1971-73, Assistant Planning Officer (Western Isles), 1973-74; Director of Planning and Development, Western Isles Islands Council, 1974-87. Recreations: reading; music; films; history;

travel. Address: (b.) Council Offices, Dingwall, Ross & Cromarty, IV15 9QN; T.-0349 63737.

Hay, Ann Catherine, OBE. Secretary, Scottish Conservative and Unionist Association, since 1981; Deputy Director, Scottish Conservative Party, since 1990; b. Forres. Educ. Forres Academy. Agent, Edinburgh Pentlands Conservative Association, 1963-65; National Organiser, Scottish Young Conservatives, 1965-68; Secretary, Federation of Conservative Students, 1969-72; Agent, High Peak (Derbyshire) Conservative Association, 1973-76; Deputy Director, Scottish Conservative Party, 1976-81. Recreations: reading; music; sewing; DIY. Address: (b.) Suite 1/1, 14 Links Place, Leith, Edinburgh, EH6 7EZ; T.-031-555 2900.

Hay, Francis (Frank) Walker Christie, OBE, DL, MA (Hons). Deputy Lieutenant, Banffshire, since 1988; Member, National Council, Royal British Legion Scotland; Member, Committee of Management, Legion Housing Scotland; b. 20.3.23, Aberdeen; m., Margaret Anne Castel; 2 s.; 1 d. Educ. Robert Gordon's College, Aberdeen; Aberdeen University. Commissioned into Reconnaissance Corps, 1943; gazetted Captain, 1947; Teacher of History, 1950-58; Special Assistant, Turriff Academy, 1958-63; Principal Teacher of History, Breadalbane Academy, Banff Academy, 1963-74; Assistant Rector, Banff Academy, 1974-88; Member, Banffshire Education Committee, 1961-75. Recreations: furniture making; amateur dramatics. Address: (h.) 11 Fife Street, Banff, AB45 1JB; T.-0261 812285.

Hay, J. Iain, FRICS, IRRV. Vice-Chairman, Royal Institution of Chartered Surveyors in Scotland, since 1989; Consultant to Knight Frank & Rutley, since 1991; J. Iain Hay, Chartered Surveyors, since 1992; b. 17.7.44, Ayr; m., Elizabeth; 2 d. Educ. Kelvinside Academy. Thomas Binnie & Hendry, Chartered Surveyors, 1962-66; Dunbarton County Assessors Office, 1962-69; Bovis Homes, 1969-70; Senior Surveyor, Millar Macrae and Stewart, 1970-72, Partner, 1972-86; Partner, Knight Frank & Rutley, 1986-91; Director, Montrose Estates (1982) Ltd., since 1986. Past President, Property Agents International. Recreations: golf; gardening. Address: (h.) Castle House, Drymen, Glasgow; T.-0360 60550.

Hay, James Taylor Cantlay, MBE, BSc (Hons), DTech, FInstPet, AAPG. Oil and Gas Consultant; Governor, Robert Gordon's Institute of Technology, Aberdeen, since 1981; Member, Aberdeen Beyond 2000, since 1986; Director, International Drilling Technology Centre, since 1991; Chairman, Offshore Command Training Organisation, since 1991; b. 13.6.35, Huntly; m., Mary Gordon Davidson; 1 s.; 2 d. Educ. Banchory Academy; Aberdeen University. Geologist, Iraq Petroleum Co. Ltd., Iraq, 1958-66; Head of Geology, Abu Dhabi Petroleum Co. Ltd., Abu Dhabi, 1967-71; Lecturer in Geology, Aberdeen University, 1971-74; Senior Production Geologist, Burmah Oil, London, 1974-76; various management roles, BNOC, Aberdeen and Glasgow, 1977-80; General Manager, BNOC/Britoil, Aberdeen, 1980-87; General Manager, BP Exploration, Aberdeen, 1988-91. Recreations: golf; shooting. Address: (h.) 67 Fountainhall Road, Aberdeen; T.-0224 645955.

Hay, John McWhirter. Project Sponsor, Scottish Courts Administration, since 1988; b. 27.4.43, Glasgow; m., Mary Wilkie Munro; 3 d. Educ. Clydebank High School. Clerical Officer: Glasgow Sheriff Court, 1960-63, Dumbarton Sheriff Court, 1963-65; Second Class Depute, Glasgow Sheriff Court, 1965-71; First Class Depute, Ayr Sheriff Court, 1971-80; Sheriff Clerk, Dunfermline, 1980-88. Captain, Troon St. Meddans Golf Club, 1975; Captain, Dunfermline Golf Club, 1989-91. Recreations: versatile sportsman, first love golf (single figure handicap, since 1972). Address: (b.) Scottish Courts

Administration, 39 Lauriston Street, Edinburgh; T.-031-229 9200.

Hay, Kenneth McLennan, BEM, ISM, KCLJ, KMLJ, FSA(Scot). Commissioner to Lord Erroll Clan Hay Society, since 1978; Secretary-General, The Monarchist League; Chairman, Royal Celtic Society; President, St. Andrew Society; b. 20.2.18, Edinburgh; m., 1, Irene Mary Roberts; 2, Fiona Dubois MacDonald; 1 s. (deceased). Educ. Flora Stevenson School, Edinburgh. War service, 1939-46: Royal Signals, Scotland, War Office, Burma; retired Executive, GPO; Member, National Committee, Post Office and Civil Service Sanatorium Society; a Governor, Benenden Chest Hospital; Honorary Vice-President, Edinburgh Gaelic Choir; President, St. Andrew Society; former Secretary-General, Grand Commandery Lochore, Military and Hospitaller Order of St. Lazarus of Jerusalem. Publication: Story of the Hays. Recreations: hill-walking; singing; dancing; literature; history; theatre; arts. Address: (h.) 12 St. Peter's Place, Edinburgh, EH3 9PH; T.-031-228 1376.

Hay, Michael James, BSc (Hons), DipEd. Head Teacher, Tynecastle High School, since 1987; b. 8.3.47, Newport Pagnell; m., Rosalind Margaret Gibling; 1 s.; 1 d. Educ. Perth Academy; Edinburgh University. Teacher of Mathematics, Royal High School, 1968-71; Principal Teacher of Mathematics: John Watson's School, 1971-73, Leith Academy, 1973-79; Assistant Head Teacher, Penicuik High School, 1979-83; Depute Head Teacher, Tynecastle High School, 1983-87. Secretary, Lothian Branch, Headteachers Association of Scotland; Chair, Lothian Region SCAMP Steering Group. Recreations: music (organist and choirmaster); hill-walking; recreational computing. Address: (b.) Tynecastle High School, McLeod Street, Edinburgh, EH11 2NJ; T.-031-337 3488.

Hay, Sheriff Principal Robert Colquhoun, CBE, MA, LLB, WS. Sheriff Principal of North Strathclyde, since 1989; b. 22.9.33, Glasgow; m., Olive Black; 2 s.; 2 d. Educ. Edinburgh University. Legal practice, 1956-63, 1968-76; Depute Procurator Fiscal, Edinburgh, 1963-68; Chairman, Industrial Tribunals (Scotland), 1976-81, President, 1981-89; Commissioner of Northern Lights, since 1989, Vice Chairman, 1991-92; Member, Sheriff Court Rules Council, since 1990. Address: (b.) Sheriff Principal's Chambers, Sheriff Court House, St. James Street, Paisley, PA3 2HW; T.-041-887 5291.

Hay, Robert King Miller, BSc, MSc, PhD, MIBiol. Director, Agricultural Scientific Services, Scottish Office Agriculture and Fisheries Department, since 1990; b. 19.8.46, Edinburgh; m., Dorothea Harden Vinycomb; 2 s.; 1 d. Educ. Forres Academy, Moray; Aberdeen University; University of East Anglia. AFRC Research Fellow, Edinburgh University, 1971-74; Lecturer in Crop Production: University of Malawi, 1974-76, Edinburgh University, 1976-77; Lecturer in Environmental Sciences, Lancaster University, 1977-82; Leverhulme European Fellow, Agricultural University of Norway, 1981; Head of Plant Sciences, Scottish Agricultural Colleges, Ayr, 1982-90; British Council Research Fellow, University of Western Australia, 1989. Publications: three books; 50 scientific papers. Address: (h.) 16 Polton Road, Lasswade, EH18 1AA.

Hay, Professor Robert Walker, BSc, PhD, CChem, FRSC, FRSE. Professor of Chemistry, St. Andrews University, since 1988; b. 17.9.34, Stirling; m., Alison Laird; 1 s.; 3 d. Educ. Stirling High School; Glasgow University. Assistant Lecturer, Glasgow University, 1959; subsequently worked at Esso Research; Lecturer, Senior Lecturer and Reader, Victoria University, Wellington, New Zealand, 1961; Reader, Stirling University, 1971; Professor, Stirling University, 1984. Publications: Bioinorganic Chemistry, 1984; numerous sci-

entific papers. Recreations: walking; travel; caravanning; reading. Address: (b.) Chemistry Department, St. Andrews, KY16 9AJ; T.-0334 76161.

Hay, William Flett, CBE (1986). President, Scottish Fishermen's Federation, since 1982; Member, Sea Fish Industry Authority, since 1983; b. 7.10.29, Findochty; m., Sheila Reid; 1 s.; 1 d. Educ. Portsoy School. Took up sea going career in the fishing industry at the age of 14; took command of own vessel, 1954; retired from active sea going career, 1984; Chairman, Scottish White Fish Producers' Association, 1976-82. Recreation: bowling. Address: (h.) Mara Vista, Marine Terrace, Portsoy, Banffshire; T.-0261 42454.

Hayes, Sir John Osler Chattock, KCB, OBE. Lord Lieutenant of Ross and Cromarty, Skye and Lochalsh, 1977-88; Deputy Chairman, Gordonstoun School, 1977-86; b. 9.5.13; m., Hon. Rosalind Mary Finlay; 2 s.; 1 d. Educ. Royal Naval College, Dartmouth. War service, 1939-45, Atlantic/HMS Repulse/Singapore/Russian Convoys/Malta; Real Admiral, Naval Secretary to First Lord of Admiralty, 1962-64; Vice Admiral/Rear Admiral, Flag Officer 2nd in command Western Fleet, 1964-66; Vice Admiral, Flag Officer Scotland and Northern Ireland, 1966-68; Member, Queen's Bodyguard for Scotland (Royal Company of Archers), since 1969; President, King George's Fund for Sailors, Scotland, 1968-79; Vice Patron, Royal National Mission for Deep Sea Fishermen, since 1968. Publication: Face the Music: a sailor's story, 1991. Recreations: music; writing; walking. Address: (h.) Wemyss House, Nigg, Tain, Ross and Cromarty, IV19 1QW; T.-Nigg 212.

Hayes, Peter Clive, BMSc, MB, ChB (Hons), MRCP, MD. Senior Lecturer, Edinburgh University, and Honorary Consultant Physician, since 1990; b. 19.1.57, Stockport; m., Sharon Jane Hayes; 1 s.; 1 d. Educ. Royal High School, Edinburgh; Dundee University. Registrar in Medicine, Ninewells Hospital, Dundee, 1982-85; Research Fellow and Honorary Lecturer, Liver Unit, Kings College Hospital, London, 1985-86; Lecturer in Medicine, Edinburgh University, 1986-90. Recreations: fishing; squash; cricket. Address: (b.) Department of Medicine, Royal Infirmary, Edinburgh, EH3 9YW; T.-031-229 2477, Ext. 3165.

Hayman, David. Actor, Director, Film-maker; Artistic Director, 7:84 Scottish People's Theatre; b. Glasgow; m., Alice Griffin; 2 s. Educ. Kingsridge Senior Secondary School, Drumchapel; Royal Scottish Academy of Music and Drama. Address: (b.) 302 Buchanan Street, Glasgow, G2 3LB; T.-041-331 2219.

Heading, Robert Campbell, BSc, MD, FRCP. Consultant Physician, Edinburgh Royal Infirmary, since 1975; Senior Lecturer in Medicine, Edinburgh University, since 1975; b. 3.7.41, Stepps, Lanarkshire; m., Patricia Mary Goldie; 2 s.; 1 d. Educ. Birkenhead School; King Edward's School, Birmingham; Edinburgh University. Address: (h.) 20 Frogston Road West, Edinburgh, EH10 7AR; T.-031-445 1552.

Heald, Professor David Albert, BA, ACMA. Professor of Accountancy, Aberdeen University, since 1990; Specialist Adviser, Treasury and Civil Service Committee, House of Commons, since 1989; Visiting Fellow, Department of Government, London School of Economics, since 1990; b. 25.9.47, York. Educ. Nunthorpe Grammar School, York; Leicester University; Jordanhill College. Accountant, Raleigh Industries, 1969-70, British Steel Corporation, 1971-72; Lecturer in Economics, Glasgow College of Technology, 1972-78; Lecturer in Economics, later in Management Studies, Glasgow University, 1978-90. Labour Parliamentary candidate, Roxburgh, Selkirk and Peebles, 1979. Publications:

several books and numerous articles, including: Making Devolution Work; Financing Devolution within the UK; A Study of the Lessons from Failure; Public Expenditure: its defence and reform; Financing a Scottish Parliament: options for debate. Recreations: theatre; cinema; everything French; squash; boating on the Moray Firth; hoping for the next Grand Slam. Address: (b.) Department of Accountancy, Aberdeen University, Edward Wright Building, Aberdeen, AB9 2TY; T.-0224 272213.

Healy, Raymond Michael, BSc. Headmaster, Lourdes Secondary School, Glasgow, since 1987 (Rector, Our Lady's High School, Cumbernauld, 1976-86); b. 8.7.40, Glasgow; m., Margaret Bradburn; 2 s. Educ. St. Aloysius College, Glasgow; Glasgow University; Jordanhill College of Education. Research Department: Babcock & Wilcox Ltd., Renfrew, 1961-62, Sandeman Bros., Glasow, 1962-63; Teacher: St. Margaret Mary's Secondary School, Glasgow, 1964-65, St. Aloysius College, Glasgow, 1965-69; Principal Teacher of Chemistry, St. Aloysius College, Glasgow, 1969-72; Assistant Headteacher, St. Andrew's High School, Clydebank, 1972-74; Depute Headteacher, St. Patrick's High School, Dumbarton, 1974-76. Member, Scottish Central Committee on Science, 1978-81. Recreation: golf. Address: (b.) Lourdes Secondary School, 47 Kirriemuir Avenue, Glasgow, G52 3DF.

Heaney, Henry Joseph, MA, FLA. University Librarian and Keeper of the Hunterian Books and MSS, Glasgow University, since 1978; b. 2.1.35, Newry, Northern Ireland; m., Mary Elizabeth Moloney. Educ. Abbey Grammar School, Newry; Queen's University, Belfast. Assistant Librarian, Queen's University, Belfast, 1959-62; Librarian, Magee University College, Londonderry, 1962-69; Deputy Librarian, New University of Ulster, 1967-69; Assistant Secretary, Standing Conference of National and University Libraries, 1969-72; Librarian: Queen's University, Belfast, 1972-74, University College, Dublin, 1975-78. Member, Advisory Committee on Public Library Service, Northern Ireland, 1965; Chairman, NI Branch, Library Association, 1966, 1973; Trustee, National Library of Scotland, 1980-91; Chairman, British Library Ad Hoc Working Party on Union Catalogues, 1982; Member: British Library Board, since 1989, British Library Reference Division Advisory Committee, 1982-89, British Library Lending Division Advisory Committee, 1983-86, British Eighteenth Century Short Title Catalogue Committee, since 1983, Standing Committee, University Libraries Section, IFLA, 1986-91; Trustee, National Manuscripts Conservation Trust, since 1989; Editor, World List of Abbreviations of Organisations; President, Scottish Library Association, 1990. Address: (b.) Glasgow University Library, Hillhead Street, Glasgow, G12 8QE; T.-041-330 5633.

Hearne, John Michael, BMus, MMus. Publisher (Longship Music); Past Chairman, Scottish Society of Composers; Freelance Composer and Professional Singer; Chairman, Scottish Music Advisory Committee, BBC; Member, Central Music Advisory Committee, BBC; Lecturer, Aberdeen College of Education, 1970-87; b. 19.9.37, Reading; m., Margaret Gillespie Jarvie. Educ. Torquay Grammar School; St. Luke's College, Exeter; University College of Wales, Aberystwyth. Teaching, Rugeley, Staffordshire, 1959-60; Warehouseman/Driver, Torquay, 1961-64; Teaching: Tonlistarskoli Borgarfjardar, Iceland, 1968-69, UCW Aberystwyth, 1969-70; Composer, vocal, instrumental and incidental music; Member, John Currie Singers; McEwen Commission, Glasgow University, 1979; President, Garioch Lions Club, 1984-85; Chorus Manager, Aberdeen International Youth Festival, since 1978; won Radio Forth Trophy, 1985, for most outstanding work on Edinburgh Festival Fringe; Chairman, Gordon Forum for the Arts; Conductor, Stonehaven and District Choral Society.

Recreations: motoring and travel (1954 Daimler Roadster). Address: (h.) Smidskot, Fawells, Keith-Hall, Inverurie, AB51 OLN; T.-065 182 274.

Heasman, Michael Anthony, FRCPEdin, FFCM, FFPHM, DPH. Director, Information Services Division, Scottish Health Service, Common Services Agency, 1974-86; Expert in Health Statistics, World Health Organisation, 1965-88; Honorary Senior Lecturer, Department of Community Medicine, Edinburgh University, 1976-86; b. 9.9.26, Colchester; m., Barbara Nelly Stevens; 1 s.; 1 d. Educ. Felsted School; St. Mary's Hospital, London University. RAF Medical Branch, 1948-53; Research Fellowships, London School of Hygiene, 1954-56; Medical Statistician, General Register Office, London, 1956-61; Senior Medical Officer, Ministry of Health, 1961-65; Principal Medical Officer, Scottish Home and Health Department, 1965-74. Recreations: hill-walking; literature. Address: (h.) 1 Monkrigg Steading, Haddington, East Lothian, EH41 4LB.

Heatly, Sir Peter, CBE, DL, BSc, CEng, FICE. Chairman, Peter Heatly & Co. Ltd., since 1958; Chairman, Scottish Sports Council, 1975-87; Chairman, Commonwealth Games Federation, 1982-90; b. 9.6.24, Edinburgh; m., Mae Calder Cochrane. Educ. Leith Academy; Edinburgh University. Structural Designer, Redpath Brown & Co. Ltd., 1946; Lecturer in Civil Engineering, Edinburgh University, 1948. Chairman, International Diving Committee, 1984-88. Recreations: swimming; gardening; travel. Address: (h.) Lanrig, Balerno, Edinburgh, EH14 7AJ; T.-031-449 3998.

Hector, Gordon Matthews, CMG (1966), CBE (1961), MA (Oxon). Vice President, The St. Andrew Society; Secretary to Assembly Council, General Assembly of Church of Scotland, 1980-85; b. 9.6.18, Aberdeen; m., Dr. Mary Forrest Gray; 1 s.; 2 d. Educ. St. Mary's School, Melrose; Edinburgh Academy; Lincoln College, Oxford. HM Colonial Administrative Service and Overseas Civil Service, 1946-66: District Commissioner, Kenya, Secretary, Kenya Road Authority, Secretary to Government of Seychelles, 1952-55, Acting Governor, 1953, Deputy Resident Commissioner and Government Secretary, Basutoland (now Lesotho), 1956-64, Deputy British Government Representative, Lesotho, 1965-66; Aberdeen University: Clerk to University Court, 1967, Deputy Secretary, 1976-80. OBE, 1955. Fellow, Commonwealth Fund, 1939; Burgess of Guild, Aberdeen; Chairman, West End Community Council, Edinburgh, 1986-89; Court of Directors, Edinburgh Academy, 1967-75; Chairman, Great North of Scotland Railway Association; Chairman, Scottish Council, Victoria League, 1983-88; Member, sometime Chairman, Board of Managers, Oakbank List D School, 1969-90. Recreations: town and country walking; railways ancient and modern; grandchildren. Address: (h.) 4 Montgomery Court, 110 Hepburn Gardens, St. Andrews, KY16 9LT; T.-0334 73784.

Hedderwick, Mairi Crawford, DA (Edin). Illustrator, Writer and Public Speaker; b. 2.5.39, Gourock; 1 s.; 1 d. Educ. St. Columba's School, Kilmacolm; Edinburgh College of Art; Jordanhill College of Education. Art Teacher, mid-Argyll primary schools, 1962; Hebridean "dropping out", crofting, child rearing, 1964-73; part-time art teaching 1979; part-time lecturing, Inverness Technical College, 1985-86; part-time work for HIDB with Highlands and Islands community co-operatives, 1986-88. Recreations: a day outside ending round a table with friends, food and wine. Address: Isle of Coll, Argyll, PA78 6TB.

Hedley, James, BA (Hons), DipEd, Hon.MCGLI, FRSA. Principal, Inverness College, since 1979; b. 1.11.34, Newcastle upon Tyne; m., Barbara Wilson; 2 d. Educ. Heaton Grammar School; King's College, Durham. Lecturer, Stockton-Billingham Technical College, 1959-67; Head of

Department, Inverness Technical College, 1968-72; Vice-Principal, SE Northumberland Technical College/North Tyneside College of Further Education, 1973-79. Member, Highlands and Islands Area Manpower Board, 1982-85; Honorary Member, City and Guilds of London Institute, since 1983; Member, Manpower Services Committee, Scotland, 1985-88; Member, Scottish Examination Board, 1986-90; Member, Forestry Training Council, Education Scotland, since 1987; Member Convocation, Heriot-Watt University, 1991-94. Recreations: theatre; music; swimming; cricket; Newcastle United FC. Address: (b.) 3 Longman Road, Inverness, IV1 1SA; T.-Inverness 236681.

Heggie, Douglas Cameron, MA, PhD, FRAS, FRSE. Reader in Mathematics, Edinburgh University, since 1985; b. 7.2.47, Edinburgh; m., Linda Jane Tennent; 2 d. Educ. George Heriot's School, Edinburgh; Trinity College, Cambridge. Research Fellow, Trinity College, Cambridge, 1972-76; Lecturer in Mathematics, Edinburgh University, 1975-85. Council Member, Royal Astronomical Society, 1982-85; President, Commission 37, International Astronomical Union, 1985-88. Publications: Megalithic Science; scientific papers on dynamical astronomy. Recreations: family life; walking; music. Address: (b.) Edinburgh University, Department of Mathematics, King's Buildings, Edinburgh, EH9 3JZ; T.-031-650 5035.

Heller, Martin Fuller Vernon. Actor, since 1947; b. 20.2.27, Manchester; m., Joyce Allan; 2 s.; 4 d. Educ. Rondebosch Boys High School, Cape Town; Central School of Speech Training and Dramatic Art, London. Compass Players, 1948-52; repertory seasons and/or individual productions at following Scottish theatres: St. Andrews Byre, Edinburgh Gateway, Glasgow Citizens' (eight seasons), Edinburgh Royal Lyceum, Edinburgh Traverse, Dundee Repertory, Perth Repertory, Pitlochry Festival; Founder Member, Prime Productions, 1986; appeared in England at Morecambe, Preston, Carlisle, Birmingham, Coventry, Leicester and Hammersmith; extensive television and radio work; Equity: Member, Scottish Committee, National Council, three times; Member, Scottish Arts Council, 1975-82 (latterly Chairman, Drama Committee); Board Member, Scottish Youth Theatre; Board Member, Pitlochry Festival Theatre; Governor, Royal Scottish Academy of Music and Drama, since 1982. Recreations: politics; history; listening to music. Address: (h.) 54 Hermiston, Currie, Midlothian, EH14 4AQ; T.-031-449 4055.

Helms, Professor Peter Joseph, MB, BS, PhD, FRCP. Professor of Child Health, Aberdeen University, since 1991; Consultant Paediatrician, since 1982; b. 26.6.47, Melbourne; m., Kathleen Mary; 1 s.; 3 d. Educ. Wimbledon College; Royal Free Hospital School of Medicine; London University. SHO, Hospital for Sick Children, Great Ormond Street, 1976; Lecturer in Paediatrics, Charing Cross Hospital Medical School, 1977-78; Research Fellow, Institute of Child Health, London, 1978-81; National Heart and Lung Institute, London, 1981-82; Senior Lecturer, Institute of Child Health, 1982-91; Honorary Consultant Paediatrician, Hospital for Sick Children, Great Ormond Street, 1982-91. Recreations: music; hill-walking; European history. Address: (b.) Department of Child Health, Foresterhill, Aberdeen, AB9 4ZD; T.-0224 681818.

Hemingway, Dennis, BSc, FSS, AFIMA. Secretary, Scottish Nursery Nurses' Board, since 1974; Consultant, Education Training and Administrative Services, since 1988; b. 28.6.35, Wakefield; m., Rosalie; 1 s.; 3 d. Educ. Normanton Grammar School; Leeds University. Technical Engineer, Bristol Aeroplane Company, 1955-60; Assistant Lecturer, Lecturer and Senior Lecturer, Bristol Technical College, 1960-65; Deputy Secretary, then Secretary, Union of Lancashire and Cheshire Institutes, 1965-74; Chief Officer, Scottish Technical Education Council, 1974-85; Depute Director, Scottish Vocational Education Council, 1985-87. Chairman, Ayrshire Branch, Leukaemia Research Fund; President, Dundonald Historical Society. Recreations: bridge; sailing; swimming. Address: (h.) 6 Kilnford Crescent, Dundonald, Kilmarnock, KA2 9DW; T.-0563 850057.

Hemingway, Professor R. Gordon, MSc, PhD. Professor of Veterinary Animal Husbandry, Glasgow University Veterinary School, 1969-90; b. 6.4.25, Sheffield; m., Dorothy E. Adam; 2 d. Educ. King Edward VII School, Sheffield; Leeds University. Ministry of Agriculture and Fisheries, 1946-48; Royal Agricultural College, Cirencester, 1948-53; joined Glasgow University, 1953. Past Chairman: Agriculture Group, Society of Chemical Industry, Scottish Group, Nutrition Society. Recreations: golf; gardening; grandchildren. Address: (h.) Eaglesfield, Milndavie Road, Strathblane, Glasgow, G63 9EL; T.-0360 70044.

Hemmings, Douglas Thorley, OBE, DPA, FBIM. Chief Executive Officer, Cumnock and Doon Valley District Council, since 1975; b. 29.12.26, Leeds; m., Aloisia; 1 s.; 1 d. Educ. Ayr Academy. Ayr County Council, 1952-75. Member, Board of Management, Cumnock and Doon Enterprise Trust; President, Burns Memorial Homes, Mauchline. Address: (h.) 2 Broadwood Park, Ayr; T.-Alloway 42742.

Henderson, Andrew Kerr, MB, ChB, FRCP. Consultant Physician, County Hospital, Oban, since 1977; Postgraduate Tutor in Medicine, since 1980; Honorary Clinical Lecturer, Glasgow University, since 1981; b. 1.3.46, Hawick; m., Doreen Innes Wilkinson; 1 s.; 2 d. Educ. Glasgow Academy; Glasgow University. Medical Registrar, Western Infirmary, Glasgow; Medical Registrar/Senior Registrar, Glasgow Royal Infirmary. Chairman, Counties Branch, Scottish Schoolboys' Club. Recreations: gardening; hill-walking. Address: (h.) Birkmoss, North Connel, Argyll; T.-Connel 379.

Henderson, Douglas Mackay, CBE, BSc, FLS, FRSE, VMH. Administrator, Inverewe Garden, National Trust for Scotland, since 1987; Queen's Botanist in Scotland, since 1987; b. 30.8.27, Blairgowrie; m., Julia Margaret Brown; 1 s.; 2 d. Educ. Blairgowrie High School; Edinburgh University. Scientific Officer, Department of Agriculture, Scotland, 1948-50; Research Botanist, Royal Botanic Garden, Edinburgh, 1950-70; Curator, Royal Society of Edinburgh, 1978-87; Secretary, International Association of Botanical Gardens, 1969-81; Regius Keeper, Royal Botanic Garden, Edinburgh, 1970-87; Honorary Professor, Edinburgh University, since 1982. Recreations: natural history; painting; sailing; cooking. Address: (h.) Inverewe House, Poolewe, Wester Ross, IV22 2LQ; T.-044 586 200.

Henderson, Elizabeth Brebner. Member, Fife Regional Council; a Director, Royal Scottish National Orchestra, since 1986; Chairman, Glenrothes College Council, since 1990; b. 23.5.14, Aberdeen; m., David McCreath (deceased); 1 s.; 1 d. Educ. Middle School, Aberdeen; Cregg College, Aberdeen. President, Old People's Welfare (Glenrothes); Founder Chairman, Glenrothes Citizens: Advice Bureau. Recreations: golf; swimming; walking; reading. Address: (b.) Fife Regional Council, Glenrothes, Fife; T.-0592 754411, Ext. 6536.

Henderson, Elizabeth Kidd, MA (Hons), MEd (Hons). Member, Church of Scotland Education Committee and Finance Committee, Board of Education; Headmistress, Westbourne School, 1970-88; b. 25.5.28, Dunfermline. Educ. Dunfermline High School; Edinburgh University; St. Andrews University. Mathematics Teacher, Morrison's Academy, Crieff; Second Master, Mathematics, Dundee High School; Principal Teacher of Mathematics, Aberdeen High

School; former Secretary, Mathematics Panel, Scottish Examination Board; President, Scottish Area, Secondary Heads Association; President, Glasgow Mathematical Association. Chairman, Community Council. Publication: Modern Mathematics for Schools (Co-author). Recreations: walking; golf. Address: (h.) 16 George Reith Avenue, Glasgow, G12 0AN; T.-041-334 8545.

Henderson, Most Rev. George Kennedy Buchanan, MBE, BA, JP. Primus, Scottish Episcopal Church, since 1990; Bishop of Argyll and the Isles, since 1977; b. 5.12.21, Oban; m., Isobel Fergusson Bowman. Educ. Oban High School; Durham University. Assistant Curate, Christ Church, Glasgow, 1943-48; Chaplain, Bishop of Argyll and the Isles, 1948-50; Rector, St. Andrew's, Fort William, 1950-77; Canon, St. John's Cathedral, Oban, 1962; Dean of Argyll, 1974. Honorary Burgess of Fort William, 1973; Honorary Sheriff, 1974. Address: Bishop's House, Achnalea, Onich, by Fort William, PH33 6SA; T.-Onich 240.

Henderson, Graeme Macdonald, BA, LLB, DipLP. Advocate, since 1987; b. 28.2.60, Edinburgh. Educ. Royal High School; Edinburgh University. Hon Secretary, The Eccentric Flamingoes. Recreations: rugby; cricket; golf; hockey. Address: (h.) 18 Leopold Place, Edinburgh, EH7 5LB; T.-031-557 0368.

Henderson, John Harley, JP. Member, City of Dundee District Council, since 1974 (Convener of Housing, since 1984); Teacher of Mathematics, St. John's High School, Dundee, since 1976; b. 17.8.41, Dundee; m., Peggy Henderson; 1 s.; 1 d. Educ. Lawside Academy, Dundee; Dundee College of Technology. Former Divisional Council Secretary, AUEW-TASS; Dundee District Council: former Secretary and Leader, Administration Group, former Convener of Cleansing, former Convener of Planning and Development; Member, Housing Committee, COSLA. Address (h.) 24 Burrelton Gardens, Dundee; T.-0382 811982.

Henderson, Merryn Sinclair, OBE, RGN, FBIM. Director of Contracts and Standards, Shetland Health Board, since 1991, Chief Area Nursing Officer, since 1974, Executive Member, since 1991; b. 3.10.37, Liverpool; m., William Henderson. Educ. Waterloo Park School; United Liverpool Hospitals Nurse Training School. Staff nurse, 1960; surgical ward sister, 1961-71; Nursing Officer and Acting Senior Nursing Officer, Shetland Hosptals, 1971-74. Former Member: Shetland Children's Panel, Children's Panel Advisory Committee; President, Royal College of Nursing Shetland Branch, 1975-77. Address: (h.) Vanby, 40 Twageos Road, Lerwick, Shetland.

Henderson, Major Richard Yates, TD, JP, BA (Oxon), LLB. Lord Lieutenant, Ayrshire and Arran, since 1991; b. 7.7.31, Nitshill; m., Frances Elizabeth Chrystal; 3 s. (inc. 1 s. dec.); 1 d. Educ. Rugby; Hertford College, Oxford; Glasgow University. Royal Scots Greys, 1950-52; TA Ayrshire (ECO) Yeomanry, 1953-69 (Major); Deputy Lieutenant, Ayrshire and Arran, 1970-90; Partner, Mitchells Roberton, Solicitors, 1958-90, Consultant, since 1991; Member, Queen's Bodyguard for Scotland (Royal Company of Archers). Chairman, SSAFA/FHS, Ayrshire. Recreations: shooting; tennis; golf. Address: (h.) Blairston, by Ayr; T.-0292 41601.

Henderson, Stewart Alexander, RIBA, FRIAS. Director of Technical Services, Edinburgh District Council; b. 18.1.47, Glasgow; m., Gillian Wallace; 1 s.; 1 d. Educ. Falkirk High School; Glasgow School of Art. Private practice, Glasgow; Principal Architect, Stewartry District; Depute Director of Architectural Services, Stornoway; Chief Architect, Clydesdale District; Chief Architect, Scottish & Newcastle. Council Member, RIAS, EAA. Recreations: shooting; stalk-

ing; fishing. Address: (b.) 329 High Street, Edinburgh; T.-031-225 2424, Ext. 5300.

Henderson, Thomas Wilson. Director, John Turnbull & Sons Ltd., Hawick, since 1983; Member, Ettrick and Lauderdale District Council, since 1974; Provost of Selkirk, since 1978; b. 28.9.41, Selkirk; m., Catherine Helen Herbert; 2 s. Educ. Selkirk Public School; Selkirk High School; Scottish College of Textiles; Paisley College of Technology. Served apprenticeship as dyer with George Roberts & Co. Ltd., Selkirk, 1957-61; Dyer, Grays Carpets, Ayr, 1961-70; Assistant Manager, John Turnbull & Sons Ltd., Hawick, 1978-83; involved in management buy-out, 1983; Member, Selkirk Town Council, 1973-75; Corporate Member, Society of Dyers and Colourists; holder of various offices, Transport and General Workers Union, since 1970; Organiser, Scottish National Party, Ayr Constituency, 1967-70. Recreations: hill-walking; horse-riding; reading; folk music; jazz; football; cricket. Address: (h.) Triglav, 29 Shawpark Crescent, Selkirk; T.-0750 20821.

Henderson, Sheriff William Crichton, MA, LLB. Sheriff of Tayside, Central and Fife, at Stirling, since 1972; b. 10.6.31.

Henderson, William Leonard Edgar, BSc (Hons). Principal, Falkirk College of Technology, since 1984; b. 9.5.39, Kilmarnock; m., Janette Anne; 2 d. Educ. Camphill School, Paisley; London University. Lecturer, Engineering and Associated Subjects, Anniesland College, 1966-68; Lecturer, Engineering Subjects, Stow College/Glasgow College of Technology, 1968-70; Senior Lecturer in Engineering, Anniesland College, 1970-74; Head, Department of Science and Mathematics, Cardonald College, 1974-77; Depute Principal, Kingsway Technical College, Dundee, 1977-84; Member, Council for Tertiary Education in Scotland, 1979-83; Member/Convener, Mathematics Panel, SCEEB, 1975-81; Member,SCCC, 1987, MEC, 1987; Member, SCOTVEC NC Committee, 1987. Recreations: walking; microelectronics. Address: (b.) Falkirk College of Technology, Grangemouth Road, Falkirk, FK2 9AD; T.-0324 24981.

Hendrie, Eric. Convener of Education, Grampian Regional Council, since 1990; b. 11.9.25, Glasgow; m., Isabel; 1 s.; 1 d. Educ. Lambhill School, Glasgow; Royal Technical College, Glasgow. Councillor: Aberdeen Corporation, 1970-75, Grampian Regional Council, since 1975. Address: (h.) 37 New Park Road, Aberdeen, AB2 6UT; T.-0224 691723.

Hendry, Professor Alan, BSc (Hons), PhD, CEng, FICeram, FIM, MInstP, FRSA. Professor of Metallurgy and Engineering Materials, Strathclyde University, since 1988 (Reader in Ceramics, 1985-88); b. 29.1.47, Ochiltree; m., Jean Carey Kerr; 1 s.; 1 d. Educ. Cumnock Academy; Strathclyde University. Postdoctoral Research Associate, Newcastle University, 1971-75; Research Officer, Midlands Region, CEGB, 1975-76; Lecturer in Metallurgy and Assistant Director, Wolfson Research Group for High Strength Materials, Newcastle University, 1976-85; President, Scottish Association for Metals; Member, Materials Group, Institution of Mechanical Engineers; Member, Materials Science and Engineering Commission, SERC, 1989-92; Member, Academy of Ceramics. Address: (h.) Ardleven, 23 Campbell Drive, Bearsden, Glasgow, G61 4NF; T.-041-942 3169.

Hendry, Professor Emeritus Arnold William, BSc, PhD, DSc, FICE, FIStructE, FRSE. Professor of Civil Engineering, Edinburgh University, 1964-88; b. 10.9.21, Buckie; m., Elizabeth Lois Alice Inglis; 1 s.; 1 d. Educ. Buckie High School; Aberdeen University. Assistant Civil Engineer, Sir William Arrol & Co. Ltd., Glasgow, 1941-43; Lecturer in Civil Engineering, Aberdeen University, 1943-49; Reader in

Civil Engineering, King's College, London, 1949-51; Professor of Civil Engineering and Dean, Faculty of Engineering, Khartoum University, 1951-57; Professor of Building Science, Liverpool University, 1957-63. Recreations: walking; DIY; bird-watching. Address: (h.) 146/6 Whitehouse Loan, Edinburgh, EH9 2AN; T.-031-447 0368.

Hendry, Joy McLaggan, MA (Hons), DipEd. Editor, Chapman Magazine, since 1972; Writer; b. 3.2.53, Perth; m., Ian Montgomery. Educ. Perth Academy; Edinburgh University. Former teacher; Co-Editor, Chapman, 1972-76, Sole Editor, since 1976; Deputy Convener, Scottish Poetry Library Association, 1983-88; Convener, Committee for the Advancement of Scottish Literature in Schools; Member AdCas; Scottish National Theatre Steering Committee; Campaign for a Scottish Assembly; writes poetry; gives lectures and talks and performances of poetry and song; radio critic, The Scotsman; theatre reviewer. Publications: Scots· The Way Forward; Poems and Pictures by Wendy Wood (Editor); The Land for the People (Co-Editor); Critical Essays on Sorley MacLean (Co-Editor); Critical Essays on Norman MacCaig (Co-Editor); Gang Doun wi a Sang (play). Recreations: going to theatre; cinema; reading. Address: 4 Broughton Place, Edinburgh, EH1 3RX.

Hendry, Professor Leo Brough, MSc, MEd, PhD, FBPS. Professor of Education, Aberdeen University, since 1989; b. 12.11.35, Glasgow; m., Philomena Walsh; 2 d. Educ. Hermitage Academy, Helensburgh; Jordanhill College of Education, Glasgow; Bradford University; Leicester University; Aberdeen University. School Teacher in Scottish and English schools, including two posts as Head of Department, 1957-64; Lecturer in Education and Physical Education, College of St. Mark and St. John's, Chelsea, London University Institute, 1964-66; Head of Human Movement Studies, Trinity and All Saints' Colleges, Leeds University Institute, 1966-71; Lecturer in Education, then Senior Lecturer, Aberdeen University, 1971-88; appointed Head, Education Department, 1988. Member, Scottish Council for Research in Education, 1983-86. Publications: School, Sport, Leisure: three dimensions of adolescence, 1978; Adolescents and Leisure, 1981; Growing Up and Going Out, 1983; Personality and Performance in Physical Education and Sport (Co-author), 1974; Physical Education in England (Co-author), 1976; Towards Community Education (Co-author), 1980; The Nature of Adolescence (Co-author), 1990; book chapters; research articles. Recreations: golf; writing; broadcasting; presenting papers at international conferences. Address: (b.) Department of Education, Aberdeen University, Aberdeen, AB9 2UB; T.-0224 272729 and 272731.

Hendry, Melville Richard McIntyre, MA. Depute Director, Scottish Examination Board, since 1975; b. Falkirk; m., Isobel H. Allan; 3 d. Educ. Falkirk High School; Edinburgh University; Moray House College of Education. Principal Teacher, Kilsyth Academy, 1961-69; Examination Officer, Scottish Examination Board, 1969-71; Assistant Head Teacher, Whitehill Secondary School, Glasgow, 1971-73; Depute Head Teacher/Acting Rector, Kilsyth Academy, 1973-75. Recreations: golf; travel; gardening. Address: (h.) 5B Highfield Road, North Berwick, East Lothian; T.-0620 3049.

Hendry, Stephen, Professional Snooker Player; b. 13.1.69. Scottish Amateur Champion, 1984, 1985; won: Rothmans Grand Prix, 1987, MIM Britannia British Open, 1988, Benson and Hedges Masters, 1989, UK Open Championship, 1989, World Championship, 1990, Scottish Professional, 1986, 1987, 1988. World Ranking 1990/91: 1.

Henning, Richard Henry, BSc (Hons). Director, North East Fife Enterprise Trust, since 1990; b. 8.2.59, Banbridge, N. Ireland; m., Kelli; 1 s. Educ. Methodist College, Belfast; Queens University, Belfast. Engineering geologist, 1981-85; Technical Marketing Co-ordinator, Hughes Tool Company, 1985-87; UK Sales and Marketing Manager, Longman Catermill, 1987-90. Director, NEFET Enterprises; Director, St. Andrews Heritage Trading Company. Address: (b.) 3 Riverside Court, Cupar, KY15 5DJ; T.-0334 56360.

Henriksen, Henry Neil, BSc, MEd. Rector, The James Young High School, since 1982; b. 2.9.33, Edinburgh; m., Edith Robb; 2 s. Educ. Royal High School, Edinburgh; Edinburgh University; Strathclyde University. Taught at Portobello, Falkirk High, Forrester; Depute Head, Penicuik High School. Recreations: television; climbing Allermuir. Address: (h.) 16 Redford Loan, Edinburgh, EH13 0AX; T.-031-441 2282.

Henry, Gordon Edward, DA, MCSD. Director, Aberdeen Tourist Board, since 1983; b. 23.9.37, Elgin; m., Elizabeth Browne; 2 s. Educ. Elgin Academy; Grays School of Art; Aberdeen College of Education. Art Teacher, Lecturer and Freelance Designer, 1960-63; Aberdeen University Press: Staff Designer, 1963-69, Design Manager, 1969-71, Company Director, 1971-75; City of Aberdeen: Depute Director PR, 1975-77, Director of Information and Tourism, 1977. Director, North East Co-ordinating Committee for Tourism and Gordon Tourist Board; Chairman, Grampian Initiative Tourism Task Force. Recreations: painting; golf; swimming; reading. Address: (b.) St. Nicholas House, Aberdeen, AB9 1DE; T.-0224 276276.

Henry, Captain Michael Charles, FNI, DL, RN (Rtd.) Deputy Lieutenant, Dunbartonshire, since 1989; Director, Merchants House of Glasgow, since 1990; b. 4.6.28, London; m., Nancie Elma Nicol; 2 s.; 3 d. Educ. Royal Naval College, Dartmouth. Naval career, Cadet to Captain, 1942-78; submarine specialist; commanded HM Submarines Seraph, Trump and Resolution, Britain's first Polaris submarine; fired first British missile, Cape Canaveral, and conducted first deterrent patrol, 1968; commanded 10th (Polaris) Submarine Squadron, Faslane, and Queen's Harbour Master, Clyde, 1972-74; commanded HMS Hampshire, 1975-76; Director of Naval Operations and Trade, 1976-78; Marine Manager, British National Oil Corporation, Aberdeen, 1978-80; Naval Regional Officer Scotland and Northern Ireland, Glasgow, 1980-90. Recreation: sailing. Address: (h.) Aldavhu, Garelochhead, Dunbartonshire, G84 0EL; T.-0436 810533.

Henry, Professor Peter (formerly H.P. Zuntz), MA (Oxon), DipEd (Leeds). Professor of Slavonic Languages and Literatures, Glasgow University, 1975-91, Emeritus, since 1991; b. 21.4.26, Marburg, Germany; m., Brenda Grace Lewis (m. diss.); 1 s.; 3 d. Educ. St. Knud's Skole, Copenhagen; Mellemskole, Birkerod, Denmark; St. Edward's School, Oxford; St. John's College, Oxford. Left Germany, 1936; Denmark, 1936-39, then Britain; Royal Tank Regiment, 1943-47; Senior Master, St. John's College Choir School, Cambridge, 1952; Russian Instructor, Joint Services School for Linguists, Coulsdon, 1952-54; Senior German Master, Haverfordwest Grammar School, 1954-57; Lecturer in Russian, Liverpool University, 1957-63; Senior Lecturer in Charge, Department of Russian Studies, Hull University, 1963-74. Editor, Scottish Slavonic Review, since 1983. Publications: Modern Russian prose composition; edited texts (Pushkin, Chekhov, Bunin, Paustovsky; two-volume anthology of Soviet satire; Gazeta: Clippings from the Soviet Press (with K. Young); A Hamlet of His Time: Vsevolod Garshin; translations: V. Garshin: From the Reminiscences of Private Ivanov and Other Stories (with L. Tudge); also stories by Sholokhov, Paustovsky, Tendryakov, etc. Recreations: travel;

music; theatre. Address: (b.) 53 Southpark Avenue, Glasgow University, Glasgow, G12 8QQ; T.-041-339 8855, Ext. 5599.

Henshelwood, James, JP, FISMM, MCIM, MBIM, AMNI. Director, Glasgow Chamber of Commerce, since 1976; Director, Bridgegate Trust, since 1982; Director, Mayfest Ltd., since 1983; Director, Glasgow Bute Benevolent Society; Member, St. John Association of Scotland; Member, Social Security Appeal Tribunals; Member, Central Advisory Committee on Justices of the Peace; b. 18.2.22, Glasgow; m., Mavis Irene Watson (deceased); 3 s.; 2 d. Educ. Allan Glen's School; Whitehill Senior Secondary School; Royal Technical College, Glasgow. Joined Merchant Navy as cadet, 1938, and "swallowed the anchor" in 1953 as Master Mariner; Special Services, RNR; Independent Councillor, Johnstone, 1966-69 (Burgh Treasurer); President, Chartered Institute of Marketing, Strathclyde Branch; Immediate Past Chairman, Nautical Institute, West of Scotland; Governor, RNLI; Member, Scottish Retirement Council. Recreations: golf; sailing; walking. Address: (h.) 72 Globe Court, Calderwood, East Kilbride, Glasgow, G74 3QZ; T.-03552 38851.

Hepburn, Mary, BSc, MD, MRCGP, MRCOG. Senior Lecturer in Women's Reproductive Health and Consultant Obstetrician and Gynaecologist, since 1990; b. 14.4.49, London. Educ. Anderson's Institute, Lerwick; Perth Academy; Edinburgh University. Trained as a general practitioner, then as an obstetrician and gynaecologist in a variety of places. Recreations: predictably – hill-walking; sailing; swimming in the Western Baths; also a few other less healthy pursuits. Address: (b.) Royal Maternity Hospital, Rottenrow, Glasgow, G4 0NA; T.-041-552 3400.

Hepburn, Professor Ronald William, MA, PhD. Professor of Moral Philosophy, Edinburgh University, since 1975; b. 16.3.27, Aberdeen; m., Agnes Forbes Anderson; 2 s.; 1 d. Educ. Aberdeen Grammar School; Aberdeen University. Assistant, then Lecturer, Department of Moral Philosophy, Aberdeen University, 1952-60; Visiting Associate Professor, New York University, 1959-60; Professor of Philosophy and Head of Department, Nottingham University, 1960-64; Professor of Philosophy, Edinburgh University, 1964-75; Stanton Lecturer, Cambridge University, 1965-68; Heslington Lecture, York University, 1970; Margaret Harris Lectures on Religion, Dundee University, 1974. Publications: Christianity and Paradox, 1958; Wonder and Other Essays, 1984. Recreation: hill-walking. Address: (b.) Department of Philosophy, David Hume Tower, George Square, Edinburgh, EH8 9JX; T.-031-667 1011.

Herbert, Rodney Andrew, BSc, PHD, CBiol, MIBiol. Reader in Microbiology, Dundee University, since 1989; b. 27.6.44, York; m., Helen Joyce Macpherson Millard; 2 s. Educ. Archbishop Holgate's Grammar School, York; Bradford University; Aberdeen University. Research Fellow, Edinburgh University, 1970-71; Lecturer/Reader in Microbiology, Dundee University, 1971-89. General Secretary, Society for General Microbiology; Senior Visiting Scientist: British Antarctic Survey, 1976-77, Ross Sea, Antarctica, 1982-83. Recreations: music; walking; gardening. Address: (b.) Department of Biological Sciences, Dundee University, Dundee, DD1 4HN; T.-Dundee 23181, Ext. 4262.

Herbison, Rt. Hon. Margaret McCrorie, PC (1964), MA, LLD (Hon.); b. 11.3.07, Shotts. Educ. Bellshill Academy; Glasgow University. Teacher, 1930-45; MP for Lanarkshire North, 1945-70; Joint Under-Secretary of State, Scottish Office, 1950-51; Minister of Pensions and National Insurance, 1964-66; Minister of Social Security, 1966-67; Chairman, Select Committee on Overseas Aid, 1968-70; Lord High Commissioner to General Assembly of Church of Scotland, 1970; Hon. LLD, Glasgow University, 1970; Scotswoman of the Year, 1970; Member, Royal Commission on Standards

of Conduct in Public Life, 1975-76; Lay Observer, 1975-76; Chairman, Labour Party, 1956-57. Recreations: reading; gardening. Address: (h.) 8 Mornay Way, Shotts, ML7 4EG; T.-Shotts 21944.

Herd, James Peter, MBE, WS, NP. Partner, Beveridge, Herd & Sandilands, WS, Kirkcaldy, since 1951; Honorary Sheriff, Kirkcaldy, since 1987; b. 18.5.20, Kirkcaldy; m., Marjory Phimister Mitchell; 3 s.; 2 d. Educ. Edinburgh Academy; St. Andrews University; Edinburgh University. Army Service as Major, Black Watch, UK and South East Asia, 1939-46; Local Director, Royal Insurance Group, since 1951; Trustee, Kirkcaldy and District Trustee Savings Bank, 1952-83; Director, Kirkcaldy Ice Rink Limited, 1982-88; Director, Kirkcaldy Abbeyfield Society. Recreations: curling; gardening. Address: (h.) 1 East Fergus Place, Kirkcaldy, Fife, KY1 1XT; T.-0592 261616.

Herdman, John Macmillan, MA (Hons), PhD (Cantab), DipTh. Writer, since 1963; b. 20.7.41, Edinburgh; m., Dolina Maclennan. Educ. Merchiston Castle School, Edinburgh; Magdalene College, Cambridge. Creative Writing Fellow, Edinburgh University, 1977-79; Scottish Arts Council bursaries, 1976 and 1982; Scottish Arts Council Book Award, 1978; Hawthornden Writer's Fellowship, 1989; William Soutar Fellowship, 1990-91. Publications: Descent, 1968; A Truth Lover, 1973; Memoirs of My Aunt Minnie/Clapperton, 1974; Pagan's Pilgrimage, 1978; Stories Short and Tall, 1979; Voice Without Restraint: Bob Dylan's Lyrics and Their Background, 1982; Three Novellas, 1987; The Double in Nineteenth Century Fiction, 1990. Recreations: reading; walking; listening to music. Address: (h.) 18 Clyde Place, Perth, PH2 0EZ; T.-0738 33504.

Heriot, Rev. Charles Rattray, BA, JP. Minister, Brightons Parish Church, since 1967; Clerk, Falkirk Presbytery, Church of Scotland, 1980-91; former National Chaplain, Girls' Brigade, Scotland; b. 9.4.31, Glasgow; m., Audrey J.L. Scott; 1 s.; 1 d. Educ. Hyndland Senior Secondary School; Glasgow University and Trinity College. Minister, Kenmure Parish Church, 1962-67. Member, Brightons Community Council. Recreations: reading; walking. Address: The Manse, Brightons, Falkirk, FK2 0JP; T.-Polmont 712062.

Heron, Garth McAllen Drennan, BA, FIPM. General Manager, Personnel Division, Clydesdale Bank, since 1987; b. 21.5.49, Belfast; m., Louise Dick; 1 s.; 1 d. Educ. Friend's School, Lisburn; Queen's University, Belfast. Personnel Officer, United Dominions Trust Ltd., 1971-73; Personnel Manager, Alcan Aluminium Ltd., 1973-76; Personnel Manager, Bourns Ltd., Fife, 1976-78; Personnel Director, Honeywell Ltd., Bracknell, 1978-87. Elder, Cramond Kirk. Recreations: family; church; sports; cinema. Address: (h.) 567 Queensferry Road, Barnton, Edinburgh, EH4 8DU; T.-031-339 3336.

Herries, Sir Michael, OBE, MC, LLD, DLitt. Director (former Chairman), Royal Bank of Scotland Group plc; Director (former Chairman), The Royal Bank of Scotland plc; Lord Lieutenant, Dumfries and Galloway (District of Stewartry), since 1989; b. 28.2.23, Castle Douglas; m.; 2 s.; 1 d. Educ. Eton; Trinity College, Cambridge. KOSB, 1942-47, NW Europe and Middle East, Captain (Acting/Major); Jardine, Matheson & Co. Ltd., Hong Kong, Japan, Singapore, latterly as Chairman and Managing Director (retired, 1988); Chairman, Matheson & Co. Ltd., 1970-75; appointed a Director, The Royal Bank of Scotland plc, 1972; Chairman, Scottish Mortgage and Investment Trust PLC; Director, Scottish Widows' Fund and Life Assurance Society (Chairman, 1981-84); Director, Banco de Santander SA, since 1989; Chairman, Enterprise Trust for Nithsdale, Annandale, Eskdale and the Stewartry of Kirkcudbright, since 1984; Member, Royal Company of Archers, since 1973; knighted,

1975; DLitt, Heriot-Watt, 1984. Recreation: shooting; walking in the Galloway Hills. Address: (b.) 42 St. Andrew Square, Edinburgh, EH2 2YE; T.-031-556 8555.

Herron, Very. Rev. Andrew, ATCL, MA, BD, LLB, DD, LLD. Moderator, General Assembly of Church of Scotland, 1971; b. 29.9.09, Glasgow; m., Joanna Fraser Neill; 4 d. Educ. Strathbungo H.G. School; Albert Road Academy; Glasgow University and Trinity College. Minister: Linwood, 1936-40, Houston and Killellan, 1940-59; Clerk, Glasgow Presbytery, 1959-81. Baird Lecturer, 1985; William Barclay Lecturer, 1989. Publications: Record Apart, 1972; Guide to the General Assembly, 1976; Guide to Congregational Affairs, 1979; Guide to the Presbytery, 1982; Kirk by Divine Right, 1985; Guide to the Ministry, 1987; Guide to Ministerial Income, 1987; Minority Report, 1990; contributed article on Houston to Third Statistical Account. Address: (h.) 36 Darnley Road, Glasgow, G41 4NE; T.-041-423 6422.

Herschell, David John, FSA Scot. Curator, Scottish Tartans Museum, since 1990; Trustee and Executive Member, Scottish Tartans Society, 1981-90; b. 26.10.44, London; m., Hazel Joyce Giddins; 1 s.; 1 d. Editor, Tartans (Journal, Scottish Tartans Society); Convener, Junior Section, Scottish Tartans Society. Publication: Rev. Francis Edward Robinson (1833-1910) - His Background and Early Life. Recreations: Scottish history and culture; reading; walking. Address: (h.) Braidon, Ancaster Lane, Comrie, Perthshire, PH6 2DT; T.-0764 70666.

Hetherington, Professor (Hector) Alastair, Dhc (Lille), MA. Emeritus Professor in Media Studies, Stirling University, since 1987; b. 31.10.19, Llanishen, Glamorgan; m., Sheila Cameron; 2 s.; 2 d.; 1 step s.; 2 step d. Educ. Corpus Christi College, Oxford. Army, 1940-46; Glasgow Herald, 1946-50; The Guardian, 1950-75 (Foreign Editor, 1953-56, Editor, 1956-75); BBC Scotland, 1976-79; Director, Scotquest (film company), since 1982; Chairman, The Scott Trust (owners, The Guardian and Manchester Evening News), 1984-89; various films for Channel Four. Publications: Guardian Years, 1981; News, Newspapers and Television, 1985; Perthshire in Trust, 1988; News in the Regions, 1989. Recreation: hillwalking. Address: (h.) 38 Chalton Road, Bridge of Allan, Stirling, FK9 4EF; T.-0786 832168.

Hetherington, Rev. Robert MacArthur, MA, BD. Minister, Barrhead South and Levern Parish Church, since 1977; b. 29.9.37, Kilmarnock; m., Inge Olderdissen; 3 s. Educ. Kilmarnock Academy; Worcester College for Blind; Edinburgh University; Marburg University. Lecturer in Philosophy, Madras Christian College, 1965-69; Scottish Braille Press, 1969-71; Inverbrothock Parish Church, Arbroath, 1971-77. Chairman, Cleric's Group, since 1991, and Chairman, Royal National Institute for the Blind, since 1990; Member, Board of Directors, Glasgow and West of Scotland Society for the Blind, since 1978; Moderator, Presbytery of Paisley, 1988-89. Recreations: music; hill-walking. Address: 3 Colinbar Circle, Barrhead, Glasgow, G78 2BE; T.-041-880 6654.

Hewitt, David S., MA, PhD. Reader in English, Aberdeen University, since 1991; b. 22.4.42, Hawick; m., Angela Catherine Williams; 1 s.; 1 d. Educ. Melrose Grammar School; George Watson's College, Edinburgh; Edinburgh University; Aberdeen University. Aberdeen University: Assistant Lecturer in English, 1964, Lecturer, 1968, Senior Lecturer, 1982; Treasurer, Association for Scottish Literary Studies, since 1973; Editor-in-Chief, Edinburgh Edition of the Waverley Novels, 1984; President, Edinburgh Sir Walter Scott Club, 1988-89; Elder, Cathedral Church of St. Machar, Old Aberdeen; Managing Editor, New Writing Scotland, 1983-86. Publications: Scott on Himself (Editor), 1982; Literature of the North, 1983; Scott and His Influence, 1984;

Longer Scottish Poems, Vol. 2 1650-1830, 1987. Address: (b.) Department of English, Aberdeen University, Aberdeen, AB9 2UB; T.-0224 272634.

Hewitt, Margaret Irene Montague, OBE (Mil.), TD. Council Member, National Trust for Scotland, since 1987; Life Vice President and Associate of Honour, National Association of Flower Arrangement Societies of Great Britain; m., Dr. Fred Hewitt. Auxiliary Territorial Service (ATS), 1939-47; retired as Chief Commander (Lt. Col.); raised 319 West Lancashire Bn., Women's Royal Army Corps (Territorial), 1948-53; Chairman, National Association of Flower Arrangement Societies of Great Britain, 1971-73; Chairman, Perth and Kinross Members' Group, National Trust for Scotland, 1982-86 (now President). Recreations: flower arranging and decor; gardening; travel; photography; theatre; wildlife and conservation; Airedale dogs. Address: (h.) Croft Cappanach, Pitlochry, Perthshire, PH16 5JT; T.-079 682 366.

Hewitt, Peter John, BA (Hons). Director, Investment Division, Ivory & Sime plc; b. 19.2.57, Edinburgh; m., Karleen. Educ. George Heriot's School; Heriot Watt University. Research Analyst, Wood Mackenzie, Stockbrokers, 1979-81; Investment Manager, Edinburgh Investment Trust, 1981-83. Recreations: rugby; cricket; golf. Address: (b.) 1 Charlotte Square, Edinburgh, EH2 4DZ; T.-031-225 1357.

Heywood, Barry Keith, MA, LLB. Regional Procurator Fiscal, Dundee, since 1991; b. 24.7.46, Oldham; m., Mary A.; 1 s.; 1 d. Educ. Kirkcaldy High School; Edinburgh University. Procurator Fiscal Depute, Ayr, 1971-77, Glasgow, 1977-78; Procurator Fiscal, Wick, 1978-83; Assistant Procurator Fiscal, Glasgow, 1983-86; Procurator Fiscal, Inverness, 1986-91. Recreations: walking; Roman and Byzantine history; "railway buff". Address: (b.) 15 West Bell Street, Dundee, DD1 1HB; T.-0382 27535.

Hider, Calvin Fraser, MB, ChB, FFARCS. Consultant Anaesthetist, Edinburgh Royal Infirmary, since 1964; Honorary Senior Lecturer, Faculty of Medicine, Edinburgh University; b. 29.5.30, Glasgow; m., 1, Jean M.D. Dott (deceased); 3 d.; 2, Frances Ann Smithers. Educ. George Watson's Boys College, Edinburgh; Edinburgh University. Medical training, Dumfries and Galloway Royal Infirmary and Edinburgh Royal Infirmary; RNVR, Surgeon (Lt.-Cdr.), 1955-64. Recreations: sailing; sheep-breeding (Jacob). Address: (h.) Marchwell Cottage, Penicuik, Midlothian, EH26 0PX; T.-0968 72680.

Higgins, Sheriff Colin Kirk, LLB. Sheriff of North Strathclyde at Paisley, since 1990; b. 9.11.45, Slough; m., Anne Marie McMahon; 1 s.; 2 d. Educ. St. Patrick's High School, Coatbridge; Glasgow University. Law Apprentice, Coatbridge, 1967-69; Legal Assistant, Coatbridge, 1969-70; Legal Assistant, James Bell & Sons, 1970-73; Partner, Bell, Russell & Co., 1973-90. Dean, Airdrie Society of Solicitors, 1989-90. Recreations: reading; travel; walking. Address (b.) Court House, St. James' Street, Paisley; T.-041-887 5291.

Higgs, Professor Peter Ware, BSc, MSc, PhD, FRS, FRSE. Professor of Theoretical Physics, Edinburgh University, since 1980; b. 29.5.29, Newcastle-upon-Tyne; m., Jo Ann Williamson; 2 s. Educ. Cotham Grammar School, Bristol; King's College, London. Postdoctoral Fellow, Edinburgh University, 1954-56, and London University, 1956-58; Lecturer in Mathematics, University College, London, 1958-60; Lecturer in Mathematical Physics, then Reader, Edinburgh University, 1960-80. Hughes Medal, Royal Society, 1981; Rutherford Medal, Institute of Physics, 1984. Recreations: music; walking; swimming. Address: (h.) 2 Darnaway Street, Edinburgh, EH3 6BG; T.-031-225 7060.

Highgate, James Brown, CBE (1981), MA, LLB, JP. Consultant, Miller Thompson Brownlie Watson, Solicitors; former Senior Partner, Brownlie Watson & Beckett, Solicitors; b. 18.6.20, Glasgow. Educ. High School of Glasgow; Glasgow University. Served, Royal Artillery and Royal Indian Artillery, 1941-46 (demobilised as Major); appointed General Commissioner of Income Tax, 1969 (appointed Chairman, Glasgow North Division, 1981); Member, Strathclyde Advisory Board, Salvation Army, since 1970, Vice Chairman, since 1990; Joint Honorary Secretary, Scottish Conservative and Unionist Association, 1973-86 (President, 1987-89); Honorary President, Motherwell North Conservative Constituency; Elder, Park Church of Scotland, Uddingston. Recreations: golf; travel. Address: (h.) Broomlands, 24 Kylepark Drive, Uddingston, Glasgow; T.-Uddingston 813377.

Hill, Richard Inglis, BSc (Hons), FICE, FIHT. Director of Roads and Transportation, Borders Regional Council, since 1974; b. 8.5.33, Callander; m., Margaret; 2 s. Educ. McLaren High School, Callander; Royal College of Science and Technology, Glasgow. Perth and Kinross Joint County Council: student assistant, 1951-53, graduate assistant, 1954-56, Assistant Engineer, 1958-59, Senior Engineer, 1959-61, Senior Supervisory Engineer, 1961-65, Assistant County Surveyor, 1965-72; County Surveyor and Engineer, Selkirk County Council, 1972-75. Past Secretary and Chairman, Scottish Branch, County Surveyors' Society; former Secretary and Chairman, Institution of Highways and Transportation, Central and Southern Scotland Branch; Vice Chairman, Edinburgh and East of Scotland Association, Institution of Civil Engineers; Chairman, Edinburgh and East of Scotland Division, Association of Municipal Engineers. Recreations: golf; music. Address: (b.) Regional HQ, Newtown St. Boswells, Melrose, TD6 OSA; T.-St. Boswells 23301.

Hill, Professor William George, BSc, MS, PhD, DSc, FRSE, FRS. Professor of Animal Genetics, Edinburgh University, since 1983; Head, Department of Genetics, 1989-90, Institute of Cell, Animal and Population Biology, since 1990; b. 7.8.40, Hemel Hempstead; m., C. Rosemary Austin; 1 s.; 2 d. Educ. St. Albans School; London University; University of California; Iowa State University; Edinburgh University. Edinburgh University: Assistant Lecturer, 1965-67, Lecturer, 1967-74, Reader, 1974-83; Visiting Research Associate, Iowa State University, 1967-68-69-72; Visiting Professor: University of Minnesota, 1966, Iowa State University, 1978, North Carolina State University, 1979; Consultant Geneticist: Cotswold Pig Development Co., since 1965, Holstein Friesian Society, since 1978; Member, AFRC Animals Research Grant Board, since 1986. Recreations: farming; bridge. Address: (h.) 4 Gordon Terrace, Edinburgh, EH16 5QH; T.-031-667 3680.

Hillhouse, Sir (Robert) Russell, KCB. Permanent Under-Secretary of State, Scottish Office, since 1988; b. 23.4.38, Glasgow; m., Alison Fraser; 2 d. Educ. Hutchesons' Grammar School, Glasgow; Glasgow University. Entered Home Civil Service as Assistant Principal, Scottish Education Department, 1962; Principal, 1966; HM Treasury, 1971; Assistant Secretary, Scottish Office, 1974; Scottish Home and Health Department, 1977; Principal Finance Officer, Scottish Office, 1980; Under-Secretary, Scottish Education Department, 1985; Secretary, 1987. Recreation: making music. Address: (b.) St. Andrew's House, Regent Road, Edinburgh, EH1 3DG; T.-031-556 8400.

Hillier, Stephen Gilbert, BSc, MSc, PhD, MRCPath. Senior Lecturer, Department of Obstetrics and Gynaecology, Edinburgh University, since 1985, and Director, Reproductive Endocrinology Laboratory, since 1985; Member, Human Fertilisation and Embryology Authority, since 1991; b. 16.1.49, Hillingdon; m., Ameneh; 2 d. Educ. Hayes County Grammar School; Leeds University; University of Wales. Postdoctoral Research Fellow, National Institutes of Health, USA, 1976-78; Research Scientist, University of Leiden, 1978-82; Senior Lecturer, Reproductive Biochemistry, RPMS, London University, 1982-85. Member, Interim Licensing Authority for Human Fertilisation and Embryology, 1987-91; 1991 Society for Endocrinology Medal. Publication: Ovarian Endocrinology, 1991. Recreations: fly-fishing; walking. Address: (b.) Edinburgh University Centre for Reproductive Biology, 37 Chalmers Street, Edinburgh, EH3 9EW; T.-031-229 2575.

Hillman, John Richard, BSc, PhD, CBiol, FIBiol, FLS, FBIM, FRSE. Director, Scottish Crop Research Institute, since 1986; Visiting Professor, Dundee University, Edinburgh University, Glasgow University and Strathclyde University; b. 21.7.44, Farnborough, Kent; m., Sandra Kathleen Palmer; 2 s. Educ. Chislehurst and Sidcup Grammar School; University of Wales. Assistant Lecturer, 1968, and Lecturer, 1969, Physiology and Environmental Studies, Nottingham University; Lecturer, 1971, Senior Lecturer, 1977, Reader, 1980, Professor of Botany, 1982, Glasgow University. Recreations: landscaping; building renovations; horology; reading. Address: (b.) Scottish Crop Research Institute, Invergowrie, Dundee, DD2 5DA; T.-0382 562731.

Hills, Professor Sir Graham (John), PhD, DSc, LLD, FRSE, Hon DSc (Lodz and Southampton), Hon. LLD (Glasgow, Waterloo and Strathclyde). National Governor for Scotland, BBC, since 1989; President, Society of Chemical Industry, since 1991; Principal and Vice-Chancellor, Strathclyde University, 1980-91; b. 9.4.26, Leigh-on-Sea; m., Mary Jane McNaughton; 1 s.; 3 d. Educ. Westcliff High School for Boys; Birkbeck College and Imperial College, London University. Lecturer in Physical Chemistry, Imperial College, 1949-62; Professor of Physical Chemistry, Southampton University, 1962-80; Visiting Professor, University of Western Ontario, 1968; Visiting Professor and National Science Foundation Fellow, Case-Western Reserve University, Ohio, 1968-69; Visiting Professor, Buenos Aires University, 1976; Member, Advisory Council on Science and Technology, since 1987; (Non-Executive) Member, Scottish Post Office Board, since 1986; Non-Executive Director, Scottish Enterprise, since 1988; Fellow, Birkbeck College; Fellow, Royal Scottish Academy of Music and Drama; Director, Glasgow Chamber of Commerce, since 1981; President, Friends of Glasgow Cathedral, since 1987; Commander Insignia, Order of Merit of Polish People's Republic; Commander Insignia, Royal Norwegian Order of Merit. Publications: Reference Electrodes, 1961; Polarography, 1964. Recreations: music; hill-walking; European politics. Address: (b.) Sunnyside of Threepwood, Laigh Threepwood, Beith, Ayrshire, KA15 2JW.

Himsworth, Professor Richard Lawrence, MD, FRCPLond, FRCPEdin, FRCPGlas. Regius Professor of Medicine, Aberdeen University, since 1985; Honorary Consultant Physician, Aberdeen Royal Infirmary, since 1985; b. 14.6.37, London; m., Sara Margaret Tattersall; 2 s.; 1 d. Educ. Westminster School; Trinity College, Cambridge; University College Hospital, London. Lecturer in Medicine, University College Hospital Medical School, 1967-71; MRC Travelling Fellowship, Columbia University, New York, 1969-70; MRC scientific staff, Clinical Research Centre, 1971-85 (Assistant Director, 1978-82). Member, National Medical Advisory Committee Scotland, since 1990. Recreation: painting. Address: (h.) Mains of Kebbaty, Midmar, Aberdeenshire, AB51 7QL; T.-Sauchen 430.

Hind, Archie. Novelist and Playwright; b. 1928. Author of The Dear Green Place, 1966.

Hind, Valerie Margaret Doris, MBChB, PhD, FRCS (Edin), FRCS (Glas), FCOphth. Consultant Ophthalmologist, Stobhill General Hospital, Glasgow, since 1976; Hon. Clinical Senior Lecturer, Glasgow University, since 1976; Hon. Senior Lecturer, St. Andrews University, since 1987; b. 30.11.36, Stretford; m., Dr. Peter Dallas Ross. Educ. Blackpool Collegiate School for Girls; St. Andrews University; Birmingham University. Lecturer in Anatomy, Birmingham University, 1964-69; Lecturer in Ophthalmology, Glasgow University, 1970-75. Recreations: fine arts; theatre; opera. Address: (h.) 11 Falkland Street, Glasgow, G12 9PY; T.-041-339 7003; Strathview, Emma Terrace, Blairgowrie; T.-0250 872762.

Hine, Professor Harry Morrison, MA, DPhil (Oxon). Scotstarvit Professor of Humanity, St. Andrews University, since 1985; b. 19.6.48, Portsmouth; m., Rosalind Mary Ford; 1 s.; 1 d. Educ. King Edward's School, Birmingham; Corpus Christi College, Oxford. P.S. Allen Junior Research Fellow, Corpus Christi College, 1972-75; Lecturer in Humanity, Edinburgh University, 1975-85. Editor (Joint), The Classical Review, since 1987. Publication: An Edition with Commentary of Seneca, Natural Questions, Book Two, 1981. Recreations: walking; reading. Address: (h.) 33 Drumcarrow Road, St. Andrews, Fife, KY16 8SE; T.-0334 74459.

Hingston, David Robert, LLB, NP. Procurator Fiscal, Dingwall; 29.7.48, Assam, India; m., Sylvia Isobel Reid; 2 s.; 1 d. Educ. Morrison's Academy, Crieff; Edinburgh University. Private practice, Edinburgh; joined Procurator Fiscal service, 1975 (Kirkcaldy, Dunfermline, Edinburgh); seconded to Scottish Law Commission; then Edinburgh Office; Procurator Fiscal, Wick; Tutor in Criminal Law, Demonstrator Criminal Procedure. Publication: Stair Memorial Encyclopaedia (Contributor); Criminal Procedure (Co-author). Recreations: fitting 36 hours into 24; fishing. Address: (b.) Procurator Fiscal's Office, Sheriff Court House, Ferry Road, Dingwall; T.-Dingwall 62122.

Hinks, Charles Edward, BSc, PhD. Senior Lecturer, Institute of Ecology and Research Management, Edinburgh University; b. 21.10.41, Darlington; m., Ann Caborn; 1 s.; 1 d. Educ. Queen Elizabeth Grammar School, Darlington; Newcastle upon Tyne University. Research Assistant, Department of Agricultural Marketing, Newcastle upon Tyne University, 1965-68; Lecturer, School of Agriculture, Edinburgh University, 1969-90; Technical Secretary, Animal Research and Development Committee, 1978-85; Director of Studies, School of Agriculture, Edinburgh University, 1981-90; Garton Lecturer, 1989. Publications: 30 scientific papers. Recreations: golf; fishing; gardening. Address: (h.) 142 Rullion Road, Penicuik, Midlothian, EH26 9JB; T.-0968 75051.

Hirst, Michael William, LLB, CA. President, Scottish Conservative and Unionist Association, since 1989; b. 2.1.46, Glasgow; m., Naomi Ferguson Wilson; 1 s.; 2 d. Educ. Glasgow Academy; Glasgow University. Partner, Peat Marwick Mitchell & Co., Chartered Accountants, until 1983; Consultant to various companies; Partner, Hirst & Associates; contested: Central Dunbartonshire, February and October, 1974, East Dunbartonshire, 1979; MP (Conservative), Strathkelvin and Bearsden, 1983-87; Member, Select Committee on Scottish Affairs, 1983-87; Parliamentary Private Secretary, Department of Energy, 1985-87; Vice-Chairman, Scottish Conservative Party, 1987-89; Chairman, Scottish Conservative Candidates Association, 1978-81; Member, National Executive Council, British Diabetic Association; Chairman, The Park School Educational Trust; Governor, The Queen's College Glasgow and Chairman, Finance Committee; Member, Executive Committee, Princess Louise Scottish Hospital, Erskine; Elder, Kelvinside Hillhead Parish Church. Recreations: golf; hill-walking; skiing.

Address: (h.) Enderley, Baldernock Road, Milngavie, Glasgow, G62 8DU; T.-041-956 1213.

Hitchman, Professor Michael L., BSc, DPhil, CChem, FRSC, FRSA. Young Professor of Chemistry, Strathclyde University, since 1984 (Chairman, Department of Pure and Applied Chemistry, 1986-89; Vice-Dean, Faculty of Science, since 1989); b. 17.8.41, Woburn, Bedfordshire; m., Pauline J. Thompson; 1 s.; 2 d. Educ. Stratton Grammar School, Biggleswade; Queen Mary College and King's College, London University; University College, Oxford. Assistant Lecturer in Chemistry, Leicester Regional College of Technology, 1963-65; Junior Research Fellow, Wolfson College, Oxford, 1968-70; ICI Postdoctoral Research Fellow, Physical Chemistry Laboratory, Oxford University, 1968-70; Chief Scientist, Orbisphere Corporation, Geneva, 1970-73; Staff Scientist, Laboratories RCA Ltd., Zurich, 1973-79; Lecturer, then Senior Lecturer, Salford University, 1979-84. Royal Society of Chemistry: Chairman, Electroanalytical Group, 1985-88, Treasurer, Electrochemistry Group, 1984-90; Science and Engineering Research Council: Member, Chemistry and Semiconductor Committees. Publications: Ring-disk Electrodes (Co-author), 1971; Measurement of Dissolved Oxygen, 1978. Recreations: family; keep fit; walking; sailing; skiing; DIY; theatre-going. Address: (b.) Department of Pure and Applied Chemistry, Strathclyde University, 295 Cathedral Street, Glasgow, G1 1XL; T.-041-552 4400.

Hobbs, Grete. Hotelier, Inverlochy Castle, since 1969; b. Copenhagen; m., Joseph B. Hobbs (deceased); 1 s.; 1 d. Educ. Ballerup. Numerous hotel awards; Free Enterprise Award; Hotelier of the Year, 1989. Recreations: golf; bridge. Address: (b.) Inverlochy Castle, Fort William, PH33 6SN; T.-0397 702177.

Hobsbaum, Professor Philip Dennis, MA, PhD, LRAM, LGSM. Titular Professor of English Literature, Glasgow University, since 1985 (Reader in English Literature, 1979-85); b. 29.6.32, London; m., Rosemary Phillips. Educ. Belle Vue Grammar School, Bradford; Downing College, Cambridge; Sheffield University. Lecturer in English, Queen's University, Belfast, 1962-66; Lecturer, then Senior Lecturer in English Literature, Glasgow University, 1966-79. Publications: A Group Anthology (Co-Editor), 1963; The Place's Fault, 1964; In Retreat, 1966; Coming Out Fighting, 1969; Ten Elizabethan Poets (Editor), 1969; A Theory of Communication, 1970; A Reader's Guide to Charles Dickens, 1972; Women and Animals, 1972; Tradition and Experiment in English Poetry, 1979; A Reader's Guide to D.H. Lawrence, 1981; Essentials of Literary Criticism, 1983; A Reader's Guide to Robert Lowell, 1988; Wordsworth: Selected Poetry and Prose (Editor), 1989. Recreations: walking the dog; playing the piano. Address: (b.) Department of English Literature, Glasgow University, Glasgow; T.-041-339 8855.

Hodges, Desmond W.H., OBE, FRIAS. Director, Edinburgh New Town Conservation Committee, since 1972; b. 25.9.28, Dublin; m., Margaret Elisabeth Anderson; 2 d. Educ. St. Columba's College, Rathfarnham, Co. Dublin. Architect practising in Dublin and Belfast, 1957-72; Visiting Lecturer, Queen's University, Belfast, 1967-78; Consultant Architect, Methodist Church in Ireland, 1964-87. Founder Member, Ulster Architectural Heritage Society; Member, Council, Cockburn Association; Representative of Royal Incorporation of Architects on Council, National Trust for Scotland. Address: (h.) 14 Shandon Street, Edinburgh; T.-031-337 4929.

Hodgson, Allan F., MA (Hons) Econ. Chairman and Managing Director, Hodgson Martin Ltd., since 1980; b. 19.5.45, Edinburgh; m., Irene Rennie; 2 d. Educ. George Heriot's; Edinburgh University. Economist, Edinburgh

Investment Trust, 1967-70; Economist, Ivory & Sime, 1970-76; Joint Investment Secretary, Scottish Widows Fund and Life Assurance Society, 1976-80. Governor, Edinburgh College of Art; Member, Scottish Economic Council. Recreations: opera; travel; antiquarian books; golf. Address: (b.) 36 George Street, Edinburgh, EH2 2LE; T.-031-226 7644.

Hogg, Norman, MP, Cumbernauld and Kilsyth, since 1979; b. 12.3.38, Aberdeen; m., Elizabeth M. Christie. Educ. Ruthrieston Secondary School, Aberdeen. Local Government Officer, Aberdeen Town Council, 1953-67; District Officer, NALGO, 1967-79; MP, East Dunbartonshire, 1979-83; Member: Transport Users Consultative Committee for Scotland, 1977-79, Select Committee on Scottish Affairs, 1979-82; Scottish Labour Whip, 1982-83; Chairman, Scottish Parliamentary Labour Group, 1981-82; Deputy Chief Opposition Whip, 1983-87; Scottish Affairs Spokesman, 1987-88; Member, Chairman's Panel, since 1988. Recreation: music. Address: House of Commons, Westminster, London SW1A 0AA; T.-071-219 5095.

Hoggar, Stuart Gerrard, BSc, MSc, PhD. Senior Lecturer in Mathematics, Glasgow University, since 1991, and Member, Board of Studies in Information Technology, since 1989; b. 4.6.39, Leicester; m., Elisabeth Dutch. Educ. Wyggeston Boys Grammar School, Leicester; Birmingham University; Warwick University. Atomic Power Division, English Electric, Whetstone, 1960-63; Mathematics Teacher, Loughborough Grammar School, 1963-65; PhD student, 1965-68; Lecturer in Mathematics, Glasgow University, since 1968. President, Glasgow Mathematical Association, 1990-91; Founding Fellow, Institute of Combinatorics and its applications. Publications: (book) Mathematical Foundations of Computer Graphics; 23 research papers. Recreations: singing; piano; hill-walking; reading; good movies/plays. Address: (h.) 18 Highburgh Road, Glasgow, G12 9YD; T.-041-339 4802.

Hogwood, Professor Brian Walter, BA, PhD. Professor of Politics, Department of Government, Strathclyde University, since 1991; b. 29.6.50, Glasgow; m., Patricia Brearey. Educ. Hamilton Academy; Glenrothes High School; Keele University. Economics Sub-Editor, Cambridge University Press, 1974-75; appointed Lecturer in Politics, Strathclyde University, 1975; Senior Lecturer, 1985; Reader, 1988. Recreations: cooking; computing; cross-country running. Address: (b.) Department of Government, Strathclyde University, McCance Building, 16 Richmond Street, Glasgow; T.-041-552 4400, Ext. 2365.

Holloway, Rt. Rev. Richard Frederick. Bishop of Edinburgh, since 1986; b. 26.11.33.

Holmes, George Dennis, CB (1979), FRSE, FICfor. Forestry Consultant, since 1987; b. 9.11.26, Conwy; m., Sheila Rosemary; 3 d. Educ. John Bright's School, Llandudno; University of Wales, Bangor. Forestry Commission, 1948-86 (Director General, 1976-86). Chairman, Scottish Council for Spastics, since 1986; Member, Eastern Board, Bank of Scotland, since 1987; part-time Member, Scottish Legal Aid Board, since 1989; Board Chairman, International Council for Research in Agroforestry, Nairobi, since 1991. Recreations: fishing; sailing; golf. Address: (h.) 7 Cammo Road, Barnton, Edinburgh, EH4 8EF; T.-031-339 7474.

Holmes, Professor Peter Henry, BVMS, PhD, MRCVS. Head, Department of Veterinary Physiology, Glasgow University, since 1978; b. 6.6.42, Beverley; m., Ruth Helen Holmes; 2 d. Educ. Beverley Grammar School; Glasgow University. Lecturer, Senior Lecturer, Reader, Titular Professor in Veterinary Physiology, Glasgow University, since 1969; various overseas projects in East Africa, particu-

larly in Ethiopia. Recreations: sailing; hill-walking. Address: (b.) Department of Veterinary Physiology, Glasgow University Veterinary School, Bearsden Road, Glasgow; T.-041-339 8855, Ext. 5793.

Holy, Ladislav, PhD. Professor of Social Anthropology, St. Andrews University, since 1987; b. 4.4.33, Prague, Czechoslovakia; m., Alice. Educ. Charles University, Prague. Director, Livingstone Museum, Zambia, 1968-72; Lecturer and Senior Lecturer, Social Anthropology, Queen's University, Belfast, 1973-79; Reader, Social Anthropology, St. Andrews University, 1979-86. Publications: books and articles on anthropology and African and Middle Eastern societies. Address: (b.) St. Andrews University, St. Andrews KY16 9AL; T.-0334 76161.

Home of the Hirsel, Rt. Hon. Lord (Alexander Frederick Douglas-Home), KT; Life Peer; b. 2.7.03, London; m., Elizabeth Alington (deceased); 1 s.; 3 d. Educ. Eton College; Christ Church, Oxford. Minister of State, Scottish Office, 1951-55; Secretary of State: Commonwealth Office, 1955-60, Foreign Office, 1960-63; Prime Minister, 1963-64; Secretary of State, Foreign and Commonwealth Office, 1970-74. Publications: The Way The Wind Blows (autobiography), 1976; Border Reflections, 1979; Letters to a Grandson, 1984. Recreations: fishing; shooting; gardening. Address: (h.) The Hirsel, Coldstream, Berwickshire; T.-0890 2345.

Home Robertson, John David. MP (Labour), East Lothian, since 1983 (Berwick & East Lothian, 1978-83); b. 5.12.48, Edinburgh; m., Catherine Brewster; 2 s. Educ. Ampleforth College; West of Scotland Agricultural College. Farmer; Member: Berwickshire District Council, 1974-78, Borders Health Board, 1975-78; Chairman, Eastern Borders Citizens' Advice Bureau, 1976-78; Member, Select Committee on Scottish Affairs, 1979-83; Chairman, Scottish Group of Labour MPs, 1983; Scottish Labour Whip, 1983-84; Opposition Front Bench Spokesman on Agriculture, 1984-87, on Scotland, 1987-88, on Agriculture, 1988-90. Address: (b.) House of Commons, Westminster, London, SW1A 0AA; T.-071-219 4135; 0368 63679.

Homfray, John L., TD, FCA. Chairman, Iona Cathedral Trust Management Board, since 1982; b. 5.8.16, Darjeeling, India; m., Elizabeth M. Shand; 2 s.; 1 d. Educ. Sherborne. Captain, RA 80 Field Regiment, 1940-45 (mentioned in Despatches); Director, Clyde Shipping Co. Ltd., Glasgow, 1948-81; Deputy Lieutenant, Dunbartonshire, 1975-90. Lt. Col., City of Glasgow Artillery, RATA, 1953-57; Vice Chairman, Glasgow Aged Seamen Relief Fund; Director, Sailors Orphan Society of Scotland. Recreations: shooting; travelling; curling. Address: (h.) Ardballachan, Bracklinn Road, Callander, Perthshire; T.-0877 30256.

Hood, Daniel, MA (Hons), LLB (Hons), Barrister-at-Law (Gray's Inn). Educational Consultant; SCOTVEC Assessor in legal subjects, since 1984; b. 5.12.26, Glasgow; m., Avril Ballantyne; 3 s. Educ. Whitehill Senior Secondary School, Glasgow; Glasgow University; Jordanhill College; London University (External). Royal Navy, 1945-47; Marketing Officer, Nigerian Government Service, 1955-57; Head, Department of Business Studies, Falkirk College of Technology, 1962-69; Depute Principal, Dundee College of Commerce, 1969-82; Research Officer, SNP, 1984-85; Member, Tayside Regional Council, 1986-90; SNP COSLA Spokesman, 1987-90; original Member, General Teaching Council; founder Member, Past President, Scottish Further and Higher Education Association; eMember, Professional Studies Committee, Scottish Business Education Council, 1973-82; former Parliamentary and Euro candidate (SNP). Recreations: hill-walking; foreign travel; caravanning; reading; Scottish history. Address: (h.) 12 Braehead Drive, Carnoustie, Angus; T.-0241 52422.

Hood, James. MP (Labour), Clydesdale, since 1987; b. 16.5.48.

Hood, John, BSc, PhD, MBChB, MRCP(UK), MRCPath (Hons). Consultant Bacteriologist, Glasgow Royal Infirmary, since 1990; Honorary Clinical Senior Lecturer, Glasgow University, since 1991; b. 16.5.53, Irvine; m., Patricia Mary Cockburn; 1 s.; 1 d. Educ. Kilmarnock Academy; Edinburgh University. House appointments, Western General Hospital (Neurosurgery) and Royal Infirmary (Medicine), Edinburgh; general medical training, Royal Infirmary, Edinburgh, and North Manchester General Hospital; Lecturer in Bacteriology, Edinburgh University, 1981-89. Recreations: attempting to change a field into a garden; watching cricket at the Oval (infrequent); outsprinting A. Bruce Harris (Ron) at the end of half-marathons; "climbing" in Glencoe with same. Address: (h.) 155 Cunningham Drive, Giffnock, Glasgow, G46 6EW; T.-041-633 3785.

Hood, Professor Neil, FRSE, MA, MLitt. Professor of Business Policy, Department of Marketing, Strathclyde University, since 1979; b. 10.8.43, Wishaw; m., Anna Watson Clark; 1 s.; 1 d. Educ. Wishaw High School; Glasgow University. Research Fellow, Scottish College of Textiles, 1966-68; Lecturer/Senior Lecturer, Paisley College of Technology, 1968-78; Economic Adviser, Scottish Economic Planning Department, 1979; Director, Locate in Scotland, 1987-89; Visiting Professor of International Business, University of Texas, Dallas, 1981; Visiting Professor, Institute of International Business, Stockholm School of Economics, since 1982; Director, Euroscot Meat Exports Ltd., 1981-85; Economic Consultant to Secretary of State for Scotland, 1980-87; Director, Scottish Development Finance Ltd., 1984-86; Investment Adviser, Castleforth Fund Managers, 1984-87; Director, LIFE Ltd., 1984-86; Board Member, Irvine Development Corporation, 1985-87; Director, Prestwick Holdings PLC, 1986-87; Director: Lamberton (Holdings) Ltd., since 1989, GA (Holdings) Ltd., since 1990, Shanks and McEwan PLC, since 1990, First Charlotte Assets Trust PLC, since 1990, Charlotte Marketing Services, since 1991; Chairman, GRF Christian Radio, since 1988; Special Adviser on Business Development, SSEB/Scottish Power, since 1989; President, European International Business Association, 1985-86. Publications: Industrial Marketing - A Study of Textiles (Co-author), 1970; Chrysler UK: A Corporation in Transition (Co-author), 1977; The Economics of Multinational Enterprise (Co-author), 1979; European Development Strategies of US Multinationals Located in Scotland (Co-author), 1980; Multinationals in Retreat: The Scottish Experience (Co-author), 1982; Multinational Investment Strategies in the British Isles (Co-author), 1983; Industry, Policy and the Scottish Economy (Co-Editor), 1984; Transnational Corporations in the Textile Industry (Co-author), 1984; Foreign Multinationals and the British Economy (Co-author), 1987; Strategies in Global Competition (Co-Editor), 1987; Scottish Financial Sector (Co-author), 1988. Recreations: swimming; reading; gardening. Address: (h.) Teviot, 12 Carlisle Road, Hamilton, ML3 7DB; T.-0698 424870.

Hook, Professor Andrew Dunnet, MA, PhD. Bradley Professor of English Literature, Glasgow University, since 1979; b. 21.12.32, Wick; m., Judith Ann (deceased); 2 s.; 1 d. Educ. Wick High School; Daniel Stewart's College, Edinburgh; Edinburgh University; Manchester University; Princeton University. Edinburgh University: Assistant Lecturer in English Literature, 1961-63, Lecturer in American Literature, 1963-70; Senior Lecturer in English, Aberdeen University, 1970-79; CNAA: Chairman, Committee for Humanities, Member Committee for Academic Affairs; Chairman, Scottish Universities Council on Entrance English Panel; Member, Scottish Examination Board, since 1984; President, Eighteenth-Century Scotish Studies Society, 1990-

92. Publications: Scotland and America 1750-1835, 1975; American Literature in Context 1865-1900, 1983; Scott's Waverley (Editor), 1971; Charlotte Bronte's Shirley (Editor, with Judith Hook), 1974; Dos Passos: A Collection of Critical Essays (Editor), 1974; The History of Scottish Literature II, 1660-1800 (Editor), 1987. Recreations: theatre; opera; catching up on reading. Address: (b.) Department of English Literature, Glasgow University, Glasgow, G12 8QQ; T.-041-339 8855, Ext. 4226.

Hope, Colin John Filshill, OStJ, BA, FCII, FCIS, FCIT, FBIM, MCIM, DipM. Member, Council, Insurance Ombudsman Bureau, since 1981; Director, Merchants House of Glasgow, since 1988 (and 1981-87); Member, Air Transport Committee, Association of British Chambers of Commerce, 1986- 90; Governor, Keil School, 1986-91; Governor, Glasgow Educational and Marshall Trust, since 1986; Member, General Convocation, Strathclyde University, 1980-90; Member, South of Scotland Electricity Consultative Committee, 1990-91; b. 24.6.24, Dullatur; m., Jean Calder Douglas; 1 s.; 2 d. Educ. Glasgow High School; Glasgow Academy; Open University. RAF, 1942-47; joined Stenhouse & Partners, 1947; appointed Director, 1949; served in many capacities, including Managing Director, Stenhouse International; joined Norman Frizzell Scotland Ltd. as Managing Director, 1974; additionally Director, Norman Frizzell UK Ltd., 1976-81; Director, G.T. Senior, 1981-83 (Consultant, 1983-85); a Director, Glasgow Chamber of Commerce, 1979-88. Member: Scottish Consumer Council, 1979-85, Electricity Consultative Council for Scotland, 1979-87, Glasgow Airport Consultative Committee, since 1984; former Chairman, Transport Users Consultative Committee; Director, Glasgow Native Benevolent Association, 1988-91; Member, Dumbartonshire Committee, Order of St. John, since 1987. Address: (h.) Omaha, 4 Munro Drive East, Helensburgh, G84 9BS; T.-0436 73091.

Hope, Rt. Hon. Lord (James Arthur David Hope), PC. A Senator of the College of Justice, and Lord Justice General and Lord President of the Court of Session, since 1989; b. 27.6.38, Edinburgh; m., Katharine Mary Kerr; 2 (twin) s.; 1 d. Educ. Edinburgh Academy; Rugby School; St. John's College, Cambridge (BA); Edinburgh University (LLB); Hon. LLD, Aberdeen (1991). National Service, Seaforth Highlanders, 1957-59; admitted Faculty of Advocates, 1965; Standing Junior Counsel to Inland Revenue, 1974-78; QC, 1978; Advocate Depute, 1978-82; Chairman, Medical Appeal Tribunal, 1985-86; Legal Chairman, Pensions Appeal Tribunal, 1985-86; Dean, Faculty of Advocates, 1986-89. Publications: Gloag and Henderson's Introduction to Scots Law (Joint Editor, 7th edition, Assistant Editor, 8th and 9th editions); Armour on Valuation for Rating (Joint Editor, 4th and 5th editions); (Contributor) Stair Memorial Encyclopaedia of Scots Law. Address: (h.) 34 India Street, Edinburgh, EH3 6HB; T.-031-225 8245.

Hope, William, MA. Rector, Elgin High School, since 1978; b. 26.9.43, Scotland; m., Patricia Miller. Educ. Dalbeattie High School; Kirkcudbright Academy; Edinburgh University; Jordanhill College of Education. Alloa Academy: Assistant Teacher, Principal Teacher of Guidance; Assistant Rector, Lochaber High School. Chairman, Moray Branch, UNICEF; Vice Chairman, Elgin and District Branch, Cancer Relief. Recreations: umpiring hockey and cricket; fishing; public speaking. Address: (b.) Elgin High School, High School Drive, Elgin, Moray; T.-0343 545181.

Hopwood, Sylvia Elaine, MB, ChB, DPM. Psychiatrist, Tayside Region, and Honorary Lecturer, Dundee University, since 1962; b. 25.2.38, Salford; 2 d. Educ. Leeds University. Medical and neurological training, Leeds, 1960-62; psychiatric training, Dundee, 1962. Chairman, Gowrie Housing Association; Member, National Schizophrenia Fellowship and Manic Depressive Fellowship. Publications: many articles on alcoholism, depression and schizophrenia. Recreations: lace-making; embroidery; gardening. Address: (h.) 6 Strips of Craigie Road, Dundee, DD4 7PZ; T.-0382 462265.

Horden, Professor John Robert Backhouse, MA, MLitt, DHL, FSA, FSA(Scot), FRSL. Professor Emeritus of Bibliographical Studies, Stirling University; b. Warwickshire; m., Aileen Mary Douglas (deceased); 1 s. Educ. Oxford University; Cambridge University; Heidelberg University; Sorbonne; Lincoln's Inn. Former Director, Centre for Bibliographical Studies, Stirling University; former Director, Institute of Bibliography and Textual Criticism, Leeds University; former Tutor and Lecturer in English Literature, Christ Church, Oxford; Visiting Professorial appointments, Universities of Pennsylvania State, Saskatchewan, Erlangen-Nurnberg, Texas at Austin, Munster; Editor, Dictionary of Scottish Biography, since 1982; Cecil Oldman Memorial Lecturer, 1971; Marc Fitch Prize for Bibliography, 1979; founded Stirling University Press, 1985. Publications: Francis Quarles: A Bibliography of his Work to 1800, 1953; Francis Quarles' Hosanna and Threnodes (Editor), 1960; Annual Bibliography of English Language and Literature (Editor), 1967-75; English and Continental Emblem Books (22 vols.) (Editor), 1968-74; Art of the Drama, 1969; Dictionary of Concealed Authorship, Vol. 1 (Editor), 1980; initiator and first editor, Index of English Literary Manuscripts, seven volumes, 1980-90; Everyday Life in Seventeenth-Century England, 1974; Techniques of Bibliography, 1977; John Freeth: Political Ballad Writer and Inn Keeper, 1985; Bibliographia (Editor), 1991. Recreations: golf (representative honours); music; painting. Address: (b.) Department of English Studies, Stirling University, Stirling, KF9 4LA.

Horlick, Sir John (James Macdonald), 5th Bt.; b. 9.4.22; m.; 1 s.; 2 d. Educ. Eton; Babson Institute of Business Administration, USA. Captain, Coldstream Guards, Second World War; former Depute Chairman, Horlicks Ltd. Address: (h.) Tournaig, Poolewe, Achnasheen, Ross-shire.

Horn, David Bowes, BSc, PhD, CChem, FRSC, FRCPath, CBiol, FIBiol, FRSE. Head, Department of Clinical Chemistry, Western General Hospital, Edinburgh, 1966-87; Honorary Senior Lecturer in Clinical Chemistry, Edinburgh University, 1966-87; b. 18.8.28, Edinburgh; m., Shirley Kay Riddell; 2 d. Educ. Daniel Stewart's College, Edinburgh; Heriot-Watt University, Edinburgh; Edinburgh University. Senior Grade Biochemist: Vale of Leven Hospital, Alexandria, 1956, Queen Elizabeth Hospital, Birmingham, 1959; Biochemist, Royal Victoria Infirmary, Newcastle-upon-Tyne, and Honorary Lecturer, Department of Clinical Biochemistry, Newcastle-upon-Tyne University, 1959. Past Chairman, Scottish Region, Association of Clinical Biochemists (former Member, ACB National Council); Past Chairman, Scientific Services Advisory Group Clinical Chemistry Sub-Committee; Royal Society of Chemistry Representative, Mastership in Clinical Biochemistry Examination Board, 1973-88. Recreations: gardening; walking. Address: (h.) 2 Barnton Park, Edinburgh, EH4 6JF; T.-031-336 3444.

Horne, Allan Maxwell, BL. Solicitor (retired); Honorary Sheriff, Elgin, since 1981; b. 24.2.17, Brora; m., Margaret Ross; 1 d. Educ. Elgin Academy; Edinburgh University. Royal Artillery, 1940-46: commissioned 128th Field Regiment, 51st (H) Division, served as Air Observation Pilot, 1945-46, demobilised with rank of Captain; Legal Assistant, Inverness, 1946-49; Partner, Grigor & Young, Solicitors, Elgin, 1949-83, retiring as Senior Partner; Burgh Prosecutor, Elgin, 1950-75. Recreation: golf. Address: (h.) Melford, 11 Fleurs Place, Elgin; T.-Elgin 542833.

Horne, Norman John, MA (Hons). Headmaster, Harlaw Academy, Aberdeen, since 1985; b. 10.12.37, Turriff, Aberdeenshire; m., Ann Gavin; 1 s.; 2 d. Educ. Aberdeen Grammar School; Aberdeen University. Teacher of Classics, Hamilton Academy, 1961-66; Principal Classics Teacher: Nicolson Institute, Stornoway, 1966-71, Inverness Royal Academy, 1971-72; Assistant Rector, Inverness High School, 1972-77; Rector, Milne's High School, Fochabers, 1977-85. Recreations: sport (golf, table tennis); music (jazz). Address: (h.) 11 Beechwood Gardens, Westhill, Skene, Aberdeen; T.-Aberdeen 743831.

Horne, Norman Wemyss, MB, ChB, FRCPE. President, Europe Region, International Union Against Tuberculosis and Lung Disease; Chairman (Scotland), Chest, Heart and Stroke Association; b. 6.4.18, Aberdeen; m., Barbara Munro Ross; 4 s. Educ. George Watson's College, Edinburgh; Edinburgh University. Squadron Leader, RAFVR, 1941-46; Consultant Physician, City Hospital, Edinburgh (retired); Senior Lecturer in Respiratory Medicine, Edinburgh University (retired). President, British Thoracic Society, 1980-81. Recreations: gardening; music. Address: (h.) 95/5 Grange Loan, Edinburgh, EH9 2FD; T. 031-667 2149.

Horner, Rev. Alan Philip, BA, BD. Chairman, Methodist Synod in Scotland, since 1982; Methodist Minister, since 1958; b. 8.3.34, Northallerton; m., Margaret Adams; 2 d. Educ. Stockton-on-Tees Grammar School; King James I Grammar School, Bishop Auckland; Durham University; Manchester University. Ministry: Kendal, 1958-62, Harlow, 1962-68, Warrington, 1968-77, Chester, 1977-82. Recreations: walking; photography; gardening; swimming; music; poetry. Address: 7 Rowanlea Drive, Giffnock, Glasgow, G46 6BS; T.-041-633 1434.

Horner, Professor Robert Malcolm Wigglesworth, CEng, BSc, PhD, MICE, MBIM. Professor of Engineering Management, since 1986, and Head, Department of Civil Engineering, 1985-91, Dundee University; Non-executive Direcor, Atlantic Power and Gas Ltd., since 1991; b. 27.7.42, Bury; m., Beverley Anne Wesley; 1 s.; 1 d. Educ. The Bolton School; University College, London. Civil Engineer, Taylor Woodrow Construction Ltd., 1966-77; Lecturer, Department of Civil Engineering, Dundee University, 1977-83, Senior Lecturer, 1983-86. Founder Chairman, Dundee Branch, Opening Windows on Engineering; Winner, CIOB Ian Murray Leslie Award, 1980 and 1984. Recreations: squash; gardening. Address: (h.) Westfield Cottage, 11 Westfield Place, Dundee, DD1 4JU; T.-0382 25933.

Hornibrook, John Nevill, VRD, BSc, FEng, FIChemE, FInstD. Divisional Director, Roche Products Ltd., Dalry, Ayrshire, since 1981; Member, Executive Committee, Scottish Council (Development and Industry); Visiting Professor of Chemical and Process Engineering, Strathclyde University; Vice Chairman, Garnock Valley Development Executive; Governor, Paisley College of Technology; Chairman, Enterprise Ayrshire; b. 25.10.28, Gerrards Cross, Buckinghamshire; m., Dr. (Norma) Gillian Newbury; 2 d. Educ. Wellington College; Birmingham University. National Service, Royal Navy, 1949-51 (Sub-Lt., (E) RNVR, later promoted to Lt.-Cdr., RNR); Assistant Production Superintendent, Trinidad Leaseholds, BWI, 1951-55; Senior Chemical Engineer, Power Gas Corporation, 1955-58; Monsanto Chemicals Ltd., 1958-72: Senior Chemical Engineer, London, Technical Manager, Alta Labs, Bombay, Production Superintendent, Ruabon, North Wales; joined Roche Products Ltd., Dalry, 1972 (Works Manager, 1973-81). Vice-President, Institution of Chemical Engineers, 1983-85; Director, Ayrshire Chamber of Industries, since 1975; former Member, CBI Scottish Regional Council; Member, Scottish Regional Committee, Chemical Industries Association; Member, CBI Education and Training Affairs

Committee. Recreations: sailing; gardening. Address: (b.) Roche Products Ltd., Dalry, Ayrshire, KA24 5JJ; T.-029 483 2345.

Horobin, John Charles, BSc, PhD. Head of Conference and Group Services, St. Andrews University, since 1989; b. 13.2.45, Long Eaton; 1 s.; 1 d. Educ. Long Eaton Grammar School; King's College, London University; Durham University. Tutor-Organiser, WEA, Plymouth and West Devon, 1971-74; Assistant Director of Adult Education, St. Andrews University, 1974-89. Convener, Hill Land Use and Ecology Discussion Group. Address: (b.) Residence and Business Services, St. Andrews University, 79 North Street, St. Andrews, KY16 9AJ; T.-0334 76161.

Horsburgh, Charles Paton, JP, BL. Solicitor to the Council, formerly Senior Town Clerk Depute, City of Glasgow District Council; Clerk, City of Glasgow Licensing Board; b. 19.12.27, Edinburgh; m., Patricia Morris; 2 d. Educ. Queen's Park Secondary School, Glasgow; Glasgow University. Thirty years with Glasgow Corporation, rising from Apprentice Solicitor to Principal Solicitor, specialising in court work. Honorary Treasurer, Sherwood Church of Scotland, Paisley. Recreations: music; photography; motoring. Address: (b.) Town Clerk's Office, City Chambers, Glasgow, G2 1DU; T.-041-227 4504.

Horse, Harry (Horne, Richard George Anthony). Political Cartoonist; Cartoonist, Scotland on Sunday, since 1987; Book Illustrator and Caricaturist; Author; b. 9.5.60, Coventry; m., Amanda Williamson. Educ. Wrekin College, Wellington. Scottish Arts Council Writer's Award for Ogopogo, 1983; illustrated centenary edition, Jekyll and Hyde, 1986; illustrated Russian Gypsy Tales, 1986; wrote Illustrated Diary of a Plagiarist; as Musician/Songwriter formed Swamptrash, 1987. Recreations: playing music; playing cricket; Cajun music; walking with Mandy and dog. Address: 1 Linton Farm Cottage, Morebattle, Kelso, TD5 8AE; T.-05734 618.

Horsman, Graham Joseph Vivian, OBE (1977), JP, MA. Chairman, Forth Valley Health Board, 1977-85; Member, Scottish Health Service Planning Council, 1977-85; Extra-Parliamentary Commissioner Under Private Legislation Procedure (Scotland) Act, 1976-86; b. 10.11.19, London; m., Ruth Guest; 2 s.; 2 d. Educ. Whitgift School; Trinity College, Oxford. Councillor, County Borough of Reading, 1946-47; Member, Stirling and Clackmannan Hospitals Board of Management, 1966-69; Chairman, Stirling, Falkirk and Alloa Hospitals Board of Management, 1970-74; Member, Forth Valley Health Board, 1973-77; Member, Committee to Review Assessment in the Third and Fourth Years of Secondary Education in Scotland (Dunning Committee), 1975-77. Chairman, Dollar Civic Trust, 1970-78; Vice-Chairman, Scottish Association of Citizens' Advice Bureaux, 1976-78 (Council Member, 1973-78). Recreations: music; reading; walking. Address: (h.) 9 Tarmangie Drive, Dollar, Clackmannanshire; T.-Dollar 2575.

Horspool, William McKie, BSc, PhD, DSc, CChem, FRSC, FRSE. Reader in Organic Chemistry, Dundee University, since 1972; b. 12.8.36, Kilmarnock; m., Una Macfarlane Hamill; 1 s.; 1 d. Educ. Kilmarnock Academy; Strathclyde University; Glasgow University. Postdoctoral Associate, Columbia University, New York, 1964-65; Lecturer in Organic Chemistry, Queen's College, St. Andrews, 1965-72; Visiting Professor, Wisconsin University, 1974; Visiting Professor, Complutense University, Madrid, 1985. Publication: Aspects of Organic Photochemistry, 1976; Synthetic Organic Photochemistry (Editor), 1984; numerous papers in scientific journals. Recreations: gardening; DIY construction; choral singing (Treasurer, Dundee Choral Union); local church affairs (Session Clerk, Fowlis and Liff). Address: (h.) Waulkmill, Liff, Dundee, DD2 5LR.

Hoskings, Christine Mary. Secretary for Local and Region Unity, Action of Churches Together in Scotland, since 1990; b. 22.1.36, Leeds. Educ. Mary Erskine School for Girls, Edinburgh; Hoster's, London. Junior Editor, Thomas Nelson & Sons Ltd., Edinburgh; Pledged Gift Organiser, Oxfam, Scotland; Area Organiser, Oxfam, E. Scotland; Travelling Adviser, Scottish Citizens Advice Bureaux; Administrative Secretary, Scottish Churches Council, since 1973; Secretary, The Dunblane Society; Member, Leighton Library Appeal Committee. Recreations: music; family history; country dancing; sailing; camping; gardening; travel. Address: (h.) 2B Buccleuch Court, Dunblane, Perthshire, FK15 0AR; T.-0786 823588.

House, Professor Charles Randall, PhD, DSc, FRSE. Professor of Cell Physiology, Edinburgh University, since 1985; b. 16.7.38, Glasgow; 1 s.; 1 d. Educ. Queens Park School, Glasgow; Glasgow University; Birmingham University; Edinburgh University. Assistant Lecturer in Biophysics, Edinburgh University; Senior Research Associate in Biophysics, University of East Anglia; Research Associate in Neurophysiology, Columbia University, NY; Lecturer, then Reader in Physiology, Edinburgh University. Editor, Journal of Physiology; Editor, Experimental Physiology. Address: (b.) Department of Preclinical Veterinary Sciences, Edinburgh University, Edinburgh, EH9 1QH; T.-031-650 6105.

Houslay, Professor Miles Douglas, BSc, PhD, FRSE, FRSA, FIBiol, CBiol. Gardiner Professor of Biochemistry, Glasgow University, since 1984; b. 25.6.50, Wolverhampton; m., Rhian Mair; 2 s.; 1 d. Educ. Grammar School, Brewood, Stafford; University College, Cardiff; King's College, Cambridge; Cambridge University. ICI Research Fellow and Fellow, Queens' College, Cambridge, 1974-76; Lecturer, then Reader in Biochemistry, UMIST, 1976-82; Selby Fellow, Australian Academy of Science, 1984; Colworth Medal, Biochemical Society of Great Britain, 1984; Honorary Research Fellow, California Metabolic Research Foundation, since 1981; Editor in Chief, Cellular Signalling; Deputy Chairman, Biochemical Journal, 1984-89; Editorial Board, Biochimica Biophysica Acta; Committee Member, Biochemical Society, 1982-85; Member, Research Committee, British Diabetic Association, 1986-91; Chairman, Grant Committee A, Cell and Disorders Board, Medical Research Council, 1989-92; Member, Scientific and Medical Grant Committee, Scottish Home and Health Department, 1991-94; Member, Advisory Board for External Appointments, London University, 1990-92. Publication: Dynamics of Biological Membranes; over 200 scientific papers. Address: (b.) Department of Biochemistry, Glasgow University, Glasgow, G12 8QQ; T.-041-339 8855, Ext. 4624.

Housley, Edward, MB, ChB, FRCPEdin, FRCP. Consultant Physician, Edinburgh Royal Infirmary, since 1970; Honorary Senior Lecturer, Department of Medicine, Edinburgh University, since 1970; b. 10.1.34, Chester, USA; m., Alma Mary; 1 d. Educ. Mundella Grammar School, Nottingham; Birmingham University. Postgraduate training, Department of Medicine, Birmingham University and McGill University, Montreal; Chairman, MRCP (UK) Part I Examining Board. Recreation: crossword puzzles. Address: (h.) 16 Sunbury Place, Edinburgh, EH4 3BY.

Houston, Major General David, CBE. Lord Lieutenant of Sutherland, since 1991.

Houston, David Charles, BSc, DPhil. Senior Lecturer, Department of Zoology, Glasgow University, since 1985; b. 2.8.46, London. Educ. University College School; Bristol University; Oxford University. Research Fellow, Edinburgh University, 1972-75; Lecturer, Glasgow University, 1975-85. Council Member, British Ornithologists' Union, 1980-91;

Member, Science Advisory Committee, Nature Conservancy Council, 1986-91; Council Member, RSPB, since 1990; Vice-President, Zoological Society of Glasgow and West of Scotland. Recreations: gardening; photography. Address: (h.) Karian, Dumgoyne, Killearn, G63 9LA; T.-0360 50662.

Houston, Professor George Frederick Barclay, MA, BLitt. Professor, Department of Political Economy, Glasgow University, since 1970; b. 26.10.20, Edinburgh; m., 1, Lilias Adam (deceased); 2, Jean Blackley; 1 s.; 3 d. Educ. George Heriot's School; Edinburgh University; Balliol College, Oxford. Lecturer, 1951, Senior Lecturer, 1966, in Agricultural Economics, Glasgow University; Consultant: FAO, OECD, SOEC, HIDB; Member, British Wool Marketing Board. Publications: Third Statistical Account of Dumfriesshire (Editor); Agrarian Change in the Scottish Highlands (Co-author). Recreations: golf; swimming. Address: (b.) Department of Political Economy, Glasgow University, Glasgow; T.-041-339 8855.

Houston, Rev. Graham Richard, BSc (Hons), BD (Hons), MTh. Chaplain, Heriot-Watt University, since 1990; b. 3.5.50, Glasgow; m., Irene Elizabeth Robertson; 1 s.; 2 d. Educ. Hutchesons' Boys' Grammar School, Glasgow; Strathclyde University; Aberdeen University. Assistant, project, Govan, 1972-73; Assistant Minister, Palmerston Place Church, Edinburgh, 1976-77; Minister, Kildonan and Loth Church, Sutherland, 1978-82; Minister, Letham St. Mark's Church, Perth, 1982-90. Recreations: squash; golf; cricket. Address: (h.) 3 Ramsay Place, Penicuik, Midlothian, EH26 9JS; T.-0968 672752.

Houston, Stewart Robertson, LLB. Procurator Fiscal, Lanark, since 1981; b. 6.1.48, Hamilton; 3 d. Educ. Lanark Grammar School; Edinburgh University. Law Apprentice, then Solicitor, J. & A. Hastie, SSC, Edinburgh, 1970-73; Depute City Prosecutor, Edinburgh, 1973-75; Depute Procurator Fiscal, Edinburgh, 1975-76; Legal Assistant, Crown Office, 1976-77; Depute Procurator Fiscal, Edinburgh, 1977-78; Depute Procurator Fiscal, Dumbarton, 1979-81. Chairman, local branch, Guide Dogs for the Blind. Recreations: badminton; swimming; walking; modern languages. Address: (h.) Kirkfield, 21 Rowhead Terrace, Biggar, Lanarkshire; T.-0899 20418.

Houstoun, Andrew Beatty, OBE, MC, DL, JP. Vice President, Scottish Landowners Federation, since 1984; Scottish Member, European Landowners Organisation, 1976-86; b. 15.10.22, Cranleigh; m., Mary Elizabeth Spencer-Nairn; 4 s. Educ. Harrow. Regular Army, 1941-56; retired as Major, 1st The Royal Dragoons; farming, Angus and Perthshire, since 1956; commanded Fife and Forfar Yeomanry/Scottish Horse (TA), 1962-65; Angus County Councillor, 1966-75 (Vice Chairman, Education Committee); Convener, Scottish Landowners Federation, 1979-82; Chancellor's Assessor, Dundee University Court, since 1981; Vice Lord Lieutenant, Angus, since 1986. Address: Lintrathen Lodge, Kirriemuir, Angus, DD8 5JJ; T.-057 56 228.

Howard, Ian, MA (Hons), ARSA. Head of Painting, Duncan of Jordanstone College of Art, Dundee, since 1986; b. 5.11.52, Aberdeen; m., Ruth D'Arcy; 2 d. Educ. Aberdeen Grammar School; Edinburgh College of Art; Edinburgh University. Travelling scholarship to Italy, 1976; part-time Lecturer in Painting, Gray's School of Art, Aberdeen, 1977 (appointed full-time, 1980); Scottish Arts Council Award, 1979, Bursary, 1985-86; numerous one-man and group exhibitions. Recreations: reading; music; cooking. Address: (h.) 66 Camphill Road, Broughty Ferry, Dundee; T.-Dundee 79395.

Howatt, Anthony Philip Reid, MA, DipAppLing. Senior Lecturer, Department of Applied Linguistics, Edinburgh University, since 1984; b. 17.6.38, Sheffield; m., Cynthia Helen Howatt; 1 step d. Educ. George Watson's College, Edinburgh; Edinburgh University. Senior Linguistics Assistant, Stockholm, 1963-65; Assistant Lecturer, Department of Applied Linguistics, Edinburgh University, 1965-68; Lecturer, 1968-84. President, TESOL Scotland, since 1987. Publications: several books on linguistics. Address: (b.) 14 Buccleuch Place, Edinburgh, EH8 9LN; T.-031-650 3498.

Howe, Professor James Alexander Macgregor, MA, PhD. Head, Department of Artificial Intelligence, Edinburgh University, since 1978 (Professor of Artificial Intelligence, since 1985); b. 7.7.37, Glasgow; m., Nan Harvie Bell; 1 s.; 2 d. Educ. Kelvinside Academy, Glasgow; St. Andrews University; Cambridge University. Senior Assistant in Research, Laboratory of Experimental Psychology, Cambridge University, 1964-66; Research Fellow, Lecturer, Senior Lecturer, Reader, Department of Artificial Intelligence, Edinburgh University, 1967-85; Chairman, IKBS Advisory Group, Alvey Directorate; Chairman, SERC/DTI Systems Engineering Sub-Committee; Founder and Chairman, Artificial Intelligence Applications Institute, Edinburgh University; Member, Ordnance Survey's Science and Technology Advisory Committee. Recreations: skiing; curling; gardening; golf. Address: (h.) 26 Essex Road, Edinburgh, EH4 6LJ; T.-031-339 5390.

Howell, John, BEng, PhD, CEng, MIEE. Senior Lecturer, Department of Mechanical Engineering, Glasgow University, since 1990; b. 25.2.54, St. Albans; m., Susan Tryner; 1 s.; 1 d. Educ. Hatfield School; Sheffield University; Glasgow University. Member, Control and Dynamics Group, Atomic Energy Establishment, Winfrith, 1975-84; Lecturer in Control Engineering, Glasgow University, 1984-90. Recreation: walking. Address: (b.) Department of Mechanical Engineering, Glasgow University, Glasgow; T.-041-339 8855.

Howgego, Joseph, MA (Hons) (Cantab). HM Chief Inspector of Schools, since 1982; b. 4.4.33, Crewe; m., Anne Barbara; 4 s. Educ. Manchester Grammar School; Queens' College, Cambridge. Teaching posts: Birkenhead School, 1955-61; King's School, Chester, 1961-64; King George V School, Southport, 1964-67; HM Inspector of Schools, 1968-82. Chairman, Gullane, Aberlady and Drem Community Council, 1975-77. Recreations: golf; walking; music (choral singing). Address: (h.) Bank House, Main Street, Gullane, East Lothian, EH31 2HD; T.-0620 842348.

Howie, Andrew Law, CBE, FRAgrS. Chairman, Robert Howie & Sons, since 1982; Chairman, Scottish Milk Marketing Board, since 1982; b. 14.4.24, Dunlop; m., Joan Duncan; 2 s.; 2 d. Educ. Glasgow Academy. Joined Robert Howie & Sons, 1941; War Service, RN; became Director, 1965; President, Scottish Compound Feed Manufacturers, 1968-70 and 1983-85; President, Compound Animal Feed Manufacturers National Association, 1971-72; Director, Scottish Corn Trade, 1976-78; Vice-President/Feed, UK Agricultural Supply Trade Association, 1980-81; Chairman, Scottish Council, UKASTA, 1985-87; Director, Scottish Milk Marketing Board, since 1980; Member, CBI Scottish Council, since 1989. Recreations: golf; gardening. Address: (h.) Newmill House, Dunlop, Kilmarnock, KA3 4BQ; T.-0560 84936.

Howie, Sir James William, Kt (1969), LLD, MD, FRCP, FRCPath, FIMLS, Hon. ARCVS; b. 31.12.07, Oldmeldrum, Aberdeenshire; m., Isabella Winifred Mitchell; 2 s.; 1 d. Educ. Robert Gordon's College, Aberdeen; Aberdeen University. Specialised in bacteriology as applied to infectious diseases and agriculture; RAMC, 1939-45, Nigeria and War Office; Professor of Bacteriology, Glasgow University, 1951-63; Medical Director, Public Health Laboratory Service, 1963-

73; Honorary Physician to the Queen, 1965-68; Past President: BMA, Royal College of Pathologists, Association of Clinical Pathologists, Institute of Sterile Services Management. Recreations: golf; music. Address: (h.) 34 Redford Avenue, Edinburgh, EH13 0BU; T.-031-441 3910.

Howie, John Cameron, IPFA, IRRV. Chief Executive, Stewartry District Council, since 1988; b. 22.9.41, Perth; m., Kathleen N.; 1 d. Educ. Perth Academy. Chief Accountant, Perth and Kinross Joint County Council, 1967; Depute County Treasurer, Ross and Cromarty County Council, 1970; County Treasurer, Kirkcudbright County Council, 1972; Director of Finance and Housing, Stewartry District Council, 1975-88. Recreations: golf; swimming; all sports; reading. Address: (h.) Kinclaven, Hardgate, Castle Douglas, DG7 3LD.

Howie, Professor John Garvie Robertson, MD, PhD, FRCPE, FRCGP. Professor of General Practice, Edinburgh University, since 1980; b. 23.1.37, Glasgow; m., Elizabeth Margaret Donald; 2 s.; 1 d. Educ. High School of Glasgow; Glasgow University. Registrar, Laboratory Medicine, Western Infirmary, Glasgow, 1962-66; General Practitioner, Glasgow, 1966-70; Lecturer/Senior Lecturer in General Practice, Aberdeen University, 1970-80; Member: Biomedical Research Committee, SHHD, 1977-81, Health Services Research Committee, SHHD, 1982-86, Chief Scientist Committeee, SHHD, since 1987, Committee on the Review of Medicines, since 1986; Chairman, Heads of Departments of General Practice Group. Publication: Research in General Practice. Recreations: golf; gardening; music. Address: (h.) 4 Ravelrig Park, Balerno, Midlothian, EH14 7DL; T.-031-449 6305.

Howie, Professor John Mackintosh, MA, DPhil, DSc, FRSE. Regius Professor of Mathematics, St. Andrews University, since 1970; b. 23.5.36, Chryston, Lanarkshire; m., Dorothy Joyce Miller; 2 d. Educ. Robert Gordon's College, Aberdeen; Aberdeen University. Assistant in Mathematics, Aberdeen University, 1958-59; Assistant, then Lecturer in Mathematics, Glasgow University, 1961-67; Senior Lecturer in Mathematics, Stirling University, 1967-70; visiting appointments: Tulane University, 1964-65, State University of New York at Buffalo, 1969-70, University of Western Australia, 1968, Monash University, 1979, Northern Illinois University, 1988; Dean of Science, St. Andrews University, 1976-79. President, Edinburgh Mathematical Society, 1972-73; Vice-President, London Mathematical Society, 1984-86 and since 1990; Convener, SCEEB Mathematics Panel, 1970-73; Chairman, Scottish Central Committee on Mathematics, 1975-81; Member, Committee to Review Examinations (Dunning Committee), 1975-77; Chairman, Governors, Dundee College of Education, 1983-87; Keith Prize, Royal Society of Edinburgh, 1979-81; Chairman, Committee to review Fifth and Sixth Years (Howie Committee), since 1990. Publications: An Introduction to Semigroup Theory, 1976; Automata and Languages, 1991; papers in mathematical journals. Recreations: music; gardening. Address: (b.) Mathematical Institute, St. Andrews University, North Haugh, St. Andrews, KY16 9SS; T.-0334 76161.

Howie, Professor Peter William, MD, FRCOG, FRSE. Professor of Obstetrics and Gynaecology, Dundee University, since 1981 (Dean, Medicine and Dentistry, since 1990); b. 21.11.39, Aberdeen; m., Anne Jardine Quigg; 1 s.; 1 d. Educ. High School of Glasgow; Glasgow University. Astor Foundation Research Fellow, Royal College of Pathologists, 1970-71; Lecturer, then Senior Lecturer, Department of Obstetrics and Gynaecology, Glasgow University, 1971-78; Clinical Consultant, Medical Research Council Reproductive Biology Unit, Edinburgh, 1978-81. Recreations: golf; watching sport. Address: (h.) 8 Travebank Gardens, Monifieth, Dundee, DD5 4ET; T.-0382 534802.

Howie, William Forbes, DL, JP, BSc, CEng, MIEE, BA. Chairman, Supplementary Benefit Appeal Tribunal, Stirling and Falkirk, 1973-88; Justice of the Peace, since 1974; Deputy Lieutenant, Stirling and Falkirk District, since 1981; General Commissioner of Income Tax, since 1983; b. 13.8.20, Falkirk; m., Janet M. Campbell; 2 s.; 1 d. Educ. Falkirk High School; Glasgow University; Open University. RAF, during Second World War (demobbed as Flight Lieutenant); Managing Director, Thomas Laurie & Co. Ltd., 1956-81; appointed Chairman, Children's Panel Advisory Committee, Falkirk, 1970; Past Chairman, Forth Valley Scouts; former Session Clerk St. Andrews Church, Falkirk; set up Stirling and District Amateur Football Association, 1951 (its first Secretary); set up Falkirk Section, Scottish Wildlife Trust, 1984. Recreations: golf; bowls; colour photography; gardening; wildlife. Address: 12 Gartcows Crescent, Falkirk, FK1 5QH; T.-Falkirk 24128.

Howitt, Lewis Finnigan, MB, ChB, DPH, FFCM, FRCP. Consultant Public Health Medicine, Lothian Health Board, since 1986; b. 27.5.28, Aberdeen; m., Sheila Helen Elizabeth Burns; 1 s.; 1 d. Educ. Aberdeen Central School; Aberdeen University. Medical Officer, RAF; Medical Officer, Counties of Roxburgh and Selkirk Public Health Department; Medical Officer, then Senior Medical Officer, City of Edinburgh Public Health Department; Deputy Medical Officer of Health, Counties of Midlothian and Peebles Public Health Department; Senior Medical Officer, Scottish Home and Health Department. Recreations: gardening; golf. Address: (h.) 27 Cluny Drive, Edinburgh, EH10 6DT; T.-031-447 5849.

Ho-Yen, Darrel Orlando, BMSc (Hons), MBChB, MD, MRCPath. Consultant Microbiologist, Raigmore Hospital, Inverness, since 1987; Director, Scottish Toxoplasma Reference Laboratory, since 1987; Honorary Clinical Senior Lecturer, Aberdeen University, since 1987; b. 1.5.48; m., Jennifer Nicholls; 2 s. Educ. Dundee University. Ninewells Hospital and Medical School, Dundee, 1974-83; Regional Virus Laboratory, Ruchill Hospital, Glasgow, 1983-87. Publications: Better Recovery from Viral Illnesses; Diseases of Infection (Co-author); Unwind; Human Toxoplasmosis (Co-author). Address: (b.) Microbiology Department, Raigmore Hospital, Inverness, IV2 3UJ; T.-0463 234151, Ext. 206.

Hubbuck, Professor John Reginald, MA (Cantab), MA, DPhil (Oxon), FRSE, FRSA. Professor of Mathematics, Aberdeen University, since 1978 (Head, Department of Mathematical Sciences); President, Edinburgh Mathematical Society, 1985-86; b. 3.5.41, Girvan; m., Anne Neilson; 1 s.; 1 d. Educ. Manchester Grammar School; Queens' College, Cambridge; Pembroke College, Oxford. Fellow: Gonville and Caius College, Cambridge, 1970-72, Magdalen College, Oxford, 1972-78. Recreation: hill-walking. Address: (h.) 8 Fonthill Terrace, Aberdeen, AB1 2UR; T.-0224 588738.

Huckle, Derek Arthur, CA, FBIM, FIIM, FCCA. Principal, Fife College of Technology, since 1984; b. 25.1.30, Newtown St. Boswells; m., Janette; 2 d. Educ. Galashiels Academy. National Service, 1954-56; paper making, 1956-70; further education, since 1970. Member, Committees, Institute of Chartered Accountants of Scotland, British Institute of Management, Institution of Industrial Managers, SCOTVEC. Address: (b.) Fife College of Technology, St. Brycedale Avenue, Kirkcaldy, KY1 1EX; T.-0592 268591.

Hudson, Christopher Sydney, DSO (and Bar), FBIM, CIPM; b. 1.8.16, Tunbridge Wells; m., Ruth Julia Risse; 1 d. Educ. privately, in Switzerland. Army Service, Royal Fusiliers and SOE, 1940-45 (Lt.-Col.); Control Commission for Germany (British and US Sectors), 1946-53; Personnel Manager in overseas companies, Shell International

Petroleum Co., Israel, Trinidad, Zaire, Algeria; seconded to International Labour Organisation, Geneva, 1966; Executive in charge of Personnel, Training and Industrial Relations, Bank of Scotland, 1968-80. Croix de Guerre with Palme. Recreations: golf; swimming. Address: (h.) Invereil House, North Berwick, East Lothian, EH39 5DH; T.-0620 3646.

Hudson, Rev. Eric Vallance, LTh. Minister, Westerton Fairlie Memorial Church, since 1990; b. 22.2.42, Glasgow; m., Lorna Mary Miller; 1 d. Educ. Paisley Grammar School; Wollongong High School, NSW; Christ's College, Aberdeen and Aberdeen University. Sub-Editor, D.C. Thomson & Co. Ltd., Dundee, 1961-66; Senior Assistant Minister, New Kilpatrick Parish Church, Bearsden, 1971-73; Minister, Kintore Parish Church, 1973-78; Religious Programmes Officer, Scottish Television, 1978-89. Address: 3 Canniesburn Road, Bearsden, Glasgow, G61 1PW.

Huggins, Martin, MA. Co-Founder and Principal, Edinburgh School of English, since 1969; b. 11.4.39, Edinburgh; m., 1, Astrid Chalmers Watson (m. diss.); 2, Margot Learmond; 2 d. Educ. George Watson's College; Edinburgh University. Chairman, Scottish Craftsmanship Association, 1977-84; Governor, Edinburgh College of Art, since 1980; Chairman, ARELS, 1984-86; Member, British Council Recognition Advisory Committee, 1984-86; Chairman, Board of Governors, Edinburgh College of Art, since 1990; President, Scottish Arts Club, 1990-92. Recreations: music; travel; lunching at the Arts Club. Address: (h.) 16 McLaren Road, Edinburgh, EH9 2BN; T.-031-667 1751.

Hughes, Professor Ian Simpson, BSc, PhD, FInstP, FRSE. Professor Emeritus, Department of Physics and Astronomy, Glasgow University; b. 1.11.30, Liverpool; m., Isobel Mary; 1 s.; 1 d. Educ. High School of Glasgow; Glasgow University. Research Fellow, Nuclear and Particle Physics, Glasgow University, 1955-57; Research Associate, Particle Physics, Duke University and Lawrence Radiation Laboratory, Berkeley, USA, 1957-58; Lecturer, Senior Lecturer, Reader, Department of Natural Philosophy, Glasgow University, 1958-71; appointed Professor, Department of Physics and Astronomy, 1971; Member, Nuclear Physics Board, Science and Engineering Research Council, 1969-73 and 1980-83 and of numerous SERC Committees. Recreations: literature - poetry, fiction, travel, history; mountaineering; music. Address: (b.) Department of Physics and Astronomy, Glasgow University, Glasgow, G12 8QQ; T.-041-339 8855.

Hughes, Professor James, BSc, CEng, MIEE, FBIM. Professor of Management, Strathclyde University, since 1989; Director of Human Relations, Thorn EMI plc, since 1984; b. 15.6.30, Ayr; m., Margaret Brown Hughes; 1 s.; 1 d. Educ. Ayr Academy; Strathclyde University. Project Manager, GEC Ltd.; general management, latterly Corporate Director Scotland, Honeywell Ltd.; Director and General Manager, Security Division, Microwave & Electronic Systems Ltd.; Director and General Manager, Tannoy Ltd.; Personnel Director, Ellerman Scotland. Recreations: music; squash; hillwalking; painting. Address: (h.) 41 Craigleith View, Edinburgh, EH4 3JY; T.-031-337 5169.

Hughes, Professor John, BSc, CEng, FIMechE, FISPO. Professor and Director, National Centre for Prosthetics and Orthotics, Strathclyde University, since 1972; b. 20.4.34, Renfrew; m., Margaret Scoular Crichton; 2 d. Educ. Camphill School; Strathclyde University. Worked in shipbuilding and engineering, 1950-63; Strathclyde University: Lecturer in Mechanical Engineering Design, 1963-67, Senior Lecturer, Bioengineering Unit, 1967-72; Past President, International Society for Prosthetics and Orthotics. Recreations: golf; gardening. Address: (b.) Strathclyde University, Curran Building, 131 St. James' Road, Glasgow, G4 OLS; T.-041-552 4049.

Hughes, Robert. MP (Labour), Aberdeen North, since 1970; b. 3.1.32; m.; 2 s.; 3 d. Educ. Powis Secondary School, Aberdeen; Robert Gordon's College, Aberdeen; Benoni High School, Transvaal; Pietermaritzburg Technical College, Natal. Engineering apprenticeship, South African Rubber Company, Natal, 1949-54; draughtsman, C.F. Wilson & Co., Aberdeen, 1954-70; Member, Aberdeen City Council, 1962-71; Chairman, Aberdeen City Labour Party, 1961-69; Member, Select Committee on Scottish Affairs, 1971; Opposition Junior Spokesman on Scottish Affairs, 1972-74; Parliamentary Under Secretary of State, Scottish Office, 1974-75; Chairman, Select Committee on Scottish Affairs, 1981; Opposition Junior Spokesman on Transport, 1981-83; Opposition Principal Spokesman on Agriculture, 1984-85, on Transport, 1985-87; Member, General Medical Council, 1976-79; Chairman, Anti Apartheid Movement, since 1976; Vice-Convenor, Scottish Group, Labour MPs, since 1989; Convenor, Scottish Group of Labour MPs, 1990-91. Address: (b.) House of Commons, London SW1A 0AA.

Hughes, Rt. Hon. Lord (William Hughes), PC (1970), CBE (1956), DL, LLD. Company Director; b. 22.1.11, Dundee; m., Christian Clancher Gordon; 2 d. Educ. Balfour Street School; Dundee Technical College. ARP Controller, Dundee, 1939-43; Armed Forces, 1943-46 (commissioned 1944, demobilised as Captain, 1946, served India, Labuan and Burma); Member, Dundee Town Council, 1933-36 and 1937-61; City Treasurer, 1946-47; Lord Provost, 1954-60; Chairman, Eastern Regional Hospital Board, 1948-60; Member, Court, St. Andrews University, 1954-63; Member, Council, Queen's College, Dundee, 1954-63; Member, Committee on Civil Juries, 1958-59; Member, Committee to Inquire into Registration of Title to Land, 1960-62; Member, North of Scotland Hydro Electric Board, 1957-64; Member, Scottish Transport Council, 1960-64; Chairman, Glenrothes Development Corporation, 1960-64; Chairman, East Kilbride Development Corporation, 1975-82; Chairman, Royal Commission on Legal Services in Scotland, 1976-80; Joint Parliamentary Under Secretary of State for Scotland, 1964-69; Minister of State for Scotland, 1969-70 and 1974-75; President, Scottish Federation of Housing Associations, since 1975; Member, Council of Europe and Western European Union, 1976-87; Hon. Member, Council of Europe, since 1987. Recreation: gardening. Address: (h.) The Stables, Ross, Comrie, Perthshire; T.-0764 70557.

Hughes, William Young, CBE. Chairman and Chief Executive, Grampian Holdings plc, since 1985 (Chief Executive, 1976-85); Deputy Chairman, Scottish Conservative Party, since 1989; b. 12.4.40, Milnrow, Lancaster; m., Anne Macdonald Richardson; 2 s.; 1 d. Educ. Firth Park Grammar School, Sheffield; Glasgow University; Strathclyde University; Heriot-Watt University. Partner, R. Gordon Drummond, 1966-70; Managing Director, MSJ Securities Ltd., 1970-76. Chairman, CBI Scotland, 1987-89; Member, Governing Council, Scottish Business in the Community. Recreations: Member, Glenbervie and Gleneagles Golf Clubs. Address: (b.) Stag House, Castlebank Street, Glasgow, G11 6DY; T.-041-357 2000.

Hughes Hallett, Professor Andrew Jonathan, BA (Hons), MSc (Econ), DPhil, FRSA. Professor of Economics, Strathclyde University, since 1989; Research Fellow, Centre for Economic Policy Research, since 1985; Consultant to World Bank, UN, EEC, etc., since 1986; b. 1.11.47, London; m., Claudia; 2 s.; 1 d. Educ. Radley College; Warwick University; LSE; Oxford University. Lecturer in Economics, Bristol University, 1973-77; Associate Professor, Erasmus University, Rotterdam, 1977-85; David Dale Professor, Newcastle University, 1985-89. Publications: four books; 102 papers. Address: (b.) 100 Cathedral Street, Glasgow, G4 OLN; T.-041-552 4400.

Hughson, A.V. Mark, MD, MB, ChB, MRCPsych, DPM. Consultant Psychiatrist, Leverndale Hospital, Glasgow, since 1990; Honorary Clinical Senior Lecturer, Glasgow University, since 1991; b. 12.3.47, Edinburgh; m., Joan Scally; 2 s. Educ. George Watson's College, Edinburgh; Glasgow University. Recreations: playing the organ (not too badly); skiing (badly). Address: (h.) 1 Cleveden Gardens, Glasgow, G12 0PU; T.-041-334 2473.

Hume, Sir Alan (Blyth), Kt, CB, MA; b. 5.1.13, Broxburn; m., Marion Morton Garrett; 1 s.; 1 d. Educ. George Heriot's School, Edinburgh; Edinburgh University. Scottish Office: entered, 1936, Under Secretary, Scottish Home Department, 1957-59, Assistant Under Secretary of State, 1959-62, Under Secretary, Ministry of Public Building and Works, 1963-64, Secretary, Scottish Development Department, 1965-73; Chairman, Ancient Monuments Board for Scotland, 1973-81; Chairman, Edinburgh New Town Conservation Committee, 1975-90. Recreations: golf; fishing. Address: (h.) 12 Oswald Road, Edinburgh, EH9 2HJ; T.-031-667 2440.

Hume, James Douglas Howden, CBE, BSc, CEng, FIMechE, Hon. LLD (Strathclyde). Chairman and Managing Director, Drimard Limited, since 1988; Non-Executive Director, Ferrum Holdings PLC; b. 4.5.28, Melbourne, Australia; m., June Katharine Spriggs; 1 s.; 2 d. Educ. Loretto; Strathclyde University; Glasgow University. Royal Artillery, 1944-46 (2nd Lt.); engineering training: James Howden & Company Limited, 1948-54, Production Engineering Limited, 1954-55; James Howden & Company Limited: Production Manager, 1955-56, appointed Director, 1957, Joint Managing Director, 1960, Managing Director, 1963; Howden Group PLC: Managing Director, 1968, Deputy Chairman and Managing Director, 1973, appointed Chairman, 1987 (resigned, November 1987). Member, Court, Strathclyde University, since 1989. Address: (b.) Drimard Limited, 22 East Lennox Drive, Helensburgh, Dunbartonshire, G84 9JD; T.-0436 75132.

Hume, John Robert, BSc, ARCST, FSA, FSA Scot. Principal Inspector of Historic Buildings, Historic Scotland; Member, Inland Waterways Amenity Advisory Council, since 1974; Member, Industrial Archaeology Sub-Committee, English Heritage, since 1985; Chairman, Seagull Trust, since 1978; Trustee, Scottish Maritime Museum, since 1983; Honorary Vice-President, Association for Industrial Archaeology. b. 26.2.39, Glasgow; m., Catherine Hope Macnab; 4 s. Educ. Hutchesons' Boys' Grammar School; Glasgow University; Royal College of Science and Technology. Assistant Lecturer, Lecturer, Senior Lecturer in Economic History, Strathclyde University, 1964-91. Member, Ancient Monuments Board for Scotland, 1981-84; Director, Scottish Industrial Archaeology Survey, 1978-84. Publications: The Industrial Archaeology of Glasgow; The Industrial Archaeology of Scotland; as Co-author: Workshop of the British Empire: Engineering and Shipbuilding in the West of Scotland; Beardmore: the History of a Scottish Industrial Giant; The Making of Scotch Whisky; A Bed of Nails: a History of P. MacCallum & Sons Ltd.; Shipbuilders to the World: a History of Harland and Wolff; Steam Entertainment; Historic Industrial Scenes: Scotland; Industrial History in Pictures: Scotland; Glasgow's Railway Stations. Recreations: photography; reading. Address: (h.) 28 Partickhill Road, Glasgow, G11 5BP.

Hume, Robert, BSc, MBChB, PhD, FRCP(Edin). Senior Lecturer, Department of Child Life and Health, Edinburgh University, since 1980; Consultant Paediatrician, Simpson Memorial Maternity Pavilion, Edinburgh, since 1980; b. 5.4.47, Edinburgh; m., Shaena Finlayson Blair; 2 d. Educ. Dalkeith High School; Edinburgh University. House Surgeon/Physician, Royal Infirmary/City Hospital, Edinburgh, 1972-73; Resident II Paediatrics, Vancouver

General Hospital, 1973-74; SHO, Royal Hospital for Sick Children, Edinburgh, 1974-75; MRC Fellow, Department of Biochemistry, Edinburgh University, 1975-78; Lecturer, Department of Child Life and Health, Edinburgh University, 1978-80. Member, Royal College of Obstetricians and Gynaecologists (Birthright) Research Advisory Committee; Medical and Dental Defence Union of Scotland Specialist Advisor. Address: (b.) Simpson Memorial Maternity Pavilion, Royal Infirmary, Lauriston Place, Edinburgh; T.-031-299 2477.

Humphrey, James Malcolm Marcus, DL, OStJ, MA, FRICS. Grand Master Mason of Scotland, 1983-88; Member, Grampian Regional Council; Deputy Lieutenant, Aberdeenshire, since 1989; b. 1.5.38, Montreal, Canada; m., Sabrina Margaret Pooley; 2 s.; 2 d. Educ. Eton College; Oxford University. Conservative Parliamentary candidate, North Aberdeen, 1966, Kincardine and Deeside, 1991; Council Member, National Farmers Union of Scotland, 1968-73; Member, Aberdeen County Council, 1970-75 (Chairman of Finance, 1973-75); Chairman of Finance, Grampian Regional Council, 1974-78 (Leader, Conservative Group, 1974-78); former Chairman, Clinterty Agricultural College Council; Member, Queen's Bodyguard for Scotland (Royal Company of Archers); Chairman, North of Scotland Board, Eagle Star Group, 1973-91. Recreations: shooting; fishing; photography. Address: (h.) Dinnet, Aboyne, Aberdeenshire.

Hunt, Rev. Trevor George, BD (Hons), CPS. Minister, linked parishes of Evie, Rendall and Firth, since 1986; b. 28.3.42, Deal, Kent; m., Pauline Hazel Keen; 1 s.; 2 d. Educ. Aberdeen University and Christ College. Scientific Assistant, National Institute for Research in Nuclear Science; Senior Electronics Techician, Imperial College of Science and Technology, then Robert Gordon's Institute of Technology. Depute Presbytery Clerk; Hon. Secretary, Christian Reformed Tapes. Address: Finstown Manse, Orkney, KW17 2EG; T.-0856 76 328.

Hunter, A. Colin J., BA. Head Teacher, Tiree High School, since 1985; b. 26.9.47, Falkirk; m., June Sinclair Stark; 2 s.; 1 d. Educ. Falkirk High School; Stirling University. Entered teaching, 1972; Teacher, Falkirk High School and Forres Academy; Principal Teacher of Biology, Whitfield High School, Dundee; Depute Head Teacher, Auchtercairn Secondary School, Gairloch. Honorary Treasurer, Stirling University Graduates Association. Recreations: gardening; golf; walking. Address: (h.) Cornaigmore Schoolhouse, Isle of Tiree, Argyll, PA77 6XA; T.-087 92 556.

Hunter, Sheriff Adam Kenneth Fisher, MA (Hons), LLB. Sheriff of North Strathclyde (formerly Renfrew and Argyll), 1953-90; b. 1920.

Hunter, Andy Robb, MA (Hons), PhD. Traditional Folk Singer/Lecturer; Lecturer, Heriot Watt University, since 1970; b. 15.1.40, Glasgow; m., Susan Marjorie; 1 s.; 1 d. Educ. Allan Glen's School, Glasgow; Aberdeen University; Stirling University. Member of first wave of Scottish folksong revival (early 50s); spent 12 months in Brittany, 1963-64, producing life-long commitment to cultural minorities; albums recorded: A Sang's a Sang; King Fareweel. Publication: Vol. IV Greig Duncan Folksong Collection (Editor). Recreations: composing songs in Scots; composing for cauld wind pipes. Address: (h.) 7 Middlebank Holdings, by Dunfermline, KY11 5QN; T.-Inverkeithing 414290.

Hunter, Archibald Sinclair, CA. Managing Partner, Glasgow, KPMG Peat Marwick, since 1983; b. 20.8.43, Glasgow; m., Pat; 2 s.; 1 d. Educ. Queen's Park School, Glasgow. Trained with Mackie & Clark, CA, Glasgow; qualified as CA, 1966; joined Thomson McLintock, 1966; Partner, 1974. Member, Council, Institute of Chartered Accountants of Scotland; Member, Master Court, Incorporation of Hammermen, Glasgow. Recreations: golf; swimming; walking. Address: (b.) 24 Blythswood Square, Glasgow, G2 4QS; T.-041-226 5511.

Hunter, Edward Anthony, BSc, MPhil. Principal Scientific Officer, Scottish Agricultural Statistics Service, Edinburgh University, since 1967; b. 12.2.43, Newcastle-upon-Tyne; m., Janet M. Bruce; 1 s.; 1 d. Educ. Lasswade Secondary School; Edinburgh University. Recreations: playing bridge; reading; jogging. Address: (b.) Scottish Agricultural Statistics Service, Edinburgh University, King's Buildings, Edinburgh; T.-031-650 4896/4900.

Hunter, George Alexander, OBE (1980), OStJ. Secretary, Commonwealth Games Council for Scotland, since 1978; Founder Governor, Scottish Sports Aid Foundation, since 1980; b. 24.2.26, Edinburgh; m., Eileen Elizabeth. Educ. George Watson's College, Edinburgh. Served with Cameronians, seconded to 17th Dogara Regiment, Indian Army, 1944-47 (Captain); Lawson Donaldson Seeds Ltd., 1942-82 (Director, 15 years); Secretary, Scottish Amateur Rowing Association, 1948-78 (President, 1978-84); Adviser, Sports Aid Foundation, since 1979; Treasurer, Commonwealth Games Council for Scotland, 1962-78; Member, Scottish Sports Council, 1976-84 (Chairman, Games and Sports Committee, 1976-84); Chairman, Scottish Standing Conference for Sport, 1977-84. Address: (h.) 139 Old Dalkeith Road, Edinburgh; T.-031-664 1070.

Hunter, James, MA (Hons), PhD. Writer, Journalist and Broadcaster; Member, Board, Highlands and Islands Enterprise; Vice-Chairman, North West Regional Board, Nature Conservancy Council for Scotland; Member, Board of Trustees, John Muir Trust; b. 22.5.48, Duror, Argyll; m., Evelyn; 1 s.; 1 d. Educ. Oban High School; Aberdeen University; Edinburgh University. Former Director, Scottish Crofters Union. Publications: The Making of the Crofting Community, 1976; Skye: The Island, 1986; The Claim of Crofting, 1991. Address: (b.) 22 Borve, Portree, Isle of Skye.

Hunter, James Albert, TD, LRCPE, LRCSE, LRFP&SG. Member, Shetland Islands Council, 1978-90 (former Chairman, Social Work Committee); b. 2.5.14, Eshaness, Shetland; m., Helena Fraser (deceased); 4 s.; 2 d. Educ. Anderson Educational Institute, Lerwick; School of Medicine, Royal Colleges, Edinburgh. Captain, Royal Army Medical Corps, 1940-46; Medical Officer: Bangour Hospital, Midlothian, 1946, Bridge of Earn Hospital, Perthshire, 1946-47; Junior Assistant Tuberculosis Officer, Edinburgh, 1947; General Practitioner, Bixter and Voe, Shetland, 1947-78. Recreations: photography; fishing. Address: (h.) Kohima, Gott, Shetland, ZE2 9SG; T.-Gott 367.

Hunter, Hon. Lord (John Oswald Mair Hunter), VRD. Senator of the College of Justice in Scotland, 1961-86; b. 21.2.13. Chairman, Scottish Law Commission, 1971-81.

Hunter, John Andrew Adam, BSc, MB, ChB, FRCPE. Consultant Physician in Rehabilitation Medicine, Lothian Health Board, since 1976; part-time Senior Lecturer in Rehabilitation Studies, Edinburgh University, since 1977 (Head, Rehabilitation Studies Unit, 1988-90); b. 20.10.43, Perth; m., Hazel Watson; 1 s.; 1 d. Educ. Bell Baxter High School, Cupar; St. Andrews University. House Officer in Medicine and Orthopaedic Surgery, 1968-69; Lecturer in Biochemistry, Rheumatism Research Centre, Manchester University, 1969-72; Senior House Officer in Medicine, University Hospitals of South Manchester, 1972-74; Lecturer in Rheumatology, Manchester Royal Infirmary and Manchester University, 1974-76; Chairman, Disability Research Committee, Chief Scientist's Office, Scottish Home and Health Department; Member, Disability Living Allowance Advisory Board, Department of Social Security; Temporary Advisor to WHO on Rehabilitation. Recreations: singing; deep sea fishing. Address: (h.) 37 Gilmour Road, Edinburgh, EH16 5NS; T.-031-667 5333.

Hunter, Professor John Angus Alexander, BA, MD, FRCPEdin. Grant Professor of Dermatology, Edinburgh University, since 1981; b. 16.6.39, Edinburgh; m., Ruth Mary Farrow; 1 s.; 2 d. Educ. Loretto School; Pembroke College, Cambridge; Edinburgh University. Research Fellow, Institute of Dermatology, London, 1967; Registrar, Department of Dermatology, Edinburgh Royal Infirmary, 1968-70; Exchange Research Fellow, Department of Dermatology, Minnesota University, 1968; Lecturer, Department of Dermatology, Edinburgh University, 1970-74; Consultant Dermatologist, Lothian Health Board, 1974-80; Member: Executive Committee of Investigative Group, British Association of Dermatologists, 1974-76; Executive Committee, British Association of Dermatologists, 1977-79; SEC, Scottish Dermatological Society, 1980-82; Specialist Advisory Committee, (Dermatology), Joint Committee on Higher Medical Training, 1980-87 (Chairman, 1986-90); Medical Appeal Tribunal, since 1982; Scottish Committee for Hospital Medical Services, 1983-85. Publications: Common Diseases of the Skin (Co-Editor); Clinical Dermatology (Co-Editor). Recreations: music; gardening; tropical fish; golf. Address: (h.) Leewood, Rosslyn Castle, Roslin, Midlothian, EH25 9PZ; T.-031-440 2181.

Hunter, Professor Laurence Colvin, CBE, MA, DPhil, FRSE. Professor of Applied Economics, Glasgow University, since 1970; b. 8.8.34, Glasgow; m., Evelyn Margaret Green; 3 s.; 1 d. Educ. Hillhead High School, Glasgow; Glasgow University; University College, Oxford. Assistant Lecturer, Manchester University, 1958-59; 2nd Lt., RAEC, 1959-61; Walgreen Postdoctoral Fellow, University of Chicago, 1961-62; joined Glasgow University as Lecturer, 1962; Vice-Principal, 1982-86; Director of External Relations, 1987-90. Council Member, ACAS, 1974-87; Chairman, Police Negotiating Board, since 1986; Council Member, Economic and Social Research Council, since 1989; Editor, Scottish Journal of Political Economy, since 1966. Recreations: golf; painting; curling. Address: (h.) 23 Boclair Road, Bearsden, Glasgow, G61 2AF; T.-041-942 0793.

Hunter, Mollie. Writer; Past Chairman, Society of Authors in Scotland; b. 30.6.22, Longniddry; m., Thomas McIlwraith; 2 s. Educ. Preston Lodge School. Freelance Journalist, until 1960; Writer of various types of fiction (fantasy, historical novels, "realism") for children of varying age groups; 25 titles published, including Talent Is Not Enough, on the craft of writing for children; travelled extensively (Australia, New Zealand, Canada, USA); Lecturer on writing for children; Writer-in-Residence, Dalhousie University, Halifax, Canada, on several occasions; awarded Arbuthnot Lectureship, 1975, and Carnegie Medal, 1975. Recreations: reading; gardening; music. Address: The Shieling, Milton, by Drumnadrochit, Inverness-shire; T.-04562 267.

Hunter, Robert Leslie Cockburn, MA, LLB, WS, FCI (Arb). Chairman, Industrial Tribunals (Scotland), 1976-85; Chairman, Social Security Appeal Tribunals, 1983-90; Lecturer in Law, Aberdeen University, 1971-89; Consultant in Labour and Social Security Law, since 1989; Member, Grampian Regional Council, since 1990; b. 31.12.34, Polmont, Stirlingshire; m., Joan Gwendolen Mappin (m. diss.); 2 s. Educ. Loretto School; St. Andrews University; Edinburgh University. National Service, Royal Signals, 1953-55; Law Apprentice, Gillespie and Paterson, WS, Patrick and James, WS, 1960-63; Assistant Solicitor, Patrick and James, WS, 1963-64; Legal Assistant, Inverness County Council, 1964-66; Lecturer in Jurisprudence, Dundee University, 1966-71; occasional Lecturer, Petroleum Training Institute,

Stavanger, Norway, 1982-84; Honorary Secretary, Aberdeen Association of University Teachers, 1974-75; Governor, Robert Gordon's Institute of Technology, 1982-88; Elder, Queen's Cross Church of Scotland, Aberdeen, since 1982. Publication: The Law of Arbitration in Scotland, 1987. Recreations: choral singing; reading (in literature, history and philosophy); cycling. Address: (h.) Primrose Cottage, Place of Tilliefoure, by Monymusk, Inverurie, Aberdeenshire, AB7 7JB; T.-Monymusk 357.

Hunter, Russell. Actor; b. 18.2.25, Glasgow. Former shipyard worker; began acting as an amateur; made professional debut with Glasgow Unity Theatre, 1947; appeared in repertory with Edinburgh Gateway, Edinburgh Traverse and Glasgow Citizens'; acted with the RSC, Bristol Old Vic and at the Old Vic, London; played title role in The Servant o' Twa Maisters, 1965, opening production of Edinburgh Civic Theatre Company; played The Pope in Galileo, also at Royal Lyceum; played The Gravedigger in Hamlet, Assembly Hall, Edinburgh Festival; took title role in Cocky, one-man play, 1969; played Jock, solo play, 1972.

Hunter, William, MA. Columnist, Glasgow Herald; b. 16.8.31, Paisley; m., Mo; 1 s.; 1 d. Educ. Paisley Grammar School; Glasgow University. Publications: The Saints; Bell the Cage!; Dear Happy Ghosts. Recreation: weeding. Address: (h.) 233 Fenwick Road, Glasgow; T.-041-638 1323.

Hunter, William Hill, CBE, CA, JP, DL. Partner, McLay, McAlister & McGibbon, CA, 1946-91, Consultant, since 1991; Director, J. & G. Grant, Glenfarclas Distillery, since 1966; b. 5.11.16, Cumnock; m., Kathleen Cole; 2 s. Educ. Cumnock Academy. Enlisted as private, RASC, 1940; commissioned Royal Artillery, 1941; Staff Captain, Middle East, 1944-46; Director: Abbey National Building Society (Scottish Advisory Board), 1966-86, City of Glasgow Friendly Society, 1966-88 (President, 1980-88); Member, CBI Scottish Council, 1978-84; Member, Institute of Directors West of Scotland Committee, 1980-91; President, Renfrew West and Inverclyde Conservative and Unionist Association, since 1972; President, Scottish Young Unionist Association, 1958-60; President, Scottish Unionist Association, 1964-65; contested (Unionist), South Ayrshire, 1959 and 1964; Hon. Treasurer, Quarrier's Homes, since 1972; Hon. Financial Advisor, Erskine Hospital, since 1980; Session Clerk, Kilmacolm Old Kirk, 1972-77; Chairman, Salvation Army Advisory Board in Strathclyde, since 1982; Chairman, Salvation Army Housing Association Scotland Ltd., 1986-91; admitted to Distinguished Order of Auxiliary Service of Salvation Army, 1981; Deacon Convener, Trades House of Glasgow, 1986-87. Recreations: gardening; golf; swimming; music. Address: (h.) Armitage, Kilmacolm, PA13 4PH; T.-050587 2444.

Hunter Blair, Francis, JP. Hill Farmer; Chairman, Galloway Cattle Society of Great Britain and Ireland, 1986-91; b. 29.10.30, Lincoln; m., Joyce Adeline Mary Graham; 4 s.; 1 d. Educ. Royal Naval College, Dartmouth; West of Scotland Agricultural College. President, Stewartry Branch, National Farmers' Union of Scotland, 1968-69; Council Member, NFU of Scotland, 1969-70; Vice President, Royal Highland and Agricultural Society of Scotland, 1987; several periods of office as Secretary and President, local agricultural shows; Past Chairman, Carsphairn Community Council; Elder, Carsphairn Kirk. Recreations: country pursuits; reading. Address: Marbrack, Carsphairn, Castle Douglas, Stewartry of Kirkcudbright; T.-Carsphairn 207.

Hunter Blair, James, DL. Landowner and Forester; SW Scotland Representative, Christies, Auctioneers, since 1984; b. 18.3.26, Ayr. Educ. Eton; Oxford. Scots Guards, 1944-48; University, 1948-50; merchant bank, London, 1951-53; managed family estate, since 1953. Past President, Royal Scottish

Forestry Society; former Vice-President, Royal Highland Society; Chairman, Historic Houses Association for Scotland. Recreations: shooting; fishing; going to the opera. Address: Blairquhan, Maybole, Ayrshire; T.-Straiton 239.

Hurford, Professor James Raymond, BA, PhD. Professor of General Linguistics, Edinburgh University, since 1979; b. 16.7.41, Reading; m., Sue Ann Davis; 2 d. Educ. Exeter School; St. John's College, Cambridge; University College, London. Assistant Professor, Department of English, University of California, Davis, 1968-71; Lecturer, then Senior Lecturer, Department of Linguistics, Lancaster University, 1972-79. Publications: Language and Number: the emergence of a cognitive system; Semantics: a coursebook (Co-author); The Linguistic Theory of Numerals. Address: (b.) Edinburgh University, Edinburgh, EH8 9YL.

Hurman, David Charles, MBChB, DTM&H, DMRT, FRCR. Consultant in Radiotherapy and Oncology, Grampian Health Board, since 1988; Visiting Consultant, Shetland Health Board, since 1988; Clinical Senior Lecturer, Aberdeen University, since 1988; b. 9.2.52, London; m., Dr. Dorothy Elizabeth McMurray; 1 s.; 1 d. Educ. Ashford County Grammar School; Liverpool University. Pre-registration and junior medical posts, Southport General Infirmary and Christiana Hartley Maternity Hospital, 1975-77; Medical Officer, Trans-Borneo Expedition, 1978; Mersey Regional Centre for Radiotherapy and Oncology, Clatterbridge Hospital, Bebington, 1979-86; Clinical Research Fellow, Cross Cancer Institute and University of Alberta, 1986-87. Recreations: foreign travel; football; cricket; hills and mountains; rock music. Address: (h.) 85 Cairnfield Place, Aberdeen, AB2 4LX; T.-0224 638411.

Hutcheson, James Forbes, BSc (Agric), NDA. Chief Agricultural Officer, Scottish Office Agriculture and Fisheries Department, since 1987; b. 1.5.34, Edinburgh; m., Irene May Taylor; 2 s.; 1 d. Educ. George Watson's Boys College; Edinburgh University. Joined DAFS as Assistant Inspector, 1958; Inspector, 1971-79; Senior Inspector/Principal Inspector, 1979-81; Assistant Chief Agricultural Officer, 1981-85; Deputy Chief Agricultural Officer, 1985-87. Recreations: golf; music; gardening. Address: (b.) Pentland House, 47 Robb's Loan, Edinburgh, EH14 1TW; T.-031-244 6029.

Hutcheson, Rev. Norman McKenzie, MA, BD. Minister, Dalbeattie with Haugh of Urr, since 1988 (Saint Andrew's Parish Church, Kirkcaldy, 1973-88); b. 11.10.48, Leven, Fife; m., Elizabeth Gilchrist Anderson; 2 d. Educ. Hillhead High School, Glasgow; Glasgow University; Edinburgh University. Member, General Assembly Committees, since 1975: Finance, Practice and Procedure, Social Responsibility, Education for the Ministry, Maintenance of the Ministry; Moderator: Kirkcaldy Presbytery, 1984, Synod of Fife, 1985. Recreations: walking; photography; Rotary. Address: The Manse, Dalbeattie, Kirkcudbrightshire.

Hutchinson, Peter, BSc, PhD, CBiol, MIBiol, MIFM. Assistant Secretary, North Atlantic Salmon Conservation Organization, since 1986; b. 26.5.56, Glasgow; m., Jane MacKellaig; 1 s.; 1 d. Educ. Queen Elizabeth's Grammar School, Blackburn; Edinburgh University. Project Co-ordinator, Surface Water Acidification; Research Biologist: Institute of Terrestrial Ecology, Edinburgh University. Recreations: golf; squash; rugby union; angling. Address: (h.) 57 Craiglea Drive, Morningside, Edinburgh.

Hutchison, David, MA, MLitt. Senior Lecturer in Communication Studies, Glasgow Polytechnic, since 1984; b. 24.9.44, West Kilbride; m., Pauleen Frew; 2 d. Educ. Ardrossan Academy; Glasgow University. Tutor/Organiser, WEA (West of Scotland), 1966-69; Teacher, Reid Kerr

College, Paisley, 1969-71; Lecturer in Communication Studies, Glasgow College of Technology, 1971-75; Member, West Kilbride District Council, 1970-75 (Chairman, 1972-75); Governor, Scottish Film Council, since 1987; Member, General Advisory Council, BBC, since 1988; author of play, Deadline, Pitlochry Festival Theatre, 1980. Publications: The Modern Scottish Theatre, 1977; Headlines: the Media in Scotland (Editor), 1978. Recreations: walking; swimming; the arts. Address: (b.) Department of Communication, Glasgow Polytechnic, Cowcaddens Road, Glasgow, G4 0BA; T.-041-331 3255.

Hutchison, Lt.-Comdr. Sir (George) Ian Clark, Kt (1954). Member, Queen's Bodyguard for Scotland (Royal Company of Archers); b. 4.1.03; m., Sheena Campbell (deceased); 1 d. Educ. Edinburgh Academy; RN Colleges. Joined Navy, 1916; Member, Edinburgh Town Council, 1935-41; rejoined Navy, 1939; MP (Unionist), Edinburgh West, 1941-59; Deputy Lieutenant, County of City of Edinburgh, 1958-84.

Hutchison, Rev. Henry, BD, BEd, MA, MLitt, PhD, DipRE, LLCM. Minister, Carmunnock Parish Church, Glasgow, since 1977; b. 4.5.23, Alloa; m., Ann Sheila Maree Ross; 1 s. Educ. Alloa Academy; Dollar Academy; Edinburgh University; Glasgow University; Jordanhill College of Education; Toronto University. War service, RAF; Minister: Erksine Church, Saltcoats, 1948-53, Crosshill-Victoria Church, Glasgow, 1953-57, St. Paul's Presbyterian Church, Peterborough, Ontario, 1957-60; Principal, Stanstead College, Quebec, 1960-63; Assistant Professor of Education, Brandon University, Manitoba, 1965-67; Lecturer in Education, Glasgow University, 1967-77; Moderator, Peterborough Presbytery, Ontario, 1959. Publications: The Church and Spiritual Healing, 1955; A Faith to Live By, 1959; The Beatitudes and Modern Life, 1960; Scottish Public Educational Documents, 1973; Kirk Life in Old Carmunnock, 1978; Carmunnock Church 1854-1947, 1979; God Believes in You!, 1980; Well I'm Blessed!, 1981, Have a Word with God, 1981; Healing through Worship, 1981; A Faith that Conquers, 1982. Recreations: music; bowls; walking. Address: 161 Waterside Road, Carmunnock, Glasgow, G76 9AJ; T.-041-644 1578.

Hutchison, Ian Somerville, OBE, JP. Chairman, Eastwood District Licensing Board; Member, Eastwood District Council (Chairman of Planning); Vice Chairman, Scottish National Housing & Town Planning Council; Member, Scottish Valuation Advisory Council, 1982-86; Member, Historic Buildings Council for Scotland, since 1983; Member, Glasgow West Conservation Trust; Managing Director, Timbertection Ltd., since 1973; b. 10.4.28, Glasgow; m., Aileen Wallace; 2 s.; 2 d. Educ. Hutchesons' Boys' Grammar School. Elected to First (Eastwood) District Council, 1967, Renfrew County Council, 1970, Eastwood District Council, 1974; Provost, Eastwood, 1974-80; Delegate, COSLA, since 1975 (Vice President, COSLA, 1979-82); Vice Chairman, Planning Exchange; Member, Renfrewshire Valuation Appeals Committee; Governor, The Queen's College, Glasgow, since 1973 (Chairman of Governors, 1980-88); Member, Management Committee, Renfrewshire Enterprise. Recreations: gardening; fishing. Address: (h.) 39 Hazelwood Avenue, Newton Mearns, Glasgow, G77 5QT; T.-041-639 2186.

Hutchison, James Kenneth, CA. Chief Executive, Scottish Sports Council, 1972-89; b. 3.7.34, Edinburgh. Educ. George Heriot's School; Edinburgh University. CA apprentice and Audit Assistant, 1952-59; RAF Officer, Secretarial Branch, 1959-63; Scottish Council of Physical Recreation: Depute Secretary, 1964-68, General Secretary, 1968-72; Trustee and Hon. Secretary, Scottish Disability Foundation; Trustee, Scottish Physical Recreation Fund; Past Chairman, Edinburgh Sports Club Ltd.; Past President, George Heriot's School (FP)

Rugby Club. Recreations: curling; golf; swimming; theatre; good food and wine. Address: (h.) 13 Douglas Crescent, Edinburgh, EH12 5BB; T.-031-337 4822.

Hutchison, Sir Peter Craft, Bt, BA. Chairman, Hutchison & Craft Ltd., Insurance Brokers, and associated/subsidiary companies; Director, Stakis plc, 1979-91; Board Member, Scottish Tourist Board, 1981-87; Vice Chairman, British Waterways Board, since 1988; Chairman, Board of Trustees, Royal Botanic Garden, Edinburgh; Chairman, Loch Lomond and Trossachs Working Party, 1991-92; b. 5.6.35, London; m., Virginia Colville; 1 s. Educ. Eton; Magdalene College, Cambridge. National Service, Royal Scots Greys (2nd Lt.); Northern Assurance Co. (London); Director of various companies; Past Chairman, Ailsa Shipbuilding Co. Ltd.; Deacon, Incorporation of Hammermen of Glasgow, 1984-85. Recreations: plant hunting; gardening; calligraphy. Address: (h.) Milton House, Milton, by Dumbarton, G82 2TU; T.-Dumbarton 61609.

Hutchison, Professor William McPhee, BSc, PhD, DSc, FIBiol, CBiol, FLS, FRSE. Emeritus Professor, Strathclyde University, since 1989 (Personal Professor in Parasitology, 1971-87); b. 2.7.24, Glasgow; m., Isabella Duncan McLaughland; 2 s. Educ. Eastwood High School; Glasgow University; Strathclyde University. Glasgow University Athletic Club Blue, 1949; University Fencing Champion, 1949; Scottish Open Fencing Champion, 1949. Robert Koch Prize, 1970; Robert Koch Medal. Recreations: reading; music; gardening; DIY. Address: (h.) 597 Kilmarnock Road, Glasgow, G43 2TH.

Hutton, Alasdair Henry, OBE, TD. Broadcaster and Consultant; Director, Scottish Agricultural College; Chairman, Crime Concern Scotland; Chairman, Disease Prevention Organisation; Chairman, Scottish Conservative Environment Committee; Chairman, Scottish Conservative European Committee; Member, Roxburgh District Advisory Committee, Scottish Borders Enterprise; Chairman, Kelso Branch, Roxburgh and Berwickshire Conservative Association; b. 19.5.40, London; m., Deirdre Mary Cassels (see Deirdre Mary Hutton); 2 s. Educ. Dollar Academy; Brisbane State High School. Trainee technician, Radio 4BH Brisbane, 1956; Clemenger Advertising, Melbourne, 1957-59; Journalist, The Age, Melbourne, 1959-61, Aberdeen Journals, 1962-64; Broadcaster, BBC, 1964-79; Member, European Parliament, 1979-89. Member, Queen's Bodyguard for Scotland (Royal Company of Archers); Honorary Member, 15th (Scottish Volunteer) Bn., The Parachute Regiment; Vice President, Kelso Branch, Royal British Legion; Trustee, Community Service Volunteers; Patron, Volonteurop; Life Member, John Buchan Society; Fellow, Industry and Parliament Trust; Honorary President, Scottish Association of CB Clubs; Patron, Kelso Laddies' Association; Member, Ancient Order of Mosstroopers; Honorary Chairman, Hawick Conservative Club. Address: (b.) Rosebank, Shedden Park Road, Kelso, TD5 7PX; T.-0573 24369.

Hutton, Deirdre Mary. Chairman, Scottish Consumer Council, since 1991; Member, National Consumer Council, since 1991; Scottish Lay Representative, General Dental Council, since 1989; Member, Rural Forum, since 1991; Vice Chairman, Borders Local Health Council, since 1991; Chairman, Broomlands School Board, since 1990; b. 15.3.49, Haddington; m., Alasdair Hutton (qv); 2 s. Educ. Sherborne School for Girls; secretarial college. Research Assistant, Glasgow Chamber of Commerce, 1976-81; seconded to Scotland is British Campaign and Scotland Says No Campaign during devolution referendum, 1979. Recreations: music; reading. Address: (h.) Rosebank, Shedden Park Road, Kelso, TD5 7PX; T.-0573 24368.

Hutton, James Thomas, ARCM. Composer; Visiting Teacher of Music, since 1960; b. 12.5.23, Glasgow; m., Anne Jamieson Bowes; 1 s. Educ. Provanside Secondary School; Glasgow University; Royal Scottish Academy of Music. Worked for Renfrewshire Education Authority, 1960-64, Lanarkshire Education Authority, since 1964; entirely self-taught Composer of orchestral music; works include two symphonies, two concert-overtures, piano concerto, chamber music, and works for brass band, solo piano and organ; has also composed and arranged music for jazz orchestras and groups. Recreation: playing jazz piano. Address· (h.) 88 Warwick, East Kilbride; T.-East Kilbride 25895.

Hyslop, Kenneth Alexander, BSc. Rector, Leith Academy, since 1983; b. 7.12.39, Edinburgh; m., Sheena Isabel Hyslop; 1 s.; 1 d. Educ. Boroughmuir Secondary School; Heriot-Watt University. Science Teacher, Currie High School, 1964-69; Newbattle High School: Principal Teacher of Science, 1969-72, Assistant Headteacher, 1972-73; Deputy Headteacher, Broughton High School, 1973-77; Headteacher, Castlebrae High School, 1977-83. Address: (b.) Leith Academy, Academy Park, Edinburgh; T.-031-554 0606.

I

Idiens, Dale, BA, DipEd. Keeper, Department of History and Applied Art, National Museums of Scotland; b. 13.5.42, Prestatyn. Educ. Wycombe High School, High Wycombe; Leicester University. Royal Scottish Museum, Department of Art and Archaeology: Assistant Keeper in Charge of Ethnography, 1964, Deputy Keeper, 1979, Keeper, 1983. Address: (b.) Royal Museum of Scotland, Chambers Street, Edinburgh; T.-031-225 7534.

Ingham, Keith Philip Dudley, BA (Hons), MA. Senior Lecturer, Department of Economics, Strathclyde University, since 1989; International Student Officer, Strathclyde Business School, since 1985; Member, Scottish Arts Council, since 1990; b. 23.4.45, Grimsby. Educ. Wintringham Boys' Grammar School, Grimsby; University of East Anglia. Teaching Assistant, Carleton University, Ottawa; Lecturer, Department of Economics, Strathclyde University; Senior Lecturer, Department of Economics, Lund University, Sweden. Publications include: Understanding the Scottish Economy. Recreations: skiing; trying to keep fit; learning to like opera. Address: (b.) Department of Economics, Strathclyde University, Glasgow, G4 0LN; T.-041-552 4400.

Ingle, Professor Stephen James, BA, MA (Econ), DipEd, PhD. Professor of Political Studies, Stirling University; b. 6.11.40, Ripon; m., Margaret Anne; 2 s.; 1 d. Educ. The Roan School, London; Sheffield University; Wellington University, NZ. Lecturer in Politics, Hull University, 1967-80; Senior Lecturer, 1980-91; Head of Department, 1985-90. Political Studies Association, 1988-89. Publications: Socialist Thought in Imaginative Literature, 1979; Parliament and Health Policy, 1981; British Party System, 1987, 1989. Recreations: reading; music; hill-walking. Address: (b.) Department of Political Studies, Stirling University, Stirling, FK9 4LA; T.-0786 67593.

Inglis, Rev. Donald Bain Carrick, MA, MEd, BD. Minister, St. Andrew's Parish Church, Turriff, since 1983; b. 17.12.41, Aberdeen; m., Yvonne M.S. Cook; 1 s.; 2 d. Educ. Aberdeen Grammar School; Aberdeen University; Aberdeen College of Education; Glasgow University. Teacher of English and History at Aberdeen and Ellon Academy, 1964-68; Educational Psychologist, then Senior Educational Psychologist, Lanarkshire, 1968-72; Assistant Minister, Bathgate High Church, 1975-77; Educational Psychologist, then Senior Educational Psychologist, Fife, 1977-83. Former Member, Executive Committee, Psychologists' Section, Educational Institute of Scotland; Convener, Education Committee, Buchan Presbytery, 1984-88. Recreations: violin playing; swimming; hill-walking; cycling. Address: St. Andrew's Manse, Balmellie Road, Turriff, Aberdeenshire, AB53 7DP; T.-Turriff 63240.

Inglis, George Finlay, CA. Director of Finance and Administration, Scottish Tourist Board, since 1988; b. 2.1.46, Edinburgh; m., Catherine; 1 s.; 1 d. Educ. Royal High School, Edinburgh. Recreations: sport; literature; good wine; good food. Address: (h.) 67 Hillpark Avenue, Edinburgh, EH4 7AL; T.-031-336 2338.

Inglis, Professor James Alistair Macfarlane, CBE (1984), MA, LLB. Professor of Conveyancing, Glasgow University, since 1979; Professor of Professional Legal Practice, since 1984; Senior Partner, McClure, Naismith, Anderson & Gardiner, Solicitors, Glasgow; Dean, Royal Faculty of Procurators in Glasgow, 1989-92; b. 24.12.28, Kilmarnock; m., Mary Elizabeth Howie; 2 s.; 3 d. Educ. Kilmarnock Academy; Fettes College; St. Andrews University; Glasgow University. Qualified as Solicitor, 1952; Member: Board of Management, Victoria and Leverndale Hospitals, 1964-74, Greater Glasgow Health Board, 1975-83; President, Rent Assessment Panel for Scotland, 1976-87; Chairman, Glasgow Hospitals Auxiliary Association, since 1985; Convener, Ad Hoc Committee, Church of Scotland, into Legal Services of Church, 1978-79; Session Clerk, Caldwell Parish Church, since 1963. Address: (h.) Crioch, Uplawmoor, Glasgow; T.-Uplawmoor 315.

Inglis, John, RSW, FSA(Scot), DA. Painter and Lecturer; b. 27.7.53, Glasgow; m., Heather; 2 s.; 2 d. Educ. Hillhead High School; Gray's School of Art. Travelling scholarships to Italy, 1976; Member, Dundee Group, 1979-84; one-man exhibitions: Aberdeen, 1976 and 1977; Glasgow, 1980, Skipton 1981, Aberdeen Hospitals, 1989, Alloa Museum, 1989; Scottish Arts Council Award, 1981; RSA Keith Prize, 1975; SAC Bursary, 1982; RSA Meyer Oppenheim Prize, 1982; RSW EIS Award, 1987; SAC Grant, 1988. Address: (h.) 21 Hillview Road, Larbert, Stirlingshire; T.-0324 558891.

Inglis, William Caldwell, MA (Hons). Rector, Largs Academy, since 1973; b. 22.12.36, Ayr; m., Helga Goldschmidt; 2 s.; 3 d. Educ. Ayr Academy; Glasgow University. Teacher of History, Irvine Royal Academy, 1959-64; Principal Teacher of History, Geography and Modern Studies, Dalmellington High School, 1964-66; Principal Teacher of History and Modern Studies, Cumnock Academy, 1966-70; Depute Rector, Auchinleck Academy, 1970-72. Founder President, Irvine Royal Academicals Rugby Football Club. Recreation: gardening; swimming. Address: (b.) Largs Academy, Flatt Road, Largs; T.-0475 675421.

Ingram, Adam Paterson. MP (Labour), East Kilbride, since 1987; b. 1.2.47.

Ingram, Hugh Albert Pugh, BA (Cantab), PhD (Dunelm). Senior Lecturer (formerly Lecturer) in Botany (Ecology), Dundee University, since 1966; Trustee, National Museums of Scotland, since 1987; Vice-Chairman (Conservation and Science), Scottish Wildlife Trust, 1982-87; b. 29.4.37, Rugby;

m., Dr. Ruth Hunter; 1 s.; 1 d. Educ. Lawrence Sheriff School, Rugby; Rugby School; Emmanuel College, Cambridge; Hatfield College, Durham. Demonstrator in Botany, University College of North Wales, Bangor, 1963-64; Staff Tutor in Natural Science, Department of Extra-Mural Studies, Bristol University, 1964-65; Member, UK Committee, International Peat Society; Member, Executive Committee, Scottish Field Studies Association, since 1989; Member, Museums and Galleries Commission Working Party on the non-national museums of Scotland, 1984-86; Editor, Journal of Applied Ecology, since 1991. Recreations: music (clarinet, piano); literature; rural history; hill-walking. Address: Johnstonfield, Dunbog, Cupar, Fife, KY14 6JG.

Inkson, Robert Henry Ewen, BSc, FSS, FIS. President, Scottish Unitarian Association, 1991-93; Head, Department of Statistics, Macaulay Institute for Soil Research, 1968-87; b. 1.10.24, Aberdeen; m., Jean Davidson McArthur. Educ. Aberdeen Central School; Aberdeen University. Macaulay Institute for Soil Research: Scientific Officer, 1948, Senior Scientific Officer, 1954, Principal Scientific Officer, 1963. Recreations: music; gardening. Address: (h.) 39 Woodend Place, Aberdeen, AB2 6AP; T.-0224 315304.

Innes, James, BSc, CEng, MICE, FIHT. Deputy Chief Road Engineer, Scottish Development Department, since 1988 (Assistant Chief Road Engineer, 1985-88); b. 7.8.44, Helmsdale; m., June Pearson; 1 s.; 1 d. Educ. Woodside Secondary School, Glasgow; Strathclyde University. Lanark County Council, 1966-67; Inverness County Council, 1967-73; Scottish Development Department, 1973-84; Department of Transport (Superintending Engineer), 1984-85. Recreation: golf. Address: (b.) Room 3/102, New St. Andrews House, Edinburgh, EH1 3SZ; T.-031-244 5178.

Innes, Norman Lindsay, BSc, PhD, DSc, FIBiol, FIHort, FRSE. Deputy Director, Scottish Crop Research Institute, since 1986 (Head, Plant Breeding Division, 1984-89); b. 3.5.34, Kirriemuir; m., Marjory Niven Farquhar; 1 s.; 1 d. Educ. Websters High School, Kirriemuir; Aberdeen University; Cambridge University. Senior Cotton Breeder: Sudan, 1958-66, Uganda, 1966-71; Head, Cotton Research Unit, Uganda, 1972; National Vegetable Research Station, Wellesbourne: Head, Plant Breeding Section, 1973-84, Deputy Director, 1977-84; Honorary Lecturer, then Honorary Professor, Birmingham University, 1973-84; Governing Board Member, International Crops Research Institute for Semi-Arid Tropics, India, 1982-88; Honorary Professor: St. Andrews University, since 1985, Dundee University, since 1988; Governing Board Member, International Potato Centre, Peru, since 1988, Chairman, since 1991; Vice-President, Association of Applied Biologists, since 1990; Chairman, British Association of Plant Breeders, 1982-84; Member, Oxfam Council of Trustees, 1982-85. Recreations: golf; photography; travel. Address: (b.) Scottish Crop Research Institute, Invergowrie, Dundee, DD2 5DA; T.-0382 562731.

Innes, Richard Threlfall, BA, LLB. Honorary Sheriff, Fife; retired Solicitor; b. 5.9.00, Kirkcaldy; m., Jean Davidson; 2 s.; 3 d. Educ. Cargilfield; Fettes; Oxford University; Edinburgh University. Former Secretary, Kirkcaldy Chamber of Commerce; former Clerk, Commissioners of Income Tax. Recreations: gardening; golf. Address: (h.) 14 Boglily Road, Kirkcaldy, Fife; T.-0592 263287.

Innes of Edingight, Sir Malcolm Rognvald, KCVO, MA, LLB, WS, FSA Scot, KStJ. Lord Lyon King of Arms, since 1981; Secretary to Order of the Thistle, since 1981; b. 25.5.38, Edinburgh; m., Joan Hay; 3 s. Educ. Edinburgh Academy; Edinburgh University. Carrick Pursuivant, 1958; Marchmont Herald, 1971; Lyon Clerk and Keeper of the Record, 1966; Member, Queen's Bodyguard for Scotland (Royal Company of Archers); President, Scottish Heraldry Society.

Recreations: archery; shooting; fishing. Address: (b.) Court of the Lord Lyon, HM New Register House, Edinburgh; T.-031-556 7255.

Ireland, James Cecil Hardin. Trustee, Scottish Rugby Union, 1951-91 (President, 1950-51); b. 10.12.03, Glasgow; m., Margaret Stewart McLean. Educ. High School of Glasgow. Singer Manufacturing Co. Ltd.; William Younger & Co. Ltd.; War service, RNVR and Royal Marines, 1940-46; Dundee Manager, William Younger & Co. Ltd.; London Manager, Scottish & Newcastle Breweries (retired, 1968); rugby international, 1925-26-27; Scottish Rugby Union Committee, 1936; international Referee, 1938-39; Chairman, four Home Unions Tours Committee, 1946-51; Honorary Vice President, South Africa Rugby Board, 1964; President, Glasgow High School Club, 1964-65; Elder, St. Columba's Church of Scotland, London, 1960-68. Recreations: spectating at all sports; renewing friendships. Address: (h.) 10 Abbots View, Polmont, FK2 0QL; T.-Polmont 713400.

Ireland, Dr. Kenneth, OBE, DUniv, BL, FRSA, FTS. Consultant, Hanover Fine Arts (Edinburgh); b. 17.6.20, Edinburgh; m., Moira Lamb; 2 s. Educ. Edinburgh Academy; Edinburgh University. Law Apprentice, Steedman Ramage & Co., WS, Edinburgh, 1938-41; War service: Royal Artillery, L. Bdr., 1941-42, Intelligence Corps, WO II, 1942-46; Lt. (TA), 1948-52; General Manager: Park Theatre, Glasgow, 1946-49, Pitlochry Festival Theatre, 1951-52; Pitlochry Festival Society Ltd.: General Manager and Secretary, 1953-57, Festival Director and Secretary, 1957-83 (retired, 1984); Board Member, Scottish Tourist Board, 1966-69; Chairman, Tourist Association of Scotland, 1967-69; Deputy Chairman, Scottish Tourist Consultative Council, 1977-83; Director, Federation of Scottish Theatre; Member: Scottish Corps of Retired Executives (SCORE/EVENT), Advisory Council for the Arts in Scotland, J.D. Fergusson Art Foundation Executive Committee. ESU Scotland Thyne Scholarship, 1970; Bill Heron Trophy, 1981 (first recipient for services to tourism). Recreations: foreign travel; theatre-going; galleries; reading. Address: (h.) 10 Ravelston Rise, Edinburgh, EH4 3LH; T.-031-346 2292.

Ireland, Sheriff Ronald David, QC. Sheriff Principal, Grampian, Highland and Islands, since 1988; b. 13.3.25, Edinburgh. Educ. George Watson's College, Edinburgh; Balliol College, Oxford (Scholar); Edinburgh University. Advocate, 1952; Clerk, Faculty of Advocates, 1957-58; Professor of Scots Law, Aberdeen University, 1958-71; QC, 1964; Dean, Faculty of Law, Aberdeen University, 1964-67; Chairman, Board of Management, Aberdeen General Hospitals, 1964-71; Sheriff, Lothian and Borders at Edinburgh, 1972-88; Director, Scottish Courts Administration, 1975-78. Address: (b.) The Castle, Inverness, IV2 3EG.

Irgens, Professor Christopher S., BEng, DipBS, MSc, MBCS, CEng. Dean, School of Information, Social and Management Sciences and Professor, Department of Computing Science, Paisley University, since 1991; b. 10.5.45, Bergen; m., Sophie Christine Tough; 2 d. Educ. Bergen Katedralskole; Liverpool University. CAD-CAM Systems Designer, Ferranti Ltd., Edinburgh, 1971-75; Systems Consultant, CSL, Edinburgh, 1975-76; Product Manager, EMMA AS, Bergen, 1976-77; Lecturer, then Senior Lecturer, Paisley College, 1979-91. Recreations: skiing; curling. Address: (b.) Department of Computing Science, Paisley University, High Street, Paisley, PA1 2BE; T.-041-848 3304.

Ironside, Leonard. Chairman, Grampian Initiative; Member, Grampian Regional Council, since 1982; Patron, Grampian Special Olympics for Handicapped; Commonwealth Professional Wrestling Champion, since 1981; Director,

Aberdeen Exhibition and Conference Centre; Director, International Downhole Drilling and Technology Centre;Director, Scottish Sub-Sea Technology Group; Director, Grampian Health Board Heart Disease Campaign; b. 16.2.50, Aberdeen. Educ. Hilton Academy, Aberdeen. Inspector, contributions agency, DHSS, since 1990. Won Commonwealth Professional Wrestling Championship at Middleweight, 1979; lost Championship, 1981; regained title, 1981; gained European Lightweight title, 1985, relinquished title, 1989. Recreations: yoga teacher; also plays tennis, squash, badminton; cycling. Address: (h.) 42 Hillside Terrace, Portlethen, Kincardineshire; T.-Aberdeen 780929.

Irvine, Andrew Robertson, MBE (1979). Rugby Player; b. 16.9.51, Edinburgh; m., Audrey; 2 d. Educ. George Heriot's School, Edinburgh; Edinburgh University. Captained George Heriot's School, Scottish Schools, Heriots FP, Edinburgh, Scotland; holds records for: most international points scored (273 for Scotland, 28 for British Lions in three tours (nine tests)) and most tries scored by a full back (10); made inter national debut against All Blacks, 1972.

Irvine, Professor John Maxwell, BSc, MSc, PhD, FInstP, ChPhys, FRAS. Principal and Vice-Chancellor, Aberdeen University, since 1991; b. 28.2.39, Edinburgh; m., Grace Ritchie; 1 s. Educ. George Heriot's School; Edinburgh University; University of Michigan; Manchester University. English-Speaking Union Fellow, University of Michigan, 1961-62; Lecturer in Theoretical Physics, Manchester University, 1964 (Senior Lecturer, 1973, Reader, 1976, Professor, 1983); Dean of Science, Manchester University, 1989. Research Associate, Cornell University, 1966-68; Head, Nuclear Theory Group, SERC Daresbury Laboratory, 1974-77. Member, Council, Institute of Physics, since 1981 (Vice President, 1982-87); Member, Council, European Physical Society, since 1989. Recreations: tennis; hill-walking. Address: (b.) Principal's Office, Aberdeen University, Regent Walk, Aberdeen, AB9 1FX; T.-0224 272134.

Irvine, Lucy. Writer; b. 1.2.56, Whitton, Middlesex; 3 s. Left full-time education aged 13. Began writing, 1982, after spending a year on an uninhabited island with a stranger; now lives in north-east Scotland. Publications: Castaway; Runaway; One is One. Recreations: reading; walking; relaxing.

Irvine-Fortescue, James William, MA (Hons), CA, JP, DL, KLJ, FSA Scot. Commissioner of Income Tax, County of Kincardine, 1957-92; Chairman, Grampian Region Valuation Appeal Committee, 1975-90; b. 7.6.17, Wilmslow; m., Margaret Guise Yates; 3 s.; 1 d. Educ. Aberdeen Grammar School; Edinburgh Academy; Aberdeen University. War Service: Royal Army Pay Corps, 1940-46, service in India and Ceylon, 1942-46 (Major and Staff Paymaster); JP and Magistrate, Kincardineshire, 1957; Member, Kincardine County Council, 1952-73; Chairman, Lower Deeside District Council, 1964-73. President, Deeside Field Club, 1981-86; a Vice President, Royal Society for Asian Affairs, 1983-88; Past President, Auchinleck Boswell Society; Past Chairman, Aberdeen Music Festival. Recreations: family history research; foreign travel. Address: (h.) Kingcausie, Maryculter, Aberdeen, AB1 0AR; T.-0224 732224.

Irving, Gordon, MA (Hons). Writer, Journalist and Broadcaster; b. 4.12.18, Annan; m., Elizabeth Dickie (deceased); 1 s. Educ. Dumfries Academy; Edinburgh University. Staff Journalist, Daily Record, Edinburgh and Glasgow; Reuters' News Agency, London; TV Guide, Scotland; The Viewer, Scotland; Freelance Writer/Journalist, since 1964; Travel Correspondent, Daily Record; Scotland Correspondent, Variety, New York. Publications: Great Scot! (biography of Sir Harry Lauder); The Good Auld Days; The Solway Smugglers; The Wit of the Scots; The Wit of Robert Burns; The Devil on Wheels; Brush Up Your Scotland; Annie

Laurie; Take No Notice and Take No More Notice! (World's Funniest Signs); The First 200 Years (Story of Dumfries and Galloway Royal Infirmary). Recreations: making video films of personal travels; motoring to Spain; collecting trivia; researching Scottish music-hall history; fighting bumbling bureaucrats. Address: (h.) 36 Whittingehame Court, Glasgow, G12 OBG; T.-041-357 2265.

Irving, John Black, BSc, MB, ChB, FRCPE. Consultant Physician, St. John's Hospital, Livingston; Honorary Senior Lecturer, Edinburgh University; Consultant Cardiologist, Edinburgh Royal Infirmary, since 1980; b. 25.11.43, Lanark; m., Elspeth Mary; 2 s.; 1 d. Educ. Selkirk High School; Edinburgh University. British Heart Foundation Research Fellow, University Department of Medicine, Edinburgh, 1970-72; Registrar, Cardiac Department, Western General Hospital, Edinburgh, 1972-74; Registrar, Edinburgh Royal Infirmary, 1974-75; Research Fellow, Department of Cardiology, University of Washington, Seattle, 1975-76; Senior Registrar in Cardiology, Edinburgh Hospitals, 1976-79. Recreations: curling; hill-walking. Address·(h.) St. John's Hospital, Howden, Livingston, EH54 6PP; T.-0506 419666.

Irving, John Bruce, BSc, MSc, PhD, FBIM, FSA Scot. Director of Information Technology, Dumfries and Galloway Regional Council, since 1986; b. 19.6.42, Lenzie; m., Margaret Anne McWilliam, MB, ChB, MFCH; 2 s.; 1 d. Educ. Lenzie Academy; Glasgow University. Owner, Bonshaw Tower, the seat of the Irving clan since 1022; research, National Engineering Laboratory, East Kilbride, 1969-78; Project Co-ordinator, then Information Systems Manager, Chloride Technical Ltd., Manchester, 1978-85. Past President: Ayrshire Philatelic Society, Dumfries Philatelic Society; awards received at national stamp exhibitions. Recreations: outdoor pursuits; family history; philately. Address: (h.) Bonshaw Tower, Kirtlebridge, Lockerbie, DG11 3LY; T.-O46 15 256.

Irving, Margaret Anne, MBChB, MFCH. Head, Department of Community Medical Services, Dumfries and Galloway Health Board, since 1990; Clinical Services Manager, Community Unit Management Team, since 1991; Scottish Chair, Medical Group, British Agencies for Adoption and Fostering, since 1990; b. 28.4.42, Glasgow; m., Dr. John Bruce Irving; 2 s.; 1 d. Educ. Bathgate Academy; Glasgow University. Registrar in Bacteriology, Western Infirmary, Glasgow; Principal in general practice, Ayrshire; CMO in Child Health, Salford Health Authority; Senior Clinical Medical Officer in Child Health, Dumfries & Galloway Health Board; Medical Adviser to Regional Adoptions and Fostering Panel. Recreations: gardening; opera. Address: (h.) Bonshaw Tower, Kirtlebridge, Lockerbie, Dumfriesshire, DG11 3LY; T.-04615 256.

Irving, Ronald Eckford Mill, MA, DPhil (Oxon). Reader in Politics, Edinburgh University, since 1981; b. 14.7.39, Glasgow; m., Christine Mary Gaudin; 4 d. Educ. Merchiston Castle School; St. Edmund Hall, Oxford. Schoolmaster, 1961-65; Lecturer in Politics: Bristol University, 1968-69, Edinburgh University, 1969-81. Publications: Christian Democracy in France, 1973; The First Indochina War: French and American Policy in Vietnam 1945-54, 1975; The Christian Democratic Parties of Western Europe, 1979. Recreations: golf; piping. Address: (h.) 76 Murrayfield Gardens, Edinburgh, EH12 6DQ; T.-031-337 3663.

Irving, W. Ronald, BCom, CA. Group Director, Christian Salvesen PLC, since 1988; b. 18.12.45, Edinburgh; m., Kate Sullivan; 1 d.; 1 d. deceased. Educ. Royal High School, Edinburgh; Edinburgh University. Chartered accountancy, 1967-70; Scottish and Newcastle Breweries PLC, 1970-73; Christian Salvesen PLC, since 1973. Publications: The Border Terrier; Your Dog. Recreations: dog showing, breeding and judging. Address: (b.) 50 East Fettes Avenue, Edinburgh, EH4 1EQ; T.-031-552 7101.

Irwin, Professor David George, MA, PhD, FSA, FRSA. Professor of History of Art and Head of Department, Aberdeen University, since 1970; b. 24.6.33, London; m., Francina Sorabji; 1 s.; 1 d. Educ. Holgate Grammar School, Barnsley; Queen's College, Oxford (Exhibitioner); Courtauld Institute of Art, London University. Lecturer in History of Fine Art, Glasgow University, 1959-70; Past President, British Society for 18th Century Studies; former Council Member, Walpole Society; former Member, Art Panel, Scottish Arts Council; Committee Member, Aberdeen Art Gallery; Committee Member, Architectural Heritage Society of Scotland; elected Member, International Association of Art Critics; won Laurence Binyon Prize, Oxford, 1956. Publications: English Neoclassical Art; Paul Klee; Visual Arts, Taste and Criticism; Winckelmann, Writings on Art; John Flaxman, Sculptor, Illustrator, Designer; Scottish Painters, At Home and Abroad, 1700 to 1900 (with Francina Irwin). Recreations: swimming; walking; travel. Address: (b.) Department of History of Art, King's College, Old Aberdeen, Aberdeen, AB9 2UB; T.-0224 272458.

Irwin, Ian Sutherland, CBE (1982). Chairman and Chief Executive, Scottish Transport Group, since 1987; b. 20.2.33.

Isaac, David Gilmour Davies, MA (Hons) (Oxon), PhD. Rector, Hutchesons' Grammar School, Glasgow, 1978-84; b. 13.7.24, Fochriw, Glamorgan; m., Sheena Reith Steele; 1 s.; 1 d. Educ. Sir Edward Lewis's School, Pengam, Glamorgan; Jesus College, Oxford (Oxford v. Cambridge association football, 1942); Edinburgh University. House Tutor and Scholarship Historian, Edinburgh Academy, 1945-62 (House Master, 1959-62); Headmaster, King Henry VIII School, Abergavenny, 1962-68; Rector, Marr College, Troon, 1968-78; Member, Headmasters' Conference, 1978-84; Council Member and Editor, Welsh Headmasters' Review; Secretary, Edinburgh Academical Football Club, 1959-62; Governor, Wellington School, Ayr; Elder, Portland Church, Troon; President, Troon Arts Guild, 1987. Recreations: golf; music; wine-making. Address: (h.) 1 Polo Gardens, Troon, Ayrshire; T.-0292 313804.

Ivory, Brian Gammell, MA (Cantab), CA. Managing Director, The Highland Distilleries Company plc, since 1988; Vice-Chairman, Scottish Arts Council, since 1988; Member, Arts Council of Great Britain, since 1988; b. 10.4.49, Edinburgh; m., Oona Mairi MacPhie Bell-Macdonald (see Oona Mairi MacPhie Ivory); 1 s.; 1 d. Educ. Eton College; Magdalene College, Cambridge. CA apprentice, Thomson McLintock, 1971-75; joined Highland Distilleries, 1976; became Director, 1978; Director, Matthew Gloag and Son Ltd., since 1987; Director, Orpar SA, since 1990; Director, Romy and Associes, since 1990; Member, Scottish Arts Council, since 1983 (Chairman, Combined Arts Committee, 1984-88). Recreations: the arts; farming; hill-walking. Address: (h.) Brewlands, Glenisla, by Blairgowrie, Perthshire, PH11 8PL; 12 Ann Street, Edinburgh, EH4 1PJ.

Ivory, Oona Mairi MacPhie, MA (Cantab), ARCM. Professional Musician; Vice Chairman, The Scottish Ballet; Governor, Royal Scottish Academy of Music and Drama; Director, Theatre Royal, Glasgow; b. 21.7.54, Ayr; m., Brian Gammell Ivory (qv); 1 s.; 1 d. Educ. King's College, Cambridge; Royal Scottish Academy of Music and Drama; Royal Academy of Music. Recreations: visual arts; sailing. Address: (h.) Brewlands, Glenisla, by Blairgowrie, Perthshire, PH11 8PL; 12 Ann Street, Edinburgh, EH4 1PJ.

Izat, Alexander John Rennie, MA. Director, United Auctions (Scotland) Ltd., since 1984; Director, Shires Investment PLC, since 1988; Partner, John Izat & Partners

(Farmers), since 1975; Director, Glasgow Investment Managers, since 1990; b. 14.7.32, London; m., Frederica Ann McNiel; 1 s.; 2 d. Educ. Glenalmond; Oriel College, Oxford. Partner, Williams de Broe & Co., Stockbrokers, 1955-75; farming at Balliliesk and Naemoor, 1975-87; farming at High Cocklaw, since 1987; former Member, Council, Scottish NFU; Past President, Fife and Kinross NFU and Kinross Agricultural Association; Director, Royal Highland Agricultural Society, since 1985; Member, Council, Glenalmond College, since 1975 (Chairman, Committee of Council, since 1989); President, Northern Area, Suffolk Sheep Society, 1989-91; Trustee, Animal Diseases Research Association, since 1988. Address: (b.) High Cocklaw, Berwick-upon-Tweed, TD15 1UZ; T.-0289 86591.

Izod, (Kenneth) John, BA (Hons), PhD. Senior Lecturer, Department of Film and Media Studies, Stirling University, since 1978; b. 4.3.40, Shepperton; m., Irene Chew Geok Keng; 1 s.; 1 d. Educ. Prince Edward School, Harare City, Zimbabwe; Leeds University. Clerk articled to Chartered Accountant, 1958-63; Projectionist, mobile cinema unit, 1963; Lecturer in English, New University of Ulster, 1969-78; Governor, Scottish Film Council; Chairman, Stirling Film Theatre, 1982-89 and since 1991. Publication: Reading the Screen, 1984; Hollywood and the Box Office 1895-1986, 1988; The Films of Nicholas Roeg, 1991. Address: (b.) Film and Media Studies, University, Stirling, FK9 4LA; T.-0786 73171.

J

Jack, Professor Robert Barr, CBE, MA, LLB. Senior Partner, McGrigor Donald, Solicitors, Glasgow, Edinburgh and London; Professor of Mercantile Law, Glasgow University, since 1978; b. 18.3.28; m., Anna Thorburn Thomson; 2 s. Educ. Kilsyth Academy; High School of Glasgow; Glasgow University. Admitted as a Solicitor in Scotland, 1951; Member: Company Law Committee, Law Society of Scotland, 1971 (Convener, 1978-85); Scottish Law Commission, 1974-77; Scottish Observer, Department of Trade's Insolvency Law Review Committee, 1977-82; Member, DOT Advisory Panel on Company Law, 1980-83; Member, Council for the Securities Industry, 1983-85; Lay Member, Council of the Stock Exchange, 1984-86; Independent Member, Board, Securities Association Ltd., since 1986; Chairman, Review Committee on Banking Services Law, 1987-89; UK Member, Panel of Arbitrators – International Centre for Settlement of Investment Disputes, since 1990; Chairman: Brownlee plc, Timber Merchants, Glasgow, 1984-86 (Director, 1974-86); Joseph Dunn (Bottlers) Ltd., Soft Drink Manufacturers, Glasgow, since 1983; Director: Bank of Scotland, since 1985; Scottish Metropolitan Property plc, since 1980 (Deputy Chairman, since 1991); Scottish Mutual Assurance Society, since 1987 (Deputy Chairman, since 1991); Clyde Football Club Ltd., since 1980; Gartmore Scotland Investment Trust PLC, since 1991; Chairman, Scottish National Council of YMCAs, 1966-73; President, Scottish National Union of YMCAs, since 1983; Governor, Hutchesons' Educational Trust, Glasgow, 1978-87 (Chairman, 1980-87); Chairman, The Turnberry Trust, since 1983. Publications: lectures and articles on various aspects of company law, the statutory regulation and self-regulation of the City, and banking and insolvency law. Recreations: golf; music; hopeful supporter of one of Glasgow's less fashionable football teams; a dedicated lover of Isle of Arran which serves, regrettably less frequently, as a retreat and restorative. Address: (h.) 39 Mansewood Road, Glasgow, G43 1TN; T.-041-632 1659; (b.) Pacific House, 70 Wellington Street, Glasgow, G2 6SB; T.-041-248 6677.

Jack, Professor Ronald Dyce Sadler, MA, PhD. Professor of Scottish and Medieval Literature, Edinburgh University, since 1987; b. 3.4.41, Ayr. Educ. Ayr Academy; Glasgow University; Edinburgh University. Department of English Literature: Assistant Lecturer, 1965, Lecturer, 1968, Reader, 1978, Associate Dean, Faculty of Arts, 1971-73; Visiting Professor, Virginia University, 1973-74; Member, Universities Central Council on Admissions, 1973-76; Pierpont Morgan Scholar, British Academy, 1976; Advising Editor, Scotia, since 1980; Member, Scottish Universities Council on Entrance, since 1981; Governor, Newbattle Abbey College, since 1984. Publications: Robert MacLellan's Jamie the Saxt (Co-Editor), 1970; Scottish Prose 1550-1700, 1972; The Italian Influence on Scottish Literature, 1972; A Choice of Scottish Verse 1560-1660, 1978; The Art of Robert Burns (Co-author), 1982; Sir Thomas Urquhart, The Jewel (Co-author), 1984; Alexander Montgomerie, 1985; Scottish Literature's Debt to Italy, 1986; The History of Scottish Literature, Volume 1, 1988; Patterns of Divine Comedy, 1989; The Road to the Never Land, 1991. Address: (b.) Department of English Literature, Edinburgh University, David Hume Tower, George Square, Edinburgh, EH8 9JX.

Jackson, Andrew James, LLB (Hons), NP. Depute Chief Executive, Lochaber District Council, since 1981; b. 28.10.54, Bellshill. Educ. Lydney Grammr School, Glos; Aberdeen University. District Solicitor, Lochaber District Council, 1979-81. Former Chairman, Fort William Round Table. Recreations: music; theatre; badminton; jogging; swimming; travelling abroad. Address: (h.) Buchandyke, 6 Sutherland Avenue, Fort William, PH33 6JT; T.-0397 702892.

Jackson, Anthony Arthur, MA, MSc, FICDDip. Senior Lecturer, School of Town and Regional Planning, Duncan of Jordanstone College, Dundee University, since 1991; Vice President (Scotland), Institute of Civil Defence, since 1991; Founding Partner, St. Andrews Economic Services (economic consultants), 1986; b. 18.6.46, London; m., Alicia; 3 d. Educ. Westminster City School; Gonville and Caius College, Cambridge; Reading University. Agricultural Economist, Malawi Government, 1968-71; St. Andrews University: Stanley Smith Senior Fellow, 1971-73, Lecturer in Economics, 1973-91; FAO/FFHC Food and Nutrition Consultant, Malawi Government, 1973-76; Warning Officer, 1975-81, and Sector Scientific Adviser, UKWMO, 1981-91; Editor, Journal of Institute of Civil Defence, 1982-89; Group Leader, Conservative Group, Fife Regional Council, 1982-86; Director, Byre Theatre, 1980-89; Diploma, Institute of Civil Defence and Gerald Drewitt Medal, 1980. Recreations: theatre; cricket; philately. Address: (h.) Creinch, Peat Inn, by Cupar, Fife, KY15 5LH; T.-033-484 275.

Jackson, David Edward Pritchett, MA, PhD (Cantab). Senior Lecturer in Arabic Studies, St. Andrews University, since 1984 (Chairman, Department of Arabic Studies, 1979-86); b. 9.12.41, Calcutta, India; m., Margaret Letitia Brown. Educ. Tynemouth School; Rossall School; Pembroke College, Cambridge. Research Fellow, Pembroke College, Cambridge, 1967-70; St. Andrews University: Assistant Lecturer, Arabic Language and Literature, 1967-68, Lecturer in Arabic Studies, 1968-84. RNR, 1972-82 (rank on leaving: Lt.-Commander). Publication: Saladin (Co-author). Recreations: the river; music; food; golf. Address: (h.) 5 River Terrace, Guardbridge, by St. Andrews, Fife, KY16 OXA.

Jackson, Eileen. Author; b. 18.4.26, Bristol; m., John Tunnard Jackson; 3 d. Short story/article writer, 1935-74; novels, since 1974; first novel, published USA, 1976, UK, 1978; 17 novels in over 60 editions and 10 languages; pseudonyms: Helen May, Linda Comer, Elizabeth Warne; also publishes as Eileen Jackson; President, Strathclyde Writers, since 1985; Lecturer. Recreations: reading; book collecting; swimming; golf; travel. Address: (h.) Girvan Lodge, Blairquhan, Maybole, Ayrshire, KA19 7QP; T.-0655 7639.

Jackson, Jack, BSc (Hons), PhD, MIBiol, CIBiol. HM Staff Inspector of Schools with responsibility for science subjects; b. 31.5.44, Ayr; m., Sheilah Margaret Fulton; 1 s.; 3 d. Educ. Ayr Academy; Glasgow University; Jordanhill College of Education. Demonstrator, Zoology Department, Glasgow University, 1966-69; Lecturer in Zoology, West of Scotland Agricultural College, 1969-72; Assistant Teacher of Biology, Cathkin High School, 1972-73; Principal Teacher of Biology, Ayr Academy, 1973-83. Senior Examiner and Setter, Scottish Examination Board, 1978-83; Director, Board, Scottish Youth Theatre, 1979-82; Member, Scottish Council, Institute of Biology, 1980-83. Recreations: family life; gardening; hill-walking; conservation. Address: (b.) HM Inspector of Schools' Office, 231 Corstorphine Road, Edinburgh; T.-031-316 4639.

Jackson, Michael Herbert, BA, PhD, CBiol, MIBiol, FRSH, MREHIS, MIEH. Head, Division of Environmental Health, Strathclyde University, since 1991 and Senior Lecturer, since 1986; b. 17.7.40, Hornchurch; m., Diana Evans; 2 d. Educ. Nantwich and Acton Grammar School; Open University; Strathclyde University. Lecturer in Environmental Health, Strathclyde University, 1977-86; previously public health inspector and environmental health officer. President, Strathendrick Speakers Club. Recreations: gardening; reading; holidaying. Address: (b.) Department of Civil Engineering, Strathclyde University, John Anderson Building, Glasgow, G4 0NG; T.-041-552 4400, Ext. 3437.

Jackson, Richard Dodds, MA, DipEd. Assistant Secretary (Vocational Education and Sport), Scottish Office Education Department, since 1990; b. 13.9.37, Galashiels; m., Brenda Routledge Jackson; 1 s.; 1 d. Educ. St. Mary's School, Melrose; Royal High School, Edinburgh; St. Andrews University; Moray House College of Education. Teacher of English, Broughton Secondary School, Edinburgh, and Daniel Stewart's College, Edinburgh, 1961-70; HM Inspector of Schools and FE Colleges, 1970-75; Scottish Education Department: Temporary Principal, Arts Branch, 1975-78; Assistant Secretary, Social Work Services Group, 1978-82; Deputy Director (Personnel and Supplies), Scottish Prison Service, 1982-86; Assistant Secretary (Primary Health Care), Scottish Home and Health Department, 1986-90. Recreations: theatre and opera work. Address: (b.) St. Andrew's House, Regent Road, Edinburgh; T.-031-244 2455.

Jackson, Robert Penman, MIBM. Director of Public Works, City of Dundee District Council, since 1984; b. 2.4.47, Dunfermline; m., Helen Paxton; 1 s.; 1 d. Educ. Beath Senior High School, Cowdenbeath; Napier College of Science and Technology, Edinburgh. RSAS Diploma. Burgh Surveyor and Sanitary Inspector, Lochgelly Town Council, 1971-75; Assistant Director of Technical Services, Dunfermline District Council, 1975-84. Honorary Secretary, Lochgelly Old Folks' Reunion Committee. Recreation: golf. Address: (b.) 353 Clepington Road, Dundee; T.-Dundee 23141, Ext. 4729.

Jacobs, Raymond Alexander. Golf Correspondent, Glasgow Herald, since 1963; b. 13.1.31, Accrington. Educ. Loretto School. Recreation: catching up. Address: (b.) 195 Albion Street, Glasgow, G1 1QP; T.-041-552 6255.

Jahoda, Professor Gustav, MSc, PhD, FBPS, FBA. Emeritus Professor of Psychology, Strathclyde University; b. 11.10.20, Vienna; m., Jean Catherine Buchanan (deceased); 3 s.; 1 d. Educ. London University. Oxford Extra-Mural Delegacy; Manchester University; University of Ghana; Glasgow University. Past President (now Fellow), International Association for Cross-Cultural Psychology. Recreations: fishing; gardening. Address: (b.) Department of Psychology, Strathclyde University, 155 George Street, Glasgow, G1 1RD; T.-041-552 4400.

Jamal, Goran A., MB, ChB (Hons), MD, PhD, MRCP. Consultant, Department of Neurology, Southern General Hospital, Glasgow, since 1988; Senior Clinical Lecturer, Glasgow University, since 1989; Senior Lecturer in Neuroscience, Strathclyde Region, since 1989; b. 19.7.53, Iraqi Kurdistan; m., Dr. Vian M.S. Anber; 1 d. Educ. Central Secondary School, Baghdad; Glasgow University. Research Fellow, Glasgow University Department of Neurology, 1981-86; Senior Registrar, Department of Neuroscience, St. Bartholomew's Hospital and London University, 1986-88. Chairman, Kurdish Relief Association. Publications: several chapters in books and more than 60 papers. Recreation: member, Pond Leisure Club, Glasgow. Address: (b.) Department of Neurology, I.N.S., Southern General Hospital, Glasgow, G51 4TF; T.-041-445 2466.

James, C. Peter, PPIWPC (Dip), FIWEM. Director, Solway River Purification Board, 1954-87; b. 30.4.27, Manchester; m., Grace Irene; 1 s.; 1 d. Educ. Sale Grammar School; Manchester College of Technology. Trainee Inspector, Lancashire Rivers Board, 1943-51; District Inspector, Yorkshire Ouse River Board, 1951-54. President, Institute of Water Pollution Control, 1980-81 (Honorary Treasurer, 1981-87);Joint Editor, Institution of Water and Environmental Management Journal, since 1989; Sidney Bedell Award, American Water Pollution Control Federation; President, Dumfries Rotary Club, 1984-85; President, Dumfries Burns Club, 1986-87; awarded Queen's Silver Jubilee Medal, 1977. Recreations: haaf-net fishing; photography; gardening; wine making. Address: (h.) Gullsway, Glencaple, Dumfries, DG1 4RF; T.-Glencaple 285.

James, David Sheard, MB, ChB, DipEd, DCH, DPM, FRCPsych, FRCP (Glas). Consultant Child Psychiatrist, Royal Hospital for Sick Children, Glasgow, since 1971; Honorary Clinical Senior Lecturer, Child and Adolescent Psychiatry, Glasgow University, since 1991; b. 19.2.39, Harrogate; m., Hilary; 1 s.; 2 d. Educ. Warwick School; Sheffield University. Paediatrics, Sheffield Children's Hospital; Registrar in Psychiatry, Mapperley Hospital, Nottingham; Research Registrar, United Sheffield Hospitals; Senior Registrar, Child Psychiatry, Birmingham Children's Hospital and Charles Burns Clinic. Publication: Families Without Hope (Co-author), 1975. Recreations: motor vehicles; model railway. Address: (h.) Waterside, Lochlibo Road, Uplawmoor, Glasgow, G78 4AA; T.-Uplawmoor 269.

James, Professor Keith, BSc, PhD, DSc, FIBiol, FRCPath, FRSE. Professor in Immunology, Edinburgh University, since 1991; b. 15.3.38, Cumbria; m., Valerie Spencer Jubb; 3 s. Educ. Whitehaven Grammar School; Birmingham University. Research Fellow, Birmingham University, 1962-64; Research Assistant, University of California, 1964-65; Senior Lecturer, Edinburgh University, 1965-77, Reader, 1977-91; Consultant in Immunology and Biotechnology for Scottish National Blood Transfusion Service, since 1987. Past Chairman, Treasurer and Education Secretary, British Society for Immunology (now a Trustee); serves on the editorial board of a number of journals. Publications: Introducing Immunology (Co-author); numerous scientific papers. Recreations: hill-walking; photography. Address: (h.) 23

Crosswood Crescent, Balerno, Edinburgh, EH14 7LX; T.-031-449 5583.

James, Mary Charlotte, BA (Hons). Headmistress, St. Leonards School, St. Andrews, since 1988; b. 2.4.44, Bilston, Staffs; m., Lawrence Edwin James; 2 s. Educ. St. Leonards School; York University; St. Anne's College, Oxford. Head of History, Casterton School, Kirkby Lonsdale, 1979-84; Headmistress, Queen Ethelburga's School, Harrogate, 1984-88. Member, Scottish Council, ISCO; Member, Scottish Council, ISIS. Recreations: reading; cooking; walking; sleeping. Address: St. Leonards House, St. Andrews, Fife; T.-0334 72126.

James, Thomas William, Director of Public Affairs, Scottish Power, since 1990; b. 23.8.40, Motherwell; m., Anne Fiona MacDonald; 2 d. Educ. Dalziel High School. Journalist, Glasgow Herald; The Scotsman: Journalist, Parliamentary Correspondent, Political Correspondent, Chief Political Correspondent; Scottish Political Editor, Sunday Standard; SSEB: Press Officer, Public Relations Officer, Director of Public Affairs. Recreations: walking; bird watching; music; theatre; clay pigeon shooting. Address: (b.) Spean Street, Cathcart, Glasgow G44 4BE; T.-041-637 7177.

James, Professor (William) Philip (Treharne), MA, MD, DSc, FRCP, FRCPEdin, FRSE. Director, Rowett Research Institute, Aberdeen, since 1982; Research Professor, Aberdeen University, since 1983; b. 27.6.38, Liverpool; m., Jean Hamilton Moorhouse; 1 s.; 1 d. Educ. Bala School, North Wales; Ackworth School, Yorkshire; University College, London. Senior House Physician, Whittington Hospital, London, 1963-65; Clinical Research Scientist, Medical Research Council Tropical Metabolism Research Unit, Kingston, Jamaica, 1965-68; Harvard Research Fellow, Massachusetts General Hospital, 1968-69; Wellcome Trust Research Fellow, MRC Gastroenterology Unit, London, 1969-70; Senior Lecturer, Department of Human Nutrition, London School of Hygiene and Tropical Medicine, and Honorary Consultant, UCH, 1970-74; Assistant Director, MRC Dunn Nutrition Unit, and Honorary Consultant Physician, Addenbrooke's Hospital, Cambridge, 1974-82. Sir David Cuthbertson Lecturer; Van den Berghs & Jurgens Reporting Award; Amos Memorial Lecturer; Sir Thomas Middleton Memorial Lecturer; Sir Stanley Davidson Memorial Lecturer; Minshull Lecture; Member, COMA and its Sub-Committees; Technical Advisory Panel on Surveillance Health; Advisory Committee on Novel Foods and Processes; Member, Research Consultative Committee on Food Safety and Applied Nutrition, Ministry of Agriculture;President, National Food Alliance; Chairman, Coronary Prevention Group; Chairman, WHO Committee on Nutrition Policy, 1989; Chairman, FAO Commission on National Energy Needs, 1987-88; author, WHO report on Nutrition and European Health; author, FAO book on human energy requirements. Address: (b.) Rowett Research Institute, Greenburn Road, Bucksburn, Aberdeen, AB2 9SB; T.-0224 712751.

Jameson, John, FBIM. Firemaster, Strathclyde Fire Brigade, since 1991; b. 12.4.46, Chapelhall; m., Helen Mulvey; 1 s.; 1 d. Educ. St. Aloysius and St. Patrick's High School, Coatbridge. Lanarkshire Fire Brigade, 1965-70; Glasgow Fire Service, 1970-75; Strathclyde Fire Brigade: joined 1975, Assistant Firemaster, 1987-88, Deputy Firemaster, 1988-91. Fire Brigade Long Service and Good Conduct Medal, 1985; Strathclyde Regional Council Medal for Bravery, 1987; Churchill Fellowship, 1983. Recreations: historic buildings; golf. Address: (h.) 69 Woodvale Avenue, Bearsden, Glasgow, G62 2NX; T.-041-942 8604.

Jameson, John Valentine McCulloch, JP, DL, BSc, FRICS. Member, Dumfries and Galloway Regional Council, since

1974 (Convener, 1983-90); Partner, G.M. Thomson & Co., Chartered Surveyors, since 1970; b. 5.10.33, Twynholm, Stewartry of Kirkcudbright; m., Mary Irene Butters; 1 s.; 2 d. Educ. Rugby School; College of Estate Management (External). Commissioned 4/7 Royal Dragoon Guards, 1952-54; Shell Petroleum Co., London, 1954-57; Richard Costain (Canada) Ltd., Toronto, 1958-64. Member and Bailie, Gatehouse-of-Fleet Town Council, 1970-75; Chairman, Finance Committee, Dumfries and Galloway Regional Council, 1974-83; Chairman, Dumfries and Galloway Tourist Association, 1978-82; Chairman, Royal Institution of Chartered Surveyors in Scotland, 1981-82; Council Member, National Trust for Scotland, 1980-84; Board Member, Dumfries & Galloway Enterprise Co. Ltd.; Treasurer, Anwoth and Girthon Kirk Session. Recreations: golf; shooting; squash; hill-walking. Address: (h.) Hillfoot, Gatehouse-of-Fleet; T.-0557 814389.

Jamie, David Mitchell, FRICS, MRTPI. Director of Planning, Lothian Regional Council, since 1986; b. 11.8.41, Edinburgh; m., Eileen; 1 s.; 1 d. Educ. North Berwick High School; Heriot-Watt University; Edinburgh College of Art. Chartered Surveyor in private practice, Edinburgh and Glasgow, 1959-67; Town Planner in local government, since 1967. Chairman, Planning and Development Division, RICS in Scotland, 1986-88. Recreations: sailing; skiing; theatre. Address: (b.) 12 St. Giles Street, Edinburgh, EH1 1PT; T.-031-229 9292.

Jamie, Kathleen, MA. Writer; b. 13.5.62, Johnstone. Educ. Currie High School; University of Edinburgh. Writer-in-Residence, Midlothian District Libraries, 1987-89; poet and travel writer. Recreations: running; loud reggae music. Address: c/o Bloodaxe Books Ltd., PO Box 1SN, Newcastle-upon-Tyne NE99 1SW; T.-091-232 5988.

Jamieson, Alexander James, BSc, ARCST. Rector, Larbert High School, since 1981; b. 9.5.33, Falkirk; m., Elizabeth; 1 s.; 2 d. Educ. Falkirk High School; Strathclyde University; Glasgow University; Jordanhill College. RAF, 1955-58 (Flt. Lt.), 1955-58; Teacher of Science, Larbert High, 1958-63; Assistant Principal, Physics, High School of Stirling, 1963-65; Principal Teacher of Science, Bo'ness Academy, 1965-69; Larbert High School: Principal Teacher of Chemistry, 1969-73, Assistant Rector (Senior School), 1973-78, Depute Rector, 1978-81. Elder, Erskine Parish Church. Recreations: badminton; swimming; family. Address: (h.) 35 Slamannan Road, Falkirk, FK1 5NF; T.-Falkirk 22460.

Jamieson, David. Honorary Sheriff, South Strathclyde, Dumfries and Galloway, since 1976; b. 10.8.17, Glasgow; m., Pauline Bainbridge; 1 d. Educ. Albert Road Academy, Glasgow; Glasgow University. Six years in HM Forces during Second World War; former practising Solicitor in Hamilton. Publications: Uddingston, The Village (parts one to five), 1974-84; Uddingston in Picture Postcards, 1984. Recreation: local history. Address: (b.) 22 Clydesdale Street, Hamilton; T.-Hamilton 281767.

Jamieson, David Stewart Burns, MA, FInstP, MIPM. Director, Edinburgh Venture Enterprise Trust (EVENT), since 1990; b. 8.8.38, Monkseaton; m., Patricia Anne; 1 s.; 1 d. Educ. St. Paul's School, London; Trinity College, Cambridge University. British Petroleum Company: various personnel posts, 1960-75; Personnel Manager, BP Oil Ltd., 1975-80; Personnel Manager, BP Petroleum Development, Aberdeen, 1980-87; personnel management in London and Glasgow, 1987-90. Member, Council, Institute of Petroleum, since 1986, Chairman, Education and Training Committee, 1984-90. Recreations: arts; church; local history; golf; watching football. Address: (b.) 30 Rutland Square, Edinburgh, EH1 2BW; T.-031-229 8928.

Jamieson, Rev. Gordon David, MA, BD. Minister, Barnhill St. Margaret's Parish Church, Dundee, since 1986; b. 1.3.49, Glasgow; m., Annette Sutherland; 1 s.; 1 d. Educ. Hamilton Academy; Edinburgh University. Assistant Minister, Tron Kirk, Edinburgh, 1973-74; Minister, The Schaw Kirk, Drongan, 1974-79; Minister, Elie Parish Church linked with Kilconquhar and Colinsburgh Parish Church, 1979-86. Recreations: reading; walking. Address: Barnhill St. Margaret's Manse, Invermark Terrace, Broughty Ferry, Dundee.

Jardine, Sir (Andrew) Rupert (John) Buchanan-, 4th Bt, MC, DL. Landowner; b. 2.2.23; m., Jane Fiona Edmonstone (m. diss.); 1 s.; 1 d. Educ. Harrow; Royal Agricultural College. Retired Major, Royal Horse Guards; Joint Master, Dumfriesshire Foxhounds, 1950; Deputy Lieutenant, Dumfriesshire, 1978. Address: (h.) Dixons, Lockerbie, Dumfriesshire.

Jardine, Ian William, BSc, PhD. Regional Director (North East Scotland), Scottish Natural Heritage, since 1992; b. 22.5.59, Edinburgh; m., Anne Daniel. Educ. Royal High School, Edinburgh; Durham University; Leeds University. Joined Scottish Office, 1984; worked in various departments, including Scottish Development and Industry Departments; Private Secretary to Ian Lang MP; involved in setting-up of urban partnership initiatives and management of Castlemilk Partnership. Recreations: acting; gardening; natural history. Address: (b.) 17 Rubislaw Terrace, Aberdeen, AB1 1XE; T.-0224 642863.

Jardine, Sheriff James Christopher Macnaughton, BL. Sheriff, of Glasgow and Strathkelvin at Glasgow, since 1979 (from 1969 of North Strathclyde at Dumbarton, and of Stirling, Dunbarton and Clackmannan at Dumbarton); b. 18.1.30, Glasgow; m., Vena Kight; 1 d. Educ. Glasgow Academy; Gresham House; Glasgow University. Lt., RASC, 1950-52; admitted as Solicitor in Scotland, 1953; in practice as principal (Nelson & Mackay), from 1955; Partner, McClure Naismith Brodie & Co., Glasgow, 1956-69; Secretary, Glasgow University Graduates Association, 1956-66; Member, Business Committee, Glasgow University General Council, 1964-67; a Vice-President, Sheriffs Association, 1976-79; Member, Joint Probation Consultative Committee for Strathclyde Region, since 1981. Recreations: enjoyment of theatre, opera and music; swimming. Address: (b.) Sheriffs' Chambers, Sheriff Court of Glasgow and Strathkelvin, 1 Carlton Place, Glasgow, G5; T.-041-429 8888.

Jardine, Leslie Thomas, LLB. Director of Economic Development, Dumfries and Galloway Regional Council, since 1986; b. 4.6.49, Dumfries; m., Angela; 1 s. Educ. Dumfries Academy; Glasgow University. Law apprentice, then Legal Assistant, Dumfries County Council, 1972-75; Policy Planning Assistant, then Regional Public Relations Officer, Dumfries and Galloway Regional Council, 1975-86. Solicitor. Recreation: riding (Chairman, Dumfries and Galloway Branch, British Horse Society). Address: (b.) 118 English Street, Dumfries; T.-0387 61234.

Jardine, William Graham, BSc, MSc, PhD, ScD, FGS. Reader, Department of Geology and Applied Geology, Glasgow University, since 1978; b. 13.3.27, Glasgow; m., Elizabeth Ann Garven; 3 s.; 1 d. Educ. Allan Glen's High School, Glasgow, 1939-44; Glasgow University; McGill University, Canada; Emmanuel College, Cambridge. National Service, 1950-52 (2nd Lt., Royal Signals, GHQ Signals Regiment, Suez Canal Zone); Soil Survey, Scotland: Scientific Officer, 1955-58, Senior Scientific Officer, 1958-59; Glasgow University: Lecturer, Department of Geology, 1959-66, Senior Lecturer, 1966-78. Council Member, Geological Society of Glasgow, 1961-64; Quaternary Research Association (of Britain): Secretary, 1970-74, Vice-

President, 1974-76; Secretary-General, Tenth Congress, International Union for Quaternary Research (INQUA), Birmingham, 1977; President, INQUA Sub-Commission on Shorelines of NW Europe, 1977-82; INQUA Sub-Committee, British National Committee for Geology, 1966-82; President, Glasgow Archaeological Society, 1981-84; Editorial Advisory Board, Quaternary Science Reviews, 1984-87; E.J. Garwood Fund, Geological Society of London, 1963; Member, Congregational Board, 1961-81, and Kirk Session, since 1978, Westerton (Bearsden) Church of Scotland. Recreation: Westerton Male Voice Choir. Address: (b.) Department of Geology and Applied Geology, Glasgow University, Glasgow, G12 8QQ; T.-041-339 8855, Ext. 5443.

Jarman, Richard Neville, MA (Oxon). Managing Director, Scottish Opera, since 1991; b. 24.7.49, Sawbridgeworth. Educ. King's School, Canterbury; Trinity College, Oxford. Publicity Officer/Assistant to Administrative Director, English National Opera, 1971-76; Touring Officer: Dance, Arts Council of GB, 1976-77; Artistic Assistant/Administrator, Edinburgh International Festival, 1978-84; General Administrator, English National Opera, 1984-90. Fellow, Royal Society of Arts. Recreations: theatre; music; travel; gardening. Address: (b.) c/o Scottish Opera, 39 Elmbank Crescent, Glasgow, G2 4PT; T.-041-248 4567.

Jarrett, Professor Oswald, BVMS, PhD, MRCVS. Professor, Department of Veterinary Pathology, Glasgow University, since 1979; b. 19.3.40, Glasgow; 2 s. Educ. Lenzie Academy; Glasgow University. Lecturer, Glasgow University, 1965-79. Address: (b.) Department of Veterinary Pathology, Bearsden, Glasgow, G61 1QH; T.-041-330 5773.

Jarvie, Norman Dobson, MB, ChB, FRCGP, DObstRCOG. General Practitioner, Crieff; Chairman, National Medical Advisory Committee, since 1990; b. 31.3.36, Glasgow; m., Dr. Anne Jarvie; 2 s.; 1 d. Educ. Rutherglen Academy; Glasgow University. Medical Officer to Crieff Cottage Hospital, Ardvreck School and Morrison's Academy, since 1964; Chairman, Local Medical Committee, Perth and Kinross Division, 1978-80; President, Perth and Kinross Division, BMA, 1980; Chairman, Scottish Association of General Practitioner Community Hospitals, 1981-85; General Practitioner Tutor, Dundee University; Chairman, Scottish Council, Royal College of General Practitioners, 1987-90; Provost, East Scotland Faculty, RCGP, 1987-90. Recreations: sailing; golf. Address: (b.) Health Centre, Crieff, PH7 3SA; T.-0764 2456.

Jarvis, Geoffrey, FRIBA, FRIAS. Architect in private practice; Consultant in historic buildings; b. 9.1.28, London; m., Rosalind Bailey; 2 s.; 2 d. Educ. Kelvinside Academy; Glasgow Academy; Glasgow School of Architecture. Worked for two years in Philadelphia and New York (Marcel Breuer); returned to Glasgow, setting up in private practice; Consultant to National Trust for Scotland, 1972-87; principal works include Culzean Country Park Centre; Clan Donald Centre, Skye; Chatelherault, Hamilton; Edinburgh Castle Visitor Reception Feasibility Study; Past Chairman, Glasgow Tree Lovers' Society; Founder, former Honorary Secretary and Chairman, New Glasgow Society; Co-Founder and Vice-Chairman, Clyde Fair International, 1972-73; RIBA national award, Regenerating Scotland Award, three Europa Nostra Diplomas of Merit; two Civic Trust Awards; Co-founder, Clydebuilt, 1991; Chairman, Glasgow Buildings Guardian Committee. Recreations: travel and sight-seeing; local and Scottish history; Glasgow; family. Address: (b.) 7 Fitzroy Place, Glasgow, G3 7RH; T.-041-226 4981.

Jarvis, Professor Paul Gordon, PhD, Fil dr, FRSE, FIBiol, FIChFor. Professor of Forestry and Natural Resources, Edinburgh University, since 1975; b. 23.5.35, Tunbridge Wells; m., Margaret Susan Gostelow; 1 s.; 2 d. Educ. Sir Anthony Brown's School, Brentwood; Oriel College, Oxford. PhD study, Sheffield University, 1957-60; Postdoctoral Fellow, NATO, Institute of Plant Physiology, Uppsala University, 1960-62; Fil dr, Uppsala University, 1963; Senior Lecturer in Plant Physiology, Royal College of Agriculture, Uppsala; Aberdeen University: Lecturer in Botany, 1966-72, Senior Lecturer, 1972-75. Council Member, Society for Experimental Biology, 1977-80, Vice President, since 1990; Commissioner, Countryside Commission for Scotland, 1976-78; Council Member, National Trust for Scotland, since 1987; Trustee, John Muir Trust, since 1989; Member, Governing Body, Scottish Crops Research Institute, 1977-86; Co-Founder and Sectional Editor, Plant, Cell and Environment; Co-Founder, Current Advances in Ecological Sciences; serves on various other editorial and review boards. Address: (h.) Belmont, 47 Eskbank Road, Dalkeith, Midlothian, EH22 3BH; T.-031-663 8676.

Jarvis, Roland John, CBE, CBIM. Managing Director and Group Chief Executive, Low and Bonar PLC, since 1984; b. 23.6.32, London; m., Louise; 2 s.; 2 d. Educ. Royal Liberty School. Ford Motor (Planning and Analysis), 1965; Group Comptroller, AEI/GEC, 1967; Financial Controller, Chrysler, 1970; Financial Director, Crane Fruehauf, 1972; TI Raleigh Industries: Financial Director, 1976-80, Managing Director, 1980-84. Recreations: tennis; golf; music. Address: (b.) Bonar House, Faraday Street, Dundee, DD1 9JA.

Jarvis, William. Solicitor; Honorary Sheriff, since 1962; Clerk to Lieutenancy; b. 19.4.11, Dunfermline; m., Helen Dalrymple; 2 s. Educ. Dunfermline High School; Edinburgh University. Partner, Wilson & Jarvis, Solicitors, Alloa, 1937-86; Member, National Health Executive Council, 1963-73; Member, Forth Valley Health Board, 1973-78; Honorary Secretary, Clackmannanshire Boy Scouts Association, 15 years; Honorary Treasurer, Alloa YMCA, 25 years; Elder, West Church, Alloa, since 1947; Founder Member and Past Chairman, Abbeyfield (Alloa and District) Society; President, Alloa Rotary Club, 1961. Recreation: bowling. Address: (h.) Greycraigs, 142 Claremont, Alloa; T.-Alloa 212466.

Jasinski, Alfons B., DA, RSW. Artist; Principal Teacher of Art, St. Andrew's High School, Kirkcaldy, since 1989; b. 14.9.45, Falkirk; m., Ann E.M. Conlan; 1 s.; 2 d. Educ. St. Modan's High School, Stirling; Edinburgh College of Art. Travelling Scholarship to Italy, 1969; began teaching, Balwearie High School, Kirkcaldy, 1969; Latimer Award, RSA, 1975; one-man exhibitions: Loomshop, 1971-72-74-76-80-82, Kirkcaldy Art Gallery, 1974, The Scottish Gallery, 1976, 1986, Cornerstone, Dunblane, 1976, Gallery 22, Cupar, 1984; works in various public and private collections. Address: (h.) 15 Normand Road, Dysart, Fife, KY1 2XN; T.-0592 52505.

Jaspan, Andrew, BA. Editor, Scotland on Sunday, since 1989; b. 20.4.52, Prestbury. Educ. Beverley Grammar School; Manchester University. Sub-Editor, Daily Telegraph; Foreign News Desk, The Times; Assistant News Editor, Sunday Times; Editor, Sunday Times Scotland. Recreations: reading; squash; walking; psephology. Address: (b.) North Bridge, Edinburgh, EH1; T.-031-243 3475.

Jauncey, Hon. Lord (Charles Eliot Jauncey), QC (Scot), BA, LLB. Lord of Appeal in Ordinary, since 1988; Senator of the College of Justice in Scotland, 1979-88; b. 8.5.25. Sheriff Principal of Fife and Kinross, 1971-74.

Jay, Xanthe, BSc, MSc. Environmental Charter Co-ordinator, Grampian Regional Council; b. b. 3.11.58, London. Educ. Cranbrook School; University of East Anglia; Manchester University. Former Co-ordinator, Friends of the Earth (Scotland). Recreations: gardening; cycling; hill-walking.

Address: (b.) Woodhill House, Westburn Road, Aberdeen, AB9 2LU; T.-0224 664737.

Jeeves, Professor Malcolm Alexander, MA, PhD (Cantab), FBPsS, FRSE. Vice-President, Royal Society of Edinburgh, 1990-93; Professor of Psychology, St. Andrews University, since 1969, and Director, Medical Research Council Cognitive Neuroscience Research Group, 1983-88; Vice-Principal, St. Andrews University, 1981-85; b. 16.11.26, Stamford, England; m., Ruth Elisabeth Hartridge; 2 d. Educ. Stamford School; St. John's College, Cambridge University. Lt., 1st Bn., Sherwood Foresters, BAOR, 1945-48; Exhibitioner, St. John's College, Cambridge, 1948-52; research and teaching, Cambridge and Harvard Universities, 1952-56; Lecturer, Leeds University, 1956-59; Professor and Head, Department of Psychology, Adelaide University, 1959-69 (Dean, Faculty of Arts, 1963-64); Member: Council, SERC, 1985-89, Neuroscience and Mental Health Board, MRC, 1985-89, Council, Royal Society of Edinburgh, 1985-88; Chairman, Executive Committee, International Neuropsychological Symposium, since 1986; Editor, Neuropsychologia; Cairns Memorial Lecturer, Australia, 1986; New College Lecturer, University of NSW, 1987. Honorary Sheriff, Fife, since 1986. Publications: Analysis of Structural Learning (Co-author); Psychology Survey No. 3 (Editor); Experimental Psychology: An introduction for biologists; The Effects of Structural Relations upon Transfer (Co-author); Thinking in Structures (Co-author); Behavioural Science and Christianity (Editor); Free to be Different (Co-author); Psychology and Christianity: The View Both Ways; The Scientific Enterprise and Christian Faith; Psychology: Through the eyes of faith (Co-author); Mind Fields. Recreations: walking; music; fishing. Address: (b.) Department of Psychology, St. Andrews University, St. Andrews, KY16 9JU; T.-0334 76161.

Jeffares, Professor Alexander Norman, MA, PhD, DPhil, Ddel'U, DLitt, FAHA, FRSE, FRSL, FRSA. Professor of English Studies, Stirling University, 1974-86; Honorary Professor, since 1987; Managing Director, Academic Advisory Services Ltd.; Director, Colin Smythe Ltd.; b. 11.8.20, Dublin; m., Jeanne Agnes Calembert; 1 d. Educ. The High School, Dublin; Trinity College, Dublin; Oriel College, Oxford. Lecturer in Classics, Trinity College, Dublin, 1943-45; Lector in English, Groningen University, 1946-48; Lecturer in English Literature, Edinburgh University, 1949-51; Professor of English Language and Literature, Adelaide, 1951-56; Professor of English Literature, Leeds, 1957-74. Secretary, Australian Humanities Research Council, 1954-57; Honorary Fellow, Australian Academy of Humanities; Founding Chairman, Association for Commonwealth Literary and Language Studies, 1966-68 (Honorary Life Fellow); Founding Chairman, International Association for Study of Anglo-Irish Literature, 1968-70 (Honorary Life President, since 1973); Member, Scottish Arts Council (Chairman, Literature Committee, 1977-83, Vice Chairman, 1980-84); Member, Arts Council of GB, 1980-84; Chairman, National Book League Scotland, 1985-87, Book Trust Scotland, 1987-89; Board Member, Book Trust, 1987-89; President, International PEN, Scottish Centre, 1986-89; Vice-President, Royal Society of Edinburgh, 1988-89; Vice-Chairman, Muckhart Community Council, 1979-86; Chairman of Judges, McVitie Prize, 1988-91. Publications: Yeats: Man and Poet; Seven Centuries of Poetry; The Scientific Background (Co-author); A Commentary on the Poems of Yeats; A Commentary on the Plays of Yeats (Co-author); History of Anglo-Irish Literature; Restoration Drama; New Commentary on Poems of Yeats; Brought up in Dublin (poems); Brought up to Leave (poems); An Irish Childhood (Co-Editor); A Jewish Childhood (Co-Editor); Yeats: a new biography; Yeats's Poems; Yeats's Vision; Yeats: the love poems; Always Your Friend (Co-Editor); Swift, the selected poems; Images of Imagination (essays). Recreations: draw-

ing; painting; restoring old houses. Address: (h.) Craighead Cottage, Fife Ness, Crail, Fife; T.-0333 50898.

Jefferson, Gordon Cort, BSc, MSc, PhD, FRPharmS. Secretary, Scottish Department, Royal Pharmaceutical Society of Gt. Britain, since 1988 (Head, Department of Pharmacy, Heriot-Watt University, 1983-88); Member, National Pharmaceutical Advisory Committee; b. 12.9.35, Edenfield, Lancs; m., Jean Margaret Perkin; 2 s. Educ. Bacup and Rawtenstall Grammar School; Lancaster Royal Grammar School; Manchester University. Benger Research Fellow, then Teaching Assistant, Department of Pharmacology, Manchester University, 1960-62; Lecturer in Pharmacology, then Senior Lecturer, Department of Pharmacy, Heriot-Watt College/University, 1962-83. Recreations: golf; railway history; amateur interest in architecture. Address: (h.) 5 Cherry Tree Crescent, Balerno, Edinburgh, EH14 5AY; T.-031-449 3549.

Jeffery, Professor Jonathan, MA, BSc, DPhil, DSc, CChem, FRSC, CBiol, FIBiol, FRSA, FRSE. Professor of Biochemistry, Aberdeen University, since 1983; b. 29.7.35, Liverpool; m., Christa Torriano-Williams; 2 d. Educ. Liverpool Institute High School; Jesus College, Oxford University. Research Biochemist, ICI, 1962-66; Aberdeen University: Lecturer in Chemical Pathology, 1966-72, Lecturer in Biochemistry, 1972-74, Senior Lecturer in Biochemistry, 1974-83. Recreations: country walks; some interest in theatre, visual arts and music. Address: (b.) Department of Molecular and Cell Biology, Aberdeen University, Marischal College, Aberdeen, AB9 1AS; T.-0224 272000.

Jeffrey, Rev. Eric William Sinclair, MA, JP. Minister, Bristo Memorial Church, Craigmillar, Edinburgh, since 1978; b. 12.2.29, Coatbridge; m., Carol Elizabeth Dover Wilson; 4 s.; 2 d. Educ. High School of Glasgow; Glasgow University and Trinity College. Missionary in Malawi, 1954-69; Minister, Dalmeny and Abercorn, 1969-78. Recreations: playing double bass; cricket umpire; golf. Address: 3 Spence Street, Edinburgh, EH16 5AG; T.-031-668 2722.

Jeffrey, Ian William McDonald, PhD, FDS, LDS, RCSEdin. Senior Lecturer in Conservative Dentistry, Dundee University, since 1978; b. 11.1.31, Edinburgh; m., Jean McKenzie; 2 s.; 1 d. Educ. George Heriot's, Edinburgh; John Bright Grammar School, Llandudno; Edinburgh University. National Service, Egypt, 1953-55; Colonial Service, Uganda, 1955-58; Registrar, Eastern Regional Hospital Board, 1959-60; Lecturing Staff, Dundee University, since 1960; Examiner, Royal College of Surgeons, Edinburgh; Visiting Lecturer, Nairobi University. Recreations: mountaineering; travel; house and car maintenance; photography. Address: (h.) Norwood, McKenzie Street, Carnoustie, Angus; T.-Carnoustie 52405.

Jeffrey, John J., BSc (Hons), BA (Ed), DipEd, CEng, MRINA. Depute Principal, Inverness College, since 1978; b. 29.7.35, Greenock; m., Norma May McGregor; 1 s.; 2 d. Educ. Greenock High School; Strathclyde University; Open University; Aberdeen University; Paisley College of Technology. Began career as apprentice/design draughtsman, Scott Lithgow (Shipbuilders), 1950-61; Nuclear power design Engineer, English Electric, Leicester, 1961-63; Lecturer in Naval Architecture/Engineering, then Senior Lecturer, Kirkcaldy College of Technology, 1963-67; Second Depute Principal, Aberdeen Technical College, 1967-70. Recreations: golf; tennis; computing. Address: (b.) Inverness College, 3 Longman Road, Longman South, Inverness; T.-0463 236681.

Jeffrey, Robin, ARCST, BSc, PhD, CEng, MIChemE. Managing Director, Engineering Resources Division, Scottish Power, since 1991; b. 19.2.39, Kirkintilloch; m., Barbara; 2

s.; 1 d. Educ. Lenzie Academy; Kelvinside Academy; Royal College of Science and Technology, Glasgow; Glasgow University; Cambridge University. Babcock and Wilcox, Renfew, 1956-60 and 1964-79; joined SEEB, 1979. Recreations: squash; tennis; real tennis; skiing. Address: (h.) 71D Partickhill Road, Glasgow; T.-041-357 3079.

Jeffreys-Jones, Rhodri, BA (Wales), PhD (Cantab), FRHistS. Reader in History, Edinburgh University, since 1990; b. 28.7.42, Carmarthen; 2 d. Educ. Ysgol Ardudwy; University of Wales; Cambridge University; Michigan University; Harvard University. Tutor: Harvard, 1965-66, Fitzwilliam College, Cambridge, 1966-67; Assistant Lecturer, then Lecturer, then Senior Lecturer, Edinburgh University, 1967-90; Fellow, Charles Warren Center for the Study of American History, Harvard, 1971-72. Publications: Violence and Reform in American History; American Espionage: From Secret Service to CIA; Eagle Against Empire: American Opposition to American Imperialism 1914-82 (Editor); The Growth of Federal Power in American History (Joint Editor); The CIA and American Democracy; North American Spies (Joint Editor). Recreations: snooker; vegetable gardening. Address: (b.) Department of History, Edinburgh University, William Robertson Building, George Square, Edinburgh, EH8 9JY; T.-031-667 1011.

Jenkins, David, BMus, PhD. Academic Registrar, Moray House College of Education, since 1984; b. 30.5.44, Dundee; m., Dr. Janet Jenkins; 2 s.; 1 d. Educ. Perth Academy; Edinburgh University. Assistant Teacher, Tynecastle Secondary School, Edinburgh, 1968-70; Lecturer, then Vice-Principal, Callendar Park College of Education, Falkirk, 1970-82; Lecturer and Clerk to Board of Studies, Moray House College of Education, 1982-84. Recreations: music; gardening. Address: (h.) 18 Blacket Place, Edinburgh, EH9 1RL; T.-031-667 2885.

Jenkins, Rev. Gordon Fraser Campbell, MA, BD, PhD. Assistant Secretary, Board of Ministry, Church of Scotland, since 1991; b. 9.1.41, Glasgow; m., Linda Victoria McGuinness; 1 s.; 1 d. Educ. Whitehill Secondary School, Glasgow; Glasgow University. Minister, North Parish Church, Dunfermline, 1968-88; Deputy Secretary, Department of Education, Church of Scotland. Recreations: sport and opera. Address: (h.) 15 Dean Ridge, Gowkhall, Dunfermline; T.-0383 851078.

Jenkins, Robin, MA. Novelist; b. 11.9.12. Author of: Happy for the Child, The Thistle and the Grail, The Cone-Gatherers, Guests of War, The Missionaries, The Changeling, Some Kind of Grace, Dust on the Paw, The Tiger of Gold, A Love of Innocence, The Sardana Dancers, A Very Scotch Affair, The Holy Tree, The Expatriates, A Toast to the Lord, A Far Cry from Bowmore, A Figure of Fun, A Would-be Saint, Fergus Lamont, The Awakening of George Darroch, Just Duffy, Poverty Castle.

Jennett, Professor Bryan, MD, FRCS. Professor of Neurosurgery, Glasgow University, 1968-91 (Dean, Faculty of Medicine, 1981-86); Member, Court, Glasgow University, 1987-91; b. 1.3.26, Twickenham, Middlesex; m., Professor Sheila Jennett (qv); 3 s.; 1 d. Educ. King's College, Wimbledon; King George V School, Southport; Liverpool University. Lecturer in Neurosurgery, Manchester University; Rockefeller Travelling Fellow, University of California; Hunterian Professor, Royal College of Surgeons of England. Member, Medical Research Council, 1979-83; Member, Chief Scientist Committee, Scotland; Rock Carling Fellow. Publications: Epilepsy After Non-Missile Head Injuries; Introduction to Neurosurgery; High Technology Medicine - Benefits and Burdens. Recreations: writing; cruising under sail. Address: (h.) 83 Hughenden Lane, Glasgow, G12 9XN.

Jennett, Professor Sheila, MD, PhD, FRCPGlas. Titular Professor in Physiology, Glasgow University, 1985-91; b. 28.1.26, Liverpool; m., Professor Bryan Jennett (qv); 3 s.; 1 d. Educ. Aigburth Vale High School, Liverpool; Liverpool University. Junior hospital appointments in surgery, spinal injuries, geriatrics and respiratory medicine, 1949-62; Lecturer, then Senior Lecturer, then Reader in Physiology, Glasgow University, 1963-85. Committee Member, Physiological Society, 1981-85. Recreations: sailing; music; walking. Address: (h.) 83 Hughenden Lane, Glasgow, G12 9XN.

Jennings, James, JP. Convener, Strathclyde Regional Council, since 1986; Honorary Sheriff, Kilmarnock, since 1991; Chairman, Police Negotiating Board, since 1990; b. 2, Margaret Mary Hughes, JP; 2 d. Educ. St. Palladius School, Dalry; St. Michael's College, Irvine. Steel industry, 1946-79. Member: Ayr County Council, 1958, Strathclyde Regional Council, 1974 (Vice-Convener, 1982-86); Chairman: Ayr CC Police and Law Committee, 1964-70, Ayrshire Joint Police Committee, 1970-75, North Ayrshire Crime Prevention Panel, 1970-82, Police and Fire Committee, Strathclyde Regional Council, 1978-82; contested Perth and East Perthshire, 1966; Vice-President, St. Andrew's Ambulance Association; Patron, Association of Youth Clubs in Strathclyde; Honorary President: Scottish Retirement Council, Princess Louise Scottish Hospital (Erskine Hospital); Honorary Vice-President: SNO Chorus, Royal British Legion Scotland (Dalry and District Branch); JP, Cunninghame, 1969 (Chairman, Cunninghame Justices Committee, since 1974); Vice-Chairman, Official Side, Police Negotiating Board, 1984-86, Chairman, 1986-88; Chairman, Garnock Valley Development Executive, since 1988. Recreation: local community involvement. Address: (h.) 4 Place View, Kilbirnie, KA25 6BG; T.-Kilbirnie 3339.

Jennings, Kevin, MB, FRCP. Consultant Cardiologist, Aberdeen Royal Infirmary, since 1983; b. 9.3.47, Charleville, Eire; m., Heather; 2 s.; 1 d. Educ. Downside; St. Bartholomew's Hospital, London. Registrar: King's College Hospital, London, London Chest Hospital; Senior Registrar, Freeman Hospital, Newcastle-upon-Tyne. Recreations: theatre; ballet; golf; windsurfing. Address: 58 Rubislaw Den South, Aberdeen, AB2 6AX; T.-Aberdeen 311466.

Jessop, Thomas Findlay. Collector of Customs and Excise, Glasgow, since 1989; Registrar of Shipping, since 1989; Receiver of Wreck, since 1989; b. 19.8.34, Edinburgh; m., Elizabeth; 1 s.; 1 d. Educ. George Heriot's School, Edinburgh; Edinburgh University. Royal Navy (National Service), 1954-56; Officer of Customs and Excise, 1956-72; Surveyor of Customs and Excise, 1972-78; Assistant Collector of Customs and Excise, 1978-86; Senior Principal, Alcoholic Drinks Policy, 1986-89. Recreations: sailing; gardening; badminton (when time permits). Address: (h.) Spinningdale, 3 Barrcraig Road, Bridge of Weir, PA11 3HG.

Jimack, Professor Peter David, BA, PhD. Professor of French, Stirling University, since 1972; b. 29.9.30, London; m., Christine Mary; 1 s.; 3 d. by pr. m. Educ. Tottenham Grammar School; Southampton University. Assistant Master: Churcher's College, Petersfield, 1954-57, Cotham Grammar School, Bristol, 1957-58; Birmingham University: Assistant Lecturer, 1959-61, Lecturer, 1961-66, Senior Lecturer, 1966-72. Recreations: gardening; swimming; watching films. Address: (h.) 6 Banavie Road, Glasgow, G11 5AN; T.-041-334 5926.

Johnsen, Konrad W.M., BCom, CA (SA). Chief Executive, Howden Group PLC, since 1987; b. 20.11.42, South Africa; m., Dorothy; 2 d. Educ. Selborne College, South Africa; Rhodes University, Grahamstown; University of

Witwatersrand. Trained as Accountant, Thomson McLintock, Johannesburg and London; joined Howden in South Africa, 1973; transferred to UK, 1984. Recreations: golf; tennis; skiing. Address: (b.) Old Govan Road, Renfrew, PA4 0XJ; T.-041-885 2245.

Johnson, Professor Brian Frederick Gilbert, FRSC, FRS, BSc, MA, PhD. Crum Brown Professor of Inorganic Chemistry, Edinburgh University, since 1991; b. 11.9.38, Northampton; m., Christine; 2 d. Educ. Northampton Grammar School; Nottingham University. Lecturer: Manchester University, 1965-67, University College, London, 1967-70; Lecturer, then Reader, Cambridge University, 1970-90; Fitwilliam College: Fellow, 1970-90, President and Acting Master, 1988-90, Hon. Fellow, since 1991. Recreations: hiking; painting. Address: (b.) Department of Chemistry, Edinburgh University, West Mains Road, Edinburgh, EH9 3JJ; T.-031-650 4706.

Johnson, David (Charles), MA, BA, PhD. Composer; Musical Historian; Cellist, McGibbon Ensemble, since 1979; 27.10.42, Edinburgh; 1 s. Educ. Aberdeen University; St. John's College, Cambridge. Tutor, Edinburgh University Music Faculty, since 1988; Member, Scottish Music Information Centre Advisory Committee, since 1983; Postdoctoral Fellowship, Music Faculty, Edinburgh University, 1979-80; awarded Scottish Arts Council Writer's Bursary, 1979; compositions include four operas, an orchestral suite, chamber music, songs, a piano concerto, church music. Publications: Music and Society in Lowland Scotland, 1972; Scottish Fiddle Music in the 18th Century, 1984; contributions to the New Grove Dictionary of Music, 1981; contributions to The Story of Scotland, 1989; The Scots Cello Book, 1990. Address: (h.) 1 Hill Square, Edinburgh, EH8 9DR; T.-031-667 7054.

Johnson, James Henry, DipArch, ARIAS. Executive Director, Edinburgh Old Town Renewal Trust, since 1991; b. 21.5.33, Southend-on-Sea; m., Krystyna Maria Anna Dobraczynska; 1 s.; 2 d. Educ. King Edward VI School, Southampton; Northern Polytechnic, London. Architect, Cumbernauld Development Corporation, 1961-63; Lecturer/Senior Lecturer/Reader, Strathclyde University, 1963-83; Director, Assist housing rehabilitation unit, 1973-83; Member, Assist architects' co-operative, 1983-86; Director, Edinburgh Old Town Committee for Conservation and Renewal, 1986-91. Board Member, WASPS. Recreation: self-build restoration of Galloway stables. Address: (b.) EOTRT, 8 Advocates Close, 357 High Street, Edinburgh, EH1 1PS; T.-031-225 8818.

Johnson, Sir Ronald (Ernest Charles), Kt (1970), CB (1962), MA (Cantab). Retired Civil Servant; b. 3.5.13, Portsmouth; m., Elizabeth Gladys Nuttall; 2 s.; 1 s. deceased. Educ. Portsmouth Grammar School; St. John's College, Cambridge. RNVR, Intelligence Eastern Fleet, 1944-45; entered Scottish Office, 1935; Secretary, Scottish Home and Health Department, 1963-72; Secretary of Commissions for Scotland, 1972-78. Chairman, Civil Service Savings Committee for Scotland, 1963-78; Member, Scottish Records Advisory Council, 1975-81; Member, Committee on Administration of Sheriffdoms, 1981-82; Chairman, Fire Service Research and Training Trust, 1976-89; President, Edinburgh Bach Society, 1973-86; President, Edinburgh Society of Organists, 1980-82; JP, Edinburgh, since 1971. Recreation: church organ. Address: (h.) 14 Eglinton Crescent, Edinburgh, EH12 5DD; T.-031-337 7733.

Johnson, Roy Arthur, CA, MIPA. Partner, Coopers & Lybrand Deloitte, Glasgow, since 1966, and Cork Gully, Glasgow, since 1981; Council Member, Institute of Chartered Accountants of Scotland, 1984-90 (Convener, Finance and General Purposes Committee, 1986-90); b. 3.3.37, Wanstead,

Essex; m., Heather Campbell; 2 s. Educ. Lancing College. Deacon, Incorporation of Cordiners, Glasgow, 1976-77; Deacon Convener, Trades House of Glasgow, 1990; Director, Glasgow Chamber of Commerce, since 1988 (Convener, Finance and Taxation Committee, since 1990); Chairman, Prince's Trust Community Volunteers – Strathclyde Region, 1991. Recreations: golf; gardening; photography. Address: (b.) Kintyre House, 209 West George Street, Glasgow; T.-041-248 2644.

Johnson-Marshall, Professor Emeritus Percy Edwin Alan, CMG, DipArch, MA, RIBA, FRTPI, RIBA, DistTP. Professor of Urban Design and Regional Planning, Edinburgh University, 1964-85; Partner, Percy Johnson-Marshall and Partners, 1960-90; b. 20.1.15, Ajmer, India; m., April Bridger; 3 s.; 4 d. Educ. Queen Elizabeth School, Kirkby Lonsdale; School of Architecture, Liverpool University. Various posts, local government, 1936-38; Senior Planning Architect, Coventry City Council, 1938-41; War Service, Royal Engineers, India and Burma, 1941-46; Advisor to Government of Burma for National Outline Plan, 1945-46; Regional Planning Officer, Ministry of Town and Country Planning, 1946-48; Planner in charge, London's Comprehensive Development Areas, LCC, 1949-59; Senior Lecturer, then Reader, Edinburgh University, 1959-64. Member: RIBA Council, 1951-75, RTPI Council, 1950-75, RIAS Council, 1964-74; former Vice-President, International Society for City and Regional Planners; Consultant on Human Settlements, UN Stockholm Conference on Environment; Member, Commonwealth Human Ecology Council, since 1973; Vice President, 1st International Congress on Planning of Major Cities, Mexico City, 1981. Recreations: reading; writing; travel. Address: (h.) Bella Vista, 64 The Causeway, Duddingston, Edinburgh, EH15 3PZ; T.-031-661 2019.

Johnston, Alan Charles Macpherson, BA (Hons) (Cantab), LLB. Queen's Counsel (1980); b. 13.1.42, Stirling; m., Anthea Jean Blackburn; 3 s. Educ. Edinburgh Academy; Loretto School; Jesus College, Cambridge; Edinburgh University. Advocate, 1967; Standing Junior Counsel, Scottish Home and Health Department, 1972; Advocate Depute, 1978-82; Chairman: Industrial Tribunal, 1982-85, Medical Appeal Tribunal, 1985-89; Treasurer, Faculty of Advocates, 1977-89, Dean, Faculty of Advocates, since 1989. Publication: Introduction to Law of Scotland 7th Edition (Joint Editor). Address: (h.) 3 Circus Gardens, Edinburgh; T.-031-225 1862.

Johnston, Alastair J.C., OBE, BSc, CEng, FIProdE, FBIM. Managing Director, Gates Rubber Co. Ltd.; Chairman, Holden and Fisher Ltd.; Director, Duncan Honeyman Ltd.; Member, CBI Scottish Council; Deputy Chairman, Dumfries and Galloway Enterprise Company; b. 16.9.28, Dundee; m., Morag Campbell; 2 s. Educ. Harris Academy, Dundee; St. Andrews University. Apprenticeship, Caledon Shipyard, Dundee; Industrial Engineering Manager, North British Rubber Co., Edinburgh; Plant Manager, Armstrong Cork Co., Gateshead; Director and General Manager, William Briggs Ltd., Dundee; Managing Director: Permanite Ltd., Waltham Abbey, Trident Equipment Ltd., Ware. Address: (h.) 8 Ravelston Park, Edinburgh, EH4 3DX; T.-031-332 8409.

Johnston, Sheriff Alexander Graham, LLB, BA. Sheriff of Glasgow and Strathkelvin, at Glasgow, since 1985 (Grampian, Highland and Islands, 1982-85); b. 16.7.44.

Johnston, David Scott, OBE, BA, FRAgS. Chief Executive, National Farmers' Union of Scotland, since 1989; b. 18.12.32, Dundee; m., Sheila Kirkby; 3 s. Educ. Harris Academy, Dundee; Rutherford Grammar School, Newcastle; Hatfield College, Durham University. Economics Researcher, Tube Investments, Birmingham, until 1957; joined NFU of Scotland as Assistant Secretary, 1957 (Deputy General

Secretary, 1972-78); UK Representative, General Experts Committee, COPA, three years; Member of Praesidium, COPA. Recreation: mountaineering. Address: (b.) 17 Grosvenor Crescent, Edinburgh, EH12 5EN; T.-031-337 4333.

Johnston, Frederick Patrick Mair, MA. Chairman, Johnston Press PLC (formerly F. Johnston & Co. Ltd.), since 1973; Chairman, Dunn & Wilson Ltd., since 1976; b. 15.9.35, Edinburgh; m., Elizabeth Ann Jones; 2 s. Educ. Morrison's Academy, Crieff; Lancing College, Sussex; New College, Oxford. Editorial Department, Liverpool Daily Post and Echo, 1959; Assistant Secretary, The Times Publishing Co. Ltd., 1960; Company Secretary, F. Johnston & Co. Ltd., 1969. Chairman, Central Scotland Manpower Committee, 1976-83; Member, Press Council, 1974-88; President, Scottish Newspaper Proprietors' Association, 1976-78; Treasurer, Society of Master Printers of Scotland, 1981-86; President, The Newspaper Society, 1989-90; Director, Scottish Mortgage & Trust plc, since 1991. Recreations: reading; travelling. Address: (b.) 53 Manor Place, Edinburgh, EH3 7EG; T.-031-225 3361.

Johnston, George Hermiston, Dip., Youth and Community Work. Director, Scottish Standing Conference of Voluntary Youth Organisations, since 1992; b. 22.11.36. Director, Clermiston Centre and Youth Secretary, Edinburgh YMCA, 1964-70; General Secretary, Belfast YMCA, 1970-74; Training Officer, Northern Ireland Association of Youth Clubs, 1974-76, Director, 1976-92. Former Vice-Chairman, Voluntary Youth Network for Northern Ireland (Youthnet); Past President, European Confederation of Youth Clubs. Recreations: photography; music; walking; art. Address: (b.) SSCVYO, Central Hall, West Tollcross, Edinburgh, EH3 9BP; T.-031-229 0339.

Johnston, Grenville Shaw, OBE, TD, KCSG, DL, CA. Chartered Accountant, since 1968; Territorial Army Officer, 1964-89 (Lt. Col.); b. 28.1.45, Nairn; m., Marylyn Jean Picken; 2 d. Educ. Blairmore School; Fettes College. Qualified in Edinburgh with Scott Moncrieff Thomson & Sheills; Thomson McLintock & Co., Glasgow, 1968-70; joined family firm, W.D. Johnston & Carmichael, Elgin, 1970; Senior Partner, 1975. Commanding Officer, 2nd 51st Highland Volunteers, 1983-86; Deputy Lieutenant of Moray, since 1980; Knight Commander, Order of St. Gregory, 1982, for work for Pluscarden Abbey; OBE for services to Territorial Army; Chairman, Grampian Committee, Royal Jubilee Trusts, 1982-91; a Director, Moray, Badenoch and Strathspey Enterprise Company Ltd.; Member, Cairngorm Recreation Trust Ltd.; Governor, Gordonstoun School; Governor, Butterstone School; Chairman, Moray Venture Capital Fund Ltd.; Director: Moray Enterprise Trust, Moray & Nairn Newspaper Co. Ltd. Recreations: shooting; fishing; hockey; running; golf; skiing. Address: (h.) Spynie Kirk House, Spynie, By Elgin, Moray, IV30 3XJ.

Johnston, Professor Ian Alistair, BSc, PhD, FRSE. Professor of Comparative Physiology (Personal Chair), Director, Gatty Marine Laboratory, St. Andrews University, since 1985 (Chairman, Department of Biology and Preclinical Medicine); b. 13.4.49, Barking, Essex; m., Dr. Rhona S. Johnston. Educ. Addey and Stanhope Grammar School, London; Hull University. NERC Postdoctoral Research Fellow, Bristol University, 1973-75; Lecturer in Physiology, St. Andrews University, 1976-84; Reader, 1984-85; Visiting Senior Lecturer, Department of Veterinary Physiology, Nairobi University, 1981; Visiting Scientist, British Antarctic Survey base, Signy Island, South Orkneys, 1983-84; awarded Scientific Medal, Zoological Society of London. Recreations: photography; walking; music. Address: (b.) Department of Biology and Preclinical Medicine, St. Andrews University, St. Andrews, KY16 8LB; T.-0334 76161, Ext. 7104.

Johnston, James George, BSc (Hons). Headteacher, Leverhulme Memorial School, Leverburgh, Harris, since 1984; b. 1.5.54, Glasgow; m., Marilyn; 1 s. Educ. Cumbernauld High School; Glasgow University. Recreations: golf; fishing; reading; voluntary work. Address: The Schoolhouse, Leverburgh, Harris, Western Isles; T.-0859 82208.

Johnston, James Kenneth Buchanan, TD, BL. Former Senior Partner, Brown Mair Mackintosh & Co., Solicitors, Glasgow; Past Chairman, Royal Yachting Association Scotland; b. 4.9.15, Stirling; 1 d. Educ. Stirling High School; Glasgow University. Organist and Choirmaster, 1930-39; Service in Territorial Army, 1936-39; War Service in Middle East and Far East, 1939-44 (rank of Lt.-Col.); graduated a Solicitor, 1945. Commodore, Royal Scottish Motor Yacht Club, 1968-71, Hon. Commodore, since 1987; Legal Adviser, Royal Yachting Association Scotland; awarded RYA Award, 1983, for services to yachting. Address: (h.) 47 Poplar Avenue, Newton Mearns, Glasgow; T.-041-639 7238.

Johnston, John Robert, BSc, PhD, FIBiol. Reader, Department of Bioscience and Biotechnology, Strathclyde University, since 1983; b. 6.10.34, Leven, Fife; m., Janet Bonthrone Reekie; 3 s. Educ. Buckhaven High School; St. Andrews University. Teaching Associate, University of California, Berkeley; Research Scientist, Brewing Research Foundation, Nutfield, Surrey; Royal Society Latin America Exchange Fellow, 1970-71, Mexico City; Lecturer, then Senior Lecturer, Strathclyde University, 1964-83; Visiting Professor, University of California, Berkeley, 1987-91; Vice-President, Royal Philosophical Society of Glasgow, 1987-90. Recreations: outdoor activities; theatre and music; community affairs. Address: (h.) 83 Castlehill Road, Bearsden, Glasgow, G61 4DX; T.-041-942 1461.

Johnston, Peter William, MA, LLB, FRSA. Chief Executive and Secretary, Institute of Chartered Accountants of Scotland, since 1989; b. 8.2.43, Peebles; m., Patricia Sandra; 1 s.; 1 d. Educ. Larbert High School; Glasgow University. Partner, MacArthur & Co., Solicitors, Inverness, 1971-76; Procurator Fiscal Service, 1976-89. Recreations: music; languages; sailing. Address: (b.) 27 Queen Street, Edinburgh, EH2 1LA; T.-031-225 5673.

Johnston, Robin Alexander, BSc, MB, BCh, BAO, MD, FRCS (Edin). Consultant Neurosurgeon, since 1985; Honorary Clinical Senior Lecturer, Glasgow University, since 1990; b. 30.3.49, Belfast; m., Ann. Educ. Belfast Royal Academy; Queens University, Belfast. Various surgical posts, UK, 1974-77; neurosurgical training, Belfast, Dallas, Glasgow, 1977-85. Recreations: golf; clay pigeon shooting. Address: (b.) Institute of Neurological Sciences, Southern General Hospital, Glasgow; T.-041-445 2466.

Johnston, Sir Russell, KB (1985), MA (Hons). MP (Liberal Democrat), Inverness, Nairn and Lochaber (formerly Inverness), since 1964; b. 28.7.32, Edinburgh; m., Joan Graham Menzies; 3 s. Educ. Carbost Public School; Portree High School; Edinburgh University; Moray House College of Education. National Service: commissioned into Intelligence Corps and 2nd i/c British Intelligence Unit, Berlin, 1958-59; History Teacher, Liberton Secondary School, Edinburgh, 1961-63; Research Assistant, Scottish Liberal Party, 1963-64; Joint Parliamentary Adviser, Educational Institute of Scotland, 1964-70; Member, Royal Commission on Local Government in Scotland, 1966-69; Parliamentary Spokesman for Scottish National Federation for the Welfare of the Blind, since 1967; Parliamentary Representative, Royal National Institute for the Blind, since 1977; Member, Select Committee on Scottish Affairs, 1969; Parliamentary Adviser, Scottish Police Federation, 1971-75; Scottish Liberal Party: elected to Executive, 1961, and

Organisation Committee, 1962, Vice Chairman, 1965, Chairman, 1970-74, Leader, 1974-88, President, since 1988; Liberal Party Spokesman on Education, 1964-66, on Foreign Affairs, 1970-75 and 1979-85, on Scotland, 1970-73, 1975-83, 1985-88, on Devolution, 1975, on Defence, 1983-88; Member, European Parliament, 1973-75 and 1976-79; Vice President, European Liberal Group and Group Spokesman on Regional Policy, 1973-75; Vice President of the Parliament's Political Committee, 1976-79; Member, Western European Union Assembly and Representative to Council of Europe, 1984-85, and since 1987; Interim Leader, Scottish Social and Liberal Democrats, 1988; Deputy Leader, Social and Liberal Democrats, since 1988; Vice President, ELDR, since 1989. Recreations: reading; photography; shinty (Vice Chief, Camanachd Association, 1987-90). Address: (h.) House of Commons, London, SW1A OAA; T.-071-219 5180.

Johnston, Thomas Lothian, MA, PhD, DL, FRSA, FRSE, CBIM, DrHC, DEd, LLD, DUniv, FEIS. Chairman, Scottish Committee, Royal Society of Arts; Director: First Charlotte Assets Trust, Hodgson Martin Ltd., Scottish Life Assurance Company; Chairman, Academic Residences in Scotland plc; b. 9.3.27, Whitburn; m., Joan Fahmy; 2 s.; 3 d. Educ. Hawick High School; Edinburgh University; Stockholm University. Lecturer in Political Economy, Edinburgh University, 1953-65; Professor of Economics, Heriot-Watt University, 1966-76; Vice-Chancellor, Heriot-Watt University, 1981-88; Chairman, Manpower Services Committee for Scotland, 1977-80; Scottish Chairman, Industry Year, 1986, and Industry Matters, 1987-89; academic appointments in other countries: Illinois University, 1957, 1962-63, Queen's University, Canada, 1965, Western Australian Institute of Technology, 1979, Visiting Professor, International Institute for Labour Studies, Geneva, 1973. Publications: Collective Bargaining in Sweden, 1962; Economic Expansion and Structural Change, 1963; The Structure and Growth of the Scottish Economy (co-author), 1971; Introduction to Industrial Relations, 1981. Recreations: gardening; walking. Address: (h.) 14 Mansionhouse Road, Edinburgh, EH9 1TZ; T.-031-667 1439.

Johnston, Very Rev. William Bryce, MA, BD, DD, DLitt. Minister, Colinton Parish Church, 1964-91; Chaplain to The Queen in Scotland, 1981-91, Extra Chaplain, since 1991; b. 16.9.21, Edinburgh; m., Ruth Margaret Cowley; 1 s.; 2 d. Educ. George Watson's College, Edinburgh; Edinburgh University. Chaplain to the Forces, 1945-49; Minister: St. Andrew's Church, Bo'ness, 1949-55, St. George's Church, Greenock, 1955-64; Chaplain, HM Prison, Greenock, 1959-64; Convener, General Assembly Committees: Adult Christian Education, 1970-72, Church and Nation, 1972-76, Inter-Church Relations, 1979-81; Moderator of the General Assembly, 1980; Cunningham Lecturer, New College, 1968-71; Visiting Lecturer in Social Ethics, Heriot-Watt University, 1966-88; Member, Broadcasting Council for Scotland, 1983-87. Publications: translations of Karl Barth and John Calvin; Ethics and Defence (Contributor). Recreations: organ-playing; bowls. Address: (h.) 15 Elliot Road, Edinburgh, EH14 1DU; T.-031-441 3387.

Johnston, William Greer, MBA, CA. Managing Director, Sutherland Transport and Trading Co. Ltd., since 1969; Member, Highland Health Board, 1983-91; b. 10.12.40, Old Kilpatrick; m., Moira Alice Haldane Smith; 3 s.; 1 d. Educ. Clydebank High School; Glasgow University. Qualified Chartered Accountant, 1962; various posts in accounting firms, then in engineering and car retail distribution, 1962-69; Member, Highland Regional Council, 1974-78 (Chairman, Education Committee); District Councillor, 1974-80 (Chairman, Environmental Health and Leisure and Recreation); Chairman, Caithness and Sutherland Local Health Council, since 1991. Chairman, Scripture Union Scotland, 1979-84; Treasurer, Scripture Union International,

since 1985. Recreations: photography; stamp collecting; family. Address: (h.) Beannach, Lairg, Sutherland; T.-0549 2113.

Johnston, William John, BSc (Hons), DipEd(Tech). Rector, Aberdeen Grammar School, since 1987; b. 17.8.47, Kilmarnock; m., Katie Mary Maclean; 3 d. Educ. Spier's School, Beith; Glasgow University. Marketing Assistant, ICI Silicones, 1969-70; Teacher: Cranhill Secondary, 1971-73, Perth High School, 1973-75; Assistant Principal Teacher, Glenrothes High School, 1975-78; Principal Teacher, Millburn Academy, 1978-81; Assistant Rector, Kingussie High School, 1981-84; Depute Rector, Culloden Academy, 1984-87. Address: (b.) Aberdeen Grammar School, Skene Street, Aberdeen; T.-0224 642299.

Johnstone, Alastair William Ross, BA. Managing Director, Morgan Grenfell (Scotland) Limited; b. 30.7.58, Manchester; m., Lesley Ann; 1 d. Educ. Kelvinside Academy, Glasgow; Stirling University. Assistant Manager, Bank of America NT and SA; Company Secretary, Morgan Grenfell (Scotland) Limited; Manager, Morgan Grenfell & Co. Limited, Edinburgh Branch. Recreations: golf; skiing; cigarette card collecting. Address: (b.) 35 St. Andrew Square, Edinburgh, EH2 2AD; T.-031-556 6982.

Johnstone, Professor Alexander Henry, BSc, PhD, DipREd, CChem, FRSC. Professor in Science Education, Glasgow University, since 1990 (Head, Science Education Research Group, since 1972); Director, Centre for Science Education, Glasgow University, since 1989; b. 17.10.30, Edinburgh; m., Martha Y. Cuthbertson; 2 s. Educ. Leith Academy; Edinburgh University; Glasgow University; Moray House College of Education. Commissioned, Royal Corps of Signals; Assistant Teacher of Chemistry, George Watson's College, Edinburgh; Head, Chemistry Department, High School of Stirling; Lecturer, then Senior Lecturer in Chemistry, then Reader in Chemical Education, Glasgow University. Vice-President, Royal Society of Chemistry (President, Education Division); Consultant to Consultative Committee on the Curriculum. Recreations: hill-walking; photography; archaeology; lay preaching. Address: (b.) Department of Chemistry, The University, Glasgow, G12 8QQ; T.-041-339 8855, Ext. 5172.

Johnstone, Professor Eve Cordelia, MD, FRCP, FRCPsych, DPM. Professor of Psychiatry, Edinburgh University; Honorary Consultant Psychiatrist; Honorary Member, Scientific Staff, Medical Research Council; b. 1.9.44, Glasgow. Educ. The Park School, Glasgow; Glasgow University. Junior hospital appointments, 1968-72; Lecturer in Psychological Medicine, Glasgow University, 1972; Member, Scientific Staff, Medical Research Council, 1974-89. Publications: 160 papers. Recreations: cultivating plants; playing bridge; foreign travel. Address: (b.) Kennedy Tower, Royal Edinburgh Hospital, Edinburgh; T.-031-447 2011.

Johnstone, Ian Temple, MA (Cantab), LLB (Edin), WS, NP. Senior Partner (retired), Biggart Baillie & Gifford, WS (formerly Baillie & Gifford WS); b. 25.2.23, Edinburgh; m., Frances Ferenbach; 3 d. Educ. Edinburgh Academy; Corpus Christi College, Cambridge; Edinburgh University. Royal Artillery, 1942-46 (final rank of Staff Captain after transfer to Q Movements Burma Command); qualified, 1949; Director, Friends Provident Life Office, since 1964; Director, Inch Kenneth Kajang Rubber PLC, since 1970; Chairman, Baillie Gifford Shin Nippon PLC, since 1985; Past President, Scottish Lawn Tennis Association; Council Member, Lawn Tennis Association, 1969-76; former Treasurer, Society of Writers to HM Signet; Council Member, Edinburgh Festival Society, 1989-92. Recreations: following sport - football, tennis, cricket, rugby; listening to music; photography; gentle hill-walking. Address: 45 Moray Place, Edinburgh, EH3; T.-031-225 2021.

Johnstone, John Raymond, CBE, BA, CA. Chairman, Forestry Commission, since 1989; Chairman, Murray Johnstone Ltd., since 1984 (Managing Director, 1968-88); b. 27.10.29, London; m., Susan Sara; 5 step s.; 2 step d. Educ. Eton; Trinity College, Cambridge. Investment Analyst, Robert Fleming & Co. Ltd., London, 1955-60; Partner (CA), Brown, Fleming & Murray (later Whinney Murray & Co.), 1960-68; Director: Dominion Insurance Co. Ltd., since 1973 (Chairman, since 1978); Scottish Financial Enterprise, since 1986 (Chairman, since 1989); Summit Group PLC (Chairman, since 1989); Glasgow Cultural Enterprises Ltd., since 1988; Murray Income PLC, since 1989; Murray International PLC, since 1989; Murray Smaller Markets PLC, since 1989; Murray Ventures PLC, since 1984; Murray Enterprise PLC, since 1989; Chairman, Murray Split Capital Trust PLC, since 1991; Director, Scottish Amicable Life Assurance Society, since 1971 (Chairman, 1983-85); Member, Scottish Economic Council; Hon. President, Scottish Opera. Recreations: fishing; shooting; opera; farming. Address: (h.) Wards, Gartocharn, Dunbartonshire.

Johnstone, Professor William, MA (Hons), BD. Professor of Hebrew and Semitic Languages, Aberdeen University, since 1980; Minister, Church of Scotland, since 1963; b. 6.5.36, Glasgow; m., Elizabeth M. Ward; 1 s.; 1 d. Educ. Hamilton Academy; Glasgow University; Marburg University. Lecturer in Hebrew and Semitic Languages, Aberdeen University, 1962-72, Senior Lecturer, 1972-80, Dean, Faculty of Divinity, 1983-87; President, Society for Old Testament Study, 1990. Recreation: alternative work. Address: (h.) 37 Rubislaw Den South, Aberdeen, AB2 6BD; T.-Aberdeen 316022.

Jolly, Douglas, BSc (Hons). Rector, Viewforth High School, since 1981; Council Member, Headteachers' Association of Scotland; b. 30.6.38, Dundee; m., Elizabeth Smith; 2 d. Educ. Grove Academy, Broughty Ferry; St. Andrews University. Principal Teacher of Physics, Lawside Academy, 1964-72; Assistant Rector, Craigie High School, 1972-75; Depute Rector, Arbroath High School, 1975-81; Member, Central Committee for Science Teaching in Scotland, 1972-75. Elder, Markinch Parish Church. Recreations: golf; gardening; travel. Address: (h.) 16 Orchard Drive, Glenrothes, Fife; T.-Glenrothes 757039.

Jones, Professor Charles, MA, BLitt. Forbes Professor of English Language, Edinburgh University, since 1990; b. 24.12.39, Glasgow; m., Isla Shennan. Educ. St. Aloysius College, Glasgow; Glasgow University. Lecturer in Linguistics, Hull University, 1964-67; Lecturer, Department of English Language, Edinburgh University, 1967-78; Professor of English Language, Durham University, 1978-90. Convenor, Scots Language Resource Centre Association. Recreation: breeding Soay sheep. Address: (h.) Laggan Cottage, Faladam, Midlothian, EH37 5SU; T.-0875 33 652.

Jones, David Adams, MA, MSc, DipStat, FSS. Director, Information and Statistics Division, Scottish Health Service, since 1986; b. 23.4.33, Fochriw; m., Fiona Janet Hill; 2 s.; 1 d. Educ. The Lewis School, Pengam, Glamorgan; Jesus College, Oxford. Lt., Royal Navy; Industrial Statistician, British Nylon Spinners; Lecturer in Statistics, UWIST; Statistician and Chief Statistician, Welsh Office; Director of Statistics, Scottish Health Service. Recreations: squash; hillwalking. Address: (b.) Trinity Park House, Edinburgh; T.-031-552 6255.

Jones, Professor Douglas Samuel, MBE, MA, DSc, HonDSc, FIMA, FRSE, FRS, CEng, FIEE, CMath. Ivory Professor of Mathematics, Dundee University, since 1964; Past President, Institute of Mathematics and its Applications; b. 10.1.22, Corby, Northamptonshire; m., Ivy Styles; 1 s.; 1 d. Educ. Wolverhampton Grammar School; Corpus Christi College, Oxford. Flt.-Lt., RAF; Commonwealth Fellow, Massachusetts Institute of Technology; Lecturer, Manchester University; Professor, Keele University; Visiting Professor, New York University; Member, University Grants Committee; Chairman, Mathematics Committee; Computer Board; Member, Open University Visiting Committee; won Van der Pol Gold Medal; Keith Prize, RSE; Naylor Prize, LMS; Honorary Fellow of Corpus Christi College, Oxford. Recreation: not answering questionnaires. Address: (b.) Department of Mathematics and Computer Science, The University, Dundee, DD1 4HN; T.-Dundee 23181.

Jones, Rev. Edward Gwynfai, BA (Hons). Minister, St. Rollox Church of Scotland, Glasgow, since 1967; b. 20.5.37, Aberystwyth, Wales; m., Elspeth Mary Margretta; 2 d. Educ. Pontardawe Grammar School, Wales; Durham University; Westminster Theological College, Cambridge. Minister, Tow Law Presbyterian Church, Co. Durham, 1964-67. Address: 42 Melville Gardens, Bishopbriggs, Glasgow, G64 3DE; T.-041-772 2848.

Jones, Keith Greig, LLB. Director of Legal Services and Depute Chief Executive, Kincardine and Deeside District Council, since 1985; b. 10.9.48, Edinburgh; m., Margaret. Educ. Aberdeen Grammar School; Aberdeen University. Various appointments in private legal practice, 1969-75; joined Law and Administration Department, Kincardine and Deeside District Council, 1975. Address: (b.) Viewmount, Stonehaven, AB3 2DQ; T.-0569 62001.

Jones, Professor Peter (Howard), MA, FRSE, FRSA. Professor of Philosophy, Edinburgh University, since 1984; Director, Institute for Advanced Studies in the Humanities, since 1986; b. 18.12.35, London; m., Elizabeth Jean Roberton; 2 d. Educ. Highgate School; Queens' College, Cambridge. Regional Officer, The British Council, London, 1960-61; Research Scholar, Cambridge University, 1961-63; Assistant Lecturer in Philosophy, Nottingham University, 1963-64; Edinburgh University: Lecturer in Philosophy, 1964-77, Reader, 1977-84; Visiting Professor of Philosophy: Rochester University, New York, 1969-70, Dartmouth College, New Hampshire, 1973, 1983, Carleton College, Minnesota, 1974, Oklahoma University, 1978, Baylor University, 1978; Distinguished Foreign Scholar, Mid-America State Universities, 1978; Visiting Fellow, Humanities Research Centre, Australian National University, 1984; Trustee, National Museums of Scotland, since 1987; Trustee, University of Edinburgh Development Trust; Governor, Morrison's Academy, Crieff, since 1984; Founder Member, The Hume Society, 1974. Publications: Philosophy and the Novel, 1975; Hume's Sentiments, 1982; A Hotbed of Genius, 1986; Philosophy and Science in the Scottish Enlightenment, 1988; The Science of Man in the Scottish Enlightenment, 1989; Adam Smith Reviewed, 1992; Rousseau and Liberty, 1992. Recreations: opera; chamber music; the arts; architecture. Address: (b.) Institute for Advanced Studies in the Humanities, Hope Park Square, Edinburgh, 8; T.-031-650 4671.

Jones, Rev. William Gerald, MA, BD, ThM. Minister, Kirkmichael with Straiton St. Cuthbert's, since 1985; b. 2.11.56, Irvine; m., Janet Blackstock. Educ. Dalry High School; Garnock Academy, Kilbirnie; Glasgow University; St. Andrews University; Princeton Theological Seminary, Princeton, New Jersey. Assistant Minister, Glasgow Cathedral, 1983-85. Freeman Citizen of Glasgow, 1984; Member, Incorporation of Gardeners of Glasgow, 1984; Convener, Administration Committee, Presbytery of Ayr, 1988-91; Member, General Assembly Panel on Worship, 1987-91; Member, Council, Church Service Society, since 1986; Member, Committee to Nominate the Moderator of the General Assembly, 1988-92; Member, Societas Liturgica (West Germany), since 1989. Publication: Prayers for the

Chapel Royal in Scotland, 1989. Recreations: music; reading; writing; travel. Address: The Manse, Kirkmichael, Maybole, Ayrshire, KA19 7PJ; T.-Kirkmichael 286.

Jordan, Gerard Michael, CEng, BEng, CEng, MIMechE. Director, AEA Technology, Dounreay, since 1987; b. 25.9.29; m., Vera Peers; 1 s.; 1 d. Educ. Grange School, Birkenhead; Liverpool University. Marine Engineering Officer, 1950-55; Group Engineer, Thomas Hedley Ltd., 1956-59; UKAEA: Principal Professional and Technical Officer, 1959-73, Band Grade Officer, 1973-80, Assistant Director (Safety and Reliability Directorate), 1980, Assistant Director (Engineering and Safety, Dounreay), 1980-84, Deputy Director (Engineering, Northern Division), 1984-85, Director of Engineering (Northern Division), 1985-87. Recreations: hobby electronics; DIY; fishing. Address: (b.) AEA Technology, Thurso, Caithness, KW14 7TZ.

Jordan, Professor Grant, MA. Professor of Politics, Aberdeen University, since 1990; b. 12.10.48, Forfar; m., Susan Allardice; 1 s.; 2 d. Educ. Forfar Academy; Aberdeen University. Entered market research, 1971; moved to Keele University, 1973, Aberdeen University, 1974. Recreations: books; skiing; Montrose FC. Address: (b.) Department of Politics and International Relations, Aberdeen University, Aberdeen, AB9 2TY; T.-0224 272722.

Jordan, Col. Howard Alfred John, MBE, FCIT. Chief Executive, Scottish Engineering, since 1980; b. 26.3.36, Edinburgh; m., Patricia Ann Tomlin; 1 s.; 1 d. Army, 1954-80; Lt. Col., Royal Corps of Transport; service in UK (including Northern Ireland), Singapore, BAOR; commanded 154 (Lowland) Transport Regiment RCT(V). Chairman, Carmunnock Community Council, since 1980; Chairman, Strathclyde Group, National Council for Conservation of Plants and Gardens, since 1983; Honorary President, Carmunnock British Legion, since 1980; Member, Lowland TA Council, since 1981; Member, CBI Scotland Employment Committee (now Training and Enterprise Committee), since 1981; County Comdt., Glasgow and Lanarkshire ACF, since 1988. Address: (b.) 105 West George Street, Glasgow, G2 1QL; T.-041-221 3181.

Joughin, Sir Michael, CBE, JP, CBIM, FRAgS. Chairman, Scottish Hydro Electric plc, since 1990; Chairman, North of Scotland Hydro-Electric Board, 1983-90; Member, South of Scotland Electricity Board, 1983-88; Member, Bank of Scotland East of Scotland Board, since 1990; Farmer, since 1952; b. 26.4.26, Devonport; m., 1, Lesley Roy Petrie; 2, Anne S.H. Hutchison; 1 s.; 1 d. Educ. Kelly College, Tavistock, Devon. Royal Marines, 1944-52 (Lt.); seconded, Fleet Air Arm, 1946-49 (ditched off Malta, 1949, invalided, 1952). Chairman, North of Scotland Milk Marketing Board, 1974-83; Past Chairman, Grassland and Forage Committee, JCC; Chairman, Scottish Agricultural Development Council, 1971-80; Chairman, Governors, North of Scotland College of Agriculture, 1969-72; President, National Farmers Union of Scotland, 1964-66; Deputy Lieutenant, County of Moray, 1974-80; Governor: Rowett Research Institute, Aberdeen, 1968-74, Scottish Plant Breeding Station, 1969-74, Animal Diseases Research Association, Edinburgh, 1969-74; Chairman, Governors, Blairmore Preparatory School, near Huntly, 1966-72; Member: Scottish Constitutional Committee (Douglas-Home Committee), 1969-70, Intervention Board for Agricultural Produce, 1972-76, National Economic Development Council for Agriculture, 1967-70; Past Chairman, NEDC Working Party on Livestock; Member: Agricultural Marketing Development Executive Committee, 1965-68, British Farm Produce Council, 1965-66; former Member: Selection Committee, Nuffield Farming Scholarships, Awards Committee, Massey-Ferguson National Award for Services to UK Agriculture; Chairman: North of Scotland Grassland Society, 1970-71, Elgin Market Green

Auction Co., 1969-70; Founder Presenter, Country Focus (farming programme), Grampian Television, 1961-64 and 1967-69; Captain, 11th Bn., Seaforth Highlanders (TA), 1952-53. Recreation: sailing. Address: (h.) Elderslie, Findhorn, Moray; T.-0309 690277.

Jowitt, Professor Paul William, PhD, DIC, BSc(Eng), ACGI, CEng, MICE. Professor of Civil Engineering Systems, Heriot-Watt University, since 1987 (Head, Civil Engineering Department, 1989-91; Head, Civil and Offshore Engineering, since 1991; Editor, Civil Engineering Systems, since 1985; b. 3.8.50, Doncaster; m., Jane Catriona Urquhart; 1 s.; 1 d. Educ. Maltby Grammar School; Imperial College. Lecturer in Civil Engineering, Imperial College 1974-86 (Warden, Falmouth Hall, 1980-86); Director, Tynemarch Systems Engineering Ltd., 1984-91 (Chairman, 1984-86). Recreations: painting; Morgan 3-wheelers; restoring old houses. Address: (h.) 22 Fountainhall Road, The Grange, Edinburgh, EH9 2LW; T.-031-667 5696.

Jung, Roland Tadeusz, BA, MA, MB, BChir, MD, MRCS, LRCP, MRCP, FRCPEdin, FRCPLond. Consultant Physician (Specialist in Endocrinology and Diabetes), since 1982; Honorary Reader, Dundee University, and Clinical Director of General Medicine, Dundee Unit; b. 8.2.48, Glasgow; m., Felicity King; 1 d. Educ. St. Anselm's College, Wirral; Pembroke College, Cambridge; St. Thomas Hospital and Medical School, London. MRC Clinical Scientific Officer, Dunn Nutrition Unit, Cambridge, and Honorary Senior Registrar, Addenbrooke's Hospital, Cambridge, 1977-79; Senior Registrar in Endocrinology and Diabetes, Royal Postgraduate Medical School, Hammersmith Hospital, London, 1980-82. Publication: Endocrine Problems in Oncology (Co-Editor), 1984; Colour Atlas of Obesity, 1990. Recreation: gardening. Address: (b.) Department of Medicine, Ninewells Hospital and Medical School, Dundee; T.-Dundee 60111.

K

Kamm, Antony, MA. Freelance Editor and Writer; b. 2.3.31, London; m., Eileen Dunlop (qv). Educ. Charterhouse; Worcester College, Oxford. Editorial Director, Brockhampton Press, 1960-72; Senior Education Officer, Commonwealth Secretariat, 1972-74; Managing Editor (Children's Books), Oxford University Press, 1977-79; Consultant to UNESCO and other international organisations, 1963-76; part-time Lecturer in Publishing Studies, Stirling University, since 1988; Chairman, Children's Book Group, The Publishers Association, 1963-67, and of Children's Book Circle, 1963-64; played cricket for Middlesex, 1952. Publications include: Choosing Books for Younger Children, 1976; Scotland, 1989; A Dictionary of British and Irish Authors, 1990; (with Eileen Dunlop): Edinburgh, 1982; The Story of Glasgow, 1983; Kings and Queens of Scotland, 1984; and other information books for children on Scottish themes; several anthologies. Recreations: work; watching sport on TV. Address: (h.) 46 Tarmangie Drive, Dollar, FK14 7BP; T.-0259 42007.

Kane, Jack, OBE, JP, DL, Dr hc (Edin). Honorary Vice-President, Age Concern Scotland, since 1986; Honorary

President: Workers Educational Association (SE Scotland), Craigmillar Festival Society, Jack Kane Centre; b. 1.4.11, Addiewell, Midlothian; m., Anne Murphy; 1 s.; 2 d. Educ. Bathgate Academy. Librarian, 1937-55; War Service, Royal Artillery, 1940-46; District Secretary, Workers Educational Association (SE Scotland), 1955-76; Chairman, South of Scotland Electricity Consultative Council, 1977-80; Chairman, Board of Trustees, National Galleries of Scotland, 1975-80; Councillor, Edinburgh, 1938-75 (Bailie, 1947-51, Lord Provost, 1972-75). Recreations: reading; walking. Address: (h.) 88 Thirlestane Road, Edinburgh, EH9 1AS; T.-031-447 7757.

Kane, Patrick Mark, MA (Hons). Lead Singer, Hue and Cry (pop group), since 1985; Rector, Glasgow University, since 1990; Writer and Broadcaster; b. 10.3.64, Glasgow; m., Joan McAlpine; 1 d. Educ. St. Ambrose RC Secondary, Coatbridge; Glasgow University. Worked in London as a freelance writer; returned to Scotland to start professional music career with brother Gregory; achieved Top 10 and Top 20 singles and albums successes, 1987-89; Columnist, The Scotsman, then The Herald; Contributing Editor, Edinburgh Review. Recreations: being with family, listening to music; reading abstruse social theory.

Karolyi, Otto Jozsef, BMus, AMusTCL. Senior Lecturer in charge of Music, Stirling University, since 1978; b. 26.3.34, Paris; m., Benedikte Uttenthal; 1 s. Educ. Champagnat French-Hungarian School, Budapest; Werboczy and Berzsenyi Gymnasiums, Budapest; Bela Bartok Conservatoire, Budapest; Akademie fur Musik und darstellende Kunst, Wien; Trinity College of Music, London; London University. Freelance writing; WEA Tutor, ILEA and Oxford districts; Tutor, Extra-Mural Department, London University; Director of Music, Hampden House School; Music Therapist, St. John's Hospital, Stone and Napsbury Hospital, St. Albans; Visiting Lecturer, London University, Imperial College of Science and Technology; Tutor and Head, Department of Musicianship, Watford School of Music; part-time Tutor and Counsellor, Open University; Senior Lecturer, City of Leeds College of Music. Publications: Introducing Music; Modern British Music. Recreations: languages; literature; the arts. Address: (b.) Stirling University, Stirling; T.-0786 73171.

Kay, Sir Andrew Watt, Kt (1973). Regius Professor of Surgery, Glasgow University, 1964-81; b. 14.8.16.

Kay, Christian Janet, MA, AM, DipGenLing. Senior Lecturer in English Language, Glasgow University, since 1989 (Head, Department of English Language, since 1989); Editor, Historical Thesaurus of English, since 1975; b. 4.4.40, Edinburgh. Educ. Mary Erskine School, Edinburgh; Edinburgh University; Mount Holyoke College, USA. Teacher, Folk University of Sweden, 1965-68; Research Assistant, Glasgow University, 1969-79; part-time Editor, Collins Publishers, 1975-79; Lecturer, Glasgow University, 1979-89. Recreations: opera; classical music; novel-reading; films. Address: (b.) Glasgow University, Glasgow, G12 8QQ; T.-041-339 8855.

Kay, Elizabeth Jane, BDS, MPH, FDSRCPS, PhD. Senior Lecturer in Dental Public Health, Dundee University, since 1990; b. 10.3.59, South Africa; m., Dr. D.B. Northridge. Educ. Edinburgh University; Glasgow University. Research Fellow, Edinburgh University, 1982; Lecturer in Community Health, Glasgow University, 1986; former Adviser to Scottish Health Education Group; devised and launched two major dental health education initiatives. President, Behavioral Science in Dentistry Group (Scotland). Recreations: horse-riding (one-day eventing); skiing. Address: (h.) 17 Crown Road North, Glasgow, G12 9HD; T.-041-339 3297.

Kay, Michael, BSc, PhD. Principal Scientific Officer, Rowett Research Institute, since 1974; Head, Animal and Feed Technology Department and Vice-Dean, Scottish Agricultural College's Centre in Aberdeen; b. 10.3.38, York; m., Moira G. Kay; 1 s.; 1 d. Educ. St. Peter's School, York; Leeds University; Aberdeen University. Joined Rowett Research Institute, 1963. Recreations: sport; gardening; DIY. Address: (b.) School of Agriculture, 581 King Street, Aberdeen, AB9 1UD; T.-0224 480291.

Kay, William, MA. Freelance Broadcaster/Writer/Producer; b. 24.9.51, Galston, Ayrshire; m., Maria Joao de Almeida da Cruz Dinis; 1 s.; 2 d. Educ. Galston High School; Kilmarnock Academy; Edinburgh University. Producer, Odyssey series, Radio Scotland; produced about 40 documentaries on diverse aspects of working-class oral history; Writer/Presenter, TV documentaries, including Miners, BBC Scotland; Presenter, Kay's Originals, Scottish TV. Commandeur d'Honneur, Commanderie du Bontemps de Medoc et des Graves; won Australasian Academy of Broadcast Arts and Sciences Pater award, 1987, 1988; Silver Medal, International Radio Festival of New York, 1990. Publications: Odyssey: Voices from Scotland's Recent Past (Editor); Odyssey: The Second Collection (Editor); Knee Deep in Claret: A Celebration of Wine and Scotland (Co-author); Made in Scotland (poetry); Jute (play for radio); Scots - The Mither Tongue; They Fairly Mak Ye Work (for Dundee Repertory Theatre); Lucky's Strike (play for radio); The Dundee Book. Recreations: the weans; languages; films; Dundee United. Address: (h.) 72 Tay Street, Newport on Tay, Fife, DD6 8AP.

Kaye, Professor Stanley Bernard, BSc, MD, FRCP. Professor of Medical Oncology, Glasgow University, since 1985; b. 5.9.48, Leeds; m., Anna Catherine; 2 s.; 1 d. Educ. Roundhay School, Leeds; London University (Charing Cross Hospital). Junior hospital medical posts in London, 1972-78; Cancer Research Campaign Research Fellowship, 1978-80; Visiting Staff Specialist, Ludwig Institute, Sydney, 1980; Senior Lecturer, Department of Medical Oncology, Glasgow University, 1981-85. Recreations: several sports played badly, including tennis, golf, football. Address: (h.) 11 Milverton Avenue, Bearsden, Glasgow; T.-041-942 4920.

Kayne, Steven Barry, PhD, MBA, BSc, MRPharmS, MCPP, DAgVetPharm, MIPharmM, MBIM. Homoeopathic and Veterinary Pharmacist; b. 8.6.44, Cheltenham Spa; m., Sorelle; 2 s. Educ. Westcliff High School; Aston University; Strathclyde University; Glasgow University. Part-time Lecturer; Pharmacy Tutor to UK Faculty of Homoeopathy; Member, UK Faculty of Homoeopathy Council and Education Committee; Member, Faculty of Homoeopathy (Scotland) Council and Education Committee; Pharmacy Research Advisor to British Homoeopathic Association; Chairman, Education, Training and Information Committee, Epilepsy Association of Scotland. Recreations: walking in Spey Valley; watching rugby; photography. Address: (h.) 79 Milverton Road, Whitecraigs, Giffnock, Glasgow; T.-041-638 3216.

Keane, Sheriff Francis Joseph, PhL, LLB. Sheriff of Glasgow and Strathkelvin, since 1984; b. 5.1.36, Broxburn; m., Lucia Corio Morrison; 2 s.; 1 d. Educ. Blairs College, Aberdeen; Gregorian University, Rome; Edinburgh University. Partner, McCluskey, Keane & Co., 1959; Procurator Fiscal Depute, Perth, 1961, Edinburgh, 1963; Senior PF Depute, Edinburgh, 1971; Senior Legal Assistant, Crown Office, Edinburgh, 1972; Procurator Fiscal, Airdrie, 1976; Regional Procurator Fiscal, South Strathclyde, Dumfries and Galloway, 1980. President, Procurators Fiscal Society, 1982-84. Recreations: music; tennis; walking; painting. Address: (b.) Sheriff's Chambers, PO Box 23, 1 Carlton Place, Glasgow, G5 9DA; T.-041-429 8888.

Keane, Professor Simon Michael, MA, LLB, PhD, CA. Professor of Accountancy, Glasgow University, since 1983; b. 8.4.33, Glasgow; m., Mary; 1 d. Educ. St. Aloysius College; Glasgow University. Investigating Accountant, Admiralty, 1965-67; Lecturer, Glasgow College of Commerce, 1967-69; Glasgow University: Lecturer, 1969-81, Reader, 1981-83. Publications: Efficient Market Hypothesis, 1980; Stock Market Efficiency, 1983. Recreations: golf; painting. Address: (b.) 67 Southpark Avenue, Glasgow, G12; T.-041-339 8855.

Kearney, Sheriff Brian, MA, LLB. Sheriff of Glasgow and Strathkelvin, since 1977; b. 25.8.35.

Kee, Professor A. Alistair, MA, BD, STM, PhD. Professor of Religious Studies and Head, Department of Theology and Religious Studies, Edinburgh University (Head, Department of Religious Studies, Glasgow University, 1976-88); b. 17.4.37, Alexandria; m., Anne Paterson; 1 s.; 1 d. Educ. Clydebank High School; Glasgow University; Union Theological Seminary, New York. Lecturer: University College of Rhodesia, 1964-67, Hull University, 1967-76; Senior Lecturer, then Reader, Glasgow University, since 1976; Visiting Professor, Augusta College, Georgia, 1982-83; Director, SCM Press Ltd.; delivered Jaspers Lectures, Ripon Hall, Oxford, 1975; Ferguson Lectures, Manchester University, 1986. Publications: The Way of Transcendence; A Reader in Political Theology; Constantine Versus Christ; Being and Truth; Domination or Liberation; The Roots of Christian Freedom; Marx and the Failure of Liberation Theology; From Bad Faith to Good News. Address: (b.) Department of Theology and Religious Studies, Edinburgh University, New College, Mound Place, Edinburgh, EH1 2LX; T.-031-225 8400.

Keeble, Neil Howard, BA, DPhil, FRHistS. Reader in English, Stirling University, since 1988; b. 7.8.44, London; m., Jenny Bowers; 2 s.; 1 d. Educ. Bancroft's School, Woodford Green; St. David's College, Lampeter; Pembroke College, Oxford. Foreign Lektor, Department of English, University of Aarhus, Denmark, 1969-72; Lecturer in English, Aarhus, 1972-74; Lecturer in English, Stirling University, 1974-88. Publications: Richard Baxter: Puritan Man of Letters; The Literary Culture of Nonconformity in later seventeenth-century England; The Autobiography of Richard Baxter (Editor); The Pilgrim's Progress (Editor); John Bunyan: Conventicle and Parnassus (Editor); A Handbook of English and Celtic Studies in the United Kingdom and the Republic of Ireland (Editor); Calendar of the Correspondence of Richard Baxter (Co-Compiler). Recreations: books and book-collecting; films (especially Westerns); the Midi; gardening. Address: Duncraggan House, Airthrey Road, Stirling, FK9 5JS; T.-0786 73758.

Keenan, J. Melvin. Assistant Secretary, Banking Insurance and Finance Union, since 1989; Member, Sea Fish Industry Authority, 1981-90; b. 13.6.49, Falkirk; m., Nancy; 2 s. Educ. St. Modan's High School, Stirling; Stow College, Glasgow; Esk Valley Technical College. Inveresk Paper Co., 1964-70; BP Chemicals International Ltd. and BP Oil Ltd., 1970-76; Aberdeen District Officer, Transport and General Workers Union, 1977-89; Member, Offshore Petroleum Industry Training Board, 1984-89; Member, Oil Industry Advisory Committee to Health and Safety Commission, 1984-89; Member, EEC Joint Committee on Social Problems in Sea Fishing, 1978-89; Trustee, Scottish Trawler Fishermen's Pension Scheme, 1981-90. Publications: Fishing: The Way Forward (Co-author), 1980; The Future Through the Keyhole (Co-author), 1988; Ethics and Efficiency (Co-author), 1991. Recreations: country life; poetry. Address: (b.) 7 Buchanan Street, Glasgow, G1 3HL; T.-041-221 6475.

Keenan, Peter. Boxer; b. 1929, Glasgow; m., Cissy; 1 s.; 2 d. Won Scottish Flyweight title, 1948, before turning professional; won two Lonsdale belts outright; British Champion, 1951-53, 1954-59; Empire Champion, 1955-59; European Champion, 1951-52, 1953; failed to beat Vic Toweel, 1952, for World title; promoted boxing in Glasgow for a number of years.

Keir, Professor Hamish Macdonald, BSc, PhD, DSc, CBiol, FIBiol, CChem, FRSC, FRSE. Macleod-Smith Professor of Biochemistry, Aberdeen University, since 1968 (Vice-Principal, 1982-84); Vice-Chairman, Governors, Macaulay Land Use Research Institute, since 1987; Chairman, Board of Governors, Rowett Research Institute, since 1989; b. 5.9.31, Moffat; m., 1, Eleanor Campbell; 1 s.; 2 d.; 2, Linda Gerrie; 1 d. Educ. Ayr Academy; Glasgow University; Yale University. Hon. Secretary, The Biochemical Society, 1970-77, Chairman, 1986-89; Member, Cell Board, Medical Research Council, 1970-74; Scottish Home and Health Department, BRC, 1974-78; Ethical and Research Committees, Grampian Health Board; Science and Engineering Research Council (Biology), 1980-84; University Grants Committee (Biology), 1984-90; Royal Society – British National Committee for Biochemistry, 1986-90; Board of Governors, North of Scotland College of Agriculture, 1976-91; Tenovus – Scotland, Grampian Region, 1980-86; Board of Governors, Longridge Towers School, since 1988; Committees of the International Union of Biochemistry, 1974-82; Chairman, Natural Environment Research Council, Institute of Marine Biochemistry, 1969-84; Chairman, Universities of Scotland Purchasing Consortium, since 1988; President, European Union of Societies for Experimental Biology, since 1989; European Science Foundation, since 1989; President, Council, Federation of European Biochemical Societies, 1980-83. Recreations: piano; golf; travel. Address: (b.) Department of Molecular and Cell Biology, Aberdeen University, Marischal College, Aberdeen, AB9 1AS; T.-0224 273121.

Keith of Kinkel, Baron (Henry Shanks Keith), PC (1976). Life Peer; Lord of Appeal in Ordinary, since 1977; b. 7.2.22. QC (Scot), 1962; Sheriff Principal of Roxburgh, Berwick and Selkirk, 1970-71; Senator of the College of Justice in Scotland, 1971-77.

Kelbie, Sheriff David, LLB (Hons); Sheriff of Grampian, Highland and Islands, at Aberdeen and Stonehaven, since 1986 (North Strathclyde, at Dumbarton, 1979-86); b. 28.2.45, Inverurie; m., Helen Mary Smith; 1 s.; 1 d. Educ. Inverurie Academy; Aberdeen University. Passed Advocate, 1968; Associate Lecturer, Heriot-Watt University, 1971-76; Secretary, Scottish Congregational College, 1974-82; Member, UK/Ireland Committee of Christian Aid, 1986-90. Recreations: sailing; reading. Address: (h.) 38 Earlspark Drive, Bieldside, Aberdeen.

Kellas, Professor James Grant, MA, PhD, FRHistS. Professor in Politics, Glasgow University, since 1984; b. 16.5.36, Aberdeen; m., Norma Rennie Craig; 2 s.; 1 d. Educ. Aberdeen Grammar School; Aberdeen University; London University. Tutorial Fellow in History, Bedford College, London University, 1961-62; Assistant in History, Aberdeen University, 1962-64; Glasgow University: Lecturer in Politics, 1964-73; Senior Lecturer, 1973-77, Reader, 1977-84. Member, Study of Parliament Group. Publications: Modern Scotland, 1968, 1980; The Scottish Political System, 1973, 1975, 1984, 1989; The Politics of Nationalism and Ethnicity, 1991. Recreations: mountaineering; music. Address: (b.) Department of Politics, Glasgow University, Glasgow, G12 8RT; T.-041-339 8855.

Kelly, Barbara Mary, DipEd. EOC Commissioner in Scotland; Chairman, Rural Forum Scotland; Member,

Scottish Economic Council; Chairman, Rural Affairs Advisory Committee, BBC Scotland; Member, Scottish Enterprise Board; Member, Priorities Board, MAFF; Journalist and Broadcaster; Partner in dairy farming enterprise; b. 27.2.40, Dalbeattie; m., Kenneth A. Kelly (qv); 1 s.; 2 d. Educ. Dalbeattie High School; Kirkcudbright Academy; Moray House College. Past Chairman, Scottish Consumer Council; former Member, National Consumer Council; former Vice-Chairman, SWRI; Duke of Edinburgh's Award: former Chairman, Scottish Advisory Committee and former Member, UK Advisory Panel; Vice-Chairman, Rural Forum, Scotland; Past Chairman, Dumfries and Galloway Area Manpower Board, Manpower Services Commission; Trustee, Scottish Children's Bursary Fund. Recreations: painting; music. Address: (h.) Barncleugh, Irongray, Dumfries, DG2 9SE; T.-0387 73210.

Kelly, James, BA, PhD, FIPM. Senior Lecturer, Department of Human Resource Management, Strathclyde University, since 1987; b. 6.7.36, Port Glasgow; m., Ann; 2 d. Educ. Port Glasgow High School; Strathclyde University; Warwick University; Oxford University. Time-served bricklayer, 1952-62; employee relations officer, 1965-71; Lecturer, Warwickshire, 1971-75; Lecturer in Personnel Management, Strathclyde University, 1975-87. Vice Chairman, West of Scotland Branch, IPM. Recreations: bike rider; Greenock Morton supporter. Address: (h.) 33 Tantallon Avenue, Gourock; T.-0475 35882.

Kelly, Kenneth Archibald. Dairy Farmer; b. Glasgow; m., Barbara Mary Prentice (see Barbara Mary Kelly); 1 s.; 2 d. Educ. Glasgow Academy; Sedbergh; West of Scotland College of Agriculture. Elected to Stewartry County Council, 1969, Dumfries and Galloway Regional Council, 1974 (Vice-Chairman, Planning; Chairman, Public Protection); Past Chairman, North British Hereford Breeders Association; Past President, Dumfries Rugby Club; Elder, Irongray Kirk. Recreations: shooting; fishing; curling; music; sailing. Address: (h.) Barncleugh, Irongray, Dumfries, DG2 9SE; T.-0387 73210.

Kelly, Very Rev. Linus. Superior of Passionist House, Prestonpans, since 1986; Parish Priest, Prestonpans, since 1986; b. 15.3.28, Dublin. Educ. Synge Street Christian Brothers School, Dublin; UCD. Entered Passionist Noviciate, Enniskillen, 1947; professed a Passionist, 1948; ordained Priest, 1954; St. Mungo's Retreat, Townhead, Glasgow, 1956; Catholic Missions in Botswana, 1958-86; Regional Vicar, Botswana Mission, 1978-84. Recreations: sport; reading; theatre. Address: St. Gabriel's, West Loan, Prestonpans, E. Lothian.

Kelly, Michael, CBE (1983), OStJ, JP, BSc(Econ), PhD, LLD, DL. Public Relations Consultant, since 1984; Chairman, Royal Scottish Society for the Prevention of Cruelty to Children, since 1987; Director, Celtic Football Club, since 1990; Member, National Arts Collection Fund, since 1990; b. 1.11.40, Glasgow; m., Zita Harkins; 1 s.; 2 d. Educ. St Joseph's College, Dumfries. Assistant Lecturer in Economics, Aberdeen University, 1965-67; Lecturer in Economics, Strathclyde University, 1967-80; Lord Provost of Glasgow, 1980-84; Rector, Glasgow University, 1984-87; Director: SITE Ltd.; Drumkinnon Development Company; Clyde Cablevision Ltd.; British Tourist Authority Medal for services to tourism, 1984; Robert Burns Award from University of Old Dominion, Virginia, for services to Scottish culture, 1984; Scot of the Year, 1987; Radio Scotland News Quiz Champion, 1986, 1987; Radio Scotland Christmas Quiz Champion, 1987; Honorary Mayor of Tombstone, Arizona; Kentucky Colonel, 1983. Recreations: supporting Celtic; philately; philumeny. Address: (b.) 95 Bothwell Street, Glasgow, G2 7HY; T.-041-204 2580.

Kelly, Patrick Joseph, BSc, CEng, MICE. Scottish Officer, National Union of Civil and Public Servants, since 1986; Member, STUC General Council, since 1986; b. 26.10.50, Glasgow; m., Rhona Marie; 2 d. Educ. St. Mungo's Academy; Glasgow University. Civil Engineer, 1973-86; National Executive, NALGO, 1979-86. Address: (b.) 6 Hillside Crescent, Edinburgh, EH7 5DY.

Kelman, James. Novelist and Short Story Writer; b. 1946, Glasgow. Books include: Not Not While the Giro; The Bus Conductor Hines; A Chancer; Greyhound for Breakfast (1987 Cheltenham Prize); A Dissatisfaction (James Tait Black Memorial Prize, 1989; short-listed for Booker Prize); The Burn.

Kelnar, Christopher J.H., MA, MD, FRCP, DCH. Consultant Paediatric Endocrinologist, Royal Hospital for Sick Children, Edinburgh, since 1983; Senior Lecturer, Department of Child Life and Health, Edinburgh University, since 1983; b. 22.12.47, London; m., Alison; 1 s.; 2 d. Educ. Highgate School, London; Trinity College, Cambridge; St. Bartholomew's Hospital, London. Research Fellow, Paediatric Endocrinology, Middlesex Hospital, London, 1979-81; Senior Registrar, Hospital for Sick Children, Great Ormond Street, London, and Tutor, Institute of Child Health, London, 1981-83. Publications: The Sick Newborn Baby, 1981 (2nd edition, 1986); chapters and papers on paediatric endocrinology. Recreations: music; gardening. Address: (b.) Royal Hospital for Sick Children, Sciennes Road, Edinburgh, EH9 1LF; T.-031-667 1991.

Kelso, David Elliot, BSc, MEd, FIPM, FBIM. HM Staff Inspector, Scottish Office Education Department; b. 25.3.45, Glasgow; m., Dorothy Louise Christie; 1 s.; 2 d. Educ. St. Joseph's College, Dumfries; Edinburgh University; Glasgow University; Dundee University. Personnel Officer, Singer (UK) Ltd., Clydebank, 1968-69; Personnel Manager, Rank Organisation, Kirkcaldy, 1969-71; Lecturer in Management, Glasgow College, 1971-73; Senior Lecturer, Dundee College of Commerce, 1973-76; Head, Department of Commerce and Business Studies, Falkirk College, 1976-83; Assistant Principal, 1983-85; HMI, 1985-90. Recreations: running; esperanto; hill-walking. Address: (h.) Lomond, St. Mary's Drive, Dunblane, Perthshire; T.-0786 822605.

Kelty, William. Chairman, General Purposes Commitee, Grampian Regional Council, since 1978; b. 4.3.16, Keith; m., Margaret Rogers; 1 s.; 1 d. Educ. Keith Grammar School; Newstead School, Perthshire; Royal Technical College, Glasgow. Elected, Keith Town Council, 1946 (Chairman, Water Services; Dean of Guild); Chairman, Keith Football Club; twice Chairman, Keith Rotary Club; Chairman, Keith Swimming Pool Fund. Address: (h.) 43 Moss Street, Keith, AB5 3HH.

Kemball, Professor Emeritus Charles, CBE, MA, ScD, HonDSc, CChem, FRSC, MRIA, FRSE, FRS. Emeritus Professor of Chemistry, Edinburgh University, since 1983; b. 27.3.23, Edinburgh; m., Kathleen Purvis Lynd; 1 s.; 2 d. Educ. Edinburgh Academy; Trinity College, Cambridge. Fellow, Trinity College, 1946-54 (Junior Bursar, 1949-51, Assistant Lecturer, 1951-54); Demonstrator in Physical Chemistry, Cambridge University, 1951-54; Professor of Physical Chemistry, Queen's University, Belfast, 1954-66 (Dean, Faculty of Science, 1957-60, Vice-President, 1962-65); Professor of Chemistry, Edinburgh University, 1966-83 (Dean, Faculty of Science, 1975-78). President, Royal Institute of Chemistry, 1974-76; President, Royal Society of Edinburgh, 1988-91; Meldola Medal, RIC, 1951; Corday-Morgan Medal, 1958; Tilden Lecturer, 1960; Surface and Colloid Chemistry Award, Chemical Society, 1972; Ipatieff Prize, American Chemical Society, 1962; Gunning-Victoria Jubilee Prize, Royal Society of Edinburgh, 1976-80.

Recreations: hill-walking; card games; wine-making. Address: (h.) 24 Main Street, Tyninghame, Dunbar, East Lothian, EH42 1XL; T.-0620 860710.

Kemp, Professor Alexander George, MA (Hons). Professor of Economics, Aberdeen University, since 1983; b. Blackhall, Drumoak, Aberdeenshire. Educ. Robert Gordon's College, Aberdeen; Aberdeen University. Economist, Shell International Petroleum, London, 1962-64; Lecturer in Economics, Strathclyde University, 1964-65; Lecturer, then Senior Lecturer, then Reader, Aberdeen University, 1966-83. Specialist Adviser to House of Commons Select Committee on Energy; Economic Consultant to Secretary of State for Scotland; Consultant to: UN Centre for Transnational Corporations, Commonwealth Secretariat, World Bank. Publications: 100 books and papers on petroleum economics. Address: (b.) Department of Economics, King's College, Aberdeen, AB9 2TY; T.-0224 272168.

Kemp, Arnold, MA. Editor, Glasgow Herald, since 1981; b. 15.2.39; 2 d. Educ. Edinburgh Academy; Edinburgh University. Sub-Editor: The Scotsman, 1959-62, The Guardian, 1962-65; The Scotsman: Production Editor, 1965-70, London Editor, 1970-72, Deputy Editor, 1972-81. Recreations: music; reading; theatre. Address: (b.) 195 Albion Street, Glasgow, G1; T.-041-552 6255.

Kemp, Professor Martin John, MA, FRSA, HRSA, HFRIAS, FBA. Professor of the History and Theory of Art, St. Andrews University, since 1981 (Associate Dean, 1983-87); Provost, St. Leonard's College; b. 5.3.42, Windsor; m., Jill Lightfoot; 1 s.; 1 d. Educ. Windsor Grammar School; Cambridge University; London University. Lecturer: Dalhousie University, Nova Scotia, 1965-66, Glasgow University, 1966-81. Trustee: National Galleries of Scotland, 1982-87, Victoria and Albert Museum, London, 1985-89; Honorary Professor of History, Royal Scottish Academy, since 1985; Honorary Fellow, Royal Institute of Architects in Scotland; Member, Institute for Advanced Study, Princeton, 1984-85; Slade Professor, Cambridge University, 1988; Benjamin Sonnenberg Visiting Professor, Institute of Fine Arts, New York University, 1988; Chair, Association of Art Historians, since 1989; Chairman of Board, Graeme Murray Gallery, Edinburgh. Publications: Leonardo da Vinci: The Marvellous Works of Nature and Man (1981 Mitchell Prize for Best First Book in Art History); The Science of Art, 1990. Recreation: sport (especially hockey). Address: (h.) Orillia, 45 Pittenweem Road, Anstruther, Fife; T.-0333 310842.

Kendell, Professor Robert Evan, MD, FRCP, FRCPsych. Chief Medical Officer, Scottish Office Home and Health Department; b. 28.3.35, Rotherham; m., Ann Whitfield; 2 s.; 2 d. Educ. Mill Hill School; Cambridge University; King's College Hospital Medical School. Visiting Professor, University of Vermont College of Medicine, 1969-70; Reader in Psychiatry, Institute of Psychiatry, London University, 1970-74; Professor of Psychiatry, Edinburgh University, 1974-91, and Dean, Faculty of Medicine, 1986-90. Gaskell Medal, Royal College of Psychiatrists, 1967; Paul Hoch Medal, American Psychopathological Association, 1988. Publications: The Classification of Depressive Illnesses, 1968; The Role of Diagnosis in Psychiatry, 1975; Companion to Psychiatric Studies (Editor), 1983 and 1988. Recreations: walking up hills; overeating. Address: (h.) 3 West Castle Road, Edinburgh, EH10 5AT.

Kemp, Professor Angus Johnston, MA, PhD, Officier dans l'Ordre des Palmes Academiques. Professor of French Language and Literature, Glasgow University; b. 9.8.40, Port Charlotte; m., Marjory McCulloch Shearer; 2 d. Educ. Bearsden Academy; Glasgow University. Glasgow University: Assistant Lecturer in French, 1965, then Lecturer,

Senior Lecturer, Reader; former Secretary, British Branch, International Arthurian Society. Publications: books on Christine de Pizan. Address: (b.) French Department, Glasgow University, Glasgow; T.-041-339 8855.

Kennedy, Professor Arthur Colville, MD, FRCP(Lond), FRCPE, FRCP(Glas), FRCPI, FRSE, FACP(Hon.), FRACP (Hon.). Consultant Physician, Royal Infirmary, Glasgow, 1959-88; Muirhead Professor of Medicine, Glasgow University, 1978-88; President, Royal College of Physicians and Surgeons of Glasgow, 1986-88; b. 22.10.22, Edinburgh; m., Agnes White Taylor; 1 s. (deceased); 2 d. Educ. Whitehill School, Glasgow; Glasgow University. Medical Officer, RAFVR, 1946-48; junior NHS posts, 1948-57; Lecturer in Medicine, Glasgow University, 1957; Senior Lecturer, 1961; Reader, 1966; Titular Professor, 1969; responsible for establishment of Kidney Unit, Glasgow Royal Infirmary, 1959; Chairman, MRC Working Party in Glomerulonephritis, 1976-88; Member, Executive Committee, National Kidney Research Fund, 1976-83; Expert Adviser to WHO on Renal Disease; Adviser to EEC on Nephrology in Developing Countries; Chairman, Professional and Linguistic Assessments Board (PLAB), GMC, 1987-89; President, Royal Medico-Chirurgical Society of Glasgow, 1971-72; President, European Dialysis and Transplant Association, 1972-75; President, Scottish Society of Physicians, 1983-84; President, Harveian Society of Edinburgh, 1985; Member, Greater Glasgow Health Board, 1985-89; Member, General Medical Council, since 1989; President, British Medical Association, 1991-92. Recreations: gardening; walking; reading; photography. Address: (h.) 16 Boclair Crescent, Bearsden, Glasgow, G61 2AG; T.-041-942 5326.

Kennedy, Charles Peter, MA (Hons). MP (SLD, formerly SDP), Ross, Cromarty and Skye, since 1983; President, Liberal Democrats, since 1989; b. 25.11.59, Inverness. Educ. Lochaber High School, Fort William; Glasgow University; Indiana University. President, Glasgow University Union, 1980-81; Winner, British Observer Mace for Student Debating, 1982; Journalist, BBC Highland, Inverness, 1982; Fulbright Scholar, Indiana University (Bloomington Campus), 1982-83. Chairman, SDP Council for Scotland, 1986-88; SDP Spokesman on Health and Social Services, and Scotland, 1983-87; Alliance Election Spokesman, Social Security, Jan.-June, 1987; Member, Select Committee on Social Services, 1985-87; SLD Interim Joint Spokesman, Social Security, 1988; SLD Spokesman, Trade and Industry, 1988-89; Liberal Democrat Spokesman, Health, since 1989; Member, Select Committee on House of Commons Televising, 1988; occasional journalist and broadcaster. Recreations: reading; writing. Address: (b.) House of Commons, London, SW1A 0AA; T.-071-219 5090.

Kennedy, Frederick John, OBE, LLB. Regional Reporter, Strathclyde Regional Council; b. 22.6.40, Grantham; m., Eleanor Mae Watson; 1 s.; 1 d. Educ. High School of Glasgow; Glasgow University. Private, industrial and local government legal practice; former Reporter to the Children's Panel, City of Glasgow; former Director of Administration, Fife Regional Council. Recreations: golf; reading; gardening. Address: (b.) McIver House, 51 Cadogan Street, Glasgow, G2; T.-041-227 6171.

Kennedy, Professor Gavin, BA, MSc, PhD, FCIM. Professorial Fellow, Esmee Fairbairn Research Centre, Heriot-Watt University; Managing Director, Negotiate Ltd., Edinburgh; b. 20.2.40, Collingham, Yorkshire; m., Patricia Anne; 1 s.; 2 d. Educ. London Nautical School; Strathclyde University. Lecturer: Danbury Management Centre, NE London Polytechnic, 1969-71, Brunel University, 1971-73. Lecturer, National Defence College, Latimer, 1972-74; Senior Lecturer in Economics, Strathclyde University, 1973-85. Publications: Military in the Third World, 1974; Economics of Defence, 1975; Bligh, 1978 (Yorkshire Post Book of the Year, 1979); Death of Captain Cook, 1978; Burden Sharing in NATO, 1979; Mathematics for Innumerate Economists, 1982; Defence Economics, 1983; Invitation to Statistics, 1983; Everything is Negotiable, 1984; Negotiate Anywhere, 1985; Macro Economics, 1985; Superdeal, 1985; The Economist Pocket Negotiator, 1987; Captain Bligh: the man and his mutinies, 1988; Do We Have A Deal?, 1991; Simulations for Training Negotiators, 1991. Recreation: reading. Address: (h.) 22 Braid Avenue, Edinburgh; T.-031-447 3000.

Kennedy, Professor Peter Graham Edward, MB, BS, PhD, MD, DSc, MRCPath, FRCPLond, FRCPGlas. Burton Professor of Neurology and Head of Department, Glasgow University, since 1987; Consultant Neurologist, Institute of Neurological Sciences, Southern General Hospital, Glasgow, since 1986; b. 28.3.51, London; m., Catherine Ann; 1 s.; 1 d. Educ. University College School, London; University College, London; University College Medical School. Medical Registrar, University College Hospital, 1977-78; Hon. Research Assistant, MRC Neuroimmunology Project, University College, London, 1978 80; Research Fellow, Institute of Virology, Glasgow University, 1981; Registrar and Senior Registrar, National Hospital for Nervous Diseases, London, 1981-84; Assistant Professor of Neurology, Johns Hopkins University School of Medicine, 1985; "New Blood" Senior Lecturer in Neurology and Virology, Glasgow University, 1986-87. BUPA Medical Foundation "Doctor of the Year" Research Award, 1990; Linacre Medal and Lectureship, Royal College of Physicians of London, 1991; Member, Medical Research Advisory Committee, Multiple Sclerosis Society; Chairman, Research Committee, Scottish Motor Neurone Disease Association. Publication: Infections of the Nervous System (Co-author). Recreations: reading and writing; music; astronomy; tennis; walking in the country. Address: (b.) Institute of Neurological Sciences, Southern General Hospital, Glasgow, G51; T.-041-445 2466.

Kennedy, Peter Norman Bingham, TD, CA, DL. Investment Director, since 1979; Landowner, since 1980; b. 11.10.42, Kings Lynn; m., Priscilla Ann; 4 d. Educ. Rugby. Qualified as CA, 1967; worked for R.C. Greig & Co., Alex. Lawrie Factors Ltd. and Duncan Lawrie Ltd.; Managing Director, Gartmore Scotland Limited, since 1988. Served with Ayrshire Yeomanry/Queen's Own Yeomanry (TA), 12 years; Chairman, River Doon Fishery Board, since 1980; Deputy Lieutenant, Ayrshire and Arran. Address: (b.) Charles Oakley House, 125 West Regent Street, Glasgow, G2 2SG; T.-041-248 3972.

Kennedy, Professor Robert Alan, BA, PhD, FBPS, FRSE. Professor of Psychology, Dundee University, since 1972; b. 1.10.39, Stourbridge; m., Elizabeth Wanda. Educ. King Edward VI Grammar School, Stourbridge; Birmingham University. Senior Tutor, then Lecturer, Melbourne University; Lecturer, Queen's College, St. Andrews; Lecturer, then Senior Lecturer, Dundee University. Publications: Studies in Long-Term Memory; The Psychology of Reading; scientific papers. Recreations: hill-walking; playing the piano. Address: (h.) 2 Norwood Crescent, Dundee; T.-0382 67348.

Kent, Rev. Arthur Francis Stoddart. Minister, Monkton and Prestwick North Parish Church, since 1981; b. 30.1.34, Glasgow; m., Isla Glen McLean; 2 d. Educ. Hutcheson's Boys' Grammar School; Glasgow University and Trinity College. Minister: United Church of Jamaica and Grand Cayman, 1965-73; Bellshill West Parish Church, 1973-81. Recreations: gardening; golf. Address: 40 Monkton Road, Prestwick, KA9 1AR; T.-Prestwick 77499.

Kermack, Sheriff Stuart Ogilvy, BA (Oxon), LLB. Sheriff of Tayside, Central and Fife, at Forfar and Arbroath, since

1971; b. 9.7.34, Edinburgh; m., Barbara Mackenzie; 3 s.; 1 d. Educ. Glasgow Academy; Jesus College, Oxford; Glasgow University. Called to Scottish Bar, 1958; Sheriff, Elgin and Nairn, 1965. Address: (h.) 7 Littlecauseway, Forfar, Angus; T.-Forfar 64691.

Kernohan, Robert Deans, OBE, MA. Editor, Life and Work, The Record of the Church of Scotland, 1972-90; Journalist, Writer and occasional Broadcaster; b. 9.1.31, Mount Vernon, Lanarkshire; m., Margaret Buchanan Bannerman; 4 s. Educ. Whitehill School, Glasgow; Glasgow University; Balliol College, Oxford. RAF, 1955-57; Editorial Staff, Glasgow Herald, 1957-67 (Assistant Editor, 1965-66, London Editor, 1966-67); Director-General, Scottish Conservative Central Office, 1967-71; Freelance Journalist and Broadcaster, 1972. Chairman, Federation of Conservative Students, 1954-55; Conservative Parliamentary candidate, 1955, 1959, 1964; Member, Newspaper Panel, Monopolies and Mergers Commission, 1987; Member, Ancient Monuments Board for Scotland, since 1990; Elder, Cramond Kirk, Edinburgh. Publications: Scotland's Life and Work, 1979; William Barclay, The Plain Uncommon Man, 1980; Thoughts through the Year, 1985; Our Church, 1985; The Protestant Future, 1991. Recreations: rugby-watching; travel; pontification. Address: (h.) 5/1 Rocheid Park, Edinburgh, EH4 1RP; T.-031-332 7851.

Kerr, Allan MacDonald, LLB. Solicitor; Director of Law and Administration, Nairn District Council, since 1984, and Chief Executive, since 1989; b. 10.6.53, Glasgow; m., Mairi; 2 s. Educ. Bishopbriggs High School; Glasgow University. Law apprentice, later qualified Assistant, McGettigan & Co., Solicitors, Glasgow, 1976-78; Principal Legal Assistant, later Solicitor, Western Isles Islands Council, 1978-82; Clerk of Court, Motherwell District, 1982-84. Recreations: family; motoring; reading. Address: (b.) The Court House, High Street, Nairn; T.-0667 55523.

Kerr, David Alexander, MC, TD, JP, DL; b. 30.9.16, Inverkip; m., Elizabeth Phoebe Coxwell Cresswell; 1 s.; 1 d. Educ. Canford School. Joined Westburn Sugar Refineries Ltd., Greenock, 1936; joined 5/6 Bn., Argyll & Sutherland Highlanders, 1936; mobilised, 1939, serving in France, Belgium, North Africa, Italy, Palestine and Syria; MC, 1945; mentioned in Despatches; Territorial Decoration, 1948; returned to Westburn, 1946; Technical Director, 1949; Refinery Director, 1955; Joint Managing Director, 1960; Managing Director, 1967; Chairman, 1972; Director, The Sankey Sugar Company Ltd., 1965; Managing Director, Maubre Sugars Ltd., 1972; Director, Tate & Lyle Refineries Ltd., 1976-79; retired, 1979. County Commissioner, County of Renfrew Scout Association, 1964-70, County Chairman, 1971-73; Area President, since 1976; Chief Commissioner for Scotland, 1977-81; Honorary Chief Commissioner, since 1981; a County Vice-President, Renfrewshire Girl Guides Association. Recreations: garden; philately; photography. Address: (h.) Whitefarland, 88 Octavia Terrace, Greenock, PA16 7PY; T.-Gourock 31980.

Kerr, Finlay, MB, ChB, DObsRCOG, FRCPEdin, FRCPGlas. Consultant Physician, Raigmore Hospital, Inverness, since 1976; Honorary Senior Lecturer, Aberdeen University, since 1976; Board Director, Highland Hospice, 1985-90 (Chairman, Board of Directors, 1985-87); b. 8.8.41, Edinburgh; m., Margaret Ann Carnegie Allan; 1 s.; 2 d. Educ. Keil School; Glasgow University. House Physician and Surgeon, Western Infirmary, Glasgow; House Physician, Ruchill Hospital, Glasgow; House Surgeon, Queen Mother's Hospital, Glasgow; Senior House Officer, Western Infirmary, Glasgow; Fellow, University of Southern California; Lecturer in Medicine, then Senior Registrar in Medicine, Edinburgh Royal Infirmary. Recreations: sailing; skiing; walking. Address: (h.) The Birks, 2 Drummond Place, Inverness.

Kerr, Francis Robert Newsam, OBE, MC, DL, JP; b. 12.9.16, Ancrum; m., Anne Frederica Kitson; 2 s.; 1 d. Educ. Ampleforth College. Officer, Royal Scots (Lt-Col.), retired, 1960. Address: (h.) New Howden, Jedburgh, TD8 6QP; T.-0835 64193.

Kerr, John, CA. Director, Scottish Association of Young Farmers' Clubs, since 1985; b. 17.5.46, Tarbolton; m., Mary Paterson; 1 s.; 2 d. Educ. Ayr Academy; Institute of Chartered Accountants of Scotland. Indentured to McClelland Moores & Co., Glasgow, 1963-68; qualified CA, 1968; Audit Senior, McClelland Moores & Co., 1968-70; joined William Grant & Sons Ltd., Paisley, 1970; appointed Chief Accountant, 1973; resigned, 1985. Chairman of Council, Scottish Young Farmers, 1976-77; Chairman, European Committee for Young Farmers, 1980-82. Recreations: family; reading; amateur drama; gardening; home decorating. Address: (b.) Young Farmers' Centre, Ingliston, Edinburgh, EH28 8NE.

Kerr, Rev. Philip John, PhB, STL. Roman Catholic Priest; Vice-Rector and Lecturer in Systematic Theology, Gillis College, Edinburgh, since 1986; b. 23.4.56, Edinburgh. Educ. Holy Cross Academy; St. Augustine's High School, Edinburgh; Scots College and Gregorian University, Rome. Assistant Priest, St. Francis Xavier's, Falkirk, 1980-82; Lecturer in Systematic Theology, St. Andrew's College, Drygrange, 1982-86. Secretary: Joint Commission for Doctrine (CofS/RC); Joint Study Group (Scottish Episcopal Church/RC). Recreations: squash; walking. Address: Gillis College, 113-115 Whitehouse Loan, Edinburgh, EH9 1BB; T.-031-447 2807.

Kerr, Robert James, MA (Hons), PhD. Rector, Peebles High School, since 1986; b. 14.6.47, Jedburgh; m., Isobel Grace Atkinson; 2 s.; 1 d. Educ. Kelso High School; Edinburgh University. Assistant Teacher, Lochaber High School, 1973-75; Assistant Principal Teacher of Geography, Forrester High School, 1976-77; Principal Teacher of Geography, Douglas Ewart High School, 1977-82; Assistant Rector, Elgin High School, 1982-85; Depute Rector, Forres Academy, 1985-86. Recreations: fishing; rugby supporter; hill-walking/mountainering; ornithology; skiing; travel. Address: (h.) Enniskerry, Eshiels, Peebles, EH45 8NA; T.-0721 22131.

Kerr, William John Stanton, BDS, FDS, RCSEdin, MDS, FFD, RCSIrel, DOrthRCS, FDS RCPS Glas. Reader in Orthodontics, Glasgow Dental Hospital and School, since 1988; Honorary Consultant in Orthodontics, since 1978; b. 12.7.41, Belfast; m., Marie-Francoise; 1 d. Educ. Campbell College, Belfast; Queen's University, Belfast. Address: (b.) Glasgow Dental Hospital and School, 378 Sauchiehall Street, Glasgow, G2 3JZ; T.-041-332 7020.

Kerr, Lt.-Col. (Rtd.) William Walker. General Secretary, Scottish Central Council Branch, British Red Cross Society, since 1985; b. 17.4.30, Haddington; m., Jacqueline Mary Sanctuary; 1 s.; 1 d. Educ. Knox Academy, Haddington; Royal Military Academy, Sandhurst. Army, Royal Highland Fusiliers, 1948-80. Recreations: hill-walking; skiing; swimming; bird-watching; stamp-collecting. Address: (b.) Alexandra House, 204 Bath Street, Glasgow, G2 4HL; T.-041-332 9591.

Kerrigan, Herbert Aird, QC, MA, LLB (Hons); b. 2.8.45, Glasgow; 1 s. Educ. Whitehill School, Glasgow; Aberdeen University; Keele University; Hague Academy. Admitted to Faculty of Advocates, 1970; Lecturer in Criminal Law and Criminology, Edinburgh University, 1969-73; Lecturer in Scots Law, Edinburgh University, 1973-74; Visiting Professor, University of Southern California, since 1979; Member, Longford Commission, 1972; Church of Scotland: Elder, 1967 (now at Greyfriars Tolbooth and Highland Kirk),

Reader, 1969, elected Member, Assembly Council, 1981-85; Vice-President, Edinburgh Royal Infirmary Samaritan Society, since 1989; called to the English Bar (Middle Temple), 1990; joined Chambers of Edmund Lawson, QC, 1991; appointed QC in Scotland, 1992. Publications: An Introduction to Criminal Procedure in Scotland, 1970; Ministers for the 1980s (Contributor), 1979; The Law of Contempt (Contributing Editor), 1982. Recreation: travel. Address: (h.) 20 Edinburgh Road, Dalkeith, Midlothian, EH22 1JY; T.-031-660 3007.

Khan, Kabir-Ur-Rahman, BA (Hons), LLB, LLM, PhD. Senior Lecturer, Department of Public International Law, Edinburgh University, since 1982 (Lecturer, 1965-81); b. 2.2.25, Firozpur Jhirka, India; m., Isobel Thomson; 1 d. Educ. Raj Rishi College, Alwar; Government College, Ajmere; Agra University; Sind University; Open University; London University. Barrister-at-Law, Gray's Inn, 1955; Advocate, High Court of Pakistan, Lahore, 1958-61. Member and Co-Chairman, Edinburgh Inter-Faith Association. Publications: The Law and Organisation of International Commodity Agreements; research papers relating to international law of development. Recreations: walking; keep fit; Urdu poetry. Address: (h.) 5 Heriot Row, Edinburgh, EH3 6HU; T.-031-556 2229.

Kidd, Professor Cecil, BSc, PhD, FIBiol, FRSA. Regius Professor of Physiology, Aberdeen University, since 1984; b. 28.4.33, Shotley Bridge, Co. Durham; m., Margaret Winifred; 3 s. Educ. Queen Elizabeth Grammar School, Darlington; King's College, Newcastle-upon-Tyne; Durham University. Demonstrator in Physiology, King's College, Newcastle-upon-Tyne; Lecturer/Senior Lecturer/Reader in Physiology, Senior Research Associate in Cardiovascular Studies, Leeds University. Recreations: squash; gardening. Address: (b.) School of Biomedical Sciences, Marischal College, Aberdeen University, Aberdeen; T.-0224 273004.

Kidd, David Hamilton, LLB, LLM, WS, NP. Partner, Biggart Baillie & Gifford, WS, since 1978; b. 21.9.49, Edinburgh; m., Geraldine Stephen; 2 s. Educ. Edinburgh Academy; Edinburgh University. Research Assistant, Law Faculty, Queen's University, Belfast, 1976-77. Former Secretary, Scottish Legal Computer Research Trust; Society for Computers and Law: Council Member, 1982-84, Secretary, since 1984; Member, Practice Management Committee, Law Society of Scotland, since 1981. Recreations: cycling; skiing; sailing. Address: (b.) 10 Glenfinlas Street, Edinburgh, EH3 6YY; T.-031-226 5541.

Kidd, Frank Forrest, CA, ATII. Partner, Coopers & Lybrand Deloitte, Chartered Accountants, since 1979; b. 4.5.38, Dundee; m., Beryl Ann Gillespie; 2 s.; 2 d. Educ. George Heriot's School; Ballards. CA Apprentice, 1955-60; Partner, Wylie & Hutton, 1962-79; Honorary Professor, Department of Accountancy and Business Law, Stirling University; President, Institute of Chartered Accountants of Scotland, 1988-89. Recreations: squash; golf; walking. Address: (b.) Erskine House, P.O. Box 90, 68/73 Queen Street, Edinburgh, EH2 4NH; T.-031-226 4488.

Kidd, Professor Ian Gray, MA (St. Andrews), MA (Oxon). Emeritus Professor of Greek, St. Andrews University; b. 6.3.22, Goretty, Chandernagore, India; m., Sheila Elizabeth Dow; 3 s. Educ. Dundee High School; St. Andrews University; Queen's College, Oxford. St. Andrews University: Lecturer in Greek, 1949, Senior Lecturer, 1965; Visiting Professor, University of Texas at Austin, 1965-66; Member, Institute for Advanced Study, Princeton, 1971-72; St. Andrews University: Personal Professor of Ancient Philosophy, 1973-76, Professor of Greek, 1976-87, Provost of St. Leonard's College, 1978-83, Chancellor's Assessor, University Court, since 1989; Member, Institute for Advanced

230 WHO'S WHO IN SCOTLAND

Study, Princeton, 1979-80; Hon. Fellow, St. Leonard's College, since 1987; Hon. Fellow, Institute for Research in Classical Philosophy and Science, Pittsburgh, USA, since 1989. Publication: Posidonius, Vol. I, The Fragments, 1972, 1989, Vol. II, and The Commentary, 1989. Recreations: music; reading. Address: (h.) Ladebury, Lade Braes Lane, St. Andrews, Fife, KY16 9EP; T.-0334 74367.

Kidd, Jean Buyers, BA, DipMusEd, LRAM, ARCM. Music Director, Junior and Youth Choruses, Scottish National Orchestra, since 1978; b. Macduff, Banffshire; widow. Educ. Buckie High School; Royal Scottish Academy of Music; Open University. Taught in various Glasgow schools and for many years, Principal Teacher of Music, Bellahouston Academy; former Conductor, Bellahouston Music Society; gave instruction in music and drama to women in Duke Street Prison; former Secretary, Scottish Certificate of Education Examination Board. Recreations: reading; playing chamber music; gardening; craft work. Address: (h.) Carolside, Gowanlea Road, Comrie, Perthshire, PH6 2HD; T.-Comrie 70856.

Kidd, Mary Helen (May), MA. Member, Scottish Consumer Council, since 1991; National Vice-Chairman, Scottish Women's Rural Institutes, since 1987; Member, Advisory Board, Scottish Agricultural College, Edinburgh, since 1991; m., Neil M.L. Kidd; 2 s. Educ. Brechin High School; Edinburgh University. Partner in family farming business. Recreations: playing piano and organ; creative writing. Address: (h.) Holehill of Kirkbuddo, Forfar, Angus, DD8 3NQ; T.-030 782 318.

Kiddie, Charles, BSc (Hons). Rector, Auchterarder High School, since 1985; b. 3.4.49, Dundee; m., Esther Linda Power; 2 s. Educ. Harris Academy, Dundee; Aberdeen University; University of Kansas; Dundee College of Education. Teacher, Forfar Academy; Principal Teacher, Breadalbane Academy, Aberfeldy; Assistant Head Teacher, Whitfield High School, Dundee; Adviser in Social Subjects, Tayside Regional Council. Recreation: family. Address: (b.) Auchterarder High School, Auchterarder, Perthshire; T.-0764 62182.

Kiely, John, BSc, MSc. HM Inspector of Schools, 1961-85; b. 27.6.25, Tugby, Leicestershire; m., Mary Macdonald; 3 s.; 1 d. Educ. Bicester County School; Bristol University. Instructor-Lt., Royal Navy, 1945-48. Assistant Master, King Edward VII School, Sheffield, 1950-51; Second Mathematics Master, Grimsby Wintringham Grammar School, 1952-55; Senior Lecturer, Royal Naval College, Dartmouth, 1955-58; Head, Mathematics Department, Blundells School, Tiverton, 1958-61. Recreations: reading; gardening. Address: (h.) Suffolkhill House, 28 Dalbeattie Road, Dumfries, DG2 7PL; T.-Dumfries 63429.

Kilgour, Professor Alistair Crichton, BSc, PhD, FBCS, CEng. Professor, Computer Science Department, Heriot-Watt University, Edinburgh, since 1989; b. 14.8.40, Glasgow; m., Margaret; 3 s. Educ. Allan Glen's School, Glasgow; Glasgow University. Scientific Programmer, English Electric Computers Ltd., 1963-66; Research Associate, Computer-Aided Design Project, Edinburgh University, 1966-74; Lecturer/Senior Lecturer, Computing Science Department, Glasgow University, 1974-89. Recreations: theatre; films; reading; telephones. Address: (b.) Heriot-Watt University, Department of Computer Science, Riccarton, Edinburgh, EH14 4AS; T.-031-449 5111.

Kilgour, Walter B., LLB, DPA, MBIM, NP. Director of Administration, Strathkelvin District Council, since 1985; b. 31.3.53, Glasgow; m., Linda M.; 1 d. Educ. Hutchesons' Boys' Grammar School; Glasgow University. Solicitor, Renfrew District Council, 1975; Senior Solicitor, Motherwell District Council, 1978; Principal Solicitor, Central Regional Council, 1980; Depute District Secretary, Falkirk District Council, 1982. Address: (b.) Tom Johnston House, Kirkintilloch, G66 4TJ; T.-041-776 7171.

Killeen, Jan Mary, BSc, DipASS, CertEd. Director, Scottish Action on Dementia, since 1988; Secretary, Scottish Dementia Appeal, since 1990; Honorary Secretary, Dementia Services Development Trust, since 1989; b. 5.7.46, Farnborough, Kent; m., Damian Killeen; 2 s. Educ. London University; University College, Swansea; Leeds University. Library Assistant, BBC, 1965-66; Housing Welfare Officer, Lambeth Borough Council, 1969-70; Community Development Officer, Coventry Corporation, 1970-73; Community Development Officer, Doncaster Metropolitan Borough Council, 1975-78; Doncaster Metropolitan Institute for Higher Education; Lecturer, 1973-79, Tutor, 1979-81; Co-ordinator, Scottish Action on Dementia, 1985-88; Training Officer, Age Concern Scotland, 1981-89. Publications: several in the field of social policy and dementia and service development in day care. Recreation: walking on the beach after dinner. Address: (b.) 33 Castle Street, Edinburgh EH2 3DN; T.-031-220 4886.

Killham, Kenneth Stuart, BSc (Hons), PhD. Senior Lecturer in Soil Microbiology, since 1990; b. 1.3.57, Formby; m., Pauline Jane. Educ. Merchant Taylors School, Crosby; Sheffield University. Research Fellow, University of California, Berkeley, 1981-83; Lecturer in Soil Microbiology, Aberdeen University, 1983-90. Recreations: sailing; hill-walking; cross-country skiing. Address: (h.) East Lodge, Westhall, Oyne, Grampian; T.-04645 651.

Killick, Roger John, BSc, MBA, PhD, CBiol, MIBiol. Secretary, Scottish Crop Research Institute, since 1988; b. 27.5.45, London; m., E. Marion Smith; 1 s.; 1 d. Educ. Purley County Grammar School for Boys; London University; Birmingham University; Dundee University. Research Geneticist, Scottish Plant Breeding Station, 1969-82; Assistant to Director, Scottish Crop Research Institute, 1982-88. Recreations: hill-walking; swimming; watching ballet. Address: (h.) Hilltops, 19 Sidlaw Terrace, Birkhill, Dundee, DD2 5PY; T.-0382 580396.

Kimbell, Professor David Rodney Bertram, MA, DPhil, LRAM, FRSA. Professor of Music, Edinburgh University, since 1987 (Professor of Music, St. Andrews University, 1979-87); b. 26.6.39, Gillingham, Kent; m., Ingrid Else Emilie Lubbe; 1 s.; 2 d. Educ. Dartford Grammar School; Kent College, Canterbury; Worcester College, Oxford. Lecturer in Music, Edinburgh University, 1965-78. Publication: Verdi in the Age of Italian Romanticism, 1981; Italian Opera, 1991. Recreations: walking; miscellaneous sports. Address: (h.) 3 Bellevue Crescent, Edinburgh, EH3 6ND; T.-031-556 5480.

Kinane, Denis Francis, BDS, PhD, FDS RCS(Edin). Senior Lecturer in Periodontology, Glasgow University, since 1988; Honorary Consultant in Periodontology, since 1990; b. 29.1.57, Edinburgh; m., Celina Alice; 1 s.; 2 d. Educ. Edinburgh University. Lecturer in Periodontology and Community Dentistry, Dundee University, 1983. Sir Wilfred Fish Research Award, 1987; Member, Council, British Society of Periodontology. Recreation: squash. Address: (b.) Department of Oral Medicine and Pathology, Glasgow Dental Hospital, 378 Sauchiehall Street, Glasgow, G2 3JZ; T.-041-332 7020, Ext. 207.

Kincraig, Hon. Lord (Robert Smith Johnston), QC (Scot), BA (Hons), LLB. Senator of the College of Justice in Scotland, 1972-88; Chairman, Parole Review Body for Scotland; b. 10.10.18, Glasgow; m., Margaret Joan Graham; 1 s.; 1 d. Educ. Strathallan; St. John's College, Cambridge;

Glasgow University. Member, Faculty of Advocates, 1942; Advocate-Depute, 1953-55; QC (Scot), 1955; Home Advocate Depute, 1959-62; Sheriff of Roxburgh, Berwick and Selkirk, 1964-70; Dean, Faculty of Advocates, 1970-72. Recreation: gardening. Address: (h.) Westwood Cottage, Southfield Farm, Longniddry, EH32 0PL; T.-Longniddry 53583.

King, Charles, MA (Hons). Member, Grampian Regional Council, since 1986; Member, Council, Association of Scottish Literary Studies, 1971-88; b. 29.10.19, Edinburgh; m., Vera Gall Thomson; 1 s.; 2 d. Educ. Trinity Academy, Edinburgh; Edinburgh University; Moray House College of Education. Served in Army, Shetland, Orkney, Malta; taught, Scottish schools; appointed Adviser in English, Aberdeen City, then Grampian Region; retired, 1985; edited Twelve Modern Scottish Poets, 1971, 1986; Twelve More Modern Scottish Poets (Co-Editor), 1986. Recreations: golf; Scottish country dancing; travel. Address: (h.) 36 Hammerfield Avenue, Aberdeen; T.-0224 310403.

King, David Neden, MA, DPhil, CertEd. Senior Lecturer in Economics, Stirling University, since 1987; b. 10.4.45, Birmingham; m., Victoria Susan Robinson; 2 s. Educ. Gresham's School, Norfolk; Magdalen College, Oxford; York University. Consultant Economist, Royal Commission on the Constitution, 1971-72; Economics Master and Head of Economics, Winchester College, 1972-78; Lecturer, Stirling University, 1978-87; Economic Adviser, Department of the Environment, 1987-88. Conductor, Stirling University Choir. Publications: Rates or Prices? (Co-author); Financial and Economic Aspects of Regionalism and Separatism; Taxes on Immovable Property; Fiscal Decentralisation (Co-editor); Fiscal Tiers: the economics of multi-level government; An Introduction to National Income Accounting; Microeconomics (Co-author); Banking and Money; The Complete Works of Robert and James Adam; Local Government Economics in Theory and Practice (Editor); Economics (Co-author). Recreations: architecture; music. Address: (b.) Department of Economics, Stirling University, Stirling, FK9 4LA; T.-0786 67475.

King, Elspeth Russell, MA, FMA. Director, Dunfermline Heritage Trust, since 1991; b. 29.3.49, Lochore, Fife. Educ. Beath High School; St. Andrews University; Leicester University. Curator, People's Palace, Glasgow, 1974-91, with responsibility for building up the social history collections for the city of Glasgow. Address: (b.) People's Palace, Glasgow Green, Glasgow, G40 1AT; T.-041-554 0223.

King, Emeritus Professor James Lawrence, MA, PhD, FIMA. Professor (Emeritus), Edinburgh University, since 1983; Governor, Strathallan School, Perthshire; b. 14.2.22, London; m., Pamela Mary Ward Hitchcock; 1 s.; 1 d. Educ. Latymer Upper School; Jesus College, Cambridge. Navy Department, 1942-68 (Admiralty Research Laboratory, 1942-61; Chief Scientist, Naval Construction Research Establishment, Dunfermline, 1961-68); Regius Professor of Engineering, Edinburgh University, 1968-83. Recreation: walking. Address: (h.) 16 Lyne Park, West Linton, Peeblesshire.

King, Robert Lees Lumsden. Secretary, Post Office Users' Council for Scotland, since 1988; Secretary, Scottish Advisory Committee on Telecommunications, since 1988; b. 23.3.49, Peebles; m., Yvonne Mary Black. Educ. Leith Academy. Department of Agriculture and Fisheries for Scotland, 1966-70; Department of Environment, 1970-72; Forestry Commission, 1972-79; Nature Conservancy Council, 1979-88. Recreations: country life; shooting; reading; travel. Address: (b.) 43 Jeffrey Street, Edinburgh, EH1 1DN; T.-031-244 5576.

Kinloch, Dorothy Craig, DipDomSc. Principal Teacher of Home Economics, McLaren High School, Callander, since 1969; Chief Commissioner of Scotland, The Scout Association, since 1988; b. 3.8.43, Glasgow. Educ. Whitehill Secondary School, Glasgow; Glasgow and West of Scotland College of Domestic Science. Taught, Westwood Secondary School, Easterhouse, Glasgow, four years; Member, first SCCC for Home Economics; Member, first Joint Working Party on Home Economics; became involved in Scouting in 1960 and has held numerous appointments, including United Kingdom Headquarters Commissioner for Cub Scouts; led UK contingent to 17th World Jamboree, Korea, 1991. Recreations: opera; reading; entertaining friends. Address: (h.) 3 Julia Cottages, Callander, Perthshire, FK17 8AE; T.-0877 30238.

Kinloch, Maggie, DSD. Artistic Director, Byre Theatre, St. Andrews, since 1989; b. 9.7.54, Largs. Educ. Largs Academy; Ardrossan Academy; Royal Scottish Academy of Music and Drama; Glasgow University; Jordanhill College of Education. Teacher of Speech and Drama, Strathclyde Region, 1976-80; Head of Drama, Glasgow Arts Centre, 1980-85; Assistant Director, TAG Theatre Company, Glasgow, 1985-87; Associate Director, Annexe Theatre Company, Glasgow, and freelance Director, 1987-89. Address: (b.) Byre Theatre, Abbey Street, St. Andrews, Fife; T.-0334 76288.

Kinnaird, Alison, MA, FGE. Glass Engraver and Artist; Clarsach Player; b. 30.4.49, Edinburgh; m., Robin Morton; 1 s.; 1 d. Educ. George Watson's Ladies College; Edinburgh University. Freelance glass artist, since 1971; exhibitions in Edinburgh, 1978, 1981, 1985, in London, 1988; work in many public and private collections; professional musician, since 1970; has produced three LPs as well as film and TV music; served on Council, Scottish Craft Centre, 1974-76; Council, SSWA, 1975-76; Member, BBC Scottish Music Advisory Committee, 1981-84; Member, BBC Broadcasting Council for Scotland, 1984-88; awarded SDA/CCC Craft Fellowship, 1980; Glass-Sellers of London Award, 1987. Recreations: children; cooking; garden. Address: (h.) Shillinghill, Temple, Midlothian, EH23 4SH; T.-Temple 328.

Kinnis, William Kay Brewster, MA, BL, PhD, DPA. Solicitor and Notary Public; Senior Partner, Miller Jackson, Solicitors, Lenzie, since 1982; Partner, Murdoch Jackson, Solicitors, Glasgow, since 1963 (Senior Partner, since 1987); Director, East Neuk Properties Ltd., Kilrymont Properties Ltd., Culdee Properties Ltd., Madras Properties Ltd., Swilcan Properties Ltd.; b. 5.1.33, St. Andrews; m., Agnes Inglis Erskine, MA; 2 d. d. Educ. Hamilton Academy; Glasgow University; London University (External). Partner: MacArthur Stewart & Orr, Solicitors, Oban and Lochgilphead, 1959-62; Town Clerk and Burgh Chamberlain, Lochgilphead, 1960-62; Council Member, Royal Faculty of Procurators, 1980-83; Governor, Baillie's Institution, since 1983. Choral Scholar, Glasgow University, 1954-58; Choirmaster, Lochgilphead Parish Church, 1959-62; Reader, Church of Scotland, since 1960; Member, Church of Scotland Practice and Procedure Committee. Recreations: choral singing; swimming; reading; travel. Address: (b.) 10 Woodside Place, Glasgow, G3 7QJ; T.-041-332 9207.

Kinross, Lord (Christopher Patrick Balfour), LLB, WS. Solicitor, since 1975; b. 1.10.49, Edinburgh; m., Susan Jane Pitman; 2 s. Educ. Eton College; Edinburgh University. Member, Royal Company of Archers, Queen's Bodyguard for Scotland; James IV Association of Surgeons. Recreation: pistol, rifle and shotgun shooting; deer stalking; military vehicle restoration. Address: (b.) 16 Charlotte Square, Edinburgh; T.-031-225 8585.

Kinsey, Richard, LLB, BA Soc/Psych. Reader in Criminology, Edinburgh University; Writer and Broadcaster;

b. 14.11.47, Northwich; m., Maureen; 3 d. Educ. William Hulme's Grammar School, Manchester; Leeds University. University Lecturer since 1973. Former Chair, Scottish Council for Civil Liberties. Publications include: Police Powers and Politics, 1984; Losing the Fight Against Crime, 1987; Crime and the Quality of Life in Scotland, 1992. Recreations: socialism and three-wheeled Morgans. Address: (h) Romanno Bank, Romanno Bridge, Peeblesshire; T.-0968 60357.

Kirby, Professor Gordon William, MA, PhD, ScD, CChem, FRSC, FRSE. Regius Professor of Chemistry, Glasgow University, since 1972; b. 20.6.34, Wallasey; 2 s. Educ. Liverpool Institute High School; Liverpool Technical College; Gonville and Caius College, Cambridge. Imperial College, London: 1851 Exhibition Senior Studentship, 1958-60, Assistant Lecturer, 1960-61, Lecturer, 1961-67; Professor of Organic Chemistry, Loughborough University of Technology, 1967-72. Corday-Morgan Medal and Prize, Royal Society of Chemistry, 1969; Tilden Lectureship, Royal Society of Chemistry, 1974-75. Recreation: hill-walking. Address: (b.) Department of Chemistry, Glasgow University, Glasgow, G12 8QQ; T.-041-339 8855, Ext. 4416/4417.

Kirk, David, MA, BM, BCh, DM, FRCS (Eng), FRCS-RCPS (Glas). Consultant Urological Surgeon, Greater Glasgow Health Board, since 1982; Honorary Clinical Lecturer, Glasgow University, since 1984; b. 26.5.43, Bradford; m., Gillian Mary Wroot; 1 s.; 2 d. Educ. King Edwards School, Birmingham; Balliol College, Oxford; Oxford University Clinical Medical School. Resident House Physician and House Surgeon, Radcliffe Infirmary, Oxford; University Demonstrator, Oxford; clinical surgical posts, Oxford and Bristol; Arris and Gale Lecturer, Royal College of Surgeons (England), 1980-81; surgical Registrar appointment, Sheffield; academic surgical research, Sheffield University; Senior Registrar in General Surgery, then in Urology, Bristol. Secretary/Treasurer, 1983-85, Chairman, 1985-88, Scottish Urological Oncology Group; Council Member, Urology Section, Royal Society of Medicine, 1984-87; Council Member, British Association of Urological Surgeons, 1988-91; Chairman, Prostate Forum. Recreations: skiing; hill-walking; classical music. Address: (h.) Woodend, Prospect Road, Dullatur, Glasgow, G68 0AN; T.-0236 720778.

Kirk, Gordon, MA, MEd. Principal, Moray House College of Education, since 1981; Chairman, Scottsh Council for Research in Education, since 1984; Chairman, Educational Broadcasting Council, Scotland, since 1985; b. 8.5.38, Dunfermline; m., Jane D. Murdoch; 1 s.; 1 d. Educ. Camphill Secondary School, Paisley; Glasgow University. Lecturer in Education, Aberdeen University, 1965-74; Head, Education Department, Jordanhill College of Education, 1974-81; Member, Munn Committee on the Curriculum of the Secondary School, 1974-77; Member: General Teaching Council for Scotland, since 1984, Consultative Committee on the Curriculum, since 1984, Council for National Academic Awards, since 1979. Publications: Scottish Education Looks Ahead (Assistant Editor), 1969; Curriculum and Assessment in the Scottish Secondary School, 1982; Moray House and Professional Education (Editor), 1985; The Core Curriculum, 1986; Teacher Education and Professional Development, 1988; Handbook of Educational Ideas and Practices (Associate Editor), 1990; Professional Issues in Education series (Co-Editor). Recreations: walking; golf; bridge. Address: (h.) Craigroyston, Broadgait, Gullane, East Lothian; T.-0620 843299.

Kirk, James, MA, PhD, DLitt, FRHistS. Reader in Scottish History, Glasgow University, since 1991; b. 18.10.44, Falkirk. Educ. Stirling High School; Edinburgh University. Lecturer in Scottish History, Glasgow University, 1972-89; Senior Lecturer, 1989-91; David Berry Prize, Royal Historical Society, 1973; Wolfson Award, 1977; British Academy Major Research Awards, 1989-92. President, Scottish Church History Society, 1989-92; Hon. Secretary, Scottish Record Society, since 1973; Hon. Secretary, Scottish Society for Reformation History, since 1980; Member, Council, Scottish History Society, 1989-92; Section Editor, Royal Historical Society, Annual Bibliography of British and Irish History; Recreations: living in Wester Ross; viticulture. Address: (h.) Woodlea, Dunmore, Stirlingshire, FK2 8LY; T.-032483 240.

Kirk, James Foster, BSc. Rector, Tain Royal Academy, since 1979; b. 31.8.41, Bellshill; m., Margo McFarlane; 1 s.; 1 d. Educ. Hamilton Academy; Glasgow University. Entered teaching, 1963; promoted to Principal Teacher of Science, then Principal Teacher of Guidance, then Assistant Rector; moved from Lanarkshire to Highlands, 1975. Recreations: gardening; golf; hill-walking. Address: (h.) The Barn House, Delny, Invergordon, Ross-shire; T.-Kildary 2564.

Kirkbride, George, CEng, FICE, FIHTE, FIBM, Eur.Ing. Director of Roads, Grampian Regional Council, since 1983; b. 26.5.33, Willington; 1 s.; 2 d. Educ. Aireborough Grammar School; Bradford Technical College. Pupil, Aireborough Urban District Council, 1949-54; Senior Engineer, Bradford Corporation, 1956-59; Senior Engineer, then Chief Assistant, Crewe Borough, 1959-66; Principal Engineer, then Project Coordinator, Wolverhampton Borough, 1966-72; Depute City Engineer, Dundee City, 1972-75; Regional Roads Engineer, Fife Regional Council, 1975-83. Past President, FUMPO; County Surveyors' Society: Member, 1992 Group, Secretary, European Liaison Group; Fellow, Dundee College of Technology. Recreations: cycling; swimming. Address: (b.) Woodhill House, Westburn Road, Aberdeen; T.-Aberdeen 682222.

Kirkhill, Baron (John Farquharson Smith). Life Peer; b. 7.5.30. Lord Provost, Aberdeen, 1971-75; Minister of State, Scottish Office, 1975-78; Chairman, North of Scotland Hydro-Electric Board, 1979-82; Member, Council of Europe, since 1987.

Kirkness, Professor Colin Maitland, BMedBiol, MBChB, FRCS(Edin), FCOphth, FRCS (Glas). Tennent Professor of Ophthalmology, Glasgow University, since 1991; b. 5.5.49, Kirkwall. Educ. Fraserburgh Academy; Aberdeen University. Resident Surgical Officer and Senior Resident, Moorfields Eye Hospital, London, 1980; Lecturer, 1983, Senior Lecturer and Director, 1989, Pocklington Eye Transplant Unit, Institute of Ophthalmology, London; Honorary Consultant, Moorfields Eye Hospital, 1987. Publications: books on ophthalmology; papers. Address: (b.) Tennent Institute, 38 Church Street, Glasgow, G11 6NT; T.-041-339 8822, Ext. 4640.

Kirkwood, Archy, BSc, NP. MP (Liberal Democrat), Roxburgh and Berwickshire, since 1983; b. 22.4.46, Glasgow; m., Rosemary; 1 s.; 1 d. Educ. Cranhill School; Heriot-Watt University. Former Personal Assistant to Rt. Hon. David Steel (qv); Solicitor. Recreation: music. Address: (b.) House of Commons, London, SW1A OAA; T.-071-219 3000.

Kirkwood, Hon. Lord (Ian Candlish Kirkwood), QC (Scot). Senator of the College of Justice, since 1987; b. 8.6.32. Advocate, 1957; QC, 1970; Chairman, Medical Appeal Tribunal in Scotland.

Kirkwood, Ralph C., BSc, PhD, FRSE. Reader in Biology, Strathclyde University, since 1981; b. 6.7.33, Glasgow; m., Mair Enid; 3 s. Educ. Jordanhill College School, Glasgow; Glasgow University; University of Wales, Aberystwyth. Lecturer, Botany Department, West of Scotland Agricultural College, 1959-64; Strathclyde University: Lecturer, Biology Department, 1964-72, Senior Lecturer, 1972-81; Member,

Regional Advisory Committee, Scottish Agricultural College; Vice-Chairman, NCSS South-West Regional Board; Member, Fellowship Committee, Institute of Biology. Publication: Target sites for herbicide action (Editor). Recreations: sailing; photography; natural history; walking. Address: (b.) Department of Bioscience and Biotechnology, Todd Centre, Strathclyde University, Glasgow, G1 1XW; T.-041-552 4400.

Kitchen, John Philip, MA, BMus, PhD (Cantab), FRCO, LRAM. Lecturer in Music, Edinburgh University, since 1987 (Lecturer in Music, St. Andrews University, 1976-87); Harpsichord Tutor, Royal Scottish Academy of Music and Drama; Concert Organist, Harpsichordist, Pianist; b. 27.10.50, Airdrie. Educ. Coatbridge High School; Glasgow University; Cambridge University. Harpsichordist/Organist, Scottish Early Music Consort, Stanesby Recorder Trio, St. Andrews Baroque Trio; BBC and commercial recordings; music reviewer. Recreations: more music; entertaining; doing housework. Address: (b.) Faculty of Music, Alison House, 12 Nicolson Square, Edinburgh, EH8 9DF; T.-031-650 2432.

Klein, Bernat, CBE, FCSD, Hon. FRIAS. Chairman and Managing Director, Bernat Klein Ltd., since 1981; b. 6.11.22, Senta, Yugoslavia; m., Margaret Soper; 1 s.; 2 d. Educ. Senta, Yugoslavia; Bezalel School of Arts and Crafts, Jerusalem; Leeds University. Designer: Tootal, Broadhurst, Lee, 1948-49, Munrospun, Edinburgh, 1949-51; Chairman and Managing Director, Colourcraft, 1952-62; Managing Director, Bernat Klein Ltd., 1962-66; Chairman and Managing Director, Bernat Klein Design Ltd., 1966-81. Member, Design Council, 1962-68; Member, Royal Fine Art Commission for Scotland, 1981-87. Publications: Eye for Colour, 1965; Design Matters, 1975. Recreations: tennis; reading. Address: High Sunderland, Galashiels; T.-0750 20730.

Kleinpoppen, Professor Hans, DipPhys, Dr re nat & habil, FInstPhys, FRAS, FRSA, FRSE, Fellow, American Physical Society. Professor of Experimental Physics, Stirling University, since 1968; b. 30.9.28, Duisburg, Germany. Educ. Giessen University; Heidelberg University; Tuebingen University. Visiting Fellow, Colorado University, 1967; Visiting Associate Professor, Columbia University, New York, 1968; Stirling University: Head, Physics Department, 1970-72, Director, Institute of Atomic Physics, 1975-81, Head, Unit of Atomic and Molecular Physics, School of Natural Sciences, since 1989. Visiting Professor, Bielefeld University, since 1979. Publication: Physics of Atoms and Molecules (Series Editor); Director, three International Summer Schools; Chairman, several International Conferences on Atomic Physics. Address: (b.) Unit of Atomic and Molecular Physics, Stirling University, Stirling.

Klopper, Emeritus Professor Arnold, MB, ChB, MD, PhD, FRCOG. Professor of Reproductive Endocrinology, Aberdeen University, 1976-87; Consultant Obstetrician and Gynaecologist, since 1960; b. 8.2.22, Ventersburg, South Africa; m., Mary Katherine Turvey. Educ. Brebner College, Bloemfontein, South Africa; Witwatersrand University, Johannesburg. Hospital residency appointments, Johannesburg and London; Clinical Research Fellow, MRC, Guy's Hospital, and Clinical Endocrinology Research Unit, Edinburgh; appointed to permanent senior scientific staff, MRC, Obstetric Medicine Research Unit, Aberdeen, 1958; Aberdeen University: Senior Lecturer, 1966, Reader, 1972. Honorary Fellow, National Obstetrical Societies, USA, Italy, Finland and Singapore. Publications: Fetus and Placenta; Placental Proteins. Recreations: fishing; shooting; training dogs; watching other people work. Address: (h.) Sea Cottage, Newtonhill, AB3 2PU.

Knight, Alanna, FSA Scot. Novelist; b. Co. Durham; m., Alistair Knight; 2 s. Educ. Jesmond High School. Writing career began, 1965; novels: Legend of the Loch, 1969 (RNA First Novel Award), The October Witch, 1971, This Outward Angel, 1971, Castle Clodha, 1972, Lament for Lost Lovers, 1972, The White Rose, 1974, A Stranger Came By, 1974, The Wicked Wynsleys, 1977; historical novels: The Passionate Kindness, 1974, A Drink for the Bridge, 1976, The Black Duchess, 1980, Castle of Foxes, 1981, Colla's Children, 1982, The Clan, 1985; Estella, 1986; detective novels: Enter Second Murderer, 1988, Blood Line, 1989, Deadly Beloved, 1989, Killing Cousins, 1990, A Quiet Death, 1991, To Kill A Queen, 1992; plays: The Private Life of R.L.S., 1973, Girl on an Empty Swing, 1977; non-fiction: The Robert Louis Stevenson Treasury, 1985; RLS in the South Seas, 1986; radio short stories, plays and documentaries. Recreations: walking; reading; creative knitting. Address: (h.) 24 March Hall Crescent, Edinburgh, EH16 5HL; T.-031-667 5230.

Knight, Joan, OBE. Artistic Director, Perth Theatre, since 1968; b. 27.9.24, Walton-Le-Dale, Lancashire. Educ. Lark Hill Convent School. Trained, Bristol Old Vic Theatre School; Director and Administrator, Castle Theatre, Farnham, five years; Director, Ludlow Festival, three years; Director of Productions, Pitlochry Festival Theatre, two years; freelance productions from Bristol Old Vic, Birmingham Repertory, Nottingham Playhouse, Royal Lyceum, Edinburgh, Traverse Theatre, Yvonne Arnaud Theatre, Scottish Theatre Company, etc. Recreations: cooking; swimming; walking. Address: (b.) Perth Theatre, High Street, Perth.

Knill-Jones, Jennifer Gillian, MB, BS, LRCP, MRCS, MRCPsych. Consultant Psychiatrist, since 1986; b. 15.8.36, Stockton-on-Tees; 3 d. Educ. Sutton High School; St. Bartholomew's Hospital Medical School. House Officer posts, Luton and Dunstaple Hospital, Elizabeth Garrett Anderson Hospital, London, St. Bartholomew's Hospital, London; Clinical Assistant, Gartnavel Royal Hospital, Glasgow; Senior Registrar in Psychiatry, Greater Glasgow Health Board. Recreations: walking; Scottish country dancing. Address: (b.) Parkhead Hospital, Salamanca Street, Glasgow, G32; T.-041-554 7951.

Knops, Professor Robin John, BSc, PhD, FRSE. Professor of Mathematics, Heriot-Watt University, Edinburgh, since 1971 (Vice Principal, since 1988); b. 30.12.32, London; m., Margaret; 4 s.; 2 d. Educ. Nottingham University. Nottingham University: Assistant Lecturer in Mathematics, 1956-59, Lecturer in Mathematics, 1959-62; Newcastle-upon-Tyne University: Lecturer in Applied Mathematics, 1962-68, Reader in Continuum Mechanics, 1968-71; Head, Department of Mathematics, Heriot-Watt University, 1971-83; Visiting Professor: Cornell University, 1967 and 1968; University of California, Berkeley, 1968; Pisa University, 1974; Ecole Polytechnique Federale Lausanne, Switzerland, 1980; Royal Society of Edinburgh: Council Member, since 1982, Executive Committee Member, 1982-86, Meetings Secretary, 1982-87, Chief Executive Editor, Proceedings A, 1982-87, Curator, since 1987; President, Edinburgh Mathematical Society, 1974-75; President, International Society for the Interaction of Mechanics and Mathematics, since 1991. Publications: Uniqueness Theories in Linear Elasticity (Co-author), 1971; Theory of Elastic Stability (Co-author), 1973. Recreations: walking; reading. Address: (b.) Department of Mathematics, Heriot-Watt University, Edinburgh, EH14 4AS; T.-031-449 5111.

Knox, Col. Sir Bryce Muir, KCVO, MC (and Bar), CStJ, TD, BA (Cantab); b. 4.4.16, Edinburgh; m., Patricia Mary Dunsmuir; 1 s.; 1 d. Educ. Stowe; Trinity College, Cambridge. County of Ayr: Deputy Lieutenant, 1953, Vice Lieutenant, 1970-74, Ayrshire and Arran Lord Lieutenant, 1974-91; Chairman, W. & J. Knox Ltd., Kilbirnie, 1970-78;

Vice-Chairman, Lindustries Ltd., 1979 (Director, 1953-79); served with Ayrshire (ECO) Yeomanry, 1939-45, North Africa and Italy (CO, 1953-56, Hon. Col., 1960-71); Honorary Colonel, Ayrshire Yeomanry Squadron, Queen's Own Yeomanry, 1971-77; President, Royal Highland Agricultural Society of Scotland, 1990-91. Publications: brief historical notes of the Ayrshire Yeomanry; History of the Eglinton Hunt. Recreation: country sports. Address: (h.) Martnaham Lodge, by Ayr, KA6 6ES; T.-Dalrymple 204.

Knox, Professor James David Edgar, MD, FRCPEdin, FRCGP. Professor and Head, Department of General Practice, Dundee University, since 1970; NHS Principal, Medical School Teaching Practice, Westgate Health Centre, Dundee, since 1979; b. 12.3.27, Edinburgh; m., Catherine Mary Bell; 1 s.; 1 d. Educ. George Watson's College, Edinburgh; Edinburgh University. Medical Officer, RAF Medical Branch, 1950-55; Registrar posts, Royal Infirmary and Northern General Hospital, Edinburgh, 1955-60; Principal, NHS general practice, West Granton Medical Group, Edinburgh, 1963-70. Former Member, Professional and Linguistic Assessment Board, GMC. Publications: Presentations in Primary Care, 1985; On Call, 1989. Recreations: fishing; music. Address: (h.) 369 Blackness Road, Dundee; T.-0382 67635.

Knox, John, BA, BD. General Secretary, Scottish National Council of YMCAs, since 1992; b. 28.1.35, Larne, Co. Antrim; m., Patricia Ringland; 1 s.; 1 d. Educ. Larne Grammar School; Queen's University, Belfast; Edgehill College; London University. Methodist Minister, Dublin, Donegal and Belfast, 1959-69; General Secretary, Methodist Youth Department, Ireland, 1969-78; Associate Secretary, Irish Council of Churches, 1978-82; Chief Officer, Scottish Standing Conference of Voluntary Youth Organisations, 1982-92. Recreations: gardening; mountain walking; music. Address: (b.) Central Hall, West Tollcross, Edinburgh, EH3 9BP; T.-031-229 0339.

Knox, John, RSA, RGI, RSW. Head of Painting Studios, Glasgow School of Art, since 1981; Secretary, Royal Scottish Academy, since 1990; b. 16.12.36; m.; 1 s.; 1 d. Educ. Lenzie Academy; Glasgow School of Art. Staff, Duncan of Jordanstone College of Art, Dundee, 1965-81; work in several permanent collections; Member, Scottish Arts Council, 1974-79; Member, Board of Trustees, National Galleries of Scotland, 1982-87.

Knox, Professor John Henderson, BSc, PhD, DSc, FRSC, CChem, FRSE, FRS. Director, Wolfson Liquid Chromatography Unit, Edinburgh University, since 1972 (Emeritus Professor of Physical Chemistry and Honorary Fellow since 1984); b. 21.10.27, Edinburgh; m., Josephine Anne Wissler; 4 s. Educ. George Watson's Boys College, Edinburgh; Edinburgh University; Cambridge University. Edinburgh University: Lecturer, 1953-66, Reader, 1966-74, Professor, 1974-84. Recreations: skiing; hill-walking; sailing. Address: (h.) 67 Morningside Park, Edinburgh; T.-031-447 5057.

Knox, Robert, MA, LLB, WS. Senior Partner, Boyd, Jameson, Edinburgh, since 1983; Solicitor, since 1959, Partner, since 1962; Solicitor to Ministry of Defence (Army) in Scotland, since 1980; Honorary Consul for Belgium in Edinburgh, since 1982; Member, High Constabulary, Port of Leith, since 1989; b. 23.5.35, Paisley; m., Jill Mackness; 2 s.; 1 d. Educ. Paisley Grammar School; Glasgow University; Manchester University; Edinburgh University. Member, Lord Maxwell's Committee on Civil Jurisdiction and Enforcement. Recreations: gardening; photography; foreign travel; music; painting; railways past and present; model railways. Address: (b.) 89 Constitution Street, Leith, Edinburgh; T.-031-554 3333.

Knox, Roger Thompson, BSc, MSc, CEng, MBCS. Senior Lecturer, Faculty of Textiles, Heriot-Watt University, since 1983; Tutor, Open University, since 1979; b. 29.10.42, Dundee; m., Mary Simpson; 2 s.; 3 d. Educ. Harris Academy, Dundee; St. Andrews University; Heriot-Watt University. Trainee Programmer, NCR; Technical Analyst/Programmer, Edinburgh Corporation; Lecturer, Moray House Centre for Computer Education; Senior Lecturer, Department of Management, Scottish College of Textiles. Former Director of Training, Scottish National Party. Publication: How Scotland Voted, 1989. Recreations: traditional music; Scots language. Address: (h.) 65 Station Road, Ratho Station, Midlothian, EH28 8QP; T.-031-333 1235.

Knox, William. Author and Journalist; b. 20.2.28, Glasgow; m., Myra Ann McKill; 1 s.; 2 d. Educ. Eastwood School. Deputy News Editor, Evening News, Glasgow, 1957; Scottish Editor, Kemsley Newspapers, Glasgow, 1957-60; News Editor, Scottish Television, 1960-62; Freelance Author and Broadcaster, since 1962; author of about 60 books, including novels of crime, sea and adventure; awarded Police Review Award for best novel of British police procedures, 1987 (The Crossfire Killings); Presenter Crime Desk, STV, 1977-88; William Knox Collection established Boston University, USA; Past President and Honorary Member, Association of Scottish Motoring Writers; former Member, Scottish Committee, Society of Authors; Past President, Eastwood Rotary Club; Honorary Editor, Scottish Lifeboat, RNLI; Fellow, Paul Harris Foundation, Rotary International, 1989. Recreations: motoring; photography; dogs. Address: (h.) 55 Newtonlea Avenue, Newton Mearns, Glasgow, G77 5QF.

Knox, William James. Chairman (UK), Federation of Small Businesses, since 1989; b. 4.8.44, Glasgow; m., Ann May; 1 d. Educ. Greenock High School; Reid Kerr College, Paisley. Partner, A.F. McPherson & Co., Builders and Merchants, since 1962; Board Member, Scottish National Federation of Building Trade Employers, 1970-79; Member, Social Security Tribunal, 1978-84; Director, Morton Football and Athletic Club, 1986-89; Chairman, Morton Development Club, 1986-89; Member, Executive, Scottish Constitutional Convention, 1989-90. Recreations: football; bowling; photography; canals. Address: (h.) 3 Moorfield Road, Gourock, PA19 1DD; T.-0475 33327.

Konstam, Peter George, OBE, MD (Frankfurt), FRCSEdin. Honorary Sheriff, Orkney Islands; b. 19.4.08, Frankfurt-on-Main, Germany; m., Dr. Sheila Ritchie; 1 s. Educ. Lessing Gymnasium, Frankfurt; Berlin University; Frankfurt University. Senior Registrar to Professor of Surgery, Aberdeen University; Major, RAMC; Associate Professor of Surgery, Ibadan University; Consultant Surgeon, Orkney Hospitals (retired, 1974). Recreations: piano playing; reading; gardening. Address: (h.) Thule, St. Ola, Orkney Isles; T.-Kirkwall 2821.

Kristiansen, Professor Bjorn, BSc, MSc, PhD. Robertson Professor of Bioprocess Technology, Strathclyde University, since 1990; Director, Strathclyde Fermentation Centre, since 1988; b. 1.2.47, Baerum, Norway; m., Joan Linden Kristiansen; 2 s.; 2 d. Educ. UMIST; Imperial College. Address: (b.) Department of Bioscience and Biotechnology, Strathclyde University, 16 Richmond Street, Glasgow, G1 1XQ.

Kuenssberg, Nicholas Christopher D., BA (Hons) (Oxon), FCIS, CBIM. Director and Chief Executive, Dawson International Plc, since 1991; Non-executive Director, Scottish Power Plc, since 1984; Director, Standard Life Assurance Company, since 1988; b. 28.10.42, Edinburgh; m., Sally Robertson; 1 s.; 2 d. Educ. Edinburgh Academy; Wadham College, Oxford. Director, J. & P. Coats Ltd., 1978-91; Director, Coats Patons Plc, 1985-91. Recreations: languages; opera; travel. Address: (b.) Dawson Intrnational Plc, 9 Charlotte Street, Edinburgh, EH2 4DB.

L

Kyle, James, CBE, DSc, MCh, FRCS. Chairman, Grampian Health Board; Surgeon, Aberdeen Royal Infirmary, 1959-89; Chairman, Scottish Joint Consultants Committee, 1984-89; President, Aberdeen Medico-Chirurgical Society, 1989-90; b. 26.3.25, Ballymena, Northern Ireland; m., Dorothy Elizabeth Galbraith; 2 d. Educ. Ballymena Academy; Queen's University, Belfast. Scholarship to Mayo Clinic, USA, 1950; Tutor in Surgery, Royal Victoria Hospital, Belfast, 1952; Lecturer in Surgery, Liverpool University, 1957; Senior Lecturer in Surgery, Aberdeen University, 1959-60. Member, Grampian Health Board, 1973-77; Chairman, Scottish Committee for Hospital Medical Services, 1976-79; elected Member, General Medical Council, since 1979; Chairman, Representative Body, British Medical Association, 1984-87. Publications: Peptic Ulcer; Pye's Surgical Handicraft; Crohn's Disease; Scientific Foundations of Surgery. Recreations: Fellow, Royal Philatelic Society, London; licensed radio amateur, GM4 CHX. Address: (h.) Grianan, 74 Rubislaw Den North, Aberdeen, AB2 4AN; T.-Aberdeen 317966.

Kyle, Peter McLeod, MBChB, FRCS(Edin), FRCS(Glas), FCOphth. Consultant Ophthalmologist, Greater Glasgow Health Board, since 1982; Honorary Clinical Senior Lecturer, Glasgow University, since 1985; Member, Medical Appeal Tribunals, Scotland, since 1986; b. 19.8.51, Rutherglen; m., Valerorie Anne Steele; 1 s.; 2 d. Educ. High School of Glasgow; Glasgow University. Lecturer in Ophthalmology, Glasgow University, 1980-84. Ophthalmic Adviser, Queens College, Glasgow, since 1985; Vice-Chairman, Examination Council, British Orthopic Society, since 1990. Recreations: walking; skiing. Address: (h.) 36 Sutherland Avenue, Glasgow; T.-041-427 4400.

Kyle, Robert, MBE, DL, NP. Honorary Sheriff, Strathclyde, at Airdrie; Deputy Lieutenant, County of Dunbarton; b. 28.3.19, Strathaven; m., Pauline Watson; 3 s.; 1 d. Educ. Strathaven Academy; Hamilton Academy; Glasgow University. War service, six years; Legal Assistant, Kilmarnock Town Council, 1946-48; Depute Town Clerk, Airdrie Town Council, 1948-52; Town Clerk, Kirkintilloch Town Council, 1952-68; Town Clerk and Manager, Cumbernauld Town Council, 1968-74; Chief Executive, Cumbernauld and Kilsyth District Council, 1974-81. Past President: Dumbartonshire Golf Union, Kirkintilloch & District Agricultural Society, Strathaven Golf Club, Rotary Club of Kirkintilloch. Recreations: golf; angling. Address: (h.) 23 Middlemuir Road, Lenzie, Glasgow, G66 4NA; T.-041-776 1861.

Kynoch, George Alexander Bryson, BSc. MP (Conservative), Kincardine and Deeside, since 1992; b. 7.10.46, Keith; m., Dr. Rosslyn Marget McDevitt; 1 s.; 1 d. Educ. Cargilfield School, Edinburgh; Glenalmond College, Perth; Bristol University. Plant Engineer, ICI Ltd., Nobel Division, 1968-71; G. and G. Kynoch PLC, 1971-92, latterly as Group Executive Director; Non-Executive Director: Kynoch Group PLC, Aaadvark Clear Mine Ltd., since 1992; Member, Aberdeen and District Milk Marketing Board, 1988-92; Director, Moray Badenoch and Strathspey Local Enterprise Co. Ltd., 1991-92; Chairman, Scottish Woollen Publicity Council, 1983-90; President, Scottish Woollen Industry, 1990-91; Vice Chairman, Northern Area, Scottish Conservative and Unionist Association, 1991-92. Recreations: golf; skiing; travel. Address: (b.) House of Commons, London, SW1A 0AA; T.-071-219 5808.

Lacy, Rev. David William, BA, BD. Minister, Henderson Parish Church, Kilmarnock, since 1989; b. 26.4.52, Inverness; m., Joan Stewart Robertson; 1 s.; 1 d. Educ. Aberdeen Grammar School; High School of Glasgow; Strathclyde University; Glasgow University and Trinity College. Assistant Minister, St. George's West, Edinburgh, 1975-77; Minister, Knightswood: St. Margaret's, Glasgow, 1977-89. Recreations: boating; caravanning; snooker; golf. Address: 52 London Road, Kilmarnock, Ayrshire, KA3 7AJ; T.-0563 23113.

Laidlaw, Basil Henderson, BSc, MSc, AH-WC, FIMA, MBCS. Vice Principal, Bell College of Technology, Hamilton, since 1986; b. 10.6.40, Edinburgh; m., Catherine Alexandra Currie; 2 d. Educ. Kirkcaldy High School; Edinburgh University; Heriot-Watt University; St. Andrews University. Lecturer, Kirkcaldy Technical College, 1968-72; Senior Lecturer, then Head, Department of Mathematics and Computing, Bell College of Technology, 1972-86. Recreations: chess; rugby (spectator); football; films; theatre. Address: (b.) Almada Street, Hamilton, ML3 0JB; T.-0698 283100.

Laidlaw, Professor James Cameron, MA, PhD. Part-time Professor of French, Aberdeen University (Professor of French, 1975-89); b. 3.3.37, Ecclefechan; m., Elizabeth Fernie Bosomworth; 1 s.; 2 d. Educ. George Watson's College, Edinburgh; Edinburgh University; Trinity Hall, Cambridge. Research Fellow, Trinity Hall, Cambridge, 1961-63; Lecturer in Medieval French, Queen's University, Belfast, 1963-65; University Assistant Lecturer (from 1969 University Lecturer) in French, and Fellow, Trinity Hall, Cambridge, 1965-74; Visiting Fellow, Gonville and Caius College, Cambridge, 1986-87; Visiting Fellow, Victoria University of Wellington, New Zealand, 1990-91; Vice-Principal, Aberdeen University, 1984-86. Member Arts Sub-Committee, University Grants Committee, 1980-89; Honorary Secretary, Modern Humanities Research Association, 1961-67. Publications: The Future of the Modern Humanities (Editor), 1969; The Poetical Works of Alain Chartier, 1974. Recreations: walking; cycling. Address: (h.) Orchard Walls, Traquair, Innerleithen, EH44 6PU; T.-Innerleithen 831227.

Laing, Professor Ernest William, MA, PhD, FInstP, FRSE. Titular Professor, Department of Physics and Astronomy, Glasgow University; b. 12.2.31, Braine-Le-Comte, Belgium; m., Olive Jean Guild Melville; 2 s. Educ. John Neilson School, Paisley; Glasgow University. Senior Scientific Officer, UKAEA Harwell, 1957-60; Glasgow University: Lecturer, 1960-66, Senior Lecturer, 1966-76, Reader, 1976-80, Titular Professor, since 1980. Publication: Plasma Physics, 1979. Recreation: music. Address: (b.) Department of Physics and Astronomy, Glasgow University, Glasgow, G12 8QQ; T.-041-330 4464.

Laing, James Findlay, MA (Hons). Under Secretary, Scottish Office Environment Department, since 1988; b. 7.11.33, Nairn; m., Christine Joy Canaway; 1 s. Educ. Nairn Academy; Edinburgh University. Assistant Principal and Principal, Scottish Office, 1957-68; Principal, HM Treasury, 1968-71; Assistant Secretary, Scottish Office, 1972-79; Under Secretary, Industry Department for Scotland, 1979-88. Recreations: squash; chess. Address: (b.) New St. Andrew's House, Edinburgh, EH1 3SZ; T.-031-244 4052.

Laing, Marshall George, MA, LLB. Solicitor; Honorary Sheriff; b. 31.1.23, Aberdeen; m. Educ. Robert Gordon's

College, Aberdeen; Aberdeen University. Legal Assistant: Guild & Guild, WS, Edinburgh, 1949-50, Davidson & Garden, Aberdeen, 1950-55, Wilkinson & Grist, Hong Kong, 1955-59, J.L. Anderson & Co., Cupar, 1960-62; Partner: Craig and Geddes, Dumfries, 1962-76, Symons & MacDonald, Dumfries, 1976-88 (Consultant, since 1988). Recreation: golf. Address: (h.) 3 Richmond Avenue, Dumfries; T.-Dumfries 53871.

Laing, Robin, BSc. Director, Scottish Association for Mental Health, since 1991; Mental Health Worker, since 1986; b. 12.2.53, Edinburgh; m., Jan; 1 s.; 2 d. Educ. Bathgate Academy; Edinburgh University. Lothian Allelon Society, 1981-86; Scottish Association for Mental Health, since 1986. Address: (h.) 4 Cliftonhall Mains, Newbridge, Edinburgh, EH28 8LQ; T.-031-229 9687.

Laird, Alexander Peddie, BL, SSC, NP. Consultant, Bell & Scott, WS, Edinburgh; b. 14.6.24, Edinburgh; m., Elizabeth Anne Melrose; 2 d. Educ. Daniel Stewart's College, Edinburgh; Edinburgh University. Joined Army, 1943; commissioned, Royal Artillery; served with 51 (Highland) Division, 1944, and with 6th Airborne Division, 1944-46, in Europe and Palestine; served with Air Observation Post, Royal Artillery, 1946-47, in Palestine; demobilised as Captain, 1947; set up in private practice, 1951. Elder, Cramond Kirk (former Session Clerk). Recreations: golf; walking; gardening. Address: (h.) 2 Barnton Avenue, Edinburgh, EH4 6AP.

Laird, David Logan, FRICS, JP, DL. Solicitor; Partner, Thorntons WS, since 1985; Chartered Surveyor and Consultant, Smiths Gore; Member, Scottish National Heritage (Regional Chairman, North East Region), since 1992; b. 13.4.37, St. Andrews; m., Ann Ruth Thorley; 2 s.; 1 d. Educ. Bell Baxter School, Cupar; Edinburgh University; Edinburgh College of Agriculture. Partner, Clark Oliver Dewar & Webster, SSC, 1971-85. Deputy Lieutenant, Angus, since 1989; Member, Nature Conservancy Council for Scotland, 1990-92. Recreations: stalking; gardening; shooting; fishing. Address: (h.) West Memus, Forfar, Angus, DD8 3TY; T.-030 786 251.

Laird, Endell Johnston. Director and Editor-in-Chief, Daily Record and Sunday Mail; Editorial Director (SDR), Mirror Group Newspapers plc; b. 6.10.33, Forfar; m., June Stanners Keenan; 1 s.; 2 d. Educ. Forfar Academy. Worked for Dundee Courier, Daily Express, Evening Times, Daily Record. Recreations: golf; bridge. Address: Daily Record, Anderston Quay, Glasgow, G3 8DA.

Laird, James Steel, MA, LLB. Solicitor; Partner, McGrigor Donald & Co. (now McGrigor Donald) since 1961; b. 6.9.32, Kilmarnock; 2 d. Educ. Prestwick High School; Ayr Academy; Glasgow University. Served legal apprenticeship, McGrigor Donald & Co., from 1952. Chairman, Pollok School Company (Craigholme School). Recreation: golf. Address: (h.) 30 Norwood Drive, Whitecraigs, Glasgow.

Lally, Patrick James, JP, DL, HRGI. Leader, City of Glasgow District Council, since 1986 (Convenor, Policy and Resource Committee, since 1986); Chairman, Glasgow Cultural Enterprises, since 1988; b. Glasgow; m., Margaret Beckett McGuire; 2 s. Elected, Corporation of Glasgow, 1966-75 (Deputy Leader of Corporation, 1972-75); elected City of Glasgow Council, 1974-77, since 1980; City Treasurer, 1984-86; Director, Greater Glasgow Tourist Board and Convention Bureau; Director, Scottish Exhibition and Conference Centre; Director, Glasgow Local Enterprise Company; Hon. Member, Royal Glasgow Institute of Fine Arts; Director, Mayfest International Arts Festival; Director, Citizens Theatre; Chairman, Glasgow International Jazz Festival; Director, 7:84 Theatre Company. Recreations:

enjoying the arts; reading; watching TV and football. Address: (b.) City Chambers, George Square, Glasgow; T.-041-227 4100.

Lamb, Professor John, CBE, BSc, MSc, PhD, DSc, FInstP, FAcoustSocAmerica, HonFInstAcoustics, FIEE, FEng, FRSE. James Watt Professor of Electronics and Electrical Engineering, Glasgow University, since 1961; b. 26.9.22, Accrington; m., Margaret May Livesey; 2 s.; 1 d. Educ. Accrington Grammar School; Manchester University. Ministry of Supply, 1943-46; Lecturer, 1946-56, Reader, 1956-61, in Electrical Engineering, Imperial College, London University; Assistant Director, Department of Electrical Engineering, Imperial College, London University, 1958-61; Vice-Principal, Glasgow University, 1977-80; Member, National Electronics Council, UK, 1963-78; Member, Council for National Academic Awards, 1964-70; Chairman, Scottish Industry/University Liaison Committee in Engineering, 1969-71; President, British Society of Rheology, 1970-72; Council Member, Royal Society of Edinburgh, 1980-83, 1986-89, Vice President and Council Member, since 1989; Member, British National Committee for Radio Science, 1983-87; Scientific Adviser, Industry Department for Scotland, since 1987. Recreations: walking; wine-making; music. Address: (h.) 5 Cleveden Crescent, Glasgow, G12 OPD; T.-041-339 2101.

Lamb, Professor Joseph Fairweather, MB, ChB, BSc, PhD, FRCPEdin, FRSE, FRSA. Chandos Professor of Physiology, St. Andrews University, since 1969; Chairman, Save British Science Society, since 1986; Senior Secretary, Physiological Society, 1982-85; b. 18.7.28, Brechin; m., 1, Olivia Jane Horne; 3 s.; 1 d.; 2, Bridget Cecilia Cook; 2 s. Educ. Brechin High School; Edinburgh University. National Service, 1947-49; House Surgeon, Dumfries Royal Infirmary, 1955-56; House Physician, Eastern General Hospital, Edinburgh, 1956; Research Scholar, then Lecturer, Edinburgh University, 1957-61; Lecturer, then Senior Lecturer, Glasgow University, 1961-69; Editor, Journal of Physiology, 1968-74; Examiner, College of Surgeons of Edinburgh, Glasgow, London; Examiner, Universities of Aberdeen, Dundee, Edinburgh, Bristol, Leeds, Southampton, Lagos, Malaysia, etc. Publication: Essentials of Physiology, 1980. Recreations: boat-building; sailing; amateur radio. Address: (h.) Kenbrae, 23 Millbank, Cupar, KY15 5DP.

Lamb, Colonel Tom Bell Maxwell, OBE, CStJ, MA, FSA (Scot), DL. Retired Colonel, HM Forces; Deputy Lord Lieutenant, Argyll & Bute, since 1987; b. 23.11.18, Lanark; m., Sheina Barclay Dempster; 2 s.; 1 d. Educ. Lanark Secondary School; Heriot-Watt College. Commercial Bank of Scotland, 1935-38; Chartered Bank of India, 1938-39; Regular Officer, Queen's Own Cameron Highlanders, 1940-70; staff, Stirling University, 1970-75; Controller, The Burn, Edzell, 1975-84. Croix de Guerre, 1945; Meritorious Service Decoration (Singapore), 1964; mentioned in Despatches, 1945; Commander of St. John, 1982. Recreation: golf (Member, R. & A.). Address: (h.) Seafield, Kilchattan Bay, Isle of Bute; T.-Kilchattan Bay 682.

Lambert, John, FMS, FBIM, FIIM. Regional Manager Scotland, Chusid Lander, Human Resource Consultants, Glasgow, since 1986; b. 17.4.34, Blyth, Northumberland; m., Constance; 2 d. Educ. Blyth Grammar School; Rutherford College of Technology, Newcastle. Managerial appointments in general management, personnel and management services; Manager, O. & M. Consultancy Services, Co-operative Wholesale Society, 1969-72; Head, Personnel and Management Services, Burgh of Greenock, 1973-75; Director, Personnel and Management Services, Renfrew District Council, 1975-80; General Manager, RTITB, Livingston Motec, 1980-84; Director, Scotland and Northern Ireland, British Institute of Management, 1984-86. Captain,

Largs Golf Club, 1984-85; President, Associated Clubs of Clyde, 1986-87. Recreations: golf; photography; music. Address: (h.) 72 Greenock Road, Largs, Ayrshire; T.-0475 672402.

Lambie, David, BSc (Hons), DipEd, FEIS. MP (Labour), Cunninghame South, 1970-92; b. 13.7.25, Saltcoats; m., Netta Merrie; 1 s.; 4 d. Educ. Ardrossan Academy; Glasgow University; Geneva University. Teacher, Glagow Corporation, 1950-70. Secretary, All Party Committee for Energy Studies, since 1980; chaired Select Committee on Scottish Affairs, 1981-87; UK Member, Council of Europe and Western European Union, since 1987; Chairman, PLP Aviation Committee, since 1988. Recreation: watching junior football. Address: (h.) 11 Ivanhoe Drive, Saltcoats, Ayrshire, KA21 6LS; T.-0294 64843.

Lamond, June Rose. Member, Grampian Regional Council, since 1978; Member, Grampian Health Board, 1975-87; b. 12.6.33, Aberdeen; m., James A. Lamond, MP; 3 d. Educ. Aberdeen Demonstration School; Aberdeen College of Commerce. Member, Aberdeen District Council, 1974-77. Recreation: tennis. Address: (h.) 15 Belvidere Street, Aberdeen; T.-Aberdeen 638074.

Lamont, Colin C., MA, PhD. Headteacher, Ross High School, Tranent, since 1989; b. 6.10.44, Glasgow; m.; 2 s. Educ. Robert Gordon's College, Aberdeen; Aberdeen University; Edinburgh University. Teacher, Merchiston Castle School, Edinburgh; Principal Teacher, Robert Gordon's College, Aberdeen; Adviser in English, Renfrew Division, Strathclyde; Headteacher, Gracemount High School, Edinburgh. Address: (b.) Ross High School, Well Wynd, Tranent, East Lothian, EH33 2EQ; T.-0875 610433.

Lamont, Rev. Stewart Jackson, BSc, BD. Minister, Church of Scotland, since 1972; Freelance Journalist and Broadcaster (Religious Affairs Correspondent, Glasgow Herald), since 1980; b. 8.1.47, Broughty Ferry; m., Larisa V. Gaydakova. Educ. Grove Academy, Broughty Ferry; St. Andrews University. General Council Assessor, St. Andrews University Court, 1970-82; Producer, BBC Religious Department, 1972-80; Freelance Radio and Television Presenter and Producer; part-time Minister, Abernyte, 1980-82. Publications: The Third Angle, 1978; Is Anybody There?, 1980; Religion and the Supernatural (Co-author), 1985; Religion Inc. (Scientology), 1986; Scotland 2000 (BBC TV, 1987; Church and State, 1989; In Good Faith, 1989; The Swordbearer: John Knox, 1991; Glasgow Herald Book of Glasgow (Contributor). Winner, Scottish Schools Debating Competition, 1965; President of the Union, St. Andrews, 1969. Recreations: cooking; music; foreign travel. Address: 3 Doune Quadrant, Glasgow, G20 6DN; T.-041-946 3629.

Lamont, William David Dawson, CA, IRRV. Director of Finance, Argyll & Bute District Council, since 1990; b. 14.11.49, Irvine; m., Eleanor; 1 s.; 1 d. Educ. Irvine Royal Academy; Institute of Chartered Accountants of Scotland (Glasgow University). Trained and worked as chartered accountant with Alexander Sloan & Company, Glasgow, 1966-73; Depute Burgh Chamberlain, Royal Burgh of Irvine, 1973-75; Depute Director of Finance, Argyll & Bute District Council, 1975-90. Treasurer, Ardrishaig Parish Church. Recreations: family; travel; music; messing about in boats. Address: (b.) Department of Finance, Kilmory, Lochgilphead, PA31 8RT; T.-0546 604220.

Lamont-Brown, Raymond, MA, AMIET, MJS, FSA (Scot). Author and Broadcaster; Lecturer, Centre for External Services, St. Andrews University, since 1978, Centre for Continuing Education, Dundee University, since 1988; Founder, Japan Research Projects, since 1965; b. 20.9.39, Horsforth, Leeds; m., Dr. Elizabeth Moira McGregor. Educ.

Wheelwright Grammar School, Dewsbury; Bradford Technical College; SOAS; Nihon Daigaku, Japan. Honorary Secretary/Treasurer, Society of Authors in Scotland, 1982-89; Past President, St. Andrews Rotary Club; Vice-Chairman, St. Andrews Community Council, since 1988; Chairman, Arthritis Care Liaison Committee (Central, Fife and Tayside), since 1991; Member, Council, Arthritis Care, since 1991. Publications: 42 published books, including Discovering Fife; Phantoms of the Sea; The Life and Times of Berwick-upon-Tweed; The Life and Times of St. Andrews; Royal Murder Mysteries; Scottish Epitaphs; Scottish Superstitions; Scottish Traditions and Festivals. Address: (h.) Crawford House, 132 North Street, St. Andrews, Fife, KY16 9AF; T.-0334 74897.

Lamprell-Jarrett, Peter Neville, KCSG, KCHS, PPIAAS, FIAS, FFB, FSA(Scot), FRSA. Partner, Archard & Partners, Architects and Surveyors, since 1954; b. 23.6.19, Margate; m., Kathleen Furner; 1 s.; 1 d. Educ. Vernon House Preparatory School; Cliftonville College. Architectural Assistant, LCC (later GLC) Housing Department, 1947-49; Deputy Controller of Works, Land Settlement Association, 1950-54; President, Incorporated Association of Architects and Surveyors, 1967-68; Kt. Commander, Equestrian Order Holy Sepulchre of Jerusalem, 1974; Kt. Commander, Pontifical Order of St. Gregory the Great, 1975; responsible for design of many Catholic schools and churches; Freeman, City of London; Life Vice President, London Caledonian Catholic Association; Past Chairman, Archdiocese of Westminster Catholic Parents and Electors Association. Recreations: painting; walking; fishing; classical music. Address: (h.) Carrick House, Carrick Castle, by Lochgoil, Argyll, PA24 8AF; T.-Lochgoilhead 394.

Landale, David William Neil, MA (Oxon), DL. Secretary and Keeper of the Records, Duchy of Cornwall, since 1987; b. 27.5.34, London; m., (Norah) Melanie; 3 s. Educ. Eton College; Balliol College, Oxford. Black Watch, Royal Highland Regiment, 1952-54; Jardine Matheson & Co. Ltd., 1958-75, served in Hong Kong, Thailand, Taiwan and Japan (Director, 1967-75); Director, Matheson & Co. Ltd., 1975; Chairman, T.C. Farries & Co. Ltd., 1982. Member, Royal Company of Archers, Queen's Bodyguard for Scotland, since 1966. Recreations: all countryside pursuits; theatre; reading (history). Address: (h.) Dalswinton, Dumfries; T.-0387 74 208.

Lander, Ronald, BSc. Chairman and Managing Director: Scotlander plc, since 1985, Scetlander Ltd., since 1986; Director, Centre for Entrepreneurial Development, Glasgow University, 1985-88; b. 5.8.42, Glasgow; m., Elizabeth Stirling; 2 s. Educ. Allan Glen's School; Glasgow University. Chairman and Managing Director, Lander Grayburn & Co. Limited, 1970-83; Deputy Managing Director, Lander Alarm Company (Scotland) Limited, 1975-79; Managing Director, Lander Alarms Limited and Lander Alarms (Scotland) Limited, 1979-85; Chairman, Lander & Jess Limited, 1983-87. Member, CBI Scottish Council, 1977-83 and 1984-90; founding Chairman, CBI Scotland's Smaller Firms' Working Group, 1977-80; founder Member, CBI Industrial Policy Committee, London, 1978-86; Chairman, Scottish Fire Prevention Council, 1979-80; Member, Glasgow University Appointments Committee, since 1979; CBI Representative, Home Office/CBI/TUC Joint Committee on Prison Industries, 1980-87; Industrial Member, Understanding British Industry, Scotland, 1981-89; Member, Council, Scottish Business School, 1982-87; Director, British Security Industry Association Council, 1984-85; Governor, Scottish Sports Aid Foundation, 1985-88; Vice-Chairman, CBI Scotland Education and Training Committee, 1986-87; Member: Kincraig Committee (review of parole system and related matters), 1987-89, Manpower Services Committee for Scotland (later the Training Agency), 1987-88; founder Chairman, Local Employer Network (LENS) Scottish Co-ordinating Committee, 1987; Chairman, CBI Scotland Education and Training Committee, 1987-89; Director, SCOTVEC, since 1987; Member, CBI Business/Education Task Force (the Cadbury Report), 1988; Member, Scottish Consultative Council on the Curriculum, 1988-91; Vice-Convener, Scottish Education/Industry Committee, 1988-91; founder Member, Glasgow Action, since 1985; Member, Secretary of State for Scotland's Crime Prevention Committee, 1984-87; Companion IEE, 1986; Board Member, Glasgow Development Agency, since 1991; Visiting Professor, Glasgow University, since 1991; National Judge, National Training Awards, 1989-91. Address: (b.) 1 Bowmont Gardens, Glasgow, G12 9LR; T.-041-357 1659.

Lane, Professor David Philip, BSc, PhD. Professor of Molecular Oncology, Department of Biochemistry, Dundee University, since 1990; Director, Cancer Research Campaign Cell Transformation Group, since 1990; b. 1.7.52, London; m., Professor Ellen Birgitte Lang; 1 s.; 1 d. Educ. John Fisher School, Purley; University College, London. Lecturer in Zoology, then Lecturer in Biochemistry, Imperial College, London; Principal Scientist, Imperial Cancer Research Fund, South Mimms. Publications: (book) Antibodies, a laboratory manual; 100 articles. Recreations: walking; tennis; motor bikes. Address: (b.) CRC Laboratories, Dundee University, Dundee, DD1 4HN; T.-0382 307920.

Lang, Lt.-Gen. Sir Derek, KCB (1967), DSO (1944), MC (1941), DL; b. 7.10.13, Guildford; 1 s.; 1 d. Educ. Wellington College; RMC, Sandhurst. Director of Army Training, 1964-66; GOC-in-C, Scottish Command, and Governor of Edinburgh Castle, 1966-69. President, Army Cadet Force Association (Scotland), 1974-86. Recreations: golf; fishing; shooting; music. Address: (h.) Templeland, Kirknewton, Midlothian, EH27 8DJ; T.0506 883211.

Lang, Ian Bruce, OStJ, BA. MP (Conservative) Galloway and Upper Nithsdale, since 1983 (Galloway, 1979-83); Secretary of State for Scotland, since 1990 (Minister of State, Scottish Office, 1987-90, Parliamentary Under Secretary of State, Scottish Office, 1986-87, and at Department of Employment, 1986); b. 27.6.40, Glasgow; m., Sandra Caroline Montgomerie; 2 d. Educ. Lathallan School; Rugby School; Sidney Sussex College, Cambridge. Member, Select Committee on Scottish Affairs, 1979-81; Honorary President, Scottish Young Conservatives, 1982-84; Trustee, Glasgow Savings Bank and West of Scotland TSB, 1969-82; Lord Commissioner of HM Treasury, 1983-86; Scottish Whip, 1981-83; Vice-Chairman, Scottish Conservative Party, 1983-87; Member, Queen's Bodyguard for Scotland (Royal Company of Archers), since 1974; Insurance Broker and Company Director, 1962-81. Address (b.) House of Commons, Westminster, London, SW1A OAA.

Langford, Professor David Anthony, MCIOB, MSc, MPhil, MBIM. Barr Professor of Construction, Strathclyde University, since 1991; b. 6.5.50, Notingham; m., Victoria; 1 d. Educ. Barstable School, Basildon; Bristol Polytechnic; Aston University; Cranfield School of Management. MSc Course Director, Department of Building Technology, Brunel University, 1975; Director of Postgraduate Studies, Bath University, 1987. Address: (b.) Department of Civil Engineering, Strathclyde University, Glasgow, G4 0NG; T.-041-552 4400.

Lansdowne, 8th Marquess of (George John Charles Mercer Nairne Petty-Fitzmaurice), PC (1964); b. 27.11.12; m., 1, Barbara Chase (deceased); 2 s.; 1 d.; 1 d. deceased; 2, Polly Carnegie (m. diss.); 3, Gillian Ann Morgan (deceased). Educ. Eton; Christ Church, Oxford. Served Second World War (Major, 1944); Lord-in-Waiting to The Queen, 1957-58; Minister of State for Colonial Affairs, 1962-64, and for

Commonwealth Relations, 1963-64; Member, Queen's Bodyguard for Scotland (Royal Company of Archers); Chairman, Victoria League in Scotland, 1952-56. Address: (h.) Meikleour House, Perthshire.

Larkin, Professor Maurice John Milner, MA, PhD. Professor of Modern European History, Edinburgh University, since 1976; b. 12.8.32, Harrow on the Hill; m., Enid Thelma Lowe; 1 s.; 1 d. Educ. St. Philip's Grammar School, Birmingham; Trinity College, Cambridge. Assistant Lecturer, then Lecturer, Glasgow University, 1958-65; Lecturer, then Senior Lecturer, then Reader, Kent University, 1965-76. Publications: Gathering Pace: Continental Europe 1870-1945, 1969; Church and State after the Dreyfus Affair, 1974; Man and Society in Nineteenth-Century Realism, 1977; France since the Popular Front, 1988. Recreations: bird-watching; music; films. Address: (b.) History Department, Edinburgh University, Edinburgh, EH8 9JY; T.-031-650 3754.

Larner, Professor John Patrick, MA, FRHistA. Titular Professor of History, Glasgow University, since 1979; b. 24.3.30, London; m., Christina Ross (deceased); 2 s. Educ. Finchley Grammar School; New College, Oxford. Rome Medieval Scholar, British School of Rome, 1954-57; Lecturer, Glasgow University, 1957-79. Publications: Lords of Romagna, 1965; Culture and Society in Italy, 1971; Florentine Society 1382-1494, 1972; Italy in the Age of Dante, 1980. Recreations: hill-walking; photography. Address: (b.) Department of Medieval History, The University, Glasgow, G12 8QQ; T.-041-339 8855.

Last, Professor Frederick Thomas, DSc, ARCS, FRSE. Applied Biologist; Honorary Professor, Forestry and Natural Resources, Edinburgh University, since 1972; Visiting Professor, Agriculture and Environmental Science, Newcastle upon Tyne University, since 1986; b. 5.2.28, Wembley; m., Pauline Mary Cope; 2 s. Educ. Haberdashers' Aske's Hampstead School; Imperial College of Science and Technology, London. Rothamsted Experimental Station, Herts, 1950-61; Chief Plant Pathologist to Government of Sudan, 1956-58; Head, Mycology and Bacteriology, Glasshouse Crops Research Institute, Sussex, 1961-69; Visiting Professor, Pennsylvania State University, 1969-70; Member of Directorate, Institute of Terrestrial Ecology, Midlothian, 1970-86; Commissioner, Red Deer Commission, 1981-86. Publications: Tree Physiology and Yield Improvement (Joint Editor), 1976; Land and its Uses, Actual and Potential: An Environmental Appraisal (Joint Editor), 1986; Acidic Deposition, Its Nature and Impacts (Joint Editor). Recreations: gardening; philately; travelling. Address: (h.) Furuly, Seton Mains, Longniddry, East Lothian, EH32 0PG; T.-0875 52102.

Last, Professor Rex William, BA, MA, PhD, FRSA. Professor of Modern Languages, Dundee University, since 1981; b. 30.6.40, Ipswich; m., Oksana S.; 3 s.; 1 d. Educ. Northgate Grammar School, Ipswich; Hull University. Lecturer, Senior Lecturer, Reader in Modern German Literature, Hull University; Honorary Life Member, Association for Literary and Linguistic Computing; Director, Lochee Publications. Publications: books on Hans Arp, Erich Kastner, E.M. Remarque, German Dadaist literature, computer applications in language teaching, study skills, PC systems programming, computer security. Address: (h.) Oak Villa, New Alyth, PH11 8NN; T.-082 83 2154.

Lauderdale, Earl of (Patrick Francis Maitland), BA (Hons) (Oxon). Company Director; b. 17.3.11, Walsall; m., Stanka Lozanitch; 2 s.; 2 d. Educ. Lancing College; Brasenose College, Oxford. Journalist, Fleet Street, 1934-39; War Correspondent, Poland, 1939; Balkans/Danubian Correspondent, The Times, 1939-41; War Correspondent, the

Pacific, News Chronicle, 1941-43; Foreign Office, 1943-45; Editor, The Fleet Street Letter Service, 1945-51; MP (Conservative), Lanark, 1951-59; Peer, since 1968; Chairman, Lords Energy Committee, 1974-79; Founder/Deputy Chairman, Parliamentary Group for Energy Studies, since 1983; Guardian, Shrine of Our Lady of Walsingham, since 1963 (now Emeritus); Chairman, Parliamentary 'Church in Danger' Group, since 1988; Hereditary Bearer of the National Flag of Scotland. Recreations: reading; travel; pilgrimages to St. Mary's, Haddington. Address: (h.) 12 St. Vincent Street, Edinburgh; T.-031-556 5692.

Laughland, Andrew William, FRFPSGlas, FRCSEdin, FRCOG. Consultant Obstetrician and Gynaecologist, Glasgow Royal Maternity Hospital and Victoria Infirmary, since 1963; b. 8.2.27, Glasgow; m., Anne Packe Johnstone. Educ. High School of Glasgow; Glasgow University. DADMS 1st Infantry Division, 1952-53; Tutor, Department of Obstetrics and Gynaecology, Liverpool University, 1958-59. Member, Council, Royal College of Obstetricians and Gynaecologists, 1970-76. Recreations: hill-walking; fishing; gardening. Address: (h.) 27 Sutherland Avenue, Glasgow, G41 4HG; T.-041-427 1704.

Laurenson, Arthur Bruce, OBE, FRSA. Consultant; Chairman, Shetland Catch Ltd., since 1992; Director, Shetland Enterprise Company, since 1991; Director, Blackhill Industrial Estate Ltd., since 1980; b. 22.7.31, Lerwick; m., Janet S. Mullay; 2 d. Educ. Anderson High School. Assistant Clerk and Collector, Lerwick Harbour Trust, 1947-64; appointed Clerk and Treasurer, 1968; General Manager and Clerk, 1972; Consultant, since 1991. Honorary Sheriff; Member, Lerwick Lifeboat Committee. Recreations: crofting; breeding Shetland ponies; gardening. Address: (h.) Vatnagarth, 2 Lovers Loan, Lerwick, Shetland, ZE1 0BA; T.-0595 2799.

Laurenson, James Tait, FCA. Managing Director, Adam & Company Group PLC, since 1984; Non-Executive Director: United Scientific Holding PLC, since 1972, The Life Association of Scotland, since 1991; Chairman, Nippon Assets Investments SA, since 1983; b. 15.3.41, Farnborough; m., Hilary Josephine; 1 s.; 3 d. Educ. Eton College; Magdalene College, Cambridge. Ivory & Sime PLC: joined 1968; Partner, 1970; Director, 1975; left 1983; Chairman, Tayburn Design Group Limited, 1983-89.Deputy Chairman, Erskine Stewart's Melville Governing Council, since 1990. Recreations: tennis; gardening; skiing; shooting; stalking. Address: (b.) 22 Charlotte Square, Edinburgh, EH2 4DF; T.-031-225 8484.

Laurie, Ian Cameron, FIH, MRSH. Chief Executive, Bearsden and Milngavie District Council, since 1985; b. 18.1.40, Bishopbriggs; m., Jean; 1 s. Educ. Bishopbriggs High School; Glasgow School of Building. Accountancy Assistant, then Housing Manager, Burgh of Kirkintilloch, 1963-74; Director of Housing, Strathkelvin District Council, 1974-85. Clerk to Lord Lieutenant of Dunbartonshire. Recreations: bowling; curling; music; reading; calligraphy. Address: (b.) 100 Milngavie Road, Bearsden, Glasgow, G61 2TQ; T.-041-942 2262.

Laurie, Thomas, OBE, FRICS. Chartered Quantity Surveyor; b. 11.11.38, Wishaw; m., Jennifer Rose; 1 s.; 2 d. Educ. Hamilton Academy; Glasgow College of Technology; College of Estate Management. Member, Scottish Arts Council, 1977-84; Council Member, Scottish Civic Trust, since 1987; Council Member, John Wheatley College, Glasgow, since 1990; Chairman, Glasgow Folk and Traditional Arts Trust; Director, Glasgow Mayfest; Chairman, Workshop and Artists Studio Provision (Scotland) Ltd. Recreations: traditional singing; hill-walking; theatre; col-

lecting contemporary art. Address: (h.) 21 Dunglass Avenue, Scotstoun, Glasgow, G14 9ED; T.-041-959 4025.

Laver, Professor John David Michael Henry, MA (Hons), DipPh, PhD, FBA, FIOA. Professor of Phonetics, Centre for Speech Technology Research, Edinburgh University, since 1985; Director, Centre for Speech Technology Research, Edinburgh University, 1984-89, Chairman, since 1989; b. 20.1.38, Nowshera, Pakistan; m., Sandy Hutcheson; 3 s.; 1 d. Educ. Churcher's College, Petersfield; Edinburgh University. Assistant Lecturer, then Lecturer in Phonetics, Ibadan University, 1963-66 (Exchange Lecturer, Edinburgh University, 1964-65); Lecturer, then Senior Lecturer in Phonetics, Edinburgh University, 1966-80; Reader in Phonetics, 1980-84; Visiting Assistant Professor, Department of Linguistics, University of California, 1971; Visiting Research Fellow, Macquarie University, Sydney, 1982; Information Technology Fellowship, Edinburgh, 1983-84. Publications: Communication in Face to Face Interaction (Joint Editor), 1972; Phonetics in Linguistics (Joint Editor), 1973; Voice Quality, 1979; The Phonetic Description of Voice Quality, 1980; The Cognitive Representation of Speech (Joint Editor), 1981; The Prospect of Future Speech Technology (Co-author), 1987; Proceedings of the European Conference on Speech Technology (Co-Editor), 1987; Aspects of Speech Technology (Co-Editor), 1988; The Gift of Speech. Address: (b.) Centre for Speech Technology Research, Edinburgh University, 80 South Bridge, Edinburgh; T.-031-650 2784.

Laverock, Edward, MA, LLB. Retired Solicitor; b. 21.10.19, Dunlop; m., Helen Moffat Harries Mackison; 1 s.; 1 d. Educ. Hutchesons' Grammar School, Glasgow; Glasgow University. Partner, J. & W. Buchan, Peebles, 1945-86 (Senior Partner, 1954-86); Town Clerk, Peebles, 1948-75. Honorary Sheriff, since 1983. Address: (h.) Craigmount, Bonnington Road, Peebles; T.-0721 20314.

Law, Graham Couper, MA (Cantab), ARSA, RIBA, FRIAS. Former Partner, The Law & Dunbar-Nasmith Partnership, Architects; b. 28.9.23, Glasgow; m., Isobel Evelyn Alexander Drysdale; 1 s.; 3 d. Educ. Merchiston Castle School; Kings College, Cambridge. Royal Engineers, 1941-46; ARIBA, 1951; Council Member: Edinburgh Architectural Association, 1964-69, Royal Incorporation of Architects in Scotland, 1965-67; Member: Architects Registration Council, 1967-75, ARCUK Professional Purposes Committee, 1967-73; Chairman, Workshop and Artists Studio Provision (Scotland) Ltd., 1977-81; Member, RIAS Investigation Committee, 1979-85; Associate, Royal Scottish Academy, 1980. Recreations: drawing; skiing; fishing; shooting. Address: (b.) 16 Dublin Street, Edinburgh, EH1 3RE; T.-031-556 8631.

Law, Hamish T., BSc, PhD. Senior Lecturer, Department of Orthopaedic Surgery, Edinburgh University, since 1982; Vice-President, International Society for Hybrid Microelectronics, 1986-89; b. 7.7.27, Dundee; m., Emma Emmerson. Educ. Elgin Academy; Edinburgh University. Research Laboratory, British Thomson-Houston Co. Ltd., Rugby; Ferranti Ltd., Edinburgh (Chief Engineer, Valve Department); Varian Associates, Palo Alto, California (Senior Scientist); Ferranti Ltd., Edinburgh (Manager, Microelectronics Department); Director, Orthopaedic Bio-Engineering Unit, Princess Margaret Rose Hospital, Edinburgh; Member, Kirk Session, Cramond Kirk; President, Rotary Club of Edinburgh, 1989-90. Publication: Upper Limb Deficiencies in Children - Surgical Prosthetic and Orthotic Management; numerous papers. Recreations: sailing; curling; music. Address: (h.) 8 Learmonth Terrace, Edinburgh, EH4 1PQ; T.-031-332 5795.

Law, James, QC, MA, LLB. Queen's Counsel, since 1971; b. 7.6.26, Irvine; m., Kathleen Margaret Gibson (see Kathleen Margaret Law); 2 s.; 1 d. Educ. Kilmarnock Academy; Girvan High School; Glasgow University. Admitted to Faculty of Advocates, 1951; Advocate Depute, 1957-64; Member, Criminal Injuries Compensation Board, since 1970. Address: 7 Gloucester Place, Edinburgh, EH3 6EE; T.-031-225 2974.

Lawrence, John Henry, FCA. Honorary Sheriff, Kilmarnock; b. 4.5.05, Cardiff; m., Kathleen Clare Craig; 3 s. Educ. Cardiff High School. Senior Clerk, Deloitte & Co., CA, London, 1929-37; Assistant Secretary, Richardsons Westgarth & Co., Wallsend, 1938-42; Director and Secretary, Glenfield & Kennedy Ltd., Kilmarnock, 1942-70; former Council Member, Glasgow Management Association; Past Chairman, Glasgow Branch, Institute of Office Management; former Director, Kilmarnock Chamber of Industries; former Member, Taxation Committee, CBI; former Committee Member, Athlone Foundation; former Secretary and President, Kilmarnock Rotary Club; former Director, Ayrshire Branch, British Red Cross Society; former Chairman, Ayrshire Branch, English Speaking Union. Recreations: music; golf; bridge. Address: (h.) 10 Wilson Avenue, Troon, KA10 7AF; T.-0292 312776.

Lawrie, Frank James. Deputy Director, Historic Buildings and Monuments, Scotland, since 1988; b. 30.10.45, Edinburgh; m., Ann Macamon Kerr; 2 s.; 1 d. Educ. Royal High School, Edinburgh. Executive Officer, Department of Agriculture and Fisheries for Scotland, 1964-70; Higher Executive Officer, Scottish Office Finance Division, 1970-78; Senior Executive Officer, 1978-81; Principal, Department of Agriculture and Fisheries for Scotland, 1981-88. Recreations: railway archaeology; cricket; golf. Address: (b.) 20 Brandon Street, Edinburgh, EH3 5RA; T.-031-244 3078.

Lawrie, Nigel Gilbert, BSc, PhD. Head Teacher, Port Glasgow High School, since 1985; b. 2.6.47, Edinburgh; m., Janet Clark Warnock; 1 d. Educ. Bearsden Academy; Strathclyde University. Chemistry Teacher, Hermitage Academy, Helensburgh, 1972-75; Principal Teacher of Chemistry, Dunoon Grammar School, 1975-81; Assistant Head Teacher, Garnock Academy, 1981-84; Depute Head Teacher, Castlehead High School, Paisley, 1984-85. Chief Moderator for Social and Vocational Skills, Scottish Examination Board, 1985-88; President, Scottish Association for Teachers of Social and Vocational Skills, 1984-88. Recreations: reading; gardening; football. Address: (b.) Port Glasgow High School, Marloch Avenue, Port Glasgow; T.-0475 705921.

Lawson, Alexander Adamson Hutt, MD, FRCPEdin. Consultant Physician, Fife Health Board, since 1969; Honorary Senior Lecturer, Edinburgh University, since 1979; Medical Adviser, War Pensions Appeal Tribunal, Scotland, since 1979; b. 30.7.37, Dunfermline; m., Barbara Helen Donnet; 3 s.; 1 d. Educ. Dunfermline High School; Edinburgh University. Consultant Member, Clinical Teaching Staff, Faculty of Medicine, Edinburgh University, since 1971; Postgraduate Tutor in Medicine, West Fife, 1973-81; Medical Assessor, General Medical Council, since 1982; Member, Fife Health Board, 1981-91 (Vice-Chairman, 1989-91); President, Scottish Society of Physicians, 1989-90; President, West Fife Medical Society, 1982-83; Life Trustee, Carnegie Dunfermline Trust and Carnegie United Kingdom Hero Fund, since 1980; Life Trustee, Carnegie United Kingdom Trust, since 1983; Member, Committee of Safety, Efficacy and Adverse Reactions of Drugs (Committee, Safety of Medicines, DHSS, London), 1982-84; Member, Specialist Advisory Committee (UK) HCMT - General (Internal) Medicine, 1984-88; UK Representative to European Union of Medical Specialties, Monospecialty Committee for General Medicine, since 1986. Publications: Common Acute

Poisonings; Acute Poisoning in Principles and Practice of Medicine; Toxicology and Drug Monitoring in Chemical Diagnosis of Disease; scientific papers. Address: (h.) 2 Park Avenue, Dunfermline, Fife, KY12 7HX; T.-Dunfermline 726435.

Lawson, Rev. Alexander Hamilton, THM, ThD, FPhS. Minister, Kilbowie Parish Church, Clydebank, 1955-88; b. 16.9.21, Toronto, Canada; m., Martha Stevenson Macdonald; 1 s.; 1 d. Educ. Coatbridge Senior Secondary School; Glasgow University and Trinity College; American Bible College, Chicago; Metropolitan College of Law, St. Albans. RAF, 1941-46; Minister, Prestonpans Grange, 1950-55; Moderator, Dumbarton Presbytery, 1970-71; Member, Education Committee, General Assembly, eight years; served 15 years on Dunbartonshire Education Committee (Chairman, General Sub-Committee, 1967-70); Joint Chairman, Religious Education/EIS Group, 1963-74; Governor, Hamilton College of Education, 1967-72; Member, British Atlantic Committee and Representative Speaker, International Conferences, Wolfheze, 1983, and Amsterdam, 1986;Leader, fact-finding mission to South AFrica, 1986. Publication: The Moral Challenge of Defence Controversy in Our Nuclear Era. Recreations: watercolour and oil paintings; Probus; Vice-President, Riverside Church Men's Bowling Club; President and Secretary, Trinity College 1950 Club; reading; gardening. Address: 1 Glebe Park, Mansewood, Dumbarton, G82 3HE; T.-Dumbarton 42030.

Lawson, David Hamilton, MD, FRCPEdin, FRCPGlas, FFPM, FCP. Consultant Physician, Glasgow Royal Infirmary, since 1973; Visiting Professor, Strathclyde University, since 1976; Visiting Scientist, Boston Collaborative Drug Surveillance Program, USA, since 1970; b. 27.5.39, Glasgow; m., Alison Diamond; 3 s. Educ. High School of Glasgow; Glasgow University. Junior doctor positions, Royal Infirmary and Western Infirmary, Glasgow; Senior Scientist, Boston Collaborative Drug Surveillance Program, Boston. Committee on Review of Medicines, DHSS, London: Member, since 1979, Vice Chairman, 1985-86, Chairman, since 1987; Member, Committee on Safety of Medicines, DofH, London, since 1987; Member, Health Services Research Committee, Office of Chief Scientist, Scottish Home and Health Department, 1984-88. Publications: Clinical Pharmacy and Hospital Drug Management (Co-Editor); Current Medicine 2 (Editor), Current Medicine 3 (Editor). Recreations: hill-walking; ornithology; photography. Address: (h.) 43 Drumlin Drive, Milngavie, Glasgow, G62 6NF; T.-041-956 2962.

Lawson, Fettes Grafton. Retired Solicitor (Lawson, Coull & Duncan, Dundee); Honorary Sheriff, Tayside, Central and Fife at Dundee; b. 27.6.18, Dundee; m., Lily Norrie Latto; 1 s.; 2 d. Educ. Alloa Academy. Apprenticeship, 1937 (War Service, 1939-45); qualified, 1946; retired, 1987. Dean, Faculty of Procurators and Solicitors in Dundee, 1973-75. Recreations: reading; walking; gardening. Address: (h.) 2 Taypark, 30 Dundee Road, West Ferry, Dundee, DD5 1LX.

Lawson, John Philip, BSc, FEIS. Chairman, Scottish Youth Hostels Association, since 1980; Headteacher, St. Joseph's School, Linlithgow, since 1974; b. 19.8.37, Bathgate; m., Diana Mary Neal. Educ. St. Mary's Academy, Bathgate; Edinburgh University; Moray House College of Education. Teacher, West Lothian, since 1962; Member, West Lothian Children's Panel, 1972-81; Member, SYHA National Executive, since 1966; Vice-Chairman, SYHA, 1975-80; Member, International Youth Hostel Federation delegation to China, 1984; awarded Richard Schirrmann Medal by German Youth Hostels Association, 1988; a Director, Scottish Rights of Way Society Ltd., since 1979; a Director, Gatliff Hebridean Hostels Trust, since 1988; President, West Lothian Headteachers Association, 1986-88; President, Federation of

Youth Hostels Associations in the European Community, since 1990. Recreations: hill-walking; classical music; reading. Address: (h.) 25 Bolam Drive, Burntisland, Fife, KY3 9HP; T.-0592 872132.

Lawson, Rev. Kenneth Charles, MA. National Adult Adviser (Group Relations), Department of Education, Church of Scotland, since 1984; b. 24.12.34, Agadir, Morocco; m., Mary Elizabeth Anderson; 3 s. Educ. Royal High School, Edinburgh; Preston Lodge School; Stranraer High School; Edinburgh University. Assistant Minister, Brechin Cathedral; Sub-Warden, St. Ninian's Training Centre, Crieff; Minister: Paisley South, Cumbernauld St. Mungo. Recreations: walking; reading; painting. Address: (b.) Group Relations Office, St. Colm's Education Centre and College, 20 Inverleith Terrace, Edinburgh, EH3 5NS; T.-031-332 0343.

Laybourn, Professor Peter John Robert, MA (Cantab), PhD. Titular Professor in Electronics and Electrical Engineering, Glasgow University, since 1985, and Head, Department of Electronics and Electrical Engineering; b. 30.7.42, London; m., Ann Elizabeth Chandler; 2 d. Educ. William Hulme's Grammar School; Bristol Grammar School; Clare College, Cambridge. Research Assistant, Leeds University, 1963-66; Research Fellow, Southampton University, 1966-71; Lecturer, then Senior Lecturer, then Reader, Glasgow University, 1971-85; Honorary Editor, Part J, IEE Proceedings. Recreations: sailing; boat-building; plant collecting. Address: (h.) Ashgrove, Waterfoot Row, Thorntonhall, Glasgow; T.-041-644 3992.

Lazarowicz, Mark. Member, Edinburgh District Council, since 1980 (Leader, Labour Group, since 1986). Address: (h.) 2/5 Clovenstone Gardens, Edinburgh EH14 3ED; T.-031-442 2196.

Leach, Donald, BSc, FIMA, CPhys, MInstP, CEng, MBCS, FRSA. Principal, Queen Margaret College, Edinburgh, since 1985; b. 24.6.31, Croydon; m., June Valentine Reid; 2 s.; 1 d. Educ. John Ruskin Grammar School, Croydon; London University (External). Pilot Officer, Navigator, RAF, 1951-53; Physicist, British Jute Trade Research Association, Dundee, 1955-65; Technical Director, A.R. Bolton & Co. Ltd., Edinburgh, 1965-66; Napier College: Lecturer and Senior Lecturer in Mathematics, 1966-68, Head, Department of Mathematics and Computing, 1968-74, Assistant Principal/Dean, Faculty of Science, 1974-85. Member, South-Eastern Regional Hospital Board, 1969-74, and Lothian Health Board, 1977-81; Member: Scottish Health Service Common Services Agency's Advisory Panel on Information Processing, 1979-86, Scottish Health Service Planning Council's Information and Computer Systems Advisory Group, 1981-86, Computer Steering Committee (Chairman), 1981-86; Institute of Mathematics: Council Member, 1978-81, Chairman, Scottish Branch, 1980-83, Member, Joint IMA-Royal Society of London Mathematical Education Committee, 1981-84; Council for National Academic Awards: Member, Combined Studies Science Board, 1975-79, Science Technology and Society Board, 1979-82 (Chairman, 1981-82), Interfaculty Studies Board, 1981-85, Committee for Science and Technology, 1981-84, Committee for Scotland, since 1987; Chairman, Science Technology and Society Association, 1982-85; Chairman, Mathematics and Computing Course Committees, SCOTEC/SCOTBEC, 1981-85; Hon. Secretary, Committee of Principals and Directors of Scottish Central Institutions (COPADOCI), 1985-88, Chairman, since 1988; Member, Council for Professions Supplmentary to Medicine, since 1985; Member, Executive, Scottish Council (Development and Industry), since 1987; Member, Board of Directors, Edinburgh Chamber of Commerce, since 1991; Liberal candidate, West Edinburgh, 1959, East Fife, 1961; Labour candidate, West Perthshire, 1970. Recreations: badminton; walking; skiing; cooking.

Address: (h.) 8 Ravelston House Park, Edinburgh, EH4 3LU; T.-031-332 3826.

Leake, Professor Bernard Elgey, BSc (Hons), PhD, DSc. Professor of Geology and Keeper of the Geological Collections in the Hunterian Museum, Glasgow University, since 1974; b. 29.7.32, Grimsby; m., Gillian Dorothy Dobinson; 5 s. Educ. Wirral Grammar School; Liverpool University. Leverhulme Postdoctorate Research Fellow, Liverpool University, 1955-57; Lecturer in Geology, then Reader, Bristol University, 1957-74. Lyell Medal, Geological Society, 1977; President, Geological Society, 1986-88, Treasurer, 1981-85 and since 1989. FRSE. Address: (b.) Glasgow University, Glasgow; T.-041-339 8855, Ext. 5345.

Leckie, George Andrew, BA (Hons), CA. Partner, Ernst & Young, CA, since 1979; b. 8.10.48, Giffnock; m., Robyn; 4 d. Educ. Stirling High School; Strathclyde University. Joned predecessor firm of Ernst & Young in Glasgow as trainee; qualified CA, 1972; became Technical Manager for Scotland; transferred to E. & Y., Dundee, 1978; became Partner, 1979. Member, Council, Institute of Chartered Accountants of Scotland, 1988-91. Recreations: golf; cooking; photography; DIY. Address: (b.) City House, 16 Overgate, Dundee, DD1 9PN; T.-0382 202561.

LeComber, Peter George, BSc, PhD, DSc, FInstPhys, FIEE, FRSE. Harris Professor of Physics, Dundee University; b. 19.2.41, Ilford, Essex; m., Joy Smith; 1 s.; 1 d. Educ. Leicester University. Research Fellow, Purdue University, USA, 1965-67; SERC Research Fellow, Leicester University, 1967-68; Lecturer, Dundee University, 1968. Awarded Maxwell Premium by IEE, 1983; Duddell Medal, I. of P., 1984; Rank Prize for Opto-Electronics, 1988; Consultant to a number of companies. Recreations: fishing; music; photography. Address: (b.) Department of Applied Physics and Electronic and Manufacturing Engineering, Dundee University, Dundee, DD1 4HN; T.-Dundee 23181.

Lederer, Peter J. Managing Director, Gleneagles Hotels plc, since 1987; General Manager, The Gleneagles Hotel, since 1983; Director, Guinness Enterprises, since 1987; b. 30.11.50; m., Marilyn Ruth MacPhail. Four Seasons Hotels, Canada, 1972-79; Vice President, Wood Wilkings Ltd., Toronto, 1979-81; General Manager, Plaza Group of Hotels, Toronto, 1981-83. Governor: Ardvreck School, Crieff, Duncan of Jordanston College of Art, Dundee; Director, Scottish Enterprise Tayside Ltd.; Chairman, Scottish Tourism Training Forum; Chairman, Hotel and Catering Benevolent Association Scotland; MBIM; FHCIMA. Recreations: Matthew and Mark. Address: (b.) The Gleneagles Hotel, Auchterarder, Perthshire, PH3 1NF; T.-0764 62231.

Ledger, Philip Stevens, CBE, FRSE, HonLLD (Strathclyde), MA, MusB, FRCM, HonRAM, FRNCM, HonGSM, FRCO. Principal, Royal Scottish Academy of Music and Drama, since 1982; b. 12.12.37, Bexhill-on-Sea; 1 s.; 1 d. Educ. Bexhill Grammar School; King's College, Cambridge. Master of the Music, Chelmsford Cathedral, 1962-65; East Anglia University: Director of Music, 1965-73, Dean, School of Fine Arts and Music, 1968-71; Conductor, Cambridge University Musical Society, 1973-82; Director of Music and Organist, King's College, Cambridge, 1974-82; Editor, Anthems for Choirs 2 and 3; Composer/Editor, Six Carols with Descants. Publication: The Oxford Book of English Madrigals (Editor). Recreations: swimming; theatre. Address: (b.) Royal Scottish Academy of Music and Drama, 100 Renfrew Street, Glasgow, G2 3DB; T.-041-332 4101.

Ledingham, Major James Norman, TD, DL, MA, LLB. Retired Farmer and Solicitor; Deputy Lieutenant, Sutherland, since 1964; b. 12.11.11, Perth; m., Helen Matheson Murray; 1 d. Educ. Allan Glen's School, Glasgow; Strathallan School;

Glasgow University. Trained and qualified as Solicitor, 1934-39; joined TA, 1938; 2nd Bn., Glasgow Highlanders HLI, 1939; Co. Commander, 1941-42; attached Commando Mountain Warfare School, Wales, 1943; posted as Signal Officer to Lovat Scouts, 1944; Italian Campaign, 1944-45; wounded; mentioned in Despatches; Chairman, Sutherland TA Association, since 1964; Sutherland NFU Representative, 1970-76; Vice President, Scottish Mountaineering Club, 1979-81; Sutherland Member, N. Committee, T.A. & A.F., 1970-82. Recreations: mountaineering; golf. Address: (h.) Kintradwell, Brora, Sutherland, KW9 6LU; T.-040 8621251.

Lee, Professor Clive Howard, MA, MLitt (Cantab). Professor of Historical Economics, Aberdeen University, since 1991; Editor, Scottish Economic and Social History, since 1989; b. 21.4.42, Leeds; m., Christine Ann. Educ. West Leeds High School; Fitzwilliam College, Cambridge. Assistant Lecturer to Professor, Aberdeen University, since 1966. Publications include: The British Economy since 1700: a macroeconomic perspective, 1986; British Regional Employment Statistics 1841-1971, 1979. Recreations: watching and playing football; gardening; going to pub. Address: (b.) Department of Economics, Aberdeen University, Regent Walk, Aberdeen; T.: 0224 272198.

Lee, Professor Michael Radcliffe, MA, DM, DPhil (Oxon), FRCP, FRCPE, FRSE. Professor of Clinical Pharmacology, Edinburgh University, since 1984; b. 21.11.34, Manchester; m., Judith Ann Horrocks; 1 s.; 1 d. Educ. Manchester Grammar School; Brasenose College, Oxford. Beit Memorial Fellow for Medical Research; Lecturer in Medicine, Oxford University; Lecturer in Medicine, St. Thomas's Hospital Medical School; Medical Director, then Managing Director, Weddel Pharmaceuticals Ltd.; Senior Lecturer in Clinical Pharmacology, Leeds University. Publications: books on medicine and hypertension. Recreations: gardening; walking; old trains; old books. Address: (b.) Department of Clinical Pharmacology, Royal Infirmary, Edinburgh; T.-031-229 2477, Ext. 3316.

Lee, Professor William Robert, MD, FRCPath, FRSE, FCOphth. Titular Professor in Ophthalmic Pathology, Glasgow University, since 1979; b. 14.10.32, Manchester; m., Noelle; 2 d. Educ. William Hulme's Grammar School, Manchester; Manchester University. Registrar in Morbid Anatomy, Westminster Hospital, London, 1964-65; Lecturer in Morbid Anatomy, Glasgow University, 1965-68; Senior Lecturer and Honorary Consultant, 1968-79. Alexander Werhner Piggot Memorial Fellowship (MRC), 1969-70; Claffey Medal, University of Sydney, 1983; Ida Mann Medal, Oxford, 1985. Recreations: curling; music; water colours. Address: (h.) High Craigton, Stockiemuir Road, Milngavie, Glasgow; T.-041-956 3286.

Lees, Rev. Andrew Paxton, BD (Hons). Minister, Knightswood St. Margaret's Parish Church, Glasgow, since 1989; b. 26.11.51, Glasgow; m., Carole Mattocks; 1 s.; 1 d. Educ. Dundee High School; Daniel Stewart's College; Edinburgh University and New College. Assistant, then Associate Minister, Old Parish Church of Peebles linked with Eddleston, 1983-84, and linked with Lyne and Manor, 1984-87; Minister, Ashton Church, Gourock, 1987-89. Recreations: motor rallying; pipe-smoking; malt whisky tasting. Address: (h.) 26 Airthrey Avenue, Glasgow, G14 9LT; T.-041-959 1094.

Lees, David Arthur Russell, MB, ChB, DObstRCOG, FRCOG. Consultant Gynaecologist and Obstetrician, Raigmore Hospital, Inverness, and Honorary Clinical Lecturer, Aberdeen University; b. 16.1.48, Elgin; m., Marie Sinclair Bruce; 4 s. Educ. Hamilton Academy; Glasgow University. Registrar in Obstetrics and Gynaecology, Robroyston and Stobhill Hospitals, Glasgow; Senior Registrar

in Obstetrics and Gynaecology, Stobhill Hospital and Queen Mother's Hospital, Glasgow. Adviser for Special Needs, Inverness Area Scouts; Scout Association Medal of Merit. Recreation: Scouting. Address: (h.) Crofthill, Daviot (West), Inverness IV1 2XQ; T.-0463 772230.

Lees, James George Grahame, MA, LLB, NP. Partner, McLean & Stewart, Solicitors, Dunblane, since 1974; Convener, Personnel Committee and Member, Judicial Commission, Assembly Council and Retirements Scheme Committee, General Assembly of the Church of Scotland; b. 22.6.46, Perth; m., Hazel Margaret Raffan; 1 s.; 2 d. Educ. Dundee High School; St. Andrews University; Edinburgh University. Solicitor, J. & F. Anderson, WS, Edinburgh, 1969-72; Solicitor, McLean & Stewart, Solicitors, Dunblane, since 1972. Elder, Dunblane Cathedral Church of Scotland. Recreations: walking; badminton; tennis; photography; fishing. Address: (h.) Northbank, St. Margaret's Drive, Dunblane, FK15 0DP; T.-Dunblane 822928.

Lees, Robert Ferguson, LLB. Regional Procurator Fiscal, Lothian and Borders, since 1991; b. 15.9.38, Bellshill; m., Elizabeth. Educ. Bellshill Academy; Strathclyde University. Entered Procurator Fiscal Service, 1972; Legal Assistant, Paisley, 1972-75; Legal Assistant/Senior Legal Assistant/Senior Depute Procurator Fiscal, Glasgow, 1975-81; Assistant Procurator Fiscal, Dundee, 1982-88; Regional Procurator Fiscal, North Strathclyde, 1989-91. Recreations: music; travel; foreign languages. Address: (b.) Procurator Fiscal's Office, 3 Queensferry Street, Edinburgh, EH2 4RB; T.-031-226 4962.

Le Gassick, Lt. Col. Cyril Norman, MBE. Former Regional Representative Grampian, National Trust for Scotland; b. 9.4.25, Gillingham; m., Jean; 1 s.; 1 d. Educ. Maidstone School. Regular Army Officer, Royal Corps of Signals, 1946-80; Chief Signal Officer HQ Scotland (Army), 1970-73; Comd. Radio Group, HQ, BAOR, 1973-75. FSA Scot. Recreations: game fishing; shooting; painting. Address: (h.) Pinewood, Pitcaple, Inverurie, Aberdeenshire, AB51 9EE; T.-Pitcaple 681634.

Leggate, Peter James Arthur, JP, FRICS. Chartered Surveyor, since 1967; Chairman, Lowland Insurance Brokers Ltd.; Director: Isla Lands Ltd., Isla Mines Ltd., James Gammell & Son Ltd.; b. 17.10.43; m., Jennifer Susan Gammell; 1 s.; 1 d. Educ. Wrekin College. Qualified as Chartered Surveyor, 1967; Kenneth Ryden & Partners, 1967-70; P.G. Matineau, Jedburgh, 1970-72; Founder, P.J. Leggate & Co., Edinburgh, 1973-79 (Sole Principal, since 1979). Recreations: horses; sailing; skiing. Address: (h.) Birkhill, Earlston, Berwickshire, TD4 6AR.

Legge, Joseph Smith, MD, FRCPEdin. Consultant in Thoracic Medicine, Grampian Health Board, since 1977; Honorary Senior Lecturer, Aberdeen University, since 1977; b. 12.11.43, Portessie, Banffshire; m., Sandra Leisk; 1 s.; 1 d. Educ. Buckie High School; Aberdeen University. Recreations: golf; photography. Address: (h.) 76 Fountainhall Road, Aberdeen; T.-0224 639590.

Leiper, Joseph, MA, DipEd, ACII. Rector, Oldmachar Academy, since 1983; b. 13.8.41, Aberdeen; m., Moira Taylor; 2 d. Educ. Aberdeen Grammar School; Aberdeen University. Inspector, Commercial Union Assurance, until 1967; Aberdeen University, 1967-72; Aberdeen College of Education, 1971-72; Teacher of English, since 1972. Recreations: hockey; sailing; jogging. Address: (b.) Oldmachar Academy, Jesmond Drive, Bridge of Don, Aberdeen, AB2 8ZJ; T.-0224 820887.

Leishman, Marista Muriel, MA, FRSA. Director, The Insite Trust; b. 10.4.32, Beaconsfield; m., Murray Leishman (qv);

1 s.; 3 d. Educ. St. George's School, Ascot; St. Andrews University. First Head of Education, National Trust for Scotland, 1979-86; National Training Award winner for Insite. Recreations: music; painting; writing; hill-walking; gardening. Address: Hunter's House, 508 Lanark Road, Edinburgh, EH14 5DH; T.-031-453 4716.

Leishman, Robert Murray, MA. Analytical Psychotherapist; formerly Minister, Church of Scotland; b. 4.8.31, Edinburgh; m., Marista M. Reith (see Marista Muriel Leishman); 1 s.; 3 d. Address: Hunter's House, 508 Lanark Road, Edinburgh, EH14 5DH; T.-031-453 4716.

Lello, Glenn Edward, BDS, FDSRCS, LRCP, MRCS, MB, BCh, FRCS, PhD, MKGChir. Senior Consultant Maxillofacial Surgeon, since 1990; Senior Lecturer; b. 31.1.47, Pretoria; m., Judith Farquharson; 1 s.; 2 d. Consultant, Rochester University, 1977-79, Zurich University, 1979-82; Senior Specialist, Witwatersrand University, 1982-85; Professor/Head of Department, Medical University, South Africa, 1985-88; Consultant, Manchester University, 1988-90; Senior Consultant, Maxillofacial Surgery, Edinburgh, since 1990. Publications: 38 scientific articles; seven chapters. Recreations: squash; skiing; watersports. Address: (b.) Department of Maxillofacial Surgery, City Hospital, Greenbank Drive, Edinburgh, EH10 5SB.

Lenman, Bruce Philip, MA (Aberdeen), MLitt, LittD (Cantab), FRHistSoc. Reader in Modern History, St. Andrews University, since 1983; b. 9.4.38, Aberdeen. Educ. Aberdeen Grammar School; Aberdeen University; St. John's College, Cambridge. Assistant Professor, Victoria University, Canada, 1963; Lecturer in Imperial and Commonwealth History, Queen's College, Dundee (St. Andrews University), 1963-67; Lecturer, Dundee University, 1967-72; United College, St. Andrews: Lecturer, Department of Modern History, 1972-78, Senior Lecturer, 1978-83; British Academy Fellow, Newberry Library, Chicago, 1982; John Carter Brown Library Fellow, Brown University, Providence, RI, 1984; Harrison Professor, College of William & Mary, VA, 1988-89. Publications: Esk to Tweed, 1975; An Economic History of Modern Scotland 1660-1976, 1977 (Scottish Arts Council Award); The Jacobite Risings in Britain 1689-1746, 1980 (Scottish Arts Council Award); Scotland 1746-1832, 1981; The Jacobite Clans of the Great Glen 1650-1784, 1984; The Jacobite Cause, 1986; The Jacobite Threat (Co-author), 1990. Recreations: golf; squash; badminton; Scottish country dancing; hill-walking. Address: (b.) Department of Modern History, St. Andrews University, St. Andrews, KY16 9AL; T.-0334 76161.

Lennie, Daniel, JP. Convener and Labour Group Leader, Midlothian District Council, since 1986; Chairman, Midlothian Constituency Labour Party, 1986-88; b. 6.2.47, Edinburgh; m., Thelma Halliday; 2 s.; 1 d. Educ. St. Margaret's School, Loanhead; St. David's School, Dalkeith. Chairman, Midlothian District Licensing Board, 1981-86; AUEW: Shop Steward, 1973-80, Convener, 1977-80, Bertrams Ltd., Edinburgh; Chairman, Bonnyrigg/Lasswade Community Council, 1978-80; Chairman, Bonnyrigg/Lasswade Labour Party, since 1979; Member, AEU Parliamentary Panel, since 1988. Recreations: politics; writing bad doggerel. Address: (h.) 10 Sherwood Walk, Bonnyrigg, Midlothian, EH19 3NL; T.-031-660 3492.

Leonard, Robert Charles Frederick, BSc, MD, MB, BS, MRCP, FRCPEdin. Senior Lecturer in Clinical Oncology, Edinburgh University, since 1983; Honorary Consultant Physician, Lothian Health Board, since 1983; b. 11.5.47, Merthyr Tydfil; m., Tania Smith; 3 d. Educ. Merthyr Tydfil County Grammar School; Charing Cross Hospital Medical School, London. House Officer, Charing Cross, West London and Fulham Hospitals, 1971-73; Senior House Officer,

Hammersmith Hospital, 1973; Medical Registrar, Oxford Hospitals, 1974-76; Leukaemia Research Fund Fellow, Oxford University, 1976-79; Senior Registrar and University Lecturer, Royal Victoria and General Hospitals, Newcastle-upon-Tyne, 1979-82; Cancer Research Campaign Travelling Fellow, Dana Farber Cancer Institute and Harvard Medical School, Boston, 1982. Recreations: classical music; reading; soccer. Address: (h.) 19 Craigcrook Road, Edinburgh, EH4 3NQ.

Leonard, Tom. Poet and Critic; b. 22.8.44, Glasgow; m., Sonya Maria O'Brien; 2 s. Educ. Lourdes Secondary School, Glasgow; Glasgow University. Writer in Residence, Paisley Central Library, 1985-87 and 1988-89. Publications: Intimate Voices, 1984 (Joint Winner, Saltire Society Book of the Year); Radical Renfrew (Editor), 1990. Recreations: swimming; snooker.

Leonard, Wilfred. Member, Island Policy Committee, Scottish Accident Prevention Council; b. 9.5.12, Humberton, Brafferton, Yorkshire; m., Margaret Ross (deceased); 1 s.; 2 d. Educ. Brafferton Church of England School. Staffordshire County Police, 1935-67 (retired in rank of Inspector); Member, Inverness County Council, 1973-74; Past Chairman: Harris District Council, South Harris Agricultural Society, Harris Council of Social Service; former Member: Highlands and Islands Consultative Council; Highlands and Islands Manpower Board, MSC; Member, Western Isles Islands Council, 1974-86 (Chairman, Planning and Development, 1980-86). Recreation: gardening. Address: (h.) Cnoc-Na-Ba, Finsbay, Isle of Harris; T.-Manish 232.

Le Roux, Joan Catherine. Member, Argyll and Clyde Health Board, since 1981; b. 23.4.30, Edinburgh; m., Peter Hugo Le Roux; 3 s. Educ. Mary Erskine College. Member, Argyll and Bute Health Council, 1975-80 (Chairman, 1977-79); Chairman, Argyll Conservative Association, 1976-78 (President, 1978-80); Vice-Chairman, Conservative Women's Scottish Council, 1981-82; Member, Dunoon and Cowal Cancer Research Committee, since 1968 (Chairman, 1982-89). Recreations: reading; sewing; music. Address: (h.) Berrybum, Dunoon, Argyll; T.-0369 2028.

Leslie, Allan Eunson, FRSH, MREHIS. Director of Environmental Health, Orkney Islands Council, since 1975; b. 15.11.41, Garmouth, Morayshire; m., Vivia Mary Stewart. Educ. Mackie Academy, Stonehaven; Harris Academy, Dundee; Strathclyde University. Assistant Sanitary Inspector, Kincardine County Council, 1964-70; Area Sanitary Inspector, Sutherland County Council, 1970-72. Recreations: gardening; walking; sea fishing; bowls; bridge; reading. Address: (b.) Orkney Islands Council, Environmental Health Department, Council Offices, School Place, Kirkwall, Orkney Isles; T.-0856 3535, Ext. 2801.

Leslie, David James, BArch, RIBA, PRIAS. Architect; Principal, The David Leslie Partnership; b. 15.5.32, Glasgow; m., Olive; 2 s.; 1 d. Educ. Hillhead High School; Glasgow School of Architecture. Qualified, 1957; Registered Architect, 1959; Partner, Walter Underwood & Partners, 1964-91; President, Royal Incorporation of Architects, 1987-89; Honorary Secretary, Glasgow Institute of Architects, 1979-82, President, 1984-86; Governor, Glasgow School of Art; Director, Glasgow Chamber of Commerce; Elder, Netherlee Church, Glasgow; Convener, Festival of Architecture in Scotland, 1984; Convener, Scotstyle Group. Publication: Glasgow Revealed (Co-author). Recreations: singing; painting; photography. Address: (b.) 3 La Belle Place, Glasgow, G3 7LH; T.-041-332 7227.

Leslie, Professor Frank Matthews, JP, BSc, PhD, FIMA, FInstP, FRSE. Professor of Mathematics, Strathclyde University, since 1982; Chairman, British Liquid Crystal

Society, 1987-91; b. 8.3.35, Dundee; m., Ellen Leitch Reoch; 1 s.; 1 d. Educ. Harris Academy; Queen's College, Dundee; Manchester University. Assistant Lecturer, Manchester University, 1959-61; Research Associate, MIT, USA, 1961-62; Lecturer, Newcastle University, 1962-68; Visiting Assistant Professor, Johns Hopkins University, USA, 1966-67; Strathclyde University: Senior Lecturer, 1968-71, Reader, 1971-79, Personal Professor, 1979-82; Consultant, RSRE Malvern; Annual Award, British Society of Rheology, 1982. Recreations: golf; hill-walking. Address: (b.) Department of Mathematics, Strathclyde University, Livingstone Tower, 26 Richmond Street, Glasgow, G1 1XH; T.-041-552 4400.

Leslie, John, MRPharmS. Chairman, Orkney Health Board, since 1991; b. 1.1.35, Kirkwall; m., Evelyn MacGillivray; 1 s. Educ. Kirkwall Grammar School; Robert Gordon's Institute of Technology, Aberdeen. Member, NHS Executive Council for Orkney, 1968-74; Chairman, Kirkwall Chamber of Commerce, 1973-74; Member, Orkney Health Board, 1979-85 and since 1987. Past President, Kirkwall Rotary Club. Recreations: participating in amateur music and drama groups; simple electronics/computing. Address: (h.) Failte, Bignold Park Road, Kirkwall, Orkney; T.-0856 874002.

Leslie, William, TD, BA (Cantab), LLB, WS. Chairman (full-time), The Industrial Tribunals (Scotland), since 1976; b. 13.4.26, Aberdeen; m., 1, Priscilla Anne Forgie Ross-Farrow (m. diss.); 2, Elizabeth Jennis Bowden-Smith; 2 s.; 1 d. Educ. Loretto School; Sidney Sussex College, Cambridge; Aberdeen University. Apprentice, Davidson & Garden, Advocates, Aberdeen, 1950-53; Assistant with, then Partner in, John C. Brodie & Sons, WS, Edinburgh (subsequently Brodie, Cuthbertson & Watson, WS, and Brodies, WS), 1953-75. Lt., Seaforth Highlanders, attached 2nd Bn., KOSB, 1945-47; The Gordon Highlanders, TA, 1948-67 (Major, TD). Publication: Industrial Tribunal Practice in Scotland, 1981. Recreations: fishing; skiing; singing; music. Address: (h.) 4 Oswald Road, Edinburgh, EH9 2HF.

Lessels, Norman, CA. Partner, Chiene & Tait, CA, since 1980; Chairman, Standard Life Assurance Company; Chairman, Cairn Energy PLC; Director, Havelock Europa PLC; Governor, BUPA; Director, Securities and Investments Board; Director, Bank of Scotland; Director, Scottish Eastern Investment Trust PLC; Director, The Murrayfield plc; Director, Scottish Homes; b. 2.9.38, Edinburgh; m., Christine Stevenson; 1 s. Educ. Edinburgh Academy. Partner, Ernst & Whinney, until 1980; President, Institute of Chartered Accountants of Scotland, 1987-88. Recreations: golf; music; bridge. Address: (b.) 3 Albyn Place, Edinburgh; T.-031-225 7515.

Lessnoff, Michael Harry, MA, BPhil. Reader in Politics, Glasgow University, since 1986; b. 23.1.40, Glasgow. Educ. High School of Glasgow; Glasgow University; Balliol College, Oxford. Assistant Principal, Department of Education and Science, 1965-66; Lecturer, then Senior Lecturer, Department of Politics, Glasgow University, 1966-86; Visiting Associate Professor, College of William and Mary, Williamsburg, USA, 1977-78. Won Snell Exhibition, 1963. Publications: The Structure of Social Science, 1974; Social Contract, 1986; Social Contract Theory, 1990. Recreations: literature; art; science; travel. Address: (h.) 58 White Street, Glasgow, G11 5EB; T.-041-334 1799.

Levein, Charles Peter Alexander, MA, PhD. Chief Research Officer, Scottish Office, since 1988; b. 16.5.40, Devonport; 1 s.; 2 d. Educ. Dunfermline High School; Edinburgh University. Demonstrator, Geography Department, Edinburgh University; Research Officer, Central Planning Research Unit, Scottish Development Department; Senior Research Officer, WC Scotland Planning Team; Principal Research Officer, Scottish Office Urban Deprivation Unit. Recreations: golf; bowls; tennis. Address: (h.) 45 The Wynd, Dalgety Bay, Fife; T.-0383 822952.

Leven and Melville, Earl of (Alexander Robert Melville). Lord Lieutenant, Nairn; Company Director; President, British Ski Federation, 1981-85; Honorary President, Scottish National Ski Council; Chairman, Governors, Gordonstoun School, 1971-89; b. 13.5.24, London; m., Susan Steuart-Menzies; 2 s.; 1 d. Educ. Eton. Coldstream Guards, 1942-52 (retired as Captain); ADC to Governor General of New Zealand, 1951-52; Convener, Nairn County Council, 1970-74. Recreations: shooting; fishing; skiing. Address: (h.) Glenferness House, Nairn, IV12 5UP; T.-0309 651202.

Lever, Professor William Fred, MA, DPhil. Professor in Urban Studies, Glasgow University, since 1982; b. 17.4.43, Accrington; m., Marian Frances Hardman; 1 s.; 2 d. Educ. Accrington Grammar School; St. Peter's College, Oxford. Tutor in Geography, Oxford University, 1965-67; Lecturer, Reader, in Urban Studies, Glasgow University, 1967-82. Publications: Industrial Relocation and Employment Change; The City in Transition; Industrial Change in the UK; Social and Economic Change in Metropolitan Areas. Recreations: travel; theatre; skiing. Address: (h.) 34 Kirkhouse Road, Blanefield, Glasgow; T.-0360 70536.

Levi, Professor Anthony Herbert Tigar, MA (Oxon), DPhil (Oxon), STL. Emeritus Professor of French Language and Literature, St. Andrews University; b. 30.5.29, London; m., Honor Marjorie Riley; 2 d. Educ. Prior Park College; Oxford University; Munich University. Member, Jesuit Order, 1949-71; Lecturer, Reader, Professor, Warwick University, 1965-71; Lecturer, Christ Church, Oxford, and Tutor, Campion Hall, Oxford, 1965-71. Publications: French Moralists: The Theory of the Passions 1585-1649, 1964; Religion in Practice, 1966; Erasmus, The Praise of Folly (Editor), 1971; Humanism in France, 1970; The Writer and the Artist in France, 1974; Collected Works of Erasmus (Vol. 27 and 28), 1986; The St. James Guide to French Literature, Vol. I and Vol. II, 1991. Address: (h.) Gibliston Farmhouse, Colinsburgh, Leven, Fife, KY9 1JS; T.-033-334 219.

Levison, Rev. Christopher Leon, MA, BD (Hons). Minister, Oakshaw Trinity Church, since 1991; Minister, Paisley High Church, 1983-91; Moderator, Paisley Presbytery, 1991-92; b. 7.4.47, Gorebridge, Midlothian; m., Rosemary Anne Milne Logan; 2 d. Educ. George Watson's College; Kirkcaldy High School; St. Andrews University; Edinburgh University. Assistant Minister, South Leith, 1971-73; Minister, Coltness Memorial Church, Newmains, 1973-78 (also Community Councillor); Associate Chaplain, Aberdeen University, 1978-83. Manager and Trustee, Kibble List D School. Recreations: sailing; hill-walking. Address: 178 Glasgow Road, Paisley, PA1 3LT; T.-041-889 3316.

Lewis, William Garry, BSc, EdBDip. Head Teacher, Possilpark Secondary School, Glasgow, since 1983; b. 2.8.29, Glasgow; m., Sylvia; 2 s. Educ. Hyndland Secondary School; Glasgow University; Jordanhill College of Education. Recreations: photography; gardening. Address: (b.) 32 Carbeth Street, Glasgow, G22 5PT; T.-041-336 8375.

Liddell, Colin. Public Affairs Director, Scotland, United Distillers, since 1986; b. 28.8.47, Falkirk; m., Sheena Wood Mackay. Educ. Denny High School. Journalist, Johnston Newspaper Group, 1964-66; Editor, Linlithgow Journal & Gazette, 1967-69; Journalist, Scotsman Publications, 1969-77; Senior Press Officer, Scottish Development Agency, 1977-82; PR Director, then Chief Executive, Charles Barker Scotland, 1982-86. Non-Executive Director: The Scottish Ballet, Barclays Bank (Scottish Regional Board); Member, Task (Sick Kids) Appeal. Recreations: golf; gardening.

Address: (h.) Friarbank, Manse Road, Linlithgow, West Lothian; T.-0506 843734.

Liddell, Donald John, LLB (Hons). Chief Executive, East Kilbride District Council, since 1988; (Director of Administration and Legal Services, Clydesdale District Council, 1984-88); b. 20.3.50, Hamilton; m., Veronica; 1 s.; 2 d. Educ. Hamilton Academy; Glasgow University. Legal Apprentice/Assistant, Livingston Development Corporation, 1971-75; Legal Assistant/Officer, Clydesdale District Council, 1975-84. Address: (b.) Civic Centre, East Kilbride, G74 1AB; T.-East Kilbride 71202.

Liddell, Helen Lawrie, BA. Director of Corporate and Public Affairs, Scottish Daily Record and Sunday Mail Ltd., since 1991 (Director of Personnel and Public Affairs, 1988-91); b. 6.12.50, Coatbridge; m., Dr. Alistair H. Liddell; 1 s.; 1 d. Educ. St. Patrick's High School, Coatbridge; Strathclyde University. Head, Economic Department, STUC, 1971-76; Scottish Secretary, Labour Party, 1977-88; Labour candidate, East Fife, 1974; Economics Correspondent, BBC, 1976-77. Publication: Elite, 1990. Address: (h.) Glenisla, Main Road, Langbank, Renfrewshire; T.-Langbank 344.

Liddell, John Chalmers, MA, LLB. Depute Chief Executive, Grampian Regional Council, since 1979; b. 25.3.46, Dumfries; m., Laura; 2 s.; 1 d. Educ. High School of Glasgow; St. Andrews University. Depute County Clerk, Berwickshire, 1972; Assistant Director of Administration, Borders Region, 1975; Depute Director of Law and Administration, Grampian Region, 1975. Chairman, Aberdeen Ski Club. Recreations: skiing; golf. Address: (b.) Woodhill House, Westburn Road, Aberdeen, AB9 2LU.

Lilley, Professor David Malcolm James, FRSE. Professor of Molecular Biology, Dundee University, since 1989; b. 28.5.48, Colchester; m., Patricia Mary; 2 d. Educ. Gilberd School, Colchester; Durham University. Joined Biochemistry Department, Dundee University, 1981; awarded Colworth Medal by Biochemical Society, 1982. Publications: over100 scientific papers. Recreation: foreign languages. Address: (b.) Department of Biochemistry, Dundee University, Dundee, DD1 4HN; T.-0382 23181.

Lilwall, Nicholas Brier, BSc, MA, PhD. Head, Rural Resource Management Department, The Scottish Agricultural College, Edinburgh, since 1985; b. 15.8.37, Liverpool; m., Anne; 2 s.; 1 d. Educ. Truro School, Cornwall; Leeds University; Minnesota University. Assistant Lecturer, Leeds University, 1964-66; Research Assistant, Minnesota University, 1967-71; Economist, Edinburgh School of Agriculture, since 1971. Recreation: tennis. Address: (b.) The Scottish Agricultural College, West Mains Road, Edinburgh, EH9 3JG; T.-031-667 1041.

Lincoln, Professor Dennis W., DSc. Director, Medical Research Council Reproductive Biology Unit, Edinburgh, since 1982; b. 21.7.39, Gt. Ellingham; m., Rosemary A. Barrell; 1 s.; 1 d. Educ. Nottingham University; Cambridge University. Research Fellow, Corpus Christi College, Cambridge, 1966-67; Lecturer, Reader, Faculty of Medicine, Bristol University. Honorary Professor, Faculty of Medicine, Edinburgh University, since 1985. Recreation: ornithology. Address: (b.) Centre for Reproductive Biology, 37 Chalmers Street, Edinburgh, EH3 9EW; T.-031-229 2575.

Lincoln, Peter, DDA. Actor and Director; Head of Movement Studies, Royal Scottish Academy of Music and Drama; b. 1.8.46, Falkirk; m., Jan; 3 s.; 1 d. Educ. Broughton School; RSAMD; Ecole Jacques Lecoq, Paris. Member, Scottish Arts Council, since 1989 (Chairman, Dance and Mime Committee, since 1989); Visiting Lecturer, Californian Institute of the Arts, Los Angeles, 1989. Edinburgh Fringe First Winner, 1984. Recreations: sports; film; theatre; walking. Address: (h.) 18 Orleans Avenue, Jordanhill, Glasgow, G14 9NF; T.-041-959 4671.

Lindop, George Black McMeekin, BSc, MB, ChB, MRCPath. Senior Lecturer and Honorary Consultant in Histopathology, Glasgow University, and Honorary Consultant in Histopathology, Western Infirmary, Glasgow, since 1979; b. 28.3.45, Glasgow; m., Sharon Ann Cornell; 2 s.; 1 d. Educ. Hillhead High School; Glasgow University. Senior House Officer/Registrar, then Lecturer/Honorary Senior Registrar, Department of Histopathology, Western Infirmary, Glasgow; Consultant Histopathologist, Ayrshire and Arran Health Board; Consulting Editor, Histology/Histopathology. Recreations: sport; the outdoors; music; cinema. Address: (b.) Department of Pathology, Western Infirmary, Glasgow; T.-041-339 8822.

Lindsay, Alistair, MA, LLB, NP, FSA Scot. Editor, Clan Lindsay Society Publications, since 1947; Consultant, Stewarts, Nicol, D. & J. Hill (Partner, 1948-82); b. 5.2.23, Glasgow; m., Agnes Calder Hamilton Neilson; 1 s.; 1 d. Educ. Pollokshields Secondary School; Larkhall Academy; Glasgow University. Governor, Baillies Institution Free Public Library, six years; Secretary, Old Glasgow Club, 12 years; Secretary, (Glasgow) Ballad Club, 24 years; Life Member, Glasgow Art Gallery and Museums Association; Director: Barloch Proprieters Ltd., Popular Properties Ltd. Publication: The Laird of Barloch 1632-1984, 1985. Recreations: genealogy; local history. Address: (h.) Brucewell, Midtoun, St. Johns Town of Dalry, Castle Douglas; T.-064 43 306.

Lindsay, Frederic, MA (Hons). Writer; b. 12.8.33, Glasgow; m., Shirley; 1 s.; 3 d. Educ. North Kelvinside Senior Secondary School; Glasgow University; Jordanhill College; Edinburgh University. Worked as library assistant, teacher, lecturer; since becoming full-time writer in 1979, has published four novels: Brond, 1984, Jill Rips, 1987, A Charm Against Drowning, 1988, After the Stranger Came, 1992; has written plays for Scottish Youth Theatre; radio plays for children; adapted Brond as serial for Channel 4. Member, Scottish Arts Council Literature Committee. Recreations: cinema; theatre; television; reading; walking in the Pentlands. Address: (h.) 2a Hopelands Road, Silverburn, Penicuik, EH26 9LH; T.-0968 784 98.

Lindsay, James, CBE, BL, CA. Honorary President, Scottish Golf Union, since 1960; Honorary Sheriff, Falkirk; b. 31.10.12, Larbert; m., Margaret Craig Wyllie; 4 s.; 1 d. Educ. Falkirk High School; Glasgow University. Macfarlane Lang & Co. Ltd.: Accountant and Secretary, 1937-57, Director, 1955-73; Director, United Biscuits Ltd., 1957-73; Chairman, The Cake and Biscuit Alliance, 1970-73; President, Scottish Golf Union, 1958-60. Recreations: golf; gardening. Address: (h.) 8 Neilson Street, Falkirk, FK1 5AQ; T.-Falkirk 22248.

Lindsay, John Maurice, CBE, TD, DLitt, HonFRIAS. Consultant, Scottish Civic Trust (Director, 1967-83); Secretary-General, Europa Nostra, 1983-91; b. 21.7.18; m., Aileen Joyce Gordon; 1 s.; 3 d. Educ. Glasgow Academy; Scottish National Academy of Music. Drama Critic, Scottish Daily Mail, 1946-47; Music Critic, The Bulletin, 1946-60; Border Television: Programme Controller, 1961-62, Production Controller, 1962-64, Features Executive and Chief Interviewer, 1964-67. Atlantic-Rockefeller Award, 1946; Editor: Scots Review, 1949-50, The Scottish Review, 1975-85; Member, Historic Buildings Council for Scotland, 1976-87; Council Member, Association of Scottish Literary Studies, since 1983, President, since 1988; Trustee, New Lanark Conservation Trust, since 1985; Trustee, National Heritage Memorial Fund, 1980-84; HonDLitt, Glasgow, 1982. Publications: poetry: The Advancing Day, 1940;

Perhaps To-morrow, 1941; Predicament, 1942; No Crown for Laughter: Poems, 1943; The Enemies of Love: Poems 1941-45, 1946; Selected Poems, 1947; Hurlygush: Poems in Scots, 1948; At the Wood's Edge, 1950; Ode for St. Andrew's Night and Other Poems, 1951; The Exiled Heart: Poems 1941-56, 1957; Snow Warning and Other Poems, 1962; One Later Day and Other Poems, 1964; This Business of Living, 1969; Comings and Goings: Poems, 1971; Selected Poems 1942-72, 1973; The Run from Life, 1975; Walking Without an Overcoat, Poems 1972-76, 1977; Collected Poems, 1979; A Net to Catch the Winds and Other Poems, 1981; The French Mosquitoes' Woman and other diversions and poems; Requiem for a Sexual Athlete; Collected Poems 1940-90; prose: Pocket Guide to Scottish Culture; The Scottish Renaissance; The Lowlands of Scotland: Glasgow and the North; Robert Burns: The Man, His Work, The Legend; Dunoon: The Gem of the Clyde Coast; The Lowlands of Scotland: Edinburgh and the South; Clyde Waters: Variations and Diversions on a Theme of Pleasure; The Burns Encyclopedia; Killochan Castle; By Yon Bonnie Banks: A Gallimaufry; Environment: A Basic Human Right; Portrait of Glasgow; Robin Philipson; History of Scottish Literature; Lowland Scottish Villages; Francis George Scott and the Scottish Renaissance; The Buildings of Edinburgh (Co-author); Thank You For Having Me: A Personal Memoir; Unknown Scotland (Co-author); The Scottish Castle: A Constable Guide; Count All Men Mortal: The Story of the Scottish Provident Institution; Victorian and Edwardian Glasgow; An Illustrated Guide to Glasgow; The Comic Poems of William Tennant (Co-editor); Edinburgh Past and Present (Co-author); The Youth and Manhood of Cyril Thornton (Editor); The Scottish Dog (Co-author); A Pleasure of Gardens (Co-author); The Scottish Quotation Book (Co-author); The Music Quotation Book (Co-author). Recreations: music; walking. Address: (h.) 7 Milton Hill, Milton, Dumbarton, G82 2TS; T.-Dumbarton 62655.

Lingard, Joan Amelia. Author; Chairperson, Society of Authors in Scotland, 1982-86; Convenor, Scottish Writers Against the Bomb; b. Edinburgh; 3 d. Educ. Bloomfield Collegiate School, Belfast; Moray House College of Education, Edinburgh. First novel published, 1963; has also written plays for TV, including 18-part series, Maggie, adapted from quartet of teenage books; Council Member, Scottish Arts Council, 1980-84 (Member, Literature Committee, 1980-84); novels: Liam's Daughter, 1963; The Prevailing Wind, 1964; The Tide Comes In, 1966; The Headmaster, 1967; A Sort of Freedom, 1968; The Lord on our Side, 1970; The Second Flowering of Emily Mountjoy, 1979; Greenyards, 1981; Sisters By Rite, 1984; Reasonable Doubts, 1986; The Women's House, 1989; 24 children's books. Recreations: reading; walking; travelling. Address: (b.) David Higham Associates, 5-8 Lower John Street, Golden Square, London, W1R 4HA.

Lingard, Robin Anthony, MA, FTS. Director of Training and Social Development, Highlands and Islands Enterprise, since 1991; Member, Scottish Tourist Board, since 1988; b. 19.7.41, Enfield; m., Margaret; 2 d. Educ. Felsted School; Emmanuel College, Cambridge. Joined Ministry of Aviation, 1963; Private Secretary to Joint Parliamentary Secretary, Ministry of Technology, 1966-68; appointments, Department of Industry, DTI, etc., to 1984; Head, Enterprise Unit, Cabinet Office, 1984-85; Head, Small Firms and Tourism Division, Department of Employment, 1985-87; full-time Board Member, Highlands and Islands Development Board, 1988-91. Member, NEDO Sector Group on Tourism and Leisure; Member, Management Board, Prince's Trust and Royal Jubilee Trusts. Recreations: watching birds; walking; reading; aviation history. Address: (h.) Kinnairdie House, Dingwall, IV15 9LL; T.-0349 61044.

Linklater, John Richard Gordon. Literary Editor, Glasgow Herald, since 1988, Theatre Critic, since 1991; b. 29.1.52, Dumfries; 1 s.; 1 d. Educ. Royal High School, Edinburgh; Stirling University; Glasgow University. Fife Free Press, Kirkcaldy, 1975-76; Evening Express, Aberdeen, 1976-78; joined Glasgow Herald, 1978 (Education Correspondent, 1980-86). Specialist Writer of the Year, Scottish Press Awards, 1985; Fulbright Fellow in Professional Journalism, 1987; Chairman, Scottish Committee, National Council for the Training of Journalists, 1988-90; Member, Book Awards Committee, Scottish Arts Council, since 1989. Recreations: music; reading; chess; Hibernian FC. Address: (b.) 195 Albion Street, Glasgow, G1 1QP; T.-041-552 6255.

Linklater, Karl Alexander, BVM&S, PhD, FRCVS. Director, Scottish Agricultural Colleges Veterinary Investigation Service, since 1986; Member, Veterinary Products Committee, since 1990; Director, Animal Diseases Research Association, since 1991; b. 1.9.39, Stromness, Orkney; m., Margaret Carr Gibb; 1 s.; 1 d. Educ. Robert Gordon's College, Aberdeen; Edinburgh University. General veterinary practice, Tarland, Aberdeenshire, 1962-66; North of Scotland College of Agriculture, Aberdeen, 1966-67; Royal (Dick) School of Veterinary Studies, Edinburgh University, 1967-73; East of Scotland College of Agriculture, St. Boswells, 1973-86. President, Sheep Veterinary Society, 1983-85; President, Association of Veterinary Teachers and Research Workers (Scotland), 1988-90; Alan Baldry Award, 1982. Recreations: sport; gardening; sheep breeding. Address: (h.) Bridge Park, Old Bridge Road, Selkirk; T.-0750 20571.

Linklater, Magnus Duncan. Editor, The Scotsman, since 1988; b. 21.2.42, Harray, Orkney; m., Veronica Lyle; 2 s.; 1 d. Educ. Eton College; Cambridge University. Reporter, Daily Express, Manchester, 1965-66; London Evening Standard: Diary Reporter, 1966-67, Editor, Londoner's Diary, 1967-69; Sunday Times: Editor, Spectrum, 1969-72, Editor, Colour Magazine, 1972-75, News Editor/Features Editor, 1975-83; Managing Editor, The Observer, 1983-86; Editor, London Daily News, 1986-87. Publications: Hoax: the Howard Hughes-Clifford Irving Affair (Co-author); Jeremy Thorpe: A Secret Life (Co-author); The Falklands War (with Sunday Times Insight team); Massacre - the story of Glencoe; The Fourth Reich - Klaus Barbie and the Neo-Fascist Connection (Co-author); Not With Honour - the inside story of the Westland Affair (Co-author); For King and Conscience – John Graham of Claverhouse, Viscount Dundee (Co-author). Recreations: tennis; cricket; fishing. Address: (b.) 20 North Bridge, Edinburgh, EH1 1YT; T.-031-225 2468.

Linklater, Marjorie; b. 19.3.09, Edinburgh; m., Eric Linklater (deceased); 2 s.; 2 d. Educ. St. George's School, Edinburgh; Downe House, Newbury, Berkshire; Royal Academy of Dramatic Art, London. Stage career ended, 1930, after appearing in three plays in West End; returned to Scotland and married Eric Linklater, 1933; SSAFA Representative, 1942-45; Member, Ross and Cromarty County Council, 1953-69; served on Inverness Hospital Board; Member, Scottish Arts Council, 1957-63; former Member, Advisory Council, HIDB; Council Member, European Architectural Heritage Year, 1972-75; joined Scottish National Party, 1979, having progressed from Conservative via Liberal; as Chairman of Orkney Heritage Society, 1977-81, led "No Uranium" campaign to prevent uranium mining in Orkney; Secretary, Stormy Bank Group opposed to dumping nuclear waste in seabed off Orkney; founder Chairman, Pier Arts Centre Management Committee; helped to initiate Orkney Folk Festival; Hon. Vice President, St. Magnus Festival. Recreation: the arts. Address: (h.) 20 Main Street, Kirkwall, Orkney, KW15 1BU; T.-0856 3619.

Linkston, Alexander Millar, IPFA. Chief Executive Officer/Director of Finance, West Lothian District Council, since 1990; b. 13.12.49, Bathgate; m., Margaret Cuddihy; 2 d. Educ. Lindsay High School, Bathgate; Glasgow College of Commerce. Joined West Lothian County Council as trainee accountant, 1965. Secretary, West Lothian Municipal Bank; Treasurer, Forth Valley Tourist Board; Secretary, Linlithgow Grange Rotary Club. Recreations: horse riding; swimming; Rotary. Address: (b.) District Headquarters, South Bridge Street, Bathgate, EH48 1TT; T.-0506 53631.

Lisgo, John, BSc (Econ) (Hons), DipEd (Hons). Principal, Jewel and Esk Valley College, Edinburgh, since 1986 (Lauder Technical College, Dunfermline, 1983-86); b. 8.7.40, Seaham, Durham; m., Norma Ranson Peel; 1 s. Educ. Ryhope School, Sunderland; London School of Economics and Political Science; Durham University. Assistant Teacher of History and Mathematics, Boldon Secondary School, 1962-63; Assistant Lecturer in Economics, then Liaison Officer for Adult Education, Monkwearmouth College of Further Education, 1963-72; Stevenson College of Further Education: Senior Lecturer in Social Studies, 1972-75, Head, Department of Language and Social Studies, 1975-80, Assistant Principal, 1980-83. Vice Chairman, Association of Principals (Scotland); Member, Scottish School of Further Education Advisory Board; Board Member, Craigmillar Opportunities Trust; Board Member, Midlothian Campaign. Recreation: swimming. Address: (b.) 24 Milton Road East, Edinburgh, EH15 2PP; T.-031-669 8461.

Lister-Kaye, Sir John, 8th Bt. of Grange. Naturalist, Author, Lecturer; Member, International Committee, World Wilderness Foundation, since 1984; Chairman, Scottish Committee, RSPB, 1985-92; Member, Committee for Scotland, NCC, 1989-90; NW Regional Chairman, NCCS, 1991; NW Regional Chairman, Scottish Natural Heritage, since 1992; b. 8.5.46; m., 1, Lady Sorrel Deirdre Bentinck; 1 s.; 2 d.; 2, Lucinda Anne Law. Educ. Allhallows School. Founded Field Studies Centre, Highlands, 1970; founder Director, Aigas Trust, 1979. Publications: The White Island, 1972; Seal Cull, 1979; The Seeing Eye, 1980. Address: (h.) Aigas House, Beauly, Inverness-shire, IV4 7AD.

Lithgow, Sir William (James), 2nd Bt. of Ormsary, DL, LLD, CEng, FRINA, CBIM. Industrialist; Farmer; Chairman, Lithgows Limited, since 1959 (Director, since 1956); b. 10.5.34; m., 1, Valerie Helen Scott (deceased); 2, Mary Claire Hill; 2 s.; 1 d. Educ. Winchester College. Chairman, Hunterston Development Company Limited, 1987 (Director, since 1971); Director: Campbeltown Shipyard Ltd., Landcatch Limited, Lithgows Limited, Lithgows Pty Limited; Chairman, Scott Lithgow Drydocks Ltd., 1967-78; Vice-Chairman, Scott Lithgow Ltd., 1968-78; Chairman, Western Ferries (Argyll) Ltd., 1972-85; Director, Bank of Scotland, 1962-86. Member: British Committee, Det Norske Veritas, since 1966, Greenock District Hospital Board, 1961-66, General Board (Royal Service Nominee), Nat. Physical Lab., 1963-66; Honorary President, Students Association, and Member, Court, Strathclyde University, 1964-69; Member: Executive Committee, Scottish Council Development and Industry, 1969-85, Scottish Regional Council, CBI, 1969-76, Clyde Port Authority, 1969-71, West Central Scotland Plan Steering Committee, 1970-74, Board, National Ports Council, 1971-78, Scottish Milk Marketing Board, 1979-83; Chairman, Iona Cathedral Trustees Management Board, 1979-83; Council Member, Winston Churchill Memorial Trust, 1979-83; Member, Queen's Body Guard for Scotland (Royal Company of Archers), 1964; Fellow, Scottish Council Development and Industry. Recreations: rural life; invention; photography. Address: (b.) PO Box 7, Lochgilphead, Argyll PA31 8JH; T.-08803 244.

Little, John Anthony, BSc, MSc, PhD, CEng, MICE, FGS. Senior Lecturer, Department of Civil and Offshore Engineering, Heriot Watt University, since 1986; SERC Co-ordinator, Geotechnics and Pavement Engineering, since 1990; Member, Committee, SERC Environmental Civil Engineering Committee, since 1990; Member, Committee, Scottish Geotechnical Group, since 1990; b. 24.11.48, Catterick; m., Gail; 1 s.; 2 d. Educ. Chatham House Grammar School, Ramsgate; University College of Wales, Aberystwyth; Durham University; City University. Geotechnical engineering appointments, 1972-76; Senior Lecturer, Hatfield Polytechnic, 1976-86. Publications: 40 papers. Recreations: hill-walking; running. Address: (b.) Department of Civil and Offshore Engineering, Heriot Watt University, Riccarton, Edinburgh, EH14 4AS; T.-031-449 5111.

Little, Keith, MB, ChB, MD, FRCP, FRCSEdin. Consultant in Accident and Emergency Medicine, Edinburgh Royal Infirmary; b. 26.4.43, Yeadon, Yorkshire; m., Margaret R.; 2 s.; 2 d. Educ. Dalbeattie High School; Dumfries Academy; Edinburgh Medical School. First posts in Edinburgh; moved to Derby as a Registrar in Accident and Emergency Medicine; Consultant, Chester Royal Infirmary, 1974-78. Chairman, Scottish Committee, Medical Commission on Accident Prevention. Publication: Accident and Emergency Resuscitation (Co-author). Recreations: golf; tennis. Address: (b.) Accident and Emergency Department, Royal Infirmary, Edinburgh; T.-031-229 2477.

Littlejohn, Professor David, BSc, PhD, CChem, FRSC. UNICAM Professor of Analytical Chemistry, Strathclyde University, since 1988; b. 1.5.53, Glasgow; m., Lesley Shaw MacDonald. Educ. Duncanrig Secondary School, East Kilbride; Strathclyde University. Technical Officer, ICI Petrochemicals Division, Wilton, Middlesborough, 1978-80; Lecturer/Senior Lecturer in Chemistry, Strathclyde University, 1981-88. Awarded 15th SAC Silver Medal by Royal Society of Chemistry, 1987; joint Editor in Chief, Talanta, International Journal of Pure and Applied Analytical Chemistry, 1989-91. Publications: 85 research papers, 10 reviews. Address: (b.) Department of Pure and Applied Chemistry, Strathclyde University, 295 Cathedral Street, Glasgow, G1 1XL; T.-041-552 4400.

Littlejohn, William Hunter, DA, RSA, RSW, RGI. Head of Fine Art, Gray's School of Art, Aberdeen, 1980-85; b. 16.4.29, Arbroath. Educ. Arbroath High School; Dundee College of Art. Art Teacher: Angus Schools, 1953-56, Arbroath High School, 1956-66; Lecturer, then Head of Painting, Gray's School of Art, 1970-80. Address: (h.) 16 Colvill Place, Arbroath, Angus; T.-Arbroath 74402.

Livingstone, Andrew Hugh, BSc (Hons), DipEd. Rector, St. Columba's School, Kilmacolm, since 1987; b. 7.12.44, Campbeltown; m., Christine Margaret Henderson (deceased); 1 s.; 1 d. Educ. Campbeltown Grammar School; Aberdeen University; Glasgow University. Assistant Teacher, High School of Glasgow, 1968-70; Principal Teacher of Mathematics, Paisley Grammar School, 1970-78; Assistant Rector, Williamwood High School, 1978-83; Depute Rector, Paisley Grammar School, 1983-87. Treasurer, Scottish Mathematical Council, 1978-83. Recreations: golf; bridge; walking. Address: (h.) 38 Lanfine Road, Paisley, PA1 3NL; T.-041-840 2125.

Livingstone, Jeremy Rae Braithwaite, MB, ChB, FRCSEdin, FRCOG. Consultant Obstetrician and Gynaecologist, Simpson Memorial Maternity Pavilion and Royal Infirmary, Edinburgh, since 1968; President, Edinburgh Obstetrical Society, 1986-88; b. 24.9.32, Simla, India; m., Diana Marjorie Cox; 4 d. Educ. Clifton Hall School, Newbridge; Clifton College, Bristol; Edinburgh University. House Officer appointments, Bangour General Hospital and Royal Hospital for Sick Children, Edinburgh; National Service, Royal Navy, 1957-59; training posts, Bangour

General Hospital, 1960-62, and Edinburgh, 1962-68; Council Member, Royal College of Obstetricians and Gynaecologists, representing Scottish members, 1972-75; seconded as Chairman, Department of Obstetrics and Gynaecology, King Faisal Specialist Hospital and Research Centre, Riyadh, 1975-77; Civil Consultant in Obstetrics and Gynaecology, Royal Navy in Scotland; Past President, Honorary Treasurer and Secretary, Edinburgh Obstetrical Society; Chairman, Lothian Division, Obstetrics and Gynaecology, 1981-84. Publication: Farquharson Textbook of Operative Surgery (Contributor). Recreations: golf; reading; music. Address: (h.) 2 Lennox Street, Edinburgh, EH4 1QA; T.-031-332 2038.

Livingstone, Rognvald Maitland, BA, PhD, NDA, NDAgrE, CBiol, MIBiol. Private Consultant, resource development; Deputy Convener, Grampian Regional Council; b. 27.1.35, Aberdeen; m., Rona Scholes; 2 s.; 2 d. Educ. Aberdeen Grammar School; North of Scotland College of Agriculture; Essex Institute of Agriculture; Aberdeen University; Open University. Military service, Royal Armoured Corps; agricultural research service, since 1958; Managing Director, Rowett Research Services, 1985-90; Governor, North of Scotland College of Agriculture, 1987-90. Recreations: skiing; swimming; hill-walking; gardening; reading. Address: (h.) Kirkstane House, Skene, Aberdeenshire, AB32 6XX; T.-0224 743586.

Livingstone of Bachuil, Alastair, MA, LLB, FSA Scot. Baron of Bachuil; b. 1.9.14, Blantyre, Nyasaland; m., Valerie Collins; 2 s.; 3 d. Educ. Loretto School; Edinburgh University; Cambridge University. Sudan Political Service, 1938-40; 1940-43: commissioned into West Yorkshire Regiment in Khartoum, later Brigade Intelligence Officer, 9th Indian Infantry Brigade, active service in Eritrea and Western Desert; seconded to Palestine Government as Assistant District Commissioner, 1943-47; Executive, Iraq Petroleum Company Ltd., 1948-73. Chairman, Lismore Community Council, 1977-80; Member, Convention of the Baronage of Scotland; Hereditary Keeper of the Pastoral Staff of Saint Moluag; Chairman, 1745 Association; Co-editor, Muster Roll of Prince Charles Edward Stuart's Army, 1746. Recreations: genealogy; Scottish history; country pursuits. Address: (h.) Bachuil, Isle of Lismore, Argyll; T.-063 176 256.

Lloyd, Charles Heywood, BSc, PhD, MIM. Reader, Department of Dental Prosthetics and Gerontology, Dundee University, since 1989; b. 15.9.47, Sinoia, Southern Rhodesia; m., Elizabeth Ann Mead; 1 s.; 2 d. Educ. Milton School, Bulawayo; Ellesmere Port Grammar School; Birmingham University. Research Associate, Department of Physical Metallurgy, Birmingham University, 1972-76; Lecturer, 1976-85, Senior Lecturer, 1985-89, Department of Dental Prosthetics and Gerontology, Dundee University. Recreations: philately; golf; beer. Address: (b.) Department of Dental Prosthetics and Gerontology, Dundee University, Dundee DD1 4HN; T.-0382 26041.

Lloyd, Douglas Mathon Gent, BSc, DSc (Bristol), DSc (St Andrews), CChem, FRSC, FRSE. Honorary Reader in Chemistry, St. Andrews University, since 1985; b. 19.7.20, Bristol; m., Lydia Morris. Educ. Colston's School, Bristol; Bristol University. Lecturer, Senior Lecturer, Reader, St. Andrews University, 1947-85; Provost of St. Leonard's College, St. Andrews University, 1973-78. Member, Council, Chemical Society, 1974-77; Member, Council, Royal Society of Chemistry, 1985-88; Member, Perkin Division Council, Royal Society of Chemistry, 1983-86. Publications: 200 papers; eight books. Recreations: organist; travel (especially by sea); interest in wine and theatre. Address: (b.) Department of Chemistry, Purdie Building, St. Andrews University, St. Andrews, KY16 9ST; T.-0334 76161.

Lloyd, Michael Gregory, BA, MSc. Senior Lecturer, Department of Land Economy, Aberdeen University, since 1989; b. 28.11.52, Bridgend; m., Siobhan Canavan; 2 s. Educ. Bridgend Boys Grammar School; Sheffield University; Aberdeen University. Lecturer, Department of Land Economy, Aberdeen University, 1978-89; Chairman, Regional Studies Association, Scottish Branch, since 1989; Reviews Editor, Journal of Property Research, since 1990. Publications: The Impact of Oil on the Aberdeen Economy (Co-author); Land Development and the Infrastructure Lottery (Co-author). Recreations: hill-walking; jogging; reading. Address: (b.) Department of Land Economy, Aberdeen University, Kings College, Old Aberdeen, AB9 2UF; T.-0224 272359.

Lloyd-Jones, Glyn Robin, MA, BA. Author and Novelist; Adviser, Education Department, Dunbartonshire, 1972-89; Director, Eljay Educational Consultancy; Director, Cellulloyd Films Ltd.; b. 5.10.34, London; m., Sallie Hollocombe; 1 s.; 2 d. Educ. Blundell's School, Tiverton; Selwyn College, Cambridge University; Jordanhill College of Education. Teaching in Scottish secondary schools; Director, Curriculum Development Centre, Clydebank; English-Speaking Union Thyne Travel Scholarship to America, 1974; President, Scottish Association of Writers, 1981-86. Publications: children's: Where the Forest and the Garden Meet, 1980; novels: Lord of the Dance (Winner, BBC/Arrow First Novel Competition, 1983); The Dreamhouse, 1985; education books: Assessment: From Principles to Action, 1985; How to Produce Better Worksheets, 1985; non-fiction: Argonauts of the Western Isles, 1989. Recreations: mountaineering; sea-canoeing; wind-surfing; photography. Address: (h.) 26 East Clyde Street, Helensburgh, G84 7PG; T.-0436 72010.

Loasby, Brian John, BA, MLitt. President, Scottish Economic Society, 1987-90; Honorary/Emeritus Professor of Economics, Stirling University, since 1984; b. 2.8.30, Kettering; m., Judith Ann Robinson; 2 d. Educ. Kettering Grammar School; Emmanuel College, Cambridge. Assistant in Political Economy, Aberdeen University, 1955-58; Bournville Research Fellow, Birmingham University, 1958-61; Tutor in Management Studies, Bristol University, 1961-67; Lecturer in Economics, then Senior Lecturer, then Professor of Management Economics, Stirling University, 1967-84. Member, Council, Royal Economic Society, 1981-86. Publications: The Swindon Project, 1973; Choice, Complexity and Ignorance, 1976; The Mind and Method of the Economist, 1989; Equilibrium and Evolution, 1991. Address: (h.) 8 Melfort Drive, Stirling, FK7 0BD; T.-0786 72124.

Lochhead, Liz. Poet and Playwright; b. Motherwell. Educ. Glasgow School of Art. Combined teaching art and writing for eight years; became full-time writer after selection as first holder, Scottish/Canadian Writers' Exchange Fellowship, 1978; former Writer in Residence, Tattenhall Centre, Chester. Publications include: Memo for Spring, Islands, Grimm Sisters, Dreaming Frankenstein, True Confessions; plays include: Blood and Ice, Dracula, Same Difference, Sweet Nothings, Now and Then, True Confessions.

Lockett, Patrick Gordon, CA. Partner, Ernst & Young, since 1979; Director, Cumbernauld Development Corporation, since 1989; b. 3.5.46, Glasgow; m., Erica; 1 s.; 1 d. Educ. Wellington College, Berkshire; Harvard Business School. Partner, Whinney Murray & Co., 1979. Governor, Cargilfield School. Recreations: field sports; tennis; travel. Address: (h.) Swindridgemuir, Dalry, Ayrshire; T.-0294 832079.

Lockhart, Sheriff Brian Alexander, BL. Sheriff, Glasgow and Strathkelvin, since 1981; b. 1.10.42, Ayr; m., Christine Ross Clark; 2 s.; 2 d. Educ. Glasgow Academy; Glasgow

University. Partner, Robertson Chalmers and Auld, Solicitors, 1967-79; Sheriff, North Strathclyde, at Paisley, 1979-81. Recreations: fishing; golf; squash; family. Address: (h.) 18 Hamilton Avenue, Glasgow, G41; T.-041-427 1921.

Lockhart of the Lee, Angus Hew; b. 17.8.46, Dunsyre; m., Susan Elizabeth Normand; 1 s.; 1 d. Educ. Rannoch School, Perthshire; North of Scotland College of Agriculture. Recreations: shooting; skiing. Address: (h.) Newholm, Dunsyre, Lanark; T.-0968 82254.

Lockhead, Moir, IEng, MCIT, MIRTE. Chairman and Managing Director, GRT Holdings PLC, since 1989; b. 25.4.45, Sedgefield; m., Audrey; 3 s.; 1 d. Educ. West Cornforth Secondary School; Darlington Technical College; Middlesborough Polytechnic. Former Head of Engineering, Strathclyde Passenger Transport Executive; joined Grampian Regional Transport as General Manager, 1985. Address: (b.) 395 King Street, Aberdeen, AB9 1SP; T. 0224 637047.

Lockley, Stephen Randolph, BSc, CEng, MICE, FICT, MIMunE, MIHT, DipTE. Director General, Strathclyde Passenger Transport Executive, since 1986; b. 19.6.43, Manchester; m., Angela; 2 d. Educ. Morecambe Grammar School; Manchester University. Highway and Planning Engineer, Lancashire County Council, 1964-72; Transportation and Planning Engineer, Lanarkshire County Council, 1972-75; Strathclyde Regional Council: Principal Engineer (Transportation), 1975-77, Depute Director of Policy Planning, 1977-80, Principal Executive Officer, 1980-86. Address: (b.) Consort House, 12 West George Street, Glasgow, G2 1HN; T.-041-332 6811.

Logan, Andrew, SDA, NDA, FIHort. Farmer; Governor, Scottish Crop Research Institute, since 1986; Director, Scottish Nuclear Stock Association, since 1983; Member, Horticultural Development Council, since 1986; Chairman, Dorward Gray Ltd.; b. 24.3.40, Cupar; m., M.L. Fleming; 3 s.; 1 d. Educ. Strathallan School; Edinburgh School of Agriculture. Director: Fifegro, 1973-79, Elba, 1979-84, Central Farmers, 1974-83; Chairman, Soft Fruit and Field Vegetable Committee, Scottish NFU, 1979-83; Member, Scottish Agricultural Development Council, 1983-86; Governor: National Vegetable Research Station, 1977-87; Strathallan School, since 1986; Director, East of Scotland Growers, 1987-89; Member, Home Grown Cereals Authority Research and Development Committee, 1987-89; Director, Scotfresh, 1984-89; Governor, Institute of Horticultural Research, 1987-89; Member, Scottish Agricultural Research and Development Advisory Council, 1987-90; Director, Futursky, since 1988; Director, Top Hat Holdings, since 1989. Recreations: skiing; golf. Address: (h.) Dairsie Mains, Cupar, Fife; T.-Cupar 52808.

Logan, James, OBE, CChem, MRIC. Vice-Chairman, Scottish Arts Council, 1984-88; Member, Arts Council of Great Britain, 1984-88; Director, Scotland the What? comedy revue, since 1970; b. 28.10.27, Haddington; m., Anne Brand; 1 s.; 1 d. Educ. Robert Gordon's Institute. Former Member, Senior Scientific Staff, Macaulay Institute for Soil Research; former Appeal Administrator, Aberdeen Maritime Museum; Founder/Chairman, Friends of Aberdeen Art Gallery and Museums; Committee Member, Aberdeen Arts Sub-Committee; Chairman, Voluntary Service Aberdeen. Queen's Silver Jubilee Medal. Recreation: theatre. Address: 53 Fountainhall Road, Aberdeen, AB2 4EU; T.-0224 646914.

Logan, Jimmy. Actor/Manager; Comedian; b. 4.4.28, Glasgow. One of five children who appeared on stage as The Logan Family; toured as an accordionist, juvenile lead and comedian's feed; for many years starred in Five Past Eight (summer revue) and numerous pantomimes; wrote and pro-

duced Lauder (one-man show); nine appearances at Royal performances.

Logan, Joseph A. Managing Director, The Scotsman Publications Limited, since 1989. Managing Director, Aberdeen Journals Limited, 1982-83; Managing Director, Newcastle Chronicle and Journal Ltd., 1985-89. President, Scottish Daily Newspaper Society. Address: (b.) 20 North Bridge, Edinburgh, EH1 1YT; T.-031-225 2468.

Logan, Robert James, MBE, JP. Vice-Chairman, Lanarkshire Health Board, since 1983; b. 19.4.21, Carnwath; m., Mary Ann Brown Watt. Educ. St. Mary's School, Melrose; Edinburgh Academy. Lanark Branch President and Area Executive Member, National Farmers Union of Scotland; member, Board of Management, Southern Lanark Hospitals, 1962; joined Lanarkshire Health Board, 1974; Member, State Hospital Management Committee, since 1976. Recreations: reading; walking; sport; sea motor boat cruising. Address: (h.) Loganlea, Eastshield, Carnwath, ML11 8LP; T.-Carnwath 840200.

Logan, Rev. Robert James Victor, MA, BD. Minister, Crown Church, Inverness, since 1970; Clerk, Synod of the Southern Highlands, since 1976; Clerk, Inverness Presbytery, since 1980; b. Kilmarnock. Educ. Dundee High School; St. Andrews University; Edinburgh University. Assistant Minister, Auld Kirk of Ayr, 1962-64; Minister, Newton Parish Church, Dalkeith, 1964-70; Member, Church Boundaries' Commission, 1974-75; Clerk, Synod of Moray, 1972-75; Convener, Nomination Committee, General Assembly, 1979-82; Chairman, successful group applying for franchise to operate Moray Firth Radio, 1979-81. Publication: The Lion, The Pit and the Snowy Day. Recreations: classical music; opera; bridge; reading history. Address: (h.) 39 Southside Road, Inverness, IV2 4XA; T.-0463 231140.

Logan, Rt. Rev. Vincent, DipRE. Roman Catholic Bishop of Dunkeld, since 1981; b. 30.6.41, Bathgate. Educ. Blairs College, Aberdeen; St. Andrew's College, Drygrange. Ordained Priest, 1964; Assistant Priest, St. Margaret's, Edinburgh, 1964-66; Corpus Christi College, London, 1966-67; Chaplain, St. Joseph's Hospital, Rosewell, Midlothian, 1966-67; Adviser in Religious Education, Archdiocese of St. Andrews and Edinburgh, 1967; Parish Priest, St. Mary's, Ratho, 1977-81; Vicar Episcopal for Education, Edinburgh, 1978. Address: Bishop's House, 29 Roseangle, Dundee, DD1 4LS; T.-0382 24327.

Logan, (William) Bruce, BA (Cantab), LLB, NP, WS. Partner, W. & J. Burness, WS, Solicitors, since 1969; b. 7.9.41, Forfar; m., Jennifer Mary; 3 d. Educ. Fettes College, Edinburgh; Cambridge University; Edinburgh University. Hon. Secretary, Scottish Arts Club, since 1983; Director, Art in Partnership Scotland Ltd.; Secretary, Edinburgh Galleries Association. Recreations: music; contemporary art; cycling; walking. Address: (b.) 16 Hope Street, Edinburgh; T.-031-226 2561.

Logie, John Robert Cunningham, MB, ChB, PhD, FRCS, FRCSEdin. Consultant General Surgeon, Inverness Hospitals, since 1981; b. 9.9.46, Aberdeen; m., Sheila C. Will. Educ. Robert Gordon's College, Aberdeen; Trinity College, Glenalmond; Aberdeen University. House Officer, then Senior House Officer, then Lecturer, Department of Surgery, then Senior Registrar, Aberdeen Royal Infirmary. Recreations: rugby refereeing; garden; railways; ornamental waterfowl. Address: (h.) The Darroch, Little Cantray, Culloden Moor, Inverness, IV1 2AG.

Long, Hamish Arthur, BSc, PhD. Director, Scottish Examination Board, since 1990 (Assistant Director, 1986-89); b. 21.9.41, Edinburgh; m., Elizabeth Anne Stephen; 1 s.;

1 d. Educ. Daniel Stewart's College; Edinburgh University; Moray House College of Education. X-ray crystallographic research, Edinburgh University, 1963-66; Technical Officer, ICI, 1966-67; Science Teacher/Special Assistant, North Berwick High School, 1968-72; Principal Teacher of Science, Dunbar Grammar School, 1972-73; Examination Officer, then Senior Examination Officer, then Statistics and Development Officer, Scottish Examination Board, 1973-86. Recreations: music; gardening; painting. Address: (b.) Ironmills Road, Dalkeith, Midlothian, EH22 1LE; T.-031-663 6601.

Lonie, James William Laing, MA. Assistant Secretary, Scottish Education Department, since 1987; b. 24.6.41, Falkirk; m., Nuala Clare Ward. Educ. Falkirk High School; Edinburgh University; Gonville and Caius College, Cambridge. HM Treasury, 1967-76; joined Scottish Office, 1976. Recreations: music; walking; languages. Address: (b.) New St. Andrews House, Edinburgh; T.-031-224 5111.

Lord, Geoffrey, OBE, MA, AIB, FRSA. Secretary and Treasurer, Carnegie UK Trust, since 1977; Chairman, The Unemployed Voluntary Action Fund, since 1990; President, Centre for Environmental Interpretation; b. 24.2.28, Rochdale; m., Jean; 1 s.; 1 d. Educ. Rochdale Grammar School; Bradford University. Midland Bank Ltd., 1946-58; Greater Manchester Probation and After-Care Service, 1958-76 (Deputy Chief Probation Officer, 1974-76); Vice-President, Selcare Trust; Chairman, Pollock Memorial Missionary Trust; Honorary Fellow, Manchester Polytechnic, 1987. Publications: The Arts and Disabilities, 1981; Interpretation of the Environment, 1984. Recreations: the arts; philately; walking; enjoying life. Address: (h.) 9 Craigleith View, Edinburgh.

Lorimer, A. Ross, MD, FRCP, FRCPGlas, FRCPEdin. Honorary Professor, Glasgow University; Consultant Physician and Cardiologist, Glasgow Royal Infirmary, since 1970; b. 5.5.37, Bellshill; m., Fiona Marshall; 3 s. Educ. Uddingston Grammar School; High School of Glasgow; Glasgow University. Recreations: reading; walking. Address: (b.) Department of Cardiology, Royal Infirmary, Glasgow.

Lorimer, Hew Martin, OBE, HonLLD, RSA. Sculptor in stone; b. 22.5.07, Scotland. Educ. Loretto School; Edinburgh College of Art. Former PRO, The British Council, Scotland; Royal Scottish Academician (retired), now Senior Academician; Fellow, Royal Society of British Sculptors (retired); Past Chairman, St. Andrews Preservation Trust; Representative in Fife, National Trust for Scotland. Recreations: music; foreign travel. Address: (h.) Kellie Castle, Pittenweem, Fife, KY10 2RF.

Lothian, Professor Niall, BA, CA. Grant Thornton Professor of Accounting and Head, Department of Accountancy and Finance, Heriot-Watt University, since 1987; b. 27.2.48, Edinburgh; m., Carol Miller; 1 s.; 1 d. Educ. Daniel Stewart's College, Edinburgh; Heriot-Watt University. Lecturer, then Senior Lecturer, Department of Accountancy and Finance, Heriot-Watt University, 1973-87; Visiting Professor: IMEDE, Lausanne, 1979-80, INSEAD, Fontainebleau, 1984; Consultant, United Nations Industrial Development Organisation, Vienna, since 1980. Publications: Accounting for Inflation: Issues and Managerial Practices, 1978; Audit Quality and Value for Money, 1983; How Companies Manage R. & D., 1984; Corporate Performance Indicators, 1987. Address: (b.) Department of Accountancy and Finance, Heriot-Watt University, PO Box 807, Riccarton, Edinburgh, EH14 4AT; T.-031-449 5111.

Lothian, 12th Marquess of (Peter Francis Walter Kerr), KCVO, DL; b. 8.9.22, Melbourne, near Derby; m., Antonella Newland; 2 s.; 4 d. Educ. Ampleforth College, York; Christ Church, Oxford. Parliamentary Under Secretary, Ministry of Health, 1964; Parliamentary Under Secretary, Foreign and Commonwealth Office, 1970-72; Lord in Waiting, 1972-73; Lord Warden of the Stannaries, 1977-83. Knight of Malta; Ensign, Queen's Bodyguard for Scotland; Chairman of Council, Scottish Branch, British Red Cross, 1973-83. Recreations: music; shooting. Address: Ferniehirst Castle, Jedburgh, Roxburghshire; T.-0835 64021.

Louden, Richard Cameron, MA (Hons), DipEd. Divisional Education Officer, Dunbarton Division, Strathclyde Regional Council, since 1990. Educ. Dunfermline High School; Edinburgh University; Moray House College of Education. Depute Director of Education, Dunbarton County Council, 1972-75; Senior Education Officer, Renfrew Division, Strathclyde, 1975-82; Depute Director of Education, SRC, 1982-89. Former Member, Consultative Committee on the Curriculum. Address: (b.) Regional Offices, Garshake Road, Dumbarton; T.-Dumbarton 27303.

Loudon, John Alexander, LLB, NP, SSC. Solicitor, Messrs J. & A. Hastie, SSC, Edinburgh (Senior Partner); Member, Council, Law Society of Scotland; b. 5.12.49, Edinburgh; m., Alison Jane Bruce Laird; 1 s. Educ. Edinburgh Academy; Dundee University. Apprenticeship, Tindal, Oatts and Roger, Solicitors, Glasgow. Secretary, Scottish Division, British Hotels Restaurants & Caterers Association; Secretary, Edinburgh and Lothians Decorators' Association. Recreations: skiing; shooting. Address: (b.) 43 York Place, Edinburgh, EH1 3HT; T.-031-556 7951.

Loudon, John Bruce, MB, ChB, FRCPsych, DPM. Consultant Psychiatrist, Royal Edinburgh Hospital, since 1978 (Deputy Physician Superintendent, since 1980); Honorary Senior Lecturer, Department of Psychiatry, Edinburgh University, since 1978; b. 12.8.43, Edinburgh; m., Susan Mary Lay; 3 s. Educ. Edinburgh Academy; Edinburgh University. Address: (b.) Andrew Duncan Clinic, Morningside, Edinburgh, EH10 5HF; T.-031-447 2011.

Loughran, Thomas Joseph, MA, BA (Hons). Head Teacher, Holy Cross RC High School, Hamilton, since 1986; b. 26.8.38, Airdrie; m., Maireen Keddilty; 2 s.; 1 d. Educ. Our Lady's High School, Motherwell; Glasgow University. Strathclyde University. Depute Head Teacher, St. Margaret's RC High School, Airdrie, 1976-78; Head Teacher, St. Andrew's RC High School, East Kilbride, 1978-86. Recreations: football; wine-making. Address: (b.) Holy Cross RC High School, Muir Street, Hamilton, ML3 6EY; T.-Hamilton 283888.

Lovat, Sheriff Leonard Scott, BL. Sheriff of South Strathclyde, Dumfries and Galloway, at Hamilton, since 1978; b. 28.7.26, Gourock; m., Elinor Frances McAlister (deceased); 1 s.; 1 d. Educ. St. Aloysius' College, Glasgow; Glasgow University. Solicitor, 1948; in partnership, 1955-59; also Assistant to Professor of Civil Law, Glasgow University, 1954-63; Procurator Fiscal Depute, Glasgow, 1960; Cropwood Fellow, Institute of Criminology, Cambridge University, 1971; Senior Assistant Procurator Fiscal, Glasgow and Strathkelvin, 1976. Member, Board of Governors, St. Aloysius' College, Glasgow; Member, Board of Governors, The Garnethill Centre, Glasgow; Member, West of Scotland Committee, Council of Christians and Jews. Publication: Climbers' Guide to Glencoe and Ardgour (two volumes), 1959 and 1965. Recreations: music; mountaineering; bird-watching. Address: (h.) 38 Kelvin Court, Glasgow, G12 OAE; T.-041-357 0031.

Lovat, 17th Baron (Simon Christopher Joseph Fraser), DSO (1942), MC, TD, JP, DL, LLD. 24th Chief of Clan Fraser of Lovat; b. 9.7.11; m., Rosamond Broughton; 4 s.; 2 d. Educ. Ampleforth; Magdalen College, Oxford. Served Second World War (Captain, Lovat Scouts, 1939, Lt.-Col.,

1942, Brig., Commandos, 1943; wounded); Under Secretary of State for Foreign Affairs, 1945. Croix de Guerre; Norway Cross. Address: (h.) Balblair, Beauly, Inverness-shire.

Love, Charles Marshall, FCIB, FCIB (Scotland), MCIM. Chief Executive, Clydesdale Bank PLC, since 1992; b. 27.10.45, Gorebridge; m., June; 1 s.; 1 d. Educ. Musselburgh Grammar School. TSB North West, 1976-83; TSB England and Wales, 1983-89; Managing Director, Banking Services, TSB Bank, 1989-90; Regional Director, Northern Region, TSB Bank, 1990-91; Chairman, TSB Asset Finance, 1989-92; Branch Banking Director, TSB Bank, 1991-92; Chief Executive, TSB Bank Scotland, 1990-92. Deputy Chairman, Committee of Scottish Clearing Bankers, since 1991; Member, CBI Scottish Council, 1990-92. Recreations: reading; music; theatre. Address: (b.) Clydesdale Bank PLC, 30 St. Vincent Place, Glasgow, G1 2HL; T.-041-248 7070.

Love, Frances Mary. Director, Scottish Marriage Guidance Council, since 1987; Tutor and Lecturer, Scottish Human Relations and Counselling Course, since 1986; Organisational Consultant, SIHR, since 1986; b. 2.7.38, Edinburgh; m., James Love; 1 d. Educ. Broughton Secondary School. Edinburgh Public Library Service; voluntary playleader, Edinburgh Toddlers Playcentres; Pre-School Playgroup Association: playgroup supervisor, fieldworker, Scottish Adviser; General Secretary, Pre-School Playgroups Association; Executive Officer/Company Secretary, Scottish Council for Opportunities in Play Experience (SCOPE). Member, Management Board, Scottish Council of Voluntary Organisations; Member, Executive Committees, Scottish Child & Family Alliance and Scottish Council for Single Parents. Recreations: gardening; reading; theatre; dress-making. Address: (b.) 26 Frederick Street, Edinburgh; T.-031-225 5006.

Love, Professor Philip Noel, CBE (1983), MA, LLB. Professor of Conveyancing and Professional Practice of Law, Aberdeen University, since 1974 (Dean, Faculty of Law, 1979-82, and since 1991; Vice-Principal, 1986-90); Member, Scottish Law Commission, since 1986; b. 25.12.39; m., Isabel Leah; 3 s. Educ. Aberdeen Grammar School; Aberdeen University. Admitted Solicitor in Scotland, 1963; Advocate in Aberdeen, since 1963; Partner, Campbell Connon & Co., Solicitors, Aberdeen, 1963-74 (Consultant, since 1974); Law Society of Scotland: Council Member, 1975-86, Vice-President, 1980-81, President, 1981-82; Chairman, Scottish Conveyancing and Executry Services Board, since 1991; Local Chairman, Rent Assessment Panel for Scotland, since 1972; Member, Joint Standing Committee on Legal Education in Scotland, 1976-85 (Chairman, 1976-80); Chairman, Secretary of State for Scotland's Expert Committee on House Purchase and Sale, 1982-84; Chairman, Registers of Scotland Customer Advisory Group, since 1990; Governor, Institute of Occupational Medicine, since 1990; Vice-President, Scottish Law Agents Society, 1970; Member, Rules Council, Court of Session, since 1968; Council Member, International Bar Association, 1983-87; Chairman, Aberdeen Home for Widowers' Children, since 1971; President, Aberdeen Grammar School FP Club, 1987-88; Member, Joint Ethical Committee, Grampian Health Board, since 1984 (Chairman, since 1986); Honorary Sheriff, Grampian, Highland and Islands, since 1978; Member, Butterworths Editorial Consultative Board for Scotland, since 1990. Recreations: rugby (golden oldies version now!); keep fit. Address: (h.) 3A Rubislaw Den North, Aberdeen, AB2 4AL; T.-Aberdeen 313339.

Love, Robert Malcolm, MA (Hons). Controller of Drama, Scottish Television, since 1979; b. 9.1.37, Paisley. Educ. Paisley Grammar School; Glasgow University; Washington University, St. Louis. Actor and Director, various repertory companies, including Nottingham Playhouse, 1962-65;

Producer, Thames TV, 1966-75, including Public Eye, Van Der Valk; freelance Producer, 1976-79, including Thames TV, LWT, Seacastle Film Productions, Scottish TV. Awards including: Commonwealth Festival, New York TV and Film Festival, Chicago Film Festival, Scottish Radio and Television Industries; nominated for International Emmy, New York, 1982; productions for Scottish include Taggart and Take the High Road. Recreations: reading; music; theatre; travel. Address: (b.) Scottish Television, Cowcaddens, Glasgow.

Loveless, Norman Ernest, MA, PhD. University Fellow, Dundee University; b. 9.10.21, London; m., Pamela May Ross; 2 s. Educ. Northern Grammar School, Portsmouth; Edinburgh University. Experimental Assistant, Mine Design Department, Admiralty, 1940-41; Radar Officer, RAF, 1941-47; student, 1947-51; Lecturer in Psychology, St. Andrews University, 1951-52; Lecturer in Industrial Health, Medical School, Newcastle, 1952-59; joined Dundee University as Lecturer, 1959. Recreation: oil painting. Address: (h.) The Limes, Coupar Angus Road, Birkhill, Dundee, DD2 5QE; T.-0382 580425.

Low, Alistair James, BSc, FFA. Director, William M. Mercer Fraser Ltd., Actuaries and Employee Benefit Consultants, since 1986; Non-Executive Director, Scottish Widows Fund, since 1984; Chairman, General Committee, Royal and Ancient Golf Club; b. 2.8.42, Dundee; m., Shona Wallace; 2 s.; 1 d. Educ. Dundee High School; St. Andrews University. Partner, Duncan C. Fraser & Co., Consulting Actuaries, 1968-86. Recreations: golf; skiing; bridge. Address: (h.) Thornfield, Erskine Loan, Gullane, East Lothian; T.-0620 843454.

Low, Bet, ARSA, RSW, RGI. Freelance Artist; b. 27.12.24, Gourock. Educ. Greenock Academy; Glasgow School of Art; Hospitalfield College of Art. Joined Unity Theatre Company, set designing etc., 1946; exhibited in international exhibition, Warsaw, 1954; co-founder and exhibitor, first open-air exhibition on railings at Botanic Gardens, Glasgow; worked part-time as art therapist, early 60s; Co-Founder and Co-Director, New Charing Cross Gallery, Glasgow, 1963-68; major retrospective exhibition, Third Eye Centre, 1985; has held many exhibitions in Britain and Ireland and taken part in hundreds of mixed exhibitions in Britain, Europe and Australia. Recreations: island bagging; beach-combing; reading everything from poetry to thrillers to labels on sauce bottles; meeting people; silence; just pottering. Address: 53 Kelvinside Gardens, Glasgow, G20 6BQ; T.-041-946 1377.

Low, Professor Donald Alexander, MA, BPhil, PhD, FRSE, FSA Scot. Professor of English Studies, Stirling University, since 1990; Director, Centre for Scottish Literature and Culture, since 1988; b. 14.5.39, Greenock; m., Sheona Grant MacCorquodale; 1 s.; 1 d. Educ. Greenock Academy; George Heriot's; Hawick High School; St. Andrews University; Cambridge University. Lecturer in English, St. Andrews University, 1966-72; Lecturer in English, Stirling University, 1972-76. Publications: Robert Burns: The Critical Heritage (Editor), 1974; Critical Essays on Robert Burns (Editor), 1975; That Sunny Dome, 1977; Thieves' Kitchen: The Regency Underworld, 1982; Robert Burns: The Kilmarnock Poems (Editor), 1985; Robert Burns, 1986; The Scots Musical Museum, 1990; The Songs of Robert Burns, 1992. Recreations: travel; music. Address: (h.) 17 Chalton Road, Bridge of Allan, Stirlingshire; T.-0786 832661.

Low, Ian Campbell, BSc, CA, LLD. Chairman, J.T. Inglis & Sons Ltd., since 1945; b. 15.12.12, Newport, Fife; m., Nora Bolton; 2 d. Educ. Fettes College; St. Andrews University. Deputy Chairman, then Chairman, Low & Bonar PLC, Dundee, 1937-77; Chairman, Dundee and London Investment Trust PLC, 1950-87. Recreations: shooting; fishing; gardening. Address: (h.) Holly Hill, 69 Dundee Road, Broughty Ferry, Dundee, DD5 1NA; T.-0382 79148.

Low, Sir James (Richard) Morrison-, 3rd Bt, DL, DFH, CEng, MIEE. Director, Osborne & Hunter Ltd., Glasgow, 1956-89; b. 3.8.25; m., Ann Rawson Gordon; 1 s.; 3 d. Educ. Ardvreck; Harrow; Merchiston; Faraday House, London. Royal Corps of Signals, 1943-47 (Captain). President, Electrical Contractors Association of Scotland, 1982-84; Director, National Inspection Council of Electrical Installation Contractors, 1982-88 (Chairman, Scottish Committee, 1982-88); Chairman, Electrical Industry Liaison Committee, 1986-88; Chairman, Fife Area Scout Council, 1966-84; Chairman, Cupar Branch, East Fife Conservative Association, 1965-78; Trustee, TSB, 1960-80; President, Elecrical Contractors Association of Scotland, 1982-84; DL, Fife, 1978. Address: (h.) Kilmaron Castle, Cupar, Fife.

Low, William, CBE, JP, CBIM. Chairman, Scottish Enterprise Tayside, since 1991; Chairman, Dundee Heritage Trust, since 1986; Director, Dundee Enterprise Trust, since 1987; b. 12.9.21, Dundee; m., Elizabeth Ann Stewart Sime; 2 s. Educ. Merchiston Castle School, Edinburgh. Chairman, Don & Low (Holdings) Ltd., 1975-89; Chairman, UBI Scotland, 1984-89; Chairman, European Association for Textile Polyolefins, 1982-85; Chairman, British Polyolefin Association, 1971-73 and 1978-79; President, Dundee & Tayside Chamber of Commerce & Industry, 1973-74. Past President, Scottish Lawn Tennis Association; Provost, Burgh of Kirriemuir, 1973-75; appointed Fellow, Scottish Council (Development & Industry), 1989. Recreations: shooting; fishing; golf; gardening. Address: (h.) Herdhill Court, Kirriemuir, Angus, DD8 5LG; T.-0575 72215.

Lowden, Professor Gordon Stuart, MA, LLB, CA. Chairman, Dundee Port Authority, since 1979; Past President, Institute of Chartered Accountants of Scotland; Director, Dundee and London Investment Trust PLC, since 1981; b. 22.5.27, Bangkok; m., Kathleen; 2 s.; 1 d. Educ. Dundee High School; Strathallan School; St. John's College, Cambridge; St. Andrews University. Trained with Moody Stuart & Robertson, CA, Dundee; became Partner, 1959; part-time Lecturer/Senior Lecturer, Dundee University, 1955-83; Honorary Professor, Department of Accountancy and Business Finance, Dundee University, since 1987; Member, Board of Governors, Strathallan School. Recreations: golf; watching rugby; bridge. Address: (h.) 169 Hamilton Street, Barnhill, Dundee, DD5 2RE; T.-0382 78360.

Lowe, Janet, BA (Hons), MBA, MIPM. Secretary and Registrar, Duncan of Jordanstone College of Art, since 1988; Convener, ACRA, Scottish Branch, since 1991; b. 27.9.50, South Normanton; m., Donald Thomas Stewart. Educ. Swanwick Hall Grammar School; Hull University; Dundee University. Immigration Officer, Home Office, 1973-76; Administrative Assistant, Hull University, 1976-80; Administrator, Lothian Region Social Work Department, 1980-83; Napier Polytechnic of Edinburgh, 1983-88, latterly as Assistant Academic Registrar. Recreations: hill-walking; literature; film; theatre. Address: (b.) Duncan of Jordanstone College of Art, Perth Road, Dundee, DD1 4HT; T.-0382 23261.

Lowe, John Duncan, MA, LLB. Crown Agent, since 1991; b. 18.5.48, Alloa; m., Jacqueline M.; 2 s. Educ. Hamilton Academy; Glasgow University. Procurator Fiscal Depute, Kilmarnock, 1974-77; Legal Assistant, Crown Office, 1977-79; Senior Procurator Fiscal Depute, Glasgow, 1979-80; Assistant Procurator Fiscal, Glasgow, 1980-83; Assistant Solicitor, Crown Office, 1983-84; Deputy Crown Agent, 1984-88; Regional Procurator Fiscal, Lothian and Borders, 1988-91. Address: (b.) 5/7 Regent Road, Edinburgh; T.-031-557 3800.

Lowe, Martin John Brodie, BSc, PhD. Secretary to Edinburgh University, since 1990 (Secretary and Registrar, St. Andrews University, 1981-89); b. 10.4.40, Dorking; m., Janet MacNaughtan; 3 s.; 1 d. Educ. Dunfermline High School; St. Andrews University. British Council Officer, with service in Tanzania and South India, 1965-69; Strathclyde University: Administrative Assistant, 1969-71, Assistant Registrar, 1971-73, Secretary to Senate, 1973-81. National Council, Voluntary Service Overseas, 1976-83; Honorary Secretary, then Chairman, Glasgow and West of Scotland VSO Committee, 1973-81. Recreations: piping; hill-walking; family interests. Address: (b.) Old College, South Bridge, Edinburgh, EH8 9YL; T.-031-650 2143.

Lowson, David Murray, CSS, MA; b. 24.4.20, Carnoustie; m., Catherine Russell Mitchell; 1 s. Educ. Logie School, Dundee; Liverpool University. Toolmaker (after apprenticeship), until 1947; course in youth and community work, 1947-48; course in social science, 1949-51; Probation Officer, 1951-59; Assistant Governor, Prison Service, England, 1959-62; Lecturer, Liverpool University, 1962-80. Member, Parole Board, England and Wales, 1973-76; Member, Parole Board for Scotland, until 1989; Warden, University Hall, Liverpool, 1970-80, Liverpool University Settlement, 1963-68; Chairman, Peterlee Community Association, 1955. Recreations: outdoor activities. Address: (h.) 87 High Street, Carnoustie, Angus, DD7 7EA; T.-Carnoustie 52189.

Lucas, Walter Pollock. Company Director; Member, Renfrew District Council, since 1984; b. 17.2.17, Port Glasgow; m., Doreen Ada Bromley; 2 s.; 1 d. Educ. Greenock High School; Herds Commercial College, Greenock; George Commercial College, Greenock. Joined Territorial Army, 1938, as a Gunner, 77th Field Regiment of Artillery; evacuated from Dunkirk, 1940; commissioned, Glasgow Highlanders (9th Bn., HLI), 1941; drafted to India, 1942; seconded to 7/17 DOGRA Regiment, stationed at Fort Salop, North West Frontier; posted to IAOC, 1944, Bombay, as Company Commander, Indian Military Wing; returned to UK, 1945. Vice-Chairman, Paisley Conservative Association, 1980-82; Honorary President, Paisley South Conservative Association, since 1985 (Chairman, 1982-85); Elder, Paisley Abbey Church, since 1960; Member, Renfrew District Council, 1974-80. Recreations: golf; fresh water fishing. Address: (h.) The Grange, 106 Corsebar Road, Meikleriggs, Paisley, PA2 9PY; T.-041-889 8554.

Ludlam, Christopher A., BSc (Hons), MB, ChB, PhD, FRCP, FRCPath. Consultant Haematologist, Edinburgh Royal Infirmary, since 1980; Director, Edinburgh Haemophilia Reference Centre, since 1980; part-time Senior Lecturer in Medicine, Edinburgh University, since 1980; b. 6.6.46, Edinburgh. Educ. Edinburgh University. MRC Research Fellow, 1972-75; Senior Registrar in Haematalogy, University Hospital of Wales, Cardiff, 1975-78; Lecturer in Haematology, University of Wales, 1979. Address: (b.) Department of Haematology, Royal Infirmary, Edinburgh; T.-031-229 2477.

Lumsden, James Alexander, MBE, TD, BA, LLB, DL. Director, Bank of Scotland, 1958-85; Director, Scottish Provident Institution, 1968-85; b. 24.1.15, Arden, Dunbartonshire; m., Sheila Cross; 3 s. Educ. Cargilfield School, Edinburgh; Rugby School; Corpus Christi College, Cambridge; Glasgow University. Territorial Army, 1937-46; Partner, Maclay Murray & Spens, Solicitors, Glasgow and Edinburgh, 1947-82; Director of certain Investment Trust companies managed by Murray Johnstone Ltd., 1967-85; Director, Burmah Oil, 1957-76; Commissioner of Income Tax, County of Dumbarton, 1964-90; Member, Committee on Company Law, 1960-62; Fellow, Law Society of Scotland and Royal Faculty of Procurators, Glasgow. Recreations: shooting; fishing; other country pursuits. Address: (h.)

Bannachra, by Helensburgh, Dunbartonshire, G84 9EF; T.-Arden 653.

Lumsden, Professor Keith Grant, MA, PhD. Professor and Director, Esmee Fairbairn Research Centre, Heriot-Watt University, Edinburgh, since 1975; Member, Board of Directors, Hewlett Packard Ltd., since 1982; b. 7.1.35, Bathgate; m., Jean Baillie MacDonald; 1 s. Educ. Bathgate Academy; Edinburgh University; Stanford University, California. Instructor, Department of Economics, then Assistant Professor, Graduate School of Business, Stanford University, 1960-67; Research Associate, Stanford Research Institute, 1965-71; Director, Stanford University Conference: NDTE, 1966, RREE, 1968; Associate Professor, Graduate School of Business, Stanford University, 1968-75; Visiting Professor of Economics, Heriot-Watt University, 1969-70; Director: Economics Education Project, 1969-74, Behavioral Research Laboratories, 1970-72, Capital Preservation Fund Inc., 1971-75, Nielsen Engineering Research Inc., 1972-75; Member, American Economic Association Committee on Economic Education, 1978-81; Academic Director, Service and Transport Executive Programme (STEP), since 1979; Professor of Economics, Advanced Management College, Stanford University, since 1971; Affiliate Professor of Economics, INSEAD, France; Member, Economics Education 14-16 Project, Manchester University; Member, Advisory Council, David Hume Institute, since 1984. Publications: The Free Enterprise System, 1963; The Gross National Product, 1964; International Trade, 1965; Microeconomics: A Programmed Book, 1966; Macroeconomics: A Programmed Book, 1966; New Developments in the Teaching of Economics (Editor), 1967; Excess Demand and Excess Supply in World Tramp Shipping Markets, 1968; Recent Research in Economics Education (Editor), 1970; Basic Economics: Theory and Cases, 1973; Efficiency in Universities: The La Paz Papers (Editor), 1974; Economics Education in the United Kingdom, 1980; Economics: a distance learning study programme, 1991. Recreations: tennis; deep sea sports fishing. Address: (h.) 40 Lauder Road, Edinburgh, EH9 1UE.

Lumsden, William Hepburn Russell, DSc, MD, DTM, DTH, FIBiol, FRCPEdin, FRSE. Scientific and Medical Writer; b. 27.3.14, Forfar; m., Pamela Kathleen Bartram; 2 s.; 1 d. (deceased). Educ. Queen Elizabeth's Grammar School, Darlington; Glasgow University; Liverpool University. MRC Fellow in Tropical Medicine, 1938-41; active service, Malaria Field Laboratories, RAMC, 1941-46; Yellow Fever (subsequently East African Virus) Research Institute, Entebbe, 1947-57; Director, East African Trypanosomiasis Research Organisation, Tororo, 1957-63; Lecturer, Department of Bacteriology, Edinburgh University Medical School, 1963-64; Senior Lecturer, Department of Animal Health, Royal (Dick) School of Veterinary Studies, Edinburgh University, 1964-68; Visiting Professor, Toronto University, 1968; Professor of Medical Protozoology, London School of Hygiene and Tropical Medicine, London University, 1968-79; Senior Editor, Advances in Parasitology, 1978-82; Council Member, Royal Society of Tropical Medicine and Hygiene, 1969-73, 1974-77; Council Member, Royal Zoological Society of Scotland, 1967-68; Member, Expert Advisory Panel on Parasitic Diseases (Trypanosomiasis), WHO, 1962-84; Member, Trypanosomiasis Panel, Ministry of Overseas Development, 1973-79; Member, International Malaria Review Teams, Bangladesh, 1978, Nepal, 1979, Sri Lanka, 1980; Editing Secretary, Berwickshire Naturalists' Club, 1988-91. Publications: Techniques with Trypanosomes, 1973; Biology of the Kinetoplastida (Editor), 1976 and 1979. Recreations: trout fishing; hill-walking. Address: (h.) 16A Merchiston Crescent, Edinburgh, EH10 5AX; T.-031-447 2702.

Lunan, Charles Burnett, MD, FRCOG, FRCS. Consultant Obstetrician, Royal Maternity Hospital, Glasgow, since 1977; Consultant Gynaecologist, Royal Infirmary, Glasgow, since 1977; b. London; m., Helen Russell Ferrie; 2 s.; 1 d. Educ. High School of Glasgow; Glasgow University. Lecturer, Obstetrics and Gynaecology, Aberdeen University, 1973-75; Senior Lecturer, University of Nairobi, 1975-77; WHO Consultant, Family Planning Programme, Bangladesh, 1984-85. Treasurer, 1982-90, Vice-President, 1990-91, President, since 1991, Royal Medico-Chirurgical Society of Glasgow; Secretary, Glasgow Obstetrical and Gynaecological Society, 1978-82. Recreations: gardening; photography; hill-walking. Address: (h.) 1 Moncrieff Avenue, Lenzie, Glasgow, G66 4NL; T.-041-776 3227.

Lunan, Duncan Alasdair, MA (Hons), FBIS, DipEd. Author; b. 24.10.45; m., Linda Joyce Donnelly (m. diss.). Educ. Marr College, Troon; Glasgow University. Management Trainee, Christian Salvesen (Managers) Ltd., 1969-70; self-employed (Author), 1970-78 and since 1980; Manager, Astronomy Project, Glasgow Parks Department, 1978-79; SF Critic, Glasgow Herald, 1971-82 and since 1985; regular astronomy column in various papers and magazines; Council Member, Association in Scotland to Research into Astronautics (ASTRA), since 1963 (President, 1966-72, 1978-85, and since 1990; Secretary, 1985- 89). Publications: Man and the Stars, 1974; New Worlds for Old, 1979; Man and the Planets, 1983; Starfield (Editor), 1989. Recreation: folk music. Address: c/o Campbell, 16 Oakfield Avenue, Hillhead, Glasgow, G12 8JE; T.-041-339 2558.

Lunn, George Michael, BSc, DipHWU. Chairman and Chief Executive, The Whyte & Mackay Group PLC; Chairman, Wm. Muir (Bond 9) Ltd.; b. 22.7.42, Stirling; m., Jennifer Burgoyne; 3 s.; 1 d. Educ. Kelvinside Academy; Glasgow University; Heriot-Watt University. North of Scotland Distilling Co. Ltd., 1965-68; Distillers Co. (Carbon Dioxide) Ltd., 1968-70; PA Management Consultants, 1970-72; British Carpets Ltd., 1972-78; joined Whyte & Mackay Distillers Ltd., 1978. Council Member, Scotch Whisky Association, since 1986; Governor, Kelvinside Academy, since 1987; Board Member, Glasgow Development Agency; Chairman, West of Scotland Branch, Institute of Directors. Recreations: golf; tennis; sailing. Address: (b.) Whyte & Mackay, Dalmore House, 310 St. Vincent Street, Glasgow, G2 5RG; T.-041-248 5771.

Lusby, John Martin, MHSM, DipHSM. General Manager, Lothian Health Board, since 1990, Executive Director, since 1991; b. 27.4.43, Cottingham; m., Clare Gargan; 1 s.; 1 d. Educ. Marist College, Hull; USHAW College, Durham. Entered NHS, 1961; District Administrator, 1981-84, District General Manager, 1984-90, Executive Director, 1990, Doncaster Health Authority. Recreations: reading; music; walking. Address: (h.) 95/6 Grange Loan, Edinburgh, EH9 2ED.

Luscombe, Rt. Rev. Lawrence Edward, OStJ, MA, MPhil, LLD, DLitt, CA, FRSA, FSA Scot. Primus of the Scottish Episcopal Church, 1985-90, and Bishop of Brechin, 1975-90; b. 10.11.24; m., Dr. Doris Morgan; 1 d. Educ. Kelham College; King's College, London; Dundee University. Indian Army, 1942-47; Major; Chartered Accountant, 1952; Partner, Galbraith Dunlop & Co. (later Watson and Galbraith), CA, 1953-63; Curate, St. Margaret's, Glasgow, 1963-66; Rector, St. Barnabas', Paisley, 1966-71; Provost, St. Paul's Cathedral, Dundee, 1971-75. Honorary Canon, Trinity Cathedral, Davenport, Iowa, since 1983; Member, Education Committee, Renfrew County Council, 1967-71; Chairman, Governing Body: Glenalmond College, Edinburgh Theological College, 1985-90; Governor: Lathallan School, Dundee College of Education; Chairman, Inter-Anglican Finance Committee, since 1989; Member, Tayside Regional

Health Board; Member, Court of Corporation of Sons of the Clergy. Address: (h.) Woodville, Kirkton of Tealing, by Dundee, DD4 0RD; T.-Tealing 331.

Lyall, Fiona Jane, DL, MB, ChB, DPH. Family Doctor, Laurencekirk, since 1959; Director, Grampian Television PLC, since 1980; Deputy Lieutenant, Kincardineshire, since 1985; b. 13.4.31, Inverness; m., Dr. Alan Richards Lyall; 1 s.; 1 d. Educ. Inverness Royal Academy; Aberdeen University. Former Member, Laurencekirk Burgh Council; former Kincardine County and Grampian Regional Councillor; Member, Grampian Health Board, 1974, and Kincardine & Deeside Health Council, 1974; Member, Children's Panel Advisory Committee, 1974; Member, Grampian Valuation Appeals Committee; Member, Prince's and Royal Jubilee Trust for Grampian; Treasurer, Action Research for Crippled Child. Recreations: skiing; riding; gardening. Address: Melrose Bank, Laurencekirk, AB3 1AL; T.-05617 220.

Lyall, Ian Alastair, DSC, VRD, DL, FICS; b. 16.3.17, Bangor, Co. Down; m., Eileen Patricia Bennet; 1 d. Educ. Hillhead High School, Glasgow; College of Nautical Studies, Glasgow. Chairman and Managing Director, Roxburgh Henderson & Co. Ltd., 1967-80; Director: British & Burmese Steam Navigation Co. Ltd., 1971-80, Henderson Line Ltd., 1971-80; President, Glasgow Chamber of Commerce, 1978-79; Hon. Consul, Republic of Philippines, since 1965; retired Lt. Commander, RNR, 1963. Recreations: sailing; fishing; shooting. Address: (h.) 21 Chapelacre, Helensburgh, G84 7SH; T.-0436 73976.

Lyall, Michael Hodge, MB, ChB, ChM, FRCSEdin. Consultant Surgeon, Tayside Health Board, since 1975; Honorary Senior Lecturer, Dundee University, since 1975; b. 5.12.41, Methilhill, Fife; m., Catherine B. Jarvie; 3 s. Educ. Buckhaven High School; St. Andrews University. President, Tayside Division, Ileostomy Association of Great Britain; Past President, North Fife Rotary Club. Recreation: computing. Address: (h.) 26 Linden Avenue, Newport on Tay, Fife, DD6 8DU.

Lyddon, William Derek Collier, CB, DLitt, BA, RIBA, DipTP, FRTPI. Chairman, The Planning Exchange; Chairman, Management Committee, Edinburgh School of Environmental Design; Chief Planner, Scottish Development Department, 1967-85; Honorary Professor, Heriot-Watt University; Governor, Edinburgh College of Art; b. 17.11.25, Loughton, Essex; m., Marian Louise Kaye Charlesworth; 2 d. Educ. Wrekin College; University College, London. Depute Chief Architect Planner, Cumbernauld Development Corporation; Chief Architect Planner, Skelmersdale Development Corporation. President, International Society of City and Regional Planners, 1981-84. Address: (h.) 38 Dick Place, Edinburgh; T.-031-667 2266.

Lyell, 3rd Baron (Charles Lyell), Bt. Parliamentary Under-Secretary of State, Northern Ireland Office, 1984-89; b. 27.3.39. Educ. Eton; Christ Church, Oxford. Scots Guards, 1957-59; CA; Opposition Whip, 1974-79; Government Whip, 1979-84; Member, Queen's Bodyguard for Scotland (Royal Company of Archers); DL, Angus, 1988. Address: (h.) Kinnordy House, Kirriemuir, Angus.

Lyle, Lt.-Col. (Archibald) Michael, DL, JP, MA, BA. Landowner and Farmer; b. 1.5.19; m., Hon. Elizabeth Sinclair; 4 d. (1 dec.). Educ. Eton College; Trinity College, Oxford. Hon. Attache, Rome, 1938-39; served 1939-45 with The Black Watch RHR (wounded Normandy, 1944, discharged with wounds, 1946); Lt.-Col., The Scottish Horse RAC (TA), 1953-56; Chairman, T&AFA, 1959-64; Member, Royal Company of Archers, since 1946; Member, Perth and Kinross County Council, 1946-74, Tayside Regional Council, 1974-79; Chairman, Perth College of Further Education, since 1978; JP, Perth, 1950; DL, Perthshire, 1961; Vice Lord Lieutenant, Perth and Kinross, since 1984. Recreations: fishing; shooting; music. Address: Riemore Lodge, Dunkeld, Perthshire; T.-035 04 205.

Lyle, David Angus, MA, LLB, FBIM, FCIS, SSC, NP. Company Secretary, Scottish Enterprise, since 1990; b. 7.9.40; m., Dorothy Ann Clark; 1 s.; 3 d. Educ. George Watson's College, Edinburgh; Edinburgh University. Account Executive, Advertising Agencies, London; Indentured, Edinburgh Corporation; Solicitor, Lloyds and Scottish Finance Ltd., Edinburgh; Depute County Clerk, East Lothian County Council; Director of Administration and Law, Dumfries and Galloway Regional Council; Agency Secretary, Scottish Development Agency. Recreations: shooting; golf; bridge. Address: (h.) Ravelston, Glencairn Road, Kilmacolm, Renfrewshire; T.-050587 2321.

Lynch, Alexander McKay, ACMA, MCIT. Deputy Director/Financial Controller, ScotRail, since 1988; b. 6.10.49, Greenock; m., Christina Keenan; 2 d. Educ. St. Columba's High School, Greenock; Central College of Commerce and Distribution, Glasgow. BR management posts since 1976; Finance and Planning Manager, ScotRail, 1985-88. Honorary President, Railway Staff Association, Scotland. Recreations: youth football; TV; music. Address: (b.) ScotRail House, 58 Port Dundas Road, Glasgow; T.-041-335 3302.

Lyons, Sheriff Hamilton, BL. Temporary Sheriff, since 1984; b. 3.8.18, Gourock; m., Jean Cathro Blair; 2 s. Educ. Gourock High School; Greenock High School; Glasgow University. Practised as Solicitor in Greenock, 1940-66; Sheriff, Stornoway and Lochmaddy, 1966-68; Sheriff, North Strathclyde (formerly Renfrew and Argyll), 1968-84. Council Member, Law Society of Scotland, 1950-66 (Vice-President, 1962-63); Member: Law Reform Committee for Scotland, 1954-64, Committee of Inquiry on Children and Young Persons, 1961-64, Committee of Enquiry on Sheriff Courts, 1963-67, Sheriff Courts Rules Council, 1952-66, Scottish Probation Advisory and Training Council, 1959-69. Recreation: family. Address: (h.) 14 Cloch Road, Gourock, PA19 1AB; T.-0475 32566.

Lyons, Professor Terence John, MA, DPhil, FRSE, FRSA. Professor (Colin MacLaurin Chair) of Mathematics, Edinburgh University, since 1985; b. 4.5.53, London; m., Barbara C. Epsom; 1 s.; 1 d. Educ. St. Joseph's College, West Norwood; Cambridge University; Oxford University. Junior Research Fellow, Jesus College, Oxford, 1979-81; Hedrick Visiting Assistant Professor, UCLA, 1981-82 (Fulbright Visiting Scholar); Lecturer in Mathematics, Imperial College of Science and Technology, London, 1981-85. Address: (b.) Department of Mathematics, James Clerk Maxwell Building, King's Buildings, Edinburgh, EH9 3JZ; T.-031-650 5084.

Mc/Mac

McAleese, Professor Ray, MA, PhD, MIInfSc. Director, Institute for Computer Based Learning, Heriot Watt University, since 1990; b. 22.3.44, Coleraine; m., Dr. Sybil McAleese; 2 s. Educ. Coleraine Academical Institution; Trinity College, Dublin. Aberdeen University: Research Fellow, 1973, Lecturer, 1975, Senior Lecturer, 1982. Elder, Church of Scotland; Council Member, SRHE, AETT. Publications: books on educational technology. Recreations: golf; water colour painting; photography; arguing. Address: (h.) 242 Colinton Road, Edinburgh, EH14 1DL; T.-031-443 9209.

McAllion, John, MA (Hons). MP (Lab), Dundee East, since 1987; b. 13.2.48, Glasgow; m., Susan Jean; 2 s. Educ. St. Augustine's Secondary, Glasgow; St. Andrews University. Teacher, History and Modern Studies, St. Saviour's Secondary, Dundee, 1973-78, Social Studies, Balgowan List D School, Dundee, 1978-82; Research Assistant to Bob McTaggart, MP, 1982-86; Regional Councillor, 1984-87; Convener, Tayside Regional Council, 1986-87. Member, Scottish Executive, Labour Party, 1986-88; Senior Vice Chairperson, Dundee Labour Party, 1986, 1987. Recreations: football; reading; music. Address: (h.) 3 Haldane Street, Dundee, DD3 0HP; T.-0382 826678.

McAlpine, Thomas, BSc, CEng, MIEE. Business Consultant; b. 23.9.29, Motherwell; m., Isobel Lindsay; 2 s.; 1 d. Educ. Dalziel High School, Motherwell; Strathclyde University. National Service, REME, 1952-54 (2nd Lt.); Chief Engineer, Belmos Co. Ltd., Bellshill, 1954-58; Chief Development Engineer, Mine Safety Appliances, Glasgow, 1958-62; Managing Director: Rowen Engineering Co. Ltd., Glasgow, 1962-71, Chieftain Industries PLC, Livingston, 1971-85. Former Executive Vice Chairman Administration, Scottish National Party (former Vice President, SNP); Parliamentary candidate, Clydesdale (Lanark), 1974, 1979, 1983, Dumfries, 1987. Recreations: when young, played rugby, swimming and tennis. Address: (h.) Millrig House, Millrig Road, Wiston, by Biggar, Lanarkshire, ML12 6HT; T.-Lamington 683.

McAndrew, Nicolas, CA. Managing Director, Murray Johnstone Ltd., since 1988; b. 9.12.34, London; 2 s.; 1 d. Educ. Winchester College. National Service (The Black Watch) commission, 1953-55; articled clerk, Peat Marwick Mitchell, 1955-61; qualified CA, 1961; S.G. Warburg & Co. Ltd., Merchant Bankers, 1962-78; became Chairman, Warburg Investment Management Ltd., and Director, Mercury Securities Ltd.; Managing Director, N.M. Rothschild & Sons Ltd., Merchant Bankers, 1979-88. Master, Worshipful Company of Grocers, 1978-79. Recreations: fishing; shooting; golf. Address: (h.) Blairquhosh House, Blanefield, by Glasgow, G63 9AJ; T.-0360 70232.

McArdle, Colin S., MD, FRCS, FRCSEdin, FRCSGlas. Consultant Surgeon, University Department of Surgery, Glasgow Royal Infirmary, since 1981; Honorary Professor, Glasgow University, since 1991; b. 10.10.39, Glasgow; m., June M.C. Merchant; 2 s.; 1 d. Educ. Jordanhill College School; Glasgow University. Senior Registrar in General Surgery, Western Infirmary, Glasgow, 1972-75; Consultant Surgeon: Victoria Infirmary, Glasgow, 1975-78, Glasgow Royal Infirmary, 1978-80. Address: (h.) 4 Collylinn Road, Bearsden, Glasgow.

MacArthur, Rev. Allan Ian, BD, JP. Minister, Lochcarron Parish, since 1973; Member, Crofters Commission, 1984-90; District Councillor, since 1984; b. 22.5.28, Marvig, Isle of Lewis; m., Effie Macleod; 1 s.; 6 d. Educ. Nicolson Institute,

Stornoway; Glasgow University and Trinity College. Meteorologist, Air Ministry and Falkland Islands Dependencies Survey, Antarctica; teaching; Minister of Religion and Presbytery Clerk. Member, Local Health Council; former Secretary and Vice-Chairman, Community Council. Address: Church of Scotland Manse, Lochcarron, Ross-shire, IV54 8YD; T.-05202 278.

Macarthur, Charles Ramsay, QC (Scot). Sheriff of Tayside, Central and Fife, 1981-91.

McArthur, Douglas B., BSc (Hons). Managing Director, Radio Advertising Bureau, since 1992; Director, Balgray Communications Group Ltd. and subsidiaries, since 1984; b. 17.3.51, Dundee; m., Elizabeth M.A.; 3 d. Educ. Kirkton High School, Dundee; Glasgow University. Marketing management roles, Proctor and Gamble, Scottish & Newcastle, Campbell's Soups Ltd., Radio Clyde; marketing and advertising consultancy roles with Hall Advertising and Baillie Marshall Advertising. Director, Drumchapel Opportunities Ltd.; Member, Scottish Arts Council (Chairman, Drama Committee). Recreations: swimming; music; visual arts; drama. Address: (h.) 33 Victoria Crescent Road, Glasgow, G12 9DD.

Macarthur, Edith. Actress; b. Ardrossan, Ayrshire. Educ. Ardrossan Academy. Began career, 1948, with Wilson Barrett Company, then Perth Repertory, Gateway Theatre Company, Citizens' Theatre, Glasgow, Bristol Old Vic, Royal Shakespeare Company, Ochtertyre Theatre, Royal Lyceum Theatre Company, West End; television work includes The Borderers, Sunset Song, Weir of Hermiston, Sutherland's Law; the "lady laird" in Take the High Road, 1980-86; recent stage appearances: solo-performance play, Marie of Scotland, Jamie the Saxt and The Thrie Estates for the Scottish Theatre Company at Edinburgh Festivals and Warsaw International Festival, 1986, Judith Bliss in Hay Fever, Royal Lyceum Theatre, 1987, Charley's Aunt, Death of a Salesman, Royal Lyceum, 1988, Daphne Laureola, Pygmalion, Pride and Prejudice, Pitlochry Festival Theatre, 1988; The Cherry Orchard, Royal Lyceum, 1989; The Cherry Orchard, The Circle, Arsenic and Old Lace, Pitlochry, 1990; Driving Miss Daisy, Perth, 1991; Cinderella, Glasgow and Edinburgh, 1990, 1991. Recreations: music; books. Address: c/o Larry Dalzell Associates Ltd., Suite 12, 17 Broad Court, London, WC2B 5QN.

McArthur, John Duncan, BSc (Hons), MB, ChB (Hons), DM, FRCPGlas, MRCP, MRCPEdin. Consultant Physician and Cardiologist, Western Infirmary and Gartnavel General Hospital, Glasgow, since 1978; Honorary Clinical Senior Lecturer, Glasgow University, since 1978; b. 7.1.38, Hamilton; m., Elizabeth A. Bowie; 2 s.; 1 d. Educ. Hamilton Academy; Glasgow University. Junior doctor, Royal Infirmary, Glasgow, and in Ayrshire, 1963-67; St. Colm's College, Edinburgh, 1967-68; Missionary, Church of Scotland, working as Cardiologist at Christian Medical College Hospital, Vellore, India, 1968-73; Senior Registrar, Glasgow Teaching Hospitals, 1974-78. Elder, Killermont Parish Church; Council Member, Interserve, Scotland. Recreations: DIY; gardening. Address: (h.) 8 Durness Avenue, Bearsden, Glasgow, G61 2AQ; T.-041-942 7330.

Macartney, Rev. William Macleod, MA; b. 11.10.12, Partick; m., Jessie H.I. Low; 1 s.; 2 d. Educ. George Watson's; Edinburgh University; Zurich University. Ordained, 1938; Missionary in Africa, 1938-45; former Minister: Bridge of Weir; Elgin; St. Machar's Cathedral, Old Aberdeen; Hutton and Fishwick; Vienna Community Church; former Member, Health Boards, Elgin and Borders; former Convener, Church of Scotland Publications Committee. Publications: Dr. Aggrey; The Church and the Underdog. Recreations: fishing;

writing. Address: (h.) Couttie Cottage, Coupar Angus, PH13 9HF; T.-0828 28152.

Macartney, W.J. Allan, MA, BLitt, PhD. Staff Tutor, Social Sciences, The Open University in Scotland, since 1975; Honorary Fellow, Edinburgh University, since 1981; Member, National Executive Committee, Scottish National Party, since 1984, Vice President, since 1990; b. 1941, Accra, Ghana; m., J.D. Anne Forsyth; 2 s.; 1 d. Educ. Elgin Academy; Tuebingen University; Marburg University; Edinburgh University; Glasgow University. Teacher, Eastern Nigeria, 1963-64; Lecturer, University of Botswana, Lesotho and Swaziland, 1966-74; Executive Member, Unit for the Study of Government in Scotland, Scottish Self-Government College, Saint Andrew Society; Church of Scotland Elder, since 1979; Member, Church and Nation Committee, since 1989; Parliamentary candidate (SNP), 1970, 1979, 1983, 1987 (International Relations Spokesperson, 1982-91, Agriculture, Forestry, Fisheries and Rural Affairs, since 1991); Euro candidate, 1989. Publications: Readings in Boleswa Government, 1971; The Referendum Experience, 1981; Islands of Europe, 1984; Self-Determination in the Commonwealth, 1987; Towards 1992, 1989; Asking the People, 1992. Recreations: music; languages; walking; vexillogy. Address: (b.) 60 Melville Street, Edinburgh, EH3 7HF; T.-031-226 3851.

Macaskill, Allan Nicolson. Member, Argyll and Bute District Council, since 1977; Founder Member, 87 Group; b. 10.2.43, Stirling; m., Elizabeth Dawn; 1 s.; 1 d. Educ. Oban High School; Glasgow High School; Anniesland College of Further Education. Recreations: reading; sport, especially athletics. Address: (h.) Ullinish, Balvicar Farm, by Oban; T.-08523 221.

MacAskill, Norman Alexander, OBE, JP. Vice-Chairman, Crofters Commission, 1966-86; b. 1.11.24, Lochinver; m., Joan Logan Brown; 2 s. Educ. Lochinver Public School; Golspie High School. Customs and Excise Officer; Social Welfare Officer, North West Sutherland; former Secretary, North and West Sutherland Council of Social Service; former Chairman: Sutherland Tourist Organisation, Sutherland Valuation Appeals Committee; Member, Scottish Rent Assessment Panel. Recreations: fishing; music; history; archaeology. Address: (h.) 8 Cruamer, Lochinver, Lairg, Sutherland; T.-057 14 291.

Macaulay, Rev. Donald, OBE, JP. Former Minister, Park, Isle of Lewis; former Convener, Western Isles Council; b. 25.2.26, Great Bernera; m., Catherine Macleod; 3 s.; 3 d. Educ. Great Bernera School; Aberdeen University. Several years a fisherman; Member: Ross and Cromarty County Council, 1969-75, Lewis District Council, 1969-75; Member, COSLA Policy Committee, 1975-82; Member, Western Isles Enterprise. Recreations: fishing; travel; local history; silviculture. Address: Garymilis, Great Bernera, Isle of Lewis; T.-0851 74341.

McAvoy, Thomas McLaughlin. MP (Labour), Glasgow Rutherglen, since 1987; b. 14.12.43, Rutherglen; m., Eleanor Kerr; 4 s. Member, Strathclyde Regional Council, 1982-87.

McBryde, Professor William Wilson, LLB, PhD, LLD. Professor of Scots Law, Dundee University, since 1987, Deputy Principal, since 1991; Solicitor, since 1969; b. 6.7.45, Perth; m., Joyce Margaret Gossip; 1 s; 2 d. Educ. Perth Academy; Edinburgh University. Apprentice and Assistant, Morton, Smart, Macdonald & Milligan, WS, Edinburgh, 1967-70; Court Procurator, Biggart, Lumsden & Co., Glasgow, 1970-72; Lecturer in Private Law, Glasgow University, 1972-76; Member, Scottish Law Commission Working Party on Contract Law, since 1975; Senior Lecturer in Private Law, Aberdeen University, 1976-87; Specialist

Parliamentary Adviser to House of Lords Select Committee on the European Communities, 1980-83; Member, Scottish Consumer Council, 1984-87; Member, Scottish Advisory Committee on Arbitration, since 1986; Director, Scottish Universities' Law Institute, since 1989; Honorary Sheriff, Tayside, Central and Fife, at Dundee, since 1991. Recreations: walking; photography. Address: (b.) Faculty of Law, Dundee University, Dundee, DD1 4HN; T.-0382 23181.

McCabe, Primrose Smith, CA. Partner, Primrose McCabe & Co., CA, Linlithgow, since 1987; Member, Council, Institute of Chartered Accountants of Scotland, since 1988; Member, Commission for Local Authority Accounts, since 1988; Non-executive Director, Dunfermline Building Society, since 1990; b. 21.9.40, Gorebridge; m., Ernest Henry Elfred McCabe. Educ. Ayr Academy. Trained CA, Stewart Gilmour & Co., Ayr, 1958-63; joined Romanes & Munro as Qualified Assistant, 1963; progressed through manager ranks to Partner, Deloitte Haskins & Sells, 1981; Hon. Treasurer, YWCA, seven years until 1987; set up own practice, 1987; first Convener, General Practitioners Committee, ICAS. Recreations: walking dogs; dress-making. Address: (b.) Regent House, Regent Centre, Linlithgow, EH49 7HU; T.-0506 842466.

MacCaig, Norman, OBE, MA, DLitt (Edinburgh), DUniv (Stirling), Lld (Dundee), FRSE, FRSC, ARSA. Poet; b. 14.11.10, Edinburgh; m., Isabel; 1 s.; 1 d. Educ. Royal High School, Edinburgh; Edinburgh University. Former schoolteacher; former Writer in Residence, Edinburgh University; former Reader in Poetry, Stirling University; publications of poetry: Far Cry, 1943, The Inward Eye, 1946, Riding Lights, 1955, The Sinai Sort, 1957, A Common Grace, 1960, A Round of Applause, 1962, Measures, 1965, Surroundings, 1966, Rings on a Tree, 1968, A Man in my Position, 1969, The White Bird, 1973, The World's Room, 1974, Tree of Strings, 1977, The Equal Skies, 1980, A World of Difference, 1983; Selected Poems, 1971; Penguin Modern Poets 21, 1972; Old Maps and New (selected poems), 1978; Collected Poems, 1985; Voice-over, 1988; Collected Poems (paperback), 1988; New Collected Poems, 1990; Queen's Gold Medal for Poetry, 1986; eight Scottish Arts Council awards, two Society of Authors awards; Heinemann Award, Cholmondely Award. Recreations: literature; music; fishing. Address: 7 Leamington Terrace, Edinburgh, EH10 4JW; T.-031-229 1809.

McCall, James, BSc, MEd, PhD, CPsychol, AFBPsS. Vice-Principal, Jordanhill College of Education, since 1983; b. 14.7.41, Kilmarnock; m., Mary Elizabeth Stuart Maclean; 3 s. Educ. Kilmarnock Academy; Glasgow University; Aberdeen University; Jordanhill College of Education. Teacher of Science, Hillhead High School, Glasgow; Principal Teacher of Physics, Queen's Park Secondary School, Glasgow; Lecturer in Educational Psychology, Aberdeen College of Education; Head, Psychology Department, Jordanhill College of Education; Member, Board of Governors, Glasgow School of Art, since 1986; Member, CNAA Committee on Teacher Education, since 1989. Publications: Techniques for the Assessment of Practical Skills in Foundation Science, 1983; Techniques for Assessing Process Skills in Practical Science, 1988; Teacher Education in Europe, 1990; How to assess open-ended practical investigations in Biology, Chemistry and Physics, 1991. Recreations: bridge; golf. Address: (b.) Jordanhill College of Education, Southbrae Drive, Glasgow, G13 1PP; T.-041-950 3220.

McCall, Kathleen Mary, DL, LRAM. Deputy Lieutenant for Borders Region, District of Tweeddale, since 1988; President, Tweeddale Branch, British Red Cross Society, since 1983; Member, Scottish Council, BRCS, since 1990; b. 20.2.33, Karachi; m., J.A.G. McCall, CMG. Educ. Calder

Girls' School, Seascale; Royal Scottish Academy of Music and Drama. Held various teaching posts; voluntary offices with Red Cross in Nigeria. Recreations: music; walking; the arts. Address: (h.) Burnside, West Linton, EH46 7EW; T.-0968 60488.

McCall-Smith, Alexander, LLB, PhD. Senior Lecturer, Faculty of Law, Edinburgh University, since 1974; Associate Dean, since 1991; Author; b. 24.8.48, Zimbabwe; m., Dr. Elizabeth Parry; 2 d. Educ. Christian Brothers' College, Bulawayo; Edinburgh University. Lecturer, Queen's University, Belfast, 1973-74; Lecturer, then Senior Lecturer, Edinburgh University, since 1974; Head, Department of Law, University of Botswana, 1981; Professor of Law, Southern Methodist University, Dallas, Texas, 1988. Publications: (non-fiction): Law and Medical Ethics (Co-author); Butterworth's Medico-Legal Encyclopaedia (Co-author); The Criminal Law of Botswana (Co-author); fiction: Children of Wax; numerous books for children. Recreations: wind instruments; reading; travel. Address: (h.) 16A Napier Road, Edinburgh, EH10 5AY; T.-031-229 6083.

MacCallum, Alasdair Norman, BSc (Hons). Chief Executive, Don & Low Holdings, since 1986; Non-Executive Chairman, Chessbourne Ltd., Unilith Ltd., Lassalle Engineering Ltd.; Chairman, CBI Scotland, since 1991; b. 27.1.36, Connel, Argyll; m., Helga Diana; 1 s.; 1 d. Educ. Keil School; Glasgow University. National Service Commission, Royal Artillery; Unilever, six years; Culter Guard Bridge Paper Co. Ltd., seven years; Devro Ltd. (Production Director, Managing Director), 14 years; Baxters of Fochabers (Managing Director), one year. Vice-Chairman, Montrose Harbour Trust; Member, Montrose Life Boat Committee. Recreations: angling; shooting; gardening; theatre; music; reading. Address: (h.) Inverossie, Rossie Braes, Montrose, DD10 9TJ; T.-0674 73013.

McCallum, Sir Donald Murdo, CBE, DL, BSc, DSc, LLD, DUniv, FEng, FIEE, FRAeS, CBIM, FRSE. Chairman, Scottish Council Development and Industry, since 1985; Director, Ferranti plc, 1970-87; Chairman, Scottish Committee, Universities Funding Council, 1989-91; Chairman, Laser Ecosse Ltd., since 1990; b. 6.8.22, Edinburgh; m., 1, Barbara Black (deceased); 1 d.; 2, Margaret Illingworth (nee Broadbent). Educ. George Watson's Boys' College; Edinburgh University. Admiralty Signal Establishment, 1942-46; Standard Telecommunication Laboratories, 1946; joined Ferranti, 1947; General Manager, Ferranti Scottish Group, 1968-85; Chairman, Scottish Tertiary Education Advisory Council, 1984-87; Trustee, National Library of Scotland; Governor: Napier Polytechnic of Edinburgh, Edinburgh College of Art; Member, Scottish Economic Council. Recreations: fishing; photography. Address: (h.) 46 Heriot Row, Edinburgh, 3; T.-031-225 9331.

MacCallum, Professor James Richard, BSc, PhD, DSc, CChem, FRSC, FRSE. Professor of Polymer Chemistry, St. Andrews University; b. 3.5.36, Kilmartin; m., Eleanor Margaret Thomson; 2 s.; 1 d. Educ. Dumfries Academy; Glasgow University. Technical Officer, ICI Fibres Division, 1961-62; ICI Research Fellow, Aberdeen University, 1962-63; Lecturer, St. Andrews University, 1964. Elder, St. Leonards Church, St. Andrews. Recreation: golf. Address: (h.) 9 Cairnsden Gardens, St. Andrews, Fife; T.-0334 73152.

Maccallum, Norman Ronald Low, BSc, PhD, CEng, FIMechE. Reader in Mechanical Engineering, Glasgow University, since 1982; b. 18.2.31, Walston, Lanarkshire; m., Mary Bentley Alexander; 1 s.; 2 d. Educ. Allan Glen's School, Glasgow; Glasgow University. Assistant in Mechanical Engineering, Glasgow University, 1952-55; National Service, Royal Navy, 1955-57 (final rank: Sub-Lt.); Lecturer in Mechanical Engineering, Glasgow University,

1957-61; Performance Engineer, Rolls-Royce Ltd. (Scottish Group), 1961-62; Lecturer in Mechanical Engineering, then Senior Lecturer, Glasgow University, 1962-72. Joint Session Clerk, Trinity St. Paul's Church, Cambuslang. Recreation: singing. Address: (h.) 43 Stewarton Drive, Cambuslang, Glasgow, G72 8DQ.

McCann, James Aloysius, MA, LLB. Solicitor and Notary Public; Senior Tutor (Professional Legal Practice), Glasgow University, 1981-91; b. 14.8.39, Glasgow; m., Jane Marlow; 3 s.; 1 d. Educ. St. Mungo's Academy, Glasgow; Glasgow University. Former Member, Legal Aid Central Committee; Dean, Faculty of Dunbartonshire Solicitors, 1986-88; Convenor for Law Society PQLE Advocacy Training Courses, 1983-91; a founding Director, Legal Defence Union in Scotland, 1987, Chairman, since 1990; Member, Law Society of Scotland Legal Aid Committee; Reporter, Scottish Legal Aid Board (Co-opted Member, Criminal Applications Committee, since 1987); appointed Honorary Sheriff at Dumbarton, 1990; Temporary Sheriff, 1991. Recreations: sailing/windsurfing; chess; music. Address: (b.) 499 Kilbowie Road, Clydebank.

McCann, Peter Toland McAree, CBE (1977), OStJ, DL, JP, BL. Solicitor and Notary Public, since 1947; b. 2.8.24, Glasgow; m., Maura Eleanor Ferris; 1 s. Educ. St. Mungo's Academy, Glasgow; Glasgow University. Councillor, Corporation of Glasgow, 1961-75; River Bailie, 1962; Magistrate, 1963-66; Police Judge, 1967-74; JP, since 1967; Lord Lieutenant, 1975-77; Lord Provost, City of Glasgow District, 1975-77; Depute Lieutenant, since 1977; Chairman, St. Thomas More Society for Lawyers, 1960; Chairman, McCann Committee for Provision of Secondary Education for Physically Disabled Children, 1968; awarded two Golden Swords from HRH Prince Fawaz of Saudi Arabia, 1977-78; awarded Silver and Golden Swords from City of Jeddah, 1975-78; awarded Medal of King Faisal of Saudi Arabia, 1976. Recreations: music; history; model railways; collecting model cars and model soldiers. Address: (h.) Craig En Ross, 31 Queen Mary Avenue, Crosshill, Glasgow, G42 8DS.

McCarrison, Robert, BSc, CBiol, FIBiol. Rector, Marr College, Troon, since 1978; b. 3.11.37, Oxford; m., Janet M. Gibson; 1 s.; 1 d. Educ. Ayr Academy; Glasgow University; Institute of Biology. Assistant Science Teacher, Principal Teacher (Biology), Assistant Rector, Cumnock Academy, 1959-76; Depute Rector, James Hamilton Academy, Kilmarnock, 1976-78. Past President: Ayrshire Science Teachers Association, Ayrshire Biology Panel, Rotary Club of Troon; Treasurer, Kingcase Parish Church, Prestwick. Recreations: golf (Prestwick St. Nicholas); curling (Troon Portland). Address: (b.) Marr College, Dundonald Road, Troon; T.-0292 311082.

McCarthy, James, BSc. Lecturer/Conservation Consultant; Deputy Director (Scotland), Nature Conservancy Council, 1975-91; b. 6.5.36, Dundee; m.; 2 s.; 1 d. Educ. Harris Academy, Dundee; Aberdeen University; University of East Africa, Kampala. Military Service, 1954-56 (Royal Marines, commissioned Black Watch, seconded King's African Rifles); Leverhulme Scholar, Makerere College, Kampala, 1959-61; Assistant Conservator of Forests, Tanzania, and Lecturer in Forest Ecology, Forest Training School, 1961-63; Deputy Regional Officer (North England), Nature Conservancy, 1963-69. Churchill Fellow, USA, 1976; Nuffield/Leverhulme Fellow, 1988; Assessor, Scottish Environmental Education Council. Recreation: cross-country skiing. Address: (h.) 6a Ettrick Road, Edinburgh; T.-031-229 1916.

McClellan, John Forrest, MA, Hon. FDIT. Director, Scottish International Education Trust, since 1986; Member, Management Committee, Hanover (Scotland) Housing

Association, since 1986; b. 15.8.32, Glasgow; m., Eva Maria Pressel; 3 s.; 1 d. Educ. Aberdeen Grammar School; Aberdeen University. 2nd Lt., Gordon Highlanders and Nigeria Regiment, Royal West African Frontier Force, 1954-56; entered Civil Service, 1956; Assistant Principal, Scottish Education Department, 1956-59; Private Secretary to Permanent Under Secretary of State, Scottish Office, 1959-60; Principal, Scottish Education Department, 1960-68; Civil Service Fellow, Glasgow University, 1968-69; Scottish Education Department: Assistant Secretary, Schools Division, 1969-71, Assistant Secretary, Higher Education Division, 1971-77; Assistant Under Secretary of State, Scottish Office, 1977-80; Under Secretary, Industry Department for Scotland, 1980-85 (retired). Publication: Then A Soldier (novel), 1991. Recreations: gardening; walking. Address: (h.) Grangeneuk, West Linton, Peeblesshire; T.-West Linton 60502.

McClelland, Thomas Henry, BAgr, CBiol, MIBiol, FRAgS. Head, Sheep Research and Development, Scottish Agricultural Colleges; b. 10.5.34, Belfast; m., Maureen Mardon; 1 s.; 2 d. Educ. Belfast Royal Academy; Queen's University of Belfast. Lecturer, Greenmmount Agricultural College, Northern Ireland, 1959-68; Research Scientist, Animal Breeding Research Organisation, 1968-75; Head, Animal Production Department (Beef and Sheep), West of Scotland Agricultural College, 1975-86. Former Member, Hill Farming Research Organisation governing body; Director, FASL. Recreations: reading; gardening; sport. Address: (b.) SAC Edinburgh, Bush Estate, Penicuik, Midlothian, EH26 0QE; T.-031-445 4811.

McClements, Rev. Duncan Elliott, MA, BD, MTh. Minister, Grahamston United Church, since 1976; Clerk, Falkirk Presbytery, since 1990; b. 28.8.40, Glasgow; m., Dorothy Jean Easton; 1 s.; 1 d. Educ. Daniel Stewart's College; Edinburgh University. Minister, Hurlford Reid Memorial Church, 1967-76. Chairman, Kirkcare Housing Association, 1980-84. Recreations: reading; gardening; walking. Address: (h.) 30 Russel Street, Falkirk, FK2 7HS; T.-0324 24461.

McClure, David, RSA, RSW, RGI. Painter and Printmaker; b. 20.2.26, Lochwinnoch; m., 1, Joyce D. Flanigan (deceased); 2 s.; 1 d.; 2, Angela Bradbury. Educ. Queen's Park School, Glasgow; Glasgow University; Edinburgh University; Edinburgh College of Art. Travelling scholarship, Italy and Spain, 1951-52; staff, Edinburgh College of Art, 1953-55; Fellow of College, 1955-57, travelling and painting in Italy and Sicily; Senior Lecturer, Duncan of Jordanstone College of Art, until 1983 (Head of Painting, 1983-87); one-man exhibitions since 1957 in Edinburgh, Palermo, London, Birmingham, Perth, etc. Publication: John Maxwell (monograph), 1976. Recreations: collecting bric-a-brac; the pianoforte; etymology. Address: (h.) 16 Strawberrybank, Dundee, DD2 1BJ; T.-0382 66959.

McCluskey, Baron (John Herbert McCluskey), QC (Scot). Senator of the College of Justice in Scotland, since 1984; Life Peer; b. 12.6.29. Sheriff Principal of Dumfries and Galloway, 1973-74; Solicitor General for Scotland, 1974-79.

McColgan, Elizabeth. Athlete; b. 24.5.64, Dundee; m., Peter Conor McColgan. Educ. University of Alabama. Gold medallist, Commonwealth Games (10,000 metres), 1986, World Championships, 1991; Silver medallist, World Cross-Country Championships, 1987; Silver medallist, Olympic Games (10,000 metres), 1988; Silver medallist, World Indoor Championships, 1989; Gold medallist (10,000 metres) and Bronze medallist (3,000 metres), Commonwealth Games, 1990.

McColl, James Hamilton, NDH, SDH, SHM. Horticulturalist; b. 19.9.35, Kilmarnock; m., Billie; 1 s.; 1 d. Educ. Kilmarnock Academy; West of Scotland Agricultural College. Staff Member, WSAC, Auchincruive, Ayr, 1956-59; Assistant Head Gardener, Reading University Botanic Garden, 1959-61; Horticultural Adviser/Lecturer, Shropshire Education Authority, 1961-67; Horticultural Adviser: MAFF, Leicestershire, Northants and Rutland, 1967-73, North of Scotland College of Agriculture, 1973-78; PRO, Morrison Bowmore Distillers Ltd.; Co-Presenter, The Beechgrove Garden, BBC TV Scotland, 1978-89; former Trustee, Royal Botanic Gardens, Edinburgh. Recreations: golf; music; rugby. Address: (h.) Ayrshire House, Oldmeldrum, Aberdeenshire; T.-065 12 3955.

McConnell, Professor Ian F., BVMS, MA, PhD, BVMS, MRCPath, MRCVS, FRSE. Professor of Veterinary Pathology, Edinburgh University, since 1983; b. 6.11.40, Glasgow; m., Anna; 3 s.; 2 d. Educ. St. Aloysius' College, Glasgow; Glasgow University. Wellcome Trust Postdoctoral Research Fellow, Department of Immunology, AFRC Institute of Animal Physiology, Babraham, Cambridge, 1970-72; Research Fellow, Clare Hall, Cambridge, 1970-72; Senior Lecturer in Immunology, Royal Postgraduate Medical School, London University, 1972-75; Senior Scientist, MRC Unit on Mechanisms in Tumour Immunity, The Medical School, Cambridge; Member, Governing Body, Institute of Animal Health. Recreation: hill-walking. Address: (b.) Department of Veterinary Pathology, Edinburgh University, Royal (Dick) School of Veterinary Studies, Summerhall, Edinburgh, EH9 1QH; T.-031-650 6164.

McConnell, Jack Wilson, BSc, DipEd. Leader of the Administration, Stirling District Council, since 1990 (Member, since 1984); Teacher, Lornshill Academy, Alloa; b. 30.6.60, Irvine. Educ. Arran High School; Stirling University. President, Students Association, Stirling University, 1980-82; Labour Group Secretary, Stirling District Council, 1984-88; Chair, Stirling District Arts Council, 1984-86; Chair, Leisure and Recreation Committee, 1986-88, Equal Opportunities Committee, 1986-90; Stirling District Council Treasurer, since 1988; Member, COSLA Rural Affairs Committee, since 1988; Parliamentary candidate, Perth and Kinross, 1987; Member, Labour Party Scottish Executive, since 1989; Chair, Board of Directors, Stirling Windows Ltd., since 1988. Publication: Proposals for Scottish Democracy, 1989. Address: (h.) 10A Argyll Avenue, Stirling; T.-0786 79470.

McConnell, Walter Scott, OBE, FRPharmS, PhC. Community Pharmacist, since 1962; Director, Ayrshire Pharmaceuticals Ltd., since 1964; Past Chairman, Pharmaceutical General Council (Scotland); Member, Local Review Committee, HM Prison, Dungavel; b. 7.4.36, Kilmarnock; m.; 1 s.; 3 d. Educ. Kilmarnock Academy; Royal Technical College, Glasgow. Recreations: curling; golf. Address: (h.) 27 Mauchline Road, Hurlford, Kilmarnock, KA1 5AB; T.-0563 25393.

McCool, Thomas Joseph, BSc (Hons), FRSA. Chief Executive, Scottish Vocational Education Council, since 1986; b. 1.3.39, Bellshill; m., Anne McGurk; 2 d. Educ. Our Lady's High School, Motherwell; Glasgow University; Jordanhill College of Education. Various teaching appointments, 1961-71; Assistant Director of Education, then Depute Director, Renfrewshire, 1971-76; Divisional Education Officer, Renfrew Division, Strathclyde, 1976-86. Member, Munn Committee, 1975-78; Member, Scottish Certificate of Education Examination Board, 1978-86; Chairman, Scottish Central Committee on Guidance, 1981-86; Member, SCDI Policy Review Committee; Member, Educational Broadcasting Council for Scotland; Member, Universities' Funding Council – Scottish Committee. Recreations: golf; swimming; reading. Address: (b.) Hanover House, Douglas Street, Glasgow, G2 7NQ; T.-041-242 2052.

MacCormack, Professor Geoffrey Dennis, BA, LLB, MA, DPhil. Professor of Jurisprudence, Aberdeen University, since 1971; b. 15.4.37, Canterbury; 1 d. Educ. Parramatta High School, Sydney; Sydney University; Oxford University. Recreation: walking. Address: (b.) Department of Jurisprudence, Aberdeen University, Aberdeen; T.-0224 27 2418.

McCormick, David. Vice-Chairman, Nith Valley Co-operative Society; Director, Dumfries and Galloway Enterprise Company; Trustee, Lockerbie Air Disaster Fund; b. 5.5.18, Kirkconnel; m., Mary-Ann Edgar Carruthers; 1 s.; 1 d. Educ. Sanquhar Academy. Started in coal-mining, 1934; Underground Deputy, 1954-65; Training Department, NCB, Barony Colliery, 1965-78; elected to Dumfries and Galloway Regional Council, 1978; former Vice Chairman, Policy Committee, and Chairman, Training Committee; Chairman, Dumfries and Galloway Emergencies and Disaster Fund. Recreations: gardening; photography; motoring. Address: (h.) 21 Libry Street, Kelloholm, Kirkconnel, Dumfriesshire, DG4 6RS; T.-Kirkconnel 67401.

MacCormick, Professor (Donald) Neil, MA, LLD, Hon. LLD (Uppsala), FRSE, FBA. Regius Professor of Public Law, Edinburgh University, since 1972; Vice President, International Association for Legal and Social Philosophy, since 1991; Vice President, Royal Society of Edinburgh, since 1991; b. 27.5.41, Glasgow; m., Karen (Caroline) Rona Barr; 3 d. Educ. High School of Glasgow; Glasgow University; Balliol College, Oxford. Lecturer in Jurisprudence, Queen's College, Dundee, 1965-67; Fellow, Balliol College, Oxford, 1967-72; Oxford University: CUF Lecturer, 1968-72, Pro-Proctor, 1970-71; Dean, Faculty of Law, Edinburgh University, 1973-76 and 1985-88; Senate Assessor, University Court, 1982-85; Member, Broadcasting Council for Scotland, 1985-89. President, Oxford Union, 1965; Executive Member, Scottish National Party, 1978-81, Council Member, 1978-84 and since 1989. Publications: as author or editor, books on philosophy of law, political philosophy, etc. Address: (h.) 19 Pentland Terrace, Edinburgh, EH10 6AA; T.-031-447 7945.

McCormick, John. Controller, BBC Scotland, since 1992; b. 24.6.44. Former school teacher; joined BBC as Education Officer, 1970; Secretary of the BBC, 1987-92.

McCosh, Professor Andrew Macdonald, BSc, DBA, HonMBA, CA. Professor of the Organisation of Industry & Commerce, Edinburgh University, since 1986; b. 16.9.40, Glasgow; m., Anne; 3 d. Educ. Edinburgh Academy; Edinburgh University; Harvard University; Manchester University. Teaching Fellow in Economics, Harvard College, 1964; Assistant Professor, then Associate Professor of Accounting, University of Michigan, 1966-71; Research Assistant, Visiting Professor of Business Administration, Harvard Business School, 1964-75; Professor of Management Accounting, Manchester Business School, 1971-85. Director, Financial Control Research Institute. Recreations: mountaineering; fishing; golf. Address: (b.) Department of Business Studies, William Robertson Building, 50 George Square, Edinburgh, EH8 9JY; T.-031-650 3801.

McCosh, James, LLB, DL. Solicitor, since 1976; b. 28.8.48, Irvine; m., Sheila Joan Loudon; 2 s. Educ. Wellington College; Dundee University. Deputy Lieutenant, since 1982; Secretary/Treasurer, Dalry Farmers Society. Address: (h.) Kaimhill, 10 Bowfield Road, West Kilbride; T.-0294 822752.

McCrae, William Morrice, MB, ChB, FRCPE, FRCP(G). Consultant Physician, Royal Hospital for Sick Children, Edinburgh, 1965-91; Senior Lecturer, Department of Child Life and Health, Edinburgh University, 1965-91; b. 11.3.32, Hurlford; m., Jennifer Jane Graham. Educ. Kilmarnock Academy; Glasgow University. House Physician/House Surgeon, Royal Infirmary, Glasgow; Captain, RAMC; Hall Fellow in Medicine, `Glasgow University; Lecturer, Department of Child Health, Glasgow University. Recreations: gardening; history. Address: (h.) Seabank House, Aberdour, Fife.

McCreadie, Robert Anderson, LLB, PhD. Lecturer in Law, Edinburgh University, since 1978; Vice Chairman, Scottish Liberal Democrats, since 1988; Member, Executive Committee, Scottish Constitutional Convention, since 1989; b. 17.8.48, St. Andrews. Educ. Madras College, St. Andrews; Edinburgh University; Christ's College, Cambridge. Lecturer, Dundee University, 1974-78. Member: Scottish Consumer Council, 1977-82, Social Security Appeal Tribunals, since 1987, DTI Appeals Panel, since 1989; Labour Parliamentary Candidate, Edinburgh South, 1983; joined Scottish Liberal Party, 1985; Parliamentary Candidate: Livingston, 1987, Glasgow Central, 1989; Chairman, Scottish Constitutional Convention's Constitutional Working Group, since 1989; Member, Executive Committee, Child Poverty Action Group, 1974-76; Chairman, Scottish Legal Action Group, 1980-82. Publication: You and Your Rights: An A to Z Guide to the Law in Scotland, 1984 (Joint Editor). Recreations: music; Scottish history; walking. Address: (h.) 40 Marchmont Crescent, Edinburgh EH9 1HG; T.-031-667 1383.

McCreath, Thomas Crawford, JP, DL. Farmer; b. 28.6.29, Whithorn; 3 s.; 1 d. Educ. Fettes College. Nuffield Farming Scholar, to New Zealand and Australia, 1956; farming, since 1948; Member, County Council and District Council; Past Chairman, SWS Grassland Society and Milk Records Association; General Commissioner of Income Tax. Recreations: music; walking; sailing; trout fishing. Address: (h.) Garlieston Home Farm, Garlieston, Newton Stewart, DG8 8HF; T.-098 86 267.

McCrone, Iain Alistair, CBE (1987), SDA. Farmer and Company Director; b. 29.3.34, Glasgow; m., Yvonne Findlay; 4 d. Educ. Glasgow Academy; Trinity College, Glenalmond; West of Scotland Agricultural College. Farming on own account, since 1956; Managing Director, McCrone Farmers Ltd., since 1958; began fish farming, 1968; Director, Highland Trout Co. (now McConnell Salmon Ltd.); Director, Otter Ferry Salmon Ltd., since 1974; Member, Fife Regional Council, 1978-82; Parliamentary candidate (Conservative), Central Fife, 1979; Council Member, National Farmers Union of Scotland, 1977-82; Board Member, Glenrothes Development Corporation, since 1980; Member, Fife Health Board, 1983-91; Nuffield Farming Scholar, 1966; President, Scottish Conservative and Unionist Association, 1985-87. Recreations: golf; rugby (spectator). Address: (h.) Cardsknolls, Markinch, Fife, KY7 6LP; T.-0337 30267.

McCrone, Robert Gavin Loudon, CB, MA, MSc, PhD, LLD, FRSE. Secretary, Scottish Office Environment Department, since 1987; Chief Economic Adviser, Scottish Office, since 1972; Visiting Professor of Economics, Glasgow University, since 1988; b. 2.2.33, Ayr; m., Alexandra Bruce Waddell; 2 s.; 1 d. Educ. St. Catharine's College, Cambridge; University of Wales; Glasgow University. Fisons Ltd., 1959-60; Lecturer in Economics, Glasgow University, 1960-65; Fellow, Brasenose College, Oxford, 1965-70; Consultant, UNESCO, 1964; Member, NEDC Working Party on Agricultural Policy, 1967-68; Adviser, House of Commons Select Committee on Scottish Affairs, 1969-70; Senior Economic Adviser, Scottish Office, 1970-72; Under Secretary, 1972-80; Secretary, Industry Department for Scotland, 1980-87. Council Member: Economic and Social Research Council, 1986-89, Royal Economic Society, 1977-82, Scottish Economic Society, 1982-91; Visiting Professor, Strathclyde University, 1983-86. Publications: The Economics of Subsidising Agriculture, 1962; Scotland's

Economic Progress 1951-60, 1963; Regional Policy in Britain, 1969; Scotland's Future, 1969. Recreation: walking. Address: (b.) St. Andrews House, Regent Road, Edinburgh; T.-031-244 4047.

McCrorie, Ian, BSc. Chorusmaster, Scottish Festival Singers, since 1991; Assistant Rector, Greenock Academy, since 1975; b. 6.5.41, Greenock; m., Olive Simpson Bolton; 2 s. Educ. Greenock Academy; Glasgow University. Founded Toad Choir, Greenock, which appeared in numerous BBC Songs of Praise programmes (and won 1975 National Choral Competition, Royal Albert Hall, London); this choir became the nucleus of the Scottish Philharmonic Singers (1976-91); Organist and Choirmaster, Mid Kirk of Greenock, since 1964; former Assistant to Arthur Oldham, Edinburgh Festival Chorus; has been Choral Director, International Festival of Youth Orchestras, Aberdeen; conducted at Festivals in France and Poland, and took SPS to Israel and the London Proms; President and Convener of Cruising, Clyde River Steamer Club; author of numerous books and articles on Clyde and West Highland steamers. Recreations: as above! Address: (h.) 72 Newton Street, Greenock; T.-0475 26689.

McCubbin, Henry. Member (Labour), Scotland North East, European Parliament, since 1989; b. 15.7.42.

McCue, William, OBE (1982), LRAM, ARAM. Bass Singer; b. 17.8.34, Allanton, Shotts; m., Patricia Carrick; 1 d. Educ. Calderhead High School; Royal Scottish Academy of Music; Royal Academy of Music. Began professional singing career in 1960; his work has included opera, oratorio, recital, concert, cabaret, pantomime and stage musical, radio and TV; has travelled throughout the world, making numerous visits to USA, Canada, USSR, Iceland, Europe and Israel; has made various recordings of Scots songs and Negro spirituals; Director, Scottish Singers Company; Honorary Life Member, Saltire Society; former Member, Scottish Arts Council. Recreations: watching all sport; listening to all kinds of music; gardening; escaping to the Scottish countryside. Address: (h.) Sweethope House, Bothwell, Glasgow, G71 8BT; T.-0698 853241.

McCulloch, Ian, DA, ARSA. Painter; b. 4.3.35, Glasgow; m., Margery Palmer; 2 s. Educ. Eastbank Academy; Glasgow School of Art. Elected Member, Society of Scottish Artists, 1964; elected Associate, Royal Scottish Academy, 1989; paintings in many private and public collections; numerous one-man and group exhibitions; 1st prize, Stirling Smith Biennial, 1989; winner, Glasgow International Concert Hall Mural Competition, 1989-90. Recreation: university teaching. Address: (h.) 51 Victoria Road, Lenzie, Glasgow, G66 5AP; T.-041-776 1053.

McCulloch, Professor James, BSc, PhD. Professor of Neuroscience, Glasgow University, since 1988; b. 7.4.51, Irvine; m., Mailis Christina; 2 s. Educ. Spiers School, Beith; Glasgow University. Lecturer, 1978-86, Reader, 1986-88, Glasgow University; Secretary, International Society for Cerebral Blood Flow and Metabolism, since 1989. Publications: three books; 135 scientific papers. Recreation: squash. Address: (b.) Glasgow University, Bearsden Road, Glasgow, G61 1QH; T.-041-339 8855, Ext. 5828.

McCunn, Archibald Eddington, OBE, BSc (Hons), CEng, MIMechE, FBIM. Director: A.E. McCunn Consultants Ltd., McConnell Salmon Ltd.; Hon. Vice-President, Scottish Salmon Growers Association; Board Member, Nature Conservancy Council for Scotland (South West); Trustee, Argyll and Bute Countryside Trust; Board Member, Highlands and Islands Development Board, 1985-89; b. 27.5.27, Motherwell; m., Olive Isobel Johnston; 1 s.; 1 d. Educ. Dalziel High School; Strathclyde University. Engineering management, Colvilles Ltd./ BSC, 1952-63;

Senior Consultant, Inbucon/AIC, 1963-67; Divisional Chairman, Stenhouse Industries, 1967-71; Divisional Chairman/Consultant, Grampian Holdings plc, 1971-89. Recreations: painting; music; walking; gardening. Address: (h.) 2 McIntosh Way, Motherwell, ML1 3BB; T.-0698 53500.

McCutcheon, Rev. George Alexander, MA. Minister of Religion, since 1948; Clerk, Presbytery of Stirling, since 1984; b. 18.1.19, Gourock; 1 s.; 1 d. Educ. High School of Glasgow; Glasgow University and Trinity College, Glasgow. Commissioned Cameronians (Scottish Rifles), 1940; demobilised Hon. Major, 1946; Minister: Barony Church, Auchinleck, 1948-67, Clackmannan Parish Church, 1967-84. Recreations: golf; music. Address: (h.) Ashfield, 13 Harviestoun Road, Dollar, FK14 7HG; T.-0259 42609.

McDaid, Professor Seamus, CA, MBA. Professor of Accounting and Head, Department of Finance and Accounting, Glasgow Polytechnic, since 1988; b. 23.7.52, Glasgow; m., Alice; 2 d. Educ. St. Mungo's Academy; Glasgow University; Strathclyde University. Qualified as CA, 1974; trained with Wylie & Bisset, CA; worked for Coopers & Lybrand; joined Glasgow College as Lecturer, 1976; Senior Lecturer, 1980. Recreations: football; badminton. Address: (h.) 4 Hexham Gardens, Maxwell Park, Glasgow, G41 4AQ; T.-041-423 1066.

McDevitt, Professor Denis Gordon, DSc, MD, FRCP, FRCPI, FRCPEd, FFPM. Professor of Clinical Pharmacology, Dundee University Medical School, since 1984; Honorary Consultant Physician, Tayside Health Board, since 1984; President, Association of Physicians of Great Britain and Ireland, 1987-88; Civil Consultant in Clinical Pharmacology, RAF, since 1987; Member, Medicines Commission, since 1986; b. 17.11.37, Belfast; m., Anne McKee; 2 s.; 1 d. Educ. Campbell College, Belfast; Queen's University, Belfast. Assistant Professor of Medicine and Consultant Physician, Christian Medical College, Ludhiana, North India, 1968-71; Senior Lecturer in Clinical Pharmacology and Consultant Physician, Queen's University Medical School, 1971-76; Merck International Fellow in Clinical Pharmacology, Vanderbilt University, Nashville, Tennessee, 1974-75; Reader in Clinical Pharmacology, Queen's University Medical School, 1976-78; Professor of Clinical Pharmacology, Queen's University of Belfast and Consultant Physician, Belfast Teaching Hospitals, 1978-83. Chairman, Clinical Section, British Pharmacological Society, 1985-88 (Secretary, 1978-82). Recreations: golf; classical music. Address: (h.) 1 Godfrey Street, Barnhill, Dundee, DD5 2QZ.

McDonald, Rev. Alexander, BA, CMIWS. General Secretary, Department of Ministry, Church of Scotland, since 1988; b. 5.11.37, Bishopbriggs; m., Essdale Helen McLeod; 2 s.; 1 d. Educ. Bishopbriggs Higher Grade School; Whitehill Senior Secondary School, Glasgow; Glasgow University and Trinity College. Management in timber trade, 1952-54; RAF, 1954-56; management in timber trade, 1956-58, motor trade, 1958-62; student, 1962-68; Minister, St. David's Bathgate, 1968-74, St. Mark's, Old Hall, Paisley, 1974-88. Trustee, Scottish Television Staff Trust; wide range of involvement with Boys' Brigade in Scotland, Scottish Spastics, mentally handicapped children, ACCORD, Christian Aid and many others; regular broadcaster. Recreations: reading; walking; fishing. Address: Church of Scotland, 121 George Street, Edinburgh, EH2 4YN; T.-031-225 5722.

Macdonald, Rev. Alexander, MA, BD. Minister, Neilston Parish Church, since 1984; b. 10.3.42, Dulnain Bridge; m., Wendy Jeanette Sloan; 1 s.; 1 d. Educ. Grantown Grammar School; Edinburgh University. Ordained Assistant, Auld Kirk of Ayr, 1966-68; Minister: Old High Kirk, Kilmarnock, 1968-78, St. Andrew's Church, Paisley, 1978-84. Honorary

Secretary, West of Scotland Bible Society, since 1974; Moderator, Presbytery of Paisley, 1990-91. Recreations: walking; reading. Address: The Manse, Neilston, Glasgow, G78 3NP; T.-041-881 1958.

Macdonald, Sheriff Alistair Archibald, MA, LLB, DL, KHS. Sheriff of Grampian, Highland and Islands, at Kirkwall and Lerwick, since 1968; b. 8.5.27, Edinburgh; m., Jill Russell; 1 s.; 1 d. Educ. Broughton School; Edinburgh University. Army Service, Intelligence Corps, 1945-48; called to Scottish Bar, 1954; Sheriff Substitute of Caithness, Sutherland, Orkney and Shetland, at Lerwick, 1961-68; Deputy Lieutenant of Shetland, since 1986. Address: (h.) Westhall, Shetland Isles; T.-Lerwick 2711.

Macdonald, Alister Gordon, BSc, PhD, DSc. Reader in Physiology, Aberdeen University, since 1984; b. 25.1.40, London; m., Jennifer; 1 s.; 2 d. Educ. Boys' High School, Trowbridge, Wiltshire; Bristol University. University of East Anglia, 1963-69; joined Aberdeen University as Lecturer in Physiology, 1969. Publications: Physiological Aspects of Deep Sea Biology, 1975; Physiological Aspects of Anaesthetics and Inert Gases, 1978. Recreations: hill-walking; badminton; music. Address: (b.) Division of Physiology, Marischal College, Aberdeen, AB9 1AS; T.-Aberdeen 273021.

Macdonald, Angus David, MA (Hons) (Cantab), DipEd. Headmaster, Lomond School, Helensburgh, since 1986; b. 9.10.50, Edinburgh; m., Isabelle Marjory Ross; 2 d. Educ. Portsmouth Grammar School; Cambridge University; Edinburgh University. Assistant Teacher, Alloa Academy, 1972-73; Assistant Teacher, Edinburgh Academy, 1973-82 (Exchange Teacher, King's School, Parramatta, NSW, 1978-79); George Watson's College, Edinburgh: Principal Teacher of Geography, 1982, Deputy Principal, 1982-86. Recreations: outdoor recreation; sport; piping; gardening. Address: 8 Millig Street, Helensburgh, Dunbartonshire; T.-0436 72472.

Macdonald, Angus John, BSc, PhD, FSA Scot. Senior Lecturer, Department of Architecture, Edinburgh University, since 1988 (Lecturer, 1970-88); writer on architectural structures and architectural history, since 1975; b. 17.1.45, Edinburgh; m., Patricia Clare Scott. Educ. George Heriot's School, Edinburgh; Edinburgh University. Partnership with Patricia Macdonald specialising in recording, principally by means of aerial photography, aspects of the landscape and environment. Publications include: Wind Loading on Buildings; Above Edinburgh and South-East Scotland; The Highlands and Islands of Scotland. Recreations: music; hill-walking. Address: (b.) Department of Architecture, Edinburgh University, 20 Chambers Street, Edinburgh, EH1 1JZ; T.-031-650 2319.

Macdonald, Angus Stewart, CBE, DL, FRAgS; b. 7.4.35, Edinburgh; m., Janet Ann Somerville; 3 s. Educ. Conon Bridge School; Gordonstoun School. Chairman, Scottish Agricultural Development Council, 1980-85; Past Chairman, former Vice President and former Treasurer, Royal Highland and Agricultural Society; Director, British Wool Marketing Board and associated companies; Chairman, Reith & Anderson (Tain and Dingwall) Ltd.; Chairman, Gordonstoun School; Governor, Aberlour School; former Director, Hill Farming Research Organisation; Trustee, Macaulay Institute, MacRobert Trust; Member, Highlands and Islands Development Board; Crown Commissioner for Crown Estates in Scotland; Member, Queen's Bodyguard for Scotland (Royal Company of Archers). Recreation: field sports. Address: Torgorm, Conon Bridge, Dingwall, Ross-shire; T.-0349 61365.

MacDonald, Calum Alasdair. MP (Labour), Western Isles, since 1987; b. 7.5.56, Stornoway. Address: (b.) House of Commons, London, SW1; T.-071-219 4609.

MacDonald, Caroline Mary, BSc, PhD. Senior Lecturer, Immunology Department, Strathclyde University, since 1989; b. 4.9.51, Edinburgh; m., Alastair MacDonald; 2 d. Educ. Glasgow High School for Girls; Glasgow University. Lecturer, Strathclyde University, 1983-89. Secretary and Treasurer, European Society for Animal Cell Technology. Recreations: family; gardening; travel. Address: (b.) Department of Immunology, Strathclyde University, Todd Centre, Glasgow, G4 0NR; T.-041-552 4400, Ext. 3829.

MacDonald, Colin Cameron, BA. Assistant Secretary, Management and Organisation Division, Scottish Office (Assistant Secretary, Housing, 1988-91; Chief Research Officer, 1981-88); b. 13.7.43, Glasgow; m., Kathryn Campbell; 1 s.; 1 d. Educ. Allan Glen's School; Strathclyde University. Scottish Development Department: Research Officer, Research Services, 1967-70, Senior Research Officer, Research Services, 1970-71, Principal Research Officer, Central Planning Research Unit, 1971-75; Senior Principal Research Officer, Scottish Office Central Research Unit, 1975-81. Recreations: tennis; fishing; music. Address: (b.) Room 31, James Craig Walk, Edinburgh; T.-031-244 3878.

MacDonald, David N., BSc (Hons), DipEd. Head Teacher, Langholm Academy, since 1980; b. 4.11.42, Edinburgh; m., Sandra Crerar-Gilbert; 2 d. Educ. Royal High School, Edinburgh; Heriot-Watt College, Edinburgh. Assistant Teacher of Mathematics: Boroughmuir Secondary School, 1965, Liberton Secondary School, 1966-68; Principal Teacher of Mathematics, Annan Academy, 1968-73; Depute Rector, Annan Academy, 1973-80. Address: (h.) Sorbie Cottage, Drove Road, Langholm, DG13 0JW; T.-03873 80531.

Macdonald, Donald Alistair, OBE, DipSoc, AAPSW. Mental Welfare Commissioner, Scotland, since 1984; b. 18.2.28, Larbert; m., Grace Catherine; 1 s.; 2 d. Educ. Larbert High School; Edinburgh University. Senior Psychiatric Social Worker, Renfrewshire Mental Hospitals; Senior Case Work Supervisor, then Training Officer, Staffordshire County Council; Deputy County Welfare Officer, Derbyshire County Council; Director of Social Work, Roxburgh County Council; Director of Social Work, Borders Regional Council (retired). Recreations: gardening; golf; walking. Address: (h.) Northumbria, Darnick, Melrose, Roxburghshire, TD6 9AJ; T.-089682 2250.

MacDonald, Professor Donald Gordon, RD*, ADC, BDS, PhD, FRCPath, FDSRCPS(G). Professor in Oral Medicine and Pathology, Glasgow University, since 1991; Consultant Oral Pathologist, Glasgow Dental Hospital, since 1974; b. 5.7.42, Glasgow; m., Emma Lindsay Cordiner; 2 s. Educ. Kelvinside Academy, Glasgow; Glasgow University. Assistant, then Lecturer, Glasgow University, 1964-69; Visiting Associate Professor in Oral Pathology, University of Illinois, 1969-70; Lecturer, Senior Lecturer, Reader in Oral Medicine and Pathology, Glasgow University, 1970-91; Editor, Glasgow Dental Journal, 1969-75; Honorary Consultant Forensic Odontologist, Strathclyde Police, since 1976; Vice President, Association of Head and Neck Oncologists of Great Britain, 1987-90; President, British Society for Oral Pathology, 1988-91. Recreations: Royal Naval Reserve; golf. Address: (h.) 2 Dougalston Gardens South, Milngavie, Glasgow; T.-041-956 2075.

MacDonald, Donald John, BSc. Rector, Nicolson Institute, Stornoway, since 1989 (Rector, Thurso High School, 1980-89); b. 25.5.39, Glasgow; 1 s.; 2 d. Educ. Hill's Trust School, Glasgow; Lionel School, Lewis; Govan High School, Glasgow; Glasgow University; Jordanhill College of

Education. Teacher of Science, Govan High School; Principal Teacher of Physics: Kirkwall Grammar School, Govan High School; Assistant Head, Linwood High School; Depute Rector, Dingwall Academy; Assistant Divisional Education Officer, Highland Region. Address: (h.) The Rectory, 1 Goathill Road, Stornoway, Isle of Lewis.

MacDonald, Donald John, BA, MREHIS. Chief Food and Dairy Officer, Scottish Office Agriculture and Fisheries Department, since 1990; b. 14.3.48, Dingwall; m., Jane E. Munro. Educ. Dingwall Academy; Inverness College of Further and Higher Education; Aberdeen University; Open University. Environmental Health Officer: Kincardine and Deeside District Council, 1970-76, Inverness District Council, 1976-84; Food and Dairy Officer, SOAFD, 1984-90. Recreations: geology; walking; literature. Address: (b.) Room 113, Pentland House, 47 Robb's Loan, Edinburgh; T.-031-244 6427.

MacDonald, Donald Murray, AIB (Scot). Retired Bank Manager; Honorary Sheriff, since 1984; b. 10.6.32, Inverness; m., Irene Foubister Kemp; 2 d. Educ. Inverness Royal Academy. Entered service of Union Bank of Scotland Ltd., 1947; worked in a number of offices throughout Scotland; appointed Accountant, Stornoway Branch, Bank of Scotland, 1971; Assistant Manager, Kirkwall, 1973; Manager, Lochmaddy and Benbecula, 1977; Manager, Portree, 1982 (retired 1986). Treasurer, Portree Angling Association; Treasurer, Church of Scotland, Portree; President, Portree and District Rotary Club. Recreations: gardening; piping; stalking. Address: (h.) Hillview, Hill Place, Staffin Road, Portree, Isle of Skye, IV51 9HP.

McDonald, Sir Duncan, Kt (1983), CBE (1976), DEng, DSc, BSc, FEng, FH-WC, Hon.FIEE, CBIM, SMIEEE, FRSE, FRSA. Director: General Accident Fire & Life Assurance Corporation plc; Barclays Bank, Scotland; Northern Rock Building Society, Scotland; b. 20.9.21, Inverkeithing; m., Jane Anne Guckian; 3 s.; 1 d. Educ. Inverkeithing Public School; Dunfermline High School; Edinburgh University. Early experience, British Thomson Houston, Rugby (Head, R & D., BTH transformer interests); appointed Chief Transformer Designer, Bruce Peebles, Edinburgh, 1954; became Chief Engineer of company, 1959; Managing Director, 1962; following merger, joined Board, C.A. Parsons, 1969, and Board, Retrofle Parsons Group, 1973; became Chief Executive of Group; first Group Managing Director, Northern Engineering Industries plc, 1977; appointed Chairman and Chief Executive, 1980; Honorary Fellow, Heriot-Watt College, 1962; DSc Heriot-Watt University, 1982; Honorary Fellow, Institution of Electrical Engineers, 1984; awarded first Hon. Doctorate of Engineering by Newcastle upon Tyne University, 1984; Fellow, Scottish Council (Development and Industry). Recreations: golf; fishing; gardening. Address: (h.) Duncliffe, Kinellan Road, Edinburgh, EH12 6ES; T.-031-337 4814.

Macdonald, Rev. Finlay Angus John, MA, BD, PhD. Minister, Jordanhill Parish Church, Glasgow, since 1977; b. 1.7.45, Watford; m., Elizabeth Mary Stuart; 2 s. Educ. Dundee High School; St. Andrews University. Assistant Minister, Bo'ness Old Kirk, 1970-71; Minister, Menstrie Parish Church, 1971-77; Junior Clerk and Treasurer, Stirling and Dunblane Presbytery, 1973-77; Convener, Church of Scotland Working Group on Children and Communion, 1980-82; Convener, Advance Planning Group, Church of Scotland Youth Education Committee, 1982-84; Co-Editor and Contributor, Children at the Table, 1982; Convener, Legal Questions Committee, Board of Practice and Procedure, 1984-85, 1986-88; Vice-Convener, Business Committee, General Assembly, 1985-88; Chairman, Jordanhill College School PTA Action Committee, 1986-88; first Convener, Board of Managers, Jordanhill School, 1987-88; Member,

Board of Governors, Jordanhill College, since 1988; Convener, General Assembly Board of Practice and Procedure, since 1988; Convener, General Assembly Business Committee, since 1989. Recreations: music; angling; reading; gardening. Address: (h.) 96 Southbrae Drive, Glasgow, G13 1TZ; T.-041-959 1310.

Macdonald, Gibson Torbett. Provost, Kyle and Carrick District Council, 1984-88 and since 1992; b. 21.1.33; m., Muirkirk; m., Mary Hastings Logan Lambie; 1 s.; 1 d. Educ. Kilmarnock Academy. National President, Junior Chamber Scotland; Executive Vice President, Junior Chamber International; Chairman, Ayr Branch, Ayr Conservative Association; Chairman, Ayr Conservative Constituency; Town Councillor, Royal Burgh of Ayr; District Councillor, Kyle and Carrick District (held Convenership of Planning, Employment and Policy and Resources Committees); Chairman, Culzean Country Park Joint Committee; Member, COSLA Planning and Town Twinning Committees. Treasurer, Ayrshire Decorative and Fine Arts Society; President, Ayr Town Twinning Association; Secretary, Franco Scottish Society (Ayrshire); President, Ayr Chamber of Commerce, 1990-92; Dean of Guildry, 1991-92. Recreations: bowling; bridge; computing; philately. Address: (h.) 14 Belmont Avenue, Ayr, KA7 2JN.

Macdonald, 8th Baron, (Godfrey James Macdonald of Macdonald). Chief of the Name and Arms of Macdonald; b. 28.11.47; m., Claire Catlow; 1 s.; 3 d. Address: (h.) Kinloch Lodge, Isle of Skye.

Macdonald, Gus. Managing Director, Scottish Television; Television Journalist; b. 20.8.40, Larkhall; m., Teen; 2 d. Educ. Allan Glen's School, Glasgow. Marine engineer, Stephens, Linthouse, 1955-62; Circulation and Publicity Manager, Tribune, 1963-65; Investigative Journalist, The Scotsman, 1965-67; Editor, Financial Scotsman, 1966-67; Investigative Bureau, World in Action, Granada, 1967-69; Editor/Executive Producer, World in Action, 1969-75; successively Head of Current Affairs, Head of Regional Programmes, Head of Features, Granada; Writer/Presenter, Camera: Early Photography, 1979-80, MacDiarmid: Hammer and Thistle; Presenter, variously, World in Action, What the Papers Say, Devil's Advocate, Union World; Election and Party Conference coverage; BAFTA Award, current affairs; National Viewers and Listeners' Association Award, 1985; founder Chairman, Edinburgh International Television Festival, 1976; Visiting Professor, Film and Media Studies, Stirling University, 1985-89; Executive, Edinburgh International Film Festival; Governor, National Film and Television School; Fellow, Royal Society of Arts. Publications: Grierson: Television and Documentary, 1977; Camera: Victorian Eyewitness, 1979. Recreations: words; music; pictures; exploring Scotland. Address: (b.) Scottish Television, Cowcaddens, Glasgow, G2 3PR.

Macdonald, Ian Hamish, OBE, FIB (Scot), CBIM. Director, Scottish Power PLC (formerly South of Scotland Electricity Board), since 1987; Chairman: Clairmont PLC, First Edinburgh Homes PLC, EFM Dragon Trust PLC, Clan Donald Lands Trust, Scottish Council Foundation; Director: Macdonald Orr Ltd., TSB Northern Ireland PLC, Morgan Grenfell Scotland Ltd.; Member, Court, Edinburgh University; b. 30.12.26, Inverness; m., Patricia Lace; 1 d. Educ. Inverness Royal Academy; Inverness Technical College. RAFVR, 1944; Queen's Own Cameron Highlanders, 1945 (Hon. Captain, 1948); Mercantile Bank, 1948-59; The Hongkong and Shanghai Banking Corporation: Manager, 1959-72, General Manager, India, 1972-73, General Manager International, 1973-80, Executive Director, 1980-83; Chairman, Hongkong Bank of Canada, 1981-83; Chief General Manager, TSB Scotland, 1983-86, and TSB Scotland PLC, 1986-87; Director, TSB Group PLC, 1986-87.

Recreations: fishing; golf; bridge. Address: (h.) Minewood Cottage, 11 Abercromby Drive, Bridge of Allan, FK9 4EA.

Macdonald, Professor Ian Robert, MA, PhD. Professor in Spanish, Aberdeen University, since 1991 (Convener, Board of Studies in Arts and Social Sciences); b. 4.5.39, The Hague; m., Frances Mary; 3 s. Educ. Whitgift School; St. Andrews University. United Steel Cos. Ltd., 1961-64; research student, 1964-65; Lecturer, then Senior Lecturer, Aberdeen University, 1965-90. Recreations: walking; digging; carpentry. Address: (h.) 47 North Deeside Road, Peterculter, Aberdeen; T.-0224 732284.

McDonald, Professor Janet B.I., MA, FRSE. Professor of Drama, Glasgow University, since 1979; b. 28.7.41, Netherlee, Renfrewshire; m., Ian James McDonald; 1 d. Educ. Hutchesons' Girls' Grammar School; Glasgow University. Member, Governing Body, Royal Scottish Academy of Music and Drama, since 1979; Member, Board, Citizens' Theatre, 1979-82 and since 1989 (Chair, since 1991); Chairman, Drama and Theatre Board, Council for National Academic Awards, 1981-85; Chairman, Standing Committee of University Departments of Drama, 1982-85; Chairman, Drama Committee, Scottish Arts Council, 1985-88; Chair, Creative and Performing Arts Committee, CNAA, 1989-91; Fellow, Royal Society of Arts. Address: (b.) 53 Hillhead Street, Glasgow, G12 8QE; T.-041-339 8855.

MacDonald, Rev. Kenneth Mackinnon, CertTheo. Free Church Minister, Rosskeen (Invergordon and Alness), since 1984; b. 9.1.35, Skinidin, Skye; m., Reta Cromarty; 2 s.; 2 d. Educ. Portree High School; Free Church College. Army, Seaforth Highlanders, Egypt, Germany, Aden, 1953-55; Uniformed Branch, HM Customs and Excise, Glasgow Docks, London Heathrow, Aberdeen and Stornoway, 1957-80; Free Church College, 1980-84. Member, Western Isles Council, 1973-76; Chairman, Western Isles Branch, Mentally Handicapped Action Committee, 1977-80; Member, Western Isles Children's Panel, 1977-80; capped seven times for Scotland as amateur footballer. Recreations: football; athletics. Address: Rosskeen Free Church Manse, Rosskeen, Invergordon, IV18 OPP; T.-0349 85 2406.

MacDonald, Margo. Political Presenter, Scottish Television; b. Hamilton; m., Jim Sillars; 1 step s.; 2 d.; 1 step-d. Educ. Hamilton Academy; Dunfermline College. Teacher, 1963-65; barmaid and mother, 1965-73; Member of Parliament, 1973-74; Broadcaster/Writer, 1974-78; Director, Shelter, Scotland, 1978-81; Radio Forth: Broadcaster, 1981-83, Editor, Topical Programmes, 1983-85.

Macdonald, Rev. Professor Murdo Ewen, MA, BD, DD (St. Andrews), DD (McGill University). Emeritus Professor, Trinity College, Glasgow University; b. 28.8.14, Isle of Harris; 2 s. Educ. Sir Edward Scott School, Harris; Kingussie Secondary School; St. Andrews University. Minister, Portree, Isle of Skye, 1939-40; Chaplain to 4th Camerons, 1940-42; Chaplain to 2nd Paras, 1942; wounded and taken prisoner, North Africa, and spent rest of War in Germany (acted as Chaplain to American Air Force); awarded Bronze Star; Pollock Lecturer in Preaching, Canada; Syme Lecturer in Theology and Preaching, Lutheran Colleges, USA; Ferrie Lecturer in Preaching and Theology, Australia. Publications: Vitality of Faith; Need to Believe; Call to Obey; Crisis of Belief; Call to Communicate; Lost Provinces of Religion. Recreations: mountain climbing (completed Munroes). Address: (h.) 24 Falkland Street, Glasgow, G12; T.-041-334 2087.

Macdonald, Norman Malcolm. Writer and Dramatist; b. 24.7.27, Thunder Bay, Canada; m., Mairi F. Educ. Nicolson Institute; Newbattle Abbey College. New Zealand Air Force, 1949-57; journalism and administration at various periods;

Administrator, Fir Chlis (Gaelic theatre company), 1978-80; Secretary, Sabhal Mor Ostaig Gaelic College, 1982-83. Publications: Calum Tod (novel); Fad (poetry); The Shutter Falls, Anna Chaimbeul, The Catechist, The Brahan Seer, Sublime Savage, Aimhreit Aignis, The Teuchtar's Tale (plays); Call Na h'Iolaire, Clann-Nighean a Sgadain (historical); The Shutter Falls (television). Recreation: walking. Address: 14 Tong, Isle of Lewis.

Macdonald, Peter Cameron, DL, SDA. Vice-President, Scottish Landowners' Federation, since 1990 (Convener, 1985-88); Farmer, since 1961; Director, J. Dickson & Son, Gunmakers, since 1968; b. 14.12.37, Edinburgh; m., Barbara Helen Drimmie Ballantyne; 2 step-s. Educ. Loretto; East of Scotland College of Agriculture. Council Member: Scottish Landowners Federation, since 1976, Blackface Sheepbreeders Association, 1970-74; Member, Forth River Purification Board, 1979-87; Director, Royal Highland and Agricultural Society of Scotland, 1985; Deputy Lieutenant, West Lothian, since 1987. Recreations: fishing; shooting; golf. Address: Colzium Farm, Kirknewton, Midlothian, EH27 8DH; T.-0506 880607.

Macdonald, Rev. Peter James, BD, DipMin. Minister, Kirkcaldy Torbain (former National Young Adult Adviser, Church of Scotland); b. 22.3.58, Dumbarton; m., Lesley Ann Orr; 2 s. Educ. Vale of Leven Academy; Trinity College, Glasgow; New College, Edinburgh. Assistant Minister, The Old Kirk of Edinburgh, West Pilton, 1985-86. Recreations: various sports; cinema; theatre; reading; listening to music. Address: 91 Sauchenbush Road, Kirkcaldy, KY2 5RN; T.-0592 263015.

McDonald, Hon. Lord (Robert Howat McDonald), MC (1944), MA, LLB. Senator of the College of Justice in Scotland, 1973-89; b. 15.5.16, Paisley; m., Barbara Mackenzie. Educ. John Neilson Institution, Paisley; Glasgow University. Admitted Solicitor, 1938; KOSB, 1939-46 (mentioned in Despatches); admitted, Faculty of Advocates, 1946; QC (Scot), 1957; Sheriff of Ayr and Bute, 1966-71; Member, Criminal Injuries Compensation Board, 1964-71; Chairman, Mental Welfare Commission for Scotland, 1964-83; Chairman, General Nursing Council for Scotland, 1970-73. Address: (h.) 5 Doune Terrace, Edinburgh, EH3 6EA.

Macdonald, Roderick, BSc(Agri), MSc. Member, Scottish Land Court, since 1986; b. 6.2.27, Benbecula; m., Elizabeth MacLeod; 3 d. Educ. Portree High School; Aberdeen University; Michigan State University, USA. Bayer Agriculture, 1952-54; Lands Division, Department of Agriculture and Fisheries for Scotland, 1954-67 and 1972-86, latterly as Assistant Chief; Head, Land Development Division, Highlands and Islands Development Board, 1967-72; appointed Gaelic Speaking Member, Scottish Land Court, 1986. Church Elder. Recreations: golf; fiddle playing; fishing. Address: 19 Cherrytree Loan, Balerno, Edinburgh; T.-031-449 3600.

Macdonald, Vice-Admiral Sir Roderick (Douglas), KBE (1978). Painter; b. 25.2.21, Java; m., 1, Joan Willis (m. diss.); 2 s.; 1 s. deceased; 2, Pamela Bartosik. Educ. Fettes (Captain, Scottish Schoolboys' rugby, 1937-38). Entered Royal Navy, 1939; served at sea throughout War, 1939-45; Comd. six HM ships, one minesweeper and two frigate squadrons; Cyprus (Despatches, 1957); Commander, Naval Forces Borneo, 1965 (CBE); Captain of the Fleet, 1970; COS to C-in-C, Naval Home Command, 1973-76; ADC to The Queen, 1975; COS to Comdr., Allied Naval Forces Southern Europe, 1976-79. Chieftain, Skye Highland Games; President, Skye Piping Society; Fellow, Nautical Institute (Vice-President, 1976-85); Trustee, Clan Donald Lands Trust; President, Inverness Sea Cadets Unit; own exhibitions, Naples, Edinburgh (2), London

(5). Recreations: sailing; Highland bagpipe, gardening. Address: (h.) Ollach, Braes, Skye, IV51 9LJ.

MacDonald, Professor Ronald, BA, MA, PhD. Robert Fleming Professor of Finance and Investment, Dundee University, since 1989; b. 23.4.55, Glasgow. Educ. Falkirk High School; Heriot Watt University; Manchester University. Midland Bank Fellow in Monetary Economics, Loughborough University, 1982-84; Lecturer in Economics, Aberdeen University, 1984-88; Senior Lecturer, 1988-89. Publications: Floating Exchange Rates; International Money: theory evidence and institutions (Co-author); five co-edited books; 70 journal articles. Recreations: music; photography; hill-walking. Address: (b.) Department of Economics and Management, Dundee University, Dundee, DD1 4HN; T.-0382 307378.

McDonald, Sheena Elizabeth, MA. Broadcaster/Journalist. Educ. George Watson's Ladies' College; Edinburgh University; Bristol University. Chairman, Traverse Theatre Board of Management; Director, Scottish Film Council; Committee Member, Association for Business Sponsorship of the Arts (Scotland); Member, Edinburgh Festival Council. Recreations: writing; travel; swimming. Address: (b.) Curtis Brown, 162/8 Regent Street, London.

MacDonald, Professor Simon Gavin George, MA, PhD, FInstP, FRSE. Professor of Physics, Dundee University, 1973-88 (Head, Department of Physics, 1979-85); Chairman, Statistics Committee, Universities Central Council on Admissions, since 1989; b. 5.9.23, Beauly, Inverness-shire; m., Eva Leonie Austerlitz; 1 s.; 1 d. Educ. George Heriot's, Edinburgh; Edinburgh University. Junior Scientific Officer, Royal Aircraft Establishment, Farnborough, 1943-46; Lecturer in Physics, St. Andrews University, 1948-57; Senior Lecturer in Physics: University College of the West Indies, 1957-62, St. Andrews University, 1962-67; Dundee University: Senior Lecturer in Physics, 1967-73, Dean of Science, 1970-73, Vice-Principal, 1974-79; Member, Scottish Universities Council on Entrance, 1969-82 (Vice-Convener, 1973-77, Convener, 1977-82); Chairman, Technical Committee, UCCA, 1979-83; Deputy Chairman, UCCA, 1983-89; Chairman, Board of Directors, Dundee Repertory Theatre, 1975-89. Publications: Problems and Solutions in General Physics; Physics for Biology and Premedical Students; Physics for the Life and Health Sciences. Recreations: bridge; golf; fiction writing. Address: (b.) 10 Westerton Avenue, Dundee, DD5 3NJ; T.-0382 78692.

McDonald, William, JP, CA. Bursar, The Carnegie Trust for the Universities of Scotland, since 1990; b. 9.11.29, Perth; m., Anne Kidd Laird McDonald; 1 s.; 1 d. Educ. Perth Academy. Secretary, South Mills and Grampian Investment, Dundee, 1957-62; The Company of Merchants of the City of Edinburgh: Chamberlain, 1962-90, Secretary, 1971-90; Clerk and Treasurer, Incorporation of Guildry in Edinburgh, 1975-90; Joint Secretary, Scottish Council of Independent Schools, 1978-90. Scout Association: Deputy Chief Commissioner of Scotland, 1977-79, Honorary Treasurer, Scotland, since 1989; Captain, Ward VIII, High Constables of Edinburgh, since 1990; Chairman, Scottish Environmental and Outdoor Education Centres, since 1987; Member, Lothian Region Valuation Appeal Committee, since 1989. Recreations: Scout Association; bridge; golf. Address (h.) 1/3 Wyvern Park, The Grange, Edinburgh, EH9 2JY; T.-031-662 4145.

Macdonald, William Alexander, JP, AIB. Honorary Sheriff, since 1972; b. 9.1.21, Banffshire; m., Millicent M. Brodie. Educ. Turriff Academy; Banff Academy. Joined Trustee Savings Bank, 1939; RAF, 1941-46; Manager, Trustee Savings Bank: Stornoway, 1949-52, Peterhead, 1952-84. Chairman: Peterhead Scottish Week, Peterhead Health Centre Patients Participation Group, Buchan Crime Prevention Panel,

Peterhead Aged and Infirm Committee; Treasurer, Frank Jack Court (Housing Association); Session Clerk, Peterhead Old Parish Church, since 1954; Past President, Peterhead Rotary Club. Recreation: gardening. Address: (h.) 6 Kinmundy Road, Peterhead, AB42 6AY; T.-0779 72103.

McDonald, Very Rev. William James Gilmour, MA, BD, Hon. DD (Edinburgh). Minister, Mayfield Parish Church, Edinburgh, since 1959; Moderator, General Assembly of Church of Scotland, 1989-90; b. 3.6.24, Edinburgh; m., Patricia Watson; 1 s.; 2 d. Educ. Daniel Stewart's College; Edinburgh University; Gottingen University. Royal Artillery and Indian Artillery, 1943-46; Parish Minister, Limekilns, 1953-59. Convener, Committee on Education for the Ministry, 1974-78; Convener, Assembly Council, 1984-87. Recreations: cycling; music; cinema. Address: 26 Seton Place, Edinburgh, EH9 2JT; T.-031-667 1286.

MacDonell of Glengarry, Air Cdre. Aeneas Ranald Donald, CB, DFC. 22nd Chief of Glengarry; Member, Standing Council of Scottish Chiefs; Trustee, Clan Donald Lands Trust; Trustee, Finlaggan Trust; b. 15.11.13, Baku, Russia; m., 1, Diana Dorothy Keane; 2 s.; 1 d.; 2, Lois Eirene Frances Streatfeild; 1 s.; 1 d. Educ. Hurtspierpoint College; Royal Air Force College, Cranwell. RAF Officer, 1931-64; seconded to Fleet Air Arm, 1935-37; Flying Instructor, 1938-39; Air Ministry; Officer Commanding Spitfire Squadron during Battle of Britain; POW, Germany, 1941-45; Chief Flying Instructor, RAF College, Cranwell; Air Attache, Moscow, 1956-58; Director of Management and Work Study, Ministry of Defence, 1960-64; retired from RAF; Construction Industry Training Board, 1967-72; Head, Commercial Department, Industrial Society, 1972-76; Partner, John Courtis & Partners, Management Selection Consultants; finally retired and moved to Scotland, 1981. Honorary President, Ross and Cromarty Branch, Soliders', Sailors' and Airmen's Families Association. Recreation: bird watching. Address: (h.) Elonbank, 23 Castle Street, Fortrose, Ross-shire, IV10 8TH; T.-0381 20121.

Macdonell, Rev. Alasdair William, MA, BD. Minister, Haddington: St. Mary's, since 1979; b. 28.9.27, Prince Albert, Canada; m., Margaret Stiven; 1 s.; 4 d. Educ. Dundee High School; Fettes College; Pembroke College, Cambridge; New College, Edinburgh. Student Assistant, Kirk of the Canongate, Edinburgh; Assistant Minister, High Kirk of St. Giles; Minister: Uddingston Burnhead, 1955-63, Tarves and Barthol Chapel, Aberdeenshire, 1963-79. Chairman, Whitekirk and Haddington Pilgrimage. Recreations: fiddling (Leader, Haddington Fiddles); hill-walking. Address: St. Mary's Manse, 21 Sidegate, Haddington, EH41 4BZ; T.-062 082 3109.

Macdougall, Alasdair Iain, RD, BSc, MB, ChB, FRCPEdin, FRCPGlas. Consultant Physician, Stobhill General Hospital, Glasgow, since 1968; Honorary Clinical Lecturer, Glasgow University, since 1968; m., Dr. Mary C. Macdougall; 1 s.; 2 d. Educ. Whitehill Secondary School; Glasgow University. Member, Scientific Staff, Medical Research Council, 1953-58; Lecturer in Materia Medica and Therapeutics, Glasgow University, 1964-68. Surgeon Commander, RNR (retired); former Principal Medical Officer, Clyde Division, RNR; Elder, Church of Scotland. Publications: papers on clinical pharmacology, hypertension and renal disease. Recreations: hill-walking; swimming; gardening; opera. Address: (h.) 6 Kelvin Crescent, Bearsden, Glasgow; T.-041-942 2850.

McDougall, Professor Bonnie S., BA, MA, PhD. Professor of Chinese, Edinburgh University, since 1990; b. 12.3.41, Sydney; m., A. Hansson; 1 s. Educ. University of Sydney. Lecturer in Chinese, University of Sydney; Nuffield Fellow, London University; Visiting Lecturer, Harvard University; editor, translator and teacher, Peking; Professor of Modern

Chinese, University of Oslo. Council Member, British Association of Chinese Studies. Recreations: reading; travelling. Address: (b.) Department of East Asian Studies, Edinburgh University, 8 Buccleuch Place, Edinburgh, EH8 9JT; T.-031-650 4227.

McDougall, Jack Craig, CBE, RIBA, FRIAS, FRSA, FFB, FBIM. Director of Architectural and Related Services, Strathclyde Regional Council, 1981-91; b. 10.4.32, Glasgow; m., Elspeth Liddell Nixon; 1 s.; 1 d. Educ. Allan Glen's School, Glasgow; Glasgow School of Art. Depute County Architect: Lanarkshire County Council, 1966, Renfrewshire County Council, 1967; Senior Depute County Architect, Renfrewshire, 1972; Depute Director of Architectural and Related Services, Strathclyde Regional Council, 1974-81. Former Council Member, RIAS; President, Association of Chief Architects of Scottish Local Authorities; Elder, Church of Scotland, since 1974. Recreations: caravanning; visiting European capital cities; interest in wine. Address: (h.) 42 Beech Avenue, Newton Mearns, Glasgow, G77 5PP; T.-041-639 4114.

MacDougall, John William, JP, FIIM. Leader of Administration, Fife Regional Council, since 1987 (Chairman, Policy and Resources Committee); Leader, majority group, COSLA, since 1989; b. 8.12.47, Dunfermline; m., Catherine; 1 s.; 1 d. Educ. Templehall Secondary Modern; Rosyth Dockyard College; Fife College; Glenrothes College. Board Member: Glenrothes Development Corporation, Fife Enterprise Company. Recreations: DIY; sport. Address: (b.) Fife House, North Street, Glenrothes, Fife; T.-0592 754411, Ext. 6209.

MacDougall, Robert Hugh, MB, ChB, DMRT, FRCS, FRCR. Head, Department of Clinical Oncology, Lothian Health Board, and Honorary Senior Lecturer in Clinical Oncology, Edinburgh University, since 1986; Honorary Senior Lecturer, St. Andrews University; b. 9.8.49, Dundee; m., Moira Jean Gray; 1 s.; 2 d. Educ. High School of Dundee; St. Andrews University; Edinburgh University. Demonstrator in Anatomy, St. Andrews University; Registrar in Surgery, Aberdeen Royal Infirmary; Lecturer in Clinical Oncology, Edinburgh University; Consultant Radiotherapist and Oncologist, Tayside Health Board. Recreations: curling; fishing; reading. Address: (b.) Department of Clinical Oncology, Western General Hospital, Edinburgh.

McDowall, Stuart, CBE, MA. Senior Lecturer in Economics, St. Andrews University, 1967-91, now Honorary Senior Lecturer; Deputy Chairman, Central Arbitration Committee, since 1976; Member, Local Government Boundary Commission for Scotland, since 1982; Member, Monopolies and Mergers Commission, 1985-90; b. 19.4.26, Liverpool; m., Margaret B.W. Gyle; 3 s. Educ. Liverpool Institute; St. Andrews University. Master, United College of St. Salvator and St. Leonard, 1976-80. Secretary, Scottish Economic Society, 1970-76; Member, Committee of Inquiry into Powers and Functions of the Islands Councils of Scotland, 1982-84; Arbitrator for ACAS, since 1975. Recreations: golf; hill-walking; gardening; music. Address: (h.) 10 Woodburn Terrace, St. Andrews, Fife, KY16 8BA; T.-0334 73247.

MacDowell, Professor Douglas Maurice, MA, FRSE. Professor of Greek, Glasgow University, since 1971; b. 8.3.31, London. Educ. Highgate School; Balliol College, Oxford. Schoolmaster, 1954-58; Manchester University: Assistant Lecturer, 1958-61, Lecturer, 1961-68, Senior Lecturer, 1968-70, Reader, 1970-71; Visiting Fellow, Merton College, Oxford, 1969; President, Glasgow Centre, Classical Association of Scotland, 1973-75, 1977-79, 1982-84, 1988-90; Chairman, 1973-76, and Vice President, since 1976, Scottish Hellenic Society; Chairman, Council, Classical Association of Scotland, 1976-82. Publications: Andokides:

On the Mysteries, 1962; Athenian Homicide Law, 1963; Aristophanes: Wasps, 1971; The Law in Classical Athens, 1978; Spartan Law, 1986; Demosthenes: Against Meidias, 1990. Address: (b.) Glasgow University, Glasgow, G12 8QQ.

MacEachern, Ian Ferguson, ACMA, DMS, MBIM, MIIM. Depute Principal, Cardonald College, since 1989; b. 15.7.36, Alexandria; m., Aileen Forsyth; 2 s. Educ. Vale of Leven Academy; Scottish College of Commerce. Clydebank College: Senior Lecturer, 1972-78, Head, Department of Business Administration, 1978-89. Member, Board, National Examinations Board in Supervisory Management. Recreations: golf; jogging; dog exhibiting. Address: (h.) Carn-Dearg, Luss, Alexandria, Dunbartonshire; T.-043-686 673.

McEachran, Colin Neil, QC, MA, LLB, JD. QC, since 1981; b. 14.1.40, Glasgow; m., Kathrine Charlotte; 2 d. Educ. Glenalmond College; Merton College, Oxford; Glasgow University; University of Chicago. Advocate, since 1968; Advocate Depute, 1974-77; QC, 1981; Member, Scottish Legal Aid Board, since 1990; part-time Chairman, Medical Appeal Tribunal. Captain, Scottish Rifle Association; Vice Chairman, Commonwealth Games Council for Scotland. Recreations: target shooting; hill-walking. Address: 1 Saxe Coburg Place, Edinburgh; T.-031-332 6820.

McEwan, Helen Purdie, MD, FRCOG, FRCSGlas. Consultant Obstetrician and Gynaecologist, Royal Infirmary and Royal Maternity Hospital, Glasgow, since 1972; President, Royal Medico Chirurgical Society, Glasgow, 1984-85; b. 8.8.38, Glasgow. Educ. Jordanhill College School; Glasgow University. Member of Council, Royal College of Obstetricians and Gynaecologists; Member, Advisory Board, Women's Health Concern. Recreations: visiting Western Highlands and Islands; music. Address: (h.) 47 Westland Drive, Glasgow, G14 9PE.

McEwan, Iain, MA (Hons). Rector, Pitlochry High School, since 1986; b. 26.10.39, Perth; m., Nancy Graham; 2 d. Educ. Blairgowrie High School; Aberdeen University. Teacher of History, Lenzie Academy, 1963-67; Principal Teacher of History, Arbroath Academy, 1967-74, Morgan Academy, 1974-81; Depute Rector, Pitlochry High School, 1981-86. Convener, SEB History Panel, 1980-82; Vice President, Scottish Schoolboys' Hockey Association, 1985-87; Vice-Chairman (Administration), Scottish Youth Hockey Board, 1987-89; Hon. Vice-President, Scottish Hockey Union and SYHB. Recreations: photography; hockey; historic aircraft. Address: (h.) 7 Fenton Terrace, Pitlochry, Perthshire; T.-0796 2188; (b.) East Moulin Road, Pitlochry, Perthshire; T.-0796 2900.

McEwan, Robert Peter, CA. Director: Scottish Consultants International Ltd. (Chairman), Bell and Bain Ltd., Echo Hotels Ltd., Scotia House Ltd., Smith and Telford Ltd., Bridgegate Trust Ltd., Quality Street Ltd., High School of Glasgow, Glasgow Cathedral Precinct Ltd., Scottish Development Finance Ltd.; Chairman, The Quality Street Corporation Ltd.; b. 21.9.23, Glasgow; m., Mary (Mollie) Howden; 1 s. Educ. High School of Glasgow. Binder Hamlyn, CA, London; Chief Accountant, Sentinel (Shrewsbury) Ltd.; Divisional Director, PA Management Consultants Ltd.; Director of Industry Services, then Director of Finance and of Property Management, Scottish Development Agency. Recreations: golf; gardening. Address: 29 Huntly Gardens, Glasgow, G12 9AX; T.-041-334 9654.

McEwan, Sheriff Robin Gilmour, QC, LLB, PhD. Sheriff of Ayr, since 1988 (of Lanark, 1982-88); Temporary Judge, Court of Session and High Court of Justiciary, since 1991; b. 12.12.43, Glasgow; m., Sheena McIntyre; 2 d. Educ. Paisley Grammar School; Glasgow University. Faulds Fellow in Law, Glasgow University, 1965-68; admitted to Faculty of

Advocates, 1967; Standing Junior Counsel, Department of Energy, 1974-76; Advocate Depute, 1976-79; Chairman, Industrial Tribunals, 1981; Member, Scottish Legal Aid Board, since 1989. Publications: Pleading in Court, 1980; A Casebook on Damages (Co-author), 1983; Contributor to Stair Memorial Encyclopaedia of the Laws of Scotland, 1986. Recreations: formerly: football, boxing; now: golf, skating. Address: (b.) Sheriff Court, Ayr, KA7 1DR; T.-Ayr 268474.

McEwen, Professor James, MB, ChB, FRCP (Glasgow), FFPHM, FFOM, DIH. Henry Mechan Professor of Public Health, Glasgow University, since 1989; Consultant in Public Health Medicine, Greater Glasgow Health Board; b. 6.2.40, Stirling; m., Elizabeth May Archibald; 1 s.; 1 d. Educ. Dollar Academy; St. Andrews University. Lecturer in Industrial Medicine, Dundee University; Senior Lecturer in Community Medicine, Nottingham University; Chief Medical Officer, The Health Education Council; Professor of Community Medicine, King's College, University of London. Recreations: church; gardening. Address: (b.) 2 Lilybank Gardens, Glasgow G12 8RZ. T.-041-330 5013.

McEwen, John, MB, ChB, PhD, FRCPE, FFPM. Medical Director, Drug Development (Scotland) Ltd., since 1983; Honorary Senior Lecturer, Dundee University, since 1983; Honorary Consultant, Tayside Health Board, since 1984; b. 11.4.43, Uddingston; m., Veronica Rosemary Iverson; 1 s.; 1 d. Educ. Ecclesfield Grammar School; St. Andrews University. Resident Physician/Surgeon, Dundee Hospitals, 1966-67; Lecturer in Therapeutics, Dundee University, 1969-75; Visiting Fellow in Clinical Pharmacology, Vanderbilt University, Tennessee, 1972-74; Head of Clinical Pharmacology, Hoechst, UK, 1975-82. Recreations: keyboard instruments; hill-walking; choral singing. Address: (h.) 1 Osborne Place, Dundee, DD2 1BE; T.-Dundee 641060.

McEwen, Martin, LLB, DLitt, AIH, MBIM, NP. Academic Registrar, Edinburgh College of Art, since 1991; Director, Scottish Ethnic Minorities Research Unit, since 1985; b. 21.12.43, Edinburgh; m., Jessica; 2 d. Educ. George Heriot's School; Aberdeen University; Edinburgh University; Heriot Watt University. District Officer/Assistant Secretary for Protectorate Affairs, Solomon Islands, 1967-70; Legal Assistant and Assistant Solicitor, Dunfermline Burgh, 1970-72; Assistant Conciliation Officer, Race Relations Board, 1972-74; Lecturer in Planning and Housing Law, Edinburgh College of Art/Heriot Watt University, 1974-86; Senior Lecturer, 1986-90. Recreations: squash; chess; tennis; walking. Address: (h.) 9 Ross Gardens, Edinburgh; T.-031-667 3725.

McEwen, Robert Rule (Robin), BL. Solicitor; Honorary Sheriff, Inverness, since 1984; b. 31.1.07, Inverness; m., 1, Elsie Ellis; 2, Marion Pringle or Jack; 1 s. Educ. Inverness Royal Academy; St. Peter's School, York; Edinburgh University. Partner, Stewart, Rule & Co., 1930-67, Rule MacEwen & Co., 1967-77; Consultant, MacLeod & MacCallum, 1977-81; War Service: RAOC, France and Germany, 1944-45 (mentioned in Despatches); Member, Inverness Town Council, 1950-56 (Magistrate and Chairman, Planning Committee); Member, Northern Regional Hospital Board, 1953-56; Dean, Faculty of Solicitors of the Highlands, 1976-79; Chairman, Federation of Scottish Film Societies, 1955; Chairman, Inverness Civic Trust, 1967-72; Chairman, Highlands and Islands Film Guild, 1974-77; Chairman, The Balnbin Trust, 1974-87, Hon. President, since 1987; Member, National Trust Advisory Committee on Culloden; Chairman, Inverness Liberal Association, 1980-81. Address: (h.) Brangan Cottage, 7 Crown Circus, Inverness, IV2 3NH; T.-0463 225385.

McFadden, Jean Alexandra, JP, MA, LLB, DL. President, Convention of Scottish Local Authorities, since 1990; Leader,

Glasgow District Council, since 1992; Lecturer in Law, Glasgow University and Strathclyde University; Vice Lord Lieutenant, City of Glasgow, since 1980; b. 26.11.41, Glasgow; m., John (deceased). Educ. Hyndland Secondary School; Glasgow University; Strathclyde University. Principal Teacher of Classics, Strathclyde schools, 1967-86; entered local government as Member, Cowcaddens Ward, Glasgow Corporation, 1971; Glasgow District Council: Member, Scotstoun Ward, 1984, Chairman, Manpower Committee, 1974-77, Leader, Labour Group, 1977-86, Leader of the Council, 1980-86. Convener, Scottish Local Government Information Unit, since 1984; Senior Vice-President, Convention of Scottish Local Authorities, 1988-90; Member, Board, Scottish Development Agency, since 1989; Chairman, Mayfest, since 1983. Recreations: cycling; theatre; walking; golf. Address: (h.) 16 Lansdowne Crescent, Glasgow G20 6NG; T.-041-334 3522.

McFadyen, Thomas, MB, ChB. Senior Medical Officer, Erskine Hospital, since 1978; b. 30.11.39, Glasgow. Educ. Allan Glen's School; Glasgow University. Appointments, Glasgow Royal Infirmary, Law Hospital, Carluke and Royal Alexandra Infirmary, Paisley. Recreation: golf. Address: (h.) Tigh-Na-Coille, Erskine Hospital, Bishopton, PA7 5PU; T.-041-812 7555.

McFall, John, BSc (Hons), BA, MBA. MP (Labour), Dumbarton, since 1987; b. 4.10.44, Glasgow; m., Joan Ward; 3 s.; 1 d. Schoolteacher, Assistant Head Teacher, 1974-87; Opposition Whip, 1989-91; Visiting Professor, Strathclyde Business School. Address: (b.) House of Commons, Westminster, London.

MacFarlane, Professor Alistair George James, CBE, PhD, DSc, MA, ScD, FIEE, FEng, FRS. Principal and Vice-Chancellor, Heriot-Watt University, since 1989; b. 1931, Edinburgh; m., Nora; 1 s. Educ. Hamilton Academy; Glasgow University. Metropolitan-Vickers Electrical Company Ltd.: Electronic Engineer, Radar and Servo Division, Group Leader, Moving Target Indication and Receiver Laboratories; Lecturer, Electrical Engineering, Queen Mary College, London University, 1959 (Reader, 1965); UMIST: Reader in Control Engineering, 1966, Professor of Control Engineering, 1969; Cambridge University: Chair, Engineering, 1974, Head, Information Engineering Division, Fellow, Selwyn College, 1974 (Vice-Master, 1980-88); Chairman, Cambridge Control Limited; Editor, International Journal of Control. Member: SERC Computer Board, Joint Policy Committee for National Facilities for Advanced Research Computing, Advisory Committee on Safety of Nuclear Installations. American Society of Mechanical Engineers Centennial Medal, 1980; Sir Harold Hartley Medal, Institute of Measurement and Control, 1982. Address: (b.) Heriot-Watt University, Riccarton, Edinburgh EH14 4AS.

Macfarlane, Rev. Alwyn James Cecil, BA, MA; b. 14.6.22, Edinburgh; m., Joan Cowell Harris; 1 s.; 1 d. Educ. Cargilfield School, Edinburgh; Rugby School; New College, Oxford; New College, Edinburgh. Captain, 6th Black Watch, North Africa, Italy and Greece, 1940-45; entered Ministry, Church of Scotland, 1951; Minister: Fodderty and Strathpeffer, 1952-59, St. Cuthbert's Church, Edinburgh (Associate), 1959-63, Portobello Old, Edinburgh, 1963-68, Newlands (South), Glasgow, 1968-85; Associate Minister, The Scots' Church, Melbourne, 1985-88. Chaplain to The Queen in Scotland; Member, The Queen's Household in Scotland. Recreations: photography; travel. Address: 4/9 Belhaven Place, Edinburgh.

MacFarlane, Professor Colin John, BSc, CEng, FRINA, MIMarE. Lloyd's Register Professor of Subsea Engineering, Strathclyde University, since 1986; Governor, Centre for Advanced Maritime Studies, since 1988; b. 4.3.50, Inverkip;

m., Sheila Gardner; 1 s.; 1 d. Educ. Uddingston Grammar School; Strathclyde University. P&O Steam Navigation Company and Three Quays Marine Services, 1973-80; BP Engineering (specialist naval architect), 1981-86. Recreations: family; reading; gardening. Address: (b.) Strathclyde University, Department of Ship and Marine Technology, 100 Montrose Street, Glasgow; T.-041-552 4400.

MacFarlane, Rev. David Cockburn, MA. Minister, Old Parish Church of Peebles, since 1970, with Eddleston Parish Church, since 1977, with Lyne and Manor Parish Church, since 1984; b. 10.6.31, Glasgow; m., Penelope Margaret Broadfoot; 3 s. Educ. High School of Glasgow; Glasgow University and Trinity College. Assistant Minister, Dunblane Cathedral, 1956-58; Minister, Aberlady Parish Church, 1959-70; Moderator: Haddington and Dunbar Presbytery, 1968-69, Melrose and Peebles Presbytery, 1977-78; Warden of Neidpath, 1984; President, Peebles Rotary Club, 1974-75. Publications: Aberlady Parish Church, 1967; The Old Parish Church of Peebles, 1973. Recreations: public speaking; reading; painting. Address: (h.) Old Parish Church Manse, Innerleithen Road, Peebles, EH45 8BD; T.-0721 20568.

Macfarlane, Neil Gerard, FRICS, IRRV, FBIM. Director of Estates, Strathclyde Regional Council, since 1987; b. Glasgow; m., Agnes Beatrix; 2 d. Educ. St. Mungo's Academy, Glasgow; Royal College of Science and Technology. Assessor's and Estates Departments, Corporation of City of Glasgow; appointed Head of Estates, Strathclyde Regional Council, 1974, Director, 1987. Executive Member, Scottish Branch, Local Authority Valuers Association; Member, Divisional Committee, General Practice Division, Scottish Branch, RICS. Recreations: bowling; walking; light music. Address: (b.) 20 India Street, Glasgow, G2 4PF; T.-041-204 2900.

Macfarlane of Bearsden, Lord, (Norman (Somerville) Macfarlane), HRSA, HRGI, Hon. FRIAS, Hon. LLD (Strathclyde, 1986; Glasgow, 1988). Chairman, Macfarlane Group (Clansman) PLC; Chairman, United Distillers PLC, since 1987; Joint Deputy Chairman, Guinness PLC, since 1989 (Chairman, 1987-89); Chairman, Arthur Bell Distillers plc, since 1989; b. 5.3.26; m., Marguerite Mary Campbell; 1 s.; 4 d. Educ. High School of Glasgow. Commissioned, Royal Artillery, 1945, served Palestine, 1945-47; founded N.S. Macfarlane & Co. Ltd., 1949 (became Macfarlane Group (Clansman) PLC, 1973); Underwriting Member of Lloyd's, since 1978; Chairman: The Fine Art Society PLC, since 1976, American Trust PLC, since 1984 (Director, since 1980); Director: Clydesdale Bank PLC, since 1980, General Accident Fire and Life Assurance Corporation plc, since 1984; Edinburgh Fund Managers plc, since 1980, Glasgow Chamber of Commerce, 1976-79; Member: Council, CBI Scotland, 1975-81, Board, Scottish Development Agency, 1979-87; Chairman, Glasgow Development Agency; Vice Chairman, Scottish Ballet, 1983-87 (Director, since 1975); Director, Scottish National Orchestra, 1977-82; President, Royal Glasgow Institute of Fine Arts, 1976-87; Member, Royal Fine Art Commission for Scotland, 1980-82; Scottish Patron, National Art Collection Fund, since 1978; Governor, Glasgow School of Art, 1976-87; Trustee: National Heritage Memorial Fund, since 1984, National Galleries of Scotland, since 1986; Director, Third Eye Centre, 1978-81; Chairman, Governors, High School of Glasgow, since 1979; Member, Court, Glasgow University, 1979-87; President: Stationers' Association of GB and Ireland, 1965, Company of Stationers of Glasgow, 1968-70, Glasgow High School Club, 1970-72; knighted, 1982; created a Life Peer, 1991; Lord High Commissioner to General Assembly of Church of Scotland, 1992. Recreations: golf; cricket; theatre; art. Address: (b.) Macfarlane Group (Clansman) PLC, Sutcliffe Road, Glasgow G13 1AH; (h.) 50 Manse Road, Bearsden, Glasgow.

Macfarlane, Professor Peter Wilson, BSc, PhD, FBCS. Professor in Medical Cardiology, Glasgow University, since 1991; b. 8.11.42, Glasgow; m., Irene Grace Muir; 2 s. Educ. Hyndland Senior Secondary School, Glasgow; Glasgow University. Glasgow University: Assistant Lecturer in Medical Cardiology, 1967, Lecturer, 1970, Senior Lecturer, 1974, Reader, 1980; President, 5th International Congress on Electrocardiology, Glasgow, 1978; Chairman, 15th Annual Conference, International Society of Computerised Electrocardiography, 1990; Author/Editor, ten books. Recreations: playing football; running half-marathons; playing violin. Address: (h.) 12 Barrcraig Road, Bridge of Weir, PA11 3HG; T.-Bridge of Weir 614443.

Macfarlane, Rev. Thomas Gracie, BSc, PhD, BD. Minister, South Shawlands Parish Church, Glasgow, since 1968; b. 10.6.27, Glasgow; m., Davina Shaw Robertson; 3 s. Educ. Allan Glen's School; Royal Technical College; Glasgow University. Research Metallurgist, 1948-53; ordained, 1956; served under Foreign Mission Committee, Church of Scotland, 1956-61, as Missionary with United Church of Central Africa in Rhodesia; Minister, St. James', Falkirk, 1961-68. Address: (h.) 0/2, 19 Corrour Road, Glasgow, G43 2DY; T.-041-632 7966.

Macfarlane, Professor Thomas Wallace, DDS, DSc, FRCPath, FDSRCPSGlas. Professor in Oral Microbiology, Glasgow University, since 1991; Honorary Consultant in Oral Microbiology; b. 12.12.42, Glasgow; m., Nancy McEwan; 1 s. Educ. Hyndland Senior Secondary School; Glasgow University. Assistant Lecturer, Dental Histology and Pathology, 1966-69; trained in Medical Microbiology and Histopathology, Glasgow Royal Infirmary; Lecturer in Oral Medicine and Pathology, 1969-77; organised and ran the diagnostic service in Oral Microbiology, Glasgow Dental Hospital and School; Senior Lecturer in Oral Medicine and Pathology and Consultant in Oral Microbiology, 1977; Reader in Oral Medicine and Pathology, 1984-91. Recreations: music; reading; painting; walking. Address: (b.) Oral Microbiology Unit, Dental Hospital and School, 378 Sauchiehall Street, Glasgow, G2 3JZ; T.-041-332 7020.

McFarlane, William Stewart, CA. President, Glasgow Chamber of Commerce, since 1990; b. 26.3.33, Glasgow; m., Sandra; 1 d. Educ. High School of Glasgow. Trained as Chartered Accountant, Wilson Stirling (now Touche, Ross & Co.), Glasgow; Parlane McFarlane CA, 1957-58; National Service (Second Lieutenant, Royal Corps of Signals), 1959-60; Partner, McFarlane, Son & Co., CA, 1961-62 (merged with Dickson, McFarlane & Robinson, CA, 1963-84, merged with Wylie & Bisset, CA, since 1985). Member, Council, Institute of Chartered Accountants of Scotland, 1971-76; Institute's representative, directorate of Glasgow Chamber of Commerce, 1970-88; Deputy President, Glasgow Chamber of Commerce, 1988-90; Past Finance Convener, Scottish Golf Union; Past Treasurer, Scottish Squash Rackets Association; Captain, Association of Golf Club Secretaries, 1980; Director, The Park School (Glasgow) Limited; Member, Master Court of the Incorporation of Masons of Glasgow; Member, Rotary Club of Charing Cross. Recreation: golf; curling; swimming; squash. Address: (b.) 30 George Square, Glasgow G2 1EQ; T.-041-204 2121.

McGarry, Very Rev. James, SDB, BD, LRAM, DSW, CQSW. Parish Priest, St. Paul's Catholic Church, Muirhouse, Edinburgh, since 1984; b. 23.8.48, Motherwell. Educ. Our Lady's High School, Motherwell; Pontifical University of Maynooth, Ireland; Glasgow University. Became Member, Salesians of St. John Bosco, 1966; qualified with Licentiate in Piano Teaching, Royal Academy of Music, 1970; ordained to priesthood, 1975; gained qualification in social work, 1980; Depute Head in charge of Social Work, St. John Bosco's List D School, 1980-83. Recreations: music; reading; cycling;

photography; computing; squash. Address: St. Paul's Catholic Church, 4 Muirhouse Avenue, Edinburgh EH4 4UB; T.-031-332 3320.

McGeough, Professor Joseph Anthony, FRSE, BSc, PhD, DSc, CEng, FIMechE, FIEE, MIM. Regius Professor of Engineering and Head, Department of Mechanical Engineering, Edinburgh University, 1983-91; Honorary Professor, Nanjing Aeronautical Institute, China, since 1991; b. 29.5.40, Kilwinning; m., Brenda Nicholson; 2 s.; 1 d. Educ. St. Michael's College; Glasgow University; Aberdeen University. Research Demonstrator, Leicester University, 1966; Senior Research Fellow, Queensland University, Australia, 1967; Research Metallurgist, International Research and Development Co. Ltd., Newcastle-upon-Tyne, 1968-69; Senior Research Fellow, Strathclyde University, 1969-72; Lecturer in Engineering, Aberdeen University, 1972-77 (Senior Lecturer, 1977-80, Reader, 1980-83). Chairman, Dyce Academy College Council, 1980-83; Honorary Vice-President, Aberdeen University Athletic Association, since 1981; Chairman, Edinburgh and S.E. Scotland Panel, IMechE, since 1988; Vice-Chairman, Scottish Branch, IMechE, 1991-93; Hon. President, Lichfield Science and Engineering Society, 1987-88. Publications: Principles of Electrochemical Machining, 1974; Advanced Methods of Machining, 1988; Processing of Advanced Materials, 1991. Recreations: gardening; golf; athletics. Address: (h.) 39 Dreghorn Loan, Colinton, Edinburgh, EH13 0DF; T.-031-441 1302.

McGettrick, Professor Andrew David, BSc, PhD, FBCS, FIEE, CEng. Head, Computer Science Department, Strathclyde University, 1984-90; Chairman, UK Committee of Professors of Computer Science, 1991-93; b. 15.5.44, Glasgow; m., Sheila Margaret Girot; 5 s.; 1 d. Educ. St. Aloysius College, Glasgow; Glasgow University; Peterhouse, Cambridge. Strathclyde University: Lecturer, 1969-80, Reader in Computer Science, 1980, Personal Professor, 1983, Full Professor, 1986. Editor, Addison Wesley's International Computer Science Series, 1980; Chairman, Computing Panel, Scottish Universities Council on Entrance, 1984-90; Member, Scottish Universities Council on Entrance, since 1990; Member, Safety Critical Systems Committee, IEE. Publications: Algol 68, A First and Second Course; An Introduction to the Definition of Programming Languages; Program Verification Using ADA; Graded Problems in Computer Science. Recreations: squash; running. Address: (b.) Computer Science Department, Strathclyde University, Livingstone Tower, 26 Richmond Street, Glasgow; T.-041-552 4400.

McGettrick, Bartholomew John, KHS, FRSA, BSc (Hons), MEd (Hons). Principal, St. Andrew's College of Education, since 1985; Member, Scottish Consultative Council on the Curriculum, since 1988 (Deputy Chairman, since 1991); Member, General Teaching Council for Scotland, since 1986; Member, various CNAA committees; Chairman, Committee on Assessment 5-14; b. 16.8.45, Glasgow; m., Elizabeth Maria McLaughlin; 2 s.; 2 d. Educ. St. Aloysius' College, Glasgow; Glasgow University. Teacher and Head, Department of Geography, St. Aloysius' College, Glasgow, 1968-72; Educational Psychologist, Scottish Centre for Social Subjects, 1972-75; Assistant Principal, then Vice-Principal, Notre Dame College of Education (latterly St. Andrew's College of Education), 1975-85. Chairman, Catholic Education Commission for Scotland, 1981-87; Member, Council for Educational Technology, 1982-86; Member, SCOTVAC, 1984-88; Chairman, Committee of Principals of Colleges of Education, 1990-92; Vice-Chairman, Association Catholique Internationale des Institutions de Sciences de L'Education, 1990-92; Chairman, Board of Governors, St. Aloysius' College, Glasgow; Recreations: sports (squash,

rugby). Address: (h.) 174 Carmunnock Road, Glasgow, G44 5AJ; T.-041-637 8112.

McGhee, John (Ian). Head of Exports, Publicity and Technology Division, The Scottish Office Industry Department; b. 12.9.46, Irvine; m., Linda Christine Whalley; 2 d. Educ. Cumnock Academy; Glasgow University. Board of Trade Investment Grant Office, 1967, Business Statistics Office, 1969; Scottish Development Department, 1971; Scottish Office Management Services Unit, 1974; Department of Agriculture and Fisheries for Scotland - EEC and international fisheries agreements, 1981; Deputy Director, Locate in Scotland, 1986-88. Recreations: reading; music; golf. Address: (b.) The Scottish Office Industry Department, Alhambra House, 45 Waterloo Street, Glasgow, G2 6AT; T.-041-248 2855.

McGhee, Very Rev. Michael James. Priest, since 1960; Parish Priest, Leith, since 1987; b. 14.1.37, Birkenhead. Educ. St. Anselm's. School Chaplain, 1960-79; parochial ministry: Dublin, 1960-81, Leeds, 1981-87. Recreations: music; theatre; reading. Address: St. Mary's, Star of the Sea, 106 Constitution Street, Leith, EH6 6AW, T.-031-554 2482.

McGhee, Rev. Robert, DD. Minister, Falkirk St. Andrew's West, since 1990 (Falkirk St. Andrew's, 1972-90); b. 29.7.29, Port Glasgow; m., Mary Stevenson Cunningham; 1 s.; 2 d. Educ. Port Glasgow High School; Greenock High School; Glasgow University and Trinity College. Trained as cashier/bookkeeper, 1945-54; RAF, 1947-49; ordained and inducted to Pulteneytown St. Andrew's, Wick, 1959; Minister, Wick St. Andrew's and Thrumster, 1961-66; Minister, Newbattle, Dalkeith, 1966-72; Convener, Board of Social Responsibility, Church of Scotland, 1985-89 (Convener, Community Care, Social Responsibility, 1977-85); Chairman, Lord's Day Observance Society, Scotland, 1970-74; President, Scottish Evangelistic Council, 1982-85; Moderator: Presbytery of Caithness, 1964-65, Presbytery of Falkirk, 1983-84, Synod of Forth, 1985-86. Address: St. Andrew's West Manse, 1 Maggie Woods Loan, Falkirk, FK1 5SJ; T.-Falkirk 23308.

McGhie, James Marshall, QC, LLB (Hons). Queen's Counsel, since 1983; part-time Chairman, Medical Appeal Tribunals, since 1987; b. 15.10.44, Perth; m., Ann M. Cockburn; 1 s.; 1 d. Educ. Perth Academy; Edinburgh University. Address: (b.) Advocates Library, Parliament House, High Street, Edinburgh; T.-031-226 5091.

McGibbon, Alistair, MA, MEd. Rector, Woodlands High School, Falkirk, since 1983; b. 3.10.37, Glasgow; m., Jean Ronald; 2 s.; 1 d. Educ. North Kelvinside School; Glasgow University; Stirling University. Teaching appointments in Glasgow, Guildford, Perth (Western Australia), Papua New Guinea, Central Region. Recreations: golf; Church activities. Address: (b.) Woodlands High School, Rennie Street, Falkirk, FK1 5AL; T.-0324 29615.

McGill, Rt. Rev. Stephen, PSS, STL. Bishop of Paisley, 1968-88; b. 4.1.12, Glasgow. Educ. St. Aloysius College, Glasgow; Blairs College, Aberdeen; Institut Catholique, Paris. Staff, Le Grand Seminaire, Bordeaux, 1939, Le Grand Seminaire, Aix-en-Province, 1940; Spiritual Director, then Rector, Blairs College, Aberdeen, 1940-60; Bishop of Argyll and the Isles, 1960-68. Recreations: caligraphy; golf. Address: 13 Newark Street, Greenock, PA16 7UH.

McGillivray, Rev. (Alexander) Gordon, MA, BD, STM. Clerk, Edinburgh Presbytery, Church of Scotland, since 1973; Depute Clerk, General Assembly, since 1971; b. 22.9.23, Edinburgh; m., Winifred Jean Porter; 2 s.; 2 d. Educ. George Watson's Boys' College, Edinburgh; Edinburgh University; Union Theological Seminary, New York. Royal Artillery,

1942-45; Assistant Minister, St. Cuthbert's Parish Church, Edinburgh; Minister: Waterbeck Church, 1951-58, Nairn High Church, 1958-73. Recreation: golf. Address: 7 Greenfield Crescent, Balerno, Midlothian, EH14 7HD; T.-031-449 4747.

Mcgilvray, Professor James William, MA, MLitt. Professor of Economics, Strathclyde University, since 1975; Director, Fraser of Allander Institute, 1980-86; b. 21.2.38, Glasgow; m., Alison Ann; 1 s.; 1 d. Educ. St. Columba's College, Dublin; Edinburgh University. Recreations: gardening; squash; shooting. Address: (b.) 100 Cathedral Street, Glasgow, G4 0LN; T.-041-552 4400.

Mcgirr, Professor Edward McCombie, CBE, BSc, MD, FRCP, FRCPEdin, FRCPGlas, FFCM, FACP (Hon.), FRSE. Chairman, Scottish Council for Postgraduate Medical Education, 1979-85; Emeritus Professor, Glasgow University, since 1981 (Dean of Faculties, since 1992); b. 15.6.16, Hamilton; m., Diane Curzon Woods; 1 s.; 3 d. Educ. Hamilton Academy; Glasgow University. RAMC, 1941-47, including posts as graded physician and specialist in medicine ; appointments in University Department of Medicine, Glasgow Royal Infirmary, 1947-78, latterly Muirhead Chair of Medicine, Glasgow University, and Physician in charge of wards, Glasgow Royal Infirmary; Dean, Faculty of Medicine, Glasgow University, 1974-81; Administrative Dean and Professor of Administrative Medicine, Glasgow University, 1978-81. President, Royal College of Physicians and Surgeons of Glasgow, 1970-72; Chairman, Scottish Health Service Planning Council, 1978-84; Honorary Physician to the Army in Scotland, 1975-81; sometime Member: Greater Glasgow Health Board, National Radiological Protection Board, General Nursing Council for Scotland, National Board for Nursing, Midwifery and Health Visiting; Past President, Royal Medico-Chirurgical Society of Glasgow; Chairman, Scottish Council for Opportunities for Play Experience (SCOPE), 1985-87; Chairman, Clyde Estuary Amenity Council, 1986-90. Recreations: reading; curling. Address: (h.) Anchorage House, Bothwell, by Glasgow, G71 8NF; T.-0698 852194.

Mcglynn, Archie Smith, BA (Hons), MPhil, DipComm. HM Chief Inspector of Schools, since 1987; b. Tarbert, Argyll; m., Leah Sutherland Ross; 1 s.; 1 d. Educ. Tarbert Secondary School; Campbeltown Grammar School; Strathclyde University; Glasgow University. Industry and commerce, 1962-64 and 1966-67; Teacher in schools and further/higher education colleges, 1964-69; Depute Principal, Glenrothes College, 1969-75; HM Inspector of Schools, 1976-87. Recreations: hedgehog preservation; following Fife Flyers. Address: (b.) Room 4/35, New St. Andrew's House, Edinburgh; T.-031-244 4569.

Mcglynn, Rt. Rev. Lord Abbot (James Aloysius) Donald, OCSO, STL, SLJ. Monk, Order of Cistercians of Strict Observance, since 1952; Abbot of Nunraw, since 1969; b. 13.8.34, Glasgow. Educ. Holyrood School, Glasgow; St. Bernardine's School, Buckinghamshire; Gregorian University, Rome. President, Scottish Council of Major Religious Superiors, 1974-77; President, British Isles Regional Council of Cistercian Abbeys, 1980-84; Chairman, Union of Monastic Superiors, 1985-89; Official Roman Catholic Visitor to the General Assembly, Church of Scotland, 1976 and 1985; Commandeur Ecclesiastique, Military & Hospitaller Order of St. Lazarus of Jerusalem, 1985; Patron, Friends of the Beatitudes, Madras; Patron, Haddington Pilgrimage of St. Mary & the Three Kings. Recreations: iconography; farm work; computer printing. Address: Sancta Maria Abbey, Nunraw, Garvald, Haddington, EH41 4LW; T.-062 083 223.

McGovern, John Gerard, JP, BSc, MRSC. Headteacher, Our Lady's High School, Broxburn, since 1978; b. 16.1.34, Cambuslang; m., Elizabeth Kearney; 2 s.; 3 d. Educ. Our Lady's High School, Motherwell; Glasgow University. National Service, Royal Signals (awarded GSM (Cyprus)); Teacher of Science (Chemistry), Our Lady's High School, Motherwell; Principal Teacher of Science/Chemistry, St. David's High School, Dalkeith; Depute Headteacher: Our Lady's High School, Broxburn, St. David's, Dalkeith. Address: (h.) 57 Staunton Rise, Dedridge, Livingston, West Lothian; T.-0506 414880.

McGowan, Rev. Andrew T.B., BD, STM, PhD. Minister, Trinity Possil and Henry Drummond Church, Glasgow, since 1988; b. 30.1.54, Glasgow; m., June S. Watson; 3 s. Educ. Uddingston Grammar School; Aberdeen University; Union Theological Seminary, New York. Assistant Minister, St. Cuthbert's, Edinburgh, 1978-80; Minister: Mallaig and the Small Isles, 1980-86, Causewayend Church, Aberdeen, 1986-88. Member, Council, Rutherford House, Edinburgh; Director, Bible Training Institute, Glasgow. Recreations: hillwalking; chess; guitar. Address: 35 Springfield Road, Bishopbriggs, Glasgow, G64; T.-041-772 1456.

McGowan, Daniel, MILAM. Director of Community Services, Cumbernauld and Kilsyth District Council, since 1989 (Director of Leisure and Recreation, 1978-89); b. 23.9.41, Coatbridge; m.; 4 s.; 1 d. Educ. St. Patrick's High School, Coatbridge; Coatbridge Technical College. Chairman, Scottish Swimming Coaches Association, since 1980. Recreations: swimming; golf. Address: (b.) Council Offices, Bron Way, Cumbernauld, G67 1DZ; T.-02367 22131.

McGowan, Professor David Alexander, MDS, PhD, FDSRCS, FFDRCSI, FDSRCPSG. Dean of Dental Education, since 1990, and Professor of Oral Surgery, Glasgow University, since 1977; Consultant Oral Surgeon, Greater Glasgow Health Board, since 1977; b. 18.6.39, Portadown, Co. Armagh; m., Margaret Vera Macaulay; 1 s.; 2 d. Educ. Portadown College; Queen's University, Belfast. Oral surgery training, Belfast and Aberdeen, 1961-67; Lecturer in Dental Surgery, Queen's University, Belfast, 1968; Lecturer, then Senior Lecturer and Deputy Head, Oral and Maxillofacial Surgery, London Hospital Medical College, 1968-77. Postgraduate Adviser in Dentistry, Glasgow University, 1977-90; Chairman, Dental Committee, Scottish Council for Postgraduate Medical Education, 1980-90; Dean, Dental Faculty, and Member of College Council, Royal College of Physicians and Surgeons of Glasgow, 1989-92; Member, General Dental Council; Member, Dental Education Advisory Council; Member, National Dental Advisory Committee; former Council Member, British Association of Oral and Maxillofacial Surgeons. Recreations: sailing; music. Address: (b.) Department of Oral Surgery, Glasgow Dental Hospital and School, 378 Sauchiehall Street, Glasgow, G2 3JZ; T.-041-332 7020, Ext. 318.

McGowan, Ian Duncan, BA. Librarian, National Library of Scotland, since 1990 (Secretary of the Library, 1988-90); b. 19.9.45, Liverpool; m., Elizabeth Ann Weir; 2 d. Educ. Liverpool Institute; Exeter College, Oxford. Assistant Keeper, National Library of Scotland, 1971-78; Keeper (Catalogues and Automation), 1978-88. Address: (b.) National Library of Scotland, George IV Bridge, Edinburgh, EH1 1EW; T.-031-226 4531.

McGowan, John, LLB. Solicitor, since 1967; Temporary Sheriff, since 1986; b. 15.1.44, Kilmarnock; m., Elise Smith; 2 s. Educ. St. Joseph's Academy, Kilmarnock; Glasgow University. Admitted Solicitor, 1967; Council Member, Law Society of Scotland, 1982-85. Recreations: golf; tennis; curling; cricket; listening to music. Address: (h.) 19 Auchentrae Crescent, Ayr.

McGowan, Stuart Watson, MB, ChB, FFARCS, DA. President, Scottish Society of Anaesthetists, 1991; Consultant Anaesthetist, Dundee Teaching Hospitals, 1964-91; b. 31.7.29, Uddingston; m., Mabel Wilson; 1 s.; 1 d. Educ. Hutchesons' Boys Grammar School, Glasgow; Glasgow University. President, North-East of Scotland Society of Anaesthetists, 1972; President, Dundee Speakers Club, 1972; President, Dundee Medical Club, 1991. Recreations: golf; music; travel. Address: (h.) 41 Whitefauld Road, Dundee, DD2 1RJ; T.-0382 65281.

McGown, Archibald M. Director, Scottish Retirement Council, since 1987; b. 15.11.33, Paisley; m., Janet Robertson; 1 s.; 2 d. Educ. Rutherglen Academy. Managing Director, Elvestead Canned Meat Co. Ltd., 1976-86. Vice Chairman, Royal Scottish Automobile Club. Recreations: curling; bowling. Address: (b.) Alexandra House, 204 Bath Street, Glasgow, G2 4HL; T.-041-332 9427.

McGrain, Daniel Fergus, MBE (1983). Footballer; b. 1.5.50, Glasgow. Former Celtic and Scotland Captain; first club, Maryhill Juniors; signed for Celtic, 1967; first cap against Wales, 1973; played in two World Cups – West Germany, 1974, Spain, 1982; played in seven Scottish Cup Finals; played more than 600 games for Celtic.

McGrath, Gerald, JP, DL, FBCO, DCLP. Optometrist; Chair, Planning and Development, Strathclyde Regional Council, since 1990 (Councillor, since 1969); b. 3.9.27, Glasgow; m., Esther; 2 s.; 4 d. Educ. St. Mungo's Academy; Stow College. Member, General Optical Council; President, British College of Optometrists. European Silver Medal of Merit. Recreation: drawing. Address: 6 Observatory Road, Glasgow, G12; T.-041-339 2262.

McGrath, John. Playwright; Theatre, Film and TV Director; Artistic Director, 7:84 Theatre Company (Scotland), 1973-88; Producer/Director, Freeway Films, since 1982; b. 1.6.35, Birkenhead; m., Elizabeth MacLennan; 2 s.; 1 d. Educ. Alun Grammar School, Mold, Clwyd; St. John's College, Oxford. Playwright (more than 35 plays produced professionally in UK and abroad); Writer of film screenplays for feature films and TV plays; Director in theatre and TV; Poet and Songwriter; plays for theatre including Events While Guarding the Bofors Gun, The Cheviot, The Stag and the Black, Black Oil, Blood Red Roses, Border Warfare, John Brown's Body. Visiting Judith E. Wilson Fellow, Cambridge, 1979 and 1989; recent film and television productions: Border Warfare, John Brown's Body, The Dressmaker. Publications: A Good Night Out (lectures); The Bone Won't Break. Address: (b.) Freeway Films, 67 George Street, Edinburgh, EH2 2JG; T.-031-225 3200.

McGrath, Professor John Christie (Ian), BSc, PhD. Regius Professor of Physiology, Glasgow University, since 1991; b. 8.3.49, Johnstone; m., Wilma Nicol; 1 s.; 1 d. Educ. John Neilson Institution, Paisley; Glasgow University. Glasgow University: Research Fellow in Pharmacology and Anaesthesia, 1973-75, Lecturer, 1975-83, Senior Lecturer, 1983-88, Reader, 1988-89, Titular Professor, 1987-91. Sandoz Prizewinner, British Pharmacological Society, 1980; Pfizer Award for Biology, 1983. Recreations: running; politics; travel. Address: (b.) Institute of Physiology, Glasgow University, Glasgow; T.-041-330 4483.

McGregor, Rev. Alistair Gerald Crichton, QC, BD, BA, LLB, WS. Minister, North Leith Parish Church, Edinburgh, since 1987; Temporary Sheriff, 1984-87; b. 15.10.37, Sevenoaks, Kent; m., Margaret Dick Lees or McGregor; 2 s.; 1 d. Educ. Charterhouse; Pembroke College, Oxford;

Edinburgh University. Solicitor; Advocate; QC; former Standing Junior Counsel to Queen's and Lord Treasurer's Remembrancer, to Scottish Home and Health Department and to Scottish Development Department; Past Chairman, Discipline Committee, Potato Marketing Board; former Clerk, Rules Council, Court of Session; former Tutor in Scots Law, Edinburgh University; Chairman, Family Care, 1983-88; Director, Apex (Scotland) Ltd. Publication: Obscenity (Co-author). Recreations: squash; tennis; swimming; travel; cinema. Address: (h.) 22 Primrose Bank Road, Edinburgh, EH5; T.-031-551 2802.

McGregor, Bobby, MBE (1964). Swimmer; b. 3.4.44, Helensburgh. Educ. Falkirk High School; Glasgow College of Architecture. Silver Medal, 4 x 100 m. relay, European Championships, 1962; Gold Medal, 100 m. freestyle, European Championships, 1966; Silver Medal, 110 yards freestyle, Commonwealth Championships, 1962; Silver Medal, 110 yards freestyle, Commonwealth Championships, 1966; Silver Medal, 100 m. freestyle, Olympic Games, 1964.

MacGregor, Professor Bryan Duncan, BSc, MSc, PhD, MRTPI. MacRobert Professor of Land Economy, Aberdeen University, since 1990 (Head, Department of Land Economy, since 1990); b. 16.10.53, Inverness. Educ. Inverness Royal Academy; Edinburgh University; Heriot Watt University; Cambridge University. Lecturer, Department of Land Management, Reading University, 1981-84; Lecturer, Department of Town and Regional Planning, Glasgow University, 1984-87; Deputy, then Property Research Manager, Prudential Portfolio Managers, 1987-90. Recreations: hill-walking; football; literature; music; thinking. Address: (b.) Department of Land Economy, St. Mary's, King's College, Aberdeen University, Aberdeen, AB9 2UF; T.-0224 272356.

McGregor, Rev. Charles Cameron, BA. Parish Priest, Banchory/Aboyne, since 1982; b. 6.9.26, Buckie. Educ. Our Lady's High School, Motherwell; Blairs College, Aberdeen; Allen Hall, St. Edmund's College, Ware. Army Service, 1945-48; ordained Priest, St. Bridget's, Baillieston, 1954; Parish Priest, Inverurie, 1956-62, Kincorth, 1962-72; Cathedral Administrator, Aberdeen, 1972-82; Dean, St. Mary's, since 1979; Dean, St. Columba's, since 1982; Broadcaster, BBC, 1958-84; Religious Adviser, Grampian TV, 1965-85; Army Chaplain, TAVR, 1965-72, 1st Bn., Lowland Volunteers; Chairman, Scottish Catholic International Aid Fund, since 1988. Recreations: reading; theatre; historical buildings; Doric prose and verse. Address: (h.) Corsee Cottage, High Street, Banchory, AB3 3RP; T.-03302 2835.

McGregor, Rev. Duncan James. Minister, parishes of Channelkirk and Lauder Old, since 1982; b. 17.7.35, Edinburgh; m., Constance Anne Aitchison; 3 s. Educ. Edinburgh Academy; Edinburgh University and New College. Worked in paper trade, then in insurance; Secretary: Scottish Anglers' Association, 1966-82, Anglers' Co-operative Association (Scotland), 1972-78, Scottish Joint Committee for Anglers, 1967-80; called to Ministry, 1982. Life Member, Scottish Anglers' National Association and Anglers Co-operative Association (Scotland); Moderator, Presbytery of Melrose and Peebles, 1988-89. Recreations: golf; angling; walking; reading. Address: The Manse of Lauder, Lauder, Berwickshire; T.-05782 320.

MacGregor of MacGregor, Brigadier Sir Gregor, 6th Bt. 23rd Chief of Clan Gregor; b. 22.12.25; m., Fanny Butler; 2 s. Educ. Eton. Commissioned, Scots Guards, 1944; commanding 1st Bn., Scots Guards, 1966-69; Col. Recruiting, HQ Scotland, 1971; Lt.-Col. commanding Scots Guards, 1971-74; Defence and Military Attache, British Embassy, Athens, 1975-78; Comdr., Lowlands, 1978-80; Grand Master Mason of Scotland, since 1988; Member, Queen's Bodyguard for Scotland (Royal Company of Archers). Address: (h.) Bannatyne, Newtyle, Blairgowrie, Perthshire.

McGregor, Iain. Honorary Secretary, Scottish Anti Common Market Council, since 1982; b. 19.3.37, Stirling. Educ. Selkirk High School; Kelso High School. Army Service, REME; International Trade Exhibitions Publicist, London; Editor, BIPS International Photo-Feature Agency; Journalist, Fleet Street and provinces; Writer and Lecturer in Journalism, Asia, Europe, North America; Founding Director, Institute for Christian Media (Canada); Member, Social Credit Secretariat; Editor, The Patriot for Scotland; Council Member, Heritage Society of Scotland. Recreations: local history; travel; music; theatre; film; books. Address: (h.) 170 Portobello High Street, Edinburgh, EH15 1EX.

MacGregor, Ian George Stewart, OBE, MA, MEd, FBIM. Partner, MacGregor & Partners, European Language School Advisers; b. 29.12.24, Newcastle-upon-Tyne. Educ. Altrincham Grammar School; Bell-Baxter School, Cupar; St. Andrews University; Edinburgh University; New York University. Assistant Principal, Ministry of Finance, Government of Northern Ireland, 1947-50; Teacher, Buckhaven High School, 1952-53 and 1954-55 (Teaching Fellowship in Psychology, New York University, 1953-54); Principal Administrative Assistant, Edinburgh Corporation Education Department, 1955-59; Assistant Director of Education, Aberdeenshire, 1959-64; Senior Depute Director of Education, West Lothian, 1964-70; Rector, Bathgate Academy, 1970-88. General Council Assessor, Edinburgh University Court; Recreations: Scouting; photography; Rotary; travel. Address: (h.) 20 Stewart Avenue, Bo'ness, EH51 9NL; T.-0506 822462.

Macgregor, James Duncan, OBE, MD,FFPHM, DPH, DTM&H. Unit Medical Officer, Perth and Kinross, Tayside Health Board, since 1981; Honorary Senior Clinical Lecturer, Department of Community Medicine, Dundee University, since 1982; b. 21.8.27, Invergowrie, Perthshire; m., Rita Moss; 2 s.; 1 d. Educ. Perth Academy; St. Andrews University. House Officer posts, Perth Royal Infirmary and Royal Northern Infirmary, Inverness, 1950-51; joined HM Colonial Medical Service, 1951; posted to Sierra Leone as General Duty MO; transferred to South Pacific Health Service as Senior Medical Officer, 1956; retired from the Overseas Service, 1975, as Director of Medical Services, Solomon Islands; Chief Administrative Medical Officer, Shetland Health Board, 1975; moved to Tayside Health Board as District MO. Red Cross Voluntary Medical Services Medal. Recreations: gardening; hill-walking. Address: (h.) 74 Glasgow Road, Perth, PH2 OPG; T.-Perth 24493.

Macgregor, Janet Elizabeth, OBE, BSc, MB, ChB, MD, FRCPath, FRCOG. Director, Harris Birthright Research Centre, Aberdeen University, since 1988; b. 12.1.20, Glasgow; m., Professor A.G. Macgregor (deceased); 3 s.; 1 d. Educ. Bearsden Academy; Glasgow University. Captain, RAMC, 1943-45; Medical Officer, Maternity and Child Welfare, Glasgow, Sheffield and Edinburgh, 1946-59; Research Fellow, Department of Obstetrics and Gynaecology, Aberdeen University, 1960-66; Medical Assistant, Grampian Health Board, 1966-73; appointed Senior Lecturer, Aberdeen University, 1973. Member, Cytology Sub-Committee, Royal College of Pathologists, 1980-82; Chairman and President, British Society for Clinical Cytology, 1977-83; Member, Medical Advisory Committee, Women's National Cancer Control Campaign, since 1977; Member, IARC (WHO) Study Group on Cervical Cancer, 1978-84; Fellow, International Academy of Cytology, since 1963. Address: (h.) Ardruighe, Clachan, Isle of Seil, Argyll; T.-085-23-427.

Macgregor, Jimmie, DA. Radio and Television Presenter, Author, and Lecturer; b. 10.3.32. Educ. Springburn Academy; Glasgow School of Art. Forefront of British folk music revival for more than 20 years; numerous radio and television appearances, and tours, Britain and abroad; more than 20 albums recorded; own daily radio programme for last nine years; regular TV series on long-distance walks; various books on folk songs and the outdoors; has written theme music, illustrated books; gives regular lectures and slide shows; Life Member, Scottish Wildlife Trust, Friends of Loch Lomond, Scottish Youth Hostels Association; President, Friends of River Kelvin; Hon. Vice-President, Scottish Conservation Projects. Recreations: collecting paintings, pottery, furniture, glass; the outdoors; wildlife; hill-walking; theatre; art; music; antiques; old cars. Address: (b.) BBC, Queen Margaret Drive, Glasgow.

McGregor, John Cummack, BSc (Hons), MB, ChB, FRCS, FRCSEdin. Consultant Plastic and Reconstructive Surgeon, Lothian Region, based at Regional Plastic Surgery Unit, Bangour General Hospital, since 1980; b. 21.4.44, Paisley; m., Moira Imray; 1 s.; 1 d. Educ. Paisley Grammar School; Glasgow University. Initial medical and surgical training, Paisley Royal Alexandra Infirmary, Western Infirmary, Glasgow, Stobhill Hospital, Glasgow, Nottingham City Hospital, Canniesburn Plastic Surgery Unit, Glasgow and Bangour General Hospital. Recreations: tennis; badminton; golf; cacti collecting; budgerigar breeding/showing. Address: (b.) Department of Plastic Surgery, Bangour General Hospital, West Lothian; Murrayfield Hospital, 122 Corstorphine Road, Edinburgh, EH12 6UD.

McGregor, Margaret Morrice, MA, JP. Chair, Edinburgh District Council Women's Committee, since 1988; b. 22.10.43, Aberdeen; m., Michael McGregor; 2 s.; 2 step d. Educ. Aberdeen Academy; Aberdeen University. Member: Edinburgh Accident Prevention Council; Edinburgh New Town Conservation Committee; Edinburgh Health Council; Royal Zoological Society of Scotland. Recreations: reading; chess; music; hill-walking; painting. Address: (h.) 6 Corstorphine House Terrace, Edinburgh, EH12 7AE; T.-031-334 1842.

McGrigor, Captain Sir Charles Edward, 5th Bt. A Vice-President, RNLI; Member, Queen's Bodyguard for Scotland (Royal Company of Archers); a Deputy Lieutenant, Argyll and Bute; b. 5.10.22; m., Mary Bettine (eldest daughter of the late Sir Archibald Edmonstone, 6th Bt. of Duntreath); 2 s.; 2 d. Educ. Eton. Joined Army, 1941; Rifle Brigade, North Africa, Italy, Austria (mentioned in Despatches); ADC to Duke of Gloucester, 1945-47.

Macgruer, Michael, RIBA, ARIAS. Director of Architectural Services, Lochaber District Council, since 1986 (District Architect, 1984-86); b. 26.2.51, Inverness; m., Sheena Robertson; 1 s.; 1 d. Educ. Grantown Grammar School; Lochaber High School; Mackintosh School of Architecture, Glasgow. Glasgow District Council: student architect, 1969-77; Project Architect, 1977-83. Address: (b.) Lochaber House, High Street, Fort William; T.-0397 703881.

McGuire, Edward, ARCM, ARAM. Composer; b. 15.2.48, Glasgow. Educ. Royal Academy of Music, London; State Academy of Music, Stockholm. Won National Young Composers Competition, 1969; Rant selected as test piece for 1978 Carl Flesch International Violin Competition; Proms debut, 1982, when Source performed by BBC SSO; String Quartet chosen for 40th Anniversary Concert, SPNM, Barbican, 1983; frequent commissions and broadcasts including Trilogy: Rebirth-Interregnum-Liberation (New Music Group), Euphoria (EIF/Fires of London), Life Songs (John Currie Singers), Songs of New Beginnings (Paragon Ensemble), Quintet II (Lontano); Peter Pan (Scottish Ballet);

plays flute with Whistlebinkies folk group. Address: c/o Scottish Music Information Centre, 1 Bowmont Gardens, Glasgow, G12; T.-041-334 6393.

McHardy, George Jamieson Ross, MA, MSc, BM, FRCPE, FRCP(Lond). Consultant Clinical Respiratory Physiologist, Lothian Health Board, since 1965; Consultant Physician, City Hospital, Edinburgh, since 1966; Senior Lecturer (part-time), Edinburgh University, since 1966; b. 17.11.30, Edinburgh; m., Dr. Valentine Urie Dewar; 2 s.; 1 d. Educ. Wellington College; Brasenose College, Oxford; Middlesex Hospital Medical School. House appointments, Middlesex Hospital, London; National Service (Flt. Lt., RAF Medical branch); Medical Registrar, Middlesex and Hammersmith Hospitals; Tutor in Medicine, Postgraduate Medical School, London, 1964; US Public Health Service Fellow, Department of Environmental Medicine, Johns Hopkins University, Baltimore, 1965. Councillor, Royal College of Physicians of Edinburgh, 1977 and 1981; on Steering Committee, "Fit for Life" Campaign, 1977-82; President, Scottish Thoracic Society, 1986-88; Chairman, Lothian Area Medical Committee, since 1988. Publications: Davidson's Textbook of Medicine, 15th edition (Contributor); papers on medical subjects. Recreations: music; sailing; skiing. Address: (h.) 6 Ettrick Road, Edinburgh, EH10 5BJ; T.-031-229 9026.

McHarg, William Wilson, OBE, MC, TD, MA, LLB, DL. Retired Solicitor and Racecourse Manager; b. 29.8.18, Ayr; m., Janet; 1 s.; 1 d. Educ. Irvine Royal Academy; Glasgow University. Royal Artillery, 1939-46 (demobolised with rank of Major); TA Service, 1947-62 (last rank: Brevet Colonel); Solicitor, 1947-80; Racecourse Manager and Clerk of the Course, 1947-88; Deputy Lieutenant, since 1975. Recreation: horse-racing. Address: (h.) 29 Earls Way, Doonfoot, Ayr, KA7 4HF; T.-0292 41350.

McIldowie, James Robert, MA, LLB, NP. Solicitor, since 1962; Honorary Sheriff, since 1986; b. 24.9.37, Crieff; m., Isabella Junor (June) Anderson; 2 d. Educ. Morrison's Academy, Crieff; Edinburgh University. Apprentice and Assistant in Edinburgh; joined McLean & Stewart, Dunblane and Callander, 1962; became a Partner, 1963; now Senior Partner. Former Secretary and Treasurer, Highland Pony Society. Recreations: golf; music; theatre; all sports. Address: (b.) 51-53 High Street, Dunblane, Perthshire; T.-0786 823217.

McIlvanney, William. Novelist; b. 1936, Kilmarnock. Educ. Kilmarnock Academy; Glasgow University. Former school teacher. Novels include: Remedy is None (joint winner, Geoffrey Faber Memorial Award, 1967) and Docherty (Whitbread Award for Fiction, 1975).

McIlwain, Alexander Edward, CBE, MA, LLB, WS, SSC. Senior Partner, Leonards, Solicitors, Hamilton and Strathaven; Honorary Sheriff, South Strathclyde, Dumfries and Galloway, at Hamilton, since 1981; b. 4.7.33, Aberdeen; m., Moira Margaret Kinnaird; 3 d. Educ. Aberdeen Grammar School; Aberdeen University. Commissioned, Royal Corps of Signals, 1957-59; Burgh Prosecutor then District Prosecutor, Hamilton, 1966-76; Dean, Society of Solicitors of Hamilton, 1981-83; Chairman, Legal Aid Central Committee, 1985-87; President, Law Society of Scotland, 1983-84; Member: Central Advisory Committee for Scotland on Justices of the Peace; Lanarkshire Health Board; Supreme Court Committee, Scottish Legal Aid Board; Scottish Committee, The Scout Association; The Scout Council (UK); Honorary Member, American Bar Association; Honorary Vice President, Scottish Lawyers for Nuclear Disarmament; Chairman, Lanarkshire Scout Area, since 1981; Temporary Sheriff, since 1984. Recreations: work; gardening; golf. Address: (h.) 7 Bothwell Road, Uddingston, Glasgow; T.-0698 813368.

MacInnes, Donald, BA, MBA. Chief Executive, Dunbartonshire Enterprise, since 1991; b. 8.8.47, Isle of Harris; m., Catherine; 3 s.; 1 d. Educ. Inverness Royal Academy; Strathclyde University. Former building society manager and development surveyor. Recreation: sailing. Address: (h.) 83 Woodend Drive, Jordanhill, Glasgow; T.-041-950 1374.

MacInnes, Hamish, OBE, BEM. Writer and Designer; b. 7.7.30, Gatehouse of Fleet. Educ. Gatehouse of Fleet. Mountaineer with numerous expeditions to Himalayas, Amazon and other parts of the world; Deputy Leader, 1975 Everest SW Face Expedition; film Producer/Advisor/safety expert, with Zinnemann, Connery, Eastwood, Putnam, etc.; Advisor, BBC TV live outside broadcasts on climbing; author of 20 books on travel and adventure, including two autobiographies and fiction; designed the first all-metal ice axe, Terodactyl ice climbing tools, the MacInnes stretchers; Founder, Search and Rescue Dog Association; Honorary Member, Scottish Mountaineering Club; former President, Alpine Climbing Group; world authority on mountain rescue; Doctor of Laws (Hons), Glasgow University; Hon. DSc, Aberdeen University; President, Guide Dogs Adventure Group; Leader, Glencoe Mountain Rescue Team. Recreations: as above. Address: (h.) Glencoe, Argyll; T.-08552 258.

McInnes, Sheriff John Colin, QC, BA (Hons) (Oxon), LLB. Advocate; Sheriff, Tayside, Central and Fife, since 1974; b. 21.11.38, Cupar, Fife; m., Elisabeth Mabel Neilson; 1 s.; 1 d. Educ. New Park School, St. Andrews; Cargilfield School, Edinburgh; Merchiston Castle School, Edinburgh; Brasenose College, Oxford; Edinburgh University. 2nd Lt., 8th Royal Tank Regiment, 1956-58; Lt., Fife and Forfar Yeomanry, Scottish Horse, TA, 1958-64; Advocate, 1963; Director, R. Mackness & Co. Ltd., 1963-70; Chairman, Fios Group Ltd., 1970-72; Parliamentary candidate (Conservative), Aberdeen North, 1964; Tutor, Law Faculty, Edinburgh University, 1965-72; in practice, Scottish Bar, 1963-72; Sheriff of Lothian and Peebles, 1972-74. Member, St. Andrews University Court, 1983-91; Chairman, Fife Family Conciliation Service, 1988-90; Member and Vice-President, Security Service Tribunal, since 1989. Publication: Divorce Law and Practice in Scotland, 1990. Recreations: fishing; shooting; hill-walking; photography. Address: (h.) Parkneuk, Blebocraigs, Cupar, Fife; T.-0334 85 366.

McInnes, William McKenzie, MSc, PhD, CA. Director of Research, Institute of Chartered Accountants of Scotland, since 1992; b. 24.5.42, Hawick; m., Christine Mary; 1 s.; 1 d. Educ. George Watsons College, Edinburgh; Durham University; Glasgow University. Management Accountant, IBM (UK) Ltd., 1966-68; Lecturer, Kirkcaldy Technical College, 1968-70; Audit Senior, Coopers and Lybrand, Bermuda, 1970-72; Senior Lecturer, Newcastle upon Tyne Polytechnic, 1974-76; Lecturer, then Senior Lecturer, Strathclyde University, 1976-91. Recreations: golf; tennis; music; Sunday School teaching. Address: (b.) 27 Queen Street, Edinburgh, EH2 1LA; T.-031-225 5673.

McInroy, Charles Colquhoun. Secretary/Treasurer, Queen's Nursing Institute Scotland, since 1983; b. 24.11.21, Edzell; m., Beryl Patricia Moody; 2 s.; 2 d. Educ. Loretto. Army, Queen's Bays, Royal Tank Regiment, and Staff (Captain), 1940-47; Scottish Equitable Life Assurance Society, 1948-81 (Staff Manager). Past Chairman, North Berwick School Council; former Captain, North Berwick Golf Club; former Treasurer, St. Baldred's Episcopal Church, North Berwick. Publication: Scottish Equitable Landmarks 1831-1981, 1981. Recreations: golf; bridge; books. Address: (h.) Arnhall, Fidra Road, North Berwick, EH39 4NE; T.-0260 2762.

McIntosh, Rev. Colin George, MA, BD (Hons). Minister, Dunblane Cathedral, since 1988 (St. John's-Renfield Church, Glasgow, 1976-88); b. 5.4.51, Glasgow; m.; Linda Mary Henderson; 2 d. Educ. Govan High School; Glasgow University. Assistant Minister, Corstorphine, Edinburgh, 1975-76. Stanley Mair Memorial Lecturer, Glasgow University, 1984. Recreations: gardening; music; reading. Address: (h.) Cathedral Manse, The Cross, Dunblane, FK15 0AQ.

McIntosh, David Bainbridge, MA, FIPM. General Manager, Scottish National Blood Transfusion Service, since 1990 (Director, Scottish Health Service Management Development Group, 1987-90); b. 28.10.46, Oxford; m., Judith Mary Mitchell; 4 d. Educ. Edinburgh Academy; Christ Church, Oxford; London School of Economics. Industrial Relations Adviser, Coats Patons (UK) Ltd., 1972-73; Personnel Manager: J. & P. Coats (UK) Ltd., 1974-79, J. & P. Coats Ltd., 1979-81; Mill Manager: Comphanhia De Linha Coats & Clark LDA Portugal, 1981-84, Hilos Cadena SA Colombia, 1984-87. Member, Advisory Board, Scottish Quality Management Centre; former Chief Instructor, Loch Earn Sailing School; Past Chairman, Glasgow and West of Scotland Outward Bound Association. Recreations: golf; sailing; skiing; squash; fishing. Address: (b.) Ellen's Glen Road, Edinburgh, EH17 7QT; T.-031-664 2317.

Macintosh, Farquhar, CBE, MA, DipEd, DLitt, FEIS, FScotvec. Chairman, Sabhal Mor Ostaig, since 1991; Chairman, Scottish Examination Board, 1977-90; b. 27.10.23, Isle of Skye; m., Margaret M. Inglis; 2 s.; 2 d. Educ. Portree High School; Edinburgh University; Glasgow University; Jordanhill College of Education. Taught, Greenfield Junior Secondary School, Hamilton, Glasgow Academy and Inverness Royal Academy; Headmaster: Portree High School, Oban High School; Rector, Royal High School, Edinburgh, 1972-89; Member, Highlands and Islands Development Consultative Council and Convener, Education Sub-Committee, 1965-82; Chairman, Jordanhill Board of Governors, 1970-72; Chairman, BBC Secondary Programme Committee, 1972-80; Chairman, School Broadcasting Council for Scotland, 1981-85; Vice-Chairman, School Broadcasting Council for UK, 1984-86; Member, Court, Edinburgh University, 1976-91; Gaelic Correspondent, Weekly Scotsman, 1953-57. Recreations: hill-walking; sea fishing; Gaelic. Address: 12 Rothesay Place, Edinburgh, EH3 7SQ; T.-031-225 4404.

McIntosh, Professor Francis George, BSc, MSc, CEng, MIEE, FRSA. Professor of Electronic and Electrical Engineering, Robert Gordon Institute of Technology, since 1984 (Assistant Principal and Dean of Science and Technology, since 1988); b. 19.3.42; 1 d. Previously Head, School of Electronic and Electrical Engineering, RGIT. Member, CNAA Electronic Electrical and Control Board, until 1987; Consultant, Board Member, Aberdeen I. Tech Ltd.; Member, IEE Accreditation Committee. Address: (b.) RGIT, Schoolhill, Aberdeen, AB9 1FR; T.-0224 633611.

McIntosh, Iain Redford. Sculptor; b. 4.1.45, Peterhead; m., Freida; 2 d. Educ. Peterhead Academy; Gray's School of Art. Recreation: sculpture. Address: (h.) Powmouth, by Montrose; T.-Bridge of Dun 346.

Macintosh, Joan, CBE (1978). Chairman, Scottish Child Law Centre, since 1989; b. 23.11.19. Chairman, Scottish Consumer Council, 1975-80; Vice-Chairman, National Consumer Council, 1976-84; Lay Observer for Scotland, 1982-89.

McIntosh, Neil William David, CBE, ACIS, MIAM, FIPM, FRSA. Chief Executive, Dumfries and Galloway Regional Council, since 1985; b. 30.1.40, Glasgow; m., Marie Elizabeth

Lindsay. Educ. King's Park Senior Secondary School, Glasgow. O. and M. Trainee, Honeywell Controls Ltd., Lanarkshire, 1959-62; O. and M. Assistant, Berkshire, Oxford and Reading Joint Management Services Unit, 1962-64; O. and M. Officer, Stewarts and Lloyds Ltd., Lanarkshire, 1964-66; Senior O. and M. Officer, Lanark County Council, 1966-69; Establishment/O. and M. Officer, Inverness County Council, 1969-75; Personnel Officer, Highland Regional Council, 1975-81; Director of Manpower Services, Highland Regional Council, 1981-85; Clerk, Dumfries Lieutenancy, 1985. Recreations: bowling; hill-walking; antique bottle collecting; local history; youth work. Address: (b.) Regional Council Offices, English Street, Dumfries; T.-0387 61234.

Macintosh, Robert Macfarlan, MA, LLB. Solicitor; Chairman, Rent Assessment Committee, Glasgow, since 1966; Honorary Sheriff Substitute, Dumbarton, since 1975; b. 16.6.17, Dumbarton; m., Ann McLean Kelso; 1 s. Educ. Dumbarton Academy; George Watson's College, Edinburgh; Glasgow University. Qualified as Solicitor, 1949; Local Secretary, Dumbarton Legal Aid Committee, 1950-84; Chairman: Dunbartonshire Rent Tribunal, 1960, Glasgow Rent Tribunal, 1974; Clerk to Commissioners of Income Tax, East and West Dunbartonshire, since 1973; President, Dumbarton Burns Club; Captain, Cardross Golf Club. Recreation: golf. Address: (h.) Ardmoy, Peel Street, Cardross, Dunbartonshire.

McIntyre, Alasdair Duncan, BSc, DSc, FRSE, FIBiol, FRSA. Chairman, Marine Forum for Environmental Issues, since 1990; President, Scottish Marine Biological Association, since 1988; Emeritus Professor of Fisheries and Oceanography, Aberdeen University, since 1986; Council Member, Nature Conservancy Council for Scotland, since 1991; Board Member, NCIS Research and Development Board, since 1991; Council Member, Marine Conservation Society, since 1991; b. 17.11.26, Helensburgh; m., Catherine Helen; 1 d. Educ. Hermitage School, Helensburgh; Glasgow University. Senior Principal Scientific Officer in charge of environmental team, Marine Laboratory, Aberdeen, 1973-79; Deputy Director, Department of Agriculture and Fisheries for Scotland, Marine Laboratory, Aberdeen, 1979-83; Director of Fisheries Research for Scotland, 1983-86; Co-ordinator, UK Fisheries Research and Development, 1986; Editor, Fisheries Research. Recreations: reading; food and wine; walking. Address: (h.) 63 Hamilton Place, Aberdeen, AB2 4BW; T.-0224 645633.

McIntyre, Archibald Dewar, MB, ChB, DPH, FFCM, FRCPE, DIH, DTM&H. Principal Medical Officer, Scottish Home and Health Department, since 1977; b. 18.2.28, Dunipace; m., Euphemia Hope Houston; 2 s.; 2 d. Educ. Falkirk High School; Edinburgh University. Senior Medical Officer, Overseas Civil Service, Sierra Leone; Depute Medical Officer of Health, Stirling County Council; Depute Secretary, Scottish Council for Postgraduate Medical Education; Senior Medical Officer, Scottish Home and Health Department. Recreations: gardening; photography. Address: (h.) Birchlea, 43 Falkirk Road, Linlithgow, EH49 7PH; T.-0506 842063.

Macintyre, Iain Melfort Campbell, MB, ChB, MD, FRCSE. Consultant Surgeon, Edinburgh, since 1979; b. 23.6.44, Glasgow; m., Tessa Lorna Mary Millar; 3 d. Educ. Daniel Stewart's College, Edinburgh; Edinburgh University. Lecturer in Surgery, Edinburgh University, 1974-78; Visiting Professor, University of Natal, 1978-79; Council of Europe Travelling Fellow, 1986; Member, Council, Royal College of Surgeons of Edinburgh, since 1991; Member, National Medical Advisory Committee, since 1992. Recreations: historical postcards; photography; tennis; skiing. Address: (b.) Department of Surgery, Western General Hospital, Edinburgh; T.-031-332 2525.

McIntyre, Very Rev. Professor John, CVO, MA, BD, DLitt, DD, DHL, Dr hc, FRSE. Professor of Divinity, Edinburgh University, 1956-86; Honorary Chaplain to The Queen in Scotland, 1974-86 (Extraordinary Chaplain, since 1986); Dean of the Order of the Thistle, 1974-89; b. 20.5.16, Glasgow; m., Jessie Brown Buick; 2 s.; 1 d. Educ. Bathgate Academy; Edinburgh University. Ordained, 1941; Locum Tenens, Parish of Glenorchy and Inishail, 1941-43; Minister, Fenwick, Ayrshire, 1943-45; Hunter Baillie Professor of Theology, St. Andrew's College, Sydney University, 1946-56; Principal, St. Andrew's College, 1950-56; Principal Warden, Pollock Halls of Residence, Edinburgh University, 1960-71; Acting Principal and Vice-Chancellor, Edinburgh University, 1973-74, 1979; Principal, New College, and Dean, Faculty of Divinity, 1968-74; Moderator, General Assembly of the Church of Scotland, 1982; Convener, Board of Education, Church of Scotland, 1983-87; former Council Member and Vice President, Royal Society of Edinburgh. Publications: St. Anselm and his Critics, 1954; The Christian Doctrine of History, 1957; On the Love of God, 1962; The Shape of Christology, 1966; Faith, Theology and Imagination, 1987. Recreation: travel. Address: (h.) 22/4 Minto Street, Edinburgh, EH9 1RQ; T.-031-667 1203.

Macintyre, Lorn, BA (Hons), PhD. Freelance Writer; b. 7.9.42, Taynuilt, Argyll; m., Mary. Educ. Stirling University; Glasgow University. Columnist, Glasgow Herald; Novelist and Short Story Writer; publications include Cruel in the Shadow and The Blind Bend in Chronicles of Invernevis Series. Recreation: work. Address: (h.) Priormuir, by St. Andrews, Fife; T.-0334 76428.

McIntyre, Robert Douglas, MB, ChB, DPH, DUniv, JP, FSC. Honorary Consultant, Stirling Royal Infirmary, since 1974; Chancellor's Assessor, Stirling University, 1978-88; b. 15.12.13, Dalziel; m., Letitia S. MacLeod; 1 s. Educ. Hamilton Academy; Daniel Stewart's College; Edinburgh University; Glasgow University. Consultant Chest Physician, Stirling and Clackmannan Counties, 1951-79; MP, Motherwell and Wishaw, 1945; Chairman, SNP, 1948-56; President, SNP, 1958-80; Honorary Treasurer, Royal Burgh of Stirling, 1958-64; Provost of Stirling, 1967-75; Freeman, Royal Burgh of Stirling. Recreations: sailing; conversation. Address: (h.) 8 Gladstone Place, Stirling. T.-Stirling 73456.

MacIver, Donald John Morrison, MA (Hons). President, An Comunn Gaidhealach, 1985-90; Researcher and Adviser in Bilingual Education, Western Isles Islands Council, since 1989 (Principal Teacher of Gaelic, Nicolson Institute, 1973-89); former Director, National Gaelic Arts Project; b. 12.11.42, Stornoway; m., Alice Macleod; 1 s. Educ. Nicolson Institute; Aberdeen University. Teacher of Gaelic, 1968-73. Member, Gaelic Books Council; Director, Acair Publishing Co.; former Editor, Sruth (newspaper of An Comunn Gaidhealach). Publications: Gaelic Oral Composition; Gaelic Language Practice; Gaelic O-Grade Interpretation; Sgriobh Seo; Feuch Seo; Feuch Freagairt; Faic Is Freagair; Camhanaich; Eadar Peann Is Paipear; Coinneach Odhar; Grian is Uisge. Recreations: writing (prose and poetry); computing; reading poetry; gardening; Coronation Street. Address: (h.) 32 Goathill Road, Stornoway, Isle of Lewis, PA87 2NL; T.-0851 702582.

MacIver, Duncan Malcolm, CBE. Deputy Director, Scottish Prison Service, 1978-86 (retired); b. 7.5.22, Meerut, India; m., Jessie D.T. Neilson; 2 s.; 1 d. Educ. McLaren High School, Callander. Served in Black Watch and Royal Scots, 1939-47, in Ceylon, India and Burma (14th Army), rank of Sgt.; joined Scottish Prison Service as a prison officer, 1948; promoted to Governor grade, 1960; Assistant Governor, Polmont and Barlinnie; Deputy Governor, Polmont and Perth; Governor: Castle Huntly Borstal, 1969-70, Aberdeen Prison, 1970-73; Assistant Inspector of Prisons, 1973-75; Governor

(HQ), 1975-76; Governor, Edinburgh Prison, 1976-78; Controller of Operations (Deputy Director), Scottish Prison Service. Recreations: golf; gardening. Address: (h.) 3 Caiystane Drive, Edinburgh; T.-031-445 1734.

MacIver, Ian, BSc, DipEd, MSc, PhD. Principal, Coatbridge College, since 1989; b. 25.11.38, Stornoway; m., Anne Maureen Ramsay; 3 s.; 2 d. Educ. Nicolson Institute, Stornoway; Portree High School; Glasgow University. Secondary school teacher, 1962-64; studied and taught, University of Alberta, University of Chicago, and York University, Toronto, 1964-73; returned to Scotland and held posts, Langside College, 1973-74, Jordanhill College, 1975-76, James Watt College, 1977-82, Anniesland College, 1982-89. Elder, Free Church of Scotland. Recreations: distance running; reading; loafing. Address: (b.) Coatbridge College, Kildonan Street, Coatbridge, ML5 3LS; T.-0236 22316.

MacIver, Matthew M., MA, MEd. Rector, Royal High School, Edinburgh, since 1989; b. 5.7.46, Isle of Lewis; m., Katrina; 1 s.; 1 d. Educ. Nicolson Institute, Stornoway; Edinburgh University; Moray House College. History Teacher, 1969-72; Principal Teacher of History, Craigmount High School, 1972-80; Assistant Rector, Royal High School, 1980-83; Depute Head Teacher, Balerno High School, 1983-86; Rector, Fortrose Academy, 1986-89. Chairman, Joint Working Party on Classical Studies, since 1988; Member, Gaelic Television Committee, since 1991; Member, Board of Governors, Moray House Institute of Education. Recreation: Gaelic culture. Address: (h.) 21 Durham Road, Edinburgh, EH15 1NY; T.-031-669 5029.

MacIver, Roy, MA, LLB. Secretary General, Convention of Scottish Local Authorities, since 1986; b. 15.10.42, Stornoway; m., Anne; 3 s. Educ. Nicolson Institute, Stornoway; Edinburgh University; Glasgow University. Legal Assistant, Paisley Corporation; Solicitor/Administrator, Dunfermline Town Council, 1970-72; Assistant County Clerk (Lewis), Ross and Cromarty County Council, 1972-75; Chief Executive, Western Isles Islands Council (Comhairle nan Eilean), 1974-86. Recreation: jazz. Address: (b.) Rosebery House, 9 Haymarket Terrace, Edinburgh; T.-031-346 1222.

Mackay, Angus Victor Peck, MA, BSc (Pharm), PhD (Cantab), MB, ChB, FRCPsych, FRCP (Ed). Physician Superintendent, Argyll and Bute Hospital, and MacKintosh Lecturer in Psychological Medicine, Glasgow University, since 1980; Hon. Senior Lecturer, Department of Psychology, St. Andrews University; Chairman, Research and Clinical Section, Royal College of Psychiatrists (Scotland), since 1981; Psychiatric Representative, Committee on Safety of Medicines, DHSS, since 1983; b. 4.3.43, Edinburgh; m., Elspeth M.W. Norris; 2 s.; 2 d. Educ. George Heriot's School, Edinburgh; Edinburgh University; Churchill and Trinity Colleges, Cambridge. MRC Research Fellow, Cambridge; Member, senior clinical staff, MRC Neurochemical Pharmacology Unit, Cambridge, with appointment as Lector in Pharmacology, Trinity College (latterly, Deputy Director of Unit). Deputy Chairman, Health Services Research Committee of the Chief Scientist for Scotland; Member, Research Committee, Mental Health Foundation; Chairman, Argyll and Clyde Area Psychiatric Sub-Committee; Member, Scottish Executive, Royal College of Psychiatrists. Recreations: rowing; sailing; rhododendrons. Address: (h.) Tigh an Rudha, Ardrishaig, Argyll; T.-0546 3272.

McKay, Sheriff Archibald Charles, MA, LLB. Sheriff of Glasgow and Strathkelvin, since 1979; b. 18.10.29; m., Ernestine Maria Tobia; 1 s.; 3 d. Educ. St. Aloysius' College, Glasgow; Glasgow University. Solicitor, Glasgow, 1957; established own firm of solicitors, 1961; President, Glasgow Bar Association, 1967-68; appointed to the bench, 1978. Recreations: flying light aircraft; motor cycling; amateur radio; tennis. Address: (h.) 96 Springkell Avenue, Pollokshields, Glasgow, G41 4EL; T.-041-427 1525.

Mackay, Charles, CB, BSc, MSc, FIBiol. Chief Agricultural Officer, Department of Agriculture and Fisheries for Scotland, 1975-87; b. 12.1.27, Kinloch, Sutherland; m., Marie A.K. Mitchell; 1 s.; 1 d. Educ. Strathmore School; Lairg Higher Grade Public School; Aberdeen University; Kentucky University. DAFS: Temporary Inspector, 1947-48, Assistant Inspector, 1948-54, Inspector, 1954-64, Senior Inspector, 1964-70, Technical Development Officer, 1970-73, Deputy Chief Agricultural Officer, 1973-75. Recreations: fishing; golf. Address: (h.) 4/3 Craufurland, Edinburgh, EH4 6DL; T.-031-339 8770.

Mackay, Colin Hinshelwood, MA (Hons), FSA Scot. Political Editor, Scottish Television PLC, 1973-92 (Presenter, Ways and Means, 1973-86); Member, Scottish Arts Council, since 1988; b. 27.8.44, Glasgow; m., Olive E.B. Brownlie; 2 s. Educ. Kelvinside Academy, Glasgow; Glasgow University; Jordanhill College of Education. Reporter/Presenter: Border Television Ltd., 1967-70, Grampian Television Ltd., 1970-73; Presenter of political programmes, including all elections and by-elections, STV, since 1973; ITV Commentator: Papal Visit to Scotland, 1982, CBI Conference, Glasgow, 1983. Winner, Observer Mace, 1967 (British Universities Debating Championship); Member, two-man British Universities Canadian Debating Tour, 1967; Commonwealth Relations Trust Bursary to Canada, 1981. Publications: Kelvinside Academy: 1878-1978, 1978; The Scottish Dimension in Central and Eastern Canada, 1981. Recreations: music (especially opera); reading; writing.

McKay, David Sutherland. General Manager, JVC Manufacturing UK Ltd., since 1988; Director, SETG Ltd., since 1984; Chairman, TTP Ltd., since 1989; b. 28.8.38, Wick; m., Catherine Margaret; 2 d. Educ. Wick High School; Robert Gordon's College. Apprenticeship in control engineering; Design Engineer, British Oxygen Co.; joined Honeywell Control Systems as Design Engineer; appointed Technical Director, 1983. Member, Design Council. Recreation: worrying about cost of sailing. Address: (h.) Green Garth, Nethan Glen, Crossford, ML8 5QU; T.-Crossford 309.

Mackay, Professor David William, CBiol, FIBiol, FIWEM, FBIM, MIFM. Chief Officer, North East River Purification Board, since 1990; Visiting Professor, Institute of Aquaculture, Stirling University, since 1992; Board Member, Scottish Marine Biological Association, since 1991; b. 6.4.36, Stirling; m., Maureen. Educ. High School of Stirling; Strathclyde University; Paisley College. Experimental Officer, Freshwater Fisheries Laboratory, Pitlochry; Freshwater Biologist, then Marine Survey Officer, Clyde River Purification Board; Principal Environmental Protection Officer, Government of Hong Kong; Depute Director, Clyde River Purification Board; Head of Environmental Services, Ove Arup and Partners, Hong Kong; General Manager and Clerk, North East River Purification Board, Aberdeen. Vice President and Secretary, Scottish Anglers National Association, 1970-89. Recreations: farming; scuba diving; fishing. Address: (b.) NERPB, Greyhope House, Greyhope Road, Torry, Aberdeen, AB1 3RD; T.-0224 248338.

Mackay, Donald George, MA. Honorary Research Fellow, Aberdeen University, 1989-91; Under Secretary, Scottish Office, 1983-88; b. 25.11.29, Dundee; m., Elizabeth Ailsa Barr; 2 s.; 1 d. Educ. Morgan Academy, Dundee; St. Andrews University. Scottish Home Department, 1953; Assistant Private Secretary to Secretary of State for Scotland, 1959; Assistant Secretary, Royal Commission on the Police, 1962-64; Secretary, Royal Commission on Local Government in Scotland, 1966-69; Scottish Development Department, 1969-

79 and 1985-88; Department of Agriculture and Fisheries for Scotland, 1979-85. Recreations: hill-walking; photography; music. Address: (h.) 38 Cluny Drive, Edinburgh, EH10 6DX; T.-031-447 1851.

MacKay, Professor Donald Iain, MA, FRSE. Chairman, PEIDA plc, since 1976; Professorial Fellow, Heriot-Watt University, since 1982; b. 27.2.37, Kobe, Japan; m., Diana Marjory Raffan; 1 s.; 2 d. Educ. Dollar Academy; Aberdeen University. Professor of Political Economy, Aberdeen University, 1971-76; Professor of Economics, Heriot-Watt University, 1976-82; Director, Grampian Holdings; Vice President, Scottish Association of Public Transport; Member, Scottish Economic Council; Economic Consultant to Secretary of State for Scotland; Governor, National Institute of Economic and Social Research. Recreations: tennis; bridge. Address: (h.) Newfield, 14 Gamekeepers Road, Edinburgh; T.-031-336 1936.

Mackay, Donald John, MA, FBIM. Chief Executive, Harris Tweed Association, since 1982; Chairman, CEDP, since 1991; b. 8.6.30, North Uist; m., Rhona MacLeod; 3 d. Educ. Portree High School; Aberdeen University; London University. District Commissioner and Private Secretary/Aide de Camp to Governor, Sierra Leone, 1954-58; Highland Area Officer, Scottish Agricultural Organisation Society, 1958-61; Staff and Management Training Officer, AEA, Dounreay, 1961-63; Personnel and Training Officer, British Aluminium, 1964-65; Director, An Comunn Gaidhealach, 1965-70; Personnel and External Affairs Manager, Primary Division, British Aluminium, 1970-82. Member, Red Deer Commission, 1966-74; Member, Highland Disablement Advisory Committee, since 1970; Member, Highland Area Group, Scottish Council, since 1971; Member, North of Scotland Electricity Council, 1981-84; Secretary, CBI Highland Area Group, 1978-87, Chairman, 1988; Member, HIDB Consultative Council, 1978-81; Member, Nature Conservancy Council Scottish Advisory Committee, 1979-86; MSC Chairman, Highlands & Islands, 1981-88; Member, Executive Committee, Scottish Council, since 1982; Chairman, CNAG, 1984-86; Chairman, Albyn Housing Society, 1979-83; Director, Fearann Eilean Iarmain, since 1972; Member, Industrial Tribunal Panel, since 1986; Deputy Chairman, Sabhal Mor Ostaig, 1981-85; Member, Highland River Purification Board, 1981-83; Member, Highland Health Board, since 1991. Recreations: sailing; shooting; fishing; Gaelic. Address: (h.) Kildonan, Teandalloch, Beauly, by Inverness; T.-0463 231 270.

Mackay, Rev. Canon Douglas Brysson. Rector, Church of the Holy Rood, Carnoustie, since 1972; Synod Clerk, Diocese of Brechin, since 1981; Canon, St. Paul's Cathedral, Dundee since 1981; b. 20.3.27, Glasgow; m., Catherine Elizabeth; 2 d. Educ. Possil Senior Secondary School; Edinburgh Theological College. Precentor, St. Andrew's Cathedral, Inverness, 1958; Rector, Gordon Chapel, Fochabers, 1961 (also Priest-in-Charge, St. Margaret's Church, Aberlour, 1964); Canon, St. Andrew's Cathedral, Inverness, 1965; Synod Clerk, Diocese of Moray, Ross, Caithness, 1965; Honorary Canon, St. Andrew's Cathedral, Inverness, 1972; Convenor of Youth, Moray Diocese, 1965; Brechin Diocese: Convenor, Social Service Board, 1974, Convenor, Joint Board, 1974, Convenor, Administration Board, 1982; Chairman, Truth and Unity Movement, 1980-87. President, British Red Cross, Carnoustie, 1974-82; President, British Legion, Carnoustie, 1981; Vice-Chairman, Carnoustie Community Care, 1981; Chairman, Carnoustie Community Council, 1979-81; President, Carnoustie Rotary Club, 1976. Recreations: golf; snooker; reading; music. Address: Holyrood Rectory, Carnoustie, DD7 6AB; T.-Carnoustie 52202.

Mackay, Eileen Alison, MA. Under Secretary, The Scottish Office Environment Department; b. 7.7.43, Helmsdale, Sutherland; m., A. Muir Russell (qv). Educ. Dingwall Academy; Edinburgh University. Research Officer, Department of Employment, 1965-72; Principal: Scottish Office, 1972-78, HM Treasury, 1978-80; Adviser, Central Policy Review Staff, Cabinet Office, 1980-83; Assistant Secretary, Scottish Development Agency and New Towns Division, Industry Department for Scotland, 1983-87; Rural Environment and Nature Conservation Division, Scottish Development Department, 1987-88; Under Secretary, Housing and Local Government, SDD, 1988-91. Address: (b.) St. Andrews House, Edinburgh.

Mackay of Talmine, Rev. Hugh, KCLJ, MA, FSAScot, CF(ACF). Minister, Duns Parish Church, since 1967; Clerk, Synod of the Borders, since 1982; b. 5.1.30, Edinburgh. Educ. Daniel Stewart's College, Edinburgh; Edinburgh University and New College. Student Assistant, Canongate Kirk, Edinburgh, 1955-57; Senior Assistant, St. Machar's Cathedral, Old Aberdeen, 1957-58; Minister, St. Bride's Parish Church, Glasgow, 1958-67. Chaplain to Moderator of General Assembly, 1972-73; Founder Chairman, Duns Community Council, 1977-78; Principal Chaplain, ACF Scotland, since 1987; Chancellor of Grand Bailiwick of Scotland, Order of St. Lazarus of Jerusalem, 1988-91; Depute Grand Master of Grand Lodge of Scotland, 1988-91; Third Grand Principal, SG Royal Arch Chapter; Grand Prior, Great Priory of the Temple & Malta. Recreations: singing; drawing; Heraldry; too many other things. Address: Manse of Duns, Berwickshire, TD11 3DP; T.-Duns 83755.

Mackay, Ian Munro, BComm, CA. Principal, MacKay & Co., Chartered Accountants, Golspie and Dornoch, since 1979; Honorary Sheriff, Dornoch Sheriff Court, since 1985; b. 14.9.47, Brora; m., Maureen; 2 s.; 1 d. Educ. Golspie High School; Edinburgh University. Trained as CA in Edinburgh, qualifying in 1973; has worked in the profession since, spending three years in United Arab Emirates, returning to UK in 1979 to set up own practice. Auditor, Treasurer, Secretary of several local charities and sporting organisations; Secretary, Dornoch Curling Club; President, Sutherland Curling Province; Treasurer, Brora Ice Rink Club. Recreations: curling; local history; garden; following most sports. Address: (h.) 4 Sutherland Road, Dornoch, Sutherland; T.-0862 810333.

Mackay, James Alexander, MA. Author and Journalist; Numismatic and Philatelic Correspondent, Financial Times, since 1972; Editor, the Burns Chronicle, 1978-91, and The Burnsian, 1986-89; b. 21.11.36, Inverness; m., Joyce May Greaves. Educ. Hillhead High School, Glasgow; Glasgow University. Lt., RA Guided Weapons Range, Hebrides, 1959-61; Assistant Keeper, Department of Printed Books, British Museum, in charge of philatelic collections, 1961-71; returned to Scotland as a full-time Writer, 1972; Editor-in-Chief, IPC Stamp Encyclopedia, 1968-72; Columnist on antiques, Financial Times, 1967-72, philately and numismatics, 1972-85; Trustee, James Currie Memorial Trust, since 1987; Publisher of books on philately and postal history; author of 140 books on aspects of the applied and decorative arts, numismatics, philately, postal history; Scottish books include Robert Bruce, King of Scots, 1974; Rural Crafts in Scotland, 1976; Scottish Postmarks, 1978; The Burns Federation 1885-1985, 1985; The Complete Works of Robert Burns, 1986; The Complete Letters of Robert Burns, 1987; Burnsiana, 1988; Burns-Lore of Dumfries and Galloway, 1988; Burns at Ellisland, 1989; Scottish Post Offices, 1989; Burns A-Z, 1990; Kilmarnock, 1992. Recreations: travel; languages; music (piano-playing); photographing post offices. Address: (h.) 75/5 Lancefield Quay, Glasgow, G3 8HA; T.-041-221 2797.

Mackay of Clashfern, Lord (James Peter Hymers), Baron (1979), PC (1979), FRSE, Hon. FRICE. Lord High Chancellor of Great Britain, since 1987; b. 2.7.27, Edinburgh; m., Elizabeth Gunn Hymers; 1 s.; 2 d. Educ. George Heriot's School, Edinburgh; Edinburgh University. Lecturer in Mathematics, St. Andrews University, 1948-50; Major Scholar, Trinity College, Cambridge, in Mathematics, 1947, taken up, 1950; Senior Scholar, 1951; BA (Cantab), 1952; LLB Edinburgh (with distinction), 1955; admitted, Faculty of Advocates, 1955; QC (Scot), 1965; Standing Junior Counsel to: Queen's and Lord Treasurer's Remembrancer, Scottish Home and Health Department, Commissioners of Inland Revenue in Scotland; Sheriff Principal, Renfrew and Argyll, 1972-74; Vice-Dean, Faculty of Advocates, 1973-76; Dean, 1976-79; Lord Advocate of Scotland, 1979-84; a Senator of the College of Justice in Scotland, 1984-85. Part-time Member, Scottish Law Commission, 1976-79; Hon. Master of the Bench, Inner Temple, 1979; Fellow, International Academy of Trial Lawyers, 1979; Fellow, Institute of Taxation, 1981; Director, Stenhouse Holdings Ltd., 1976-77; Member, Insurance Brokers' Registration Council, 1977-79; a Commissioner of Northern Lighthouses, 1975-84; Hon. LLD: Edinburgh, 1983, Dundee, 1983, Strathclyde, 1985, Aberdeen, 1987, Birmingham, 1990; Hon. DCL, Newcastle, 1990; Hon. Doctor of Laws, College of William and Mary, 1989; Hon. Fellow, Trinity College, Cambridge, 1989; Hon.LLD, Cambridge, 1989; Hon. Fellow, Royal College of Surgeons, Edinburgh, 1989; Fellow, American College of Trial Lawyers, 1990; a Lord of Appeal in Ordinary, 1985-87. Recreation: walking. Address: Lord Chancellor's Residence, House of Lords, London, SW1A 0PW; T.-01-219 3232.

MacKay, John, OBE, MB, ChB, FRCGP. Retired General Medical Practitioner; Member, National Board for Nursing, Midwifery and Health Visiting for Scotland; Member, General Medical Council; Member, Scottish National Board for Nursing, Midwifery and Health Visiting; b. 24.7.26, Glasgow; m., Matilda MacLennan Bain; 2 s.; 2 d. Educ. Govan High School; Glasgow University. Junior House Doctor, Victoria Infirmary and Southern General Hospital, Glasgow, 1949; Ship's Surgeon, 1950; Assistant in General Practice, Govan, 1951-52 (Principal, since 1953); Member, Board of Management, Glasgow South West Hospitals, prior to 1973; Tutor, University Department of General Practice, Glasgow; part-time Medical Referee, Scottish Home and Health Department; Honorary Life Manager, Govan Weavers Society; Member, Scottish General Medical Services Committee. Recreations: angling; golf; gardening. Address: (h.) Moorholm, Barr's Brae, Kilmacolm, Renfrewshire, PA13 4DE; T.-Kilmacolm 3234.

Mackay, John, TD, MA, FInstD. General Manager, Royal Mail Scotland, N. England and N. Ireland, since 1986; Board Member, Royal Mail Letters, Scottish Post Office Board, since 1985; b. 14.9.36, St. Andrews; m., Barbara Wallace; 1 s.; 2 d. Educ. Madras College; Dunfermline High School; Kirkcaldy High School; Edinburgh University. Army (Lt., East Anglian Regiment), 1959-63; TA, 1964-86, Royal Engineers (Postal and Courier), Colonel; Post Office: Assistant Postal Controller, Wales, N. Ireland, 1963-68, Principal, Post Office HQ, 1968-76, Controller (Personnel and Finance), Eastern Region, 1977-79, Director Philately, Post Office HQ, 1979-84, Controller Royal Mails Scotland, 1985-86. Recreations: golf; reading; walking dog; convivial company. Address: (b.) West Port House, Edinburgh, EH3 9HS; T.-031-228 7400.

MacKay, John Angus, MA. Director, Gaelic Television Fund, since 1991; Director, Comunn Na Gaidhlig, since 1985; Chairman, Trustees, The Gaelic College, since 1987; b. 24.6.48, Shader, Stornoway; m., Maria F.; 3 s. Educ. Nicolson Institute; Aberdeen University; Jordanhill College. Aberdeen

Circulation Rep., D.C. Thomson, 1970-71; Jordanhill College, 1971-72; Teacher, 1972-77; Field Officer, then Development Officer, then Senior Administrative Officer, HIDB, 1977-85. Chairman, Gaelic Youth Radio Trust; Director, Acair (Gaelic publishing company). Recreations: reading; skiing; swimming; running. Address: (h.) Druimard, Arnol, Isle of Lewis; T.-0851 71479.

McKay, John Henderson, CBE (1987), BA (Hons), PhD, Dr h.c. (Edinburgh). Secretary, Royal Caledonian Horticultural Society, since 1988; Lord Provost of Edinburgh, 1984-88; b. 12.5.29, Kirknewton; m., Catherine Watson Taylor; 1 s.; 1 d. Educ. West Calder High School; Open University. Labourer and Clerk, Pumpherston Oil Co. Ltd., 1948-50; National Service, Royal Artillery, 1950-52; Customs and Excise, 1952-85. Secretary, Royal Caledonian Horticultural Society. Recreations: gardening; reading; listening to music. Address: (h.) 2 Buckstone Way, Edinburgh, EH10 6PN; T.-031-445 2865.

MacKay of Ardbrecknish, Lord (John Jackson MacKay), BSc, DipEd, JP. Chairman, Sea Fish Industry Authority, since 1990; b. 15.11.38, Lochgilphead; m., Sheena Wagner; 2 s.; 1 d. Educ. Dunoon Grammar School; Campbeltown Grammar School; Glasgow University; Jordanhill College of Education. Member, Oban Town Council, 1969-74; Member, Argyll Water Board, 1969-74; Principal Teacher of Mathematics, Oban High School, 1969-79; MP for Argyll, 1979-83, for Argyll & Bute, 1983-87; Parliamentary Private Secretary to Secretary of State for Scotland, 1982; Parliamentary Under Secretary of State, Scottish Office, 1987-82; Chief Executive, Scottish Conservative Party, 1987-90; Justice of the Peace for Argyll and Bute. Recreations: fishing; sailing. Address: (h.) Innishail, 51 Springkell Drive, Pollokshields, Glasgow, G41 4EZ.

Mackay, John M., MBE. General Manager, Northern Lighthouse Board, since 1977; b. 26.7.28, London; m., Martha; 1 s.; 1 d. Educ. Winchester House, Brackley; RN Colleges, Dartmouth and Greenwich. After training, service in RN General Service ships, 1949-51; service in RN Surveying Service at sea, 1951-67; Commander RN (retd.); Ministry of Defence, 1967-77. Recreations: gardening; Austin Seven. Address: (b.) 84 George Street, Edinburgh, EH2 3DA.

McKay, Rev. Johnston Reid, MA (Glasgow), BA (Cantab). Senior Producer, Religious Programmes, BBC, since 1987; b. 2.5.42, Glasgow. Educ. High School of Glasgow; Glasgow University; Cambridge University. Assistant Minister, St. Giles' Cathedral, 1967-71; Church Correspondent, Glasgow Herald, 1968-70; Minister, Bellahouston Steven Parish Church, 1971-78; frequent Broadcaster; Governor, Paisley College; Minister, Paisley Abbey, 1978-87; Editor, The Bush (newspaper of Glasgow Presbytery), 1975-78; Chairman, Scottish Religious Advisory Committee, BBC, 1981-86. Publications: From Sleep and From Damnation (with James Miller), 1970; Essays in Honour of William Barclay (Joint Editor), 1976; Through Wood and Nails, 1982. Recreations: good music and bad golf. Address: (b.) 41 Stakehill, Largs, KA30 9NH; T.-0475 672960.

MacKay, Professor Norman, MD, FRCP(Glas), FRCP(Edin). Dean of Postgraduate Medicine and Professor of Postgraduate Medical Education, Glasgow University, since 1989; Consultant Physician, Victoria Infirmary, Glasgow, since 1974; b. 15.9.36, Glasgow; m., Grace Violet McCaffer; 2 s.; 2 d. Educ. Govan High School; Glasgow University. Honorary Secretary: Royal College of Physicians and Surgeons of Glasgow, 1973-83, Standing Joint Committee, Scottish Royal Colleges, 1978-82, Conference of Royal Colleges and Faculties in Scotland, since 1982; Speciality Adviser in Medicine, West of Scotland Committee of Postgraduate Medical Education, 1982-89; President,

Royal Medico-Chirurgical Society of Glasgow, 1982-83; Member, Area Medical Committee, Greater Glasgow Health Board, 1987-89; President, Southern Medical Society, 1989-90. Recreations: gardening; walking; golf; association football. Address: (h.) 4 Erksine Avenue, Dumbreck, Glasgow, G41 5AL; T.-041-427 1900.

Mackay, Peter, MA. Secretary, Scottish Office Industry Department, since 1990; b. 6.7.40, Arbroath; m., Sarah Holdich; 1 s.; 2 d. Educ. Glasgow High School; St. Andrews University. Teacher, New South Wales, Australia, 1962-63; Assistant Principal, Scottish Development Department, 1963; Private Secretary to Ministers of State, Scottish Office, 1966-68; Principal, Scottish Home and Health Department, 1968-73; Private Secretary to Secretaries of State for Scotland, 1973-75; Assistant Secretary, 1975; Head, Local Government Division, Scottish Development Department, 1979-83; Director for Scotland, Manpower Services Commission, 1983-85; on secondment from Scottish Office to Department of Employment, London, 1985, Under Secretary, Scottish Education Department (Further and Higher Education, Arts and Sport), 1987-89; Principal Establishment Officer (Director of Personnel), Scottish Office, 1989-90. Nuffield Travelling Fellowship, 1978-79. Recreations: Scotland; easy mountaineering; dinghy sailing; sea canoeing; tennis. Address: (h.) 6 Henderland Road, Edinburgh, EH12 6BB; T.-031-337 2830.

Mackay, Robert D.C., MA, DipEd. Rector, Glenrothes High School, since 1976; b. 5.2.30, Longforgan; m., Lorna J. Davis; 2 s. Educ. Perth Academy; Edinburgh University; University of Dijon; Moray House College of Education. Royal Army Education Corps, 1953-55; Teacher of Modern Languages, Airdrie Academy, 1955-58, and Perth Academy, 1958-64; Principal Teacher, 1964-71, Depute Rector, 1971-76, Graeme High School, Falkirk. Past President, Headteachers' Association of Scotland; Member, Heriot-Watt University Court; Past President, Glenrothes Rotary Club. Recreation: mainly caravanning. Address: (h.) 7 Culzean Crescent, Kirkcaldy, KY2 6UZ; T.-0592 200682.

Mackay, Robert Ostler. Solicitor, since 1930; Notary Public, since 1955; b. 25.12.07, Greenock; m., 1, Dorothy Lilian Johnson (deceased); 2, Irene Isobel Ray Anderson; 1 s.; 2 d. Educ. Greenock Academy; Alyth Public School; Blairgowrie High School; Edinburgh University. Partner: J.C. Richards & Morrice, Solicitors, Fraserburgh, 1939-45, Ferguson & Petrie, Solicitors, Duns, 1945-85; Honorary Sheriff, Lothian and Borders, at Duns, since 1981; Council Member, Law Society of Scotland, 1958-79 (Vice-President, 1967-68); Life Member, Cairngorm Club. Address: (h.) Nethercraigs, Tighnabruaich, Argyll; T.-0700 811 368.

Mackay, William Kenneth, BSc, CEng, FICE, FIHT, FRSA, MCIT. Director, JMP Consultants Ltd. (formerly Jamieson Mackay & Partners), since 1965; Commissioner, Royal Fine Arts Commission for Scotland, since 1981; Board Member, Clyde Port Authority, since 1985; b. 6.6.30, Moyobamba, Peru. Educ. Hillhead High School, Glasgow; Glasgow University. Engineer, NCB, West Fife Area, 1954-57; Senior Engineer, Fife County Council, 1957-59; Group Engineer, Cumbernauld New Town Development Corporation, 1959-65; Consultant, since 1965; Past Chairman, Scottish Branch, Institution of Highways and Transportation; former Member, Planning and Transport Research Advisory Council to UK Government. Recreations: swimming; walking. Address: (b.) JMP (Consultants) Ltd., 20 Royal Terrace, Glasgow, G3 7NY; T.-041-332 3868.

McKean, Charles Alexander, BA, FRSA, FSA Scot, HonFRIBA. Secretary, Royal Incorporation of Architects in Scotland, since 1979; b. 16.7.46, Glasgow; m., Margaret Yeo; 2 s. Educ. Fettes College; Bristol University. RIBA:

Secretary, London Region, 1968-76; Secretary, Eastern Region, 1972-79; Secretary, Community Architecture, 1976-79; Architectural Correspondent, The Times, 1977-83; Trustee, Thirlestane Castle; author of architectural guides to Edinburgh, Dundee, Stirling, London, Cambridge, Moray, Central Glasgow, Banff and Buchan; General Editor, RIAS/Landmark Trust Guides to Scotland. Publications: The Scottish Thirties; Edinburgh: Portrait of a City. Recreations: books; glasses; gardens; stately homes. Address: (b.) 15 Rutland Square, Edinburgh, EH1; T.-031-229 7545.

McKechnie, George. Editor, Glasgow Evening Times, since 1980; b. 28.7.46, Edinburgh; m., Janequin Claire Seymour Morris; 2 s. Educ. Portobello High School, Edinburgh. Reporter: Paisley & Renfrewshire Gazette, 1964-66, Edinburgh Evening News, 1966, Scottish Daily Mail, 1966-68, Daily Record, 1968-74; Deputy News Editor/News Editor, Sunday Mail, 1974-76; Assistant Editor, Evening Times, 1976-80. Recreation: reading. Address: (b.) 195 Albion Street, Glasgow, G1 1QP; T.-041-552 6255.

McKee, Professor (James Clark St. Clair) Sean, BSc, MA, PhD, DSc, FIMA. Professor of Mathematics, Strathclyde University, since 1988; b. 1.7.45, Belfast. Educ. George Watson's College, Edinburgh; St. Andrews University; Dundee University; Oxford University. NCR Research Fellow, 1970-72; Lecturer in Numerical Analysis, Southampton University, 1972-75; Fellow, Hertford College, Oxford, 1975-86; Professor of Industrial Mathematics, Strathclyde University, and Consultant Mathematician, Unilever Research, 1986-88. Member, Educational Committee, ECMI; Committee Member, Scottish Branch, Institute of Mathematics and Its Applications; Member, IMA Programmes Committee. Publications: 75 papers; Industrial Numerical Analysis (Co-Editor), 1986; Vector and Parallel Computing (Co-Editor), 1989. Recreations: climbing Munros; golf; theatre; running conferences. Address: (b.) Department of Mathematics, Strathclyde University, Glasgow, G1 1XH; T.-041-552 4400.

McKee, John Joseph, KSG, JP, MA (Hons), FEIS. Vice Chairman, Scottish Catholic International Aid Fund; b. 11.11.05, Johnstone; m., Margaret M.A. McGuire; 2 s.; 1 d. Educ. St. Mungo's Academy, Glasgow; Glasgow University. Forty-five years' teaching service in Glasgow, latterly as Headteacher, Holyrood Secondary School, 1959-71; Education Officer to Roman Catholic Hierarchy of Scotland, 1971-82; Secretary, Catholic Education Commission Scotland, 1972-82; Member of Justice and Peace Commission for Scotland, since 1974. Recreation: gardening. Address: (h.) 30 Lanton Road, Glasgow, G43 2SR; T.-041-633 0070.

McKellar, Kenneth, BSc. Singer, Composer, Writer; b. 23.6.27, Paisley. Gave first concert in local hall, aged 13; continued singing while at school, university and during his first two years working in forestry; has made numerous records of classical and popular music; numerous tours, especially in Australia and New Zealand; has appeared a number of times at the London Palladium.

McKelvey, William. MP (Labour), Kilmarnock and Loudoun, since 1979; b. 1934.

McKelvie, Campbell John, BSc (Hons), ARCST, FBIM, MICE, MIMBM, CEng. Director of Building and Works, Strathclyde Region; b. 1.2.32, Tarbert, Argyll; m., Rhona Paton Smith; 2 s. Educ. Marr College, Troon; Glasgow University; Royal College of Science and Technology. Private sector, 1955-75; Senior Depute Head of Direct Works, Strathclyde Region, 1975-79. Recreations: golf; curling; bridge. Address: (b.) Philip Murray Road, Bellshill, Lanarkshire; T.-Bellshill 749121.

McKenna, Rosemary, DCE, JP. Provost, Cumbernauld and Kilsyth District Council, since 1988; Convener, COSLA Equal Opportunities Committee, since 1986; Member, Board, Cumbernauld Development Corporation, since 1984; b. 8.5.41, Lochwinnoch; m., James Stephen McKenna; 3 s.; 1 d. Educ. St. Augustine's Secondary School, Glasgow; St. Andrew's College, Bearsden. Taught in various primary schools, since 1974; Leader of Council, Cumbernauld and Kilsyth, 1984-88; Chair, Scottish Local Authorities New Towns Forum, 1988-89; Secretary, COSLA Labour Group, since 1986; Board Member, Cumbernauld Theatre Trust; Board Member, Cumbernauld ITEC; Executive Member and Chair, Powers Working Party, Scottish Constitutional Convention. Recreations: reading; cooking. Address: (h.) 9 Westray Road, Cumbernauld, G67 1NN.

Mackenzie, A(lexander) Graham, MA, ALA. Librarian, St. Andrews University, 1976-89; b. 4.12.28, Glasgow; m., E. Astrid MacKinven; 1 s.; 1 d. Educ. Hutchesons' Boys' Grammar School; Glasgow University. Keeper of Science Books, Durham University Library, 1952-60; Sub-Librarian, Nottingham University Library, 1960-61; Deputy Librarian, Brotherton Library, Leeds University, 1961-63; Librarian, Lancaster University, 1963-76, and Director, Library Research Unit, 1970-76. Honorary Treasurer, SCONUL, 1982-89. Recreations: sailing; Scottish country dancing; Baroque music; golf. Address: (h.) Doocot Lodge, 7 Doocot Road, St. Andrews, Fife, KY16 8QP.

MacKenzie, Angus Alexander, CA. Chartered Accountant, since 1955; b. 1.3.31, Nairn; m., Catherine; 1 d. Educ. Inverness Royal Academy; Edinburgh University. National Service, RAF, 1955-57; in private practice as CA Assistant in Edinburgh, 1957-59, Inverness, 1959-61; commenced in practice on own account, 1961; Chairman, Highland Group, Riding for the Disabled Association; Director, PLM Helicopters Ltd. Recreations: shooting; stalking; hill-walking; gardening. Address: (h.) Tigh an Allt, Tomatin, Inverness-shire; T.-Tomatin 270.

MacKenzie, Archibald MacIntosh, DL. Assistant Chief Constable, British Transport Police, since 1983; Vice Lord Lieutenant, Dunbartonshire, since 1990; b. 3.6.33, Inveraray; m., Margaret Young Ritchie; 1 s.; 1 d. Educ. Hermitage School, Helensburgh. Chairman, Dumbarton Branch, Royal National Lifeboat Institution; Vice Convenor, Scottish Lifeboat Council; Chairman, Scottish Lifeboat Executive Committee; Member, Committee of Management, Royal National Lifeboat Institution; Elder, Church of Scotland. Recreations: sailing; golf; reading; classical music. Address: (h.) Millerston, 10 Boghead Road, Dumbarton; T.-Dumbarton 63654.

Mackenzie, Major Colin Dalzell, MBE, MC, DL. Vice Lieutenant, Inverness-shire, since 1986; b. 23.3.19, Fawley; m., Lady Anne Fitz Roy; 1 s.; 3 d. Educ. Eton; RMC, Sandhurst. Page of Honour to King George V, 1932-36; joined Seaforth Highlanders, 1939; ADC to Viceroy of India, 1945-46; Deputy Military Secretary to Viceroy of India, 1946-47; retired, 1949; TA, 1950-56; Inverness County Council, 1949-52; Director, various companies. Recreation: fishing. Address: (h.) Farr House, Inverness, IV1 2XB; T.-Farr 202.

Mackenzie, Colin Scott, DL, BL, NP. Procurator Fiscal, Stornoway, since 1969; Director, Harris Tweed Association Ltd., since 1979; Vice Lord Lieutenant of Islands Area, Western Isles, since 1984; b. 7.7.38, Stornoway; m., Christeen E.D. MacLauchlan. Educ. Nicolson Institute; Fettes College; Edinburgh University. Burgh Prosecutor, Stornoway, 1971-75; JP Fiscal, 1971-75; Deputy Lieutenant and Clerk to Lieutenancy of the Western Isles, 1975; Founder President, Stornoway Flying Club, 1970; Founding Dean, Western Isles

Faculty of Solicitors; elected Council Member, Law Society of Scotland, 1985; Convener, Criminal Law Committee, 1991-92; Elder, Church of Scotland, since 1985; Member, Board of Social Responsibility, Church of Scotland; Convener, Assembly Study Group on Young People and the Media, 1991-93; author of article on Lieutenancy, Stair Memorial Encyclopaedia of Law of Scotland, 1987; President, Stornoway Rotary Club, 1977; Chairman, Lewis Pipe Band, since 1978. Recreation: fishing. Address: (h.) Park House, Matheson Road, Stornoway, Lewis; T.-Stornoway 2008.

McKenzie, Hamish, BSc, MB, ChB, PhD, MRCPath. Senior Lecturer in Medical Microbiology, Aberdeen University, since 1989; b. 28.2.49, Aberdeen; m., Janet Carmichael McDonald. Educ. Grangemouth High School; Strathclyde University; Glasgow University. Address: (b.) Department of Medical Microbiology, University Medical Buildings, Foresterhill, Aberdeen, AB9 2ZD; T.-0224 681818, Ext. 52446.

MacKenzie, Hugh D., MA (Hons), FEIS, JP. Headteacher, Craigroyston Community High School, since 1972; Director, Craigroyston Curriculum Project, since 1980; b. 29.5.33, Edinburgh; m., Helen Joyce; 1 s.; 1 d. Educ. Royal High School; Edinburgh University; Moray House College of Education, Edinburgh. Education Officer, RAF, 1956-58; Assistant Teacher, Niddrie Marischal Junior Secondary School and Falkirk High School, 1958-62; Principal Teacher: Broxburn Academy, 1962-64, Liberton High School, 1964-70; Deputy Headteacher, Craigmount High School, 1970-72; Scottish Representative, Northern Regional Examination Board, 1973-88; Vice-Chairman, Lothian Regional Consultative Committee, 1984-87; a Director, Royal Lyceum Theatre, Edinburgh, since 1985, Scottish Community Education Council, 1985-88; President, Royal High School Rugby Club; President and Founder Member, Edinburgh Golden Oldies Rugby Club. Recreations: rugby; squash; golf; ornithology; philately; jazz. Address: (h.) 3 Beechwood Mains, Edinburgh.

MacKenzie, Ian Kenneth, OBE, JP. Chairman, Red Deer Commission, since 1984; Chairman, Highlands and Islands Development Consultative Council, 1988-91; Landowner; b. 1.3.31, Nairn; m., Margaret Vera Matheson; 2 s.; 2 d. Educ. Inverness Royal Academy. Member, Scottish Agricultural Consultative Panel; Member, Secretary of State's Panel of Arbiters; Director, Royal Highland and Agricultural Society of Scotland, 1980-84. Recreation: field sports. Address: Culblain, 46 Southside Road, Inverness, IV2 4XA; T.-0463 231894.

Mackenzie, Rev. Ian Murdo. Church of Scotland Minister; Writer, Broadcaster, Organist; b. 3.8.31, Fraserburgh; m., Elizabeth Alice Whitley; 1 s.; 1 d. Educ. Strichen School; Fettes College; Edinburgh University. Assistant Organist, St. Giles Cathedral, 1952-58; Editor, The Student, Sooth and Breakthrough; Founder Member, Telephone Samaritans Scotland, 1960; Columnist, Edinburgh Evening Dispatch; Conductor, Calton Singers; Music Organiser, Iona Abbey; Assistant Minister, St. Giles, 1960-62; Founder, Edinburgh University CND, 1962; Scottish Secretary, Student Christian Movement, 1962-63; Assistant General Secretary, Student Christian Movement, 1963-64; Secretary, University Teachers Group, 1963-65; Religious Adviser and Executive Producer, Religious Programmes, ABC TV, 1964-68; LWT, 1968-69; conceived and produced From Inner Space, Looking for an Answer, Don't Just Sit There, Question '68, Roundhouse; Religious Columnist, The Times, 1966-68; Minister, Peterhead Old Parish Church, 1969-73; Presenter, For Christ's Sake and What The Religious Papers Say, Grampian TV; Chairman, Scottish Religious Panel, IBA, 1970-72; Head of Religious Programmes, BBC Scotland,

1973-89; conceived Eighth Day, Voyager, Angles, Gates to Space, The Quest; Writer/Presenter, He Turned Up, Channel Four, 1990; Baird Lectures on Church Music, 1990; Presenter/Improviser on hymns, Radio Scotland, 1990-91. Publications: Vision and Belief; various papers, articles and essays. Recreations: concert-going; politician-watching; cathedrals; animals; hot baths; writing letters; drawing wonderfully bad cartoons. Address: (h.) 1 Glenan Gardens, Helensburgh, Dunbartonshire, G84 8XT; T.-0436 73429.

MacKenzie, James Alexander Mackintosh, CB, FEng, FICE, FIHT. Chief Road Engineer, Scottish Development Department, 1976-88; b. 6.5.28, Inverness; m., Pamela D. Nixon; 1 s.; 1 d. Educ. Inverness Royal Academy. Miscellaneous local government appointments, 1950-63; Chief Resident Engineer, Durham County Council, 1963-67; Deputy Director, North Eastern Road Construction Unit, Department of Transport, 1967-71 (Director, 1971-76). Recreations: golf; fishing. Address: (h.) 2 Dean Park, Longniddry, East Lothian, EH32 OQR; T.-Longniddry 52643.

Mackenzie, John Saffery, OBE. Managing Director, Alloa Brewery Co. Ltd., since 1975; b. 10.6.35, Barnet, Herts; m., Yvonne Elizabeth D'Albiac; 1 s.; 2 d. Educ. Cranleigh School. National Service, 1953-55, 2nd Lt., Queen's Royal Surrey Regiment; Lambert Brothers Ltd., 1955-59; Balfour Williamson Ltd., 1959-62; Allied Breweries Ltd., since 1962. Chairman, Visitors Division, XIII Commonwealth Games, Edinburgh, 1986; Trustee: YWCA Scottish National Council, Saints and Sinners Club Scotland; Founder Director, Quality Scotland Foundation; Vice Chairman, Biggar Museum Trust; Director, Craigmillar Opportunities Trust; Council Member, CBI Scotland. Recreations: rugby (watching these days); gardening; family. Address: (h.) The Old Manse, Elsricke, Biggar, Lanarkshire, ML12 6QZ.

MacKenzie, Kenneth John, MA, AM. Under Secretary, Scottish Office, since 1985; b. 1.5.43, Glasgow; m., Irene Mary Hogarth; 1 s.; 1 d. Educ. Birkenhead School; Pembroke College, Oxford; Stanford University, California. Assistant Principal, Scottish Home and Health Department; Principal, Scottish Education Department; Principal Private Secretary to Secretary of State for Scotland; Assistant Secretary, Scottish Economic Planning Department and Scottish Office Finance Division; Under Secretary, Principal Finance Officer, Scottish Home and Health Department and Scottish Office Agriculture and Fisheries Department; Convener, Congregational Board, St. Cuthbert's Parish Church, Edinburgh; Hon. President, Edinburgh Civil Service Dramatic Society. Address: (b.) Pentland House, 47 Robb's Loan, Edinburgh, EH14 1TW.

MacKenzie, Malcolm Lackie, MA (Hons), MEd. Senior Lecturer in Education, Glasgow University; b. 5.7.38, Clydebank. Educ. Clydebank High School; Glasgow University. Assistant Teacher of English and History, Bearsden Academy, 1961-64; Lecturer in Education, Jordanhill College of Education, 1964-67; joined Department of Education, Glasgow University, 1967; Member, Council of Management, British Educational Administration Society, 1972-76; Member, Working Party set up by CCC on Communication and Implementation of Aims in Secondary Education, 1972-74; Past Chairman, Scottish Association for Educational Management and Administration; Member, Working Party on Educational Policy-making, Administration and Management, Council for Educational Technology for UK, 1974-77; Member, Scottish Central Committee on English, 1978-80; Co-Director, Scottish Schools Councils Research Project, 1976-80; Member, National Advisory Committee on Education, Conservative Party, 1962-82; Chairman, Glasgow and Strathclyde Universities Staff Conservative Association, since 1986;

Member, Scottish Consultative Council on the Curriculum, 1990-91; Member, Education Committee, CBI (Scotland), since 1990. Address: (h.) 64 Polwarth Street, Hyndland, Glasgow, G12 9TL; T.-041-357 2038.

McKenzie, Rev. Morris Glyndwr, BA, LLB. Barrister and Solicitor, Supreme Court of New Zealand; Minister, South Ronaldsay and Burray, since 1978; b. 10.2.28, Invercargill, New Zealand; m., Janette Zena Lewis. Educ. John McGlashan College, Dunedin, New Zealand; Victoria University College, Wellington, New Zealand; University of Otago, Dunedin, New Zealand; St. Mary's College, St. Andrews. New Zealand: Ministry of Social Security, 1947-48, Ministry of Labour, 1948-55, Ministry of Works, 1956-74, District Solicitor, Ministry of Works, Dunedin, 1965-71, District Solicitor, Ministry of Works, Auckland, 1971-74; student, 1974-76; Assistant Minister, St. James, Forfar, 1976-77. Moderator, Orkney Presbytery, 1983-84. Recreations: walking; cycling; travel; reading; music; wine-making. Address: Manse of South Ronaldsay and Burray, St. Margaret's Hope, Orkney; T.-St. Margaret's Hope 288.

Mackenzie, Stuart D., DPE, DYCS, DMS, MBA. Executive Director of Community Services, Stirling District Council; b. 14.8.46, Glasgow; m., Anita. Educ. Eastbank Academy, Glasgow; Jordanhill College of Education; Glasgow College of Technology; Strathclyde University. Activities Organiser, Scottish Association of Boys Clubs, 1968-70; Area Organiser, Glasgow Education Department, 1970-72; Lecturer, Jordanhill College, 1972-77; Depute Director of Leisure and Recreation, Cunninghame District Council, 1977-82. Executive Committee: Scottish Sports Association for the Disabled, 1975-82, Association of Directors of Leisure, Recreation and Tourism, 1982-91 (Honorary Chairman, 1988-90). Recreations: DIY; walking; video filming; driving. Address: (b.) Beechwood House, St. Ninians Road, Stirling, FK8 2AD; T.-Stirling 50403, Ext. 125.

McKenzie, Rev. William Moncur, DA. Minister, Laurieknowe Troqueer Parish Church, Dumfries, since 1977; b. 30.12.28, Glasgow; m., Margaret Semple Scott; 1 s.; 2 d. Educ. King's Park Secondary School, Glasgow; Glasgow School of Art; Jordanhill Teacher Training College; Trinity College, Glasgow; St. Colm's Missionary College, Edinburgh. Art Teacher in Glasgow, 1951-55; ordained Minister, 1958; Assistant, St. Mary's, Govan; District Missionary, Lubwa, Northern Rhodesia, Livingstonia Mission, Church of Scotland, 1959-65; integrated into United Church of Zambia, 1965; transferred to Kashinda, Mporokoso, 1968, for lay training and Bible translation; left Zambia, 1977. Chaplain, HM Prison, Dumfries, since 1983, ICI Dumfries, since 1978; Secretary/Exegete for Chibemba Bible, Zambia (published, 1983); Committee Member, National Bible Society of Scotland, since 1978. Recreations: walking; camping; gardening. Address: The Manse, Troqueer Road, Dumfries, DG2 7DF; T.-0387 53043.

Mackenzie, William Roderick Simon, ARICS. Member, North East Fife District Council, since 1984 (Chairman, Finance and General Purposes Committee); President, Zoological Society of Glasgow and West of Scotland; Chairman, St. Andrews and North East Fife Tourist Board, since 1985; Vice-Chairman, Scottish Confederation of Tourism, since 1991; Vice-Chairman, Fife Marriage Counselling Service; b. 2.3.30, Glasgow; m., Margaret Borland Maclachlan; 2 s.; 1 d. Educ. Pollokshields Senior Secondary School, Glasgow; Royal College of Science and Technology, Glasgow. Assistant Quantity Surveyor, Muirhead, Muir & Webster, Glasgow, 1948-64; Quantity Surveyor, Cumbernauld New Town Development Corporation, 1964-69; Senior Quantity Surveyor, Fife County Council, 1969-74; Buildings Office, Dundee University, since 1974. Recreations: writing plays; amateur dramatics; gar-dening; visiting zoos. Address: (h.) 3 Tarvit Gardens, Cupar, Fife, KY15 5BT; T.-Cupar 52660.

Mackenzie-Robinson, Mhairi Philippa, BA (Hons). Administrator, Edinburgh Festival Fringe, since 1986; b. 10.9.59, Edinburgh. Educ. St. Margaret's School for Girls, Edinburgh; Durham University. Associate Administrator, Edinburgh Festival Fringe, 1982-86. Address: (b.) Fringe Office, 180 High Street, Edinburgh, EH1 1QS; T.-031-226 5257/9.

McKenzie Smith, Ian, RSA, PRSW, LLD, FSA (Scot), FMA; City Arts Officer, City of Aberdeen, since 1989 (Director, Aberdeen Art Gallery and Museums, 1968-89); b. 3.8.35; m., Mary Rodger Fotheringham; 2 s.; 1 d. Educ. Robert Gordon's College, Aberdeen; Gray's School of Art, Aberdeen; Hospitalfield College of Art, Arbroath. Teacher of Art, 1960-63; Education Officer, Council of Industrial Design, Scottish Committee, 1963-68. Work in permanent collections: Scottish National Gallery of Modern Art, Scottish Arts Council, Arts Council of Northern Ireland, Contemporary Art Society, Aberdeen Art Gallery and Museums, Glasgow Art Gallery and Museums, Abbot Hall Art Gallery, Kendal, Hunterian Museum, Glasgow, Nuffield Foundation, Carnegie Trust, Strathclyde Education Authority, Lothian Education Authority, Royal Scottish Academy, Department of the Environment. Member, Scottish Arts Council, 1970-77; President, RSW, 1988; Deputy President, RSA, 1990-91, Treasurer, since 1990; Governor: Edinburgh College of Art, 1976-88, Robert Gordon's Institute of Technology, 1989; FSS; FRSA. Address: (h.) 70 Hamilton Place, Aberdeen, AB2 4BA; T.-0224 644531.

Mackenzie-Stuart, Lord (Alexander John Mackenzie-Stuart); b. 18.11.24; m., Anne Burtholme Millar; 4 d. Educ. Fettes College; Sidney Sussex College, Cambridge; Edinburgh University (LLB). Admitted Faculty of Advocates (Scottish Bar), 1951; Honorary Keeper, Advocates' Library, 1969; Sheriff-Principal of Aberdeen, Kincardine and Banff, 1971; Senator of the College of Justice, 1972; Judge of the Court of Justice of the European Communities, 1973; elected President of the Court, 1984; retired from Court of Justice, 1988; since retirement, Woodrow Wilson Center for International Scholars, Washington; lectures on Community Law and other matters in UK and Europe; President, British Academy of Experts; Honorary Doctorates: Stirling, Exeter, Edinburgh, Glasgow, Aberdeen, Cambridge, Birmingham; Prix Bech for services to Europe, 1989; Honorary Bencher, Middle Temple, King's Inn, Dublin; created Life Baron, 1988, as Lord Mackenzie-Stuart of Dean; FRSE; President, British Academy of Experts. Address: (h.) 7 Randolph Cliff, Edinburgh, EH3 7TZ; T.-031-225 1089.

McKerrell, Douglas Gordon, LLB. Partner, Kidstons, since 1991; Partner, Maclay Murray & Spens, 1976-91; b. 18.8.44, Edinburgh; m., Elizabeth Anne Brown; 3 s.; 1 d. Educ. Royal High School, Edinburgh; High School of Glasgow; Glasgow University. After training and qualifying, spent several years in private practice in London and Glasgow; joined Maclay Murray & Spens, 1975; Tutor/Senior Tutor, Finance and Investment, Diploma in Legal Practice, Glasgow University, 1980-89; Chairman, Rent Assessment Panel for Scotland, 1980-89; Director, Scottish Music Information Centre and ICMC Glasgow, since 1990; Chairman, Scottish SPCA, since 1988. Publication: The Rent Acts: A Practitioner's Guide, 1985. Recreations: music; theatre; cinema; collecting records. Address: (b.) 16 Gordon Street, Glasgow; T.-041-221 6551.

Mackey, Professor James Patrick, PhD, LPh, BD, STL, DD, BA. Thomas Chalmers Professor of Theology, Edinburgh University, since 1979; b. 9.2.34; m., Hanorah Noelle Quinlan; 1 s.; 1 d. Educ. Mount St. Joseph College, Roscrea; National University of Ireland; Pontifical University,

Maynooth; Queen's University, Belfast; Oxford University; London University; Strasbourg University. Lecturer in Philosophy, Queen's University, Belfast, 1960-66; Lecturer in Theology, St. John's College, Waterford, 1966-69; Associate Professor and Professor of Systematic and Philosophical Theology, San Francisco University, 1969-79; Visiting Professor: California University, Berkeley, 1974, Dartmouth College, New Hampshire, 1989; Member, Centre for Hermeneutical Studies, Berkeley, 1974-79; Dean, Faculty of Divinity, Edinburgh University, 1984-88. Publications: The Modern Theology of Tradition, 1962; Life and Grace, 1966; Tradition and Change in the Church, 1968; Contemporary Philosophy of Religion, 1968; Morals, Law and Authority (Editor), 1969; The Church: Its Credibility Today, 1970; The Problems of Religious Faith, 1972; Jesus: The Man and the Myth, 1979; The Christian Experience of God as Trinity, 1983; Religious Imagination (Editor), 1986; Modern Theology: A Sense of Direction, 1987; New Testament Theology in Dialogue, (Co-Author), 1987; Introduction to Celtic Christianity, 1989. Recreations: yachting; rediscovery of original Celtic culture of these islands. Address: (h.) 10 Randolph Crescent, Edinburgh EH3 7TT; T.-031-225 9408.

McKichan, Duncan James, OBE, BL. Solicitor; Partner, Maclay Murray & Spens, 1952-91; Honorary Consul for Canada; Dean, Royal Faculty of Procurators in Glasgow, 1983-86; b. 28.7.24, Wallington, Surrey; m, Leila Campbell Fraser; 2 d. Educ. George Watson's College, Edinburgh; Solihull School; Downing College, Cambridge; Glasgow University. Royal Navy, 1943-46; qualified as Solicitor, 1950. Recreations: gardening; walking; sailing; skiing. Address: (h.) Invermay, Queen Street, Helensburgh; T.-0436 74778.

Mackie, John T., CEng, FIMinE, FBIM. Regional Opencast Director, Scotland, British Coal Corporation, since 1990; b. 27.12.28, Kirkcaldy; m., Rose; 1 s. Educ. Kirkcaldy High School; Heriot Watt University. Director, Coal Trades Benevolent Association; Member of Council, CBI Scotland. Recreations: golf; curling. Address: (b.) 160 Glasgow Road, Edinburgh; T.-031-317 7300.

Mackie, Michael James, BMedBiol, MBChB, MD, FRCP, FRCPath. Consultant Haematologist, since 1981; Area Director, Haematology Services, since 1991; b. 17.11.48, Aberdeen; 1 s.; 1 d. Educ. Robert Gordon's College, Aberdeen; Aberdeen University. Junior appointments in Aberdeen and Canada; Consultant and Senior Lecturer, Liverpool University, 1981-86; Consultant Haematologist, Western General Hospital, Edinburgh, since 1986. Recreation: tennis. Address: (b.) Department of Haematology, Western General Hospital, Crewe Road, Edinburgh; T.-031-332 2525, Ext. 4201.

MacKie, Professor Rona McLeod, MD, MRCP, FRCPGlas, FRCPLond, FRCPath, FRSE, FInstBiol. Professor of Dermatology, Glasgow University, since 1978; Honorary Consultant Dermatologist, Greater Glasgow Health Board, since 1978; b. 22.5.40, Dundee; m., Dr. Euan MacKie; 1 s.; 1 d. Educ. Laurelbank School, Glasgow; Glasgow University. Registrar, Department of Dermatology, Western Infirmary, Glasgow, 1970-71; Lecturer in Dermatology, Glasgow University, 1971-72; Consultant Dermatologist, Greater Glasgow Health Board, 1972-78. Recreation: skiing. Address: Department of Dermatology, Glasgow University, Glasgow, G11 6NU; T.-041-339 8855, Ext. 4006.

Mackie-Campbell, Peter Lorne, DL, JP. Chairman, Tarbert Harbour Authority, since 1956; Company Director; b. 6.3.25, Edinburgh; m., Gillian Coats; 1 s. (deceased); 1 d. Educ. Eton; Magdalen College, Cambridge. RAF, 1943; The Rifle Brigade, 1945-54; management, Stonefield Farms, 1954-89; Argyll County Council, NFU of Scotland, SLF (Convener),

various land development companies. Member, Queen's Bodyguard for Scotland (Royal Company of Archers). Recreations: photography; bird-watching; gardening. Address: (h.) Stonefield House, Tarbert, Argyll; T.-0880 820342.

McKillop, Professor James Hugh, BSc, MB, ChB, PhD, FRCP. Muirhead Professor of Medicine, Glasgow University, since 1989; Honorary Consultant Physician, Glasgow Royal Infirmary, since 1982; b. 20.6.48, Glasgow; m., Caroline A. Oakley; 2 d. Educ. St. Aloysius' College, Glasgow; Glasgow University. Hall Fellow in Medicine, then Lecturer in Medicine, Glasgow University, 1974-82; Postdoctoral Fellow, Stanford University Medical Center, California, 1979 and 1980; Senior Lecturer in Medicine, Glasgow University, 1982-89. Watson Prize Lectureship, Royal College of Physicians and Surgeons of Glasgow, 1979; Harkness Fellowship, Commonwealth Fund of New York, 1979-80; Robert Reid Newall Award, Stanford University, 1980; Honorary Treasurer, Scottish Society of Experimental Medicine, 1982-87; Honorary Secretary, British Nuclear Cardiology Group, 1982-87; Symposium Editor, Scottish Medical Journal, since 1984; Council Member, British Nuclear Medicine Society, since 1985 (Hon. Secretary, 1988-90), President, since 1990. Recreations: music (especially opera); history. Address: (h.) 10 Kirklee Circus, Glasgow, G12 OTW; T.-041-339 7000.

McKinlay, Professor David Gemmell, BSc, PhD, ARCST, CEng, FICE, FASCE, FGS, FRSE. Professor Emeritus, Strathclyde University; Geotechnical Consultant; b. 23.8.24, Glasgow; m., Muriel Lees Donaldson; 1 s.; 1 d. Educ. Allan Glen's School, Glasgow; Royal Technical College, Glasgow; Glasgow University. War Service, commissioned RNVR; County Engineer's staff, Dumfries County; civil engineering consultancy; teaching and research, Royal College of Science and Technology, then Strathclyde University. Member, Subsidence Compensation Review Committee, 1984; Council Member, Institution of Civil Engineers, 1979-82, 1983-86; Chairman, Ground Engineering Group Board, 1981-86; Governor, Rotary International District 123, 1987-88. Recreations: estate development; freshwater fishing; travel. Address: (h.) Spylawbank, Burn Road, Darvel, KA17 ODB; T.-0560 22552.

MacKinlay, Gordon Alexander, MB, BS, LRCP, FRCSEdin, FRCSEng. Senior Lecturer in Clinical Surgery, Edinburgh University, since 1980; Consultant Surgeon, Royal Hospital for Sick Children, Edinburgh, since 1980; b. 25.4.46, Dunfermline; m., Genevieve Anne Bailey; 1 s.; 2 d. Educ. Tiffin School, Kingston-upon-Thames; Charing Cross Hospital Medical School, London University. Senior House Officer appointments, 1970-74; Registrar in General Surgery, Wycombe General Hospital, 1974-76; Senior Registrar to the paediatric surgery units, Edinburgh, 1976-80; Senior Medical Officer, later Consultant, Red Cross Children's Hospital, Cape Town, 1977-78; Senior Paediatric Surgeon, Tawam Hospital, Abu Dhabi, 1982-83. Director, Scottish Children's Tumour Register. Publications on paediatric surgery. Recreations: skiing; travel. Address: (h.) Marhaba, Johnsburn Park, Balerno, Midlothian, EH14 7NA; T.-031-449 5979.

McKinney, Alan. National Director, Scottish Decorators' Federation; Director of Organisation and Headquarters, Scottish National Party, 1977-90; b. 16.10.41, Glasgow; m., Elma; 1 s.; 1 d. Educ. Brechin High School. Time-served refrigeration engineer before entering politics full-time as National Organiser, SNP, 1977; former Election Agent, Dundee East; former elected Member, NEC. Played football for Brechin City. Recreation: golf. Address: (b.) 41 York Place, Edinburgh; T.-031-557 9345.

McKinnon, David Douglas, BSc, FFA, FIMA. Director, General Manager and Actuary, Scottish Mutual Assurance Society, 1982-90, Director, since 1991; b. 18.7.26, Larbert; m., Edith June Kyles; 1 s.; 2 d. Educ. High School of Stirling; Glasgow University. Faculty of Actuaries: Fellow, since 1951, President, 1979-81; Member of Council, International Actuarial Association, 1972-89 and Secretary for the UK, 1975-89; Member, Investment Advisory Committee, Glasgow University Court, since 1982; Chairman, Associated Scottish Life Offices, 1988-90; Member, Board of Association of British Insurers, 1988-90; Session Clerk, Larbert West Church, 1968-87; Vice-Chairman, Church of Scotland Trust, 1984-89, Chairman, since 1991; Member, Church of Scotland Assembly Council, since 1987; Member, Trinity College (Glasgow) Financial Board, since 1977; President, Falkirk and District Battalion, The Boys' Brigade, 1972-77. Recreations: golf; gardening. Address: (h.) 4 Carronvale Road, Larbert, Stirlingshire; T.-0324 562373.

MacKinnon, Major John Farquhar, MC, DL, JP; b. 27.1.18, Melbourne; m., Sheila Pearce (deceased); 1 s.; 1 d. (deceased); 2, Mrs Anne Swann. Educ. Geelong, Australia; Corpus Christi College, Cambridge (MA). Army, Queen's Own Cameron Highlanders, 1939-46 (Major); twice wounded; Middle East, 1940-41; ADC, Governor General, Union of South Africa, 1942; Staff, UK, 1943-46 (left service due to wounds); Staff TA, 1949-54; ICI Ltd., 1949-73, Regional Manager; Secretary, British Field Sports Society, Berwickshire, 1974-80; Elder, Kirk of Lammermuir; JP, 1966; Deputy Lieutenant, Berwickshire, since 1987. Recreations: shooting; fishing. Address: (h.) Craigie Lodge, Longformacus, by Duns, Berwickshire; T.-Longformacus 251.

MacKinnon, Niall I., MA (Hons), DipEd. Head Teacher, Braidfield High School, Clydebank, since 1985; b. 6.4.39, Daliburgh, South Uist; m., Eileen; 2 s.; 2 d. Educ. Portree High School; Glasgow University. Teacher, Hillhead High School, 1962-69; Principal Teacher of Classics, Hermitage Academy, 1969-76; Assistant Head Teacher, then Depute Head Teacher, Vale of Leven Academy, 1976-85. Publication: Discovering the Greeks (Co-author), 1977. Recreations: golf; bridge. Address: (b.) Braidfield High School, Queen Mary Avenue, Clydebank, G81 2LR; T.-041-952 3265.

Mackinnon, Roderick, JP. Member, Western Isles Islands Council, since 1986; b. 9.8.28, Castlebay, Isle of Barra; m., Katie-Ann Haggerty-MacKinnon; 1 s.; 1 d. Educ. Castlebay Secondary School; Liverpool College of Technology. Entered Merchant Navy, 1946; qualified as foreign-going Master Mariner, 1961; first command, 1966; became oil marketing executive, 1968; retired, 1983. Honorary Agent: Royal Alfred Seafarers' Society, The Sailors' Children's Society; Deputy Launching Authority, RNLI Castlebay Station; Hon. Agent, Shipwrecked Mariners' Society; Member, Transport Users' Consultative Committee for Scotland. Recreations: fishing; sailing; writing; community work. Address: (h.) Faire Rhum, Brevig, Castlebay, Isle of Barra, PA80 5UN; T.-Castlebay 242.

Mackintosh, Rev. Aeneas. Information Officer and Communication Adviser, Scottish Episcopal Church; b. 1.7.27, Inverness; m., Eileen Mary Barlow; 4 s. Educ. Inverness Royal Academy; Kelham Theological College. Precentor, St. Andrew's Cathedral, Inverness, 1952-55; Curate, St. Augustine's, Wisbech, 1955-57; Rector: St. Matthew, Possilpark, 1957-61, Holy Trinity, Haddington, 1961-65; Town Councillor, Haddington, 1962-65; Diocesan Inspector of Church Schools, 1963; Team Priest, St. John's, Princes Street, Edinburgh, 1965-69, and Rector, St. John's, 1969-81; Rector, St. Baldred's, North Berwick, and St. Aidan's, Gullane, 1981-87; Canon, St. Mary's Cathedral,

Edinburgh, 1975-87; Tutor, Diocese of Edinburgh TM, 1974-87. Address: 31 St. Albans Road, Edinburgh, EH9.

Mackintosh of Mackintosh, Lachlan Ronald Duncan, OBE, JP. 30th Chief of Clan Mackintosh, since 1957; Lord Lieutenant of Inverness, Lochaber, Badenoch and Strathspey, since 1985; Member, Highland Regional Council, since 1974; b. 27.6.28, Camberley; m., Mabel Cecilia Helen ("Celia") Bruce; 1 s.; 2 d.; 1 d. deceased. Educ. R.N. College, Dartmouth. Seaman Officer, Specialist in Communications, Royal Navy, retiring as Lt.-Cdr., 1963; President, Clan Chattan Association, since 1958; Chairman, Highland Exhibitions Ltd., 1964-85; Vice President, Scottish Conservative and Unionist Association, 1969-71; Member, Inverness County Council, 1970-75; Chairman, Inverness Prison Visiting Committee, 1973-86. Address: Moy Hall, Tomatin, Inverness, IV13 7YQ; T.-Tomatin 211.

Mackintosh, Peter, MIEDO, FInstP. Director of Development, Highland Regional Council, since 1980; b. 7.6.39, Nairn; m., Una; 2 s. Educ. Roses Academic Institute, Nairn. Architectural Assistant: Inverness County Council, 1958-60, Fife County Council, 1960-62; Ross and Cromarty County Council. Senior Architectural Assistant, 1962-72, Assistant Development Officer, 1972-75; Highland Regional Council: Divisional Development Officer, 1975-78, Assistant Director of Development, 1978-80. Chairman, Clan Chattan Association. Recreations: walking; gardening; travel; world affairs; family activities. Address: (b.) Regional Buildings, Glenurquhart Road, Inverness, IV3 5NX; T.-0463 234121.

McLachlan, Alastair Stevenson, MA (Hons). Rector, Lornshill Academy, Alloa, since 1988; b. 7.8.40, Glasgow; m., Anne Rutherford; 1 s.; 1 d. Educ. High School of Glasgow; Glasgow University. Recreations: family; golf; after-dinner speaking; singing. Address: (b.) Lornshill Academy, Tullibody Road, Alloa, FK10 2ES; T.-0259 214331.

Maclachlan, Alistair Andrew Duncan, BA (Hons). Rector, Forres Academy, since 1982; b. 14.3.46, Perth; m., Alison M.S. Love; 2 s. Educ. Perth Academy; Strathclyde University. Teacher in various schools, 1969-71; Principal Teacher of Economics and Business Studies, 1971-74; Assistant Rector, Keith Grammar School, 1974-78; Depute Rector, Elgin High School, 1978-82; Member, SCCC. Secretary and Treasurer, Keith Agricultural Show, 1972-82; Chairman, Elgin Squash Club, since 1982. Recreations: keeping fit; squash; reading; music. Address: (h.) 82 Duncan Drive, Elgin, Moray, IV30 2NH; T.-Elgin 542193.

Maclaren, Allan, MA, PhD. Senior Lecturer in Historical Sociology, Department of History, Strathclyde University; b. 3.11.37, Brechin; m., Marcia Nott; 2 s. Educ. Robert Gordon's College, Aberdeen; Aberdeen University. Worked in printing and publishing industry; former Lecturer, Department of Political Economy, Aberdeen University. Main publications: Religion and Social Class, 1974; Social Class in Scotland (Editor), 1976. Recreations: yachting; photography. Address: (b.) Department of History, Strathclyde University, Glasgow, G1.

McLaren, Bill, MBE (1979). Rugby Union Commentator, BBC; b. 16.10.23. Played wing forward for Hawick; had trial for Scotland but forced to withdraw because of illness; became reporter on local newspaper; first live radio broadcast, Glasgow v. Edinburgh, 1953; former teacher of physical education.

MacLaren, Duncan MacGregor, MA (Hons), MTh. Director, Scottish Catholic International Aid Fund (SCIAF), since 1986; b. 22.3.50, Dumbarton. Educ. Clydebank High School; Glasgow University; New College, Edinburgh

University. Assistant Principal, English Section, Institut auf dem Rosenberg, Switzerland, 1973-74; Researcher, Historical Dictionary of Scottish Gaelic, Glasgow University, 1974-75; Researcher, House of Commons, 1975-77; Press Officer, SNP, Edinburgh, 1977-83; Education/Promotion Officer, SCIAF, Glasgow, 1983-86. Member, Third Order of St. Dominic; Chair, Scottish Development Education Centre. Publications: Amannan; Dialogue for Development (Editor); Focus on Peace and Justice. Recreation: hill-walking in the Highlands. Address: (b.) 5 Oswald Street, Glasgow, G1 4QR; T.-041-221 4447.

MacLaren, Iain Ferguson, MB, ChB, FRCSEdin, FRCS. Consultant Surgeon, Royal Infirmary, Edinburgh, since 1974; b. 28.9.27, Edinburgh; m., Dr. Fiona Barbara Heptonstall; 1 s.; 1 d. Educ. Edinburgh Academy; Fettes College; Edinburgh University. Captain, RAMC, Egypt, 1950-52; Surgical Registrar, Royal Hospital for Sick Children, Edinburgh, 1956-58; Senior Surgical Registrar, Royal Infirmary, 1959-63 and 1964-67; Fellow in Surgical Research, Hahnemann Medical College and Hospital, Philadelphia, 1963-64; Consultant Surgeon, Deaconess Hospital, Edinburgh, 1967-85; Vice-President, Royal College of Surgeons of Edinburgh, 1983-86 (Council Member, 1977-83 and since 1987); Fellow, Royal Medical Society (Honorary Treasurer, 1979-85); Chairman, Royal Medical Society Trust, since 1985; Honorary Pipe-Major, Royal Scottish Pipers' Society, 1959-62; Honorary Secretary: Harveian Society of Edinburgh, 1968-87, Aesculapian Club, since 1978; Hon. Secretary, Royal College of Surgeons of Edinburgh, 1972-77. Recreations: music; the study of military history; all aspects of Scottish culture. Address: (h.) 3 Minto Street, Edinburgh, EH9 1RG; T.-031-667 3487.

McLaren, John James, FREHIS, MIEH. Director of Technical Services, Roxburgh District Council, since 1985; b. 2.4.40, Melrose; m., Katharine Parkin; 2 s. Educ. Melrose Grammar School; Galashiels Academy; Heriot-Watt College. City of Aberdeen Council, 1961-63; Reading Borough Council, 1963-67; Goole Rural District Council, 1967-71; Burgh Surveyor, Melrose Town Council, 1971-75; Roxburgh District Council, since 1975. Past President, Royal Environmental Health Institute of Scotland. Recreations: walking; gardening; dry fly fishing. Address: (b.) High Street, Hawick, Roxburghshire, TD9 9EF; T.-0450 75991.

McLatchie, Cameron, OBE, LLB. Chairman and Chief Executive, Scott & Robertson PLC, since 1988 (renamed British Polythene Industries PLC, 1990); Board Member, Scottish Enterprise; b. 18.2.47, Paisley; m., Helen Leslie Mackie; 2 s.; 1 d. Educ. Boroughmuir School, Edinburgh; Largs High School; Ardrossan Academy; Glasgow University. Whinney Murray & Co., Glasgow, 1968-70; Thomas Boag & Co. Ltd., Greenock, 1970-75; Chairman and Managing Director, Anaplast Ltd., Irvine, 1975-83; this company purchased by Scott & Robertson. Recreations: bridge; golf. Address: (b.) 96 Port Glasgow Road, Greenock; T.-0475 45432.

Maclauchlan, Alasdair Boyd, MSc, MIMinE, CEng. Chief Executive, Anderson Group PLC, since 1989; b. 20.3.46; m., Moira Harvey Yuill; 2 s. Educ. Keil School, Dumbarton; Strathclyde University. Terex Limited, 1969-83; Managing Director, Dowty Mining Equipment Limited, 1983-89. Recreations: gardening; golf; squash; motor racing. Address: (b.) Broad Street, Glasgow; T.-041-554 1800.

McLaughlin, Andrew James, BSc (Hons), MSc, MPharmS. Chief Administrative Pharmaceutical Officer, Ayrshire and Arran Health Board, since 1978; b. 8.1.44, Greenock; m., Sheila; 2 d. Educ. St. Columba's High School, Greenock; Glasgow University; Heriot Watt University. Community pharmacy, Boots The Chemist; hospital pharmacy, Hairmyres

Hospital, East Kilbride; Principal Pharmacist, Western Infirmary, Glasgow; Member, National Pharmaceutical Advisory Committee; Chairman, National Pharmacy Audit Committee; Chairman, Ayrshire Branch, Royal Pharmaceutical Society. Recreations: golf; hill-walking; photography. Address: (h.) 40 Bathurst Drive, Alloway, Ayr, KA7 4QY; T.-0292 42404.

McLaughlin, Eleanor Thomson, JP. Lord Provost and Lord Lieutenant of Edinburgh, 1988-92; b. Edinburgh; m., Hugh McLaughlin; 1 s.; 2 d. Former Deputy Chairman, Edinburgh District Council, and former Chairman, Housing Committee. Address: (b.) City Chambers, Edinburgh, EH1 1YJ.

McLaughlin, Mary, MA. Head Teacher, Notre Dame High School, Glasgow, since 1989; m., William J. McLaughlin; 1 d. Educ. St. Patrick's High School, Coatbridge; Glasgow University; Notre Dame College of Education. Principal Teacher of Modern Languages, St. Margaret's High, Airdrie; Assistant Head Teacher, Taylor High School, New Stevenston. Recreations: reading; music; cycling; walking. Address: (b.) 160 Observatory Road, Glasgow, G12 9LN; T.-041-339 3015.

Maclay, Baron (Joseph Paton Maclay), 3rd Baron; Bt. Deputy Lieutenant, Renfrewshire, since 1986; b. 11.4.42; m., Elizabeth Anne Buchanan; 2 s.; 1 d. Educ. Winchester; Sorbonne. Managing Director: Denholm Maclay Co. Ltd., 1970-83, Denholm Maclay (Offshore) Ltd., Triport Ferries (Management) Ltd., 1975-83; Deputy Managing Director, Denholm Ship Management Ltd., 1982-83; Director: Milton Shipping Co. Ltd., 1970-83, Marine Shipping Mutual Insurance Company, 1982-83; President, Hanover Shipping Inc., 1982-83; Director: British Steamship Short Trades Association, 1978-83, North of England Protection and Indemnity Association, 1976-83; Chairman, Scottish Branch, British Sailors Society, 1979-81; Vice-Chairman, Glasgow Shipowners & Shipbrokers Benevolent Association, 1982-83; Director, Denholm Ship Management (Holdings) Ltd., since 1991; Director, BIMCO, since 1991. Address: (h.) Duchal, Kilmacolm, Renfrewshire.

McLean, Rev. Andrew Thomas, BA, BD. Chaplain, Strathclyde University, since 1985; b. 1.2.50, Abadan, Iran; m., Alison Douglas Blair; 1 s.; 1 d. Educ. Bearsden Academy; Clydebank Technical College; Stirling University; Edinburgh University. Co-operative Insurance Society, 1967-70; Partner, Janus Enterprises, 1970-72; Probationer, Loanhead, 1979-80; Minister, Aberdeen Stockethill, 1980-85. Convener, Church of Scotland Board of Social Responsibility; Recreations: sound recording; running; photography; parachuting. Address: Chaplaincy Centre, Strathclyde University, John Street, Glasgow; T.-041-553 4144.

McLean, Angus, BL, SSC. Solicitor; Honorary Sheriff, Argyll (Dunoon); b. 26.10.12, Kilmartin, Argyll; m., Celia Jane Oliver; 1 s.; 1 d. Educ. Dunoon Grammar School; Glasgow University. Solicitor (Corrigall Ritchie & McLean, Dunoon), 1935; Royal Artillery, 1940-46; seconded Indian Army, 1942, Major (DAAG), 1945. Member, Council, Law Society of Scotland, 1950-74 (Vice President, 1964); Past President, Dunoon Business Club and Dunoon Rotary Club. Publications: History of Dunoon; Place Names of Cowal. Recreations: travel; gardening. Address: (h.) 21 Ravelston Dykes, Edinburgh, EH4 3JE; T.-031-332 4774.

MacLean, Charles Hector, BL, AE, DL. Former Senior Partner, Montgomerie & Co., Solicitors, Glasgow; Chairman, Association for Relief of Incurables in Glasgow and West of Scotland, since 1964; Deputy Lieutenant, County of Renfrew, since 1987; b. 9.12.13, Glasgow; m., Rachael Malcolm Hutchesson; 2 s.; 2 d. Educ. Canford School; Glasgow University. Pilot Officer, 602 Squadron Auxiliary Air Force,

1936; mobilised, 1939; severely wounded, 1940, as Flt. Commander in Battle of Britain; released in rank of Wing Commander, 1945; re-commissioned as wing Commander, RAuxAF to raise and command 3602 Fighter Control Unit. Vice President, Officers Association, Scottish Branch; Member, Committee, Earl Haig Fund Scotland. Address: (h.) 71 Lochwinnoch Road, Kilmacolm, Renfrewshire.

Maclean, Sir Donald, FBCO. Vice Chairman, Scottish Conservative Party, 1989-91; President, Scottish Conservative and Unionist Association, 1983-85; Ophthalmic Optician, since 1952; b. Annan; widower; 1 s.; 1 d. Educ. Morrison's Academy, Crieff; Heriot-Watt, Edinburgh. Ophthalmic Optician in Edinburgh, Newcastle, Perth and now Ayr; Chairman, Ayrshire Local Optical Committee, 1986-88; former Member, Transport Users Local Consultative Committee; Chairman, Ayr Constituency Conservative Association, 1971-75; Chairman, West of Scotland Area Council, Scottish Conservative Association, 1977-78-79; Member, National Union Executive Committee, 1979-89 (Member, GP Committee, 1983-85); Elder, Church of Scotland; Past President, West Highland Steamer Club; Liveryman of the Worshipful Copany of Spectacle Makers; Freeman, City of London. Recreations: photography; reading. Address: (h.) 22 Woodend Road, Alloway, Ayr.

McLean, Donald, FRICS. Commercial Director, Cumbernauld Development Corporation, since 1984; b. 20.2.45, Hamilton; m., Nancy; 2 s. Educ. Hamilton Academy. Lanark CC, 1962-68; West Lothian CC, 1968-69; Ronald Lyon Group, 1969-73; Dundee Corporation, 1970-73; Forth Ports Authority, 1973-74; Livingston Development Corporation, 1974-80; Northampton Development Corporation, 1980-84. Member, Dunbartonshire Valuation Appeal Committee. Recreations: golf; gardening; walking; reading; rugby. Address: (b.) Cumbernauld House, Cumbernauld; T.-0236 721155.

Maclean, Donnie M., DipTechEd. Director, An Comann Gaidhealach, since 1987; b. 5.9.36, Coll, Isle of Lewis; m., Lynn Kemp; 2 s.; 1 d. Educ. Back Public School; Nicolson Institute, Stornoway; Duncan of Jordanstone College of Art, Dundee; Moray House College of Education, Edinburgh. Fisherman; Civil Servant; Teacher; Producer, BBC Scotland; National Organiser, Scottish Civic Entertainment Association. Playwright. Recreations: drama; photography; the arts; crofting; fishing. Address: (h.) 7A Coll, Back, Isle of Lewis; T.-Back 260.

Maclean of Dunconnel, Sir Fitzroy Hew, 1st Bt, CBE (Mil). 15th Hereditary Keeper and Captain of Dunconnel; b. 11.3.11; m., Hon. Mrs Alan Phipps; 2 s. Educ. Eton; Cambridge. Entered Foreign Office, 1933; served Second World War, Queen's Own Cameron Highlanders and Special Air Service Regiment (Brigadier commanding British Military Mission to Yugoslav partisans, 1943-45); MP (Conservative), Lancaster, 1941-59, Bute and North Ayrshire, 1959-74; Parliamentary Under Secretary of State for War and Financial Secretary, War Office, 1954-57; Member, UK Delegation to North Atlantic Assembly, 1962-74; Member, Council of Europe and WEU, 1972-74; Hon. LLD, Glasgow, 1969, Dundee, 1984; Croix de Guerre, France; Order of Kutuzov, USSR; Partisan Star, 1st Class, Yugoslavia; Order of the Yugoslav Star with Ribbon; Order of Merit, Yugoslavia; President, British Yugoslav Society; Past President, Great Britain-USSR Association; author of works of military history and other books. Address: (h.) Strachur House, Strachur, PA27 8BX.

Maclean, Sheriff Hector Ronald. Sheriff of Lothian and Borders at Linlithgow, since 1988; b. 6.12.31.

MacLean, Ian Teasdale, MA, LLB. Solicitor; Senior Partner, Mackie & Dewar, since 1982 (Partner, since 1968); Honorary Treasurer, Aberdeen YMCA, since 1970; b. 3.6.40, Stornoway; m., Lavinia May Symonds; 1 s.; 1 d. Educ. Nicolson Institute, Stornoway; Aberdeen University. Qualified as Solicitor, 1964, after three years' indenture with Morice & Wilson, Advocates in Aberdeen; salaried Solicitor, J.D. Mackie & Dewar, Advocates in Aberdeen, 1965-68. Address: (b.) 18 Bon-Accord Square, Aberdeen; T.-0224 596341.

MacLean, Ian Hamish, MBChB, FFPHM. Chief Administrative Medical Officer and Director of Public Health, Dumfries and Galloway Health Board, since 1989; Honorary Clinical Senior Lecturer, Glasgow University, since 1989; b. 9.10.47, Bishop's Stortford, Herts; m., Anne; 1 s.; 1 d. Educ. Felsted School; Dundee University. Consultant in Public Health Medicine, Borders Health Board, 1980-89. Recreations: music; sailing; flying; house restoration; photography. Address: (b.) Dumfries and Galloway Health Board, Nithbank, Dumfries, DG1 2SD; T.-0387 46246.

McLean, Jack, DA, MSIAD. Journalist and Broadcaster; b. Irvine, Ayrshire. Educ. Allan Glen's School, Glasgow; Edinburgh College of Art. Apprentice Welder, 1962-65; various jobs until 1968; Studio Artist, uncertificated Art Teacher, 1968-70; Edinburgh Art College; Jordanhill College of Education; Teacher of Art in Glasgow schools, until 1988; began writing with Times Educational Supplement with regular column; Columnist, The Scotsman, 1967-81; Columnist, Glasgow Herald, since 1981; Scottish Vice-Chairman and National Executive Member, National Union of Students, 1970-74; Member, Scottish Council, Educational Institute of Scotland, 1981-82; Member, Strathclyde Regional Council Education Committee, 1986-88. Commendation, Scottish Press Awards, 1985, 1986; Runner-up, Columnist of the Year, British Press Awards, 1985; Scottish Feature Writer of the Year, 1989; commended Columnist of the Year, 1989. Recreations: drinking in public houses (see A. Hind); flashy dressing; not playing tennis. Address: Glasgow Herald, 195 Albion Street, Glasgow, G1 1QP; T.-041-423 0380, 041-552 6255.

McLean, John David Ruari, CBE, DSC, Croix de Guerre. Typographer and Author; b. 10.6.17, Minnigaff; m., Antonia Maxwell Carlisle; 2 s.; 1 d. Educ. Dragon School, Oxford; Eastbourne College. Royal Navy, 1940-45; Tutor in Typography, Royal College of Art, 1948-51; Typographic Adviser, Hulton Press, 1953-60; The Observer, 1960-62; Art Editor, The Connoisseur, 1962-73; Founder-Partner, Rainbird, McLean Ltd., 1951-58; Founder Editor, Motif, 1958-67; Honorary Typographic Adviser to HM Stationery Office, 1966-80; Senior Partner, Ruari McLean Associates Ltd., 1960-81; Trustee, National Library of Scotland, 1981. Publications include: Modern Book Design, 1958; Victorian Book Design and Colour Printing, 1963; Magazine Design, 1969; Jan Tschichold, Typographer, 1975; The Thames & Hudson Manual of Typography, 1980; Benjamin Fawcett, Engraver and Colour Printer, 1988; Edward Bawden, war artist, and his letters home 1940-45 (Editor), 1989; Nicolas Bentley drew the pictures, 1990. Recreations: sailing; acquiring books. Address: (h.) Pier Cottage, Carsaig, Isle of Mull; T.-Pennyghael 216.

Maclean, John Robert, DL; b. 24.5.51, Lossiemouth; m., Veronica Mary Lacy Hulbert-Powell; 1 s.; 2 d. Educ. Milton Abbey School. Commissioned into Queen's Own Highlanders, 1971; left Army, 1978, and returned home to farm via Royal Agricultural College, Cirencester; Deputy Lieutenant, County of Moray, since 1987; Member, Royal Company of Archers (Queen's Bodyguard for Scotland), since 1988; Chairman, Elgin Branch, Earl Haig Fund; Member, Committee, Highland Branch, Scottish Landowners

Federation. Recreations: shooting; field sports. Address: (h.) Westfield House, near Elgin, Moray.

MacLean, Hon. Lord (Ranald Norman Munro MacLean), BA, LLB, LLM. Senator of the College of Justice, since 1990; Queen's Counsel, since 1977; b. 18.12.38, Aberdeen; m., Pamela Ross; 2 s.; 1 d. Educ. Inverness Royal Academy; Fettes College, Edinburgh; Cambridge University; Edinburgh University; Yale University. Advocate, 1964; Advocate Depute, 1972-75; Advocate Depute (Home), 1979-82. Recreations: hill-walking; bird watching. Address: (h.) 23 Rothesay Terrace, Edinburgh, EH3 7RY; T.-031-225 5240.

Maclean, Sir Robert (Alexander), KBE (1973), Kt (1955), LLD. Honorary Life President, A.F. Stoddard & Co. Ltd.; Deputy Lieutenant, Renfrewshire; b. 11.4.08, Cambuslang; m., Vivienne Neville Bourke; 2 s.; 2 d. Educ. High School of Glasgow. Partner, later a Senior Partner, James Templeton & Co., Glasgow, 1937-45; Chairman, A.F. Stoddard & Co. Ltd., 1946-83. Chairman, Glasgow Junior Chamber of Commerce, 1940; President, Glasgow Chamber of Commerce, 1956-58; Chairman, Scottish Council of Chambers of Commerce, 1960-62; President, Association of British Chambers of Commerce, 1966-68; Regional Controller (Scotland), Board of Trade, 1944-46; Regional Controller, Factory and Storage Control, 1941-44; Chairman, Scottish Industries Exhibitions, 1949, 1954, 1959; Chairman, Scottish Exports Committee, 1966-70; Chairman, Scottish Industrial Estates Corporation, 1955-72; President, British Industrial Exhibition, Moscow, 1966; Member, BNEC, 1966-70; Member, Scottish Aerodromes Board, 1950-61; Member, Export Council for Europe, 1960-64; Vice-Chairman, Scottish Board for Industry, 1952-60; a Vice-President, Scottish Council (Development and Industry), 1955-82. Recreations: golf; fishing. Address: (h.) South Branchal Farm, Bridge of Weir, Renfrewshire, PA11 3SJ; T.-Kilmacolm 2162.

MacLean, Sorley, MA (Hons). Poet; b. 1911, Osgaig, Raasay; m., Renee Cameron; 3 d. Educ. Portree High School; Edinburgh University. Teacher of English, Portree and Tobermory; Head, English Department, Boroughmuir School, Edinburgh; Headmaster, Plockton High School; Writer in Residence, Edinburgh University, 1973-75; Filidh (Resident Poet), Sabhal Mor Ostaig, 1975-76; author of: 17 Poems for 6d (with Robert Garioch), 1940; Dain do Eimhir, 1943; Four Points of a Saltire (Co-author), 1970; Poems to Eimhir (translated from the Gaelic by Iain Crichton Smith), 1971; Reothairt is Contraigh, Spring Tide and Neap Tide, Selected Poems 1932-72, 1977.

Maclean, William James, DA, RSA, FSA Scot. Lecturer in Fine Art, Duncan of Jordanstone College of Art, Dundee, since 1982; b. 12.10.41, Inverness; m., Marian Forbes Leven; 2 s.; 1 d. Educ. Inverness Royal Academy; HMS Conway; Grays School of Art, Aberdeen. Postgraduate and Travel Scholarship, Scottish Education Trust Award, Visual Arts Bursary, Scottish Arts Council; Benno Schotz Prize; one-man exhibitions in Rome, Glasgow, Edinburgh and London; group exhibitions in Britain, Europe and North America; represented in private and public collections including Arts Council, British Museum, Scottish National Gallery of Modern Art, Fitzwilliam Museum, Cambridge, and several Scottish galleries. Address: (h.) Bellevue, 18 Dougall Street, Tayport, Fife.

MacLeary, Alistair Ronald, MSc, DipTP, FRICS, FRTPI, FBIM, FRSA. Member, Lands Tribunal for Scotland; MacRobert Professor of Land Economy, Aberdeen University, 1976-89 (Dean, Faculty of Law, 1982-85); President, Planning and Development Division, Royal Institution of Chartered Surveyors, 1984-85; b. 12.1.40, Glasgow; m., Claire Leonard; 1 s.; 1 d. Educ. Inverness Royal Academy; College of Estate Management; Heriot-Watt University; Strathclyde University. Assistant Surveyor, Gerald Eve & Co., Chartered Surveyors, 1962-65; Assistant to Director, Murrayfield Real Estate Co. Ltd., 1965-67; Assistant Surveyor and Town Planner/Partner, Wright & Partners, 1967-76; seconded to Department of the Environment, London, 1971-73; Member, Committee of Inquiry into the Acquisition and Occupancy of Agricultural Land, 1977-79; Member, Home Grown Timber Advisory Committee, Forestry Commission, 1981-87; Chairman, Board of Education, Commonwealth Association of Surveying and Land Economy, 1981-90; Editor, Land Development Studies, 1986-90; Member, Natural Environment Research Council, 1988-91. Recreations: shooting; skiing; hill-walking. Address: (h.) St. Helen's, St. Andrew's Road, Ceres, Fife, KY15 5NQ; T.-033 482 8862.

MacLeay, Very Rev. John Henry James, MA. Dean of Argyll, since 1987; Rector, St. Andrew's, Fort William, since 1978; Canon, St. John's Cathedral, Oban, since 1980; b. 7.12.31, Inverness; m., Jane Speirs Cuthbert; 1 s.; 1 d. Educ. St. Edmund Hall, Oxford. Ordained Deacon, 1957; Priest, 1958; Curate: St. John's, East Dulwich, 1957-60, St. Michael's, Inverness, 1960-62; Rector, St. Michael's, Inverness, 1962-70; Priest-in-Charge, St. Columba's, Grantown-on-Spey and St. John's, Rothiemurchus, 1970-78. Recreations: fishing; reading; visiting churches and cathedrals. Address: St. Andrew's Rectory, Parade Road, Fort William, PH33 6BA; T.-0397 2979.

MacLehose of Beoch, Baron (Crawford Murray MacLehose), KT (1983), GBE (1976), KCMG (1971), KCVO (1975), DL, Hon. LLD (York, 1983, Strathclyde, 1984). Chairman, School of Oriental and African Studies, 1983-91; Chairman, Scottish Trust for the Physically Disabled and Margaret Blackwood Housing Association, 1983-91; Life Peer; 16.10.17; m.; 2 d. Educ. Rugby; Balliol College, Oxford. Served Second World War (Lt., RNVR); joined Foreign Service, 1947; Governor and C-in-C, Hong Kong, 1971-82. Address: (h.) Beoch, Maybole, Ayrshire.

McLeish, Henry Baird. MP (Labour), Central Fife, since 1987; b. 15.6.48.

McLellan, Rev. Andrew Rankin Cowie, MA, BD, STM. Minister, St. Andrew's and St. George's, Edinburgh, since 1986; b. 16.6.44, Glasgow; m., Irene L. Meek; 2 s. Educ. Kilmarnock Academy; Madras College, St. Andrews; St. Andrews University; Glasgow University; Union Theological Seminary, New York. Assistant Minister, St. George's West, Edinburgh, 1969-71; Minister, Cartsburn Augustine, Greenock, 1971-80; Minister, Viewfield, Stirling, 1980-86; Member, Inverclyde District Council, 1977-80; Tutor, Glasgow University, 1978-82; Honorary Secretary, Church and Nation Committee, General Assembly, 1988-91; Chaplain, HM Prison, Stirling, 1982-85; Chairman, George Street Association of Edinburgh. Recreations: golf; family; theatre; travel; books. Address: 25 Comely Bank, Edinburgh, EH4 1AJ; T.-031-332 5324.

McLellan, Douglas Richard, MD, MRCPath, DFM. Consultant Pathologist, Victoria Infirmary, Glasgow, since 1989; Honorary Senior Lecturer, Glasgow University, since 1989; b. 13.6.55, Glasgow; m., Caitriona; 3 s. Educ. High School of Glasgow; Glasgow University. Registrar in Pathology, Southern General Hospital, Glasgow, 1978-81; Honorary Senior Registrar in Neuropathology (MRC Head Injury Project), Institute of Neurological Sciences, Glasgow, 1981-84; Senior Registrar in Pathology, Western Infirmary, Glasgow, 1984-89. Recreations: bibliomania; Celtology. Address: (h.) 9 Selborne Road, Jordanhill, Glasgow, G13 1QG.

McLellan, James Alexander, LLB. Director of Administration, Argyll and Bute District Council, since 1978; b. 23.12.50, Lochgilphead; m., Alexis; 2 s.; 1 d. Educ. Keil School; Glasgow University. Recreations: fishing; rugby; gardening. Address: (b.) Kilmory, Lochgilphead, Argyll, PA31 8RT; T.-0546 2127.

McLelland, John, BVMS, MVSc, PhD, MRCVS. Reader, Department of Preclinical Veterinary Sciences, Edinburgh University, since 1981; b. 11.6.37, Kilmarnock; m., Morar; 1 s.; 2 d. Educ. Kilmarnock Academy; Glasgow Academy; Glasgow University; Liverpool University. Pig Industry Development Authority Scholar, Veterinary Hospital, Glasgow University, 1962-63; Egg Marketing Board Scholar, Department of Veterinary Anatomy, Liverpool University, 1964; Assistant Lecturer, then Lecturer, Department of Veterinary Anatomy, Liverpool University, 1964-72; Lecturer, then Senior Lecturer, Department of Veterinary Anatomy, Edinburgh University, 1972-81; Chairman, Sub-Committee on Systema Digestorium, International Committee on Avian Anatomical Nomenclature. Publications: Outlines of Avian Anatomy (Co-author), 1975; Form and Function in Birds (Co-editor), 1979, 1981, 1985, 1989; An Introduction to the Functional Anatomy of the Limbs of the Domestic Animals (Co-author), 1984; Birds: Their Structure and Function (Co-author), 1984; A Colour Atlas of Avian Anatomy, 1990. Recreations: cooking; travel. Address: (h.) 117/10 W. Savile Terrace, Edinburgh; T.-031-662 4588.

MacLennan, David Neall, BSc, FIOA. Deputy Director, Marine Laboratory, since 1986; b. 26.9.40, Aberdeen; m., Sheila Cormack; 1 s.; 1 d. Educ. Robert Gordon's College; Aberdeen University. Scientific Officer, AERE Harwell, 1962-67; Marine Laboratory, 1967-73; Head Office, Department of Agriculture and Fisheries for Scotland, 1973-75; returned to Marine Laboratory, 1976. Chairman, ICES Fish Capture Committee, 1986-89. Recreation: bridge. Address: (h.) 2 Stronsay Avenue, Aberdeen; T.-0224 876544.

Maclennan, Professor Duncan, MA, MPhil. Professor of Urban Economics and Finance, Glasgow University; Director, Centre for Housing Research, since 1983; Economic Adviser to OECD, Paris, since 1981; Director, Joseph Rowntree Memorial Trust Housing Finance Research Programme, since 1987; Board Member, Scottish Homes, since 1988; b. 12.3.49, Glasgow; 1 s.; 1 d. Educ. Allan Glen's Secondary School; Glasgow University. Lecturer in Applied Economics, Glasgow University, 1974-76; Lecturer in Political Economy, Aberdeen University, 1976-78; Lecturer in Applied Economics, Glasgow University, 1979-82; Chairman, National Steering Group for Care and Repair. Past President, Allan Glen's Rugby Club. Recreations: watching rugby; gardening; housework. Address: (b.) Centre for Housing Research, 25 Bute Gardens, Glasgow; T.-041-339 8855.

MacLennan, Finlay, QPM, FBIM. Deputy Chief Constable, Northern Constabulary, since 1985; Member, National Broadcasting Council for Scotland, 1987-91; b. 10.4.36, Harris; m., Barbara Patricia; 1 s.; 1 d. Educ. Portree High School; Garnett College, London. National Service, Cameron Highlanders, 1956-58; Metropolitan Police, 1958-85. Member, Board of Management, YMCA, Lambeth, 1979-82. Recreations: squash; shooting; hill-walking; sailing; fishing. Address: (b.) Police Headquarters, Perth Road, Inverness, IV2 3SY; T.-0463 239191.

Maclennan, Robert Adam Ross. MP (Lib. Dem.), Caithness and Sutherland; Lib. Dem. Spokesman on Home Affairs and the Arts, since 1988; Barrister-at-Law; b. 26.6.36, Glasgow; m., Helen Cutter Noyes; 2 s.; 1 d. Educ. Glasgow Academy; Balliol College, Oxford; Trinity College, Cambridge;

Columbia University, New York. Parliamentary Private Secretary to Secretary of State for Commonwealth Affairs, 1967; Opposition Spokesman on Scottish Affairs and Defence, 1970; Parliamentary Under-Secretary of State, Department of Prices and Consumer Protection, 1974; Opposition Spokesman on Foreign Affairs, 1979; Founder Member, SDP, 1981, and author of party's constitution; Parliamentary Spokesman on Agriculture, 1981, Home Affairs, 1983, Economic Affairs, 1987; elected Leader, SDP, 1987. Recreations: music; theatre; books. Address: (b.) House of Commons, London, SW1A 0AA; T.-071-219 4133.

MacLennan, Professor William Jardine, MD, FRCP, FRCPEdin, FRCPGlas. Professor of Geriatric Medicine, Edinburgh University, since 1986; Honorary Consultant Physician in Geriatric Medicine, Lothian Health Board, since 1986; b. 11.2.41, Glasgow; m., Fiona Hannah Campbell; 2 s. Educ. Hutchesons' Boys' Grammar School; Glasgow University. House Physician, Stobhill Hospital, Glasgow 1964; Hansen Research Scholar, then Assistant Lecturer, then Lecturer, Department of Materia Medica, Glasgow University, 1965-69; Senior Registrar in Geriatric Medicine, Stobhill General Hospital and Glasgow Western Infirmary, 1969-71; Senior Lecturer in Geriatric Medicine, Southampton University, 1971-80; Senior Lecturer, then Reader in Geriatric Medicine, Dundee University, 1980-86; Convener of Trustees, Dementia Services Development Centre; Member, Council of Professions Supplementary to Medicine; Chairman, Scientific Committee, British Geriatrics Society. Publications: books on clinical care of the elderly, drugs in the elderly and bone disease in the elderly, metabolic and endocrine disorders in the elderly. Recreations: hill-walking; ship-modelling; playing classical guitar badly. Address: (h.) 26 Caiystane Avenue, Fairmilehead, Edinburgh; T.-031-445 1755.

MacLeod, Andrew Kenneth, BA. Chief Executive, Scottish Fisheries Protection Agency, since 1991; b. 28.3.50, Elgin; m., Sheila Janet; 2 d. Educ. Fettes College, Edinburgh; St. John's College, Oxford. Nuffield College, Oxford, 1971-74; National Economic Development Office, 1974-78; Economic Adviser, Manpower Services Commission, Office for Scotland, 1978-83; Economic Adviser/Principal, Scottish Office, 1983-90; Head, Fisheries Division III, 1990-91. Address: (b.) Pentland House, 47 Robb's Loan, Edinburgh, EH14 1TW; T.-031-244 6059.

MacLeod, Archibald, OBE, NDA, NDD. Member, Red Deer Commission, since 1989; Chairman, Crofters Commission, 1986-89; b. 23.3.28, Kames, Argyll; m., Sheena Fleming Ferguson; 2 s.; 1 s deceased. Educ. Greenock High School; West of Scotland Agricultural College. Research Assistant, West of Scotland Agricultural College, 1949-53; Officer-in-Charge, Lephinmore Research Farm, Hill Farming Research Organisation, 1953-56; Senior Adviser (North Argyll), West of Scotland Agricultural College, 1956-66; Head of Advisory Services, Argyll Area, 1966-86. Past President: Oban Rotary Club, Oban Speakers Club; founder Chairman, West Cowal YFC; Honorary Vice-President, Lorn Agricultural Society. Recreations: shooting; curling; gardening; reading. Address: (h.) Craigielea, Kames, By Tighnabruaich, Argyll, PA21 2AE.

MacLeod, Calum Alexander, CBE, MA, LLB, LLD. Chairman, Britannia Life Ltd., since 1989; Chairman, The Harris Tweed Association Ltd., since 1984; Chairman, Aberdeen Petroleum PLC, since 1982; Chairman, Abtrust Scotland Investment Company PLC, since 1986; Chairman, Albyn of Stonehaven Ltd., since 1973; Deputy Chairman, Grampian Television PLC, since 1982; Deputy Chairman, Scottish Eastern Investment Trust PLC, since 1988; Director, Callanish Ltd., since 1986; Director, Bradstock Blunt (Scotland) Ltd., since 1990; Aberdeen Board Member, Bank of Scotland, since 1980; b. 25.7.35, Stornoway; m., Elizabeth M. Davidson; 2 s.; 1 d. Educ. Nicolson Institute; Glenurquhart School; Aberdeen University. Partner, Paull & Williamsons, Advocates, Aberdeen, 1964-80; Member, White Fish Authority, 1973-80; Member, North of Scotland Hydro-Electric Board, 1976-84; Member, Highlands and Islands Development Board, 1984-91; Chancellor's Assessor, Aberdeen University, 1984-90; Chairman of Governors, Robert Gordon's College, since 1981; Chairman, Scottish Council of Independent Schools, 1988-91; Chairman, SATRO North Scotland, 1986-90. Recreations: golf; motoring; hill-walking; reading; music. Address: (h.) 6 Westfield Terrace, Aberdeen, AB2 4RU; T.-0224 641614.

Macleod, Rev. Professor Donald, MA. Professor of Systematic Theology, Free Church College, since 1978; Editor, The Monthly Record, 1977-90; Vagrant Preacher, since 1978; b. 24.11.40, Ness, Isle of Lewis; m., Mary Maclean; 3 s. Educ. Nicolson Institute, Stornoway; Glasgow University; Free Church College. Ordained Guy Fawkes Day, 1964; Minister: Kilmallie Free Church, 1964-70, Partick Highland Free Church, Glasgow, 1970-78. Recreations: dreaming about cricket, fishing and gardening; Gaelic music. Address: (h.) 84 Craiglea Drive, Edinburgh; T.-031-447 6269.

Macleod, Donald Angus David, MB, ChB, FRCS Edin. Consultant General Surgeon, since 1976; Chairman, Lothian Health Board Basic Surgical Training Committee, 1986-91; b. 4.3.41, Selkirk; m., Lucile Janette Kirkpatrick; 1 s.; 2 d. Educ. Gordonstoun; Edinburgh University. Assistant Director of Studies (Surgery), Edinburgh Postgraduate Board for Medicine, 1976-86; Chairman, Scottish Committee, Medical Commission for Accident Prevention, 1980-85; Chairman, West Lothian Medical Staff Committee, 1986-89; Member, West Lothian Unit Management Team, 1987-89; Hon. Medical Adviser, Scottish Rugby Union, since 1969; Member, International Rugby Football Board Medical Advisory Committee, since 1978; Vice-Chairman, Medical Advisory Committee, 13th Commonwealth Games, Scotland, 1984-86; Chairman, Sports Medicine and Sports Science Consultative Group, Scottish Sports Council, since 1990. Recreation: orienteering. Address: (h.) The Haining, Woodlands Park, Livingston, West Lothian, EH54 8AT.

MacLeod, Donald Ian Kerr, RD*, MA, LLB, WS. Partner, Shepherd & Wedderburn, WS, since 1964; b. 19.4.37, Edinburgh; m., Mary St. Clair Bridge; 1 s.; 2 d. Educ. Aberdeen Grammar School; Aberdeen University; Edinburgh University. Apprentice, MacPherson & Mackay, WS, 1957-60; Assistant, Shepherd & Wedderburn, 1960-64; Solicitor in Scotland to HM Customs and Excise and Department of Employment, since 1970, and Health and Safety Executive, since 1974. Lt.-Cdr. RNR (Retd.); Member, Court of Session Rules Council and Rules of Court Review Group; Past President, East District, Scottish Hockey Association; Church Elder. Recreations: hockey (Class 1 international umpire); golf. Address: (b.) 16 Charlotte Square, Edinburgh, EH2 4YS; T.-031-225 8585.

MacLeod, Duncan James, CBE (1986), CA. Chartered Accountant; b. 1.11.34, Edinburgh; m., Joanna Bibby; 2 s.; 1 d. Educ. Eton College. Qualified CA, 1958; Partner, Brown Fleming & Murray, 1960; Managing Partner, Glasgow, Ernst & Whitney, 1985-89; Director: Bank of Scotland, 1973-91, Scottish Provident Institution, since 1975, Weir Group Plc, since 1976, Harry Ramsden's Plc, since 1989, Motherwell Bridge Holdings Ltd., since 1990; Member, Scottish Industrial Development Advisory Board, 1980 (Chairman, 1989); Member, Scottish Tertiary Education Advisory Council, 1984-87. Chief, Glasgow Skye Association. Recreations: golf; shooting. Address: (b.) 50 George Square, Glasgow, G2 1RR; T.-041-552 3456.

McLeod, Helen R. General Secretary, The Girls' Brigade Scotland, since 1981; b. 2.9.44, Glasgow. Educ. Hyndland Secondary School; Jordanhill College of Education. Local government officer, 1961-78; community education worker, 1980-81. Secretary, Strathclyde Conference of Voluntary Youth Organisations. Recreations: music; photography; reading. Address: (b.) Boys' Brigade House, 168 Bath Street, Glasgow, G2 4TQ; T.-041-332 1765.

MacLeod, Professor Iain Alasdair, BSc, PhD, CEng, FICE, FIStructE. Professor of Structural Engineering, Strathclyde University, since 1981; b. 4.5.39, Glasgow; m., Barbara Jean Booth; 1 s.; 1 d. Educ. Lenzie Academy; Glasgow University. Design Engineer, Crouch and Hogg, Glasgow, 1960-62; Assistant Lecturer in Civil Engineering, Glasgow University, 1962-66; Design Engineer, H.A. Simons Ltd., Vancouver, 1966-67; Structural Engineer, Portland Cement Association, Illinois, 1968-69; Lecturer in Civil Engineering, Glasgow University, 1969-73; Professor and Head, Department of Civil Engineering, Paisley College of Technology, 1973-81; Chairman, Scottish Branch, Institution of Structural Engineers, 1985-86; Vice-President, Institution of Structural Engineers, 1989-90; Member, Standing Committee on Structural Safety, since 1989. Recreations: climbing; sailing. Address: (b.) Department of Civil Engineering, Strathclyde University, 107 Rottenrow, Glasgow; T.-041-552 4400.

Macleod, Ian Buchanan, BSc, MB, ChB, FRCSEdin. Consultant Surgeon, Royal Infirmary, Edinburgh, since 1969; Honorary Senior Lecturer, Department of Clinical Surgery, Edinburgh University, since 1969; Surgeon to the Queen in Scotland, since 1987; b. 20.5.33, Wigan; m., Kathleen Gillean Large; 1 s.; 1 d. Educ. Wigan Grammar School; Edinburgh University. House Surgeon and House Physician, Royal Infirmary, Edinburgh, 1957-59; National Service, RAMC, Malaya, Singapore, Nepal, 1959-61; appointments, Department of Clinical Surgery, Edinburgh University and Royal Infirmary, Edinburgh, since 1961. Editor, Journal, Royal College of Surgeons of Edinburgh, 1982-87. Publications: Principles and Practice of Surgery (Co-author), 1985; Farquharson's Text Book of Operative Surgery (Contributor), 1986; Companion to Medical Studies (Contributor), 1981, 1985. Recreations: golf; photography. Address: (h.) Derwent House, 32 Cramond Road North, Edinburgh, EH4 6JE; T.-031-336 1541.

MacLeod, Rev. Ian Ingram Scott, MA, BD. Minister, Church of Scotland (retired); Chaplain, Little Cairnie Hospital, Arbroath, since 1986; b. 8.8.25, Leeds; m., Alice L. Duncan; 2 d. Educ. Biggar High School; Dollar Academy; Edinburgh University; Aberdeen University. Army Service, Royal Artillery, 1944-47, finally Staff Captain; Assistant, St. Francis in the East, Bridgeton, Glasgow, 1952-54; Minister, Jamestown Parish, Dunbartonshire, 1954-59; Minister, St. Andrews, Arbroath, 1959-91. Recreations: tennis; languages; travel; walking. Address: (h.) Clunie, 13 Trinity Fields Crescent, Brechin, Angus, DD9 6YF; T.-0356 625599.

MacLeod, Professor James Summers, LLM, CA, FTII. Partner, Ernst & Young, Edinburgh, since 1973; Professor, Department of Accountancy, Edinburgh University, since 1986; b. 3.8.41, Dumfries; m., Sheila Stromier; 2 s.; 1 d. Educ. Dumfries Academy; Glasgow University. Lecturer, Edinburgh University, 1965-68; Lecturer, Heriot Watt University, 1968-71; joined Arthur Young (now Ernst & Young), 1971. Publication: Taxation on Insurance Business (Co-author), 3rd edition, 1992. Recreations: bridge; music; reading. Address: (h.) 2 Bonaly Road, Edinburgh; T.-031-441 4144.

MacLeod of MacLeod, John. 29th Chief of Clan MacLeod; b. 10.8.35.

McLeod, John, FRAM. Composer, Conductor and Lecturer; Visiting Lecturer in Composition, Napier Polytechnic of Edinburgh; Course Director, Composing for Film and Television, London College of Music; b. 8.3.34, Aberdeen; m., Margaret Murray; 1 s.; 1 d. Educ. Aberdeen Grammar School; Royal Academy of Music, London. Director of Music, Merchiston Castle School, 1974-85; Visiting Lecturer, RSAMD, 1985-89; Ida Carroll Research Fellow, Royal Northern College of Music, 1988-89; Guest Conductor: Scottish National Orchestra, Scottish Chamber Orchestra, BBC Scottish Symphony Orchestra; Associate Composer, Scottish Chamber Orchestra, 1980-82; Guinness Prize for British Composers, 1979; Radio Forth Award for Composition, 1981; UK Music Education Award, 1982. Recreations: reading; films; theatre; art galleries; walking. Address: (h.) 9 Redford Crescent, Colinton, Edinburgh, EH13 OBS; T.-031-441 3035.

Macleod, Rev. John, MA. Minister, Free Church of Scotland congregation of Duthil-Dores, since 1983; b. 1.1.39, Shawbost, Isle of Lewis; m., Mary Macarthur. Educ. Nicolson Institute, Stornoway; Aberdeen University; Aberdeen College of Education. Torry Academy, Aberdeen: Assistant Teacher of General Subjects, 1961-66, Principal Teacher of Modern Studies, 1966-80. Recreations: gardening; local history. Address: Free Church Manse, Tomatin, Inverness-shire.

MacLeod, Rev. John, MA, DipTh. Minister, Tarbat Free Church of Scotland, Portmahomack, since 1978; b. 14.5.48, Fearn; m., Veda Joy Morrison; 6 s.; 1 d. Educ. Tain Royal Academy; Aberdeen University; Free Church College, Edinburgh. Standard Life Assurance Co., 1969-71; Free Church Missioner to Students, Aberdeen, 1974-75; Free Church Lecturer in Religious Studies, Aberdeen College of Education, 1974-75; Preacher, Highland Church, Vancouver, 1976; Preacher, Free Church of Scotland Western Charge, Prince Edward Island, 1977-78; Convener, Psalmody Committee, Free Church of Scotland, 1982-84; Chairman, Moray Firth Radio Christian Council, 1983-88; Publicity Officer, Free Presbytery of Ross, since 1984; Clerk, Training of the Ministry and Admissions Committee, Free Church of Scotland, since 1986; Clerk, Free Presbytery of Ross, since 1990. Recreations: squeezing quarts into pint pots and getting blood out of stones. Address: Free Church Manse, Portmahomack, Tain, Ross-shire, IV20 1YL; T.-086287 467.

Macleod, John Alasdair Johnston, DL, MRCGP, DCH, DObsRCOG. General Practitioner, North Uist, since 1973; Secretary, Western Isles Local Medical Committee (GP), 1977-91; Deputy Lieutenant, Western Isles, since 1979; b. 20.1.35, Stornoway; m., Lorna Jean Ferguson; 2 s.; 1 d. Educ. Nicolson Institute; Keil School; Glasgow University. National Service, Royal Navy, 1957-59; hospital posts, Glasgow and London, 1963-73; Non-Executive Director, Olscot Ltd., since 1969; trainer in general practice, since 1975; Visiting Professor, Department of Family Medicine, University of North Carolina, since 1985. Member, Committee of North Uist Highland Gathering; Fellow, Royal Society of Medicine; Admiralty Surgeon and Agent, 1974-91; author of papers and articles, singly and jointly, on aspects of isolated practice. Recreations: boating; horticulture; photography; time-sharing. Address: (h.) Tigh-Na-Hearradh, Lochmaddy, Isle of North Uist, PA82 5AE; T.-08763 224.

Macleod, John Francis Matheson, MA, LLB, NP. Solicitor in Inverness, since 1959; Dean, Faculty of Solicitors of the Highlands, 1988-91; Chairman, Crofters Commission, 1978-86; Member, Council, Law Society of Scotland, since 1988; b. 24.1.32, Inverness; m., Alexandra Catherine; 1 s. Educ. Inverness Royal Academy; George Watson's College; Edinburgh University. Solicitor, Fife County Council, 1957-59; in private practice, since 1959; Parliamentary candidate (Liberal): Moray and Nairn, 1964, Western Isles, 1966;

Chairman, Highland Region, Scottish Liberal Party, until 1978; former Vice-Chairman, Broadcasting Council for Scotland. Address: (b.) 28 Queensgate, Inverness; T.-0463 239393.

Macleod, John Murray, MA. Freelance Journalist and Broadcaster; b. 15.4.66, Kilmallie, Inverness-shire. Educ. Jordanhill College School, Glasgow; James Gillespie's High School, Edinburgh; Edinburgh University. Columnist, The Herald and The Scotsman; also writer of interviews/profiles. Scottish Journalist of the Year, 1991; Young Scottish Journalist of the Year, 1991-92. Recreations: cycling; corresponding; photography; Dr Who; applied Free Presbyterianism. Address: (h.) 84 Craiglea Drive, Edinburgh, EH10 5PH; T.-031-447 6269.

MacLeod, Emeritus Professor Malcolm, MD (Hons), FRCPEdin. Professor Emeritus in Renal Medicine, Aberdeen University; b. 9.12.16, Glasgow; m., Elizabeth Shaw Ritchie; 1 s. Educ. Nicolson Institute, Stornoway; Aberdeen University. Military Service, Africa, India, SE Asia, 1940-46 (Medical Specialist, RAMC); Lecturer, Senior Lecturer, Reader in Medicine, 1947-80; Personal Professor in Renal Medicine, Aberdeen University, 1981; Honorary Consultant Physician, Aberdeen Royal Infirmary, 1955-82 and Honorary Consultant in charge, Medical Renal Unit, 1966-82; President, Scottish Society of Physicians, 1980. Recreation: natural history. Address: (h.) 76 Hamilton Place, Aberdeen, AB2 4BA; T.-0224 635537.

Macleod, Rev. Murdo Alexander, MA. Minister, Stornoway Free Church, since 1984; Moderator, Lewis Presbytery, Free Church of Scotland, 1984-85; b. 15.10.35, Stornoway; m., Annie Bella Nicolson; 5 s.; 1 d. Educ. Nicolson Institute, Stornoway; Aberdeen University; Free Church College. Minister: Drumchapel Free Church, Glasgow, 1966-72, Dingwall Free Church, 1972-78, Greyfriars, Inverness, 1978-84. Recreations: walking; talking. Address: Free Church Manse, Stornoway, Lewis; T.-Stornoway 2279.

Macleod, Murdoch, MBE, JP. General Manager, Secretary and Treasurer, Stornoway Pier and Harbour Commission, since 1975; Honorary Sheriff; b. 11.8.32, Shawbost, Isle of Lewis; m., Crisybil; 1 s.; 1 d. Educ. Nicolson Institute, Stornoway. Ross and Cromarty Council: Highways Department, 1955-57, Education Department, 1957-65; Stornoway Town Council: Town Clerk's Department, 1965-68, Town Clerk, 1968-75. Deputy Chairman, Transport Users Consultative Committee for Scotland; Past Chairman, District Courts Association; Chairman, Western Isles Justices Committee; Chairman, Scottish Port Members, British Ports Federation; Chairman, Western Isles Arts Guild, Western Isles District of Scottish Community Drama Association; Director, Western Isles Development Fund Ltd.; Vice-Chairman, Lewis Pipe Band; Member, British Airways Consumer Council for Highlands and Islands; Chairman, League of Friends, Stornoway Hospitals and Homes. Recreations: fair weather golf; reading. Address: (h.) 46 Barony Square, Stornoway, Isle of Lewis; T.-0851 3024.

MacLeod, Sheriff Norman Donald, QC, MA, LLB. Sheriff Principal of Glasgow and Strathkelvin, since 1986; Commissioner of Northern Lighthouses, since 1986; b. 6.3.32, Perth; m., Ursula Jane Bromley; 2 s.; 2 d. Educ. Mill Hill School; George Watson's Boys College; Edinburgh University; Hertford College, Oxford. Called to the Bar, 1956; District Officer and Crown Counsel, Colonial Service, East Africa, 1957-63; at the Bar, 1963-67; Sheriff at Glasgow, 1967-86. Recreation: rustic pursuits. Address: (b.) 1 Carlton Place, Glasgow, G5 9DA; T.-041-429 8888.

MacLeod, Peter, AIB (Scot). Retired Banker; Honorary Sheriff, Oban, since 1988; b. 9.6.33, Ruaig, Isle of Tiree; m., Jean MacDonald Buchanan; 2 s. Educ. Oban High School. Served as Captain, Royal Signals, AER; joined Royal Bank of Scotland, 1949; Bank Manager: Tobermory, Kinlochleven, Wick, Oban. Past Commodore, Royal Highland Yacht Club. Publication: History of Royal Highland Yacht Club, 1881-1986. Recreations: sailing; genealogy; island wandering; immortal memories; impromptu ceilidhs. Address: (h.) The Wheelhouse, Ganavan, Oban, Argyll; T.-0631 63577.

MacLeod, Rev. Roderick, MA (Hons), BD, PhD. Minister, Cumlodden, Lochfyneside and Lochgair, Argyll, since 1985; b. 24.6.41, Lochmaddy. Educ. Paible Secondary School; Portree High School; Edinburgh University. Minister, Berneray, North Uist, 1966-85; Member: Western Isles Islands Council, 1974-82, Western Isles Health Board, 1975-79; Clerk, Uist Presbytery, 1981-85; Mackinnon Memorial Lecturer, Cape Breton College, 1979; Visiting Scholar, Harvard Divinity School, 1981; Editor, Gaelic Supplement, Life and Work, since 1980; Founder, Cruisgean (Gaelic newspaper); author of several Gaelic books; writes and broadcasts on Highland affairs in Gaelic and English. Recreations: walking; shinty. Address: Furnace, Inveraray, Argyll, PA32 8XU.

MacLeod, Rev. William, BSc, ThM. Minister, Partick Free Church, since 1976; b. 2.11.51, Stornoway; m., Marion Johnston; 1 s. Educ. Nicolson Institute; Aberdeen University; Free Church College; Westminster Theological Seminary, USA. Chaplain to Free Church Eventide Home, 1976-79; Free Church Lecturer in Religious Studies, Jordanhill College of Education, 1977-83; Moderator, Glasgow Presbytery, Free Church, 1983-84; Exit Examiner in Theology, Free Church College, 1981-86; Chairman, Lord's Day Observance Society, Glasgow Branch, 1979-90; Convener, Church Extension Committee, Free Church, 1984-85. Recreations: reading; gardening; angling. Address: 64 Woodend Drive, Glasgow; T.-041-959 5648.

Macleod Nicol, Nancy, RGN, ONC, RCNT, RNT. Head, Continuing Education Department, Lothian College of Nursing and Midwifery, since 1991; b. 31.7.39, Edinburgh. Educ. Mary Erskine School for Girls, Edinburgh; Jordanhill College of Education, Glasgow. Staff nurse to senior nursing officer, 1962-84; held teaching posts, South Lothian College of Nursing and Midwifery, from 1986; elected Member, National Board for Nursing Midwifery and Health Visiting; President, Clan Macleod Society of Scotland. Publication: Basic Management for Staff Nurses, 1991. Recreations: genealogy; walking; gardening. Address: (h.) Muiravonside, 25 Coltbridge Avenue, Edinburgh, EH12 6AF; T.-031-337 8353.

McLevy, Harry. Regional Officer, Amalgamated Engineering Union, since 1985; Member, General Council, Scottish TUC, since 1986; b. 28.8.36, Dundee; m., Doris Laburn; 3 s.; 1 d. Educ. Logie Junior Secondary. Address: (b.) 145 West Regent Street, Glasgow; T.-041-248 7131.

McLusky, Donald S., BSc, PhD. Senior Lecturer in Biology, Stirling University, since 1977 (Head, Department of Biological Science, 1985); Council Member, Editor of Bulletin, Estuarine and Coastal Sciences Association, since 1983; b. 27.6.45, Harrogate; m., Ruth Alicia Donald; 1 s.; 2 d. Educ. Latymer Upper School, London; Aberdeen University; Stirling University. Stirling University: Assistant Lecturer, 1968-70, Lecturer, 1970-77; Council Member, Scottish Marine Biological Association, 1976-82 and 1985-91; Member, Central Region Valuation Appeal Committee. Publications: Ecology of Estuaries, 1971; Physiology and Behaviour of Marine Organisms, 1977; The Estuarine Ecosystem, 1989; The Natural Environment of the Estuary and Firth of Forth, 1987; North Sea – Estuarine Interactions,

1990. Recreations: walking; swimming; travel. Address: (h.) Ardoch Cottage, Strathyre, Callander, FK18 8NF; T.-08774 309.

McMahon, Hugh Robertson, MA (Hons). Member (Labour), European Parliament, Strathclyde West, since 1984; b. 17.6.38, Saltcoats; m., Helen Paterson Grant; 1 s.; 1 d. Educ. Stevenson High School; Ardrossan Academy; Glasgow University. Schoolteacher in Ayrshire (Largs High, Stevenston High, Irvine Royal Academy, Mainholm Academy); Assistant Head, Ravenspark Academy, 1971-84. Recreation: golf. Address: (b.) Abbeymill Business Centre, Paisley, PA1 1JN; T.-041-889 9990.

McMahon, Michael Kenneth Cowan, BA, PhD, DipLing. Senior Lecturer in English Language, Glasgow University, since 1987; b. 7.8.43, Winchester; m., Rev. Janet P.H. MacMahon; 1 s.; 1 d. Educ. Hymers College, Hull; Durham University; Glasgow University; Reading University. Lecturer in Phonetics and Linguistics, Jordanhill College, Glasgow, 1968-72; Lecturer in Linguistics and Phonetics, Glasgow University, 1972-83, Lecturer in English Language, 1983-87. Member, Council, International Phonetic Association; Member, Executive Committee, Henry Sweet Society; Archivist, British Association of Academic Phoneticians. Publications include: Basic Phonetics, 1988. Recreations: music; running. Address: (h.) 6 Jubilee Gardens, Bearsden, Glasgow, G61 2RT; T.-041-942 3671.

McMahon, Rev. Robert James, BD. Minister, Crossford with Kirkfieldbank, since 1976; b. 28.1.27, Glasgow; m., Jessie Millar Steele; 3 s.; 3 d. Educ. Strathbungo School; Glasgow University. Journalist, Glasgow, 1943-56; student 1953-59; ordained by Glasgow Presbytery, 1959; Missionary, Church of Scotland, Seoni, Central India, 1960-75 (Minister, United Church of Northern India and from 1970 of the Church of North India). Moderator, Lanark Presbytery, 1982. Publication: To God Be The Glory (account of the Evangelical Fellowship of India 1951-1971). Address: The Manse, Crossford, Carluke, ML8 5RE; T.-055-586 415.

McManus, Colin Francis, QFSM, BA, MIFireE. Commandant, Scottish Fire Service Training School, since 1988; b. 15.9.40, Stalybridge; m., Dorothy; 2 d. Educ. Xaverian College, Manchester. Fire service career, 1959-86, starting in Cheshire and ending in Greater Manchester as Deputy Chief Fire Officer, 1981-86; joined Fire Service College as Senior Course Director, then Head of Command Studies. Recreations: golf; gardening. Address: (b.) Scottish Fire Service Training School, Gullane, East Lothian; T.-0620 842236.

McManus, John, DSC, PhD, ARCS, DIC, FRSE, CGeol, MIEnvSci. Reader in Geology, St. Andrews University, since 1988; Honorary Director, Tay Estuary Research Centre, since 1979; b. 5.6.38, Harwich; m., J. Barbara Beveridge; 2 s.; 1 d. Educ. Harwich County High School; Imperial College, London University. Assistant, then Lecturer, St. Andrews University, 1964-67; Lecturer, Senior Lecturer, Reader, Dundee University, 1967-88; UNESCO Representative, International Commission on Continental Erosion, 1980-84 and since 1986; Member, Nature Conservancy Council (Scotland) S.E. Region Board; former Member, Council, Estuarine and Brackish Water Sciences Association; former Treasurer, British Sedimentological Research Group; Consultant on Coastal Erosion and Protection to four Regional Councils; Associate Editor, Continental Shelf Research. President: Cupar Choral Association, 1968-78, Cupar Amateur Opera, since 1978. Recreations: music; bird-watching; swimming; stamp collecting. Address: (b.) Department of Geography and Geology, Purdie Building, St. Andrews University, St. Andrews, Fife, KY16 9ST.

McManus, Rev. Matthew Francis. Parish Priest, Kilwinning; Convenor, Association of Scottish Local Health Councils, since 1983; b. 22.9.40, Rutherglen. Educ. Sacred Heart High School, Girvan; St. Andrew's College, Drygrange. Ordained, 1965, Assistant Priest, St. Margaret's, Ayr; Parish Priest, New Cumnock, Kirkconnel and Sanquhar, 1976-81, Kirkcudbright, 1981-88; Chairman, Dumfries and Galloway Local Health Council, 1985-87; Chairman, Castle Douglas District CAB, 1984-87; Chairman, Stewartry Council of Voluntary Service, 1985-88; Chairman, Stewartry School Council, 1985-87; Member, Scottish Consumer Council, 1983-90; Member, Complaints Committee, Law Society of Scotland, since 1985; Secretary, Association of Vocations Directors of Scotland, since 1987. Address: St. Winin's, St. Winning's Lane, Kilwinning, KA13 6EP; T.-Kilwinning 52276.

McMaster, Brian John, CBE. Director, Edinburgh International Festival, since 1991; b. 9.5.43. General Administrator, subsequently Managing Director, WNO, 1976-91.

McMaster, Gordon James, MP, MIHort, CertEd. MP (Labour), Paisley South, since 1990; b. 13.2.60, Johnstone. Educ. Johnstone High School; Langside College; West of Scotland Agricultural College, Jordanhill College. Began career as apprentice gardener, 1976; Lecturer, then Senior Lecturer in Horticulture, Langside College, 1980-89; Co-ordinator, Growing Concern (Strathclyde), 1989-90. Former Member, Renfrew District Council (Leader, 1988-90). Recreations: gardening; reading; writing. Address: (h.) 36 Bevan Grove, Johnstone, PA5 8TP; T.-041-848 9004.

MacMillan, Professor Andrew, MA, FRIAS, RIBA, RSA. Professor of Architecture and Head, Mackintosh School of Architecture, Glasgow University, since 1973; b. 11.12.28, Glasgow; m., Angela Lillian McDowell; 1 s.; 3 d. Educ. North Kelvinside Secondary School; Glasgow School of Architecture. Glasgow Corporation, 1945-52; East Kilbride Development Corporation, 1952-54; joined Gillespie Kidd & Coia, 1954 (Partner, 1966); has served as a Member of: CNAA Architecture Board, ARCUK Board of Architectural Education, Scottish Arts Council WASPS Board, GIA Education Committee; Vice President for Education, RIBA; Vice President, Prince and Princess of Wales Hospice, 1981; RIBA Bronze Medal, 1965; RIBA Award for Architecture, four times; RSA Gold Medal, 1975; Concrete Society Award, 1978; Carpenter Award, 1982, 1983; various Saltire Society and Civic Trust awards; Member, Forum, Scottish Churches Architectural Heritage Trust; Patron, Arts Education Trust, since 1988. Recreations: travel; sailing; water colour. Address: (b.) Mackintosh School of Architecture, Glasgow University and Glasgow School of Art, 177 Renfrew Street, Glasgow, G3 6RQ; T.-041-332 9797.

MacMillan, George Gordon, MA (Cantab). Chief of Clan MacMillan; Deputy Lieutenant, Renfrewshire; b. 20.6.30, London; m., (Cecilia) Jane Spurgin; 2 s. Educ. Aysgarth School; Eton; Trinity College, Cambridge. Schoolmaster, Wellington College, 1953-63; Lecturer, Trinity College, Toronto, 1963-64; Lecturer, Bede College, Durham, 1965-74. Owner, small historic house with gardens and woods open to the public. Address: (h.) Finlaystone, Langbank, Renfrewshire, PA14 6TJ; T.-Langbank 285.

MacMillan, Hector. Playwright; b. 1929, Glasgow. Author of: The Rising, Dundee Repertory Theatre, 1973; The Sash, Pool Theatre, Edinburgh, 1973; The Royal Visit, Dundee Repertory, 1974; The Gay Gorbals, Traverse, Edinburgh, 1976; Oh What A Lovely Peace, Scottish Youth Theatre, Edinburgh, 1977; Past Chairman, Scottish Society of Playwrights.

Macmillan, Sheriff Iain Alexander, CBE, LLD, BL. Sheriff of South Strathclyde, Dumfries and Galloway, at Hamilton, since 1981; b. 14.11.23, Oban; m., Edith Janet McAulay; 2 s.; 1 d. Educ. Oban High School; Glasgow University; Scottish Commercial College. RAF (France, Germany, India), 1944-47; Solicitor (Sturrock & Co., Kilmarnock), 1952-81; Council Member, Law Society of Scotland, 1964-79 (President, 1976-77); Chairman, Lanarkshire Branch, Scottish Association for the Study of Delinquency, since 1986. Recreations: golf; hill-walking; photography; music. Address: (h.) 2 Castle Drive, Kilmarnock, Ayrshire; T.-0698 282957.

McMillan, John Boyd, BSc. Rector, Invergordon Academy, since 1986; b. 16.12.41, Irvine; m., Kathleen Miller; 2 s. Educ. Irvine Royal Academy; Glasgow University; Jordanhill College of Education. Mathematics Teacher: Irvine Royal Academy, 1964-67, Gloucester School, Hohne, 1967-72, Invergordon Academy, 1972-74; Principal Teacher of Mathematics, Thurso High School, 1974-82; Assistant Rector, Alness Academy, 1982-86; In-Service Training Co-ordinator, HRC, Inverness, 1986; President, Highland Secondary Heads Association; Chairman, Highland Education Industry Liaison Committee; President, Highland Secondary Heads Association, 1988-90; President, Invergordon Highland Gathering. Football Blue. Recreations: gardening; public speaking. Address: (b.) Invergordon Academy, Academy Road, Invergordon, IV18 0LD; T.-0349 852362.

Macmillan, (John) Duncan, MA, PhD. Reader, Department of Fine Art, Edinburgh University; Curator, Talbot Rice Gallery and University Collections, Edinburgh University, since 1979; b. 7.3.39, Beaconsfield; m., Vivien Rosemary Hinkley; 2 d. Educ. Gordonstoun School; St. Andrews University; London University; Edinburgh University. Lecturer, then Senior Lecturer, Department of Fine Art, Edinburgh University; Chairman, Scottish Society for Art History. Recreation: walking. Address: (h.) 20 Nelson Street, Edinburgh; T.-031-556 7100.

MacMillan, John MacFarlane Bute, MBE, MC. Chairman, Taste of Scotland Scheme Ltd.; Chairman, The Murrayfield PLC; b. 12.8.17, Rothesay; m., Rosaline Daphne May Spencer; 1 s.; 1 d. Educ. Allan Glen's School, Glasgow. Regular Army Officer, Royal Artillery, 1939-57; General Manager, then Managing Director, D.S. Crawford Ltd., 1958-62; Director, United Biscuits (Holdings) Ltd., 1962-82; Chairman, D.S. Crawford Ltd., 1979-82; Chairman, UB Restaurants Ltd., 1979-82. Recreations: bird-watching; walking; swimming; tennis. Address: (h.) 24 Cammo Gardens, Edinburgh, EH4 8EQ; T.-031-339 6501.

McMillan, Joyce Margaret, MA (Hons), DipEd. Journalist and Theatre Critic; Social/Political Columnist, Scotland on Sunday, since 1989; Radio Critic, Glasgow Herald, since 1983; Scottish Theatre Critic, The Guardian, since 1984; b. 29.8.52, Paisley. Educ. Paisley Grammar School; St. Andrews University; Edinburgh University. Theatre Reviewer, BBC Radio Scotland and The Scotsman, 1979-81; Theatre Critic, Sunday Standard, 1981-83. Secretary, NUJ Freelance Branch, Edinburgh. Recreations: food; drink; films; music; talking politics; playing with babies. Address: 8 East London Street, Edinburgh, EH7 4BH; T.-031-557 1726.

Macmillan, Marie Alpine, JP. Chairman, Western Isles Health Board, since 1979; b. 26.4.24, Stornoway; m., Ian M. Macmillan, LDS, RFPS; 1 s.; 1 d. Educ. Hyndland School, Glasgow; West of Scotland Commercial College, Glasgow. Member: Office of Electricity Regulation Northern Scotland Consumers Committee, Supplementary Benefit Appeals Tribunal, National Insurance Appeals Tribunal, Justices Committee. Recreations: reading; sewing; golf. Address: (h.) 22 Matheson Road, Stornoway, Isle of Lewis; T.-0851 2760.

Mcmillan, Michael Dale, BSc, LLB, NP. Partner, Macdonalds Sergeants, Solicitors, East Kilbride and Glasgow, since 1971; b. 15.2.44, Edinburgh; m., Isobel Ross Mackie; 2 s.; 1 d. Educ. Edinburgh Academy; Edinburgh University. Secretary: East Kilbride Chamber of Commerce, 1971-86, East Kilbride Chamber of Trade, since 1971; Member, East Kilbride Development Corporation, 1979-84; Secretary, Pilgrim Legal Users' Group, since 1985; Captain, East Kilbride Golf Club, 1979; Chairman, Strathaven Academy School Board, since 1991; President, East Kilbride Burns Club, since 1989. Recreations: golf; sailing; skiing. Address: (h.) Bonnanhill House, Sandford, Strathaven, Lanarkshire; T.-Strathaven 21210.

McMillan, William Alister, BL. Solicitor, since 1955; b. 19.1.34, Ayr; m., Elizabeth Anne; 3 d. Educ. Strathallan; Glasgow University. Clerk of the Peace, County of Ayr, 1974-75; Honorary Sheriff, Ayr; Governor, Strathallan School. Recreations: sailing; golf; philately. Address: (h.) Afton Lodge, Mossblown, by Ayr; T.-0292 520 710.

Macmillan, Rt. Rev. William Boyd Robertson, MA, BD, HonLLD (Dundee), Hon. DD (Aberdeen). Minister, Dundee Parish Church (St. Mary's), since 1978; Convener, Board of Practice and Procedure, 1984-88, and of Business Committee, 1985-88, General Assembly, Church of Scotland; Moderator, General Assembly, 1991-92; Chaplain in Ordinary to The Queen in Scotland, since 1988; b. 3.7.27, Keith; m., Mary Adams Bisset Murray. Educ. Royal High School, Edinburgh; Aberdeen University. Royal Navy, 1946-48; Aberdeen University, 1948-54 (President, SRC, 1953-54); Minister: St. Andrew's Church, Bo'ness, 1955-60, Fyvie Parish Church, 1960-67, Bearsden South Church, 1967-78. President, Church Service Society; Chaplain, City of Dundee District Council; Freeman of Dundee, 1991. Recreations: golf; reading. Address: Manse of Dundee, 371 Blackness Road, Dundee, DD2 1ST; T.-0382 69406.

Macnab of Macnab, Hon. Mrs. Chairman, Scotland's Gardens Scheme, since 1983; b. 6.6.36, Edinburgh; m., J.C. Macnab of Macnab (qv); 2 s.; 2 d. Address: (h.) West Kilmany House, Cupar, KY15 4QW.

Macnab of Macnab, James Charles – The Macnab. Senior Consultant, Hill Samuel Investment Services Ltd., since 1982; 23rd Chief, Clan Macnab; b. 14.4.26, London; m., Hon. Diana Mary Anstruther-Gray (see Hon. Mrs. Macnab of Macnab); 2 s.; 2 d. Educ. Radley College; Ashbury College, Ottawa. Served, RAF and Scots Guards, 1944-45; Lt., Seaforth Highlanders, 1945-48; Assistant Superintendant and Deputy Superintendant, Federation of Malaya Police Force, 1948-57; Captain, Seaforth Highlanders (TA), 1960-64; managed family estate and farms, 1957-82; County Councillor, Perth and Kinross Joint County Council, 1964-75; District Councillor, Perth, 1961-64; JP, 1968-86; Member, Central Regional Council, 1978-82; Member, Queen's Bodyguard for Scotland (Royal Company of Archers). Address: (h.) West Kilmany House, Kilmany, Cupar, Fife, KY15 4QW.

Macnab, Joan Catherine Mackenzie, BSc, PhD, FRCPath. Senior Scientist, Medical Research Council Institute of Virology, Glasgow University, since 1980; Honorary Lecturer, Glasgow University, since 1976; b. Netherlee, Glasow; m., Alastair James Macnab; 3 s. Educ. Glasgow High School for Girls; Glasgow University. Early minor appointments in NHS and on grants; Research Assistant to Professor Guido Pontecorvo (Genetics), Glasgow University; Scientist, MRC Institute of Virology. Publications: numerous papers on the role of viruses in oncogenic disease. Recreations: skiing; squash; hill-walking; landscape gardening; horticulture. Address: Medical Research Council, Institute of Virology, Glasgow University, Glasgow, G11 5JR; T.-041-339 8855.

McNair, James Burt Oliver, BSc (Hons), DipEd. Headteacher, Waverley Secondary School, since 1976; b. 20.7.33, Bargeddie, Lanarkshire; m., Muriel Eadie; 1 s.; 2 d. Educ. Woodside Secondary School, Glasgow; Glasgow University. Taught, Gambia High School; Principal Teacher of Physics and Assistant Head, North Kelvinside Secondary School; Depute Head, John Street Secondary School; Chairman, SED Joint Working Party on Social and Vocational Skills; Convener, Education Committee, Headteachers' Association of Scotland; Member, Scottish Examination Board; Chairman, Drumchapel Citizens' Advice Bureau, 1981-84; Chairman, Scripture Union - Scotland; Director, Drumchapel Community Business; Director, Glasgow Compact. Publication: Basic Knowledge Physics. Address: (b.) 120 Summerhill Road, Glasgow, G15 7LD; T.-041-944 1171.

Macnair, John Bennett, JP. Member, East Lothian District Council, 1977-89; b. 28.6.25, Haltwhistle; m., D. Patricia Eldridge; 2 s.; 1 d. Educ. Edinburgh Academy; North Berwick High School; Trinity Academy; Edinburgh and East of Scotland College of Agriculture. Royal Navy, 1942-46. Member, North Berwick Town Council, 1964-75 (Provost, 1971-75); Member, East Lothian County Council, 1967-75 (Vice-Chairman, Education Committee, 1970-75). Chairman, North Berwick Rugby Club; President, North Berwick British Legion; Chairman, North Berwick Boy Scout Executive; Past President, North Berwick Rotary Club. Recreations: shooting; boating; golf; working sheep dogs. Address: (h.) Gilsland, North Berwick, East Lothian.

Macnair, Terence Crawford, LLB, NP. Solicitor, since 1967; Honorary Sheriff, North Strathclyde, since 1988; b. 16.12.42, Kingston, Jamaica; m., Ishbel Ross Hunter; 1 s. Educ. High School of Glasgow; Glasgow University. Town Clerk, Lochgilphead, 1970-75; Partner, MacArthur Stewart & Orr, 1970-81; Senior Partner, since 1981; Assistant Clerk, Tarbert Harbour Authority, since 1970; Clerk, Awe District Salmon Fishery Board, since 1979; President, Oban Rotary Club, 1988-89; Past Chairman, Oban Tennis and Squash Club; Secretary/Treasurer, Oban and District Licensed Trade Association, since 1977. Recreations: tennis; squash; golf; curling; bridge; music. Address: (b.) Boswell House, Oban; T.-0631 62215.

Mcnair, Thomas Jaffrey, CBE, MD, FRCSEdin, FRCSEng, FRCPEdin, FRCP & S Glas, FRACS (Hon). President, Royal College of Surgeons of Edinburgh, 1985-88; b. 1.3.27, Edinburgh; m., Dr. Sybil M.D. Wood; 1 s.; 1 d. Educ. George Watson's College; Edinburgh University. Consultant Surgeon, Eastern General Hospital, Edinburgh, 1961-64, Chalmers Hospital, Edinburgh, 1964-81, Royal Infirmary, Edinburgh, 1961-87; Surgeon to the Queen in Scotland, 1977-87. Recreation: golf. Address: (h.) Easter Carrick, Chapel Green, Earlsferry, Leven, Fife, KY9 1AD; T.-0333 330244.

McNally, Rt. Rev. Anthony Joseph. Rector, Gillis College, Edinburgh, since 1987; Vicar General, Archdiocese of St. Andrews and Edinburgh, since 1985; b. 27.5.32, Edinburgh. Educ. Blairs College, Aberdeen; Seminaire St. Sulpice, Paris. Ordained Priest, 1955; Assistant Priest, Methil, Fife, 1955-63; Missioner, Calabar and Bauchi Province, Nigeria, 1963-67; Assistant Priest, Bonnybridge, 1967-72; Parish Priest, Burntisland, 1972-80, St. Peter's, Morningside, 1980-85; Parish Priest, Musselburgh, and Vicar General, Archdiocese, 1985. Recreations: reading; walking. Address: (b.) 113 Whitehouse Loan, Edinburgh, EH9 1BB; T.-031-447 2807.

McNaught, Peter Cairn, MA, MLitt, FRSA. Principal, Craigie College of Education, Ayr, 1976-87; b. 29.5.25, Glasgow; m., Else Kristine Sandvad; 1 s.; 1 d. Educ. Hutchesons' Boys' Grammar School, Glasgow; Glasgow

University. Teacher, Queen's Park and Hutchesons' Boys' Grammar Schools, Glasgow, 1952-58; Lecturer in English, Moray House College of Education, Edinburgh, 1958-60; Principal Lecturer in English, Aberdeen College of Education, 1960-61; Moray House College of Education: Principal Lecturer in Educational Methods and Senior Assistant Principal, 1961-70, Vice-Principal, 1970-75. Vice-Chairman, Scottish Council for the Validation of Courses for Teachers; Member, General Teaching Council for Scotland; Vice-Chairman, West Sound; Chairman, STV Education Committee; Member, STV Staff Trust; United Kingdom Award, Council for Educational Technology, 1982; Visiting Professor in English Studies, Strathclyde University, 1988. Recreations: swimming; walking; travel. Address: (b.) Department of Continuing Education, Strathclyde University, Glasgow, G1 1XQ.

Macnaughton, Edwin George, OBE, JP, MA (Hons). Honorary Sheriff; b. 9.5.02, Aberfeldy; m., Annie Meffan (deceased); 2 d. Educ. Breadalbane Academy; Glasgow University. Assistant Teacher: Airdrie Academy, 1923-27, Dalziel High School, 1927-30; Principal Teacher of Classics: Uddingston Grammar School, 1930-32, Airdrie Academy, 1932-44; Headmaster, St. John's Grammar School, Hamilton, 1944-50; Rector, Hamilton Academy, 1950-67. Joint Author: Approach to Latin series, 1938-53, A New Approach to Latin, I, 1973, II, 1974. Address: (h.) 1A Dunchattan Grove, Troon, Ayrshire; T.-0292 316877.

Macnaughton, Rev. Gordon Fraser Hay, MA, BD. Chaplain, Dundee University, since 1991 (Minister, Fenwick Parish Church, 1985-91); Convener, Volunteer Group, Scottish Churches World Exchange; b. 27.3.58, Glasgow; m., Isabel Carole Marks; 1 d. Educ. Glasgow Academy; Glasgow University; Edinburgh University. Assistant Minister, Newlands (South), Glasgow, 1981-85. Coach, Dundee University RFC, since 1991. Recreations: rugby; wildlife conservation; golf. Address: (h.) 10 Springfield, Dundee, DD1 4JE; T.-0382 23766.

McNaughton, John Ewen, OBE, JP, FRAgS. Chairman, Scotch Quality Beef & Lamb Association, since 1981; Member, British Wool Marketing Board, since 1975; Member, Panel of Agricultural Arbiters, since 1973; Member, Red Deer Commission, since 1975; b. 28.5.33, Edinburgh; m., Jananne Ogilvie Honeyman; 2 s.; 2 d. Educ. Cargilfield; Loretto. Born and bred a hill sheep farmer; after a short spell in America, began farming at Inverlochlarig with father; served on Council, NFU of Scotland; Council Member, Scottish Agricultural Arbiters Association. Elder, Church of Scotland. Recreations: yachting; stalking. Address: Inverlochlarig, Balquhidder, Locheamhead, Perthshire, FK19 8PH; T.-087 74 232.

Macnaughton, Professor Sir Malcolm Campbell, MD, LLD, FRCPGlas, FRCOG, FRSE, FSLCOG (Hon.), FACOG (Hon.), FFARCS (Hon.), FRACOG (Hon.). Professor of Obstetrics and Gynaecology, Glasgow University, 1970-90; b. 4.4.25, Glasgow; m., Margaret-Ann Galt; 2 s.; 3 d. Educ. Glasgow Academy; Glasgow University. RAMC, 1949-51; Lecturer in Obstetrics and Gynaecology, Aberdeen University, 1957-61; Senior Lecturer, St. Andrews University, 1961-66; Consultant, Eastern Regional, 1966-70. Member, Chief Scientist Committee, SHHD; Member, Biomedical Research Committee and Health Service Research Committee, SHHD; Member, MRC Grant Committee and Cell Systems Board, MRC; Member, Scientific Committee, Hospital Recognition Committee, RCOG; President, RCOG, 1984-87. Chairman, Scottish Perinatal Mortality Advisory Group. Recreations: walking; fishing; curling. Address: (h.) 15 Boclair Road, Bearsden, Glasgow, G61 2AF; T.-041-942 1909.

McNay, W. Gordon, OBE, DL, JP, BL; b. 11.12.25, Wishaw; m., Margaret C. MacKay. Educ. Wishaw High School; Glasgow University. Depute Town Clerk, Burgh of Airdrie, 1952-53; Senior Depute Town Clerk, Burgh of Motherwell and Wishaw, 1953-63; Town Clerk, Burgh of East Kilbride, 1963-75; Chief Executive, East Kilbride District Council, 1975-88. Deputy Lieutenant, County of Lanark; Honorary Freeman, East Kilbride District. Recreations: golf; photography; philately. Address: (h.) Solbakken, 17 Kibblestane Place, Strathaven, ML10 6EL; T.-0357 20889.

MacNeacail, Aonghas. Writer; b. 7.6.42, Uig, Isle of Skye; m., Gerda Stevenson (qv); 1 s. Educ. Portree High School; Glasgow University. Writer's Fellowships: Sabhal Mor Ostaig, Skye, 1977-79; An Comunn Gaidhealach, 1979-81; Ross and Cromarty District Council, 1988-90; Scottish Arts Council Writer's Bursary, 1983; Grampian Television Poetry Award; Gaelic Books Council Manuscript for Publication Award; Scottish Association for the Speaking of Verse Diamond Jubilee Award; An Comunn Gaidhealach/National Mod Literary Prize. Publications: Poetry Quintet, 1976; imaginary wounds, 1980; Seeking Wise Salmon, 1983; The Great Snowbattle, 1984; The Avoiding, 1986; Rock and Water, 1990; A Writer's Ceilidh (for Neil Gunn), 1991; Atoms of Delight (play), 1991. Recreations: reading; walking. Address: (h.) 1 Roseneath Terrace, Edinburgh, EH9 1JS; T.-031-229 5652.

McNee, Sir David Blackstock, Kt, QPM, FBIM, FRSA, KStJ. President, National Bible Society of Scotland; Non-Executive Director and Adviser to a number of public limited companies; b. 23.3.25; m., Isabella Clayton Hopkins; 1 d. Educ. Woodside Senior Secondary School, Glasgow. Joined City of Glasgow Police, 1946; Deputy Chief Constable, Dunbartonshire Constabulary, 1968; Chief Constable: City of Glasgow Police, 1971-75, Strathclyde Police, 1975-77; Commissioner, Metropolitan Police, 1977-82. Honorary Vice-President, Boys' Brigade, since 1980; Vice-President, London Federation of Boys Clubs, since 1982; Patron, Scottish Motor Neurone Association, since 1982; Freeman, City of London, 1977; President, Glasgow City Committee, Cancer Relief, since 1987. Recreations: fishing; golf; music.

MacNee, William, MB, ChB, MD (Hons), FRCP(Glas), FRCP(Edin). Senior Lecturer, Edinburgh University and Consultant Physician, Lothian Health Board, since 1987; b. 18.12.50, Glasgow; m., Edna Marina Kingsley; 1 s.; 1 d. Educ. Coatbridge High School; Glasgow University. House Physician/House Surgeon, Glasgow and Paisley, 1975-76; SHO/Registrar in Medicine, Western Infirmary/Gartnavel Hospitals, Glasgow, 1976-79; Registrar in Respiratory Medicine, City Hospital, Edinburgh, 1979-80; MRC Research Fellow/Honorary Registrar, Department of Respiratory Medicine, Royal Infirmary, Edinburgh, 1980-82; Lecturer, Department of Respiratory Medicine, City Hospital, Edinburgh, 1982-83; Senior Registrar, Respiratory Medicine/Medicine, Lothian Health Board, 1983-87; MRC Research Fellow, University of British Columbia, Vancouver, 1985-86. Member, Council, Scottish Thoracic Society, since 1990. Recreations: music; theatre; squash. Address: (b.) Unit of Respiratory Medicine, City Hospital, Greenbank Drive, Edinburgh, EH10 5SB; T.-031-447 1001.

Macneil of Barra, Ian Roderick, BA, LLB, FSA Scot. Wigmore Professor of Law, Northwestern University, Chicago, since 1980; b. 20.6.29, New York City; m., Nancy C. Wilson; 2 s.; 1 d. Educ. Scarborough School; Vermont University; Harvard University. Lt., AUS, 1951-53; Commissioned Officer, USAR, 1950-67; practised law, 1956-59; Member, Cornell Law School Faculty, 1959-72, 1974-80; Visiting Professor, University College, Dar es Salaam, 1965-67, Duke Law School, 1971-72; Professor of Law and

Member, Centre for Advanced Studies, Virginia University, 1972-74; Visiting Fellow, Centre for Socio-Legal Studies, Wolfson College, Oxford, 1979, and Edinburgh University Faculty of Law, 1979, 1987; Visiting Professor, Harvard University, 1988-89; Guggenheim Fellow, 1978-79. Member, Standing Council of Scottish Chiefs. Recreations: tennis; reading; historical studies. Address: (h.) Kisimul Castle, Isle of Barra, PA80; T.-Castlebay 300.

McNeil, Neil, MB, ChB, DPH, DPA, FFCM, FFPHM, MRE-HIS. Unit Consultant in Public Health Medicine/Director of Community Medicine/Unit Medical Officer/District Medical Officer, Lanarkshire Health Board, since 1976; Honorary Senior Clinical Lecturer, Department of Public Health, Glasgow University, since 1973; b. 4.6.31, Glasgow; m., Florence Ward Butterworth; 2 s.; 1 d. Educ. Govan High School; Glasgow University. SHO, Senior Resident, House Physician and House Surgeon, Western Infirmary, Glasgow, 1956-58; Hall Fellow, Glasgow University, 1958-60; Registrar, Western Infirmary, Glasgow, 1960-61; Divisional Medical Officer of Health, City of Glasgow, 1962-65; Principal Lecturer in Health Education and Medical Officer, Jordanhill College, Glasgow, 1965-68; Medical Officer of Health, North-East Hampshire, and Honorary Consultant, Aldershot, 1968-69; Medical Officer, Scottish Home and Health Department, 1969-73; Honorary Lecturer, Departments of Materia Medica and Community Medicine, Glasgow University, 1973-74; Consultant Epidemiologist, Communicable Diseases (Scotland) Unit, Ruchill Hospital, 1973-74; Senior Medical Officer, Scottish Home and Health Department, 1974-76. Dr. MacKinlay Prize in Public Health and Preventive Medicine, Glasgow University, 1962. Publications on community medicine, environmental medicine, public health, immunisation and infectious disease control. Recreations: tennis; photography; natural history; Gaelic language and culture; Scottish history and archaeology. Address: (h.) Claddach, 25 Waterfoot Road, Newton Mearns, Glasgow, G77 5RU; T.-041-639 5165.

McNeill, Graeme Peter, MB, ChB, PhD, FRCPE. Consultant Cardiologist, Tayside Health Board and Honorary Senior Lecturer, Dundee University, since 1982; b. 27.9.44, Dundee; m., Dr. Karalyn E.M. McNeill; 1 s.; 3. Educ. Daniel Stewart's College; Dundee High School; St. Andrews University. Lecturer in Medicine, McGill University, Montreal, 1975-76; Lecturer in Medicine and Cardiology, Dundee University, 1976-82. Publications: books on heart disease; research papers on diagnosis and treatment of coronary disease and heart rhythm disturbances. Recreations: running; music; reading. Address: (h.) Bendochy House, Coupar Angus, Perthshire, PH13 9HU; T.-0828 27751.

MacNeill, Hector Fletcher, MA. Honorary Sheriff of North Strathclyde at Campbeltown, since 1981; b. 28.9.18, South Knapdale, Argyll; m., Iona Mary Pursell; 1 s.; 2 d. Educ. Keil School; Edinburgh University. RNVR, 1939-46; in action with HMS Hotspur at Battles of Narvik, Matapan and Crete; commanded HM Frigate Keats, 1945-46; Assistant Master, Campbeltown Grammar School, 1947-53, Oban High School, 1953-56; Head Master, Campbeltown primary schools, 1956-83. Member, crew, Campbeltown Lifeboat, 1950-53; President, Campbeltown Horticultural Society, 1963-84; Commodore, Campbeltown Sailing Club, 1968-69; Chairman, Campbeltown Sea Cadets, 1978-83; Member, Presbytery of South Argyll. Recreations: gardening; sailing; woodworking; climbing in Scotland. Address: (h.) Davaar House, Campbeltown, Argyll, PA28 6RE; T.-0586 52349.

McNeill, Ian Cameron, DSc, PhD, BSc. Reader in Chemistry, Glasgow University, since 1977; b. 29.4.32, Glasgow; m., Jessie Morton Howard; 2 s.; 1 d. Educ. Allan Glen's School, Glasgow; Glasgow University. Assistant in Chemistry, Glasgow University, 1956; ICI Research Fellow,

Londonderry Laboratory for Radiochemistry, Durham University, 1958; Lecturer in Chemistry, then Senior Lecturer, Glasgow University, 1961-77. Member, Editorial Board, Polymer Degradation and Stability; Committee Member, Polymer Degradation Discussion Group; Elder, Church of Scotland. Recreations: hill-walking; photography; classical music. Address: (b.) Department of Chemistry, Glasgow University, Glasgow, G12 8QQ; T.-041-339 8855, Ext. 441.

MacNeill, Malcolm Torquil, BL, FSA Scot. Honorary Sheriff, Grampian, Highland and Islands; b. 29.11.19, Bowmore; m., Morag Mackinnon; 2 s.; 1 d. Educ. Dunoon Grammar School; Glasgow University. War Service, The Cameronians (Scottish Rifles), 1939-46 (to Major); Territorial Army, The Cameronians and Parachute Regiment, 1947-52 (to Major); Legal Assistant, Scottish Office, 1950; Procurator Fiscal Depute, 1951; Procurator Fiscal: Moray and Nairn, 1961, Aberdeenshire, 1969; Regional Procurator Fiscal, 1975. Marriage Guidance Counsellor, 1956. Recreations: golf; curling; photography. Address: (h.) 56 Gray Street, Aberdeen; T.-0224 316854.

McNeill, Sheriff Peter Grant Brass, PhD, MA (Hons), LLB, QC. Sheriff of Lothian and Borders at Edinburgh, since 1982; b. 3.3.29, Glasgow; m., Matilda Farquhar Rose; 1 s.; 3 d. Educ. Hillhead High School, Glasgow; Morrison's Academy, Crieff; Glasgow University. Law apprentice, Biggart Lumsden & Co., Glasgow, 1952-55; Carnegie Fellowship, 1955; Faulds Fellowship, 1956-59; Scottish Bar, 1956; Honorary Sheriff Substitute of Lanarkshire, and of Stirling, Clackmannan and Dumbarton, 1962; Standing Junior Counsel to Scottish Development Department (Highways), 1964; Advocate Depute, 1964; Sheriff of Lanarkshire, subsequently of Glasgow and Strathkelvin, at Glasgow, 1965-82; President, Sheriffs' Association, 1982-85; Chairman, Council, Stair Society, 1990; Chairman, Scottish Legal History Group, 1990. Publications: Balfour's Practicks (Editor), 1962-63; An Historical Atlas of Scotland c. 400 - c. 1600 (Co-Editor), 1975; Adoption of Children in Scotland, 1982, 2nd ed., 1986. Recreations: legal history; gardening; book-binding. Address: (b.) Sheriffs' Chambers, Sheriff Court House, Lawnmarket, Edinburgh, EH1 2NS; T.-031-226 7181.

MacNeill, Seumas, MA, MInstP. Principal, The College of Piping, since 1945; Editor, The Piping Times, since 1950; b. 12.9.17, Glasgow; m., Janet Boyd; 1 s. Educ. Hyndland School; Glasgow University. Physicist, Royal Technical College, Glasgow, 1940-41; Lecturer, Natural Philosophy Department, Glasgow University, 1941-82. Honorary Secretary, Glasgow District, SYHA, 1943-45. Publications: Tutor for the Bagpipe, Parts 1, 2 and 3 (Co-author); Piobaireachd, the Classical Music for the Bagpipe; Piobaireachd and its Interpretation (Co-author). Recreations: hill-walking; bridge; physics. Address: (h.) 22 Mosshead Road, Bearsden, Glasgow; T.-041-334 3587.

McNeillage, James Kean, CA, FCT. General Manager Finance, Clydesdale Bank PLC, since 1988; b. 7.10.40, Glasgow; m., Gillian; 2 d. Educ. Daniel Stewart's College. Peat Marwick, 1966-69; Christian Salvesen PLC, 1969-82; The Distillers Company PLC, 1983-87; Lilley PLC, 1987-88. Address: (b.) 30 St. Vincent Place, Glasgow, G1 2HL; T.-041-223 2101.

McNicol, George Paul, MD, PhD, FRSE, FRCP, FRCPG, FRCPE, FRCPath, HonFACP, FRSA, Hon.DSc (Wabash Coll.) Principal and Vice-Chancellor, Aberdeen University, 1981-91; b. 24.9.29, Glasgow; m., Susan Moira Ritchie; 1 s.; 2 d. Educ. Hillhead High School, Glasgow; Glasgow University. House Surgeon, Western Infirmary, Glasgow, 1952; House Physician, Stobhill General Hospital, Glasgow, 1953; Regimental MO, RAMC, 1953-55; Assistant,

Department of Materia Medica and Therapeutics, and Registrar, University Medical Unit, Stobhill General Hospital, 1955-57; University Department of Medicine, Glasgow Royal Infirmary: Registrar, 1957-59, Honorary Senior Registrar, 1961-65; Lecturer in Medicine, 1963-65; Honorary Consultant Physician, 1966-71; Senior Lecturer in Medicine, 1966-70; Reader in Medicine, 1970-71; Professor of Medicine and Honorary Consultant Physician, Leeds General Infirmary, 1971-81; Chairman, Board, Faculty of Medicine, Leeds University, 1978-81; Harkness Fellow, Commonwealth Fund, Department of Internal Medicine, Washington University, 1959-61; Honorary Clinical Lecturer and Honorary Consultant Physician, Makerere UC Medical School Extension, Kenyatta National Hospital, Nairobi, 1965-66. Former Member, Advisory Council on Misuse of Drugs; Chairman, Part I Examining Board, Royal College of Physicians (UK); Member of Council, Committee of Vice-Chancellors and Principals of the Universities of the UK, 1989-91; Chairman, Medical Advisory Committee, CVCP, 1985-91; Member, Committee on Academic Standards and International Advisory Committee (European Sub-Group), CVCP; Member, Advisory Committee for Medical Training, European Community, since 1987; Member of Council, Association of Commonwealth Universities, 1988-91. Recreations: skiing; sailing. Address: (h.) Chanonry Green, Kincurdie Drive, Rosemarkie, Ross-shire, IV10 8SJ; T.-0381 21211.

McNicoll, David Rollo, OBE, MA. Chairman, Scottish Environmental Education Council, since 1991; b. 11.8.29, Kirriemuir; m., Vera E.F. Thow; 1 s.; 1 d. Educ. Pollokshields Secondary School, Glasgow; Glasgow University. RAF, 1947-49; teaching in primary and secondary schools, Glasgow, 1953-66; Senior Lecturer, Hamilton College of Education, 1966-69; Principal Examiner (History), Scottish Examination Board, 1967-69; HM Inspector of Schools, 1969-88; Secretary and Chief Officer, Consultative Committee on the Curriculum, 1979-87; Chief Executive, Scottish Consultative Council on the Curriculum, 1987-91. Address: (h.) 40 Gordon Road, Edinburgh, EH12 6LU.

McNicoll, Professor Iain Hugh, BA, PhD. Professor of Applied Economics, Strathclyde University, since 1987; Research Professor, Fraser of Allander Institute, since 1989; b. 24.6.51, Glasgow; m. Educ. St. Mungo's Academy, Glasgow; Stirling University. Leverhulme Research Fellow, Industrial Science, Stirling University, 1974-76; Lecturer, Business Studies, Edinburgh University, 1976-79; Fellow/Senior Fellow, Director of Research, Acting Director/Director, Fraser of Allander Institute, 1979-89. Publications: two books; six monographs; 40 academic journal and book articles. Recreations: hi-fi; golf; astronomy. Address: (b.) Department of Economics, Strathclyde University, 100 Cathedral Street, Glasgow; T.-041-552 4400.

McNulty, Howard, BPharm, PhD, FRPharmS. Chief Administrative Pharmaceutical Officer, Greater Glasgow Health Board, since 1990; b. 8.11.46, Colne; m., Laura Jean; 1 s.; 2 d. Educ. Nelson Secondary Technical School, Lancs; Bradford University. Began career as pharmacist, Timothy White's/Boots, 1969; joined Greater Glasgow Health Board as District Pharmaceutical Officer, Western District, 1983. Recreations: watching cricket; rugby. Address: (h.) 14 Coronation Way, Bearsden, Glasgow, G61 1DA; T.-041-942 8427.

McOwan, Rennie, FSA Scot. Writer and Broadcaster; b. Stirling; m., Agnes Mooney; 3 s.; 1 d. Educ. Alva Academy. Reporter, Stirling Journal; Sub-Editor, Kemsley Newspapers, Daily Record; Public Relations, Roman Catholic Church; Sub-Editor, Features Writer, Scotsman Publications; Assistant Publicity Secretary, National Trust for Scotland. Correspondent in Scotland for NC News Agency,

Washington, and RNS Agency, New York; Scottish Arts Council Lecturer under Writers in Schools scheme; Tutor to writing groups; Contributor to newspapers and magazines in Britain and overseas. Publications: Light on Dumyat; The White Stag Adventure; Walks in the Trossachs and the Rob Roy Country; The Green Hills; Kilchurn Castle: A History; contributed to: Walking in Scotland; Poetry of the Scottish Hills; Speak to the Hills; Wild Walks; The Story of Scotland; Discover Scotland; Great Walks, Scotland; Classic Coastal Walks of Britain; On Foot Through History. Recreations: mountaineering; Scottish history and literature. Address: 7 Williamfield Avenue, Stirling, FK7 9AH; T.-0786 61316.

McPartlin, Sheriff Noel, MA, LLB. Sheriff of Grampian, Highland and Islands, at Elgin, since 1985; b. 25.12.39.

McPhail, Rev. Andrew Montgomery, BA. Minister, Ayr: Wallacetown, since 1968; b. 1.8.36, Kilwinning; m., Ann Bryden Stirrat Logan; 2 s.; 1 d. Educ. Irvine Royal Academy; Glasgow University; Open University. Assistant, Irvine: Fullarton, 1966-68; Moderator, Ayr Presbytery, 1985-86. Recreations: golf; films; music. Address: 87 Forehill Road, Ayr, KA7 3JR, T.-Ayr 269161.

Macphail, Sheriff Iain Duncan, QC, MA (Hons), LLB. Member, Scottish Law Commission, since 1990; b. 24.1.38; m., Rosslyn Graham Lillias Hewitt; 1 s.; 1 d. Educ. George Watson's College; Edinburgh University; Glasgow University. Admitted Faculty of Advocates, 1963; practice, Scottish Bar, 1963-73; Faulds Fellow in Law, Glasgow University, 1963-65; Lecturer in Evidence and Procedure, Strathclyde University, 1968-69, Edinburgh University, 1969-72; Standing Junior Counsel to Scottish Home and Health Department and Department of Health and Social Security, 1971-73; Extra Advocate-Depute, 1973; Sheriff of Glasgow and Strathkelvin (formerly Lanarkshire), 1973-81; Sheriff of Tayside, Central and Fife at Dunfermline and Alloa, 1981-82; Sheriff of Lothian and Borders at Linlithgow, 1982-88, at Edinburgh, 1988-89. Chairman, Scottish Association for the Study of Delinquency, 1978-81. Publications: Evidence, 1987; Sheriff Court Practice, 1988. Recreations: music; theatre; reading; writing. Address: (b.) Scottish Law Commission, 140 Causewayside, Edinburgh, EH9 1PR; T.-031-668 2131.

McPhee, Rev. Duncan Cameron, MA, BD. Secretary-Depute, Department of National Mission, Church of Scotland, since 1978; b. 26.10.28, Glasgow; m., Elizabeth Anderson MacGregor; 1 s.; 3 d. Educ. Borden Grammar School, Sittingbourne; Glasgow University. Assistant Minister, Barony of Glasgow, 1953-55; Minister: Dalrymple, 1955-61, Airdrie Broomknoll, 1961-78. Assistant Clerk, Hamilton Presbytery, 1964-72; Clerk, 1972-78. Recreations: music; walking. Address: (b.) 121 George Street, Edinburgh, EH2 4YN; T.-031-225 5722.

McPhee, George, BMus, FRCO, DipMusEd, RSAM, Hon. FRSCM. Senior Lecturer, Royal Scottish Academy of Music and Drama; Organist and Master of the Choristers, Paisley Abbey, since 1963; b. 10.11.37, Glasgow; m., Margaret Ann Scotland; 1 s.; 2 d. Educ. Woodside Senior Secondary School, Glasgow; Royal Scottish Academy of Music and Drama; Edinburgh University. Studied organ with Herrick Bunney and Fernando Germany; Assistant Organist, St. Giles' Cathedral, 1959-63; joined staff, RSAMD, 1963; Conductor, Scottish Chamber Choir, 1971-75; Conductor, Kilmarnock and District Choral Union, 1975-84; since 1971, has completed 12 recital tours of the United States and Canada; has been both Soloist and Conductor with Scottish National Orchestra; numerous recordings and broadcasts; has taken part in numerous music festivals as Soloist; Adjudicator; Examiner, Associated Board, Royal Schools of Music; Special Commissioner, Royal School of Church Music; Silver

Medal, Worshipful Company of Musicians. Recreations: golf; walking. Address: (h.) 17 Main Road, Castlehead, Paisley, PA2 6AJ; T.-041-889 3528.

Macpherson, Sheriff Alexander Calderwood, MA, LLB. Sheriff of South Strathclyde, Dumfries and Galloway, at Hamilton, since 1978; b. 14.6.39.

McPherson, Professor Andrew Francis, BA, DPSA, FEIS. Co-Director, Centre for Educational Sociology, and Professor of Sociology, Edinburgh University; b. 6.7.42, Louth; 1 s.; 1 d. Educ. Ripon Grammar School; Queen's College, Oxford. Lecturer, Glasgow University, 1965-68; Edinburgh University: Research Fellow, 1968-72, Lecturer, 1972-79, Senior Lecturer, 1979-83, Reader, 1983-89, Professor, since 1989. Publications: The Scottish Sixth, 1976; Tell Them from Me, 1980; Reconstructions of Secondary Education, 1983; Governing Education, 1988. Address: (h.) 11 Dalrymple Crescent, Edinburgh.

Macpherson, Rev. Colin Campbell Reith, MA, BD. Minister, St. Margaret's Parish Church, Dunfermline, since 1966; b. 8.6.31, Edinburgh. Educ. Aberdeen Grammar School; Merchiston Castle School, Edinburgh; Aberdeen University; Cambridge University; Gottingen University. Assistant Minister, Auld Kirk, Ayr, 1958-59; Minister, West Church, Inverurie, 1959-66. Recreations: books; conversation; walking; visiting stately homes and gardens. Address: 38 Garvock Hill, Dunfermline, Fife; T.-Dunfermline 723955.

McPherson, Duncan James, MA, SDA. Farmer; Convener, Highland Regional Council; b. 29.10.30, Santos, Brazil; m., Vivian Margaret; 1 s.; 1 d. Educ. Robert Gordon's College, Aberdeen; Aberdeen University. Member, Cromarty Town Council, 1964-75, Ross and Cromarty County Council, 1972-75; Vice President, COSLA, since 1990; Vice-President, Scottish Council (Development and Industry), since 1990; Member, NCC (Scotland); President, Rosemarkie Golf Club; Chairman, Cromarty Firth Port Authority. Recreations: golf; curling; formerly rugby (Scottish trialist, 1951-56). Address: Cromarty Mains, Cromarty, Ross-shire; T.-038 17 232.

Macpherson, Ian, CA. Chief Executive, Watson & Philip plc, Dundee, since 1988, Chairman and Chief Executive, since 1989; Non-Executive Chairman, Low & Bonar PLC, since 1990; Member, Court, Dundee University, since 1991; Member, Council, Institute of Directors, since 1991; b. 25.3.36; m., Margaret; 1 s.; 1 d. Educ. Morrison's Academy, Crieff. Deputy Chief Executive, British Linen Bank, 1982-88. Recreation: golf. Address: (b.) Watson & Philip plc, PO Box 89, Blackness Road, Dundee, DD1 9PU; T.-0382 27501.

Macpherson, Ian George, BSc, DipEd. Rector, Eastwood High School, since 1977; b. 29.4.37, Perth; m., Gillian Brian; 2 s. Educ. Perth Academy; St. Andrews University; Edinburgh University; Moray House College of Education. Assistant Teacher of Physics, George Heriot's School, Edinburgh, 1959-62; Principal Teacher of Science, Dornoch Academy, Sutherland, 1962-64; Principal Teacher of Physics, Liberton High School, Edinburgh, 1964-69; Adviser in Science, Renfrewshire, 1969-73; Headmaster, Barrhead High School, 1973-77. Member, Strathclyde Executive, Headteachers' Association of Scotland. Recreations: yachting; Ocean Youth Club; Rotary. Address: (h.) 20A Park Road, Paisley, PA2 6JW; T.-041-884 2807.

McPherson, James Alexander Strachan, CBE, MA, BL, LLB, FSA Scot, JP. Lord Lieutenant, Grampian Region (Banffshire), since 1987; Senior Partner, Alexander George & Co., Solicitors, Macduff; Chairman, JP Advisory Committee, Banff and Buchan, since 1987; Honorary Sheriff, Grampian, Highland and Islands at Banff, since 1972; b. 20.11.27, Wormit, Fife; m., Helen Marjorie Perks; 1 s.; 1 d.

Educ. Banff Academy; Aberdeen University. Member, Macduff Town Council and Banff County Council, 1958-75; Provost of Macduff, 1972-75; Convener, Banff County Council, 1970-75; Member, Grampian Health Board, 1974-82; Member, Post Office Users National Council for Scotland, 1976-80; Member, Police Advisory Board for Scotland, 1974-86; Member, Grampian Regional Council, 1974-90; Governor, Scottish Police College, 1974-86. Recreations: reading; sailing; swimming. Address: (h.) Dun Alastair, 126 Gellymill Street, Macduff; T.-Macduff 32377.

Macpherson of Drumochter, Lord ((James) Gordon Macpherson), 2nd Baron, JP, FRES, FRSA, FZS. Chairman and Managing Director, Macpherson, Train & Co. Ltd., since 1964; Chairman, A.J. Macpherson & Co. Ltd., since 1973; b. 22.1.24; m., 1, Dorothy Ruth Coulter (deceased); 2 d.; 1 s. deceased; 2, Catherine MacCarthy; 1 s.; 2 d. Educ. Loretto; Wells House, Malvern. RAF, 1939-45. Freeman, City of London. Address: (h.) Kyllachy, Tomatin, Inverness-shire.

Macpherson, John Hannah Forbes, CBE, OStJ, CA. Chairman, Scottish Mutual Assurance Society, since 1971; Chairman, TSB Scotland plc, since 1984; Director, TSB Group plc, since 1985; Deputy Chairman, Hill Samuel Bank Ltd., since 1991; b. 23.5.26, Glasgow; m., Margaret Graham Roxburgh; 1 s. Educ. Glasgow Academy; Merchiston Castle School, Edinburgh. Royal Naval Volunteer Reserve, 1943; Apprentice CA, Wilson Stirling & Co., 1947 (qualified, 1949); Partner, Wilson Stirling & Co. (subsequently Touche Ross & Co.), 1956-86; Chairman: Glasgow Junior Chamber of Commerce, 1965; Scottish Industrial Estates Corporation, 1972, Irvine Development Corporation, 1976; President, Glasgow Chamber of Commerce, 1980; Director, Scottish Metropolitan Property plc, 1986; Governor, Merchiston Castle School, 1988; Deputy Chairman, Glasgow Development Agency, 1990; Member, Charity Appeals Committee for Prince and Princess of Wales Hospice, Institute of Neurological Sciences Research; Director, Merchants House and Glasgow Native Benevolent Society; Trustee, Scottish Civic Trust; Member of Court, Glasgow University, 1987. Recreations: travel; gardening; reading. Address: (h.) 16 Collylinn Road, Bearsden, Glasgow; T.-041-942 0042.

MacPherson, Margaret Hope, MA. Children's Author; b. 29.6.08, Colinton; m., Duncan MacPherson; 7 s. Educ. St. Denis School, Edinburgh; Edinburgh University. Married, farmed, brought up family; local government, 1945-49; Member, Commission of Inquiry into Crofting, 1951-54 (wrote minority report); Secretary, Skye Labour Party, 1961-84. Publications (children's books): Shinty Boys, 1963; The Rough Road, 1965; Ponies for Hire, 1967; The New Tenants, 1968; Battle of the Braes, 1970; The Boy on the Roof, 1972. Recreations: gardening; watching shinty; football; swimming. Address: (h.) Ardrannach, Torvaig, Portree, Skye; T.-0478 2758.

Macpherson, Peter, FRCP, FRCR, DTCD, FLS. President, British Society of Neuroradiologists; President, Botanical Society of the British Isles; retired Consultant Neuroradiologist, Institute of Neurological Sciences; b. 10.10.25, Inveraray; m., Agnes Cochrane Davidson; 4 d. Educ. Inveraray Grammar School; Keil School, Dumbarton; Anderson College, Glasgow. House Surgeon, Royal Infirmary, Stirling; Junior Hospital Medical Officer, Robroyston Hospital, Glasgow; Chest Physician, Argyll; Registrar/Senior Registrar, Western Infirmary, Glasgow. Commodore, Oban Sailing Club, 1958-60; President, Glasgow Natural History Society, 1979-81 and 1983-86; Honorary Secretary, Botanical Society of the British Isles, Committee for Scotland, since 1977; Honorary Plant Recorder for Lanarkshire, since 1979; Elder, Church of Scotland, since 1957. Recreations: natural history; sailing.

Address: (h.) Ben Alder, 15 Lubnaig Road, Glasgow; T.-041-632 0723.

Macpherson, Stuart Gowans, MB, ChB, FRCS. Senior Lecturer in Surgery, Glasgow University, since 1977; Honorary Consultant Surgeon, Western Infirmary, Glasgow, since 1977; b. 11.7.45, Glasgow; m., Norma Elizabeth Carslaw; 2 s.; 1 d. Educ. Allan Glen's School, Glasgow; Glasgow University. Surgical training and experience in West of Scotland, with postgraduate training at Harvard Medical School, Boston. Recreations: golf; travelling; reading; family. Address: (b.) Department of Surgery, Western Infirmary, Glasgow, G11 6NT; T.-041-339 8822, Ext. 4710.

Macpherson of Cluny (and Blairgowrie), The Honourable Sir William, KB (1983), TD, MA. 27th Hereditary Chief of the Clan Macpherson (Cluny-Macpherson); b. 1.4.26; m., Sheila McDonald Brodie; 2 s.; 1 d. Educ. Summer Fields, Oxford; Wellington College; Trinity College, Oxford. Scots Guards, 1944-47 (Captain); 21st Special Air Service Regiment (TA), 1951-65 (Lt.-Col. Commanding, 1962-65); Honorary Colonel, 21st SAS, 1983-91. Called to the Bar, Inner Temple, 1952; Queen's Counsel, 1971 83; Recorder of the Crown Court, 1972-83; Member, Senate and Bar Council, 1979-83; Bencher, Inner Temple, 1978; Judge of the High Court of Justice (of England and Wales), Queen's Bench Division, 1983; Honorary Member, Northern Circuit, since 1987. Member, Queen's Bodyguard for Scotland (Royal Company of Archers), since 1976, Brigadier, 1989; Vice President, Royal Scottish Corporation. Recreations: golf; fishing; rugby football. Address: (h.) Newton Castle, Blairgowrie, Perthshire; (b.) Royal Courts of Justice, Strand, London, WC2.

Macphie, Charles Stewart. Chairman and Managing Director, Macphie of Glenbervie Ltd., since 1965; Director, Grampian Enterprise Ltd.; Governor, Rowett Research Institute; Farmer; b. 22.9.29, Baltimore, Maryland; m., Elizabeth Margaret Jill Pearson; 1 s.; 1 d. Educ. Dalhousie Castle School; Rugby. Chairman of Governors, Oxenfoord Castle School; Trustee, Kincardineshire Royal Jubilee Trust. Address: (h.) Glenbervie, Kincardineshire; T.-05694 226.

McQuaid, John, MA (Hons), MEd, PhD. Composer and Psychologist; b. 14.3.09, Lochgelly; m., Mary Darkin; 1 s.; 1 d. Educ. St. Mungo's Academy, Glasgow; Glasgow University; Edinburgh University. Taught, 1935-40; War Service, 1941-46 (Intelligence Corps), Africa and SE Asia; taught, 1946-51; Psychologist, 1952-77; studied music under Erik Chisholm; numerous broadcasts and public performances of compositions (piano, chamber music, orchestra, etc.); Visiting Lecturer, Galway University, 1971. Address: (h.) St. Anne's, 8 Ardrossan Road, Saltcoats, KA21 5BW; T.-0294 63737.

Macquaker, Donald Francis, MA (Oxon), LLB. Chairman, Scottish Health Service Common Services Agency, 1987-91; Chairman, Greater Glasgow Health Board, 1983-87; Partner, T.C. Young & Son, Writers, Glasgow, since 1957; Director, Lithgows Limited, since 1987; b. 21.9.32, Stair; m., Susan Elizabeth Finlayson; 1 s.; 1 d. Educ. Winchester College; Trinity College, Oxford; Glasgow University. Former Member, Board of Management, Glasgow Royal Maternity Hospital and Associated Women's Hospitals (latterly Vice-Chairman); Chairman, Finance and General Purposes Committee, Greater Glasgow Health Board, 1974-83. Recreations: shooting; fishing; gardening. Address: (h.) Blackbyres, by Ayr; T.-0292 41088.

MacQueen, Professor Jack (John), MA (Glasgow), MA (Cantab), Hon DLitt. Endowment Fellow and Professor Emeritus, Edinburgh University, since 1988; b. 13.2.29, Springboig; m., Winifred W. MacWalter; 3 s. Educ.

Hutchesons' Boys Grammar School; Glasgow University; Christ's College, Cambridge. RAF, 1954-56 (Pilot Officer, Flying Officer); Assistant Professor of English, Washington University, St. Louis, Missouri, 1956-59; Edinburgh University: Lecturer in Medieval English and Scottish Literature, 1959-63, Masson Professor of Medieval and Renaissance Literature, 1963-72; Director, School of Scottish Studies, 1969-88; Professor of Scottish Literature and Oral Tradition, 1972-88. Publications: St. Nynia, 1961, 1990; Robert Henryson, 1967; Ballattis of Luve, 1970; Allegory, 1970; Progress and Poetry, 1982; Numerology, 1985; Rise of the Historical Novel, 1989; Scotichronicon III and IV (with W. MacQueen), 1989; Oxford Book of Scottish Verse (with T. Scott), 1966; A Choice of Scottish Verse 1470-1570 (with W. MacQueen), 1972; Humanism in Renaissance Scotland (Co-author), 1990. Recreations: walking; occasional archaeology; music. Address: (b.) School of Scottish Studies, 27 George Square, Edinburgh, EH8 9LD; T.-031-650 3059.

McQueen, James Donaldson Wright, MA, PhD. Chief Executive, Scottish Dairy Trade Federation; UK Representative, ASSILEC (European Dairy Association); Member, CBI National Council; Member, Advisory Committee for Scotland and N. Ireland, Understanding British Industry; b. 14.2.37, Dumfries; m., Jean Evelyn Brown; 2 s.; 1 d. Educ. King's Park School, Glasgow; Glasgow University. Assistant Lecturer, Department of Geography, Glasgow University, 1960-61; Junior Manager, Milk Marketing Board (England and Wales), 1961-62; Scottish Milk Marketing Board, 1963-89, Deputy Managing Director, 1985-89; Member, CBI Scottish Council, 1987-89; Director, Taste of Scotland Scheme Ltd., 1984-89. Recreations: golf; gardening; photography. Address: (h.) Ormlie, 53 Kingston Road, Bishopton, Renfrewshire, PA7 5BA; T.-Bishopton 862380.

Macqueen, Julie-Ann, OBE, CQSW, BA, SNNEB. Director, Scottish Council for Single Parents, 1967-88; b. 30.4.28, Palestine. Educ. Convent of Our Lady of Sion, Jerusalem, London, Shropshire; Edinburgh University; Open University; Dean College, Edinburgh. Nursery Nurse in Edinburgh, 1946-54; between 1954 and 1967, held the posts of Personnel Officer, Crawfords Biscuit Factory, Leith, School Welfare Officer, Dundee and Senior Social Worker, Scottish Child Care Office, Glasgow. Convenor, Macqueen Appeal Trust, Walpole Housing Association, Edinburgh Sitter Service of Scottish Council for Single Parents; Committee Member, Claremont Park Trust, Home Link and Supported Accommodation Committee of Scottish YWCA Housing Association; a Vice-President, National Out of School Alliance. Recreations: reading; listening to music; housing; photography; France. Address: (h.) 7 North Park Terrace, Edinburgh, EH4 1DP.

MacRae, Duncan Keith, MA, LLB, NP. Partner, Jardine Donaldson, Solicitors, Stirling, since 1963; b. 24.9.30, Glenshiel, Ross-shire; m., Edith Watson; 2 s. Educ. Plockton; Aberdeen University. Flying Officer, RAF; Partner, McCulloch & MacRae, Solicitors, Grantown-on-Spey, 1956-62; Member, Council, Scottish Law Agents' Society, since 1976 (President, 1988-89, Hon. Life Member of Council, 1989); Local Secretary, Macmillan Cancer Relief Society; Director, Stirling Ice Rink Co. Ltd. Recreations: curling; shooting; hill-walking; fishing. Address: (b.) 80 Port Street, Stirling, FK8 2LR; T.-Stirling 50366.

McRae, Ian Knox. Chief Executive, Cowal Enterprise Trust, since 1991; b. 15.12.36, Dunoon; m., Margaret; 1 d. Educ. Dunoon Grammar School. China merchant, 1960-90. Past President, Cowal Round Table, Dunoon Rotary Club; Past Chairman, Dunoon & District Angling Club. Recreations: water colour painting; fly fishing; natural history; cooking.

Address: (h.) The Palms, Alexandra Parade, Dunoon, Argyll; T.-0369 4455.

MacRae, John C., BSc, PhD. Head, Physiological Sciences Division, Rowett Research Institute, since 1985; b. 10.7.42, Skelmersdale, Lancashire; m., Eileen E.; 2 s. Educ. Ormskirk Grammar School; Newcastle University. Research Scientist, Applied Biochemistry Division, Department of Scientific and Industrial Research, Palmerston North, New Zealand, 1968-71; Research Scientist, Hill Farming Research Organisation, Penicuik, 1972-77; Head, Department of Energy Metabolism, Rowett Research Institute, 1978-85. Member, Editorial Board, British Journal of Nutrition, 1977-83; Committee Member, Scottish Group, Nutrition Society, 1973-75 and 1983-86. Recreations: sport (golf, cricket); family life. Address: (b.) Rowett Research Institute, Greenburn Road, Bucksburn, Aberdeen; T.-Aberdeen 712751.

MacRae, Rev. Malcolm Herbert, MA. Minister, Coalsnaughton Parish Church, since 1986; b. 27.9.45, Lima, Peru. Educ. Inverness High School; Arbroath High School; Free Church College, Edinburgh; Aberdeen University. Minister, West Free, Coatbridge, 1971; Associate Minister, Dunblane Cathedral, 1984; Minister, South Mull, 1985. Leader, Link Study Group on Theology and Philosophy; Editor, Link. Recreations: sport; sailing; cine-photography; painting. Address: Longriggs Manse, Coalsnaughton, FK13 6LG; T.-0259 50272.

Macrae, Col. Sir Robert Andrew Alexander Scarth, KCVO, MBE (1953). Lord Lieutenant of Orkney, 1972-90; Farmer; b. 14.4.15; m., Violet Maud Maclellan; 2 s. Educ. Lancing; RMC, Sandhurst. Commissioned Seaforth Highlanders, 1935; active service, BEF 1940 (PoW, 1940-45), NW Europe, 1945 (Despatches, 1945), Korea, 1952-53, East Africa, 1953-54; retired from Army, 1968; farming in Orkney, since 1967; Councillor, Orkney CC, 1970-74; Member, Orkney Islands Council, 1974-78; Vice-Chairman, Orkney Hospital Board, 1971-74; Orkney Health Board, 1974-79; Honorary Sheriff, Grampian Highlands and Islands, 1974; JP, 1975. Recreations: sailing; gardening (watching the cabbages being blown out to sea). Address: (h.) Grindelay, Orphir, Orkney, KW17 2RD; T.-0856 81 228.

MacRobert, John Carmichael Thomas, MA (Cantab), LLB (Glasgow), NP. Solicitor; Honorary Sheriff; b. 26.4.18, Edinburgh; m., Anne Rosemary Millar; 1 s.; 2 d. Educ. Craigflower; Rugby; Queens' College, Cambridge; Glasgow University. Captain, Royal Artillery (Despatches, Burma); Member, Council, Law Society of Scotland, 1965-77; Scottish Office Working Parties on Planning Reform and "Planning Exchange"; Hon. Sheriff, 1969; Hon. Solicitor, subsequently Trustee, now Vice President, Scottish Civic Trust; Hon. President (Past Chairman), Paisley South Conservatives. Recreations: sailing; country sports; gardening. Address: (h.) Failte, Colintraive, Argyll; T.-070 084 239.

McSherry, John Craig Cunningham, LLB (Glasgow), NP. Solicitor, since 1974; b. 21.10.49, Irvine; 2 s. Educ. Ardrossan Academy; Glasgow University. President, University Law Society, 1971-72; Partner, McSherry Halliday, Solicitors; Chairman, Largs and District Citizens' Advice Bureau, 1976-83; Council Member, Law Society of Scotland, 1982-85; Honorary Legal Adviser, Largs CAB and Saltcoats CAB. Recreations: music; skiing; gardening; curling; golf. Address: (b.) 23 Aitken Street, Largs, Ayrshire; T.-0475 686944.

McSwan, Malcolm, OBE, CA. Managing Director, Racal-MESL Ltd., since 1983; Director, Wolfson Microelectronics Ltd., since 1984; Chairman, Central Scotland Woodlands Ltd., since 1989; b. 31.8.39, Glasgow; m., Juliet Cowper-Jackson; 2 s. Educ. Royal High School, Edinburgh. Trustee, Central Scotland Countryside Trust. Recreations: renovation;

trees. Address: (b.) Lochend Industrial Estate, Newbridge, Midlothian; T.-031-333 2000.

MacSween, Iain MacLean, BA (Econ), MPhil. Chief Executive, Scottish Fishermen's Organisation, since 1982; b. 20.9.49, Glasgow; m., Jean Gemmill Martin; 3 s.; 1 d. Educ. Knightswood Secondary School; Strathclyde University; Glasgow University. Fisheries Economics Research Unit, 1973-75; Department of Agriculture and Fisheries for Scotland, 1975-77; Scottish Fishermen's Organisation, since 1977; President, European Federation of Fishermen's Organisations. Address: (b.) 601 Queensferry Road, Edinburgh, EH2 6EA; T.-031-339 7972.

MacSween, Malcolm D., MA (Hons), BLitt. Head Teacher, Abronhill High School, Cumbernauld, since 1978; b. 10.10.34, Torridon, Ross and Cromarty. Educ. Golspie High School; Glasgow University. Teacher, Glasgow schools, 1959-71; Assistant Head Teacher, Shawlands Academy, 1971-75; Depute Head Teacher, Stanely Green High School, Paisley, 1975-78. Elder, Church of Scotland. Recreations: bowls; reading; walking; visiting places of interest in UK. Address: (b.) Abronhill High School, Larch Road, Cumbernauld, Glasgow.

MacSween, Professor Roderick Norman McIver, BSc, MD, FRCPGlas, FRCPEdin, FRCPath, FRSE, FIBiol. Professor of Pathology, Glasgow University, since 1984; Honorary Consultant Pathologist, Western Infirmary, Glasgow, since 1970; b. 2.2.35, Kinloch, Lewis; m., Marjory Pentland Brown; 1 s.; 1 d. Educ. Inverness Royal Academy; Glasgow University. Successively Lecturer, Senior Lecturer, Reader and Titular Professor in Pathology, Glasgow University, 1965-84; Physician/Research and Education Associate, Colorado University Medical Center, Denver, 1968-69; Honorary Fellow, South African Society of Pathologists, 1982; Otago Savings Bank Visiting Professor, Otago University, 1983; Hans Popper Lecturer in Liver Pathology, Columbia University College of Physicians and Surgeons, New York, 1988. President, Royal Medico-Chirurgical Society of Glasgow, 1978-79; Honorary Librarian, Royal College of Physicians and Surgeons, Glasgow; President, International Academy of Pathology, British Division, 1988-90; Editor, Histopathology (Journal). Publications: Muir's Textbook of Pathology, 13th edition (Co-Editor); Pathology of the Liver, 3nd edition (Co-Editor); Recent Advances in Histopathology, Nos. 11-15; Recent Advances in Hepatology, No. 1. Former Captain, Dunaverty and Machrihanish Golf Clubs. Recreations: golf; gardening; opera; hill-walking; more golf! Address: (b.) University Department of Pathology, Western Infirmary, Glasgow, G11 6NT; T.-041-339 8822, Ext. 4732.

McTaggart, Dick, MBE (1985). Boxer; b. 1935, Dundee. Suffered only 24 defeats in 634 contests; Olympic Gold Medallist, Melbourne, 1956; Olympic Bronze Medallist, Rome, 1960; British Empire Lightweight Champion, 1958; European Lightweight Champion, 1961; British Empire Silver Medallist, 1962.

MacTaggart, Kenneth Dugald, BA, PhD. Senior Economist, Highlands and Islands Enterprise, since 1988; b. 15.4.53, Glasgow; m., Caroline McNicholas; 2 d. Educ. Allan Glen's School, Glasgow; Glasgow University; Paisley College; Aston University. Economic research, Aston University, 1976-80; Editor, Export Times, London, 1980-84; Editor, Property International, London and Bahrain, 1984-87; Director, Inc Publications, London, 1987-88. Recreations: hill-walking; piano; photography. Address: (h.) The Sutors, 28 Broadstone Park, Inverness, IV2 3LA; T.-0463 233717.

MacThomas of Finegand, Andrew, FSA Scot. 19th Chief of Clan MacThomas, since 1970; b. 28.8.42, Edinburgh; m.,

Anneke Cornelia Susanna Kruyning; 1 s.; 1 d. Educ. in Scotland, then St. Edward's, Oxford. Worked in public affairs, 1982-87, Government relations, since 1987. Member, Standing Council of Scottish Chiefs; President, Clan MacThomas Society; Vice-President, Clan Chattan Association. Recreation: travel. Address: c/o Barclays Bank, Hide Hill, Berwick-upon-Tweed.

MacVicar, Angus, MA, DUniv. Author; b. 28.10.08, Argyll; m., Jean Smith McKerral (deceased); 1 s. Educ. Campbeltown Grammar School; Glasgow University. Reporter, Campbeltown Courier, 1931-33; Freelance Author; Army Service, 1940-45 (Captain, RSF); Freelance Author, Journalist, Radio and TV Scriptwriter; published 71 books, including adult novels, children's novels, adult and children's non-fiction, plays; Honorary Sheriff-Substitute, Argyll, 1965; Doctorate, Stirling University, 1985. Recreations: golf; gardening; amateur drama. Address: (h.) Achnamara, Southend, Campbeltown, Argyll, PA28 6RW; T.-0586 83 228.

McVicar, George Christie, DipMusEd, RSAM; Hon.FTSC. Chairman, Scottish Amateur Music Association, since 1982; Examiner, Trinity College of Music, 1979-91; Founder and Director, New Saltire Singers, since 1990; Convenor, Saltire Scots Song Competitions, since 1986; b. 17.3.19, Dumbarton. Educ. Dumbarton Academy; Royal Scottish Academy of Music and Drama. Teacher of Music, Dunbartonshire Schools, 1946-54; Lecturer in Music, Moray House College of Education, 1954-56; Adviser in Music to Stirlingshire and subsequently Central Region, 1956-79. Adjudicator Member, British Federation of Music Festivals. Publications: The Saltire Scottish Song Book (formerly Oxford Scottish Song Book); Saltire Two-Part Song Book; The New Scottish Song Book. Address: (h.) 22 Queen Street, Stirling, FK8 1HN; T.-0786 72074.

McVie, John, BL, WS, NP. Consultant, McVies WS; Honorary Sheriff-Substitute, Lothian and Borders; b. 7.12.19, Edinburgh; m., Lindsaye Woodburn Mair; 1 s.; 1 d. Educ. Royal High School; Edinburgh University. Captain, 7/9th Bn., The Royal Scots, 1940-46 (Signal Officer, North West Europe); mentioned in Despatches; Town Clerk, Royal Burgh of Haddington, 1951-75. Recreations: fishing; golf; motoring. Address: (h.) Ivybank, Haddington, East Lothian; T.-062-082 3727.

MacWalter, Ronald Siller, BMSc (Hons), MB, ChB (Hons), MRCP(UK). Consultant Physician in Medicine for the Elderly, Royal Victoria Hospital, Dundee, since 1986; Honorary Senior Lecturer in Medicine, Dundee University, Ninewells Hospital, Dundee, since 1986; b. 14.12.53, Broughty Ferry; m., Sheila Margaret Nicoll; 2 s. Educ. Harris Academy, Dundee; Dundee University. Registrar in Medicine and Haematology, Department of Clinical Pharmacology, Ninewells Hospital, Dundee; Senior Registrar in General Medicine and Geriatric Medicine, Nuffield Department of Medicine, John Radcliffe Hospital, Oxford. Publication: Aids to Clinical Examination. Recreations: gardening; DIY; watercolour painting; music; skiing; swimming. Address: (h.) Ellangowan, 8 Hillcrest Road, Dundee, DD2 1JJ; T.-0382 66125.

McWilliam, James, OBE, MA (Hons), DipEd. Rector, Lochaber High School, 1970-88; Chairman, Highland Health Board, 1983-91; b. 4.10.27, Portsoy, Banffshire; m., Helen C. Brodie; 3 d. Educ. Fordyce Academy, Banffshire; Glasgow University. Teacher of English, Calderhead School, Shotts, 1951; National Service (Royal Army Education Corps), 1951-53; Teacher, Coatbridge High School, 1953; Special Assistant, Beath High School, Cowdenbeath, 1958; Principal Teacher of English, Campbeltown Grammar School, 1961-70. Member, Highland Health Board, since 1978 (Chairman, Practitioners' Committee, 1981); Honorary Sheriff,

Grampian, Highlands and Islands, since 1978; Past President: Lochaber Rotary Club, Lochaber EIS, Highland Secondary Headteachers Association. Recreations: music; TV; golf (occasionally). Address: (h.) 19 Seafield Street, Portsoy, Banff; T.-0261 43148.

McWilliam, Rev. Thomas Mathieson, MA, BD. Minister, Lylesland Parish Church, Paisley, since 1980; b. 12.11.39, Glasgow; m., Patricia Jane Godfrey; 1 s.; 1 d. Educ. Eastwood Secondary School; Glasgow University; New College, Edinburgh. Assistant Minister, Auld Kirk of Ayr, 1964-66; Minister: Dundee St. David's North, 1966-72, East Kilbride Greenhills, 1972-80; Convener, Youth Education Committee, General Assembly, 1980-84; Moderator, Paisley Presbytery, 1985-86; Convener, Board of Practice and Procedure, General Assembly, since 1992. Recreations: sea angling; walking; reading; gardening; bowling. Address: (h.) 36 Potterhill Avenue, Paisley, PA2 8BA; T.-041-884 2882.

M

Maan, Bashir Ahmed, JP, DL. Honorary Research Fellow, Glasgow University, since 1988; b. 22.10.26, Maan, Pakistan; 1 s.; 3 d. Educ. D.B. High School, Quila Didar Singh; Punjab University. Involved in the struggle for creation of Pakistan as a student, 1943-47; organised rehabilitation of refugees from India in Maan and surrounding areas, 1947-48; emigrated to UK and settled in Glasgow, 1953; Founder Secretary, Glasgow Pakistan Social and Cultural Society, 1955-65 (President, 1966-69); Member, Executive Committee, Glasgow City Labour Party, 1969-70; Vice-Chairman, Glasgow Community Relations Council, 1970-75; Member, Glasgow Corporation, 1970-75 (Magistrate, City of Glasgow, 1971-74; Vice-Chairman, then Chairman, Police Committee, 1971-75); Member, National Road Safety Committee, 1971-74 and Scottish Accident Prevention Committee, 1971-75; Member, BBC Immigrant Programmes Advisory Committee, 1972-80; Convenor, Pakistan Bill Action Committee, 1973; contested East Fife Parliamentary seat, February 1974; President, Standing Conference of Pakistani Organisations in UK and Eire, 1974-77; Police Judge, City of Glasgow, 1974-75; Member, City of Glasgow District Council, 1975-84; Deputy Chairman, Commission for Racial Equality, 1977-80; Member, Scottish Gas Consumers Council, 1978-81; Bailie, City of Glasgow, 1980-84; Member, Greater Glasgow Health Board, since 1981; Deputy Lieutenant, Glasgow, since 1982; Founder Chairman, Scottish Pakistani Association, 1984-91; Judge, City of Glasgow District Courts; Chairman, Strathclyde Community Relations Council, since 1986; a Governor, Jordanhill College of Further Education, 1987-91; Chairman, Mosque Committee, Islamic Centre, Glasgow, 1986-91. Recreations: golf; reading. Address: (h.) 8 Riverview Gardens, Glasgow, G51 8EL; T.-041-429 7689.

Mabon, Rt. Hon. Dr. Dickson, PC (1977), KStL, MB, ChB, DHMSA, MFHom, FRSA, FInstPet, FInstD. Chairman, Ashtree & Son Ltd.; Deputy Chairman, Cairn Energy plc; Director, East Midlands Electricity Generation Ltd.; Director, Independent Power Generators Ltd.; b. 1.11.25, Glasgow; m., Elizabeth Zinn; 1 s. Educ. North Kelvinside School; Glasgow

University. MP, Greenock and Port Glasgow, 1955-83; Joint Parliamentary Under Secretary of State for Scotland, 1964-67; Minister of State for Scotland, 1967-70; Minister of State for Energy, 1976-79; Treasurer, Parliamentary Group for Energy Studies. Address: (h.) 2 Sandringham, Largs, KA30 8BT; T.-0475 672293.

Machin, Professor George Ian Thom, MA, DPhil, FRHistS. Professor of British History, Dundee University, since 1989; b. 3.7.37, Liverpool; m., Dr. Jane Margaret Pallot; 2 s. Educ. Silcoates School, near Wakefield; Jesus College, Oxford. Research Student and Tutor, Oxford University, 1958-61; Assistant Lecturer, then Lecturer in History, Singapore University, 1961-64; Lecturer in Modern History, St. Andrews University, 1964-67; Lecturer, then Senior Lecturer, then Reader, Dundee University, 1967-89; Course Tutor, Open University in Scotland, 1971-82. Member, History Panel, Scottish Universities Council on Entrance, since 1990; Observer, Scottish Education Board, since 1991; sometime External Examiner, Universities of Cambridge, St. Andrews, Aberdeen, Hull, Sussex; Treasurer, Abertay Historical Society, 1966-73; Treasurer, Dundee Branch, Historical Association, since 1981; Elder, Church of Scotland, since 1981. Publications: The Catholic Question in English Politics 1820 to 1830, 1964; Politics and the Churches in Great Britain 1832 to 1868, 1977; Politics and the Churches in Great Britain 1869 to 1921, 1987; The Liberal Governments 1905-15, 1991. Recreations: the arts; hill-walking; photographing historic sign-posts. Address: (h.) 50 West Road, Newport-on-Tay, Fife, DD6 8HP; T.-0382 543371.

Maciocia, Mario G.A. Chairman and Chief Executive, Alma Holdings, since 1988; Chief Executive, Alma Confectionery Ltd., since 1985; Director, Continental Sweets NV, since 1985; b. 17.5.49, Kirkcaldy; m., Hilary Anne; 2 s.; 1 d. Educ. St. Andrews High School; George Watson's College; Heriot Watt University. Recreations: cricket; fishing; shooting; skiing; rugby. Address: (h.) Pittormie, Dairsie, Fife; T.-0334 870374.

Mack, Donald William, MA. Depute Senior Chief Inspector of Schools, since 1988; b. 9.5.32, Dunfermline; m., Catherine; 1 s.; 1 d. Educ. Allan Glen's School, Glasgow; Glasgow University. History Teacher in Glasgow; Lecturer in History, Jordanhill College of Education; Principal Lecturer in Social Studies, Hamilton College of Education; HMI, since 1974. Recreations: art history; languages; travel. Address: (b.) Room 4/115, New St. Andrew's House, St. James Place, Edinburgh; T.-031-244 4521.

Mack, Douglas Stuart, MA, PhD. Lecturer, Stirling University, since 1986; General Editor, Association for Scottish Literary Studies, 1980-90; General Editor, Stirling Edition of James Hogg, since 1990; President, The James Hogg Society, since 1982; b. 30.1.43, Bellshill; m., Wilma Stewart Grant; 2 s. Educ. Uddingston Grammar School; Glasgow University; Stirling University. Research Assistant, National Library of Scotland, 1965-66; Assistant Librarian, St. Andrews University, 1966-70, Stirling University, 1970-86; Editor of various books by James Hogg. Recreations: watching Hamilton Accies; sailing on paddle steamers. Address: (h.) 2 Law Hill Road, Dollar, FK14 7BG; T.-Dollar 42452.

Mack, Jimmy. Broadcaster and Journalist; Presenter, The Jimmy Mack Show, Radio Clyde 2, since 1990; b. 26.6.34, Greenock; m., Barbara; 1 s.; 1 d. Educ. Lenzie Academy; Bathgate Academy. Insurance Inspector, Guardian Royal Exchange Assurance Co., 1956-70; Producer and Presenter, various programmes, BBC Radio Medway, Kent, 1970-79; Presenter, Radio 1 Club, BBC Radio 1, 1967-70; Presenter, The Early Show, Night Ride, Junior Choice, BBC Radio 2, 1971-76; Producer, You and Yours, Woman's Hour, In

Britain Now, BBC Radio 4, 1977-78; Presenter, The Jimmy Mack Show and Jimmy Mack's Old Gold, BBC Radio Scotland, 1979-89; Presenter, Top Club and Best Years of Their Lives, Grampian TV, 1980-84; Presenter, Scotland Today, Scottish TV, 1984-85; Presenter, I Believe You Believe, BBC TV, 1986. Television and Radio Industries Club of Scotland Award for best live radio programme, 1986. Publication: Jimmy Mack Show Book, 1984. Recreation: photography. Address: (b.) Radio Clyde, Clydebank Business Park, Glasgow, G81 2RX; T.- 041-306 2200.

Mackie, Professor Andrew George, MA, PhD, FRSE, FIMA. Professor of Applied Mathematics, Edinburgh University, 1968-88; b. 7.3.27, Tain; m., Elizabeth Maud Hebblethwaite; 1 s.; 1 d. Educ. Tain Royal Academy; Edinburgh University; Cambridge University; St. Andrews University. Lecturer, Dundee University, 1948-50; Bateman Research Fellow and Instructor, California Institute of Technology, 1953-55; Lecturer: Strathclyde University, 1955-56, St. Andrews University, 1956-62; Professor of Applied Mathematics, Victoria University of Wellington, New Zealand, 1962-65; Research Professor, Maryland University, 1966-68; Visiting Professor, California Institute of Technology, 1984 and University of New South Wales, Australia, 1985; Vice-Principal, Edinburgh University, 1975-80; Chairman, Scottish Mathematical Council, 1980-84; President, Edinburgh Mathematical Society, 1982-83. Publication: Boundary Value Problems, 1965. Recreation: golf. Address: (h.) 47 Cluny Drive, Edinburgh, EH10 6DU; T.-031-447 2164.

Mackie of Benshie, Baron (George Yull Mackie), CBE, DSO, DFC, LLD. Farmer; SLD Spokesman, House of Lords, on Agriculture and Scottish Affairs; Member, Council of Europe and Western European Union; b. 10.7.19, Aberdeen; m., 1, Lindsay Lyall Sharp; 1 s. (deceased); 3 d.; 2, Mrs Jacqueline Lane. Educ. Aberdeen Grammar School; Aberdeen University. Bomber Command and Air Staff, 1944. Contested South Angus, 1959; Vice-Chairman (Organisation), Scottish Liberal Party, 1959-64; MP (Liberal), Caithness and Sutherland, 1964-66; Chairman, Scottish Liberal Party, 1965-70; contested Caithness and Sutherland, 1970; contested NE Scotland, European Parliamentary Election, 1979; Member, EEC Scrutiny Committee (D), House of Lords; Executive, Inter-Parliamentary Union; Chairman, Industrial Appeal Committee, Pitlochry Festival Theatre, 1979; Chairman, Angus Committee, Salvation Army, 1976-84; Rector, Dundee University, 1980-83. Recreations: golf; shooting; social life. Address: (h.) Cortachy House, by Kirriemuir, Angus; T.-Cortachy 229.

Mackie, Joyce Grant, BA, DipCE. Vice-President, National Trust for Scotland, since 1988; Partner, farming business, since 1963; b. 7.5.40, Forfar; m., Bruce Stephen Mackie; 2 s.; 2 d. Educ. St. Margaret's School for Girls, Aberdeen; Moray House College of Education. Teacher, Dalmilling School, Ayr, 1961-63. National Trust for Scotland: Member, Council, 1974-79, 1985-90, Member, Executive Committee, 1976-86; Member, Aberdeen Committee, Scottish Children's League (RSSPCC); Trustee, David Gordon Memorial Trust, since 1977; Director, Lathallan Preparatory School, Montrose, since 1979, Chairman, since 1990; Member, Council, Glenalmond College, since 1991; Member, Church of Scotland Nomination Committee, 1985-88. Recreations: gardening; art; tennis; Scotland. Address: (h.) Balquhindachy, Methlick, Ellon, Aberdeenshire AB41 0BY; T.-06514 373.

Mackie, Sir Maitland, Kt (1982), JP. Lord Lieutenant of Aberdeenshire, 1975-87; Farmer; b. 16.2.12.

Mackie, Maitland, CBE, BSc, MA. Farmer; Chairman, Farmdata, since 1979; b. 21.9.37, Aberdeen; m., Dr. Halldis Mackie; 1 s.; 2 d. Educ. Aberdeen Grammar School;

Aberdeen University. Member, Scottish Agricultural Development Council; Former Chairman, Food and Animal Committees, Agricultural and Food Research Council; Vice-President, National Farmers Union of Scotland; Chairman, Scottish Pig Industry Initiative; Director, Grampian Enterprise Ltd.; former Director, Aberdeen & District Milk Marketing Board. Recreations: skiing; sailing; Norway. Address: Westertown, Rothienorman, Aberdeenshire; T.-04675 466.

Mackie, Marie Watson-Watt, MA (Hons), EdB (Dip). National Chairman, Scottish Women's Rural Institutes, since 1987; Council Member, Scottish Association of Young Farmers Clubs, since 1987; Council Member, Rural Forum (Scotland), 1987-90; b. Kilmarnock; m., Alex. O. Mackie, MA, FSA Scot. Educ. Kilmarnock Academy; Glasgow University. Secondary Teacher, Borders, 15 years; County Federation Chairman, SWRI, Roxburghshire, 1975-81; National Vice-Chairman, SWRI, 1981-87; Member, Women's National Commission, 1987-89; former Executive Member, Scottish Institute of Adult Education; Producer, Lecturer and Adjudicator, amateur drama; Chairman, Roxburghshire Drama Association; Britain in Bloom Judge, 1975-84. Recreations: interior design; 19th-century pottery; Samoyed dogs; enjoying the countryside of Scotland. Address: (h.) Linton Downs, Kelso, Roxburghshire.

Macklon, Alan Edward Stephen, BSc, PhD. Project Leader, Plants Division, Macaulay Land Use Research Institute; b. 2.10.36, Dover; m., Bridget Jessamine Carr; 4 s. Educ. Cambridgeshire High School for Boys; Nottingham University; Aberdeen University. Joined Macaulay Institute for Soil Research, 1962; spent a year as Research Associate, Washington State University, 1966-67. Recreation: gardening. Address: (b.) Macaulay Land Use Research Institute, Craigiebuckler, Aberdeen, AB9 2QJ; T.-Aberdeen 318611.

Maddox, Christopher Edward Ralph, BSc, PhD, CBiol, MIBiol, DipManEd. Principal, Scottish College of Textiles, Galashiels, since 1988 (Vice Principal, Queen Margaret College, Edinburgh, 1983-88); b. 21.11.40; m., Janet; 2 s. Educ. Priory School, Shrewsbury; Birmingham University. MRC Research Fellow, Warwick University, 1965-66; Senior Lecturer, Luton College of Technology, 1966-67; Senior Lecturer, then Principal Lecturer, then Assistant Dean of Studies, Manchester Polytechnic, 1967-77; Head, Department of Molecular and Life Sciences, Dundee College of Technology, 1977-83. Member, SCOTEC Committees for Biology and Medical Laboratory Sciences, 1978-83; Member, Council, Scottish Branch, Institute of Biology, 1979-82; Member, CNAA Combined Studies Board, 1983-87; Member, CNAA Health Studies Committee, 1987-89; Member, Health Visiting Joint Committee, UK Central Council for Nursing, Midwifery and Health Visiting, 1983-88; Director, Scottish Borders Enterprise Company, since 1990. Recreations: reading; watching sports. Address: (b.) Scottish College of Textiles, Galashiels, TD1 3HF; T.-0896 3351.

Madsen, Johan, BA, MBA, DipM, MBIM, MCIM. Managing Director, Garnock Valley Development Executive Ltd., since 1988; Director, Ayrshire Marketing Ltd., since 1991; b. 15.4.40, Aarhus, Denmark; m., Dr. Sheila Madsen; 2 d. Educ. Open University; Strathclyde University; Chartered Institute of Marketing. Manager, subsidiary of Danish company, 1969-72; Sales Manager for Scotland, Stimorol (UK) Ltd., 1972-86. Recreations: music; photography. Address: (b.) 44 Main Street, Kilbirnie, Ayrshire; T.-0505 685455.

Maguire, Brian Robert, LLB. Procurator Fiscal, Oban, since 1990; b. 8.7.50, Lennoxtown; m., Evelyn Manson; 1 s.; 1 d. Educ. St. Aloysius College, Glasgow; Glasgow University. Entered Procurator Fiscal service, 1975; Depute, Ayr, Greenock, Glasgow. Recreations: reading; skiing; horse-rid-

ing, researching the Zulu wars. Address: (b.) Procurator Fiscal Office, Sheriff Court, Albany Street, Oban; T.-0631 64088.

Maguire, Sheriff John, PhD, LLB, QC. Sheriff Principal, Tayside, Central and Fife, since 1990; b. 30.11.34, Kirkintilloch; m., Eva O'Hara; 2 s.; 2 d. Educ. St. Ninian's High School, Kirkintilloch; St. Mary's College, Blairs; Pontifical Gregorian University, Rome; Edinburgh University. Standing Junior Counsel, Ministry of Public Buildings and Works, 1962-68; Sheriff at Airdrie, 1968-73; Sheriff at Glasgow, 1973-90; Secretary, Sheriffs Association, 1982-87, President, 1988-90. Co-Founder and Chairman, PHEW, 1985-90. Recreations: reading; thinking about doing the garden. Address: (b.) Sheriff Principal's Chambers, Perth Sheriff Court, Tay Street, Perth; T.-Perth 205406.

Magnusson, Magnus, MA (Oxon), FRSE, FRSA, FSA Scot. Writer and Broadcaster; Chairman, Scottish Natural Heritage, since 1992; b. 12.10.29, Reykjavik, Iceland; m., Mamie; 1 s.; 3 d. Educ. Edinburgh Academy; Jesus College, Oxford. Reporter, Scottish Daily Express; Features Writer, The Scotsman; Co-Presenter, Tonight, BBC TV, 1964-65; Presenter: Chronicle, Cause for Concern, Checkpoint, All Things Considered, Mainly Magnus, BC - The Archaeology of the Bible Lands, Living Legends, Vikings!, Mastermind; Rector, Edinburgh University, 1975-78.

Maher, Professor Gerard, LLB, BLitt. Professor of Law, Strathclyde University, since 1991; Advocate; b. 26.3.53, Lanark; m., Joan Tennison Cunningham. Educ. St. Patrick's, Coatbridge; Glasgow University; Queen's College, Oxford. Lecturer in Law, Edinburgh University, 1976-79; Lecturer, then Senior Lecturer, Glasgow University, 1980-91. Recreations: playing golf; watching football. Address: (b.) Law School, Strathclyde University, Glasgow, G4 0RQ; T.-041-552 4400.

Maher, Michael Alexander Ramsey, JP, ABTI. Convener, Tweeddale District Council; b. 14.5.18, Glasgow; m., Ellaretta Eckford Montgomery; 1 s.; 1 d. Educ. St. Mungo's Academy, Glasgow. Served with 157 Field Ambulance (TA), RAMC, seven years; Training Officer in Civil Defence, Peeblesshire County Council; transferred to Borders Regional Council on re-organisation; held post of Registrar of Births, Deaths and Marriages for Peebles and District; Treasurer, H. Ballantyne Memorial Institute, Walkerburn, 30 years; Chairman: Walkerburn Community Council, Walkerburn OAP Association, St. James Church Parish Council, Innerleithen; Member, COSLA Economic Affairs Committee; Past President, Probus (Innerleithen, Walkerburn and Traquair); Member: Scottish Borders Tourist Board, Scottish National Housing and Town Planning, Tweeddale District Licensing Board; Treasurer, Tweeddale Crime Prevention Panel; Chairman, Tweeddale Emergency Committee. Recreations: gardening; painting; marquetry. Address: (h.) 2 Park Avenue, Walkerburn, Peebles-shire; T.-Walkerburn 272.

Mahmood, Tahir Ahmed, MB, BSc, DObstRCP, MD, MRCOG. Consultant Obstetrician and Gynaecologist, Forth Park Hospital, Kirkcaldy, since 1990; Clinical Senior Lecturer, Obstetrics and Gynaecology, Aberdeen University, since 1990; Hon. Secretary, Division of Obstetrics and Gynaecology and Paediatrics, Fife, since 1991; b. 7.10.53, Pakistan; m., Aasia Bashir; 2 s. Educ. King Edward Medical College, Lahore, Punjab University. Senior Registrar/Clinical Lecturer, Raigmore Hospital, Inverness and Aberdeen Royal Infirmary/Aberdeen Maternity Hospital, 1986-90. Member, Scottish Hospital Staffing Review Committee, sub-speciality of obstetrics and gynaecology, 1986-88; Member, Minimal Invasive Surgery Subgroup and Clinical Resource Management – Procurement Group for Acute Unit, Fife, 1991-92. Recreations: squash; jogging; reading; history;

walking. Address: (b.) Forth Park Hospital, 30 Bennochy Road, Kirkcaldy, Fife; T.-0592 261155.

Main, Professor Brian G.M., BSc, MBA, MA, PhD. Professor of Economics, Edinburgh University, since 1991 (Head, Department of Economics, since 1991); b. 24.8.47, St. Andrews; m., June Lambert; 2 s. Educ. Buckhaven High School; St. Andrews University; University of California, Berkeley. Lecturer, then Reader in Economics, Edinburgh University, 1976-87; Professor of Economics and Chairman, Department of Economics, St. Andrews University, 1987-91. Recreation: fishing. Address: (b.) Department of Economics, Edinburgh University, George Square, Edinburgh, EH8 9JY; T.-031-650 8361.

Main, Carol B.L.D., BA. Secretary, National Association of Youth Orchestras, since 1979; Scottish Representative, Live Music Now, since 1984; Classical Music Editor, The List, since 1985; b. 21.12.58, Kirkcaldy; m., Colin Heggie; 1 d. Educ. Kirkcaldy High School; Edinburgh University. Freelance music critic, mainly with Glasgow Herald. Board Director, Edinburgh Festival Fringe Society. Address: (b.) Ainslie House, 11 St. Colme Street, Edinburgh, EH3 6AG; T.-031-225 4606.

Main, Kirkland, ARSA, RSW, DA, FEIS. Head, School of Drawing and Painting, Edinburgh College of Art, and Deputy Principal, since 1991; b. 1.7.42, Edinburgh; m., Geraldine Francis; 1 d. Educ. Daniel Stewart's College; Edinburgh College of Art. Assistant to Vice Principal, Edinburgh College of Art, 1980-83 (Governor, 1979-85); Member, Central Institutions Staffs Salaries Committee, 1977-81; Member, Scottish Joint Negotiating Committee, Further Education, 1982-87; Chairman, Association of Lecturers in Scottish Central Institutions, 1982-86. Address: (h.) 15 Cramond Village, Edinburgh, EH4 6NU.

Main, Sir Peter (Tester), ERD, MD, LLD (Hon.), FRCPE, CBIM. Director, Scottish Development Agency, 1986-91; Director, W.A. Baxter & Sons Ltd., 1985-91; b. 21.3.25, Aberdeen; m., 1, Margaret Tweddle (deceased); 2 s.; 1 d.; 2, May Heatherington McMillan. Educ. Robert Gordon's College; Aberdeen University. House Surgeon, Aberdeen Royal Infirmary, 1948-49; Captain, RAMC, 1949-51; Medical Officer with Field Ambulance (Suez), 1956; Lt. Col., RAMC (AER), retired 1964; general practice, 1953-57; The Boots Co. PLC: joined Research Department, 1957; Director of Research, 1968; Managing Director, Industrial Division, 1979; Director, 1973-85, Vice Chairman, 1980-81, Chairman, The Boots Co. PLC, 1982-85. Member, National Economic Development Council, 1984-85; Chairman, Committee of Inquiry into Teachers' Pay and Conditions, Scotland, 1986; Governor, Henley Management College, 1983-86. Recreations: fishing; shooting; Scottish music. Address: Lairig Ghru, Dulnain Bridge, Grantown-on-Spey, PH26 3NT; T.-047985 264.

Mair, Alexander, MBE (1967). Chairman, RGIT Offshore Survival Centre Ltd., since 1988; Governor, Robert Gordon's College, Aberdeen, since 1988; b. 5.11.22, Echt; m., Margaret Isobel. Educ. Skene Central School; School of Accountancy, Glasgow. Company Secretary, Grampian TV, 1961-70; appointed Director, 1967; Director and Chief Executive, 1970-87. President, Aberdeen Chamber of Commerce, 1989-91; Chairman, Aberdeen International Football Festival, 1988-91. Recreations: golf; skiing; gardening. Address: (h.) Ravenswood, 66 Rubislaw Den South, Aberdeen, AB2 6AX; T.-0224 317619.

Mair, Alistair S.F., MBE, BSc, FBIM. Chairman, since 1991, Managing Director, since 1977, Caithness Glass PLC; Chairman, CBI Scotland, 1989-91, and Member, CBI Council; b. 20.7.35, Drumblade; m., 1, Anne Garrow

(deceased); 2, Mary Bolton; 4 s.; 1 d. Educ. Robert Gordon's College, Aberdeen; Aberdeen University. Rolls Royce, Glasgow, 1957-71: graduate apprentice, PA to General Manager, Production Control Manager, Product Centre Manager; RAF, 1960-62 (short-service commission, Technical Branch); Managing Director, Caithness Glass Ltd., 1971-75; Marketing Director, Worcester Royal Porcelain Co., 1975-76. Non-Executive Director, Grampian Television, since 1986; Director, Drambuie Group PLC; Governor, Morrison's Academy, Crieff. Recreations: gardening; walking; current affairs. Address: (h.) Dungora, Heathcote Road, Crieff, Perthshire, PH7 4AG; T.-0764 2191.

Mair, Henry. Poet; b. 4.3.45, Kilmarnock; m., Etta; 1 s.; 1 d. Educ. St. Joseph's High School, Kilmarnock. Originator, 1972, and Secretary, Scottish National Open Poetry Competition; guest, USSR Writers' Union, 1980. Publications: I Rebel, 1970; Alone I Rebel, 1974; Flowers in the Forest, 1978; The Prizewinners, 1987. Address: (h.) 42 Tollerton Drive, Irvine, Ayrshire; T.-Irvine 76381.

Mair, William Wallace, MA. Secretary, Faculty of Actuaries in Scotland, since 1974; Secretary, Associated Scottish Life Offices; b. 19.6.49, Bellshill; m., Sandra Cunningham; 1 s.; 1 d. Educ. Uddingston Grammar School; Glasgow University. Assistant Secretary, Royal Institution of Chartered Surveyors, 1969-72; Secretary, Scottish National Federation of Building Trades Employers, 1972-73. Recreations: badminton; cricket; hill-walking; lay preaching. Address: (b.) 23 St. Andrew Square, Edinburgh, EH2 1AQ; T.-031-557 1575.

Maitland-Carew, The Hon. Gerald Edward Ian, DL; b. 28.12.41, Dublin; m., Rosalind Averil Speke; 2 s.; 1 d. Educ. Harrow School. Army Officer, 15/19 The Kings Royal Hussars, 1960-72; looked after family estates, since 1972; Member, Royal Company of Archers; Chairman, Lauderdale Hunt; Chairman, Lauderdale and Galawater Branch, Royal British Legion Scotland; Deputy Lieutenant, Ettrick and Lauderdale and Roxburgh, 1989; elected Member, Jockey Club, 1989; Member, Border Area, TA Committee. Recreations: racing; hunting; shooting. Address: (h.) Thirlestane Castle, Lauder, Berwickshire; T.-05782 254.

Makgill Crichton Maitland, Major John David. Lord Lieutenant of Renfrewshire, since 1980; b. 10.9.25.

Makin, Professor Brian, BSc, PhD, CEng, FIEE, FInstP. Watson-Watt Professor of Electrical Engineering, Dundee University, since 1974; b. 28.12.35, Sheffield; m., Hazel Phillips; 3 s. Educ. High Storrs Grammar School, Sheffield; Southampton University. Scientific Assistant, Avco-Everett, Massachusetts, 1962-63; Project Engineer, W.G. Pye, Cambridge, UK, 1964-66; Lecturer, then Senior Lecturer, Department of Electrical Engineering, Southampton University, 1966-74. Address: (b.) Department of APEME, The University, Dundee, DD1 4HN; T.-Dundee 23181, Ext. 4394.

Makower, Michael, MA, DipOR, FInstPet. Senior Lecturer, Department of Management Science, Stirling University, since 1967; Organiser, Edinburgh Finance and Investment Seminar, since 1967; Organiser, Glasgow Discussion Group on Finance and Investment, since 1970; Vice-Chairman, Association for Management Education and Training in Scotland, since 1989; b. 12.9.36; m., Selina Elizabeth Barran; 3 d. Educ. Cambridge University; London School of Economics. 2nd Lt., Corps of Royal Engineers, 1954-56; Senior Scientific Officer, British Iron and Steel Research Association, 1960-63; Lecturer in Operational Research, Edinburgh University, 1963-67. Trustee, Arthur Smith Memorial Trust. Recreation: timpanist. Address: (b.) Department of Management Science, Stirling University, Stirling, FK9 4LA; T.-0786 67363.

Maksymiuk, Jerzy. Principal Conductor, BBC Scottish Symphony Orchestra, since 1983; b. 9.4.36, Grodno, Poland; m., Irena Kirjacka. Educ. Warsaw Academy of Music. Opera House, Warsaw, 1969, conducting Mozart, Stravinsky and modern works; Director, National Radio Orchestra of Poland, 1972-74; former Music Director, Polish Chamber Orchestra; Composer of music for Polish films. Winner of Polish Cultural Awards for composition and for forming Polish Chamber Orchestra; Polish Cross; awarded Hon. Doctorate in Music, Strathclyde University, 1990. Address: (b.) BBC, Queen Margaret Drive, Glasgow, G12 8DG; T.-041-330 2355/3.

Malcolm, David, MA, LLB. Honorary Sheriff, since 1976; b. 20.6.15, Cromarty; m., Helen Liddell Menzies; 2 s. Educ. Cromarty Higher Grade Public School; Fortrose Academy; Glasgow University. 2nd Bn., Glasgow Highlanders and 9th Gurkha Rifles, 1939-46 (attained rank of Major); Partner, J.M. & J. Mailer, Solicitors, Stirling, 1949-81, retiring as Senior Partner; Dean, Stirling Society of Solicitors and Procurators, 1973-75. Honorary Vice-President (and Past Chairman), Stirling and District Choral Union, since 1984; Past President: Stirling Rotary Club, Stirling Bowling Club, Borestone and Stirling Curling Club, Stirling Probus Club, Stirling Burns Club; Elder, St. Columba's Church, Stirling, since 1950. Recreations: bowls; curling; choral singing; music. Address: (h.) 55 Snowdon Place, Stirling, FK8 2JY; T.-0786 73949.

Malcolm, Robin Neill, DL, JP. Chairman, Argyll & Bute Countryside Trust, since 1990; Member, SW Board, Scottish Natural Heritage, since 1992; Board Member, Argyll & Isles Enterprise, since 1990; b. 11.2.34, Edinburgh; m., Susan Freeman; 2 s.; 2 d. Educ. Eton; North of Scotland College of Agriculture. National Service, A&SH, 1953-54; TA Service, 8th A&SH, 1955-63; shipping and shipbuilding in London and Glasgow, 1955-63; farming, since 1963; Convener, Highlands and Islands Committee, NFU of Scotland, 1972-74; President, SAOS Ltd., 1983-86; Member, Argyll and Bute District Council, 1976-92. Recreations: shooting; swimming. Address: (h.) Duntrune Castle, Kilmartin, Argyll; T.-054 65 283.

Malcolmson, Peter, OBE, CQSW. Administration Manager, Shetland Oil Industries Group; former Director of Social Work, Shetland Islands Council; b. 27.7.39, Lerwick; m., Grace Eleanor Robson; 2 s.; 2 d. Educ. Anderson High School, Lerwick; Moray House College, Edinburgh. Social Worker, 1963-70. Recreations: swimming; distance running; guizing and sailing Viking Longship. Address: (h.) Skersund, Upper Sound, Lerwick, Shetland Isles, ZE1 0RQ.

Mallard, Professor John Rowland, BSc, PhD, DSc, FInstP, CEng, FIEE, FRCPath, FRSE. Professor of Medical Physics and Head of Department, Aberdeen University and Grampian Health Board, since 1965; b. 14.1.27; m., Fiona Mackenzie Lawrance; 1 s.; 1 d. Educ. Nottingham University. President, Hospital Physicists Association, 1972-73; Founder President, International Union of Physical Engineering Sciences in Medicine, 1982-85; Founder President, European Society of Magnetic Resonance in Medicine, 1983-85; Member, International Commission of Radiation Units and Measurements, since 1985; President, Biological Engineering Society, 1978-79; Founder Trustee, Society of Magnetic Resonance in Medicine and Biology, 1982-86; President, International Organisation of Medical Physics, 1979-82. Publications: Brain Tumour Detection, 1961; Medical Radioisotope Visualization, 1966; In-vivo NMR Imaging in Medicine, 1980; Royal Society Wellcome Foundation Prize Lecture: NMR Imaging in Medicine, 1986; Medical Imaging: a tool of our destiny, 1988; Science and Technology in Europe (Contributor), 1990. Address: (b.) Aberdeen University, Aberdeen, AB9 2ZD.

Mallinson, Edward John Harold, MPharm, MPS, FBIM, FRSH. Chief Administrative Pharmaceutical Officer, Lanarkshire Health Board, since 1984; b. 15.3.50, Bingley; m., Diana Gray; 2 d. Educ. Bradford Grammar School; Bradford University. Staff Pharmacist (Ward Pharmacy Services), Bradford Royal Infirmary, 1973-78; District Pharmaceutical Officer, Perth and Kinross District, 1978-83. Chairman, Scottish Chief Administrative Officers, 1990-92; Royal Pharmaceutical Society of Great Britain: Hon. Secretary, Bradford & District Branch, 1978, Hon. Secretary, Dundee & Eastern Scottish Branch, 1979-83, Hon. Secretary and Treasurer, Lanarkshire Branch, since 1984; Member of Council, Royal Society of Health; Vice Chairman and Secretary, Pharmaceutical Group, Royal Society of Health, 1986-89; Chairman, Strathclyde Police/Lanarkshire Health Board Drug Liaison Committee, 1985-91; Member, General Synod, Scottish Episcopal Church; Secretary, Lanarkshire Branch, British Institute of Management, 1989-91, now Chairman. Recreations: genealogy; learning Gaelic; walking and cooking. Address: (h.) Malden, North Dean Park Avenue, Bothwell, Glasgow, G71 8HH; T.-0698 852973.

Malone, Desmond Noel Scott, MB, ChB, FRCPEdin. Consultant Physician, Department of Medicine, Milesmark Hospital, Dunfermline, since 1973; Honorary Senior Lecturer, Edinburgh University, since 1981; b. 12.12.34, Edinburgh; m., Kathleen Helena Murray; 2 s.; 2 d. Educ. Mount St. Mary's College, near Sheffield; Edinburgh University Medical School. House Physician, Peel Hospital, Galashiels; Flight Surgeon, Royal Canadian Airforce, Winnipeg; Research Fellow and Registrar, Northern General Hospital, Edinburgh; Medical Registrar, then Senior Medical Registrar, Western General Hospital, Edinburgh. Past Chairman, Fife Area Medical Committee; Past President, West Fife Medical Society. Recreations: fishing; windsurfing. Address: (h.) 2 Dalmeny View, Dalgety Bay, Fife, KY11 5LU; T.-0383 822532.

Manca, Gianni. Partner, Manca, Amenta, Biolato, Corrao & C., Rome, Milan and Edinburgh; b. 21.7.24, Genoa; m., Paola Graziadei; 2 s.; 1 d. Educ. University of Rome (LLD). Admitted to Bar (Italy), 1953; Member, Italian delegation to Council of the Bars and Law Societies of the European Community, 1978-88 (CCBE); Vice President, CCBE, 1989, President, 1990. Recreations: golf; fishing; shooting; stamp collecting. Address: (b.) Orchard Brae House, 30 Queensferry Road, Edinburgh, EH4 2HG; T.-031-315 2344.

Manlove, Colin Nicholas, MA, BLitt, DLitt. Reader in English Literature, Edinburgh University, since 1984; b. 4.5.42, Falkirk; m., Evelyn Mary Schuftan; 2 s. Educ. Dollar Academy; Edinburgh University. Assistant Lecturer in English Literature, Lecturer, Edinburgh University, 1967-84. Publications: Modern Fantasy; Literature and Reality 1600-1800; The Gap in Shakespeare; The Impulse of Fantasy Literature; Science Fiction: ten explorations; C.S. Lewis: his literary achievement; Critical Thinking: a guide to interpreting literary texts; Christian fantasy: from 1200 to the present. Recreations: walking; DIY. Address: (h.) 92 Polwarth Terrace, Edinburgh, EH11 1NN; T.-031-337 1641.

Mann, Lt. Col. Charles John Howell, OBE, OStJ, TD, DL, MB, BS, DPH, FSA(Scot). Medical Practitioner, since 1949; b. 21.2.26, London; m., Dr. Evelyn M.F. Mann; 1 s. (dec.); 2 d. Educ. Epsom College; St. Mary's Hospital Medical School, London. Chairman, St. Andrew's Ambulance Association, Aberdeen; Hon. Medical Adviser, RNLI, Aberdeen. Recreations: gardening; walking; fishing; shooting. Address: (h.) Altmore, Murtle Den Road, Milltimber, Aberdeen; T.-0224 867682.

Mann, Gordon Laurence, DipTP, MRTPI, MInstPet. Director of Physical Planning, Dumfries and Galloway

Regional Council, since 1987 (Director of Planning, Shetland Islands Council, 1980-87); b. 28.4.48, Dundee. Address: (b.) English Street, Dumfries, DG1 2DD; T.-0387 61234.

Manners, Professor David John, MA, PhD, ScD, DSc, FRSC, FInstBiol, FRSE. Emeritus Professor of Biochemistry, Heriot-Watt University; b. 31.3.28, Castleford; m., Gweneth Mary Chubbock; 2 s.; 1 d. Educ. Grammar School, Castleford; Fitzwilliam House, Cambridge. Lecturer, then Reader in Chemistry, Edinburgh University, 1952-65; awarded Meldola Medal, Royal Institute of Chemistry, 1957; Alsberg-Schoch Memorial Award, American Association of Cereal Chemists, 1984; Award of Merit, Japanese Society of Starch Science, 1989. Recreations: philately; military history. Address: (h.) 165 Mayfield Road, Edinburgh, EH9 3AY.

Manning, Professor Aubrey William George, BSc, DPhil, FInstBiol, Dr (h c) (Toulouse), FRSE. Professor of Natural History, Division of Biological Sciences, Edinburgh University, since 1973; b. 24.4.30, London; m.; 3 s., inc. 2 by pr. m. Educ. Strode's School, Egham; University College, London; Merton College, Oxford. Research, 1951-54; National Service, Royal Artillery, 1954-56; Lecturer, then Reader in Zoology, Edinburgh University, 1956-73; Secretary-General, International Ethological Committee, 1971-79; President, Association for the Study of Animal Behaviour, 1981-84; Member, Scottish Advisory Committee, Nature Conservancy Council, 1982-89; Member, Advisory Committee on Science, NCC, 1985-89; Chairman of Council, Scottish Wildlife Trust, since 1990. Publication: An Introduction to Animal Behaviour, 1992; research papers in biological journals. Recreations: woodland conservation; walking; architecture. Address: (h.) The Old Hall, Ormiston, East Lothian; T.-Pencaitland 340536.

Manojlovic-Muir, Ljubica, BSc, PhD, CChem, FRSC. Reader in Chemistry, Glasgow University, since 1989; b. 31.10.31, Topola, Yugoslavia; m., Dr Kenneth W. Muir; 1 s.; 1 d. Educ. Arandjelovac Gimnazia, Yugoslavia; University of Belgrade. Scientific Officer, Boris Kidrich Institute of Nuclear Sciences, Vincha, Belgrade, 1955-67; 1967-72: Research Fellow, Brookhaven National Laboratory, Upton, New York, Northwestern University, Evanston, Illinois, University of Sussex; Lecturer, Chemistry, Glasgow University, since 1972. Member: Royal Society of Chemistry, British Crystallographic Association. Publications: 182 papers published in chemistry journals. Recreations: reading; music; gardening; hill walking. Address: Department of Chemistry, Glasgow University, Glasgow G12 8QQ; T.-041-339 8855, Ext. 4506.

Mansfield and Mansfield, 8th Earl of (William David Mungo James Murray), JP, DL; b. 7.7.30; m., Pamela Joan Foster; 2 s.; 1 d. Educ. Eton; Christ Church, Oxford. National Service, Malayan Campaign; called to Bar, Inner Temple, 1958; Barrister, 1958-71; Member, British Delegation to European Parliament, 1973-75; Minister of State, Scottish Office, 1979-83; Minister of State, Northern Ireland Office, 1983-84; Director: General Accident Fire and Life Assurance Corporation Ltd., 1972-79, and since 1985; The American Trust Ltd., since 1985; Pinneys of Scotland Ltd., 1985-89; Ross Breeders Ltd., since 1989; Hon. President, St. Andrews Society of Glasgow, since 1972; President, Royal Scottish Country Dance Society, since 1977; First Crown Estate Commissioner, since 1985. Address: (h.) Scone Palace, Perthshire, PH2 6BE.

Manson, Alexander Reid, CBE, SDA. Farmer; Chairman, Buchan Meat Producers Ltd., since 1982; Member, Meat and Livestock Commission, since 1986; General Commissioner of Income Tax, since 1991; Past President, Federation of Agricultural Cooperatives; b. 2.9.31, Oldmeldrum; m., Ethel Mary Philip; 1 s.; 2 d. Educ. Robert Gordon's College; North of Scotland College of Agriculture. Member, Oldmeldrum Town Council, 1960-65; founder Chairman, Aberdeen Beef and Calf Ltd., 1962; Past President, Scottish Agricultural Organisation Society Ltd.; Member, Williams Committee of Enquiry, 1989. Recreations: golf; bird-watching. Address: (h.) Kilblean, Oldmeldrum, Inverurie, AB5 ODN; T.-Oldmeldrum 2226.

Manson, George Inglis, OBE, MB, ChB. Honorary Sheriff, Arbroath, since 1989; b. 8.6.22, Fordoun; m., Helen Johnston; 3 d. Educ. Mackie Academy; Aberdeen University. Assistant in general practice, Peterhead, 1944-48, then Principal, 1948-86; Medical Officer, HM Prison, Peterhead, 1955-87, International Twist Drill Company, Peterhead, 1955-87. Sometime Member and Chairman, former North-East Aberdeenshire Hospitals Board of Management; JP since 1965. Recreations: golf; reading. Address: (h.)12 Brothock Meadows, Letham Grange, Arbroath, DD11 4RL.

Manson, Richard U., MIH. General Manager, State Hospital, Carstairs, since 1990; b. 2.5.51, Glasgow; m., Barbara; 1 s.; 1 d. Educ. Shawlands Academy; Glasgow College of Commerce; Glasgow College of Building. District Housing Manager, then Management Auditor, Glasgow District Council, 1979-87; Operations Director, Quality Street Ltd., 1987-89; Managing Director, Homesense Ltd., 1989-90. Recreations: golf; music; the arts. Address: (b.) State Hospital, Carstairs, Lanark ML11 8RP; T.-0555 840293.

Manson, Thomas Mortimer Yule, MA, DipEd, LLD. Member, Shetland Islands Council, 1982-90; b. 9.2.04, Lerwick. Educ. Anderson Educational Institute; Edinburgh University; Moray House College of Education. Trained and qualified as a teacher; entered family printing and newspaper business, 1929; on father's death in 1941, became Proprietor, T. & J. Manson, Lerwick, and Editor, Shetland News (closed, 1963); Reporter, Radio Shetland, 1979-82; Bandmaster, local Boys' Brigade, seven years; Shetland County Scout Commissioner, 14 years (awarded Silver Acorn by Chief Scout); Conductor, Lerwick Brass Band, five years; Secretary, Lerwick Orchestral Society, 42 years; Chairman, Shetland Civic Society, 12 years. Recreation: music. Address: (h.) 93 Gilbertson Road, Lerwick, Shetland; T.-0595 4632.

Manwaring, Gaye Melodie Anne, MBE, BSc, PhD, FRSA. Coordinator of Tertiary Education, Northern College of Education, since 1987; Director, Medical Open Learning Service, since 1987; b. 15.10.45, Margate; m., Andrew Henry Wilson. Educ. Exeter University; Edinburgh University. Research Fellow, Glasgow University, 1969-75; Senior Lecturer in Educational Technology, Dundee College of Education, 1975-87. Former Governor, SCET; Member, various Committees of SCET, CET, CNAA; work with MSC, Open Tech, National Extension College, Open College, British Council, SOED. Recreations: theatre; gardening; reading; friends; cats. Address: (b.) Northern College of Education (Dundee Campus), Gardyne Road, Dundee, DD5 1NY; T.-0382 453433.

Mappin, Rev. Michael Graeme, BA. Minister, Bower linked with Watten, since 1970; Clerk, Presbytery of Caithness, since 1975; b. 16.3.32, Essex; m., Catherine; 4 s.; 2 d. Educ. Radley College; Pembroke College, Cambridge. Assistant Curate, St. Paul's and St. George's Episcopal Church, Edinburgh, 1960-62; Rector, St. Mungo's Episcopal Church, Balerno, 1962-69; Assistant Minister, Corstorphine Old Parish Church, 1969-70. Recreations: cabinet making; gardening; music. Address: The Manse, Watten, by Wick, Caithness; T.-Watten 220.

Mar, 13th Earl of, and Kellie, 15th Earl of (John Francis Hervey Erskine). Premier Viscount of Scotland; Hereditary Keeper of Stirling Castle; Lord Lieutenant of Clackmannan, since 1966; b. 15.2.21; m., Pansy Constance Thorne; 3 s.; 1 d. Educ. Eton; Trinity College, Cambridge. Major, Scots Guards (retired, 1954); Major, Argyll and Sutherland Highlanders (TA) (retired, 1959); Vice-Convener, Clackmannan County Council, 1961-64; Chairman, Forth Conservancy Board, 1957-68; Chairman, Clackmannanshire T&AFA, 1961-68; Member, Queen's Bodyguard for Scotland (Royal Company of Archers). Address: (h.) Claremont House, Alloa, Clackmannanshire.

Maran, Professor Arnold George Dominic, MB, ChB, MD, FRCS, FACS, FRCP, FRCS (Eng). Professor of Otolaryngology, Edinburgh University, since 1988; Secretary, Royal College of Surgeons; Consultant Surgeon, Royal Infirmary and City Hospital, Edinburgh, since 1974; b. 16.6.36, Edinburgh; m., Anna; 1 s.; 1 d. Educ. Daniel Stewart's College; Edinburgh University; University of Iowa. Trained in Otolaryngology in Edinburgh and America; former Consultant Otolaryngologist, Tayside Health Board, and Professor of Otolaryngology, West Virginia University. Ten Visiting Professorships to foreign universities. Publications: four books and 110 scientific papers. Recreations: golf; music; travel. Address: (h.) 15 Cluny Drive, Edinburgh, EH10 6DW; T.-031-447 8519.

Marjoribanks, Gerald Brian, BA, LRAM, ALAM. Officer for Scotland, Independent Broadcasting Authority, since 1983; b. 22.7.42, Falkirk; m., Kathleen; 2 s.; 2 d. Educ. Falkirk High School; Edinburgh College of Speech and Drama; Open University. Sports Presenter, Sportsreel, Sportscene, Sportsound, BBC Scotland, 1966-83; Lecturer in Drama, Notre Dame College of Education, 1967-79; Co-ordinator of Learning Resources, Dunfermline College of Physical Education, 1979-80; Head of Public Relations, Cumbernauld Development Corporation, 1980-83. Recreations: drama adjudication; badminton; photography. Address: (h.) Underwood, 33 Maggie Wood's Loan, Falkirk, FK1 5HR.

Marjoribanks, Sir James Alexander Milne, KCMG (1965), MA. HM Diplomatic Service, 1934-71; b. 29.5.11, Edinburgh; m., Sonya Patricia Stanley de Brandon (deceased); 1 d. Educ. Edinburgh Academy; Edinburgh University; Strasbourg University. Served in Peking, Hankow, Marseilles, Jacksonville, New York, Bucharest, Canberra, Luxembourg, Bonn, Brussels, London; Under-Secretary of State, Foreign Office, 1962-65; Ambassador to European Communities, 1965-71. Director, Distillers PLC, 1971-76; Member, Edinburgh University Court, 1976-80; Governing Member, Caledonian Research Foundation; Chairman, Scotland in Europe, 1979-91; Member, Committee for European Community Cultural Co-operation. Recreation: hill-walking. Address: Lintonrig, Kirk Yetholm, Kelso; T.-057 382 384.

Marker, Cdr. John (Iain) Hamilton, VRD (and bar), BA, MLitt, FIL, FRMetS, RNR (Rtd.). Depute Principal, Napier College of Commerce and Technology, 1974-87; b. 23.9.24, Greenock; m., Elizabeth Urie Macfarlane. Educ. Ulverston Grammar School; Kings College, Durham University. Assistant Master, Middlesex County Secondary School, 1952-54; Assistant Lecturer in Economics, Kingston College of Advanced Technology, 1954-57; Assistant Lecturer/Lecturer in Economics, Isleworth Polytechnic, 1957-62; Head of Department, West London College, 1962-68; Head of Department, then Depute Principal, Edinburgh College of Commerce, 1968-74. Recreations: golf; reading; gardening. Address: (h.) 2 Cherry Tree Gardens, Balerno, Midlothian, EH14 5SR; T.-031-449 3936.

Marker, William Bennett, MA, MEd. Field Officer, Scottish Committee for Staff Development in Education, 1987-91; b. 5.2.28, Greenock; m., Anne Margaret Manthorpe; 1 s.; 1 d.

Educ. Ulverston Grammar School; Wadham College, Oxford. Assistant Teacher, Purbrook Park High School, 1954-56; Assistant Housemaster, Woodbridge School, 1956-58; Senior History Master, Queen Elizabeth School, Kirkby Lonsdale, 1958-67; Schoolmaster Fellow, Hull University, 1967; Lecturer/Senior Lecturer in History, Jordanhill College of Education, 1967-72 (Principal Lecturer (In-service), 1972-75); Assistant Principal (In-service Education), 1976-86. Member, National Committee for the In-service Training of Teachers, 1976-85; Member, Scottish Council for the Validation of Courses for Teachers, 1983-86. Recreations: hill-walking; theatre-going. Address: (h.) 2 Huntly Drive, Bearsden, Glasgow, G61 3LD; T.-041-942 6756.

Markland, John A., MA, PhD, ACIS. Chief Executive, Fife Regional Council, since 1986; b. 17.5.48, Bolton; m., Muriel Harris; 4 d. Educ. Bolton School; Dundee University. Demographer, Somerset County Council, 1974-76; Senior Professional Assistant, Tayside Regional Council; Personal Assistant to Chief Executive, then Assistant Chief Executive, Fife Regional Council, 1979-86. Recreations: golf; swimming; cycling. Address: (b.) Fife House, North Street, Glenrothes, Fife; T.-0592 754411.

Marks, Frederick Charles, OBE, MA, LLB, FBIM. Deputy Chairman, Local Government Boundary Commission for Scotland; Chairman, Key Housing Services Ltd.; b. 3.12.34, Bellshill; m., Agnes M. Bruce; 3 s.; 1 d. Educ. Wishaw High School; Glasgow University. Depute Town Clerk, Dunfermline, 1963-68; Town Clerk, Hamilton, 1968-75; Chief Executive, Motherwell, 1974-83; General Manager, Scottish Special Housing Association, 1983-89. Address: (h.) Dunkeld, 33 Townhill Road, Dunfermline, KY12 0JD; T.-0383 723501.

Marnoch, Hon. Lord (Michael Stewart Rae Bruce), QC (Scot). Senator of the College of Justice, since 1990; b. 26.7.38. Advocate, 1963; QC, 1975; Advocate Depute, 1983-86.

Marnoch, Derek George, BSc, ACMA. Chief Executive, Aberdeen Chamber of Commerce, since 1983; b. 30.10.35, Aberdeen; m., Kathleen Howard; 3 s. Educ. Aberdeen Grammar School; Aberdeen University. Recreation: golf. Address: (h.) The Gables, Kirk Road, Stonehaven, AB3 2DX; T.-0569 62709.

Marr, Derek Shepherd. Firemaster, Tayside Fire Brigade, since 1990; Zone Fire Commander Designate, Northern Zone Civil Defence, since 1990; Secretary, Scottish Chief & Assistant Chief Fire Officers Association, since 1991; b. 6.7.48, Arbroath; m., Edna; 1 s.; 1 d. Educ. Arbroath High School. Joined fire service, 1967. Chairman, Tayside Fire Liaison Panel; COSLA Adviser to Protective Services Committee; Council Member, Chief & Assistant Chief Fire Officers Association. Recreations: reading; golf. Address: (b.) Fire Brigade Headquarters, Blackness Road, Dundee.

Marr, Norman G., OStJ, DipArch, ARIBA, FRIAS. Consultant Architect/Planner; Director of Planning and Development, Kincardine and Deeside District Council, 1975-92; b. 19.5.37, Aberdeen. Educ. Aberdeen Grammar School; Scott Sutherland School of Architecture, Aberdeen. Architectural Assistant, Aberdeen County Council, 1961-66; Senior Research Assistant, Corporation of the City of Aberdeen, Town Planning Department, 1967-69 (Principal Development Assistant, 1970-75). Organist and Choirmaster, Denburn Parish Church, Aberdeen, since 1956; Secretary, Scottish Federation of Organists, 1970-92; Vice-Chairman, Friends of St. Machar's Cathedral, Aberdeen, and Friends of the Kirk of St. Nicholas, Aberdeen. Recreations: organ playing/building; swimming; marathon running; hill-walking. Address: (h.) 63 Devonshire Road, Aberdeen, AB1 6XP.

Marrian, Ian Frederic Young, MA, CA. Deputy Secretary, Institute of Chartered Accountants of Scotland, since 1991 (Director of Education, since 1981); b. 15.11.43, Kilwinning; m., Moira Selina McSwan; 1 s.; 2 d. Educ. Royal Belfast Academical Institution; Queens University, Belfast; Edinburgh University. Qualified as CA, 1969; Deloitte Haskins & Sells: audit practice, Rome, 1969-72, London, 1972-73, Audit Partner, Edinburgh, 1973-78, Technical Partner, London, 1978-81. Recreations: gardening in the grand scale; wines. Address: (h.) Bowerhouse, Dunbar, EH42 1RE; T.-031-479 4815.

Marrian, Valerie Jean, MB, ChB, FRCP(Lond), FRCP(Edin), DCH. Consultant Paediatrician, since 1967; Honorary Senior Lecturer in Child Health, since 1967; b. 16.8.32, London; m., Douglas Fraser Hooper. Educ. Mary Erskine School, Edinburgh; Edinburgh University. Member, Children's Panel Advisory Committee, 1971-74; Member, Scottish Sports Council, 1974-80, Vice-Chairman, 1980-88; Member, The Sports Council, 1983-88. Recreations: skiing; classical music; opera; dog obedience/agility; cats. Address: (h.) 25 Hamilton Place, Perth, PH1 1BD; T.-0738 21018.

Marsh, John Haig, BA, MEng, PhD, CEng, MIEE. Senior Lecturer, Department of Electronics and Electrical Engineering, Glasgow University, since 1990; b. 15.4.56, Edinburgh; m., Annabel Christine Mitchell. Educ. Glasgow Academy; Cambridge University; Liverpool University; Sheffield University. Lecturer, Glasgow University, 1986-90. Member, IEE Professional Group on Optical Devices and Systems, since 1988; Director, NATO Advanced Study Institute Waveguide Optoelectronics, 1990, Glasgow. Publications: 70 scientific papers; book: Waveguide Optoelectronics (Co-editor). Recreations: hill-walking; steward, Woodlands Methodist Church; classical music; cooking; malt whisky. Address: (h.) 43 Strathcona Gardens, Glasgow, G13 1DN; T.-041-954 0903.

Marshall, David. MP (Labour), Glasgow Shettleston, since 1979; b. 1941.

Marshall, Enid Ann, MA, LLB, PhD, Assoc. RICS, ACIArb, FRSA. Solicitor; Reader in Business Law, Stirling University, since 1977; Editor, Scottish Law Gazette, since 1983; Chairman, Social Security Appeal Tribunal, Stirling and Falkirk, since 1984; b. 10.7.32, Boyndie, Banffshire. Educ. Banff Academy; Bell-Baxter School, Cupar; St. Andrews University. Apprentice Solicitor, 1956-59; Lecturer in Law, Dundee College of Technology, 1959-72; Lecturer, then Senior Lecturer, in Business Law, Stirling University, 1972-77. Departmental Editor, Arbitration Section, Journal of Business Law, since 1976. Publications: General Principles of Scots Law; Scottish Cases on Contract; Scottish Cases on Agency; Scottish Cases on Partnerships and Companies; Scots Mercantile Law; Gill on Arbitration; Charlesworth and Cain Company Law (Scottish Editor); Notes on the Law of Property in Scotland (Editor, 3rd edition); M.C. Oliver's Company Law (10th and 11th editions). Recreations: veganism; animal welfare. Address: (h.) 24 Easter Cornton Road, Stirling, FK9 5ES; T.-Stirling 78865/67285.

Marshall, George Howard Stirling, MBA. Managing Director, Business & Employment Skills Training Ltd., since 1988; b. 24.8.47, Bath; m., Helen Barbara; 2 s. Educ. County Secondary School, Portland, Dorset. Established BEST as training provider, 1988. Fellow, British Institute of Management; Fellow, Institute of Training and Development; Fellow, Institute of Administrative Management; Member, Scottish Council, CBI. Recreations: walking; reading. Address: (h.) 42 Morrishill Drive, Beith, Ayrshire, KA15 1LS; T.-05055 2993.

Marshall, Professor Ian Howard, MA, BD, PhD (Aberdeen), BA (Cantab). Professor of New Testament Exegesis, Aberdeen University, since 1979; b. 12.1.34, Carlisle; m., Joyce Elizabeth; 1 s.; 3 d. Educ. Aberdeen Grammar School; Aberdeen University; Cambridge University; Gottingen University. Assistant Tutor, Didsbury College, Bristol; Methodist Minister, Darlington; Lecturer, then Senior Lecturer and Reader in New Testament Exegesis, Aberdeen University. Publications: Kept by the Power of God; Luke: Historian and Theologian; The Origins of New Testament Christology; New Testament Interpretation (Editor); The Gospel of Luke; I Believe in the Historical Jesus; The Epistles of John; Acts; Last Supper and Lord's Supper; Biblical Inspiration; 1 and 2 Thessalonians; Jesus the Saviour; 1 Peter. Address: (b.) Department of New Testament, King's College, Aberdeen, AB9 2UB; T.-0224 272388.

Marshall, Professor Mary Tara, MA, DSA, DASS. Director, Dementia Services Development Centre, Stirling University; b. 13.6.45, Darjeeling, India. Educ. Mary Erskine School for Girls; Edinburgh University; London School of Economics; Liverpool University. Child Care Officer, London Borough of Lambeth, 1967-69; Social Worker, Personal Service Society, Liverpool, 1970-74; Research Organiser, Age Concern, Liverpool, 1974-75; Lecturer in Social Studies, Liverpool University, 1975-83; Director, Age Concern Scotland, 1983-89. Publication: Social Work with Old People, 1983. Recreations: photography; bird-watching. Address: (b.) Dementia Services Development Centre, Stirling University, Stirling, FK9 4LA; T.-0786 67740.

Marshall, Susan Muriel, ALAM. Reporter to the Children's Panel, Western Isles Islands Area, since 1990; b. 8.6.49, St. Andrews; m., John Lawrence Marshall; 2 d. Educ. St. Denis School, Edinburgh; Edinburgh College of Speech & Drama. Q. & M. analyst, 1970-74; Member, Western Isles Children's Panel, 1976-90, Chairman, 1983-90. Recreations: walking; cooking; France. Address: (b.) 10 Harbour View, Stornoway, Isle of Lewis; T.-0851 706317.

Marshall, William Alexander, OStJ. Chief Executive, Kincardine and Deeside Enterprise Trust, since 1991; Chairman, Braemar Civic Amenities Trust, since 1986; Hon. Warden, Nature Conservancy Council, since 1977; b. 26.6.35, Aberdeen; m., Dora; 3 s. Educ. Aberdeen Grammar School. F. Duack & Son (Aberdeen), Senior Partner, 1957-91; Managing Director, Marshall Mountain & Ski Equipment Ltd., 1965-76, Scorpion Outdoor Sports Ltd., 1967-76; founder Leader, Aberdeen Mountain Rescue Team, 1964-74. Recreations: mountaineering; cross country skiing; photography. Address: (h.) Mountain Cottage, Chapel Brae, Braemar; T.-03397 41695.

Martin, Daniel, MA, BSc, PhD, FRSE, FIMA. Honorary Lecturer in Mathematics, Glasgow University, since 1980; b. 16.4.15, Carluke. Educ. High School of Glasgow; Glasgow University. Lecturer in Mathematics, Royal Technical College, Glasgow, 1938-47; Scientific Officer, Air Navigation Section, Royal Aircraft Establishment, Farnborough, 1941-45; Lecturer/Senior Lecturer in Mathematics, Glasgow University, 1947-80; Snell Visitor to Balliol College, Oxford, 1975-76. President, Glasgow Mathematical Association, 1958-59; President, Edinburgh Mathematical Society, 1960-61; former Assessor, Church of Scotland's selection schools for candidates for the Ministry. Publications: Solving Problems in Complex Numbers, 1968; An Introduction to Vector Analysis (Reviser), 1970; Maniford Theory: an introduction for mathematical physicists, 1991. Recreations: theology; local history; Gaelic. Address: (b.) Department of Mathematics, Glasgow University, Glasgow, G12 8QW; T.-041-339 8855, Ext. 6537.

Martin, David McLeod, DA, RSW, RGI. Painter; b. 30.12.22, Glasgow; m., Isobel Agnes Fowlie Smith; 4 s. Educ. Govan High School; Glasgow School of Art; Jordanhill College of Education. RAF, 1942-46. Principal Teacher, Hamilton Grammar School, 1973-83; retired early to paint full-time; exhibits regularly in Scotland; exhibited RA, 1984; numerous group shows; one man shows, Glasgow, Edinburgh, Perth, Greenock, Newcastle, Stenton, London; former Vice President, RSW. Address: (h.) The Old Schoolhouse, 53 Gilmour Street, Eaglesham, Glasgow, G76 0LG.

Martin, David Weir, BA (Econ). Member (Labour), European Parliament, for Lothians, since 1984; Vice-President, European Parliament, since 1989; b. 26.8.54, Edinburgh; m., Margaret Mary Cook; 1 s.; 1 d. Educ. Liberton High School; Heriot-Watt University. Worked as stockbroker's assistant and animal rights campaigner; became Lothian Regional Councillor, 1982; Vice-President, National Playbus Association; Member, Board of Governors, Road Industry Training Board, Livingston MOTEC; Member, Committee, Advocates for Animals; Director, St. Andrew Animal Fund; Member, West Lothian Develoment Council. Recreations: soccer; reading. Publication: Bringing Common Sense to the Common Market – A Left Agenda for Europe. Address: (h.) 7 Mortonhall Park Gardens, Edinburgh, EH17 8SL; T.-(b.) 031-557 0936.

Martin, Ged, BA, MA, PhD. Director, Centre of Canadian Studies, Edinburgh University, since 1983; President, British Association for Canadian Studies, since 1990; Co-Editor, British Review of New Zealand Studies, since 1988; b. 22.5.45, Hornchurch; m., Ann Barry. Educ. Royal Liberty School, Romford; Magdalene College, Cambridge. Research Fellow, Magdalene College, Cambridge, 1970-72, Australian National University, 1972-77; Lecturer, then Statutory Lecturer, University College, Cork, 1977-83. Canadian High Commissioner's Award for Service to British-Canadian Relations, 1989. Publications: nine books, including Canada's Heritage in Scotland (Co-author), 1989. Recreations: reading and writing history; music; talking to cats. Address: (b.) 21 George Square, Edinburgh, EH8 9LD; T.-031-667 1011, Ext. 6801.

Martin, Graham Douglas Cameron, MA, MLitt, PhD, FIL. Senior Lecturer in German, Strathclyde University, since 1990 (Lecturer, 1970-90); b. 28.1.37, Liverpool. Educ. Merchant Taylors' School, Crosby; Cambridge University; Trinity College, Dublin. Assistant Lecturer in German, Strathclyde University, 1967-70. Member of Council, Institute of Linguists, since 1987; President, Scottish Society of Institute of Linguists, since 1987. Publication: book on Liechtenstein education system; several articles. Recreations: theatre-going; walking. Address: (h.) 12 Crown Gardens, Glasgow, G12 9HL; T.-041-334 5940.

Martin, Graham Dunstan, MA, BLitt (Oxon), GradCertEd. Senior Lecturer, French Department, Edinburgh University, since 1982; b. 21.10.32, Leeds; m., 1, Ryllis E. Daniel; 2 s.; 1 d.; 2, Anne M. Crombie; 2 s. Educ. Leeds Grammar School; Oxford University. Teacher: Robert Clack Technical School, Dagenham, 1956, Great Yarmouth Grammar School, 1959; Assistant, Centre Pedagogique Regional, Montpellier, 1962; Teacher, Colchester Royal Grammar School, 1964; Junior Lecturer, then Lecturer, French Department, Edinburgh University, 1965-82. Publications: Paul Valery's Cimetiere Marin, 1971; Language, Truth and Poetry, 1975; The Architecture of Experience, 1981; Shadows in the Cave, 1990; novels: Giftwish, 1980; Catchfire, 1981; The Soul Master, 1984; Time-Slip, 1986; The Dream Wall, 1987; Half a Glass of Monshine, 1988. Address: (b.) French Department, Edinburgh University, 60 George Square, Edinburgh, EH8 9JU; T.-031-650 1000, Ext. 8409.

Martin, Rev. James, MA, BD, DD. Minister, High Carntyne, Glasgow, 1954-87; b. 21.1.21, Motherwell; m., Marion Gordon Greig; 2 d. Educ. Dalziel High School, Motherwell; Glasgow University. Minister, Newmilns West Church, 1946-54; Convener, Publications Committee, General Assembly, 1978-83 and Board of Communications, 1983-87. Publications: Did Jesus Rise from the Dead?; The Reliability of the Gospels; Letters of Caiaphas to Annas; Suffering Man, Loving God; The Road to the Aisle; People in the Jesus Story; A Plain Man in the Holy Land; Listening to the Bible; William Barclay: A Personal Memoir; My Friend Bobby; It's You, Minister; It's My Belief; Travels in the Holy Land; God-Collared. Recreations: football; tennis; conversation. Address: 9 Magnolia Street, Wishaw; T.-Cambusnethan 385825.

Martin, James B., BA (Econ). General Secretary, Educational Institute of Scotland, since 1988; b. 6.12.53, Stirling; m., Anne; 1 s.; 1 d. Educ. Larbert High School; Heriot-Watt University; Moray House College of Education. Teacher, Falkirk High School, 1975-79; Field Officer, then Assistant Secretary, EIS, 1979-88. Board Member, Forth Valley Enterprise; Executive Member, European Trade Union Committee for Education; Member, European Committee, World Confederation of Organisations of the Teaching Profession; Member, SCDI Executive; Member, Standing Committee on Crime Prevention; Convener, STUC Education and Training Committee. Recreations: Hibernian FC; football. Address: (b.) 46 Moray Place, Edinburgh; T.-031-225 6244.

Martin, James Davidson, MA, BD, PhD. Senior Lecturer in Hebrew and Old Testament, St. Andrews University, since 1977 (Chairman, Department of Biblical Criticism and Hebrew, 1983-90; Dean, Faculty of Divinity, 1986- 90); b. 4.5.35, Stirling; m., Frances Margaret Stewart; 1 s.; 2 d. Educ. High School of Stirling; Glasgow University. Minister, Dunscore (Dumfries), 1962-66; Glasgow University: Assistant in Old Testament Language and Literature, 1966-68, Lecturer in Hebrew, 1968-69; ordained to priesthood of Scottish Episcopal Church, 1989. Publication: The Book of Judges. Address: (h.) 22 Kilrymont Road, St. Andrews, Fife; T.-0334 77361.

Martin, John S.B., BSc. Assistant Secretary, Transport and Local Roads Division, Scottish Office, since 1989; b. 7.7.46, West Kilbride; m., Catriona Meldrum; 1 s.; 1 d. Educ. Bell-Baxter High School, Cupar; St. Andrews University. Assistant Principal, SED, 1968-73; Private Secretary to Parliamentary Under Secretary of State, 1971-73; Principal, SED/CS/SHHD, 1973-79; Rayner Scrutinies, Consultative Committee on the Curriculum/SDD Planning, 1979-80; Assistant Secretary, Highlands and Tourism Division, SEPD/IDS, 1980-84; Housing Division 1, SDD, 1984-89. Recreations: tennis; cricket; philately. Address: (b.) New St. Andrews House, Edinburgh; T.-031-244 4146.

Martin, Michael John. MP (Labour), Glasgow Springburn, since 1979; Chairman, Scottish Grand Committee, since 1987; b. 3.7.45, Glasgow; m., Mary McLay; 1 s.; 1 d. Educ. St. Patrick's Boys' School, Glasgow. Member, Glasgow Corporation, 1973-74, and Glasgow District Council, 1974-79. Member, Speaker's Panel of Chairmen, since 1987; Fellow, Parliament and Industry Trust; Secretary, British-Italian Parliamentary Group. Recreations: hill-walking; study-ing history of Forth and Clyde Canal; listening to pipe band music. Address: (h.) 144 Broomfield Road, Glasgow, G21 3UE; T.-041-558 2975.

Martin, Robert, MC, BL. Consultant Solicitor, Wright & Crawford, Paisley, retired; Honorary Sheriff; b. 5.2.17, Wishaw; m., Dr. Jan J. Martin; 1 s.; 1 d. Educ. Dalziel High School, Motherwell; Glasgow University. War Service, 1940-46: Field Artillery and Parachute Brigade, Singapore, India,

Middle East, Italy, Greece, France, Germany (commissioned, 1940). Honorary Vice-President, Paisley Branch, Save the Children Fund; Governor, Imperial Cancer Research Fund. Recreations: golf; swimming. Address: (h.) The Willows, 12 Crosbie Wood, Paisley, PA2 OSG; T.-041-884 2113.

Martin, Robert (Roy) Logan, QC, LLB. Advocate, since 1976; Barrister, since 1990; b. 31.7.50, Glasgow; m., Fiona Frances Neil; 1 s.; 2 d. Educ. Paisley Grammar School; Glasgow University. Solicitor, 1973-76; Member, Sheriff Courts Rules Council, 1981-84; Standing Junior Counsel, Department of Employment (Scotland), 1983-84; Advocate-Depute, 1984-87; admitted to Bar of New South Wales, 1987; Queen's Counsel, 1988; called to the Bar, Lincoln's Inn, 1990; Chairman (part-time), Industrial Tribunals, since 1990; Chairman, Scottish Planning, Local Government and Environmental Bar Group, since 1991. Honorary Secretary, The Wagering Club, 1982-91. Recreations: shooting; skiing. Address: (h.) Hardengreen House, Dalkeith, EH22 3LF; T. 031-660 5997.

Martin-Bates, Robert Stuart, BL. Honorary Sheriff, Perth, since 1989; b. 8.5.21, Perth; m., Ursula Louise Sarena; 2 s. Educ. Glenalmond College; Edinburgh University. Private practice as solicitor in Perth and Pitlochry, 1948-90; Burgh Prosecutor, Crieff, 1960-74; Depute Burgh Prosecutor, Perth, 1963-74. Member and Past Moderator, Perth Society of High Constables, since 1957; Past President, Society of Solicitors of the City and County of Perth; Member, Committee, Perth Model Lodging House Association, 1950-85 (Chairman, 1968-85); Member, Committee, Perthshire & Kinrosshire Society for the Blind, 1979-89, including three years as Chairman. Recreations: golf; gardening; reading. Address: (h.) Immeriach, Glencarse, Perth, PH2 7NF; T.-073886 284.

Marwick, Ewan, MA. Secretary and Chief Executive, Glasgow Chamber of Commerce; Secretary, Association of Scottish Chambers of Commerce, since 1982; b. 23.4.52, Edinburgh; m., Helen Daw; 4 s.; 1 d. Educ. Daniel Stewart's College; Edinburgh University. Postgraduate research and consultancy work; Assistant Secretary, Royal Institution of Chartered Surveyors (Scottish Branch); Depute Secretary, Glasgow Chamber of Commerce, 1980-82; Chairman, UK Certification and International Trade Formalities Committee, since 1991; UK Representative, Regional Policy Committee, European Chambers of Commerce; Non-Executive Director, Edinburgh Financial and General Holdings Ltd.; a director, Glasgow Opportunities and Glasgow Compact; Secretary, Glasgow Posts and Telecommunications Advisory Committees; Member, Scottish Advisory Committee on Telecommunications; Hon. Secretary, Saints and Sinners Club of Scotland. Address: (b.) Glasgow Chamber of Commerce, 30 George Square, Glasgow, G2 1EQ; T.-041-204 2121.

Marwick, George Robert, SDA, DL, JP. Chairman, Swannay Farms Ltd., since 1972; Chairman, Campbeltown Creamery (Holdings) Ltd., 1974-90; Deputy Lieutenant, County of Orkney, since 1976; Member, Countryside Commission for Scotland, 1978-86; b. 27.2.32, Edinburgh; m., 1, Hanne Jensen; 3 d.; 2, Norma Gerrard. Educ. Port Regis; Bryanston; Edinburgh School of Agriculture. Councillor, local government, 1968-78; Vice-Convener, Orkney County Council, 1970-74, Convener, Orkney Islands Council, 1974-78; Chairman, North of Scotland Water Board, 1970-73; Member, Scottish Agricultural Consultative Panel, since 1972 (formerly Winter Keep Panel, 1964-72); Director, North Eastern Farmers Ltd., since 1968; Director, Orkney Islands Shipping Co., 1972-87; Council Member, National Trust for Scotland, 1979-84. Recreations: shooting; tennis; motor sport. Address: (h.) Swannay House, by Evie, Orkney; T.-085-672 365.

Mason, Christopher Michael, MA, PhD. Leader, Strathclyde Liberal Democrat Group, since 1986; Member, Strathclyde Regional Council, since 1982; Lecturer in Politics, Glasgow University, since 1966; b. 8.3.41, Hexham; m., Stephanie Maycock; 2 d. Educ. Marlborough College; Magdalene College, Cambridge. Alliance candidate, Glasgow, European Elections, 1984; PPC candidate (Liberal Democrat), Glasgow Hillhead; Chairman, Scottish Liberal Party, 1987-88; Member, Scottish Constitutional Convention, since 1989. Publication: Effective Management of Resources; The International Politics of the North Sea, 1979. Recreation: sailing. Address: (h.) 18 Randolph Road, Glasgow, G11 7LG; T.-041-339 2840.

Mason, Professor David Kean, CBE, BDS, MD, Hon. DChD, FRCS, FDS, FRCPath, Hon. FFD, Hon. FDS. Professor of Oral Medicine, Glasgow University, since 1967; Dean of Dental Education, 1980-90; Honorary Consultant Dental Surgeon, since 1965; b. 5.11.28, Paisley; m., Judith Armstrong; 2 s.; 1 d. Educ. Paisley Grammar School; Glasgow Academy; St. Andrews University; Glasgow University. RAF Dental Branch, 1952-54; Registrar in Oral Surgery, Dundee, 1954-56; Senior Lecturer in Dental Surgery and Pathology, Glasgow University, 1964-67; Honorary Consultant Dental Surgeon, Glasgow, 1964-67; Chairman, National Dental Consultative Committee, 1976-80 and since 1983; Member: Medicines Commission, 1976-80, Dental Committee, MRC, 1973-83, Physiological Systems Board, MRC, 1976-80, GDC, since 1976, Dental Strategy Review Group, 1980-81, Dental Review Working Party, UGC, 1986-87, WHO Expert Committee on Oral Health, since 1991; Convener, Dental Council, RCPSGlas, 1977-80; John Tomes Prize, RCS England, 1979. Publications: Salivary Glands in Health and Disease (Co-author); Introduction to Oral Medicine (Co-author); Self Assessment: Manuals I and II (Co-Editor); Oral Manifestations of Systemic Disease. Recreations: golf; tennis; gardening; enjoying the pleasure of the countryside. Address: (h.) Greystones, Houston Road, Kilmacolm, Renfrewshire; T.-Kilmacolm 2001.

Mason, Derek Stevens, CBE (1986), JP, FRICS, FFB. Chairman, Scottish Special Housing Association, 1981-89; Partner, John Baxter, Dunn and Gray, Chartered Quantity Surveyors, since 1970; Governor (Vice-chairman, 1987), Hutchesons' Educational Trust, since 1972; b. 21.5.34, Glasgow; m., Jeanette; 2 s.; 1 d. Educ. Allan Glen's School, Glasgow; Royal Technical College (part-time). RICS: Chairman, West of Scotland Junior Sub-Branch, 1965-66, Chairman, Scottish Junior Branch, 1966-67; Councillor, Glasgow Corporation, 1970 and 1972-75, Glasgow District Council, 1974-84 (Deputy Leader, Conservative Group, 1977-80, Bailie, 1977-80); Chairman, Glasgow Sports Promotion Council, 1977-80 (Hon. Vice-President, since 1980); Preceptor, Hutchesons' Hospital, 1978-80; JP, since 1977; Member, Master Court, Incorporation of Masons of Glasgow, since 1983, Collector, 1989-90, Deacon, 1991-92; Member, Merchants House of Glasgow. Recreations: reading; current affairs; watching Clyde FC. Address: (h.) Carinya, 77 Newlands Road, Glasgow, G43 2JP; T.-041-649 2665.

Mason, Douglas C., BSc. Member, Glenrothes Development Corporation, since 1985; Parliamentary Research Assistant, since 1979; Freelance Journalist, since 1977; b. 30.9.41, Dunfermline. Educ. Bradford Grammar School; St. Andrews University. Conservative Party Organising Secretary, 1969-77; Member, Fife County Council, 1967-70; Member, Kirkcaldy District Council, 1974-88; Member, Scottish Housing Advisory Committee, 1978-80; contested Central Fife, General Election, 1983; Vice-Convener, General Council Business Committee, St. Andrews University. Domestic Policy Adviser, Adam Smith Institute, since 1984. Publications: Allocation and Transfer of Council Houses (Co-author), 1980; The Qualgo Complex, 1984; Revising the Rating System, 1985; Room for Improvement, 1985; University Challenge, 1986; Time to Call Time, 1986; Ex Libris, 1986; Expounding the Arts, 1987; Licensed to Live, 1988; A Home for Enterprise, 1989; Privatizing the Posts, 1989. Recreations: books; music. Address: (h.) 84 Barnton Place, Glenrothes, Fife; T.-0592 758766.

Mason, Gavin John Finlay, MA, LLB. Solicitor; Secretary and Legal Adviser, Strathclyde Passenger Transport Executive, since 1984; b. 15.5.31, Bargeddie, Lanarkshire; m., Patricia Hunter Anderson; 1 s.; 1 d. Educ. Hamilton Academy; Glasgow University. Solicitor in private practice, until 1979, then local government service. Address: (h.) 3 Newark Drive, Glasgow, G41 4QJ; T.-041-423 7496.

Mason, Jeanette Miller. Deputy Chairman, Irvine Development Corporation, since 1991 (Member, 1983-91); Member, Scottish Transport Users Consultative Committee, since 1987; Member, Office of Electricity Regulation, since 1992; b. 12.10.35, Glasgow; m., Derek S. Mason, CBE, JP (qv); 2 s.; 1 d. Educ. Strathbungo. Member, Scottish Committee, IBA, 1972-77; Children's Panel (Glasgow), 1971-77; Member, Scottish Gas Consumers' Council, 1982-86; Councillor, Strathclyde Regional Council, 1978-86; Chairman, Strathclyde Lunch Committee, Action Research for the Crippled Child, 1985-87, Chairman, Special Events Committee, since 1990; Member, DSS Appeals Tribunal, since 1987; Panel Member for Scotland, Gas Consumers Council, since 1986. Recreations: current affairs; politics; reading; gardening. Address: (h.) Carinya, 77 Newlands Road, Glasgow, G43 2JP; T.-041-649 2665.

Mason, Professor Emeritus John Kenyon French, CBE, MD, LLD, FRCPath, DMJ. Regius Professor of Forensic Medicine, Edinburgh University, 1973-85; b. 19.12.19, Lahore; m., Elizabeth Latham (deceased); 2 s. Educ. Downside School; Cambridge University; St. Bartholomew's Hospital. Regular Officer, Medical Branch, RAF, following War Service; Consultant in charge, RAF Department of Aviation and Forensic Pathology, 1957-73. President, British Association in Forensic Medicine, 1981-83; Swiney Prize in Jurisprudence, 1978. Publication: Forensic Medicine for Lawyers, 2nd Edition; Law and Medical Ethics, 3rd Edition (Co-author); Medico-legal Aspects of Reproduction and Parenthood; Human Life and Medical Practice. Address: (h.) 66 Craiglea Drive, Edinburgh, EH10 5PF; T.-031-447 2301.

Mason, Keith Stirling, LLB (Hons), NP. Chief Administrative Officer, Dunfermline District Council, since 1991; Clerk of the Peace, Dunfermline, since 1991; b. 4.6.55, Montrose. Educ. Kirkcaldy High School; Edinburgh University. Legal apprenticeship, Dundas & Wilson, CS, Edinburgh; Legal Assistant, Dunfermline District Council, 1979-82, Senior Legal Assistant, 1982-85; Principal Solicitor, 1985-91. Clerk to Standing Conference of Local Authorities in the Forth Estuary. Recreations: squash; public transport systems; Church elder; Crusaders leader. Address: (b.) City Chambers, Kirkgate, Dunfermline; T.-0383 722711.

Mason, Rev. Canon Kenneth Staveley, BD, BSc, ARCS. Principal, Coates Hall (Theological College of the Scottish Episcopal Church); Canon, St. Mary's Cathedral, Edinburgh; Pantonian Professor of Theology, since 1989; b. 1.11.31, Winnipeg, Canada; m., Barbara Thomson; 1 s.; 1 d. Educ. Imperial College of Science and Technology, London; Wells Theological College. Vicar, Allerthorpe with Thornton and Melbourne, Diocese of York, 1963-69; Sub-Warden and Librarian, St. Augustine's College, Canterbury, 1969-76; Director and Principal, Canterbury School of Ministry, 1976-89; Examining Chaplain to Archbishop of Canterbury, 1977-91. Recreation: bird watching. Address: (b.) Coates Hall, Rosebery Crescent, Edinburgh EH12 5JT; T.-031-337 3838.

Mason, Peter James, MSc, CEng, FICE, FIHT, MCIT, DipTE. Director of Highways, Lothian Regional Council, since 1981; b. 20.7.33, Newton Abbott; m., Janet Mary Terrill; 1 d. Educ. Watford Boys' Grammar School. Joint Deputy (Planning and Transportation), South Yorkshire County Council, 1973-81. Recreations: gardening; walking. Address: (b.) 19 Market Street, Edinburgh, EH1 1BL; T.-031-469 3637.

Massie, Allan Johnstone, BA, FRSL. Author and Journalist; Member, Scottish Arts Council; b. 16.10.38, Singapore; m., Alison Langlands; 2 s.; 1 d. Educ. Drumtochty Castle; Trinity College, Glenalmond; Trinity College, Cambridge. Schoolmaster, Drumtochty Castle, 1960-71; taught EFL, 1972-75; Creative Writing Fellow, Edinburgh University, 1982-84, Glasgow and Strathclyde Universities, 1985-86; Editor, New Edinburgh Review, 1982-84; Fiction Reviewer, The Scotsman, since 1975; Television Critic, Sunday Standard, 1981-83 (Fraser of Allander Award, Critic of the Year, 1982); Sports Columnist, Glasgow Herald, 1985-88; Columnist, Sunday Times, since 1987. Publications: (novels): Change and Decay in all around I see; The Last Peacock; The Death of Men (Scottish Arts Council Book Award); One Night in Winter; Augustus; A Question of Loyalties; The Hanging Tree; Tiberius; The Sins of the Fathers; (non-fiction): Muriel Spark; Ill Met by Gaslight; The Caesars; Portrait of Scottish Rugby; Colette; 101 Great Scots; Byron's Travels; Glasgow; (as Editor): Edinburgh and the Borders in Verse; (radio play): Quintet in October; (play) The Minstrel and the Shirra. Recreations: reading; watching rugby, cricket, racing; walking the dogs. Address: (h.) Thirladean House, Selkirk, TD7 5LU; T.-Selkirk 20393.

Massie, Leslie Alexander, MA, LLB, CM, PJK (Malaysia). Advocate, since 1953; b. 20.5.10, Aberdeen; m., Margot N. Hesketh; 1 d. Educ. Robert Gordon's College, Aberdeen; Aberdeen University. General legal practice as Solicitor in Scotland, 1936-37; Examining Officer's Commission, HM Coal Commission and HM Sasine Office, Scotland, 1938-39; enlisted as private, Royal Scots, 1939; commissioned 2nd Lt., Royal Scots Fusiliers, 1940-42; Captain and Adjutant, 15th (Scottish) Division Infantry Training Battle School, 1943-44; passed SC Military Staff College, Camberley, 1945; Staff Officer (Major), General Headquarters South East Asia Command, XIV Army, 1945; promoted Lt.-Col., Royal Scots Fusiliers, 1945; President, Superior Court (Military) and State Legal Advsier, Malay States of Kedah and Perlis, 1945-46; Assistant Judge-Advocate General GHQ South East Asia Command, 1946-47; President, War Crimes Court, South East Asia, 1947-48; demobilised Army, 1948; passed entry to HM Colonial Legal Service and gazetted as Federal Counsel to Government of Malaya, 1948; later, Senior Federal Counsel; Member, State Executive Council and State Legislative Council in several Malay States and British Settlements; called to Scottish Bar, 1953; took part in deliberations in respect of British Settlement of Malacca, HM Reid Constitutional Commission, 1957; Solicitor-General, Federation of Malaysia, 1959-60; returned to UK, 1961. Recreations: golf; bowling; gardening. Address: (h.) 9 Whitehouse Terrace, Edinburgh, EH9 2EU; T.-031-667 6462.

Masson, Alastair H.B., BA, MB, ChB, FRCSEdin, FFARCS. President, British Society of the History of Medicine; Consultant Anaesthetist, Edinburgh Royal Infirmary (retired); b. 30.1.25, Bathgate; m., Marjorie Nan Paisley-Whyte; 3 s.; 1 d. Educ. Bathgate Academy; Edinburgh University. Visiting Professor of Anesthesiology, South Western Medical School, Dallas, Texas, 1962-63. President, Scottish Society of Anaesthetists, 1978-79; Honorary Archivist, Royal College of Surgeons, Edinburgh; President, Scottish Society of the History of Medicine, 1984-87. Recreations: golf; hill-walking; music; travel. Address: (h.) 13 Osborne Terrace, Edinburgh.

Masters, Christopher, BSc (Hons), PhD, AKC. Chief Executive, Christian Salvesen PLC, since 1989; b. 2.5.47, Northallerton; m., Gillian Mary Hodson; 2 d. Educ. Richmond School; King's College, London; Leeds University. Shell Research BV/Shell Chemicals UK Ltd., 1971-77; joined Christian Salvesen as Business Development Manager, 1979; transferred to Christian Salvesen Inc., USA, 1982, as Director of Planning; Managing Director, Christian Salvesen Seafoods, 1983; Managing Director, Industrial Services Division, 1985; appointed a Director, Christian Salvesen PLC, 1987. Member, Scottish Economic Council, since 1991, Scottish Council of CBI, since 1988, Scottish Board of Young Enterprise, since 1986; Member, Governing Council, Queen Margaret College, since 1991. Recreations: wines; clocks. Address: (b.) 50 East Fettes Avenue, Edinburgh, EH4 1EQ; T.-031-552 7101.

Masterton, Gavin George, FIB (Scot). General Manager, Bank of Scotland, since 1986; b. 19.11.41, Dunfermline; m., Sheila; 3 d. Educ. Dunfermline High School; Harvard University (AMP). Began banking career with British Linen Bank, 1957; branch banking for several years, then to various Head Office functions; appointed Assistant General Manager; initiated bank's move into management buy-out market. Recreations: gardening; walking. Address: (b.) Uberior House, 61 Grassmarket, Edinburgh; T.-031 243 5750.

Mather, Alexander Smith, BSc, PhD. Senior Lecturer, Department of Geography, Aberdeen University, since 1982; Editor, Scottish Geographical Magazine; b. 17.9.43, Aberdeen; m., Grace MacArthur; 1 s. Educ. Maud School; Peterhead Academy; Aberdeen Grammar School; Aberdeen University. Department of Geography, Aberdeen University: Assistant Lecturer, 1967, Lecturer, 1970. Publications: academic papers and monographs; Land Use; Global Forest Resources. Recreation: hill-walking. Address: (b.) Department of Geography, Aberdeen University, Aberdeen, AB9 2UF; T.-0224 272354.

Mather, John, FSCA, FCIS, FCIT. Managing Director, Clyde Port Authority, since 1980; b. 17.12.36, Glasgow. Clyde Navigation Trust (which became Clyde Port Authority): joined, 1953, Director Finance and Marketing, 1974, Deputy Managing Director, 1977; Chairman, Ardrossan Harbour Co. Ltd.; Member, British Ports Federation Board of Directors; Member, Council, Company and Commercial Accountants; President of World Ports, International Association of Ports and Harbors; Visiting Professor, Strathclyde University Department of Engineering. Address: (b.) 16 Robertson Street, Glasgow, G2 8DS; T.-041-221 8733.

Matheson, Alexander, OBE, JP, MRPharmS. Convener, Western Isles Islands Council, 1982-90; Member, Western Isles Health Board, since 1972 (Vice-Chairman, since 1991); Member, Stornoway Trust, since 1967; b. 16.11.41, Stornoway; m., Irene Mary Davidson, BSc, MSc; 2 s.; 2 d. Educ. Nicolson Institute, Stornoway; Robert Gordon's Institute of Technology, Aberdeen. Member: Stornoway Town Council, 1967-75 (Provost, 1971-75), Ross and Cromarty County Council, 1967-75; Chairman, Stornoway Trust, 1971-81; Member, Stornoway Pier and Harbour Commission, since 1967 (Chairman, 1970-71 and since 1991); Chairman, Development Services, Western Isles Islands Council, 1974-80; Vice-Convener, Western Isles Islands Council, 1980-83; Honorary Sheriff, since 1972; Parliamentary candidate (Labour), 1979; Chairman, Lewis Development Fund (now Western Isles Development Fund), since 1972; President, Islands Commission of the Conference of Peripheral Maritime Regions of Europe, 1987-91; Director, Western Isles Enterprise, since 1991; Director, Harris Tweed Association Ltd., since 1991. Address: (h.) 33 Newton Street, Stornoway, Isle of Lewis; T.-0851 2082.

Matheson, Allen Short, FRIBA, PPRIAS, MRTPI. Senior Partner, Matheson Gleave Partnership, Architects and Interior Designers, since 1983; b. 28.2.26, Port-Said, Egypt; m., Catherine Anne; 2 s. Educ. George Watson's College; Edinburgh College of Art. Past President, Royal Incorporation of Architects in Scotland; Past Chairman, Scottish Construction Industry Group; former Vice-Chairman, Board of Governors, Glasgow School of Art; former Director, Glasgow Chamber of Commerce; Past Chairman, Joint Standing Committee of Architects, Surveyors and Building Contractors; Member, Royal Fine Art Commission for Scotland. Address: (b.) 10 Lynedoch Crescent, Glasgow, G3 6EW; T.-041-332 6025.

Matheson, Andrew James, BSc, PhD. Director of Manpower, NHS in Scotland Management Executive, since 1990; b. 13.10.37, Inverness; m., Muriel Oliver Davidson; 3 d. Educ. Inverness Royal Academy; Edinburgh University. Research Fellow, Department of Electrical Engineering, Glasgow University, 1962-65; Lecturer, then Senior Lecturer, Department of Chemistry, Essex University, 1965-75; Principal, Scottish Office, 1975-89; Assistant Secretary, since 1989. Recreations: Church organist; choral singing; Munros compleated. Address: (b.) St. Andrews House, Edinburgh, EH1 3DE; T.-031-244 2233.

Matheson, Very Rev. James Gunn, MA, BD. Moderator, General Assembly of the Church of Scotland, 1975-76; Minister, Portree, 1973-79; b. 1.3.12.

Mathewson, David Carr, BSc, CA. Merchant Banker; Director, Noble Grossart Limited, since 1989; b. 26.7.47, Broughty Ferry; m., Jan McIntyre; 1 s.; 1 d. Educ. Daniel Stewart's College, Edinburgh; St. Andrews University. Deloitte Haskins & Sells, Edinburgh, 1968-72; Williams Glyn & Co., London, 1972-75; Nedbank Group, South Africa, 1976-86; Noble Grossart Limited, since 1986; Director, Quicks Group plc, since 1991. Recreations: family interests; golf; skiing; athletics. Address: (b.) 48 Queen Street, Edinburgh, EH2 3NR; T.-031-226 7011.

Mathewson, George Ross, CBE, BSc, PHD, MBA, LLD, FRSE, CEng, MIEE, CBIM. Deputy Group Chief Executive, Royal Bank of Scotland Group plc, Royal Bank of Scotland plc, since 1990; Director, Strategic Planning and Development, Royal Bank of Scotland Group plc, Royal Bank of Scotland plc, since 1987; Director: Scottish Investment Trust Ltd., since 1981, EFTPOS UK Ltd., since 1988, Scottish Financial Enterprise, since 1988, Royal Bank Group Services Ltd., since 1987, Citizens Financial Group, since 1989, Royal Scottish Assurance plc, since 1989, Royal Santander Financial Services SA, since 1989, Direct Line Insurance plc, since 1990; b. 14.5.40, Dunfermline; m., Sheila Alexandra Graham Bennett; 2 s. Educ. Perth Academy; St. Andrews University; Canisius College, Buffalo, New York. Assistant Lecturer, St. Andrews University, 1964-67; Systems Engineer (various positions), Bell Aerospace, Buffalo, New York, 1967-72; ICFC: Executive in Edinburgh Area Office, 1972-81, Area Manager, 1974-79, Director and Assistant General Manager, 1979-81; Chief Executive, Scottish Development Agency, 1981-87. Recreations: tennis; skiing; geriatric rugby; golf; business. Address: (h.) 29 Saxe Coburg Place, Edinburgh, EH3 5BP.

Mathie, Hugh Alexander, MA, MEd. Rector, McLaren High School, Callander, since 1985; b. 30.7.35, Dundee; m., Margaret Black; 2 s.; 1 d. Educ. Morgan Academy, Dundee; St. Andrews University. Teacher of Classics, Kilsyth Academy and Kirkton High School, Dundee; Principal Teacher of Classics, Kilsyth Academy and Cumbernauld High School; Assistant Rector, Depute Rector, Greenfaulds High School; Rector, Kilsyth Academy. Recreations: hill-walking; golf. Address: (h.) Welwyn, Firpark Terrace, Cambusbarron, Stirling; T.-Stirling 72900.

Mathieson, John George, CBE, TD, DL, BL. Solicitor; Senior Partner, Thorntons, WS, Dundee and Arbroath; b. 15.6.32, Argyll; m., Shirley Bidder; 1 s.; 1 d. Educ. George Watson's College, Edinburgh; Glasgow University. Territorial Army, 1951-76: Commanding Officer The Highland Regiment RA (T), 1967-69, TA Colonel for Highlands, 1972-76, Chairman, Highlands TA Association, 1976-82. Commenced practice as Solicitor, Glasgow, 1955; joined practice of Clark Oliver, Arbroath, 1957; Chairman, Arbroath Branch, Royal British Legion and Earl Haig Fund; Deputy Lieutenant, Angus, 1977; Chairman, Royal Artillery Council for Scotland; Honorary President, Angus Bn., Boys' Brigade; Elder, Colliston Parish Church. Recreations: shooting; skiing; golf; gardening. Address: (h.) Willanyards, Colliston, Arbroath, Angus; T.-02489 286.

Matthews, Baird, BL. Solicitor in private practice, since 1950; Honorary Sheriff, Kirkcudbright and Stranraer; b. 19.1.25, Newton Stewart; m., Mary Thomson Hope; 2 s.; 1 d. Educ. Douglas Ewart High School, Edinburgh University. Commissioned, Royal Scots Fusiliers, 1944; demobilised as Captain, 1st Bn., 1947; Partner, A. B. & A. Matthews, Solicitors, Newton Stewart, since 1950; Clerk to General Commissioners of Income Tax, Stranraer and Newton Stewart Districts, from 1952; Burgh Prosecutor, Newton Stewart, from 1968; Depute Procurator Fiscal for Wigtownshire, 1970; Chairman, Board of Local Directors, General Accident Fire and Life Assurance Corporation, 1988; Dean of Faculty of Stewartry of Kirkcudbright Solicitors, 1979; Dean of Faculty of Solicitors of the District of Wigtown, 1983; Chairman, Appeals Tribunal, 1984. Recreations: golf; curling. Address: (b.) Bank of Scotland Buildings, Newton Stewart, Wigtownshire; T.-0671 3013.

Matthews, Edward. Director, Edinburgh Council of Social Service, since 1974; b. 11.9.37, Brentford, Middlesex; m., Ann Patricia; 1 s.; 1 d. Educ. Finchley Grammar School; St. Edmund's College, Ware. Curate and Borstal Chaplain, 1961-66; Assistant Director, then Deputy Director, Richmond Fellowship, 1966-74; Member, Lothian Health Board, 1983-87; Winston Churchill Fellowship, 1973; Secretary, Edinburgh Lodging House Association; Executive Committee Member: Edinburgh University Settlement, SACRO, Edinburgh Cyrenians, Edinburgh Council for Single Homeless, Old Town Housing Association; Member, Board of Directors: Scottish Council for Voluntary Organisations; Edinvar Housing Association; Trustee, Waverley Care Trust. Recreations: woodwork; badminton; gardening. Address: (b.) Edinburgh Council of Social Service, 11 St. Colme Street, Edinburgh, EH3 6AG; T.-031-225 4606.

Matthews, Professor John Burr Lumley, MA, DPhil, FRSE. Director, NERC Dunstaffnage Marine Laboratory; Director and Secretary, Scottish Marine Biological Association; Honorary Professor, Stirling University, since 1984; b. 23.4.35, Isleworth; m., Jane Rosemary; 1 s.; 2 d. Educ. Warwick School; Oxford University. Research Scientist (Zooplankton), Oceanographic Laboratory, Edinburgh, 1961-67; Senior Lecturer, Department of Marine Biology, then Professor of Marine Biology, University of Bergen, 1967-84; Visiting Professor, University of British Columbia, 1977-78. Recreations: cross country skiing; gardening; wine-making. Address: (h.) Grianaig, Rockfield Road, Oban, PA34 5DH; T.-0631 62734.

Matthews, Herbert Eric, MA (Oxon), BPhil (Oxon). Head, Department of Philosophy, Aberdeen University, since 1989; Senior Lecturer in Philosophy, since 1973; b. 24.10.36, Liverpool; m., Hellen Kilpatrick Matthews; 2 s. Educ. Liverpool Institute High School for Boys; St. John's College,

Oxford. Lecturer, Department of Logic, Aberdeen University, 1963. Publications: numerous articles in learned journals; translations of works of German philosophy; The Philosophy of Thomas Reid (Editor); Philosophy and Health Care (Editor). Recreations: cinema; reading; walking; cycling. Address: (b.) Department of Philosophy, Aberdeen University, Aberdeen, AB9 2UB; T.-0224 272367.

Mattock, Professor John Nicholas, MA, PhD. Professor of Arabic and Islamic Studies, Glasgow University, since 1987; b. 6.1.38, Horsham. Educ. Christ's Hospital; Pembroke College, Cambridge. Research Fellow, Pembroke College, Cambridge, 1963-65; Lecturer in Arabic and Islamic Studies, then Senior Lecturer, Glasgow University, 1965-87. Member, Editorial Board, Journal of Arabic Literature, since 1970; British Representative, European Union of Arabists and Islamists, since 1986; President, European Union of Arabists and Islamists, since 1990. Address: (b.) Department of Arabic and Islamic Studies, Glasgow University, Glasgow, G12 8QQ; T.-041-339 8855, Ext. 5586.

Mauchline, John, PhD, DSc, CBiol, FIBiol, FRSE. Research Biologist, Scottish Marine Biological Association, since 1962; UK Editor, Marine Biology, since 1977; b. 1.7.33, Motherwell; m., Isobel Hopkins Warden; 1 s.; 2 d. Educ. High School of Glasgow; Glasgow University. Research Biologist, UKAEA, 1958-62. Visiting Professor, University of Tokyo, 1976; Visiting Scholar, Memorial University of Newfoundland, 1987. Recreations: fly fishing; painting. Address: (b.) Dunstaffnage, Marine Research Laboratory, P.O. Box 3, Oban, PA34 4AD; T.-Oban 62244.

Maughan, Ronald John, BSc, PhD. Senior Lecturer, University Medical School, Aberdeen University, since 1987; b. 14.10.51, Aberdeen; 1 d. Educ. Robert Gordon's College; Aberdeen University. Lecturer, then Senior Lecturer, Liverpool Polytechnic, 1978-80; Lecturer, Aberdeen University, 1980-87. Publications: 200 papers and other works. Recreation: work. Address: (b.) University Medical School, Foresterhill, Aberdeen, AB9 2ZD; T.-0224 681818, Ext. 52482.

Maund, Robert Graham, BSc, DipTP, FRTPI. Director of Physical Planning, Strathclyde Regional Council, since 1984; b. 10.11.38, Cheshire; m., Judith L.; 3 s.; 1 d. Educ. Manchester University. City of Manchester: trainee graduate engineer, various planning posts, Assistant City Planning Officer; Greater Manchester Council: Assistant County Planning Officer, Deputy County Planning Officer. Recreations: walking; cross-country running; photography; listening to music; reading; theatre. Address: (b.) Strathclyde House, 20 India Street, Glasgow, G2 4PF; T.-041-227 3626.

Maver, Professor Thomas Watt, BSc (Hons), PhD, FInstE, FRSA, HonFRIAS. Professor of Computer Aided Design, Department of Architecture and Building Science, Strathclyde University, since 1982 (Head of Department, 1983-85, 1988-91); b. 10.3.38, Glasgow; m., Avril Elizabeth Cuthbertson; 2 d. Educ. Eastwood Secondary School; Glasgow University. Special Research Fellow, Engineering Faculty, Glasgow University, 1961-67; Strathclyde University: Research Fellow, School of Architecture, 1967-70, Director, Architecture and Building Aids Computer Unit, Strathclyde, since 1970; Visiting Professor, Department of Architecture, Technical University, Eindhoven; Past Chairman, Design Research Society; Royal Society Esso Gold Medal, 1989. Recreations: family; farming. Address: (h.) 8 Kew Terrace, Glasgow, G12; T.-041-339 7185.

Mavor, Professor John, BSc, PhD, DSc (Eng), FRSE, FIEEE, CPhys, FInstP, CEng, FIEE. Dean, Faculty of Science & Engineering, Edinburgh University, since 1989; Chair of Electrical Enginering, Edinburgh University, since 1986

(Head, Department of Electrical Engineering, 1984-89; Chairman, School of Engineering, 1987-89); first holder, Lothian Chair of Microelectronics, 1980-86; b. 18.7.42, Kilwinning; m., Susan Christina; 2 d. Educ. Bromley Technical High School; City University; London University. AEI Research Laboratories, London, 1964-65; Texas Instruments Ltd., Bedford, 1968-70; Emihus Microcomponents Ltd., Glenrothes, 1970-71; joined Edinburgh University, 1971. Recreations: gardening; hill-walking. Address: (b.) Department of Electrical Engineering, Edinburgh University, King's Buildings, Edinburgh, EH9 3JL; T.-031-650 5646.

Maxton, John Alston. BA (Oxon), DipEd (Oxon). MP (Labour), Glasgow Cathcart, since 1979; b. 5.5.36, Oxford; m., Christine Elspeth; 3 s. Educ. Lord Williams Grammar School, Thame; University College, Oxford. Lecturer in Social Studies, Hamilton College of Education, before entering Parliament; Chairman, Association of Lecturers in Colleges of Education in Scotland, 1974-78; Member, Scottish Select Committee, 1980-83, Public Accounts Committee, 1983-84; Opposition Treasury and Scottish Whip, 1984-85; Opoosition Scottish Front Bench Spokesperson on Health, Local Government and Transport, 1985-87, on Industry and Local Government Finance, since 1987. Recreations: listenng to jazz (Director, Glasgow International Jazz Festival); running. Address: (h.) 37 Larch Grove, Hamilton, ML3 8NF; T.-0698 43847.

Maxwell, Donald, MA. Professional Singer; b. 12.12.48, Perth. Educ. Perth Academy; Edinburgh University. Former Teacher of Geography; since 1976, professional Singer with British opera companies and orchestras; Principal Baritone, Scottish Opera, 1978-82; Principal Baritone, Welsh National Opera, 1982-85; guest appearances, Royal Opera House, London, as well as France, Belgium, Germany, Canada, Argentina, USA, Italy, Japan. Recreations: railways; watching cricket. Address: (h.) c/o 6 Murray Crescent, Perth.

Maxwell, Gordon Stirling, MA, FSA, FSA Scot. Archaeologist and Author; b. 21.3.38, Edinburgh; m., Kathleen Mary King; 2 d. Educ. Daniel Stewart's College, Edinburgh; St. Andrews University. Investigator (Archaeological), Royal Commission on the Ancient and Historical Monuments of Scotland, 1964-86; Head of Field Survey, RCAHMS, since 1986. Publications: Rome's North-West Frontier: The Antonine Wall (Co-author), 1983; The Impact of Aerial Reconnaissance on Archaeology (Editor), 1983; The Romans in Scotland, 1989; A Battle Lost: Romans and Caledonians at Mons Graupius, 1990. Recreations: archaeology; gardening; aviation; Scottish literature. Address: (h.) Micklegarth, 72A High Street, Aberdour, Fife, KY3 0SW; T.-0383 860796.

Maxwell, Ingval, DA, RIBA, FRIAS, FSA Scot. Assistant Director of Works, Historic Scotland, since 1985; b. 28.5.44, Penpont; m., Susan Isabel Maclean; 1 s.; 1 d. Educ. Dumfries Academy; Duncan of Jordanstone College of Art, Dundee. Joined Ministry of Public Buildings and Works as Architect, 1969; Area Architect, then Principal Architect, Ancient Monuments Branch, 1972-85; RIBA Research Award, 1970-71; RIAS Thomas Ross Award, 1988; Chairman, Scottish Vernacular Buildings Working Group; Member, Great Britain Technical Forum; Member,RIAS Conservation Working Group; Member, SDA Conservation Bureau Advisory Panel, 1989-91. Recreations: photography; astronomy; aircraft; farm buildings. Address: (h.) 135 Mayfield Road, Edinburgh, EH9 3AN.

Maxwell, Hon. Lord (Peter Maxwell), QC, BA, LLB. Senator, College of Justice, 1973-88; Chairman, Scottish Law Commission, 1981-88; b. 21.5.19, Edinburgh; m., Alison Susan Readman; 1 s.; 2 d. Educ. Wellington College; Balliol

College, Oxford; Edinburgh University. Argyll and Sutherland Highlanders and Royal Artillery, 1939-46; called to Scottish Bar, 1951; QC, 1961; Sheriff Principal, Dumfries and Galloway, 1970-73; Member, Royal Commission on Legal Services in Scotland, 1976-80. Address: (h.) 19 Oswald Road, Edinburgh, EH9 2HE; T.-031-667 7444.

Maxwell, Thomas Jefferson, BSc, PhD. Director, Macaulay Land Use Research Institute, since 1987 (Head, Animal Production Department, Hill Farming Research Organisation, 1981-87); Honorary Research Professor, Aberdeen University; b. 7.10.40, Aspatria, Cumbria; m., Christine Patrick Speedie; 1 s.; 1 d. Educ. Silcoates School, Wakefield; Edinburgh University. Specialist Animal Production Adviser, East of Scotland College of Agriculture, 1967-70; Research Scientist, Animal Production Department, Hill Farming Research Organisation, 1970-81. Recreations: reading; squash; hill-walking; choral singing. Address: (b.) Macaulay Land Use Research Institute, Craigiebuckler, Aberdeen.

Maxwell Davies, Sir Peter, KB (1987), MusB (Hons). Composer; Founder and President, St. Magnus Festival, Orkney; Associate Conductor/Composer, Scottish Chamber Orchestra, since 1985; Conductor/Composer, BBC Philharmonic Orchestra, since 1992; b. 8.9.34, Manchester. Educ. Leigh Grammar School; Royal Manchester College of Music; Manchester University. Director of Music, Cirencester Grammar School, 1959-62; Harkness Fellowship, Princeton University, 1962-64; Professor of Composition, Royal Northern College of Music, Manchester, until 1980; Founder and Artistic Director, Fires of London, 1971-87; Artistic Director, Dartington Summer School of Music, 1979-84; President, Composers Guild of GB, since 1986; Honorary Doctor of Music, Edinburgh University, 1979, Honorary Doctor of Law, Aberdeen University, 1981. Address: (b.) c/o Mrs Judy Arnold, 50 Hogarth Road, London, SW5; T.-01-370 1477.

Maxwell-Irving, Alastair Michael Tivey, BSc, CEng, MIEE, MBIM, AMICE, FSAScot. Antiquarian and Archaeologist; b. 1.10.35, Witham, Essex; m., Esther Mary Hamilton, MA, LLB. Educ. Lancing College; London University. General Electric Company, 1957; English Electric Company, 1960; Assistant Factor, Annandale Estates, 1966; Weir Pumps Ltd., 1979-91; founder Member and Secretary, 1975-78, Central Scotland Branch, British Institute of Management; Member, Scottish Section Committe, Antiquarian Horological Society, since 1988. Publications: Genealogy of the Irvings of Dumfries, 1965; The Irvings of Dumfries, 1968; Lochwood Castle, 1968; Early Firearms and their Influence on the Military and Domestic Architecture of the Borders, 1974; Cramalt Tower: Historical Survey and Excavations, 1977-79, 1982; Borthwick Castle: Excavations 1979, 1982; Andrew Dunlop (Clockmakers' Company 1701-32), 1984; Hoddom Castle: A Reappraisal of its Architecture and Place in History, 1989. Recreations: architecture and history of the Border towers of Scotland; archaeology; family history and genealogy; Florence and the art and architecture of Tuscany; horology; heraldry; photography; gardening. Address: (h.) Telford House, Blairlogie, Stirling, FK9 5PX.

Maxwell-Scott, Dame Jean (Mary Monica), DCVO (1984). Lady in Waiting to Princess Alice, Duchess of Gloucester, since 1959; b. 8.6.23. VAD Red Cross Nurse, 1941-46; great-great grand-daughter of Sir Walter Scott. Address: (h.) Abbotsford, Melrose, Roxburghshire, TD6 9BQ.

Maxwell-Scott, Patricia Mary, OBE. Honorary Sheriff of Selkirk, since 1971; b. 11.3.21, Curragh, Dublin; m., Harold Hugh Christian Boulton. Educ. Convent des Oiseaux, Westgate on Sea, Kent. ATP, 1942-45. President, Borders Branch, Save the Children Fund; President, Spastics

312   WHO'S WHO IN SCOTLAND

Association (Borders); President, Roxburgh Branch, BRCS. Great-great-great grand-daughter of Sir Walter Scott. Recreations: travelling; reading. Address: (h.) Abbotsford, Melrose, TD6 9BQ; T.-0896 2043.

May, David Jeans, MA (Hons). Rector, Craigie High School, Dundee, since 1990; b. 28.12.45, Aberdeen; m., Anne Elizabeth Raeside Eastop; 1 s.; 1 d. Educ. Robert Gordon's College, Aberdeen; Aberdeen University; Jordanhill College of Education. Teacher of Modern Studies and History, St. Columba's, Gourock, 1973-74; Assistant Principal Teacher of Social Subjects, Castlehead High, Paisley, 1974-78; Principal Teacher of Modern Studies/Economics, Grange Secondary, Glasgow, 1978-84; Assistant Head Teacher, Dunoon Grammar School, 1984-87; Deputy Rector, Montrose Academy, 1987-90. Convener, SEB Modern Studies Panel; Member, Secretary of State for Scotland's Working Group on Environmental Education. Recreations: golf; tennis; squash; gardening. Address: (h.) Evanston, Lamondfauld Lane, Hillside, Montrose, DD10 9HY; T.-067 483 673.

May, Douglas James, LLB. Queen's Counsel, since 1989; b. 7.5.46, Edinburgh. Educ. George Heriot's; Edinburgh University. Advocate, 1971; Temporary Sheriff, since 1990; Parliamentary Candidate (Conservative), Edinburgh East, 1974, Glasgow Cathcart, 1983. Recreations: golf; photography; travel. Address: (b.) Advocates' Library, Parliament House, Edinburgh; T.-031-226 5071.

May, Malcolm Stuart, BA, BD, STM, CQSW. Chief Executive, Dundee Voluntary Action, since 1979; b. 9.9.40, Isle of Shapinsay, Orkney; m., Alison Wood; 1 s.; 1 d. Educ. Kilmarnock Academy; The Gordon Schools, Huntly; Hamilton Academy; Queen's University, Belfast; Glasgow University; Union Theological Seminary, New York. Assistant Minister, The Old Kirk, West Pilton, Edinburgh, 1966-68; staff, Iona Community, Glasgow, 1968-72; social work training, 1972-73; Training Officer, Scottish Council for Voluntary Organisations, 1973-78. Recreations: reading; choral singing; wine-making. Address: (b.) Castlehill House, 1 High Street, Dundee, DD1 1TD; T.-0382 21545.

May, Ranald Stuart, MA, BComm. Senior Lecturer in Economics, St. Andrews University, since 1978; b. 1.5.32, Dundee; m., Jennifer Alison Shewan. Educ. Grove Academy, Dundee; St. Andrews University; Queen's University, Canada. Ft.-Lt., RAF, 1956-59; Finance Officer and Economic Adviser, Shell International Petroleum Company, London and Shell-BP Petroleum Development Company, Nigeria, 1959-63; St. Andrews University: Shell Fellow in Economic Development, 1963-70, Lecturer in Economics, 1970-78. Treasurer, Scottish Economic Society; Arbitrator to ACAS, since 1975. Recreations: golf; gardening. Address: (h.) St. Andrews University, St. Andrews, Fife.

Mayfield, Hon. Lord (Ian MacDonald), MC (1945), QC (Scot). Senator of the College of Justice in Scotland, since 1981; b. 26.5.21. Sheriff Principal of Dumfries and Galloway, 1973; President, Industrial Tribunals for Scotland, 1973-81.

Mearns, Anne, MA (Hons), DipTP, MRTPI. Depute Town Clerk (Corporate Policy Development), Glasgow District Council, since 1989; b. 20.8.47, Glasgow. Educ. Hyndland Secondary School; Glasgow University; Strathclyde University. Planning Assistant, Coatbridge Burgh, 1969; Planner, Lanark County Council, 1969-73; Senior Planner (Research), Glasgow Corporation, 1973-75; Supervisory Planner (Policy Analysis), 1975-78, Assistant Chief, 1978-79, Chief Planner (Policy and Intelligence), 1979-87, Chief Corporate Planner, Town Clerk's Office, 1987-89, Glasgow District Council. Member, Editorial Board, British Urban and Regional Information Systems Association; Member,

Council, West of Scotland Branch, Royal Institute of Public Administration. Recreations: cities; canine rambles; cultural and cerebral pursuits; clarsach. Address: (b.) City Chambers, Glasgow, G2 1DU; T.-041-227 5718.

Meek, Brian Alexander, OBE, JP. Columnist, Glasgow Herald; Deputy Chairman, Livingston Development Corporation, since 1986; Director, Capital Publicity Ltd., since 1987; Member, Conservative Group, Lothian Regional Council, since 1973 (Regional Convener, 1982-86); Vice President, Scottish Conservative and Unionist Association, since 1989; b. 8.2.39, Edinburgh; m., Frances C. Horsburgh; 1 s.; 1 d. Educ. Royal High School, Edinburgh; Edinburgh Secretarial College. Joined Scotsman Publications as trainee, then Sub-Editor, Features Writer; transferred to Express Newspapers as Feature Writer, Leader Writer and Rugby Correspondent; elected, Edinburgh Corporation, 1969; Leader, Conservative Group, 1970-72; elected as Bailie, 1972; elected, Lothian Regional Council and Edinburgh District Council, 1973; Member, Education Board, Merchant Company. Recreations: golf; theatre. Address: (b.) Lothian Regional Council, Parliament Square, Edinburgh; T.-031-229 9292.

Meek, Donald Eachann MacDonald, MA (Cantab), MA, PhD (Glas), FRHistS. Senior Lecturer in Celtic, Edinburgh University, since 1990; b. 16.5.49, Glasgow; m., Rachel Jane Rogers; 2 d. Educ. Oban High School; Glasgow University; Emmanuel College, Cambridge. Lecturer in Celtic, Edinburgh University, 1979-90. Assistant Editor, Historical Dictionary of Scottish Gaelic, Glasgow University, 1973-79; Honorary Secretary, Gaelic Society of Glasgow, 1974-79; Member, Gaelic Advisory Committee to Broadcasting Council for Scotland, 1976-78; Member, Gaelic Panel, National Bible Society of Scotland, since 1978; Reviser, since 1986, latest edition of Gaelic Bible; Baptist lay preacher. Publications: books include Mairi Mhor nan Oran, 1977; The Campbell Collection of Gaelic Proverbs and Proverbial Sayings, 1978; Island Harvest: A History of Tiree Baptist Church, 1988. Recreations: family activities; getting to know the Highlands. Address: (h.) 38 Fauldburn, East Craigs, Edinburgh, EH12 8YH; T.-031-339 1738.

Meikle, Robert Baxter, MA, DipEd. Rector, Alness Academy, since 1975; b. 8.6.33, Kirkliston, West Lothian; m., Adrianne Margaret Stewart; 1 s.; 1 d. Educ. Broxburn High School; Edinburgh University; Moray House College of Education. Sergeant, RAEC, 1956-58; Teacher of Geography and Special Assistant, Bell-Baxter High School, Cupar, 1958-64; Principal Teacher of Geography, then Assistant Rector, Montrose Academy, 1964-75. Chairman, Highland Region Computer Working Party, 1980-84; Chairman, Saltburn Community Council. Publication: Windows on the Geography of Scotland, 1972-73. Recreations: golf; fell-walking; music; photography; art; the works of Robert Burns. Address: (b.) Alness Academy, Alness, Ross and Cromarty; T.-0349 883341.

Mein, William Main, MA (Hons). HM Inspector of Schools, since 1972; b. 1.7.38, Nairn; m., Dorothy Robertson Steele; 2 d. Educ. Nairn Academy; Edinburgh University; Moray House College of Education. Teacher of Mathematics, Robert Gordon's College, Aberdeen, 1961-65; Principal Teacher of Mathematics, Invergordon Academy, 1965-68; Principal Teacher of Mathematics, then Assistant Headteacher, Dingwall Academy, 1968-72. Elder, Crown Church, Inverness. Recreations: angling; photography; gardening.

Meldrum, James, MA. Head, Investment Assistance Division, Scottish Office Industry Department, since 1991; b. 9.8.52, Kirkintilloch. Educ. Lenzie Academy; Glasgow University. Administration Trainee/HEO (Admin), Scottish Office, 1973-79; Principal grade posts, Scottish Economic

Planning Department, Scottish Development Department, Scottish Office Personnel Division, 1979-86; Deputy Director, Scottish Courts Administration, 1986-91. Address: (b.) Magnet House, 59 Waterloo Street, Glasgow, G2 7BT; T.-041-242 5801.

Mellon, Sir James, KCMG, MA. Chairman, Scottish Homes, since 1989; Chairman, MF Corporation (Europe) Ltd., since 1991; Vice-President, English-Speaking Union Scotland, since 1991; Member, Board of Governors, Napier Polytechnic of Edinburgh, since 1989; Director, Scottish American Investment Company PLC, since 1989; b. 25.1.29, Glasgow; m., 1, Frances Murray (dec.); 2, Philippa Shuttleworth; 1 s.; 3 d. Educ. Glasgow University. Department of Agriculture for Scotland, 1953-60; Agricultural Attache, Copenhagen and The Hague, 1960-63; Foreign Office, 1963-64; Head of Chancery, Dakar, 1964-66; UK Delegation to European Communities, 1967-72; Counsellor, 1970; Foreign and Commonwealth Office: Head, Science and Technology Department, 1973-75, Commercial Counsellor, East Berlin, 1975-76, Head, Trade Relations and Export Department, 1976-78; High Commissioner in Ghana and Ambassador to Togo, 1978-83; Ambassador to Denmark, 1983-86; Director-General for Trade and Investment, USA, and Consul General, New York, 1986-88. Publication: A Danish Gospel, 1986. Recreations: music; theatre; golf. Address: (b.) Thistle House, 91 Haymarket Terrace, Edinburgh, EH12 5HE; T.-031-313 0044.

Melrose, Rev. James Henderson Loudon, MA (Hons), BD (Hons), MED, FSA(Scot). Lecturer, Jordanhill College of Education, since 1982; Minister of Religion (Moderator, Presbytery of Hamilton, 1987); Lecturer, Extra Mural Department, Glasgow University, since 1972; b. 24.3.30, Glasgow; m., Henrietta Spence Patrick; 3 s. Educ. Forfar Academy; Glasgow University and Trinity College. Ordained Assistant, Barony of Glasgow, 1955-57; Minister, Larbert East, 1958-63; Principal Teacher of Religious Education, 1963-66; Lecturer, Craigie College of Education, 1966-70; Principal Lecturer in Religious Education, Hamilton College of Education, 1970-82. Member, COPE Committee, 1981-85; Member, General Assembly Committee on Education, 1977-81; Vice-Chairman and Chairman, Scottish Covenanters Memorial Association. Recreations: walking; golf; natural history. Address: (b.) Jordanhill College of Education, Southbrae Drive, Glasgow, G13 1PP; T.-01-959 1232.

Melville, Ian Dunlop, MB, ChB, FRCPGlas, FRCPLond. Consultant Neurologist, Institute of Neurological Sciences, Glasgow, 1965-88; Honorary Clinical Lecturer, Glasgow University, 1968-88; b. 9.11.27, Glasgow; m., Eliza Duffus; 1 s.; 3 d. Educ. Shawlands Academy; Glasgow University. RAF Medical Branch; Medical Registrar, Glasgow Royal Infirmary; Academic Registrar, National Hospital for Nervous Diseases, London; Clinical Research Fellow, Medical Research Council, London; Senior Medical Registrar, Glasgow. Member, Council of Management, Quarrier's Village, Bridge of Weir; Editor, Bulletin of Royal College of Physicians and Surgeons, Glasgow. Recreations: golf; photography; watercolour painting. Address: (h.) 9 Mirrlees Drive, Glasgow, G12 OSH; T.-041-339 7085.

Melvin, Thomas. District Head Postmaster, Glasgow, since 1991; b. 5.9.52, Glasgow; m., Cecilia; 1 s. Educ. Possilpark Secondary. Joined Post Office as counter clerk, 1968. Recreations: sport; DIY. Address: (b.) 1-5 George Square, Glasgow, G2 1AA; T.-041-242 4100.

Mennie, Alastair Douglas, LLB, PhD, FSA Scot. Advocate, since 1982; part-time Lecturer in International Private Law; b. 2.10.57, Aberdeen. Educ. Aberdeen Academy; Aberdeen University. Publications: Domicile Flowcharts, 1991; numer-

ous articles in law journals. Address: (h.) 25 Panmure Place, Edinburgh, EH3 9HP; T.-031-229 5604.

Mennie, William Patrick, BL, NP. Partner, Grigor & Young, Solicitors, Elgin and Buckie, since 1964 (Senior Partner, since 1984); b. 11.10.37, Elgin; m., Patricia Leslie Bogie; 2 s.; 1 d. Educ. Elgin Academy; Edinburgh University. Solicitor, 1960; part-time Town Clerk, Dufftown, 1973-75; part-time Depute Procurator Fiscal, Elgin, 1966-74; Member, Property Marketing Committee, Law Society of Scotland, since 1985. Recreation: game shooting. Address: (h.) Innesmill, Urquhart, Elgin; T.-0343 842643.

Menzies, Duncan A.Y., QC, MA (Oxon), LLB. Queen's Counsel, since 1991; b. 28.8.53, Edinburgh; m., Hilary Weston; 2 s. Educ. Edinburgh Academy; Cargilfield; Glenalmond; Wadham College, Oxford; Edinburgh University. Advocate, 1978; Standing Junior Counsel to The Admiralty, 1984-91. Parliamentary Candidate, Midlothian, 1983, Edinburgh Leith, 1987; founder, Scottish Wine Society, 1976; Chairman, Ptarmigan Wines Ltd. Recreations: shooting; golf; wines. Address: (h.) Leaston House, Humbie, East Lothian; T.-Humbie 219.

Menzies, George Macbeth, BA, LLB. Partner, W. & J. Burness, Solicitors, since 1974; b. 18.4.43, Edinburgh; m., Patricia Mary; 1 s.; 2 d. Educ. Edinburgh Academy; Corpus Christi College, Oxford; Edinburgh University. Past Chairman, North British Steel Group (Holdings) PLC; Non-Executive Director, Cairn Petroleum Oil & Gas Ltd., 1986-88; Chairman, Fruitmarket Gallery, 1984-88; President, Edinburgh Academical Football Club, 1990-92; Chairman, Endeavour Training (Scotland) Ltd., since 1983. Recreations: walking; contemporary arts; rugby. Address: (b.) 16 Hope Street, Edinburgh; T.-031-226 2561.

Menzies, Gordon, MA (Hons), DipEd. Independent Producer (retired Head of Educational Broadcasting, BBC Scotland); b. 30.7.27, Logierait, Perthshire; m., Charlotte; 2 s.; 1 d. Educ. Breadalbane Academy, Aberfeldy; Edinburgh University. Producer/Director, Who Are the Scots?, 1971; The Chiel Amang Us, 1974, Ballad Folk, 1975, History Is My Witness, 1976, Play Golf with Peter Alliss, 1977, Scotch and Wry, 1978-79, Two Views of Burns, 1979, Barbara Dickson in Concert, 1981-84-86, The World of Golf, 1982, The Celts, 1987, Play Better Golf with Peter Alliss, 1989, Scotch and Wry Hogmanay, 1980-91; Editor, The Afternoon Show, 1981-85; Play Snooker with Dennis Taylor, 1990; Play Bridge with Zia, 1991. Publications: Who Are the Scots?, 1971; The Scottish Nation, 1972; History Is My Witness, 1976; Play Golf, 1977; The World of Golf, 1982; Scotch and Wry, 1986; Double Scotch and Wry, 1988; Play Better Golf, 1989. Recreations: golf; snooker; curling; theatre. Address: (h.) 8 Ingleside, Lenzie, Glasgow, G66 4HN.

Menzies, John Maxwell. Chairman, John Menzies PLC, since 1952; b. 13.10.26; m., Patricia Eleanor Dawson; 4 d. Educ. Eton. Lt., Grenadier Guards; Member, Berwickshire County Council, 1954-57; Director: Scottish American Mortgage Co., 1959-63, Standard Life Assurance Co., 1960-63, Vidal Sassoon Inc., 1969-80, Gordon & Gotch plc, 1970-85, Atlantic Assets Trust, 1973-88, Independent Investment Co. plc, since 1973 (Chairman, since 1983), Fairhaven International, 1980-88, Rocky Mountains Oil & Gas, 1980-85, Ivory & Sime plc, 1980-83, Personal Assets PLC, since 1981, Bank of Scotland, since 1984, Guardian Royal Exchange, since 1985, Malcolm Innes & Partners Ltd., since 1989. Trustee, Newsvendors' Benevolent Institution, since 1974 (President, 1968-74); Member, Royal Company of Archers, Queen's Bodyguard for Scotland. Recreations: farming; shooting; reading; travel. Address: (b.) 108 Princes Street, Edinburgh, EH2 3AA; T.-031-225 8555.

Menzies, Neil Graham Finlay, BSc, FRSA. Scottish Affairs Adviser, ICI, since 1982; b. 14.10.41, Meikleour; m.; 2 d. Educ. Lower School of John Lyon, Harrow; St. Andrews University. Voluntary Service Overseas, Nigeria, 1964-66; ICI: Teesside, 1966-68, various positions in production, personnel, etc., 1968-82. Member, Executive, Scottish Council; Director, Prince's Scottish Youth Business Trust; Member, Executive, Scottish Business in the Community; Director, ASSET; Director, APL. Address: (b.) ICI Scottish Affairs, Grangemouth Works, Earls Road, Grangemouth; T.-0324 494990.

Mercer, John, MA, DipEd. Headmaster, Belmont House School, since 1972; b. 11.8.40, Glasgow; m., Eileen Margaret; 2 s.; 1 d. Educ. Eastwood Senior Secondary School; Glasgow University; Jordanhill College of Education. Teacher of English/History, Mossvale Secondary School, Paisley, 1962-66; Head Teacher of English, Belmont House School, 1966-72. Elder and former Session Clerk, Mearns Parish Kirk; President, Eastwood Rotary Club, 1986-87. Recreations: golf; skiing; walking; reading; palaeontology. Address: (b.) Belmont House School, Newton Mearns, Glasgow, G77 5DU; T.-041 639 2922.

Mercer, Roger James, MA, FSA, FSA Scot, MIFA. Secretary, Royal Commission for the Ancient and Historical Monuments (Scotland); b. 12.9.44, London; m., Susan; 1 s.; 1 d. Educ. Harrow County Grammar School; Edinburgh University. Inspector of Ancient Monuments, AM Division, Department of the Environment, London, 1969-74; Lecturer and Reader, Department of Archaeology, Edinburgh University, 1974-89. Treasurer, Society of Antiquaries of Scotland, 1977-87; Chairman, Scottish Group, Institute of Field Archaeologists; Vice President, Society of Antiquaries of Scotland, 1988-91; Vice President, Prehistoric Society, 1987-91; Vice-President, Council for British Archaeology, 1991-94. Recreations: music; reading; learning. Address: (b.) RCAHMS, 54 Melville Street, Edinburgh.

Merchant, Bruce Alastair, OBE, LLB. Solicitor; Partner, South, Forrest, Mackintosh & Merchant, Inverness, since 1971; Vice-Chairman, Highland Health Board, 1981-91 (Vice Chairman, 1987-91); b. 17.5.45, Edinburgh; m., Joan Isobel Sinclair Hamilton; 1 s.; 2 d. Educ. Inverness Royal Academy; Aberdeen University. Council Member, Law Society of Scotland, 1982-88 (Convener, Guarantee Fund Committee, 1984-87, Convener, Finance Committee, 1987-88); Member; Board of Management for Inverness Hospitals, 1971-74, Inverness Local Health Council, 1975-81. Address: (h.) 3 Crown Circus, Inverness; T.-0463 239980.

Merrills, Austin, OBE. Chairman, Ireland Alloys (Holdings) Ltd., since 1971; Director, Johnston Press PLC, since 1985; Member, Lloyd's, since 1978; b. 15.4.28, Sheffield; m., Daphne Olivia Coates; 1 s.; 2 d. Educ. King Edward VII School, Sheffield; Sheffield University. Council Member, Bureau International de la Recuperation; Governor, Glasgow School of Art; Member, Scottish Industrial Development Advisory Board; Council Member, British Secondary Metals Association. Address: (b.) PO Box 18, Hamilton, ML3 0EL; T.-0698 822461.

Merrylees, Andrew, BArch, DipTP, RSA, RIBA, FRIAS, FCSD. Architect; Principal, Andrew Merrylees Associates, since 1985; b. 13.10.33, Newmains; m., Maie Crawford; 2 s.; 1 d. Educ. Wishaw High School; Strathclyde University. Sir Basil Spence, Glover and Ferguson: joined, 1957, Associate, 1968, Partner, 1972; awards: RIBA Bronze Medal, Saltire Award, Civic Trust Award, Art in Architecture Award, Royal Scottish Academy Gold Medal. Recreations: painting; cooking; tennis; walking. Address: (b.) Quadrant, 17 Bernard Street, Edinburgh, EH6 6PW; T.-031-555 0688.

Meston, Professor Michael Charles, MA, LLB, JD. Professor of Scots Law, Aberdeen University, since 1971; b. 13.12.32, Aberdeen; m., Dorothea Munro; 2 s. Educ. Robert Gordon's College, Aberdeen; Aberdeen University; Chicago University. Lecturer in Private Law, Glasgow University, 1959-64; Aberdeen University: Senior Lecturer in Comparative Law, 1964-68, Professor of Jurisprudence, 1968-71; Dean, Faculty of Law, 1970-73 and 1988-91; Honorary Sheriff, Grampian Highland and Islands, since 1972; Vice Principal, Aberdeen University, 1979-82; Trustee, National Museum of Antiquities of Scotland, 1982-85; Governor, Robert Gordon's College, Aberdeen; Member, Grampian Health Board, 1985-91. Publications: The Succession (Scotland) Act 1964; The Matrimonial Homes (Family Protection) (Scotland) Act 1981; The Scottish Legal Tradition, 1991. Recreations: golf; photography. Address: (h.) 4 Hamilton Place, Aberdeen, AB2 4BH; T.-Aberdeen 641554.

Michie, Professor David Alan Redpath, RSA, RGI, RWA, DA, FRSA. Professor, Heriot Watt University, 1988-90; Head, School of Drawing and Painting, Edinburgh College of Art, 1982 90; b. 30.11.28, St. Raphael, France; m., Eileen Anderson Michie; 2 d. Educ. Hawick High School; Edinburgh College of Art. Travelling Scholarship, Italy, 1954-55; Lecturer, Grays School of Art, Aberdeen, 1957-61; Lecturer, Edinburgh College of Art, 1961 (Vice Principal, 1974-77). President, Society of Scottish Artists, 1961-63; Member, General Teaching Council for Scotland, 1975-80; Member, Court, Heriot-Watt University, 1979-82; Council Member, British School at Rome, 1980-85; Guthrie Award, RSA, 1964; David Cargill Prize, RGI, 1977; Lothian Region Award, 1977; Sir William Gillies Award, 1980; RGI Prize, 1990; one-man exhibitions, Mercury Gallery, London, six times, 1966-83, Lothian Region Chambers, 1977, The Scottish Gallery, 1980, Loomshop Gallery, Lower Largo, 1981, 1987, Mercury Gallery, Edinburgh, 1986; Artists' Self Portraits, Tate Gallery, 1989. Address: (h.) 17 Gilmour Road, Edinburgh, EH16 5NS.

Michie, (Janet) Ray. MP (Lib. Dem.), Argyll and Bute, since 1987; b. 4.2.34; m.; 3 d. Educ. Aberdeen High School for Girls; Lansdowne House School, Edinburgh; Edinburgh School of Speech Therapy. Former Area Speech Therapist, Argyll and Clyde Health Board. Address: (b.) House of Commons, SW1A 0AA.

Micklem, Professor Henry Spedding, MA, DPhil (Oxon). Professor of Immunobiology, Edinburgh University, since 1988 (Reader in Zoology, 1973-88); b. 11.10.33, Oxford; m., Lisel Ruth Thomas; 3 s. 1 d. Educ. Rugby School; Oriel College, Oxford. Scientific Staff, Medical Research Council; Research Fellow, Institut Pasteur, Paris; Academic Staff, Department of Zoology, Edinburgh University; Visiting Professor, Department of Genetics, Stanford University; Visiting Fellow, Department of Pathology, New York University Medical School. Address: (b.) Division of Biological Sciences, Edinburgh University, West Mains Road, Edinburgh, EH9 3JT; T.-031-650 5496.

Middleton, Francis, MA, LLB; b. 21.11.13, Rutherglen; m., Edith Muir; 2 s.; 1 d. Educ. Rutherglen Academy; Glasgow University. Solicitor, 1937; Indian Army, 1939 (11 Sikh Regiment); injured, 1942; Judge Advocate General's Branch, 1942-45; 1st Class Interpreter, Urdu, Examiner for India in Punjabi; Advocate, 1946; Sheriff, 1948-78. Serves on boards of various charitable bodies. Recreations: reading; walking; gardening; water divining. Address: (h.) 20 Queens Court, Helensburgh, G84 7AH; T.-0436 78965.

Middleton, Rev. Jeremy Richard Hunter, LLB, BD. Parish Minister, Davidson's Mains, since 1988; b. 19.3.53, Kilbarchan; m., Susan Margaret; 3 s. Educ. Charterhouse;

Edinburgh University. Parish Minister, Kildrum, Cumbernauld, 1980-88. Address: 1 Hillpark Terrace, Edinburgh; T.-031-336 3078.

Middleton, Robert, JP. Convener, Grampian Regional Council, since 1990; Chairman, Labour Party in Scotland, 1986-87; b. 28.7.32, Aberdeen; m., Audrey Ewen; 2 s. Educ. Aberdeen Grammar School. Started apprenticeship with Post Office Telephones, 1948; Aberdeen Town Council: elected, 1961, appointed Magistrate, 1963, Chairman of Magistrates, 1965-66, Chairman, Education Committee, 1966-69; contested Banffshire as Labour candidate, 1966; contested Aberdeen South, 1974 (twice) and 1983; elected, Grampian Regional Council, 1975. Publication: North Sea Brose. Recreations: golf; reading; writing not very good poetry; travel; bridge; bowls. Address: (h.) 9 Stronsay Avenue, Aberdeen, AB2 6HX; T.-0224 313366.

Middleton, Ruth Charlotte, LLB. Secretary/Director, Ark Housing Association Ltd., since 1978; b. 9.9.42, Edinburgh; m., Norman A. Middleton; 1 s.; 1 d. Educ. Berwickshire High School; Edinburgh University. Legal practice, 1965-78. Address: 8 Balcarres Street, Edinburgh, EH10 5JB; T.-031-447 9027.

Midgley, Professor John Morton, BSc, MSc, PhD, CChem, FRCS, FRPharmS. Professor of Pharmacy, Strathclyde University, since 1984 (Chairman and Head of Department, 1985-90); b. 14.7.37, York; m., Jean Mary Tillyer; 2 s. Educ. Nunthorpe Grammar School, York; Manchester University; London University. Demonstrator, Manchester University, 1959-61; Assistant Lecturer, School of Pharmacy, London University, 1962-65; Research Associate, Massachusetts Institute of Technology, 1965-66; Lecturer, then Senior Lecturer, School of Pharmacy, London University, 1966-83; Member: Committee on the Review of Medicines, since 1984, British Pharmacopoeia Committee, since 1985, Committee on the Safety of Medicines, since 1990, Council of Royal Pharmaceutical Society of GB, since 1991, Science and Engineering Research Council Pharmacy Panel, since 1985. Recreations: fly fishing; fisheries management; training labradors; gardening; music. Address: (b.) Strathclyde University, Department of Pharmacy, Royal College, 204 George Street, Glasgow, G1 1XW; T.-041-552 4400, Ext. 2125.

Milburn, Professor George Henry William, PhD, CChem, FRSC, FBIM, Dr (h.c.), FRSA. Head, Department of Applied Chemical and Physical Sciences, Napier Polytechnic of Edinburgh, since 1973; b. 25.11.34, Wallasey; m., Jean Muriel; 1 s.; 1 d. Educ. Wallasey Grammar School; Leeds University. Short service commission, Royal Corps of Signals, 1959-63; Staff Demonstrator, Leeds University, 1963-66; Research Fellow, Sydney University, 1967-68; Senior Scientific Officer, Agricultural Research Council, 1968-69; Lecturer, Plymouth Polytechnic, 1969-70; Senior Lecturer, Sheffield Polytechnic, 1970-73. Scientific Adviser for Lothian Region; Member, Scottish College of Textiles Academic Council; Honorary Doctorate, Technical University, Budapest, 1988. Publications: more than 50 scientific publications including a textbook on crystal structure analysis. Recreations: golf; bridge; photography. Address: (h.) 9 Orchard Court, Longniddry, East Lothian; T.-0875 53228.

Miles, Rex Stafford, MB, ChB, FRCPath. Senior Lecturer, Edinburgh University, since 1976; Honorary Consultant, Lothian Health Board, since 1976; b. 16.11.42, Beeston, Nottinghamshire; m., Janice Isabel Martin; 3 s.; 1 d. Educ. Southwell Minster Grammar School; Edinburgh University. House Physician, Edinburgh Royal Infirmary; House Surgeon, Peel Hospital, Galashiels; Registrar in Bacteriology, Edinburgh University; Lecturer and Honorary Senior

Registrar in Bacteriology, Dundee University. Recreations: golf; photography; Border history. Address: (b.) Edinburgh University Medical School, Teviot Place, Edinburgh, EH8 9AG; T.-031-229 2477.

Millan, Rt. Hon. Bruce, PC, CA. European Commissioner, since 1989; b. 5.10.27, Dundee; m., Gwendoline May Fairey; 1 s.; 1 d. Educ. Harris Academy, Dundee. MP, Glasgow Craigton, 1959-83, Glasgow Govan, 1983-88; Parliamentary Secretary for the RAF, 1964-66; Parliamentary Secretary, Scottish Office, 1966-70; Minister of State, Scottish Office, 1974-76; Secretary of State for Scotland, 1976-79; Opposition Spokesman on Scottish Affairs, 1979-83. Address: (h.) 10 Beech Avenue, Glasgow, G41; T.-041-427 6483.

Millan, Professor Charles Gordon, MA, PhD. Professor of French Studies, Strathclyde University, since 1991 (Director, Languages for Business Unit, since 1990); b. 25.9.46, Kirkcaldy; m., Margaret Anne Robbie; 1 s.; 1 d. Educ. Kirkcaldy High School; Merrywood Grammar School, Bristol; Edinburgh University. Temporary Lecturer, French Department, Edinburgh University, 1971; Teacher, Broughton High School, Edinburgh, 1972-76; Lecturer, then Senior Lecturer, Strathclyde University, 1976-91. Recreations: reading; cinema. Address: (h.) 32 Broughton Place, Edinburgh, EH1 3RT.

Millan, William Robert, LLB, NP. Director of Administrative and Legal Services, Roxburgh District Council, since 1986; Clerk of the Peace (Roxburgh Commission Area), since 1986; Clerk to the Licensing Board and District Court, since 1986; b. 17.8.52, Glasgow; m., Margaret Hamilton McCulloch; 1 s.; 1 d. Educ. Hillhead High School; Glasgow University. Bannatyne, Kirkwood, France & Co., Writers, Glasgow, 1973-75; Senior Legal Assistant, Cumnock and Doon Valley District Council, 1975-79; Depute Director of Administrative and Legal Services, Roxburgh District Council, 1979-86. Recreations: reading; DIY; gardening; skiing; badminton; golf; vintage cars. Address: (b.) District Council Offices, High Street, Hawick, TD9 9EF; T.-0450 75991.

Millar, Helen Jean, MA. Member, Air Transport Users Committee, since 1991; Member, Quality Council Food from Britain, since 1990; Member, Advisory Committee on Novel Foods and Processes, since 1991; Member, Glasgow Local Health Council, since 1991; Member, European Commission Consumer's Consultative Commission; Lecturer in charge, Children's Panel Training, Glasgow University, since 1980; b. 10.10.31, Glasgow; 3 s.; 2 d. Educ. Craigholme School, Glasgow; Glasgow University. Chairman, Consumers in European Community Group, 1988-91; Chairman, Consumer's Committee for Scotland, 1980-89; Member and Vice-Chairman, Scottish Consumer Council, 1979-87; Chairman, Strathclyde Children's Panel, 1979-81; Vice-Chairman, New Glasgow Society, 1980-87; Founder Member, Board, Tron Theatre Club, Glasgow. Recreations: theatre; arts in general; Glasgow; arguing. Address: (h.) 33 Aytoun Road, Glasgow, G41; T.-041-423 4152.

Millar, Henry Rankin, MB, ChB, BMedBiol (Hons), FRCPsych. Consultant Psychiatrist, Ross Clinic, Aberdeen, since 1991; b. 23.4.47, Aberdeen; m., Frances Morgan; 3 d. Educ. Aberdeen Grammar School; Aberdeen University. House Officer, Aberdeen Royal Infirmary, 1972-73; Junior Fellow in Community Medicine and Honorary Senior House Officer in Medicine, Aberdeen University and Aberdeen Royal Infirmary, 1973-74; Senior House Officer/Registrar in Psychiatry, Royal Edinburgh Hospital, 1975-77; Senior Registrar and Lecturer, Dundee Psychiatric Services and Dundee University, 1977-80; Consultant Psychiatrist, Southern General Hospital, Glasgow, 1980-91. Recreations:

golf; walking. Address: (h.) 237 Fenwick Road, Giffnock, Glasgow; T.-041-638 1178.

Millar, James Lauder, CBE, CA. Chairman and Chief Executive, William Low & Co. PLC, since 1990; Chairman, Invergordon Distillers Ltd., since 1990; b. 4.8.30, Dundee; m., Joan Marjorie Smith; 2 s.; 2 d. Educ. Morgan Academy, Dundee. CA indentureship, 1947-52; National Service, RAF, 1953-55; professional practice, 1955-58; joined William Low & Co., 1958. Chairman, SCRI, since 1990; Chairman, Dundee Enterprise Trust, since 1990; Chairman, Dundee Industrial Association, since 1985. Recreations: sailing; cycling; hill-walking. Address: (b.) Baird Avenue, Dryburgh, Dundee; T.-0382 814022.

Millar, Professor Keith, BA, PhD, CPsychol, FBPsS. Professor of Behavioural Science, Medical Faculty, Glasgow University, since 1984; b. 27.6.50, Dundee; m., Dr. Margaret Elspeth Reid; 1 step s. Educ. Dundee High School; Stirling University; Dundee University. Research Scientist, MRC Applied Psychology Unit, Cambridge, 1976-79; Lecturer, Department of Psychiatry, University Hospital and Medical School, Nottingham, 1979-84; Senior Lecturer, Behavioural Sciences Group, Medical Faculty, Glasgow University, 1984-88. Publications: papers and edited book on topics relating psychology to medicine. Recreations: reading; travelling; idleness; procrastination. Address: (h.) 33 West Chapelton Crescent, Bearsden, Glasgow, G61 2DE; T.-041-942 4978.

Millar, Mary Armour, MB, ChB, FRCPGlas, FRCR. Consultant Radiologist, Victoria Infirmary, Glasgow, since 1972; b. 10.8.39, Glasgow. Educ. Queen's Park Senior Secondary School; Glasgow University. Resident House Officer: Stobhill Hospital, Glasgow Royal Infirmary; Victoria Infirmary: Registrar in Medicine, Registrar in Radiology, Senior Registrar. Medical Advisor, Overseas Missionary Fellowship in Scotland; Member, Congregational Board, Sandyford Henderson Memorial Church. Recreations: reading; gardening; hill-walking. Address: (h.) 1 Rosslea Drive, Giffnock, Glasgow, G46 6JW; T.-041-638 3036.

Millar, Peter Carmichael, OBE, MA, LLB, WS. Deputy Keeper of Her Majesty's Signet, 1983-91; Chairman, Church of Scotland General Trustees, 1973-85; Chairman, Mental Welfare Commission for Scotland, 1983-91; Chairman, Medical Appeal Tribunals, since 1991; b. 19.2.27, Glasgow; m., Kirsteen Lindsay Carnegie; 2 s.; 2 d. Educ. Aberdeen Grammar School; Glasgow University; St. Andrews University; Edinburgh University. Royal Navy, 1944-47; Partner, W. & T.P. Manuel, WS, 1954-62; Partner, Aitken Kinnear & Co., WS, 1963-87; Partner, Aitken, Nairn WS, since 1987; Clerk, Society of Writers to HM Signet, 1964-83. Recreations: golf; hill-walking; music. Address: (h.) 25 Cramond Road North, Edinburgh, EH4 6LY.

Millar, William McIntosh, OBE, BL. Solicitor; Partner and latterly Consultant, McClure Naismith Anderson & Gardiner, Solicitors, Glasgow, 1955-92; Editor, Journal of the Law Society of Scotland, 1983-89; b. 10.9.25, Edinburgh; 3 s.; 2 d. Educ. Glasgow Academy; Fettes College; Glasgow University. Royal Signals. 1943-47 (Captain, 1947); Secretary, Fife Kinross & Clackmannan Charitable Society, 1955-88 (President, 1961-62, and Patron, 1985); Chairman, Strathclyde Housing Society Ltd. and 11 associated housing societies, 1966-75; Member, Scottish Housing Advisory Committee, 1970-75; Founder Member, Scottish Federation of Housing Associations, 1976-78; Trustee, Scottish Housing Associations Charitable Trust, 1980-91 (Chairman, since 1985); Director, Citizens Theatre Ltd. and Chairman, Close Theatre Club, 1969-72; Governor, Royal Scottish Academy of Music and Drama, 1969-90; Chairman, Scottish Early Music Association, 1984-91. Recreations: music; writing;

avoiding golf and politics; learning about crofting. Address: (h.) 5 Reef, Uig, Isle of Lewis, PA86 9HU; T.-0851 75 245.

Miller, Alan Cameron, MA, LLB, FCIT. Advocate; Past Chairman (Scotland), Institute of Transport; b. 10.1.13, Killin, Perthshire; m., Audrey Main; 1 s.; 1 d. Educ. Fettes College; Edinburgh University. Member, Faculty of Advocates, since 1938; Royal Navy, 1940-45; Sheriff, Fort William, 1946-52; Legal Adviser (Scotland) to: British Transport Commission, 1952-62, British Railways Board, 1962-72. Voluntary Tutor, Fettes College. Recreations: golf; music. Address: (h.) 42 Great King Street, Edinburgh; T.-031-556 3800.

Miller, Alan Douglas, LLB (Hons), DipLP. Reporter to Children's Panel, Dumfries and Galloway Region, since 1990; Secretary, Association of Children's Reporters, since 1990; b. 30.11.59, Edinburgh; m., Alison; 1 s.; 1 d. Educ. Stewart's/Melville College, Edinburgh; Edinburgh University. Private legal practice followed by Assistant and Area Reporter posts, Strathclyde Region. Church of Scotland elder. Recreations: music; reading; food; family; friends. Address: (b.) 3 Newall Terrace, Dumfries, DG1 1LN; T.-0387 60390.

Miller, Alastair Robert John Dunlop, BSc, MAg, NDA, FRAgS. Farmer; Chairman, Top Hat Holdings Ltd.; b. 5.3.37, Tranent; m., Margaret Eileen Lees-Brown; 3 d. Educ. Edinburgh Academy; Rugby; Edinburgh University; Purdue University, USA. Scottish Horticulture Medal. Recreations: golf; travel. Address: (h.) Ferrygate, North Berwick, East Lothian.

Miller, Professor Andrew, MA, BSc, PhD, FRSE, FIBiol. Professor of Biochemistry, Edinburgh University, since 1984; Vice-Dean of Medicine, since 1991; b. 15.2.36, Kelty, Fife; m., Rosemary S.H. Fyvie; 1 s.; 1 d. Educ. Beath High School; Edinburgh University. Assistant Lecturer in Chemistry, Edinburgh University, 1960-62; Postdoctoral Fellow, CSIRO, Melbourne, and Tutor in Chemistry, Ormond College, Melbourne University, 1962-65; Staff Scientist, MRC Laboratory of Molecular Biology, Cambridge, 1965-66; Lecturer in Molecular Biophysics, Oxford University and (from 1967) Fellow, Wolfson College, 1966-83; on secondment as first Director, European Molecular Biology Laboratory, Grenoble Antenne, France, 1975-80. Committee Member: British Biophysical Society, 1972-74, SERC Synchrotron Radiation Facility Committee, 1979-82, Biological Sciences Committee, 1982-85, Neutron Beam Research Committee, 1982-85; Council Member, Institut Laue-Langevin, 1981-85; Member: MRC Joint Dental Committee, 1984-86, UGC Biological Sciences Committee, 1985-89; (part-time) Director of Research, European Synchrotron Radiation Facility, Grenoble, 1986-91; Member, Advisory Board, AFRC Food Research Institute, since 1985; Member, UFC Advisory Groups on Biological Sciences and Pre-clinical Medicine, since 1989; Member, Scientific Council, Grenoble University, since 1989. Address: (b.) Biochemistry Department, Edinburgh University Medical School, Hugh Robson Building, George Square, Edinburgh, EH8 9XD; T.-031-650 3718.

Miller, Andrew, MA, FLA. Director of Libraries, Glasgow City Council, since 1981; b. 25.12.36, Hamilton; m., Jean Main Freeland; 2 d. Educ. St. John's Grammar School; Hamilton Academy; Glasgow and West of Scotland Commercial College. Assistant, Hamilton Public Libraries and Glasgow District Libraries; Depute Burgh Librarian, Motherwell and Wishaw, 1963-74; Depute Director of Libraries, Glasgow District Council, 1974-81. Chairman of Council and Past President, Scottish Library Association; Past President, Strathclyde Librarians' Club. Recreations: reading; travelling; public speaking; planning. Address: (b.)

Mitchell Library, North Street, Glasgow, G3 7DN; T.-041-221 7030.

Miller, Rev. Charles W., MA. Minister, Fowlis Easter and Liff Parish Church, since 1980; Chaplain, Royal Dundee Liff Hospital, since 1980; b. 4.2.26, Kinross; m., Isabella Russell Stewart, MA; 3 s. Educ. St. Mary's School, Dunblane; McLaren High School, Callander; Aberdeen University; St. Andrews University. Assistant Minister, Auld Kirk of Ayr, 1953-54; Minister: Torthorwald, Dumfries, 1953-59, Munro Church, Rutherglen, 1959-65, Cruden, Aberdeenshire, 1965-72, Anstruther Parish Church, 1972-80; former Convener: Overseas Committee, Dumfries Presbytery; Church and Nation and Social Responsibility Committees, Aberdeen Presbytery; Social Responsibility Committee, St. Andrews Presbytery; Member, Scottish Churches Consultative Committee on Road Safety; Member, Governing Council, Institute of Advanced Motorists, since 1964 (President, Scottish Churches Association); Chairman, Royal Dundee Liff Hospital League of Friends. Recreations: caravanning; swimming; landscape painting. Address: 14 Liff Park, Liff, Dundee, Angus; T.-0382 580033.

Miller, Sheriff Colin Brown, LLB, SSC. Sheriff of South Strathclyde, Dumfries and Galloway, since 1991; b. 4.10.46, Paisley; m., Joan Elizabeth Blyth; 3 s. Educ. Paisley Grammar School; Glasgow University. Partner, McFadyen & Semple, Solicitors, Paisley, 1971-91 (Senior Partner, 1987-91); Council Member, Law Society of Scotland, 1983-91 (Convener, Conveyancing Committee, 1986-89; Convener, Judicial Procedure Committee, 1989-91; Chairman, Working Party on Rights of Audience in Supreme Courts, 1990-91); Member, Joint Law Society Committee with Keeper of Registers, 1982-91; Chairman, Blythswood Housing Association Ltd., 1981-91; Honorary Legal Adviser, Waverley Steam Navigation Co., 1976-91. Recreations: sailing (PS Waverley); Clyde steamers; railways; photography. Address: (b.) Sheriff's Chambers, Hamilton Sheriff Court, Almada Street, Hamilton; T.-0698 282957.

Miller, Sir Donald John, BSc, FEng, FIMechE, FIEE. Chairman, Scottish Power (formerly SSEB), since 1982; b. 9.2.27, London; m., Fay G. Herriot; 1 s.; 2 d. Educ. Banchory Academy; Aberdeen University. Metropolitan-Vickers, 1947-53; British Electricity Authority, 1953-55; Preece Cardew & Rider (Consulting Engineers), 1955-66; Chief Engineer, North of Scotland Hydro-Electric Board, 1966-74; Director of Engineering, SEEB, 1974; appointed Deputy Chairman, 1979. Chairman, Power Division, IEE, 1977. Recreations: gardening; walking; sailing. Address: (h.) Puldohran, Gryffe Road, Kilmacolm, Renfrewshire; T.-Kilmacolm 3652.

Miller, Douglas Hamilton, TD, MREHIS, MIWM. Director of Environmental Health, Banff and Buchan District Council, since 1974; b. 15.3.33, Dunfermline; m., Jean Elizabeth; 2 s.; 3 d. Educ. Dunfermline High School; Heriot-Watt, Edinburgh. Apprentice, then Assistant Burgh Surveyor, Lochgelly, 1950-55; Group Hygienist, RAF, 1956-58; Assistant Sanitary Inspector, Perth, 1958-60; Assistant, then District Sanitary Inspector, then Depute County Sanitary Inspector and Master of Works, then Director of Environmental Health and Master of Works, Banff County Council, 1960-74. Founder Member and Past Chairman, Banff Round Table; founder Chairman, Banff Branch, Institute of Advanced Motorists; Past President, Banff Rotary Club; Administrative Officer in Specialist Medical Unit, TA (Major); Elder, Church of Scotland. Recreations: snooker; golf. Address: (h.) Broadcroft, 15 Bellevue Road, Banff, AB45 1BJ; T.-0261 812213.

Miller, Edward, CBE, MA, MEd, MLitt. Director of Education, Strathclyde Regional Council, 1974-88; b. 30.3.30, Glasgow; m., Margaret T. McLean; 2 s. Educ.

Eastbank Academy; Glasgow University. Junior Depute Director of Education, West Lothian, 1959-63; Senior Assistant Director of Education, Stirlingshire, 1963-66; Depute and Senior Depute Director of Education, Glasgow, 1966-74. Recreations: swimming; boating; reading; golf; gardening. Address: (h.) 58 Heather Avenue, Bearsden, Glasgow, G61 3JG.

Miller, Hugh Craig, BSc, MB, ChB, FRCPEdin. Consultant Cardiologist, Edinburgh Royal Infirmary, since 1975; b. 7.4.42, Edinburgh; m., Isobel Margaret; 1 s.; 1 d. Educ. George Watson's College; Edinburgh University. Registrar, Edinburgh Royal Infirmary, 1969-72; Senior Registrar, Brompton Hospital, London, 1972-75; Research Fellow, Duke University, North Carolina, 1973-74; Fulbright Scholar. Recreations: skiing; sailing. Address: (h.) 12 Dick Place, Edinburgh; T.-031-667 4235.

Miller, Professor Hugh Graham, BSc, PhD, DSc, FICFor, FIBiol, FRSE, FRSA. Professor and Head, Department of Forestry, Aberdeen University, since 1984; b. 22.11.39, Ndola, Zambia; m., Thelma Martin; 1 s.; 1 d. Educ. Kaptagat School, Kenya; Strathallan School; Sutton High School; Aberdeen University. Joined Department of Peat and Forest Soils, Macaulay Institute for Soil Research, 1986. Awarded Institute of Foresters Silvicultural Prize, 1974; selected for International Union of Forest Research Organization's Scientific Achievement Award, 1981. Recreation: curling. Address: (b.) Department of Forestry, Aberdeen University, St. Machar Drive, Aberdeen, AB9 2UD; T.-0224 272666.

Miller, Ian George Tweedie, BSc, APIMA, MBCS, CEng, FRSA. Principal, North Glasgow College, since 1990; Chairman, Skill (Scotland), since 1992; b. 5.8.42, Hamilton; m., Una; 1 s.; 1 d. Educ. George Heriot's, Edinburgh; Heriot Watt University. Research Assistant, Hatfield Polytechnic; Lecturer, Computer Science, Strathclyde University; Director, Computer Centre, Paisley College; Depute Principal, Stevenson College. Recreations: golf; bowling. Address: (b.) 110 Flemington Street, Glasgow, G21 4BX; T.-041-558 9001.

Miller, Ian Harper Lawson, MA (Hons), LLB. Partner, Burnett and Reid, Advocates and Solicitors, Aberdeen, since 1986; b. 16.1.54, Aberdeen; m., Sheila Matthews Howie; 2 d. Educ. Robert Gordon's College, Aberdeen; Aberdeen University. Member, Sheriff Court Rules Council, since 1987. Recreations: reading; music. Address: (h.) 25 Rubislaw Den South, Aberdeen, AB2 6BD; T.-0224 317042.

Miller, Rev. Ian Hunter, BA, BD. Minister, Bonhill, since 1975; b. 30.5.44, Johnstone; m., Joan Elizabeth Parr; 2 s. Educ. Johnstone High School; Glasgow University; Open University. Travel agent, latterly Branch Manager, A.T. Mays, 1962-69; Assistant Minister, Renfrew Old Kirk, 1974-75. Moderator, Dumbarton Presbytery, 1985-87 (Convener, Planning Committee, since 1985). Recreations: golf; badminton; music; drama. Address: Bonhill Manse, 1 Glebe Gardens, Bonhill, Alexandria, G83 9HR; T.-Alexandria 53039.

Miller, Ian James, MA, LLB. Secretary and Academic Registrar, Napier Polytechnic of Edinburgh, since 1987; b. 21.10.38, Fraserburgh; m., Sheila Mary Hourston; 1 s.; 2 d. Educ. Fraserburgh Academy; Aberdeen University; Edinburgh University. Private legal practice, 1963-68; Senior Legal Assistant, Inverness County Council, 1968-70; Depute County Clerk, then County Clerk, Ross and Cromarty County Council, 1970-75; Chief Executive, Inverness District Council, 1975-77; Director of Law and Administration, Grampian Regional Council, 1977-84; Director, Kildonnan Investments Ltd., Aberdeen, 1984-87. Recreations: golf; curling. Address: (b.) 219 Colinton Road, Edinburgh, EH14 1DJ; T.-031-444 2266.

Miller, Dr. Jack Elius, OBE, JP, OStJ, FRCGP. Consultant Occupational Medical Officer, since 1965; Director, The Medical Insurance Agency Ltd., since 1978; Director and Chairman, Echo Publications Ltd., since 1988; Trustee, The Cameron Fund (London), since 1981; b. 7.3.18, Glasgow; m., Ida Warrens; 1 s. Educ. Hillhead High School; Glasgow University. General Medical Practitioner in Glasgow (retired); Captain, Royal Army Medical Corps, 1944-46; Chairman (founder Member), Glasgow Marriage Guidance Council, 1956-61 (Hon. Vice-President, since 1961); Hon. Vice-President, Scottish Marriage Guidance Council, since 1967; Chairman, Scottish General Services Committee, 1969-72; Chairman, Association of Jewish Ex-Servicemen and Women of Scotland, 1952-61 and 1964-68; President, Glasgow Jewish Representative Council, 1969-72; Member, Council, BMA, 1964-81 (National Treasurer, 1972-81; Gold Medallist, 1982); Freeman, City of London; Member, Board of Deputies of British Jews, 1979-88; Vice-President, Prince and Princess of Wales Hospice, since 1981; Co-Chairman, Scottish Jewish Archives Committee, since 1986. Recreations: travel; reading; communal affairs. Address: (h.) 38 Fruin Court, Fruin Avenue, Newton Mearns, Glasgow, G77 6HJ; T.-041-639 7869.

Miller, James, CBE (1986), MA, FCIOB, FCIArb, CBIM. Chairman and Managing Director, The Miller Group Ltd. (formerly James Miller & Partners) since 1970; Director, Life Association of Scotland Ltd., since 1981; Director, British Linen Bank Ltd., since 1983; Member, Advisory Board, British Petroleum; President, FCEC, since 1990; Treasurer, Merchant Company of Edinburgh, since 1990; Chairman, Court, Heriot-Watt University, since 1990; b. 1.9.34, Edinburgh; m., 1, Kathleen Dewar (deceased); 2, Iris Lloyd-Webb; 1 s.; 3 d. Educ. Edinburgh Academy; Harrow School; Balliol College, Oxford. National Service, Royal Engineers. James Miller & Partners Ltd.: joined, 1958, appointed Director, 1960; Scottish Representative, Advisory Committee to the Meteorological Services, since 1980; Chairman, Federation of Civil Engineering Contractors, 1985-86; Deacon Convener, Incorporated Trades of Edinburgh, 1974-77; President, Edinburgh Chamber of Commerce, 1981-83; Assistant on Court of Merchant Company of Edinburgh, 1982-85. Recreation: shooting. Address: (b.) The Miller Group Ltd., Miller House, 18 South Groathill Avenue, Edinburgh, EH4 2LW; T.-031-332 2585.

Miller, James David Frederick, DUniv (Stirling), MA (Cantab), CBIM, FIPM. Vice-Chairman, Wolverhampton and Dudley Breweries; Chairman, SCOTVEC; Member, Council, British Institute of Management; b. 5.1.35, Wolverhampton; m., Saffrey Blackett Oxley; 2 s.; 1 s. (deceased); 1 d. Educ. Edinburgh Academy; Emmanuel College, Cambridge; London School of Economics. National Service, Argyll and Sutherland Highlanders, Cameron Highlanders, commissioned in South Staffords, 1953-55. Council Member, Outward Bound Ltd.; Member, Court, Stirling University, 1978-84; Vice-Chairman, Royal National Orchestra; Director, Edinburgh Academy, 1985; Commissioner, Queen Victoria School, Dunblane, 1987; Member, CBI Employee Involvement Panel; Governor, Scottish College of Textiles, since 1989. Recreations: gardening; tennis; golf. Address: (b.) 6 Belford Terrace, Edinburgh, EH4 3DG; T.-031-315 2882.

Miller, Professor James Douglas, MD, PhD, FRCSEdin, FRCSGlas, FACS, FRCPEdin. Professor of Surgical Neurology, Edinburgh University, since 1981 (Chairman, Department of Clinical Neurosciences); b. 20.7.37, Glasgow; m., Margaret Scott Rainey; 2 s. Educ. Glasgow Academy; Glasgow University. Surgical Senior House Officer and

Registrar, Glasgow, 1962; Neurosurgical Registrar, Institute of Neurological Sciences, Glasgow, 1965; Medical Research Council Fellow, Department of Surgery, Glasgow University, 1967; Senior Registrar in Neurosurgery, Institute of Neurological Sciences, Glasgow, 1969; US Public Health Service Fellow in Neurosurgery, University of Pennsylvania, 1970; Senior Lecturer in Neurosurgery, Glasgow University, 1971; Professor of Neurosurgery, Virginia Commonwealth University, USA, 1975. Recreation: hill-walking. Address: (h.) 36 Cluny Drive, Edinburgh, EH10 6DX; T.-031-447 5828.

Miller, Rev. John Stewart Abercromby Smith, MA, BD, STM. Minister, Morningside United Church, Edinburgh, since 1980; b. 3.5.28, Gibraltar; m., Lorna Vivien Fraser; 1 s.; 1 d. Educ. Lanark Grammar School; Edinburgh University; Union Theological Seminary, New York. Assistant Minister, St. Giles' Cathedral, Edinburgh, 1953-54; Minister: St. Andrew's, Hawick, 1954-59, Sandyhills, Glasgow, 1959-67, Mortlach and Cabrach, Banffshire, 1967-75, North Morningside, Edinburgh, and Morningside Congregational Church, 1975-80; Visiting Instructor, Columbia Theological Seminary, Georgia, 1986; Honorary Associate Minister, Peachtree Presbyterian Church, Atlanta, 1986; Chaplain, Sea Cadet Corps. Recreations: reading; listening to music; exploring Britain. Address: (h.) 1 Midmar Avenue, Edinburgh; T.-031-447 8724.

Miller, Professor Kenneth, LLB, LLM, PhD. Professor of Law, Strathclyde University, since 1992; b. 11.12.51, Paisley; m., Margaret MacLeod. Educ. Paisley Grammar School; Strathclyde University; Queen's University, Canada. Lecturer in Law, then Senior Lecturer, Strathclyde University, 1975-91; Deputy General Editor, Stair Memorial Encyclopaedia of the Laws of Scotland, since 1990; Member, Employment Law Committee, Law Society of Scotland. Publications: Employment Law in Scotland (Co-author); Property Law (Co-author). Recreations: reading; golf; theatre. Address: (b.) Law School, Strathclyde University, 173 Cathedral Street, Glasgow; T.-041-552 4400.

Miller, Richard King, BA (Hons); LLB (Hons). Queen's Counsel, since 1988; b. 19.8.49, Edinburgh; m., Lesley Joan Rist; 2 s. Educ. Edinburgh Academy; Magdalene College, Cambridge; Edinburgh University. Advocate, since 1975; Temporary Sheriff, since 1988. Recreations: fishing; shooting; tennis; walking; reading; collecting fine works of literature; wine. Address: (h.) Leahurst, 16 Gillespie Road, Colinton, Edinburgh; T.-031-441 3737.

Miller, Ronald Andrew Baird, CBE (1985), CA, BSc. Executive Chairman, Dawson International PLC, since 1982; b. 13.5.37, Edinburgh. Non-Executive Director: Christian Salvesen PLC, Scottish Amicable Life Assurance Society, Securities Trust of Scotland. Address: (b.) Dawson International PLC, 9 Charlotte Square, Edinburgh, EH2 4DR.

Miller, Ronald Murdoch. Scottish Officer, Equal Opportunities Commission, since 1978; b. 16.3.33, Dundee; m., Phyllis; 1 s. Educ. Morgan Academy. War Service, Korea/Japan, 1951-53; Youth and Community Worker, Gloucestershire; Deputy Youth and Community Officer, Suffolk; Community Development Officer, Holland (Lincolnshire); Education Researcher (Curriculum), Lanarkshire. Recreations: gardening; curling; golf. Address: (b.) St. Andrew House, 141 West Nile Street, Glasgow, G1 2RN; T.-041-332 8018.

Miller, Stanley Scott, MB, ChB, ChM, FRCS. Consultant General and Paediatric Surgeon, since 1976; Honorary Senior Lecturer in Surgery, Aberdeen University, since 1976; b. 24.12.38, Whitley Bay; 2 s.; 3 d. Educ. Robert Gordon's College; Aberdeen University. Research Fellow, Department of Surgery, Aberdeen University, 1970; Senior Surgical Registrar, Aberdeen Royal Infirmary, 1970-74; Resident Assistant Surgeon, Hospital for Sick Children, Great Ormond Street, London, 1975. Member, Executive, British Association of Paediatric Surgeons, 1983. Recreations: fishing; skiing; golfing. Address: (h.) 1 St. John's Wood, Maryculter, Aberdeen, AB1 0BE; T.-0224 735508.

Miller, Stewart O. Director, Miller Farms (Balbeggie); Honorary Member, Perth Branch Committee, National Farmers' Union of Scotland (Branch Chairman, 1955); Director, East of Scotland Farmers, 1960-91; Member, Tayside Regional Council, 1978-86; b. 2.4.18, Errol; m., Betty L. Penny; 1 s.; 1 d. Educ. Perth Academy. Started work on farm, 1933; took over farm, 1943; Member, Perth and Kinross County Council, 1958-75 (Chairman, Housing Committee, 1967-75); elected, Perth Branch Committee, National Farmers' Union of Scotland, 1950 (Branch Chairman, 1955); elected, Council, NFU of Scotland; served on various local committees, local Health Board, Perth Presbytery. Address: (h.) Rosefield, Balbeggie, Perth, PH2 6AT; T.-Kinrossie 236.

Miller, Professor Timothy John Eastham, PhD, BSc, MIEE, CEng, SMIEEE. Lucas Professor in Power Electronics, Glasgow University, since 1989; b. 25.9.47, Wigan; m., Janet Ann; 3 d. Educ. Atlantic College; Glasgow University; Leeds University. Research Fellow, Department of Electrical and Electronic Engineering, Leeds University, 1973-77; joined Corporate Research and Development Center, General Electric, NY, 1979, Manager, Power Electronics Control Program, 1983-86; appointed GEC Titular Professor in Power Electronics, Glasgow University, 1986. Publications: two textbooks and reference book; 60 papers. Recreation: racing cyclist. Address: (b.) Department of Electronics and EE, Glasgow University, Glasgow, G12 8QQ; T.-041-330 4922.

Miller, Professor William L., MA, PhD. Edward Caird Professor of Politics, Glasgow University, since 1985; b. 12.8.43, Glasgow; m., Fiona Thomson; 2 s.; 1 d. Educ. Aberdeen Grammar School; Royal High School, Edinburgh; Edinburgh University; Newcastle University. Formerly Lecturer, Senior Lecturer and Professor, Strathclyde University; Visiting Professor, Virginia Tech., Blacksburg, Virginia, 1983-84; also taught at Universities of Essex and Cologne; frequent Contributor to Press and TV; Member, Editorial Boards: Electoral Studies, Political Studies. Publications: Electoral Dynamics, 1977; The End of British Politics?, 1981; The Survey Method in the Social and Political Sciences, 1983; Elections and Voters, 1987; The Quality of Local Democracy, 1988; How Voters Change, 1990; Media and Voters, 1991. Address: (b.) Department of Politics, Glasgow University, G12 8RT; T.-041-339 8855.

Milligan, Eric. Convener, Lothian Regional Council, since 1990; b. 27.1.51, Edinburgh; m., Janis. Educ. Tynecastle High School; Napier College of Commerce and Technology. Edinburgh District Councillor, 1974-78; Lothian Regional Councillor, since 1978; Chairman, Finance Committee, 1980-82, 1986-90; President, COSLA, 1988-90. Address: (h.) 22 Hailes Grove, Edinburgh, EH13 ONE; T.-031-441 1528.

Milligan, Hon. Lord (James George Milligan), QC (Scot). Senator of the College of Justice, since 1988; b. 10.5.34. Advocate, 1959; QC, 1972; Advocate Depute, 1971-78.

Mill Irving, Robert Martin. Marine Superintendent, Scottish Fisheries Protection Agency; b. 18.6.37, Suez; m., Alison Machray Loudon; 1 s.; 2 d. Educ. Merchiston Castle; Thames Nautical Training College. Joined Shell Tanker Company as Apprentice, 1955; Department of Agriculture and Fisheries for Scotland: Second Officer, 1966, First Officer, 1971,

Commanding Officer, 1977, Assistant Marine Superintendent, 1981. Recreation: riding. Address: (h.) Station House, Gifford, East Lothian; T.-062081 404.

Mills, Colin Frederick, MSc, PhD, CChem, FRSC, FRSE. Director, Postgraduate Studies, Rowett Research Institute, since 1986 (Head, Biochemistry Division, 1966-86); b. 8.7.26, Swinton, Lancashire; m., D. Beryl; 1 d. Educ. Altrincham Grammar School; Reading University; London University. ARC Unit for Micronutrient Research, Long Ashton Research Station, Bristol University, 1946-47; Assistant Lecturer in Biochemistry, Wye College, London University, 1947-51; joined Rowett Research Institute, 1951. Member, WHO/FAO Experts Committee on Trace Elements in Human Nutrition; Chairman, International Committee for Symposia on Trace Elements in Man and Animals; Royal Society for Chemistry John Jeye Gold Medallist (Environmental Studies). Recreations: music; sailing. Address: (b.) Rowett Research Institute, Bucksburn, Aberdeen, AB2 9SB; T.-0224 712751.

Mills, Derek Henry, BSc, MSc, PhD, FIFM, FLS. Lecturer, Senior Lecturer and University Fellow, Department of Forestry and Natural Resources, Edinburgh University, 1965-91; b. 19.3.28, Bristol; m., Florence Cameron; 1 s.; 1 d. Educ. Clifton House; Harrogate Grammar School; Queen Mary College, London University. RAF, 1947-49; Scientific Officer, Oceanographic Laboratory, Edinburgh, 1954-56; Assistant Scientist, Fisheries Research Board of Canada, 1956-57; Senior Scientific Officer, Freshwater Fisheries Laboratory, Pitlochry, 1957-65. Consultant Biologist to Anglers' Co-operative Association; Fisheries Adviser to Scottish Hydro-Electric; Member, Tweed River Purification Board, 1983-86; Editor, Journal of Aquaculture and Fisheries Management; Member, Training Committee, Institute of Fisheries Management; Member, Council of Management, International Committee and Scientific Advisory Panel, Atlantic Salmon Trust; Member, Council, L'Association de Defense du Saumon Atlantique; Trustee, Tweed Foundation; Member, SE Regional Board, Nature Conservancy Council, Scotland, since 1991. Publications: Salmon and Trout; Introduction to Freshwater Ecology; Scotland's King of Fish; Salmon Rivers of Scotland (Co-author); Salmon in Iceland (Co-author); The Fishing Here is Great; Ecology and Management of Atlantic Salmon; Freshwater Ecology: Principles and Applications (Co-author); Tweed Towards 2000 (Editor); Strategies for the Rehabilitation of Salmon Rivers (Editor). Recreations: angling; hill-walking; photography; Address: (h.) 37 Granby Road, Edinburgh, EH16 5NP; T.-031-667 4931.

Mills, Harold Hernshaw, BSc, PhD. Principal Finance Officer, Scottish Office, since 1988; b. 2.3.38, Greenock; m., Marion Elizabeth Beattie. Educ. Greenock High School; Glasgow University. Cancer Research Scientist, Roswell Park Memorial Institute, Buffalo, New York, 1962-64; Lecturer, Chemistry Department, Glasgow University, 1964-69; Principal, Scottish Home and Health Department, 1970-76; Assistant Secretary: Scottish Office, 1976-81, Privy Council Office, 1981-83, Scottish Development Department, 1983-84; Under Secretary, Scottish Development Department, 1984-88. Address (b.) Scottish Office, New St. Andrew's House, Edinburgh, EH1 3TB; T.-031-244 4714.

Mills, Kenneth Leslie George, MA, BSc, MB, BChir, FRCS, FRCSEdin, FRCSCanada. Consultant Orthopaedic Surgeon, since 1968; b. 16.8.29, Birmingham; 2 d. Educ. High School of Glasgow; Cambridge University; Westminster Hospital, London. Medical Officer, RAF; Senior Lecturer in Orthopaedic Surgery, Dundee University. Publications: Guide to Orthopaedics (Trauma), 1979; Colour Atlas of Accidents and Emergencies, 1984. Address: (h.) 29

Craigiebuckler Avenue, Aberdeen, AB1 7SL; T.-0224 314077.

Milne, Brian, MB, ChB, FRCOG. Consultant Gynaecologist and Obstetrician, Highland Health Board (based at Raigmore Hospital, Inverness), since 1978; Clinical Senior Lecturer, Aberdeen University, since 1978; b. 9.1.42, Elgin; m., Mary I.B.; 2 s. Educ. Keith Grammar School; Aberdeen University. House Officer and Senior House Officer appointments, Aberdeen Royal Infirmary; Registrar appointments, Raigmore Hospital, Inverness and Southern General Hospital, Glasgow; Senior Registrar, Obstetrics and Gynaecology, Leicester Royal Infirmary, 1974-78. Recreations: golf; curling. Address: (h.) Muirfield House, 28 Muirfield Road, Inverness; T.-0463 222134.

Milne, George, BSc (Hons), MEd. Headteacher, Peterhead Academy since 1991; b. 4.6.49, Aberdeen; m., Elizabeth Kerr; 2 s.; 1 d. Educ. Aberdeen Grammar School; Aberdeen University. Maths Teacher, 1972-81; Principal Teacher of Maths, Peterhead Academy, 1981-84; Assistant Head Teacher, then Depute Head, Mintlaw Academy, 1984-91. Recreations: Rotary activities; golf; reading. Address: (b.) Peterhead Academy, Prince Street, Peterhead, AB42 6QQ; T.-0779 72231.

Milne, John Alexander, BA, BSc (Hons), PhD. Head, Animals and Grazing Ecology Division, Macaulay Land Use Research Institute (formerly Hill Farming Research Organisation), since 1988; b. 22.11.43, Edinburgh; m., Janet Erskine; 1 s. Educ. Edinburgh Academy; Edinburgh University; London University; Open University. Joined Hill Farming Research Organisation, 1970. Editor, British Journal of Nutrition. Address: (b.) Pencaitland, Roslin, Midlothian, EH25 9RF.

Milne, Robert Hughes, MCIM. Managing Director, Aberdeen Fish Curers and Merchants Association Ltd., since 1987 (Chief Executive/Secretary, 1983-87); b. 4.6.39, Pittenweem; m., Helen Wilma Masson; 1 s. Educ. Waid Academy, Anstruther. Assistant Chief Fisheries Advisor, then Regional Officer, Herring Industry Board, 1962-73; Development Officer/Secretary, then Secretary General, Scottish Federation of Fishermen's Co-operatives Ltd., Fishing Co-operative Trading (Scotland) Ltd. and Fishing Co-operatives (Manufacturing) Ltd., 1973-83. Served, European Community Social Problems Fisheries Committee, European Community Advisory Committee on Fisheries and Association of European Agricultural and Fisheries Co-operatives, 1973-83; Member, Isle of Man Government's Commission of Inquiry, 1982-83; Secretary, Scottish Fish Merchants Federation Ltd., since 1984; Member, Sea Fish Industry Authority Research and Development Committee and Sea Fish Training Council, since 1983. Chairman, Aberdeen Fish Festival Committee; Burgess of Guild, City of Aberdeen; Council Member, Aberdeen Chamber of Commerce; Vice Chairman, Grampian Region Fisheries Committee. Recreations: gardening; church activities. Address: (b.) South Esplanade West, Aberdeen, AB9 2FJ; T.-0224 897744.

Milne Home, John Gavin, JP, TD, FRICS. Lord Lieutenant, Dumfries and Galloway, 1988-91; Chartered Surveyor and Land Agent; b. 20.10.16, Dumfriesshire; m., Rosemary Elwes; 2 s.; 1 d. Educ. Wellington College; Trinity College, Cambridge. Served 4th Bn., King's Own Scottish Borderers, 1938-45; Factor, Buccleuch Estates Ltd., on Eskdale, Liddesdale and Branxholm Estates, 1945-74; Member, Dumfries County Council, 1949-74; Chairman, Dumfries and Galloway Region, British Field Sports Society, 1976-88. Recreations: country sports; nature study. Address: Kirkside of Middlebie, Lockerbie, Dumfriesshire, DG11 3JW; T.-05763 204.

Milner, Professor A.D., MA, DipPsych, PhD. Professor of Neuropsychology, St. Andrews University, since 1990 (Chairman, Department of Psychology, 1983-88); b. 16.7.43, Leeds. Educ. Bradford Grammar School; Lincoln College, Oxford. Research Worker, Institute of Psychiatry, London, 1966-70; Lecturer, then Senior Lecturer, St. Andrews University, 1970-85, Reader, 1985-90. Address (b.) Psychological Laboratory, St. Andrews University, St. Andrews, KY16 9JU; T.-0334 76161.

Milner, Professor Arthur John Robin Gorell, BA (Cantab). Professor of Computation Theory, Edinburgh University, since 1984; b. 13.1.34, Yealmpton; m., Lucy; 2 s.; 1 d. Educ. Eton; King's College, Cambridge. National Service, 2nd Lt., Royal Engineers, 1952-54; student, 1954-58; Mathematics Teacher, Marylebone Grammar School, 1959-60; Ferranti Ltd., 1960-63; Mathematics Lecturer, The City University, 1963-68; Research Fellow, University College, Swansea, 1968-70; Research Associate, Artificial Intelligence Laboratory, Stanford University, 1971-72; joined Edinburgh University as Lecturer, 1973. Elected Fellow of the Royal Society, 1988; Founding Member, Academia Europaea, 1988; Distinguished Fellow, British Computer Society, 1989; Hon. Doctorate of Science, Chalmers University of Technology, Gothenburg, 1988; ACM A.M. Turing Award, 1991. Publications: Edinburgh LCF (Co-author); A Calculus of Communicating Systems; Communication and Concurrency; Definition of Standard ML (Co-author); Commentary on Standard ML (Co-author). Recreations: music (oboe and piano); carpentry; walking. Address: (h.) 2 Garscube Terrace, Edinburgh, EH12 6BQ; T.-031-337 4823.

Milton, Professor Anthony Stuart, MA, DPhil (Oxon), DSc (Oxon), FRSA. Professor of Pharmacology and Head of Department, Aberdeen University, since 1973; b. 15.4.34, London; m., Elizabeth Amaret Freeman; 1 s.; 2 d. Educ. Cranleigh School; St. Catherine's College, Oxford. Lecturer, Dartmouth College Medical School, USA, 1959-60; Research Fellow: Stanford University Medical Center, USA, 1960-61, Edinburgh University, 1961-63; Lecturer, then Senior Lecturer, School of Pharmacy, London University, 1966-73. Recreation: breeding and showing Border Terrier dogs. Address: (h.) Stone Cottage, Baillieswells Road, Bieldside, Aberdeen, AB1 9BQ; T.-0224 868651.

Minto, 6th Earl of (Gilbert Edward George Lariston Elliot-Murray-Kynynmound), OBE (1986), JP. Brigadier, Queen's Bodyguard for Scotland (Royal Company of Archers); Chairman, Scottish Council on Alcohol, since 1973; Deputy Lieutenant, Borders Region, Roxburgh, Ettrick and Lauderdale, since 1983; Convenor, Borders Regional Council, since 1990; b. 19.6.28; m., 1, Lady Caroline Child-Villiers (m. diss.); 1 s.; 1 d.; 2, Mary Elizabeth Ballantine (deceased); 3, Mrs Caroline Larlham. Educ. Eton; Sandhurst. Former Captain, Scots Guards. Address: (h.) Minto, Hawick.

Miquel, Raymond Clive, CBE (1981). Chairman, Scottish Sports Council, since 1987; b. 28.5.31. Managing Director, Arthur Bell & Sons Ltd., 1968-85.

Misra, Prem Chandra, BSc, MBBS, DPM (RCP&S, Edin and Glas), FAGS. Deputy Physician Superintendent, Gartloch and Parkhead Hospitals, Glasgow, since 1984; Clinical Senior Lecturer, Glasgow University, since 1976; b. 24.7.41, Lucknow, India; m., Sandhya; 1 s.; 2 d. Educ. KK Degree College and King George's Medical College, Lucknow, India; Lucknow University. Rotating Intern, King George's Medical College Hospital, Lucknow, 1967; Demonstrator, Department of Human Physiology, Lucknow University, 1967; Resident Senior House Officer, General Medicine and Geriatrics, Wigan and Leigh Group of Hospitals, 1968-69; Resident House Surgeon, General Surgery, Wigan Royal

Infirmary, 1968-69; Resident House Physician, General Medicine, Whelley Hospital, Wigan, 1969-70; Resident Senior House Officer in Psychiatry, then Resident Registrar in Psychiatry, Bolton District General Hospital, 1970-73; Senior Psychiatric Registrar (Midland Area Consultant Training Scheme), Hollymoor Hospital, Birmingham, 1973-76; Consultant Psychiatrist, Solihull Area Health Authority, 1976; appointed Consultant Psychiatrist, Glasgow Royal Infirmary and Duke Street Hospital, 1976; Consultant in Charge, Acorn Street Day Hospital, 1979. President, Indian Association of Strathclyde, since 1981; Member, Executive Committee: Strathclyde Community Relations Council, 1981-85, Scottish Council for Racial Equality, 1982; Member, Social and Welfare Committee, CRC, for Ethnic Groups and Vietnam Refugees, 1982; awarded Ludwika Bierkoskigo Medal by Polish Medical Association for "outstanding contributions in the prevention and treatment of disabilities"; Secretary, Division of Psychiatry, Eastern District of Glasgow, since 1980; Member: Executive Committee, British Society of Research on Sex Education, International Scientific Committee on Sexuality and Handicap, International Advisory Board of Israel Society of Clinical and Experimental Hypnosis; Executive Committee Member, European Society of Hypnosis; Member, International Committee of Sexologists; Justice of the Peace; President, British Society of Medical and Dental Hypnosis (Scottish Branch), 1987-89. Publications: Modern Trends in Hypnosis; research papers. Address: (b.) Gartloch Hospital, Gartcosh, Glasgow, G69 8EJ; T.-041-771 0771.

Mitcalfe, Kirsteen, BA. Deputy Lieutenant of Moray, since 1991; Member, Gordonstoun School Board of Governors, since 1982; b. 23.7.36, Edinburgh; m., Hugh Mitcalfe; 4 d. Educ. Oxenfoord Castle School; Open University. Recreations: skiing; tennis; reading. Address: (h.) Milton Brodie, Forres, Moray, IV36 0UA; T.-0343 85281.

Mitchell, Rev. Alexander Bell, BD, DipTechEd.. Minister, St. Leonard's Church, Dunfermline, since 1981; Chairman, Executive Committee, Fife Marriage Counselling Service, 1986-90; b. 28.6.49, Baillieston; m., Elizabeth Brodie; 1 s.; 2 d. Educ. Uddingston Grammar School; New College, Edinburgh. Mechanical Engineer, Motherwell Bridge and Engineering, 1965-70; student, 1970-72; Teacher, Uddingston Grammar School, 1972-75; theology degree, 1975-79; Assistant Minister, Dunblane Cathedral, 1979-81. Chaplain, RAF Pitreavie, 1982-88. Recreations: badminton; hill-walking. Address: 12 Torvean Place, Dunfermline, KY11 4YY; T.-Dunfermline 721054.

Mitchell, Archie Mackenzie, MITSA. Director of Trading Standards, Tayside Regional Council, since 1980; b. 23.3.35, Cupar; m., Kathleen; 2 s.; 1 d. Educ. Bell-Baxter High School, Cupar. Trainee Inspector of Weights and Measures, Fife, 1953-58; Inspector of Weights and Measures, Glasgow, 1959; Ayr County: District Inspector, 1959-69, Depute Chief Inspector, 1969-75; Chief Inspector Consumer Protection (Ayr Sub-Region), Strathclyde, 1975-77; Depute Director, Grampian, 1977-80. Honorary Secretary, Society of Directors of Trading Standards in Scotland, 1982-86; Adviser on Trading Standards to COSLA and LACOTS, 1986-90. Recreations: curling; cricket; rugby. Address: (b.) Duncarse, 381 Perth Road, Dundee, DD2 1PR; T.-Dundee 67778.

Mitchell, Christopher Reginald, FRICS. Principal Quantity Surveyor, PSA Projects, since 1985; Head of Profession QS, since 1991; b. 17.5.47, Insen, Aberdeenshire; m., Rosemary Helen Hunter, CA; 2 s. Educ. Peebles High School; Boroughmuir School, Edinburgh. Apprentice QS, Edinburgh, 1966-70; Quantity Surveyor, Ministry of Public Buildings and Works (later PSA), Rosyth and Edinburgh, 1970-91. Recreation: curling. Address: (b.) PSA Projects, Argyle

House, 3 Lady Lawson Street, Edinburgh, EH3 9SD; T.-031-222 6244.

Mitchell, David William, CBE. Director, Mallinson-Denny (Scotland) Ltd., since 1980; Chairman, Cumbernauld New Town, since 1987; b. 4.1.33, Glasgow; m., Lynda Guy; 1 d. Educ. Merchiston Castle School. Member, Western Regional Hospital Board, 1965-73; Member, Glasgow Rating Valuation Appeal Committee, 1970-74; Council Member, CBI Scotland, 1979-85; Executive Member, Scottish Council (Development and Industry), since 1979; President, Scottish Timber Trade Association, 1980-82; Executive Member, Institute of Directors in Scotland, since 1983; President, Scottish Conservative and Unionist Association, 1980-82; Treasurer, Scottish Conservative Party, since 1990. Recreations: golf; shooting; fishing. Address: (h.) Dunmullen House, Blanefield, Stirlingshire, G63 9AJ; T.-0324 483294.

Mitchell, Rev. Duncan Ross, BA (Hons), BD (Hons). Minister, St. Andrews Church, West Kilbride, since 1980; b. 5.5.42, Boddam, Aberdeenshire; m., Sandra Brown; 2 s.; 1 d. Educ. Hyndland Senior Secondary School, Glasgow; Strathclyde University; Glasgow University. Worked in insurance industry, four years; Minister, Craigmailen UF Church, Bo'ness, 1972-80; Convener, Assembly Youth Committee, UF Church, 1974-79; Member: Scottish Joint Committee on Religious Education, 1974-79, Multilateral Conversation in Scotland, 1976-79, Board of Social Responsibility, Church of Scotland, 1983-86;Ardrossan Presbytery: Convener, World Mission and Unity, 1984-88, Convener, Stewardship and Finance, since 1988; Convener, General Assembly Board of World Mission and Unity, Local Involvements Committee, and Executive Member of the Board, since 1987; Church of Scotland Delegate to Council of Churches for Britain and Ireland Assembly. Address: St. Andrew's Manse, 7 Overton Drive, West Kilbride; T.-0294 823142.

Mitchell, Iain Grant, LLB (Hons), FSA Scot, FRSA. Advocate, since 1976; b. 16.11.51, Edinburgh. Educ. Perth Academy; Edinburgh University. Called to Scottish Bar, 1976; Advisor in Scots Law to Lawtel (Prestel Legal Database), since 1983; Past President, Diagnostic Society of Edinburgh; former Vice-President, Edinburgh University Conservative Association; Conservative candidate, Falkirk West, General Election, 1983, and Kirkcaldy, General Election, 1987; Chairman, Trust for an International Opera Theatre of Scotland; Vice-Chairman, Scottish Baroque Ensemble Ltd.; Board Member, Sinfonia of Scotland; Member, Scottish Committee, Royal Institute of International Affairs; Member, Conservative Group for Europe and the European Movement. Recreations: music and the arts; photography; cinema; walking; history; travel; writing; finding enough hours in the day. Address: (b.) Advocates Library, Parliament House, High Street, Edinburgh; T.-031-226 5071.

Mitchell, James F.O., MD, DLO, FRCSEdin. Senior Consultant Ear, Nose and Throat Surgeon, Tayside Area (retired); Consultant Otolaryngologist, Dundee, Angus and Perth NHS, 1951-87; b. 7.9.21, Edinburgh; 3 s. Educ. George Heriot's School, Edinburgh; Edinburgh University. Army Service, RAMC, 1945-48, Egypt and Palestine, latterly as Major. Chairman, Area Medical Committee, 1981-83; Chairman, British Medical Association, Angus, 1964, and Dundee, 1978. Dundee Chairman, British Subaqua Club, 1969. Recreations: swimming; skiing; caravanning; ornithology; golf; fishing. Address: (h.) 19 Rockfield Crescent, Dundee; T.-0382 66092.

Mitchell, Sheriff (James Lachlan) Martin. Sheriff of Lothian and Borders at Edinburgh, since 1978; b. 13.6.29, Inverness. Educ. Cargilfield; Sedbergh; Edinburgh University. National Service (RN), 1954-55; Sub Lt. (S), RNVR, 1954; Permanent Reserve, 1956-74; Commander, RNR, 1966;

retired, 1974; Law Apprentice, 1950-53; Member, Faculty of Advocates, 1957; in practice, 1957-74; Standing Junior Counsel in Scotland to the Admiralty Board, 1963-74; Temporary Sheriff, 1971; Sheriff of Lothian and Peebles, 1974, and as a floating Sheriff, 1974-78; Honorary Sheriff at Inverness, 1983; Governor, Cargilfield School, 1966-91. Recreations: fishing; photography; the gramophone. Address: (b.) Sheriffs' Chambers, Sheriff Court, Lawnmarket, Edinburgh, EH1 2NS; T.-031-226 7181.

Mitchell, John, BSc. Head Teacher, Kilsyth Academy, since 1985; b. 4.1.45, Kirkintilloch; m., Irene; 1 s.; 1 d. Educ. Lenzie Academy; Glasgow University. Taught in Glasgow; Principal Teacher of Physics, Balfron High School and Bishopbriggs High School; Assistant Head Teacher, Kilsyth Academy; Deputy Head Teacher, Knightswood Secondary School. Address: (h.) Kilsyth Academy, Balmalloch, Kilsyth, G65 9NF; T.-0236 822244.

Mitchell, (John) Angus (Macbeth), CB, CVO, MC, LLD(Hon). Chairman of Court, Stirling University, since 1984; Chairman, Scottish Action on Dementia, since 1986; Member, Historic Buildings Council for Scotland, since 1988; b. 25.8.24, Ootacamund, India; m., Ann Williamson; 2 s.; 2 d. Educ. Marlborough College; Brasenose College, Oxford. Royal Armoured Corps (Captain), 1943-46; Scottish Office, 1949-84; Principal Private Secretary to Secretary of State for Scotland, 1958-59; Under Secretary, Social Work Services Group, 1969-74; Secretary, Scottish Education Department, 1976-84. Order of Orange-Nassau, 1946; Chairman, Scottish Marriage Guidance Council, 1965-69; Vice-Convener, Scottish Council of Voluntary Organisations, 1986-91; Member, Commission for Local Authority Accounts in Scotland, 1985-89. Publications: Scottish Office Ministers 1885-1985; Procedures for the Reorganisation of Schools in England, 1986. Recreations: old Penguins; gravestones; maps. Address: (h.) 20 Regent Terrace, Edinburgh, EH7 5BS; T.-031-556 7671.

Mitchell, John Gall, QC, MA, LLB. Social Security (formerly National Insurance) Commissioner, since 1979; b. 5.5.31, Edinburgh; m., 1, Anne Bertram Jardine (deceased); 3 s.; 1 d.; 2, Margaret Galbraith. Educ. Royal High School, Edinburgh; Edinburgh University. Advocate, 1957; Standing Junior Counsel, Customs and Excise, Scotland, 1964-70; a Chairman, Industrial Tribunals, Scotland, 1966-80; Honorary Sheriff of Lanarkshire, 1970-74; Chairman, Supreme Court Legal Aid Committee, 1974-79; a Chairman, Pensions Appeal Tribunals, Scotland, 1974-80. Address: (h.) Rosemount, Park Road, Eskbank, Dalkeith, Midlothian; T.-031-663 2557.

Mitchell, John Logan, QC, LLB (Hons). Queen's Counsel, since 1987; Advocate Depute, 1981-85; b. 23.6.47, Dumfries; m., Christine Brownlee Thomson; 1 s.; 1 d. Educ. Royal High School, Edinburgh; Edinburgh University. Called to Bar, 1974; Standing Junior Counsel to Forestry Commission; Standing Junior Counsel, Department of Agriculture and Fisheries. Address: (h.) 17 Braid Farm Road, Edinburgh; T.-031-447 8099.

Mitchell, Lyn, BSc (SocSci), MMedSci, RGN, SCM, RSCN, RNT. Chief Executive Officer, National Board for Nursing, Midwifery and Health Visiting for Scotland, since 1986; b. 26.4.40, Elgin; m., David Mitchell; 1 step s.; 1 step d. Educ. Elgin Academy; Edinburgh University; Nottingham University. Ward Sister: Sheffield Children's Hospital, Aberdeen Royal Infirmary; Nurse Teacher, Foresterhill College, Aberdeen; Senior Health Education Officer, Grampian Health Board; Lecturer, Department of Nursing Studies, Edinburgh University; Nursing Adviser, Scottish Health Education Group. Publication: Teaching for Health.

Address: (b.) 22 Queen Street, Edinburgh, EH2 1JX; T.-031-226 7371.

Mitchell, Peter Crichton, QPM. Deputy Chief Constable, Strathclyde Police, since 1985; b. 24.7.38, Stonehaven; m., Mary; 1 s.; 2 d. Educ. Pitlochry High School; Glasgow College. Lanarkshire Contabulary, 1959-75; Strathclyde Police, since 1975. Recreations: photography; gardening; golf; music. Address: (b.) 173 Pitt Street, Glasgow, G2 4JS; T.-041-204 2626.

Mitchell, Very Rev. Ronald Gerard, DGA, BD. Rector, Montfort House, Barrhead, Glasgow, since 1988; Episcopal Vicar for Religious, Diocese of Paisley, since 1988; b. Belfast. Educ. St. Mary's CB Grammar School, Belfast; Queen's University, Belfast; Heythrop College, London University. Northern Ireland Civil Service, 1960-66; Member, Montfort Missionary Society, since 1966. Recreation: walking. Address: Montfort House, Darnley Road, Barrhead, Glasgow, G78 1TA; T.-041-881 1440.

Mitchell, Ross, MA, DSA, FHSM, MIPM. Associate Director, Scottish Hospital Advisory Service, since 1987 (Secretary, Lothian Health Board, 1981-87); b. Glasgow; m., Marion; 1 s. Educ. Hillhead High School, Glasgow; Glasgow University; Manchester University. Eastern Regional Hospital Board: National Administrative Trainee, 1956-58, Administrative Assistant, 1958-60, Work Study Officer, 1960-61; Hospital Secretary, Bridge of Earn Hospital, 1961-65; Deputy Secretary and Treasurer, East Fife Board of Management, 1965-69; Secretary and Treasurer, West Lothian Board of Management, 1969-73; Secretary, Fife Health Board, 1973-81. Recreations: squash; golf; tennis. Address: (h.) 43 Braehead Road, Edinburgh, EH4 6BD; T.-031-339 1279.

Mitchell, Professor Ross Galbraith, MD, FRCPEdin, DCH. Professor of Child Health, Dundee University, 1973-85, now Emeritus; Member, General Medical Council, 1983-85; b. 18.11.20; m., June Phylis Butcher; 1 s.; 3 d. Educ. Kelvinside Academy, Glasgow; Edinburgh University. Surgeon Lt., Royal Naval Volunteer Reserve, 1944-47; junior medical posts, Edinburgh, Liverpool and London, 1947-52; Rockefeller Research Fellow in Physiology, Mayo Clinic, USA, 1952-53; Lecturer in Child Health, St. Andrews University, 1952-55; Consultant Paediatrician, Dundee Teaching Hospitals, 1955-63; Professor of Child Health, Aberdeen University, 1963-72. Chairman, Editorial Board, Mac Keith Press, since 1980; Chairman, Scottish Advisory Council on Child Care, 1966-68; Dean, Faculty of Medicine and Dentistry, Dundee University, 1978-81; Chairman, Aberdeen Association of Social Service, 1971-72; President, Scottish Paediatric Society, 1982-84; President, Harveian Society of Edinburgh, 1982-83; Vice-Chairman, Scottish Child and Family Alliance, since 1985. Recreations: fishing; gardening; languages. Address: (h.) Craigard, Abertay Gardens, Barnhill, Dundee, DD5 2SQ; T.-0382 76983.

Mitchell, Ruthven, BSc (Hons), MB, ChB, MD, FRCPath, FRCPGlas, FRCPEdin. Regional Director, Glasgow and West of Scotland Blood Transfusion Service, since 1978; b. 28.3.36, Cambuslang; m., Eleanor Forbes Burnside; 1 s.; 1 d. Educ. Hamilton Academy; Glasgow University. Glasgow Royal Infirmary: Medical and Surgical House Officer, 1961-62, Senior House Officer in Pathology, 1962-63, Registrar in Pathology, 1963-65, University Lecturer in Pathology, 1965-68; Consultant Pathologist, Ministry of Health, Tanzania, 1965-67; Deputy Medical Director, Glasgow and West of Scotland Blood Transfusion Service, 1968-78. Recreations: gardening; fishing. Address: (h.) 2 Byron Court, Sweethope Farm Steading, Bothwell, Lanarkshire; T.-0698 853255.

Mitchell, Thomas. Lord Provost, City of Dundee, since 1984; b. 4.9.41, Dundee; m., Gertrude Brown; 2 s. Educ. St. John's High School, Dundee. Elected, City of Dundee District Council, 1980. Recreations: football; hill-walking. Address: (b.) City Chambers, Dundee, DD1 3BY; T.-Dundee 23141.

Mitchison, Professor John Murdoch, ScD, FRS, FRSE. Professor Emeritus and University Fellow, Edinburgh University (Professor of Zoology, 1963-88); b. 11.6.22; m., Rosalind Mary Wrong; 1 s.; 3 d. Educ. Winchester College; Trinity College, Cambridge. Army Operational Research, 1941-46; Research Scholar, then Fellow, Trinity College, Cambridge, 1946-54; Lecturer, then Reader in Zoology, Edinburgh University, 1953-62; Member, Edinburgh University Court, 1971-74, 1985-88; Dean, Faculty of Science, 1984-85; Member, Academia Europaea; Member, Scottish Marine Biological Association, 1961-67; Executive Committee Member, International Society for Cell Biology, 1964-72; Member: Biological Committee, SRC, 1972-75, Royal Commission on Environmental Pollution, 1974-79, Science Board, SRC, 1976-79, Working Group on Biological Manpower, DES, 1968-71, Advisory Committee on Safety of Nuclear Installations, Health and Safety Executive, 1981-84; President, British Society for Cell Biology, 1974-77. Publication: The Biology of the Cell Cycle. Address: (h.) Great Yew, Ormiston, East Lothian, EH35 5NJ; T.-Pencaitland 340530.

Mitchison, Naomi, CBE. Writer; b. 1.11.97, Edinburgh; m., Dick Mitchison; 3 s.; 2 d. Educ. Dragon School, Oxford; St. Anne's College, Oxford. Member: Argyll County Council, 1945-65, Highland Panel, 1945-65, Highland and Island Advisory Council, 1965-75; contested Scottish Universities Parliamentary constituency for Labour; author of about 80 books, including: The Corn King and the Spring Queen; Blood of the Martyrs; The Bull Calves; The Big House; Lobsters on the Agenda; Five Men and a Swan; Cleopatra's People; volumes of autobiography; The Cleansing of the Knife; Images of Africa; Memoirs of a Space Woman; Travel Light; Early in Orcadia; A Girl Must Live. Address: (h.) Carradale House, Carradale, Campbeltown, Argyll.

Mitchison, Professor Rosalind Mary, MA. Professor of Social History, Edinburgh University, 1981-86; b. 11.4.19, Manchester; m., J.M. Mitchison (qv); 1 s.; 3 d. Educ. Channing School, Highgate; Lady Margaret Hall, Oxford. Assistant Lecturer, Manchester University, 1943-46; Tutor, Lady Margaret Hall, Oxford, 1946-47; Assistant: Edinburgh University, 1954-57, Glasgow University, 1962-63; Lecturer, Glasgow University, 1966-67; Lecturer, then Reader, Edinburgh University, 1967-81. President, Scottish History Society, 1981-84. Publications: A History of Scotland, 1970; British Population Change since 1860, 1977; Life in Scotland, 1978; Lordship to Patronage: Scotland 1603-1745, 1983; Sexuality and Social Control: Scotland 1660-1780 (Co-author), 1989. Recreation: walking. Address: (h.) Great Yew, Ormiston, East Lothian, EH35 5NJ; T.-Pencaitland 340530.

Mithen, Dallas Alfred, CB, BSc, FICFor. President, Institute of Chartered Foresters, 1984-86; Chairman, Forestry Training Council, since 1984; b. 5.11.23; m., 1, Peggy Clarke (deceased); 2, Avril Teresa Dodd; 1 s.; 1 d. Educ. Maidstone Grammar School; University College of North Wales, Bangor. Fleet Air Arm, 1942-46; joined Forestry Commission as District Officer, 1950; Deputy Surveyor, New Forest, and Conservator, SE (England), 1968-71; Senior Officer, Scotland, 1971-75; Head, Forest Management Division, Edinburgh, 1975-76; Commissioner for Harvesting and Marketing, Forestry Commission, 1977-83. Trustee, Central Scotland Countryside Trust, since 1985; President, Forestry Section, BAAS, 1985. Recreations: swimming; walking; gardening. Address: (h.) Kings Knot, Bonnington Road, Peebles, EH45 9HF; T.-0721 20738.

Moffat, Alistair Murray, MA (Hons), MPhil. Director of Programmes, Scottish Television, since 1990; b. 16.6.50, Kelso; m., Lindsay Thomas; 1 s.; 2 d. Educ. Kelso High School; St. Andrews University; Edinburgh University; London University. Ran Edinburgh Festival Fringe, 1976-81; Arts Correspondent/Producer/Controller of Features, Scottish Television. Publications: The Edinburgh Fringe, 1978; Kelsae - A History of Kelso from Earliest Times, 1985; Remembering Charles Rennie Mackintosh, 1989. Recreations: sleeping; supporting Kelso RFC. Address: (b.) Scottish Television, Cowcaddens, Glasgow, G2 3PR.

Moffat of that Ilk, Francis, MC, JP, DL, FSA Scot. Chief of the Name and Arms of Moffat; Deputy Lieutenant, County of Dumfries, since 1957; b. 21.3.15, Moffat; m., Margaret Carrington; 2 d. Educ. Shrewsbury School; Trinity College, Cambridge. Farming in Roxburghshire, 1937-40; War Service, 1940-45: Major, King's Own Scottish Borderers, severely wounded in Germany, 1945; Farmer and Landowner, Dumfriesshire, 1946-76; succeeded father as County Councillor for Moffat and Wamphray, 1948; President, Moffat Show Society, 1950-57 (Honorary President, since 1957); Member, Association of County Councils in Scotland, 1961-75; Vice-Convener, Dumfries County Council, 1961-69, Convener, 1969-75; Chairman: SW Scotland Joint Planning Working Party, 1969-72, SW Scotland Industrial Development Authority, 1972-75; Member, Board of Management, Small Industries Council for Rural Areas of Scotland, 1972-75; Member, Committee for European Investment in Scotland, 1972-74; Member, Scottish Consultative Committee, Scottish Council (Development and Industry), 1972-75; Council Member, Galloway Cattle Society, 1961-72; President, Dumfriesshire Conservative Association, 1978-85. Recreations: historical and genealogical research; walking; reading. Address: (h.) Redacres, Moffat, Dumfriesshire, DG10 9JT; T.-0683 20045.

Moffat, Leslie Ernest Fraser, BSc, MB, ChB, FRCS. Consultant Urological Surgeon, since 1986; Clinical Senior Lecturer, Aberdeen University; b. 23.11.49, Lanark; m., Elaine Elizabeth Theakston; 3 d. Educ. Lanark Grammar School; Edinburgh University. Professorial house officer posts, Edinburgh; SHO, Department of Surgery, Royal Infirmary, Edinburgh; Rotating Surgical Registrar, Edinburgh, 1977-79; Urological Senior Registrar, Glasgow teaching hospital, 1982-86. Recreation: country life. Address: (h.) Tillery House, Udny, Ellon, Aberdeenshire; T.-06513 2898.

Moir, Alan C., MA (Hons), DipEd. Headteacher, Ayr Academy, since 1989; b. 18.4.47, Elgin; m., Margaret Aird; 2 s. Educ. Aberdeen Grammar School; Aberdeen University. Teacher, Belmont Academy, Ayr, 1971-76; Principal Teacher of History, Auchinleck Academy, 1976-83; Assistant Headteacher, then Depute Headteacher, Carrick Academy, 1983-89. Session Clerk, Prestwick South Church. Recreations: music; reading; gardening. Address: (h.) 98 Ayr Road, Prestwick, KA9 1RR; T.-0292 76883.

Moir, Alexander Thomas Boyd, MB, ChB, BSc, PhD, FRCPEdin, FRCPGlas, FRCPath, MFOM, MFPHM, FIBiol, FIFST. Director and Deputy Chief Scientist, Chief Scientist Office, Scottish Office Home and Health Department; b. 1.8.39, Bolton; m., Isabel May Sheehan; 1 s.; 2 d. Educ. George Heriot's School, Edinburgh; Edinburgh University. Intern appointment, New York City Hospitals; MRC Scientific/Clinical Scientific Staff, Honorary Registrar/Senior Registrar, Honorary Fellow, Edinburgh University; Senior/Principal Medical Officer, Scottish Home and Health Department. Recreations: playing games; listening to music; reading. Address: (b.) Scottish Office Home and Health Department, St. Andrews House, Edinburgh, EH1 3DE; T.-031-556 8400.

Moir, Dorothy Carnegie, MB, ChB, MD, FFCM. Chief Administrative Medical Officer, Forth Valley Health Board, since 1988; Community Medicine Specialist, since 1979; Honorary Senior Clinical Lecturer in Public Health, Aberdeen University; Honorary Senior Clinical Lecturer, Department of Public Health, Glasgow University; b. 27.3.42, Aberdeen; m., Alexander D. Moir; 3 s. Educ. Albyn School for Girls, Aberdeen; Aberdeen University. Research Fellow in Therapeutics and Pharmacology, 1966-69; Lecturer in Community Medicine, 1970-79. Address: (b.) 33 Spittal Street, Stirling.

Moir, Rev. Ian Andrew, MA, BD. Church of Scotland Adviser for Urban Priority Areas, since 1991; Minister, Old Kirk of Edinburgh, 1983-91; b. 9.4.35, Aberdeen; m., Elizabeth; 3 s. Educ. Aberdeen Grammar School; Aberdeen University. Sub-Warden, St. Ninian's Training Centre, Crieff, 1959-61; Superintendent, Pholela High School, Natal, 1962-73; Assistant Secretary, Church of Scotland Overseas Council, 1974-83. Recreations: walking; golf. Address: (h.) 47 Millersneuk Drive, Lenzie, G66 5JE.

Mole, George Alexander (Sandy). Vice President, National Farmers Union of Scotland, since 1990; Director, Coastal Grains Ltd., since 1988; Director, Scottish Agricultural and Rural Centre Ltd., since 1992; b. 7.6.43, Duns; m., Jean Mitchell; 1 s.; 2 d. Educ. St. Mary's, Melrose; Merchiston Castle. NFU of Scotland: President, Mid and East Berwick; Convener, Cereals Committee; Member, EEC Commission Cereals Advisory Committee; Chairman, AFRC Cereal Consultative; Member, Home Grown Cereals Authority R. & D. Committee; Member, Institute of Brewing Cereal Publicity. Recreations: golf; shooting. Address: Greenburn, Reston, Eyemouth, TD14 5LP.

Mollison, Professor Denis, MA, PhD. Professor of Applied Probability, Heriot-Watt University, since 1986; Chairman, Mountain Bothies Association, since 1978; Trustee, John Muir Trust; b. 28.6.45, Carshalton; m., Jennifer Hutton; 1 s.; 3 d. Educ. Westminster School; Trinity College, Cambridge. Research Fellow, King's College, Cambridge, 1969; Lecturer in Statistics, Heriot-Watt University, 1973. Elected Member of Council, National Trust for Scotland, 1979-84. Address: (h.) The Laigh House, Inveresk, Musselburgh, EH21 7TD; T.-031-665 2055.

Monaghan, Rt. Rev. James. Titular Bishop of Cell Ausaille and Auxiliary Bishop of St. Andrews and Edinburgh (retired); b. 11.7.14, Bathgate. Educ. St. Aloysius', Glasgow; St. Mary's, Blairs; Scots College, Valladolid; St. Kieran's, Kilkenny. Ordained Priest, 1940; Assistant: St. Andrew's, Ravelston, Edinburgh, 1940-42, St. Margaret Mary's, Edinburgh, 1942-47; Chaplain, Little Sisters of the Poor, Edinburgh, 1947-59; Parish Priest, Holy Cross, Edinburgh, 1959; President, Scottish Catholic Communications Commission, 1970-77. Address: 252 Ferry Road, Edinburgh, EH5 3AN.

Monagan, Thomas John, IPFA. Town Clerk and Chief Executive, City of Glasgow District, since 1991; b. 24.11.46, Airdrie; m., Anna-Frances; 3 s. Educ. St. Patrick's High School, Coatbridge. Qualified as an accountant, 1970; held various appointments in Finance Department before becoming Senior Depute Town Clerk, 1988. Recreations: golf; opera. Address: (b.) City Chambers, Glasgow, G2 1DU; T.-041-227 4501.

Moncreiff, 5th Baron (Harry Robert Wellwood Moncreiff), Bt; b. 4.2.15; m., Enid Marion Watson Locke (deceased); 1 s. Educ. Fettes College, Edinburgh. Lt.-Col. (Hon.), RASC (retired). Address: (h.) Tulliebole Castle, Fossoway, Kinross-shire.

Moncrieff, Charles William Kemley, BSc, MA. Rector, Annan Academy, since 1984; b. 12.7.42, Edinburgh; m., Helen Grantham; 1 s.; 1 d. Educ. Ross High School; Edinburgh University; Heriot-Watt University; Moray House College of Education. Teacher of Mathematics and Science: Daliburgh Secondary School, South Uist, Knox Academy, Haddington; Principal Teacher of Mathematics: David Kilpatrick Secondary School, Edinburgh, Gracemount High School, Edinburgh; Assistant Rector, Banff Academy; Depute Rector, Dumfries Academy. Address: (b.) Annan Academy, St. John's Road, Annan, DG12 6AP; T.-Annan 2954.

Mone, Rt. Rev. John Aloysius. Bishop of Paisley, formerly Titular Bishop of Abercorn and Auxiliary Bishop of Glasgow; b. 22.6.29, Glasgow. Educ. Holyrood Secondary School; Seminaire St. Sulpice and Institut Catholique, Paris. Ordained Priest, 1952; Assistant: St. Ninian's, Knightswood, Glasgow, 1952-75, Our Lady and St. George, Glasgow, 1975-79; Parish Priest, St. Joseph's, Tollcross, Glasgow, 1979-84. National Chairman, Catholic Marriage Advisory Council, 1981; Chairman, Scottish Catholic International Aid Fund, 1975-77; President, National Justice and Peace Commission, 1987; President/Treasurer, Scottish Catholic International Aid Fund, since 1985.

Monelle, Raymond, MA, BMus, PhD, ARCM. Writer on music; Composer; Music Critic, The Independent and Opera Magazine; Senior Lecturer in Music, Edinburgh University; b. 19.8.37, Bristol; 2 d. Educ. Bristol Grammar School; Pembroke College, Oxford; Royal College of Music. Address: (h.) 3 Livingstone Place, Edinburgh, EH9 1PB.

Monro, Sir Hector, AE, DL, JP. MP (Conservative), Dumfries, since 1964; Under Secretary of State, Scottish Office, since 1992; Farmer; b. 4.10.22, Edinburgh; m., Lady (Anne) Monro; 2 s. Educ. Canford School; Cambridge University; Dundee School of Economics. RAF, 1941-46; Royal Auxiliary Air Force, 1946-53, Honorary Air Commodore, since 1981, Inspector since 1990; Member, Dumfries County Council, 1952-67 (Chairman, Planning Committee and Joint Police Committee); Scottish Conservative Whip, 1967-70; Lord Commissioner, HM Treasury, 1970-71; Minister of Health and Education, Scottish Office, 1971-74; Opposition Spokesman on Scottish Affairs, 1974-75, Sport, 1974-79; Minister of Sport and Rural Affairs, 1979-81; Member, Nature Conservancy Council, 1982-91; Member, Area Executive, NFU, since 1964; Member, Council, National Trust for Scotland, since 1983; Vice-President, Scottish Rugby Union, 1975, President, 1976-77; Member, Queen's Bodyguard for Scotland (Royal Company of Archers); President: NSRA, since 1987, ACU, 1983-90. Recreations: rugby; golf; flying; vintage cars; country sports. Address: (h.) Williamwood, Kirtlebridge, Lockerbie, Dumfriesshire; T.-04615 213.

Montagu-Smith, Group Captain Arthur. Deputy Lieutenant, Morayshire, 1970-91; b. 17.7.15; m., Elizabeth Hood Alexander; 1 s.; 1 d. Educ. Whitgift School; RAF Staff College. Commissioned RAF, 1935; Adjutant 99 Squadron, 1938-39; served Second World War, European Theatre, North Africa and Mediterranean; Flt. Cdr., 264 Squadron, 1940, and 221 Squadron, 1941; OC 248 Squadron, 1942-43; Battle of Britain Gold Rosette, 1940; mentioned in Despatches, 1942; Deputy Director, RAF Training, USA (Washington), 1944; OC 104 Wing, France, 1945; Hon. ADC, Governor, N.I., 1948-49; Air Adviser, New Delhi, 1949-50; RAF Representative, Chiefs of Staff Committee, UN, New York, 1951-53; HM Air Attache, Budapest, 1958-60; retired at own request, 1961; Regional Executive, Small Industries Council and Scottish Development Agency, 1962-80; Member, Elgin District Council, 1967-75; Member, Moray TAFA, 1961-68; Director, Elgin and Lossiemouth Harbour Company, 1966-90; Hon. County Representative, Moray and Nairn, RAF

Benevolent Fund, since 1964; Chairman, Elgin and Lossiemouth Scottish SPCA, 1971-82; Past President, Victoria League, Moray and Nairn; Past Chairman, Moray Association of Youth Clubs. Recreations: outdoor interests; travel; animal welfare. Address: (h.) Woodpark, by Elgin, Moray; T.-034 384 2220.

Monteith, Lt.-Col. Robert Charles Michael, OBE, MC, TD, JP, DL, OStJ. Vice-Lieutenant of Lanarkshire, since 1964; b. 25.5.14, London; m., Mira Elizabeth Fanshawe; 1 s. Educ. Ampleforth College. CA, Edinburgh; served with Lanarkshire Yeomanry, 1939-45; contested Hamilton Division, 1950 and 1951; County Councillor (Lanarkshire), 1949-74; Chairman, Clydesdale District Council, 1974-84; Member, Mental Welfare Commission for Scotland, 1962-84; Member, East Kilbride Development Corporation, 1972-76; Member, Queen's Bodyguard for Scotland (Royal Company of Archers); Member, SMO Knights of Malta, 1956. Recreations: shooting; curling. Address: (h.) Cranley, Cleghorn, Lanark, T.-0555-870 330.

Monteith, Rev. William Graham, MA, BD, BPhil. Minister, Hoy & Walls linked with Flotta and Fara, since 1985; Convener, Business Committee, Presbytery of Orkney, since 1986; b. 14.11.46, Glasgow; m., Angela Mary Faulkner; 1 s. Educ. Ross High School, Tranent; Edinburgh University; York University. Assistant Minister, St. Andrew's, Drumchapel, 1973-74; Minister, Berwick Wallace Green Church, 1974-85. Hon. Treasurer, Orkney Disability Forum; Director and Company Secretary, Hoy Teleservice Centre. Publications: Disability, Faith and Acceptance, 1987; various papers and articles. Recreations: table games; music; philosophy; lazing around beaches. Address: The Manse of the South Isles, Green Hill, Longhope, Stromness, Orkney, KW16 3PG; T.-0856 70 325.

Montgomery, Sir (Basil Henry) David, 9th Bt, JP, DL. Chairman, Forestry Commission, 1979-89; b. 20.3.31. Deputy Lieutenant, Perth and Kinross, since 1975.

Montgomery, Daniel David William, BSc. Director of Commercial Services, Electrical Contractors' Association of Scotland; Director and Secretary, Scottish Joint Industry Board, since 1975; Director, Scottish Electrical Contractors' Insurance Ltd., since 1975; b. 24.9.37, Banton, Stirlingshire; m., Joan Elizabeth Allan; 2 s. Educ. Kilsyth Academy; Glasgow University; Royal College of Science and Technology; Heriot-Watt University. Student apprentice, Fairfield Shipbuilding and Engineering Co. Ltd. and Rolls-Royce Ltd.; graduate training, then Organisation and Methods Officer, Joseph Lucas Ltd., Birmingham, and Uniroyal, Edinburgh; joined Electrical Contractors Association of Scotland, 1965, as Assistant to the Chief Executive. Territorial Army Commission, Royal Engineers, 1963-67. Recreations: golf; hill-walking; reading. Address: (b.) Bush House, Bush Estate, Midlothian, EH26 0SB; T.-031-445 5577.

Montgomery, Rev. Robert Aitken. Parish Minister, Quarrier's Village, since 1986; Hon. President, Abbeyfield Quarrier's Society; b. 25.7.27, Ruthwell, Dumfries; m., Elizabeth Hay; 2 s. Educ. Hutchesons' Grammar School; Glasgow University and Trinity College. Parish Minister: Portsoy, 1955, Fordyce, 1972. Moderator: Presbytery of Fordyce, 1965, of Strathbogie and Fordyce, 1972, of Greenock, 1983; Chairman, various Committees, County of Banff and Grampian Region, until 1978; Chairman, Abbeyfield Quarrier's Society. Recreations: fishing; hill-walking. Address: The Manse, Quarrier's village, Bridge of Weir, Renfrewshire; T.-0505 690498.

Moody, Geoffrey Howard, BDS, PhD, FDS RCS Edin, MRCPath, DFM. Senior Lecturer, Oral Pathology, Edinburgh University, since 1987; Consultant Pathologist, Lothian Health Board, since 1987; Member, Dental Council, and Convener, Dental Examinations Committee, Royal College of Surgeons of Edinburgh, since 1988; b. 13.6.43, Stafford; m., Alison Birse; 2 s.; 1 d. Educ. Melville College, Edinburgh; Edinburgh University. Lecturer, Edinburgh University, 1970-79; Lecturer, University of Papua New Guinea, 1979-81; Lecturer/Senior Lecturer, Edinburgh University, since 1981; Forensic Dentist, Lothians and Borders Police, since 1988. Recreations: Church works; trout fishing; hill-walking; DIY. Address: (b.) Department of Oral Medicine and Pathology, Old Surgeons Hall, High School Yard, Edinburgh, EH1 1NR; T.-031-650 2382.

Moon, Brenda Elizabeth, MA, MPhil, FLA. Librarian, Edinburgh University, since 1980; b. 11.4.31, Stoke on Trent. Educ. Oxford University. Assistant Librarian, Sheffield University, 1955-62; Sub-Librarian, then Deputy Librarian, Hull University, 1962-79. Recreations: walking; gardening; canal cruising. Address: (b.) Edinburgh University Library, George Square, Edinburgh; T.-031-650 3378.

Moonie, Lewis George. MP (Labour), Kirkcaldy, since 1987; b. 25.2.47.

Moore, Andrew F., BL. Director, Scottish Chambers of Commerce, since 1989; b. 5.12.39, Leven; m., Anne MacGregor; 2 s.; 1 d. Educ. Buckhaven High School; Edinburgh University. Examiner, Estate Duty Office, Edinburgh, 1958-63; Assistant, then Depute Secretary, Scottish Council for Commercial Education, 1963-73; Depute Chief Officer, Scottish Business Education Council, 1973-80; Chief Officer, SCOTBEC, 1980-87; seconded to Stirling University, 1987-89. Governor, Scottish Council for Educational Technology, 1976-84; Director, Filmhouse, Edinburgh, 1980-85; Honorary Treasurer, British Association for Commercial and Industrial Education, 1979-81; President, Pedagogical Committee, International Society for Business Education and Member, ISBE/SIEC Executive, since 1980; Treasurer, Levenmouth Enterprise Trust; Member, Scottish Council for Research in Education, 1984-87; Hon. Secretary, Scottish Students' Song Book Committee Ltd.; Session Clerk, Scoonie Kirk, Leven; President, Leven YMCA; Member: Council, Association of British Chambers of Commerce; Executive Committee, Scottish Business in the Community; Executive Committee, Scottish Council (Development & Industry); Forces Resettlement Committee for Scotland. Recreations: golf; youth work; Rotary International; foreign travel. Address: (h.) Annandale, Linksfield Street, Leven, Fife; T.-0333 25164.

Moore, George, LLB (Hons). Solicitor; Joint Senior Partner, Hamilton Burns Moore, since 1973; b. 7.11.47, Kilmarnock; m., Ann Beattie; 2 s.; 1 d. Educ. High School of Glasgow; Glasgow University. Member, Glasgow and North Argyll Legal Aid Committee, 1979; Reporter to Scottish Legal Aid Board, 1986; part-time Chairman, Industrial Tribunals in Scotland, 1986; Member, Sheriff Court Rules Council, 1987. Recreations: tennis; golf; windsurfing. Address: (b.) 13 Bath Street, Glasgow, G2 1HY; T.-041-353 2121.

Moore, Kenneth William, BSc, PhD. Agricultural Research, Education and Advisory Services Division, Scottish Office Agriculture and Fisheries Department, since 1990; b. 31.5.41, Glasgow; m., Sheila Blackwood; 2 d. Educ. Allan Glen's School, Glasgow; Glasgow University. Joined Civil Service, 1967; variously responsible for Land Tenure Reform, Health Services, Scottish Development Agency; Finance Officer, Scottish Education Department, 1980-83, and Department of Agriculture and Fisheries for Scotland, 1983-84; Head, Local Government Division, 1984-87; Head, Housing (Private Sector) Division, 1987-90. Recreations: hill-walking; mathematics and computing; cycling; language and languages;

bird-watching; music. Address: (h.) 22 Morningside Park, Edinburgh; T.-031-447 2051.

Moore, Michael Ritchie, BSc, PhD, DSc. Reader in Medicine and Therapeutics, Glasgow University, since 1989; b. 24.1.44, Glasgow; m., Alice Briscoe; 1 s.; 2 d. Educ. Falkirk High School; Glasgow University. Glasgow University: Research Assistant, Department of Medicine, 1967, Department of Materia Medica, 1970, Research Fellow, 1973, Lecturer in Materia Medica, 1975, in Medicine, 1978; Senior Lecturer in Medicine, 1982; Chief Professional Officer, Groote Schuur Hospital, Cape Town, 1982; Senior Research Fellow, MRC/UCT Porphyrias Unit, Cape Town University, 1983. Chairman, Kilsyth Community Council, 1985; Chairman, Lanarkshire Local Health Council, 1991; Secretary Director, Clock Theatre, Kilsyth, 1984; Committee Member, Tetrapyrrole Discussion Group, 1975; Secretary, Committee on Review of Porphyrinogenicity (Corp), 1987. Publications: Disorders of Porphyrin Metabolism, 1987; Porphyria, Drug Lists, 1991. Recreations: rock climbing and hill-walking; photography; amateur dramatics; gardening; motor sport. Address: (b.) Porphyrias Unit, University Department of Medicine and Therapeutics, Western Infirmary, Glasgow, G11 6NT; T.-041-339 8822.

Moore, Rev. William Haisley, MA. Secretary for Scotland, Boys Brigade, since 1990; b. 9.7.35, Donaghadee; m., Geraldine Ann Moorhead; 1 s.; 2 d. Educ. Bangor Grammar School; Magee University College, Londonderry; Dublin University; Presbyterian College, Belfast. Chaplain to the Forces, attached Royal Highland Fusiliers, 1966-70; Minister, Church of Scotland, 1970-90. Convener, Church of Scotland Youth Education Committee. Recreations: golf; gardening. Address: (b.) Boys Brigade, Scottish HQ, Carronvale House, Larbert, FK5 3LH; T.-0324 562008.

Moorhouse, Professor Robert Gordon, MA, PhD, CPhys, FInstP, FRSE. Titular Professor, Department of Physics and Astronomy (formerly Department of Natural Philosophy), Glasgow University, since 1968; b. 14.3.26, Huddersfield; m., Peggy Gee; 1 s. Educ. Huddersfield College; Cambridge University. Research Fellow and Lecturer, Natural Philosophy, Glasgow University, 1950-61; Principal Scientific Officer, Rutherford-Appleton Laboratory (Science and Engineering Research Council), 1961-67; Reader, Glasgow University, 1967-68. Publication: The Pion-Nucleon System (Co-author). Address: (b.) Department of Physics and Astronomy, Glasgow University, Glasgow, G12 8QQ; T.-041-339 8855.

Moos, Khursheed Francis, MB, BS, BDS, FRCSEdin, FDS RCS (Eng, Edin), FDS RCPS (Glas). Consultant Oral and Maxillofacial Surgeon; President, British Association of Oral and Maxillofacial Surgeons, since 1991; Vice Dean, Faculty of Dental Surgery, Royal College of Physicians and Surgeons of Glasgow, since 1989; b. 1.11.34, London; m., Katharine Addison; 2 s.; 1 d. Educ. Dulwich College; Guy's Hospital, London; Westminster Hospital. National Service, RADC, Lt., 1959, Capt., 1960; Registrar in Oral Surgery, Mount Vernon Hospital, Middlesex, 1966-67; Senior Registrar, Oral Surgery, University of Wales, Cardiff, 1967-69; Consultant Oral Surgeon, S. Warwicks and Coventry Hospitals, 1969-74; Consultant Oral and Maxillofacial Surgeon, Canniesburn Hospital, Glasgow, since 1974; Civilian Consultant to Royal Navy, since 1976; Down Surgical Prize, 1988. Publications include contributions to books and various papers. Recreations: music; natural history; philately; Eastern philosophy; gardening. Address: (h.) 43 Colquhoun Street, Helensburgh, Dunbartonshire, G84 9JW; T.-0436 73232.

Mole, George Alexander (Sandy). Vice President, NFU of Scotland, since 1990; Director, Coastal Grains Ltd., since 1988; Director, Scottish Agricultural and Rural Centre Ltd., since 1992; b. 7.6.43, Duns; m., Jean Mitchell; 1 s.; 2 d. Educ. St. Mary's, Melrose; Merchiston Castle. President, Mid and Easst Berwick, NFU of Scotland; Convener, Cereals Committee, NFU of Scotland; Member, EEC Commission Cereals Advisory Committee; Chairman, AFRC Cereal Consultative; Member, Home Grown Cereals Authority R. & D. Committee; Member, Institute of Brewing Cereal Publicity. Recreations: golf; shooting. Address: (h.) Greenburn, Reston, Eyemouth, TD14 5LP.

Moray, Earl of (Douglas John Moray Stuart), BA, FRICS. Chairman, Moray Estates Development Co., since 1974; b. 13.2.28, Johannesburg; m., Malvina Dorothea Murray; 1 s.; 1 d. Educ. Hilton College, Natal; Trinity College, Cambridge. Address: (h.) Darnaway Castle, Forres, Moray.

More, Magnus, MA, BSc, DipEd. Director of Education, Fife Regional Council, since 1985; b. 2.2.34, Wick; m., Audrey; 3 s. Educ. Wick High School; St. Andrews University/Dundee College of Education. Teacher, Oban High School, 1959-62; Principal Teacher, Queen Anne High School, Dunfermline, 1962-67; Assistant Director of Education, Aberdeen County Council, 1967-69; Fife County Council: Assistant Director of Education, 1969-71, Senior Assistant Director of Education, 1971-75, Senior Depute Director of Education, 1975-84. Adviser to COSLA Education and Social Work Committees; Member, Board of Governors, Scottish Centre for Children with Motor Impairments; Member: Convocation, Heriot-Watt University; National Committee on Staff Development and Appraisal; Past President, Association of Directors of Education in Scotland; Scotland. Recreations: swimming; golf; gardening. Address: (b.) Fife House, North Street, Glenrothes, Fife, KY7 5LT.

Moreland, John Scotland, OBE, BSc, CEng, FIMechE. Board Member, Cumbernauld Development Corporation, since 1976; Director, Scottish Nuclear Ltd., since 1990; Visiting Professor, Glasgow University, since 1990; b. 6.5.31, Bellshill; m., May; 2 s.; 1 d. Educ. Dalziel High School, Motherwell; Glasgow University. Early career in engineering design and production management; Motherwell Bridge Group, 1967-82: Production Director, General Manager of Motherwell Brige Offshore, latterly Group Marketing Director; BP Exploration/Britoil, 1982-90: Construction Manager then Project Manager for Clyde offshore oil field development, latterly Venture Manager for all BP non-operated oil fields in UK continental shelf. Recreations: theatre; opera; music; climbing mountains. Address: (h.) 24 Falkland Street, Glasgow, G12 9PR; T.-041-334 5676.

Morgan, Edwin (George), OBE, MA, Hon. DLitt (Loughborough, Glasgow, Edinburgh), Hon.DUniv (Stirling). Freelance Writer (Poet, Critic, Translator), since 1980; Emeritus Professor of English, Glasgow University, since 1980; Visiting Professor of English, Strathclyde University, 1987-90; Honorary Professor, University College of Wales, Aberystwyth, since 1990; b. 27.4.20, Glasgow. Educ. Rutherglen Academy; High School of Glasgow; Glasgow University. War Service, Royal Army Medical Corps, 1940-46; Glasgow University: Assistant Lecturer in English, 1947, Lecturer, 1950, Senior Lecturer, 1965, Reader, 1971, Titular Professor, 1975; received Cholmondeley Award for Poets, 1968; Hungarian PEN Memorial Medal, 1972; Scottish Arts Council Book Awards, 1968, 1973, 1977, 1978, 1983, 1985, 1988, 1991; Saltire Society and Royal Bank Scottish Literary Award, 1983; Soros Translation Award (New York), 1985. Publications: (poetry): The Vision of Cathkin Braes, 1952, Beowulf, 1952, The Cape of Good Hope, 1955, Poems from Eugenio Montale, 1959, Sovpoems, 1961, Collins Albatross Book of Longer Poems (Editor), 1963, Starryveldt, 1965, Emergent Poems, 1967, Gnomes, 1968, The Second Life, 1968, Proverbfolder, 1969, Twelve Songs, 1970, The

Horseman's Word, 1970, Scottish Poetry 1-6 (Co-Editor), 1966-72; Glasgow Sonnets, 1972, Wi the Haill Voice, 1972, The Whittrick, 1973, From Glasgow to Saturn, 1973, Fifty Renascence Love-Poems, 1975, Rites of Passage, 1976, The New Divan, 1977, Colour Poems, 1978, Platen: Selected Poems, 1978, Star Gate, 1979, Scottish Satirical Verse (Editor), 1980, Poems of Thirty Years, 1982, Grafts/Takes, 1983, Sonnets from Scotland, 1984, Selected Poems, 1985, From the Video Box, 1986, Themes on a Variation, 1988; Tales from Limerick Zoo, 1988; Collected Poems, 1990; Hold Hands Among the Atoms, 1991; prose: Essays, 1974, East European Poets, 1976, Hugh MacDiarmid, 1976, Twentieth Century Scottish Classics, 1987; Nothing Not Giving Messages, 1990; Crossing the Border, 1990; Evening Will Come They Will Sew The Blue Sail, 1991; plays: The Apple-Tree, 1982, Master Peter Pathelin, 1983. Address: (h.) 19 Whittingehame Court, Glasgow, G12 OBG; T.-041-339 6260.

Morgan, Professor Henry Gemmell, BSc, MB, ChB, FRCPEdin, FRCPGlas, FRCPath, FRSE. Honorary Senior Research Fellow, Glasgow University; Professor of Pathological Biochemistry, Glasgow University, 1965-88; Director, Institute of Biochemistry, Glasgow Royal Infirmary, 1967-88; President, Association of Clinical Biochemists, UK, 1985-87; b. 25.12.22, Dundee; m., Margaret Duncan; 1 d. Educ. Merchiston Castle School, Edinburgh; St. Andrews University. Local Defence Volunteers/Home Guard, 1940-44; Lecturer/Senior Lecturer in Pathology, St. Andrews University, 1948-65; Research Fellow, Johns Hopkins Medical School, Baltimore, 1956; Adviser to SHDD, WRHB, GGHB, London University etc.; Chairman, Medical Staff Committee, Glasgow Royal Infirmary, since 1984; former External Examiner, Universities of Dublin, Leeds and Newcastle; Secretary, Forfarshire Medical Association, 1960-65. Recreation: travel abroad; politics. Address: (h.) Firwood House, 8 Eaglesham Road, Newton Mearns, Glasgow, G77 5BG; T.-041-639 4404.

Morgan, Tom, CBE, DL, OStJ, JP, NDD, CDD; b. 24.2.14, Aberdeenshire; m., Mary Montgomery McLauchlan (deceased); 2 s. Educ. Longside School; North and West of Scotland Colleges of Agriculture. Unigate PLC, 38 years (Regional Director, Scotland); Councillor, City of Edinburgh Corporation, 1954-71, City of Edinburgh District Council, 1977-84; City Treasurer, 1968-71; Lord Provost and Lord Lieutenant, 1980-84; Chairman, Edinburgh Military Tattoo and Edinburgh International Festival, 1980-84. Recreations: golf; gardening. Address: (h.) 400 Lanark Road, Edinburgh, EH13 0LX; T.-031-441 3245.

Morison, Hon. Lord (Alastair Malcolm Morison), QC, MA, LLB. Senator of the College of Justice, since 1985; b. 12.2.31, Edinburgh; m., Birgitte Hendil; 1 s., 1 d. by pr. m. Educ. Winchester College; Edinburgh University. Advocate, 1956. Recreation: fishing. Address: (h.) 6 Carlton Terrace, Edinburgh, EH7 5DD; T.-031-556 6766.

Morison, Hugh, MA, DipEd. Under Secretary, Industry Department for Scotland, since 1988; b. 22.11.43, Bognor Regis; m., Marion H. Smithers; 2 d. Educ. Chichester High School for Boys; St. Catherine's College, Oxford. Assistant Principal, Scottish Home and Health Department, 1966-69; Private Secretary to Minister of State, Scottish Office, 1969-70; Principal: Scottish Education Department, 1971-73, Scottish Economic Planning Department, 1973-79 (seconded to Offshore Supplies Office, Department of Energy, 1974-75); Assistant Secretary, Scottish Economic Planning Department, 1979-82; Gwilym Gibbon Research Fellow, Nuffield College, Oxford, 1982-83; Assistant Secretary, Scottish Development Department, 1983-84; Under Secretary, Scottish Home and Health Department, 1984-88. Non-Executive Director, the Weir Group PLC. Publication:

The Regeneration of Local Economies, 1987. Publications: The Regeneration of Local Economics, 1987; Dauphine (Co-author), 1991. Recreations: cycling; hill-walking; archaeology. Address: (b.) Alhambra House, 45 Waterloo Street, Glasgow, G2 6AT; T.-041-242 5466.

Morley, Kenneth Donald, BMedBiol (Hons), MB, FRCPEdin, FRACP. Consultant General Physician and Rheumatologist, since 1982; b. 16.4.49, Ripon; m., Susan Margaret Bell Tawse; 2 s.; 1 d. Educ. Dame Allan's Boys School, Newcastle; Aberdeen University. Formerly General Medical Registrar, Christchurch Hospitals, New Zealand; Arthritis and Rheumatism Council Copeman Research Fellow and Honorary Senior Registrar, Hammersmith Hospital, London. Recreations: family; DIY; gardening; hill-walking. Address: (h.) 9 Burnside Road, Invergowrie, Dundee; T.-0382 562673.

Morley, William Neil, RD–, MB, ChB, FRCPEdin, FRCPGlas. Consultant Dermatologist; Civil Consultant to Royal Navy, since 1976; Consultant, Western Infirmary and Royal Hospital for Sick Children, Glasgow, since 1963; Member, Medical Appeal Tribunal, DSS, since 1977; b. 16.2.30, Bradford; m., Dr. Patricia Morley; 3 s.; 1 d. Educ. Merchiston Castle School; Edinburgh University. House Surgeon and Physician, Edinburgh Royal Infirmary; Surgeon Lt., RNVR, HMS Falcon, Malta; Assistant, Department of Medicine, Edinburgh University; Registrar and Senior Registrar, Dermatology Department, Edinburgh Royal Infirmary. Past President and Secretary, Royal Medical Society; President, Scottish Dermatological Society, 1985-88. Publication: Colour Atlas of Paediatric Dermatology. Recreations: golf; gardening. Address: (h.) Parkhall, Balfron, Glasgow, G63; T.-Balfron 40124.

Morrell, David William James, MA, LLB. Scottish Legal Services Ombudsman; b. 26.7.33, Glasgow; m., Margaret; 2 s.; 1 d. Educ. George Watson's Boys' College, Edinburgh; Edinburgh University. Administrative Assistant, Durham University, 1957-60; Assistant Registrar and Appointments Officer, Exeter University, 1960-64; Senior Assistant Registrar, Essex University, 1964-66; Academic Registrar, Strathclyde University, 1966-73; Registrar and Secretary, 1973-89. Consultant to OECD Programme on Management in Higher Education, 1989-90; Governor, Paisley College of Technology, 1990-94. Recreations: hill-walking; fishing; swimming; history and environment. Address: (b.) 2 Greenside Lane, Edinburgh, EH1 3AH.

Morris, Alexander Watt, BSc (Hons), MInstP. Principal, Edinburgh Tutorial College and American School of Edinburgh, since 1976; b. 24.11.46, Dunfermline; m., Moira Joan Watson; 1 s. Educ. Dunfermline High School; Edinburgh University. Began teaching career, Musselburgh Grammar School, 1972; Head of Physics, George Watson's Ladies College, 1973 (and to George Watson's College on merger of the schools); founded Edinburgh Tutorial College and American School of Edinburgh. Recreations: good food; hifi; cricket; skiing. Address: (b.) 29 Chester Street, Edinburgh, EH3 7EN; T.-031-225 9888.

Morris, Arthur McGregor, MA, MB, BChir (Cantab), FRCSEdin, FRCSEng. Consultant Plastic Surgeon, Tayside Health Board, since 1975; Honorary Senior Lecturer in Surgery, Dundee University, since 1975; b. 6.5.41, Heswall, Wirral; m., Victoria Margaret Whitaker; 1 s.; 1 d. Educ. Dulwich College; Selwyn College, Cambridge; Guy's Hospital. Plastic Surgery Registrar, Canniesburn Hospital, Glasgow, 1972; Plastic Surgery Senior Registrar, Bangour General Hospital, 1972-75. Chairman, Scottish Committee for Hospital Medical Services, since 1989; Member, Scottish Joint Consultants Committee, since 1983. Publications: complications of plastic Surgery and malignant melanoma topics.

Recreations: golf; curling; photography; bee-keeping. Address: (b.) Tayside Plastic Surgery Unit, Dundee Royal Infirmary, Dundee; T.-Dundee 23125.

Morris, Arthur Stephen, BA, MA, PhD. Reader, Department of Geography, Glasgow University; b. 26.12.36, Broadway, Worcestershire; m., Estela C.; 1 s.; 1 d. Educ. Chipping Campden; Exeter College, Oxford University; University of Maryland; University of Wisconsin. Instructor/Assistant Professor, Western Michigan University, 1964-67; joined Glasgow University as Lecturer, 1967. Publications: South America, 1979; Latin America, 1981. Recreations: gardening; music; sailing. Address: (h.) The Old Manse, Shandon, near Helensburgh; T.-041-339 8855.

Morris, Professor Christopher David, BA, DipEd, MIFA, FSA, FSA Scot. Professor of Archaeology, Glasgow University, since 1990; b. 14.4.46, Preston; m., Dr. Colleen E. Batey. Educ. Queen Elizabeth's Grammar School, Blackburn; Durham University; Oxford University. Assistant Lecturer, Hockerill College of Education, Bishops Stortford, 1968-72; Lecturer, then Senior Lecturer in Archaeology, 1972-88, Reader in Viking Archaeology, 1989-90, Durham University; Member, Ancient Monuments Board for Scotland, since 1990. Council Member, Society of Antiquaries of Scotland, Glasgow Archaeological Society. Recreations: classical music; opera; theatre; walking; skiing. Address: (b.) Department of Archaeology, 10 The Square, Glasgow University, Glasgow, G12 8QQ; T.-041-339 8855, Ext. 5690/4422.

Morris, Jean Daveena Ogilvy, CBE, MA, MEd, OSStJ. Chairman, Parole Board for Scotland, since 1980; b. 28.1.29, Kilmarnock; m., Rev. William J. Morris (qv); 1 s. Educ. Kilmarnock Academy; St. Andrews University. Clinical Psychologist: Royal Hospital for Sick Children, Edinburgh, St. David's Hospital, Cardiff, and Church Village, Pontypridd; Member, Bailie and Convener of Housing, Peterhead Town Council; Member, Aberdeen County Council; Columnist, Aberdeen Press and Journal; Chairman, Christian Action Housing Association; Member, Scottish Federation of Housing Associations; Chairman, Government Committee on Links Between Housing and Social Work (Morris Committee); Chairman, Local Review Committee, Barlinnie Prison; Vice Chairman, Glasgow Abbeyfield Society; Vice Chairman, TSB Foundation; Director, Scottish Advisory Board, Abbey National; Chairman, Scotia House Development Company. Badminton Blue, St. Andrews University. Recreations: swimming; holidays in France. Address: (h.) 94 St. Andrews Drive, Glasgow, G41 4RX; T.-041-427 2757.

Morris, Professor John Llewelyn, BSc, PhD, FIMA, CMath. Professor of Computer Science, Dundee University, since 1986; b. 19.9.43, Newtown, Wales; 2 s.; 1 d. Educ. Tywyn Grammar School; Leicester University; St. Andrews University. NCR Postdoctoral Fellow, Dundee University, 1967-69; Lecturer, Dundee University, 1969-75; Associate Professor, then Professor, University of Waterloo, Ontario, 1975-86. Publications: Computers and Computing (Co-author), 1973; Computational Methods in Elementary Numerical Analysis, 1983. Address: (b.) Dundee University, Dundee, DD1 4HN.

Morris, Richard Graham Michael, MA, DPhil. Reader in Neuroscience, Edinburgh University, since 1989; b. 27.6.48, Worthing; m., Hilary Ann; 2 d. Educ. St. Albans, Washington DC; Marlborough College; Cambridge University; Sussex University. Addison Wheeler Fellow, Durham University, 1973-75; SSO, British Museum (Natural History), 1975-77; Researcher, BBC Television, 1977; Lecturer, St. Andrews University, 1977-86; MRC University Research Fellow, 1983-86. Member, MRC Neurosciences Grants Committee,

1981-85; Hon. Secretary, Experimental Psychological Society, 1985-89; Chairman, Brain Research Association, since 1990. Publications: 80 papers; one book (Editor). Recreation: sailing. Address: (b.) Department of Pharmacology, Edinburgh University, 1 George Square, Edinburgh, EH8 9JZ; T.-031-650 3518/4353.

Morris, Professor Robert Lyle, BSc, PhD. Professor of Parapsychology, Edinburgh University, since 1985; b. 9.7.42, Canonsburg, Pennsylvania; m., Joanna Du Barry; 2 d. Educ. Crafton High School; University of Pittsburgh; Duke University. Research Fellow, Duke University, 1969-71; Research Co-ordinator, then Research Associate, Psychical Research Foundation, 1971-74; Lecturer in Parapsychology, University of California, Santa Barbara, 1974-78; Lecturer, School of Social Sciences, University of California, Irvine, 1978-80; Reseach Coordinator, Communication Studies Laboratory, and Senior Research Scientist, School of Computer and Information Sciences, Syracuse University, 1980-85. Member, Council, Parapsychological Association; Member, Council, British Society for Psychical Research. Publication: Foundations of Parapsychology: Exploring the Boundaries of Human Capability (Co-author), 1986. Address: (h.) 2 Strathalmond Green, Edinburgh, EH4 8AQ; T.-031-339 6461.

Morris, William, BA, FIOP. Principal, Anniesland College, 1981-89; b. 15.5.24, Aberdare, Wales; m., Pauline; 1 s.; 2 d. Educ. Aberdare Boys' Secondary School; Cardiff School of Art; Garnet College, London; London School of Printing and Graphic Arts; Open University. Compositor/Typographer; Royal Artillery, 1942-45; Lecturer in Typography, LSP&GA, 1951-58; Head, Department of Typography and Related Subjects; Depute Principal, Glasgow College of Building and Printing; Board Member, Printing and Publishing Industry Training Board, 1968-82; Member, City and Guilds of London Institute; Board Member and Director, Scottish Vocational Education Council, 1987-91; Immediate Past Chairman and Committee Member, Association of Principals of Colleges (Scottish Branch); Associate Member, Association of Colleges of Further and Higher Education; Immediate Past Chairman and Committee Member, Association of College Management (Scottish Branch); Secretary to the Vestry, St. Cyprian's Church, Lenzie. Recreations: golf; gardening; painting. Address: (h.) 26 Laurel Avenue, Lenzie, Kirkintilloch, Glasgow, G66 4RU; T.-041-776 2716.

Morris, Rev. William James, JP, BA, BD, PhD, LLD, DD, Hon. FRCP&SGlas. Minister, Glasgow Cathedral, since 1967; Chaplain in Ordinary to The Queen in Scotland, since 1969; Chairman, Iona Cathedral Trust, since 1979; Dean, Chapel Royal in Scotland, since 1991; b. 22.8.25, Cardiff; m., Jean Daveena Ogilvy Howie (see Jean Daveena Ogilvy Morris); 1 s. Educ. Cardiff High School; University of Wales (Cardiff and Aberystwyth); Edinburgh University. Ordained, 1951; Assistant, Canongate Kirk, Edinburgh, 1949-51; Minister, Barry Island and Cadoxton Presbyterian Church of Wales, 1951-53; Minister: St. David's, Buckhaven, 1953-57, Peterhead Old Parish Church, 1957-67; Chaplain, Peterhead Prison, 1963-67; Chaplain to Lord High Commissioner, 1975-76; Moderator, Deer Presbytery, 1965-66; Chaplain: Strathclyde Police, Glasgow Academy, High School of Glasgow, Glasgow District Council, Trades House of Glasgow, Glasgow YMCA, West of Scotland Engineers Association, Royal Scottish Automobile Club, Order of St. John; Member, Independent Broadcasting Authority, 1979-84 (Chairman, Scottish Advisory Committee); Member, Convocation, Strathclyde University; Honorary President, Glasgow Society of Social Service. Publication: A Walk Through Glasgow Cathedral, 1986. Recreation: being good, careful, and happy (not always simultaneously). Address: (h.) 94 St. Andrews Drive, Glasgow, G41 4RX; T.-041-427 2757.

Morrison, Alexander Fraser, BSc (Hons). Chairman and Managing Director, Morrison Construction Group Ltd., since 1984; b. 20.3.48, Dingwall; m., Patricia Janice Murphy; 1 s.; 2 d. Educ. Tain Royal Academy; Edinburgh University. Morrison Construction Group, since 1970; Managing Director, 1976-84. Chairman, Scottish Section, Federation of Civil Engineering Contractors; Member, Board of Governors, Edinburgh College of Art; Member Designate, Highlands and Islands Enterprise; Director, Aberforth Split Level Trust plc; Director, Investors in People; winner, 1991 Scottish Business Achievement Award. Recreations: rugby; golf; skiing; opera; theatre; art. Address: (b.) Morrison House, 12 Atholl Crescent, Edinburgh, EH3 8HA; T.-031-228 4188.

Morrison, Rev. Alistair Hogarth, BTh, DipYCS. Minister, Church of St. Mark, Paisley, since 1989 (Minister, Elgin High Church, 1985-89); b. 12.9.43, Glasgow; m., Grace; 1 s.; 1 d. Educ. Jordanhill College School; Aberdeen University. City of Glasgow/Strathclyde Police, 1962-81 (Inspector). Strathclyde Medal for Bravery, 1975. Recreation: hill-walking. Address: 36 Newtyle Road, Paisley, PA1 3JX; T.-041-889 4279.

Morrison, Andrew Neil, QFSM, MIFireE, DipEdTech. Firemaster, Grampian Region, since 1985; b. 8.9.37, Arbroath; m., Kathleen; 1 s. Educ. Arbroath High School; Dundee College of Technology. Armourer, REME, serving in Malaya, Singapore and Berlin (gained GSM and clasp), joined Fire Service, 1962, with Tayside (then Angus) Fire Brigade; joined Grampian as Deputy Firemaster, 1980. President, Chief and Assistant Chief Fire Officers' Association; Scottish Regional Representative to Institution of Fire Engineers. Recreations: golf; curling; swimming. Address: (b.) 19 North Anderson Drive, Aberdeen, AB9 2TP; T.-0224 696666.

Morrison, Rev. Angus Wilson, MA, BD. Minister, Kildalton and Oa Parish, Islay, since 1989 (Minister, Braid Parish Church, Edinburgh, 1977-89); b. 14.2.34, Glasgow; m., Isobel M.S. Taylor; 1 s.; 2 d. Educ. Epsom College, Surrey; Trinity College, Oxford; New College, Edinburgh. Minister: Whithorn, 1961-67, Cults West, Aberdeen, 1967-77; various periods of service on General Assembly Committees, including Overseas Council, Inter-Church Relations, Board of Education and Selection Schools; Observer for World Alliance of Reformed Churches, Vatican Council II, 1963. Recreations: travel; family. Address: The Manse, Port Ellen, Isle of Islay, PA42 7DB; T.-0496 2447.

Morrison, Professor Arnold, BA, MEd, FBPsS, CPsychol. Emeritus Professor of Education, Stirling University, since 1984; Educational Consultant, since 1986; b. 29.3.28, Birmingham; m., Katharine Neil; 2 s.; 1 d. Educ. Birmingham College of Arts and Crafts; Birmingham University. Schoolmaster, 1952-62; Lecturer, Moray House College of Education, 1962-66; Lecturer, Edinburgh University, 1966-70; Senior Lecturer, Dundee University, 1970-75; Professor of Education, Stirling University, 1975-84; Member, General Teaching Council for Scotland, 1976-79; Member, University Grants Committee, 1977-82; Member, Consultative Committee on the Curriculum, 1980-86. Recreations: mountaineering; genealogy. Address: (h.) 4 Victoria Place, Stirling, FK8 2QX; T.-0786 74053.

Morrison, David Donald Corbett, BA (Hons), DipComm, MCIM. Managing Director, Dundee Industrial Association Ltd., since 1985; Managing Director, Dundee Enterprise Trust Ltd., since 1987; b. 23.1.44, Durness, Sutherland; 2 s. Educ. Dornoch Academy; Strathclyde University. Special Assistant Teacher of Commerce, Cults Academy, 1967-72; Management Accountant, HIDB, 1972-78; Senior Development Manager, Caithness and Sutherland, Highlands and Islands Development Board, 1978-82; Marketing

Manager, Kestrel Subsea Systems Ltd., 1982-85. Recreations: hill-walking; keep-fit; reading; Gaelic. Address: (h.) Roseneath, Monikie, Dundee, DD5 3QA; T.-Newbigging 244.

Morrison, James, ARSA, RSW, DA, DUniv (Stirling). Painter in oil and watercolour; b. 11.4.32, Glasgow; m., Dorothy McCormack; 1 s.; 1 d. Educ. Hillhead High School; Glasgow School of Art. Taught part-time, 1955-58; won Torrance Memorial Prize, RGI, 1958; Visiting Artist, Hospitalfield, 1962-63; Council Member, SSA, 1964-67; staff, Duncan of Jordanstone College of Art, 1965-87; won Arts Council Travelling Scholarship to Greece, 1968; painting in various regions of France, 1976-82; numerous one-man exhibitions since 1956, in Scotland, London, Italy, West Germany, Canada; four works in private collection of Duke of Edinburgh and numerous other works in public and private collections; several group exhibitions since 1980 in UK and Europe. Publication: Aff the Squerr. Recreation: playing in a chamber music group. Address: (h.) Craigview House, Usan, Montrose, Angus; T.-Montrose 72639.

Morrison, Rev. Mary Brown, MA (Hons), BD (Hons), DipEd, DipRelEd. Minister, Carmichael/Covington/Pettinain, since 1992; Regional Organiser for Evangelism, 1986-91; b. 10.9.35, Edinburgh; m., Peter K. Morrison; 1 s.; 3 d. Educ. James Gillespie's High School for Girls; Edinburgh University. Teacher, Dalkeith High School; Minister, Townhill Parish Church, Dunfermline, 1978-86. Recreations: knitting; walking; theatre; collecting china; country dancing; family. Address: (h.)The Manse, Thankerton, Biggar, ML12 6PA.

Morrison, Nigel Murray Paton, QC. Queen's Counsel, since 1988; b. 18.3.48, Paisley. Educ. Rannoch School. Called to the Bar of England and Wales, Inner Temple, 1972; admitted to Scottish Bar, 1975; Assistant Editor, Session Cases, 1976-82; Assistant Clerk, Rules Council, 1978-84; Clerk of Faculty, Faculty of Advocates, 1979-86; Standing Junior Counsel to Scottish Development Department (Planning), 1982-86; Temporary Sheriff, since 1982; Chairman, Social Security Appeal Tribunals, 1982-91; Second (formerly Junior) Counsel to the Lord President of the Court of Session, 1984-89; First Counsel to the Lord President, since 1989; Counsel to Secretary of State under Private Legislation Procedure (Scotland) Act 1936, since 1986; Chairman, Medical Appeal Tribunals, since 1991; Trustee, National Library of Scotland, since 1989. Publication: Stair Memorial Encyclopaedia of the Laws of Scotland (Contributor). Recreations: music; riding; Scottish country dancing; walking. Address: 9 India Street, Edinburgh EH3 6HA; T.-031-225 2807.

Morrison, Peter, MA, LLB. Singer and Solicitor; b. 14.8.40, Greenock; m., Irene; 1 s.; 1 d. Educ. Greenock Academy; Glasgow University. Town Clerk's Department: Paisley, 1965, Clydebank, 1966-68; private legal practice thereafter; established own legal practice, 1977; began professional singing engagements at University; passed BBC audition, 1969, and began solo broadcasts; first television series, Castles in the Air, 1971; numerous radio, television and theatre appearances in UK and abroad. Recreations: golf; tennis; non-participating cricket and rugby supporter. Address: (b.) 65 Bath Street, Glasgow; T.-041-331 1029.

Morrison, Peter Angus. Member, Crofters Commission, since 1984; Director, Lewis Land Services Ltd.; b. 31.12.45, Isle of Lewis; m., Murdina; 2 d. Educ. Shawbost School; Lews Castle College. Mechanical engineering apprenticeship, then draughtsman, William Beardmore & Co., Glasgow; contracts draughtsman, John Brown Engineering, Clydebank; Lecturer in Mechanical Engineering, Springburn College of Engineering; Senior Lecturer, Engineering Department, Lews

Castle College. Recreation: travel. Address: (h.) 52 Newmarket, Stornoway, Lewis; T.-0851 5338.

Morrison, Rev. Roderick, MA, BD. Minister, High Church, Stornoway, Lewis, since 1981; b. 3.7.43, Lochmaddy; m., Christina Ann MacDonald; 1 s.; 1 d. Educ. Lochportan Public School; Glasgow University and Trinity College. Assistant Minister, Drumchapel Old Parish Church, Glasgow, 1973-74; Minister, Carinish Parish Church, North Uist, 1974-81. Recreations: sailing; fishing; shooting. Address: High Church Manse, 1 Goathill Road, Stornoway, Isle of Lewis; T.-Stornoway 3106.

Morrison, Professor Ronald, BSc, MSc, PhD. Professor of Software Engineering, St. Andrews University, since 1985; b. 15.4.46, Glasgow; m., Ann Margaret MacDonald; 1 s.; 1 d. Educ. Eastbank Academy, Glasgow; Strathclyde University; Glasgow University; St. Andrews University. Systems Programmer, Glasgow University, 1968-71; Senior Research Fellow, Lecturer, Reader, St. Andrews University, 1971-85. Past President, Scottish Cross Country Union. Recreations: cross country running; golf. Address: (h.) 8 Trinity Place, St. Andrews, KY16 8SG; T.-0334 75649.

Morrison, William Garth, BA, CEng, MIEE, DL. Farmer; Chief Scout, since 1988; Chief Commissioner of Scotland, The Scout Association, 1981-88; b. 8.4.43, Edinburgh; m., Gillian Cheetham; 2 s.; 1 d. Educ. Pangbourne College; Pembroke College, Cambridge. Service, Royal Navy, 1961-73, retiring with rank of Lt.; farming, since 1973; Member, Lothian Region Children's Panel, 1976-83 (Chairman, Midlothian/East Lothian Area Panel, 1978-81); Lamp of Lothian Trustee, 1978; Member, Lothian, Borders and Fife Committee, Prince's Trust, 1979, Lothian and Borders Committee, Prince's and Royal Jubilee Trusts, 1983-88; Member, Society of High Constables of Holyroodhouse, 1979; Deputy Lieutenant, East Lothian, 1984; Member, Scottish Community Education Council, since 1988. Recreations: golf; sailing; Scouting. Address: West Fenton, North Berwick, East Lothian; T.-0620 842154.

Morrison, Professor William Russell, BSc, PhD, DSc, FIFST, FRSE. Professor of Food Science, Strathclyde University; b. 14.1.32, Glasgow; 2 s.; 1 d. Educ. High School of Glasgow; Royal College of Science and Technology. Address: (b.) Department of Bioscience and Biotechnology, Strathclyde University, 131 Albion Street, Glasgow, G1 1SD; T.-041-552 4400, Ext. 2209.

Morrocco, Alberto, RSA, RSW, RP, RGI, LLD, DUniv. Painter, since 1938; b. 14.12.17, Aberdeen; 2 s.; 1 d. Educ. Sunnybank School, Aberdeen; Gray's School of Art, Aberdeen. Former Member, Grants Committee, Scottish Arts Council; former Member, Royal Fine Art Commission for Scotland. Carnegie Award, Royal Scottish Academy: Guthrie Award, San Vito Romano Prize. Address: Binrock, 456 Perth Road, Dundee; T.-0382 69319.

Morrow, Digby Wilson, LLB, CA. Chief Executive, Sidlaw Group plc, since 1988; b. 4.5.49, Barrhead; m., Margaret; 2 s.; 1 d. Educ. Paisley Grammar School; Glasgow University. European Controller, then Assistant VP Operations, Gray Tool Co., 1973-80; Finance Director, IMS Ltd., Singapore, 1980-83; Group Controller, Flopetrol Schlumberger, Paris, 1983-85; Finance Director, Sidlaw Group plc, 1985-88. Chairman, Tayside Committee, Scottish Council Development and Industry; Member, Scottish Council, CBI. Recreations: sailing; golf; hill-walking. Address: (b.) Sidlaw Group plc, Nethergate Centre, Dundee; T.-0382 23161.

Morsbach, Helmut, MSc, PhD. Reader in Social Psychology, Glasgow University, since 1983; b. 2.8.37, Rondebosch, South Africa; 2 d. Educ. Bonn University;

Stellenbosch University; Hamburg University; Cape Town University. Lecturer in Psychology, Rhodes University, Grahamstown, South Africa, 1964-67; Assistant Professor in Psychology, International Christian University, Tokyo, 1967-69; Lecturer, then Senior Lecturer in Social Psychology, Glasgow University, since 1969. Visiting Professor, International Christian University, 1972, 1987, 1989-90; Volkswagen Foundation Grant for studies on Japan, 1977-80; Snell Visitor, Balliol College, Oxford, 1982. Recreation: gliding. Address: (b.) Department of Psychology, Glasgow University, Glasgow, G12 8RT; T.-041-339 8855, Ext. 5085.

Morton, Rev. Alasdair J., MA, BD, DipEd, DipRE, FEIS. Minister, Maxton linked with Newtown St. Boswells, since 1991; General Secretary, Department of Education, Church of Scotland, 1977-91; b. 8.6.34, Inverness; m., Gillian M. Richards; 2 s.; 2 d. Educ. Bell-Baxter School, Cupar; St. Andrews University; Hartford Theological Seminary. District Missionary/Minister, Zambia (Northern Rhodesia), 1960-65; Chaplain and Religious Education Lecturer, Malcolm Moffat Teachers' College, Serenje, Zambia, 1966-67; Principal, David Livingstone Teachers' College, Livingstone, Zambia, 1968-72; Minister, Greyfriars Parish Church, Dumfries, 1973-77. Recreations: choral singing; gardening. Address: (b.) 121 George Street, Edinburgh, EH2 4YN; T.-031-225 5722.

Morton, Rev. Andrew Reyburn, MA, BD. Deputy General Secretary, Board of World Mission and Unity, Church of Scotland, since 1988; b. 24.5.28, Kilmarnock; m., Marion Armstrong Chadwin; 2 s.; 2 d. Educ. Kilmarnock Academy; Glasgow University; Edinburgh University; University of Bonn. Scottish Secretary, Student Christian Movement, 1953-56; Minister, Moncreiff Parish, East Kilbride, 1956-64; Chaplain, Edinburgh University, 1964-70; Warden, Wolfson Hall and Co-ordinating Warden, Halls of Residence, Glasgow University, 1970-74; Social Responsibility Secretary and, latterly, Secretary, Division of Community Affairs and Assistant General Secretary, British Council of Churches, 1974-81; Secretary, Inter-Church Relations Committee and Assistant Secretary, Overseas Council, subsequently Assistant Secretary, Board of World Mission and Unity, Church of Scotland, 1982-88. Recreation: walking. Address: (h.) 11 Oxford Terrace, Edinburgh, EH4 1PX; T.-031-332 6592.

Morton, 22nd Earl of (John Charles Sholto Douglas), DL; b. 19.3.27. Lord-Lieutenant, West Lothian, since 1985.

Morton of Shuna, Baron (Hugh Drennan Baird Morton), QC (Scot). Senator of the College of Justice, since 1988; Life Peer; b. 10.4.30. Advocate, 1965; QC, 1974.

Morton, William F., MA (Hons). Rector, Coltness High School, Wishaw, since 1974; b. 28.3.32, Glasgow; m., Ena Nicol; 1 d. Educ. Bishopbriggs Higher Grade School; Albert Secondary School, Glasgow; Glasgow University. Hamilton Academy: Teacher, 1956, Special Assistant, 1961, Principal Teacher of English, 1968; Assistant Head Teacher, Hamilton Grammar School, 1973-74. Secretary, Lanarkshire County English Committee, 1971-74; Examiner for Higher Grade English, Scottish Examination Board, 1972-75; Honorary Vice-President, Hamilton Golf Club, since 1981 (Captain, 1976-78); President, Lanarkshire Golf Association, 1974. Address: (h.) The Coach House, Woodlands Gate, Wishaw, Lanarkshire; T.-0698 384790.

Morton, William John Keirs, DipTP, MRTPI. Chief Executive, Forth Valley Enterprise, since 1990; b. 14.6.49, Glasgow; m., Jan; 2.; 1 d. Educ. Bearsden Academy; Glasgow College of Art. Planning Assistant, Royal Burgh of Inverness, 1973-75; Project Officer, East Kilbride Development Corporation, 1975-76; SDA, 1976-87, latterly as Project Manager (Coatbridge Project); Chief Executive, Aberdeen Beyond 2000, 1987-89; Head of Urban Regeneration, SDA,

1989-90. Recreations: family; travel; cycling; reading. Address: (b.) Laurel House, Laurelhill Business Park, Stirling, FK7 9JQ; T.-0786 51919.

Mosco, Les, BSc, FInstPS, MBIM. Head of Purchasing Supply, Scottish Office, since 1990; b. 15.7.54, Manchester; m., Barbara; 1 s.; 1 d. Educ. Queen Elizabeth Grammar School, Middleton, Manchester; Sheffield University. Formerly with British Coal. Recreations: walking; squash. Address: (b.) Room 2/26, New St. Andrews House, Edinburgh; T.-031-244 4833.

Moule, Rev. Gerald Christopher, BA, BD. Minister, Moffat linked with Wamphray, since 1975; b. 31.8.45, Guildford; m., Patricia Rosemary Parker; 1 s.; 2 d. Educ. Edinburgh Academy; Kelvinside Academy, Glasgow; St. Andrews University; Newcastle upon Tyne University; New College, Edinburgh. Chartered Accountancy articles with Chalmers, Impey & Co., London; Assistant Minister, West Church of St. Nicholas, Aberdeen, 1973-75; Moderator, Presbytery of Annandale and Eskdale, 1980-81 and 1988-89; Secretary and Treasurer, Scottish Journal of Theology. Recreations: cricket; swimming; travel; hill-walking; gardening. Address: St. Andrew's Manse, Moffat, Dumfriesshire, DG10 9EJ; T.-Moffat 20128.

Mowat, Bill, MA (Hons), FInstPet. Member, Highland Regional Council, since 1978; Trustee, Wick Harbour, since 1978; b. 13.5.43, Thurso. Educ. Wick High School; Edinburgh University. Vice-President, Scottish Union of Students, 1965-66; Editor, Caithness Courier, 1966-68; Reporter, Daily Record, since 1968; Director, John O'Groats Crafts Ltd., since 1974; Honorary Secretary, Highland Branch, NUJ, 1975-78; Vice-President, Inverness Trades Council, 1977-78. Address: (h.) Balquholly, John O'Groats, Caithness; T.-0955 81360.

Mowat, James Rennie, BSc, FEng, FIMinE. Chairman, Invercoe Engineering Ltd., since 1990; Chairman, Butters Engineering Services Ltd., since 1990; Board Member, East Kilbride Development Corporation, since 1990; b. 7.5.36, Glasgow; m., Gillian; 3 s. Educ. High School of Glasgow; Royal Technical College, Glasgow; Administrative Staff College, Henley. Various technical and managerial appointments, Anderson Strathclyde (Managing Director, 1980-89); Non-Executive Director: Invercoe Engineering Ltd., Butters Engineering Services Ltd., Fortune Engineering Ltd., Starkstrom (Scotland) Ltd. Past President: Scottish Engineering, Mining Institute of Scotland; Director, Glasgow Chamber of Commerce. Recreations: sailing; occasional golf. Address: 3 Gardenside Avenue, Uddingston, Glasgow, G71 7BU; T.-0698 813565.

Mowat, Sheriff Principal John Stuart, MA, LLB, QC. Sheriff Principal of South Strathclyde, Dumfries and Galloway, since 1988; b. 30.1.23, Manchester; m., Anne Cameron Renfrew; 2 s.; 2 d. Educ. High School of Glasgow; Merchiston Castle School; Glasgow University. Served RAF Transport Command, 1942-46 (Flt.-Lt.); Journalist, 1947-52; Advocate, 1952-60; Sheriff of Fife and Kinross, at Dunfermline, 1960-72, at Cupar and Kinross, 1972-74, of Glasgow and Strathkelvin, 1974-88; Chairman, Sheriff Court Rules Council, since 1989; Office-Bearer, Scottish Liberal Party, 1954-58; Parliamentary candidate, Caithness and Sutherland, 1955; Secretary, Sheriffs Association, 1968-75 (President, 1988); Trustee: Carnegie Dunfermline Trust, 1967-74, Carnegie United Kingdom Trust, 1970-74. Recreations: golf; curling; watching football. Address: (h.) 31 Westbourne Gardens, Glasgow, G12 9PF; T.-041-334 3743; Afton, Port Wemyss, Isle of Islay.

Mowat, Norman Ashley George, MB, ChB, MRCP (UK), FRCP, FRCP (Edin). Consultant Physician and Gastroenterologist, Aberdeen Teaching Hospitals, since 1975; Clinical Senior Lecturer in Medicine, Aberdeen University, since 1975; b. 11.4.43, Cullen; m., Kathleen Mary Cowie; 1 s.; 2 d. Educ. Fordyce Academy; Aberdeen University. House Officer, then Senior House Officer, then Registrar, Aberdeen Teaching Hospitals, 1966-72; Lecturer in Medicine, Aberdeen University, 1972-73; Lecturer in Gastroenterology and Research Associate, Medical College of St. Bartholomew's, London, 1973-75. Visiting Physician to Shetland Islands; publications include Integrated Clinical Sciences: Gastroenterology (Co-Editor), 1985. Recreations: sailing; golf; soccer; reading; photography. Address: (h.) Bucholie, 13 Kings Cross Road, Aberdeen, AB2 4BF; T.-0224 319223.

Mowat, William George, JP. Honorary Sheriff, Caithness; Chairman, Caberfeidh Court, Royal British Legion Housing Association Ltd., since 1978; Chairman, Caithness Voluntary Group, since 1991; b. 12.5.28, Lybster; m., Aline Cameron Johnston; 3 d. Educ. Robert Gordon's College, Aberdeen. Provost of Wick, 1967-75; Chairman, Royal Burgh of Wick Community Council, 1977-91; Member, Caithness County Council, 1957-75. Vice Chairman, Civilian Committee, ATC Wick Squadron; Chairman, Friends of Hempriggs Residential Home, Wick; Elder, Church of Scotland. Recreations: golf; flying; used to fish a little. Address: (h.) Buchollie, Coronation Street, Wick, KW1 5LS; T.-0955 4794.

Muir, Alastair James, BA (Hons). Chief Executive, Clydebank Economic Development Company, since 1989; b. 21.10.57, Paisley; m., Dr. Sarah Louise Davidson; 1 d. Educ. John Neilson, Paisley; Paisley College. Centre for Study of Public Policy, Strathclyde University, 1984-86; Depute Chief Executive, ASSET, 1986-89. Recreations: skiing; sailing; hill-walking. Address: (b.) Phoenix House, 7 South Avenue, Clydebank, G81 2LG; T.-041-951 1131.

Muir, Rev. Frederick Comery, MA, BD, ThM, ARCM, ARSCM. Minister, Stepps Parish Church, since 1983; b. 26.11.32, Glasgow; m., Christine Elizabeth Dickie; 1 s.; 1 d. Educ. Kelvinside Academy; Glasgow University; Princeton Theological Seminary. Assistant Minister, Cathcart South Church, Glasgow, 1957-58; Teaching Fellow, Princeton Theological Seminary, 1959-60; Minister: St. James' Church, Lossiemouth, 1961-72, Whitehill Parish Church, Stepps, 1972-83. Instructor of Music, Gordonstoun School, 1967-71; Conductor, Strathkelvin Choral Society, 1973-78; Chairman, Scottish Committee, Royal School of Church Music, 1986-89; President, Glasgow Society of Organists, 1983-84. Recreations: music-making; hill-walking. Address: 20 Alexandra Avenue, Stepps, Glasgow, G33 6BP; T.-041-779 2504.

Muir, Sir John (Harling), 3rd Bt, TD. Director, James Finlay & Co. Ltd., 1946-81; Member, Queen's Bodyguard for Scotland (Royal Company of Archers); b. 7.11.10; m.; 5 s.; 2 d. Educ. Stowe. Served Second World War (demobilised with rank of Major). Address: (h.) Bankhead, Blair Drummond, by Stirling.

Muir, Trevor. Chief Executive, Midlothian District Council, since 1987; b. 10.7.49, Glasgow; m., Christine Ann; 1 s.; 1 d. Educ. High School of Glasgow; Langside College; Strathclyde University. Scottish Special Housing Association, 1973-77; City of Glasgow District Council, 1977-81; Director of Housing, City of Aberdeen District Council, 1981-87. Recreations: squash; family life. Address: (b.) Midlothian House, Buccleuch Street, Dalkeith, Midlothian, EH22 1DN.

Muirshiel, 1st Viscount (John Scott Maclay), KT (1973), CH (1962), CMG (1944), PC (1952), DL. Lord Lieutenant of Renfrewshire, 1967-80; Secretary of State for Scotland, 1957-62; b. 26.10.05; m., Betty L'Estrange Astley (deceased).

Educ. Winchester; Trinity College, Cambridge. MP, Montrose Burghs, 1940-50, Renfrewshire West, 1950-64; Minister of Transport and Civil Aviation, 1951-52; Minister of State for Colonial Affairs, 1956-57; President, Assembly of WEU, 1955-56; Director, Clydesdale Bank, 1970-82; Hon. LLD: Edinburgh, 1963, Strathclyde, 1966, Glasgow, 1970. Address: (h.) Knapps Wood, Kilmacolm, Renfrewshire, PA13 4NQ; T.-Kilmacolm 2770.

Muir Wood, Professor David, MA, PhD, CEng, MICE. Cormack Professor of Civil Engineering, Glasgow University, since 1987; Associate, Geotechnical Consulting Group, since 1983; b. 17.3.49, Folkestone; m., Helen Rosamond Piddington; 2 s. Educ. Royal Grammar School, High Wycombe; Peterhouse, Cambridge. William Stone Research Fellow, Peterhouse, Cambridge, 1973-75; Royal Society Research Fellow, Norwegian Geotechnical Institute, Oslo, 1975; Fellow, Emmanuel College, Cambridge, 1975-87; University Lecturer in Soil Mechanics, Cambridge University, 1975-87. British Geotechnical Society Prize, 1978. Publications: Offshore Soil Mechanics (Co-author); Pressuremeter Testing (Co-author); Soil Behaviour and Critical State Soil Mechanics. Recreations: music; travel; walking. Address: (b.) Department of Civil Engineering, Rankine Building, Glasgow University, Glasgow, G12 8LT; T.-041-339 8855.

Mullen, Ian M., BSc, MRPharmS. Healthcare Consultant and Freelance Writer; b. 11.5.46, Stirling; m., Veronica Drummond; 2 s.; 1 d. Educ. St. Modan's High School, Stirling; Heriot-Watt University. Registered MPS, 1970; self-employed community pharmacist, since 1971; elected to Pharmaceutical General Council, 1974; Vice-Chairman, 1983; Chairman, Pharmaceutical General Council (Scotland), 1986-88; Vice-Chairman, National Pharmaceutical Consultative Committee, 1987-89; Member, UK Advisory Committee on Borderline Substances, 1986-89; Vice-Chairman, Forth Valley Health Board, 1989-91; Director, Common Services Agency of the NHS in Scotland, 1991-95; Member Scottish Aids Research Appeal; contributor to all-party Parliamentary Group on Aids; Director, Central Scotland Chamber of Commerce, 1990-94; Chairman, St. Andrew's School Board, 1990-94. Recreations: walking; golf; swimming. Address: (h.) Ardenlea, 11 Arnothill, Falkirk, FK1 5RZ; T.-0324 21806.

Mulrine, Stephen, MA (Hons). Poet and Playwright; Senior Lecturer in Historical Studies, Glasgow School of Art, since 1983 (Lecturer, 1969-83); Extra-Mural Lecturer in Creative Writing, Glasgow University, since 1970; b. 13.3.37, Glasgow; m., Elizabeth S.K. Lees; 2 s.; 1 d. Educ. St. Mungo's Academy; Glasgow University; Edinburgh University. Member, Board of Directors, Glasgow Citizens' Theatre, since 1971; Member, Drama Committee, Scottish Arts Council, 1983-88; author of six television plays, including The Silly Season (Play for Today), BBC 1, and The House on Kirov Street, BBC; numerous radio plays including serials Deacon Brodie and Mary, Queen of Scots; theatre and poetry criticism; translations from Russian. Recreations: theatre-going; reading. Address: (h.) 132 Kingswood Drive, Glasgow, G44 4RB; T.-041-649 2183.

Munn, Charles William, BA, PhD, DipIB (Scot). Chief Executive, Chartered Institute of Bankers in Scotland; b. 26.5.48, Glasgow; m., Andrea Cuthbertson; 1 s.; 1 d. Educ. Queen's Park Secondary School, Glasgow; Langside College; Strathclyde University; Glasgow University; Jordanhill College. British Linen Bank, 1964-67; Glasgow College of Technology, Department of Finance and Accounting, 1975-78; Senior Lecturer in Economic History, Glasgow University, 1978-88. Editor, The Scottish Banker; Member, Church of Scotland Church and Nation Committee. Publications: Clydesdale Bank: the First 150 Years, 1988;

The Scottish Provincial Banking Companies 1747-1864, 1981. Recreation: golf. Address: (b.) 19 Rutland Square, Edinburgh, EH1 2DE; T.-031-229 9869.

Munn, Sir James, OBE, MA, DEd, LLD, DUniv. University Commissioner, since 1988; b. 27.7.20, Bridge of Allan; m., Muriel Jean Millar Moles; 1 d. Educ. Stirling High School; Glasgow University. Indian Civil Service, 1941-48; various teaching appointments, Glasgow, 1949-57; Principal Teacher of Modern Languages, Falkirk High School, 1957-66 (Depute Rector, 1962-66); Principal Examiner in Modern Languages, Scottish Examination Board, 1965-66; Rector: Rutherglen Academy, 1966-70, Cathkin High School, 1970-83; Member, University Grants Committee, 1973-82; Member, Consultative Committee on the Curriculum, 1968-80, Chairman, 1980-87; Chairman, Committee to review the Structure of the Curriculum at S3 and S4, 1975-77; Member of Court, Strathclyde University, 1983-91; Manpower Services Commission/Training Commission Chairman for Scotland, 1984-88, Chairman, GB, 1987-88. Address: (h.) 4 Kincath Avenue, High Burnside, Glasgow, G73 4RP; T.-041-634 4654.

Munn, Professor Walter Douglas, MA, PhD, DSc, FRSE. Thomas Muir Professor of Mathematics, Glasgow University, since 1973; b. 24.4.29, Kilbarchan; m., Margaret Clare Barlow. Educ. Marr College, Troon; Glasgow University; St. John's College, Cambridge. Scientific Officer, Royal Naval Scientific Service; Assistant in Mathematics, then Lecturer in Mathematics, Glasgow University; Visiting Assistant Professor, Tulane University; Senior Lecturer in Computing Science, then Senior Lecturer in Mathematics, Glasgow University; Professor of Mathematics, Stirling University. Recreations: music; gardening; hill-walking. Address: (b.) Department of Mathematics, Glasgow University, Glasgow, G12 8QW; T.-041-339 8855, Ext. 4207.

Munro, Alexander, MB, ChB, ChM, FRCS. Consultant General Surgeon, Raigmore Hospital, Inverness, since 1978; Clinical Senior Lecturer in Surgery, Aberdeen University, since 1978; b. 5.6.43, Ross and Cromarty; m., Maureen E. McCreath; 2 s.; 1 d. Educ. Fortrose Academy; Aberdeen University. Training in General Surgery at Registrar and Senior Registrar level, Aberdeen Hospitals, 1971-78; specialist training, St. Mark's Hospital, 1977. Recreation: gardening. Address: (h.) 23 Eriskay Road, Inverness; T.-Inverness 223804.

Munro, Angus Cunningham, BSc, PhD. Director, Scottish Antibody Production Unit, since 1984; b. 12.1.44, Dundee; m., Christine Renwick; 2 s.; 1 d. Educ. Harris Academy, Dundee; Edinburgh University. Senior Scientist and Project Manager, Beecham Pharmaceuticals, 1969-74; Principal Scientist, Glasgow and West of Scotland Blood Transfusion Service, 1974-84. Recreations: music; astronomy; collecting. Address: (b.) Scottish Antibody Production Unit, Law Hospital, Carluke, Lanarkshire, ML8 5ES; T.-0698 351161.

Munro, Professor Colin Roy, BA, LLB. Professor of Constitutional Law, Edinburgh University, since 1990; Assistant Editor, Public Law, since 1988; Chief Examiner, London University LLB (External) Degree, since 1991; b. 17.5.49, Aberdeen; m., Ruth Elizabeth Pratt; 1 s.; 1 d. Educ. Aberdeen Grammar School; Aberdeen University. Lecturer in Law, Birmingham University, 1971-72, Durham University, 1972-80; Senior Lecturer in Law, then Reader in Law, Essex University, 1980-85; Professor of Law, Manchester University, 1985-90. Publications: Television, Censorship and the Law; Studies in Constitutional Law. Recreations: sport; cinema and theatre; real ale. Address: (b.) Faculty of Law, Old College, South Bridge, Edinburgh, EH8 9YL; T.-031-650 2056.

Munro, Rev. David Peacock, MA, BD, STM. Minister, Bearsden North Church, since 1967; Clerk, Presbytery of Dumbarton, since 1986; b. 7.9.29, Paisley; m., Jessie Scott McPherson; 3 d. Educ. Paisley Grammar School; Glasgow University; Union Theological Seminary, New York. Minister, Aberluthnott Parish Church, 1953-56, Castlehill Church, Ayr, 1956-67. Vice Convener, General Assembly Council, 1988-90, Convener, since 1990; Chairman, General Assembly Board of Education, 1974-79; Convener, General Assembly Education Committee, 1981-85; Editor, Children of the Way (Sunday School Programme), Year One, 1981. Publication: Preface to Teaching. Recreations: golf; gardening. Address: North Manse, 8 Collylinn Road, Bearsden, Glasgow; T.-041-942 0366.

Munro, Donnie, Guitarist and Lead Singer, Runrig; Rector, Edinburgh University; b. Skye; m.; 3 children. Formerly Art Teacher, Inverness and Glasgow.

Munro, Graeme Neil, MA. Director, Historic Scotland, since 1990; b. 28.8.44, Edinburgh; m., Nicola Susan Wells (qv); 1 s.; 1 d. Educ. Daniel Stewart's College, Edinburgh; St. Andrews University. Assistant Principal, Scottish Development Department, 1968-72; Principal, Scottish Development Department and Scottish Home and Health Department, 1972-79; Assistant Secretary, Department of Agriculture and Fisheries for Scotland, SHHD, and Central Services, 1979-90. Recreations: walking; reading; local history; gardening; swimming. Address: (b.) 20 Brandon Street, Edinburgh, EH3 5RA; T.-031-244 3068.

Munro, Jean Mary, BA (Hons), PhD. Chairman, Council, Scottish History Society; b. 2.12.23; m., Robert William Munro. Educ. London University; Edinburgh University. WRNS, 1944-47; freelance historical researcher; Member, Council, National Trust for Scotland, 1964-69 and since 1987 (Executive, 1968-80); Chairman, Council, Scottish Genealogy Society, 1983-86 (Vice-President, since 1987); Chairman, Council, Scottish Local History Forum, 1984-88. Publications (as Jean Dunlop): the British Fisheries Society; the Clan Chisholm; the Clan Mackenzie; the Clan Gordon; the Scotts; the Clan Mackintosh; (with R.W. Munro): Tain through the Centuries; The Scrimgeours; The Acts of the Lords of the Isles. Recreations: reading; walking. Address: (h.) 15a Mansionhouse Road, Edinburgh, EH9 1TZ; T.-031-667 4601.

Munro, Jennifer Margaret Cochrane, MA (Hons), DipRE. Headmistress, St. Denis and Cranley School, Edinburgh, since 1984; b. 13.8.37, Edinburgh. Educ. St. Denis and Cranley School, Edinburgh; Edinburgh University; Moray House College of Education. History Teacher, Kelso High School, Ottawa (Ontario), James Gillespie's (Edinburgh); History and Deputy Head, St. Denis and Cranley. Elder, Church of Scotland; President, Scottish Women's Hockey Association, 1980-83; player, manager or delegate to IFWHA tournaments and conferences. Recreations: European travel; history; gardening. Address: (b.) St. Denis and Cranley, Ettrick Road, Edinburgh, EH10 5BJ; T.-031-229 1500.

Munro, Professor J. Forbes, MA, PhD. Professor in Economic History, since 1990, and Clerk of Senate, since 1991, Glasgow University; b. 15.3.40, Grantown-on-Spey. Educ. Dingwall Academy; Edinburgh University; Wisconsin University. Lecturer in Economic History, then Senior Lecturer, then Reader, Glasgow University, 1965-90. Editor, Journal of African History, 1982-87; Dean of Social Sciences, Glasgow University, 1987-89. Publications: Colonial Rule and the Kamba, 1975; Africa and the International Economy, 1976; Britain in Tropical Africa, 1984. Recreation: curling. Address: (b.) 4 University Gardens, Glasgow University, Glasgow, G12 8QQ.

Munro, John Forbes, MB, ChB (Hons), FRCPEdin. Consultant Physician, Eastern General and Edenhall Hospitals, since 1968; part-time Senior Lecturer, Edinburgh University, since 1974; b. 25.6.33, Edinburgh; m., Elizabeth Jean Durell Caird; 3 d. Educ. Edinburgh Academy; Chigwell School, Essex; Edinburgh University. Registrar and Senior Registrar, Edinburgh Royal Infirmary, 1962-68. Recreations: art; gardening. Address: (h.) Backhill, Carberry, near Musselburgh, East Lothian; T.-031-663 4935.

Munro, Rev. John Pringle Lorimer, MA (Cantab), BD, PhD. Asia Secretary, Church of Scotland Board of World Mission and Unity, since 1990; Minister, St. Vigeans, linked with Knox's, Arbroath, 1986-90; b. 11.5.47, Edinburgh; m., Patricia Ann Lawson; 1 s.; 1 d. Educ. Edinburgh Academy; Christ's College, Cambridge; New College, Edinburgh University. Chaplain, Stirling University, 1977-82; Lecturer, St. Paul's United Theological College, Limuru, Kenya, 1983-85. Recreations: the study of Third World theology; piano; angling. Address: 50A Craigmillar Park, Edinburgh, EH16 5PS; T.-031-667 6476.

Munro, Kathleen Margaret, BA, RGN, SCM, DN, PWT, RNT, DNT, FET (Cert). Senior Lecturer, Curriculum Development, Queen Margaret College, Edinburgh, since 1989; Member, National Board for Nursing, Midwifery and Health Visiting for Scotland, since 1983; Member, Queen's Nursing Institute, Scotland, since 1991; b. 6.12.52, Glasgow. Educ. Eastwood High School, Glasgow; Open University. Chairman, District Nursing Joint Committee, 1989-90. Recreations: exhibits and breeds Lochanbrae flatcoated retrievers; badminton; walking; drawing; painting. Address: (h.) 29 Fairmile Avenue, Edinburgh, EH10 6RL; T.-031-445 2052.

Munro, Kenneth Alexander, MA. Head, Office in Scotland, Commission of the European Communities, since 1988; b. 17.12.36, Glasgow; m., Elizabeth Coats Forrest McCreanor; 2 d. Educ. Hutchesons' Boys' Grammar School; Glasgow University. Economic research, Scottish American Investment Company, 1963-66; Senior Research Officer, ETU, 1966-67; Secretary, Economic Development Committee, NEDO, 1967-69; Industrial Relations Manager, Ford Motor Co., 1969-74; joined Commission of the European Communities, 1974. Recreations: walking; swimming; cinema; theatre. Address: (b.) 9 Alva Street, Edinburgh, EH2 4PH; T.-031-225 2058.

Munro, Nicola Susan, BA (Hons). Head, Urban Policy Division, Scottish Office Industry Department, since 1989; b. 11.1.48, Hitchin; m., Graeme Neil Munro (qv); 1 s.; 1 d. Educ. Harrogate Grammar School; Warwick University. Joined Scottish Office, 1970. Recreations: travel; reading; gardening. Address: (b.) New St. Andrews House, Edinburgh, EH1 3TA; T.-031-244 4624.

Munro of Foulis, Captain Patrick, TD (1958), DL (1949). 30th Chief of Clan Munro; Vice Lieutenant of Ross and Cromarty, 1968-77; b. 30.8.12; m., Eléanor Mary French; 3 s.; 1 d. Educ. Imperial Service College, Windsor; Sandhurst. 2nd Lt., Seaforth Highlanders, 1933; Captain, 1939; served Second World War (POW); Farmer and Landowner; Honorary Sheriff of Ross and Cromarty. Address: (h.) Foulis Castle, Evanton, Ross-shire.

Munro, Robert William. Author and Journalist; b. 3.2.14, Kiltearn, Ross-shire; m., Jean Mary Dunlop. Educ. Edinburgh Academy. War Service, Seaforth Highlanders and Inter-Services Public Relations Directorate (India), 1940-46; Editorial Staff, The Scotsman, 1933-59 and 1963-69; Editor-in-Chief, Highland News Group, 1959-63; Chairman, Edinburgh Press Club, 1955-57 (President, 1969-71); Honorary Editor, Clan Munro Association, 1939-71 (Vice-

President, since 1963); former Council Member: Society of Antiquaries of Scotland, Scottish History Society, Scottish Genealogy Society; Trustee, National Museum of Antiquities of Scotland, 1982-85. Publications: Donald Monro's Western Isles of Scotland and Genealogies of the Clans 1549 (Editor), 1961; Tain Through the Centuries (Co-author, with wife), 1966; The Glorious Privilege: The History of The Scotsman (Co-author), 1967; Kinsmen and Clansmen, 1971; The Northern Lighthouses, 1976; Highland Clans and Tartans, 1977; Edinburgh and the Borders, 1977; The Munro Tree 1734, 1978; Scottish Lighthouses, 1979; Taming the Rough Bounds, Knoydart 1745-1784, 1984; Acts of the Lords of the Isles 1336-1493 (Co-author, with wife), 1986. Recreations: historical research and writing; walking; visiting islands. Address: (h.) 15A Mansionhouse Road, Edinburgh, EH9 1TZ; T.-031-667 4601.

Munro, Shona, BSc (Hons), DipEd, MAppSci. Director, Edinburgh Book Festival, since 1991; b. 7.9.57, Edinburgh. Educ. James Gillespie's High School, Edinburgh; Aberdeen University; Jordanhill College; Glasgow University. Depute, then Co-Director, Edinburgh Book Festival, 1987-91. Board Member, Winged Horse Touring Productions. Recreations: reading; cinema; walking; sport. Address: (b.) Scottish Book Centre, 137 Dundee Street, Edinburgh, EH11 1BG; T.-031-228 5444.

Murchison, Lilian Elizabeth, MB, ChB, PhD, FRCPE, FRCP(Lond). Consultant Physician and Honorary Clinical Senior Lecturer in Medicine, Aberdeen University, since 1976; b. 29.4.36, Aultbea. Educ. Invergordon Academy; Edinburgh University; Glasgow University. Member, Scientific Staff, Atheroma Research Unit, Western Infirmary, Glasgow, 1963-68; Senior Tutor/Senior Registrar, Department of Medicine, Queen's University, Belfast, 1969-71; Lecturer, Department of Therapeutics and Clinical Pharmacology, Aberdeen University, 1971-76. Recreations: overseas travel; hill-walking. Address: (h.) 9 Highgate Gardens, Aberdeen, AB1 2TZ; T.-0224 588532.

Murchison, Maurine, OBE, MA (Hons). Chairman, Children's Panel Advisory Committee, Highland Region, 1980-85; Member, Consultative Committee on the Curriculum, 1980-87; Member, Highlands and Islands Development Consultative Council, 1978-86; Member, Police Advisory Board for Scotland, since 1985; b. 25.11.35, London; m., Dr. Murdoch Murchison (qv); 3 s.; 2 d. Educ. James Allen's Girls School, Dulwich; Edinburgh University. Secondary school teaching, 1958-60; homemaker and mother, since 1960; Member, Inverness County Children's Panel, 1971-75 (Chairman, 1972-75); Chairman, Highland Region Children's Panel, 1975-80; Member, Inverness Prison Visiting Committee, 1984-85; Member, Panel for Appeals Tribunal, set up under Social Work Scotland Act 1968, since 1983; Assessor under Race Relations Act, since 1982; Church Representative, Grampian Education Committe; Trustee, Aberdeen School of Christian Studies; Conciliator, Grampian Family Conciliation Service, 1988. Recreations: embroidery; group Bible study; reading (ethics and theology). Address: (h.) Riverdale, 22 Hillview Road, Cults, Aberdeen, AB1 9HB; T.-0224 868327.

Murchison, Murdoch, MB, ChB, DObstRCOG, DPH, DIH, FFCM. Chief Administrative Medical Officer and Director of Public Health Medicine, Grampian Health Board, since 1984; Honorary Clinical Senior Lecturer, Aberdeen University, since 1984; b. 27.10.33, Aultbea, Ross-shire; m., Maurine Tallach (see Maurine Murchison); 3 s.; 2 d. Educ. Invergordon Academy; Edinburgh University. Medical Officer of Health, Inverness County Council and Inverness Burgh Council; Community Medicine Specialist and District Medical Officer, Highland Health Board; Police Surgeon, Northern Constabulary; Medical Officer, Highland and Islands Fire Brigade. Member, Community Medicine Consultative Committee UK; Past Chairman, Scottish Committee for Community Medicine, BMA; Past President, Scottish Society for Community Medicine. Recreations: hill-walking; gardening. Address: Riverdale, 22 Hillview Road, Cults, Aberdeen, AB1 9HB; T.-Aberdeen 868327.

Murdoch, Brian Oliver, BA, PhD, AMusTCL. Senior Lecturer in German, Stirling University, since 1975 (Head, Department of German, 1982-90); b. 26.6.44, London; m., Ursula I. Riffer; 1 s.; 1 d. Educ. Sir George Monoux Grammar School, Walthamstow; Exeter University; Goettingen University; Freiburg University; Jesus College, Cambridge. Lecturer in German, Glasgow University; Assistant/Associate Professor of German, Illinois University; Lecturer in German, Stirling University. Visiting Fellow, Trinity Hall, Cambridge, 1989; Editor, Scottish Papers in Germanic Studies, since 1981. Recreations: jazz; numismatics; books. Address: (b.) German Department, Stirling University, Stirling, FK9 4LA; T.-0786 73171, Ext. 7546.

Murdoch, Eileen, OBE, MA. Headmistress, St. Augustine's High School, Edinburgh, since 1977; b. Edinburgh. Educ. Holy Cross Academy; Edinburgh University; Craiglockhart College. President, CHAS, 1988-90; President, HAS, 1990-91. Recreation: choral singing. Address: (b.) St. Augustine's High School, Broomhouse Road, Edinburgh; T.-031-334 6801.

Murdoch, Professor George, MBChB, FRCS (Edin), DSc. Professor Emeritus of Orthopaedic Surgery, since 1966; Visiting Professor, Strathclyde University; b. 30.11.20, Denny; m., Elizabeth Ann Rennie; 2 s.; 3 d. Educ. Falkirk High School; St. Andrews University. Squadron Leader, RAF; Consultant Orthopaedic Surgeon; Professor of Orthopaedic Surgery, Dundee University. Travelling Fellow, World Health Association; Honorary Fellow, International Society for Prosthetics and Orthotics. Publications: papers on surgery, prosthetics, orthotics; Editor of three books on prosthetics, orthotics. Recreations: reading; writing. Address: (h.) Pitfour Castle, Flat 3, St. Madoes, Perthshire, PH2 7NJ.

Murdoch, John, FCMA, JDipMA, CIPFA. Director of Finance and Management Services, Irvine Development Corporation, since 1972; b. 31.12.34, Glassford; m., Ann McTaggart Jack; 3 s.; 1 d. Educ. Hamilton Academy; School of Accountancy (Correspondence Courses). Bank Clerk, Bank of Scotland, Hamilton, 1951-53 and 1955-58; National Service, Cameronians (Scottish Rifles), 1953-55; Trainee Cost Accountant, Colvilles Steel Industry, Motherwell, 1958-63; Budget Controller, East Kilbride Development Corporation, 1963-68; Financial Controller, Irvine Development Corporation, 1968-72. Recreations: lay preaching; writing; fungi-hunting; bird-watching. Address: (b.) Irvine Development Corporation, Perceton House, Girdle Toll, Irvine, Ayrshire; T.-Irvine 214100.

Murdoch, Rev. William M., BSc, BD, STM, PhD. Chaplain to Aberdeen University, since 1991; b. 9.3.51, Edinburgh; m., Dr. Helen B. Murdoch; 1 s.; 1 d. Educ. Ashville College, Harrogate; Aberdeen University; Union Theological Seminary, New York. Research Assistant, Aberdeen University, 1973-76; Minister, Barthol Chapel with Tarves, 1980-91. Recreations: hill-walking; skiing; travel; cooking; fine wine. Address: (b.) Chaplaincy Centre, 25 High Street, Old Aberdeen, AB2 3EE; T.-0224 272137.

Murphy, Hayden. Poet, Writer/Journalist; b. 12.8.45, Dublin; 2 d. Educ. CBS, Limerick; Blackrock College, Dublin; Trinity College, Dublin (without taking degree). Editor, Broadsheet (Poetry Prose & Graphics), 1967-78; retrospective exhibition, National Library of Scotland, 1983; theatre criticism and reviewing, since 1975; literary criticism and reviewing, since 1970. Publications: Poems, 1966; Places of Glass, 1981 (poetry); Poet of Structure, 1971; Imagination's Autograph 1972 (drama, RTE); Slates, 1992; contributions in anthologies including Penguin Irish Verse. Recreations: reading while walking and hiding in Dumfries and Galloway. Address: 103 Cartvale Road, Cathcart, Glasgow G42 9RW; T.-041-649 4290.

Murphy, Herbert Edward Harnett, OBE, ACIT. Director, Public Affairs Scotland, Automobile Association, since 1990; Regional Director, Scotland and Northern Ireland, Automobile Association, 1974-90; b. 31.8.32, Dublin; m., Susan Gillian Hall; 2 s. Educ. Repton School, Derbyshire; Trinity College, Dublin. Member, Transport Committee, Glasgow Chamber of Commerce; Member, Transport Action Scotland Committee. Recreations: sailing; golf; hill-walking. Address: (h.) 20 Donaldfield Road, Bridge of Weir, Renfrewshire, PA11 3JG; T.-0505 613118.

Murphy, Sheriff James Patrick, BL. Sheriff of Glasgow and Strathkelvin, since 1989; (Sheriff of North Strathclyde, 1976-89); b. 24.1.32.

Murphy, James Barrie, MB, ChB, DPM, FRCPsych. Physician Superintendent and Honorary Clinical Lecturer, Gartnavel Royal Hospital, Glasgow; b. 27.7.42, Glasgow; m., Jean Wynn Kirkwood; 1 s.; 1 d. Educ. High School of Glasgow; Glasgow University. Consultant Psychiatrist, Dykebar Hospital, Paisley, 1973-80. Address: (b.) Gartnavel Royal Hospital, 1055 Great Western Road, Glasgow, G12 0XH; T.-041-334 6241.

Murphy, Peter Alexander, MA, MEd. Rector, Whitfield High School, Dundee, since 1976; b. 5.10.32, Aberdeen; m., Margaret Christie; 3 s.; 1 d. Educ. Aberdeen Grammar School; Aberdeen University. Assistant Principal Teacher of English, Aberdeen Grammar School, 1963-65; Principal Teacher of English, Summerhill Academy, Aberdeen, 1965-71; Head Teacher, Logie Secondary School, Dundee, 1971-76. Chairman, Carnoustie Branch, Labour Party; Elder, Carnoustie Church. Publication: Life and Times of Logie School (Co-author). Recreations: hill-walking; hockey; bee-keeping; gardening. Address: (h.) Ashlea, 44 Burnside Street, Carnoustie, Angus; T.-Carnoustie 52106.

Murphy-Black, Tricia, MSc, PhD, RM, RGN, RCNT. Research Fellow, Nursing Research Unit, Edinburgh University, since 1985; Chairman, Midwifery Committee, National Board for Nursing, Midwifery and Health Visiting, since 1992; b. 29.3.46, Cork. Educ. Our Lady's Priory, Haywards Heath; Manchester University. Former midwifery sister. UK Member, Royal College of Midwives Council, since 1982; Chairman, Royal College of Midwives Council, 1989-90. Publications: Antenatal Group Skills Training; Midwifery: excellence in nursing, the research route. Recreations: gardening; Celtic knotwork. Address: (h.) Mauldslie Hill Cottage, Temple, Midlothian, EH23 4TB; T.-087 530 235.

Murray, Rev. Alexander, MA. Minister, Associated Presbyterian Churches of Scotland, since 1989 (first Moderator); Minister, Free Presbyterian Church of Scotland, 1954-89; Member, Highland Regional Council, since 1986 (and 1975-78); b. 1.11.25, Invershin, Sutherland; m., Marjory Graham; 3 s.; 4 d. Educ. Bonar Bridge H.G. School; Selwyn College, Cambridge; Glasgow University. RAFVR, 1944-47; Moderator, Synod of FP Church, 1960 and 1978; Clerk, Foreign Missions Committee, 1977-89; Member, Education Committee, Ross and Cromarty County Council, 1960-70, Member of the Council, 1970-75; Chairman, Social Work Committee, Highland Regional Council; Secretary, Applecross Committee, 1965-75. Recreations: loch and sea fishing; swimming. Address: APC Manse, Saval Road, Lairg, IV27 4EH; T.-0549 2176.

Murray, Alexander George, KStG, KLJ, BSc, FBSC(Lond), FSA Scot. National Director, Crossroads (Scotland) Care Attendant Schemes, since 1981; m., Margaret Elizabeth; 1 d. Educ. Whitehill School, Glasgow; Glasgow University. Former Scottish Manager, British subsidiary of Chase Manhatten Bank of America; formed several companies in investment/credit field. Led first Scottish delegation to UNESCO, 1955-56; established Scottish Worldfriends Society and became its first National Director; active in Highland societies; Scot of the Year, 1986; Founder and Convener, Caledonian Country Dancing Clubs; former Secretary, West of Scotland Refugee Committee; Past President, East Kilbride Sea Cadet Corps; Member, Organising Committee, East Kilbride National Mod, 1974-75; Provincial Grand Master Mason. Publications: A History of Scottish Contra Dancing; 40 Popular Scottish Dances. Recreations: bowling; swimming; walking. Address: (h.) Failte, 51 Eaglesham Road, Clarkston, Glasgow, G76 7TR.

Murray, Athol Laverick, PhD, MA, LLB, FRHistS, FSA Scot. Vice-President, Society of Antiquaries of Scotland; Keeper of the Records of Scotland, 1985-90; b. 8.11.30, Tynemouth; m., Irene Joyce Cairns; 1 s.; 1 d. Educ. Lancaster Royal Grammar School; Jesus College, Cambridge; Edinburgh University. Research Assistant, Foreign Office, 1953; Scottish Record Office: Assistant Keeper, 1953-83, Deputy Keeper, 1983-84. Recreations: historical research; bowling. Address: (h.) 33 Inverleith Gardens, Edinburgh, EH3 5PR; T.-031-552 4465.

Murray, David Edward. Chairman and Managing Director, Murray International Holdings; Chairman, The Rangers Football Club plc; b. 14.10.51, Ayr; m., Louise; 2 s. Educ. Fettes College; Broughton High School. Young Scottish Business Man of the Year, 1984; Hon. Doctorate, Heriot-Watt University, 1986; Chairman, UK 2000 (Scotland), 1987; Governor, Clifton Hall School, 1987. Recreations: sports sponsorship; snooker; collecting wine. Address: (b.) South Gyle, Edinburgh; T.-031-317 7000.

Murray, Donald, MA. Head Teacher, Sir Edward Scott School, Tarbert, Isle of Harris, since 1981; b. Port of Ness, Isle of Lewis; 2 d. Educ. Nicolson Institute, Stornoway; Glasgow University. Teacher, Calder Street Secondary School, Glasgow; Teacher, Achnamara Residential School, Argyll; Principal Teacher of Guidance, Victoria Drive Secondary School, Glasgow; Assistant Head Teacher (Curriculum), Kingsridge Secondary School, Glasgow. Recreations: angling; gardening; reading. Address: (h.) Balranald, West Tarbert, Isle of Harris; T.-0859 2339.

Murray, Donald Alexander Keith. Farmer; Director, Royal Highland and Agricultural Society, since 1989; b. 11.7.43, Inverness; m., Muriel Goldie; 1 s.; 1 d. Educ. Dalhousie School; Strathallan School; North of Scotland College of Agriculture. President, Shetland Pony Stud Book Society, 1982; President, Caithness Agricultural Society, 1986. Recreations: indoor bowling; pony club activities. Address: (h.) Borgie House, Castletown, Thurso, KW14 8SN; T.-084 782 204.

Murray, Rev. Douglas Millar, MA, BD, PhD. Lecturer in Church History, Glasgow University, since 1989; b. 1946, Edinburgh; m., Dr. Freya M. Smith. Educ. George Watson's College, Edinburgh; Edinburgh University; New College, Edinburgh; Fitzwilliam and Westminster Colleges, Cambridge. Minister: St. Bride's Church, Callander, 1976-80, John Ker Memorial Church in deferred union with Candlish Church, Edinburgh, 1980-81, and Polwarth Church, 1981-89. Editor, Liturgical Review, 1979-81; Associate

Editor, Scottish Journal of Theology, 1981-87; Convener, Panel on Doctrine, General Assembly, Church of Scotland, 1986-90. Publication: Studies in the History of Worship in Scotland (Co-Editor). Recreations: golf; Scottish country dancing; hill-walking. Address: 7 Newark Drive, Glasgow, G41 4QJ; T.-041-423 7276.

Murray, Eleanor Leslie, MB, ChB, FRCOG, FRCPath. Consultant Pathologist, Vale of Leven Hospital, Alexandria, since 1980; Postgraduate Education Clinical Tutor, Dunbartonshire, since 1989; Honorary Clinical Senior Lecturer, Glasgow University, since 1990; b. 30.5.43, Greenock; m., Andrew Baxter; 1 s.; 2 d. Educ. Greenock Academy; Glasgow University. JHO and SHO posts, 1966-70; Registrar in Obstetrics and Gynaecology, Royal Maternity and Royal Samaritan Hospitals, Glasgow, 1970-72; Registrar, then Lecturer in Gynaecological Pathology, Western Infirmary, Glasgow, 1972-80. Recreations: gardening; reading; opera. Address: (h.) Dam of Aber, Gartocharn, Dunbartonshire, G83 8NQ; T.-038 983 395.

Murray, Frank McDonald, BSc (Hons), CEng, FIMinE. Managing Director, ICI Nobel's Explosives Co., since 1988; b. 7.9.36, Dunfermline; m., Nancy McDermott; 1 s.; 1 d. Educ. Kirkcaldy High School; Edinburgh University. Coal mining/gold mining, 1957-62; joined ICI as explosives engineer, 1962. President, Ayrshire Chamber of Industries, 1986-87; President, Federation of European Explosives Manufacturers. Recreation: golf. Address: (b.) Nobel House, Stevenston, Ayrshire; T.-0294 87447.

Murray, Gordon, BSc (Hons), PhD. Director, Scottish Courts Administration, since 1986; b. 25.8.35, Aberdeen; m., Janet Yerrington; 2 s.; 1 d. Educ. Kirkcaldy High School; Edinburgh University. Research Fellow, Atomic Energy Authority of Canada, 1960-62, UKAEA, 1962-65; Lecturer in Physics, Manchester University, 1965-69; Principal, Scottish Home and Health Department, 1970-77; Assistant Secretary, Scottish Education Department, 1977-79, Central Services, 1979-86. Recreations: reading; walking. Address: 26 Royal Terrace, Edinburgh, EH7 5AH; T.-031-556 0755.

Murray, Gordon Lindsay Kevan. Partner, W.J. Burness WS, since 1982; Secretary, Scottish National Orchestra Society Ltd., 1985-90, Director, since 1990; b. 23.5.53, Glasgow; m., Susan Patricia; 1 s.; 3 d. Educ. Lenzie Academy; Edinburgh University. President, Scottish Young Lawyers Association, 1977-78. Address: (b.) 16 Hope Street, Charlotte Square, Edinburgh, EH2 4DD; T.-031-226 2561.

Murray, Iain McInnes, BSc (Hons), MEd (Hons). Head Teacher, Wishaw High School, since 1989; b. 1.3.46, Glasgow; m., Marilyn Crichton; 1 s. Educ. Allan Glen's High School, Glasgow; Glasgow University. Teacher of Physics, Paisley Grammar, 1969-72; Assistant Principal Teacher of Science, Castlehead High, 1972-73; Principal Teacher of Physics, Caldervale High, Airdrie, 1973-81; Assistant Head Teacher, Vale of Leven, Alexandria, 1981-86; Depute Head Teacher, Braidfield High, Clydebank, 1986-89. Recreations: golf; bridge; computing. Address: (h.) 12 Balmuildy Road, Bishopbrigs, Glasgow, G64 3BS; T.-041-772 5855.

Murray, Isobel (Mary), MA, PhD. Writer and Book Reviewer; Senior Lecturer in English, Aberdeen University, since 1974; b. 14.2.39, Alloa; m., Bob Tait. Educ. Dollar Academy; Edinburgh University. Assistant Lecturer, then Lecturer, Department of English, Aberdeen University; books include several editions of Oscar Wilde, introductions to new editions of J. MacDougall Hay's Gillespie, Ian MacPherson's Shepherd's Calendar and Robin Jenkins's Guests of War; edited, Beyond This Limit: Selected Shorter Fiction of Naomi Mitchison; A Girl Must Live: stories and poems by Naomi Mitchison; Ten Modern Scottish Novels (with Bob Tait),

1984; wide range of book reviews, especially for The Scotsman, since 1962, and new fiction for Financial Times, 1968-81. Address: (b.) Department of English, King's College, Old Aberdeen, Aberdeen, AB9 2UB; T.-Aberdeen 272644.

Murray, Professor James, BSc, ARCST, CEng, FIMechE, FIProdE, FBIM. Assistant Principal, Napier Polytechnic, since 1974; b. 25.7.30, Glasgow; m., Emily Lamb Beveridge; 1 s.; 1 d. Educ. Allan Glen's School, Glasgow; Glasgow University. Development Engineer, Ferranti, Edinburgh; Lecturer, Department of Mechanical Engineering, Heriot Watt University; Head, Department of Production Engineering, Napier Polytechnic. Former Member, Council, SCOTVEC; Past Chairman, IProdE Scotland Region and CEI Scotland. Recreations: watching rugby; light rail transport. Address: (b.) Napier Polytechnic of Edinburgh, Colinton Road, Edinburgh, EH10 5DT; T.-031-455 7832.

Murray, Professor James Lothian, BSc, MSc, FIMechE, CEng, FRSA. Professor of Computer Aided Engineering, Heriot-Watt University, since 1985 (Director, CAE Centre, since 1982); b. 11.6.38, Loanhead; m., Anne Walton; 1 d. Educ. Lasswade Senior Secondary School; Heriot-Watt University. Student apprentice, then Design Engineer, Ferranti Ltd., 1956-66; Heriot-Watt University: Lecturer in Engineering Design, 1966-78, Senior Lecturer in Design and Manufacture, 1978-85, Head, Department of Mechanical Engineering, 1984-89, Director, CAE Centre, since 1982. Member, Academic Board, Napier Polytechnic. Recreation: hill-walking. Address: (b.) Department of Mechanical Engineering, Heriot-Watt University, Edinburgh, EH14 4AS; T.-031-449 5111.

Murray, Rev. John James, DipTh. Minister, Free St. Columba's Church, Edinburgh, since 1989 (Minister, Oban Free High Church, 1978-89); b. 11.9.34, Dornoch; m., Cynthia MacPhee; 1 s.; 1 d. Educ. Dornoch Academy; Edinburgh University; Free Church College. Worked with insurance company before joining Banner of Truth Trust, 1960, as Assistant Editor; Secretary, Reformation Translation Fellowship, 1962-89; Clerk, Argyll and Lochaber Presbytery, 1979-89; Editor, The Bulwark, 1977-80. Address: Free Church Manse, 10 Esslemont Road, Edinburgh, EH16 5PX; T.-031-667 4730.

Murray, John Kenneth, BCom, CA. Partner, Price Waterhouse, since 1985; Chairman, Aberdeen Enterprise Trust, since 1992; b. 9.8.51, Bridge of Allan; m., Morag; 1 s.; 1 d. Educ. Dollar Academy; Edinburgh University. Trained as CA with Price Waterhouse, Glasgow; Manager, Price Waterhouse, Edinburgh; Partner, Price Waterhouse, Aberdeen. Recreations: golf; shooting; cricket. Address: (h.) Bogarn House, Inchmarlo, Banchory; T.-03302 4476.

Murray, Jonathan Aidan Muir, BSc, MB, ChB, FRCS, FRACS, MD. Consultant Ear Nose and Throat Surgeon, Edinburgh, since 1983; part-time Senior Lecturer in Otolaryngology, since 1984; b. 16.8.51, Edinburgh; 2 s.; 2 d. Educ. Daniel Stewart's College, Edinburgh; Edinburgh University. Address: (h.) 7 South Learmonth Gardens, Edinburgh, EH4 1EY; T.-031-332 9484.

Murray, Professor Kenneth, BSc, PhD, FRS, FRSE, FRCPath. Professor of Molecular Biology, Edinburgh University, since 1976; b. 30.12.30, East Ardsley; m., Noreen E. Parker (see Noreen Elizabeth Murray). Educ. Henry Mellish Grammar School; Birmingham University. Postdoctoral work, Stanford University, California, 1959-64; MRC Scientific Staff, Cambridge, 1964-67; joined Edinburgh University, 1967; leave of absence at European Molecular Biology Laboratory, Heidelberg, 1979-82. Recreations: musical appreciation; reading. Address: (b.) Institute of Cell and

Molecular Biology, Edinburgh University, Mayfield Road, Edinburgh, EH9 3JR; T.-031-650 5387.

Murray, Leonard G., JP, BL. Former Senior Partner, Levy & McRae, Solicitors; b. 16.8.33, Glasgow; m., Elizabeth Wilson; 3 s. Educ. St. Mungo's Academy, Glasgow; Glasgow University. Director, Murray Inns Ltd. After-dinner speaker; founder Director, Speakeasy (Scotland) Ltd., 1987. Recreation: golf. Address: (h.) 77 Roman Court, Bearsden, Glasgow, G61 2NW.

Murray, Professor Maxwell, BVMS, DVM, FRCPath, FRSE, PhD. Professor of Veterinary Medicine, Glasgow University, since 1985; b. 3.5.39, Glasgow; m., Christine Madelaine; 1 s.; 2 d. Educ. Shawlands Senior Secondary School; Glasgow University. Animal Health Trust Research Scholarship, 1962-63; Lecturer in Veterinary Pathology, University of Nairobi, 1963-65; Lecturer in Veterinary Pathology, then Senior Lecturer, Glasgow University, 1965-75; Senior Scientist, International Laboratory for Research on Animal Diseases, Nairobi, 1975-85. Recreations: family; football; philosophy. Address: (b.) Department of Veterinary Medicine, Glasgow University Veterinary School, Bearsden Road, Bearsden, Glasgow, G61 1QH; T.-041-339 8855, Ext. 5734.

Murray, Myles, BSc (Hons). Head Teacher, St. Thomas Aquinas Secondary School, Glasgow, since 1982; b. 1938, Glasgow. Educ. Our Lady's High School, Motherwell; Glasgow University. Former Depute Head Teacher, Holy Cross High School, Hamilton. Address: (b.) St. Thomas Aquinas Secondary School, 80 Westland Drive, Glasgow, G14 9PG; T.-041-954 5905.

Murray, Professor Noreen Elizabeth, FRS, PhD, FRSE. Professor, Institute of Cell and Molecular Biology, Edinburgh University; b. 26.2.35, Burnley; m., Kenneth Murray (qv). Educ. Lancaster Girls' Grammar School; King's College, London; Birmingham University. Research Associate, Department of Biological Sciences, Stanford University, 1960-64; Research Fellow, Botany School, Cambridge, 1964-67; Edinburgh University: Member, MRC Molecular Genetics Unit, Department of Molecular Biology, 1968-74, Lecturer, then Senior Lecturer, Department of Molecular Biology, 1974-80; Group Leader, European Molecular Biology Laboratory, Heidelberg, 1980-82; joined Edinburgh University as Reader, 1982. Recreation: gardening. Address: (b.) Institute of Cell and Molecular Biology, Edinburgh University, Mayfield Road, Edinburgh, EH9 3JR; T.-031-650 5374.

Murray, Patrick, VRD, WS. Landowner; b. 13.5.11, Edinburgh; m., Doris Herbert Green; 2 d. Educ. Ardvreck, Crieff; Marlborough College. Royal Naval Volunteer Reserve, 1935-55 (Commander); Partner, Murray, Beith & Murray, WS, Edinburgh, 1937-77. Recreations: gardening; forestry. Address: (h.) Townhead of Cavers, Hawick, Roxburghshire, TD9 8LJ; T.-0450 73604.

Murray, Rt. Hon. Lord (Ronald King Murray), PC (1974), MA, LLB. Senator of the College of Justice in Scotland, since 1979; b. 15.6.22; m., Sheila Winifred Gamlin. Educ. George Watson's College; Edinburgh University; Jesus College, Oxford. Advocate, 1953; QC, 1967; MP (Leith), 1970-79; Lord Advocate, 1974-79. Assessor, Edinburgh University Court, since 1981 (Vice-Chairman of Court, since 1990); Member, Scottish Records Advisory Council. Recreation: sailing. Address: (h.) 31 Boswall Road, Edinburgh, EH5 3RP; T.-031-552 5602.

Murray, William Hutchison, OBE. Author and Mountaineer; b. 18.3.13, Liverpool; m., Anne Burnet Clark. Educ. Glasgow Academy. Union Bank of Scotland, until 1939; Captain, HLI, Western Desert (Prisoner of War, 1942-45); Leader, Scottish Himalayan Expedition, 1950; Deputy Leader, Everest Expedition, 1951; Leader, NW Nepal Expedition, 1953; Commissioner, Countryside Commission for Scotland, 1968-80; Mungo Park Medal, RSGS, 1950; Literary Award, USA Education Board, 1954; Honorary Doctorate, Stirling University, 1975; DLitt, Strathclyde University, 1991. Publications: Mountaineering in Scotland, 1947; Rock Climbs, Glencoe and Ardgour, 1949; Undiscovered Scotland, 1951; Scottish Himalayan Expedition, 1951; Story of Everest, 1953; Five Frontiers, 1959; The Spurs of Troodos, 1960; Maelstrom, 1962; Highland Landscape, 1962; Dark Rose the Phoenix, 1965; The Hebrides, 1966; Companion Guide to West Highlands, 1968; The Real MacKay, 1969; The Islands of Western Scotland, 1973; The Scottish Highlands, 1976; The Curling Companion, 1981; Rob Roy MacGregor, 1982; Scotland's Mountains, 1987. Recreations: mountaineering; sailing. Address: Lochwood, Loch Goil, Argyll.

Murray-Smith, Professor David James, MSc, PhD, CEng, FIEE, MInstMC. Titular Professor in Electronics and Electrical Engineering, Glasgow University; b. 20.10.41, Aberdeen; m., Effie Smith; 2 s. Educ. Aberdeen Grammar School; Aberdeen University; Glasgow University. Engineer, Inertial Systems Department, Ferranti Ltd., Edinburgh, 1964-65; Glasgow University: Assistant, Department of Electrical Engineering, 1965-67, Lecturer, 1967-77, Senior Lecturer, 1977-83, Reader, 1983-85. Past Chairman, United Kingdom Simulation Council; Member, various committees, Institution of Electrical Engineers; Advisory Director, Scottish Engineering Training Scheme Ltd. Recreations: hill-walking; photography; strong interest in railways. Address: (b.) Department of Electronics and Electrical Engineering, Glasgow University, Glasgow, G12 8QQ; T.-041-339 8855.

Murrie, Sir William Stuart, GCB (1964), KBE (1952), Hon. LLD (Dundee); b. 19.12.03, Dundee; m., Eleanore Boswell (deceased). Educ. Harris Academy, Dundee; Edinburgh University; Balliol College, Oxford. Scottish Office, 1927-35; Department of Health for Scotland, 1935-44; Under Secretary, Offices of War Cabinet, 1944; Deputy Secretary (Civil), Cabinet Office, 1947; Deputy Under Secretary of State, Home Office, 1948-52; Secretary: Scottish Education Department, 1952-57, Scottish Home Department, 1957-59; Permanent Under Secretary of State for Scotland, 1959-64; Chairman, Board of Trustees, National Galleries of Scotland, 1972-75; Member, Council on Tribunals, 1965-77; General Council Assessor, Edinburgh University Court, 1967-75. Address: (h.) 7 Cumin Place, Edinburgh, EH9 2JX; T.-031-667 2612.

Musgrave, Ralph Gilbert, BSc, PhD, IPM. Director of Management and Information Services, Lothian Regional Council, since 1986; b. 10.4.39, Edinburgh; m., Patricia E. Smith; 2 s. Educ. Broughton High School, Edinburgh; Edinburgh University. ICI Ltd., 1965; Lecturer, Falkirk College of Technology, 1966-71; Depute Director of Education, East Lothian County Council, 1971-75; Assistant Director of Education, Lothian Regional Council, 1975-86. Recreations: rugby; golf. Address: (b.) Lothian Regional Council, George IV Bridge, Edinburgh, EH1 1UQ; T.-031-229 9292.

Musson, John Nicholas Whitaker, MA (Oxon). Scottish Director, Independent Schools Careers Organisation, since 1987 (Warden, Glenalmond College, 1972-87); b. 2.10.27; m., Ann Priest; 1 s.; 3 d. Educ. Clifton College; Brasenose College, Oxford. Served as Guardsman and Lt., Lancashire Fusiliers, 1945-48; HM Overseas Service, 1951-59 (District Officer, N. Nigeria and Lecturer, Institute of Administration, Nigeria); British Petroleum Co., London, 1959-61; Assistant Master and Housemaster, Canford School, Dorset, 1961-72.

Scottish Division Chairman, Headmasters' Conference, 1981-83. Recreations: hill-walking; history; fine arts. Address: (h.) 47 Spylaw Road, Edinburgh, EH10 5BP; T.-031-337 0089.

Mutch, Alexander Fyvie, CBE, JP. Member, Grampian Regional Council, 1974-90 (first Convener, 1974-82); b. 23.3.24, Aberdeen; m., Freda Mutch; 1 d. Educ. Aberdeen Central School. Convener, Aberdeen Corporation Cleansing Committee, 1963; Vice-Chairman, North-East Water Board, 1968-70; Magistrate, Aberdeen, 1967; Senior Magistrate, 1968; Chairman, Aberdeen Licensing Court, 1968; Member, Aberdeen University Court, 1974-82; Chairman, South Aberdeen Conservative Association, 1964-68 (President, 1968-72); Senior Vice-President, Conservative Party in Scotland, 1972-73 (President, 1973-74); Leader, Conservative Group, Aberdeen Town Council, 1974-75; Governor, Robert Gordon's College, Aberdeen, 1968-70 and since 1974; Honorary President, Grampian-Houston Association; Honorary Citizen, Houston, Texas. Address: (h.) 28 Salisbury Terrace, Aberdeen; T.-Aberdeen 591520.

Mutch, William Edward Scott, OBE, BSc, PhD, FRSE, FICFor. Forestry and Land Use Consultant; b. 14.8.25, Salford; m., Margaret Isobel McKay; 1 d. Educ. Royal High School, Edinburgh; Edinburgh University. HM Colonial Service (Forest Department, Nigeria, as Assistant Conservator of Forests and Silviculturist), 1946; Research Assistant, Oxford University, 1952; Lecturer in Forestry, Edinburgh University, 1953. Head, Department of Forestry and Natural Resources, Edinburgh University, 1981-87; President, Institute of Chartered Foresters, 1982-84 (Institute Medal, 1986); Member: Countryside Commission for Scotland, 1988-92; National Forestry Research Advisory Committee; Nature Conservancy Council, 1988-91; NCC for Scotland, 1991-92; Scottish Natural Heritage, Chairman S.E. Scotland, since 1992; Director, Central Scotland Woodlands Ltd., since 1989. Publication: Farm Woodland Management. Recreations: cabinet making; travel; painting. Address: (h.) 19 Barnton Grove, Edinburgh, EH4 6EQ; T.-031-339 1400.

Myatt, Mary Elizabeth, BSc (Hons). Headmistress, The Park School, Glasgow, since 1986; b. 4.1.41, Belfast; m., Thomas Myatt. Educ. Omagh Academy; Queen's University, Belfast. Head, Mathematics Department: Dungannon High School for Girls, 1963-66, International School of Hamburg, 1966-68, Ashleigh House School, Belfast, 1968-70, Maida Vale High School, London, 1970-71; Wellington School, Ayr: Head, Mathematics Department, 1971-86, Director of Studies, 1984-86. Area Chairman, National Association of Ladies' Circles, 1978-79. Recreations: bridge; golf. Address: (b.) 25 Lynedoch Street, Glasgow, G3 6EX; T.-041-332 0426.

Myles, David Fairlie, CBE. Hill Farmer; Member, North of Scotland Hydro-Electric Board, 1985-89; Member, Angus District Council, since 1984; Member, Angus Tourist Board, since 1984; Chairman, Dairy Produce Quota Tribunal for Scotland, since 1984; Member, Potato Marketing Board, since 1988; b. 30.5.25, Cortachy, Kirriemuir; m., Janet I. Gall; 2 s.; 2 d. Educ. Brechin High School. Auctioneer's clerk, 1941-43; Royal Marines, 1943-46; Tenant Hill Farmer, since 1946; Director of auction company, 1963-81; Member, Transport Users Consultative Committee for Scotland, 1973-79; Council Member, NFU of Scotland, 1970-79 (Convener, Organisation and Publicity Committee, 1976-79); Member, Meat Promotion Executive, MLC, 1975-79; Chairman, North Angus and Mearns Constituency Conservative Party, 1971-74; MP (Conservative), Banff, 1979-83; Joint Secretary, Backbench Conservative Agriculture Committee, 1979-83; Secretary, Backbench Conservative European Committee, 1980-83; Member, Select Committee on Agriculture and Select Committee on European Legislation, 1979-83. Elder, Edzell-Lethnot Parish Church. Recreations: curling; traditional Scottish fiddle music; works of Robert Burns. Address:

(h.) The Gorse, Dunlappie Road, Edzell, Brechin, DD9 7UB; T.-035 64 207.

Myles, William Mackay Stanley, TD (with bar). Senior Partner, Myles Brothers, Wholesale Ironmongers, Edinburgh, since 1954; Member, Executive Committee, National Trust for Scotland, since 1988; b. 6.3.27, Edinburgh; m., Margaret Shiela Grace Bruce; 3 s. Educ. Sciennes and James Clark's, Edinburgh; Bell-Baxter, Cupar. Royal Scots, 1945-66; India & Pakistan 1st Bn., 1946-47, 7/9 and 8/9 TA Bns., 1948-66, as Rifle Company Commander, 1951-66; Member, Regimental Council, since 1977; Mountaineering Council of Scotland: Training Officer, 1974-90, Hon. Secretary, 1977-83, Vice-President, 1984-88; Chairman, The Royal Scots Club, Edinburgh, since 1977; Chairman, Edinburgh West End Community Council; Director, Lord Roberts Workshops for Disabled Ex-Servicemen; Council Member, Earl Haig Fund; Member, Church of Scotland Committee on Artistic Matters; Elder, Church of Scotland; Director, Drumsheugh Baths Club Ltd., Edinburgh, since 1972; President, Rotary Club of Edinburgh, 1983-84. Recreations: hill-walking; swimming; painting in oils; gardening. Address: (h.) 12 Douglas Crescent, Edinburgh, EH12 2BB; T.-031-337 4781.

N

Nandy, Kashinath, BSc, MSc (Calcutta), MSc (Edinburgh), PhD, FRAS, FRSE. Deputy Chief Scientific Officer, Royal Observatory, Edinburgh, 1977-86; Visiting Professor, Rome University, 1987; b. 1.12.27, Santipur, West Bengal, India; m., Smritilekha; 1 d. Educ. Calcutta University; Edinburgh University. Observatory Assistant, Presidency College Observatory, Calcutta, 1952-59; received International Astronomical Union Grant for Studies Abroad, 1959-60; held Robert Cormack Bequest Fellowship (Royal Society of Edinburgh), 1960-63; Royal Observatory, Edinburgh: Research Fellow, 1963-68, Principal Scientific Officer, 1968-72, Senior Principal Scientific Officer, 1972-77. Fellow, Royal Astronomical Society; Member, International Astronomical Union; Honorary Fellow, Edinburgh University, 1973-87; Honorary Research Fellow, University College, London, 1979-86, re-elected, 1989; elected Fellow, Royal Society of Edinburgh, 1973; Fellow, Royal Society of Liege, 1980. Recreations: reading; travel; photography; surfing. Address: (h.) 36 West Mains Road, Edinburgh, EH9 3BG; T.-031-667 6131.

Narayan, K.M. Venkat, MBBS, DGM, MSc, MRCP, MFCM, MIHE. Consultant Public Health Physician, Grampian Health Board, since 1989; Clinical Senior Lecturer, Aberdeen University, since 1989; b. 14.9.56, Bangalore; m., Asha Krishaswamy. Educ. Bishop Cotton Boys' School, Bangalore; St. John's Medical College, Bangalore; Edinburgh University. Resident Medical Officer, Ruwais Hospital, Abi Dhabi; SHO, Basildon Hospital, St. Andrew's Hospital, Billericay; Registrar, Dryburn Hospital, Durham; Registrar/Senior Registrar, Grampian Health Board. Member, Board of Directors, Grampian Heart Campaign. Recreations: swimming; theatre. Address: (b.) 1-7 Albyn Place, Aberdeen, AB9 8QP; T.-0224 589901.

Nathanson, Vivienne Hilary, MB, BS. Scottish Secretary, British Medical Association, since 1990; b. 9.3.55, Liverpool. Educ. Birkenhead High School GPDST; Middlesex Hospital Medical School; London University. Medical Registrar, Ysbyty Glan Clwyd, Bodelwyddan, 1981-84; BMA: Management Trainee, 1984-86, Assistant Secretary, 1986-89. Recreations: opera; bridge; photography. Address: (b.) 3 Hill Place, Edinburgh, EH8 9EQ; T.-031-662 4820.

Naumann, Laurie M. Director, Scottish Council for Single Homeless, since 1978; b. 1943, Saffron Walden; m., Barbara; 2 s.; 3 d. Educ. Edinburgh, Gloucester and Nuremberg Rudolf Steiner; Leicester University. Furniture maker, Gloucestershire; Probation and After Care Officer, Leeds; Social Worker, Edinburgh. Council of Europe Social Fellowship to Finland to study services for the drunken offender, 1976; jointly won Rosemary Delbridge Memorial Trophy for influencing Parliament to legislate, 1983; Secretary, Care in the Community Scottish Working Group and Hamish Allan Trust; Board Member, Kingdom and Old Town Housing Associations. Recreations: travel; reading; walking; woodwork. Address: (h.) St. Ann's, Alexander III Street, Kinghorn, Fife, KY3 9SD.

Naylor, Arthur, MA, MEd, PhD, MBA. Assistant Principal, St. Andrew's College of Education, Bearsden, since 1986; b. 27.2.49, Glasgow; m., Valerie Jean Fox; 2 s.; 1 d. Educ. Holyrood Secondary School, Glasgow; Glasgow University; Jordanhill College of Education. Teacher and Assistant Principal Teacher, 1972-75; Principal Teacher: St. Margaret's High, Paisley, 1975-76 (until amalgamation), Turnbull High, Bishopbriggs, 1976-81; St. Andrew's College of Education: Lecturer in Educational Science, 1981-84, Head of Department, 1984-86. Member of wide-ranging advisory committees on guidance, 1981-84, and on undergraduate and postgraduate teacher education, since 1984. Recreations: local history; swimming; walking; reading. Address: (b.) St. Andrew's College of Education, Bearsden, G61 4QA; T.-041-943 1424.

Naylor, Graham John, MB, ChB, BSc, DPM, MD, FRCPsych. Reader in Psychiatry, Dundee University, since 1980; Honorary Consultant, Royal Dundee Liff Hospital, since 1970; b. 13.2.40, Sheffield; m., Pamela Hilda Moody. Educ. Firth Park Grammar School, Sheffield; Sheffield University. Consultant Psychiatrist, Royal Dundee Liff Hospital, 1970-72; Senior Lecturer, Department of Psychiatry, Dundee University, 1972-80. Address: (b.) Department of Psychiatry, Ninewells Hospital and Medical School, Dundee; T.-Dundee 60111.

Neil, James Wilson McDowell, MA. Principal, Dumfries and Galloway College of Technology, since 1981; b. 16.6.39, Airdrie; m., Halina Adams; 2 s.; 2 d. Educ. Airdrie Academy; Glasgow University. Lecturer, Coatbridge College, 1962-66; Senior Lecturer, Telford College, 1966-70; Depute Principal, Moray College, 1970-80. Convener, ACFHE in Scotland, since 1984. Recreations: hill-walking; eating. Address: (h.) Vendaceburn, Lockerbie; T.-0387 810719.

Neill, David Lindsay. Master Mariner; Ship's Captain, since 1973; Captain, P.S. Waverley, since 1975; b. 21.5.44, Glasgow; m., Jean Shaw Thomson McLachlan; 1 s.; 2 d. Educ. various schools; Glasgow School of Nautical Studies. Deck Apprentice, 1960-64; Ship's Navigating Officer, 1964-70; Ferry Manager (Isle of Skye), 1970-71; Ship's Navigating Officer, 1971-73. Life Member, Paddle Steamer Preservation Society. Recreations: out of door. Address: (b.) Waverley Excursions Ltd., Anderston Quay, Glasgow, G3 8HA; T.-041-221 8152.

Neill, Gordon Webster McCash, DSO, SSC, NP, FInstD. Solicitor and Notary Public; Honorary Sheriff; b. Arbroath;

m., Margaret Mary Lamb; 1 s.; 1 d. Educ. Edinburgh Academy. Legal apprenticeship, 1937-39; Pilot, RAF, 1939-46 (DSO, French Croix de Guerres with silver gilt star and silver star); Partner, Neill & Gibb, SSC, 1947; Chairman, Dundee Area Board, British Law Insurance Co. Ltd., 1954; Principal, Neill & Mackintosh, SSC, 1967; Consultant, Thorntons WS, 1989; Past Chairman, Scottish Gliding Association and Angus Gliding Club Ltd.; Past President, Chamber of Commerce, Arbroath Rotary Club and Society of Solicitors and Procurators in Angus. Recreations: gliding; shooting; fishing. Address: (h.) 29 Duncan Avenue, Arbroath, Angus DD11 2DA; T.-0241 72221.

Neill, Rev. William George, MA, BD. Minister, St. Andrew's Church, Ayr, since 1986; b. 19.8.45, Edinburgh; m., Marjory Joyce Reid; 2 s.; 2 d. Educ. George Heriot's School; Edinburgh University. Assistant, Crown Court Church, London, 1970-71; Blackbraes and Shieldhill Church, Falkirk, 1971-75; Scotstoun East Church, Glasgow, 1975-80; North Leith Parish Church, 1980-86. Editor, Church Service Society Record, 1982-86; Robert Lee Lecturer, 1984. Recreations: hill-walking; photography; music; philosophy; politics. Address: (h.) 31 Bellevue Crescent, Ayr, KA7 2DP; T.-0292 262621.

Neill, William Wilson, MA (Hons). Poet; b. 22.2.22, Prestwick; m., Doris Marie; 2 d. (by pr. m.). Educ. Ayr Academy; Edinburgh University. Served, RAF; won Sloane Verse Prize and Grierson Verse Prize while at Edinburgh University; Teacher; crowned Bard, Aviemore Mod, 1969; former Editor, Catalyst; former Editor, Lallans (Scots Language magazine); SAC Book Award, 1985; broadcasts, essays in Scotland's three tongues. Publications: Scotland's Castle, 1969; Poems, 1970; Four Points of a Saltire (Co-author), 1970; Despatches Home, 1972; Buile Shuibhne, 1974; Galloway Landscape: Poems, 1981; Cnu a Mogaill: Poems, 1983; Wild Places: Poems, 1985; Blossom, Berry, Fall: Poems 1986; Making Tracks: Poems, 1988. Address: (h.) Burnside, Crossmichael, Castle Douglas, DG7 3AP; T.-055-667 265.

Neilson, Rev. Peter, MA, BD. National Adviser in Mission and Evangelism, Church of Scotland, since 1986, and Director of Training, St. Ninian's Centre, Crieff, since 1992; b. 8.1.48, Lanark; m., Dorothy Jane; 3 d. Educ. Hamilton Academy; Glasgow University; Edinburgh University. Assistant Minister, Dunblane Cathedral, 1972-75; Minister, Mount Florida Parish Church, 1975-86. Recreation: singing. Address: (b.) St. Ninian's Centre, Crieff, PH7 4BG; T.-0764 3766.

Nelson, John, MBE, TD, JP, DL. Convener, Stewartry District Council, since 1976; Chairman, Solway River Purification Board, since 1986; b. 26.12.18, Irongray, Dumfries; m., Margaret M.C. Shedden; 4 s. Educ. Castle Douglas High School. Farming, 1934-84, except for War years spent with Royal Artillery and Indian Mountain Artillery in Burma; NFU Committee Member, 40 years (Chairman, Stewartry Area, 1960-61); County Councillor, 1971-74; appointed Deputy Lieutenant, 1983. Recreation: horse riding. Address: (h.) Greentop, 4 Castle View, Castle Douglas; T.-Castle Douglas 3143.

Nelson, (Peter) Frederick, BSc, CEng, MIEE. Chairman, Scottish Sports Association, since 1990; Member, Scottish Sports Council, since 1990; b. 2.9.52, Glasgow; m., (Caroline) Ann; 3 s. Educ. John Neilson; Strathclyde University. President, Scottish Canoe Association, 1980-90; Member, Commonwealth Games Council for Scotland, since 1982. Recreations: canoeing; walking; DIY. Address: (h.) 11 Barnton Park Place, Edinburgh, EH4 6ET; T.-031-336 4779.

Neumann, Jan, CBE, BSc, FEng, FIMechE, FIMarE, MIES. Director, Scottish Nuclear Ltd.; b. 26.6.24, Prague; m., Barbara Joyce Gove; 2 s. Educ. Friends' School, Great Ayton; London University. Flight Engineer, RAF; Design Engineer, English Electric Co., Rugby; various engineering design and management positions in Yarrow Admiralty Research Department; Director, YARD Ltd., 1969-88 (Managing Director, 1978-87); Director, Yarrow PLC, 1978-86; Board Member, SEEB, 1986-88; received Denny Gold Medal, IMarE, and Thomas Lowe Gray Prize, IMechE. Recreations: swimming; bowls. Address: (h.) 38 Norwood Park, Bearsden, Glasgow, G61 2RZ.

Newall, Stephen Park, DL, Hon. LLD (Strathclyde). Chairman, Court, University of Strathclyde, since 1988; Chairman: Kanthal Limited, since 1980, Bulten Limited, since 1980, Shuna Shipping Ltd., since 1986; Deputy Lieutenant, Dunbartonshire, since 1985; b. 12.4.31, Bearsden, Dunbartonshire; m., Gay Sommerville Craig; 4 s.; 1 d. Educ. Loretto. Commissioned and served with Parachute Regiment, National Service, 1949-51; Sales Manager, A.P. Newall & Co., 1951-57; Managing Director, Bulten-Kanthal Stephen Newall Co. Ltd., 1957-80. Chairman, Epilepsy Association of Scotland, 1982-86; Chairman, Finance Committee, University of Strathclyde, 1985-88; Council Member, Quarrier's Homes, 1983-88; Council Member, Scottish Business School, 1983-85; Secretary of State for Scotland's Nominee on Court of Cranfield, since 1985; Deacon Convener, Trades of Glasgow, 1983-84. Recreations: farming; hill-walking; sailing; music. Address: (h.) Rowaleyn, Rhu, Dunbartonshire; T.-0436 820 521.

Newbould, Peter, BSc, BAgr, DPhil. Assistant Director, Macaulay Land Use Research Institute; b. 24.9.31, Lincoln; m., Doreen Wilson; 1 s.; 1 d. Educ. Priory School, Shrewsbury; Queen's University, Belfast; Lincoln College, Oxford. Research Assistant, Department of Agriculture, Oxford University; ARC Radiobiological Laboratory (subsequently Letcombe Laboratory): Scientific Officer, Senior Scientific Officer, Principal Scientific Officer, Head of Field Studies Section; Senior Principal Scientific Officer, Plants and Soils Department, Hill Farming Research Organisation; Member, Editorial Board, Journal of the Science of Food and Agriculture. Recreations: gardening; photography; reading. Address: (b.) Craigiebuckler, Aberdeen, AB9 2QJ; T.-0224 318611.

Newell, Professor Alan F., BSc, PhD, FIEE, CEng, FBCS. NCR Professor of Electronics and Microcomputer Systems, Dundee University, since 1980 (Director, Dundee University Microcomputer Centre, since 1980); b. 1.3.41, Birmingham; m., Margaret; 1 s.; 2 d. Educ. St. Philip's Grammar School; Birmingham University. Research Engineer, Standard Telecommunication Laboratories; Lecturer, Department of Electronics, Southampton University. Recreations: family life; skiing; sailing. Address: (b.) Micro Centre, Department of Mathematics and Computer Science, The University, Dundee, DD1 4HN; T.-Dundee 23181.

Newis, Kenneth, CB, CVO, MA. Chairman, Queen's Hall (Edinburgh) Ltd.; Vice Chairman of Council, Cockburn Association; Director, Cockburn Conservation Trust; Trustee, RSAMD Trust; b. 9.11.16, Crewe; m., Kathleen Barrow; 2 d. Educ. Manchester Grammar School; St. John's College, Cambridge. HM Office of Works, London, 1938-70; Under Secretary, Scottish Development Department, 1970-73; Secretary, 1973-76. Recreation: music. Address: (h.) 11 Abbotsford Park, Edinburgh, EH10 5DZ; T.-031-447 4138.

Newlands, Rev. George McLeod, MA, BD, PhD. Professor of Divinity, Glasgow University, since 1986 (Dean, Faculty of Divinity, 1988-90); Principal, Trinity College, since 1991; 12.7.41, Perth; m., Mary Elizabeth Wallace; 3 s. Educ. Perth Academy; Edinburgh University; Heidelberg University; Churchill College, Cambridge. Assistant Minister, Muirhouse, Edinburgh, 1969; Lecturer in Divinity, Glasgow University, 1969; University Lecturer in Divinity, Cambridge, 1973; Dean, Trinity Hall, Cambridge, 1982. Publications: Hilary of Poitiers, 1978; Theology of the Love of God, 1980; The Church of God, 1984; Making Christian Decisions, 1985. Recreations: walking; sailing; golf. Address: (h.) 14 Gt. George Street, Glasgow, G12 8NA; T.-041-334 4712.

Newlands, William Jeffrey, MB, ChB, FRCSEdin. Consultant Ear, Nose and Throat Surgeon, Grampian Health Board and Orkney and Shetland Health Boards, since 1981; Clinical Senior Lecturer in Otolaryngology, Aberdeen University, since 1981; b. 9.9.29, Edinburgh; m., Patricia Kathleen St. Quintin Gee; 2 s.; 2 d. Educ. Daniel Stewart's College, Edinburgh; Edinburgh University. House Physician and House Surgeon, Western General Hospital, Edinburgh, 1952-53; Captain, RAMC, 1953-55; specialist training, 1958-65, Royal Infirmary, Edinburgh, Western Infirmary, Glasgow, Royal National Throat, Nose and Ear Hospital, London; Otolaryngologist, Brown Clinic, Calgary, 1966; Consultant ENT Surgeon: Grampian Health Board, 1967-77, County Hospital, Uddevalla, Sweden, 1977-78, Lothian Health Board, 1978-79; Professor of Otolaryngology, King Faisal University College of Medicine, Saudi Arabia, 1979-81. Examiner in Otolaryngology, Part 2 Examination, FRCSEdin. Recreations: travel; music. Address: (h.) 4 Camperdown Road, Aberdeen, AB2 4NU; T.-0224 633784.

Newton, Ray William, MB, ChB, FRCPEdin. Consultant Physician in charge of diabetes, Ninewells Hospital, since 1977; Senior Lecturer in Medicine, Ninewells Hospital Medical School, since 1983; Senior Lecturer in Clinical Pharmacology, Dundee University, since 1978; b. 8.12.44, Cockermouth; m., Sylvia Spreng; 3 s. Educ. Cockermouth Grammar School; Edinburgh University. Medical Registrar, Royal Infirmary, Edinburgh, 1970-74; Senior Registrar, Ninewells Hospital, Dundee, 1974-77; Chairman, National Youth Diabetes Project, since 1983; Tayside Regional Adviser, Royal College of Physicians of Edinburgh, since 1986; Specialty Adviser in Medicine, Tayside Region, since 1987; Chairman, Scottish Committee, British Diabetic Association; Secretary, Scottish Society of Physicians, 1978-83. Publication: Endocrinology - The New Medicine (Editor), 1983. Recreations: President, Forthill Sports Club; Member, Royal and Ancient Golf Club. Address: (h.) 70 Seafield Road, Broughty Ferry, Dundee, DD1 3AQ; T.-0382 76239.

Nicholson, Sheriff Principal (Charles) Gordon (Brown), QC, MA, LLB. Sheriff Principal of Lothian and Borders, since 1990; Commissioner, Scottish Law Commission, 1982-89; b. 11.9.35, Edinburgh; m., Hazel Mary Nixon; 2 s. Educ. George Watson's College, Edinburgh; Edinburgh University. Admitted to Faculty of Advocates, 1961; Advocate Depute, 1968-70; Sheriff of Dumfries and Galloway, at Dumfries, 1970-76; Sheriff of Lothian and Borders, at Edinburgh, 1976-82. Honorary President, Scottish Association for the Study of Delinquency; Hon. President, Scottish Association of Victim Support Schemes. Publication: The Law and Practice of Sentencing in Scotland, 1981 (2nd edition, 1992). Recreation: music. Address: (h.) 1A Abbotsford Park, Edinburgh, EH10 5DX; T.-031-447 4300.

Nicholson, Peter Alexander, LLB (Hons). Managing Editor, W. Green, The Scottish Law Publisher, since 1989; General Editor, Scots Law Times; Scottish Editor, Current Law; General Editor, Green's Weekly Digest, since 1986; b. 22.5.58, Stirling; m., Morag Ann Fraser; 1 s.; 1 d. Educ. St. David's RC High School, Dalkeith; Edinburgh University. Admitted as Solicitor, 1981. Chairman of Four Churches (Ecumenical) Council, Slateford, 1988-89. Recreations:

choral singing; gardening; keeping fit. Address: (h.) 1 Buckstone Row, Edinburgh, EH10 6TW; T.-031-445 4311.

Nickson, Sir David Wigley, KBE (1987), CBE (1981), DL, CBIM, FRSE. Chairman, Clydesdale Bank, since 1991 (Director, since 1981); Chairman, Scottish Enterprise, since 1990 (Scottish Development Agency, from 1988); Chairman, Top Salaries Review Body, since 1989; President, Confederation of British Industry, 1986-88 (Chairman, CBI in Scotland, 1979-81); Chairman, Countryside Commission for Scotland, 1983-86; Director, Scottish & Newcastle Breweries plc (Chairman, 1983-89); Director, General Accident Fire and Life Assurance Corporation plc; Director, Edinburgh Investment Trust; b. 27.11.29, Eton; m., Helen Louise Cockcraft; 3 d. Educ. Eton College; Royal Military Academy, Sandhurst. Commissioned, Coldstream Guards, 1949-54; William Collins: joined, 1954, Director, 1961-85, Joint Managing Director, 1967, Vice-Chairman, 1976-83, Group Managing Director, 1979-82; Director: Scottish United Investors plc, 1970-83, Radio Clyde Ltd., 1982-85; Chairman, Pan Books, 1982-83. Member: Scottish Industrial Development Advisory Board, 1975-80, Scottish Economic Council, since 1980, Scottish Committee, Design Council, 1978-81; Chairman, Atlantic Salmon Trust; Vice-Chairman, Association of Scottish District Fishery Boards; Brigadier, Queen's Bodyguard for Scotland (Royal Company of Archers); Deputy Lieutenant, Stirling and Falkirk, since 1982. Recreations: fishing; bird-watching; the countryside. Address: (h.) Renagour House, Aberfoyle, Stirling, FK8 3TF; T.-Aberfoyle 275.

Nicol, Alexander David, CA. Director and Deputy Chief Executive, British Linen Bank Ltd.; Managing Director, Capital Leasing Ltd.; Managing Director, British Linen Assets plc; b. 11.7.38, Kirkcaldy; m., Sheila Giffen; 1 s.; 2 d. Educ. Buckhaven High School; Harvard AMP. Managing Director, NEI Peebles, 1976-83. Member, General Teaching Council for Scotland; Member, Edinburgh University Advisory Committee on Business Studies. Address: (b.) 4 Melville Street, Edinburgh, EH3 7NZ; T.-031-243 8304.

Nicol, Rev. Douglas Alexander Oag, MA, BD (Hons). General Secretary, Church of Scotland Department of National Mission; b. 5.4.48, Dunfermline; m., Anne Wilson Gillespie; 2 s.; 1 d. Educ. Kirkcaldy High School; Edinburgh University; Glasgow University. Assistant Warden, St. Ninian's Centre, Crieff, 1972-76; Minister, Lochside, Dumfries, 1976-82; Minister, St. Columba, Kilmacolm, 1982-91. Chairman, Board of Directors, National Bible Society of Scotland, 1984-87; Convener, Board of National Mission, Church of Scotland, 1990-91. Recreations: family life; hill-walking. Address: (h.) 24 Corbiehill Avenue, Blackhall, Edinburgh, EH4 5DR; T.-031-336 1965.

Nicol, Rev. John Chalmers, MA, BD, MHSM, DipHSM. Minister, Holy Trinity Church, Bridge of Allan, since 1985; b. 6.4.39, Greenock; m., Anne Morrison Macdonald; 1 s.; 1 d. Educ. Greenock Academy; Glasgow University; Princeton Theological Seminary. Assistant Minister, Westwood Parish Church, East Kilbride, 1964-65; Minister: St. Andrews Scots Church, Temperley, Buenos Aires, 1965-69, Bonnyrigg Parish Church, 1970-75; Secretary, Edinburgh Local Health Council, 1975-78; Principal Administrative Assistant, Argyll and Clyde Health Board, 1978-85. Recreations: fishing; wine-making; Charles Rennie Mackintosh. Address: 29 Keir Street, Bridge of Allan, Stirling, FK9 4QJ; T.-0786 832093.

Nicol, Rev. Thomas James Trail, LVO, MBE, MC, DD. Minister, Church of Scotland; Extra Chaplain to The Queen, since 1979; b. 24.1.17, Skelmorlie, Ayrshire; m., Mary Barnfather Taylor; 2 d. Educ. Edinburgh Academy; Dundee High School; Glasgow Academy; Aberdeen Grammar School; Aberdeen University. OCTU and Commission, Black

Watch, 1939-42; ordained as Chaplain to the Forces, 1942; RAChd, 1942-46, attached 51 (H) Division; Minister, St. Luke's, Broughty Ferry, 1946-49; regular commission, RAChd, 1949-72; Assistant Chaplain-General, HQ Scotland, 1967-72; Minister, Crathie, 1972-77; Domestic Chaplain in Scotland to the Queen, 1972-79. Recreations: hill-walking; gardening; golf. Address: (h.) Beech Cottage, Dalginross, Comrie, Perthshire, PH6 2HB; T.-0764 70430.

Nicol, William, CBE, BSc, FCIOB, FInstR. Chairman, Scottish Committee, and Member of Council, CNAA; former Chairman and Managing Director, Craig-Nicol Limited; b. 9.9.24, Glasgow; m., Margaret Jean McNeill; 2 s.; 1 d. Educ. High School of Glasgow; Gresham House; Glasgow University. President, Glasgow Master Wrights and Builders' Association, 1953-54; Chairman, Glasgow Local Joint Apprenticeship Committee, 1952-61; Chairman, Scottish Building Apprenticeship Council, 1959-67; Member, Board of Governors, Jordanhill College of Education, 1959-67; Deacon, Incorporation of Wrights in Glasgow, 1963-64; Director, Glasgow Chamber of Commerce, 1965-70 (Chairman, Education Committee); Founder Chairman, Scottish Branch, Chartered Institute of Building, 1963-65 (National President, 1970-71, Honorary Treasurer, 1972-76); Member, Construction Industry Training Board, 1964-85 (Chairman, Building Committee, 1967-72); President, Scottish National Federation of Building Trades' Employers, 1969-70 and 1972-73; Governor, Glasgow College of Building and Printing, 1966-75 (first Chairman, Board of Governors) and Vice-Chairman, then Chairman, new College Council, 1976-82; Vice-Chairman, Scottish Technical Education Council, 1973-78, Chairman, 1978-85; Chairman, British Refrigeration Association, 1975-77, President, 1986-88; Chairman, Commercial Section, CECOMAF, 1974-77 (President, CECOMAF, 1979-83); Committee Member, Scottish Branch, Institute of Refrigeration, 1977-81 (elected Vice-Chairman, 1979); Member, Heating, Ventilating, Air Conditioning and Refrigeration Equipment - Economic Development Committee, NEDO, 1984-87; Governor, Glasgow Polytechnic, since 1985; Chairman, Sector Board 4, SCOTVEC, since 1989. Recreations: gardening; walking; reading; music; bridge. Address: (h.) 27 Burnhead Road, Glasgow, G43 2SU; T.-041-637 4097.

Nicoll, Douglas Alexander Smith, JP. Honorary Sheriff, Forfar; b. 24.6.18, Forfar; m., Ella Mary Grant (deceased); 1 s.; 2 d. Educ. Forfar Academy. Partner, joinery manufacturing firm, Forfar, from 1936; Managing Director and Chairman upon retirement, 1972; Member, Forfar Town Council, seven years; served on Magistrates' Bench, three years; served on Steering Committee for Community Councils in Angus; Elder, Church of Scotland. Recreations: music; bowling. Address: (h.) Dunvegan, 11 Turfbeg Avenue, Forfar, DD8 3LJ; T.-0307 63232.

Nicoll, Eric Hamilton, CBE, FSA Scot, BSc (Hons), FICE, FIWEM (Dip). Deputy Chief Engineer, Scottish Development Department, 1976-85; b. 15.5.25, Edinburgh; m., Helen Elizabeth Barnes; 1 s.; 1 d. Educ. George Heriot's School, Edinburgh; Edinburgh University. Engineering Assistant: Midlothian County Council Roads Department, 1945-46, Edinburgh Corporation Water Department, 1946-51; Chief Assistant County Engineer, Midlothian County Council, 1951-62; Scottish Development Department: Engineering Inspector, 1962-68, Senior Engineering Inspector, 1968-72, Assistant Chief Engineer, 1972-75. US Water Pollution Control Federation Arthur Sidney Bedell Award, 1985. Publication: Small Water Pollution Works: Design and Practice, 1988. Recreations: wood sculpture; music; antiquities. Address: (h.) 35 Wardie Road, Edinburgh, EH5 3LJ.

Nicolson, Alasdair George, MA (Hons). Assistant Principal, Jordanhill College of Education, since 1976; b. 6.12.26, Stepps, Lanarkshire; m., Sylvia Hall; 1 d. Educ. Coatbridge High School; Glasgow University. Teacher/Principal, Modern Studies and History, Airdrie High School, 1951-61; Lecturer in Modern Studies, then Head, Modern Studies Department, Jordanhill College of Education, 1961-76; Principal Examiner, Modern Studies, SCEEB, 1965-74; Member, BBC Schools Broadcasting Council Advisory Committee, 1968-74; Member, STV Education Advisory Committee, since 1981; Member, Scottish Central Committee Social Subjects, 1974-81; Chairman, Scottish Council, United Nations Association, 1982-89; Chairman, Saltire Education Committee, 1970-76; Chairman, Association of Lecturers in Colleges of Education in Scotland, 1969-72; Chairman, Association for Liberal Education, 1969-72; Executive Member, Council for Education in the Commonwealth, since 1979; Vice Chairman, Scottish Environmental Education Council; Chairman, West of Scotland District, WEA, since 1982. Publications: The Cold War, 1972; World Today (Co-author); Europe Today (Co-author); Britain Today (Co-author). Recreations: swimming; travel. Address: (h.) 12 Somerford Road, Bearsden, Glasgow, G61 1AS; T.-041-942 4933.

Nicolson, David M., CA. Office Managing Partner, KPMG Peat Marwick, Edinburgh, since 1988; b. 22.4.42, Edinburgh; m., Elizabeth Finlay Smith; 1 s.; 1 d. Educ. Royal High School, Edinburgh. Qualified as CA with Robertson & Maxtone Graham, Edinburgh, 1964; Peat Marwick Mitchell & Co., London, 1964-67; returned to Robertson & Maxtone Graham, 1967 (now KPMG Peat Marwick). President, Edinburgh Junior Chamber of Commerce, 1975-76; Vice President, Edinburgh Chamber of Commerce and Manufactures, since 1990; Member of Council, Institute of Chartered Accountants of Scotland, since 1987. Recreations: golf; tennis; skiing; gardening. Address: (b.) Saltire Court, 20 Castle Terrace, Edinburgh, EH1 2EG; T.-031-222 2000.

Nicolson, Ronald Samuel, MChemA, FIFST, CChem, FIWEM, FRSC. Regional Chemist, Public Analyst and Agricultural Analyst, Strathclyde Regional Council; b. 8.1.30, Toronto; m., Jean; 1 s.; 3 d. Educ. Larkhall Academy; Royal Technical College, Glasgow. Laboratory Assistant, Lanark County Council Public Analyst Laboratory, 1946-53; National Service, 1953-55; Senior Analyst, A. Dargie, Consultant Public Analyst, Dundee, 1953-56; Public Analyst, City of Dundee, and County Analyst, Angus, Fife, Perth and Kinross, 1956-73; Corporation Chemist and Public Analyst, Corporation of Glasgow, 1973-74. Chairman, Scottish Food Coordinating Committee; Member, Food Advisory Committee; Elder, Church of Scotland. Recreations: bowling; country dancing. Address: (b.) 8 Elliot Place, Glasgow, G3 8EJ; T.-041-227 2380.

Nimmo, Ian Atholl, MA (Cantab), PhD (Edin). University Teacher, since 1963; b. 22.11.40, Calcutta; m., Anne Elizabeth Mary Bauermeister; 1 s.; 1 d. Educ. Rugby; Emmanuel College, Cambridge. President, Scottish Squash Rackets Association, 1987-89; Treasurer, Scottish Sports Association, since 1990. Recreations: angling; hill-walking; running; squash. Address: (h.) Airlie Lodge, 5 Whitehouse Terrace, Edinburgh, EH9 2EU; T.-031-447 4735.

Nimmo, Myra A., BSc, PhD. Assistant Principal, Jordanhill College of Education, since 1991; Member, Scottish Sports Council, since 1990; b. 5.1.54, Edinburgh; m., Dr. J.A. Macaskill; 2 s. Educ. Westbourne School for Girls; Glasgow University. Temporary Lecturer, Glasgow University, 1978-80; Wellcome Research Fellow, 1980-82; Lecturer in Physiology, Queen's College, Glasgow, 1982-84, Senior Lecturer in Physiotherapy and research, 1984-87, Acting Head, Department of Physiotherapy, 1987-88; Assistant

Director, Scottish Vocational Education Department, 1988-91. Olympic athlete. Recreation: general fitness. Address: (b.) Jordanhill College of Education, Southbrae Drive, Glasgow, G13 1PP; T.-041-950 3530.

Nimmo Smith, William Austin, QC, BA, LLB. Advocate, since 1969; Scottish Law Commissioner, since 1988; b. 6.11.42, Edinburgh; m., Dr. Jennifer Nimmo Smith; 1 s.; 1 d. Educ. Eton; Balliol College, Oxford; Edinburgh University. Standing Junior Counsel, Department of Employment, 1977-82; QC, 1982; Advocate Depute, 1983-86; Chairman, Medical Appeal Tribunals and Vaccine Damage Tribunals, 1986-91; Member (part-time), Scottish Law Commission, since 1988. Recreations: hill-walking; music. Address: (h.) 29 Ann Street, Edinburgh, EH4 1PL.

Nisbet, Hugh Haddow, MA (Hons), DipEd. Headteacher, Paisley Grammar School, since 1989; b. 20.4.40, Barrhead; m., Lilian; 1 s.; 1 d. Educ. Paisley Grammar School; Glasgow University. Teacher, Crookston Castle Secondary School, Glasgow, 1963-69; Principal Teacher of History, Glenwood Secondary School, Glasgow, 1969-71; Assistant Head Teacher: Riverside Secondary School, Glasgow, 1971-75, Crookston Castle Secondary School, 1975-77; Headteacher, Stanely Green High School, Paisley, 1977-89. Recreations: reading; tropical fish-keeping; junior football; golf. Address: (b.) Paisley Grammar School, Glasgow Road, Paisley, PA1 3RP; T.-041-889 3484.

Nisbet, John Andrew, BSc, MSc, CEng, MICE, FCIT, MBIM. Chief Executive, Dumbarton District Council, since 1989; b. 20.6.44, Haverfordwest; m., Patricia Phillips; 1 s.; 2 d. Educ. Milford Haven Grammar School; University College of Swansea; Birmingham University. Transport Economist, Economist Intelligence Unit, 1969-70; Transport Planner: Monmouthshire CC, 1970-71, Glamorgan CC, 1971-74; County Transportation Officer, West Glamorgan CC, 1974-75; Planning Manager, Strathclyde PTE, 1975-86; Chief Engineer, Strathclyde Buses, 1986-88; Director of Services, Broadland District Council, 1988. Recreations: jogging; swimming; croquet; hill-walking; music and drama. Address: (b.) Crossleb House, Argyll Avenue, Dumbarton; T.-0389 65100.

Nisbet, Professor John Donald, OBE, MA, BEd, PHD, FEIS. Professor of Education, Aberdeen University, 1963-88; b. 17.10.22, Rosyth; 1 s.; 1 d. Educ. Dunfermline High School; Edinburgh University; Aberdeen University. RAF, 1943-46; Teacher, 1946-48; Lecturer, 1949-63; Visiting Professor, San Jose, 1961, 1964, Monash, Australia, 1974, Waikato, New Zealand, 1978. Chairman: Educational Research Board, 1972-75, Scottish Committee on Primary Education, 1974-80, Scottish Council for Research in Education, 1975-78; President, British Educational Research Association, 1975; Editor, British Journal of Educational Psychology, 1967-74; Editor, Studies in Higher Education, 1979-84; Editor, World Yearbook of Education, 1985. Recreations: golf; orienteering. Address: (h.) 7 Lawson Avenue, Banchory, AB31 3TW; T.-03302 3145.

Niven, Catharine, BSc, AMA, FSA(Scot). Curator, Inverness Museum and Art Gallery, since 1984; b. 23.9.52, Denbigh; m., Roger Niven. Educ. Loughton High School; Leicester University. Freelance archaeologist, working in Britain and Scandinavia; Keeper of Antiquities, Rotherham Museum, 1979-81; Assistant Curator (Archaeology), Inverness Museum and Art Gallery, 1981-84. Recreation: music. Address: (b.) Castle Wynd, Inverness, IV2 3ED; T.-0463 237114.

Niven, Peter Stuart Buchanan, LLB. Secretary – Legal Education, Law Society of Scotland; b. 18.8.57, Edinburgh; m., Lynne Temporal. Educ. George Watson's College,

Edinburgh; Edinburgh University. Apprenticed to Robson, McLean & Paterson, WS, 1978-80; Qualified Assistant: Fyfe Ireland & Co., WS, 1980-82; Shepherd & Wedderburn, WS, 1982-84. Member, Vestry, Old St. Paul's Scottish Episcopal Church, since 1983. Recreations: tennis; choral singing; listening to good music; eating out. Address: (h.) 14 Wolseley Crescent, Edinburgh; T.-031-659 6229.

Niven, Stuart Matthew, BSc, DipEd. Director, Scottish School of Further Education, and Senior Assistant Principal, Jordanhill College of Education; b. 1.3.36, Clydebank; m., Jean K. McPhee; 1 s.; 1 d. Educ. Clydebank High School; Glasgow University. Teacher of Mathematics and Physics: Clydebank High School, 1959, Stow College of Engineering, 1961; Head, Department of Mathematics and Physics, Kilmarnock College, 1964; Jordanhill College of Education: Lecturer in Mathematics, 1967, Senior Lecturer in Further Education, 1968, Principal Lecturer, 1970. Member, CNAA Further Education Board, 1978-84; Chairman, Editorial Board, Journal for Further and Higher Education in Scotland, 1976-83; Chairman, National Liaison Committee on Training of Teachers of Nursing, Midwifery and Health Visiting, 1983-88; Member, National Board for Scotland and the UK Central Council for Nursing, Midwifery and Health Visiting, since 1989; Vice-President for Europe, International Vocational Education and Training Association, since 1990. Publications: Vocational Further Education in Scotland, 1982; Professional Development of Further Education Lecturers in Scotland: Towards Comprehensive Provision, 1987. Recreation: golf. Address: Jordanhill College of Education, 76 Southbrae Drive, Glasgow, G13 1PP; T.-041-950 3121.

Nixon, Christopher William, NDA, CertEd. Principal, Oatridge Agricultural College, since 1985; b. 7.11.45, Grappenhall; m., Susan Doreen Presley; 1 s.; 2 d. Educ. Normain College, Chester; Harper Adams Agricultural College. Lecturer in Agriculture/Extra Mural Lecturer, Newton Rigg, Penrith; Lecturer in Sheep Production/Senior Lecturer, Extra Mural, Bishop Burton; Depute Principal, Oatridge Agricultural College. Address: (h.) Bridgehill Farm, Harthill, Shotts, Lanarkshire, ML7 5TR; T.-0501 51257.

Nixon, Mary MacKenzie, OBE, MA (Hons), DipEd. Archivist, Scottish Girl Guides Association, 1979-90; b. Port Arthur, Canada. Educ. High School of Stirling; St. Andrews University. Assistant English Teacher, Riverside School, Stirling; Responsible Assistant, History, High School of Stirling, Falkirk High School; Responsible Assistant, English, Falkirk High School; Head, English Department, Grangemouth High School. Girl Guides Association: County Camp Adviser and Chairman, Training Committee, Stirlingshire; Scotland: Ranger Adviser, Training Adviser, Deputy Scottish Chief Commissioner; Co-ordinator, Silver Jubilee Scheme for Unemployed; Chairman, Netherurd Committee, Scottish Girl Guides Association Training Centre, 1981-85. Recreations: genealogy; archaeology; poetry. Address: (h.) Gartlea, 19 Station Road, Bannockburn, FK7 8LE.

Noble, Sheriff David, MA, LLB, WS, JP. Sheriff at Oban, Campbeltown and Fort William, since 1983; b. 11.2.23, Inverness; m., Marjorie Scott Smith; 2 s.; 1 d. Educ. Inverness Royal Academy; Edinburgh University. RAF Bomber Command, 1942-46; Miller Thomson & Robertson, WS, Edinburgh, 1950-83. Recreation: sailing. Address: (h.) Woodhouselee, North Connel, Argyll; T.-Connel 678.

Noble, David Hillhouse, LLB. Chief Executive, Skye and Lochalsh District Council, since 1974; b. 27.4.48, Paisley; m., Hilary; 1 s.; 2 d. Educ. Greenock Academy; Glasgow University. Legal and Administrative Assistant, Argyll County Council, 1972-73; Senior Legal and Administrative

Assistant, Inverness County Council, 1973-74. Address: (b.) Tigh na Sgire, Park Lane, Portree, IV51 9EP; T.-0478 2341.

Noble, Rev. George Strachan, DipTh. Minister, Newarthill linked with Carfin, since 1972; b. 29.9.31, Inverallochy, near Fraserburgh; m., Mary Kinsman Addison; 1 s.; 1 d. Educ. Inverallochy Public School; Fraserburgh Academy; Glasgow University; Aberdeen University. Apprentice Auctioneer, fish trade, Fraserburgh, 1948-50; Royal Artillery, 1950-52; Auctioneer, 1952-59; Manager and Director, fishing boat management/fish-selling firm, Fraserburgh, 1959-66; divinity student, 1966-71; Probationer Assistant Minister, Fraserburgh Old Parish Church, 1971-72. Member, Church and Nation Committee and Health and Healing Committee, Church of Scotland. Address: The Manse, Church Street, Newarthill, Motherwell, ML1 5HS; T.-0698 860316.

Noble (or Nobail), Sir Iain, Bt. of Ardkinglas and Eilean Iarmain, OBE, MA. Chairman, Noble and Company Ltd.; b. 8.9.35, Berlin. Educ. in China, Argentina and England; University College, Oxford. Scottish Council (Development and Industry), 1964-69; Noble Grossart Ltd., Edinburgh, 1969-72. Chairman, Seaforth Maritime Ltd., 1972-77; Director: Adam and Company plc, since 1983, New Scotland Insurance Group PLC, since 1986, and other companies; Proprietor, Fearann Eilean Iarmain; Member, Edinburgh University Court, 1970-73; Co-founder, Governor and Trustee, College of Sabhal Mor Ostaig, 1974-84; Chairman, Club Gniomhachas nan Gaidheal, 1989-90; Scotsman of the Year Award, 1982 (Knights Templar); Editor, Sources of Finance, 1967-69. Recreations: deasbad, comhradh, orain is ceol le deagh chompanaich. Address: An Oifig, Eilean Iarmain, An t-Eilean, Sgitheanach, IV43 8QR; T.-047 13-266; 5 Darnaway Street, Edinburgh, EH3.

Noble, Lillias Mary, BEd. Director, LEAD-Scotland (Linking Education and Disability), since 1988; b. 11.9.54, Vancouver. Educ. Larkhall Academy; Hamilton College of Education; Strathclyde University. Teacher of English and Assistant Principal Teacher, Thurso High School, 1975-80; Assistant Principal Teacher, Wester Hailes Education Centre, 1980-85; Save the Children Fund (Scotland), 1985-88. Recreations: escaping to the West Coast; reading feminist literature. Address: (b.) LEAD-Scotland, Queen Margaret College, Clerwood Terrace, Edinburgh, EH12 8TS; T.-031-339 5408.

Noble, Sir (Thomas Alexander) Fraser, Kt (1971), MBE (1947), MA, LLD, FRSE; b. 29.4.18, Cromdale; m., Barbara A.M. Sinclair; 1 s.; 1 d. Educ. Nairn Academy; Aberdeen University. Indian Civil Service, 1940-47; Lecturer in Political Economy, Aberdeen University, 1948-57; Secretary, Carnegie Trust for Scottish Universities, 1957-62; Vice-Chancellor, Leicester University, 1962-76; Principal, Aberdeen University, 1976-81; Past Chairman of numerous public service committees, including Scottish Standing Conference of Youth Service Organisations, Home Office Advisory Committee for Probation and After Care, Television Research Committee; Chairman, UK Committee of Vice Chancellors, 1970-72; former Member of Council, Association of Commonwealth Universities. Recreations: golf; listening to music. Address: (h.) Hedgerley, Victoria Street, Nairn; T.-Nairn 53151.

Noble, Timothy Peter, MA, MBA. Director: Noble & Company Ltd., Waverley Mining Finance plc, Independent Insurance Co. Ltd.; Chairman, Business Archives Council of Scotland; b. 21.12.43; m., Elizabeth Mary Aitken; 2 s.; 1 d. Educ. University College, Oxford; Gray's Inn, London; INSEAD, Fontainebleau. Recreations: wine; astronomy; spectrology; skiing; tennis; bridge. Address: (h.) Ardnahane, Barnton Avenue, Edinburgh; T.-031-336 3565.

Noel-Paton,(Frederick) Ranald, BA. Group Managing Director, John Menzies plc, since 1986; b. 7.11.38, Bombay; m., Patricia Anne Stirling; 4 d. Educ. Rugby School; McGill University. Investment Analyst, Greenshields Inc., 1962-63; Management Trainee, United Biscuits, 1964; various posts, British United Airways Ltd., 1965-70; various senior executive posts, British Caledonian Airways, 1970-86 (General Manager, West Africa, 1975-79, General Manager, Far East, 1980-86, Director, Caledonian Far East Airways, 1984-86); Director: Pacific Assets Trust plc, since 1986, General Accident Group plc, since 1987, Royal Bank of Scotland Group plc, since 1988, Macallan Glenlivet plc, since 1990. Recreations: fishing; walking; bird-watching; the arts. Address: (b.) 108 Princes Street, Edinburgh, EH2 3AA; T.-031-225 8555.

Nolan, Paul Walter. Chairman, Social Work Committee, Lothian Regional Council, since 1986; Secretary, Lothian Labour Group, since 1982; b. 4.8.50, Edinburgh; m., Kathleen McVey; 1 s.; 2 d. Youth work and social work, 1965-80; full-time politician, since 1980; Chairman, Craigmillar Festival Society; Chairman, Craigmillar Opportunities Trust; Chairman, Jack Kane Centre. Recreations: swimming; walking. Address: (h.) 8 Niddrie Marischal Crescent, Edinburgh; T.-031-657 1309.

Norris, Derrick S., BSc (Hons), FBCS, CEng. Director of Information Technology, Glasgow City Council, since 1979; b. 17.3.40, Liverpool; m., Pamela Anne; 1 s.; 1 d. Educ. Liverpool Institute; Liverpool University. Statistician/Programmer, Associated Octel, 1963-67; Senior Computer Assistant, Cheshire County Council, 1967-69; Senior Systems Analyst, Lancashire County Council, 1969-74; Deputy Computer Manager, Devon County Council, 1974-78; Assistant County Treasurer (Computer Services), Northamptonshire County Council, 1978-79. Recreations: swimming; walking; Stock Market; DIY. Address: (b.) 112 Ingram Street, Glasgow, G1 1ET; T.-041-227 4067.

North, Michael James, MA, PhD. Reader in Biochemistry, Stirling University, since 1989; b. 20.1.48, London; m., Barbara Lockwood; 1 d. Educ. East Barnet Grammar School; Hertford College, Oxford; Newcastle upon Tyne University. SRC Postdoctoral Fellow, Leicester University and Essex University, 1973-75; Lecturer in Biochemistry, Stirling University, 1975-85; Senior Lecturer, 1985-89. Convener, Scottish Branch, Society for General Microbiology, since 1988; Editor, Journal of General Microbiology, since 1989. Publication: Biochemical Protozoology (Joint Editor). Recreations: gardening; music; supporting Tottenham Hotspur FC. Address: (b.) Department of Biological and Molecular Sciences, Stirling University, Stirling, FK9 4LA; T.-0786 67764.

Norwell, Peter Smith, OBE, TD, JP. Honorary Sheriff, Perth; b. 14.4.12, Perth; m., Elisabeth May Edwards; 3 d. Educ. Dollar Academy. Lt.-Col., RASC, 1944; Secretary, Perthshire Territorial Army Association, 1960-62; Assistant Secretary, Angus, Perthshire and Fife Territorial Army Association, 1962-67; Managing Director, Norwells Perth Footwear Ltd., 1935-60; Town Councillor, Perth, 1946-52; Chairman, Perth Theatre Company, 1968-72. Address: (h.) Dura Den, Pitcullen Terrace, Perth, PH2 7EQ; T.-Perth 26789.

Oakley, Charles A., CBE, JP, LLD. Honorary President, Glasgow College of Technology, since 1985; Chairman, Central College of Commerce, Glasgow, since 1966; Honorary President, Scottish Film Council, since 1939; Hon. President, Citizens Theatre, Glasgow; b. 30.9.00, Portsmouth; m., Dr. Agnes Stewart (deceased); 2 d. Educ. Devonport High School; Glasgow University. Apprentice, John Brown's Shipyard, 1919-24; qualified naval architect; Lecturer in Industrial Psychology, Glasgow University, 1930-72 (seconded to Civil Service, 1939-53); Scottish Area Officer, Air Ministry; Scottish Controller, Ministry of Aircraft Production, 1940-45; also Controller, North of Ireland, 1944-45; Scottish Controller, Board of Trade, 1945-53; President, Glasgow Chamber of Commerce, 1963-65; President, Association of Scottish Chambers of Commerce, 1966-68. Publications including: Men at Work, 1946; The Second City, 1946.

O Baoill, Colm J.M., MA, PhD. Senior Lecturer in Celtic, Aberdeen University, since 1980; b. 22.9.38, Armagh; m., Frances G.R. O Boyle; 3 d. Educ. St. Patrick's College, Armagh; Queen's University, Belfast. Assistant Lecturer in Celtic, Queen's University, Belfast, 1962-65; Lecturer in Celtic, Aberdeen University, 1966-80. Publications: Bardachd Shilis Na Ceapaich, 1972; Eachann Bacach and Other Maclean Poets, 1979. Address: (h.) 19 King's Crescent, Old Aberdeen, Aberdeen; T.-Aberdeen 637064.

O'Brien, Francis Aloysius, BL, NP. Honorary Sheriff, Dumfries, since 1971; b. 30.8.07, Dumfries; m., Ellen Drysdale Johnstone; 2 d. Educ. St. Joseph's College, Dumfries; Edinburgh University. Depute Procurator Fiscal, 1941-62; Burgh Prosecutor, 1941-44. Dumfries Guild of Players, since 1924: Secretary, 17 years, Treasurer, 3 years, Master, 1973-78, Honorary Life Member, since 1957; Secretary/Treasurer, Dumfries Property Owners, 1941-57; Governor, St. Joseph's College, Dumfries, 1960-82; Dean of Faculty (Dumfriesshire), 1975-77. Recreations: golf; drama. Address: (h.) Belmont, Whinnyhill, Dumfries, DG2 8HE; T.-New Abbey 354.

O'Brien, Sir Frederick William Fitzgerald, KB, QC, MA, LLB. Sheriff Principal, Lothian and Borders, 1978-89; Commissioner, Northern Lighthouse Board, 1965-89; Convener of Sheriffs Principal, 1972-89; b. 19.7.17, Edinburgh; m., Audrey Muriel Owen; 2 s.; 1 d. Educ. Royal High School, Edinburgh; Edinburgh University. Called to Scottish Bar, 1947; QC, 1960; Commissioner, Mental Welfare Commission, 1962-65; Senior Advocate Depute, Crown Office, 1964-65; Sheriff Principal, Caithness, Sutherland, Orkney and Shetland, 1965-75; Interim Sheriff Principal, Aberdeen, Kincardine and Banff, 1969-71; Sheriff Principal, North Strathclyde, 1975-78; Interim Sheriff Principal, South Strathclyde, 1981; Member, Scottish Medical Practices Committee, 1973-76; Member, Scottish Records Advisory Council, 1974-83; Chairman, Sheriff Court Rules Council, 1975-81; Convener, General Council Business Committee, Edinburgh University, 1980-84; Past President, Royal High School FP Club (Honorary President, since 1980); Chairman, Edinburgh Sir Walter Scott Club, 1989. Recreations: music; golf. Address: (h.) 22 Arboretum Road, Edinburgh, EH3 5PN; T.-031-552 1923.

O'Brien, Most Rev. Keith Michael Patrick, BSc, DipEd. Archbishop of St. Andrews and Edinburgh, since 1985; b. 17.3.38, Ballycastle, Northern Ireland. Educ. Saint Patrick's, Dumbarton; Holy Cross Academy, Edinburgh; Edinburgh University; St. Andrew's College, Drygrange; Moray House College of Education. Teacher, St. Columba's High School, Fife; Assistant Priest, Kilsyth, then Bathgate; Spiritual

Director, St. Andrew's College, Drygrange; Rector, Blairs College, Aberdeen; ordained Archbishop by Cardinal Gray, 1985. Recreations: music; walking. Address: Saint Bennet's, 42 Greenhill Gardens, Edinburgh, EH10 4BJ.

Odoni, Professor Robert W.K., BSc (Econ), PhD (Cantab). Professor of Pure Mathematics, Glasgow University, since 1989; b. 14.7.47, London; m., Josephine Ann; 2 s.; 1 d. Educ. Queen Elizabeth Grammar School, Barnet; Exeter University: Downing College, Cambridge. Temporary Lecturer in Pure Mathematics, Liverpool University, 1971-72; Research Fellow, Glasgow University, 1972-73;Exeter University: Lecturer in Pure Mathematics, 1973-79, Reader in Number Theory, 1979-85, Professor of Number Theory, 1985-89. Editorial Adviser, London Mathematical Society. Publications: 50 research papers. Recreations: country walks; swimming; cricket; music; literature; history; languages. Address: (b.) Department of Mathematics, University Gardens, Glasgow, G12 8QW; T.-041-339 8855, Ext. 5179.

O'Farrell, Professor Patrick Neil, BA, PhD, MIPI. Professor of Economics, Heriot-Watt University, since 1986; b. 18.4.41; m.; 3 d. Educ. Trinity College, Dublin. Assistant in Geography, Trinity College, Dublin, 1963-65; Assistant Lecturer and Lecturer in Geography, Queen's University, Belfast, 1965-70; Lecturer in Geography, New University of Ulster, 1971-73; Lecturer, Senior Lecturer and Reader in Planning, UWIST, 1973-86. Recreations: golf; talking; music. Address: (b.) Heriot-Watt University, Riccarton, Edinburgh, EH14 4AS.

Ogden, Professor Raymond William, MA, PhD, FRSE. George Sinclair Professor of Mathematics, Glasgow University, since 1984 (Head of Department, since 1986); b. 19.9.43, Lytham; m., Susanne; 2 s.; 2 d. Educ. Leamington College; Gonville and Caius College, Cambridge. Science Research Council Research Fellow, East Anglia University, 1970-72; Lecturer, then Reader in Mathematics, Bath University, 1972-80; Professor of Mathematics, Brunel University, 1981-84. Publication: Non-linear Elastic Deformations, 1984. Recreations: playing squash; walking; music; gardening. Address: (b.) Department of Mathematics, Glasgow University, Glasgow, G12 8QW; T.-041-339 8855.

Ogilvie, Lorna Margaret, BSc, MSc, FRMetS. Headmistress, St. Margaret's School for Girls, Aberdeen, since 1989; b. 22.3.47, Edinburgh. Educ. Mary Erskine School for Girls; Edinburgh University; University of Calgary; Moray House College of Education. Geography Teacher, Inverness High School, 1972-73; Head of Geology and Teacher of Geography, Royal Russell School, Croydon, 1973-82; Assistant Rector, Morrison's Academy, Crieff, 1982-88. Recreations: Scottish country dancing; skiing; golf; theatre; travel; reading. Address: (b.) 17 Albyn Place, Aberdeen, AB9 1RH; T.-0224 584466.

Ogilvie, Margaret Elizabeth. Owner/Gardener, Pitmuies Gardens, since 1966; b. 21.12.29, Co. Down; m., Douglas Farquhar Ogilvie (deceased); 1 s.; 2 d. Educ. Central School of Art and Crafts, London. Prior to marriage, advertising manager and book designer/typographer; National Trust for Scotland: Member of Council (twice), Member, Executive Council, 10 years; Member, Gardens Committee and Countryside Advisory Committee; Member, Council, Scottish Landowners Federation; Member, Council, APRS; Member, Scottish Council for National Parks; Member, Committee, Scottish Museums of Year Award. Recreations: riding; skiing; music; travelling. Address: (h.) House of Pitmuies, by Forfar, Angus; T.-024 12 245.

Ogilvie-Laing of Kinkell, Gerald, NDD, ARBS. Sculptor; b. 11.2.36; 3 s.; 1 d. Educ. Berkhamsted School; RMA, Sandhurst. Commissioned Fifth Fusiliers, 1955-60; resigned

commission and attended St. Martin's School of Art, 1960-64; lived in New York, 1964-69; Artist in Residence, Aspen Institute for Humanistic Studies, Colorado, 1966; moved to north of Scotland, 1969, and restored ruins of Kinkell Castle; Civic Trust Award, 1971; established a tapestry workshop in north of Scotland; Visiting Professor, University of New Mexico, 1976-77; set up bronze foundry, Kinkell Castle, to produce own work; Member, Art Committee, Scottish Arts Council, 1978-80; Professor of Sculpture, Columbia University, New York, 1986-87; appointed Commissioner, Royal Fine Art Commission for Scotland, 1987; divides time between north of Scotland and New York; public sculpture includes Callanish, 1971; Frieze of the Wise and Foolish Virgins, 1980; Fountain of Sabrina, 1982; Conan Doyle Memorial, 1991; Axis Mundi, 1991. Address: (h.) Kinkell Castle, Ross and Cromarty, IV7 8AT; T.-0349 61485.

Ogilvy, Sir David (John Wilfrid), 13th Bt, DL. Farmer and Landowner; Deputy Lieutenant, East Lothian, since 1971; b. 3.2.14; m., Penelope Mary Ursula Hills; 1 s. Educ. Eton; Trinity College, Oxford. RNVR, 1939-45. Address: (h.) Winton Cottage, Pencaitland, East Lothian, EH34 5AT.

Ogle, Ian Henry, CA. Audit Partner (Glasgow), Ernst & Young; Director: CBI Scottish Council, Scottish Chamber Orchestra; Member, Governing Council, SCOTBIC; President, Glasgow Chamber of Commerce; b. 26.4.34, London; 2 s.; 2 d. Educ. Glasgow Academy. Arthur Young: Executive Partner, 1975-78, Managing Partner, 1978-85, Regional Managing Partner, 1985-86. Recreations: golf; swimming; orchestral music. Address: (b.) George House, 50 George Square, Glasgow, G2 1RR; T.-041-552 3456.

O'Grady, Richard John Peard, MA (Hons). Director/Secretary, Zoological Society of Glasgow and West of Scotland, since 1972; b. 6.7.49, Cambridge; m., Maria Ann; 2 s. Educ. King's School, Bruton; Dundee University. Weekly pets feature, Daily Record, since 1976; D. of E. Inspector of Zoos, since 1982; Member, Clyde/Calders Conservation Committee. Recreations: family; son's hobbies: visiting zoos, parks, reserves; natural history. Address: (b.) Glasgow Zoo, Calderpark, Uddingston, Glasgow, G71 7RZ; T.-041-771 1185.

Ogston, Rev. David Dinnes, MA, BD. Minister, St. John's Kirk of Perth, since 1980; b. 25.3.45, Ellon, Aberdeenshire; m., Margaret Macleod; 2 d. Educ. Inverurie Academy; King's College and Christ's College, Aberdeen. Assistant Minister, St. Giles' Cathedral, Edinburgh, 1969-73; Minister, Balerno, 1973-80. Publication: White Stone Country; Dry Stone Days. Recreations: late-night films on TV; Greek and Russian Ikons. Address: 15 Comely Bank Perth; T.-Perth 21755.

Ogston, Professor Derek, MA, MD, PhD, DSc, FRCPEdin, FRCP, FIBiol, FRSE, FRSA. Professor of Medicine, Aberdeen University, since 1983 (Dean, Faculty of Medicine, 1984-87; Vice-Principal, since 1987); b. 31.5.32, Aberdeen; m., Cecilia Marie; 1 s.; 2 d. Educ. King's College School, Wimbledon; Aberdeen University. Aberdeen University: Lecturer in Medicine, 1962-69, Senior Lecturer in Medicine, 1969-75, MRC Travelling Fellow, 1967-68, Reader in Medicine, 1975-76, Regius Professor of Physiology, 1977-83. Publications: Haemostasis: Biochemistry, Physiology and Pathology (Joint Editor), 1977; The Physiology of Hemostasis, 1983; Antifibrinolytic Drugs: Chemistry, Pharmacology and Clinical Usage, 1984; Venous Thrombosis: Causation and Prediction, 1987. Recreation: gardening. Address: (h.) 64 Rubislaw Den South, Aberdeen, AB2 6AX; T.-Aberdeen 316587.

O'Halloran, Sir Charles Ernest, KB. Chairman, Citizens Advice Scotland, 1988-90; b. 26.5.24, Liverpool; m., Annie Rowan; 1 s.; 2 d. Educ. Conway Central School, Birkenhead.

Member, Ayr Town Council, 1953-74 (Provost, 1964-67); Member, Strathclyde Regional Council, 1974-82 (Convener, 1978-82); Freeman, Ayr Burgh, 1975; Chairman, Irvine Development Corporation, 1983-85. Recreations: golf and walking (can be the same). Address: (h.) 40 Savoy Park, Ayr, KA7 2XA; T.-0292 266234.

Olcayto, Ender, BSc, MSc, PhD. Electronics and Telecommunications engineer; Senior Lecturer, Department of Electronic and Electrical Engineering, Strathclyde University; b. 4.6.40, Turkey; m., Joan St. John; 2 s. Educ. Turkey; Manchester University and UMIST. Turkish PO Research Laboratories, 1967-70; National Service, Turkish Armed Forces, 1970-71; Principal Engineer, Plessey Telecommunications Research Ltd., 1971-73; Lecturer, then Senior Lecturer, Strathclyde University, since 1973. Recreations: cycling; painting; sailing. Address: (h.) Barbreck, 1 Granville Street, Helensburgh, G84 7HN; T.-0436 75190.

Oliver, Ian Thomas, QPM, LLB, MPhil, PhD. Chief Constable, Grampian Police; b. 24.1.40, London; m., Elsie; 2 s.; 1 d. Educ. Grammar School, Hampton, Middlesex; Nottingham University; Strathclyde University. RAF, 1959-61; Constable to Superintendent, Metropolitan Police, 1961-77; Northumbria Police: Chief Superintendent, 1977, Assistant Chief Constable (Management Services), 1978; Chief Constable, Central Scotland, 1979. Clerk/Treasurer, Sir James Duncan Medal Trust; Churchill Fellow, 1986. Publication: Police, Government and Accountability, 1987. Address: (b.) Police Headquarters, Queen Street, Aberdeen; T.-Aberdeen 639111.

Oliver, James Kenneth Murray. Farmer; Honorary Vice President, Royal Highland and Agricultural Society of Scotland, since 1962; b. 1.2.14, Hawick; m., Rhona Mary Purdom Wilkinson; 1 s.; 1 d. Educ. Merchiston Castle, Edinburgh. Army, 1939-46; Chairman, Oliver Homes (Manufacturing); as racehorse trainer, trained almost 1,000 winners under National Hunt Rules; rode winner, Scottish Grand National, 1950; trained five winners, Scottish Grand National; four times runner-up, Grand National; trained winners for the Queen Mother; Director, Doncaster Bloodstock Sales Ltd.; Secretary, Teviotdale Farmers Club. Recreations: hunting; racing; golf; tennis; squash; gardening. Address: (h.) Hassendean Bank, Hawick; T.-0450 87 216.

Oliver, Professor Michael Francis, CBE, MD, MDhc (Bologna and Stockholm), FRCP, FRCPEdin, FFCM, FACC, FRSE. Director, Wynn Institute for Metabolic Research, London, and Honorary Professor, National Heart and Lung Institute, London; Duke of Edinburgh Professor of Cardiology, Edinburgh University, 1979-89; Senior Cardiologist and Physician, Edinburgh Royal Infirmary, 1978-89; b. 3.7.25, Borth; m., 1, Margaret Y. Abbey; 2 s.; 1 s. (deceased); 1 d.; 2, Helen L. Daniel. Educ. Marlborough College, Wiltshire; Edinburgh University. Consultant Physician, Royal Infirmary, and Senior Lecturer in Medicine, Edinburgh University, 1961; Reader in Medicine, 1973; Personal Professor of Cardiology, 1977; Member, Scientific Board, International Society of Cardiology, 1968-78 (Chairman and Council on Atherosclerosis); Chairman, British Atherosclerosis Group, 1970-75; Member, Cardiovascular Panel, Government Committee on Medical Aspects of Food Policy, 1971-74 and 1982-84; UK Representative, Advisory Panel for Cardiovascular Diseases, World Health Organisation, since 1972; Chairman, BBC-Medical Advisory Group in Scotland, 1975-81; Council Member, British Heart Foundation, 1976-84; Convener, Cardiology Committee, Scottish Royal Colleges, 1978-81; President, British Cardiac Society, 1981-85; President, Royal College of Physicians of Edinburgh, 1985-88; Chairman, Honorary Advisory Panel, Cardiovascular Conditions for

Fitness to Drive, 1983-90; Purkinje Medal, 1981; Polish Cardiac Society Medal, 1984; FRACP, 1988; FRCPI, 1988. Publications: 300 medical and scientific papers and five books. Recreations: questioning; all things Italian. Address: (h.) Barley Mill House, Pencaitland, East Lothian, EH34 5EP.

Olver, Professor Richard Edmund, BSc, MB, FRCP, FRCPE. James Mackenzie Professor of Child Health, Dundee; b. 26.10.41, Ayr; m.; 2 s.; 2 d. Educ. London University. House Officer and Senior House Officer posts, St. Thomas's, Addenbrookes and Brompton Hospitals, 1966-69; Lecturer, Senior Lecturer, Reader, Department of Paediatrics, University College, London, 1969-85; MRC Travelling Fellow, Cardiovascular Research Institute, San Francisco, 1973-74; Consultant Paediatrician, University College Hospital, London, 1975-85. Address: (b.) Dundee University, Dundee.

O'Malley, Thomas John, BSc (Hons), DipEd. Headmaster, St. David's High School, Dalkeith, since 1975; Chairman, Lothian Regional Consultative Committee on Secondary Education, 1983-87; Chairman, Catholic Headteachers' Association of Scotland, 1984-86; Member, Scottish Consultative Council on the Curriculum, 1986-91; b. 7.4.37, Edinburgh; m., Maureen; 1 s.; 2 d. Educ. Holy Cross Academy, Edinburgh; Edinburgh University; Moray House College of Education. Assistant Teacher, Holy Cross Academy, 1960-63; Principal Teacher of Chemistry, St. Mary's Academy, Bathgate, 1963-67; Principal Teacher of Physical Sciences, Lawrence Park Collegiate Institute, Toronto, 1967-69; Principal Teacher of Chemistry, St. Anthony's Secondary School, Edinburgh, 1969-72; Assistant Head Teacher, Holyrood High School, Edinburgh, 1972-75. Member: Munn Committee, 1975-77, Archbishop O'Brien's Advisory Committee on Education. Recreations: Direector, Hibernian FC; golf; hill-walking. Address: (b.) Abbey Road, Dalkeith, EH22 3AD; T.-031-663 1961.

O'Neill, Basil, MA, BPhil. Senior Lecturer, Department of Philosophy, Dundee University, since 1976; President, Scottish Phenomenology Society, since 1986; b. 22.8.36, Wallasey; m., Louise; 1 s.; 1 d. Educ. King's School, Chester; Balliol College, Oxford. Technical Services (Sales), British Calculating Machines, 1958-60; Junior Lecturer in Philosophy, Trinity College, Dublin, 1962-65; Lecturer in Philosophy, Dundee University, 1965-76. Recreation: climbing. Address: (b.) Department of Philosophy, Dundee University, Dundee, DD1 4HN; T.-0382 23181.

O'Neill, Professor John Cochrane, BA, BD, PhD. Professor of New Testament Language, Literature and Theology, Edinburgh University, since 1985; b. 8.12.30, Melbourne; m., Judith Beatrice Lyall; 3 d. Educ. Melbourne Church of England Grammar School; Melbourne University; Ormond College Theological Hall; University of Gottingen; Clare College, Cambridge. Senior Tutor in History, Melbourne University, 1953-55; Lecturer in New Testament Studies, Ormond College Theological Hall, Melbourne, 1960-64; Dunn Professor of New Testament Language, Literature and Theology, Westminster College, Cambridge, 1964-85. Publications: Paul's Letter to the Romans, 1975; The Bible's Authority: a portrait gallery of thinkers from Lessing to Bultmann, 1991. Recreations: swimming; walking. Address: (h.) 9 Lonsdale Terrace, Edinburgh, EH3 9HN; T.-031-229 6070.

O'Neill, Martin (John), BA (Econ). MP (Labour), Clackmannan, since 1983 (East Stirlingshire and Clackmannan, 1979-83); b. 6.1.45; m., Elaine Samuel; 2 s. Educ. Trinity Academy, Edinburgh; trades union and evening classes; Heriot-Watt University; Moray House College of Education. President, Scottish Union of Students, 1970-71; school teacher, 1974-79; Tutor, Open University, 1976-79.

Member, Select Committee, Scottish Affairs, 1979-80; Opposition Spokesman, Scottish Affairs, 1980-84; Opposition Spokesman on Defence, 1984-88; Shadow Defence Secretary, since 1988. Recreations: watching football; reading; listening to jazz; cinema. Address: (b.) 19 Mar Street, Alloa, FK10 1HR; T.-0259 721536.

O'Reilly, Denis St. John, MSc, MD, MRCPath. Consultant Clinical Biochemist, Royal Infirmary, Glasgow, since 1984; b. 30.3.51, Cork; m., Margaret M.P. Lucey; 2 s.; 1 d. Educ. Presentation Brothers College, Cork; University College, Cork; Birmingham University. Registrar, Queen Elizabeth Medical Centre, Birmingham, 1978; Senior Registrar, Bristol Royal Infirmary, 1978-84; Ainsworth Scholar-Research Fellow, Norsk Hydro Institute for Cancer Research, Oslo, 1982. Recreation: hill-walking. Address: (h.) 47 Strathblane Road, Milngavie, G62 8HA.

Ormiston, Linda, MA, DRSAMD. Mezzo Soprano Singer; b. 15.1.48, Motherwell. Educ. Dalziel High School, Motherwell; Glasgow University; Royal Scottish Academy of Music and Drama; London Opera Centre. Freelance Singer, since 1980; sung all over Britain and France, Belgium, Italy, Germany, Austria, Holland and Yugoslavia; sings regularly at Glyndebourne; also well-known in lighter vein and as a member of The Music Box; recordings include HMS Pinafore and Ruddigore with New Sadlers Wells Opera and Tell Me Pretty Maiden; recently made debut in New York and Vancouver; recent appearances with Opera North, Leeds. Member, Scottish Arts Council. Recreations: playing the piano; skating; golf. Address: (h.) 39 Colinhill Road, Strathaven, ML10 6HF.

Orr, David Campbell, MA. Director, Scottish Federation of Housing Associations, since 1990; Chair, Young Homelessness Group, since 1992; b. 27.3.55, Kirkconnel; m., Carol; 1 s.; 2 d. Educ. Dundee University. Deputy Warden, Iona Community, Community House, 1976-77; Team Leader, then Co-ordinator, Centrepoint, Soho, 1977-86; Director, Newlon Housing Trust, 1986-90. Recreations: watching sport – playing badly; cinema. Address: (b.) 40 Castle Street North, Edinburgh, EH2 3BN; T.-031-226 6777.

Orr, Gillean McNeill, MIPM, MBIM. Executive Director, Highland Perthshire Development Company Ltd., since 1991; Director, Locus Trading Ltd., Aberfeldy, since 1992; b. 16.7.38, Glasgow; m., Patricia Margaret Scott; 3 d. Educ. Kelvinside Academy. Hardie, Caldwell, Ker & Hardie, CAs, Glasgow, 1956-59; Shell-Mex and BP Ltd., 1960-75; BP Oil Ltd., 1976-88; Glasgow Opportunities Enterprise Trust, 1989-90. Recreations: brown trout fishing; golf; skiing; supporting Scottish rugby Grand Slam efforts. Address: (h.) Ballinduin, Strathtay, Pitlochry, PH9 0LP; T.-Strathtay 460.

Orr, Ian, MPS. Pharmacist; Honorary Sheriff, South Strathclyde, Dumfries and Galloway, since 1980; Lord Cornet (Standard Bearer), Lanark, since 1961; b. 14.3.26, Lanark; m., Dora Hickey; 1 s. Educ. Lanark Grammar School; Strathclyde University. National Service, RAMC, Egypt, 1947-49. Past President, Lanark Rotary Club; President, Dante Alighieri Society (Diploma Di Benemerenza and Silver Medal). Recreations: fox-hunting; golf; foreign travel. Address: (h.) Gezira, St. Patrick's Road, Lanark; T.-0555 2810.

Orr, John, OBE, BA, DipFM, FBIM. Deputy Chief Constable, Dumfries and Galloway, since 1990; b. 3.9.45, Kilmarnock; m., Joan; 2 s.; 1 d. Educ. James Hamilton Academy, Kilmarnock; Open University; Glasgow University. Entered police as cadet, Renfrew and Bute, 1961. Recreations: Rotary; reading; gardening; angling. Address: (b.) Police Headquarters, Loreburn Street, Dumfries, DG1 1HP; T.-0387 52112.

Orr Ewing, Major Edward Stuart, DL, JP. Lord Lieutenant, Wigtown District, since 1989; b. 28.9.31, London; m., 1, F.A.B. Farquhar (m. dissolved); 2, Diana Mary Waters; 1 s.; 2 d. Educ. Sherborne; RMCS, Shrivenham. Black Watch RHR, 1950-69 (Major); Farmer and Landowner, since 1964. Recreations: country sports; skiing; sailing; painting. Address: (h.) Dunskey, Portpatrick, Stranraer; T.-Portpatrick 211.

Orr Ewing, Major Sir Ronald Archibald, 5th Bt; b. 14.5.12; m., Marion Hester; 2 s.; 2 d. Educ. Eton; Sandhurst. Scots Guards, 1932-53 (Major); DL, Perthshire, 1963; JP, Perthshire; Grand Master Mason of Scotland, 1965-69. Address: (h.) Cardross, Kippen, Stirling, FK8 3DY.

Osborne, Hon. Lord (Kenneth Hilton Osborne), QC (Scot). Senator of the College of Justice, since 1990; b. 9.7.37. Advocate, 1962; QC, 1976; Chairman, Local Government Boundary Commission, since 1990.

Osler, Douglas Alexander, MA (Hons), DipRE. HM Chief Inspector of Schools, Scottish Office Education Department; b. 11.10.42, Edinburgh; m., Wendy I. Cochrane; 1 s.; 1 d. Educ. Royal High School, Edinburgh; Edinburgh University; Moray House College of Education. Assistant Teacher of History/Careers Master, Liberton Secondary School, Edinburgh, 1965-68; Principal Teacher of History, Dunfermline High School, 1968-74. English Speaking Union Fellowship to USA, 1966; International Visitor Program to USA, 1989. Publications: Queen Margaret of Scotland; Sources for Modern Studies, Volumes 1 and 2. Address: (b.) Room 4/107, New St. Andrew's House, Edinburgh.

Owen, Professor David Gareth, MA, BD (Hons), PhD, FICE, CEng. Professor of Offshore Engineering, Heriot-Watt University, since 1986; b. 6.11.40, Brecon, Wales; m., Ann Valerie Wright; 2 d. Educ. Christ College, Brecon; Downing College, Cambridge. Graduate Engineer, John Laing & Son, London; Aerospace Engineer, Marconi Space and Defence Systems, Portsmouth; Lecturer in Civil Engineering, Heriot-Watt University; Visiting Professor, University of New Hampshire; Senior Lecturer, Department of Offshore Engineering, Heriot-Watt University. Recreations: music; travelling; skiing. Address: (h.) 7 Oak Lane, Edinburgh, EH12 6XH; T.-031-339 1740.

Owen, Professor Douglas David Roy, MA, PhD. Professor of French, St. Andrews, 1972-88; b. 17.11.22, Norton, Suffolk; m., Berit Mariann; 2 s. Educ. Cambridge and County High School; Nottingham High Pavement School; Nottingham University; St. Catharine's College, Cambridge. St. Andrews University: Lecturer, 1951-64, Senior Lecturer, 1964-71, Reader, 1971-72; General Editor, Forum for Modern Language Studies. Publications: Fabliaux (Joint Editor), 1957; The Evolution of the Grail Legend, 1968; The Vision of Hell, 1970; Arthurian Romance: Seven Essays (Editor), 1970; Two Old French Gauvain Romances (Joint Editor), 1972; The Song of Roland (Translator), 1972 (new edition, 1990); The Legend of Roland, 1973; Noble Lovers, 1975; Chretien de Troyes, Arthurian Romances (Translator), 1987; A Chat Round the Old Course, 1990; Guillaume le Clerc, Fergus of Galloway (Translator), 1991. Recreation: golf. Address: (h.) 7 West Acres, St. Andrews, KY16 9UD; T.-St. Andrews 73329.

Owens, Agnes. Author; b. 24.5.26, Milngavie; m., Patrick Owens; 2 s.; 4 d. Educ. Bearsden Academy. Worked in shops, factories and offices; came to writing by accident; author of Gentlemen of the West (Autumn Book Award, 1984) and Like Birds in the Wilderness; short stories in Lean Tales, The Seven Deadly Sins and The Seven Cardinal Virtues; wrote a play with Liz Lochhead which toured Scotland for three months. Recreations: walking; reading. Address: (h.) 21 Roy

348   WHO'S WHO IN SCOTLAND

Young Avenue, Balloch, Dunbartonshire; T.-Alexandria 50921.

Oxby, Dennis, BA, CA. Management Consultant; b. 18.8.55, Helensburgh. Educ. Dumbarton Academy; Strathclyde University. Director: Scottish Exhibition Centre Ltd. (Managing Director, since 1991), SSA Investment Company Ltd., Associated Events and Exhibitions Ltd., Scottish Exhibition and Conference Centre Ltd., Greater Glasgow Tourist Board and Convention Bureau Ltd., SEC Exhibitions Ltd. Recreation: hitting head off numerous brick walls. Address: (h.) 15 Riverview Drive, The Waterfront, Glasgow; T.-0836 737754.

P

Pacione, Professor Michael, MA, PhD. Professor of Geography, Strathclyde University, since 1990 (Head, Department of Geography, since 1986); b. 14.10.47, Dundee; m., Christine Hopper; 1 s.; 1 d. Educ. Lawside Academy, Dundee; Dundee University. Lecturer in Geography, Queens University, Belfast, 1973-75; Lecturer, Senior Lecturer, Reader, Strathclyde University, Glasgow, 1975-89. Publications: two books; editor of 13 books; 70 research papers. Recreations: sport; travel; photography. Address: (b.) Department of Geography, Strathclyde University, 50 Richmond Street, Glasgow, G1 1XH; T.-041-552 4400.

Pack, Professor Donald Cecil, CBE, MA, DSc, FIMA, FEIS, FRSE. Emeritus Professor, Strathclyde University, since 1986; b. 14.4.20, Higham Ferrers; m., Constance Mary Gillam; 2 s.; 1 d. Educ. Wellingborough School; New College, Oxford. Ordnance Board, Cambridge, 1941-43; Armament Research Department, Ministry of Supply, Fort Halstead, 1943-46; Lecturer in Mathematics, St. Andrews University, 1947-52; Visiting Research Associate, Maryland University, 1951-52; Lecturer in Mathematics, Manchester University, 1952-53; Professor of Mathematics, Strathclyde University, 1953-82 (Vice-Principal, 1968-72); Honorary Professor, 1982-86. (First) Hon. Member, European Consortium for Mathematics in Industry, 1988; Chairman, Scottish Certificate of Education Examination Board, 1969-77; Chairman, Committee of Inquiry into Truancy and Indiscipline in Scottish Schools, 1974-77 ("Pack Report" published by HMSO, 1977); Hon. President, National Youth Orchestra of Scotland (Chairman from foundation, 1978-88); Member, Scottish Arts Council, 1980-85; Member, UK Committee for European Music Year 1985 and Chairman, Scotland Advisory Committee, 1983-86; Member: General Teaching Council for Scotland, 1966-73, Dunbartonshire Education Committee, 1960-66; Governor, Hamilton College of Education, 1976-81; Council Member, Royal Society of Edinburgh, 1960-63; Honorary Treasurer and Council Member, Institute of Mathematics and its Applications, 1964-72; Member, International Advisory Committee on Rarefied Gas Dynamics Symposia, 1976-88; Member, British National Committee for Theoretical Mechanics, 1973-78; Council Member, Gesellschaft fuer angewandte Mathematik und Mechanik, 1977-83; Guest Professor: Technische Universitat, Berlin, 1967, Bologna University and Politechnico Milan, 1980, Technische Hochschule, Darmstadt, 1981; other visit-

ing appointments, Warsaw University, 1977, Kaiserslautern University, 1980-84. Past President: Edinburgh Mathematical Society, Glasgow Mathematical Association; President, Milngavie Music Club, since 1983. Recreations: music; gardening; golf. Address: (h.) 18 Buchanan Drive, Bearsden, Glasgow, G61 2EW; T.-041-942 5764.

Pagan, Graeme Henry, BL, WS. Solicitor, Hosack & Sutherland, Oban, since 1960; Chairman, Oban Housing Association, since 1971; Honorary Sheriff of North Strathclyde at Oban, since 1988; b. 20.3.36, Cupar; m., Heather; 1 s.; 2 d. Educ. New Park, St. Andrews; Bedford School; Edinburgh University. Part-time Procurator Fiscal, Oban, 1970-79; Regional Organiser, Shelter Campaign for the Homeless, 1968-75; Member, Committee, Oban Abbeyfield Society; Organiser, Scottish Solicitors Will Aid; Chairman, Argyll and Bute Liberal Democrats. Recreations: family; jazz; sport; malt whisky; politics; walking in the Highlands. Address: (h.) Neaveton, Oban, Argyll; T.-0631 63737.

Pagan, Rev. John, FRSA, FSA Scot. Parish Minister, St. Michael's, Dumfries, since 1978, also of Caerlaverock, since 1983; Chaplain, Dumfries Academy, since 1978; b. 23.4.25, Maryport, Cumberland; m., Frederica Janet Emmerson Anderson; 2 s.; 1 d. Educ. Creighton School, Carlisle; Westminster College, Cambridge. Student Assistant Minister, Balquidder, 1953-53; Ordained Minister, Presbyterian Church, Newbiggin-by-the-Sea, Northumberland, 1957; Robert Stewart Memorial Church, Newcastle upon Tyne, 1961; Presbyterian Congregation in Watford, 1968. Area Padre for SW Scotland, British Legion; Chaplain to various Scottish societies and Burns associations, Dumfries Cornets Club and Guild Nychburris Festival Association. Recreations: historical research; Burnsiana; bowls. Address: St. Michael's Manse, 39 Cardoness Street, Dumfries, DG1 3AL; T.-0387 53849.

Page, Professor Alan Chisholm, LLB, PhD. Professor of Public Law, Dundee University, since 1985 (Head, Department of Law, since 1986); b. 7.4.52, Broughty Ferry; m., Sheila Duffus; 1 s.; 1 d. Educ. Grove Academy; Edinburgh University. Lecturer in Law, University College, Cardiff, 1975-80; Senior Lecturer in Law, Dundee University, 1980-85. Publications: Legislation; Investor Protection. Recreation: mountaineering. Address: (h.) Westlands, Westfield Road, Cupar, Fife, KY15 5DR.

Page, Christopher Nigel, BSc, PhD, FLS. Principal Scientific Officer, Royal Botanic Garden, Edinburgh, since 1971; Honorary Lecturer, Department of Botany, Edinburgh University, since 1983; b. 11.11.42, Gloucester; m., 1, Pauline Ann (m. diss.); 1 s.; 2 d.; 2, Jane Clare; 1 d. Educ. Cheltenham Grammar School; Kings College, Durham; Newcastle-upon-Tyne University. NATO Overseas Research Fellow, Queensland University, 1968-70; Department of Rural Economy, Oxford University, 1970-71. Nuffield/Leverhulme Overseas Travel Fellow, 1976-77; Tutor, Scottish Field Studies Council, since 1973; Editor, British Fern Gazette, 1974-84; Specialist Adviser and Chairman, Conifer Conservation Committee, International Union for the Conservation of Nature, since 1986; Honorary Life Vice President, British Pteridological Society, since 1991. Publications: The Ferns of Britain and Ireland, 1982; Biology of Pteridophytes, 1984; Ferns (New Naturalist), 1988. Recreations: photography; walking; writing. Address: (h.) 17 Silverknowes Crescent, Edinburgh, EH4 5JE; T.-031-336 1142.

Page, Rev. Ruth, MA, BD, DPhil. Senior Lecturer, Faculty of Divinity, Edinburgh University, since 1989; Central Committee Member, World Council of Churches, since 1991; b. 15.9.35, Dundee. Educ. Harris Academy, Dundee; Stirling

High School; St. Andrews University; University of Otago; Oxford University. Schoolteacher 1958-68; ordained, Presbyterian Church of New Zealand, 1975; received into ministry of Church of Scotland, 1981; Lecturer in Theology, University of Otago, 1975; Lecturer in Divinity, Edinburgh University, 1979. Publications: Ambiguity and the Presence of God; The Incarnation of Freedom and Love. Recreations: gardening; walking; reading. Address: (b.) New College, Mound Place, Edinburgh, EH1 2LX; T.-031-225 8400.

Page Croft, Hugo Douglas. Managing Director, Wholesale, Scottish & Newcastle Breweries Ltd.; b. 23.5.44, Herts; m., Dawn; 3 s.; 1 d. Educ. Shrewsbury. Founder Director to MD, Moray Firth Maltings, 1967-86; MD, William Younger & Co., 1986-88; Director, Scottish & Newcastle Breweries PLC, since 1988; Chairman, Scottish Brewers, William Younger & Co., since 1988; Chairman, Newcastle Breweries Ltd., Home Brewery PLC, Matthew Brown PLC. Member, CBI Scottish Council; Member, Policy Review Committee, SCD&I. Recreation: shooting. Address: (b.) Abbey Brewery, Holyrood Road, Edinburgh; T.-031-556 2591.

Paine, Nigel, Chief Executive, Scottish Council for Educational Technology, since 1990; b. 25.4.52. Educ. Haberdasher's Aske's Hatcham Boys' School; Reading University; East Anglia University. English Speaking Union Thyne Scholar, 1984; Trustee, National Extension College, since 1987; Member, Training and Development Lead Body, since 1989; Member, BBC Education Broadcasting Council for Scotland, since 1989; Fellow, Institute of Training and Development. Recreations: running; reading; writing. Address: 74 Victoria Crescent Road, Dowanhill, Glasgow G12 9JN; T.-041-334 9314.

Palmer, Godfrey Henry Oliver, MIBiol, BSc, PhD, DSc, FIBrew. University Reader, International Centre for Brewing and Distilling, Heriot-Watt University, since 1977; Research Consultant; Visiting Professor and Research Scholar, University of Kyoto, Japan, 1991; b. 9.4.40, Elizabeth, Jamaica; m., Margaret Ann Wood. Educ. Shelbourne Secondary Modern School; Highbury County School; Leicester University; Edinburgh University; Heriot-Watt University. Technician, 1958-61; Brewing Research Foundation, 1968-77. Publication: Cereal Science and Technology, 1989. Recreations: reading; watching cereal fields; education of deprived children; friends; ball games; music. Address: (b.) Heriot-Watt University, Department of Biological Sciences, International Centre for Brewing and Distilling, Edinburgh; T.-031-449 5111.

Palmer, John Carrington, BSc, PhD. Chief Executive Officer, Citizens Advice Scotland, since 1986; b. 24.11.50, Nakuru, Kenya; m., Nicoline; 2 s. Educ. Marlborough College; LSE. Anthropological research, Kenya, 1973-75; Course Co-ordinator, Open University, 1978-80; Voluntary Service Overseas (Field Director, Kenya), 1980-83; VSO Programme Management Officer, London, 1983-86. Director, Scottish Education and Action for Development; Director, Energy Action Scotland. Recreations: cycling; walking; rugby; skiing; Woodcraft Folk. Address: (b.) 26 George Square, Edinburgh, EH8 9LD.

Palmer, Robert Allen, BA (Hons). Director of Performing Arts, Glasgow City Council, since 1991; Director, Glasgow Cultural Capital of Europe 1990 and Festivals Director, Glasgow City Council, 1987-91; Theatre Director, since 1971; b. 3.6.47, Toronto; m., Lynn Susan Winston; 1 s.; 1 d. Educ. Forrest Hill Collegiate; York University; Central London Polytechnic. Teacher of English and Drama, Inner London Education Authority and Surrey County Council, 1970-72; Director, Theatre Centre for Young People, 1971-73; Director, Theatremakers, MacRobert Arts Centre, Stirling, 1973-75; Director, Theatre Workshop, Edinburgh, 1975-80;

Drama and Dance Director, Scottish Arts Council, 1980-87. Member, Advisory Panel for Drama and Dance, British Council, 1980-87. Recreations: cooking; walking; music. Address: (h.) 28 Cathkin Road, Glasgow, G42.

Panton, John, MBE. Professional Golfer; b. 9.10.16, Pitlochry. Won PGA Match-Play Championship, 1956 (Runner-up, 1968); PGA British Seniors', 1967-69; World Seniors', 1967 (defeated Sam Snead for title); Silver King, 1950; Daks, 1951; North British-Harrogate, 1952; Goodwin Foursomes, 1952; Yorkshire Evening News, 1954; Gleneagles-Saxone Am.-Pro. Foursomes, 1956; Woodlawn Invitation Open (West Germany), 1958-59-60; leading British player, Open Championship, 1956; Leader, PGA Order of Merit (Vardon Trophy), 1951; won Scottish Professional Championship, seven times (and joint Champion, once); Ryder Cup player, 1951-53-61; awarded Golf Writers' Trophy, 1967; Hon. Professional, Royal and Ancient Golf Club, St. Andrews.

Park, Ian Michael Scott, CBE, MA, LLB. Partner, Paull & Williamsons, Advocates, Aberdeen, since 1961, Consultant, since 1991; Member, Criminal Injuries Compensation Board, since 1983; Council Member, Law Society of Scotland, 1974-85; b. 7.4.38, Aberdeen; m., Elizabeth M.L. Struthers; 2 s. Educ. Aberdeen Grammar School; Aberdeen University. Assistant to, subsequently Partner in, Paull & Williamsons; Member, Society of Advocates in Aberdeen, since 1962; sometime part-time Assistant, Department of Public Law, Aberdeen University; President, Law Society of Scotland, 1980-81; Chairman, Aberdeen Citizens Advice Bureau, until 1988; Secretary, Aberdeen Granite Association, 1962-84; frequent broadcaster on legal topics. Recreations: golf; gardening. Address: (h.) 46 Rubislaw Den South, Aberdeen.

Parker, Cameron Holdsworth, BSc. Managing Director, Lithgows Limited, since 1984; b. 14.4.32, Dundee; m., Marlyne Honeyman; 3 s. Educ. Morrison's Academy, Crieff; Glasgow University. Managing Director, latterly also Chairman, John G. Kincaid & Co. Ltd., Greenock, 1967-80; Chairman and Chief Executive, Scott Lithgow Ltd., Port Glasgow, 1980-83; Board Member, British Shipbuilders, 1977-80, 1981-83; Chief Executive, Prosper Enginering Ltd., Irvine, 1983-84. Liveryman, Worshipful Company of Shipwrights; Member, Council, CBI Scotland. Recreation: golf. Address: (b.) Netherton, Langbank, Renfrewshire, PA14 6YG; T.-047554 692.

Parker, Nicholas Sherren, MA (Cantab), FCA. Chartered Accountant; Partner, Coopers & Lybrand Deloitte, since 1978 (Partner in charge, Corporate Finance Scotland); b. 11.6.46, Edinburgh; m., Julia Caroline Hamilton Dunlop; 1 s.; 2 d. Educ. Edinburgh Academy; St. Catharine's College, Cambridge. Governor, Oxenfoord School. Recreations: shooting; golf; squash; fishing. Address: (h.) Erskine House, 68/73 Queen Street, Edinburgh, EH2 4NH; T.-031-226 4488.

Parkins, James J., BSc (Hons), PhD, CBiol, FIBiol. Head, University Department, Glasgow Veterinary School, since 1991; University Farm Academic Co-ordinator, since 1990; b. 27.7.45, Tynemouth; m., Elma; 1 s.; 1 d. Educ. Wolverhampton Grammar School; Glasgow University. Lecturer in Veterinary Animal Husbandry, 1970; Senior Lecturer, 1983, Reader, 1990, Glasgow University Veterinary School. Publications: over 100 papers. Recreations: the country; golf; music. Address: (b.) Glasgow University Veterinary School, Bearsden Road, Glasgow, G61 1QH; T.-041-339 8855, Ext. 5720.

Parnell, Brian K., BSc, ACGI, DipTP, FRTPI. Head, Department of Planning, Glasgow School of Art, 1976-87; Planning Consultant; Visiting Professor, Centre for Planning, Strathclyde University, since 1991; b. 18.12.22, Brighton; 2

s.; 1 d. Educ. Varndean School, Brighton; London University; Edinburgh College of Art. Captain, EME, 1943-47; Department of Planning, Midlothian County Council, 1949-57; Depute Planning Officer, Stirling County Council, 1957-64; joined Glasow School of Art, 1964; Commissioner, Countryside Commission for Scotland, 1968-80; part-time Planning Inquiry Reporter, Scottish Office, since 1982. Chairman, Association of Scientific Workers (Scottish Area), 1949-69; Member, Board of Governors, Heriot-Watt College, 1954-56; Chairman, Scottish Branch, Royal Town Planning Institute, 1972-73; Executive Committee Member, National Trust for Scotland, 1973-83; Trustee, Scottish Civic Trust, since 1985. Recreations: sailing; swimming; hill-walking; travel. Address: (h.) 15 Park Terrace, Stirling, FK8 2JT; T.-0786 65714.

Parr, Professor John Brian, BSc (Econ), MA, PhD. Titular Professor in Applied Economics, Glasgow University, since 1989 (Secretary, Centre for Urban and Regional Research, 1978-88); Chairman, British Section, Regional Science Association, 1981-85; b. 18.3.41, Epsom; m., Pamela Jean Harkins; 2 d. Educ. Henry Thornton School; London University; University of Washington Instructor, University of Washington, 1966; Assistant Professor/Associate Professor, University of Pennsylvania, 1967-75; joined Glasgow University as Lecturer, 1975. Editor, Papers of the Regional Science Association, 1968-75; Associate Editor, Journal of Regional Science, since 1978; Co-Editor, European Research in Regional Science, since 1990; Member, Board of Management, Urban Studies, since 1981. Publications: Christaller Central Place Structures (Co-author); Regional Policy: Past Experience and New Directions (Co-Editor); Analysis of Regional Structure: Essays in Honour of August Losch (Co-Editor); Market Centers and Retail Location (Co-author). Address: (b.) Department of Social and Economic Research, Glasgow University, Glasgow, G12 8RT; T.-041-339 8855, Ext. 4724.

Parratt, Professor James Roy, BPharm, MSc, PhD, DSc, MD (h.c.), MRCPath, DipRelStudies (Cantab), FRPharmS, FESC, FIBiol, FRSE. Professor of Cardiovascular Pharmacology, Strathclyde University, since 1983 (Head, Department of Physiology and Pharmacology, 1986-90); b. 19.8.33, London; m., Pamela Joan Lyndon Marels; 2 s.; 1 d. Educ. St. Clement Danes Holborn Estate Grammar School; London University. Spent nine years in Nigeria as Head of Pharmacology, Nigerian School of Pharmacy, then in Physiology, University Medical School, Ibadan; joined Strathclyde University, 1967; appointed Reader, 1970; Personal Professor, Department of Physiology and Pharmacology, 1975-83. Chairman, Cardiac Muscle Research Group, 1980-83; Gold Medal, Szeged University, 1975; Honorary Member, Hungarian Pharmacological Society, 1983; Honorary Doctorate, Albert Szent-Gyorgi Medical University, Hungary, 1989; Chairman, Universities and Colleges Christian Fellowship, 1984-90; former Vice-Chairman, Scripture Union; Past Chairman, SUM Fellowship; Lay Preacher, Baptist Unions of Scotland and Great Britain; Honorary President, Baptist Lay Preachers Association of Scotland, 1985-90. Recreation: music. Address: (h.) 16 Russell Drive, Bearsden, Glasgow, G61 3BD; T.-041-942 7164.

Parry, Kenneth Michael, OBE, MB, ChB, FRCPEdin, FFCM, FRCGP, DCH. Secretary, Scottish Council for Postgraduate Medical Education, since 1970; b. 28.5.29, Manchester; m., Maureen Anne Jones; 2 s.; 1 d. Educ. Bristol Grammar School; Bristol University. Senior Administrative Medical Officer, Eastern Regional Hospital Board, 1967-70; Council of Europe Medical Fellow, 1974; William Pickles Lecturer, Royal College of General Practitioners, 1977; Australian Universities Commonwealth Senior Fellow, 1980; Honorary Secretary, Association for Study of Medical Education, 1984-91. Recreations: music; painting. Address: (h.) 9 Moray Place, Edinburgh, EH3 6DS; T.-031-226 3054.

Parry-Jones, Professor William Llywelyn, MA, MD (Camb), BChir, FRCPsych, FRCP Glas, DPM Eng. Professor of Child and Adolescent Psychiatry, Glasgow University, since 1987; Honorary Consultant Psychiatrist, Greater Glasgow Health Board, since 1987; Supernumerary Fellow, Linacre College, Oxford, since 1987; b. 22.6.35, Ilford; m., Brenda Griffiths; 1 s.; 2 d. Educ. Llangefni Grammar School; Gonville and Caius College, Cambridge; London Hospital Medical College, London University. Lecturer in Psychiatry, Oxford University, 1969; Fellow, Linacre College, Oxford, 1969; Consultant in Adolescent Psychiatry, Highfield Adolescent Unit, Warneford Hospital, Oxford, 1972; Visiting Fellow, Gonville and Caius College, 1991. Publications include: The Trade in Lunacy, 1972. Recreations: collecting antiquarian medical books; travel; gardening. Address: (b.) Royal Hospital for Sick Children, Yorkhill, Glasgow, G3 8SJ; T.-041-339 8888, Ext. 4223.

Parsons, Professor Ian, BSc, PhD, FRSE. Professor of Mineralogy, Edinburgh University, since 1988; b. 5.9.39, Manchester; m., Brenda Mary Reah; 3 s. Educ. Beckenham and Penge Grammar School; Durham University. DSIR Research Fellow, Manchester University, 1963-64; Aberdeen University: Assistant Lecturer, 1964-65, Lecturer, 1965-77, Senior Lecturer, 1977-83, Professor, 1983-88. Former Member, NERC Geological Sciences Research Grants Committee and Geological Sciences Training Awards Committee; Vice-President, Mineralogical Society, 1981; Member, NCC Committee for Scotland, 1985-90. Recreations: skiing; hill-walking; music. Address: (b.) Department of Geology and Geophysics, Edinburgh University, West Mains Road, Edinburgh, EH9 3JW; T.-031-667 1081.

Parsons, Professor John William, BSc, PhD, FIBiol. Dean of Biological Science, 1989, and Professor of Soil Science, Aberdeen University, since 1981; b. 20.7.33, Wallasey; m., Gillian Mary; 3 s. Educ. Oldershaw Grammar School; Reading University. Postdoctoral Fellow, Delaware University, 1958-60; Lecturer and Senior Lecturer, Aberdeen University, 1960-81; Visiting Research Fellow, CSIRO Soils Division, Adelaide, 1972-73. Governor, Strathallan School; Member, Board of Management, Scottish Crop Research Institute. Recreations: hill-walking; reading. Address: (b.) Department of Plant and Soil Science, Aberdeen University, Aberdeen, AB9 2UD; T.-0224 272692.

Paternoster, Rev. Canon Michael Cosgrove, MA. Rector, St. James' Episcopal Church, Aberdeen, since 1990; Honorary Canon, St. Paul's Cathedral, Dundee, since 1981; b. 13.5.35, East Molesey, Surrey; m., Careth Osborne. Educ. Kingston Grammar School; Pembroke College, Cambridge; Cuddesdon Theological College. Deacon, 1961; Priest, 1962; Curate, St. Andrew's, Surbiton, 1961-63; Chaplain to Anglican students in Dundee, 1964-68; Secretary, Fellowship of St. Alban and St. Sergius, 1968-71; Rector, St. James', Dollar, 1971-75; Rector, St. James's, Stonehaven, 1975-90; Secretary, Inter-Church Relations Committee, Scottish Episcopal Church, 1975-82; Member, Doctrine Committee, Scottish Episcopal Church, 1980-91; Aberdeen and N.E. Wing Chaplain, Air Training Corps. Publications: Thou art There Also, 1967; Stronger Than Death, 1972. Recreations: reading; sketching; bird-watching; listening to music. Address: 31 Gladstone Place, Aberdeen, AB1 6UX; T.-0224 322631.

Paterson, Professor Alan Alexander, LLB (Hons), DPhil (Oxon). Professor of Law, Strathclyde University, since 1984; b. 5.6.47, Edinburgh; m., Alison Jane Ross Lowdon; 2 s.; 1 d. Educ. Edinburgh Academy; Edinburgh University;

Pembroke College, Oxford. Research Associate, Oxford Centre for Socio-Legal Studies, 1972-73; Lecturer, Law Faculty, Edinburgh University, 1973-84; Visiting Professor, University of New Mexico Law School, 1982, 1986. Former Chairman, Scottish Legal Action Group; Chairman, British and Irish Legal Education and Technology Association; Chairman, Legal Advice Group, Citizens Advice Scotland. Publications: The Law Lords, 1982; The Legal System of Scotland (Co-author), 1986. Address: (b.) Strathclyde University Law School, 173 Cathedral Street, Glasgow, G4 ORQ; T.-041-552 4400, Ext. 3341.

Paterson, Colin Ralston, MA, DM, MSc, FRCP, FRCPath. Senior Lecturer in Biochemical Medicine, Dundee University, since 1969; Honorary Consultant, Tayside Area Health Board, since 1971; b. 5.10.36, Manchester; m., Sally Hellier; 1 s.; 2 d. Educ. Shrewsbury School; Brasenose College, Oxford; University College Hospital. House Physician, University College Hospital; House Surgeon, Leeds General Infirmary; Assistant Lecturer, Clinical Investigation Unit, Leeds University; Medical Registrar, York. Van den Berghs and Jurgens Nutrition Award, 1972; Chairman, Brittle Bone Society. Publications: Metabolic Disorders of Bone, 1975; Textbook of Physiology and Biochemistry, 9th edition (Co-author), 1976; Textbook of Physiology, 10th edition (Co-author), 1980; Essentials of Human Biochemistry, 1983; Bone Disease in the Elderly (Co-author), 1984; Textbook of Physiology, 11th edition (Co-author), 1988. Address: (b.) Department of Biochemical Medicine, Ninewells Hospital, Dundee, DD1 9SY; T.-0382 632517.

Paterson, David Murray, BA, MSocSci. Deputy General Secretary (Scotland), Banking, Insurance and Finance Union, since 1979; b. 26.2.43, Glasgow; m., Janet Beaumont Shepherd; 1 d. Educ. High School, Clydebank; Strathclyde University; Birmingham University. Member: STUC General Council, since 1983, Scottish Economic Council, since 1988, Scottish Industrial Development Advisory Board, since 1988, Scottish Examination Board, 1979-88, Ardrossan, Saltcoats and Stevenston Enterprise Trust, since 1986; Extra-Parliamentary Commissioner for Private Legislation, since 1990. Address: (b.) 7 Buchanan Street, Glasgow, G1 3HL; T.-041-221 6475.

Paterson, George Marshall, FBIM, FITD, FIPM. Depute Secretary (Manpower), Convention of Scottish Local Authorities, 1986-90 (Personnel Director, Central Regional Council, 1974-86); Lay Member, Industrial Tribunals; Honorary Lecturer, Stirling University; b. 29.4.31, Falkirk; m., Pearl Dow; 1 s.; 1 d. Educ. Falkirk Technical School. Entered local government service, 1945. Honorary President, Larbert Amateur Operatic Society; Scottish Area Representative for Region No. 3, National Operatic and Dramatic Association; Elder, Larbert Old Church; Director/Secretary, East Stirlingshire FC. Recreations: involvement in the amateur operatic movement; golf. Address: (h.) 3 Dobbie Avenue, Larbert, Stirlingshire, FK5 3EP; T.-Larbert 66172.

Paterson, Lt. Col. Howard Cecil, TD, FSA Scot, FRSA. International Tourism Consultant; Senior Partner, Tourism Advisory Services; Chairman, Scottish International Gathering Trust; b. 16.3.20, Edinburgh; m., Isabelle Mary; 1 s. Educ. Daniel Stewart's College, Edinburgh; Edinburgh College of Art. Army, 1939-49; combat duties during War; personnel selection afterwards; Territorial Army, 1949-70; serves on East Scotland TAVR Committee; Scottish Personnel Manager, Jute Industries Ltd., Dundee, 1949-51; Organising Secretary, Scottish Country Industries Development Trust, 1951-66; Senior Director, Scottish Tourist Board, 1966-81. Chairman, Taste of Scotland Ltd., 1984-86; Vice-Chairman, John Buchan Society; Member,

Scottish Committee, British Horse Society; Vice-Chairman, Trekking and Riding Society of Scotland. Publications: Tourism in Scotland; Flavour of Edinburgh (with Catherine Brown). Recreations: fishing; shooting; riding; writing; gardening; natural history; history. Address: (h.) Dovewood, West Linton, Peeblesshire, EH46 7DS; T.-0968 60346.

Paterson, (James Edmund) Neil, MA. Author; b. 31.12.15, Greenock; m., Rosabelle MacKenzie; 2 s.; 1 d. Educ. Banff Academy; Edinburgh University. Lt., RNVR minesweepers, 1940-45; variously Member, Chairman of Production, Director, Consultant, Films of Scotland, 1954-79; Governor, British Film Institute, 1958-60; Chairman, Literature Committee, Scottish Arts Council, 1967-76; Member, Planning Committee, National Film School, 1969; Governor, Pitlochry Festival Theatre, 1966-76; Governor, National Film School, 1970-80; Member, Arts Council of GB, 1974-76; Director, Grampian Television, 1960-86; Atlantic Award in Literature, 1946; American Film Academy Award, 1959; author of: The China Run, Behold Thy Daughter, And Delilah, Man on the Tight-Rope, The Kidnappers; various stories and screenplays. Recreations: golf; fishing; bridge. Address: (h.) St. Ronans, Crieff, Perthshire; T.-0764 2615.

Paterson, Rev. (James) Roy (Herkless), MA. Minister, Cairns Church, Milngavie, since 1964; b. 22.2.28, Brechin; m., Elizabeth Moyra Wright; 3 s. Educ. Merchiston Castle School; Edinburgh University. National Service, Royal Signals, 1945-47; Assistant Minister, West Church of St. Nicholas, Aberdeen, 1953-55; Minister, Craigie Parish Church, Perth, 1955-64. Publications: Meeting the Mormons; A Faith for the Year 2000. Recreations: golf; photography. Address: 4 Cairns Drive, Milngavie, Glasgow, G62 8AJ; T.-041-956 1717.

Paterson, Sheriff James Veitch, MA (Oxon), LLB (Edin). Sheriff of Lothian and Borders at Jedburgh, Selkirk and Duns, since 1963; b. 16.4.28; m., Ailie Campbell Clark Hutchison (see Ailie Campbell Clark Paterson); 1 s.; 1 d. Educ. Edinburgh Academy; Lincoln College, Oxford; Edinburgh University. Admitted Faculty of Advocates, 1953. Recreations: fishing; shooting; gardening. Address: (h.) Sunnyside, Melrose, Roxburghshire; T.-Melrose 2502.

Paterson, John Gordon, MB, ChB, DRCOG, DCM, FFCM. Consultant in Public Health Medicine, Grampian Health Board, since 1977; Honorary Senior Lecturer, Aberdeen University, since 1977; National Co-ordinator and Quality Assurance Manager, Scottish Health Service Breast Feeding Programme, since 1991; b. 19.11.41, Blackburn. Educ. Queen Elizabeth's School, Blackburn; Edinburgh University. Hospital posts in East Lothian and Edinburgh, followed by General Practitioner appointments in North Berwick and Selkirk; transferred to public health duties, 1973, as Assistant Medical Officer of Health, Roxburgh and Selkirk; Scottish Health Service Fellow in Community Medicine, 1974-77. Deputy President, Grampian Branch, British Red Cross Society. Address: (h.) Bracken Cottage, Schivas, Ythanbank, near Ellon, Aberdeenshire, AB41 0UE; T.-035 87 284.

Paterson, Rev. John Love, MA, BD, STM, FSA Scot. Minister, St. Michael's Parish Church, Linlithgow, since 1977; b. 6.5.38, Ayr; m., Lorna Begg (see Lorna Marion Paterson). Educ. Ayr Academy; Glasgow University; Edinburgh University; Union Theological Seminary, New York. Minister: Presbyterian Church of East Africa, 1964-72, St. Andrew's, Nairobi, 1968-72; Chaplain, Stirling University, 1973-77. Moderator, West Lothian Presbytery, 1985. Recreation: gardening. Address: St. Michael's Manse, Linlithgow, West Lothian; T.-0506 842195.

Paterson, Very Rev. John Munn Kirk, ACII, MA, BD, DD. Minister Emeritus, St. Paul's Church, Milngavie; b. 8.10.22,

Leeds; m., Geraldine Lilian Parker; 2 s.; 1 d. Educ. Hillhead High School; Edinburgh University. Pilot, RAF, 1940-46; Insurance official, 1946-58; ordained Minister, Church of Scotland, 1964; Minister, St. John's Church, Bathgate, 1964-70; Minister, St. Paul's Church, Milngavie, 1970-87. Moderator, General Assembly, Church of Scotland, 1984-85; Life Member, Chartered Insurance Institute; Hon. Doctorate, Aberdeen University, 1986. Recreations: fishing; hill-walking. Address: (h.) 58 Orchard Drive, Edinburgh, EH4 2DZ; T.-031-332 5876.

Paterson, Lorna Marion, MA. General Secretary, Church of Scotland Woman's Guild, since 1985; b. 26.1.38, Unst; m., Rev. John L. Paterson (qv). Educ. Inverurie Academy; Aberden University; Aberdeen College of Education. Teacher of English, History, Geography and Religious Education, 1960-62; Teacher of English, 1962-66; Administrative Assistant, Strathclyde University, 1966-68; Deputy Academic Registrar, then Education Administrator, Stirling University, 1970-85. Guider (Division Commissioner, West Lothian, 1982-85); Secretary, Linlithgow Arts Guild, 1979-84. Recreations: singing; homemaking; church activities; the arts; people. Address: (h.) St. Michael's Manse, Kirkgate, Linlithgow, EH49 7AL; T.-031-225 5722.

Paterson, Robert Archibald, MA, LLB. Solicitor of the Church of Scotland, since 1968; Law Agent to the General Assembly, since 1971; Secretary, Scottish Churches Committee, since 1989; b. Tarbolton; m., Jean Marshall Stewart; 2 d. Educ. Ayr Academy; Edinburgh University. Qualified Assistant, then Partner, James M. & A. Inglis & Wilkie, Solicitors, Kilmarnock, 1956-64; Principal Assistant, Law Department, Church of Scotland, 1964-67. Recreations: the Scottish scene; hill-walking; travel; music. Address: (b.) 121 George Street, Edinburgh, EH2 4YN; T.-031-225 5722.

Paterson, (Thomas) Michael, DA. Artist; Educational Television Consultant; b. 14.4.38, Kirkcaldy; m., Joan; 1 s.; 2 d. Educ. George Watson's Boys' College; Edinburgh College of Art; Moray House College of Education. Teacher of Art, Waid Academy, Anstruther, 1960-64; Special Assistant, George Heriot's, Edinburgh, 1964-67; Head of Art, Marr College, Troon, 1967-69; Lecturer and Programme Director, College Television Service, Craigie College of Education, 1969-80; Assistant Head of Educational Programmes, Scottish Television, 1981-89, Head of Education, 1989-91. ETA: Chairman (Scotland), 1979-80, National Executive, since 1978; RTS Awards Convener, 1981-86, Chairman, Scottish Centre, and Member of Council, 1986-88; Member, Publicity Committee, General Assembly, Church of Scotland, 1983-86; Member, Board of Communication, 1986-90, Convener, A/V Production Unit, Church of Scotland, 1986-88. Publication: A Primary Art Course (Co-author). Recreations: golf; travel; gardening; reading. Address: (h.) 1 Laurelbank Road, Maybole, KA19 8BE.

Paterson, Rev. William, BD. Minister, Craigmillar Park Church, Edinburgh, since 1984; b. 5.6.36, Airdrie; m., Evelyn Jean Davie Marshall; 1 s.; 1 d. Educ. Glasgow Academy; Glasgow University. Director, Robert Paterson and Sons Ltd., Airdrie, 1958-72; divinity student, 1971-76; Minister: St. Machar's Ranfurly Church, Bridge of Weir, 1977-84. Director, Society for the Relief of the Destitute Sick. Recreations: music; motoring; travel. Address: 14 Hallhead Road, Edinburgh, EH16 5QJ; T.-031-667 1623.

Paterson, William, BSc (Eng), CEng, MRAeS. Engineer in Chief, Northern Lighthouse Board, since 1987; b. 24.7.40, Neilston; m., Margaret Quirie Forrest Gerrard; 2 s.; 2 d. Educ. Paisley Grammar School; Strathclyde University. Radio Officer, Merchant Navy; Technician, then Engineer, Civil Aviation Authority; Head, Radio Department, Northern Lighthouse Board. Recreation: fair weather golf. Address: (b.) 84 George Street, Edinburgh, EH2 3DA; T.-031-226 7051.

Paterson, Professor William Edgar, MA (Hons), MSc, PhD. Salvesen Professor of European Institutions and Director, Europa Institute, Edinburgh University, since 1990; Chairman, University Association for Contemporary European Studies, since 1989; b. 26.9.41, Blair Atholl; m., Phyllis McDowell; 3 s.; 2 d. Educ. Morrisons Academy, Crieff; St. Andrews University. Lecturer in International Relations, Aberdeen University, 1967-70; Warwick University: Volkswagen Lecturer in German Politics, 1970-75, Senior Lecturer, 1975-82, Reader, 1982-89, Professor and Chairman of Politics Department, 1989-90. Founder and Past Chairman, Association for the Study of German Politics. Recreations: reading; walking. Address: (b.) Europa Institute, Edinburgh University, Old College, South Bridge, Edinburgh, EH8 9YL; T.-031-650 2040.

Paterson, Wilma, DRSAM. Freelance Composer/Writer/Journalist; b. 23.4.44, Dundee; 1 s.; 1 d. Educ. Harris Academy; Royal Scottish Academy of Music. Composition study with Luigi Dallapiccola in Florence; writes all types of music (chamber, orchestral, incidental); music reviews for Glasgow Herald and The Independent; broadcasts and writes on food, plants, travel. Publications: A Country Cup; Was Byron Anorexic?; Shoestring Gourmet; Flowers and Herbs of the Bible; Lord Byron's Relish; Salmon & Women, The Feminine Angle. Address: 27 Hamilton Drive, Glasgow, G12 8DN; T.-041-339 2711.

Paterson-Brown, June, MBChB. Commonwealth Chief Commissioner, Girl Guides Association, 1985-90; Vice-Chairman, Princes Trust, since 1982; Non-Executive Director, Border Television plc, since 1980; b. 8.2.32, Edinburgh; m., Peter Neville Paterson-Brown (qv); 3 s.; 1 d. Educ. Esdaile School; Edinburgh University. Medical Officer, Family Planning and Well Woman's Clinics, 1959-85; Past Chairman: County of Roxburghshire Youth Committee, Roxburgh Duke of Edinburgh Award Committee; Scottish Chief Commissioner, Girl Guides Association, 1977-82; Chairman, Borders Region Children's Panel Advisory Committee, 1982-85; Chairman, Scottish Standing Conference of Voluntary Youth Organisations, 1983-85; Trustee, MacRobert Trusts, since 1987; Deputy Lieutenant, Roxburgh, Ettrick and Lauderdale, since 1990. Address: (h.) Norwood, Hawick, Roxburghshire; T.-0450 72352.

Paterson-Brown, Peter Neville, MBChB, DObst RCOG. Medical Practitioner, since 1957; b. 23.3.51, Hawick; m., June Garden (see June Paterson-Brown); 3 s.; 1 d. Educ. Merchiston Castle School; Edinburgh University. Medical Adviser, Red Cross Scotland, since 1981; Member, Scottish Committee, Medical Commission on Accident Prevention, since 1978; Vice President, React, since 1991. Publication: A Matter of Life or Death. Recreations: skiing; shooting; golf; fishing. Address: (h.) Norwood, Hawick, Roxburghshire; T.-0450 72352.

Patience, Rev. Donald, MA. Minister, Kilmaurs: St. Maurs-Glencairn, since 1963; b. 28.6.28, Blair Atholl; m., Flora Bell Edgar; 1 s.; 1 d. Educ. Kingussie School; St. Andrews University. Assistant, St. Ninian's, Stirling, 1953-54; Chaplain, RAF, 1954-57; Minister, Burns Church, Kilsyth, 1958-63. Moderator, Irvine and Kilmarnock Presbytery, 1981-82; Moderator, Synod of Ayr, 1982-83. Publication: The Kirk at Kilmaurs. Recreations: history (particularly of the clans and tartans); hill-walking; jogging; participated in Glasgow Marathon 1982. Publication: The Kirk at Kilmaurs. Address: The Manse, 9 Standalane, Kilmaurs, Ayrshire; T.-Kilmarnock 38289.

Patience, Donald MacAngus, BSc (Hons). Director Investment, Scottish Enteprise Agency, since 1982; b. 10.3.37, Fearn, Ross and Cromarty; m., Patricia Anne; 3 d. Educ. Tain Royal Academy; St. Andrews University. Research Scientist, General Electric Co., 1960-64; Production Manager, EMI, Middlesex, 1964-67; Area Manager, Liverpool then London, Investors in Industry PLC, 1967-80; Director and Manager, Finance Corporation for Industry, 1980-82. Recreations: tennis; swimming; reading; Stock Exchange investment. Address: (h.) Fir Tops, 2 Camstradden Drive East, Bearsden, Glasgow, G61 4AH; T.-041-943 1236.

Paton, Alasdair Chalmers, BSc, CEng, FICE, MIWEM. Chief Engineer, Scottish Office Environment Department, since 1991; b. 28.11.44, Paisley; m., Zona G. Gill; 1 s.; 1 d. Educ. John Neilson Institution, Paisley; Glasgow University. Assistant Engineer, Clyde Port Authority, 1967-71; Assistant Engineer, DAFS, 1971-72; Senior Engineer, SDD, 1972-77; Engineer, Public Works Department, Hong Kong Government, 1977-80; Senior Engineer, then Principal Engineer, SDD, 1980-87; Deputy Chief Engineer, 1987-91. Recreations: Rotary; sailing; golf. Address: (b.) 27 Perth Street, Edinburgh; T.-031-244 3035.

Paton, David Romer, FRICS, IRRV, FSA (Scot). Chartered Surveyor; b. 5.3.35, Aberdeen; m., Juliette Burney; 2 s. Educ. Gordonstoun School; Keble College, Oxford. Scottish Director, Leslie Lintott & Associates, 1979-86, Consultant, 1986-89; Immediate Past President, Aberdeen Chamber of Commerce; Past Chairman, Gordon Conservative and Unionist Association; Past Chairman, Royal Northern & University Club; Chairman: Association of Scottish Chambers of Commerce, Aberdeen Beyond 2000, North East Scotland Preservation Trust, Don District Salmon Fishery Board, Grampian-Houston Association; Vice-Chairman, Aberdeen Harbour Board; President, Friends of Grampian Stones; Secretary of State Appointee, North East River Purification Board; Minister of State Appointee, HMG Salmon Advisory Committee; Director, Aberdeen Chamber of Commerce; Member, Board of Management, Association of British Chambers of Commerce; Member, Aberdeen Harbour Board; Director, Scottish Business in the Community; Member, Grampian Initiative; Member, Committee, Architectural Heritage Society of Scotland; Member of Council, Association of Scottish District Salmon Fishery Boards; Member, St. John's Hospital Committee; Director, Aberdeen Maritime Museum Appeal Co. Ltd.; Director, Aberdeen Salmon Company Ltd. Recreations: fishing; conservation; music; bridge. Address: Grandhome, Aberdeen, AB22 8AR; T.-0224 722202.

Paton, George, MA, MEd, FEIS, FITD. Director, Scottish Council for Educational Technology, 1986-90; b. 5.12.31, Rutherglen; m., 1, Barbara Thomson (deceased); 2 s.; 2, J. Honor Smith. Educ. Rutherglen Academy; Glasgow University. National Service, RAEC, 1953-55; Schoolteacher, 1955-61; Lecturer in English, Jordanhill College of Education, 1961-63; Principal Lecturer in English, then Assistant Principal, Dundee College of Education, 1963-69; Principal, Hamilton College of Education, 1970-81; Assistant Principal, Jordanhill College of Education, 1981-82; Depute Director, Scottish Council for Educational Technology, 1982-86. President, International Council for Educational Media, 1989-91; Member, Library Information Service Committee (Scotland), 1984-91; Executive Committee Member, Commonwealth Institute in Scotland, since 1985; Governor, David Livingstone Memorial Trust, since 1971; former Convener, Education Committee, General Teaching Council for Scotland; Member, Consultative Committee on the Curriculum, 1980-83; Member, SCE Examination Board, 1977-81; Past President, Association of Higher Academic Staff in Colleges of Education in Scotland; Elder, Church of

Scotland. Recreations: singing; drama; gardening. Address: (h.) 16 Old Bothwell Road, Bothwell, Glasgow, G71 8AW.

Paton, Rev. Iain Ferguson, BD, FCIS. Minister, Newlands South, Glasgow, since 1985; b. 28.1.41, Edinburgh; m., Marjorie Vickers Macdonald; 1 s.; 1 d. Educ. George Watson's College, Edinburgh; Edinburgh University. Royal Bank of Scotland Ltd., 1957-66; Assistant Secretary, John Menzies (Holdings) Ltd., 1966-68; Senior Registrar, Charlotte Registrars Ltd., 1968-70; Secretary, Scottish Sports Council, 1970-75; Faculty of Divinity, Edinburgh University, 1975-79; Assistant Minister, St. Ninians Church, Corstorphine, 1979-80; Minister, Banchory-Ternan West Parish Church, 1980-85. Address: Newlands South Manse, 24 Monreith Road, Glasgow, G43 2NY; T.-041-632 2588.

Paton, Robert Michael, BSc, PhD, CChem, MRSC. Senior Lecturer, Chemistry Department, Edinburgh University, since 1987; b. 13.3.44, Epsom; m., Susan Cockburn; 1 s.; 1 d. Educ. Epsom College; St. Andrews University. Research Scientist, ICI Corporate Laboratory, 1970-73; Lecturer, Liverpool University, 1972-73, Edinburgh University, 1973-87; Visiting Scientist, Queensland University, 1988. Recreations: rugby; cricket; golf; hill-walking. Address: (h.) 29 Hatton Place, Edinburgh, EH9 1UA; T.-031-667 1601.

Paton, William, BSc (Hons). Director of Operations, National Engineering Laboratory; b. 29.11.41, Kilwinning; m., Elizabeth Anne; 2 s. Educ. Douglas Ewart School, Newton Stewart; Glasgow University. Consulting Geophysicist, Seismograph Services Ltd., 1963; Management Trainee, Colvilles Ltd., Ravenscraig, 1964; Research Scientist in Materials, NEL, 1965-76; Offshore Supplies Office, 1976-77; Divisional Manager, Materials Engineering Division, then Controller, Design, Materials and Systems Department, NEL, 1977-87. Recreation: golf. Address: (b.) National Engineering Laboratory, East Kilbride, Glasgow; T.-East Kilbride 20222.

Patrick, James McIntosh, RSA, LLD, ROI, ARE. Artist and Landscape Painter; b. 4.2.07, Dundee; m., Janet Watterston (deceased); 1 s.; 1 d. Educ. Morgan Academy, Dundee; Glasgow School of Art. Guthrie Award, RSA, 1935; paintings in numerous national and municipal collections; Hon. LLD, Dundee, 1973; Fellowship, Duncan of Jordanstone College of Art. Address: (h.) The Shrubbery, Magdalen Yard Road, Dundee.

Patterson, Professor Edward McWilliam, BSc, PhD, FRSE, FIMA. Professor of Mathematics, Aberdeen University, since 1965; b. 30.7.26, Whitby; m., 1, Joan Sibald Maddick (deceased); 2, Elizabeth McAllan Hunter; 1 d. Educ. Northallerton Grammar School; Ripon Grammar School; Whitby County School; Lady Lumley's Grammar School, Pickering; Leeds University. Research Demonstrator in Mathematics, Sheffield University, 1949-51; Lecturer in Mathematics: St. Andrews University, 1951-56, Leeds University, 1956-59; Aberdeen University: Senior Lecturer in Mathematics, 1960-64, Dean, Faculty of Science, 1981-84; Royal Society Visiting Professor, Malaya University, 1973; awarded MakDougall-Brisbane Prize, Royal Society of Edinburgh, 1962; Vice-President, IMA, 1973-74; President, Edinburgh Mathematical Society, 1964-65; Council Member, London Mathematical Society, 1976-80. Publications: Topology, 1956; Elementary Abstract Algebra (Co-author), 1965; Solving Problems in Vector Algebra, 1968. Address: (b.) Department of Mathematical Sciences, Edward Wright Building, Dunbar Street, Aberdeen, AB9 2TY; T.-0224 272758.

Patterson, Walter Moffat, MSc, BSc. HMI (Higher Education); b. 14.6.45, Airdrie; m., Colleen McCrone; 1 s.; 1 d. Educ. Coatbridge High School; Strathclyde University.

Lecturer in Statistics, Paisley College; Development Officer, Glacier Metal Co., Kilmarnock, 1973-74; Lecturer in Statistics, Paisley College, 1974-83; Senior Lecturer in Information Technology, MEDC, Paisley College, 1983-86. Recreations: gardening; computing; golf. Address: (b.) Room 4/100, New St. Andrews House, Edinburgh, EH1 3SY; T.- 031-244 4528.

Pattison, David Arnold, BSc, PhD. Director of Leisure and Tourism Consulting, Cobham Resource Consultants; Hon. Vice-President, Scottish Youth Hostels Association; Hon. Professor, Queen Margaret College, Edinburgh; b. 9.2.41, Kilmarnock; m., Anne Ross Wilson; 2 s.; 1 d. Educ. Kilmarnock Academy; Glasgow University. Planning Assistant, Ayr County Council, 1963-64; PhD studies, Glasgow University, 1964-66; Planning Assistant, Dunbarton County Council, 1966-67; Lecturer, Strathclyde University, 1967-70; Head of Tourism, Highlands and Islands Development Board, 1970-81; Chief Executive, Scottish Tourist Board, 1981-85; Director Leisure & Tourism Consulting, Ernst & Young, 1985-89. External Examiner for postgraduate tourism courses, Strathclyde University, 1981- 84. Recreations: reading; watching soccer and rugby; golf; gardening. Address: (h.) 7 Cramond Glebe Gardens, Cramond, Edinburgh, EH4 6NZ.

Pattison, Rev. Kenneth John, MA, BD, STM. City Centre Chaplain, St. Andrew's and St. George's Church, Edinburgh, since 1990; formerly Chaplain, Glasgow Royal Infirmary; b. 22.4.41, Glasgow; m., Susan Jennifer Brierley Jenkins; 1 s.; 2 d. Educ. Lenzie Academy; Glasgow University; Union Theological Seminary, New York. Missionary of Church of Scotland/Minister, Church of Central Africa Presbyterian, Malawi, 1967-77; Principal, Kapeni Theological College, Blantyre, Malawi, 1975-77; Minister, Park Parish Church, Ardrossan, 1977-84. Recreations: gardening; hill-walking. Address: (h.) 46 Berridale Avenue, Cathcart, Glasgow, G44 3AE; T.-041-637 2697.

Pattullo, David Bruce, CBE, BA, FIB (Scot), FRSE. Governor and Group Chief Executive, Bank of Scotland, since 1991; Director (Non-Executive): British Linen Bank, since 1977, Standard Life, since 1985, Bank of Wales PLC, since 1986, NWS Bank, since 1986; Group Chief Executive and a Deputy Governor, Bank of Scotland, 1988-91; b. 2.1.38, Edinburgh; m., Fiona Jane Nicholson; 3 s.; 1 d. Educ. Belhaven Hill School; Rugby; Hertford College, Oxford. National Service commission, Royal Scots (seconded to West Africa); joined Bank of Scotland, 1961; winner, first prize, Institute of Bankers in Scotland, 1964; Investment Services Department, 1967-71; Deputy Manager, Bank of Scotland Finance Co. Ltd., 1971-73; Chief Executive, Group Merchant Banking Activities, 1973-78; Deputy Treasurer, Bank of Scotland, 1978; Treasurer and General Manager, 1979-88; Chairman, Committee of Scottish Clearing Bankers, 1987-89; Fellow and President, Institute of Bankers in Scotland. Recreation: tennis. Address: (b.) Bank of Scotland, Head Office, The Mound, Edinburgh, EH1 1YZ; T.-031-243 5555.

Paul, Rev. Iain, BSc, PhD, BD, PhD, SOSc. Minister, Craigneuk and Belhaven Church, Wishaw, 1976-90; b. 15.6.39, Glasgow; m., Elizabeth Henderson Findlay Russell; 1 s.; 1 d. Educ. Govan High School; Strathclyde University; Bristol University; Edinburgh University. Postdoctoral research, Sheffield University, 1967-69; Lecturer in Chemistry, Queen Elizabeth College, London University, 1969-71; Assistant Minister, St. Conal's linked with St. Mark's, Kirkconnel, 1974-75; Member, Center of Theological Inquiry, Princeton, USA, 1980-81. Publications: Science, Theology and Einstein, 1982; Science and Theology in Einstein's Perspective, 1985; Knowledge of God, Calvin, Einstein, Polyani, 1987; One World – Changing Perspectives on Reality (Co-Editor), 1990. Recreations: writing books; reading; music. Address: 116 Tryst Road, Stenhousemuir, Larbert, FK5 4QJ; T.-0324 562641.

Paul, Professor James, DipArch, DipTP, FRIBA, FRIAS, FRTPI, AILA, Hon. FRBS. Professor of Architecture, Duncan of Jordanstone College of Art/Dundee University, since 1983; b. 7.10.29, Toronto; m., Elizabeth; 4 s. Educ. Banff Academy; School of Architecture, Aberdeen; School of Town Planning, Royal Technical College, Glasgow. Architect/Planner, Corporation of City of London, 1954-56; School of Architecture, Dundee: Lecturer, 1956, Senior Lecturer, 1959, Head of School, since 1965; private practice: James Parr and Partners, 1957-59, Johnston and Baxter, 1959- 62 (Partner), Baxter, Clark and Paul Architects, 1962-79 (Partner), James Paul Associates, since 1979. Address: (b.) Department of Architecture, Duncan of Jordanstone College of Art/Dundee University, 13 Perth Road, Dundee; T.-0382 23261, Ext. 260.

Paul, Professor John P., BSc, PhD, ARCST, CEng, FIMechE, FISPO, cFBOA, FRSA, FRSE. Professor and Head, Bioengineering Unit, Strathclyde University, since 1978; Hon. Senior Research Fellow, Glasgow University, since 1989; b. 26.6.27, Sunderland; m., Elizabeth R. Graham; 1 s.; 2 d. Educ. Aberdeen Grammar School; Allan Glen's School, Glasgow; Royal College of Science and Technology, Glasgow; Glasgow University. Successively Research Assistant, Lecturer and Senior Lecturer in Mechanics of Materials, Royal College of Science and Technology, subse- quently Strathclyde University, 1949-69; Visiting Professor, West Virginia University, 1969-70; Reader, then Personal Professor, Bioengineering Unit, Strathclyde University, 1970- 78. Elected President, International Society of Biomechanics, 1987. Publications: Computing in Medicine (Senior Editor), 1981; Biomaterials in Artificial Organs (Senior Editor), 1984; Disability (Co-Editor), 1979; Total Knee Joint Replacement (Co-Editor), 1988. Recreations: formerly rugby; gardening; home maintenance; light reading. Address: (h.) 25 James Watt Road, Milngavie, Glasgow, G62 7JX; T.-041-956 3221.

Paul, Michael Anthony, BA, BSc, PhD, CGeol, FGS. Senior Lecturer, Heriot Watt University, since 1986; Deputy Head, Department of Civil and Offshore Engineering, since 1991; b. 25.11.48, Ealing; m., Angela. Educ. St. Nicholas Grammar School, Northwood; University of East Anglia. Lecturer in Engineering Geology, Heriot Watt University, 1974-86. Address: (b.) Department of Civil and Offshore Engineering, Heriot Watt University, Edinburgh, EH14 4AS; T.-031-449 5111, Ext. 4412.

Paul, Robert, SDA, DipM, MBA. Course Leader, HND Business Studies, since 1984, and Senior Lecturer in Marketing, since 1986, Scottish College of Textiles; b. 8.6.35, Hamilton; m., Sheila M. Collins; 2 s.; 1 d. Educ. Hamilton Academy; West of Scotland Agricultural College; Strathclyde University. Manager, Almada Dairy Farm, Hamilton; Sales Representative, Ranks, Hovis, McDougal Ltd.; Marketing Officer, Department of Agriculture and Fisheries for Scotland; Lecturer, Central College of Commerce, Glasgow. Recreations: swimming; gardening. Address: (h.) 22 Morning Hill, Peebles, EH45 9JS; T.-0721 20406.

Paul, Ronald, MA, DipEd. Headmaster, Currie High School, since 1970; b. 6.8.32, Edinburgh; m., Nancy Crawford Logan; 3 s. Educ. Boroughmuir School, Edinburgh; Edinburgh University; Moray House College of Education. Commissioned, RAF, 1955-58; Teacher of Geography, Edinburgh, 1958-65; Principal Teacher, Boroughmuir, 1965- 67; Headmaster, James Clark School, Edinburgh, 1968-70. Church Elder; President, Edinburgh Rotary Club, 1982-83; Past President, Lothian Headteachers and Headteachers Association of Scotland; Member, Scottish Examination

Board. Recreations: family; travel; reading; music; oil painting. Address: (b.) Currie High School, Dolphin Avenue, Currie, EH14 5RD; T.-031-449 2165.

Pawley, Professor G. Stuart, MA, PhD, FRSE. Professor of Computational Physics, Edinburgh University, since 1985; b. 22.6.37, Ilford; m., Anthea Jean Miller; 2 s.; 1 d. Educ. Bolton School; Corpus Christi College, Cambridge. Lecturer, Edinburgh University, 1964; Reader, 1970; Personal Chair, 1985; Guest Professor, Aarhus University, Denmark, 1969-70. Recreations: choral singing; mountain walking. Address: (b.) Physics Department, Kings Buildings, Edinburgh University, EH9 3JZ; T.-031-650 5300.

Payne, Professor Peter Lester, BA, PhD, FRHistS. Professor of Economic History, Aberdeen University, since 1969; b. 31.12.29, London; m., Enid Christine Rowntree; 1 s.; 1 d. Educ. Brockley County School, London; Nottingham University. Visiting Lecturer in American Economic History, Johns Hopkins University, 1957-58; Lecturer in Economic and Social History, Nottingham University, 1958-59; Colquhoun Lecturer in Business History, Glasgow University, 1959-69; Senior Lecturer in Economic History, Glasgow University, 1964-69; Sherman Fairchild Distinguished Scholar, California Institute of Technology, Pasadena, 1977-78. Member: Business Archives Council, since 1959; Business Archives Council of Scotland. Publications include: Rubber and Railways in the Nineteenth Century; British Entrepreneurship in the Nineteenth Century; Colvilles and the Scottish Steel Industry; The Early Scottish Limited Companies; The Hydro. Recreations: philately; woodwork. Address: (h.) 68 Hamilton Place, Aberdeen, AB2 4BA; T.-0224 644874.

Peacock, Professor Sir Alan Turner, Kt (1987), DSC, MA, Hon. DUniv (Stirling), Hon. DEcon (Zurich), Hon. DScEcon (Buckingham), HonDUniv (Brunel), HonLLD (St. Andrews), HonLLD (Dundee), HonDSc (Edinburgh), FBA, FRSE. Research Professor in Public Finance, Esmee Fairbairn Centre, Heriot-Watt University, since 1985; Executive Director, David Hume Institute, Edinburgh, 1985-91; Chairman, Scottish Arts Council, 1986-92; Chairman, Academic Advisory Council, Institute of Economic Affairs, since 1991; b. 26.6.22, Ryton-on-Tyne; m., Margaret Martha Astell-Burt; 2 s.; 1 d. Educ. Grove Academy; Dundee High School; St. Andrews University. Royal Navy, 1942-45; Lecturer in Economics, St. Andrews, 1947-48; Lecturer, then Reader in Economics, London School of Economics, 1948-56; Professor of Economic Science, Edinburgh University, 1956-62; Professor of Economics, York University, 1962-78 (Deputy Vice Chancellor, 1963-69); Professor of Economics, University College, Buckingham, 1978-80; Principal, then Vice Chancellor, Buckingham University, 1980-84; Chief Economic Adviser, Department of Trade and Industry (on secondment), 1973-76; Member, Royal Commission on the Constitution, 1970-73; Member, Inquiry into Retirement Provision, 1983-85; SSRC Council, 1972-73; President, International Institute of Public Finance, 1966-69; Chairman, Committee on Financing the BBC, 1985-86; Chairman, Rowntree Inquiry on Takeovers, 1989-91; Head, UN Advisory Mission to Russia on Social Protection, 1992; Scottish Free Enterprise Award, 1987. Publications: 25 books, over 200 articles on economic questions. Recreations: attempting to write music; jogging; hill-walking. Address: (h.) Clinton Grange, 104/4 Whitehouse Loan, Edinburgh, EH9 2AN; T.-031-447 5917.

Peacock, Noel A., BA (Hons), MA. Head, Department of French, and Senior Lecturer in French, Glasgow University; b. 28.9.45, King's Lynn; m., Sandra M. Keenan; 1 s. Educ. King Edward VII Grammar School, King's Lynn; University College, Cardiff. Lecturer in French, Glasgow University, 1970-89; Member, Modern Languages Panel, Scottish

Universities Council on Entrance, since 1988. Publications: four books on Moliere. Recreations: sport (particularly cricket, football, tennis); theatre. Address: (b.) French Department, Glasgow University, Glasgow, G12 8QL; T.-041-339 8855.

Peacock, Peter James. Member, Highland Regional Council, since 1982 (Vice-Convener and Chairman, Finance Committee); Training, Organisation and Policy Consultant; Chairman, Scottish Library and Information Committee, since 1991; Board Member, Centre for Highlands and Islands Policy Studies; Board Member, National Conservancy Council for Scotland (N.W. Region); b. 27.2.52, Edinburgh; 2 s. Educ. Hawick High School; Jordanhill College of Education, Glasgow. Community Worker, Orkney Islands, 1973-75. Co-author, Vice-Chairman, subsequently Chairman of successful applicant group for Independent Local Radio franchise, Moray Firth; Member, Scottish Valuation Advisory Committee; former Area Officer, Highlands, Islands, Grampian, Scottish Association of Citizens Advice Bureaux. Recreations: ornithology; watching rugby union; challenging conventional thought. Address: (h.) 68 Braeside Park, Balloch, Inverness; T.-0463 790371.

Peaker, Professor Malcolm, DSc, PhD, FZS, FLS, FIBiol, FRSE. Director, Hannah Research Institute, Ayr, since 1981; Hannah Professor, Glasgow University, since 1981; b. 21.8.43, Stapleford, Nottingham; m., Stephanie Jane Large; 3 s. Educ. Henry Mellish Grammar School, Nottingham; Sheffield University; University of Hong Kong. ARC Institute of Animal Physiology, 1968-78; Head, Department of Physiology, Hannah Research Institute, 1978-81. Member, Editorial Board: Journal of Dairy Science, 1975-78, International Zoo Yearbook, 1978-82, Journal of Endocrinology, 1981; Editor, British Journal of Herpetology, 1977-81. Publications: Salt Glands in Birds and Reptiles, 1975; Avian Physiology (Editor), 1975; Comparative Aspects of Lactation (Editor), 1977; Physiological Strategies in Lactation (Co-Editor), 1984. Recreations: vertebrate zoology; natural history; golf; grumbling about bureaucrats. Address: (h.) Hannah Research Institute, Ayr, KA6 5HL.

Pearson, Brigadier Alastair Stevenson, CB (1958), DSO, OBE, MC, KStJ, TD. Lord Lieutenant of Dunbartonshire, 1979-90; Keeper of Dumbarton Castle, since 1981; b. 1.6.15; m.; 3 d. Educ. Kelvinside Academy; Sedbergh. Served Second World War (Lt.-Col., 1942); ADC to The Queen, 1956-61; Hon. Colonel, 15th (Scottish) Bn., The Parachute Regiment (TA), 1963-77 and 1983-89. Address: (h.) Tullochan, Gartocharn, by Alexandria, Dunbartonshire, G83 8ND.

Pearson, Donald William Macintyre, BSc (Hons), MB, ChB, FRCP(Glas), FRCP(Edin). Consultant Physician, Aberdeen Teaching Hospitals, since 1984; Clinical Senior Lecturer, Aberdeen University, since 1984; b. 5.9.50, Kilmarnock; m., Margaret J.K. Harris; 2 s.; 1 d. Educ. Cumnock Academy; Glasgow University. Registrar, University Department of Medicine, Glasgow Royal Infirmary; Lecturer in Medicine with Aberdeen University, Raigmore Hospital, Inverness; Senior Registrar in General Medicine, Diabetes and Endocrinology, Grampian Health Board. Past President, New Cumnock Burns Club. Recreations: music; Scottish poetry and literature. Address: (b.) Diabetic Clinic, Woolmanhill, Aberdeen Royal Infirmary, Aberdeen; T.-0224 681818, Ext. 55491.

Pearson, Francis Salmond Gillespie, MA (Oxon). Painter in oils, since 1984; b. 31.7.35, Edinburgh. Educ. Fettes College, Edinburgh; University College, Oxford; Edinburgh University. National Service, Cameron Highlanders; Assistant Master, Harrow School, 1960-61 and 1967-73; Member, Faculty of Advocates, since 1964; Headmaster, Truro

Cathedral School, 1974-79; Head of Arts and Languages, Welbeck College, 1979-83. Trustee, Hopetoun House Preservation Trust. Address: (h.) 28 Douglas Crescent, Edinburgh, EH12 5BA; T.-031-225 4736.

Pearson, Keith Philip, MA (Cantab), CertEd, DipEstHisp. Headmaster, George Heriot's School, since 1983; b. 5.8.41, Preston; 2 d. Educ. Preston Grammar School; Madrid University; St. Catharine's College, Cambridge. Assistant Teacher, then Head of Modern Languages, Rossall School, 1964-72; Head of Modern Languages, then Deputy Principal, George Watson's College, 1972-83. Member, HMC; twice Member, SCCML; Member, Scottish Consultative Council on the Curriculum, 1987-91. Recreations: sport; hill-walking; music; DIY; foreign travel. Address: (h.) 11 Pentland Avenue, Edinburgh, EH13 0HZ; T.-031-441 2630.

Peart, Geoff, BA, MA, MRTPI. Director of Development and Planning, Central Regional Council, since 1991; b. 25.10.46, Jarrow; m., Kathryn; 1 s.; 1 d. Educ. Dame Allan's Boys Grammar School, Newcastle upon Tyne; Southampton University; Nottingham University. Member, Scottish Office/COSLA Scottish Statistical Liaison Committee, 1975-91; Technical Adviser to Scottish Office/COSLA Local Government Finance Distribution Committee, 1985-91; Member, COSLA European Policy Advisory Group, 1989-91; Member, Royal Town Planning Institute Retail Working Party, 1986-87. Recreations: hill-walking; squash; cricket; reading. Address: (b.) Viewforth, Stirling; T.-Stirling 442989.

Peat, Jeremy Alastair, BA, MSc. Senior Economic Adviser, Scottish Office, since 1985; b. 20.3.45, Haywards Heath; m., Philippa Ann; 2 d. Educ. St. Paul's School, London; Bristol University; University College London. Economic Assistant/Economic Adviser, Ministry of Overseas Development, 1969-77; Economic Adviser, Manpower Services Commission, 1978-80; Head, Employment Policy Unit, Ministry of Finance and Development Planning, Government of Botswana, 1980-84; Economic Adviser, HM Treasury, 1984-85. Recreations: walking; reading; tennis; listening to music. Address: (b.) Room 5/27, New St. Andrews House, Edinburgh, EH1 3TA; T.-031-244 5104.

Peat, William Wood Watson, CBE, JP, FRAgS. Farmer; National Governor for Scotland, BBC, and Chairman, Broadcasting Council for Scotland, 1984- 89; b. 14.12.22, Denny; m., Jean McHarrie; 2 s.; 1 d. Educ. Denny Public School. Lt., Royal Signals, NW Europe and India, 1940-46; Broadcaster; National Chairman, subsequently President, Scottish Association of Young Farmers Clubs; Member, Stirling County Council, 1959-75 (Vice Convener, 1967-70); Council Member, NFU of Scotland, 1959-78 (President, 1966-67); Member, Scotish River Purification Advisory Committee, 1960-79; Board of Management, RSNH, 1960-72; General Commissioner of Income Tax, since 1962; Chairman, Scottish Advisory Committee, Association of Agriculture, 1974-79 (Vice-President, since 1979); Council, Hannah Research Institute, 1963-82; Council Member, Scottish Agricultural Organisation Society Ltd., since 1963 (President, 1974-77); Member, British Agricultural Council, 1974-84; Member, Board of Management, Oatridge Agricultural College, 1967-75; Governor, West of Scotland Agricultural College (Chairman, 1983-88); Chairman, Scottish Agricultural Colleges Ltd., 1987-90; Director, FMC plc, 1974-83; Member, Central Council for Agricultural and Horticultural Co-operation, 1967-83; Member, Co-operative Development Board, 1983-89; Member, Board of Management, British Farm Produce Council, 1964-83; BFP Committee, Food from Britain, 1984-87; Chairman, BBC Scottish Agricultural Advisory Committee, 1971-76. Recreations: amateur radio; flying. Address: (h.) 61 Stirling Road, Larbert, FK5 4SG.

Peddie, Richard L., MA, MEd, AFBPsS. Hon. Lecturer, Strathclyde University, since 1988; formerly Vice Principal, Craigie College of Education; b. 11.6.28, Grangemouth; m., Nan K. Bell; 1 s.; 2 d. Educ. Grangemouth High School; Glasgow University. Royal Signals Officer, Allied Supreme HQ (SHAPE), 1951-53; Teacher, Stirlingshire, 1953-56; Educational Psychologist, Ayrshire, 1956-59; Lecturer, Jordanhill College, 1959-64; Head, Psychology Department, Assistant Principal, Vice-Principal, Craigie College of Education, 1964-88; Member, General Teaching Council for Scotland, 1970-78; External Examiner in Education, London University Institute, 1971-76; External Examiner, Hamilton College of Education, 1977-80; Member, Scottish Examination Board, 1980-84; Member, Education Committee, British Psychological Society, 1964-68; Chairman, Glasgow University Educational Colloquium, 1966-67; Chairman, Association of Lecturers in Colleges of Education in Scotland (ALCES), 1967-69; Captain, 51 (H) Infantry Division Signals Regiment (TA), 1953-60; Vice-Chairman, Ayr Children's Panel, 1970-74; Member, Scottish Council for Research in Education, 1962-78; Member, Executive Committee, Scottish Division of Educational and Child Psychology, since 1979; Chairman, Association of Higher Academic Staff in Colleges of Education, 1984-87; Paul Harris Fellow, Rotary Award, 1986; Church of Scotland Elder. Recreations: reading; Rotary; driving; very occasional golf; tennis. Address: (h.) 14 Glenpark Place, Alloway, Ayr, KA7 4SQ; T.-0292 41996.

Peden, Hugh Andrew Mair, JP, MA, LLB, NP. Retired Senior Partner, Peden and Patrick, Solicitors, Glasgow; b. 7.11.20, Glasgow; m., Grace Joyce Parker (deceased); 1 s.; 1 d. Educ. High School of Glasgow; Glasgow University. Served in 11 Group Fighter Command, RAF, 1941-46; qualified as a Solicitor and became a Partner in family law firm, 1951; between 1955 and 1975, at various times a Councillor for Mearns and Properties Convener, Eastwood District Council; Past Chairman, Mearns Ratepayers Association; former Secretary and Past Chairman, East Renfrewshire Liberal Association; Liberal Party Parliamentary Agent, seven consecutive General Elections since 1959, Eastwood (formerly East Renfrewshire). Recreations: politics; supporting Queens Park FC (of which a member for more than 25 years); reading. Address: (h.) Milrig, Glebe Road, Newton Mearns, Glasgow.

Peden, Professor George Cameron, MA, DPhil. Professor of History, Stirling University, since 1990; b. 16.2.43, Dundee; m., Alison Mary White; 3 s. Educ. Grove Academy, Broughty Ferry; Dundee University; Brasenose College, Oxford. Sub-Editor, Dundee Evening Telegraph, 1960-68; mature student, 1968-75; Tutorial Assistant, Department of Modern History, Dundee University, 1975-76; Temporary Lecturer, School of History, Leeds University, 1976-77; Lecturer in Economic and Social History, then Reader in Economic History, Bristol University, 1977-90. Publications: British Rearmament and the Treasury 1932-39, 1979; British Economic and Social Policy: Lloyd George to Margaret Thatcher, 1985; Keynes, The Treasury and British Economic Policy, 1988. Recreation: hill-walking. Address: (h.) Ardvurich, Leny Feus, Callander, FK17 8AS; T.-0877 30488.

Peden, Professor James McKenzie, BSc, MEng, PhD, CEng, MIChemE. Director of Horizontal Well Technology Unit, Heriot Watt University, since 1991; Shell UK Ltd. Research Professor in Petroleum Engineering, since 1986; Director, Petroleum International Training and Consultancy, since 1987; b. 27.9.47, Edinburgh; m., Jacqui Watson. Educ. Darwen Grammar School; Boroughmuir Senior Secondary School; Heriot Watt University. Process technologist, research engineer, sales development officer, postgraduate student, petroleum engineer, 1970-78; joined Heriot Watt University as Lecturer, Department of Petroleum

Engineering, 1978. Publications: 70 scientific papers; co-author of books on drilling management and petroleum technology. Recreations: golf; fly fishing. Address: (h.) Dunella, Station Road, Kinross, KY13 7TH; T.-0577 62708.

Peggie, Robert Galloway Emslie, CBE, FCCA, FBCS. Commissioner (Ombudsman) for Local Administration in Scotland, since 1986; b. 5.1.29, Bo'ness; m., Christine; 1 s.; 1 d. Educ. Lasswade High School. Trainee Accountant, 1946-52; Accountant in industry, 1952-57; Edinburgh Corporation, 1957-72: O. and M. Officer, Assistant City Chamberlain, Deputy City Chamberlain, Reorganisation Steering Committee; Chief Executive, Lothian Regional Council, 1974-86. Member, Court, Heriot-Watt University (Convener, Finance Committee). Recreation: golf. Address: (b.) 5 Shandwick Place, Edinburgh, EH2 4RG; T.-031-229 4472.

Pelham Burn, Angus Maitland, JP, DL. Director, Bank of Scotland, since 1977; Director, Scottish Provident, since 1975; Director, Aberdeen Trust PLC, since 1985; Director, Abtrust Scotland Investment Company, since 1989; b. 13.12.31, London; m., Anne; 4 d. Educ. Harrow; North of Scotland College of Agriculture. Hudson's Bay Company, 1951-58; Farmer and Company Director, since 1958; Member, Kincardine County Council, 1967-75 (Vice Convener, 1973-75); Member, Grampian Regional Council, since 1974; Member, Accounts Commission for Scotland, since 1980 (Deputy Chairman, since 1987); Chairman, Aberdeen Airport Consultative Committee, since 1986; Director, Aberdeen Association for Prevention of Cruelty to Animals, since 1975; Chairman, Order of St. John Committee, Aberdeen, since 1992; Council Member, Winston Churchill Memorial Trust, since 1984; Member, Queen's Bodyguard for Scotland (Royal Company of Archers), since 1968; Vice Lord Lieutenant, Kincardineshire, since 1978. Recreations: gardening; photography; deer-stalking. Address: (b.) 68 Station Road, Banchory, AB31 3JS; T.-033 02 3343.

Penman, David Roland, DA (Edin), DipTP (Edin), FRTPI, ARIAS. Director of Planning, Perth and Kinross District Council, since 1975; b. 6.6.36, Manchester; m., Tamara Scott; 2 s.; 1 d. Educ. George Watson's Boys' College, Edinburgh; Edinburgh College of Art. Assistant Architect, private practices, 1960-67; Partner, Bamber Hall & Partners, Edinburgh, 1967-71; Depute County Planning Officer, Argyll County Council, 1971-73; County Planning Officer, Perth & Kinross Joint County Council, 1973-75. Chairman, RTPI Scotland, 1984, Member of Council, 1978-85; President, Dundee Institute of Architects, 1988, Member of Council, 1980-90; Chairman, Scottish Urban Archaeological Trust, 1990-91; Vice-Chairman, Duncan of Jordanstone College of Art; Vice-Chairman, Scottish Conservation Projects Trust; Council Member, National Trust for Scotland. Recreations: hill-walking; art galleries; theatre; DIY; Scots history; travel. Address: (h.) 17 Gannochy Road, Perth, PH2 7EF; T.-0738 27775.

Penman, Ian Dalgleish, CB (1987), MA. Chief Executive, Scottish Homes, April-October 1991; Deputy Secretary, Central Services, Scottish Offices, 1984-91; b. 1.8.31, Glasgow; m., Elisabeth Stewart Strachan; 3 s. Educ. High School of Glasgow; Glasgow University; Balliol College, Oxford. RAF Education Branch, 1955-57; HM Treasury, 1957-58; joined Scottish Office, 1958; Private Secretary to Parliamentary Under Secretary of State, 1960-62; Principal, Scottish Development Department, 1962-70; Assistant Secretary, Establishment Division, 1970-72, Police Division, 1972-78; Under Secretary, Scottish Development Department, 1978-84. Recreations: swimming; travel; music. Address: (h.) 4 Wardie Avenue, Edinburgh, EH5 2AB; T.-031-552 2180.

Penn, Ian Devis, CBiol, FIBiol, AIMLS. Depute Principal, Dumfries and Galloway College of Technology, since 1983;

b. 20.3.40, Bromley; m., Valerie Jane Rolston; 1 s.; 1 d. Educ. Colfe's Grammar School, London; North East Surrey College of Technology. Laboratory technician; Assistant Lecturer in Biology, Chelmsford, Essex; Lecturer B in Biology, Bristol Technical College; Senior Lecturer in Science, then Head, Department of Science, Stevenson College, Edinburgh. Institute of Biology: Chairman, Education Division, 1984-86, Chairman, Scottish Branch, 1985-8; Secretary, Dumfries Baptist Church, since 1989. Recreation: gardening. Address: (h.) Nithsdale, Edinburgh Road, Dumfries; T.-0387 62269.

Pennington, Christopher Royston, BSc (Hons), MB, ChB, MRCP, MD, FRCPEdin. Consultant Physician (Medicine and Gastroenterology), since 1979; Honorary Senior Lecturer in Medicine, Dundee University, since 1979; Examiner, MRCP (UK), since 1986; b. 22.2.46, Chard; m., Marcia Jane Barclay; 1 d. Educ. Shebbear College; Manchester University. House Officer, Manchester Royal Infirmary, 1970-71; Registrar in Medicine, Aberdeen Royal Infirmary, 1971-74; Lecturer in Medicine, Dundee University, 1974-79. External Examiner in Medicine, Aberdeen University, 1983-86. Publication: Therapeutic Nutrition: A Practical Guide, 1988. Address: (h.) Balnagowan, Braehead, Invergowrie, Dundee.

Penrose, Hon. Lord (George William Penrose), QC (Scot). Senator of the College of Justice, since 1990; b. 2.6.38. Advocate, 1964; QC, 1978; Procurator to General Assembly of Church of Scotland, 1984-90.

Penrose, Professor Oliver, BSc, PhD, FRS, FRSE. Professor of Mathematics, Heriot-Watt University, since 1986; b. 6.6.29, London; m., Joan Lomas Dilley; 2 s.; 1 d. Educ. Central Collegiate Institute, London, Ontario; University College, London; Cambridge University. Mathematical Physicist, English Electric Co., Luton, 1953-56; Research Associate, Yale University, 1955-56; Lecturer, then Reader in Mathematics, Imperial College, London, 1956-69; Professor of Mathematics, Open University, 1969-86. Publications: Foundations of Statistical Mechanics, 1970; 55 papers. Recreations: music; chess. Address: (b.) Department of Mathematics, Heriot-Watt University, Riccarton, Edinburgh, EH14 4AS; T.-031-451 3225.

Pentland, Brian, BSc, MB, ChB, FRCPE. Consultant Neurologist in Rehabilitation Medicine, since 1982; Senior Lecturer in Orthopaedic Surgery and Neurosciences, Edinburgh University, since 1983; b. 24.6.49, Glasgow; m., Gillian Mary Duggua; 4 s. Educ. Liberton High School, Edinburgh; Edinburgh University. Junior hospital appointments in Edinburgh, Cumbria and Dundee; formerly Lecturer in Neurology in Edinburgh. Recreation: hill-walking. Address: (b.) Astley Ainslie Hospital, Grange Loan, Edinburgh, EH9 2HL; T.-031-447 6271.

Peoples, Robin (Robert John), MA (Hons). Artistic Director, Brunton Theatre, since 1992; b. 9.9.54, Londonderry; m., Lamorna Hutchison; 1 s.; 1 d. Educ. Foyle College, Derry; St. Andrews University. Youth and community work in Northern Ireland; taught at University of Erlangen-Nuremberg, West Germany; awarded Scottish Arts Council Director's Bursary; directed and designed with various theatre companies throughout Scotland; Artistic Director, Scottish Youth Theatre, 1983-91; Member, New Beginnings Board, New Initiatives Awards Committee; Patron, Voluntary Arts Network. Recreations: theatre; painting; reading. Address: (b.) Brunton Theatre, Musselburgh, EH21 6AA; T.-031-665 3711.

Peploe, Denis Frederic Neil, RSA, DA. Artist; b. 25.3.14, Edinburgh; m., Elizabeth Marion Barr; 1 s.; 1 d. Educ. Edinburgh Academy; Edinburgh College of Art. Fellowship, Edinburgh College of Art, 1939-40; War Service, 1940-46

(RA, Intelligence Corps, SOE); Lecturer, Edinburgh College of Art, 1954-79; elected ARSA, 1956, RSA, 1966; Governor, Edinburgh College of Art, 1982. Recreations: hill-walking; mycology. Address: (h.) 18 Mayfield Gardens, Edinburgh; T.-031-667 6164.

Percy, Professor John Pitkeathly, CA, FRSA. Senior Partner, Grant Thornton, Scotland, since 1991; Non-Executive Director: W. & J.R. Watson (Holdings) Ltd., MacDonald Orr Ltd., Caledonian Bank PLC; b. 16.1.42, Southport; m., Sheila; 2 d. Educ. Edinburgh Academy; Edinburgh University. Managing Partner, Grant Thornton, London, 1981-88; Honorary Professor of Accounting, Aberdeen University, 1988. Freeman, City of London; Member, British Academy of Experts; Elder, St. Cuthbert's Church of Scotland; President, Institute of Chartered Accountants of Scotland, 1990-91. Recreations: golf; fishing. Address: (h.) 30 Midmar Drive, Edinburgh; T.-031-447 3645.

Percy-Robb, Professor Iain Walter, MB, ChB, PhD, FRCPEdin, FRCPath. Professor in Pathological Biochemistry, Glasgow University, since 1984; b. 8.12.35, Glasgow; m., Margaret E. Cormie; 2 s.; 2 d. Educ. George Watson's College, Edinburgh; Edinburgh University. Various clinical posts, 1959-63; research scholar, 1963-65; Lecturer, then Senior Lecturer, then Reader, Edinburgh University, 1965-84; MRC International Travelling Research Fellow, 1972-73; Visiting Associate Professor of Medicine, Cornell University Medical Center, New York, 1972-73; Australian Postgraduate Federation in Medicine Lecturer, 1981; Distinguished Visiting Professor in Medicine, University of Adelaide, 1984; Director, InforMed Software Ltd., Glasgow University. Recreations: golf; gardening. Address: (h.) Rossendale, 7 Upper Glenburn Road, Bearsden, Glasgow.

Perfect, Hugh Epton, BSc. Senior Assistant Principal, Moray House, Heriot-Watt University; b. 9.4.41, London; m., Susan; 2 d. Educ. Haberdasher's Askes' School, Hampstead; Imperial College, London. Teacher, Windsor Grammar School; Lecturer, Bulmershe College of Education, Reading; Lecturer/Senior Lecturer, Biology Department, Moray House College of Education. Recreations: badminton; gardening; micro-computers. Address: (b.) Moray House College of Education, Holyrood Road, Edinburgh, EH8 8AQ; T.-031-558 6168.

Perks, Professor Robert William, BA, MSc, FCMA, MBIM. Professor of Accountancy, Aberdeen University, since 1988; b. 19.7.44, Wolverhampton. Educ. Chipping Sodbury Grammar School; Reading University; Strathclyde University. Accountancy Trainee, English Electric and British Rail; Management Accountant, Abbey National Building Society; Lecturer in Accountancy, Dundee College of Technology, then Strathclyde University; Foundation Professor of Accounting, Queen's University, Belfast, 1980-85; Vice Principal and Finance Director, Middlesex Polytechnic, 1985-88. Recreations: politics; accountancy. Address: (b.) Department of Accountancy, Aberdeen University, Aberdeen; T.-0224 272205.

Perman, Raymond John, BA, MBA. Managing Director, Insider Publications Ltd., since 1985; b. 22.8.47, London; m., Fay Young; 3 s. Educ. Hemel Hempstead Grammar School; St. Andrews University; Open University; Edinburgh University. Oxford Mail, 1969-71; The Times, 1971-75; The Scotsman, 1975-76; Scottish Correspondent, Financial Times, 1976-81; Deputy Editor, Sunday Standard, 1981-83. Address: 43 Queensferry Street Lane, Edinburgh, EH2 4PF; T.-031-225 8323.

Perrie, Walter, MA, MPhil. Poet and Critic; b. 5.6.49, Quarter. Educ. Hamilton Academy; Edinburgh University; Stirling University. Full-time writer since 1975; six collec-

tions of poetry, one of which, A Lamentation for the Children, won a Scottish Arts Council book award; critical writings on aesthetics, philosophy of language, Hugh MacDiarmid, W.H. Auden, Muriel Spark and Lord Byron; held Scottish-Canadian writer's exchange fellowship, 1984-85; has lectured widely in Europe and North America; received a Gregory Award for poetry and bursaries from the Merrill-Ingram Foundation (New York) and Scottish Arts Council; Editor, Margin, a quarterly of arts and ideas, 1986-90; author, Roads that Move: a journey through Eastern Europe, 1991; Writer in Residence, Stirling University, 1991. Address: The Square Inch, Lower Granco Street, Dunning, PH2 0SQ.

Perry, Professor Clive Graham, MA (Cantab), Hon. MA (Leicester). Festival Director, Pitlochry Festival Theatre, since 1986; Professor and Head, Department of Drama, Queen Margaret College, Edinburgh, since 1990; b. 17.3.36, Harrow. Educ. Wolverhampton Grammar School; Harrow County Grammar School; Cambridge University. Awarded Thames TV Scholarship to regional theatre, 1960-61; Assistant Director, Derby Playhouse; Associate Director, Castle Theatre, Farnham; Director of Productions, Phoenix Theatre, Leicester; Director, Royal Lyceum Theatre, Edinburgh, 1966-76 (Director of Theatres in Edinburgh, 1971-76); Director, Birmingham Repertory Theatre, 1976-86. Recreation: theatre. Address: (b.) Pitlochry Festival Theatre, Port-Na-Craig, Pitlochry, PH16 5DR; T.-0796 3054.

Perth, 17th Earl of (John David Drummond), PC (1957); b. 13.5.07; m., Nancy Seymour Fincke; 2 s. Educ. Downside; Cambridge University. Lt., Intelligence Corps, 1940; War Cabinet Offices, 1942-43; Ministry of Production, 1944-45; Minister of State for Colonial Affairs, 1957-62; First Crown Estate Commissioner, 1962-77; Member, Court, St. Andrews University, 1967-86; Trustee, National Library of Scotland, since 1968. Hon. LLD; Hon. FRIBA; Hon. FRIAS. Address: (h.) Stobhall, by Perth.

Peter, Andrew Lowson, BSc (Hons), FRICS. Controller of Estates Services, City of Glasgow District Council, since 1986; b. 27.10.35, Glasgow; m., Elisabeth Stewart; 1 s.; 2 d. Educ. Hutchesons Grammar School; North East London Polytechnic. Senior Field Survey Officer, Ministry of Overseas Development, Zambia; Chief Surveyor, African/Arabian States Consulting Organisation; Chief Surveyor, EDI Ltd; Principal Surveyor, Estates Department, Strathclyde Regional Council. Chairman, Royal Institution of Chartered Surveyors in Scotland, 1989-90 (Chairman, Education and Membership Committee, 1985-88); Member, Council, Royal Institution of Chartered Surveyors, since 1981. Recreations: squash; swimming; golf; badminton. Address: (b.) 116 West Regent Street, Glasgow G2 2RW; T.-041-332 9700.

Peterken, Laurence Edwin, CBE, MA. General Manager, Greater Glasgow Health Board, since 1986; b. 2.10.31, London; m., 1, Hanne Birgithe Von Der Recke (deceased); 1 s.; 1 d.; 2, Margaret Raynal Blair; 1 s.; 1 d. Educ. Harrow School (Scholar); Peterhouse, Cambridge (Scholar). Pilot Officer, RAF Regt., Adjt. No. 20 LAA Sqdn., 1950-52; Service Divisional Manager, Hotpoint Ltd., 1961-63; Commercial Director, then Managing Director, British Domestic Appliances Ltd., 1963-68; Director, British Printing Corporation Ltd., 1969-73; Managing Director, Fashion Multiple Division, Debenhams Ltd., 1974-76; Management Auditor, 1976-77; Controller, Operational Services, GLC, 1977-85; President, GLC Chief Officers' Guild, 1983-85; Acting Director, Royal Festival Hall, 1983-85. Recreations: opera; swimming. Address: (h.) 25 Kingsborough Gardens, Glasgow, G12 9NH.

Peters, David Alexander, MA, DSA, FHSM. General Manager, Borders Health Board, since 1985; b. 18.10.38,

Glasgow; m., Moira Cullen Macpherson; 2 s.; 1 d. Educ. King's Park School, Glasgow; Glasgow University; Manchester University. Hospital Secretary, Greenock Royal Infirmary, Eye Infirmary, ENT Hospital, 1963-66; Eastern Regional Hospital Board, Dundee: Principal Administrative Assistant, 1966-68, Assistant Secretary, 1968-71, Principal Assistant Secretary, 1971-74; District Administrator, Renfrew District, Argyll and Clyde Health Board, 1974-81; Secretary, Borders Health Board, 1981-85. Recreations: curling; tennis; sailing; golf; gardening. Address: (h.) Wildcroft, Gattonside, Melrose, TD6 9NP.

Peters, Kenneth Jamieson, CBE, JP, DL, FRSA, FSA Scot, Assoc. MCIT. Member, British Railways (Scottish) Board, since 1982; Member, Girobank, Scotland Board, 1984-90; Vice-Chairman, Peterhead Bay Authority, since 1989; Director, Aberdeen Journals Ltd., 1960-90; b. 17.1.23, London; m., Arunda Merle Jane Jones. Educ. Aberdeen Grammar School; Aberdeen University. Served Second World War; commissioned Queen's Own Cameron Highlanders; also King's Own Scottish Borderers; editorial staff, Scottish Daily Record and Evening News Ltd., 1947-51; Assistant Editor, Aberdeen Evening Express, 1951-52; Assistant Editor, Manchester Evening Chronicle, 1952-53; Editor, Aberdeen Evening Express, 1953-56; Editor, Press and Journal, Aberdeen, 1956-60; Managing Director, Aberdeen Journals Ltd., 1960-80, Chairman, 1980-81; Director: Thomson North Sea, 1981-88, Thomson Scottish Petroleum, 1981-86, Thomson Forestry Holdings, 1982-88, Highland Printers Ltd., 1968-83; President, Scottish Daily Newspaper Society, 1964-66 and 1974-76; Member, Press Council, 1974-77; Director, Thomson Regional Newspapers, 1974-81; Director, Aberdeen Association of Social Service, 1973-78; Member, Executive, Scottish Council (Development and Industry), 1982-88 (Chairman, Aberdeen and North-East Committee, 1982-88); Fellow, SCDI, 1989; Member, Scottish Advisory Committee, British Council, 1967-84; National Committee Member, Films of Scotland, 1970-82; Burgess of Guild, City of Aberdeen, 1963. Publications: The Northern Lights, 1978; Burgess of Guild, 1982; Great North Memories, Vol. 1 and Vol. 2 (Editor). Recreations: walking; cricket; rugby football. Address: 47 Abergeldie Road, Aberdeen, AB1 6ED; T.-0224 587647.

Peterson, George Sholto, NP. Solicitor and Notary Public, since 1956; Honorary Sheriff, since 1982; b. 18.9.27, Lerwick; m., Dorothy Hilda Spence; 2 s.; 4 d. Educ. Lerwick Central Public School; Edinburgh University. Secretary, The Shetland Trust; Factor for the Marquess of Zetland; Senior Partner, Tait & Peterson, Solicitors and Estate Agents, Lerwick; Dean, Faculty of Solicitors in Shetland; Honorary Pastor, Ebenezer Church, Lerwick. Recreations: studying theology; reading; fishing. Address: (b.) Bank of Scotland Buildings, Lerwick, Shetland; T.-0595 3010.

Pethrick, Professor Richard Arthur, BSc, PhD, DSc, FRSC, FRSE. Professor in Chemistry, Strathclyde University, since 1983; b. 26.10.42; m., Joan Knowles Hume; 1 s. Educ. North Gloucestershire College, Cheltenham; London University; Salford University. Editor: British Polymer Journal, Polymer Yearbook, Polymer International; Member, Polymer Committee, European Science Foundation; Member, Committee, MACRO Group, 1979-84. Address: (h.) 40 Langside Drive, Newlands, Glasgow, G43 2QQ; T.-041-552 4400.

Petrie, Professor James Colquhoun, MB, ChB, FRCPEdin, FRCP, FFPM. Professor of Clinical Pharmacology, Department of Medicine and Therapeutics, Aberdeen University, since 1985; Honorary Consultant Physician, Aberdeen Teaching Hospitals, since 1971; b. 18.9.41, Aberdeen; m., Dr. M. Xanthe P.; 2 s.; 2 d. Educ. Anieres, Geneva; Robert Gordon's College, Aberdeen; Aberdeen

University. Senior Lecturer, 1971-81, Reader, 1981-85, Aberdeen University. Chairman, Lecht Ski Company, since 1976. Recreations: ski; golf; fishing. Address: (b.) Department of Medicine and Therapeutics, Aberdeen Royal Infirmary, Foresterhill, Aberdeen, AB9 2ZB; T.-0224 681818.

Pettigrew, Paul James, MA, MSC, MRTPI, FRSA, MTS. Chief Executive, Dumfries and Galloway Enterprise, since 1991; b. 13.1.52, Glasgow; m., Yvonne Le Brun; 2 d. Educ. Hutchesons' Grammar School; Edinburgh University; Aston University. Senior Planning Officer, Greater Manchester Council; various posts in Development Board for Rural Wales. Churchill Fellow, 1986. Recreations: tennis; football; Clyde FC; French; squash; badminton. Address: (h.) 16 Laurieknowe, Dumfries, DG2 7AJ; T.-0387 66833.

Peyton Jones, Professor Simon Loftus, MA (Cantab), DipCompSci. Professor of Computing Science, Glasgow University, since 1989; b. 18.1.58, Cape Town, South Africa; m., Dorothy Helen. Educ. Marlborough College; Trinity College, Cambridge. Systems Engineer, Beale Electronic Systems Ltd, 1980-82; University College London: Lecturer in Computer Science, 1982-86, Senior Lecturer in Computer Science, 1986-89. Publication: The Implementation of Functional Programming Languages, 1987. Recreations: cycling; reading; singing. Address: (b.) Department of Computing Science, University of Glasgow, Glasgow G12 8QQ; T.-041-330 4500.

Philip, Alistair Erskine, MA, PhD, FBPsS, CPsychol. Head of Area Clinical Psychology Service, Lothian Health Board, since 1980; Member, State Hospital Management Committee, since 1980; NHS National Assessor in Clinical Psychology, since 1980; Honorary Senior Lecturer, Edinburgh University, since 1980; b. 10.7.38, Aberdeen; m., Betty J. McKay; 1 s.; 2 d. Educ. Aberdeen Grammar School; Aberdeen University; Edinburgh University. Scientific staff, MRC Unit for Epidemiological Studies in Psychiatry, Edinburgh University, 1963-71; Head, Psychology Department, Bangour Village Hospital, 1971-80; Committee Member, Clinical Division, British Psychological Society, 1971-81; Chairman, Clinical Psychology Sub-Committee, National Consultative Committee of Scientists in Professions Allied to Medicine, 1981-85; Temporary Adviser to WHO, 1985. Publications: numerous books, chapters and articles on psychological topics. Recreations: playing hockey; golf; going to auctions. Address: (h.) 37 Meggetland Terrace, Edinburgh, EH14 1AP; T.-031-443 2447.

Philip, Rev. George M., MA. Minister, Sandyford-Henderson Memorial Church, since 1956; b. 11.11.25, Bucksburn, Aberdeenshire; m., Patricia Joy Morrison; 2 s.; 1 d. Educ. Bucksburn School; Central Secondary School, Aberdeen; Aberdeen University. Able seaman, Royal Navy, 1943-47; qualified as Member, Institute of Bankers in Scotland, 1949; licensed by Aberdeen Presbytery, 1953. Moderator, Glasgow Presbytery, 1979-80. Publications: Commentary on the Apostles Creed; School of Discipleship; Commentary on Book of Job; Commentary on Ecclesiastes; Kingdom against Kingdom; Daily Bible Reading Notes. Recreation: gardening. Address: 66 Woodend Drive, Glasgow, G13 1TG; T.-041-954 9013.

Philip, Michael Stuart, OBE, MA (Oxon), BSc, FICF. Overseas Forestry Consultant; b. 4.11.26, London; m., Audrey Elizabeth Rae; 1 s.; 1 d. Educ. Bancroft's; Kings College, London; Keble College, Oxford. Assistant Conservator of Forests, Uganda, 1947-60; Forest Ecologist, Uganda, 1960-62; Conservator of Forests (Research), Uganda, 1962-64; Lecturer, then Senior Lecturer in Forestry, Aberdeen University, 1964-82; Associate Professor of Forestry, Dar-es-Salaam University, 1977-79; Reader in Forestry, Aberdeen University, 1982-88. Trustee, Scottish

Forestry Trust, 1983-88; Team Leader, Nepal-UK Forestry Research Project, Kathmandu, Nepal, 1988-91. Publication: Measuring Trees and Forests. Recreations: gardening; fishing. Address: (h.) Luton Cottage, Bridgeview Road, Aboyne, AB34 5HB; T.-03398 86086.

Philips, Douglas John, MHSM, DipHSM. General Manager, Argyll and Dumbarton Unit, Argyll and Clyde Health Board, since 1989; b. 30.4.53, Edinburgh; m., Morag S. Hall. Educ. Dalkeith High School. Formerly General Manager, Northern Unit, Highland Health Board. Recreations: hill-walking; rambling; cycling; gardening; reading fiction; music; Coronation Street. Address: (h.) Windsong, 3 Cedar Grove, Cardross, G82 5JW; T.-0389 841748.

Phillips, John Clifford, BSc, FIMA, FRSA, MBIM, CMath. Principal, The Queen's College, Glasgow, since 1991; b. 29.1.43, Dyfed; m., Anne Margaret; 1 s.; 1 d. Educ. Llandello Grammar School; University of Wales, Aberystwyth. Lecturer, Lancashire Polytechnic, 1967-69, Leeds Polytechnic, 1969-71; Leeds Polytechnic: Senior Lecturer, 1971-77, Principal Lecturer, 1977-86, Head, School of Mathematics and Computing, 1986-87, Dean, Faculty of Engineering and Computing, 1987-88, Senior Executive, External Development, 1988-90. Former Member, North Yorkshire County Council. Recreations: reading; walking; architectural conservation. Address: (b.) The Queen's College, Glasgow, 1 Park Drive, Glasgow, G3 6LP; T.-041-337 4010.

Phillips, John H., MA, PhD. Director of Biology teaching and Reader in Biochemistry, Edinburgh University, since 1988; b. 19.2.41, York; m., Kerstin B. Halling; 2 d. Educ. Leighton Park School, Reading; Christ's College, Cambridge. Lecturer in Biochemistry, Makerere University, Uganda, 1967-69; scientific staff, MRC Laboratory of Molecular Biology, Cambridge, 1969-74; Department of Biochemistry, Edinburgh University, since 1974. Recreations: natural history; Scottish mountains; visits to Sweden. Address: (h.) 46 Granby Road, Edinburgh, EH16 5NW; T.-031-667 5322.

Pickard, Willis Ritchie, MA (Hons), Hon. LLD (Aberdeen). Editor, Times Scottish Education Supplement, since 1977; Rector, Aberdeen University, 1988-90; b. 21.5.41, Dunfermline; m., Ann; 2 d. Educ. Daniel Stewart's College; St. Andrews University. The Scotsman: Leader Writer, 1967-72, Features Editor, 1972-77. Former Member, Scottish Arts Council; Chairman, Children's Book Committee for Scotland; Chairman, Book Trust Scotland; Liberal candidate, East Fife, 1970 and February, 1974. Address: (b.) 37 George Street, Edinburgh, EH2 2HN; T.-031-220 1100.

Pickett, Professor James, BSc (Econ), MLitt. Professor and Director, David Livingstone Institute, Strathclyde University, since 1973; b. 7.6.29, Greenock; m., Janet C. Hamilton; 1 s.; 2 d. Educ. Greenock Academy; School of Economics, Dundee; Paris University; Glasgow University. Statistician, Dominion Bureau of Statistics, Canada; Lecturer, Strathclyde University; Visiting Professor, Saskatchewan University; Special Economic Adviser, UN Economic Commission for Africa; Senior Lecturer and Professor, Strathclyde University. Regular Consultant to UN, OECD, and EEC, and Adviser to African Development Bank. Recreations: photography; walking; listening to music; long-suffering support of Greenock Morton. Address: (b.) Strathclyde University, Livingstone Tower, 26 Richmond Street, Glasgow, G1 1XH; T.-041-552 4400.

Pidgeon, Professor Carl R., BSc, PhD, FRSE. Professor of Semiconductor Physics and Deputy Head, Physics Department, Heriot Watt University; b. 27.11.37, London; 1 s.; 1 d. Educ. Reading University. Staff Member, National Magnet Laboratory, MIT, 1964-71; Reader in Physics, Heriot

Watt University, 1971-83. Recreations: golf; skiing. Address: (b.) Physics Department, Heriot Watt University, Edinburgh.

Pighills, Christopher David, MA (Cantab). Headmaster, Strathallan School, Perth, since 1975; b. 27.11.37, Bradford. Educ. Rydal School, North Wales; Christ's College, Cambridge. Assistant Master/Housemaster, Fettes College, 1960-75. Recreations: shooting; dog training; hill-walking; working. Address: (b.) Strathallan School, Perth, PH2 9EG; T.-0738 812546.

Pignatelli, Frank, MA, MEd, FBIM. Director of Education, Strathclyde Regional Council, since 1988; Visiting Professor of Education, Glasgow University, since 1989; b. 22.11.46, Glasgow; m., Rosetta; 1 s.; 1 d. Educ. St. Mungo's Academy, Glasgow; Glasgow University. Chairman, Scottish Advisory Group on Technical and Vocational Initiative; Member, UK National Steering Group on TVEI; Member, CBI UK Policy Group on Understanding British Industry; Consultant to Egyptian Government on Vocational Education; Consultant to Queensland Catholic Education Commission; Member, Council, Association of Directors of Education in Scotland; Director and Member, Scottish Consultative Council on the Curriculum; President, British Institute of Management, Renfrewshire Branch; Chairman, Royal Institute of Public Administration, Glasgow and West of Scotland Branch. Recreations: genealogy; reading. Address: (b.) Strathclyde Regional Council, Department of Education, 20 India Street, Glasgow, G2 4PF; T.-041-227 2359.

Pike, (Kathryn) Lorna, MA (Hons). Editor, Dictionary of the Older Scottish Tongue, since 1986; b. 8.8.56, Fort William. Educ. Lochaber High School, Fort William; Edinburgh University. Editor, Concise Scots Dictionary, 1979-83; Assistant Editor, Dictionary of the Older Scottish Tongue, 1984-86. Secretary, Scottish Text Society. Recreations: riding; photography; handicrafts. Address: (b.) 27 George Square, Edinburgh, EH8 9LD; T.-031-650 4147.

Pilcher, Rosamunde. Author; b. 22.9.24, Lelant, Cornwall. Began publishing short stories in Woman and Home, 1945; since then has published hundreds of short stories and 25 novels, including Sleeping Tiger, Under Gemini, Wild Mountain Thyme, The Carousel, Voices in Summer, The Shell Seekers, September; play, The Dashing White Sergeant. Address: (h.) Over Pilmore, Invergowrie, by Dundee; T.-Longforgan 239.

Pinkerton, Group Captain George Cannon, OBE, DFC, AE, DL, JP; b. 11.6.09, Rayleigh: m., Margaret Angela Weddell (m. diss.); 1 s.; 1 d. Educ. Glasgow High School. Farming, 1926-1939; RAF Fighter Command and Air Defence, 1939-45; returned to farming, 1945; former Member, Renfrewshire County Council; former Member, Paisley and District Hospital Board; County Representative, RAF Benevolent Fund. Recreation: sailing. Address: (h.) South Mains, Houston, Renfrewshire, PA6 7BD; T.-0505 612250.

Pippard, Professor Martin John, BSc, MB, ChB, MRCPath, FRCP. Professor of Haematology, Dundee University, since 1989; Honorary Consultant Haematologist, Tayside Health board, since 1989; Honorary Consultant Haematologist, Tayside Health Board, since 1989; b. 16.1.48, London; m., Grace Elizabeth; 2 s.; 1 d. Educ. Buckhurst Hill County High School; Birmingham University. House Physician and House Surgeon, 1972-73; Senior Medical House Officer, 1973-75; Research Fellow, Nuffield Department of Clinical Medicine, Oxford, 1975-78; MRC Travelling Research Fellow, University of Washington, Seattle, 1978-80; Wellcome Trust Research Fellow and Clinical Lecturer, Nuffield Department of Clinical Medicine, 1980-83; Consultant Haematologist, MRC Clinical Research Centre and Northwick Park Hospital, 1983-88. Recreations:

gardening; fell-walking. Address: (b.) Department of Haematology, Ninewells Hospital and Medical School, Dundee, DD1 9SY; T.-0382 60111.

Pirie, Henry Ward, OStJ, MA, LLB. Crossword Compiler, Glasgow Herald, and various publications; b. 13.2.22, Edinburgh; m., Jean Jardine; 4 s. Educ. George Watson's College; Edinburgh University. Royal Scots; Indian Army (Grenadiers), 1944; Advocate, 1947; Standing Junior Counsel to the Admiralty in Scotland, 1951; Sheriff-Substitute of Lanarkshire, at Airdrie, 1954-55; Sheriff-Substitute (late Sheriff) of Lanarkshire, at Glasgow, 1955-74. Past president: Glasgow and West of Scotland Watsonian Club, The Lenzie Club. Recreations: opera; bridge; dog-walking. Address: (h.) 16 Poplar Drive, Lenzie, Glasgow, G66 4DN.

Pirie, Professor Hugh Munro, BVMS, PhD, MRCVS, FRCPath. Professor, Department of Veterinary Pathology, Glasgow University, since 1982; Secretary, European Association of Establishments for Veterinary Education, 1988-92; Chairman, Veterinary Panel, Royal College of Pathologists, 1988-92; b. 10.4.36, Glasgow; m., Myrtle Elizabeth Stewart Levack; 1 d. Educ. Coatbridge High School; Glasgow University. Scientific Editor, Research in Veterinary Science, 1981-88; British Council Specialist, Argentina, 1982, Ethiopia, 1986-88; President, Association of Veterinary Teachers and Research Workers, 1984. Recreations: travel; gardening; hill-walking; swimming; gastronomy. Address: (h.) North East Corner, Buchanan Castle Estate, Drymen, G63 0HX; T.-0360 60781.

Pirie, Sheriff Iain Gordon, MA, LLB. Sheriff of Glasgow and Strathkelvin, since 1982; b. 15.1.33, Dundee; m., Dr. Sheila B. Pirie; 2 s.; 1 d. Educ. Harris Academy, Dundee; St. Andrews University. Procurator Fiscal, Dumfries, 1971-76, Ayr, 1976-79; Sheriff of South Strathclyde, Dumfries and Galloway, 1979-82. Address: (b.) Sheriff Court, 1 Carlton Place, Glasgow, G5 9DA; T.-041-429 8888.

Pirie, John McDonald Strachan, CA. Managing Director, Milk Marketing Division, Scottish Milk Marketing Board, since 1991 (Finance Director, 1983, Secretary, 1988); b. 17.11.38, Ayr; m., Rosetta; 1 s.; 2 d. Educ. Ayr Academy; Glasgow University. Address: (b.) Underwood Road, Paisley; T.-041-887 1234.

Pitt, Professor Douglas Charles, BA, MA, PhD, FBIM. Professor of Organisational Analysis, Strathclyde University, since 1989, and Head, Human Resource Management; b. 13.7.43, Greenock; m., Jean Hamilton Spowart. Educ. Varndean Grammar School, Brighton; Exeter University; Manchester University. Executive Officer, Civil Service, 1961-64; Lecturer, then Senior Lecturer and Reader, Strathclyde University, 1973-89. Current research interest: telecommunications deregulation in Britain and the USA. Publications: The Post Office Telecommunications Function, 1980; Public Administration: An Introduction, 1980; Government Departments: An Organisational Analysis, 1981; The Computer Revolution in Public Administration, 1984. Recreations: German; riding; swimming; fishing; skiing; sailing; traditional jazz; bluegrass; opera. Address: (h.) 19 Waterfoot Road, Newton Mearns, Glasgow, G77 5RU; T.-041-639 5359.

Pittock Wesson, Joan Hornby, BA (Hons), MA, PhD. Senior Lecturer in English, Aberdeen University, since 1978; Director, Centre for Cultural History; Director, Institute for Cultural Studies; b., Featherstone; m., 1, Malcolm John Whittle Pittock; 2, Harry Chamberlain Wesson; 1 s. Educ.Normanton High School for Girls; Manchester University. Assistant Lecturer in English, Aberdeen University, 1964; Lecturer, 1966; Founder Editor, British Journal for Eighteenth Century Studies; President, British

Society for Eighteenth Century Studies, 1980-82. Publications include: The Ascendary of Taste: the achievement of Joseph and Thomas Warton, 1973; Aberdeen and Enlightenment (Co-editor), 1988; Interpretation and Cultural History (Co-editor), 1991. Recreation: walking. Address: (b.) Institute for Cultural Studies, Aberdeen University, Aberdeen: T. 0224 272629.

Playfair-Hannay of Kingsmuir, Patrick Armour. Farmer; b. 12.7.29, Banstead; m., Frances Ann Robertson; 1 s.; 1 d. Educ. Oundle. National Service, commissioned into RASC; planting tea and rubber in Ceylon, seven years; took up farming in the Border country, 1956. Chairman, Association for Protection of Rural Scotland. Recreation: shooting. Address: Clifton on Bowmont, Kelso, Roxburghshire; T.-057 382 227.

Playle, Colin, BA (Hons). Regional Chairman, British Gas Scotland, since 1991; b. 13.5.33, Grimsby; m., Patricia Margaret Playle; 2 d. Educ. University College, London. Joined British Gas, 1957. Chairman, Combined Heat and Power Association, since 1991; Companion of Institution of Gas Engineers, 1991. Recreations: skiing; ornithology; modern literature. Address: (b.) British Gas Scotland, Granton House, 4 Marine Drive, Edinburgh, EH5 1YB; T.-031-559 5000.

Plotkin, Professor Gordon David, BSc, PhD. Professor in Computer Science, Edinburgh University; Director, Laboratory for the Foundation of Computer Science; b. 9.9.46, Glasgow; m., Lynda Margaret; 1 s. Educ. Glasgow HIgh School for Boys; Glasgow University; Edinburgh University. Lecturer, then Reader, Edinburgh University; British Petroleum Venture Research Fellow, 1981-88; Director, Laboratory for the Foundation of Computer Science; Member, Academia Europaea; Editor, Information and Control, Mathematical Structures in Computer Science; Series Editor, Oxford University Press. Recreations: chess; hill-walking. Address: (b.) Department of Computer Science, King's Buildings, Edinburgh University, Edinburgh; T.-031-667 1081, Ext. 2775.

Pollacchi, Derek Albert Paterson, Chief Executive Designate, Royal Scottish National Hospital and Community Trust, since 1991; Unit General Manager, Mental Handicap Services, Forth Valley Health Board, since 1987; b. 23.7.51, Dunbarton; m., Jean Lindsay Mullan; 2 d. Educ. St. Mungo's Academy, Glasgow. Director of Administrative Services, Lennox Castle Hospital/Stobhill General Hospital and Associated Community Health Services, 1984-87. Recreations: swimming; badminton; hill-walking; reading. Address: (b.) Royal Scottish National Hospital, Old Denny Road, Larbert, FK5 4SD; T.-0324 556131.

Pollen, Roger Alan, ARCM. Managing Director, Scottish Ensemble, since 1988; Member, Management Committee, Scottish International Piano Competition, since 1986; b. 5.8.62, Belfast. Educ. Royal Belfast Academical Institution; City of Belfast School of Music; Royal Scottish Academy of Music and Drama. Freelance Cellist, since 1984; Musical Director, T. Flynn Productions Ltd., 1985; Co-ordinator, Scottish Piano Competition, 1986; Orchestra Manager, Scottish Chamber Orchestra, 1986-88. Recreations: collecting vintage and classic cars; sailing; skiing; swimming; hill-walking; walking; tree planting. Address: (h.) 22 Hamilton Drive, Hillhead, Glasgow, G12.

Pollock, Sheriff Alexander, MA (Oxon), LLB. Sheriff of Tayside, Central and Fife, at Stirling, since 1991; Advocate, since 1973; b. 21.7.44, Glasgow; m., Verena Francesca Gertraud Alice Ursula Critchley; 1 s.; 1 d. Educ. Rutherglen Academy; Glasgow Academy; Brasenose College, Oxford; Edinburgh University; Perugia University. Partner, Bonar Mackenzie & Kermack, WS, 1971-73; called to Scottish Bar,

1973; Conservative candidate: West Lothian, General Election, February 1974, Moray and Nairn, General Election, October 1974; MP, Moray and Nairn, 1979-83, Moray, 1983-87; Parliamentary Private Secretary to Secretary of State for Scotland, 1982-86; PPS to Secretary of State for Defence, 1986-87; Advocate Depute, 1990-91. Member, Queen's Bodyguard for Scotland (Royal Company of Archers), since 1984. Recreations: walking; music. Address: (h.) Drumdarrach, Forres, Moray.

Pollock, John Denton, BSc, FEIS. General Secretary, The Educational Institute of Scotland, 1975-88; b. 21.4.26, Kilmarnock; m., Joyce Maragret Sharpe; 1 s.; 1 d. Educ. Ayr Academy; Royal Technical College, Glasgow; Glasgow University; Jordanhill College of Education. Commissioned Royal Engineers, 1945-48. Teacher, Mauchline Secondary School, 1951-59; Head Teacher, Kilmaurs Secondary School, 1959-65; Rector, Mainholm Academy, Ayr, 1965-74; General Secretary Designate, EIS, 1974. Forestry Commissioner, 1978-91; Chairman, Scottish Labour Party, 1959 and 1971; Chairman, STUC, 1981-82 (Vice-Chairman, 1980-81); Member, General Council, STUC, 1975-87; Member, Annan Committee on Future of Broadcasting, 1974-77; Member, Manpower Services Committee Scotland, 1977-88; Member, Employment Appeal Tribunal, since 1991; Board Member, Network Scotland, since 1991; Member, National Broadcasting Council for Scotland, 1985-89; member, World Executive, 1986-90, and Chairman, European Committee, 1980-90, World Confederation of Organisations of the Teaching Profession; Vice President, European Trade Union Committee for Education, 1989-90; Honorary member, National Union of Teachers (E. & W.), since 1988; Honorary Vice-President, Ulster Teachers Union, since 1989; Honorary Vice-President, South West District, SYHA, since 1985. Address: (h.) 52 Douglas Road, Longniddry, East Lothian.

Polwarth, Lord (Henry Alexander Hepburne-Scott), TD, DL, FRSE. Vice-Lord-Lieutenant, Borders Region, 1975-91; Member, Queen's Bodyguard for Scotland (Royal Company of Archers); Chartered Accountant; b. 17.11.16; m., 1, Caroline Margaret Hay (m. diss.); 1 s.; 3 d.; 2, Jean Jauncey; 2 step s.; 1 step d. Educ. Eton College; King's College, Cambridge. Served Second World War as Captain, Lothians and Border Yeomanry; former Partner, Chiene and Tait, CA, Edinburgh; Governor, Bank of Scotland, 1966-72, Director, 1974-87; Chairman, General Accident, Fire & Life Assurance Corporation, 1968-72; Director, ICI Ltd., 1969-72, 1974-81; Director, Halliburton Co., 1974-87; Director, Canadian Pacific Ltd., 1975-86; Director, Sun Life Assurance Co. of Canada, 1975-84; Minister of State, Scottish Office, 1972-74; Chairman, later President, Scottish Council (Development and Industry), 1955-72; Chairman, Scottish Forestry Trust, 1987-89; Member, Franco-British Council, 1981-89; Chairman, Scottish National Orchestra Society, 1975-79; Chancellor, Aberdeen University, 1966-86; Hon. LLD: St. Andrews, Aberdeen; Hon. DLitt, Heriot-Watt; DUniv, Stirling. Address: Easter Harden, Hawick; T.-Hawick 72069.

Ponton, Professor John Wylie, BSc, PhD, FIChemE, FEng. ICI Professor of Chemical Engineering, Edinburgh University, since 1989; b. 2.5.43, Edinburgh; m., Katherine Jean Victoria Eachus. Educ. Melville College, Edinburgh; Edinburgh University. Recreations: engineering; music. Address: (b.) Department of Chemical Engineering, Edinburgh University, EH9 3JL; T.-031-650 4860.

Poodle, Thomas, CEng, MICE, MIWEM. Assistant Director (Chief Engineer), Clyde River Purification Board, since 1989; b. 25.7.43, Denny; m., Joan; 1 s.; 1 d. Educ. Denny High School; Graeme High School, Falkirk; Strathclyde University. Clyde River Purification Board: Assistant Hydrologist, 1968-75, Hydrologist, 1975-88. Member, British Standards Technical Committee. Recreations: sailing; skiing. Address:

(b.) Rivers House, Murray Road, East Kilbride, Glasgow, G75 0LA; T.-03552 38181.

Poole, Sheriff Isobel Anne, LLB. Sheriff of Lothian and Borders; b. 9.12.41, Oxford. Educ. Oxford High School for Girls; Edinburgh University. Advocate. Recreations: country; arts; gardens; friends. Address: (b.) Sheriffs' Chambers, Sheriff Court, Edinburgh, EH1 2NS.

Pope, Professor Peter F., MA, BCom. Touche Ross Professor of Accounting, Strathclyde University, since 1985; b. 28.5.54, Blackpool; m., Donna; 2 s. Educ. St. Mary's College, Crosby; Lancaster University; Liverpool University. Accounting Assistant, GEC Distribution Ltd., 1976-77; Lecturer in Accounting and Finance, Liverpool University, 1978-84. Recreations: sports; music. Address: (b.) Department of Accounting and Finance, Strathclyde University, 100 Cathedral Street, Glasgow, G12 0PT; T.-041-552 4400.

Portchmouth, Rev. Roland John, NDD, ATD. Minister, Church of Scotland, since 1980; b. 4.9.23, London; m., Susan Mary; 1 s.; 3 d. Educ. Kilburn Grammar School; Harrow and Hornsey Colleges of Art; Edinburgh University. Royal Navy, 1942-46; Art Teacher, 1951-61; Lecturer in Art Education and Senior Lecturer in Art, 1961-68. Artist (paintings exhibited, Royal Academy and other London and provincial galleries); work includes permanent exhibition of religious paintings, Peebles Old Parish Church, cover designs and poems for Life and Work magazine, book illustrations, prints of Scottish churches, scripts and sets of religious dramas, poems in New Writing Scotland. Publications: Creative Crafts for Today, 1969; Secondary School Art, 1971; Poetry, 1972; All Kinds of Paper Crafts, 1972; Working in Collage, 1973; Making Things from the Beach, 1973; The Creatures of the Carp, 1977. Address: Glenvegan, Braehead, Avoch, The Black Isle, Ross-shire, IV9 8QL; T.-0381 21028.

Porteous, Brian William, BSc (Hons), MILAM, DipILAM. Director of Operations, Scottish Sports Council, since 1989; Member, Board, National Coaching Foundation, since 1990; b. 6.2.51, Falkirk; m., Shena; 3 s. Educ. Falkirk High School; St. Andrews University; Moray House College of Education; Loughborough University of Technology. Joined Scottish Sports Council as Development Officer, 1979. Honorary Secretary, British Orienteering Federation, 1974-76. Publication: Orienteering, 1979. Recreations: golf; orienteering; amateur opera/musicals; caravanning. Address: (h.) Rannoch Lodge, 11a Mansion Road, North Berwick, East Lothian, EH39 4PG; T.-0620 3482.

Pounder, Professor Derrick John, MB, ChB, FRCPA, FFPathRCPI, FCAP, MRCPath. Professor of Forensic Medicine, Dundee University, since 1987; b. 25.2.49, Pontypridd; m., Georgina Kelly; 1 s.; 2 d. Educ. Pontypridd Boys' Grammar; Birmingham University. Senior Lecturer (Forensic Pathology), University of Adelaide; Deputy Chief Medical Examiner, Edmonton, Alberta, and Associate Professor, Universities of Alberta and Calgary, 1985-87. Freeman of Llantrisant. Recreations: photography; medieval architecture; almost lost causes. Address: (b.) Department of Forensic Medicine, Royal Infirmary, Dundee, DD1 9ND; T.-0382 200794.

Power, James Patrick, MA (Hons), BA (Hons). Secretary, Headteachers' Association of Scotland; b. 2.2.27, Renfrew; m., E. Patricia Currie; 1 d. Educ. St. Mirin's Academy, Paisley; Glasgow University; London University; Jordanhill College of Education. Teacher: St. Columba's High School, Greenock, 1948-52, St. Joseph's Academy, Kilmarnock, 1952-56; Principal Teacher of Science, Sacred Heart High School, Girvan, 1956-60; Principal Teacher of Mathematics, St. Joseph's Academy, Kilmarnock, 1960-63; Head,

Department of Mathematics and Science, Ayr Technical College, 1963-74; Mathematics Tutor, Open University, 1971-75; Adviser in Mathematics, County of Lanark, 1974-75; Rector, St. Columba's High School, Gourock, 1975-88. Chairman, Scottish Central Committee on Mathematics, 1981-86; Member: Scottish Education/Industry Committee, 1984-86, CNAA Committee in Scotland, 1983-87, Catholic Education Commission, 1978-87; Chairman, Central Support Group on Mathematics; Chairman, 5-14 Review and Development Group for Mathematics; President, Gourock Rotary Club, 1984-85; Hon. Vice-President, Ayr Amateur Opera Company. Address: (b.) Jordanhill College of Education, Southbrae Drive, Glasgow, G13 1PP; T.-041-950 3298.

Poyser, Norman Leslie, BPharm, PhD, DSc. Research Scientist; Senior Lecturer and Director of Studies, Edinburgh University; b. 9.8.47, Nottingham; m., Moira A.; 1 s.; 1 d.; 2 step d. Educ. High Pavement Grammar School, Nottingham; School of Pharmacy, London University; Edinburgh University. Lecturer, Edinburgh University, 1975-87. Sandoz Prize. Publication: Prostaglandins in Reproduction. Recreations: bridge; tennis; watching sport on television; going to theatre and concerts. Address: (h.) 5 Buckstone Close, Edinburgh, EH10 6XA; T.-031-445 4781.

Prag, Thomas Gregory Andrew, MA, FBIM. Managing Director, Moray Firth Radio; b. 2.1.47, London; m., Angela; 3 s. Educ. Westminster School; Brasenose College, Oxford. Joined BBC, 1968, as Studio Manager; Producer, BBC Radio Oxford; Programme Organiser, BBC Radio Highland; first Chief Executive, Moray Firth Radio, 1981. President, Inverness and District Choral Society; Trustee, Highland Community Foundation; Council Member, Radio Academy. Recreations: good intentions towards restoration of 1950 Daimler; keeping clock collection wound; family; growing vegetables; chasing deer off vegetables. Address: (b.) Moray Firth Radio, PO Box 271, Inverness, IV3 6SP.

Preece, Paul Edward, MD, FRCSEdin, FRCS. Senior Lecturer in Surgery, Dundee University, since 1978; Honorary Consultant Surgeon, Tayside Health Board, since 1978; b. 21.10.40, Great Malvern; m., Heather Margaret Angell; 2 d. Educ. Worcester Cathedral King's School; Welsh National School of Medicine, Cardiff. Pre-registration House Officer, Cardiff and Newport, 1966-67; Senior House Officer posts, Oxford, Bristol and Birmingham, 1968-70; Rotational Surgical Registrar, South Wales, 1971-72; Tenovus and Medical Research Council Research Fellow, 1973-74; Lecturer in Surgery, Welsh National School of Medicine, 1975-77. Council of Europe Fellowship, Germany, 1975. Recreations: music; vintage cars. Address: (h.) 11 Marchfield Road, Dundee, DD2 1JG; T.-0382 68126.

Prentice, Rev. George, BA, BTh, ASTA, AIST(LS). Minister, Martyrs' Church, Paisley, since 1969; b. 21.7.32, Motherwell; m., Janet Dunsmuir; 1 s.; 1 d. Educ. Wishaw High School; Glasgow University and Trinity College. Civil Service, 1949-58; National Service, RAF, 1951-53; student, 1958-63; Minister, Townhead Parish Church, Coatbridge, 1964-69; Moderator, Presbytery of Paisley, 1982-83; Moderator, Synod of Clydesdale, since 1988. Publication: Church and Congregation. Recreations: teaching swimming; examining life-saving; following football; reading. Address: 12 Low Road, Castlehead, Paisley; T.-041-889 2182.

Prescott, Professor Laurie F., MA, MB, BChir, MD, FRCPEdin, FRSE, FRCP, FFPM. Honorary Consultant Physician, Edinburgh Royal Infirmary, since 1969; Professor of Clinical Pharmacology, Edinburgh University, since 1985; b. 13.5.34, London; m.; 1 s.; 3 d. Educ. Hitchin Boys Grammar School; Cambridge University; Middlesex Hospital Medical School, London. Research Fellow, Johns Hopkins

Hospital, Baltimore, 1963-65; Lecturer in Therapeutics, Aberdeen University, 1965-69; Senior Lecturer in Clinical Pharmacology, Edinburgh University, 1969-74, Reader, 1974-85. British Pharmacological Society Lilly Prize, 1978. Recreations: music; walking; gardening; sailing. Address: (h.) Redfern, 24 Colinton Road, Edinburgh, EH10 5EQ; T.-031-447 2571.

Preston, Ian Mathieson Hamilton, BSc, PhD, FEng, MInstP, FIEE. Chief Executive, Scottish Power, since 1990; Deputy Chairman, South of Scotland Electricity Board, 1983-90; b. 18.7.32, Bournemouth; m., Sheila Hope Pringle; 2 s. Educ. Kilmarnock Academy; Glasgow University. University Assistant Lecturer, 1957-59; joined SSEB as Assistant Reactor Physicist, 1959; various appointments until Chief Engineer, Generation Design and Construction Division, 1972; Director General, Central Electricity Generating Board, Generation Development and Construction Division, 1977-83. Chairman, British Hydromechanics Research Association, 1985-89. Recreations: angling; gardening. Address: (b.) Scottish Power plc, Cathcart House, Spean Street, Glasgow, G44 4BE; T.-041-637 7177.

Preston-Thomas, Rev. Canon Colin Barnabas Rashleigh. Priest, Scottish Episcopal Church, since 1954; b. 11.6.28, Exford, Somerset; m., Barbara Anne Davidson. Educ. Bristol Grammar School; King's College, London; Edinburgh Theological College. Curate, St. David's, Pilton, 1953-54; Precentor, Perth Cathedral, 1954-60; Prison Chaplain, Perth, 1955-60; Rector: Rosyth with Inverkeithing, 1960-72, St. John's Forfar, 1972-82, Holy Trinity, Pitlochry, with Kilmaveonaig, Blair Atholl, since 1982; Synod Clerk, St. Andrews Diocese; Canon, Perth Cathedral, since 1968; Diocesan Secretary, 1980-90. Recreations: theatre; music. Address: The Parsonage, Perth Road, Pitlochry, PH16 5DJ; T.-Pitlochry 2176.

Prettyman, James Arthur, CEng, MIEE. Executive Director, Leith Enterprise Trust, since 1984; President, Motherwell Bridge Projects Ltd. (Canada), since 1982; Director and General Manager, Motherwell Bridge Pipe Ltd., since 1970; b. 19.3.31, Hatfield, Hertfordshire; m., Wendy Bell; 2 d. Educ. North Western Polytechnic, London; Hatfield Polytechnic. Student Apprentice/Production Engineer, de Havilland Aircraft; Sub-Lieutenant, Royal Navy (Fleet Air Arm); Management Trainee/Production Superintendent, Brush Electrical Engineering Co. (now Hawker Siddeley); Unit Engineer, Glacier Metal; Manufacturing Manager, Ampep Products; Director, Motherwell Bridge Group. Member, Citizens Advice Management Group; Past President, Leith Rotary Club. Recreations: fitness; swimming; hill-walking. Address: (b.) 47 Queen Charlotte Street, Leith, Edinburgh; T.-031-553 5566.

Price, Professor Gareth Glyn, MA, DPhil. Professor and Chief Executive, St. Andrews Management Institute, since 1989 (on secondment from Shell); b. 29.1.35, Cardiff; m., Maureen Ann; 1 s.; 2 d. Educ. Canton High School, Cardiff; Chipping Campden Grammar School; Pembroke College, Oxford. Commissioned, RAF; Shell Research, 1962-64; Shell International Petroleum Co., since 1964; Head of Energy Economics, SIPC, 1981; Senior Consultant, 1983. Recreation: golf. Address: (h.) 24 Golf Place, St. Andrews, Fife.

Price, Rev. Peter Owen, CBE, QHC, BA, FPhS. Minister, Blantyre Old Parish Church, Glasgow, since 1985; b. 18.4.30, Swansea; m., 1, Margaret Winifred Trevan (deceased); 3 d. Educ. Wyggeston School, Leicester; Didsbury College, Bristol; Open University. Chaplain, Royal Navy, 1960-84, latterly Principal Chaplain, Church of Scotland and Free Churches (Naval), Ministry of Defence, 1981-84. Recreations: clay pigeon shooting; rugby; warm water sailing. Address: The Manse of Blantyre, High Blantyre, Glasgow, G72 9UA; T.-0698 823130.

Prickett, Professor (Alexander Thomas) Stephen, MA, PhD, DipEd, FAHA. Regius Professor of English Language and Literature, Glasgow University, since 1990; b. 4.6.39, Freetown, Sierra Leone; m., Maria Angelica; 2 d. Educ. Kent College, Canterbury; Trinity Hall, Cambridge; University College, Oxford. English Teacher, Methodist College, Uzauakoli, E. Nigeria, 1962-64; Lecturer/Reader, Sussex University, 1967-82; Professor of English, Australian National University, Canberra, 1983-89. Publications: Do It Yourself Doom, 1962; Coleridge and Wordsworth: the Poetry of Growth, 1970; Romanticism and Religion, 1976; Victorian Fantasy, 1979; Words and the Word: language poetics and Biblical interpretation, 1986; England and the French Revolution, 1988. Recreations: walking; skiing; tennis; drama. Address: (b.) Department of English Literature, Glasgow University, Glasgow; T.-041-339 8855.

Pride, Stephen James, BSc, PhD. Reader in Mathematics, Glasgow University, since 1987; b. 8.1.49, Melbourne. Educ. Hampton High School, Melbourne; Monash University, Melbourne; Australian National University, Canberra. Research Fellow, Open University, 1974-78; Temporary Lecturer in Mathematics, King's College, London University, 1978-79; Lecturer in Mathematics, Glasgow University, 1979-87. Member, Editorial Board, London Mathematical Society. Publications: more than 45 articles on group theory. Recreations: sport and outdoor activities; travelling; cinema. Address: (h.) 54 Airlie Street, Glasgow, G12 9SN; T.-041-339 7395.

Priest, Professor Eric Ronald, BSc, MSc, PhD, FRSE. Professor of Theoretical Solar Physics, St. Andrews University, since 1983; b. 7.11.43, Birmingham; m., Clare Wilson; 3 s.; 1 d. Educ. King Edward VI School, Birmingham; Nottingham University; Leeds University. St. Andrews University: Lecturer in Applied Mathematics, 1968, Reader, 1977. Recreations: bridge; walking; swimming; swingnastics; children. Address: (b.) Mathematical and Computational Sciences Department, St. Andrews University, St. Andrews, KY16 9SS; T.-0334 76161.

Pringle, Derek Hair, CBE, PhD, DSc, CPhys, FInstP, FRSE, Hon. FRCSE, FRSA. Chairman, Borders Health Board, since 1989; Chairman, SEEL Limited, Livingston, since 1980; Director: Melville Street Investments plc, since 1984, Amersham International PLC, 1978-87; Chairman, Bioscot Limited, Edinburgh, 1983-86; b. 8.1.26, Edinburgh; m., Anne Collier Caw; 3 s.; 1 d. Educ. George Heriot's School, Edinburgh; Edinburgh University. Research Physicist, Ferranti Ltd., Edinburgh, 1948-59; Nuclear Enterprises Ltd., Edinburgh: Technical Director, 1960-76, Managing Director, 1976-78, Chairman, 1978-80. Member, National Radiological Protection Board, 1969-81; Member, Court, Heriot-Watt University, 1968-77; President, Edinburgh Chamber of Commerce, 1979-81; Chairman, Association of Scottish Chambers of Commerce, 1985-87; Vice President, Royal Society of Edinburgh, 1985-88; Trustee, National Museums of Scotland, since 1985. Recreations: golf; gardening. Address: (h.) Earlyvale, Eddleston, Peeblesshire EH45 8QX; T.-072-13-231.

Pringle, Reginald Vincent, MA, MLitt. Librarian, Aberdeen University, since 1988; b. 23.12.42, Edinburgh; m., Pamela Margaret; 3 s. Educ. George Heriot's School; Edinburgh University. Associate Librarian, St. Andrews University, 1981-88. Project Director, Grampian Information, since 1990. Recreation: music. Address: (h.) 47 Malcolm's Mount, Stonehaven, AB3 2SR; T.-0569 66405.

Pringle, Robert, MB, ChB, ChM, FRCS(Eng), FRCS(Edin), FRCS(Glas). Consultant Surgeon, Ninewells Hospital, Dundee, since 1974; Honorary Senior Lecturer, Dundee University, since 1967; Member, Council, Medical and Dental Defence Union of Scotland, since 1979; b. 23.8.27, Paisley; m., Margaret Anne Mitchell; 1 s.; 2 d. Educ. Camphill School, Paisley; Glasgow University. RAF, 1951-55 (Squadron Leader); Hall Fellow in Surgery, then Registrar in Surgery, Glasgow Royal Infirmary, 1956-59; Senior Registrar in Surgery, Royal Victoria Infirmary, Newcastle upon Tyne, 1960-63; First Assistant in Surgery, Newcastle upon Tyne University, 1963-64; Senior Lecturer in Surgery, St. Andrews University, 1964-67; Consultant Surgeon, Dundee Royal Infirmary, 1964-74. Chairman, Surgical Section, National Medical Consultative Committee, since 1987. Publications: papers and books on various gastroenterological, surgical and scientific topics. Recreations: flying; piano; golf; cycling. Address: (h.) Taynuilt, Kilspindie, Rait, Perthshire, PH2 7RX; T.-0821 670289.

Pritchard, Kenneth William, BL, WS, SSC. Secretary, The Law Society of Scotland, since 1976; Secretary, Scottish Council of Law Reporting, since 1976; Clerk, Registrar of Examiners, since 1976; b. 14.11.33, London; Honorary Sheriff, Dundee; m., Gretta Murray; 2 s.; 1 d. Educ. Dundee High School; Fettes College; St. Andrews University. National Service, Argyll and Sutherland Highlanders, 1955-57; 2nd Lt., 1956; TA, 1957-62 (Captain); joined J. & J. Scrimgeour, Solicitors, Dundee, 1957; Senior Partner, 1970-76; Member: Sheriff Court Rules Council, 1973-76, Lord Dunpark's Committee considering Reparation upon Criminal Conviction, 1973-77; Hon. Visiting Professor, Law School, Strathclyde University; Hon. Member, Law Institute of Victoria, 1985; Hon. Member, Law Society of New Zealand, 1987; Hon. Member, Faculty of Procurators and Solicitors in Dundee; Governor, Moray House College of Education, 1982-86; Member, National Trust for Scotland Jubilee Appeal Committee, 1980-82; Member, University Court of Dundee; President, Dundee High School Old Boys Club, 1975-76. Recreation: golf. Address: (h.) 36 Ravelston Dykes, Edinburgh, EH4 3EB; T.-031-332 8584.

Procter, Robert Hendy, MA. Secretary, Scottish Council, The Scout Association, since 1982; b. 22.1.31, Alloa; m., Elizabeth Rosemary; 1 s.; 2 d. Educ. Fettes College; Trinity Hall, Cambridge. Commissioned, Royal Corps of Signals (2nd Lt.), 1950; Patons & Baldwins Ltd., 1954-79 (General Manager, from 1969); Director, John Gladstone & Co. Ltd., Galashiels, 1980-82. General Commissioner of Income Tax, Clackmannan Division, 1976-80; Honorary Sheriff, Tayside Central and Fife, at Alloa, 1975; Edinburgh Diocese training for ministry, 1988-91; Member, Christ Church Morningside Ministry Team, 1991. Recreations: hill-walking; choral singing. Address: (h.) 2 Braid Avenue, Morningside, Edinburgh, EH10 6DR; T.-031-447 1140.

Proctor, David Maxwell, OBE, CStJ, MB, ChB, FRCSEdin, DL; b. 19.5.21, Aberdeen; m., Laura Lillias Marr; 4 s. Educ. Robert Gordon's College, Aberdeen; Aberdeen University. Formerly Consultant i/c Accident and Emergency Department, Aberdeen Royal Infirmary, Clinical Senior Lecturer in Traumatic Surgery and Deputy Director, Institute of Environmental and Offshore Medicine, Aberdeen University. Recreations: gardening; complaining. Address: (h.) 1 Royfold Crescent, Aberdeen, AB2 6BH; T.-0224 314263.

Prophit, Professor Penny, BSN, MSN, DNSc, PhD. Professor of Nursing Studies and Head of Department, Edinburgh University, since 1983; b. 7.2.39, Monroe, Louisiana. Educ. The Catholic University of America; St. Louis University. Associate Professor and Chairperson of Psychiatric-Mental Health Nursing Department, University of Southern Mississippi, 1974-75; Associate Professor and Chairperson of Graduate Research, The Catholic University of America, Washington DC, 1975-78; Professor, Catholic University of Louvain/Leuven, Belgium, 1978-83; Director, Nursing Research Unit, Edinburgh University, 1983-84. Consultant, World Health Organisation; Mental Welfare Commissioner for Scotland, 1986-90. Recreations: playing piano; golf; jogging; writing poetry and short stories. Address: (h.) 51 Thirlestane Road, Edinburgh, EH9 1AP; T.-031-447 2148.

Prosser, (Leslie) Charles, DFA, DAEd. Secretary, Royal Fine Art Commission for Scotland, since 1976; b. 27.10.39, Harrogate; m., Coral; 1 s.; 2 d. Educ. Bath Academy of Art at Corsham Court; Slade School of Fine Art, London University. Assistant Lecturer in Fine Art, Blackpool School of Art, 1962-64; Fine Art research, Royal Academy, Stockholm, 1964-65; Lecturer in Fine Art, Leeds/Jacob Kramer College of Art, 1965-76; research in Art Education, Leeds University, 1974-75. Leverhulme European Arts Research Award, 1964. Recreations: Scottish dancing and hill-walking. Address: (h.) 28 Mayfield Terrace, Edinburgh, EH9 1RZ; T.-031-668 1141.

Prosser, Hon. Lord QC, MA (Oxon), LLB. Senator of the College of Justice in Scotland and Lord of Session, since 1986; b. 23.11.34, Edinburgh; m., Vanessa Lindsay; 2 s.; 2 d. Educ. Edinburgh Academy; Corpus Christi College, Oxford; Edinburgh University. Advocate, 1962; Queen's Counsel, 1974; Vice-Dean, Faculty of Advocates, 1979-83, Dean of Faculty, 1983-86. Chairman, Royal Lyceum Theatre Company; Chairman, Scottish Historic Buildings Trust; Chairman, Royal Fine Art Commission for Scotland. Address: 7 Randolph Crescent, Edinburgh, EH3 7TH; T.-031-225 2709.

Proudfoot, Thomas A., BSc. Rector, Girvan Academy, since 1982; b. 28.2.33, Irvine; m., V. Audrey Howlett; 1 d. Educ. Carrick Academy, Maybole; Glasgow University; Jordanhill College of Education. National Service, Royal Signals; Mathematics Teacher, Irvine Royal Academy and Ravenspark Academy; Assistant Rector, Kilmarnock Academy; Depute Rector, Carrick Academy, Maybole. Elder, Church of Scotland. Recreations: DIY; gardening; walking. Address: (h.) 8 Ainslie Road, Girvan, KA26 OAY.

Proudfoot, Professor V. Bruce, BA, PhD, FSA, FRSE, FRSGS, FSA Scot. Professor of Geography, St. Andrews University; b. 24.9.30, Belfast; m., Edwina Valmai Windram Field; 2 s. Educ. Royal Belfast Academical Institution; Queen's University, Belfast. Research Officer, Nuffield Quaternary Research Unit, Queen's University, Belfast, 1954-58; Lecturer in Geography: Queen's University, Belfast, 1958-59, Durham University, 1959-67; Hatfield College, Durham: Tutor, 1960-63, Librarian, 1963-65; Visiting Fellow, University of Auckland and Commonwealth Visiting Fellow, Australia, 1966; Alberta University, Edmonton: Associate Professor, 1967-70, Professor, 1970-74; Co-ordinator, Socio-Economic Opportunity Studies and Staff Consultant, Alberta Human Resources Research Council, 1971-72. General Secretary, Royal Society of Edinburgh, since 1991 (Convener, Earth Sciences Committee, 1983-85, Vice-President, 1985-88, Convener, Grants Committee, 1988-91); Chairman, Society for Landscape Studies, 1979-83; Vice-President, Society of Antiquaries of Scotland, 1982-85; President, Section H, BAAS, 1985; Chairman, Rural Geography Study Group, Institute of British Geographers, 1980-84; Hon. Editor, Royal Scottish Geographical Society, since 1978; Hon. President, Scottish Association of Geography Teachers, 1982-84; Trustee, National Museum of Antiquities of Scotland, 1982-85. Recreation: gardening. Address: (h.) Westgate, Wardlaw Gardens, St. Andrews, KY16 9DW; T.-0334 73293.

Provan, James Lyal Clark. Chairman, McIntosh of Dyce Ltd., McIntosh Donald Ltd.; European Consultant; Member (Conservative), European Parliament, NE Scotland, 1979-89; Farmer; b. 19.12.36, Glenfarg, Perthshire; m., Roweena Adele Lewis; 2 s.; 1 d. Educ. Ardvreck School, Crieff; Oundle School, Northants; Royal Agricultural College, Cirencester. National Farmers Union of Scotland: Area President, Kinross, 1965, Fife and Kinross, 1971; Tayside Regional Councillor, 1978-81; Member, Tay River Purification Board, 1978-81; European Democratic (Conservative) Spokesman on Agriculture and Fisheries, 1981-87; Questor of European Parliament, 1987-89; former Executive Director, Scottish Financial Enterprise. Recreations: country pursuits; sailing; flying; politics; agriculture. Address: Wallacetown, Bridge of Earn, Perth, PH2 8QA; T.-0738 812243.

Punter, Professor David Godfrey, BA, MA, PhD. Professor of English Studies, Stirling University, since 1988; b. 19.11.49, London; m., Caroline Mary Case-Punter; 1 s.; 2 d. Educ. John Lyon School, Harrow; Fitzwilliam College, Cambridge. Lecturer, University of East Anglia, 1973-84; Professor, Fudan University, Shanghai, 1983; Senior Lecturer, University of East Anglia, 1984-86; Director, Development of University English Teaching Project, 1985-86; Professor, Chinese University of Hong Kong, 1986-88. Publications: eight books; 31 articles; 26 chapters contributed; two books edited. Recreations: child-minding; dog-minding; walking; squash. Address: (b.) Stirling University, Stirling, FK9 4LA; T.-0786 73171, Ext. 2362.

Purser, John Whitley, MA, PhD. Composer and Lecturer; Poet, Playwright and Broadcaster; b. 10.2.42, Glasgow; 1 s.; 1 d. Educ. Fettes College; Glasgow University; Royal Scottish Academy of Music and Drama. Part-time Lecturer in English Literature, Glasgow University, 1981-85; Manager, Scottish Music Information Centre, 1985-87; compositions include two operas, numerous orchestral and chamber works; three books of poetry, The Counting Stick, A Share of the Wind and Amoretti; four radio plays and two radio series, A Change of Tune and Scotland's Music. Recreations: numerous. Address: (b.) 29 Banavie Road, Glasgow, G11 5AW; T.-041-339 5292.

Purslow, Christopher George, BArch, RIBA, FRSA. Director of Architecture and Related Services, City of Glasgow, since 1988; b. 27.3.46, Shrewsbury. Educ. High School, Newcastle under Lyme; Bristol University. Courtaulds Ltd., Coventry, 1967; Tarmac Ltd., Wolverhampton, 1968; Philip Johnson, Architect, New York, 1969; Rice/Roberts, Architects, London, 1972; LB of Islington, 1974; Borough Architect, Islington, 1983-88. Recreations: theatre; music; mountains; architecture. Address: (b.) 20 Trongate, Glasgow, G1 5EY; T.-041-227 5379.

Purves, David, BSc, PhD. Editor, Lallans Magazine, since 1987; Playwright; b. 9.4.24, Selkirk; m., Lilian Rosemary; 3 s. Educ. Galashiels Academy; Edinburgh University. Head, Trace Element Department, Edinburgh School of Agriculture, 1956-82; Supervisor, Central Analytical Department, 1982-87; author of Trace Element Contamination of the Environment, 1977; poetry collection: Thrawart Threipins, 1976; many poems in Scots published; Past Preses, Scots Language Society. Address: (h.) 8 Strathalmond Road, Edinburgh, EH4 8AD; T.-031-339 7929.

Purves-Hume, Ian Campbell, FBIM. Director, Royal Scottish Agricultural Benevolent Institution, since 1990; b. 22.7.38, London; m., Jill Cairns Fairbairn; 2 d. Educ. Ottershaw; Royal Military Academy, Sandhurst. Army Officer, Argyll and Sutherland Highlanders, 1958-90, to rank of Brigadier. Recreations: walking; bird-watching. Address: (b.) RSABI, Ingliston, Edinburgh, EH28 8NB; T.-031-333 1023.

Purvis, John Robert, CBE, MA (Hons). International Business Consultant (Managing Partner, Purvis & Co.), since 1973; Member for Scotland, IBA, 1985-89; Director, James River UK Holdings Ltd., since 1984; Vice President, Scottish Conservative and Unionist Association, 1987-89; b. 6.7.38, St. Andrews; m., Louise Spears Durham; 1 s.; 2 d. Educ. Glenalmond; St. Andrews University. 2nd Lt., Scots Guards, 1956-58; First National City Bank (Citibank NA), London, New York City, Milan, 1962-69; Treasurer, Noble Grossart Ltd., Edinburgh, 1969-73; Director and Secretary, Brigton Farms Ltd., 1969-86; Managing Director, Founder, Owner, Gilmerton Management Services Ltd., since 1973; Member, European Parliament, Mid Scotland and Fife, 1979-84 (Deputy Chief Whip, Group Spokesman on Monetary Affairs, Energy, Research and Technology) Vice Chairman, European Parliament Delegation to the Gulf States; Chairman, IBA Scottish Advisory Committee, 1985-89. Member of Council, St. Leonards School, St. Andrews, 1981-89; Chairman, Economic Affairs Committee, Scottish Conservative and Unionist Association, since 1986; Member, Scottish Advisory Committee on Telecommunications, since 1990. Recreations: Italy and Scotland. Address: Gilmerton House, Dunino, St. Andrews, KY16 8NB; T.-0334 75830.

Puxty, Professor Anthony Grahame, BA, MA, PhD, ACIS, MBIM. Professor of Accounting and Finance, Strathclyde University, since 1987; b. 17.5.46, Shoeburyness; m., Jenifer Mary; 2 s. Educ. Southend-on-Sea High School for Boys; Lancaster University. Insurance Officer, Provident Life Association, 1963-68; Assistant Accountant, First National Credit Co., 1968-70; Scotia Investments, 1970-71; Accountant/Chief Accountant, advertising agency, 1971-73; Financial Accountant, Ruberoid Contracts, 1973-74; Lecturer, Sheffield University, 1976-87. Recreations: music; swimming. Address: (h.) The Lindens, 9 Victoria Road, Helensburgh, G84 7RT; T.-0436 76878.

Pyper, Mark Christopher Spring-Rice, BA. Headmaster, Gordonstoun School, since 1990; b. 13.8.47, Seaford; m., Jennifer L.; 1 s.; 2 d. Educ. Winchester College; Oxford University; London University. Assistant Master, Stoke Brunswick School, East Grinstead, 1966-68; Assistant Master, then Joint Headmaster, St. Wilfrid's School, Seaford, 1969-79; Registrar, Housemaster, then Deputy Headmaster, Sevenoaks School, 1979-90; Director, Sevenoaks Summer Festival, 1979-90. Address: (h.) Headmaster's House, Gordonstoun School, Elgin, IV30 2RF; T.-0343 830445.

Q

Quinault, Francis Charles, BSc, PhD. Assistant Principal for External Affairs, St. Andrews University, since 1987; Senior Lecturer, Department of Psychology; b. 8.5.43, London; m., Wendy Ann Horton; 1 s.; 2 d. Educ. Dulwich College; St. Catharine's College, Cambridge; Bristol University. Ford Foundation Scholar, Oslo University, 1969-70. Member, National Committee for the Training of University Teachers, 1981-87. Recreations: theatre; singing; hill-walking. Address: (b.) College Gate, St. Andrews University, St. Andrews, KY16 9AJ; T.-0334 76161.

R

Racey, Professor Paul Adrian, MA, PhD, DSc, FIBiol. Professor of Zoology, Aberdeen University, since 1985 (Head of Department, since 1987); b. 7.5.44, Wisbech, Cambridgeshire; m., Anna Priscilla Notcutt; 3 s. Educ. Ratcliffe College, Leicester; Downing College, Cambridge. Rothamsted Experimental Station, Harpenden, 1965-66; Zoological Society of London, 1966-70; Unit of Reproductive Biology, Liverpool University, 1970-73; joined Department of Zoology, Aberdeen University, 1973. Recreations: riding; sailing; shooting. Address: (b.) Department of Zoology, Aberdeen University, Tillydrone Avenue, Aberdeen, AB9 2TN; T.-0224 272858.

Radford, Professor Peter F., DPE, MSc, PhD. Professor and Head, Department of Physical Education and Sports Science, Glasgow University (Director, Department of Physical Education and Recreation, 1976-87); b. 20.9.39, Walsall; m., Margaret M. Beard; 1 d. Educ. Tettenhall College, Wolverhampton; Cardiff College of Education; Purdue University, Indiana; Glasgow University. Assistant Professor, McMaster University, School of Physical Education and Athletics, Hamilton, Ontario, 1967-75. Member, Scottish Sports Council, 1983-90; Chairman, Scottish Consultative Group on Sports Medicine and Sports Science, 1984-90; Chairman, Sports Council Drug Abuse Advisory Group, since 1991 (Member, since 1988); Member, International Working Group on Anti-Doping in Sport, since 1991; Chairman, Review of Coaching in Sport in UK, since 1989; UK Delegate to Council of Europe's Monitoring Group, European Anti-Doping in Sport Convention, since 1990; Member, National Sports Medicine Institute Management Committee, since 1991; holder of world record, 200 metres and 220 yards, 1960; Bronze Medal, 100 metres and 4 x 100 metres Relay, Olympic Games, Rome, 1960; British 100 metres record, set in Paris, 1958, remained unbroken for 20 years. Address: (b.) Department of Physical Education and Sports Science, Glasgow University, Glasgow, G12 8LT; T.-041-330 5429.

Rae, Hugh Crauford. Novelist; b. 22.11.35, Glasgow; m., Elizabeth Dunn; 1 d. Educ. Knightswood School. Prolific popular novelist; author of more than 50 tiles, under a variety of pseudonyms, including Stuart Stern, James Albany and Jessica Stirling; books include (as Hugh C. Rae) Skinner, The Marksman, The Shooting Gallery, Harkfast and Privileged Strangers and (as Jessica Stirling) The Spoiled Earth, The Hiring Fair, The Dark Pasture, Treasures on Earth, Creature Comforts, Hearts of Gold, The Good Provider, The Asking Price, The Wise Child, The Welcome Light. Recreation: golf. Address: (h.) Drumore Farm Cottage, Balfron Station, Stirlingshire.

Rae, Rita Emilia Anna, LLB (Hons). Advocate. Educ. St. Patrick's High School, Coatbridge; Edinburgh University. Apprentice, Biggart, Lumsden & Co., Glasgow, 1972-74; Assistant Solicitor: Balfour & Manson, Edinburgh, 1974, Biggart, Baillie & Gifford, Glasgow, 1974-76; Solicitor and Partner, Ross Harper & Murphy, Glasgow, 1976-81; Advocate, 1982. Recreations: theatre; driving; walking; opera; music. Address: (h.) 73 Fotheringay Road, Glasgow; T.-041-423 0781.

Rae, Scott Alexander, LLB (Hons), WS, NP. Partner, Morton Fraser Milligan WS, Edinburgh, since 1970; b. 17.12.44, Edinburgh; m., Annabel Riach; 3 s. Educ. Daniel Stewarts College, Edinburgh; Edinburgh University. Sometime Tutor and Course Leader, Edinburgh University; Law Society of Scotland Examiner in Taxation and Chairman, Board of Examiners; Member, VAT Tribunal (Scotland); Clerk, Incorporated Trades of Edinburgh; Council

Member, International Academy of Estate and Trust Law. Recreations: fishing; gardening. Address: (b.) 15-19 York Place, Edinburgh; T.-031-556 8444.

Raeburn, James B., FCIS. Director, Scottish Print Employers' Federation and Scottish Newspaper Publishers' Association, since 1984; b. 18.3.47, Jedburgh; m., Rosemary Bisset; 2 d. Educ. Hawick High School. Edinburgh Corporation, 1964-69; Roxburgh County Council, 1969-71; Electrical Contractors' Association of Scotland, 1972-83 (Secretary, 1975-83). Consultative Member, The Press Council, 1984-90; Director, Press Standards Board of Finance Ltd., since 1990; Director, Advertising Standards Board of Finance Ltd., since 1988. Recreations: golf; squash. Address: (b.) 48 Palmerston Place, Edinburgh, EH12 5DE; T.-031-220 4353.

Raeburn, Emeritus Professor John Ross, CBE, FRSE, FIBiol, BSc, MA, PhD. Consultant; b. 20.11.12, Kirkcaldy; m., Mary Roberts; 1 s.; 3 d. Educ. Manchester Grammar School; Edinburgh University; Cornell University. Professor, Agricultural Economics, Nanking University, 1936-37; Research Officer, Oxford University, 1938-39; Statistician, then Head of Agricultural Plans Branch, Ministry of Food, 1939-46; Senior Research Officer, Oxford University, 1946-49; Reader in Agricultural Economics, London University, 1949-59; Professor and Head, Department of Agriculture, Aberdeen University, 1959-78; Principal, North of Scotland College of Agriculture, 1963-78; Consultant to World Bank, since 1979; Vice-President, International Association of Agricultural Economists, 1964-70; President, Agricultural Economics Society, 1964-65. Publications: Agriculture: Foundations, Principles and Development; The History of the International Association of Agricultural Economists (Co-author). Recreations: travel; gardening; photography. Address: (h.) 30 Morningfield Road, Aberdeen, AB2 4AQ; T.-0224 314010.

Raffe, David James, BA, BPhil. Reader in Education, Edinburgh University, since 1985 (Co-Director, Centre for Educational Sociology, since 1987); b. 5.5.51, Felixstowe; m., Shirley Paine; 1 s.; 1 d. Educ. The Leys School; New College, Oxford; Nuffield College, Oxford. Edinburgh University: Research Fellow, Centre for Educational Sociology, 1975-79, Lecturer in Education, 1979-85; Deputy Director, Centre for Educational Sociology, 1979-87. Publications: Reconstructions of Secondary Education, 1983; Fourteen to Eighteen, 1984; Education and the Youth Labour Market, 1988. Recreations: squash; hill-walking. Address: (b.) 7 Buccleuch Place, Edinburgh, EH8 9LW; T.-031-650 4191.

Rafferty, George Campbell, BSc, MRCVS, DL. Veterinary Surgeon in general practice, since 1948; b. 1.3.26, Glasgow; m., Jane Lilian Sarsons; 2 s.; 2 d. Educ. Rutherglen Academy; Royal Dick Veterinary College. Qualified, 1948; in practice: Suffolk, 1948-49, Hampshire, 1949-50, Fife, 1951-52, Strathspey, since 1953; appointed Veterinary Zoo Inspector, 1984; Deputy Lieutenant, Inverness-shire, since 1985; Honorary Vice-President, Strathspey Farmers Club. Recreation: work. Address: Seaforth, Seafield Avenue, Grantown-on-Spey, Morayshire; T.-0479 2847.

Rahman, Mohammad Zalilur, MB, BS, FRCPsych, DTM&H. Consultant Psychiatrist, since 1977; Honorary Clinical Senior Lecturer, Glasgow University, since 1986; Chairman, North Division of Psychiatry, Greater Glasgow Health Board, since 1989; Deputy Physician Superintendent, Woodilee/Stoneyetts Hospital, since 1989; President, University Mosque D'awatul Islam Trust (Scotland) Ltd.; b. 14.11.30, Bangladesh; m., Dr. Syeda K. Nahar; 1 s. Educ. Dhaka University; Edinburgh University. Graduated in medicine, Dhaka; GP in Bangladesh; emigrated to UK, 1969; for-

mer Psychiatric Tutor, Royal College of Psychiatrists; Convener, Working Party on Manpower and Training, Substance Misuse Section, Royal College of Psychiatrists; Treasurer, Psychosomatic Society, Glasgow; former Vice Chairperson, Strathclyde Community Relations Council; President, Bengali and Arabic School, Glasgow; Member and Past President, Bangladesh Association, Glasgow; former Member, Broadcasting Council for Scotland; Member, Senate, Glasgow University, 1990-93. Recreations: gardening; travelling; reading. Address: (h.) Lynedoch, Larch Avenue, Lenzie, Glasgow, G66 4HT; T.-041-776 6428.

Rainey, John Bruce, BSc, MB, ChB, ChM, FRCSEdin. Consultant Surgeon, St. John's Hospital, Howden, Livingston, since 1988; Senior Lecturer in Surgery, Edinburgh University, since 1988; b. 18.5.52, Belfast; m., Dr. Linda Margaret King; 2 s.; 1 d. Educ. Royal Belfast Academical Institution; Edinburgh University. Trained in general surgery; Examiner in surgery and accident and emergency medicine for Royal College of Surgeons of Edinburgh. Aris and Gale Lecturer, Royal College of Surgeons of England, 1985. Recreations: family; sport; history and military history. Address: (h.) 9 Blackford Hill View, Edinburgh, EH9 3HD; T.-031-667 6216.

Ralston, Andrew Dunlop, BL, NP. Consultant, Macnair Clyde & Ralston, Solicitors, Paisley; Honorary Sheriff of North Strathclyde, at Paisley, since 1976; b. 22.5.23, Glasgow; m., Jane Neilson Burns; 3 s. Educ. Allan Glen's School, Glasgow; Glasgow University. Honorary Secretary, Scottish Baptist College, 1966-83. Recreation: gardening. Address: (b.) 43 High St, Paisley, PA1 2AJ; T.-041-887 5181.

Ralston, Ian B.M., MA, PhD, FSA, FSA Scot, MIFA. Senior Lecturer in Archaeology, Edinburgh University, since 1990; Director, Centre for Field Archaeology, since 1991; b. 11.11.50, Edinburgh; m., Sandra M. Webb; 1 s.; 1 d. Educ. Edinburgh Academy; Edinburgh University. Research Fellow in Archaeology, Aberdeen University, 1974-77; Lecturer in Geography/Archaeology, Aberdeen University, 1977-85; Lecturer in Archaeology, Edinburgh University, 1985-90. Hon. Chairman, Institute of Field Archaeologists, 1991-92. Publications: Introduction to British Prehistory (Co-author); Les Enceintes Du Limousin; 75 papers and reports. Recreation: family life. Address: (b.) Centre for Field Archaeology, Appleton Tower, Crichton Street, Edinburgh, EH8 9LE; T.-031-650 4138.

Ramsay, Major General Charles Alexander, CB, OBE. Landowner and Farmer, since 1965; Chief Executive, Caledonian Eagle, since 1991; b. 12.10.36, North Berwick; m., Hon. Mary Margaret Hastings MacAndrew; 2 s.; 2 d. Educ. Eton; Sandhurst. Commissioned Royal Scots Greys, 1956; Staff College, Canada, 1967-68; Commanded Royal Scots Dragoon Guards, 1977-79; Commander 12th Armoured Brigade, 1980-82; Dep DMO MOD, 1983-84; GOC Eastern District, 1984-87; Director, General Army Organisation and Territorial Army, 1987-89; resigned from Army; Chairman, Eagle Enterprises Ltd. (Bermuda), The Wine Company (Scotland) Ltd.; Director, John Menzies Plc, Grey Horse Properties Ltd., Edinburgh Military Tattoo Ltd., Potomac Holdings Inc (USA), Morningside Holdings Inc (USA); Colonel, The Royal Scots Dragoon Guards, 1992; Member, Royal Company of Archers (Queen's Bodyguard for Scotland). Recreations: field sports; equitation; travel; motoring. Address: (h.) Bughtrig, Coldstream, Berwickshire, TD12 4JP; T.-089 084 678.

Ramsay, John Neville David. Retired Chairman, John G. Borland & Peat Ltd., Glasgow; Board Member, Clyde Port Authority, 1983-89; b. 18.5.24, Glasgow; m., Olive Doreen; 1 s. Educ. Hutchesons' Boys Grammar School, Glasgow. Joined Anchor Line Ltd., Glasgow, 1940; War Service, RAF (home, North Africa, Italy), 1942-47; John G. Borland & Peat Ltd., Shipbrokers: joined, 1947, appointed Director, 1959, Managing Director, 1978, Chairman, 1980; President, Glasgow and Clyde Shipping Association, 1983; Director, Glasgow Chamber of Commerce, since 1983. Recreations: angling; painting; gardening; music. Address: (h.) Ash Ford, 17 Brackenrig Crescent, Waterfoot, Eaglesham, G76 0HF; T.-041-644 4234.

Ramsay, Rev. Robert John, LLB (Hons), NP, BD. Minister, Glenisla with Kilry with Lintrathen, since 1986; b. 28.10.51, Alyth; m., Sheila Margaret Ball; 2 d. Educ. Blairgowrie High School; Edinburgh University; St. Mary's College, St. Andrews. Apprentice Solicitor and Tutor in Constitutional Law, Dundee University, 1973-75; Lecturer in Private Law, Dundee University, 1975-79; Head, Department of Legal Studies, Administrative College, Port Moresby, Papua New Guinea, 1979-82; Assistant Minister, Kirriemuir Old Church, 1985-86. Honorary Treasurer, Fellowship of Reconciliation in Scotland; Depute Clerk, Angus Presbytery, since 1990. Recreations: music; reading; travel. Address: The Manse, Bridgend of Lintrathen, Kirriemuir, Angus; T.-05756 226.

Ramsey, Professor Peter Herbert, MA, DPhil. Professor of History, Aberdeen University, since 1966; b. 19.11.25, Barnet; m., Priscilla Telford; 3 d. Educ. Mill Hill School; Worcester College, Oxford. Assistant, Glasgow University, 1951-55; Lecturer, Bristol University, 1955-65. Publications: Tudor Economic Problems, 1963; The Price Revolution in Sixteenth Century England, 1971. Recreations: reading; music. Address: (h.) Goose Croft House, Kintore, Aberdeenshire; T.-Kintore 32337.

Randall, John Norman, BA, MPhil. Assistant Secretary, Housing Division 1, Scottish Office Environment Department, since 1989; b. 1.8.45, Bromley, Kent; 1 s.; 1 d. Educ. Bromley Grammar School; Bristol University; Glasgow University. Department of Economic Affairs; Scottish Office. Recreation: hill-walking. Address: (b.) St. Andrews House, Edinburgh, EH1 3DD; T.-031-244 2014.

Rankeillour, Rt. Hon. The Lord. Peer; Member, House of Lords, since 1968; Rear Commodore, House of Lords Yacht Club; Farmer and Landowner; b. 29.5.35. Educ. Ampleforth College. Recreations: agricultural and horticultural equipment/machinery inventor; shooting, hunting, and landscaping on the grand scale. Address: (h.) The Achaderry Estate, Roy Bridge, Western Inverness-shire; T.-Spean Bridge 206.

Rankin, Alick Michael, CBE (1986). Chairman, Scottish & Newcastle plc, since 1989; Director: Christian Salvesen PLC, since 1986, Bank of Scotland, since 1987, Sears plc, since 1991, British Linen Bank Group, since 1991, Scottish Financial Enterprise, since 1991, Securities Trust of Scotland plc, since 1991, High Gosforth Park PLC, since 1988; b. 23.1.35, London; m., Suzetta Nelson; 1 s.; 3 d. Educ. Eton College; Oxford University. Scots Guards, 1953-55; investment banking, Toronto, 1956-59; Scottish & Newcastle Breweries plc, since 1960. Immediate Past President, The Brewers' Society. Recreations: fishing; shooting; golf; tennis. Address: (b.) Abbey Brewery, 111 Holyrood Road, Edinburgh, EH8 8YS; T.-031-556 2591.

Rankin, Professor David W.H., MA, PhD, FRSE. Professor of Structural Chemistry, Edinburgh University, since 1989 (Head, Chemistry Department, since 1990); b. 8.6.45, Birkenhead; m., Stella M. Thomas; 3 s.; 1 d. Educ. Birkenhead School; King's College, Cambridge. Edinburgh University: ICI Research Fellow, 1969, Demonstrator, 1971, Lecturer, 1973, Reader, 1980, Professor, 1989. Publication: Structural Methods in Inorganic Chemistry, 1986. Address: (b.) Department of Chemistry, Edinburgh University, West Mains Road, Edinburgh, EH9 3JY; T.-031-650 4728.

Rankin, Emeritus Professor Robert Alexander, MA, PhD, ScD, FRSAMD, FRSE. Emeritus Professor of Mathematics, Glasgow University, since 1982; b. 27.10.15, Garlieston, Wigtownshire; m., Mary Ferrier Llewelyn; 1 s.; 3 d. Educ. Whithorn School; Fettes College; Clare College, Cambridge. Fellow, Clare College, 1939-51; War work on rockets, 1940-45; Lecturer, Cambridge University, 1945-51; Assistant Tutor, Clare College, 1947-51; Mason Professor of Pure Mathematics, Birmingham University, 1951-54; Professor of Mathematics, Glasgow University, 1954-82 (Clerk of Senate, 1971-78, Dean of Faculties, 1985-88). Vice-President, Royal Society of Edinburgh, 1960-63; Keith Prize, RSE, 1961-63; Member, Secretary of State's Advisory Council on Education, 1959-61; Honorary President, Gaelic Society of Glasgow, since 1969; Vice-President, London Mathematical Society, 1966-68; LMS Senior Whitehead Prize, 1987; President, Edinburgh Mathematical Society, 1957-58 and 1978-79, Honorary member, since 1990. Recreations: music; hill-walking; Gaelic studies. Address: (h.) 98 Kelvin Court, Glasgow, G12 OAH; T.-041-339 2641.

Rankin, Thomas John, MA, AdvDipEd, FCollP. Head Teacher, Sgoil Dhalabroig, South Uist, since 1981; b. 29.3.47, Glasgow; m., Jean Helen Adams; 2 d. Educ. Strathbungo Secondary School, Glasgow; Glasgow University. Teacher, Bernard Street Junior Secondary School, Glasgow; Teacher, Chizongwe Secondary School, Chipata, Zambia; Deputy Head, Kabulonga School for Boys, Lusaka, Zambia; Examinations Officer, i/c Cambridge School Certificate and London University External Degree Examinations, Ministry of Education, Lusaka; Acting Headmaster, Libala Secondary School, Lusaka; Teacher: West Derby Comprehensive School, Liverpool, Chryston High School, near Glasgow. Address: (b.) Sgoil Dhalabroig, Dalabrog, Isle of South Uist, PA81 5SS; T.-08784 276.

Ransford, Tessa, MA. Director, Scottish Poetry Library; Poet; Editor, Lines Review; b. 8.7.38, Bombay; 1 s.; 3 d. Educ. St. Leonard's School, St. Andrews; Edinburgh University; Craiglockhart College of Education. Publicity Department, Oxford University Press, 1958; in Pakistan as wife of missionary, 1960-68; Assistant to the Director, Scottish Institute of Adult Education, 1982-83; books of poetry: Poetry of Persons, 1975, While It Is Yet Day, 1976, Light of the Mind, 1980, Fools and Angels, 1984; Shadows from the Greater Hill, 1987; A Dancing Innocence, 1988; Seven Valleys, 1991; first prize, Jubilee poetry competition, Scottish Association for the Speaking of Verse, 1974; Scottish Arts Council Book Award, 1980; Howard Sergeant Award for services to poetry, 1989; Founder and Organiser, School of Poets (open learning workshop for practising poets). Recreation: hill-walking. Address: (b.) Scottish Poetry Library, Tweeddale Court, 14 High Street, Edinburgh, EH1 1TE; T.-031-557 2876.

Rea, John Malcolm, OBE, BA, MSc, CQSW. Director-General, Quarriers, since 1991; Vice-Chairman, Children's Hospice Association of Scotland, since 1992; Provincial Mission Board Convenor, Scottish Episcopal Church, since 1992; b. 28.2.44, Bradford; m., Della; 1 s.; 1 d. Educ. Bradford and Circencester Grammar Schools; Durham University; Newcastle University; Stirling University. Principal Adviser for Children, Newcastle Social Services, 1973-76; Scottish Director (Child Care), Barnardos, 1976-91; founding Chairman, Edinburgh Stopover, 1981-85; founding Vice-Chair, Scottish Child and Family Alliance, 1982-87; Consultant to Lambeth Conference, 1988; Management Group, Anglican International Family Network, since 1988; Scottish Consultant, Charities Effectiveness Review Trust, since 1991; Member, Anglican International Refugees Network, since 1991. Recreations: voluntary work; tennis; sailing; skiing; walking; travel; church social and political action. Address: (h.) Beaconhill, Kirknewton, Midlothian, EH27 8AA; T.-0506 880637.

Read, Professor Paul, BSc, MSc, PhD, CBiol, FIBiol, MIWEM. Associate Head, Department of Biological Sciences, Napier University, since 1990; b. 1.1.48, Saffron Walden; m., Jane. Educ. Palmers Grammar School, Grays; Hull University; Aston University. Research Technician, Essex Water Authority, 1969-70; Research Assistant, University of Aston, 1971-72; Research Fellow, then Lecturer, Napier College, 1972-82; Senior Lecturer, Napier Polytechnic, 1982-90. Forty publications. Recreations: offshore sailing/cruising; gardening; hill-walking. Address: (b.) Department of Biological Sciences, Napier University, Colinton Road, Edinburgh, EH10 5DT; T.-031-455 2625.

Readman, Hope, OBE. Chairman of Council, Scottish Branch, British Red Cross Society, 1986-90; b. 18.4.29, Glasgow; m., Lt.-Col. Ian R. Readman, MC (deceased); 2 s.; 1 d. Educ. Southover Manor School. British Red Cross Society: enrolled Perth Branch, 1959, President, Perth and Kinross Branch, 1974-84, Vice Chairman, Scottish Council, 1984-86; Member, Central and Tayside War Pensions Committee, 1975-80; Member, MSC Employment for Disabled, 1983-85; Member, Scottish Veterans' Garden City Association, since 1981; Elder, Dunblane Cathedral; Jubilee Medal; VMSM (three bars). Recreations: music; reading; cooking; sewing. Address: (h.) Gateside of Glasingall, Dunblane, Perthshire; T.-Dunblane 824248.

Reavley, Edwin, BJur, DipCrim. Head, Atmospheric and General Environment Protection Division, Scottish Office Environment Division, since 1989; b. 9.10.43, Oxford; m., Coral Hilary; 4 d. Educ. Huddersfield New College; Magdalen College School, Oxford; Sheffield University; Cambridge University. Joined Scottish Office, 1970. Recreations: horses; tennis; theatre; walking. Address: (h.) 19 Nelson Street, Edinburgh, EH3 6LJ; T.-031-556 7312.

Redding, Penelope Jane, MB, BS, MRCS, LRCP, MRCPath. Consultant Bacteriologist, Victoria Infirmary, Glasgow, since 1984; Honorary Clinical Lecturer, Glasgow University, since 1985; b. 21.11.50, London; m., Christopher John Vincent (deceased); 2 s. Educ. Lycee Francais de Londres; University College, London/Westminster Hospital Medical School. House Surgeon, Gynaecology, Queen Mary's, Roehampton, 1974; House Physician, Medicine, St. Stephen's, Fulham, 1975; Rotating SHO, Pathology, Westminster Hospital, 1975-76; Assistant Lecturer, Microbiology, St. Thomas's Hospital, 1976-77; Registrar, Bacteriology and Immunology, Western Infirmary, 1977-80 (Senior Registrar, 1980-84). Publication: Handbook of Intensive Care (Contributor), 1983. Recreations: skiing; swimming; dress-making; opera; ballet. Address: (b.) Bacteriology Department, Victoria Infirmary, Glasgow, G42 9TY; T.-041-649 4545.

Redpath, Jean, MBE, DUniv (Stirling), DMus (St. Andrews). Singer; b. 28.4.37, Leven. Educ. Leven; Buckhaven; Edinburgh University. Singer of traditional Scottish music with particular interest in Burns; has sung in every state in the USA, where she tours several times a year; lectures at summer school, Stirling University, each year; numerous radio and TV appearances, UK, USA and Australia; Kentucky Colonel. Recreations: singing!; photography. Address: resident in Fife.

Reed, Professor Peter, BA, RIBA, FRIAS, FRSA. Professor of Architecture, Strathclyde University, since 1986; Vice Principal of the University, since 1992; b. 31.1.33, Hayes, Middlesex; m., Keow Chim Lim; 2 d. Educ. Southall Grammar School; Manchester University; Open University. Commissioned Officer, RAF, 1960-61; Assistant Lecturer,

University of Hong Kong, 1961-64; Architect in practice, Malaysia, 1964-70; joined Strathclyde University, 1970. Governor, Glasgow School of Art, since 1982; Director, Glasgow West Conservation Trust, since 1990; Chairman, Council, Charles Rennie Mackintosh Society, since 1991. Recreations: opera; Italian language and culture; wine; cricket. Address: (b.) Department of Architecture and Building Science, Strathclyde University, 131 Rottenrow, Glasgow, G4 0NG; T.-041-552 4400.

Rees, Alan Tait, MA (Cantab), CQSW. Assistant Director, Edinburgh Council of Social Service, since 1976; b. 4.8.31, Shanghai, China; m., Alison Margaret; 2 s.; 2 d. Educ. Kingswood School, Bath; Gonville and Caius College, Cambridge; London School of Economics; University College, Swansea. Community Development Officer, Tanzania; Lecturer in Youth and Community Studies, Moray House College; Organising Secretary, Board for Information in Youth and Community Service, Scotland; Senior Community Development Officer, Council of Social Service for Wales. Chairman, Scotland Yard Adventure Centre, Edinburgh; Member, Scottish Committee, British Association of Social Workers; Trustee, Seagull Trust; Secretary, Handicabs (Lothian); Member, Transport Users Consultative Committee for Scotland; Treasurer, Scottish Community Transport Group. Recreations: gardening; painting; DIY. Address: (h.) 20 Seaforth Drive, Edinburgh, EH4 2BZ; T.-031-332 7317.

Rees, Professor Elmer Gethin, BA (Cantab), PhD (Warwick), MA (Oxon), FRSE. Professor, Department of Mathematics, Edinburgh University, since 1979; b. 19.11.41, Llandybie, Wales; m., Mary Elene; 2 s. Educ. Llandeilo Grammar School; St. Catharine's College, Cambridge; Warwick University. Lecturer, Department of Pure Mathematics, Hull University, 1967-69; Member, Institute for Advanced Study, Princeton, 1969-70; Lecturer, Department of Pure Mathematics, University College of Swansea, 1970-71; Tutorial Fellow, St. Catherine's College, Oxford and Lecturer in Mathematics, Oxford University, 1971-79. Publications: Notes on Geometry; Homotopy Theory. Address: (h.) 23 Blacket Place, Edinburgh, EH9 1RJ; T.-031-667 2747.

Rees, Jennifer Linda, BSc, MBIM. Head, Department of Management Studies, Scottish College of Textiles, since 1989; b. 2.7.51, Edinburgh; m., Richard; 1 s.; 1 d. Educ. George Watson's Ladies College, Edinburgh; Edinburgh University. Operational Research Analyst, then Statistical Quality Control Manager, Scottish & Newcastle Breweries Ltd.; Lecturer, Department of Business Studies, Edinburgh University. Recreations: swimming; skiing; playing piano badly. Address: (b.) Scottish College of Textiles, Galashiels, TD1 3HF.

Rees, Jonathan Stephen, ARCM. Artistic Director, Scottish Ensemble, since 1987; b. 22.1.61, Welwyn Garden City; m., Louise Clare Aston. Educ. Yehudi Menuhin School; Juilliard School, New York. Appearances at Gstaad Festival and tour of Holland as soloist, 1976; 1978: scholarships from Countess of Munster Trust, Martin Scholarship Fund, Royal Society of Arts, prize winner in BBC TV Young Musician of the Year Competition, first prize in Royal Overseas League Competition; solo performances in USA and UK, 1979-83; Rotary International Scholar, 1980; 1983-87: Co-Principal Violinist, Academy of St. Martin-in-the-Fields, recipient of Young Concert Artists Trust Award, British recipient, EEC award for young artists (given by Sponsorship of Trade and Industry, Switzerland); 1990: first disc made as Artistic Director, Scottish Ensemble, Virgin Classics, first disc made as soloist, Virgin Classics. Recreations: sailing; skiing; golf; walking; keeping wife happy. Address: (b.) Scottish

Ensemble, Millworks, Field Road, Busby, Glasgow, G76 8SE.

Reeves, Philip Thomas Langford, RSA, RSW, RE, RGI, ARCA. Artist; b. 7.7.31, Cheltenham; m., Christine MacLaren; 1 d. Educ. Naunton Park School, Cheltenham; Cheltenham School of Art; Royal College of Art, London. Lecturer in Graphic Design, Glasgow School of Art, 1954-70 (Head of Printmaking, 1970-91). Address: (h.) 13 Hamilton Drive, Glasgow, G12 8DN; T.-041-339 0720.

Regent, Peter. Writer and Sculptor; b. 8.12.29, Bury St. Edmunds; m., Karola Hood Zurndorfer; 1 d. Educ. Thetford Grammar School; Keble College, Oxford. Nigerian Government Service, 1954-56; Head of African Section/Research Director, Hansard Society, 1956-59; Staff Tutor in Government, Police Staff College, Bramshill, 1959-65; Head, Department of Liberal and Complementary Studies, Duncan of Jordanstone College of Art, Dundee, 1965-75. Member, North East Fife District Council, since 1984; Parliamentary candidate (Liberal/Alliance), North Tayside, 1987. Publication: Laughing Pig (short stories), 1984. Recreation: walking abroad. Address: (h.) Windhover House, Woodmuir Crescent, Newport-on-Tay, Fife; T.-0382 543192.

Reiach, Alan, OBE, RIBA, RSA, RSW. Architect; b. 2.3.10, London; m., Patricia Anne; 1 s.; 1 d. Educ. Edinburgh Academy; Edinburgh College of Art. Apprenticed to Sir Robert Lorimer; Travelling Scholarship to USA, 1935-36; worked in office of Robert Atkinson, London, 1936-37; Architect Planner, Scottish Office, 1940-46; ran own practice, 1949-65, then with Eric Hall & Partners; retired, 1975; Consultant, 1975-80. Publication: Building Scotland (Co-author), 1940. Recreation: painting. Address: (b.) Messrs Reiach & Hall, 6 Darnaway Street, Edinburgh; T.-031-225 8444.

Reid, Rev. Albert Brown, BSc, BD. Minister, Trinity Parish Church, Dundee, since 1981; b. 19.1.40, Monifieth, Angus; m., Mary McDonald Pattie; 1 s.; 2 d. Educ. Grove Academy, Broughty Ferry; St. Andrews University; New College, Edinburgh. Assistant, Wallacetown Parish Church, 1964-66; Minister: Cairns Church, Lanark, 1966-72, Letham Kirk, Perth, 1972-81. Recreations: golf; hill-walking; photography. Address: 75 Clepington Road, Dundee; T.-0382 457430.

Reid, Daniel, OBE, MD, FRCPGlas, FFPHM, FRSH, DPH. Director, Communicable Diseases (Scotland) Unit, since 1969; Visiting Professor, Strathclyde University, since 1989; Honorary Clinical Senior Lecturer, Department of Infectious Diseases, Glasgow University, since 1969; Honorary Senior Lecturer, Edinburgh University, since 1991; since 1969; b. 5.2.35, Glasgow; m., Eileen Simpson (deceased); 2 d. Educ. Allan Glen's School, Glasgow; Glasgow University. House Surgeon, Victoria Infirmary, Glasgow; House Physician, Southern General Hospital, Glasgow; House Surgeon, Stobhill Hospital, Glasgow; Lt./Captain, Royal Army Medical Corps (attached Royal Northumberland Fusiliers, Hong Kong); Registrar, University Department of Infectious Diseases, Ruchill Hospital, Glasgow; Senior Registrar, Epidemiological Research Laboratory, London. Forbes Fellow, Fairfield Hospital, Melbourne, 1982; Chairman, Advisory Group on Infection, Scottish Health Services Planning Council. Address: (b.) Communicable Diseases (Scotland) Unit, Ruchill Hospital, Glasgow, G20; T.-041-946 7120.

Reid, David C., MA, MEd. Rector, Kinross High School, since 1985; b. 4.9.43, Motherwell; m., Alison W. Ewing; 1 s.; 1 d. Educ. Wishaw High School; Glasgow University; Jordanhill College; Edinburgh University. Teacher of English, Kirkcaldy High School, 1966-71; Principal Teacher of English, Currie High School, 1971-80; Assistant Rector,

Inverkeithing High School, 1980-85. Member/Chairman, English Panel, Scottish Examination Board, 1976-82; Member, IBA Educational Advisory Council (Schools Panels), 1975-86; Chairman, Joint Working Party (English "S" Grade), 1982-83; Member, Grampian Television Schools Advisory Committee. Recreations: hill-walking; angling; conversation; reading; Scottish traditional architecture. Address: (b.) Kinross High School, Kinross, Kinross-shire, KY13 7AW; T.-0577 62430.

Reid, Professor Gavin Clydesdale, MA, MSc, PhD. Professor in Economics, St. Andrews University, since 1991; b. 25.8.46, Glasgow; m., 1, Margaret Morrice or McGregor (m. diss.); 1 s.; 1 step-s.; 2, Maureen Johnson or Bagnall; 2 d.; 1 step.-s. Educ. Lyndhurst School; Frimley and Camberley Grammar School; Aberdeen University; Southampton University; Edinburgh University. Lecturer, Senior Lecturer, Reader in Economics, Edinburgh University, 1971-91; Visiting Associate Professor: Queen's University, Ontario, 1981-82, Denver University, Colorado, 1984; Visiting Scholar, Darwin College, Cambridge, 1987-88; Leverhulme Trust Research Fellowship, 1989. Review Editor, 1981-87, Editorial Board, since 1986, Scottish Journal of Political Economy. Publications: The Kinked Demand Curve Analysis of Oligopoly, 1981; Theories of Industrial Organization, 1987; The Small Entrepreneurial Firm (Co-author), 1988; Classical Economic Growth, 1989. Recreations: music; reading; running; badminton. Address: (b.) St. Andrews University, St. Salvator's College, St. Andrews, Fife, KY16 9AL; T.-0334 76161.

Reid, Harry William, BA (Hons). Deputy Editor, Glasgow Herald, since 1983; b. 23.9.47, Glasgow; m., Julie Davidson (qv); 1 d. Educ. Aberdeen Grammar School; Fettes College; Oxford University. The Scotsman: Education Correspondent, 1973-77, Features Editor, 1977-81; Sports Editor, Sunday Standard, 1981-82; Executive Editor, Glasgow Herald, 1982-83. Recreations: reading; walking; supporting Aberdeen Football Club. Address: (h.) 15 Albion Buildings, Ingram Street, Glasgow; T.-041-552 8403.

Reid, Jimmy. Journalist and Broadcaster; b. 1932. Former Engineer; prominent in campaign to save Upper Clyde Shipbuilders; former Convener of Shop Stewards, AUEW; former (Communist) Member, Clydebank Town Council; joined Labour Party and contested Dundee East, General Election, 1979; Rector, Glasgow University, 1971-74.

Reid, John, PhD. MP (Labour), Motherwell North, since 1987; b. 8.5.47, Bellshill; m., Catherine McGowan; 2 s. Educ. St. Patrick's Senior Secondary School, Coatbridge; Stirling University. Scottish Research Officer, Labour Party, 1980-83; Political Adviser to Rt. Hon. Neil Kinnock, 1983-85; Scottish Organiser, Trade Unionists for Labour, 1986-87. Recreations: crosswords; football; reading. Address: (b.) Parliamentary Office, 114 Manse Road, Newmains, ML2 9BD; T.-0698 383866.

Reid, Rev. John Kelman Sutherland, CBE, TD, MA, DD. Member, Editorial Board, Scottish Journal of Theology, since 1948; Member, Church of Scotland Board of World Mission and Unity, since 1961; b. 31.3.10, Leith; m., Margaret Winifrid Brookes (deceased). Educ. George Watson's College, Edinburgh; Edinburgh University; Heidelberg University; Basel University; Marburg University; Strasburg University. Professor of Philosophy, Calcutta University, 1935-37; Minister, Craigmillar Park Parish Church, Edinburgh, 1939-52; Chaplain to the Forces with Parachute Regiment, 1942-46; Professor of Theology, Leeds University, 1952-61; Chaplain, Territorial Army, 1948-62; Professor of Systematic Theology, Aberdeen University, 1961-76. Publications: Calvin's Theological Treatises (Editor and Translator), 1954; The Biblical Doctrine of the Ministry,

1955; The Authority of Scripture, 1957; Calvin's Concerning the Eternal Predestination of God (Editor and Translator), 1961; Our Life in Christ, 1963; Presbyterians and Unity, 1966; Christian Apologetics, 1969. Recreation: golf. Address: (h.) 8 Abbotsford Court, 18 Colinton Road, Edinburgh, EH10 5EH; T.-031-447 6855.

Reid, Professor John Low, MA, DM, FRCP. Regius Professor of Medicine and Therapeutics, Glasgow University, since 1989; Consultant Physician, Western Infirmary; b. 1.10.43, Glasgow; m., Randa Pharaon; 1 d. Educ. Fettes College; Oxford University. MRC Research Fellow, Royal Post Graduate Medical School, London, 1970-73; Travelling Fellow, US National Institutes of Health, Washington, USA, 1973-75; Senior Wellcome Fellow in Clinical Science and Reader in Clinical Pharmacology, Royal Post Graduate Medical School, London, 1975-78; Regius Professor of Materia Medica, Glasgow University, 1978-89; Editor, Journal of Hypertension. Publications: Lecture Notes in Clinical Pharmacology (Co-author); Clinical Science, 1982-84 (Editor); Handbook of Hypertension (Editor). Recreations: outdoors; gardening. Address: (b.) Gardiner Institute, Western Infirmary, Glasgow; T.-041-339 8822.

Reid, Margaret E., MA, PhD. Senior Lecturer, Medical Sociology, Glasgow University, since 1988; b. 28.9.46, Chorleywood; m., Professor Keith Millar; 1 s. Educ. Aberdeen Girls' High School; Aberdeen University. Research Assistant, Aberdeen University, 1970-71; Lecturer, Glasgow University, 1973-88; Visiting Fellow, University of Wisconsin, 1981-82. Member: Advisory Board, National Perinatal Epidemiology Unit, Healthy Cities Glasgow Women's Health Working Party. Recreations: travel; visual arts. Address: (h.) 33 West Chapelton Crescent, Bearsden, Glasgow, G61 2DE; T.-041-330 4040.

Reid, Norman, BSc, PhD, FRSC. Rector, Bathgate Academy, since 1988; b. 18.11.43, Edinburgh; m., Gillian; 4 d. Educ. George Watson's College; Edinburgh University; Glasgow University. Teaching, 1966-75; Research Fellow in Education, 1975-80; Teaching, since 1980. RSC Medal for Services to Education, 1982. Recreations: gardening; sport (formerly!); church youth work; music (playing). Address: (h.) Hazelbank, 83 Marjoribanks Street, Bathgate, EH48 1QH; T.-0506 53366.

Reid, Patricia Maureen, BL. Chairman, Programme and Training, The Girl Guides Association, since 1990; Member and Director, Scottish Community Education Council; b. 29.8.39, Glasgow; m., Graham Douglas Melville Reid; 1 s.; 1 d. Educ. Laurel Bank School, Glasgow; Glasgow University. Qualified as Solicitor, 1961; employed as an Associate in private practice. County Commissioner, City of Glasgow Girl Guides, 1979-82; Scottish Chief Commissioner, 1982-87. Address: (h.) 64 Crown Road North, Glasgow, G12 9HW; T.-041-357 1351.

Reid, Professor Peter, BA, RIBA, FRIAS, FRSA. Professor of Architecture, Strathclyde University, since 1986; Vice Principal of the University, since 1992; b. 31.1.33, Hayes, Middlesex; m., Keow Chim Lim; 2 d. Educ. Southall Grammar School; Manchester University; Open University. Commissioned Officer, RAF, 1960-61; Assistant Lecturer, University of Hong Kong, 1961-64; Architect in practice, Malaysia, 1964-70; joined Strathclyde University, 1970. Governor, Glasgow School of Art, since 1982; Director, Glasgow West Conservation Trust, since 1990; Chairman of Council, Charles Rennie Mackintosh Society, since 1991. Recreations: opera; Italian language and culture; wine; cricket. Address: (b.) Department of Architecture and Building Science, Strathclyde University, 131 Rottenrow, Glasgow, G4 0NG; T.-041-552 4400.

Reid, Robert Russell, JP. Chairman, Argyll and Clyde Health Board, since 1991; Member, Argyll and Bute District Council, since 1975; Honorary Sheriff; Farmer; b. 26.12.32, Campbeltown; m., Rebecca Simpson Hunter; 3 s.; 1 d. Educ. Campbeltown Grammar School; Thorpe House; Rothesay Academy. Address: (h.) Ardmaleish Farm, Rothesay, Bute, PA20 0QL; T.-0700 503058.

Reid, Seona Elizabeth, BA, FRSA. Director, Scottish Arts Council, since 1990; b. 21.1.50, Paisley. Educ. Park School, Glasgow; Strathclyde University; Liverpool University. Business Manager, Theatre Royal, Lincoln, 1972-73; Press Officer, Northern Dance Theatre, Manchester, 1973-76; PRO, Ballet Rambert, London, 1976-79; freelance arts consultant, 1979-81; Director, Shape, London, 1981-87; Assistant Director, Greater London Arts, 1987-90. Recreations: walking; the arts. Address: (b.) 12 Manor Place, Edinburgh, EH3 7DD; T.-031-226 6051.

Reid, William James, ACII, FBIBA. Chairman and Chief Executive, C.E. Heath (Scotland) Ltd. and Heath Collins Halden (Scotland) Ltd.; Director, Scotsure MBI Ltd.; b. 18.9.32, Edinburgh; m., Patricia; 2 s. Educ. George Heriot's School. Director, Collins Halden & Co. Ltd., 1960-68; Joint Managing Director, 1968-72; Chairman and Chief Executive, 1972-78; Director, Halden McQuaker & Co. Ltd., Glasgow, 1964-73; Director, Collins Halden & Burnett Ltd., Aberdeen, 1962-74; Director, Hogg Robinson Ltd., London, 1978-84; Chief Executive, Hogg Robinson (Scotland) Ltd., 1978-84. President, Insurance Society of Edinburgh, 1978-79; Chairman, Corporation of Insurance Brokers Scotland, 1969-70; Member, National Council, Corporation of Insurance Brokers, 1968-71. Address: (h.) Ravensworth, 38 Pentland Avenue, Edinburgh, EH13 0HY; T.-031-441 3942.

Reid, Sheriff William Macpherson, MA, LLB. Sheriff of Tayside, Central and Fife, since 1983; b. 6.4.38.

Reilly, David Paul Taylor, MB, ChB, MRCP, MRCGP, FFHom. Consultant Physician, Glasgow Homoeopathic Hospital, since 1990; Honorary Senior Lecturer in Medicine, Glasgow Royal Infirmary, since 1991; Education Director, Faculty of Homoeopathy in Scotland, since 1985; b. 4.5.55. Ran a music business, 1970-73; Glasgow University, 1973-78; training in alternative therapies, 1978-86; Research Fellow, Research Council for Complementary Medicine and Medical Research Council, University Department of Medicine, Glasgow Royal Infirmary and Senior Registrar in Medicine, 1987-90. RAMC Memorial Prize. Publications: The Frontiers of Science (Co-author); scientific papers. Recreations: living; loving; laughing; looking; literating; longing; lounging. Address: (b.) Glasgow Homoeopathic Hospital, 1000 Great Western Road, Glasgow, G12 0NR; T.-041-339 2786.

Reith, David Stewart, LLB, NP, WS. Partner, Lindsays WS, Solicitors, Edinburgh, since 1976; b. 15.4.51, Edinburgh; m., Elizabeth Julia Hawkins; 1 d. Educ. Edinburgh Academy; Fettes College; Aberdeen University. Director, Scottish Historic Buildings Trust, since 1985; Secretary: Lothian Building Preservation Trust, since 1984, Ponton House Association, Edinburgh, since 1982; Honorary Solicitor and Treasurer, Architectural Heritage Society of Scotland. Recreations: curling; swimming; photography; wine. Address: (h.) The Studio, 1 Ravelston Park, Edinburgh, EH4 3DX; T.-031-343 2341.

Remp, Stephen Edward, BA, MA. Chairman and Chief Executive, Ramco Oil Services plc, since 1977; b. 5.5.47, California, USA; m., Janine Beverley; 2 s. Educ. American International School; Claremont Men's College; John Hopkins University. Saltire Award, 1977, and Civic Trust Award, 1977 (Harthill Castle); Scottish Business

Achievement Award, 1984; Burgess of Guild of City of Aberdeen. Recreations: skiing; tennis; shooting; swimming; beekeeping; music. Address: (b.) Hareness Circle, Altens Industrial Estate, Aberdeen, AB1 4LY; T.-0224 879554.

Renfrew, Rt. Rev. Charles McDonald, PhL, STL. Assistant Bishop in Glasgow (Titular See Abula), since 1977; b. 21.6.29, Glasgow. Educ. St. Aloysius College, Glasgow; Scots College, Rome; Gregorian University, Rome. Ordained Priest in Rome, 1953; Assistant Priest, Immaculate Conception, Glasgow, 1953-56; Professor of English and Music, and Bursar, St. Mary's College, Blairs, 1956; first Rector, St. Vincent's College, Langbank, 1961; Chaplain to Sisters of Notre Dame, Glasgow, and Vicar General of Glasgow, 1974; ordained Titular Bishop of Abula, 1977; Head, Commission for Pastoral and Social Care, since 1984; Member, Kidney Research Committee Scotland and Second Chance Committee Scotland. Publications: St. Vincent's Prayer Book; Rambling Through Life; Pageant of Holiness. Recreations: classical music; history of Glasgow. Address: 70 Mansionhouse Gardens, Glasgow, G41; T.-041-649 2228.

Rennie, Archibald Louden, CB, LLD. Chancellor's Assessor, St. Andrews University, 1985-89; Vice-Chairman, Advisory Committee on Distinction Awards, since 1985; Member, Scottish Records Advisory Council, since 1985; Member, Council on Tribunals, and its Scottish Committee, 1987-88; Trustee, Lockerbie Air Disaster Appeal, 1988-91; Chairman, Disciplined Services Pay Review Committee, Hong Kong, 1988; b. 4.6.24, Guardbridge, Fife; m., Kathleen Harkess; 4 s. Educ. Madras College, St. Andrews; St. Andrews University. Experimental Officer, Minesweeping Research Division, 1944-47; joined Department of Health for Scotland, 1947; Private Secretary to Secretary of State for Scotland, 1962-63; Assistant Secretary, Scottish Home and Health Department, 1963-69; Registrar General for Scotland, 1969-73; Under Secretary, Scottish Economic Planning Department, 1973-77; Secretary, Scottish Home and Health Department, 1977-84. Chairman, Blacket Association, 1971-73. Recreations: sailing; sea-fishing; walking; bird-watching. Address: (h.) Well Wynd House, South Street, Elie, Fife, KY9 1DN; T.-0333 330741.

Rennie, James Alexander Norris, MD, FRCP. Consultant Physician (Rheumatology), since 1979; b. 28.1.47, Dunfermline; m., Margaret; 2 s.; 1 d. Educ. Dunfermline High School; Aberdeen University. Lecturer, Department of Medicine, Aberdeen University, 1973-76; Senior Registrar, General Medicine/Rheumatology, Glasgow, 1976-79. Recreations: DIY; china painting; football. Address: (h.) 13 Belvidere Street, Aberdeen, AB2 4QS; T.-Aberdeen 632172.

Rennie, Robert, LLB, PhD. Partner, Ballantyne & Copland, Solicitors, Motherwell, since 1972; b. 30.6.47, Glasgow; m., Catherine Mary; 1 s.; 3 d. Educ. Lenzie Academy; Glasgow University. Apprentice then Legal Assistant, Bishop Milne Boyd & Co., Solicitors, Glasgow; joined Ballantyne & Copland as Legal Assistant, 1971; Member, Law Society of Scotland Conveyancing Committee, Publications Committee, Complaints Committee and various working parties; Trustee, Lanarkshire Spastics Association; Member, Local Interview Committee, Prince's Scottish Youth Business Trust; Director and Secretary, Taggarts (Motor Holdings) Limited. Recreation: classical music. Address: (b.) Torrance House, Knowetop, Motherwell, ML1 2AF; T.-0698 66200.

Renshaw, David, BSc, MSc, PhD, CEng, MIEE, MGTCS. Senior Lecturer, Department of Electrical Engineering, Edinburgh University, since 1989; Technical Manager, VLSI Vision Ltd., since 1990; b. 20.7.47, Edinburgh; m., Ann MacDougall. Educ. Edinburgh Rudolf Steiner School; George Watson's College; Edinburgh University. Research Mathematician, Switzerland; Schoolteacher; Research

Fellow; University Lecturer. Recreations: reading; music; woodturning; gardens and wildlife; walking. Address: (b.) Department of Electrical Engineering, Edinburgh University, King's Buildings, Edinburgh; T.-031-650 5566.

Renshaw, Professor Eric, BSc, ARCS, DipStats, MPhil, PhD. Professor of Statistics, Strathclyde University, since 1991; b. 25.7.45, Preston; m., Anne Renshaw. Educ. Arnold School, Blackpool; Imperial College, London; Manchester University; Sussex University; Edinburgh University. Lecturer, then Senior Lecturer in Statistics, Edinburgh University, 1969-91. Publication: Modelling Biological Populations in Space and Time. Recreations: skiing; golf; hill-walking; photography. Address: (b.) Department of Statistics and Modelling Science, Livingstone Tower, Strathclyde University, 26 Richmond Street, Glasgow, G1 1XU; T.-041-552 4400.

Renton, Rev. Ian Paterson, OStJ, FSA Scot, JP. Minister, St. Colm's Parish Kirk, Dalry, Edinburgh, since 1966; b. 22.3.26, Kirkcaldy; m., Ann Gordon Mutter Macpherson; 2 s.; 1 d. Educ. Sinclairtown and Viewforth Schools, Kirkcaldy; Newbattle Abbey College; Glasgow University; St. Mary's College, St. Andrews. Shipping Clerk, Robert Wemyss & Co., Kirkcaldy, 1941-44; Sergeant, 3rd Bn., Scots Guards, 1944-47; Ministry of Labour, Kirkcaldy, 1947-48; Newbattle Abbey College, 1948-50; Youth Clubs Organiser, Roxburghshire, 1950-53; divinity studies, 1953-58; Assistant Minister, North Kirk, Aberdeen, 1958-60; Minister, St. Mark's Church, Greenwich, London, 1960-66. Member, Edinburgh City Education Committee, 1970-76; Governor: Moray House College, 1971-79, Donaldson's School, Edinburgh, 1972-75, Newbattle Abbey College, 1973-76; Member, General Assembly Committee on Education, 1973-79; Joint Chairman, Scottish Joint Committee on Religious Education, 1974-79; Member, Lothian Region Education Committee, 1977-78; Member, Edinburgh Children's Panel, 1971-74; Executive Member, Broadcasting Council, Radio Forth, 1976-79; Member, DHSS Social Security Tribunal, 1978-84; Member, Church of Scotland Board of Education, 1983-85; Member, Committee on Medical Ethics, Lothian Health Board, since 1984; regular Contributor, BBC, STV, Radio Forth, since 1973; Moderator, Edinburgh Presbytery, 1989-90; Chaplain to Astley Ainslie Hospital, Edinburgh. Recreations: climbing; golfing; gardening; drystane diking; archaeological excavation, Byzantine site, Shelomi, Israel. Address: Roseneath, Newbattle Terrace, Edinburgh, EH10 4SF.

Renton, Janice Helen, LLB. Deputy Commissioner for Local Administration in Scotland, since 1991; Deputy Local Government Adjudicator for Scotland, since 1990; b. 20.4.47, Falkirk. Educ. Bo'ness Academy; Edinburgh University. Legal Assistant, Clackmannan County Council, 1969; Depute Reporter, Children's Panel, Glasgow Corporation, 1971; Senior Legal Assistant, Aberdeen County Council, 1972; Depute Director of Law and Administration, Grampian Regional Council, 1974; Senior Depute Director of Administration, City of Edinburgh, 1976-84; joined Commissioner's Office, 1989. Secretary, Edinburgh International Festival Society, 1982-84. Recreations: eating; talking. Address: (h.) 57 Philip Avenue, Linlithgow, EH49 7BH.

Renton, Joan Forrest, DA, RSW. President, Society of Scottish Artists and Artist Craftsmen, 1990-93; President, Scottish Society of Women Artists, 1988-90; Vice President, Scottish Arts Club, 1988-90; b. 11.8.35; m., Ronald Renton (qv); 2 s.; 1 d. Educ. Dumfries Academy; Shawlands Academy, Glasgow; Hawick High School; Edinburgh College of Art. Practising artist, painting in watercolours and oils; Teacher of Art, Lothian Region, until 1983. Recreations:

music; gardening. Address: (h.) 9 Lennox Row, Trinity, Edinburgh, EH5 3JP; T.-031-552 1209.

Renton, Stuart, MBE, ARSA, DA, FRIBA, FRIAS. Architect; Senior Partner, Reiach and Hall, Architects, Edinburgh and Glasgow, 1982-91; b. 15.9.29, Edinburgh; m., Ethnie Sloan; 1 s.; 1 d. Educ. Royal High School, Edinburgh; Edinburgh College of Art. Military Service, RAF and RAFVR; Partner, Alan Reiach and Partners, 1959; Partner, Reiach and Hall, 1965; External Examiner, several universities; Assessor for architectural awards schemes; Member, Visiting Board Panel, RIBA Education Board, 1984-92; Governor, Edinburgh College of Art, since 1985. Recreations: skiing; game fishing. Address: (b.) 6 Darnaway Street, Edinburgh, EH3 6BG; T.-031-225 8444.

Renwick, Professor John Peter, MA, PhD, DLitt, Officier des Palmes Academiques. Professor of French, Edinburgh University, since 1980; b. 25.5.39, Gillingham; m., Claudette Gorse; 1 s.; 1 d. Educ. Gillingham Grammar School; St. Bartholomew's Grammar School, Newbury; St. Catherine's College, Oxford; Sorbonne; British Institute in Paris (Leverhulme Research Scholar). Assistant Lecturer, then Lecturer, Glasgow University, 1964-66; Fellow, Churchill College, Cambridge, 1966-72; Maitre de Conferences Associe, Departement de Francais, Universite de Clermont-Ferrand, 1970-71, 1972-74; Professor of French, New University of Ulster, 1974-80 (Pro-Vice-Chancellor, 1978-80). Publications: La destinee posthume de Jean-Francois Marmontel, 1972; Marmontel, Memoires, 1972; Marmontel, Voltaire and the Belisaire affair, 1974; Marmontel, Correspondence, 1974; Catalogue de la bibliotheque de Jean-Baptiste Massillon, 1977; Voltaire et Morangies, ou les Lumieres l'ont echappe belle, 1982; Chamfort devant La Posterite, 1986; Catalogue de la Bibliotheque du Comte D'Espinchal, 1988; Language and Rhetoric of the Revolution, 1990. Address: (b.) 60 George Square, Edinburgh, EH8 9JU.

Rettie, James Philip, CBE, TD. Farmer; Partner, Crossley and Rettie; Director, Edinburgh and Glasgow Investment Co.; Trustee, Scottish Civic Trust, since 1982; b. 7.12.26, Dundee; m., 1, Helen Grant; 2, Diana Harvey; 2 s.; 1 d. Educ. Trinity College, Glenalmond. Royal Engineers, 1945-48. Chairman, Sea Fish Industry Authority, 1981-87; Chairman, William Low & Co. PLC, 1980-85. Hon. Colonel, 117 and 277 FD 8QNS RE (V), 1983-89. Recreations: shooting; gardening; walking. Address: (h.) Hill House, Ballindean, Inchture, Perthshire, PH14 9QS; T.-082 886 337.

Rew, Malcolm McIntosh, BD (Hons), CPS, DCD, DMS, MBIM. Minister, Albany Deaf Church of Edinburgh, since 1988; b. 17.3.48, Dundee; m., Susan Feidt; 2 d. Educ. Fettes College, Edinburgh; St. Andrews University; Edinburgh University. Former Minister, Pitsligo Parish Church; Governor, Donaldson's School for the Deaf, since 1989; Chaplain, HM Prison, Saughton, since 1990. Recreations: chess; swimming. Address: (h.) 11 Brandon Street, Edinburgh, EH3 5DX; T.-031-557 1487.

Reynolds, Professor Sian, BA, MA. Professor of French, Stirling University, since 1990; Translator; b. 28.7.40, Cardiff; m., Peter France; 3 d. Educ. Howell's School, Llandaff; St. Anne's College, Oxford. Lecturer and Senior Lecturer, Sussex University, 1974-89; Lecturer, Edinburgh University, 1989-90. Publications: Women, State and Revolution (Editor); Britannica's Typesetters; translations. Address: (b.) Stirling University, Stirling, FK9 4LA; T.-0786 73171.

Rhind, William, MA (Hons), BSc. Honorary Sheriff, Grampian, Highlands and Islands; b. 11.9.07, Inverurie; m., Georgia L. Ollason; 1 d. Educ. Inverurie Academy; Aberdeen University; Aberdeen Teacher Training College. Anderson High School, Lerwick: Principal Teacher of Mathematics,

1931-47, Deputy Headmaster, 1947-52, Headmaster, 1952-70. Recreations: bridge; music; reading; angling. Address: (h.) Kelda, 6 Lovers Loan, Lerwick, Shetland; T.-0595 2238.

Richards, Professor Bryan Edward, BSc (Eng), DIC, PhD, CEng, FRAeSoc, AFAIAA. Mechan Professor of Aerospace, Glasgow University, since 1980; b. 30.6.38, Hornchurch; m., Margaret Owen; 2 s.; 2 d. Educ. Palmer's School, Grays; Queen Mary College, London University. Aerodynamicist, Bristol Aeroplane Company, Filton, 1960-62; Research Assistant, Imperial College, London University, 1962-66; Assistant Professor, Associate Professor, Professor, Von Karman Institute, Belgium, 1967-79; Head, Department of Aerospace Engineering, Glasgow University, 1980-90; Dean of Engineering, 1984-87. Publications: 110 articles. Recreations: sailing; hill-walking. Address: (h.) Ravenswood, 32 Suffolk Street, Helensburgh, G84 9PA; T.-0436 72112.

Richards, Glyn, BA, BD, MA, BLitt. Senior Lecturer in Religious Studies, Stirling University, since 1976 (Head, Department of Religious Studies, 1977-90); b. 6.8.23, Rhymney; m., Helga; 2 s.; 2 d. Educ. Rhymney Grammar School; University of Wales; McMaster University; Oxford University. Minister of Religion; Extra Mural Lecturer, University of Wales; Tutor, McMaster University, Canada; Lecturer, Carleton University, Ottawa; Senior Lecturer, Stirling University; Visiting Lecturer, International Christian University, Tokyo; Founder and Editor, Scottish Journal of Religious Studies; General Editor, Themes in Comparative Religion. Publications: The Development of Theological Liberalism, 1957; The Philosophy of Gandhi, 1981; A Sourcebook of Modern Hinduism, 1984; Towards a Theology of Religions, 1989; Beyond Tragedy: an anthology, 1991. Recreations: travel; golf; reading. Address: (b.) Department of Religious Studies, Stirling University, Stirling; T.-Stirling 73171.

Richards, John Deacon, CBE, AADip, DUniv, RSA, RIBA, PPRIAS. Architect; Deputy Chairman, Scottish Homes; b. 7.5.31, Shanghai; m., Margaret Brown; 1 s.; 3 d. Educ. Cranleigh School, Surrey; Architectural Association School of Architecture, London. Member, Royal Fine Art Commission for Scotland, 1975-89; Agrement Board, 1980-83; Member, Williams Committee on National Museums and Galleries, 1981; Gold Medallist, RSA, 1972; Past President, Royal Incorporation of Architects in Scotland, 1983-85; Trustee, National Galleries of Scotland, 1986-90. Recreation: country life. Address: (h.) Lady's Field, Whitekirk, East Lothian; T.-Whitekirk 206.

Richardson, Professor John Stuart, MA, DPhil. Professor of Classics, Edinburgh University, since 1987; b. 4.2.46, Ilkley; m., Patricia Helen Robotham; 2 s. Educ. Berkhamsted School; Trinity College, Oxford. Lecturer in Ancient History, Exeter College, Oxford, 1969-72, St. Andrews University, 1972-87; Priest, Scottish Episcopal Church, since 1980; Anglican Chaplain, St. Andrews University, 1980-87; Team Priest, St. Columba's, Edinburgh, since 1987. Publications: Roman Provincial Administration, 1976; Hispaniae, 1986; papers on ancient history. Recreation: choral singing. Address: (h.) 29 Merchiston Avenue, Edinburgh EH10 4PH; T.-031-228 3094.

Richardson, Michael John, BSc, MSc. Assistant Director and Head, Potato and Plant Health Division, Agricultural Scientific Services, Department of Agriculture and Fisheries for Scotland, since 1979; b. 10.7.38, St. Albans; m., Barbara Anne Cooper; 2 s. Educ. St. Albans County Grammar School; Nottingham University. School teacher, Ripley, Derbyshire, 1959-60; Research Associate, Trent Polytechnic, Nottingham, 1961-64; Plant Pathologist, SOAFD, since 1964. Editor, Transactions of the British Mycological Society; Chairman, Scottish Gliding Union. Recreations: gliding; gardening;

mycology. Address: (b.) SOAFD, Agricultural Scientific Services, East Craigs, Edinburgh, EH12 8NJ; T.-031-244 8895.

Richardson, Penny (Penelope Jane), MA, DipGS, Certificate in Community Education. Director, Scottish Association of Health Councils, since 1990; b. 31.7.46, Edinburgh. Educ. Edinburgh University; Edinburgh College of Commerce; Moray House College of Education. Secretary/PA, then General Manager, Traverse Theatre, 1968-74; Articled Clerk, London, 1974-75; Community Animateur, Third Eye Centre, Glasgow, 1976; General Manager, Theatre Workshop, Edinburgh, 1977-82; various consultancies and short term posts, 1983-88; Secretary, West Lothian Health Council, 1988-90. Founder Member, Cervical Smear Campaign; Vice-Chair, Scottish Convention of Women; Chair, Public Health Alliance in Scotland. Address: (b.) 21 Torphichen Street, Edinburgh, EH3 8HX; T.-031-229 2344.

Riches, Professor John Kenneth, MA. Professor of Divinity and Biblical Criticism and Head, Department of Biblical Studies, Glasgow University; b. 30.4.39, London; m., Renate Emmy Thermanx; 2 s.; 1 d. Educ. Cranleigh School; Corpus Christi College, Cambridge. Assistant Curate, St. Edmund's, Norfolk, 1965-68; Chaplain, Fellow and Director of Studies in Theology, Sidney Sussex College, Cambridge, 1968-72; Lecturer, Department of New Testament Language and Literature, Glasgow University, 1973-86; Senior Lecturer, Department of Biblical Studies, Glasgow University, 1986-91. Publications: Jesus and the Transformation of Judaism; The World of Jesus. Recreations: hill-walking; third world trading. Address: (h.) Viewfield, Balmore, Torrance, Glasgow, G64 4AE; T.-0360 20254.

Richmond, Professor John, MD, FRCPE, FRCP, FRCPSG, FRCPI, FACP(Hon), FFPM(Hon), FRCSE, FFPHM(Hon), FCP(SA)(Hon), FRACP(Hon). President, Royal College of Physicians of Edinburgh, 1988-91; Emeritus Professor of Medicine, Sheffield University, since 1989; b. 30.5.26, Doncaster; m., Jenny Nicol; 2 s.; 1 d. Educ. Doncaster Grammar School; Edinburgh University. Junior hospital appointments, Edinburgh and Northants, 1948-49, 1952-53; RAMC, 1949-50; rural general practice, Galloway, 1950-52; Lecturer, Senior Lecturer, Reader in Medicine, Edinburgh University, 1954-73; Professor of Medicine, Sheffield University, 1973-89 (Dean of Medicine, 1985-88). Senior Censor and Senior Vice-President, Royal College of Physicians of London, 1984-85; Chairman, MRCP (UK) Examining Board, 1984-88; Member, Board of Advisors in Medicine, London University, since 1984; External Advisor, Chinese University of Hong Kong, since 1982; Member, Council of Management, Yorkshire Cancer Research Campaign, since 1989; Member, Sheffield Health Authority, 1981-84; Member, Department of Health Clinical Standards Advisory Group, since 1991; Member, Scottish Advisory Board, British Council, since 1991. Recreations: photography; gardening. Address: (h.) 15 Church Hill, Edinburgh.

Richmond, John Kennedy, JP, DL. Chairman, Glasgow Airport Consultative Committee, since 1979; b. 23.4.37, Glasgow; m., Elizabeth Margaret; 1 s.; 1 d. Educ. King's Park Secondary School. Conservative Member, Glasgow Corporation, 1963-75; Member, Glasgow District Council, 1975-84; Deputy Lord Provost, 1977-80; Conservative Group Leader, 1975-77. Recreations: tennis; music; travel. Address: (h.) 84 Merrylee Road, Newlands, Glasgow, G43 2QZ; T.-041-637 7705.

Rickets, Brigadier Reginald Anthony Scott. Managing Director, Irvine Development Corporation, since 1981; Director, Ayrshire Chamber of Industries (President, 1986); Trustee, Scottish Maritime Museum (Irvine); President, Ayrshire Chamber of Industry and Commerce, since 1989;

Director, Enterprise Ayrshire, since 1990; Executive Member, Scottish Council Development and Industry; b. 13.12.29, Weybridge; m., Elizabeth Ann Serjeant; 1 s.; 1 d. Educ. St. George's College, Weybridge; Royal Military Academy, Sandhurst. 2nd Lt., RE, 1949; served with Airborne, Armoured and field Engineers, UK, Cyrenaica, Egypt, Malaya, Borneo, Hong Kong and BAOR; special employment military forces, Malaya, 1955-59; Staff College, Camberley, 1962; Brigade Major, BAOR, 1963-66; Gurkha Independent Field Squadron, 1966-68; Directing Staff, Army Staff College, 1968-70; Commandant, Gurkha Engineers, 1970-73; Chief of Staff, Berlin, 1973-77; Brigadier Chief Engineer, UK Land Forces, 1978-81. Recreation: sailing (DTI Ocean Skipper, RYA Coach/Examiner, Commodore REYC, 1979). Address: (b.) Irvine Development Corporation, Perceton House, Irvine, KA11 2AL; T.-0294 214100.

Ricketts, Rev. Henry Martin, MA, BD; b. 8.8.11, Dundee; m., 1, Margaret Calthorpe Emslie (deceased); 1 s.; 2, Ethel Isabel Morrison. Educ. Morgan Academy, Dundee; St. Andrews University; University of Goettingen. Member, Walker Trust Excavation Team, Istanbul, 1935-36, excavating Palace of Justinian; Minister, Craigiebuckler Parish Church, Aberdeen, 1939-81; Convener, Church of Scotland Committee on Social Service, 1966-71; Chairman, Royal Scottish Society for Prevention of Cruelty to Children, 1979-87, Vice President, since 1989. Recreations: gardening; fishing. Address: (h.) 306 Queen's Road, Aberdeen, AB1 8DT; T.-0224 315783.

Rickman, Professor Geoffrey Edwin, MA, DPhil (Oxon), FBA, FSA. Professor of Roman History, St. Andrews University, since 1981; b. 9.10.32, Cherat, India; m., Ann Rosemary Wilson; 1 s.; 1 d. Educ. Peter Symonds' School, Winchester; Brasenose College, Oxford. Junior Research Fellow, Queen's College, Oxford; St. Andrews University: Lecturer in Ancient History, Senior Lecturer, Professor; Visiting Fellow, Brasenose College, Oxford. Council Member, Society for Promotion of Roman Studies; Member, Faculty of Archaeology, History and Letters, British School at Rome (Chairman, 1984-87). Publications: Roman Granaries and Storebuildings, 1971; The Corn Supply of Ancient Rome, 1980. Recreations: opera; swimming. Address: (h.) 56 Hepburn Gardens, St. Andrews, Fife; T.-St. Andrews 72063.

Riddle, Gordon Stewart, MA. Principal and Chief Ranger, Culzean Country Park, since 1976 (Deputy Administrator, Culzean Castle and Country Park, since 1982); b. 2.10.47, Kelso; m., Rosemary Robb; 1 s.; 1 d. Educ. Kelso High School; Edinburgh University; Moray House College of Education. Biology and History Teacher, Lasswade High School, 1970-71; National Ranger Training Course, 1971-72; Ranger and Depute Principal, Culzean Country Park, 1972-75; National Park Service (USA) Training Course, 1978; Winston Churchill Travelling Fellowship, USA, 1981. Publication: The Kestrel; Seasons with the Kestrel. Recreations: sport; gardening; birds of prey; photography; hill-walking; music; writing. Address: (h.) Swinston, Culzean Country Park, by Maybole, Ayrshire; T.-06556 662.

Riddle, Robert William, OBE. General Secretary, Royal British Legion Scotland/Earl Haig Fund (Scotland)/Officers' Association (Scottish Branch), since 1983; b. 19.1.33, Galashiels; m., Ann Mary Munro Millar; 3 d. Educ. Stonyhurst. 2nd Lt., King's Own Scottish Borderers, 1953; Staff College, 1963; Brigade Major, 157 (L) Brigade TA, Glasgow, 1964; Commanding Officer, 1st Bn., King's Own Scottish Borderers, 1971; Military Secretary, CINC BAOR, 1974; Colonel AQ 3rd Armoured Division, 1977; Brigadier Scottish Division, 1980; retired, 1983. Colonel, 2nd Bn., 52nd Lowland Volunteers (TA); Member, Queen's Bodyguard for Scotland (Royal Company of Archers). Recreations: field sports; golf; tennis. Address: (h.) Old Harestanes, Blyth Bridge, West Linton, Peeblesshire, EH46 7AH; T.-07215 2255.

Ridgway, John Rae, RFO, JP, FSA Scot. Councillor, Orkney Islands Council, since 1985 (Chairman, Roads and Transportation Committee, since 1989); b. 23.8.35, Edinburgh; m., Janette Catherine; 1 s.; 1 d. Educ. Janette Catherine; 1 s.; 1 d. Educ. Boroughmuir School, Edinburgh. District Manager, British Airways, 1956-89; Proprietor, Ridgway Travel and Holiday Centre, since 1989. Recreation: country life. Address: (h.) Old Schoolhouse, Kirkbister, Orphir, Orkney; T.-0856 81 202.

Riemersma, Rudolph Arend, BSc, MSc, PhD. Assistant Director, Cardiovascular Research Unit, Edinburgh University, since 1975 (British Heart Foundation Senior Lecturer in Cardiac Biochemistry, since 1979); b. 9.5.43, Hengelo, Netherlands; m , Eva J. Nieuwenhuis; 1 s.; 1 d. Educ. Charlois Lyceum, Rotterdam; Leyden University; Edinburgh University. Biochemist, Department of Cardiology, Academic Hospital, Utrecht; postgraduate research, Royal Postgraduate Medical School, Hammersmith Hospital, London; Research Fellow, Edinburgh University, 1973. Former Vice-President, European Society of Clinical Investigation. Recreations: orienteering; skiing; hill-walking; botany. Address: (b.) Cardiovascular Research Unit, Hugh Robson Building, George Square, Edinburgh; T.-031-650 3699.

Rifkind, Malcolm Leslie, QC, LLB, MSc. Secretary of State for Defence, since 1992; Secretary of State for Transport, 1990-92; MP (Conservative), Edinburgh Pentlands, since 1974; b. 21.6.46, Edinburgh; m., Edith Amalia Steinberg; 1 s.; 1 d. Educ. George Watson's College, Edinburgh; Edinburgh University. Lecturer, University of Rhodesia, 1967-68; called to Scottish Bar, 1970; Opposition Front-Bench Spokesman on Scottish Affairs, 1975-76; Member, Select Committee on European Secondary Legislation, 1975-76; Chairman, Scottish Conservatives' Devolution Committee, 1976; Joint Secretary, Conservative Parliamentary Foreign and Commonwealth Affairs Committee, 1977-79; Member, Select Committee on Overseas Development, 1978-79; Parliamentary Under-Secretary of State, Scottish Office, 1979-82; Parliamentary Under-Secretary of State, Foreign and Commonwealth Office, 1982-83; Minister of State, Foreign and Commonwealth Office, 1983-86; Secretary of State for Scotland, 1986-90. Address: (b.) House of Commons, London, SW1.

Rinning, Andrew, Secretary, Red Deer Commission, since 1990; b. 15.9.49, Balerno; m., Jeanette Legg; 1 s.; 1 d. Educ. Currie Senior Secondary School. Department of Agriculture and Fisheries for Scotland, 1969-75; Scottish Office Finance Division, 1975-78; Scottish Development Department, 1978-82; Scottish Office Finance Division, 1982-85; Assistant Private Secretary to Secretaries of State for Scotland, 1985-88; Scottish Office Finance Division, 1988-90. Recreations: curling; gardening; golf. Address: (b.) Knowsley, 82 Fairfield Road, Inverness, IV3 5LH; T.-0463 231751.

Risk, Sheriff Douglas James, MA, LLB. Sheriff of Grampian, Highland and Islands at Aberdeen and Stonehaven, since 1979; b. 23.1.41; m., Jennifer Hood Davidson; 3 s.; 1 d. Educ. Glasgow Academy; Gonville and Caius College, Cambridge; Glasgow University. Admitted Advocate, 1966; Standing Junior Counsel to Scottish Education Department, 1975; Sheriff of Lothian and Borders at Edinburgh, 1977-79; Honorary Lecturer, Faculty of Law, Aberdeen University, since 1981. Address: (b.) Sheriff Court House, Exchequer Row, Aberdeen, AB9 1AP; T.-Aberdeen 572780.

Risk, Robert Neil, LLB. Director of Administration, Shetland Islands Council, since 1989; b. 14.2.58, Glasgow; m., Alison Jane. Educ. Shawlands Academy, Glasgow; Dundee University. Apprenticeship, McClure Naismith Anderson & Gardner, 1980-82; Legal Assistant, Principal Legal Assistant, Depute Director of Administration, Shetland Islands Council, 1982-89. Recreations: skiing; volleyball; music; photography. Address: (h.) Nordlys, Shurton Brae, Gulberwick, Shetland; T.-0595 5851.

Risk, Sir Thomas Neilson, BL, LLD (Glasgow), FRSE; b. 13.9.22, Glasgow; m., Suzanne Eiloart; 4 s. Educ. Kelvinside Academy, Glasgow; Glasgow University. Flt. Lt., RAF, 1941-46; RAFVR, 1946-53; Partner, Maclay, Murray & Spens, Solicitors, 1950-81; Governor, Bank of Scotland, 1981-91; Chairman, Standard Life Assurance Company, 1969-77; Director, Shell UK Ltd., since 1983; Director, MSA (Britain) Ltd., since 1958; Director, The Merchants Trust plc, since 1973; Director, British Linen Bank Limited, 1977-91 (Governor, 1977-86); Director, Bank of Wales, 1986-91; Director, Howden Group, 1971-87; Chairman, Scottish Financial Enterprise, 1986-89; Director, Barclays Bank, 1983-85; Member, Scottish Economic Planning Council, 1983-91; Member, National Economic Development Council, 1987-91; Member, Scottish Industrial Development Board, 1972-75; Trustee, Hamilton Bequest. Address: (h.) 10 Belford Place, Edinburgh, EH4 3DH.

Ritchie, Adam B., BSc, FMA. Curator, Dundee Art Galleries and Museums, since 1982; b. 24.10.43, Lewes; m., Ann M. Educ. Hemel Hempstead Grammar School; Gosforth Grammar School; Weston Super Mare Grammar School; Leicester University. Assistant Keeper of Biology, Leicester Museum; Keeper of Natural Museum, Dundee Museum; Depute Curator, Dundee Art Galleries and Museums. Recreations: travel; hill-walking; wildlife photography. Address: (h.) 43 Albany Terrace, Dundee; T.-0382 25733.

Ritchie, Alastair Newton Bethune; b. 30.4.21, London; m., Isobel Sinclair; 1 s.; 1 d. Educ. Harrow School; Corpus Christi College, Cambridge. Scots Guards, 1940-58; campaign North-West Europe, 1944-45; wounded; mentioned in Despatches; active service, Malaya and Far East, 1947-49; Canadian Army Staff College, 1951; Assistant Military Attache, Canada, 1952-53; active service, Canal Zone, Egypt, 1954; retired as Major, 1958; Argyll and Sutherland Highlanders TA, 1966-68; Partner, Drunkie Farms, Callander, 1967-81; Partner, Sheppards and Chase, Stock and Money Brokers and Member, Stock Exchange, 1960-85; Member, Stirling District Council, 1977-90; Member, Queen's Bodyguard for Scotland (Royal Company of Archers), since 1966; Deputy Lieutenant, Central Region (Stirling and Falkirk), since 1979. Recreations: gardening; fishing; music. Address: (h.) Avonbeith, Callander, Perthshire, FK17 8BN; T.-0877 30078.

Ritchie, Anthony Elliot, CBE, MA, DSc, MD, FCSP, FRCPEd, FRSE, LLD. Secretary and Treasurer, Carnegie Trust for the Universities of Scotland, 1969-86; b. 30.3.15, Edinburgh; m., Elizabeth Lambie Knox; 1 s.; 3 d. Educ. Edinburgh Academy; Aberdeen University; Edinburgh University. Carnegie Scholar, Lecturer and Senior Lecturer in Physiology, Edinburgh University, 1941-48; Professor of Physiology, St. Andrews University, 1948-69; Honorary Consultant, Eastern Regional Hospital Board, 1950-69; Chairman, Scottish Committee on Science Education, 1970-78; Chairman, Scottish University Entrance Board, 1963-69; Member, British Library Board, 1973-80; Member, Houghton Committee on Teachers' Pay; Trustee, National Library of Scotland, Carnegie Trust; Royal Society of Edinburgh: Fellow, 1951, General Secretary, 1966-76, Bicentenary Gold Medal, 1983; Hon. DSc (St. Andrews); Hon. LLD (Strathclyde). Recreations: reading; hill-walking; mechanics;

electronics. Address: (h.) 12 Ravelston Park, Edinburgh, EH4 3DX; T.-031-332 6560.

Ritchie, Astrid Ilfra, JP, MA, DipSocAdmin. Member, Scottish Community Education Council; Chairman, Scottish Adult Basic Education Forum; Member, Scottish Examination Board; Chairman, Scottish Conservative Party Education Policy Committee; Party Spokeswoman on Education in Scotland; b. 19.4.36, Edinburgh; m., 1, Martin Huggins (m. dissolved); 2 d.; 2, Professor David Scarth Ritchie. Educ. Harrogate College; Edinburgh University. Former Lothian Regional Councillor; former Editor, Focus on Social Work and Service in Scotland; former Member, Broadcasting Council for Scotland; former Member, Mental Welfare Commission for Scotland; former Member, General Teaching Council. Address: (h.) 11 Ann Street, Edinburgh, EH4 1PL; T.-031-332 1455.

Ritchie, Ian Charles Stewart, MA (Cantab). Managing Director, Scottish Chamber Orchestra, since 1984; Artistic Co-Director, St. Magnus Festival, Orkney, since 1989; b. 19.6.53, London; m., Angela Mary Reid; 2 d. Educ. Stowe School; Royal College of Music; Trinity College, Cambridge; Guildhall School of Music and Drama. Promotion Manager, Universal Edition (Music Publishers), 1976-79; General Manager, City of London Sinfonia, 1979-84; Artistic Director, City of London Festival, 1983-84; Member, Advisory Panel on Music, Arts Council of GB, 1983-86; Council Member, National Youth Orchestra of Scotland; Trustee, Scottish Musicians' Benevolent Fund; Director, St. Mary's Music School, Edinburgh; Chairman, Association of British Orchestras; Council Member, Society for the Promotion of New Music. Recreations: playing various sports; solving crosswords. Address: (h.) 25/7 St. James Square, Edinburgh, EH1 3AY.

Ritchie, Professor James McPherson, MA, DrPhil, DLitt. Professor, Department of German, Aberdeen University, since 1987; b. 10.7.27; m.; 2 s.; 1 d. Educ. Aberdeen University; University of Tubingen. Lecturer, Glasgow University, 1954-61; Associate Professor, University of Newcastle, NSW, Australia, 1961-65; Reader, Hull University, 1965-70; Professor, Sheffield University, 1970-87. Recreation: playing the clarinet. Address: (b.) Department of German, Aberdeen University, Aberdeen.

Ritchie, John Douglas, CA. Partner, Pannell Kerr Forster, since 1985; b. 9.10.52, Edinburgh; m., Joan Moira. Educ. George Watson's College. Barstow & Millar, CA, 1971-85 (Partner, 1978-85); Member, National Board for Nursing, Midwifery and Health Visiting for Scotland, since 1988; Member, Management Committee, Viewpoint Housing Association, since 1991; Trustee, Viewpoint Trust, since 1991. Address: (b.) 16 Rothesay Place, Edinburgh, EH3 7SQ; T.-031-225 3688.

Ritchie, Rev. Malcolm Alexander. Minister, Kilbrandon and Kilchattan, 1982-90; b. 8.6.20, Beckenham, Kent; m., Heather Peebles Brown; 2 s.; 1 d. Educ. Dulwich College; King's College, Wimbledon; Edinburgh University and New College. Commissioned, Royal Regiment of Artillery, 1941; honorary rank of Captain, 1946; licensed to preach, 1950; Children's Evangelist and Staff Worker, Scripture Union Scotland, 1950; Parish Minister: Broughty Ferry – St. James's, 1955-59, Strathblane, 1969-82; Chairman, Waldensian Missions Aid Society in Scotland, 1979-89; preached, centenary service of Scripture Union, Assembly Hall, Edinburgh, 1957; Moderator, Presbytery of Lorn and Mull, 1988-89. Recreations: boats; music; gardening. Address: Roadside Cottage, Tayvallich, Argyll.

Ritchie, Professor William, BSc, PhD, FRSGS, FRSE, FRICS. Vice Principal, since 1980, Professor of Physical Geography, since 1979, Aberdeen University (Head, Department of Geography, 1982-90); b. 22.3.40, Wishaw; m., Elizabeth Armstrong Bell; 2 s.; 1 d. Educ. Wishaw High School; Glasgow University. Research Assistant, Glasgow University, 1963; Assistant Lecturer, Lecturer, Senior Lecturer, Professor, Aberdeen University, since 1964; Dean, Faculty of Social Sciences, 1988; Visiting Professor/Research Scientist, Lousiana State University. Sometime Member: Nature Conservancy Advisory Committee for Scotland, Scottish Examination Board, Council of Royal Society of Edinburgh; Past Chairman, Royal Scottish Geographical Society (Aberdeen); Chairman, SCOVACT, since 1989; Vice-Chairman, SOTEAG; Member, Environmental Committee, American Association of Petroleum Geologists; Trustee, National Library of Scotland. Address: (b.) Department of Geography, Aberdeen University, Old Aberdeen; T.-0224 272328.

Ritson, Bruce, MD, FRCPsych, FRCP(Ed), DipPsych. Consultant Psychiatrist, Royal Edinburgh Hospital, since 1972; Senior Lecturer in Psychiatry, Edinburgh University, since 1972; Consultant, Royal Edinburgh Hospital, since 1972; b. 20.3.37, Elgin; m., Eileen Carey; 1 s.; 1 d. Educ. Edinburgh Academy; Edinburgh University, Harvard University. Trained in medicine, Edinburgh; postgraduate training in psychiatry, Edinburgh, Harvard and California; Director, Sheffield Region Addiction Unit, 1968-71; at present Consultant with special responsibility for alcohol-related problems; Consultant to World Health Organisation on several occasions. Chairman, Howard League in Scotland; Executive Committee, Medical Council on Alcoholism; Secretary, Substance Misuse Section, Royal College of Psychiatrists; Member, Advisory Group on Alcohol Problems to Health and Safety Executive, EEC. Recreations: friends; squash; theatre. Address: (b.) Andrew Duncan Clinic, Royal Edinburgh Hospital, Morningside Park, Edinburgh; T.-031-447 2011.

Rizvi, Mohammad Bin Ashiq, MA (Econ), LLB, AInstAM, JP. Member, Lothian Regional Council, since 1986 (Member, Justice of Peace Committee, Conservative Spokesman on Health and Member, Joint Liaison Committee with Lothian Health Board); b. 15.12.36, Amroha, India; m., Yasmin; 2 d. Educ. India; Karachi University; London University. Began as Teacher with ILEA, 1963; joined insurance group, 1964, and remained until 1986; took early retirement to devote full time to politics; held various offices in Scottish Conservative Party; first non-white Regional Councillor in UK; Executive Council Member, Stevenson College; Director, Theatre Workshop; Executive Member, Council of Social Services; Executive Member, Lothian Racial Equality Council; Secretary and Trustee, Central Mosque and Islamic Centre. Recreations: tennis; cricket; reading. Address: (h.) 5 Fox Covert Avenue, Edinburgh, EH12 6UQ; T.-031-334 5389.

Roach, Professor Alan Colin, BSc, PhD, FRSC, CChem. Head, Department of Chemistry and Chemical Engineering, Paisley University, since 1990; Dean, School of Science and Technology, since 1989; b. 16.6.42, Hull; m., Anne Bolton; 1 s.; 2 d. Educ. Greenock High School; Glasgow University; Oxford University. Lecturer in Theoretical Chemistry, Manchester University, 1968-70; Lecturer in Physical Chemistry, Paisley College, 1970-79, Senior Lecturer, 1979-90. Recreations: walking; running; rowing; politics. Address: (h.) 93 Octavia Terrace, Greenock; T.-0475 30213.

Roach, Professor Gary Francis, BSc, MSc, PhD, DSc. Professor of Mathematics, Strathclyde University, since 1979 (Dean, Faculty of Science, since 1982); b. 8.10.33, Penpedairheol, South Wales; m., Isabella Grace Willins Nicol. Educ. University College, South Wales and Monmouthshire; London University; Manchester University. RAF (Education Branch), Flying Officer, 1955-58; Research

Mathematician, British Petroleum Co. Ltd., 1958-61; Lecturer, Manchester University Institute of Science and Technology, 1961-66; Visiting Professor, University of British Columbia, 1966-67; Strathclyde University: Lecturer, 1967-70, Senior Lecturer, 1970-71, Reader, 1971-79. Fellow, Royal Astronomical Society; Fellow, Institute of Mathematics and its Applications; Fellow, Royal Society of Arts; Fellow, Royal Society of Edinburgh; Past President, Edinburgh Mathematical Society. Recreations: mountaineering; photography; philately; gardening; music. Address: (b.) Department of Mathematics, Strathclyde University, Livingstone Tower, 26 Richmond Street, Glasgow, G1 1XH; T.-041-552 4400, Ext. 3800.

Roads, Elizabeth Ann, MVO, FSA (Scot). Lyon Clerk and Keeper of the Records, since 1986; b. 5.7.51; m., Christopher George William Roads; 2 s. Educ. Lansdowne House School, Edinburgh; Cambridge College of Technology; Study Centre for Fine Art, London. Christie's, Art Auctioneers, 1971-74; Court of the Lord Lyon, 1975-86; temporarily Linlithgow Pursuivant Extraordinary, 1987. Recreations: history; reading; countryside activities. Address: (h.) 9 Denham Green Place, Edinburgh; T.-(b.) 031-556 7255.

Robb, Professor Alan, DA, MA, RCA. Head, School of Fine Art, Duncan of Jordanstone College of Art, Dundee, since 1983; b. 24.2.46, Glasgow; m., Cynthia J. Neilson; 1 s.; 1 d. Educ. Robert Gordon's College, Aberdeen; Grays School of Art; Royal College of Art. Assistant Art Master, Oundle School, 1972-75; Crawford School of Art: Lecturer in Painting, 1975-78, Head of Painting, 1978-80, Head of Fine Art, 1980-83. Member, Fine Art Panel, CNAA, 1986-87; Specialist Advisor, CNAA, since 1987; Director, Art in Partnership and WASPS; Director, British Health Care Arts Centre; first one-man exhibition, New 57 Gallery; exhibitions, 1973 and 1976; Arts Council touring two-man exhibition, 1978-79; regularly exhibits in Scotland. Publication: Irish Contemporary Art, 1980. Address: (b.) Duncan of Jordanstone College of Art, Perth Road, Dundee, DD1 4HT.

Robb, Colin Denholm, BSc (Econ) (Hons). Member, East Kilbride District Council, since 1979 (Leader of the Council; Chairman, Policy and Resources and Economic Development Committees); Board Member, East Kilbride Development Corporation, 1983-86 and since 1989; Board Member, Lanarkshire Development Agency, since 1991; Lecturer in Economics, Bell College, Hamilton, since 1978; b. 14.10.46, Rutherglen; m., Mariet; b. 1 s.; 1 d. Educ. Rutherglen Academy; Glasgow College of Technology; Strathclyde University (postgraduate degree course). Leader, Labour Group, and Chairman, Policy and Resources Committee, East Kilbride District Council, 1980-83. Recreations: reading; hill-walking; photography. Address: (h.) 22 Loch Torridon, East Kilbride, G74 2ET; T.-East Kilbride 24337.

Robb, Kenneth Richard, LLB (Hons), NP. Solicitor; Partner, Marshall, Wilson, Dean & Turnbull, Falkirk; b. 3.9.54, Larbert; m., Susan Margaret Ringrose; 1 d. Educ. Falkirk High School; Edinburgh University. Private legal practice, since 1976; Member, Council, Law Society of Scotland, since 1987; Member, Castlemilk Law Centre Management Committee; Trustee, Scottish Child Law Centre. Recreations: history; hill-walking; gardening. Address: (h.) 9 Bryanston Drive, Dollar, Clackmannanshire; T.-0259 43430.

Robbins, Oliver Charles Gordon, BA (Hons), MIProdE, MIED. Depute Principal, Cambuslang College of Further Education, since 1984; b. 28.4.36, Edinburgh; m., Andrewena Henderson Briggs; 4 s.; 1 d. Educ. Bellevue Secondary School; Open University; Napier College. Apprentice engineer, 1952-57; draughtsman, 1957-60; design draughtsman, Rolls Royce/Ferranti Ltd., 1960-69; Lecturer, Senior Lecturer,

Head of Department, Moray College of FE. Recreations: caravanning; martial arts. Address: (h.) 11 Strathaven Road, Lesmahagow, Lanarkshire; T.-Lesmahagow 894617.

Roberts, Rev. Maurice Jonathon, BA, BD. Minister, Ayr Free Church of Scotland, since 1974; b. 8.3.38, Timperley, Cheshire; m., Alexandra Macleod; 1 d. Educ. Lymm Grammar School; Durham University; London University; Free Church College. Schoolteacher, 14 years; Minister, 16 years; former Editor, Free Church youth magazine; former Convener, Public Questions Committee, Free Church; Editor, Banner of Truth magazine, since 1988. Recreation: reading. Address: (b.) Free Church Manse, 8 Inverkar Road, Ayr, KA7 2JT; T.-0292 266043.

Roberts, Professor Richard Henry, BA (Hons), MA, PhD. Professor of Divinity, St. Andrews University, since 1991; Director, Institute for Religion and the Human Sciences, St. Andrews University, since 1991; b. 6.3.46, Manchester; m., Audrey Butterfield; 1 s. Educ. William Hulme's Grammar School, Manchester; Lancaster University; Cambridge University; Edinburgh University; Tubingen University. Lecturer in Theology and Religious Studies, Leeds University, 1975-76; Lecturer in Systematic Theology, Durham University, 1976-89; M.B. Reckitt Research Fellow, Lancaster University, 1989-91. Publications: Hope and its Hieroglyph: a critical decipherment of Ernst Bloch's Principle of Hope, 1989; A Theology on its Way?, 1991. Recreations: hill-walking; music; foreign travel. Address: (b.) St. Mary's College, St. Andrews University, St. Andrews, KY16 9JU; T.-0334 76161, Ext. 7143.

Roberts, Professor Ronald John, BVMS, MRCVS, PhD, FRCPath, FIBiol, FRSE. Professor of Aquatic Pathobiology and Director, Institute of Aquaculture, Stirling University, since 1971; b. 28.3.41; m., Helen Macgregor; 2 s. Educ. Campbeltown Grammar School; Glasgow University. Lecturer, Glasgow University, 1964-71; Consultant: Department of Agriculture and Fisheries for Scotland, 1967-70, Overseas Development Administration, since 1974, United Nations, since 1976; World Bank, since 1989; Council Member, Royal Society of Edinburgh, 1980-83; Buckland Professor of Fisheries, Buckland Foundation, 1985; BVA Dalrymple-Champnys Medallist, 1990; Scientific Director, Machrihanish Marine Environmental Research Laboratory; Director, Stirling Salmon; Editor, Journal of Fish Diseases, Aquaculture and Fishery Management. Publications: Fish Pathology; Handbook of Salmon and Trout Diseases; Recent Advances in Aquaculture; Diseases of Asian Catfishes (Co-author). Recreations: golf at Machrihanish Golf Club; squash; forestry; rhododendron culture. Address: (b.) Institute of Aquaculture, Stirling University, Stirling; T.-Stirling 73171.

Roberts, Stewart Muir, OBE, DL, JP, FEIS, BA, MA. Honorary Sheriff, Ettrick and Lauderdale; Governor, Merchiston Castle School, 1962-90; b. 4.2.08, Selkirk; m., Marguerite Hugh Considine; 1 s.; 2 d. Educ. Merchiston Castle School; Clare College, Cambridge; Scottish Woollens' Technical College, Galashiels. Director, George Roberts & Co. Ltd., 1936-62 (Managing Director, 1956-62); Director, Roberts, Thorburn and Noble, 1962-73; Army Service, 1943-46; Standard Bearer, Royal Burgh of Selkirk, 1934; Member, Selkirk Town Council, 1935-75 (Provost, 1955-61); Member, Selkirk County Council, 1937-75 (Chairman, County Education Committee, 1948-75); Member and Chairman, Education Committee, Borders Regional Council, 1974-78; Vice-Convenor, Borders Regional Council, 1974-78. Recreations: golf; fishing; curling; bee-keeping. Address: (h.) Tweedknowe, Selkirk; T.-0750 20224.

Robertson, Alistair John, BMedBiol (Hons), MB, ChB, MRCPath, MIAC. Consultant in Administrative Charge, Perth and Kinross Unit Laboratories, since 1982; Consultant

Histopathologist, Tayside Health Board, since 1982; Honorary Senior Lecturer in Pathology, Dundee University, since 1982; b. 29.6.50, Aberdeen; m., Frances Elizabeth Smith. Educ. Aberdeen Grammar School; Aberdeen University. House Physician, Ninewells Hospital, Dundee, 1975; House Surgeon, Aberdeen Royal Infirmary, 1976; Senior House Officer in Pathology, Ninewells Hospital, 1976; Lecturer in Pathology, Ninewells Hospital, 1977. Recreations: golf; curling; caravanning; philately; photography. Address: (b.) The Laboratory, Rose Crescent, Perth Royal Infirmary, Perth; T.-Perth 23311.

Robertson, Alistair Raeburn, RD (and clasp), DPA, DSA, FHSM, FBIM. Director, Strathcarron Hospice, since 1991; b. 29.5.33, Glasgow; m., Mary Gilchrist Smith; 2 s.; 1 d. Educ. Hyndland Senior Secondary School; Glasgow University; Manchester University. Corporation of Glasgow Education Department, 1949-56; Royal Navy, 1951-53; miscellaneous appointments, Scottish Health Service, 1956-71; Group Secretary and Treasurer, Board of Management for Angus Hospitals, 1971-74; District Administrator, South Eastern District, Greater Glasgow Health Board, 1974-85; Acting Secretary, Greater Glasgow Health Board, 1985-86; General Manager, Forth Valley Health Board, 1986-91. Royal Naval Reserve, 1951-79, Captain (Retd); Member, National Board for Nursing, Midwifery and Health Visiting for Scotland. Recreations: curling; sailing; gardening. Address: (b.) Strathcarron Hospice, Randolph Hill, Denny, FK6 5HJ; T.-0324 826222.

Robertson, Andrew Ogilvie, LLB. Partner, T.C. Young & Son, Solicitors and Notaries, since 1968; Secretary, Erskine Hospital, since 1976; Secretary, Clydeside Federation of Community Based Housing Associations, since 1978; Secretary, The Briggait Company Ltd., 1982-88; Director, Glasgow Chamber of Commerce, since 1982; Chairman, Post Office Users Council for Scotland, since 1988; b. 30.6.43, Glasgow; m., Sheila Sturton; 2 s. Educ Glasgow Academy; Sedbergh School; Edinburgh University. Director, Merchants House of Glasgow, 1978-85 and 1988. Recreations: climbing; skiing; sailing; running; fishing. Address: (b.) 30 George Square, Glasgow, G2 1LH; T.-041-221 5562.

Robertson, Rev. Archibald, MA, BD, DipREd. Minister, Eastwood Parish Church, Glasgow, since 1977; Chaplain, Royal Hospital for Sick Children, Glasgow, since 1972; b. 16.12.33, Newburgh, Fife; m., Christina Duncan Isles; 1 s. Educ. Bellahouston Academy; Trinity Academy, Edinburgh; Hyndland Senior Secondary, Glasgow; Glasgow University; Jordanhill College of Education, Glasgow. Minister, Whiteinch Baptist Church, Glasgow, 1957-60; Teacher of Religious Education, 1960-70; Minister, Queen's Park West, 1970-77. Recreations: philately; reading; holidaying in Saltzburg; jigsaw puzzles. Address: (h.) 54 Mansewood Road, Glasgow, G43 1TL; T.-041-632 0724.

Robertson, Avril Margaret, HCIMA. Director, Strathclyde Region Catering Services, since 1988; b. 17.7.35, Edinburgh; 2 s. Educ. Eastwood Secondary School; Queen's College, Glasgow. Began career as assistant housekeeper, 1956; former domestic science teacher and catering manager; Principal Officer (Catering), Strathclyde Regional Council, 1982-88. Member, Advisory Committee, Glasgow College of Food Technology; Member, Governing Body, Queen's College, Glasgow. Recreations: walking; reading; studying Portuguese; gardening. Address: (h.) 2 Rosehill Drive, Condorrat, Cumbernauld, Glasgow; T.-0236 738130.

Robertson, Brenda Margaret, JP. Member, Orkney Islands Council, since 1974; Member, Children's Panel Advisory Committee; Vice-Chairman, Highlands and Islands Fire Board; b. 8.9.24, Scarborough; m., John MacDonald Robertson, BL, NP; 1 s.; 1 d. Educ. Scarborough Girls' High School; University College, St. Andrews. Wartime service, WRNS (Naval Intelligence); formerly: District Commissioner for Guides, Stromness and West Mainland; Member, Stromness Town Council, 1961-74; Orkney County Councillor; Member, Executive Council, NHS; Governor, Aberdeen College of Education. Recreations: reading; arts generally. Address: (h.) Berridale, Stromness, Orkney.

Robertson, Rev. Charles, MA, JP. Minister, Canongate Kirk, since 1978; Chaplain to The Queen, since 1991; b. 22.10.40, Glasgow; m., Alison Margaret Malloch; 1 s.; 2 d. Educ. Camphill School, Paisley; Edinburgh University. Assistant Minister, North Morningside Church, Edinburgh, 1964-65; Minister, Kiltearn, Ross and Cromarty, 1965-78. Secretary, Panel on Worship, General Assembly; Church of Scotland Representative on Joint Liturgical Group; Chaplain to Lord High Commissioner, 1990, 1991; Chaplain to: Donnachaidh Society, New Club, Moray House College; President, Church Service Society, since 1988; Chairman, Board, Queensberry House Hospital; Governor, St. Columba's Hospice, Edinburgh; Director, Whitedael Housing Association; Lecturer, St. Colm's College; Justice of the Peace, City of Edinburgh; Member, Broadcasting Standards Council; Trustee, Edinburgh Old Town Trust. Recreations: books; music. Address: Manse of Canongate, Edinburgh, EH8 8BR; T.-031-556 3515.

Robertson, Sheriff Daphne Jean Black, WS, MA, LLB. Sheriff of Glasgow and Strathkelvin, since 1979; b. 31.3.37.

Robertson, Rev. Fergus Alexander, MA, BD. Minister, New Restalrig Parish Church, Edinburgh; b. 25.4.45, Malvern; m., A. Valery Macrae; 3 d. Educ. George Heriot's School, Edinburgh; Edinburgh University; St. Andrews University. Assistant Minister, West Pilton, Edinburgh; Minister, Dalneigh and Bona Church, Inverness. Moderator, Inverness Presbytery, 1984-85. Recreations: swimming; skiing. Address: 19 Abercorn Road, Edinburgh, EH8 7DP; T.-031-661 4045.

Robertson, George F., FRICS, FCIArb. Partner, Robertson and Dawson, Chartered Surveyors, Edinburgh, since 1970; President, Rent Assessment Panel for Scotland, since 1987; Lay Member, Scottish Solicitors Discipline Tribunal, since 1976; b. 14.7.32, Edinburgh; m., Anne McGonigle; 3 d. Educ. George Heriot's School, Edinburgh; Heriot-Watt College, Edinburgh. Chartered Surveyor; Arbiter; Lecturer (part-time), School of Architecture, Edinburgh College of Art/Heriot-Watt University, 1964-84; Chairman, Joint Standing Committee of Architects, Surveyors and Building Contractors in Scotland, 1976-78; Chairman, Board of Governors, Leith Nautical College, 1976-78; Chairman, Scottish Branch, Royal Institution of Chartered Surveyors, 1984-85; Director, Queensberry House Hospital, Edinburgh, 1983-86; Chairman, Scottish Building Contract Committee, 1983-88; Board Member, Scottish Development Agency, 1987-91; Hon. Secretary, Royal Institution of Chartered Surveyors in Scotland, 1988-90. Recreations: working; gardening; hill-walking; Greece; researching Scottish market crosses. Address: (h.) Gladsheil, Campbell Court, Longniddry, East Lothian, EH32 0NR.

Robertson, George Islay MacNeill, MA. MP (Labour), Hamilton, since 1978; Deputy Opposition Spokesman on Foreign and Commonwealth Affairs, since 1981; b. 12.4.46, Port Ellen, Islay; m., Sandra Wallace; 2 s.; 1 d. Educ. Dunoon Grammar School; Dundee University; St. Andrews University. Tayside Study Economics Group, 1968-69; Scottish Organiser, General, Municipal, Boilermakers Union, 1969-78; Chairman, Scottish Labour Party, 1977-78; Member, Scottish Executive, Labour Party, 1973-79; PPS to Secretary of State for Social Services, 1979; Opposition Spokesman on Scottish Affairs, 1979-80, on Defence, 1980-

81, on Foreign and Commonwealth Affairs, since 1981; Principal Spokesman on Europe, since 1985; Member of Board, Scottish Development Agency, 1976-78, Scottish Tourist Board, 1974-76; Board of Governors, Scottish Police College, 1975-78; Vice Chairman, British Council; Council Member, Royal Institute of International Affairs; Council Member, National Trust for Scotland, 1976-80, 1983-85; Member, Governing Body, Great Britain/East Europe Centre; Member, Steering Committee, Konigswinter Conference; Council Member, British Atlantic Committee. Recreations: family; photography. Address: (h.) 3 Argyle Park, Dunblane, Perthshire.

Robertson, George Slessor, MD, FFARCS, SBStJ. Consultant Anaesthetist, since 1969; Honorary Senior Lecturer in Anaesthesia, Aberdeen University; b. 30.12.33, Peterhead; m., Audrey E. McDonald; 1 s.; 2 d. Educ. Peterhead Academy; Aberdeen University. Early medical training, Aberdeen, London and Winnipeg. Publications: papers on the ethical dilemmas of non-treatment decisions in the demented elderly. Recreations: golf; hill-walking; picture-framing. Address: (b.) Department of Anaesthesia, Royal Infirmary, Foresterhill, Aberdeen, AB9 2ZB; T.-0224 681818.

Robertson, Harry, IPFA. Director of Finance and Depute Chief Executive, Perth and Kinross District Council, since 1981; b. 7.9.49, Dunfermline; m., Rosemary Elizabeth; 2 s. Educ. Dunfermline High School; Glasgow College of Commerce. Trainee Accountant, Burgh of Burntisland; Accountancy Assistant, Assistant Town Chamberlain, Depute Town Chamberlain, Burgh of Barrhead; Depute Director of Finance, Perth and Kinross District Council. Secretary/Treasurer, Perth Repertory Theatre Ltd.; Chairman, Scottish Branch, CIPFA, 1987-88; Treasurer, Perthshire Tourist Board. Recreations: golf; theatre; badminton. Address: (b.) 2 High Street, Perth, PH1 5PH; T.-Perth 39911.

Robertson, Maj.-Gen. Ian Argyll, CB (1968), MBE (1947), MA, DL. Deputy Lieutenant, Highland Region (Nairn), 1973-88; b. 17.7.13, Richmond, Surrey; m., Marjorie Violet Isobel Duncan; 2 d. Educ. Winchester College; Trinity College, Oxford. Commissioned Seaforth Highlanders, 1934; commanded 1st Bn., 1954-57; commanded School of Infantry, 1963-64; commanded 51 Highland Division, 1964-66; retired, 1968. Vice-Chairman and Chairman, Royal British Legion Scotland, 1971-74. Recreations: golf; gardening. Address: (h.) Brackla House, Nairn; T.-Cawdor 220.

Robertson, Ian Barr, MA, LLB. Solicitor (retired); Advocate in Aberdeen; Member, Grampian Regional Council, 1974-86 (Chairman, Transportation and Roads Committee, 1978-86); Honorary Sheriff, Grampian, Highland and Islands, at Stonehaven; b. Aberdeen; m., Vi L. Johnston; 2 s.; 1 d. Educ. Mackie Academy; Fettes College; Aberdeen University. King's Regiment and KAR, 1939-46 (Captain); Partner, Cunningham & Robertson, Solicitors, Stonehaven, 1951-89; Joint Town Clerk, then Town Clerk, Stonehaven, 1957-75; President, Society of Town Clerks in Scotland, 1973-75; Member, Aberdeen Harbour Board, 1975-86; Member, Peterhead Bay Authority, 1978-88; Past President, Stonehaven Rotary Club; Elder, Stonehaven South. Recreations: golf; country sports. Address: (h.) 15 Bath Street, Stonehaven; T.-Stonehaven 62879.

Robertson, Ian Macbeth, CB, LVO, HRSA, Hon. DLitt (Heriot-Watt). Chairman, Board of Governors, Edinburgh College of Art, 1981-88; b. 1.2.18, Crookedholm, Ayrshire; m., Anne Stewart Marshall. Educ. Melville College; Edinburgh University. Served, Middle East and Italy, Royal Artillery and London Scottish, 1940-46; entered Scottish Office, 1946; Private Secretary to Minister of State, 1951-52, and to Secretary of State for Scotland, 1952-55; Under Secretary, Scottish Office, Scottish Development Department

and Scottish Education Department, 1963-78; Secretary of Commissions for Scotland, 1978-83; JP, Edinburgh, 1978. Member, Williams Committee on National Museums and Galleries in Scotland, 1979-81; Chairman, Scottish United Services Museum Advisory Committee, 1970-85; Director, Royal Lyceum Theatre Company, 1978-85. Address: (h.) 8 Colinton Road, Edinburgh, EH10 5DS; T.-031-447 4636.

Robertson, Hon. Lord (Ian Macdonald Robertson), TD (1946), BA, LLB, QC. Senator of the College of Justice in Scotland, 1966-87; Chairman of Governors, Merchiston Castle School, since 1970; b. 30.10.12, Edinburgh; m., Anna Love Glen; 1 s.; 2 d. Educ. Merchiston Castle School, Edinburgh; Balliol College, Oxford; Edinburgh University. Admitted Faculty of Advocates, 1939; served War of 1939-45, 8th Bn., The Royal Scots (The Royal Regiment) - commissioned 1939; Captain/Staff Officer, 44th Lowland Infantry Brigade (15th Scottish Division); Normandy and North West Europe, 1944-45; mentioned in Despatches; Advocate Depute, 1949-51; QC, 1954, Sheriff Principal of Ayr and Bute, 1961-66; Sheriff Principal of Perth and Angus, 1966; Chairman, Medical Appeals Tribunal, 1957-63; Chairman, Scottish Joint Council for Teachers Salaries, 1965-81; Chairman, Scottish Valuation Advisory Council, 1977-86; UK Representative on Central Council, International Association of Judges, 1974-87; General Council Assessor, Edinburgh University Court, 1967-81; Chairman, Edinburgh Centre of Rural Economy and Edinburgh Centre for Tropical Veterinary Medicine, 1967-86; Governor, Merchiston Castle School, 1954-90; Captain, Honourable Company of Edinburgh Golfers at Muirfield, 1970-72. Recreation: golf. Address: (h.) 13 Moray Place, Edinburgh, EH3 6DT; T.-031-225 6637.

Robertson, John Davie Manson, OBE (1978), BL. Chairman, Robertson Group of Companies, since 1980; Director, Stanley Services Ltd., since 1987; Chairman, Highland Health Board, since 1991; Chairman, SCOTMEG, since 1985; b. 6.11.29, Golspie; m., Elizabeth Amelia Macpherson; 2 s.; 2 d. Educ. Kirkwall Grammar School; Edinburgh University. Board Member, Highlands and Islands Enterprise, 1990; Trustee, TSB Scotland Foundation; Honorary Vice Consul for Denmark, 1972; Honorary Consul, Federal Republic of Germany, 1976; Honorary Sheriff, Grampian, Highland and Islands, 1977; Chairman, Orkney Health Board, 1983-91; Member, Highlands and Islands Development Consultative Council, 1988-91; Chairman, Highlands and Islands Savings Committee, 1975-78; Chairman, Children's Panel for Orkney, 1971-76; Chairman, Children's Panel, Orkney Advisory Committee, 1977-82; Member, Board of Management, Orkney Hospitals, 1970-74; Member, Rent Assessment Panel for Scotland, 1973-85. Royal Order of Knight of Dannebrog, 1982; Cavelier's Cross of the Order of Merit, 1986. Publication: Uppies and Doonies, 1967; An Orkney Anthology, 1991. Recreations: fishing; rough shooting. Address: (h.) Spinningdale House, Spinningdale, Sutherland, IV24 3AD; T.-0862 88223.

Robertson, John William, MA. Secretary, British Linen Bank Ltd., since 1986; Solicitor, since 1971; b. 12.11.43, Dunfermline; m., Alice Rudland; 1 s.; 3 d. Educ. Dunfermline High School; Edinburgh University. Assistant Law Secretary, Bank of Scotland, 1975; Manager, Law Department, Bank of Scotland, London, 1978; Assistant Secretary, British Linen Bank Ltd., 1983. Address: (h.) 52 Findhorn Place, Edinburgh, EH9 2NS; T.-031-667 4229.

Robertson, Sir Lewis, CBE, FRSE, FRSA. Chairman: Lilley plc, since 1986, Stakis plc, since 1991, Havelock Europa plc, since 1989; Chairman, Girobank Scotland, 1984-90; b. 28.11.22, Dundee; m., Elspeth Badenoch; 3 s.; 1 d. Educ. Trinity College, Glenalmond. Apprentice Chartered Accountant, 1939-42; RAF Intelligence, 1942-46; entered family textile business, 1946; appointed Managing Director, Robertson Industrial Textiles, 1954; first Managing Director, Scott & Robertson, 1965 (Chairman, 1968); resigned, 1970; Chief Executive, Grampian Holdings, Glasgow, 1971-76 (also Deputy Chairman, 1972-76); Non-Executive Director, Scottish & Newcastle Breweries, 1975-87; Chairman: Triplex Lloyd plc, 1982-90, Borthwicks plc, 1985-89; Director, Whitman International, Geneva, 1987-90; Chairman, Scottish Board (and UK Council Member), British Institute of Management, 1981-83; Chairman, Eastern Regional Hospitals Board, 1960-70; Member, Committee of Enquiry into the Relationship of the Pharmaceutical Industry with the NHS, 1965-67; Member, Monopolies (later Monopolies and Mergers) Commission, 1969-76; Deputy Chairman and first Chief Executive, Scottish Development Agency, 1976-81; Member, Scottish Economic Council, 1977-83; Member, Restrictive Practices Court, since 1983; Member, Scottish Post Office Board, 1984-90; Trustee, since 1963, Member, Executive Committee, since 1964, Chairman, since 1990, Carnegie Trust for the Universities of Scotland; Member, Court, Dundee University, 1967-70 (first Finance Chairman); Council Member, Scottish Business School, 1978-83; Chairman, Scottish Arts Council, and Member, Arts Council of GB, 1970-71; Chairman, Scottish Advisory Committee, British Council, 1978-87; Council Member, Scottish History Society, 1984-89; first Chairman, Policy Committee, Scottish Episcopal Church, 1974-76; Trustee, Foundation for the Study of Christianity and Society, 1983-89; Member, Advisory Board, Edinburgh Edition of the Waverley Novels, since 1986; Director, Friends of Royal Scottish Academy, since 1986; Honorary Doctorate of Laws, Dundee University, 1971. Recreations: work; foreign travel; computer use; music. Address: 32 Saxe Coburg Place, Edinburgh, EH3 5BP; T.-031-332 5221.

Robertson, Noel Farnie, CBE, MA, BSc, PhD, FRSE, FIBiol. Vice Chairman, Board of Trustees, Royal Botanic Garden, Edinburgh; b. 24.12.23, Dundalk; m., Doreen Colina Gardner; 2 s.; 2 d. Educ. Trinity Academy; Edinburgh University; Trinity College, Cambridge. Plant Pathologist, West African Cacao Research Institute, Ghana, 1946-48; Lecturer, Plant Pathology, Cambridge University, 1948-59; Professor of Botany, Hull University, 1959-69; Professor of Agriculture, Edinburgh University, and Principal, East of Scotland College of Agriculture, 1969-83. Recreations: gardening; natural history. Address: (h.) Woodend, Juniper Bank, Walkerburn, Peebles-shire, EH43 6DE; T.-089 687 523.

Robertson, Raymond. MP (Conservative), Aberdeen South, since 1992.

Robertson, Richard Ross, RSA, FRBS, DA. Sculptor; b. 10.9.14, Aberdeen; m., Kathleen May Matts; 2 d. Educ. Paisley Grammar School; Glasgow School of Art; Aberdeen Art School. Work exhibited in Aberdeen public parks and several public buildings in city and county of Aberdeen; also exhibited in several private collections in Britain, America and Holland; retired Lecturer in Sculpture, Gray's School of Art, Aberdeen. Recreations: carving; gardening; walking. Address: (h.) Creaguir, Woodlands Road, Rosemount, Blairgowrie, Perthshire; T.-0250 4970.

Robertson, Robert, CBE, JP, FEIS. Member, Strathclyde Regional Council, 1974-86; b. 15.8.09, Shapensay, Orkney; m., Jean Murdoch Moffatt; 1 s.; 1 d. Educ. Forres Academy; Royal Technical College, Glasgow. Local government service since 1952; Convener, former Renfrewshire County Council; Chairman, former Renfrewshire Education Committee, 13 years; Chairman, Standing Committee for the Supply and Training of Teachers in Further Education (Robertson Report); Member, Board of Governors, Jordanhill College of Education; Member, various College Councils. Recreations: fishing; painting. Address: (h.) 24 Broadwood

Park, Alloway, Ayrshire; T.-0292 43820; Castlehill, near Maybole, Ayrshire; T.-029 250 337.

Robertson, Lord Provost Robert, JP, LLD. Lord Provost, City of Aberdeen, since 1988; m., Susan. Joined Aberdeen Corporation, 1965, as Labour Member; Grampian Regional Councillor, 1975-79; joined Aberdeen City Council, 1979; Housing Convener, 1980-84; Policy Convener, 1984-87.

Robertson, Roderick. Managing Director, Robertsons of Tain Ltd.; Honorary Sheriff, Tain and Dingwall, 1976; b. 24.8.35, Tain; m., Elizabeth Martin Steele; 1 s. Educ. Tain Royal Academy. Agricultural engineering, 1951-56; Army, 1956-59; commenced business (agricultural engineering), 1959; elected, Tain Town Council, 1965 (Chairman of Development, Dean of Guild and Senior Bailie); JP, 1975; appointed Member, Valuation Appeal Committee, Ross and Cromarty, Skye and Lochalsh, 1980; Director, Royal Highland and Agricultural Society of Scotland, since 1979; Director, Ross and Cromarty Enterprise, since 1991; Chairman, Justice of the Peace Committee, Ross and Cromarty, 1980; Chairman, Local Royal British Legion Housing Association, 1984; Chairman, Tain Community Council. Recreations: flying; shooting; fishing; judo. Address: (h.) Viewfield Farm, Tain, Ross-shire, IV19 1PX; T.-0862 892151.

Robertson, Sidney Park, MBE, TD, JP, DL, BCom. Director, S. & J.D. Robertson Group Ltd. (Chairman, 1965-79); Honorary Sheriff, Grampian, Highlands and Islands, since 1969; Vice Lord Lieutenant of Orkney, 1987-90; b. 12.3.14, Kirkwall; m., Elsa Miller Croy; 1 s.; 1 d. Educ. Kirkwall Grammar School; MIBS; Edinburgh University. Commissioned, Royal Artillery, 1940 (Despatches, NW Europe, 1945); managerial posts, Anglo-Iranian Oil Co., Middle East, 1946-51; Manager Operations/Sales, Southern Division, Shell-Mex and BP, 1951-54; founder, Robertson firm, 1954; Major Commanding 861 (Independent) Light Anti-Aircraft Battery RA (Orkney and Zetland), TA, 1956-61; Lt. Col. Commanding Lovat Scouts, 1962-65; Brigadier, CRA 51st Highland Division, 1966-67; Chairman, Orkney Hospitals Board of Management/Orkney Health Board, 1965-79; DL, 1968; Honorary Area Vice-President (Orkney), Royal British Legion, since 1975; Honorary Colonel, 102 (Ulster and Scottish) Light Air Defence Regiment, Royal Artillery, 1975-80; Hon. Colonel Commandant, Royal Regiment of Artillery, 1977-80; Vice President, National Artillery Association, since 1977; Chairman, Royal Artillery Council of Scotland, 1980-84; Honorary President, Orkney Bn., Boys' Brigade; Vice-President, RNLI, since 1985; Freedom of Orkney, 1990. Recreations: travel; hill-walking; angling. Address: (h.) Daisybank, Kirkwall, Orkney; T.-0856 2085.

Robertson, Stanley. Ballad Singer and Story-teller; b. 8.6.40, Aberdeen; m., Johnann Mann; 4 s.; 2 d. Educ. Frederick Street Junior Secondary School; Aberdeen Commercial College (part-time). TV and radio work in folklore and educational programmes; subject of thesis; written about in at least 10 folk books; 1st prize, BBC Listener's Corner; guest Lecturer at many universities. Publications: Exodus to Alford; Nyakim's Windows; Fishooses; Fishooses 2. Recreations: piping; reading. Address: (h.) 101 Marchburn Drive, Northfield, Aberdeen.

Robertson, Sue, BA, MSocSci. Director, Scottish Council for Single Parents, since 1988; b. 12.7.50, Carlisle; m., Paul Hare; 1 s.; 2 d. Educ. Penrith Queen Elizabeth Grammar School; Oxford University; Birmingham University. Senior Economic Assistant, Scottish Economic Planning Department, 1973-78; Co-ordinator, Scottish Women's Aid, 1978-83; Training Officer, Scottish Council for Single Parents, 1983-88. Founder Member, Culdion Housing Association; Committee Member, Walpole Housing

Association. Recreations: hill-walking; cycling; reading. Address: (b.) 13 Gayfield Square, Edinburgh, EH1 3NX; T.-031-556 3899.

Robins, Professor David John, BSc, PhD, DSc, CChem, FRSC. Professor of Chemistry, Glasgow University, since 1990; b. 12.8.45, Purley; m., Helen Dorothy Skinner; 1 s.; 1 d. Educ. Purley Grammar School; Exeter University. NIH Postdoctoral Fellowship, University of Pittsburgh, 1969-71; SRC Fellowship, Surrey University, 1971-72; Tutorial Fellow in Organic Chemistry, Reading University, 1973-74; Lecturer in Organic Chemistry, Glasgow University, 1974-87, Senior Lecturer, 1987-88, Reader, 1988-90. Recreations: badminton; gardening; music; hill-walking; cycling. Address: (b.) Department of Chemistry, Glasgow University, Glasgow, G12 8QQ; T.-041-339 8855.

Robins, John F. Company Secretary, Animal Concern (Scotland), since 1988 (Company Secretary, Scottish Anti-Vivisection Society, 1981-88); Co-ordinator, Scottish Animal Rights Network, since 1983; Managing Director, Ethical Promotions Ltd., since 1988; Co-ordinator, Save Scotland's Seals Funds, since 1988; b. 2.1.57, Glasgow; m., Mary E.; 1 s.; 1 d. Educ. St. Ninian's High School. Co-ordinator, Glasgow Energy Group, 1978-80; Green Party activist and candidate, 1978-81; Delegate, Anti-Nuclear Campaign, 1978-81; Vice-Chair, Friends of the Earth (Scotland) Ltd., 1981-82. Recreations: campaigning against hunting, shooting and fishing; catching up on lost sleep. Address: (b.) 62 Old Dumbarton Road, Glasgow, G3 8RE; T.-041-334 6014.

Robinson, David Beattie, BLitt, MA (Oxon). Senior Lecturer in Greek, Edinburgh University, since 1972; b. 28.4.35, Manchester; m., H. Mairi J. Robinson; 1 s.; 1 d. Educ. Manchester Grammar School; Balliol College, Oxford. Lecturer, St. John's College, Oxford, 1957-58; joined Edinburgh University, 1958. Publication: OCT Plato (Co-editor). Recreations: literature; music; walking. Address: (h.) 127 Grange Loan, Edinburgh, EH9 2HB.

Robinson, Helen Mairi Johnstone, MA. Dictionaries Editor, W. & R. Chambers, since 1990; Research Associate, Edinburgh Edition of the Waverley Novels, 1987-91; Kerr-Fry Award holder, Edinburgh University, 1985-90; b. 21.1.45, Glasgow; 1 s.; 1 d. Educ. George Watson's Ladies' College, Edinburgh; Edinburgh University. Scottish National Dictionary: Junior Assistant Editor, 1966, Assistant Editor, 1967, Senior Assistant Editor, 1972; Editor-in-Chief, Concise Scots Dictionary, 1973-85; Member, Advisory Committee, Private Papers of James Boswell, Yale University, since 1987. Publication: Concise Scots Dictionary, 1985. Recreations: music; theatre; reading; travel. Address: (b.) 43-45 Annandale Street, Edinburgh.

Robinson, Stanley Scott, MBE (Mil), TD, BL, SSC. Sheriff of Grampian, Highland and Islands (retired); Honorary Sheriff of Inverness; Honorary Sheriff of Angus; b. 27.3.13, Edinburgh; m., Helen Annan Hardie; 3 s. Educ. Boroughmuir School, Edinburgh; Edinburgh University. Admitted Solicitor, 1935; TA commission, 1936; War service, Royal Artillery, 1939-45; Major; mentioned in Despatches (2); France and Belgium, 1939-40, France and Germany, 1944-45; admitted SSC, 1962; Vice President, Law Society of Scotland, 1970-72; appointed Sheriff, Fort William/Skye/Inverness/Western Isles, 1972; retired, 1985. Publications: Law of Inderdict, 1987; Law of Game and Salmon Fishing, 1990; Encyclopedia of Laws of Scotland (Contributor). Recreations: bowling; caravanning. Address: (h.) Drumalin House, 16 Drummond Road, Inverness, IV2 4NB; T.-0463 233488.

Robson, Agnes, MA. Head, Urban Policy Divsion, Scottish Office Industry Department, since 1990; b. 6.10.46,

Edinburgh; 1 s. Educ. Holy Cross Academy; Edinburgh University. Civil Servant, since 1968; Head, Energy Division, 1988-89; Head, Nuclear Energy Division, 1989-90. Recreations: music; theatre. Address: (b.) New St. Andrews House, Edinburgh.

Robson, Euan Macfarlane, BA, MSc, MICA. Scottish Manager, Gas Consumers' Council, since 1986; b. 17.2.54, Northumberland; m., Valerie; 1 d. Educ. Trinity College, Glenalmond; Newcastle-upon-Tyne University; Strathclyde University; Durham University. Teacher, 1976-79; Deputy Secretary, Gas Consumers' Northern Council, 1981-86. Member, Northumberland County Council, 1981-89; Honorary Alderman, Northumberland CC, since 1989; Liberal/SDP Alliance candidate, Hexham, 1983, 1987. Address: (h.) Elmbank, Tweedsyde Park, Kelso, TD5 7RF; T.-0573 25279.

Robson, Professor James Scott, MB, ChB (Hons), MD, FRCPEdin, FRCP. Emeritus Piofessor; Professor of Medicine, Edinburgh University, 1977-86; Physician in charge, Medical Renal Unit, Edinburgh Royal Infirmary, 1959-86; b. 19.5.21, Hawick; m., Mary Kynoch MacDonald; 2 s. Educ. Hawick High School; Edinburgh University; New York University. RAMC (Captain), India, Palestine and Egypt, 1945-48; Rockefeller Research Fellow, Harvard University, 1949-50; Edinburgh University: Senior Lecturer in Therapeutics, 1959, Reader in Therapeutics, 1961, in Medicine, 1968; Honorary Associate Professor of Medicine, Harvard, 1962; Merck Sharpe & Dome Visiting Professor to Australia, 1968. President, Renal Association, London, 1977-80; sometime Member, Editorial Board, and Deputy Chairman, Clinical Science and other medical journals; Member, Biomedical Research Committee, SH&HD; Chairman, Sub-Committee in Medicine, National Medical Consultative Committee. Publications: Companion to Medical Studies (Co-Editor); many scientific papers on renal physiology and disease. Recreations: gardening; theatre; reading; contemporary art; writing. Address: (h.) 1 Grant Avenue, Edinburgh, EH13 ODS; T.-031-441 3508.

Robson, Robert, MA (Hons). Festival Director, Mayfest, since 1990; b. 21.12.54, Hamilton; m., Annette Liddle; 2 s. Educ. Hamilton Academy; Glasgow University. Community drama worker with Easterhouse Festival Society, 1978-83; Artistic Director, Cumbernauld Theatre, 1983-90. Recreations: family; theatre; reading; music; football; mokre work. Address: (h.) 12 Moray Gardens, Westerwood, Cumbernauld, G68 0HY.

Robson, Professor William Wallace, FRSE, MA (Oxon). Professor Emeritus of English Literature, Edinburgh University; b. 20.6.23, Plymouth; m., Anne-Varna Moses; 2 s. Educ. Leeds High School and Modern School; New College, Oxford. Assistant Lecturer, King's College, London, 1944-46; Lecturer, Lincoln and Queen's Colleges, Oxford, 1944-46; Fellow, Lincoln College, Oxford, 1948-70; Professor of English, Sussex University, 1970-72; Visiting Professor: University of Southern California, 1953, Adelaide University, 1956, Delaware University, 1963-64; Elizabeth Drew Professor, Smith College, USA, 1968-69; Visiting Fellow: All Souls College, Oxford, 1981, New College, Oxford, 1985. Publications: Critical Essays, 1966; The Signs Among Us, 1968; Modern English Literature, 1970; The Definition of Literature, 1982; A Prologue to English Literature, 1986. Recreations: non-strenuous games of many kinds. Address: (b.) Department of English Literature, Edinburgh University, David Hume Tower, George Square, Edinburgh, EH8; T.-031-667 1011.

Rochester, Professor Colin Herbert, BSc, PhD, DSc, CChem, FRSC, FRSE. Baxter Professor of Chemistry, Dundee University, since 1980; b. 20.3.37, Coventry; m.,

Jennifer Mary Orrell; 2 s.; 2 d. Educ. Hymers College, Hull; Royal Liberty School, Romford; King's College, London University. Nottingham University: Assistant Lecturer in Physical Chemistry, 1962-64, Lecturer, 1964-72, Reader, 1972-80. Publication: Acidity Functions, 1970. Recreations: fossil collecting; swimming. Address: (b.) Chemistry Department, The University, Dundee, DD1 4HN; T.-0382 23181.

Rochford, Professor Gerard, BA, BSc. Psychoanalytical Psychotherapist; b. 17.12.32, Dorking; m., Anne Prime; 3 s.; 7 d. Educ. Worcester Royal Grammar School; Hull University; Oxford University. Medical Research Council, 1960-63; Lecturer in Psychology: Aberdeen University, 1963-67, Hong Kong University, 1967-70; Lecturer/Senior Lecturer, 1970-78, Professor of Social Work Studies, 1978-88, Aberdeen University. Member, Scottish Association of Psychoanalytical Psychotherapists. Recreations: family; friends; poetry. Address: (h.) 47 Waverley Place, Aberdeen; T.-Aberdeen 644873.

Roddin, John Begbie. Director of Policy and Resources, Scottish Fisheries Protection Agency, since 1991; b. 26.8.48, Musselburgh; m., Isobel Walker; 2 s.; 1 d. Educ. Musselburgh Grammar School. Clerical Officer, Executive Officer, Higher Executive Officer, Department of Agriculture and Fisheries for Scotland; Senior Executive Officer, Scottish Office Manpower Division, 1978; Principal, Scottish Office Efficiency Unit, 1985; Scottish Development Department, 1987. Recreations: sailing; angling; walking; reading. Address: (h.) 3 Ormelie Terrace, Edinburgh, EH15 2EX; T.-031-669 4348.

Rodger, Alan, BSc, MB, ChB, DMRT, FRCSEdin, FRCR. Consultant Radiation Oncologist, Western General Hospital, Edinburgh, since 1981; b. 9.6.46, Kirkcaldy. Educ. Kirkcaldy High School; Edinburgh University. Pre-registration hospital posts, Royal Infirmary, Edinburgh, and Victoria Hospital, Kirkcaldy, 1971-72; junior hospital training course in surgery, Royal Infirmary, Edinburgh, 1972-75; Registrar post in Radiotherapy, Western General Hospital, Edinburgh, 1975-77; University Lecturer in Radiotherapy, Western General Hospital, Edinburgh, and MRC Cyclotron Unit, 1977-80; Project Investigator, M.D. Anderson Hospital and Tumour Institute, Houston, 1980-81. Member, several SHHD committees and working parties, and committees of Royal College of Radiologists. Recreations: preparation and eating of good food; good wines; opera sopranos; history and architecture. Address: (h.) 1 Laverockbank Road, Trinity, Edinburgh; T.-031-552 5699.

Rodger of Earlsferry, Rt. Hon. Lord (Alan Ferguson Rodger), QC, MA, LLB, DCL. Lord Advocate, since 1992; b. 18.9.44. Educ. Kelvinside Academy, Glasgow; Glasgow University; New College, Oxford. Fellow, New College, Oxford, 1970-72; Member, Faculty of Advocates, 1974; Clerk of Faculty, 1976-79; Advocate Depute, 1985-88; Home Advocate Depute, 1986-88; Member, Mental Welfare Commission for Scotland, 1981-84; UK Delegation to CCBE, 1984-89; Maccabaean Lecturer, British Academy, 1991; Solicitor General for Scotland, 1989-92. Recreation: walking. Address: (b.) Crown Office, Regent Road, Edinburgh, EH7 5BL; T.-031-557 3800.

Rodger, Albert Alexander, BSc (Eng), PhD, CEng, MICE, FGS. Senior Lecturer, Department of Engineering, Aberdeen University, since 1989; b. 12.5.51, Greenock; m., Jane Helen Whyte; 2 d. Educ. Duncanrig Senior Secondary School; Aberdeen University. Lecturer, Department of Engineering, Aberdeen University, 1976-77; Project Scientist, Cementation Research Ltd., 1977-79; Lecturer, Aberdeen University, 1977-89. Council Member, Aberdeen Association of Civil Engineers. Recreations: swimming; computing. Address: (b.) King's College, Aberdeen, AB9 2UE; T.-0224 272984.

Rodger, James McPhail, BSc, MEd. Headmaster, Portree High School, since 1971; b. 15.9.33, Cleland, Lanarkshire; m., Jessie Tyre Crawford; 4 d. Educ. Wishaw High School; Glasgow University; Jordanhill College. Flying Officer, RAF, 1956; Teacher of Mathematics, Hamilton Academy, 1959-64; Principal Teacher of Mathematics and latterly Depute Headmaster, Carluke High School, 1964-71. Member, Consultative Committee on the Curriculum, 1980-83. Professional footballer: Glasgow Rangers, 1952-55, St. Mirren, 1955-62, Heart of Midlothian, 1962-65. Recreations: bridge; golf; hill-walking; gardening; reading. Address: (b.) Portree High School, Portree, Isle of Skye; T.-0478 2030.

Rodger, Willie, ARSA, DA (Glas). Printmaker; b. 3.3.30, Kirkintilloch; m., Anne Charmian Henry; 2 s.; 2 d. Educ. Lenzie Academy; Glasgow School of Art. Visualiser, London advertising agency, 1953-54; Art Teacher, Lenzie Acacady, 1955-68; Head, Art Department, Clydebank High School, 1968-87. Artist in Residence, Sussex University, 1971; first prize, Scottish Design Centre Awards, 1975; Saltire Awards for Art in Architecture, 1984-89. Recreations: gardening; jazz; fishing. Address: Stenton, Bellevue Road, Kirkintilloch, Glasgow, G66 1AP; T.-041-776 2116.

Rodgers, Professor Eamonn Joseph, BA (Hons), MA, PhD. Professor of Spanish and Latin-American Studies, Strathclyde University, since 1990; b. 4.6.41, Belfast; m., Valerie Ann Goodman; 2 s. Educ. St. Mary's Grammar School, Belfast; Queen's University, Belfast. Junior Lecturer in Spanish, Trinity College, Dublin, 1964-66; Lecturer, 1966-78; Senior Lecturer, 1978-89. Publication: From Enlightenment to Realism: The Novels of Galdos 1870-1887, 1987. Recreations: country walks; music. Address: (b.) Strathclyde University, Glasgow, G1 1XH; T.-041-552 4411.

Roger, Alan Stuart, MBE (Mil), JP. Vice-President, National Trust for Scotland, since 1984; Council Member, Contemporary Art Society, 1980-90; Chairman, Bonsai Kai, since 1965; b. 27.4.09, London. Educ. Loretto School; Trinity College, Oxford. Partner, Norris Oakley Bros. and Director, various public companies, 1933; BRC and St. John Ambulance, France, 1940; Ministry of Supply mission to India, 1940-41; Indian Army, 1941-45 and War Office, 1945-52, serving India, Persia, Iraq, Hong Kong; Director of various public companies in UK and Portugal, 1953-79. Trustee, National Galleries of Scotland, 1967-82; Trustee, Crarae Garden Trust; Member, Countess of Perth's Committee for Awards to Museums and Galleries, 1987-91. Recreations: gardening; reading. Address: (h.) Dundonnell, by Garve, Ross & Cromarty; T.-085 483 206.

Roger, Peter Charles Marshall, CA. Director, Speirs & Jeffrey Ltd., since 1974; b. 11.4.42, Glasgow; m., Fiona Ann Murray; 2 s.; 1 d. Educ. Glasgow High School. Qualified CA, 1964; Thomson McLintock & Co., 1964-71; joined Speirs & Jeffrey Ltd., 1971. Recreation: golf. Address: (b.) 36 Renfield Street, Glasgow, G2 1NA; T.-041-248 4311.

Rogers, Rev. Dr. James Murdoch, BA (Hons), BD, DCult. Minister, Roseangle Ryehill Church, Dundee, since 1980; b. 22.11.28, Limavady, Northern Ireland; m., Doris Young; 2 s. Educ. Coleraine Academical Institution; Queen's University, Belfast; Presbyterian College, Belfast. Minister, Second Presbyterian Church, Saintfield, 1955-65; Moderator, Down Presbytery; Secretary, Irish Council of Churches, 1963-65; Minister, Ryehill Church, Dundee, 1965-80; Chairman, Hospitals Sub-Committee, Home Board, Church of Scotland; Vice-Convener, Overseas Council, 1977-80; Chairman, Departmental Board of Overseas Missions and Inter-Church Relations, 1977-83; Convener, Board of World Mission and

Unity, Church of Scotland, 1984-88; Vice President, British Council of Churches, 1987-90; Member, Central Committee, World Council of Churches, 1988-91; Leader, Scottish Delegates, General Assembly of World Council, Canberra, 1991; Exchange Preacher, National Council of Churches, USA; Moderator, Presbytery of Dundee, 1988-89; Chairman, Churches Together in Dundee, since 1991; Chaplain, Scout Association, City of Dundee; Church of Scotland Chaplain and Parish Minister, Dundee University; Member, Board of Directors, Royal Dundee Blindcraft Products, since 1966, President and Chairman of the Board, since 1990; Chairman, Joint Committee, RDBP and Lord Roberts Workshops. Recreations: golf; gardening; photography; travel; Rotarian. Address: (h.) 15 West Park Road, Dundee, DD2 1NU; T.-Dundee 67460.

Rogers, Mary Elizabeth, MA, MS, PhD. Senior Lecturer, Biological Sciences, Edinburgh University, since 1991; Director of Studies, since 1989; b. 11.11.41, Bitton. Educ. Gardenhurst School, Burnham-on-Sea; Oxford University. University Demonstrator, then Lecturer, Edinburgh University. Publications: Looking at Vertebrates, 1986; papers in journals. Recreations: hill-walking; travel; swimming; tennis; reading; baroque music. Address: (h.) 72 Great King Street, Edinburgh, EH3 6QU.

Rogerson, Robert William Kelly Cupples, OBE, BArch, FRIBA, FRIAS, FSA Scot, MRSH. Vice Chairman, Scottish Council on Disability, 1987-89; Chairman, Committee on Access for Scotland, 1980-89; Council Member, National Trust for Scotland, 1980-86; b. 14.5.17, Glasgow; m., Mary Clark MacNeill; 1 s.; 1 d. Educ. High School of Glasgow; Strathclyde University. Architect in private practice, 1955-56 and 1958-82 (Partner, Watson Salmond & Gray, 1949-58); Lecturer, School of Architecture, Glasgow School of Art; Past Chairman, Glasgow Building Guardian Committee; Past Chairman, RIAS Trustees of The Hill House, Helensburgh; Founder and Chairman, Glasgow Summer School; former Member, Committee on Artistic Matters, Church of Scotland. Publications: A Place at Work (Co-author); Jack Coia, His Life & Work. Recreations: gardening; travelling abroad. Address: (h.) 49 Roman Court, Roman Road, Bearsden, Glasgow, G61 2NW; T.-041-942 3997.

Rolfe, Mervyn James, JP. Deputy Leader of the Administration, Tayside Regional Council, since 1990, and Convener, Education Committee, since 1986; Member, Executive Committee, COSLA, since 1990; b. 31.7.47, Wisbech; m., Christine; 1 s. Educ. Buckhaven High School. Civil servant, until 1983; Co-ordinator, Dundee Resources Centre for the Unemployed, 1983-87; Vice-Chair, Dundee Trades Council, 1981-82; Governor, Dundee (now Northern) College of Education, since 1986; Member, Dundee University Court, since 1986; Member, Scottish Community Education Council, 1986-88; Member, General Teaching Council, since 1986; Member, Scottish Committee for Staff Development in Education, 1987-91; Board Member, Scottish Enterprise, Tayside, since 1991; Member, Scottish Cooperative Development Committee, since 1984; Member, Dundee Heritage Trust, since 1986; Executive Member, Campaign for a Scottish Assembly, 1989-91. Recreations: reading; politics. Address: (h.) 17 Mains Terrace, Dundee; T.-0382 450073.

Rolfe, William David Ian, PhD, FRSE, FGS, FMA. Keeper of Geology, National Museums of Scotland, since 1986; b. 24.1.36; m., Julia Mary Margaret Rayer; 2 d. Educ. Royal Liberty Grammar School, Romford; Birmingham University. Geology Curator, University Lecturer, then Senior Lecturer in Geology, Hunterian Museum, Glasgow University, 1962-81; Deputy Director, 1981-86. President, Geological Society of Glasgow, 1973-76; Editor, Scottish Journal of Geology, 1967-72; President, Edinburgh Geological Society, 1989-91;

President, Palaeontological Association, 1992-94. Recreations: visual arts; walking; swimming; music. Address: 4A Randolph Crescent, Edinburgh, EH3 7TH; T.-031-226 2094.

Rooke, Matthew Andre Paul, MA (Hons). Music Director, Scottish Arts Council, since 1991; b. 14.2.63, Oxford; m., Georgina Verity Dawson. Educ. St. Andrews University; Berklee College of Music. Music Officer, Arts Council of G.B., 1989-91. Recreation: cookery. Address: (b.) 12 Manor Place, Edinburgh, EH3 7PD; T.-031-225 6051.

Rorke, Professor John, CBE, PhD, BSc, CEng, FIMechE, FRSE. Professor Emeritus, formerly Professor of Mechanical Engineering, Heriot-Watt University, 1980-88, and Vice-Principal, 1984-88; b. 2.9.23, Dumbarton; m., Jane Craig Buchanan; 2 d. Educ. Dumbarton Academy; Royal Technical College, Glasgow. Lecturer, Strathclyde University, 1946-51; Assistant to Engineering Director, Alexander Stephen & Sons Ltd., 1951-56; Technical Manager, then General Manager and Engineering Director, William Denny & Bros. Ltd., 1956-63; Technical Director, then Sales Director, Managing Director and Chairman, Brown Bros. & Co. Ltd. and Chairman, John Hastie of Greenock Ltd., 1963-78; Managing Director, Vickers Offshore Group, 1978 (Director of Planning, Vickers PLC, 1979-80). President, Institution of Engineers and Shipbuilders in Scotland, 1985-87; Chairman, Institute of Offshore Engineering Group, since 1990. Recreations: bridge; golf. Address: (h.) 3 Barnton Park Grove, Edinburgh; T.-031-336 3044.

Rose, David, BA, NDA, CertEd. Principal, The Barony College, Dumfries, since 1980; b. 6.7.40, Denton, Manchester; m., Pauline Anne Rose; 1 s.; 1 d. Educ. Seale-Hayne College of Agriculture; Open University. Assistant Farm Manager, Wiltshire, 1962-66; Lecturer in Agriculture, Cumbria College of Agriculture and Forestry, 1967-70; Senior Lecturer in Agriculture, Bishop Burton College of Agriculture, 1970-74; Vice-Principal, Oatridge College of Agriculture, 1974-80. Recreation: hill-walking. Address: (b.) Parkgate, Dumfries; T.-038 786 251.

Rose, Professor Richard, BA, DPhil. Director and Professor of Public Policy, Centre for the Study of Public Policy, Strathclyde University, since 1976; b. 9.4.33; m., Rosemary J.; 2 s.; 1 d. Educ. Clayton High School, Missouri, USA; Johns Hopkins University; London School of Economics; Lincoln and Nuffield Colleges, Oxford University. Political public relations, Mississippi Valley, 1954-55; Reporter, St. Louis Post-Dispatch, 1955-57; Lecturer in Government, Manchester University, 1961-66; Professor of Politics, Strathclyde University, 1966-82; Consultant Psephologist, The Times, Independent Television, Daily Telegraph, STV, UTV, etc., since 1964; American SSRC Fellow, Stanford University, 1967; Visiting Lecturer in Political Sociology, Cambridge University, 1967; Director, ISSC European Summer School, 1973; Secretary, Committee on Political Sociology, International Sociological Association, 1970-85; Founding Member, European Consortium for Political Research, 1970; Member: US/UK Fulbright Commission, 1971-75, Eisenhower Fellowship Programme, 1971; Guggenheim Foundation Fellow, 1974; Visiting Scholar: Woodrow Wilson International Centre, Washington DC, 1974, Brookings Institute, Washington DC, 1976, American Enterprise Institute, Washington, 1980, Fiscal Affairs Department, IMF, Washington, 1984; Visiting Professor, European University Institute, Florence, 1977, 1978; Visitor, Japan Foundation, 1984; Hinkley Professor, Johns Hopkins University, 1987; Guest Professor, Wissenschaftzentrum, Berlin, 1988; Ransone Lecturer, University of Alabama, 1990; Consultant Chairman, NI Constitutional Convention, 1976; Home Office Working Party on Electoral Register, 1975-77; Co-Founder, British Politics Group, 1974;

Convenor, Work Group on UK Politics, Political Studies Association, 1976-88; Member, Council, International Political Science Association, 1976-82; Keynote Speaker, Australian Institute of Political Science, Canberra, 1978; Technical Consultant, OECD; Director, ESRC (formerly SSRC) Research Programme, Growth of Government, 1982-86; Honorary Vice President, Political Studies Association, UK, 1986; Editor, Journal of Public Policy, since 1985 (Chairman, 1981-85); Foreign Member, Finnish Academy of Science and Letters, 1985. Publications: The British General Election of 1959 (Co-author), 1960; Must Labour Lose? (Co-author), 1960; Politics in England, 1964; Studies in British Politics (Editor), 1966; Influencing Voters, 1967; Policy Making in Britain (Editor), 1969; People in Politics, 1970; European Politics (Joint Editor), 1971; Governing Without Consensus – An Irish Perspective, 1971; International Almanack of Electoral History (Co-author), 1974; Electoral Behaviour – A Comparative Handbook (Editor), 1974; Lessons From America (Editor), 1974; The Problem of Party Government, 1974; The Management of Urban Change in Britain and Germany (Editor), 1974; Northern Ireland – A Time of Choice, 1976; Managing Presidential Objectives, 1976; The Dynamics of Public Policy (Editor), 1976; New Trends in British Politics (Joint Editor), 1977; Comparing Public Policies (Joint Editor), 1977; What is Governing? – Purpose and Policy in Washington, 1978; Elections Without Choice (Joint Editor), 1978; Can Government Go Bankrupt? (Co-author), 1978; Britain – Progress and Decline (Joint Editor), 1980; Do Parties Make a Difference?, 1980; Challenge to Governance (Editor), 1980; Electoral Participation (Editor), 1980; Presidents and Prime Ministers (Joint Editor), 1980; Understanding the United Kingdom, 1982; United Kingdom Facts (Co-author), 1982; The Territorial Dimension in United Kingdom Politics (Joint Editor), 1982; Fiscal Stress in Cities (Joint Editor), 1982; Understanding Big Government, 1984; The Nationwide Competition for Votes (Co-author), 1984; Public Employment in Western Nations, 1985; Voters Begin to Choose (Co-author), 1986; Patterns of Parliamentary Legislation (Co-author), 1986; The Welfare State East and West (Joint Editor), 1986; Ministers and Ministries, 1987; Taxation By Political Inertia (Co-author), 1987; The Post-Modern President – The White House Meets the World, 1988; Ordinary People in Public Policy, 1989; Training Without Trainers? (Co-author), 1990; The Loyalty of Voters (Co-author), 1990. Recreations: architecture (historical, Britain; modern, America); music; writing. Address: (b.) CSPP, Strathclyde University, Livingstone Tower, Glasgow, G1 1XH; T.-041-552 4400.

Rosebery, 7th Earl of (Neil Archibald Primrose), DL; b. 11.2.29; m., Alison Mary Deirdre Reid; 1 s.; 4 d. Educ. Stowe; New College, Oxford. Address: (h.) Dalmeny House, South Queensferry, West Lothian.

Rosie, Professor Aeneas Murdoch, BSc, MSc, PhD, FIEE, CEng. Professor of Telecommunications, Strathclyde University, since 1973; b. 6.6.31, Wick; 1 s.; 1 d. Educ. Wick High School; Glasgow University; Birmingham University. Engineer, Pye Radio Co., Cambridge; Research Fellow, Birmingham University; Lecturer, Senior Lecturer, Reader, Queen's University of Belfast. Recreation: sailing. Address: (h.) Mill Bridge, Rhu Road Higher, Helensburgh; T.-0436 72625.

Rosie, George. Freelance Writer and Broadcaster; b. 27.2.41, Edinburgh; m., Elizabeth Ann Burness; 2 s.; 1 d. Educ. Trinity Academy, Edinburgh; Edinburgh School of Architecture. Editor, Interior Design magazine, 1966-68; freelance magazine writer, 1968-76; Scottish Affairs Correspondent, Sunday Times, 1976-86; Reporter, Channel 4 TV series Down the Line, 1986-87, Scottish Eye, 1988; Reporter/Writer, The Englishing of Scotland, 1988, Selling Scotland, 1989;

Scotching the Myth, 1990; Losing the Heid, 1991; Editor, Observer Scotland, 1988-89; award winner, RSPB birds and countryside awards, 1988. Publications: British in Vietnam, 1970; Cromarty, 1975; The Ludwig Initiative, 1978; Hugh Miller, 1982; The Directory of International Terrorism, 1986; as contributor: Headlines, the Media in Scotland, 1978; Scottish Government Yearbook, 1982; Scotland, Multinationals and the Third World, 1982; World Offshore Oil and Gas Industry Report, 1987; stage plays: The Blasphemer, 1990; Carlucco and the Queen of Hearts, 1991 (winner, Fringe First, The Independent Theatre Award). Recreation: hill-walking. Address: (h.) 70 Comiston Drive, Edinburgh, EH10 5QS; T.-031-447 9660.

Rosin, Leslie, BL. Company Director; Member: Eastwood District Council, since 1984 (Vice Chairman, Chairman of Finance and General Purposes, Chairman of Direct Services); Strathclyde Regional Council, 1986-90; b. 31.8.31, London; m., Hilary Langman; 1 s.; 2 d. Educ. Hutchesons' Grammar School; Glasgow University. Immediate Past Chairman, Eastwood Conservative Association. Recreation: harpsichord maker. Address: (h.) 26 Glenpark Avenue, Glasgow, G46 7JF; T.-041-638 3333.

Ross, Alastair Robertson, OStJ, DA, ARSA, FRBS, FSA Scot, FRSA, MBIM. Artist; Lecturer in Fine Art, Duncan of Jordanstone College of Art, Dundee, since 1966; Honorary Lecturer, Dundee University, since 1969; Vice President, Royal Society of British Sculptors, 1988-90; Council Member, British School at Rome, since 1990; b. 8.8.41, Perth; m., Kathryn Margaret Greig Wilson; 1 d. Educ. St. Mary's Episcopal School, Dunblane; McLaren High School, Callander; Duncan of Jordanstone College of Art, Dundee. SED Postgraduate Scholarship, 1965-66; Dickson Prize for Sculpture, 1962; Holokrome (Dundee) Sculpture Prize and Commission, 1962; SED Travelling Scholarship, 1963; Royal Scottish Academy Chalmers Bursary, 1964; Royal Scottish Academy Carnegie Travelling Scholarship, 1965; Duncan of Drumfork Scholarship, 1965; award winner, Paris Salon, 1967; Medaille de Bronze, Societe des Artistes Francais, 1968; Professional Member, Society of Scottish Artists, 1969; Medaille D'Argent, 1970; Membre Associe, Societe des Artistes Francais, 1970; Scottish Representative and Member, Council, Royal Society of British Sculptors, since 1972; Sir Otto Beit Medal, Royal Society of British Sculptors, 1988; Freeman, City of London, 1989; Sir William Gillies Bequest Award, Royal Scottish Academy, 1989; Council Member, Society of Scottish Artists, 1972-75; exhibited work widely in UK and abroad; work in: Scottish Arts Council Collection, Dundee Education Authority Collection, private collections in Austria, Switzerland, Egypt, USA, Norway, Bahamas, Canada, Portugal, India, UK. Recreations: genealogy; heraldry; travel. Address: (h.) Ravenscourt, 28 Albany Terrace, Dundee, DD3 6HS; T.-0382 24235.

Ross, Alexander (Sandy), LLB, CYCW. Controller, Arts and Entertainment, Scottish Television, since 1986; b. 17.4.48, Grangemouth; 1 s.; 1 d. Educ. Grangemouth High School; Edinburgh University; Moray House College. Apprentice lawyer, 1971-73; Lecturer, Paisley College, 1974-75; Producer, Granada TV, 1978-86. Member, Edinburgh Town Council, 1971-74; Member, Edinburgh District Council, 1974-78; President, Moray House Students Union, 1976. Recreations: golf; music; reading; watching football. Address: (h.) 7 Murrayfield avenue, Edinburgh, EH12 6AU; T.-031-337 3679.

Ross, Rev. Andrew Christian, MA, BD, STM, PhD. Senior Lecturer in Ecclesiastical History, Edinburgh University, since 1966 (Principal of New College and Dean, Faculty of Divinity, 1978-84); b. 10.5.31, Millerhill, Lothian; m., I. Joyce Elder; 4 s.; 1 d. (deceased). Educ. Dalkeith High School; Edinburgh University; Union Theological Seminary,

New York. RAF, 1952-54; Minister, Church of Central Africa Presbyterian (Malawi), 1958-65; Chairman, Lands Tribunal of Nyasaland, then Malawi Government, 1963-65; Vice Chairman, National Tenders Board, Nyasaland, then Malawi Government, 1963-65. Member, University Court, 1971-73; Convener, Student Affairs Committee, 1977-83; Kerr Lecturer, Glasgow University, 1984; Lecturer, Assembly's College, Belfast, 1985. Publication: John Philip: Missions, Race and Politics in South Africa. Recreation: coaching and watching football. Address: (h.) 27 Colinton Road, Edinburgh; T.-031-447 5987.

Ross, Colin Hamish, CA. Chairman, Edinburgh Fund Managers PLC, since 1991; b. 16.9.40, St. Andrews; m., Elaine Gemmel Taylor; 3 s.; 1 d. Educ. Fettes College. Recreations: golf; bridge; fishing. Address: (b.) 4 Melville Crescent, Edinburgh, EH3 7JB; T.-031-226 4931.

Ross, Rev. David Sinclair, BSc, MSc, PhD, BD. Minister, Old Parish Church, Peterhead, since 1978; Church of Scotland Representative, Grampian Regional Education Committee, 1981-90; b. 24.7.45, Aberdeen; 2 s. Educ. Aberdeen Academy; Aberdeen University; Glasgow University. Research Chemist, West Germany, 1971-74. Port Chaplain, Peterhead, since 1992; President, Peterhead Rugby FC; Chaplain, HM Prison, Peterhead, 1980-88; Chaplain, RAF Buchan. Recreations: choral singing; rugby; trout fishing. Address: 1 Hawthorn Road, Peterhead, AB42 6DW; T.-0779 72618.

Ross, Rt. Hon. Lord (Donald MacArthur Ross), PC, MA, LLB. President of the Second Division of the Court of Session and Lord Justice Clerk, since 1985; a Senator of the College of Justice, since 1977; Lord High Commissioner to the General Assembly of the Church of Scotland, 1990 and 1991; b. 29.3.27, Dundee; m., Dorothy Margaret Annand; 2 d. Educ. High School of Dundee; Edinburgh University. Advocate, 1952; QC, 1964; Vice-Dean, Faculty of Advocates, 1967-73; Dean of Faculty, 1973-76; Sheriff Principal of Ayr and Bute, 1972-73; Member, Scottish Committee, Council of Tribunals, 1970-76; Member, Committee on Privacy, 1970; Deputy Chairman, Boundary Commission for Scotland, 1977-85. Member, Court, Heriot-Watt University, 1978-90, Chairman, 1984-90. Hon. LLD, Edinburgh, Dundee; Hon. DUniv, Heriot-Watt; FRSE. Recreation: gardening; walking. Address: Parliament House, Edinburgh, EH1 1RQ; T.-031-225 2595.

Ross, Donald Forrester, MA, CA. Deputy General Treasurer, Church of Scotland, since 1975; Secretary, Church of Scotland Trust, since 1975; b. 14.6.42, Aberdeen; m., Dorothy Reid Nelson; 2 s. Educ. Aberdeen Grammar School; Aberdeen University. CA Apprentice, G. & J. McBain, CA, Aberdeen, 1963-67; Audit Assistant, Thomson McLintock, CA, Glasgow, 1967-69; Assistant Treasurer, Church of Scotland, 1969-75. Recreation: golf. Address: (b.) 121 George Street, Edinburgh, EH2 4YN; T.-031-225 5722.

Ross, Duncan, MBE. Principal, Benmore Centre for Outdoor Education, since 1975; Commissioner, Countryside Commission for Scotland, 1972-88; Vice-Chairman and former Chairman, Scottish Mountain Leader Training Board; Member, Scottish Mountain Safety Group, since 1988; b. 29.4.33, Sandbank, Argyll; m., Kathryn Dilworth. Educ. Moray House College of Education, Edinburgh. Pilot, RAF, 1951-57; Instructor, National Mountain Training Centre, Glenmore Lodge, 1963-71; Deputy Principal, Benmore Centre for Outdoor Education, 1971-75. Recreations: mountaineering; sailing; skiing; nature study and conservation; reading. Address: (h.) Ardmhor, Hunter Street, Dunoon, Argyll, PA23 8DZ; T.-0369 6578.

Ross, Elizabeth Allan, MA, DipLib. General Secretary, Disablement Income Group Scotland, since 1990; b. 22.1.46, Galashiels. Educ. Kelso High School; Edinburgh University; Strathclyde University. Librarian, Lauder Technical College, Dunfermline, 1967-69; Assistant Librarian: Heriot-Watt University, 1969-76, Glasgow University, 1977-79; Scottish Legal Life Assurance Society, 1981-83; National Secretary, YWCA of Scotland, 1984-90. Recreations: reading; music; people; church work. Address: (b.) 5 Quayside Street, Edinburgh, EH6 6EJ; T.-031-555 2811.

Ross, Ernest. MP (Labour), Dundee West, since 1979; Chair, PLP Foreign Affairs Committee; Member, Employment Select Committee; b. 27.7.42, Dundee; m., June; 2 s.; 1 d. Educ. St. John's Junior Secondary School. Apprentice Marine Fitter, Caledon Shipyard; Quality Control Inspector/Engineer, Timex. Recreations: football; cricket. Address: (b.) Constituency Office, 13 Cowgate, Dundee; T.-0382 200329.

Ross, Graham Tullis, LVO, OBE. Chairman, Edinburgh Old Town Renewal Trust, since 1991; Chairman, Edinburgh Old Town Charitable Trust, since 1990; b. 5.7.28, Edinburgh; m., Margot; 1 s.; 2 d. Educ. George Watson's College, Edinburgh. Director, Macvitties Guest & Co. Ltd., Edinburgh, 1955-65; Managing Director, Macvitties Guest (Edinburgh), A.F. Reid (Glasgow), 1965-71; Managing Director, A.A. Laing Ltd. and Ross Restaurants Ltd., 1971-76; Managing Director, D.S. Crawford (Catering) Ltd., 1976-82; Director, Scottish Business in the Community, 1982-90. Chairman, Scottish Hotel and Catering Institute, 1968-72; Chairman, Napier College Advisory Committee, 1970-85. Recreation: hill-walking. Address: (h.) 20 Munro Drive, Edinburgh; T.-031-225 8818.

Ross, Helen Elizabeth, BA, MA (Oxon), PhD (Cantab), FBPsS, CPsychol, FRSE. Reader in Psychology, Stirling University, since 1983; b. 2.12.35, London. Educ. South Hampstead High School; Somerville College, Oxford; Newnham College, Cambridge. Assistant Mistress, schools in London and Oxfordshire, 1959-61; Research Assistant and student, Psychological Laboratory, Cambridge University, 1961-65; Lecturer in Psychology: Hull University, 1965-68, Stirling University, 1969-72; Senior Lecturer in Psychology, Stirling University, 1972-83; Research Fellow, DFVLR Institute for Aerospace Medicine, Bonn, 1980-81; Leverhulme Fellowship, 1983-84; Member, S.E. Regional Board, Nature Conservancy Council for Scotland. Publications: Behaviour and Perception in Strange Environments, 1974; E.H. Weber: The Sense of Touch (Co-translator), 1978. Recreations: skiing; curling; hill-walking; traditional music. Address: (b.) Department of Psychology, Stirling University, Stirling, FK9 4LA; T.-0786 73171.

Ross, John Alexander. President, National Farmers' Union of Scotland, 1990; b. 19.2.45, Stranraer; m., Alison Jean Darling; 2 s.; 1 d. Educ. George Watson's College, Edinburgh. NFU of Scotland: Convener, Hill Farming Sub-Committee, 1984-90, Convener, Livestock Committee, 1987-90, Vice-President, 1986-90, Wigtown Area President, 1985-86. Chairman, Stranraer School Council, 1980-89; Session Clerk, Portpatrick Parish Church, 1975-80; Elder, Church of Scotland; Director, Animal Diseases Research Association. Recreations: golf; curling. Address: (b.) National Farmers' Union of Scotland, 17 Grosvenor Crescent, Edinburgh, EH12 5EN; T.-031-337 4333.

Ross, John Graham, DSO, MBE, TD, DL. Solicitor, Honorary Sheriff, Dundee, since 1971; Deputy Lieutenant, City of Dundee, since 1975; b. 13.4.21, Dundee; m., Kathleen Mary Pain (deceased); 3 s.; 1 d. Educ. Dundee High School. Commissioned, Black Watch (RHR), 1939-41, Parachute Regiment, 1941-46, 15th Bn., Parachute Regiment (TA), 1949-53; former Partner, Ross Strachan & Co., Solicitors,

Dundee, 1949. Recreation: gardening. Address: (h.) Nether Ridge, Rockcliffe, by Dalbeattie, DG5 4QF.

Ross, Lindsay Glenn, PhD, BSc. Senior Lecturer, Institute of Aquaculture, Stirling University, since 1987; b. 11.6.45, Sunderland; m., Dr. Barbara Ross; 1 d. Educ. Bede Collegiate School for Boys; Wolverhampton Polytechnic; Stirling University. Early technical career with ICI, Union International, and Department of Pharmacy, Manchester University; professional guitarist for a year; Lecturer in Biology, then Lecturer in Aquaculture, Stirling University, 1977-87. Publications: scientific papers. Recreations: landscape gardening; music; drawing; photography. Address: (h.) West Lodge, Boquhan, Kippen, Stirlingshire; T.-0786 87651.

Ross, Philip Wesley, TD, MB, ChB, MD, FRCP, FRCPath, CBiol, FIBiol, FLS. Consultant, Edinburgh Royal Infirmary, and Reader in Medical Microbiology, Edinburgh University; b. 6.6.36, Aberdeen; m., Stella Joyce Shand; 2 s.; 1 d. Educ. Turriff Academy; Robert Gordon's College, Aberdeen; Aberdeen University. Senior Warden, Edinburgh University, 1972-83. Lt.-Col., RAMC (TA); Officer Commanding Medical Division and Edinburgh Detachment 205 Scottish General Hospital, 1975-80; Scottish Chairman, Institute of Biology; Examiner, Royal College of Surgeons, Edinburgh, Royal College of Pathologists; Chairman, Lothian Area Division of Laboratory Medicine, 1986-89; Elder, Duddingston Kirk, Edinburgh. Publications: textbooks and papers in scientific and medical journals on streptococci, diseases of mouth, throat and genital tract, antibiotics and cross infection. Recreations: music; playing church organs (formerly organist in three Aberdeen churches); walking; tennis. Address: (h.) 18 Old Church Lane, Duddingston Village, Edinburgh, EH15 3PX; T.-031-661 5415.

Ross, Thomas Alexander, KStJ, BL, PhD. Former Senior Partner, Russel & Aitken, WS, Falkirk, Edinburgh and Denny; Honorary Sheriff, Tayside, Central and Fife; b. 18.7.06, Selkirk; m., Eleanor Tyson; 1 s. Educ. Selkirk School; Edinburgh University. Director of Administration, Far Eastern Bureau of Political Intelligence, Department of the Foreign Office in Delhi and Chungking, 1944; Governor, Christ's Hospital. Recreations: travelling; shooting. Address: (b.) Russel & Aitken, WS, King's Court, Falkirk; T.-Falkirk 22888.

Ross, William, FRICS. Director of Economic Development and Estates, City of Edinburgh District Council, since 1984; b. 2.2.41, Rutherglen; m., Margaret; 2 s.; 1 d. Educ. Rutherglen Academy; Glasgow University. Trainee, London County Council; Negotiator, Hillier Parker May and Rowden; Valuer, Glasgow Corporation; District Surveyor, British Rail Property Board; Group Development Surveyor, Maxwell Property Development Company; self-employed; Principal Surveyor (Development), Grampian Regional Council; Depute Director of Estates, Edinburgh District Council. Recreations: gardening; chess; family. Address: (b.) 375 High Street, Edinburgh; T.-031-225 2424, Ext. 5800.

Ross Stewart, David Andrew, OBE, BA (Cantab). Chairman, Scottish Provident Institution; b. 30.11.30, Edinburgh; m., Susan Olive Routh; 2 s. Educ. Rugby School; Cambridge University. Assistant General Manager, Alex. Cowan & Sons (NZ) Ltd., 1959-62; General Manager, Alex. Cowan & Sons (Stationery) Ltd., 1962-66; General Manager, Spicers (Stationery) Ltd., 1966-68; Managing Director, John Bartholomew & Son Ltd., 1968-89. Chairman, St. Andrew Trust plc; Chairman, West Lothian Enterprise Ltd.; Chairman, EFM Income Trust plc; Director, East of Scotland Industrial Investments plc; Member, Scottish Advisory Board, Abbey National; Member, Trade Development Committee, Scottish Council (Development and Industry). Recreations: fishing;

gardening; golf. Address: (b.) 13 Blacket Place, Edinburgh, EH9 1RN; T.-031-667 3221.

Round, Professor Nicholas Grenville, MA, DPhil. Stevenson Professor of Hispanic Studies, Glasgow University, since 1972; b. 6.6.38, Looe, Cornwall; m., Ann Le Vin; 1 d. Educ. Launceston College; Pembroke College, Oxford. Lecturer, then Reader in Spanish, Queen's University, Belfast, 1962-72; Warden, Alanbrooke Hall, Queen's University, Belfast, 1970-72. Publications: Unamuno: Abel Sanche: A Critical Guide, 1974; The Greatest Man Uncrowned: A Study of the Fall of Alvaro de Luna, 1986; Tirso de Molina: Damned for Despair, 1986; Re-Reading Unamuno (Editor), 1989; On Reasoning and Realism, 1991. Recreations: reading; drawing; politics; hillwalking; music; all aspects of Cornwall. Address: (h.) 11 Dougalston Avenue, Milngavie, Glasgow; T.-041-956 2507.

Rowan, John O'Donnell, PhD, CPhys, FInstP, CEng, FIEE, FIPSM. Deputy Director, West of Scotland Health Boards Department of Clinical Physics and Bio-Engineering, since 1983; Honorary Clinical Senior Lecturer in Clinical Physics, Glasgow University, since 1991; Member, National Panel of Assessors for NHS Scientists in Scotland, since 1982; b. 5.4.36, Glasgow; m., Anne Kerr Wotherspoon; 2 d. by pr. m. Educ. Victoria Drive Senior Secondary School, Glasgow; Glasgow University. Research Physicist, Barr and Stroud, Glasgow, 1961-63; Electronics Engineer, Scottish Research Reactor Centre, East Kilbride, 1963-66; West of Scotland Health Boards Department of Clinical Physics and Bio-Engineering: Senior Physicist, 1966-71, Principal Physicist, 1971-81, Top Grade Physicist, 1981-83. Honorary Treasurer, Scottish Branch, Institute of Physics, 1972-77; Honorary Secretary, Hospital Physicists Association, 1976-78, and President, 1982-84; Deputy Editor, Physics in Medicine and Biology, 1980-82; President, Institute of Physical Sciences in Medicine, 1982-84; Member, Scottish Health Service National Scientific Services Advisory Committee, since 1989. Address: (b.) 11 West Graham Street, Glasgow; T.-041-332 6061.

Rowan-Robinson, Professor Richard Jeremy, MA, LLM. Professor, Department of Land Economy, Aberdeen University, since 1989; b. 29.3.44, Edinburgh; m., Yvonne Joan Elizabeth; 2 s. Educ. University of Kent; Aberdeen University; Law Society College of Law. Assistant Solicitor, LB of Redbridge, 1966; Senior Assistant Solicitor, LB of Hillingdon, 1969; Deputy Clerk, Westmorland County Council, 1972; Solicitor, Lake District Special Planning Board, 1975; Lecturer, then Senior Lecturer, Department of Land Economy, Aberdeen University, 1978-89. Address: (b.) Department of Land Economy, Aberdeen University, St. Mary's, King's College, Old Aberdeen; T.-0228 272358.

Rowe, Michael, BA (Hons). Director (Scotland), Advisory Conciliation and Arbitration Service, since 1989; b. 30.5.37, Stoke-on-Trent; m., Kathleen Marie; 2 s. Educ. High School, Newcastle-under-Lyme; St. Catherine's College, Oxford University. Various posts, Department of Employment, 1961-70; First Secretary, UK Delegation to European Communities in Brussels, 1970-72; various posts, London, 1972-81; Benefit Manager, Scotland, Department of Employment, 1981-87; Deputy Director Scotland, Employment Service, 1987-89. Recreations: family; involvement in youth club activities; enjoying good food and wine. Address: (b.) Advisory, Conciliation and Arbitration Service, 123 Bothwell Street, Glasgow; T.-041-204 2677.

Rowley, Professor David Ian, MB, ChB, BMedBiol, MD, FRCS. Professor of Orthopaedic and Trauma Surgery, Dundee University, since 1988; b. 4.7.51, Dewsbury; m., Ingrid Ginette; 1 s.; 1 d. Educ. Wheelwright Grammar School, Dewsbury; Aberdeen University; Sheffield University.

Lecturer in Orthopaedic Surgery, Sheffield University, 1981; Senior Lecturer in Orthopaedic Surgery, Manchester University, and Senior Lecturer in Orthopaedic Mechanics, Salford University, 1985-88. Orthopaedic Editor, Journal of Royal College of Surgeons of Edinburgh; Chairman, Training Panel, Biological Engineering Society; Editor, International Journal of Orthopaedic Surgery; Examiner, Royal College of Surgeons, Edinburgh. Recreations: gardening; reading history. Address: (h.) Marclann Cottage, Kellie Castle, Arbroath; T.-0241 76466.

Rowlings, Professor Cherry, BA, DipSAS. Professor of Social Work, Stirling University, since 1991; Vice-President, European Regional Group, International Association of Schools of Social Work, since 1991; b. 10.11.44, Bristol. Educ. York University; Oxford University. Social Worker/Team Leader, Croydon and Lewisham, 1969-74; Research Officer/Senior Research Fellow, Oxford and Keele Universities, 1974-80; Lecturer/Senior Lecturer in Social Work, Bristol University, 1980-91; Senior Research Fellow, Kent University, 1988-91. Recreations: walking; gardening; reading; music; theatre. Address: (b.) Stirling University, Stirling, FK9 4LA; T.-0786 73121.

Rowson, John Tyldesley, BSc, CEng, FICE, FIHT. Director of Engineering, Fife Regional Council, since 1984; b. 4.4.38, Pendleton, Lancs; m., Diana Valerie Snelson; 2 s.; 1 d. Educ. Bolton School; Manchester University. Early appointments in Bolton, Macclesfield and Manchester; appointed Assistant City Engineer, Dundee, 1972; Depute Director of Roads, Tayside Region, 1975. Board Member, Association of Municipal Engineers; Chairman, County Surveyors' Society (Scottish Branch); Past Chairman, Dundee Branch, Institution of Civil Engineers and AME (Scotland). Recreations: golf; garden. Address: (b.) Fife Regional Council, Fife House, North Street, Glenrothes, Fife; T.-0592 754411.

Roxburgh, Andy, DPE. Scottish Football Association National Coach, since 1986, and Technical Director, since 1975; b. 5.8.43, Glasgow; m., Catherine; 1 s. Educ. Bellahouston Academy; Jordanhill College. Primary school Head Teacher, three years; professional footballer, 10 years; clubs: Partick Thistle, Clydebank, Falkirk; Coach, Clydebank, two years. Member, FIFA Technical Committee. Recreations: music; reading; golf. Address: (b.) 6 Park Gardens, Glasgow; T.-041-332 6372.

Roxburgh, John Hampton, DPE. Technical Administrator, Scottish Rugby Union, since 1974; b. 20.6.38, Glasgow; m., Irene; 1 s.; 1 d. Educ. Jordanhill College School; Jordanhill College of Education. Taught in various Glasgow schools as Assistant Teacher of PE; transferred to further education; Head of Physical Education, Barmulloch College of Further Education. Captained Jordanhill, nine seasons; represented Glasgow in three positions; appointed SRU Advisory Coach, 1968. Recreation: golf. Address: (b.) Scottish Rugby Union, Murrayfield, Edinburgh, EH12 5PJ; T.-031-337 9551.

Roxburgh, William, MA, FRICS. Partner, Gooch & Wagstaff (Chartered Surveyors and International Property Consultants), since 1983; b. 7.5.48, Bearsden; m., Susannah Mary Grizel Douglas Don; 1 s.; 2 d. Educ. Eton College; Pembroke College, Cambridge. Partner, Gale Heath & Co., Chartered Surveyors, 1976-83. Member of Council: National Trust for Scotland, Scottish Wildlife Trust; Freeman of London; Freeman of Glasgow. Recreations: aviculture; ornithology; golf; country pursuits. Address: (h.) Cantyhall, Ladybank, Fife, KY7 7RU; T.-Letham 212.

Roxburghe, 10th Duke of (Guy David Innes-Ker), b. 18.11.54; m., Lady Jane Meriel Grosvenor; 2 s.; 1 d. Educ. Eton; Sandhurst; Magdalene College, Cambridge. Address: (h.) Floors Castle, Kelso.

Roy, Rev. Alan John, BSc, BD, MA. Minister, Stobswell Parish Church, Dundee, since 1985; b. 27.12.34, Edinburgh; m., Roma Mary Hutchison Finlayson; 2 s.; 1 d. Educ. Daniel Stewart's College, Edinburgh; Edinburgh University; Swedish Theological Institute, Jerusalem. Missionary, Church of Scotland, with the United Church of Zambia, 1961-72, first as District Minister, Serenje, then as Tutor, Ministerial Training College, Mindolo, Kitwe; Minister, Park, Dundee, 1972-76; became Minister, United Congregation of Stobswell, 1976. Chairman, Dundee Branch, Leprosy Mission; Vice Chairman, Crossroads Care Attendant Scheme (Dundee); Moderator, Dundee Presbytery, 1991-92. Recreations: golf; stamp collecting. Address: (h.) 23 Shamrock Street, Dundee, DD4 7AH; T.-Dundee 459119.

Roy, Rev. Alistair Anderson, MA, BD. Minister, Wick Bridge Street Church, since 1955; Member, Caithness District Council, since 1982; Member, Scottish Constitutional Convention, since 1989; b. 13.4.27, Oldmeldrum; m., Jean Morrison McIntosh; 2 s. Educ. Elgin Academy; Aberdeen University. Secretary, Royal Burgh of Wick Community Council. Address: Mansefield, Miller Avenue, Wick, KW1 4DF; T.-Wick 2822.

Roy, Kenneth. Editor, The Journalist's Handbook (quarterly review of the media), since 1985; Columnist, Scotland on Sunday, since 1988; b. 26.3.45, Falkirk; m., Margaret H. Campbell; 2 s. Local journalism, 1962-1965; Glasgow Herald, 1965-67; public relations, 1967-69; Editor, Scottish Theatre magazine, 1969-72; Anchorman/Reporter, BBC Scotland, 1972-80; Managing Director, West Sound, 1980-82. Scottish Press Awards: Critic of the Year, 1990; runner-up, Feature Writer of the Year, 1991. Publications: Travels in a Small Country, 1987; Conversations in a Small Country, 1989; The Best of Scotland on Sunday (Editor), 1990. Address: (b.) Carrick Media, 2/7 Galt House, 31 Bank Street, Irvine, KA12 0LL; T.-0294 311322.

Roy, Lindsay Allan, BSc. Rector, Inverkeithing High School, since 1989; b. 19.1.49, Perth; m., Irene Elizabeth Patterson; 2 s.; 1 d. Educ. Perth Academy; Edinburgh University. Assistant Rector, Kirkcaldy High School, 1983-86; Depute Rector, Glenwood High School, Glenrothes, 1986-89; Chairman, Modern Studies Association, 1976-79; Chairman, Modern Studies Panel, Scottish Examination Board, 1980-83; Member, Consultative Committee on the Curriculum Central Committee for Social Subjects, 1978-85. Recreation: angling. Address: (b.) Inverkeithing High School, Hillend Road, Inverkeithing, Fife; T.-0383 414551.

Roy, Ronald Robert, MA (Hons). Chief Executive, Greater Glasgow Tourist Board and Convention Bureau, since 1991; b. 20.1.42, Stirling; m., Lai Ching; 1 s.; 1 d. Educ. High School of Stirling; Glasgow University. British Tourist Authority, 1965-74, latterly Manager, Germany, Switzerland, Austria; Sales Director, Germany, Trusthouse Forte Hotels, 1976-79; Business Travel Manager, USA, then Marketing Manager, London, British Tourist Authority, 1979-84; V.P., Intermediary Marketing, Holiday Inns Inc., Memphis. Recreations: reading; golf; travel. Address: (b.) 39 St. Vincent Place, Glasgow, G1; T.-041-204 4480.

Royan, Bruce, BA (Hons), ALA, MBA. Director of Information Services and University Librarian, Stirling University, since 1989; Principal Consultant, Infologistix Ltd., since 1988; b. 22.1.47, Luton; m., Ann Elisabeth Wilkins; 1 s.; 1 d. Educ. Dunstable Grammar School; North West Polytechnic; Glasgow University. Systems Development Manager, British Library, 1975-77; Head of Systems, National Library of Scotland, 1977-85; Director, Singapore Integrated Library Automation Service, 1985-88. Secretary, Working Party on Access to the National Database, 1980-83; Member, Council, Library Association of Singapore, 1987-

88; Member, Inter-University Committee on Computing, since 1989. Recreations: choral singing; Scottish country dancing; hill-walking; travel. Address: (b.) Stirling University, Stirling, FK9 4LA; T.-0786 73171.

Royle, Trevor Bridge, MA. Author and Broadcaster; Chairman, Society of Authors in Scotland; Defence Correspondent, Scotland on Sunday; b. 26.1.45, Mysore, India; m., Dr. Hannah Mary Rathbone; 3 s. Educ. Madras College, St. Andrews; Aberdeen University. Editor, William Blackwood & Sons Ltd.; Literature Director, Scottish Arts Council, 1971-79; Council Member, Scottish National Dictionary Association; Scottish Arts Council Book Award, 1983. Publications: We'll Support You Evermore: The Impertinent Saga of Scottish Fitba' (Co-Editor), 1976; Jock Tamson's Bairns (Editor), 1977; Precipitous City: The Story of Literary Edinburgh, 1980; A Diary of Edinburgh, 1981; Edinburgh, 1982; Death Before Dishonour: The True Story of Fighting Mac, 1982; The Macmillan Companion to Scottish Literature, 1983; James and Jim: The Biography of James Kennaway, 1983; The Kitchener Enigma, 1985; The Best Years of their Lives: The Post-War National Service Experience, 1986; War Report: The War Correspondents' View of Battle from the Crimea to the Falklands, 1987; The Last Days of the Raj, 1989; A Dictionary of Military Quotations, 1989; Anatomy of a Regiment, 1990; radio plays: Magnificat, 1984; Old Alliances, 1985; Foreigners, 1987; Huntingtower, 1988; A Man Flourishing, 1988; In Flanders Fields: Scottish poetry and prose of the First World War, 1990; The Pavilion on the Links (radio play), 1991; Buchan of Tweedsmuir (stage play), 1991. Recreations: rugby football; hill-walking; music. Address: (h.) 6 James Street, Edinburgh, EH15 2DS; T.-031-669 2116.

Ruckley, Charles Vaughan, MB, ChM, FRCSEdin. Consultant Surgeon, Royal Infirmary, Edinburgh, since 1971; Reader, Edinburgh University, since 1989; b. 14.5.34, Wallasey; m., Valerie Anne Brooks; 1 s.; 1 d. Educ. Wallasey Grammar School; Edinburgh University. Research Fellow, University of Colorado, 1967-68. Secretary/Treasurer, Vascular Surgical Society of Great Britain and Ireland; Member, Council, Association of Surgeons of Great Britain and Ireland. Recreations: angling; music; skiing. Address: (b.) Vascular Surgery Unit, Royal Infirmary, Edinburgh; T.-031-229 2477.

Runciman, H.L.I. (Peter), CBE, BSc, FIQ. Chairman, Shanks & McEwan Group plc, since 1981; Chairman, Scottish Eastern Investment Trust plc, since 1989; Director, British Steel plc; Director, Scottish National Trust plc; b. 9.10.28, Argentina; m., Rosemary Janet Hadfield; 3 d. Educ. Kings College, London. Chloride Batteries Ltd., 1959-61; Tarmac Group, 1961-80; Shanks & McEwan Group plc, since 1980. Past President, Glasgow Chamber of Commerce; President, Glasgow and West of Scotland Outward Bound Association; Scottish Chairman, Aims of Industry. Recreations: fishing; gardening; opera. Address: (b.) 22 Woodside Place, Glasgow, G3; T.-041-331 2614.

Runciman, William Chisholm, LLB. Director, National Playing Fields Association – Scotland, since 1987; b. 15.11.41, Greenock; m., Eileen; 2 s. Educ. Greenock Academy; Edinburgh University. Police Officer in Edinburgh and Lothian & Borders, retiring in 1987 as Chief Superintendent. Recreations: mountaineering; fishing; photography. Address: (h.) 22 Swanston Grove, Edinburgh, EH10 7BW; T.-031-225 4307.

Rundell, David Richard, BSc, MSc, MIS. Director of Computing Services, Heriot-Watt University, since 1990; b. 5.9.48, Plymouth; 3 d. Educ. Harwich County High, Harwich, Essex; St. Andrews University; Heriot-Watt University. Statistician, Medical School, Edinburgh University, 1970-76;

Applications Team, Regional Computing Centre, University of Bath, 1976-79; User Services Manager, Computer Centre, Heriot-Watt University, 1979-90. Chairman, School Board, The Royal High School. Address: (b.) Computer Centre, Heriot-Watt University, Riccarton, Edinburgh EH14 4AS; T.-031-449 5111.

Runnalls, Graham Arthur, BA, MA, DipGenLing, DLitt. Reader in French, Edinburgh University; b. 21.11.37, Exmouth; m., Anne K.; 2 d. Educ. Exmouth Grammar School; Exeter University. Assistant Lecturer in French, Exeter University, 1962-63; Lecturer in French, North London Polytechnic, 1963-66; joined Edinburgh University as Lecturer, 1966. Honorary President, International Society for the Study of Medieval Theatre. Recreations: opera; sport, especially tennis and running. Address: (h.) 85A Colinton Road, Edinburgh, EH10 5DF; T.-031-337 1737.

Rusby, Sir Cameron, KCB, LVO. Chief Executive, Scottish Society for the Prevention of Cruelty to Animals, 1983-91; Legislative Adviser to the Society, since 1991; b. 20.2.26, Sliema, Malta; m., Marion Elizabeth Bell; 2 d. Educ. Wootton Court School, near Canterbury; Royal Naval College, Dartmouth. Thirty nine years in Royal Navy, reaching rank of Vice Admiral; retired, 1982. Recreations: sailing; skiing; equitation. Address: c/o Bank of Scotland, 70 High Street, Peebles, EH45 8AQ.

Rush, Christopher, MA (Hons). Writer; Teacher, George Watson's College, Edinburgh, since 1972; b. 23.11.44, St. Monans; m., Patricia Irene Boyd; 1 s.; 1 d. Educ. Waid Academy; Aberdeen University. Has won two Scottish Arts Council bursaries, two SAC book awards, twice been short-listed for Scottish Book of the Year Award; shortlisted for McVitie Scottish Writer of the Year, 1988; Screenwriter, Venus Peter (based on own book). Publications include: Peace Comes Dropping Slow; A Resurrection of a Kind; A Twelvemonth and A Day; Two Christmas Stories; Into the Ebb; With Sharp Compassion; Venus Peter Saves the Whale; Last Lesson of the Afternoon. Recreations: music; reading; long-distance travel; walking by the sea. Address: (h.) 2 Peel Terrace, Edinburgh, EH9 2AY; T.-031-667 1248.

Russell, Sheriff Albert Muir Galloway, CBE, QC, BA (Oxon), LLB. Sheriff, Grampian, Highland and Islands, at Aberdeen, 1971-91; b. 26.10.25, Edinburgh; m., Margaret Winifred Millar; 2 s.; 2 d. Educ. Edinburgh Academy; Wellington College; Brasenose College, Oxford; Edinburgh University. Lt., Scots Guards, 1944-47; Member, Faculty of Advocates, 1951; Standing Junior Counsel to Board of Trade, Department of Agriculture and Forestry Commission; QC (Scot), 1965; Vice Chairman, Board of Management, Southern Group of Hospitals, Edinburgh, 1966-70; Governor, Moray House College of Education, 1965-70. Recreations: golf; music. Address: (h.) Tulloch House, 1 Aultbea, Ross-shire, IV22 2JA.

Russell, Rev. Archibald, MA. Minister, Duror linked with Glencoe, 1979-90; b. 17.11.24, Cleland, Lanarkshire; m., Elma Sandeman Watson; 2 s. Educ. Wishaw High School; Glasgow University. Assistant, South Dalziel Parish Church, Motherwell; Minister: Holyrood Abbey, Edinburgh, St. Mark's Lancefield, Glasgow, Anderston Parish Church, Glasgow; first Community Minister of Church of Scotland (based at Drumchapel, Glasgow). Founder Editor, Drumchapel News. Recreations: gardening; local history. Address: (h.) 4 Bonnytoun Avenue, Linlithgow, West Lothian, EH49 7JS; T.-0506 84 2530.

Russell, David Colin Dalziel, MA (Hons), FBIM. Chief Executive, Coats Industrial (Coats Viyella), since 1990; b. 30.1.41, Edinburgh; m., Heather; 2 s.; 1 d. Educ. Glenalmond College; Gonville and Caius College, Cambridge. Joined J.

& P. Coats Ltd. as management trainee, 1963; Technical Director, J. & P. Coats Ltd., 1988-90. Recreations: golf; walking; fishing; gardening. Address: (b.) 155 St. Vincent Street, Glasgow, G2 5PA; T.-041-221 8711.

Russell, David Michael, MSc (Eng), BSc (Eng), AKC, CEng, MIEE. HM Inspector of Schools (Further and Higher Education), since 1976; b. 18.6.34, Runwell, Essex; m., Lena; 1 s.; 1 d. Educ. St. Clement Danes Grammar School; King's College, London University; Birmingham University. RAF, 1953-55; Executive Engineer, Cable and Wireless Ltd., 1960-62; Engineer, Decca Radar Ltd., 1962-64; Assistant Professor, American University of Beirut, 1964-67; Senior Lecturer, Middlesex Polytechnic, 1967-70; Technical Consultant, NEC (Japan), Beirut, 1970-72; Senior/Principal Lecturer, Plymouth Polytechnic, 1972-76. Recreations: Member, Edinburgh Festival Chorus and Edinburgh Grand Opera. Address: (h.) 27 Murrayfield Gardens, Edinburgh, EH12 6DG; T.-031-337 5016.

Russell, George, MB, ChB, FRCP. Consultant Paediatrician, Grampian Health Board, since 1969; Honorary Senior Lecturer in Child Health, Aberdeen University, since 1970; Clinical Services Co-ordinator, Maternity and Children's Services, Foresterhill Hospitals Unit, since 1989; b. 2.7.36, Insch; m., Gillian Douglas Simpson; 2 s.; 2 d. Educ. Robert Gordon's College; Aberdeen University. Junior hospital appointments, Aberdeen teaching hospitals; Research Fellow, University of Colorado; Lecturer in Child Health, Aberdeen University; Professor of Paediatrics, University of Riyad, Saudi Arabia. Regional Adviser in Paediatrics, British Paediatric Association, since 1988; Chairman, Scottish Cystic Fibrosis Group, since 1988; Member, British Paediatric Association Working Party on Cystic Fibrosis. Recreations: walking; photography; DIY. Address: (h.) 12 Pinewood Avenue, Aberdeen, AB1 8NB; T.-0224 315448.

Russell, George Stuart, OBE, BL, CA, WS. Former Senior Partner, Strathern and Blair WS; b. 21.1.14, Edinburgh; m.; 1 s.; 3 d. Educ. Edinburgh Academy; Belhaven Hill; Harrow; Edinburgh University. CA, 1937; served Second World War, 1939-45 (Lt. Col.); then pursued a legal career; Fiscal, WS Society, 1973-79; closely involved in work of National Trust for Scotland, 1951-82, now Councillor Emeritus; Treasurer, Iona Community, 1947-65; President, Edinburgh Abbeyfield Society; Vice President, UK, Abbeyfield Society, 1975-83; Trustee, Edinburgh Old Town Trust, Lothian Building Preservation Trust and Scottish Churches Architectural Heritage Trust; Member, Queen's Bodyguard for Scotland (Royal Company of Archers). Recreations: fishing; walking. Address: 59 Braid Road, Edinburgh, EH10; T.-031-447 6009.

Russell, Rev. John, MA. Minister, Tillicoultry Parish Church, since 1978; b. 29.5.33, Glasgow; m., Sheila Spence; 2 s. Educ. Cathedral School, Bombay; High School of Glasgow; Glasgow University. Licensed by Glasgow Presbytery, 1957; ordained by United Church of Canada, 1959; Assistant Minister: Trinity United Church, Kitchener, Ontario, 1958-60, South Dalziel Church, Motherwell, 1960-62; Minister: Scots Church, Rotterdam, 1963-72, Southend Parish Church, Kintyre, 1972-78; Member of various General Assembly Committees, since 1972; Convener, General Assembly's Committee on Unions and Readjustments, 1987-90; Convener, Parish Reappraisal Committee, since 1990. Recreations: travel; reading. Address: The Manse, Dollar Road, Tillicoultry, Clackmannanshire, FK13 6PD; T.-0259 50340.

Russell, Professor Michael John, BSc, PhD, CEng, FIMM. Dixon Professor of Applied Geology, Glasgow University, since 1989; b. 12.4.39, Sutton; m., Sheila Margaret; 2 s.; 2 d. Educ. Chigwell School; London University; Durham University. Works Chemist Improver, 1959-60; UNA

Volunteer Geologist, British Solomon Islands, 1963-65; Exploration Geologist, Falconbridge Nickel Mines Ltd., Yukon, 1965; Lecturer Department of Geology, University of Ghana, 1971; joined Strathclyde University as Assistant Lecturer, 1969. Distinguished Lecturer, Institution of Mining and Metallurgy, 1988. Recreations: cycling; reading; art appreciation. Address: (h.) Clober Farm, Milngavie, Glasgow, G62 7HW; T.-041-956 3871.

Russell, Michael William, MA. Independent Television Producer; b. 9.8.53; m., Cathleen Macaskill; 1 s. Educ. Marr College, Troon; Edinburgh University. Creative Producer, Church of Scotland, 1974-77; Director, Cinema Sgire, Western Isles, 1977-81; Founder and first Director, Celtic Film and Television Festival, 1980; Secretary General, Association for Film and Television in the Celtic Countries, 1981-83; Chief Executive, Network Scotland Ltd., 1983-91. Parliamentary candidate (SNP), Clydesdale, 1987; Executive Vice Convenor in charge of Publicity, SNP, 1987-91; Chairman, Save a Life in Scotland Campaign, 1986-88; Trustee, Celtic Film and TV Association, since 1990. Recreation: cookery. Address: (h.) 3 The Terrace, Tillietudlem, by Lesmahagow, Lanarkshire, ML11 9PN; T.-Crossford 276.

Russell, Peter MacLeod, MA. Assistant Secretary, Scottish Office Home and Health Department, since 1986; b. 22.1.51, Edinburgh; m., Patricia Anne Kelly; 4 s.; 1 d. Educ. Royal High School, Edinburgh; Edinburgh University. Entered Scottish Office, 1973; Private Secretary to Parliamentary Under Secretary of State, 1976-78; Principal, 1978-86: Royal Commission on Legal Services in Scotland, 1978-80, SDD, 1980-84, Industry Department for Scotland, 1985-86. Recreation: Scouting. Address: (b.) St. Andrews House, Edinburgh, EH1 3DE; T.-031-244 2154.

Russell, Robin Irvine, MD, PhD, FRCPEdin, FRCPGlas, FACN. Consultant in Charge, Gastroenterology Unit, Royal Infirmary, Glasgow, since 1970; Consultant Physician, Royal Infirmary, Glasgow, and Glasgow University, since 1970; b. 21.12.36, Wishaw; m., Ann Tindal Wallace; 1 s.; 1 d. Educ. Glasgow University. Lecturer, Department of Clinical Medicine, Glasgow University; Member, medical and scientific staff, Medical Research Council Gastroenterology Unit, London. Chairman, British Digestive Diseases Foundation (Scotland). Publications: Elemental Diets; Investigative Tests and Techniques in Gastroenterology; Nutrition in Gastro-Intestinal Disease. Recreations: golf; travel; literature; music. Address: (h.) 28 Ralston Road, Bearsden, Glasgow, G61 3BA; T.-041-942 6613.

Russell, Sheriff Terence Francis, BL. Sheriff, North Strathclyde, at Kilmarnock, since 1983; b. 12.4.31, Glasgow; m., Mary Ann Kennedy; 2 d. Educ. St. Mungo's Academy, Glasgow; Glasgow University. Solicitor, Glasgow, 1955-58; Bombay High Court, 1958-63, Glasgow, 1963-81; Sheriff, North Strathclyde, at Oban and Campbeltown and Grampian, Highland and Islands, at Fort William, 1981-83. Recreations: gardening; painting.

Russell, Thomas, BSc (Hons), MB, ChB, FRCS Edin, FRCS Glas. Consultant Neurosurgeon, since 1987; Senior Lecturer in Neurosurgery, Edinburgh University, since 1989; b. 8.3.50, Lanark; m., Donna; 1 d. Educ. Wishaw High School; Glasgow University. MRC Fellow in Neurosurgery, Institute of Neurological Sciences, Glasgow; Senior Registrar, Neurosurgery, Bristol; Exchange Neurosurgical Resident, Memphis; Consultant Neurosurgeon, Western General Hospital, Edinburgh. Recreation: photography. Address: (h.) 69 Craiglockhart Road North, Edinburgh, EH14 1BS; T.-031-443 2679.

Russell, Professor William C., BSc, PhD, FRSE. Professor of Biochemistry, St. Andrews University, since 1984; b. 9.8.30, Glasgow; m., 1, Dorothy Ada Brown (deceased); 1 s.; 1 d.; 2, Reta McDougall. Educ. Allan Glen's School, Glasgow; Glasgow University. Locke Research Fellow, Institute of Virology, Glasgow, 1959-63; Eleanor Roosevelt International Cancer Fellow, Toronto University, 1963-64; Member, MRC Scientific Staff, National Institute for Medical Research, London, 1964-84; Head, Division of Virology, 1977-84. Editor, Journal of General Virology, 1972-77; Convener, Virus Group, Society for General Microbiology, 1984-89; Member, Council, Society for General Microbiology, 1988-91. Address: (b.) Department of Biochemistry and Microbiology, St. Andrews University, Irvine Building, North Street, St. Andrews, KY16 9AL; T.-0334 76161.

Rutherford, Alan Gray, BSc, PhD, CChem, CEng, FRSA, MRSC, MInstE. Scotch Whisky Production Director, United Distillers plc, since 1988; b. 9.10.42, Cramlington; m., Roslyn Anne Moore; 1 s.; 1 d. Educ. Gosforth Grammar School, Newcastle upon Tyne; Sheffield University; Newcastle upon Tyne University. Cookson Group of companies, three years; Scottish & Newcastle Breweries, 14 years, latterly as Group Personnel Director; joined Distillers Company Ltd. as Head of Development, 1984. Executive Member, Scottish Council Development & Industry; Council Member, Scotch Whisky Association; President, Malt Distillers' Association of Scotland; Hon. Col., 15 Para (TA); Member, Parachute Regimental Council; President, Ayrshire Branch, Parachute Regimental Association; Trustee, Airborne Forces Charities Development Trust. Recreations: TA; hill-walking; rugby football. Address: (b.) United Distillers plc, 33 Ellersly Road, Edinburgh, EH12 6JW; T.-031-337 7373.

Rutherford, Rev. Brian Craig, BSc, BD. Minister, Mastrick Parish, Aberdeen, since 1990; Councillor, Aberdeen District Council, since 1992; b. 8.6.47, Glasgow; m., Jean Walker; 2 s. Educ. King's Park Secondary School, Glasgow; Glasgow University; Edinburgh University. Assistant Minister, Carrick Knowe Parish, Edinburgh, 1976-77; Minister, Strathbrock Parish, West Lothian, 1977-83; Minister, Greyfriars/St. Ann's Church, Trinidad, 1983-87; General Treasurer, Blantyre Synod, Church of Central Africa Presbyterian, Blantyre, Malawi, 1988-89. Former Member, Edinburgh Corporation, Edinburgh District Council (JP, 1977-80), West Lothian District Council; Member, Aberdeen District Council, since 1992. Address: (h.) 13 Beechgrove Avenue, Aberdeen, AB2 4EZ; T.-0224 638 011.

Rutherford, William Hay, MA, LLB. Advocate in Aberdeen, since 1949; Consultant, Raeburn Christie & Co. (Partner, 1978-87); Honorary Sheriff, Grampian, Highland and Islands, since 1974; b. 9.11.16, Forres; m., Dr. Jean Aitken Steel Wilson; 1 s.; 2 d. Educ. Forres Academy; Aberdeen University. Law Apprentice, James & George Collie, Advocates, Aberdeen, 1936-39; 51st Highland Division, Royal Signals, 1939-46 (taken prisoner, St. Valery, France, 1940; held prisoner, Stalag VIIIB, Upper Silesia, 1940-45); Legal Assistant, John Angus, Advocate, Aberdeen, 1946-61; Partner, Christie, Buthlay & Rutherford, Advocates, Aberdeen, 1962-78; President, Society of Advocates, Aberdeen, 1985-86; Session Clerk, Kirk of St. Nicholas (City Kirk of Aberdeen), since 1954; President, Royal Northern Agricultural Society, 1980. Recreations: country walking and wildlife study. Address: 38 Gladstone Place, Queen's Cross, Aberdeen.

Rutherfurd, Richard Napier, JP, BSc (Eng), MB, ChB, MRCGP. Honorary Sheriff; b. 13.5.02, Glasgow; m., Elinor D. Jackson (deceased); 2 s.; 1 d. Educ. Glasgow Academy; Sedbergh School; Glasgow University. Sir William Arrol, 1921-28; Engineer, Central Argentine Railway, 1928-31;

Western Infirmary, Glasgow/Royal Hospital for Sick Children, Yorkhill, 1938-39; general practice: Rothesay, 1939, West Kirkby, Cheshire; Captain, RAMC, UK and Egypt, 1942-45; general practice, Kirkcudbright, 1946-70. Last Provost of Royal Burgh of Kirkcudbright. Recreations: sailing; tennis; climbing. Address: (h.) Wester Oakley, Kirkcudbright, DG6 4AH; T.-0557 30410.

Ruthven, Ian Scott, MB, ChB, FRCPEdin, FRCPGlas, DObstRCOG. Consultant Paediatrician, Ayrshire and Arran Health Board, since 1969; Postgraduate Tutor, South Ayrshire Hospitals, 1981-87; b. 9.3.37, Glasgow; m., Louisa Mary Jolly; 1 s.; 2 d. Educ. High School of Glasgow; Glasgow University. Junior hospital appointments, various Glasgow hospitals and in New Jersey, USA. Chairman, Ayrshire Paediatric Division and Past Chairman Ayrshire and Arran Committee for Hospital Medical Services; Chairman, Ayrshire and Arran Division, BMA, 1987-88; Member, Paediatric Committee, Royal College of Physicians and Surgeons of Glasgow. Recreations: golf; angling; hill-walking. Address: (h.) Westholme, 10 Victoria Drive, Troon, KA10 6EN; T.-0292 313006.

Ryden, Kenneth, MC, DL, FRICS; b. 15.2.17, Blackburn; m., Catherine Kershaw Wilkinson; 2 s. Educ. Queen Elizabeth's Grammar School, Blackburn. Served Second World War, Royal Engineers, attached Royal Bombay Sappers and Miners, in India, Burma and Assam, 1940-46; retired Captain (MC and Bar, despatches, 1945); Ministry of Works, Scotland, 1946-47; attached UK High Commission, India, 1947-50; Senior Estate Surveyor, Scotland, 1950-59; Founder and Senior Partner, Kenneth Ryden & Partners, Chartered Surveyors, 1959-74; Member, Board, Housing Corporation, 1971-77; Member, Lothian Region Valuation Appeal Panel, 1965-90 (Chairman, 1987-90); Director, Thistle Foundation, since 1990; Member, Scottish Solicitors' Discipline Tribunal, since 1985. FRCPE, 1985; Master, Company of Merchants of City of Edinburgh, 1976-78; Liveryman, Chartered Surveyor's Company; DL, Edinburgh, 1978. Recreations: golf; fishing; Scottish art. Address: 19 Belgrave Crescent, Edinburgh, EH4 3AJ; T.-031-332 5893.

S

Salmon, Thomas Graham, MA, LLB, Hon.FRIAS, SSC, JP. Factor, Lockerby Trust, since 1959; Chairman, Davidson Clinic (Edinburgh) Trust, since 1973; Chairman, Scottish Anti-Common Market Council, since 1976; Trustee, Scottish Cinematograph Trade Benevolent Fund; b. 21.7.10, Edinburgh; m., Annie (Nancy) Hunter Waters; 2 s.; 1 d. Educ. George Watson's Boys' College, Edinburgh; Edinburgh University. Solicitor, 1934; private practice until retirement in 1981; was Secretary/Treasurer: Edinburgh Section, Cinematograph Exhibitors' Association, Society of Scottish Artists, Scottish Society of Women Artists, Edinburgh Architectural Association, Treasurer, Scottish Modern Arts Association, and Legal Adviser, Scottish Branch, CEA; twice Chairman, South Edinburgh Branch, Scottish Liberal Party; Army, during War; Staff Captain A (Legal) Scottish Command, 1945-46; served Council, Law Society of Scotland; former Vice-President, SSC Society. Recreations:

Scottish activities; gardening; modest tartan collecting. Address: 9 South Gray Street, Edinburgh, EH9 1TE; T.-031-668 1358.

Salmon, Professor Trevor Charles, MA (Hons), MLitt, PhD. Jean Monnet Professor of European Integration Studies, St. Andrews University, since 1990; b. 7.9.48, Cambridge; m., June Veronica Miller; 1 d. Educ. Soham Grammar School; Aberdeen University. Lecturer in Politics, National Institute of Higher Education, Limerick, 1973-78; Lecturer in International Relations, then Senior Lecturer, St. Andrews University, 1978-90. Chairman, Scottish Branch, Royal Institute of International Affairs, since 1991. Recreations: Church of Scotland; politics; golf. Address: (h.) 14 Morton Crescent, St. Andrews, KY16 8RA; T.-0334 72044.

Salmond, Alexander Elliot Anderson, MA (Hons). Economist; MP (SNP), Banff and Buchan, since 1987; National Convener, Scottish National Party, since 1990; b. 31.12.54, Linlithgow; m., Moira McGlashan. Educ. Linlithgow Academy; St. Andrews University. Vice-President: Federation of Student Nationalists, 1974-77, St. Andrews University SRC, 1977-78; Founder Member, SNP 79 Group, 1979; Assistant Agricultural and Fisheries Economist, DAFS, 1978-80; Economist, Royal Bank of Scotland, 1980-87. Recreations: golf; reading. Address: (b.) 17 Maiden Street, Peterhead, AB42 6EE; T.-0779 70444.

Salmond, Rev. James Sommerville, BA, BD, MTh, ThD. Minister, Holytown Parish Church, since 1979; b. 13.1.51, Broxburn; m., Catherine F. Wildy; 1 s.; 4 d. Educ. West Calder High School; Whitburn Academy; Leeds University; Edinburgh University; Central School of Religion. Serves on the Committees of Scottish Reformation Society, National Church Association, etc. Publications: Evangelicals within the Kirk 1690-1843; Moody Blues. Recreations: field sports; riding. Address: The Manse, Holytown, Motherwell; T.-Holytown 832622.

Salter, Professor Stephen Hugh, MA (Cantab), FRSE. Professor of Engineering Design, Edinburgh University, since 1986; b. 7.12.38, Johannesburg; m., Professor Margaret Donaldson. Educ. Framlingham College; Sidney Sussex College, Cambridge. Apprentice aircraft fitter and tool-maker; Research Assistant, Department of Psychology, Cambridge University; Research Fellow, then Lecturer, Department of Artificial Intelligence, then Reader in Mechanical Engineering, Edinburgh University. Recreations: photography; inventing and designing instruments and tools. Address: (b.) Department of Mechanical Engineering, Mayfield Road, Edinburgh University, Edinburgh, EH9 3JL; T.-031-650 5703.

Saltoun, Lady (Flora Marjory Fraser). Chief of Clan Fraser; b. 18.10.30; m., Captain Alexander Ramsay of Mar; 3 d. Address: (h.) Cairnbulg Castle, Fraserburgh, Aberdeenshire, AB43 5TN.

Salzen, Professor Eric Arthur, BSc, PhD, FBPsS, FRSE. Professor of Psychology, Aberdeen University, since 1973 (Head, Department of Psychology, 1977-88); b. 28.4.30, London; m., Heather Ann Fairlie; 2 d. Educ. Wanstead County High School; Edinburgh University. Assistant in Zoology, Edinburgh University, 1954-55; Scientific Officer, HM Overseas Civil Service, 1955-56; Research Assistant and Lecturer in Psychology, Durham University, 1956-60; Lecturer in Zoology, Liverpool University, 1960-64; Associate Professor and Professor of Psychology, Waterloo University, Ontario, 1964-68; Senior Lecturer and Reader in Psychology, Aberdeen University, 1968-73. Recreation: travel. Address: (b.) Psychology Department, King's College, Aberdeen University, Aberdeen; T.-0224 272230.

Sampson, Colin, CBE, QPM. HM Chief Inspector of Constabulary for Scotland, since 1991; b. 26.5.29; m., Kathleen Stones; 2 s. Educ. Stanley School, Wakefield; Leeds University. Joined Police Force, 1949; Comdt., Home Office Detective Training Scheme, Wakefield, 1971-72; Assistant Chief Constable, West Yorkshire, 1973; Deputy Chief Constable, Notts, 1976; Chief Constable, West Yorkshire, 1983-89; HM Inspector of Constabulary, 1989-90. CBIM, 1987; OStJ, 1988; DUniv Bradford, 1988; Hon. LLD, Leeds, 1990. Recreations: choral music; walking; gardening. Address: St. Andrew's House, Edinburgh, EH1 3DE.

Sandeman, Mary. Singer; b. 10.7.47, Edinburgh; 2 s. Educ. St. Denis School, Edinburgh. Began to learn Gaelic and singing at aged 10; gained diploma in domestic science, secretarial training, National Institute of Broadcasting (Canada); worked in TV Department, Heriot-Watt University; in 1981, had a "No 1" hit record in nine countries with song called Japanese Boy under the stage name of Aneka. Recreations: travel; theatre; keeping fit. Address: (h.) 80 Braemar Avenue, Dunblane, Perthshire; T.-0786 825303.

Sandeman, Robert John, LLB, NP, WS, DL. Solicitor, since 1979; Deputy Lieutenant, Stirling and Falkirk Districts, since 1986; Chairman, Southern Area Committee, Highland TA&VRA, since 1991; b. 8.1.29, India; m., Enid; 1 s.; 1 d. Educ. Trinity College, Glenalmond; RMA, Sandhurst; Glasgow University. Infantry Officer, 1948-76; Second-in-Command, 1st Bn., The Royal Scots (The Royal Regiment), 1965-67; staff appointments, 1967-76; retired from Regular Army as Major, 1976; law student, 1976-79; commanded Number One Company, Home Service Force (Black Watch); Territorial Army, 1982-85. Member, Queen's Bodyguard for Scotland (Royal Company of Archers), since 1967; Director, Glasgow, Stirlingshire and Sons of the Rock Society, since 1986; Chairman, Stirling Members' Centre, National Trust for Scotland, since 1990. Recreations: archery; hill-walking; shooting. Address: (h.) Khyber House, Upper Glen Road, Bridge of Allan, FK9 4PX; T.-0786 832180.

Sandeman, The Hon. Mrs (Sylvia Margaret). Chairman, Scottish Spinal Cord Injury Association, since 1988; Member, Scottish Council on Disability; b. 29.7.49, Irvine; m., Ronald L. Sandeman; 1 d. Educ. Downe House, Newbury. Former Member: Scottish Sports Council, Scottish Consumer Council, Post Office Users Council for Scotland. Recreation: sailing. Address: (h.) Rosgaradh, West Dhuhill Drive, Helensburgh, G84 9AW; T.-0436 75105.

Sanders, Samuel Chandrarajan, MBBS, FRCP, DMJ. Consultant Physician, Geriatric Medicine, Glasgow West, since 1976; Honorary Senior Clinical Lecturer, Geriatric Medicine, Glasgow University, since 1977; b. 1.7.32, Jaffna, Sri Lanka; m., Irene Saravanamuttu; 1 s.; 2 d. Educ. Jaffna College, Sri Lanka; Ceylon University. Resident HO, Ceylon, 1957-58; varied experience in medicine, surgery, neuro-surgery, public health and forensic medicine, Sri Lanka, 1958-70; postgraduate training, forensic medicine and clinical therapeutics, Glasgow University, Guy's Hospital, London and Edinburgh Royal Infirmary, 1971-72; Registrar, then Senior Registrar, Glasgow Western District, 1973-76. Recreations: sport; reading; fishing. Address: (h.) 28 Hillfoot Drive, Bearsden, Glasgow, G61 3QF; T.-041-942 9388.

Sanderson, Arthur Norman, MBE, MA, DipEd. Regional Director, The British Council, Glasgow, 1986-89; b. 3.9.43, Glasgow; m., Issy Halliday; 1 s.; 1 d. Educ. Glasgow Academy; Fettes College; Corpus Christi College, Oxford; Moray House College of Education. Tutor in Maths and English, Foso Training College, Ghana, 1966-68 (VSO); Economics and Careers Master, Daniel Stewart's College, 1969-73; British Council: Assistant Director, Kano, Nigeria, 1974-76, Regional Director, Recife, Brazil, 1976-80, Far East and Pacific Department, London, 1980-83, Assistant, then Acting Representative, Ghana, 1983-86; Director, Enugu, Nigeria, 1989-91; Director, South India (Madras), since 1991. Recreations: hill-walking; jogging; golf; languages; Scottish country dancing; classical music. Address: (h.) 57 St. Andrew's Drive, Glasgow, G41 5HQ.

Sanderson, Eric Fenton, LLB, CA. Director, The British Linen Bank Ltd., since 1984, Chief Executive, since 1989; Non-Executive Director, Airtours PLC, English and Overseas Properties plc, British Railways Board, Melville Street Investments PLC, United Artists Communications Scotland Ltd.; b. 14.10.51, Dundee; m., Patricia Ann Shaw; 3 d. Educ. Morgan Academy, Dundee; Dundee University. Qualified CA with Touche Ross & Co.; joined British Linen Bank Ltd., 1976. Recreations: gardening; photography. Address: (b.) 4 Melville Street, Edinburgh, EH3 7NZ; T.-031-243 8301.

Sanderson, Professor Jeffrey John, BSc, PhD. Professor of Theoretical Plasma Physics, St. Andrews University, since 1985 (Reader in Applied Mathematics, 1975-85); b. 25.4.37, Birmingham; m., Mirjana Adamovic; 1 s.; 1 d. Educ. George Dixon Grammar School, Birmingham; Birmingham University; Manchester University. Research Associate, Maryland University, 1961-64; Theoretical Physicist, English Electric Co., Whetstone, 1964-66; Lecturer, then Senior Lecturer in Applied Mathematics, St. Andrews University, 1966-75; Visiting Professor, Department of Physics, College of William and Mary, USA, 1976-77. Publications: Plasma Dynamics (Co-author), 1969; Laser Plasma Interactions (Joint Editor), 1979. Recreations: chess; Scottish country dancing; five-a-side football; cricket. Address: (b.) North Haugh, St. Andrews, KY16 9SS; T.-0334 76161, Ext. 8135.

Sanderson, Stewart Forson, MA. Hon. Harold Orton Fellow, Leeds University, since 1983; Member, Scottish Arts Council, 1983-88 (Chairman, Literature Committee); b. 23.11.24, Blantyre, Malawi; m., Alison M. Cameron; 2 s.; 1 d. Educ. George Watson's College; Edinburgh University. RNVR, 1943-46; Secretary-Archivist and Senior Research Fellow, School of Scottish Studies, 1952-60; Director, Institute of Dialect and Folk Life Studies, Leeds University, 1960-83; Royal Gustav Adolfs Academy, since 1968; Visiting Professor of Folklore and Folklife, University of Pennsylvania, 1974; Chairman, School of English, Leeds University, 1980-83; President, Folklore Society, 1970-73; Council, Society for Folk Life Studies, 1974-79; Governor, British Institute of Recorded Sound, 1979-83; Committee, Leeds City Museums, 1979-84; British Library Committee, National Sound Archive, since 1983; Hon. Secretary, Kelso Arts Appreciation Society, since 1989. Publications: Hemingway, 1961; The Secret Commonwealth, 1976; Linguistic Atlas of England, 1978; Studies in Linguistic Geography, 1985; Word Maps, 1987. Recreations: music; fly-fishing; gardening. Address: (h.) Primside Mill Farmhouse, Kelso, Roxburghshire, TD5 8PR; T.-Yetholm 678.

Sanderson, William. Farmer; Director, Royal Highland and Agricultural Society of Scotland; b. 9.3.38, Lanark; m., Netta; 4 d. Educ. Dalkeith High School. Past Chairman, South Midlothian and Lothians and Peeblesshire Young Farmers Clubs; Past Chairman, Dalkeith Agricultural Society; President, Royal Caledonian Curling Club, 1984-85; Past President, Oxenfoord and Edinburgh Curling Clubs; Scottish Curling Champion, 1971 and 1978 (2nd, World Championship, 1971). Recreations: curling; exhibiting live-stock. Address: (h.) Blackshiels Farm, Blackshiels, Pathhead, Midlothian; T.-Humbie 288.

Sanderson, Very Rev. William Roy, MA, DD. Minister, Church of Scotland; Extra Chaplain to The Queen in Scotland, since 1977 (Chaplain-in-Ordinary, 1965-77); b. 23.9.07, Leith; m., Muriel Easton; 3 s.; 2 d. Educ. Fettes College; Oriel College, Oxford; New College, Edinburgh. Ordained, 1933; Assistant Minister, St. Giles' Cathedral, 1932-34; Minister: St. Andrew's, Lochgelly, 1935-39, The Barony of Glasgow, 1939-63, Stenton with Whittingehame, 1963-73; Moderator, Glasgow Presbytery, 1958 and Haddington and Dunbar Presbytery, 1972-74; Moderator, General Assembly, 1967; Hon. DD (Glasgow), 1959; Chairman, Scottish Religious Advisory Committee, BBC, 1961-71; Member, Central Religious Advisory Committee, BBC and ITA, 1961-71; Governor, Fettes College, 1967-77; Honorary President, Church Service Society; President, New College Union, 1975. Recreations: reading; walking. Address: (h.) 1A York Road, North Berwick, EH39 4LS; T.-0620 2780.

Sanderson of Bowden, Lord (Charles Russell Sanderson), KB. Life Peer; Chairman, Scottish Conservative Party, since 1990; Director: Illingworth Morris, Scottish Mortgage and Trust, since 1990; Chairman, Hawick Cashmere Co., since 1990; b. 30.4.33, Melrose; m., Frances Elizabeth Macaulay; 2 s.; 2 d. Educ. St. Mary's School, Melrose; Glenalmond College; Bradford University; Scottish College of Textiles. Commissioned, Royal Signals; Partner, Charles P. Sanderson, 1958-87; former Director, Clydesdale Bank, Johnston of Elgin; former Chairman, Shires Investment PLC and Edinburgh Financial Trust; President, Scottish Conservative and Unionist Association, 1977-79; Chairman, National Union of Conservative and Unionist Associations Executive Committee, 1981-86; Minister of State, Scottish Office, 1987-90; Chairman, Eildon Housing Association, 1976-83; DL. Recreations: golf; amateur dramatics. Address: (h.) Becketts Field, Bowden, Melrose, Roxburgh.

Sandham, Andrew, BDS, LDSRCS, FDSRCS, DOrth, PhD. Senior Lecturer in Orthodontics, Edinburgh University, since 1982; Consultant Orthodontist (Head, Clinical Department of Orthodontics), Edinburgh Dental School, since 1982; b. 22.1.43, Mansfield, Nottinghamshire. Educ. King Edward VI School, Stourbridge; Durham University. Dentist, Norwegian Health Service, 1966-67; House Surgeon, Birmingham and London, 1967-68; Registrar, Birmingham Dental Hospital, 1968-71; Lecturer in Children's Dentistry and Orthodontics, Dundee University, 1971-74; Lecturer in Orthodontics, Birmingham University, 1974-76; Consultant Orthodontist: Fife Health Board, 1976-78, Birmingham Area Health Authority, 1978-82. Examiner, Royal College of Surgeons, Edinburgh. Recreations: travel; fine art; aviation. Address: (b.) Edinburgh University Dental School, Chambers Street, Edinburgh, EH1 1JA; T.-031-225 9511.

Sandilands, Robert Ian, MA. Director General (and Deputy Chief Executive), National Farmers' Union of Scotland, since 1989 (Deputy Director and General Secretary, 1978-89): b. 23.9.34, Dumfries; m., Frances Margaret Elliot; 1 s.; 2 d. Educ. Langholm Academy; Dumfries Academy; Edinburgh University. Caterpillar Tractor Company Ltd., Tannochside, 1957-60; Secretary, Lanark Area Executive, NFU of Scotland, 1960-72. Recreations: golf; photography; walking. Address: (b.) 17 Grosvenor Crescent, Edinburgh, EH12 5EN; T.-031-337 4333.

Sanford, Professor Anthony John, BSc, PhD, ABPsS, CPsychol. Professor of Psychology, Glasgow University, since 1982 (Head, Department of Psychology, 1983-86); b. 5.7.44, Birmingham; m., Linda Mae Moxey; 1 d. Educ. Waverley Grammar School; Leeds University; Cambridge University. MRC Research Scholar, Applied Psychology Unit, Cambridge; Postdoctoral Research Fellow, then Lecturer in Psychology, Dundee University; Senior Lecturer, then Reader in Psychology, Glasgow University. Gifford Lecturer in Natural Theology, Glasgow, 1983. Publications: Understanding Written Language (Co-author); Models, Mind and Man; Cognition and Cognitive Psychology; The Mind of

Man. Recreations: hill-walking; industrial archaeology; music; cooking. Address: (b.) Department of Psychology, Glasgow University, Glasgow; T.-041-339 8855.

Sang, Christopher T.M., MB, ChB, FRCSEdin, MRCP. Consultant Cardiothoracic Surgeon, Lothian Health Board, since 1982; b. 14.6.43, Georgetown, Guyana; m., Jean Cowan; 1 s.; 2 d. Educ. George Watson's College, Edinburgh; Edinburgh University. General surgery training, Edinburgh, and general medicine and cardiology training, Edinburgh and Canada, 1966-73; cardiovascular and thoracic surgery training, Toronto, Edinburgh, London (Guy's) and Baltimore (Johns Hopkins), 1973-82. Address: (h.) 29 Blackford Hill Grove, Edinburgh, EH2 3HA; T.-031-667 6046.

Sangster, Professor Alan John, BSc (Eng), MSc, PhD, CEng, FIEE. Professor, Electromagnetic Engineering, Heriot Watt University, since 1990; b. 21.11.40, Aberdeen; m., Barbara Macleod Wilkie; 1 s.; 1 d. Educ. Aberdeen Grammar School; Aberdeen University. Research Engineer, Ferranti Ltd, Edinburgh, 1964-69; Plessey Radar Ltd., 1969-72; Lecturer, Heriot Watt University, 1972-79, Senior Lecturer, 1979-86, Reader, 1986-90. Publications: 50 papers. Recreation: golf. Address: (b.) Electrical and Electronic Engineering Department, Heriot Watt University, Edinburgh; T.-031-225 6465.

Sangster, Rev. Ernest George, MA, BD, ThM. Minister, Alva Parish Church, since 1990; b. 19.6.32, Lumphanan, Aberdeenshire; m., Alison Margaret Runcie; 2 s.; 2 d. Educ. Robert Gordon's College, Aberdeen; Aberdeen University; Union Theological Seminary, Richmond, Virginia; Oriel College, Oxford. Chaplain, St. Andrews Colleges, St. Andrews University, 1961-65; Minister, Beechgrove Church, Aberdeen, 1966-76, Blackhall St. Columba's, Edinburgh, 1976-90. Recreations: reading; music; golf; hill-walking. Address: St. Serf's Manse, Ochil Road, Alva, FK12 5JT; T.-0259 60262.

Sankey, Catharine Elizabeth, BSc, CMIBiol, MILAM. Director, Scottish Environmental Education Council, since 1987; Honorary Lecturer, Department of Environmental Science, Stirling University, since 1987; b. 23.5.53, Dundee; m., Stephen Sankey. Educ. Redland High School, Bristol; Southampton University. Lecturer in Biology, Yeovil College, Somerset, 1977-80; Education Officer, Countryside Education Trust, Beaulieu, 1980-85. Member, IUCN NW Europe Committee, Commission on Education and Training; Member, Secretary of State for Scotland's Working Group on Environmental Education, 1990-92. Publications: Loch Lomond Landscapes, 1985; Eigg: an Island Landscape, 1987. Recreations: the great outdoors, especially Scotland; mountaineering; offshore sailing; traditional knitting and music; natural and local history. Address: (b.) Department of Environmental Science, Stirling University, FK9 4LA; T.-0786 50001.

Sarkar, Professor Susanta, BTech (Hons), DCT, PhD, CEng, MIStructE. Professor and Head, Department of Civil Engineering, Surveying and Building, Dundee Institute of Technology, since 1978; b. 22.9.34, West Bengal; m., Delphine; 2 s. Educ. Indian Institute of Technology; Leeds University. Postdoctoral Fellow, Leeds University; Senior Scientific Officer and Head of Concrete Structures, Structural Engineering Research Centre, 1965-68; Senior Lecturer/Acting Head, Department of Civil Engineering, National University of Singapore, 1968-71; Director of Studies, Civil Engineering, Hatfield Polytechnic, 1971-78. Past Chairman, Tayside Community Relations Council; Past Chairman, Dundee Voluntary Association. Recreations: travelling; photography; squash; badminton. Address: (h.) Carphin, 81 Camphill Road, Broughty Ferry, Dundee, DD5 2NA; T.-0382 730777.

Sarson, William C.T., BSc (Hons), MEd. Rector, Mintlaw Academy, since 1981; b. 23.9.38, Edinburgh; m., Lorna E. Black; 3 s. Educ. Lasswade Senior Secondary School; Edinburgh University. Production Engineer, Honeywell Controls, Newhouse; Physics Master, Edinburgh Academy; Principal Teacher of Physics and Assistant Head Teacher, Liberton High School; Depute Rector, Douglas Ewart High School, Newton Stewart. Recreations: swimming; hill-walking; computing. Address: (b.) Station Road, Mintlaw, Peterhead, AB42 8FN; T.-07712 2994.

Saunders, Professor Alison Marilyn, BA, PhD. Professor of French, Aberdeen University, since 1990; b. 23.12.44, Darlington. Educ. Wimbledon High School GPDST; Durham University. Lectrice, the Sorbonne, 1968-69; Lecturer in French, Aberdeen University, 1970-85; Senior Lecturer in French, 1985-90. Recreations: swimming; gardening; DIY; cooking; antiquarian book-collecting. Address: (h.) 1 Orchard Walk, Old Aberdeen, Aberdeen; T.-0224 494806.

Saunders, Professor David Stanley, BSc, PhD. Professor of Insect Physiology, Edinburgh University, since 1990; b. 12.3.35, Pinner; m., Jean Margaret Comrie Doughty; 3 s. Educ. Pinner County Grammar School; King's College, London; London School of Hygiene and Tropical Medicine. Joined academic staff, Zoology Department, Edinburgh, 1958; Visiting Professor: Stanford University, California, 1971-72, North Carolina University, 1983. Publications: Insect Clocks; Introduction to Biological Rhythms. Recreations: cycling; gardening; photography. Address: (b.) Institute of Cell, Animal and Population Biology, West Mains Road, Edinburgh, EH9 3JT.

Saunders, Francis William, MBE, ERD, JP, CEng, MICE, MCIOB. Member, Central Regional Council; b. 2.7.06, Liverpool; m., Mary Winifred Service. Educ. Glasgow Academy; Royal Technical College, Glasgow. Civil Engineer, private and public appointments, 1923-39; commissioned, Royal Engineers Regular Army Reserve, 1936; Army service, BEF (France), MEF (Western Desert, Palestine, Transjordan), CMF (Italy, Greece), 1939-47 (mentioned in Despatches); Regular Army Reserve (rank of Lt.-Col.), 1947-61; Civil Engineer, public service, 1947-49; travelled privately in Antipodes, 1949-50; private practice as Civil Engineer, 1950-91. Former Member, Stirling Town Council; President, Glasgow Branch, Royal Engineers Association. Recreations: travel; domestic life. Address: (h.) 1 Royal Gardens, Stirling, FK8 2RJ; T.-Stirling 73975; 37 Shoregate, Crail, KY10 3SU; T.-Crail 50690.

Savage, Rev. Gordon Matthew Alexander, MA, BD. Minister, Maxwelltown West, Dumfries, since 1984; Clerk, Presbytery of Dumfries and Kirkcudbright, since 1987; b. 25.8.51, Old Kilpatrick; m., Mairi Janet MacKenzie; 2 s. Educ. Glasgow Academy; Edinburgh University. Assistant Minister: Dyce Parish Church, 1975-76, Dunblane Cathedral, 1976-77; Minister: Almondbank, Tibbermore and Logiealmond, 1977-84. Junior Chaplain to Moderator, General Assembly, 1982; Junior Clerk, Perth Presbytery, 1980-83. Recreations: railways; model railways; music. Address: Maxwelltown West Manse, 11 Laurieknowe, Dumfries, DG2 7AH; T.-0387 52929.

Savin, John Andrew, MA, MD (Cantab), FRCP, FRCPEdin, DIH. Consultant Dermatologist, Edinburgh Royal Infirmary, since 1971; Senior Lecturer, Dermatology Department, Edinburgh University, since 1971; President, Section of Dermatology, Royal Society of Medicine; b. 10.1.35, London; m., Patricia Margaret Steel; 2 s.; 2 d. Educ. Epsom College; Trinity Hall, Cambridge; St. Thomas's Hospital, London. Royal Naval Medical Service, 1960-64; Registrar to Skin Department, St. George's Hospital, London; Senior Registrar, St. John's Hospital for Diseases of the Skin, and St. Thomas's

Hospital, London; Co-Editor, Recent Advances in Dermatology; Associate Editor, British Journal of Dermatology; former Secretary, Scottish Dermatological Society. Recreations: golf; literature. Address: (h.) 86 Murrayfield Gardens, Edinburgh; T.-031-337 7768.

Saxon, Professor David Harold, MA, DPhil, DSc, CPhys, FInstP. Kelvin Professor of Physics, Glasgow University, since 1990; b. 27.10.45, Stockport; m., Margaret Flitcroft; 1 s.; 1 d. Educ. Manchester Grammar School; Balliol College, Oxford; Jesus College, Oxford. Research Officer, Nuclear Physics Department, Oxford University, 1969-70; Research Associate, Columbia University, New York, 1970-73; Rutherford Appleton Laboratory, Oxon: Research Associate, 1974-75, Senior Scientific Officer, 1975-76, Principal Scientific Officer, 1976-89. Address: (b.) Department of Physics and Astronomy, Glasgow University, Glasgow, G12 8QQ; T.-041-330 4673.

Schaffer, Professor Heinz Rudolph, BA, PhD, FBPsS. Professor of Psychology, Strathclyde University, since 1970; b. 21.7.26, Berlin; m., Evelyn Blanche; 1 s.; 1 d. Educ. Ackworth School, Yorkshire; Birkbeck College, London. Research Psychologist, Tavistock Clinic, London, 1951-55; Principal Psychologist, Royal Hospital for Sick Children, Glasgow, 1955-63; Lecturer, then Senior Lecturer and Reader, Strathclyde University, 1964-70; Nuffield Fellowship, North Carolina University, 1971; Van Leer Fellowship, Jerusalem, 1976. Council Member, Social Science Research Council, 1976-78; President, Section J, British Association for the Advancement of Science, 1984-85; Chairman, Association for Child Psychology and Psychiatry, 1986-87. Recreations: walking; travelling. Address: (h.) 89 Roman Court, Bearsden, Glasgow, G61 2NW; T.-041-942 0197.

Schaw-Miller, Jean-Clare. Deputy Lieutenant, West Lothian; Scottish Chief Commissioner, The Girl Guide Association (Scotland), since 1987; Member, Scottish Youth Work Forum, SCEC, since 1991; b. 22.2.37, Hambrook, Gloucestershire; m., Robert Grant Schaw-Miller; 1 s.; 1 d. Educ. Clifton High School for Girls, Bristol; Edinburgh College of Domestic Science. The Girl Guide Association: former District and County Commissioner, West Lothian; Deputy Training Adviser for Scotland, 1976-79; International Adviser for Scotland, 1981-84; elected Member, UK GGA, 1977-84; UK Executive Committee, 1981-84; Deputy Scottish Chief Commissioner, 1986-87; Member, The Prince's Trust and Royal Jubilee Trusts Committee for Lothian and Borders, 1983-89; Chairman, South East Scotland Training Association, 1979-85; WRVS Family Welfare Organiser (Scotland), 1985-86. Recreations: gardening; reading; walking. Address: (h.) Newgardens, Dalmeny, South Queensferry, West Lothian, EH30 9TF; T.-031-331 4612.

Scheunemann, Professor Dietrich F.G., MA, Dr.phil. Professor of German, Edinburgh University, since 1990; b. 16.9.39, Schlawe, Germany; 2 s. Educ. Free University of Berlin; Yale University; University of Heidelberg. Taught, University of Heidelberg and Free University of Berlin; Reader in German and Comparative Literature, 1985, Chairman of German, 1987, Sussex University. Address: (b.) Department of German, Edinburgh University, David Hume Tower, Edinburgh, EH8 9JX; T.-031-667 1011.

Schlesinger, Philip Ronald, BA, PhD. Professor of Film and Media Studies, Stirling University, since 1989; b. 31.8.48, Manchester; m., Sharon Joy Rose; 2 d. Educ. North Manchester Grammar School; Queen's College, Oxford; London School of Economics. Thames Polytechnic: Lecturer, 1974, Senior Lecturer, 1977, Principal Lecturer, 1981; Head, Division of Sociology, 1981-88, Professor of Sociology,

1987-89; Social Science Research Fellow, Nuffield Foundation, 1982-83; Jean Monnet Fellow, European University Institute, Florence, 1985-86; Co-Editor, Media, Culture and Society, since 1982. Publications: Putting 'Reality> Together, 1978, 1987; Televising 'Terrorism>, 1983; Communicating Politics, 1986; Media, Culture and Society, 1986; Los Intelectuales en la Sociedad de la Informacion, 1987; Media, State and Nation, 1991. Recreations: the arts; walking; travel. Address: Department of Film and Media Studies, Stirling University, Stirling FK9 4LA; T.-0786 67520.

Schofield, Rev. Melville Frederick, MA. Chaplain to Western General and Associated Hospitals, Edinburgh, since 1988; b. 3.10.35, Glasgow; m., Christina Skirving Crookston. Educ. Irvine Royal Academy; Dalkeith High School; Edinburgh University and New College. Ordained Assistant, Bathgate High, 1960-61; Minister, Canal Street, Paisley, 1961-67; Minister, Laigh Kirk, Kilmarnock, 1967-88. Former Moderator, Presbytery of Irvine and Kilmarnock; former Moderator, Synod of Ayr; radio and TV broadcaster; Past President, No. 0 Kilmarnock Burns Club. Recreations: international Burns engagements; golf; after-dinner speaking. Address: (h.) 25 Rowantree Grove, Currie, Midlothian, EH14 5AT; T.-031-449 4745.

Schroder, Martin, BSc, PhD, DIC, MRSC, CChem. Reader in Chemistry, Edinburgh University, since 1991; Member, Inorganic Chemistry Sub-Committee, Science and Engineering Research Council, since 1990; b. 14.4.54, Taplow; m., Dr. Leena-Kreet Kore Schroder. Educ. Slough Grammar School; Sheffield University. Senior Demonstrator, Department of Chemistry, Edinburgh University, 1982-83, Lecturer in Inorganic Chemistry, 1983-91; Visiting Professor, University of Toronto, 1990. Corday Morgan Medal and Prize, Royal Society of Chemistry, 1989; Royal Society of Edinburgh Support Research Fellowship, 1991. Recreations: cricket; music. Address: (b.) Department of Chemistry, West Mains Road, Edinburgh University, Edinburgh, EH9 3JJ; T.-031-650 4761.

Schuster, Ida. Actress; b. Glasgow; m., Dr. Allan Berkeley; 2 s. Founder Member, Glasgow Jewish Institute Players; appeared in leading roles in Glasgow Unity Theatre; played Leah in The Dybbuk, Jewish Arts Festival; Member, Pitlochry Festival Theatre Company, 1974; directed and acted for Glasgow University Arts Theatre; has worked extensively in Scottish theatre, including the Citizens' Theatre, where she acted under five consecutive directorial regimes; one of the original cast of John Byrne's The Slab Boys; three Edinburgh Festivals; recent appearances at Glasgow Citizens' Theatre and Mayfest (in The Steamie); film work including a leading role in Passing Glory, 1986. Address: (h.) 1 Arran Drive, Giffnock, Glasgow, G46 7NL; T.-041-638 6767.

Sclater, Robert Chalmers. Director of Harbours, Orkney Islands Council, since 1989; Oil Pollution Officer, Orkney, since 1989; Executive Director, Orkney Towage Company, since 1989; Master Mariner; b. 7.8.41, Kirkwall; m., Anna Margaret; 1 s.; 2 d. Educ. Kirkwall Grammar School; Leith Nautical College; Robert Gordon's Institute of Technology. Merchant Navy, 1956-76; Marine Officer/1st Class Pilot, Orkney Islands Council, 1976-85; Depute Director of Harbours and Pilotage Superintendent, 1985-89. Member, Orkney Maritime Planning Committee; Kirkwall Sea Cadets Management Committee; DLA, RNLI, for Kirkwall Lifeboat; Elder, St. Magnus Cathedral. Recreations: swimming; gardening; walking. Address: (b.) Council Offices, Kirkwall, Orkney, KW15 1NY.

Scobie, Rev. Andrew John, MA, BD. Minister, Cardross Parish Church, since 1965; Convener, General Assembly's Panel on Worship, 1986-90; Member, Joint Liturgical Group,

1987-91; b. 9.7.35, Windygates; m., Elizabeth Jeannette; 1 s.; 1 d. Educ. Whitehill Senior Secondary School, Glasgow; Glasgow University (Medal in Systematic Study); Gottingen University; Tubingen University; Marburg University. Assistantship, New Kilpatrick Church, Bearsden; Moderator, Dumbarton Presbytery, 1973-74; Convener, General Assembly's Parish Education Commitee, 1978-80. Chairman or Vice-Chairman, Cardross Community Council, since inception; Former Member, British Council of Churches; Former Co-Chairman, Presbytery of Dumbarton/Archdiocese of Glasgow Liaison Group; involved in wide range of ecumenical initiatives including Swanwick Consultation, 1987. Publications: Studies in the Historical Jesus (Translator); contributions to New Ways to Worship, 1980, Prayers for Sunday Services, 1980, Three Orders for Holy Communion, 1986, Songs of God's People, 1988; Worshipping Together, 1991. Recreations: golf; photography; wine making; visual arts. Address: The Manse, Cardross, Dumbarton G82 5LB; T.-0389 841289.

Scobie, William Galbraith, MB, ChB, FRCSEdin, FRCSGlas. Consultant Paediatric Surgeon, Lothian Health Board, since 1971; part-time Senior Lecturer, Department of Clinical Surgery, Edinburgh University, since 1971; Assistant Director, Edinburgh Postgraduate Board for Medicine, since 1986; b. 13.10.36, Maybole; m., Elizabeth Caldwell Steel; 1 s.; 1 d. Educ. Carrick Academy, Maybole; Glasgow University. Registrar, General Surgery, Kilmarnock Infirmary; Senior Registrar, Royal Hospital for Sick Children, Glasgow; Senior Registrar, Hospital for Sick Children, London; Senior Paediatric Surgeon, Abu Dhabi, 1980-81. Recreations: fishing; golf; gardening; music. Address: (h.) 598 Queensferry Road, Edinburgh, EH4 6AT; T.-031-339 2306.

Scothorne, Professor Raymond John, BSc, MD, FRSE, FRCSG. Regius Professor of Anatomy, Glasgow University, 1973-90; b. 13.6.20, Nottingham; m., Audrey Gillott; 1 s.; 2 d. Educ. Royal Grammar School, Newcastle-upon-Tyne; Leeds University; Chicago University. Lecturer in Anatomy, Leeds University, 1944-50; Senior Lecturer, Glasgow University, 1950-60; Professor of Anatomy, Newcastle-upon-Tyne University, 1960-73. Anatomical Society of Gt. Britain and Ireland: Honorary Secretary, 1967-71, President, 1971-73; President, British Association of Clinical Anatomists, 1986-89; Foundation Editor, Clinical Anatomy, since 1988. Recreations: the countryside; labrador dogs. Address: (b.) Southern Knowe, Friars Brae, Linlithgow, West Lothian, EH49 6BQ.

Scothorne, Richard Mark, MA, MPhil. Economic Development Manager, Lothian Regional Council, since 1987; b. 17.7.53, Glasgow; m., Dr. Sarah Gledhill. Educ. Royal Grammar School, Newcastle upon Tyne; St. Catharine's College, Cambridge; Edinburgh University. Various posts, Gloucester City Council, Grampian Regional Council and Lothian Regional Council, 1977-86; Scottish Director, British Shipbuilders Enterprise Ltd., 1986-87. German Marshall Fellowship (USA), 1986. Publication: The Vital Economy (Co-author), 1990. Recreations: mountaineering; travelling; Scottish arts. Address: (h.) 8 Royal Terrace, Linlithgow, EH49 6HQ; T.-0506 844992.

Scott, Alan W.A., AIB (Scot). Secretary, The Committee of Scottish Clearing Bankers. Address: (b.) 19 Rutland Square, Edinburgh, EH1 2DD; T.-031-229 1326.

Scott, Alexander, MA, MSc, PhD. Professor of Economics, Heriot-Watt University, since 1989; b. 7.3.45, Lerwick; m., Anne Elliot; 3 d. Educ. Anderson Educational Institute; Boroughmuir Secondary; Edinburgh University. Research Assistant, Edinburgh University, 1967-70; Research Fellow, Heriot-Watt University, 1970-89; Tutor, Open University,

1971-75; Director, The Polecon Co., 1972-89; External Examiner, CNAA, 1981-85; Member, Joint Working Party on Economics, Scottish Examination Board, 1989-90; Chairman, Southfield Housing Society, 1977-80. Publications: Economics in Action (Co-author); Running the British Economy (Co-author); numerous papers. Recreations: squash; hill-walking; swimming; music. Address: (b.) The Esmee Fairbairn Research Centre, Heriot-Watt University, Riccarton, Edinburgh; T.-031-451 3090.

Scott, Bill, RSA. Sculptor; Head, School of Sculpture, Edinburgh College of Art (Lecturer, since 1962); b. 16.8.35, Moniaive; m., Phyllis Owen Scott; 1 s.; 2 d. Educ. Dumfries Academy; Edinburgh College of Art. One-man exhibitions: Compass Gallery, 1972, Stirling Gallery, 1974, New 57 Gallery, 1979, Lamp of Lothian, 1980, Art Space Gallery, 1980; numerous group exhibitions. Address: (h.) 45 St. Clair Crescent, Roslin, Midlothian, EH25 9NG.

Scott, Donald Bruce, MD, FRCPEdin, FFARCS. Consultant Anaesthetist, Edinburgh Royal Infirmary, 1959-86; President, European Society of Regional Anaesthesians, 1982-89; b. 16.12.25, Sydney; m., Joan Isobel White; 4 s.; 2 d. Educ. Hove Grammar School; Edinburgh University. Colonial Medical Service, Ghana, four years; training in anaesthesia, Edinburgh, six years; Consultant, NHS, Edinburgh Royal Infirmary, since 1959. Past President, Scottish Society of Anaesthetists; Past President, Obstetric Anaesthetists Association. Publication: Handbook of Epidural Anaesthesia (Co-author); Techniques of Regional Anaesthesia. Recreations: golf; food and wine. Address: (h.) 1 Zetland Place, Edinburgh, EH5 3HU; T.-031-552 3317.

Scott, Esme (Lady Scott), CBE, WS, MA, LLB, NP. Chair, Volunteer Development Scotland; Member, Securities and Investments Board; Member, Court, Edinburgh University; Member, Scottish Committee, Council on Tribunals; Member, Social Security Advisory Committee; b. 7.1.32, Edinburgh; m., 1, Ian Macfarlane Walker (deceased); 1 s.; 2, Kenneth Bertram Adam Scott, KCVO, CMG; 1 step-s.; 1 step-d. Educ. St. George's School for Girls, Edinburgh; Edinburgh University. Lawyer; Vice Chairman, National Consumer Council, 1984-87; Chairman, Scottish Consumer Council, 1980-85; Member, Equal Opportunities Commission, 1985-90; Past Chair, Scottish Association of Citizens Advice Bureaux. Address: (h.) 13 Clinton Road, Edinburgh.

Scott, Rev. Gideon George, MA, BD, ThM. Minister, St. David's North, Dundee, since 1973, linked with Albany-Butterburn, since 1986; b. 6.8.35, Alexandria; m., Jean Logan Russell Carlile; 2 s. by pr. m. Educ. Dumbarton Academy; Glasgow University; Princeton Theological Seminary. Assistant: St. Stephen's Blythswood, Glasgow, 1961, West Second-Avenue Presbyterian Church, Columbus, Ohio, 1962; Locum Preacher, Rosneath, St. Modan's, 1962; Teacher of Religious Education, Vale of Leven Academy, 1962; Minister, Wester Coates, Edinburgh, 1963-73; Extra-Mural Lecturer in Religion, Dundee University, 1978-79, 1982-83. Secretary, Scottish Church Theology Society, 1966-71. Recreations: listening to classical music; reading. Address: 2 Anstruther Road, Maryfield, Dundee; T.-0382 456579.

Scott, Gordon Ramsay, OBE, BSc, MS, PhD, FRCVS. Honorary Fellow, Edinburgh University; Consultant Virologist, Food and Agricultural Organisation, since 1963; b. 6.7.23, Arbroath; m., Joan Henderson Walker; 1 s.; 2 d. Educ. Arbroath High School; Royal (Dick) Veterinary College, Edinburgh; Wisconsin University. Private practice, 1946-49; Virologist, Veterinary Laboratory, Kabete, Kenya, 1950-52 (Head, Virus Section, 1952-56); Head, Division of Virus Diseases, East African Veterinary Research Organisation, 1956-62; Acting Director, EAVRO, Kenya,

1959, 1962; Lecturer, Senior Lecturer, then Reader in Tropical Veterinary Medicine, Edinburgh University, 1963-90. Recreations: biometry; travel. Address: (h.) 2/12 Craufurdland, Braepark Road, Edinburgh, EH4 6DL.

Scott, Rev. Ian Gray, BSc, BD, STM. Minister, Greenbank Parish Church, Edinburgh, since 1983; b. 31.5.41, Kirkcaldy; m., Alexandrina Angus; 1 d. Educ. Kirkcaldy High School; St. Andrews University; Union Theological Seminary, New York. Assistant Minister, St. Mungo's, Alloa, 1965-66; Minister: Holy Trinity Church, Bridge of Allan, 1966-76, Holborn Central, Aberdeen, 1976-83; Convener, Panel on Doctrine, General Assembly, 1978-82; part-time Lecturer, Faculty of Divinity, Aberdeen University, 1977-79; founder Member, Ministry and Psychotherapy Group; Convener, Committee on Education for the Ministry, Church of Scotland, since 1992; Vice-Convener, Board of Education, 1988-91; President, Stirling Bn., Boys' Brigade. Recreations: reading; photography; caravanning; golf (so called). Address: 112 Greenbank Crescent, Edinburgh, EH10 5SZ; T.-031-447 4032.

Scott, James Archibald, CB, LVO, MA (Hons). Executive Director, Scottish Financial Enterprise, since 1991 (Chief Executive, Scottish Development Agency, 1990-91); b. 5.3.32, Jaffa, Palestine; m., Dr. Elizabeth A.J. Buchan-Hepburn; 3 s.; 1 d. Educ. Dollar Academy; St. Andrews University; Queen's University, Ontario. RAF Aircrew, 1954-56; joined Commonwealth Relations Office, 1956; First Secretary, UK High Commission, New Delhi, 1958-62 and UK Mission to UN, New York, 1962-65; transferred to Scottish Office, 1965; Private Secretary to Secretary of State for Scotland, 1969-71; Assistant Secretary, Scottish Development Department, 1971; Under-Secretary, Industry Department for Scotland, 1976-84; Secretary, Scottish Education Department, 1984-87; Secretary, Industry Department for Scotland, 1987-90. Recreations: music; golf. Address: (b.) 91 George Street, Edinburgh, EH2 3ES; T.-031-225 6990.

Scott, James Inglis. Director, Dunfermline Building Society, since 1961 (Chairman, since 1981); b. 14.8.24, Dunfermline; m., Mabel Easson; 1 s.; 2 d. Educ. Merchiston Castle School. James Scott Electrical Group, 1947-78 (Director, 1955-78). Life Trustee: Carnegie Dunfermline Trust, since 1963 (Chairman, 1983-86); Carnegie United Kingdom Trust, since 1970; President, Electrical Contractors Association of Scotland, 1969-71. Address: (h.) 7/3 Rocheid Park, East Fettes Avenue, Edinburgh, EH9 1RP; T.-031-332 8991.

Scott, Jean Grant, BSc (Hons), PGCE, MIBiol. Headmistress, St. George's School for Girls, since 1986; b. 7.10.40, Helmsdale; m., John Scott (deceased); 2 s. Educ. George Watson's Ladies College, Edinburgh; Wellington School, Ayr; Glasgow University; London University Institute of Education. Research Biologist, Glaxo Laboratories Ltd., 1962-65, ICI, Alderley Edge, 1966-67; Lecturer in Biology (part-time), Newcastle-under-Lyme College of Further Education, 1969-70; Teacher of Biology (part-time), Dr. Challoner's High School for Girls, Little Chalfont, 1970-76; Teacher of Biology, Northgate Grammar School, Ipswich, 1976-77; Teacher of Biology, Head of Biology and Senior Mistress, Ipswich High School GPDST, 1977-86. Member, Committee for Biological Sciences, Cambridge University Local Examinations Syndicate, 1982-87; Teacher Moderator for "A" level Social Biology, Cambridge Board, 1983-86. Recreations: skiing; loch fishing; holidays in France; theatre; concerts. Address: (b.) St. George's School for Girls, Garscube Terrace, Edinburgh, EH12 6BG; T.-031-332 4575.

Scott, John, DL, JP. Member, Orkney Islands Council, since 1962; Director, Orkney Islands Shipping Company, since 1962; b. 3.9.21, Papa Stronsay; m., Margaret Ann Pottinger; 4 d. Educ. Stromness Academy. Home Guard; Auxiliary in Charge, HM Coastguard, Westray (retired); Army Cadet Force (Honorary Captain, retired); President, Local Committee, National Farmers Union; Secretary, Westray Baptist Church, 1943-86. Recreations: flying (PPL); sailing; golf; badminton. Address: (h.)Leckmelm, Annfield Crescent, Kirkwall, Orkney, KW15 1NS; T.-0856 3917.

Scott, Rev. John, LTh. Minister, St. Fillan's Church, Aberdour, since 1975; b. 21.6.31, Edinburgh; m., Catherine McLurg; 2 s.; 1 d. Educ. Royal High School, Edinburgh; Edinburgh University. Printing trade, 1947-63; Assistant Minister, Paisley Abbey, 1968-70; Minister, Viewfield Church, Stirling, 1970-75. Chairman, Aberdour Community Council, 1984-87; Moderator, Synod of Fife, 1985-86; Moderator, Presbytery of Dunfermline, 1986-87. Recreation: reading. Address: The Manse, Aberdour, Fife; T.-Aberdour 860349.

Scott, John Andrew Ross, JP. Member, Borders Regional Council, since 1985 (Chairman, Planning and Development Committee, 1989-90); Chief Reporter, Southern Reporter, since 1986; b. 6.5.51, Hawick; m., Christine Evans Collie; 2 s Educ. Hawick High School. Worked on father's farm, 1966-74; Journalist, Hawick News, 1977-78, Tweeddale Press Group, since 1978; first SDP Member, Roxburgh District Council (1980-85) and Borders Regional Council; Chairman, Roxburgh District Licensing Board, 1984-85; first Chairman, Borders Area Party, SDP, 1981-84; Assistant Secretary, Roxburgh and Berwickshire Liberal Democrats, 1988-89. Recreations: broadcasting; writing; music; travel; tennis. Address: (h.) 8 Union Street, Hawick, Roxburghshire; T.-0450 76324.

Scott, John Hamilton. Farmer; Vice Lord-Lieutenant, Shetland; Chairman, Wool Growers of Shetland Ltd.; Chairman, Shetland Crofting, Farming and Wildlife Advisory Group; Member, N.E. Scotland Board, Nature Conservancy Council for Scotland; b. 30.11.36; m., Wendy Ronald; 1 s.; 1 d. Recreations: hill-climbing; Up-Helly-Aa; music. Address: (h.) Gardie House, Bressay, Shetland, ZE2 9EL.

Scott, Rev. John Miller, MA, BD, DD, FSA (Scot). Minister, St. Andrew's Scots Memorial Church, Jerusalem, 1985-88; b. 14.8.22, Glasgow; m., Dorothy Helen Loraine Bushnell; 2 s.; 1 d. Educ. Hillhead High School; Glasgow University and Trinity College. War Service, Egypt, Italy, India, 1942-46; Assistant Minister, Barony of Glasgow, 1948-49; Minister: Baxter Park Parish, Dundee, 1949-54; High Kirk of Stevenston, 1954-63; Kirk of the Crown of Scotland (Crown Court Church, Westminster), 1963-85; Moderator, Presbytery of England, 1971, 1979; Moderator, Presbytery of Jerusalem, 1986-88; Chairman, Israel Council, 1986-88; various periods of service on General Assembly Committees; Representative, World Alliance of Reformed Churches, Ecumenical Patriarchate, Istanbul, 1988. President, Caledonian Society of London, 1983-84; instituted Kirking Service for Scottish MPs and peers, 1966; Member, UNA Religious Advisory Committee, 1983-85. Recreations: travel; historical research; reading; gardening. Address: (h.) 8 Woodland Way, Kingoodie, Invergowrie, Dundee, DD2 5DZ; T.-0382 562751.

Scott, Professor Michael George, BA (Econ), PhD. Scottish Amicable Professor of Entrepreneurial Studies, Stirling University, since 1987; b. 26.4.38, Harrogate. Educ. Queen Elizabeth Grammar School, Wakefield; Manchester University; Edinburgh University. Executive Officer, Civil Service, 1959-65; Principal Lecturer, Newcastle Polytechnic, 1971-84; Lecturer, Durham University Business School, 1984-87; Director, Scottish Enterprise Foundation, Stirling University, since 1987. Director, Forth Valley Enterprise, since 1991. Recreations: fine art and antiques; archaeology and local history. Address: (b.) Scottish Enterprise Foundation, Stirling University, Stirling, FK9 4LA; T.-0786 67333.

Scott, Mora Joan, DL, MB, ChB. Deputy Lieutenant, Morayshire, since 1983; President, Moray District, Scottish Children's League, since 1968; retired General Practitioner; b. 9.10.17, Beckenham; m., Gordon Islay Scott (deceased); 1 s.; 2 d. Educ. Albyn School, Aberdeen; Aberdeen University. Past President, Elgin Soroptimist Club; Chairman, RSSPCC Elgin District, since 1983. Recreations: fishing; gardening. Address: St. Michael's, Northfield Terrace, Elgin, Moray; T.-Elgin 543832.

Scott, Paul Henderson, CMG, MA, MLitt. Rector, Dundee University, since 1989; Member, National Executive Committee, SNP, since 1989; Convener, Advisory Council for the Arts in Scotland, since 1981; Vice-President, Scottish Centre, PEN International, since 1983; Member of Councils: Association for Scottish Literary Studies, Saltire Society and Scots Language Society; b. 7.11.20, Edinburgh; m., B.C. Sharpe; 1 s.; 1 d. Educ. Royal High School, Edinburgh; Edinburgh University. HM Forces, 1941-47 (Major, RA); HM Diplomatic Service in Foreign Office, Warsaw, La Paz, Havana, Montreal, Vienna, Milan, 1947-80. Publications: 1707, The Union of Scotland and England, 1979; Walter Scott and Scotland, 1981; John Galt, 1985; The Age of MacDiarmid (Co-Editor), 1980; In Bed with an Elephant: the Scottish Experience, 1985; A Scottish Postbag (Co-Editor), 1986; The Thinking Nation, 1989; Towards Independence – essays on Scotland, 1991. Recreation: skiing. Address: (h.) 33 Drumsheugh Gardens, Edinburgh, EH3 7RN; T.-031-225 1038.

Scott, Peter David, MIFireE. Firemaster, Lothian and Borders Fire Brigade, since 1989; b. 1946, Glasgow; m.; 1 s.; 1 d. Joined Lothian and Borders Fire Brigade, 1963. Recreations: golf; swimming; rugby. Address: (b.) Lauriston Place, Edinburgh, EH3 9DE.

Scott, Sheriff Richard John Dinwoodie, MA, LLB. Sheriff of Lothian and Borders at Edinburgh, since 1986 (of Grampian, Highland and Islands, at Aberdeen and Stonehaven, 1977-86); Honorary Reader, Aberdeen University, 1980-86; b. 28.5.39, Manchester; m., Josephine Moretta Blake; 2 d. Educ. Edinburgh Academy; Edinburgh University. Lektor, Folkuniversitet of Sweden, 1960-61; admitted to Faculty of Advocates, 1965; Standing Junior Counsel, Ministry of Defence (Air), 1969; Parliamentary candidate, 1974. Address: (b.) Sheriffs' Chambers, Sheriff Court House, Edinburgh, EH1 2NS; T.-031-226 7181.

Scott, Roger Davidson, BSc, PhD, CPhys, FInstP. Director, Scottish Universities Research and Reactor Centre, since 1991; b. 17.12.41, Lerwick; m., Marion McCluckie; 2 s.; 1 d. Educ. Anderson Institute, Lerwick; Edinburgh University. Demonstrator, Edinburgh University, 1965-68; Lecturer, then Depute Director, SURRC, 1968-91. Recreations: watching football; walking dogs; home maintenance. Address: (b.) Scottish Universities Research and Reactor Centre, East Kilbride, Glasgow, G75 0QU; T.-03552 20222, Ext. 2609.

Scott, Thomas Hardy, BPhil, DPS. Adviser for Scotland, Cancer Relief Macmillan Fund, since 1984; b. 11.5.32, Dundee; m., Dorothy K. Shields; 2 s.; 2 d. Educ. Sedbergh School; Edinburgh University; St. Andrews University. Assistant Minister, St. Giles Cathedral, Edinburgh, 1959-61; Minister, Bonnybridge Parish Church, 1961-66; Chaplain, Heriot-Watt University, 1966-79; Hospice Director, Strathcarron Hospice, Denny, 1979-91. Chairman, Edinburgh Council of Social Service, 1974-77; Chairman, Joint Committee on Alcohol Related Problems, Lothian Health Board and Social Work Department, 1978-81; Member,

Scottish Health Service Advisory Council, since 1989. Recreation: golf. Address: (b.) Cancer Relief Macmillan Fund, 9 Castle Terrace, Edinburgh, EH1 2DP; T.-031-229 3276.

Scott, Tom, MA, PhD. Writer; b. 6.6.18, Glasgow; m., Margaret Heather Fretwell; 1 s.; 2 d. Educ. Hyndland School, Glasgow; Madras College, St. Andrews; Edinburgh University. Began life in building trade, St. Andrews, 1934; War Service (Nigeria, 1941-43); after few jobs in bookshops in London, freelance Writer until belated University studies via Newbattle Abbey College (under Edwin Muir); first published poem in Poetry London, 1940; first volumes, Seeven Poems O Maister Francis Villon, An Ode Til New Jerusalem, The Ship and Ither Poems; then At the Shrine O The Unkent Sodger, Brand the Builder, The Tree, The Dirty Business; edited Oxford Book of Scottish Verse (with John MacQueen), Some Late Medieval Scottish Poets, the Penguin Book of Scottish Verse; for children, Tales of King Robert the Bruce and Tales of Sir William Wallace; criticism: Dunbar, An Exposition of the Poems. Recreations: surviving; ornithology; music. Address: (h.) 3 Duddingston Park, Edinburgh.

Scott, Walter, CBE, DA, RIBA, FRIAS. Architect, Scott & McIntosh, Edinburgh, since 1964; Member, Borders Health Board, since 1983; b. 26.1.26, Musselburgh; m., Irene Duncan; 1 s.; 2 d. Educ. Musselburgh Grammar School; Edinburgh College of Art; Heriot-Watt University. Royal Engineers, 1944-47 (Captain); joined Architect's Department, South Eastern Regional Hospital Board, 1957; founded Scott & McIntosh, 1964; Member, RIAS Council, 1957-60; President, Scottish Conservative Association, 1970-71; President, Old Musselburgh Club, 1972. Recreations: rugby football; gardening; curling. Address: (h.) The Dell, Gordon, Berwickshire; T.-057381 335.

Scott, William Andrew Black, MA, FFA. General Manager and Deputy Chief Executive, Scottish Provident, since 1988; b. 4.2.38, Dumfries; m., Marion Gow; 1 s.; 1 d. Educ. Preston Lodge; Edinburgh University. Assistant Actuary, 1965; Deputy Actuary, 1969; Secretary, 1975; Assistant General Manager and Secretary, 1980. Recreations: golf; railways. Address: (b.) 6 Andrew Square, Edinburgh, EH2 2YA; T.-031-556 9181.

Scott, Professor William Talbot, MA, PhD, DipEd, CertEd. Professor and Head, Department of Communication, Glasgow Polytechnic, since 1984; b. 28.2.42, Glasgow; m., Wendy Elizabeth Murray; 1 s.; 1 d. Educ. Woodside Secondary, Glasgow; Glasgow University; Sheffield University. Features Writer, D.C. Thomson & Co.; Lecturer/Senior Lecturer/Principal Lecturer in Communication Studies, Sheffield City Polytechnic. Chairman, Appeals Committee, Epilepsy Association of Scotland. Publication: The Possibility of Communication, 1990. Recreations: running; gardening. Address: (b.) Department of Communication, Glasgow College, Cowcaddens Road, Glasgow, G4 0BA; T.-041-331 3260.

Scott Brown, Ronald, MA, LLB. Director, Aberdeen Trust PLC, since 1983, Chairman, 1989-91; Director, Abtrust Fund Managers and Abtrust Management Ltd., since 1987; b. 14.2.37, Madras; m., Jean Leslie Booth; 3 s. Educ. Aberdeen Grammar School; Aberdeen University. Qualified Solicitor, 1961; Assistant, then Partner, Brander & Cruickshank, Advocates, 1961-83. Member, Board of Governors, Northern College of Education, since 1983; Member, Court, Aberdeen University, since 1990. Address: (b.) 10 Queen's Terrace, Aberdeen, AB9 1QJ; T.-0224 631999.

Scott-Dempster, Ronald, BL, WS. Writer to the Signet (Consultant), since 1974; Honorary Sheriff, Perthshire, since 1958; b. 8.5.98, Perth; m., Ann Reid; 1 s.; 2 d. Educ. Perth

Academy; Edinburgh University. Lt., Royal Field Artillery, 1916-19; wounded, 1917; Partner, Robertson Dempster & Co., WS, 1924-74; Chairman, Court of Referees, 1933-38; Registrar, Diocese of St. Andrews, 1928-74; Treasurer, Perthshire Nursing Federation, 1933-58; Treasurer, Perth Royal Infirmary, 1938-49; Secretary, Territorial Army Association, Perthshire, 1939-49; Lt.-Col., Army Welfare, Perthshire, 1943-50; Director, General Accident Assurance Co., 1948-74, Yorkshire General Life Assurance, 1950-62, English Insurance Co., 1962-77, Grampian Properties Ltd., 1967-77; Consultant, Condie Mackenzie & Co., WS, 1974-91; Deer Consultant, 1977-82; Convener, Executive Council, Scottish Episcopal Church, 1959-67 (Trustee, 1960-91); Vice-Chairman, Perth Branch, Royal British Legion since formation; Life Member, Gaelic Society of Perth and Royal Scottish Pipers Society. Recreations: golf; deer stalking; gardening; piping; hill-walking. Address: (h.) Tayhill, Dunkeld, Perthshire; T.-03502 277.

Scott Elliot, Lt. Col. Alastair William. Regimental Secretary, Argyll & Sutherland Highlanders, since 1987; Commandant, Argyll & Sutherland Highlanders Bn. ACF, since 1990; b. 25.11.34, Berwick upon Tweed; m., Andrena Christian Anderson; 2 s. Educ. Wellington College. Joined Army, 1953; served as a regular officer until 1987; commanded 1 A&H, 1974-77. Recreations: golf; shooting. Address: (h.) Shoreland, Fintry Road, Kippen, by Stirling; T.-078687 261.

Scrimgeour, John Beocher, MB, ChB, DObst, RCOG, FRCOG, FRCS(Edin). Consultant Obstetrician and Gynaecologist, since 1972; Honorary Senior Lecturer in Obstetrics and Gynaecology, Edinburgh University, since 1972; b. 22.1.39, Elgin; m., Joyce Morrin; 1 s.; 1 d. Educ. Hawick High School; Edinburgh University. General Practitioner, Edinburgh, 1963-65; Senior House Officer: Stirling Royal Infirmary, 1965, and Registrar, Eastern General Hospital, Edinburgh, 1966-69; Senior Registrar, Edinburgh Royal Infirmary, 1970-72; Senior Secretary, Edinburgh Obstetrical Society, 1980-85; Chairman, Area Division of Obstetrics and Gynaecology, 1984-88; Member, Council, Royal College of Obstetricians and Gynaecologists, 1976-81. Publication: Towards the Prevention of Fetal Malformation, 1978. Recreations: gardening; golf; tennis. Address: (h.) 4 Kinellan Road, Edinburgh, EH12 6ES; T.-031-337 6027.

Seafield, 13th Earl of (Ian Derek Francis Ogilvie-Grant), b. 20.3.39; m., 1, Mary Dawn Mackenzie Illingworth (m. diss.); 2 s.; 2, Leila Refaat. Educ. Eton. Address: (h.) Old Cullen, Cullen, Banffshire.

Seager, Professor David Lewis, BSc, PhD. Deputy Chairman and Technical Director, Lewis C. Grant Ltd., since 1990; Visiting Professor in Mechanical Engineering, Edinburgh University, since 1991; b. 6.3.41, Bournemouth; m., Margaret Lythgoe; 3 s. Educ. Fettes College; Glasgow University; Cambridge University. Development Engineer, Sikorsky Aircraft, 1967-68; Research Engineer, Westinghouse Electric, 1968-72; Lecturer in Engineering, Aberdeen University, 1972-75; Technical Director, then Managing Director, Lewis C. Grant Ltd., Kirkcaldy, 1975-90; Honorary Fellow, Edinburgh University, 1984-91; Non-Executive Director, Forsbergs Inc., USA, 1987-90. Recreations: linguistics; theatre; cross-country skiing. Address: (h.) 20 Lady Helen Street, Kirkcaldy, KY1 1PR; T.-0592 51035.

Seagrave, David Robert, LLB (Hons), SSC, NP. Solicitor and Notary Public; Council Member, Law Society of Scotland, 1981-87; Partner, Seagrave & Co., Solicitors, Dumfries; b. 29.4.43, Berwick-on-Tweed; m., Fiona Lesley Thomson; 1 s.; 1 d. Educ. Newcastle-upon-Tyne; Glasgow University. Banking, insurance, police; Secretary, Enterprise Trust for Nithsdale, Annandale/Eskdale and the Stewartry. Recreations: choral singing; shooting; fishing; golf. Address: (h.) Amulree, Islesteps, Dumfries; T.-Dumfries 64523.

Sealey, Barry Edward, CBE, BA (Hons) (Cantab), CBIM. Director: David A. Hall Ltd., Warburtons Ltd., Albacom plc, The Caledonian Brewing Company Ltd., Scottish Equitable Life Assurance Society, Scottish American Investment Trust plc, Morago Ltd., and other companies; Chairman, In-Spec Manpower and Inspection Services Ltd.; b. 3.2.36, Bristol; m., Helen Martyn; 1 s.; 1 d. Educ. Dursley Grammar School; St. John's College, Cambridge. RAF, 1953-55. Joined Christian Salvesen as trainee, 1958; joined Board, Christian Salvesen PLC (responsible for Food Services Division), 1969; appointed Managing Director, 1981, Deputy Chairman and Managing Director, 1987; retired from Christian Salvesen, 1990. Council Member, The Industrial Society. Address: (h.) 4 Castlelaw Road, Edinburgh, EH13 0DN.

Searle, Jack, MSc, MRTPI, ARIAS. Director of Planning, Tayside Regional Council, since 1990; b. 28.3.38, London; m., Joyce Davidson; 2 d. Educ. Tottenham Grammar School; Northern Polytechnic, London; Edinburgh University. Private practice, 1962-66; MSc, Edinburgh University, 1966-67; Dundee City Planning Department, 1967-75 (Depute Director, 1972-75); Depute Director of Planning, Tayside RC, 1975-90. Recreations: hill-walking; glass; reading. Address: (b.) Tayside House, Crichton Street, Dundee; T.-0382 23281.

Seaton, Professor Anthony, BA, MD (Cantab), FRCPLond, FRCPEdin, FFOM. OMS Professor of Environmental and Occupational Medicine, Aberdeen University, since 1988; b. 20.8.38, London; m., Jillian Margaret Duke; 2 s. Educ. Rossall School, Fleetwood; King's College, Cambridge; Liverpool University. Assistant Professor of Medicine, West Virginia University, 1969-71; Consultant Chest Physician, Cardiff, 1971-77; Director, Institute of Occupational Medicine, Edinburgh, 1978-90. Editor, Thorax, 1977-82. Publications: Occupational Lung Diseases; Respiratory Diseases. Recreations: rowing; painting. Address: (h.) 8 Avon Grove, Cramond, Edinburgh, EH4 6RF; T.-031-336 5113.

Seaton, Anthony Victor, MA (Oxon), BA. Senior Lecturer in Tourism and Marketing Behaviour, Strathclyde University, since 1991; b. 15.3.43, Birmingham; m., Claudia Florence; 1 s.; 2 d. Educ. Wolverhampton Grammar School; Wadham College, Oxford. Worked in brand management/advertising, Procter and Gamble, 1966-72; Teacher, Huddersfield Polytechnic, 1972-73, Newcastle Polytechnic, 1973-91; Lecturer in Media Studies/Popular Culture, Open University, 1976-91. Publications: The travel journals of George Clayton Atkinson in Iceland 1833 (Editor); The occupational practices and idealogies of travel page editors, 1990. Recreations: antiquarian book collecting; travel; 1960s pop music.

Seaton, Robert, MA, LLB. Secretary of the University, Dundee University, since 1973; b. 2.8.37, Clarkston, Renfrewshire; m., Jennifer Graham Jack; 2 s.; 2 d. Educ. Eastwood Secondary School; Glasgow University; Balliol College, Oxford; Edinburgh University. Administrative Assistant, then Senior Administrative Officer, then Assistant Secretary, Edinburgh University, 1962-73. Director, Dundee University Research Limited. Recreations: tennis; squash; golf. Address: (h.) Dunarn, 29 South Street, Newtyle, Angus, PH12 8UQ; T.-Newtyle 330.

Sedgley, Jeffrey P., BA (Hons), MSc, MA. Head Teacher, Lionel School, Isle of Lewis, since 1990; b. 15.3.44, Birmingham; 1 s.; 1 d. Educ. Sheldon Heath School, Birmingham; Keele University. Teacher in Lewis and Shetland, 1971-75; Depute Head Teacher, Lionel School, 1975-90. Chairman, Lewis and Harris Local Health Council, since 1986; Secretary, Western Isles Executive, EIS, since

1988. Recreations: reading; cooking; visiting Italy. Address: (h.) 23 Adabrock, Port of Ness, Isle of Lewis; T.-0851-81-453.

Sefton, Rev. Henry Reay, MA, BD, STM, PhD. Master of Christ's College, Aberdeen, since 1982; Senior Lecturer in Church History, Aberdeen University, since 1991; Moderator, Synod of Grampian, since 1991; b. 15.1.31, Rosehearty. Educ. Brechin High School; St. Andrews University; Glasgow University; Union Theological Seminary, New York. Assistant Minister, Glasgow Cathedral, 1957-58, St. Margaret's, Knightswood, Glasgow, 1958-61; Acting Chaplain, Hope Waddell Training Institution, Nigeria, 1959; Associate Minister, St. Mark's, Wishaw, 1962; Minister, Newbattle, 1962-66; Assistant Secretary, Church of Scotland Department of Education, 1966-72; Lecturer in Church History, Aberdeen University, 1972-90. Moderator, Aberdeen Presbytery, 1982-83; Chairman, Association of University Teachers (Scotland), 1982-84. Recreations: hill-walking; church architecture; stamp and coin collecting. Address: (h.) 25 Albury Place, Aberdeen, AB1 2TQ; T.-0224 572305.

Semple, Peter d'Almaine, MD, FRCPGlas, FRCPEdin. Consultant Physician and Chest Specialist, Inverclyde District, since 1979; b. 30.10.45, Glasgow; m., Judith Mairi Abercromby; 2 d. Educ. Belmont House; Loretto School; Glasgow University. Various training posts, Glasgow and Dundee teaching hospitals; Consultant Physician, Inverclyde Royal Hospital, 1979; former Postgraduate Medical Tutor, Inverclyde District; Honorary Clinical Senior Lecturer, Glasgow University. Chairman, Medical Audit Sub-Committee, Scottish Office; President, Greenock and District Faculty of Medicine; Past Chairman, West of Scotland Branch, British Deer Society. Recreations: golf; field sports; windsurfing. Address: (h.) Allandale, 11 Barrhill Road, Gourock, PA19 1JX; T.-0475 32720.

Semple, Walter George, BL, NP, ACI Arb. Solicitor; Partner, Bird Semple Fyfe Ireland, WS, Solicitors; b. 7.5.42, Glasgow; m., Dr. Lena Ohrstrom; 3 d. Educ. Belmont House, Glasgow; Loretto School; Glasgow University. President, Glasgow Juridical Society, 1968; Tutor and Lecturer (part-time), Glasgow University, 1970-79; Council Member, Law Society of Scotland, 1976-80; Chairman, Scottish Lawyers European Group, 1978-81; Member, Commission Consultative des Barreaux Europeens, 1978-80, 1984-87; President, Association Internationale des Jeunes Avocats, 1983-84; Chairman, Scottish Branch, Institute of Arbitrators, 1989-91; Director: Alexanders Holdings plc, Lex Mundi Limited (USA). Recreations: golf; fishing; skiing; music. Address: (h.) 47 Newark Drive, Glasgow, G41 4QA; T.-041-423 7095.

Semple, William David Crowe, CBE, BSc (Hons), DipEd, FBIM. Director of Education, Lothian Regional Council, since 1974; b. 11.6.33, Grangemouth; m., Margaret; 1 s.; 1 d. Educ. Grangemouth High School; Falkirk High School; Glasgow University; Jordanhill College, Glasgow; London University. Education Officer, Northern Rhodesia, 1958-64; Zambia: Deputy Chief Education Officer, 1964-66, Chief Education Officer, 1966-67, Acting Director of Technical Education, 1967-68; Edinburgh Corporation: Assistant Director of Education, 1968-70, Depute Director of Education, 1970-74. Member: University Grants Committee, 1983-89, Scottish Council for Tertiary Education, 1979-83, UK National Committee for UNESCO, 1981-86; Chairman, Scottish Television Educational Advisory Committee, 1979-85; General Secretary, Association of Directors of Education; Member, Howie Committee, 1990-92. Recreation: gardening. Address: (b.) 40 Torphichen Street, Edinburgh; T.-031-229 9166.

Sessford, Rt. Rev. George Minshull, MA. Bishop of Moray, Ross and Caithness, since 1970; b. 7.11.28, Aintree; m., Joan G.M. Black; 3 d. Educ. Oulton High School; Liverpool Collegiate; St. Andrews University; Lincoln Theological College. Ordained Deacon, 1953; Ordained Priest, 1954; Assistant Curate, St. Mary's Cathedral, Glasgow, 1953-58; Anglican Chaplain, Glasgow University, 1955-58; Priest in Charge, Cumbernauld New Town, 1958-66; Rector, Forres, 1966-70. Recreations: sailing; donkey breeding. Address: Spynie House, 96 Fairfield Road, Inverness, IV3 5LL; T.-0463 231059.

Sewell, Professor John Isaac, BSc, PhD, CEng, FIEE. Professor of Electronic Systems, Glasgow University, since 1985 (Dean, Faculty of Engineering, since 1990); b. 13.5.42, Kirkby Stephen; m., Ruth Alexandra Baxter; 1 d. Educ. Kirkby Stephen Grammar School; Durham University; Newcastle-upon-Tyne University. Lecturer, Senior Lecturer, Reader, Department of Electronic Engineering, Hull University, 1968-85. Publications: 97 papers. Recreations: swimming; climbing. Address: (h.) 16 Paterson Place, Bearsden, Glasgow, G61 4RU; T.-041-943 0729.

Sewell, Major Morley Hodkin, MA, PhD, VetMB, MRCVS. Director, Centre for Tropical Veterinary Medicine, since 1990; Reader in Veterinary Parasitology, Edinburgh University, since 1980; b. 1.9.32, Sheffield; m., Cynthia Margaret-Rose Hanson; 1 s.; 3 d. Educ. King Edward VII School, Sheffield; Cambridge University. Colonial Office Research Scholar, Cambridge, 1957-59; Veterinary Research Officer, Government of Nigeria, 1959-63; Lecturer, then Senior Lecturer, then Reader, Edinburgh University, since 1963. Local Preacher, Methodist Church, since 1958; Circuit Steward, Edinburgh and Forth Circuit; Vice-Chairman, Action Partners. Recreations: Church; politics; travel. Address: (h.) 14 Craigiebield Crescent, Penicuik, Midlothian.

Seymour, Professor Philip Herschel Kean, BA, MEd, PhD. Professor of Cognitive Psychology, Dundee University, since 1988; b. 9.3.38, London; m., Margaret Jean Dyson Morris; 2 s.; 2 d. Educ. Kelly College, Tavistock; Exeter College, Oxford; St. Andrews University. Dundee University: Lecturer, 1966-75, Senior Lecturer, 1975-82, Reader, 1982-88. Chairman, Scottish Dyslexia Association, 1982-85. Publications: Human Visual Cognition, 1979; Cognitive Analysis of Dyslexia, 1986. Address: (b.) Department of Psychology, Dundee University, Dundee; T.-Dundee 23181.

Shackleton, Rev. William, MA (Hons). Minister, Wellpark West, Greenock, since 1983; b. 19.10.27, Glasgow; m., Margaret Mackenzie Brown; 1 s.; 2 d. Educ. Preston Grammar School; Edinburgh University. Assistant, then Minister, St. Francis-in-the-East, Glasgow, 1955-83. Chairman, Church House Youth Club, Bridgeton; President, Bridgeton Business Club; President, Regnal League of Men's Circles. Recreations: writing; golf. Address: 45 Denholm Street, Greenock; T.-0475 21974.

Shand, Jimmy, MBE. Musician and Scottish Country Dance Band Leader; b. 28.1.08, East Wemyss; m., Anne Anderson; 2 s. Educ. East Wemyss School. Has played the accordion and led Scottish danceband at thousands of concert and theatre performances at home and overseas; numerous recordings; several thousand broadcasts. Recreations: motor bikes; sailing.

Shanks, Duncan Faichney, RSA, RGI, RSW. Artist; b. 30.8.37, Airdrie; m., Una Brown Gordon. Educ. Coatdyke Grammar School; Glasgow School of Art. Part-time Lecturer, Glasgow School of Art, until 1979; now full-time painter; one-man shows: Stirling University, Scottish Gallery, Fine Art Society, Talbot Rice Art Gallery, Edinburgh University, Crawford Centre, Maclaurin Art Gallery, Glasgow Art

Gallery, Fine Art Society, touring exhibition (Wales); taken part in shows of Scottish painting, London, 1986, Toulouse, Rio de Janeiro, 1985, Wales, 1988; Scottish Arts Council Award; Latimer and MacAulay Prizes, RSA; Torrance Award, Cargill Award, MacFarlane Charitable Trust Award, RGI; May Marshall Brown Award, RSW; tapestry commissioned by Coats Viyella, woven by Edinburgh Tapestry Company, presented to Glasgow Royal Concert Hall, 1991. Recreations: music; gardening.

Shanks, Rev. Norman James, MA, BD. Lecturer in Practical Theology, Glasgow University, since 1988; Convener, Acts Commission on Justice, Peace, Social and Moral Issues, since 1991; b. 15.7.42, Edinburgh; m., Ruth Osborne Douglas; 2 s.; 1 d. Educ. Stirling High School; St. Andrews University; Edinburgh University. Scottish Office, 1964-79; Chaplain, Edinburgh University, 1985-88; Chairman, Edinburgh Council of Social Service, 1985-88; Chairman, Secretary of State's Advisory Committee on Travelling People, 1985-88; Convener, Church and Nation Committee, Church of Scotland, 1988-92; Member, Broadcasting Council for Scotland, since 1988; Member, Scottish Constitutional Convention and Executive Committee, since 1989. Recreations: armchair cricket; occasional golf. Address: (h.) 1 Marchmont Terrace, Glasgow, G12 9LT; T.-041-339 4421.

Shanks, Thomas Henry, MA, LLB. Solicitor and Notary Public, since 1956; Honorary Sheriff, Lanark, since 1982; b. 22.10.30, Lanark; m., Sheila Dales Hunter (deceased); 1 s.; 1 d. Educ. Lanark Grammar School; Glasgow University. Intelligence Corps (National Service), 1954-56. Depute Clerk of Peace, County of Lanark, 1961-74; Chairman, Royal Burgh of Lanark Community Council, 1977-80 and 1983-86; Captain, Lanark Golf Club, 1962; Lord Cornet, 1968; Secretary, Lanark Lanimer Committee; Secretary, Clydesdale Upperward Society; Preses, Cairns Church, Lanark. Recreation: golf. Address: (h.) Clydesholm Braes, Lanark.

Shanks, William Alexander, IEng, MIM, MIQA. Manager, Materials Testing Laboratories, Strathclyde University, since 1983; b. 10.9.27, Lanark; m., Margaret Lockhart Wallace; 1 s. Educ. Lanark Grammar School; Royal Technical College, Glasgow. Apprentice Metallurgist/Metallurgist, Colvilles Ltd., 1945-56; National Service, RAF, 1946-49; Company Metallurgist/Specialist Production Engineer, Honeywell Controls Ltd., 1956-64; Senior Research Assistant/Laboratory Head/Manager – Technical Services and Contracts, Scottish Research Laboratories, British Steel Corporation, 1964-83. Member, BSI Committees; Member of Council, Scottish Association for Metals; former Hon. Secretary and Director, Scottish Gliding Union. Recreations: golf; gardening; music. Address: (b.) Division of Mechanics of Materials, Strathclyde University, James Weir Building, 75 Montrose Street, Glasgow, G1 1XJ; T.-041-552 4400.

Sharp, Alexander McLean, JP. Chairman, Fife Regional Planning and Development Committee, since 1974; Chairman, Scottish National Housing and Town Planning Association, since 1982; Chairman, Planning Committee, COSLA, since 1980; Chairman, National Housing and Planning Council (UK), 1988-89; Vice Chairman, Planning Forum, UK, since 1990; b. 13.10.33, Lochgelly; m., Betty Gray; 2 s.; 1 d. Educ. Lochgelly Junior Secondary School. Former Member, Lochgelly Town Council (Provost of Lochgelly, 1973-75); Member, Dunfermline Advisory Board for Justices of the Peace, since 1973; Chairman: Cowdenbeath School Council, Lochgelly Centre Management Committee, Mossmorran/Braefoot Bay Petrochemical Liaison Committee; Vice Chairman, Forth Road Bridge Board; Member, Glenrothes Development Corporation, 1978-84; Deputy Chairman, SDA Consultative Committee; Chairman, Central District, Gas Consumer Council; Citizen of the Year,

Lochgelly, 1987. Recreations: golf; fishing; local interests. Address: (h.) 119 Main Street, Lochgelly, Fife; T.-Lochgelly 780508.

Sharp, Professor David William Arthur, MA, PhD, CChem, FRSC, FRSE. Professor of Chemistry, Glasgow University, since 1968; Director, Office for International Programmes, Glasgow University, since 1988; Convener, Scottish Council for the Validation of Courses for Teachers, 1983-89; b. 8.10.31, Folkestone; m., 1, Margaret Cooper; 1 s.; 2 d.; 2, Mary Mercer. Educ. Harvey Grammar School, Folkestone; Sidney Sussex College, Cambridge. Lecturer, Imperial College, London, 1957-61; Strathclyde University, latterly as Professor, 1965-68; Chairman, Scottish Council for Educational Technology, 1975-81; Council Member, Scottish Universities Council on Entrance, 1974-83; Chairman, Committee of Heads of University Chemistry Departments, 1979-81; Governor, Jordanhill College, 1971-79; Member, Scottish Examination Board, 1977-84; Council Member, Royal Society of Chemistry, 1974-77; Member, Council, Royal Society of Edinburgh, 1985-88. Publications: A New Dictionary of Chemistry (Editor); Penguin Dictionary of Chemistry (Editor); J. Fluorine Chemistry (Editor). Recreation: walking. Address: (b.) Department of Chemistry, Glasgow University, Glasgow, G12 8QQ; T.-041-330 5290.

Sharp, Sir George, Kt (1976), OBE, JP, DL. Chairman, Glenrothes Development Corporation, 1978-86; Member, Economic and Social Committee, EEC, 1982-86; b. 8.4.19; m., Elsie May Rodger; 1 s. Educ. Buckhaven High School. Fife County Council: Member, 1945-75, Chairman, Water and Drainage Committee, 1955-61, Chairman, Finance Committee, 1961-72, Convener, 1972-75; Convener, Fife Regional Council, 1974-78; President: Association of County Councils, 1972-74, COSLA, 1975-78; Chairman: Kirkcaldy District Council, 1958-75, Fife and Kinross Water Board, 1967-75, Forth River Purification Board, 1955-67 and 1975-78, Scottish River Purification Advisory Committee, 1967-75, Scottish Tourist Consultative Council, 1979-82; Vice-Chairman, Forth Road Bridge Committee, 1972-78; Member, Scottish Water Advisory Committee, 1962-69, Committee of Enquiry into Salmon and Trout Fishing, 1963, Scottish Valuation Advisory Committee, 1972, Committee of Enquiry into Local Government Finance, 1974-76, Scottish Development Agency, 1975-80, Royal Commission on Legal Services in Scotland, 1978-80; Director, Grampian Television, 1975-89; Member, Scottish Board, National Girobank, 1982-90; Managing Trustee, Municipal Mutual Insurance Ltd., since 1979. Recreations: golf; reading; gardening; football spectating. Address: (h.) Strathela, 56 Station Road, Thornton, Fife; T.-Glenrothes 774347.

Sharp, John Clarkson Macgregor, MB, ChB, DPH, FFCM, MRCPGlas. Consultant Epidemiologist, Communicable Diseases (Scotland) Unit, Ruchill Hospital, Glasgow, since 1971; b. 20.6.31, New Stevenston, Lanarkshire; m., Elizabeth Anthony Stevenson; 2 d. Educ. Daniel Stewart's College; Edinburgh University. Hospital appointments, Plymouth, Dartford and Bangour; general practice, Edinburgh and Motherwell; Senior Medical Officer, Public Health Department, Edinburgh; Depute County Medical Officer, West Lothian. Honorary Medical Adviser, Scottish Rugby Union. Recreations: golf; curling. Address: (b.) Communicable Diseases (Scotland) Unit, Ruchill Hospital, Glasgow, G20 9NB; T.-041-946 7120.

Sharp, Leslie, QPM, LLB, FBIM. Chief Constable, Strathclyde Police, since 1991; b. 14.5.36, London; m., Audrey Sidwell; 4 d. Educ. Finchley County Grammar School; University College, London. MRC, 1952-54; Middlesex Regiment, 1954-56; Metropolitan Police, 1956-80; Assistant and Deputy Chief Constable, West Midlands Police, 1980-88; Chief Constable, Cumbria Constabulary,

1988-91. Recreations: angling; cricket umpire; water colour painting; gardening. Address: (b.) 173 Pitt Street, Glasgow, G2 4JS; T.-041-204 2626.

Sharratt, John, DPA, DCA, MITSA. Chief Trading Standards Officer, Borders Regional Council, since 1988; Education Secretary, Institute of Trading Standards Administration (Scottish Branch), 1985-91, Chairman, since 1991; b. 16.8.47, Manchester; m., Yvonne; 4 s. Educ. Horwich Secondary School; Bell College of Technology. Trainee, Lancashire CC, 1964-69; Senior Trading Standards Officer, Glasgow Corporation/Strathclyde RC, 1969-79; Assistant Divisional Trading Standards Officer, 1979-84, Principal TSO (Research, Development and Training), 1984-88, Strathclyde RC. Education Secretary, Institute of Trading Standards Administration (Scottish Branch), since 1988. Recreations: squash; golf; fishing; watching rugby. Address: (b.) County Buildings, Jedburgh, TD8 6AR; T.-0835 63377.

Shaw, Rev. Alexander James, MA, BD. Minister, Ardclach with Auldearn and Dalmore, Nairn, since 1984; b. 6.6.42, Perth; m., Elspeth Margaret Walker; 2 s. Educ. Perth Academy; Edinburgh University. Worked with General Accident Fire and Life Assurance Corporation; Minister, West Parish Church, Cowdenbeath, 1968-84. Member, Board of Social Responsibility, Church of Scotland; Chairman, Moray Firth Radio Christian Council; Chaplain, (Nairn) Air Training Corps; Member, Presbyterian and Reformed Renewal Ministries, Oklahoma City; Reviewer of religious books. Recreations: reading; running; leading pilgrimages to the Holy Land. Address: The Manse, Auldearn, Nairn, IV12 5SX; T.-Nairn 53180.

Shaw, Rev. Alistair Neil, MA (Hons), BD (Hons). Minister, Laigh Kirk, Kilmarnock, since 1988 (Minister, Relief Parish Church, Bourtreehill, Irvine, 1982-88); b. 6.7.53, Kilbarchan; m., Brenda Bruce; 2 d. Educ. Paisley Grammar School; Glasgow University. Recreations: foreign travel; ancient history; swimming. Address: 1 Holmes Farm Road, Kilmarnock, KA1 1TP; T.-Kilmarnock 25416.

Shaw, Professor Douglas William David, MA, LLB, BD, DD, WS. Professor of Divinity, St. Andrews University, since 1979 (Dean, Faculty of Divinity, 1983-86, Principal, St. Mary's College, since 1986); Minister, Church of Scotland, since 1960; b. 25.6.28, Edinburgh; m., Edinburgh Academy; Loretto; Ashbury College, Ottawa; St. John's College, Cambridge; Edinburgh University. Practised law as WS (Partner, Davidson and Syme, WS, Edinburgh), 1952-57; Assistant Minister, St. George's West Church, Edinburgh, 1960-63; Official Observer, Second Vatican Council, Rome, 1962; Lecturer in Divinity, Edinburgh University, 1963-79; Principal, New College, and Dean, Faculty of Divinity, Edinburgh, 1973-78; Visiting Fellow, Fitzwilliam College, Cambridge, 1978; Visiting Lecturer, Virginia University, 1979. Publications: Who is God?, 1968; The Dissuaders, 1978. Recreations: squash; golf; hill-walking. Address: (h.) 40 North Street, St. Andrews, Fife, KY16 9AQ; T.-0334 77254.

Shaw, Rev. Duncan, BD (Hons), MTh. Minister, St. John's, Bathgate, since 1978; b. 10.4.47, Blantyre; m., Margaret S. Moore; 2 s.; 1 d. Educ. St. John's Grammar School, Hamilton; Hamilton Academy; Trinity College, Glasgow University. Assistant Minister, Netherlee Parish Church, Glasgow, 1974-77. Clerk, West Lothian Presbytery, since 1982 (Moderator, 1989-90). Recreations: gardening; travel (in Scotland). Address: St. John's Parish Church Manse, Mid Street, Bathgate, EH48 1QD; T.-Bathgate 53146.

Shaw, Professor John Calman, CBE, BL, CA, FCMA, MBCS. Deputy Governor, Bank of Scotland, since 1991; b. 10.7.32, Perth; m., Shirley Botterill; 3 d. Educ. Strathallan;

Edinburgh University. Qualified as Chartered Accountant, 1954; Partner, Graham, Smart & Annan, CA, Edinburgh, latterly Deloitte Haskins & Sells, 1960-1987; Executive Director, Scottish Financial Enterprise, 1986-90; President, Institute of Chartered Accountants of Scotland, 1983-84; Johnstone Smith Professor of Accountancy, Glasgow University, 1977-83. Director: Scottish Mortgage and Trust PLC, Scottish American Investment Company PLC, TR European Growth Trust PLC, US Smaller Companies Trust PLC; Director, Scottish Enterprise; Member, Scottish Industrial Development Advisory Board; Member, Universities Funding Council; Lay Director, Scottish Chamber Orchestra; Deputy Chairman, Edinburgh Festival Society; Trustee, David Hume Institute; author of various texts and publications on accountancy. Recreations: music; walking; travel. Address: (b.) The Mound, Edinburgh, EH1 1YZ.

Shaw, John Campbell, BSc, MSc, MRTPI. Managing Director, East Kilbride Development Corporation, since 1990; b. 2.8.49, Belfast; m., Sheila Kerr Thomson; 2 d. Educ. Grosvenor High School, Belfast; Queens University, Belfast; Heriot-Watt University, Edinburgh. Lanarkshire County Council, 1973-75; Motherwell District Council, 1975-78; East Kilbride Development Corporation, since 1978: Head of Planning, 1982, Technical Director, 1986. Board Member, Lanarkshire Development Agency; Member, Town and Country Planning Association; contributor to various international symposia on matters relating to new or expanded community development. Recreations: squash; tennis; golf; watersports. Address: (b.) Atholl House, East Kilbride, G74 1LU; T.-03552 41111.

Shaw, Mark Robert, BA, MA, DPhil. Keeper of Natural History, National Museums of Scotland, since 1983; b. 11.5.45, Sutton Coldfield; m., Francesca Dennis Wilkinson; 2 d. Educ. Dartington Hall School; Oriel College, Oxford. Research Assistant (Entomology), Zoology Department, Manchester University, 1973-76; University Research Fellow, Reading University, 1977-80; Assistant Keeper, Department of Natural History, Royal Scottish Museum, 1980-83. Recreations: field entomology; family life. Address: (h.) 48 St. Albans Road, Edinburgh, EH9 2LU; T.-031-667 0577.

Shaw, Richard Wright, MA. Principal, Paisley University, since 1987; b. 22.9.41, Preston; m., Susan Angela; 2 s. Educ. Lancaster Royal Grammar School; Sidney Sussex College, Cambridge. Assistant Lecturer in Management, then Lecturer in Economics, Leeds University, 1964-69; Lecturer in Economics, then Senior Lecturer, Stirling University, 1969-84; part-time Lecturer, Glasgow University, 1978-79; Visiting Lecturer, Newcastle University, NSW, 1982; Head, Department of Economics, Stirling University, 1982-84; Professor and Head, Department of Economics and Management, Paisley College, 1984-86; Vice Principal, 1986. Director, Renfrewshire Enterprise. Recreations: walking; listening to music. Address: (b.) Paisley College, High Street, Paisley, PA1 2BE; T.-041-848 3000.

Shaw, Professor Susan Angela, MA (Cantab). Professor, Department of Marketing, Strathclyde University; former Professor of Marketing, Stirling University; General Secretary, Federation Europeenne De La Salmoniculture, 1986-88; b. 1.6.43, Bristol; m., Richard Shaw; 2 s. Educ. Kingswood Grammar School, Bristol; Girton College, Cambridge. Marketing Executive, ICI Fibres; Lecturer in Economics, Stirling University. Publications: The World of Business (Co-author); Marketing for Fish Farmers; Salmon Economics and Marketing (Co-author); Marketing the Products of Aquaculture. Recreations: hill-walking; opera. Address: (b.) Department of Marketing, Strathclyde

University, Stenhouse Buulding, 173 Cathedral Street, Glasgow, G4 0RQ.

Shaw-Dunn, Gilbert, BSc, MBChB, FRCP Glas, MRCPsych. Consultant Psychiatrist, Greater Glasgow Health Board, since 1985; b. 20.1.49, Glasgow. Educ. Hillhead High School, Glasgow; Glasgow University. Trained, Glasgow Royal Infirmary and Royal Edinburgh Hospital; Consultant in psychiatry of old age, Leverndale Hospital, Glasgow. Recreations: domesticity; dog-walking; computing; reading. Address: (h.) 2 Buchlyvie Road, Ralston, Paisley, Renfrewshire.

Shaw-Stewart, Sir Houston (Mark), 11th Bt, MC (1950), TD. Vice Lord Lieutenant, Strathclyde Region (Eastwood, Renfrew and Inverclyde Districts), since 1980; b. 24.4.31; m., Lucinda Victoria Fletcher; 1 s. Educ. Eton. Coldstream Guards, 1949; 2nd Lt., Royal Ulster Rifles, Korea, 1950; Ayrshire Yeomanry, 1952; Member, Queen's Bodyguard for Scotland (Royal Company of Archers). Address: (h.) Ardgowan, Inverkip, Renfrewshire, PA16 0DW.

Shaw-Stewart, Lady (Lucinda Victoria), FRSA. National Trust for Scotland: Member, Executive Committee, since 1985, Member, Curatorial Committee, since 1982, Member, Merchandising Committee, since 1985; Trustee, Wallace Collection, since 1987; b. 29.9.49, Harrogate; m., Sir Houston Shaw-Stewart Bt; 1 s. Educ. Cranborne Chase School; diploma from Study Centre for the History of the Fine and Decorative Arts. Freelance Lecturer in Fine and Decorative Arts, 1969-82; National Trust for Scotland: London Representative, 1978-82, Member, Council, 1983-88. President, Inverclyde Branch, Save the Children Fund; Honorary Vice President, Ardgowan Hospice, Greenock; Member, Council of Management, Formakin Trust. Address: (h.) Ardgowan, Inverkip, Renfrewshire PA16 0DW; T.-0475 521226.

Shearer, Magnus MacDonald, JP. Lord Lieutenant of Shetland, since 1982; Honorary Consul for Sweden in Shetland and Orkney, since 1958; Honorary Consul for Federal Republic of Germany in Shetland, 1972-87; b. 27.2.24; m., Martha Nicolson Henderson; 1 s. Educ. Anderson Educational Institute, Shetland; George Watson's College, Edinburgh. Royal Navy, Atlantic, Mediterranean and Far East, 1942-46; Royal Artillery TA, commissioned 2nd Lt., 1949; TARO, rank Captain, 1959; Honorary Secretary, Lerwick Branch, RNLI, since 1968; Member, Lerwick Town Council, 1963-69; Deputy Lieutenant of Shetland, 1973. Recreations: reading; bird watching; ships. Address: (h.) Birka, Cruester, Bressay, Shetland, ZE2 9EL; T.-0595 82 363.

Shedden, Alfred Charles, MA, LLB. Managing Partner, McGrigor Donald, since 1985; b. 30.6.44, Edinburgh; m., Irene; 1 s.; 1 d. Educ. Arbroath High School; Aberdeen University. McGrigor Donald: Apprentice, 1967-69, Assistant, 1969-70, Partner, 1971. Director, Scottish Financial Enterprise, since 1989; Chairman, Legal Resources Group, since 1991. Address: (b.) Pacific House, 70 Wellington Street, Glasgow; T.-041-248 6677.

Sheehan, Sheriff Albert Vincent, MA, LLB. Sheriff of Tayside, Central and Fife, at Falkirk, since 1983; b. 23.8.36, Edinburgh; m., Edna Georgina Scott Hastings; 2 d. Educ. Bo'ness Academy; Edinburgh University. 2nd Lt., 1st Bn., Royal Scots (The Royal Regiment), 1960; Captain, Directorate of Army Legal Services, 1961; Depute Procurator Fiscal, Hamilton, 1961-71; Senior Depute Procurator Fiscal, Glasgow, 1971-74; Deputy Crown Agent for Scotland, 1974-79; Scottish Law Commission, 1979-81; Sheriff of Lothian and Borders, at Edinburgh, 1981-83. Leverhulme Fellow, 1971. Publications: Criminal Procedure in Scotland and France, 1975; Criminal Procedure, 1990. Recreations: naval history; travel; curling. Address: (b.) Sheriff Court House, Falkirk; T.-Falkirk 20822.

Sheehan, Michael John, BSc (Econ), PhD, FBIS. Director, Strategic and Political Analysis Ltd., since 1988; Senior Lecturer in International Relations, Department of Politics and International Relations, Aberdeen University, since 1990; Director, Aberdeen University Space Policy Research Unit, since 1991; b. 26.6.54, London. Educ. Cardinal Vaughan School, Kensington; University College of Wales, Aberystwyth. Lecturer in International Relations, Aberdeen University, 1979-86; Research Associate, International Institute in Strategic Studies, 1986-87. Publications: The Arms Race; The Economist Pocket Guide to Defence; Arms Control: theory and practice; A Bibliography of Arms Control Verification. Recreations: hill-walking; war-gaming; Aberdeen Football Club. Address: (b.) Department of Politics and International Relations, Aberdeen University, Regent Walk, Aberdeen, AB9 2UB; T.-0224 272726.

Shelton, Richard Graham John, BSc, PhD. Officer-in-Charge, DAFS Freshwater Fisheries Laboratory, Pitlochry, since 1982; b. 3.7.42, Aylesbury; m., Freda Carstairs; 2 s. Educ. Royal Grammar School, High Wycombe; St. Andrews University. Research work, Burnham-on-Crouch Laboratory, MAFF, 1968-72; Assistant to Controller of Fisheries Research and Development, MAFF Fisheries Laboratory, Lowestoft, 1972-76 and (from 1974) DAFS Marine Laboratory, Aberdeen; worked on the population ecology of Crustacea, 1976-82. Recreations: shooting; fishing; steam model railways. Address: (b.) DAFS, Freshwater Fisheries Laboratory, Faskally, Pitlochry, PH16 5LB; T.-0796 2060.

Shepherd, David Arnot, JP, BSc, FRICS, IRRV. Senior Partner, J. & E. Shepherd, Chartered Surveyor, since 1963; b. 28.2.30, Dundee; m., Irene; 2 s.; 3 d. Educ. High School of Dundee; Mill Hill School, London; London University. Commissioned 2nd Lt., Royal Engineers, 1949. President, Property Owners and Factors of Scotland, 1963; President, Rating and Valuation Association, 1968; Member, Glenrothes Development Corporation, 1970-76; Member, Scottish Local Government Property Commission, 1973-76; Member, Lands Tribunal for Scotland, 1987-89. Recreations: skiing; golf; swimming; travel. Address: (b.) 13 Albert Square, Dundee; T.-0382 200454.

Shepherd, Rev. Henry Arthur, MA, BD. Minister, Balerno, since 1980; b. 27.5.33, Kilmarnock; m., Joyce Margaret Cameron Hardy; 1 s.; 1 d. Educ. Kilmarnock Academy; Edinburgh University; Basel University. Assistant Lecturer in New Testament, Edinburgh University, 1959-62; Minister, Ruthrieston West Church, Aberdeen, 1962-72; Assistant Secretary, Department of Education, Church of Scotland, 1972-80. Convener, Nomination Committee, 1985-88; Vice Convener, Education for the Ministry Commitee, 1989-92. Recreations: gardening; music. Address: The Manse, 3 Johnsburn Road, Balerno, Midlothian; T.-031-449 3830.

Shepherd, Professor James, BSc, MB, ChB, PhD, MRCPath, FRCP (Glas). Professor in Pathological Biochemistry, Glasgow University, since 1987 (Reader, 1984-87); b. 8.4.44, Motherwell; m., Janet Bulloch Kelly; 1 s.; 1 d. Educ. Hamilton Academy; Glasgow University. Lecturer, Glasgow University: Biochemistry, 1968-72, Pathological Biochemistry, 1972-77; Assistant Professor of Medicine, Baylor College of Medicine, Houston, Texas, 1976-77; Senior Lecturer in Pathological Biochemistry, Glasgow University, 1977-84; Visiting Professor of Medicine, Geneva University, 1984. Address: (b.) Department of Biochemistry, Royal Infirmary, Glasgow, G4 OSF; T.-041-552 3535, Ext. 5279.

Shepherd, Robert Horne (Robbie), AScA. Freelance Broadcaster, since 1976; b. 30.4.36, Dunecht, Aberdeen; m., Agnes Margaret (Esma); 1 s. Educ. Robert Gordon's College, Aberdeen. Left school at 15 to work in accountant's office; National Service, two years; joined fish firm as Assistant Accountant, then with fish group for 13 years as Management Accountant; left to become self-employed in that capacity; now full-time on radio and television. Recreations: golf; gardening; traditional music. Address: (h.) 15 Balgownie Crescent, Bridge of Don, Aberdeen.

Sherrard, Rev. (Henry) Dane, BD. Minister, Buckhaven Parish Church, since 1976; b. 13.3.46, Watford; m., Rachel Joan Hammerton. Educ. Dundee High School; St. Andrews University. President, SRC, St. Andrews, 1965-66; Vice President, Scottish Union of Students, 1966; Assistant, Abronhill Parish Church, 1970; Church of Scotland Minister, Northern Italy (responsible for Seamen's Mission), 1971-76. Area Board Member, MSC, 1983- 88; Chairman, Aberhill Youth Project, 1979-82; Chairman, Levenmouth Council of Social Service, 1978-82; in 1983, began employment scheme which led to Buckhaven Parish Church Agency, 1983-91, and Buckhaven Theatre; Moderator, Presbytery of Kirkcaldy, 1988-89; Member, Board, Community Business Scotland, since 1991. Recreations: theatre and music; a passion for Gilbert and Sullivan and cricket. Address: Buckhaven Theatre, Lawrence Street, Buckhaven, KY8 1BQ; T.-0592 715577.

Sherrington, Professor David Colin, BSc, PhD, FRSC, CChem, FRSE. Professor of Polymer Chemistry, Department of Pure and Applied Chemistry, since 1987; b. 5.3.45, Liverpool; m., Valerie. Educ. Waterloo Grammar School; Liverpool University. Lecturer, then Senior Lecturer, Strathclyde University, 1971-84; Polymer Science Area Head, Unilever Research, 1984-87; Reader, Strathclyde University, 1987. Editor, Reactive Polymers. Recreation: angling. Address: (h.) 10 Hawthorne Avenue, Lenzie, Glasgow, G66 4RA; T.-041-776 1747.

Sherwood, Professor John Neil, DSc, PhD, CChem, FRSC, FRSE. Burmah Professor of Physical Chemistry, Strathclyde University, since 1983; Deputy Principal, since 1988; b. 8.11.33, Redruth, Cornwall; m., Margaret Enid Shaw; 2 d. Educ. Aireborough Grammar School; Bede College, Durham University. Research Fellow, Hull University, 1958-60; Lecturer and Reader, Strathclyde University, 1960-83. Recreations: hill-walking; photography; gardening. Address: (b.) Department of Pure and Applied Chemistry, Strathclyde University, Glasgow, G1 1XL; T.-041-552 4400.

Shiach, Sheriff Gordon Iain Wilson, MA, LLB, BA (Hons). Sheriff of Lothian and Borders, at Edinburgh, since 1984; b. 15.10.35, Elgin; m., Margaret Grant Smith; 2 d. Educ. Lathallan; Gordonstoun; Edinburgh University; Open University. Admitted Advocate, 1960; practised as Advocate, 1960-72; Sheriff of Fife and Kinross, at Dunfermline, 1972-79; Sheriff of Lothian and Borders, at Linlithgow, 1979-84; Hon. Sheriff, Elgin, since 1986; Member: Council of Sheriffs' Association, 1989-92; Standing Committee on Criminal Procedure, 1989-92; Board, Lothian Family Conciliation Service, since 1989; Parole Board for Scotland, since 1990. Recreations: walking; swimming; music; art; theatre. Address: (b.) Sheriff Court House, Lawnmarket, Edinburgh, EH1 2NS; T.-031-226 7181.

Shirreffs, Murdoch John, MB, ChB, DObstRCOG, MRCGP. General Medical Practitioner and Medical Hypnotherapist, Aberdeen, since 1974; b. 25.5.47, Aberdeen; m., Jennifer McLeod. Educ. Aberdeen Grammar School; Aberdeen University. General Practice Trainer, since 1977; Secretary, Grampian Division, British Medical Association, since 1978; Member, BMA Scottish Council. Past President,

North of Scotland Veterans' Hockey Club. Recreations: hockey; opera and classical music; big band jazz; curling; DIY; gardening; food and wine; travel. Address: (h.) 72 Gray Street, Aberdeen, AB1 6JE; T.-0224 321998.

Short, Agnes Jean, BA (Hons), MLitt. Writer; b. Bradford, Yorkshire; m., Anthony Short (qv); 3 s.; 2 d. Educ. Bradford Girls' Grammar School; Exeter University; Aberdeen University. Various secretarial, research and teaching jobs, both in UK and abroad; took up writing, 1966; 17 novels, most of which have a Scottish setting; also short stories and radio; Constable Award, 1976. Recreations: dog-walking; whisky-tasting; good food; small hills. Address: (h.) Khantore, Crathie, by Ballater, Aberdeenshire, AB3 5TJ.

Short, Anthony, BSc (Econ), MA, BLitt. Reader in International Relations, Aberdeen University, since 1977 (Warden, Dunbar Hall, 1967- 89); b. 26.6.29, Singapore; m., Agnes Russell (see Agnes Jean Short); 3 s.; 2 d. Educ. Hele's School, Exeter; University College, Exeter; London School of Economics; University of Virginia; St. Catherine's, Oxford. National Service, Malaya, 1947-49; Lecturer, Bristol University, 1957-60; Lecturer, University of Malaya 1960-66; Visiting Fellow, Senior Lecturer, Reader, Department of Politics, Aberdeen University. Publications: The Communist Insurrection in Malaya 1948-60; The Origins of the Vietnam War. Recreations: malt whisky; wood gathering; temperate hill-walking. Address: (h.) Khantore, Crathie, by Ballater, Aberdeenshire, AB3 5TJ.

Short, Emeritus Professor David Somerset, MD, PhD, FRCP, FRCPEdin. Honorary Consultant Physician, Grampian Health Board, since 1983; Emeritus Professor in Clinical Medicine, Aberdeen University, since 1983; b. 6.8.18, Weston-super-Mare, Avon; m., Joan Anne McLay; 1 s.; 4 d. Educ. Bristol Grammar School; Cambridge University; Bristol University. RAMC, 1944-47; Senior Registrar in Medicine/Cardiology, Bristol, National Heart Hospital, London Hospital and Middlesex Hospital, London, 1948-59; Consultant Physician, Aberdeen Hospitals and Senior Lecturer, Aberdeen University, 1960-83; former Physician to The Queen in Scotland. Recreation: walking. Address: (h.) 48 Victoria Street, Aberdeen, AB9 2PL; T.-0224 645853.

Sibbald, Alexander, BSc. Headteacher, Hazlehead Academy, since 1984; b. 8.4.38, Edinburgh; m., Christina W.M. Mallinson; 1 s.; 1 d. Educ. George Heriot's School; Edinburgh University. Assistant Teacher of Science, Lindsay High School, Bathgate, 1961-63; Lecturer, Regent Road Institute, Edinburgh, 1963-66; Principal Teacher of Science, Castlebrae High School, Edinburgh, 1966-75; Assistant Head/Depute Head, Whitburn Academy, West Lothian, 1975-80; Head Teacher, Kemnay Academy, 1981-84. Recreations: wide range of sports; car restoration. Address: (b.) Groat's Road, Aberdeen; T.-Aberdeen 310184.

Sibbett, Professor Wilson, BSc, PhD. Professor of Physics, St. Andrews University, and Chairman, Department of Physics, since 1985; b. 15.3.48, Portglenone, N. Ireland; m., Barbara Anne Brown; 3 d. Educ. Ballymena Technical College; Queen's University, Belfast. Postdoctoral Research Fellow, Blackett Laboratory, Imperial College, London, 1973-76; Lecturer in Physics, then Reader, Imperial College, 1976-85. Member, Physics Committee, Science and Engineering Research Council; Member, Optoelectronics Sub-committee, SERC; Editorial Board Member, Journal of Physics B; Fellow, Royal Society of Edinburgh. Recreation: golf (to low standard). Address: (b.) Department of Physics and Astronomy, St. Andrews University, North Haugh, St. Andrews, KY16 9SS; T.-0334 76161.

Sidgwick, Richard Twining, JP, DL, MSc, FRICS. Partner, West Highland Estates Office, since 1974; b. 17.7.44, Crossmichael; m., Alison Janet Baggallay; 1 s.; 2 d. Educ. Fort Augustus Abbey School; Reading. Director, Lochaber Limited, 1991; Chairman, British Field Sports Society, Highland Region, 1987; Chairman, Shiel District Fishery Board, 1990; Chairman, West Lochaber Deer Management Group, 1990. Recreations: country sports; gardening. Address: (h.) Inverlair Lodge, Roy Bridge, Inverness-shire, PH31 4AR; T.-039785 246.

Sillars, Evelyn Murdoch, MBE, JP, MA. Member, Cunninghame District Council, since 1974; Member, HIDB Consultative Council, since 1975; Director, Caledonian MacBrayne Ltd.; b. 24.11.23, Ayr; m., Douglas A. Sillars; 4 d. Educ. Ayr Academy; Glasgow University. Intelligence Section, Foreign Office (War Service); Teacher of English and Religious Education; former Honorary Secretary, Scottish Committee, War on Want; County Councillor, holding post of County Convener at time of reorganisation (only woman to hold such appointment in Scotland); District Councillor for Arran; Executive Member, Arran Council of Social Service; Executive Member, Arran Tourist Association; Centre Organiser for Red Cross; Church Elder. Recreations: music; bridge; bowling. Address: (h.) Lichfield Lodge, Brodick, Isle of Arran; T.-0770 2246.

Sillars, James. MP (SNP), Glasgow Govan, 1988-92; b. 4.10.37, Ayr; m., Margo MacDonald (qv); 1 s.; 3 d. Educ. Ayr Academy. Member, Ayr Town Council and Ayr County Council Education Committee, 1960s; Member, Western Regional Hospital Board, 1965-70; Head, Organisation Department, Scottish TUC, 1968-70; MP, South Ayrshire, 1970-79. Recreation: reading.

Sime, Martin, MA. Director, Scottish Council for Voluntary Organisations, since 1991; b. 23.9.53, Edinburgh. Educ. George Heriot's; St. Andrews University; Edinburgh University. Social and Economic History Researcher, 1976-78; Sheep Farmer, 1978-81; Freelance Researcher, 1982; Project Manager, Sprout Market Garden, 1983-85; Development/Principal Officer (Day Services), Scottish Association for Mental Health, then Director, 1985-91; Member, Executive Committee, Edinburgh Association for Mental Health; Council Member, Scottish Business in the Community. Recreations: cinema; food; bridge. Address: (b.) 18/19 Claremont Crescent, Edinburgh, EH7 4QD; T.-031-556 3882.

Simmers, Brian Maxwell, CA. Managing Director, Scottish Highland Hotels, since 1963; b. 26.2.40, Glasgow; m., Constance Ann Turner; 3 s. Educ. Glasgow Academy; Larchfield; Loretto. President, Glasgow Academical Club; Governor, Glasgow Academy; Honorary Secretary, Rugby Internationals' Golfing Society. Played rugby for Scotland (seven caps) and Barbarians. Recreations: rugby; golf; shooting; skiing. Address: (b.) 98 West George Street, Glasgow, G2 1PW; T.-041-332 3033.

Simmers, Graeme Maxwell, OBE, CA. Chairman, Scottish Highland Hotels Group Ltd., since 1972; b. 2.5.35, Glasgow; m., Jennifer M.H. Roxburgh; 2 s.; 2 d. Educ. Glasgow Academy; Loretto School. Qualified CA, 1959; commissioned Royal Marines, 1959-61. Former Partner, Kidsons Simmers CA; Member, Scottish Tourist Board, 1979-86; Chairman, HCBA (Scotland), 1984-86; Past Chairman, Board of Management, BHRCA; Elder and Treasurer, Killearn Kirk; Governor, Queen's College, Glasgow, and Loretto School; Past Chairman, Championship Committee, Royal and Ancient Golf Club of St. Andrews. Recreations: rugby; golf; skiing; literary society. Address: (h.) Kincaple, Boquhan, Balfron, near Glasgow, G63 ORW; T.-0360 40375.

Simpson, Andrew Rutherford, MB, ChB, D(Obst)RCOG. Principal, general practice, since 1967; b. 13.7.32, Hawick; m., Helen Margaret Douglas; 3 d. Educ. Merchiston Castle School, Edinburgh; Edinburgh University. BMA: Member, Scottish Council, 1972; Past Chairman, Scottish Borders Division, 1980, Representative for Borders on Scottish Council, since 1972; Past President, now Medical Officer and Life Member, Hawick Rugby Club; Past President, Hawick Callants Club; Chairman, Douglas Haig Court. Recreations: rugby involvement; golf; philately. Address: (h.) Netherfield, Buccleuch Road, Hawick, TD9 0EL; T.-0450 72459.

Simpson, David, CBE, DSc, CEng, FIEE. Chairman, Spider Systems Ltd.; Chairman, Simpson Research Ltd.; Chairman, Albacom PLC; b. 23.11.26, Ceres; m., Janice Ann; 1 s.; 2 d. Educ. Bell Baxter School, Cupar; Dundee Technical College; Stanford University. R. & D. Engineer, Marconi, 1952-56; Managing Director, Microcell Electronics, 1956-60; General Manager, Hughes Microelectronics, 1960-62; Managing Director, Hewlett Packard Ltd., 1962-70; Director, George Kent Ltd., 1970-76; President, Gould Corp., Chicago, 1976-88; Chairman, various UK companies, 1988-92. Recreations: hill-walking; wood-carving. Address: (h.) Elvingston House, Tranent, East Lothian; T.-0875 52878.

Simpson, David James, MIEIE, IEng. Principal, Shetland College of FE, since 1988; b. 29.5.30, Tiverton, Cheshire; m., Joan Johnson; 2 d. Educ. Davies College, Chester; Wigan College of Technology. UKAEA Design Headquarters, 1956-61; Michelin Tyre, 1961-62; Further Education Lecturer, 1962-88. Address: (b.) Shetland College of FE, Gressy Loan, Lerwick, Shetland, ZE1 0BB; T.-0595 5514.

Simpson, Eric William McIntyre, DipEdTech, ALA. Chairman, Glasgow and West Hospital Broadcasting Service, since 1975; Co-ordinator, Learning Resources, Anniesland College, since 1988; freelance broadcaster; b. 18.2.45, Glasgow. Educ. Victoria Drive School, Glasgow; Strathclyde University. Former Administrative Director, Glasgow and West Hospital Broadcasting Service; SCOTVEC Subject Assessor for National Certificate; Member, National Working Party on Resource Based Learning; Radio Judge, Television and Radio Industries Club of Scotland Radio Awards, 1987, 1988. Recreations: reading; spectator sports; listening to radio. Address: (h.) 11 Victoria Park Drive South, Glasgow, G14.

Simpson, George Alexander. Chairman, Thainstone House Hotel Ltd., Glegg & Thomson Ltd., Carden Place Investments Ltd.; b. 13.1.43; m., Lorraine; 1 s.; 1 d. Educ. Peterhead Academy. Founded Kildonnan Investments Ltd., late '60s; sold, 1989; founded Craigendarroch Group, 1983; Director, North of Scotland Radio Ltd. (Northsound). Recreations: golf; swimming; football. Address: (h.) 22 Rubislaw Den North, Aberdeen, AB2 4AN; T.-0224 644202.

Simpson, Gordon Russell, DSO and bar, LVO, TD. Stockbroker; b. 2.1.17, Tayport; m., Marion Elizabeth King, deceased; 2 s. Educ. Rugby. Member, Edinburgh Stock Exchange, 1938; Partner, Bell Cowan & Co.; Lothians and Border Horse, 1939-46, commanding 2nd Regiment, 1944-46; Chairman, Edinburgh Stock Exchange, 1961-63; Chairman, Scottish Stock Exchange, 1965-66; President, Council of ASE, 1971-73; Deputy Chairman, The Stock Exchange, 1973-78; Director, General Accident, 1967-87, Chairman, 1979-87. DL, Central Region, Stirling and Falkirk Districts; Member of Court, Stirling University, 1980-88; Commissioner, Queen Victoria School; Member, Board, Scottish Chamber Orchestra; Member, Executive Committee, Scottish Veterans Garden City Association; Kirk Elder. Recreations: music; skiing; archery; tennis. Address: Bell Lawrie White, 7 Drumsheugh Gardens, Edinburgh, EH3 7QH.

Simpson, Professor Hugh Walter, MB, ChB, MD, PhD, FRCPath, FRCP(Glas). Professor in Pathology, Glasgow University, since 1988; Head of Pathology, Glasgow Royal Infirmary, since 1984; b. 4.4.31, Ceres, Fife; m., Myrtle Emslie (see Myrtle Simpson); 3 s.; 1 d. Educ. Bryanston; Edinburgh University. Leader of numerous expeditions to polar and tropical regions; awarded Polar Medal and Mungo Park Medal. Recreation: skiing. Address: (h.) 7 Cleveden Crescent, Glasgow, G12 0PD; T.-041-357 1091.

Simpson, Ian Christopher, LLB. Sheriff of South Strathclyde, Dumfries and Galloway, since 1988, at Airdrie, since 1991; b. 5.7.49, Edinburgh; m., Christine Margaret Anne Strang; 2 s. Educ. Glenalmond; Edinburgh University. Admitted to Faculty of Advocates, 1974. Captain, Scottish Universities Golfing Society, 1989; President, All Sphere Club, 1989-90. Recreation: golf. Address: (b.) Airdrie Sheriff Court, Graham Street, Airdrie, ML6 6EE; T.-0236 751121.

Simpson, Rev. James Alexander, BSc (Hons), BD, STM. Minister, Dornoch Cathedral, since 1976; b. 9.3.34, Glasgow; m., Helen Gray McCorquodale; 3 s.; 2 d. Educ. Eastwood Secondary School; Glasgow University; Union Seminary, New York. Minister: Grahamston Church, Falkirk, 1960-66, St. John's Renfield, Glasgow, 1966-76. Publications: There is a time to ....; Marriage Questions Today; Doubts are not Enough; Holy Wit; Laughter Lines; The Master Mind; Dornoch Cathedral; More Holy Wit; Keywords of Faith. Recreations: golf; photography; writing. Address: Cathedral Manse, Dornoch, IV25 3HN; T.-086 2810296.

Simpson, James White, BSc, MCIT, MRIN. Divisional Manager, Marine Services, Forth Ports Authority, since 1986 (Port Manager, Grangemouth, 1982-86); Director, Forth Estuary Towage Ltd., since 1986; b. 30.8.44, St. Andrews; m., Barbara Hutton; 1 s.; 1 d. Educ. Grangemouth High School; Buckhaven High School; Leith Nautical College; Plymouth Polytechnic. Cadet, Furness Prince Lines, 1961-64; Navigating Officer: Shaw Savill Line, 1965-68, Overseas Containers Ltd., 1969-70; Assistant Harbour Master, then Assistant to Port Superintendent, Grangemouth, 1973-77; Port Superintendent, Leith and Granton, 1978-82. Recreation: sailing. Address: (b.) Forth Ports Authority, Tower Place, Leith, EH6 7DB; T.-031-554 6473.

Simpson, Professor John Alexander, MD Hon. (Glasgow), FRCPLond, FRCPEdin, FRCPGlas, FRSE. Emeritus Professor of Neurology, Glasgow University, since 1987 (Professor of Neurology, 1965-87); Senior Neurologist, Institute of Neurological Sciences, Southern General Hospital, Glasgow, 1965-87; Consultant Neurologist, Civil Service Commission, 1974-87; b. 30.3.22, Greenock; m., Dr. Elizabeth M.H. Simpson; 2 s.; 1 d. Educ. Greenock Academy; Glasgow University. Surgeon-Lieutenant, RNVR; Registrar in Medicine, Southern General Hospital, Glasgow; Lecturer in Medicine, Glasgow University; MRC Research Fellow, National Hospital for Nervous Diseases, London; Senior Lecturer in Medicine, Glasgow University; Consultant Physician, Western Infirmary, Glasgow; Reader in Neurology, Edinburgh University. President, Association of British Neurologists, 1985-86; Past Chairman, Scottish Epilepsy Association; former Consultant Neurologist to British Army in Scotland; Editor, Journal of Neurology, Neurosurgery and Psychiatry. Recreations: violinist (Glasgow Chamber Orchestra and Scottish Fiddle Orchestra); painting; sailing. Address: (h.) 87 Glencairn Drive, Glasgow, G41 4LL; T.-041-423 2863.

Simpson, John Moir, FRICS, FCIArb. Senior Partner, John M. Simpson & Co., Chartered Quantity Surveyors; Senior Partner, Wilkie & Simpson, Chartered Surveyors; b. 29.1.28; m., Elizabeth Russell Faulds; 1 s.; 1 d. Educ. Whitehill Secondary School, Glasgow; Royal Technical College,

Glasgow. Chief Quantity Surveyor, Cumbernauld Development Corporation, 1965-69. Chairman, Advisory Panel, Glasgow College of Building and Printing, since 1965; Chairman, Valuation Appeals Committee (North Strathclyde); former Member, Cumbernauld Development Corporation; Chairman, Cumbernauld Information and Technology Board; Vice-Chairman, Cumbernauld CAB, since 1976; Member, Board of Management, Cumbernauld and Kilsyth Enterprise Trust; Member, Cumbernauld International Sports Trust; Past President, Cumbernauld Rotary Club and Cumbernauld Burns Club; Member, Executive Committee, Glasgow Association of Burns Clubs. Recreations: bowling; curling. Address: (h.) 17 Glen View, Cumbernauld, Glasgow, G67 2DA; T.-0236 722933.

Simpson, Myrtle Lillias. Author and Lecturer; Member, Scottish Sports Council; Past Chairman, Scottish National Ski Council; b. 5.7.31, Aldershot; m., Professor Hugh Simpson (qv); 3 s.; 1 d. Educ. 19 schools (father in Army). Writer/Explorer; author of 12 books, including travel, biography, historical and children's; first woman to ski across Greenland; attempted to ski to North Pole (most northerly point reached by a woman unsupported); numerous journeys in polar regions on ski or canoe; exploration in China and Peru; Mungo Park Medal. Recreations: climbing; skiing; canoeing. Address: (h.) 7 Cleveden Crescent, Glasgow, G12 0PD; T.-041-357 1091.

Simpson, Patrick William, CA. Chairman, Lothian Building Preservation Trust; Director, The Queen's Hall (Edinburgh); Member: Edinburgh New Town Conservation Committee, Queen's Nursing Institute Scotland, Scotland's Gardens Scheme; General Commissioner of Income Tax; b. 14.3.22, Edinburgh; m., Elizabeth Wilson (deceased); 1 s.; 1 d. Educ. Rugby. Royal Artillery and Ayrshire Yeomanry, N. Africa and Italy, 1941-46; Partner, Chiene & Tait, CA, 1952-87. Former Board Member, Scottish Opera and Edinburgh Festival Society. Recreations: music; skiing; painting. Address: (h.) 23 Moray Place, Edinburgh, EH3 6DA; T.-031-225 8020.

Simpson, Robert Keith, FCCA, IPFA. Scottish Audit Adviser to Chartered Institute of Public Finance and Accountancy, since 1989; b. 26.7.43, Barrow-in-Furness; m., Brenda Mary Baines; 2 s. Educ. Barrow-in-Furness Grammar School. Accountant, Barrow-in-Furness County Borough Council, 1959-72; Principal Auditor, Bristol City Council, 1972-74; Chief Auditor, Avon County Council, 1974-77; Assistant Director of Finance, South Yorkshire County Council, 1977-82; Depute Controller of Audit, Commission for Local Authority Accounts in Scotland, 1982-85; Controller of Audit, Commission for Local Authority Accounts in Scotland, 1985-89. Former Editor, Audit Bulletin, CIPFA. Publications: Internal Audit in the Public Sector; Audit in the Public Sector (Co-author). Recreations: golf; archery; hill-walking. Address: (h.) Cerna, 69 Dirleton Avenue, North Berwick; T.-0620 4288.

Sinclair, Alan, MA (Hons), MBA. Chief Executive, The Wise Group, since 1987; Chairman, Energy Action Scotland, since 1986; b. 18.9.54, Bellshill. Educ. Our Lady's High School, Motherwell; St. Andrews University; Edinburgh University. Chairman, Scottish Education & Action for Development, 1978-79; Director, Heatwise Glasgow, 1983-86; Non-Executive Director, Main Tool Company, since 1989; appointed Fellow, German Marshall Fund, 1989; Director, Heatwise Enterprises, since 1986. Recreations: cross-country skiing; hill-walking; squash; not being rude about pot noodles. Address: (b.) 8 Elliot Place, Glasgow, G3 8EP; T.-041-248 3993.

Sinclair, Alexander, OBE, DL, FCII. President, The Golf Foundation, since 1991; b. 6.7.20, West Kilbride; m.,

Elizabeth Tennant; 2 s.; 1 d. Educ. Ardrossan Academy. Clerk, Norwich Union, 1938-40; Royal Artillery, 1940-46; joined Alexander Stenhouse Insurance Brokers, 1957 (Director, 1962); Chairman, British Insurance Brokers Association in Scotland, 1985; retired, 1985. Deputy Lieutenant, Lanarkshire, 1988; Captain, Royal & Ancient Golf Club, 1988-89; Chairman, R. & A. Selection Committee, 1969-75; President, European Golf Association, 1981-83; President, Scottish Golf Union, 1976-77; former Scottish golf internationalist and Scottish golf captain; awarded Frank Moran Award, 1979, for contribution to golf; West of Scotland Champion, 1950; semi-finalist, Scottish Amateur Championship, 1947-56; Lanarkshire Champion, three times; Scottish Senior Champion, 1979-84. Recreations: golf; curling; painting. Address: (h.) 17 Blairston Avenue, Bothwell, G71 8RZ; T.-0698 853359.

Sinclair, Professor Allan MacDonald, PhD, FRSE. Professor in Mathematical Analysis, Edinburgh University, since 1991 (Reader in Mathematics, 1977-91); b. 11.7.41, Johannesburg, South Africa; m., Patricia Margaret Bush; 1 s.; 1 d. Educ. Parktown Boys' High School, Johannesburg; Witwatersrand University; Newcastle-upon-Tyne University. Senior Lecturer, 1968-72, and Professor, 1972-73, in Mathematics, Witwatersrand University; Lecturer in Mathematics, Edinburgh University, 1973-77; Visiting Professor, California University, Los Angeles, 1978-79. Recreations: hill-walking; sculpture. Address: (b.) Department of Mathematics, Edinburgh University, James Clark Building, King's Buildings, Mayfield Road, Edinburgh, EH9 3JZ; T.-031-667 1081, Ext. 2812.

Sinclair, 17th Lord (Charles Murray Kennedy St. Clair), CVO. Lord Lieutenant, Dumfries and Galloway Region (District of Stewartry), 1982- 89; Extra Equerry to the Queen Mother, since 1953; Member, Queen's Bodyguard for Scotland (Royal Company of Archers); b. 21.6.14; m., Anne Lettice Cotterell; 1 s.; 2 d. Educ. Eton; Magdalene College, Cambridge. Served Second World War (mentioned in Despatches); retired Major, Coldstream Guards. Address: (h.) Knocknalling, St. John's Town of Dalry, Castle Douglas, Kirkcudbrightshire.

Sinclair, Rev. David Ian, BSc (Soc Sci), BD, DipSW. Minister, Martyrs Parish Church, since 1990; b. 23.1.55, Bridge of Allan; m., E. Mary Jones; 1 s.; 1 d. Educ. High School of Stirling; Aberdeen University; Bristol University; University College, Cardiff; Edinburgh University. National President, Student Christian Movement, 1975-76; Community Social Worker, Livingston, 1980-84; Assistant Minister, Dunblane Cathedral, 1987-88. Recreations: music; photography; armchair sport. Address: 49 Irvine Crescent, St. Andrews, Fife; T.-0334 72948.

Sinclair, Derek Urquhart, MA (Hons), MB, ChB, MRCGP, DPM. Senior Medical Officer, Scottish Home and Health Department, since 1988 (Medical Officer, 1987-88); b. 10.10.40, Falkirk; m., Dorothy Aalbregt; 1 s.; 2 d. Educ. Grangemouth High School; Falkirk High School; Glasgow University. Norwegian State Stipendiary, University of Oslo, 1965-66; Principal in general practice, Falkirk, 1972-86; Deputy Police Surgeon, Central Scotland Police, 1972-86; Regional Medical Officer, Scottish Home and Health Department, 1986-87. Recreations: gardening; walking; fishing. Address: (b.) St. Andrews House, Edinburgh, EH1 3DE; T.-031-244 2274.

Sinclair, Eric T.A., MA, DipEd. Rector, Kirkwall Grammar School, since 1991; b. 20.9.48, Edinburgh. Educ. Bell Baxter High School, Cupar; St. Andrews University; Edinburgh University; Moray House College. Taught, Teacher Training Colleges, Cameroon, Nigeria; Head of English, English High School, Istanbul; Assistant Rector, Forres Academy; Depute

Rector, Bridge of Don Academy. Address: (h.) Inganess Cottage, St. Ola, Kirkwall, Orkney.

Sinclair, Isabel Lillias, MA, BL, QC. Honorary Sheriff of Lothian and Borders, since 1979; b. Glasgow; m., J. Gordon MacDonald, BL. Educ. Shawlands Academy; Glasgow University. Newspaperwoman, 1933-46; Scottish Editor, BBC Woman's Hour, 1948; called to Scottish Bar, 1949; appointed Queen's Counsel, 1964; Sheriff Substitute, Lanarkshire at Airdrie, 1966-68; Sheriff of Lothian and Borders at Selkirk and Peebles, then Peebles and Edinburgh, 1968-79. Address: 30 Ravelston Garden, Edinburgh EH4 3LE; T.-031-337 9797.

Sinclair, Martin Fraser, MA, CA. Partner, Chiene & Tait, CA, since 1973; Director, Albyn Trust Ltd., since 1973; Director, NESSCO (Aberdeen) Ltd., since 1982; Director, Lawrie & Symington Ltd., since 1991; b. 18.7.45, Greenock; m., Patricia Anne Ogilvy Smith; 1 s.; 2 d. Educ. Edinburgh Academy; Edinburgh University. Apprentice, Chiene & Tait, CA; qualified, 1970; Peat Marwick Mitchell & Co., Vancouver, 1970-73. President, Institute of Chartered Accountants Benevolent Association, 1983-84 (Member, Property Committee, since 1979). Athletics Blue, Edinburgh University; Captain, Scottish Universities Athletics Team, 1969. Recreations: skiing; squash; orienteering. Address: (b.) 3 Albyn Place, Edinburgh, EH2 4NQ; T.-031-225 7515.

Sinfield, Professor Robert Adrian, BA, DipSocAdmin. Professor of Social Policy, Edinburgh University, since 1979; b. 3.11.38, Wallington, Surrey; m., Dorothy Anne Palmer; 2 d. Educ. Mercers' School, London; Balliol College, Oxford; London School of Economics. Assistant Lecturer/Lecturer/Senior Lecturer/Reader in Sociology, Essex University, 1965-79; Visiting Lecturer in Social Work, Bryn Mawr College and Columbia University, 1969-70; consultancies, OECD, 1965-68, 1970, 1983 and UN, 1970-71; Scientific Adviser to DHSS Chief Scientist, since 1980; Convener and Co-Founder, Unemployment Unit, 1981-91; Chair, Social Policy Association, 1986-89. Publications: The Long-Term Unemployed, 1968; Which Way for Social Work?, 1969; Industrial Welfare, 1971; The Workless State (Co-Editor), 1981; What Unemployment Means, 1981; Excluding Youth (Co-author), 1991. Address: (h.) 12 Eden Lane, Edinburgh, EH10 4SD; T.-031-447 2182.

Singleton, Major John Francis Maxwell, MA, DL. Deputy Lieutenant, Kincardineshire; b. 26.8.16, Colwall; m., Jean Osborne (deceased); 1 s.; 2 d. Educ. Uppingham; Pembroke College, Cambridge. Commissioned Royal Artillery, 1938; served Second World War, BEF, MEF, CMF, BLA; Instructor, Mons Officer Cadet School, 1949-52; Malayan emergency, 1953-54. Vice Chairman, NE TAVRA; County Commissioner for Scouts, Kincardineshire. Recreations: cricket and hockey (represented Army at both); golf; shooting. Address: Scotston of Kirkside, St. Cyrus, Montrose.

Sischy, Sheriff Mark, MA, LLB, SSC, NP. Sheriff at Glasgow and Strathkelvin, since 1990; Past President, Society of Solicitors in the Supreme Courts of Scotland; b. 14.7.45, Johannesburg; m., Judith Lewis; 2 d. Educ. George Watson's College, Edinburgh; Edinburgh University. Recreation: armchair sportsman.

Skene, Hugh Crawford. Scottish Composer; b. 24.2.19; m., Barbara Land; 1 d. Educ. Bristol. War Service as Camouflage Officer; graduated, 1949; Director of Orchestra, Buxton College; Founder Member and Musical Director, Buxton Opera Group; Director of Orchestras, City of Norwich School, 1953-73; compositions during this period include Derbyshire Rhapsody, Symphony from East Anglia and the cantata Birthday of Jesus; Musical Director, St. Cecilia Chorus and Orchestra, 13 years; returned to Scotland

(Hamilton Grammar School), 1973; Musical Director, Blantyre Choral Society and West End Sinfonia; retired from education service, 1983; later compositions include opera on Dumas' The Black Tulip, A Highland Symphony, Hebridean Poem, Concertino for Double Bass and orchestra, Song of the Psalms, various ensembles and fanfares; Fanfare '88, Edinburgh Festival, 1988; Flute Concerto; Saxophone Concerto; Three Islands Idylls; Barlow Caprice. Recreation: exploring and photographing remote Scotland. Address: (h.) Crowhills, by Hamilton, Lanarkshire, ML3 7XP; T.- Chapelton 303.

Skett, Paul Geoffrey, BSc (Hons), FilDr. Senior Lecturer in Pharmacology, Glasgow University, since 1988; Associate Schools Liaison Officer, since 8. 15.7.52, Liverpool; m., Barbara Ann; 2 d. Educ. Park High School, Birkenhead; Liverpool University. Ciba-Geigy Fellow, Karolinska Institute, Stockholm, 1973-77; Lecturer in Medical Chemistry, Karolinska Institute, 1977-78; Lecturer in Pharmacology, Glasgow University, 1978-88. Publications: 100 papers, including Introduction to Drug Metabolism (Co-author). Recreations: family; environment; photography; reading. Address: (b.) Department of Pharmacology, West Medical Building, Glasgow University, Glasgow, G12 8QQ; T.-041-339 8855.

Skinner, Professor Andrew, MA, BLitt, FRSE, FRSA. Daniel Jack Professor of Political Economy, since 1985, Vice-Principal, since 1991, Glasgow University; b. 11.1.35, Glasgow; m., Margaret Mary Robertson. Educ. Keil School, Dumbarton; Glasgow University; Cornell University, New York. Address: (h.) Glen House, Cardross, G82 5ES; T.-038 9841 603.

Skinner, Angus, MBA, BSc, CQSW. Chief Inspector of Social Work Services, Scotland, since 1992; Chief Social Work Adviser to Secretary of State for Scotland, since 1991; b. 9.1.50, Pakistan; m., Kate; 1 s. Educ. Daniel Stewart's, Edinburgh; Edinburgh University; London University; Strathclyde University. Cheshire County Council, 1971-72; Kent County Council, 1973-75; Lothian Region Social Work Department, 1976-88; Borders Region Social Work Department, 1988-91. Recreations: whenever possible. Address: (h.) 37 Hadfast Road, Cousland, Midlothian; T.- 031-663 6151.

Skinner, Basil Chisholm, OBE, MA, FSA. Former Director of Extra-Mural Studies, Edinburgh University; b. 1923, Edinburgh; m., Lydia Mary Mackinnon; 2 s. Educ. Edinburgh Academy; Edinburgh University. Army Service, Yorkshire Yeomanry and Intelligence Corps; Librarian, Glasgow School of Art, 1951-54; Assistant Keeper, Scottish National Portrait Gallery, 1954-66; joined Edinburgh University as Lecturer, 1966; Council Member, National Trust for Scotland, 1970-75; Governor, Edinburgh Academy, 1973-75; Vice-President, Society of Antiquaries of Scotland, 1975-78; Member, Board of Trustees, National Museum of Antiquities, 1975-78; Trustee, Sir Patrick Geddes Memorial Trust, since 1981; Past Chairman, Hopetoun House Preservation Trust; Past Chairman, Conservation Committee, Scottish Development Agency; recipient, George Waterston Memorial Award, 1982. Publications: Scottish History in Perspective, 1966; Scots in Italy, 1966; Lime Industry in Lothian, 1970. Recreations: gardening; walking; travel. Address: (h.) Southfield Farm, Duddingston, Edinburgh, EH15 1SR; T.-031-669 2041.

Skinner, Robert Gordon, LLB (Hons). Advocate, since 1987; part-time Chairman, Social Security Appeals Tribunal, since 1988; part-time Chairman, Disability Appeals Tribunal, since 1991; b. 14.6.57, Glasgow; m., Eileen Mary Judith Paterson; 2 s. Educ. Bishopbriggs High School; Glasgow University. Law Apprentice, Hughes, Dowdall & Co., Solicitors, Glasgow; Solicitor, Dorman Jeffrey & Co.,

Solicitors, Glasgow, 1980-86; called to the Bar, 1987. Recreations: football; swimming; golf; opera. Address: (h.) 17 Hamilton Avenue, Pollokshields, Glasgow.

Skorupski, Professor John Maria, MA, PhD. Professor of Moral Philosophy, St. Andrews University, since 1990; b. 19.9.46, Italy; m., Barbara Mary; 2 d. Educ. St. Benedict's, Ealing; Christ's College, Cambridge. Visiting Lectureships, Nigeria and Belgium, 1971-74; University of Wales Research Fellow, University College of Swansea, 1974-76; Lecturer in Philosophy, Glasgow University, 1976-84; Professor of Philosophy, Sheffield University, 1984-90. Fellow, Royal Society of Edinburgh. Publications: Symbol and Theory, 1976; John Stuart Mill, 1989; English Language Philosophy 1750-1945, 1993. Recreations: music; walking; skiing. Address: (h.) Ceader Lodge, Hepburn Gardens, St. Andrews, KY16 9LP; T.-0334 77590.

Slane, John Kerr, BSc. Factory Manager, Tarka Controls Ltd., Inverness, since 1984; Chairman, Highland Area Group, CBI; b. 16.2.53, Dundee; m., Linda Jean. Educ. Morgan Academy; Dundee College of Technology. Member, Inverness College Council. Recreation: hill-walking. Address: (b.) Tarka Controls Ltd., Lochiel Road, Inverness, IV2 3XR; T.-0463 237311.

Slater, Basil Crandles Smith, OBE, MD, FRCP, FRCGP, FFCM, Hon. MCFP (Canada). Community Medical Specialist, Royal Infirmary, Edinburgh; former Director, Scottish Health Services Planning Unit, Scottish Home and Health Department; b. 26.7.28, Broxburn; m., Jean Wallace Simpson; 2 s.; 1 d. Educ. Armadale Public School; Bathgate Academy; Edinburgh University. House Physician, Edinburgh Royal Infirmary, 1952; House Surgeon, Bangour General Hospital, 1953; Surgeon Lieutenant, RNVR, 1953-55; General Practitioner, Harrow, Middlesex and Dalkeith, Midlothian, 1955-75; joined Scottish Home and Health Department, 1975. Former Honorary Secretary and Vice Chairman of Council, Royal College of General Practitioners; former Regional Adviser in General Practice, North West Metropolitan Region; former Vice-President, Section of General Practice, Royal Society of Medicine; first Civilian Consultant in General Practice to Royal Navy. Recreations: bridge (average); bowling (reasonable); fireside sitting (well). Address: (b.) Royal Infirmary, Lauriston Place, Edinburgh; T.-031-229 2477, Ext. 2006.

Slater, Carolyn Louttit (Buchanan), LLB. Director (formerly Secretary), Royal Institution of Chartered Surveyors in Scotland, since 1987; Executive Manager, Surveyors Holdings Ltd. (Scotland), since 1989; Member, Board of Directors, Edinburgh Chamber of Commerce, since 1989; Member, Scottish Conveyancing and Executry Servicesd Board, since 1991; b. 22.12.47, Glasgow; m., John Cameron Slater. Educ. Hutchesons' Girls' Grammar School, Glasgow; Glasgow University. Apprentice Solicitor and Legal Assistant, Glasgow, 1968-74; Lecturer, Department of Land Economics, Paisley College of Technology, 1974-78; Secretary (Legal Education), Law Society of Scotland, 1978-87. Address: (b.) 9 Manor Place, Edinburgh, EH3 7DN; T.- 031-225 7078.

Slater, Peter Anderson, MB, ChB, FRCSEdin. Consultant Orthopaedic Surgeon, Grampian Health Board, since 1978; b. 6.9.41, Aberdeen; m., Isobel; 1 s. Educ. Prince of Wales School, Nairobi; Aberdeen University. House Officer, Aberdeen Royal Infirmary, 1966-67; Lecturer in Pathology, Aberdeen University, 1967-68; Senior House Officer, General Surgery, Aberdeen Royal Infirmary, 1968-70; Registrar, General Surgery, South Teesside Hospitals, 1970-72; Registrar in Orthopaedics, South Birmingham Hospitals, 1972-75; Senior Registrar in Orthopaedics, Aberdeen Royal Infirmary, 1975-78; Consultant in Orthopaedic Surgery,

Stracathro Hospital, 1978-91. Board Member, National Centre for Education and Training in Prosthetics and Orthotics, Strathclyde University. Recreations: DIY; reading science fiction. Address: (h.) 6 Argyll Street, Brechin, Angus, DD9 6JL; T.-035 62 2554.

Slater, Professor Peter James Bramwell, BSc, PhD, DSc, FIBiol, FRSE. Kennedy Professor of Natural History, St. Andrews University, since 1984; b. 26.12.42, Edinburgh; m., Elisabeth Vernon Smith; 2 s. Educ. Edinburgh Academy; Glenalmond; Edinburgh University. Demonstrator in Zoology, Edinburgh University, 1966-68; Lecturer in Biology, Sussex University, 1968-84. Secretary, Association for the Study of Animal Behaviour, 1973-78, President, 1986-89; European Editor, Animal Behaviour, 1979-82; Editor, Advances in the Study of Behavior. Recreations: walking; ornithology; music; disarmament. Address: (b.) Department of Biology and Preclinical Medicine, St. Andrews, Fife; T.-0334 76161, Ext. 7218.

Slaven, Professor Anthony, MA, BLitt, FRHistS. Professor of Business History, Glasgow University, since 1979 (Head, Department of Economic History, since 1979); Director, Centre for Business History in Scotland, since 1987; b. 5.10.37, Blantyre; m., Isabelle Dunsheath Cameron; 1 s.; 2 d. Educ. Hamilton Academy; Glasgow University. Assistant Lecturer, Glasgow University, 1960-62; Lecturer in Geography, Queensland University, 1962-64; Glasgow University: Lecturer in Economic History, 1965-70, Colquhoun Lecturer in Business History, since 1969, Senior Lecturer in Economic History, 1970-79. Secretary/Treasurer, Association of Business Historians; Member, Editorial Board, Scottish Economic and Social History. Publications: The Development of the West of Scotland; Shipbuilding - A Review of UK Statistics; Dictionary of Scottish Business Biography (Co-Editor). Recreations: walking; golf; DIY. Address: (b.) Department of Economic History, 4 University Gardens, Glasgow University, G12 8QQ; T.-041-339 8855, Ext. 4669.

Slavin, William J., MA, STL, CPsychol. Co-ordinator, Scottish Drugs Forum, since 1986; b. 17.1.40, Bristol. Educ. Blairs College, Aberdeen; Scots College, Rome; Glasgow University. Assistant Priest, Broomhill, Glasgow, 1965-70; Educational Psychologist, Glasgow Child Guidance Service, 1970-75; Deputy Director, Jessore Training Centre, Bangladesh, 1975-80; Secretary, RC Justice and Peace Commission, 1980-85; Assistant Chaplain, Barlinnie Prison. Recreation: An rud Gaidhealach. Address: (b.) 5 Oswald Street, Glasgow, G1 5QR; T.-041-221 1175.

Slawson, Keith Brian, BSc, MB, ChB, FFARCS. Consultant Anaesthetist, Western General Hospital, Edinburgh, since 1966; Honorary Senior Lecturer, Edinburgh University, since 1975; b. 7.9.33, Birmingham; m., Nan; 1 s.; 1 d. Educ. Bradford Grammar School; Edinburgh University. MRC Scientific Assistant, Department of Therapeutics, Edinburgh Royal Infirmary, 1962-63; Lecturer in Anaesthesia, Edinburgh University, 1963-66. Honorary Medical Officer, Scottish Rugby Union. Recreation: caravanning. Address: (h.) 27 Craigmount View, Edinburgh; T.-031-339 4786.

Sleeman, Professor Brian David, BSc, PhD, DSc, CMaths, FIMA, FRSE. Professor of Mathematics, Dundee University, since 1978; b. 4.8.39, London; m., Juliet Mary Shea; 2 s.; 1 d. Educ. Tiffin Boys School; Battersea College of Technology; London University. Department of Mathematics and Computer Science, Dundee University: Assistant Lecturer, 1965-67, Lecturer, 1967-71, Reader, 1971-78. Chairman, Scottish Branch, Institute of Mathematics and its Applications, 1982-84; Member, General Synod, Scottish Episcopal Church, 1984-90; President, Edinburgh Mathematical Society, 1988-89. Publications: Multiparameter

Spectral Theory in Hilbert Space, 1978; Differential Equations and Mathematical Biology, 1983. Recreations: choral music; hill-walking. Address: (b.) Department of Mathematics and Computer Science, Dundee University, Dundee, DD1 4HN; T.-0382 23181.

Sleeman, Professor Derek Henry, BSc, PhD. Professor of Computing Science, Aberdeen University, since 1986; b. 11.1.41, Penzance; m., Margaret G. Rankine; 1 d. Educ. Penzance Grammar School; King's College, London. Leeds University: Computing Assistant, 1965-67, Lecturer in Computational Science, 1967-82, Associate Director, Computer Based Learning Project, 1969-82; Visiting Scientist: Rutgers University, 1979, Carnegie-Mellon University, 1980-81; Senior Consultant, Teknowledge, Palo Alto, CA, 1983-86; Senior Research Associate/Associate Professor, Stanford University, 1982-86. Secretary, SS AISB, 1979-82. Publications: 70 technical papers, including Intelligent Tutoring Systems (Co-Editor). Recreations: hill and coastal path walking; medieval architecture; photography. Address: (b.) Computing Science Department, King's College, Aberdeen University, Aberdeen, AB9 2FX; T.-0224 272288.

Sleigh, Professor James Douglas, MB, ChB, FRCPath, FRCPGlas. Professor of Bacteriology, Glasgow University, since 1989; Consultant Bacteriologist, Glasgow Royal Infirmary, since 1979; b. 5.7.30, Glasgow; m., Rosemary Margaret Smith; 2 s. Educ. Glasgow Academy; Glasgow University. House appointments, Glasgow Western Infirmary, 1953-54; Pathologist, RAMC, 1954-56; Registrar in Bacteriology, Glasgow Western Infirmary, 1956-58; Lecturer in Bacteriology, Edinburgh University, 1958-65; Consultant Clinical Pathologist, Dunbartonshire Hospitals, 1965-69; Senior Lecturer in Bacteriology, Glasgow University, 1969-84; Reader, 1984-89; Consultant Bacteriologist, Glasgow Western Infirmary, 1969-79. Publication: Notes on Medical Bacteriology (Co-author). Recreations: seeking non-existent bargains; spending time on Arran. Address: (h.) Clynder, 5 Sutherland Avenue, Glasgow, G41 4JJ; T.-041-427 1486.

Sloan, Andrew Kirkpatrick, QPM, BA. Chief Constable, Strathclyde, 1985-91; b. 27.2.31, Dumfries; m., Agnes Sofie Storvik; 3 d. Educ. Kirkcudbright Academy; Dumfries Academy; Open University. Royal Navy, 1947-55; West Yorkshire Police, 1955-76 (Chief Superintendent); Assistant Chief Constable, Lincolnshire Police, 1976-79; National Co-ordinator, Regional Crime Squad (England and Wales), 1979-81; Deputy Chief Constable, Lincolnshire Police, 1981-83; Chief Constable, Bedfordshire Police, 1983-85. FSA Scot. Recreation: walking. Address: c/o Royal Bank of Scotland, 151 High Street, Dumfries, DG1 2RA.

Sloan, Professor David McPheator, BSc, MSc, PhD, DSc. Professor of Mathematics, Strathclyde University; b. 24.12.38, Cronberry; m., Margaret Templeton Kirk; 3 s.; 1 d. Educ. Cumnock Academy; Glasgow University; Keele University; Strathclyde University. Mathematician, English Electric Co., Stafford, 1962-64; Lecturer, Stafford Polytechnic, 1964-65; Lecturer, Senior Lecturer, Reader, Professor, Strathclyde University, from 1965. Recreations: hill-walking; folk music; reading. Address: (b.) Department of Mathematics, Strathclyde University, Glasgow; T.-041-552 4400, Ext. 3819.

Sloane, Professor Peter James, BA (Econ), PhD. Professor of Political Economy, Aberdeen University, since 1984; b. 6.8.42, Cheadle Hulme; m., Avril Mary Urquhart; 1 s. Educ. Cheadle Hulme School; Sheffield University; Strathclyde University. Assistant Lecturer and Lecturer, Strathclyde University. Assistant Lecturer and Lecturer, Aberdeen University, 1966-69; Lecturer in Industrial Economics, Nottingham University, 1969-75; Economic Adviser, Department of Employment Unit for

Manpower Studies (on secondment), 1973-74; Professor of Economics and Management, Paisley College, 1975-84. Member, Economic and Social Research Council, 1979-85; Council Member, Scottish Economic Society, since 1983. Publications: Sex Discrimination in the Labour Market, 1976; Women and Low Pay, 1980; Sport in the Market?, 1980; Equal Employment Issues, 1981; Tackling Discrimination in the Workplace, 1982; Labour Economics, 1985. Recreation: sport. Address: (b.) Department of Economics, Aberdeen University, Edward Wright Building, Dunbar Street, Old Aberdeen, Aberdeen, AB9 2TY.

Smail, Peter James, MA, BM, BCh, FRCP, DCH. Consultant Paediatrician, Grampian Health Board, since 1980; Honorary Senior Lecturer in Child Health, Aberdeen University, since 1980; b. 10.10.43, Harrow; m., Janice Lockhart; 3 s.; 1 d. Educ. Merchant Taylors', Northwood; St. John's College, Oxford; Oxford Clinical Medical School. Paediatric House Officer, Inverness Hospitals, 1970; Medical Registrar, Royal Cornwall Hospital (Treliske), 1972; Lecturer in Child Health, Dundee University, 1975; Fellow in Paediatric Endocrinology, University of Manitoba, Winnipeg, 1979. Member, Health Services Human Growth Hormone Committee, 1982-87; Secretary, Scottish Study Group for the Care of Young Diabetics, 1984-89. Recreations: Member, Aberdeen Bach Choir; Lay Clerk, St. Andrew's Cathedral, Aberdeen. Address: (b.) Royal Aberdeen Children's Hospital, Aberdeen, AB9 2ZG; T.-0224 681818, Ext. 53102.

Small, Christopher. Writer; b. 15.11.19, London; 3 d. Educ. Dartington Hall; Pembroke College, Oxford. Journalist and miscellaneous writer; Literary Editor and Dramatic Critic, Glasgow Herald, 1955-80. Publications: Ariel Like A Harpy: Shelley, Mary & Frankenstein; The Road to Miniluv: George Orwell, the State & God; The Printed Word. Recreation: gardening. Address: (h.) 26 Bell Place, Edinburgh, EH3 5HT; T.-031-332 6591.

Small, Professor John Rankin, CBE, BSc (Econ), FCCA, FCMA. Professor, Department of Accountancy and Finance, Heriot-Watt University, since 1967; Chairman, Commission for Local Authority Accounts in Scotland, since 1983; b. 28.2.33, Dundee; m., Catherine Wood; 1 s.; 2 d. Educ. Harris Academy; Dundee School of Economics. Industry and commerce; Lecturer; Edinburgh University; Senior Lecturer, Glasgow University. Consultant to various organisations; Council Member, Chartered Association of Certified Accountants (President, 1982-83); Vice-Principal, Heriot-Watt University, 1974-78, 1987-90, Deputy Principal, since 1990; Chairman, National Appeal Panel for Entry to Pharmaceutical Lists (Scotland), since 1987. Recreation: golf. Address: (b.) Heriot-Watt University, Grassmarket, Edinburgh; T.-031-225 8432.

Small, Ramsay George, MB, ChB, FFCM, FRCPE, DPH. Chief Administrative Medical Officer, Tayside Health Board, 1986-89 (retired); Honorary Senior Lecturer in Community Medicine, Dundee University, 1974-89; b. 5.2.30, Calcutta; m., Aileen Stiven Masterton; 4 s. Educ. Harris Academy, Dundee; St. Andrews University. Assistant Medical Officer of Health, Ayr County Council, 1958-61; Senior Assistant Medical Officer of Health, then Principal Medical Officer, City of Dundee, 1961-74; Community Medicine Specialist, Tayside Health Board, 1974-85. Faculty Adviser, Scotland, Faculty of Community Medicine, 1980-83, Convener Scottish Affairs Committee, 1983-86; Member, National Medical Consultative Committee and Member, Board, Faculty of Community Medicine, 1985-89; Member, Council, Royal College of Physicians of Edinburgh, 1987-90; President, Baptist Union of Scotland, 1972-73; Chairman, Eastern Regional Postgraduate Medical Education Committee, 1980-83; Secretary, Broughty Ferry Baptist Church, since 1969.

Recreations: bird-watching; music. Address: 46 Monifieth Road, Broughty Ferry, Dundee, DD5 2RX; T.-Dundee 78408.

Small, Very Rev. Robert Leonard, CBE, MA, DD. Honorary President, Age Concern Scotland; Minister of Religion (retired); b. 12.5.05, North Berwick; m., Jane Hay McGregor; 3 s.; 1 d. Educ. North Berwick High School; Edinburgh University and New College. Minister: St. John's, Bathgate, 1931-35, West High, Kilmarnock, 1935-44, Cramond Kirk, Edinburgh, 1944-56, St. Cuthbert's, Edinburgh, 1956-75; Convener, Church of Scotland Committees: Huts and Canteens, Temperance and Morals, Social and Moral Welfare, Stewardship and Budget; Moderator, General Assembly, 1966; Chaplain to The Queen, since 1967; Member, Scottish Advisory Committee on Treatment of Offenders, 1950-66; Chairman, Parole Board for Scotland, 1967-73. Vice-President, Edinburgh Scout Council; Vice-President, Edinburgh Council of Girl Guides; Honorary Vice-President, Boys' Brigade; Regional Chaplain to Air Training Corps, since 1953; OBE, 1957; Chairman, Age Concern Scotland, 1981-83; Chairman, Edinburgh Parkinson's Disease Society; Vice-President, Royal Blind Asylum and School; Vice-President, Scottish National Institution for the War Blinded. Address: (h.) 5 Craighill Gardens, Edinburgh, EH10 5PY; T.-031-447 4243.

Smart, Graham Noel Johnston, DL, MIFM. Chairman and Managing Director, Jos. Johnston & Sons Ltd., Montrose, since 1968; b. 11.6.39, Dundee; m., Christine Maclean; 1 s.; 2 d. Educ. Cargilfield and Fettes; St. Edmund Hall, Oxford. Chairman: Montrose Branch, RNLI; Esk District Salmon Fishery Board; Member, Fisheries Committee, Secretary of State for Scotland; Past Chairman and Executive Council Member, Salmon Net Fishing Association of Scotland. Deputy Lieutenant, County of Angus, since 1989. Recreations: flying; sailing; skiing; shooting; sport spectating. Address: (h.) Kinnaber House, Montrose, Angus.

Smillie, Ian R.D., BL. Chief Executive, Kyle and Carrick District Council, since 1983; b. 13.9.39, Kilmarnock; m., Margaret; 2 d. Educ. Kilmarnock Academy; Glasgow University. Private practice, 1958-68; Royal Burgh of Ayr, 1968-74 (latterly as Assistant Town Clerk); Director of Administration, Kyle and Carrick District Council, 1974-83. Chairman, BACT, 1981; Dean, Ayr Faculty of Solicitors, 1989-90; Director, Freeport Scotland Limited; Director, Ayrshire Hospice. Address: (b.) Burns House, Burns Statue Square, Ayr, KA7 1UT; T.-0292 281511.

Smith, Professor Adam Neil, MD, FRCSE, FRCPE, FIBiol, FRSE. Wade Professor of Surgical Studies, RCSEd, since 1986; formerly Consultant Surgeon, Gastro-Intestinal Unit, Edinburgh (retired); b. 27.6.26, Hamilton; m., Sibyl Mary Veitch Johnstone; 1 s.; 3 d. Educ. Lanark Grammar School; Glasgow University. Academic and Health Service appointments, since 1948; Lecturer in Surgery, Glasgow University; Medical Research Council Fellow; Reader, Edinburgh University and Western General Hospital. Vice-President and Council Member, Royal College of Surgeons of Edinburgh; Council Member, Association of Coloproctology; President, British Group for Research into Pelvic Function and Disease; former Surgical Traveller, James IV Surgical Association. Recreation: golf. Address: (h.) 105 Trinity Road, Edinburgh; T.-031-552 3836.

Smith, Sir Alan, Kt (1982), CBE (1976), DFC (1941) and Bar (1942), DL, JP. President, Dawson International plc, Kinross, since 1982; Chairman, Quayle Munro PLC, Edinburgh, since 1982; b. 14.3.17, South Shields; m., 1, Margaret Stewart Todd (deceased); 2, Alice Elizabeth Moncur; 3 s.; 2 d. Educ. Bede College, Sunderland. Self-employed, 1931-36; Unilever, 1936-39; RAF, 1939-45; Managing Director, Todd & Duncan Ltd., Kinross, 1946-60;

Chairman and Chief Executive, Dawson International, Kinross, 1960-82. Board Member, Scottish Development Agency, 1982-87; Kinross Burgh Councillor, 1952-65; Provost of Kinross, 1959-65; Tayside Regional Councillor, 1979-90; Financial Convenor, Tayside Region, 1980-86. Recreations: work; sailing. Address: (h.) Ardgairney House, Cleish, by Kinross; T.-05775 265.

Smith, Alan Gordon Rae, MA, PhD, FRHistS. Reader in Modern History, Glasgow University, since 1985; b. 22.12.36, Glasgow; m., Isabel Robertson; 1 s.; 1 d. Educ. Glasgow High School; Glasgow University; University College, London. Research Fellow, Institute of Historical Research, London University, 1961-62; Assistant in History, 1962-64, then Lecturer, Glasgow University, 1964-75; Senior Lecturer in Modern History, 1975-85; Review Editor, History (Journal of the Historical Association), 1984-87; Member, Council, Royal Historical Society, since 1990. Publications: The Government of Elizabethan England, 1967; The New Europe, 1969; Science and Society in the Sixteenth and Seventeenth Centuries, 1972; Servant of the Cecils: The Life of Sir Michael Hickes, 1977; The Emergence of a Nation State: The Commonwealth of England 1529-1660, 1984; The Anonymous Life of William Cecil, Lord Burghley, 1990; The Last Years of Mary Queen of Scots, 1990. Recreation: watching sport. Address: (h.) 5 Cargil Avenue, Kilmacolm, Renfrewshire; T.-Kilmacolm 2055.

Smith, Alexander. Member (Labour), Scotland South, European Parliament, since 1989; b. 2.12.43.

Smith, Alistair Fairley, MA, MD, FRCPEdin, FRCPath. Senior Lecturer in Clinical Biochemistry, Edinburgh University, since 1971; Consultant Clinical Biochemist, Edinburgh Royal Infirmary, since 1971; Director, Clinical Biochemistry Servicesd, Lothian Area, since 1991; b. 5.10.35, Edinburgh; m., Carol Ann; 1 s.; 1 d. Educ. Bootham School, York; Clare College, Cambridge. House Officer posts, London Hospital, 1960-61; House Officer and Junior Assistant Pathologist posts, Addenbrookes' Hospital, Cambridge; Lecturer in Clinical Chemistry, Edinburgh University, 1965-71. Publications: Lecture Notes on Clinical Chemistry (Co-author); Multiple Choice Questions on Clinical Chemistry (Co-author). Recreations: golf; bridge. Address: (b.) Department of Clinical Chemistry, Royal Infirmary, Edinburgh, EH3 9YW; T.-031-229 2477, Ext. 3182.

Smith, Allan Keppie. CBE, BSc, FIMechE, FEng, FWeldI. Managing Director, Babcock Thorn Ltd., Rosyth Royal Dockyard PLC, since 1987; Chairman, Integrated Graduate Development Scheme Management Committee, Paisley College of Technology, since 1990; Member, Scottish Industry Development Advisory Board, since 1984; b. 18.5.32, Kincardineshire; m., May Love; 1 s.; 3 d. Educ. Stonehaven Mackie Academy; Aberdeen University. Joined Army for National Service, 1953; commissioned, REME, 1954; Babcock & Wilcox: joined as Graduate Trainee, 1955, appointed Industrial Engineering Manager, Renfrew Works, 1965, appointed Production Director, Renfrew Works, 1974, appointed Managing Director, Renfrew and Dumbarton Works, 1976; appointed Director, Babcock International Group PLC, 1989. Past President, Scottish Engineering Employers Association; Past Chairman, Council of the Welding Institute. Recreations: clay pigeon shooting. Address: (h.) The Forts, Hawes Brae, South Queensferry EH30 9TE; T.-031-319 1668.

Smith, Professor Brian Clive, BA, MA, PhD. Professor of Political Science and Social Policy, Dundee University, since 1989; b. 23.1.38, London; m., Joan Baselow; 1 s.; 1 d. Educ. Colfe's Grammar School; Exeter University; McMaster University, Canada. Lecturer in Politics, Exeter University;

Lecturer in Public Administration, Civil Service College, 1970-72; Senior Lecturer/Reader in Politics, Bath University, 1972-89. Publications include: Decentralisation; Bureaucracy and Political Power. Recreations: walking; opera. Address: (b.) Dundee University, Dundee, DD1 4HN; T.-0382 23181.

Smith, Sheriff Charles, MA, LLB, NP. Sheriff of Tayside, Central and Fife, at Cupar, since 1991, at Perth, 1986-91; b. 15.8.30, Methil; m., Janet Elizabeth Hurst; 1 s.; 1 d. Educ. Perth Academy; St. Andrews University. Solicitor, 1956; private practice as Principal, 1962-82; Member, Perth Town Council, 1966-68; Interim Depute Procurator Fiscal, 1974-82; Tutor, Dundee University, 1980-82; Member, Council, Law Society of Scotland (Convener, various Committees), 1977-82; Temporary Sheriff, 1977-82; Honorary Tutor, Dundee University, since 1982; Sheriff of Glasgow and Strathkelvin, 1982-86; Member, Council, Sheriffs' Association, 1987-90. Recreations: tennis; golf; bridge. Address: (b.) c/o Sheriff Clerk, Sheriff Court, Cupar, KY15 4LX; T.-0334 52121.

Smith, C. Christopher, MB, FRCP. Consultant Physician, General Medicine, Aberdeen Royal Infirmary and Consultant in charge, Regional Infection Unit, City Hospital, Aberdeen, since 1973; Honorary Senior Lecturer, Aberdeen University, since 1973, and Member, Senatus Academicus, since 1988; b. 16.5.39, West Indies; m., Sheila Anne Calder, MRCPsych; 2 s., 1 d. by pr. m. Educ. Lodge School, Barbados; Edinburgh University. Registrar, Department of Medicine, Edinburgh Royal Infirmary; Registrar, Thoracic Medicine, then Senior Registrar, Infectious Diseases, City Hospital, Edinburgh; Senior Registrar, Department of Therapeutics, Edinburgh Royal Infirmary; former Member, Part I MRCP Examination Board, RCPS; Examiner, MRCP Part II; Chairman, Specialty Advisory Committee, (JCHMT) on Infection and Tropical Medicine; Visitor for JCHMT accreditation in internal medicine, infection/tropical medicine, and community/public health medicine; Member, Aberdeen and N.E. Scotland Postgraduate Medical Education Committee; author of papers, chapters and leading articles on topics on medicine, infection, post-infective phenomena, and antimicrobial chemotherapy; Visiting Lecturer, Hong Kong, Singapore, Malaya, Kenya, Zimbabwe, Cape Town, 1986-89. Recreations: watching cricket; golf; live theatre; jazz music; Winston Churchill's literary output and his biographies. Address: (b.) Wards 25/26, Aberdeen Royal Infirmary, Foresterhill, Aberdeen, AB2; T.-Aberdeen 681818.

Smith, David Bruce Boyter, MA, LLB, NP. Director and Chief Executive, Dunfermline Building Society, since 1987; b. 11.3.42, St. Andrews; m., Christine Anne; 1 s.; 1 d. Educ. High School, Dunfermline; Edinburgh University. Legal training, Balfour & Manson, Edinburgh; admitted Solicitor, 1968; Solicitor, Standard Life Assurance Co., 1969-73; Dunfermline Building Society: Secretary, 1974-81, General Manager (Admin.), 1981-86, Deputy Chief Executive, 1986. Past Chairman, Scottish Liaison Committee, Building Societies Association; Member, Council, NHBC (Scotland); Vice-Chairman, Care and Repair National Committee, Scotland; Deputy Chairman, Glenrothes Development Corporation; Director, South Fife Enterprise Trust; Director, Fife Enterprise Ltd.; Member, Secretary of State's Expert Committee on Valuations and Surveys; Member, Court, Edinburgh University; Life Trustee, Carnegie Trust. Recreations: golf; sailing; the arts. Address: (b.) 12 East Port, Dunfermline, Fife; T.-0383 721621.

Smith, Sheriff David Buchanan, MA, LLB. Sheriff of North Strathclyde at Kilmarnock, since 1975; b. 31.10.36, Paisley; m., Hazel Mary Sinclair; 1 s.; 1 d. Educ. Paisley Grammar School; Glasgow University; Edinburgh University. Advocate, 1961; Standing Junior Counsel to Scottish Education Department, 1968-75; Tutor, Faculty of Law,

Edinburgh University, 1964-72; Trustee, Scottish Curling Museum Trust, since 1980. President, Kilmarnock and District History Group. Publications: Curling: An Illustrated History, 1981; The Roaring Game: Memories of Scottish Curling, 1985; contributions to The Laws of Scotand: Stair Memorial Encyclopedia, Vol. 6. Recreations: Scotland - history and culture; curling; music. Address: (b.) Sheriff Court House, Kilmarnock, KA1 1ED; T.-0563 20211.

Smith, Sir David Cecil, Kt, MA, DPhil, FRS, FRSE. Principal and Vice-Chancellor, Edinburgh University, since 1987; m.; 1 d. Educ. St. Paul's School, London; Queen's College, Oxford. Browne Research Fellow, Queen's College, Oxford, 1956-59; Harkness Fellow, University of California, Berkeley, 1959-60; University Lecturer, Department of Agriculture, Oxford University, 1960-74; Fellow and Tutor, Wadham College, Oxford, 1964-74; Melville Wills Professor of Botany, Bristol University, 1974-80; Sibthorpian Professor of Rural Economy, Oxford University, 1980-87. President, British Lichen Society, 1972-74; President, British Mycological Society, 1980; President, Society for Experimental Biology, 1983-85. Publication: The Biology of Symbiosis (Co-author), 1987. Address: Old College, Edinburgh University, Edinburgh, EH8 9YL; T.-031-650 2151.

Smith, Very Rev. David Macintyre Bell Armour, MA, BD, DUniv, JP. Minister, Logie, 1965-89; Moderator, General Assembly of the Church of Scotland, 1985; b. 5.4.23, Fort Augustus; m., Mary Kulvear Cumming; 3 s. Educ. Monckton Combe; Peebles High School; St. Andrews University. Minister, Warrender Church, Edinburgh, 1951-61; Exchange Preacher, USA, 1958 and 1961; Minister, Old Partick, Glasgow, 1961-65; Moderator, Stirling and Dunblane Presbytery, 1972-73; Moderator, Perth and Stirling Synod, 1975-76; Vice Convener, Joint Working Party, Church of Scotland, 1980-82; Convener, Church of Scotland Board of Education, 1979-83; Church of Scotland Representative, Stirlingshire Education Committee, 1969-79; Governor, Moray House College of Education, 1983; Member, Central Regional Education Committee, since 1986; Member, Church of Scotland Board of Practice and Procedure, since 1982; Member, Assembly Council, since 1989; Member, Board of Practice and Procedure, 1982-90; Honorary Brother, Guildry of Stirling, 1986. Recreations: philately; gardening. Address: (h.) 28 Millar Place, Stirling, FK8 1XD; T.-Stirling 75085.

Smith, Douglas Murray, MA (Hons). Rector, Dumfries Academy, since 1980; b. 2.10.39, Glasgow; m., Patricia Katherine Petrie; 2 d. Educ. Hutchesons' Boys Grammar School; Glasgow University. Co-author of mathematics text books. Recreation: sport. Address: (b.) Dumfries Academy, Dumfries; T.-0387 52846.

Smith, (Edward) Alistair, CBE, MA, PhD. Director, Aberdeen University Overseas Office, since 1990 (Director, Aberdeen University University Development Trust, 1982-90); Deputy Chairman, Scottish Conservative Party, 1981-86; b. 16.1.39, Aberdeen. Educ. Aberdeen Grammar School; Aberdeen University. Lecturer in Geography, Aberdeen University, 1963-88; President, Scottish Conservative and Unionist Association, 1979-81; Member, Grampian Health Board, 1983-91; Board Member, SCOTVEC, since 1989; Member, Committee for Scotland, Nature Conservancy Council, 1989-91; Member, N.E. Regional Committee, Nature Conservancy Council, 1991-92. Publications: Europe: A Geographical Survey of the Continent (Co-author), 1979; Scotland's Future Development (Contributor), 1983. Recreations: travel; photography; music. Address: (h.) 68A Beaconsfield Place, Aberdeen, AB2 4AJ; T.-0224 642932.

Smith, Elaine Constance. Actress; b. 2.8.58, Baillieston; m., Robert Morton; 1 d. Educ. Braidhurst High School,

Motherwell; Royal Scottish Academy of Music and Drama; Moray House College of Education. Teacher of Speech and Drama, Firrhill High School, Edinburgh, 1979-82; joined 7:84 Theatre Company, 1982; moved to Wildcat Stage Productions, 1982; since 1986, worked with Borderline Theatre Co., Royal Lyceum, Dundee Rep., Tron Theatre; TV work includes City Lights and Naked Video; plays Mary Nesbitt in Rab C. Nesbitt (BBC2); original cast member, The Steamie. Vice-Chair, Scottish Actors Equity; Board Member, Scottish Youth Theatre; Chairperson, Scottish Arts for Nicaragua. Recreations: swimming; aerobics; reading. Address: (b.) c/o 17 Kilmaurs Road, Newington, Edinburgh; T.-031-667 8905.

Smith, Gordon Matthew, DCA, MITSA. Director of Trading Standards, Dumfries and Galloway Regional Council, since 1982; b. 10.11.44, Ayr; m., Moyra; 1 s.; 1 d. Educ. Ayr Academy. Trainee Trading Standards Officer, Ayr County Council, 1962-66; Trading Standards Officer: Lindsey (Lincolnshire) County Council, 1966-68, Lanark County Council, 1968-72; District Trading Standards Officer, 1972-75; Senior Trading Standards Officer, Strathclyde Regional Council, 1975-79; Assistant Chief Trading Standards Officer, Central Regional Council, 1979-82. Recreations: golf; curling; badminton. Address: (b.) 1 Newall Terrace, Dumfries, DG1 1LN; T.-0387 60091.

Smith, Grahame Francis, MA, PhD. Senior Lecturer, Department of English Studies, Stirling University, since 1970, and Head, School of Arts, since 1989; b. 30.5.33, London; m., Angela Mary; 2 s.; 1 d. Educ. Woodside Senior Secondary School, Glasgow; Aberdeen University; Cambridge University. Taught at California University, Los Angeles, 1963-65, University College, Swansea, 1965-70; secondment to Malawi University, 1982-83. Publications: Dickens, Money and Society, 1968; The Novel and Society: From Defoe to George Elliot, 1984; The Achievement of Graham Greene, 1985. Recreations: cinema; opera; jazz; walking. Address: (b.) Department of English Studies, Stirling University, Stirling, FK9 4LA; T.-078686 3171.

Smith, Rev. G. Richmond N.R.K., OBE, MA, BD. Minister, Church of Scotland, since 1952; b. 2.3.27, Rendall, Orkney; m., Agnes Margaret Elliott Longden. Educ. Anderson Educational Institute, Lerwick; Edinburgh University. Minister: East Parish, Peterhead, 1952-60, West High Parish, Kilmarnock, 1960-65; Theological Secretary, World Alliance of Reformed Churches, Geneva, 1965-83; retired to Scotland, 1983. Recreations: ornithology; archaeology. Address: (h.) Aignish, Kippford, by Dalbeattie, DG5 4LL; T.-Kippford 624.

Smith, Hamilton, BSc, PhD, CChem, FRSC, FRCPath, FRSE. Titular Professor of Forensic Medicine (Toxicology), Glasgow University, since 1987; b. 27.4.34, Stirling; m., Jacqueline Ann Spittal. Educ. Kilsyth Academy; Glasgow University. Glasgow University: MRC Fellow, 1960, Special Research Fellow, 1963, Lecturer in Forensic Medicine Department, 1964, Senior Lecturer, 1973, Reader, 1984. Publication: Glaister's Medical Jurisprudence and Toxicology, 13th edition. Recreations: golf (New Club, St. Andrews, Crail Golfing Society); gardening. Address: (b.) Department of Forensic Medicine and Science, Glasgow University, Glasgow, G12 8QQ; T.-041-339 8855.

Smith, Hugh, DipWEM. Assistant Director (Chief Inspector), Clyde River Purification Board, since 1989; b. 23.2.47, Glasgow; m., Jessie; 1 s.; 1 d. Educ. Glenwood Secondary School; Stow College; Paisley College of Technology. Junior Chemist, BSC, Motherwell, 1963-65; Clyde River Purification Board: Junior Chemist, 1965-69, Assistant Inspector, 1969-76, Senior Assistant Inspector, 1976-79, Divisional Inspector, 1979-89. Member, Scottish

Industrial Waste Panel. Recreations: golf; badminton. Address: (b.) Rivers House, Murray Road, East Kilbride, Glasgow, G75 0LA; T.-03552 38181.

Smith, Iain Crichton, OBE, LLD (Dundee), DLitt (Glasgow), DLitt (Aberdeen), MA (Hons). Writer; b. 1.1.28, Glasgow; m., Donalda Gillies Logan; 2 step s. Educ. Nicolson Institute, Stornoway; Aberdeen University. Teacher, Oban High School, 1955-77; full-time Writer, since 1977; Member, STV Gaelic Advisory Committee; Fellow, Royal Literary Society; books in English: 10 novels, six volumes of short stories, 13 volumes of poetry; books in Gaelic: two novels, five volumes of short stories, four volumes of poetry; translations from Gaelic into English; numerous radio plays in both languages; Poetry Book Society Choice and three recommendations; eight Arts Council awards; awards for Gaelic plays and short stories; award for Gaelic television play; PEN Award, 1970; Scotsman Short Story Award, 1983; Commonwealth Poetry Prize (European Section), 1986; Travelling Scholarship, Society of Authors, 1987. Recreation: reading detective stories. Address: Tigh Na Fuaran, Taynuilt, Argyll; T.-Taynuilt 463.

Smith, Iain William, BA Hons. Member, Fife Regional Council, since 1982; Leader, Opposition SLD Group, since 1986; Constituency Agent, N.E. Fife Liberal Democrats; Chair, Scottish Liberal Democrat Councillors and Campaigners, since 1988; b. 1.5.60, Gateside, Fife. Educ. Bell Baxter High School, Cupar; Newcastle-upon-Tyne University. Advice Worker, then Centre Manager, Bonnethill Advice Centre, Dundee, 1982-85; Agent Organiser, North East Fife Liberal Association. Recreations: watching football, cricket, etc.; real ale. Address: (b.) Waterend Road, Cupar, Fife, KY15 5HP; T.-0334 56361.

Smith, Ian Croy, CA. General Manager, Argyll & Clyde Health Board, since 1985; b. 24.9.37, Stornoway; m., June Patricia McCalman. Educ. Nicolson Institute, Stornoway; Glasgow University. Assistant Regional Treasurer, Western Regional Hospital Board, 1972-74; District Finance Officer, Ayrshire & Arran Health Board, 1974-77; Treasurer, South Tyneside Health Authority, 1977-79; Treasurer, Argyll & Clyde Health Board, 1979-85. Recreations: music; gardening. Address: (b.) Gilmour House, Gilmour Street, Paisley; T.-041-887 0131.

Smith, James Aikman, TD, BA, LLB. Advocate; Honorary Sheriff, since 1976; b. 13.6.14, Kilmarnock; m., Katharine Ann Millar; 3 d. Educ. Glasgow Academy; Oxford University; Edinburgh University. Admitted Faculty of Advocates, 1939; served Royal Artillery, 1939-46 (Lt. Col., 1944), North Africa, Italy and Austria; Despatches, Bronze Star US; Sheriff Substitute, Renfrew and Argyll, 1948-52, Roxburgh, Berwick and Selkirk, 1952-57, Aberdeen, Kincardine and Banff, 1957-68; Sheriff of Lothians and Borders, 1968-76; President, Sheriffs' Association, 1969-72; Member, UK Departmental Committee on Probation Service, 1959-62; Member, After Care Council (Scotland), 1962-65; UK Delegate to UN Congress on Crime, Japan, 1970; Chairman, Edinburgh and East of Scotland Branch, English Speaking Union, 1970-74; Vice-President, Cairngorm Club, 1962-65; Chairman, Allelon Society, 1970-76; Elder, Church of Scotland, since 1948; has served on various General Assembly Committees. Recreations: hill-walking; gardening; travel. Address: (h.) 16 Murrayfield Avenue, Edinburgh, EH12 6AX; T.-031-337 8205.

Smith, James David, OBE, MA, LLB. Retired Solicitor; Honorary Sheriff of North Strathclyde at Greenock, since 1976; b. 27.10.19, Dumbarton; m., Margaret McGregor Grant; 2 s. Educ. Dumbarton Academy; Glasgow University. Commissioned Highland Light Infantry, 1940; Town Clerk, Dumbarton, 1951-67; Chief Executive, Corporation of Greenock, 1967-75; Visiting Lecturer in Law, Paisley College of Technology, 1976-87. Address: (h.) 42 Octavia Terrace, Greenock, PA16 7SR; T.-0475 23788.

Smith, Jeremy J., BA, MPhil, PhD, AKC. Senior Lecturer in English Language, Glasgow University, since 1990; Director, Institute for Historical Dialectology, since 1992; b. 18.10.55, Hampton; m., Elaine Patricia Higgleton. Educ. Kingston Grammar School; King's College, London; Jesus College, Oxford; Glasgow University. College Lecturer in English Language, Keble College, Oxford, 1978-79; Lecturer in English Language, Glasgow University, 1979-90. Secretary, Teachers of Old English in Britain and Ireland. Publications: numerous papers on language and English studies. Recreations: hill-walking; opera. Address: (b.) Department of English Language, Glasgow University, Glasgow, G12 8QQ; T.-041-339 8855, Ext. 5684.

Smith, Rt. Hon. John, QC, MA, LLB. MP (Labour), Monklands East, since 1983 (North Lanarkshire, 1970-83); Leader of the Opposition, since 1992; b. 13.9.38, Dalmally, Argyll; m., Elizabeth Margaret Bennett; 3 d. Educ. Dunoon Grammar School; Glasgow University. Called to Scottish Bar, 1967; QC (Scot), 1983; Parliamentary Under Secretary of State for Energy, 1974-75; Minister of State for Energy, 1975-76; Minister of State, Privy Council Office, 1976-78; Secretary of State for Trade, 1978-79; Member, Shadow Cabinet, since 1979; Principal Opposition Spokesman on Treasury and Economic Affairs; Vice Chairman, Great Britain-USSR Association; a Governor, Ditchley Foundation; National President, Industrial Common Ownership Movement. Recreations: opera; hill-walking. Address: (h.) 21 Cluny Drive, Edinburgh, EH10 6DW; T.-031-447 3667.

Smith, John Michael, BA (Hons), DipEd, MBIM. Rector, Berwickshire High School, since 1982; b. 7.2.40, Barnsley; m., Elspeth Sheena; 2 d. Educ. Queen Elizabeth Grammar School, Wakefield; Durham University; Westminster College, Oxford. Assistant Teacher of Classics and RE, 1962-67; Head of Classics, Wallsend Upon Tyne Grammar School, 1967-70; Senior Housemaster, Dalziel High School, 1970-73; Depute Rector, Berwickshire High School, 1973-82. Methodist Church Lay Preacher, since 1960; Secretary, Berwick Upon Tweed Methodist Church Circuit. Recreations: walking; golf; reading spy thrillers; camping abroad. Address: (b.) Berwickshire High School, Duns; T.-0361 83710.

Smith, Rev. John Murdo. Minister, Lochmaddy and Trumisgarry, Uist, since 1963; b. 29.8.27, Shader, Isle of Lewis; m., Mary Margaret Macpherson; 1 s.; 2 d. Educ. Airidhantuim School, Isle of Lewis; Skerry's College, Glasgow; Glasgow University; Aberdeen University. National Service, RAF, 1945-48; Minister, South Uist Howmore, 1956-63; Moderator, Uist Presbytery, 1957, 1973, 1982 (Presbytery Clerk, 1959-71); updated North Uist part, Statistical Account of Scotland; Chaplain, Lochmaddy Hospital, since 1963, Hon. Port Chaplain, British Sailors Society, Lochmaddy, since 1963. Recreations: fishing; hill-walking. Address: (h.) The Manse, Lochmaddy, North Uist.

Smith, Joseph Raymond, OBE, BSc (Econ), MSc, MA. Institute Secretary, Dundee Institute of Technology, since 1983; b. 21.12.28, High Wycombe; m., Jean Margaret Hughes; 1 s.; 1 d. Educ. Royal Grammar School, High Wycombe; LSE. Chief Education Officer, HQ Land Forces, Hong Kong, 1969-72; Lt. Col., Officer Education Branch, 1972-76; Col., Directorate of Army Education, MoD, 1976-78; Col./Chief Inspector, Army Education, 1978-79; Brigadier/Chief Education Officer HQ UK Land Forces, 1979-82; Brigadier/Chief Education Officer, HQ BAOR, 1982-83. Recreations: reading; walking; bird-watching. Address: (b.) 40 Bell Street, Dundee, DD1 1HG; T.-0382 23291.

Smith, Professor Keith, BA, PhD, FRSE. Professor of Environmental Science, Stirling University, since 1986; b. 9.1.38, Marple; m., Muriel Doris Hyde; 1 s.; 1 d. Educ. Hyde County Grammar School; Hull University. Tutor in Geography, Liverpool University, 1963-65; Lecturer in Geography, Durham University, 1965-70; Strathclyde University: Senior Lecturer, 1971-75, Reader, 1975-82, Personal Professor, 1982-84, Professor and Head of Department, 1984-86. Drapers' Company Visiting Lecturer, Adelaide University, 1978; Visiting Principal Scientist, Illinois State Water Survey, 1988; Visiting Professor of Geography, University of Illinois, 1988. Publications: Water in Britain; Principles of Applied Climatology; Human Adjustment to Flood Hazard; Environmental Hazards. Recreations: hill-walking; badminton. Address: (b.) Department of Environmental Science, Stirling University, Stirling, FK9 4LA; T.-0786 67842.

Smith, Professor Lawrence D., BSc. Professor of Agricultural Economics, Glasgow University, since 1989; b. 1939, Bedfordshire; m., Evelyn Mavis Stead; 1 s.; 2 d. Educ. Bedford Modern School; Wye College, London University; Linacre College, Oxford. Departmental Lecturer, Agricultural Economics Research Institute, Oxford University, 1963-66; Lecturer, Senior Lecturer, Reader in Agricultural Economics, Department of Political Economy, Glasgow University. Recreation: gardening. Address: (b.) Department of Political Economy, Glasgow University, Glasgow; T.-041-339 8855.

Smith, Professor Lorraine Nancy, BScN, MEd, PhD. Professor of Nursing Studies, Glasgow University, since 1990 (Head of Department, since 1990); b. 29.6.49, Ottawa; m., Christopher Murray Smith; 1 s.; 1 d. Educ. Hillcrest High School, Ottawa; University of Ottawa; Manchester University. Co-opted to English National Board, 1988-90; Member, Scottish Alcohol Advisory Group, since 1991; Member, Clinical and Biomedical Research Committee (Scotland), since 1992. Recreations: reading; bridge; sailing. Address: (b.) 68 Oakfield Avenue, Glasgow University, Glasgow, G12 8LS; T.-041-339 8855, Ext. 5498.

Smith, Martin, CBE, FRICS. President, Glasgow Chamber of Commerce, 1984-86; Senior Partner, Doig & Smith, Chartered Quantity Surveyors, 1977-87; Honorary Secretary, RICS in Scotland, 1979-88; b. 16.7.22, Glasgow; m., Margaret Emma; 2 s. Educ. Coatbridge High School. Qualified ARICS, 1948; Chairman, RICS in Scotland, 1974-75; Chairman, Scottish Building Contract Committee, 1975-81; Elder, Church of Scotland; Deacon, Incorporation of Gardeners, 1964-65. Recreations: gardening; golf. Address: (b.) 34 Langside Drive, Newlands, Glasgow, G43 2QQ; T.-041-637 9683.

Smith, Michael A., BA, MBA. Marketing and Distribution Director, Scottish Power plc, since 1990; Director, Electricity Association Ltd., since 1991; Director, Caledonian Gas Ltd., since 1992; b. 8.2.51, Manchester; m., Ninuk Indrawaty; 2 s.; 2 d. Educ. St. Bede's College, Manchester; University of Wales; Manchester Business School. Thorn EMI, 1982-90, latterly as Group Planning Manager. Director, Quality Scotland Foundation, since 1991. Recreations: family; music. Address: (b.) Scottish Power plc, Cathcart House, Spean Street, Glasgow, G44 4BE; T.-041-637 7177.

Smith, Nigel R. Managing Director, David Auld Valves Ltd., since 1976; Member, Executive, Scottish Engineering Employers Association, 1985-90; Member, Broadcasting Council for Scotland, 1986-90; Member, BBC General Advisory Council, since 1991; b. 9.6.41, Girvan; m., Jody; 2 s.; 2 d. Educ. Dollar Academy. Lt., 4/5 Bn., Royal Scots Fusiliers (TA), 1960-67; staff and management appointments, Bowater Paper, Richard Costain, Rank Hovis McDougall. Member, Camden Council Community Relations Committee,

1966-69. Recreations: hill-walking; offshore sailing; opera and choral; reading, particularly biography. Address: (b.) David Auld Valves, Cowlairs Industrial Estate, Finlas Street, Glasgow, G22 5DQ; T.-041-557 0515.

Smith, Philip Morgans, BSc, PhD, FLS. Convener, Honours School of Botany, Edinburgh University, since 1990; b. 5.2.41, Halesowen; m., Eira; 2 s. Educ. Halesowen Grammar School; Birmingham University. Harkness Fellow, Commonwealth Fund, New York; Lecturer/Senior Lecturer in Botany, Edinburgh University; various examining appointments/offices, Scottish Examination Board and related Scottish Office services, since 1970. Past President, Botanical Society of Scotland; Director, Botany of the Lothians Survey. Recreations: canal boating; watching trains; singing; painting. Address: (h.) 7 Clayhills Park, Balerno, Midlothian, EH14 7BH; T.-031-449 4345.

Smith, Ralph Alastair Randall, AMA, FSA Scot. Keeper of Technology, Glasgow Museums, since 1981; b. 6.12.43, Manchester; m., Ruth Kathleen Geddes; 1 s. Educ. Melville College, Edinburgh. Department of Technology, Royal Museum of Scotland, 1963-70; Keeper, Museum of Science and Engineering, Newcastle, 1970-73; Assistant Keeper, 1973-76, Depute Keeper, 1976-81, Department of Technology, Glasgow. Publications: Railways in Scotland, 1980; A Guide to the Museum of Transport, Glasgow, 1980, 1988; Scottish Angling Guide, 1986. Recreations: fishing; collecting old fishing tackle. Address: (b.) Museum of Transport, Kelvin Hall, Glasgow; T.-041-357 3929.

Smith, Rev. Ralph Colley Philip, MA, STM. Director of Audio Visual Productions, Church of Scotland, 1985-91; part-time Chaplain, Edinburgh Northern Hospital Group; Minister, Church of Scotland, since 1960; b. 11.3.31, Edinburgh; m., Florence; 2 s. Educ. Edinburgh Academy; St. Andrews University; Edinburgh University; Union Seminary, New York. Minister, Gallatown Church, Kirkcaldy; Religious Broadcasting Assistant, then Producer, Religion, Television, BBC Scotland; Associate Minister, New Kilpatrick Parish Church, Bearsden. Recreations: cello; bowls; golf. Address: (h.) 2 Blackford Hill View, Edinburgh, EH9 3HD.

Smith, Robert Haldane, CA. Chairman and Chief Executive, Morgan Grenfell Development Capital Limited and Director, Morgan Grenfell & Co. Limited and Morgan Grenfell (Scotland) Limited; b. 8.8.44, Glasgow; m., Alison Marjorie Bell; 2 d. Educ. Allan Glen's School, Glasgow; Glasgow University. Articled to Robb Ferguson & Co., CA, Glasgow, 1963-68; qualified CA, 1968; ICFC, now 3i, 1968-82; General Manager (Corporate Finance Division), The Royal Bank of Scotland plc, 1983-85; Managing Director, National Commercial & Glyns, 1983-85; Managing Director, Charterhouse Development Capital Limited and Executive Director, Charterhouse Bank Limited, 1985-89; current Directorships include: Bristow Helicopter Group Limited, TIP Europe PLC, MFI Furniture Group Ltd.; Member, Board of Trustees, National Museums of Scotland; Commissioner, Museums and Galleries Commission. Publication: Managing Your Company's Finances (Co-author). Recreations: amateur drama; public speaking; spectator sports; historic and listed buildings; music. Address: (h.) 4 Lauder Road, Edinburgh; T.-031-667 1400.

Smith, Robert Lupton, OBE, JP, FRICS. Director, Association for the Protection of Rural Scotland, since 1981; Chartered Surveyor in private practice, since 1954; b. 26.4.24, Cheadle Hulme; m.; 3 d. Educ. George Watson's College; College of Estate Management; Heriot-Watt College. Chairman, Scottish Junior Branch, RICS, 1952; Member, Scottish Executive Committee, RICS, 1952-60; elected, Edinburgh Town Council, 1962-74 and Edinburgh District Council, 1974-77; Governor, Edinburgh College of Art, 1963-

89; fought European Election, 1979, as Liberal; Deputy Traffic Commissioner, 1974-78; Chairman, Good Neighbours Housing Association, 1984-87; Scottish Liberal Party: Chairman, Executive Committee, 1971-74, Chairman, 1974, President, 1976-82; Council Member, Royal Scottish Geographical Society, since 1957; Chairman, Scottish Liberal Club, 1984-91; Director, Cockburn Conservation Trust Ltd., 1976-90. Recreations: visiting Orkney; reading; looking at fine art. Address: (h.) Charleston, Dalguise, near Dunkeld, PH8 0JX; T.-03502 8968.

Smith, Robert S., MA (Hons), DipEd. Head Teacher, Cumnock Academy, since 1989; b. 18.10.40, St. Monans; m., Roslyn Hulme; 1 s.; 1 d. Educ. Waid Academy, Anstruther; St. Andrews University; Aberdeen University; Aberdeen College of Education. Classics Teacher, Airdrie Academy, 1963-67; Principal Teacher of Classics: Armadale Academy, 1967-70, Dumbarton Academy, 1970-74; Assistant/Depute Head Teacher, Clydebank High School, 1974-78; Head Teacher, Allan Glen's Secondary, 1978-89. Chairman, Scottish Executive, Professional Association of Teachers, 1989-90 (Council Member, 1989-92). Publications: Discovering the Greeks; Discovering Greek Mythology. Recreation: country activities. Address: (b.) Cumnock Academy, Ayr Road, Cumnock, Ayrshire; T.-0290 21228.

Smith, Roger. Writer and Editor; b. 28.11.38, London; 2 d. Educ. Latymer Upper School, London. Editor, The Great Outdoors, 1977-86; Editor, Environment Now, 1987-89; Editor, Scottish World, 1989-90; Past Chairman, Scottish Wild Land Group; elected Council Member, National Trust for Scotland. Publications: Penguin Book of Orienteering, 1981; The Winding Trail, 1981; Outdoor Scotland, 1981; Weekend Walking, 1982; Visitor's Guide to Scottish Borders, 1983; Jet Guide to Scotland's Countryside, 1985; The Great Outdoors Book of the Walking Year, 1988; Classic Walks in Scotland (Co-author), 1988. Recreations: hill-walking; running; orienteering; Scottish history. Address: (h.) Stevensons Building, High Street, Burrelton, Blairgowrie, PH13 9NX; T.-08287 577.

Smith, Roger Galbraith, MB, ChB, FRCPEdin, FRCPLond. Consultant Physician in Geriatric Medicine, Royal Victoria Hospital, Edinburgh, and Honorary Senior Lecturer in Geriatric Medicine, Edinburgh University, since 1989; b. 7.7.42, Edinburgh; m., Margaret Lawson; 1 s.; 1 d. Educ. George Watson's College, Edinburgh; Edinburgh University. Surgeon Lieutenant, Royal Navy, 1967-72; Senior Registrar in Geriatric Medicine, 1973-76; Senior Lecturer, Department of Geriatric Medicine, Edinburgh University, 1976-89. Member, Board of Directors, Queensberry House Hospital, Edinburgh. Recreations: golf; curling. Address: (h.) 56 Alnwickhill Road, Edinburgh; T.-031-664 1745.

Smith, Professor Stanley Desmond, BSc, PhD, FRS, FRSE, DSc. Professor of Physics and Head of Department, Heriot-Watt University, since 1970; Chairman, Edinburgh Instruments Ltd., since 1971; b. 3.3.31, Bristol; m., Gillian Anne Parish; 1 s.; 1 d. Educ. Cotham Grammar School; Bristol University; Reading University. SSO, RAE, Farnborough, 1956-58; Research Assistant, Department of Meteorology, Imperial College, London, 1958-59; Lecturer, then Reader, Reading University, 1960-70; Head, Department of Physics, Heriot-Watt University, since 1970. Member: Advisory Council for Applied Research and Development, 1985-87, Defence Scientific Advisory Council, 1985-91, SERC Astronomy and Planetary Science and Engineering Boards, 1985-88, Council, Institute of Physics, 1984-87. Recreations: tennis; skiing; mountaineering; golf; raising the temperature. Address: (h.) 29D Gillespie Road, Colinton, Edinburgh, EH13 0NW; T.-031-441 7225.

Smith, Professor Stanley William, MA, PhD (Cantab). Professor and Head of English, Dundee University, since 1989 (Reader in English, 1988-89); b. 12.1.43, Warrington; 2 s.; 1 d. Educ. Boteler Grammar School, Warrington; Jesus College, Cambridge. Assistant Lecturer in English, Aberdeen University, 1967-68; Lecturer in English, Dundee University, 1968-84; Senior Lecturer, 1984-88; Visiting Professor, University of Florence, 1987; Chair, Council for University English, since 1991. Publications: A Sadly Contracted Hero: The Comic Self in Post-War American Fiction, 1981; Inviolable Voice: History and Twentieth Century Poetry, 1982; 20th Century Poetry, 1983; W.H. Auden, 1985; Edward Thomas, 1986; W.B. Yeats, 1990; General Editor, Longman Critical Reader series and Longman Studies in 20th-century Literature series. Recreations: the arts; politics; chess; travel. Address: (b.) English Department, The University, Dundee, DD1 4HN; T.-0382 307411.

Smith, W. Gordon. Writer; b. 13.12.28, Edinburgh. Journalist; Radio/TV Producer, BBC, 25 years; author of plays: Vincent; Jock; Knox; Sweeter Than All The Roses; A North British Working Man's Guide to the Arts; Wizard; On the Road to Avizandum; Marie of Scotland; Xanadu.

Smith, William Angus, BEM, JP. Chairman, Education Committee, Shetland Islands Council, since 1975 (Vice Chairman, Housing Committee, 1982-85); Vice-Chairman, Lerwick Harbour Trust; b. 20.8.19, Burra Isle, Shetland; m., Daisy Manson; 3 s. Educ. Anderson Educational Institute. Engineer, British Telecomms, 1937-83; Royal Signals, UK, Middle East, Burma, India, Germany, 1940-46; Member, Lerwick Town Council and Zetland County Council, 1967-75; Member, Lerwick Harbour Trust, since 1967 (except for short break); Provost of Lerwick, 1971-74; Member, Shetland Islands Council, since 1975; Member, Shetland Area Health Board, 1974-89; Member, Electricity Consultative Council for North of Scotland District, 1974-90; Member, Clickimin Recreational Trust. Recreations: crosswords; reading. Address: (h.) 14 Bruce Crescent, Lerwick, Shetland, ZE1 0PB; T.-0595 2121.

Smith, William Anthony. Director, Scottish Office Training Unit, 1982-86; b. 14.9.28, Edinburgh; m., Maureen Enid Graham; 2 s.; 2 d. Educ. George Heriot's School, Edinburgh. Various executive posts, Department of Health and Social Security; Senior O. & M. Officer, HM Treasury; Head of O. & M. Unit, Scottish Office; UN Consultant in Management, Costa Rica, and in Organisation Development, Iran; Personnel Manager, Scottish Office. Past Chairman, Edinburgh Oxfam Committee. Publication: Poets and Peasants, 1978. Recreations: part-time antiquarian and second-hand bookseller; wine-making; reading and writing about avocados. Address: (h.) 5 Stirling Road, Edinburgh; T.-031-552 1850.

Smith, William Leggat, CBE, MC, TD, JP, DL, BA (Oxon), LLB, LLD; b. 30.1.18, Kilmarnock; m., Yvonne Menna Williams; 1 s.; 2 d. Educ. Glasgow Academy; Queen's College, Oxford; Glasgow University. Commissioned (TA), Cameronians (Scottish Rifles), 1939; served Second World War in UK, Europe, USA; Solicitor, 1947-86; Chairman, Governors, Glasgow Academy, 1972-80; Deacon Convener, Trades of Glasgow, 1964-65; Dean, Royal Faculty of Procurators in Glasgow, 1976-79; Member, Reviewing Committee on Export of Works of Art, 1980-82; Convener, Retirement Scheme of Church of Scotland, 1976-80; Chairman, Charles Rennie Mackintosh Society, 1985-88; Chairman, Indigent Gentlewomen of Scotland Fund, since 1985; Chairman, Glasgow School of Art, 1975-88. Recreations: gardening; salmon fishing. Address: (h.) The Cottage, Clachan of Campsie, Glasgow; T.-0360 311434.

Smith, William Wilson Campbell, MA (Cantab), LLB (Glas). Partner, Biggart Baillie & Gifford, WS, Solicitors,

Glasgow and Edinburgh, since 1974; b. 17.5.46, Glasgow; m., Elizabeth Margaret Richards; 2 d. Educ. Glasgow Academy; St. Catharine's College, Cambridge; Glasgow University. Qualified as a Solicitor, 1972; Assistant Solicitor, Herbert Smith & Co., London, 1972-73. Member, various committees, Law Society of Scotland; Member, Joint Insolvency Examination Board; Deacon, Incorporation of Barbers, Glasgow, 1989-90; Trustee, Glassford Sheltered Housing Trust. Recreations: croquet; golf; barbershop singing. Address: (b.) 105 West George Street, Glasgow, G2 1QP; T.-041-221 7020.

Smout, Professor Thomas Christopher, MA, PhD, FRSE, FRSA, FBA. Director, St. John's House Institute for Advanced Historical Studies, St. Andrews University since 1991; Professor of Scottish History, 1980-91; b. 19.12.33, Birmingham; m., Anne-Marie; 1 s.; 1 d. Educ. Leys School, Cambridge; Clare College, Cambridge. Department of Economic History, Edinburgh University 1975-79. Member, Board, Scottish Natural Heritage; Trustee, National Museums of Scotland; Member, Royal Commission on the Ancient and Historic Monuments of Scotland. Address: (b.) St. Andrews University, St. Andrews, Fife.

Smylie, Henry Gordon, MB, ChB, MD, FRCPath. Senior Lecturer, Department of Bacteriology, Aberdeen University, and Honorary Consultant, Grampian Health Board, Aberdeen Hospitals, since 1964; b. 31.7.26, Aberdeen; m., Evelyn Allan Gray; 4 s. Educ. Robert Gordon's College; Aberdeen University. Variously employed in the newspaper, clothing and building industries, farming and forestry; three years' volunteer service, Royal Navy, 1944-47; undergraduate, 1948-54; several months in general practice, then Probationer Lecturer, Bacteriology, Aberdeen University, 1955; Governor, Robert Gordon's College, since 1981. Recreations: swimming; cycling; gardening. Address: (h.) Birken Lodge, Bieldside, Aberdeen; T.-Aberdeen 861305.

Smyth, Professor John Crocket, OBE, BSc, PhD, DipEd, CBiol, FIBiol, FLS, FRSA. Emeritus Professor of Biology, Paisley College, since 1988; Honorary Professor (Environmental Education), Stirling University, since 1988; Chairman, Scottish Environmental Education Council, 1983-91, President, since 1991; Chairman, Secretary of State for Scotland's Working Group on Environmental Education, 1990-92; b. 21.3.24, Edinburgh; m., Elizabeth Wallace Learmond; 1 s.; 1 d. Educ. George Watson's College; Edinburgh University. Assistant Lecturer in Zoology, Edinburgh University; Lecturer to Head, Department of Biology, Paisley College; Commissioner, Countryside Commission for Scotland, 1990-92; Vice-President, Royal Zoological Society of Scotland; Charter Award for 1989, Institute of Biology, and former Secretary and Chairman, Scottish Branch; Member, Steering Committee, IUCN Commission on Education and Communication; Tree of Learning Award, 1990; Chairman, N.W. Europe Committee, 1980-85; Member, Loch Lomond Park Authority. Address: (h.) Glenpark, Johnstone, Renfrewshire, PA5 0SP; T.-0505 20219.

Smyth, Professor John Fletcher, MA, MB, BChir, MD (Cantab), MSc (Lond), FRCPE, FRCP. Professor of Medical Oncology, Edinburgh University, since 1979 (Head, Department of Clinical Oncology, since 1980); Honorary Director, Imperial Cancer Research Fund Medical Oncology Unit, Edinburgh University, since 1980; b. 26.10.45, Dursley; m., Catherine Ellis; 2 d. Educ. Bryanston School; Trinity College, Cambridge. Trained, St. Bartholomews Hospital, Royal Postgraduate Medical School and Institute of Cancer Research, London; National Cancer Institute, Bethesda; University of Chicago; Honorary Consultant Physician, Royal Marsden Hospital and Senior Lecturer, Institute of Cancer Research, London, 1976-79. Governor, Bryanston School.

Recreations: flying; music. Address: (h.) 18 Inverleith Avenue South, Edinburgh, EH3 5QA; T.-031-552 3775.

Smyth, Michael Jessop, MA, PhD, FRAS, FRSE. Senior Lecturer, Department of Astronomy, Edinburgh University, since 1965; b. 12.11.26, Hounslow; m., Mary Florence Isabel Speyer; 2 s. Educ. Hounslow College; Selwyn College, Cambridge. Lecturer in Astronomy, Edinburgh University, 1950-54; Assistant Director and Acting Director, Dunsink Observatory, Dublin, 1954-59; Lecturer in Astronomy, Edinburgh University, 1959-65. Member, British National Committee for Astronomy. Recreations: travel; photography; hill-walking; swimming; gardening; wine-making. Address: (b.) Royal Observatory, Edinburgh, EH9 3HJ; T.-031-668 8100.

Snaith, David William, MSc, PhD, CEng, MIM, CChem, FRSC. Principal, Stow College, Glasgow, since 1983; b. 30.6.40, Birmingham; m., Susan Willoughby Tucker; 1 s.; 2 d. Educ. Kings Norton Grammar School, Birmingham; Aston University. Research Chemist, Birmingham Small Arms Co. Ltd.; Assistant Lecturer in Chemistry, Matthew Boulton Technical College, Birmingham, 1965; Lecturer in Chemistry, Ipswich Civic College, 1969; Deputy Head, Department of Science and Technology, North Lindsey College of Technology, Scunthorpe, 1974; Head, Department of Science, North East Liverpool Technical College, 1980. Royal Society of Chemistry: Assistant Secretary, East Anglian Section Committee, 1972-74, Chairman, Southumbria Section, 1977-78. Recreations: hill-walking; photography; music; rifle shooting. Address: (b.) Stow College, 43 Shamrock Street, Glasgow, G4 9LD; T.-041-332 1786.

Sneader, Walter, BSc, PhD, MRPharmS. Honorary President, Glasgow Jewish Representative Council, since 1989 (President, 1986-89); Chairman, West of Scotland Council of Christians and Jews, 1987-89; Senior Lecturer in Pharmaceutical Chemistry, Strathclyde University; b. 2.11.39, Glasgow; m., Myrna Joan Levine; 2 s.; 1 d. Educ. Glasgow High School; Glasgow University. After a period with National Research Council of Canada, joined Strathclyde University; Member, National Pharmaceutical Advisory Committee; former Executive Member, Glasgow Board of Jewish Education; former Hon. Secretary, Jewish Representative Council; Member, BBC Religious Advisory Committee, since 1989; elected Member, Jewish Board of Deputies, 1988. Publications: Drug Discovery: The Evolution of Modern Medicines, 1985; Drug Development: From Laboratory to Clinic, 1986. Address: (b.) Department of Pharmaceutical Sciences, Strathclyde University, Glasgow, G1 1XW; T.-041-552 4400.

Snedden, Charles, OBE, OStJ, JP. Director, J. Robertson (Builders) Ltd., Bo'ness; Director and Board Member, Scottish Homes, since 1988; Member, University Court, Stirling; b. 28.3.32, Bo'ness; m., Margaret Kidd; 1 s.; 1 d. Educ. Bo'ness Academy. Joined Bo'ness Town Council and West Lothian County Council, 1959; Provost of Bo'ness, 1964-75; former Member, Council of Management, Scottish Special Housing Association (Depute Chairman); Convener, Central Regional Council, 1986-90; Honorary President: Bo'ness United FC, Kinneil Colliery Silver Band, West Lothian Golf Club; Trustee and Director, Bo'ness Heritage Trust. Recreations: gardening; reading. Address: Pennvael, 2 Deanburn Grove, Bo'ness, West Lothian, EH51 0NA; T.-0506 822355.

Sneddon, Ian Naismith, OBE (1969), BSc, DSc, BA, MA, FRS, FRSE, FIMA, FRSA. Honorary Senior Research Fellow and Emeritus Professor of Mathematics, Glasgow University; Vice-Chairman, Advisory Council, Scottish Opera; Vice-Chairman, Board of Directors, Citizens' Theatre, Glasgow;

b. 8.12.19, Glasgow; m., Mary Campbell Macgregor; 2 s.; 1 d. Educ. Hyndland School, Glasgow; Glasgow University; Trinity College, Cambridge. Junior Scientific Officer, Ministry of Supply, 1942-45; William Bryce Fellow, Glasgow University, 1945-46; Lecturer in Natural Philosophy, Glasgow University, 1946-50; Professor of Mathematics, University College of North Staffordshire, 1950-56; Simson Professor of Mathematics, Glasgow University, 1956-85. Hon DSc: Warsaw University, Heriot-Watt University, Hull University; Kelvin Medal, Glasgow University; Makdougall-Brisbane Prize, Royal Society of Edinburgh, 1959; Eringen Medal, Society of Engineering Science, 1979; Copernicus Medal, Polish Academy of Sciences, 1973; Gold Medal for Culture (Poland), 1983; Member, Order of the Long Leaf Pine (North Carolina), 1964; Commander, Order of Polonia Restituta, 1969; Commander, Order of Merit of Poland, 1979. Recreations: music; painting in oils; photography. Address: (h.) 19 Crown Terrace, Glasgow, G12 9ES; T.-041-339 4114.

Sole, David Michael Barclay, BA (Hons). Rugby Player; b. 8.5.62, Aylesbury; m., Jane; 1 s.; 1 d. Educ. Trinity College, Glenalmond; Exeter University. Has played rugby for Scotland since 1986 (38 caps); also British Lions and Barbarians; Captain of Scotland, 1989-91; tour to New Zealand; 1991 World Cup. Address: (b.) 33 Ellersley Road, Edinburgh; T.-031-337 7373.

Solomon, Sally Elizabeth, BSc, PhD. Senior Lecturer and Head, Poultry Research Group, Department of Veterinary Anatomy, Glasgow Veterinary School; b. 19.4.44, Glasgow; m., Dr. Roger Tippett. Educ. Rothesay Academy; Woodside Secondary School; Glasgow University. Assistant Lecturer, Veterinary Histology, 1968; Lecturer, 1972. Chairman, Social Committee, European Poultry Congress 1994; Treasurer, West of Scotland Microscopy Group; Council Member, WPSA; Member, EC Working Party on egg quality. Publications: 78 papers; two books. Recreations: walking; swimming; pottery; gardening. Address: (b.) Poultry Research Group, Department of Veterinary Anatomy, Bearsden Road, Glasgow, G61 1QH; T.-041-339 8855.

Somerville, Donald Robert, LLB, NP. Director of Legal Services, Inverness District Council, since 1984; b. 19.3.53, Edinburgh; m., Margaret; 3 d. Educ. Scotus Academy, Edinburgh; Edinburgh University. Law Apprentice/Legal Assistant, private practice, 1974-77; Principal Legal Assistant, West Lothian District Council, 1977-84. Recreations: hill-walking; jogging; following the Hearts. Address: (b.) Town House, Inverness; T.-0463 239111.

Sommerville, John Kenneth, CA. Partner, French & Cowan, CA, Glasgow, since 1970; Council Member, Institute of Chartered Accountants of Scotland, 1984-90; Council Member, Association of Accounting Technicians, since 1989; b. 1.3.42, Glasgow; m., Iris Alexa Hutchison; 3 d. Educ. Kelvinside Academy. Member, Board of Governors, Kelvinside Academy, since 1976 (Chairman of Board, since 1985). Recreations: golf; skiing; running. Address: (b.) Pegasus House, 375 West George Street, Glasgow, G2 4LH; T.-041-221 2984.

Soulsby, John Allan, MA, PhD. Senior Lecturer in Biogeography, St. Andrews University, since 1975; b. 18.1.35, Grosmont; m., Evelyn Margaret Coutts; 1 s.; 1 d. Educ. Whitby Grammar School; Aberdeen University; Dublin University. Junior Lecturer, Dublin University, 1961-64; Lecturer, St. Andrews University, 1964-75; Visiting Professor, University of Missouri, 1968-69; Professor of Earth Sciences, University of Malawi, 1976-79 (Dean of Science, 1978). Member, Council, Royal Scottish Geographical Society. Recreations: golf; hill-walking; jazz. Address: (b.) Department of Geography and Geology, St. Andrews University, St. Andrews, KY16 9ST; T.-0334 76161, Ext. 8293.

Souter, Ian Patrick, MA, CA. Partner, Ernst & Young, since 1975; b. 15.3.43, Aberdeen; m., May; 1 s.; 1 d. Educ. Aberdeen Grammar School; Aberdeen University. Qualified CA, 1967; joined Whinney Murray & Co., London, 1967; Partner, 1975; established Aberdeen Office, Whinney Murray, 1975; Member, Board of Governors, RGIT, since 1987 (Deputy Chairman); Member, Council, ICAS, 1988-91; Chairman, Grampian Committee, ICAS, 1988-91. Recreations: sport; holidays in France. Address: (b.) Ernst & Young, 50 Huntly Street, Aberdeen, AB9 1XN; T.-0224 640033.

Southam, Professor John Chambers, MA, MD, FRCPath, FDS. Professor of Oral Medicine and Pathology, Edinburgh University, since 1977; Secretary, Faculty of Dental Surgery, Royal College of Surgeons Edinburgh, since 1991; b. 3.2.34, Leeds; m., Susan; 1 s.; 1 d. Educ. Leeds Grammar School; Cambridge University; Leeds University. Lecturer, Oral Pathology, Sheffield University, 1963-70; Lecturer, Dental Surgery, Edinburgh University, 1970-71; Senior Lecturer, 1971-77. Member, General Dental Council, 1984-94. Publication: Oral Pathology (Co-author). Recreations: gardening; walking; travel; Scouting. Address: (h.) 13 Corstorphine House Avenue, Edinburgh, EH12 7AD; T.-031-334 3013.

Southcott, Barry John, BSc (Econ), AMSIA. Director, British Investment Trust; Managing Director, Marketable Securities, British Coal Pension Fund, now CIN Management Ltd., since 1975; b. 27.3.50, London; m., Lesley Anne Parkinson. Educ. Latymer Upper School; Bradford University. Phillips & Drew, 1971-75; British Coal Pension Fund, since 1975. Recreations: tennis; football; music. Address: (b.) 4 Melville Crescent, Edinburgh.

Soutter, Patrick Eliot, BL, NP. Retired Solicitor; Chairman, Department of Health and Social Security Appeal Tribunal, Hamilton, 1980-91; Honorary Sheriff, Hamilton, since 1984; b. 13.4.19, Hamilton; m., Muriel Gettings Johnston; 1 d. Educ. Hamilton Academy; Glasgow University. RAF (Pilot), 1939-45; joined family legal business, 1951; retired as Senior Partner, 1984; Secretary and Treasurer, Hamilton Golf Club, since 1951 (now Joint Secretary and Treasurer). Recreations: golf (played for Glasgow University and Lanarkshire County); fishing; curling. Address: (h.) The Linn, Woodhead Gardens, Bothwell, Lanarkshire; T.-0698 853123.

Spalding, Julian, BA, FMA. Director, Glasgow Museums and Art Galleries, since 1989; b. 15.6.47, London; 1 s. Educ. Chislehurst and Sidcup Grammar School for Boys; Nottingham University. Art Assistant: Leicester Museum & Art Gallery, 1970-71, Durham Light Infantry Museum & Arts Centre, 1971-72; Keeper, Mappin Art Gallery, 1972-76; Depute Director, 1976-82; Director of Arts, Sheffield City Council, 1982-85; Director, Manchester City Art Galleries, 1985-89; Director, National Museum of Labour History, 1987-89. Member, Arts Council of GB, 1978-82; Founder, Art Galleries Association, 1976; Director, Guild of St. George, since 1983; Director, Mayfest, since 1989; Member, Crafts Council, since 1986; Member, British Council, since 1987; Advisory Member, new British Library. Publications: L.S. Lowry, 1979; Three Little Books on Painting, 1984; various exhibition catalogues. Recreations: cycling; gardening; painting. Address: (b.) Art Gallery and Museum, Kelvingrove, Glasgow, G3 8AG; T.-041-357 3929.

Spawforth, David Meredith, MA (Oxon). Headmaster, Merchiston Castle School, since 1981; b. 2.1.38, Wakefield; m., Yvonne Mary Gude; 1 s.; 1 d. Educ. Silcoates School; Hertford College, Oxford. Assistant Master, Winchester

College, 1961-64; Housemaster, Wellington College, 1964-80; BP Education Fellow, Keble College, Oxford, 1977. Recreations: travel - especially France and Italy; theatre; walking. Address: (b.) Merchiston Castle School, Colinton, Edinburgh.

Spear, Professor Walter Eric, PhD, DSc, FRS, FRSE, FInstP. Professor of Physics, Carnegie Laboratory of Physics, Dundee University, since 1968; b. 20.1.21, Frankfurt/Main, West Germany; m., Hilda Doris King; 2 d. Educ. London University. Lecturer in Physics, Leicester University, 1953; Visiting Professor: Purdue University, 1957-58, N. Carolina University, 1965-66; Reader in Physics, Leicester University, 1967-68. Max Born Prize, 1977; Europhysics Prize, 1977; Makdougal-Brisbane Medal, Royal Society of Edinburgh, 1981. Rank Prize for Optoelectronics, 1988; Rumford Medal, Royal Society, 1990. Recreations: music; languages; literature. Address: (b.) Carnegie Laboratory of Physics, Dundee University, Dundee, DD1 4HN; T.-0382 23181, Ext. 4563.

Speirs, John A.A., CA, FRICS. Managing Partner, Speirs Gumley; b. 16.3.37, Glasgow; m., Dorothea Ross Kelly; 1 s.; 1 d. Educ. Merchiston Castle School, Edinburgh. Chairman, Scottish Junior Branch, Royal Institution of Chartered Surveyors, 1969-70; President, Property Owners & Factors Association, Glasgow, 1979-81; Deputy Chairman, West of Scotland TSB, 1982-83; Board Member, TSB Scotland PLC, 1986-89; Member, East Kilbride Development Corporation, since 1987; Deacon, Incorporation of Weavers in Glasgow, 1973-74; Governor, Glasgow School of Art, 1982-88; Deacon Convener, Trades of Glasgow, 1985-86; Member of Court, Glasgow University, since 1987; Trustee, Trades Hall of Glasgow Trust. Recreations: angling; shooting; sailing. Address: (h.) Clifton, Moor Road, Strathblane, by Glasgow, G63 9EX; T.-Blanefield 70424.

Speirs, Norman Thomas, BSc, MB, ChB, DMRD, FACI. Consultant Radiologist, Lothian Health Board, since 1958; b. 31.8.24, London; m., Dorothy Glen; 1 d. Educ. George Watson's Boys' College; Edinburgh University. House Surgeon, Royal Infirmary, Edinburgh; Captain, RAMC; specialist training in Radiology; various Registrar appointments, Edinburgh; retired Consultant Radiologist, Princess Margaret Rose Orthopaedic Hospital, Edinburgh, and Roodlands Hospital, Haddington; entered part-time private practice (now at Murrayfield Hospital, Edinburgh). Past Chairman, Scottish Association of Amateur Cinematographers; elected to National Council, Institute of Amateur Cinematographers (IAC) and awarded its Fellowship, 1981; National Chairman, IAC, 1990-92. Address: (h.) 5 Blackbarony Road, Edinburgh, EH16 5QP; T.-031-667 6662.

Speirs, William MacLeod. Deputy General Secretary, Scottish TUC; b. 8.3.52, Dumbarton; m., Lynda; 1 s.; 1 d. Educ. John Neilson High School, Paisley; Strathclyde University. Chairperson, 7:84 Theatre Co. (Scotland); Chairperson, Scottish Friends of Palestine; Governor, Glasgow College of Technology. Recreations: watching St. Mirren FC; playing football and cricket. Address: (b.) STUC, 16 Woodlands Terrace, Glasgow, G3 6DF; T.-041-332 4946.

Spence, Professor Alastair Andrew, MD, FCAnaes, FRCP Glas, FRCSEdin, FRCSP (Hon). Professor of Anaesthetics, Edinburgh University, since 1984; Honorary Consultant Anaesthetist, Royal Infirmary, Edinburgh; President, President, College of Anaesthetists; b. 18.9.36, Glasgow; m., Maureen Isobel Aitchison; 2 s. Educ. Air Academy; Glasgow University. Professor and Head, University Department of Anaesthesia, Western Infirmary, Glasgow, 1969-84; Editor, British Journal of Anaesthesia, 1973-83; Hunterian Professor, Royal College of Surgeons of England, 1974; Joseph Clover Lecturer, 1990. Recreations: golf; gardening. Address: (h.) Harewood, Kilmacolm, PA13 4HX; T.-Kilmacolm 2962.

Spence, James William, KFO (Norway), BSc, MNI, AICS, MRIN, DL. Master Mariner, since 1971; Shipbroker, since 1975; Company Director, since 1977; b. 19.1.45, St. Ola, Orkney; m., Margaret Paplay Stevenson; 3 s. Educ. Leith Nautical College, Edinburgh; Robert Gordon's Institute of Technology, Aberdeen; University of Wales, Cardiff. Merchant Navy, 1961-74 (Member, Nautical Institute, 1972, Member, Royal Institute of Navigation, 1971); Micoperi SpA, 1974-75 (Temporary Assistant Site Co-ordinator on Scapa Flow Project); John Jolly (Shipbrokers, Stevedores, Shipping and Forwarding Agents) since 1975 (Manager, 1975, Junior Partner, 1976-77, Proprietor and Managing Director, since 1977). Vice-Consul for Norway, 1976, Consul, 1978; Vice-Consul for the Netherlands, 1978; Member, Kirkwall Community Council, 1978-82; Member, Orkney Pilotage Committee, 1979-88; Chairman, Kirkwall Port Employers' Association, 1979-87 (Member, since 1975); Station Honorary Secretary, RNLI, Kirkwall Lifeboat, 1987 (Deputy Launching Authority, 1976-87); Chairman, Pier Arts Centre Trust, 1989-91 (Trustee, 1980-91); Vice-Chairman, Association of Honorary Norwegian Consuls in the UK and Ireland, 1991. Recreations: oenology; equestrian matters; Orcadian history. Address: (h.) Alton House, Kirkwall, Orkney KN15 1NA; T.-0856 2268.

Spence, Professor John, ARCST, BSc, MEng, PhD, DSc, CEng, FIMechE. Chairman and Head, Department of Mechanical Engineering, Strathclyde University, since 1987 (Trades House of Glasgow Professor of Mechanics of Materials, since 1982); b. 5.11.37, Chapelhall; m., Margaret Gray Hudson; 2 s. Educ. Airdrie Academy; Royal College of Science and Technology; Sheffield University. Engineering apprenticeship, Stewarts & Lloyds (now British Steel Corporation); Senior Engineer, then Head of Stress Analysis, Babcock & Wilcox Research Division; Strathclyde University: Lecturer, 1966, Senior Lecturer, Reader. Serves on several national committees, including Institution of Mechanical Engineers, SERC and British Standards Institution. Address: (b.) Department of Mechanical Engineering, Strathclyde University, 75 Montrose Street, Glasgow, G1 1XJ; T.-041-552 4400, Ext. 2324.

Spence, Roger Norman Abbot, Managing Director, Royal Lyceum Theatre Company, since 1983; b. 28.9.47, Lincoln; m., Judith Marie Mohekey. Educ. Lincoln Grammar School; Lincoln College of Art. Early career in production and as Lighting Designer in theatre, opera and ballet; General Manager, The Scottish Ballet, 1975-80; Administrative Director, Tynewear Theatre Company, 1980-83. Vice President, Theatrical Management Association; Board Director: Edinburgh Capital Group, Scottish International Children's Festival, National Council for Drama Training, Scottish Arts Lobby (SALVO), Federation of Scottish Theatre. Address: (h.) 21 Glencairn Crescent, Edinburgh EH12 5BT; (b.) Royal Lyceum Theatre Company, Grindlay Street, Edinburgh EH3 9AX; T.-031-337 8330.

Spence, William Arthur, QPM, LLB, BA. Deputy Chief Constable, Tayside Police, since 1988; b. 20.11.43, Ellon; m., Hazel; 2 d. Educ. Ellon Academy; Strathclyde University; Open University. Constable, Renfrew and Bute Constabulary, 1962, to Assistant Chief Constable, Strathclyde Police, 1986. Member, Home Office Joint Working Group on Racial Attacks and Harassment; Member, Funding Panel, Scottish Victim Support; Scottish Liaison Officer in European football matters; Member, Secretary of State's Crime Prevention Committee and Chairman, Crime Prevention Working Group; Past Chairman, Crime Prevention Working Committee. Recreations: reading; gardening; theatre. Addsress: (b.) Tayside Police, PO Box 59, West Bell Street, Dundee, DD1 9JU; T.-0382 23200.

Spencely, John Despenser, MA, BArch, DipTP, RIBA, PPRIAS, MRTPI, FCIArb. Partner, Reiach and Hall, since 1978; Director, Buildings Investigation Centre, since 1985; b. 5.10.39, Westerham, England; m., Marilyn Anne Read; 1 d. (by pr. m.). Educ. Bryanston School; Cambridge University; Edinburgh University. Architect and Town Planner, Reiach and Hall, since 1965; Director, CASCO (Consultants in Urban Renewal), 1987-89. Member: Council, RIAS, since 1977, Council, RIBA, 1987-91; former Member, Scottish Building Contract Committee; President: Edinburgh Architectural Association, 1984-86, Royal Incorporation of Architects in Scotland, 1989-91; Member, Advisory Committee on Arbitration to Scottish Law Commission; Honorary Fellow, Faculty of Social Sciences, Edinburgh University, since 1989; Freeman of the City of London; Liveryman, Worshipful Company of Arbitrators. Recreations: sailing; reading; collecting some unfashionable 20th century authors; making jam. Address: (b.) 6 Darnaway Street, Edinburgh EH3 6BG; T.-031-225 8444.

Spencer, Rt. Rev. Alfred Raymond, OSB. Abbot, Pluscarden Abbey, Elgin, since 1966; b. 28.6.15, Scopwick, Lincoln. Educ. Panton College, Lincoln; Franciscan Friary, Crawley. Joined Capuchin Franciscan Order, 1934; Priest, 1941; pastoral work in England and Wales; Assistant Novice Master, Pantasaph, North Wales, five years; transferred to Benedictine Abbey, Prinknash, 1951; Novice Master, 1953; elected Conventual Prior of Pluscarden, 1966 (Priory given status of Abbey, 1974); confirmed as first Abbot. Address: Pluscarden Abbey, Elgin, Moray, IV30 3UA; T.-034 389 257.

Spiers, Rev. John McLaren, LTh. Minister, Orchardhill Church, Giffnock, since 1977; b. 12.12.43, Edinburgh; m., Janet Diane Watson; 2 d. Educ. George Watson's College, Edinburgh; Glasgow University. Trainee, Scottish Union and National Insurance Company, 1961-65; University, 1966-71; Probationer Assistant, Drumchapel Old Parish Church, Glasgow, 1971-72; Minister, South Church, Barrhead, 1972-77. Recreations: music; art; family life; various sports. Address: 23 Huntly Avenue, Giffnock, Glasgow, G46 6LW.

Spilg, Walter Gerson Spence, MB, ChB (Hons), FRCPath, FRCPG. Consultant Pathologist, Victoria Infirmary, Glasgow, since 1972, in Administrative Charge, since 1986; Honorary Clinical Lecturer, Glasgow University, since 1973; b. 27.10.37, Glasgow; m., Vivien Anne Burns; 1 s.; 2 d. Educ. Hutcheson's Boys' Grammar School, Glasgow; Glasgow University. Registrar in Pathology, Glasgow Royal Infirmary, 1965-68; Senior Registrar in Pathology, Victoria Infirmary, Glasgow, 1968-69; Lecturer in Pathology, Glasgow University (Western Infirmary), 1969-72. Member, Greater Glasgow Health Board Area Medical Sub-Committee in Laboratory Medicine; Chairman, Laboratory Medicine Committee, West of Scotland Committee for Postgraduate Medical Education; Member, Forensic Pathology Liaison Committee. Recreations: bridge; golf. Address: (h.) 98 Ayr Road, Newton Mearns, Glasgow, G77 6EJ; T.-041-639 3130.

Spratt, Col. Douglas Norman, CBE, TD, DL. Partner, Cameo of Edinburgh, since 1984; b. 18.9.20, Ramsgate; m., Margaret; 1 d. Educ. Sir Roger Manwood's Grammar School, Sandwich, Kent. President, Edinburgh Branch, Institute of Marketing; Honorary Col., 71 (Scottish) Engineer Regiment (V); Chairman, Friends of the Reserve Forces Association, Scotland; Vice Chairman, Action Research in Scotland (Chairman, Edinburgh Committee); Member, High Constables of Edinburgh; Deputy Lieutenant, City of Edinburgh; Member of the Military Attaches London; Lighting Director, Edinburgh Military Tattoo. Recreations: fishing; sailing. Address: (h.) 6 Fernielaw Avenue, Edinburgh, EH13 0EE; T.-031-441 1962.

Sprent, Professor Janet I., BSc, ARCS, PhD, DSc, FRSE. Professor of Plant Biology, Dundee University, since 1989; b. 10.1.34, Slough; m., Emeritus Professor Peter Sprent. Educ. Slough High School; Imperial College, London; Tasmania University. Has spent 23 years at Dundee University; research focussed on nitrogen fixing legumes, both tree and crop species; currently involved in international collaboration, mainly in Africa and Brazil; Dean of Science and Engineering, 1987-89. Publications: three books and over 100 chapters/papers. Recreations: flying; hill walking. Address: Department of Biological Sciences, Dundee University, Dundee DD1 4HN; T.-0382 23181, Ext. 4279.

Sprent, Professor Peter, BSc, PhD, FRSE. Statistician and Author; Professor of Statistics, Dundee University, 1972-85, Professor Emeritus, since 1985; b. 28.1.23, Hobart, Australia; m., Janet Irene Findlater. Educ. Hutchins School, Hobart, Tasmania; Tasmania University; London University. Lecturer in Mathematics, Tasmania University, 1948-57; Statistician, East Malling Research Station, 1958-67; Senior Lecturer in Statistics, Dundee University, 1967-72. Sometime Member, Editorial Boards, Journal of Royal Statistical Society, Journal of American Statistical Association, Biometrics. Publications: seven books and many papers on statistics and related topics. Recreations: aviation; golf; hill-walking. Address: (h.) 32 Birkhill Avenue, Wormit, Newport-on-Tay, DD6 8PW; T.-0382 541706.

Sprigge, Professor Timothy Lauro Squire. Emeritus Professor of, and Endowment Fellow at, Edinburgh University, since 1989 (Professor of Logic and Metaphysics, 1979-89); b. 14.1.32, London; m., Giglia Gordon; 1 s.; 2 d. Educ. Gonville and Caius College, Cambridge. Lecturer in Philosophy, University College, London, 1961-63; Lecturer, then Reader in Philosophy, Sussex University, 1963-79. Publications: The Correspondence of Jeremy Bentham, Volumes 1 and 2; Facts, Words and Beliefs; Santayana: An Examination of his Philosophy; The Vindication of Absolute Idealism; Theories of Existence; The Rational Foundations of Ethics. Recreation: backgammon. Address: (b.) Philosophy Department, David Hume Tower, Edinburgh University, George Square, Edinburgh; T.-031-650 1000.

Sprot of Haystoun, Lt.-Col. Aidan Mark, MC, JP. Lord Lieutenant, Tweeddale, since 1980; Landowner (Haystoun Estate) and Farmer, since 1965; b. 17.6.19, Lilliesleaf. Educ. Belhaven Hill; Stowe. Commissioned, Royal Scots Greys, 1940; served Palestine, 1941-42, Western Desert, 1942-43, Italy, 1943-44, NW Europe, 1944-45; continued serving with Regiment in Germany until 1952, Libya, Egypt and Jordan, 1952-55, UK, 1955-58, Germany, 1958-62; Adjutant, 1944-45; Commanding Officer, 1959-62; retired, 1962. County Councillor, Peeblesshire, 1963-75; DL (Peeblesshire), 1966-80; Member, Queen's Bodyguard for Scotland (Royal Company of Archers), since 1950; County Director, Peeblesshire Branch, Red Cross, 1966-74, Patron, since 1983; County Commissioner, Peeblesshire Scout Association, 1968-73; Honorary Secretary, Royal Caledonian Hunt, 1964-74; President, Lowlands of Scotland TA&VRA, 1986-89; President, Lothian Federation of Boys' Clubs, since 1989. Recreations: country sports; motor cycle touring. Address: (h.) Crookston, by Peebles, EH45 9JQ; T.-Kirkton Manor 209.

Sprott, Gavin Chappell, MA. Head, Working Life Section, National Museums of Scotland and Curator, Scottish Agricultural Museum, Ingliston; b. 23.7.43, Dundee; m., Maureen Turnbull; 2 s.; 1 d. Educ. Edinburgh University. Research Assistant, Scottish Country Life Section, National Museum of Antiquities of Scotland, 1972-79. Recreations: cycling; walking. Address: (b.) National Museums of Scotland, Queen Street, Edinburgh, EH2; T.-031-225 7534.

Squire, Geoffrey, DFA, ARSA, RSW, RGI. Portrait and Landscape Painter; Senior Lecturer, Glasgow School of Art, 1971-88 (retired); b. 21.2.23, Cleckheaton; m., Jean Marie; 1 s.; 1 d. Educ. Heckmondwike Grammar School; Leeds College of Art; Ruskin School, Oxford; Slade, London. Fleet Air Arm, Europe and Far East, 1942-46. Lecturer, Glasgow School of Art, 1948; elected ARSA, 1977, RGI, 1980, RSW, 1983. Recreation: vintage motoring. Address: (h.) The Studio, Links Place, Elie, Fife.

Squire, Rachel Anne, BA, CQSW. MP (Labour), Dunfermline West, since 1992; b. 13.7.54, Carshalton, Surrey; m., Allan Mason. Educ. Godolphin and Latymer Girls' School; Durham University. Social Worker, Birmingham Social Services, 1975-81; National Union of Public Employees, 1981-92. Recreations: archaeology; swimming. Address: (h.) 125 Whitelaw Drive, Bathgate, West Lothian; T.-0506 56753.

Stachura, Peter Desmond, MA, PhD, FRHistS. Reader in Modern History, Stirling University, since 1983; b. 2.8.44, Galashiels; m., Kay Higgins; 1 s.; 1 d. Educ. St. Mirin's RC Academy, Paisley; Glasgow University; East Anglia University. Research Fellow, Institut for Europaische Geschichte, Mainz, Germany, 1970-71; Lecturer in History, Stirling University, 1971-83. Publications: Nazi Youth in the Weimar Republic; The Weimar Era and Hitler: a critical bibliography; The Shaping of the Nazi State (Editor); The German Youth Movement, 1900-1945; Gregor Strasser and the Rise of Nazism; The Nazi Machtergreifung (Editor); Unemployment and the Great Depression in Weimar Germany (Editor); The Weimar Republic and the Younger Proletariat: an economic and social analysis; Political Leaders in Weimar Germany: a biographical study; Themes of Modern Polish History. Recreations: supporting Celtic FC; discovering Poland; gardening. Address: (h.) Ashcroft, Chalton Road, Bridge of Allan, FK9 4EF; T.-0786 832793.

Stair, 13th Earl of (John Aymer Dalrymple), KCVO (1978), MBE (1941). Captain General, Queen's Bodyguard for Scotland (Royal Company of Archers), 1973-88; b. 9.10.06; m., Davina Bowes-Lyon; 3 s. Educ. Eton; Sandhurst. Colonel (retired), Scots Guards. Address: (h.) Lochinch Castle, Stranraer, Wigtownshire.

Stanforth, Professor Anthony William, BA, MA, Drphil. Professor of Languages, Heriot-Watt University, since 1981 (Head, Department of Languages, 1981-89; Dean, Faculty of Economic and Social Studies, 1989-92); b. 27.7.38, Ipswich; m., Susan Margaret Vale; 2 s. Educ. Ipswich School; King's College, Newcastle (Durham University); Marburg University. Earl Grey Memorial Fellow, Newcastle-upon-Tyne University, 1962-64; Assistant Lecturer, Manchester University, 1964-65; Lecturer, Senior Lecturer, Newcastle-upon-Tyne University, 1965-81; Visiting Assistant Professor, Wisconsin University, 1970-71. Fellow, Royal Society of Arts. Recreation: opera. Address: (b.) Department of Languages, Heriot-Watt University, Riccarton, Edinburgh, EH14 4AS; T.-031-449 5111.

Stanley, Alexander, MA. General Secretary, Scottish Secondary Teachers' Association, since 1985; b. 1.4.45, Wolverhampton. Educ. Wolverhampton Grammar School; Queen's College, Dundee; St. Andrews University. Principal Teacher of History, Rockwell High School, Dundee, 1972-84. Held various offices within SSTA. Recreations: gardening; reading; horse-racing (viewing). Address: (b.) 15 Dundas Street, Edinburgh, EH3 6QG; T.-031-556 5919/0605.

Stanley-Whyte, Rev. John James, FRGS, FSA (Scot). Minister, Church of Scotland, since 1952; Chairman, Scottish Naval, Military and Air Force Bible Society, since 1989; b. 28.7.23, Liverpool; m., Elinor Mary Barclay; 1 s. Educ. Royal College of Surgeons, Edinburgh; Edinburgh University and New College. Royal Navy, 1942-46; Royal Navy Chaplain, 1952, including Fleet Chaplain, Far East Station and Korea, 1952-54; Deputy Editor, Navy News, 1954-55; Director, Sailors' Festival, Loch Fyne, 1958; Moderator, Mid Argyll Presbytery, 1961; Moderator, Synod of Argyll and the Isles, 1962; Extra-Chaplain, Moderator of the General Assembly, 1959; various parish ministries; former Director, National Bible Society of Scotland. Recreations: golf; gardening. Address: (h.) Croft Cottage, Croft Road, Markinch, Fife, KY7 6EQ; T.-0592 758570.

Stanners, Ian Cram, FRICS. Chartered Quantity Surveyor; Chairman, Royal Institution of Chartered Surveyors in Scotland, 1986-87; b. 30.11.38, Glasgow; m., Louise Robertson; 2 d. Educ. Hutchesons' Boys' Grammar School. Chairman, Quantity Surveyors Divisional Committee, Scottish Branch, RICS, 1980-81; Vice Chairman, Scottish Building Contract Committee. Honorary Vice-President, Clyde Amateur Rowing Club. Recreations: rowing; curling. Address: (b.) 21 Woodlands Terrace, Glasgow, G3 6DF; T.-041-332 6032.

Stansfeld, John Raoul Wilmot, JP, DL, MA (Oxon), MIFM. Director, Joseph Johnston & Sons Ltd., since 1962; b. 15.1.35, London; m., Rosalinde Rachel Buxton; 3 s. Educ. Eton; Christ Church, Oxford. Lt., Gordon Highlanders, 1954-58; Chairman, North Esk District Salmon Fishery Board, 1967-80; Esk Fishery Board Committee, 1980-85; Vice Chairman, Association of Scottish District Salmon Fishery Boards, 1970-85; Director and Chairman, Montrose Chamber of Commerce, since 1984; Editor, Salmon Net Magazine, 1978-85; Chairman, Scottish Fish Farmers Association, 1970-73; Secretary, Diocese of Brechin, 1968-76. Member, Royal Company of Archers (Queen's Bodyguard for Scotland). Recreations: reading; jigsaw puzzles; trees. Address: (h.) Dunninald, Montrose, Angus, DD10 9TD; T.-0674 72666.

Stansfield, David Ashton, BSc, PhD. Senior Lecturer in Biochemistry, Dundee University, since 1974; Warden, Belmont Hall, since 1974; b. 28.10.34, Rochdale; 3 s. Educ. Hulme Grammar School, Oldham; University College of North Wales, Bangor. Assistant Lecturer, Aberdeen University, 1960-63; Lecturer and Senior Lecturer in Biochemistry, Queens College, Dundee, and Dundee University, 1963-74. Former Chairman, Dundee Liberal Association; Chairman, Dundee Liberal Democrat Association. Recreations: photography; jazz; politics. Address: (h.) 7 Hawkhill Place, Dundee; T.-0382 307252.

Stapleton, Anna Louise. Drama and Dance Director, Scottish Arts Council, since 1987; b. 20.10.49, Hitchin, Herts. Educ. Michael Hall School, Forest Row; New College of Speech and Drama, London. Company/Stage Manager for a range of theatres, 1972-77; Administrator, 1978-82, for Belt and Braces Theatre Company, Liverpool Everyman, Half Moon Theatre and others; Arts Development Officer (Drama), Greater London Arts Association, 1983-87. Recreations: travel; reading; walking; wine; friends. Address: (b.) 12 Manor Place, Edinburgh, EH3 7DD; T.-031-226 6051.

Starszakowna, Norma, DA. Textile Designer/Artist; Course Director, Textiles and Fashion, Duncan of Jordanstone College of Art, since 1984; b. 9.5.45, Crosshill; m., Andrew Taylor; 2 s. Educ. Kirkcaldy High School; Duncan of Jordanstone College of Art. Design and production of printed and dyed textiles for fashion and interior; commissioned work includes Crest Hotel, Antwerp, and General Accident HQ, Perth; exhibited widely, UK and abroad. SAC Award, 1977; Saltire Art in Architecture Award, 1983. Recreations: reading; travel; snorkelling. Address: (h.) 9 Fort Street, Magdalen Green, Dundee, DD2 1BS; T.-0382 644654.

Steedman, Robert Russell, RSA, RIBA, FRIAS, ALI, DA, MLA. Partner, Morris and Steedman, Architects and Landscape Architects; b. 3.1.29, Batu Gajah, Malaysia; m., 1, Susan Scott (m. diss.); 1 s.; 2 d.; 2, Martha Hamilton. Educ. Loretto School; School of Architecture, Edinburgh College of Art; Pennsylvania University. Governor, Edinburgh College of Art, since 1974; Commissioner, Countryside Commission for Scotland, since 1980; ARSA, 1973, Academician, 1979; Council Member, RSA, 1981 (Deputy President, 1982-83, Secretary, since 1983); Commissioner, Royal Fine Art Commission for Scotland, since 1983; former Member, Council, RIAS; nine Civic Trust Awards, 1963-78; British Steel Award, 1971; RIBA Award for Scotland, 1974; European Heritage Medal, 1975; Association for the Protection of Rural Scotland, 1977; Borders Region Award, 1984. Address: (h.) 11B Belford Mews, Edinburgh; T.-031-225 1697.

Steel, Very Rev. David, MA, BD, DD, LLD. Minister Emeritus, St. Michael's, Linlithgow, since 1977; b. 5.10.10, Hamilton; m., Sheila E.N. Martin; 3 s. (eldest son: Sir David Steel, PC, MP (qv)); 2 d. Educ. St. John's Grammar School, Hamilton; Peterhead Academy; Robert Gordon's College, Aberdeen; Aberdeen University. Minister: Denbeath, Fife, 1936-41, Bridgend, Dumbarton, 1941-46; Associate Secretary, Foreign Mission Committee, Edinburgh, 1946-49; Minister, St. Andrew's, Nairobi and East Africa, 1949-57; Locum, St. Cuthbert's, Edinburgh, 1957-58; Minister, St. Michael's, Linlithgow, 1959-76; Moderator, General Assembly of the Church of Scotland, 1974-75; Visiting Preacher and Lecturer: in America, 1953-87, Lausanne, 1978, Tanzania, 1980; Vice-President: Boys' Brigade, National Bible Society of Scotland, West Lothian Historical and Amenity Society; Member, National Committee, ESU. Publications: History of St. Michael's; The Belief; Preaching through the Year. Recreations: trout fishing; travel. Address: (h.) 39 Newbattle Terrace, Edinburgh, EH10 4SF; T.-031-447 2180.

Steel, Rt. Hon. Sir David (Martin Scott), PC (1977). MP, Tweeddale, Ettrick and Lauderdale, since 1983 (Roxburgh, Selkirk and Peebles, 1965-83); Leader, Liberal Party, 1976-88; b. 31.3.38, Kirkcaldy; m., Judith MacGregor; 3 s.; 1 d. Educ. Prince of Wales School, Nairobi; George Watson's College, Edinburgh; Edinburgh University (MA, LLB). Assistant Secretary, Scottish Liberal Party, 1962-64; Interviewer, BBC TV Scotland, 1964-65; Presenter, weekly religious programme, STV, 1966-67, for Granada, 1969, for BBC, 1971-76; Liberal Chief Whip, 1970-75; Sponsor, Private Member's Bill to reform law on abortion, 1966-67; President, Anti-Apartheid Movement of Great Britain, 1966-69; Chairman, Shelter, Scotland, 1969-73; Member, British Council of Churches, 1971-75; Vice-President, Liberal International, since 1978; Rector, Edinburgh University, 1982-85; Chubb Fellow, Yale, 1987; Hon. DUniv (Stirling), 1991; awarded Freedom of Tweeddale, 1988, and Ettrick and Lauderdale, 1990; DL, 1989; contested Central Italy seat, European elections, 1989. Publications: Boost for the Borders, 1964; Out of Control, 1968; No Entry, 1969; The Liberal Way Forward, 1975; Militant for the Reasonable Man, 1977; High Ground of Politics, 1979; A House Divided, 1980; Border Country (with Judy Steel), 1985; The Time Has Come (with David Owen), 1987; Mary Stuart's Scotland (with Judy Steel), 1987; Against Goliath, 1989. Recreations: angling; vintage motoring. Address: (b.) House of Commons, London, SW1A 0AA; T.-071-219 3373.

Steel, David Robert, MA, DPhil. Director of Administration, NHS in Scotland, since 1990; b. 29.5.48, Oxford; m., Susan Elizabeth Easton; 1 s.; 1 d. Educ. Birkenhead School; Jesus and Nuffield Colleges, Oxford. Lecturer in Public Administration, Exeter University, 1972-84; Assistant Director, National Association of Health Authorities, 1984-86; Secretary, Health Board Chairmen's and General Managers' Groups and SCOTMEG, 1986-90. Address: (b.) St. Andrew's House, Edinburgh, EH1 3DE; T.-031-244 2223.

Steel, Major Sir (Fiennes) William Strang, 2nd Bt, DL, JP; b. 24.7.12; m., Joan Henderson (deceased); 2 s.; 1 d. (deceased). Educ. Eton; Sandhurst. Retired Major, 17/21st Lancers; Member, Forestry Commission, 1958-73; Convener, Selkirk County Council, 1967-75. Address: (h.) Philiphaugh, Selkirk.

Steele, Alexander Allison, OBE (1986). Honorary Sheriff, Perth, since 1985; b. 5.10.25, Oakley, Fife; m., Patricia Joyce Hipkins; 1 s.; 2 d. Educ. Boroughmuir Secondary School. Entered Scottish Home Department, 1942; Royal Navy, 1943-46; Scottish Court Service (Sheriff Clerk's Branch), 1950; Sheriff Clerk: Dingwall, 1969-71, Perth, 1971-81, Dundee, 1981-85; Member, Lord Stewart's Committee on Alternatives to Prosecution, 1977-83; Honorary Life Member, Society of Sheriff Court Auditors. Recreations: gardening; swimming; wine-making. Address: (h.) Lyndhurst, Hillend Road, Perth; T.-0738 26611.

Steele, George Thomas, MA (Hons). Rector, Johnstone High School, since 1975; b. 19.8.39, Newquay; m., Janet Mary Craig; 4 d. Educ. Hutchesons' (Boys) Grammar School; Glasgow University; Jordanhill College of Education. Teacher, Queen's Park Secondary School, 1962-65; Teacher, Hutchesons' (Boys') Grammar School, 1965-67; Principal Teacher of Classics, Whitburn Academy, 1967-71; Assistant Head Teacher, then Depute Head Teacher, Hillpark Secondary School, 1971-75. Member, Advisory Council on Misuse of Drugs to Home Office, 1977-83; Member, GGHB Liaison Committee on Alcohol and Drug Misuse, 1977-85. Recreations: DIY; reading; walking; holidays abroad. Address: (b.) Johnstone High School, Beith Road, Johnstone; T.-Johnstone 22173.

Steele, Rev. Leslie McMillan, MA, BD (Hons). Minister, Galashiels Old Parish & St. Paul's, since 1988 (Gardner Church, Macduff, 1973-88); b. 13.12.47, Edinburgh; m., Lillias Margaret Franks; 4 d. Educ. George Heriot's, Edinburgh; Edinburgh University. Assistant Minister, St. Columba's, Largs, 1972-73. Recreation: DIY. Address: Old Parish Manse, Barr Road, Galashiels, TD1 3HX; T.-0896 2320.

Steele, Thomas Graham. Director: Radio Forth, Radio Tay; b. 11.5.45, Lanark; m., Fiona MacAuslane; 1 s.; 1 d. Educ. Larkhall Academy, Larkhall; Skerry's College, Glasgow. Lobby Correspondent, Scottish Daily Mail; TV and Radio Presenter, BBC Glasgow; Producer, BBC Local Radio; Broadcaster, Radio Clyde; Head of News and Current Affairs, Radio Forth; Director of Programmes (Group); Creator, Festival City Radio. Recreations: sailing; walking; reading; conversation. Address: (b.) Forth House, Forth Street, Edinburgh; T.-031-556 9255.

Steer, Christopher Richard, BSc (Hons), MB, ChB, DCH, FRCPE. Consultant Paediatrician; Clinical Tutor, Department of Child Life and Health, Edinburgh University; Hon. Senior Lecturer, Department of Child Life and Health, Aberdeen University; Hon. Senior Lecturer, Department of Biochemistry, St. Andrews University; Clinical Director of Obstetrics, Gynaecology and Paediatrics; b. 30.5.47, Clearbrook, near Plymouth; m., Patricia Mary Lennox. Educ. St. Olaves and St. Saviours Grammar School, London; Edinburgh University. Publications: Textbook of Paediatrics (Contributor); Treatment of Neurological Disorders (Contributor). Recreation: our garden. Address: (b.) Paediatric Unit, Victoria Hospital, Kirkcaldy, Fife; T.-0592 261155.

Stein, Rev. Jock, MA, BD. Joint Warden, Carberry Tower, since 1986 (Minister, Steeple Church, Dundee, 1976-86); b. 8.11.41, Edinburgh; m., Margaret E. Munro; 3 d. Educ. Sedbergh School; Cambridge University; Edinburgh University. Work Study Officer, United Steel Companies, Sheffield; Assistant Warden, St. Ninian's Lay Training Centre, Crieff; publishing and lay training, Presbyterian Church of East Africa. Publications: Ministers for the '80s (Editor); Our One Baptism; In Christ All Things Hold Together (Co-author); Ministry and Mission in the City; Mission and the Crisis of Western Culture (Editor); Scottish Self-Government: Some Christian Viewpoints (Editor). Recreations: music; skiing. Address: Carberry Tower, Musselburgh, EH21 8PY.

Steiner, Eleanor Margaret, MB, ChB, DPH, MFCM, MRCGP, MICGP. Associate General Practitioner at Appin and Easdale, formerly Principal in general practice; Executive Member, Scottish Child Law Centre; Medical Member, Disability Appeals Tribunal; b. 21.5.37, Glasgow; m., Mark Rudie Steiner (qv); 1 s. Educ. Albyn School, Aberdeen; Aberdeen University. Surgical Assistant, Freiburg; worked in hospitals, Switzerland, Canada, USA; Departmental Medical Officer/Senior Medical Officer, Aberdeen City; Organiser, Family Planning Services, Aberdeen; Member, Rubella Working Party; Adviser, Aberdeen Telephone Samaritans; Assistant, Psychiatry, Murray Royal Hospital, Perth; Contributor, Scientific Congress, Institute of Advanced Medical Sciences, Moscow. Recreations: sailing; hill-walking; international contacts. Address: (h.) Atlantic House, Ellenabeich, Isle of Seil, by Oban, Argyll, PA34 4RF; T.-Balvicar 593.

Steiner, Mark Rudie, LLB, NP. Legal Consultant and Defence Lawyer; Member, Scottish Consumer Council; part-time Chairman, Social Security Appeal Tribunal and Disability Appeal Tribunal; Scottish Representative, Consumers in the European Community Group; Member, Potato Marketing Board Consumer Liaison Committee; Member, National Pharmaceutical Consultative Committee Working Group on Quality Assurance; m., Dr. Eleanor Steiner, DPH, MFCM, MRCGP, MICGP; 1 s. Educ. Aberdeen University. Editor, Canadian Broadcasting Corporation, Toronto and Montreal; Editor, Swiss Broadcasting Corporation, Berne; Procurator Fiscal in Scotland; Partner and Director of various firms and companies; Past Chairman, Perth Community Relations Council; Delegate, Scottish Council for Racial Equality; Chairman, Central Scotland Society of Conservative Lawyers; neutral observer at various overseas political trials; contributor to various international journals; retired Principal, Goodman Steiner & Co., Defence Lawyers and Notaries in Central Scotland. Recreations: sailing; developing international exchanges. Address: (h.) Atlantic House, Ellenabeich, Isle of Seil, by Oban, Argyll, PA34 4RF; T.-Balvicar 593.

Stell, Geoffrey Percival, BA, FSA, FSA Scot. Head of Architecture, Royal Commission on the Ancient and Historical Monuments of Scotland, since 1991; b. 21.11.44, Keighley; m., Evelyn Florence Burns; 1 s.; 1 d. Educ. Keighley Boys' Grammar School; Leeds University; Glasgow University. Historic Buildings Investigator, RCAHMS, since 1969; one-time Chairman, Scottish Vernacular Buildings Working Group; Chairman, Scottish Urban Archaeological Trust; one-time Vice-President, Council for Scottish Archaeology. Publications include: Dumfries and Galloway, 1986; Monuments of Industry (Co-author); Buildings of St. Kilda (Co-author); Loads and Roads in Scotland (Co-editor); The Scottish Medieval Town (Co-editor); Galloway, Land and Lordship (Co-editor). Recreations: gardening; music; travel, particularly in Scotland and France. Address: (h.) Beechmount, Borrowstoun, Bo'ness, West Lothian, EH51 9RS; T.-0506 822441.

Stenhouse, Andrew John, DA, ARSA. Artist; b. 30.5.54, Renfrew. Educ. John Neilson High School, Paisley; Duncan of Jordanstone College of Art, Dundee. Sculptor/painter/audio artist; helped to develop Scottish Sculpture Workshop; helped to set up and develop Edinburgh Sculpture Workshop; many exhibitions in Britain, Ireland, France, Korea, USA, Canada, etc. Recreations: music of all types; gliding. Address: (h.) 13 Kirk Street, Markinch, Fife, KY7 6DU; T.-0592 758846.

Stenlake, Professor John Bedford, CBE, PhD, DSc, Hon. DSc (Strathclyde), FRPharmS, CChem, FRSC, FRSE. Honorary Professor, Strathclyde University, since 1982; Chairman, British Pharmacopoeia Commission, 1980-89; Member, Medicines Commission, since 1984; b. 21.10.19, Ealing; m., Anne Beatrice Holder; 5 s.; 1 d. Educ. Ealing Grammar School; School of Pharmacy, London. Pilot, RAF, 1942-45; Demonstrator, Assistant Lecturer, Lecturer in Pharmaceutical Chemistry, School of Pharmacy, London, 1945-52; Senior Lecturer in Pharmaceutical Chemistry, Royal College of Science and Technology, Glasgow, 1952-61; Professor of Pharmacy, Strathclyde University, 1961-82. Member, Committee on Safety of Medicines, 1970-79; author of more than 100 papers, reviews and articles concerned with original research in medicinal chemistry. Recreations: reading; gardening. Address: (h.) Mark Corner, Twynholm, Kirkcudbright.

Stephen, Alex, FCCA. Chief Executive, City of Dundee District Council, since 1991; b. 17.9.48, Dundee; m., Joyce; 1 s.; 1 d. Local government since 1970. Recreation: voluntary work. Address: (b.) 21 City Square, Dundee; T.-0382 23141.

Stephen, Rev. Donald Murray, TD, MA, BD, ThM. Minister, Marchmont St. Giles' Parish Church, Edinburgh, since 1974; b. 1.6.36, Dundee; m., Hilda Swan Henriksen; 2 s.; 1 d. Educ. Brechin High School; Richmond Grammar School, Yorkshire; Edinburgh University; Princeton Theological Seminary. Assistant Minister, Westover Hills Presbyterian Church, Arkansas, 1962-64; Minister, Kirkoswald, 1964-74; Chaplain, TA, 1965-85 (attached to 4/5 Bn., RSF, 205 Scottish General Hospital, 2nd Bn., 52nd Lowland Volunteers); Convener, Committee on Chaplains to Her Majesty's Forces, General Assembly, 1985-89. Recreations: golf; curling. Address: 19 Hope Terrace, Edinburgh, EH9 2AP; T.-031-447 2834.

Stephen, Eric John. Farmer; Director, Aberdeen and Northern Marts Ltd., since 1986; Director, Aberdeen and Northern Estates Ltd., since 1987; b. 2.1.38, Turriff; 1 s.; 3 d. Educ. Inverurie Academy. Member, Scottish Agricultural Wages Board; former Convener, Employment and Technology Committee, National Farmers Union of Scotland; Elder, Auchterless Parish Church, 29 years; Past President, Aberdeen and Kincardine Executive, NFU of Scotland; Past President, Royal Northern Agricultural Society; Vice President, Aberdeen Fatstock Club; President, Turriff Show, 1992. Recreation: bowling. Address: Lower Thorneybank, Rothienorman, Inverurie, AB5 8XT; T.-08884 233.

Stephen, Professor Frank H., BA, PhD. Professor, Department of Economics, Strathclyde University, since 1990 (Senior Lecturer, 1979-86, Reader, 1986-90); Managing Editor, Journal of Economic Studies, since 1982; b. 20.11.46, Glasgow; m., Christine Leathard; 2 d. Educ. Queen's Park Secondary School, Glasgow; Strathclyde University. Research Officer, then Head, Economics Department, STUC, 1969-71; Lecturer, Department of Economics, Strathclyde University, 1971-79. Publications: The Performance of Labour-Managed Firms (Editor), 1982; Firms Organisation and Labour (Editor), 1984; The Economic Analysis of Producers' Cooperatives, 1984; The Economics of the Law,

1988. Address: (b.) Department of Economics, Strathclyde University, Glasgow; T.-041-552 4400.

Stephen, Professor Kenneth William, BDS, DDSc, HDDRCPS, FDSRCS. Professor of Community Dental Health, Glasgow University, since 1984 (Head, Department of Oral Medicine and Pathology, since 1980); Consultant-in-charge, Glasgow School of Dental Hygiene, since 1979; b. 1.10.37, Glasgow; m., Anne Seymour Gardiner; 1 s.; 1 d. Educ. Hillhead High School, Glasgow; Glasgow University. General Dental Practitioner, 1960-64; House Officer, Department of Oral Surgery, Glasgow Dental Hospital, 1964-65; Lecturer, Department of Conservative Dentistry, 1965-68, Lecturer, Department of Oral Medicine and Pathology, Glasgow University, 1968-71; Visiting Lecturer, Department of Oral Physiology, Newcastle-upon-Tyne University, 1969-70; Senior Lecturer, Department of Oral Medicine and Pathology, Glasgow University, 1971-80; Reader, 1980-84. Co-President, European Organisation for Caries Research, 1978-79. Recreations: swimming; hill-walking; skiing; gardening. Address: (b.) Dental School, 378 Sauchiehall Street, Glasgow, G2 3JZ; T.-041-332 7020.

Stephen, Pamela Judith, BSc (Hons), MB, ChB, MRCP. Consultant in Geriatric Medicine, Perth Royal Infirmary, since 1984; Honorary Senior Lecturer, Department of Medicine, Dundee University, since 1984; b. 29.1.51, Falkirk. Educ. Mary Erskine School for Girls, Edinburgh; Edinburgh University. Pre-registration House Officer and Senior House Officer, Edinburgh, 1975-77; Medical Registrar, Falkirk, 1977-80; Registrar in Rehabilitation Medicine, Edinburgh, 1980-81; Lecturer, Department of Geriatric Medicine, Edinburgh University, 1982-84. Recreations: classical music; theatre and the arts; gardening; travel. Address: (b.) Geriatric Unit, Perth Royal Infirmary, Perth, PH1 1NX; T.-0738 23311.

Stephens, Professor William Peter, MA, BD, DesSR. Professor of Church History, Aberdeen University, since 1986 (Dean, Faculty of Divinity, 1987-89, Provost, Faculty of Divinity, 1989-90); Methodist Minister, since 1958; b. 16.5.34, Penzance. Educ. Truro School; Clare College, Cambridge, and Wesley House, Cambridge; Universities of Lund, Strasbourg, Muenster. Assistant Tutor, Hartley Victoria College, Manchester, 1958-61; Minister and University Chaplain, Nottingham University, 1961-65; Minister, Shirley Methodist Church, Croydon, 1967-71; Chair of Church History, Hartley Victoria College, Manchester, 1971-73; Chair of Historical and Systematic Theology, Wesley College, Bristol, 1973-80; Research Fellow, then Lecturer in Church History, Queen's College, Birmingham, 1980-86. Secretary, Society for the Study of Theology, 1963-77. Publications: The Holy Spirit in the Theology and Martin Bucer; Faith and Love; Methodism in Europe; The Theology of Huldrych Zwingli. Recreations: squash; tennis; hill-walking; skiing; swimming; theatre. Address: (b.) Faculty of Divinity, King's College, Aberdeen University, Aberdeen; T.-0224 272383.

Stevely, Professor William Stewart, BSc, DPhil, DipEd, FIBiol. Vice Principal, Paisley University (formerly Paisley College), since 1992; b. 6.4.43, West Kilbride; m., Sheila Anne Stalker; 3 s.; 2 d. Educ. Ardrossan Academy; Glasgow University; Oxford University. Lecturer and Senior Lecturer in Biochemistry, Glasgow University, 1968-88; Professor and Head, Department of Biology, Paisley College, 1988-92. Address: (b.) Paisley University, High Street, Paisley; T.-041-848 3000.

Steven, John Douglas, MB, ChB, FRCOG. Consultant Obstetrician and Gynaecologist, Stirling Royal Infirmary, since 1981; Member, Scottish Council, British Medical Association; b. 20.4.46, Perth. Educ. Douglas Ewart High School, Newton Stewart; Edinburgh University. Registrar in Obstetrics and Gynaecology, Western General Hospital, Edinburgh; Senior Registrar, Obstetrics and Gynaecology, Ninewells Hospital, Dundee. Address: (b.) Stirling Royal Infirmary, Stirling, FK8 2AU; T.-0786 73151.

Stevenson, Rev. Andrew Lockhart, LLB, MLitt, DPA, FPEA. Parish Minister, Balmerino with Wormit, since 1984; b. 12.12.26, Beith; m., Jane Wilson Begg; 1 s.; 2 d. Educ. Spier's School, Beith; Scottish School of Physical Education, Jordanhill; London University; Aberdeen University. National Service, RAF, 1946-48; Teacher, Ayrshire, London and Glasgow, 1948-57; Principal Physical Education Teacher, Aberdeen Grammar School, 1957-66; Lecturer/Senior Lecturer (PE), Aberdeen College of Education, 1966-81. Governor, Aberdeen College of Education, 1976-81; President, Scottish Physical Education Association; Member, Aberdeen District Council, 1976-84 (Convener, Housing, Building and General Purposes Committee, 1979-80). Address: The Manse, 5 Westwater Place, Wormit, Fife, DD6 8NS; T.-Newport-on-Tay 542626.

Stevenson, Professor David, BA, PhD, DLitt. Professor in Scottish History, St. Andrews University, since 1991 (Reader in Scottish History, 1990-91); b. 30.4.42, Largs; m., Wendy B. McLeod; 2 s. Educ. Gordonstoun; Dublin University; Glasgow University. Aberdeen University: Lecturer in History, 1970-80, Senior Lecturer in History, 1980-84; Reader in Scottish History, 1984-90. Honorary Secretary, Scottish History Society, 1976-84; Fellow, Royal Historical Society. Publications: The Scottish Revolution 1637-44, 1973; Revolution and Counter-Revolution in Scotland 1644-51, 1977; Alasdair MacColla and the Highland Problem in the 17th Century, 1980; Scottish Covenanters and Irish Confederates, 1981; The Government of Scotland under the Covenanters 1637-51, 1982; Scottish Texts and Calendars (with Wendy B. Stevenson), 1987; The Origins of Freemasonry, 1988; The First Freemasons: The Early Scottish Lodges and their members, 1988; The Covenanters: the National Covenant and Scotland, 1988; King's College, Aberdeen, 1560-1641, 1990. Address: (b.) Department of Scottish History, St. Andrews University, St. Andrews, KY16 9AL.

Stevenson, David Deas, CBE, BCom, CA. Managing Director, Edinburgh Woollen Mill, since 1970; b. 28.11.41, Hawick; m., Alix Jamieson; 2 d. Educ. Langholm Academy; Dumfries Academy; Edinburgh University. British Steel Corporation, 1966-67; Langholm Dyeing Co., 1967-70. Recreations: squash; horses; running. Address: (b.) Waverley Mills, Langholm, Dumfriesshire, DG13 OEB; T.-0541 80611.

Stevenson, Gerda, DDA. Actress, Singer, Writer, Book Illustrator, Theatre Director; b. 10.4.56, West Linton; m., Aonghas MacNeacail; 1 s. Educ. Peebles High School; Royal Academy of Dramatic Art, London. Has performed with (among others) 7:84 Theatre Co., Scottish Theatre Company (most notably as Queen Anne in Jamie the Saxt), Royal Lyceum Theatre, Edinburgh; performed one-woman play, Barry, Traverse Theatre, Edinburgh; Jock Tamson's Bairns, Communicado Theatre Company, 1990; television work includes Clay, Smeddum and Greenden, Square Mile of Murder, Grey Granite, Around Scotland, The Celts, Horizon, Battered Baby (all BBC), The Old Master and Taggart (STV), The Stamp of Greatness (Channel 4); extensive radio work includes title roles in The Bride of Lammermoor and Catriona; Producer, BBC Radio Scotland; performs regularly as singer and story-teller with her sister, Savourna Stevenson; directed Uncle Jesus, Edinburgh Festival Fringe, 1987; Assistant Director, Royal Lyceum, Edinburgh, Autumn 1987. Vanbrugh Award, RADA; wrote and illustrated children's book, The Candlemaker and other stories, 1987. Recreation: walking in the country. Address: (h.) 1 Roseneath Terrace, Marchmont, Edinburgh, EH9 1JS; T.-031-229 5652.

Stevenson, James Edward Mackenzie, MA, LLB, NP. Solicitor; Honorary Sheriff Substitute, South Strathclyde, Dumfries and Galloway, at Dumfries; b. 9.11.19, Lockerbie; m., Maureen Mary; 2 s.; 2 d. Educ. Lockerbie Academy; George Watson's Boys College; Edinburgh University. Captain, 131st Field Regiment, RA, Second World War; Town Clerk and Chamberlain: Burgh of Lochmaben, 1949-75, Burgh of Lockerbie, 1957-75. Director, South of Scotland Ice Rink, Lockerbie; Clerk, Lockerbie Branch, Earl Haig Fund; Secretary, Abbeyfield Lockerbie & District Society Ltd. Recreations: golf; curling. Address: (h.) Fairfield, St. Brydes Terrace, Lockerbie, Dumfriesshire.

Stevenson, John Meikle, BSc, FInstD, FBIM. Farmer; Chairman, Royal Scottish Agricultural Benevolent Institution; b. 20.1.31, Aberlady; m., Eileen A.; 2 s.; 1 d. Educ. Trinity College, Glenalmond; Aberdeen University. Councillor, East Lothian County Council, 1961-66; President, East Lothian, National Farmers' Union, 1968-69; Council Member, NFU, 1966-70; Member, Governing Body, British Society for Research in Agricultural Engineering, since 1968; Chairman, Committee, Scottish Centre of Agricultural Engineering, since 1987; Governor, East of Scotland College of Agriculture. Recreations: shooting; fishing; gardening; golf. Address: Luffness Mains, Aberlady, East Lothian, EH32 OPZ; T.-Aberlady 212.

Stevenson, John S.K., MB, ChB, FRCGP, D(Obst)RCOG. Former Senior Lecturer, Department of General Practice, Edinburgh University; b. 28.8.29, West Kilbride; m., Helen L. Howes; 3 s.; 1 d. Educ. Ayr Academy; Glasgow University. Principal, general practice, Stevenston, Ayrshire, 1958-68; Member, NHS Executive Council for Ayrshire, 1963-68; Member, Edinburgh and District Council on Alcoholism, 1969-73; Honorary Treasurer, Association of University Teachers of General Practice, 1972-81; Member, BBC Scotland Medical Advisory Group, 1976-84; BBC Scotland Radio Doctor, 1976-78; Member, Biomedical Research Committee, Chief Scientist Organisation, SHHD, 1983-85. Recreations: reading; theatre; golf. Address: (h.) 30 Moston Terrace, Edinburgh, EH9 2DE; T.-031-667 4405.

Stevenson, Peter David, MA (Cantab). Chairman, Mackays Stores (Holdings) PLC, since 1991; b. 6.3.47, Edinburgh; m., The Hon. Susan Blades; 1 s.; 1 d. Educ. Edinburgh Academy; Trinity College, Cambridge. Director: William Low PLC, Scottish Nuclear Ltd. and EFT Group PLC. Address: (b.) 28 Rutland Square, Edinburgh, EH1 2BW; T.-031-229 0550.

Stevenson, Robert Orr, BA, FCIS. Secretary, Scottish Homes (formerly Secretary, Scottish Special Housing Association); b. 27.4.33, Glasgow; m., Anne. Educ. Trinity College, Glenalmond; Christ's College, Cambridge. Beaverbrook Newspapers Ltd.: General Manager, Sunday Express; General Manager, Daily Express; Group General Manager, Scotland; Director and General Manager, Felixstowe Dock and Railway Company (Chief Executive, Port of Felixstowe); Managing Director, A.M. Tweedie & Co. Ltd. Recreations: golf; opera. Address: (h.) 14/1 East Parkside, Edinburgh, EH12 5XL; T.-031-667 9642.

Stevenson, Ronald, FRMCM. Composer and Pianist; Broadcaster; Author; b. 6.3.28, Blackburn; m., Marjorie Spedding; 1 s.; 2 d. Educ. Royal Manchester College of Music; Conservatorio Di Santa Cecilia, Rome. Senior Lecturer, Cape Town University, 1963-65; BBC Prom debut in own 2nd Piano Concerto, 1972; Aldeburgh Festival recital with Sir Peter Pears, 1973; Busoni documentary, BBC TV, 1974; BBC Radio Scotland extended series on the bagpipe, clarsach and fiddle music of Scotland, 1980-84; Artist in Residence: Melbourne University, 1980, University of W. Australia, 1982, Conservatory of Shanghai, 1985; York University, 1987; published and recorded compositions:

Passacaglia for Piano, two Piano Concertos, Violin Concerto (commissioned by Menuhin), Prelude, Fugue and Fantasy for Piano, Prelude and Fugue for Organ, In Memoriam Robert Carver, St. Mary's May Songs, A Child's Garden of Verse (BBC commission), Voces Vagabundae; Salute to Nelson Mandela (march for brass band). Publication: Western Music. Recreations: hill-walking; reading poetry, biographies and politics. Address: (h.) Townfoot House, West Linton, Peeblesshire; T.-0968 60511.

Stevenson, Ronald Harley, MA, LLB. Chief Executive, Highland Regional Council, since 1981; b. 6.1.34, Dunfermline. Educ. Dunfermline High School; Edinburgh University. County Clerk, Caithness County Council, 1967-75; Joint Director of Law and Administration, Highland Regional Council, 1975-81. Address: (b.) Regional Buildings, Inverness; T.-Inverness 234121.

Stevenson, Sir Simpson, LLD. Provost, Inverclyde District Council, 1984-88; Chairman, Scottish Health Services Common Services Agency, 1983-87; b. 18.8.21, Greenock; m., Jean Holmes Henry. Educ. Greenock High School. Provost of Greenock, 1962-65; Chairman, Western Regional Hospital Board, 1967-73; Chairman, Greater Glasgow Health Board, 1973-83; knighted, 1976; Hon. LLD, Glasgow University, 1982; Member, Royal Commission on NHS, 1976-79. Address: (h.) The Gables, Reservoir Road, Gourock; T.-0475 31774.

Stevenson, Struan John Stirton. Farmer and Director, J. & R. Stevenson Ltd., Ballantrae; Leader of the Administration, Kyle & Carrick District Council, 1986-88 (Chairman, Policy and Resources Committee, 1986-88); Chairman, Conservative Group, COSLA, 1986-88; Chairman, Carrick, Cumnock and Doon Valley Conservative Constituency Association, 1982-89; b. 4.4.48, Ballantrae; m., Pat; 2 s. Educ. Strathallan; West of Scotland Agricultural College (Diploma in Agriculture). Elected, Girvan District Council, 1971-75. Parliamentary Candidate (Conservative), South Edinburgh, 1992. Recreations: contemporary art collector; photography. Address: (h.) Balig House, Ballantrae, Girvan, KA26 OJY; T.-046583 214.

Stevenson, William Trevor, CBE, DL, FCIT; b. 21.3.21, Peebles; m., Alison Wilson Roy. Educ. Edinburgh Academy. Apprentice Engineer, 1937-41; Engineer, 1941-45; entered family food manufacturing business, Cottage Rusks, 1945; Managing Director, 1948-54; Chairman, 1954-59; Chief Executive, Cottage Rusks Associates, 1965-69; Regional Director, Ranks Hovis McDougall, 1969-74; Director, various companies in food, engineering, hotel and aviation industries, since 1974; Chairman, Alex. Wilkie Ltd., 1977-90; founder Chairman, Gleneagles Hotels, 1981-83; Chairman, Scottish Transport Group, 1981-86; Chairman, Hodgson Martin Ventures Ltd., 1982-87; Master, Company of Merchants of City of Edinburgh, 1978-80; Vice President, Edinburgh Chamber of Commerce, 1983-87. Recreations: flying; sailing; curling. Address: (h.) 45 Pentland View, Edinburgh, EH10 6PY; T.-031-445 1512.

Stewardson, Raymond Richard, BA (Hons). Headteacher, Castlehead High School, Paisley, since 1989; b. 26.9.37, Huyton, Merseyside; m., Aileen Agnes Mackie; 1 s.; 1 d. Educ. Prescot Grammar School; Sheffield University; London University (External). Assistant Teacher; Principal Teacher of Geography; Assistant Head Teacher; Depute Rector; Rector, John Neilson High School, 1983-89, when merged with Castlehead High School. Recreations: swimming; gardening. Address: (b.) Castlehead High School, Camphill, Canal Street, Paisley, PA1 2HL; T.-041-887 4261.

Stewart, A.J. (Ada F. Kay). Playwright and Author; b. 5.3.29, Tottington, Lancashire. Educ. Grammar School,

Fleetwood: ATS Scottish Command; first produced play, 1951; repertory actress, 1952-54; BBC TV Staff Writer/Editor/Adaptor, Central Script Section, 1956-59; returned to Scotland, 1959, as stage and TV writer; winner, BBC New Radio Play competition, 1956; The Man from Thermopylae, presented in Festival of Contemporary Drama, Rheydt, West Germany, 1959, as part of Edinburgh International Festival, 1965, and at Masquers' Theatre, Hollywood, 1972; first recipient, Wendy Wood Memorial Grant, 1982; Polish Gold Cross for achievements in literary field. Publications: Falcon - The Autobiography of His Grace, James the 4, King of Scots, 1970; Died 1513-Born 1929 - The Autobiography of A.J. Stewart, 1978; The Man from Thermopylae, 1981. Recreation: work. Address: 15 Oxford Street, Edinburgh, 8.

Stewart, Alan George. Chief Executive, Alloa and Clackmannan Enterprise Ltd., since 1991; b. 21.8.49, Glasgow; m., Allison; 1 s.; 2 d. Educ. Hutchesons', Glasgow; Glasgow School of Art. Manager of Planning, Victoria, Australia; Policy Unit, SDA; Head of Policy and Planning, Clackmannan District Council. Recreations: family; work; walking; photography. Address: (b.) Alloa Business Centre, The Whins, Whins Road, Alloa, FK10 3SA.

Stewart, Alasdair Duncan, CA. Finance Director, Scottish Nuclear Ltd.; b. 24.2.33, Perth; m., Audrey Jean Lind Stewart; 3 s. Educ. Perth Academy. J. & R. Morison & Co., Perth, 1950-59; Stewarts & Lloyds Ltd., Birmingham and Glasgow, 1959-67; P-E Consulting Group, 1967-72; joined North of Scotland Hydro-Electric Board, 1972; Financial Director, North of Scotland Hydro Electric Board, 1975-89. Recreations: sailing; walking; badminton. Address: (b.) Minto Building, 6 Inverlair Avenue, Glasgow, G44 4AD; T.-041-663 1166.

Stewart, Sheriff Alastair Lindsay, BA (Oxon), LLB(Edin). Sheriff of Tayside, Central and Fife at Dundee, since 1990; b. 28.11.38, Aberdeen; m., 1, Annabel Claire Stewart (m. diss.); 2 s.; 2, Sheila Anne Mackinnon. Educ. Edinburgh Academy; St. Edmund Hall, Oxford; Edinburgh University. Admitted to Faculty of Advocates, 1963; Tutor, Faculty of Law, Edinburgh University, 1963-73; Standing Junior Counsel to the Registrar of Restrictive Trading Agreements, 1968-70; Advocate Depute, 1970-73; Sheriff of Lanarkshire (later South Strathclyde, Dumfries and Galloway) at Airdrie, 1973-79; Sheriff of Grampian, Highland and Islands at Aberdeen and Stonehaven, 1979-90. Chairman, Scottish Association of Family Conciliation Services, 1986-89. Publications: Sheriff Court Practice (Contributor), 1988; The Scottish Criminal Courts in Action, 1990. Recreations: music; reading; walking. Address: (b.) Sheriffs' Chambers, Sheriff Court House, PO Box 2, 6 West Bell Street, Dundee, DD1 9AD; T.-0382 29961.

Stewart, Alexander Donald, BA, LLB, WS. Solicitor; Partner, McGrigor Donald, Glasgow; Director, Clyde Cablevision Limited; Deputy Chairman, Scottish Amicable Life Assurance Society; b. 18.6.33, Edinburgh; m., Virginia Mary Washington; 1 s.; 5 d. Educ. Wellington College, Berkshire; Oxford University; Edinburgh University. Hon. Consul of Thailand in Scotland; DL, Perthshire. Recreations: music; field sports; winter sports. Address: (h.) Ardvorlich, Lochearnhead, Perthshire.

Stewart, Alexander Reavell Macdonald, FRICS, FRVA, ACIArb. Chartered Surveyor; Chairman, Scottish Branch, Royal Institution of Chartered Surveyors, 1985-86; b. 14.2.29, Bearsden; m., Keris Duguid Keir; 2 s.; 2 d. Educ. Merchiston Castle School. President: Property Owners and Factors Association Glasgow, 1968-69, National Federation of Property Owners Scotland, 1978-80. Recreations: trout fish-

ing; piping. Address: (b.) 21 Winton Lane, Glasgow; T.-041-332 2752.

Stewart, Andy. Entertainer; Song Writer; b. 30.12.33, Glasgow. Numerous theatre seasons and concert tours in UK and USA, Canada, Australia, New Zealand, South Africa; toured with White Heather Club; Hogmanay shows for BBC TV, Scottish Television and Grampian Television; TV specials including Andy Stewart Show and White Heather Club; 13 Sauchie Street series (radio); wrote the song A Scottish Soldier, and other ballads and monologues.

Stewart, Archibald Ian Balfour, CBE, BL (Dist), FSA (Scot). Retired Solicitor; Honorary Sheriff; b. 19.5.15, Campbeltown; m., Ailsa Rosamund Mary Massey; 3 s. Educ. Cheltenham College; Glasgow University. Solicitor, 1938; Town Clerk, Lochgilphead, 1939-46, Campbeltown, 1947-54; Procurator Fiscal of Argyll at Campbeltown, 1941-74; Temporary Sheriff, 1975-88; Secretary, Clyde Fishermen's Association, 1941-70; Churchill Fellow, 1966; President, Scottish Fishermen's Federation, 1970-75; Hon. President, Clyde Fishermen's Association and Scottish Fishermen's Federation; former Director, Scottish Fishermen's Organisation and Scottish Board, Phoenix Insurance Co. Ltd.; Past President, Kintyre Antiquarian Society; Past Chairman, Argyll and Bute National Insurance Committee, Kintyre Employment Committee; Adviser, North East Atlantic Fisheries Conference, UN Law of Sea Conference; Editor, Kintyre Antiquarian and Natural History Society Magazine. Recreations: local history; genealogy; wine; gardening; idling. Address: (h.) Askomel End, Campbeltown, Argyll, PA28 6EP; T.-0586 52353.

Stewart (nee Muir), Professor Averil M., BA, FCOT, TDip, SROT. Chairman, Occupational Therapists Board, Council for Professions Supplementary to Medicine, since 1986; Head, Department of Occupational Therapy, Queen Margaret College, Edinburgh, since 1986; b. 7.4.43, Edinburgh; m., J. Gavin Stewart. Educ. Dunfermline High School; Occupational Therapy Training Centre, Edinburgh. Lecturer, Glasgow School of Occupational Therapy, 1972-74; Senior Occupational Therapist, Head and District Occupational Therapist, Worthing District, 1975-83; Educational Development Officer, Council for Professions Supplementary to Medicine (secondment), 1978-80; Senior Lecturer, Department of Occupational Therapy, Queen Margaret College, 1983-86. Member, Vice-Chairman and Chairman, Occupational Therapists Board, CPSM, since 1980. Publications: Occupational Therapy Teaching Resources in UK; Occupational Therapy in Psychiatry (Contributor). Recreations: wilderness travel; gardening. Address: (b.) Queen Margaret College, Edinburgh, EH12 8TS.

Stewart, Clement A., MA, MEd. Rector, Portlethen Academy, since 1986; b. 9.1.41, Strichen. Educ. Aberdeen Grammar School; Aberdeen University. Teacher of Mathematics, Aberdeen Grammar School, 1963-70; Dunoon Grammar School: Principal Teacher of Mathematics, 1970-72, Assistant Rector, 1972-74, Depute Rector, 1974-77; Head Teacher, Lochgilphead High School, 1977-86. Address: (h.) Kilmory, 12 Martin Avenue, Stonehaven, Kincardineshire, AB3 2LZ; T.-0569 63852.

Stewart, David Roger, TD, MA, BA (Hons), FEIS. Honorary Sheriff, Selkirk, since 1983; b. 3.2.20, Glasgow; m., Gwyneth Ruth Morris; 2 s.; 1 d. Educ. Hyndland Secondary School; Glasgow High School; Glasgow University; London University. Army, 1939-46; Schoolmaster, 1947-65 (Kelvinside Academy, Galashiels Academy); Rector, Selkirk High School, 1965-81; Member: Selkirk Town Council, 1971-75, Borders Education Committee, 1975-81, Borders Regional Council, 1982-86; TA, 1939-64; Chairman, Selkirk Committee, Cancer

Research Campaign. Recreations: golf; caravanning; gardening. Address: (h.) Cairncoed, Hillside Terrace, Selkirk, TD7 4ND; T.-0750 21755.

Stewart, Rt. Hon. Donald James, PC. MP (Scottish National Party), Western Isles, 1970-87; b. 17.10.20, Stornoway; m., Christina MacAulay. Educ. Nicolson Institute, Stornoway. Town and County Councillor, 1951-70; Provost of Stornoway, 1958-64 and 1968-70; Honorary Sheriff. Recreations: photography; fishing; gardening. Address: (h.) Hillcrest, 41 Goathill Road, Stornoway; T.-0851 2672.

Stewart, Douglas Fleming, MA, LLB, WS, NP, FSA Scot. Solicitor (Scotland), Crown Estate Commissioners, 1970-91; Partner, J.F. Anderson, WS, since 1961; Secretary, Stewart Society, 1968-87; b. 22.5.27, Sydney, Australia; m., Catherine Coleman; 2 d. Educ. George Watson's College, Edinburgh; Edinburgh University. RAF, 1945-48; Member, Business Committee, General Council, Edinburgh University, 1961-69; Session Clerk, Braid Church, Edinburgh, 1979-91; Treasurer, Friends of the Royal Scottish Museum, 1972-90; Council Member, Royal Celtic Society, since 1981; President, Watsonian Club, 1989-90. Recreation: swimming. Address: (b.) 48 Castle Street, Edinburgh, EH2 3LX; T.-031-225 3912.

Stewart, Ena Lamont. Playwright; b. 10.2.12, Glasgow; m., Jack Stewart (deceased); 1 s. Educ. Woodside School, Glasgow; Esdaile School, Edinburgh. Assistant, Public Library, Aberdeen, 1930-34; Medical Secretary, Radcliffe, Lancashire, 1934-37; Secretary/Receptionist, Royal Hospital for Sick Children, Glasgow, 1937-41; Baillie's Reference Library, Glasgow: Assistant Librarian, 1953-57, Librarian-in-charge, 1957-66; author of plays: Starched Aprons, Men Should Weep, The Heir to Ardmally, Business in Edinburgh, After Tomorrow (unperformed), Walkies Time, Knocking on the Wall, Towards Evening, High Places. Recreations: reading; listening to music. Address: (h.) 5a Monkton Road, Prestwick, KA9 1AP; T.-0292 79827.

Stewart, Francis John, MA (Oxon), LLB, TD. Writer to the Signet (retired); Member, Queen's Bodyguard for Scotland (Royal Company of Archers); b. 11.5.17, Edinburgh; m., Olga Margaret Mounsey; 3 s.; 1 d. Educ. Cargilfield School, Edinburgh; Loretto School; Trinity College, Oxford; Edinburgh University. 1st Bn., Lothians and Borders Yeomanry; Senior Partner, Murray Beith & Murray, WS, Edinburgh (retired); Past Chairman of Governors, Loretto School; Honorary Consul for Principality of Monaco, 1964-85; Chevalier of the Order of St. Charles. Recreation: gardening. Address: (b.) 39 Castle Street, Edinburgh; T.-031-225 1200.

Stewart, Sir Frederick Henry, KB, BSc, PhD, FRSA, DSc Hon. (Aberdeen, Leicester, Heriot-Watt, Durham, Glasgow), FRS, FRSE, FGS. Professor Emeritus, Edinburgh University, since 1982; Trustee, British Museum (Natural History), 1983-88; Council Member, Scottish Marine Biological Association, 1983-89; b. 16.1.16, Aberdeen; m., Mary Florence Elinor Rainbow. Educ. Fettes College, Edinburgh; Robert Gordon's College, Aberdeen; Aberdeen University; Emmanuel College, Cambridge. Mineralogist, Research Department, Imperial Chemical Industries, 1941-43; Lecturer in Geology, Durham University, 1943-56; Regius Professor of Geology and Mineralogy, Edinburgh University, 1956-82; Member, Council for Scientific Policy, 1967-71 (Assessor, 1971-73); Chairman, Natural Environment Research Council, 1971-73; Chairman, Advisory Board for the Research Councils, 1974-79; Member, Advisory Council for Research and Development, 1976-79; University Grants Committee Earth Sciences Review, 1986-87. Lyell Fund Award, 1951 and Lyell Medal, 1970, Geological Society of London; Mineralogical Society of America Award, 1952; Clough Medal, Edinburgh Geological Society; Sorby Medal,

Yorkshire Geological Society. Publications: The British Caledonides, 1963; Marine Evaporites, 1963. Recreations: fishing; collecting fossil fish. Address: (h.) 79 Morningside Park, Edinburgh, EH10 5EZ; T.-031-447 2620; House of Letterawe, Lochawe, Argyll, PA33 1AH; T.-083-82 329.

Stewart, George Girdwood, CB, MC, TD, BSc, FICFor, Hon. FLI. Cairngorm Estate Adviser to Highlands and Islands Enterprise, since 1988; Forestry Consultant to National Trust for Scotland, since 1989 (Regional Representative for Central and Tayside, 1984-88); Chairman, Scottish Wildlife Trust, 1981-87; Member, Countryside Commission for Scotland, 1981-88; Member, Environment Panel, British Railways Board, 1980-90; Associate Director, Oakwood Environmental, since 1990; Member, Cairngorm Recreation Trust, since 1986; President, Scottish National Ski Council, since 1988; b. 12.12.19, Glasgow; m., Shelagh Jean Morven Murray; 1 s.; 1 d. Educ. Kelvinside Academy, Glasgow; Glasgow University; Edinburgh University. Royal Artillery, 1940-46 (mentioned in Despatches); Forestry Commission: District Officer, 1949-60, Assistant Conservator, 1960-67, Conservator (Glasgow), 1967-69, Commissioner, Forest and Estate Management, 1969-79. Commanding Officer, 278 (Lowland) Field Regiment RA (TA), 1956-59; President, Scottish Ski Club, 1971-75; Vice President, National Ski Federation of Great Britain, 1975-78; Fellow, Royal Society of Arts. Recreations: skiing; tennis; studying Scottish painting. Address: (h.) Stormont House, 11 Mansfield Road, Scone, Perth, PH2 6SA; T.-0738 51815.

Stewart, Ian William. Governor, Dundee College of Technology, since 1985; b. 24.3.23, Edinburgh; m., Jane Alison Cunningham; 2 s. Educ. Merchiston Castle School. Pilot, RAF, 1941-46; William Low & Co., PLC, 1946-88 (Managing Director, 1959-83, Deputy Chairman, 1983-88); President, Dundee and Tayside Chamber of Commerce and Industry, 1984-85; Board Member, SCOTVEC, 1985-88. Recreations: golf; gardening. Address: (h.) Greenbank, Barry, Carnoustie, Angus; T.-0241 53043.

Stewart, James Blythe, MA, LLB. Advocate; Senior Lecturer in Law, Heriot-Watt University, since 1976; b. 22.4.43, Methil. Educ. Buckhaven High School; Edinburgh University. Research Assistant, Faculty of Law, St. Andrews University, 1966-67; Assistant Lecturer in Law, then Lecturer, Heriot-Watt University, 1967-76. Recreations: bowls; golf; football spectating. Address: (h.) 3 Comely Bank Terrace, Edinburgh, EH4 1AT; T.-031-332 8228.

Stewart, Rev. James Charles, MA, BD, STM. Minister, Kirk of St. Nicholas, Aberdeen, since 1980; b. 29.3.33, Glasgow. Educ. Glasgow Academy; St. Andrews University; Union Theological Seminary, New York. Assistant Minister, St. John's Kirk of Perth, 1969-74; Minister: St. Andrew's Church, Drumchapel, 1964-74, East Church of St. Nicholas, Aberdeen, 1974-80; Secretary, General Assembly's Committee on Public Worship and Aids to Devotion, 1976-82; Chairman, Aberdeen Civic Society, 1979-81; Chairman, Third World Centre, Aberdeen. Address: (h.) 48 Gray Street, Aberdeen; T.-0224 34056.

Stewart, John Allan. MP (Conservative), Eastwood, since 1983 (East Renfrewshire, 1979-83); b. 1.6.42, St. Andrews; m., Susie Gourlay; 1 s.; 1 d. Educ. Bell Baxter High School, Cupar; St. Andrews University; Harvard University. Lecturer in Political Economy, St. Andrews University, 1965-70; Confederation of British Industry: Head, Regional Development Department, 1971, Deputy Director (Economics), 1973, Scottish Secretary, 1976, Scottish Director, 1978; Under Secretary of State, Scottish Office, 1981-86, since 1990. Recreations: bridge; reading; hedgehogs. Address: (b.) House of Commons, London, SW1A 0AA; T.-071-219 5110.

Stewart, John Barry Bingham, OBE, BA, CA. Past Chairman, Martin Currie Ltd.; b. 21.2.31, Edinburgh; m., Ailsa Margaret Crawford. Educ. The Leys School, Cambridge; Magdalene College, Cambridge. Accountancy training, Edinburgh; worked in London, United States and Canada; joined Martin Currie, 1960; Independent Member, Scottish Agricultural Wages Board. Recreations: fishing; shooting; golf; skiing. Address: 18 Hope Terrace, Edinburgh, EH9 2AR; T.-031-447 1626.

Stewart, Sheriff John Hall, LLB. Sheriff of Strathclyde, Dumfries and Galloway, at Airdrie, since 1985; b. 15.3.44, Bellshill; m., Marion MacCalman; 1 s.; 2 d. Educ. Airdrie Academy; St. Andrews University. Admitted Solicitor, 1971; Advocate, 1978. President, Uddingston RFC. Address: (b.) Sheriff's Chambers, Sheriff Court House, Graham Street, Airdrie, ML6 6EE; T.-Airdrie 751121.

Stewart, Kathleen Margaret, MA, LLB, WS, NP. Partner, McGrigor Donald, Solicitors, Edinburgh, Glasgow and London, since 1988 (Partner, Balfour & Manson, Solicitors, Edinburgh, 1983-87); b. St. Andrews. Educ. Bell Baxter High School, Cupar; St. Andrews University; Sweet Briar College, USA; Edinburgh University. Assistant Lawyer (Corporate Department) in London firm of commercial lawyers, 1975-79, and Scottish firms of commercial lawyers, 1980-83. Committee Member, Edinburgh Committee, Institute of Directors; Member, Company Law Panel, CBI; Member, EEC Sub-Committee, Company Law Committee, Law Society of Scotland. Recreations: horse riding; tennis; squash; bad bridge. Address: (b.) Erskine House, Queen Street, Edinburgh; T.-031-226 7777.

Stewart, Rev. Norma Drummond, MA, MEd, DipTh, BD. Minister, Strathbungo Queen's Park Church, Glasgow, since 1979; b. 20.5.36, Glasgow. Educ. Hyndland Secondary School, Glasgow; Glasgow University; Bible Training Institute, Glasgow; Trinity College, Glasgow. Teacher, Garrioch Secondary School, Glasgow, 1958-62; Missionary, Overseas Missionary Fellowship, West Malaysia, 1965-74; ordained to ministry, Church of Scotland, 1977. Selection School Assessor; Convener, Education for the Ministry Committee, Glasgow Presbytery; Member, Church of Scotland Panel on Doctrine; occasional Lecturer in Old Testament, Glasgow University; Participant in Congress on World Evangelisation, Manila, 1989; Member, World Mission and Unity Committee, Glasgow Presbytery; Pastoral Adviser, Glasgow Presbytery. Recreation: research in Old Testament studies. Address: 5 Newark Drive, Glasgow, G41 4QJ; T.-041-423 4818.

Stewart, Norman MacLeod, BL, SSC. President, Law Society of Scotland, 1985-86; Senior Partner, Allan, Black & McCaskie, Solicitors, Elgin, since 1984; b. 2.12.34, Lossiemouth; m., Mary Slater Campbell; 4 d. Educ. Elgin Academy; Edinburgh University. Training and Legal Assistant, Alex. Morison & Co., WS, Edinburgh, 1954-58; Legal Assistant: McLeod, Solicitor, Portsoy, 1958-59, Allan, Black & McCaskie, Solicitors, Elgin, 1959-61 (Partner, 1961); Council Member, Law Society of Scotland, 1976-87 (Convener, Public Relations Committee, 1979-81, and Professional Practice Committee, 1981-84). Past President, Elgin Rotary Club; Past Chairman, Moray Crime Prevention Panel; Member, Committee, Police Dependants' Trust (Grampian); President, Edinburgh University Club of Moray, 1987-89. Recreations: walking; golf; music; Spanish culture. Address: (h.) Argyll Lodge, Lossiemouth, Moray; T.-034381 3150.

Stewart, Patrick Loudon McIain, LLB, WS, DL. Senior Partner, Stewart Balfour & Sutherland, Solicitors, since 1982; Secretary, Clyde Fishermen's Association, since 1970; b. 25.7.45, Campbeltown; m., Mary Anne McLellan; 1 s.; 1 d.

Educ. Edinburgh Academy; Edinburgh University. Partner, Stewart Balfour & Sutherland, Campbeltown, 1970; former Executive Member, Scottish Fishermen's Federation, and Director, Scottish Fishermen's Organisation Ltd.; member of many Scottish fishing industry committees; Chairman, Argyll & Bute Trust; District Officer, Highlands District, Sea Cadet Corps; Member, Sea Cadet Council; Cadet Forces Medal. Recreations: sailing; shooting; youth work. Address: Craigadam, Campbeltown, Argyll, PA28 6EP; T.-0586 52161.

Stewart, Peter Duns, MD, FRCPath, DL. Deputy Lieutenant, Dunbartonshire, since 1973; b. 11.7.15, Oban; m., Doreen M. King; 2 d. Educ. Oban High School; Edinburgh University. Service in RAMC (Regular) - general duties, then Pathologist, 1937-59; Consultant Pathologist, Vale of Leven District General Hospital, 1959-80; Member, Argyll and Clyde Health Board, 1975-83; Territorial Army, 1960-67; Army Cadet Force, 1968-77; Medical Officer, Dunbartonshire BRCS, 1967-80, County Director, 1980-83. Recreation: fishing. Address: (h.) Burnside House, 38 Campbell Street, Helensburgh, G84 8YG; T.-Helensburgh 72612.

Stewart, Robert Armstrong, BA, DipTP, FRTPI. Director of Physical Planning and Development, Moray District Council, since 1979; b. Stirling. Planning Assistant, Lanark County Council, 1968-69; Planner, Glasgow, 1969-70; Senior Assistant, then Group Leader: Development Control, West Lothian County, 1970-75; Depute Director: Planning, East Lothian District, 1975-79. Address: (b.) District Headquarters, High Street, Elgin; T.-Elgin 545121.

Stewart, Robin Reith Wittet, MA, DSA, FHSM. General Manager, Highland Health Board, since 1985 (Secretary, 1974-84); Member, Hospital Committee, EEC, 1980-88; b. 11.8.35, Cambridge; m., Sara Sutherland; 2 d. Educ. George Watson's College, Edinburgh; Edinburgh University; Cambridge University; Manchester University. Depute Secretary and Treasurer, Glasgow Royal Infirmary, 1963-70; Secretary, Northern Regional Hospital Board, 1970-74. Church of Scotland Elder; former President, Inverness and District Choral Society; Past Chairman, Scottish Division, Institute of Health Service Management; former Treasurer, Inverness District Sports Council. Recreations: choral singing; golf; watching rugby. Address: (h.) 20 Crown Avenue, Inverness, IV2 3NF; T.-0463 236493.

Stewart, Roger Alfred, MA, MBA, ACIS. Commercial Manager, Lothian Health Board, since 1989; Chairman, Scottish Health Boards' Income Generation Group, since 1989; b. 13.10.48, London; m., Frances Abercromby; 2 d. Educ. St. Marylebone Grammar School, London; St. Andrews University; Union College, NY; Edinburgh University. Administrator, Scottish Special Housing Association, Edinburgh, 1973-75; Assistant Secretary, Queen Margaret College, Edinburgh, 1976-88. Elected Member of Council, National Trust for Scotland, 1986-91. Address: (h.) 66 South Trinity Road, Edinburgh, EH5 3NX; T.-031-552 7467.

Stewart, William F., MA, DipEd, BA (Hons). Rector, Belmont Academy, Ayr, since 1975; b. 25.1.33, Dreghorn; m., Marion McMillan; 3 d. Educ. Irvine Royal Academy; Glasgow University. Irvine Royal Academy: Teacher (Maths), Special Assistant Teacher (Maths), Principal Assistant (Maths), Principal Teacher (Maths), Depute Rector. President, Headteachers Association of Scotland, 1989-90; Headteacher Representative, Ayr College Council; Executive Member, Kyle and Carrick Sports Council; Member, UCCA Executive. Recreation: golf. Address: (b.) Belmont Academy, Belmont Road, Ayr; T.-0292 281733.

Stewart, William Jeffrey McMillan, LLB (Hons), LLM, NP. Senior Lecturer in Law, Strathclyde University, since 1986; Consultant, MacMillans, Solicitors, Glasgow, since 1988; b. 7.9.58, Glasgow. Educ. Clydebank High School; Glasgow University. Trained with D. Douglas Mackie & Co.; qualified as Solicitor, 1981; practised with McClure Naismith, Ross Harper and Murphy. Publications: Skiing and the Law; Introduction to Delict; A Casebook on Delict. Recreations: skiing; computing; music. Address: (b.) Strathclyde University, Law School, 16 Richmond Street, Glasgow, G1 1XQ.

Stiff, John Barry, QFSM, GradIFireE. Firemaster, Dumfries and Galloway Fire Brigade, since 1984; b. 17.5.43, Sunderland; m., Catherine Ann; 2 s.; 1 d. Educ. Sunderland County Borough Boys' Technical School. Joined Sunderland Fire Brigade, 1964; South Western Area Fire Brigade, Scotland, 1972; Dumfries and Galloway, 1975. Recreations: cars; caravanning; wood-turning. Address: Dumfries and Galloway Fire Brigade Headquarters, Brooms Road, Dumfries, DG1 2DZ; T.-0387 52222.

Still, Ronald McKinnon, MB, ChB, FRCOG. Consultant Obstetrician and Gynaecologist, since 1967; Honorary Senior Clinical Lecturer, Glasgow University, since 1967; b. 12.5.43, Helensburgh; 1 s.; 2 d. Educ. Hermitage School, Helensburgh; Glasgow University. House Surgeon/House Physician, Royal Infirmary, Glasgow, 1956-57; Captain, RAMC, seconded Malaya Military Forces, 1957-60; Registrar, Queen Mother's Hospital/Stobhill General Hospital, Glasgow; Senior Registrar, Glasgow Teaching Hospitals. Recreations: golf; music. Address: (h.) 9/5 Whistlefield Court, 2 Canniesburn Road, Bearsden, Glasgow, G61; T.-041-942 3097.

Still, Rev. William. Minister, Gilcomston South Church, Aberdeen, since 1945; Chairman of Trustees, Rutherford House Study Centre, since 1981; b. 8.5.11, Aberdeen. Educ. Aberdeen University and Christ's College. Fish worker in family business; Teacher of music, pianoforte, singing, choral work; Cadet, Salvation Army College, London; Assistant Minister, Springburnhill Parish Church, Glasgow. President, Inter-Varsity Fellowship, 1975-76; President, local University Christian Union, on several occasions. Recreations: walking; music; gardening; art; architecture. Address: 18 Beaconsfield Place, Aberdeen; T.-Aberdeen 644037.

Stimson, Professor William Howard, BSc, PhD, CBiol, FIBiol, FRSE. Professor of Immunology and Head, Department of Immunology, Strathclyde University, since 1981; Research Director/Executive Director, Rhone-Poulenc Diagnostics Ltd., Glasgow; Director, Aquaculture Diagnostics Ltd., Glasgow; b. 2.11.43, Liverpool; m., Jean Scott Baird; 1 s.; 1 d. Educ. Prince of Wales School, Nairobi; St. Andrews University. Research Fellow, Department of Obstetrics and Gynaecology, Dundee University, 1970-72; Lecturer, then Senior Lecturer, Biochemistry Department, Strathclyde University, 1973-80. Patron, Scottish Motor Neurone Disease Association; holder, Glasgow Loving Cup, 1982-83; Member, Editorial Boards, six scientific journals. Recreations: mechanical engineering; walking. Address: (b.) Department of Immunology, Strathclyde University, 31 Taylor Street, Glasgow, G4 ONR; T.-041-552 4400, Ext. 3729.

Stirling, George Scott, MB, ChB, FRCPGlas, FRCPsych, DPM. Former Medical Administrator, Crichton Royal Hospital, Dumfries; b. 20.4.26, Aberdeen; m., Yvonne; 1 s.; 1 d. Educ. Robert Gordon's College, Aberdeen; Aberdeen University. House Physician, Royal Cornhill Hospital, Aberdeen; Medical Branch, RAF; House Physician, Woodend General Hospital, Aberdeen; Fellow in Psychiatry, Crichton Royal, Dumfries; Past Chairman, Forensic Section, Scottish Division, Royal College of Psychiatrists; Member,

Parole Board for Scotland; Council of Europe Travelling Fellow; former Vice-Chairman, SASD (Dumfries). Recreations: fishing; gardening. Address: (h.) Phyllis Park, Murraythwaite, Dalton, Lockberie, DG11 1DW.

Stirling of Garden, Col. James, CBE, TD, FRICS. Lord Lieutenant of Stirling and Falkirk, since 1983; b. 8.9.30.

Stirling, Joe. Editor, Scottish Field, since 1988; b. 19.9.35, Glasgow. Educ. Shawlands Academy. Publisher, 1952-59; Advertising Agent, 1959-70; Fine Arts Consultant, 1970-81; Freelance Journalist, 1981-86; Deputy Editor, Scottish Field, 1987. Past President, Glasgow Press Club. Recreations: reading; writing; fishing; the company of friends. Address: (b.) The Plaza Tower, East Kilbride, Glasgow, G74 1LW.

Stirling, Robin Colin Baillie, OBE, JP; b. 6.4.25, Bo'ness; m., Jean R. Hendrie, MA. Educ. Dalziel High School, Motherwell. Editor: Motherwell Times, 1957-85, Motherwell Times Series, 1959-85. Former Secretary, Lanarkshire Branch, NUJ; elected Life Member, NUJ, 1985; Guild of British Newspaper Editors: former Scottish Secretary, Chairman, 1967-70; NCTJ: Member, Scottish Training Committee, 1961-85, Chairman, Scottish Committee, 1978-81. Convener, Motherwell Guild of Help, since 1953; Chairman, Strathclyde Police P Division Crime Prevention Panel, 1976-84; Member: Management Committee, Motherwell and Wishaw CAB, since 1971 (Chairman, 1978-80), Motherwell and District Christian Aid Committee 1970-82; Honorary Vice President: Motherwell ASC, since 1986, Motherwell CC, since 1985, Lanarkshire Little Theatre; President, Motherwell Probus Club, 1987-88; Founder Chairman, Motherwell and District Music Society (Chairman, since 1984). Recreations: gardening; music (including jazz); steam locomotives; Motherwell FC; Scottish Opera; cinema organs. Address: (h.) 37 The Loaning, Motherwell ML1 3HE; T.-63762.

Stirling, William Norman, IPFA, DPA, FCIT. Unit Finance Manager, Greater Glasgow Health Board, since 1991; b. 26.2.36, Glasgow; m., Edith; 1 s.; 3 d. Educ. Hamilton Academy; Glasgow College of Commerce; Glasgow University. Lanark County Council, 1953-58; Midlothian County Council, 1958-59; Clydebank Town Council, 1959-61; Motherwell and Wishaw Town Council, 1961-73 (Town Chamberlain and Collector of Rates, Local Taxation Officer and Manager, Municipal Bank, 1970-73); Director, Strathclyde Passenger Transport Executive, 1973-86; Scottish Manager, CSL Group Ltd., 1986-90. Director, National Transport Tokens Ltd.; Past Chairman, Scottish Branch, CIPFA. Recreations: golf; Robert Burns. Address: (h.) and (b.) 10 Crawford Gardens, High Burnside, Glasgow, G73 4JP; T.-041-634 2728.

Stirling of Fairburn, Roderick William Kenneth, TD, JP. Lord Lieutenant, Ross and Cromarty and Skye and Lochalsh, since 1988; Landowner and Estate Manager; Member, Red Deer Commission, 1964-89; Chairman, Highland Region Valuation Appeal Committee, 1983-91; Chairman, Scottish Salmon and White Fish Co. Ltd., 1980-91; b. 17.6.32; m., Penelope Jane Wright; 4 d. Educ. Wellesley House; Harrow; Aberdeen University. National Service, Scots Guards, 1950-52 (commissioned, 1951); TA service, Seaforth and Queen's Own Highlanders, 1953-69 (retired with rank of Captain); Member, Regional Advisory Committee to Forestry Commission, 1964-85; Local Director, Eagle Star Insurance Co., 1966-85; Director, Moray Firth Salmon Fishing Co. Ltd.; Member, Highland River Purification Board, 1975-90; Ross and Cromarty County Councillor, 1970-74 (Chairman of Highways, 1973-74); Member, Ross and Cromarty District Council, since 1984; Member, Highland Committee, Scottish Landowners Federation (Chairman, 1974-79); Junior Vice President, Scottish Accident Prevention Society. Recreations:

wild life management; gardening; curling. Address: (h.) Arcan, Muir of Ord, Ross-shire; T.-Urray 207.

Stiven, Frederic William Binning, ARSA, MCSD, DA. Constructivist, Designer and Teacher; Head of Design, Grays School of Art, Aberdeen, 1982-87; b. 25.4.29, Cowdenbeath; m., Jenny Paton; 2 s.; 2 d. Trained Edinburgh College of Art. Constructivist work in numerous public and private collections; exhibited in Edinburgh, Glasgow, Leeds, London, Bergen, Helsinki, Venice and New York; freelance Designer; Royal Scottish Academy Gillies Award, 1985. Address: (h.) Sheallagan, Golf Course Road, Rosemount, Blairgowrie, Perthshire; T.-0250 4863.

Stobie, David Henry, BSc, MSc, CEng, MIMechE, DMS, FBIM. Head, Department of Management Studies, Napier Polytechnic, since 1984; Chairman, Edinburgh Branch, British Institute of Management, 1988-91, Vice-President, since 1991; b. 21.10.41, Edinburgh; m., June Moffat; 1 s.; 1 d. Educ. Tynecastle Senior Secondary School, Edinburgh; Heriot-Watt University, Edinburgh. Production Planning Engineer, Ferranti Ltd., 1965; various line management positions, Hewlett-Packard Ltd., 1966-73; Works Manager, Hall and Hall Ltd., 1973-74; Senior Systems Analyst, Hewlett-Packard Ltd., 1974-75; joined Napier as Lecturer, 1975. Recreations: hill-walking; classical music; wine-tasting. Address: (b.) Napier Management Centre, Napier Polytechnic of Edinburgh, EH10 5BR; T.-031-444 2266.

Stobo, James, OBE, DL, FRAgS. Farmer; President, Animal Diseases Research Association, since 1980; Chairman of Governors, Longridge Towers School, since 1982; Chairman, Scottish Seed Potato Development Council, since 1988; Chairman, Moredun Animal Health Ltd.; b. 9.12.34, Lanark; m., Pamela Elizabeth Mary Herriot; 1 s.; 2 d. Educ. Edinburgh Academy. Farming, since 1951; Past Chairman and President, Scottish Association of Young Farmers Clubs; Member, Home-Grown Cereals Authority, 1971-76; President, National Farmers' Union of Scotland, 1973-74; Director, John Hogarth Ltd., Kelso Mills; Member, Secretary of State for Scotland's Panel of Agricultural Arbiters. Vice-President: Scottish National Fat Stock Club, Royal Smithfield Club; Deputy Lieutenant, County of Berwick, 1987. Recreations: game shooting; photography. Address: Nabdean, Berwick-upon-Tweed, TD15 1SZ; T.-0289 86224.

Stockdale, Elizabeth Joan Noel, MB, ChB, DMRD, FRCR. Consultant Radiologist, Royal Aberdeen Children's Hospital and Aberdeen Royal Infirmary, since 1980; Clinical Senior Lecturer, Aberdeen University, since 1980; b. Chippenham; m., Christopher Leo Stockdale; 2 s.; 1 d. Educ. Aberdeen University. House Surgeon, Aberdeen Royal Infirmary; Senior House Surgeon, Professorial Surgical Unit, Hospital for Sick Children, Great Ormond Street; Registrar, St. George's Hospital; Senior Registrar, Royal National Orthopaedic Hospital, Royal Marsden Hospital, Atkinson Morley's Hospital. Recreations: theatre; classical music; travel. Address: (h.) 1 Grant Road, Banchory, Kincardineshire, AB31 3UW; T.-03302 3096.

Stoddart, Charles Norman, LLB, LLM, PhD, SSC. Sheriff of North Strathclyde at Paisley, since 1988; b. 4.4.48, Dunfermline; m., Anne Lees; 1 d. Educ. Dunfermline High School; Edinburgh University; McGill University. Private practice as Solicitor, 1972-73; Lecturer in Scots Law, Edinburgh University, 1973-80; private practice as Solicitor, 1980-88. Publications: The Law and Practice of Legal Aid in Scotland (3rd ed., 1990); A Casebook on Scottish Criminal Law (Co-author); Cases and Materials on Scottish Criminal Procedure (Co-author); Criminal Warrants, 1991. Recreations: skiing; foreign travel. Address: (b.) Paisley Sheriff Court, St. James Street, Paisley; T.-041-887 5291.

Stodart of Leaston, Rt. Hon. Lord (James Anthony Stodart), PC (1974); b. 6.6.16, Exeter; m., Hazel Usher. Educ. Wellington. MP (Conservative), Edinburgh West, 1959-74; Joint Under Secretary of State, Scottish Office, 1963-64; Parliamentary Secretary, later Minister of State, Ministry of Agriculture, Fisheries and Food, 1970-74; Chairman: Agricultural Credit Corporation Ltd., 1975-87, Committee of Enquiry into Local Government in Scotland, 1980, Manpower Review of Veterinary Profession in UK, 1984-85. Publication: Land of Abundance: a study of Scottish agriculture in the 20th century. Recreations: music; golf; preserving a sense of humour. Addresses: Lorimers, North Berwick; Leaston, Humbie, East Lothian.

Stone, Professor Frederick Hope, MB, ChB, FRCP, FRCPsych. Professor of Child and Adolescent Psychiatry, Glasgow University, 1977-86; Consultant Psychiatrist, Royal Hospital for Sick Children, Glasgow, since 1954; b. 11.9.21, Glasgow; m., Zelda Elston, MA; 2 s.; 1 d. Educ. Hillhead High School, Glasgow; Glasgow University. Acting Director, Lasker Mental Hygiene Clinic, Hadassah, Jerusalem, 1952-54; World Health Organisation Visiting Consultant, 1960, 1964; Member, Kilbrandon Committee, 1963-65; Secretary General, International Association of Child Psychiatry, 1962-66; Member, Houghton Committee on Adoption, 1968-72; Chairman, Scottish Division, Royal College of Psychiatrists, 1981-84; President, Young Minds; Chairman, Strathclyde Children's Panel Advisory Committee, since 1988. Publication: Child Psychiatry for Students (Co-author). Address: (h.) 14A Hamilton Avenue, Pollokshields, Glasgow, G41 4JF; T.-041-427 0115.

Stone, Gordon Victor, MBChB, FFCM, MFCMI, DCM. Chief Administrative Medical Officer/Director of Public Health Medicine, Highland Health Board, since 1989; b. 4.10.45, London; m., Aileen S. Wilson; 1 s.; 1 d. Educ. Aberdeen Grammar School; Aberdeen University; Edinburgh University. Medical Officer, RAF, 1970-75; Scottish Health Service Fellow in Community Medicine, 1975-78; Specialist in Community Medicine, Grampian Health Board, 1978-89. Recreations: golf; skiing. Address: (b.) Reay House, Old Edinburgh Road, Inverness, IV2 3HG; T.-0463 239851.

Stone, Sheriff Marcus, MA, LLB. Sheriff of Lothian and Borders, at Linlithgow, since 1984; b. 22.3.21, Glasgow; m., Jacqueline Barnoin; 3 s.; 2 d. Educ. High School of Glasgow; Glasgow University. Served Second World War; admitted Solicitor, 1949; admitted Faculty of Advocates, 1965; Sheriff of North Strathclyde, at Dumbarton, 1971-76; Sheriff of Glasgow and Strathkelvin, at Glasgow, 1976-84. Publications: Proof of Fact in Criminal Trials, 1984; Cross-examination in Criminal Trials, 1988; Fact-Finding for Magistrates, 1990. Recreations: swimming; music. Address: (b.) Sheriff Court House, Court Square, Linlithgow, EH49 7EQ; T.-Linlithgow 684 2922.

Stone, Professor Trevor W., BPharm, PhD, DSc. Professor and Head of Pharmacology, Glasgow University, since 1989; b. 7.10.47, Mexborough; m., Anne Corina. Educ. Mexborough Grammar School; London University; Aberdeen University. Lecturer in Physiology, Aberdeen University, 1970-77; Senior Lecturer/Reader in Neuroscience, then Professor of Neuroscience, London University, 1977-88. Editor, British Journal of Pharmacology, 1980-86. Publications: Microiontophoresis and Pressure Ejection, 1985; Purines: Basic and Clinical Aspects, 1990. Recreations: photography; snooker; working. Address: (b.) Department of Pharmacology, Glasgow University, Glasgow, G12; T.-041-330 4481.

Storey, Gerald Francis, BSc, CEng, FICE, FIHT. Consulting Engineer; former Assistant Chief Engineer, Scottish Development Department; b. 14.5.27, Edinburgh;

m., Marjorie Purves; 1 s.; 1 d. Educ. George Heriot's School; Edinburgh University. Argyll County Council; Air Ministry Works Directorate; Macartney Ltd., Contractors; Department of Agriculture and Fisheries; Ministry (now Department) of Transport; seconded to Scottish Office, since 1962. Past Chairman, Scottish Branch, Institution of Highways and Transport; former Member, Road Engineering Board, Institution of Civil Engineers. Recreations: golf; motoring. Address: (h.) Cruivan, 7 Lodgehill Park, Nairn, IV12 4SA; T.-0667 53120.

Storie, Roy G., MA (Hons), DipEd. Headteacher, Prestwick Academy, since 1987; b. 16.9.34, Edinburgh; m.; 1 s.; 1 d. Educ. Royal High School; Edinburgh University; Moray House College of Education. Address: (b.) Prestwick Academy, Newdykes Road, Prestwick, KA9 2LB.

Stormonth Darling, Sir Jamie Carlisle, Kt, CBE, MC, TD, WS, LLB, MA, Hon. FRIAS, DUniv (Stirling), Hon. LLD (Aberdeen). Vice-President, Scottish Conservation Projects Trust (President, 1983-88); b. 18.7.18, Battle, Sussex; m., Mary Finella Gammell, BEM, DL; 1 s.; 2 d. Educ. Winchester College; Christ Church, Oxford; Edinburgh University. 2nd Lt., KOSB (Territorial), 1937: Adjutant, 1941, to Lt.-Col. Commanding 52nd (L) Division; Reconnaissance Regiment, RAC, 1945-46; studied law, Edinburgh University, 1946-49; appointed Chief Executive as Secretary, then Director, National Trust for Scotland, 1949-83, then Vice-President (Emeritus). Concerned with various Scottish charities such as Scottish Churches Architectural Heritage Trust, Scotland's Gardens Scheme, Pollok Trust (Glasgow), Edinburgh Old Town Trusts. Recreations: gardening; countryside; golf. Address: (h.) Chapelhill House, Dirleton, North Berwick, EH39 5HG; T.-062 085 296.

Stormonth Darling, Lady (Mary Finella), BEM, DL (East Lothian). Chairman, New Generation Housing Association, since 1987; b. 15.4.24, Farnborough; m., Sir Jamie Carlisle Stormonth Darling, qv; 1 s.; 2 d. Educ. Southover Manor School, Lewes; Architectural Association, London. Special Operations Executive (SOE), 1942-45. Designed own house, 1974; Elder, Dirleton Kirk and Convener, Fabric Committee, since 1976; Member, Church and Nation Committee, Church of Scotland, 1978-86; Convener, Sub-Committee on International Interests, 1982-84; Member, British Council of Churches, 1980-83; voluntary and charitable work. Recreations: painting, sculpting and gardening. Address: Chapelhill House, Dirleton, North Berwick, EH39 5HG; T.-062 085 296.

Storrar, George Alexander, MC, BSc, JP. Farmer; Honorary Sheriff; b. 17.9.18, Collessie, Fife; m., Leila Barrie Orchison; 1 s.; 2 d. Educ. Perth Academy; Edinburgh University. Army, 1939-46: Fife and Forfar Yeomanry and Royal Tank Regiment - Major; France, 1940, NW Europe, 1944-46; mentioned in Despatches (2). Trustee, Cupar Savings Bank; Director, Scottish Plant Breeding Station; Member, Fife Valuation Appeal Court; President, Cupar Rotary Club, 1967-68; Trustee, Cupar TSB. Address: (h.) Halhill, Leckiebank Road, Auchtermuchty, Fife; T.-Auchtermuchty 28603.

Stother, Ian G., MA, MB, BChir, FRCSEdin, FRCSGlas. Consultant Orthopaedic Surgeon, Glasgow Royal Infirmary and Nuffield McAlpin Clinic, Glasgow, since 1978; b. Lytham; m., Jacqueline; 2 d. Educ. King Edward VII School, Lytham; Kings College, Cambridge; St. George's Hospital Medical School, London. Honorary Clinical Senior Lecturer, Glasgow University; Honorary Lecturer, Bioengineering Unit, Strathclyde University; Examiner, Royal College of Physicians and Surgeons of Glasgow; Orthopaedic Adviser, Dance School of Scotland and Scottish Ballet. Recreations:

classic cars; golf. Address: (h.) 13 Moncrieff Avenue, Lenzie, Glasgow; T.-041-776 5330.

Stott, Rt. Hon. Lord (George Gordon Stott), PC (1964), QC (Scot), MA, LLB, DipEd; b. 22.12.09; m., Nancy Braggins; 1 s.; 1 d. Educ. Edinburgh Academy; Edinburgh University. Advocate, 1936; QC (Scot), 1950; Advocate Depute, 1947-51; Sheriff of Roxburgh, Berwick and Selkirk, 1961-64; Lord Advocate, 1964-67; Senator of the College of Justice, 1967-85. Editor, Edinburgh Clarion. Recreations: Mozart; reading; keeping a diary. Address: (h.) 12 Midmar Gardens, Edinburgh; T.-031-447 4251.

Stout, George Alexander, MA (Hons). Company Director; b. 9.11.27, Dundee; m., Dorothy Smith; 1 s.; 3 d. Educ. Morgan Academy, Dundee; Edinburgh University. Director: Fleming Claverhouse Investment Trust PLC, since 1977, Advent Technology p.l.c., since 1981, Advent Capital Limited, since 1985, XCL Sunrisie Inc., since 1990; Adviser, Joseph Johnston & Sons Ltd , since 1987; Honorary Visiting Professor, Dundee University. Recreations: golf; curling; gardening; photography; music; travel. Address: (h.) Achmore, Victoria Street, Monifieth, DD5 4HP.

Stoward, Professor Peter John, MA, MSc, DPhil, FInstBiol, DipRMS, FRSE. Professor of Histochemistry, Dundee University; b. 27.1.35, Birmingham; m., Barbara Essex Lewis (deceased); 1 d. Educ. King Edward's School, Birmingham; Oriel College, Oxford. Assistant Lecturer, University of Aston in Birmingham, 1958-61; Research Assistant, Department of Human Anatomy, Oxford University, 1961-63 and 1965-67; International Research Fellow, National Institutes of Health, Bethesda, Maryland, 1964, 1965; Lecturer, Nuffield Department of Orthopaedic Surgery, Oxford University, 1967-68; Senior Lecturer in Anatomy, Dundee University, 1968-75; Reader in Histology, Dundee University, 1975-89; Acting Head, Department of Anatomy, Dundee University, 1987-88; Head, Department of Anatomy, 1988-91; Visiting Professor, Pavia University, Italy, since 1980; Editor, Histochemical Journal, since 1967. Diocesan Reader, Scottish Episcopal Church. Publications: Histochemistry: The Widening Horizons (Co-author), 1981; Histochemistry of Secretory Processes (Co-author), 1977. Recreations: sailing; walking; the performing arts; reading. Address: (b.) Department of Anatomy and Physiology, The University, Dundee, DD1 4HN; T.-0382 23181.

Strachan, Graham Robert, CBE (1977), DL, FEng, FIMechE, FIMarE. Director, Scott Lithgow Ltd., since 1984; b. 1.11.31; m., Catherine Nicol Liston; 2 s. Educ. Trinity College, Glenalmond; Trinity College, Cambridge. Apprentice Engineer, 1950-55; National Service, RNVR, 1955-57; John Brown & Co. (Clydebank) Ltd., 1957-63; John Brown Engineering Ltd.: Director and General Manager, 1966, Managing Director, 1968, Group Managing Director, 1975, Deputy Chairman, 1983-84; Director: British Smelter Constructions Ltd., 1968-73, CJB Offshore Ltd., 1975-80, John Brown & Co. (Overseas) 1976-84; Chairman: JBE Offshore Ltd., 1976-81, JBE Gas Turbines, 1976-84, Stephens of Linthouse Ltd., 1982-84. Member: CBI Oil Steering Group, 1975-79, Executive Committee, Scottish Engineering Employers' Association, 1966-82; Vice-President, Scottish Council (Development and Industry), since 1983; Director, Glasgow Chamber of Commerce, since 1978; Member, Court, Strathclyde University, 1979-83. Recreations: skiing; golf; early jazz. Address: (h.) The Mill House, Strathblane, Stirlingshire; T.-Blanefield 70220.

Strachan, John, JP, MA, LLB. Senior Partner, Davidson & Garden, Advocates, Aberdeen, since 1969, and Peterkins, Advocates, Aberdeen, since 1990; Director, William Wilson Holdings Ltd., since 1979; Director, Osprey Communications P.L.C., since 1982; b. 9.8.29, Fraserburgh; m., Margaret

Cheyne (deceased); 1 s.; 2 d. Educ. Fraserburgh Academy; Aberdeen University. National Service, 1954-56 (Sub Lt., RNVR); Partner, Davidson & Garden, Advocates, 1958. Recreations: shooting; fishing. Address: (h.) 5A Rubislaw Den North, Aberdeen, AB2 4AL; T.-0224 317284.

Strang, Gavin Steel, BSc (Hons), DipAgriSci, PhD. MP (Labour), East Edinburgh, since 1970; b. 10.7.43, Dundee; m., Bettina Smith; 1 s. Educ. Morrison's Academy, Crieff; Edinburgh University. Parliamentary Under Secretary of State, Department of Energy, February to October, 1974; Parliamentary Secretary, Ministry of Agriculture, 1974-79. Recreations: golf; swimming; the countryside. Address: (h.) 80 Argyle Crescent, Edinburgh, EH15 2QD; T.-031-669 5999.

Strang Steel, Malcolm Graham, BA (Cantab), LLB, WS. Partner, W. & J. Burness, WS, since 1973; Member, Council, Law Society of Scotland, 1984-90; Chairman, Scottish Dyslexia Trust; b. 24.11.46, Selkirk; m., Margaret Philippa Scott; 1 s.; 1 d. Educ. Eton; Trinity College, Cambridge; Edinburgh University. Sometime Chairman, Albyn Housing Society Ltd. Recreations: shooting; fishing; skiing; tennis; reading. Address: (b.) 16 Hope Street, Edinburgh, EH2 4DD; T.-031-226 2561.

Strathmore and Kinghorne, Mary, Countess of, DL. Deputy Lieutenant for Angus; b. 31.5.32, London; m., 17th Earl of Strathmore and Kinghorne (deceased); 1 s.; 2 d. Deputy Lieutenant. Address: (h.) c/o Glamis Castle, Forfar, Angus.

Straton, Timothy Duncan, TD, CA, ATII. Partner, Scott-Moncrieff Thomson & Shiells, CA; Treasurer, Scottish Society for the Prevention of Cruelty to Animals; b. 1.10.42, Edinburgh; m., Gladys Margaret George; 1 s.; 1 d. Educ. Edinburgh Academy. Honorary Treasurer, Bruntsfield Links Golfing Society. Recreations: driving; photography; golf. Address: (b.) 17 Melville Street, Edinburgh, EH3 7PH; T.-031-226 6281.

Street, Margaret Dobson; b. 18.10.20, Hawick; m., Richard Andrew Rutherford Street (deceased); 2 s. Educ. Hawick High School; Alva Academy. Civil Servant, 1938-48; Ministry of Labour and National Service, 1938-47; Ministry of National Insurance (Inspectorate), 1947-48; voluntary work since 1948, apart from freelance writing on household and conservation topics; Honorary Secretary (Past Chairman), Leith Civic Trust; Convener, Friends of North Carr Lightship; Saltire Society Representative, Council, National Trust for Scotland; Secretary, Mungo Park Commemoration Committee; Trustee, Robert Hurd Memorial Fund; Vice-Chairman, Edinburgh Branch, Saltire Society; Member, Steering Committee, Brownsbank; Member, Executive Committee, Scottish Peat and Land Development Association; Appeal Convener, Wallace Statue, Dryburgh. Recreations: promotion of Scottish cultural activity; conservation; good cooking. Address: (h.) 115 Trinity Road, Edinburgh; T.-031-552 2409.

Stronach, Professor Ian MacDonald, MA, MEd, PhD. Professor of Education, Stirling University, since 1991; b. 16.3.45, Aberdeen; m., Kathleen Mary; 1 s.; 2 d. Educ. Aberdeen Grammar School; Aberdeen University; Bristol University; Glasgow University; University of East Anglia. Taught in Scotland and Zambia, 1968-77; Senior Research Fellow, Jordanhill College, until 1984; Lecturer, Centre for Applied Research in Education, University of East Anglia, until 1991. Address (b.) Department of Education, Stirling University, Stirling, FK8 2QP; T.-0786 73171.

Stuart, Charles Murray. Chairman, Scottish Power PLC, since 1992; Vice Chairman and Director, Hill Samuel Bank

Ltd., since 1992; b. 28.7.33, Gourock; m., Netta Caroline; 1 s.; 1 d. Educ. Glasgow Academy; Glasgow University. MB Group PLC (formerly Metal Box), 1981-90, latterly as Executive Chairman; Director and Chief Financial Officer, Berisford International plc, 1990-91. Recreations: sailing; ballet; theatre. Address: (b.) Cathcart House, Spean Street, Glasgow, G44 4BE; T.-041-637 7177.

Stuart, Michael John, BSc (Hons). Head Teacher, Kincorth Academy, since 1991; b. 24.11.46, Fraserburgh; m., Daniele Bathier; 2 s.; 1 d. Educ. Fraserburgh Academy; Aberdeen University. Assistant Teacher of Geography, Fraserburgh Academy, 1970-71, Kelvinside Academy, 1971-72; Principal Teacher of Geography, Greenwood Academy, Irvine, 1972-82; AHT, Loudoun Academy, Kilmarnock, 1982-90; Depute Head Teacher, Carrick Academy, 1990-91. Recreations: golf; angling; hill-walking. Address: (h.) Lorien, 12 Barclay Park, Aboyne, AB34 5JF; T.-03398 86687.

Stuart-Smith, Deryk Aubrey, BSc, MD, FRCPGlas, FRCPEdin. Senior Lecturer, Department of Medicine, Glasgow University, since 1970; Consultant Physician, Western Infirmary, Glasgow, since 1970 (Director, Bone Metabolism Research Unit, since 1971); b. 12.4.27, Simla, India; m., Anne Bennoch; 1 s.; 3 d. Educ. Bishop Cotton School; Glasgow University. Publication: Diagnostic Procedures in Disorders of Calcium Metabolism. Recreations: gardening; theatre; science fiction; science fact. Address: (h.) 30 Dolphin Road, Maxwell Park, Glasgow, G41 4DZ; T.-041-423 2430.

Stubb, Ian Michael, LLB, CA, FTII. Partner, Maclay Murray & Spens, Solicitors, Glasgow and Edinburgh, since 1973; b. 14.11.43, Birmingham; m., Joan Baird Crowther; 2 s.; 1 d. Educ. Marr College, Troon; Glasgow University. Thomson McLintock, Glasgow, 1965-68; Apprentice/Assistant, Maclay Murray & Spens, 1968-73. Council Member, Institute of Chartered Accountants of Scotland, 1986-92; Past Chairman, Board of Examiners, Law Society of Scotland; Senior Tutor, Wills Trusts and Executries, Glasgow University, 1980-86. Address: (h.) Suffolk Lodge, Methven Road, Whitecraigs, Glasgow, G46; T.-041-639 6580.

Sturgeon, David, BL. Registrar and Deputy Secretary, Heriot-Watt University, since 1967; b. 10.12.35, Kilwinning; m., Nancy McDougall; 2 s.; 1 d. Educ. Dalry High School, Ayrshire; Glasgow University. National Service (RASC - War Office), 1957-59; Trainee Actuary, Scottish Widows Fund, 1959-61; Administrative Assistant, Royal College of Science and Technology (later, Strathclyde University), 1961-67. Secretary and Treasurer, Edinburgh Society of Glasgow University Graduates, since 1971. Recreations: golf; music (particularly Scottish country dance music). Address: (h.) 10 Dalhousie Road, Eskbank, Midlothian, EH22 3AS; T.-031-663 1059.

Sturrock, Alexander Muir, MBE, TD; Croix de Guere, WS, NP, BA (Oxon); b. 21.9.13, Edinburgh; m., Mary Percival Walsh; 1 s.; 2 d. Educ. Edinburgh Academy; Exeter College, Oxford; Edinburgh University. Commissioned, 1939, KOSB posted 6 KOSB; served in Europe until 1945; Adjutant, 6 KOSB, DAA and QMG, 44 (Lowland) Brigade, DAAG 15 (Scottish) Division; rejoined 4 KOSB (TA), 1947; Burgh Prosecutor, Royal Burgh of Jedburgh; Clerk, Jedburgh District Council; Clerk, River Tweed Commissioners, 1950-82. Recreations: (used to be!) rugby; tennis; golf; shooting; fishing. Address: (h.) Elm Bank, Jedburgh, TD8 6QF; T.-0835 62400.

Sturrock, Robert Ralph, MB, ChB, DSc. Reader in Anatomy, Dundee University, since 1981; b. 1.7.43, Dundee; m., Norma Duncan; 1 d. Educ. Dundee High School; St.

Andrews University. House Surgeon, Perth Royal Infirmary, 1967-68; House Physician, Stirling Royal Infirmary, 1968; Demonstrator, then Lecturer, Anatomy Department, Dundee University, 1968-77; Visiting Associate Professor of Neuroanatomy, Iowa University, 1976; Senior Lecturer, Dundee, 1977-81. Symington Memorial Prize in Anatomy, 1978. Recreations: reading; running; swimming; hill-walking. Address: (h.) 6 Albany Terrace, Dundee; T.-0382 23578.

Subak-Sharpe, Professor John Herbert, CBE, FInstBiol, BSc, PhD, FRSE. Professor of Virology, Glasgow University, since 1968; Honorary Director, MRC Virology Unit, Institute of Virology, Glasgow, since 1968; b. 14.2.24, Vienna; m., Barbara Naomi Morris; 2 s.; 1 d. Educ. Humanistisches Gymnasium, Vienna; Birmingham University. Assistant Lecturer, Glasgow University, 1954-56; Member, ARC scientific staff, AVRI Pirbright, 1956-61; Visiting Fellow, California Institute of Technology, 1961; Member, MRC Experimental Virus Unit scientific staff, Glasgow, 1961-68; Visiting Professor, NIH, Bethesda, 1967-68. Visiting Fellow, Clare Hall, Cambridge, 1986; elected Member (Past Chairman, Course and Workshops Committee), EMBO, since 1969; Trustee (former Secretary and Vice-President), Genetical Society, since 1971; Chairman, MRC Training Awards Panel, 1986-89; Member, Governing Body, West of Scotland Oncological Organisation, since 1974, and Governing Body, Animal Virus Research Institute, Pirbright, 1986-88; Member, Scientific Advisory Group, Equine Virology Research Foundation, since 1987; Member, Medical Research Council Cell Biology and Disorders Board, 1988-92. Recreations: travel; bridge. Address: (h.) 17 Kingsborough Gardens, Hyndland, Glasgow, G12 9NH; T.-041-339 1863.

Suckling, Professor Colin James, BSc, PhD, DSc, CChem, FRSC, FRSA, FRSE. Professor of Chemistry, Strathclyde University, since 1984; b. 24.3.47, Birkenhead; m., Catherine Mary Faulkner; 2 s.; 1 d. Educ. Quarry Bank High School, Liverpool; Liverpool University. Lecturer, Department of Pure and Applied Chemistry, Strathclyde University, 1972; Royal Society Smith and Nephew Senior Research Fellow, 1980. Convener, RSE Chemistry Committee, 1989-91; Member of Council, RSE, since 1989. Publications: Chemistry Through Models (Co-author), 1978; Biological Chemistry (Co-author), 1980; Enzyme Chemistry, Impact and Applications (Co-author), 1984, 1989. Recreations: music; horn playing. Address: (b.) Department of Pure and Applied Chemistry, Strathclyde Universtiy, 295 Cathedral Street, Glasgow, G1 1XL; T.-041-552 4400.

Suddaby, John Trevor, MA. Deputy Secretary, Edinburgh University, since 1987; b. 28.3.34, Horbury; m., Margaret Helen Steventon; 1 s.; 1 d. Educ. Bradford Grammar School; Jesus College, Cambridge. National Service (Intelligence Corps), 1955-57; Assistant Research Officer, Ministry of Defence, 1958-62; on administrative staff, Edinburgh University, since 1962. Recreations: music; mountain-walking. Address: (h.) Old College, South Bridge, Edinburgh, EH8 9YL; T.-031-650 1000.

Suess, Nigel M., MA, FCIB, FCCA. Director: The British Linen Bank Ltd., since 1979, The Murrayfield p.l.c., since 1982, Lothian Homes Ltd., since 1986, Anglo Scottish Properties p.l.c., since 1991; b. 13.12.45, Chelmsford; m., Maureen Ferguson; 1 d. Educ. Chigwell School; Gonville and Caius College, Cambridge. N.M. Rothschild & Sons Ltd., 1967-77 (Assistant Director, 1974-77); joined The British Linen Bank Ltd., 1978. Recreations: mountaineering; chess; ornithology. Address: (b.) 4 Melville Street, Edinburgh, EH3 7NS; T.-031-453 1919.

Sugden, Chris, BA. Rector, Buckie High School; b. 25.5.46, Paignton; m., Lynne; 1 s.; 1 d. Educ. Newcastle upon Tyne University. Gordonstoun School, Moray; Castlebrae High School, Edinburgh; Knox Academy, Haddington; Harlaw Academy, Aberdeen. Recreations: exploration and outdoor activities. Address: (b.) Buckie High School, West Cathcart Street, Buckie, AB56 1QB; T.-Buckie 32605.

Sugden, Professor David Edward, MA, DPhil. Professor, Department of Geography, Edinburgh University, since 1987; b. 5.3.41, Paignton; m., Britta Valborg Stridsberg; 2 s.; 1 d. Educ. Warwick School; Jesus College, Oxford. Scientific Officer, British Antarctic Survey, 1965-66; Lecturer/Reader, Department of Geography, Aberdeen University, 1966-86. Recreations: hill-walking; gardening; squash. Address: (b.) Department of Geography, Edinburgh University, Edinburgh, EH8; T.-031-650 2521.

Sullivan, John, BA, MA. Senior Lecturer in Russian, St. Andrews University, and Chairman of Department, since 1990; b. 2.11.37, Sheffield; m., Veronica Margaret Jones; 2 s.; 1 d. Educ. Firth Park Grammar School, Sheffield; Manchester University. Lecturer in Russian, St. Andrews University, 1964-83. Publications include: An Unpublished Religious Songbook of Mid Eighteenth Century Russia; Russian Love Songs in the Early Eighteenth Century, three volumes. Recreations: golf; ornithology. Address: (h.) Thorncroft, 1 Hepburn Gardens, St. Andrews, Fife; T.-0334 72614.

Susskind, Werner, MB, ChB, FRCPGlas, FRCPEdin. Consultant Dermatologist, Victoria Infirmary, Glasgow, since 1965; Honorary Senior Clinical Lecturer in Dermatology, Glasgow University, since 1966; b. 29.4.33, Hamburg; m., Shirley Banks; 2 s. Educ. Hillhead High School, Glasgow; Glasgow University. Recreations: choral singing; photography; golf. Address: (h.) 1B Ramsay Court, Eaglesham Road, Newton Mearns, by Glasgow, G77 5DJ; T.-041-639 3265.

Sutherland, Alistair. Vice Chairman, North of Scotland Milk Marketing Board, since 1990; b. 8.1.46, Orkney; m., Judith A.; 1 s.; 2 d. Educ. Nairn Academy. Joined family farming business on leaving school; former Chairman, Highland Region Young Farmers Clubs; Past President, Moray and Nairn NFU; writes on dairy farming for Agribusiness. Winner, Roy Watherston Award, 1973. Recreations: reading; writing; showing dairy cattle; antiques; travel. Address: (h.) Bankhead, Brodie, Morayshire; T.-030 94 232.

Sutherland, David George Carr, CBE, MC and bar, TD. Landowner and Farmer, since 1962; Consultant, Control Risks Group Ltd., since 1985; b. 2.10.20, London; m., 1, Jean Henderson; 2, Christine Hotchkiss; 1 s.; 2 d. Educ. Eton; Sandhurst. War Service, Black Watch and Special Air Service Regiment, Dunkirk, Western Desert, Aegean, Adriatic; wounded; mentioned in Despatches; Greek War Cross; command and staff appointments, 1945-55, including British Military Mission to Greece, instructor at Sandhurst, Gold Staff Officer at The Queen's Coronation; retired from the Army, 1955; Ministry of Defence, 1955-80; commanded 21 SAS Regiment, Artists Rifles, TA, 1956-60; Deputy Lieutenant for Tweeddale, since 1974; Non-Executive Director, Asset Protection International Ltd., 1981-85. Member, Queen's Bodyguard for Scotland, Royal Company of Archers, since 1949; Fellow, Royal Geographical Society. Recreations: fishing; shooting; walking. Address: Ferniehaugh, Dolphinton, West Linton; T.-Dolphinton 82257.

Sutherland, David I.M., MA, MEd, FRSA. Registrar, The General Teaching Council for Scotland, since 1985; b. 22.1.38, Wick; m., Janet H. Webster; 2 s. Educ. Aberdeen Grammar School; Aberdeen University; University of Zurich. Teacher of Modern Languages, Aberdeen Grammar School, 1962-66; Lecturer in Education, Stranmillis College of Education, Belfast, 1966-69; Lecturer in Educational

Psychology, Craigie College of Education, Ayr, 1969-72; Assistant Director of Education, Sutherland County Council, 1972-75; Divisional Education Officer (Inverness), then Depute Director of Education, Highland Regional Council, 1975-85. Chairman: Scottish Television Educational Advisory Committee, Broadcasting and the Curriculum Liaison Group; Assessor: Council for National Academic Awards (Committee for Teacher Education), Joint Committee of Colleges of Education in Scotland; Member: Scottish Education Department Planning Group on Teacher Supply, Project Committee on Appointment Procedures for Promoted Staff in Schools, Scottish Association for Educational Management and Administration, Scottish Educational Research Association, Professional Advisory Committee to Department of Education, Stirling University. Recreations: golf; walking; theatre; reading. Address: (b.) 5 Royal Terrace, Edinburgh, EH7 5AF; T.-031-556 0072.

Sutherland, Donald Gilmour, CA. Regional Managing Partner – South, Ernst & Young, since 1990; b. 15.4.40, Edinburgh; m., Linda Malone; 2 s.; 1 d. Educ. George Watson's College. Joined Brown Fleming & Murray, London, 1963; Partner, Whinney Murray & Co., Glasgow, 1968, Edinburgh, 1974; Managing Partner, Ernst & Whinney, Edinburgh, 1985; Regional Managing Partner, 1987; Director, Murray Johnstone Ltd., Murray International Trust plc, Murray Income plc, Murray Smaller Markets Trust plc, 1987-89; Regional Managing Partner – North, Ernst & Young, 1989-90; Director, Standard Life Assurance Company, since 1990; Vice-Chairman, Governing Council, George Watson's College. Recreations: conservation: golf; antiques. Address: (b.) 39 Melville Street, Edinburgh, EH3 7JL; T.-031-226 4621.

Sutherland, Elizabeth (Elizabeth Margaret Marshall). Writer; Curator, Groam House Museum, Rosemarkie, since 1982; b. 24.8.26, Kemback, Cupar; m., Rev. John D. Marshall; 2 s.; 1 d. Educ. St. Leonard's Girls' School, St. Andrews; Edinburgh University. Social Worker for Scottish Episcopal Church, 1974-80; author of: Lent Term (Constable Trophy), 1973, The Seer of Kintail, 1974, Hannah Hereafter (Scottish Arts Council Book Award), 1976, The Eye of God, 1977, The Weeping Tree, 1980, Ravens and Black Rain: The Story of Highland Second Sight, 1985, The Gold Key and The Green Life, 1986. Recreations: Highland history; Gaelic language; gardening; the Picts; walking. Address: (h.) 17 Mackenzie Terrace, Rosemarkie, Ross-shire, IV10 8UH; T.-Fortrose 20924.

Sutherland, Countess of (Elizabeth Millicent Sutherland). Chief of Clan Sutherland; b. 30.3.21; m., Charles Noel Janson; 2 s.; 1 s. (deceased); 1 d. Educ. Queen's College, London; abroad. Land Army, 1939-41; Laboratory Technician, Inverness and London, 1941-45. Address: (h.) Dunrobin Castle, Sutherland; House of Tongue, Lairg, Sutherland.

Sutherland, George Roberton (Roy), MB, ChB, FRCPEdin, FRCPGlas, FRCR, DMRD. Consultant Radiologist in administrative charge, Glasgow Royal Infirmary, Stobhill General Hospital, and associated hospitals; Honorary Clinical Lecturer, Glasgow University, since 1974; Consultant Radiologist, Nuffield McAlpine Hospital, Glasgow and Bon Secours Nursing Home, Glasgow, since 1981; b. 15.12.31, Glasgow; m., Lorna Hunter Murray; 2 d. Educ. George Heriot's School, Edinburgh; Edinburgh University. Former Honorary Secretary, Dunbartonshire Division, BMA; President, Scottish Radiological Society; Council Member, Scottish Thoracic Society; Chairman, Hospital Medical Committee, Northern District, Glasgow; Member, Area Medical Committee Executive, Glasgow; Deputy Chairman, Senior Medical Staffing Committee, Glasgow; Chairman, Ethical Committee, Glasgow Northern

Hospitals; Member, Sub-Committee in Radiology, National Medical Consultative Committee; Member, Faculty Board, Royal College of Radiologists and Chairman, Computer Advisory Committee; Chairman, Scottish Standing Committee, Royal College of Radiologists; Member, Symposium Committee, Royal College of Physicians and Surgeons, Glasgow; Governor, Queens College Glasgow; Elder, St. George's Tron, Glasgow. Recreations: electronics; amateur radio, repairing old motor cars, or any other mechanical or electrical device; classical music; photography; gardening; golf. Address: (h.) 22 Montrose Drive, Bearsden, Dunbartonshire; T.-041-942 7802.

Sutherland, Hamish Watson, MB, ChB, FRCOG. Clinical Reader (former Acting Head), Department of Obstetrics and Gynaecology, Aberdeen University; Consultant, Grampian Area Health Board; b. 20.10.33, Kinross; m., Frances Cairns; 2 s. Educ. Dollar Academy; St. Andrews University. Resident appointments, Dundee Royal Infirmary; RAMC, 1959-61; Clinical Officer, British Military Hospital, Munster and Hostert; Senior House Officer/Registrar, Dundee, Falkirk and Glasgow; Lecturer/Honorary Senior Registrar, Department of Obstetrics and Gynaecology, Aberdeen University, 1965 (Senior Lecturer, 1970); Representative, Scottish Medical Schools, Central Midwives Board for Scotland, 1979-83; Secretary of State appointee, UK Central Council for Nursing, Midwifery and Health Visiting, 1983, reappointed 1988; former Member, Scottish Executive Committee, Royal College of Obstetricians and Gynaecologists; Past Chairman, Diabetic Pregnancy Study Group, European Association for the Study of Diabetes; Chairman, Piper Alpha Memorial Appeal Fund. Publications: Carbohydrate Metabolism in Pregnancy and the Newborn (four volumes) (Editor); Perspectives in Pre-pregnancy Counselling and Care (Editor). Recreations: sport; art. Address: (h.) Redstones, 9 Marchbank Road, Bieldside, Aberdeen, AB1 9DJ; T.-Aberdeen 867017.

Sutherland, Ian Douglas, FRICS. Partner, D.M. Hall & Son, Chartered Surveyors, since 1975; b. 23.10.45, Colombo, Ceylon; m., Kathryn; 1 s.; 1 d. Educ. St. Bees School, Cumberland. Address: (b.) 13-15 Morningside Drive, Edinburgh, EH10 5LZ; T.-031-452 8811.

Sutherland, James, CBE (1974), MA, LLB, LLD. McClure Naismith Anderson & Gardiner, Solicitors, Glasgow, Edinburgh and London (Partner, 1951-87, Consultant, 1987-90); b. 15.2.20; m., 1, Elizabeth Kelly Barr; 2 s.; 2, Grace Williamson Dawson. Educ. Queens Park Secondary School, Glasgow; Glasgow University. Royal Signals, 1940-46; Examiner in Scots Law, 1951-55, and Mercantile Law and Industrial Law, 1968-69, Glasgow University; Chairman, Glasgow South National Insurance Tribunal, 1964-66; Member, Board of Management, Glasgow Maternity and Women's Hospitals, 1964-74 (Chairman, 1966-74); Council Member, Law Society of Scotland, 1959-77 (Vice-President, 1969-70, President, 1972-74); Council Member, International Bar Association, since 1972 (Chairman, General Practice Section, 1978-80, Secretary General, 1980-84, President, 1984-86); Vice-Chairman, Glasgow Eastern Health Council, 1975-77; Council Member, General Dental Council, 1975-89; Deacon, Incorporation of Barbers, Glasgow, 1962-65; Dean, Royal Faculty of Procurators in Glasgow, 1977-80; Member, Court, Strathclyde University, since 1977. Recreation: golf. Address: (h.) Greenacres, 20/1 Easter Belmont Road, Edinburgh, EH12 6EX; T.-031-337 1888.

Sutherland, Margaret Helen. Rector, Dornoch Academy, since 1989; b. 15.11.28. Educ. Wishaw High School; West of Scotland Agricultural College; Jordanhill College of Education. Lecturer, Cumberland/Westmorland Farm School; Assistant Teacher of Science, West Lothian; Depute Head, Beauly Secondary School; Head Teacher, Farr Secondary School, Bettyhill. Founder President, Soroptimist

International of Easter Ross; Past Chairman, Ross and Cromarty Conservative Association. Recreations: golf; gardening; Soroptimists; charity work. Address: (h.) Runachloie; Drummuie Terrace, Golspie, Sutherland.

Sutherland, Hon. Lord (Ranald Iain Sutherland), QC (Scot). Senator of the College of Justice, since 1985; b. 23.1.32. Advocate Depute, 1962-64, 1971-77; QC (Scot), 1969.

Sutherland, Sinclair Stewart, MB, ChB, DPM, FRCPsych. Consultant Psychiatrist, Lanarkshire Health Board, since 1985; Physician Superintendent, Hartwood Hospital, Shotts, since 1985; b. 4.1.30, Carluke; m., 1, Margaret Helen Christina Strachan; 3 s.; 2, Dr. Alice Andries; 1 s. Educ. Wishaw High School; Aberdeen University. General Practitioner, Shetland Isles and Aberdeenshire, 1957-60; Psychiatry trainee posts, North Eastern Regional Hospital Board, 1960-65; Research Fellow in Psychiatry, Harvard University, 1964; Consultant Psychiatrist, Greater Glasgow Health Board, Deputy Physician Superintendent, Woodilee and Stoneyetts Hospitals, Glasgow, and Honorary Clinical Lecturer, Glasgow University, 1966-85. Worked with Scottish and Glasgow Marriage Guidance Councils, since 1972; Group Discussion Leader, Lanarkshire MGC, since 1986; Chairman, Lanarkshire MGC, 1990. Recreations: golf; motor cycling; clarinet. Address: (h.) Egmont, 51 Belhaven Terrace, Wishaw; T.-0698 372632.

Sutherland, Sir William George MacKenzie, Kt. (1988), QPM. Chief Constable, Lothian and Borders Police, since 1983; b. 12.11.33, Inverness; m., Jennie Abbott; 2 d. Educ. Inverness Technical High School. Cheshire Police, 1954-73; Surrey Police, 1973-75; Hertfordshire Police, 1975-79; Chief Constable, Bedfordshire Police, 1979-83. Recreations: squash; hill-walking. Address: (b.) Police Headquarters, Fettes Avenue, Edinburgh, EH4 1RB; T.-031-311 3131.

Sutherland, William James, IPFA, FCMA. Group Financial Controller, Scottish Power plc, since 1990; b. 10.6.35, Glasgow; m., Fiona Mackay Begg; 3 s.; 1 d. Educ. Victoria Drive Senior Secondary School, Glasgow; Strathclyde University. Glasgow Corporation, 1952-61; Depute Town Chamberlain, Burgh of Bearsden, 1961-64; Town Chamberlain: Burgh of Bishopbriggs, 1964-68, Burgh of Cumbernauld, 1968-75; Depute Director of Finance, Strathclyde Regional Council, 1975-82; Chief Financial Officer, South of Scotland Electricity Board, 1982-90. Recreations: golf; table tennis. Address: (b.) Scottish Power plc, Spean Street, Glasgow, G44 4BE; T.-041-637 7177.

Sutter, Art. Presenter/Broadcaster, BBC Radio Scotland, since 1985; Grampian Television (chat show), since 1989; b. 27.8.41, Airdrie; m., Janette; 2 d. Educ. Airdrie Academy. Studied piano/organ/voice; most of career spent in Scotch whisky industry (sales); before joining BBC was Sales Manager Scotland, Buchanan's Whisky; regular vocalist, BBC Radio Orchestra, from 1979. Recreations: golf; badminton; gardening. Address: (b.) BBC Scotland, Queen Margaret Drive, Glasgow, G12 8DG; T.-041-330 2874.

Suttie, James Michael Peter, MRTPI. Director of Planning and Development, Banff and Buchan District Council, since 1980; b. 24.3.48, Arbroath; m., Sylvia; 1 s.; 2 d. Educ. Dundee High School; Duncan of Jordanstone College of Art, Dundee. Principal Planning Officer, Dundee Corporation, 1973-75; Principal Planning Assistant, Tayside Regional Council, 1975; Chief Assistant Planning Officer, Fife Regional Council, 1975-80. Recreations: golf; hill-walking; orienteering; driving. Address: (b.) Town House, Low Street, Banff; T.-0261 812521.

Swaffield, Professor John Arthur, BSc, MPhil, PhD, CEng, MRAeS, FIWEM, MCIBSE. Professor of Building Services Engineering, Heriot-Watt University, Edinburgh, since 1985; b. 4.3.43, Aberystwyth; m., Jean Winnan; 2 d. Educ. Ardwyn Grammar School, Aberystwyth; Bristol University. Research Fellow, Mechanical Engineering Department, City University, London, 1966-70; Deputy Head, Systems Laboratory, British Aircraft Corporation, Filton, Bristol, 1970-72; Lecturer and Senior Lecturer, Department of Building Technology, Brunel University, 1972-83; Reader in Mechanical Engineering, Brunel University, 1983-85. Recreations: skiing; hill-walking; cinema; political/military history. Address: (b.) Department of Building, Heriot-Watt University, Riccarton, Edinburgh, EH14 4AS; T.-031-449 5111.

Swanson, Alexander James Grenville, MB, ChB, FRCS Edin. Consultant Orthopaedic Surgeon, since 1980; Acting Head, Department of Orthopaedic Surgery, Dundee University, 1986-88; b. 18.10.41, Ecclefechan; 2 s. Educ. Dingwall Academy; St. Andrews University. Postgraduate training: St. Andrews, 1967-68, Edinburgh, 1968-69, Glasgow, 1969-70, Edinburgh, 1970-74, Dunfermline, 1974-75; Lecturer, then Senior Lecturer and Honorary Consultant, Dundee University, 1975-83. Recreations: downhill skiing; cross-country skiing; travel. Address: (b.) Department of Orthopaedic and Traumatic Surgery, Royal Infirmary, Dundee, DD1 9ND; T.-0382 23125.

Swanson, Kenneth M., BSc, PhD, JP, DL. Farmer; Assistant Director, Technology, Dounreay Nuclear Power Development Establishment, 1986-91; b. 14.2.30, Canisbay, Caithness; m., Elspeth J.W. Paton; 2 s.; 1 d. Educ. Wick High School; St. Andrews University. Flying Officer, Pilot, RAF, 1952; Lecturer in Physics, University of Wales, 1955; joined UKAEA, Dounreay, on Fast Reactors, 1958; appointed JP, 1970; DL, Caithness, 1977; Chairman, Caithness Jobs Commission, 1988; Director, Caithness and Sutherland Local Enterprise Company, 1990. Author of papers and patents on the development of plutonium fuels for electricity production. Address: Knockglass, Westfield, Thurso; T.-084 787 201.

Swapp, George David, OBE, DL, MA (Hons), DipEd. Deputy Lieutenant, Kincardineshire, since 1990; Member, Grampian Regional Council, since 1986; b. 25.5.31, Labuan (of Aberdeen parents); m., Eva Jane MacNab; 2 s.; 2 d. Educ. Mackie Academy, Stonehaven; Aberdeen University. RAF Staff College, graduate and directing staff, 1965-68; Ministry of Defence (Training Policy), 1971-74 and 1978-80; promoted Wing Commander, 1971; Board Chairman, RAF Officer and Aircrew Selection Centre, 1974-78; Head, RAF Officer Training Establishment, Bracknell, 1980-83; retired from RAF, 1983. Member, North East River Purification Board; President, Stonehaven Branch, Royal British Legion; Committee Member, Stonehaven Heritage Society; Chairman, Stonehaven Harbour Committee; Church Elder. Recreations: hill-walking; sailing; local history; geography; protection and enhancement of amenities and woodlands. Address: (h.) 9 Urie Crescent, Stonehaven, AB3 2DY; T.-Stonehaven 64124.

Sweeney, Sister Dorothea, MA (Hons), BA (Hons), PhD. Vice Principal, St. Andrew's College of Education, since 1985; b. Glasgow. Educ. Notre Dame High School, Glasgow; Glasgow University; Notre Dame College of Education; Bedford College and LSE, London University; Strathclyde University. Assistant Teacher of English, Our Lady & St. Francis Secondary School, Glasgow, 1960-63; entered Congregation of Sisters of Notre Dame, Sussex, 1963; Assistant Teacher of English, Notre Dame High School, London, 1966-67; Notre Dame College of Education: Lecturer, Department of Psychology, 1970-76, Senior Lecturer, Department of Educational Science, 1976-80,

Assistant Principal, 1980-85. Member, Board of Governors, St. Andrew's College, since 1980; Member, CNAA Inservice Education Board, 1982-87, and Committee for Teacher Education, 1987-89; Member, National Inter-College Committee for Educational Research, 1982-89; Convener, School Boards, Headteacher Training, Steering Committee, 1988-89; School Boards Members Training, 1989-90; Training Consultant, National Staff Development & Appraisal Training, 1991-92. Recreations: creative writing; dance; music; art; sport; drama; technology. Address: (b.) St. Andrew's College of Education, 6 Duntocher Road, Bearsden, Glasgow, G61 4QA; T.-041-943 1424.

Sweeney, William John, DRSAM. Composer; b. 5.1.50, Glasgow; m., Susannah Conway; 1 s.; 1 d. Educ. Knightswood Secondary School; Royal Scottish Academy of Music and Drama; Royal Academy of Music. Studied clarinet and composition, 1967-72; principal compositions: Heights of Maccu Piccu, 1978, String Quartet, 1981, Maqam, 1983, Nine Days, 1976; Sunset Song, 1985, An Rathad Ur, 1988. Executive Committee Member, Musicians' Union. Recreation: a quiet pint in the Dowanhill Bar. Address: (h.) 37 Lawrence Street, Glasgow, G11 5HD; T.-041-334 9987.

Swift, David, BA, FIPM, MBA. Director Personnel, Scottish Enterprise, since 1990; b. 10.1.44, Wetherby; m., Janette; 1 s.; 1 d. Educ. Foxwood School, Leeds; Strathclyde University. Management Trainee, Western Regional Hospital Board; Management Services Officer, SSEB; Stirling County Council; Chief Personnel Officer, Dunfermline District Council; joined SDA as Head of Personnel, 1977. Recreations: tennis; theatre. Address: (h.) 2H Buccleuch Court, The Haining, Dunblane, Perthshire; T.-0786 825990.

Swinfen, Professor David Berridge, MA, DPhil, FRHistS. Professor of Commonwealth History, Dundee University, since 1990 (Head, Department of Modern History, since 1988); b. 8.11.36, Kirkcaldy; m., Ann Pettit; 2 s.; 3 d. Educ. Fettes College, Edinburgh; Hertford College, Oxford. Assistant Lecturer in Modern History, then Lecturer, Queen's College, Dundee, 1963-75; Director, School of American Studies, Dundee University, 1970-85; Senior Lecturer, Modern History, Dundee University, 1975-90. Recreation: music. Address: (h.) 14 Cedar Road, Broughty Ferry, Dundee, DD5 3BB; T.-0382 76496.

Swinney, John Ramsay, MA. National Secretary, Scottish National Party, since 1986; b. 13.4.64, Edinburgh. Educ. Forrester High School, Edinburgh; Edinburgh University. Research Officer, Scottish Coal Project, 1987-88; Senior Management Consultant, Development Options Ltd., since 1988; Secretary, Young Scottish Nationalists, 1982-84; SNP: Assistant National Secretary, 1984-86, Acting National Secretary, 1986, Member, National Executive Committee, since 1983; Joint Editor, "Activist" publications, 1985-86; SNP Prospective Parliamentary candidate, Tayside North. Publication: Defending a Free Scotland (Co-author), 1986. Recreations: reading; classical music. Address: (h.) 50 Thornwood Avenue, Glasgow, G11 7PG; T.-041-334 8707.

Swinton, Major General Sir John, KCVO, OBE, JP. Lord Lieutenant, Berwickshire, since 1989; Brigadier, Queen's Bodyguard for Scotland (Royal Company of Archers), since 1977; Honorary Colonel, 2nd Bn., 52nd Lowland Volunteers, 1983-90; National Chairman, Royal British Legion Scotland, 1986-89; Council Member, Commonwealth Ex-Servicemen's League, since 1984; Vice Chairman, Scottish National War Memorial, since 1988; Chairman, Thirlestane Castle Trust, 1984-90; Trustee, Army Museums Ogilby Trust, 1978-91; Chairman, Berwickshire Civic Society, since 1982; Member, Central Advisory Committee on War Pensions, 1986-89; Trustee, Royal British Legion Scotland Housing Association, since 1989; President, Lowland TA & VRA, since 1992;

Chairman, St. Abbs Head National Nature Reserve Joint Management Committee, since 1991; b. 21.4.25, London; m., Judith Balfour Killen; 3 s.; 1 d. Educ. Harrow School. Enlisted Scots Guards, 1943; commissioned, 1944; served NW Europe (twice wounded); Malaya, 1948-51 (Despatches); ADC to Field Marshal Sir William Slim, Governor General of Australia, 1953-54; Regimental Adjutant, Scots Guards, 1960-62; Adjutant, RMA, Sandhurst, 1962-64; comd. 2nd Bn., Scots Guards, 1966-68; Lt.-Col. commanding Scots Guards, 1970-71; Commander, 4th Guards Armoured Brigade, BAOR, 1972-73; Brigadier, Lowlands and Commander, Edinburgh and Glasgow Garrisons, 1975-76; GOC London District and Major General comd. Household Division, 1976-79. Coordinator for Scotland, Duke of Edinburgh's Award 25th Anniversary Appeal, 1980 (Honorary Liaison Officer for the Borders, 1983-85); Chairman, Roxburgh and Berwickshire Conservative Association, 1983-85. Address: (h.) Kimmerghame, Duns, Berwickshire; T.-0361 83277.

Sword, Ian Pollock, BSc, PhD, CChem, FRSC, FBIM. Chairman/Managing Director, Inveresk Research International, since 1979; Chairman, Inveresk Clinical Research, since 1988; Director, SGS (UK) Ltd., since 1989; b. 6.3.42, Kilmarnock; m., Flora Collins; 2 s.; 1 d. Educ. Coatbridge High School; Glasgow University. Princeton University, New Jersey, 1967-69; Oxford University, 1969-70; Huntingdon Research Centre, 1970-73; Inveresk Research International, since 1973. Publications: editor of two books: scientific papers. Recreations: music; golf. Address: (b.) Inveresk Research International Ltd., Tranent, EH33 2NE: T.-0875 614545.

Syme, James, MB, ChB, FRCPEdin, FRCPGlas, FRCPLond. Consultant Paediatrician, Edinburgh, since 1965; Honorary Senior Lecturer, Edinburgh University, since 1970; Vice President, Royal College of Physicians of Edinburgh, 1985-89; b. 25.8.30, Fife; m., Pamela; 1 s.; 1 d. Educ. Edinburgh University. Captain, RAMC, 1955-57: Registrar and Senior Registrar posts, up to Consultant appointment, 1965; former Secretary, Royal College of Physicians of Edinburgh. Recreations: gardening; antiquarian interests. Address: (h.) 13 Succoth Park, Edinburgh, EH12 6BX: T.-031-337 6069.

Symington, Rev. Alastair Henderson, MA. BD. Minister, New Kilpatrick Parish Church, Bearsden, since 1985; b. 15.4.47, Edinburgh; m., Eileen Margaret Jenkins; 2 d. Educ. Daniel Stewart's College, Edinburgh; Edinburgh University; Tubingen University, West Germany. Assistant Minister, Wellington Church, Glasgow, 1971-72; Chaplain, RAF, 1972-76; Minister, Craiglockhart Parish Church, Edinburgh, 1976-85. Contributor, Scottish Liturgical Review. Publications: Westminster Church Sermons, 1984: Reader's Digest Family Guide to the Bible (Co-author), 1985. Recreations: golf; rugby; music; computing. Address: 51 Manse Road, Bearsden, Glasgow, G61 3PN: T.-041-942 0035.

T

Tait, A. Margaret, BSc. Member, Scottish Legal Aid Board; Member, Lothian Health Council; Executive Member, British

Federation of University Women; b. 8.10.44, Edinburgh; m., J. Haldane Tait; 1 s.; 1 d. Educ. George Watson's Ladies' College, Edinburgh; Edinburgh University; Jordanhill College of Education. Teacher of Mathematics, Bellahouston Academy, Glasgow; Member, Edinburgh Children's Panel; Secretary, Scottish Association of Children's Panels; Chairman, Dean House Children's Home, Edinburgh; Volunteer, Edinburgh Citizens' Advice Bureau; Convener, Public Affairs Sub-Committee, Edinburgh University Business Committee; Member, Edinburgh Youth Orchestra Committee; formerly Secretary of State's Nominee to General Teaching Council; Past Chairman, Dean Orphanage and Cauvin's Trust, Edinburgh. Recreations: golf; music; country walks; speaking in Spanish; entertaining. Address: (h.) 6 Ravelston House Park, Edinburgh, EH4 3LU; T.-031-332 6795.

Tait, Professor Andrew, BSc, PhD. Director, Wellcome Unit of Molecular Parasitology, since 1988; Titular Professor, Glasgow University, 1989-92, Professor of Veterinary Parasitology, since 1992; b. 2.4.43, Banstead; m., Dr. S.M. Grant; 1 s. Educ. Dartington Hall School, Totnes; Edinburgh University. Post-Doctoral Research Fellow, Edinburgh University, 1969-72, 1974-77; Research Associate, Colorado University, USA, 1972-74; Edinburgh University: Wellcome Research Fellow in Tropical Medicine, 1977-81, Wellcome Senior Lecturer, 1981-87; Glasgow University: Honorary Lecturer, Department of Zoology, 1981-87, Wellcome Senior Lecturer, 1987-88. Publications: author of over 50 scientific publications. Member: Genetical Society, British Section of the Society of Protozoology, British Society of Parasitology; Editorial Board Member, Parasite Immunology and Experimental Parasitology. Recreations: antique toy collecting; DIY. Adddress: 57 Dowanside Road, Glasgow G12 9DL; T.-041-357 0390.

Tait, Professor Elizabeth Joyce, BSc, PhD, FRSA, MIEEM. Professor, Environmental and Technology Management, Strathclyde University, since 1991; b. 19.2.38, Edinburgh; m., Alex. D. Tait; 1 s.; 2 d. Educ. Glasgow High School for Girls; Glasgow University; Royal College of Science and Technology. Lecturer and Senior Lecturer, Open University, 1979-91 (Director, Centre for Technology Strategy, 1990-91). Founder Member and Council Member, Institute of Ecology and Environmental Management. Address: (b.) Strathclyde Graduate Business School, 130 Rottenrow, Glasgow, G4 0GE; T.-041-553 6121.

Tait, Eric, MBE, BSc (Eng), MPhil. Director, European Operations, Pannell, Kerr, Forster, since 1989; b. 10.1.45, Edinburgh; m., Jane; 1 s.; 1 d. Educ. George Heriot's School; London University; Royal Military Academy, Sandhurst; Cambridge University. Commissioned, 2nd. Lt., Royal Engineers, 1965; mentioned in Despatches; GSO3 HQ 39 Infantry Brigade, 1976; student, Advanced Staff Course, RAF Staff College, Bracknell, 1977; GSO2 SD HQ1 (BR) Corps, 1977-79; Officer Commanding 7 Field Squadron, RE, 1979-81; Lt. Col., 1982; Directing Staff, Staff College, Camberley, 1982; retired from active list, 1983. Member, Executive, Scottish Council (Development and Industry), 1984-89; Secretary, Institute of Chartered Accountants of Scotland, 1984-89. Recreations: swimming; hill-walking; reading. Address: (b.) 16 Rothesay Place, Edinburgh, EH3 7SQ; T.-031-225 3688.

Tait, Emeritus Professor Eric Alexander, BSc. Honorary Sheriff, Kincardine and Deeside, since 1983; Emeritus Professor, Aberdeen University; b. 26.2.22, Edinburgh; m., Margaret Anna Rowter (deceased); 2 s.; 2 d. Educ. King Alfred's Grammar School, Wantage; Aberdeen University. War Service, 1940-46 (Captain, Royal Artillery); student, 1946-50; Colonial Service, Geological Survey, Nigeria, 1950-61 (Principal Geologist); Department of Geology and Mineralogy, Aberdeen University, 1961-82 (Professor and Head of Department, 1972-82). Member, Stonehaven Town Council, 1965-71; Chairman, Stonehaven Community Council, 1975-78; Chairman, Mackie Academy School Council, 1975-82; Vice-Chairman, Kincardine and Deeside Conservative Association, 1975-91; Director, Kincardine and Deeside Branch, British Red Cross Society, 1981-91; Member, Grampian Health Board, 1983-91. Recreations: travel; reading. Address: (h.) Hingston, 83B Cameron Street, Stonehaven, AB3 2HF; T.-0569 62872.

Tait, Ivan Ballantyne, TD, KStJ, KLJ, FRCS, FRCSEdin, FRCSGlas. Physician in Administrative Charge, Genito-Urinary Medical Services in the West of Scotland; b. 14.9.28, Stepps, Lanarkshire; m., Jocelyn Mary Connel Leggatt; 1 s.; 1 d. Educ. Glasgow Academy; Daniel Stewart's College; Edinburgh University; St. Mary's Hospital, London; University of Kentucky. National Service, RMO 2/10 PMO Gurkha Rifles, mentioned in Despatches, 1953; Col., L/R AMC (V); Representative Knight of Justice, Scottish Priory of the Order of St. John; Liveryman, Worshipful Society of Apothecaries; Freeman, City of London; Hammerman, Freeman, City of Glasgow; late Honorary Surgeon (TA) to The Queen. Recreations: TA; charitable societies. Address: (h.) 6 Lennox Row, Edinburgh, EH5 3HN.

Tankel, Henry I., OBE, MD, FRCSEdin, FRCSGlas. Surgeon, Southern General Hospital, Glasgow, 1962-91; Chairman, Glasgow Board of Jewish Education, 1985-90; b. 14.1.26, Glasgow; m., Judith Woolfson; 2 s.; 2 d. Educ. High School of Glasgow; Glasgow University. Fulbright Scholar, 1954-55; President, Glasgow Jewish Representative Council, 1974-77; Chairman, Glasgow Hospital Medical Services Committee, 1974-79; Board of Science and Education, 1978-81; President, United Synagogues of Scotland, 1978-85; Treasurer, Scottish Committee for Hospital Medical Services, 1978-91; Member, National Panel of Specialists, 1978-82 and 1987-91; invited to address General Assembly of Church of Scotland, 1984; Chairman, Scottish Joint Consultants Committee, since 1989; Member, Scottish Health Service Advisory Council, since 1989. Recreations: walking; making model boats. Address: (h.) 26 Dalziel Drive, Glasgow, G41 4PU; T.-041-423 5830.

Tannahill, Andrew James, MB, ChB, MSc, FFPHM. General Manager, Health Education Board for Scotland, since 1991; b. 28.4.54, Inchinnan; m., Carol Elizabeth Fyfe. Educ. John Neilson Institution; Glasgow University; Edinburgh University. Lecturer in Pathology, Glasgow University; Senior Registrar in Community Medicine, Lothian Health Board/Honorary Clinical Tutor, Edinburgh University; Regional Specialist in Community Medicine, East Anglian Regional Health Authority/Associate Lecturer, Cambridge University; Senior Lecturer in Public Health Medicine, Glasgow University/Honorary Consultant in Public Health Medicine, Greater Glasgow Health Board. Publications: Health Promotion: models and values (Co-author); papers on health education. Recreations: countryside and bird-watching; music; theatre; photography; drawing and painting. Address: (b.) Health Education Board for Scotland, Woodburn House, Canaan Lane, Edinburgh, EH10 4SG; T.-031-447 8044.

Tasker, George Leith, CA. Senior Partner, Bird, Simpson & Co., CA, Dundee; b. 28.9.30, Dundee; m., Norma Croll; 3 d. Educ. Morgan Academy, Dundee; Cambridge University. CA training, 1947-53; National Service, RAF, 1953-55; commissioned into RAF Intelligence as interpreter (Russian); Qualified Assistant, Norman J. Bird & Co., CA, 1955-57 (became Partner, 1957, Senior Partner, 1979); Council Member, Institute of Chartered Accountants of Scotland, 1982-88. Former Council Member, Dundee Civic Trust; Treasurer, Dundee Chamber Music Club; Elder, Church of

Scotland; Governor, Duncan of Jordanstone College of Art, Dundee; President, Boys' Brigade, Dundee Bn. Recreations: music; theatre; travel abroad; art; fishing. Address: (h.) Hammersrang, Pitroddie, Perthshire, PH2 7RJ; T.-082 17 279.

Tavener, Alan, MA, ARCO, ARCM. Director of Music, Strathclyde University, since 1980; Artistic Director, Cappella Nova, since 1982; b. 22.4.57, Weston-Super-Mare; m., Rebecca Jane Gibson. Educ. City of Bath Boys' School; Brasenose College, Oxford. Conducted several world premieres of choral works. Recreations: architecture; exhibitions; theatre; food and drink. Address: (b.) Strathclyde University, Livingstone Tower, Richmond Street, Glasgow, G1 1XH; T.-041-552 4400, Ext. 3444.

Taylor, Rev. Alan Hunter Stuart, BA (Hons), MA (Hons), BD. Minister, Brydekirk and Hoddam, Ecclefechan, since 1987; b. 28.3.26, Wick; m., Margaret Riddell McNay; 2 d. Educ. Morrison's Academy, Crieff; St. Andrews University; London University. Royal Signals and Intelligence Corps, Far East, 1944-48; teaching appointments, John Watson's School, Edinburgh, and Coatbridge High School; Assistant Minister, Auld Kirk of Ayr, 1957-58, Minister: Dryfesdale Parish Church, Lockerbie, 1958-65, Aberlour and Craigellachie, 1965-75, Holm, Orkney, 1975-87. Recreations: music; miscellaneous reading; art; gardening; golf; hill-walking. Address: The Manse of Brydekirk and Hoddam, Ecclefechan, Lockerbie, Dumfriesshire; T.-057 63 357.

Taylor, Rev. Andrew Stark, ThB, FPhS. Minister, Union Church, Greenock, since 1959; b. 3.11.28, Glasgow; m., Mary McEwan; 1 d. Educ. Govan Senior Secondary School; Glasgow University and Trinity College. Staff, Donaldson Brothers and Black Ltd., Shipping Agents, 1944-54; Assistant Minister: Linthouse Church, 1955-57, St. Nicholas Church, Glasgow, 1957-59. Address: 72 Forsyth Street, Greenock; T.-0475 21092.

Taylor, Anthony Edward, BA, IPFA. Director of Finance, Fife Regional Council, since 1987; b. 13.4.43; m., Joan Elizabeth; 3 s. (2 by pr. m.); 1 d. Educ. Cowbridge Grammar School, Glamorgan; University College of Wales, Aberystwyth. Research Officer, Lancashire and Merseyside Industrial Development Association, 1966-68; Economist, Cardiff City Council, 1968-70; Assistant Chief Accountant, then Head of Economics Unit, Brighton County Borough Council, 1970-74; Chief Budget Officer, Brighton Borough Council, 1974-79; Assistant Director of Finance, Sandwell Metropolitan Borough Council, 1979-82; Senior Depute Director of Finance, Tayside Regional Council, 1982-87. Vice Chairman, CIPFA Scottish Branch; Chairman, CIPFA Scottish Weekend School; Member, COSLA Accountancy Training Advisory Group; Company Treasurer, Forth Bridge Centenary Trust; Member, CIPFA (Scotland) Education and Training Executive. Recreations: history; castles; gardening; horse-riding; philately. Address: (b.) North Street, Glenrothes, Fife; T.-0592 754411.

Taylor, Charles Edwin, CBE, BSc, PhD, FRSE, FIBiol. Director, Scottish Crop Research Institute, 1972-86; President, Association of Applied Biologists, 1989; NATO Senior Research Fellow, Istituto di Nematologia Agraria CNR, Bari, Italy; b. 11.9.23, Oystermouth; 1 d. Educ. Cardiff High School; University College, Cardiff. Pilot, RAF, 1943-46; Lecturer in Applied Zoology, Nottingham University School of Agriculture, 1949-56; Senior Entomologist, Federation of Rhodesia and Nyasaland, 1956-59; Head, Zoology Section, Scottish Horticultural Research Institute, 1959-72. President, European Society of Nematologists, 1980-84; Editor, Nematalogica, since 1990. Address: (b.) Westcroft, Longforgan, Dundee, DD2 5EX; T.-082 622 243.

Taylor, David John, MB, BS, MD, FRCOG. Reader, Obstetrics and Gynaecology, Dundee University; Honorary Consultant Obstetrician and Gynaecologist, Ninewells Hospital, Dundee, since 1979; b. 10.8.47, Gateshead; m., Pamela; 1 s.; 2 d. Educ. St. Aidan's Grammar School, Sunderland; Newcastle upon Tyne University. House Officer, Royal Victoria Infirmary, Newcastle upon Tyne, 1970-71; Newcastle Vocational Rotation in Obstetrics and Gynaecology, 1971-75; Member, scientific staff, MRC Reproduction and Growth Unit, 1975-77; First Assistant, Department of Obstetrics and Gynaecology, Newcastle upon Tyne, 1977-79; Joint Director, EEC Concerted Action into Maternal Alcohol Consumption and its Effects on Pregnancy Outcome and Child Development, 1985. Recreations: golf; badminton; watching all sports. Address: (b.) Department of Obstetrics and Gynaecology, Ninewells Hospital and Medical School, Dundee, DD1 9SY; T.-0382 60111, Ext. 2500.

Taylor, Rev. Howard, BSc (Hons), BD (Hons). Minister, St. David's Church, Knightswood, Glasgow, since 1986; Part-time Lecturer in Apologetics, Glasgow Bible College, since 1989; b. 6.6.44, Stockport; m., Eleanor Clark; 3 s. Educ. Gravesend Technical School, Kent; Nottingham University; Edinburgh University. Maths and Physics Teacher, Malawi University; Missionary in Malawi (minister of town and rural African churches, theological teacher, teacher of African languages to missionaries); Minister, Toward and Innellan Churches, Argyll. Publications: In Christ All Things Hold Together; World Hope in the Middle East; The Delusion of Unbelief in a Scientific Age; Faith and Understanding; Israel – People of God. Recreations: hill walking; reading; classical music. Address: 60 Southbrae Drive, Glasgow G13 1QD; T.-041-959 2904.

Taylor, Rev. Ian, BSc, MA, LTh, DipEd. Minister, Abdie & Dunbog and Newburgh, since 1983; b. 12.10.32, Dundee; m., Joy Coupar, LRAM; 2 s.; 1 d. Educ. Dundee High School; St. Andrews University; Durham University; Sheffield University; Edinburgh University. Teacher, Mathematics Department, Dundee High School; Lecturer in Mathematics, Bretton Hall College of Education; Senior Lecturer in Education, College of Ripon and York St. John; Assistant Minister, St. Giles' Cathedral, Edinburgh. Secretary, History of Education Society, 1968-73; extensive work in adult education (appreciation of music and the arts); Director, Summer Schools in Music, St. Andrews University, 1974-82; numerous courses for Edinburgh and Hull Universities and WEA; has played principal roles in opera and operetta; Producer, Gilbert and Sullivan Society of Edinburgh, 1979-87; compiled Theatre Music Quiz series, Radio Tay; presented own operetta, My Dear Gilbert…My Dear Sullivan, BBC; Writer of revues and documentary plays with music, including Tragic Queen (Mary Queen of Scots), St. Giles' Cathedral, Edinburgh Festival Fringe, 1982, and John Knox (Church of Scotland Video). Publications: How to Produce Concert Versions of Gilbert Sullivan; The Gilbert and Sullivan Quiz Book; The Opera Lover's Quiz Book. Address: The Manse, Cupar Road, Newburgh, Fife, KY14 6HA; T.-0337 40275.

Taylor, James, OBE, MC, TD, JP. Retired Farmer; b. 6.12.08; m., Margaret Stewart MacLean; 3 s. Educ. Campbeltown Grammar School. Served with 8th Bn., Argyll and Sutherland Highlanders, 1926-36, commissioned 1936; war service, 1939-44 with 8th A&SH; OC, 1943-44; staff appointment, 1944-45; OC, 8th A&SH, 1951-52 (TA); Argyll County Councillor, 1958-75 (Convener, 1972-75); Argyll and Bute District Councillor, 1975-85 (Chairman of Planning); Freeman, Argyll and Bute, 1985; former Chairman, Argyll Agricultural Executive Committee; Lt. Col., 1944; Brevet Col., 1952. Recreation: golf. Address: (h.) CNOC Araich Southend, Campbeltown, Argyll, PA28 6RQ; T.-0586 83 632.

Taylor, John A., BSc (Econ), MSc (Econ). Senior Lecturer in Public Management, Strathclyde University, since 1989; b. 18.4.44, Ashbourne. Educ. Alsop Grammar School, Liverpool; LSE. Local government officer; Lecturer and Director, Centre for Local Research, Teesside Polytechnic; Research Fellow, Newcastle upon Tyne University. Chair, Joint Universities Council Research Group on Information and Communication Technology and Public Administration. Publications on standards of conduct in local government, corporate computer networking, information and communication technologies. Address: (h.) Barnaig, Beauclere Street, Alva, FK12 5LE; T.-0259 760339.

Taylor, John McDowall, IPFA, MBIM. City Chamberlain, City of Aberdeen District Council, since 1988; b. 12.2.40, Kilwinning; m., Maureen Agnes Graham Taylor; 2 d. Educ. City Public Senior Secondary School, Glasgow. Various finance posts, Glasgow Corporation, 1956-66; Chief Assistant, then Deputy Borough Treasurer, Dover Borough Council, 1966-71; Principal Accountant, then Assistant Controller of Financial Services, LB of Harrow, 1971-74; Chief Officer, Finance, LB of Ealing, 1974-77; Depute City Chamberlain, then Senior Depute, City of Aberdeen District Council, 1977-88. Director, Aberdeen International Football Festival. Recreations: golf; football; travel; exotic cooking. Address: (b.) Town House, Broad Street, Aberdeen; T.-0224 276276.

Taylor, Rt. Rev. John Mitchell, MA. Bishop of Glasgow and Galloway; b. 23.5.32, Aberdeen; m., Edna Elizabeth Maitland; 1 s.; 1 d. Educ. Banff Academy; Aberdeen University; Theological College, Edinburgh. Curate, St. Margaret's, Aberdeen; Rector: Holy Cross, Knightswood, Glasgow, St. Ninian's, Pollokshields, Glasgow, St. John the Evangelist, Dumfries; Canon, St. Mary's Cathedral, Glasgow. Recreations: angling; hill-walking; sketching; music. Address: Bishop's House, 25 Quadrant Road, Glasgow, G43 2QP.

Taylor, John Murray, MA, DipEd. Principal, Clackmannan College, since 1987; b. 18.7.42; m., Katie Forsyth; 2 d. Educ. Banchory Academy; Aberdeen University. Teacher, Dunfermline High School, 1965-70; Principal Teacher of Classics, Kirkcudbright, Liberton, Callander, 1970-78; Assistant Director of Education, Central Region, 1978-87. Recreations: amateur operatics; cycling; skiing; railways; DX radio. Address: (b.) Clackmannan College of Further Education, Branshill Road, Alloa, FK10 3BT; T.-0259 215121.

Taylor, Rt. Rev. Maurice, STD. Bishop of Galloway, since 1981; b. 5.5.26, Hamilton. Educ. St. Aloysius College, Glasgow; Our Lady's High School, Motherwell; Pontifical Gregorian University, Rome. Royal Army Medical Corps, UK, India, Egypt, 1944-47; Assistant Priest: St. Bartholomew's, Coatbridge, 1951-52, St. Bernadette's, Motherwell, 1954-55; Lecturer, St. Peter's College, Cardross, 1955-65; Rector, Royal Scots College, Spain, 1965-74; Parish Priest, Our Lady of Lourdes, East Kilbride, 1974-81. Episcopal Secretary, Bishops' Conference of Scotland; Vice President, Catholic Institute for International Relations. Publications: The Scots College in Spain, 1971; Guatemala, A Bishop's Journey, 1991. Address: 8 Corsehill Road, Ayr, KA7 2ST; T.-Ayr 266750.

Taylor, Michael Alan, BA, MSc, MEd, PhD. Principal, Telford College, Edinburgh, since 1985; b. 22.12.45, London; m., Maureen Brown. Educ. Sir George Monoux Grammar School, Walthamstow; Middlesex Polytechnic; Lancaster University; Liverpool University; Keele University. Teacher, London secondary schools, 1968-71; Lecturer, Chorley College of Education, 1971-73; Senior and Principal Lecturer, Ulster Polytechnic, 1973-76; Head, School of Social Sciences

and Dean, North East Wales Institute of Higher Education, 1976-82 (Director, Institute of Health Education); Depute Principal, Telford College, 1982-84. Recreations: mountaineering; canoeing; skiing; cycling. Address: (b.) Telford College of Further Education, Crewe Toll, Edinburgh, EH4 2NZ; T.-031-332 2491.

Taylor, Michael George, MA (Hons). Rector, St. Joseph's College, Dumfries, since 1982; b. 22.2.43, Coleraine; m., Eileen Forde; 1 s.; 2 d. Educ. St. Aloysius' College, Glasgow; Glasgow University. Head, History Department, St. Conval's High School, Cumnock, 1970-71; Head, History Department, then Assistant Rector, St. Andrew's Academy, Saltcoats, 1971-81; seconded to Chief Executive's Department, Strathclyde Regional Council, 1981-82. President, Ayrshire History Teachers' Association, 1978-81; Member, Catholic Education Commission, 1984-87 and since 1989; Member, Scottish Parent Teacher Council Executive Committee; Vice Chairman/Chairman, Dumfries Schools' Council, 1987-88; Hon. President, St. Joseph's College Past Pupils' Association, St. Joseph's College Parents' and Friends' Association. Recreations: reading; education; historical research. Address: (b.) St. Joseph's College, Craigs Road, Dumfries, DG1 4UU; T.-0387 52893.

Taylor, Michael Thomas, MA, MEd. Rector, Dyce Academy, Aberdeen, since 1980; b. 17.2.47, Newcastle upon Tyne; m., Sheena Robertson; 1 s.; 2 d. Educ. Rutherford Grammar School, Newcastle upon Tyne; Trinity College, Cambridge; Aberdeen University. Teacher of Chemistry, Cannock Grammar School, 1969-75; Ellon Academy: Principal Teacher of Guidance, 1975-76, Assistant Head Teacher, 1977-78, Depute Rector, 1978-80. Secretary, Newmachar Community Council; Elder, Newmachar Parish Church. Recreations: hill-walking; music. Address: (h.) Loch-An-Eilan, Newmachar, Aberdeen; T.-065 17 2234.

Taylor, Peter Bruce, MB, ChB, FFARCS. Consultant Anaesthetist, since 1979; Honorary Senior Lecturer in Anaesthesia, Dundee University, since 1979; b. 30.6.44, Newcastle-upon-Tyne; m.; 1 s.; 1 d. Educ. Aberdeen Grammar School; Aberdeen University. Short Service commission, RAF, 1968-74; Anaesthetic Registrar, Aberdeen Royal Infirmary, 1974-75; Anaesthetic Senior Registrar, Nottingham AHA, 1976-79; Instructor in Anaesthesia, Michigan University Hospital, 1977-78. Linkman (Tayside), Association of Anaesthetists of GB and Ireland; Director and President, Dundee Bridge Club; Life Master, Scottish Bridge Union. Recreations: duplicate bridge; reading; philately (specialist in Machin definitives). Address: (b.) Anaesthetic Department, Ninewells Hospital, Dundee, DD1 9SY; T.-Dundee 60111, Ext. 2475.

Taylor, Sheriff Robert Richardson, MA, LLB, PhD, QC. Sheriff Principal of Tayside Central and Fife, 1975-90; Chairman, Sheriff Courts Rules Council, 1982-89; b. 16.9.19, Glasgow; m., Martha Birgitta Bjorkling; 2 s.; 1 d. Educ. Glasgow High School; Glasgow University. Called to Scottish Bar, 1944; called to Bar (Middle Temple), 1948; Lecturer in International Private Law, Edinburgh University, 1947-69; Sheriff Principal, Stirling Dumbarton & Clackmannan, 1971-75; contested (Unionist and National Liberal), Dundee East, 1955, Dundee West, 1959 and 1963; Chairman, Central and Southern Region, Scottish Conservative Association, 1969-71; Chairman, Northern Lighthouse Board, 1985-86. Recreations: lapidary; mineral collecting. Address: (h.) 51 Northumberland Street, Edinburgh, EH3 6JQ; T.-031-556 1722.

Taylor, Ross Jenkins, MD, FRCGP, DCH. Senior Lecturer, Department of General Practice, Aberdeen University, since 1978; General Medical Practitioner, Grampian Health Board, since 1980; b. 16.4.43, Glasgow; m., Armida Mary Craig; 2

s.; 2 d. Educ. Thurso High School; Aberdeen University Medical School. RAF Medical Branch, 1965-73; House Officer, Stracathro Hospital, Brechin, 1966-67; Honorary Registrar in Paediatrics, St. George's Hospital, London, 1970; Lecturer, Department of General Practice, Aberdeen University, 1973-78; Academic Member, NHS Prescription Pricing Authority, 1980-83. Butterworth Gold Medal, RCGP, 1977. Recreation: music. Address: (b.) Department of General Practice, Aberdeen University, Foresterhill Health Centre, Westburn Road, Aberdeen, AB9 2AY; T.-0224 681818, Ext. 53993.

Taylor, Professor Samuel Sorby Brittain, BA, PhD. Professor of French, St. Andrews University, since 1977; b. 20.9.30, Dore and Totley, Derbyshire; m., Agnes McCreadie Ewan; 2 d. Educ. High Storrs Grammar School, Sheffield; Birmingham University; Paris University. Royal Navy, 1956-68 (Sub Lt., RNVR); Personnel Research Officer, Dunlop Rubber Co., 1958-60; Institut et Musee Voltaire, Geneva, 1960-63; St. Andrews University: Lecturer, 1963, Reader, 1972, Personal Chair, 1977; Chairman, National Council for Modern Languages, 1981-85; Member, Executive Committee, Complete Works of Voltaire, since 1970; Project Leader, Inter-University French Language Teaching Research and Development Project, 1980-88; Chairman, Scottish Joint Working Party for Standard Grade in Modern Languages, 1982-84. Recreations: athletics timekeeping; photography. Address: (b.) Department of French, St. Andrews University, St. Andrews, Fife; T.-0334 76161, Ext. 485.

Taylor, Stephen Derek, BA (Hons), DipURP, MRTPI. Planning and Environment Consultant, W.S. Atkins Scotland, since 1991; Hon. Secretary, Royal Town Planning Institute Scotland, since 1991; b. 26.6.61, Southend; m., Mairead Ferguson. Educ. Strathclyde University; University of Wales, Aberystwyth. City Engineer's Department, Westminster Council, London, 1982; Roads Department, Tayside Regional Council, 1983-85; TVL Keski Suomi, Finland, 1986; Planning Department, Renfrew District Council, 1989-91. Voluntary Service, Guyana, 1987. Recreations: sporting. Address: (b.) Claremont House, 20 North Claremont Street, Glasgow, G3 7LE; T.-041-331 1252.

Taylor of Gryfe, Lord (Thomas Johnston Taylor), Hon. LLD (Strathclyde); b. 27.4.12, Glasgow; m., Isobel. Educ. Bellahouston Academy. Member, Board, Scottish Television, 1968-83; Director: Whiteaway Laidlaw (Bankers), since 1971, Friends Provident, 1972-83, Scottish Metropolitan Property, 1972-88; Member, International Advisory Board, Morgan Grenfell, 1972-88; Chairman, Forestry Commission, 1967-72; Chairman, Economic Forestry, 1972-82; Chairman, Scottish Railways Board, 1969-80; Chairman, Wolfson Trust (Scotland), since 1975; Trustee, Dulverton Trust, since 1979; Chairman, Scottish Peers Association, since 1988. Recreation: golf. Address: (h.) 33 Seagate, Kingsbarns, Fife, KY16 8SR; T.-033 488 430.

Taylor, William Gordon, MA, DipTP, MRTPI, FBIM, FIIM. Director, Economic Development and Planning, Fife Regional Council, since 1985; b. 13.2.43, Edinburgh; m., Margaret Frances Carrick McKinnon; 1 s.; 1 d. Educ. George Watson's College; Edinburgh University; Heriot-Watt University. Planning Assistant, Edinburgh Corporation; Area Planning Officer, Fife County Council; Assistant City Planning Officer, Dundee Corporation; Depute Planning Officer, then Director of Economic Development and Planning, Fife Regional Council. Board Member, Fife Enterprise Company; Past Chairman, Scottish Society of Directors of Planning; Advisor, EEC Environment Directorate; Advisor on industry and the environment, WHO; External Examiner, Dundee University. Recreations: golf; walking; music; current affairs. Address: (h.) Langdale, 55 Main Street, Dairsie, Fife, KY15 4SR; T.-0334 870503.

Teasdale, Professor Graham Michael, MB, BS, MRCP, FRCSEdin, FRCSGlas. Professor and Head, Department of Neurosurgery, Glasgow University, since 1981; Consultant Neurosurgeon, Institute of Neurological Sciences, Glasgow, since 1975; b. 23.9.40, Spennymoor; m.; 3 s. Educ. Johnston Grammar School, Durham; Durham University. Postgraduate clinical training, Newcastle-upon-Tyne, London and Birmingham, 1963-69; Assistant Lecturer in Anatomy, Glasgow University, 1969-71; specialist training in surgery and neurosurgery, Southern General Hospital, Glasgow, 1971-75; Senior Lecturer, then Reader in Neurosurgery, Glasgow University, 1975-81. Editor, Society of British Neurosurgeons. Publication: The Management of Head Injuries. Recreations: hill-walking; inshore fishing. Address: (b.) University Department of Neurosurgery, Institute of Neurological Sciences, Southern General Hospital, Glasgow; T.-041-445 2466.

Tebbutt, Michael Laurence, MBIM. Administrator, Culzean Castle and Country Park, and National Trust Representative in Ayrshire, since 1982; b. 23.7.31, Stamford; m., Hazel Taylor; 4 d. Educ. Stamford School, Lincolnshire. Royal Navy, 1950-57; Outward Bound Trust, 1957-61; Joint Iron Council, 1961-64; Stevenage Youth Trust, 1964-67; National Federation of Young Farmers Clubs, 1967-69; Comptroller, Knebworth House and Country Park, 1970-72; Administrator, Weston Park, 1972-82. Vice-President, Wrekin Decorative and Fine Art Society; Chairman, Ayrshire Decorative and Fine Arts Society. Recreations: sailing; mountaineering; music; heritage; photography. Address: Culzean Castle, Maybole, Ayrshire; T.-06556 274.

Tedder, Rt. Hon. Lord (John Michael Tedder), MA, ScD, PhD, DSc, FRSE. Purdie Professor of Chemistry, St. Andrews University, since 1969; b. 4.7.26, London; m., Peggy Eileen Growcott; 2 s.; 1 d. Educ. Dauntsey's School, Wiltshire; Magdalene College, Cambridge; Birmingham University. Research Fellow: Birmingham University, 1950-52, Ohio State University, 1952-53, Edinburgh University, 1953-55; Lecturer, then Reader, Sheffield University, 1955-64; Roscoe Professor of Chemistry, Dundee University, 1964-68. Member, Board of Management, Macaulay Institute of Soil Research, 1979-87. Publication: Basic Organic Chemistry, Parts 1-5 (Co-author); Valence Theory (Co-author); The Chemical Bond (Co-author); Radicals (Co-author); numerous papers. Recreation: music. Address: (h.) Little Rathmore, Kennedy Gardens, St. Andrews, Fife; T.-St. Andrews 73546.

Tedford, Professor David John, BSc, PhD, ScD, ARCST, CEng, FIEE, SMIEEE, CPhys, FInstP, FRSE, FRSA, Order of Merit of Poland. Professor of Electrical Engineering (Foundation Chair), Strathclyde University, since 1972, and Special Adviser to the Principal, since 1991; b. 12.7.31, Coatbridge; m., Mary White Gardner; 3 s.; 1 d. Educ. Coatbridge High School; Royal Technical College; Glasgow University. Research Engineer, Ferranti Ltd., Edinburgh, 1955-57; joined Strathclyde University as Lecturer, 1957; Deputy Principal, 1982-84, Vice-Principal, 1986-88, Deputy Principal (International Affairs), 1988-91. Member: British National Committee and Executive Committee, CIGRE; Board, Engineering Design Research Centre; Council, Royal Society of Edinburgh; Education Committee and International Relations Committee, Royal Society; Standing Conference on University Entrance; Scottish Examination Board; Convener, Scottish Universities Council on Entrance; Chairman, Governing Council, Bell College of Technology, Hamilton. Recreations: hill-walking; tennis; music; amateur astronomy. Address: (b.) Department of Electronic and Electrical Engineering, Strathclyde University, Royal College Building, 204 George Street, Glasgow, G1 1XW; T.-041-552 4400, Ext. 2071.

Telfer, Walter Little, CA. Chief Executive International, Low & Bonar PLC; Chairman and President, Bonar Inc., Canada; b. 3.3.36, Milngavie; m., Margaret Esther Lilias; 1 s.; 1 d. Educ. Elgin Academy; Glasgow University. Joined Low and Bonar, 1975; appointed to parent Board, 1982. Address: (h.) Mara Lodge, Bellwood, Dundee Road, Perth, PH2 7AL; T.-0738 38623.

Templeton, Professor Allan, MD, FRCOG. Professor of Obstetrics and Gynaecology, Aberdeen University, since 1985; b. 28.6.46, Glasgow; m., Gillian Constance Penney; 3 s.; 1 d. Educ. Aberdeen Grammar School; Aberdeen University. Junior hospital posts in obstetrics and gynaecology, Aberdeen, 1969-75; Lecturer and Senior Lecturer in Obstetrics and Gynaecology, Edinburgh University, 1976-85. Recreation: mountaineering. Address: (h.) Knapperna House, Udny, Aberdeenshire, AB4 0SA; T.-06513 2481.

Tennant, George, BSc, PhD, CChem, FRSC, FRSE. Reader in Organic Chemistry, Edinburgh University, since 1977; b. 22.2.36, Glasgow; 1 s.; 1 d. Educ. Whitehill Senior Secondary School, Glasgow; Glasgow University. ICI Research Fellow, Aberdeen University, 1961-63; Lecturer: Queen's College, St. Andrews, 1963-65, Edinburgh University, 1965-76; Senior Lecturer, Edinburgh University, 1976-77; Head of Organic Chemistry, 1979-80, 1981-84. Secretary, Heterocyclic Group, Royal Society of Chemistry, 1976-79; Chairman, Edinburgh and SE Scotland Section, Royal Society of Chemistry, 1981-83. Recreations: sport; music; art. Address: (b.) Department of Chemistry, Edinburgh University, West Mains Road, Edinburgh, EH9 3JJ; T.-031-667 1081.

Tennant, Iain Mark, KT (1986). Chairman, Grampian Television PLC, 1968-89 (Vice-Chairman, 1960-68); Director, Caledonian Associated Cinemas PLC, 1950-90; Director, Clydesdale Bank PLC, 1969-89; Director, Abbey National Building Society (Chairman, Scottish Advisory Board, 1969-89); Director, Moray and Nairn Newspaper Company Ltd.; Crown Estate Commissioner, 1969-89; Honorary Director, Seagram Company Ltd., Montreal; Lord Lieutenant of Morayshire; Lord High Commissioner to the General Assembly of the Church of Scotland, 1988, 1989; b. 11.3.19, North Berwick; m., Lady Margaret Ogilvy; 2 s.; 1 d. Educ. Eton College; Magdalene College, Cambridge. Learned about film production, Welwyn Garden City Film Studios; served in Egypt with 2nd Bn., Scots Guards, 1940-42; became Intelligence Officer, 201 Guard's Brigade; captured at the surrender of Tobruk; prisoner of war, Italy and Germany, until 1945; Founder Member, Moray Sea School, 1949; Council Member, Outward Bound Trust, 15 years; joined Board, Gordonstoun School, 1951 (Chairman, 1957-72); Member, Moray and Nairn County Council, 1956-64 (latterly Vice-Chairman, Education Committee); Member, The Times Publishing Co. Ltd., 1962-66; Member, Board, Cairngorm Sports Development Ltd., 1964-76; appointed Chairman, local Disablement Advisory Committee, 1964; Chairman, Glenlivet and Glen Grant Distilleries Ltd., 1964-70; Chairman, Glenlivet Distillers Ltd., 1970-77; Trustee, King George's Jubilee Trust, London, 1967-71; FRSA, 1971; Trustee, Churchill Trust, 1973-76; Member, Board, Courage Ltd., 1974-77; Chairman, Seagram Distillers Ltd. (in London), 1977-82; CBIM, 1983. Recreations: shooting; fishing. Address: (b.) Innes House, Elgin, Moray; T.-Lhanbryde 2410.

Terry, Peter Brian, MB, ChB, MD, FRCS Edin, MRCOG. Consultant Obstetrician and Gynaecologist, since 1986; b. 3.6.52, Hillingdon; m., Gillian Margaret; 3 s. Educ. Merchant Taylors'; Edinburgh University Medical School. SHO, Simpson Memorial Maternity Pavilion, Edinburgh, 1977; Cumberland Infirmary, Carlisle, 1978; Registrar, Obstetrics and Gynaecology, Dudley Road Hospital, Birmingham, 1979;

Research Registrar, 1982; Senior Registrar, Obstetrics and Gynaecology, Aberdeen, 1983; Consultant, 1986. Recreations: gardening; golf; walking. Address: (h.) 60 Forest Road, Aberdeen, AB2 4RP; T.-0224 317560.

Thimbleby, Professor Harold William, BSc, MSc, PhD, MIEE, CEng, FRSA. Professor of Information Technology, Stirling University, since 1988; b. 19.7.55, Rugby; m., Prudence; 3 s.; 1 d. Educ. Rugby; Queen Elizabeth College, London. Expert in user interface design; British Computer Society Medal, 1987. More than 100 publications. Address: (b.) Stirling University, Stirling, FK9 4LA; T.-0786 67421.

Thin, David Ainslie, BSc. Chairman and Managing Director, James Thin Ltd., since 1962; Chairman, Book Tokens Ltd., since 1987; b. 9.7.33, Edinburgh; m., Elspeth J.M. Scott; 1 s.; 2 d. Educ. Edinburgh Academy; Loretto School; Edinburgh University. President, Booksellers Association of GB and Ireland, 1976-78. Recreations: golf; travelling; reading. Address: (h.) 60 Fountainhall Road, Edinburgh, EH9 2LP; T.-031-667 2725.

Thoday, Keith Lawrence, BVetMed, PhD, DVD, MRCVS. Senior Lecturer in Veterinary Medicine, Edinburgh University, since 1988; b. 18.4.48, Blackpool; m., Sheena Caroline Elizabeth Stuart-King; 2 d. Educ. Baines Grammar School, Poulton-Le-Fylde; Royal Veterinary College, London University. House Surgeon, Royal Veterinary College, 1971-73; private practice, Wembley, 1973-77; Lecturer in Veterinary Medicine, Edinburgh University, 1977-88. Chairman, Continuing Education Committee, British Small Animal Veterinary Association, 1986-89; Chairman, Dermatology Board, Royal College of Veterinary Surgeons, 1988-90; Woodrow Award, 1989. Publications: papers on veterinary dermatology and endocrinology. Recreations: fresh water angling; folk music. Address: (b.) Department of Veterinary Clinical Studies, Edinburgh University, Royal (Dick) School of Veterinary Studies, Summerhall, Edinburgh, EH9 1QH; T.-031-650 1000.

Thomas, Professor David Brynmor, MB, BS, BSc, DSc, FRCP Edin, FRC Path, FIBiol, FRSE. Bute Professor of Anatomy and Experimental Pathology, St. Andrews University, since 1973; b. 11.10.30, Wales; m., Elizabeth Elma Flanagan; 1 s. Educ. University College, London; University College Hospital Medical School. President, Anatomical Society of Great Britain and Ireland; President-Elect, European Federation for Experimental Morphology; Secretary, International Federation of Associations of Anatomists; Member, International Committee on Morphological Sciences; Member, Editorial Board, Journal of Anatomy; Fellow, Royal Society of Medicine. Recreations: golf; music; photography; walking. Address: (b.) Bute Medical Buildings, Queen's Terrace, St. Andrews, KY16 9TS; T.-0334 76161, Ext. 7106.

Thomas, Professor Lyn Carey, MA, DPhil (Oxon), FIMA. Professor of Management Science, Edinburgh University, since 1985 (Head, Department of Business Studies, 1987-90); b. 10.8.46, Dowlais; m., Margery Wynn Bright; 2 s.; 1 d. Educ. Lewis School, Pengam; Jesus College, Oxford. Research Fellow, University College, Swansea, 1971-74; Lecturer in Decision Theory, then Senior Lecturer, Manchester University, 1974-85; Senior NRC Fellow, Naval Postgraduate School, Monterey, California, 1982-83; Editor, IMA Journal of Mathematics Applied in Business and Industry. Publications: Games, Theory and Applications, 1984; Operational Research Techniques, 1986. Recreations: reading; rugby; rambling. Address: (b.) Department of Business Studies, William Robertson Building, 50 George Square, Edinburgh; T.-031-650 3798.

Thomas, Professor Michael Frederic, MA, PhD, FGS, FRSE. Professor of Environmental Science, Stirling University, since 1980; b. 15.9.33, London; m., Elizabeth Anne Dadley (deceased); 1 s.; 1 d. Educ. Royal Grammar School, Guildford; Reading University. Assistant Lecturer in Geography, Magee University College, Londonderry, 1957-60; Lecturer, Ibadan University, Nigeria, 1960-64; Lecturer, then Senior Lecturer, St. Andrews University, 1964-79; visiting appointments, Universities of Canterbury (New Zealand), New South Wales, Natal, and Sierra Leone. Council Member, Royal Scottish Geographical Society; Past Chairman, British Geomorphological Research Group; Member, Scottish Environmental Education Council Management Committee. Publication: Tropical Geomorphology, 1974. Recreations: listening to music; hill-walking; travel. Address: (b.) Department of Environmental Science, Stirling University, Stirling, FK9 4LA; T.-0786 67840.

Thomas, Professor Michael James, BSc, MBA, FRSA, FCIM. Professor of Marketing and Head of Department, Strathclyde University, since 1987; b. 15.7.33; m.; 1 s.; 1 d. Educ. University College London; Indiana University. Metal Box Co. Ltd., London, 1957-60; Syracuse University Management School, 1960-71; Lancaster University, 1972-86. Recreation: ornithology. Address: (b.) Strathclyde University, Glasgow, G4 ORQ.

Thomas, Professor Phillip Charles, BSc, PhD, FIBiol, CBiol. Principal and Chief Executive, The Scottish Agricultural College, since 1990; Professor of Agriculture, Glasgow University, since 1987; Honorary Professor, Edinburgh University, since 1991; b. 17.6.42, Pontypool; m., Pamela Mary Hirst; 1 s.; 1 d. Educ. Abersychan Grammar School; University College of North Wales, Bangor. Lecturer, Department of Animal Nutrition and Physiology, Leeds University, 1966-71; Research Scientist, Hannah Research Institute, Ayr, 1971-87; Principal, West of Scotland College, Ayr, 1987-90. Publications: Nutritional Physiology of Farm Animals, 1983; Silage for Milk Production, 1983. Recreations: watching the garden grow; rugby coaching. Address: (b.) The Scottish Agricultural College, Central Office, West Mains Road, Edinburgh, EH9 3JG.

Thomason, Edward, OBE, ACII. Convener, Shetland Islands Council, 1986-91; Chairman, Sullom Voe Association; b. 12.8.22, Lerwick; m., Dinah. Educ. Anderson Educational Institute, Lerwick. Councillor, since 1960; Convener, Zetland County Council, 1970-73. Recreations: fiddle and accordion music; writing magazine articles. Address: (h.) 14 Mounthooly Place, Lerwick, Shetland; T.-0595 2901.

Thompson, Professor Alan Eric, MA (Hons), PhD. Emeritus Professor of the Economics of Government, Heriot-Watt University; b. 16.9.24; m., Mary Heather Long; 3 s.; 1 d. Educ. Edinburgh University. Edinburgh University: Assistant in Political Economy, 1952-53, Lecturer in Economics, 1953-59 and 1964-71; Professor of the Economics of Government, Heriot-Watt University, 1972-87; MP (Labour), Dunfermline, 1959-64; Member, Royal Fine Art Commission for Scotland, 1975-80; Chairman, Northern Offshore Maritime Resources Study, 1974-83; Governor, Newbattle Abbey College, 1975-85 (Chairman, 1980-83); Member, Local Government Boundaries Commission for Scotland, 1975-80; Member, Scottish Council for Adult Education in HM Forces, since 1973; BBC National Governor for Scotland, 1975-79; Governor, Leith Nautical College, 1981-85; Trustee, Bell's Nautical Trust, 1981-85; Parliamentary Adviser, Pharmaceutical General Council (Scotland), since 1984. Publication: Development of Economic Doctrine (Co-author), 1980. Recreation: writing

children's stories and plays. Address: (h.) 11 Upper Gray Street, Edinburgh, EH9 1SN; T.-031-667 2140.

Thompson, Colin, CBE, DUniv, FRSE, MA, FMA. Writer, Lecturer and Broadcaster on art and museums; b. 2.11.19, Berkhamstead; m., Jean A.J. O'Connell; 1 s.; 1 d. Educ. Sedbergh; King's College, Cambridge; Chelsea Polytechnic. War Service, FS Wing (CMP) and GCHQ, 1941-45; Lecturer, Bath Academy of Art, Corsham, 1948-54; joined National Gallery of Scotland as Assistant Keeper, 1954; Director, National Galleries of Scotland, 1977-84. Member, Scottish Arts Council, 1976-83; Member, Edinburgh Festival Society, since 1979; Chairman, Scottish Museums Council, 1984-87; Chairman, Board of Governors, Edinburgh College of Art, 1989-91; Trustee, Buccleuch Heritage Trust. Publications: Pictures for Scotland, 1972; Hugo Van Der Goes and the Trinity Panels in Edinburgh (Co-author), 1974; Exploring Museums: Scotland, 1990. Address: (h.) Edenkerry, Lasswade, Midlothian, EH18 1LW; T.-031-663 7927.

Thompson, David George, MITSA, MAPEA, DCA, FBIM. Director of Trading Standards, Highland Regional Council, since 1986; b. 20.9.49, Lossiemouth; m., Veronica; 1 s.; 3 d. Educ. Lossiemouth High School. Trainee, then Trading Standards Officer, Banff, Moray and Nairn Joint CC, 1967-73; Assistant Chief Trading Standards Officer, Ross & Cromarty County Council, 1973-75; Chief Trading Standards Officer, Western Isles Islands Council, 1975-83; Depute Director of Trading Standards, Highland Regional Council, 1983-86. Secretary/Treasurer, Scottish Branch, Institute of Trading Standards Administration, 1985-87, Chairman, 1988-89; Secretary/Treasurer, Society of Directors of Trading Standards in Scotland, 1987-89, Chairman, since 1991. Recreations: golf; DIY; reading; Speakers' Club. Address: (h.) Balnafettack Guest House, Leachkin Road, Inverness; T.-0463 221555.

Thompson, Francis George, FIElecIE, MASEE, TEng, FSA Scot. Author of books on Highland subjects; Senior Lecturer, Lews Castle College, Stornoway; Director, Western Isles Development Fund; b. 29.3.31, Stornoway; m., Margaret Elaine Pullar; 1 s.; 3 d. Educ. Nicolson Institute, Stornoway. From 1946: supply maintenance electrician, technical writer, assistant publicity manager, lecturer; has held various offices within An Comann Gaidhealach, including editorship of Sruth, bilingual newspaper, 1967-71; books include: Harris and Lewis, 1968; Harris Tweed, 1969; Highlands and Islands, 1974; Crofting Years, 1985; Shell Guide to Northern Scotland, 1987; The Western Isles, 1988; Discovering Speyside, 1990. Recreation: writing! Address: Am Fasgadh, 5 Rathad na Muilne, Stornoway, Lewis; T.-0851 3812.

Thompson, Graham L.,BSc. Managing Director, United Distillers UK plc, since 1990; b. 7.7.44, Birmingham; m., Gwendoline Ann. Educ. Solihull School; Leeds University. Brand Manager, Pedigree Petfoods, 1973-75, Senior Buyer, 1975-77; General Manager Purchasing, Arthur Bell & Sons, 1977-78, General Manager Administration, 1978-86, Administration Director, 1986-87; Operations Director, Arthur Bell Distillers, 1987-90; Director, Edward Dillon & Co. Ltd. Recreation: sport. Address: (h.) Glengyle, Comrie Road, Crieff, PH7 4BW; T.-0764 4821.

Thompson, John Robert, LLB, NP. Director of Administration, Inverclyde District Council, since 1981; Clerk, Inverclyde Licensing Board and District Court; Clerk of the Peace; Solicitor; b. 23.5.38, Glasgow; 1 s.; 1 d. Educ. Hutchesons' Grammar School; Glasgow University. Address: (b.) Municipal Buildings, Clyde Square, Greenock, PA15 1LY; T.-0475 24400.

Thomson, Alan James Reid, FCIBS, MIPM. General Manager, Bank of Scotland, since 1990; b. 28.10.35, Airdrie;

m., Eileen Isobel Millar; 1 s.; 1 d. Educ. Robert Gordon's College, Aberdeen. Bank of Scotland, since 1952; Staff Manager, 1974; Assistant General Manager (Staff), 1978. Member, Scotland and N. Ireland Advisory Committee, Understanding British Industry; a Vice President and Convenor, Education Committee, Chartered Institute of Bankers in Scotland; Member, General Convocation, Heriot-Watt University. Recreations: golf; swimming. Address: (b.) Bank of Scotland Head Office, The Mound, Edinburgh, EH1 1YZ; T.-031-243 5480.

Thomson, Rev. Alexander, BSc, BD, MPhil, PhD. Minister, Rutherglen Old Parish Church, since 1985; b. 25.4.47, Motherwell; m., Ann Fraser Smith; 2 s. Educ. Brandon High School and Dalziel High School, Motherwell; Glasgow University; Edinburgh University; Aberdeen University. Industrial Chemist, Dalziel Steel Works, Motherwell; Assistant Minister, New Kilpatrick Church, Bearsden, 1973-75; Minister: St. Columba's, Kilbirnie, 1975-82, Ardler, Kettins, Meigle, 1982-85. Publication: Tradition and Authority in Science and Theology, 1987. Address: 31 Highburgh Drive, Rutherglen, Glasgow; T.-041-647 6178.

Thomson, Alexander McEwan, SSC, NP. Solicitor; b. 13.11.17, Dublin; m., Marjorie May Wood; 2 s.; 1 d. Educ. Daniel Stewart's College; George Heriot's School; Edinburgh University. Partner, Drummond & Reid, 1960-69 and Drummond & Co., WS, 1969-83 (Senior Partner, 1970-83); retired, 1983; Solicitor to General Teaching Council for Scotland, 1966-83; Solicitor to Edinburgh (subsequently Lothian Regional) Assessor; President, Society of Solicitors in the Supreme Courts of Scotland, 1979-82. Recreation: gardening. Address: (h.) The Steading, Leithhead, by Kirknewton, West Lothian; T.-0506 883393.

Thomson, Colin, BSc (Hons), PhD, FRSC. Reader in Theoretical Chemistry, St. Andrews University, since 1978 (Senior Lecturer, 1970-88); Regional Director for Research, National Foundation for Cancer Research, since 1977; Director, Association for International Cancer Research, since 1984; b. 6.7.37, Whitby, Yorkshire; m., Maureen Margaret Green; 2 s.; 2 d. Educ. Whitby Grammar School; Leeds University. Postdoctoral Research Fellow, California University, 1961-63; Postdoctoral (NATO) Research Fellow, Cambridge University, 1963-64; Lecturer in Theoretical Chemistry, St. Andrews University, 1964-70; Committee Member, SERC Computational Chemistry Committee, since 1983; Editor, RSC specialist reports. Recreations: jazz and dance band musician; walking; sailing. Address: (h.) 12 Drumcarrow Road, St. Andrews, KY16 8SE; T.-0334 74820.

Thomson, David Kinnear, CBE, TD, CStJ, JP, DL. President, Perth Festival of the Arts, 1985-90; Honorary Sheriff, Perth and Kinross, since 1969; b. 26.3.10, Perth. Educ. Perth Academy; Strathallan School. Member, Committee of Management, Trustee Savings Bank, Perth/Tayside, 1959-83; Lord Provost of Perth, 1966-72; Member: Scottish Economic Planning Council, 1968-74, Scottish Council (Development and Industry), 1968-75; Member, IBA, 1969-75; Director, Scottish Opera, 1967-79; Director, Scottish Transport Group, 1972-78; Chairman, Tayside Health Board, 1973-77; Member, Cancer Research Committee (Perth), 1967-87. Recreations: walking; golf; listening to music. Address: (h.) Fairhill, Oakbank Road, Perth.

Thomson, Professor Derick S., MA (Aberdeen), BA (Cantab), DLitt (Univ. of Wales), FRSE. Professor of Celtic, Glasgow University, 1963-91; b. 5.8.21, Stornoway; m., Carol Galbraith; 5 s.; 1 d. Educ. Nicolson Institute, Stornoway; Aberdeen University; Cambridge University; University College of North Wales, Bangor. Taught at Edinburgh, Glasgow and Aberdeen Universities before returning to Glasgow as Professor, 1963; Chairman, Gaelic

Books Council, 1968-91; President, Scottish Gaelic Texts Society; former Member, Scottish Arts Council; first recipient, Ossian Prize, 1974; author of numerous books and articles, including An Introduction to Gaelic Poetry, The Companion to Gaelic Scotland, European Poetry in Gaelic and collections of Gaelic poetry, including collected poems Creachadh na Clarsaich; Editor, Gairm, since 1952. Address: (h.) 19 Bemersyde Avenue, Glasgow, G43; T.-041-632 7880.

Thomson, Duncan, MA, PhD. Keeper, Scottish National Portrait Gallery, since 1982; b. 2.10.34, Killearn; m., Julia Jane Macphail; 1 d. Educ. Airdrie Academy; Edinburgh University; Edinburgh College of Art; Moray House College of Education. Teacher of Art; Assistant Keeper, Scottish National Portrait Gallery. Publication: The Life and Art of George Jamesone, 1974. Recreations: literature; walking; looking. Address: (b.) Scottish National Portrait Gallery, 1 Queen Street, Edinburgh, EH2 1JD; T.-031-556 8921.

Thomson, Sir (Frederick Douglas) David, Bt, BA. Chairman, Britannia Steamship Insurance Association Limited, since 1986 (Director, since 1965); Director, Life Association of Scotland Ltd., since 1970; Director, Cairn Energy PLC, since 1971; Chairman, Through Transport Marine Mutual Assurance Association (Bermuda) Ltd., since 1983 (Director, since 1973); Director, Danae Investment Trust Ltd., since 1979; Chairman, Jove Investment Trust PLC, since 1983; Director, Martin Currie Pacific Trust PLC, since 1985; Chairman, Abtrust New European Investment Trust PLC, since 1990; Chairman, Castle Cairn Investment Trust Company PLC, since 1990; Director, G. & G. Kynoch PLC, since 1991; Director, The Murrayfield PLC, since 1991; Member, Royal Company of Archers (Queen's Bodyguard for Scotland); b. 14.2.40, Edinburgh; m.; 2 s.; 1 d. Educ. Eton; University College, Oxford. Recreations: shooting; skiing; tennis. Address: (h.) Old Caberston, Walkerburn, Peeblesshire; T.-089687 206.

Thomson, Geddes, MA (Hons). Teacher and Writer; b. 20.9.39, Dalry; m., Lucy Faulkner; 2 s. Educ. Dalry High School; Glasgow University. Principal Teacher of English, Allan Glen's School, Glasgow, 1972-89; Shawlands Academy, Glasgow, since 1989; Extra-Mural Lecturer, Department of Adult and Continuing Education, Glasgow University, since 1985. Publications include: A Spurious Grace, 1981; Identities (Editor), 1981; The Poetry of Edwin Morgan, 1986. Recreations: supporting Partick Thistle; fishing; browsing in bookshops. Address: (h.) 48 Windyedge Crescent, Glasgow, G13 1YF; T.-041-959 5277.

Thomson, George Buchanan, FIB (Scot). Honorary Treasurer, Scottish Civic Trust, since 1976; Director, Clydesdale Development Company, since 1988; Director, Association for the Relief of Incurables, since 1987; b. 10.1.24, Glasgow; m., Margaret Irene Williams. Educ. Eastwood Secondary School. Joined Union Bank of Scotland, 1940; War Service, 1942-46 with RAF (Navigator, Bomber Command); held various banking appointments, 1947-86; retired as Assistant General Manager (Branch Administration, West), Bank of Scotland; Past President, Institute of Bankers in Scotland; Director, Ian Skelly Holdings Ltd., 1986-89. Convener, Board of Stewardship and Finance, Church of Scotland. Recreations: curling; bowling. Address: (h.) Kingswood, 26 Waverley Avenue, Helensburgh, G84 7JU; T.-0436 72915.

Thomson, Gordon MacKenzie, MA (Hons), CA. Deputy Chief Executive, Institute of Chartered Accountants of Scotland, since 1991; Member, Fife Health Board, since 1991; b. 28.5.47, Glasgow; m., Sandra; 1 s.; 2 d. Educ. Hutchesons' Boys' Grammar School; Glasgow University. Group Finance Director, Alma Holdings Ltd., 1983-91.

Recreations: tennis; reading; watching sport. Address: (b.) 27 Queen Street, Edinburgh; T.-031-225 5673.

Thomson, Iain Marshall, FIA (Scot). Managing Director, Lawrie and Symington, since 1990; formerly Director, United Auctions Ltd.; b. 28.9.38, Stirling; 2 d. Educ. Lanark Grammar School; George Watson's College, Edinburgh. Joined Macdonald, Fraser and Co. Ltd., 1955, appointed Director, 1970, Joint Managing Director, 1976; Council Member, Institute of Auctioneers and Appraisers in Scotland, since 1972, Vice President, 1986-88, President, 1988-90; Vice President, Royal Highland and Agricultural Society of Scotland, since 1990; appointed by Secretary of State for Scotland to Panel of Arbiters, 1983; Past Chairman, Perth and District Junior Agricultural Club. Recreations: golf; fishing. Address: (b.) Muirglen, Lanark, ML12 9AX.

Thomson, Rev. Iain Urquhart, MA, BD. Minister, Parish of Skene, since 1972; Clerk, Presbytery of Gordon, since 1988; b. 13.12.45, Dundee; m., Christine Stewart Freeland; 1 s.; 2 d. Educ. Harris Academy, Dundee; Inverness Royal Academy; Aberdeen University and Christ's College. Recreations: golf; football; other sporting activities. Address: The Manse, Skene, Aberdeenshire, AB32 6XX; T.-0224 743277.

Thomson, John Aidan Francis, MA, DPhil, FRHistS. Reader in Mediaeval History, Glasgow University, since 1983; b. 26.7.34, Edinburgh; m., Katherine J.V. Bell; 1 s.; 1 d. Educ. George Watson's Boys' College, Edinburgh; Edinburgh University; Balliol College, Oxford. Glasgow University: Assistant in Mediaeval History, 1960, Lecturer, 1961, Senior Lecturer, 1974. President, Glasgow Archaeological Society, 1978-81. Publications: The Later Lollards 1414-1520, 1965; Popes and Princes 1417-1517, 1980; The Transformation of Mediaeval England 1370-1529, 1983; Towns and Townspeople in the Fifteenth Century (Editor), 1988. Recreations: hill-walking; gardening. Address: (b.) Department of Medieval History, Glasgow University, Glasgow, G12 8QQ; T.-041-339 8855.

Thomson, John Alexander, MD, PhD, FRCPGlas, FRCPLond. Reader in Medicine, University Department of Medicine, Glasgow University, since 1981; Honorary Consultant Physician, Glasgow Royal Infirmary, since 1968; b. 19.4.33, Airdrie; m., Fiona Jane Reid; 2 s.; 2 d. Educ. Hamilton Academy; Glasgow University. House Physician, then House Surgeon, Glasgow Royal Infirmary, 1956-57; Royal Army Medical Corps, 1957-59 (Regimental Medical Officer, 13/18 Royal Hussars); House Surgeon, Glasgow Royal Maternity and Women's Hospital, 1959-60; McIntyre Clinical Research Scholar in Medicine, University Department of Medicine, 1960-61; Registrar in Medicine, then Senior Registrar, University Medical Unit, Glasgow Royal Infirmary, 1961-68; Senior Lecturer in Medicine and Consultant Endocrinologist, Glasgow Royal Infirmary, 1968-81. Address: (b.) University Department of Medicine, Royal Infirmary, 10 Alexandra Parade, Glasgow, G31 2ER; T.-041-552 3535.

Thomson, Rev. John Bruce, MA, BD. Minister, Scone Old Parish Church, since 1983; also Minister, St. David's, Stormontfield, since 1983; b. 14.7.44, Edinburgh; m., Margaret Anne Craigen; 1 s.; 1 d. Educ. James Gillespie's Boys' School; George Heriot's School, Edinburgh; Edinburgh University; New College, Edinburgh. Ordained Assistant, Dundee Parish Church (St. Mary's), 1971-74; Minister, Thurso West Church, 1974-83; Moderator, Caithness Presbytery, 1979-80. Contributor, BBC Radio Orkney, Radio Tay, Reflections (Grampian TV), Scotspraise (BBC TV). Recreations: swimming; golf; Rotary Club of Perth St. John's. Address: The Manse, Burnside, Scone, Perth, PH2 6LP; T.-0738 52030.

Thomson, Rev. John Morria Arnott, BD, ThM. Minister, Lanark: St. Nicholas, since 1988; b. 27.2.49, Buckhaven; m., Marlene Jeffrey Logan; 1 s.; 1 d. Educ. Irvine Royal Academy; Glasgow University; Columbia Theological Seminary, Atlanta, Georgia. Journalist, Irvine Herald; Executive Officer, Natural Environment Research Council; Finance/Administration Officer, Irvine Development Corporation; Assistant Project Co-ordinator, Wiltshire County Council; Minister, Houston and Killellan Kirk, 1978-88. Chaplain, TA; Chaplain, Lanark Lord Cornets Club; Chairman, Scotland Romania Charitable Trust. Recreations: sailing; writing; history; Romanian aid; music; National Trust for Scotland. Address: (h.) St. Nicholas Manse, 32 Braxfield Road, Lanark, ML11 9BS; T.-0555 662600.

Thomson, Professor Joseph McGeachy, LLB. Regius Professor of Law, Glasgow University, since 1991; Deputy General Editor, Stair Memorial Encyclopaedia of the Laws of Scotland, since 1985; b. 6.5.48, Campbeltown. Educ. Keil School, Dumbarton; Edinburgh University. Lecturer in Law, Birmingham University, 1970-74; Lecturer in Laws, King's College, London, 1974-84; Professor of Law, Strathclyde University, 1984-90. Recreations: opera; ballet; food and wine. Address: (h.) 140 Hyndland Road, Glasgow; T.-041-334 6682.

Thomson, Professor Kenneth James, MA, MSc, MS. Professor of Agricultural Economics, Aberdeen University, since 1986; b. 30.9.45, Aberdeen; m., Lydia. Educ. Aberdeen Grammar School; Aberdeen University; London University; Iowa State University. Lecturer and Senior Lecturer, Department of Agricultural Economics, Newcastle upon Tyne University, 1972-86. Editor, Journal of Agricultural Economics, since 1987. Publication: The Cost of the Common Agricultural Policy, 1982. Recreations: viola-playing; mountaineering. Address: (b.) School of Agriculture, 581 King Street, Aberdeen, AB9 1UD; T.-0224 480291.

Thomson, Michael Scott, FRICS, IRRV. Commercial Director, Irvine Development Corporation, since 1972; Director, Ayr United Football Club, since 1986; b. 21.5.39, Newcastle; m., Elizabeth; 1 s.; 2 d. Educ. Allan Glen's School, Glasgow. Valuation Surveyor, Glasgow City Assessor's Department and Estates Department; Deputy Commercial Director, Redditch Development Corporation. Former Chairman, Ayrshire District Manpower Committee; Member, Ayrshire Area Manpower Board; founder President, Irvine Junior Chamber; Past President, Irvine Burns Club. Recreations: golf (participant); most other sports (spectator). Address: (h.) 7 Finlas Avenue, Ayr; T.-0292 42000.

Thomson, Sheriff Nigel Ernest Drummond, MA, LLB. Sheriff of Lothian and Borders, at Edinburgh, since 1976, and at Peebles, since 1983; b. 19.6.26, Aberdeen; m., Snjolaug Magnusson; 1 s.; 1 d. Educ. George Watson's Boys' College; St. Andrews University; Edinburgh University. Called to Scottish Bar, 1953; appointed Sheriff at Hamilton, 1966; Member, Scottish Arts Council, 1978 (Chairman, Music Committee, 1979-84). Honorary President, Strathaven Arts Guild; Honorary Vice-President, Tenovus-Scotland; Honorary President, Scottish Association for Counselling, 1986-89; Chairman, Edinburgh Youth Orchestra Society. Recreations: music; woodwork; golf. Address: (h.) 50 Grange Road, Edinburgh; T.-031-667 2166.

Thomson, Rev. Peter David, MA, BD. Minister, Comrie and Strowan with Dundurn, since 1978; b. 4.11.41, St. Andrews; m., Margaret Celia Murray; 1 s.; 1 d. Educ. Dundee High School; Edinburgh University; Glasgow University; Tubingen University. Minister, Balmaclellan with Kells, 1968-78; Moderator, Kirkcudbright Presbytery, 1974-75; Convener, Nomination Committee, General Assembly, 1982-85. Chairman, New Galloway and Kells Community Council,

1976-78; Moderator, Perth Presbytery, 1988-89. Recreations: haphazardly pursued interests in photography, wildlife, music, theology, current affairs. Address: The Manse, Comrie, Perthshire, PH6 2HE; T.-0764 70269.

Thomson, Robert Scott, OBE, BSc, CChem, MRCS, FRSA. Rector, Larkhall Academy, since 1974; b. 9.6.33, Newtongrange; m., Helen Mary McIntosh; 1 d. Educ. Newbattle Secondary School; Dalkeith High School; Heriot-Watt University. Scientific Technical Officer, NCB, 1950-59; Chemistry Teacher, George Watson's College, 1963-67; Principal Teacher of Chemistry: Dalkeith High School, 1967-70, George Watson's College, 1970-74. Former Member, Scottish Consultative Council on the Curriculum; Chairman, Committee on Technology; Convener, Scottish Education Industry Committee. Recreations: reading; gardening; bowling. Address: (b.) Larkhall Academy, Cherryhill, Larkhall, ML9 1QN; T.-Larkhall 881570.

Thomson, Roy Hendry, CStJ, MA (Hons). Chairman, Scottish Liberal Democrats; Chairman, Friends of Aberdeen University Library; General Council Assessor, Court of Aberdeen University; b. 27.8.32, Aberdeen; m., Nancy; 3 d. Educ. Aberdeen Grammar School; Aberdeen University. National Service, Gordon Highlanders, 1955-57; personnel and market research, Rowntree & Co. Ltd., 1957-60; Chairman/Director, family motor business, until 1986; former Director, The Scottish Ballet (Chairman, 1983-87); former Member, City of Aberdeen District Council; Past President: Rotary Club of Aberdeen, Mountain Rescue Association, Aberdeen. Recreations: skiing; hill-walking; beekeeping. Address: (h.) 5 Baillieswells Grove, Bieldside, Aberdeen, AB1 9BH; T.-Aberdeen 861628.

Thomson, Professor Samuel J., BSc, PhD, DSc, CChem, FRSC, FRSE. Professor Emeritus, Glasgow University, since 1987; Honorary Senior Research Fellow, since 1987; Member, British Rail (Scottish) Board, since 1989; b. 27.9.22, Hamilton; m., Christina M. MacTaggart; 1 s.; 1 d. Educ. Hamilton Academy; Glasgow University. Lt., Royal Signals, 1944; Lecturer in Radiochemistry, Durham University, 1951; Lecturer, Senior Lecturer, Reader, Titular Professor, Glasgow University, 1957-87. Publications: books and papers on surface chemistry and catalysis, etc. Recreations: visual perception; reading. Address: (h.) 10 Balfleurs Street, Milngavie, Glasgow, G62 8HW; T.-041-956 2622.

Thomson, S. Kenneth, MHSM, DipHSM. Unit General Manager, Lanarkshire Health Board, Motherwell and Clydesdale Unit, since 1989; Conductor, Glasgow Gaelic Musical Association, since 1983; b. 20.8.49, Campbeltown; m., Valerie Ferguson; 1 s.; 1 d. Educ. Keil School, Dumbarton. Administrative trainee, Scottish Health Service; hospital administrator; Unit Administrator, Argyll and Clyde Health Board, Renfrew Unit; Unit General Manager, Argyll and Dumbarton Unit. National Mod Gold Medallist, 1979. Recreations: music; Gaelic language and culture; theatre; skiing; sailing. Address: (b.) Law Hospital, Carluke, Lanarkshire, ML8 5ER; T.-0698 355717.

Thomson, Stuart James, HND (Agric). General Secretary, Ayrshire Cattle Society of GB and Ireland, since 1984; Director, Cattle Services (Ayr) Ltd.; b. 29.8.54, Kirkwall; m., Carolynne Henderson; 1 s. Educ. Kirkwall Grammar School; School of Agriculture, Aberdeen. Regional Officer, North of Scotland Milk Marketing Board, 1976-84. Recreations: gardening; golf; fishing. Address: (b.) 1 Racecourse Road, Ayr, KA7 2DE; T.-Ayr 267123.

Thomson, Sir Thomas James, Kt (1991), CBE (1983), OBE (1978), MB, ChB, FRCPGlas, FRCPLond, FRCPEdin, FRCPIre. Chairman, Greater Glasgow Health Board, since 1987; b. 8.4.23, Airdrie; m., Jessie Smith Shotbolt; 2 s.; 1 d.

Educ. Airdrie Academy; Glasgow University. Lecturer, Department of Materia Medica, Glasgow University, 1953-61; Postgraduate Adviser to Glasgow Northern Hospitals, 1961-80; Honorary Secretary, RCPSGlas, 1965-73; Secretary, Specialist Advisory Committee for General Internal Medicine for UK, 1970-74; Chairman: Medico-Pharmaceutical Forum, 1978-80 (Chairman, Education Advisory Board, 1979-83); Conference of Royal Colleges and Faculties in Scotland, 1982-85; National Medical Consultative Committee for Scotland, 1982-87; President, RCPSGlas, 1982-84; Hon.FACP, 1983; Hon. LLD, Glasgow University, 1988. Publications: Dilling's Pharmacology (Co-Editor); Gastroenterology - an integrated course. Recreations: swimming; golfing. Address: (h.) 1 Varna Road, Glasgow, G14 9NE; T.-041-959 5930.

Thomson, Walter, MBE. Editor, Selkirk Advertiser, 1932-86; Rugby Writer, Sunday Post, since 1931; b. 20.3.13, Selkirk; m., Gerda; 2 d. Educ. Selkirk High School; Heriot-Watt. Army (Captain), 1940-46. Publication: Rummle Them Up!, 1989. Recreation: photography. Address: (h.) Cruachan, Murrayfield, Selkirk; T.-Selkirk 20261.

Thomson, Rev. William Halliday. Minister, Liberton Northfield Parish Church, Edinburgh, since 1987; b. 21.1.34, Kilmarnock; m., Margaret; 4 d. Educ. James Hamilton Academy; Kilmarnock Academy; Glasgow University and Trinity College. National Service, 1952-54; in commerce, 1949-59; student assistant, Riccarton Parish Church, Kilmarnock, 1963-64; Minister: Broxburn West, 1964-70, John Knox (Gerrard Street), Aberdeen, 1970-76, St. Columba's, Glenrothes, 1976-87. Recreations: swimming; hill-walking; snooker. Address: 9 Claverhouse Drive, Edinburgh, EH16 6BR.

Thornber, Iain, JP, DL, FRSA, FSA Scot, FSA. District Councillor, Morvern, Sunart and Ardgour, Lochaber, since 1988; Deputy Lieutenant, Lochaber, Inverness, Badenoch and Strathspey, since 1988; b. 3.2.48, Falkirk. Educ. Glenhurich Public School. Company Factor, Glensanda Estate, Morvern, Argyll. Life and Management Committee Member, West Highland Museum, Fort William; Member, Local Advisory Panel, Forestry Commission; Member, Morvern Red Deer Management Group; Member, Inverness Prison Visiting Committee. Publications: The Castles of Morvern; The Gaelic Bards of Morvern; Rats; The Sculptures Stones of Cill Choluimchille, Morvern; Moidart or Among the Clanranalds (Editor); Bronze Age Cairns in the Aline Valley, Morvern (Co-author). Recreations: deer stalking; salmon fishing; photography; local history research. Address: (b.) Knock House, Morvern, by Oban, PA34 5UU; T.-096 784 651.

Thorne, Roderick Hugh Frank, MA, CertEd, AdvCertEd. Head Teacher, Sanday School, Orkney, since 1984; b. 7.5.47, Maidenhead; m., Sylvia Mary Driscoll; 3 s. Educ. Leighton Park; Trinity, Cambridge; Christ Church, Oxford. Head Teacher, Fetlar, 1971-74, Fair Isle, 1976-81, Kent, 1981-84. Recreations: natural history; golf; photography. Address: (b.) Schoolhouse, Sanday, Orkney; T.-08575 404.

Thornton, James Allan, BA (Hons), MBA, MBIM, AMITD. Chief Executive, Perthshire Enterprise Co. Ltd., since 1991; Director, Clyde Chambers Ltd.; b. 7.12.51, Overtoun. Educ. Stirling University. RAF Officer; Accountant; Special Projects Officer, Ross and Cromarty District Council; Training Organiser, Highland Regional Council; Northern Manager, Mari Ltd.; Chief Executive, Barras Enterprise Trust. Recreations: hill-walking; fly-fishing; traditional and choral singing. Address: (b.) 1 High Street, Perth; T.-0738 29114.

Thornton, Jeffrey Michael, BA. Assistant Secretary, Head of Industry Policy Division, Scottish Office, since 1991;

Director, Turnkey (UK) Ltd., since 1992; b. 17.4.53, Londonderry; m., Laura Gaffney; 1 s.; 1 d. Educ. King Edward VI School, Chelmsford; Huddersfield Polytechnic. Pilot, RAF, 1972-74; Administration Trainee, Scottish Office, 1978; Private Secretary to Minister for Home Affairs, 1981-83; Assistant to Chief Executive, SDA, 1984-87; West Coast US Director, Locate in Scotland, 1987-91. Recreations: golf; skiing; badminton. Address: (b.) Alhambra House, Waterloo Street, Glasgow, G2; T.-041-242 5537.

Thornton-Kemsley, Nigel Scott, CBE (1987), DL. Member, Grampian Health Board, since 1989; Managing Director, Thornton Enterprises Ltd.; Managing Director, Thornton Farms Ltd., 1956-88; Chairman, North of Scotland College of Agriculture, 1982-88; Director, Royal Highland and Agricultural Society of Scotland, 1971-88; Director, Scottish Agricultural Colleges, 1987-88; Governor, Rowett Research Institute, 1981-88; b. 14.8.33, Chigwell, Essex; m., Judith Gay Sanders; 1 s.; 2 d. Educ. Fettes College; East of Scotland College of Agriculture. National Service: Royal Signals, 1954-56, TA 51st Highland Signal Regiment, 1957-63, 3rd Bn., Gordon Highlanders, 1963-71, OC TAVR Company; Major on retiral; Deputy Lieutenant, Kincardineshire, 1978; President, Aberdeen-Angus Cattle Society, 1981-82; Member, Scottish American Community Relations Council, 1971-80; Chairman, Council, Scottish Agricultural Colleges, 1982-84; Life Governor, Imperial Cancer Research Council, since 1978; Past President, Royal Northern Agricultural Society; Past President, Fettercairn Farmers' Club. Recreation: fishing. Address: Thornton Castle, Laurencekirk, Kincardineshire; T.-056 17 301.

Thorpe, John Elton, BA, PhD. Senior Principal Scientific Officer, Freshwater Fisheries Laboratory, Pitlochry, since 1981; b. 24.1.35, Wolverhampton; m., Judith Anne Johnson; 2 s. Educ. Kingswood School, Bath; Jesus College, Cambridge. Cambridge Expedition to British Honduras, 1959-60 (Leader); Shell International Chemical Co. Ltd., London, 1960-62; joined DAFS Freshwater Fisheries Laboratory, Pitlochry, 1963. Vice-President, Fisheries Society of British Isles, 1988-93; Editor, Journal of Fish Biology, since 1991; Member, Editorial Board: Journal of Animal Ecology, since 1988, Reviews in Fish and Fisheries, since 1989, Fisheries Management, 1978-84, and Aquaculture and Fisheries Management, since 1985; Chairman, Killiecrankie and Fincastle Community Council, 1976-78. Publications: seven books; 150 scientific papers. Recreations: travelling; Baroque music. Address: (b.) Freshwater Fisheries Laboratory, Pitlochry, Perthshire, PH16 5LW; T.-0796 2060.

Thrower, Rev. Charles George, BSc. Minister, Carnbee linked with Pittenweem, since 1970; Moderator, St. Andrews Presbytery, 1991-92; b. 22.11.37, Barton Turf, Norfolk; m., Dr. Stephanie A.M. Thrower; 1 s.; 3 d. Educ. King Edward VI School, Norwich; Britannia Royal Naval College, Dartmouth. Electrical branch training H.M.S. Girdle-Ness (Malta), 1960-61; divinity student, St. Mary's, 1961-64; pro-bationer, St. Andrews Church, Dundee, 1964-65; missionary appointment, Hampden with Falmouth, Trelawny, Jamaica, 1966-70. Synod of Fife Youth Adviser, 1971-74; Chairman, East Neuk of Fife Committee, RSSPCC, since 1974, and Member, RSSPCC Policy and Staff Committee. Recreations: water colour painting; photography; sailing; gardening; local church history. Address: The Manse, 2 Milton Place, Pittenweem, Fife, KY10 2LR; T.-0333 311255.

Thrower, James Arthur, BLitt, MA, PhD. Director, Centre for the Study of Religions and Riddoch Lecturer in Comparative Religion, Aberdeen University, since 1987; b. 5.10.36, Guisborough; m., Judith Elizabeth Gauss; 3 d. Educ. Guisborough Grammar School; St. Chad's College, Durham; St. Edmund Hall, Oxford. Staff-Tutor, Eastern District, WEA, 1962-64; Lecturer in Philosophy of Religion, Ghana University, 1964-68; Lecturer in Religious Studies, Bede College, Durham, 1968-70; Lecturer in Religious Studies, Aberdeen University, 1970 (Senior Lecturer, 1981, Head of Department, 1984-87); Visiting Professor: Helsinki University, 1974, Polish Academy of Sciences, 1976, Aligarh Muslim University, India, 1988; British Council Exchange Scholar, Leningrad University, 1976 and 1978; Visiting Scholar, Gdansk University, 1981 and 1982; British Academy exchange scholar Chinese Academy of Social Sciences, 1989; Warden, Balgownie Lodge, Aberdeen University, 1971-82. Author of a number of books and articles about the history of religions. Recreations: travel and exploration; classical music; ballet. (b.) Centre for the Study of Religions, Aberdeen University, AB9 2UB; T.-Aberdeen 272147.

Thurso, Viscount (Robin Macdonald Sinclair), 2nd Viscount, 5th Bt. of Ulbster, JP. Lord Lieutenant of Caithness, since 1973; Baron of Thurso; Chairman, Sinclair Family Trust Ltd; Chairman, Lochdhu Hotels Ltd.; Chairman, Thurso Fisheries Ltd.; Director, Stephens (Plastics) Ltd.; Founder and first Chairman, Caithness Glass Ltd.; b. 24.12.22, Kingston Vale; m., Margaret Beaumont Brokensha; 2 s.; 1 d. Educ. Eton; New College, Oxford; Edinburgh University. RAF, 1941-46; Flt.-Lt., 684 Squadron, 540 Squadron; commanded Edinburgh University Air Squadron, 1946; Member, Caithness County Council, 1949, 1952, 1955, 1958; Member, Thurso Town Council, 1957, 1960 (resigned, 1961), 1965, 1968, 1971; President, North Country Cheviot Sheep Society, 1951-54; Chairman, Caithness and Sutherland Youth Employment Committee, 1957-75; Member, Red Deer Commission, 1965-74; President, Highland Society of London, 1980-82; Council Member, Royal National Mission to Deep Sea Fishermen, 1983-85; President, Boys' Brigade, since 1985; Vice Lieutenant, Caithness, 1964-73. Recreations: fishing; shooting; amateur drama. Address: Thurso East Mains, Thurso, Caithness, KW14 8HW; T.-0847 62600.

Thyne, Malcolm Tod, MA. Headmaster, Fettes College, since 1988; b. 6.11.42, Edinburgh; m., Eleanor Christine Scott; 2 s. Educ. The Leys School, Cambridge; Clare College, Cambridge. Assistant Master, Edinburgh Academy, 1965-69; Assistant Master, Oundle School, 1969-80 (Housemaster, 1972-80); Headmaster, St. Bees School, Cumbria, 1980-88. Publications: Periodicity, Atomic Structure and Bonding (Revised Nuffield Chemistry), 1976; contributions to Revised Nuffield Chemistry Handbook for Pupils and Teachers Guides, 1978. Recreation: mountaineering. Address: (b.) Fettes College, Edinburgh, EH4 1QX; T.-031-332 2281.

Tiefenbrun, Ivor Sigmund, MBE. Managing Director, Linn Products Ltd., Glasgow; b. 18.3.46, Glasgow; m., Evelyn Stella Balarksy; 2 s.; 1 d. Educ. Strathbungo Senior Secondary School; Strathclyde University (Sixties dropout). Worked overseas, 1971-73; founded Linn Products, 1973. Chairman, Federation of British Audio, 1983-87. Recreations: thinking; music; reading; sailing. Address: (b.) Linn Products Ltd., Floors Road, Waterfoot, Eaglesham, Glasgow, G76 0EP; T.-041-644 5111.

Tierney, David A., BA (Hons). Rector, Speyside High School, Aberlour, since 1987; b. 15.1.50, Glasgow; m., Valerie Lauder; 2 s. Educ. Queen's Park School, Glasgow; Strathclyde University; Jordanhill College of Education; Glasgow University. Teacher, Govan High School, Glasgow, 1973-76; Principal Teacher of Modern Studies, Mackie Academy, 1976-83; Depute Rector, Speyside High School, 1983-87. Member, Consultative Committee on the Curriculum Central Committee for Social Subjects, 1984-86; Chairman, SEB/SCCC Joint Working Party for SCE European Studies. Recreations: hill-walking; cycling; reading; gardening. Address: (h.) Sunningdale, Elgin; T.-0343 547945.

Tilbrook, Peter John, BSc, PhD, MIEEM. Director, North West Region, Scottish Natural Heritage, since 1992; b. 12.12.38, Romford; m., Frances Carol Brander; 2 d. Educ. Royal Liberty Grammar School; Durham University; Queen Mary College, London University. Research Scientist and Base Commander, Signy Island Base, South Orkney Islands, Falkland Islands Dependencies Survey; Head, Terrestrial Ecology Section, British Antarctic Survey; Deputy Regional Officer and Regional Officer, North West Scotland, Nature Conservancy Council; Director, North West Region, Nature Conservancy Council for Scotland. Polar Medal, 1967. Recreations: hill-walking; scuba diving; squash; photography; music; gardening. Address: (h.) Rosenberg, Cromarty, Ross-shire, IV11 8YT; T.-03817 239.

Timms, Professor Peter Kenneth, MBE. Chairman, Board of Management, Glasgow University Business School, since 1991; Managing Director, Flexible Technology Ltd., Bute, since 1981; Member, Highlands and Enterprise, since 1990; Member, Scottish Industrial Development Advisory Board, since 1989; b. 2.12.43, Witney, Oxon; m., Patricia; 3 s. Educ. St. Edmund's School, Canterbury, Kent. Production Engineer, Texas Instruments Ltd., 1964; Manufacturing Engineer, then Process Engineering Manager, IBM UK Ltd., 1967; Director and General Manager, AFA Minerva, 1978. Non-Executive Director: Sea Catch plc, Murray Enterprise plc, Scottish Electronics Technology Group Ltd. Recreations: boating; travel. Address: (h.) Millbrae, Ascog, Rothesay, Bute, PA20 9ET; T.-0700 504515.

Tinsley, Emeritus Professor Joseph, BSc, PhD, FRSE, FRSC, CChem. Emeritus Professor of Soil Science, Aberdeen University, since 1981; Chairman, DAFS Residual Manurial Values Committee, since 1976; President, Aberdeen YMCA, since 1984; b. 24.7.16, Wootton Bassett; m., Mary Joan Swain; 4 d. Educ. Reading University. Assistant Agricultural Advisory Chemist, MAFF, SE Counties of England, 1938-43; Lecturer in Agricultural Chemistry, Reading University, 1943-58; Reader in Soil Science and Head of Department, Aberdeen University, 1958-71; first Professor of Soil Science, Aberdeen University, 1971-81. President, British Society of Soil Science, 1970-72. Recreations: exploring landscapes in the UK and overseas; support for Christian organisations and aid to third world countries; photography, mainly to illustrate lectures on scientific and travel topics; family interests. Address: (h.) 52 Victoria Street, Aberdeen, AB1 1XA; T.-0224 646552.

Titterington, Professor (Donald) Michael, BSc, PhD, DipMathStat, FRSE. Professor of Statistics, Glasgow University, since 1988; b. 20.11.45, Marple, Cheshire; m., Mary Hourie Philp; 1 s. Educ. High School of Stirling; Edinburgh University; Cambridge University. Lecturer, then Senior Lecturer, then Titular Professor, Department of Statistics, Glasgow University, 1972-88; visiting appointments: Princeton University, 1978, State University of New York, 1980, Wisconsin University, 1982, Australian National University, 1982; Associate Editor, Biometrika, 1979-85, Annals of Statistics, 1983-85, and Journal, American Statistical Association, 1986-88 and since 1991; Joint Editor, Journal of the Royal Statistical Society, Series B, 1986-89; Council Member, Royal Statistical Society, since 1987; elected Fellow, Institute of Mathematical Statistics, 1986; elected Member, International Statistical Institute, 1991. Publications: Statistical Analysis of Finite Mixture Distributions (Co-author); many journal articles. Recreation: being a father. Address: (b.) Department of Statistics, Glasgow University, Glasgow, G12 8QQ; T.-041-339 8855.

Tobin, Patrick Francis John, MA, PGCE. Principal, Mary Erskine School and Daniel Stewart's & Melville College, since 1989; Member, Scottish Consultative Council on the Curriculum; b. 4.10.41, London; m., Margery Ann Sluce; 1 s.; 3 d. Educ. St. Benedict's, Ealing; Christ Church, Oxford; London University. Head of Economics, St. Benedict's, Ealing, 1963-71; Head of History, Christ College, Brecon, 1971-75; Head of History, Tonbridge School, 1975-81; The King's School, Parramatta, NSW, 1980; Headmaster, Prior Park College, Bath, 1981-89. Recreations: reading; writing; canal boating; hill-walking; travel. Address: (h.) 11 Queensferry Terrace, Edinburgh, EH4 3EQ.

Tod, Stewart, DA (Edin), RIBA, FRIAS, FSA Scot. Senior Partner, Stewart Tod & Partners, Architects, Edinburgh, since 1977; b. 30.4.27, West Wemyss; m., A. Vivienne J. Nixon; 2 s.; 2 d. Educ. Buckhaven High School; Edinburgh College of Art. RAF, 1945-48; Stratton Davis & Yates, 1952-55; Falkirk District Council, 1955-57; Carr and Matthew, 1957-60; David Carr Architects, 1960-77. Committee Member, Association for the Protection of Rural Scotland; General Trustee, Church of Scotland; Member, Church of Scotland Board of Practice and Procedure. Recreation: bee-keeping. Address: (b.) 43 Manor Place, Edinburgh; T.-031-225 7988.

Todd, Professor Adrian Christopher, BTech, PhD, CEng, FIChemE, FInstPet. Professor of Petroleum Engineering, Heriot Watt University, since 1991; b. 1.4.44, Leicester; m., Valerie H. Todd; 1 d. Educ. Lutterworth Grammar School; Loughborough University of Technology. Research Scientist, Shell, 1969-72; joined Heriot Watt University as Lecturer in Chemical Engineering, 1972. Recreation: Christian activities. Address: (b.) Department of Petroleum Engineering, Heriot Watt University, Riccarton, Edinburgh; T.-031-451 3124.

Todd, Rev. Andrew Stewart, MA, BD, DD. Minister, St. Machar's Cathedral, Old Aberdeen, since 1967; Chaplain to The Queen in Scotland, since 1991; b. 26.5.26, Alloa; m., Janet Agnes Brown Smith; 2 s.; 2 d. Educ. High School of Stirling; Edinburgh University; Basel University. Assistant Minister, St. Cuthbert's, Edinburgh, 1951-52; Minister: Symington, Lanarkshire, 1952; North Leith, 1960; Member, Church Hymnary Revision Comittee, 1963-73; Convener, General Assembly's Committee on Public Worship and Aids to Devotion, 1974-78; Moderator, Aberdeen Presbytery, 1980-81; Convener, Panel on Doctrine; Member, Church Hymnary Trust; awarded Honorary Doctorate, Aberdeen University, 1982; translator of three theological books from German into English; Honorary President, Church Service Society; Honorary President, Scottish Church Society. Recreations: music; gardening. Address: 18 The Chanonry, Old Aberdeen, Aberdeen; T.-0224 483688.

Tolley, David Anthony, MB, BS (Lond), FRCS, FRCSEdin. Consultant Urological Surgeon, Western General Hospital, Edinburgh, since 1980; Honorary Senior Lecturer, Department of Surgery/Urology, Edinburgh University, since 1980; Director, Scottish Lithotriptor Centre; b. 29.11.47, Warrington; m., Judith Anne Finn; 3 s.; 1 d. Educ. Manchester Grammar School; Kings College Hospital Medical School, London University. House Surgeon and Physician, Kings College Hospital; Lecturer· in Human Morphology, Southampton University; Lecturer in Anatomy and Fulbright Fellow, University of Texas at Houston; Surgical Registrar, Hammersmith and Ealing Hospitals, London; Senior Surgical Registrar (Urology), Kings College Hospital, London; Senior Urological Registrar, Yorkshire Regional Training Scheme. Member, MRC Working Party on Urological Cancer; Past Chairman, Scottish Urological Oncology Group. Recreations: golf; motor racing; sailing. Address: (b.) Murrayfield Hospital, Corstorphine Road, Edinburgh; T.-031-334 0363.

Tongue, Christopher Hugh, MA (Cantab), DipEd. Headmaster, Keil School, since 1984; b. 2.4.43, Uppingham; m., Chelsia Hitchings; 2 s. Educ. Kingswood School, Bath; Jesus College, Cambridge; Makerere College, Uganda. Teacher: Kagumo High School, Kenya, 1966-68, Felsted

School, Essex, 1968-74, 1976-84, Diocesan College, Cape Town, 1975-76. Recreations: cricket; rugby; music. Address: (b.) Keil School, Helenslee Road, Dumbarton, G82 4AL; T.-0389 62003.

Topping, Professor Barry H.V., BSc, PhD, CEng, MBCS, MICE, MIStructE, FIMA. Professor, Department of Civil Engineering, Heriot-Watt University, Edinburgh, since 1990; b. 14.2.52, Manchester. Educ. Bedford Modern School; City University, London. Lecturer in Civil Engineering, Edinburgh University, 1978-88; Von-Humboldt Research Fellow, Stuttgart University, 1986-87; Senior Lecturer, Heriot-Watt University, 1988-89, Reader, 1989-90. Editor, Structural Engineering Review; Co-Editor, Computing Systems in Engineering. Address: (b.) Department of Civil Engineering, Heriot-Watt University, Riccarton, Edinburgh, EH14 4AS; T.-031-449 5111.

Torbet, Thomas Edgar, MB, ChB, FRCSEdin, FRCOG. Consultant Obstetrician and Gynaecologist, since 1967; Honorary Clinical Lecturer, Glasgow University, since 1967; b. 15.3.30, Bearsden; m., Helen Fiona; 1 s. Educ. Morrison's Academy, Crieff; Glasgow University. JP, East Kilbride. Recreations: sailing; skiing. Address: (h.) 10 Easter Road, Busby, Clarkston, Glasgow; T.-041-644 1099.

Torrance, Rev. Professor James Bruce, MA (Hons), BD. Professor of Systematic Theology, Aberdeen University, 1977-89 (Dean, Faculty of Divinity, 1978-81); Minister, Church of Scotland, since 1950; b. 3.2.23, Chengtu, Szechwan, West China; m., Mary Heather Aitken; 1 s.; 2 d. Educ. Royal High School, Edinburgh; Edinburgh University and New College; Marburg University; Basle University; Oxford University. RAF, 1943-45; ordained, Invergowrie, Dundee, 1954; Lecturer in Divinity and Dogmatics in History of Christian Thought, 1961, and Senior Lecturer in Christian Dogmatics, 1972, New College, Edinburgh; Visiting Professor of New Testament, Union Theological Seminary, 1960, of Theology, Columbia Theological Seminary, 1965, and Vancouver School of Theology, 1974-75; Visiting Professor in South Africa, USA, New Zealand and Australia. Convenor, Panel on Doctrine, General Assembly, 1982-86; Joint Convener, British Council of Churches Commission on Doctrine of the Trinity, 1983-89; Joint Convenor, World Alliance of Reformed Churches, Lutheran World Federation Conversations, 1985-88. Recreations: bee-keeping; fishing; swimming; gardening. Address: (h.) 3 Greenbank Crescent, Edinburgh, EH10 5TE; T.-031-447 3230.

Torrance, Very Rev. Thomas Forsyth, MBE, MA, BD, DrTheol, DLitt, DD, DrTeol, DTheol, DSc, FBA, FRSE. Emeritus Professor, Edinburgh University, since 1979; b. 30.8.13, Chengdu, Sichuan, China; m., Margaret Edith Spear; 2 s.; 1 d. Educ. Canadian School, Chengdu, China; Bellshill Academy, Lanarkshire; Edinburgh University; Basel University; Oriel College, Oxford. Minister: Alyth Barony Parish Church, 1940-47; served as Church of Scotland Chaplain, 1943-45; Minister, Beechgrove Parish Church, Aberdeen, 1947-50; Edinburgh University: Professor of Church History, 1950-52, Professor of Christian Dogmatics, 1952-79; Moderator, General Assembly of the Church of Scotland, 1976-77. Cross of St. Mark, First Class, 1970; Protoprebyter of Greek Orthodox Church (Hon.), 1973; President, Academie Internationale des Sciences Religieuses, 1972-81. Recreations: formerly golf, squash, fishing; now walking. Address: (h.) 37 Braid Farm Road, Edinburgh, EH10 6LE; T.-031-447 3224.

Toth, Professor Akos George, Dr. Jur., PhD. Professor of Law, Strathclyde University, since 1984; Jean Monnet Chair of European Law, since 1991; b. 9.2.36, Mezotur, Hungary; m., Sarah Kurucz. Educ. Budapest University; Szeged University; Exeter University. Strathclyde University:

Lecturer in Law, 1971-76, Senior Lecturer, 1976-82, Reader, 1982-84. Publications: Legal Protection of Individuals in the European Communities, 1978; The Oxford Encyclopaedia of European Community Law, 1990. Recreations: travel; music; opera; theatre; swimming; walking. Address: (b.) Strathclyde University, Law School, 173 Cathedral Street, Glasgow, G4 0RQ; T.-041-552 4400.

Toulmin, David. Hon. MLitt (Aberdeen). Writer; b. 1.7.13, Rathen, Aberdeenshire; m., Margaret Jane Willox; 3 s. Educ. five public/parish schools. From the age of 14 to 65, earned living by manual labour (farm worker); his first article was published by Farmer and Stock Breeder, 1947; wrote short stories in dialect for local newspapers and the Scots Magazine; five stories broadcast on radio by the BBC; a collection was published as Hard Shining Corn, 1972; has published a further eight books; awarded grant by the Scottish Arts Council, 1983; real name, John Reid. Recreations: writing; reading; popular music; cinema; video; television; antiquarian research. Address: (h.) 7 Pittodrie Place, Aberdeen; T.-Aberdeen 634058.

Towers, Professor Brian, BA (Corn), BSc (Econ), PhD. IPM Professor of Industrial Relations, Strathclyde Business School, since 1989; ACAS Arbitrator, since 1975; Editor, Industrial Relations Journal; b. 8.7.36, Liverpool; 1 s.; 3 d. Educ. De La Salle College, Salford; Manchester University. Senior Lecturer, Nottingham University, 1966-89. Publications include: Bargaining for Change, 1973; Handbook of Industrial Relations Practice, 1989. Recreations: music; football. Address: (b.)Department of Human Resource Management, Strathclyde Business Management School, Marland House, Richmond Street, Glasgow, G1 1XT.

Townell, Nicholas Howard, MB, BS (Lond), FRCS (Eng). Consultant General Surgeon and Urologist, Dundee and Angus Hospitals, since 1985; Honorary Senior Lecturer in Surgery, Dundee University Medical School, since 1985; b. 19.4.49, Redhill; m., Hoang Anh Vuong; 1 s.; 2 d. Educ. Davenant Foundation Grammar School; London University; Royal Free Hospital School of Medicine. Various House Surgeon, House Physician and Registrar posts; Senior Registrar in General Surgery and Urology, Royal Free Hospital. Fellow, Royal Society of Medicine. Recreations: classical music; golf; squash; hill-walking. Address: (h.) Rosebank, Hillside, Angus, DD10 9HZ; T.-067 483 296.

Trabichoff, Geoffrey Colin, AGSM, LGSM. Violinist; Leader, BBC Scottish Symphony Orchestra, since 1982; Soloist and Recitalist; b. 15.4.46, London; m., Judith Orbach; 1 step s.; 1 d. Leader, Gulbenkian Orchestra, Lisbon, 1974-76; Leader, Mannheim Chamber Orchestra, 1976-78; Leader, Hannover State Orchestra, 1978-81. Address: (h.) 40 Woodend Drive, Jordanhill, Glasgow, G13; T.-041-959 3496.

Trainer, Professor James, MA, PhD. Deputy Principal, Stirling University, and Professor of German, since 1969; b. 2.3.32; m., Barbara Herta Reinhard (deceased); 2 s.; 1 d. Educ. St. Andrews University; Free University of Berlin. Lecturer in German, St. Andrews University, 1958-67; Visiting Professor, Yale University, 1964-65; Visiting Scholar, University of California at Santa Barbara, 1989; Vice-Convener, SUCE, since 1987; Convener, SUCE Modern Languages Panel, 1979-86; Member, Inter University and Polytechnic Council, since 1983; Member, Scottish Examination Board, 1975-82; Chairman, SED Postgraduate Awards Committee, since 1989; Member, UK Fulbright Committee, since 1985; Trustee, National Library of Scotland, 1986-91; Chairman, Scottish Conference of University Teachers of German, 1978-80; Member, National Academic Audit Unit. Recreations: music; cricket; translating. Address: (b.) Stirling University, Stirling; T.-0786 73171.

Tranter, Nigel, OBE, KCLJ, DLitt, MA (Hon.). Author and Novelist, since 1935; b. 23.11.09, Glasgow; m., May Jean Campbell Grieve (deceased); 1 s. (deceased); 1 d. Educ. St. James' Episcopal School; George Heriot's, Edinburgh. Professional Writer, since 1946; published more than 100 books, including over 70 novels; Vice-Convener, Scottish Covenant Association, 1951-55; President, East Lothian Liberal Association, 1960-70; Chairman, National Forth Road Bridge Committee, 1953-57; Chairman, St. Andrew Society of East Lothian, since 1966; President, Scottish PEN, 1962-66 (now Honorary President); Chairman, Society of Authors, Scotland, 1966-70; Chairman, National Book League, Scotland, 1971-73. Vice-Chancellor, Order of St. Lazarus of Jerusalem, 1982-88; Hon. Vice-President, Scottish Association of Teachers of History; Honorary Freeman of Blackstone, Virginia, USA, 1980; BBC Radio Scot of the Year, 1989; Hon. President, Saltire Society. Recreations: walking; climbing; genealogy; castle architecture. Address: (h.) Quarry House, Aberlady, East Lothian; T.-Aberlady 258.

Travis, Christopher Douglas, BSc (Soc Sci). Executive Director, Clydesdale Development Co. Ltd., since 1991; Chairman, Lanarkshire Enterprise Training Ltd., since 1992; b. 12.5.59, Kaduna, Nigeria. Educ. Dollar Academy; Edinburgh University. Lecturer in Economics/research student, Dundee College of Technology, 1983-88; Business Counsellor, SDA, 1987-88; Economic Development Manager, Gordon District Council, 1988-91. Recreations: cooking; reading; hill-walking; golf. Address: (b.) 129 Hyndford Road, Lanark; T.-0555 65064.

Trayhurn, Professor Paul, BSc, DPhil. Head, Division of Biochemical Sciences, Rowett Research Institute, since 1988; b. 6.5.48, Exeter; m., Deborah Hartland Gigg; 3 s.; 1 d. Educ. Colyton Grammar School, Devon; Reading University; Oxford University. Graduate student, Linacre College, Oxford, 1969-72; NATO European Research Fellow, Strasbourg, 1972-73; Postdoctoral Fellow, Oxford, 1973-75; MRC Scientific/Senior Scientific Staff, Dunn Nutrition Laboratory, Cambridge, 1975-86; Professor and Heritage Scholar, University of Alberta, 1986-88. Publications: 190 scientific publications. Address: (h.) 48 Carlton Place, Aberdeen, AB2 4BQ; T.-0224 643417.

Trevarthen, Professor Colwyn Boyd, BSc, MSc, PhD. Professor of Child Psychology and Psychobiology, Edinburgh University, since 1984; b. 2.3.31, Auckland; m., Elizabeth Lee Simmons; 3 s. Educ. Auckland Grammar School; Auckland University. Research Fellow, California Institute of Technology, 1962; USPHS Postdoctoral Fellow (CNRS), Marseille, 1963-66; MRC Research Fellow, Psychological Laboratory, Cambridge University, 1966; Research Fellow in Cognitive Studies, Lecturer in Psychology, Harvard University, 1966-68; Senior Research Fellow, California Institute of Technology, 1969-70; Edinburgh University: Lecturer, 1971-72, Reader, 1973-84, Associate Dean, Social Sciences, 1974-75; Visiting Reader or Professor, La Trobe University, Auckland University, California Institute of Technology, Lagos University, Universite Libre de Bruxelles, Natal University, University of Texas at Austin, University of Utah, University of Crete; Director, Edinburgh Centre for Research in Child Development. Recreations: walking; travelling; reading; music; conversation. Address: (b.) Department of Psychology, Edinburgh University, 7 George Square, Edinburgh, EH8 9JZ; T.-031-650 3436/5.

Trotter, Alexander Richard. DL, FRSA. Convenor, Scottish Landowners Federation, 1982-85; Member, Nature Conservancy Council and Chairman, its Committee for Scotland, 1985-90; b. 20.2.39, London; m., Julia Henrietta Greenwell; 3 s. Educ. Eton College. Royal Scots Greys, 1958-68; Member, Berwickshire County Council, 1968-74 (Chairman, Roads Committee, 1972-74); Member, UK

Committee, European Year of the Environment, 1986-88; Chairman, Mortonhall Park Ltd., since 1973; Vice-Chairman, Border Grain Ltd., since 1984. Member, Queen's Bodyguard for Scotland (Royal Company of Archers). Recreations: skiing; tennis; riding; shooting. Address: Charterhall, Duns, Berwickshire, TD11 3RE; T.-089 084 301.

Trotter, William, MA. Headteacher, Craigmount High School, Edinburgh, since 1969; b. 7.5.28, Greenock; m., Sylvia Rosemary Hall; 1 s.; 1 d. Educ. Hamilton Academy; Glasgow University; Jordanhill College of Education. Teacher of Modern Languages: Airdrie Academy, 1955-58, Forest Hill School, London, 1958-61; Head of Languages Department, Sedgehill School, London, 1961-65; Lecturer in Modern Languages, High Wycombe College of Technology, 1965-67; Deputy Head, Joseph Leckie School, Walsall, 1967-69; President, Corstorphine Rotary Club, 1988-89. Recreations: reading; music; swimming; light-hearted bridge. Address: (h.) 26 Ormidale Terrace, Edinburgh, EH12 6EQ; T.-031-337 6492.

Trudgill, David L., BSc, PhD, CBiol, FBIBiol. Head, Zoology Department, Scottish Crop Research Institute, since 1972; b. 2.5.42, Leeds; m., Margaret Jean Luckraft; 3 s. Educ. Leeds Grammar School; Ulverston Grammar School; Leeds University; London University. Nematologist, Rothamsted Experimental Station, 1966-72. Chairman, European Plant Protection Organisation ad hoc committee on potato cyst nematodes. Recreations: table tennis; hill-walking; fishing. Address: (b.) Zoology Department, Scottish Crop Research Institute, Invergowrie, Dundee, DD2 5DA; T.-0382 562731.

Truman, Donald Ernest Samuel, BA, PhD, FIBiol, CBiol. Vice-Dean, Faculty of Science and Engineering, Edinburgh University, since 1989; b. 23.10.36, Leicester; m., Kathleen Ramsay; 1 s.; 1 d. Educ. Wyggeston School, Leicester; Clare College, Cambridge. NATO Research Fellow, Wenner-Gren Institute, Stockholm, 1962-63; MRC Epigenetics Research Group, Edinburgh, 1963-72; Lecturer, Department of Genetics, Edinburgh University, 1972-78; Senior Lecturer, 1978-89, Head of Department, 1984-89, Director of Biology Teaching Unit, 1985-89; Aneurin Bevan Memorial Fellow, Government of India, 1978. Publications: The Biochemistry of Cytodifferentiation, 1974; Differentiation in Vitro (Joint Editor), 1982; Stability and Switching in Cellular Differentiation, 1982; Coordinated Regulation of Gene Expression, 1986. Recreation: gardening. Address: (b.) Faculty of Science Office, West Mains Road, Edinburgh, EH9 3JY; T.-031-667 1081.

Tucker, Professor John Barry, BA, MA, PhD. Professor of Cell Biology, St. Andrews University, since 1990; b. 17.3.41, Arundel; m., Janet Stephen Murray; 1 s. Educ. Queen Elizabeth Grammar School, Atherstone; Peterhouse, Cambridge. Fulbright Travel Scholar and Research Associate, Department of Zoology, Indiana University, 1966-68; SERC Research Fellow, Department of Zoology, Cambridge, 1968-69; Lecturer in Zoology, St. Andrews University, 1969-79 (Chairman, Zoology Department, 1982-84); Reader in Zoology, 1979-90. Member: SERC Advisory Group II, 1977-80, SERC Molecular Biology and Genetics Sub-committee, 1986-89, Editorial Board of Development, 1979-88. Recreations: cycling; hill-walking; tennis; reluctant gardener. Address: (b.) Department of Biology and Preclinical Medicine, Bute Building, St. Andrews University, St. Andrews, Fife, KY16 9TS; T.-0334 76161.

Tulloch, Bruce Attwood, MA, DipEd. Honorary Sheriff, since 1988; Justice of the Peace, since 1980; b. 9.11.22, Dunfermline; m., Patricia Hunter; 2 s.; 1 d. Educ. Dunfermline High School; Edinburgh University. RAF Service, 1942-45; Headmaster: Flotta School, Orkney, 1949-51, Inchberry School, Moray, 1951-61, Inverlochy School,

Inverness-shire, 1961-82. Recreations: talking; books; music; gardening; fishing. Address: (h.) A'chruach, Duror, Appin, Argyll; T.-0631-74-297.

Tumelty, Michael, MA (Hons). Music Critic, The Herald, since 1983; b. 31.5.46, Hexham; m., Frances McGinniss; 2 s.; 1 d. Educ. St. Aloysius College, Glasgow; Aberdeen University. Postgraduate research into the music of Debussy, 1974-75; entered teaching, St. Columba's High School, Clydebank (Principal Teacher, 1980-83); served on a variety of working groups on curriculum development; freelance Music Critic, Jewish Echo, 1979-82, and Daily Telegraph, 1982-83; Member, Scottish Central Committee on Music, 1982-83. Recreations: family; avid collector of records. Address: (b.) The Herald, Albion Street, Glasgow.

Tunstall-Pedoe, Professor Hugh David, MA, MD, FRCP, FRCPE, FFCM. Professor and Director, Cardiovascular Epidemiology Unit, and Senior Lecturer in Medicine, Ninewells Hospital and Medical School, Dundee, since 1981; Honorary Consultant Cardiologist, since 1981; Honorary Specialist in Community Medicine, since 1981; b. 30.12.39, Southampton; m., Jacqueline Helen; 2 s.; 1 d. Educ. Haberdashers' Aske's School; Dulwich College; King's College, Cambridge; Guy's Hospital Medical School. Junior hospital posts, Guy's, Brompton, National Queen Square and London Hospitals; MRC Social Medicine Unit, 1969-71; Lecturer in Medicine, The London Hospital, 1971-74; Senior Lecturer in Epidemiology and Honorary Physician, and Honorary Community Physician, St. Mary's Hospital and Medical School, London, 1974-81. Chairman, European Society of Cardiology Working Group on Epidemiology and Prevention, 1983-85. Recreations: hill-walking; bee-keeping; golf. Address: (b.) Cardiovascular Epidemiology Unit, Ninewells Hospital and Medical School, Dundee, DD1 9SY; T.-0382 644255.

Turmeau, William Arthur, CBE, FRSE, BSc, PhD, CEng, FIMechE. Principal, Napier Polytechnic of Edinburgh, since 1982; b. 19.9.29, London; m., Margaret Moar Burnett; 1 d. Educ. Stromness Academy, Orkney; Edinburgh University; Moray House College of Education; Heriot-Watt University. Royal Signals, 1947-49; Research Engineer, Northern Electric Co. Ltd., Montreal, 1952-54; Mechanical Engineer, USAF, Goose Bay, Labrador, 1954-56; Contracts Manager, Godfrey Engineering Co. Ltd., Montreal, 1956-61; Lecturer, Bristo Technical Institute, Edinburgh, 1962-64; Napier College: Lecturer and Senior Lecturer, 1964-68, Head, Department of Mechanical Engineering, 1968-75, Assistant Principal and Dean, Faculty of Technology, 1975-82. Member, Scottish Economic Council, since 1988; Member, Scottish Examination Board, since 1988; Member, Council for Industry and Higher Education, since 1991; Member, Standing Conference of Rectors and Vice-Chancellors of European Universities, since 1989; Member, Council, Societe Europeene Pour La Formation Des Ingenieurs, since 1983; Member, British Council CICHE, since 1982. Recreations: modern jazz; Leonardo da Vinci. Address: (h.) 71 Morningside Park, Edinburgh, EH10 5EZ; T.-031-447 4639.

Turnbull, Wilson Mark, DipArch, MLA, MBCS, RIBA, FRIAS, FLI. Turnbull Jeffrey Partnership, Landscape Architects, since 1983; b. 1.4.43, Edinburgh. Educ. George Watson's; Edinburgh College of Art; University of Pennsylvania. Assistant Professor of Architecture, University of Southern California, 1970-74; Partner, W.J. Cairns and Partners, Environmental Consultants, 1974-82; Partner, Design Innovations Research, 1976-81; Commissioner, Countryside Commission for Scotland, 1988-92; Chairman, Edinburgh Greenbelt Initiative, 1988-91; Director, Edinburgh Greenbelt Trust, since 1991. Recreation: sailing. Address: (b.) Sandeman House, 55 High Street, Edinburgh, EH1 1SR; T.-031-557 5050.

Turner, Colin William, BSc, AKC. Rector, Glasgow Academy, since 1983; b. 10.12.33, Torquay; m., Priscilla Mary Trickett; 2 s.; 2 d. Educ. Torquay Grammar School; King's College, London University; Exeter University. Edinburgh Academy: Assistant Master, 1958, CCF Contingent Commander, 1960-74, Housemaster, 1975-82. Recreations: mountaineering; caravanning. Address: (h.) 11 Kirklee Terrace, Glasgow, G12 OTH; T.-041-357 1776.

Turner, John R., MA, MusB, FRCO. Organist and Director of Music, Glasgow Cathedral, since 1965; Lecturer, Royal Scottish Academy of Music, since 1965; Organist, Strathclyde University, since 1965; b. Halifax. Educ. Rugby; Jesus College, Cambridge. Recreations: gardening; travel. Address: (h.) 2 Cathkin Cottage, Burnside Road, Glasgow, G73 5RD; T.-041-634 3083.

Turner, Captain John Russell, OBE (1986), MCIT, MIMH, MNI. General Manager, Aberdeen Harbour Board, 1978-89; b. 17.6.30, Cheadle Hulme; m., Jean Catherine Baker; 1 s.; 2 d. Educ. Kings School, Macclesfield; Thames Nautical Training College, HMS Worcester; UMIST; Cranfield Institute of Technology Cadet, Royal Naval Reserve, 1946-47; Navigating Officer: Clan Line, P. & O., Cunard Line, 1948-57; Port of Manchester: Assistant Chief Superintending Stevedore, Dock Traffic Superintendent, Assistant Docks Manager, 1957-73; Deputy General Manager, Aberdeen Harbour Board, 1973-78. Liveryman, Honourable Company of Master Mariners, 1972, Vice Chairman, N.E. Scotland Branch, since 1992; Chairman, Fishing Ports Committee, British Ports Federation, 1983-87; Member, Management Committee, and Chairman, Medium Ports Committee, British Ports Federation, 1987-89; Council Member, Association of Pilotage Authorities, 1978-84; Vice Chairman and Co-Founder, Scottish Advisory Committee, Netherlands British Chamber of Commerce, 1975-89; Council Member, Aberdeen Chamber of Commerce, 1978-89; Vice Chairman, North of Scotland Export Club, 1982-84; Chairman, Grampian-Houston Association, 1985-87; received Freedom of the City of London, 1972; awarded John Morris Gold Medal, British Industrial Truck Association, 1965. Recreations: golf; travel; historical research; sailing. Address: (h.) Pinewood, Woodlands Road, Banchory, Kincardineshire, AB31 3ZL.

Turner, Professor Kenneth John, BSc, PhD. Professor of Computing Science, Stirling University, since 1987; b. 21.2.49, Glasgow; m., Elizabeth Mary Christina; 2 s. Educ. Hutchesons' Boys Grammar School; Glasgow University; Edinburgh University. Data Communications Designer, International Computers Ltd., 1974-76; Senior Systems Analyst, Central Regional Council, 1976-77; Data Communications Consultant, International Computers Ltd., 1977-87. Recreations: choral singing; craft work; sailing. Address: (b.) Department of Computing Science, Stirling University, Stirling, FK9 4LA; T.-0786 67420.

Turner, Malcolm, OBE, JP. Member, Strathclyde Regional Council, since 1974; Deputy Lieutenant, Dunbartonshire, since 1989; Governor, Jordanhill College, since 1989; b. 13.12.21, Clydebank; m., Margaret Balfour; 1 s. Educ. Clydebank High School. Member: Clydebank Town Council, 1957-75 (Provost, 1966-69), Dunbarton County Council, 1957-75; Member, Cumbernauld Development Corporation, 1975-83; former Chairman, Central Water Development Board. Recreations: angling; caravanning; bowling; golf. Address: (h.) 14 Mossgiel Drive, Clydebank, Dunbartonshire, G81 2BY; T.-041-952 3992.

Turner, Norman William, MILAM, ALA, FBIM, FSA(Scot). Director of Leisure Services, Motherwell District Council, since 1985; Chairman, Association of Directors of Leisure, Recreation and Tourism, since 1990; b. 12.4.48,

Portsmouth. Educ. Portsmouth Technical High School; Brighton Polytechnic. District Librarian, Motherwell District Council; Depute Director of Libraries and Museums, Falkirk District Council; Deputy District Librarian, City of Southampton District; Deputy Borough Librarian, Andover Borough Council. Former Vice-Chairman, Public Libraries Group; former Hon. Treasurer, Scottish Library Association. Recreations: season ticket holder, Motherwell FC; sport; theatre; cinema; music; natural history. Address: (b.) Motherwell District Council, PO Box 14, Civic Centre, Motherwell, ML1 1TW; T.-0698 66166.

Turner, Susan Morag, MA, DipEd, MBATOD, FISW, FCollP, FRSA. Director, Scottish Association for the Deaf, since 1991; Director, Scottish Centre for the Education of the Deaf, 1971-91; b. 5.4.35, Glasgow. Educ. Rutherglen Academy; Glasgow University; Manchester University. Teacher of hearing-impaired children, Glasgow School for the Deaf; Head Teacher: Paisley School for the Deaf, Dundee School for the Deaf; Lecturer, Professional Curriculum Support Services Department, Moray House College. Member: National Council of Special Education; Council of Management, Royal National Institute for the Deaf; Church Advisorate on Special Educational Needs. Address: (h.) 15 Bonaly Brae, Colinton, Edinburgh, EH13 0QF; T.-031-441 7520.

Turner Thomson, Ann Denise. Interior Designer; b. 23.5.29, Molesey; m., Gordon Turner Thomson; 1 s.; 3 d. Educ. Sherborne School for Girls, Dorset; St. James's Secretarial College, London. Council Member, National Trust for Scotland; Member, Council, Edinburgh International Festival; Member, Board of Directors, Art in Partnership. Recreations: theatre; opera; reading; sailing; swimming; tennis. Address: 8 Middleby Street, Edinburgh, EH9 1TD; T.-031-667 3997.

Tweedy, Brigadier Oliver Robert. Commandant, Queen Victoria School, Dunblane, since 1985, and Bursar, 1985-91; b. 4.2.30, Newbury; m., Dawn Berrange; 2 s.; 1 d. Educ. Sedbergh School; RMA, Sandhurst. Commissioned, The Black Watch, 1949; commanded 1st Bn., The Black Watch, Scotland, Northern Ireland and Hong Kong, 1971-73; Commander, British Army Advisory Team, Nigeria, 1980-82; Commander, 51 Highland Brigade, 1982-84; ADC to The Queen, 1983; retired, 1985. Recreations: golf; country pursuits. Address: (h.) Inverbraan, Little Dunkeld, Perthshire, PH8 0AD.

Tyre, Colin Jack, LLB, DESU. Advocate, since 1987; b. 17.4.56, Dunoon; m., Elaine Patricia Carlin; 2 d. Educ. Dunoon Grammar School; Edinburgh University; Universite d'Aix Marseille. Admitted as Solicitor, 1980; Lecturer in Scots Law, Edinburgh University, 1980-83; Tax Editor, CCH Editions Ltd., Bicester, 1983-86. Publications: CCH Inheritance Tax Reporter; contributor to Stair Memorial Encyclopaedia. Recreations: orienteering; golf; mountain walking; contemporary music. Address: (b.) Advocates' Library, 1 Parliament Square, Edinburgh; T.-031-226 5071.

Tyrie, Peter Robert, BSc, FHCIMA. Managing Director, Balmoral International Ltd., since 1989; b. 3.4.46, Reigate; m., Christine Mary; 3 s. Educ. Enfield Grammar School; Westminster College Hotel School. Manager, Inverurie Hotel, Bermuda, 1969-71; Resident Manager, Portman Hotel, London, 1971-73; Project Director, Pannell Kerr Forster, 1973-77; Operations Director, Penta Hotels, 1977-80; Managing Director, Gleneagles Hotels PLC, 1980-86; Main Board Director, Bell's Whisky, 1983-86; Managing Director, Mandarin Oriental Hotel Group, 1986-89. Recreations: squash; shooting; fishing; rugby; classic cars. Address: (b.) The Balmoral Hotel, Princes Street, Edinburgh, EH2 2EQ; T.-031-557 8688.

Tyrrell, Reginald Charles, DL. Farmer and Company Director, since 1970; b. 15.11.30, Essex; m., Lady Caroline Hay. Educ. Forest School. Former Director of companies in audio-visual, film and management training fields, including: Sound-Services Ltd. (Managing), Merton Park Studios Ltd. (Managing), Film Producers' Guild Ltd., Film Facilities Ltd., Management Training Ltd. Chairman, National Trust for Scotland; Vice-President, Scottish Heritage USA; Vice-Chairman, British Field Sports Society; Deputy Lieutenant, Annandale and Eskdale, and Nithsdale. Recreations: field sports; meteorology. Address: (h.) Capplegill, Moffat, Dumfries-shire, DG10 9LQ; T.-0683 20525.

U

Underwood, Rev. Geoffrey Horne, BD, FPhS. Minister, Chalmers Memorial Church, Cockenzie, since 1964; b. 6.11.28, Stockport; m., Florence; 3 s.; 1 d. Educ. Alexandra School, Stockport; Manchester University; Edinburgh University. Employed in industry and commerce, 1942-54 (National Service, 1946-49); Minister, Levenshulme URC Church, Manchester, 1958-63; Assistant, Greenbank Church, Edinburgh, 1963-64. Recreations: sailing; swimming; hillclimbing. Address: Braemar Villa, 2 Links Road, Port Seton, EH32 0HA.

Upton, Professor Anthony Frederick, MA (Oxon), AM, FRHistS. Professor of Nordic History, St. Andrews University, since 1984; b. 13.10.29, Stockton Heath, Cheshire; m., Sirkka R.; 3 s. Educ. County Boys' School, Windsor; Queen's College, Oxford. Assistant Lecturer in Modern History, Leeds University, 1952-56; St. Andrews University: Lecturer in Modern History, 1956, Senior Lecturer, 1966, Reader, 1974. Sundry offices, Labour Party in Fife and in educational bodies, e.g. St. Andrews School Council. Recreations: music; literature; politics. Address: (h.) 5 West Acres, St. Andrews, Fife.

U'ren, William Graham, BSc (Hons), DiptTP, FRTPI. Director of Planning and Technical Services, Clydesdale District Council, since 1982; b. 28.12.46, Glasgow; m., Wendy; 2 d. Educ. Aberdeen Grammar School; Aberdeen University; Strathclyde University. Planning Assistant: Clackmannan County Council, 1970-72, Lanark County Council, 1972-75; Principal and Chief Planning Officer, Clydesdale District Council, 1975-82. Past Chairman, Scottish Society of Directors of Planning. Recreations: sport; bird watching; philately. Address: (b.) District Offices, South Vennel, Lanark, ML11 7JT; T.-Lanark 61331.

Urquhart, Alistair P., OBE, MA. Chairman, Central Support Group for Music, 1986-89; Headmaster, Kincorth Academy, Aberdeen, 1971-85; b. 27.7.21, Paisley; m., May Brown (deceased). Educ. John Neilson Institute, Paisley; Glasgow University. War Service, 1941-46 (Captain, Royal Artillery); Teacher of English, then Principal Teacher, Powis Junior Secondary School, Aberdeen, 1947-61; Deputy Headmaster, Summerhill Secondary School, Aberdeen, 1962-66; Headmaster, Old Aberdeen Secondary School, 1966-71. Chairman, Scottish Central Committee on Music, 1979-86; President, Scottish Badminton Union, 1970-72; Captain,

Deeside Golf Club, 1986-88. Recreations: golf; badminton; music. Address: (h.) 15 Kingshill Road, Aberdeen; T.-Aberdeen 316100.

Urquhart, Daniel, FCCA. Director of Finance, Banff and Buchan District Council, since 1974; b. 27.4.32, Banff; m., Molly; 1 s.; 1 d. Educ. Banff Academy. Trainee Accountant, Banff County Council, 1955-59; Aberdeen Corporation: Audit Assistant, 1959-61, Accountancy Assistant, 1961-63, Senior Accountancy Assistant, 1963-67; Town Chamberlain, Fraserburgh Town Council, 1967-74. Recreations: golf; bridge; gardening. Address: (b.) St. Leonard's, Sandyhill Road, Banff; T.-Banff 2521.

Urquhart, James Macconnell, MB, ChB, FFPHM, DPH. Chairman, Management Committee, Margaret Blackwood Housing for Adult Handicapped, Dundee; Convener, National Group Retirement Councils Scotland; Commissioner, Clan Urquhart Association; b. 1.10.18, Wishaw; m., 1, May Harrison (m. diss.); 2, Nora Hanna; 1 s.; 2 d. Educ. Dumfries Academy; High School of Glasgow; Glasgow University. RAF Medical Branch, 1942-68 (retired with rank of Group Captain); War Service, India, Burma; Safety Office, Atomic Trials, Australia, 1956; OC, RAF Hospitals; Community Medicine, Northern Ireland Hospital Authority, 1968-72; Medical Superintendent, Dundee General Hospitals, 1972-75; District Medical Officer, Dundee District, 1975-83. Treasurer, Forfarshire Medical Association; Treasurer, Preparation for Retiral Council, Dundee; Trustee, Scottish Trust for Physically Disabled; Trustee, Dundee Trust for Education of Deaf; Treasurer, St. Margaret's Episcopal Church, Dundee. Recreations: reading; photography. Address: (h.) 35 Albany Terrace, Dundee, DD3 6HS; T.-0382 22928.

Urquhart, John Munro, CBE, MA, MEd, FEIS; b. 16.9.10, Gairloch; m., Adela Margaret Sutherland; 1 s.; 1 d. Educ. Lochgilphead Secondary School; Oban High School; Glasgow University. Schoolmaster, Hutchesons' Boys' Grammar School; Assistant Director of Education, Banffshire; Depute Director of Education, Glasgow; Director of Education, Selkirkshire; Director, Scottish Certificate of Education Examination Board, 1965-75; Consultant Registrar, Caribbean Examinations Council, 1977-78; President, Association of Directors of Education, 1963-64. Boy Scouts County Commissioner, Selkirkshire; edited Statistical Account of Selkirkshire, 1964; District Governor, Rotary District 102, 1980. Recreations: angling; walking; reading; gardening. Address: (h.) 29 Craiglockhart Drive South, Edinburgh, EH14 1JA; T.-031-443 3085.

Urquhart-Logie, Celia Margaret Lloyd, RGN, DMS, MBA, FBIM. Founder and Managing Director, C U Data Ltd., since 1986; b. 7.4.47, Glasgow; m., William McLellan Logie; 1 s.; 2 d.; 3 step s.; 2 step d. Educ. Strathclyde University. Member, Advisory Panel on Enterprise and Deregulation, Department of Trade and Industry, since 1988; Governor, Queens College, Glasgow, since 1988 (Chairman, since 1990); Director, Glasgow Chamber of Commerce, since 1990; Member, Board, Cumbernauld Development Corporation, since 1991; Scottish Enterprise Award by Aims of Industry, 1990. Recreations: enjoying the luxury of spending time with husband and children and being a housewife; as well as sailing. Address: (b.) 501 Crow Road, Glasgow, G11 7DN; T.-041-954 3138.

Urwin, Professor Derek William, BA, MA (Econ), PhD. Professor of Politics and International Relations, Aberdeen University, since 1990; b. 27.10.39, Consett; m., Patricia Anne Ross; 2 s. Educ. Consett Grammar School; Wolsingham Grammar School; Keele University; Manchester University. Lecturer, Strathclyde University, 1963-72; Associate Professor, University of Bergen, 1972-80; Professor,

Warwick University, 1981-90. Publications: Western Europe since 1945; The Community of Europe; From Ploughshare to Ballot Box; Politics in Western Europe Today; Centre-Periphery Structures in Europe; Scottish Political Behaviour. Recreations: walking; reading; marquetry. Address: (b.) Department of Politics and International Relations, Aberdeen University, Old Aberdeen, AB9 2TY; T.-0224 272716/272713.

Usher, John Richard, BSc (Hons), MSc, PhD, FIMA, CMath. Head, School of Computer and Mathematical Sciences, The Robert Gordon Institute of Technology, since 1983; Member, Scottish Examination Board Steering Committee for the Revision of Higher and Post-Higher, since 1987; Member, Council, Institute of Mathematics and its Applications, 1987-90 (Chairman, Scottish Branch, 1985-88); b. 12.5.44, London; m., Sheila Mary; 1 d. Educ. St. Nicholas Grammar School; Hull University; St. Andrews University. Lecturer I, then Lecturer II, Teesside Polytechnic, 1970-74; Senior Lecturer, Glasgow College of Technology, 1974-82. Recreations: bridge; hill-walking; philately. Address: (b.) School of Computer and Mathematical Sciences, Robert Gordon's Institute of Technology, St. Andrew Street, Aberdeen; T.-0224 633611, Ext. 363.

V

Valentine, Ian Balfour, CA. Scottish Managing Partner, BDO Binder Hamlyn, Chartered Accountants, since 1985; Non-Executive Board Member, Ayrshire and Arran Health Board; b. 17.10.40, Glasgow; m., Elaine; 1 s.; 1 d. Educ. Hutchesons' Boys' Grammar School. Partner, J. Wyllie Guild & Ballantine, 1965 (subsequently Binder Hamlyn). Member, Council, Institute of Chartered Accountants of Scotland and of South West Committee; Chairman, Ayrshire Association of Chartered Accountants, 1976-78; President, Junior Chamber Ayr, 1972-73; Member, Ayr Schools Council, 1976-78; Director, Federation of Scottish Junior Chambers of Commerce, 1973-74; Honorary Secretary and Treasurer, Ayr Rugby Football Club, 1979-84. Recreations: golf; rugby (as spectator); bridge; curling. Address: (b.) 64 Dalblair Road, Ayr; T.-0292 263277.

Valentine, Keith, MA, LLB. Procurator Fiscal, Stirling, since 1976; b. 10.12.32, Perth; m., Anne Florence Ritchie; 1 s.; 2 d. Educ. Perth Academy; Edinburgh University. RAF Education Branch, 1956-59 (Flt.-Lt.); Procurator Fiscal Service, since 1961, Ayr, Glasgow, Edinburgh and Crown Office; other legal experience in private practice and with General Accident Fire and Life Assurance Corporation Ltd. Founder Chairman and former Scottish Branch Representative, Executive Committee, British Association for the Study and Prevention of Child Abuse and Neglect. Recreations: golf; gardening; swimming; holidays in the sun. Address: (h.) Muircroft, Chalton Road, Bridge of Allan, FK9 4EF.

Vanderheijden, Professor Cornelius A.J.M. Professor of Strategic Management, Strathclyde University, since 1991; b. 31.10.32, Rotterdam; m., Haverkamp Henderika. Educ. Technological University, Delft. General and business planning, Shell Group; Head, Internal Consultancy, then Head, Scenario Planning, Shell International; Member, Shell's Planning Management Team. Address: (h.) Flat 7, 166 Ingram Street, Glasgow; T.-041-552 7899.

Vardy, Professor Alan Edward, BSc, PhD, EurIng, CEng, FICE, MASCE, MIAHR, FRSA. Professor of Civil Engineering, Dundee University, since 1979 (Deputy Principal, 1985-88, Vice-Principal, 1988-89); Director, Wolfson Bridge Research Unit, 1980-90; b. 6.11.45, Sheffield; m., Susan Janet; 2 s.; 1 d. Educ. High Storrs Grammar School, Sheffield; Leeds University. Lecturer in Civil Engineering, Leeds University, 1972-75; Royal Society Warren Research Fellow, Cambridge University, 1975-79. Recreations: flying; wind-surfing; skiing; music. Address: (h.) Dunholm, 512 Perth Road, Dundee, DD2 1LW; T.-Dundee 66123.

Varty, Professor E. Kenneth C., BA, PhD, DLitt, FSA, ChevOPA. Stevenson Professor of French, Glasgow University, since 1967; b. 18.8.27, Calke, Derbyshire; m., Hety Benninghoff; 2 d. Educ. Bemrose Grammar School, Derby; Nottingham University. Assistant Lecturer, then Lecturer, Keele University, 1953-61; Lecturer, then Senior Lecturer, Leicester University, 1961-67. Dean, Faculty of Arts, Glasgow, 1979-82; Visiting Lecturer, Warwick University, 1967; Visiting Professor, Jerusalem University, 1977; Visiting Research Fellow, Merton College, Oxford, 1974, and Clare Hall, Cambridge, 1983; Life Member, Clare Hall, 1985. Address: (b.) French Department, Glasgow University, Glasgow; T.-041-339 8855.

Vas, Peter, MSc, PhD, CSc, DSc, MIEEE. Professor in Engineering, Department of Engineering, Aberdeen University, since 1990; b. 1.6.48, Budapest; m., S. Vasne; 2 s. Educ. Technical University of Budapest. United Electrical Machine Works, 1973-77; Newcastle University, 1977-87; Chalmers University of Technology, Lund University of Technology, 1987-90. Publications: 85 papers; three books. Address: (b.) Department of Engineering, University of Aberdeen, Aberdeen; T.-0224 272818.

Vaughan, Barbara, BSc, MA. Chairman, Scottish Community Education Council, since 1988; Marketing Co-ordinator, Angus College of Further Education, since 1987; b. 12.2.40, Thornton Heath; m., Dr. Robin A. Vaughan; 2 s.; 2 d. Educ. St. Anne's College, Sanderstead; Nottingham University; Dundee University. Teacher, Derbyshire, 1962-64; Lecturer in Economics, Dundee Institute of Technology, 1979-83; Councillor, Tayside Region, 1980; Chairman, Further Education Sub-Committee, 1981-82; Chairman, Education Committee, 1982-86; Member, MSC Committee for Scotland, 1983-86; Commissioner, MSC, 1986; Member, Boards, Scottish Examination Board, Scottish Vocational and Education Council, Scottish Council for Educational Technology, Dundee University Court, Dundee College of Education. Recreations: addicted to quilting and gardening; politics. Address: (h.) Taymount House, Caputh, Perthshire, PH1 4JJ; T.-073 871 287.

Vernon, Kenneth Robert, CBE, BSc, FEng, FIEE, FIMechE. Deputy Chairman and Chief Executive, North of Scotland Hydro-Electric Board, 1973-88; b. 15.3.23, Dumfries; m., Pamela Hands; 1 s.; 3 d.; 1 d. deceased. Educ. Dumfries Academy; Glasgow University. BTH Co., Edinburgh Corporation, British Electricity Authority, 1948-55; South of Scotland Electricity Board, 1955-56; North of Scotland Hydro Electric Board: Chief Electrical and Mechanical Engineer, 1964, General Manager, 1966, Board Member, 1970; Director, British Electricity International Ltd., 1976-88; Board Member, Northern Ireland Electricity Service, 1979-85. Recreation: fishing. Address: (h.) 10 Keith Crescent, Edinburgh, EH4 3NH; T.-031-332 4610.

Vernon, Richard Geoffrey, BSc, PhD, FIBiol. Head, Department of Biochemistry and Molecular Biology, Hannah Research Institute; Honorary Lecturer, Glasgow University; b. 19.2.43, Maidstone; m., Mary Christine Cunliffe; 1 s.; 1 d. Educ. Newcastle High School; Birmingham University. Chairman, Scottish Branch, Nutrition Society, 1989-91; Chairman, Belmont Academy School Board; Consultant Editor, Journal of Dairy Research; Past President, Birmingham University Mountaineering Club; first ascent of Mount Mazinaw, first British ascent, Mount Nautilus. Publication: Physiological Strategies in Lactation (Joint Editor). Recreations: walking; ornithology; mountaineering; bridge; photography. Address: (h.) 29 Knoll Park, Ayr; T.-0292 42195.

Vettese, J.W., MA (Hons), DipEd. Headteacher, Liberton High School, since 1985; b. 31.5.37, Brechin; m., M.L. McLean; 1 s.; 1 d. Educ. Bathgate Academy; Edinburgh University. Assistant Teacher, Wishaw High School; Housemaster, Stratford Academy, New Jersey; Principal Teacher of Geography: Hunter High School, East Kilbride, Garrion Academy, Wishaw; Assistant Head Teacher, Upper School, Coltness High School, Wishaw; Rector, Calderhead High School, 1979-85. Address: (h.) 5 Winton Grove, Fairmilehead, Edinburgh, EH10 7AS; T.-031-445 5171.

Vickerman, Professor Keith, BSc, PhD, DSc, FLS, FRSE, FRS. Regius Professor of Zoology, Glasgow University, since 1984; Consultant Expert on Parasitic Diseases, World Health Organisation, since 1973; b. 21.3.33, Huddersfield; m., Moira Dutton; 1 d. Educ. King James Grammar School, Almondbury; University College, London (Fellow, 1985). Wellcome Lecturer in Protozoology, University College, London, 1958-63; Tropical Research Fellow, Royal Society, 1963-68; Glasgow University: Reader in Zoology, 1968-74; Professor of Zoology, 1974-84, Head, Department of Zoology, 1979-85. Publications: The Protozoa (Co-author), 1967; many papers in scientific and medical journals. Recreations: drawing and painting; gardening. Address: (h.) 16 Mirrlees Drive, Glasgow, G12 OSH; T.-041-334 2794.

Vincent, Catherine Lindsey, BA (Hons). Director of Communications, Scottish Sports Council, since 1988; b. 30.7.56, Oxford; m., Jonathan Nicholas Crook; 2 d. Educ. Rosebery Grammar School, Epsom; Newnham College, Cambridge. Research Assistant, Sheffield University, 1978; Assistant Editor, Athlone Press, 1979; Freelance Writer, 1980; Development Officer, Scottish Community Education Council, 1981; Senior Policy Analyst, Fife Regional Council, 1986. Former Chairman, Spiritual Assembly of the Baha'is of Edinburgh; former Director, Baha'i Information Scotland. Publication: Discovering Edinburgh, 1981. Recreations: reading; walking; tennis; badminton; enjoying family. Address: (b.) Scottish Sports Council, Caledonia House, South Gyle, Edinburgh, EH12 9DQ; T.-031-317 7200.

Vines, Professor David Anthony, BA, MA, PhD. Adam Smith Professor of Political Economy, Glasgow University, since 1985; Adjunct Professor of Economics, Australian National University; Board Member, Glasgow Development Agency, since 1991; Director, Analysys Ltd., since 1988; Member, Board, Channel Four Television, since 1987; Economic Consultant, Secretary of State for Scotland, since 1987; Member, Academic Panel, HM Treasury, since 1986; Research Fellow, Centre for Economic Policy Research, since 1983; Member, Board, Scottish Early Music Consort, since 1991; b. 8.5.49, Oxford; 3 s. Educ. Scotch College, Melbourne; Melbourne University. Teaching Fellow, then Research Fellow, Cambridge University, 1976-85. Publications: Macroeconomic Policy; Macroeconomic Interactions Between North and South; Stagflation; Demand Management. Recreations: hill-walking; music. Address: (b.)

Department of Political Economy, Glasgow University, Glasgow, G12 8RT; T.-041-339 8855, Ext. 4659.

W

Waddell, Professor David Alan Gilmour, MA, DPhil, FRHistS. Professor of Modern History, Stirling University, 1968-88 (Professor part-time, since 1988); b. 22.10.27, Edinburgh; m., Barbara Box; 2 s.; 1 d. Educ. Royal High School, Edinburgh; St. Andrews University; Oxford University. Lecturer, University College of the West Indies, Jamaica, 1954-59; Lecturer and Senior Lecturer, Edinburgh University, 1959-68; visiting appointments, Trinidad, Colombia and California. President, Scottish Society of the History of Medicine, 1987-90. Address: (b.) Department of History, Stirling University, Stirling, FK9 4LA; T.-0786 73171, Ext. 7582.

Waddell, Peter, PhD, MS, BS, MIMechE, MRTS, CEng. Senior Lecturer, Mechanical Engineering Division, Strathclyde University, since 1986; b. 19.7.37, Glasgow; m., Anne Goodall; 1 d. Educ. Grove and Morgan Academies, Dundee; Strathclyde University; Birmingham University. Industrial research, 1960-64; Lecturer, Strathclyde University, 1964-86; invented "image derotator", now sold worldwide; invented and patented stretchable imaging mirror. Publications: The Secret Life of John Logie Baird (Co-author), 1986; Vision Warrior (Co-author), 1990. Recreations: travel; gardening; hockey; philately; photography; history. Address: (b.) M615, James Weir Building, Strathclyde University, 75 Montrose Street, Glasgow; T.-041-552 4400, Ext. 2083.

Waddell, Ronald Muir, BA, MSc. Director, Scottish Liberal Democrats, since 1988 (Political Director, Scottish Liberal Party, 1985-88); b. 15.5.54, Glasgow; m., Sandra Grieve. Educ. Bearsden Academy; Strathclyde University; Salford University; Cranfield Institute of Technology. Chair, Scottish Young Liberals, 1981-82; Organisation Vice-Chair, Scottish Liberal Party, 1981-82, 1983-85. Recreations: hill-walking; travel; music. Address: (h.) 2 Gardenside Avenue, Uddingston, Glasgow, G71 7BU.

Wade, Professor Nicholas James, BSc, PhD. Professor of Visual Psychology, Dundee University, since 1991; b. 27.3.42, Retford, Nottinghamshire; m., Christine Whetton; 2 d. Educ. Queen Elizabeth's Grammar School, Mansfield; Edinburgh University; Monash University. Postdoctoral Research Fellow, Max-Planck Institute for Behavioural Physiology, Germany, 1969-70; Lecturer in Psychology, Dundee University, 1970-78, Reader, 1978-91. Publications: The Art and Science of Visual Illusions, 1982; Brewster and Wheatstone on Vision, 1983; Visual Allusions: Pictures of Perception, 1990; Visual Perception: an introduction, 1991. Recreations: golf; cycling. Address: (h.) 36 Norwood, Newport-on-Tay, Fife, DD6 8DW; T.-0382 543136.

Wade, Professor Terence Leslie Brian, BA, PhD, FIL. Professor in Russian Studies, Strathclyde University; b. 19.5.30, Southend-on-Sea; m., Mary Isobel McEwan; 2 d. Educ. Southend-on-Sea High School for Boys; Durham

University. National Service, Intelligence Corps, 1953-55; War Office Language Instructor, 1955-63; Lecturer, Scottish College of Commerce, Glasgow, 1963-64; Lecturer, Senior Lecturer, Reader, Professor, Strathclyde University, from 1964; Chairman, Department of Modern Languages, since 1986. Convener, West of Scotland Association of Teachers of Russian; Editor, Journal of Russian Studies, 1980-86: Chairman, Association of Teachers of Russian, 1986-89; President, Association of Teachers of Russian, 1989-90; Member, Presidium, International Association of Teachers of Russian Language and Literature, 1991-94. Publications: Russian Exercises for Language Laboratories (Co-author); The Russian Preposition "do" and the Concept of Extent; Prepositions in Modern Russian; Russia Today (Co-Editor); The Gender of Soft-Sign Nouns in Russian; A Comprehensive Russian Grammar. Address: 1 Cleveden Crescent, Glasgow, G12 OPD; T.-041-339 3947.

Waigh, Professor Roger David, BPharm, PhD, MRPharmS, CChem, FRSC. Professor of Medicinal Chemistry, Strathclyde University, since 1991; b. 8.8.44, Loughborough; m., Sally Joy Bembridge; 1 s.; 1 d. Educ. Sir George Monoux Grammar School, Walthamstow; Bath University. Lecturer, Strathclyde University, 1970-76; Lecturer, then Senior Lecturer, Manchester University, 1976-91. Recreations: bird-watching; golf; photography. Address: (b.) Department of Pharmaceutical Sciences, Strathclyde University, Glasgow, G1 1XW; T.-041-552 4400.

Waite, James A., MA. Rector, Perth Academy, since 1986; b. 9.10.42, Edinburgh; m., Sandra R. MacKenzie; 1 s.; 2 d. Educ. Royal High School, Edinburgh; Edinburgh University. Teacher of English, George Heriot's School, 1965-70; Principal Teacher of English, Campbeltown Grammar School, 1970-71; Principal Teacher of English, then Assistant Head Teacher, Boroughmuir High School, 1971-83; Depute Head Teacher, James Gillespie's High School, 1983-86. Recreations: theatre; literature; music. Address: (b.) Perth Academy, Murray Place, Perth, PH1 1NJ; T.-0738 23491.

Wake, Joseph Robert, MA, CPA. Secretary, Scotland, Central Bureau for Educational Visits and Exchanges, since 1972; b. 16.5.42, Corbridge; 1 s.; 2 d. Educ. Royal Grammar School, Newcastle upon Tyne; Edinburgh University. Teacher, Kirkcaldy High School, 1966-69, St. Modan's High School, Stirling, 1969-71; Principal Teacher of Modern Languages, Grangemouth High School, 1971-72. Recreations: cricket; philately; Scottish dancing. Address: (b.) 3 Bruntsfield Crescent, Edinburgh, EH10 4HD; T.-031-447 8024.

Wakeford, Air Marshal Sir Richard (Gordon), KCB (1976), LVO (1961), OBE (1958), AFC (1952). Chairman, MacRobert Trustees, since 1982; b. 20.4.22, Torquay; m., Anne Butler; 2 s.; 1 d.; 1 d. (deceased). Educ. Montpelier School, Paignton; Kelly College, Tavistock. Entered RAF, 1941; Coastal Command, 1941-45; Transport Command, 1945-47; Training Command, 1947-52; staff duties, including Director of Ops Staff, Malaya, 1952-58; CO, The Queens' Flight, 1958-61; IDC, 1969; Director, Service Intelligence, 1970-73; Commander, Anzuk Force Singapore, 1974-75; Deputy Chief of Defence Staff (Intelligence), 1975-78; retired Air Marshal, 1978. Director, RAF Benevolent Fund, Scotland, 1978-89; Commissioner, Queen Victoria School, Dunblane, 1980-90; Director, Thistle Foundation; Director, Cromar Nominess; Commander, Order of St. John, 1986. Recreation: fishing. Address: (h.) Earlston House, Forgandenny, Perth, Ph2 9DE; T.-0738 812392.

Walkden, Gordon Mark, BSc, PhD. Member, Kincardine and Deeside District Council, since 1984 (Vice Convener and Chairman, Policy and Resources, since 1988); Senior Lecturer and Research Scientist, Department of Geology, Aberdeen

University, since 1987; Geological Consultant to industry; b. 8.6.44, Edinburgh; m., K. Mary M. Begg; 3 c. Educ. Quintin School, London; Manchester University. Past Chairman, Banchory Community Council; scientific author and local historian. Recreations: building restoration; palaeontology. Address: (h.) Banchory, Kincardineshire.

Walker, (Alexander) Percy, DL, MB, ChB, DObstRCOG, MRCGP. Deputy Lieutenant, Ayr and Arran; b. 2.7.16, Irvine; m., Aileen G. Digby; 1 s.; 3 d. Educ. Shrewsbury School; Glasgow University. Temporary Surgeon Lt., RNVR, 1940-46; General Medical Practitioner, Ayr, 1948-81; Adjudicating Medical Officer, DHSS, 1952-87; Senior Medical Officer, Western Meeting Club, Ayr Racecourse, 1955-87. Recreations: golf; gardening; curling; sailing. Address: (h.) Maryborough Road, Prestwick, Ayrshire, KA9 1SW; T.-0292 77876.

Walker, Alexander William, JP. Honorary Sheriff, since 1970; Chairman, Finance and General Purposes Committee, Tweeddale District Council, since 1977 (Member of Council, since 1974); Chairman, Tweeddale Licensing Board, since 1975; Chairman, Tweeddale Local Sports Council; b. 10.5.24, Peebles; m., Dorothy Margaret. Educ. Kingsland School; Scottish Woollen and Worsted Technical College. D.B. Ballantyne Bros., 1939-70; Air Training Corps, 1941-43, RAF, 1943-46 (Sergeant); former Director, Sonido International Ltd. (formerly Fidelitone International Ltd.); elected, Peebles Town Council, 1960-75; Provost, 1967-70; Burgh Treasurer, 1971-75; held every office, Peebles Town Council; Member, Peeblesshire County Council, 1960-70 (Vice Chairman, Finance Committee); Vice Chairman, Tweeddale District Council, 1974-77; Warden, Neidpath Castle, 1971; former Dean, Guildry Corporation of Peebles; Honorary Member, Peebles Callants Club; Honorary Dean, Guildry Corporation of Peebles, since 1990. Recreations: football in younger days; now enjoys reading political biographies; and, of course, local government, which unfortunately is no longer local or indeed democratic. Address: (h.) Gadeni, 59 High Street, Peebles; T.-Peebles 21011.

Walker, Sir Allan Grierson, QC, MA, LLB, LLD. Sheriff Principal of Lanarkshire, 1963-74; b. 1.5.07, Dumfries; m., Audrey Margaret Glover; 1 s. Educ. Whitgift School; Edinburgh University. Practised at Scottish Bar, 1931-39; Sheriff Substitute, Selkirk and Peebles, 1942-45; Sheriff Substitute, Dumbarton, 1945-50; Sheriff Substitute, Glasgow, 1950-63; Member, Law Reform Committee for Scotland, 1964-70; Chairman, Sheriff Court Rules Council, 1972-74. Publications: The Law of Evidence in Scotland (Co-author); Purves' Scottish Licensing Laws, 7th and 8th editions. Recreations: gardening; walking. Address: (h.) 24 Moffat Road, Dumfries, DG1 1NJ; T.-0387 53583.

Walker, Professor Andrew Charles, BA, MSc, PhD, FInstP, CPhys. OCLI Professor of Modern Optics, Heriot-Watt University, since 1988; b. 24.6.48, Wembley; m., Margaret Elizabeth; 1 s.; 2 d. Educ. Kingsbury County Grammar School; Essex University. Postdoctoral Fellowship, National Research Council of Canada, 1972-74; SRC Research Fellowship, Essex University, 1974-75; Higher/Senior Scientific Officer, UKAEA Culham Laboratory, 1975-83; Lecturer/Reader, Heriot-Watt University, 1983-88. Honorary Secretary, Quantum Electronics Group, Institute of Physics, 1982-85. Recreations: music; skiing; sailing. Address: (b.) Department of Physics, Heriot-Watt University, Riccarton, Edinburgh, EH14 4AS; T.-031-451 3036.

Walker, Professor David Maxwell, CBE, QC, MA, PhD, LLD, Hon. LLD, FBA, FRSE, FRSA. Regius Professor of Law, Glasgow University, 1958-90; Honorary Senior Research Fellow, since 1990; b. 9.4.20, Glasgow; m.,

Margaret Knox, OBE. Educ. High School of Glasgow; Glasgow University; Edinburgh University; London University. HLI and Indian Army, 1939-46; Advocate, 1948; in practice, Scottish Bar, 1948-54; Professor of Jurisprudence, Glasgow University, 1954-58; Barrister (Middle Temple), 1957; QC (Scot), 1958; Dean, Faculty of Law, Glasgow University, 1956-59; Convener, School of Law, 1984-88. Chairman, High School of Glasgow Trust (School Governor). Publications: Law of Damages in Scotland; The Scottish Legal System; Law of Delict in Scotland; Law of Civil Remedies in Scotland; Law of Prescription in Scotland; Law of Contracts in Scotland; Oxford Companion to Law; Principles of Scottish Private Law (four volumes); The Scottish Jurists; Stair's Institutions (Editor); Stair Tercentenary Studies (Editor); A Legal History of Scotland, Vols. I and II. Recreations: book collecting; Scottish history; motoring. Address: (b.) Department of Private Law, Glasgow University, Glasgow, G12 8QQ; T.-041-339 8855, Ext. 4556.

Walker, David Morrison, DA, FSA, FSA Scot, HFRIAS, Hon. LLD (Dundee). Chief Inspector of Historic Buildings, Scottish Office Environment Department, since 1988; b. 31.1.33, Dundee; m., Averil Mary Stewart McIlwraith; 1 s. Educ. Morgan Academy, Dundee; Dundee College of Art. Voluntary work for National Buildings Record, Edinburgh, 1952-56; National Service, Royal Engineers, 1956-58; Glasgow Education Authority, 1958-59; Dundee Education Authority, 1959-61; Historic Buildings Branch, Scottish Office: Senior Investigator of Historic Buildings, 1961-76, Principal Investigator of Historic Buildings, 1976-78; Principal Inspector of Historic Buildings, 1978-88. Alice Davis Hitchcock Medallion, 1970. Publications: Dundee Nineteenth Century Mansions, 1958; Architecture of Glasgow (Co-author), 1968 (revised and enlarged edition, 1987); Buildings of Scotland: Edinburgh (Co-author), 1984; Dundee: An Illustrated Introduction (Co-author), 1984; St. Andrew's House: an Edinburgh Controversy 1912-1939, 1989; Central Glasgow: an illustrated architectural guide (Co-author), 1989. Address: (b.) 20 Brandon Street, Edinburgh, EH3 5RA; T.-031-244 2971.

Walker, Drew, BSc, MB, ChB, MSc, MFCM. Director of Health Planning and Public Health, Chief Administrative Medical Officer, Executive Board Member, Ayrshire and Arran Health Board, since 1991; b. 30.8.54, Bridge of Allan. Educ. Perth Academy; Edinburgh University. House Officer/SHO, 1978-80; District Medical Officer, Zimbabwe, 1980-82; Registrar/Senior Registrar in public health, 1983-87; Consultant in public health, 1987-91. National Vice President, Medical Practitioners Union, 1988-90. Recreations: football; climbing; skiing; reading Viz. Address: (h.) Schaw House, by Stair, Ayrshire.

Walker, Ernest John Munro, OBE. Chairman, Health Education Board for Scotland; b. 20.7.28, Glasgow; m., Anne; 1 s.; 2 d. Educ. Queen's Park Secondary School. Army (Royal Horse Artillery), 1946-48; Assistant Secretary, industrial textile company, 1948-58; Assistant Secretary, Scottish Football Association, 1958-77, Secretary, 1977-90. Director, Euro-Sportring; Director, Scotball Travel and Leisure Ltd.; Member: FIFA Board of Appeal, FIFA World Cup 1994 Inspection Group, UEFA Organizing Committee of the Club Competitions; Chairman, UEFA Stadia Committee; Chairman, Scottish Stadia Committee; Vice-President, Newspaper Press Fund. Recreations: golf (past Captain, Haggs Castle GC); fishing; music; travel. Address (b.) Woodburn House, Canaan Lane, Edinburgh, EH10 4SG; T.-031-447 8044.

Walker, Ian. Member, Gordon District Council, since 1984; Head Teacher, Westhill Primary School, since 1987; Chairman, Gordon Sports Council; Member: Gordon District Tourist Board, Gordon Forum for the Arts; b. 1.6.40,

Inverurie; m., Mildred Agnes Rose; 1 s.; 1 d. Educ. Daviot School; Inverurie Academy; Aberdeen College of Education. Assistant Teacher, Insch School, 1963-67; Head Teacher: Finzean School, 1967-69, Kinellar School, 1969-73; Member, Working Party on Mathematics in the Primary School, Grampian Regional Council; Elder, Church of Scotland; Chairman: Westhill and District Swimming Pool Association, Westhill Swimming Pool Trust, Lawsondale Playing Field Trust. Recreations: listening to all kinds of music, especially jazz and blues; indoor bowling; walking; watching cricket (Blue, Aberdeen College of Education); reading; theatre; films; golf. Address: (h.) 11A Arnhall Drive, Westhill, Skene, Aberdeenshire, AB32 6TZ; T.-0224 741783.

Walker, Leslie Gresson, MA, PhD, DipClinPsychol, CPsychol, AFBPsS. Senior Lecturer, Department of Mental Health, Aberdeen University, since 1989; b. 17.5.49, Glasgow; m., Mary Birnie; 2 s. Educ. Banff Academy; Aberdeen University. Clinical Psychologist, Grampian Health Board, 1974-76; Lecturer, Aberdeen University, 1976-89; elected Member, National Committee of Scientists in Professions Allied to Medicine (Clinical Psychology Sub-Committee), Scottish Home and Health Department, 1979-85; External Assessor, Children's Panel Advisory Committee, Grampian Regional Council, 1982-90; Council Member, British Society of Experimental and Clinical Hypnosis, since 1991; Consultant Editor, Contemporary Hypnosis, since 1991; Elder, Church of Scotland. Publications: three books; numerous scientific papers. Address: (b.) Department of Mental Health, Medical School, Foresterhill, Aberdeen, AB9 2ZD; T.-0224 681818, Ext. 53881.

Walker, Margaret, OBE, MA. Vice-President, Scottish Conservative & Unionist Association, 1987-89; Chairman, Scottish Committee, National Social Affairs Forum, since 1985; b. 4.5.26, Paisley; m., David Maxwell Walker (qv). Educ. Paisley Grammar School; Glasgow University. Manuscript Department, National Library of Scotland, 1948-54; Chairman, Hillhead Conservative & Unionist Association, 1982-86; West of Scotland Conservative Women's Area Committee: Vice-Chairman, 1980-81, Chairman, 1981-83; West of Scotland Conservative Area Council: Vice-Chairman, 1983-85, Chairman, 1985-87. Recreations: music; ballet; conservation; cookery. Address: (h.) 1 Beaumont Gate, Glasgow, G12 9EE; T.-041-339 2802.

Walker, Michael Giles Neish, CBE, MA (Cantab). Chairman, Sidlaw Group, since 1988 (Chief Executive, 1976-88); b. 28.8.33, Fife; m., Margaret R. Hills; 2 s.; 1 d. Educ. Shrewsbury School; St. John's College, Cambridge. National Service, Royal Dragoons, 1952-54 (2nd Lt.); TA, Fife and Forfar Yeomanry, 1954-72 (Major); joined Jute Industries Ltd., 1958 (subsequently name changed to Sidlaw Group); Director, Dundee and London Investment Trust plc, since 1982; Director, Scottish Hydro-Electric plc, since 1982; Director, First Charlotte Assets Trust PLC, since 1990. Address: (b.) Sidlaw Group plc, Nethergate Centre, Dundee, DD1 4BR; T.-0382 23161.

Walker, Vaughan, BSc, CText, ATI. Director, Scottish Textile & Technical Centre, Faculty of Textiles, Heriot Watt University, since 1986; b. 29.11.44, Sutton-in-Craven; m., Pauline Jeannie Burne. Educ. Keighley School; Bradford University. Technical Manager, Brocklehurst Whiston Ltd., 1967; Lecturer, Kidderminster College, 1969; Lecturer, then Senior Lecturer, Scottish Institute of Textiles, Galashiels, 1970-86. Secretary, Textile Institute (Scotland). Recreations: opera; gardening; industrial archaeology. Address: (b.) Scottish Textile and Technical Centre, Netherdale, Galashiels; T.-0896 2196.

Walker, William Buchanan Cowan, MA, LLB. Solicitor; Secretary, Royal Scottish Forestry Society; Farmer and

Landowner; b. 27.6.27, Callander; m., Rita Bate; 2 s.; 1 d. Educ. Dollar Academy; Edinburgh Academy; Edinburgh University. Assistant, Robert Stewart & Scott, SSC, Edinburgh; Partner, Henderson and Jackson, WS, Edinburgh; Consultant, Lindsays, WS, Edinburgh; Director, Glenbervie Estate Co. Ltd.; Director, Garvald School Ltd. Recreations: repairing old buildings; travelling; people watching. Address: (h.) Halmyre Deans, Romanno Bridge, West Linton, Peeblesshire.

Walker, William Connoll, FIPM, FBIM, FRSA. MP (Conservative), Tayside North, since 1979; b. Dundee; m., Mavis Evelyn; 3 d. Educ. Logie School. Message boy; RAF (commissioned); Training and Education Officer; Director of Personnel; Managing Director. Recreations: gliding; caravanning. Address: (h.) Candletrees, Golf Course Road, Rosemount, Blairgowrie, Perthshire; T.-0250 2660.

Walker, Professor William Farquhar, DSc, ChM, FRCS (Edin and Eng), FRSE. Consultant General Surgeon, since 1965; Emeritus Professor of Vascular Surgery, Surgery, Dundee University; b. 26.5.25, Aberdeen; m., Bettie Stanley; 2 s.; 1 d. Educ. Forfar Academy; St. Andrews University. RAF, 1949-51; Senior Lecturer in Surgery (Consultant), Dundee Royal Infirmary, 1956-75. President, Association of Surgeons of Great Britain and Ireland, 1984; President, Vascular Society of Great Britain and Ireland, 1989; Chairman, Distinction Awards Committee Scotland, 1990. Recreations: golf; fishing; gardening. Address: (h.) 438 Blackness Road, Dundee; T.-0382 68179.

Walker-Naddell, Alexander, KStJ, ERD, QHS, JP, DL, FRCS, FRCPS, FSA Scot, FRSA. Consultant Orthopaedic and Neuro Surgeon; Hon. Colonel, 304 General Hospital "City of Glasgow" TAVR; b. 25.12.10, Glasgow; m., Iris Elaine Harris; 1 s.; 2 d. Educ. Bellahouston Academy; Glasgow University and St. Mungo College. Qualified in medicine, 1938; War Service, 1939-45; appointed Surgeon, Glasgow Royal Infirmary, 1946; volunteered service to Army; appointed Surgeon in command, S Division, 4 General Hospital, 1952-62; JP, City of Glasgow, 1962; Deputy Lieutenant, City of Glasgow, since 1963; Director, Humane Society, 20 years; District Court Judge, City of Glasgow, to 1981; Fellow, Royal Society of Medicine. Publications: The Slipped Disc and Aching Back of Man, 1985; Fight Old Age, 1987; Migraine – Control and Cure; papers on the medical aspects of atomic warfare, and migraine. Recreations: golf; water polo. Address: 22 Sandyford Place, Charing Cross, Glasgow, G3 7NG; T.-041-221 7571.

Walkingshaw, Francis, NP. Solicitor; Procurator Fiscal, District of Wigtown, since 1983; b. 9.12.42, Edinburgh; m., Penelope Marion Theodosia Brooks McKissock; 2 s. Educ. George Watson's College, Edinburgh. Private practice; joined Procurator Fiscal service, 1975. Dean, Faculty of Wigtown District Solicitors, 1985-87. Recreations: shooting; fishing; food and wine. Address: (b.) Sheriff Court House, Lewis Street, Stranraer; T.-0776 4321.

Wallace, Alan John, FRICS. Commercial Manager, East Kilbride Development Corporation, since 1990; b. 9.7.51, Motherwell; m., Mary; 1 s.; 1 d. Educ. Wishaw High School. Valuation Surveyor, Lanark County Council, 1969-75; Estates Surveyor, Motherwell District Council, 1975-78; Depute Commercial Director, Livingston Development Corporation, 1978-90. Recreation: golf. Address: (b.) East Kilbride Development Corporation, Atholl House, East Kilbride, G74 1LU; T.-03552 41111.

Wallace, Archibald Duncan, MB, ChB. Medical Practitioner, Campbeltown, since 1950; Hon. Sheriff of North Strathclyde at Campbeltown, since 1980; b. 4.1.26, Glasgow; m., Rona B. MacLennan; 1 s.; 2 d. Educ. High School of

Glasgow; Glasgow University. Sector Medical Officer, Argyll and Clyde Health Board, until 1988; Civilian MO to RAF Machrihanish, until 1988. Chairman, Campbeltown Branch, RNLI; Past President, Campbeltown Rotary Club; Past Captain, Machrihanish Golf Club. Recreations: golf; gardening. Address: (h.) Lilybank House, Low Askomil, Campbeltown; T.-0586 52658.

Wallace, Professor David Alexander Ross, BSc, PhD, FRSA, FRSE. Professor of Mathematics, Strathclyde University, since 1986 (Professor, Stirling University, 1973-86); b. 24.11.33, Cupar. Educ. Stranraer High School; St. Andrews University; Manchester University. Instructor: Princeton University, 1958-59, Harvard University, 1959-60; Research Fellow, then Lecturer, Glasgow University, 1960-65; Senior Lecturer, Aberdeen University, 1965-73. Recreations: culture; tennis; swimming; skiing; badminton. Address: (b.) Department of Mathematics, Strathclyde University, Livingstone Tower, 26 Richmond Street, Glasgow, G1 1XH; T.-041-552 4400.

Wallace, Professor David James, BSc, PhD, FRSE, FRS. Tait Professor of Mathematical Physics, Edinburgh University, since 1979; Director, Edinburgh Parallel Computing Centre; Chairman, Science Board and Member, Council, SERC, since 1990; b. 7.10.45, Hawick; m., Elizabeth Anne Yeats; 1 d. Educ. Hawick High School; Edinburgh University. Harkness Fellow, Princeton University, 1970-72; Lecturer in Physics, 1971-78, Reader, 1978-79, Southampton University; Maxwell Medal, Institute of Physics, 1980. Recreations: running; eating at La Potiniere. Address: (b.) Physics Department, The University, Mayfield Road, Edinburgh, EH9 3JZ; T.-031-650 5250.

Wallace, George, DPA, MInstAM (Dip), FMS, FIPM. Director of Personnel, Perth and Kinross District Council, since 1975; Personnel Officer, Perth and Kinross Recreational Facilities Ltd., since 1987; Personnel Adviser, Perthshire Tourist Board, since 1983; b. 5.7.34, Glasgow; m., Elizabeth Hall Graham; 1 s.; 1 d. Educ. Albert Senior Secondary School; Glasgow University. National Service, RAF, 1952-54; Glasgow Corporation, 1954-64; Renfrew County Council, 1964-65; Western Regional Hospital Board, 1965-68; Lanark County Council, 1968-71; LAMSAC, 1971-73; Perth and Kinross Joint County Council, 1973-75. Panel Chairman, British Standards Institution; Elder, Church of Scotland. Recreation: amateur radio. Address: (b.) 2 High Street, Perth, PH1 5PH; T.-0738 39911.

Wallace of Campsie, Baron (George Wallace), JP, DL. Life President, Wallace, Cameron (Holdings) Ltd., since 1981; b. 13.2.15; m. Educ. Queen's Park School, Glasgow; Glasgow University. Solicitor, since 1950; Honorary Sheriff, Hamilton, since 1971; Chairman, East Kilbride and Stonehouse Development Corporation, 1969-75; Member, South of Scotland Electricity Board, 1966-68; Member, Board, Scottish Development Agency, 1975-78; President, Glasgow Chamber of Commerce, 1974-76; Chairman, Scottish Executive Committee, British Heart Foundation, 1973-76; Patron, Scottish Retirement Council, since 1975. Address: (h.) 14 Fernleigh Road, Newlands, Glasgow, G43 2UE.

Wallace, James Fleming, QC, MA, LLB. Counsel (Draftsman), Scottish Law Commission, since 1979; b. 19.3.31, Edinburgh; m., Valerie Mary Lawrence (deceased); 2 d.; 2, Linda Ann Lilleker. Educ. Edinburgh Academy; Edinburgh University. National Service, 1954-56 (2nd Lt., Royal Artillery); TA (Lt., Royal Artillery), 1956-60; practised at Scottish Bar, 1957-60; Parliamentary Draftsman and Legal Secretary to Lord Advocate, 1960-79. Publications: The Businessman's Lawyer (Scottish Supplement); Stair Memorial Encyclopaedia (Contributor). Recreations: hill-walking; choral singing; golf; badminton. Address: (h.) 24 Corrennie Gardens, Edinburgh, EH10 6DB; T.-031-447 1224.

Wallace, James Robert, MA (Cantab), LLB (Edinburgh). MP (Lib. Dem., formerly Liberal), Orkney and Shetland, since 1983; Liberal Parliamentary Spokesman on Energy and Fisheries, 1983-85, on Defence and Fisheries, 1985-88; Chief Whip, Liberal Party, 1987-88; first Chief Whip, Social and Liberal Democrats, since 1988; Lib. Dem. Spokesman on Employment and Fisheries, since 1988; Advocate, since 1979; b. 25.8.54, Annan; m., Rosemary Janet Fraser; 2 d. Educ. Annan Academy; Downing College, Cambridge; Edinburgh University. Called to Scottish Bar, 1979; contested Dumfries, 1979, and South of Scotland Euro Constituency, 1979; Member, Scottish Liberal Party Executive, 1976-85 (Vice-Chairman, Policy, 1982-85); Honorary President, Scottish Young Liberals, 1984-85. Publication: New Deal for Rural Scotland (Co-Editor), 1983. Recreations: golf; reading; travelling (especially between London and the Northern Isles). Address. (h.) Northwood House, Tankerness, Orkney, KW17 2QS; T.-0856 86 383.

Wallace, John Anderson. Chief Executive, Tayside Regional Council, 1982-90; b. 10.7.29, Perth; m., Mary; 1 s.; 1 d. Educ. Perth Academy; Edinburgh University. Solicitor, private practice, 1951-54; Solicitor: Dundee Corporation, 1954-60, Cumbernauld Development Corporation, 1960-66; Depute Town Clerk, Dundee Corporation, 1966-75; Depute Chief Executive, Tayside, 1975-82. Recreations: bowls; wine-making; music. Address: (h.) Corrymeela, 17 Fintry Place, Broughty Ferry, Dundee, DD5 3BG; T.-Dundee 78833.

Wallace, John David, MA, DipEd, FSA Scot. International Arbiter and Secretary, Arbiters Commission, Federation Internationale des Echecs; President, Scottish Junior Chess Association, 1986-89; Council Member, Scottish Chess Association; b. 21.11.21, Bulford; m., Jenefer M.H. Bell (deceased); 1 s.; 1 d. Educ. Tonbridge School; St. Andrews University. Army Service, 1940-46 (Captain, Royal Artillery); teaching appointments in Orkney and Fife, 1954-73; Assistant Rector, Madras College, St. Andrews, 1971-73; founding Headmaster, Abbotsgrange Middle School, Grangemouth, 1974-84. Recreations: bridge; chess; curling; hill-walking. Address: (h.) Kirkheugh Cottage, The Shorehead, St. Andrews, Fife, KY16 9RG.

Wallace, Thomas, BSc. President, Scottish Secondary Teachers' Association, 1987-89; b. 12.11.41, Glasgow; m., Kathleen May Macqueen; 1 d. Educ. Allan Glen's School; Glasgow University; Jordanhill College. Teacher, 1966; Principal Teacher (Physics), Riverside Secondary, 1971, Albert Secondary, 1984, Springburn Academy, 1988. Elected Vice-President, SSTA, 1974; Vice-President, 1985; elected to General Teaching Council for Scotland, 1979 (re-elected 1983 and 1987); Convener, GTC Supply Committee, 1987; appointed by Secretary of State to Scottish Committee for Staff Development in Education, 1987. Recreation: bagpipes. Address: (h.) 40 Rowallan Gardens, Glasgow, G11 7LJ; T.-041-334 2436.

Wallace, Professor William Villiers, MA, FRHistS. Director, Institute of Soviet and East European Studies, Glasgow University, since 1979; Dean, Faculty of Social Sciences, Glasgow University, since 1989; b. 15.12.26, Glasgow; m., Gulli Fyfe; 2 s.; 1 d. Educ. Hutchesons' Boys' Grammar School; Glasgow University; London University. RNVR, 1944-47; appointments in History, Pittsburgh University, London University, Aberdeen University, Durham University, 1953-67; Professor of History, New University of Ulster, 1967-79. Address: (b.) Institute of Soviet and East European Studies, Glasgow University, 29 Bute Gardens, Glasgow, G12 8RS; T.-041-330 4579.

Walls, Professor Andrew Finlay, OBE, MA, BLitt, FSA Scot. Director, Centre for the Study of Christianity in the Non-Western World, since 1982; b. 21.4.28; m., Doreen Mary Harden; 1 s.; 1 d. Librarian, Tyndale House, Cambridge, 1952-57; Lecturer in Theology, Fourah Bay College, Sierra Leone, 1957-62; Head, Department of Religion, Nigeria University, 1962-65; Aberdeen University: Lecturer in Church History, 1966-69, Senior Lecturer, 1969, first Head, Department of Religious Studies, and Riddoch Lecturer in Comparative Religion, 1970, Reader, 1975, Professor of Religious Studies, 1979-85, Emeritus Professor, 1985; Honorary Professor, Edinburgh University, since 1987; Visiting Professor of World Christianity, Yale University, 1988; Co-opted Member, Aberdeen Education Committee, 1971-74; Aberdeen City Councillor, 1974-80; Convener, Arts and Recreation, COSLA, 1978-80; Chairman, Council for Museums and Galleries in Scotland, 1978-81; Vice-Chairman, Committee of Area Museums Councils, 1980-81; Member, Williams Committee on the future of the national museums, 1979-82; Trustee, National Museum of Antiquities of Scotland, 1982-85; Member, Museums Advisory Board for Scotland, 1984-85; Trustee, National Museums of Scotland, 1985-87; Methodist Preacher; Past Chairman, Disablement Income Group, Scotland; President, British Association for the History of Religions, 1977-80; Secretary, Scottish Institute of Missionary Studies; Editor, Journal of Religion in Africa, 1967-86; Committee Member, European Ethnological Research Centre; Henry Martyn Lectures, Cambridge University, 1988; Margaret Harris Lectures, Dundee University, 1989. Address: (b.) Centre for the Study of Christianity in the Non-Western World, Edinburgh University, New College, Mound Place, Edinburgh, EH1 2LX; T.-031-225 8400.

Walsh, David Brian, MB, ChB, MRCPath. Consultant in Clinical Chemistry, Tayside Health Board, since 1973; Honorary Senior Lecturer in Biochemical Medicine, Dundee University, since 1973; Honorary Senior Lecturer in Biochemistry, St. Andrews University; b. 3.7.41, Douglas, Isle of Man; m., Maureen; 2 d. Educ. William Hulme's Grammar School, Manchester; Victoria University of Manchester. House Officer posts, St. Woolos Hospital, Newport; Senior House Officer posts in Clinical Pathology, London Hospital and Llandough Hospital, Cardiff; Lecturer in Pathology, Manchester University; Senior Registrar in Chemical Pathology, United Manchester Hospitals. Recreations: photography; family. Address: (b.) Department of Biochemical Medicine, Ninewells Hospital, Dundee, DD2 9SY.

Walsh, Professor Patrick Gerard, MA, PhD, FRSE. Professor of Humanity, Glasgow University, since 1972; b. 16.8.23, Accrington; m., Eileen Benson Quin; 4 s.; 1 d. Educ. Preston Catholic College; Liverpool University. Lecturer in Ancient Classics, University College, Dublin, 1952-59; Lecturer, Reader, Professor, Department of Humanity, Edinburgh University, 1959-72. Recreations: tennis; travel. Address: (h.) 17 Broom Road, Glasgow, G43 2TP; T.-041-637 4977.

Walsh, Sadie Delores, MB, ChB, MRCPEdin, FRCPEdin. Consultant Physician, Royal Victoria Hospital and Corstorphine Hospital, Edinburgh, since 1980; b. 14.10.32, Kingston, Jamaica; m., John Nuttall; 2 d. Educ. Edinburgh University. House Physician, Roodland General Hospital; House Surgeon, Dumfries and Galloway Royal Infirmary; House Physician, Royal Hospital for Sick Children, Edinburgh; Registrar posts, Respiratory Unit, City Hospital, Edinburgh; general medicine, Western General Hospital, Edinburgh; Registrar, Haematology, Edinburgh Royal Infirmary; Registrar, Geriatric Medicine, Royal Victoria Hospital, Edinburgh; Consultant Physician, Geriatric Medicine, Fife Health Board, 1975-80. Recreations: hill-walking; skiing; swimming. Address: (h.) 8 S.W. Northumberland Street Lane, Edinburgh, EH3 6JD; T.-031-556 7632.

Walters, Dafydd B., LLB (Hons), LLM (Lond), ACIArb. Senior Lecturer, Faculty of Law, Edinburgh University; Vice-Chairman, Scottish Council for Arbitration; b. 16.9.35, Bexley, Kent; m. Educ. Erith Grammar School; King's College, London. National Service (Army, commissioned), 1954-56; Economics and Statistical Research Division, Unilever, 1956-57; theological and legal training, 1957-63; public sector law teaching, 1963-67; joined Faculty of Law, Edinburgh University, 1967. Assessor in Comparative Law, Faculty of Advocates; attached to Legal Service, Commission of the European Communities; Visiting Professor, Universite Libre de Bruxelles, and Research Officer, Council of the European Bars, 1991-92. Address: (b.) Faculty of Law, Old College, Edinburgh University, Edinburgh, EH8 9YL; T.-031-650 2050.

Walters, Professor David Gareth, BA, PhD. Professor of Hispanic Studies, Glasgow University, since 1991; b. 1.1.48, Neath; m., Christine Ellen Knott; 1 s.; 1 d. Educ. Rhondda County Grammar School for Boys; University College, Cardiff. Temporary Lecturer in Spanish, Leeds University, 1972-73; Lecturer in Hispanic Studies, then Senior Lecturer, Glasgow University, 1973-91. Publications: books on Francisco de Quevedo and Francisco de Aldana; numerous articles on Spanish poetry. Recreations: music; playing the piano; poetry; travel; antiques. Address: (h.) 32 Golf View, Bearsden, Glasgow, G61 4HJ; T.-041-942 4948.

Walton, Professor Ewart Kendall, BSc, PhD, FRSE. Professor of Geology, St. Andrews University, 1968-88, Emeritus Professor, since 1988; b. 28.11.24, Ashington, Northumberland; m., 1, Margaret; 1 s.; 1 d.: 2, Susan Clare. Educ. Bedlington Secondary School, Northumberland; King's College, Durham. Assistant, Glasgow University, 1951-54; Lecturer, then Reader, Edinburgh University, 1954-68; Master, United College, St. Andrews, 1972-76. President, Association of Teachers of Geology, 1978-80; Member, Scottish Advisory Committee, NCC, 1982-85; Member, Geology Panel, Scottish Examination Board, 1982-85. Address: (b.) Department of Geography and Geology, Division of Geology, Purdie Building, St. Andrews, Fife, KY16 9ST; T.-0334 76161.

Walton, Professor Henry John, MD, PhD, FRCPE, FRCPsych, DPM, Hon.MD Uppsala, New University of Lisbon. Physician; Professor of International Medical Education, Edinburgh, since 1986; b. 15.2.24, South Africa; m., Sula Wolff. Educ. University of Cape Town; London University; Columbia University, NY; Edinburgh University. Registrar in Neurology and Psychiatry, University of Cape Town, 1946-54; Head, Department of Psychiatry, 1957-60; Senior Registrar, Maudsley Hospital, London, 1955-57; Senior Lecturer in Psychiatry, then Professor of Psychiatry, Edinburgh University, 1962-85; Editor, Medical Education, since 1976; President, Association for Medical Education in Europe, 1972-86, Hon. Life President, since 1986; President, World Federation for Medical Education, since 1983; frequent Consultant to WHO. Publications: as Editor: Small Group Psychotherapy, 1974; Dictionary of Psychiatry, 1985; as Co-Editor: Newer Developments in Assessing Clinical Competence, 1986; as Co-Author: Alcoholism, 1988; Report of the World Conference on Medical Education, 1988. Recreations: literature; visual arts, particularly Western painting and Chinese and Japanese art. Address: Edinburgh University, Teviot Place, Edinburgh, EH8 9AG; T.-031-226 3125.

Walton, John Christopher, BSc, PhD, DSc. Reader in Chemistry, St. Andrews University, since 1986; b. 4.12.41,

St. Albans; m., Jane Lehman; 1 s.; 1 d. Educ. Watford Grammar School for Boys; Sheffield University. Assistant Lecturer: Queen's College, St. Andrews, 1966-67, Dundee University, 1967-69; Lecturer in Chemistry, United College, St. Andrews, 1969-80; Senior Lecturer, 1980-86. Director, Good Health Association (Scotland) Ltd.; Elder, Seventh-day Adventist Church. Recreations: music; philosophy. Address: (b.) Department of Chemistry, St. Andrews University, St. Andrews, Fife, KY16 9ST; T.-0334 76161.

Walton, Kenneth D., BMus, GMusRNCM, ARCO. Director – Public Relations, Greater Glasgow Tourist Board and Convention Bureau, since 1989; b. 20.2.58, Paisley; m., Janis H. Goodfellow; 2 d. Educ. Paisley Grammar School; Glasgow University; Royal Northern College of Music, Manchester. Tutor in Music, Glasgow University, 1982-83; Lecturer in Academic Studies, Royal Scottish Academy of Music and Drama, 1985-86, and 1988-89; on music staff, Hutchesons' Grammar School, 1987-88; Manager, Scottish Music Information Centre, 1988-89. Member, BBC Music Advisory Committee (Scotland); President, Glasgow Society of Organists, 1985-86; Secretary and Treasurer, Scottish Musicians Benevolent Fund, 1988-89; Member, Board of Directors, Chorus International Festival, since 1989; Music Critic, Daily Telegraph, 1983-91. Recreations: gardening; golf. Address: (h.) 38 Lancaster Avenue, Beith, Ayrshire, KA15 1AR; T.-Beith 3511.

Wannop, Professor Urlan Alistair, MA, MCD, MRTPI. Professor of Urban and Regional Planning, Strathclyde University, since 1981; b. 16.4.31, Newtown St. Boswells; 1 s.; 1 d. Educ. Aberdeen Grammar School; Edinburgh University; Liverpool University. Appointments in public and private practice, 1956-68; Team Leader, Coventry-Solihull-Warwickshire Sub-Regional Planning Study, 1968-71; Director, West Central Scotland Plan, 1972-74; Senior Deputy Director of Planning, Strathclyde Regional Council, 1975-81; Vice-Chairman, Planning Committee, Social Science Research Council, 1978-82; Member, Parliamentary Boundary Commission for Scotland, since 1983. Address: (h.) 43 Lomond Street, Helensburgh, G84 7ES; T.-0436 74622.

Ward, Brian James, BSc (Hons). Production Director, Shell UK Exploration and Production, since 1990; b. 20.11.46, Chatham; m., Shirley Joan Ward Martin; 2 s. Educ. University of East Anglia. Joined Shell as a petroleum engineer, 1968; various appointments, 1969-90, in the Far East, Africa, Europe and South America. Burgess of the Guild, Aberdeen. Recreations: golf; rugby; hill-walking; computers. Address: (b.) 1 Altens Farm Road, Nigg, Aberdeen, AB9 2HY; T.-0224 882410.

Ward, David Romen, MA, CertEd. Rector, Hutchesons' Grammar School, since 1987; b. 21.12.35, Newcastle upon Tyne; m., Stella Barbara Anderson; 1 s.; 2 d. Educ. St. Mary's, Melrose; Sedbergh School; Emmanuel College, Cambridge. Assistant Master: Winchester College, Wellington College; Senior History Master, City of London School; Deputy Headmaster, Portsmouth Grammar School; Head Master, Hulme Grammar School. Member, Admiralty Interview Board. Publications: Fall of Metternich and the Revolution of 1848; British Foreign Policy 1815-1865; Explorations. Address: (h.) 192 Nithsdale Road, Glasgow, G41 5EU; (b.) Hutchesons' Grammar School, Beaton Road, Glasgow, G41 4NW; T.-041-423 2933.

Ward, Dorothy May Blair, MB, ChB. Principal in general practice, Glasgow, since 1966; Hospital Practitioner, Geriatric Medicine, Cowglen Hospital, Glasgow, since 1974; b. 27.8.28, York; m., Thomas B. Begg; 1 s.; 2 d. Educ. Paisley Grammar School; Glasgow University. Member and Past Chairman, Joint Committee, Postgraduate Training for General Practice; Member and Past Chairman, Glasgow Local Medical Committee; Member, Scottish Council, BMA; Member, General Medical Services Committee, BMA; Member, General Medical Council; President, Medical Women's International Association. Address: (h.) 3 Montgomery Drive, Giffnock, Glasgow, G46 6PY.

Ward, Professor John Macqueen, CA, Companion, IEE. Resident Director, Scotland and North of England, IBM United Kingdom Ltd., since 1990; Professor, Heriot Watt University; b. 1.8.40, Edinburgh; m., Barbara Macintosh; 1 s.; 3 d. Educ. Edinburgh Academy; Fettes College. Joined IBM UK Ltd. at Greenock plant, 1966; worked in France and UK; appointed European Director of Information Systems, 1975, and Havant Site Director, 1981. Vice-Chairman, Scottish CBI; Director, IIP Scotland; Director, Greater Easterhouse Development Corporation; Director, Edinburgh Venture and Enterprise Trust; Director, Edinburgh Vision; Member, Scottish CBI Council; Member, SBC Executive Council; Member, Scottish Committee, Association of Business Sponsorship of the Arts; Member, Education Board, Institute of Chartered Accountants. Address: (b.) 21 St. Andrew Square, Edinburgh, EH2 1AY; T.-031-556 9292.

Ward, Maxwell Colin Bernard, MA. Partner, Baillie Gifford & Co., since 1975; Director, Scottish Equitable Life Assurance Society, since 1988; b. 22.8.49, Sherborne; m., Sarah Marsham; 2 s.; 1 d. Educ. Harrow; St. Catharine's, Cambridge. Trainee, Baillie Gifford & Co., 1971-75. Board Member, Scottish Council for Spastics. Recreations: tennis; squash; bridge; country pursuits. Address: (h.) The Old Manse, Crichton, Pathhead, Midlothian, EH27 5XA; T.-0875 320702.

Ward, Rev. Michael John, BSc (Hons), BD (Hons). Parish Minister, St. Madoes and Kinfauns Church, since 1983; b. 23.8.56, Barrow-in-Furness; m., Jean Gallan. Educ. Galashiels Academy; Edinburgh University. Assistant Minister, Auchtertool with Burntisland, 1982-83. Church Representative, Scottish Churches' Action for World Development. Recreations: contemporary art; theatre and cinema; philately; sports. Address: St. Madoes Manse, Glencarse, Perth, PH2 7NF; T.-0738 86 387.

Wardell, Gareth. Producer-Director, Jam Jar Films, since 1985; Founder, Arts Education Trust; b. 26.10.46, Edinburgh. Educ. Royal Scottish Academy of Music and Drama; Glasgow University; Jordanhill College of Education. Trainee Actor and Director, various repertory companies; Teacher of Speech and Drama, John Street Secondary School, Glasgow; Lecturer in Speech and Drama, Moray House College of Education, Edinburgh; Founder/Artistic Director, Scottish Youth Theatre/Young Playwrights Festival; Head of Youth Programmes, BBC TV and Radio (N.I.). Recreations: friends; landscape gardening. Address: c/o Jam Jar Films, Balerno, Edinburgh, EH14 7DH; T.-031-449 7227.

Wardlaw, Professor Alastair Connell, MSc, PhD, DSc, FRSE. Professor of Microbiology, Glasgow University, since 1970; b. 20.1.30, Port of Spain; m., Jacqueline Shirley Jones; 1 s.; 2 d. Educ. Manchester Grammar School; Manchester University. Research Fellow, Western Reserve University, Cleveland, Ohio, 1953-55; Sir Alexander Fleming Research Fellow, St. Mary's Hospital, London, 1955-58; Research Fellow and Research Member, Connaught Laboratories, Toronto, 1958-66; Professor of Microbiology, Toronto University, 1966-70. Member, Marshall Aid Commemoration Commssion. Publications: Sourcebook of Experiments for the Teaching of Microbiology; Practical Statistics for Experimental Biologists; Pathogenesis and Immunity in Pertussis. Recreations: ceramics; gardening; cycle-camping. Address: (h.) 92 Drymen Road, Bearsden, Glasgow, G61 2SY; T.-041-942 2461.

Wardlaw, Rev. Elliot G.S., BA, BD, DipMin. Minister, Bathgate: St. David's Parish Church, since 1984; Chairman, Board of Directors, BAIT Ltd.; Chairman, West Lothian Community Trust; Convener, Church and Community Committee, West Lothian Presbytery; b. 12.10.56, Edinburgh. Educ. Edinburgh Academy; Edinburgh University. Address: St. David's Manse, 70 Marjoribanks Street, Bathgate, West Lothian; T.-0506 53177.

Warlow, Professor Charles Picton, BA, MB, BChir, MD, FRCP (Lond), FRCP (Edin). Professor of Medical Neurology, Edinburgh, since 1987; Honorary Consultant Neurologist, Lothian Health Board; b. 29.9.43; m.; 2 s.; 1 d. Educ. Cambridge University. Lecturer in Medicine, Aberdeen University, 1971-74; Registrar and Senior Registrar in Neurology, National Hospitals for Nervous Diseases, London, and University College Hospital, London, 1974-76; Clinical Lecturer in Neurology, then Clinical Reader, Oxford University, 1976-86. Recreations: sailing; photography; theatre. Address: 3 Mortonhall Hall Road, Edinburgh, EH9 2HS.

Warner, Sheriff Graeme Christopher, LLB, WS, NP. Sheriff of Grampian, Highland and Islands, at Aberdeen and Stonehaven, since 1992; in private practice as a Solicitor, 1969-91; b. 20.10.48, Glasgow; m., Rachel Kidd Gear; 1 s.; 1 d. Educ. Strathallan; Edinburgh University. Recreation: skiing. Address: (b.) Sheriff Court House, Aberdeen; T.-0224 645132.

Warren, Alastair Kennedy, TD, MA. Chairman, Nithsdale Council of Voluntary Service, 1988-91; Director, Solway Community Business, 1987-91; Chairman, Loch Arthur Village for Mentally Handicapped Adults, since 1985; Trustee, Dumfries and Galloway Care Trust, since 1989; Freelance Journalist; b. 17.7.22, Glasgow; m., Ann Lindsay Maclean; 2 s. Educ. Laurel Bank School; Glasgow Academy; Loretto School; Glasgow University. Served at home and overseas, HLI, 1940-46 (from private to Major); Management Trainee, Stewarts and Lloyds, 1950-53; Glasgow Herald: joined, 1954, Business Editor, 1961-63, City Editor, 1964-65, Editor, 1965-74; Regional Editor, Scottish and Universal Newspapers Ltd., Southern Region, 1974-76; Editor, Dumfries and Galloway Standard, 1976-86. Served with 5/6th Bn., HLI (TA), 1947-63; first Chairman, Stewartry Mountaineering Club, 1976-78; Provost, Royal Burgh of New Galloway and Kells Parish, 1978-81. Recreations: hill-walking; running; swimming; poetry; conversation. Address: (h.) Rathan, High Street, New Galloway, Castle Douglas, DG7 3RN; T.-New Galloway 257.

Waterman, Professor Peter George, BPharm (Hons), PhD, FLS, DSc. Professor in Phytochemistry, Department of Pharmacy, Strathclyde University, since 1987; b. 28.4.46, Langley, Kent; m., Margaret Humble. Educ. Judd School, Tonbridge; London University. Postgraduate Research Assistant, London University, 1968-69; Lecturer, Senior Lecturer, Reader, Department of Pharmacy, Strathclyde University, 1969-87. Pharmaceutical Society Young Scientist of the Year Award, 1979; Phytochemical Society of Europe Tate & Lyle Award for contribution to Phytochemistry, 1984; Executive Editor, Journal of Biochemical Systematics and Ecology. Recreations: travel; walking. Address: (b.) Phytochemistry Research Laboratories, Department of Pharmacy, Strathclyde University, Glasgow, G1 1XW; T.-041-552 4400.

Waters, Donald Henry. Chief Executive and Director, Grampian Television PLC, since 1987; b. 17.12.37, Edinburgh; m., June Leslie Hutchison; 1 s.; 2 d. Educ. George Watson's, Edinburgh; Inverness Royal Academy. Director, John M. Henderson and Co. Ltd., 1972-75; Grampian Television PLC: Company Secretary, 1975, Director of Finance, 1979; Director: Moray Firth Radio Ltd., 1982,

Glenburnie Properties Ltd., 1976, Cablevision Scotland PLC, 1987-91. Recreations: gardening; travel. Address: (h.) Balquhidder, 141 North Deeside Road, Milltimber, Aberdeen, AB1 0JS; T.-Aberdeen 867131.

Waters, Rev. Robert, MA. General Secretary, Congregational Union of Scotland, since 1971; b. 8.7.30, Edinburgh; m., Magdalene Forrest; 1 s.; 1 d. Educ. Boroughmuir School, Edinburgh; Edinburgh University; Scottish Congregational College; Chicago University. Recreation: trout fishing. Address: (b.) 340 Cathedral Street, Glasgow, G1 2BQ; T.-041-332 7667.

Waterworth, Keith Robinson. Traffic Commissioner and Licensing Authority for Scottish Traffic Area, since 1989; b. 23.11.42, Barnoldswick. Educ. Ermysteads Grammar School. Air Ministry; Ministry of Defence; Ministry of Housing and Local Government; Department of Environment; Department of Transport. Recreations: wine club; Scotch Malt Whisky Society; cooking; theatre; National Hunt racing. Address: (b.) 83 Princes Street, Edinburgh, EH2 5ER; T.-031-225 5494.

Watkins, Trevor Francis, BA, PhD, FSA, FSA Scot. Senior Lecturer, Department of Archaeology, Edinburgh University, since 1979; b. 20.2.38, Epsom, Surrey; m., Antoinette Marie; 1 s.; 2 d. Educ. Kingston Grammar School; Birmingham University. Research Fellow, Birmingham University; Lecturer, Edinburgh University. Honorary Secretary, British Institute of Archaeology at Ankara; Council Member, British School of Archaeology in Iraq; Director, Scottish Field School of Archaeology. Recreations: walking; bird-watching; music. Address: (b.) Department of Archaeology, Edinburgh University, 19 George Square, Edinburgh, EH8 9JZ; T.-031-667 1011.

Watkinson, Geoffrey, MD, BS (Lond), FRCP (Lond), FRCPGlas. Consultant Physician, Glasgow Nuffield Hospital; former Physician and Gastroenterologist, Western Infirmary, Garnavel General Hospital and Southern General Hospital, Glasgow; b. 12.5.21, Bolton; m., Marie Christine; 1 s.; 1 d. Educ. Southgate County School; St. Bartholomew's Hospital, London. House Physician and Senior Registrar, Medical Professorial Unit, St. Bartholomew's Hospital; Medical Branch, RAF (Wing Commander); Leeds University, 1948-60, latterly as Senior Lecturer in Medicine and Honorary Consultant; Physician, Leeds General Infirmary and St. James Hospital, Leeds; Rockefeller Travelling Fellowship in Medicine, 1953-54 (Mayo Clinic, Minnesota); Consultant, York Group of Hospitals, 1961-68, latterly as Senior Physician and Chairman, Medical Division. Council Member, Association of Physicians of Great Britain and Ireland; Member, National Committee of the Review of Medicines, 1979-83; Member, Awards Committee for Scotland, 1982-85; Senior Examiner, Membership Examination, Royal College of Physicians of Glasgow and London; Phillip Bushell Lectureship in Australian Gastroenterology, 1969; Council Member and Past President, British Society of Gastroenterology; Secretary General, President and latterly Honorary President, World Organisation of Gastroenterology. Recreations: music; photography; gardening. Address: (h.) 14 Southview Road, Blanefield, Glasgow, G63 9JG; T.-0360 70689.

Watson, Adam, BSc, PhD, DSc, FRSE. Senior Principal Scientific Officer and Leader of grouse research team, Institute of Terrestrial Ecology, since 1971; b. 14.4.30, Turriff; m., Jenny; 1 s.; 1 d. Educ. Aberdeen University. Demonstrator in Zoology, McGill University, Montreal, 1952-53; Zoologist on Baird expedition to Baffin Island, 1953; Assistant Lecturer in Zoology, Aberdeen University, 1953-55; Teacher of Science, Aberdeen Academy, 1957; Senior Research Fellow, Aberdeen University, 1957-60; Senior Scientific Officer, then Principal Scientific Officer,

Nature Conservancy, 1961-66; Officer in charge, Nature Conservancy Council Mountain and Moorland Ecology Station, Banchory, 1966-71; Neill Prize, Royal Society of Edinburgh, for "outstanding contribution to natural history". Recreations: mountaineering; skiing. Address: (h.) Clachnaben, Crathes, Banchory, AB3 3JE.

Watson, Professor Alan Albert, JP, MA, MB, BS, FRCP, FRCPath, DMJ, DTM&H. Regius Professor of Forensic Medicine, Glasgow University, since 1985; Honorary Consultant in Forensic Medicine, Greater Glasgow Health Board, since 1978; Committee Member, Forensic Medicine (Scotland) Committee, since 1982; b. 20.2.29, Reading; m., Jeannette Anne Pitts; 3 s. Educ. Reading School; St. Mary's Hospital, London; Queens' College, Cambridge. Lecturer in Pathology, Glasgow University, 1964-69; University Senior Assistant Pathologist, Cambridge University, 1969-71; elected Fellow of Queen's College and Assistant Director of Studies, 1970; Consultant in Forensic Medicine, SE Asia Region, Delhi, WHO, 1977. Hon. President, Scottish Band of Hope Union. Recreations: Church activities (Baptist lay preacher). Address: (b.) Department of Forensic Medicine and Science, Glasgow University, Glasgow, G12 8QQ; T.-041-339 8855.

Watson, Alexander Bell, MA, MEd, FBIM, FSA Scot. Director of Education, Tayside Regional Council, since 1990; b. 20.5.45, Airdrie; m., Jean; 3 s. Educ. Airdrie Academy; Glasgow University; Jordanhill College of Education. Teacher of Classics, Morrison's Academy, Crieff, 1968; Principal Teacher of Classics: Portree High School, 1971, McLaren High School, Callander, 1973; Assistant Director of Education: Central, 1975, Strathclyde, 1983; Senior Depute Director of Education, Central, 1986. Vice-President, Association of Directors of Education in Scotland. Recreations: music; reading; fishing; Scottish heritage; DIY. Address: (h.) Belmont, Lour Road, Forfar, DD8 2BB; T.-0307 62718.

Watson, Antony Charles Harington, MB, ChB, FRCSEdin. Consultant Plastic Surgeon, Lothian Health Board, since 1972; part-time Senior Lecturer, Department of Clinical Surgery, Edinburgh University, since 1972; President, British Association of Plastic Surgeons, 1991; Hon. Treasurer, Royal College of Surgeons of Edinburgh; b. 14.10.36, London; m., Anne Henderson Spence; 1 s.; 3 d. Educ. Barnard Castle School; Edinburgh University. Surgical training, Edinburgh and Florida. Council Member, British Association of Plastic Surgeons, since 1984; Examiner for Fellowship, Royal College of Surgeons of Edinburgh; Fellowship in Accident and Emergency Medicine and in Specialist Assessment in Plastic Surgery; Secretary, Scottish Melanoma Group, 1980-84. Recreations: playing and listening to music; boating; painting and sculpture; spending time with the family. Address: (h.) 6 Duncan Street, Edinburgh, EH9 1SZ; T.-031-667 4022.

Watson, Edward Paul, MBII. President, Scottish Licensed Trade Association, since 1986; Vice Chairman, Forth Wines Ltd., since 1986; b. 10.9.25, Aberdeen; m., Isabella Jean Stewart; 2 s.; 1 d. Educ. Aberdeen Grammar School. United Africa Co. (Unilever), Nigeria and Ghana, 1951-66; Proprietor, Park Hotel, Aberdeen, 1966-71; Proprietor, The Grill, Aberdeen, since 1971. Recreations: golf; photography. Address: (h.) 71 Morningfield Road, Aberdeen, AB2 4AP.

Watson, Professor George Alistair, BSc, MSc, PhD, FIMA. Professor, Department of Mathematics and Computer Science, Dundee University, since 1988; b. 30.9.42, Aberfeldy; m., Hilary Mackay; 1 d. Educ. Breadalbane Academy; Edinburgh University; Australian National University. Demonstrator, Computer Unit, Edinburgh University, 1964-66; Dundee University: Research Fellow,

then Lecturer, Mathematics Department, 1969-82; Senior Lecturer, Mathematical Sciences Department, 1982-84; Reader, Department of Mathematics and Computer Science, 1984-88. Recreation: gardening. Address: (h.) 7 Albany Road, West Ferry, Dundee, DD5 1NS; T.-Dundee 79473.

Watson, Hamish, MFH, TD, MD, FRCPEdin, FRCP, FAAC. Consultant Physician and Cardiologist, Tayside Area, 1964-85; Chairman, Section of Cardiology, Department of Medicine, Dundee University, 1964-85; Postgraduate Dean and Director of Postgraduate Medical Education, 1970- 85; b. 26.6.23, Edinburgh; m., Lesley Leigh Dick Wood; 1 s. (deceased); 2 d. Educ. George Watson's College; Edinburgh University. President, Association of European Paediatric Cardiologists, 1963-70; Assistant Editor, British Heart Journal, 1964-68; Member, Scientific Board, International Society of Cardiology and Chairman, Council of Paediatric Cardiology, 1966-72; Convenor, Cardiology Committee, Royal College of Physicians of Edinburgh, 1969-75; Member, Specialist Advisory Committee on Cardiovascular Diseases, 1970-74; Member, Scottish Council for Postgraduate Medical Education, 1970-85; Convenor, Working Party on Training for Blood Transfusion Service, 1973-74; Convenor, Working Party on part-time Training in Medicine, 1977-85; Trustee, Royal College of Physicians of Edinburgh since 1973; Chairman, Standing Committee, Conference of Postgraduate Deans and Directors of Postgraduate Medical Education of Universities of UK, 1975-79; Chairman, UK Hospital Junior Staff Group Council, 1959-62; Chairman, Scottish Hospital Junior Staff Group Council, 1955-62. RMO, The Scottish Horse RAC (TA), 1952-57, and Fife and Forfar Yeomanry/Scottish Horse, 1957-67; RAMC: Garrison Medical Officer, Northern Territories, Nigeria, British West Africa, 1945-48; Senior Medical Specialist, 1952-78, Territorial Efficiency Decoration, 1966. Member, Masters of Foxhounds Association, since 1985. Publications: numerous books and scientific papers on heart disease. Recreations: fox-hunting; polo; fishing; horticulture; farming. Address: (h.) Nethermains of Kinnaird, Inchture, Perthshire, PH14 9QX; T.-0828 86303.

Watson, Harry Duff, MA, BA, DipEd. Director and Senior Editor, Dictionary of the Older Scottish Tongue, Edinburgh University, since 1985; b. 17.6.46, Crail; m., Susan Margaret Saul; 2 s. Educ. Waid Academy, Anstruther; Edinburgh University; University College, London. Teacher of English/English as a Foreign Language, Scotland, England, Sweden, West Germany, 1970-79; appointed Editor, Dictionary of the Older Scottish Tongue, 1979. Past Senior Vice-President, Scottish Swedish Society; Member, Council, Scottish Text Society; Member, Board, Scottish Studies, Edinburgh University. Publication: Kilrenny and Cellardyke. Recreations: reading; writing; music; genealogy; languages. Address: (h.) 14 Braehead Grove, Edinburgh, EH4 6BG; T.-031-339 6911.

Watson, Hugh, QPM. Commandant, Scottish Police College, Tulliallan Castle, since 1991; b. 24.2.38, Edinburgh; m., Evelyn Scrimger; 1 s.; 2 d. Educ. Dunfermline High School. RAF, 1955-58; Lothian and Peebles Constabulary, 1958-75; Lothian and Borders Police, 1975-91; Assistant Chief Constable, 1984-91. Recreations: gardening; reading; DIY. Address: (b.) Tulliallan Castle, Kinardine-on-Forth, KY10 4BE; T.-031-332 2707.

Watson, Professor John, BSc, ARCST, PhD, DSc. Professor in Biochemistry, Strathclyde University, since 1988 (Reader, 1985-88); b. 17.6.42, Glasgow; m., Anne Brown; 2 d. Educ. Whitehill Secondary, Glasgow; Glasgow University; Strathclyde University. MRC Research Fellow, Glasgow University; Lecturer, Senior Lecturer, Reader, Professor, Strathclyde University. Recreations: golf; swimming; skiing; reading. Address: (b.) Bioscience and Biotechnology,

Strathclyde University, Todd Centre, Glasgow, G4 0NR; T.-041-552 4400, Ext. 3825.

Watson, Captain John J. Chief Executive, Dundee Port Authority, since 1986; Director, British Ports Federation; Chairman, Group 2 Ports, British Ports Federation; Chairman, Marine Safety Sub-Committee, COPSSEC; Member, International Association of Ports and Harbours; Vice-President, Dundee & Tayside Chamber of Commerce & Industry; Member, Tayside Branch, Scottish Council (Development & Industry); Master Mariner; b. 19.1.39, Barr, Ayrshire; m., Maureen; 1 s. Educ. Girvan High School; Strathclyde University, Glasgow. Merchant Navy, 1954-66; British Transport Docks Board, 1966-80; Harbourmaster, Dundee Port Authority, 1980-86. Former District Commissioner for Scouting, Boothferry; Past President, Goole & District Junior Chamber. Recreations: shooting; golf; fishing. Address: (h.) 39 Elie Avenue, Broughty Ferry, Dundee, DD5 3SF; T.-0382 738151.

Watson, Lewis McIntosh, BSc, PhD, CPhys. Senior Lecturer in Metallurgy and Engineering Materials, Strathclyde University, since 1988; Co-ordinator, Metco Strathclyde, since 1984; b. 21.8.40, Denby Dale; m., Ewa Maria Gworek; 2 s.; 2 d. Educ. Lenzie Academy; Glasgow University; Strathclyde University. Research Fellow, Senior Research Fellow in Metal Physics, 1967-73; Lecturer in Metallurgy and Engineering Materials, 1973-88. Publications: 62 scientific papers; two conference proceedings books. Recreations: golf; DIY. Address: (b.) Department of Metallurgy and Engineering Materials, Strathclyde University, Glasgow, G1 1XN; T.-041-552 4400, Ext. 3131.

Watson, Michael Goodall, BA (Hons). MP (Labour), Glasgow Central, since 1989; b. 1.5.49, Cambuslang; m., Lorraine Therese McManus. Educ. Dundee High School; Heriot-Watt University. Development Officer, WEA East Midlands District, 1974-77; Industrial Officer, ASTMS, 1977-79; Regional Officer, ASTMS (latterly MSF), 1979-89. Member, Scottish Executive Committee, Labour Party, 1987-90. Publication: Rags to Riches: the official history of Dundee United FC. Recreations: watching Dundee United FC; jogging; reading, especially political biographies. Address: (b.) 58 Fox Street, Glasgow, G1 4AU; T.-041-204 4738.

Watson, Roderick, MA, PhD. Poet; Literary Critic and Writer; Reader in English, Stirling University; b. 12.5.43, Aberdeen; m., Celia Hall Mackie; 1 s.; 1 d. Educ. Aberdeen Grammar School; Aberdeen University; Peterhouse, Cambridge. Lecturer in English, Victoria University, British Columbia, 1965-66; collections of poetry include Trio and True History on the Walls; other books include The Penguin Book of the Bicycle, The Literature of Scotland, MacDiarmid, and The Poetry of Norman MacCaig. Recreation: cycling. Address: (h.) 19 Millar Place, Stirling; T.-Stirling 75971.

Watt, Alison, BA (Hons). Painter; b. 11.12.65, Greenock. Educ. Glasgow School of Art. Prizes: British Institution Fund, 1st prize for painting, 1986; winner, John Player Portrait Award, 1987; Armour Prize for still life painting, Glasgow School of Art, 1987; Elizabeth Greenshields Foundation Award, 1989; commissioned to paint HM Queen Elizabeth the Queen Mother for National Portrait Gallery; recent exhibitions: one-woman show, Scottish Gallery, London; one-woman show, Glasgow Art Gallery and Museum, Kelvingrove.

Watt, Archibald, JP, MA, MEd, FEIS, FSA Scot. Honorary Sheriff, Grampian, Highlands and Islands, since 1979; b. 20.5.14, Aberdeen; m., 1, Anne D.M. Ashton (deceased); 2, Elizabeth P. White; 1 d. Educ. Robert Gordon's College, Aberdeen; Aberdeen University; Aberdeen College of Education. Teacher of English, Elgin Academy, 1938; Flt.-Lt., RAF Administrative and Special Duties Branch and RAF Regiment, 1941-46; Mackie Academy: Principal Teacher of English, 1949, Deputy Rector, 1962, retired, 1977; Organist, HM Prison, Aberdeen, 1930-38; WEA Organiser for Adult Education, Elgin, 1946-49; WEA Tutor in Psychology, 1946-51; Founder and Organising Secretary, Stonehaven Music Club, since 1949; Member, National Council, and Chairman, Regional and District Committees, Scottish Community Drama Association, 1949-67; Member, National Executive and District Chairman, School Library Association in Scotland, 1952-73; Elder, Church of Scotland, since 1954; Chairman and/or Member, Kincardine District Committee, EIS, 1956-77; Member, Joint Consultative Committee, Kincardine County Council, 1965-77; Queen's Jubilee Medal, 1977; Organist and Clerk, Congregational Board, South Church, Stonehaven, since 1976; Director, Kinneff Old Church Preservation Trust Ltd., since 1979; Founder Member and President, Stonehaven Probus Club, 1981-82; Committee Member, National Trust for Scotland (Kincardine and Deeside Centre), 1984-88; Member, Aberdeen Choral Society, since 1978, and Aberdeen Proms Chorus, since 1985; Chairman, Stonehaven Heritage Society, since 1988; author of Reading Lists for the Secondary School, 1966; Highways and Byways Round Stonehaven, 1976; Highways and Byways Round Kincardine, 1985; A Goodly Heritage, 1991. Recreations: concert and theatre-going; travel; antiquities and archaeology; brass bands; research; golf; choral singing. Address: (h.) Rutlands, Arduthie Road, Stonehaven; T.-Stonehaven 62712.

Watt, Archibald Scott, LCH, SRCH. Member, Borders Regional Council, since 1974; Member, Lothian and Borders Police Board, since 1974; Member, Borders Health Board, since 1974; Member, Tweed River Purification Board; b. 21.8.29, Loanhead, Midlothian; m., Mary Corbett McNairn Brown; 1 d. RAF, 1947-49; Chiropodist, in private practice, since 1957; elected, Peebles Town Council and Peeblesshire County Council, 1973; TA, 1960-62; Past President, Peebles Rotary Club. Recreations: photography; archery. Address: East Rectory, Tweed Brae, Peebles; T.-Peebles 20803.

Watt, Brian, MD, FRCPath, CBiol, FIBiol. Consultant Bacteriologist, City Hospital, Edinburgh, since 1982; Honorary Senior Lecturer, Department of Bacteriology, Edinburgh University, since 1974; Area Director of Medical Microbiology Services, Lothian Health Board, since 1991; b. 6.12.41, Edinburgh; m., Hilary Watt; 2 d. Educ. Rudolf Steiner School; Edinburgh University. Lecturer, Department of Bacteriology, Edinburgh University, 1968-73; Consultant Microbiologist, Western General Hospital, 1973-82. Recreations: fishing; gardening; golf; tennis; singing. Address: (h.) Silverburn House, by Penicuik, Midlothian; T.-Penicuik 72085.

Watt, Graham B.A., MA, LLB. Secretary, Scottish Power plc, since 1990; b. 20.3.37, Edinburgh; m., Carolyn Kelso; 1 s.; 1 d. Educ. Fettes College, Edinburgh; Glasgow University. Coats Viyella plc, 1961-88: number of secretarial appointments, then managing number of group subsidiaries at home and abroad; Administrative Director and Secretary, Lilley plc, 1988-90. Recreations: gardening; golf; music. Address: (b.) Cathcart House, Spean Street, Glasgow G44 4BE.

Watt, Hamish, JP, Hon. LLD (Aberdeen). Rector, Aberdeen University, since 1985; b. 27.12.25, Keith; m., Mary N. Grant; 1 s.; 2 d. Educ. Keith Grammar School; St. Andrews University. MP, Banffshire, 1974-79. Recreation: travel. Address: (h.) Mill of Buckie, Buckie; T.-Buckie 32591.

Watt, James Affleck Gilroy, MB, ChB, MD, FRCPEdin, FRCPsych, DPM. Consultant Psychiatrist, Gartnavel Royal Hospital, since 1971; b. 14.7.34, near Edinburgh; m., Shirley Camilla Wilson (m. diss.); 2 s.; 1 d. Educ. Lasswade Senior

Secondary School; Edinburgh University. House Officer in Neurosurgery, Medicine and Neurology, 1958-60; Junior Medical Specialist, RAMC, 1960-64 (BAOR); Registrar in Psychiatry, Bangour, 1964-66; Research Fellow in Psychiatry, Edinburgh, 1966-69; Lecturer in Psychiatry, Dundee, 1969-71. Recreations: skiing; chess; glass engraving; windsurfing. Address: (b.) Gartnavel Royal Hospital, 1055 Great Western Road, Glasgow, G12; T.-041-334 6241.

Watt, Jim, MBE (1980). Boxer; b. 18.7.48, Glasgow. Turned professional, 1968; British Lightweight Champion, 1972-73, 1975-77; European Lightweight Champion, 1977-79; World Lightweight Champion, 1979-81; four successful defences of World title; Freedom of Glasgow, 1981.

Watt, Robert Strachan, CBE, MA, FBCS. Chairman, Livingston Development Corporation, since 1982; Chairman, Scotbyte Computers Ltd., since 1979; Director, Lothian and Edinburgh Enterprise Ltd.; b. 13.10.32, Aberdeen; m., Lorna Beattie; 1 s.; 2 d. Educ. Robert Gordon's College; Aberdeen University. Member, Glenrothes Development Corporation, 1971-78 (Deputy Chairman, 1978-81); Chairman, Management Committee, Scottish New Towns Computer Service, 1977-81; Member, Whitley Council, 1975-81; Council Member, British Computer Society, 1968-69; Elder, Cramond Kirk; Honorary President, Livingston Voluntary Organisations Council; Trustee, Livingston Youth Trust; Member, Edinburgh Airport Consultative Committee. Recreations: golf; tennis. Address: (b.) Kirkton South, Kirkton Campus, Livingston, EH54 7AJ.

Watt, William Percy, JP, NCIA. Dairy Farmer; Chairman, Planning Committee, Moray District Council, since 1984 (Member, since 1978); Scottish Member, United Kingdom Seeds Executive, 1978-89; b. 29.4.29, Keith; m., Elizabeth Shand; 4 d. Educ. Keith Grammar School; North of Scotland College of Agriculture. President, National Farmers Union of Scotland, 1976-77; former Member, Intervention Board for Agricultural Produce. Address: (h.) Auchoynanie, Keith, Moray; T.-05422 2566.

Watts, John, MA, MSc, PhD. Rector, St. Kentigern's RC Academy, Blackburn, since 1988; b. 23.6.39; m., Moira McCallum; 3 s.; 3 d. Educ. Oxford University; Glasgow University. Teacher, 1960-74; Head Teacher, Daliburgh Primary/Secondary School, South Uist, 1974-81; Head Teacher, Bishop Challoner RC Secondary School, Birmingham, 1981-88. Recreations: reading; Gaelic language and culture; family caravanning. Address: (b.) St. Kentigern's Academy, West Main Street, Blackburn, West Lothian, EH47 7LX; T.-0506 56404.

Waugh, Alan, BSc (Hons), DipEd. Head Teacher, Penicuik High School, since 1992; b. 9.2.49, Loanhead; m., Margo Watt; 1 s.; 1 d. Educ. Lasswade Senior Secondary School; Edinburgh University. Head of Chemistry, then Assistant Head Teacher, Lasswade High School Centre, 1976-86; Depute Head Teacher, James Gillespie's High School, 1986-92. Address: (b.) Penicuik High School, Carlops Road, Penicuik, EH26 9EP; T.-Penicuik 674165.

Weatherhead, Alexander Stewart, OBE, TD, MA, LLB. Solicitor; Partner, Tindal Oatts, Solicitors, Glasgow, since 1960; b. 3.8.31, Edinburgh; m., Harriett Foye; 2 d. Educ. Glasgow Academy; Glasgow University. Royal Artillery, 1950-52; TA, 1952; Lt. Col. Commanding 277 (A&SH) Field Regiment, RA (TA), 1965-67, The Lowland Regiment, RA (T), 1967 and Glasgow and Strathclyde Universities OTC, 1970-73; Colonel, 1974; TAVR Colonel, Lowlands (West), 1974-76; ADC (TAVR) to The Queen, 1977-81; Honorary Colonel, Glasgow and Strathclyde Universities OTC, since 1982; Chairman, Lowlands TAVRA, since 1990; Council Member, Law Society of Scotland, 1971-84 (Honorary Vice-

President, 1983-84); Member, Royal Commission on Legal Services in Scotland, 1976-80; Council Member, Society for Computers and Law, 1973-86 (Chairman, 1981-84); Temporary Sheriff, since 1985. Recreations: tennis; sailing; reading; music. Address: (h.) 52 Partickhill Road, Glasgow, G11 5AB; T.-041-334 6277.

Weatherhead, Anne E., MB, ChB, MRCPsych. Medical Officer, Mental Welfare Commission for Scotland, since 1984; b. 3.5.37, Kirriemuir; m., Rev. James L. Weatherhead (qv); 2 s. Educ. Cheltenham Ladies' College; Edinburgh University. Trained in psychiatry, Sunnyside Royal Hospital, Montrose, with earlier medical training in Vancouver, Canada. Former National Vice-President, Woman's Guild, Church of Scotland; Elder, St. Giles Cathedral, Edinburgh. Recreations: music; art. Address: (h.) 28 Castle Terrace, Edinburgh.

Weatherhead, Rev. James Leslie, MA, LLB. Principal Clerk, General Assembly of the Church of Scotland, since 1985; b. 29.3.31, Dundee; m., Dr. Anne Elizabeth Shepherd (see Anne E. Weatherhead); 2 s. Educ. High School of Dundee; Edinburgh University and New College, Edinburgh. Temporary Sub-Lt., RNVR (National Service), 1955-56. Licensed by Presbytery of Dundee, 1960, Presbytery of Ayr, 1960; Assistant Minister, Auld Kirk of Ayr, 1960-62; Minister: Trinity Church, Rothesay, 1962-69, Old Church, Montrose, 1969-85. Member, Broadcasting Council for Scotland, 1978-82. Recreations: music; sailing. Address: (b.) Church of Scotland Offices, 121 George Street, Edinburgh, EH2 4YN; T.-031-225 5722.

Weatherston, William Alastair Paterson, MA (Hons). Under Secretary, Scottish Office Education Department, since 1989; b. 20.11.35, Peebles; m., Margaret Jardine; 2 s.; 1 d. Educ. Peebles High School; Edinburgh University. Assistant Principal, Department of Health for Scotland and Scottish Education Department, 1959-63; Private Secretary to Permanent Under Secretary of State, Scottish Office, 1963-64; Principal, Scottish Education Department, 1964-72; Cabinet Office, 1972-74; Assistant Secretary, Scottish Home and Health Department, 1974-77; Scottish Education Department, 1977-79; Central Services, Scottish Office, 1979-82; Director, Scottish Courts Administration, 1982-86; Fisheries Secretary, Department of Agriculture and Fisheries for Scotland, 1986-89. Recreations: reading; music. Address: (b.) Scottish Office Education Department, 43 Jeffrey Street, Edinburgh, EH1 1DN; T.-031-244 5322.

Weatherstone, Robert Bruce, CA, TD. Chairman, Lothian Health Board, 1986-90; Director, Lothian Region Transport plc; b. 14.5.26, Bangor; m., Elaine Fisher; 1 s.; 1 d. Educ. Edinburgh Academy; Dollar Academy; Edinburgh University. Director/Secretary, J.T. Salvesen Ltd., Grangemouth, 1954-62; Director and Member, Management Committee, Christian Salvesen Ltd., 1962-83; served in TA, latterly as Colonel, for more than 20 years; Trustee and Chairman, Executive Committee, Leonard Cheshire Foundation, 1987-91; Chairman, Mental Care Committee, since 1991. Recreations: hill-walking; ornithology. Address: (h.) 27 Ravelston Garden, Edinburgh, EH4 3LE; T.-031-337 4035.

Weaver, John Patrick Acton, MA, BA (Hons), BSc, BM Bch, DM, MCh, FRCSEdin, FRCS. Consultant Urologist, Dundee Royal Infirmary; Honorary Senior Lecturer in Surgery, Dundee University; b. 17.11.27, Oxford; m., Mary Catherine Bainbridge Robinson; 2 s.; 1 d. Educ. Ampleforth; Trinity College, Oxford; Guy's Hospital. Demonstrator in Biochemistry, Oxford University; House Surgeon, Guy's Hospital; Senior Surgical Registrar, Royal Victoria Infirmary, Newcastle-upon-Tyne; Lecturer in Surgery, Newcastle-upon-

Tyne University. Recreation: gardening. Address: (b.) 229 Strathmartine Road, Dundee; T.-Dundee 89383.

Webb, David John, MD, MRCP (UK). Senior Lecturer in Medicine, Edinburgh University, since 1990; Director, Clinical Research Centre and Honorary Consultant Physician, Western General Hospital, Edinburgh, since 1990; b. 1.9.53, Greenwich; m., Dr. Margaret Jane Cullen. Educ. Dulwich College, London; London University: Royal London Hospital. Junior hospital appointments, 1977-79; Medical Registrar, Royal London rotation, 1979-82; MRC Research Fellow, MRC Blood Pressure Unit, Glasgow, and Honorary Lecturer, Glasgow University, 1982-85; Lecturer in Pharmacology and Clinical Pharmacology, St. George's Hospital Medical School, London, and Honorary Medical Senior Registrar, St. George's Hospital, London, 1985-89. Executive Member, British Hypertension Society, since 1991; Honorary Trustee and Joint Research Director, High Blood Pressure Foundation and Endocrine Research Trust, since 1991. Recreations: opera; bridge; summer and winter mountaineering. Address: (h.) 26 Inverleith Gardens, Edinburgh, EH3 5PS; T.-031-332 1205.

Webb, Professor Jeffrey R.L., BSc, DPhil, FRSE. Titular Professor in Mathematics, Glasgow University, since 1987 (Reader, 1982-87); b. 19.12.45, Stourport-on-Severn; m., Angela Millard; 1 s.; 1 d. Educ. King Charles I School, Kidderminster; Sussex University. Royal Society European Programme Fellowship, 1970-71; Science Research Council Fellowship, Sussex University, 1971-73; Lecturer in Mathematics, Glasgow University, 1973-78 and 1979-82; Visiting Associate Professor, Indiana University, 1978-79; Visiting Professor, Tulane University, New Orleans, 1982. Member, Editorial Board, Glasgow Mathematical Journal. Recreations: chess; books; listening to music. Address: (b.) Mathematics Department, Glasgow University, Glasgow, G12 8QW; T.-041-339 8855, Ext. 5181.

Webster, Brian Charles, BA, PhD. University Lecturer in Theoretical Chemistry, since 1967; b. 20.6.39, Bournemouth; m., Mary Blaker; 1 s.; 3 d. Educ. Bournemouth School; Magdalen College, Oxford. Expert on behaviour of excess electrons and positive muons in matter; Chairman, Fifth International Meeting on Excess Electrons, 1979; Member, European Committee, Fifth International Meeting on Muon Spectroscopy, 1990; invited Professor, University of Paris. Publications: scientific papers; Chemical Bonding Theory, 1990. Recreations: fine arts; clarsach playing; hill-walking. Address: (h.) 31 Thomson Drive, Bearsden, Glasgow, G61 3PA; T.-041-942 7234.

Webster, David. Producer/Director, This is Scotland (stage and screen promotions); Director, Highland Theatre and Highland Discovery Centre, Oban. Address: (h.) Corriebeg, Oban, Argyll, PA34 5DU; T.-0631 63794.

Webster, David Pirie, DPE, LCSP (Phys). Author; Chairman, Commonwealth Games Council for Scotland; Director of Leisure, Recreation and Tourism, Cunninghame District Council, 1975-87; b. 18.9.28, Aberdeen; 4 s.; 2 d. Educ. Crowlees Boys School; Aberdeen Training College; Woolmanhill College. Senior Technical Representative, Scottish Council of Physical Recreation, 1954-72; Head of Facilities Planning Division, Scottish Sports Council, 1972-74; Director/Administrator, Magnum Leisure Centre, 1974-75. Director of Weightlifting, Commonwealth Games; Secretary General, World Federation of Heavy Events Athletes. Recreations: writing (more than 30 books); Highland Games; fitness and weight training. Address: (h.) 43 West Road, Irvine, Ayrshire, KA12 8RE; T.-0294 72257.

Webster, Derek Adrian, CBE (1979). Chairman and Editorial Director, Scottish Daily Record and Sunday Mail Ltd., 1974-87; Director, Mirror Group Newspapers, 1974-87; Director, Clyde CableVision Ltd., 1982-86; b. 24.3.27; m., Dorothy Frances Johnson; 2 s.; 1 d. Educ. St. Peter's, Bournemouth. Royal Navy, 1944-48; Reporter, Western Morning News, 1943; Staff Journalist, Daily Mail, 1949-51; joined Mirror Group, 1952; Northern Editor, Daily Mirror, 1964-67; Editor, Daily Record, 1967-72. Vice Chairman, Age Concern Scotland, 1977-83; Member, Press Council, 1981-84 (Joint Vice Chairman, 1982-84); Honorary Vice President, Newspaper Press Fund. Recreations: photography; travel. Address: (h.) 32 Athole Gardens, Dowanhill, Glasgow, G12 9BD; T.-041-339 6239.

Webster, Jack (John Barron). Author and Journalist; Columnist, The Herald; b. 8.7.31, Maud, Aberdeenshire; m., Eden Keith; 3 s. Educ. Maud School; Peterhead Academy; Robert Gordon's College, Aberdeen. Reporter, Turriff Advertiser; Reporter/Sub Editor, Aberdeen Press & Journal/Evening Express; Chief Sub-Editor, Scottish Sunday Express; Feature Writer, Scottish Daily Express; Feature Writer, Sunday Standard. Publications: The Dons, 1978; A Grain of Truth, 1981; Gordon Strachan, 1984; Another Grain of Truth, 1988, 'Tis Better to Travel, 1989; Alistair MacLean (biography), 1991; television films: The Roup, 1985; As Time Goes By, 1987; Northern Lights, 1989; Webster Goes West, 1991. Address: (b.) The Herald, 195 Albion Street, Glasgow, G1; T.-041-552 6255.

Webster, Michael, BA (Hons), DMS, MBIM. Principal, Perth College of Further Education, since 1991; b. 7.12.45, Manchester; m., Christine Lesley Roberts. Educ. Chethams School; Moseley Hall Grammar School; Exeter University. Merchandise distributor, 1962-68; Lecturer in Social Sciences, Bridgenorth College of Further Education, 1972-80; Head, Business and General Studies, Bridgenorth College, 1980-84; Shropshire County Co-ordinator, Technical and Vocational Education Initiative, 1984-86; Adviser 14-19 Education, Shropshire LEA, 1986-88; Principal Adviser, Shropshire LEA, 1988-91. Recreations: hill-walking; skiing; cinema; theatre. Address: (b.) Perth College of Further Education, Crieff Road, Perth, PH1 2NX; T.-Perth 21171.

Webster, Professor Robin Gordon Maclennan, MA (Cantab), MA (Arch), RIBA, ARIAS. Professor of Architecture and Head of School, Scott Sutherland School of Architecture, Robert Gordon's Institute of Technology, Aberdeen, since 1984; Senior Partner, Robin Webster & Associates, Aberdeen, since 1984; Commissioner, Royal Fine Art Commission for Scotland, since 1990; b. 24.12.39, Glasgow; m., Katherine S. Crichton; 1 s.; 2 d. Educ. Glasgow Academy; Rugby School; St. John's College, Cambridge. Assistant, Gillespie Kidd & Coia, Architects, Glasgow, 1963-64; National Building Agency, London, 1965-67; Senior Partner, Spence and Webster, Architects, 1972-84; Lecturer, Bartlett School of Architecture, 1969-74; Visiting Lecturer, Washington University, St. Louis, 1975, Cambridge University, 1976-77, and Mackintosh School, Glasgow School of Art, 1978-84. Winner, New Parliamentary Building Competition, Westminster, 1972; 1st prize, New York Waterfront Competition, 1988; Chairman, Association of Scottish Schools of Architecture, 1986-90; President, Aberdeen Society of Architects, 1989-91. Recreations: drawing and painting; sailing. Address: (b.) Scott Sutherland School of Architecture, RGIT, Garthdee Road, Aberdeen; T.-0224 313247.

Webster, G.E. (Ted), FRICS. Managing Partner Scotland, Richard Ellis, Chartered Surveyors; b. 28.2.48, Glasgow; m.; 3 children. Joined Richard Ellis, Glasgow, 1975, admitted to partnership, 1985. Recreations: Glasgow Art Club; Pollok and Western Gailes Golf Clubs. Address: (b.) Pacific House, 70 Wellington Street, Glasgow; T.-041-204 1931.

Weeple, Edward John, MA. Under Secretary, Scottish Office Industry Department, since 1990; b. 15.5.45, Glasgow; 3 s.; 1 d. Educ. St. Aloysius' College, Glasgow; Glasgow University. Entered DHSS, London, 1968; Assistant Principal, 1968-73 (Private Secretary to Minister of Health, 1971-73); Principal, 1973-78; transferred to Scottish Office, 1978; Principal (Industrial Development Division, SEPD), 1978-80; Assistant Secretary, Scottish Home and Health Department, 1980-85; Assistant Secretary, Department of Agriculture and Fisheries for Scotland, 1985-90. Address: (h.) 19 Lauder Road, Edinburgh; T.-031-668 1150.

Weir, Alan David, MBA, CA. Finance Officer, Glasgow University, since 1982; b. 25.11.37, Edinburgh; m., Alys Taylor Macdonald; 2 s. Educ. Mill Hill; Edinburgh University; Strathclyde University. National Service (commissioned), Black Watch (RHR) and 4th QONR; served Articles with Touche Ross, London; commercial and industrial experience at Board level. Recreations: golf; hill-walking. Address: (h.) 3 Dumgoyne Drive, Bearsden, Glasgow, G61 3AP; T.-041-942 7936.

Weir, Hon. Lord (David Bruce Weir), QC (Scot), MA, LLB. Senator of the College of Justice in Scotland, since 1985; b. 19.12.31. Advocate Depute, 1979-82; Chairman, Medical Appeal Tribunal, 1972-77; Chairman, Pensions Appeals Tribunal for Scotland, 1978-84.

Weir, Professor Donald Mackay, MB, ChB, FRCPEdin, MD (Hons). Professor of Microbial Immunology, Edinburgh University, since 1983; Honorary Consultant, Lothian Health Board, since 1967; b. 16.9.28, Edinburgh; m., Dr. Cecelia Caroline Blackwell; 3 s. Educ. Edinburgh Academy; Edinburgh University. Research Fellow, Medical Research Council, Rheumatism Research Unit, 1957-61; Edinburgh University: Lecturer, Department of Bacteriology, 1961-67, Senior Lecturer, 1967-78, Reader, 1978-83. Publications: Immunology, An Outline for Students of Medicine and Biology; Handbook of Experimental Immunology (Editor); Principles of Infection and Immunity in Patient Care (Co-author, with wife). Recreation: sailing. Address: (h.) 36 Drummond Place, Edinburgh; T.-031-556 7656.

Weir, Professor Jamie, MB, BS, FRCPEdin, DMRD, FRCR. Consultant Radiologist, Aberdeen Royal Infirmary, since 1976; Professor of Clinical Radiology, Aberdeen University, since 1991; b. 22.9.45, Woking. Educ. King's College School, Wimbledon; Middlesex Hospital Medical School. House Physician, then House Surgeon, Middlesex Hospital, 1969; Senior House Officer, Ipswich Hospital, 1970-71; Registrar, then Senior Registrar, Radiology, Middlesex Hospital (latterly also Harefield Hospital), 1971-75. Publications: Atlas of Radiological Anatomy (Co-author); Atlas of Clinical Echocardiography (Co-author). Recreation: golf. Address: (b.) Radiology Department, Aberdeen Royal Infirmary, Foresterhill, Aberdeen; T.-0224 681818.

Weir, Robin Loudon. Honorary Sheriff; retired hotelier; b. 17.7.19, Muar, Malaya; m., Dorothy Isabella Urquhart; 2 s.; 1 d. Educ. Bellahouston Academy, Glasgow; Glasgow University. Address: (h.) Rose Cottage, Scorrybreck, Coolin Hills Estate, Portree, Isle of Skye; T.-0478 2135.

Weir, Tom. Journalist and Photographer. Former Ordnance Surveyor; climbed in the Himalayas and began professional photography; author of several books on climbing and Scotland; Presenter, Weir's Way, Scottish Television.

Weir, William, FRAgS. Director, Ross & Weir, Dairy and Livestock Farmers; Chairman, Blackshaw Farm Park Ltd.; Director, Scottish Milk Marketing Board, since 1982; b. 9.8.24, Lugar, Ayrshire; m., Margaret Ross; 1 s.; 2 d. Educ. Patna and Dalmellington Schools. Past President: World

Federation of Ayrshire Cattle Societies, Ayrshire Cattle Society of Great Britain and Ireland; Past Chairman, Scottish Dairy Council; former Director, Cattle Services, Ayr Ltd. Recreations: occasional game of curling; watching football and athletics. Address: Wheatrig, Kilmaurs, Kilmarnock, Ayrshire; T.-0563 38231.

Weir, Viscount (William Kenneth James Weir), BA. Chairman, The Weir Group PLC, since 1966; Vice-Chairman, St. James' Place Capital plc, since 1985; Director, BICC plc, since 1977; Director, Canadian Pacific Limited; b. 9.11.33, Glasgow; m., 1, Diana MacDougall (m. diss.); 2, Jacqueline Mary Marr (m. diss.); 3, Marina Sevastopoulo; 2 s.; 1 d. Educ. Eton; Trinity College, Cambridge. Member, London Advisory Committee, Hongkong and Shanghai Banking Corporation, since 1980; Deputy Chairman, Charterhouse J. Rothschild PLC, 1983-85; Member, Court, Bank of England, 1972-84; Co-Chairman, RIT and Northern PLC, 1982-83; Director, 1970, Chairman, 1975-82, Great Northern Investment Trust Ltd.; Member, Scottish Economic Council, 1972-85; Director, British Steel Corporation, 1972-76; Member, Queen's Bodyguard for Scotland (Royal Company of Archers). Recreations: shooting; golf; fishing. Address: (h.) Rodinghead, Mauchline, Ayrshire; T.-Fiveways 233.

Welsh, Andrew Paton, MA (Hons), DipEd. MP (SNP), Angus East, since 1987; National Vice-President, SNP, since 1987; b. 19.4.44, Glasgow; m., Sheena Margaret Cannon (see Sheena Margaret Welsh); 1 d. Educ. Govan High School; Glasgow University. Member, Stirling District Council, 1974; MP (SNP), South Angus, 1974-79; SNP Parliamentary Spokesman on Housing, 1974-78 and since 1987, Self-Employed and Small Businesses, 1975-79 and since 1987, Agriculture, 1975-79 and since 1987, Parliamentary Chief Whip, 1977-79 and since 1987; SNP Executive Vice Chairman for Administration, 1979-83; Member, National Executive Committee, SNP, since 1983; Parliamentary candidate, East Angus, 1983; Member, Church and Nation Committee, Church of Scotland, 1984-85; Member, Dundee University Court, 1984-87; Provost, Angus District Council, 1984-87; Member, Angus District Health Council; Member, SCOTVEC Public Administration and Moderating Committees. Recreations: music; horse riding. Address: (h.) 22 Monymusk Road, Arbroath, Angus; T.-0241 76291.

Welsh, Frederick Wright, JP. Chairman, Community Services Committee, Dundee District Council, since 1990; Convenor of Housing, Dundee District Council, since 1992; National Chair, Association of Direct Labour Organisations, 1991-92; Director, Local Government Information Unit, 1991-92; Director/Chairman, Taywide Services, Dundee, since 1991; Member, Central Advisory Committee on Justices of the Peace, since 1991; Member, Justices Committee, Dundee District; Member, Scottish Housing Forum; Member, Post Office and Telecommunications Advisory Committee for Tayside; b. Dundee; m., Margaret; 3 s. Educ. Rockwell Secondary School, Dundee. Member, Dundee Corporation, 1973-75 (Convener, Public Libraries, Museums and Art Galleries, 1973-75); Member, Tayside Regional Council, 1974-77 (Labour Group Chief Whip and Further Education Opposition Spokesman, 1974-77); Chair, Dundee East Constituency Labour Party; Member, Dundee District Council, since 1977; Member, Central Committee, Gas Consumers Council for Scotland; Member, Perth Prison Visiting Committee; Member, Management Committee, Dundee Resources Centre for Unemployed; Chairman, ADLO Scottish Region and Member, National Council, ADLO; Vice Convener, COSLA Miscellaneous Services Committee; Depute Chair, Heat Development (Dundee) Ltd., since 1986; Member, Fire Services Scotland Examination Board, 1973-75; Member, British Standards Institute OC/4 Committee. Recreations: gardening; DIY; watching all sports;

walking. Address: (h.) 2 McKinnon Street, Dundee, DD3 6JN; T.-0382 27669.

Welsh, Gerard F.G., LLB. Regional Solicitor, Lothian Regional Council, since 1982; b. 20.2.41, Uddingston; m., Elizabeth Anne Wilde; 1 s.; 1 d. Educ. Our Lady's High School, Motherwell; Glasgow University. Apprenticeship, Scottish Gas Board; Legal Assistant and Principal Legal Assistant, Midlothian County Council; Assistant Director of Administration, Lothian Regional Council. Chairman, Society of Directors of Administration in Scotland, 1989-90. Recreations: rugby; golf; cricket. Address: (b.) ! Parliament Square, Edinburgh, EH1 1RF; T.-031-469 3444.

Wemyss and March, Earl of (Francis David Charteris), KT (1966), Hon. LLD (St. Andrews), Hon. DUniv (Edinburgh), JP, BA. Lord Lieutenant, East Lothian, 1967-87; b. 19.1.12, London; m., Mavis Lynette Gordon Murray (deceased); 1 s.; 1 d.; 1 s. (deceased); 1 d. (deceased). Educ. Eton; Balliol College, Oxford. Commissioned, Lovat Scouts (TA), 1932-44; Basutoland Administrative Service, 1937-44; War Service, African Auxiliary Pioneer Corps, Middle East, 1941-44; Chairman, Council, National Trust for Scotland, 1947-67 (President, 1967-91); Chairman, Scottish Churches Council, 1964-71; Chairman, Royal Commission on Ancient and Historical Monuments of Scotland, 1949-84; Vice-President, Marie Curie Memorial Foundation; President, Royal Scottish Geographical Society, 1958-62; President, National Bible Society of Scotland, 1960-83; Lieutenant, Queen's Bodyguard for Scotland (Royal Company of Archers). Recreations: countryside and conservation. Address: (h.) Gosford House, Longniddry, East Lothian; T.-Aberlady 200.

Wemyss, Robert Duncan, MA (Hons), MSc, MRTPI. Director of Economic Development and Planning, Western Isles Islands Council, since 1988; b. 28.3.48, Inverness; m., Marilyn Helen; 1 s.; 1 d. Educ. Inverness High School; Aberdeen University; Heriot-Watt University. Planning Assistant, Royal Burgh of Ayr, 1972-75; Assitant Director, Planning, Cumnock and Doon Valley District Council, 1975-88. Recreations: hill-walking; ornithology; photography. Address: (h.) Willowglen House, Stornoway, Isle of Lewis; T.-0851 2515.

West, Peter William Alan, MA. Secretary to the University, Strathclyde University, since 1990; b. 16.3.49, Edinburgh; m., Margaret Clark; 1 s.; 1 d. Educ. Edinburgh Academy; St. Andrews University. Administrator, Edinburgh University, 1972-77; Assistant Secretary, Leeds University, 1977-83; Deputy Registrar, Strathclyde University, 1983-89. Recreations: family; tennis; France; wine. Address: (b.) Strathclyde University, McCance Building, 16 Richmond Street, Glasgow, G1 1XQ; T.-041-552 4400, Ext. 2240.

West, Professor Thomas Summers, CBE, BSc, PhD, DSc, FRSC, FRSE, FRS. Former Director, Macaulay Institute for Soil Research, Aberdeen; b. 18.11.27, Peterhead; m., Margaret O. Lawson; 1 s.; 2 d. Educ. Tarbat School, Portmahomack; Tain Royal Academy; Aberdeen University; Birmingham University. Lecturer in Chemistry, Birmingham University, 1955-63; Imperial College of Science and Technology, London: Reader in Chemistry, 1963-65, Professor of Chemistry, 1965-75. Meldola Medal, Royal Institute of Chemistry; Gold Medal, Society of Analytical Chemistry; President, Society for Analytical Chemistry, 1969-71; Honorary Secretary, Royal Society of Chemistry, 1972-75; President, Analytical Division, International Union of Pure and Applied Chemistry, 1979-81; Secretary General, IUPAC, 1983-91; Honorary Research Professor, Aberdeen University, since 1983. Recreations: gardening; motoring; reading; music; fishing. Address: (h.) 31 Baillieswells Drive, Bieldside, Aberdeen, AB1 9AT; T.-0224 868294.

Westcott, Michael John Herbert, BSc (Hons) (Glasgow), Hon. MA (Edinburgh). University Administrative Fellow, Edinburgh University; b. 16.4.19, Plymouth. Educ. Hillhead High School; Glasgow University. Ministry of Home Grown Timber Production, 1940-43; Army (Royal Signals), 1943-48 (retired as Major); Colonial Service, Sierra Leone (Administrative Officer), 1948-61; Administrative Officer, Edinburgh University, 1962-86. Chairman, Friends of the Buckhaven Theatre; Vice-Chairman, Royal Lyceum Theatre Club; Honorary President, Edinburgh and SE Scotland VSO Group. Recreations: walking; theatre; music. Address: (h.) 2 Kilgraston Court, Kilgraston Road, Edinburgh, EH9 2ES; T.-031-447 8282.

Westwood, Alan, BSc, MSc, PhD, CChem, MRSC, FRCPath. Top Grade Scientist and Head, Department of Paediatric Biochemistry, Royal Hospital for Sick Children, Edinburgh, since 1979; Honorary Senior Lecturer, Edinburgh University, since 1981; b. 2.3.48, Luton; m., Jennifer Anne; 1 s.; 1 d. Educ. Luton Technical School; Liverpool University; Birmingham University. Clinical Biochemist: Broadgreen Hospital, Liverpool, 1969, Birmingham Children's Hospital, 1970, Liverpool Royal Infirmary, 1976, Edinburgh Royal Hospital for Sick Children, 1979. Chairman, Scottish Region, Association of Clinical Biochemists, 1984-87 (Member of Association Council, 1982-85). Recreations: tennis; curling; microcomputing. Address: (h.) Fawnspark, Loanstone, by Penicuik, Midlothian, EH26 8PH; T.-Penicuik 78407.

Whaley, Professor Keith, MB, BS, MD, PhD, FRCP, FRCPath. Professor, Department of Pathology, Glasgow University, since 1984; Honorary Consultant in Clinical Immunology; b. 2.9.42, Redcar; m., Mairearad Campbell Whyte; 2 s. Educ. Middlesbrough High School; Newcastle-upon-Tyne University. SHO/Registrar, Medicine/Rheumatology, Centre for Rheumatic Diseases, Glasgow, 1967-69; MRC Research Fellow, then Lecturer, Immunopathology, Glasgow University, 1969-74; Assistant Professor of Medicine, Medical College, Virginia, 1974-76; Lecturer, then Senior Lecturer, then Reader, Glasgow University, 1976-84. Publications: Methods in Complement for Clinical Immunologists; Complement in Health and Disease. Recreations: sailing; jogging; gardening; reading. Address: (b.) Pathology Department, Western Infirmary, Glasgow; T.-041-339 8822, Ext. 4210.

Whaling, Frank, MA, ThD, PhD, AAABI, FIBA, FRAS, FWLA, FABI, MIPSP. Senior Lecturer, Religious Studies, Edinburgh University, since 1984; b. 5.2.34; m., Patricia Hill; 1 s.; 1 d. Educ. Christ's College, Cambridge; Wesley House, Cambridge; Harvard University. Minister: Methodist Church, Birmingham, 1960-62; Methodist Church, India, 1962-66; Methodist Church, Eastbourne, 1966-69; Teaching Fellow, Harvard University, 1972-73; Special Teacher in Religious Studies, Edinburgh University, 1973-84; Director: Edinburgh-Farmington Project, Edinburgh and Oxford, 1977-81; Edinburgh-Cook Project, Edinburgh and Gloucester, 1981-83; Council Member, Shap Working Party, London, since 1973; Chairman/President, Scottish Working Party on Religion in Education, since 1975; Council Member, Christian Education Movement in Scotland, since 1979; Chairman, Scottish Churches China Group, since 1986; Chairman, Edinburgh Inter-Faith Association, since 1987; Chairman, Scottish Inter-Faith Symposium, since 1988; Fulbright Fellow, Harvard University, 1981; British Council awards, 1982 and 1984; British Academy Fellow to China, 1982 and 1987; Commonwealth Foundation Award to India, 1985; Moray Trust Award, 1987. Publications: An Approach to Dialogue: Hinduism and Christianity, 1966; The Rise of the Religious Significance of Rama, 1980; John and Charles Wesley in the Classics of Western Spirituality, 1981; The World's Religious Traditions: Current Perspectives in Religious Studies, 1984; Contemporary Approaches to the

Study of Religion: The Humanities, 1984, and The Social Sciences, 1985; Religions of the World, 1985; Christian Theology and World Religions: A Global Approach, 1986; Religion in Today's World, 1987; Compassion Through Understanding, 1990. Address: (h.) 29 Ormidale Terrace, Murrayfield, Edinburgh, EH12 6EA.

Wheater, Roger John, OBE, CBiol, FIBiol, FRSA, FRSE. Director, Royal Zoological Society of Scotland, since 1972; b. 24.11.33, Brighton; m., Jean Ord Troup; 1 s.; 1 d. Educ. Brighton, Hove and Sussex Grammar School; Brighton Technical College. Commissioned, Royal Sussex Regiment, 1953; served Gold Coast Regiment, 1953-54; 4/5th Bn., Royal Sussex Regiment (TA), 1954-56; Colonial Police, Uganda, 1956-61; Chief Warden, Murchison Falls National Park, 1961-70; Director, Uganda National Parks, 1970-72; Member, Co-ordinating Committee, Nuffield Unit of Tropical Animal Ecology; Member, Board of Governors, Mweka College of Wildlife Management, Tanzania; Director, National Park Lodges Ltd.; Member, Uganda National Research Council; Vice Chairman, Uganda Tourist Association; Council Member, 1980, and President, 1988-91, International Union of Directors of Zoological Gardens; Council Member, 1974, and Vice Chairman, 1980, The National Federation of Zoological Gardens of Great Britain and Ireland; Chairman, Anthropoid Ape Advisory Panel, 1977; Member, International Zoo Year Book Editorial Board, 1987; President, Association of British Wild Animal Keepers, 1984; Chairman, Membership and Licensing Committee, since 1984; Chairman, Working Party on Zoo Licensing Act, 1981-84; Council Member, Zoological Society of London, since 1991; Member of Council, National Trust for Scotland, 1973-78, Executive Committee, 1982-87; Chairman, Cammo Estate Advisory Committee, 1980; Member, Proceedings B Editorial Board, Royal Society of Edinburgh, 1988-91; ESU William Thyne Scholar, 1975; Assessor, Council, Scottish Wildlife Trust, 1973; Consultant, World Tourist Organisation (United Nations), 1980; Member, Secretary of State for Scotland's Working Group on Environmental Education, since 1990; Vice-Chairman, Edinburgh Branch, English Speaking Union, 1977-81; President, Edinburgh Special Mobile Angling Club, 1982-86. Recreations: country pursuits; painting; gardening. Address: (b.) Scottish National Zoological Park, Edinburgh, EH12 6TS; T.-031-334 9171.

Wheatley, Denys Neville, BSc, PhD, DSc, FRCPath, CBiol, FIBiol. Reader in Cell Pathology, Aberdeen University, since 1981; b. 18.3.40, Ascot; m., Pamela Snare; 2 d. Educ. Windsor Grammar School; London University. Research Fellow, Aberdeen University, 1964; MRC Travelling Fellow, Wisconsin University, 1968-69; US Public Health Service supported Fellowship, 1969-70; Research Fellow, then Lecturer in Pathology, then Senior Lecturer, Aberdeen University, 1970-81. Director and Scientific Consultant, Biocure Ltd. Recreations: music; hill-walking; rowing. Address: (b.) Department of Pathology, University Medical Buildings, Foresterhill, Aberdeen, AB9 2ZD; T.-0224 681818.

Wheatley, Sheriff John Francis, BL. Sheriff, Perthshire and Kinross-shire, at Perth, since 1980; b. 9.5.41, Edinburgh; m., Bronwen Catherine Fraser; 2 s. Educ. Mount St. Mary's College, Derbyshire; Edinburgh University. Called to Scottish Bar, 1966; Standing Counsel to Scottish Development Department, 1968-74; Advocate Depute, 1974-78. Recreations: music; gardening. Address: Braefoot Farmhouse, Fossoway, Kinross-shire; T.-Fossoway 212.

Wheelans, James Dunn, CBE, MBE (Mil), BL. Honorary Sheriff, Selkirk, since 1979; b. 19.1.13, Hawick; m., Catherine Laidlaw Sanderson. Educ. Hawick High School; Edinburgh University. Legal Assessor to Scottish Land Court, 1936; War Service, TA, 1939-45 (active service, Europe, demobilised in

rank of Lt. Col.); entered private legal practice, Galashiels, 1946; part-time Secretary, Scottish Woollen Technical College, 1949-79; elected to Council, Law Society of Scotland, 1958: Vice-president, 1971-72, President, 1974-76; retired from active legal practice, 1982. Recreations: fishing; gardening; hill-walking; photography. Address: (h.) Lillieslea, Lilliesleaf, Melrose; T.-083 57 304.

Wheeler, Sir (Harry) Anthony, Kt (1988), OBE, PPRSA, Hon. RA, Hon. RHA, Hon. RGI, Hon. DDes, Hon. RBS, PPRIAS, FRIBA, FRSA, BArch, MRTPI, DipTP. Consultant, Wheeler & Sproson, Architects and Town Planners, Edinburgh and Kirkcaldy, since 1986; b. 7.11.19, Stranraer; m., Dorothy Jean Campbell; 1 d. Educ. Stranraer High School; Glasgow School of Architecture; Strathclyde University. War Service, Royal Artillery, 1939-46; John Keppie Scholar and Sir Rowand Anderson Studentship, RIBA Grissell Medallist, Neale Bursar; Assistant to City Architect, Oxford, to Sir Herbert Baker & Scott, London; Senior Architect, Glenrothes Development Corporation; began private practice in Fife; Senior Lecturer, Dundee School of Architecture, 1952-58; Saltire Awards and Commendations (22), Civic Trust Awards and Commendations (12); Trustee, Scottish Civic Trust, 1970-83; Member, Royal Fine Art Commission for Scotland, 1967-85; President, Royal Scottish Academy, 1983-90. Recreations: sketching and water colours; fishing; music; drama; gardens. Address: (h.) Hawthornbank House, Dean Village, Edinburgh, EH4 3BH.

Wherrett, Professor Brian Spencer, BSc, PhD, FInstP, FRSE. Chair of Theoretical Optoelectronics, Heriot-Watt University, since 1986; b. 8.5.46, Bromley; m., Shirley Ruth; 1 s.; 1 d. Educ. Westcliff High School; Reading University. Lecturer, Department of Physics, Heriot-Watt University, 1971; promoted to Senior Lecturer and Reader; Visiting Professor, North Texas State University, 1981-82; Past Chairman, SERC Committee on Atomic, Molecular and Plasma Physics and Optical Sciences. Recreations: golf; squash. Address: (b.) Department of Physics, Heriot-Watt University, Riccarton, Edinburgh, EH14 4AS; T.-031-451 3039.

Whitby, Professor Lionel Gordon, MA, PhD, MD, BChir, FRCP, FRCPEdin, FRCPath, FRSE, FIBiol. Emeritus Professor; Professor of Clinical Chemistry, Edinburgh University, 1963-91; Honorary Consultant in Clinical Chemistry, South Eastern Regional Hospital Board, 1963-74, and Lothian Health Board, 1974-91; b. 18.7.26, London; m., Joan Hunter Sanderson; 1 s.; 2 d. Educ. Eton College; King's College, Cambridge. MRC Scholar for Training in Research, Biochemistry Department, Cambridge University, 1948-51; Fellow, King's College, Cambridge, 1951-55; junior hospital appointments, Middlesex Hospital, London, etc., 1956-58; Registrar in Chemical Pathology, then Assistant Lecturer, Royal Postgraduate Medical School, London, 1958-60; Rockefeller Travelling Fellowship in Medicine, National Institutes of Health, Bethesda, 1959-60; University Biochemist, Addenbrooke's Hospital, Cambridge, 1960-63; Fellow, Peterhouse, Cambridge, 1961-62; Dean, Faculty of Medicine, Edinburgh University, 1969-72 and 1983-86. Visiting Professor of Chemical Pathology, Royal Postgraduate Medical School, 1974; Vice-Principal, Edinburgh University, 1979-83; Member, General Medical Council, 1986-91; Medical Laboratory Technicians Board, Council for Professions Supplementary to Medicine, since 1978. Publications: Lecture Notes on Clinical Chemistry (Co-author); Principles & Practice of Medical Computing (Co-editor); scientific papers. Recreations: gardening; photography. Address: (h.) 51 Dick Place, Edinburgh, EH9 2JA; T.-031-667 4358.

White, Campbell, BL. Senior Partner, Wright Johnston & Mackenzie, since 1988; b. 4.2.35, Blantyre; m., Helen Fairbairn Borthwick; 1 s.; 4 d. Educ. Kirkcudbright Academy; Glasgow University. Former Chairman, F.J.C. Lilley PLC; former Chairman, W.H. Lowrie Ltd.; Secretary, Whithorn Trust; Secretary, Scottish Plant Owners Association. Recreations: golf; shooting; fishing. Address: (h.) 226 Fenwick Road, Giffnock, Glasgow; T.-041-638 3900.

White, David J., BSc (Hons), PhD, JP. Rector, Garnock Academy, since 1974; b. 13.12.32, New York; m., Cecilia Wilson; 1 s.; 3 d. Educ. Strathclyde University; Glasgow University. Member, Saltcoats Town Council/Chair, Cunninghame District Council, 1964-77; Member, Irvine Development Corporation, 1975-77; Member, Consultative Committee on the Curriculum, 1976-83; Chair, Education, for the Industrial Society Project, 1977-83; Chair, European Association of Teachers in Scotland, since 1989. Address: (h.) 30 Mulgrew Avenue, Saltcoats, Ayrshire, KA21 6HP; T.-0294 62568.

White, Duncan Bryce, OBE. Sheriff Clerk, Edinburgh, since 1981; Commissary Clerk, Edinburgh, since 1981; Sheriff Clerk of Chancery, since 1981; Regional Sheriff Clerk, Sheriffdom of Lothian and Borders, since 1986; b. 3.2.32, Airdrie; m., Ivie White Neill; 2 d. Educ. Coatbridge High School. HM Treasury, 1953; HM Exchequer, 1954; Sheriff Court, Aberdeen, 1955; Sheriff Court, Glasgow, 1961; Sheriff Court, Dunblane, 1964; Principal Training Officer, Scottish Court Service, 1974. Recreations: golf; hill-walking. Address: (h.) Mylnhurst, Old Doune Road, Dunblane, Perthshire; T.-0786 822582.

White, Glenda Ann, BA (Hons), MEd (Hons), DCE. Chief Inspector of Schools, Department of Education, Strathclyde Regional Council (HM Inspector of Schools, 1985-90); b. 5.4.45, Wallasey. Educ. Queen Elizabeth's Girls' Grammar School, Barnet; Open University; Glasgow University; Manchester University. Teaching appointments, four primary schools in Liverpool and Glasgow, including Assistant Headteacher, Commonhead Primary School, Easterhouse, 1966-72; Lecturer, Callander Park College of Education, Falkirk, 1972-74; Lecturer/Senior Lecturer, Jordanhill College of Education, Glasgow, 1974-85. Member, Education Advisory Committee, Independent Television Commission; Associate Secretary, Hillhead Baptist Church. Recreations: hill-walking; theatre; music. Address: (h.) 72 Great George Street, Glasgow, G12 8RU; T.-041-339 0893.

White, Graham, BSocSci, DipEd. Director, The Environment Centre, since 1983; Author and Editor, Scottish Environmental Handbook, since 1989; b. 2.9.48, St. Helens. Educ. Cowley Grammar School, St. Helens; Bradford University; Leeds University. Director of Community Media, InterAction Trust, 1971-74; Youth and Community Director, Islington Bus Company, 1974-76; travelled and worked in USA, 1976-79; worked for Volunteers Environmental Resource Centre as Manager and Education Officer, 1979-83. Publication: The Nature of Scotland (Co-author). Recreations: mountaineering; fly fishing; scuba diving. Address: (b.) The Environment Centre, Drummond High School, Cochran Terrace, Edinburgh, EH7 4QP; T.-031-557 2135.

White, Eur. Ing. James Francis, CEng, FICE, FIHT, Eur.Ing. Director of Roads and Transport, Tayside Regional Council, 1986-91 (Senior Depute Director, 1977-86); b. 14.9.30, St. Andrews; m., Winifred Rose Gourlay Robertson; 3 s. Educ. Madras College, St. Andrews; Dundee Technical College. Apprentice road surveyor, Fife County Council, 1948-53; Engineer and Divisional Surveyor, Perth and Kinross County Council, 1953-63; Divisional Surveyor, Hereford County Council, 1963-66; Depute County Surveyor, then County Surveyor, Ross and Cromarty County Council, 1966-75; Depute Director of Roads, Highland Regional Council, 1975-77. Chairman, North of Scotland Branch, Institution of Highways and Transportation, 1976-77; Chairman, Dundee Branch, Institution of Civil Engineers, 1988-89. Recreations: gardening; golf. Address: (h.) 138 Strathern Road, Broughty Ferry, Dundee, DD5 1BQ; T.-Dundee 76249.

White, John, BA, MIFireE. Firemaster, Fife Regional Council, since 1988; b. 23.3.36, Rosewell; 1 s.; 1 d. Educ. Lasswade Secondary; West Calder High School; Open University. South Eastern Fire Brigade, 1959; Grampian Fire Brigade, 1969; Fife Fire Brigade, 1979. Recreations: golf; hill-walking. Address: (b.) Fife Fire & Rescue Service Headquarters, Strathore Road, Thornton, Kirkcaldy; T.-0592 774451.

White, Robert I.K., BSc, FRICS. Chief Estates Officer, Scottish Office, since 1985; b. 22.2.36, Comrie; m., Constance M. Jackson; 2 s. Educ. Larbert High School; Edinburgh University. Ministry of Public Buildings and Works/PSA, 1962-85, serving in Glasgow, Newcastle, London, Germany and Edinburgh; Chairman, GP Division, RICS in Scotland, 1991-92. Recreations: golf; curling; gardening. Address: (b.) Room 39a, James Craig Walk, Edinburgh, EH1 3SZ; T.-031-244 3629.

White, Professor Stephen Leonard, MA, PhD, DPhil. Professor of Politics, Glasgow University, since 1991; b. 1.7.45, Dublin; m., Ishbel MacPhie; 1 s. Educ. St. Andrew's College, Dublin; Trinity College, Dublin; Glasgow University; Wolfson College, Oxford. Lecturer in Politics, Glasgow University, 1971-85, Reader, 1985-91. Examiner, Certificate of Sixth Year Studies (Modern Studies), Scottish Examination Board, since 1985; Joint Editor, Coexistence. Publications include: Britain and the Bolshevik Revolution, 1980; Origins of Detente, 1986; The Bolshevik Poster, 1988; Gorbachev and After, 1991. Address: (h.) 11 Hamilton Drive, Glasgow, G12 8DN; T.-041-334 9541.

Whitelaw, Brian Murray, LLB, DipLP, NP. Depute Chief Executive, Caithness District Council, since 1990; Solicitor and Notary Public; b. 25.12.53, Glasgow; m., Joan Harte; 1 s.; 2 d. Educ. St. Columba's, Clydebank; Strathclyde University. Trainee Solicitor, 1981-83; Assistant Solicitor, Borders Regional Council, 1983-85; Senior Solicitor, Dumbarton District Council, 1985-86; Principal Solicitor, Dumbarton District Council, 1986-90. Recreations: pistol shooting; photography; drinking whisky. Address: (b.) Caithness District Council, Market Square, Wick, KW1 4AB; T.-0955 3761.

Whitelaw, Ian Macleod. Assistant Secretary, Department of Agriculture and Fisheries for Scotland, since 1984; b. 20.9.42, Edinburgh; m., Rhoda Margaret Thomson; 1 s.; 1 d. Educ. Royal High School, Edinburgh. Scottish Education Department, 1961-71; Secretary, Scottish Agricultural Development Council, 1971-74; DAFS, since 1974. Recreations: sport; history (Scottish/military); hill-walking. Address: (b.) Department of Agriculture and Fisheries for Scotland, Pentland House, 47 Robbs Loan, Edinburgh, EH14 1TW; T.-031-556 8400, Ext. 6335.

Whitelaw, James Weir, MB, ChB, FRCPEdin, FRCPath, DPath. Consultant Haematologist, Southern General Hospital, Glasgow, since 1960; Chairman, Scottish Committee for Hospital Medical Services, 1986-89; Honorary Clinical Lecturer, Glasgow University; b. 9.7.29, Hull; 1 s.; 1 d. Educ. Paisley Grammar School; Glasgow University. House Physician and House Surgeon, Royal Alexandra Infirmary, Paisley; Captain, RAMC; Senior Registrar, Pathology Department, Western Infirmary, Glasgow; Consultant

Haematologist, Southern General Hospital, Glasgow; Honorary Clinical Lecturer, Glasgow University. Recreations: travel; bowling. Address: (b.) Department of Haematology, Southern General Hospital, Glasgow, G51 4TF; T.-041-445 2466, Ext. 4119.

Whitelaw, Robert George, MA, MD, FRCOG, DL. Deputy Lieutenant, Fife, since 1969; Honorary Sheriff, since 1978; b. 29.4.13, Motherwell; m., Cicely Mary Ballard; 1 s. Educ. Wishaw High School; Glasgow University. Consultant Obstetrician and Gynaecologist, West Fife Group of Hospitals, 1956-78; External Examiner, Edinburgh University, 1967-71; Examiner: Central Midwives Board for Scotland, General Nursing Council for Scotland, Royal College of Surgeons of Edinburgh, PLAB. Past President, Fife Branch, BMA; Past President, Dunfermline Rotary Club. Publications: various papers, mainly on obstetrical and gynaecological subjects. Recreations: golf; photography; travel. Address: (h.) 64 Garvock Hill, Dunfermline, Fife, KY12 7UU; T.-0383 721209.

Whiten, David Andrew, BSc, PhD, FBPS. Reader in Psychology, St. Andrews University, since 1990; b. 20.4.48, Grimsby; m., Dr. Susie Challoner; 2 d. Educ. Wintringham School, Grimsby; Sheffield University; Bristol University; Oxford University. Research Fellow, Oxford University, 1972-75; Lecturer, St. Andrews University, 1975-90; Visiting Professor, Zurich University, 1992. Publications: Machiavellian Intelligence (Co-author), 1988; Natural Theories of Mind, 1991; Foraging Strategies of Monkeys, Apes and Humans (Co-author), 1992. Recreations: painting; walking; wildlife; good-lifing. Address: (b.) Department of Psychology, St. Andrews University, St. Andrews, KY16 9JU.

Whitfield, Professor Charles Richard, MD, FRCOG, FRCPGlas. Regius Professor of Midwifery, Glasgow University, since 1976; Consultant Obstetrician, Queen Mother's Hospital, Glasgow, and Consultant Gynaecologist, Western Infirmary, Glasgow, since 1976; b. 21.10.27, India; m., Marion Douglas McKinney; 1 s.; 2 d. Educ. Campbell College, Belfast; Queen's University, Belfast. Resident appointments, Belfast Teaching Hospitals, 1951-53; RAMC 1953-64 (Senior Specialist in Obstetrics and Gynaecology, 1959-64); Consultant Obstetrician and Gynaecologist, Belfast Teaching Hospitals, 1968-74; Professor of Obstetrics and Gynaecology, Manchester University, 1974-76. Publication: Dewhurst's Postgraduate Textbook of Obstetrics and Gynaecology (Editor). Recreations: trying to remember what they were. Address: (h.) 23 Thorn Road, Bearsden, Glasgow, G61.

Whiting, Professor Brian, MD, FRCPGlas, FFPM. Titular Professor (Clinical Pharmacology), Glasgow University, since 1986; Dean, Faculty of Medicine, since 1992; Head, Division of Clinical Pharmacology, Department of Medicine and Therapeutics, 1989-91; Consultant Physician (Clinical Pharmacology), since 1972, now at Western Infirmary, Glasgow; Chairman, Glasgow Clinical Pharmacology Group, 1986-91; b. 6.1.39, Manchester; 2 d. Educ. Stockport Grammar School; Glasgow University. Research and hospital posts, Stobhill General Hospital, Department of Materia Medica, 1965-77; Visiting Professor of Clinical Pharmacology, University of California, San Francisco, 1978-79; returned to Glasgow, 1979; Director, Clinical Pharmacokinetics Laboratory, Department of Materia Medica, Stobhill General Hospital, Glasgow, 1980-91; Treasurer, Clinical Section, British Pharmacological Society, 1987-91. Publication: Lecture Notes on Clinical Pharmacology (Co-author). Recreations: painting; music; mountaineering. Address: (h.) 2 Milner Road, Glasgow, G13 1QL; T.-041-959 2324.

Whitley, Rev. Laurence Arthur Brown, MA, BD. Minister, Montrose Old Parish, since 1985 (Busby East and West, 1975-85); b. 19.9.49, Port Glasgow; m., Catherine MacLean MacFadyen; 1 s.; 1 d. Educ. Edinburgh Academy; Edinburgh University; St. Andrews University. Assistant Minister, St. Andrews, Dundee, 1974-75. Parliamentary candidate (SNP), Dumfriesshire, February and October, 1974. Recreation: Heautontimorumenosis. Address: (h.) 2 Rosehill Road, Montrose, Angus, DD10 8ST; T.-Montrose 72447.

Whitson, Angus Grigor Macbeath, LLB. Past Chairman, Council, Scottish Tartans Society; Honorary Secretary, Angus Branch, British Red Cross Society, 1969-88; Company Director and Insurance Broker; b. 17.3.42, Dundee; m., Elizabeth Marjorie Greville; 2 s.; 1 d. Educ. Loretto School; Edinburgh University. Solicitor, Angus, 1966-77; Clerk to the Justices of the Peace for Angus, 1970-76. Recreations: fishing; shooting; sailing; curling; drinking fine spirits and wines. Address: (h.) The Kirklands, by Montrose, Angus.

Whitson, Harold A., CBE, BA; b. 20.9.16, Esher; m., Rowena Pitt; 1 s.; 2 d. Educ. Rugby School; Trinity College, Cambridge. Royal Engineers, 1940-46; Melville, Dundas and Whitson Ltd., 1946-82; East Kilbride Development Corporation, 1962-79; President, Glasgow Chamber of Commerce, 1967-68; Chairman, Irvine Development Corporation, 1979-82; former Director, Scottish National Orchestra; Fellow, Royal Society of Arts. Recreations: gardening; shooting. Address: (h.) Edmonston House, Biggar, ML12 6QY; T.-0899 20063.

Whittemore, Professor Colin Trengove, BSc, PhD, DSc, NDA, CBiol, FIBiol. Head, Institute of Ecology and Resource Management, Edinburgh University, since 1990, and Professor of Agriculture and Rural Economy, since 1990; b. 16.7.42, Chester; m., Chris; 1 s.; 3 d. Educ. Rydal School; Newcastle-upon-Tyne University. Lecturer in Agriculture, Edinburgh University and Head, Animal Production, Advisory and Development, Edinburgh School of Agriculture; Professor of Animal Production, Head, Animal Division, Edinburgh School of Agriculture. Sir John Hammond Memorial Prize for scientific contribution to an understanding of nutrition and growth; Oxford University Blackman Lecture; Royal Agricultural Society of England Gold Medal for research; Mignini Oscar; David Black Award. Recreations: skiing; riding. Address: (b.) Edinburgh University, School of Agriculture, West Mains Road, Edinburgh, EH9 3JG; T.-031-667 1041.

Whittington, Graeme Walter, BA, PhD. Reader in Geography, St. Andrews University, since 1982 (Chairman, Department of Geography and Geology, since 1987); b. 25.7.31, Cranleigh. Educ. King Edward VI Royal Grammar School, Guildford; Reading University. St. Andrews University: Assistant, 1959; Lecturer, 1962, Senior Lecturer, 1972; Visiting Lecturer, Natal University, 1971; Member, British Association Committee on Ancient Fields, 1958-73. Publications: Environment and Land Use in Africa (Co-Editor); An Historical Geography of Scotland (Co-Editor). Recreations: gardening; classical music. Address: (h.) 3 Leonard Gardens, St. Andrews, Fife, KY16 8RD; T.-0334 76807.

Whyte, Donald, JP, FHG, FSG. Consultant Genealogist, Author and Lecturer; b. 13.3.26, Newtongrange; m., Mary Burton; 3 d. Educ. Crookston School, Musselburgh; Institute of Heraldic and Genealogical Studies, Canterbury. Agricultural and horticultural work, 1940-68; professional genealogist, 1968-76; Member, Kirkliston and Winchburgh District Council, 1964-75 (Chairman, 1970-73); Member, West Lothian County Council, 1970-75; founder Member and Vice-President, Scottish Genealogy Society; President, Association of Scottish Genealogists and Record Agents, since 1981. Publications: Kirkliston: A Short Parish History; Dictionary of Scottish Emigrants to USA; Introducing Scottish Genealogical Research; Dictionary of Scottish Emigrants to Canada before Confederation; Walter MacFarlane: Clan Chief and Antiquary. Address: (h.) 4 Carmel Road, Kirkliston, EH29 9DD; T.-031-333 3245.

Whyte, Duncan, CA, ATII. Financial Director, Scottish Power plc, since 1988; b. 27.7.46, Falkirk; m., Marion; 1 s. Educ. Kilsyth Academy. Qualified as CA, 1968; Arthur Anderson & Co., 1969-83 (Managing Partner, Edinburgh Office, 1980-83); Financial Director, Kwik-Fit Holdings PLC, 1983-88. Recreations: squash; golf; general sport; reading (history). Address: (b.) Cathcart House, Spean Street, Glasgow, G44 4BE.

Whyte, Rev. Iain Alexander, BA, BD, STM. National Secretary for Scotland, Christian Aid, since 1990; Minister, Blairhill Dundyvan Parish Church, Coatbridge, 1987-90; Convener, Africa Committee, Board of World Mission and Unity, Church of Scotland, 1987-91; b. 3.9.40, Stirling; m., Isabel Helen Martin; 2 s.; 1 d. Educ. Sherborne School, Dorset; St. Peter's College, Oxford; Glasgow University; Union Theological Seminary, NY. Assistant Minister, Kildrum, Cumbernauld, 1967-69; Minister and Youth Worker in Ghana, 1969-71; Chaplain to Overseas Students in Glasgow, 1971-74; Lecturer, Falkirk Technical College, 1974-75; Minister, Merksworth Parish Church, Paisley, 1976-81; Chaplain, St. Andrews University, 1981-87. Scottish Churches Representative, Board, Christian Aid, 1980-86 (Chairman, Christian Aid Middle East Committee, 1982-86); Chairman, Scottish Churches Council Race and Community Relations Group, 1981-83; Scottish Representative, Britain/Zimbabwe Society; former Chair, Glasgow Anti-Apartheid Group. Recreations: travel; squash; watching St. Mirren; numismatics; candle-making. Address: (h.) 34 Shandon Crescent, Edinburgh, EH11 1QF; T.-031-337 3559.

Whyte, Rev. James, BD, DipCE. Parish Minister, Broom, Newton Mearns, since 1987; b. 26.4.46, Glasgow; m., Norma Isabella West; 1 s.; 2 d. Educ. Glasgow; Jordanhill College; Glasgow University. Trained as planning engineer; studied community education (Glasgow and Boston, Mass., USA); Community Organiser with Lamp of Lothian Collegiate Trust, Haddington; Organiser of Community Education, Dumbarton, 1971-73; Assistant Principal Community Education Officer, Renfrew Division, Strathclyde Region, 1973-77; entered ministry, Church of Scotland, 1977; Assistant Minister: Barrhead Arthurlie, 1977-78, St. Marks, Oldhall, Paisley, 1978-80; Minister, Coupar Angus Abbey, 1981-87. Recreations: gardening; reading. Address: Manse of Broom, 3 Laigh Road, Newton Mearns, Glasgow, G77; T.-041-639 2916.

Whyte, Very Rev. Professor James Aitken, MA, LLD, DD. Moderator, General Assembly of the Church of Scotland, 1988-89; Professor of Practical Theology and Christian Ethics, St. Andrews University, 1958-87; b. 28.1.20, Leith; m., Elisabeth Wilson Mill (deceased); 2 s.; 1 d. Educ. Daniel Stewart's College, Edinburgh; Edinburgh University. Ordained and commissioned as Chaplain to the Forces, 1945; Minister: Dunollie Road Church, Oban, 1948-54, Mayfield North Church, Edinburgh, 1954-58; Dean of Divinity, St. Andrews University, 1968-72; Principal, St. Mary's College, 1978-82; Kerr Lecturer, Glasgow University, 1969-72; Croall Lecturer, Edinburgh University, 1972-73; Hon. LLD, Dundee University, 1981; Hon.DD, St. Andrews University, 1989; President, Society for the Study of Theology, 1983-84; Margaret Harris Lecturer, Dundee University, 1990. Address: (h.) 13 Hope Street, St. Andrews, Fife; T.-St. Andrews 72323.

Whyte, Robert, MB, ChB, FRCPsych, DPM. Consultant Psychotherapist, Carswell House, Glasgow, since 1979; b.

1.6.41, Edinburgh; m., Susan Frances Milburn; 1 s.; 1 d. Educ. George Heriot's, Edinburgh; St. Andrews University. House Officer in Surgery, Arbroath Infirmary, 1966; House Officer in Medicine, Falkirk and District Royal Infirmary, 1967; Trainee in Psychiatry, Dundee Psychiatric Services, 1967-73; Consultant Psychiatrist, Duke Street Hospital, Glasgow, 1973. Past Chairman, Scottish Association of Analytical Psychotherapists; Member, Scottish Institute of Human Relations. Address: (h.) Waverley, 70 East Kilbride Road, Busby, Glasgow, G76 8HU; T.-041-644 1659.

Wickham-Jones, Caroline R., MA, MIFA, FSA, FSA Scot. Secretary, Society of Antiquaries of Scotland, since 1988; Archaeologist; b., 25.4.55, Middlesborough. Educ. Teesside High School; Edinburgh University. Freelance archaeologist with research interests in early (postglacial) settlement of Scotland and in stone tools; most recent project: excavation of mesolithic settlement site on Rhum; Council Member, Institute of Field Archaeologists, 1986-90; Trustee, John Muir Trust, since 1989. Recreations: travel; wilderness walking; socialising. Address: (b.) Society of Antiquaries of Scotland, Royal Museum of Scotland, Queen Street, Edinburgh, EH2; T.-031-225 7534, Ext. 327.

Wigglesworth, Rev. Chris, MBE, BSc, PhD, BD. General Secretary, Church of Scotland Board of World Mission and Unity, since 1987; b. 8.4.37, Leeds; m., Ann Livesey; 1 s.; 3 d. Educ. Grangefield Grammar School, Stockton-on-Tees; University College, Durham; New College, Edinburgh. Church of North India, 1967-72; St. Andrew's and St. Columba's Church, Bombay, 1972-79; University Lecturer in Practical Theology, Aberdeen, 1979-86. Recreations: painting; surviving. Address: (h.) 12 Leven Terrace, Edinburgh; T.-031-228 6335.

Wight, John James. Farmer; Director, Royal Highland and Agricultural Society of Scotland, since 1981; Council Member, British Charolais Cattle Society, since 1984; b. 3.5.38, Crawford; m., Netta S.S. Struthers; 2 s.; 1 d. Educ. Biggar High School. Member, NFU Committee, Biggar; Member, Biggar Show Committee; former Member, NFU Council; former Council Member, North British Hereford Herd Book Society; Past President, Coulter Curling Club. Recreations: curling; golf. Address: Midlock, Crawford, Biggar, Lanarkshire, ML12 6UA; T.-08642 230.

Wight, Robin A.F., MA, FCA. Regional Executive Chairman – Scotland, Coopers & Lybrand, since 1989; b. 5.6.38, Edinburgh; m., Sheila; 3 s.; 1 d. Educ. Dollar Academy; Magdalene College, Cambridge. Partner, Coopers & Lybrand, since 1971; Regional Partner, Scotland, 1977-89; Member, Executive Committee, 1978-87; Member, Governing Board, since 1987. Recreations: skiing; golf; reading; theatre. Address: (h.) 22 Regent Terrace, Edinburgh; T.-031-556 2100.

Wightman, Very Rev. William David, BA (Hons). Provost, St. Andrews Cathedral, Aberdeen, since 1991, also Priest-in-Charge, St. Ninian's, Aberdeen; Hon. Canon, Christchurch Cathedral, Hartford, Conn., since 1991; b. 29.1.39, Leicester; m., Karen Elizabeth Harker; 2 s.; 2 d. Educ. Alderman Newton's Grammar School, Leicester; George Dixon Grammar School, Birmingham; Birmingham University; Wells Theological College. Ordained Deacon, 1963; ordained Priest, 1964. Director, Training for Ministry (Diocese of Aberdeen and Orkney), since 1989. Recreations: fishing; swimming; choral music. Address: (h.) 15 Morningfield Road, Aberdeen, AB2 4AP; T.-0224 314765.

Wild, John Robin, JP, BDS, DPD. Deputy Chief Dental Officer, Scottish Home and Health Department, since 1987 (Chief Administrative Dental Officer, Borders Health Board, 1974-87; Regional Dental Postgraduate Adviser, SE Regional

Committee for Postgraduate Medical Education, 1982-87); b. 12.9.41, Scarborough; m., Eleanor Daphne Kerr; 1 s.; 2 d. Educ. Sedbergh School; Edinburgh University; Dundee University. General Dental Practitioner, Scarborough, 1965-71; Dental Officer, East Lothian, 1971-74; Honorary Member, clinical teaching staff, Edinburgh Dental School, since 1975; Fellow, Edinburgh University; Past Chairman, Scottish Council, British Dental Association. Recreations: vintage cars (restoration and driving); music; gardening; photography. Address: (h.) Braehead House, St. Boswells, Roxburghshire; T.-0835 23203.

Wildgoose, James Richmond, BSc, DPhil. Chief Agricultural Economist (Senior Economic Adviser), Scottish Office, since 1990; b. 17.4.49, Edinburgh; m., Charlotte Dorothy; 1 s.; 1 d. Educ. Melville College; Edinburgh University;   Oxford   University.   Economic Assistant/Economic Adviser, Ministry of Agriculture, Fisheries and Food, 1976-86; Administrative Principal, MAFF Tropical Foods Division, 1986-90; Admnistrative Principal, Scottish Office (SDD), 1990. Recreations: local Baptist church; playing piano; music; walking. Address: (b.) Room 137, Pentland House, Robb's Loan, Edinburgh; T.-031-244 6128.

Wilkie, Rev. James Lindsay, MA, BD. Secretary for relations with churches in Africa and the Caribbean, Board of World Mission and Unity, Church of Scotland, since 1984; b. 30.1.34, Dunfermline; m., Dr. Irene A. Wilkie; 1 s.; 3 d. Educ. Aberdeen Grammar School; Aberdeen University and Christ's College. Assistant Minister, St. Machar's Cathedral, Aberdeen, 1959-60; District Missionary and Minister, United Church of Zambia, 1961-70; Chaplain, University of Zambia, 1970-76; Africa Secretary, then Divisional Secretary and Deputy General Secretary, British Council of Churches, 1976-84; member of team which translated Bible into Chinamwanga language of Zambia. Recreation: DIY. Address: (h.) 7 Comely Bank Avenue, Edinburgh, EH4 1EW; T.-031-343 1552.

Wilkie, Lydia. Secretary, Scottish Committee of the Council on Tribunals, since 1989; b. 3.5.56, Edinburgh; m., Michael McConnell; 1 s.; 1 d. Educ. George Watson's College; Glasgow University. Seconded to present post from Scottish Office. Recreations: drawing and painting; horse riding; reading. Address: (b.) 20 Walker Street, Edinburgh; T.-031-220 1236.

Wilkie, Neil Keith, MA (Hons). Headteacher, Gairloch High School, since 1978; b. 5.4.39, Perth; m., Margaret Rawlinson; 1 s. Educ. Perth Academy; Dundee University; Dundee College of Education; East of Scotland College of Agriculture. Sugar planter, Trinidad, six years; resumed academic studies, 1966; Teacher of History and Modern Studies, then Principal Teacher of History, Golspie High School, 1972-78. Elder, Gairloch and Dundonnell Parish Church; Member, Gairloch Community Council. Recreations: sport; fishing; gardening. Address: (h.) Rohallion, Achtercairn, Gairloch, Ross-shire; T.-0445 2221.

Wilkie, Professor (William) Roy, MA. Professor, Department of Human Resource Management, Strathclyde University, since 1974; b. 10.6.30, Rutherglen; m., Jill Henzell; 1 s.; 3 d. Educ. Rutherglen Academy; Aberdeen University. Lecturer and Senior Lecturer, Department of Administration, Strathclyde University, 1963-66; Director & J. Denholm (Management) Ltd., 1966-70; Reader and Head, Department of Administration, Strathclyde University, 1966-73. Publications: The Concept of Organization, 1974; Managing the Police, 1986. Recreations: swimming; movies; jazz; reading. Address: (b.) Graham Hill Building, 50 Richmond Street, Glasgow; T.-041-552 4400.

Wilkin, Andrew, BA, MA, MIL. Senior Lecturer in Italian Studies, Strathclyde University, since 1986 (Associate Dean, Faculty of Arts and Social Studies, since 1986); b. 30.5.44, Farnborough, Kent; m., Gaynor Carole Gray; 1 s.; 1 d. Educ. Royal Naval School, Malta; Manchester University; Open University. Assistant Lecturer in Italian Studies, then Lecturer, Strathclyde University, 1967-86; Governor, Craigie College of Education, 1985-91; invested with insignia of Cavaliere dell'Ordine Al Merito della Repubblica Italiana, 1975. Publications: papers in Italian language and literature, contemporary Italian affairs, Italian migration to Scotland. Recreations: travel; motorcycling; reading; Scottish history. Address: (b.) Department of Modern Languages, Strathclyde University, Glasgow, G1 1XH; T.-041-552 4400, Ext. 3914.

Wilkins, Professor Malcolm Barrett, BSc, PhD, DSc, AKC, FRSE. Regius Professor of Botany, Glasgow University, since 1970 (Dean, Faculty of Science, 1985-87); b.27.2.33, Cardiff; m., Mary Patricia Maltby; 1 s.; 1 d. (deceased). Educ. Monkton House School, Cardiff; King's College, London University. Lecturer in Botany, King's College, London, 1958-64; Lecturer in Biology, then Professor of Biology, East Anglia University, 1964-67; Professor of Plant Physiology, Nottingham University, 1967-70. Rockefeller Foundation Fellow, Yale University, 1961-62; Corporation Research Fellow, Harvard University, 1962-63; Darwin Lecturer, British Association for the Advancement of Science, 1967; elected Corresponding (Honorary) Member, American Society of Plant Physiologists, 1984; Chairman, Life Science Working Group, European Space Agency, 1987-89; Trustee, Royal Botanic Garden, Edinburgh, since 1990. Recreations: sailing; fishing; model engineering. Address: (b.) Botany Department, Glasgow University, Glasgow, G12 8QQ; T.-041-339 8855.

Wilkinson, Alexander Birrell, MA, LLB. Sheriff of Glasgow and Strathkelvin at Glasgow, since 1991; b. 2.2.32, Perth; m., Wendy Imogen Barrett; 1 s.; 1 d. Educ. Perth Academy; St. Andrews University; Edinburgh University. Advocate, 1959; practised at Scottish Bar, 1959-69; Lecturer in Scots Law, Edinburgh University, 1965-69; Sheriff of Stirling, Dunbarton and Clackmannan, at Stirling and Alloa, 1969-72; Professor of Private Law, Dundee University, 1972-86 (Dean, Faculty of Law, 1974-76 and 1986); Sheriff of Tayside, Central and Fife at Falkirk, 1986-91; a Chairman, Industrial Tribunals (Scotland), 1972-86; Chancellor, Dioceses of Brechin and of Argyll and the Isles, Scottish Episcopal Church; Chairman, Scottish Marriage Guidance Council, 1974-77; Chairman, Legal Services Group, Scottish Association of CAB, 1979-83. Publications: Gloag and Henderson's Introduction to the Law of Scotland, 8th and 9th editions (Co-Editor); The Scottish Law of Evidence. Recreations: collecting books and pictures; reading; travel. Address: (h.) 25 Glencairn Crescent, Edinburgh, EH12 5BT; T.-031-346 1797.

Wilkinson, Andrew Peter Descarrieres, BSc, MB, ChB, DipObstRCOG. Senior Partner, general practice, Castle Douglas, since 1982; Governor, Strathallan School, since 1987; Vice Chairman, Dumfries and Galloway Health Board, since 1989; b. 19.2.44, Edinburgh; m., Patricia Jane Elliot; 2 s.; 1 d. Educ. Strathallan School; Edinburgh University. Former HO and SHO, Edinburgh; general practice, since 1972. Member: Dumfries and Galloway Health Board, since 1987; Scottish Council, BMA, 1980-90; Scottish General Medical Services Committee, 1981-91; Chairman, Castle Douglas Branch, Royal Scottish Society for the Prevention of Cruelty to Children, since 1982. Recreations: gardening; shooting; sailing. Address: Lochbank, Castle Douglas, Kirkcudbright; T.-0556 3413.

Wilkinson, Professor Paul, MA. Professor of International Relations, St. Andrews University, and Director, Research

Institute for the Study of Conflict and Terrorism; Writer on conflict and terrorism; b. 9.5.37, Harrow, Middlesex; m., Susan; 2 s.; 1 d. Educ. John Lyon School; University College, Swansea; University of Wales. RAF, 1959-65; Assistant Lecturer in Politics, University College, Cardiff, 1966-68; University of Wales: Lecturer, 1968-75, Senior Lecturer, 1975-77, Reader in Politics, 1978-79; Professor of International Relations, Aberdeen University, 1979-89; Editorial Adviser, Contemporary Review; Editor, Terrorism and Political Violence; Member, Editorial Board, Conflict Quarterly, Security Handbook, Social Intelligence, and Violence and Aggression; Editor, Key Concepts in International Relations; Scottish Free Enterprise Award, 1982; Honorary Fellow, University College, Swansea, 1986; Special Consultant, CBS America and BBC, since 1989; Aviation Security Adviser to IFAPA, 1988. Publications: Social Movement, 1971; Political Terrorism, 1974; Terrorism and the Liberal State, 1986 (revised edition); The New Fascists, 1983; Terrorism: Theory and Practice (Co-author), 1979; British Perspectives on Terrorism (Editor), 1981; Contemporary Research on Terrorism (Joint Editor), 1987. Recreations: modern art; poetry; walking. Address: (b.) Department of International Relations, St. Andrews University, St. Andrews, KY16 9TR; T.-0334 76161.

Wilkinson, Professor Peter Charles, MD, FRSE, FIBiol. Titular Professor in Bacteriology and Immunology, Glasgow University, since 1982; Honorary Consultant in Immunology, Western Infirmary, Glasgow, since 1970; b. 10.7.32, London; m., Eileen Mary Baron; 2 s.; 1 d. Educ. London Hospital Medical College; London University. House appointments, London Hospital, 1956-58; Flt.-Lt., RAF (Medical Officer), 1958-60; Lecturer in Bacteriology, London Hospital Medical College, 1960-63; Lecturer and Senior Lecturer in Bacteriology and Immunology, Glasgow University, 1964-77; MRC Travelling Fellow, Swiss Research Institute, 1967-69; Reader, Glasgow University, 1977-82; Visiting Professor, Rockefeller University, New York, 1979. Publications: Chemotaxis and Inflammation; A Dictionary of Immunology (Co-author). Recreations: various interests in the arts. Address: (h.) 26 Randolph Road, Glasgow, G11 7LG.

Wilkinson, Rev. William Brian, MA (Hons), BD (Hons). Minister, East Church, Kirkwall, since 1987; b. 14.4.42, Edinburgh; m., Janet Cameron Inglis. Educ. Peterhead Academy; High School of Stirling; Edinburgh University. Assistant Minister, Gilmerton Parish Church, Edinburgh, 1967-69; Minister: Carnock Parish Church, Fife, 1969-74, Christ's Church, Dunollie, Oban, 1974-83, Kilmore and Oban Parish Church (Senior Colleague), 1984-87. Deputy Chairman, Royal National Mission to Deep Sea Fishermen, since 1990. Recreations: Gaelic and English choral singing; book (Highland) collecting; walking. Address: East Manse, Kirkwall, Orkney; T.-0856 5469.

Wilkinson, (William) Roderick, DAA, FIPM. Novelist and Scriptwriter; b. 31.3.17, Glasgow; 1 s.; 2 d. Educ. North Kelvinside Secondary, Glasgow. Director of advertising agency, 1946-59; Director of Personnel, 1959-80. Publications: 10 books, fiction and non-fiction; plays, articles and stories. Recreation: fishing. Address: (h.) 61 Norwood Park, Bearsden, Glasgow, G61 2RZ; T.-041-942 2185.

Will, David Houston, BL, NP. Vice-President, FIFA, since 1990; Chairman, FIFA Referees Committee, Players Status Committee and Legal Matters Committee; Member, FIFA Executive Committee, World Cup Organising Committee and Security Committee; b. 20.11.36, Glasgow; m., Margaret; 2 d. Educ. Brechin High School; Edinburgh University. Chairman, Brechin City FC, 1966-91; appointed to SFA Council, 1970; President, SFA, 1984-89; Vice-President, UEFA, 1986-90. Recreations: golf; curling. Address: (h.) Norandale, 32 Airlie Street, Brechin, Angus; T.-03562 2273.

Will, Ronald Kerr, WS. Retired Solicitor; b. 22.3.18, Edinburgh; m., Margaret Joyce Stevenson; 2 s. Educ. Merchiston Castle School; Edinburgh University. Served King's Own Scottish Borderers, 1940-46 (Major); mentioned in Despatches; WS, 1950; former Senior Partner, Dundas & Wilson, CS, Edinburgh; Deputy Keeper of Her Majesty's Signet, 1975-83; Director, Scottish Equitable Life Assurance Society, 1965-88 (Chairman, 1980-83); Director, Scottish Investment Trust PLC, 1963-88; Member, Council on Tribunals, 1971-76 and Chairman, Scottish Committee; Governor, Merchiston Castle School, 1953-76. Recreations: gardening; shooting; fishing. Address: (h.) Chapelhill Cottage, Dirleton, North Berwick, East Lothian; T.-062 085 338.

Willett, Professor Frank, CBE, MA, FRSE. Director, Hunterian Museum & Art Gallery, Glasgow, 1976-90; b. 18.8.25, Bolton; m., Mary Constance Hewitt; 1 s.; 3 d. Educ. Bolton Municipal Secondary School; University College, Oxford. Keeper of Ethnology and General Archaeology, Manchester Museum, 1950-58; Government Archaeologist, Nigeria, 1958-63; Leverhulme Research Fellow, 1964; Research Fellow, Nuffield College, Oxford, 1964-66; Professor of Art History, African Studies and Interdisciplinary Studies, Northwestern University, Evanston, Illinois, 1966-76; Visiting Fellow, Clare Hall, Cambridge, 1970-71; Hon. Corresponding Member, Manchester Literary and Philosophical Society, since 1958; Vice Chairman, Scottish Museums Council, 1986-89; Fellow, Royal Anthropological Institute. Publications: Ife in the History of West African Sculpture, 1967; African Art: An Introduction, 1971; Treasures of Ancient Nigeria, Co-author, 1980. Recreation: walking. Address: (h.) 583 Anniesland Road, Glasgow, G13 1UX; T.-041-959 3424.

Williams, Sir Alwyn, Kt, PhD, FRS, FRSE, MRIA, FGS, Hon. FRCPS, Hon. DSc, Hon. LLD. Honorary Research Fellow, Department of Geology, Glasgow University (Principal and Vice-Chancellor, Glasgow University, 1976-88); Non-Executive Director, Scottish Daily Record and Sunday Mail Ltd., 1984-90; b. 8.6.21, Aberdare, Wales; m., Edith Joan Bevan; 1 s.; 1 d. Educ. Aberdare Boys' Grammar School; University College of Wales, Aberystwyth. Commonwealth Fund Fellow, US National Museum, 1948-50; Lecturer in Geology, Glasgow University, 1950-54; Professor of Geology, Queen's University, Belfast, 1954-74; Lapworth Professor of Geology, Birmingham University, 1974-76; Chairman, Scottish Hospital Endowments Research Trust, since 1989; Member, Scottish Tertiary Education Advisory Council, 1984-86; President, Palaeontological Association, 1968-70; President, Royal Society of Edinburgh, 1985-88; Trustee and Chairman, Board of British Museum (Natural History), 1971-79; Chairman, Committee on National Museums and Galleries of Scotland, 1979-81; Honorary Fellow, Geological Society of America, since 1970; Foreign Member, Polish Academies of Science, since 1981; Hon. DSc, Universities of Wales, Queen's (Belfast) and Edinburgh; Hon. DCL, Oxford; Hon. LLD, Glasgow, Strathclyde. Address: (h.) 25 Sutherland Avenue, Pollokshields, Glasgow, G41 4HG; T.-041-427 0589.

Williams, Arthur, OBE, MRPharmS. Chief Administrative Pharmaceutical Officer, Grampian, Orkney and Shetland Health Boards, since 1981; b. 5.11.32, Tarleton, near Preston; m., Barbara; 1 s.; 1 d. Educ. Hutton Grammar School, near Preston; School of Pharmacy, Leicester. Senior Pharmacist, United Manchester Hospitals, 1957-59; Chief Pharmacist: Jewish Hospital, 1959-62, Macclesfield Hospital, 1962-66; Group Chief Pharmacist to Area Pharmaceutical Officer, 1966-81. Merck, Sharp and Dohme Award, 1979; Evans Gold Medal, 1991; Evans Award for Innovation (Scotland), 1991. Recreations: gardening; fell-walking; natural history. Address: (b.) Department of Pharmacy, Aberdeen Royal

Infirmary, Foresterhill, Aberdeen, AB9 2ZB; T.-0224 589901, Ext. 75135.

Williams, Professor Bryan Peter, BA (Hons), MA, CQSW. Professor of Social Work and Head, Department of Social Work, Dundee University; b. 18.11.45, Northampton; m., Anne Rosemary Dysart; 1 d. Educ. Northampton and Weston-Super-Mare Grammar Schools; Hull University; Bristol University. UK Atomic Energy Authority, 1963-66; residential social worker, Chile voluntary service, 1966-67; school-teacher, 1967-68; probation officer, 1973-76; Lecturer in Social Work, Dundee University, 1976-89. Member, Review Committee on Parole and Related Issues, 1988-89; Member, Council, Central Council for Education and Training in Social Work and Chair, UK Standards Panel; Member, Scottish Committee, Central Council for Education and Training in Social Work; Member, Council, Scottish Association for the Care and Resettlement of Offenders, since 1982 (Chair, 1990). Publications: books and papers on research into social work and criminal justice. Recreations: mountaineering; skiing; rock climbing; sea canoeing; all types of music. Address: (b.) Department of Social Work, Dundee University, Dundee, DD1 4HN; T.-0382 307651.

Williams, Professor Howard Peter, MSc. Professor, Management Science Department, Strathclyde University, since 1990; b. 27.2.54, St. Albans. Educ. Exeter University; Newcastle upon Tyne University. Economist, ICI Plant Protection Division, International Wool Secretariat, British Ship Research Association; Senior Research Fellow, Newcastle-upon-Tyne University. Member, Scottish Advisory Committee on Telecommunications, Glasgow Advisory Committee on Posts and Telecommunications. Recreations: windsurfing; water; music; breadmaking. Address: (b.) Department of Management Science, Livingstone Tower, Strathclyde University, Glasgow, G1 1XH; T.-041-552 4400, Ext. 3153.

Williams, John Rosser, MA, PhD. Senior Lecturer in German, St. Andrews University, since 1987; b. 4.3.40, Worcester; m., Elizabeth; 2 s. Educ. Royal Grammar School, Worcester; St. John's College, Oxford; Heidelberg University. Lecturer in German Language and Literature, UMIST, 1963-64; St. Andrews University, since 1964; international prize for verse translation, 1982. Hon. President, St. Andrews RFC, 1979-82. Publications: Goethe's Faust, 1987; numerous papers. Recreations: golf; gardening; skating; hill-walking; travel; cricket; rugby; music; humour. Address: (b.) Department of German, St. Andrews University, St. Andrews, KY16 9PH.

Williams, Professor Morgan Howard, BSc Hons, PhD, FBCS, FRSA. Professor of Computer Science, Heriot-Watt University, since 1980 (Head of Department, 1980-88); b. 15.12.44, Durban; m., Jean Doe; 2 s. Educ. Grey High School, Port Elizabeth; Rhodes University, Grahamstown. Physicist in Antarctic Expedition, 1968-69; Rhodes University: Lecturer in Computer Science, 1970-72, Senior Lecturer, 1972-77, Professor and Head of Department, 1977-80. Address: Computer Science Department, Heriot-Watt University, 79 Grassmarket, Edinburgh, EH1 2HJ; T.-031-225 6465, Ext. 550.

Williamson, David, CBE, BL. Honorary President, SSC (a club for the youth of Scotland), Chairman, 1964-89; Chairman, North Merchiston Club, Edinburgh, since 1982; Trustee, Stanley Nairne Memorial Trust, since 1969; b. 13.1.20, Edinburgh; m., Agnes Margaret. Educ. George Heriot's School, Edinburgh; Edinburgh University. Army Service, 1940-46 (Gunner, Lance Bombadier, Bombadier, Sergeant, Officer Cadet, Second Lieutenant, Lieutenant, Captain); Keeper of the Registers of Scotland, 1973-82 (supervised introduction of Registration of Title to Scotland,

1981); Honorary Member, Law Society of Scotland, since 1982; received Keystone Gold Award for services to Boys' Clubs, 1985. Publications: Registration of Title Practice Book (Co-author); The Story of the Scottish Schoolboys' Club (Editor and Co-author); Stanley Nairne, The Boys' Club Pioneer. Recreations: walking; enjoying countryside; reading; appreciating music (including opera); watching rugby. Address: (h.) 10 Homeross House, Mount Grange, Edinburgh, EH9 2QX; T.-031-447 3050.

Williamson, Douglas Guthrie, BSc, PhD. Senior Lecturer in Chemistry, Aberdeen University, since 1980; Member, Transport Users Consultative Committee for Scotland, since 1987; Vice Chairman, Scottish Consumer Council, 1987-89; b. 2.6.37, Edinburgh; m., Alison J. Donaldson. Educ. Paisley Grammar School; Glasgow University. Research Fellow (DSIR), Glasgow and Cambridge Universities, 1963-65; Lecturer in Chemistry, Aberdeen University, 1965-80. Secretary, Aberdeen Consumer Group, 1978-83. Recreations: hill-walking; gardens. Address: (h.) 150 Broomhill Road, Aberdeen, AB1 6HY; T.-0224 586847.

Williamson, Duncan. Author, Storyteller and Singer; b. 11.4.28, Furnace; m., Dr. Linda J. Williamson; 4 s.; 5 d. Educ. Furnace Primary. One of Scotland's travelling people. Publications: Fireside Tales of the Traveller Children, 1983; The Broonie, Silkies and Fairies, 1985; A Thorn in the King's Foot: folktales of the Scottish travelling people, 1987; Tell Me a Story for Christmas, 1987; May the Devil Walk Behind Ye: Scottish travellers' tales, 1989; Don't Look Back, Jack!, 1990; The Genie and the Fisherman, and other tales of the travelling people, 1991; Tales of the Seal People, 1992. Address: (h.) Falfield Bank, Peat Inn, Fife, KY15 5LL; T.-033484 474.

Williamson, Professor Edwin Henry, MA, PhD. Professor of Hispanic Studies, Edinburgh University, since 1990; b. 2.10.49, Gibraltar; m., Susan Jane Fitchie; 2 d. Educ. Edinburgh University. Lecturer in Spanish, Trinity College, Dublin, 1974-77; Lecturer in Spanish, Birkbeck College, London, 1977-90. Publications: The Half-Way House of Fiction: Don Quixote and Arthurian Romance, 1984; El Quijote Y Los Libros de Caballerias, 1991; The Penguin History of Latin America, 1992. Recreations: theatre; art; film; hill-walking. Address: (b.) Department of Hispanic Studies, Edinburgh University, David Hume Tower, George Square, Edinburgh, EH8 9JX; T.-031-650 3673.

Williamson, Professor James, CBE, MB, ChB, FRCPEdin, DSc (Hon.). Past President, British Geriatrics Society; Past Chairman, Age Concern Scotland; Professor Emeritus, Geriatric Medicine, Edinburgh University; b. 22.11.20, Wishaw; m., Sheila Mary Blair; 3 s. Educ. Wishaw High School; Glasgow University. General medical training in Glasgow hospitals; general practice; training in respiratory medicine, becoming Consultant in Edinburgh, 1954; converted to geriatric medicine, 1959; Consultant, Edinburgh, until 1973; first occupant, Chair of Geriatric Medicine, Liverpool University; first occupant, Chair of Geriatric Medicine, Edinburgh University, 1976-86; Visiting Professor to several North American medical schools. Recreations: reading; walking. Address: (h.) 14 Ann Street, Edinburgh, EH4 1PJ; T.-031-332 3568.

Williamson, Rev. Magnus James Cameron. Minister, Fetlar linked with Yell, since 1982; b. 9.9.34, Nesting, Shetland; m., Eunice Winifred Mary Williamson; 3 s.; 1 d. Educ. Lerwick; Aberdeen. Lay Missionary: Eday, Orkney, 1965-73, Yell and Fetlar, 1973-82. Past Chairman, Yell and Fetlar School Council; Member, Yell Community Council and Old Haa Trust. Recreation: gardening. Address: The Manse, Mid Yell, Shetland, ZE2 9BN; T.-0957 2283.

Williamson, Raymond MacLeod, MA, LLB. Solicitor, since 1968 (Partner, MacRoberts, Solicitors, Glasgow and Edinburgh, since 1972); Governor, High School of Glasgow; Member, Council, Law Society of Scotland; b. 24.12.42, Glasgow; m., Brenda; 1 s.; 1 d. Educ. High School of Glasgow; Glasgow University. Chairman, Royal Scottish Orchestra, 1985-91. Recreation: music. Address: (h.) 11 Islay Drive, Ryelands, Newton Mearns, Glasgow, G77 6UD; T.-041-639 4133.

Williamson, Richard John. Editor, Evening Express, Aberdeen, since 1986; b. 14.12.35, Dunphail, Moray; m., Lesley Paterson Mutch; 1 s.; 1 d. Educ. Forres Academy. Trustee, Chris Anderson Trust, Aberdeen. Recreations: reading; walking. Address: (b.) Lang Stracht, Mastrick, Aberdeen; T.-0224 690222.

Williamson, W. David, MA. Rector, Whitburn Academy, since 1990; b. 4.6.47, Glasgow; m., Margaret McLaren; 1 s.; 2 d. Educ. Allan Glens School, Glasgow; Glasgow University; Jordanhill College. Teacher, then Principal Teacher of Modern Studies, John Neilson High School, Paisley, 1969-78; Assistant Headteacher, Castlebrae High School, Edinburgh, 1978 83; Depute Headteacher, Portobello High School, Edinburgh, 1983-90. Recreations: hill-walking; running. Address: (h.) 4 House O'Hill Road, Edinburgh; T.-031-332 7009.

Willock, Professor Ian Douglas, MA, LLB, PhD. Professor of Jurisprudence, Dundee University. Educ. Aberdeen University. Address: (b.) Department of Law, Dundee University, Dundee; T.-0382 23181.

Wills, Jonathan W.G., MA (Hons), PhD. Writer and Broadcaster; Illustrator and Painter; Editor, Shetland Times, 1987-90; b. 17.6.47, Oxford; m., Lesley M. Roberts; 3 s.; 1 d. Educ. Warwick School; Anderson Educational Institute, Lerwick; Edinburgh University. Reporter, Shetland Times, 1969; Warden and boatman, Noss National Nature Reserve, 1970; Rector, Edinburgh University (first student Rector), 1971; Scottish and NI Organiser, Third World First (Oxfam), 1972; Boatman, Muckle Flugga Lighthouse, Unst, 1974; Reporter, Shetland Times, 1976; Senior Producer/Presenter, BBC Radio Shetland, 1977; News Editor, Shetland Times, 1981; Scottish Correspondent, The Times, 1982; Producer, BBC Radio Scotland, 1983; Freelance and Research Assistant to Alex. Falconer, MEP, 1984; Tutor, Media Studies, STUC and individual trade unions, 1984; Senior Reporter, Shetland Times, 1985; Fraser Press Award, 1981-82, for work on Shetland Times; Labour candidate, Orkney and Shetland, 1974 (twice). Publications: (children's books) Magnus Pole, 1975; Linda and the Lighthouse, 1976. Recreations: sailing other people's boats; ornithology; painting; gardening. Address: (h.) Sundside, Bressay, Shetland, ZE2 9ER.

Wilson, Alan Oliver Arneil, MB, ChB, DPM, FRCPsych. Consultant in private practice, Murrayfield Hospital and Montgomery Clinic, Edinburgh; Consultant Psychiatrist, Bangour Hospitals, 1977-89; former Member, Clinical Teaching Staff, Faculty of Medicine, Edinburgh University; Past Member and Past President, Board of Directors, World Association for Psychosocial Rehabilitation; Consultant (in Scotland), Ex-Services Mental Welfare Society; b. 4.1.30, Douglas; m., Dr. Fiona Margaret Davidson; 3 s. Educ. Biggar High School; Edinburgh University. RAMC, 1953-55; psychiatric post, Stobhill General Hospital, Glasgow, and Garlands Hospital, Carlisle, 1955-63; Consultant Psychiatrist and Deputy Physician Superintendent, St. George's Hospital, Morpeth, 1963-77. Joint Honorary Secretary, Northern Counties Psychiatric Association; Chairman, Group for Study of Rehabilitation and Community Care, Scottish Division, RCPsych; Member, Ethics Committee, World Association for Social Psychiatry; Chairman, Psychosocial Rehabilitation

Scotland. V.M. Bekhterev Medal awarded by Bekhterev Psychoneurological Research Institute, St. Petersburg. Recreations: golf; folk singing; guitar; "blethering"; former Hibernian FC footballer. Address: (h.) 14 Cammo Hill, Edinburgh, EH4 8EY; T.-031-339 2244.

Wilson, Brian, MA (Hons), FSA (Scot). MP (Labour), Cunninghame North, since 1987; b. 13.12.48, Dunoon; m., Joni Buchanan; 1 s.; 1 d. Educ. Dunoon Grammar School; Dundee University; University College, Cardiff. Journalist; Publisher and Founding Editor, West Highland Free Press; Contributor to The Observer, Glasgow Herald, Scotland on Sunday, etc.; first winner, Nicholas Tomalin Memorial Award for Journalism; contested Ross and Cromarty, Oct., 1974, Inverness, 1979, Western Isles, 1983; front-bench spokesman on Scottish Home Affairs etc., since 1988; Parliamentary Adviser to Scottish Professional Footballers Association. Address: (h.) 219 Queen Victoria Drive, Glasgow; T.-041-959 1758.

Wilson, Brian, LLB. Chief Executive, Inverness District Council, since 1978; Clerk, Highland River Purification Board, since 1989; b. 20.2.46, Perth; m., Isobel Esson; 3 d. Educ. Buckie High School; Aberdeen University. Management trainee, 1966-68; Apprentice, then Legal Assistant, Banff County Council, 1969-72; Senior Legal Assistant, Inverness County Council, 1972-73; Depute County Clerk, Banff County Council, 1973-75; Director of Administration and Legal Services, Banff and Buchan District Council, 1975-78. Hon. Secretary: Inverness Town Twinning Committee, since 1979, SOLACE, Scottish Branch, since 1986; Clerk, JP Advisory Committee (Inverness). Recreations: family; garden; fishing. Address: (b.) Town House, Inverness, IV1 1JJ; T.-0463 239111.

Wilson, Sir Charles Haynes, Kt (1965). Principal and Vice-Chancellor, Glasgow University, 1971-76; b. 16.5.09.

Wilson, Conrad. Music Critic, The Scotsman, 1963-91 (also restaurant reviewer, 1981-91); freelance music reviewer and feature writer, The Herald, since 1991; b. 7.11.32, Edinburgh; 1 s.; 1 d. Educ. Daniel Stewart's College, Edinburgh. Music Critic, Evening Dispatch, Edinburgh, 1954-58; Music Editor, Philips Records, Holland, 1958-61; Cultural Correspondent, The Scotsman, London Office, 1961-63. Programme Editor, Edinburgh Festival, 1966-82; freelance Music Lecturer, since 1964; Chairman, Critics' Committee, European Music Year, Arts Council of GB, 1985; Co-Director, Ramsay Head Press, since 1987. Publications: A Critic's Choice, 1966; Scottish Opera, the First Ten Years, 1972; Collins Encyclopedia of Music (revised), 1976; Good Food Facts (Co-author), 1986; Where to Eat Well in Scotland, 1988; Collins Dictionary of Music (revised), 1988; music section, Guinness Encyclopaedia of Music. Address: (h.) 10 Leslie Place, Edinburgh; T.-031-343 2866.

Wilson, David Rowan, OBE. Honorary Sheriff, Wigtown; retired Solicitor; b. 1.11.13, Hamilton; m., Helen Kirkland Benson; 1 s. Educ. Hamilton Academy; Glasgow University. Qualified as Solicitor, 1936; Depute County Clerk, then County Clerk, Wigtownshire, 1948-75; Chief Executive, Wigtown District Council, 1975-78. Justice of the Peace, Wigtown District. Recreations: golf; curling. Address: (h.) Benachie, Cairnryan Road, Stranraer; T.-0776 2307.

Wilson, David Steel, DipM. Chef/Proprietor, The Peat Inn, since 1972; b. 21.1.36, Bishopbriggs; m., Patricia Ann; 1 s.; 1 d. Educ. Bishopbriggs High School; Glasgow College of Commerce. Sales/Marketing Manager in industry, 1967-71; trainee chef, 1971-72. Master Chef of G.B.; Chef Laureate. Recreations: travel; art; sport; music; theatre. Address: (b.) The Peat Inn, by Cupar, Fife, KY15 5LH; T.-033 484 206.

Wilson, Forrest. Children's Author and Crossword Compiler; b. 6.12.34, Renfrew; m., Jean Anderson; 1 d. Educ. Renfrew High School. British Oil and Cake Mills, 1959-68; Scottish Milk Marketing Board, 1968-77; began writing, 1966, full-time, since 1977; creator of Super Gran and author of Super Gran series of books (12), The Adventures of ABC Mob, Brain Benders, Farm Crosswords; Scottish Arts Council Lecturer under Writers in Schools Scheme and Young Authors' Project. Recreations: theatre-going; composing music; playing petanque. Address: (h.) 5 Meadowpark Drive, Ayr, KA7 2LH.

Wilson, Gerald, CB, MA. Secretary, Scottish Office Education Department, since 1988; b. 7.9.39, Edinburgh; m., Margaret; 1 s.; 1 d. Educ. Holy Cross Academy; Edinburgh University. Assistant Principal, Scottish Home and Health Department, 1961-65; Private Secretary, Minister of State for Scotland, 1965-66; Principal, Scottish Home and Health Department, 1966-72; Private Secretary to Lord Privy Seal, 1972-74; to Minister of State, Civil Service Department, 1974; Assistant Secretary, Scottish Economic Planning Department, 1974-77; Counsellor, Office of the UK Permanent Representative to the Economic Communities, Brussels, 1977-82; Assistant Secretary, Scottish Office, 1982-84; Under Secretary, Industry Department for Scotland, 1984-88. Recreation: music. Address: (b.) New St. Andrew's House, Edinburgh, EH1 3SY; T.-031-244 4409.

Wilson, Gordon, MA (Hons), DipEd. Head Teacher, Shawlands Academy, Glasgow, since 1983; b. 9.6.33, Glasgow; m., Sybil Scott Ewing; 2 d. Educ. Allan Glen's School, Glasgow; Glasgow University; Jordanhill College of Education. Teacher of Geography: Shawlands Academy, 1960-64; Langside College, 1964-66; Hyndland Secondary School: Principal Teacher of Geography, 1966-71, Assistant Head Teacher, 1971-74, Depute Head Teacher, 1974-75; Head Teacher, John Street Secondary School, 1975-83. Past President, Headteachers' Association of Scotland. Recreations: badminton; golf. Address: (b.) Shawlands Academy, 31 Moss-side Road, Glasgow, G41 3TR; T.-041-632 1154.

Wilson, Gordon McAndrew, MA, PhD, FRSA. Principal, Craigie College of Education, since 1988; b. 4.12.39, Glasgow; m., Alison Rosemary Cook; 2 s.; 1 d. Educ. Eastwood Secondary School; Glasgow University; Jordanhill College of Education. Teacher of History and Modern Studies: Eastwood Secondary School, 1963-65, Eastwood High School, 1965-67; Lecturer in Social Studies, Hamilton College of Education, 1967-73 (Head of Department, 1973-81); Principal Lecturer in Inservice Education, then Assistant Principal, Jordanhill College of Education, 1981-88; Member, Board, Scottish Council for Research in Education; Member, Educational Broadcasting Council for Scotland; Chairman, Standing Committees on Research and on Learning Resources, JCCES; Chairman, Review and Development Group 1 on Language 5-14, SCCC; Member, Committee on Curriculum and Examinations S5-S6, 1990-92. Publications: Teaching Local History in Lanarkshire, 1972; Alexander McDonald, Leader of the Miners, 1982; Dictionary of Scottish Business Biography (Contributor), 1986. Recreations: reading; gardening; walking; music. Address: (b.) Craigie College of Education, Beech Grove, Ayr, KA8 0SR; T.-0292 260321/4.

Wilson, Hamish Robert McHattie, MA (Aberdeen), MA, PhD (Cantab), AHSM. Director of Contracts, Grampian Health Board, since 1991 (Unit General Manager, 1987-90); b. 19.1.46, Aberdeen. Educ. Robert Gordon's College, Aberdeen; Aberdeen University; Emmanuel College, Cambridge. Entered Health Service administration, 1972; held posts with Grampian Health Board in planning, primary care and as Secretary. Member, Scottish Society of the History of Medicine; Chairman, Scottish Divisional Council, Institute of Health Services Management. Recreations: music; reading; theatre; cinema; good food and wine. Address: (b.) 1 Albyn Place, Aberdeen; T.-Aberdeen 589901.

Wilson of Langside, Baron (Henry Stephen Wilson), PC, QC, LLB. Advocate, since 1946; House of Lords Spokesman for SDP on Scottish Legal Affairs; b. 21.3.16, Glasgow; m., Jessie Forrester Waters. Educ. High School of Glasgow; Glasgow University. Army, 1939-46 (Regimental Officer, HLI and RAC); called to Scottish Bar, 1946; Labour candidate, Dumfries, 1950, 1955, West Edinburgh, 1951; Sheriff, Greenock, 1955-56, Glasgow, 1956-65; Solicitor-General for Scotland, 1965-67; Lord Advocate, 1967-70; Sheriff, Glasgow, 1971-75, Sheriff Principal, Glasgow and Strathkelvin, 1975-77. Recreations: gardening; hill-walking. Address: (h.) Dunallan, Kippen, Stirlingshire, FK8 3HL; T.-Kippen 210.

Wilson, Professor Herbert Rees, BSc, PhD, FInstP, FRSA, FRSE. Professor Emeritus; Professor of Physics, Stirling University, 1983-90; b. 28.1.29, Nefyn, Wales; m., Elizabeth Turner; 1 s.; 2 d. Educ. Pwllheli Grammar School; University College of North Wales, Bangor. Research Scientist, Wheatstone Physics Laboratory, King's College, London, 1952-57; Lecturer in Physics, Queen's College, Dundee, 1957-64; Research Associate, Children's Cancer Research Foundation, Boston, 1962; Senior Lecturer and Reader in Physics, Dundee University, 1964-83; Head, Physics Department, 1983-88, Head, Division of Physics and Chemistry, 1988-89, Stirling University. Publication: Diffraction of X-Rays By Proteins, Nucleic Acids and Viruses. Recreations: travel; theatre; art. Address: (h.) Lower Bryanston, St. Margaret's Drive, Dunblane, FK15 ODP; T.-0786 823105.

Wilson, Ian Crawford, OBE, JP, BCom, IPFA. Chief Executive, Inverclyde District Council, since 1974; b. 10.4.36, Glasgow. Educ. Dalziel High School; Edinburgh University. Depute County Treasurer, Berwickshire County Council, 1968-71; Town Chamberlain, Greenock Corporation, 1971-74. Recreations: sailing; hill-walking. Address: (b.) Municipal Buildings, Greenock; T.-0475 24400.

Wilson, Ian Dunn. Farmer; Chairman, Scottish Dairy Council, 1990-91; Member, Council, Scottish Agricultural Organisation Society; Director, Scottish Milk Marketing Board, since 1988; Panel Member, Scottish Agricultural Arbiters Association; b. 25.4.46, Edinburgh; m., Agnes Jane; 1 s.; 1 d. Educ. Trinity College, Glenalmond; Royal Agricultural College, Cirencester. Recreations: golf; shooting. Address: Drum, Beeswing, Dumfries, DG2 8PB; T.-0387 76240.

Wilson, Ian Matthew, CB, MA. Secretary of Commissions for Scotland, since 1987 (Under Secretary, Scottish Education Department, 1977-86); b. 12.12.26, Edinburgh; m., Anne Chalmers (deceased); 3 s. Educ. George Watson's College; Edinburgh University. Assistant Principal, Scottish Home Department, 1950; Private Secretary to Permanent Under Secretary of State, Scottish Office, 1953-55; Principal, Scottish Home Department, 1955; Assistant Secretary: Scottish Education Department, 1963, Scottish Home and Health Department, 1971; Assistant Under Secretary of State, Scottish Office, 1974-77. Address: (h.) 1 Bonaly Drive, Edinburgh, EH13 OEJ; T.-031-441 2541.

Wilson, Brigadier James, CBE. Executive Director, Edinburgh Old Town Trust, 1987-90; Chief Executive, Livingston Development Corporation, 1977-87; b. 12.3.22, Irvine; m., Audrie Veronica Haines; 3 d. Educ. Irvine Royal Academy; Edinburgh Academy. Served Royal Artillery, 1941-77. Chairman, Soldiers, Sailors and Airmen's Families

Association, West Lothian; President, Royal Artillery Association Scotland; Vice Chairman, Royal Artillery Council for Scotland; Member, Lothian Area Committee, Lowland Territorial Auxiliary and Volunteer Reserve Association. Recreations: golf; bridge. Address: (h.) 2 The Gardens, Aberlady, East Lothian.

Wilson, James Wiseman, OBE, SBStJ. Director, Wilforge Foundation, since 1970; Director, Sealed Air Corporation (UK) Ltd., since 1980; Director, Wilson Management Ltd., since 1970; b. 31.5.33, Glasgow; m., Valerie Grant; 1 s.; 3 d. Educ. Trinity College, Glenalmond; Harvard Business School. Marketing Director, Scottish Animal Products, 1959-63; Sales Director, then Managing Director, then Chairman, Robert Wilson & Sons (1849) Ltd., 1964-85. National Trust for Scotland: Member of Council, 1977-82 and 1984-89, President, Ayrshire Members' Centre; Chairman, Management Committee, Scottish Civic Trust; Honorary President, Skelmorlie Golf Club and Irvine Pipe Band; won Aims of Industry Free Enterprise Award (Scotland), 1980. Recreations: golf; backgammon; skiing; bridge; travelling. Address: (h.) Skelmorlie Castle, Skelmorlie, Ayrshire, PA17 5EY; T.-0475 521127.

Wilson, Janette Sylvia, LLB, NP. Depute Solicitor, Church of Scotland, since 1981; b. 15.1.51, Inverness; m., Stuart Ronald Wilson. Educ. Inverness Royal Academy; Edinburgh University. Law Apprentice, then Assistant, Dundas & Wilson, CS, Edinburgh, 1973-77; Assistant, then Partner, Ross Harper & Murphy, Edinburgh, 1977-81. Member, Law Society Public Service and Commerce Group. Recreations: keeping fit; gardening. Address: (b.) 121 George Street, Edinburgh; T.-031-225 5722.

Wilson, John Melville, RIBA, FRIAS, DipTP, MRTPI, FIH. Director of Housing, City of Edinburgh District Council, since 1983; b. 11.9.31, Uphall; m., Mary H.; 2 d. Educ. Lenzie Academy; Clydebank High School; Glasgow School of Architecture; Strathclyde University. Senior Architect, SSHA, 1968-72; Assistant Director of Housing, Edinburgh Corporation, 1972-75; Depute Director of Housing, City of Edinburgh, 1975-83. Recreations: swimming; curling; hill-walking. Address: (b.) 23 Waterloo Place, Edinburgh, EH1 3BH; T.-031-225 2424.

Wilson, Professor Leslie Blakett, BSc, DSc, CEng, FBCS. Professor and Head, Computing Science and Mathematics Department, Stirling University, since 1979 (Chairman, Board of Studies for Science, 1984-87, Deputy Head, School of Management, since 1990); b. 1.11.30, Newcastle-upon-Tyne; m., Patricia Kinair; 2 d. Educ. Newcastle Royal Grammar School; Durham University. Scientific Officer/Senior Scientific Officer, Naval Construction Research Establishment, Dunfermline, 1951-64; Lecturer/Senior Lecturer in Computing Science, Newcastle-upon-Tyne University, 1964-79; Visiting Associate Professor, Waterloo University, Canada, 1974; Visiting Professor, New Mexico State University, 1989-90. Publications: Information Representation and Manipulation Using Pascal; Computational Combinatorics; Comparative Programming Languages: A Conceptual Approach. Recreations: bridge; cinema; fell-walking; golf. Address: (b.) Computing Science and Mathematics Department, Stirling University, Stirling, FK9 4LA; T.-Stirling 67420.

Wilson, Professor Peter Northcote, CBE, BSc, MSc, Dip. Animal Genetics, PhD, CBiol, FIBiol, FRSE, FRSA. Emeritus Professor of Agriculture and Rural Economy, Edinburgh University; Scientific Director, Edinburgh Centre for Rural Research, since 1990; b. 4.4.28, Beckenham, Kent; m., Maud Ethel Bunn; 2 s.; 1 d. Educ. Whitgift School, Croydon; Wye College, London University; Edinburgh University. Lecturer in Agriculture, Makerere College, East Africa; Senior

Lecturer in Agriculture, Imperial College of Tropical Agriculture, Trinidad; Professor of Tropical Agriculture, University of West Indies; Head of Biometrics, Unilever Research Laboratory, Bedford; Agricultural Development Director, SLF Ltd., Liverpool; Chief Agricultural Adviser, BOCM Silcock Ltd., Basingstoke. Past President, British Society of Animal Production; Past Vice President, Institute of Biology; Chairman, Frank Parkinson Agricultural Trust, since 1978. Publications: Agriculture in the Tropics (Co-author); Improved Feeding of Cattle and Sheep (Co-author). Recreations: walking; photography; natural history. Address: (b.) Crew Building, Kings Buildings, West Mains Road, Edinburgh, EH9 3JG.

Wilson, Ralph Stewart, BSc. Headteacher, Armadale Academy, since 1985; b. 10.7.35, Callander; m., Mary Eleanor Voller; 2 s. Educ. McLaren High School; Glasgow University; Jordanhill College of Education. Instructor Officer, Royal Navy, 1957-63; Teacher, Jedburgh Grammar School, 1963-67; Principal Teacher/Depute Headteacher, Armadale Academy, 1967-73; Rector, Bannerman High School, 1973-77; Principal, Wester Hailes Education Centre, 1977-82; Director, Scottish Community Education Council, 1982-85. Vice-Chairman, Board, West Lothian Youth Theatre. Recreations: crosswords; music; hill-walking; gardening. Address: (h.) Aasly, Bowyett, Torphichen, Bathgate, EH48 4LZ; T.-0506 53475.

Wilson, Robert Gordon, BL, LLD. National Convener, Scottish National Party, 1979-90; Solicitor; b. 16.4.38, Glasgow; m., Edith M. Hassall; 2 d. Educ. Douglas High School for Boys; Edinburgh University. National Secretary, SNP, 1963-71; Partner, law firm, 1965-74; MP, Dundee East, 1974-87; own law business, since 1988. Rector, Dundee University, 1983-86; Chairman, Marriage Counselling (Tayside); Governor, Dundee Institute of Technology. Recreation: reading; sailing; walking. Address: (h.) 48 Monifieth Road, Dundee, DD5 2RX.

Wilson, Roy. General Manager, Pitlochry Festival Theatre, since 1961; b. St. Andrews. Educ. Burgh School and Madras College, St. Andrews. Proprietor, grocer's business, St. Andrews, 1953-59; Assistant Manager, Pitlochry Festival Theatre, 1959-61. Recreations: plays and theatre in general; most forms of classical music, with particular interest in choral singing; listening to records; reading. Address: (h.) Kilrymont, Bruach Lane, Pitlochry, Perthshire, PH16 5DG; T.-Pitlochry 2897.

Wilson, R. Ross, BSc, PhD, MInstP, CPhys. Managing Director, James Howden Group Technology, since 1989; Visiting Professor, Mechanical Engineering, Strathclyde University, since 1985; b. 13.3.47, Glasgow; m., Margaret; 2 s. Educ. Hamilton Academy; Glasgow University. Research Officer, then Vibration Group Leader, Central Electricity Research Laboratories, CEGB; Section Head, Design Analysis, Corporate Engineering Laboratory, British Steel; Design Manager, then Technical Director, James Howden Ltd. Recreations: golf; reading; gardening. Address: (b.) Old Govan Road, Renfrew, PA4 8XJ; T.-041-886 6711.

Wilson, Thomas Black, BSc (Hons), MBCS. Principal, Glasgow College of Building and Printing, since 1989; b. 23.12.43, Airdrie; m., Barbara Smith; 1 s.; 1 d. Educ. Cumnock Academy; Glasgow University; Jordanhill College. Principal Teacher, Prestwick Academy, 1969-74; Head, Computing Department, Ayr College, 1974-84; Depute Principal: Barmulloch College, Glasgow, 1984-86, Cardonald College, Glasgow, 1986-89. Member, Scottish Central Committee (Mathematics), 1975-82. Recreations: reading; writing; music. Address: (b.) 60 North Hanover Street, Glasgow, G1 2BP; T.-041-332 9969.

Wilson, Emeritus Professor Thomas Brendan, CBE, MA, BMus, ARCM. Composer; b. 10.10.27, Trinidad, Colorado; m., Margaret Rayner; 3 s. Educ. St. Mary's College, Aberdeen; Glasgow University; Royal College of Music. RAF, 1945-48; Glasgow University: Lecturer in Music, Extra-Mural Studies, 1957, Reader in Music, Extra-Mural Studies, 1972, Professor, 1977; Member, Scottish Arts Council, 1966-72; Past Chairman, Composers Guild; President, Scottish Society of Composers; Member, Advisory Commitee, Scottish Music Information Centre; elected Member, Royal Society of Musicians; compositions include orchestral, choral-orchestral, chamber-orchestral, opera (including The Confessions of a Justified Sinner), ballet, brass band, vocal music of different kinds, and works for a wide variety of chamber ensembles and solo instruments; numerous commissions; Hon. Doctorate of Music, Glasgow University, 1991; Fellow, Royal Scottish Academy of Music and Drama, since 1991. Recreations: golf; talking shop. Address: (h.) 120 Dowanhill Street, Glasgow, G12 9DN; T.-041-339 1699.

Wilson, Professor William Adam, MA, LLB, FRSE. Lord President Reid Professor of Law, Edinburgh University, since 1972; b. 28.7.28, Glasgow. Educ. Hillhead High School, Glasgow; Glasgow University. Solicitor, 1951-60; Lecturer in Scots Law, Edinburgh University, 1960-72. Recreation: walking. Address: (h.) 2 Great Stuart Street, Edinburgh; T.-031-225 4958.

Wilson, William Murray, MB, ChB, MRCGP. General Medical Practitioner, Dalry, Ayrshire, 1949-89; Medical Advisor, Roche Products, Dalry, Ayrshire, since 1965; Medical Referee, Cunninghame District Council, since 1972; Member, Ayrshire and Arran Health Board; b. 19.1.25, Glasgow; m., Elizabeth Carbine; 3 s. Educ. Eastwood Secondary School; Glasgow University. Past Chairman, Local Medical Committee/GP Committee, Area Medical Committee, BMA Ayrshire Division; former Member, General Medical Services Committee, London and Edinburgh; Elder, St. Margaret's Church, Dalry; former Member, Education for the Ministry Committee, Church of Scotland; Honorary Lecturer, British Red Cross Society, St. Andrew's Ambulance Association. Recreations: travel; photography. Address: (h.) 22 Courthill Street, Dalry, Ayrshire, KA24 5AN; T.-Dalry 832165.

Wilson, Rev. William Stewart, DA. Minister, Kirkcudbright, since 1980; b. 8.3.34, Stromness; m., Sheila Stevens; 1 s.; 1 d. Educ. Stromness Academy; Gray's School of Art; Aberdeen University. Soldier (Instructor, RAEC), two years; Schoolteacher, five years; islander (Fair Isle), nine years; Schoolteacher, four years. Adviser, Committee on Artistic Matters, Church of Scotland. Publication: Shipwrecks of Fair Isle, 1970. Recreations: painting; drama; ornithology. Address: 6 Bourtree Avenue, Kirkcudbright; T.-0557 30489.

Wilson, W. Stewart, BSc. Rector, Banchory Academy, since 1978; b. 15.5.37, Aberdeen; m., Elizabeth Gorrod; 1 s.; 1 d. Educ. Aberdeen Grammar School; Aberdeen University. Teacher, Aberdeen Grammar School, 1961-66; Principal Teacher of Mathematics, then Deputy Rector, Banchory Academy, 1966-78. Elder and Clerk, Congregational Board, Banchory Ternan West Parish Church; Past President: Banchory and District Round Table, Rotary Club of Banchory Ternan; Past Chairman, Kincardine and Deeside National Trust Members' Centre; former Scottish Headquarters Scout Commissioner for Adult Leader Training, now Assistant Chief Commissioner for Scotland. Recreations: philately; Robert Burns - his life and works; antique maps of Kincardineshire. Address: (h.) Ibiscus, Rosehill Crescent, Banchory; T.-033-02 3194.

Wilson Smith, Lt. Col. John Logan, OBE. Regimental Secretary, The Royal Scots, since 1983; b. 4.7.27, Harrow; m., Ann Winifred Lyon Corsar; 3 d. Educ. Wellington College. Commissioned, 1946; Lt. Col., 1972; retired, 1977; Chairman, The Royal Scots Association; Director, The Royal Scots Regimental Shop Ltd.; President, SSAFA and FHS, Edinburgh and Midlothian. Recreations: forestry; shooting; fishing. Address: (h.) Cumledge, Duns, Berwickshire, TD11 3TB.

Wiltshire, James Phillip, OBE (1987), BA, PhD. Member, Ayrshire and Arran Health Board, 1982-91; b. 9.5.24, Sheffield; m., Janet Eleanor; 1 s.; 1 d. Educ. Maltby Grammar School; Queens' College, Cambridge. Joined ICI as Research Chemist, Paints Division, Slough, 1947; seconded to Canadian Industries Ltd., Toronto, 1960-62; Research Manager, Nobel Division, ICI, Stevenston, 1969; Policy Group Member, Corporate Laboratory, ICI, Runcorn, 1971; Research and Personnel Director, Nobel's Explosives Co. Ltd., Stevenston, 1973; a CBI Representative, Manpower Services Committee for Scotland, 1980-82; retired from ICI, 1982; Chairman, Ayrshire Area Manpower Board, 1983-88; Past Chairman, Ayrshire Marriage Guidance Council; former Treasurer, Ayrshire Council on Alcoholism; former Representative, CBI Scotland, on Community Business Scotland; former Member, Scottish Technical Education Council. Recreations: sailing; hill-walking; a little music and opera. Address: (h.) Burnswood, 20 Greenfield Avenue, Alloway, Ayr, KA7 4NW; T.-0292 41502.

Windsor, Malcolm L., PhD, FRSC. Secretary, North Atlantic Salmon Conservation Organization, since 1984; b. 12.4.38, Bristol; m., Sally; 2 d. Educ. Cotham Grammar School, Bristol; Bristol University. Researcher, University of California, 1965-67; fisheries research, Humber Laboratory, Hull, 1967-75; Fisheries Adviser to Chief Scientist, Ministry of Agriculture and Fisheries, London, 1975-84. Secretary, Society for the Preservation of Duddingston Village. Publication: book on fishery products. Recreations: local conservation work; jazz; walking. Address: (b.) 11 Rutland Square, Edinburgh, EH1 2AS; T.-031-228 2551.

Windsor, Col. Rodney Francis Maurice, CBE, DL. Farmer; b. 22.2.25, Redhill; m., Deirdre Chichester; 2 s.; 1 d. Educ. Tonbridge School. Enlisted Royal Armoured Corps, 1943; commissioned The Queen's Bays, 1944-52; Captain, 1949; ADC to CINC and High Commissioner Austria, 1949-50; served in North Irish Horse (TA), 1959-67; Lt. Col. Commanding, 1964-67; Colonel TA N. Ireland, 1967-71; ADC (TA) to HM The Queen, 1970-75; Member, Highland TA Association, 1971-77; Member, Banff and Buchan District Valuation Appeal Committee, since 1982 (Deputy Chairman, since 1989); Deputy Lieutenant, Aberdeenshire, since 1989. Recreations: field sports; golf. Address: (h.) Byth House, New Byth, Turriff, Aberdeenshire, AB5 7XN; T.-08883 230.

Winney, Robin John, MB, ChB, FRCPEdin. Consultant Renal Physician, Edinburgh Royal Infirmary, since 1978; b. 8.5.44, Dunfermline. Educ. Dunfermline High School; Edinburgh University. Recreations: badminton; curling. Address: (h.) 74 Lanark Road West, Currie, Midlothian, EH14 5JZ.

Winning, Most Rev. Thomas Joseph, STL, DCL, DD, FEIS, KCHS. Archbishop of Glasgow and Metropolitan, since 1974; President, Bishops' Conference of Scotland, since 1985; b. 3.6.25, Wishaw. Educ. Our Lady's High School, Motherwell; St. Mary's College, Blairs; St. Peter's College; Scots College; Gregorian University, Rome. Ordained Priest, Rome, 1948; Assistant Priest, Chapelhall, 1949-50; Rome (DCL, "Cum Laude"), 1953; Assistant Priest, St. Mary's Hamilton, 1953-57; Cathedral, Motherwell, 1957-58;

Chaplain, Franciscans of the Immaculate Conception, Bothwell, 1958-61; Diocesan Secretary, Motherwell, 1956-61; Spiritual Director, Scots College, Rome, 1961-66; Advocate of the Sacred Roman Rota, 1965; Parish Priest, St. Luke's Motherwell, 1966-70; Officialis and Vicar Episcopal, Motherwell Diocese, 1966-70; first President, Scottish Catholic Marriage Tribunal, 1970; nominated Titular Bishop of Louth and Bishop Auxiliary, 1971, and ordained by James Donald Scanlan, Archbishop of Glasgow, November, 1971; Parish Priest, Our Holy Redeemer's Clydebank, 1972-74; translated to Glasgow as Archbishop, 1974; Honorary DD (Glasgow), 1983; awarded Glasgow Loving Cup, 1983; Grand Prior of Scotland, Equestrian Order of the Holy Sepulchre of Jerusalem, 1989. Recreations: watching football; listening to music. Address: (h.) 40 Newlands Road, Glasgow, G43 2JD; T.-041-226 5898.

Winter, Charles M., FIB (Scot). Group Chief Executive, Royal Bank of Scotland Group p.l.c., since 1985; b. 21.7.33, Dundee; m., Audrey Hynd; 1 s.; 1 d. Educ. Harris Academy, Dundee. Joined Royal Bank of Scotland, 1949; Director, 1981; Director, Royal Bank of Scotland Group, 1981; President, Institute of Bankers in Scotland, 1981-83; Director, Lloyds & Scottish PLC, 1983-84, Chairman, Committee of Scottish Clearing Bankers, 1983-85 and 1989-91; Member, Board of Governors, Leith Nautical College, 1979-82; Treasurer, Commonwealth Games, Scotland, 1986; Chairman, Steering Committee, Inter-Alpha Group of Banks, 1986; Senior Vice-President, Edinburgh Chamber of Commerce and Manufactures. Recreations: golf; choral music. Address: (b.) Royal Bank of Scotland Group p.l.c., 42 St. Andrew Square, Edinburgh; T.-031-556 8555.

Winton, Alexander, QFSM, MIFireE. HM Chief Inspector of Fire Services for Scotland, since 1990; b. 13.7.32, Perth; m., Jean; 2 s. Perth and Kinross Fire Brigade, 1958; Instructor, Scottish Fire Service Training School, 1962; Lancashire County Fire Brigade, 1967; East Riding of Yorkshire Fire Brigade, 1970; Angus Area Fire Brigade, 1973; Tayside Fire Brigade, 1975; Deputy Firemaster, Tayside Fire Brigade, 1981; Firemaster, 1985-89. Recreations: golf; curling. Address: (h.) 5 Ferndale Drive, Broughty Ferry, Dundee, DD5 3DB; T.-Dundee 78156.

Wishart, David, BSc, PhD, CEng. Assistant Secretary, Scottish Office Education Department, since 1984; b. 5.7.43, London; m., Doreen Pamela Craig Wishart; 3 s. Educ. Kilburn Grammar School; Truro School; St. Andrews University. Statistician, Civil Service Department, London, 1970-75; Principal, Scottish Office, 1975-77; Chief Statistician, Scottish Office, 1977-81; Director of Statistics, Scottish Office, 1981-84. Fellow: British Computer Society, Royal Statistical Society (Vice President, 1986-88), Royal Society of Arts; Director, Wishart Society. Recreations: cricket; skiing; opera. Address: (h.) 16 Kingsburgh Road, Edinburgh, 12; T.-031-337 1448.

Wishart, Ruth. Columnist, The Scotsman, since 1986; Broadcaster, BBC Radio, since 1989 (Presenter, Headlines); b. Glasgow; m., Rod McLeod. Educ. Eastwood Senior Secondary School. TV Editor, Daily Record, 1970-73; Woman's Editor, Daily Record, 1973-78; Assistant Editor, Sunday Mail, 1978-82; Assistant Editor, Sunday Standard, 1982-83; Freelance Writer, 1983-86; Senior Assistant Editor, The Scotsman, 1986-88. Member, Scottish Advisory Committee, British Council; Director, Assembly Theatre; Member, Scottish Committee, ABSA. Recreations: theatre; travel; curling. Address: (h.) Wilson Court, Wilson Street, Glasgow.

Withers, John Alexander (Jack), FCIL. Librarian and Writer-in-Residence, Scottish-German Centre/Goethe Institut, since 1974; Writer; b. Glasgow; m., Beate (Bea) Haertel.

Educ. North Kelvinside School; Jordanhill College of Education (Youth and Community Diploma). Left school at 14; worked in garage, electrical industry, labouring, National Service, unemployment, razor-blade salesman; long periods abroad, wandering, wondering, working: France, FRG, Italy, Scandinavia, Spain, North Africa; youth worker; freelance writer; ski instructor; librarian; Scottish republican and radical; plays for radio, TV, theatre; James Kennoway Screenplay Award (shared); Scottish Arts Council Awards; short stories published in numerous journals in UK, Denmark and West Germany; Editor, Two Tongues – Two Cities; book: Glasgow Limbo. Address: (h.) 16 Belmont Crescent, Glasgow; T.-041-339 9492.

Witney, Professor Brian David, BSc, MSc, PhD, CEng, FIMechE, FIAgrE. Director, Scottish Centre of Agricultural Engineering, since 1987, and Vice-Dean, Scottish Agricultural College, since 1990; b. 8.6.38, Gloucester; m., Maureen M.I. Donnelly; 1 s.; 2 d. Educ. Daniel Stewart's College, Edinburgh; Edinburgh University; Durham University; Newcastle University. Senior Research Associate, Newcastle upon Tyne University, 1962-66; Research Fellow, US Army Research Office, Duke Univ., 1966-67; Senior Scientific Officer, Military Engineering Experimental Establishment, Christchurch; Head, Agricultural Engineering Department, East of Scotland College of Agriculture, Edinburgh, 1970-86. President, Institution of Agricultural Engineers, 1988-90. Publication: Choosing and Using Farm Machines. Address: (b.) Scottish Centre of Agricultural Engineering, Bush Estate, Penicuik, Midlothian, EH26 0PH; T.-031-445 2147.

Wolfe, William Cuthbertson, CA, JP. Member, National Council, Scottish National Party, since 1991; b. 22.2.24; 2 s.; 2 d. Educ. Bathgate Academy; George Watson's College, Edinburgh. Army Service, 1942-47, NW Europe and Far East; Air OP Pilot. Hon. Publications Treasurer, Saltire Society, 1953-60; Scout County Commissioner, West Lothian, 1960-64; Hon. President (Rector), Students' Association, Heriot-Watt University, 1966-69; contested (SNP) West Lothian, 1962, 1964, 1966, 1970, Feb. and Oct. 1974, 1979, North Edinburgh, Nov. 1973; Chairman, SNP, 1969-79, President, 1980-82; Treasurer, Scottish CND, 1982-85; Secretary, Scottish Poetry Library, 1985-91. Publication: Scotland Lives. Address: Burnside Forge, Burnside Road, Bathgate, West Lothian, EH48 4PU; T.-0506 54785.

Wolfe Murray, Stephanie. Managing Director, Canongate Press PLC; b. 27.4.41, Blandford, Dorset. Educ. England; Florence; Paris; m., Angus; lived in Leeds and Invernessshire, having four sons there. Chair, Scottish Publishers Association; Council Member, Book Trust, Scotland. Recreations: walking; reading. Address: (h.) 20 Leonard's Bank, Edinburgh; T.-031-220 3800.

Wolfram, Professor Julian, BSc, CEng, PhD, FRINA. Total Oil Marine Chair of Offshore Research and Development, Heriot-Watt University, since 1990; b. 2.8.46, London; m., Margaret Mary Lockhart; 1 s., 1 d., by pr. m. Educ. Gordonstoun; Reading University; Newcastle University. Research and Development Officer, Vickers Shipbuilders Ltd.; Lecturer (latterly Senior Lecturer) in Naval Architecture, Sunderland Polytechnic; Lecturer (latterly Senior Lecturer) in Marine Technology, Strathclyde University; Tutor, Open University; Chief Examiner, Ship Structures and Dynamics, Engineering Council; Consultant to several companies in the marine field. Publications: over 20 technical papers. Recreations: sailing; squash; hill walking. Address: (b.) Heriot-Watt University, Edinburgh EH14 4AS; T.-031-449 5111.

Wolrige Gordon, Captain Robert. Member, Grampian Regional Council, 1978-86 (Deputy Chairman, Planning,

WHO'S WHO IN SCOTLAND 477

1982-86); b. 20.9.28, Esslemont; m., Rosemary Jane Abel Smith; 1 s.; 1 d. (deceased). Educ. Eton College; Royal Military Academy, Sandhurst. Enlisted Grenadier Guards, 1947; commissioned, 1948; Captain, 1953; retired, 1959; Member, Aberdeenshire County Council, 1961-74 (Chairman, Accident Prevention and Civil Defence Committee); Chairman, Gordon Constituency Conservative Association, 1988-90; Grand Master Mason of Scotland, 1974-79; Member, Representative Church Council, 1959-82; Member, Diocesan and Provincial Synod, Scottish Episcopal Church. Recreations: shooting; fishing; history. Address: (h.) Esslemont, Ellon, Aberdeenshire; T.-Ellon 20234.

Wong, Professor Henry H.Y., BSc, PhD, DIC, CEng, FRAeS. Professor, Department of Aeronautics and Fluid Mechanics, Glasgow University; Adviser to the Guangdong Higher Education Bureau, China, since 1985; Adviser to Glasgow University on Chinese Affairs, since 1986, and "Concurrent" Professor, Changsha Institute of Technology, since 1989; Senior Research Fellow, since 1987; b. 23.5.22, Hong Kong; m., Joan Anstey; 2 s.; 1 d. Educ. St. Stephen College, Hong Kong; Jiao-Tong University, Shanghai; Imperial College, London; Glasgow University. Assistant Lecturer, Jiao-Tong University, 1947-48; Engineer, Armstrong Siddeley, 1949; Structural Engineer, Hunting Percival Aircraft, 1949-51; Senior Structural Engineer, de Havilland Aircraft, 1952-57; Senior Lecturer, Hatfield Polytechnic, 1957-59; Lecturer, Senior Lecturer, then Reader in Aeronautics and Fluid Mechanics, Glasgow University, from 1960; Economic and Technological Consultant to Shantou Special Economic Zone, China, since 1988. Former Treasurer and Vice-Chairman, Kilmardinny Music Circle; Chairman, Glasgow Summer School, since 1979. Recreations: reading; music; painting; swimming. Address: (h.) 77 Antonine Road, Bearsden, Glasgow; T.-041-942 8346.

Wood, Arthur Murdoch Mactaggart, OBE, MA, LLB. General Secretary, RSSPCC, since 1968; b. 15.12.37, Kilbarchan; 2 s.; 2 d. Educ. George Watson's College, Edinburgh; Edinburgh University. Standard Life Assurance Company, 1960-61; Assistant Secretary, RSSPCC, 1961-68. Address: (b.) RSSPCC, Melville House, 41 Polwarth Terrace, Edinburgh, EH11 1NU; T.-031-337 8539.

Wood, Brian Charles Thallon, BL (Dist.), NP. Solicitor, since 1955; Partner, Charles Wood & Son, Solicitors, Kirkcaldy, since 1956; Honorary Sheriff; b. 8.8.34, Kirkcaldy; m., Tessa; 1 s.; 1 d. Educ. Fettes; Edinburgh University. Part-time Chairman, Industrial Tribunals, 1972-77; part-time Chairman, Rent Assessment Committee, 1987. Recreations: gardens; skiing; mending anything. Address: (b.) 37 Kirk Wynd, Kirkcaldy, Fife; T.-0592 261621.

Wood, Brian James, JP, BSc (Hons). Rector, Mearns Academy, since 1989; b. 6.12.49, Banff; m., Doreen A. Petrie; 1 s.; 1 d. Educ. Banff Academy; Aberdeen Academy; Aberdeen University; Aberdeen College of Education. Teacher of Physics, George Heriot's School, Edinburgh, 1972-75; Mackie Academy, 1975-89, latterly as Depute Rector. Member, Kincardine and Deeside District Sports Council, since 1989; Elder, Church of Scotland. Recreations: sport; reading; music; travel; theatre; DIY. Address: (h.) 13 Edinview Gardens, Stonehaven; T.-0569 63888.

Wood, Brian James Barry, PhD, BSc, CChem, FRSC, FIFST, FRSA. Reader, Department of Bioscience and Biotechnology, Strathclyde University, since 1981; b. 11.7.34, Birmingham. Educ. Kings Norton Grammar School, Birmingham; Birmingham University. Research Biochemist, University of California at Davis, 1959-62; Scientist, Unilever Ltd., Bedford, 1962-68; Strathclyde University: Lecturer, 1968-75, Senior Lecturer, 1975-81; Technical Director, Bean Products Ltd., 1981-84. Representative, Forth and Clyde

Canal Society on Glasgow Urban Wildlife Group. Recreations: gardening; Lenzie Rugby FC; work. Address: (b.) Division of Applied Microbiology, Strathclyde University, Glasgow, G1 1XW; T.-041-552 4400.

Wood, George Alexander McDougall, BA. Senior Lecturer in English Studies, Stirling University, since 1975; Executive Editor, Edinburgh Edition of the Waverley Novels, since 1986; b. 9.8.38, Hyde. Educ. William Hulme's Grammar School, Manchester; University College, London. Research Assistant, English Department, University College, London, 1962; Librarian, Osborn Collection, Yale University, 1962-66; Fellow, Silliman College, Yale University, 1965-66; Assistant Professor of English, University of California, Santa Barbara, 1966-68; Lecturer, Stirling University, 1968-75. Recreation: railways. Address: (h.) Burn O'Vat, Haining, Dunblane, Perthshire; T.-Dunblane 4878.

Wood, Professor Hamish Christopher Swan, BSc, PhD, CChem, FRSC, FRSE. Professor of Organic Chemistry, Strathclyde University, since 1969; b. 8.5.26, Hawick; m., Jean Dumbreck Mitchell; 1 s.; 1 d. Educ. Hawick High School; St. Andrews University. Lecturer in Chemistry, St. Andrews University, 1950-51; Research Fellow, Australian National University, 1951-53; Lecturer, Senior Lecturer and Reader, Strathclyde University, 1953-69 (Vice-Principal, 1984-86); Member, Universities Funding Council, since 1989; Chairman, Governing Body, Glasgow Polytechnic, since 1987. Address: (b.) Thomas Graham Building, Strathclyde University, 295 Cathedral Street, Glasgow, G1 1XL; T.-041-552 4400.

Wood, Ian Clark, CBE (1982), LLD, BSc, CBIM. Chairman and Managing Director, John Wood Group PLC, since 1967; Chairman, J.W. Holdings, since 1982; b. 21.7.42, Aberdeen; m., Helen Macrae; 3 s. Educ. Robert Gordon's College, Aberdeen; Aberdeen University. Joined family business, John Wood & Sons, 1964; Member, Scottish Economic Council; Fellow, Royal Society of Arts; Member, Offshore Industry Board and Offshore Industry Export Advisory Group; Member, Scottish Sub-Committee, University Funding Council; Board Director, Royal Bank of Scotland; Member, Aberdeen Beyond 2000; Chairman, Grampian Enterprise Ltd.; Member, National Training Task Force; Grampian Industrialist of the Year, 1978; Young Scottish Businessman of the Year, 1979; Hon. LLD, 1984. Recreations: squash; family; art. Address: (b.) John Wood Group PLC, John Wood House, Greenwell Road, East Tullos, Aberdeen; T.-0224 875464.

Wood, Jack Williamson, FRICS, FRVA. Regional Assessor and Electoral Registration Officer, Strathclyde Regional Council, since 1981, and Community Charge Registration Officer, since 1987; President, Scottish Assessors' Association; Visiting Professor, Paisley College, since 1991; b. 15.3.33, Rutherglen; m., Wilma; 2 d. Educ. Rutherglen Academy; Royal College of Science and Technology. Assistant Chief Surveyor, Glasgow, 1964-75; Strathclyde Region: Depute Assessor, 1975-79, Senior Depute Assessor, 1979-81. Recreations: sport (golf); music; literature. Address: (b.) Strathclyde House II, 20 India Street, Glasgow; T.-041-249 4300.

Wood, Michael, BSc (Hons), DipCarto, FRGS. Senior Lecturer in Geography (Cartography), Aberdeen University, since 1983; b. 25.6.41, Insch; m., Margaret Russell Lochhead Barr; 2 d. Educ. Aberdeen Grammar School; Aberdeen University; Glasgow University. Research Assistant, then Assistant Lecturer, Department of Geography, Glasgow University, 1964-69; Lecturer, Department of Geography, Aberdeen University, 1969-83; External Examiner for National Certificates in Cartography, Surveying and Planning in Britain, 1971-78; Council Member, British Cartographic

Society, since 1971 (President, 1982-84); Member, UK Committee for Cartography, since 1990; President, Society of Cartographers, since 1991; Vice-President, International Cartographic Association, 1991-95. Publications: Surveying and Mapping for Field Scientists (Co-author), 1988; papers on cartography and map reading; numerous maps. Recreations: hill-walking; skiing. Address: (b.) Department of Geography, Elphinstone Road, Aberdeen, AB9 2UF; T.- 0224 272332.

Wood, Robert Anderson, BSc, MB, ChB, FRCPEdin. Consultant Physician, Perth Royal Infirmary, since 1972; Senior Lecturer in Pharmacology and Therapeutics, Dundee University, since 1972; Councillor, Royal College of Physicians of Edinburgh, since 1990; b. 26.5.39, Edinburgh. Educ. Edinburgh Academy; Edinburgh University. Address: (h.) Ballomill House, Abernethy, Perthshire; T.-Abernethy 201.

Wood, Stephen Charles, MA, BA (Hons), FSA(Scot). Keeper, Scottish United Services Museum, Edinburgh Castle, since 1983; b. 29.1.52, Wells, Somerset; 1 s. Educ. The Blue School, Wells; Bishop Wordsworth's School, Salisbury; Birkbeck College, London University. Curator, Department of Uniform, National Army Museum, London, 1971-83. Publications: The Scottish Soldier, 1987; In the Finest Tradition, 1988; The Auld Alliance, 1989; The Legendary 51st, 1990. Recreations: travel; gastronomy; country matters. Address: (b.) Edinburgh Castle, Edinburgh; T.-01-225 7534.

Wood-Gush, Professor David Grainger Marcus, PhD, BSc, DipAnimGen, FRSE. Honorary Professor, Institute of Ecology and Resource Management, Edinburgh University, since 1978; b. 20.11.22, Dordrecht, South Africa; m., Eola Langham Godden; 1 s.; 1 d. Educ. St. Andrews College, Grahamstown, South Africa; Witwatersrand University, Johannesburg; Edinburgh University. Senior Principal Scientific Officer (Special Merit), AFRC, and Head, Ethology Department, AFRC Poultry Research Centre, Edinburgh, 1952-78. Former Chairman, Association for the Study of Animal Behaviour; former President, Society for Veterinary Ethology. Publications: The Behaviour of the Domestic Fowl; Elements of Ethology. Recreations: reading; swimming; hill-walking; historic building preservation. Address: (h.) 26 Nelson Street, Edinburgh, EH3 6LJ; T.-031-556 6488.

Woodruff, Professor Sir Michael (Francis Addison), Kt (1969), DSc, MD, MS, FRCS, FRCSE, FRACS, Hon. FACS, FRSE, FRS. Professor Emeritus, Surgery, Edinburgh University; b. 3.4.11, London; m., Hazel Gwenyth Ashby; 2 s.; 1 d. Educ. Wesley College, Melbourne; Queens College, Melbourne University. House Physician and House Surgeon, Royal Melbourne Hospital; Captain, Australian Army Medical Corps (PoW, Singapore); Tutor in Surgery, Sheffield University, 1946; Senior Lecturer in Surgery, Aberdeen University, 1948; Professor of Surgery, Otago University, 1953, Edinburgh University, 1957-76; research worker, MRC Clinical and Population Cytogenetics Unit, Edinburgh, 1976-86. President, The Transplantation Society, 1972-74. Publications: Deficiency Diseases in Japanese Prison Camps; Surgery for Dental Students; The Transplantation of Tissues and Organs; On Science and Surgery; The Interaction of Cancer and Host; Cellular Variation and Adaptation in Cancer, 1990. Recreations: sailing; music; tennis. Address: (h.) The Bield, 506 Lanark Road, Juniper Green, Edinburgh, EH14 5DH; T.-031-453 3653.

Woods, Adrian Charles, MA. Director, Policy and Planning, Scottish Enterprise, since 1991; b. 22.9.55, London. Educ. Farnham Grammar School; Slough Grammar School; St. Andrews University. Joined SDA, 1981; Area Programme Development Team, Glasgow, 1981-84; Head, Oil and Gas Division, Aberdeen, 1984-88; Head, Policy and Projects,

Lanarkshire, 1988-89; Assistant Director, Employment and Special Initiatives, 1989-91. Recreation: golf. Address: (b.) 120 Bothwell Street, Glasgow; T.-041-248 2700.

Woodward, Professor John Frank, BSc, CEng, EurIng, FICE, FBIM. Vice Principal, Paisley University; Visiting Professor, Glasgow Business School, since 1970; b. 23.6.33, London; m., Marjorie Isobel; 4 d. Educ. City of Leicester Boys School; Glasgow University. Engineer, latterly Director, associate company, Taylor Woodrow Group, 1956-67; Reader in Management Science, Stirling University, 1968-81. Recreations: field sports; hill-walking. Address: (b.) Paisley University, High Street, Paisley, PA1 2BE; T.-041-848 3000.

Wooldridge, Ian, BA (Hons). Artistic Director, Royal Lyceum Theatre Company, Edinburgh, since 1984; b. 11.8.46, Swansea. Educ. King Henry VIII School, Coventry; Cardiff University; Bristol University. Stage Manager and Teacher of Drama, 1968-72; Associate Director, Dark and Light Theatre Company, Brixton, 1972-75; freelance Theatre Director and Drama Consultant, Lothian Region Education Authority, 1975-78; Artistic Director, TAG Theatre Company, Glasgow, 1978-84. Address: (b.) Royal Lyceum Theatre, Grindlay Street, Edinburgh, EH3 9AX; T.-031-229 7404.

Woolman, Stephen E., LLB. Advocate, since 1987; b. 16.5.53, Edinburgh; m., Dr. Helen F. Mackinnon; 2 d. Educ. George Heriot's School; Aberdeen University. Lecturer in Law, Edinburgh University, 1978-87 (Associate Dean, Faculty of Law, 1981-84); Official Visitor, University of Melbourne, 1984; Governor, George Heriot's School, 1985-87; Standing Junior Counsel to Office of Fair Trading in Scotland, since 1991. Introduction to the Scots Law of Contract, 1987. Recreation: cinema. Address: (b.) Advocates' Library, Parliament House, Edinburgh.

Workman, Professor Paul, BSc, PhD. Cancer Research Campaign Professor of Experimental Cancer Therapy, Glasgow University, since 1991; Director, Laboratory Research, Department of Medical Oncology, Cancer Research Campaign Beatson Laboratories, Glasgow University, since 1991; Chairman, New Drug Development Co-ordinating Committee, European Organisation for Research and Treatment of Cancer, since 1991; b. 30.3.52, Workington; m., Elizabeth May; 1 s.; 1 d. Educ. Workington County Grammar School; Leicester University; Leeds University. Staff Scientist, MRC Clinical Oncology and Radiotherapeutics Unit, Cambridge University, 1976-90. Past President, EORTC Pharmacology and Molecular Mechanisms Group; Member, Cancer Research Campaign Phase I/II Clinicals Committee; European School of Oncology Prize for research in cancer chemotherapy, 1985. Recreations: family; hiking; sport; music; theatre; reading; food and wine. Address: (b.) Cancer Research Campaign Beatson Laboratories, Glasgow University, Glasgow, G12 8QQ; T.-041-330 4886.

Worrall, Ernest Paterson, MB, ChB, FRCPsych, DPM. Consultant Psychiatrist: Southern General Hospital, Glasgow, since 1980, Ross Hall Hospital, Glasgow, since 1984, Bon Secours Hospital, Glasgow; b. 28.10.42, Hamilton; m., Jean Price; 1 s.; 1 d. Educ. Hamilton Academy; Glasgow University. Lecturer in Psychiatry, Dundee University, 1973-75; Senior Lecturer in Psychological Medicine, Glasgow University, 1975-80. Recreations: cycling; bowling. Address: (b.) Department of Psychiatry, Southern General Hospital, Glasgow, G51 1TF; T.-041-445 2466.

Worthington, Tony, BA, MEd. MP (Labour), Clydebank and Milngavie, since 1987; front-bench Scottish Spokesman on Education, Employment and Training and Social Work;

b. 11.10.41, Hertfordshire; m., Angela; 1 s.; 1 d. Educ. City School, Lincoln; London School of Economics; York University; Glasgow University. Recreations: running; fishing; gardening. Address: (h.) 24 Cleddans Crescent, Hardgate, Clydebank; T.-0389 73195.

Wotherspoon (John Munro) Iain, TD, DL. Senior Partner, MacAndrew & Jenkins, WS, since 1954; Deputy Lieutenant, Districts of Lochaber, Inverness, Badenoch and Strathspey, since 1982, and Clerk, since 1985; b. 19.7.24, Inverness; m., Victoria Avril Jean Edwards; 2 s.; 2 d. Educ. Inverness Royal Academy; Loretto School; Trinity College, Oxford; Edinburgh University. Lt., Royal Signals, Europe and Burma, 1944-46; TA, 1948-78; Lt.-Col. commanding 51 (Highland) Division Signals, 1963-70; Col. Dep. Cdr. 13 Signals Gp., 1970-72; Hon. Col. 32 (Scottish) Signal Regiment, 1972-78; ADC to The Queen, 1971-76; WS, 1950; Solicitor and Land Owner. Recreations: shooting; fishing; stalking. Address: (h.) Maryfield, 62 Midmills Road, Inverness, IV2 3QL; T.-0463 233642.

Wray, James. MP (Labour), Glasgow Provan, since 1987; b. 28.4.38.

Wren-Lewis, Professor Simon, MA (Cantab), MSc. Professor of Macroeconomic Modelling, Strathclyde University, since 1990; b. 11.7.53, London; m., Joanna; 2 s. Educ. Latymer Upper School; Clare College, Cambridge. Economist, HM Treasury, 1974-81; Research Fellow, National Institute for Economic and Social Research, 1981-90. Recreations: gardening; walking. Address: (b.) Economics Department, Strathclyde University, 100 Cathedral Street, Glasgow, G4 0LN; T.-041-552 4400, Ext. 3851.

Wright, Dan W., EurIng, MBE, BSc, CEng, FIMechE, ANRAeS, MSAE. Managing Director, Fleming Thermodynamics Ltd., since 1983; b. 10.6.49, Glasgow; m., Christine Williamson; 1 s.; 1 d. Educ. Hamilton Academy; Glasgow University. Ford Motor Company; Howden Compressors; Leyland Vehicles; Ogle Design (Chief Engineer/Associate Director). Member, Department of Trade and Industry panel on deregulation of industry); Member, Board of Governors, Glasgow School of Art; Member, Business Development Committee, Scottish Council Development and Industry; Committee Member, IMechE Automobile Division (Scottish Centre). Recreations: shooting; fishing; driving cars and trucks. Address: (b.) Fleming Thermodynamics Ltd., 1 Redwood Court, East Kilbride, G74 5PF; T.-03552 26600.

Wright, David Frederick, MA (Cantab). Senior Lecturer in Ecclesiastical History, Edinburgh University, since 1973; b. 2.10.37, Hayes, Kent; m., Anne-Marie; 1 s.; 1 d. Educ. Christ's College, Cambridge; Lincoln College, Oxford. Edinburgh University: Lecturer, 1964-73, Associate Dean, Faculty of Divinity, 1972-76, Dean, since 1988, Member, University Court, 1984-87; External Examiner, Universities of Sussex, Liverpool, Durham, Cambridge, etc.; Member, Council of Management, Keston College; Chairman, Tyndale Fellowship for Biblical and Theological Research; Associate Editor, Tyndale Bulletin; Editor, Scottish Bulletin of Evangelical Theology; Member of Praesidium, International Congress on Calvin Research. Publications: Common Places of Martin Bucer, 1972; Essays in Evangelical Social Ethics (Editor), 1979; Lion Handbook History of Christianity (Consultant Editor), 1977; New Dictionary of Theology (Joint Editor), 1988; The Bible in Scottish Life and Literature (Contributor and Editor), 1988; Chosen by God: Mary in Evangelical Perspective (Contributor and Editor), 1989. Recreations: walking; gardening; DIY. Address: (h.) 5 Lockharton Gardens, Edinburgh, EH14 1AU; T.-031-443 1001.

Wright, David John, MB, BS, FFARCS. Consultant Anaesthetist, Western General Hospital, Edinburgh, since 1979; b. 13.4.44, Oswestry; m., Bronwen; 2 s.; 1 d. Educ. Bristol Grammar School; St. Bartholomew's Hospital Medical College, London. Honorary Secretary, Scottish Society of the History of Medicine. Address: (h.) 20 Lennox Row, Edinburgh, EH5 3JW; T.-031-552 3439.

Wright, Douglas Stewart. Director, Keep Scotland Beautiful, since 1973; Chairman, Beautiful Scotland in Bloom, since 1983; Deacon, Free Church of Scotland; b. 22.7.32, Glasgow; m., May Carswell; 1 s.; 2 d. Educ. Albert Road Academy, Pollokshields. Representative, Scottish Field, 1947-58; National Service, 1st Bn., Cameronians Scottish Rifles (Malaya), 1950-52; General Manager, The Scottish Farmer, 1959-66; Appeals Director, Scottish Council for the Care of Spastics, 1966-73. Committee Member, Stars Organisation for Spastics (Scotland); Past President, Glasgow Haggis Club (No. 33). Recreations: dog walking; specialist in China Tea Clippers; bee-keeping. Address: (b.) Cathedral Square, Dunblane, Perthshire, FK15 0AQ; T.-0786 823202.

Wright, Sir Edward (Maitland), Kt (1977). Research Fellow, Aberdeen University, since 1976; b. 1906. Principal and Vice-Chancellor, Aberdeen University, 1962-76.

Wright, Professor George, BSc, MPhil, PhD. Professor of Business Administration, Strathclyde Graduate Business School, since 1991; b. 24.11.52, Louth; m., Josephine Elizabeth; 2 s. Educ. Queen Elizabeth II Grammar School; NE London Polytechnic; Brunel University. Research Assistant, Brunel University, 1974-79; Research Fellow, Huddersfield Polytechnic, 1979-81; Senior Lecturer, City of London Polytechnic, 1981-86; Reader, then Professor, Bristol Business School, 1986-91. Publications: seven books; 60 journal articles. Recreation: renovating and driving a Triumph 2500S. Address: (b.) Strathclyde Graduate Business School, 130 Rottenrow, Glasgow, G4 0GE; T.-041-553 6000.

Wright, George Gordon. Publisher; b. 25.6.42, Edinburgh. Educ. Darroch Secondary School; Heriot Watt College. Started publishing as a hobby, 1969; left printing trade, 1973, to develop own publishing company; founder Member, Scottish General Publishers Association; Past Chairman, Scottish Young Publishers Society. Publications: MacDiarmid: An Illustrated Biography, 1977; A Guide to the Royal Mile, 1979; Orkney From Old Photographs, 1981; A Guide to Holyrood Park and Arthur's Seat, 1987. Recreations: history of Edinburgh; photography; jazz. Address: (h.) 25 Mayfield Road, Edinburgh, EH9 2NQ; T.-031-667 1300.

Wright, Professor Howard David, BEng, PhD, CEng, FIStructE, MICE. Professor of Structures (in association with Thorburns), Strathclyde University, since 1991; b. 5.10.52, Holmes Chapel; m., Elizabeth Mary Warren Baynham; 2 s.; 1 d. Educ. Sandbach School; Sheffield University. Assistant Engineer, 1974-78; Structural Engineer, Boots the Chemists, 1978-82; Lecturer in Structural Design, University of Wales, Cardiff, 1982-91. Council Member, Institution of Structural Engineers, 1988-91; Committee Member, Building Standards Advisory Board, since 1991. Publications: papers on composite construction and engineering education. Recreations: hill-walking; music; mechanics. Address: (b.) Department of Civil Engineering, 109 Rottenrow, Glasgow, G4 0NG; T.-041-552 4400, Ext. 3251.

Wright, Rev. Iain Alastair Mackay, RD, BA, BD. Director, CARE in Scotland, since 1989; b. 19.9.57, Edinburgh; m., Caroline Louise Read; 2 s. Educ. George Watson's College; Edinburgh University. Assistant Minister, St. Columba's, Pont Street, London, 1982-84; Minister, Falkland l.w. Freuchie, 1984-89. Lt. RNR; served on staff of FOSNI during Gulf War, awarded Reserve Decoration; Freeman Citizen of Glasgow. Recreations: reading; philately. Address: CARE in Scotland, 3 Royal Exchange Court, Glasgow, G1 3DB; T.-041-221 7212.

Wright, Ian William Weir, BSc, DRCST, CEng, MIChemE, CChem, MRIC. Chief Inspector, HM Industrial Pollution Inspectorate, since 1985; b. 22.4.35, Glasgow; m., Mary Stirling; 1 s.; 1 d. Educ. Allan Glen's School, Glasgow; Strathclyde University.Production Chemist, UKAEA, Windscale Works, 1959-63; Chemical Engineer, Scottish Pulp & Paper Mills, 1963-71 (Deputy Technical Manager); HM Industrial Pollution Inspectorate, since 1971. Recreations: DIY; gardening; reading; motoring. Address: (b.) 27 Perth Street, Edinburgh, EH3 5RB; T.-031-244 3056.

Wright, Rev. Kenyon Edward, MA, BA, BSc, MTh. Director, Kairos (Centre for Social and Environmental Studies), since 1990; Consultant on Justice and Peace to ACTS (Action of Churches Together in Scotland); Chair, Executive, Scottish Constitutional Convention; Co-ordinating Secretary, The Christian Peace Conference (International); Canon Emeritus and Companion of the Order of the Cross of Nails, Coventry Cathedral; b. 31.8.32, Paisley; m., Betty Robinson; 3 d. Educ. Paisley Grammar School; Glasgow University; Cambridge University. Missionary in India, 1955-70; Director, Ecumenical Social and Industrial Institute, Durgapur, India, 1963-70; Director, Urban Ministry, Coventry Cathedral, 1970-74; Canon Residentiary and Director of International Ministry, Coventry Cathedral, 1974-81; General Secretary, Scottish Churches Council and Director, Scottish Churches House, 1981-90. Recreations: reading; walking; travel; living life to the full. Address: (b.) Kairos, 122/124 Norse Road, Glasgow, G14 9EH; T.-041-954 0262.

Wright, Professor Michael, LLB, LLM, FBIM, FPIM. Assistant Principal, Napier Polytechnic of Edinburgh, since 1983; b. 24.5.49, Newcastle-upon-Tyne; m., Pamela Stothart; 2 s.; 1 d. Educ. Durham Johnston Grammar School; Bearsden Academy; Birmingham University. Lecturer, Bristol Polytechnic, 1970-79; Head of Department, Glasgow Polytechnic, 1980-83; Vice-President, Institute of Personnel Management, 1991-93; Elder, Balerno Parish Church. Recreation: sport. Address: (b.) Napier Polytechnic, Sighthill Court, Edinburgh, EH11 4BN; T.-031-455 3381.

Wright, Professor Norman Gray, BVMS, MRCVS, PhD, DVM, FRCPath, FRSE, FIBiol. Dean, Faculty of Veterinary Medicine, since 1991, and Professor of Veterinary Anatomy, Glasgow University, since 1975; b. 19.8.39, Kilmarnock; m., Irene Anne Wright; 2 s. Educ. Kilmarnock Academy; Glasgow University. General veterinary practice, Kilmarnock, 1962-63; Assistant Lecturer/Lecturer/Senior Lecturer, Department of Veterinary Pathology, Glasgow University, 1963-75; awarded G. Norman Hall Gold Medal, Royal College of Veterinary Surgeons, 1975. Recreations: fishing; boating. Address: (h.) 50 Kilmardinny Crescent, Bearsden, Glasgow; T.-041-942 3944.

Wright, Right Rev. Roderick, Bishop of Argyll and The Isles, since 1991; b. 28.6.40, Glasgow. Educ. St. Gerard's Secondary School, Glasgow; St. Mary's College, Blairs; St. Peter's College, Cardross. Ordained Priest, 1964; Assistant Priest: St. Laurence, Drumchapel, 1964-66, St. Jude, Barlanark, 1966-69; Spiritual Director and Procurator, Blairs, 1969-74; incardinated, Diocese of Argyll and The Isles, 1974; Assistant Priest: Dunoon, 1974-76, Fort William, 1976-80; Parish Priest: Ardkenneth, South Uist, 1980-87, Corpach and Caol, 1987-90; nominated Bishop of Argyll and The Isles, 1990. Address: Bishop's House, Esplanade, Oban, PA34 5AB.

Wright, Very Rev. Ronald (William Vernon) Selby, CVO, ChStJ, TD, MA, DD, FRSE, JP. Chaplain, Edinburgh Castle and to the Governor, 1959-90; Chaplain, Queen's Bodyguard for Scotland (Royal Company of Archers), since 1973; Extra Chaplain to the Queen, since 1978 (Chaplain, 1961-78); b., 12.6.08, Glasgow. Educ. Edinburgh Academy; Melville College, Edinburgh; Edinburgh University and New College. Minister of the Canongate, 1937-77; Chaplain, 7/9 Royal Scots, 1938-42, 1946-48; Senior Chaplain, 52 Lowland Division, 1942-43; 1O Indian Division, 1944-45; Honorary Senior Chaplain to the Forces, since 1945; Founder Warden, St. Giles (later Canongate) Boys' Club, 1927-78; Moderator: Edinburgh Presbytery, 1963, General Assembly, 1972-73; Radio Padre, BBC, 1942-47; Extra-ordinary Director, Edinburgh Academy, since 1973. Publications: Asking them Questions; Take Up God's Armour; Another Home. Address: (h.) The Queen's House, 36 Moray Place, Edinburgh, EH3 6BX; T.-031-226 5566.

Wright, Tom, BA (Hons). Writer; b. 8.3.23, Glasgow. Educ. Coatbridge High School; Strathclyde University. Served apprenticeship in embossing and stained glass; Army, 1943-47; served in Europe and Far East, including Japan; began to publish poems and short stories after demobilisation; had first play performed, Edinburgh Festival, 1960; author of There Was A Man; began to write radio and television drama, 1963; former Creative Writing Fellow; former Script Editor, BBC Scotland Drama Department; has also been Script Editor and Story Line Editor, Take The High Road, STV; won Festival Fringe Award, 1984, for Talk of the Devil; Past Chairman, Scottish Committee, Writers' Guild, and Scottish Society of Playwrights. Recreation: listening to music. Address: 318 Churchill Drive, Glasgow, G11.

Wyke, John Anthony, MA, PhD, VetMB, MRCVS, FRSE. Director, Beatson Institute for Cancer Research, since 1987; Honorary Professor, Glasgow University; b. 5.4.42, Cleethorpes. Educ. Dulwich College; Cambridge University; Glasgow University; London University. Leukemia Society of America Fellow, Universities of Washington and Southern California, 1970-72; Staff Scientist, Imperial Cancer Research Fund, 1972-85; Assistant Director of Research, 1985-87. Address: (b.) Beatson Institute for Cancer Research, Garscube Estate, Switchback Road, Bearsden, Glasgow, G61 1BD; T.-041-942 9361.

Wylie, Rt. Hon. Lord (Norman Russell Wylie), PC (1970), VRD (1961), BA (Oxon), LLB (Glas). Senator of the College of Justice in Scotland, 1974- 90; b. 26.10.23, Elderslie; m., Gillian Mary Verney; 3 s. Educ. Paisley Grammar School; St. Edmund Hall, Oxford (Hon. Fellow, since 1975); Glasgow University; Edinburgh University. Fleet Air Arm, 1942-44 (subsequently RNR, Lt.-Cdr, 1954). Admitted Faculty of Advocates, 1952; Standing Junior Counsel to Air Ministry, 1956; Advocate Depute, 1958; QC, 1964; Solicitor General for Scotland, April to October, 1964; MP (Conservative), Edinburgh Pentlands, 1964-74; Lord Advocate, 1970-74. Chairman, Scottish National Committee, English Speaking Union of Commonwealth, 1978-84; Trustee, Carnegie Trust for Universities of Scotland, since 1975. Recreations: shooting; sailing. Address: (h.) 30 Lauder Road, Edinburgh; t.-031-667 8377.

Wylie, Ronald James, OBE, CA, JDipMA. Executive Director, Young Enterprise - Scotland; b. 31.8.30, Edinburgh; m., Brenda Margaret Wright; 2 s. Apprentice, John M. Geoghegan & Co. Ltd., 1947-52; National Service, 1953-55; Tullis Russell & Co. Ltd.: Cost Accountant, 1955-59, Accountant, 1959-62, Secretary, 1962-72, joined Board, 1971, Joint Managing Director, 1973-81, Chief Executive, 1981-85. Elder, Dysart Kirk; former Council Member, British Paper and Board Industry Federation. Recreation: sailing. Address: 123 Dysart Road, Kirkcaldy, KY1 2BB.

Wylie, Rev. William Andrew, MA. Human Resources Consultant; b. 17.5.27, London; m., Jennifer Barclay Mack; 4 d. by pr. m. Educ. Glasgow Academy; Glasgow University and Trinity College. Royal Navy, 1944-47; Chaplain, Clyde Division, RNVR, 1954-59; Minister: Stepps, 1953-59, Scots Kirk, Lausanne, 1959-67; General Secretary, Scottish Churches Council, 1967-71; Minister, St. Andrew's and St. George's, Edinburgh, 1972-85; Chaplain, Inverclyde Industrial Mission, 1985-86; elected Hon. Fellow, Institute of Petroleum, 1990; elected Burgess of Aberdeen, 1990; Chaplain to the oil industry, 1986-91; Chairman of Governors, Aiglon College, Switzerland, 1984-91; Governor, Fettes College, 1978-85. Recreations: hill-walking; golf; broadcasting; music. Address: (h.) Chesterhills, Boarhills, by St. Andrews, Fife.

Wyllie, George. Artist; b. 1921, Glasgow. Installations; performances; events; best known for "paper boat" installation and exhibition, Glasgow, Liverpool, London and New York, 1989-90; Visiting Lecturer, Glasgow School of Art; Associate, Royal Scottish Academy; Hon. DLitt, Strathclyde University, Glasgow.

Wyllie, Gordon Malcolm, LLB, FSA Scot, NP, WS. Partner, Biggart Baillie & Gifford; Clerk to the Trades House of Glasgow and to Grand Antiquity Society of Glasgow; Clerk to General Commissioners of Inland Revenue, Glasgow North and South Divisions; b. Newton Mearns. Educ. Dunoon Grammar School; Glasgow University. Honorary Treasurer, Edinburgh Summer School in Ancient Greek; Director, Bailford Trustees Ltd.; Chairman, Edinburgh Subscription Ball Committee; wrote Scottish contribution to International Bar Association's International Dictionary of Succession Terms. Recreations: music; history and the arts generally; country walks; foreign travel. Address: (b.) 105 West George Street, Glasgow; T.-041-221 7020.

Wyllie, James Hogarth, BA, MA. Senior Lecturer in International Relations and Director, Postgraduate Strategic Studies Programme, Aberdeen University, since 1979; International Affairs Analyst, Grampian Television, since 1989; Member, JDM Marketing Associates, Aberdeen, since 1992; b. 7.3.51, Dumfries; 2 s. Educ. Sanquhar Academy; Dumfries Academy; Stirling University; Lancaster University. Research Officer, Ministry of Defence, 1974-75; Tutor in Politics, Durham University, 1975-77; Lecturer in Politics, University of East Anglia, 1977-79; freelance journalism; frequent current affairs comment and analysis, BBC Radio; Commonwealth Fellow, University of Calgary, 1988. Publications: Influence of British Arms; European Security in the Nuclear Age; Economist Pocket Guide to Defence (Co-author); International Politics since 1945 (Contributor). Recreations: travelling; cinema; badminton; walking; cycling. Address: (b.) Department of Politics and International Relations, Aberdeen University, Aberdeen, AB9 2TY; T.-0224 272725.

Wyllie, Rt. Rev. Hugh Rutherford, MA. Moderator, General Assembly of Church of Scotland, 1992-93; Minister, Hamilton Old Parish Church, since 1981; b. 11.10.34, Glasgow; m., Eileen E. Cameron, MA; 2 d. Educ. Hutchesons' Grammar School; Glasgow University. Bank of Scotland, 1951-53 (AIBS); RAF, 1953-55; student, 1956-62; Assistant, Glasgow Cathedral, 1962; Minister: Coatbridge Dunbeth, 1965, Cathcart South, 1972; Convener, Stewardship and Budget Committee, General Assembly, 1978-83; Convener, Board of Stewardship and Finance, General Assembly, 1983-86; Convener, Assembly Council, General Assembly, 1987-91; Moderator, Presbytery of Hamilton, 1989. Recreations: gardening; DIY. Address: Mansewood, Union Street, Hamilton, ML3 6NA; T.-0698 420002.

Wynd, Andrew H.D., DipSW (CQSW). Executive Officer, Scottish Spina Bifida Association, since 1989; b. 7.10.53, Hamilton. Educ. Bellshill Academy; Stirling University. Local government officer; Senior Officer, National Voluntary Childcare Organisation. Past Chair, Scottish Association of Voluntary Service Co-ordinators; Chair, Strathclyde Regional Council Pre-five Voluntary Sector Forum; Member, Executive, Scottish Council on Disability. Address: (b.) Scottish Spina Bifida Association, 190 Queensferry Road, Edinburgh, EH4 2BW; T.-031-332 0743.

Y

Yang, Eric Shih-Jung, BSc, MSc, PhD, CEng, FIEE, FIOA. Reader, Department of Electrical and Electronic Engineering, Heriot-Watt University, since 1985; m., Fei Jeannette; 1 d. Educ. Hong Kong University; Queen Mary College, London University. Senior Scientific Officer, British Rail, 1970-72; Lecturer, then Senior Lecturer, Heriot-Watt University, 1972-85. Publications: Low-Noise Electrical Motors, 1981; Machinery Noise Measurement (Co-author), 1985; Handbook of Electric Machines (Co-author), 1987. Address: (h.) 14 Cherry Tree Park, Balerno, Edinburgh, EH14 5AJ; T.-031-449 2069.

Yarrow, Sir Eric Grant, MBE, DL, CEng, MRINA, FRSE. Chairman, Clydesdale Bank PLC, 1985-91 (Director, since 1962); Director, National Australia Bank Ltd., 1987-91; b. 23.4.20, Glasgow; m., 1, Rosemary Ann Young (deceased); 1 s. (deceased); 2, Annette Elizabeth Francoise Steven (m. diss.); 3 s.; 3, Joan Botting; 3 step d. Educ. Marlborough College; Glasgow University. Served engineering apprenticeship, G. & J. Weir, 1938-39; Royal Engineers, 1939-45; served Burma, 1942-45 (Major, RE, 1945); Yarrow & Co. Ltd. (later Yarrow PLC): Assistant Manager, 1946, Director, 1948, Managing Director, 1958-67, Chairman, 1962-85, President, 1985-87; Director, Standard Life Assurance Company, 1958-91; Hon. President, Executive Committee, Princess Louise Scottish Hospital, Erskine; Council Member, Royal Institution of Naval Architects, since 1957 (Vice President, 1965, Honorary Vice President, 1972); Member, General Committee, Lloyd's Register of Shipping, 1960-89; Deacon, Incorporation of Hammermen in Glasgow, 1961-62; Chairman, Yarrow (Shipbuilders) Ltd., 1962-79; Officer (Brother), Order of St. John, since 1965; Deputy Lieutenant, County of Renfrewshire, since 1970; Prime Warden, Worshipful Company of Shipwrights, 1970-71; Council Member, Institute of Directors, 1983-90; President, Smeatonican Society of Civil Engineers, 1983-84; President, The Marlburian Club, 1984; President, Scottish Area, Burma Star Association, since 1990; Vice President, Royal Highland and Agricultural Society for Scotland, since 1990. Recreations: golf; shooting. Address: (h.) Cloak, Kilmacolm, Renfrewshire, PA13 4SD; T.-Kilmacolm 2067.

Yellowlees, Gideon, JP, FSA Scot. Chairman, Roxburgh District Council, since 1988; b. 17.8.20, Jedburgh; m., Jean; 1 d. Educ. Jedburgh Grammar School; Hawick High School. RAF, 1940-46, intelligence; Councillor, Jedburgh Town Council, 1959-75 (Provost, Royal Burgh of Jedburgh, 1969-75); Councillor, Roxburgh District Council, since 1979;

Chairman/Vice Chairman, Scottish District Court, 1984-88; Chairman/Vice Chairman, Scottish Borders Tourist Board, 1986-90; President, Jedburgh Rotary Club, 1975; President, Jedforest Instrumental Band, 1960-92. Recreations: horse riding and training. Address: (h.) Ridgevale, Galahill, Jedburgh, Roxburghshire; T.-0835 62292.

Yemm, Professor Robert, BDS, BSc, PhD, FDS RCS(Edin). Professor and Head, Department of Dental Prosthetics and Gerontology, Dundee University, since 1984; b. 31.1.39, Bristol; m., Glenys Margaret; 1 s.; 1 d. Educ. Bristol Grammar School; Bristol University. Lecturer in Dental Prosthetics, Bristol University; Associate Professor, Department of Oral Biology, Alberta University; Lecturer in Dental Medicine (Oral Biology), then Dental Prosthetics, Bristol University; Senior Lecturer (Honorary Consultant), Dental Prosthetics, Dundee University. Recreation: sailing. Address: (h.) 10 Birkhill Avenue, Wormit, Newport-on-Tay, Fife, DD6 8PX; T.-0382 541819.

Young, Daniel Greer, MB, ChB, FRCSEdin, FRCSGlas, DTM&H. Reader in Paediatric Surgery, Glasgow University, since 1984; Honorary Consultant Paediatric Surgeon, since 1967; President, British Association of Paediatric Surgeons; b. Skipness, Argyll; m., Agnes Gilchrist Donald; 1 s.; 1 d. Educ. Wishaw High School; Glasgow University. Resident Assistant Surgeon, Hospital for Sick Children, London; Senior Lecturer, Institute of Child Health, London University; Honorary Consultant Surgeon, Hospital for Sick Children, London, and Queen Elizabeth Hospital, Hackney, London; Senior Lecturer and Head, Department of Paediatric Surgery, Glasgow University, Honorary Consultant Surgeon, Royal Hospital for Sick Children and Stobhill General Hospital, Glasgow. Honorary Secretary, Lanarkshire Division, British Medical Association; Past President, Royal Medico-Chirurgical Society of Glasgow; Honorary President, Scottish Spina Bifida Association; Member of Council, Royal College of Physicians and Surgeons; Chairman, Intercollegiate Board in Paediatric Surgery; Honorary Member: Hungarian Paichatree Surgical Association, South African Paediatric Surgical Association, American Surgical Paediatric Association. Recreations: curling; fishing; gardening. Address: (b.) Department of Paediatric Surgery, Royal Hospital for Sick Children, Yorkhill, Glasgow, G3 8SJ; T.-041-339 8888, Ext. 4169.

Young, Lt.-Gen. Sir David (Tod), KBE (1980), CB (1977), DFC (1952). Chairman, Cairntech Ltd., Edinburgh, since 1983; b. 17.5.26, Edinburgh; m., 1, Joyce Marian Melville (deceased); 2 s.; 2, Joanna Myrtle Oyler (nee Torin). Educ. George Watson's College, Edinburgh. Commissioned The Royal Scots, 1945; Brevet Lt.-Col., 1964; Mil. Assistant, MoD, 1964-67; commanded 1st Bn., The Royal Scots, 1967-69; Col. GS, Staff College, 1969-70; Commander, 12 Mechanized Brigade, 1970-72; Deputy Military Secretary, MoD, 1972-74; Commander Land Forces, Northern Ireland, 1975-77; Director of Infantry, MoD, 1977-80; GOC Scotland and Governor, Edinburgh Castle, 1980-82; Colonel, The Royal Scots, 1975-80; Colonel Commandant: Scottish Division, 1980-82, Ulster Defence Regiment, 1986-91; Honorary Colonel, Northern Ireland Regiment Army Air Corps, 1988. Member, Scottish Committee, Marie Curie Foundation, since 1983 (Chairman, 1986); President, Army Cadet Force Association Scotland, since 1984; HM Commissioner, Queen Victoria School, since 1984; Chairman, St. Mary's Cathedral Workshop, since 1986; Member, Board of Governors, St. Columba's Hospice, since 1986. Recreations: golf; sports; music. Address: c/o Adam & Company plc, 22 Charlotte Square, Edinburgh, EH2 4DF.

Young, George Bell, CBE, CStJ, CBIM, FInstM. Managing Director, East Kilbride Development Corporation, 1968-90; b. 17.6.24; m., 1, Margaret Wylie Boyd (deceased); 1 s.; 2,

Joyce Marguerite McAteer. Educ. Queens Park School, Glasgow. RNVR, 1942-45 (Lt., destroyers and mine-sweepers); Journalist and Feature Writer, Glasgow Herald, 1945-48; North of Scotland Hydro-Electric Board, 1948-52; Chief Executive (London), Scottish Council (Development and Industry), 1952-68; Council Member, National Trust for Scotland, 1974-79; Director, Royal Caledonian Schools, 1957-85; Chairman, East Kilbride and District National Savings Committee, 1968-78; Trustee, Strathclyde Scanner Campaign; President, British Heart Foundation Scottish Appeal, since 1975; Chairman, East Kilbride Committee, Order of St. John, 1977-87; Honorary Secretary, Saints and Sinners Club of Scotland, 1982-88, Chairman, 1990-91; Chairman, BIM Scotland, 1988-91; Member, British Railways (Scottish) Board, since 1985; Hon. Freeman, East Kilbride, 1990; formed George Young Associates, East Kilbride, 1990. Address: (h.) 4 Newlands Place, East Kilbride, G74 1AE.

Young, Howard Anthony, MB, BS, FRCS. Consultant Otolaryngologist, Grampian Health Board, since 1978; Clinical Senior Lecturer in Otolaryngology, Aberdeen University, since 1978; Visiting Surgeon, Mount Elizabeth Hospital, Singapore, and Orkney and Shetland Health Boards, since 1978; b. 3.9.45, Swinton. Educ. Manchester Grammar School; Newcastle upon Tyne University. House Surgeon and Physician, Royal Victoria Hospital, Newcastle upon Tyne; Demonstrator in Pathology, Newcastle upon Tyne University; Resident in Neurosurgery and Plastic Surgery, Newcastle General Hospital; SHO, Royal National Throat, Nose and Ear Hospital, London; Registrar Otolaryngology, Royal Victoria Hospital, Newcastle; Senior Registrar, Ninewells Hospital and Medical School, Dundee; Honorary Lecturer, Dundee University. Recreations: travel; golf; ornithology; fishing. Address: (h.) Holme Rose, 18 Edgehill Road, Aberdeen, AB2 4JH; T.-0224 324554.

Young, Hugh Kenneth, CA, FIB (Scot). General Manager and Secretary and Member, Management Board, Bank of Scotland; b. 6.5.36, Galashiels; m., Marjory Bruce Wilson; 2 s.; 1 d. Educ. Edinburgh Academy. National Service, 1959-61; commissioned as 2nd Lt., Royal Scots, now Company Commander No. 5 (HSF) Company, 2nd Bn. 52nd Lowland Volunteers, TA; with ICFC Ltd., 1962-67; with Schroders Ltd. group, 1967-73, latterly as Manager, J. Henry Schroder Wagg & Co. Ltd.; Local Director in Edinburgh, Edward Bates & Sons Ltd., 1973-75; joined Bank of Scotland, 1975; Head of Corporate Finance, Bank of Scotland Finance Company Ltd., 1976; Director, The British Linen Bank Ltd., 1978-84 (Deputy Chief Executive, 1982-84). Director: Bank of Scotland (Jersey) Ltd., 1986 (Chairman), Bank of Wales (Jersey) Ltd., 1986, Scottish Agricultural Securities Corporation PLC, 1988. Recreations: squash; tennis; hillwalking. Address: (b.) The Mound, Edinburgh, EH1 1YZ; T.-031-243 5562.

Young, Ian Macrae, BSc, CertEd, CBiol, MIBiol. Educational Adviser, Health Education Board for Scotland, since 1983; b. 20.7.46, Glasgow; m., Anne Crawford; 2 s. Educ. Rutherglen Academy; Paisley College of Technology. Teacher of Science, Camphill High School, Paisley, 1969; Principal Teacher of Biology, Renfrew High School, 1972; Adviser in Science, Renfrew and Argyll and Bute Divisions, Strathclyde Region, 1978. Publications: The Science of Life (series of biology texts). Recreations: folk song; photography; running. Address: (b.) Health Education Board for Scotland, Woodburn House, Canaan Lane, Edinburgh, EH10 4SG; T.-031-447 8044.

Young, James Douglas, BA (Hons), PhD. Senior Fellow, School of Arts, Stirling University, since 1992; Fellow, Royal Historical Society, since 1991; b. 3.4.31, Grangemouth; m., Lorna Margaret Robertson; 1 s.; 1 d. Educ. Dundas Secondary

School, Grangemouth; Stirling University. Prominent activist, Labour League of Youth; former Secretary, Grangemouth Trades Council; student, Newbattle College, Dalkeith; scholarship, Ruskin College, Oxford; Lecturer in Scottish History, Stirling University, 1970-89; Reader in History, 1990-91; Labour historian; resigned from Labour Party, 1977, to join Scottish Labour Party; founding Organiser, Scottish Socialist Party, 1988. Publications include: The Rousing of the Scottish Working Class, 1979; Making Trouble, 1987; Socialism since 1889: a biographical history, 1988; John Maclean: Clydeside socialist, 1992. Recreations: walking; travelling; relaxing with malt whisky. Address: (h.) 8 Tarbert Place, Polmont, Falkirk; T.-0324 712155.

Young, James McMicken, FIB, FBIM. Member, Clyde Port Authority; Member, Edinburgh Company of Merchants; Treasurer, Scottish Association of Victim Support Schemes; Joint General Manager, Bank of Scotland, 1973-85; b. 4.10.25, Stranraer; m., Lillian Frances Judith Maran; 1 s.; 1 d. Educ. Stranraer Academy; Stranraer High School. Bank of Scotland: Assistant Manager, London Chief Office, 1965, Assistant Secretary, 1968, Assistant General Manager, Bank of Scotland, and Manager, Bank of Scotland Finance Co. Ltd. (now British Linen Bank Ltd.), 1972, Director, Bank of Scotland Finance Co. Ltd., 1973; Director: British Linen Bank Ltd., British Linen Assets PLC, Capital Leasing Ltd. Recreation: tennis; reading. Address: (h.) 23 Succoth Park, Edinburgh, EH12 6BX; T.-031-337 5479.

Young, John Henderson, OBE (1980), JP, MBIM, MIEx, DL. Leader of the Opposition, Glasgow District Council, since 1988 (Council Member, since 1974); Deputy Lieutenant, Glasgow, since 1981; Chairman, Association of Scottish Conservative Councillors, since 1991; Bailie/Magistrate of Glasgow; b. 21.12.30, Glasgow; m., Doris Paterson; 1 s. Educ. Hillhead High School, Glasgow; Scottish College of Commerce. RAF, 1949-51. Councillor, Glasgow Corporation, 1964-73, Glasgow District Council, since 1974; Leader, Glasgow City Council, 1977-79; Parliamentary candidate (Conservative), Rutherglen, 1966; Chairman, Cathcart Conservatives, 1964-65, 1968-71, 1987-88; Chairman, Glasgow Conservative Euro Constituency, since 1987; Vice-Chairman, Glasgow Conservatives, 1969-72; Public Relations Consultant; Vice-Chairman, Scottish Pakistani Association; Kentucky Colonel, 1984; Member, Glasgow Sports Promotion Council; Member, Post Office Advisory Committee; Governor, Hutchesons' Educational Trust, since 1991. Recreations: tennis; reading; history; animal welfare; meeting people. Address: (h.) 4 Deanwood Avenue, Muirend, Glasgow, G44 3RJ; T.-041-637 9535.

Young, John Maclennan, OBE (1987), JP. Convener, Caithness District Council, since 1974; Member, Highland Regional Council, 1974-90; b. 6.6.33, Thurso. Educ. Thurso Miller Academy. Farmer; Member, Caithness County Council, 1961-75; Member, Caithness Western District Council, 1961-75; Chairman, Housing Committee, 1968-73, and Planning Commitee, 1973-75, Caithness County Council; Conservative candidate, Caithness and Sutherland, 1970. Address: (h.) Sordale, Halkirk, Caithness; T.-Halkirk 228.

Young, Margaret Rose, JP, MPAH (Scot). Hypnotherapist and Counsellor; Honorary Sheriff; b. 5.1.51, Canada; m., Simon George Young; 3 d. Educ. St. Mary's School, Calne; St. Andrews University. Recreations: reading; music; theatre; walking. Address: (h.) Tarrel, by Tain, Ross-shire, IV20 1SL; T.-086 287 248.

Young, Mark Richard, BSc, PhD, FRES, MIBiol, CBiol. Senior Lecturer, Aberdeen University, since 1989; Member, North East River Purification Board, since 1984; Bulletin Editor, British Ecological Society, since 1985; Chairman, National Reserves Committee, Scottish Wildlife Trust, since

1990; b. 27.10.48, Worcester; m., Jennifer Elizabeth Tully; 1 s.; 1 d. Educ. Kings School, Worcester; Birmingham University. Lecturer, Aberdeen University, 1973-89. Recreations: natural history; walking; ball sports; visiting Hebridean islands. Address: (b.) Department of Zoology, Aberdeen University, Tillydrone Avenue, Aberdeen, AB9 2TN; T.-0224 272880.

Young, Raymond Kennedy, OBE, BArch, ARIAS. Regional Director – North, Scottish Homes; b. 23.1.46, Newcastle-upon-Tyne; m., Jean; 3 s. Educ. High School of Glasgow; Strathclyde University. Strathclyde University Research Group, 1971-74; Housing Corporation, Glasgow Office, 1974-78; Director, Scotland, The Housing Corporation, 1978-89. Recreations: music; theatre; railway modelling; no sports. Address: (b.) South Inch Business Centre, Shore Road, Perth, PH2 8BW; T.-0738 34772.

Young, Robert W.J., BSc (Hons), PhD, CEng, MICE. HM Inspector of Schools (Staff Inspector), since 1970; b. 14.3.36, Falkirk; m., Cynthia; 2 d. Educ. Melville College, Edinburgh; Edinburgh University. Civil Engineer, British Rail, 1958-61; Edinburgh University, 1961-70, with period of secondment to Khartoum University, Sudan. Recreations: wind-surfing; sailing; skiing; bridge. Address: (b.) Room 3/19, Scottish Education Department, New St. Andrews House, St. James Centre, Edinburgh; T.-031-556 8400, Ext. 4534.

Young, Roger, BSc, MBA. Chief Executive, Scottish Hydro-Electric plc, since 1988; b. 14.1.44, Edinburgh; m., Susan; 1 s.; 2 d. Educ. Gordonstoun School; Edinburgh University; Cranfield Business School. Address: (b.) 16 Rothesay Terrace, Edinburgh, EH3 7SE; T.-031-225 1361.

Young, Professor Stephen, BCom, MSc. Professor of International Business, Strathclyde University, since 1987; b. 20.8.44, Berwick upon Tweed; 1 s.; 1 d. Educ. Berwick Grammar School; Liverpool University; Newcastle upon Tyne University. Lecturer, Dar-es-Salaam Technical College, 1966-67; Economist, Ministry of Agriculture and Cooperatives, Dar-es-Salaam, 1967-68; Manager, International Economics Department, Milk Marketing Board, 1969-73; Lecturer/Senior Lecturer, Paisley College of Technology, 1973-79; Senior Lecturer, Department of Marketing, Strathclyde Business School, 1980-87 (Director, Strathclyde International Business Unit, from 1983); Directorships: Scotmex Ltd., Strathclyde Technology Transfer Ltd., The Licensing Centre Ltd., Ecosse Ltd. Recreations: mountaineering; swimming; cycling. Address: (h.) 65 Russell Place, Linwood, Renfrewshire, PA3 3SS; T.-0505 2762.

Young, Sheriff Sir Stephen Stewart Templeton, 3rd Bt. Sheriff of North Strathclyde, since 1984; b. 24.5.47; m.; 2 s. Educ. Rugby; Trinity College, Oxford; Edinburgh University. Sheriff, Glasgow and Strathkelvin, 1984.

Young, Rev. William Galbraith, MA (Hons), BD, PhD. Retired Bishop, Church of Pakistan; retired Minister, Church of Scotland; b. 10.10.17, Greenock; m., Elizabeth Crawford Wiseman; 1 s.; 2 d. Educ. Greenock Academy; Oban High School; Glasgow University. Private, RAMC, 1940-45 (War service overseas, India, Iraq, Persia, Cyprus); Missionary, Church of Scotland, Punjab, Pakistan, 1947-77; Principal, Murree Language School, 1954-55; Vice-President, West Pakistan Christian Council, 1963-64; Editor, Urdu Textbook Project, Theological Education Fund, 1963-77; Professor of Church History, Gujranwala Theological Seminary, 1966-70; Church of Pakistan: Bishop, 1970-77, Chairman, Liturgical Commission, 1970-77, Deputy Moderator, 1974-77; Minister, Resolis and Urquhart Parish Church, 1977-85; Moderator, Chanonry and Dingwall Presbytery, 1979-80; Moderator, Synod of Ross, Sutherland and Caithness, 1981-82;

Chairman, Sialkot Inter-Aid Committee (Flood and Refugee Relief), 1973-77; Vice-Chairman, East Ross and Black Isle Council of Social Service, 1980-82. Publications: Handbook of Source Materials for Students of Church History up to 650 AD, 1969; Patriarch, Shah and Caliph, 1974; Church of Pakistan - Experimental Services, 1974; The Parish of Urquhart and Logie Wester, 1984; Life and Witness Through Sixty Years of Change, 1991; various publications in Urdu. Recreations: (when young) tennis; (now) choral singing; walking; reading; listening to music. Address: (h.) 29 Ferry Brae, North Kessock, Inverness, IV1 1YH; T.-046 373 581.

Younger of Leckie, 3rd Viscount (Edward George Younger), OBE (1940); b. 21.11.06; m., Evelyn Margaret McClure (deceased); 3 s.; 1 d. Educ. Winchester; New College, Oxford. Served Second World War; Colonel, Argyll and Sutherland Highlanders (TA); Lord Lieutenant, Stirling and Falkirk, 1964-79. Address: (h.) Leckie, Gargunnock, Stirling.

Younger of Prestwick, Rt. Hon. Lord (George Kenneth Hotson Younger), TD, DL. Chairman, Royal Bank of Scotland Group plc, since 1991; MP (Conservative), Ayr, 1964-92; b. 22.9.31; m., Diana Rhona Tuck; 3 s.; 1 d. Educ. Cargilfield School, Edinburgh; Winchester College; New College, Oxford. Argyll and Sutherland Highlanders, 1950-51; 7th Bn., Argyll and Sutherland Highlanders (TA), 1951-65; Honorary Colonel, 154 (Lowland) Transport Regiment, RCT T&AVR, 1977-85; Director: George Younger & Son Ltd., 1958-68, G. Thomson & Co. Ltd., Leith, 1962-66, Maclachlans Ltd., 1968-70, Tennant Caledonian Breweries, since 1977; Non Executive Director: Royal Bank of Scotland Group plc, 1989, Murray International Trust PLC, 1989, Murray Smaller Markets Trust PLC, 1989, Murray Income Trust PLC, 1989, Murray Ventures PLC, 1989, Scottish Equitable Life Assurance Society, 1990, Siemens Plessey Electronic Systems Ltd., 1990 (Chairman), Banco de Santander SA, 1991; Chairman, Ayrshire Community Airport Project Ltd., 1991; contested North Lanarkshire, 1959; Unionist Candidate, Kinross and West Perthshire, 1963 (stood down in favour of Sir Alec Douglas-Home); Scottish Conservative Whip, 1965-67; Parliamentary Under-Secretary of State for Development, Scottish Office, 1970-74; Minister of State for Defence, 1974; Secretary of State for Scotland, 1979-86; Chairman, Conservative Party in Scotland, 1974-75 (Deputy Chairman, 1967-70); Secretary of State for Defence, 1986-89; President, National Union of Conservative and Unionist Associations, 1987-88. Brigadier, Queen's Bodyguard for Scotland (Royal Company of Archers); DL, Stirlingshire, 1968. Recreations: music; tennis; sailing; golf. Address: (b.) 42 St. Andrew Square, Edinburgh EH2 2YE; T.-031-556 8555.

Younger, John David Bingham, DL. Managing Director, Broughton Brewery Ltd., since 1979; b. 20.5.39, Doune; m., Anne Rosaleen Logan; 1 s.; 2 d. Educ. Eton College; Royal Military Academy, Sandhurst. Argyll and Sutherland Highlanders, 1957-69; Scottish and Newcastle Breweries, 1969-79; Broughton Brewery Ltd., since 1979; Deputy Lieutenant, Tweeddale, 1987. Chairman, Board of Governors, Belhaven Hill School Trust, 1988; Chairman, Scottish Borders Tourist Board, 1989; Member, A&SH Regimental Trust and Committee, 1985. Recreation: country pursuits. Address: (h.) Kirkurd House, Blyth Bridge, Peeblesshire, EH46 7AH; T.-0721 52 223.

Younger, Sheriff Robert Edward Gilmour, MA, LLB. Sheriff of Tayside, Central and Fife, at Stirling and Alloa, since 1987; b. 25.9.40, Stirling; m., Helen Jane Hayes; 1 s.; 1 d. Educ. Winchester; New College, Oxford; Edinburgh University; Glasgow University. Advocate, 1968-79; Sheriff of Glasgow and Strathkelvin, at Glasgow, 1979-82, and of Tayside, Central and Fife, at Stirling and Falkirk, 1982-87.

Recreations: out of doors. Address: (h.) Old Leckie, Gargunnock, Stirling; T.-Gargunnock 213.

Youngson, Alexander John, CBE, MA, DLitt, Hon.FRIAS. Chairman, Royal Fine Art Commission for Scotland, 1983-90; b. 28.9.18, Pakistan; m., Elizabeth Gisborne Naylor; 1 s.; 1 d. Educ. Aberdeen Grammar School; Aberdeen University. Fleet Air Arm, 1939-45; Lecturer, St. Andrews University, 1948-50; Lecturer, Cambridge University, 1950-58; Fellow, Emmanuel College; Professor, Edinburgh University, 1958-74; Director, Research School, Social Sciences, Australian National University, 1974-80; Professor, University of Hong Kong, 1980-82. Publications: Possibilities of Economic Progress, 1959; The Making of Classical Edinburgh, 1966; After the Forty Five, 1970; The Prince and the Pretender, 1985. Recreation: gardening. Address: (h.) Flat 2, The Warren, Hummel Road, Gullane, East Lothian, EH31 2BG; T.-0620 843100.

Youngson, George Gray, MB, ChB, PhD, FRCSEdin. Consultant Surgeon, Royal Aberdeen Children's Hospital and Aberdeen Royal Infirmary, since 1985; Honorary Senior Lecturer in Clinical Surgery, Aberdeen University, since 1985; b. 13.5.49, Glasgow; m., Sandra Jean Lister; 1 s.; 2 d. Educ. Buckhaven High School; Aberdeen University. House Officer to Professor George Smith, 1973; Research Fellow, 1975; Registrar in General Surgery, 1975-77; Senior Resident in Cardiac and Thoracic Surgery, University Hospital, London, Ontario, 1979; Lecturer in Clinical Surgery, Aberdeen University, 1981; Clinical Fellow, Paediatric Surgery, Hospital for Sick Children, Toronto, 1983; Lecturer in Surgical Paediatrics and Transplantation, Aberdeen University, 1984. Recreations: sport (tennis and squash); music (piobaireachd, guitar). Address: (h.) 10 Kennerty Park, Peterculter, Aberdeen.

Yule, William. Honorary Sheriff, Tayside, Central and Fife, since 1976; b. 16.2.08, Kirkcaldy; m., Joan Kininmonth; 1 s. Educ. Kirkcaldy High School; George Watson's Boys' College, Edinburgh. President: Wholesale Grocers Association of Scotland, 1955-56, Kirkcaldy Rotary Club, 1957-58; Chairman, East Fife Hospitals Board of Management, 1963-68; Commissioner of Income Tax, 1964-78. Address: (h.) 16 Victoria Gardens, Kirkcaldy, KY1 1DJ; T.-Kirkcaldy 263356.

Z

Zealley, Andrew King, MB, ChB, FRCP, FRCPsych, DPM. Medical Director, Royal Edinburgh Hospital and Mental Health Unit, Lothian Health Board, since 1984; Consultant Psychiatrist, Lothian Health Board, since 1971; b. 28.10.35, Stockton-on-Tees; m., Dr. Helen Elizabeth Zealley (qv); 1 s.; 1 d. Educ. Sherborne School; Edinburgh University. Chairman, Lothian Area Medical Committee, 1978-88; Chairman, Lothian Area Ethics of Medical Research Committee, since 1988. Publication: Companion to Psychiatric Studies, 5th edition (Co-editor). Recreations: running; sailing; skiing. Address: (h.) Viewfield House, Tipperlinn Road, Edinburgh, EH10 5ET; T.-031-447 5545.

Zealley, Helen Elizabeth, MD, FRCPE, FFPHM. Chief Administrative Medical Officer and Director of Public Health, Lothian Health Board, since 1988; Honorary Senior Lecturer, Edinburgh University, since 1988; b. 10.6.40; m., Dr. Andrew Zealley (qv); 1 s.; 1 d. Educ. St. Albans High School; Edinburgh University. Member, Council, Royal College of Physicians, Edinburgh; Member, Board, Faculty of Public Health Medicine; Hon. President, Lothian Branch, British Association of Early Childhood. Recreations: family and home; sailing; skiing; travel. Address: (b.) Lothian Health Board, 148 Pleasance, Edinburgh, EH8 9RS; T.-031-229 5888.

Ziervogel, Mark Allan, BSc, MB, ChB, DMRD, FRCR. Consultant Paediatric Radiologist, Royal Hospital for Sick Children, Glasgow, since 1978; b. 25.12.36, Pietersburg, South Africa; m., Toni Levick; 1 s.; 1 d, Educ. Pretoria Boys' High School; Natal University; Glasgow University. Cattle farming, South Africa; hospital appointments, Glasgow, Stirling and New Plymouth (New Zealand). Honorary Lecturer in Radiodiagnosis, Glasgow University. Recreations: cycling; tandem touring with wife; squash; music, food and wine. Address: (h.) Robinsfield, Balmore Road, Bardowie, Milngavie, Glasgow, G62 6ER; T.-0360 22268.